LEMPRIERE'S CLASSICAL DICTIONARY

LEMPRIERE'S CLASSICAL DICTIONARY

J. Lemprière, DD

BRACKEN BOOKS
LONDON

This edition published 1984 by Bracken Books
an imprint of Bestseller Publications Ltd.
Princess House, 50 Eastcastle Street
London W1N 7AP, England

Reprinted 1990

ISBN 0-946495-12-2

Printed and bound in Finland

A CHRONOLOGICAL TABLE

FROM THE

CREATION OF THE WORLD TO THE FALL OF THE ROMAN EMPIRE IN THE WEST, AND IN THE EAST.

	Before Christ.*
The world created in the 710th year of the Julian period	4004
The deluge	2348
The tower of Babel built, and the confusion of languages	2247
Celestial observations are first made at Babylon	2234
The kingdom of Ægypt is supposed to have begun under Misraim, the son of Ham, and to have continued 1663 years, to the conquest of Cambyses	2188
The kingdom of Sicyon established	2089
The kingdom of Assyria begins	2059
The birth of Abraham	1996
The kingdom of Argos established under Inachus	1856
Memnon, the Ægyptian, is said to have invented letters, 15 years before the reign of Phoroneus	1822
The deluge of Ogyges, by which Attica remained waste above 200 years, till the coming of Cecrops	1764
Joseph sold into Ægypt by his brethren	1728
The chronology of the Arundelian marbles begins about this time, fixing here the arrival of Cecrops in Attica, an epoch which other writers have placed later by 26 years	1582
Moses born	1571
The kingdom of Athens begun under Cecrops, who came from Ægypt with a colony of Saites. This happened about 780 years before the first Olympiad	1556
Scamander migrates from Crete, and begins the kingdom of Troy	1546
The deluge of Deucalion in Thessaly	1503
The Panathenæa first celebrated at Athens	1495
Cadmus comes into Greece, and builds the citadel of Thebes	1493
The first Olympic games celebrated in Elis by the Idæi Dactyli	1453
The first five books of Moses written in the land of Moab, where he dies the following year, aged 110	1452
Minos flourishes in Crete, and iron is found by the Dactyli by the accidental burning of the woods of Ida in Crete	1406
The Eleusinian mysteries introduced at Athens by Eumolpus	1356
The Isthmian games first instituted by Sisyphus, king of Corinth	1326
The Argonautic expedition. The first Pythian games celebrated by Adrastus, king of Argos	1263
Gideon flourishes in Israel	1245
The Theban war of the seven heroes against Eteocles	1225
Olympic games celebrated by Hercules	1222
The rape of Helen by Theseus, and 15 years after, by Paris	1213
Troy taken after a siege of 10 years. Æneas sails to Italy	1184
Alba Longa built by Ascanius	1152
Migration of the Æolian colonies	1124
The return of the Heraclidæ into Peloponnesus, 80 years after the taking of Troy. Two years after, they divide the Peloponnesus among themselves; and here, therefore, begins the kingdom of Lacedæmon under Eurysthenes and Procles	1104
Saul made king over Israel	1095
The kingdom of Sicyon ended	1088
The kingdom of Athens ends in the death of Codrus	1070
The migration of the Ionian colonies from Greece, and their settlement in Asia Minor	1044
Dedication of Solomons's temple	1004
Samus built	986
Division of the kingdom of Judah and Israel	975
Homer and Hesiod flourished about this time, according to the Marbles	907
Elias the prophet taken up into heaven	896
Lycurgus, 42 years old, established his laws at Lacedæmon, and, together with Iphitus and Cleosthenes, restores the Olympic games at Elis, about 108 years before the era, which is commonly called the first Olympiad	884
Phidon, king of Argos, is supposed to have invented scales and measures, and coined silver at Ægina. Carthage built by Dido	869
Fall of the Assyrian empire by the death of Sardanapalus, an era placed 80 years earlier by Justin	820
The kingdom of Macedonia begins, and continues 646 years, till the battle of Pydna	814
The kingdom of Lydia begins, and continues 249 years	797
Triremes first invented by the Corinthians	786

* In the following table, I have confined myself to the more easy and convenient eras of before, (B.C.) and after (A.D.) Christ. For the sake of those, however, who do not wish the exclusion of the Julian period, it is necessary to observe, that as the first year of the Christian era always falls on the 4714th of the Julian years, the number required either before or after Christ, will easily be discovered by the application of the rules of substraction or addition.

For the following methods of converting years B.C. into Olympiads, and finding the year of Rome, the editor desires to acknowledge himself indebted to Dr. Butler, who has given them in the introduction to his useful and popular work upon ancient and modern geography:

To find the Olympiad, substract the given year B.C. from 776, divide the remainder by 4, and to the quotient add 1 for the current Olympiad, and 1 for the current year of it.

To find the year of Rome, substract the given year B.C. from 753, and to the remainder add 1 for the current year.

	B.C.
The monarchical government abolished at Corinth, and the Prytanes elected	779
Corœbus conquers at Olympia, in the 28th Olympiad from the institution of Iphitus. This is vulgarly called the first Olympiad, about 23 years before the foundation at Rome	776
The Ephori introduced into the government of Lacedæmon by Theopompus	760
Isaiah begins to prophesy	757
The decennial archons begin at Athens, of which Charops is the first	754
Rome built on the 20th of April, according to Varro, in the year 3961 of the Julian period	753
The rape of the Sabines	750
The era of Nabonassar king of Babylon begins	747
The first Messenian war begins, and continues 19 years, to the taking of Ithome	743
Syracuse built by a Corinthian colony	732
The kingdom of Israel finished by the taking of Samaria by Salmanasar king of Assyria. The first eclipse of the moon on record March 19th, according to Ptolemy	721
Candaules murdered by Gyges, who succeeds to the Lydian throne	718
Tarentum built by the Parthenians	707
Corcyra built by the Corinthians	703
The second Messenian war begins, and continues 14 years, to the taking of Ira, after a siege of 11 years. About this time flourished the poets Tyrtæus and Archilochus	685
The government of Athens intrusted to annual archons	684
Alba destroyed	665
Cypselus usurps the government of Corinth, and keeps it for 30 years	659
Byzantium built by a colony of Argives or Athenians	658
Cyrene, built by Battus	630
The Scythians invade Asia Minor, of which they keep possession for 28 years	624
Draco establishes his laws at Athens	623
The canal between the Nile and the Red Sea begun by king Necho	610
Nineveh taken and destroyed by Cyaxares and his allies	606
The Phœnicians sail round Africa, by order of Necho. About this time flourished Arion, Pittacus, Alcæus, Sappho, &c	604
The Scythians are expelled from Asia Minor by Cyaxares	596
The Pythian games first established at Delphi. About this time flourished Chilo, Anacharsis, Thales, Epimenides, Solon, the prophet Ezekiel, Æsop, Stersichorus	591
Jerusalem taken by Nebuchadnezzar, on the 9th of June, after a siege of 18 months	587
The Isthmian games restored, and celebrated every first and 3rd year of the Olympiads	582
Death of Jeremiah the prophet	577
The Nemean games restored	568
The first comedy acted at Athens by Susarion and Dolon	562
Pisistratus first usurped the sovereignty at Athens	560
Cyrus begins to reign. About this time flourished Anaximenes, Bias, Anaximander, Phalaris and Cleobulus; also the prophet Daniel	559
Crœsus conquered by Cyrus. About this time flourished Theognis and Pherecydes	548
Marseilles built by the Phocæans. The age of Pythagoras, Simonides, Thespis, Xenophanes, and Anacreon	539
Babylon taken by Cyrus.	538
The return of the Jews by the edict of Cyrus, and the rebuilding of the temple	536
The first tragedy acted at Athens on the waggon of Thespis	535
Learning encouraged at Athens, and a public library built	526
Ægypt conquered by Cambyses	525
Polycrates, of Samus put to death	522
Darius Hytaspes chosen king of Persia. About this time flourished Confucius, the celebrated Chinese philosopher	521
The tyranny of the Pisistratidæ abolished at Athens	510
The consular government begins at Rome after the expulsion of the Tarquins, and continues independent 461 years, till the battle of Pharsalia	509
Sardis taken by the Athenians and burnt, which became afterwards the cause of the invasion of Greece by the Persians. About this time flourished Heraclitus, Parmenides, Milo, the wrestler, Aristagoras, &c	504
The first dictator, Lartius, created at Rome	498
The Roman populace retire to mount Sacer	493
The battle of Marathon	490
The battles of Thermopylæ, August the 7th, and Salamis, October the 20th. About this time flourished Æschylus, Pindar, Charon, Anaxagoras, Zeuxis, Aristides, &c	480
The Persians defeated at Platæa and Mycale on the same day, 22nd September	479
The 300 Fabii killed at Crimera, July 17th	477
Themistocles, accused of conspiracy, flies to Xerxes	471
The Persians defeated at Cyprus, and near Eurymedon	470
The third Messenian war begins and continues ten years	465
Ægypt revolts from the Persians under Inarus, assisted by the Athenians	463
The Romans send to Athens for Solon's laws. About this time flourished Sophocles, Nehemiah the prophet, Plato the comic poet, Aristarchus the tragic, Leocrates, Thrasybulus, Pericles, Zaleucus, &c	454
The first sacred war concerning the temple at Delphi	448
The Athenians defeated at Chæronæa by the Bœotians	447
Herodotus reads his history to the council of Athens, and receives public honors in the 39th year of his age. About this time flourished Empedocles, Hellanicus, Euripides, Herodicus, Phidias, Artemones, Charondas, &c.	445
A colony sent to Thurium by the Athenians	444
Comedies prohibited at Athens, a restraint which remained in force for three years	440
A war between Corinth and Corcyra	439
Meton begins here his 19 years' cycle of the moon	432
The Peloponnesian war begins, May the 7th, and continues about 27 years. About this year flourished Cratinus, Eupolis, Aristophanes, Meton, Euctemon, Malachi the last of the prophets, Democritas, Gorgias, Thucydides, Hippocrates, &c	431
The history of the Old Testament finishes about this time. A plague at Athens for five years	430
A peace of 50 years made between the Athenians and Lacedæmonians, which is kept only during six years and ten months, though each continued at war with the other's allies	421
The scene of the Peloponnesian war changed to Sicily. The Agrarian law first moved at Rome	416
Ægypt revolts from the Persians, and Amyrtæus is appointed king	414

	B.C.
The Carthaginians enter Sicily, where they destroy Selinus and Himera, but they are repulsed by Hermocrates	409
The battle of Ægospotamos. The usurpation of Dionysius	405
Athens taken by Lysander, on the 24th of April. The end of the Peloponnesian war, and the appointment of 30 tyrants over the conquered city. About this time flourished Parrhasius, Protagoras, Lysias, Agathon, Euclid, Cebes, Telestes, &c	404
Cyrus the younger killed at Cunaxa. The glorious retreat of the 10,000 Greeks, and the expulsion of the 30 tyrants from Athens by Thrasybulus	401
Socrates put to death	400
Agesilaus, of Lacedæmon's expedition into Asia, against the Persians. The age of Xenophon, Ctesias, Zeuxis, Antisthenes, Evagoras, Aristippus of Cyrene, and Archytas	396
The Corinthian war begun by the alliance of the Athenians, Thebans, Corinthians and Argives, against Lacedæmon	395
The Lacedæmonians, under Pisander, defeated by Conon at Cnidus; and, a few days after, the allies are defeated at Coronæa, by Agesilaus	394
The battle of Allia, July 17th, and the taking of Rome by the Gauls	390
Dionysius besieges Rhegium, and takes it after 11 months. About this time flourished Plato, Philoxenus, Damon, Pythias, Iphicrates, &c	388
The Greek cities of Asia tributary to Persia, by the peace of Antalcidas, between the Lacedæmonians and Persians.	387
The war of Cyprus finished by a treaty, after it had continued two years	385
The Lacedæmonians defeated in a sea-fight at Naxus, September 20th by Chabrias. About this time flourished Philistus, Isæus, Isocrates, Arete, Philolaus, Diogenes the Cynic, &c	377
Artaxerxes sends an army under Pharnabazus, with 20,000 Greeks, commanded by Iphicrates	374
The battle of Leuctra, July 8th, in which the Lacedæmonians are defeated by Epaminondas, the general of the Thebans	371
The Messenians, after a banishment of 300 years, return to Peloponnesus	370
One of the consuls at Rome elected from the Plebeians	367
The battle of Mantinea, gained by Epaminondas, a year after the death of Pelopidas	363
Agesilaus assists Tachos, king of Ægypt. Some of the governors of Lesser Asia revolt from Persia	362
The Athenians are defeated at Methone, the first battle that Philip of Macedon ever won in Greece	360
Dionysius the Younger is expelled from Syracuse by Dion. The second Sacred War begins, on the temple of Delphi being attacked by the Phoceans	357
Dion put to death, and Syracuse governed seven years by tyrants. About this time flourished Eudoxus, Lycurgus, Ibis, Theopompus, Ephorus, Datames, Philomelus, &c	354
The Phocians, under Onomarchus, are defeated in Thessaly by Philip	353
Ægypt is conquered by Ochus	350
The Sacred War is finished by Philip taking all the cities of the Phocians	348
Dionysius recovers the tyranny of Syracuse, after ten year's banishment	347
Timoleon recovers Syracuse, and banishes the tyrant	343
The Carthaginians defeated by Timoleon, near Agrigentum. About this time flourished Speusippus, Protogenes, Aristotle, Æschines, Xenocrates, Demosthenes, Phocion, Mamercus, Icetas, Stilpo, Demades, &c	340
The battle of Cheronæa, August 2, in which Philip defeats the Athenians and Thebans, &c	338
Philip of Macedon killed by Pausanias. His son Alexander, in the following year, enters Greece, destroys Thebes, &c	336
The battle of the Granicus, on the 22nd of May	334
The battle of Issus in October	333
Tyre and Ægypt conquered by the Macedonian prince, and Alexandria built	332
The battle of Arbela, October 2nd	331
Alexander's expedition against Porus. About this time flourished Appelles, Callisthenes, Bagoas, Parmenio, Philotas, Memnon, Dinocrates, Calippus, Hyperides, Philetus, Lysippus, Menedemus, &c.	327
Alexander dies on the 21st of April. His empire is divided into four kingdoms. The Samian war, and the reign of the Ptolemies in Ægypt	323
Polyperchon publishes a general liberty to all the Greek cities. The age of Praxiteles, Crates, Theophrastus, Menander, Demetrius, Dinarchus, Polemon, Neoptolemus, Perdiccas, Leosthenes	320
Syracuse and Sicily usurped by Agathocles. Demetrius Phalereus governs Athens for ten years	317
Eumenes delivered to Antigonus by his army	315
Seleucus takes Babylon, and here begins the era of the Seleucidæ	312
The conquests of Agathocles in Africa	309
Democracy established at Athens by Demetrius Poliorcetes	307
The title of kings first assumed by the successors of Alexander	306
The battle of Ipsus, where Antigonus is defeated and killed by Ptolemy, Seleucus, Lysimachus, and Cassander. About this time flourished Zeno, Pyrrho, Philemon, Megasthenes, Crantor, &c.	301
Athens taken by Demetrius Poliorcetes, after a year's siege	296
The first sun-dial erected at Rome by Papirius Cursor, and the time first divided into hours	293
Seleucus, about this time, built about forty cities in Asia, which he peopled with different nations. The age of Euclid the mathematician, Arcesilaus, Epicurus, Bion, Timocharis, Erasistratus, Aristyllus, Strato, Zenodotus, Arsinoe, Lachares, &c.	291
The Athenians revolt from Demetrius	287
Pyrrhus expelled from Macedon by Lysimachus	286
The Pharos of Alexandria built. The Septuagint supposed to be translated about this time	284
Lysimachus defeated and killed by Seleucus. The Tarentine war begins, and continues ten years. The Achæan league begins	281
Pyrrhus, of Epirus, goes to Italy to assist the Tarentines	280
The Gauls, under Brennus, are cut to pieces near the temple of Delphi. About this time flourished Dionysius the astronomer, Sostratus, Theocritus, Dionysius Heracleotes, Philo, Aratus, Lycophron, Persæus, &c.	278
Pyrrhus, defeated by Curius, retires to Epirus	274
The first coining of silver at Rome	269
Athens taken by Antigonus Gonatas, who keeps it twelve years	268
The first Punic war begins, and continues for twenty-three years. The chronology of the Arundelian marbles composed. About this time flourished Lycon, Crates, Berosus, Hermachus, Helenus, Clinias, Aristotimus, &c.	264
Antiochus Soter defeated at Sardis by Eumenes of Pergamus	262
The Carthaginian fleet defeated by Duilius	260

	B.C.
Regulus defeated by Xanthippus. Athens is restored to liberty by Antigonus	256
Aratus persuades the people of Sicyon to join the Achæan league. About this time flourished Cleanthes, Homer junior, Manetho, Timæus, Callimachus, Zoilus, Duris, Neanthes, Ctesibius, Sosibius, Hieronymus, Hanno, Laodice, Lysias, Ariobarzanes	251
The Parthians under Arsaces, and the Bactrians under Theodotus, revolt from the Macedonians	250
The sea-fight of Drepanum	249
The citadel of Corinth taken by Aratus, on the 12th of August	243
Agis, king of Sparta, put to death for attempting to settle an Agrarian law. About this period flourished Antigonus Carystius, Conon of Samus, Eratosthenes, Apollonius of Perga, Lacydes, Amilcar, Agesilaus, one of the ephori, &c.	241
The plays of Livius Andronicus first acted at Rome	240
Amilcar passes with an army into Spain, with Annibal his son	237
The temple of Janus shut at Rome, the first time since Numa's reign	235
The Sardinian war begins, and continues three years	234
Original manuscripts of Æschylus, Euripides, and Sophocles, lent by the Athenians to Ptolemy for a pledge of fifteen talents	233
Tho first divorce known at Rome, being that of Sp. Carvilius. Sardinia and Corsica conquered	231
The Roman ambassadors first appeared at Athens and Corinth	228
The war between Cleomenes and Aratus begins, and continues for five years	227
The colossus of Rhodes thrown down by an earthquake. The Romans first cross the Po, pursuing the Gauls, who had entered Italy. About this time flourished Chrysippus, Polystratus, Euphorion, Archimedes, Valerius Messala, C. Nævius, Aristarchus, Apollonius, Philochorus, Aristoleus, Fabius Pictor, the first Roman historian, Phylarchus, Lysiades, Agro, &c.	224
The battle of Sellasia	222
The Social War between the Ætolians and Achæans, assisted by Philip	220
Saguntum taken by Annibal	219
The second Punic war begins, and continues seventeen years	218
The battle of the lake Thrasymenus, and, next year, that of Cannæ, May 21	217
The Romans begin the Auxiliary war against Philip in Epirus, which is continued at intervals for fourteen years	214
Syracuse taken by Marcellus, after a siege of three years	212
Philopœmen defeats Machanidas at Mantinea	208
Asdrubal is defeated. About this time flourished Plautus, Archagathus, Evander, Teleclus, Hermippus, Zeno, Sotion, Ennius, Hieronymus of Syracuse, Tlepolemus, Epicydes	207
The battle of Zama	202
The first Macedonian war begins, and continues nearly four years	200
The battle of Panius, in which Antiochus defeats Scopas	198
The battle of Cynoscephale, in which Philip is defeated	197
The war of Antiochus the Great begins, and continues three years	192
Lacedæmon joined to the Achæan league by Philopœmon	191
The luxuries of Asia brought to Rome in the spoils of Antiochus	189
The laws of Lycurgus abrogated for a while at Sparta by Philopœmen	188
Antiochus the Great defeated and killed in Media. About this time flourished Aristophanes of Byzantium, Asclepiades, Tegula, C. Lælius, Aristonymus, Hegesinus, Diogenes the Stoic, Critolaus, Masinissa, the Scipios, the Gracchi, Thoas, &c.	187
A war, which continues for one year, between Eumenes and Prusias, till the death of Annibal	184
Philopœmen defeated and killed by Dinocrates	183
Numa's books found in a stone coffin at Rome	179
Perseus sends his ambassadors to Carthage	175
Ptolemy's generals defeated by Antiochus, in a battle between Pelusium and mount Cassius. The second Macedonian war	171
The battle of Pydna, and the fall of the Macedodian empire. About this period flourished Attalus, the astronomer, Metrodorus, Terence, Crates, Polybius, Pacuvius, Hipparchus, Heraclides, Carneades, Aristarchus, &c.	168
The first library erected at Rome, with books obtained from the plunder of Macedonia	167
Terence's Andria first acted at Rome	166
Time measured at Rome by a water machine, invented by Scipio Nasica, 134 years after the introduction of sun-dials	159
Andriscus the Pseudophilip, assumes the royalty in Macedon	152
Demetrius, king of Syria, defeated and killed by Alexander Balas	150
The third Punic war begins. Prusias, king of Bithynia, put to death by his son Nicomedes	149
The Romans make war against the Achæans, which is finished the next year by Mummius	148
Carthage is destroyed by Scipio, and Corinth by Mummius	147
Viriathus is defeated by Lælius, in Spain	146
The war of Numantia begins, and continues for eight years	141
The Roman army of 30,000, under Mancinus, is defeated by 4000 Numantines	138
The restoration of learning at Alexandria, and universal patronage offered to all learned men by Ptolemy Physcon. The age of Satyrus, Aristobulus, Lucius Accius, Mnaseas, Antipater, Diodorus the peripatetic, Nicander, Ctesibius, Sarpedon, Micipsa, &c.	137
The famous embassy of Scipio, Metellus, Mummius, and Panætius, into Ægypt, Syria and Greece	136
The history of the Apocrypha ends. The Servile War in Sicily begins, and continues for three years	135
Numantia taken. Pergamus annexed to the Roman empire	133
Antiochus Sidetes killed by Phraates. Aristonicus defeated by Perpenna	130
Demetrius Nicator defeated at Damascus by Alexander Zebina	127
The Romans make war against the pirates of the Baleares. Carthage is rebuilt by order of the Roman senate	123
C. Gracchus killed	121
Dalmatia conquered by Metellus	118
Cleopatra assumes the government of Ægypt The age of Erymnæus, Athenion, Artemidorus, Clitomachus, Apollonius, Herodicus, L. Cælius, Castor, Menecrates, Lucilius, &c.	116
The Jugurthine war begins, and continues for five years	111
The famous sumptuary law at Rome, which limited the expenses of eating every day	110
The Teutones and Cimbri begin the war against Rome, and continue it for eight years	109
The Teutones defeat 80,000 Romans on the banks of the Rhone	105
The Teutones defeated by C. Marius at Aquæ Sextiæ	102
The Cimbri defeated by Marius and Catulus	101
Dolabella conquers Lusitania	99

Event	B.C.
Cyrene left by Ptolemy Apion to the Romans	97
The Social war begins, and continues three years, till finished by Sylla	91
The Mithridatic war begins and continues twenty-six years	89
The civil wars of Marius and Sylla begin, and continue six years	88
Sylla conquers Athens, and sends its valuable libraries to Rome	86
Young Marius is defeated by Sylla, who is made dictator	82
The death of Sylla. About this time flourished Philo, Charmidas, Asclepiades, Apelicon, L. Sisenna, Alexander Polyhistor, Plotius Gallus, Diotimus, Zeno, Hortensius, Archias, Posidonius, Geminus, &c	78
Bythinia left by Nicomedes to the Romans	75
The Servile war, under Spartacus, begins, and, two years after, the rebel general is defeated and killed by Pompey and Crassus	73
Mithridates and Tigranes defeated by Lucullus	69
Mithridates conquered by Pompey in a night battle. Crete is subdued by Metellus, after a war of two years	66
The reign of the Seleucidæ ends in Syria on the conquest of the country by Pompey	65
Catiline's conspiracy detected by Cicero. Mithridates kills himself	63
The first triumvirate in the persons of J. Cæsar, Pompey, and Crassus. About this time flourished Apollonius of Rhodes, Terentius Varro, Tyrannion, Aristodemus of Nysa, Lucretius, Dionysius the grammarian, Cicero, Antiochus, Spurinus, Andronicus, Catullus, Sallust, Timagranes, Cratippus, &c	60
Cicero banished from Rome, and recalled the next year	58
Cæsar passes the Rhine, defeats the Germans, and invades Britain	55
Crassus is killed by Surena in June	53
Civil war between Cæsar and Pompey	50
The battle of Pharsalia about May 12th	48
Alexandria taken by Cæsar	47
The war of Africa. Cato kills himself. This year is called the year of Confusion, because the calendar was corrected by Sosigenes, and the year made to consist of fifteen months, or 445 days	46
The battle of Munda	45
Cæsar murdered	44
The battle of Mutina. The second triumvirate composed of Octavius, Antony, and Lepidus. Cicero put to death. The age of Sosigenes, C. Nepos, Diodorus Siculus, Trogus Pompeius, Didymus the scholiast, Varro the poet, &c.	43
The battle of Philippi	42
Pacorus, general of Parthia, defeated by Ventidius, fourteen years after the disgrace of Crassus, and on the same day	39
Pompey the Younger defeated in Sicily by Octavius	36
Octavius and Antony prepare for war	32
The battle of Actium on the 2nd of September. The era of the Roman emperors properly begins here	31
Alexandria taken, and Ægypt reduced into a Roman province	30
The title of Augustus given to Octavius	27
The Ægyptians adopt the Julian year. About this time flourished Virgil, Manilius, Dioscorides, Asinius, Pollio, Mæcenas, Agrippa, Strabo, Horace, Macer, Propertius, Livy, Musa, Tibullus, Ovid, Pylades, Bathyllus, Varius, Tucca, Vitruvius, &c.	25
The conspiracy of Muræna against Augusta	22
Augustus visits Greece and Asia	21
The Roman ensigns recovered from the Parthians by Tiberius	20
The secular games celebrated at Rome	17
Lollius defeated by the Germans	16
The Rhæti and Vindelici defeated by Drusus	15
The Pannonians conquered by Tiberius	12
Some of the German nations conquered by Drusus	11
Augustus corrects the calendar, by ordering the twelve ensuing years to be without intercalation. About this time flourished Damascenus, Hyginus, Flaccus the grammarian, Dionysius of Halicarnassus, and Dionysius the geographer	8
Tiberius retires to Rhodes for seven years	6
Our Saviour is born, four years before the vulgar era, in the year 4710 of the Julian period, A.U.C. 749, and the fourth of the 193rd Olympiad	4
	A.D.
Tiberius returns to Rome	2
The leap year corrected, having formerly been every third year	4
Ovid banished to Tomos	9
Varus defeated and killed in Germany by Arminius	10
Augustus dies at Nola, August the 19th, and is succeeded by Tiberius. The age of Phædrus, Asinius Gallus, Velleius Paterculus, Germanicus, Cornel, Celsus, &c.	14
Twelve cities in Asia destroyed by an earthquake	17
Germanicus, poisoned by Piso, dies at Antioch	19
Tiberius goes to Capræa	26
Sejanus disgraced	31
Our Saviour crucified on Friday, April the 3rd. *This event is put four years earlier by some chronologists*	33
St. Paul converted to Christianity	35
Tiberius dies at Misenum near Baiæ on March the 16th, and is succeeded by Caligula. About this period flourished Valerius Maximus, Columella, Pomponius Mela, Appion, Philo Judæus, Artabanus, and Agrippina	37
St. Matthew writes his gospel	39
The name of Christians first given, at Antioch, to the followers of our Saviour	40
Caligula murdered by Chæreas, and succeeded by Claudius	41
The expedition of Claudius into Britain	43
St. Mark writes his gospel	44
Secular games celebrated at Rome	47
Caractacus carried in chains to Rome	51
Claudius succeeded by Nero	54
Agrippina put to death by her son Nero	59
The first persecution against the Christians	64
Seneca, Lucan, and others, put to death	65

	A.D.
Nero visits Greece. The Jewish war begins. The age of Persius, Q. Curtius, Pliny the elder, Josephus, Frontinus, Burrhus, Corbulo, Thrasea, Boadicea, &c	66
St. Peter and St. Paul put to death	67
Nero dies, and is succeeded by Galba	68
Galba put to death. Otho, defeated by Vitellius, kills himself. Vitellius is defeated by Vespasian's army	69
Jerusalem taken and destroyed by Titus	70
The Parthians revolt	77
The death of Vespasian, and succession of Titus. Herculaneum and Pompeii destroyed by an eruption of Mount Vesuvius, November 1st	79
Death of Titus, and succession of Domitian. The age of Sil. Italicus, Martial, Appollonius Tyanæus, Valerius Flaccus, Solinus Epictetus, Quintilian, Lupus, Agricola, &c	81
The Capitoline games instituted by Domitian, and celebrated every fourth year	86
Secular games celebrated. The war with Dacia begins and continues fifteen years	88
The second persecution of the Christians	95
Domitian put to death by Stephanus, &c. and succeeded by Nerva. The age of Juvenal, Tacitus, Statius, &c	96
Nerva dies, and is succeeded by Trajan	98
Pliny, proconsul of Bithynia, sends Trajan an account of the Christians	102
Dacia reduced to a Roman province	103
Trajan's expedition against Parthia. About this time flourished Florus, Suetonius, Pliny junior, Philo, Byblius, Dion, Prusæus, Plutarch, &c	106
The third persecution of the Christians	107
Trajan's column erected at Rome	114
Trajan dies, and is succeeded by Adrian	117
The fourth persecution of the Christians	118
Adrian builds a wall in Britain	121
Adrian visits Asia and Ægypt for seven years	126
He rebuilds Jerusalem, and raises there a temple to Jupiter	130
The Jews rebel, and are defeated after a war of five years, and all banished	131
Adrian dies, and is succeeded by Antoninus Pius. In the reign of Adrian flourished Theon, Phavorinus, Phlegon Trallianus, Aristides, Aquila, Salvius Julian, Polycarp, Arrian, Ptolemy, &c.	138
Antoninus defeats the Moors, Germans, and Dacians	145
The worship of Serapis brought to Rome	146
Antoninus dies, and is succeeded by M. Aurelius and L. Verus, the last of whom reigned nine years. In the reign of Antoninus flourished Maximus Tyrius, Pausanias, Diophantus, Lucian, Hermogenes, Polyænus, Appian, Artemidorus, Justin the martyr, Apuleius, &c	161
A war with Parthia, which continues three years	162
A war against the Marcomanni, which continues five years	169
Another which continues three years	177
M. Aurelius dies, and Commodus succeeds. In the last reign flourished Galen, Athenagoras, Tatian, Athenæus, Montanes, Diogenes Laertius	180
Commodus makes peace with the Germans	181
Commodus put to death by Martia and Lætus. He is succeeded for a few months by Pertinax, who is murdered, 193, and four rivals arise, Didius Julianus, Pescennius Niger, Severus, and Albinus. Under Commodus flourished J. Pollux, Theodotion, St. Irenæus, &c	192
Niger is defeated by Severus at Issus	194
Albinus defeated in Gaul, and killed at Lyons, February the 19th	198
Severus conquers the Parthians	200
The fifth persecution against the Christians	202
Severus visits Britain, and two years after builds a wall there across from the Frith of Forth	207
Severus dies at York, and is succeeded by Caracalla and Geta. In his reign flourished Tertullian, Minutius Felix, Papinianus, Clemens of Alexandria, Philostratus, Plotianus, and Bulas	211
Geta is killed by his brother Caracalla	212
The Septuagint discovered. Caracalla murdered by Macrinus. Oppian flourished	217
Opilius Macrinus killed by the soldiers, and succeeded by Heliogabalus	218
Alexander Severus succeeds Heliogabalus. The Goths then exacted an annual payment on condition that they should not invade or molest the Roman empire. The age of Julius Africanus	222
The Arsacidæ of Parthia are conquered by Artaxerxes, king of Media, and their empire destroyed	229
Alexander defeats the Persians	234
The sixth persecution against the Christians	235
Alexander killed, and succeeded by Maximinus. At that time flourished Dion Cassius, Origen, and Ammonius	235
The two Gordians succeed Maximinus, and are put to death by Pupienus, who is soon after destroyed, with Balbinus, by the soldiers of the younger Gordian	236
Sabinianus defeated in Africa	240
Gordian marches against the Persians	242
He is put to death by Philip, who succeeds, and makes peace with Sapor the next year.	244
About this time flourished Censorius, and Gregory Thaumaturgus	244
Philip killed and succeeded by Decius. Herodian flourished	249
The seventh persecution against the Christians	250
Decius succeeded by Gallus	251
A great pestilence over the empire	252
Gallus dies, and is succeeded by Æmilianus, Valerianus, and Gallienus. In the reign of Gallus flourished St. Cyprian and Plotinus	254
The eighth persecution against the Christians	257
The empire is harassed by thirty tyrants successively	558
Valerian is taken by Sapor and flayed alive	260
Odenatus governs the east for Gallienus	264
The Scythians and Goths defeated by Cleodamus and Athenæus	267
Gallienus killed, and succeeded by Claudius. In this reign flourished Longinus Paulus, Samosatenus, &c	268
Claudius conquers the Goths, and kills 300,000 of them. Zenobia takes possession of Ægypt	269
Aurelian succeeds	270
The ninth persecution against the Christians	272
Zenobia defeated by Aurelian at Edessa	273
Dacia ceded to the Barbarians by the emperor	274

	A.D.
Aurelian killed, and succeeded by Tacitus, who died after a reign of six months, and was succeeded by Florianus, and, two months after, by Probus	275
Probus makes an expedition into Gaul	277
He defeats the Persians in the east	280
Probus is put to death and succeeded by Carus, and his sons Carinus and Numerianus	282
Diocletian succeeds	284
The empire attacked by the Barbarians of the north. Diocletian takes Maximianus as his imperial colleague	286
Britain recovered after a tyrant's usurpation of ten years. Alexandria taken by Diocletian	296
The tenth persecution against the Christians, which continues ten years	303
Diocletian and Maximinianus abdicate the empire, and live in retirement. They are succeeded by Constantius Chlorus and Galerius Maximianus, the two Cæsars. About this period flourished J. Capitolinus, Arnobius, Gregory, and Hermogenes, the lawyers, Ælius Spartianas, Hierocles, Flavius Vopiscus, Trebellius Pollio, &c	304
Constantius dies, and is succeeded by his son	306
At this time there were four emperors, Constantine, Licinius, Maximianus, and Maxentius	308
Maxentius defeated and killed by Constantine	312
The emperor Constantine begins to favour the Christian religion	319
Licinius defeated and banished by Constantine	324
The first general Council of Nice, composed of 318 bishops, who sit from June the 19th to August the 25th	325
The seat of the empire removed from Rome to Constantinople	328
Constantinople solemnly dedicated by the emperor on the 11th of May	330
Constantine orders all the heathen temples to be destroyed	331
The death of Constantine, and the succession of his three sons, Constantinus, Constans, and Constantius. In the reign of Constantine flourished Lactantius, Athanasius, Arius, and Eusebius	337
Constantine the Younger defeated and killed by Constans at Aquileia	340
Constans killed in Spain by Magnentius	350
Gallus put to death by Constantius	354
One hundred and fifty cities of Greece and Asia ruined by an earthquake	358
Constantius and Julian quarrel, and prepare for war; but the former dies the next year, and leaves the latter sole emperor. About this time flourished Ælius Donatus, Eutropius, Libanius, Ammianus, Marcellinus, Iamblichus, St. Hilary, &c	360
Julian dies, and is succeeded by Jovian. In Gregory's reign flourished Gregory Nazianzenus, Themistius, Aurelius, Victor, &c	363
Upon the death of Jovian, and the succession of Valens and Valentinian, the empire is divided, the former being emperor of the east, and the other of the west	364
Gratian taken as partner in the western empire by Valentinian	367
Firmus, tyrant of Africa defeated	373
Valentinian the Second succeeds Valentinian the First	375
The Goths permitted to settle in Thrace, on being expelled by the Huns	376
Theodosius the Great succeeds Valens in the eastern empire. The Lombards first leave Scandinavia, and defeat the Vandals	379
Gratian defeated and killed by Andragathius	383
The tyrant Maximus defeated and put to death by Theodosius	388
Eugenius usurps the western empire, and is two years after defeated by Theodosius	392
Theodosius dies, and is succeeded by his sons, Arcadius in the east, and Honorius in the west. In the reign of Theodosius flourished Ausonius, Eunapius, Pappus, Theon, Prudentius, St. Austin, St. Jerome, St. Ambrose, &c	395
Gildo, defeated by his own brother, kills himself	398
Stilicho defeats 200,000 of the Goths at Fesulæ	405
The Vandals, Alani, and Suevi, permitted to settle in Spain and France by Honorius	406
Theodosius the Younger succeeds Arcadius in the east, having Isdegerdes, king of Persia, as his guardian, appointed by his father	408
Rome plundered by Alaric, king of the Visigoths, August the 24th	410
The Vandals begin their kingdom in Spain	412
The kingdom of the Burgundians is begun in Alsace	413
The Visigoths found a kingdom at Toulouse	414
The Alani defeated and extirpated by the Goths	417
The kingdom of the French begins on the Lower Rhine	420
The death of Honorius, and succession of Valentinian the Third. Under Honorius flourished Sulpicius Severus, Macrobius, Anianus, Panodorus, Stobæus, Servius the commentator, Hypatia, Pelagius, Synesius, Cyrill, Orosius, Socrates, &c	423
Theodosius establishes public schools at Constantinople, and attempts the restoration of learning	425
The Romans take leave of Britain and never return	426
Pannonia recovered from the Huns by the Romans. The Vandals pass into Africa	427
The French defeated by Ætius	428
The Theodosian code published	435
Genseric, the Vandal, takes Carthage, and begins the kingdom of the Vandals in Africa	439
The Britons abandoned by the Romans, make their celebrated complaint to Ætius against the Picts and Scots, and, three years after, the Saxons settle in Britain, upon the invitation of Vortigern	446
Attila, king of the Huns, ravages Europe	447
Theodosius the Second dies, and is succeeded by Marcianus. About this time flourished Zosimus, Nestorius, Theodoret, Sozomen, Olympiodorus, &c	450
The city of Venice first began to be known	452
Death of Valentinian the Third, who is succeeded by Maximus for two months, by Avitus for ten, and, after an interregnum of ten months, by Majorianus	454
Rome taken by Genseric in July. The kingdom of Kent first established	455
The Suevi defeated by Theodoric on the Ebro	456
Marcianus dies, and is succeeded by Leo, surnamed the Thracian. Vortimer defeated by Hengist at Crayford, in Kent	457
Severus succeeds in the western empire	461
The paschal cycle of 532 years invented by Victorius of Aquitain	463
Anthemius succeeds in the western empire, after an interegnum of two years	467
Olybrius succeeds Anthemius, and is succeeded, the next year, by Glycerius, and Glycerius by Nepos	472

	A.D.
Nepos is succeeded by Augustulus. Leo junior, son of Ariadne, though an infant, succeeds his grandfather Leo, in the eastern empire, and, some months after, is succeeded by his father Zeno	474
The western empire is destroyed by Odoacer, king of the Heruli, who assumes the title of king of Italy. About this time flourished Eutyches, Prosper, Victorius, Sidonius Apollinaris	476
Constantinople partly destroyed by an earthquake, which lasted forty days at intervals	480
The battle of Soissons and victory of Clovis over Siagrius the Roman general	485
After the death of Zeno in the east, Ariadne married Anastasius, surnamed the Silentiary, who ascends the vacant throne	491
Theodoric, king of the Ostrogoths, revolts about this time, and conquers Italy from the Heruli. About this time flourished Boethius and Symmachus	493
Christianity embraced in France by the baptism of Clovis	496
The Burgundian laws published by king Gondebaud	501
Alaric defeated by Clovis at the battle of Vorcillè, near Poitiers	507
Paris made the capital of the French dominions	510
Constantinople besieged by Vitalianus, whose fleet is burned with a brazen speculum by Proclus	514
The computing of time by the Christian era, first introduced by Dionysius	516
Justin the First, a peasant of Dalmatia, makes himself emperor	518
Justinian the First, nephew of Justin, succeeds. Under his glorious reign flourished Belisarius, Jornandes, Paul the Silentiary, Simplicius, Dionysius, Procopius, Proclus, Narses, &c	527
Justinian publishes his celebrated code of laws, and, four years after, his digest	529
Conquest of Africa by Belisarius, and that of Rome, two years after	534
Italy is invaded by the Franks	538
The Roman consulship suppressed by Justinian	542
A great plague, which arose in Africa, desolates Asia and Europe	543
The beginning of the Turkish empire in Asia	545
Rome taken and pillaged by Totila	547
The manufacture of silk introduced from India, into Europe, by monks	551
Defeat and death of Totila, the Gothic king of Italy	552
A dreadful plague over Africa, Asia, and Europe, which continues for fifty years	558
Justin the Second, son of Vigilantia, the sister of Justinian, succeeds	565
Part of Italy conquered by the Lombards from Pannonia, who form a kingdom there	568
Tiberius the Second, an officer of the imperial guards, is adopted, and soon after succeeds	578
Latin ceases to be the language of Italy about this time	581
Maurice, the Cappadocian, son-in-law of Tiberius, succeeds	582
Gregory the First, surnamed the Great, fills St. Peter's chair at Rome. The few men of learning who flourished towards the latter end of this century, were Gildas, Agathias, Gregory of Tours, the father of French history, Evagrius, and St. Augustin the monk	590
Augustin the Monk, with 40 others, comes to preach Christianity in England	597
About this time the Saxon Heptarchy began in England	600
Phocas, a simple centurion, is elected emperor, after the revolt of the soldiers, and the murder of Maurice and of his children	602
The power of the Popes begins to be established by the concessions of Phocas	606
Heraclius, an officer in Africa, succeeds, after the murder of the usurper Phocas	610
The conquests of Chosroes, king of Persia, in Syria, Ægypt, Asia Minor, and, afterwards, his siege of Rome	611
The Persians take Jerusalem with the slaughter of 90,000 men, and, the next year, they over-run Africa	614
Mahomet, in his 53rd year, flies from Mecca to Medina, on Friday, July the 16th, which forms the first year of the Hegira, the era of the Mahometans	622
Constantinople is besieged by the Persians and Arabs	626
Death of Mahomet	632
Jerusalem taken by the Saracens, and, three years after, Alexandria and its famous library destroyed	637
Constantine the Third, son of Heraclius, in partnership with Heracleonas, his brother by the same father, assumes the imperial purple. Constantine reigns 103 days, and, after his death, his son. Constantine's son Constans is declared emperor, though Heracleonas, with his mother Martina, wished to continue in possession of the supreme power	641
Cyprus taken by the Saracens	648
The Saracens take Rhodes, and destroy the Colossus	653
Constantine the Fourth, surnamed Pogonatus, succeeds, on the murder of his father in Sicily. Constantinople first besieged by the Arabs	668
The Saracens ravage Sicily	669
Constantinople besieged by the Saracens, whose fleet is destroyed by the Greek fire	673
Justinian the Second succeeds his father Constantine In his exile of ten years the purple was usurped by Leontius and Absimerus Tiberius. His restoration happened 704. The only men of learning in this century were Secundus, Isidorus, Theophylactus, Geo. Pisides, Callinicus, and the venerable Bede	685
Pepin engrosses the power of the whole French monarchy	690
Africa finally conquered by the Arabs	709
Bardanes, surnamed Philippicus, succeeds at Constantinople, on the murder of Justinian	711
Spain is conquered by the Saracens. Accession of Artemius, or Anastasius the Second, to the throne	713
Anastasius abdicates, and is succeeded by Theodosius the Third, who, two years after, yields to the superior influence of Leo the Third, the first of the Isaurian dynasty	716
A second, but unsuccessful siege of Constantinople by the Saracens	717
The Tax called Peterpence, begun by Ina king of Wessex, to support a college at Rome	727
Saracens defeated by Charles Martel between Tours and Poictiers, in October	732
Constantine the Fifth, surnamed Capronymus, succeeds his father Leo	741
Dreadful pestilence for three years over Europe and Asia	746
The computation of years from the birth of Christ first used in historical writings	748
Learning encouraged by the race of Abbas, Caliph of the Saracens	749
The Merovingian race of kings ends in France	750
Bagdad built, and made the capital of the Caliphs of the house of Abbas	762
A violent frost for 150 days from October to February	763
Monasteries dissolved in the east by Constantine	770

	A.D.
Pavia taken by Charlemagne, which ends the kingdom of the Lombards, after a duration of 206 years	774
Leo the Fourth, son of Constantine, succeeds, and five years after, is succeeded by his wife Irene and his son Constantine the Sixth	775
Irene murders her son and reigns alone. The only men of learning in this century were Johannes Damascenus, Fredegaire, Alcuinus, Paulus Diaconus, and George the monk	797
Charlemagne is crowned Emperor of Rome and of the western empire. About this time the Popes separate themselves from the princes of Constantinople	800
Egbert ascends the throne of England, but the total reduction of the Saxon Heptarchy is not effected till 26 years after	801
Nicephorus the First, great treasurer of the empire, succeeds	802
Stauracius, son of Nicephorus, and Michael the First, surnamed Rhangabe, the husband of Procopia, sister of Stauracius, assume the purple	811
Leo the Fifth, the Armenian, though but an officer of the palace, ascends the throne of Constantinople	813
Learning encouraged among the Saracens by Alamon, who made observations on the sun, &c.	816
Michael the Second, the Thracian, surnamed the Stammerer, succeeds, after the murder of Leo	821
The Saracens of Spain take Crete, which they call Candia	823
The Almagest of Ptolemy translated into Arabic, by order of Alamon	827
Theophilus succeeds his father Michael	829
Origin of the Russian monarchy	839
Michael the Third succeeds his father Theophilus with his mother Theodora	842
The Normans get possession of some cities in France	853
Michael is murdered, and succeeded by Basil the First, the Macedonian	867
Clocks first brought to Constantinople from Venice	872
Basil is succeeded by his son Leo the Sixth, the philosopher. In this century flourished Mesué, the Arabian physician Eginhard, Rabanus, Albumasar, Godescalchus, Hincmarus, Odo, Photius, John Scotus, Anastasius the librarian, Alfraganus, Albategni, Reginon, John Asser. Oxford University founded about this time by Alfred the Great	886
Paris besieged by the Normans, and bravely defended by Bishop Goslin	887
Death of Alfred, king of England, after a reign of 30 years	900
Alexander, brother of Leo, succeeds, with his nephew Constantine the Seventh, surnamed Porphyrogenitus	911
The Normans establish themselves in France under Rollo	912
Romanus the First, surnamed Lecapenus, general of the fleet, usurps the throne, with his three sons, Christopher, Stephen, and Constantine the Eighth	919
Fiefs established in France	923
Saracen empire divided by usurpation into seven kingdom	936
Naples seized by the Eastern emperors	942
The sons of Romanus conspire against their father, and the tumults this occasioned produced the restoration of Porphyrogenitus	945
Romanus the Second, son of Constantine the Seventh, by Helena, the daughter of Lecapenus succeeds	959
Romanus, poisoned by his wife Theophana, is succeeded by Nicephorus Phocas the Second, whom the empress, unable to reign alone under the title of protectress of her young children, had married	963
Italy conquered by Otho, and united to the German empire	964
Nicephorus, at the instigation of Theophana, is murdered by John Zimisces, who assumes the purple	969
Basil the Second, and Constantine the Ninth, the two sons of Romanus by Theophana, succeed on the death of Zimisces	975
The third or Capetian race of kings in France begins July 3d	987
Arithmetical figures brought into Europe from Arabia by the Saracens	991
The empire of Germany first made Elective by Otho III. The learned men of this century were Eudes de Cluni, Azophi, Luitprand, Alfarabius, Rhazes, Geber, Abbo, Aimoin Gesbert	996
A general massacre of the Danes in England, Nov. 13th	1002
Old churches about this time rebuilt in a new manner of architecture	1004
Flanders inundated in consequence of a violent storm	1014
The Normans first invade Italy	1018
Constantine becomes sole emperor on the death of his brother	1025
Romanus the Third, surnamed Argyrus, a patrician, succeds, by marrying Zoe, the daughter of the late monarch	1028
Zoe, after prostituting herself to a Paphlagonian money lender, causes her husband Romanus to be poisoned, and afterwards marries her favorite, who ascends the throne under the name of Michael the Fourth	1034
The kingdoms of Castile and Arragon begin	1035
Zoe adopts for her son Michael the Fifth, the trade of whose father (careening vessels) had procured him the surname of Calaphates	1041
Zoe, and her sister Theodora, are made sole empresses by the populace, but after two months, Zoe, though 60 years old, takes, for her third husband, Constantine the Tenth, who succeeds	1042
The Turks invade the Roman empire	1050
After the death of Constantine, Theodora recovers the sovereignty, and 19 months after, adopts as her successor, Michael the Sixth, surnamed Stratioticus	1054
Isaac Comnenus the First, chosen emperor by the soldiers	1057
Isaac abdicates, and, when his brother refuses to succeed him, appoints his friend Constantine the Eleventh, surnamed Ducas	1059
Jerusalem conquered by the Turks from the Saracens	1065
The crown of England is transferred from the head of Harold by the battle of Hastings, October 14th, to William the Conqueror, duke of Normandy	1066
On the death of Ducas, his wife Eudocia, instead of protecting his three sons, Michael, Andronicus, and Constantine, usurps the sovereignty, and marries Romanus the Third, surnamed Diogenes	1067
Romanus being taken prisoner by the Turks, the three youug princes ascend the throne, under the name of Michael Parapinaces the Seventh, Andronicus the First, and Constantine the Twelfth	1071
The general Nicephorus Botaniates the Third, assumes the purple	1078

	A.D.
Doomsday-book begun to be compiled from a general survey of the estates of England, and finished in six years	1080
Alexius Comnenus the First, nephew of Isaac the First, ascends the throne. His reign is rendered illustrious by the pen of his daughter, the princess Anna Comnena. The Normans, under Robert of Apulia, invade the eastern empire	1081
Asia Minor finally conquered by the Turks	1084
Accession of William the Second to the English throne	1087
The first crusade	1096
Jerusalem retaken by the crusaders on the 15th of July. The only learned men of this century were Avicenna, Guy d'Arezzo, Glaber, Hermannus, Franco, Peter Damiani, Michael Celularius, Geo. Cedrenus, Berenger, Psellus Marianus, Scotus, Arzachel, William of Spires, Suidas, Peter the Hermit, Sigebert, &c	1099
Henry the First succeeds to the throne of England	1100
Learning revived at Cambridge	1110
John, or Calojohannes, son of Alexius, succeeds at Constantinople	1118
The order of Knights Templars instituted	1118
Accession of Stephen to the English crown	1135
Manuel, son of John, succeeds at Constantinople	1143
The second crusade	1147
The canon law composed by Gratian, after 24 years' labour	1151
The party names of Guelfs and Gibbelines begin in Italy	1154
Henry the Second succeeds in England	1154
The Teutonic order begins	1164
Conquest of Ægypt by the Turks	1169
The famous council of Clarendon in England, January the 25th. Conquest of Ireland by Henry II	1172
The dispensing of justice by circuits first established in England	1176
Alexius the Second succeeds his father Manuel	1180
English laws digested by Glanville	1181
From the disorders of the government, on account of the minority of Alexius, Andronicus, the grandson of the great Alexius is named Guardian, but he murders Alexius and ascends the throne	1183
Andronicus is cruelly put to death, and Isaac Angelus, a descendant of the great Alexius by the female line, succeeds	1185
The third crusade, and siege of Acre	1188
Richard the First succeeds his father Henry in England	1189
Saladin defeated by Richard of England in the battle of Ascalon	1192
Alexius Angelus, brother of Isaac, revolts, and usurps the sovereignty, by putting out the eyes of the emperor	1195
John succeeds to the English throne. The learned writers of this century were Peter Abelard, Anna Comnena, St. Bernard, Averroes, William of Malmesbury, Peter Lombard, Otho Frisingensis, Maimonides, Humenus, Wernerus, Gratian, Jeoffry of Monmouth, Tzetzes, Eustathius, John of Salisbury, Simeon of Durham, Henry of Huntingdon, Peter Comestor, Peter of Blois, Ranulph Glanville, Roger Hoveden, Companus of Newburg	1199
Constantinople is besieged and taken by the Latins, and Isaac is taken from his dungeon and replaced on the throne with his son Alexius. This year is remarkable for the fourth crusade...	1203
The father and son are murdered by Alexius Mourzoufle, and Constantinople is again besieged and taken by the French and Venetians, who elect Baldwin, count of Flanders, emperor of the east. In the meantime, Theodore Lascaris makes himself emperor of Nice; Alexius, grandson of the tyrant Andronicus, becomes emperor of Trebizond; and Michael, an illegitimate child of the Angeli, founds an empire in Epirus	1204
The emperor Baldwin is defeated by the Bulgarians, and next year is succeeded by his brother Henry	1205
Reign and conquests of the great Zingis Khan, first emperor of the Moguls and Tartars, till the time of his death 1227	1206
Aristotle's works imported from Constantinople are condemned by the council of Paris	1209
Magna Charta granted to the English barons by king John	1215
Henry the Third succeeds his father John on the English throne	1216
Peter of Courtenay, the husband of Yolanda, sister of the two last emperors Baldwin and Henry, is made emperor by the Latins	1217
Robert, son of Peter Courtenay, succeeds	1220
Theodore Lascaris is succeeded on the throne of Nice by his son-in-law, John Ducas Vataces	1222
John of Brienne and Baldwin the Second, son of Peter, succeeded on the throne of Constantinople	1228
The inquisition, which had been begun in 1204, is now entrusted to the Domimicans	1233
Baldwin alone	1237
Origin of the Ottomans	1240
The fifth crusade	1248
Astronomical tables composed by Alphonso the Eleventh of Castille	1253
Ducas Vataces is succeeded on the throne of Nice by his son Theodore Lascaris the Second	1255
The Tartars take Bagdad, and finish the Saracen empire	1258
Lascaris succeeded by his son, John Lascaris, a minor	1259
Michael Palæologus, son of the sister of the queen of Theodore Lascaris ascends the throne, after the murder of the young prince's guardian	1260
Constantinople is recovered from the Latins by the Greek emperors of Nice	1261
Edward the First succeeds to the English throne...	1272
The famous Mortmain act passes in England	1276
Eight thousand French murdered during the Sicilian vespers on the 30th March	1282
Wales conquered by Edward, and annexed to England	1283
Michael Palæologus dies, and his son Andronicus, who had already reigned nine years conjointly with his father, ascends the throne. The learned men of this century are, Gervase, Diceto, Saxo, Walter of Coventry, Accursius, Antony of Padua, Alexander Halensis, William of Paris, Peter de Vignes, Matthew Paris, Grosseteste, Albertus, Thomas Aquinas, Bonaventura, John Joinville, Roger Bacon, Cimabue, Durandus, Henry of Ghent, Raymond Lulli, Jacob Voraigne, Albertet, Dun Scotus, Thebit	1283
A regular succession of English parliaments from this time	1293
The Turkish empire begins in Bithynia	1298

	A.D.
The mariner's compass invented or improved by Flavio	1302
The Swiss Cantons begin	1307
Edward the Second succeeds to the English crown	1307
Translation of the holy see to Avignon, which continues 68 years, till the return of Gregory the Eleventh	1308
Andronicus adopts, as his colleagues, Manuel, and his grandson, the younger Andronicus. Manuel dying, Andronicus revolts against his grandfather, who abdicates	1320
Edward the Third succeeds in England	1327
The first comet observed, the course of which is described with exactness, in June	1337
About this time flourished Leo Pilatus, a Greek professor at Florence, Barlaam, Petrarch, Boccace, and Manuel Chrysoloras, and at this period may be fixed the era of the revival of Greek literature in Italy	1339
Andronicus is succeeded by his son John Palæologus, in the ninth year of his age. John Cantacuzene, who had been left guardian of the young prince, assumes the purple. First passage of the Turks into Europe	1341
The knights and burgesses of Parliament first sit in the same house	1342
The battle of Crecy, August 26	1346
Seditions of Rienzi at Rome, and his elevation to the tribuneship	1347
Order of the Garter in England established April 23rd	1349
The Turks first enter Europe	1352
Cantacuzene abdicates the purple	1355
The battle of Poictiers, September 19th	1356
Law pleadings altered from French into English as a favour from Edward III. to his people, in his 50th year	1362
Rise of Timour, or Tamerlane, to the throne of Samarcand, and his extensive conquests till his death, after a reign of 35 years	1370
Accession of Richard II. to the English throne	1377
Manuel succeeds his father John Palæologus	1391
Accession of Henry the Fourth in England. The learned men of this century were Peter Apono, Flavio, Dante, Arnoldus Villa, Nicholas Lyra, William Occam, Nicephoras Gregoras, Leontius Pilatus, Matthew of Westminster, Wickliff, Froissart, Nicholas Flamel, &c.	1399
Henry the Fourth is succeeded by his son Henry the Fifth	1413
Battle of Agincourt, October 25th	1415
The island of Madeira discovered by the Portuguese	1420
Henry the Sixth succeeds to the throne of England. Constantinople is besieged by Amurath the Second, the Turkish emperor	1422
John Palæologus the Second succeeds his father Manuel	1424
Cosmo de Medici recalled from banishment, and the rise of that family at Florence	1434
The famous pragmatic sanction settled in France	1439
Printing discovered at Mentz, and improved gradually in twenty-two years	1440
Constantine, one of the sons of Manuel, ascends the throne after his brother John	1448
Mahomet the Second, emperor of the Turks, besieges and takes Constantinople on the 29th of May. Fall of the eastern empire. The captivity of the Greeks, and the extinction of the imperial families of the Comneni and Palæologi. About this time the House of York in England began to aspire to the crown, and, by their ambitious views, to deluge the whole kingdom in blood. The learned men of the fifteenth century were Chaucer, Leonard Aretin, John Huss, Jerome of Prague, Poggio, Flavius Blondus, Theodore Gaza, Frank Philelphus, Geo. Trapezuntius, Gemistus Pletho, Laurentius Valla, Ulugh Beigh, John Guttemberg, John Faustus, Peter Schœffer, Wesselus, Peurbachius, Æneas Sylvius, Bessarion, Thomas à Kempis, Argyropulus, Regiomontanus, Platina, Agricola, Pontanus, Ficinus, Lascaris, Tiphernas, Annius of Viterbo, Merula, Savonarola, Picus, Politian, Hermolaus, Grocyn, Mantuanus, John Colet, Reuchlin, Lynacre, Alexander ab Alexandro, Demetrius, Chalcondyles, &c.	1453

RULES OF PRONUNCIATION.

---o---

THE consonants *c*, *s*, and *t*, immediately preceded by the accent, and standing before *i*, followed by another vowel, have the sound of *sh*; as in *Phocion* (fo'sheun), *Accius* (ak'sheus), *Helvetii* (helve'shei, &c., &c.

C., following an accented syllable, has also the same sound before *eu* and *yo*, as in *Caduceus* (kadu'-sheus), *Sicyon* (sish'eon), &c.

Exceptions. T, when preceded by *s* or *x*, has its hard sound, as in *Sestius*, *Sextius*. When *si* or *zi*, immediately preceded by an accented vowel, is followed by a vowel, the *s* or *z* generally takes the sound of *zh*, as *Mœsia* (me'zhea), *Hesiod* (he'zheod), *Elysium* (elizh'eum), *Sabazius* (saba'zheus). The exceptions are *Asia*, *Sosia*, *Theodosia*, *Lysias*, *Tysias* and a few others.

X, ending an accented syllable, and standing before *i* followed by a vowel, has the sound of *ksh*; as in Alexia (alek'shea).

In some proper names, *t* preserves its true sound; as, *Ætion*, *Amphictyon*, *Androtion*, *Eurytion*, *Gration*, *Harpocration*, *Hippotion*, *Iphition*, *Metion*, *Ornytion*, *Palluntion*. *Philistion*, *Polytion*, *Sotion*, *Stration*, and a few others; but *Helphæstion* and *Theodotion*, are Anglicized, and the last syllable pronounced like the same in *question*, *commotion*. In the words *Æsion*, *Dionysion*, and *Iasion*, the *s* takes the sound of *z*, but not of *zh*.

In words ending in *eia*, *eii*, *eium*, and *eius*, with the accent on the *e*, the *i* following the accent is to be understood as articulating the following vowel like *y* consonant; as, *Elege'ia* (eleje'ya), *Pompe'ii* (pompe'yi), *Pompe'ium* (pompe'yum), *Pompe'ius* (pompe'yus). The same rule also applies to words ending in *ia*, preceded by *a* or *o* having the accent upon it, as *Acha'ia* (aka'ya), *Lato'ia* (lato'ya), and likewise to words having the accent on a vowel, followed by *ia*, even when these letters do not end the word, as *Ple'iades* (ple'yadez).

The letters *yi*, followed by a vowel, generally represents the Greek diphthong *υι*, and form but one syllable; as *Harpyia*, pronounced *Harpy'ya*, or, as some prefer, *Harpwy'a*; *Ilythia*, pronounced in four syllables, *Ilithy'ya*, not *Ilithyi'a*, as in Walker.

The diphthongs *æ* and *œ*, ending a syllable with the accent on it, are pronounced like long *e*, in *Cæsar* (se'zar); but when followed by a consonant in the same syllable, like short *e*, as in *Dædalus* (ded'alus).

In Greek and Latin words which begin with uncombinable consonants, the first letter is silent; thus, *C* in *Cneus* and *Ctesiphon*, *M* in *Mneus*, *P* in *Psyche* and *Ptolemy*, *Ph* in *Phthia*, and *T* in *Tmolus* are not sounded.

The termination *eus* in most Greek proper names correspond to *εύς*, and is then to be pronounced in one syllable, as, *Orpheus*, pronounced *Or'phuse*.—(*Worcester*.)

The necessity of attending to the quantity of the vowel in the accented syllable has sometimes produced a division of words that does not seem to convey the actual pronunciation. Thus, *Sulpitius*, *Anicium*, *Artemisium*, &c., being divided into *Sulpit'ius*, *Anic'ium*, *Artemis'ium*, &c., we fancy the syllable after the accent deprived of a consonant closely united with it in sound, and which, from such a sound, derives an aspirated sound equivalent to *sh*. But as the sound of *t*, *c*, or *s*, in this situation, is so generally understood, it was thought more eligible to divide the words in this manner, than into *Sulpi'tius*, *Ani'cium*, *Artemi'sium*, as in the latter mode the *i* wants its shortening consonant, and might, by some speakers, be pronounced as it generally is in Scotland, like *ee*. The same may be observed of *c* and *g* when they end a syllable, and are followed by *e* and *i*, as in Acera'tus, Acida'lia, Tigelli'nus, Teg'yra, &c., where the *c* and *g* ending a syllable, we at first sight think them to have their hard sound; but by observing the succeeding vowel, we soon perceive them to be soft, and only made to end a syllable in order to determine the shortness of the vowel that precedes it.—(*Walker*).

A
CLASSICAL DICTIONARY,
&c., &c.

AARAS'SUS, a city of Pisidia. *Artemid. ap Strab.* l. 12. It is probably the ARIASIS of *Ptolemy.*

A'BA, or A'BÆ, a town of Phocis, famous for an oracle of Apollo, surnamed Abæus. The inhabitants, called Abantes, were of Thracian origin. After the ruin of their country by Xerxes, they migrated to Eubœa, which from them was called Abantis. Some of them passed afterwards from Eubœa into Ionia. *Herodot.* 8. c. 33.—*Paus.* 10 c. 55.——A city of Caria.——A city of Arabia Felix.——A mountain of Armenia Major. *Plin.* 5. c. 24. *Strab.* 10.——A daughter of Xenophanes, who by her address procured from Antony and Cleopatra the government of Olbus, a city of Cilicia. *Strabo*, l. 14.

ABACÆ'NA, or ABACÆ'NUM, a town at the north-east of Sicily, near Messana. *Diod.* 14.——A city of Media. *Ptol.*

AB'ADIR, the name of the stone presented to Saturn by Ops or Rhea, instead of his children.

A'BÆ, a place of Lycia, where there was a temple dedicated to Apollo. *Scol. in Sophocl. Æd. Tyr.*

ABÆ'US, the name of a temple consecrated to Apollo at Abæ.——A surname of Apollo.

ABAG'ARUS, a king of the Osrhoëni and Edesseni, who surrendered to Severus. *Herodian.*——A king of Persia, subdued by the emperor Severus. *Spart.*

AB'ALA, a town of Africa, not far from the Red Sea. *Plin.* 6. c. 29.—A bay near it was called Abalites. ——A harbour to which Cæsar fled when fighting with Pompey. *Appian.* 5. *Civil. Bell.*

AB'ALI, a people of India. *Plin.* 9. c. 19.

AB'ALUS, an island in the German ocean, where, as the ancients supposed, amber dropped from the trees. *Plin.* 37. c. 2.—If a man was drowned there, and his body never appeared above the water, propitiatory sacrifices were offered to his manes during a hundred years.

ABA'NA, a place of Capua. *Cic. contra Rull.*—It is generally supposed, however, that this is an error; and that it ought to be Albana. *Vide Cic. pro. Leg. Agrar.*——A river of Syria washing the walls of Damascus. 2 *Kings*, 12.—*Cluver. Geog.* l. 5. c. 22.

ABAN'DUS, a river of Æthiopia, falling into the Nile, above the island of Meroe. By some it is called Abanhus; by *Ptolemy*, Astapus.

ABAN'NÆ, or ABAN'NI, a people of Africa, subdued by Theodosius. *Amm. Marcel.* l. 29.

ABAN'TA, a city near Parnassus, sacred to Apollos. *Phaverinus.*

ABAN'TES, a people of Peloponnesus, who built a town in Phocis, called Aba after their leader Abas, whence also their name. They afterwards went to Eubœa. They were a warlike people; and it is said that they never suffered their hair to grow but on the hinder part of their head, that their enemies might not seize them by the forehead in battle. *Vid*, ABA. *Strab.* 10. *Ovid. Met.* 15. v. 164. —*Hom. Il.* 2. v. 536.—*Herodot.* 1. c. 146.——A people near Pontus. *Orpheus in Argonaut.*

ABAN'TIAS, or ABANTIADES, a patronymic given to the descendants of Abbas king of Argos, such as Acrisius, Danaë, Perseus, Atalanta, &c. *Ovid. Met.* 4. v. 607.

ABAN'TIDAS, a man who made himself master of Sicyon, after he had murdered Clinias, the father of Aratus. He was himself soon after assassinated. —B.C. 251.—*Plut. in Arat.*

ABAN'TIS, or ABAN'TIAS, an ancient name of the island of Eubœa. *Vid.* ABA.—*Plin.* 4. c. 12.——A country of Epirus, inhabited by a colony of the Abantes of Eubœa, whom a storm had forced on this coast on their return from the Trojan war. *Paus.* 5. c. 22.

ABAOR'TÆ, a people near the river Indus. *Plin.* 6. c. 20.

ABAR'ATHA, a town of Taprobane. *Ptol.*

ABARA'ZA, a city of Syria, between Cyra and Edessa. *Anton. in Itin.*

ABARBA'REA, one of the Naiades, mother of Æsepus and Pedasus by Bucolion, Laomedon's eldest son. *Homer Il.* 6. v. 22.

ABARBI'NA, a city of Hyrcania. *Ptol.*

ABAR'IMON, a country of Scythia, near mount Imaüs. The inhabitants were called Abari or Abares. They had toes behind their heels, and could breathe no air but that of their native country *Plin.* 7. c. 2.

ABARI'NUS, now Navarino, a town of Messenia.

AB'ARIS, a man killed by Perseus. *Ovid. Met.* 5. v. 86.——A Rutulian killed by Euryalus. *Virg. Æn.* 9. v. 344.——A Scythian, son of Seuthes, received a flying arrow from Apollo, with which he gave oracles, and transported himself wherever he pleased. He is supposed to have lived about the third Olympiad. He visited several parts of Greece, and laid the foundation of Proserpine's temple at Lacedæmon. He is said to have returned to the Hyperborean countries from Athens without eating, and to have made the Trojan Palladium with the bones of Pelops. Some suppose that he wrote treatises in Greek: but only the titles are now extant: such as, a history of the oracles of the places which he had visited; an account of Apollo's travels among the Hyperboreans, and the nuptials of the Hebrus. It is reported that there is a Greek manuscript of his epistles to Phalaris, in the library of Augsburg. But there were probably two persons of that name. *Herodot.* 4. c. 36.—*Strab.* 7.—*Paus*, 3. c. 13.—*Vossius de P. Gr.* 16.—*Maussacus ad Harpocrat.* p. 8.—*Plato, in Charm.*—*Fabric. Bib. Gr.*

ABAR'NUS, a city of the Phocians. *Hesyck.*——A city and region of Pariana, near the Propontis. *Steph.*

AB'ARUS, an Arabian prince, who perfidiously deserted Crassus in his expedition against Parthia. *Appian. in Parth.*—He is called Mezeres by *Florus*, 3. c. 11., and Ariamnes by *Plutarch. in Crass.*

A'BAS, a mountain in Syria, in which the Euphrates rises.——A river of Armenia Major, where Pompey routed the Albani. *Plut. in Pomp.*——A son of Metanira, or Melaninia, changed into a lizard for laughing at Ceres. *Ovid Met.*5.126.——The eleventh king of Argos, son of Belus, some say of Lynceus and Hypermnestra, was famous for his genius and valor. He was father of Prœtus and Acrisius, by Ocalea, and built Abæ. He reigned twenty-three years, B. C. 1384.—*Servius* 3.*Æn.* 286.—*Euseb. in Chron.*—*Paus.* 2. c. 16. l. 10. c. 35.—*Hygin.* 170. 273. 244. *Apollod.* 2. c. 2.——A Trojan, lost in the storm which drove Æneas to Carthage. *Virg. Æn.* 1. v. 121.——A Latin chief who assisted Æneas against Turnus, and was killed by Lausus. *Virg. Æn.* 10 v. 170,, &c.——A Greek, slain by Æneas during the Trojan war. The conqueror carried away his brazen shield, which he afterwards deposited in the temple of Apollo with an inscription. *Virg. Æn.* 3. v. 286.——A Trojan, son of Eurydamas, slain by Diomedes. *Hom. Il.* 5. v. 148.——

A Centaur, famous for his skill in hunting. *Ovid. Met.* 12. v. 306.——A soothsayer, to whom the Spartans erected a statue in the temple of Apollo, for his services to Lysander. *Diod.* 1.—*Paus.* 10. c. 9.——A sophist who wrote two treatises, one on history, the other on rhetoric. The time at which he lived is unknown.——A son of Neptune and Arethusa. *Apollod.* 1. c. 25. *Hygin.* 157. Apollodorus mentions another, son of Melampus.——A man who wrote an account of Troy. He is quoted by Servius in *Virg. Æn.* 9.

AB'ASA, an island in the Red Sea, near Æthiopia. *Paus.* 6. c. 26.

ABASE'NI, a nation of Arabia. *Steph.*

ABASI'TIS, a part of Mysia. *Strab.*

ABASSE'NA, or ABASSIN'IA—*Vid.* Abyssinia.

ABAS'SUS, a town of Phrygia. *Liv.* 38. c. 15.

ABASTA'NI, a people near the Indus. *Arrian*, l. 6.

ABAS'TOR, one of the horses which drew Plutus's chariot. *L. Girald. de Mus.*—*Bocc. Gen. D.*—*Claudian de Pros.* 1. v. 286.

ABATH'UBA, a town of Marmarica. *Ptol.*

AB'ATOS an island in the lake near Memphis, in Ægypt, abounding with flax and papyrus. It was the burial place of Osiris, and was celebrated for its antiquity. The annual increase of the Nile was first observed there; and the spot was held in such high veneration, that only the priests were permitted to go there; whence, probably, the name applied to those temples inaccessible to the vulgar (ὰ *non* βαίνω, *ascendo*). The *penetrale* of the Latins bore the same signification, and was guarded with the same sanctity. *Fest. de Verb. Sig.*—*Seneca, N. Q.* 3. c. 2.—*Lucan.* 10. v. 323.

AB'BA, a city of Africa near Carthage. *Polyb.* 1. 14.

AB'BARUS, or AB'GARUS, a name peculiar to the Arabian kings, as that of Ptolemy was to the Ægyptians.

AB'DADA, a city of Galatia. *Ptol.*

ABDAGE'SES, a noble Parthian. *Tac. Ann.* 6. 36.

ABDALON'IMUS, one of the descendants of the kings of Sidon, so poor, that, to maintain himself, he worked in a garden. When Alexander took Sidon, he made him king in the room of Strato, the deposed monarch, and enlarged his possessions, on account of his great disinterestedness, by the addition of some neighbouring provinces. *Justin*, 11. c. 10.—*Diod*, 17.—*Q. Curt.* 4. c. 1.—He is called by *Diodorus*, Ballonimus; by *Plutarch*, Alynomus.

ABDE'RA, according to *Strabo*, Abdara, according to *Ptolemy*, a town of Hispania Bætica, built by the Carthaginians on the shores of the Mediterranean, in the modern kingdom of Grenada. *Plin.* 3. c. 1. *Ptol.* 2. c. 4. *Strab.* 3.——A maritime city of Thrace, built by Hercules, in memory of Abderus, one of his favourites, and afterwards beautified by the Clazomenians and Teians. Some suppose that Abdera, the sister of Diomedes, built it, because some of the medals of this town bear on one side the head of a woman. The air was so unwholesome, and the inhabitants of such a sluggish disposition, that stupidity was commonly called *Abderitica mens.*—Abdera gave birth to Democritus, Protagorus, Anaxarchus, and Hecatæus. *Mela.* 2. c. 2.—*Cic. ad Attic.* 4. ep. 16.—*Herodot.* 1. c. 168.—*Mart.* 10. ep. 25.—*Plin.* 4. c. 11. l. 5. c. 1.—*Philostr. Ic.* 2. c. 25.—*Hippoc.* 3.—*Cluv. Geogr.* 1. 4. c. 14.

ABDE'RIA, a town of Spain, better known by the name of Abdera. *Apollod.* 2. c. 5.—*Mela.* 1. 2. c. 8.

ABDERI'TES, a people of Pæonia, who were obliged to leave their country on account of the great number of rats and frogs which infested it. *Justin.* 15. c. 2.

ABDE'RUS, a native of Opus, in Locris, son of Erimus, arm-bearer to Hercules, was torn to pieces by the mares of Diomedes, which the hero had entrusted to his care when going to war against the Bistones. Hercules built a city near the tomb of his friend, which in honour of his name he called Abdera. *Apollod.* 2. c. 5.—*Philostrat.* 2. c. 25.

AB'DUS, a Parthian eunuch, who conspired against Artabanus, but was poisoned by him. *Tac. Ann.* 6. c. 21.

ABE'A, a city of Messenia. *Ptol.*

ABE'ACUS, a king of the Siraces, a people at the foot of Caucasus. *Strabo.* 11.

ABEA'TÆ, a people of Achaia, probably the inhabitants of Abia. *Paus.* 4. c. 30.—*Plin.* 4. c. 6.

ABEL'LA, now Avella, a town of Campania, the inhabitants of which were called Abellani. It was famous for its nuts, called *avellanæ*, and also for its apples. *Virg. Æn.* 7. v. 740.—*Justin.* 20. c. 5.—*Sil.* 8. v. 544.—*Plin.* 15. c. 22.—*Cluv. Geog.* 1. 3. c. 29.

ABELLI'NUM, now Avellino, a town of Campania, upon the river Sabatus; the people were called Abellinates. *Cluv. Geog.* 1. 3. c. 28. *Plin.* 3. c. 11.

ABEL'LIO, the name under which the Gauls paid adoration to the sun. *Is. Vossius*, 2. *de Idol.* 17.

AB'ELUX, a noble of Saguntum, who favoured the party of the Romans against Carthage. *Liv.* 22. c. 22.

ABEN'DA, a town of Caria, the inhabitants of which were the first who raised temples to the city of Rome as a divinity. *Liv.* 45. c. 6.

ABEO'NA, (ab *abeo*), a divinity whom the Romans invoked when going to undertake a journey. *Augustin Civ. D.* 4. c. 21.

ABE'RA, a town of Arabia Deserta.

ABER'IDES, a heathen god, the same as Saturn, the son of Cœlus and Vesta.

ABES'AMIS, a city of the Omani in Arabia Felix. *Plin.* 6. 28.

ABES'TE, a city of Arachosia. *Id.*6. c. 23.

A'BIA, in Homer, Æpea, formerly Ira, a maritime town of Messenia, one of the seven cities promised to Achilles by Agamemnon. It was called after Abia, daughter of Hercules and nurse of Hyllus. *Paus.* 4. c. 30. *Strab.* 8.—*Hom. Il.* 9. v. 294.

ABIADE'NE, a province of Assyria, near the Tigris.

AB'ICE or AB'ICA, a region of Pontus, near the mouth of the Borysthenes.

AB'IDA, a city of Cœlesyria. *Ptol.*

AB'IGAS, a river of Mauritania. *Procopius.*

A'BII, a nation between Scythia and Thrace. They lived chiefly upon milk; were fond of celibacy, and enemies to war; and, according to Homer, they deserved to be called the justest nation upon earth. *Strab.* 7.—*Hom. I.* 13. v. 6.—According to *Curtius*, 7. c. 6. they surrendered to Alexander, after they had maintained their independence since Cyrus.—*Arrian.* 1. 4. c. 1. § 1.

AB'ILA, or AB'YLA, a mountain of Africa, at the entrance of the Mediterranean, in that part which is nearest to the opposite mountain called Calpe, on the coast of Spain, only eighteen miles distant. These two mountains were called the columns of Hercules, and were said to have been united, till the hero separated them, and made a communication between the Mediterranean and Atlantic seas. *Strab.* 3.—*Mela.* 1. c. 5.—*Plin.* 3.—*Cluv. Geog.* 1. 1. c. 12.

ABILON'CÆ, a people of Syria. *Polyb.* 1. 5.

ABILU'UM, a city of Germany. *Ptol.*

ABI'NA, a city of Susiona. *Id.*

ABI'SA, a city of Arabia Felix. *Id.*

ABISA'MA, a city of Arabia Felix. *Id.*

ABIS'ARES, an Indian prince who offered to surrender to Alexander. *Strabo*, 1. 15. calls him Abisarus; *Diodorus*, Embisarus; and *Arrian*, Ambisarus, Abiasares, or Abissares. *Curt.* 1. 8. c. 12. *Arrian*, 1. 4. c. 27. 1. 5. c. 20.

ABISON'TES, some inhabitants of the Alps. *Plin.* 3. c. 20.

ABIS'TAMES, or ABISTAM'ENES, a præfect of Cappadocia under Alexander the Great. *Curt.* 2. c. 4.

ABLE'TES, a people of Asia Minor, near Troy. *Strab.*

ABLI'ALA, a city of Albania. *Ptol.*

AB'NOBA, mountains of Germany, now Abenow, or the black mountains, where are the sources of the Danube. *Tac. G.* 1. 3. c. 5. 1. 4. c. 16.

ABO'BUS, a surname given to Adonis by the inhabitants of Perga, in Pamphylia. *Hesyck.*

ABOBRI'CA, a town of Lusitania. *Plin.* 4. c. 20.——A town of Spain, called by *Mela*, 1. 3. c. 1., Adobrica.

ABOC'CIS, a town of Æthiopia. *Plin.* 6. c. 29.

ABODI'ACUM, or ABUDI'ACUM, a city of Vindelicia. *Ptol.*

ABŒ'CRITUS, a Bœotian general, killed with a thousand men, in a battle at Chæronea, against the Ætolians. *Plut. in Aral.*

ABOLA'NI, a people of Latium, near Alba. *Plin.* 5. c. 5.

ABOL'LA, a town of Sicily. *Steph.*—*Suidas.*

AB'OLUS, a small river of Sicily. *Plut. in Timol.*

ABONITEI'CHOS, a town of Galatia. *Arrian in Peripl.*

ABORA'CA, a town of Asiatic Sarmatia, near the Euxine sea. *Strabo.*

ABORIEN'SE, a town of Africa Propria. *Plin.* 4. c. 5.

ABORIG'INES, the original inhabitants of Italy; or, according to others, a nation whom Saturn conducted into Latium, where they taught the use of letters to Evander, the king of the country. Their posterity was called Latini, from Latinus, one of their kings; and they assisted Æneas against Turnus. Rome was built in their country. The word signifies *without origin*, or whose *origin is not known*, and is generally applied to the original inhabitants of any country. *Liv.* 1. c. 1., &c.—*Dionys. Hal.* 1. c. 10.—*Justin.* 43. c. 1.—*Plin.* 3. c. 5.—*Aurel. Vict.* 10. 12. 13.—*Strab.* 5.—*Cluv. Geog.* 1. 3. c. 34.

ABOR'RAS, or according to *Ptolemy*, Chaboras, a river of Mesopotamia which falls into the Euphrates below Thapsacus. *Strab.* 16.

A'BOS, or A'BA, a mountain of Armenia, where the ancients place the sources of the Araxes and of the Euphrates.

AB'OTIS, a city of Egypt. *Steph.—Suidas.*

AB'RACES, a general of Artaxerxes. *Xenoph. Cyrop.*

ABRADA'TAS, a king of Susa, who, when his wife Panthea had been taken prisoner by Cyrus, and treated with humanity and respect, surrendered himself and his troops to the conqueror. He was killed in the first battle which he undertook in the cause of Cyrus, and his wife stabbed herself on his corpse. Cyrus raised a monument on their tomb. The history of Abradatas and Panthea forms one of the most interesting parts of Xenophon's writings. For simplicity and elegance, as well as for pathetic and unaffected description, it ranks among the finest passages of antiquity. *Xenoph. Cyrop.* 5, 6, &c.

ABRAG'ANA, a city of the Seres. *Ptol.*

ABREN'TIUS, a man made governor of Tarentum by Hannibal. He betrayed his trust to the enemy, to gain the favours of a beautiful woman, whose brother was in the Roman army. *Polyæn.* 8. c. 24.

ABRETTE'NE, the ancient name of Mysia, from the nymph Abretia. *Plin.* 5. 33.

ABRETTE'NUS, a surname of Jupiter, in Mysia. His priest named Cleon was first a noted robber, and then an officer under Antony and Augustus.

ABRINA'TÆ, a people of Pontus. *Steph.*

ABRINCA'TUI, a people of Gallia Lugdunensis. *Plin.* 4. 18.—*Ptol.*

ABROCO'MES, son of Darius, was in the army of Xerxes, when he invaded Greece. He was killed at Thermopylæ. *Herodot.* 7. c. 224. *Plut. in Cleom.*

ABRODIÆ'TUS, a name given to Parrhasius the painter, on account of his sumptuous manner of living. *Vid.* Parrhasius.

A'BRON, an Athenian, who wrote some treatises on the religious festivals and sacrifices of the Greeks. The titles only of his works are preserved, and quoted as respectable authority by several mythologists. *Suidas.*——A grammarian of Rhodes, who taught rhetoric at Rome.——A grammarian, who wrote a treatise on Theocritus.——A Spartan, son of Lycurgus, the orator. *Plut. in* 10. *Orat.*——A native of Argos, rendered infamous by his debauchery.

ABRO'NIUS SI'LO, a Latin poet, in the Augustan age. He wrote some fables. *Senec.*

ABRONY'CHUS, an Athenian, very serviceable to Themistocles in his embassy to Sparta. *Thucyd.* 1. c. 91.—*Herodot.* 8. c. 21.

ABRO'TA, the wife of Nisus, the youngest of the sons of Ægeus. As a monument to her chastity, Nisus, after her death, ordered the garments which she wore to become the models of fashion for the females of Megara. *Plut. Quest. Græc.*

ABRO'TONUM, the mother of Themistocles. *Plut. in Them.*——A town of Africa, near the Syrtes. *Cluver. Geog.* 1. 6. c. 4.—*Plin.* 5. c. 4.——A harlot of Thrace. *Plut. in Arat.*

ABRUP'OLIS, an ally of Rome, driven from his possessions by Perseus, the last king of Macedonia. *Liv.* 42. c. 13. & 41.

A'BRUS, a city of the Sapæ in Thrace. Some suppose that this passage wants correction. *Paus.* 7. c. 10.

ABSAN'DER, the nineteenth king of Athens, reigned ten years. According to others, Acastus was the nineteenth king.

AB'SARUS, a river of Iberia, or of Armenia Minor, called by *Ptolemy* Apsorrus.

ABSE'US, a giant, son of Tartarus and Terra, destroyed by the thunder of Jupiter. *Hygin. Præf. Fab.*

ABSIN'THII or APSIN'THII, a people on the coasts of Pontus, where there is also a mountain of the same name. *Herodot.* 6. c. 34.

AB'SORIS, a town in the island of Minerva, founded by the Colchians, who went in pursuit of Medea. *Hygin. Fab.* 23.

AB'SORUS or ABSYR'TIS, called in the plural Absyrtides, islands in the Adriatic, or near the west of Istria, where Absyrtis was killed, whence their name. *Strab.* 7.—*Lucan.* 3. v. 190.—*Philost.* 2. c. 11.—*Apollod.* 1. c. 9.—*Plin.* 3. c. 26.

ABSYR'TUS, a son of Æetes king of Colchis, and Hypsea. His sister Medea, as she fled away with Jason, tore his body to pieces, and strewed his limbs in her father's way to stop his pursuit. The place where he was killed was called Tomos. *Strab.* 7.—*Seneca in Medeâ.*—*Plin.* 3. c. 21. & 26.—*Hygin. Fab.* 23.—*Apollod.* 1. c. 9.—*Flacc.* 8. v. 261. —*Ovid. Trist.* 3. el. 9.—*Cic. de Nat. D.* 3. c. 19. ——A small river of Istria, near which Absyrtus was murdered. *Lucan.* 3. v. 190.

ABU'DIUS RU'SO, a Roman who wished to unite his daughter to the son of Sejanus, but was banished. *Tac. Ann.* 6. c. 30.

AB'ULA, a town of Hispania Tarraconensis, now *Avila. Ptol.*

ABULI'TES, a governor of Susa, who betrayed his trust to Alexander, and was rewarded with a province. *Curt.* 5. c. 2.—*Diod.* 17.

ABU'BUS, or rather Abus, the classic name of the *Humber* in England.

ABYDE'NUS, a disciple of Aristotle, too much indulged by his master. He wrote some historical treatises on Cyprus, Delus, Arabia, and Assyria. *Phil. Jud. Joseph contr. Ap.*

ABY'DON, a region of Macedonia. *Steph.—Suidas.*

ABY'DOS, a town of Egypt, known for the famous temple of Osiris, and for the residence of Memnon. It was situated on the west bank of the Nile, between Ptolemais and Thebes, and is now called Madfune or Abutich. *Cluver. Geog.* 6. c. 2.—*Plin.* 5. c. 9.—*Plut. de Isid. & Osir.*—*Mela*, 1. c. 19, & 11. c. 2.——A city of Asia opposite Sestus in Europe, with which, from the narrowness of the Hellespont, it seemed to those who approached it by sea to form only one town. It was built by the Milesians, by permission of king Gyges; but no longer exists. Its coasts abounded with excellent oysters. It was famous for the loves and melancholy fate of Hero and Leander, and for the bridge of boats which Xerxes built there across the Hellespont. The inhabitants being besieged by Philip, the father of Perseus, devoted themselves to death with their families, rather than fall into the enemy's hands. *Liv.* 31. c. 18.—*Lucan.* 2. v. 674. —*Justin.* 2. c. 13.—*Musæus in Her. et Leand.*—*Flacc.* 1. v. 285.—*Ovid. Trist.* 1. el. 9.—*Virg. Geog.* 1. v. 207.—*Cluv. Geog.* 1. 4. c. 14.——A city of Iapygia in Italy. *Steph.*

AB'YLA, a town of Syria. *Plin.* 5. c. 18.

AB'YLA, *vid.* Abila.

ABYL'LI, a people near the Nile. *Steph.*

AB'YLON or AB'YDON, a city of Egypt. *Athen.* 13.

ABYSSIN'IA, a large kingdom of Africa, in Upper Æthiopia, where the Nile takes its rise. The inhabitants are said to be of Arabian origin, and were little known to the ancients. *Cluv. Geog.* 1. 6. c. 9.

ABYSTÆ'I, a people of Lybia. *Phavorin.*

ABYS'TRUM, a city of Magna Græcia, now Ursimaro. *Ptol.*

ABZIRITA'NUM, a town of Africa. *Plin.* 5. c. 4.

ABZO'Æ, a people near the Scythian Ocean. *Id.* 6. c. 13.

A'CA, a city of Phœnicia, afterwards Ptolemais. *Id.* 5. 19.

AC'ABE, a mountain on the borders of Egypt near the Arabian Gulph. *Ptol.*

ACABE'NE, a region of Mesopotamia. *Id.*

ACACAL'LIS, a nymph, mother of Phylander and Phylacis by Apollo. These children were exposed to the wild beasts in Crete, but a goat gave them her milk, and preserved their life. *Paus.* 10. c. 16. ——A daughter of Minos, mother of Cydon, by Mercury; and of Amphithemis, by Apollo. *Paus.* 8. c. 53.—*Apollon.* 4. v. 1493.

ACACE'SIUM, a town of Arcadia, built by Acacus, son of Lycaon. Mercury, surnamed Acacesius, because brought up by Acacus as his foster father, was worshipped there. *Paus.* 8. c. 3. 36. &c.

ACACHU'MA, a city of Ethiopia. *Ptol.*

ACA'CIUS, a rhetorician, in the age of the Emperor Julian. *Suidas.*

ACADE'MIA, a place near Athens, surrounded with high trees, and adorned with spacious covered walks, belonging to Academus, from whom the name is derived. Here Plato opened his school of philosophy, and from this, every place sacred to learning has ever since been called *Academia*. To exclude profaneness and dissipation from a spot so solemnly dedicated to literature, it was even forbidden to laugh there. It was called *Academia vetus*, to distinguish it from the *second Academy* founded by Arcesilaus, who made some few alterations in the Platonic philosophy, and from the *third*, which was established by Carneades. *Cic. de Div.* 1. c. 3.—*Diog.* 3.—*Ælian V. H.* 3. c. 35.

ACADE'MUS, an Athenian, who discovered to Castor and Pollux where Theseus had concealed their sister Helen, for which they amply rewarded him. *Plut. in Thes.*

ACADE'RA, a city of India. *Curt.* 8. c. 10.

ACADI'NA or A'CIS, a fountain of Sicily, sacred to the Palici. Near its sacred stream the inhabitants assembled to try the veracity of oaths. They were written on wooden tablets, which were thrown into the fountain, and if they sunk the oaths were considered as true. *Macrob. Sat.* 5. c. 19.—*Sil. Ital.* 14. v. 221.—*Alex.* 5. c. 10.

AC'ADRA, a town of Arabia Felix. *Ptol.*

AC'ADRÆ, a people of Asia who inhabited the provinces now called Quicheu and Huquan, in China.

ACALAN'DRUS or ACALYN'DRUS, a small river of Lucania, falling into the bay of Tarentum. *Plin.* 3. c. 11.

AC'ALE, a city of Arabia Felix. *Ptol.*

ACAL'LE, or according to *Pausanias*, Acalis, a daughter of Minos and Pasiphae, probably the same as Acacallis. *Apollod.* 3. c. 1.

AC'ALUS, the nephew of Dædalus, called also Talus. *Vid.* Talus.

ACAMAN'TIDES, a philosopher of Heliopolis. *Suidas.*

ACAMAN'TIS, the name of one of the tribes of Athens, called after Acamas. *Id.*——An ancient name of Crete, from the promontory Acamas. *Steph.*

ACAMAN'TIUS, a philosopher of Heliopolis. *Suidas.*

ACAMAR'CHIS, one of the Oceanides. *Diod. Sic.* 6.

AC'AMAS, son of Theseus and Phædra, went with Diomedes to demand Helen from the Trojans after her elopement from Menelaus. In his embassy he had a son called Munitus, by Loadice, the daughter of Priam. He was engaged in the Trojan war, where he distinguished himself by his valor, and was in the number of those who were concealed in the wooden horse. At the sacking of the unfortunate city, he discovered his own son by Loadice, and not only saved his life, but that of Æthra, who had made the child known to him, and who had brought him up with maternal care. He afterwards built the town of Acamantium in Phrygia, and, on his return to Greece, called a tribe after his own name at Athens. *Paus.* 10. c. 26.—*Q. Calab.* 12.—*Hygin.* 108.—*Tzetzes in Lycoph.*—*Tryphiodor.*—*Parthen. Erot.* 16.—*Schol. Euripid. in Herc. Inf.*——A son of Antenor, known by his valor in the Trojan war. *Q. Cal.* 10. v. 168.—*Hom. Il.* 11. v. 60.——A Thracian auxiliary of Priam, in the Trojan war. *Hom. Il.* 11.——The most western promontory of Cyprus, now called Holy Epiphany. The whole island was called from it Acamantis. *Plin.* 5 c. 32.

ACAMP'SIS, a river of Colchis. *Arrian.*

ACAN'THA, a nymph loved by Apollo, and changed into the flower Acanthus. *Plin.* 24. c. 12.—*Dioscorid.* 3. c. 12 & 13.—*Hesychius.*

ACAN'THINE, an island of the Arabian Gulf. *Ptol.*

ACAN'THON, a mountain of Ætolia. *Plin.* 4. c. 2.

ACAN'THUS, a town of Caria. *Mela*, 1. c. 16.——A town near mount Athos, now Erisso, belonging to Macedonia; or according to others, to Thrace. It was founded by a colony from Andrus. It was from this place that Xerxes in his expedition against Greece, cut a canal to communicate with the Sinus Singiticus, not to sail round mount Athos. *Diod.* 2.—*Thucyd.* 4. c. 84.—*Mela*, 2. c. 2. ——A town in Ægypt, at the south of Memphis, on the western banks of the Nile. *Strab.* 17.——A town in Asia near the river Ninus. It was anciently called Dulopolis. *Plin.* 5. c. 28.——An island mentioned by *Plin.* 5. c. 32.——A son of Antonous and Hippodamia, changed into a bird. *Calphurn. ec.* 6. v. 7.—*Antonin.* 7.

ACAPEA'TÆ, a people near the Palus Mæotis. *Plin.* 6. c. 7.

AC'APIS, a river of Asia.

AC'ARA, a town of Pannonia.——A town in Italy. *Strab.* 5.

ACARAS'SUS, a city of Lycia. *Steph.*

ACA'RIA, a fountain of Corinth, near which Iolas cut off the head of Eurystheus. *Strab.* 8.

ACARNA'NIA, anciently Curetis, a country of Epirus, at the north of the Ionian sea, divided from Ætolia by the Achelous. The inhabitants were so addicted to pleasure, that *porcus Arcanas* became proverbial. Their horses were famous for swiftness as well as for beauty. The country received its name from Acarnas. *Plin.* 2. c. 90. 1. 4. c. 1. —*Strab.* 7. & 9.—*Paus.* 8. c. 24.—*Lucian. in Dial. Meretr.*—*Macrob. Sat.* 1. c. 12.—*Mela*, 2. c. 4.—*Cluv. Geog.* 1. 4. c. 7.——A city not far from Syracuse. *Cic. in Pison.* 40.——A country of Egypt. *Serv. in Æn.* 5. v. 298.

ACAR'NAS and AMPHOT'ERUS, sons of Alcmæon and Callirrhoe. Alcmæon being murdered by the brothers of Alphesibœa his former wife, Callirrhoe requested of Jupiter, that her children, who were still in the cradle, might suddenly grow up to punish their father's murderers. This was granted. *Vid.* Alcmæon. *Paus.* 8. c. 24.—*Ovid. Met.* v. 414.

ACAR'NAS or ACAR'NAN, a stony mountain of Attica. *Senec. in Hippol.* v. 20.

ACAR'NE, a town near Magnesia. *Plin.* 4. c. 9.

ACAR'RA, a city of Achaia. *Steph.*

AC'ASIS, probably the same as Acalis. *Vid.* Acalle.

ACAS'TA, one of the Oceanides. *Hes. Theog.* v. 356.

ACAS'TUS, son of Peleus, king of Iolchis, by Anaxibia, married Astydamia or Hyppolyte, who fell in love with Peleus, son of Æacus, when in banishment at her husband's court. Peleus rejecting the guilty addresses of Hippolyte, was accused before Acastus of attempts upon her virtue, and soon after, at a chase, he was tied to a tree, and cruelly exposed to wild beasts. Vulcan, by order of Jupiter, delivered Peleus; who returned to Thessaly, and put to death Acastus and his wife. Acastus had accompanied his relation Jason to Colchis, and at his return succeeded Peleus, in whose honour he instituted funeral games, the first, it is said, ever celebrated on such an occasion. He pursued his sisters, who had destroyed their father (*Vid.* Peleus); and made war against Admetus, who had hospitably afforded them protection. His dexterity in the chase has been mentioned as one of his great qualities. *Vid.* Peleus and Astydamia. *Pindar* 4. *Nem.*—*Ovid. Met.* 8. v. 306. 1. 11. c. 409. *Heroid.* 13. v. 25.—*Apollod.* 1. c. 9. &c.——The second Archon at Athens.

ACATHAR'TUS, a bay in the Red Sea. *Strab.* 16.

AC'ATON, a mountain of Ætolia.

AC'CA LAUREN'TIA, the wife of Faustulus, the shepherd of king Numitor's flocks, brought up Romulus and Remus, who had been exposed on the banks of the Tiber. From her wantonness she was called *Lupa*, (a prostitute,) whence originated the fable that Romulus was suckled by a she wolf. *Dionys. Hal.* 1. c. 18.—*Liv.* 1. c. 4.—*Aul. Gel.* 6. c. 7.—*Servius in Virg.* 1. *Æn.* 277.—*Vossius de Id.* 1 c. 12.—The Romans yearly celebrated certain festivals (*Vid. Laurentalia*) in honor of another prostitute of the same name. *Plut. Quæst. Rom. et in Romul.*——A companion of Camilla. *Virg. Æn.* 11. v. 820.

AC'CA TARUN'TIA, the wife of Taruntius, a noble

Etrurian, probably the one whose fabulous history is related by *Plutarch*. Vid. *Scalig. in Varron. de LL.* p 78.

ACCABICONTICHIT'Æ, a people of Mauritania, their town was called Accabicontichos, or Accabicus Murus. *Steph.*

ACCHIT'Æ, a people of Arabia near the Red Sea. *Plin.* 6. c. 28. *Stephanus* calls them Acheni.

AC'CI, a town of Hispania Tarraconensis. *Ptol.*

AC'CIA or A'TIA, daughter of Julia, the sister of Cæsar, and M. Atius Balbus, was the mother of Augustus, and died about forty years B.C. *Suet. in Aug.* 4.——A city of Corsica.

AC'CIA VARIO'LA, an illustrious female whose cause was eloquently pleaded by Pliny. *Plin.* 6. ep. 33.

AC'CILA, a town of Sicily. *Liv.* 24. c. 35.

ACCI'SI, a people near the Palus Mæotis. *Plin.* 6. c. 7.

ACCITA'NA, a colony of Hispania Citerior. *Id.* 3. c. 3.

AC'CIUS L. or AT'TIUS, a Roman tragic poet, whose roughness of style Quintilian has imputed to the unpolished age in which he lived. He translated some of the tragedies of Sophocles, but of his numerous pieces only some of the names are known. The consul Junius Brutus cultivated his acquaintance, and not only raised a statue to his honor in the temple of the Muses, but inscribed on the temples and public monuments of Rome the verses of his friend. His popularity was great, not only among the nobles, but among the people, whom he entertained by the effusions of his muse. Some few of his verses are preserved in Cicero, and other writers, and may be seen to the number of seven hundred and ninety-nine in the collection of the Latin poets. He died about one hundred and eighty years B. C. *Horat.* 2. ep. 1. v. 56. —*Ovid. Am.* 1. el. 15. v. 19.—*Quintil.* 10. c. 1.—*Cic. ad Att. & in Br.* 18. *De Orat.* 3. c. 16.—*Macrob. Sat.* 1, 7.—*Vos. de Poet. Lat.* c. 1. p. 67., &c.—*Fabric. B. L.* 4. c. 1. p. 659.—*Hamberger.* part i. p. 404.—*Sax. Onom.* 1. p. 138.—*Harles. Not. Lit. Rom.* v. 1. p. 98.——A famous orator of Pisaurum in Cicero's age. *Cic. Brut.* 78.—Some considered this person the same as the poet. *Vid. Harles Lit. Rom.* v. 2. p. 112.

AC'CIUS LA'BEO, a foolish poet, who translated some of the books of Homer's Iliad into Latin verse. He was a favorite of Nero. *Pers. Sat.* 1. 4. & 50.

AC'CIUS TUL'LIUS, a prince of the Volsci, very inimical to the Romans. Coriolanus, when banished by his countrymen, fled to him, and led his armies against Rome. *Liv.* 2. c. 37.—*Plut. in Coriol.*

AC'CO, a general of the Senones in Gaul. *Cæs. Bell. Gall.* 6. c. 4. &. 44.——An old woman who went mad on seeing her deformity in a looking-glass. *Hesych.*—*Cœl. Rhod.* 16. c. 2.

AC'CUA, a town in Italy. *Liv.* 24. c.20.

ACCUSO'RIUM COLO'NIA. *Vid.* Acusio Colonia.

A'CE, a maritime town in Phœnicia, called also Ptolemais, from a king of Ægypt, and now Acre It was a colony of Claudius Cæsar, and, in modern history, is famous for the many sieges which it sustained during the crusades, alternately against the Saracens and of the Christians. It is now an inconsiderable town, about twenty-four miles from Tyre, and forty-five from Jerusalem, and frequented only by a few merchant ships. *C. Nep. in Datam.* c. 5.—*Cluver. Geog.* 1. 5. c. 21.——A place of Arcadia, near Megalopolis, where Orestes was delivered from the persecution of the furies, who had a temple there. *Paus.* 8. c. 34.

AC'EDUM, now Ceneda, a town of the Veneti. *Ptol.*

AC'ELA, a town of Lycia, so called from Acelus, a son of Hercules and Malis, the attendant of Omphale. *Steph.*

AC'ELUM, a town of the Veneti, now Azolo. But in most copies of *Ptolemy* it is Acedum.

AC'EMA, a mountain of the Alps, in which the Varus has its source. *Plin.* 3 c. 5.—Some read Cema.

ACEN'IPO, a town of Hispania Bætica. *Ptol.*

ACER'ATUS, a soothsayer, who alone remained at Delphi, when the approach of Xerxes frightened away the inhabitants. *Herodot.* 8. c. 37.

ACER'BAS, a priest of Hercules at Tyre, who married Dido. *Vid.* Sichæus. *Justin.* 18. c. 4. *Virg. Æn.* 1. v. 343.

ACERI'NA, a colony of the Brutii in Magna Græcia, taken by Alexander of Epirus. *Liv.* 8. c. 24.

ACERO'NIA, an attendant of Agrippina, who was slain in attempting to save the life of her mistress. *Tacit. Annal.* 14. c. 5.

ACER'RÆ or ACER'RA, an ancient town of Campania, near the river Clanius. It still subsists, and the frequent inundations from the river which terrified its ancient inhabitants, are now prevented by large drains. *Virg. G.* 2. v. 225.—*Liv.* 8. c. 17.—*Cluv. Geog.* 1. 3. c. 29.

ACERSEC'OMES, a surname of Apollo, and also of Bacchus. The word ἀκερσεκόμης, signifies unshorn. *Juv.* 8. v. 128.

ACERVI'TIS, a town of Thrace, afterwards called Calatis. *Plin.* 4. c. 11.

A'CES, a river of Asia. *Herodot.* 3. c. 117.

AC'ESÆ, a city of Macedonia, the inhabitants were called Acesæi. *Steph.*

ACESAM'ENÆ, a city of Macedonia, so called from Acessamenus of Pieria. *Id.*

ACESAN'DER, the writer of a history of Cyrene, mentioned by the Scholiast on *Apollonius Argon.* and on *Pindar, Pyth.* 4.—*Voss. His. Gr.* 1. 3.

AC'ESAS, or ACE'SIUS, a native of Patara, famed for his skill in embroidery. He, together with Helicon of Carystus, made a peplum for Minerva Polias. *Erasm. in Adag.*

ACE'SIA, part of the island of Lemnos, which received this name from Philoctetes, whose wound was cured there. *Philostr.*

ACE'SIAS, an ignorant physician, whose want of skill gave rise to the proverb *Acesias medicatus est. Erasm. in Adag.*

ACESI'NE, a river of Sicily; the Asines of *Pliny* 3. c. 8., and Onabalæ of *Appian.*—*Thucyd.* 4. c. 25.

ACESI'NES, a name of the Tanais. *Steph.*

ACESI'NUS, a river of Persia falling into the Indus, and forming the eastern boundary of the ancient kingdom of Porus. Its banks produced reeds of such an uncommon size, that a piece between two knots served as a boat to cross the water.—*Justin.* 12. c. 9.—*Plin.* 4. c. 12.

ACE'SIUS, a surname of Apollo in Elis and Attica, given to him as a god of medicine. *Paus.* 6. c. 24.

ACESODO'RUS, an historian. *Vid.* Acestodorus.

ACESSÆ'US, a sailor who excused his dilatoriness in setting out on his voyages, by saying that he was waiting for the moon. Hence the proverb *Acessæi luna*, to express delay. *Erasm. in Adag.*

ACES'TA, a town on the western shores of Sicily, called after king Acestes, and known also by the names of Segesta and Ægesta. It was built according to Virgil, by Æneas, who left here part of his followers, as he was going to Italy. *Virg. Æn.* 5. v. 746.

ACESTÆ'I, the inhabitants of Acesta, in Sicily. *Steph.*—*Plin.* 3. c. 8.

ACES'TE, the nurse of the daughters of Adrastus. *Stat. Thebaid.* 1.

ACES'TES, son of Crinisus and Egesta, was king of the country near Drepanum in Sicily. He aided Priam in the Trojan war, kindly entertained Æneas during his voyage, and assisted him to bury his father on mount Eryx. In commemoration of this event, Æneas built the city of Acesta. *Virg. Æn.* 5. v. 746, &c.——A river of India, near which Alexander founded the city of Bucephala.

ACES'TIUM, a woman who saw the sacred office of torch-bearer in the festivals of Ceres successively conferred on her father Xenocles, her grandfather and her brother of the name of Sophocles, her great grandfather Leon, her husband Themistocles, and her son Theophrastus. *Paus.* 1. c. 37.

ACESTODO'RUS, a Greek historian, who mentions the review which Xerxes made of his forces before the battle of Salamis. *Plut. in Themist. Stephanus* mentions an historian of Megalopolis, called Acesodorus; he was probably the same person.

ACES'TOR, a writer on the city of Cyrene, mentioned by the Scholiast on *Apollonius, Argonaut.* 2.

ACESTOR'IDES, an Athenian Archon.——A Corinthian governor of Syracuse. *Diod.* 19.——A writer who published four books of fables, *de quâque urbe. Tzetz. Chiloph.* 7. *His.* 144.

ACES'TORUS or ACES'TOR, a tragic poet of Thrace, surnamed Saces. *Scholiast in Aristoph.*

ACE'TES, a son of Phœbus and Perseis, was king of the Colchians. He received Phryxus kindly, and gave him his daughter Chalciope. *Apollod.* 1. *Bibl.*——One of Evander's attendants. *Virg. Æn.* 11. v. 30.

ACE'UM, a town of Colchis, on the banks of the Phasis.

ACHABY'TOS, a lofty mountain in Rhodes, where Jupiter had a temple. *Diod. Sic.*

ACHÆ'A, a surname of Pallas, whose temple in Daunia was defended by dogs, which, as historians report, fawned upon the Greeks, but fiercely attacked all other persons. *Aristot. de Mirab.* Ceres was called Achæa, from her lamentations (ἀχεα,) for the loss of Proserpine. *Plut. in Isid. & Osir.*——A town of Asiatic Sarmatia, near the Euxine sea. *Ptol.* According to *Ovid*, *de Pont.* 4. *el.* 10. it seems to have been a colony of the Orchomenians.

ACHÆ'Æ PETRÆ, rocks hewn from the mountain out of which the river Jordanus flows, and on which the city of Samos was built. *Strabo.* 8.

ACHÆ'I, the descendants of Achæus, at first inhabited the country near Argos, but being expelled by the Heraclidæ, 80 years after the Trojan war, they retired among the Ionians, whose twelve cities they seized and kept. The names of these cities were Pellene, Ægira, Ægæ, Bura, Tritœa, Ægion, Rhypæ, Olenos, Helice, Patræ, Dyme, and Pharæ. The inhabitants of these three last began a famous confederacy, 284 years B.C. which continued formidable upwards of 130 years, under the name of the *Achæan league*, and was most illustrious whilst supported by the splendid virtues and abilities of Aratus and Philopœmen. Their arms, with the assistance of Philip of Macedon, were directed against the Ætolians for three years; and they grew powerful by the accession of the neighbouring states of Peloponnesus. After the conquest of Macedonia, however, the Romans interfered more arrogantly in the affairs of Greece, and the Achæans, after insulting the ambassadors of the republic, manifested a degree of resistance, which, if directed by wisdom and unanimity, might have withstood foreign invasion, but which shrunk beneath the formidable legions of Rome; and thus the country was enslaved, and the Achæan league destroyed, B.C. 147. The Achæans had extended the borders of their country by conquest, and even planted colonies in Magna Græcia. The name of *Achæi* is generally applied to all Greeks indiscriminately, by the poets, *Vid.* Achaia. *Herodot.* 1. c. 145. l. 8. c. 36.—*Stat. Theb.* 2. v. 164.—*Polyb. Liv.* 1. 27, 32., &c. *Plut. in Philop.*—*Plin.* 4. c. 5.—*Ovid. Met.* 4. v. 605.—*Paus.* 7. c. 1., &c.——A people of Asia, on the northern borders of the Euxine sea. *Ovid de Pont.* 4. el. 10. v. 27.

ACHÆ'IA, a hill near Carystus. *Steph.*

ACHÆ'IUM, a place of Troas, near Tenedus. *Strab.* 8.

ACHÆM'ENES, an ancient king of Persia, among the progenitors of Cyrus the Great. His descendants, called Achæmenides, formed a separate tribe in Persia, of which the kings were members. Cambyses, son of Cyrus, on his death-bed, charged his nobles, and particularly the Achæmenides, not to suffer the Medes to recover their former influence in the state, and abolish the power of Persia. *Herodot.* 1. c. 125. l. 3. c. 65. l. 7. c. 11.—*Horat.* 2. od. 12. v. 21.——A Persian, made governor of Ægypt by Xerxes, and slain by Inaros, B.C. 484. *Herodot.* 7. 7.——A people of Africa Propria. *Ptol.*

ACHÆME'NIA, part of Persia, called after Achæmenes, whence Achæmenius. *Horat.* 3. od. 1. v. 44. *Epod.* 13. v. 12.

ACHÆMEN'IDES, one of the companions of Ulysses, abandoned on the coast of Sicily, where Æneas, on his voyage to Italy, found him. *Virg. Æn.* 3. v. 614.—*Ovid Ib.* 417. *Met.* 14. v. 163. *Pont.* 2. el. 2. v. 25.

ACHÆ'ORUM LI'TUS, a harbour in Cyprus. *Strab.* ——A harbour in Troas.——A harbour in Æolia. ——A harbour in Peloponnesus.——A harbour on the Euxine. *Paus.* 1. c. 34.

ACHÆ'ORUM STA'TIO, a place on the coast of the Thracian Chersonesus, where Polyxena was sacrificed to the shade of Achilles, and where Hecuba killed Polymnestor, who had murdered her son Polydorus.

ACHÆ'US, a king of Lydia, hanged by his subjects for his extortion. *Ovid in Ib.*——A son of Xuthus of Thessaly. He fled, after the accidental murder of a man, to Greece, and the inhabitants were called, from him, Achæi. He afterwards returned to Thessaly. *Strab.* 8.—*Paus.* 7. c. 1.——A tragic poet of Eretria, son of Pythodorus, who wrote forty-three tragedies, of which some of the titles are preserved. Of these only one obtained the prize. He lived some time after Sophocles, and Euripides is said by *Athenæus*, 6. p. 270., to have borrowed from his tragedies. *Sax. Onom.* l. p. 34.—*Voss. de Poet. Græc.* c. 5. p. 27.—*Fabric. Bib. Græc.* v. 2. p. 79.——Another poet of Syracuse, who wrote ten tragedies. Fragments of the tragedies of both or one of these poets may be seen in Grotius, *Frag. Trag. et Com.* p. 441.—*Fabric. Bibl. Græc. ibid.*——An historian who wrote before Pindar; he is praised by the Scholiast on *Pindar, Olymp. Od.* 7.—*Fabric. ibid.*——A river which falls into the Euxine. *Arrian. in Peripl.*——A relation of Antiochus the Great, appointed governor of all the king's provinces beyond Taurus, aspired to the sovereign power, which he disputed for eight years with Antiochus. He was at last betrayed by a Cretan, and put to death. *Polyb.* 8.——A youth who slew Hipparinus, tyrant of Syracuse. *Parthen. in Amat.*——A foolish person, surnamed Callicon. *Eustath. Od.* 10.

ACHA'IA, called also Hellas, a country of Greece, situated between Epirus, Thessaly, the Ægean sea, and Peloponnesus. It contained, anciently the districts of Attica, Bœotia, Doris, Ætolia, Locris, and Phocis, and now forms part of Livadia. It was originally called Œgialus, (*shore*,) from its situation. The Ionians called it Ionia when they settled there, and it received the name of Achaia from the Achæi, who dispossessed the Ionians. By Achaia, when conquered by the Romans, is generally understood the greater part, or the whole of the Peloponnesus, with Græcia Propria. *Vid.* Achaia. A small part of Phthiotis, of which Alos was the capital, was also called Achaia. *Hom. Il.* 2. v. 684.—*Herod.* 1. c. 145.—*Cluv. Geog.* l. 4. c. 7.—*Pomp. Mela.* l. 2. c. 4.

ACHAIC'ARUS, a prophet of the Bosporani. *Strab.* 16.

ACHA'ICUM BEL'LUM. *Vid.* Achæi.

ACHA'IS, a region of Lydia, near the Pactolus. *Steph.*——A town, called also Heraclea, at the east of the Caspian sea. *Plin.* 6. c. 16.

ACHALDÆ'US, a general, slain by Aristomenes. *Paus.* 4.

ACH'AME, a people of the interior of Africa. *Ptol.*

ACHAMAN'TIS, a daughter of Danaus. *Hygin. Fab.* 170.

ACH'AMAS, one of Vulcan's workmen. *Val. Flacc.* 1. v. 583.

ACH'ANA, a river of Arabia Felix. *Plin.* 6. c. 28.

ACHA'NI or ACHAR'NI, a people near Scythia. *Steph.*

ACH'ARA, a town near Sardis. *Strab.* 14.

ACHAR'ACA or CHAR'ACA, a village near the city of Nysa, where were temples dedicated to Pluto and Juno. *Strab.* 12 & 14.

ACHAR'BAS or ACER'BAS. *Vid.* Sichæus.

ACHAREN'SES, a people near Syracuse, now *Carrane. Cic. in Verr.* 3.

ACHARITA'NUM, a town of Africa Propria. *Plin.* c. 4.

ACHAR'NÆ, a village of Attica, belonging to the tribe of Æneis. Aristophanes has given this name to one of his comedies, and has represented the inhabitants as uncouth and slovenly. Pindar bestows high encomiums on their women. *Paus.* 1. c. 31.—*Aristoph. Achar. Pind.* 2. *Nem.*—*Stat. Theb.* 12. v. 623.—*Thucyd.* c. 19.—*Cluv.* l. 4. c. 8.

ACHAR'NIS, a man slain by the partisans of Marius, who had received orders to put to death all whom their leader did not salute. *Plut. in Mar.* —*Lucan.* 2. v. 113.

ACHAR'RÆ, a city of Thessaly.

ACH'ASA, a region of Scythia beyond the Imaus. *Ptol.*

ACHATA'GIA, a region of India, between the Indus and Ganges.

ACHAT'ARA, a city of the Sinæ. *Ptol.*—The Greek M.S. of *Ptolemy* has Acadra.

ACHA'TES, a friend of Æneas, whose fidelity was so exemplary that *Fidus Achates* became a proverb. *Virg. Æn.* 1. v. 163. 316. *Servius in Æn.* 1. v. 178.——A river on the southern coast of Sicily at the east of Gela, from which the jewel called Agate derives its name. *Plin.* 37. c. 10.——A river falling into the African sea; now *Drillo. Diod. Sic.*

ACHELO'IDES, a patronymic given to the Syrens, the daughters of Achelous. *Ovid. Met.* 5. v. 552.

ACHELO'RIUM, a small river of Thessaly. *Polyæn.* 8.

ACHELO'US, the son of Oceanus or Sol, by Terra or Tethys, was god of the river of the same name in Epirus. He was one of the suitors of Dejanira, and in his contest with Hercules first changed himself into a serpent, and afterwards into an ox. Hercules broke off one of his horns, which was taken up by the nymphs, filled with fruit and flowers, and presented to the goddess of plenty. Some say that Achelous was changed into a river after the victory of Hercules; but Strabo explains the fable, by relating the frequent inundations of the river, and the consequent disputes of the neighbouring nations of Ætolia and Acarnania concerning the extent of their borders; till the causes of their quarrel were removed by the labours of their hero, who confined by strong dikes and solid banks, the waters in their proper channel, and exhibited the horn of plenty in the fertility which soon covered their fields. The Achelous rises in Mount Pindus, and after dividing Ac rnania from Ætolia falls into the Ionian sea. The sand and mud which it carries down have formed some islands at its mouth. This river is said by some authors to have sprung from the earth after the deluge, *Herodot.* 2. c. 10. 7. c. 126.—*Strab.* 10.—*Ovid. Meta.* 8. fab. 5. l. 9. Fab. 1. *Heroid.* 1. ep. 9. & 15. *Amor.* 3. el. 6. v. 35.—*Apollod.* 1. c. 3. &. 7.—l. 2. c. 7.—*Hygin. præf. fab.*—*Servius in G. Virg.* 1. v. 8.—*Sophocl. in Trach.*—*Plut de Flum.*—*Mela*, l. 2. c. 4.—*Cluver* l. 4. c. 8.——A river of Arcadia falling into the Alpheus.——A river flowing from Mount Sipylus. *Paus.* 8. c. 38.

ACHE'LUS, a person mentioned by *Flaccus* 3. v. 138. But some read Ethelus.

ACH'EMES, a ruler of Egypt. A.M. 3477.

ACH'EMON or **ACH'MON**, brother of Bassalus, a native of Africa, was punished by Hercules for ridiculing his hairy appearance, μέλας πυγή, &c.; from whence arose the proverb, *Ne in melampygum incidas. Suidas.*—*Nazianzenus.*

ACHER'DUS, a tribe of Attica, hence the epithet Acherdusius, in *Demosthenes.*

ACH'ERÆ, a town of the Insubres, now Acreano. *Polyb.*

ACHERI'NI, a people of Sicily. *Cic.* 3. *in Verr.*

ACHE'RIUS or **HARE'LIUS**, an orator in the time of Augustus. *Cœl. Rhodig.* 15. c. 11.

ACH'ERON, a river of Thesprotia in Epirus, falling into the Ionian sea opposite Corcyra, at the west of the bay of Ambracia. Homer calls it one of the rivers of hell, and the fable has been adopted by all succeeding poets, who make the god of the stream the son of Ceres, without a father; and say that he concealed himself in hell for fear of the Titans, and was changed into a bitter stream, over which the souls of the dead were first conveyed. Some make him son of Titan, and suppose that he was plunged into hell by Jupiter, for supplying the Titans with water. The word Acheron is often taken for hell itself. *Horat.* l. od. 3, v. 36. *Virg. G.* 2. v. 492.—*Æn.* 2. v. 295. &c.—*Strab.* 7.—*Lucan.* 3. v. 16.—*Sil.* 2.—*Silv.* 6. v. 80.—*Liv.* 8. c. 24.—*Cluver.* l. 4. c. 10.——A river of Elis in Peloponnesus. Another on the Riphæan mountains. *Orpheus.* Also a small river in the country of the Brutii in Italy, falling into the Tyrrhene sea. *Justin.* 12. c. 2.——A river of Bithynia, afterwards Sonautes, flowing into the Euxine sea near Heraclea. Hercules is said to have dragged Cerberus from hence. *Cluver.* l. c. 3. 31.

ACHERON'TIA, a town of Apulia, called Nidus by Horace, 3. od. 4. v. 14. from its elevated situation. It is now Matera. Its inhabitants were called Acherontini. *Cluver.* l. 3. c. 29.

ACHER'RES, a king of Ægypt, successor to the Pharaoh who reigned in the time of Moses.

ACHERU'SIA, Palus, a lake of Egypt, near Memphis, over which, as Diodorus, lib. 2. relates, the bodies of the dead were conveyed. The boat was called Baris, and the ferryman Charon. Hence arose the fable of Charon and the Styx, &c. afterwards imported into Greece by Orpheus, and adopted as part of the religion of the country.——A lake of Epirus, and another in Calabria; from which circumstance, Alexander, king of the Molossi, was deceived by the ambiguity of an oracle. The monarch had been warned to flee from the borders of the Acherusia; and when he sought repose and safety in Italy, the prediction of the oracle was fatally verified by his being slain on the banks of the Calabrian Acherusia. *Justin.* 12. c. 2.—*Cluver.* l. 3. c. 30.——A place or cave in Chersonesus Taurica, where Hercules is reported to have dragged Cerberus out of hell. *Xenoph. Anab.* 6.—*Plin.* 6. c. 1. l. 27. c. 2.—*Ovid. Met.* 7. v. 409.

ACHE'TUS, a river of Sicily, now Fiume di Noto *Sil.* 14.

ACHIDA'NA, a river of Carmania. *Ptol.* Some read Achindana.

ACHIL'LAS, a general of Ptolemy, who perfidiously murdered Pompey the Great. He was put to death by Ganymedes the eunuch, who was in the confidence of Arsinoe, the sister of the monarch. *Hirt. B. Alex.* 4.—*Plut. in Pomp. Lucan.* 8. v. 538.

ACHILLE'A, or Ἀχίλλειος δρόμος, Achilleius cursus, a peninsula near the mouth of the Borysthenes. *Mela.* 2. c. 1.—*Herodot.* 4. c. 55 & 76.——An island at the mouth of the Ister, in which, according to some authors, was the tomb of Achilles, over which it is said birds never flew. *Plin.* 10. c.29.—*Athen.* 2. c. 2.—It is called by the Turks Janitzari. *Mela.* 2. 9.—*Cluver.* 5. c. 18.——A fountain of Miletus, the waters of which were salt at its source, but afterwards became sweet.

ACHILLEIEN'SES, a people near Macedonia. *Xenoph. Hist. Græc.* 3.

ACHILLE'IS, an unfinished poem of Statius, in which he describes the education and memorable actions of Achilles. *Vid.* Statius.

ACHIL'LES, the son of Peleus and Thetis, was the bravest of all the Greeks who took part in the Trojan war. During his infancy, Thetis plunged him into the Styx, and made every part of his body invulnerable, except the heel, by which she held him. The care of his education was entrusted to the Centaur Chiron, who taught him the arts of war and music. He was taught eloquence by Phœnix, whom he ever after loved and respected. Thetis, to prevent him from going to the Trojan war, where she knew he was to perish, privately sent him to the court of Lycomedes, where he was disguised in the dress of a female; and, by his familiarity with the king's daughters, made Deidamia mother of Neoptolemus. As Troy could not be taken without the aid of Achilles, Ulysses was commissioned by the Greeks to go to the court of Lycomedes, and, in the habit of a merchant, the artful prince exposed jewels and arms for sale, Achilles, chusing the arms, discovered his sex, and accompanied his countrymen to the war. Vulcan, at the request of Thetis, made him a strong suit of armour, which was proof against all weapons. Having plundered several cities, and distinguished himself by superior valour in the plains of Troas, the hero was insolently robbed by Agamemnon of his favorite mistress Briseis, who had fallen to his lot at the division of the booty of Lyrnessus. For this affront he refused to appear in the field, till the unfortunate death of his friend Patroclus recalled him to action and to revenge. *Vid.* Patroclus. He slew Hector, tied the corpse by the heels to his chariot, and dragged it three times round the walls of the city. After thus avenging the death of his friend, he yielded to the entreaties and tears of Priam, and permitted him to ransom Hector's body. In the tenth year of the war, Achilles was charmed with Polyxena; and as he solicited her hand in the temple of Minerva, it is said that Paris, by the advice and direction of Apollo, aimed an arrow at his vulnerable heel, of which wound he died. His body was buried at Sigæum, and divine honors were paid to him. It is said that after the taking of Troy, the ghost of Achilles appeared to the Greeks, and demanded of them Polyxena, who was accordingly sacrificed upon his tomb by his son Neoptolemus. Some authors assert that Polyxena was so grieved at his death, that she killed herself on his tomb. The Thessalians yearly sacrificed a black and white bull on his tomb. It is reported that he married Helen after the siege of Troy; but others relate that this marriage happened in the island of Leuce. *Vid.* Leuce. Some ages after the Trojan war, Alexander, marching to the conquest of Persia, offered sacrifices on the tomb of Achilles, and admired a hero who had found a Homer to publish his fame to posterity. *Xenoph. de Venat.—Plut. in Alex. De facie in Orbe Lun. De music. De amic. mult. Quæst. Græc.—Scholiast. Aristoph. in Nub. Eustath. in Iliad.* 1. &c.—*Quint. Calab.* 3. &c.—*Tzetzes in Lycoph.—Parthenius Erot.* 21. *Quint. Smyrnæus,* 3.—*Philostr. in Heroid.* 19.—*Claud in Stilic.* 1.—*Propert.* 2. el. 8. & 20.—*Paus.* 3. c. 18. &c.—*Diod.* 17.—*Stat. Achill.—Ovid. Met.* 12. fab. 3. &c. *Trist.* 3. el. 5. v. 37. &c.—*Virg. Æn.* 1. v.472. &c.—*Apollod.* 3. c. 13.—*Hygin.* fab. 96 & 110.—*Strab.* 14.—*Plin.* 35. c. 15.—*Max. Tyr. Orat.* 27.—*Horat.* 1. od. 8. &c.—*Hom. Il. & Od.*—*Dictys. Cret.* 1, 2, 3, &c.—*Dares Phryg.*—*Juv.* 7. v. 210.—*Apollon. Argon.* 4. v. 869. There is a fine statue of this hero in the Borghese collection, now removed to Paris, and a dying head, in the collection at Florence.——A man who received Juno when she fled from Jupiter's courtship.——A son of Jupiter and Lamia, declared by Pan to be fairer than Venus.——A man who instituted ostracism at Athens.

ACHIL'LES TA'TIUS, a native of Alexandria, in the age of the emperor Claudius, originally a pagan, but converted to Christianity, and afterwards made a bishop. He wrote a mixed history of great men, a treatise on the sphere, tactics, a romance on the loves of Clitophon and Leucippe, &c. Some manuscripts of his works are preserved in the Vatican and Palatinate libraries. The best editions of his works are that in 12mo. L. Bat. 1640, and that of Leipzig, 1776. *Sax. Onomast.* 1. p. 372.—*Voss. de Scient. Mathem.* c. 33. sec. 29. p. 166.—*Fabr. Bib. Græc.* vol. 8. p. 130.—*Montucla. Histor. Mathes.* V. 1. l. 5. sec. 5. p. 312. English versions have been published as follows: London, 1577, 4to. Oxon, 1638, 8vo. London, 1720, 12mo.

ACHILLE'UM, a town and promontory of Asiatic Sarmatia, now Capo di Croce.——A town of Troas, near the tomb of Achilles, built by the Mytelenenans, *Plin.* 5. c. 30.——A harbour of Laconia, near the promontory of Tænarus. *Pausan.*——A castle near Smyrna.——A place of Sicily.——A village and harbour of Mesene. *Steph.*——A place before Tanagræa in Bœotia. *Plut.*

ACHILLE'US, or ACHIL'LEUS, a Roman general employed in Ægypt in the reign of Diocletian, who rebelled, and for five years maintained the imperial dignity at Alexandria. Diocletian at last marched against him; and because he held out during a long siege, ordered him to be devoured by lions. *Vopiscus.—Pomp. Lœtus.*——A eunuch in the reign of Domitian, beheaded at Tarracini.

ACHI'VI, the name of the inhabitants of Argos and Lacedæmon, before the return of the Heraclidæ, by whom they were expelled from their possessions, 80 years after the Trojan war. Being without a home they drove the Ionians from Ægialus, seized their twelve cities, and called the country Achaia. The fugitive Ionians were received by the Athenians. The appellation of Achivi is indiscriminately applied by the ancient poets, especially by Homer, to all the Greeks, and thence the difficulty of assigning proper limits to the country inhabited by a doubtful or a wandering race. *Paus.* 7. c. 1. &c.—*Mela,* l. 1. c. 18. & l. 2. c. 2. *Vid.* Achaia.

ACHILLI'NUS, or rather Acilenus, a soldier of Belisarius, who sustained alone an attack of the Goths. *Procop.*

ACHIR'OE, a daughter of the Nile, who bore two daughters to Sithon, king of Thrace. One gave her name to Pallenæa in Thrace; the other to Rhætea in Troas.

ACHIS'ARIS, a town of which the inhabitants were called Achisarmi. *Plin.* 6. c. 30.

ACHLADÆ'US, a Corinthian general killed by Aristomenes. *Paus.* 4. c. 19.

ACH'NÆ, a city of Thessaly.——A city of Bœotia. *Steph.*

ACHI'NE, the ancient name of the island of Casus, near Rhodes. *Plin.* 5. c. 31.

ACHO'ALI, a people of Arabia Felix. *Plin.* 6. c. 28.

ACH'OLA, a city of Africa; probably the Acilla of Hirtius, and the Acholla of Livy.

ACHO'LIUS, an historian in the age of Valerian, Claudius and Aurelian. *Vopisc. in Aurel.* c. 17.—*Voss. de Hist. Lat.* 2. c. 4.

ACHOL'LA, a city of Lybia, not far from the Syrtes; called by Appian, Cholla. *Steph.—Mela,* l. 1. c. 7.

ACHOLO'E, one of the Harpies. *Hygin.* 14.

ACH'OMÆ, and ACHOME'NI, a people of Arabia Felix. *Steph.*

ACHO'RUS, the name of the third and fourth kings of Ægypt.

ACHRADI'NA, the citadel of Syracuse, taken by Marcellus.——An island in its vicinity. *Cicer. Verr.* 6.—*Plut. in Marcel.—Steph.*

ACH'RADUS, *untis,* a tribe of Attica. *Steph.*

ACHRIA'NA, a city of Hyrcania. *Id.*

ACH'RUA, a city of Arabia Felix. *Ptol.*

AC'IBI, a people of European Sarmatia, near the source of the Borysthenes.

ACICHO'RIUS, a general in the expedition which the Gauls undertook against Pæonia. *Paus.* 10. c. 10.

ACIDA'LIA, a surname of Venus, from a fountain of the same name in Bœotia, sacred to her. The Graces were said to bathe in this fountain. *Servius in Virg. Æn.* 1. v. 720.—*Ovid. Fast.* v. 4. 468.

ACID'ALUS, a fountain of Campania, the waters of which were said to cure weak eyes.

AC'IDAS, or ACIDA'SA, a river of Peloponnesus, formerly called Jardanus. *Paus.* 5. c. 5.

AC'IDON, a river of Triphylia. *Strab.* 8.

ACID'ULUS, a fountain near Venafrum in Campania. *Plin.* 13. c. 2.

ACIEN'SES, a people of Italy, near the Albani and Albenses. *Id.* 2. c. 5.

AC'ILA, called Ocila by Pliny, and Ocelis by Ptolemy, a town of Arabia, situate on the Red Sea, and now called Zidem. The ancients set sail thence for India. *Plin.* 6. c. 28.——A city of Africa. *Hirtius.* c. 33.

ACIL'IA, a plebeian family at Rome, which traced its pedigree up to the Trojans. There were two branches of this family, the Glabriones, and the Balbi; they were illustrious as senators, generals, and consuls, and are frequently mentioned with great commendation by Livy, Tacitus, Seutonius. and others. *Vid.* Acilius.——the mother of Lucan.

ACIL'IA AUGUS'TA, a town of Vindelicia, now Azelburg.

ACIL'IA LEX was enacted, A.U.C. 556, by Acilius the tribune for the establishment of the five colonies in Italy. *Liv.* 32. c. 29.—Another called also Calpurnia, A.U.C. 684. which enacted, that no person convicted of *ambitus,* or using bribes at elections, should be admitted into the senate, or hold any office.—Another, concerning such as were guilty of extortion in the provinces.

ACILISE'NE, a district of Armenia Major, between mount Taurus and the Euphrates. *Strab.*

M. ACILIUS AVIO'LA, a lieutenant of Tiberius in Gaul. Some suppose this to be the same person who, when placed on the funeral pile, awoke from a trance, but could not be saved from the flames. *Val. Max.* 1. c. 1. But this was another person. *Tacit. Ann.* 3. c. 41.——A superintendent of the aqueducts in the reigns of Vespasian and Domitian.

M. ACIL'IUS BAL'BUS was consul with Portius Cato, A.U.C. 638. It is said, that during his consulship milk and blood fell from heaven. *Plin.* 2. c. 56.—*Cic. Epist. ad. Attic.* 1. 12. 5.

C. ACIL'IUS BU'TAS, a prætor, when he had lavished away his patrimony, and was complaining of his poverty before Tiberius, was thus addressed by the emperor: *Serus, O Buta, experrectus es. Senec. Ep.* 122.

M. ACIL'IUS GLA'BRIO, a tribune of the people, who quelled the insurgent slaves in Etruria. Being consul with P. Corn. Scipio Nasica, A. U. C. 561, he conquered Antiochus at Thermopylæ, for which he obtained a triumph, and three days were appointed for public thanksgiving. He stood for the censorship against Cato, but desisted on account of the false measures used by his competitor. *Justin* 31. c. 6.—*Liv.* 30. c. 40. l. 31. c. 50. l. 35. c. 10. &c.

M. ACIL'IUS GLA'BRIO, the son of the preceding, erected a temple to Piety, which his father, when fighting against Antiochus, had vowed to this goddess. He raised a golden statue to his father, the first that appeared in Italy. The temple of Piety was built on the spot where once a woman had fed her aged father with milk, whom the senate had imprisoned, and condemned to be deprived of all aliments.—*Val. Max.* 2. c. 5.

M. ACIL'IUS GLA'BRIO, the enactor of a law against bribery.

M. ACIL'IUS GLA'BRIO, a prætor at the time when Verres was accused by Cicero. *Cic. in Verr.*

M. ACIL'IUS GLA'BRIO, a man accused of extortion, and twice defended by Cicero. He was proconsul of Sicily, and lieutenant to Cæsar in the civil wars. *Cæs. Bel. Civ.* 3. c. 15.

M. ACIL'IUS GLA'BRIO, a consul, whose son was killed by Domitian, because he fought with wild beasts. The true cause of this murder was, that young Glabrio was stronger than the emperor, and therefore envied by him. *Juv.* 4. v. 94.—There were many consuls of this name in the reigns of the later emperors.

ACIL'IUS, a Greek historian, whose compositions were translated into Latin by a writer of the name of Claudius. *Liv.* 25. c. 40. l. 35. c. 14.

ACIL'IUS, now Acelino, a river of Sicily. *Vid.* Acis.

ACIL'LA. *Vid.* Achola and Acholla.

ACI'NA, a town of Arabia. *Plin.* 6. c. 29.

ACIN'ACÆ, a people of Bactriana. *Ptol.* 6. c. 11.

ACIN'ASIS, a river of Colchis. *Arrian in Peripl.*

ACIN'IPO, a town of Hispania Bætica: Acenipo, according to Ptolemy. *Plin.* 3. c. 1.

AC'IRIS, now Agri, a river and town of Lucania, falling into the bay of Tarentum.——A city of the Brutii. *Mela,* 2. c. 6.

A'CIS, a shepherd of Sicily, son of Faunus and the nymph Simæthis. Galatea passionately loved him; upon which his rival Polyphemus, through jealousy, crushed him to death with a piece of a broken rock. The gods, pitying the fate of Acis, changed him into a stream, which rises in mount Ætna, and falls into the sea above Catana. *Ovid Met.* 13. v. 861. *Servius in Ecl. Virg.* 9. v. 39.

ACIS'CULUS, a surname of the Valerian family, having the same meaning as Dolabella. *Quintil.* 6. *Instit.* c. 3. &c.

ACITA'NI, a people of Spain. *Macrob.* 1. *Sat.* c. 19. *Vid.* Accitana.

ACITAVO'NES, a people inhabiting the Alps. *Plin.* 3. c. 20.

ACITH'IUS, a river of Sicily. *Ptol. Vid.* Acilius.

AC'ITON, an island near Crete. *Plin.* 4. c. 12.

ACLISE'NA, a city of Armenia Minor. *Strab.* 11.

AC'ME, a mistress of Septimius. *Catul. Epigr.* 46.

ACME'NÆ, nymphs of Venus, who had an altar at Olympia. *Paus.* 1. *Eliac.*

ACMO'DÆ, or ACMO'DES, the ancient name of the Scilly islands, on the coast of Britain. It was the name also of the Shetland isles, otherwise called Æmodæ.

AC'MON, the most ancient of the gods, according to some Greek mythologists, said to have existed from eternity, and to have produced Chaos. *Lactant. in Stat. Theb.* 4. v. 316. *Bocac. in Deor. gen.* 1. c. 3.——A native of Lyrnessus, who accompanied Æneas into Italy. His father's name was Clytus. *Virg. Æn.* 10. v. 128.

ACMO'NIA, an ancient town on the borders of the Thermodon, and another in Phrygia; both built, according to the accounts of the Scythians, by Acmon, one of their kings, who extended his conquests over Asia Minor. *Steph. Byz. Acmonia.*——A city of Dacia, on the Danube, according to Ptolemy.

ACMON'IDES, one of the Cyclopes. *Ovid. Fast.* 4. v. 288.

A'CO, now Acre, a town of Phœnicia. *Vid.* Ace.

ACŒ'TES, the pilot of the ship, the crew of which found Bacchus asleep, under the form of a child, in the island of Naxus, and carried him away against his will. *Ovid. Met.* 3. v. 641. *Homer in Bacc.*—*Servius in* 4. *Æn.* 469.

AC'OLA, a town of Medea on the Caspian sea. *Ptol.*

AC'OLIS, a small city in the island of Tenedus.

ACOLITA'NUM, a town of Africa Propria, towards Cyrenaica. *Plin.* 5. c. 4.

AC'ONÆ or AC'ONE, a harbour of Heraclea, in Bithynia. Some suppose the herb Aconitum received its name from this place.

ACON'TES, one of Lycaon's fifty sons. *Apollod.* 3. c. 8.

ACON'TEUS, a famous hunter, changed into a stone, by the head of Medusa, at the nuptials of Perseus and Andromeda. *Ovid. Met.* 5. v. 201.——A person killed in the wars of Æneas and Turnus. *Virg. Æn.* 11. v. 615.

ACONTIS'MA, a narrow pass in Macedonia. *Ammian.* l. 26. Antonius places it on the confines of Thrace and Macedonia.

ACON'TIUM, a town of Arcadia, so called from the sons of Lycaon.——A town of Eubœa. *Steph.*

ACON'TIUS, a youth of Cea, who, when he went to Delus to see the sacrifices of Diana, fell in love with Cydippe, a beautiful virgin. Being unable to obtain her hand, on account of the obscurity of his origin, he wrote these verses on an apple, which he threw into her bosom:

Juro tibi sanctæ per mystica sacra Dianæ,
Me tibi venturam comitem, sponsamque futuram.

Cydippe read the verses, and being compelled by the oath she had inadvertently made, since everything uttered in the presence of the goddess was considered as inviolable, at last married Acontius, with the consent of her parents. *Ovid. Her.* ep. 20.——A mountain of Bœotia, or Magnesia. *Plin.* 4. c. 7.

ACONTOB'OLI, a nation of Cappadocia, under Hippolyte, queen of the Amazons. *Apollon. Arg.* 2.

ACOR'ACA, a city of Syria, in the region of Chalybonitis. *Ptol.*

AC'ORIS, a king of Ægypt, who assisted Evagoras, king of Cyprus against Persia. *Diod.* 15.

A'CRA, a town of Eubœa. It was the name also of a town in Cyprus,—in Acarnania,—in Sicily, near the promontory Pachynus,—in Africa,—in Sarmatia, &c.——A promontory of Calabria, in Italy, now Capo di Leuca. *Vid.* Ace.

AC'RABA, a city of Mesopotamia. *Ptol.*

ACRABATA'NUS, a lake of Æthiopia.

ACRACAR'NES, or according to some, Anacyndaraxes, a king of the Assyrians, father of Sardanapalus. *Euseb. Chron.*

ACRADI'NA. *Vid.* Achradina.

A'CRÆ, a mountain of Peloponnesus. *Paus.* 2. c. 34. A city of Sicily. Acreæ, according to Ptolemy. *Sil.* 14.—*Cluver. Sic. Antiq.* l. 2.

ACRÆ'A, a daughter of the river Asterion, who gave her name to a mountain of Argolis. *Paus.* 2. c. 17.——a surname of Diana, from a temple built to her by Melampus, on a mountain near Argos.——A surname of Juno. *Strab.* 8.

ACRÆ'PHIA, a town in Bœotia; whence Apollo is called Acræphius. *Herodot.* 8. c. 135. It is called Acræphium by Strabo; Acræphnium, by Pausanias; Agriphia, by Ptolemy; and Arene, according to some, by Homer.

ACRÆ'US, a surname of Jupiter, under which he was worshipped by the inhabitants of Smyrna, according to two medals mentioned by Spon. *Misc. Erud. An.*

ACRAGALLI'DÆ, a dishonest nation living anciently near Athens. *Æsch. contra. Ctesiph.*

AC'RAGAS, a river of Sicily, now Girgenti. *Mela.* 2. c. 9. *Vid.* Acragas.——A city of Thrace. It was the name also of a town in Eubœa, in Cyprus, and in Ætolia.——A statuary of great reputation. *Plin.* 33. c. 12.

ACRAMELÆ'NA, a promontory in Bithynia, near the Bosporus. *Arrian in Peripl.*

ACRAP'AGES, a king of Assyria. *Euseb. Chron.*

ACRA'TUS, a freedman of Nero, sent into Asia to plunder the temple of the gods. *Tac. An.* 15. c. 45. l. 16. c. 23.——The genius of the bacchanals at Athens. *Paus. in Att.*

ACRAVIS'CI, a people of Lower Pannonia. *Plin.* 3. c. 25.

ACREN'SES, a people of Sicily. *Id.* 3. c. 8.

A'CRIA, now Ormoas, a town of Laconia, at the mouth of the Eurotas. *Ptol.*——A town of Spain. *Plin.* 4. c. 12.

A'CRIAS, one of Hippodamia's suitors. He built Acria. *Paus.* 6. c. 21. 3. c. 21.

AC'RIBA, a city of Peloponnesus. *Pausan. Lacon.* 9.

AC'RIDE, a town of Africa. *Diodor.* l. 20.

ACRIDOPH'AGI, an Æthiopian nation, who as the name implies, ʼακρὶς φαγεῖν fed upon locusts, and lived not beyond their 40th year. It is said that at the approach of old age, swarms of insects attacked them, and gnawed their belly and breast, till the patient, by rubbing himself, drew blood, which increased their number, and ended in his death. *Diod.* 3.—*Plin.* 11. c. 29.—*Strab.* 16.

ACRIL'LÆ, a city of Sicily, not far from Syracuse. *Steph.*—*Cluver. Sic. Ant.*

ACRI'ON, a Pythagorean philosopher of Locris. *Cic. de fin.* 3. c. 29.

ACRISIONE'US, a name given to the Argives, from Acrisius, one of their ancient kings, or from

Acrisione, a town of Argolis, called after a daughter of Acrisius, of the same name. *Virg. Æn.* 7. v. 410.

ACRISIONI'ADES, a patronymic of Perseus, from his grandfather Acrisius. *Ovid Met.* 5. v. 70.

ACRIS'IUS, son of Abas, king of Argos, by Ocalea, daughter of Mantineus. He was born at the same birth as Prœtus, with whom it is said that he quarrelled even in his mother's womb. The enmity between the brothers increased with their years, and at last, after much dissension, Acrisius prevailed, and Prœtus was driven from Argos. Acrisius had Danäe by Eurydice, daughter of Lacedæmon, and being told by an oracle, that his daughter's son should put him to death, he confined Danäe in a brazen tower, to prevent her becoming a mother. She, however, was visited by the god Jupiter, who assumed the form of a golden shower. The fruit of this intercourse was Perseus, and though Acrisius ordered her and her infant to be exposed on the sea, yet they were saved; and Perseus soon after became so famous for his actions, that Acrisius, anxious to see so renowned a grandson, went to Larissa. Here Perseus, wishing to show his skill in throwing the quoit, killed an old man, who proved to be his grandfather, whom he knew not, and thus the oracle was unhappily fulfilled. Acrisius reigned about 31 years.—*Hygin.* fab. 63.—*Ovid Met.* 4. v. 608.—*Horat.* 3. od. 16.—*Apollod.* 2. c. 2. &c.—*Paus.* 2. c. 16. &c.—*Vid.* Danäe, Perseus, Polydectes.

ACRI'TAS, a promontory of Messenia in Peloponnesus; now Capo di Gallo. *Plin.* 4. c. 5.—*Mela* 2. c. 4. & 9.——A promontory of Bithynia, according to Ptolemy, the same as Acramelæna.

A'CRO HELE'NIUS, a scholiast, with Pomponius Porphyrion, on Horace. The time at which he lived is uncertain. *Sax Onomast.* vol. 1. p. 189. —*Harles. Lit. Rom.* 1. p. 258.

ACRO'ATHON, or ACROTHOU'M, a town on the top of mount Athos, the inhabitants of which were said to live to an uncommon old age. *Mela.* 2. c. 2.—*Plin.* 8. c. 10.—*Cluver.* 1. 4. c. 10.—*Herodot.* 1. 7. c. 22.—*Thucyd.* 1. 4. c. 109.

ACROCERAU'NIUM, a lofty promontory of Epirus, with mountains called Acroceraunia, or Acroceraunii, which project in a westerly direction between the Ionian and Adriatic seas. The word is derived from ἄκρος high, and κεραυνὸς thunder; because on account of their great height they were often struck with thunder. *Lucret.* 6. v. 420.—*Plin.* 4. c. 1. *Virg. Æn.* 3. v. 506.—*Strab.* 6.—*Horat.* 1. od. 3. v. 20.—*Cluver.* 1. 4. c. 10.

ACROC'OMÆ, a people of Thrace, so called from their long hair.

ACROCORIN'THUS, a lofty mountain on the isthmus of Corinth, taken by Aratus, B.C. 243. There was a temple of Venus on the top, and Corinth was built at the bottom. *Strab.* 8. *Paus.* 2. c. 4. *Plut. in Arat.*—*Stat. Theb.* 7. v. 106.—*Cluver.* 1. 4. c. 7.—*Mela.* 1. 2. c. 4.

ACROLO'CHIAS, a promontory of Ægypt, near Pharus. *Strab.*

ACROME'RUS, called by Tacitus, *Ann.* 11. c. 16, Catumerus, a prince of the Catti.

A'CRON, a king of Cænina, killed by Romulus in single combat, after the rape of the Sabines. His spoils were dedicated to Jupiter Feretrius and his subjects were incorporated with the citizens of Rome. *Plut. in Romul.*——A physician of Agrigentum, B.C. 439, educated at Athens with Empedocles. He wrote treatises in the Doric dialect, and cured the Athenians of a plague, by lighting a fire near the houses of the infected. *Plin.* 29. c. 21.—*Plut. in Isid.*——One of the friends of Æneas killed by Mezentius. *Virg. Æn.* 10. v. 719.

ACRO'NEUS, a prince of the Phæacians *Homer Od.* 8.

ACRO'NIUS LA'CUS, the lower part of the lake of Constance in Switzerland, now Unter-see. *Mela,* 3. c. 2.

ACROPA'THOS, one of Alexander's officers, who obtained part of Media after the king's death. *Justin.* 13. c. 4.——A bay of the Caspian Sea, in Media.

ACROP'OLIS, the citadel of Athens, built on a rock, and accessible only on one side. Minerva had a temple at the bottom. *Paus. in Attic.*

ACRORE'I, a city of Triphylia. *Steph.*

ACRO'RIA, a tract of land in Elis. *Xenoph.* 7. *Gr. Hist.*

ACROT'ATUS, son of Cleomenes, king of Sparta, died before his father, leaving a son called Areus. *Paus.* 1. c. 13. 1. 3. c. 6.——Son of Areus, greatly loved by Chelidonis, wife of Cleonymus. This amour displeased her husband, who called upon Pyrrhus the Epirot to avenge his wrongs. *Plut. in Pyrrh.*

ACRO'THO'UM or ACROTHO'I. *Vid.* Acroathon.

ACROVEN'TUM, now Governo, a village of Italy, near the Po.

AC'TA, or AC'TE, the country about Attica. The word is derived from 'ακτή a shore, and is applied to Attica, as being near the sea. It is derived by some writers, from Actæus, a king, from whom the Athenians have been called Actæi. *Ovid. Met.* 1. v. 313.—*Virg. Ecl.* 2. v. 23.——A place near mount Athos, on the Ægean sea. *Thucyd.* 4. c. 109.

ACTÆ'A, one of the Nereides. *Hesiod. Theog.* 250. *Homer Il.* 18. v. 41.——A daughter of Danaus. *Apollod.* 2. c. 1.——A surname of Ceres.

ACTÆ'ON, a famous hunter, son of Aristæus and Autonoe, daughter of Cadmus, whence he is called Autoneius Heros. He saw Diana and her attendants bathing near Gargaphia, and for his rashness in approaching the place, the goddess sprinkled water over him, and he was immediately changed into a stag, and devoured by his own dogs. The ancients have procured for the curiosity of posterity, the names of the dogs who so ungratefully destroyed their unfortunate master. Ovid mentions them to the number of 35. Hyginus makes the number altogether 80. Apollodorus however, mentions only the following: Proteus, Lynceus, Banus, Amarynthus, Argus, Spartus, Bores. *Hygin.* fab. 181.—*Apollod.* 2.—*Paus.* 9. c. 2.—*Ovid. Met.* 3. fab. 3. [A small group, of Actæon defending himself from the attack of his dogs, is to be found in the British museum, among the Towneley marbles.]——A beautiful youth, son of Melissus of Corinth, whom Archias, one of the Heraclidæ, endeavoured to debauch and carry away. He was killed in the struggle, which in consequence of this, happened between his father and ravisher. Melissus afterwards drowned himself; and the country being visited soon after by a pestilence, Archias was expelled. *Plut. in Amat.*

ACTÆ'US, a powerful person who made himself master of a part of Greece, which he called Attica. His daughter Agraulos married Cecrops, whom the Athenians called their first king, though Actæus reigned before him. *Paus.* 1. c. 2. & 10. The word is of the same signification as Atticus, an inhabitant of Attica.——A mountain near the river Thermodon. *Lycoph.*——One of the Telchines. *Strab.* 10.

ACTA'NIA, now Helichland, an island in the German ocean. *Plin.* 4. c. 13.

AC'TE, a mistress of Nero, descended from Attalus. *Suet. in Ner.* 28.——One of the Horæ. *Hygin.* fab. 183.——A place near mount Athos. *Thucyd.* 4. It was the name also of a city of Acarnania, of a city of Magnesia, of a city of Ionia, of a city of the Bosporus. *Steph.*

AC'TIA, the mother of Augustus. As she slept in the temple of Apollo, she dreamt that a dragon had lain with her. Nine months after, she brought forth, having previously dreamt that her bowels were scattered all over the world. *Suet. in Aug.* 94.——A daughter of Actius Balbus and Julia, mother of Octavius, the father of Augustus. *Plut. in Aug.*——Games sacred to Apollo, in commemoration of the victory of Augustus over M. Antony at Actium. They were celebrated every third, sometimes fifth year, with great pomp, and the Lacedæmonians had the care of them. *Plut. in Ant.*—*Strab.* 7.—*Virg. Æn.* 3. v. 280. 1. 8. v. 675. ——A sister of Julius Cæsar. *Plut. in Cic.*

ACTIA'NUS, or ACCIA'NUS FUN'DUS, a place near Pisaurus; now Farnazzano.

AC'TRI, a people of the Hunni, in Asia. *Suidas.*

AC'TIS or ACTI'NUS, son of Sol, went from Greece into Ægypt, where he taught astrology, and founded the city of Heliopolis. *Diod.* 5.

ACTIS'ANES or ACTIS'ANUS, a king of Æthiopia, who conquered Ægypt, and expelled king Amasis. He was famous for the severity with which he punished robbers. *Diod.* 1.—*Cluver.* 1. 5. c. 20. *in notis.*

ACTIUM, now Capo Figalo, town and promontory of Epirus, famous for the naval victory which Augustus obtained there over Antony and Cleopatra, on the 2nd of September, B.C. 31, in honour of which the conqueror built there the town of Nicopolis, and instituted games in honor of Apollo, who had a temple there. *Vid.* Actia.—*Plut. in Anton.*—*Suet. in Aug.*—*Mela.* 2. c. 4.—*Cluver.* 4. c. 7.—*Thucyd.* 4. c. 29.——A promontory of Corcyra. *Cic. ad Att.* 7. p. 2.

ACTIUS, a surname of Apollo, from Actium, where he had a temple. *Propert.* 4. el. 6. v. 67.—*Virg. Æn.* 12. v. 93.——A poet. *Vid.* Accius.——A prince of the Volsci. *Vid.* Accius.——A centurion put to death by Tiberius. *Tac. Ann.* 6. c. 4.

ACTIUS NÆVIUS, an augur who cut a loadstone in two with a razor, before Tarquin and the Roman people, to convince them of his skill as an augur. *Flor.* 1. c. 5.—*Liv.* 1. c. 36.

ACTOR, a companion of Hercules in his expedition against the Amazons.——A son of Myrmidon and Pisidice, father of Menœtius, Eurytion, and others, by Ægina, whom he married after she became the mother of Æacus. His children conspired against him, for which he expelled them from his kingdom. *Apollod.* 1. c. 16. 1. 3. c. 25.—*Schol. Apollon. Argon.* 4 *Ovid. Trist.* 1. el. 8.——A leader of the Aurunci. *Virg. Æn.* 12. v. 93.——One of the friends of Æneas. *Id.* 9. v. 500.——A son of Neptune by Agameda. *Hygin.* fab. 14.——A son of Deion and Diomede. *Apollod.* 1. c. 9.——A son of Phorbas and Hyrmine, daughter of Epeus, who built Hyrmine or Elis, and was the father of Eurytus, and brother of Augeas. *Apollod.* 2. c. 7.——A son of Hippasus, one of the Argonauts. *Hygin.* fab. 14.——A son of Azeus, king of Aspledon and Orchomenus, and father of Astyoche. *Hom. Il.* 2.—*Paus.* 9. c. 37.——A king of Lemnos. *Hygin.* 102.

ACTORIDES, a patronymic given to Patroclus, grandson of Actor, (*Ovid. Meta.* 13. 273.) also to Erithus, son of Actor. *Id. Meta.* 5. v. 79.——Two brothers, so fond of each other, that in driving a chariot one generally held the reins and the other the whip; whence they are represented with two heads, four feet, and one body. Hercules conquered them. *Pindar.*

ACTORIS, a maid of Ulysses. *Homer. Od.* 23.

M. ACTORIUS NASO, a Roman historian. *Suet. in Jul.* 9.

ACUES, a king of Arcadia, who slew the Lacedæmonians who had treacherously taken possession of Tegea. *Polyæn.* 1. c. 11.

ACUINUS, a Roman who was desirous of aiding in the murder of Cæsar. *Appian. Bell. Civ.* 2.

ACULA or AQUULA, a town of Etruria, the inhabitants of which are called Aquenses by Pliny.

ACULEO, C. a Roman lawyer, celebrated for his extensive knowledge of the law. He was uncle to Cicero. *Cic. in Orat.* 1. c. 43.

ACUMINCUM LEGIO, a town of Lower Pannonia, near the Danube. *Ptol.* Ammianus Marcellinus, 1. 19. calls it Acunincum.

ACUMULUM, a town of Aprutium in Italy, on the river Truentus.

ACUPHIS, an ambassador from India to Alexan- *Plut. in Alex.*

ACUR, a city of India within the Ganges. *Ptol.*

ACUS, an island of the Æthiopian sea.

ACUSILAUS and DAMAGETUS, two brothers of Rhodes, who were both declared winners at the Olympic games. The Greeks strewed flowers upon Diagoras, their father, and called him happy in having such worthy sons. *Paus.* 6. c. 7.

ACUSILAUS, an historian of Argos, often quoted by Josephus, who says, that he lived a little before the expedition of the Persians into Greece. He wrote on genealogies, in a style simple and destitute of all ornament. *Cic. de Orat.* 2. c. 29—*Suidas. Joseph. contr. Apion.* p. 1034. *Ed. Colon.* 1691.——An Athenian who taught rhetoric at Rome, under Galba. *Suidas.*

ACUSIO COLONIA, a city of Gallia Narbonensis, called afterwards Gratianopolis. It is now Grenoble.

ACUTÆ, islands near the Echinades. *Strab.* 8.

ACUTIA, the wife of P. Vitellius, found guilty of treason. *Tacit. Ann.* 6. c. 47.

ACUTIA, a city of the Vaccæi in Spain, according to Stephanus, after Strabo. Most copies of Strabo, however, read Acontia.

ACUTICUS, M. a Latin poet who composed some elegies, which were attributed to Plautus. *Voss. de Poet Lat.* 1.

ACUTUS, a river of Gaul.

ACYLAS, the name of a philosopher mentioned by Suidas.

ACYLINA, a city of Illyria. *Steph.*

ACYPHAS, one of the cities of the Dorian Tetrapolis. *Id.*

ACYTTUS, an island near Cydonia in Crete. *Id.*

ADA, a sister of queen Artemisia, daughter of Pixodorus and Aphneis of Cappadocia, married Hidricus. After her husband's death she succeeded to the throne of Caria; but being expelled by her younger brother, she retired to Alindæ, which she delivered to Alexander, after adopting him as her son. *Curt.* 2. c. 8.—*Strab.* 14.—*Arrian.* 1.1. c. 23.

ADACHA, a city of Palmyrene. *Ptol.*

ADAD, one of the chief deities of the Assyrians, supposed to be the sun. They considered him as married to Atergatis, one of the goddesses under whose name they paid adoration to the moon. *Macrob. Sat.* 1. c. 23.

ADADATA, a city of Pisidia, near mount Taurus. *Strab.* 12. It is called Adada by Ptolemy.

ADÆ, *arum*, a town of Asia. *Strab.* 13.

ADÆI, a people of Arabia, bordering on Ægypt. *Ptol.*

ADÆUS, a native of Mitylene, who wrote a Greek treatise on statuaries. *Athen.* 13. Athenæus mentions another person of this name in his book περὶ διαθέσεως l. 11.——An Athenian surnamed Alectryon, from wearing a crest on his head. *Id.* 6. c. 8.

ADAMANA, a city of Cœlesyria, in Asia.

ADAMANTÆA, Jupiter's nurse in Crete, who suspended him in his cradle to a tree, that he might be found neither on the earth, in the sea, nor in heaven. To drown the infant's cries, she caused drums to be sounded around the tree. *Hygin.* fab. 139.

ADAMANTIS, a river of India without the Ganges. *Ptol.*

ADAMAS, a Trojan prince, killed by Merion. *Homer Il.* 13. v. 560.——A youth who raised a rebellion on being emasculated by Cotys, king of Thrace. *Arist. Pol.* 5. c. 10.

ADAMAS, a river in the Sinus Gangeticus. *Ptol.*

ADAMASTUS, a native of Ithaca, father of Alchæmenides. *Virg. Æn.* 3. v. 614.

ADANA, a city of Cilicia. *Ptol.*——A city near the Euphrates. *Steph.*——A city of Arabia Felix. *Id.*

ADANI, *orum*, two islands of Arabia Felix. *Ptol.*

AD AQUAS, a city of Sicily. *Antonin.*

AD AQUILAS, a place of Attica. *Paus.*——A place of Gaul near Ravenna, now Aigle.

AD ARAS, a city of Spain, between Hispalis and Corduba.

AD CASAS, a place of Italy, now St. Cassiano. *Antonin.*

AD CENTESIMUM, a place of Italy, 107 miles from Rome. *Id.*

AD DECIMUM, now il Borghetto, a town of Italy, 10 miles from Rome.

AD DRACONES, a place of Mauritania Cæsariensis.——A place of Armenia Major. *Antonin.*

AD DUOS PONTES a place of Spain, between Bracara and Asturica. *Id.*

AD FINES, now Pfin, a town of Helvetia.——A town of Belgium, now Tuin.——A town on the confines of Liburnia and Pannonia, now Samaguar.

AD FRATRES, a place of Mauritania Cæsariensis. *Antonin.*

AD GALLINAS, a villa of the Cæsars in Italy, formerly called Veientanum. *Plin.* 15. c. 30.—*Suet. in Galb.* c. 1.—*Cluver Ital. Antiq.*

AD LIPPOS, a place of Hispania Bœtica. *Antonin.*

AD MALUM, a city of Liburnia. *Id.*

AD MARCIUM, a place not far from Lauvium. *Liv.* l. 6.

AD MARTIS, a place of Italy between Narnia and Mevania. *Antonin.*——A place between Segusium and Brigantio in the Alps; perhaps the Martis vertex of Ammianus Marcellinus.

AD MORUM, a place of Spain, between Acci and Carthago Nova. *Antonin.*

AD OLIVAM, a place of Mauritania Cæsariensis. *Antonin.*

AD PALA'TIUM, a village between Tridentum and Verona, now Palazzo. *Id.*
AD PAL'UDES, a place of Arabia. *Strab.*
AD PER'TICAS, a village of Italy, near Ticinum, now S. Maria delle Pertiche.
AD PI'NUM, a place in Samnium. *Antonin.*
AD PON'TEM, a place of Spain, near Gades. *Id.*
AD PUBLICA'NOS, a place of Gallia Narbonensis. *Id.*
AD PUTE'A, a place of Spain, between Liminium and Cæsar Augusta. *Id.*
AD RE'GIAS, a place of Mauritania Cæsariensis. *Id.*
AD RO'TAM, a city of Numidia. *Antonin.* Augustin. 1. 3. contra Crescon, calls it Rotaria.
AD RU'BRAS, a place of Hispania Bætica, near the mouth of the river Anas.
AD RU'BRAS PE'TRAS, a place of Italy. *Mart.*4. *Epi.*64.
AD SAL'ICES, a place of Lower Mœsia, near the mouths of the Danube. *Antonin.*
AD SEP'TEM FRA'TRES, a city of Mauritania Tingitana, now Ceuta.
AD SEP'TIMUM, a place of Spain between Asturica and Tarraco. *Antonin.*
AD SEX IN'SULAS and AD TRES IN'SULAS, places of Mauritania Tingitana. *Id.*
AD SORO'RES now Val de Fuentes, a village of Lusitania, near Emerita. *Id.*
AD STATUAS COLOS'SAS, a place between Aretium and Clusium in Etruria. *Id.*——A place of Spain, near the Sucro.
AD TIT'ULOS, a city of Liburnia. *Antonin.*
AD TUR'REM, a city of Sardinia. *Id.*
AD TUR'RES, a city of Calabria in Italy; now Blazio.
ADAR'CHIAS or ATHA'RIAS, an aged officer, who, when his juniors were remiss in attacking the enemy at Halicarnassus, led the soldiers on himself. *Curt.* 5. c. 2.
ADAR'CHIDÆ, a nation of Lybia. *Steph.*
AD'ARI, a town of Arabia Felix. *Ptol.*
ADAR'IMA, a city of India within the Ganges. *Id.*
ADARUP'OLIS, a city of Persia. *Steph.*
ADASA'THRA, or ADISA'THRA, a city of India within the Ganges. *Ptol.*
ADAS'PII, a people at the foot of mount Caucasus, subdued by Alexander. *Justin.* 12. c. 5.—*Orosius* 9. c. 18. Arrian calls them Aspii.
AD'ATHA, a city of Armenia Major. *Ptol.*
ADAUGMAG'DUM, a city of Africa. *Antonin.*
ADBUCIL'LUS, a Gaul mentioned by Cæsar. *Bell, Civ.* 9. c. 59.
ADCANTUAN'NUS or ADCANTUI'NUS, an Aquitanian general, mentioned by Cæsar, *Bell. Gall.*3.c.22.
ADDÆ'A, a city of Mesopotamia. *Ptol.*
ADDA'NIS, a river of Carmania; called by Ptolemy Andanis, by Arrian Anamis.
ADDEPHA'GIA, *Vid.* Adephagia.
ADDIA'NUM, a city of Africa Propria.
AD'DUA, now Adda, a river of Cisalpine Gaul, falling into the Po between Placentia and Cremona. *Plin.* 2. c. 103.—*Cluver.* 1. 3. c. 31.
AD'DYMA, a town of Mauritania Cæsariensis; now Velez, according to some writers. *Ptol.*
ADEL'LUM, a town of Spain. *Antonin.*
ADEL'PHIUS, a friend of M. Antonius, whom he accompanied in his expedition into Parthia, of which he wrote the history. *Strab.* 11.—Casaubon, however, reads, ὁ Δέλλιος, and he is so called by Plutarch. The third ode of the second book of Horace is also addressed to Dellius.——A man of proconsular dignity, husband of the learned Proba Falconia.
ADE'MON, a person who raised a sedition in Mauritania, to avenge his master Ptolemy, whom Caligula had put to death. *Suet in Calig.* 35.—*Plin.* 5. c. 11.
ADEO'NA, a goddess worshipped by the heathens, because she was supposed to give men the power of going, *adeundi*, to any place. *Vid.* Abeona.
ADEPHA'GIA, ἅδος φαγεῖν the goddess of gluttony, to whom the Sicilians erected an altar and a statue in the temple of Ceres. *Athen.*4.—*Ælian.* 1. *V. H.* c. 27.
ADEPH'AGUS, a name given to Hercules and Milo of Crotona, as expressive of their voracity. *Schol. Argon. Apollon.* 1.
ADER'CON, a city of Spain. *Steph.*
A'DES or HA'DES, the god of the infernal regions among the Greeks, the same as the Pluto of the Latins. The word is derived from ἀ εἶδω *non videre*, because hell is deprived of light, and it is used by the ancient poets for the habitation of departed spirits.
ADES, a king of the Molossi, whose daughter Pirithous attempted to carry off from a place near the river Acheron; hence the fable of his descent into hell. *Plut. in Thes.*
ADES, a place of Bithynia, near Nicea. *Zonoras.*
ADE'SA, a river of Lycia. *Plin.* 5. c. 27.——A river of Germany, now Etsch. *Cluver.*
ADGANDES'TRIUS, a prince of Gaul, who sent to Rome for poison to destroy Arminius; but was nobly answered by the senate, that the Romans fought their enemies openly, and never used perfidious measures. *Tacit. An.* 2. c. 88.
ADHARNA'HA, a town of Etruria. *Liv.*
ADHER'BAL, son of Micipsa, and grandson of Masinissa, was deprived of his possessions; and after being besieged for some time at Cirta, was put to death by Jugurtha, after vainly imploring the aid of Rome, B.C. 112. *Sallust. in Jug.*
ADHER'BAS, *vid.* Sichæus.
ADIABA'TÆ, or ADIABA'RÆ, a people of Æthiopia, opposite the island of Meroe. *Plin.* 6. c. 30.
ADIABE'NE, an ancient name of Assyria. *Plin.* 5. 12. &c.—*Mela.* 1. c. 12.
ADIAB'LA, a city of Albania. *Ptol.* 5. c. 12.
ADIAN'TE, a daughter of Danaus. *Apollod.* 2. c. 11.
ADIATO'RIX, a governor of Galatia, who, to gain Antony's favour, slaughtered, in one night, all the inhabitants of the Roman colony of Heraclea in Pontus. He was taken at Actium by Augustus, and after adorning the triumph of the conqueror, was strangled in prison. *Strab.* 12. c. 14.
ADIC'ARA or IDIC'ARA, a town of Arabia.
ADIE'NUS, according to Arrian, a river near the Euxine sea.
ADILIS'IUS, or rather ADYLIS'IUS, a mountain of Greece. *Plin.* 4. c. 7.
ADIMAN'TUS, a commander of the Athenian fleet, taken by the Spartans. All the men of his fleet were put to death except Adimantus, because he had opposed the designs of his countrymen, who had intended, if victorious, to mutilate all the Spartans. *Xenoph. Hist. Græc.*—Pausanias, 4. c. 17. l. 10. c. 9. says, that the Spartans had bribed him. ——A brother of Plato. *Laert.* 3.——A Corinthian general, who reproached Themistocles on account of his exile.——A king of Phlius, struck with lightning for saying that Jupiter deserved no sacrifices. *Ovid in Ibin.* 337.
A'DIS, a city of the Carthaginians, in Africa. *Polyb.* l. 1.
ADISA'MAM, a city of Taprobane. *Ptol.*
ADISA'THRUS, a mountain of India within the Ganges: the people in the neighbourhood are called Adisathri by Ptolemy, and were probably the Xathri of Arrian.
ADIS'DARA, a town of India within the Ganges. *Ptol.*
ADME'TA, a daughter of Eurystheus, was priestess of Juno's temple at Argos. She expressed a wish to possess the girdle of Hippolyte, queen of the Amazons, and Hercules was ordered to procure it by Eurystheus, which he effected by the conquest of the Amazons. *Apollod.* 2. c. 23.
ADMETA, one of the Oceanides. *Hesiod. Theog.* v. 349.
ADME'TUS, son of Pheres and Clymene, was king of Pheræ, in Thessaly. Apollo, when banished from heaven, is said to have tended his flocks nine years, and to have obtained from the Parcæ this remarkable favor, that Admetus should never die, if another person laid down his life for him, a proof of unbounded affection which his wife Alceste cheerfully exhibited by devoting herself to death. Admetus was one of the Argonauts, and was at the chase of the Calydonian boar. Some say that Hercules brought back Alceste from hell, as a reward for the humanity and friendship with which he had treated him in his travels through Thessaly. The death of Alceste is the subject of one of the plays of Euripides. *Euripid. in Alc.*—*Val. Max.* 4. c. 6.—*Plut. in Amat.*—*Tzetzes in Lycoph.* —*Servius in Virg. Ec.* 5. v. 35.—*G.* 1. *Æn.* 6. v. 398. l. 7. v. 761.—*Fulgent. Mythol.* 1. c. 27.—*Senec. in Medea.*—*Hygin.* fab. 50, 51. & 243.—*Ovid. de Art. Am.* 3.—*Apollod.* 1. c. 8 & 9, &c.—*Tibul.* 2. el. 3. —*Paus.* 5. c. 17.——A king of the Molossi, to whom Themistocles fled for protection when banished from Athens by his countrymen.—*C. Nep. in Them.* 8.——An officer of Alexander, killed at the siege of Tyre. *Diod.* 17.——A poet in the time of Nero, ridiculed by Lucian, *in Demonaete.*
ADMINOCI'NUS, son of Bellinus, king of the Batavi, surrendered to C. Caligula. *Eutrop.* l. 7.

ADOBRI'CA, *Vid.* Abobrica.

ADO'NEUS, a name of Bacchus among the Arabians.

ADO'NIA, festivals in honour of Adonis, first celebrated at Byblus, in Phœnicia. They lasted two days, the first of which was spent in lamentations, the second in rejoicings, as if Adonis were returned to life. In some towns of Greece and Ægypt, they lasted eight days. The time of the celebration was supposed to be very unlucky. The fleet of Nicias sailed from Athens to Sicily on that day, whence many unfortunate omens were drawn. *Plut. in Nicia.—Ammian.* 22. c. 9.—*Selden de Diis. Syr.* 2. c. 11.—*Meurs. Gr. fer.*

ADO'NIS, son of Cinyras by his daughter Myrrha, (*vid.* Myrrha) was the favorite of Venus. He was fond of hunting, and received in the chase a mortal bite from a wild boar, which he had wounded. Venus flew to his relief; but all assistance was vain, and she therefore changed him into a flower called anemone. Proserpine is said to have restored him to life, on condition that he should spend six months with her, and the rest of the year with Venus. This implies the alternate return of summer and winter. Adonis is often taken for Osiris. He had temples raised to his memory, and is said by some to have been beloved by Apollo and Bacchus. *Apollod.* 3. c. 14.—*Plut. in Par.* 22. *in Niciâ.—Servius in Ec.* 8. v. 37. & 10. v. 16. —*Ammian. Marcel.* 22. c. 9.—*Selden de Syr. Diis.* —*Lucian de D. Syriâ.—Macrob. Sat.* 1. c. 21.— *Ptol. Hephœst. apud Photium.—Athen.* 10 c. 22. —*Propert.* 2. el. 13. v. 53.—*Bion. in Adon.—Hygin.* 58. 164. 248. &c.—*Ovid. Met.* 10. fab. 10.— *Musœus de Her.—Paus.* 2. 20. l. c. 41.——[There is a very beautiful statue of Adonis in the museum of the Vatican at Rome.]

ADONIS, a small river of Phœnicia, falling into the Mediterranean, below Byblus: it is called Canis and Naracebelle, by the inhabitants of the country. *Cluver.* l. 5. c. 21.

ADORIS'SUS, a city of Lycaonia, in Cappadocia. *Ptol.*

ADO'REUS, a mountain of Phrygia, from which the river Sangarius issues.

ADOR'SI, a nation near the Bosporus. *Tac. Ann.* 12. c. 15. Lipsius reads Aorsi.

A'DRA, a city of Illyricum, now Oduca.—A city of Phœnicia.—A city of Arabia Petræa.—A city of Cœlesyria. *Ptol.*

AD'RAÆ, plains now Markfelt, in Austria. *Id.*

ADRAIS'TÆ, a people of India, near the upper part of the Indus. *Arrian.* l. 5. They are called Andresti by Diodorus Siculus, l. 17.

ADRAMA, a city of Cœlesyria. *Ptol.*

ADRAMIT'Æ, a people of Arabia Felix. *Id.*—Theophrastus speaks of a place there called Adrametta.

ADRAMYT'TIS, an island of Lycia. *Steph.*

ADRAMYT'TIUM, an Athenian colony on the sea coast of Mysia, near the Caycus, and opposite the island of Lesbos. *Cluver.* 5. c. 18.—*Mela,* 1. c. 18. —*Strab.* 13.—*Thucyd.* 5. c. 1.

ADRA'NA, a river in Germany, which falls into the Visargis, and with it discharges itself into the German Ocean. *Tac. Ann.* 1. c. 56.——A city of Thrace, called also Adrena. *Steph.*

ADRA'NUM, a town of Sicily, with a river of the same name, near Ætna. The chief deity of the place was guarded by 1,000 dogs, which were said to fawn upon the inhabitants, but to attack with violence such as were guilty of impiety. Adranus was said to be the father of the gods called Palici. *Hesych.* Παλικοι.—*Diod.* 4.—*Plut. in Timol.*

ADRAP'SA, *orum,* a city of Bactriana. *Strab.* 15.

ADRAS'TA, one of the Oceanides who nursed Jupiter. *Hygin.* fab. 182.

ADRASTI'A, a fountain of Sicyon. *Paus.* 2. c. 15. ——A mountain. *Plut. in Lucul.*——A country near Troy, called after Adrastus, who built there a temple to Nemesis. Here Apollo had an oracle *Strab.* 13.——A daughter of Jupiter and Necessity, called by some Nemesis, and the punisher of injustice. The Ægyptians placed her above the moon, whence she looked down upon the actions of men. *Strab.* 13.——A daughter of Melisseus, to whom some attribute the nursing of Jupiter. She is the same as Adrasta. *Apol.* l. c. 1.

ADRAS'TII CAM'PI, a plain in Asia Minor, near the Granicus, where Alexander first defeated Darius. *Justin.* 11. c. 6.—*Cluver.* 5. c. 18.

ADRAS'TUS, son of Talaus and Eurynome was king of Argos. Polynices, being banished from Thebes by his brother Eteocles, fled to Argos, where he married Argia, daughter of Adrastus. The king assisted his son-in-law, and marched against Thebes with an army headed by seven of his most famous generals. All perished in the war except Adrastus, who, with a few men fled to Athens, and implored the aid of Theseus, who went to his assistance, and was victorious. Adrastus, after a long reign, died through grief, occasioned by the death of his son Ægialeus. A temple was raised to his memory at Sicyon, and a solemn festival annually celebrated his services to the state, and his popularity among his subjects. It was abolished by Clisthenes, tyrant of Sicyon. Adrastus had a famous horse called Arion, supposed to be the offspring of Neptune after his union with Ceres. *Virg. Æn.* 6. v. 480.—*Apollod.* 1. c. 9. l. 3. c. 7. *Homer Il.* 5.—*Stat. Theb.* 4, & 5.—*Euripid. in Sup. & Phœnis.—Æschyl. sept. contra. Theb.*—*Philostr.* 2. c. 29.—*Hygin.* fab. 68, 69, & 70.— *Paus.* 1. c. 39. l. 8. c. 25. l. 10. c. 90.—*Herodot.* 5. c. 67, &c.——A peripatetic philosopher, disciple to Aristotle. It is supposed that a copy of his treatise on harmonies is preserved in the Vatican.——A Phrygian prince, who having inadvertently killed his brother, fled to Crœsus, by whom he was humanely received, and entrusted with the care of his son Atys. In hunting a wild boar Adrastus unfortunately slew the young prince, and killed himself on his grave in despair. *Herodot.* 1. c. 35. &c.——A Lydian, who assisted the Greeks against the Persians. *Paus.* 7. c. 5.——A soothsayer in the Trojan war, son of Merops. He was killed by Diomedes. *Homer Il.* 2 & 11.——The father of Eurydice, who married Ilus, the Trojan. *Apollod.* 2. c. 12.——A king of Sicyon, who reigned four years. B.C. 1215.——A son of Hercules. *Hygin.* 242.

ADRES'TE, a female attendant of Helen. *Odys.* 4. 305.

A'DRI, a city of Arabia Petræa. *Ptol.*

A'DRIA, ADRIA'NUM, or ADRIAT'ICUM MA'RE, a sea lying between Illyricum and Italy, now called the Gulph of Venice, first made known to the Greeks by the discoveries of the Phocæans. *Herodot.* 1. c. 163.—*Horat.* 1. od. 33. l. 3. od. 3 & 9. —*Catul.* 4. 6.—*Mela.*——A town at the top of the Adriatic, at the mouth of the Po. *Liv.* 5. c. 33. —*Justin.* 20. c. c. 1.—*Cluver.* 3. c. 24.——A Roman colony in the Picenia, famed for its wine.

ADRIA'NIS, one of the tribes of Athens.

ADRIANOP'OLIS, a town of Thrace on the Hebrus. —A town of Ætolia.—A town of Pisidia.—A town of Bithynia.

ADRIANOTH'ERÆ, or ADRIA'NI, a small city of Mysia. *Philostrat.*

ADRIA'NUS, or HADRIA'NUS, the fifteenth emperor of Rome, is represented to have been an active, learned, warlike, and austere general. He came to Britain, where he built a wall between the mouth of the Tyne and the Solway Frith, eighty miles long, to protect the Britons from the incursions of the Caledonians. He killed in battle 500,000 Jews who had rebelled, and built a city on the ruins of Jerusalem, which he called Ælia. In the beginning of his reign he imitated the virtues of his adopted father and predecessor Trajan; he remitted all arrears due to his treasury for sixteen years, and publicly burnt the accompt-books, that his word might not be suspected. His peace with the Parthians proceeded from a wish of punishing the other enemies of Rome, more than from the effects of fear. During his reign he visited repeatedly the various provinces of his extensive empire, distributing justice impartially, redressing the wrongs of the oppressed, and listening to the complaints of injured innocence against the tyranny of corrupt ministers or of guilty favourites. It is said that Adrian wished to enrol Christ among the gods of Rome; but his apparent good-will towards the Christians was disproved by the erection of a statue to Jupiter on the spot where Jesus rose from the dead, and one to Venus on Mount Calvary. When the weight of his diseases became intolerable, Adrian attempted to destroy himself; and when prevented, exclaimed, that the lives of others were in his hands, but not his own. He wrote an account of his life, and published it under the name of one of his domestics. He died of a dysentery, at Baiæ, July 10, A.D. 138, in the sixty-third year of his age, after a reign of twenty-one years; and as he expired, he uttered a short but elegant address to his soul, which has been beautifully translated by Mr. Pope, beginning with the words,—

Animula, vagula, blandula,
Hospes, &c.

As he had no children by his wife Sabina, the grand niece of Trajan, he adopted Lucius Aurelius Annius Commodus Verus for his successor; stipulating that on his death, he should appoint Titus Antonius to succeed him, who was to be followed by Marcus Annius Verus, and the son of Lucius Verus. *Eutrop. Sparsian in Adrian.—Dio.—Tillemont. Hist des Emp.* [Of Adrian, who was a great encourager of the arts, there are many fine busts and statues. The best of the latter is that in the Capitol at Rome, where he is represented in the character of the high priest; and of the former the colossal bust in the Vatican at Rome, which was discovered in his mausoleum.]

ADRIA'NUS, an officer of Lucullus. *Plut. in Luc.*——A rhetorician of Tyre, in the age of M. Antonius, who wrote seven books of Metamorphoses, besides other treatises now lost.——An author in the fifth century, who wrote an introduction to the Scriptures in Greek. It was printed at Augsburg in 1602, in 4to, and a Latin translation of it may be found in the Opuscule of Lottinus, Belluno. 1650. in fol. *Sax. Onom.* 1. p. 438. *Fabr. B. G.* 1. 5.c. 38.

ADRIE'NI, a people of Arabia Felix. *Steph.*

A'DRIUS, or AR'DIUS, a mountain of Dalmatia.—*Strab.*

ADROB'ICUM, a city of Hispania Tarraconensis, now Corunna.

ADROBRI'CA or ABOBRI'CA, a city of the Artabri, in Spain. *Mela.* 3. c. 1.

ADROT'TA, a maritime city of Lydia. The inhabitants were called Adrotteni. *Steph.*

AD'RUBÆ, *Vid.* Ad Rubras.

ADRUME'TUM, called by *Strabo* Adrume, by *Stephanus* Adrumes, by *Ptolemy* Adrumetus, a town of Africa, at the south-east of Carthage, and on the shores of the Mediterranean, built by the Phœnicians. It is now called Mahometta. *Sallust. in Jug.—Cluver.* 6. c. 4.

A'DRUS, a river of Spain, according to *Antonius*, but *Ortelius* wishes to read Anas, and others Dadrus.——An ancient name of the Arotius, a river of the Ædui in Gaul.

A'DRYX. a city of the Syracusans. *Steph.*

ADUAT'ICI or ATUAT'ICI, a nation of Belgic Gaul, or modern French Flanders, between the Scheldt and the Maese, supposed to be the people of Namur, or Antwerp, or, according to others, Falais on the Mehaigne. *Cæs. B. G.* 2. c. 4.

ADU'LA, a mountain in the Rhætian Alps, near which the Rhine takes its rise, now St Gothard. *Strab.*

ADU'LIS, a town of Upper Ægypt, situate on a bay of the Arabic Gulph, called Adulicus Sinus. Here Ptolemy Evergetes had a statue with a flattering inscription. It is now called Docono or Eroco according to others. *Sax Onom.* 1. p. 112. *de Monum. Adulit.—Plin.* 6. c. 29. &c.

ADUL'TUS, an epithet for Jupiter, as Adulta was for Juno. *Plut. in Problem.*

ADU'RA, now Ayre, a city of Aquitania.

A'DUS, a city of Cilicia. *Steph.*

ADU'SA. a river of Epirus, near Appollonia.

ADYLI'SUS, or ADILLIS'IUS, a mountain of Bœotia. *Plin.* 4. c. 7.

ADYRMACH'IDÆ, a maritime people of Africa, at the west of the lake Mœris, in Ægypt. *Herodot.* 4. c. 168.

Æ'A, a huntress, changed into an island of the same name by the gods, to rescue her from the pursuit of her lover, the god of the river Phasis. The island had a town called Æa, which was the capital of Colchis, and famous for being the place where the golden fleece was preserved when Jason reached the country. *Plin.* 6. c. 4.—*Ptol.* 5. c. 10.—*Flacc.* 5. v. 426.——A town of Thessaly.—A town of Africa·——A fountain of Macedonia, near Amydon.

ÆACE'A, games celebrated at Ægina, in honour of Æacus.

ÆACIDES, a king of Epirus, son of Neoptolemus, and brother of Olympias. He was expelled by his subjects for the continual wars which he waged against Macedonia. He left a son, Pyrrhus, only two years old, whom Chaucus, king of Illyricum educated. *Paus.* 1. c. 11.—*Justin.* 17. c. 3.

ÆACIDES, a patronymic of the descendants of Æacus, such as Achilles, Peleus, Phocus, Telamon, Pyrrhus, &c. Alexander the Great was descended from them by his mother Olympias. Justin has observed that it was the fate of the illustrious heroes of that name to die young. *Justin.* 12. c. 15 & 16.—*Virg. Æn.* 1. v. 103, &c. & *Servius in loco.*

Æ'ACUS, son of Jupiter by Ægina, daughter of Asopus, was king of the island of Œnopia. which he called by his mother's name. He was highly venerated by the Athenians; for when their country was visited with a drought, they were informed by the oracle that their distresses should cease only at the intercession of Æacus. Afterwards when a pestilence destroyed the inhabitants of Ægina, Æacus entreated Jupiter to repeople his kingdom; and according to his desire, all the ants which were in an old oak were changed into men, and called by the monarch *myrmidons*, from *μύρμηξ an ant.* Æacus married Endeis, by whom he had Telamon and Peleus. He afterwards had Phoces, by Psamathe, one of the Nereids. He was a man of such integrity that the ancients have made him one of the judges of hell. *Horat.* 2. od. 13. l. 4. od. 8.—*Paus.* 1. c. 44. l. 2. c. 29.—*Ovid Met.* 1. 13. v. 25. *In Ibin.* 187.—*Propert.* 4. el. 12.—*Plut. de consol. ad Apoll.—Apollod.* 3. c. 12.—*Diod.* 4.

Æ'Æ, Æ'A, or ÆÆ'A, an island of Colchis, in the Phasis. *Vid.* Æa.—*Apollon.* 3.—*Plin.* 5. c. 30.

ÆÆ'A, a name given to Circe, because she was born at Æa. *Virg. Æn.* 3. v. 386.

Æ'A, the island of Calypso, placed in the Sicilian sea by some; and near Circeii, on the coast of Italy, by others. Calypso is thence called Ææa puella. *Propert.* 3. el. 11. v. 31.—*Servius ad Æn. loco. cit.—Mela.* 2. c. 9. The name was also given to Medea, from her birth in Colchis.——A town of Apulia. *Liv.* 24. c. 20.

ÆAME'NE, a region of the Nabatæi, in Arabia Petræa. *Steph.*

Æ'ANIS, a fountain of Macedonia, with a grove called Æanium. *Strab.* l. 3.

ÆAN'TIDES, a tyrant of Lampsacus, intimate with Darius. He married Archedice, the daughter of Hippias, tyrant of Athens. *Thucyd.* 6. c. 59.——One of the seven poets called Pleiades. *Voss. de poet. Gr.* p 64.

ÆAN'TIS, one of the tribes of Athens. *Plut. Symp.* 2.

ÆAN'TIUM, a city of Troas, where Ajax was buried, whence the name. *Bas. Fabri. Thes. Erud.—Plin.* 5. c. 30.——An island near the Thracian Chersonesus. *Id.* 4. c. 12.——A promontory of Magnesia. *Id.* 4. c. 9.

Æ'AS, now Vajussa, a river of Epirus, falling into the Ionian sea. In the fable of Io, Ovid describes it as falling into the Peneus, and meeting other rivers at Tempe. This some have supposed to be a geographical mistake of the poet. *Lucan.* 6 v. 361.—*Ovid. Met.* 1. v. 580.—*Mela,* 2. c. 5.—*Cluver.* 4. c. 10.

Æ'ATUS, son of Philip, and brother of Polyclea, was descended from Hercules. An oracle having declared that whichever of the two first touched the land after crossing the Achelous, should obtain the kingdom, Polyclea pretended to be lame, and prevailed upon her brother to carry her across on his shoulders. When they came near the opposite side, Polyclea leaped ashore from her brother's back, exclaiming that the kingdom was her own. Æatus afterwards married her, and reigned conjointly with her. Their son Thessalus gave his name to Thessaly. *Polyæn.* 8.

ÆBU'RA, now Talavera, a city of Hispania Tarraconensis. *Steph.*

ÆBU'TIUS, a Roman family name. T. Æbutius Elva, was consul A.U.C. 255., and was wounded at the battle of the lake Regillus. *Liv.* 2. c. 19. L. Æbutius was consul A.U.C. 291. Livy mentions several other persons of this name, but they were little known. *Liv.* 3. c. 6. &c.

ÆCA'NA, now Troja, a city of Daunian Apulia.

ÆCA'NI, a people of Etruria, conquered by Camillus. *Plut.*

ÆCHMAG'ORAS, a son of Hercules, by Phyllone, daughter of Alcimedon, was exposed with his mother in the woods, where Hercules, conducted by the noise of a magpie, which imitated the cries of a child, found and delivered them. *Paus.* 8. c. 12.

ÆCH'MIS, succeeded Polymnestor on the throne of Arcadia, in the reign of Theopompus of Sparta,

Paus. 8. c. 5.——A son of Briacus, waged war with the Spartans. *Id.*

ÆC'LUS, a man who migrated from Athens to Eretria after the Trojan war. *Strab.* 1. 10.

ÆCULA'NUM, now Frisento, or Laconiano, a town of the Hirpini. The people were called Æculani. *Ptol.—Plin.* 3. c. 11.

ÆDE'MON. *Vid.* Ademon.

ÆDEP'SUM. *Vid.* Ædipsus.

ÆDE'SIA, an Ægyptian woman, wife of Hermias, whose life has been written by *Suidas.*

ÆDES'SA, or EDES'SA, a town of Macedonia, near Pella. Ceranus, king of Macedonia, took it by following goats that sought shelter from the rain, and called it from that circumstance, Ægeas. It was the burying place of the Macedonian kings, and an oracle had said, that as long as the kings were buried there, so long would their kingdom exist. Alexander was buried elsewhere, and on that account some authors have said the kingdom became extinct. It is now Vodena. *Liv.—Polyb.—Justin.* 7. c. 1.—*Cluver.* 4. c. 9.

ÆDIC'ULA RIDIC'ULI, a temple raised to the god of mirth, from the following circumstance: after the battle of Cannæ, Hannibal marched to Rome, whence he was driven back by the inclemency of the weather; which caused so much joy in Rome, that the Romans raised a temple to the god of mirth. This deity was worshipped at Sparta. *Plut. in Lyc. Agid. & Cleom. Pausanias* also mentions a θεος γελωτος.

ÆDI'LES, Roman magistrates, who had the care of all buildings, baths, and aqueducts, and examined the weights and measures, that nothing might be sold without its due value. There were three different sorts, the Plebeii or Minores, the Majores, and the Cereales. The plebeian ædiles were two, first created with the tribunes, A.U.C. 260. They presided over the more minute affairs of the state, the good order, and the repairing of the streets; and they examined the plays produced on the stage, and distributed the palm of the victory to the most deserving actors. They procured all the provisions of the city, and executed the decrees of the people. The Majores and Cereales had greater privileges, though they at first shared in the labor of the plebeian ædiles; they appeared with more pomp, and were allowed to sit in public in ivory chairs. The office of an ædile was honourable, and was always the primary step to greater honors in the republic. The ædiles were at first chosen from the plebeians; but afterwards the election was made indiscriminately from the plebeians and the patricians. This office continued in existence with little variation till the age of Constantine. In some of the principle towns, the ædiles were sometimes the only magistrates, as at Arpinum, &c. *Cic. Off.* 2. 16.—*Fam.* 13. ep. 11.—*Liv.* 3. c. 55.—*Diodor.* 49. c. 43.—*Plaut. Trin.* 4.—*Juv.* 3. v. 179.—*Gell.* 10. c. 6.—*Varro de L. L.* 4. c. 14.

ÆDIP'SUS, a town on the western shores of Eubœa, now Dipso, abounding in hot baths. *Plin.* 4. c. 12.—*Strab.* 10.

ÆDIT'UUS, Valer., a Roman poet before the age of Cicero, very successful in amorous poetry and epigrams. He was preferred by some to the Greek writers for the sweetness, elegance, and delicacy of his numbers. Only ten verses of his poetry are preserved. *Varro.*

ÆDIT'UUS, the name of officers entrusted with the care of the temples at Rome, whence the name, *ædes tuiri. Fest. de Verb. Sig.*

AE'DON, the wife of Zethus, brother of Amphion, had a son called Itylus. She was so jealous of her sister Niobe, because she had more children than herself, that she resolved to murder the eldest son, who was educated with Itylus. She, by mistake, killed her own son, and was changed into a goldfinch, as she attempted to destroy herself. *Homer Od.* 19. v. 518. *Bocac. gen. Deor.*——A daughter of Pandarus the Ephesian, who married Polytechnus, an artist of Colophon.

ÆD'UI or HÆD'UI, a powerful nation of Gaul, at the west of the river Arar, known for their valor during the wars of Cæsar, and called by *Cicero* the brothers of the Romans, because they were the first of the Gauls who became the allies of Rome. When their country was invaded by this celebrated general, they were at the head of a faction in opposition to the Sequani and their partisans, and they had established their superiority in frequent battles. To support their cause, however, the Sequani obtained the assistance of Arivostus, king of Germany, and soon defeated their opponents. The arrival of Cæsar changed the face of affairs, the Ædui were restored to the sovereignty of the country, and the artful Roman, by employing one faction against the other, was enabled to conquer them all; though the insurrection of Ambiorix, and that more powerfully supported by Vercingetorix, shook for a while the dominion of Rome in Gaul, and checked the career of the conqueror. *Cæs. in Bell. G.—Cluver.* 2. c. 11.

ÆDU'SII, according to *Stephanus*, a nation near Gallia Celtica, in alliance with Rome.

ÆE'TA, or ÆE'TES, king of Colchis, son of Sol and Perseis, daughter of Oceanus, was father of Medea. Absyrtus and Chalciope, by Idyia, one of the Oceanides. He killed Phryxus, son of Athamas, who had fled to his court on a golden ram, that he might obtain possession of the fleece. The Argonauts, headed by Jason, undertook an expedition against Colchis, and by the assistance of Medea, recovered the golden fleece, though it was guarded by bulls that breathed fire, and by a venomous dragon. Their expedition has been celebrated by all the ancient poets. *Vid.* Jason, Medea, and Phryxus. *Apollod.* 1. c. 9.—*Ovid Met.* 7. v. 9, &c.—*Paus.* 2. c. 3.—*Justin.* 42. c. 2.—*Flacc. & Orph. in Argon.*

ÆE'TIAS, ÆE'TIS, and ÆE'TIA, patronymics given to Medea, as daughter of Æetes. *Ovid. Met.* 7. v. 9.

Æ'GA, an island of the Ægæan sea, between Tenedus and Chios.

Æ'GA, a daughter of Olenus, and a nurse of Jupiter, is said by some authors to have been the wife of Pan. *Hygin. Poet Astron.* 1. 2. c. 13.

Æ'GA, a promontory of Æolis, not far from the Caicus. *Strab.*

Æ'GA, a queen of the Amazons, who, according to *Festus Pompeius*, perished in, and gave her name to, the Ægæan sea.

Æ'GA, a city of Pollene. *Herod.* 7. c. 123.——A river of Phocis.——A town of Thessaly.

ÆGÆ'A, a city of Emathia.—A city of Mauritania. *Ptol.*

ÆGE'AS, or Æ'GÆ, a town of Macedonia, the inhabitants of which were called Ægeates. It is the some as Ædessa. *Vid.* Ædessa. Some writers make them different, but *Justin* proves this to be erroneous. *Plin.* 4. c. 10.——A town of Eubœa, whence Neptune is called Ægæus. *Strab.* 9. *Cluver.* 4. c. 9.—*Solin.* c. 14.

ÆGÆ'Æ, a town and seaport in the eastern parts of Cilicia. *Lucan.* 3. v. 227.——A city of Æolia. *Herod.* 1. 149.

ÆGÆ'ON, one of Lycaon's 50 sons. *Apollod.* 3. c. 8. ——The son of Cœlus and Terra, the same as Briareus. *Vid.* Briareus. It is supposed that he was a notorious pirate, chiefly residing at Æga, whence his name; and that the fable about his 100 hands arises from his having 100 men to manage his oars in his piratical excursions. *Virg. Æn.* 10. v. 565. & *Servius in loco.—Hesiod. Theog.* 149.—*Homer, Il.* 1. v. 404.—*Ovid. Met.* 2. v. 10.

ÆGÆ'UM MA'RE, now the Archipelago, part of the Mediterranean, dividing Greece from Asia Minor, and extending from north to south more than 400 miles. The principal islands amount in number to about 45, and are called, some Cyclades, some Sporades, &c. The word Ægæum is derived by some from Ægæ, a town of Eubœa; or from the number of islands which it contains that appear above the sea, as αιγες, goats; or from the promontory Æga; or from Æga, a queen of the Amazons; or from Ægeus, who is supposed to have drowned himself there. *Plin.* 4. c. 11.—*Festus de V. Sig. Varro de R. R.* 2. c. 1.—*Lucan.* 1. v. 103.—*Strab.* 7.—*Mela.* 1. c. 3. 1. 2. c. 2. &c.—*Ptol.* 3. c. 15. 1. 5. c. 2.—*Cluver. pass.*

ÆGÆ'US, a surname of Neptune, from Ægæ in Eubœa. *Strab.* 9.

ÆGÆUS, a river of Corcyra.——A plain in Phocis.

ÆGAGE'A, a mountain of Asia. *Nicand. in Theriac.* v. 218.

ÆGA'LEOS or ÆGA'LEON, a mountain of Attica, opposite Salamis, on which Xerxes sat during the engagement of his fleet with the Grecian ships in the adjacent sea. *Herodot.* 8. c. 90.—*Thucyd.* 2. c. 19.

ÆGAN, *Græc.* αἰγαν or αἰγάων, the Ægæan sea *Stat. Theb.* 5. v. 56.

ÆGAS, a place of Eubœa.——A place near Daunia in Italy. *Polyb.* 3.

ÆGATES, a promontory of Æolia, now Cane and Cavæ. *Stephan.* It is called *Artemidorus* αἰξ.——Three islands near Lilybæum, at the west of Sicily opposite Carthage, called Aræ by *Virgil, Æn.* 1. v. 109., near which the Romans under Lutatius Catulus defeated the Carthaginian fleet commanded by Hanno. This celebrated battle, fought 242 years B.C. put an end to the first Punic war. The Ægates were called Phorbantia, Hiera, and Ægusa, aud are now Levenzo, Maretamo, and Favignana. *Polyb.* 6. c. 60. &c. *Liv.* 21. c. 10. & 41. l. 22. c. 54.—*Mela,* 2. c. 7.—*Sil.* 1. v. 61. These islands are improperly called Ægades by the commentator upon *Cluverius,* 1. 3. c. 41.

ÆGEIS, a tribe of Athens, so called from Ægeus, son of Pandion. *Steph.*

Æ'GELI, a people of Media. *Stephan.*

ÆGE'LION, a town of Macedonia, taken by king Attalus. *Liv.* 31. c. 46.

Æ'GEMON, a poet who celebrated the Theban war. *Volateran.*

ÆGE'ONIS, a promontory near the mouth of the Rhyndacus. *Apollon.* l. 1.

ÆGE'RIA. *Vid.* Egeria.

ÆGES'TA, the daughter of Hippotes, was mother of Ægestus, called also Acestes. *Virg. Æn.* 1. v. 554.——An ancient town of Sicily, near mount Eryx, destroyed by Agathocles. It was sometimes called Segesta, Acesta, and Egesta. *Diod.* 10.—*Strabo.* &c. *Vid.* Acesta.

Æ'GEUS, king of Athens, son of Pandion, married Æthra, daughter of Pittheus king of Troezene. When he returned to Athens he left her pregnant, and told her, if she had a son, to send him to Athens as soon as he could lift a stone under which he had concealed his sword. Æthra became mother of Theseus, whom she accordingly sent to Athens with his father's sword, when he reached the age of manhood. At that time Ægeus lived with Medea, the divorced wife of Jason. When Theseus came to Athens, Medea attempted to poison him; but he escaped, and upon showing Ægeus the sword which he wore, discovered himself to be his son. When Theseus returned from Crete, after the death of the Minotaur, he forgot, agreeably to the engagement with his father, to hoist up white sails as a signal of his success: and Ægeus, at the sight of black sails, concluding that his son was dead, threw himself from a high rock into the sea; which, from him, as some suppose, has been called the Ægæan sea. Ægeus reigned 48 years, and died B.C. 1235. He is supposed to have first introduced the worship of Venus Urania into Attica, to render the goddess propitious to his wishes for a son. *Vid.* Theseus, Minotaurus and Medea.—*Apollod.* 1. c. 8. 9. l. 3. c. 15.—*Paus.* 1. c. 5. 22. 38. l 4. c. 2.—*Plut. in Thes.*—*Hygin.* fab. 37. 43. 79. & 173.—*Servius. in* 3 *Æn.* v. 74.——A son of Oiolycus, from whom the tribe of Ægidæ at Sparta received their name. *Herod.* 4. 149.

Æ'GIE, a town of Laconia. *Pausan.* 3. It is called Augea by *Stephanus.*——A city of Ætolia. *Dioscor.*

ÆGI'ALE, one of Phaeton's sisters, who were changed into poplars, and their tears into amber. They were called Heliades.

ÆGI'ALE, or ÆGIALE'A, a daughter of Adrastus, by Amphithea, daughter of Pronax. She married Diomedes, in whose absence during the Trojan war, she prostituted herself to her servants, and chiefly to Cometes, whom the king had left guardian of his house. At his return, Diomedes being informed of his wife's licentious conduct, abandoned his country and went to settle in Daunia. Some say that Venus implanted those vicious propensities in Ægiale, to revenge herself on Diomedes, who had wounded her in the Trojan war. *Ovid in Ib.* v. 350.—*Homer Il.* 5. v. 41?.—*Apollod.* 1. c. 9.—*Stat.* 3. *Sivl.* 5. v. 48.—*Lycoph apud Eustath.* 5. *Il.*—*Tzeztes in Lycoph.*

ÆGIALE'A or ÆGILIA, an island between Peloponnesus and Crete.——An island in the Ionian sea, near the Echinades. *Plin.* 4. c. 12.—*Herodot.* 4. c. 107.——The ancient name of Peloponnesus. *Strab.* 12.—*Mela,* 2. c. 7.

ÆGI'ALEUS, son of Adrastus by Amphithea or Demoanassa, was one of the Epigoni, *i.e.* one of the sons of those generals who were killed in the first Theban war. They went against the Thebans, who had refused to give burial to their fathers, and were victorious. They all returned home safe except Ægialeus, who was killed. That expedition is called the war of the Epigoni. *Paus.* 1. c. 43. 5.—*Apollod.* 1. c. 9. l. 3. c. 7.—*Hygin.* 79., ll c. 44. l. 2. c. 20. ——A name given to Absyrtus, brother of Medea. *Justin.* 42. c. 3.— *Cic. de N. D.* 3.—*Diod.* 4.

ÆGI'ALUS, son of Phoroneus, was entrusted with the kingdom of Achaia by king Apis when he went to Ægypt. Peloponnesus was called Ægialea from him.——A man who founded the kingdom of Sicyon, 2091 B. C. and reigned 52 years. *Suidas.*——A name given to part of Peloponnesus. *Vid.* ACHAIA.—*Paus.* 5. c. 1. l. 7. c. 1.——An inconsiderable town of Pontus.——A city of Asia Minor——A city of Thrace near the Strymon.——A mountain of Galatia.——A city of Æthiopia.

Æ'GIAS, an artisan who assisted Aratus in effecting a change in the government of Sicyon.

ÆGICORE'US, an ancient tribe of Athens. *Stephan.*—*Pollux.* l. 8.

ÆG'IDA, a town of Istria, now Capo d'Istria. *Cluver.* 3. c. 24.

ÆGI'DES, a patronymic of Theseus. *Homer Il.* 1. v. 265.

ÆG'ILA, a place in Laconia, where Aristomenes was taken prisoner by a number of religious women whom he had attacked. *Paus.* 4. c. 17.——An island near Crete, *Plin.* 4. c. 12 called Ægyla by *Dion.*——A city of Cyrene, called Augila by *Ptolemy.*

ÆGIL'IA. *Vid.* ÆGIALEA.——A place in Eubœa. *Herdot.* 6. c. 101.——A tribe at Athens. *Athen.*

ÆG'ILIPS, a city of Acarnania. *Strab.*——A place in Epirus. *Stephan.*—*Homer Il.* 2. 633.

ÆGIL'IUM, an island of the Tyrrhene sea; now Il Oiglio.

ÆGILO'DES, a bay of Laconia. *Plin.* 4. c. 5.

ÆG'ILON, an island between Crete and Laconia.——A district of Laconia——A part of a tribe of Attica, so called from Ægilus. *Athen.*—*Demosth. in Neæram.*

ÆG'ILUM, a place of Asia Minor. *Zonaras.* It was probably the same as Ægialus.

ÆGIM'IUS, an old man who lived, according to Anacreon, 200 years. *Plin.* 7. c. 48.——A king of Doris, whom Hercules assisted to conquer the Lapithæ. *Apollod.* 2. c. 7.

ÆGIM'ORUS, or ÆGIMU'RUS, an island near Libya, supposed by some to be one of the Ægates, the same which *Virgil* mentions under the name of Aræ. It is placed in the bay of Carthage by some commentators, and called Galetta. *Liv.* 29. c. 27. l. 30. c. 24.—*Plin.* 5. c. 7.

ÆGI'NA, daughter of Asopus, bore Æacus to Jupiter, who visited her in the likeness of a flame of fire. Some say that she was changed by Jupiter into the island which bears her name; though more probably the island was so called from her concealment there. *Ptol.* 3. c. 16.—*Nat. Com. Myst.* 6. c. 17.—*Plin.* 4. c. 12.—*Strab.* 8.—*Apollod.* 1. c. 9. l. 3. c. 12.—*Paus.* 2. c. 5. & 29.—*Herod.* 5. 80.——An island opposite Athens, formerly called Œnopia, and now Engia, in the part of the Ægæan sea called Saronicus Sinus, about 22 miles in circumference. The inhabitants were once destroyed by a pestilence, and the country is said to have been repeopled by ants changed into men by Jupiter, at the prayer of king Æacus. They were once a very powerful nation by sea, but cowardly gave themselves up to Darius, when he demanded submission from all the Greeks. The Athenians under Pericles made war against them, and, after taking 70 of their ships in a naval battle, expelled them from Ægina. The fugitives settled in Peloponnesus, but after the ruin of Athens by Lysander, returned to their country; they, however, never after rose to their former power or consequence. The people of Ægina were the first who coined money, which they did by the advice of Phidon. *Herodot.* 5. 6. & 7.—*Thucyd.* 1. c. 14.—*Plin.* 4. c. 12—*Paus.* 2. c. 29. l. 8. c. 44.—*Strab.* 8.—*Ælian. V. H.* 12. c. 10.—*Mela,* 2. c. 9.—*Cluver.* 4. c. 10.——The wife of Aristodemus, king of Sparta. *Herod.* 1. 6.

ÆG'INAPS, an island near Peloponnesus. *Hesych.*

ÆGINE'TA PAU'LUS, a physician born in Ægina. He flourished in the fourth, or, according to others, in the seventh century, and distinguished himself for his knowledge in surgery. His writings in Greek consist of seven books, de Re Medicâ, edited at Venice, in folio, 1528

ÆGINE'TES, a king of Arcadia, in whose age Lycurgus instituted his famous laws. *Paus.* 1. c. 5.——A town and river of Paphlagonia. *Steph.*

ÆGIN'IUM, a town of Thessaly, between the rivers Aliacmon and Peneus. *Pliny*, 4. c. 10. places it in Pieria. *Liv.* 32. c. 15. l. 36. c. 13. l 44. c. 46.

ÆGI'NUM, a town of Illyricum, called Æginium by *Stephanus*. *Plin.* 4. c. 10.

ÆGI'OCHUS, a surname of Jupiter, because, according to some authors, he was brought up by the goat Amalthæa and used her skin instead of a shield in the war of the Titans; though more properly the epithet is derived from the ægis which the god bore, αιγις ἔχω. *Lactant.* 1. *de fals. Rel.* 21.—*Homer.* 1. v. 202. & *Schol. ibi.*—*Diod.* 5.——A place of Crete, where Jupiter was nourished by the goat. *Diod. Sic* 1.

ÆG'IPAM, a town of Upper Æthiopia, on the banks of the Nile. *Plin.* 6. c. 30.

ÆG'IPAN, (αἰγίπαν *semicaper*,) a name of Pan, because he had goats' feet. The word is also applied to Faunus, to Capricornus, one of the signs of the zodiac, and to those of the rural deities whose shape partook, in some degree, of that of the goat. *Eratosth.* 28 —*Hygin. P. A.* 2. c. 13 & 28.—*Plin.* 5. c. 1. & 8.—*Voss. ad. Mel.* 1. c. 8.

ÆGIPA'NES, a nation in the middle of Africa, whose bodies were said, by ancient mythologists, to be human above the waist, whilst their lower parts were those of a goat. *Mela*, 1. c. 4. & 8.

ÆGIPLANC'TUM, a mountain mentioned by Æschylus in his Agamemnon. *Ortelius* supposes it to be near Corinth. *Æsch. Agam.* 294 Ed. *Blomf.*

ÆGI'RA, a town of Peloponnesus, situate at the west of Sicyon. It is now Scolocastro, or Xylocastro. *Mela*, 2. c. 4.——An island of Achaia. *Plin.* 4. c. 5.

ÆGIROES'SA, a town of Æolia. *Herodot.* 1. c. 149.

ÆGI'RUM, a city in the narrowest part of the island of Lesbus. It is now Genia. *Strab.*

ÆGIRU'SA, called also Ægosthena, a town of Megaris. *Paus.*

Æ'GIS, the shield of Jupiter, ἀπὸ τῆς αἰγός, a goat's skin; so called, from the goat Amalthæa, whose skin covered his shield. The goat was placed among the constellations. Jupiter gave this shield to Pallas, who placed upon it Medusa's head, which turned into stone all those who fixed their eyes upon it. *Tibull.* 2. el. 2.—*Homer Il.* 5. v. 738.—*Servius in Æn.* 2. v. 615.—*Capella.* 6.—*Stat.* 12 *Theb.* & 1 *Ach.*—*Tzetzes in Cass. Lyc.*—*Heliod. Æth.* 3.—*Albric. de D. Imag.* 8.—*Fulgent.* 2. *Myth.*—*Lucian. Philos.* 8.—*Martial.* 7. ep. 1.—*Virg. Æn.* 8. v. 352 & 435.——A tribe of Attica. *Pollux. Vid* Ægeis.

ÆGIS'TE, a city of Arabia Felix. *Ptol.*

ÆGIS'THUS, a king of Argos, was son of Thyestes, by his daughter Pelopea. After this incestuous intercourse, Pelopea married her uncle Atreus, who received into his house her natural son. As Thyestes had debauched the first wife of Atreus, Atreus sent Ægisthus to put him to death; but Thyestes discovered that he was his own son, and sent him back to murder Atreus. After this murder Thyestes ascended the throne, and banished Agamemnon and Menelaus, the sons, or as others say, the grandsons of Atreus. Ægisthus, however, was reconciled to the sons of Atreus; and when they went to the Trojan war, he was left guardian to Agamemnon's kingdoms, and of his wife Clytemnestra. Ægisthus fell in love with Clytemnestra, and murdered, at a chase, the confidant whom Agamemnon had secretly left to watch his conduct, and afterwards lived in criminal intercourse with the queen. On Agamemnon's return, the two adulterers murdered him, and by a public marriage strengthened themselves on the throne of Argos. Ægisthus was at length slain by Orestes, in the temple of Apollo, after he had reigned seven years; and his body, together with that of Clytemnestra, whom Orestes slew at the same time, was buried without the walls of the city. *Vide* Agamemnon, Thyestes, Orestes, Clytemnestra, Pylades, & Electra. *Ovid. de Rem. Am.* 161. *Trist.* 2. v. 396.—*Hygin.* fab. 87. 88. &. 258.—*Ælian. V. H.* 12. c. 42.—*Lactant. Theb.* 1. v. 684.—*Servius in Æn.* 1. v. 572.—*Tzetzes. in* 1. *Chil.* 8.—*Schol. Eurip. in Orest.* 5. & 813.—*Paus.* 2. c. 16, &c.—*Sophocl. in Electra.*—*Æschyl.* & *Senec in Aga.*—*Homer Od.* 3. & 11. Pompey used to call J. Cæsar, Ægisthus, on account of his adultery with his wife Mutia, whom he repudiated after she had borne him three children. *Suet. in Cæs.* 50.

ÆGITHAR'SUS, a promontory of Sicily. *Cluverius*, however, considers it to be a corrupt reading for Ægithallus. *Sic. Ant.* 1. 2. It is now Capo di S. Vito, or, according to others, Capo di St. Theodoro.

ÆGIT'IUM, a town of Ætolia, on a mountain eight miles from the sea. *Thucyd.* 3. c. 97.

Æ'GIUM, a town of Peloponnesus, on the bay of Corinth, now Vostitza, where Jupiter is said to have been fed by a goat, whence the name. The goddess of health, Hygieia or Salus was particularly worshipped there. *Strab.* 8.—*Liv.* 28. c 7.

ÆG'LE, the youngest daughter of Æsculapius and Lampetia.——A nymph, daughter of Sol and Neæra. *Hygin.* fab. 176.—*Paus.* 9. c. 35.—*Virgil. Ec.*——A nymph, daughter of Panopeus, beloved by Theseus after he had abandoned Ariadne. *Plut. in Thes.*

Æg'le, one of the Hesperides. *Hygin. in Præf. fab.*

Æg'le, one of the Graces, more commonly called Aglae.——A prostitute. *Mart.* 1. ep. 95.

ÆG'LES, a Samian wrestler, born dumb. Seeing some unlawful measure pursued in a contest, he broke the string which held his tongue, through the desire of discovering the fraud of the combatants, and ever after spoke with ease. *Val. Max.* 1. c. 8.—*A. Gell.* 5. c. 9.

ÆGLE'TES, a surname by which Apollo was known in the island of Anaphe. *Apoll. Argon.* 4.

ÆG'LOGE, a nurse of Nero. *Suet. in Ner.* 50.

ÆGOB'OLUS, (αἰγὸς βόλος,) a name of Bacchus at Potnia in Bœotia. The inhabitants of this place, in a state of inebriety, had murdered the priest of their favorite divinity Bacchus, for which their country was visited by a pestilence, and they were directed by the oracle to appease the god by a yearly sacrifice of a youth who had attained the age of puberty. The sacrifice was continued till the god himself at last substituted a goat, whence his surname of Ægobolus. *Paus.* 9. c. 8.

ÆGOC'EROS, or Capricornus, an animal into which Pan transformed himself when flying before Typhon, in the war waged by the gods against the giants. Jupiter made him a constellation. *Lucret.* 1. v. 613.—*Lucan.* 9. v. 536.

ÆGOC'ORIS, *Vid.* Ægicoreus.

ÆGO'LIUS, a man who entered a cave in Crete, sacred to the bees of Jupiter, and was changed into a bird. *Ant. Lib. Met.*

Æ'GON, a king of the Argives, after the failure of the race of the Heraclidæ.——A prince of Carystus in Eubœa.

Æ'gon, a river of Africa, rising in the mountains of Æthiopia.

Æ'gon, a shepherd. *Virg. Ecl.*—*Theocrit*, *Idyl.*

Æ'gon, a promontory of Lemnus.——A name of the Ægæan sea. *Flacc.* 1. v. 628.

Æ'gon, a boxer of Zacynthus, who, to display his uncommon strength, dragged a large bull by the heel from a mountain into the city. *Theocryt. Idyl.* 4.

ÆGO'NES, a people of Gallia Cisalpina, now Vicovenza. *Polyb.*

ÆGOPH'AGUS, a surname of Juno among the Lacedæmonians, because Hercules, after his victory over the children of Hippocoon, for want of other victims, sacrificed to her a goat. *Paus.* 3. c. 15.

ÆGOS'AGÆ, an Asiatic nation under Attalus, with whom he conquered Asia, and to whom he gave a settlement near the Hellespont. *Polyb.* 5.

Æ'GOS POT'AMOS, *i. e.* the goat's river, a town in the Thracian Chersonesus, with a small river of the same name, where the Athenian fleet, consisting of 180 ships, commanded by Philocles, was defeated by Lysander, on the 13th Dec. B. C. 405. *Mela*, 2. c. 2.—*Plin.* 2. c. 58.—*Paus.* 3. c. 8. & 11.—*Cor. Nep. in Lys. Alc.* & *Con.*

ÆGOS'THENA, a town of Phocis in Achaia. *Ptol.*

ÆGOS'THENA. *Vid.* Ægirusa.

ÆG'UA, a city of Hispania Bœtica, not far from Corduba. *Strab.*

ÆG'ULA, an island of the Cretan sea. *Dion. Af.*

Æ'GUS and ROSCIL'LUS, two brothers among the Allobroges, who deserted from Cæsar to Pompey. *Cæs. Bell. Civ.* 3. c. 59.

ÆGU'SA, the middle island of the Ægates, on the western coast of Sicily. *Vid.* Ægates.

ÆGUS'SA, or ÆGU'SA, an island of Libya, called by the inhabitants Catria. *Steph.*

Æ'GY, a town near Sparta, destroyed because its inhabitants were suspected by the Spartans of favoring the Arcadians. *Paus.* 3. c. 2.

ÆGYP'IUS, a Thessalian, son of Atheus, changed into a vulture by Jupiter. *Anton. Lib. Met.*

ÆGYP'SUS, or ÆGYS'SUS. a town of the Getæ, on the south side of the Danube. *Ovid. ex Pont.* 1. ep. 8. 1. 4. ep. 7.

ÆGYP'TA, a freedman of Cicero. *Cic.* 1. 16. ep. 15,

ÆGYP'TII, the inhabitants of Ægypt. *Vid.* Ægyptus.

ÆGYP'TIS, a region of Peloponnesus. *Paus in Arcad.—Steph. in Voc.* ἠλίς.

ÆGYP'TIUM MA'RE, that part of the Mediterranean sea on which is the coast of Egypt. It is called also Pharium and Parthenium by *Eustathius* and *Ammianus Marcellinus.*

ÆGYP'TUS, son of Belus, king of Africa, gave his 50 sons in marriage to the 50 daughters of his brother Danaus. Danaus, who had established himself at Argos, and was jealous of his brother, who, by following him into Greece from Ægypt, seemed envious of his prosperity, obliged all his daughters to murder their husbands on the first night of their nuptials. This perfidious deed was executed, but Hypermnestra alone spared her husband Lynceus. Even Ægyptus himself was killed by his niece Polyxena. *Vid,* Danaus, Danaides, Lynceus. Ægyptus was king, after his father, of a part of Africa, which from him has been called Ægyptus. *Hygin.* fab. 168. 170. & 273.—*Apollod.* 2. c. 1.—*Ovid. Her.* 14.—*Paus.* 7. c. 21.

Ægyp'tus, an extensive country of Africa, watered by the Nile, bounded on the east by Arabia, and on the west by Libya. It took its name from Ægyptus, the brother of Danaus. Its extent, according to modern calculation, is 180 leagues from north to south, and it measures 120 leagues along the shore of the Mediterranean; but at 50 leagues from the sea it diminishes so much as scarcely to measure 7 or 8 leagues between the mountains on the east or west. It is divided into lower, which lies near the Mediterranean, and upper, which lies towards the south. Upper Egypt was famous for the town of Thebes, but lower Ægypt was the most populous, and contained the Delta, a number of large islands, which, from their form, have been called after the fourth letter of the Greek alphabet. The greatest part of lower Ægypt has been formed by the mud and sand carried down by the Nile. The Ægyptians reckoned themselves the most ancient nation in the universe, (*vid.* Psammetichus); but some authors make them of Æthiopian origin. They were remarkable for their superstition; they paid as much honour to the cat, the crocodile, the bull, and even to onions, as to Isis. In their civil government the Ægyptians were divided into three classes or casts, the shepherds, husbandmen, and artizans, whose employments were regularly transmitted from father to son. Rain never or seldom falls in this country; the fertility of the soil is occasioned by the yearly inundation of the Nile, which rises about 25 feet above the surface of the earth, and exhibits a large plain of waters, in which are scattered here and there the towns and villages, as the Cyclades in the Ægæan sea. The air is not wholesome, but the population is notwithstanding great, and the cattle very prolific. It is said that Ægypt once contained 20,000 cities; the most remarkable of which were Thebes, Memphis, Alexandria, Pelusium, Arsinoe, Ptolemais, Panopolis, Coptos, Bubastis, and Heliopolis. It was governed by kings, who immortalized themselves by the pyramids which they raised, and the canals which they opened. The most remarkable of their monarchs was Sesostris, who extended his conquest over the greater part of Asia and Africa; but his history, and indeed the early history of the country, is so intermixed with fabulous and mythological reports, that no information derived from that quarter can be considered as authentic, at least before the age of Cambyses. The priests pretended to trace the existence of the country for many thousand years, and fondly imagined that the gods were their first sovereigns, and that their monarchy had lasted 11,340 years according to Herodotus, or 30,000 years according to Diodorus. According to the calculation of Constantine Manasses, the kingdom of Ægypt lasted 1,663 years from its beginning under Misraim the son of Ham, 2,188 B. C. to the conquest of Cambyses, 525 B.C. Ægypt revolted afterwards from the Persian power B. C. 414, and Amyrtæus then became king. After him succeeded Psammetichus, Nephereus, Acoris, Psammuthis, Nepherites, Nectanebus, &c. It was conquered by Ochus 350 B. C.; and after the destruction of the Persian power by Alexander, Ptolemy refounded the kingdom, and began to reign 323 B.C. To him succeeded Philadelphus, 284; Evergetes, 246; Philopater, 221; Epiphanes, 204; Philomater, 180 and 169, with Evergetes II. or Physcon, for 6 years; Evergetes II. 145; Lathurus Soter and his mother Cleopatra, 116; Alexander of Cyprus and Cleopatra, 106; Lathurus Soter restored, 88; Cleopatra II. 6 months, with Alexander the Second, 19 days, 81; Ptolemy, surnamed Alexander III. 80; Dionysius, surnamed Auletes, 65; Dionysius II. with Cleopatra III. 51; Cleopatra III. with young Ptolemy, 46; and in 30 B. C. the country was reduced by Augustus into a Roman province. The history of Ægypt, therefore, may be divided into three epochas: the first begins with the foundation of the empire, and ends with the conquest of Cambyses; the second ends with the death of Alexander; and the third comprehends the reign of the Ptolemies, and ends with Cleopatra, in the age of Augustus. Under the Roman empire, Ægypt, as belonging to the emperors of Constantinople, was attacked by the Saracens under Omrow, the general of Omar, who took Alexandria after a siege of 14 months, and the loss of 23,000 men, A.D. 642. The caliphs of Bagdad, after this conquest, continued masters of the country till the year 982 A.D. when the Ægyptians recovered their independence. Saladin, in the year 1171, laid the foundation of a new dynasty; and under the protection of these masters Ægypt prospered and flourished till the insurrection of the Mamelukes 1250 A.D. introduced a new system of government. Selim, emperor of Turkey, in 1517 A.D. subdued the Mamelukes; and since that time Ægypt, though occasionally torn by civil discord and partial insurrections, has submitted to the power of the Porte; and under the arbitrary government of a capricious pacha, regularly remitted its annual tribute to Constantinople. *Strab.* 17.—*Justin.* 1.—*Hirt. in Alex.* c. 24.—*Macrob. Sat.* 1. c. 12. *in Som. Scip.* 1. c. 19 & 21.—*Herodian.* 4. c. 9.—*Herodot.* 2, 3, & 7.—*Theocrit. Id.* 17. v. 79.—*Polyb.* 15.—*Diod.* 1.—*Plin.* 5. c. 1. 1. 14. c. 7. —*Marcell.* 22. c. 40.—*C. Nep. in Paus.* 3. *in Iphic. in Datam.* 3.—*Curt.* 4. c. 1.—*Juv.* 15. v. 175.—*Paus.* 1. c. 14.—*Plut. de facie in Orb. Lun. de Isid. et Osir. in Ptol. in Alex.*—*Mela,* 1. c. 9.—*Apollod.* 2. c. 1. & 5.—*Cluver.* 1. c. 4. &c.

Ægyp'tus, a minister of Mausolus, king of Caria. *Polyæn.*

Ægyp'tus, the ancient name of the Nile. *Homer. Od.* ξ. v. 258.—*Paus.* 9. c. 40.

Æ'GYS. *Vid.* Ægy.

ÆGYS'THUS. *Vid.* Ægisthus.

ÆI'ANES, a people of Greece. *Paus. in Phoc.*—*Ortelius* reads Ænianes.

ÆLA'NA, a city of Arabia Petræa, on the Arabic Gulph, part of which is called Sinus Ælaniticus from it. It is now Eltor; or according to others, Aila.

Æ'LAS, a suburb of Carthage. *Procop.* 1. 2.

ÆLETA'NI, or LALETA'NI, a people of Hispania Tarraconensis, between the Iberus and the Pyrenees. *Strab.* 3.

Æ'LIA, the wife of Sylla. *Plut. in Syll.*

Æ'lia, Catul'la, a rich and noble matron, who, at the age of 80 danced before Nero. *Xiphilinus.*

Æ'lia Peti'na, the wife of Claudius Cæsar, of the family of the Tuberones, divorced by him when he married Messalina. *Suet. in Claud.* 26.

Æ'lia, the name of some towns built or repaired by the emperor Adrian.

Æ'lia Capitoli'na. *Vid.* Hierosolyma.

Æ'lia Adria'na. *Vid.* Zama.

Æ'lia Lex, enacted by Ælius Tubero, the tribune, A.U.C. 559, to send two colonies, one into the country of the Brutii, and the other to Thurium. *Liv.* 34. c. 53.—Another, enacted, A.U.C. 568, ordaining that, in public affairs, the augurs should observe the appearance of the sky, and the magistrates, on the occurrence of ill omens, be empowered to postpone the business.—Another called Ælia

Sentia, introduced by Ælius Sextus, A.U.C. 756, which enacted, that all slaves who bore any marks of punishment received from their masters, or who had been imprisoned, might be set free, but should not rank as Roman citizens.

ÆLIA'NUS CLAU'DIUS, a Roman of Præneste, in the reign of Adrian, surnamed Meliglossus, *honey-tongued*, from the sweetness of his style. He taught rhetoric at Rome, and published treatises on animals in 17 books, on various history in 14 books, &c. in Greek, a language which he preferred to Latin. In his writings he shows himself very fond of the marvellous, and relates many stories which, besides their improbability, are frequently devoid of eloquence and purity of style. Philostratus, however, has commended his language as superior to what could be expected from a person who was neither born nor educated in Greece. Ælian died in the 60th year of his age, A.D. 140. The best editions of his works are, that of Conrad Gesner, folio, Tiguri, 1556, now very scarce, and that of Kuenius, 2 vols. 8vo. Lips. 1780. Some attribute the treatise on the tactics of the Greeks to another Ælian. For an account of the opinions which the learned have held, as to the existence of two writers of this name, see *Sax. Onom.* 1. p. 301 and 356.—*Fabr. B. G.* vol. v. 609. Saxius maintains that Ælian the tactician lived about 130. A.D., and that the sophist lived about 225 A.D.

ÆLIA'NUS MEC'CIUS, a physician mentioned by *Galen*.

Æ'LIUS, or Æ'LIA, a family in Rome, so poor that 16 lived in a small house, and were maintained by the produce of a little field. This family branched into the families of the Pacti, Tuberones, Cati, &c. *Val. Max.* 4. c. 4.

Æ'LIUS, a Roman soldier, who, when sick of a mortal disease, slew himself that he might die bravely.

Æ'LIUS ADRIA'NUS, the grandfather of the emperor Adrian. *Vid.* Adrianus.

Æ'LIUS CEL'SUS, a senator slain by Severus. *Æl. Spartian. in Sever.* 13.

Æ'LIUS CORDUE'NUS, a celebrated general under the emperor Commodus. *Æl. Spartian. in Pescen. Nig.* c. 4.

Æ'LIUS DONA'TUS. *Vide* Donatus.

Æ'LIUS GAL'LUS, a Roman knight, the first who invaded Arabia Felix. He was very intimate with Strabo the geographer, and sailed on the Nile with him to take a view of the country. It was to him that Virgil inscribed his tenth eclogue. *Plin.* 6. c. 28.—*Strab.* 2.

Æ'LIUS GRAC'ILIS, or, according to *Lipsius*, Gracchus, a lieutenant of Gallia Belgica, in the time of Nero. *Tacit. Ann.* 13. c. 53.

Æ'LIUS, LA'MIA, a præfect of Syria, detained at Rome by Tiberius through fear. *Tacit. Ann.* 6. c. 27.

Æ'LIUS LAMPRID'IUS. *Vid.* Lampridius.

Æ'LIUS MAN'TIA, the accuser of L. Libo, before the censors, when Pompey undertook the defence. *Val. Max.* 6. c. 5.

Æ'LIUS MELIS'SUS, a grammarian in the age of A. Gellius.

Æ'LIUS PÆ'TUS, son of Sextus, or Publius. As he sat in the senate house, a woodpecker perched on his head; upon which a soothsayer exclaimed, that if he preserved the bird, his house would flourish, and Rome decay; and if he killed it, the contrary must happen. Hearing this, Ælius immediately bit off the head of the bird in the presence of the senate. All the youths of his family were killed at Cannæ, but the Roman arms were soon after attended with success. *Val. Max.* 5. c. 6.

Æ'LIUS PUB'LIUS, one of the first quæstors chosen from the plebeians at Rome. *Liv.* 4. c. 54.

Æ'LIUS SATURNI'NUS, a satirist thrown down from the Tarpeian rock, for writing verses against Tiberius.

Æ'LIUS SEJA'NUS, *Vid.* Sejanus.

Æ'LIUS SERENIA'NUS, a counsellor of Severus. He was pupil of Papinianus. *Lamprid. in Alex. Sev. c. ult.*

Æ'LIUS SEX'TUS CA'TUS, a censor with M. Cethegus. He separated the senators from the people, in the public spectacles. During his consulship, the ambassadors of the Ætolians found him feasting in earthen dishes, and offered him silver vessels, which he indignantly refused, satisfied with the earthen cups, &c., which, for his virtues, he had received from his father-in-law, L. Paulus, after the conquest of Macedonia. *Plin.* 33. c. 11.—*Cic. de Orat.* He is called *cordatus homo*, by Ennius, on account of his knowledge of the civil law.

Æ'LIUS SPARTIA'NUS wrote the lives of the emperors Adrian, Antonius Pius, and M. Aurelius. He flourished A.D. 240.

Æ'LIUS SUCCES'SUS, a merchant who received the name of Pertinax from his attention to commerce. He was father of the emperor Pertinax. *Capitolin in Pertinac.* c. 1.

Æ'LIUS TU'BERO, grandson of L. Paulus, was austere in his morals, and a formidable enemy to the Gracchi. His grandson was accused before Cæsar, and ably defended by Cicero. *Cic. ep. ad. Brut.*

Æ'LIUS VE'RUS CÆ'SAR, the name assumed by L. C. Commodus Verus, after Adrian had adopted him. He was made prætor and consul by the emperor, who was soon convinced of his incapacity to discharge his public duties. He killed himself by drinking a strong cathartic medicine, and Antoninus, surnamed Pius, was adopted in his place. Ælius was father of Antoninus Verus, whom Pius adopted.

Æ'LIUS XIFID'IUS, a præfect of the treasury under Valerian. *Vopisc. Aurel.* c. 12.

Æ'LIUS, a bridge at Rome, now Ponte di S. Angelo.

AEL'LO, one of the harpies, so called from ἄελλα, a storm. *Flacc.* 4. v. 450.—*Hesiod. Th.* 267.—*Ovid. Met.* 13. v. 710.

AEL'LO, one of Actæon's dogs. *Ovid. Met.* 3. 220.

ÆLUÆ'ONES or HELVEC'ONES, according to *Tacitus Germ.* 1. 43. a people of Germany. *Ptol.*

ÆLU'RI, a people separated from Gaul by the Alps. *Suidas.*—*Zonaras.*

ÆLU'RUS, αἴλουρος, a cat, a deity worshipped by the Ægyptians, and after death embalmed, and buried in the city of Bubastis. *Herodot.* 2. c. 66. &c.—*Diod.* 1.—*Cic. de N. D.* 1.—*A. Gell.* 20. c. 7.—*Plut. in Præc.*

ÆMA'RII, the name of an illustrious family of Gaul.

ÆMARO'RUM MONS, a town of Gallia Narbonensis, now Montlimar. *Strab.*

ÆMA'THIA. *Vid.* Emathia.

ÆMA'THION. *Vid.* Emathion.

ÆMIL'IA CLA'RA, the mother of the emperor Didius Julianus. *Æl. Spart. in Did.* c. 1.

ÆMIL'IA LEX was enacted by the dictator Æmilius, A.U.C. 311. It ordained that the censorship, which was before quinquennial, should be limited to one year and a half. *Liv.* 9. c. 33.—Another enacted in the second consulship of Æmilius Mamercus, A.U.C. 391. It gave power to the eldest prætor to drive a nail in the capitol on the Ides of September. *Liv.* 7. c. 3. The driving of a nail was a superstitious ceremony, by which the Romans supposed that a pestilence could be stopped, or an impending calamity averted.—Another, a sumptuary law, enacted by M. Æmilius Lepidus. *A. Gell.* 1. 2. c. 24.

ÆMILIA'NUS C. JU'LIUS, a native of Mauritania, proclaimed emperor after the death of Decius. He marched against Gallus and Valerian, but was ininformed that they had been murdered by their own troops. He soon after shared their fate. *Pomp. Læt.*—*Eutrop.* 1. 9. [There is a bust of this emperor in the museum of the capitol at Rome.]

ÆMILIA'NUS, a proconsul of Asia, under Severus, who being declared an enemy by the emperor, fled to Cyzicum, and thence to another city, where he was slain. *Æl. Spart. in Sever.* c. 9.

ÆMIL'IUS. *Vid.* Æmylius.

ÆMIL'IUS LÆ'TUS, a præfect of the prætorian cohort under Commodus. *Lamprid. Comm.* c. 4.

ÆMIN'IUM, a town of Lusitania, now Agueda, or, according to *Varrerius*, Conimbra.

ÆMIN'IUS, a river of Spain. *Plin. ex. Varone*, l. 4. c. 22.

ÆMNES'TUS, a tyrant of Enna, was deposed by Dionysius the elder. *Diod.* 14

Æ'MON. *Vid.* Hæmon.

ÆMO'NA, a large city of Asia. *Cic. pro Flacc.*

ÆMO'NIA, a country of Greece, which received its name from or Æmon, Æmus, and was afterwards called Thessaly. Achilles is called Æmonius, as being born there. *Ovid. Trist.* 3. el. 11. 4. el. 1. *Heroid.* 13. *Fast.* 2. *de A. A.* 1.—*Catull. de Nupt. Pel.*—*Stat. Theb.* 5. *Horat.* 1. od. 37. It was also called Pyrrha, from Pyrrha, Deucalion's wife, who reigned there. The word has been applied indiscriminately to all Greece by some authors. *Plin.* 4. c. 7.—*Cluver.* 4. c. 8.——A city of Pannonia. *Plin.* 3. c. 25.——A city of Noricum. *Id.* 3. c. 14.

ÆMON'IDES, a priest of Apollo in Italy, killed by Æneas. *Virg. Æn.* 10. 537.

ÆMUS, an actor in Domitian's reign. *Juv.* 6. v. 197.

Æ'MUS, a mountain. *Vid.* Hæmus.

ÆMYL'IA, a vestal, who rekindled the fire of Vesta, which was extinguished, by putting her veil over it. *Val. Max.* 1. c. 1.—*Dion. Hal.* 2.——The wife of Africanus the elder, famous for her behaviour to her husband, when suspected of infidelity. Her daughter Cornelia was the mother of the Gracchi. *Val. Max.* 6. c. 7.

ÆMYL'IA LEP'IDA, daughter of Lepidus, married Drusus the younger, whom she disgraced by her licentious conduct. She killed herself when accused of adultery with a slave. *Tacit.* 6. c. 40.

ÆMYL'IA MU'SA, a rich freedwoman, whose property, she having died intestate, Tiberius gave to Æmylius Lepidus. *Tacc. Ann.* 2. c. 48.

ÆMYL'IA, a part of Italy, called also Flaminia. *Mart.* 6. ep. 85.——A public road leading from Placentia to Ariminum, called after the consul Æmylius, who is supposed to have made it. *Id.* 3. ep. 4.

ÆMYLIA'NA, a place of the Oretani, in Spain. *Ptol.*——A place in the suburbs of Rome.

ÆMYLIA'NUS, a name of Africanus the younger, son of P. Æmylius. In him the families of the Scipios and Æmylii were united. Many of that family bore the same name. *Juv.* 8. v. 3.——A præfect set over Ægypt by Gallienius. He wished to assume the purple; but being taken by Theodorus, he was put to death. *Trebell. in Gallien.* c. 4. and 5.——A general under Severus.

ÆMYL'II, a noble family in Rome, said to be descended from Æmylius, the son of Ascanius. Plutarch says that they were descended from Mamercus, the son of Pythagoras, surnamed Æmylius, from the sweetness of his voice, and the power and elegance of his expressions. The family was distinguished in the various branches of the Lepidi, Mamerci, and Mamercini, Barbulæ, Pauli, and Scauri. *Plut. in. Num. & Æmyl.*

ÆMYL'IUS, a beautiful youth of Sybaris, whose wife met with the same fate as Procris. *Vid.* Procris.

ÆMYL'IUS CENSORI'NUS, a cruel tyrant of Sicily, who liberally rewarded those who invented new methods of torture. Paterculus gave him a brazen horse for this purpose, and the tyrant made the first experiment upon the donor. *Plut. in Parall.* 7. c. 5.

ÆMYL'IUS LEP'IDUS, a youth to whom a statue was erected in the capitol, for saving the life of a citizen in battle. *Val Max.* 4. c. 1.

ÆMYL'IUS LEP'IDUS, a triumvir with Octavius. *Vid.* Lepidus.

ÆMYL'IUS LONGI'NUS, a deserter from the first legion, who hastened the death of the lieutenant Dillius Vocula. He was afterwards slain by the Byzantine soldiers who were in the legion. *Tac. Hist.* 4. c. 59. & 62.

ÆMYL'IUS MA'CER, a poet. *Vid.* Macer.——A poet in the age of Tiberius, who wrote a tragedy called Athens. He afterwards destroyed himself.

ÆMYL'IUS MAMER'CUS, was three times dictator; he likewise conquered the Fidenates, and took their city. He altered the time of holding the censorship from five years to one year and a half. *Liv.* 4. c. 17. 19, &c.

ÆMYL'IUS PACEN'SIS, a tribune cashiered by Galba, but restored to his rank by Otho. He was slain by the adherents of Vitellius. *Tac. Hist.* 1. c. 20. & 3. c. 73.

ÆMYL'IUS PAPINIA'NUS, son of Hostilius Papinianus, was a favourite of the emperor Severus, and governor of his sons Geta and Caracalla. Geta was killed by his brother, and Papinianus was slain by his soldiers for upbraiding him. From his school the Romans had many able lawyers, who were called Papinianists.

ÆMYL'IUS PAP'PUS, a censor, who banished from the senate P. Corn. Ruffinus, who had been twice consul, because he had at his table ten pounds of silver plate. According to Livy, he triumphed over the Gauls when consul, A.U.C. 528. *Liv.* 14.

ÆMYL'IUS PAU'LUS. *Vid.* Paulus.

ÆMYL'IUS PORCI'NA, an elegant orator. *Cic. in Brut.*

ÆMYL'IUS REC'TUS, a præfect of Ægypt, reproved by Tiberius for extortion in his province. *Dion. Nicæus. in Tiber.*

ÆMYL'IUS REGIL'LUS, conquered the general of Antiochus at sea, and obtained a naval triumph. *Liv.* 37. c31.

ÆMYL'IUS. M. SCAU'RUS, a Roman, who flourished about 100 B.C., and wrote three books concerning his own life, which he dedicated to Fusidius. *Cic. in Brut.*

ÆMYL'IUS SCAU'RUS, a noble but poor citizen of Rome, whose father was a coal merchant. He was ædile, and afterwards prætor, and fought against Jugurtha.

ÆMYL'IUS MAR'CUS, one of the last mentioned, was son-in-law to Sylla, and in his ædileship built a very magnificent theatre. *Plin.* 36. c. 15.

ÆMYL'IUS SU'RA, a writer on the Roman year.

ÆMYL'IUS, a bridge at Rome, called also Sublicius. *Juv.* 6. v. 32.

Æ'NA, a city of Arabia Felix. *Ptol.*——A city of Macedonia. *Ptol.—Suidas.*

ÆNA'RIA, an island in the bay of Puteoli, abounding with cypress trees. It was called Pithecusa by the Greeks, and is now Ischia, and was once famous for its mineral waters. *Plin.* 3. c. 6. l. 31. c. 2. —*Stat.* 3. *Sylv.* 5. v. 104. *Liv.* 8. c. 22.—*Mela*, 2. c. 9.

ÆNA'RIUM, a forest near Olenus, in Achaia, sacred to Jupiter, where the inhabitants of the country frequently held their assemblies. *Strab.* 8.

ÆNAU'TA, certain Milesian magistrates, so called from their custom of deliberating on board a ship, at some distance from the land. *Hesych.—Plut. in Quæst. Gr.*

ÆNE'A, or, ÆNEI'A, now Moncastro, a town of Macedonia, founded by Æneas, and situated on the Sinus Thermaicus, 15 miles from Thessalonica. *Liv.* 40. c. 4. l. 44. c. 10.—*Virg. Æn.* 3. v. 18.—*Herod.* 7. 123. Cassander destroyed it, and carried the inhabitants to Thessalonica, lately built. *Dion. Hal.* 1.

ÆNE'ADES, a patronymic of Ascanius. *Virg. Æn.* 9. v. 653.

ÆNE'ADÆ, a name given to the friends and companions of Æneas by *Virgil. Æn.* 1. v. 157. &c.

ÆNE'AS, a Trojan prince, son of Anchises and Venus. At the age of five years, he was placed under the care of Alcathous, the friend and companion of his father. He afterwards improved himself in Thessaly, under the celebrated Chiron. Soon after his return he married Creusa, the daughter of Priam, by whom he had a son called Ascanius. During the Trojan war, he behaved with great valor, in defence of his country, and fought with Diomedes and Achilles. Yet Strabo, Dictys of Crete, Dionysius of Halicarnassus, and Dares of Phrygia, accuse him, in conjunction with Antenor, of betraying his country to the Greeks, and of preserving his life and fortunes by this treacherous measure. When Troy was in flames, he carried away upon his shoulders his father Anchises, and the images of his household gods, leading by the hand his son Ascanius, and leaving his wife to follow behind. Some say that he retired to mount Ida, where he built a fleet of twenty ships, and whence he set sail in quest of a settlement. Strabo and others maintain, however, that Æneas never left his country, and rebuilt Troy, where he reigned, and his posterity after him. Even Homer, who lived 200 years after the Trojan war, says that the gods destined Æneas to reign over the Trojans. This passage Dionysius of Halicarnassus explains, by saying, that Homer meant the Trojans who accompanied Æneas to Italy. According to Virgil and other Latin authors, who, to make their court to the Roman emperors, traced their origin up to Æneas, and described his arrival in Italy as indubitable, he first came to the Thracian Chersonesus, where Polymnestor, one of his allies reigned. After visiting Delus, the Strophades, and Crete, he landed in Epirus, and afterwards visited Drepanum, the court of king Acestes, in Sicily, where he buried his father. Having left Sicily, he was driven on the coast of Africa, and kindly received by Dido, queen of Carthage. Dido being enamoured of him, wished to marry him; but he was commanded by the gods to abandon his new settlement, and pursue his course to Italy. In his voyage he was driven to Sicily, and thence he passed to Cumæ, where the Sybil conducted him to the infernal regions, that he might hear from his father the fates which attended him and his posterity. After a voyage of seven years, and the loss of thirteen ships, he came to the Tyber. Latinus, the king of the country, received him with hospitality, and promised him his daughter Lavinia, who had been before betrothed to Turnus by her mother Amata. To prevent this marriage, Turnus made war against Æneas and, after many battles, the war was decided by a single combat between the two rivals, in which Turnus was slain. Æneas married Lavinia, in whose honour he built the town of Lavinium, and succeeded his father-in-law on the throne. After a short reign, Æneas was killed in a battle against the Etrurians. Some say that he was drowned in the Numicus, and that his body was weighed down by his armour; upon which the Latins, not finding their king, supposed that he had been taken up to heaven, and therefore offered sacrifices to him as to a god. Dionysius of Halicarnassus fixes the arrival of Æneas in Italy in the fifty-fourth Olympiad. Some authors suppose that Æneas, after the siege of Troy, fell to the share of Neoptolemus, together with Andromache, and that he was carried to Thessaly, whence he escaped to Italy. Others say, that after he had come to Italy, he returned to Troy, leaving Ascanius seated on the throne of Latium. Æneas has been praised for his piety, and submission to the will of the gods. *Homer. Il.* 13 & 20 —*Hymn in Ven.—Apollod.* 3. c. 12.—*Diod.* 3.—*Paus.* 2. c. 33. l. 3. c 22. l. 10. c. 25. *Plut. in Romul. & Corol. Quæst. Rom.—Val. Max.* 1. c. 8.—*Flor.* 1. c. 1.—*Justin.* 20. c. 1. l. 31. c. 8. l. 43. c. 1.—*Dictys. Cret.* 5.—*Dares Phryg.* 6.—*Dion. Hal.* 1. c 11.—*Strab.* 13.—*Liv.* 1.c. 1.—*Virg. Æn. & Servius Ibid.*—*Aur. Vic*—*Ælian. V. H.* 8. c. 22.—*Propert.* 4. el. 1. v. 42.—*Ovid. Met.* 14. fab. 3. &c. *Trist.* 4. v. 798. & *Fast.* 403. & 798.—*Heroid.* 7.—*Hygin.*fab.94.—*Xenoph. Cyneg.*1.*Philostr.Her.*14.

ÆNE'AS SYL'VIUS, a son of Æneas and Lavinia, so called because his mother retired with him into the woods after his father's death. He succeeded Ascanius on the throne of Latium, being preferred by his subjects to Julius, son of Ascanius, because the kingdom of Alba was his mother's dowry.—*Liv.* 1. c. 3.

ÆNE'AS, an ambassador sent by the Lacedæmonians to Athens to treat for peace, in the eighth year of the Peloponnesian war. *Thucyd.* 4. c. 119.

ÆNE'AS TAC'TICUS, an ancient author who wrote on tactics, besides other treatises, which, according to *Ælian*, were epitomised by Cineas the friend of Pyrrhus. *Sax. Onom.* 1. p. 73.—*Fabr. B. G.* 4. p. 334—*Suidas.*

Æ'NEAS, a native of Gaza, who, from a Platonic philosopher, became a Christian, A.D. 485, and wrote a dialogue, called Theophrastus, on the immortality of the soul, and the resurrection of the body. The work was first translated into Latin, and published at Basil, 1516. Barthius has enriched it with notes. Leipzig, 4to. 1658. *Sax. Onom.* 2. p. 8 —*Fabr. B. G.* 1. p. 689.

ÆNEI'A or ÆNI'A, a place near Rome, afterwards called Janiculum. *Dion. Hal.* l. 1.——A city of Troas. *Strab.*17.——A city of Macedonia. *Vid.* Ænea

ÆNE'IS, a poem of Virgil, which has for its subject the settlement of Æneas in Italy. In this poem, the great merit of which is universally acknowledged, the author has imitated Homer; and, in the opinion of respectable critics, Homer is superior to him only because he is more ancient, and, consequently, more original. Virgil died before he had corrected the work, and at his death desired that it might be burnt. This request was, happily, not complied with. The Æneid had engaged the attention of the poet for eleven years; and in the first six books it seems that it was Virgil's design to imitate Homer's Odyssey, and in the last his Iliad. The action of the poem comprehends eight years, one of which only, the last, is really taken up by action, as the seven first are merely episodes, such as Juno's attempts to destroy the Trojans, the loves of Æneas and Dido, the relation of the fall of Troy, &c. Much and deservedly, however, as the poem is admired, it is to be observed that there are in it few or no characters of marked dignity or superior eminence. The companions of the hero are at best insignificant figures, introduced without interest, and disappearing without exciting the respect or engaging the passions of the reader. Æneas himself claims no particular attention; his history interests only as it is connected with the fates and future glories of imperial Rome. The character of Dido, her intercourse with Æneas, her passion and her sufferings, manifest, however, the glowing pencil of a master; and in this part of the poem, as well as in the description of the fall of Priam, of the destruction of Troy by the invisible gods, and of the descent into hell, and in a few other episodes, Virgil shewed himself a most successful rival of the best writers of Greece. His excellence, as Dr. Blair has judiciously observed, is tenderness. His soul was full of sensibility, and he knew how to touch the heart by a single stroke. For correctness, elegance, majestic stateliness, and tender descriptions, Virgil is, above all others, eminent; but in genius, fire, boldness, and sublimity, it must be acknowledged that he yields the palm to Homer. In the first book of the Æneid, the hero is introduced, in the seventh year of his expedition, sailing in the Mediterranean, and shipwrecked on the African coast, where he is kindly received by Dido. In the second, Æneas, at the desire of the Phœnician queen, relates the fall of Troy, and his flight through the general conflagration to mount Ida. In the third, the hero continues his interesting narration, gives a minute account of his voyage through the Cyclades, of the places where he had landed, and of the dreadful storm with which the poem opened. Dido, in the fourth book, makes public her partiality for Æneas, she is, however, slighted by the sailing of the Trojans from Carthage, and the book closes with the suicide of the disappointed queen. In the fifth book, Æneas reaches Sicily, where he celebrates the anniversary of his father's death, and thence pursues his voyage to Italy. In the sixth he visits the Elysian fields, and learns from his father the fates which attend him and his descendants the Romans. In the seventh book, the hero reaches Latium, and concludes a treaty with the king of the country, which is soon broken by the interference of Juno, who stimulates Turnus to war. The auxiliaries of the enemy are enumerated; and, in the eighth book, Æneas is assisted by Evander, and receives from Venus a shield wrought by Vulcan, on which are represented the future glory and triumphs of the Roman nation. The reader is gratified in the ninth book with the account of battles between the rival armies, and with the pathetic episode of the friendship of Nisus and Euryalus. Jupiter, in the tenth, attempts a reconciliation between Venus and Juno, who patronise the opposite parties; the fight is renewed, Pallas killed, and Turnus saved from the avenging hand of Æneas by the interposition of Juno. The eleventh book gives an account of the funeral of Pallas, and of the meditated reconciliation between Æneas and Latinus, which the sudden appearance of the enemy defeats. Camilla is slain, and the combatants are separated by the night. In the last book, Juno prevents the single combat agreed upon by Turnus and Æneas. The Trojans are defeated in the absence of their king, but, on the return of Æneas, the battle takes a different turn, a single combat ensues between the rival leaders, and the poem concludes with the death of Turnus. The unfinished state of the Æneid exercised the talents of Maphæus Vegius, in the 15th century; he with great industry and success added a thirteenth book. *Plin.* 7. c. 30. &c. For an account of Maphæus Vegius, *Vid. Sax. Onom.* 2. p. 426.—*Gyrald. de poet.*—*Voss. de poet. Lat.* c. 7. p. 78. &c.

ÆNE'SIAS, one of the Ephori at Sparta. *Thucyd.*2. c.2.

ÆNESIDE'MUS, a brave general of Argos, who when the city was besieged by Philocles, was slain in its defence. *Liv.* 32. c. 25.——A Cretan philosopher, who wrote eight books on the doctrines of his master Pyrrho. *Diog. in Pyr.*——A son of Pataicus, one of the body guards of Hippocrates. *Herod.* 7. 154.

ÆNESYPH'YRA, a harbour of Marmarica. *Ptol.*

ÆNE'SIUS, a surname of Jupiter, from mount Ænum.

ÆNE'TUS, a victor at Olympia, who in the moment of victory, died through excess of joy. *Paus.* 3. c. 18.——A person made governor of Ephesus by Demetrius, but who lost the city by means of the intrigues of Lycus and Andron. *Polyæn.* 5. c. 19.

Æ'NEUS, the father of Cyzicus.

Æ'NI, an island of the Sinus Arabicus. *Ptol.*

Æ'NI, PONS, or ŒNIPONS, a town of Noricum, now Oetingen.

Æ'NIA, a town of Perrhæbia, not far from the Achelous. *Strab.* 14.

ÆNIA'NES, a people of Thessaly, near the Sinus

Maliacus. It was probably the gentile name for the inhabitants of Ænia. *Strab.—Heliodor.—Plut. Quæst. Gr.*

ÆN'ICUS, a comic writer at Athens; some of his plays are mentioned by Pollux. *Voss de poet. Gr.* c. 6.

ÆNI'OCHI. *Vid.* Heniochi.

Æ'NIUS, a river of Perrhæbia. *Steph.*——A river of Troas. *Strab.* 2.

ÆNOBAR'BUS or AHENOBAR'BUS, the surname of Domitius. When Castor and Pollux acquainted him with a victory, he discredited them, upon which they touched his chin and beard, which instantly became of a brazen color, whence the surname given to himself and descendants.

ÆN'OCLES, a writer of Rhodes. *Athen.*

ÆNO'NA, a city of Illyricum. *Plin.* 3. c. 21. It is now Nona, according to Niger.

Æ'NOS, now Eno, an independent city of Thrace, at the eastern mouth of the Hebrus, confounded with Æneia, of which Æneas was the founder. *Mela*, 2. c. 2.

Æ'NUM, a town of Thrace, the same as Ænos.—A town of Thessaly.—A town of Æolia. *Herodot.* 6. c. 58.—A city of Crete, built by Æneas.——A small town at the west of the Sinus Arabicus. *Plin.* 6. c. 29. It is called by some Philotera, by others Philoteris. *Mela*, 3. c. 8.——A mountain in Cephallenia. *Strab.* 7.——A river and village near Ossa.

Æ'NUS, a river of Rhætia, now the Ins.

ÆNY'RA, a small town in the island of Thasus. *Herodot.* 6. c. 47.

Æ'OLI, a people of Cappadocia.

ÆO'LIA, a name given to Arne, as daughter of Æolus. Sappho is called *Æolia puella*, and lyric poetry *Æolium carmen*, because Sappho and Alcæus were natives of Lesbus in Æolia, and wrote in the Æolic dialect. *Horat.* 4. od. 3. v. 12. & od. 9. v. 12.

ÆO'LIA or Æ'OLIS, a country of Asia Minor, on the shores of the Ægæan sea, bounded by Troas on the north, and Ionia on the south. The inhabitants were of Grecian origin, and masters of many of the neighbouring islands. They had twelve, others say thirty, considerable cities, of which Cumæ and Lesbus were the most famous. They received their names from Æolus, son of Helen. They migrated from Greece about 1124 B.C. 80 years before the migration of the Ionian tribes. *Herodot.* 1. c. 26. &c.—*Strab.* 1, 2. & 6.—*Plin.* 5. c. 30.—*Mela*, 1. c. 2. & 18.—*Ptol.* 5. c. 2.—*Quintil.* 1. c. 6. l. 8. c. 3.—*Cluver.* 5. c. 18. Thessaly was anciently called Æolia. Bœotus, son of Neptune having settled there, called his followers Bœotians, and their country Bœotia.

ÆO'LIÆ or ÆOL'IDES, seven islands between Sicily and Italy; called Lipara, Hiera, Strongyle, Didyme, Ericusa, Phœnicusa, and Euonymus. They were regarded by the poets as the retreat of the winds; and *Virg. Æn.* 1. v. 52. calls them Æolia, and the kingdom of Æolus the god of the storms and winds. They sometimes bear the name of Vulcaniæ and Hephæstiades, and are known among the moderns under the general appellation of Lipari islands. *Vid.* Lipara, Hiera, &c.—*Lucan.* 5. v. 609.—*Justin.* 4. c. 1.—*Cluver.* 3. c. 41—*Mela.* 2. c. 9.

ÆOL'IDA, a city of Tenedus.——A city near Thermopylæ. *Herodot.* 8. c. 35.

ÆOL'IDES, a patronymic of Ulysses. He was so called because Anticlea, his mother, was pregnant by Sisyphus, the son of Æolus, when she married Laertes. It is also given to Athamas and Misenus, as sons of Æolus. *Ovid Met.* 4. v. 512. l. 13. v. 26.—*Horat.* 2. od. 14. v. 20.—*Virg. Æn.* 6. v. 164. & 529.

ÆO'LIUM, a town of the Thracian Chersonesus. *Steph.*

Æ'OLUS, the king of storms and winds, was the son of Hippotas. He reigned over the Æolian islands; and because he was the inventor of sails, and a great astronomer, the poets have called him the god of the winds. Æolus was indebted to Juno for his royal dignity, according to Virgil. The name seems to be derived from αἰολος, *varius*, because the winds over which he presided are ever varying. *Pliny*, 3. c. 9. l. 7. c. 56.—*Homer. Od.* 10. v. 1.—*Virg. Æn.* 1. v. 56, &c.—*Ovid. Met.* 11. v. 748. l. 14. v. 224.—*Quint. Smyrn.* 14.—*Apollon. Arg.* 4. *Diodor.* 5.—*Flacc.* 1. v. 556.——A king of Etruria, father of Macareus and Canace.——A son of Helen, often confounded with the god of the winds. He married Enaretta, by whom he had seven sons and five daughters. *Apollod.* 1.

Æ'ON, the name of the first formed woman, who married Protogonus, and instructed her children to feed upon the fruits of trees, according to the system of the Phœnicians. *Sanchon. apud. Euseb. in præp. evang.* 1.

ÆO'RA, a festival celebrated at Athens in honour of Erigone. *Hesych.* &c.

Æ'OS, son of Typhon, founded the city of Paphus, according to some authors; others attribute it to Pygmalion.

ÆPA'LIUS, a king of Greece, restored to his kingdom by Hercules. *Strab.*

ÆPA'SIUS CAM'PUS, a plain near Lepreum in Peloponnesus. *Strab.* 8.

ÆPE'A, a town of Cyprus called Soli or Soloe, in honour of Solon. *Vid.* Solon. *Plut. in Solon.*——A town of Laconia.——A town of Crete.

Æ'PIUS, a pugilist, who rendered himself ridiculous by his vain boasting. *Plut. de sui laud.*

ÆPO'LIUM or ŒPO'LIUM, a city of European Sarmatia. *Plin.* 4. c. 12.

ÆP'ULO, a general of the Istrians, who drank to excess after he had stormed the camp of Manlius. According to *Livy*, 41. c. 11. he killed himself that he might not fall into the power of the enemy. *Florus*, 2. c. 10. says, that he was taken alive by C. Claud. Pulcher.

Æ'PY, a town of Messenia, in the dominions of Nestor. *Stat. Theb.* 4. v. 180.—*Hom. Il.* 2. v. 592.

ÆP'YTUS, king of Mycenæ, son of Chresphontes and Merope, was educated in Arcadia with Cypselus, his mother's father. To recover his kingdom, he killed Polyphontes, who had married his mother against her will, and had usurped the crown. *Apollod.* 2. c. 6. *Paus.* 4. c. 8.——A king of Arcadia, son of Elatus, who forcibly entered the temple of Neptune, near Mantinea, and was struck blind by the sudden eruption of a stream of salt water from the altar. He was killed by a serpent in hunting. *Paus.* 8. c. 4 & 5.

ÆQUA'NA JU'GA, mountains in the country of the Piceni; now Montagna de Sorrento.

ÆQUESIL'ICI, a people of Hispania Tarraconensis. *Plin.* 3. c. 3. They were probably the Aquæ Silinorum of *Ptolemy*.

Æ'QUI or ÆQUIC'OLI, a people of Latium, at the east of the towns of Præneste and Tibur. They were subdued by the Romans and incorporated among the allies and citizens of Rome. *Flor.* 1. c. 11.—*Liv.* 1. c. 32. l. 2. c. 30, &c.—*Plin.* 3. c. 4.—*Virg. Æn.* 7. v. 747. l. 9. v. 684.—*Ovid Fast.* 3. v. 93.—*Dion. Hal* 2. c. 19.—*Cluver.* 3. c. 27.

ÆQUIME'LIUM, a place in Rome where the house of Melius, who aspired to sovereign power, stood. For this crime his habitation was levelled to the ground. *Liv.* 4. c. 16.

Æ'QUUM, a colony and town of Dalmatia, now Cluzzi, or, perhaps, Chognitz.

Æ'RÆ, a city of Macedonia.——A city of Ionia.——A city near the Hellespont. *Steph.*

Æ'RÆ, a people of Carmania. *Ptol.*

ÆRA'RIUS MER'GUS, a name given to the emperor Pertinax, by *Lucilius* for his avarice.

ÆRENO'SI, a people of Spain. *Polyb.* 3. *Ortelius* considers the passage as faulty. *Livy*, l. 21. c. 23. has Ausetani in this place.

ÆRET'ICA, a region of Armenia Minor. *Ptol.*

Æ'RIA or AE'RIA, a city of Gallia Narbonensis, now Aire or l'Oriol. *Plin.* 3. c. 4.——A city of Crete.——A name of the island of Thasus.

Æ'RIAS, an ancient king of Cyprus, who built the temple at Paphus. *Tac. Hist.* 2. c. 3.

AER'OPE, wife of Atreus, committed adultery with Thyestes, her brother-in-law, and had by him twins, who were murdered and placed as food before Atreus. *Ovid. Trist.* 2. v. 391.

AER'OPE, a daughter of Cepheus, violated by Mars. She died in childbed; but her child was preserved, and called Æropus. *Paus.* 8. c. 44.

ÆROPOLI'TÆ, a nation of Arabia. *Sozom.* 7. c. 15.

AER'OPUS, a general of Epirus, in the reign of Pyrrhus.——A son of Temenus. *Herod.* 8. 137.——A person appointed regent to Orestes, the infant son of Archelaus, king of Macedonia.——A son of Philip. *Herod.* 8. 139.——An officer of king Philip, banished for bringing a singer into his camp. *Polyæn.* 4. c. 2.——A mountain of Chaonia. *Liv.* 31. c. 5.

ÆRO'SA, an ancient name of the island of Cyprus. *Sex. Pomp.*

ÆSA, a city of Thrace, near Pallene. *Steph.*

ÆS'ACUS, a river of Troy, near mount Ida.—A son of Priam, enamoured of Hesperia, whom he pursued into the woods. The nymph, in her flight, was stung and killed. Æsacus, upon this, threw himself into the sea, and was changed into a cormorant by Tethys. Other authors relate that he married Sterope, and was so disconsolate at her sudden death soon after their union, that he threw himself into the sea, and was thus changed into a cormorant. *Tzetzes. in Lycoph.—Apollod.* 3.—*Ovid. Met.* 11. fab. 11.

ÆSA'GEA, a mountain mentioned by *Homer, Hymn. in Apoll.* v. 40.

ÆSA'PUS or ÆSE'PUS, a small river of Mysia, falling into the Propontis. *Plin.* 5. c. 32.—*Cluver.* 5. c. 18.

Æ'SAR or ÆSA'RAS, a small river of Magna Græcia, falling into the Ionian sea, near Crotona. *Leander* supposes it is called Hylias by *Thucydides;* it is now Eraso. *Ovid. Met.* 15. v. 23.

ÆS'ARIS, a river of Etruria, now Osari. *Plin.* 3. c. 5.

ÆSARONEN'SII, a people of Sardinia. *Ptol.*

ÆSA'RUS or ÆS'ARUS. *Vid.* Æsar.

ÆS'CHINES, an Athenian orator, the rival of Demosthenes. He flourished about 342 B.C. and boasted of his descent from a noble family, though Demosthenes reproached him as being the son of a courtezan. The rival orators were sent as ambassadors to the court of Philip, but the character of Æschines was tarnished by the acceptance of a bribe from the Macedonian prince, whose tyranny had hitherto been the subject of his declamation. When the Athenians wished to reward the patriotic labors of Demosthenes with a golden crown, Æschines impeached Ctesiphon, who proposed it; and to their subsequent dispute we are indebted for the two celebrated orations *de corona.* Æschines was defeated by his rival's superior eloquence, and banished to Rhodes; but, as he retired from the city, Demosthenes ran after him, and nobly forced him to accept a present of silver. In his banishment he repeated to the Rhodians the oration which he had delivered against Demosthenes; and after receiving much applause he was requested to repeat the answer of his antagonist. It was heard with greater marks of approbation; but, exclaimed Æschines, how much more would your admiration have been raised, had you heard Demosthenes himself speak it! Æschines died in the 75th year of his age. He wrote three orations, and nine epistles, which from their number, severally received the names of the graces, and of the muses. The orations alone are extant, and they are generally found connected with those of Lysias. An oration which bears the name of *Deliaca lex,* is said not to be his, but that of Æschines, another orator of that age. *Cic. de Orat.* 1. c. 24. 1. 2. c. 53. *in Brut.* c. 17. *Tusc.* 3. c. 63.—*Strab.* 14.—*Plut. in Demosth.*—*Diog.* 2 & 3.—*Plin.* 7. c. 30.—*Sax. Onom.* 1 p. 74.—*Fabr. B. Gr.* 2. p. 850. Diogenes mentions other persons of the same name. *Diog. Laert.* 2. 64. [There is a fine bust of this orator in the pope's museum of the Vatican at Rome.——A Neapolitan Platonic philosopher, disciple of Melanthius Rhodius. *Fabr. B. Gr.* 3. p. 160.——A philosopher, disciple of Socrates, who wrote several dialogues, some of which bore the following titles: Aspasia, Phædon, Alcibiades, Draco, Erycia, Polyænus, Telauges, &c. The dialogue entitled Axiochus, and ascribed to Plato, is supposed to be his composition. As a writer and an orator, he ranked high among the Athenians, and his style was considered as elegant and purely Attic. The best editions are that of Leovard, 1718, with the notes of Horræus, in 8vo. and that of Fischer, 8vo. Lips. 1766. *Laert. in vit.*—*Stanley's Lives.*—*Hesychius.*—*Sax Onom.* 1. p. 50.—*Fabr. B. Gr.* 2. p. 691.——A man who wrote on oratory.——An Arcadian.——A Mitylenean.——A Milesian writer.——A statuary.——A son of Nothon, an Eretrian noble, who preserved the lives of 4,000 Athenian auxiliaries. *Herodot.* 6. 100.——An Athenian quack, who used the burnt ashes of dead bodies medicinally; this preparation he called Botryon. *Plin.* 1. 28. c. 4.——An empyric of Chius, who cured Eunapius, when he was apparently at the last extremity.——Son of Sellus, a vain-glorious Athenian. *Aristoph. Vesp.* 451. & 519.

ÆS'CHRION, a Mitylenean poet intimate with Aristotle. He accompanied Alexander in his Asiatic expedition.——An Iambic poet of Samus.—*Athen.*——A physician commended by *Galen.* A treatise of his on husbandry has been quoted by *Pliny.*——A lieutenant of Archagathus, killed by Hanno. *Diod.* 20.——A person who gave his name to the tribe Æschrionia at Samus. *Herodot.* 3. c. 26.

ÆSCHYL'IDES, a man who wrote a book on agriculture. *Ælian. H. An.* 15.

ÆS'CHYLUS, son of Euphorion, and brother of Cynægirus, was a celebrated soldier and poet of Athens. He distinguished himself in the Athenian army at the battles of Marathon, Salamis, and Platæa. He wrote ninety tragedies, forty of which were rewarded with a prize, but only seven have come to us, viz. Prometheus vinctus, Septem contra Thebas, Persæ, Agamemnon, Choephoræ, Eumenides, and Supplices. It is said, that when he composed, his countenance betrayed the greatest ferocity; and, according to one of his scholiasts, when his Eumenides was represented, many children died through fear, and several pregnant women actually miscarried at the sight of the horrible masks that were introduced. His style is obscure, and he may safely be pronounced the most difficult of all the Greek classics. A few expressions of impious tendency in one of his plays, nearly proved fatal to him; he was condemned to death; but his brother Amynias, it is reported, reversed the sentence by uncovering an arm, of which the hand had been cut off at the battle of Salamis, in the service of his country, and the poet was pardoned. In his old age the poet retired to the court of Hiero in Sicily. Being informed by an oracle that he was to die by the fall of a house, he withdrew from the city into the fields, where he sat down. An eagle, with a tortoise in her bill, flew over his bald head, and supposing it to be a stone, dropped her prey upon it to break the shell, and Æschylus instantly died of the blow, in the 69th year of his age, 456 B.C. His remains were buried with great pomp by the Sicilians, near the river Gela. It is said that he wrote an account of the battle of Marathon, in elegiac verse. Among the editions of his works are that of Stanley, fol. London, 1663; that of Glasgow, 2 vols. 12mo. 1746; and that of Schutz, 2 vols. 8vo. Halæ, 1782. Dr. Butler has since republished Stanley's edition with valuable additions. But the best edition of the tragedies of the immortal poet, is that by Dr. Blomfield, late bishop of London. They are rendered valuable by the correctness of the text, which is formed from the collection of a great many MSS. and by the able illustrations and expositions which they present of the most difficult passages of this, in many cases, obscure author. *Herodot.* 2 c. 156.—*Propert.* 2. el. 34. v. 41.—*Paus.* 1. c. 14.—*Ælian. V. H.* 5. c. 19.—*Horat. Art. Poet.* 278.—*Athen.* 6.—*Quintil.* 10. c. 1.—*Plin.* 10. c. 3.—*Val. Max.* 9. c. 12.—*Sax. Onom.* 1. p. 31.—*Fabr. B. Gr.* 2. p. 165.——The twelfth perpetual archon of Athens.——A Corinthian, brother-in-law to Timophanes, intimate with Timoleon. *Plut. in Timol.*——A Rhodian, set over Ægypt with Peucestes of Macedonia. *Curt.* 4. c. 8.——A native of Cnidus, who taught Cicero rhetoric. *Cic. in Brut.* 91. & 95. *De Orat.* 175 & 182.

ÆSCULA'PIUM, a grove between Berytus and Sidon. *Strab.*——A grove in the island of Cos. *Lactant. de orig. error.*

ÆSCULA'PIUS, son of Apollo, by Coronis, was god of medicine, which art he was taught by Chiron. He was physician to the Argonauts, and is said to have restored the dead to life, among whom were Capanens son of Hipponous, Lycurgus of Nemæa, Hippolytus son of Theseus, Tyndarus of Sparta, Eriphyle wife of Amphiaraus, and Glaucus son of Minos. Pluto was displeased with the success of the physician, and complained to Jupiter, who struck Æsculapius with thunder; but Apollo, angry at the death of his son, killed the Cyclopes who had made the fatal thunderbolts. Æsculapius received divine honours after death, chiefly at Epidaurus, Pergamus, Athens, Smyrna, Cyrene, and Crete, and he had also a temple at Rome. Rome, A.U.C. 462, was delivered of a plague, and in gratitude built a temple to the god of medicine, who, as was supposed, had come there in the form of a serpent, and concealed himself among the reeds in an island of the Tyber. Goats, bulls, lambs, and pigs were sacrificed on his altars, and the cock and the serpent were sacred to him. In the temple at Epidaurus, Æsculapius was represented in a statue of gold and ivory, with a large beard, holding in his other hand a staff, round which was wreathed a serpent, and he was generally attended by a cock, the symbol of vigilance. In the midst of the temple a marble theatre was erected, and the garden round the sacred edifice was adorned with statues, and with columns, on which were inscribed the names of those who had been healed by the power of the god, the manner of their cure, and the diseases under which they laboured. Serpents were considered more particularly sacred to him, not only because the ancient physicians used them in their prescriptions, but because also they were considered as the symbol of that prudence and foresight so necessary in the medical profession. Æsculapius married Epione, by whom he had two sons, famous for their skill in medicine, Machaon and Podalirius, and four daughters, of whom Hygieia, goddess of health, is most celebrated. Some have supposed that he lived a short time after the Trojan war. Hesiod makes no mention of him. Amongst the surnames of Æsculapius, the most common are those of Philolaus, descriptive of his salutary efforts for the good of mankind; Gortynian, from his being worshipped at Gortynia in Crete; Cotyleus, from the cure he effected on the thigh of Hercules, &c. *Cicero, de Nat. D.* 3. c. 22. says there were three persons of this name; the first, a son of Apollo, worshipped in Arcadia, and considered as the inventor of the probe, and of the manner of dressing wounds; the second, a brother of Mercury, killed by a thunderbolt, and buried at Cynosura; and the third, a son of Arsippus and Arsinoe, who is said to have improved medicine by discovering the use of purges, and the manner of extracting teeth. For farther information respecting Æsculapius, or Asclepius, and the writings attributed to persons of that name, *vid. Fabr. B. Gr.* 1. p. 62. and the writers quoted by *Saxius Onom.* 1. p. 8.—*Homer. Il.* 4. v. 193. *Hymn. in Æscul.*—*Apollod.* 3. c. 10.—*Apollon.* 4. *Argon.*—*Hygin.* fab. 14. 49. 202.—*Ovid. Met.* 2. fab. 8.—*Paus.* 2. c. 11. & 27. l. 7. c. 23. l. 8. c. 25.—*Diod.* 4.—*Lactant. de fals. R.* 10.—*Tzetzes Ch.* 10. *Hist.* 349.—*Schol. Pind. in Pyth.* 3.—*Servius in Æn.* 6. v. 398. & l. 11. v. 259.—*Schol. Euripid. Alcest.* v. 1.—*Plato in Phæd.*—*Tertull.* 46.—*Apolog. de Anim.* 1.—*Nat. Com.* 4. c. 12.—*Oros.* 3. c. 22.—*Clem. Alex. Strom.*—*Lucian. Dial. de Saltat.*—*Val. Max.* 1 c. 8. [Statues of Æsculapius are to be found in almost all the collections; the finest is one of those at Florence, in the collection formed by the grand dukes of Tuscany. It is a grand and simple figure, resting its right hand upon a staff, round which is entwined the serpent.]——A governor of Sicily, who overturned a statue which was erected for the purpose of restraining the eruptions of Mount Ætna. After its overthrow the island was visited by several eruptions, and other calamities. *Olympiod.*——A philosopher, author of a work on arithmetic. *Voss. de scient. Math.* c. 50.

ÆSE'PUS, a son of Bucolion. *Homer. Il.* 6. v. 21.

ÆSE'PUS, a river. *Vid.* Æsapus.

ÆSER'NIA, a city of the Samnites, in Italy, situated near the source of the Vulturnus. It is now Sergnia or Isernia. *Liv.* 27. c. 12.—*Sil.* 8. v. 567.—*Cluver.* 3. c. 28.

ÆSERNI'NUS, a gladiator, who probably received his name from his native city Æsernia. *Cic. opt. gent.* 6. *ad Quint.* 3. ep. 4.

Æ'SIA, a river of Gallia Belgica, now Oyse.

Æ'SIAS a banker of Sicyon, by whose means Aratus took the Acrocorinthus.

ÆSIME'DES, the second decennial archon at Athens.——A naval commander of the Corcyreans.—*Thucyd.* 1. 47.

Æ'SION, a noble citizen of Athens, a panegyrist of Demosthenes. *Plut. in Demosth.*

Æ'SIS, now Esino, a small river of Italy, which separates Umbria from Picenum, and falls into the Adriatic sea. *Sil.* 8. v. 446. There was a town of the same name on the banks of the river: the cheese made there was held in great esteem by Pliny. *Cluver.* 3. c. 26. & 37.—*Mela,* 2. c. 6. *Vid.* Æsus.

ÆSI'TÆ, a people of Arabia Deserta. *Ptol.*

Æ'SIUS, a river of Bithynia. *Plin.* 5. c. 32.

Æ'SON, son of Cretheus, succeeded his father in the kingdom of Iolchus, but was soon after exiled by the intrigues of his brother Pelias. He married Alcimeda, by whom he had Jason. When Jason was grown up, he demanded his father's kingdom from his uncle, but the usurper persuaded him to go in quest of the golden fleece. *Vid.* Jason. At his return, Jason found his father very infirm; and Medea (*vid.* Medea,) at his request, drew the blood from Æson's veins, and refilled them with the juice of certain herbs which she had gathered, and immediately the old man recovered the vigor and bloom of youth. Some say that Æson killed himself by drinking bull's blood, to avoid the persecution of Pelias. *Diod.* 4.—*Apollod.* 1. c. 9.—*Ovid. Met.* 7. v. 287.—*Hygin.* fab. 12.—*Schol. Pind. ad Pyth.* 4.—*Lactant. ad* 3. *Theb.* v. 516. l. 5. v. 345.—*Val. Flacc.* 1.—*Tzetzes in Lycoph.* 175.

Æ'SON, a river of Thessaly, with a town of the same name.——A city of Magnesia. *Apollon. Scholiast.*

Æ'SON, an ambassador sent, with Eustrophus, by the Argives to conclude a treaty with the Spartans. *Thucyd.* 5. c. 40.

ÆSONEN'SES, a people of Spain, inhabitants of Æsona, now Isona, in Catalonia.

ÆSON'IDES, a patronymic of Jason, as being descended from Æson.

ÆSO'PUS, a philosopher of Cotyæum in Phrygia, originally a slave. He travelled over the greatest part of Greece and Ægypt, but chiefly resided at the court of Crœsus, king of Lydia, by whom he was sent to consult the oracle of Delphi, and to make offerings to Apollo. Æsop satirically compared the Delphians to floating sticks, which appear striking objects at a distance, but are nothing when brought near. The Delphians upon this, accused him of having secreted one of the sacred vessels of Apollo's temple, and threw him down from a rock, 561 B.C. *Maximus Planudes* has written his life in Greek; and asserts that the philosopher was short and deformed. This assertion, though considered erroneous by many, is confirmed by a half statue of Æsop, which is in the Villa Albani at Rome. This statue represents him as deformed, and is a very fine work of art. Æsop dedicated his fables to his patron Crœsus; but the work which appears now under his name, is no doubt a compilation of all the fables and apologues of wits before and after the age of Æsop, conjointly with his own. Though some attribute the original invention of fables to Æsop, yet it is most probable, as *Quintilian* observes, that Hesiod first conveyed instruction in that form. *Plut. in Solon.*—*A. Gell.* 2. c. 29.—*Phæd.* 1. fab. 2. l. 2. fab. 9.—*Sax. Onom.* 1. p. 21.—*Fabr. B. Gr* 1 p. 618.—*Herodot.* 2. c. 134.

ÆSO'PUS CLAU'DIUS, a tragic actor, very intimate with Cicero, to whom he gave instructions in oratory. He was so successful in his profession that he amassed a fortune equal to £160,000. His son was so extravagant that he dissolved precious stones to drink at his entertainment. *Fabr. ibid.*—*Horat.* 2. sat. 3. v. 239.—*Cic.* 7. *ad Fam.* 1. *ad. Att.* 11. ep. 15. *Plut. in Cic.*—*Macrob. Sat.* 2. c. 10.—*Val. Max.* c. 8. 10. l. 9. c. 1. *Plin.* 9. c. 35. l. 10. c. 51.

ÆSO'PUS, a freed man of Demosthenes. *Macrob. Sat.* 1. c. 11.——An attendant of Mithridates, who wrote a treatise on Helen, and a panegyric on his royal master.——An historian in the time of Anaximenes. *Plut. in Solon.*——An orator. *Diog.* For other persons of this name see *Fabr. B. Gr.* 1. p. 621.

ÆSO'PUS, a river of Pontus. *Strab.* 12.

ÆSTIÆ'I or ÆSTY'I, a people of Sarmatia, situated in modern Estonia, in Livonia, on the shores of the Baltic. *Tac. Germ.* c. 45.—*Cluver.* 3. c. 1.

ÆSTRÆ'UM, a town of Macedonia. *Ptol.*

ÆS'TRIA, an island in the Adriatic. *Mela,* 2. c. 9.

ÆS'ULA, a town on a mountain between Tiber and Præneste. *Horat.* 3. od. 29.

ÆSYE'TES, the name of a person from whose tomb Polites spied what the Greeks did in their ships during the Trojan war. *Hom. Il.* 2. 793.

ÆSY'MA, a city of Thrace. It was the country of Castianira, mother of Gorgytion by Priam. *Steph. Hesychius* calls it a city of Troas.

ÆSYMNE'TES, a surname of Bacchus. *Paus.* 7. c. 21.

ÆSYM'NUS, a person of Megara, who consulted Apollo to know the best method of governing his country. *Paus.* 1. c. 43.

ÆTÆÆ'I, a people of Arabia Felix, according to *Ptolemy;* they are called Ægæi by the commentators on that author.

ÆTÆI, a people of Greece. *Æschin. de fals. legat.*
ÆTARE, probably Apari, a city of Africa Propria. *Ptol.*
ÆTER'NIUS, A. a patrician and tribune of the people.
ÆTETA, a woman of Laodicea, in Syria, who was changed into a man. *Phlegon*, in his book *de Mirab.* asserts that he saw her.
ÆTHÆ'A, a town of Laconia. *Steph. ex. Thucyd.* 1.
ÆTHA'LIA, an island, called also Ilva and now Elba, on the coast of Etruria, at a short distance from Corsica. *Plin.* 3. c. 6. l. 6. c. 30. *Polybius, in fragm.* calls Lemnus by this name. *Cluver.* 3. c. 26.
ÆTHAL'IDÆ, part of the tribe Leontis. *Steph.*
ÆTHAL'IDES, a herald, son of Mercury, who was permitted to be among the dead and living at stated times, and thus become acquainted with what passed on earth. *Apollon. Argon.* l. v. 641.
ÆTHAL'OES, a stream near Troy. *Strab.*—It was probably the Aidoneus of *Pausanius*, 1. 10.
ÆTHES, a Thracian general, who pretended to desert to Lysimachus, and when he had gained his confidence, brought upon him Dromichætes, his former king, who slew Lysimachus and 100,000 of his subjects. *Polyæn.* 7. c. 25.
ÆTHIC'IA, a city and region of Thessaly, the inhabitants of which were called Æthices. *Steph.—Hesych.*
ÆTH'ICUS, a Paphlagonian mentioned by *Q. Smyrnœus*, 1. 6.
ÆTH'ICUS IS'TER, a geographer, whose work on cosmography is usually published with the Itinerary of Antoninus. His style is very uneven. The best edition is that of Simler, Basil, 1575. Stephens published the works of this writer with his edition of Dionysius Periegetes, 1646. *Harles. Not. Lit. Rom* 1. p. 211. *Sax. Onom.* 1. p. 414.
ÆTHI'ON, a man slain at the nuptials of Perseus and Andromeda. *Ovid. Met.* 5. v. 146.
ÆTHIO'PIA, an extensive country of Africa, at the south of Ægypt, divided into eastern and western by the ancients; the former division lying near Meroe, and the latter near the Mauri. The country, properly now called Abyssinia, as well as the inhabitants, were little known to the ancients, though Homer has styled them the most just of men, and has represented the gods going annually to feast in the country, as a place particularly favoured by heaven. *Diodorus*, 1. 4. says, that the Æthiopians were the first inhabitants of the earth. They were the first who worshipped the gods, for which, as some suppose, their country was never invaded by an enemy. The inhabitants are of a dark complexion, and therefore the ancients have given the name of Æthiopia to every country the inhabitants of which are of a black color. *Lucan.* 3. v. 253. &c.—*Juv.* 2. v. 23.—*Virg.* 6. *Ecl* v. 68. —*Stat. Theb.* 5. v. 426.—*Plin.* 6. c. 29.—*Paus.* 1. c. 33.—*Homer. Od.* 1. v. 22. *Il.* 1. v. 423.—*Mela*, 1. c. 10.—*Cluver.* 6. c. 6.
ÆTHIO'PIA, an epithet of Diana. *Steph.*
ÆTHIO'PIUM, a region of Lydia. *Id.*——A place of Eubœa. *Suidas.*
ÆTH'LIUS, or AETH'LIUS, son of Jupiter by Protogenia, or according to some, of Æolus, was father of Endymion. *Apollod.* 1. c. 7.——An historian of Samus. *Athen.* 14.—*Clemens in Protrept.—Etymolog.*
ÆTHON, one of the horses of the sun. *Ovid. Met.* 2. fab. 1.—A horse of Pallas, represented as shedding tears at the death of his master. *Virg. Æn.* 11. v. 89.—A horse of Hector. *Homer. Il.* 8. v. 185.—A horse of Pluto's chariot. *Claud. de Rap. Pros.* 1.——A name given to Erisichthon, from the excess of his hunger and thirst. *Ælian. V. H.* 1. —*Lycoph. in Cass.*
ÆTHRA, a daughter of Pittheus, king of Trœzene, was the mother of Theseus. *Vid.* Ægeus. She was carried away by Castor and Pollux, when they recovered their sister Helen, whom she afterwards accompanied to Troy. *Homer. Il.* 3. v 144.—*Paus.* 2. c. 31. l. 5. c. 19.—*Hygin.* fab. 37. & 79.—*Plut. in Thes.*—*Ovid Her.* 10. v. 131.—*Schol. Eurip. in Herc.*—*Tzetzes in Lycoph.*—*Quint. Calab.* 13.—*Parthen. in Erot.* 16.——One of the Oceanides, wife of Atlas. She is more generally called Pleione. *A. Gell.* 13. c. 9.
ÆTHRE'A, an ancient name of the island of Rhodes. The inhabitants were called Ætrei. *Steph.*
ÆTHU'SA, a daughter of Neptune by Amphitrite, or Alcyone, beloved by Apollo. *Apollod.* 3.—*Paus.* 9. c. 20.

ÆTHU'SA, an island near Lilybæum, the same as Ægusa; though *Ptolemy* makes them names of different islands. *Fazellus* places Æthusa between Melita and Africa; It is now Limera. *Plin.* 3. c. 1.
Æ'TIA, the name of a poem of Callimachus *de causis et rationibus sacrorum.* *Mart.* 10. epigr. 4.
ÆTIN'IUM, a town of Macedonia, called Athenæum by *Livy*, l. 38. c. 1. It is now Atino.
AE'TION, a painter, whose picture of Alexander going to celebrate his nuptials with Roxane was so much admired when exhibited at the Olympic games, that the president bestowed upon him the hand of his daughter. *Cic. Brut.* 18.
Æ'TIUM, a corporate town of Italy. *Frontin.*
Æ'TIUS, or AETIUS, a Greek physician, some of whose works are extant. *Voss. de Philos.* c. 21.
Æ'TIUS LA'BEO. *Vid.* Labeo.
ÆT'NA, a mountain of Sicily, now Gibello, famous for its volcano, the largest in the world, which, for about 3000 years, has thrown out fire at intervals. It is two miles in perpendicular height, measures 100 miles round at the base, with an ascent of 30 miles, and its crater forms a circle of 3½ miles in circumference. *Pindar* is the first who mentions an eruption of Ætna; and the silence of *Homer* on the subject is considered as a proof that the fires of the mountain were unknown in his age. From the time of Pythagoras, the supposed date of the first volcanic appearance, to the battle of Pharsalia, it is computed that Ætna has had 100 eruptions. The poets supposed that Jupiter had confined the giants under this mountain; or that it was the forge of Vulcan, where his servants the Cyclopes fabricated thunder-bolts, &c. Most of the ancient poets have described the terrors and catastrophes which accompany the eruptions of the mountain; and particularly Cornelius Severus, who has written a poem on the subject, for an account of which see *Harles Not. Lit. Rom.* 1. p. 254. & 2. p. 400—*Val. Flacc.* 2. v. 29.—*Hesiod. Theog.* v. 860.—*Virg. Æn.* 3. v. 570.—*Ovid. Met.* 5. v. 352. l. 15. v. 340.—*Ital.* 14. v. 59.—*Claud de Pros.* 1. v. 161. &c.—*Lucret.* 6. v. 639.—*Lucan.* 6. v. 293. *Mela*, 2. c. 9.—*Cluver.* 3. c. 42.——A town at the bottom of a mountain on the south side, was called Ætna, and is now Nicolosi. *Strab.* 6.
ÆT'NA, a daughter of Cœlus and Terra, mother of the gods Palici, by Jupiter. *Serv. in Æn.* 9. v. 585.
ÆTO'LIA, a country bounded by Epirus, Acarnania, and Locris, supposed to be about the middle of Greece. It received its name from Ætolus. The inhabitants were covetous and illiberal, and little known in Greece, till after the ruin of Athens and Sparta, when they acquired power and consequence in the country. They afterwards made themselves formidable, first, as the allies of Rome, and then as its enemies, till they were conquered by Fulvius. *Liv.* 26. c. 24. &c.—*Flor.* 2. c. 9.—*Strab.* 8. & 10. —*Mela.* 2. c. 4.—*Plin.* 4. c. 2.—*Paus.* 10. c. 18.—*Plut. in Flam.*—*Cœl. Rh.* 21.—*Cluver.* 4. c. 8.—Diomedes is called *Ætolius Heros*; and Apulia, where he settled *Ætoli Campi.* *Sil.* 1. v. 125. l. 9. v. 493. &c.
ÆTO'LUS, was son of Endymion and Iphianassa. Having accidentally killed Apis, son of Phoroneus, he left his country, and came to settle in that part of Greece which has been called from him Ætolia. *Apollod.* 1. c. 7 & 9.—*Paus.* 5. c. 1.
ÆTO'SA, a city of Italy. *Phlegon.*
ÆTUA'TII, or ÆTUA'TES, according to Cæsar, a people of Helvetia, now Canini or Grisones. *Strab. Cæs.* 1. 6.
ÆTULA'NE, a province of Armenia Minor. *Cluver.* 5. c. 16.
ÆTU'LIA, or ÆTULA'NE, a portion of Armenia Minor. *Ptol.*—*Voss. ad Justin.* 14. c. 1.
ÆTUS, an ancient name of the Nile. *Lycoph.*——A river of Scythia, which continually inundated the fertile fields of Prometheus, and which gave rise to the fable that an eagle ἀετὸς, fed upon his liver, which never diminished though continually devoured. *Cœl. Rhod.* 7. c. 20 &c.
ÆTYMAN'DRI, a nation of Asia. *Ptol.*
ÆVITER'NI, a name given to the heathen gods on account of their eternal existence. *Ennius.—Plin.*
ÆX, a rocky island situated between Tenedus and Chius. *Pliny*, 4. c. 11.——A city in the country of the Marsi.
ÆX, the nurse of Jupiter, changed into a constellation.
ÆXO'NE, a village of Attica according to *Strabo.*

and *Dionysius* of *Halicarnassus*. *Stephanus* and *Suidas* call it a village of the tribe Cecropis.

ÆXO'NIA, a city of Magnesia.

ÆZ'ALA, a town of Armenia Major, now Picaza. *Ptol.*

ÆZ'ANIS, a city of Phrygia Major. *Id.*

ÆZ'ARI, a nation of Marmarica. *Id.*

ÆZ'ICA, a part of Thrace. *Steph.*

A'FER, an inhabitant of Africa.——An informer under Tiberius and his successors, known also as an orator, and as the preceptor of Quintilian. He was made consul by Domitian, and died A.D. 59. *Quintil.* 12. c. 11.—*Dio.* 59.—*Tac. Ann.* 4. c. 52. ——The father of the emperor Adrian *Spartian.*

AFRA'NIA, a Roman matron, who, forgetful of female decency, frequented the forum. *Val. Max.* 8. c. 3.

AFRA'NIUS LU'CIUS, a Latin comic poet in the age of Terence, often compared to Menander, and highly commended for his vivacity and genius. The titles of some of his plays are preserved, but only 266 of his verses remain, which are to be found in the *Corpus Poetarum*. *Quint.* 10. c. 1.—*Suet. Ner.* 11. *Horat.* 2. ep. 1. v. 57.—*Cic. de Fin.* 1 c. 3. —*A. Gell.* 13. c. 8.—*Vell. Pat.* 1. c. 17.

AFRA'NIUS, a general of Pompey, in Spain. He was attacked by Cæsar, to whom he was obliged to submit. He afterwards revolted from Cæsar, and was put to death, after the battle of Zama. *Cæs. B. C.* 1. c. 8.—*Cic. ad Att.* 1. ep. 18. &c. *ad. Fam.* 16.—*Hirt. A.B.* 95.—*Suet. in Cæs.* 34.—*Plut. in Pomp.*

AFRA'NIUS Q., a man who wrote a severe satire against Nero, for which he was put to death in the Pisonian conspiracy. *Tac. Ann.* 4. c. 34.

AFRA'NIUS POTI'TUS, a plebeian, who said before Caligula, that he would willingly die if the emperor could recover from the distemper under which he labored. Caligula recovered, and Afranius was put to death that he might not forfeit his word. *Dio.*

AFRA'NIUS BUR'RHUS. *Vid.* Burrhus.

AF'RICA, called Libya by the Greeks, one of the three parts of the ancient world, and the greatest peninsula of the universe, bounded on the east by Arabia and the Red Sea, on the north by the Mediterranean, south and west by the ocean. In length, from Cape Bona in the Mediterranean, to the Cape of Good Hope, it is 4,300 miles; and in breadth, from Cape Verd in the Atlantic, to Guardafui, near Babelmandel, it is 3,500 miles. It is joined on the east to Asia by the isthmus of Suez, 60 miles long, and which some of the Ptolemies in vain endeavoured to cut through, to form a junction between the Red and the Mediterranean Seas. Africa is so immediately situated under the sun, that only the maritime parts are inhabited, and the inland country is almost barren and sandy, and infested with wild beasts. The most remarkable mountains of Africa are mount Atlas in Mauritania, and the mountains of the Moon in Abyssinia, to which may be added the peak on the island of Teneriff, the highest single mountain in the globe. The largest rivers are the Nile and the Niger, both which, at stated seasons, inundate and fertilize the neighbouring country. The whole of Africa is divided by some of the moderns into nine parts, Ægypt, Barbary, Guinea, Congo, Cafraria, Abyssinia, Nigritia, Nubia, and the adjacent islands. *Vid.* Libya. *Mela,* 1. c. 4. &c.—*Cluverius.*—*Varro, R. R.* 2. c. 1.—*Diod.* 3. 4. & 20.—*Herodot.* 2. c. 17. 26. & 32. 1. 4. c. 41. &c.—*Plin.* 5. c. 1. &c. There is a part of Africa called Propria, which lies about the middle, on the shores of the Mediterranean, and of which Carthage is the capital.

AFRICA'NUS, a blind poet commended by *Ennius.* ——A lawyer, disciple to Papinian, and intimate with the emperor Alexander. *Eutrop.* 6.——An orator mentioned by *Quintilian.*——The surname of the Scipios, from the conquest of Africa. *Vid.* Scipio.

AFRICA'NUS SEX'TUS, J., a Christian writer, who flourished A.D. 222. In his chronicle, which was universally esteemed, he reckoned 5,500 years from the creation of the world to the age of Julius Cæsar. Nothing remains of this work but what Eusebius has preserved. In a letter to Origen, Africanus proved that the history of Susanna is suppositious; and in another to Aristides, still extant, he endeavours to reconcile the seeming contradictions that appear in the genealogies of Christ which are found in the Gospels of St. Matthew and St. Luke. He is supposed to be the same who wrote nine books upon physic, agriculture, &c. *Sax. Onom.* 1. p. 353.—*Fabr. B. Gr.* 4. p. 241.

AFRICA'NUS SEX'TIUS, a noble youth deterred from marrying Silana, by Agrippina.

AF'RICUM MA'RE, is that part of the Mediterranean which is on the coast of Africa. It is called Punicum Mare by *Florus*, and Maurus Oceanus by *Juvenal*. *Mela.* 2 c. 9.—*Cluver.* 1. c. 12.

AF'RICUS, a name applied to a wind, which blew from the coast of Africa on the Mediterranean. *Virg.* 1. v. 86.—*Horat.* 1. od. 14. v. 5.

A'GA, a mountain from which the Araxes and Euphrates rise. It is called Aba by *Strabo* and *Ptolemy*. *Hermol. in Plin.* 1. 6. c. 9.

AG'ABO, a king of Æthiopia, a fratricide, of whom the historians of that country relate wonderful things.

AG'ABRA, now Cabra, a town of the Turdetani, in Spain.

AGAC'LYTUS, a powerful freed man of Verus. *Jul. Capitol. in Marc Antonin.*

AGAE'TUS, a king of Scythia.

AGAGRIA'NÆ PORT'Æ, gates at Syracuse, near which the dead were buried. *Ursinus* reads Archadinæ. *Cic. in Tusc.* 5.

AGALAS'SES, a nation of India, conquered by Alexander. *Diod.* 17.

AGAL'LIS, a woman of Corcyra, who wrote a treatise upon grammar. *Athen.* 1.—*Meurs. de lud. Gr.* p. 5.—*Voss. de Philol.* c. 2.

AGAMA'NA, a city of Mesopotamia. *Ptol.* It is probably the Agabana of *Marcellinus.*

AGAME'A, or AG'AME, a promontory and harbour near Troy. *Steph.*—*Suidas.*

AGAME'DE, a town of Lesbus. *Steph.*

AGAME'DES and TROPHO'NIUS, two architects who made the entrance to the temple of Delphi, for which they demanded of the god whatever gift was most advantageous for a man to receive. Eight days after they were found dead in their bed. Pausanias, however, mentions that the two brothers were solicited by Hyrieus, an opulent prince, to build him a place of security for his immense riches The building was raised, but a secret passage was left, which, by the removal of a particular stone, could admit the architects to the treasures. Hyrieus, discovering that his wealth decreased, laid a snare for the unknown plunderers; and when Agamedes was caught, his brother Trophonius, unable to extricate him, cut off his head to avoid a discovery of his person. *Plut. de Cons. ad Apoll.* —*Cic. Tusc.* 1. c. 47.—*Paus.* 9. c. 11. & 37.

AGAMEM'NON, king of Mycenæ and Argos, was son of Plisthenes, the son of Atreus. Homer calls him the son of Atreus, which is erroneous, upon the authority of Hesiod, Apollodorus, &c. *Vid.* Plisthenes. When Atreus was dead, his brother Thyestes seized the kingdom of Argos, and Agamemnon fled to Polyphidus, king of Sicyon, and thence to Œneus, king of Ætolia, where he was educated. Agamemnon married Clytemnestra, daughter of Tyndarus, king of Sparta, who assisted him to recover his father's kingdom. After the banishment of the usurper to Cythera, Agamemnon established himself at Mycenæ. When Helen was carried off by Paris, Agamemnon was elected commander in chief of the Grecian forces against Troy; to which expedition he furnished 100 ships, and lent 60 more to the people of Arcadia. The combined fleet was detained at Aulis, where Agamemnon sacrificed his daughter to appease Diana. *Vid* Iphigenia. During the Trojan war, Agamemnon behaved with much valour; but his quarrel with Achilles, whose mistress he took by force, was fatal to the Greeks. After the ruin of Troy, Agamemnon obtained, as his share of the spoils, the beautiful Cassandra; but he disregarded the warning of his captive, who foretold to him that his wife Clytemnestra would put him to death; and he returned to Greece. On his arrival, the queen, with her adulterer Ægisthus (*vid.* Ægisthus), prepared to murder him; and as he came from the bath, to embarrass him, she gave him a tunic, the sleeves of which were sewed together, and while he attempted to put it on, she brought him to the ground with a hatchet, and Ægisthus seconded her blows. His death was revenged by his son Orestes. *Vid.* Clytemnestra, Menelaus, and Orestes. His death forms the subject of one of the tragedies of Æschylus. The Agamemnon of Seneca, with all its faults, possesses marks of genius and sublimity. *Homer Il.* 1. 2. &c. *Odyss.* 4. &c.—*Eustath in Il. & Odyss.*—*Apollod.* 3.—*Lactant.* in 1.

Achill. 36.—*Tzetzes. Chil.* 1. *Hist.* 18.—*Lucret.* 1. v. 84.—*Nicand. apud Aton. Lib. Narr.* 27.—*Philostr Icon.* 2. c. 9 —*Lucian. in Enc. Dom.*—*Ovid. de Rem. Am.* v. 777, *Met.* 12. v. 30.—*Hygin.* fab. 88. & 97.—*Strab.* 8.—*Thucyd.* 1. c. 9.—*Ælian. V. H.* 4. c. 26.—*Dictys. Cret.* 1. 2, &c.—*Dares. Phryg.*—*Sophocl. in Elect.*—*Euripid. in Orest.*—*Senec. in Agam.*—*Paus.* 2. c. 6. 1. 9. c. 40. &c.—*Virg. Æn.* 6. v. 838.—*Mela,* 2. c. 4.

AGAMEMNO'NIA, in Attica, the station of the combined fleet which went against Troy. *Mela,* 2. c. 3.

AGAMEMNO'NIUS, an epithet applied to Orestes, as son of Agamemnon. *Virg. Æn.* 4. v. 471.

AGAMES'TOR, a perpetual archon of Athens, who reigned 24 years.

AGAME'TOR, an athlete of Mantinea, frequently honoured with the prize at Olympia. *Paus.* 6. c. 10.

AGAMID'IDES, son of Ctesippus, grandson of Hercules, reigned in some part of Greece. *Paus.* 1. 3. *de Laced. Rep.*

AGA'MIUM, a town of Gaul, now Aghem or Ghem.

AGAMNES'TOR, or AGANES'TOR, an academic philosopher. *Plut. in Deipnos. Quæst.* 4.

AG'AMUS, a city of Pontus, near Heraclea. *Steph.*

AGAM'ZUA, a town of Media. *Plin.* 6. c. 14.

AGANAG'ARA, a city of India within the Ganges. *Ptol.*

AGANGINÆ, a people in the interior of Libya. *Id.*

AGANIP'PE, a celebrated fountain in Bœotia, at the foot of mount Helicon. It flows into the Permessus, and is sacred to the muses, who from it were called Aganippedes. *Paus.* 9. c. 29.—*Propert.* 2. el. 3.—*Ovid. Met.* 5. v. 312.—*Cluver.* 4. c. 8.—*Plin.* 4. c. 7.—*Solin.* 7.

AGAPE'NOR, the commander of Agamemnon's fleet. *Homer. Il.* 2. v. 609.——The son of Ancæus, and grandson of Lycurgus, was king of Arcadia, and one of Helen's suitors. On his return from the Trojan war, his fleet was dispersed on the coast of Cyprus, where he built Paphus, and raised a temple to Venus, who was before worshipped only at Golgi. In his absence the kingdom of Arcadia fell into the hands of Hippothous, son of Cercyon. *Hom. Il.* 2.—*Hygin.* 79. & 81.—*Apollod.* 3. c. 15. —*Paus.* 8. c. 5.

AGA'PIUS, a philosoper of Alexandria, who opened a school at Byzantium. *Voss de Philol.* c. 13——A philosopher of Athens, pupil of Marinus. *Suidas.*

AGAPTOL'EMUS, a son of Ægyptus and Phœnissa, put to death by his wife Pirene. *Apollod.* 2.

A'GAR, a town of Africa. *Hirt. Bell. Afr.* 76.

AG'ARA, a town of India within the Ganges. *Ptol.*

AGARE'NI, a people of Arabia. Trajan destroyed their city called Agarum. *Strab.* 16.—*Cluver.* 5. c. 25.

AGARIS'TA, daughter of Clisthenes, was courted by all the princes of Greece. She married Megacles. *Ælian. V. H.* 12. c. 24.—*Herodot.* 6. c. 126. &c. ——A daughter of Hippocrates, who married Xantippus. She dreamed that she had brought forth a lion, and some time after became mother of Pericles. *Plut. in Pericl.*—*Herodot.* 6. c. 131.

AGARLA'VÆ, a place of Africa Propria. *Antonin.*

AGAR'RHA, a city of Susiana. *Ptol.*

AGA'RUM, a promontory of European Sarmatia. *Id.*

AG'ARUS, now Shiret, a city and a river of European Sarmatia, called Sagaris by *Ovid,* Ep. 1. 4. 10. It empties itself into the Bosphorus. *Ptol.* From this city and river the root Agaric received its name. *Plin.* 25. c. 9.

AGA'SIAS, a brave warrior of Stymphalus in Arcadia, mentioned by *Xenophon, Anab.* 1. 5.——A sculptor of Ephesus, to whom the famous Borghese gladiator is attributed.

AGAS'ICLES, king of Sparta, was son of Archidamus. He used to say that a king ought to govern his subjects as a father governs his children. *Paus.* 3. c. 7. *Plut. in Apoph.*——A man of Halicarnassus, who carried off a tripod which he won as a prize, and which had been usually dedicated by the victor to Apollo. *Herod.* 1. c. 144.

AGAS'SÆ, a city of Thessaly. *Liv.* 45. c. 27.

AGAS'THENES, father of Polyxenus, and king of Elis, was one of Helen's suitors, and concerned in the Trojan war. *Homer. Il.* 2. 624.—*Apollod.* 3. c. 11.

AGAS'THUS or ACAS'TUS, an archon of Athens.

AGAS'TROPHUS, a Trojan, wounded by Diomedes. *Homer Il.* 11. v. 338.

AG'ASUS, a harbour on the coast of Apulia, now Porto Græco. *Plin.* 3. c. 11.

AG'ATHA, a town of Gaul, near the shores of the Mediterranean, now Agde, in Languedoc. *Mela,* 2. c. 7.—*Plin.* 3. c. 4.—*Cluver.* 3. c. 29.—A city of Campania.——A city of Phocis. *Steph.*——An island of Lycia.

AGATHAR'CHIDAS, a general of Corinth in the Peloponnesian war. *Thucyd.* 2. c. 83.

AGÄTHAR'CHIDES, a Samian philosopher and historian, who wrote a treatise on stones, and a history of Persia and Phœnice, besides an account of the Red Sea, of Europe, and Asia. Some make him a native of Cnidus; and add that he flourished about 177 B.C. *Joseph cont. Ap.*—*Plut.*—*Diod.*—*Voss. in H. Gr.* 1. c. 20.—*Sax. Onom.* 1. p. 129.—*Fabr. B. Gr.* 3. p. 32.

AGATHAR'CHUS, an officer in the Syracusan fleet. *Thucydides,* 7. c. 25.——A painter, who boasted of his quickness in executing his pieces, whilst Zeuxis prided himself on his slowness. *Plut. in Alcib. & Pericl.*——A victor at Olympia, in the archonship of Heraclius. *Dion. Hal.* 4.

AGATHEM'ERUS, a geographer supposed to have lived in the age of Septimus Severus. His works have been edited by Vossius, and by Jacob. Gronovius, Lug. Bat. 1697, and lastly by Hudson in the 2nd vol. of the Geog. Min. 1703. *Sax. Onom.* 1. 350.—*Fabr. B. Gr.* 4. p. 65.

AG'ATHI DÆMO'NIS, an island of the Indian sea. *Steph.*——A river in Lower Ægypt. *Ptol.*

AGATHI'A, a city of Phocis. *Steph.*

AGA'THIAS, or AGATHI'AS, a poet and historian born at Myrina, in Asia, in the age of Justinian, of whose reign he published the history in five books. Several of his epigrams are to be found in the Anthologia His history is a sequel of that of Procopius. The best edition is that of Paris, fol. 1660. *Suidas.*—*Sax. Onom.* 2. p. 64.—*Fabr. B. Gr.* 3. c. 32.

AG'ATHO, a Samian historian, who wrote an account of Scythia.——A tragic poet, who flourished 406 B.C. The names of some of his tragedies are preserved, such as Telephus, Thyestes, &c. *Sax. Onom.* 1. p. 52.—*Fabr. B. Gr.* 2. p. 281. [A fine bust in the museum of the Capitol at Rome, bears his name inscribed on the shoulder.]——A comic poet, who lived in the same age. *Plut. in Parall.* ——A son of Priam. *Apollod.* 3.—*Homer Il.* 24. A governor of Babylon. *Curt.* 5. c. 1.——A Pythagorean philosopher. *Ælian. V. H.* 13 c. 4.——A learned and melodious musician, who first introduced songs in tragedy. *Aristot. in Poet.*——A youth of Athens loved by Plato. *Diog. Laert.* 3. c. 32.—*A. Gell.* 19. c. 11.—*Macrob. Sat.* 2. c. 2.

AG'ATHO or AGATHI'ON, an Athenian of prodigious bravery and size, in the time of Adrian and Herodes Atticus. *Philostr. in Attic.*

AGATHOCLE'A, a beautiful courtezan of Ægypt. One of the Ptolemies destroyed his wife Eurydice to marry her. She with her brother long governed the kingdom, and attempted to murder the king's son. *Plut. in Cleom.*—*Justin.* 30. c. 1.

AGATH'OCLES, son of a potter, entered into the Sicilian army, and at length reduced all Sicily under his power. Being defeated at Himera by the Carthaginians, he carried the war into Africa, where for four years he extended his conquests over his enemy. He afterwards passed into Italy, and made himself master of Crotona. He died in his 72nd year, B.C. 289, after a reign of 28 years. *Plut. in Justin.* 22. & 23.—*Polyb.* 15.—*Auson.* ep. 8.—*Diod.* 18. &c.——A son of Lysimachus, taken prisoner by the Getæ. After he was ransomed he married Lysandra, daughter of Ptolemy Lagus. His father in his old age married Arsinoe, the sister of Lysander. After her husband's death, Arsinoe, fearful for her children, attempted to murder Agathocles. Some say that she fell in love with him, and killed him because he slighted her addresses. After the death of Agathocles, 283. B.C., Lysander fled to Seleucus. *Strab.* 13. *Plut. in Pyrrh. & Demetr.*—*Paus.* 1. c. 9. & 10.——A Grecian historian of Babylon, who wrote an account of Cyzicus. *Cic. de Div.* 1. c. 24.——A Chian, who wrote on husbandry. *Varro.*—There were several other persons of this name; as, a Milesian, who wrote on rivers; an Atracian, who wrote on fishes; a Samian writer, a physician; an Athenian archon.

AGATH'OCLIS, the name of two islands in the Arabic Gulph. *Ptol.*

AGATHOER'GI, Spartans who were employed, during the year in which they left the equestrian order, in promoting the public good. *Herodot.* 1. c. 67.

AG'ATHON. *Vid.* Agatho.

AGATH'ONIS, an island of the Arabic Gulph towards Ægypt. *Ptol.*

AGATHON'YMUS wrote a history of Persia. *Plut. de Flum.*

AGATHOP'OLIS, a town at the south of Gaul, now the salubrious Montpelier.

AGATHOS'THENES, a poet, &c. *Tzetzes, Chil.* 7. *Hist.* 144. *Voss. de H. Gr.* 1. 4.

AGATHOS'TRATUS, a general, probably a Rhodian, who signally defeated the naval commander of Ptolemy. *Polyæn.* l. 5.

AGATHODÆ'MON, an Alexandrian writer on the world. *Voss. de H. Gr.* l. 4.

AGATHYL'LUS, an elegiac poet of Arcadia. *Dion. Hal.* 1.

AGATHYR'NUM, AGATHYR'IUM, or AGATHYR'SUS, a town at the north of Sicily, on the sea-shore, nearly opposite the Lipari Isles. It was said to have been founded by Agathyrnus, son of Æolus. *Ptol.—Strab.—Plin.* 3. c. 8.

AGATHYR'SI, a nation of Scythia, represented by Herodotus as civilized, and so fond of magnificence, that their garments were generally adorned with golden fillets. They received their name from Agathyrsus the son of Hercules. *Herodot.* 4. c. 10. —*Virg. Æn.* 4. v. 146.—*Mela,* 2. c. 1.—*Plin.* 4. c. 12.—*Cluver.* 4. c. 17.

AGATHYR'SUS, brother of Gelonus, a son of Hercules.—*Steph.*

AGAU'I, a northern nation who lived upon milk. *Homer. Il.* 13.

AGAU'NUM, a town of the Helvetii, now S. Mauritz.

AGA'VA, a city of the Pentapolis in Africa. *Ptol.*

AGA'VE, daughter of Cadmus and Hermione, married Echion, by whom she had Pentheus. *Vid.* Pentheus. She received divine honors after death, because she had contributed to the aid of Bacchus. *Hygin.* 184. 239. 240. 254.—*Theocrit.* 26.—*Ovid. Met.* 3. v. 725.—*Lucan.* l. v. 574.—*Stat. Theb.* 11. v. 318.—*Apollod.* 3. c. 4.——One of the Danaides, who married and murdered Lycus. *Apollod.* 1. c. 6. l. 2. c. 4. *Hygin. Præf. Fab.*—It was the name also of one of the Nereides, *Apollod.* 1.; and of a tragedy of Statius. *Juv.* 7. v. 87.—*Pers.* 1. v. 100.

AGA'VUS, a son of Priam. *Hom. Il.* 24. v. 251.

AGDAME'A, a city of Phrygia. *Socrat.—Callist.* 14.

AG'DAMI, a city of Arabia Felix. *Ptol.*

AGDES'TIS or AGDIS'TUS, a mountain of Phrygia, where Atys was buried. *Paus.* 1. c. 4.

Agdes'tis, a surname of Cybele. *Hesych.*

AGDIS'TIS, a monster, the offspring of Jupiter. *Paus.* 7. c. 17.

AGE'DI, a people of Asiatic Sarmatia. *Plin.* 6. c. 7.

AGEDIN'CUM, a town of Gallia on the borders of the Senones, now Sens. *Cæs. B. G.* 6. c. 44.

AGEDU'NUM, now Ahun, a town of Gaul, on the river Crosa.

AGELA'DAS, a celebrated statuary of Argos, in the 78th Olympiad. In the age of the Antonines, there were still to be seen, at Ægium in Achaia, an infant Jupiter and a Hercules, which were the productions of his chisel. *Plin.* 24. c. 8.—*Colum.* 10. v. 29.—*Paus.* 6. c. 8. l. 7. c. 23. l. 8. c. 42.

AG'ELAS, a Trojan, son of Phradmon, killed by Diomedes. *Homer. Il.* 8. v. 257.——An Arcadian, son of Stymphalus, who gave his name to a town and mountain of Arcadia. *Paus.* 8. c. 35.——An Athlete, who obtained a prize at the Pythian games. *Paus.* 10. c. 7.——A king of Corinth. *Vid.* Agelaus.

AGELAS'TUS, (from ἀ, *non*, and γελάω, *rideo*), a surname of Crassus, the grandfather of the rich Crassus. He only laughed once in his life, and this, it is said, was upon seeing an ass eat thistles. *Cic. de Fin.* 5. c. 30. *Plin.* 7. c. 19.—*Solin.* 4.—The name was also given to Pluto, from the sullen and melancholy appearance of his countenance. *L. Gyrald Synt.* 6.——A stone of Attica, near Eleusis, so called because Ceres sat on it when oppressed with grief in consequence of the loss of her daughter. *Apollod.* 1. c. 11. *Ovid. Fast.* 4. v. 504.

AGELA'US, the First, a king of Corinth, son of Ixion, and one of the Heraclidæ.

Agela'us the Second, a king of Corinth, who reigned 30 years. *Diod. apud Syncell.* p. 179.

Agela'us, a son of Hercules and Omphale, from whom Crœsus was descended. *Apollod.* 2. c. 7.——A servant of Priam, who preserved Paris when exposed on mount Ida. *Id.* 3. c. 12.——One of Penelope's suitors. *Homer. Odyss.* 20.

AG'ELE, a tribe of Attica. *Phavorin.*

AGELI'A, an epithet of Minerva, from her carrying off the booty, ἄγουσα λεῖαν *Cœl. Rhod.* 14. c. 18.

AGEM'ACHUS, a general of the Messenians, who retook Pheræ from the pirate Nicon. *Polyæn.* 2. c. 35.

AG'EMON, brother of Aristodemus, governed Corinth for 16 years, during the minority of Telestes. *Diod. —Paus.*

AGEM'YTHA, a city of India without the Ganges. *Ptol.*

AGEN'NUM or AGI'NUM, now Agen, a city of Aquitania, near the Garumna. *Plin.* l. 4. c. 19.—*Auson.* ep. 24. v. 79.

AGE'NOR, king of Phœnicia, was son of Neptune and Libya, and father of Cadmus, Phœnix, Cilix, and Europa. As Carthage was built by his descendants, it is called *Agenoris urbs. Virg. Æn.* l. v. 338.—*Hygin.* fab. 6.—*Ital.* l. v. 15. l. 17. v. 58.—*Apollod.* 2. c. 1. l. 3. c. 1.——A son of Jasus, and father of Argus. *Apollod.* 2. c. 10.——A son of Pleuron, father of Parthaon and Demonice, by Jocasta or Epicasta, daughter of Calydon. *Paus.* 3. c. 13.—*Apollod.* 1. c. 7.——A son of Antenor, slain in the Trojan war by Neoptolemus. *Paus.* 10. c. 27.—*Homer. Il.* 21. v. 579.——A Mitylenean, who wrote a treatise on music. *Aristox Music.* 1. 2.—*Voss. de Scient. Mathem.* c. 59.——A son of Ægyptus by Arabia, *Apollod.* 2. c. 1.——A son of Phlegeus. *Id.* 3. c. 7. Also a son of Amphion and Niobe, *Id.* 3. c. 4.; and a king of Argos, father of Crotopus.

AGENO'RIA or AGERO'NIA, a goddess among the Romans, who presided over industry, whence her name (*ab agere*). Her temple was upon mount Aventine. *Hermolaus in Plin.* 15. c. 29.—*August. de Civ.* 4. c. 11. The goddess of silence bore also the same name. *Macrob. Sat.* 1. c. 10. l. 3. c. 9.—*Plin.* 3. c. 5.—*Solin.* 1.

AGENOR'IDES, the patronymic of Cadmus, and the other descendants of Agenor. *Ovid. Met.* 3. v. 8.

AGERI'NUS, a freed man of Agrippina, accused of attempting Nero's life. *Tac. Ann.* 14. c. 7.

AGESAN'DER, a sculptor of Rhodes under Vespasian, who, in conjunction with Polydorus and Athenodorus, made a marble statue of Laocoon. *Plin.* 36. c. 5.—*Vid.* Laocoon.——An ambassador sent to Athens by the Lacedæmonians with Ramphius and Milesippus, before the Peloponnesian war. *Thucyd.* 1. c. 139.

AGESI'ANAX, the author of a commentary on Aratus. *Voss. de Scient. Math.* c. 33.

AGE'SIAS, called also Hesius and Hegesias, a Platonic philosopher, who taught the immortality of the soul. One of the Ptolemies forbad him to continue his lectures because his doctrine was so popular that many of his auditors committed suicide. *Cic. Tusc. Quæst.* 1. c. 34.——An archon at Athens Olymp. 114.——A Syracusan, son of Sostratus, a victor at Olympia. *Pind. Olymp.* 6. v. 18.

AGESIDA'MUS, a Locrian pugilist, victor at the Olympic games. *Pind. Olymp.* 10. & 11.——A Syracusan, father of Chromius. *Id. Nem.* 1. 42. & 9. 99.

AGES'IDES, a king of Lacedæmon.

AGESILA'US the First, king of Sparta, of the family of the Agidæ, was son of Dorissus, and father of Archelaus. He ascended the throne B.C. 957, and died after a reign of 44 years. In his time Lycurgus instituted his famous laws. *Herodot.* 7. c. 204. *Paus.* 3. c. 2.

Agesila'us the Second, son of Archidamus, of the family of the Proclydæ, succeeded Agis. He made war against Artaxerxes, but was recalled from Asia, to oppose the Athenians and Bœotians, and he passed over, in 30 days, that tract of country which had taken a whole year of Xerxes' expedition. He subsequently defeated his enemies at Coronea. Though deformed, of low stature, and lame, he was a brave general. He went, in his 80th year, to assist Tachus king of Ægypt, and the natives were astonished to see the Lacedæmonian general eating with his soldiers on the ground, bareheaded. Agesilaus reigned 36 years, and died 362 B.C. *Justin.* 6. c. 1.—*Plut. & C. Nepos. in Vit.—Paus.* 3. c. 9.—*Xenoph. Orat. pro. Ages.*

Agesila'us, a brother of Themistocles, sent as a spy into the Persian camp, where he killed Mardonius instead of Xerxes. He was about to be sacrificed on the altar of the sun, when, extending his hand over the blazing coals without emotion, he informed the astonished monarch that all the Athenians possessed equal fortitude; and thus, by his intrepidity, he obtained his liberation. *Plut. in Parall.*——A surname of Pluto, most probably corrupted from the epithet Agelastus.——A Greek, who wrote a history of Italy. *Plut. in Parall.* 29.——An ancestor of Leotochides. *Herodot.* 8. c. 131.

AGESINA'TES, a people of Gaul, near the Pictones. *Plin.* 4. c. 19.

AGESIP'OLIS the First, king of Lacedæmon, and son of Pausanias, obtained a great victory over the Mantineans. He reigned 14 years, and was succeeded by his brother Cleombrotus, B.C. 380. *Paus.* 3. c. 5. l. 8. c. 8.—*Xenoph. Hist. Gr.* 4. & 5.

AGESIP'OLIS the Second, son of Cleombrotus, king of Sparta, was succeeded by Cleomenes the Second, B.C. 370. *Paus* 1. c. 13. l. 3. c. 5.

AGESISTRATA, the mother of king Agis. *Plut. in Algid.*

AGESISTRATUS, the writer of a treatise, *De arche machinali. Vitruv. Præf.* l. 7.

AGES'SUS, a city of Thrace. *Steph.*

AGE'TA, a city of Upper Mœsia. *Antonin.*

AGETES or AGE'TIS, a son of Apollo by Cyrene, brother of Aristæus. He is called also Ageus or Argeus. *Justin* 13. c. 7.

AGGE'NUS UR'BICUS, the author of a work on lands and boundaries, which was first published by Turnebus, with those of Siculus Flaccus and Hyginus Gromaticus, and afterwards enriched with notes by Rigaltius. *Voss de Scient. Math.* c. 27.sec. 10

AGGRAM'MES, or according to Diodorus Siculus, Xandrames, a cruel king of the Gangarides. His father was a hairdresser, of whom the queen became enamoured, and whom she made governor to the king's children, to gratify her passion. He killed them to raise Agrammes, his son by the queen, to the throne. *Curt.* 9. c. 2.—*Diod.* 17.

AGGRI'NÆ, a people of Thrace near mount Rhodope. *Cic. in L. Pis.* 37.

AG'GYA, a place of Africa. *Augustin.*

AGI'ADÆ, a place of Lacedæmon. *Hesychius.*

A'GIAS, a soothsayer of Lacedæmon, who foretold to Lysander his success at Ægospotamos. *Paus.* 3. 11.——An historian who wrote on the affairs of Argos. *Athen.* l. 3.——An officer. *Vid.* Agis.

A'GIAS, a place of Argolis. *Diod. Sic.* 12.

AG'IDÆ, the descendants of Eurysthenes, who shared the throne of Sparta with the Proclidæ. The name is derived from Agis, son of Eurysthenes; and the family became extinct in the person of Cleomenes, son of Leonidas. *Plut.*

AG'IDOS, a city of Cyprus, between Lapatha and Aphrodisium.——A city of Sicily, between Anemurium and Arsinoe. *Strab.*

AGILA'RIA, a town of Spain, now De Campos, in Old Castille.

AGILA'US, the third king of Corinth, reigned 36 years.——One of the Ephori, almost murdered by the partisans of Cleomenes. *Plut. in Cleom.*

AGI'LIS, a man who accompanied the Tirynthian youth to the Theban war.

AG'INIS, a village of the Susii. *Arrian in Indic.*

AGIN'NA, city of Asiatic Iberia. *Ptol.*

A'GION, a mountain in Scythia. Also a place in the same country, where Æsculapius was worshipped *Steph.*

A'GIS the First, king of Sparta, succeeded his father Eurysthenes, and, after a reign of one year, was succeeded by his son Echestratus, B.C.1058. *Paus.*3.c.2.

A'GIS the Second, a king of Sparta, who waged bloody wars against Athens, and restored liberty to several Greek cities. He attempted to restore the laws of Lycurgus at Sparta, and to make an equal division of the lands of the state among his countrymen; but he was strangled by order of the Ephori. *Plut. in Algid.*—*Cic. Off.* 2. c. 23.

A'GIS the Third, a son of Archidamus, who signalized himself in the war which the Spartans waged against Epidaurus. He obtained a victory at Mantinea, and was successful in the Peloponnesian war. He reigned 27 years. *Thucyd.* 3. & 4.—*Paus.* 3.c. 8. &. 10.

A'GIS the Fourth, a son of Archidamus, king of Sparta, who, with the assistance of the Persians, endeavoured to deliver Greece from the empire of Macedonia. He was vanquished in the attempt, and slain by Antipater. *Curt.* 6. c. 1.—*Diod.* 17.—*Justin.* 12. c. 1. &c.

A'GIS the Fifth, son of Eudamidas, was strangled in prison by order of the Ephori. *Paus. Lacon.*

A'GIS, an Arcadian in the expedition of Cyrus against his brother Artaxerxes. He was perfidiously seized by Tissaphernes, and sent to the king. *Polyæn.* 7. c. 18.——A poet of Argos, who attended Alexander in his Asiatic expedition. He raised his patron to immortality, and declared that Bacchus, Hercules, and the sons of Leda, would yield to his superior merits in the assembly of the gods. *Curt.* 8. c. 5. ——A Lycian, who followed Æneas into Italy, where he was killed. *Virg. Æn.* 10. v. 751.

AGISYM'BA, an extensive region of Africa, now Zanguebar. *Ptol.*

A'GLA, a town of Spain. *Plin.* 3. c. 1.

AGLA'IA, one of the Graces, sometimes called Pasiphaë. *Hesiod. Theog.* 908.—*Paus.* 9. c. 35.—*Apollod.* 1. c. 6.—*Hygin. Præf. Fab.*——A daughter of Thestius, mother of Antiades and Onesippus, by Hercules. *Apollod.* 2 c. 35.

AG'LAIS, daughter of Megacles, a woman of gluttonous appetite. *Cœl. Rh.* l. 15. c. 19.

AGLA'ON, a fountain of Aulis. *Hesych.*

AGLAONI'CE, daughter of Hegemon, was acquainted with astronomy and eclipses, whence she boasted of her power to draw down the moon from heaven. Hence arose the proverb, τὴν Σελήνην καταϛπᾷ, applied to vain boasters. *Erasmi. Adag.*—*Schol. Apollon.* 4. *Arg.*—*Plutarch de Orac. Defect.* calls her Aganice.

AGLA'OPE, one of the Sirens.

AGLA'OPES, the name given to Æsculapius by the Laconians. *Hesych.*

AGLA'OPHON, a celebrated Greek painter in the age of Evenor, the father of Parrhasius. *Cic. De. Orat.* 3. c. 7.—*Ælian. Anim.* 17. c. 46.—*Quintil.* 12. c. 10.—*Plin.* 35. c. 8.

AGLAOS'THENES wrote a history of Naxus. *Strab.* 6.—*Voss. H. Gr.* p. 318.

AGLAU'RUS or AGRAU'LUS, daughter of Erechtheus, or, according to *Hesychius*, of Cecrops, was, with her sisters Herse and Pandrosus, entrusted with a basket by Minerva, with positive injunctions not to open it. Aglaurus, however, opened the basket, which contained the infant Erichthonius, and the goddess punished her curiosity by making her jealous of Herse, of whom Mercury was enamoured, and she was changed into a stone by the god. *Ovid. Met.* 2. v. 739. *Pollux*, however, gives a different account of her end. She had, according to Apollodorus, a daughter called Alcippe, by Mars. *Hygin.* fab. 166.—*Apollod.* 3. c. 28.—*Paus.* 1. c. 18.—*Herodot.* 8 c. 53.

AGLA'US, the poorest man of Arcadia, pronounced by the oracle more happy than Gyges, king of Lydia. *Plin.* 7. c. 46. *Val. Max.* 7. c. 1.

AGLIBO'LUS and MALACHBE'LUS, gods of Palmyrene, a city of Arabia, according to an inscription found there. *Vid. Gruter. in vet. Insc.* p. 81.

AG'MON, a faithful and valiant companion of Diomedes, changed into a swan for insulting Venus. *Ovid. Met.* 14. v. 484.

AG'NA, a woman in the age of Horace, who though deformed, had many admirers. *Horat.* 1. sat. 3. v.40.

AG'NA, a river of Mauritania Tingitana. *Ptol.*

AG'NI COR'NU, a promontory near the Bolbitic mouth of the Nile. *Strab.* 17.

AGNI'CES or AGNI'CIS, a river flowing into the Tigris. *Plin.* 6. c. 27.

AGNI'TA or AGNI'TES, a surname of Æsculapius at Sparta, where he had a statue hewn out of the plant called Agnos. *Cœl. Rhod.* 18. c. 5.—For this plant see *Pliny*, 24. c. 9.

AG'NIO, a river of Belgium, now Aa.

AG'NO or HAG'NO, one of the nymphs who nursed Jupiter. She gave her name to a fountain on mount Lycæus. *Paus.* 8. c. 31. &c.

AGNOD'ICE, an Athenian woman, who disguised her sex to learn medicine, which science she was taught by Hierophilus. *Hygin.* fab. 274.

AG'NON, son of Nicias, was present at the taking of Samus by Pericles. In the Peloponnesian war he went against Potidæa, but abandoned his expedition through disease. He built Amphipolis, the inhabitants of which afterwards revolted to Brasidas. *Thucyd.* 2. 3. &c.——A writer whose talents were employed in vilifying the power of eloquence. —*Quint.* 2. c. 17.——A native of Teus, an officer of Alexander, whose favour he lost. *Plut. quom. adult.*—*Plin.* 33. c. 3.——The father of Theramenes, a free man of Steria, in the tribe Pandionis.

AGNONI'A, a town of Thrace, near Amphipolis. *Steph.*

AGNON'IDES, a rhetorician of Athens, who accused Phocion of betraying the Piræeus to Nicanor. He was afterwards put to death. *Plut. & Nep. in Phoc.*

AG'NUS, part of the tribe Attalis, in Attica. *Hesychius* has Æolis, but read Attalis. *Meurs. de pop. Att.*

AGNO'TES, a people of Gallia Celtica, near the ocean. *Steph.*

AG'OCE, a city of Upper Æthiopia. *Plin.* 6 c. 29.

AG'OLA, a city of Upper Æthiopia, near mount Amara.

A'GON or AG'ONUS, a river of Æthiopia. *Hesych.*

AGONA'LIA or AGO'NIA, festivals at Rome, celebrated three times a year, in honor of Janus or of Agonius, on the Capitoline hill. They were instituted by Numa, and on the festive days the chief priest used to offer a ram. *Ovid Fast.* 1. v. 317.—*Varro, de L. L.* 5.—*Macrob. Sat.* 1. c. 4.

AGO'NAX or AZO'NAX, the preceptor of Zoroaster in the art of magic. *Plin.* 30. c. 1.

AGONEN'SIS PORTA, now Porta Salari, a gate at Rome, called also Collina and Quirinalis.

AGO'NES, a people of Insubria. Their country is now La Val di Gogna. *Polybius* places them between the Apennines and the Po.

Ago'nes Capitoli'ni, games celebrated at Rome, every fifth year. Prizes were then proposed for agility and strength, as well as for poetical and other literary compositions. The poet Statius recited his Thebaid at these games, but it was not received with much applause.

AGO'NIA a river of Insubria, now la Gogna.

AGO'NIS, an attendant in the temple of Venus, on mount Eryx. *Cic. Verr.* 1.

AGO'NIUS, a Roman deity, who patronized the actions of men. *Festus de V. Sig. Vid.* Agonalia.

AGONOTHE'TES, a name given by the Greeks and Latins to the judges at the exhibition of the scenic games, &c. *Tertul.—Suet. Ner.* 12.—*Spartian in Adri.* 13.

AG'ORA or AG'ORUM, a town of Italy in the Venetian territories.

Ag'ora, a town of the Thracian Chersonesus, now Malgara. *Steph.—Herod.* 7. c. 58.

AGORAC'RITUS, a sculptor of Pharus, pupil of Phidias, B.C. 450. He disputed with Alcamenes about making a statue of Venus, but was defeated. Upon this he sold his statue to strangers, that it might not remain in the city of Athens, and gave it the name of Nemesis. This statue was esteemed by *Varro* the best and most finished of all those which he had ever seen. *Plin.* 36. c. 5.—*Paus.* 1. c. 1. 18. & 33. 1. 9. c. 34.

AGORÆ'A, a name given to Minerva at Sparta. *Paus.* 3. c. 11.

AGORÆ'US, a surname of Mercury and also of Jupiter, given to them from their presiding over markets. *Paus.* 1. c. 15.

AGORA'NIS, a river which falls into the Ganges. *Arrian. de Indic.*

AGORAN'OMI, ten magistrates at Athens, who watched over the city and port, and inspected whatever was exposed to sale.

AG'OREUS, a river over which the emperor Justinian built a bridge. It was probably in Thrace, near Agora. *Hist. Misc.* 6. 16.

AGORI'TÆ, a nation of Asiatic Sarmatia. *Ptol.*

AG'OTUS, now l'Agout, a river of Aquitania.

A'GRA, a place near Athens, on the banks of the Ilissus, where the lesser Eleusinian mysteries were celebrated. Diana was also said to hunt there; whence her surname of Agræa. *Paus.* 1. c. 19.——A city of Susiana. *Ptol.*

AGRAD'ARUS, a king of Persia, afterwards called Cyrus, from the river of that name. *Strab.* 15.

A'GRÆ, a city of Arcadia. *Plin.* 4. c. 6.

AGRÆ'I or AGREN'SES, people of Arabia. *Plin.* 6. c. 28.——A people of Ætolia. *Liv.* 32. c. 34.

AG'RAGAS. *Vid.* Agrigentum. According to *Stephanus* there were four other towns of this name; one in Thrace; another in Eubœa; another in Cyprus: and another in Ætolia.

AGRA'NI, a people of Arabia Felix.

Agra'ni, a town of Babylonia. *Plin.* 6. c. 26.

AGRA'RIA LEX, was intended to distribute among the Roman people, all the land they had gained by conquest. This measure was warmly supported by the plebeians, but was vehemently resisted by the patricians, who had seized upon the conquered lands, and therefore refused to yield the fruit either of their rapine or of their brave exertions in the cause of their country. To divert the people from their favourite measure, the patricians gained over some of the tribunes, whose opposition set the matter at rest. The Agrarian law was first proposed A.U.C. 268, by the consul Sp. Cassius Vicellinus, and rejected by the senate. This produced dissension between the senate and the people; and Cassius seeing the ill success of the new regulations proposed by him; offered to distribute among the people the money which was produced from the corn of Sicily, after it had been brought to Rome and sold. This act of liberality the people refused, and tranquility was soon after re-established in the state; but the unfortunate Cassius was severely punished for his interference in the public affairs. He was accused by his enemies of aspiring to the sovereignty of the state, and though probably innocent, thrown down from the Tarpeian rock. It was proposed a second time, A.U.C. 269, by the tribune Licinius Stolo, and so great were the tumults which followed, that one of the tribunes of the people was killed, and many of the senators fined for their opposition. Mutius Scævola, A.U.C. 620, persuaded the tribune Tiberius Gracchus to propose it a third time; and though Octavius, his colleague in the tribuneship, opposed it, yet it passed into a law, and commissioners were appointed to make a division of the lands. The law at last proved fatal to the freedom of Rome, under Julius Cæsar. *Flor.* 3. c. 3. & 13.—*Cic. pro. Leg. Agr.—Dionys.* 8. c. 69. 81.—*Liv.* 2. c. 41. 44. 48. 52.

AGRAU'LE, a tribe of Athens. *Plut. in Alcib.*——A place in Sardinia belonging to the Athenians. *Steph.*

AGRAU'LIA, festivals at Athens and in Cyprus, in honor of Agraulus.

AGRAU'LUS. *Vid.* Aglaurus.——A surname of Minerva. *Harpocration.*

AGRAUONI'TÆ, a people of Illyria. *Liv.* 45. c. 26.

A'GRE, one of Actæon's dogs. *Ovid. Met.*——A town of Lydia. *Steph.*

AGRES'PHON, an author mentioned by *Suidas* as having written *περὶ ὁμωνύμων*, *i. e.* concerning celebrated men of the same name.

A'GRIA or AGA'RIA. *Vid.* Agarus.

A'GRIÆ, a people of Pæonia, between mounts Hæmus and Rhodope. *Steph.*

AGRIA'NE, a town of Cappadocia.

AGRIA'NES, a small river of Thrace. *Herodot.* 4. c. 90. The people in the same neighbourhood were called by the same name. *Id.* 5. c. 16. *Vid.* Agriæ.

AGRIAU'LÆ, a nation of Attica. *Hesych.* They were probably the Agraulæ of *Stephanus.*

AGRIC'OLA. CN. JUL. the father-in-law of the historian Tacitus, was for some years governor of Britain, and first discovered it to be an island by sailing round it. Domitian, envying his virtues, recalled him from the province, and ordered him to enter Rome in the night, that no triumph might be granted to him. Agricola obeyed, and retired to solitude and the enjoyment of the society of his friends. He died in his 56th year, A.D. 93. His life was written by Tacitus, and in it is to be found much valuable information on the early history of Britain. *Tac. in Agric.*

AGRIGEN'TUM, AG'RAGAS, or AC'RAGAS, now Girgenti, a town on the southern coast of Sicily, on mount Agragas. It was founded, according to Polybius, by a Rhodian colony, or, according to Thucydides, by a colony from Gela. The inhabitants were remarkable for their luxurious living; and the city, in its flourishing state, contained 200,000 inhabitants, who submitted without resistance to the superior power of Syracuse. The government, which was at first monarchical, became afterward democratical, and was for some time in the hands of the Carthaginians. Agrigentum was formerly celebrated for its temples of Jupiter and Hercules; the latter of which was considered one of the most finished models of antiquity, and it can even now boast of more remains of ancient art than any other town in Sicily. *Polyb.* 9.—*Strab.* 6.—*Diod.* 13.—*Virg. Æn.* 3. v. 707.—*Sil. Ital.* 14. v. 211.—*Thucyd.* 6.—*Cluver.* 3. c. 41.

A'GRII, a name of the Titans, and also of a place in Armenia. *Hesych.*

AGRIN'AGRA, a city of India within the Ganges. *Ptol.*

AGRIN'IUM, a city of Acharnania. *Polyb.* 6.—*Diod. Sic.* 19.

AGRI'ODOS, the name of one of Actæon's dogs. *Ovid. Met.* 3. fab. 2.

AGRIO'NIA, annual festivals among the Bœotians, in honour of Bacchus. They were generally celebrated in the night; and the women who were present at the solemnity made inquiries for Bacchus, and not finding him, reported that he had retired among the Muses. Upon this they amused themselves with ænigmas and difficult questions. *Plut. in Symp.* 8. c. 1.

AGRI'OPAS, a man who wrote the history of all those who obtained prizes at Olympia. *Plin.* 8. c. 22.——The father of the Cynaras who invented several useful mechanical instruments, &c. *Plin.* 7. c. 56.

AGRI'OPE, the wife of Agenor, king of Phœnicia, whom some, however, call Telephassa. *Hygin.* fab. 6. 178, 179.—*Schol. Apollon.* 3. *Arg.*—*Lactant. in Pheb.* 2.

AGRIOPH'AGI, a people of Æthiopia, who fed on the flesh of panthers and lions. *Solinus*, c. 33. *Ptolemy* mentions a people of this name in India within the Ganges.

M. AGRIP'PA VIPSA'NIUS, a celebrated Roman, who obtained a victory over S. Pompey, and favored the cause of Augustus at the battles of Actium and Philippi, where he behaved with great valor. In his expeditions in Gaul and Germany, Agrippa obtained several victories, but refused the honor of a triumph, and turned his liberality towards the embellishment of Rome, and the raising of magnificent buildings, one of which, the Pantheon, still exists. After he had retired for two years to Mitylene, in consequence of a quarrel with Marcellus, Augustus recalled him, and, as a proof of his regard gave him his daughter Julia in marriage, and left him the care of the empire during an absence of two years, which time he employed in visiting the Roman provinces of Greece and Asia. He died, universally lamented, at Rome in the 51st year of his age, 12 B.C. and his body was placed in the tomb which Augustus had prepared for himself. He had been married three times: to Pomponia, daughter of Atticus; to Marcella, daughter of Octavia; and, after being forcibly divorced from her, to Julia, by whom he had five children, Caius, and Lucius Cæsar, Posthumus Agrippa, Agrippina and Julia. [The finest statue, for there are many existing of Agrippa, is that in the possession of the Grimani family at Venice; and of the busts, which are likewise very numerous, that in the Musée Royale at Paris.

AGRIP'PA C. CÆ'SAR, his son, was adopted by Augustus, and made consul, at the age of 14 or 15. He went to Armenia on an expedition against the Persians, in which expedition he was slain.

AGRIP'PA L. CÆ'SAR, his younger brother, was likewise adopted by his grandfather Augustus; but he was soon after banished to Campania, for using seditious language against his benefactor. He was slain in his 26th year through the intrigues of Livia and Tiberius. *Virg. Æn.* 8. v. 682.—*Horat.* 1. od. 6. One of the servants of the murdered prince assumed the name of L. Cæsar Agrippa, and raised commotions. *Tac.* 2. c. 39.

AGRIP'PA POST'HUMUS, the youngest son of Agrippa, was also exposed to the cruel persecutions of Livia, and banished to the island Planasia, and afterwards murdered by order of Tiberius. *Tac. Ann.* 1. c. 3.

AGRIP'PA HERO'DES, a son of Aristobulus, grandson of the great Herod, became tutor to the grandchild of Tiberius, and was soon after imprisoned by the suspicious tyrant. When Caligula ascended the throne, he was released, presented with a chain of gold as heavy as that which had lately confined him, and made him king of Judæa. He was a popular character with the Jews; and it is said, that while they were flattering him with the appellation of god, an angel of God struck him with the lousy disease, of which he died, A.D. 43.

AGRIP'PA HERO'DES, son of the last-mentioned monarch, was the last king of the Jews, being deprived of his kingdom by Claudius, in exchange for other provinces. He was with Titus at the siege of Jerusalem, and died A.D. 94. It was before him that St. Paul pleaded with such eloquence and effect. *Juv.* 6. v. 156.—*Tac. Hist.* 2. c. 81.

AGRIP'PA FU'RIUS MEDULLI'NUS, a consul who conquered the Æqui and Volsci.

AGRIP'PA FU'RIUS PHILO, a tribune of the people.

AGRIP'PA MENEN'IUS, a Roman general, who obtained a triumph over the Sabines. He appeased the populace of Rome by the well known fable of the belly and the limbs, and instituted the office of tribune of the people, A.U.C. 261. As he died poor, his funeral was performed at the expense of the public, from which source also his daughters received dowries. *Liv.* 2. c. 32.—*Flor.* 1. c. 23.

AGRIP'PA SYL'VIUS, a son of Tiberius Sylvius, king of Latium. He reigned 33 years, and was succeeded by his son Remulus Sylvius. *Dion. Hal.* 1. c. 8.

AGRIP'PA, a native of Bithynia, known as a mathematician in the reign of Domitian. *Ptol.* 1. 7.——A sceptical philosopher. *Laert.* 1. 9.

AGRIPPEN'SES, a people of Bithynia. *Plin.* 5. c. 32.

AGRIPPI'NA VIPSA'NIA, the wife of Tiberius, repudiated by him that he might marry Julia. *Suet. in Tib.* 7.

AGRIPPI'NA, a daughter of M. Agrippa, and granddaughter of Augustus. She married Germanicus, whom she accompanied into Syria; and when Piso poisoned him, she carried his ashes to Italy, and accused his murderer. She fell under the displeasure of Tiberius, who exiled her to the island of Pandataria, and ordered her to be starved to death. She died in the place of her exile, A.D. 33, aged 46, leaving nine children. *Tac. Ann.* 1. c. 2. &c. —*Suet. in Tib.* 52. [Of the several fine statues which remain of Agrippina, the best is that in the Capitol at Rome, where there is also a fine bust of her.]

AGRIPPI'NA JU'LIA, daughter of Germanicus and Agrippina, married Cneus Domitius Ænobarbus, by whom she had Nero. After her husband's death, she married her uncle the emperor Claudius, whom she destroyed, to make Nero succeed to the throne. After many cruelties and much licentiousness, she was assassinated by order of her son. She left memoirs, which assisted Tacitus in the composition of his annals. The town which she built on the borders of the Rhine, where she was born, and which she called *Agrippina Colonia*, is the modern Cologne. *Tac. Ann.* 4. c. 75. 1. 12. c. 7. 22. &c. [There is a fine bust of her in the museum of the Capitol at Rome.]

AGRIP'PUS MEM'PHIS, a player, brought from Syria by the emperor Verus.

A'GRIS or AGRI'SA, a city of Carmania. *Ptol.*—*Steph.*

AGRIS'IUS. *Vid.* Acrisius.

AGRIS'OPE, the mother of Cadmus. *Hygin.* fab. 6.

A'GRIUS, son of Parthaon, drove his brother Œneus from the throne. He was afterwards expelled by Diomedes, the grandson of Œneus, upon which he killed himself. *Hygin.* fab. 175. & 242.—*Apollod.* 1. c. 7.—*Homer. Il.* 14. v. 117. *Anton.* lib. 37.—*Tzetzes in Lycoph.*—*Ovid. Her.* 9. v. 153.——A son of Ulysses by Circe. *Hesiod. Theog.* v. 1013. ——A centaur killed by Hercules. *Apollod.* 2. c. 5.——The father of Thersites. *Ovid. ex Pont.* 3. el. 9. v. 9.——One of Actæon's dogs. *Hygin.* fab. 181.——A giant.

AGROE'TAS, a writer on Scythian affairs, mentioned by the *Scholiast* on *Apollonius*, 1. 2, and by *Stephanus in voc.* "Αμπελος.

AG'ROLAS and HYBER'BIUS surrounded the citadel of Athens with walls, except that part which was afterwards repaired by Cimon. *Paus.* 1. c. 28.

A'GRON, a king of Illyria, who, after conquering the Ætolians, drank to such excess that he died instantly, B.C. 231. *Polyb.* 2. c. 4.

A'GRON or AR'GON, a son of Ninus, was the first of the Heraclidæ who reigned at Sardis. *Herod.* 1. c. 7.—*Cœl. Rhod.* 23. c. 5.

A'GRON, a celebrated physician, who, by lighting fires, banished the plague from Athens. *Cœl. Rhod.* 24. c. 22.

AGROS'PI, a people of Upper Æthiopia, on the banks of the Nile. *Plin.* 6. c. 30.

AGRO'SUS, a mountain on which Rome now stands. Faunus, being driven from Arcadia by Evander, retired thither, and called it Palatinus.

AGRO'TAS, a Greek orator of Marseilles.

AGROT'ERA, a sacrifice of goats offered to Diana, yearly at Athens. It was instituted by Callimachus the polemarch, who vowed to sacrifice to the goddess as many goats, as there should be enemies killed in a battle which he was going to fight against the troops of Darius, who had invaded Attica. The quantity of slain was so great, that a sufficient number of goats could not be procured; they were, therefore, limited to 500 every year, till they equalled the number of Persians slain in battle. *Cœl. Rhod.* 20. c—*Xenoph. in Cyrop.* Under this name the goddess had a temple at Ægira in Peloponnesus, *Paus.* 7. c. 26.

AGUBE'NI, a nation of Arabia Deserta, *Ptol.*

AGUILLO'NIUM, now Aiguillon, a town of Aquitania on the Garumna.

AGUNTUM, a town of Sicily. *Ptol.*——A town of Noricum, now Inneken or Doblach.

AGU'TI or **AGI'TA**, an island between Sicily and Africa. *Antonin.*

AGY'IEUS, (from ἀγυιὰ, a street,) a surname of Apollo, because sacrifices were offered to him in the public streets of Athens. *Horat.* 4. od. 6.——An Hyperborean, who in the company of Pegasus visited Phocis, and laid the foundations of the temple of Apollo at Delphi, from which circumstance the god received the name of the founder. *Paus.* 10. c. 5.

AGYL'LA, a town of Etruria, at the west of the Tiber, founded by a colony of Pelasgians, and governed by Mezentius when Æneas came to Italy. It was called Cære by the Lydians, who took possession of it. *Vid.* Cære.—*Virg. Æn.* 7. v. 652. l. 8. v. 479.

AGYLLÆ'US, a gigantic wrestler of Cleonæ, scarcely inferior in strength to Hercules. *Ovid Met.* 5. v. 148.—*Stat. Theb.* 6. v. 837.—*Lactant. in Theb.*

AGY'RIS, a tyrant of Sicily assisted by Dionysius against the Carthaginians. *Diod.* 14.——A king of Cyprus, and an ally of the Persians, slain by Evagoras. *Diod. Sic.* l. 14.

AGYR'IUM, now Agirone, a town of Sicily, on the banks of the river Simethus, where Diodorus the historian was born. The inhabitants were called Agyrinenses or Agyrini. *Diod.* 14.—*Cic. in Verr.* 2. c. 65.—*Plin.* 3. 8.

AGYR'IUS, an Athenian general, who succeeded Thrasybulus. *Diod.* 14.

AGYR'TES, a man who killed his father. *Ovid. Met.* 5. v. 148.——A piper. *Sil.* 2. *Ach.* v. 50.

AHA'LA, the surname of the family of the Servilii, at Rome.

AHAR'NA a town of Etruria. *Liv.* 10. c. 25.

AHENOBAR'BUS, *Vid.* Ænobarbus.

A'JAS, a mountain of Ægypt, near the Arabian Gulph. *Ptol.*

A'JAX, son of Telamon, was, next to Achilles, the bravest of all the Greeks at the Trojan war. He engaged in combat with Hector, with whom, at parting, he exchanged arms. After the death of Achilles, Ajax and Ulysses both urged their claim to the arms of the dead hero, but Ulysses prevailed, and obtained the prize. Ajax in his rage slaughtered a whole flock of sheep, supposing them to be the sons of Atreus, and then stabbed himself with his sword. The blood which flowed from the wound was changed into the flower hyacinth. Some say that he was killed by Paris; others, by Ulysses. His body was buried at Sigæum, some say on mount Rhætus; and his tomb was visited by Alexander, some ages after. He was vulnerable in the neck only, according to Homer; and accordingly, at the games in honour of Patroclus, Diomedes directed all his blows towards that part.—*Q. Calab.* 1. & 4 *Apollod.* 3. c. 10. & 13.—*Philostr. in Heroic.* c. 12 —*Pind. Isthm.* 6.—*Homer Il.* l. &c. *Odyss.* 11, *Dictys. Cret.* 5.—*Dares. Phryg* 9.—*Ovid Met.* 13. *Horat.* 2. sat. 3. v. 197.—*Hygin* fab. 107. & 242.—*Paus.* 1. c. 35. l. 5. c. 19.—*Herod.* 5. c. 66. l. 8. 64. l. 7. 121.

A'JAX, the son of Oileus king of Locris, was surnamed Locrian. As one of Helen's suitors, he went to the Trojan war with forty ships, at the head of the inhabitants of Opus, Scarphia, Bessa, Thronium, and the other towns of Locris. He here distingushed himself by his intrepidity, and shared the toils and the dangers of the Telamonian Ajax. The night that Troy was taken he offered violence to Cassandra, in Minerva's temple. Agamemnon, however, rescued her from his hands; and though Ulysses excited the Greeks to stone him, he escaped, and set sail for Locris. Minerva, however, resented the insult offered to her temple; the fleet of the unhappy Ajax was dispersed, and his ship set on fire. He, however, swam to a rock, and might have been preserved, had he not impiously defied the power of the offended divinities. Neptune upon this struck the rock with his trident, and the hero was precipitated into the sea, where he perished. His body was afterwards found, and the Greeks honoured his remains with funeral obsequies, and offered black sheep on his tomb The Locrians also honoured his memory with similar sacrifices; and, in compliment to his valor, their generals afterwards, in the field of battle, left a vacant space, as if to be filled by the manes of their departed hero. *Apollod.* 3. c. 21.—*Quint. Smyrn.* 4. v. 206. l. 11. v. 440.—*Servius in Virg. Æn.* 1. v. 45. l. 2. v. 414.—*Lycoph. in Cass.*—*Q. Calab.* 13. & 14.—*Conon. Narat.* 18.—*Virg. Æn.* 1. v. 43. &c.—*Homer. Il.* 2. 13. &c. *Odyss.* 4.—*Hygin.* fab. 116. & 273.—*Philostr. Icon.* 2. c. 13.—*Senec. in Agam.*—*Horat.* epod. 10. v. 13.—*Paus.* 10. c. 26. & 31. The two Ajaces were, as some suppose, placed after death in the island of Leuce, a place preserved only for the bravest heroes of antiquity.

A'JAX, a river in Magna Græcia, mentioned by *Lycophron;* it is, however, probably the river Æas to which he alludes.

AIDO'NEUS, a surname of Pluto.——A king of the Molossi, who imprisoned Theseus, because he and Pirithous offered violence to his daughter Proserpine, near the Acheron; whence arose the well known fable of the descent of Theseus and Pirithous into hell. *Plut. in Thes.*

AIDO'NEUS, a river of Phrygia. *Paus.* 10. c. 12.

A'JI, a people of India within the Ganges. *Ptol.*

AIM'YLUS, son of Ascanius, was, according to some, the progenitor of the noble family of the Æmilii at Rome.

A'IUS LOCU'TIUS, a deity at Rome, so called because a voice more than human, issuing from above Vesta's temple, pronounced, *aiebat*, that Rome would be attacked by the Gauls. Camillus, after the conquest of the Aauls, built a temple to that supernatural voice, under the name of Aius Locutius. This divinity is ridiculed by Cicero. *Liv.* 5. c. 32. & 50. *Cic. de D.* 1. c. 45. l. 2. c. 32.—*Plut. in Camil.* & *De Fort. Rom.*—*A. Gell.* 16. c. 17.

AL'ABA, a city of Hispania Citerior. *Plin.* 3, c. 3. ——A region of Spain, now Alava; the people are called Alabenses.——An island near Taprobane. *Ptol.*

ALABA'GIUM, a promontory of Carmania. *Id.*

ALABA'NA, a town of Arabia Felix. *Id.*

ALABAN'DA, *æ*, or *orum*, a town about the middle of Caria. The name was derived from Alabandus the founder, who was worshipped by the inhabitants as a god. Their voluptuousness was remarkable. *Cic. de N. D.* 3. c. 15. & 19. *Ad fam.* 13. ep. 56. & 64.—*Juv.* 3. v. 70.—*Strab.* 14—*Plin.* 37. c. 7.—*Herodot.* 7. c. 195.—*Cluv.* 5. c. 18.

ALABAN'DUS. *Vid.* Alabanda.

ALABAS'TRUM, a town of Ægypt, near which alabaster was found. *Plin.* 36. c. 7. l. 37. c. 10.

ALABAS'TRUS, a river of Troas, rising in mount Ida. *Id.* 5. c. 30.

AL'ABON, a city and river mentioned by *Stephanus;* where it was situated does not appear, but it was probably the same as Alabus.

ALABO'NA, a city of Spain near Cæsar Augusta. *Antonin.*

ALABU'RIUM, a city of Syria. *Steph.*

AL'ABUS or AL'ABIS, a small river of Sicily. *Ptol.*—*Diod. Sic.* 4.

ALACH'ROÆ, a people of Africa, called also Lotophagi. *Plin.* 5. c. 4.

ALÆ'A or ALEÆ'A, an epithet of Minerva in Peloponnesus. This name was also given to her festivals. *Paus.* 8. c. 4. 7.

A'LÆ ÆXON'IDES, a place of Attica, near Æxon: it belonged to the tribe Cecropis.

A'LÆ ARAPHEN'IDES, also a place of Attica, in the tribe Ægeis. Here was a temple and statue of Diana Taurica, mentioned by *Euripides* and *Callimachus.*

ALAÆ'I, small islands in the Arabian Gulph, abounding with tortoises. *Arrian. Peripl.*

ALÆ'SA, ALE'SA, or HALE'SA, a city of Sicily, at the mouth of the river Alæsus. *Plin.* 3. c. 8.—*Ptol.*—*Strab.*

ALÆ'US, the father of Auge, who married Hercules.

ALAGO'NIA, a city of Laconia. *Paus.* 3. c. 21. & 26.

ALA'LA, the goddess of war, sister to Mars. *Plut. de fratern. amor.*

ALALCOM'ENÆ, a city of Bœotia, near Coronea. Minerva had a temple there, whence she was called Αλαλκομενηις. The city received its name from Alalcomenes, the foster-father of Minerva. *Strab.* 9.—*Plut. Quæst. Gr.*—*Stat. Theb.* 7. v. 330.—*Homer. Il.* 4. &c.

ALALCOME'NIA, a daughter of Ogyges and Thebe, to whom the people of Haliartus in Bœotia, raised a temple after death, and paid divine honors. She was sometimes called Praxidice; and, according to *Suidas* the heads of animals were her most acceptable sacrifice. *Paus.* 9. c. 19. 33. & 39.

ALA'LIA, a town of Corsica, built by a colony of Phocæans, destroyed by Scipio, 262 B.C., and afterwards rebuilt by Sylla. *Herodot.* 1. c. 165.—*Flor.* 2. c. 2.

ALA'LIS, a city of Palmyrene, near the Euphrates. *Ptol.*

ALAMA'NES, a statuary of Athens, pupil of Phidias. *Plut.*

ALAMAN'NI. *Vid.* Alemanni.

ALAMA'TA, a city of Palmyrene, near the Euphrates. *Ptol.*

AL'AMUS, a town of Albania. *Id.*

ALA'NA, a city of Upper Æthiopia. *Plin.* 6. c. 29.

ALAN'DER, a river of Phrygia. *Liv.* 38. c. 18.

ALA'NI, a people of Sarmatia, near the Palus Mæotis, who inhabited the country now called Lithuania. *Plin.* 4. c. 12.—*Claudian. Ruf.* 1. v. 314.—*Joseph. B. J.* 7. c. 29.

ALANOR'SI. *Vid.* Agathyrsi.

ALA'NUS, a river of Scythia.——A mountain of Sarmatia. *Steph.*

ALAPE'NI, a people of Arabia Felix. *Ptol.*

ALAP'TA, (*plural,*) a place of Thrace.

ALAPUN'TIS, a city of Gallia Narbonensis, now Talart. *Antonin.*

AL'ARES, a people of Pannonia. *Tac. Ann.* 15. c. 10. Probably the name of soldiers, from *ala.*

ALARI'CUS, a famous king of the Goths, who plundered Rome in the reign of Honorius, and during his reign kept the Roman empire in continual alarm. He died, after a reign of thirteen years, A.D. 410. The body of Alaric was buried in the midst of the river Vasento, in Calabria, the waters of which had been previously drained into a different channel, and with it were deposited the spoils of plundered nations. After the river had been restored to its usual current, all those who had been employed in digging the grave were most inhumanly butchered. *Zosim.* 5.—*Claudian apud Sig.*—*Jornand.*—*Oros.*—*Prudent.*—*Petav. rat. temp.* 2.——The 10th king of the Visi-Goths, succeeded Euricus. He also took Rome, but was treacherously slain after a reign of 23 years. *Gregor. Turon.* 2. c. 35. &c.

ALARO'DII, a nation near Pontus. *Herodot.* 3. c. 94.

AL'ARUS, a river of Hyrcania, falling into the Caspian sea.

A'LAS, a region of Attica, near the Carystian rocks. *Euripid.*

ALASAR'NA, a people of Coos. *Hesych.*

AL'ASI, a town in the interior of Africa, taken by Corn. Balbus.

ALAS'TIGI or ALOS'TIGI, a people of Spain. *Plin.* 3. c. 1.

ALAS'TOR, a son of Neleus and Chloris. *Apollod.* 1. c. 9.——An arm-bearer of Sarpedon, king of Lycia, killed by Ulysses. *Homer. Il.* 5. v. 677. *Ovid. Met.* 13. v. 257.——One of Pluto's horses when he took away Proserpine. *Claudian de rapt Pros.* 1. v. 286. The name Alastores was frequently applied by the Greeks to those genii or dæmons whose machinations proved so mischievous to mankind. *Athen.* 12. c. 10.—*Plut. in Cic.*

ALA'TA, a city of Arabia Felix.——A city of Arabia Deserta. *Ptol.*

ALA'TA CAS'TRA, a military station in Britain, supposed to be the modern Edinburgh.

ALA'TIUM, or ELA'TUM, a town in the Hierapolis, near Emesa. *Hermol. in Plin.* 5. c. 23.

ALA'TRIUM or ALETRIUM, now Alatri, a city of the Hernici. The inhabitants are called Alatrinates by *Livy,* 9. c. 42; Aletrinates by *Pliny,* 3. c. 5. *Cluver.* 3. c. 27.

ALAU'DÆ, soldiers of one of Cæsar's legions in Gaul. *Suet. in Jul.* 24.

ALAU'NE or ALAU'NIA, a town of Britain. According to *Camden,* it was near Stirling.

ALAU'NI, a nation of Noricum, now part of Stiria.——A nation of Sarmatia, now Volhinia. *Ptol.*

ALAU'NIUM, a city of Gallia Narbonensis. *Antonin.*

ALAU'NIUS, a river of the Durotriges, in Britain, suppose by *Ortelius* to be the Avon, and called by *Ptolemy* Halænus.

ALAU'NUS, now Alne, a river of Northumberland.——A mountain of European Sarmatia. *Ptol.*

ALAVO'NA, now Alagon, a town of the Vascones in Spain. *Id.*

ALA'ZIR, a king of the Barcæi. *Herod.* 4. c. 164.

ALA'ZON, a river flowing from mount Caucasus into the Cyrus, and separating Albania from Iberia. *Flacc.* 6. v. 101.

ALAZO'NES, a people of Scythia. *Herod.* 4. c. 17. &52.

AL'BA SYL'VIUS, son of Latinus Sylvius, succeeded his father in the kingdom of Latium, and reigned 36 years. *Ovid. Met.* 14. v. 612.

AL'BA AUGUS'TA, a town of Gallia Narbonensis, now, probably, Viviers.

AL'BA HELVIO'RUM, now Alby, a town of Gaul on the Rhone. *Cluver.* 3. c. 9.

AL'BA JU'LIA, a town of Dacia, so called from Julia Augusta, mother of the emperor M. Aurelius. It is now Weissenburg. *Id.* 4. c. 18.

AL'BA LON'GA, a city of Latium, built by Ascanius B.C. 1152, was called Longa because it extended *along* the hill Albanus. The descendants of Æneas reigned there in the following order: 1. Ascanius, son of Æneas, eight years. 2. Sylvius Posthumus, twenty-nine. 3. Æneas Sylvius, thirty-one. 4. Latinus, fifty-one. 5. Alba, thirty-nine. 6. Atys, or Capetus, twenty-six. 7. Capys, twenty-eight. 8. Calpetus, thirteen. 9. Tyberinus, eight. 10. Agrippa, thirty-three. 11. Alladius, or Remulus, nineteen. 12. Aventinus, thirty-seven, 13. Procas, thirteen. 14. Numitor and Amulius. Ovid, Dionysius of Halicarnassus, and Livy, differ, however, in their accounts of the succession of these kings. Alba, which had long been the powerful rival of Rome, was destroyed by the Romans, 665 B.C. The inhabitants were carried away by the conquerors, and incorporated with the citizens of Rome, *Tibull.* 2. el. 5. v. 50.—*Liv.* 1. c. 3.—*Strab.* 5.—*Euseb. Chron.*—*Dion. Hal.* 1. *Ovid. Met.* 14. *Fast.* 4.—*Plin.* 3. c. 12 —*Juv.* 12. v. 72. *Varro. de R. R.* 2. c. 4.—*Cic. de Div.* 1. c. 44.

AL'BA, a city of the Marsi in Italy, of which the inhabitants were called Albenses, to distinguish them from the people of Alba Longa, called Albani.

AL'BA POMPE'IA, a town of Liguria, on the Tanarus, one of the branches of the Po. *Cluver.* 3. c. 24.

AL'BA REGA'LIS, a town of Hungary, now Stuelweissenburg. *Cluver.* 4. c. 2

AL'BA VIRGAONEN'SIS, a town of Hispania Bætica. *Plin.* 3. c. 1. There were also several small rivers called Alba.

AL'BACE, a place of Heraclea, in Caria. *Suidas in Diogenianus.*

AL'BÆ COLUM'NÆ, a place near the river Marsyas. *Herod.* 5. 118.

ALBAM'ALA, a city of Gaul, now Aumale, in Normandy.

ALBAMAR'LA, town of Gaul, probably so called from a kind of white earth called *marna* by *Pliny,* 17. c. 6. and *marga* by others.

ALBA'NA, a city, the emporium of Albania on the Caspian sea, now Bachu.——A city of Arabia Felix. *Ptol.*

ALBANEN'SES, a people of Spain. *Id.*

ALBA'NI, and ALBEN'SES, names, the former of which were applied to the inhabitants of Alba Longa, the latter to the inhabitants of Alba, a town of the Marsi. *Vid.* Alba. *Cic. ad Her.* 2. c. 28.

ALBA'NIA, a country of Asia, between the Caspian Sea and Iberia. The inhabitants were said to have their eyes all blue, and the country received its name from the whiteness of their hair. *Solin.* 25. Some assert that they followed Hercules from mount Albanus in Italy, when he returned from the conquest of Geryon. *Dion. Hal.* 1. c. 15.—*Justin.* 42. c. 3.—*Strab.* 11.—*Plin.* 8. c. 40.—*Mela,* 3. c. 5. The Caspian Sea is called Albanum, as being near Albania. *Plin.* 6. c. 13.

ALBA'NIÆ PORT'Æ, a name given to the defiles which open a communication with Albania, across Caucasus. *Flacc.* 3. v. 497.

ALBANOP'OLIS, an inland city of Macedonia.

ALBA'NUM, now Albano, a small town of Latium.——A city of Asia in Armenia Major.

ALBA'NUS, a mountain near Alba, 16 miles from Rome, where the *Latinæ feriæ* were celebrated. The Alban lake was at the foot of the mountain, and was about seven or eight miles in circumference. The neighbourhood was embellished with villas of opulent Romans. *Horat.* 2. ep. 1. v. 27. —*Propert.* 3. el. 21.——A mountain of Upper Pannonia, called Albius by *Strabo:* now Auff der Alben.——A river of Albania in Asia, flowing into the Caspian Sea.

AL'BARA, a city of Syria.

AL'BE, a city of Crete. *Steph.*

AL'BIA TEREN'TIA, the mother of Otho. *Suet.*

ALBI'CI, a people of Aquitania. *Cæsar* places them in Gallia Narbonensis, above Massilia. *Bell. Civ.* 1. c. 34. Also written Al'bici.

ALBID'IUS, a person who spent all his fortune in luxurious living. *Macrob. Sat.* 2. c. 2.

ALBIE'TÆ, a people of Latium. *Dion. Hal.* 8.

ALBI'GA, a very ancient city of Gaul, now Alby. It is called Alba Julia by *Ptolemy*. *Cæs. B. C.* 1. c. 15.

ALBIMA'NA, or ALBINIA'NA, now Alphen, a small town of Holland. *Antonin.*

ALBI'NA, a noble matron, mother of Marcellus, and disciple of St. Jerome. *Hieron. præf. in epist. ad Galat.*

ALBINGAU'NUM, a town of Liguria, now Albenga. *Mela.* 2. c. 4.

ALBINOVA'NUS CEL'SUS. *Vid.* Celsus.

Albinova'nus Pe'do, a poet contemporary with Ovid. He wrote elegies, epigrams, and heroic poetry in a style so elegant that he merited the epithet of divine. Martial, however, censures him for the indelicacy of some of his expressions. His elegy on the death of Drusus is the only one which has escaped the ravages of time, though Scaliger wishes to ascribe an elegy on the death of Mecænas to him. *Senec. Suas.* 1. ep. 122.—*Mart.* 2. epigr. 77. l. 5. epigr. 5.—*Ovid. ex Pont.* 4. ep. 10.—*Quintil.* 10. c. 5.—*Harles. Lit. Rom.*

ALBINTEME'LIUM, or AL'BIUM INTEME'LIUM, a town of Liguria, at the mouth of the Rutuba. *Tac. Hist.* 2. c. 13.—*Cluver.* 3. c. 24.

ALBI'NUS, was born at Adrumetum in Africa, and made governor of Britain by Commodus. After the murder of Pertinax, he was elected emperor by the soldiers in Britain. Severus had also been invested with the imperial dignity by his own army; and these two rivals, with about 50,000 men each, came into Gaul to decide the fate of the empire. Severus was conqueror, and he ordered the head of Albinus to be cut off, and his body to be thrown into the Rhone, A.D. 198.——A prætorian sent by the senate as ambassador to Sylla, during the civil wars. He was put to death by Sylla's soldiers. *Plut. in Syll.*——A plebeian who received the vestals into his chariot in preference to his own family, when they fled from Rome, which the Gauls had sacked. *Val. Max.* 1. c. 1.—*Liv.* 5. c. 40.—*Flor.* 1. c. 13.——A Platonic philosopher, contemporary with Galen. *Sax. Onom.* 1. p. 317. *Fabr. B. Gr.* 3. p. 157.——A præfect of Judæa. *Joseph. J. A.* 2. c. 8.——A Latin poet who wrote annals of Rome in verse. *Voss. de poet. Lat.* c. 1.——Two orators of this name are commended by *Cicero, in Brut.*——A usurer. *Horat.* The name was common among the tribunes and military officers. *Sallust. Jug.* 35.—*Liv.* 2. c. 33. l. 6. c. 40.—*Cic. Brut.* 21. & 25.

Albi'nus A. Posthumus, consul with Lucullus, A.U.C. 603, wrote a history of Rome in Greek. *A. Gell.* 11. c. 8.

AL'BION, a son of Neptune by Amphitrite, is said to have established the kingdom of Britain. He was killed by Jupiter because he opposed the passage of Hercules over the Rhone. *Mela,* 2. c. 7.——The greatest island of Europe, now called Great Britain. It was so named after Albion, or from its chalky white cliffs, which exhibit a remarkable appearance at a distance. *Plin.* 4. c. 16.—*Tac. in Agric.*

AL'BIS, a large river in Germany, falling into the German Ocean near Hamburgh. It is now the Elbe. *Lucan.* 2. v. 52.—*Mela,* 3. c. 3.—*Cluver.* 3. c. 5.

ALBIS'TRUM, an inland town of the Brutii, at the foot of the Apennines. It is now Ursomarso.

AL'BIUS, the father of a noted spendthrift. *Horat.* 1. sat. 4.——A name of the poet Tibullus. *Id.* 1. od. 33. v. 1.

ALBUCEL'LA, a city of the Vaccæi, in Hispania Tarraconensis. It is called Arbocala by *Livy,* 21. c. 5.—*Ptol.*

ALBOCEN'TII, a people of Dacia. *Ptol.*

ALBONEN'SES, a people of Illyricum. *Plin.* 3. c. 21.

ALBON'ICA, a city of Spain, between Liminium and Cæsar Augusta. *Antonin.*

ALBO'TI, a people of Macedonia. *Ptol.*

ALBUCIL'LA, an immodest and infamous woman. *Tac. Ann.* 6. c. 47.

AL'BULA, the ancient name of the river Tiber. *Virg. Æn.* 8. v. 332.—*Liv.* 1. c. 3.——A river of Picenum, flowing into the Adriatic. It is called Albulates by *Pliny,* 3. c. 13. and is now Liberata.——A stream in the country near Tibur, the waters of which were said by *Strabo* to cure wounds. *Mart.* 1. epigr. 13.

AL'BUM, a promontory of Africa. *Plin.* 3. *in. proœm.*——A promontory of Phœnicia, not far from Tyre. *Id.* 5. c. 19.

ALBU'NEA, a divinity worshipped in a grove near Tibur, thought by some to be Ino, wife of Athamas. By *Pliny,* 31. c. 2., and others, she is supposed to have been a nymph presiding over the waters of the place; and by others she is called a Sybil. *Ovid. Met.* 4. fab. 13.—*Paus.* 1.—*Lactant.* 1. c. 6. &c.——A wood near Tibur, sacred to the Muses, or, according to some, to Leucothoe, the Mantuta of the Latins. There was near it a small lake of the same name, the waters of which emitted a sulphureous smell, and possessed some medicinal properties. *Horat.* 1. od. 7. v. 12.—*Virg. Æn.* 7. v. 83.—*Tibul.* 2. el. 5. v. 69.—*Lactant.* 1. c. 6.—*Turneb.* 11. c. 26.——A river of Italy flowing into the Po. It is now Albona.

ALBU'BACIS, a river of Gallia Narbonensis, now l'Ariege.

ALBUR'NUS, now Alborna, a lofty mountain of Lucania, in which the Tanager rises. *Virg. G.* 3. v. 147. A god of the same name was worshipped here. *Tertull. adv. Gent.*——A celebrated pleader. *Senec.*

AL'BUS PA'GUS, a place near Sidon, where Antony awaited the arrival of Cleopatra. *Plut.*——A place on the Arabian Gulph. *Arrian in Peripl.*

ALBU'TIUS, a prince of Celtiberia, to whom Scipio restored his wife.——A sordid man, father of Canidia. He beat his servants before they were guilty of any offence, "lest," said he, "I should have no time to punish them when they offend." *Horat.* 2. sat. 2.——A rhetorician in the age of Seneca. *Suet. de illust. Rhet.* c. 6.

Albu'tius Syl'vius, the 5th king of Latium, who reigned 39 years. *Dion. Hal.* 1. c. 8.

Albu'tius Ti'tus, an Epicurean philosopher, made governor of Sardinia; but he grew offensive to the senate and was banished. *Varro* says that he wrote satires after the manner of Lucilius, and it is supposed that he died at Athens. *Cic. Tusc.* 5. c. 37.—*De Fin.* 1. c. 3.

ALCÆ'US, a celebrated lyric poet of Mitylene in Lesbus, florished about 600 B.C. He was the inventor of Alcaic verses, and was contemporary with the famous Sappho, to whom he paid his addresses. Of all his works, only a few fragments remain, which are to be found in Athenæus and others; but the eulogium which *Quintilian,* 10. c. 1. passes on him, sufficiently proves the loss which the world has sustained. *Herodot.* 5. c. 95.—*Horat.* 2. od. 13. l. 4. od. 9.—*Cic. Tusc.* 4. c. 33.—*Sax. Onom.* 1. p. 17.—*Fabr. B. Gr.* 2. p. 84.——A writer of the ancient comedy, who, according to *Suidas,* left ten plays, and contended with Aristophanes. *Athen.* &c.——A son of Androgeus, who went with Hercules into Thrace, and was made king of that part of the country. *Apollod.* 2. c. 5.——A son of Perseus and Andromeda, father of Amphitryon. Hercules was called Alcides from him. *Apollod.* 2. c. 4.—*Paus.* 8. c. 14.——A Lydian, grandson of Hercules, and father of Argon, the founder of the dynasty of the Heraclidæ. *Herod.* 1. c. 7.——A dissolute character mentioned by *Ælian, Var. Hist.* l. 9. c. 12.

ALCAM'ENES, one of the Agidæ, king of Sparta, celebrated for his apophthegms. He succeeded his father Teleclus, and reigned 37 years. The Helotæ rebelled in his reign. *Paus.* 3. c. 2. l. 4. c. 4. & 5. *Plut. in Apoph. Lac.* c. 32. &c.——A general of the Achæans. *Paus.* 7. c. 15.——A statuary who lived 448 B.C. and was distinguished for his beautiful statues of Venus and Vulcan. *Id.* 1. c. 19. &c.—*Quintil.* 1. c. 10.—*Plin.* 34. c. 8.——The commander of a Spartan fleet, put to death by the Athenians. *Thucyd.* 4. c. 5. & 8. c. 10.

ALCAN'DER, an attendant of Sarpedon, killed by Ulysses. *Ovid Met.* 13. v. 257.——A Lacedæmonian youth, who accidentally put out one of the eyes of Lycurgus, and was generously forgiven by him. *Plut. in Lycoph.*—*Paus.* 3. c. 18.——A Trojan killed by Turnus.—*Virg. Æn.* 9. v. 767.——A writer mentioned by Clemens Alexandrinus. *Voss. de poet. Gr.* 85.

ALCAN'DRE, the wife of Polybius, a rich native of Egyptian Thebes. *Homer. Odys.* 4. v. 126.

ALCA'NOR, a Trojan of Mount Ida, whose sons, Pandarus and Bitias followed Æneas into Italy. *Virg. Æn.* 9. v. 672.——A son of Phorus killed by Æneas. *Id.* 10. v. 338.

ALCATHE'A, the mother of Pausanias, and wife of Cleombrotus, king of Sparta. *Schol. in Aristoph. Equit.*

ALCATH'OE, a name of Megara in Attica, because rebuilt by Alcathous, son of Pelops, who reigned there. *Ovid. Met.* 7. v. 443. l. 8. v. 8. *De Art. A.* 2. v. 421. Also written Alcith'oe.

ALCATH'OUS, a son of Pelops, who being suspected of murdering his brother Chrysippus, came to Megara, when this country was ravaged by a fierce lion, to the destroyer of which Megareus the king offered his crown and daughter. Alcathous was victorious, and, in acknowledgement of his victory, raised a temple to Apollo and Diana, under the names of Agroæus and Agrotera. It was said that he was assisted by Apollo in rebuilding Megara. Festivals, called Alcathoïa, were instituted at Megara in his honor. *Paus.* 1. c. 41. & 42.—*Plut. in Parall.* 27.—*Apollod.* 3. c. 25.——The father of Automedusa, the first wife of Iphicles, king of Phylace, in Phthiotis. *Apollod.* 2. c. 13.——A Trojan, who married Hippodamia, daughter of Anchises. He was killed in the Trojan war by Idomeneus. *Homer. Il.* 12. v. 93.——A son of Parthaon, killed by Tydeus. *Apollod.* 1. c. 7. &c.——A friend of Æneas, killed in the Rutulian war. *Virg. Æn.* 10. v. 747.

AL'CE, a town of Spain, which surrendered to Gracchus. It is now called Alcazar, and is situated near the springs of the Tagus, a little above Toledo. *Liv.* 40. c. 47.——One of Actæon's dogs. *Ovid Met.* 3. fab. 2.

ALCE'NOR, an Argive, who alone, with the exception of Chromius, survived a battle fought between 300 of his countrymen and 300 Spartans. *Herodot.* 1. c. 82.

AL'CES, a river of Bithynia. *Plin.* 5. c. *ult.*

ALCES'TE, or ALCES'TIS, daughter of Pelias, and wife of Admetus, laid down her life for her husband, when she had been told by an oracle that he could never recover from a disease, except some one of his friends died in his stead. According to some authors, Hercules brought her back from hell. She had many suitors while she lived with her father. *Vid.* Admetus. *Juv.* 6. v. 651.—*Apollod.* 1. c. 9.—*Paus.* 5. c. 17. *Hygin.* fab. 50. 51. 251. —*Eurip. in Alcest.*—*Ovid. Met.* 7. fab. 3. & 4. *Heroid.* 12.—*Servius in Virg. Ecl.* 5. v. 35. *G.* 3. v. 1. *Æn.* 6. v. 398.—*Tzetzes in Lycoph.*—*Fulgent.* 1. *Myth.* 27.—*Palæph. de Incred.* 41.

AL'CETAS, a king of the Molossi, descended from Pyrrhus, the son of Achilles, expelled from his kingdom, but reinstated by the aid of Dionysius. *Diod. Sic.* 15.—*Paus.* 1 c. 11.——A king of the Epirotæ, banished by his father Arymbas, for his passionate disposition, and afterwards slain by his subjects. *Paus. in Phoc.*——A general of Alexander's army, brother to Perdiccas. *Suidas.*——The eighth king of Macedonia, who reigned 39 years. ——An historian who wrote an account of every thing that had been dedicated in the temple of Delphi. *Athen.* 1. 13.

AL'CHIDAS, a Rhodian, who became enamoured of a Cupid sculptured by Praxiteles. *Plin.* 36. c. 5.

ALCHIM'ACHUS, a celebrated painter. *Id.* 35. c. 11.

ALCHI'ONE, a mountain of Macedonia. *Id.* 4. c. 10.

ALCIBI'ADES, a famous Athenian general, son of Clinias, and nephew of Pericles, and lineally descended from Ajax. He was educated in the school of Socrates, whose lessons and example checked for a while his vicious propensities. In the Peloponnesian war he encouraged the Athenians to make an attack upon Syracuse; and he was chosen general in that expedition, together with Nicias and Lamachus. But the jealousy of the Athenians was excited by the virulence of his enemies; and Alcibiades, accused of ridiculing the mysteries of religion, was summoned to appear before the tribunals of his country. He, however, during the voyage from Sicily, secretly withdrew himself from the ship, and fled to Sparta. His abilities were here exerted against his country; but the Spartans became suspicious of his sincerity, and obliged him to fly for shelter to Tisaphernes, the Persian satrap. Alcibiades, however, could never forget that Athens gave him birth; he was soon reconciled to his country, and the Athenians entrusted him with the command of their fleets and armies, which he soon led to triumph over the Peloponnesians. The Persians also were defeated by Alcibiades, and he returned to Athens loadened with the spoils of Asia. Prosperity, however, was again succeeded by adversity; the failure of an expedition against the Hellespont was attributed to his perfidy, and he was deprived of the command. Upon this he fled to Pharnabazus, the Persian satrap, who was secretly instigated to murder his guest, by Lysander the Spartan general. Two servants were sent to destroy him, and they set on fire the cottage where he was, and killed him with darts as he attempted to make his escape. He died in the 46th year of his age, 404 B.C. after a life of perpetual difficulties. The reputation of Alcibiades has been cleared from the malevolent aspersions of his enemies, by the writings of Thucydides, Timæus, and Theopompus. *Plut. & C. Nep. in Alcib.*—*Thucyd.* 5. 6. & 7.—*Xenoph. Hist. Gr.* 1. &c.—*Diod.* 12. [Though Alcibiades lived at a period when the arts were in their most flourishing state, no authentic statue remains of him. There is, however, a bust in the Vatican at Rome inscribed with his name.]

ALCI'DÆ, Certain gods at Lacedæmon, according to *Hesychius.*

ALCID'AMAS, of Cos, father of Ctesilla, who was changed into a dove. *Ovid. Met.* 7. fab. 12.——A celebrated wrestler. *Stat. Theb.* 10. v. 500.——A philosopher and orator, who wrote a treatise on death. He was pupil to Gorgias, B.C. 424. Some of his orations are preserved in the collections of Aldus. *Cic. Tusc.* 1. c. 48.—*Quintil.* 3. c. 1.—*Plut. de Orat.*

ALCIDAME'A was mother of Bunus by Mercury.

ALCIDAM'IDAS, a general of the Messenians, who retired to Rhegium after the taking of Ithome by the Spartans. B.C. 723. *Strab.* 6.

ALCI'DAS, a Lacedæmonian, sent with 23 galleys against Corcyra, in the Peloponnesian war. *Thucyd.* 3. c. 16. &c.

ALCI'DES, a name of Hercules, from his strength, ἀλκή, or from his grandfather Alcæus.——A surname of Minerva, in Macedonia. *Liv.* 42. c. 51.

ALCID'ICE, the mother of Tyro by Salmoneus. *Apollod.* 1. c. 9.

ALCIM'ACHUS, a painter, whose pieces are mentioned by *Pliny*, 35. c. 11.——A man of Eretria, father of Euphorbus, whose treachery to his country is mentioned by *Pausanius*, 7. c. 10.

ALCIM'EDE, the wife of Æson, and mother of Jason. She was daughter of Phylacus by Clymene, daughter of Minyas, and sister of Iphiclus. *Apollon. Arg.* 1. & *Pherecydes apud Schol.*—*Hygin* fab. 14. —*Flacc.* 1. v. 296.

ALCIM'EDON, a plain of Arcadia, with a cave, the residence of Alcimedon. *Homer. Il.* 16. v. 197.—*Paus.* 8. c. 12.——An excellent carver, whose beautiful workmanship is extolled by *Virgil, Ecl.* 3. 36.

ALCIM'ENES, a tragic poet of Megara. *Suidas.*——A comic writer of Athens. *Suidas.*—*Athen.*——An Epirote, an attendant of Demetrius, noted for his strength and courage. *Plut. in Dem.*——A man killed by his brother Bellerophon. *Apollod.* 2. c. 3.——A Greek general mentioned by *Xenophon, Græc.* 4.——An Achæan, rendered eminent among his countrymen by his birth, and glorious actions. *Plut. in Dion.*

ALCIMOEN'NIS, a city of Germany. *Ptol.* It is supposed by some to be Ulm.

AL'CIMUS, a king of Lydia, of the dynasty of the Heraclidæ, of a meek and religious disposition. *Suidas in* Ξανθ.——An historian of Sicily, who wrote an account of Italy. *Athen.* 10.——An orator much celebrated in his day. *Diog.*——A son of Æacus king of Ægina, and brother of Teucer and Telamon. *Schol. Theocr.*

AL'CIMUS AVI'TUS, a Christian writer. *Vid.* Avitus.

ALCIN'OE, a daughter of Sthenelus, son of Perseus, and sister of Eurystheus. *Apollod.* 2. c. 4.——One of Jupiter's nurses, honoured with a statue in Minerva's temple at Tegea. *Paus. Arc.* 47.

ALCIN'OUS, son of Nausithous, king of Phæacia, married his niece Arete, by whom he had several sons and one daughter. His island was celebrated for its fertility; he administered justice with impartiality, and treated strangers hospitably. He kindly entertained Ulysses, who had been shipwrecked on his coast, and heard the recital of his adventures, whence arose the proverb of the stories of Alcinous, *Alcinoi apologus*, to denote improbability. *Homer Od.* 7. *Orph. in Argon.*—*Virg. G.* 2. v. 87.—*Stat.* 1. *Sylv.* 3. v. 81.—*Juv.* 5. v. 151.—*Ovid. Am.* 1. el. 10. v. 56.—*Plato de Rep.* 10.—*Apollod.* 1. c. 9.——A son of Hippocoon. *Apollod.* 3. c. 10.——A man of Elis, mentioned by *Pausanias.*——A philosopher in the second century, who wrote a book *De doctrina Platonis*, the best edition of which is the 12mo. printed Oxon. 1667. It was edited also by Heinsius, with Maximus Tyrius, Lug. Bat. 1607. *Sax. Onom.* 1. p. 294—*Fabr. B. Gr.* 5. p. 523.

AL'CIPHRON, a philosopher of Magnesia, in the age of Alexander. Some epistles in Greek that bear his name, are supposed by some to be the production of a writer of the fourth century. The best edition is that of Leipsic, 12mo. 1715, cum notis Bergleri. *Suidas.*—*Sax. Onom.* 1. p. 383.—*Fabr. B. Gr.* 1. p. 687.

ALCIP'PE, a daughter of the god Mars, by Agraulus, to whom Halirrhotius, son of Neptune, offered violence. The ravisher was killed by the offended father, and the murder is said to have occasioned the institution of the famous tribunal afterwards known under the name of the Areopagus. *Paus.* 1. c. 21. —*Apollod.* 3. c. 14.——The wife of Metion, and mother of Eupalamus. *Id.* 3. c. 16.——The daughter of Œnomaus, and wife of Evenus, by whom she had Marpessa.——A countrywoman. *Virg. Ecl.* 7.——A woman who attended Helen. *Hom. Od.* 4. v. 124.——A daughter of the giant Alcyon. *Cœl. Rhod.* 1. 14. c. 11.—*Suidas.*

ALCIP'PUS, a renowned citizen of Sparta, banished by his enemies. He married Democrite, of whom *Plutarch* speaks in *Erot.* c. 5.

AL'CIS, a daughter of Ægyptus. *Apollod.*——A name of Minerva among the Macedonians. *Liv.* 42 c. 51.——A deity worshipped by some of the German tribes. *Tac. Ger.* 43.

ALCIS'THENE, a woman celebrated for her knowledge of painting by *Pliny*, 35. c. 11.

ALCIS'THENES, a rich native of Sybaris, mentioned by *Aristotle in mirab.* Probably we should read Antisthenes.——An archon of Athens, Olymp. cii. an 1.

ALCITH'OE, a Theban woman, who ridiculed the orgies of Bacchus. She was changed into a bat, and the spindle and yarn with which she worked, into a vine and ivy. *Ovid Met.* 4 fab. 1.

ALCMÆ'ON, was son of the prophet Amphiaraus and Eriphyle. He murdered his mother, for which crime the furies persecuted him, till Phlegeus purified him, and gave him his daughter Alphesibœa in marriage. Alcmæon afterwards divorced her, and married Calirhoe, the daughter of Achelous. He was at length put to death by Alphesibœa's brothers, on account of the infamous manner he had treated their sister. *Vid.* Alphesibœa, Amphiaraus, Eriphyle. *Paus.* 5. c. 17. &c.—*Plut. de Exil.* —*Apollod.* 3. c. 7.—*Hygin.* fab. 73. & 245.—*Stat. Theb.* 2. & 4.—*Ovid. Fast.* 2. v. 44. *Met.* 9. fab. 10. ——A son of Ægyptus, the husband of Hippomedusa. *Apollod.*——A philosopher, disciple of Pythagoras, born at Crotona. He wrote on physics, and was the first who dissected animals to examine into the structure of the human frame. *Cic. de N. D.* 6. c. 27.—*Diog. Laer.* 1. 8. *in vit.*—*Clem. Strom.* 1. 1.——A son of Sillus, driven from Messenia, with the rest of Nestor's family, by the Heraclidæ. He came to Athens, and from him the Alcmæonidæ were descended. *Paus.* 1. c. 18.——A son of Megacles, sent by Crœsus to consult the oracle of Delphi. *Herodot.* 6. c. 125.——The last of the perpetual archons at Athens. He reigned 12 years. *Euseb.*

ALCMÆON'IDÆ, a noble family of Athens. They undertook for 300 talents to rebuild the temple of Delphi, which had been burnt; and they finished the work in a more splendid manner than was required, in consequence of which they gained merited popularity, and by their influence the Pythia prevailed upon the Lacedæmonians to deliver their country from the tyranny of the Pisistratidæ. *Herodot.* 5. & 6.—*Thucyd.* 6. c. 59.—*Plut. in Solon.*

ALC'MAN, an ancient lyric poet, born at Sardis, and not at Lacedæmon, as some authors suppose. He wrote in the Doric dialect, six books of verses in praise of his favorite mistress Megalostrata; he wrote also a play called Colymbosas. He flourished B.C. 670. Some fragments of his verses, nearly 60 in number, have been preserved by Athenæus, and others. *Paus.* 1. c. 41. l. 3. c. 15.—*Aristot. Hist. Anim.* 5. c. 31.—*Plin.* 11. c. 33.—*Euseb. Chron.* —*Athen.* 14.—*Ælian. V. H.* 1. c. 27, &c.—*Sax. Onom.* 1. p. 15.—*Fabr. B. Gr.* 2. p. 88.——A lyric poet of Messenia. *Voss. de poet. Gr.*—*Paus.* 3.

ALCMA'NIA, otherwise Heraclea, an inland city of Caria. *Steph.*

ALCME'NE, was daughter of Electryon, king of Argos, by Anaxo, whom Plutarch, *de Reb. Gr.* calls Lysidice and Diodorus, l. 2. Eurymede. Her father promised his crown and daughter to Amphitryon, if he would revenge the death of his sons, who had all been killed, except Licymnius, by the Teleboans, a people of Ætolia. While Amphitryon was engaged in his expedition against the Ætolians Jupiter introduced himself into Alcmena's bed, and Alcmena, in consequence, brought forth twins, Hercules, conceived by Jupiter, and Iphiclus by Amphitryon. After Amphitryon's death, Alcmena married Rhadamanthus, and retired to Ocalea in Bœotia. She is sometimes represented with three moons on her head, as a symbol of the three nights which Jupiter had spent in her company. *Pliny*, l. 35. c. 9. mentions a picture of Alcmena painted by Xeuxis. *Anton. Liber.* 83. *Hom. Schol. Od.* 11. v. 265. *Il.* 14. v. 323. l. 19.—*Ovid. Met.* 8. fab. 5 & 6.—*Antholog.* 38. c. 9.—*Euseb. in præp. Ev.* 2.—*Serv. in Virg. Æn.* 8. v. 103.—*Paus.* 1. c. 41. &c.—*Plut. in Thes. & Romul.*—*Pindar. Pyth.* 9. —*Lucian. Dial. Deor.*—*Diod.* 4.—*Hygin.* fab. 29. —*Apollod.* 2. c. 4. 7. &c.—*Plaut. in Amphit.*—*Herodot.* 2. c. 43. & 45. *Vid.* Amphitryon, Hercules, Eurystheus.

ALCOM'ENÆ, a city of Ithaca.——A city of Illyria. *Steph.*

AL'CON, a Cretan, or according to others, a son of Erechtheus, a famous archer, who one day saw his son attacked by a serpent, and aimed at it so dexterously that he killed the beast without hurting his son. *Serv.* 5.—*Ecl. Virg.*——A silversmith. *Ovid. Met.* 13. fab. 5.——A son of Hippocoon. *Paus.* 3. c. 14.——A surgeon under Claudius, who acquired opulence in his profession by his successful reduction of hernias and fractures.——A son of Mars. ——A son of Amycus. These two last were at the chase of the Calydonian boar. *Hygin.* fab. 14 & 173.——A native of Saguntum, employed by his countrymen in a fruitless embassy to Annibal, who was besieging their city. *Liv.* 21. c. 12.

ALCO'NA POMPEIA'NA, a harbour of Gallia Narbonensis. *Antonin.*

ALCYN'OE, the third priestess of Juno at Argos. *Dion. Hal.* 1

ALCY'ONE, or HALCY'ONE, daughter of Neptune, married Ceyx, who was drowned as he was going to Clarus, to consult the oracle of Apollo. When she found, on the morrow, his body washed on the shore, she threw herself into the sea, and they were both changed into birds of the same name. *Virg. G.* 1. v. 399.—*Apollod.* 1. c. 7.—*Ovid Met.* 11. fab. 10.—*Hygin.* fab. 65.——One of the Pleiades, daughter of Atlas and Plione. She was mother of the wife of Ceyx by Neptune, and changed into a constellation. *Vid.* Pleiades. *Paus.* 2. c. 30. 3. c. 18. *Apollod.* 3. c. 10.—*Hygin.* fab. 157.——The daughter of the Evenus carried away by Apollo after her marriage. Her husband pursued the ravisher, but was not able to recover her. Upon this, her parents called her Alcyone, and compared her fate to that of the wife of Ceyx. *Hom. Il.* 9. v. 558.——The wife of Meleager. *Hygin.* fab. 174.

ALCY'ONE, a town of Thessaly on the Sinus Maliacus, according to *Pliny*, 4. c. 7. Methone was built from its ruins.

ALCY'ONEUS, son of Antigonus, a youth of exemplary virtue. *Plut. in Pyrrh.*—*Diog.* 4.——A giant, brother of Porphyrion. He was killed by Hercules. His daughters, mourning his death, threw themselves into the sea, and were changed into Alcyons by Amphitrite. *Claudian. de Rapt. Pros.*—*Apollod.* 1. c. 6.

ALCYO'NIUM, a pool of immense depth, which Nero

in vain attempted to sound. *Pausanias*, l. 1. calls it *Amphiarai fons.*

ALDES'CUS, a river of European Sarmatia, rising from the Riphæan mountains, and falling into the Northern Sea. *Dion. Per.* 314.

ALDU'ABIS, *Vid.* Dubis.

A'LEA a surname of Minerva, from her temple at Tegea, built by Aleus, son of Aphidas. The statue of the goddess, made of ivory, was removed by Augustus to Rome. *Paus.* 8. c. 4. & 46.—*Stat. Theb.* 4. v. 288.—*Sylv.* 4. 6. v. 51.

A'LEA, a town of Arcadia, built by Aleus. It had three famous temples sacred to Minerva, to Bacchus, and to Diana the Ephesian. *Paus.* 8. c. 23.——A city of Thessaly.——A city of the Carpetani. *Steph.*

ALE'BAS, a tyrant of Larissa, killed by his own guards for his cruelties. *Ovid. in Ib.* 323.

ALEBECE'RII, a people of Gallia Narbonensis. *Plin.* 3. c. 4.

ALE'BION and DER'CYNUS, sons of Neptune, were killed by Hercules for stealing his oxen in Africa. *Apollod.* 2. c. 5.

ALEC'TA, a city of Gallia Narbonensis, now Alette.

ALEC'TO, one of the furies, represented armed with flaming torches, her head covered with serpents, and breathing vengeance, war, and pestilence. *Vid.* Eumenides. *Virg. Æn.* 7. v. 324, &c. l. 10. v. 41. *Claudian. ad Ruf.* 1. v. 49.

ALEC'TOR, succeeded his father Anaxagoras in the kingdom of Argos, and was father of Iphis and Capaneus. *Paus.* 2. c. 18.—*Apollod.* 3. c. 6.

ALEC'TRYON, a youth whom Mars, during his amours with Venus, stationed at the door to watch the approach of the sun. He fell asleep, and the lovers were exposed by Vulcan to the derision of all the gods. Mars was so incensed, that he changed Alectryon into a cock. *Lucian. in Alect.*

ALEC'TUS, a military præfect in the reign of Diocletian, slew Carausius, who had usurped the government of Aremorica, and was afterwards slain by Constantius Asclepiodotus. *Victor de Cæs.*

ALE'IUS CAM'PUS, a place in Lycia, where Bellerophon fell from the horse Pegasus, and wandered over the country till the time of his death. *Homer. Il.* 6. v. 201.—*Dion. Perieg.* 872.—*Ovid. in Ib.* 257.—*Herodot.* 6. c. 95.

ALEMAN'NI or ALAMAN'NI, a people of Germany, who issued from the wilds of Sarmatia upon the distant provinces of the Roman empire. The country where they settled received from them the name of Alemannia. They are first mentioned in the reign of Caracalla, who was honoured with the surname of Alemannicus, from a victory obtained over them. *Spartian in Car.*—*Claudian.* 4.—*Honor.* 449.

ALEMAN'NIA, the name of Germany in ancient times. *Vid.* Alemanni.

ALE'MON, a native of Argolis, father of Myscelus. He built Crotona. Myscelus is often called Alemonides. *Ovid. Met.* 15. v. 19 & 26.

ALEMU'SII, inhabitants of part of Attica, in whose territories there were temples dedicated to Ceres and Proserpine. *Paus. in Attic.*

A'LENS, a place in the island of Cos. *Theocr.* Also a river. *Theocr. Schol.*

A'LEO, a son of Atreus, mentioned by *Cicero, De Nat. D.* 3. c. 21.

A'LEON, a small river of Ionia, near Colophon. *Plin.* 5. c. 29. It was probably the Ales of *Pausanias*, l. 7. c. 5. &c.

ALEOPE'TRA, an island in the Mæotis.

ALE'RIA, a colony and city of Corsica. *Plin.* 3. c. 6.—*Ptol.* It was founded by Sylla, and afterwards destroyed by L. Scipio. *Florus.* 1. 2. c. 2.—*Salmas ad Solin.* p. 29.

A'LES. *Vid.* Aleon.

ALE'SA. *Vid.* Alæsa.

ALE'SIA or ALEX'IA, now Alise, a famous city of the Mandubii in Gaul, at the west of the Arar, founded by Hercules as he returned from Iberia. J. Cæsar conquered it. *Flor.* 3. c. 10.—*Cæs. B. G.* 7. c. 68.—*Vell.* 2. c. 47.

ALESI'NI, Arabians near the Persian Gulph. *Strab.*

ALE'SIUM, a town and mountain of Peloponnesus. *Paus.* 8. c. 10.—*Strab.* 8.

ALE'SIUS, one of the suitors of Hippodamia, or, according to others, a son of Gargettus.

ALE'SIUS, a town of Elis. *Steph.*——A mountain of Arcadia, not far from Mantinea. *Paus.* 1. 8.

ALES'TES, a river of Spain, now Rio di Braga.

ALE'SUS, a river of Sicily, now Pittineo.——A river of Etruria, now Sanguinaria, according to *Ortelius.*

ALE'TA, a town of Illyricum, now Mosth.——A town of Sicily, where the town of St. Mark now stands. It seems to be called Alicya by *Cicero.*

ALE'TES, a son of Ægisthus, murdered by Orestes. *Hygin.* fab. 122.

ALE'THES, son of Hippotas, the first of the Heraclidæ who was king of Corinth. His descendants reigned there for five generations, till the time of Bacchis, son of Prumnis. *Paus.* 2. c. 4.——A companion of Æneas, described as a prudent and venerable old man. *Virg. Æn.* 1. v. 125. &c.

ALE'THIA, one of Apollo's nurses.

ALE'TIS, (from ἀλῆτις, *erratrix*,) a festival at Athens, instituted in remembrance of Erigone, who wandered with a dog after her father Icarus. Some say it was observed in honour of king Temaleus, or of Ægisthus and Clytæmnestra. *Hesych.*—*Etymol. Auct.*

ALE'TIUM, a city of the Salentini, in Apulia, now Lezze. *Ptol.*

ALE'TRIUM, now Alatro, a town of Latium, the inhabitants of which are called Alétrinates. *Liv.* 9. c. 42.—*Plin.* 3. c. 5.

ALE'TUM, a town near the harbour of New Carthage in Spain. *Polyb.* 10.

ALEU'ADÆ, a royal family of Larissa in Thessaly, descended from the king Aleuas; they betrayed the independence of their country to Xerxes. The name is often applied to the Thessalians generally. *Diod.* 16.—*Herodot.* 7. c. 6. 172.—*Paus.* 3. c. 8. l. 7. c. 10.—*Ælian. Anim.* 8. c. 11.

ALEU'ADES, a people of Thessaly. *Paus. in Lacon.* —*Plut.*—*Polyæn.* 4. c. 2.

ALEU'AS, a king of Thessaly. *Herodot.* 7. c. 130. *Vid.* Aleuadæ.

A'LEUS, a son of Amphidas, king of Arcadia, famous for his skill in building temples. *Apollod.* 3. c. 16. & 17.—*Paus.* 8. c. 4 & 53.

A'LEX, a small river in the country of the Brutii. *Dionys. Perieg.* v. 367.

ALEXAM'ENUS, an Ætolian, who killed Nabis, tyrant of Lacedæmon, and was soon after murdered by the people. *Liv.* 35. c. 34.

ALEXAN'DER the First, son of Amyntas, was the 10th king of Macedonia. He killed the Persian ambassadors for their immodest behaviour to the females of his father's court, and was the first who raised the reputation of the Macedonians. He reigned 43 years, and died 451. B.C. *Justin.* 7. c. 3. *Herodot.* 5. 7, 8 & 9.

ALEXAN'DER the Second, son of Amyntas the Second, king of Macedonia, was treacherously murdered B.C. 370, by his younger brother Ptolemy, who held the kingdom for four years, and made way for Perdiccas and Philip. *Justin.* 7. c. 5.

ALEXAN'DER the Third, surnamed the Great, was son of Philip and Olympias, and was born at Pella, B.C. 355. He was the pupil of Aristotle during five years, and received his learned preceptor's instruction with becoming deference, and showed his respect for his abilities by unbounded acts of gratitude and liberality. When Philip went to war, Alexander, in his fifteenth year, was entrusted with the government of Macedonia, where he quelled a dangerous sedition, and soon after followed his father to the field, and saved his life in battle. When Philip was assassinated, he shewed his respect for his memory by punishing his murderers; and by his prudence and moderation gained the affections of his subjects. He conquered Thrace and Illyricum, and marched against Greece, which soon submitted. Thebes alone, unwilling to yield, felt the victor's vengeance. Her walls were destroyed, and her houses devoted to pillage; but the conqueror spared the descendants of the illustrious Pindar. Alexander was now unanimously chosen chief commander of the Grecian states; he declared war against the Persians, and prepared to gratify that wild ambition which had already grasped at the dominion of the universe. He crossed the Hellespont in the third year of his reign, and with about 32,000 foot and 4,000 horse he invaded Asia. The Persian were defeated at the river Granicus, and in the plains of Issus. The mother, wife, and children of Darius fell into the hands of the conqueror, who, in his conduct towards them manifested much humanity. From Issus he entered Syria, took

Tyre after an obstinate siege of seven months, and the slaughter of 2,000 of the inhabitants in cold blood, and made himself master of Palestine, Ægypt, Media, Syria, and Persia. From Ægypt he visited the temple of Jupiter Ammon, and bribed the priests, who saluted him as the son of their god, and enjoined his army to pay him divine honours. He laid the foundation of a city which he called Alexandria, on the western side of the Nile, near the coast of the Mediterranean. From Ægypt he advanced beyond the Euphrates, and the last battle which he fought with the Persians was at Arbela. This victory was more complete than the others, as the death of Darius, who was basely murdered by Bessus soon after the engagement, left him undisputed master of Persia. He afterwards conquered India, where he fought with Porus, a powerful king of the country; and after he had invaded Scythia, and visited the Indian Ocean, he retired to Babylon, loaded with the spoils of the east. He died at Babylon on the 21st of April, in the 32nd year of his age, after a reign of 12 years and 8 months of brilliant and continued success, 323 B.C. During his conquests in Asia, he founded many cities, which he called Alexandria, after his own name. When he had conquered Darius, he ordered himself to be worshipped as a god; and Calisthenes, because he refused to comply, was shamefully put to death. He murdered also, at a banquet, his friend Clitus, who had once saved his life in battle, because he preferred the exploits of Philip to those of his son. Yet, among all his extravagances, Alexander was fond of truth; and when one of his officers read to him as he sailed upon the Hydaspes, a history, in which he had too liberally panegyrized him, Alexander snatched the book from his hand, and threw it into the river, saying, "What need is there of such flattery? are not the exploits of Alexander sufficiently meritorious in themselves, without the colourings of falsehood?" He in like manner rejected the proposal of a statuary, who offered to cut mount Athos into a statue of him, and to represent him as holding a town in one hand, and pouring a river from the other. He forbade any statuary to make his statue except Lysippus, and any painter to draw his picture except Apelles. On his death he gave his ring to Perdiccas, and it was supposed that he wished to appoint him his successor. Alexander, with all his pride, was humane and liberal, easy and familiar with his friends, and a great patron of learning, as may be collected from his assisting Aristotle with a purse of money, to effect the completion of his natural history. Curtius, Arrian, and Plutarch have written an account of Alexander's life. *Diod.* 17 & 18.—*Paus.* 1. 7, 8, 9.—*Justin.* 11. & 12.—*Val. Max.*—*Strab.* 1. &c. [A very fine terminal head of Alexander is to be found in the Musée Royale at Paris, with his name inscribed on the breast; and an equestrian statue of bronze, in the Museum at Palermo, having been dug up from the ruins of Herculaneum.] ——A son of Alexander the Great, by Roxane, put to death with his mother by Cassander. *Justin.* 15. c. 2.——A man who after the expulsion of Telestes, reigned in Corinth. Twenty-five years after, Telestes dispossessed him, and put him to death.——A son of Cassander, king of Macedon, who reigned conjointly with his brother Antipater, and was prevented by Lysimachus from revenging his mother Thessalonica, whom his brother had murdered. Demetrius, the son of Antigonus, put him to death. *Justin.* 16. c. 1.—*Paus.* 9. c. 7.——A king of Epirus, brother of Olympias, and successor to Arymbas. He banished Timolaus to Peloponnesus, and made war in Italy against the Romans. He was surnamed Molossus. *Justin* 17. c. 3.—*Diod.* 16.—*Liv.* 8. c. 17 & 27.—*Strab.* 16.——A son of Pyrrhus, was king of Epirus. He conquered Macedonia, from which he was expelled by Demetrius. He recovered it by the assistance of the Acarnanians. *Justin.* 26. c. 3.—*Plut. in Pyrrh.* ——A king of Syria, driven from his dominions by Nicanor, son of Demetrius Soter, and his father-in-law Ptolemy Philometor. *Justin.* 35. c. 1 & 2.—*Joseph. Ant. Jud.* 13.—*Strab.* 17.——A king of Syria, first called Bala, was a merchant, and succeeded Demetrius. He conquered Nicanor by means of Ptolemy Physcon, and was afterwards killed by Antiochus Griphus, son of Nicanor.—*Joseph. Ant. Jud.* 13. c. 18.——A youth ordered by Alexander the Great to climb the rock Aornus, with thirty other youths. He was killed in the attempt. *Curt.* 8. c. 11.——An historian of Mindus, mentioned by *Plutarch, in Mario.*——An Epicurean philosopher. *Plut. in Deipmos.* l. 2. ——A governor of Æolia, who collected together a multitude, on pretence of shewing them an uncommon spectacle, and then confined them till they had each bought their liberty with a sum of money. *Polyæn.* 6. c. 10.——A name given to Paris, son of Priam. *Vid.* Paris.——A son of Herod by Mariamne, strangled with his brother Aristobulus, by order of his father. *Jos. Jud. Ant.* l. 16.——A Paphlagonian, who gained divine honours by his magical tricks and impositions, and likewise procured the friendship of Marcus Aurelius. He died at the age of 70.——A native of Aphrodisias, in Caria, in the third century, who wrote a commentary on the writings of Aristotle, part of which is still extant. *Voss. de Sect. Philos.* c. 17.——A poet of Ætolia, in the age of Ptolemy Philadelphus. ——A peripatetic philosopher, said to have been preceptor to Nero.——An historian of Miletus, called also Polyhistor, who wrote five books on the Roman republic. He also wrote 42 treatises on the Pythagorean philosophy, on grammar, on history, &c. B.C. 88. Of all his works, only a few fragments are preserved in Athenæus, Plutarch, Eusebius, and Pliny.——A poet of Ephesus, who wrote a poem on astronomy and geography. *Strab.* 14.——A sophist of Seleucia, in the age of Antoninus.——A physician in the age of Justinian.——A Thessalian, who, in a naval battle, gave to his soldiers a quantity of missile weapons, and ordered them to dart continually upon the enemy. *Polyæn.* 6. c. 27.——A son of Lysimachus. *Id.* 6. c. 12.——A governor of Lycia, who brought a reinforcement of troops to Alexander the Great. *Curt.* 7. c. 10.——A son of Polyperchon, killed in Asia by the Dymæans. *Diod.* 18 & 19.——A poet of Pleuron, who wrote elegies and tragedies, some fragments of which may be found in Athenæus, A. Gellius, &c. and was ranked among the seven poets who received the name of Pleiades. *Strab.* 14.—*L. Gyrald. de Poet. Hist.* 7. —*Paus.* 2. c. 22.——A Spartan, killed with 200 of his soldiers by the Argives, when he endeavoured to prevent their passing through the country of Tegea. *Diod.* 15.——A cruel tyrant of Pheræ, in Thessaly, who made war against the Macedonians, and took Pelopidas prisoner, who had been sent in the sacred character of ambassador to his court. He was murdered B.C. 357, by his wife Thebe. *Ælian. V. H.* 11. c. 9. l. 4. c. 40.—*Cic. de Inv.* 2. c. 49. *de Off.* 2. c. 9.—*Val. Max.* 9. c. 13.—*Plut. & C. Nep. in Pelop.*—*Paus.* 6. c. 5.—*Diod.* 15 & 16.—*Ovid. in Ib.* v. 321.——A son of Æropas, surnamed Lyncestes, a brave man, and favourite of Alexander the Great. *Freinshem. supplem. in Q. Curt.* l. 2.——A magician under Antoninus Pius. He was disciple of Appollonius Tyanensis. *Lucian, in vit. ejus.*

Alexan'der Ptol'emy the First, was one of the Ptolemean kings of Ægypt. His mother Cleopatra raised him to the throne, in preference to his brother Ptolemy Lathurus, and reigned conjointly with him. Cleopatra, however, expelled him, and soon after recalled him; and Alexander, to prevent a second expulsion from his kingdom, put her to death; and for his unnatural action was himself murdered by one of his subjects. *Joseph. Ant. Jud.* 13. c. 20. &c.—*Justin.* 39. c. 3 & 4.—*Paus.* 1. c. 9.

Alexan'der Ptol'emy the Second, king of Ægypt, was the son of the preceding. Falling into the hands of Mithridates, he escaped to Sylla, who restored him to his kingdom. He was murdered by his subjects a few days after his restoration. *Appian.* 1. *Bell. Civ.*

Alexan'der Ptol'emy the Third, was king of Ægypt after his brother Alexander, last mentioned. After a peaceful reign, he was banished by his subjects, and died at Tyre, B.C. 65, leaving his kingdom to the Roman people. *Vid.* Ægyptus & Ptolemæus. *Cic. pro Rull.*

Alexan'der Jannæ'us, a king of Judæa, son of Hyrcanus, and brother of Aristobulus, whose reign was rendered disgraceful by his cruelty and licentiousness. He died through excess of drinking, B.C. 79, after massacring 800 of his subjects for the entertainment of his concubines.

Alexan'der the Second, son of Aristobulus, invaded Judæa, and was conquered by Gabinius. *Jos. Ant. Jud.* l. 13. c. 19, &c.

Alexan'der Trallia'nus, a physician and philosopher of the fourth century; some of whose works in Greek are still extant.

Alexan'der Seve'rus, a Roman emperor. *Vid.* Severus.

Alexan'der Emise'nus, a man who revolted under the emperor Commodus, and miserably perished. *Lamprid. in Com.* c. 8.

ALEXAN'DRA, the name of some queens of Judæa mentioned by *Josephus*.——A nurse of Nero. *Suet. in Ner.* 50. This name was also given to Cassandra, because she was said to assist mankind by her prophecies. *Tzetzes. in Lycoph.*

ALEXANDRI'A, the name of several cities founded by Alexander, during his conquests in Asia. The most famous are:—A great and extensive city of Ægypt, built B.C. 332, by Alexander on the western side of the Delta. Alexandria was famous, among other curiosities, for the large library which the Ptolemies collected. This valuable repository was burnt by the orders of the Caliph Omar, A.D. 642; and the numerous volumes supplied fuel for 4,000 baths for six months. Alexandria has likewise been distinguished for its schools, not only of theology and philosophy, but of physic. The astronomical school, founded by Philadelphus, maintained its superior reputation for ten centuries, till the time of the Saracens. The modern town, erected upon the ruins of Alexandria, scarcely contains 6,000 inhabitants. *Curt.* 4. c. 8.—*Strab.* 17.—*Plin.* 5. c. 10.—*Quintil.* 1. c. 2.—*Stat. Syl.* 5. v. 66.—*Cæs. B. C.* 3. c. 110.——A town in Albania at the foot of mount Caucasus.——A town of Arachosia, in India.——A town on the banks of the river Indus.——The capital of Aria, between Hecatompylon and Bactra.——A town of Carmania.——A town in Cilicia, on the confines of Syria.——The capital of Margiana.——A town of Troas, on mount Ida, called, as is reported, after Alexander, the son of Priam, who there adjudged the prize of beauty to Venus. For an account of various towns of this name, see *Cluverius passim.*—*Paus.* 10. c. 12.—*Strab.* 13.—*Liv.* 35. c. 42 l. 37. c. 55.—*Curt.* 7.—*Plin.* The English form is Alexan'dria.

ALEXAN'DRI A'RÆ, the boundaries, according to some, of Alexander's victories in Asia, near the Tanais, Some authors place them on the banks of the Hyphasis, the most eastern of the branches of the river Indus. *Plin.* 5. c. 16.

ALEXAN'DRIDES, a Lacedæmonian, who married his sister's daughter, by whom he had Dorycus, Leonidas, and Cleombrotus.——A native of Delphi, of which he wrote a history. *Vos. Hist. Gr.* l. 4.——A native of Rhodes, distinguished himself at Athens by some comedies which obtained the applause of his contemporaries, and some fragments of which are preserved in *Athenæus*, 6. 8, 9, &c.—*Vos. H. Gr.* 4.

ALEXANDRI'NA A'QUA, baths in Rome, built by the emperor Alexander Severus. *Lamprid. in vit. ejus.*

ALEXANDROP'OLIS, a city of Parthia, built by Alexander the Great. *Plin.* 6. c. 25.

ALEXA'NOR, a son of Machaon, who built in Sicyon a temple to his grandfather Æsculapius, and received divine honours after death. *Paus.* 2. c. 11.

ALEXA'NUM, now Alessano, a city of the Salentini.

ALEXAR'CHUS, a Greek historian. *Plut. in Paral.* c. 7.—*Serv. Æn.* 3. v. 334. *Voss. Hist. Gr.*

ALEX'AS, of Loadicea, was recommended to M. Antony by Timagenes. Antony was induced by him to repudiate Octavia, and marry Cleopatra. Augustus punished him severely after the defeat of Antony. *Plut. in Anton.*

ALEX'IA, or ALE'SIA. *Vid.* Alesia.

ALEXI'ARES, a son of Hercules by Hebe, born at the same birth with Anicetus. *Apollod.* 2. c. 7.

Alexi'ares, a place of Bœotia, where Alexiares was born. *Paus.* 9. c. 25.

ALEXIC'ACUS, a surname given to Apollo by the Athenians, because he delivered them from the plague. *Paus.* 8. c. 42. The same surname was applied by some of the Greeks to Hercules also. *Cæl. Rhod.* 16. c. 19.—*Lactant.* 5. c. 3.—*Varro. L. L.* 6. c. 5.

ALEXI'NUS, a disciple of Eubulides, the Milesian, famous for the acuteness of his genius, and for his fondness for contention and argumentation. He died of a wound which he received from a sharply-pointed reed, as he swam across the river Alpheus. *Diog. in Eucl.*

ALEX'ION, a physician intimate with Cicero. *Cic. ad Att.* 13. ep. 25.

ALEXIP'PUS, a physician of Alexander. *Plut. in Alex.*

ALEXIR'HOE, a daughter of the river Granicus, said by some authors to be the mother of Æsacus by Priam. *Ovid. Met.* 11. v. 763.

ALEX'IS, a man of Samus, who endeavoured to ascertain by his writings, the borders of his country.——A comic poet, 336 B.C., of Thurium, who wrote 245 comedies, of which some few fragments remain. *Voss. de Poet. Gr.* 8.—*L. Gyrald. de P. Hist.* 7.—*Sax. Onom.* 1. p. 81.—*Fabr. B. Gr.* 2. p. 406.——A servant of Asinius Pollio.——A youth of whom a shepherd was deeply enamoured. *Virgil. Ecl.* 2.——A statuary, pupil of Polycletes, in the 87th Olympiad. *Plin.* 34. c. 8.——A school-fellow of Atticus. *Cic. ad Attic.* 7. ep. 2.

ALEX'ON, a native of Myndus, who wrote fables. *Diog. in Thalet.*

ALFATER'NA, the same as Nuceria, a town of Campania, beyond mount Vesuvius. *Pliny*, 3. c. 5. calls the inhabitants Alfaterni. *Diod. Sic.* 19.

ALFELLA'NI, a people of Italy. *Plin.* 3. c. 11.

P. ALFE'NUS VA'RUS, a native of Cremona, who, by his genius and application, raised himself from his original business of a cobler to the office of consul. *Horat.* 1. sat. 3. v. 130. Respecting this person see Heyne on the life of Virgil, A.U.C. 713. & *Argum. Eclog.* 6.—See also *Sax. Onom.* 1. p. 171.—*Fabr. Bib. Lat.*—*Heinneccii. Histor. Jur.* &c.

Alfe'nus Va'rus, a præfect under Vitellius. *Tac. Hist.* 1. c. 29.

ALGA'RIUM, now Algher, a city of Sardinia.

AL'GIDUM, a town of Latium, near Tusculum, about 12 miles from Rome. There is a mountain of the same name in the neighbourhood. It is now called Selva d'Algieri, and was famous for the defeat of the Æqui by Q. F. Vibulanus. *Cluver.* 3. c. 27.—*Horat.* 1. od. 21.—*Plin.* 19. c. 5.

ALIAC'MON or HALIAC'MON, a river of Macedonia, separating it from Thessaly; it falls into the Sinus Thermaicus, near Pydna. *Plin.* 4. c. 10.

A'LIÆ, islands of the Sinus Andulicus, called Eliæ, by *Strabo*. *Plin.* 6. c. 29.

ALIA'RIA, the wife of Sempronius Gracchus, who was put to death for adultery with Julia.——A city of Comagena. *Antonin.*

ALIAR'TUS, a town in Peloponnesus, on the coast of Messenia. *Stat. Theb.* 7. v. 274.

Aliar'tus, (or um), or Haliar'tus, a town of Bæotia, near the river Permessus, taken by M. Lucretius. *Liv.* 42. c. 63.

ALIB'ACA, a city of the Pentapolis in Africa. *Ptol.*

ALIC'ADRA, a city of Media. *Id.*

ALICA'NUM, a city of Pannonia. *Antonin.*

ALICHOR'DA, a city of Bactriana. *Ptol.*

AL'ICIS, a small town of Laconia.—A tribe of Athens. *Strab.*—*Diod. Sic.*

ALIC'IUM CA'PUT, now Capo dell'Alice, a promontory of Calabria.

ALIC'TUM, now Isola, a town of Istria.

ALIE'NUS CÆCI'NA, a Roman quæstor in Bæotia, appointed for his services commander of a legion in Germany, by Galba. The emperor disgraced him for his bad conduct; for which he raised commotions in the empire. *Tacit.* 1. *Hist.* c. 52.

ALI'FA or ALI'PHA, now Alifi, a town of Campania, on the banks of the Vulturnus, famous for the making of cups. *Liv.* 8. c. 25.—*Horat.* 2. sat. 8. v. 39.—*Sil.* 12. v. 526.—*Cic. Rull.* 2. c. 25.

ALILÆ'I, a people of Arabia Felix. *Diod. Sic.* 1. 3.

ALIME'LA, a region of Lycia. *Steph.*

ALIMEN'TUS C. an historian in the second Punic war, who wrote an account of Annibal in Greek, besides a treatise on military affairs. *Liv.* 21. & 30.—*Sax. Onom.* 1. p. 118.—*Ionsius. de Script. Hist. Philos.* 1. 2. c. 9.

ALI'MUS, *untis*, part of the tribe Leontis in Attica. *Steph.*

ALIN'DA, a town near the middle of Caria. *Arrian.*

ALINDO'IA, a city of Macedonia. *Steph.*

ALIPHE'RA, a town of Arcadia, situate on a hill. *Polyb.* 4. c. 77.—*Liv.* 28. c. 8. l. 32. c. 5.

ALI'PUS. *Vid.* Alypius.

ALIRRO'THIUS, a son of Neptune, who endeavoured to cut down the olive, which had sprung from Minerva's victory over his father; but he missed his aim, and cut his own legs so severely, that he instantly expired. *Servius. in Virg. G.* 1. v. 18. According to others, Alirrothius offered violence to Alcippe, daughter of Mars, for which he was put to death by her father. *Vid.* Alcippe. *Apollod.* 3.—*Paus.* 1. c. 21.

ALISAR'NA, a city of Troas. *Steph.*

ALIS'CA, a city of Pannonia. *Antonin.*

ALI'SO, now Iselburg, a town of Germany.——Now Alme, a river of Germany.

ALIS'TA, a town of Corsica. *Ptol.* It is now Porto Vecchio.

ALI'SUS, a city of Germany, on the coast of the Baltic. *Ptol.*

ALITE'RIUS, a surname of Jupiter, and also Aliteria, a surname of Ceres. *Plut. & Pollux in Aristoph.*

A'LIUM, a town of Elis, in Peloponnesus.

ALLA'DIUS, called also Remus, Aremulus, or Remulus Sylvius, son of Agrippa, and 12th king of Latium, reigned 20 years. He was killed by lightning for his impiety. *Dionys.* 1.—*Euseb. Chron.*

ALLAN'TE, a town of Macedonia, and also of Arcadia. *Steph. Pliny,* 4. c. 10. calls the inhabitants Allantenses.

ALLA'RIA or ALLO'RIA, a city of Crete. *Steph.*

ALLE'DIUS T. SEVE'RUS, a Roman knight, who married his brother's daughter, to please Agrippina.

ALLE'DIUS, a noted glutton in Domitian's reign. *Juv.* 5. v. 118.

AL'LIA, a small river of Italy, falling into the Tiber a few miles above Rome. It is celebrated in history for the defeat of the Romans on its banks by Brennus and the Gauls, on the 17th of July, B.C. 390. *Plut. in Camill.*—*Liv.* 5. c. 37.—*Flor.* 1. c. 18.—*Virg. Æn.* 7. v. 717.—*Ovid. Art. Am.* 1. v. 413.—*Lucan.* 7. v. 409.—*Cic. ad Att.* 1. ep. 4.—*Suet.* It is A'lia, according to Niebuhr.

ALLIE'NUS, a prætor of Sicily, under Cæsar. *Hirt. Afric.* 2.

AL'LIUS FUS'CUS, a man of consular dignity, slain by order of the emperor Commodus. *Lamprid in vit.*

ALLOB'ROGES, a warlike nation of Gaul, near the Rhone, in that part of the country now called Savoy, Dauphinè, and Vivarais. The Romans destroyed their city because they had assisted Annibal. Their ambassadors at Rome were allured by great promises to join in Catiline's conspiracy against his country; but they nobly refused, and discovered the plot to Cicero. *Dio.*—*Strab.* 4.—*Tacit.* 1. *Hist.* c. 66.—*Sallust. in Jug. Bell.*—*Mela,* 2. c. 7.—*Cic. in Cat.* 3. *De Div.* 1. c. 12.—*Plin.* 3. c. 4. l. 7. c. 49.—*Liv.* 21. c. 31.—*Ptol,* 2. c. 10.—*Cluv.* 2. c. 9.

ALLOBRO'GICUS, a surname of Fabius Maximus, because he conquered the Allobroges. *Juv.* 8. v. 13.—*Val. Max.* 3. c. 5. l. 6. c. 9.

AL'LOBROX, the 15th king of the Gauls. *Beros.* l. 5.——A king of the Celtæ, at the time when Pharaoh was drowned in the Red Sea. *Id. Ibid.*

ALLOB'RYGES, a people of Gaul, supposed by most authors to be the same as the Allobroges. *Polyb.* 30. c. 56.

ALLOE'RA, afterwards Attalia, a city of Lydia. *Steph.*

ALLONE'SUS, now Pelagnasi, an island on the coast of Macedonia, near the Sinus Thermaicus. *Vid.* Hallonesus.

ALLOT'RIGES, or ALTRIG'ONES, according to *Casaubon,* a nation in the southern parts of Spain. *Strab.* 2.

ALLU'TIUS. *Vid.* Albutius.

AL'MA or AL'MUS, a mountain of Upper Mœsia, near Sirmium, planted with vines by the emperor Probus, according to *Eutropius.*

AL'MA, a river of Etruria. *Antonin.*

ALMA'NA or AMIA'NA, now Albegna, a river of Etruria.

ALMAN'TIA, a town of Orestis, in Macedonia.

ALME'NE, a city on the Euxine sea. *Steph.*

AL'MO, a small river near Rome, at the south, falling into the Tiber, in which whatever was consecrated to Cybele was previously purified. The image of the goddess was there annually washed on the 25th of March. It is now called Rio d'Appio, as it crosses the Appian way *Flacc.* 8. v. 239.—*Stat.* 5. *Silv.* 1. v. 223.—*Martial.* 3. epigr. 47.—*Prudent. in H. Rom.* 5.—*Ovid. Fast.* 4. v. 387.—*Lucan.* 1. v. 600.

AL'MON, the eldest of the sons of Tyrrhus, was the first Rutulian killed by the Trojans. *Virg. Æn.* 7. v. 532.——A town of Thessaly. *Plin.* 4. c. 8.——A city of Bæotia. *Steph.*——The father of Lara, who bore the gods Lares to Mercury.

ALMO'PIA, a part of Macedonia, so called from a giant. son of Neptune and Athamantis. *Steph. Pliny,* 4. c. 10. calls the people Almopii.

AL'MUS, a son of Sisyphus. *Paus. Corinth.*

ALO'A, festivals at Athens in honour of Bacchus and Ceres. The oblations were the fruits of the earth. Ceres has been called from this, Aloas, and Alois. *Meursius. Græc. Eleus.*—*Eustath.* l. *Il.*

ALO'EUS, a giant, son of Titan and Terra, married Iphimedia, by whom Neptune had twins, Otus and Ephialtus. Aloeus educated them as his own, and from this circumstance they have been called Aloides. They grew up nine inches every month, and were only nine years old when they conspired with the giants to make war against the gods. Their tomb was shown in the age of Pausanias, at Anthedon, in Bœotia, on the borders of the Euripus. They built the town of Ascra, at the foot of Mount Helicon; and it is said that they established the worship of the three muses, Melete, Mneme and Aoide. *Paus.* 9. c. 29.—*Virg. Æn.* 6. v. 582.—*Hom. Il.* 5. v. 385. *Odys.* 11. v. 305.—*Lucan.* 6. v. 410.—*Schol. Apollon.* 1. v. 482.

ALOI'DES and ALOI'DÆ, the sons of Aloeus. *Vid.* Aloeus.

ALO'NE, an island near Cyzicus.——A city of Paphlagonia. *Steph.*——A city of Hispania Tarraconensis. *Ptol.* Some suppose it to be the modern Alicante, but it is now Guardamar.

ALO'NI, a people of Mesopotamia. *Plin.* 6. c. 26.

ALONTIGIC'ELI, a people of Spain. *Id.* 3. c. 1.

ALON'TIUM, a city of Sicily, now S. Philadelpho.

AL'OPE, daughter of Cercyon, king of Eleusis, bore a child to Neptune, and was changed by him into a fountain. The child, called Hippothoon, was preserved by some shepherds, and placed by Theseus upon his grandfather's throne. *Paus.* 1. c. 5 & 39.—*Hygin.* fab. 187.——One of the Harpies. *Hygin.* fab. 14.——A town of Thessaly. *Plin.* 4. c. 7. —*Hom. Il.* 2. v. 682.—*Liv.* 42. c. 56.——A town of Attica.——A town of Pontus where Penthesilea was born.——A town of Eubœa.——A city near Delphi.——A city of Locris. *Steph.*—*Mela,* 2. c. 2.

ALOP'ECE, an island in the Palus Mæotis, now l'Isle des Renards. *Strab.*——An island in the Ægean Sea opposite Smyrna. *Id.* 5. c. 31.——An island in the Cimmerian Bosphorus. *Plin.* 4. c. 12.——A small village of Attica, where was the tomb of Anchimolius. Socrates and Aristides were born there. *Æschin. contra Timarch.*—*Herodot.* 5. c. 63.—*Hesych.*

ALOPECONNE'SUS, a town of the Thracian Chersonesus. *Liv.* 31. c. 16.—*Mela,* 2. c. 2.

ALO'PIUS, a son of Hercules and Antiope. *Apollod.* 2. c. 35.

ALO'RUS, a city of Pæonia, in Macedonia. *Ptol.* It is called Olorus by *Pliny,* 4. c. 10. and is now Dianoro.

A'LOS, a city of Argolis. *Hesych.*——A city of Arcadia. *Steph.*——A city of Phthiotis. *Plin.* 4. c. 7.—*Strab.* 9.——A city of Thessaly. *Etymol.*

ALOSAN'GA, a city of India within the Ganges. *Ptol.*

ALO'TIA, (from ἁλωτὸς, *qui facile capi potest,*) festivals celebrated in Arcadia, in commemoration of a victory gained over Lacedæmon by the Arcadians. *Pausan. Arcad.*

ALO'US, a city of Illyria. *Steph.*

ALPE'NOR, a prophet slain by Ulysses. *Bocat.*

ALPE'NUS, the capital of Locris, at the north of Thermopylæ. *Herodot.* 7. c. 176, &c.

AL'PES, mountains that separate Italy from Gaul, Rhætia, and Germany, and are considered the highest ground in Europe. They are covered with perpetual snows; and distinguished, according to their situation, by the different names of Cottiæ, Carnicæ, Dalmaticæ, Graiæ, Juliæ, Lepontiæ, Maritimæ, Noricæ, Pannonicæ, Penninæ, Rhæticæ, Tridentinæ, Ultimæ. They were supposed for a long time to be impassable; till Hercules, according to mythologists, penetrated through their difficult defiles. Hannibal marched his army over them, and made his way through rocks, it is said, by softening and breaking them with vinegar. They were inhabited by fierce uncivilized nations, who remained unsubdued till the age of Augustus, who, to commemorate, the victory which he had obtained over them, erected a pillar in their territory. *Strab.* 4 & 5.—*Liv.* 21. c. 35.—*Juv.* 10. v. 151.—*Horat.* 2. sat. 5. v. 41.—*Lucan.* 1. v. 183.—*Tacit. Hist.* 3. c. 53.—*Mela, & Cluver. pass.* &c.

ALPE'SA, a town of Gallia Celtica. *Plin.* 3. c. 1.

ALPHABU'CELIS, a city of the Marsi, now Avez zano. *Ptol.*

ALPHE'A, a surname of Diana in Elis, given her when she deceived the gods of the Alpheus, who wished to offer her violence. *Paus.* 6. c. 22.——A surname of the nymph Arethusa, because loved by the Alpheus. *Ovid. Met.* 5. v. 487.

ALPHE'NOR, one of Niobe's sons. *Ovid. Met.* 6. fab. 6.

ALPHE'NUS. *Vid.* Alfenus.

ALPHESIBŒ'A, daughter of the river Phlegeus, married Alcmæon, son of Amphiaraus, who afterwards deserted her. *Vid.* Alcmæon. *Hygin.* fab. 244.—*Propert.* 1. el. 15. v. 15.—*Paus.* 8. c. 24.

ALPHESIBŒ'US, a shepherd, often mentioned in Virgil's eclogues.

ALPHE'US, now Orfea or Rofea, a river of Peloponnesus, which rises in Arcadia, and after passing through Elis, falls into the sea below Olympia. The god of this river fell in love with the nymph Arethusa, and pursued her until she was changed into a fountain by Diana. The fountain Arethusa is in Ortygia, a small island near Syracuse; and the ancients affirm, that the river Alpheus passes under the sea from Peloponnesus, rises again in Ortygia, and joins the stream of Arethusa. Hercules made use of the Alpheus to clean the stables of Augeas. *Strab.* 6.—*Virg. Æn.* 3. v. 694.—*Ovid. Met.* 5. fab. 10.—*Lucan.* 3. v. 176.—*Stat. Theb.* 1 & 4.—*Mela*, 2. c. 7.—*Paus.* 5. c. 7. l. 6. c. 21.—*Marcellin.* 25.—*Plin.* 2. c. 103.—*Mosch. Idyll.*—*Sil. Ital.* 3.—*Nonn.* 37.—*Claudian de Getic.*—*Melanth. de Sacrif.* 2.—*Nicand. Sam. de Flum.* 5.

AL'PHIUS or AL'FIUS, a celebrated usurer, ridiculed by *Horace*, *Epod.* 2.

AL'PHIUS AVI'TUS, a poet in the age of Severus, who wrote an account of illustrious men, and a history of the Carthaginian war. *Voss. de Hist. Lat.* l. 3.

ALPI'NUS, belonging to the Alps. *Virg. Æn.* 4. v. 442.

ALPI'NUS CORNE'LIUS, a contemptible poet, ridiculed by *Horace*, sat. 10. v. 36.

ALPI'NUS JU'LIUS, one of the chiefs of the Helvetii. *Tacit. Hist.* 1. c. 68.

ALPI'NUS MONTA'NUS, a præfect sent by Vespasian into Germany. *Tac. Hist.* 3. c. 35.

AL'PIS, a small river falling into the Danube.

ALPO'NOS, a city and mountain of Macedonia. Some, however, call it a city of Thessaly, and others of the Epicnemidian Locri.

AL'SA, a river of Forum Julii, flowing by Aquileia. *Plin.* 3. c. 8.

AL'SIUM, a maritime town of Etruria, at the west of the Tiber. There is here a villa of the Farnese family, called Palo. *Cluver.* 3. c. 26.—*Plin.* 3. c. 3. *Cic. ad Fam.* 9. ep. 6.—*Sil.* 8. v. 476.

AL'SUS, a river of Achaia in Peloponnesus, flowing from mount Sipylus. *Paus.* 7. c. 27.——A shepherd during the Rutulian wars. *Virg. Æn.* 12. v. 304.

AL'TABA, a city of Africa Propria. *Antonin.*

ALTA'NUM, a town of Catabria, now Soreto. *Id.*

AL'TAO, a city of Mauritania Cæsariensis. *Ptol.* It is called by others Atao, and is supposed to be now Calao.

ALTER'NIA, a city of the Carpetani, in Italy. *Ptol.*

AL'TES, a city of Peloponnesus. *Xen. Hist. Gr.* l. 7. It is called Altis by *Pausanias* in *Eliac.*

ALTHA, a city of Babylonia.—*Ptol.*

ALTHÆ'A, daughter of Thestius, married Œneus, king of Calydon, by whom she had many children, among whom was Meleager. When Meleager killed his two uncles, Althæa's brothers, Althæa, to revenge their death threw the log, on which his life depended, into the fire, and as soon as it was burnt Meleager expired. *Vid.* Meleager. She afterwards killed herself, being unable to survive her son. *Ovid Met.* 8. fab. 4.—*Homer. Il.* 9.—*Paus.* 8. c. 45. l. c. 10. c. 31.—*Apollod.* 1. c. 8.

ALTHÆM'ENES, a son of Cissus, or, according to *Diodorus*, of Catreus, king of Crete. Hearing that either he or his brothers were to cause the death of their father, he fled to Rhodes. Catreus went in search of his son Althæmenes; but when he landed in Rhodes the inhabitants attacked him, and he was killed by the hand of his own son. When Althæmenes knew that he had killed his father, he entreated the gods to remove him, and the earth immediately opened under his feet, and swallowed him up. *Apollod.* 3. c. 2.

ALTHE'A, a city of the Olcades, in Spain. *Steph.*

ALTHE'PUS, son of Neptune, was king of Ægypt. The country received the name of Althepia from him. *Paus.* 2. c. 30.—*Cœl. Rhod.* 12. c. 9.

ALTIL'IA, a town of Liguria, now Alteiola.

ALTI'NUM, a flourishing city of Italy, near Aquileia, famous for its wool. *Plin.* 3. c. 18.—*Martial.* 14. epigr. 25.—*Tacit. Hist.* 3. c 6.—*Eutrop.* 8. c. 5.—*Columell.* 7.—*Mela*, 2. c. 6.—*Cluv.* 3. c. 24.——A town of Lower Pannonia, on the Danube. It is now Tolna, or Bosoch, according to others.

ALTI'NUS JU'LIUS, suspected of being concerned in Piso's conspiracy, was banished by Nero to an island in the Ægean sea. *Tac. Ann.* 15. c. 71.

AL'TIS, a grove round Jupiter's temple at Olympia, where the statues of the Olympic conquerors were generally erected. *Paus.* 5. c. 20, &c.

AL'TUS, a city of Peloponnesus. *Xen. Hist. Gr.*——A place near Thessalonica. *Steph.*

ALU'ACA, a town of Media. *Ptol.*

ALUN'TIUM, a town at the mouth of the river Chydas, on the northern side of Sicily. *Plin.* 3. c. 8. *Cic. in Verr.* 4

ALUO'NA, a city of Liburnia. *Ptol.*

A'LUS, AL'UUS, or HA'LUS, a village of Arcadia, called also Fanum Æsculapii. *Paus.* 8. c. 25.

ALU'TA, now Alth, a river of Dacia, falling into the Danube. *Cluver.* 4. c. 18.

ALU'TÆ, a nation of Illyricum. *Plin.* 3. c. 21.

ALUTREN'SES, people inhabiting the Alps. *Id.* 3. c. 19.

ALU'UM, an inland town of Istria, now Albona.

ALYAT'TA, a region of Bithynia, so called from Alyattes. *Steph.*

ALYAT'TES the First, a king of Lydia, descended from the Heraclidæ. He reigned 14 years.

ALYAT'TES, the Second, king of Lydia, of the family of the Mermnadæ, was father of Crœsus. He drove the Cimmerians from Asia, made war against the Medes, and died when engaged in a war against Miletus, after a reign of 35 years. *Herodot.* l. c. 16, 17, &c.——*Strab.* 13.

AL'YBA, a country near Mysia. *Homer. Il.* 2.—*Cluver.* 5. c. 18.

AL'YBAS, otherwise Metapontium, a city of Italy.——A city of Thrace. Hence the epithet Alybantius. *Steph.*

ALYCÆ'A, a town of Arcadia. *Paus.* 8. c. 27.

ALYCÆ'US, son of Sciron, was killed by Theseus. A place in Megara received its name from him. *Plut. in Thes.*——A city of Peloponnesus. *Steph.*

ALYD'DA, now Luday, a city of Phrygia Major. *Ptol.*

ALYM'NE, a city of Phrygia Major. *Steph.*

ALY'MON, the husband of Circe.

ALYP'IUS, a person of Antioch, to whom the emperor Julian committed the care of commencing the building of the temple at Jerusalem. Two letters of Julian addressed to him are extant, from one of which it is probable that he wrote a work upon geography. There were several persons of this name. For an account of them, see *Fabr. B. Gr.* 3. p. 646.—*Sax. Onom.* 1. p. 294.

ALYS'IUS, an epithet of Bacchus, ἀπὸ τοῦ λύειν. *Cœl. Rhod.* 7. c. 15.——A name under which Jupiter was worshipped in Crete.

ALYS'SUS, a fountain of Arcadia, the waters of which could cure the bite of a mad dog. *Paus.* 8. c. 19.

ALYXOTH'OE. *Vid.* Alexirrhoe.

ALYZ'IA, a town of Acarnania, at the western mouth of the Achelous, opposite the Echinades. *Cic. ad Fam.* 16. ep. 2.

AM'AA, or AM'NIA, a city of Lusitania, now Portalegre. *Ptol.* 4. c. 22.

AMACAS'TIS, a city of India within the Ganges. *Ptol.*

AM'ACI, a people of Hispania Tarraconensis. *Id.*

AMAC'TION, a præfect of the royal cohort, in the army of Seleucus. *Polyæn. in Seleuc.* 4. c. 9.

AMAD'OCA, now Kiow, a lake and city of European Sarmatia, near the Borysthenes. *Ptol.*

AMAD'OCI, mountains and people of Sarmatia. *Stephanus* calls them a nation of Scythia, and their country. Ἀμαδόκιον. *Ptol.*

AMAD'OCUS, a king of Thrace, defeated by his an- Seuthes. *Diodorus Siculus* calls him Midocon. *Aristot.* 5. *Polit.* 10.—*Xenoph. Hell.* 4.

AMAFIN'IUS, a Roman, who first taught among his countrymen the tenets of Epicurus, which he saw embraced with avidity. *Cic. Tusc.* 4. c. 3.

AM'AGE, a queen of Sarmatia, remarkable for her justice and fortitude. *Polyæn.* 8. c. 56.

AMAICHI'UM, part of the Northern Ocean. *Plin.* 4. c. 13.

AMALOBRI'CA, a city of Spain, between Salmantica and Complutum. *Antonin.*

AMALTHÆ'A, daughter of Melissus, king of Crete, fed Jupiter with goat's milk. From this circumstance some authors have called her a goat, and have maintained that Jupiter made her a constellation, and gave one of her horns to the nymphs who had taken care of his infant years. This horn was called the horn of plenty, and had power of giving the nymphs whatever they desired. *Diod.* 3, 4, & 5.—*Ovid. Fast.* 5. v. 113.—*Strab.* 10.—*Hygin.* fab. 139.—*Paus.* 7. c. 26. [A goat, with the hand of a child, being part of a group, and thereby supposed to represent the goat Amalthea, is in the hall of the animals in the Vatican.]——A sybil of Cumæ, called also Hierophile and Demophile. She is supposed to have been the same who brought nine books of prophecies to Tarquin, king of Rome. *Varro.*—*Tibul.* 2. el. 5. v. 67. *Vid.* Sibyllæ.

AMALTHE'UM, a gymnasium which Atticus opened in his country house called Amalthea, in Epirus, and provided with everything which could furnish entertainment or convey instruction. *Cic. ad Attic.* 1. ep. 13.

AMA'NA or AMA'NUS, a part of mount Taurus, between Syria and Cilicia. A narrow defile over it, through which Darius entered Cilicia, was called Amanicæ Pylæ. *Cic. ad. Fam.* 2. ep. 10. *Ad. Att.* 5. ep. 10.—*Curt.* 3. c 4.—*Arrian.* 2.—*Plut. in Alex.*—*Lucan.* 3. v. 244.—*Mela*, 1. c. 12.

AMAN'DÆ, a people of India. *Plin.* 6. c. 19.

AMAN'DRA, a region near the Nile containing four nations, the Peucolaitæ, Alsagalitæ, Ceretæ, and Absoi. *Plin.* 6. c. 20.——A city of Æthiopia, in the dominions of king Cepheus. *Suidas.*

AMAN'DUS CN. SAL. a rebel general under Diocletian, who assumed imperial honours, and was at last conquered by Diocletian's colleague.

AMAN'ICÆ PY'LÆ. *Vid.* Amana.

AMAN'TES or AMANTI'NI, a people of Illyricum, said to be descended from the Abantes of Phocis. Their chief town, called Amantia, was on the sea coast at the south of Apollonia. *Cic. Phil.* 11. c. 11.—*Cæs. Civ.* 3. c. 40.—*Callimach.*

AMAN'TIA. *Vid.* Amantes.

AMA'NUS, a deity worshipped in Armenia and Cappadocia, and supposed to be the sun. Two other divinities, called Anaitis and Anandratus, shared the same honours. *Strab.* 11.

AMA'NUS, a mountain. *Vid.* Amana.

AM'ARA, a city of Arabia Felix, *Ptol.*——A city of Armenia. *Cedrenus.*

AMAR'ACUS, an officer of Cinyras, changed into the herb marjoram. *Servius. in Æn.* 1. v. 697.

AMARAN'TI, a people of Colchis, inhabiting mount Amarantius, whence the Phasis rises.

AMAR'DI, a nation near the Caspian Sea. *Mela*, 1. c. 2. Thoy are called Amordi by *Pliny*, 6. c. 17. and Mardi by *Ptolemy*.

AMAR'DUS, a river of Media, falling into the Caspian Sea, now probably Miana. *Ptol.* 6. c. 2.—*Plin.* 6. 2. 26.

AMA'RI FON'TES, fountains near Arsinoe on the Arabian Gulph. *Strab.*

AMARIS'PII, a nation of Bactriana. *Ptol.*

AMAR'SIAS, a sailor who sailed with Theseus to Crete, when he went against the Minotaur. *Simon. ap Plut. in vit. Thes.*

AMAR'THEAS, a native of Sais, was king of Ægypt, and reigned six years.

AMAR'TUS, a city of Greece. *Homer. Hymn. in Apoll.*

AMAR'UA or AMARU'SA, a town of Hyrcania. *Ptol.*

AMARYL'LIS, the name of a countrywoman mentioned by Theocritus and Virgil. Some suppose that the name is meant to signify Rome. *Servius*, 1. *Ecl.* v. 31.—*Politian.* 1. ep. 2.

AMARYN'CEUS, a king of the Epeans, buried at Buprasium. *Strab.* 3.—*Paus.* 3. c. 1.

AMARYN'THUS, a village of Eubœa, whence Diana is called Amarysia, and her festivals in that town Amarynthia. Eubœa is sometimes called Amarynthus. *Paus.* 1. c. 31.——A river between Arcadia and Triphylia, now Armoa.

AMARYS'IA. *Vid.* Amarynthus.

A'MAS, a mountain of Laconia. *Paus.* 3.

AMASE'NUS, a small river of Latium falling into the Tyrrhene Sea. *Virg. Æn.* 7. v. 685.

AMA'SIA, a city of Pontus. on the Iris, where Mithridates the Great, and Strabo the geographer, were born. *Strab.* 12.—*Plin.* 6. c. 3.——A town in Germany, now Marpurg. *Ptol.* Also Amasi'a.

AMA'SIA, AMIS'IA, or AMIS'IUS, a river of Germany, now the Ems, which falls into the German Ocean, near Embden. *Tacit. Ann.* 1. c. 60 & 63.—*Plin.* 4. c. 14.—*Mela*, 3. c. 3.—*Cluver.* 3. c. 5.

AMA'SIS, a man who, from a common soldier, became king of Ægypt, but died before the invasion of his country by Cambyses, king of Persia. He refused to continue in alliance with Polycrates, the tyrant of Samus, on account of his uncommon prosperity. When Cambyses came into Ægypt, he ordered the body of Amasis to be dug up, and burnt, an action which proved very offensive to the Ægyptians. *Herodot.* 1, 2, 3.——A man who led the Persians against the inhabitants of Cyrene. *Herodot.* 4. c. 201, &c.

AMAS'SI, a people near the Palus Mæotis. *Plin.* 6. c. 7.

AMAS'TRA or AMES'TRATUS, a town at the north-west of Sicily, on the Halesus, which falls into the Tyrrhene Sea. *Cic. Verr.* 3. c. 39. l. 5. c. 51.—*Sil.* 14. v. 267. The Romans besieged it for seven months, and it yielded at last after a third siege, and the inhabitants were sold as slaves. *Polyb.* 1. c. 24.

AMAS'TRIS, the wife of Dionysius, tyrant of Sicily, was sister of that Darius whom Alexander conquered. *Strab.*——A city of Paphlagonia, at the mouth of the Parthenius, on the Euxine Sea. It was formed out of four villages, and is now Famastro or Samastro. *Plin.* 2. c. 2.—*Ovid. Ibin.* 331.—*Catull.*—*Cluv.* 5. c. 17.——The wife of Xerxes, king of Persia. *Vid.* Amestris.

AMAS'TRUS, one of the auxiliaries of Perses against Æetes, king of Colchis, killed by Argus, son of Phryxus. *Flacc.* 6. v. 554.——A friend of Æneas, killed by Camilla in the Rutulian war. *Virg. Æn.* 11. v. 673.

AMA'TA, the wife of king Latinus, zealously favored the interests of Turnus. When her daughter was given in marriage to Æneas, the disappointed queen hanged herself to avoid the sight of her son-in-law. *Virg. Æn.* 7. &c.——The name of the first vestal virgin. *A. Gell.* 1. c. 12.

AMA'TÆ, a people of India. *Plin.* 6. c. 20.

AM'ATHUS, (*untis*), now Limisso, a city of Cyprus, dedicated to Venus. The island and the goddess herself are not unfrequently called Amathusia. Adonis was also worshipped here. *Steph.*—*Ovid. Met.* 10. v. 223.——*Amor.* 3. el. 15. v. 15.—*Catull.* 61. v. 51.—*Tac. Ann.* 3. c. 62.—*Plin.* 5. c. 31.—*Virg. Æn.* 10. v. 51.—*Ptol.* 5. c. 14.——A river flowing near Pylus.——A town of Laconia.

AMATHU'SIA. *Vid.* Amathus.

AMATI'NI, people of Epirus. *Cæs. Bell. Civ.* 1. 3.

AMATIS'SA, now l'Amasse, a river of Gaul.

AMAX'IA or AMAX'ITA, an ancient town of Troas. *Steph.*

AMAX'IA, a place of Cilicia, abounding with wood fit for building ships, given by Antony to Cleopatra. *Plin.* 5. c. 9.—*Strab.*

AMAZE'NES or MAZE'NES, a prince of the island Oaractas, who sailed for some time with Alexander's expedition in the east. *Arrian. in Indic.* 37.

AMAZ'ONES or AMAZON'IDES, a nation of famous women, who lived near the Thermodon, in Cappadocia. They were carefully educated in the labours of the field; their right breast was burnt off, that they might hurl a javelin with more force, and make a better use of the bow; from that circumstance, therefore, their name is derived (ἀ *non*, μαζὸς, *mamma*). They founded an extensive empire in Asia Minor, along the shores of the Euxine, and near the Thermodon. Themyscyra, or Themyscyrium, according to *Mela*, was the most celebrated of their towns; and Smyrna, Magnesia, Thyatira, and Ephesus, according to some authors, were built by them. Some authors, among whom is Strabo, deny the existence of the Amazons, but Justin and Diodorus assert it; and the latter says, that Penthesilea, one of their queens, went to the Trojan war to support the cause of Priam, and that she was killed by Achilles; and from that time the glory and military character of the Amazons gradually decayed. Their most famous actions were their expedition against Priam; and, afterwards, the assistance they gave him during the Trojan war; and their invasion of Attica, to punish Theseus, who had carried away Antiope, one of their queens. They were also conquered by Bellerophon and Hercules. Among their queens, Hippolyte, Antiope, Lampeto, Marpesia, &c. are the most renowned. Curtius says, that Thalestris, one of their queens, came to visit Alexander whilst he was pursuing his conquests in Asia. To denote the goodness of a bow or quiver, it was usual to call it Amazonian. *Virg. Æn.* 5. v. 311.—*Journand. de Reb. Get.*—c. 7.—*Philostr. Icon.* 2 c. 5.—*Justin.* 2. c. 4.—*Curt.* 6. c. 5.—*Plin.* 6. c. 7. l. 14. c. 8. l. 36. c. 5.—*Herodot.* 4. c 110.—*Strab.* 11.—*Diod* 2.—*Dion. Hal.* 4.—*Paus.* 7. c. 2. —*Plut. in Thes.*—*Apollod.* 2. c. 3 & 5.—*Hygin.* fab. 14 & 163.—*Hom. Il.* 1.—*Palæphat. de Incred. Eustath. in Il.* 1.—*Servius. in Æn.* 2.—*Ptol.* 5. c. 10.—*Mela* & *Cluver. passim.* [There is a fine representation of an Amazon in the Museum of the Capitol.]

AMAZO'NIA, a celebrated mistress of the emperor Commodus.

AMAZO'NIA, the country of the Amazons, near the Caspian Sea.

AMAZO'NIUM, a place in Attica, where Theseus obtained a victory over the Amazons.——A city of Cumæ, inhabited by Amazons.——A place in Bœotia. *Steph.*

AMAZO'NIUS, a surname of Apollo at Lacedæmon, *Paus. in. Lacon.*

AMBAR'RI, a people of Gallia Celtica, on the Arar, related to the Ædui. *Cæs. Bell. G.* 1. c. 11. *Liv.* 5. c. 34.

AMBARVA'LIA, *(ab ambiendis arvis,)* a procession round the ploughed fields, in honor of Ceres. There were two festivals of that name, celebrated by the Romans, one in the month of April, the other in July. On this occasion, a sow, a sheep, and a bull, called *ambarvaliæ hostiæ*, were immolated, and the sacrifice has sometimes been called *suovetaurilia*, from *sus, ovis*, and *taurus*. *Virg. G.* 1. 339. & 345.—*Tib.* 2. el. 1. v. 19.—*Cato. de R. R.* c. 141. —*Strab.* 5.—*Sergius. in Virg. citat.*—*Festus in Macrob.* 3. c. 5.

AMBA'SIA, now Amboise, a city of the Turones, on the Ligeris, in Gaul.

AMBAS'TÆ, a people of the Sinæ, in Asia, now comprising the provinces Chequiam, Chiamsi, and Fuquien.

AMBAS'TUM, a river in Asia. *Ptol.*

AMBA'SUM, the metropolis of the Phrygians. *Steph.*

AMBA'TÆ, a people of Asia. *Ptol.*

AMBAU'TÆ, a people inhabiting mount Paropamisus in India. *Id.*

AM'BE, a city of Arabia Felix.

AM'BENUS, a mountain of European Sarmatia. *Flacc.* 6. v. 251.

AMBIALI'TES, a people of Gallia Celtica. *Cæs. Bell. G.* 3. c. 9.

AMBIA'NUM, a town of Belgium, now Amiens. Its inhabitants conspired against J. Cæsar. *Cæs.* 2. *Bell. G.* c. 4.—*Cluver.* 2. c. 15.

AMBIA'TI, a people of Galatia. *Plin.* 5. c. 32.

AMBIATI'NUM, now Capelle, a village of Germany, where the emperor Caligula was born. *Sueton. in Cal.* 8. More correctly Ambitari'nus.

AMBIBAR'ETI, a people against whom J. Cæsar sent C. Antistius Rheginus with one legion, into winter quarters. *Cæs. Bell. Gall.* 7. 90. The country is supposed to be the modern Vivaretz.

AMBIDRA'NI, a people of Noricum, forming the eastern portion of the modern Stiria.

AMBIGA'TUS, a king of the Celtæ, in the time of Tarquinius Priscus. Seeing the great population of his country, he sent his two nephews, Sigovesus and Bellovesus, in quest of new settlements; the former towards the Hercynian woods, and the other towards Italy. *Liv.* 5. c. 34, &c.

AMBILIA'TES, a people of Gallia Celtica: their chief town is now l'Amballes.

AMBIL'ICI, a people of Noricum, occupying the western part of the modern Stiria.

AMBI'ORIX, a king of the Eburones in Gaul, and a great enemy to Rome, distinguished himself in the battles which he fought against her generals. He was at last killed in a battle with J. Cæsar, and 60,000 of his countrymen shared his fate. *Cæs. B. G.* 5. c. 11. &c.

AMBISON'TES, a people of Noricum, who occupied the country now called Carinthia.

AMBIVAR'ETI, a people of Gallia Belgica, between the Rhine and the Moselle; their country was probably the modern Brabant.

AMBIV'IUS, a person mentioned by *Cicero de Senec.*

AMBIV'IUS TUR'PIO, a comic actor, who represented some of the characters in Terence's comedies.

AM'BLADA, a town of Pisidia. *Strab.*

AM'BRA, a city of Vindelicia, now Brag.

AMBRA'CIA, a city of Epirus, the residence of king Pyrrhus. It originally bore the name of Epuia, afterwards of Paralia. Augustus, after the battle of Actium, called it Nicopolis. *Mela*, 2. c. 4.—*Plin.* 4. c. 1.—*Polyb.* 4. c. 63.—*Strab.* 10.—*Ptol.* 3. c. 14.—*Liv.* 38. c. 43 & 44.—*Cluver.* 4. c. 7.

AMBRA'CIUS SI'NUS, a beautiful bay in the Ionian Sea, near Ambracia, now called le Golfe de Larta. *Polyb.* 4. c. 63.—*Mela*, 2. c. 4.—*Flor.* 4. c. 11.—*Strab.* 10.—*Cluver.* 4. c. 7.

AM'BRACUS, a town of Epirus. *Steph.*

AM'BRI, an Indian nation. *Justin.* 12. c. 9.

AMBRO'DAX, a city of Parthia. *Ptol.*

AMBRO'NES, certain inhabitants of Gaul, who lost their possessions by the inundation of the sea, and lived upon rapine and plunder; whence the word Ambrones implied a dishonourable meaning. They were conquered by Marius. *Plut. in Mar.*—*Eutrop.* 5.—*Strab.* 4.

AMBRO'SIA, festivals observed in honor of Bacchus in some cities of Greece. They were the same as the Brumalia of the Romans.——One of the daughters of Atlas, changed into a constellation after death.—The food of the gods was called ambrosia, and their drink nectar. The word signifies immortal. The ambrosia had the power of giving immortality to all those who ate it. It was sweeter than honey, and of a most odoriferous smell; and, it is said, that Berenice, the wife of Ptolemy Soter, was saved from death by tasting ambrosia, given her by Venus. Tithonus was made immortal by eating ambrosia; and in like manner Tantalus and Pelops, who, on account of their impiety, had been driven from heaven, and compelled to die upon earth. It had the power of healing wounds, and therefore Apollo, according to Homer, saved Sarpedon's body from putrefaction, by rubbing it with ambrosia; and Venus also, according to Virgil, healed the wounds of her son with it. The gods used generally to perfume their hair with ambrosia, as Juno when she adorned herself to captivate Jupiter. and Venus when she appeared to Æneas. *Hom. Il.* 1, 14, 16, & 24.—*Lucian. de Dea Syria. Catull.* ep. 100.—*Theocrit. Id.* 15.—*Virg. Æn.* 1. v. 407. l. 12. v. 419. & *Serv. in loc.*—*Ibicus. apud. Athen.* 11. c. 39.—*Ovid. Met.* 2.—*Pindar*, 1.—*Olymp.*

AMBRO'SIUS, a celebrated bishop of Milan, obliged the emperor Theodosius to do penance for the murder of the people of Thessalonica, and distinguished himself by his writings, especially against the Arians. His three books *de Officiis*, are still extant, besides eight Latin hymns on the works of creation. His style is not inelegant, but his diction is sententious, and his opinions eccentric. He died at Milan, the 4th of April A.D. 397. His life was written by Paulinus, and dedicated to St. Augustine. The best edition of his works is that of the Benedictines, 2. vols. fol. Paris, 1686. *Sax. Onom.* 1. p. 434.—*Harles. Lit. Rom.* 1. p. 635.—*Voss. de P. Lat.*——A native of Cyzicus, slain by Peleus in a nocturnal engagement. *Val. Flac.* 3. v. 138.

AMBRUAR'ETI, a people of Gallia Lugdunensis, between the rivers Digeris and Icauna.

AM'BRYON, a man who wrote the life of Theocritus of Chius. *Diog.*—*Voss. Hist. Gr.* 3. p. 320.

AMBRY'SUS, a city of Phocis, at the south of mount Helicon, so called from a hero of the same name. *Paus.* 10. c. 35.——A city of Bœotia.

AMBUAR'ETI. *Vid.* Ambruareti.

AMBUBA'JÆ, Syrian women of immoral lives, who attended festivals and assemblies as minstrels. *Horat.* 1. sat. 2. v. 1.—*Suet. in Ner.* 27.

AMBU'LII, a surname of Castor and Pollux, at Sparta.

AMBULA'TRI, a people of Aquitania, near the Vasates.

AMBUR'BIA, (from *ambire urbem*), festivals at Rome, which consisted in a solemn procession round the walls of the city. *Jos. Scalliger* (*Castigat in Fest.*) confounds these festivals with the Ambarvalia. *Turneb.* 18. c. 17.—*Serv. in Virg.* 3. ecl. 77. —*Lucan.* 1. v. 592.

AMBUS'TUS, a surname of the Fabii. It was borne by Fabius Eburnus, because he was burnt by lightning. *Fest.*—*Plin.* 7. c. 41.

AME'LA, a city of Media. *Ptol.*

AM'ELAS, a town of Lycia. *Plin.* 5. c. 27.

AM'ELES, a river of hell, the waters of which no vessel could contain. *Plat.* 10. *de Rep.*

AMELESAG'ORAS, or MELESAG'ORAS, a very ancient historian. *Clem. Alex. Strom.* 6.—*Voss. Hist. Gr.* l. 1. c. 2.

AME'LIUS, a philosopher of Apamea, pupil of Plotinus, and master of Porphyry, or according to others, contemporary with him. *Suidas.—Voss. de Philos.* c. 17. sec. 6.

AMENA'NUS, a small river of Sicily, near mount Ætna, now Guidicello. *Strab.* 5.

AMENI'DES, a secretary of Darius, the last king of Persia. Alexander set him over the Arimaspi. *Curt.* 7. c. 3.

AMENO'PHIS, a name common to several Ægyptian kings.

AMENO'PHIS the First, succeeded Chebron, and reigned 27 years, 7 months.

AMENO'PHIS the Second, succeeded Thummosis, and reigned 30 years, 10 months.

AMENO'PHIS the Third, succeeded Ramesses, and reigned 19 years, 6 months.

AMENO'PHIS the Fourth, subdued Greece, Syria, Phœnicia, and the Scythians, and led an army into Thrace. He is called Vexores by *Justin* and *Orosius*, by others Sesostris, or rather Memnon.

AMENO'PHIS, king of Ægypt, probably called Pheron by *Herodotus*, l. 2., rendered blind for his impiety. *Euseb. African.—Joseph. cont. Apion.* l. c. 5.—*Plin.* 36. c. 7.

AMENOPH'THIS, a king of Ægypt, who reigned nine years, about the time of Ehud, judge of Israel. *Joh. Marsham. Can. Chron.*

AM'ERA, a city near the Palus Mæotis. *Procop.*

AME'RIA, a city on the south of Umbria, near the Tiber, where Sextus Roscius, so ably defended by Cicero, was born. The osiers which grew there, (*Amerinæ salices*), were, on account of their toughness and strength, very serviceable in the binding of the vines to the elms. *Columell.* 4.—*Plin.* 3. c. 14.—*Virg. G.* 1. v. 265.

AME'RIAS, a Greek grammarian, quoted and commended by Athenæus and the scholiast of Apollonius of Rhodes. *Casaub.* 1. *Lect. Th.*

AMERI'OLA, a town in Latium, the situation of which is not now known. *Plin.* 3. c. 5.

AMESI'SES, a king of Lower Ægypt, who reigned 65 years. Abraham is supposed to have visited the country in his reign.

AMES'SIS, a daughter of Amenophis, who succeeded her father, and reigned 48 years. *Manetho* calls her his sister. *Euseb. in Chron.—Joseph. cont. Apion,* l. c. 5. &c.

AMES'TRATUS. *Vid.* Amastra.

AMES'TRIS, queen of Persia, was wife of Xerxes. She cruelly treated the mother of Artiante, her husband's mistress, and cut off her nose, ears, lips, breast, tongue, and eyebrows. She also buried alive 14 noble Persian youths, to appease the deities under the earth. *Herodot.* 7. c. 61. &c. ——A daughter of Oxyartes, wife of Lysimachus. *Diod.* 20.

AMICU'SIA, an island in the Red Sea. *Steph.*

AMI'DA, called by *Ptolemy* Ammæa, a city of Mesopotamia, on the western shores of the Tigris, besieged and taken by Sapor, king of Persia. *Ammian.* 19. Also Am'ida.

AMIL'CAR, a Carthaginian general of great eloquence and cunning, surnamed Rhodanus. When the Athenians were afraid of the power of Alexander, Amilcar went to his camp, gained his confidence, and secretly transmitted an account of all his schemes to Athens. *Trogus,* 21. c. 6.——A Carthaginian, whom the Syracusans called to their assistance against the tyrant Agathocles, who besieged their city. Amilcar soon after favoured the interest of Agathocles, for which he was accused at Carthage. He died in Syracuse, B.C. 309. Some authors suppose this to be the same person as the last. *Diod.* 20.—*Justin.* 22. c. 2. 3.——A Carthaginian, surnamed Barcas, father of the celebrated Annibal. He was general of the Carthaginian forces in Sicily, during the first Punic war. After a peace had been made with the Romans, he quelled a rebellion of slaves, who had besieged Carthage, and taken many towns in Africa, and rendered themselves so formidable to the Carthaginians, that they begged and obtained assistance from Rome. After this, he passed into Spain with his son Hannibal, who was but nine years of age, and laid there the foundation of the town Barcelona. He was killed in a battle against the Vettones, B.C. 237. He had formed a plan for invading Italy, by crossing the Alps, which his son afterwards carried into execution. His restless ambition, and his eternal enmity to the Romans, proved the cause of the second Punic war. He used to say of his sons, that he kept three lions to devour the Roman power. *C. Nep. in vit.*—*Liv.* 21. c. 1.—*Polyb.* 2.—*Plut. in Annib.*——A Carthaginian general, who assisted the Insubres against Rome, and was taken prisoner by Cn. Cornelius. *Liv.* 32. c. 30. l. 33. c. 8.——A son of Anno, defeated in Sicily by Gelon, the same day that Xerxes was defeated at Salamis by Themistocles. He burnt himself, that his body might not be found among the slain. Sacrifices were offered to him. *Herodot.* 7. c. 165, &c.

AM'ILUS, a river of Mauritania, which falls into the Mediterranean, and in which elephants were said to wash themselves by moonlight. *Plin.* 8. c. 1.——A town of Arcadia. *Paus. in Arcad.*

AMIMO'NE or AMYMO'NE, a daughter of Danaus, changed into a fountain, which is near Argos, and flows into the lake Lerna. *Ovid Met.* 2. v. 240.

AMIN'EA or AMMIN'EA, a part of Campania, where the inhabitants were famous agriculturists. Its wine was highly esteemed. *Virg. G.* 2. v. 97.——A place of Thessaly.

AMIN'IAS, a noted pirate, whom Antigonus employed against Apollodorus, tyrant of Cassandrea. *Polyæn.* 4. c. 18.——Son of Pronapus, an archon at Athens. *Schol. in Aristoph. Nub. & Vesp.*——An Athenian who fought bravely at the battle of Salamis. *Herodot.* 8. c. 84 & 93.

AMIN'IUS RE'BIUS, a rich and skilful lawyer at Rome, in the consulship of Q. Volusius and P. Scipio. He opened his veins to avoid the sufferings of an old age, rendered painful by his debaucheries. *Tac. Ann.* 3. c. 30. Some read Caninius, others Caninius Rebilius.

AMIN'IUS, a river of Arcadia. *Paus.* 8. c. 30.

AMIN'OCLES, a native of Corinth, who flourished 705 B.C. He was said to be the first Grecian who built a trireme at Samus and Corinth. *Thucyd.* 1. c. 13.——A Magnesian, son of Cretinas. *Herodot.* 7. c. 190.

AM'INON, an archon at Athens, at the time of the death of Pericles. *Athen.*

AMIN'ULA, a poor city of Apulia. *Festus.*

AMIP'SIAS, a comic poet, ridiculed by Aristophanes for his insipid verses. *Voss. de poet. Gr.*

AMISE'NA, a country of Cappadocia, of which Amisus was the capital. *Strab.* 12.

AMISOD'ARUS, called Isarus by the Lycians, a companion of the pirate Chimæra. *Plut. de virt. fœm.* c. 14.

AMIS'SAS, an officer of Megalopolis, in Alexander's army. *Curt.* 10. c. 22.

AMI'SUS, a maritime city of Pontus, at the east of the Halys, now Samsoun. *Cic. Man.* 8.—*Plin.* 10. ep. 93.—*Cluv.* 5. c. 17. Also Am'isus.

AMITER'NUM, a town of Italy, the birth-place of Sallust. The inhabitants assisted Turnus against Æneas.— *Virg. Æn.* 7. v. 710.—*Plin.* 3. c. 5.—*Liv.* 28. c. 45.—*Cluver.* 3. c. 27.

AMITHA'ON or AMYTHA'ON was father of the famous prophet Melampus. *Stat. Theb.* 3. v. 451.

AMITINEN'SES, a people of Latium. *Plin.* 3. c. 5.

AMITROCH'ARES, or AMITROCHA'TES, a king of India. *Cœl. Rhod.* 18. c. 9.—*Athen.* 14.

AMMA'LO, a festival in Greece in honour of Jupiter. *Hesych.*

AMMÆ'A. *Vid.* Amida.——A city of Arabia Deserta. *Ptol.*

AMMÆD'ARA, a city of Africa, bordering on Numidia. *Ptol. Antonius* calls it Admetera.

AMMA'ITHA, city of Syria. *Lib. Notit.*

AMMIA'NUS. *Vid.* Marcellinus.——A celebrated poet, who, in one of his distichs, asserts, that it was easier to find white crows and flying tortoises than an honest rhetorician in Cappadocia. *Cœl. Rhod.* 17. c. 11.

AMMIEN'SES, a people of Spain. *Plin.* 4. c. 2. *Ptolemy* mentions their city called Ammia.

AMMI'TES, a river of Greece. *Athen.* 8.

AM'MON or HAM'MON, a name under which Jupiter was worshipped in Libya. He appeared under the form of a ram to Hercules, or, according to others, to Bacchus, who, with his army, suffered the greatest extremities, for want of water in the deserts of Africa, and shewed him a fountain. Upon this, Bacchus erected a temple to his father, under the name of Jupiter Ammon, (from ἄμμος, *arena*,) with the horns of a ram. The ram, according to some, was made a constellation. This temple was nine days' journey from Alexandria, and had a famous oracle, which, according to ancient tradition, was established about 18 centuries before the age of Augustus, by two doves, which flew away from Thebais in Ægypt, and came, one to Dodona, and the other to Libya, where the people were soon informed of their divine mission. The oracle of Hammon was consulted by Hercules, Perseus, and others; but when it pronounced Alexander to be the son of Jupiter, its long established reputation was destroyed, and in the age of Plutarch its answers were little regarded. The situation of the temple was pleasant, and there was near it a fountain, the waters of which were cold at noon and midnight, and warm in the morning and evening. There were above 100 priests in the temple, but only the elders delivered oracles. The statue of the god was brazen, but valuable on account of the emeralds and precious stones which had been melted in its formation; and it rested upon a golden pedestal. There was also an oracle of Jupiter Ammon in Æthiopia. *Ovid. Met.* 15. v. 310.—*Lucret.* 6. v. 847.—*Herodot. in Melpom. &c.*—*Curt.* 4. c. 7. &c.—*Plin.* 6. c. 29.—*Strab.* 1, 11, & 7.—*Plut. cur. Orac. edi. desierint, & in Isid.*—*Paus.* 3, c. 18. &c.—*Hygin.* fab. 133. *Poet. Astr.* 2. c. 20.—*Justin.* 1. c. 9, &c.—*Lactant. in* 3. *Theb.* 476.—*Serv. in Æn.* 4. v. 198.—*Ampelius in Mem.* 2.—*Antig. Car.* 159. [There is a fine mask of Jupiter, under this character, in the Vatican, and a bust in the Museum of the Capitol.]——A king of Libya, father of Bacchus. He gave his name to the temple of Ammon, according to *Diodorus*, 8.

AM'MON and BRO'TEAS, two brothers, famous for their skill in boxing. *Ovid. Met.* 5. v. 107.

AMMO'NIA, a name of Juno in Elis, given her as being the wife of Jupiter Ammon, though *Montfaucon* (*Antiq.* lib. 1.) considers it as a local appellation given to the goddess, from an altar raised to her honor in Libya. *Paus.* 5. c. 15.——A name of Libya. *Steph.*

AMMO'NII, a nation of Africa, who derived their origin from the Ægyptians and Æthiopians. *Herodot.* 2, 3, & 4.

AMMO'NIUM, a promontory of Arabia Felix. *Ptol.*

AMMO'NIUS, a Christian philosopher, surnamed Saccas. He opened a school of Platonic philosophy at Alexandria, 232 A.D. and had among his pupils Origen and Plotinus. His treatise, Περὶ Ὁμοίων, was published in 4to by Valckenaer, L. Bat. 1739.——An author who wrote an account of sacrifices, as also a treatise on the harlots of Athens. *Athen.* 13.——A Carthaginian general, surnamed Barcas. *Polyb.* 3.——A disciple of Proclus, in the sixth century. He wrote a commentary on Aristotle, besides a treatise *de differentiâ vocum*, published at Venice, 1497, with a Greek dictionary. There were no less than 16 persons of this name, for an account of whom see *Fabr. B. Gr.* l. 4. c. 29. (*olim.* 26.) The most eminent, after those mentioned above, were the writer of the Monotessaron and the grammarian. See also *Sax. Onom.* 1. p. 449.

AMMO'THEA, one of the Nereides. *Hesiod. Theog.*

AMNAME'THU, an island in the Indian Sea. *Ptol.*

AMNI'SUS, a port of Gnossus, at the north of Crete, with a small river of the same name, near which Lucina had a temple. The nymphs of the place were called Amnisides or Amnisiades. *Paus.* 1. c. 18.—*Hom. Od.* 19. v. 187.—*Callim in Dian.* 15.—*Spank. in loco.*——A small river of Bithynia. *Appian. de Bel. Mithr.*

AM'NUS, a king of Etruria, who reigned 25 years.

AMŒ'BEUS, an Athenian player of great reputation, who sang at the nuptials of Demetrius and Nicæa. *Polyæn.* 4. c. 6.

AMOL'BUS, a city of Magnesia.——A city of Macedonia. *Steph.*

AMOMETUS, a Greek historian. *Plin.* 6. c. 17.

A'MOR. *Vid.* Cupido.

AMOR'GES, a Persian general, killed in Caria, in the reign of Xerxes. *Herodot.* 5. c. 121.

AMOR'GUS, one of the Cyclades, at the south-east of Naxus, where Simonides was born. The Greeks had part of their dress called *Amorginæ vestes*, from a kind of red stuff which was manufactured in the island. *Steph.*—*Suidas.*—*Hesych.*—*Strab.* 10. *Cluver.* 4. c. 10.

AMO'RIA, a city of Armenia. *Procop.*

AMO'RIUM, a town of Phrygia Major. *Ptol.*

AM'PE, a city on the Red Sea. The gentile name was Ampæus. *Herod.* 6. c. 20.—*Steph.*

AMPE'LA, a town of Crete. *Plin.* 4. c. 12.

AMPELOES'SA, a town or rather region of Syria Decapolitana. *Id.* 5. c. 18.

AM'PELUS, a favourite of Bacchus, who lived on the banks of the Euphrates, in Armenia. He fell when gathering grapes, and was killed on the spot. He was made a constellation by Bacchus. *Ovid. Fast.* 3. v. 407. [In the gallery at Florence, there is a very beautiful group of Bacchus leaning on the shoulder of Ampelus. There are also many repetitions of this group elsewhere, bnt they are inferior.]

AM'PELOS, a promontory of Samus.——A town of Crete.——A town of Macedonia.——A town of Liguria.——A town of Cyrene.

AMPELU'SIA, a promontory of Mauritania. *Mela,* 1. c. 5 & 6.

AMPHA'NE, a Dorian city. *Steph.*

AMPHAPA'LIA, a city of Crete. *Strab.*

AMPHAX'IS, a town of Macedonia; the region was called Amphaxitis, and the people Amphaxitæ. *Steph.*—*Cluver.* 4.

AM'PHE, one of the Cyclades.

AMPHE'A, a city of Mipenia, taken by the Spartans. *Paus.* 4. c. 5.—*Steph.* Also Amphi'a

AMPHI'ALA, a town of Attica. *Strab.*

AMPHIALA'US, a famous dancer in the island of the Phæacians. *Hom. Od.* 8. v. 128.——A son of Neoptolemus by Andromache. *Hygin.* fab. 123.

AMPHI'ANAX, a king of Lycia, in the time of Acrisius and Prœtus. *Apollod.* 2. c. 2.

AMPHIARA'I BALNEA, a place of Attica. *Steph.*

AMPHIARAI'DES, a patronymic of Alcmæon, as being son of Amphiaraus. *Ovid. Fast.* 2. c. 43.

AMPHIARA'US, son of Oecleus, was at the chase of the Calydonian boar, and one of the Argonauts. He was famous for his knowledge of futurity, whence he is called by some, son of Apollo. He married Eriphyle, the sister of Adrastus, king of Argos, by whom he had two sons, Alcmæon and Amphilochus, When Adrastus declared war against Thebes, Amphiaraus secreted himself, that he might not go to a war in which he was doomed to perish. But Eriphyle was prevailed upon to betray him by Polynices, who gave her, for her perfidy, a famous necklace. Amphiaraus went to the war, but previously charged his son Alcmæon to put to death his mother Eriphyle, as soon as he was informed that he was killed. The Theban war proved fatal to the Argives, and Amphiaraus was swallowed up in his chariot by the earth, as he attempted to retire from the battle. The news of his death was brought to Alcmæon, who immediately executed his father's command, and murdered Eriphyle. Amphiaraus received divine honors after death, and had a celebrated temple and oracle at Oropus, in Attica. His statue was made of white marble, and near his temple was a fountain, the waters of which were ever held sacred. They only who had consulted his oracle, or had been delivered from a disease, were permitted to bathe there; after which they gratefully threw pieces of gold and silver into the stream. Those who consulted the oracle of Amphiaraus, first purified themselves, and abstained from food for 24 hours, and three days from wine; after which they sacrificed a ram to the prophet, and spread the skin upon the ground, upon which they slept in expectation of receiving in a dream the answer of the oracle. Plutarch *de Orac. Defect.* mentions, that the oracle of Amphiaraus was once consulted in the time of Xerxes, by one of the servants of Mardonius, for his master, who was with an army in Greece; and that the servant when asleep saw in a dream the priest of the temple, who upbraided him, and drove him away, and even threw stones at his head when he refused to comply. This oracle was verified in the death of Mardonius, who was soon after actually killed by the blow of a stone which he received on the head. *Cic. de Div.* 1. c. 40.—*De Leg.* 2. 13.—*Philostr. in Vit.*—*Apollon.* 2. c. 11. *Homer. Odyss.* 15. v. 243. &c.—*Hygin.* fab. 70, 73. &c. —*Diod.* 4.—*Ovid.* 9. fab. 10.—*Paus.* 1. c. 34. l. 2. c. 37. &c.—*Æschyl. Sept. contra. Theb.*—*Apollod.* 1. c. 8 & 9. l. 3. c. 6, &c.—*Strab.* 8.

AM'PHIAS, a person sent by the Epidaurians, in the eighth year of the Peloponnesian war, to reconcile the Athenians and Lacedæmonians. *Schol. in Aristoph. Equit.*——A person mentioned by *Macrobius*, sat. 7. c. 3. as having arrived at great wealth from the lowest state of poverty.

AMPHICÆ'A, called Ophitea by *Pausanias*, a town of Phocis, where Bacchus had a temple. *Herod.* 8. c. 33. Also Amphicli'a.

AMPHIC'LUS, a Trojan killed by Meges, during the siege of his country. *Homer. Il.* 16. v. 313.——A son of Agis, father of Amphisthenes of Sparta. *Paus.* 3. c. 16.

AMPHIC'RATES, an historian who wrote the lives of illustrious men. *Diog. Laert. in Aristip.* 2. c. 101.——An Athenian sophist, banished from his country. He retired to Seleucia, where he starved himself to death. Some suppose he was the same as the former. *Plut. in Lucul.—Jonsius.* 2. *de Script. Hist. Phil.* c. 15.

AMPHIC'TYON, son of Deucalion and Pyrrha, reigned at Athens after Cranaus, and first attempted to give a satisfactory interpretation of dreams, and to draw omens. Some say that the deluge happened in his age. *Justin.* 2. c. 6.——The son of Helenus, who first established the celebrated council of the Amphictyons, composed of the wisest and most virtuous men of some cities of Greece. This august assembly consisted of twelve persons, who bore the title of Pylagores, and were originally sent by the following states: the Ionians, Dorians, Perrhæbians, Bœotians, Magnesians, Phthians, Locrians, Malians, Phocians, Thessalians, Dolopes, and the people of Œta. Other cities, in process of time, sent also some of their citizens to the council of the Amphictyons, and in the age of Antonius Pius their number was increased to 30. They generally met twice every year at Delphi, and sometimes sat at Thermopylæ; though some authors assert that they always sat at Delphi in the spring, and at Anthela, near Thermopylæ, in the autumn. The object of their deliberations was the public affairs of the country; and they took into consideration all matters of difference which might exist between the states of Greece. When the Phocians plundered the temple of Delphi, the Amphictyons declared war against them, and this war was supported by all the states of Greece, and lasted ten years. In consequence of this, the Phocians, with their allies, the Lacedæmonians, were deprived of the privilege of sitting in the council of the Amphictyons, and the Macedonians were admitted in their place, for their services in support of the war. About sixty years after, when Brennus, with the Gauls, invaded Greece, the Phocians behaved with such courage, that they were restored to their former privileges. Before they proceeded to business, the Amphictyons sacrificed an ox to Apollo in the several cities which they represented. Their decisions were held so sacred and inviolable, that even arms were taken up to enforce them. Much valuable information respecting this interesting council may be derived from various parts, but especially the first volume, of Mr. *Mitford's* excellent history of Greece. *Paus. in Phocic. & Achaic.—Strab.* 8.*—Suidas—Hesych.—Æschin.*

AMPHID'AMAS, a son of Aleus, was of the family of the Inachidæ, and one of the Argonauts. *Flacc.* 1. v. 376.—*Paus.* 8. c. 5.——The father of Melanion and of the wife of Eurystheus, was son of Lycurgus and Cleophile. *Apollod.* 2. c. 17.——The father of Clysonymus, supposed to be the same mentioned by *Homer, Il.* 10. v. 268. l. 23. v. 87.——A son of Ægeus and Cleobule, one of the Argonauts. *Hygin.* fab. 14.——A son of Busiris, killed by Hercules. *Apollod.* 2. c. 5.——A warrior, who fell in a battle against the Eretrians. *Plut. in con.* 7. *Sapient.* c. 21.

AMPHID'OLI a city of Triphylia. *Steph.*

AMPHIDRO'MIA (from ἀμφίδρομος, *circum currens,*) a festival observed by private families at Athens, the fifth day after the birth of every child. It was customary to *run round* the fire with the child, to present him to the domestic gods, and to give him a name in the presence of the parents. *Meurs. Mis.—Hesychius in Verb.—Harpocration de Abort—Lys.*

AMPHIGENI'A, a town of Messenia. *Stat.* 4.—*Theb.* v. 178. Also Amphige'nia.

AMPHIL'OCHI, a people of Acharnania, in Epirus; their city was called Amphilochia, or Argos Amphilochicum, and is now Anfiolca. *Mela*, c. 4.—*Cluver.* 4. c. 7.

AMPHILO'CHIA, *Vid.* Amphilochi.——A city of Hispania Tarraconensis, now Orense. It was fonded by Teucer, and called after his companion Amphilochus. *Strabo.*

AMPHILO'CHIUS, a bishop of Iconium in Lycaonia. His writings, of which there are but few remains, were very valuable. *Fabr. B. Gr.* 8. p. 373.—*Sax. Onom.* 1. p. 381.

AMPHIL'OCHUS, a son of Amphiaraus and Eriphyle, engaged in the Theban war, where he distinguished himself. *Apollod.* 3.—*Hom Od.* 15. v. 248.—*Paus.* 2. c. 18 & 20.——A son of Alcmæon, by Manto, daughter of Tiresias. After his return from the Trojan war, he left Argos, his native country, and built Argos Amphilochicum or Amphilochia. *Cic. Pis.* 12.—*Liv.* 38. c. 5.—*Strab.* 10.—*Paus.* 2. c. 18.——An Athenian philosopher who wrote upon agriculture. *Varro de R. R.* 1.——A son of Cteatus, one of Helen's suitors, called also Amphimachus. *Apollod.* 3.

AMPHILY'SUS, a river flowing from mount Assarus, in Samus. *Steph.*

AMPHIL'YTUS, a soothsayer of Acarnania, who encouraged Pisistratus to seize the sovereign power at Athens. *Herodot.* 1. c. 62.

AMPHIM'ACHE, a daughter of Amphidamas, wife of Eurystheus. *Apollod.* 2.

AMPHIM'ACHUS, one of Helen's suitors. *Apollod.* 3. c. 10.—*Hygin.* fab. 97.—*Vid.* Amphilochus.——A son of Actor and Theronice. *Paus.* 5. c. 3.——A son of Nomion, who was at the Trojan war at the head of the Carians and the inhabitants of the banks of the Mæander. *Homer. Il.* 2.——A son of Polyxenus of Elis, in Peloponnesus. *Paus.* 5. c. 3.

AMPHIMA'LIA, a town of Crete, with a bay called Sinus Amphimalus, now Golfo di Suda or di Nicola. *Cluv.* 4. c. 12.

AMPHIM'EDON, a Lybian, killed by Perseus at the court of Cepheus. *Ovid. Met.* 5. v. 75.——One of Penelope's suitors, son of Melantheus. He was killed by Telemachus. *Homer. Od.* 22. v. 283.

AMPHIN'OME, the name of one of the Nereides, attendants of Thetis. *Hygin. in Præf. Fab.—Hom. Il.* 18. v. 44.—This name is also given to the mother of Jason by *Diodorus*, though other mythologists call her Alcimene.

AMPHIN'OMUS, son of Nisus, was one of Penelope's suitors, and was killed by Telemachus. He was the cause that the life of Telemachus was spared. *Hom. Od.* 16 & 22.——A philosopher and geometrician, commended by *Proclus*. *Comment. in Eucl.* 1.—*Voss. de Scient. Math.* c. 54. *sec.* 17.

AMPHIN'OMUS and ANA'PIUS, two brothers, who, when Catana and the neighbouring cities were in flames by an eruption from mount Ætna, saved their parents by conveying them away upon their shoulders. The fire, as it is said, spared these affectionate youths, while it consumed others by their side; and Pluto, to reward their uncommon piety, placed them after death in the island of Leuce. They received divine honours in Sicily. *Val. Max.* 5. c. 4.—*Strab.* 6.—*Ital.* 14. v. 197.—*Seneca de Benef.* 3.—*Cornel. Sever. in Ætna*, 620.—*Claudian. Ep. de Amph.*

AMPHI'ON was son of Jupiter, by Antiope, daughter of Nycteus. He was born on mount Cithæron, at the same birth with Zethus; and the two children were exposed in the woods, but their lives were preserved by a shepherd. *Vid.* Antiope. He is said to have been the inventor of music, and to have built the walls of Thebes by the sound of his lyre. Mercury was his instructor, and gave him the lyre, to which he added three strings; and he was the first who raised an altar to Mercury. Zethus and Amphion united to avenge the wrongs which their mother had suffered from the cruelties of Dirce. They besieged and took Thebes, put Lycus to death, and tied his wife Dirce to the tail of a wild bull, which dragged her over rocks and through precipices till she expired. The fable which describes Amphion as moving stones, and raising the walls of Thebes at the sound of his lyre has been explained, by supposing that he persuaded, by the force of his eloquence, a wild and uncivilized people to unite together and build a town to protect themselves against the attacks of their enemies. His tomb was shewn at Thebes in the age of the Antonines; and near it appeared some unpolished stones, which, tradition says, were drawn thither by the power of his lyre. *Vid.* Dirce, Lycus, &c. *Palæphat de Incr.* 42.—*Macrob. in Scip.—Somn.* 3.—*Boccac. in Gen. D.* 5. c. 30.—*Antimenidas,* 1. *Hist.—Pherecyd.* 10. *apud. Athen.* 12. *& Nat. Com.* 8. c. 15.—*Gyrald. de Poet. H.* 2.—*Schol. Apollon.* 1. *Argon.* —*Hom. Od.* 11.—*Apollod.* 3. c. 5 & 10.—*Paus.* 6. c. 6. l. 6. c. 20. &c.—*Propert.* 3. el. 15.—*Ovid. de Art. Am.* 3. v. 323.—*Horat.* 3. od. 11. *Art. Poet.* v. 394.—*Stat. Theb.* 1. v. 10. [The celebrated colossal group at Naples, known by the name of the "Toro Farnese," is commemorative of the punishment of Dirce, in which Amphion is one of the principal figures.]——Son of Jasus, king of Orchomenus, married Niobe, daughter of Tantalus. He has been confounded by mythologists with the son of Antiope; though Homer, in his Odyssey, distinguishes them beyond contradiction. The number of Amphion's children, according to Homer, was twelve, six of each; according to Ælian, twenty: and according to Ovid, fourteen, seven males and seven females. All these children, except Chloris, were destroyed by the arrows of Apollo and Diana, and Amphion killed himself in a fit of despair. *Vid.* Niobe. *Hom. Od.* 11. v. 261 & 282. & *Schol. ibid.* —*Diod.* 4.—*Paus.* 9. c. 36.—*Ælian. V. H.* 12. v. 36.—*Ovid. Met.* 6. fab. 5.——One of the Argonauts, son of Hyperasius, king of Pellene in Arcadia. *Flacc.* 1. v. 367.—*Schol. Apollon.* 1. v. 176.—*Hygin.* fab. 14.——A famous statuary, son of Acestor of Gnossus, in Crete. *Paus.* 10. c. 15.—*Plin.* 36. c. 10——One of the Greek generals in the Trojan war. *Homer. Il.* 13. v. 692.——A famous painter. *Plin.* 35. c. 10.——A freed man of Q. Catulus; a man of great genius. *Id.* 35. c. 18.

AMPHIP'OLES, magistrates at Syracuse, appointed by Timoleon, after the expulsion of Dionysius the younger. The office existed for above three hundred years. *Diod.* 16.

AMPHIP'OLIS, called Christopolis, or Emboli, by the Turks, a town on the Strymon, between Macedonia and Thrace. An Athenian colony under Agnon, son of Nicias, drove the ancient inhabitants, called Edonians, from the country, and built a city, which they called Amphipolis, *i.e.* a town surrounded on all sides, because the Strymon flowed all round it. It has been also called Myrica, Eïon, Novem-Viæ, and the town of Mars. It was so advantageously situated for commerce and for security, that it proved the cause of many wars between the rival states of Athens and Sparta. *Thucyd.* 4. c. 102. &c.—*Herodot.* 5. c. 126. l. 7. c. 114.—*Diod.* 11, 12, &c.—*C. Nep. in Cim.*——A town of Syria, near the Euphrates, founded by Seleucus, and called by the Syrians Turmeda. *Steph.*

AMPHIP'YROS, (from ἀμφίπυρος, *utrumque ardens,*) a surname of Diana, because she is represented as carrying a *torch* in *each* of her hands. *Sophocles in Trach.*

AMPHI'RA, an epithet of Minerva. *Lycoph.*

AMPHIRE'TUS, a man of Acanthus, who artfully escaped from pirates, who had made him prisoner. *Polyæn.* 6.

AMPHIR'OE, one of the Oceanides. *Hesiod. Theog.* v. 361.

AM'PHIS, a Greek comic poet of Athens, contemporary with Plato. Beside his comedies he wrote other pieces, all of which are now lost, though occasionally quoted by *Stobæus, Athenæus,* and the *Scholiast* of *Aratus. Gyrald. de Poet. Hist.* 7.—*Suidas.* —*Diog.*

AMPHI'SA, a river of Phocis.

AMPHIS'SA or IS'SA, a daughter of Macareus, beloved by Apollo. She gave her name to a city of Locris, in which was a temple of Minerva. *Liv.* 37. c. 5.—*Paus.* 10. c. 38.—*Strab.* 9.—*Lucan.* 3. v. 172.

AMPHIS'SA, a town of Locris, now Lambina. *Lucan.* 3. 172. &c.——A town on the eastern coast of the Brutii; it is now La Rocella. *Ovid. Met.* 15. v. 703.

AMPHISSE'NE, a country of Armenia. *Steph. ex Strab.*

AMPHIS'SUS, a son of Dryope. *Ovid. Met.* 9. v. 356.

AMPHIS'THENES, a Lacedæmonian, who became delirious whilst offering sacrifices to Diana. *Paus.* 3. c. 16.

AMPHISTI'DES, a man so naturally destitute of intellect, that he seldom remembered that he ever had a father. He wished to learn arithmetic, but never could comprehend beyond the figure 5. *Aristot. Probl.* § 10.

AMPHIS'TRATUS and RHE'CAS, two men of Laconia, charioteers of Castor and Pollux. *Strab.* 11. —*Justin.* 42. c. 3.

AMPHIS'TRATUS, a statuary. *Plin.* 36. c. 5.

AMPHITH'EA, the mother of Ægialeus, by Cyanippus; and of three daughters, Argia, Deipyle, and Ægialea, by Adrastus, king of Argos. *Apollod.* 1. ——The wife of Autolycus, by whom she had Anticlea, the wife of Laertes. *Hom. Od.* 19. v. 416.

AMPHITHEA'TRUM, a large round or oval building, where the people assembled to see the combats of gladiators, and of the wild beasts, and other exhibitions. They were generally built of wood. Statilius Taurus, in the time of Augustus, was the first who built them of stone.

AMPHITH'EMIS, a Theban general, who involved the Lacedæmonians in a war with his country. *Plut in Lys.—Paus.* 3. c. 9.

AMPHITH'EUS, a priest of Ceres at Athens, whom Aristophanes, in order to ridicule Euripides, makes a descendant of the goddess. *Aristoph. in Acharn.*

AMPHITH'OE, one of the Nereides. *Gyrald. Hist. D.* 5.—*Hygin. Fab. Præfat.*

AMPHITRI'TE, a daughter of Oceanus and Tethys, married Neptune. She became mother of Triton, and shared the divine honours of her husband, especially at Corinth, where she had a statue erected in his temple. The name is often used by the poets for the sea itself. *Varro. de L. L.* 4.—*Hesiod. Theog.* 930.—*Apollod.* 3.—*Claudian. de Rapt. Pros.* 1. v. 104.—*Ovid. Met.* 1. v. 14.—*Hygin. P. A.* 2. c. 17. [The statues of this deity are uncommon; but there is one of colossal size at the entrance of the Villa Albani, near Rome.]——One of the Nereides. *Hesiod. Theog.* 241.—*Apollod.* 1.

AMPHIT'ROPE, a part of the tribe Antiochis, not far from Cephissia. *Æsch. cont. Timarch.*

AMPHIT'RYON, a Theban prince, son of Alcæus and Hipponome. His sister Anaxo had married Electryon, king of Mycenæ, whose sons were killed by the Teleboans in battle. Electryon promised his crown, and daughter Alcmena, to him who should revenge the death of his sons upon the Teleboans. *Vid.* Alcmena. Amphitryon accordingly went to the war, and when he returned home from his expedition, he brought back to Electryon the herds which the Teleboans had taken from him in their former incursions. One of the cows having strayed from the rest, Amphitryon threw a stick at it, which struck the horns of the cow, and rebounded with such violence upon Electryon, that he was killed on the spot. Amphitryon, upon this, was obliged to leave Argolis, and to retire to Thebes with Alcmena, when Creon, king of Thebes, purified him of the murder. *Appollod.* 2. c. 4.—*Virg. Æn.* 8. v. 213.—*Propert.* 4. el. 10. v. 1.—*Hesiod. in Scut. Hercul.—Hygin.* fab. 29.—*Paus.* 8. c. 14.—*Flacc.* 1. v. 371.—*Lucan.* 9. v. 644.

AMPHITRYONI'ADES, a surname of Hercules, as the supposed son of Amphitryon. *Virg. Æn.* 8. v. 103.

AM'PHITUS, a charioteer. *Vid.* Amphistratus.——A priest of Ceres at the court of Cepheus. *Ovid. Met.* 5.

AM'PHIUS, a son of Merops the soothsayer, who, in spite of his father's prophecies, went to the siege of Troy. *Hom. Il.* 2. v. 830. Also Amphi'us.

AMPHOT'ERUS, an officer appointed commander of a fleet in the Hellespont by Alexander. *Curt.* 3. c. 1.——A son of Alcmæon. *Vid.* Acarnan.

AMPHRY'SUS, a river of Thessaly, near which Apollo, when banished from heaven, tended the flocks of king Admetus. From this circumstance the god has been called *Amphrysius,* and his priestess *Amphrysia vates. Ovid. Met.* 1. v. 580.—*Lucan.* 6. v. 367.—*Virg. G.* 3. v. 2. *Æn.* 6. v. 398. *& Servius, ibid.*——A river of Phrygia, the waters of which rendered women liable to barrenness. *Plin.* 32. c. 2.——A city of Phocis. *Steph.*

AM'PIA LABIE'NA LEX, was enacted by T. Ampius and T. Labienus, tribunes of the people, A.U.C. 693. It gave Pompey the Great the privilege of appearing in triumphal robes at the Circensian games, and with a prætexta and golden crown at the theatre.

T. AM'PIUS FLAVIA'NUS, a consul or lieutenant at Panonnia. *Tac. Hist.* 2. 86. *Fulvius Ursinus,* however, reads Tampius Flavianus.

AMPRA'CIA. *Vid.* Ambracia.

AMP'SAGA, a river which separates Mauritania Cæsariensis, on the west, from Numidia, and falls into the Mediterranean Sea at the west of Hippo. It is now called Suffegmar. *Cluver*. 6. c. 5.—*Mela*, 1. c. 6.

AMP'SALIS or AL'BA SE'QUIA, a town of Asiatic Sarmatia. *Ptol.*

AMPYC'IDES, a patronymic of Mopsus, son of Ampyx. *Ovid. Met.* 8. v. 316.

AM'PYX, a son of Pelias. *Paus.* 7. c. 18.——The father of the soothsayer Mopsus. *Ovid Met.* 5. 184. l. 8. v. 316. &c.—*Orph. in Argon.*—*Paus.* 5. c. 17. ——A noble person of Patræ. *Paus.* 1.

AMSANC'TUS, a lake in the country of the Hirpini in Italy, at the east of Capua, the waters of which were said to be so sulphureous that they infected and destroyed whatever animals approached it. It was through this place that Virgil represents the fury Alecto to have descended into hell, after her visit to the upper regions. *Virg. Æn.* 7. v. 565.—*Cic. de Div.* 1. c. 36.

AMU'DASA, a city of Byzacena, in Africa Propria.

AMU'LIUS, king of Alba, and son of Procas, was youngest brother of Numitor, whose son Lausus he slew, and consecrated his daughter Rhea Sylvia to the service of Vesta, to prevent her from ever becoming a mother. He was put to death by Romulus and Remus, who restored the crown to their grandfather Numitor. *Vid.* Ilia, Numitor, &c. *Ovid. Fast.* 3. v. 67.—*Liv.* 1. c. 3 & 4.—*Plut. in Romul.*—*Flor.* 1. c. 1.—*Dion. Hal.*—*Servius in Æn.* 1. v. 277.——A celebrated painter. *Plin.* 35. c. 10.

AMU'LIUS SERE'NUS, a captain of the prætorian cohorts, *Tac. Hist.* 1. c. 31.

AM'UN, the Ægyptian name of Jupiter, similar to the Ammon of the Greeks and Latins. *Plut. de Isid. & Osir.* &c.

A'MUS, a city of Caria. *Steph.*

AMUTHANTÆ'US, the thirty-seventh Theban king of Ægypt, who reigned 63 years. *Joh. Marsham. Can. Chron.*

AM'YCI POR'TUS, a place in Pontus, famous for the death of Amycus, king of the Bebryces. It is now Lamia or Scala marmorea. His tomb was covered with laurels, the boughs of which were said, when carried on board a ship, to cause uncommon dissensions among the sailors. *Plin.* 5. c. 32.—*Arrian.*

AMY'CLA, a daughter of Niobe, spared by Diana. *Paus.* 2. c. 22.—*Apollod.* 3. *Homer* says that all the daughters perished. *Il.* 24. *Vid.* Niobe.——The nurse of Alcibiades. *Plut.*

AMY'CLÆ, a town of Italy, between Caieta and Tarracina, built by the companions of Castor and Pollux. The inhabitants were strict followers of the precepts of Pythagoras, and, therefore, abstained from flesh. False reports having been often spread respecting the approach of the enemy, a law was passed to forbid any one to give credit to them; and the city was consequently taken. From this circumstance the epithet of *tacitæ* has been given to Amyclæ. Some discover the origin of this epithet in the submission of the inhabitants to the precepts of Pythagoras, whose scholars were enjoined some years of silence, before they were admitted to the philosopher's conversation. *Plin.* 8. c. 29. —*Virg. Æn.* 10. v. 564.—*Sidonius*, 8. ep. 6.—*Sil.* 8. v. 529.——A city of Peloponnesus, near Lacedæmon, built by Amyclas, and the birth-place of Castor and Pollux. The country was famous for dogs. Apollo, called Amyclæus, had a rich and magnificent temple there, surrounded with delightful groves. *Paus.* 3. c. 18.—*Stat. Theb.* 4. v. 223. l. 7. v. 162.—*Ital.* 2. v. 434.—*Meurs. Mis. Lacon.* 4. c. 2. *Strab.* 8.—*Virg. G.* 3. v. 345.—*Ovid. de Art. Am.* 2. v. 5.

AMYCLÆ'UM, a city and harbour of Crete. *Steph.*

AMYCLÆ'US, a statuary. *Paus.* 10. c. 13.——A surname of Apollo.

AMY'CLAS, son of Lacedæmon and Sparta, built the city of Amycla. He married Diomede, daughter of Lapithus, by whom he had Cynortas. *Tzetzes in Lycoph.*—*Apollod.* 1. c. 23. l. 3. c. 19.—*Paus.* 3. c. 1. l. 7. c. 18.——The master of a ship in which Cæsar embarked in disguise. When Amyclas wished to put back to avoid a violent storm, Cæsar discovered himself and exclaimed, *Cæsarem vehis, Cæsarisque fortunam. Lucan.* 5. v. 520.—— A Pythagorean philosopher and geometrician. *Procl.* l. 2. *in Eucl.*—*Diog. Laert. in Democ.*—— A king of Sparta.

AMYC'TERES, a monstrous nation of India. *Strab.* —*Salmas. in Solin.* p. 1006.

AM'YCUS, son of Neptune by Melia, was king of the Bebryces, and celebrated for his skill in the management of the cæstus. He challenged all strangers to a trial of strength, and Pollux, when engaged in his Argonautic expedition, accepted his challenge, and killed him. *Apollon.* 2. *Argon.*—*Theocrit. Id.* 22.—*Servius in Æn.* 5. v. 373.—*Lactant. in* 3. *Theb.* 353.—*Apollod.* 1. c. 9.——One of the companions of Æneas, who almost perished in a storm on the coast of Africa. He was killed by Turnus. *Virg. Æn.* 1. v. 225, &c.——A Trojan, likewise killed by Turnus. *Id.* 12. v. 509.——A son of Ixion and the cloud. *Ovid. Met.* 12. v. 245.

AM'YDON, a city of Pæonia, in Macedonia, which sent auxiliaries to Priam during the Trojan war. *Homer. Il.* 20. 848.—*Juv.* 3. v. 69.

AMYM'NI, a people of Epirus. *Steph.*

AMYMO'NE, daughter of Danaus, married Enceladus, whom she murdered. While hunting in the woods, she wounded a satyr, who pursued her, and offered her violence, but Neptune delivered her. It was said that she was the only one of the fifty sisters who was not condemned to fill the leaky tub with water in hell, because she had been so continually employed, by order of her father, in supplying the city of Argos with water, in a great drought. Neptune saw her thus employed, and, being enamoured of her, carried her away, and in the place where she stood, he raised a fountain, by striking a rock. The fountain has been called Amymone. She bore Nauplius to Neptune. *Propert.* 2. el. 26. v. 46.—*Apollod.* 2.—*Strab.* 8.—*Paus.* 2. c. 37.—*Ovid. Amor.* 1. v. 515.—*Hygin.* fab. 169.

AMYMO'NE, a fountain and rivulet in Peloponnesus, flowing through Argolis into the lake of Lerna. Amymone is said to have been changed into this fountain by Neptune. *Ovid. Met.* 2. v. 240.

AMYN'IAS, a horse dealer mentioned by *Aristophanes, in Nub.*

AMYN'TÆ, a nation of Thesprotia. *Steph.*

AMYN'TAS the First, was king of Macedonia, after his father Alcetas. When his son Alexander murdered the ambassadors of Megabyzus (*Vid.* Alexander,) Bubares, a Persian general, was sent with an army to avenge their death; but he married the king's daughter and defended his possessions. *Justin.* 7. c. 3.—*Herodot.* 5, 7 & 8.

AMYN'TAS the Second, was son of Menelaus, and king of Macedonia, after his murder of Pausanias. He was expelled from his throne by the Illyrians, and restored by the assistance of the Thessalians and Spartans. He afterwards made war against the Illyrians and Olynthians, and lived to a great age. He had Philip, Alexander the Great's father, by his first wife, and several other children. He reigned 24 years; and, soon after his death, his son Philip murdered all his brothers, and ascended the throne. *Justin.* 7. c. 4 & 9.—*Diod.* 14, &c.—*C. Nep. & Plut. in Pelopid.* There were other kings of Macedonia of the name, but of them few particulars are recorded in history.

AMYN'TAS, the successor of Dejotarus in the kingdom of Gallogræcia. After his death it became a Roman province. *Strab.* 12.——One of Alexander's officers. *Curt.* 2. c. 6.——Another officer, who deserted to Darius, and was killed as he attempted to seize on Ægypt. *Curt* 3. c. 9.——A son of Antiochus, who withdrew himself from Macedonia, because he hated Alexander. *Curt.*—*Arrian.*—*Diod. Sic.*——An officer in Alexander's cavalry. He was accused of conspiracy against the king, on account of his great intimacy with Philotas, but was acquitted. *Curt.* 4. c. 15. l. 6. c. 9. l. 8. c. 12.——A shepherd's name, often introduced in *Virgil's Eclogues.*——A Greek writer, who composed several works quoted by *Athenæus*, 10 & 12, and by *Ælian, H. A.* 17. c. 17.

AMYNTIA'NUS, an historian in the age of Antoninus, who wrote a treatise in commendation of Philip, Olympias, and Alexander. *Phot. Bibl. Cod.* 131.—*Voss. Hist. Græc.* 2. c. 14.

AMYN'TOR, a king of Argos, son of Phrastor. He deprived his son Phœnix of his eyes, to punish him for the violence which he had offered to Clytia, his concubine. *Hygin.* fab. 173.—*Ovid. Met.* 8. v. 307. —*Apollod.* 3.—*Homer. Il.* 9.——A general of the Dolopes. *Ovid. Met.* 12. v. 364.——A son of Ægyptus, killed by Damone, the first night of his marriage. *Hygin.* fab. 170.——A Macedonian, father of Hephæstion.

AMYR'GIUM, a plain of the Sacæ. *Steph.*

AMYRI'CUS CAM'PUS, a plain of Thessaly. *Polyb.* 3.

AM'YRIS, a man of Sybaris, who consulted the oracle of Delphi concerning the probable duration of his country's prosperity, &c.

AMYR'TUS, a king by whom Cyrus was killed in a battle. *Ctesias.*

AM'YRUS, a town of Thessaly. *Steph.*——A river mentioned by *Valerius Flaccus*, 2. v. 11.

AMYS'TIS, a river of India falling into the Ganges. *Arrian in Indic.*

AMYTHA'ON, a son of Cretheus, king of Iolcus, by Tyro. He married Idomene, by whom he had Bias and Melampus, and a daughter called Perimele. After his father's death, he established himself in Messenia, and re-established or regulated the Olympic games. Melampus is called Amythaonius, from his father Amythaon, and part of Elis is also called Amythaonia from him. *Virg. G.* 3. v. 550.—*Diod.* 4.—*Apollod.* 1.—*Hom. Od.* 11.——A son of Hippasus, who assisted Priam in the Trojan war, and was killed by Lycomedes. *Hom. Il.* 17.

AMYTHAO'NIUS. *Vid.* Amythaon.

AM'YTIS, a daughter of Astyages, whom Cyrus married. *Ctesias.*——A daughter of Xerxes, who married Megabyzus, and disgraced herself by her debaucheries.

AMY'ZON, a city of Caria, now Mezo. *Plin.* 5. c. 29.

AN'ABIS, a city of Hispania Tarraconensis, now probably Igualada in Catalonia. *Ptol.*——A village of Ægypt. *Euseb.*

AN'ABUM, a city near the Danube. *Ptol.*

AN'ACE, a city of Achaia. *Steph.*

AN'ACES, or ANACTES, a name given to Castor and Pollux among the Athenians. Their festivals were called Anacea. *Plut. in Thes.*—*Cic. N. D.* 3. c. 21.

ANACE'UM, a mountain in Attica, with a temple sacred to the Anaces. *Polyæn.* 1. c. 21.

ANACHAR'SIS, a Scythian philosopher who flourished 592 B.C. From his extensive knowledge, he has been called one of the seven wise men of Greece. When he returned to Scythia from Athens, where he had studied for some time, and had been intimate with Solon, he wished to introduce there the laws of the Athenians. This so irritated his brother, who was then on the throne, that he killed him with an arrow. Anacharsis rendered himself known by his writings, and his poems on war, the laws of Scythia, &c. Two of his letters to Crœsus and Hanno are still extant. The invention of anchors, of the potter's wheel, and of tinder has been attributed to him. Many of his apophthegms are preserved, and are remarkable for their shrewdness. He was wont to observe that the vine bore three sorts of grapes; the first productive of mirth, the second of drunkenness, and the third of repentance. When reproached by an Athenian for being a Scythian, he replied, "True, my country disgraces me, but you are a disgrace to your country." The name of Anacharsis has been rendered familiar to modern ears, by the elegant, valuable, and truly classical work of Barthelemi, called the travels of Anacharsis. *Herodot.* 4. c. 46, 47 & 48. *Plut. in Conviv.*—*Cic. Tusc.* 5. c. 32.—*Strab.* 7.—*Sax. Onom.* 1. p. 20.—*Fabr. B. Gr.* 9. p. 643.

ANACINDARAX'ES, a king of Nineveh, father of Sardanapalus. *Schol. in Aristoph. Av.*

ANAC'OLE, an island of the Ægæan sea. *Antonin.*

ANAC'REON, a famous lyric poet of Teus, in Ionia. The attack made on his country by Harpagus, the general of Cyrus, obliged him to flee with his fellow citizens to Abdera in Thrace; whence he retired to the court of Polycrates, tyrant of Samus, by whom he was kindly received. Anacreon was invited to Athens by Hipparchus, son of Pisistratus: after his death he returned to Teus, and, on the revolt of Histiæus, he again removed to Abdera, where he died. Love and wine were the constant burden of his song, and his writings possess beauties which succeeding poets have in vain attempted to equal. Uncommon sweetness, great elegance, and graces of the most fascinating nature, though dispersed with a careless hand, abound in his poems. "He flows," as Rapin has well said, "softly and easily, every where diffusing the joy and indolence of his mind through his verse, and tuning his harp to the smooth and pleasant temper of his soul." Besides odes and epigrams, Anacreon wrote elegies, hymns, and iambics; but of these only some of his odes are extant. Though only bacchanalian and love sonnets, and accompanied with a freedom often offensive to morality, yet they have been, and must continue to be, the admiration of every age and country. He lived to his 85th year, when he was choked with a grape stone. *Plato* says, that Codrus, the last king of Athens, was one of his progenitors. There was a statue of him in the citadel of Athens, representing him as an old drunken man, singing. Anacreon flourished 532 B.C. His odes were first published by H. Stephens, with an elegant translation. The best editions of his works are, that of Maittaire, 4to. London, 1725, of which only 100 copies were printed; and the very correct one of Barnes, 12mo. Cantab. 1721; to which may be added that of Brunck, 12mo. Argentor. 1778. *Paus.* 1. c. 2. 25.—*Strab.* 14.—*Ælian. V. H.* 9. c. 4.—*Cic. in Tusc.* 4. c. 33.—*Horat. Epod.* 14. v. 20.—*Plin.*— 7. c. 7.—*Herodot.* 3. c. 121 —*Maxim. Tyr.* 2.—*Sax. Onom.* 1. p. 24.—*Fabr. B. Gr.* 2. p. 91. [There is a bust of Anacreon in the Museum of the Capitol.] Also Ana'creon.

ANACTO'RIA or ANACTO'RIUM, a town of Epirus, in a peninsula on the east of the gulph of Ambracia. It was founded by a Corinthian colony, and, from its situation, proved the cause of many quarrels between the Corcyræans and Corinthians. Augustus removed the inhabitants to Nicopolis, on the shores of the Ambracian bay, after the battle of Actium. *Strab.* 10.—*Thucyd.* 1. c. 55.—*Plin.* 4. c. 1. l. 5. c. 29.——An ancient name of Miletus.

ANACTO'RIE, a woman of Lesbus, beloved by Sappho. *Ovid. Her.* 15. v. 17.

ANADYOM'ENE, a valuable painting of Venus, by Apelles, in which she was represented as rising from the sea, and wringing her wet hair. Augustus bought it of the inhabitants of Cos, where it adorned the sanctuary of Æsculapius, by remitting the hundred talents of tribute which they paid to Rome, and placed it in the temple of Julius Cæsar. The lower part of it was a little defaced, and there were, at that time, no painters in Rome able to repair it. It was said that the beautiful courtezan Phryne sat as a model to the painter. *Athen.* 13. c. 6.—*Antipat. in Anthol.* 4. c 12.—*Phurnut de N. D.* 24 —*Ovid. de A. A.* 3. v. 401.—*Plin.* 35. c. 10.

ANÆ'A, a city of Caria, opposite Samus; so called from an Amazon of that name. *Thucydides* calls the people Anaitæ, but *Stephanus*, Anæi.

ANÆ'TIA, a city of Armenia Major, washed by the Euphrates. *Plin.* 5. c. 24.

ANAGAL'LIS, a grammarian of Corcyra, called Agallis by *Athenæus*. It is probably a surname from the herb anagallis. *Suidas.*—*Casaub. in Athen.*

ANAG'NIA, now Anagni, a city of the Hernici, where Antony caused a medal to be struck when he divorced Octavia and married Cleopatra. The people are called Anagnini by *Livy* and *Pliny*, but Anagnitæ by *Diodorus Siculus*. *Virg. Æn.* 7. v. 684.—*Cic. Att.* 16. ep. 8.—*Plin.* 3. c. 5. l. 34. c. 6. —*Strab.* 5.—*Ital.* 8. v. 392. *Cluver.* 3. c. 27.

ANAGNU'TES, a people of Aquitania, now Pays d'Aunis.

ANAGO'GIA and CATAGO'GIA, the names of festivals yearly observed by the people of Eryx in Sicily, in honour of Venus. She was said, during the celebration of the Anagogia, to leave the mountain, attended by all the doves which resorted to it. After nine days the goddess and the doves returned, when the festival called Catagogia was celebrated. *Ælian. V. H.* 1. c. 15. *H. A.* 4. c. 2.

ANAG'YRUS, a place in the tribe Erechtheis, in Attica which produced an offensive plant, called Anagyris, which became more fetid the more it was touched; whence arose the proverb, *Anagyrum commovere*, to signify the bringing of misfortune on oneself. Cybele had a temple there. *Strab.* 9. —*Plin.* 27. c. 4.——A genius, who revenged himself upon an old man who had injured a grove which was sacred to him, by making the old man's concubine fall in love with his son. When he rejected her addresses, she accused him of an attempt upon her virtue, when the old man threw him down from the roof of the house, and afterwards hanged himself. *Suidas. ex Aristoph. Lysistr.*

ANAIT'ICA, a region of Armenia, so called from the goddess Anaitis. Its exact position is not now known. *Plin.* 5. c. 24.

ANAI'TIS, a goddess of Armenia. Her festivals were called *Sacarum festa*; and during their celebration, the votaries of the goddess inebriated themselves to such a degree, that scenes of the greatest lasciviousness and intemperance ensued. They were said to have been instituted by Cyrus, after his conquest of the Sacæ. *Strab.* 11.——A name of Diana among the Lydians. *Plin.* 33. c. 4.—*Paus.* 3.

ANALI'TÆ, a people of Arabia Felix. *Plin.* 6. c. 28.

ANA'LIUS, ARA'LIUS, or ARA'TIUS, the fifth king of Assyria. He reigned 40 years, to A.M. 2198. *Euseb. in Chron.*

ANAMAS'CIA, a city of Lower Pannonia. *Antonin.* It is now either Almaz or Anamatia.

AN'AMIS, a river of Carmania, falling into the Persian Gulph; it is now probably the Tsindo.

ANA'NIAS or ANA'NIUS, an Iambic poet. *Athen.*—*Voss. de Poet. Gr.* 89.

ANAPAUOM'ENOS, a fountain in the grove of Dodona, the waters of which were said to light a torch. It overflowed at midnight and was dry at mid-day. *Plin.* 2. c. 103.—*Mela,* 2. c. 3.

AN'APHE, an island which rose out of the Cretan Sea, near Thera, and received this name from the Argonauts, who, in the midst of a storm, suddenly saw the new moon. Apollo was worshipped there, and called Anaphæus. *Apollon.*—*Ovid. Met.* 7. v. 461.

AN'APHES, son of Otanes, was the leader of the Cissii, in the army of Xerxes. *Herodot.* 7. 62.

ANAPHLYS'TUS, a small village of the tribe of Antiochis, in Attica, near the sea. It was so named after a son of Troezen, and the inhabitants were said to possess a strong propensity to satire. *Aristoph.*—*Paus.* 2. c. 30.—*Strab.* 8.—*Laert. in Zenon.*

ANA'PUS, a small river of Epirus. *Thucyd.* 2. c. 82.——A river of Sicily, near Syracuse. It is now Alfeo. *Vid.* Amphinomus. *Id.* 6. c. 96.—*Ovid. Met.* 5. v. 417.—*Cluver.* 3. c. 41.

ANARI'ACÆ or ANARI'ACI, a people near the Caspian Sea. *Plin.* 6. c. 16.—*Strab.*

ANA'RIUM, a town of Armenia Major.

ANAR'TES, a people of Lower Pannonia. *Cæs. B. Gr.* 6. c. 25.

A'NAS, now Guadiana, a river of Spain which rises in New Castille, and falls into the ocean between Cape St. Vincent and Cadiz. *Strab.* 3.—*Cluver.* 2. c. 3.—*Mela,* c. 2 & 3.——A river of Sicily. *Liv.* 24.

ANAS'SUS or ANAS'TUS, now la Piave, a river in the country of the Carni, at the top of the Adriatic. *Plin.* 3. c. 18.

AN'ATHA, a city, called by *Arrian,* Tyre. *Steph.*

ANAT'ILI, a people of Gallia Narbonensis, who lived in the country now called la Crau, and la Camargue, at the mouth of the Rhone. Their town, Anatilia, is now St. Gilles. *Plin.* 3. c. 4.

AN'ATIS, now Zilia, a river of Mauritania Tingitana. *Id.* 5. c. 1.——A river of Sicily, otherwise Anas.

ANAT'OLE, one of the Horæ. *Hygin.* fab. 183.——A mountain near the Ganges, where Apollo offered violence to the nymph Anaxibia. *Plut de Mont.*

ANATO'LIUS, a native of Alexandria, where he taught the tenets of Aristotle, and was afterwards made bishop of Laodicea. He was well skilled in every department of literature, but especially in the mathematics.——A philosopher, the preceptor of Jamblichus, and contemporary with Porphyrius.——A Roman, consul with Valentinian. There were several other persons of this name. *Vid. Fab. B. G.* 3. p. 461.—*Sax. Onom.* 1. v. 373 & 375.

ANAU'CHIDAS, a Samian wrestler. *Paus.* 5. c. 27.

ANAU'DOMA, a town of the Syenitæ, in Ægypt. *Plin.* 6. c. 29.

ANAU'RUS, a small river of Thessaly, near the foot of Mount Pelion. The winds were said to respect the waters of this river. *Lucan.* 6. v. 370. *Orph. Argon.*—*Apollon.* 1 & 3.—*Callim. in Dion.*—*Apollod.* 1. c. 26.——A river near mount Ida, in Troas. *Coluth.*

ANAU'SIS, one of Medea's suitors, killed by Styrus. *Val. Flacc.* 6. v. 43.

ANA'VA, a city of Phrygia. *Steph.*

A'NAX, a son of Cœlus and Terra, father of Asterius. Miletus was called Anactoria after him. *Paus.* 1. c. 36. l. 7. c. 2.

ANAXAG'ORAS, succeeded his father Megapenthes on the throne of Argos, and shared the sovereign power with Bias and Melampus, who had cured the women of Argos of madness. *Paus.* 2. c. 18.——A Clazomenian philosopher and astronomer, was son of Hegesibulus, disciple of Anaximenes, and preceptor of Socrates and Euripides. He was also acquainted with eclipses, and travelled into Ægypt in search of information. Pericles was one of his pupils, and often consulted him in matters relating to the state. As the ideas of Anaxagoras concerning the heavens were wild and extravagant, he was accused of impiety, and condemned to die, but his scholar Pericles pleaded eloquently and successfully for him, and the sentence of death was exchanged for that of banishment. In prison, the philosopher is said to have attempted to square the circle, and determine exactly the proportion of its diameter to its circumference. He died at Lampsacus, in his 72nd year, 428 B.C., and on every anniversary of his death, a holiday, called Anaxagoreia, was granted to the children of the city. Two altars, one to Good Sense, and the other to Truth were erected on his grave. His writings were not much esteemed by his pupil Socrates. *Diog. in Vitâ.*—*Plut. in Niciâ & Pericl.*—*Cic. Acad. Q.* 4. c. 23. *Tusc.* 1. c. 43.——A statuary of Ægina. *Paus.* 5. c. 23.——A grammarian, disciple of Zenodotus. *Diog.*——An orator, disciple of Socrates. *Id. Fab. B. Gr.* 2. p. 644.——A son of Echeanax, who with his brothers Codrus and Diodorus, destroyed Hegesias, tyrant of Ephesus.

ANAXAN'DER, of the family of the Heraclidæ, was son of Eurycrates, and king of Sparta. The second Messenian war began in his reign. His son was called Eurycratidas. *Herodot.* 7. c. 204.—*Plut. in Apoph.*—*Paus.* 3. c. 3. l. 4. c. 15 & 16.——A general of Megalopolis, taken by the Thebans. *Diod. Sic.* 16.

ANAXAN'DRIDES, son of Leon, divorced his wife on account of her barrenness, and was the first Spartan who had two wives. His second wife bore him Cleomenes, and sometime after the one whom he had divorced bore him Dorieus, Leonidas, and Cleombrotus. *Herodot.* 1, 5 & 7.—*Plut. in Apoph.* 1.—*Paus.* 3. c. 3, &c.——A son of Theopompus. *Herodot.* 8. c. 131.——A comic poet of Rhodes, in the age of Philip and Alexander, was the first who introduced intrigues upon the stage. He composed 65 plays, of which 10 obtained the prize, and of which the titles of 28 remain, Of these Athenæus has preserved some fragments. He was starved to death by order of the Athenians, for satirizing their government. *Aristot. Rhet.* 3.—*Voss. de Poet. G.* 7.—*Gyrald de Poet. Hist. Dial.* 6.—*Fabr. B. Gr.* 2. p. 411.—*Sax. Onom.* 1. p. 66.——An author who wrote περι τῶν συληθ'εντων ἐν Δελφοῖς ἀναθημάτων. *Hemsterhusius,* however, maintains that the name of this person was Alexandrides. *Fabr. ibid.*

ANAXAR'CHUS, a philosopher of Abdera, one of the followers of the doctrines of Democritus, and the friend of Alexander. When the monarch had been wounded in battle, the philosopher pointed to the wound, adding, "That is human blood and not the blood of a god." The freedom of Anaxarchus offended Nicocreon, tyrant of Cyprus, who, after Alexander's death, seized the philosopher, and pounded him in a stone mortar with iron hammers. He bore this with composure, exclaiming, pound the body of Anaxarchus, for thou dost not "Pound his soul." Upon this Nicocreon threatened to cut off his tongue, but he bit it off, and spit it out into the tyrant's face. *Justin.* 12. c. 13.—*Val. Max.* 3. c. 3.—*Ovid. in Ib.* v. 571.—*Plut. in Symp.* 7.—*Diog. in Vitâ.*—*Cic. in Tusc.* 2. c. 22.——A Theban general. *Thucyd.* 8. c. 100.

ANAXAR'ETE, a girl of Salamis, nobly descended, who despised the addresses of Iphis, a youth of ignoble birth. When her lover, in despair, hanged himself at her door, she saw this sad spectacle without any emotion, and was changed into a stone by the gods. *Ovid. Met.* 14. v. 748.

ANAXE'NOR, a musician, whom M. Antony greatly honoured, and presented with the tribute of four cities. *Strab.* 14.

ANAX'IAS, a Theban general. *Paus.* 2. c. 22.

ANAXIB'IA, a daughter of Atreus, mother of seven sons and two daughters by Nestor. *Apollod.* 1.—*Paus.* 2. c. 29.——A daughter of Bias, who married Pelias, king of Iolcus; by whom she had Acastus, and four daughters, Pisidice, Pelopea, Hippothoe, and Alceste. *Apollod.* 1. c. 9. She is called daughter of Dymas, by *Hyginus,* fab. 14.

ANAXIB'IUS. a naval commander of the Byzantines.——a Lacedæmonian, præfect of the garrison of Abydus. *Polyæn.* 3. com. 44.—*Frontin.* 1. c. 4.

ANAXIC'RATES, an Athenian archon. *Paus.* 10. c. 23.

ANAXIDA'MUS, succeeded his father Zeuxidamus on the throne of Sparta *Paus.* 3. c. 7. l. 4. c. 15.

ANAX'ILAS or ANAXILA'US, a Messenian tyrant of Rhegium. He took Zancle, and was so popular during his reign, that when he died, 476 B.C., he entrusted his infant sons to the care of one of his servants, and the citizens chose rather to obey a slave than revolt from their benevolent sovereign's children. *Macrob*. 1. c. 11.—*Thucyd*. 6. c. 5.—*Justin*. 3. c. 2.—*Paus*. 4. c. 23. l. 5. c. 26.—*Herodot*. 6. c. 23. l. 7. c. 167.——A Pythagorean philosopher, banished from Italy by Augustus. *Irenæus, Epiphanius*, and *Pliny*, mention a work of his called παίγνια or *ludicra*. *Fabr. B. Gr*. 2. p. 412.——A physician mentioned by *Pliny*, 19. c. 1.——An historian who began his history with bitter invectives against former writers. *Dion. Hal*. 1.——A Lacedæmonian mentioned by *Plutarch in Alcib*.——A comic writer, about the 100th Olympiad, the names of whose plays are recorded by *Meursius*.—*Suidas*.—*Ælian*. l. 1. *Var*. c. 27.—*Fabr. ibid*.—*Sax. Onom*. 1. p. 69.

ANAXIL'IDES, an author who wrote some treatises on philosophers, and asserted that Plato's mother became pregnant by a phantom of Apollo, from which circumstance her son was called the Prince of Wisdom. *Diog. in Plat*.

ANAXIMAN'DER, a Milesian philosopher, son of Praxiades, the companion and disciple of Thales. He was the first who constructed spheres, and asserted that the earth moved round the sun, and that the moon received light from the sun, which he considered to be 28 times greater than the earth. He made the first geographical maps and sun-dials mentioned in history, and died in the 64th year of his age, B.C. 547. *Cic. Acad. Quæst*. 4. c. 37. *Div*. 1. c. 50. *N.D*. 1. c. 10.—*Diog. in Vitâ*.—*Plin*. 2. c. 79.—*Plut. Ph*.—*Fabr. B. Gr*. 2. 23. He had a son who bore his name. *Strab*. 1.—*Voss. Hist. Gr*. p. 25.—*Suidas*, 1. p. 173.—*Diog. Laert*. 2. c. 2.

ANAXIM'ENES, a philosopher, son of Eurystratus, and pupil of Anaximander, whom he succeeded in his school. He was singular in his opinions, and considered the earth as a plane, and the heavens as a solid concave sphere, on which the stars were fixed like nails, an opinion prevalent at that time, and from which originated the proverb, τί εἰ οὐρανὸς ἐμπέσοι, What if the heavens should fall! to which Horace seems to allude, 3. od. 3. v. 7. He died 504 B.C. *Lactant*. 1. c. 5.—*Cic. Acad. Quæst*. 4. c. 37. *N.D*. 1. c. 10.—*Plut. Ph*.—*Plin*. 2. c. 76.—*Fabr. B. G*. 2. p. 650.——A native of Lampsacus, son of Aristocles. He was pupil of Diogenes the cynic, and preceptor of Alexander the Great, of whose life, and of Philip's, he wrote a history. When Alexander threatened to put to death all the inhabitants of Lampsacus, because they had maintained a long siege against him, Anaximenes was sent to appease the king, who, as soon as he saw him, swore he would not grant the favour which he was going to ask. Upon this, Anaximenes begged the king to destroy the city and enslave the inhabitants, and thus saved the city from destruction. Besides the lives of Philip and his son, he wrote a history of Greece, in twelve books, all now lost. His nephew bore the same name, and wrote an account of ancient paintings. *Paus*. 6. c. 18.—*Val. Max*. 7. c. 3.—*Diog. in Vit*.—*Voss. Hist. Gr*. 1. c. 10.—*Fabr. ibid*.——A sophist of Chius, *Fabr. ibid*.

ANAXIP'OLIS, a comic poet of Thasus. *Plin*. 14. c. 14.—*Varro*, 1. 1.—*Colum*.—3. c. 1. But *Harduin* and *Vossius* have doubts as to this passage of *Pliny*.

ANAXIP'PUS, a comic writer in the age of Antigonus and Demetrius Poliorcetes. He used to say, that philosophers were wise only in their speeches, but fools in their actions. The names of four of his dramas are preserved. *Gyrald. de Poet. Hist*. 7. —*Athen*.—*Fab. B. Gr*. 2. p. 413.——A Myndian, who consecrated a statue to Hercules. *Paus. El*. 1.

ANAXIR'RHOE, a daughter of Coronus, who married Epeus. *Id*. 5. 1.

ANAX'IS, a Bæotian historian, who wrote a history down to the age of Philip, son of Amyntas. *Diod*. 5.——A son of Castor and Hilaria, who had a celebrated equestrian statue made of ebony in the temple of the Dioscuri, at Argos. *Paus*. 2. c. 22.

ANAXITHE'A, a daughter of Danaus, bore Olenus to Jupiter. *Steph. in* Ὤλενος.

ANAX'O, a virgin of Troezene, carried away by Theseus. *Plut. in Thes*.——A daughter of Alcæus and Hipponome, who married Electryon, king of Thebes, and became mother of Alcmene. *Apollod*. 2. c. 9 & 10.

ANAZAR'BUS, a city of Cilicia, on the river Pyramus, so called from the name of its founder. It produced Oppian the poet, and Dioscorides, and is called Cæsarea Augusta by *Pliny*, and Diocæsarea by *Suidas*. It is now Azar. *Plin*. 5. c. 27.—*Ptol*.

ANAZIP'OLIS. *Vid*. Anaxipolis.

ANCÆ'US, the son of Lycurgus and Antinoe, was one of the Argonauts. He was at the chase of the Calydonian boar, in which he perished. *Hygin*. fab. 173 & 248.—*Ovid. Met*. 8.——Son of Neptune and Astypalæa, was one of the Argonauts, and succeeded Tiphys as pilot of the ship Argo. He reigned in Ionia, where he married Samia, daughter of the Mæander, by whom he had four sons, Perilas, Enudus, Samus, and Alithersus, and one daughter, Parthenope. Being told by one of his servants, whom he pressed with hard labour in his vineyard, that he would never taste the produce of it, he took the cup in his hand, and called the prophet to convince him of his falsehood; when the servant uttered this well known proverb,

Πολλὰ μεταξὺ πέλει κύλικος καὶ χείλεος ἄκρου.

At that very moment Ancæus was told that a wild boar had entered his vineyard; upon which he threw down the cup, and ran to drive away the wild beast, but was killed in the attempt. *Orph. Argon*.—*Tzetzes in Lycoph*. 491. The son of Neptune is often confounded with the son of Lycurgus.

ANCALI'TES, a people of ancient Britain, near the Trinobantes, supposed to have occupied the country round Oxford and Buckingham. *Cæs. B. G*. 5. c. 21.—*Cluv*. 2. c. 21.—*Camben's Brit*.

AN'CARA, a city of Italy. *Steph*.

ANCHA'RIA or ANCA'RIA, a goddess worshipped by the Asculani. *Cœl. Rhod*. 1. 22. c. 3.—*Tertul. Apol*. c. 24. &c.

ANCHA'RIA, a family at Rome.——The name of Octavia's mother. *Plut. in Anton*.

ANCHA'RIUS, a noble Roman, killed by the partisans of Marius, during his civil wars with Sylla. *Plut in Mar*.

ANCHEM'OLUS, son of Rhætus, king of the Marrubii, in Italy, offered violence to his mother-in-law, Casperia, for which he was banished by his father. He fled to Turnus, and was killed by Pallas, in the wars of Æneas against the Rutuli. *Virg. Æn*. 10. v. 389. & *Servius, ibid*.

ANCHESI'TES, a wind which blows from Anchesa, a harbour of Epirus. *Cic. ad Att*. 7. ep. 1.—*Dion. Hal*.

ANCHE'SIUS, a mountain near Orchomenus, so called from the monument of Anchises. *Paus*. 1. 8.

ANCHES'MUS, a mountain of Attica, where Jupiter, surnamed Anchesmius had a statue.

ANCHI'ALE, ANCHIALE'A, or ANCHI'ALUS, a city on the coast of Cilicia. Sardanapalus, the last king of Assyria, built it, with Tarsus in its neighbourhood. The founder was buried there, and had a statue, under which was an inscription in the Syrian language, denoting the dissipation which distinguished him throughout his life. *Strab*. 14.—*Plin*. 5. c. 27.—*Diod*. 2.—*Athen*. 8.—*Tzetzes. Chil*. 3. *H*. 454.—*Schol. Aristoph. in Av*.

ANCHI'ALUS, a city of Thrace, on the shores of the Euxine Sea. Ovid calls it the city of Apollo, and it is now called Anchelo by the Greeks, but Kenkis by the Turks. Also a city of Epirus. *Ovid. Trist*. 1. el. 10. v. 36.—*Plin*. 4. c. 11.—*Mela*, 2. c. 2.——A famous astrologer. *Cic. de Div*.——A Greek, killed by Hector. *Homer. Il*. 5. v. 609.——A great warrior, father of Mentes. *Od*. 1. v. 180. Also a Phæacian. *Id*. 8. v. 112.

ANCHIMO'LIUS, a Spartan general, sent against the Pisistratidæ, and killed in the expedition. *Herodot*. 5. c. 63. The son of Rhætus was also sometimes called by this name. *Vid*. Anchemolus.

ANCHIN'OE, a daughter of Nilus, and wife of Belus. *Apollod*. 2. c. 1.

ANCHI'ON. *Vid*. Chionis.

ANCHI'SA or ANCHI'SE, a city of Italy. *Dion. Hal*. —*Steph*.

ANCHI'SES, a son of Capys by Themis, daughter of Ilus. He was so beautiful that Venus came down from heaven to mount Ida, to enjoy his company, and bore him a son called Æneas. When Troy was taken, Anchises became so infirm that Æneas, whom the Greeks permitted to take away whatever he esteemed most valuable, carried him through the flames upon his shoulders, and thus saved his life. He accompanied his son in his voyage towards

Italy, and died in Sicily, in the 80th year of his age. He was buried on mount Eryx by Æneas and Acestes, king of the country, and the anniversary of his death was, the following year, celebrated by his son and the Trojans on his tomb. Virgil in the sixth book of the Æneid, introduces him in the Elysian fields, relating to his son the fates which were to attend him, and the fortunes of his descendants the Romans. *Vid.* Æneas.—*Virg. Æn.* 1, 2, &c. *Hygin.* fab. 94. &c.—*Hesiod. Theog.* v. 1010.—*Apollod.*—*Servius, in Virg. Æn.* 3. v. 648.—*Eustath. in Il.* 12.—*Ovid. Fast.* 4. v. 34.—*Homer. Il.* 20. *Hymn. in Ven.*—*Xenoph. Cyneg.* c. 1.—*Dion. Hal.* 1. *de Antiq. Rom. Pausanias*, 8. c. 12. says that Anchises was buried in a mountain on Arcadia, which from him has been called Anchisia.——An archon at Athens. *Dion. Hal.* 8.

ANCHIS'IA, a mountain of Arcadia. *Vid.* Anchises.

ANCHISI'ADES, a patronymic of Æneas, as son of Anchises. *Virg. Æn.* 6. v. 348. &c.

ANCHI'TÆ, a nation of Arabia Felix. *Ptol.*

AN'CHOE, a place near the mouth of the Cephisus, with a lake of the same name. *Strab.*

AN'CHORA, a fortified place in Galatia. *Strab.* 12.

ANCHU'NIUS, a king of Thebais, in Ægypt, who reigned about the time of the birth of Moses. *Joh. Marsham. Can. Chron.*

ANCHU'RUS, a son of Midas king of Phrygia, who sacrificed himself for the good of his country, by throwing himself into a chasm, which had opened in the earth, and swallowed up many buildings. Midas erected an altar to Jupiter on the spot. *Plut. in Parall.* 5.—*Callisthen in Met.* 2.

ANCI'LE or ANCY'LE, a sacred shield, which was said to have fallen from heaven in the reign of Numa, during a pestilence. As the fate of the Roman empire depended upon the preservation of this shield, Numa ordered eleven of the same size and form to be made, to render it difficult to distinguish the true one. *Vid.* Mamurius. These shields were kept in the temple of Vesta, and an order of priests was instituted to watch over their safety. *Vid.* Salii. These verses of *Ovid* explain the origin of the word Ancyle,

Idque Ancyle vocat, quod ab omni parte recisum est,
Quemque notes oculis, angulus omnis abest.
Fast. 3. v. 377, &c.

Varro. de L. L. 5. c. 6.—*Val. Max.* 1. c. 1.—*Juv.* 2. v. 124.—*Plut. in Num.*—*Virg. Æn.* 8. v. 664.—*Dion. Hal.* 2.—*Liv.* 1. c. 20.

ANCOHARI'TIS, a region opposite Arabia Deserta, according to *Strabo*; or in Mesopotamia, according to *Ptolemy*.

AN'CON or ANCO'NA, a town of Picenum, built by the Sicilians, on the shores of the Adriatic, with a harbour in the form of a crescent or elbow, ἀγκών. A triumphal arch, erected to commemorate the beneficence of Trajan, who, at his own expense, had improved and enlarged the harbour, is still to be seen there. *Plin.* 3. c. 13.—*Lucan.* 2. v. 402.—*Sil.* 8. v. 437.—*Mela*, 2. c. 6.—*Juv.* 4. v. 40.

AN'CON, a city of the Leucosyri, in Cappadocia. *Ptol. Arrian. in Peripl.* calls it a harbour.

ANCORA'RIUS, a mountain of Mauritania Tingitana. *Ammian.*

ANCO'RE, a city of Bithynia, called afterwards Antigonia, and then Nicæa. *Steph.*

AN'CUS MAR'TIUS, the fourth king of Rome, was grandson of Numa, by his daughter. He waged a successful war against the Latins, Veientes, Fidenates, Volsci, and Sabines, joined mount Janiculum to the city by a bridge, and enclosed mounts Martius and Aventinus within the walls. He also built the town of Ostia, at the mouth of the Tiber. He appears to have inherited the valour of Romulus with the moderation of Numa. He died B.C. 616, after a reign of 24 years, and was succeeded by Tarquinius Priscus. *Dion. Hal.* 3. c. 9.—*Liv.* 1. c. 32, &c.—*Flor.* 1. c. 4.—*Virg. Æn.* 6. v. 815.—*Plut. in Tull. Host.*—*Horat.* 4. od. 7. v. 15.

AN'CUS, a river of Lusitania, flowing near Saurium, and now Rio di Soure.

ANCY'RA, a town of Galatia, at the west of the Halys, now Angouri. *Plin.* 5. c. 32.——A town of Phrygia. *Paus.* 1.——A town of Macedonia, or Illyricum. *Liv.* 38. c. 24.

ANCY'RÆ, a town of Sicily, which favoured the Carthaginians. *Diod. Sic.* 14.—*Cluv. Sic. Ant.* 2.

ANCYRE'UM, a promontory of Asia Minor, now Psomion.

ANCYR'ION, a town of Italy. *Steph.*

ANCY'RON, a city of Ægypt. *Id.*

AN'DA, a city of Africa. *Polyb.*

ANDAB'ATÆ, certain gladiators of Rome who fought blindfold, whence the proverb, *Andabatarum more*, to denote rash and inconsiderate measures. *Cic. ad Fam.* 7. ep. 10.

ANDAB'ILIS, a city of Cappadocia. *Antonin.*

ANDA'CA, a city of India, which surrendered to Alexander. *Arrian. Indic.*

ANDA'NIA, a city of Arcadia, where Aristomenes was educated. It was so called from a gulph of the same name. *Paus.* 4. c. 1 & 33.

ANDA'NIUS, a river of Carmania. *Strabo.* It is called Andanis by *Pliny*, 6. c. 23, and is now, probably, the Tisindan.

ANDA'NUM, a city of Caria. *Steph. in Bargylla.*

ANDA'RÆ, a people of India. *Plin.* 6. c. 19.

ANDAR'BA, a city of Dalmatia. *Antonin.*

ANDARIS'TUS, a town of the Pelagones, in Macedonia. *Ptol. Pliny* calls the inhabitants Andarestenes. It is now either Vostanza or Erisso.

ANDA'TIS, a town of Upper Æthiopia on the banks of the Nile. *Plin.* 6. c. 30.

ANDAUTO'NIUM, a town of Upper Pannonia. *Ptol.*

ANDE'CRIUM, an inland city of Dalmatia. *Ptol.* It is called Andretium by *Strabo.*

ANDECA'VIA, now l'Anjou, a country of Gaul, near the Turones and the ocean, on the banks of the Ligeris. *Tac. Ann.* 3. c. 41.—*Plin.* 4. c. 18.

ANDEGA'VUM, formerly Juliomagus, now Angers, a city of Gaul. *Vid.* Andecavia.

ANDE'RA, a town of Phrygia, which was said to produce stones convertible into iron by the application of fire. Cybele, called Anderina, was worshipped there. *Strab.* 13.

ANDERI'TUM, a town of the Vascones, in Spain. *Ptol.*

AN'DES, a nation of Gaul. *Cæs. B. G.* 2. c. 35. *Vid.* Andegavia.——A village of Italy near Mantua. Virgil was born here, and hence called Andinus. *Sil.* 8. v. 595.

ANDE'TRIUM. *Vid.* Andecrium.

ANDIAN'TES, A people of Lower Pannonia. *Ptol.*

ANDIZE'TII, a people of Liburnia. *Strab.* 7. *Pliny*, 3, c. 25. calls them Sandrizetii.

ANDOC'IDES, an Athenian orator, son of Leogoras. He lived in the age of Socrates, and was intimate with the most illustrious men of his age. He was often banished, but his dexterity always restored him to public favour. *Plutarch* has written his life *in* 10 *Orat.* Four of his orations are extant, and may be found in the 4th vol. of *Reiske's Oratores Græci. Fabr. B. Gr.* 2. p. 758. *Sax. Onom.* 1. p. 52.

ANDOLOGEN'SES, a people of Hispania Tarraconensis. *Plin.* 3. c. 3.

ANDOMADU'NUM or ANDONATU'NUM, a town of ancient Gaul, between the sources of the Matrona and the Arar, now Langres, in modern Champagne. *Cluver.* 2. c. 12.

ANDOM'ATIS, a river of India, falling into the Ganges. *Arrian.*

ANDORISIP'PO, a town of Hispania Bætica. *Plin.* 3. c. 1. Some read Andorisæ.

ANDRA'CA, a city of Cappadocia. *Ptol.*

ANDRÆ'MON, the father of Thoas, married Gorge daughter of Œneus, whom he succeeded on the throne of Calydon. He died at Amphissa, where his tomb was still to be seen in the age of the Antonines. *Hygin.* fab. 97.—*Paus.* 10. c. 38.—*Hom. Il.* 2 & 14.—*Apollod.* 1. c. 19 & 21.—*Ovid. Met.* 9. v. 333.

ANDRAGA'THIUS, a tyrant defeated by Gratian, A.D. 383, &c.

ANDRAG'ATHUS, a man bribed by Lysimachus to betray his country, &c. *Polyæn.* 4. c. 12.

ANDRAG'ORAS, a man who died a sudden death. *Mart.* 6. epigr. 53.

ANDRAM'YTES, a king of Lydia, one of the Heraclidæ. *Athen.*

ANDRAP'ANA, a city of India within the Ganges. *Ptol.*

ANDRASIMUN'DI, a promontory of Taprobane. *Id.*

ANDRAS'SUM, a city of Asia Minor, near Galatia. *Cedren.*

AN'DREAS, a statuary of Argos. *Paus.* 6. c. 16.——A man of Panormus, who wrote an account of all the remarkable events that had happened in Sicily. *Athen.* 14.——A son of the Peneus. Part of Bœotia, especially where Orchomenus was built, was called Andreis after him. *Paus.* 9. c. 34, &c. l. 10. c. 13.

AN'DRI, a people of Gallia Cisalpina. *Polyb.* 2.

AN'DRIA, a city of Elis.——A city of Macedonia. *Steph.*

ANDRI'ACA, a town of Media.——A town of Lycia. *Ptol.*——A town of Thrace. *Strab.*—*Plin.* 5. c. 27.

AN'DRICLUS, a mountain of Cilicia. *Strab.* 14.——A small river of Troas, falling into the Scamander. It is called Andrius by *Strabo*. *Plin.* 5. c. 27.

ANDRIS'CUS, a man who wrote a history of Naxus. *Athen.* 1.——A worthless person called Pseudophilippus, on account of his resemblance to king Philip. He incited the Macedonians to revolt against Rome, and was at last conquered by Metellus, 152 B.C. *Flor.* 2. c. 14.—*Eutrop.* 4. c. 3.

ANDRO'BIUS, a famous painter. *Plin.* 35. c. 11.

ANDROC'ALIS, a town of Upper Æthiopia. *Id.* 6. c. 29.

ANDROCLE'A, a daughter of Antipœnus of Thebes. She, with her sister Heraclea, sacrificed herself for the good of her country, when the oracle had promised the victory to her countrymen, who were engaged in a war against Orchomenus, if any one of noble birth would devote himself for the glory of the nation. The sisters received great honours after death; and Hercules, who fought on the side of Thebes, dedicated to them the image of a lion in the temple of Diana. *Paus.* 9. c. 17.

AN'DROCLES, a son of Phintas, who reigned in Messenia. *Id.* 4. c. 5, &c.——An historian of Cyprus.

ANDROCLI'DES, a noble Theban, who defended the democratical, against the encroachments of the oligarchical, power. He was killed by Leontidas.——A sophist in the age of Aurelian, who wrote an account of philosophers. *Suidas.*——A Laconian, who, being lame, was not suffered to go to war. He answered, that they ought to go into the field who thought of fighting, not of running away. *Plut. in Apoph.*—*Cœl. Rhod.* 14. c. 5.

ANDRO'CLUS, a son of Codrus, who reigned in Ionia, and took Ephesus and Samus. *Paus.* 7. c. 2.——A Dacian slave, recognised in the circus at Rome, and spared, by a lion whose wounded foot he had formerly cured in his native woods. *A. Gell.* 5. c. 14. *Ælian. H. A.* 7. c. 48.—*Senec. de Benef.* 2. c. 19.

ANDROCOT'TUS. *Vid.* Sandrocottus.

ANDROCY'DES, a physician, who wrote the following letter to Alexander:—*Vinum potaturus, Rex, memento te bibere sanguinem terræ: sicuti venenum est homini cicuta, sic et vinum. Plin.* 14. c. 5.——A painter. *Id.* 35. c. 9.

ANDROD'AMUS. *Vid.* Andromadas.

ANDRO'DUS, a Dacian slave. *Vid.* Androclus.

ANDROE'TAS, an historian of Tenedus, whose work is cited by the commentator on *Apollonius*, 1. 2.

ANDRO'GEA, a region of Persia. *Cedren.*

ANDRO'GEUS, a Greek, killed by Æneas and his friends, whom he took to be his countrymen. *Virg. Æn.* 2. v. 371.——Son of Minos and Pasiphae was famous for his skill in wrestling. He overcame every antagonist at Athens; and Ægeus, king of the country, grew so jealous of his popularity, that he caused him to be assassinated. Some say that he was killed by the wild bull of Marathon. Minos, upon this, declared war against Athens; and peace was at last re-established between the two countries, on condition that Ægeus sent yearly seven boys and seven girls to be devoured by the Minotaur. *Vid.* Minotaurus. The Athenians also established festivals by order of Minos, in honour of his son, and called them Androgea. *Hygin.* fab. 41.—*Diod.* 4.—*Virg. Æn.* 6. v. 20.—*Paus.* 1. c. 1. & 27.—*Apollod.* 2. c. 5. l. 3. c. 1 & 15.—*Plut. in Thes.*—*Catull.* 62. v. 77.

ANDROG'YNÆ, a fabulous nation of Africa, beyond the Nasamones, who were said to have the characteristics both of the male and female sex. *Lucret.* 5. v. 837.—*Liv.* 27. c. 11.—*Auson.* ep. 69. v. 12.—*A. Gell.* 9. c. 4.—*Plin.* 7. c. 2.

ANDROM'ACHE, daughter of Eetion, king of Thebes in Cilicia, married Hector, son of Priam, by whom she had Astyanax. Homer's account of her parting with Hector, who was going to a battle in which he perished, has always been deemed the most pathetic passage in the Iliad. After the taking of Troy, Andromache fell to the share of Neoptolemus, who treated her as his wife, and carried her to Epirus, but afterwards repudiated her, although she had borne him three sons, Molossus, Pielus, and Pergamus. She afterwards married Helenus, son of Priam, who, like herself, was a captive at the court of Pyrrhus. She reigned with her husband over part of the country, where she received Æneas and his followers, on their way to Italy. *Hom. Il.* 6. 22, & 24.—*Q. Calab.* 13.—*Virg. Æn.* 3. v. 486.—*Hygin.* fab. 123.—*Dares. Phryg.*—*Ovid. A.A.* 1. el. 9. v. 35. *Trist.* 5. el. 6. v. 43.—*Apollod.* 3. c. 12.—*Paus.* 1. c. 11. l. 10. c. 25.—*Eurip. & Senec. in Troad.*—*Tzetzes. in Lycoph.*——The title of a tragedy written by Ennius. *Cic. Div.* 1. c. 13.

ANDROM'ACHUS, an opulent person of Sicily, father of the historian Timæus. He assisted Timoleon in recovering the liberty of the Syracusans. *Diod.* 16.——A general of Alexander, to whom Parmenia gave the government of Cœlesyria. He was burnt alive by the Samaritans. *Curt.* 4. c. 5. & 8.——An officer of Seleucus the younger. *Polyæn.* 4. c. 17.——A physician of Crete, in the age of Nero, who wrote in elegiac verse a description of *theriaca*, a medicine of which he was the inventor. *Fabr. B. Gr.* 4. p. 357. His son was also physician to Nero, and wrote two books, περί συνθέσεως φαρμάκων, much commended by *Galen. Fabr. ibid.*—*Sax. Onom.* 1. p. 256.——A flatterer, who betrayed Crassus to the Parthians.——The father of Achæus and brother of Laodice, wife of king Seleucus. *Salmas ad Solin.* 984.——A sophist of Naples, in the age of Diocletian. *Suidas.*——A poet of Byzantium.

ANDROM'ADAS or ANDROD'AMUS, a native of Rhegium, who made the laws of the Thracians concerning the punishment of homicide, &c. *Aristot. Polit.* 1. 2.

ANDROM'EDA, a daughter of Cepheus, king of Æthiopia, by Cassiope. When she had boasted that she was fairer than Juno and the Nereides, Neptune innundated the kingdom, and sent a sea monster to ravage the country. Andromeda was ordered by the oracle to be exposed to the monster, and she was accordingly tied naked to a rock; but Perseus delivered her, changed the monster into a rock, by the exhibition of Medusa's head, and married her. This marriage was opposed by Phineus, to whom she had been betrothed; but he, after a bloody battle, was changed into a stone by Perseus. Some say that Minerva made Andromeda a constellation in heaven after death. *Vid.* Perseus, &c. *Hygin.* fab. 74. *Poet. A.* 2. c. 11.—*Cic. de N. D.* 2. c. 43.—*Apollod.* 2. c. 4.—*Manil.* 5. v. 533.—*Propert.* 3. el. 21. According to *Pliny,* l. 5. c. 31. it was at Joppa, in Judæa, where Andromeda was tied to the rock. *Euripides* composed a tragedy on this subject.

ANDRO'MON, the name of the founder of Colophon.

AN'DRON, an Argive, who is said to have travelled over the deserts of Libya without drinking. *Aristot. de Ebriet.* 1.——An officer set over the citadel of Syracuse by Dionysius. Hermocrates advised him to seize it, and revolt from the tyrant, which he refused to do. The tyrant put him to death for not discovering that Hermocrates had incited him to rebellion. *Polyæn.* 5. c. 2.——A writer of Halicarnassus, who composed some historical works, particularly a valuable genealogy, now lost, but often quoted by other authors. *Plut. in Thes.*——A native of Ephesus, who wrote an account of the seven wise men of Greece. *Diog.* 1. c. 119, &c.—*Apollon. Hist. Mir.* c. 8.—*Athen.*—*Clem. Alex. Strom.* 1.—*Euseb. de Evang. Pr.* 10.——A player on the flute, who, according to *Theophrastus*, first taught dancing and rhythm. *Cœl. Rhod.* 5. c. 4.——A Teian, whose Periplus is quoted by the scholiast on *Apollonius*, 1. 2.——An Alexandrian, who wrote a work called Χρονικά. *Athen.* 4.——A physician mentioned by *Celsus.* 5. c. 20. & *Galen*, 3.—*Athen.* 15.——A musician and geometrician, master of Marcus Antoninus. *Jul. Capit. in M. Anton. Phil.*

AN'DRON, a town of Ægypt, on the Nile. *Ptol.*

ANDRO'NA, a town of Cyrrhestica, in Syria. *Antonin.*

ANDRONI'CUS LIV'IUS. *Vid.* Livius.

ANDRONI'CUS, a peripatetic philosopher of Rhodes, who flourished 59 years B.C. He was the first who published and revised the works of Aristotle and Theophrastus. His periphrasis is extant, the best edition of which is that of Heinsius, 8vo. L. Bat. 1617. *Plut. in Syll.*—*Fabr. B. Gr.* 3. p. 464.——

A Latin poet in the age of Cæsar.——A Latin grammarian, whose life *Suetonius* has written.——One of Alexander's officers. *Curt.* 7. c. 3.——An historian who wrote an account of the actions of Alexander. *Volaterran.* l. 21.

ANDRONI'CUS CYRRHES'TES, an astronomer of Athens, who built a marble octagonal tower in honour of the eight principal winds, on the top of which was placed a Triton, with a stick in his hand, pointing to the quarter whence the wind blew.

ANDRONI'CUS TITIA'NUS, a physician mentioned by *Galen. Fabr. B. Gr.* 3. p. 464.

ANDROPH'AGI, a savage nation of European Scythia. *Herodot.* 4. c. 18. & 102.—*Mela.* 3. c. 9.

ANDROPOM'PUS, a Theban, who treacherously killed Xanthus in single combat. *Paus.* 2. c. 18.

ANDROS'THENES, one of Alexander's generals, sent with a ship to the coast of Arabia. He wrote a description of the globe, a work praised by Artemidorus of Ephesus, &c. *Arrian.* 7. c. 10.—*Strab.* 16.—*Theophrast. de Caus. Plaut.* 2. c. 7.—*Artemid. Ephes. in Epit.*——A governor of Thessaly, who favoured the interests of Pompey. He was conquered by J. Cæsar. *Cæs. B. Civ.* 3. c. 80.——A statuary of Thebes, who was engaged in beautifying the temple of Delphi. *Paus.* 10. c. 19.——A writer mentioned by *Polybius*, l. 11.

ANDRO'TION, a Greek who wrote a history of Attica, and a treatise on agriculture. *Plin.*—*Paus.* 10. c. 8.—*Ælian. V. H.* 8. c. 10. Some, however, doubt whether the writer *de re rusticâ*, mentioned by *Pliny*, is the same person as the historian. *Varro & Columel. de R. R.* l. 1.—*Fabr. B. Gr.* 2. p. 744.—*Voss. Hist. Gr.* 3. p. 322.

AN'DRUS, an island in the Ægæan sea, at the east of Eubœa, known by the different names of Epagrys, Lasia, Caurus, Hydrussa, and Nonagria. Its chief town was called Andrus. It had a harbour, near which was a temple of Bacchus, with a fountain, the waters of which, during the ides of January, were said to taste like wine. It received its name from Andrus, one of its kings, who lived in the time of the Trojan war. *Ovid. Met.* 13. v. 648. *Virg. Æn.* 3. v. 80. *Juv.* 3. v. 70.—*Plin.* 2. c. 103.—*Mela*, 1 & 2.—*Antonin. Lib. Nar.* 41.

ANEJ'ANUM, a city of Italy, now Monte Agnano. *Antonin.*

ANELON'TIS, a river near Colophon. *Paus.* 8. c. 28. Some read Alentis.

AN'EMO. *Vid. Almo.*

ANEMOLI'A, a city of Phocis, aftewards called Hyampolis. *Strab.* According to *Ptolemy*, it was a city of Bœotia.

ANEMO'SA, a village of Arcadia. *Paus.* 8. c. 35.

ANEMU'RIUM, a promontory and city of Cilicia, now Stalemura, or Scalemuro. *Mela*, 1. c. 13.

ANEMU'SA, an island of the Mediterranean. *Ptol.*

ANERŒS'TUS, a king of Gaul.

ANERI'TÆ, a people of Marmarica. *Ptol.*

ANETHUS'SA, a city of Libya. *Steph.*

ANETOR, a Phocian, who kept the sheep of Peleus. *Ovid. Met.* 11. v. 348.

ANFIN'OMUS and ANA'PIUS. *Vid.* Amphinomus.

AN'GARIS, a mountain of Palestine. *Plin.* 5. c. 13.——A town, the emporium of Bithynia. *Socr. Hist.* 3. c. 20.

AN'GE, a village of Arabia Felix. *Ptol.*

AN'GELE, part of the tribe Pandionis. *Steph.* It is now Angelocopus, or, as it is corruptly called, Ambelokipous. *Jac. Spon. Itin. Gr.* part 3. p. 69, &c.

ANGE'LIA, a daughter of Mercury. *Cœl. Rhod.* 18. c. 6.

ANGE'LION, a statuary who made a statue of Apollo. *Paus.* 2. c. 32.

ANGEL'LÆ, city of Hispania Bætica. *Antonin.*

AN'GELUS, a son of Neptune, born in Chius, of a nymph whose name is unknown. *Paus.* 7. c. 4.

ANGERO'NA, a goddess at Rome, so called *ab angendo*. She was supposed to drive away pain, and was also the goddess of silence. Her festivals were celebrated on the 21st of December, and were called Angeronalia. *Plin.*—*Macrob. Sat.* 1. c. 10.—*Solin*, &c. Also Angero'nia.

ANGI'TES, a river of Thrace, falling into the Strymon. *Herodot.* 7. c. 113.

ANGIT'IA. *Vid.* Anguitia.

ANGIT'ULA, a town and river of Calabria. *Antonin.* It is called Crissa by *Lycophron;* and is now Roccha d'Angitola.

AN'GLI, a people of Germany, at the north of the Elbe, from whom, as being a branch of the Saxons, the English have derived their name. *Tac. Germ.* 40.

ANGRIVA'RII, a people of Germany. *Ptol.*—*Tac. Ann.* 2. c. 8.

AN'GRUS, a river of Illyricum, flowing in a northern direction. *Herodot.* 4. c. 49.

ANGUIT'IA, now Selva d'Albi, a wood in the country of the Marsi, between the lake Fucinus and Alba. It is said, that serpents could not injure the inhabitants, because they were descended from Circe. *Virg. Æn.* 7. v. 759.—*Sil.* 8.

ANGULA'NI, a people of Italy. *Plin.* 3. c. 12. Their town Angulus is now Civita di St. Angelo.

ANGU'RUS, a mountain of Scythia. *Apollon. Argon.* 4.

ANGYRO'RUM URBS, a city of Ægypt. *Ptol.*

A'NIA, a Roman widow, celebrated for her beauty. When advised to marry again, she replied, "If I marry a man as affectionate as my first husband, I shall be apprehensive of losing him; and if he should prove unkind, why have him after such an indulgent one?"

ANIA'NA, a city of Mesopotamia. *Ptol.*

ANICE'TUS, a son of Hercules, by Hebe. *Apollod.* 2——A freedman who superintended the education of Nero, and afterwards became the instrument of his crimes. *Suet. in Ner.*——A freedman of Polemon of Pontus, was præfect of the royal fleet. He summoned the nations of Pontus in the name of Vitellius, took Trapezus, and slew the garrison. He was at length delivered up to Virdius Geminus by the king of the Sedochezi. *Tac Hist.* 3. c. 47.

ANI'CHÆ, a nation of India. *Ptol.*

ANIC'IA, a family at Rome, which, in the flourishing times of the republic, produced some brave and illustrious citizens.——A relation of Atticus.—*C. Nepos.*

ANIC'IUM, a town of Gaul, now Le Puy. *Cæs. B. G.* 7.

ANIC'IUS GAL'LUS triumphed over the Illyrians and their king Gentius, and was proprætor, A.U.C. 585.——A consul with Corn. Cethegus, A.U.C. 594. During his consulship, or that of a consul of the same name, there was so plentiful a vintage, that *Anicianum vinum* afterwards became expressive of wine of superior excellence. *Cic. Brut.* 83.

ANIC'IUS PRO'BUS, a Roman consul in the fourth century, famous for his humanity.

ANIC'IUS CEREA'LIS, a consul elect under Nero.

A'NIEN. *Vid.* Anio.

ANIEN'SIS JUNIO'RUM, a Roman tribe. *Liv.* 24. c. 7. *Cic. pro Planc, &c.*

ANI'GRUS, a river of Thessaly. *Ovid. Met.* 15. v. 281. The nymphs of this river were called Anigriades. *Paus.* 5. c. 6.

ANIMO'THA, a city of Arabia. *Lib. Not.*

ANI'NA, a city of India without the Ganges. *Ptol.*

ANINA'CHA, a city of India within the Ganges. *Id.*

A'NIO or A'NIEN, now Teverone, a river of Italy, which rises in the Apennines, and falls into the Tiber. It received its name, as some suppose, from Anius, a king of Etruria, who was drowned in it. *Stat.* 1. *Sylv.* 3. v. 20. *Dion. Hal.* 5. c. 37.—*Plin.* 3. c. 12.—*Virg. Æn.* 7. v. 683.—*Strab.* 5.—*Horat.* 1. od. 7. v. 13.—*Plut. de fort. Rom.*—*Propert.* 3. el. 21. v. 22. l. 4. el. 7. v. 86.

ANI'SIS or ASY'CHIS, a king of Ægypt, who reigned six years.

ANIS'TIS, a Lacedæmonian, who was in the service of Alexander the Great, and ran from Sicyon to Elis, 1,200 stadia, in one day. *Solin.* 6.

ANI'THA, a city of Arabia Petræa. *Ptol.*

ANITOR'GIS, a city of Spain, near which a battle was fought between Asdrubal and the Scipios. *Liv.* 25. c. 33.

ANIT'IUS, a curule ædile. *Plin.* 33. c. 1.

ANIT'IUS, FAUS'TUS, a consul in the reign of Diocletian. *Euseb.*

A'NIUS, son of Apollo and Rhea, was king of Delus. He had three daughters, to whom Bacchus had given the power of changing whatever they pleased into wine, corn, and oil. When Agamemnon went to the Trojan war, he wished to carry them with him to supply his army with provisions; but they complained to Bacchus, who changed them into doves. *Ovid. Met.* 13. v. 642.—*Dion. Hal.* 1.—*Diod.* 5.—*Virg. Æn.* 3. v. 80.—*Cœl. Rhod.* 7. c. 15.

A'NIUS, a place near Puteoli, now Lago Sudatorio.

AN'NA, a goddess, in whose honour the Romans instituted festivals. She was, according to some, the daughter of Belus and sister of Dido, who, after her sister's death, fled from Carthage, which Iarbas had besieged, and came to Italy, where Æneas, jealous of the tender treatment which Anna received, meditated her ruin. Anna, upon this, fled to the river Numicus, of which she became a deity, and ordered the inhabitants of the country to call her *Anna Perenna*, because she would remain for ever under the waters. Her festivals were celebrated on the 15th of March, with many rejoicings. The Romans generally sacrificed to her, to obtain a long and happy life; and hence the words *Annare et Perennare*. Some have supposed Anna to be the moon, *quia mensibus impleat annum*; others call her Themis, or Io, the daughter of Inachus; and sometimes Maia. Another more received opinion is, that Anna was an industrious old woman at Bovillæ, who, when the populace had retired to mount Sacer, brought them cakes every day; for which kind treatment the Romans, when a reconciliation was effected, decreed divine honours to her, calling her Perenna, *a perennitate cultûs*, and regarding her as one of their deities. *Ovid. Fast.* 3. v. 653, &c.—*Sil.* 8. v. 79.—*Virg. Æn.* 4. v. 9. 20. 421 & 500.—*Mart.* 4. epigr. 64. v. 16.

AN'NA COMNE'NA, a princess of Constantinople, who wrote a Greek history, in 15 books, called the Alexiad, which treated of the actions of her father Alexius, emperor of the east. The work may be read with great advantage by those whose judgment can make allowance for the partiality of a daughter. The best edition is that of Paris, folio. 1651. *Fabr. B. Gr.* 7. p. 726.—*Sax. Onom.* 2. p. 218.

ANNÆ'US a Roman family, which was subdivided into the Lucani, Senecæ, Flori, &c.

ANNA'LIS or ANNA'RIA LEX settled the age at which a citizen could be admitted to exercise the offices of the state. This law was introduced into Rome from Athens, by L. Villius, who, from that circumstance, obtained the surname of Annalis. No man could be a knight before eighteen years of age, nor could he be invested with the consular power before he had arrived at his 43rd, or afterwards, at his 25th year. *Liv.* 40. c. 43.—*Quintil.* 6. c. 3. & 86.—*Cic. Phil.* 5. &c.

ANNA'RUS, a king of Babylon, noted for his gluttony. *Alex. ab Alex.* 1. 5.

ANNES'TUS or ANES'TUM, a town of Arabia Felix, destroyed by Gallus. *Plin.* 6. c. 28.

AN'NIA CORNIFIC'IA, a younger sister of Antoninus. *Jul. Cap. in vit.*

AN'NIA FAUSTI'NA. *Vid.* Faustina.

ANNIA'NUS, a poet in the age of Antoninus and Adrian. *A. Gell.* 7. c. 7, &c.

AN'NIBAL, a celebrated Carthaginian general, son of Amilcar. He passed into Spain when nine years old, and, at the request of his father, took a solemn oath that he never would be at peace with the Romans. After his father's death, he was appointed commander of the cavalry in Spain; and upon the death of Asdrubal, he was invested with the command of all the armies of Carthage, though not yet in the 25th year of his age. In three years he subdued the whole of Spain, and took Saguntum, after a siege of eight months. This celebrated city was in alliance with the Romans, and its fall was the cause of the second Punic war. To carry on this war, Annibal levied three large armies, one of which he sent into Africa, left another in Spain, and marched at the head of the third towards Italy, over the Pyrenees, the Rhone, and the Alps, a march of above a thousand miles, which he effected in the space of five months. After gaining the top of the Alps, which had never been passed over before him but by Hercules; he conquered the uncivilized inhabitants; and, with the loss of 30,000 men, made his way so easy, by softening the rocks with fire and vinegar, (according to *Livy* and *Juvenal*,) that even his armed elephants descended the mountains without difficulty, by paths in which a man, though disencumbered of his arms, could not before walk in safety. After he had defeated P. Corn. Scipio and Sempronius, near the Rhone, the Po, and the Trebia, he crossed the Apennines, and invaded Etruria. He routed the army of the consul Flaminius near the lake Trasimenus; and soon after met the two consuls, C. Terentius and L. Æmilius, at Cannæ. His army consisted only of 40,000 foot and 10,000 horse, when he engaged the Romans in this celebrated battle. The slaughter on that fatal day was so great, that no less than 40,000 Romans, (or, according to Polybius, 70,000) were killed, and 13,000 made prisoners, and the conqueror made a bridge of the dead carcasses; and, as a sign of his victory, he sent to Carthage three bushels of gold rings, which had been taken from 5,630 Roman knights slain in the battle. Had Annibal now marched his army to the gates of Rome, it must have yielded. His delay, however, gave the enemy more spirit and boldness; and when he at last, approached the walls, he was informed that the piece of ground on which his army then stood was selling at a high price in the Roman forum. After hovering for some time round the city, he retired to Capua, the pleasures of which so enervated his soldiers, that it has been said that Capua was a Cannæ to Annibal. After the battle of Cannæ, the Romans, led on by the great Fabius, became more cautious, and Marcellus first taught the Romans that the Carthaginian general was not invincible. After many debates in the senate, it was decreed that war should be carried into Africa, to remove Annibal from the gates of Rome; and Scipio, who was the first proposer of the plan, was empowered to put it into execution. Carthage no sooner saw the enemy on their coasts, than she recalled Annibal from Italy; and that great general left, with tears in his eyes, a country which, during sixteen years, he had kept under continual alarms. He and Scipio met near Carthage; and, after a parley, in which neither would give the preference to his enemy, they determined to come to a general engagement. The battle was fought near Zama; Scipio made a great slaughter of the enemy; 20,000 were killed, and the same number made prisoners. Annibal fled to Andrometum; and thence, at the instance of the Carthaginians, he revisited his native city, from which he had been absent about 36 years. Soon after this decisive battle, the Romans granted peace to Carthage on hard conditions; and afterwards Annibal, who was jealous and apprehensive of the Roman power, fled to Syria, to king Antiochus, whom he advised to make war against Rome. Antiochus distrusting the fidelity of Annibal, and not regarding his advice, was conquered by the Romans, who granted him peace on the condition of his delivering their immortal enemy into their hands. Annibal who was apprised of this, fled to Prusias, king of Bithynia. He encouraged him to declare war against Rome, and even assisted him in weakening the power of Eumenes king of Pergamus, who was in alliance with the Romans. The senate, receiving intelligence that Annibal was in Bithynia, immediately sent ambassadors to demand him of Prusias. The king was unwilling to betray Annibal, and violate the laws of hospitality, but at the same time he dreaded the power of Rome. Annibal extricated him from his embarrassment; for when he heard that his house was besieged on every side, he took a dose of poison, which he always carried with him in a ring on his finger; and when he breathed his last, he exclaimed, *Solvamus diuturnâ curâ populum Romanum, quando mortem senis expectare longum censet.* He died in his 70th year, according to some, about 182 years B.C. That year was famous for the death of the three greatest generals of the age, Annibal, Scipio, and Philopœmen. If Annibal shone in the field, he also distinguished himself by his studies. He was taught Greek by Sosilus, a Lacedæmonian, and he even wrote some books in that language on different subjects. He also made himself as conspicuous in the government of the state as at the head of armies; and though his enemies reproached him with laughing in the Carthaginian senate while every senator was bathed in tears for the misfortunes of the country, Annibal defended himself by saying, that he, who had been bred all his life in a camp, could not be expected to possess the polished feelings of a courtier. When in Bithynia, his house was fortified like a castle, and had secret doors to afford him the means of escape. When he quitted Italy, and embarked on board a vessel for Africa, he so strongly suspected the fidelity of the pilot, who told him that the lofty mountain which appeared at a distance was a promontory of Sicily, that he killed him on the spot; but he afterwards buried him in a magnificent manner, and called the promontory by his name. The Romans have celebrated the humanity of Annibal, who, after the battle of Cannæ, sought the body of the fallen consul amidst the heaps of slain, and honoured it with a funeral becoming the dignity of Rome. He performed the same friendly offices to the remains of Marcellus and Tib. Gracchus, who had perished in the battle. The Romans entertained such a high opinion of him as a commander, that Scipio called him the greatest general that ever lived, giving the second rank to Pyrrhus the Epirot, and placing himself next to these in merit and abilities. Livy has painted the character of Annibal like an enemy; and it is much to be lamented that this celebrated historian, with inexcusable bitterness, and the most reprehensible illiberality, has withheld the tribute due to the merits and virtues of the greatest of generals. *C. Nep. in Vit.—Liv.* 21, 22, &c. —*Plut. in Flamin.* &c.—*Justin.* 32. c. 4.—*Ital.* 1, &c.—*Appian.—Florus,* 2 & 3.—*Polyb.* — *Diod.*— *Juv.* 10. v. 159. &c.—*Val. Max.*—*Horat.* 4 od. 4. epod. 16.—*Plin.* 34. c. 6. [A bronze bust of Annibal, dug up at Herculaneum, exists in the Museum at Naples.]

AN'NIBAL, the son of the great Annibal, was sent by Himilco to Lilybæum, which was besieged by the Romans, to keep the inhabitants faithful to their duty. *Polyb.* 1.——A Carthaginian general, son of Asdrubal, commonly called of Rhodes, lived about 160 years before the great Annibal. *Justin.* 19. c. 2.—*Xenoph. Hist. Gr.*——A son of Giscon, and grandson of Amilcar, sent by the Carthaginians to the assistance of Ægesta. He was overpowered by Hermocrates, an exiled Syracusan. *Justin.* 22. & 23.——A Carthaginian, surnamed Senior. He was conquered by the consul C. Sulpit. Paterculus, in Sardinia, and crucified by his countrymen for his misconduct and bad success.

AN'NIBI, mountains and people of Serica. *Ptol.*

ANNIC'ERIS, a charioteer of Cyrene, who exhibited his skill in driving a chariot before Plato and the academy. When the philosopher was sold by Dionysius, Anniceris ransomed his friend; and farther shewed his respect for learning, by establishing a sect at Cyrene, called after his name, which maintained that all good consisted in pleasure. *Cic. de Off.* 3. c. 33.—*Diog. in Plat. & Arist.—Ælian. V. H.* 2. c. 27.

ANNICHO'RI or ANNICHO'RES, a people near Persia. *Steph.*

AN'NIUS BAS'SUS, a lieutenant of the 11th legion. *Tac. Hist.* 3. c. 50.

AN'NIUS FAUS'TUS, an informer under Nero. He was put to death by Otho, at the instigation of Vibius Crispus, whose brother he had ruined. *Id. ibid.* 2. c. 10.

AN'NIUS LI'BO, a consul, uncle of M. Antoninus. *Jul. Cap. in vit. M. Ant.*

AN'NIUS MAR'CUS, a Greek orator, who had M. Antoninus for his pupil. *Id. ibid.—Philostrat.*

AN'NIUS SCAP'ULA, a noble person put to death for conspiring against Cassius. *Hirt. de bell. Alex.* 55.

AN'NON or HAN'NO, a Carthaginian general, conquered in Spain by Scipio, and sent prisoner to Rome. He was son of Bomilcar, whom Annibal sent privately over the Rhone to conquer the Gauls. *Liv.* 21. c. 27.

AN'NON, a Carthaginian, who taught birds to sing "Annon is a god," after which he restored them to liberty; but the birds lost with their slavery what they had been taught. He was banished from Carthage for taming a lion for his own amusement, which was interpreted as if he wished to aspire to sovereign power. *Plin.* 8. c. 16.—*Ælian. V. H. ult.* l. c. 30.——A Carthaginian, who wrote in the Punic language, the account of a voyage which he had made round Africa. This curious book was translated into Greek, and is still extant. *Voss. de H. Gr.* 4.—*Fabr. B. G.* 1. p. 55.—*Sax. Onom.* 1. p. 90. This name was common to many Carthaginians who signalized themselves during the Punic and Sicilian wars. *Liv.* 26, 27, &c.—*Fabr. ibid.*

ANNO'NA, the goddess of fertility among the Romans. *Salmas. ad Solin.* 250.

ANO'CHUS, a wrestler mentioned by *Pausanias.* 1. 7.

ANODEGA'TÆ, an inland city of Libya. *Ptol.*

ANO'LUS, a city of Lydia. *Steph.*

ANO'NIUM, a city of the Lepontii in Latium. *Ptol.*

ANOPÆ'A, a mountain and road near the river Asopus. *Herod.* 7. c. 216.

ANOP'OLIS, a city of Crete.

ANOY'PHES, the 10th king of Thebais, in Ægypt; he reigned 20 years.

AN'SER, a Roman poet, whom *Ovid, Trist.* 3. el. 1. v. 425., calls bold and impertinent. He reflected with severity on some of Virgil's verses, which the poet is said to have resented by playing upon the double meaning of *Anser*, in his ninth eclogue. He was a favourite of M. Antony, whom he accompanied to the siege of Mutina. *Cic. Phil.* 13. c. 5.—*Propert.* 2. el. 36.

ANSIBA'RII, a people of Germany. *Tac. Ann.* 13. c. 55.—*Cluver.* 3. c. 3.

ANTA'CÆ, a people of Asiatic Sarmatia. *Plin.* 6. c. 7.

ANTACH'ARÆ, a city of India within the Ganges. *Ptol.*

ANTACI'TES, a river of Asia, flowing into the Palus Mæotis. *Athen.—Ptol.*

ANTÆ'A, the wife of Proteus, called also Stenobœa. *Hom. Il.* 6. v. 160.——A goddess worshipped by the people of Antium, supposed to be the same as Rhea or Fortune. *Schol. Apollon.*

ANTÆ'AS, a king of Scythia, who said that the neighing of a horse was far preferable to the music of Ismenias, a famous musician, who had been taken captive. *Plut. de Alex. fort.*

ANTÆOP'OLIS, a city of Ægypt. *Steph.*

ANTÆ'US, a giant of Libya, son of Terra and Neptune. Hercules attacked him, and as he received fresh strength as often as he touched the ground, the hero lifted him up into the air, and squeezed him to death in his arms. *Lucan.* 4. v. 598.—*Stat.* 6. *Theb.* v. 893.—*Juv.* 3. v. 88.—*Senec. in Herc. Œteo.—Plut. in Thes.—Sil.* 3. v. 40. [A fine group of Hercules strangling Antæus, of large size, is in the Gallery at Florence.——A servant of Atticus. *Cic. ad Att.* 13. ep. 44.——A friend of Turnus, killed by Æneas. *Virg. Æn.* 10. v. 561. ——A physician. *Plin.* 28. c. 1.——A statuary. *Id.* 34. c. 8.

ANTAG'ORAS, a man of Cos. *Paus.* 3. c. 5.——A Rhodian poet much admired by *Antigonus. Id.* 1. c. 2.—*Plut. Symp. & Apoph.—Cœl. Rhod.* 7. c. 8. —*Gyrald. de Poet. H.* 3.

ANTAL'CIDAS of Sparta, son of Leon, was sent into Persia, where he made a peace with Artaxerxes very disadvantageous to his country, by which, B.C. 387, the hitherto independent Greek cities of Asia became tributary to the Persian monarch. *Paus.* 9. c. 1. &c.—*Diod.* 14.—*Plut. in Artax.*

ANTAN'DER, a general of Messenia, in the war against the Spartans. *Paus.* 4. c. 7.——A brother of Agathocles, tyrant of Sicily. *Justin.* 22. c. 7.

ANTAN'DRUS, now St. Dimitri, a city of Troas, inhabited by the Leleges, near which Æneas built his fleet after the destruction of Troy. It was also called Edonis, Cimmeris, Assus, and Apollonia. *Strab.* 13.—*Virg. Æn.* 3. v. 6. & *Servius ibid.*— *Mela,* 1. c. 18.—*Cluver.* 5. c. 18.

ANTAPHER'NES. *Vid.* Artaphernes.

ANTAR'ADUS, a city of Syria. *Ptol.* It was called also Constantia, and is now Tortosa.

ANTERBRO'GIUS, an ambassador to Cæsar from the Rhemi, a nation of Gaul. *Cæs. B. G.* 2. c. 3.

ANTE'IUS PUB'LIUS, was appointed governor of Syria by Nero. He was accused of sedition, and drank poison, which operating slowly, he was obliged to open his veins, and he bled to death. *Tac. Ann.* 13. c. 22, &c.

ANTE'LIA, a city of Armenia Minor. *Ptol.*

ANTEM'NÆ or ANTEM'NA, a city of the Sabines, between Rome and the Anio, whence the name (*ante amnem*). *Virg. Æn.* 7. v. 631.—*Dion. Hal.* —*Cluver.* 3. c. 27.

ANTE'NIUS or ANTHE'MIUS, a celebrated architect, distinguished for the erection of the temple of St. Sophia, at Constantinople, under the emperor Justinian. He was assisted in this laborious undertaking by Isidorus of Miletus. *Gibbon, Rom. Hist.* c. 40.

ANTE'NOR, a Trojan prince related to Priam, said to have perfidiously engaged in a secret correspondence with the Greeks. He is also said to have persuaded Ulysses to carry away the Palladium, and to have encouraged the Greeks to make the wooden horse, which, at his desire, was brought into the city of Troy, by a breach made in the walls. After the destruction of his country, Antenor migrated to Italy, and settled near the shores of the Adriatic, where he built the town of Padua. *Liv.* 1. c. 1.— *Plin.* 3. c. 13.—*Virg. Æn.* 1. v. 242. & *Servius ibid.*—*Tac. Ann.* 16. c. 21.—*Homer. Il.* 3, 7, 8, 11. *Eustath. in Il.* 3.—*Ovid. Met.* 13.—*Dictys. Cret.*

5.—*Dares. Phryg.* 6.—*Strab.* 13.—*Dion. Hal.* 1.—*Paus.* 10. c. 27.——A Cretan, who wrote a history of his country. *Ælian. An.* 17. c. 35.——A statuary *Paus.* 1. 1.

ANTENOR'IDES, a patronymic given to the three sons of Antenor, all killed during the Trojan war. *Virg. Æn.* 6. v. 484.

ANTEQUI'A or **ANTECUI'A**, a city of Spain, now S. Ander. *Ptol.*

AN'TEROS, (ἀντὶ ἔρως, *amor mutuus*), a son of Mars and Venus, was the god of mutual love and tenderness. He had a temple raised to him at Athens. *Vid.* Meles. Cupid and Anteros are often represented striving to seize a palm-tree from one another, to teach us that true love always endeavours to overcome by kindness and gratitude. These two deities were always painted in the Greek academies, to inform the scholars that it was their duty to be grateful to their teachers. *Porphyr. de Div. Rom.* —*Gyrald. Hist. D Synt.* 13.—*Cic. de N. D.* 3. c. 23.—*Paus.* 1. c. 30. l. 6. c. 23.——A name given to Apollonius, a grammarian of Alexandria, in the age of the emperor Claudius. *Suidas.*——A freedman of Atticus. *Cic. ad. Attic.* 9. ep. 14.

ANTEVOR'TA, a goddess at Rome, so called from knowing things past. *Cœl. Rhod.* 25. c. 30.—*Macrob.* Sat. 1. c. 17.

AN'TEUS, a Macedonian, of Pella, father of Leonatus.

AN'THAS, the founder of Anthea. *Paus.* 2.

ANTHE'A, a town of Achaia. *Id.* 7. c. 18.——A city of Messenia. *Id.* 4. c. 31.——A city of Trœzene. *Id.* 2. 30.——A sister of Priam, seized by the Greeks. She compelled the people of Pellene to burn their ships, and build Scione. *Polyæn.* 7. c. 47.

ANTHE'A, a daughter of Thespius, mistress of Hercules. *Apollod.* 2. c. 7.——A daughter of Amphianassa, wife of Prœtus, king of Argos. *Boccat.* 2. c. 2.

AN'THEAS, a son of Eumelus, killed in attempting to sow corn from the chariot of Triptolemus, drawn by dragons. *Paus.* 7. c. 18.

ANTHE'DON, now Talandi, a city of Bœotia, on the Euripus, so called from the flowery plains that surround it, or from Anthedon, an unknown nymph. Bacchus and Ceres had temples there, and there also was seen the tomb of the sons of Aloeus. *Mela*, 2. c. 4.—*Athen.* 7.—*Paus.* 7. c. 10. l. 9. c. 22.—*Hom. Il.* 2.—*Ovid. Met.* 13. v. 905.——A city of Syria, near Gaza. It was afterwards called Agrippias, according to *Josephus*. *Plin.* 4. c. 7.——A port of Peloponnesus. *Id.* 4. c. 5.—*Stat.* 9. v. 291.

ANTHE'LA, a town near the Asopus, near which Ceres and Amphictyon had a temple. *Herodot.* 7. c. 176.

ANTHE'LII, gods at Athens, so called from their statues being constantly exposed to the sun. *Hesych.*

AN'THEMIS, an island in the Mediterranean, the same with the Ionian Samus. *Strab.* 10,

ANTHE'MIUS. *Vid.* Antenius.

ANTHEMŒ'SIA, a daughter of the river Lycus, wife of Dascylus.

ANTHEMŒ'SIS or **ANTHEMU'SIS**, a lake in the country of Maryandini. *Apollon.* 2.

AN'THEMON, a Trojan. *Homer. Il.* 4. v. 473.——A city of Syria, on the eastern bank of the Euphrates. *Strab.* 16.

AN'THEMUS, a city of Macedonia, near Thermæ.

ANTHEMU'SIA, the same as Samus.——A country of Mesopotamia, situated at the south of Edessa.—*Cluver.* 5. c. 23.—*Strab.*—*Ptol.*

ANTHE'NA, a town of Peloponnesus. *Thucyd.* 5. c. 41.

ANTHER'MUS, a sculptor of Chius. He and his brother Bupalus made a statue of the poet Hipponax, which caused universal laughter, on account of the deformity of its countenance. The poet was, in consequence, so satirical against the statuaries, that they hanged themselves. *Plin.* 36. c. 5.

AN'THES, a native of Anthedon, who first invented hymns. *Plut. de Mus.*——A son of Neptune.

ANTHESPHO'RIA, festivals celebrated in Sicily, in honour of Proserpine, who was carried away by Pluto as she was gathering flowers. *Claud. de Rapt. Pros.*—Festivals of the same name were also observed at Argos, in honour of Juno, who was called Anthea. *Paus. Corinth.*—*Pollux. Onom.* 1. c. 1.

ANTHESTE'RIA, festivals in honour of Bacchus, celebrated in the month of February, called Anthesterion, whence the name is derived. They continued for three days, and the first was called Πιθοιγία, ἀπὸ τοῦ πίθους οἴγειν, because they tapped their barrels of liquor. The second day was called Χόες, from the measure χοά, because every individual drank of his own vessel, in commemoration of the arrival of Orestes, who, after the murder of his mother, came, without being purified, to Demophoon, or Paudion, king of Athens, and was obliged, with all the Athenians, to drink by himself, for fear of poluting the people by drinking with them before he was purified of the parricide. It was usual on that day to ride out in chariots, and ridicule those that passed by. The best drinker was rewarded with a crown of leaves, or rather of gold, and a cask of wine. The third day was called χύτροι from χύτρα, a vessel brought out full of all sorts of seeds and herbs, deemed sacred to Mercury, and therefore not touched. The slave had permission to be merry and free during these festivals; and at the end of the solemnity a herald proclaimed, Θύραζε. Κᾶρες, οὐκ ἔτ' Ἀνθεστήρια: *i. e.* Depart, ye Carian slaves, the festivals are at an end. They were also celebrated at Rome. *Ælian. V. H.* 2. c. 41.

AN'THEUS, a son of Antenor, much esteemed by Paris.——One of the companions of Æneas. *Virg. Æn.* 1. v. 514.

AN'THIAS. *Vid.* Antheas.

ANTHIP'PE, a daughter of Thestius, king of Bœotia; she bore several children to Hercules. *Apollod.* 2. c. 35.

ANTHIP'PUS, a Greek comic poet, praised by *Athenæus*. *Fabr. B. Gr.* 2. p. 413.——A Lacedæmonian, engaged in a negotiation with the Athenians. *Thucyd.* 5. c. 19.

AN'THIUM, a town of Thrace, on the borders of the Euxine Sea. It was afterwards called Apollonia. *Plin.* 4. c. 11.——A city of Italy.

AN'THIUS, *(flowery)*, a name of Bacchus, under which he was worshipped at Athens. He had also a temple at Patræ. *Paus.* 1.

AN'THO, a daughter of Amulius, king of Alba.

ANTHO'RES, a companion of Hercules, who settled in Italy, and was killed in the wars of Turnus against Æneas. *Virg. Æn.* 10. v. 778.

ANTHRA'CIA, a nymph. *Paus.* 8. c. 31.

ANTHROP'INUS, a person who, with Tisarchus and Diocles, laid snares for Agathocles, tyrant of Sicily. *Polyæn.* 5. c. 3.

ANTHROPOG'RAPHUS, a surname given to Dionysius the painter, because he employed his skill in painting men only. *Plin.* 35. c. 10.

ANTHROPOPH'AGI, a people of Scythia, who fed on human flesh. They lived near the country of the Massagetæ. *Id.* 4. c. 12. l. 6. c. 30.—*Mela*, 2. c. 1.

ANTHYL'LA, a city of Ægypt, on the Canopic mouth of the Nile, which supplied the queens of the country with shoes, or, according to *Athenæus*, 1. with girdles. *Herodot.* 2. c. 98.

ANTI'A LEX was made for the suppression of luxury at Rome. Its particulars are not known. The enactor was Antius Restio, who afterwards never supped abroad, for fear of being himself a witness of the profusion and extravagance which his law was intended to destroy, but without effect. *Macrob.* 3. c. 17.

ANTIANI'RA, the mother of Eurylus and Echion. *Apollon.* 1.

AN'TIAS, the goddess of fortune, was chiefly worshipped at Antium.——A poet. *Vid.* Furius.

ANTIBA'RUM, a city of Dalmatia, on the shores of the Adriatic. It is now Antivari.

ANTIB'OLE, one of the mouths of the Ganges. *Ptol.*

ANTICA'RIA, a city of Hispania Bætica, called also Singylia. It is now Antiquera.

ANTICAUCA'SUS, a mountain of Seleucia. *Strab.*

ANTICH'THONES, another name for the Antipodes. *Cluver.* 1. c. 5.—*Mela*, 1. c. 1. & 10.

ANTICINO'LIS, a town of Pontus. *Mela*, 1. c. 20.

ANTICI'TES. *Vid.* Antacites.

ANTICLE'A, a daughter of Autolycus and Amphithea, was pregnant of Ulysses by Sisyphus, when she was given in marriage to Laertes, king of Ithaca. It is said she killed herself when she heard a false report of her son's death, which had been raised by Nauplius. *Avienus. in Alleg. Siren.*—*Tzetzes in Lycoph.*—*Schol. Sophocl. in Ajac.*—*Lactant. in Achil. Stat.* 3. v. 76.—*Eustath. in Od.* 11. & *Hom. Od.* 11 & 19.—*Hygin.* fab. 201. 243.—*Paus.* 10. c. 29.——A woman who became mother of Periphetes, by Vulcan. *Apollod.* 3.——A daughter of Diocles, who married Machaon. *Paus.* 4. c. 30.

ANTI'CLES, an archon at Athens in the 103rd Olympiad.——A man who with Hermolaus, conspired against Alexander. *Curt.* 8. c. 6.——An Athenian commander, mentioned by *Thucydides*, 1. c. 119. ——An Athenian victor at Olympia.

ANTICLI'DES, a Greek historian, whose works are now lost. They are often quoted by *Athenæus*, and *Plutarch in Alex.—Plin.* 7. c. 61.

ANTIC'OLI, a people in the interior of Libya. *Ptol.*

ANTICONDY'LES, a people of Bœotia. *Steph.*

ANTIC'RAGUS, a mountain of Lycia, opposite mount Cragus. *Strab.* 4.

ANTIC'RATES, a Spartan who stabbed Epaminondas at the battle of Mantinea. *Plut. in Agid.*

ANTIC'YRA, two towns of Greece, the one in Phocis, on the bay of Corinth, the other near mount Œta, both famous for the hellebore which they produced. This plant was said to possess great medicinal powers in the cure of diseases, and particularly of insanity; hence the proverb *Naviget Anticyram.* The Anticyra of Phocis was anciently called Cyparissa, and had a celebrated temple of Neptune. Some writers, especially *Horace Art. P.* 300, speak of three islands of this name; but this seems to be a mistake. *Paus.* 10. c. 36.—*Horat.* 2 sat. 3. v. 166.—*Persius*, 4. v. 16.—*Strab.* 9.—*Mela*, 2. c. 3.—*Ovid. Pont.* 4. ep. 3. v. 53.—*Liv.* 26. c. 26.—*A. Gell.* 17. c. 15.——A mistress of Demetrius. *Plut. in Demetr.*

ANTIDALÆI, a people of Arabia Felix. *Plin.* 6. c. 28.

ANTID'AMAS, an historian who wrote a history of Alexander the Great. *Voss. de Hist. Gr.* 3.

ANTID'ONUS, a warlike soldier of King Philip, employed at the siege of Perinthus.

ANTIDO'RUS, a Lemnian, who deserted from Xerxes to the Greeks. *Herodot.* 8. c. 11.

ANTID'OTUS, an excellent painter, pupil of Euphranor. *Plin.* 35. c. 11.

ANTIG'ENES, one of Alexander's generals, publicly rewarded for his valour. *Curt.* 5. c. 14.——The father of Socrates, a commander of the Athenian fleet. *Thucyd.* 2. c. 23.——An historian, mentioned by *Plutarch in Alex.*——A musician. *Plin.* 16. c. 36.

ANTIGEN'IDAS, a famous musician of Thebes, pupil of Philoxenus. He taught his pupil Ismenias to despise the judgment of the populace, and when he seemed discouraged by the indifference of his auditors, he raised his spirits by saying *Mihi cane et Musis. A. Gell.* 15. c. 17. *Val. Max.* 3. c. 7.—*Pliny*, 36. c. 13. attributes to his debauchery and corrupt example the effeminate dress of the Milesians of Ionia. *Cic. in Brut.* 97.

ANTIG'ONE, a daughter of Œdipus, by his mother Jocasta. She accompanied her blind and helpless father when banished from his country; and interred by night the remains of her brother Polynices, against the orders of Creon, who commanded her to be buried alive. She however killed herself before the sentence could be executed. The death of Antigone is the subject of one of the tragedies of Sophocles, with which the Athenians were so much pleased on the first representation, that they presented the author with the government of Samus, and caused it to be acted 32 times without interruption. *Sophocl. in Antig.*—*Hygin.* fab. 67. 72. 243. 254.—*Apollod.* 3. c. 5.—*Ovid. Trist.* 3. el. 3.—*Philostrat.* 2. c. 29.—*Stat. Theb.* 12. 350. [In the gardens of the Villa Ludovisi, near Rome, there is a much-admired group of Hæmon and Antigone.]——A daughter of Eurytion, king of Phthia, in Thessaly. *Apollod.*——A daughter of Laomedon, changed into a stork for presuming to compare herself to Juno. *Ov. Met.* 6. v. 93.——A daughter of Berenice, wife of King Pyrrhus. *Plut. in Pyrrh.*

ANTIGONI'A, an inland town of Epirus, now Argiro Castro. *Plin.* 4. c. 1.—*Cluver.* 4. c. 7.——A city of Macedonia, founded by Antigonus, son of Gonatas, near the sources of the Chidorus. *Plin.* 4. c. 10.——A city of Syria, on the border of the Orontes. *Strab.* 16.——A city of Bithynia, called also Nicæa. *Id.* 12.——A city of Arcadia, anciently called Mantinea. *Paus.* 8. c. 8.——A city of Troas. *Strab.* 13.

ANTIG'ONIS, a tribe of Attica, so called from Antigonus.

ANTIG'ONUS, one of Alexander's generals, supposed to be the natural son of Philip, Alexander's father. In the division of the provinces, he received as his share, Pamphylia, Lycia and Phrygia. He united with Antipater and Ptolemy to destroy Perdiccas and Eumenes; and, afterthe death of Perdiccas, he made continual war against Eumenes, whom, after three years of various fortune, he took prisoner, and ordered to be starved to death. He afterwards declared war against Cassander, whom he conquered: and his generals had several engagements with Lysimachus. He obliged Seleucus to retire from Syria, and flee for refuge to Ægypt. Ptolemy, who had established himself in Ægypt, promised to defend Seleucus, and a new war was begun, in which Demetrius, the son of Antigonus, conquered the fleet of Ptolemy, near the island of Cyprus, and took 16,000 men prisoners, and sank 200 ships. After this famous naval battle, which happened 26 years after Alexander's death, Antigonus and his son assumed the title of kings; and their example was followed by all the rest of Alexander's generals. The power of Antigonus was now become so formidable, that Ptolemy, Seleucus, Cassander, and Lysimachus combined together to destroy him; yet Antigonus despised them, saying he would disperse them as birds. He attempted in vain to enter Ægypt, though he gained several victories over his opponents; and he at last received so many wounds at the battle of Ipsus, that he died in the 80th year of his age, 301 B.C. Antigonus was deeply engaged in the different intrigues of the Greeks. He made a treaty of alliance with the Ætolians, and was highly respected by the Athenians, to whom he showed himself very liberal and indulgent. *Strab.* 13.—*Diod.* 17. &c.—*Paus.* 1. c. 6. &c.—*Justin.* 13, 14, & 15. *C. Nep. in Eumen.—Plut. in Demetr. Eumen. & Arat.*

ANTIG'ONUS the First, surnamed Gonatas, was son of Demetrius, grandson of Antigonus, and king of Macedonia. He restored the Armenians to liberty, he conquered the Gauls, and was at last expelled by Pyrrhus, who seized his kingdom. After the death of Pyrrhus, he recovered Macedonia, and died after a reign of 36 years, leaving his son Demetrius as his successor, B.C. 243. *Justin.* 21 & 25.—*Polyb.*—*Plut. in Demetr.*

ANTIG'ONUS the Second, was guardian of his nephew, Philip, the son of Demetrius, and usurped the kingdom. He was called *Doson*, from his promising much, and giving nothing. He conquered Cleomenes, king of Sparta, and obliged him to retire into Ægypt, because he favoured the Ætolians against the Greeks. He died B.C. 221, after a reign of 11 years, leaving the crown to its lawful possessor, Philip. *Justin.* 28 & 29.—*Polyb.* 2.—*Plut in Cleom.*

ANTIG'ONUS, son of Aristobulus, king of Judæa, obtained an army from the king of Parthia, by promising him 1000 talents and 500 women. With these troops he attacked his country, and cut off the ears of Hyrcanus, to make him unfit for the priesthood. Herod, with the aid of the Romans, took him prisoner, and he was put to death by Antony. *Joseph.* 14.—*Dion. & Plut. in Anton.*——The son of Hyrcanus, was slain by Aristobulus his brother. *Joseph.* 12, &c.——An historian of Carystus, in the age of Ptolemy Philadelphus, of whose writings only one book, entitled ἱσοριῶν παραδόξων συναγωγή, is extant. He wrote also other works, quoted by *Laertus, Athenæus, Suidas*, and *Hesychius. Sax. Onom.* 1. p. 103.—*Fabr. B. Gr.* 4. p. 303.——A writer of Cumæ. His works on agriculture are commended by *Varro, Pliny*, and *Columella.*——A writer of the history of Italy, praised by *Festus* and *Dionysius* of *Halicarnassus.*——An Alexandrian grammarian.——A painter, who wrote on his art. *Plin.* 34. c. 10.——A statuary. *Id.* 34. c. 8.——A mathematician.——A physician. *Vid. Fabr. ibid.*

ANTIL'EON, a tyrant of Chalcis; after whose death the government became oligarchical. *Aristot.* 5. *Polit.* c. 12.——An author who wrote a book, περὶ χρόνων, cited by *Laertius. Julius Pollux, Onom.* 24. has also mentioned a person of this name, but whether the same or not is doubtful.

ANTILIB'ANUS, a mountain of Syria, opposite mount Libanus, near which the Orontes flows. *Plin.* 5. c. 20.—*Cluver.* 5. c. 21. *Strabo.*

ANTIL'OCHUS, a king of Messenia. *Paus.* 7.——The eldest son of Nestor, by Eurydice, accompanied his father to the Trojan war, where he distinguished himself by his great valour. He displayed his agility at the games in honour of Patroclus, where he was repeatedly rewarded with the prize. He was at last killed by Memnon, or, according to *Ovid*, by Hector. *Hom. Il.* 4, 6, 7, 13, 14, 15, 16 & 24. *Odys.* 3.—*Philostrat. in Antil.*—*Quint. Calab.* 2.—*Pind. Pyth.* 6.—*Apollod.* 1.—*Hygin.* fab. 252.——A poet, who wrote a panegyric upon Lysander, and received a hat filled with silver. *Plut. in Lys.*——An historian commended by *Dionysius* of *Halicarnassus.*

ANTIM'ACHUS, a Greek poet and musician of Ionia, in the age of Socrates, wrote a treatise on the age and genealogy of Homer. He repeated one of his compositions before a large audience; but his diction was so obscure, and his language so unintelligible, that all retired except Plato; upon which he said, *Legum nihilominus, Plato enim mihi est unus instar omnium.* The emperor Adrian was so fond of his poetry that he preferred it to Homer's. He wrote a poem on the Theban war, and before he had brought his heroes to the city of Thebes, he had filled 24 volumes. He was surnamed Clarius, from Clarus, where he was born. *Gyrald. de Poet. Hist.* 3.—*Paus.* 9. c. 35.—*Plut. in Lysand. & Timol.*—*Propert.* 2. el. 34. v. 45.—*Quintil.* 10. c. 1.——A poet, surnamed *Psecas*, because he praised himself. *Suidas.*—*Voss. de poet. Gr.*——A Trojan, whom Paris bribed to oppose the restoration of Helen to Menelaus and Ulysses. *Homer. Il.* 11. v. 123. & 12. v. 188.——A son of Hercules, by Eleuchia, the daughter of Thespius. *Apollod.* 2 & 3.——A native of Heliopolis, who wrote a poem on the creation of the world.——A lascivious person.——An historian.

ANTIM'ENES, a son of Deiphon. *Paus.* 2. c. 28.

ANTIMEN'IDAS, a Lacedæmonian ambassador to Athens. *Thucyd.* 5. c. 42.

ANTIMEN'IDES, a general who accompanied Alcæus in his expedition against Pittacus. *Arist.* 3. *Polit.* 14.—*Strab.* 13.

ANTIMNES'TUS, the father of Hierophon, an Athenian general. *Thucyd.* 3. c. 105.

ANTIN'OE, one of the daughters of Pelias. *Apollod.* 1. c. 32. *Paus.* 8. c. 11.

ANTINOEI'A, annual sacrifices and quinquennial games in honor of Antinous, instituted by the emperor Adrian, at Mantinea, where Antinous was worshipped as a divinity.

ANTINOP'OLIS, a city of Ægypt, on the eastern bank of the Nile, built by Adrian in honor of Antinous.

ANTIN'OUS, a youth of Bithynia, of whom the emperor Adrian was so extremely fond, that at his death he erected a temple to him, and wished it to be believed that he had been changed into a constellation. Some writers suppose that he was drowned in the Nile, while others assert that he offered himself at a sacrifice, as a victim, in honor of the emperor. [The statues of this favorite of Adrian are almost innumerable. He has been represented in the characters of nearly all the gods. The most celebrated is that of the Capitol; and of the equally numerous busts, that of Villa Monte Dragone near Rome.]——A native of Ithaca, and one of Penelope's suitors, who excited his companions to destroy Telemachus. When Ulysses returned home, he came to the palace, disguised in a beggar's dress, and Antinous struck him. After Ulysses had discovered himself, he killed Antinous first among the suitors. *Homer. Odyss.* 1, 16, 17, & 22.—*Propert.* 2. el. 5. v. 7.

ANTIOCHI'A, the name of a Syrian province. *Mela*, 1. c. 1.—*Plin.* 5. c. 20.——A city of Syria, once the third city of the world for beauty, size, and population. It was built by Antiochus and Seleucus Nicanor, partly on a hill and partly in a plain. It is situated on the banks of the river Orontes, and had a celebrated grove called Daphne; whence, for the sake of distinction, it has been called Antiochia near Daphne. *Dionys. Perieg.* [This city is personified in a fine statue, with the river Orontes at her feet, in the Museum of the Vatican.]——A city called also Nisibis, in Mesopotamia, built by Seleucus, son of Antiochus. It is now Nisibin.——The capital of Pisidia, 92 miles east of Ephesus.——A city on mount Cragus, in Cilicia.——A city near the river Tragues, 25 leagues from Seleucia, on the west.——A city of Margiana, called also Alexandria and Seleucia. *Plin.* 6. c. 26.——A city near mount Taurus, on the confines of Syria.——A city of Caria, on the river Mæander. *Cluver. Passim.*

ANTI'OCHIS, the name of the mother of Antiochus, the son of Seleucus.——A tribe of Athens.

ANTI'OCHUS, surnamed *Soter*, was son of Seleucus, and king of Syria and Asia. He strengthened himself on his throne by a treaty of alliance with Ptolemy Philadelphus, king of Ægypt. In his youth he became so deeply enamoured of his stepmother Stratonice, that his life was despaired of. When this was told Seleucus, he willingly gave Stratonice to his son, that his immoderate love might not cause his death. He died 291 B. C., after a reign of 19 years. *Justin.* 17. c. 2. &c.—*Val. Max.* 5.—*Polyb.* 4.—*Appian.*

ANTI'OCHUS the Second, surnamed *Theus* by the Milesians, because he put to death their tyrant Timarchus, was son and successor of Antiochus Soter. He put an end to the war which had been begun with Ptolemy; and to strengthen the peace he married Berenice, the daughter of the Ægyptian king. This so offended his wife Laodice, that she poisoned him, and then spread abroad a report that the king had died a natural death. *Vid.* Artemon. She then placed her son on the throne, and dispatched Berenice and her son, 246 B. C. *Appian.*

ANTI'OCHUS the Third, surnamed the *Great*, and brother of Seleucus Ceraunus, was king of Syria and Asia, and reigned 36 years. He was defeated by Ptolemy Philopater, at Raphia, after which he made war against Persia, and took Sardes. After the death of Philopater, he took advantage of the weak government of his infant son Epiphanes, and attempted to destroy his independence; but his guardians solicited the aid of the Romans, and Antiochus was compelled to resign his pretensions. He conquered the greatest part of Greece; but though some cities implored the aid of Rome, and gave a new turn to the state of the war, Annibal, who had taken refuge at his court, encouraged him to resist these formidable allies, and even to carry hostilities into the heart of Italy. But the measures of Antiochus were dilatory. He saw his armies defeated at Thermopylæ by Glabrio, and his conquests in Greece and Asia snatched away from his feeble hands, whilst, to avoid the disgrace of captivity, he fled into the centre of his kingdom, and agreed to confine the boundaries of his dominions east of mount Taurus, and to pay a yearly fine of 2,000 talents to the Romans. His revenues being unable to discharge this heavy imposition, he attempted to plunder the temple of Belus, in Susiana, which so incensed the inhabitants that they killed him, with his followers, 187 B. C. Antiochus was humane and liberal, the patron of learning, and the friend of merit. He had three sons, Seleucus Philopater, Antiochus Epiphanes, and Demetrius. The first succeeded him, and the two others were detained in Italy as hostages by the Romans. *Justin.* 31 & 32.—*Strab.* 16.—*Liv.* 34. c. 59.—*Flor.* 2. c. 1.—*Appian. Bell. Syr.*

ANTI'OCHUS the Fourth, surnamed *Epiphanes* or *Illustrious*, succeeded his brother Seleucus, and reigned eleven years. He destroyed Jerusalem, and showed himself so cruel in the tortures and punishments which he inflicted on the Jews, as is minutely recorded in the book of the Maccabees, that they called him *Epimanes* or *Furious*, and not *Epiphanes.* He attempted to plunder Persepolis, without effect. His character was childish and licentious, and he danced with such indecency among the stage players, that even the most dissipated blushed at the sight. *Polyb.*—*Justin.* 34. c. 3.

ANTI'OCHUS the Fifth, surnamed *Eupator*, succeeded his father Epiphanes, on the throne of Syria, 164 B. C. He made a peace with the Jews, and, in the second year of his reign, was assassinated by his uncle Demetrius, who said that the crown was lawfully his own, and that it had been wrested from his father. *Justin.* 34.—*Joseph.* 12.

ANTI'OCHUS the Sixth, king of Syria, was surnamed *Entheus* or *Noble.* His father, Alexander Bala, entrusted him to the care of Malcus, an Arabian; and he received the crown from Tryphon, in opposition to his brother Demetrius, whose character and conduct rendered him an aversion to the people. Before he had been a year on the throne, Tryphon murdered him, 143 B. C. and reigned in his place three years. *Joseph.* 13.

ANTI'OCHUS the Seventh, surnamed *Sidetes*, reigned nine years. In the beginning of his reign, he was afraid of Tryphon, and concealed himself; but he soon obtained the means of destroying his enemy. He made war against Phraates, king of Parthia, and fell in the battle which was soon after fought, about 130 B. C. *Justin* 36. c. 1.—*Appian. Bell. Syr.*

ANTI'OCHUS, the Eighth, surnamed *Gryphus*, from his *aquiline* nose, was son of Demetrius Nicanor, by Cleopatra. His brother Seleucus was destroyed by Cleopatra, and he himself would have shared the same fate, had not he discovered his mother's artifice, and compelled her to drink the poison which she had prepared for him. He killed Alexander Zebenna, whom Ptolemy had set up to oppose him on the throne of Syria, and was at last assassinated, B. C. 112. *Justin.* 39. &c.—*Joseph.*—*Appian.*

ANTI'OCHUS the Ninth, surnamed *Cyzicenus*, from the city of Cyzicus, where he received his education, was son of Antiochus Sidetes, by Cleopatra. He contended for the sovereignty with his brother Gryphus, who ceded to him Cœlesyria. He was at last conquered by his nephew Seleucus, near Antioch; and killed himself, B. C. 93. While a private man, he seemed worthy to reign; but when raised to the throne he became dissolute and tyrannical. He was fond of mechanics, and invented some useful military engines. *Appian.*—*Joseph.*

ANTI'OCHUS the Tenth, was ironically surnamed *Pius*, because he married Selena, the wife of his father and of his uncle. He was the son of Antiochus the Ninth, and expelled Seleucus, the son of Gryphus, from Syria. He was killed in a battle which he fought against the Parthians, in the cause of the Galatians. *Joseph.*—*Appian.* After his death the kingdom of Syria was torn to pieces by the factions of the royal family, and of usurpers, who, under the name of Antiochus or his relations, established themselves for a little time, as sovereigns either of Syria or Damascus, or other dependent provinces. At last, Antiochus, the son of Antiochus the Ninth, surnamed *Asiaticus*, was restored to his paternal throne by the influence of Lucullus, the Roman general on the expulsion of Tigranes, king of Armenia, from the Syrian dominions. But four years afterwards, Pompey deposed him; and observed, that he who had hid himself while a usurper sat upon his throne, was not fit to be a king. From that time, B.C. 65, Syria was a Roman province, and the race of Antiochus became extinct. *Justin* 40.

ANTI'OCHUS, a philosopher of Ascalon, famous for his writings, and the respect with which he was treated by his pupils, Lucullus, Cicero, and Brutus. *Plut. in Lucul.*—*Strab.* 16.——An historian of Syracuse, son of Xenophanes, who wrote, besides other works, a history of Sicily. This history was still extant in the age of the Antonines, and is quoted as respectable authority by *Pausanias*. *Strab.*—*Diod* 12.—*Voss. de Hist. Gr.* p. 456.——A rich king of Asia, tributary to the Romans in the age of Vespasian. *Tac. Hist.* 2. c. 81.——A sophist, who refused to take upon himself the government of a state, on account of the vehemence of his passions.——An officer in the Athenian fleet, under Alcibiades. He was conquered by Lysander. *Xenoph. Hist. Gr.*——A writer of Alexandria, who published a treatise on comic poets. *Athen.*——A sculptor, son of Illas, who is said to have made the famous statue of Pallas, preserved in the Ludovisi gardens at Rome.——A king conquered by Antony, &c. *Cæsar*, 3. *Bell. Civ.* 4.——A king of Messenia. *Paus.* 4.——A sceptic of Laodicea. *Diog. in Pyrrh.*——A learned sophist. *Philost.*——A servant of Atticus. *Cic. ad Att.* 13. ep. 33.——A hair-dresser, mentioned by *Martial*, 11. epigr. 85.——A son of Hercules by Medea. *Apollod.* 2. 1. 7.——A stage player. *Juv.* 3. v. 98.

ANTI'OPE, daughter of Nycteus, king of Thebes, was beloved by Jupiter, to whom she bore twins, Amphion and Zethus, on Mount Cithæron. She exposed them, but they were preserved by some shepherds. She then retired to Sicyon, where Epopeus, the king of the country, married her. She afterwards married her uncle Lycus. His wife Dirce, jealous of this new connection, prevailed upon her husband to deliver her into her hands, and Antiope was confined in a prison, and exposed to torments daily. After many years of imprisonment, she found means to escape, and went after her sons, who undertook to avenge her wrongs upon Lycus and Dirce. They took Thebes, put the king to death, and tied Dirce to the tail of a wild bull. *Vid.* Dirce. Bacchus, pitying her misfortunes, changed her into a fountain, and deprived Antiope of her senses. In this condition she wandered over Greece, and at last found relief in the house of Phocis, son of Ornytion, who cured her of her disorder and married her. Some authors have called Antiope daughter of Asopus, because she was born on the banks of that river. The *Scholiast* on *Apollonius*, 1. v. 735. maintains, that there were two persons of that name, one the daughter of Nycteus, and the other of Asopus, and mother of Amphion and Zethus. *Paus.* 2. c. 1. 9. c. 17.—*Ovid. Met.* 6. v. 110.—*Apollod.* 3. c. 5.—*Propert.* 3. el. 15.—*Homer. Od.* 11. v. 259.—*Hygin.* fab. 7, 8, & 155.—*Nonnus, Dionys.* 7 & 16.—*Nat. Com.* 8. c. 1. [Antiope is represented in the celebrated group at Naples, known by the name of *Il Toro Farnese*.——A daughter of Thespius or Thestius, mother of Alopius, by Hercules. *Apollod.* 2. c. 7.——A queen of the Amazons. *Vid.* Hippolyte.——A daughter of Æolus, mother of Bœotus and Hellen, by Neptune. *Hygin.* fab. 157.——A daughter of Pilon, who married Eurytus. *Id.* fab. 14.——The name of a tragedy of Pacuvius. *Pers.* 1. v. 77.

ANTIO'RUS, a son of Lycurgus. *Plut. in Lycurg.*

ANTIP'ARUS, a small island in the Ægæan Sea, opposite Parus, from which it is distant six miles.

ANTIP'ATER, son of Iolaus, was one of the generals of Alexander the Great. When Alexander invaded Asia, he left Antipater governor of Macedonia and of all Greece, and he made a successful war against the Greeks, whom the absence of Alexander had induced to rebel, and killed in battle Agis, king of Sparta. His great services were, however, ill repaid by Alexander, who grew jealous of his fame, and commanded him to appear before him at Babylon. Antipater obeyed with reluctance, and the death of Alexander, which happened soon after, was attributed to the machinations of the offended general. His sons, Cassander and Iolas, were in the camp, and, it is said by some historians, that to prevent the condemnation of their father they administered poison to the unsuspecting king. After Alexander's death, Macedonia was allotted to Antipater, against whom the Athenian's levied an army of 33,000 men, and equipped 200 ships. Their expedition was attended with much success; Antipater was routed in Thessaly, and even besieged in the town of Lamia. But when Leosthenes, the Athenian general, was mortally wounded under the walls of Lamia the fortune of the war changed; Antipater obliged the enemy to raise the siege, and soon after received a reinforcement from Craterus, from Asia, with which he conquered the Athenians, at Cranon, in Thessaly. After this defeat, Antipater and Craterus marched into Bœotia, conquered the Ætolians, and granted peace to the Athenians on the humiliating conditions which Leosthenes had formerly proposed to Antipater, when besieged in Lamia, *i.e.* that he should be absolute master over them. Besides this, he required that they should deliver into his hands the orators Demosthenes and Hyperides, whose eloquence had inflamed the minds of their countrymen against him. The conditions were accepted. A Macedonian garrison was stationed in Athens, but the inhabitants were still allowed to retain their laws and privileges. Antipater and Craterus were the first who made hostile preparations against Perdiccas. Antipater likewise assisted Eumenes, in Asia, against Antigonus, according to *Justin.* 14. c. 2. At his death, B.C. 319, he left Polyperchon master of all his possessions, and recommended that everything should be done according to his superior judgment. Antipater, like many of the great men of his age, cultivated and patronised literature; and as a proof of his learning, a letter from him to his son Cassander is highly extolled by *Cicero, Off.* 2. c. 14.—*Justin.* 9. c. 4, &c.—*Paus.* 7. c. 10.—*Curt.* 4. c. 1, &c.—*Arrian.* 1 & 7.—*Plin.* 30. c. 16.—*Val. Max.* 1. c. 7.—*Tac. Ann.* 2. c. 73.—*Diod.* 17, 18, &c.—*C. Nep. in Phoc. & Eumen.*—*Plut. in Eumen. Alex. &c.*——A son of Cassander, king of Macedonia, and son-in-law of Lysimachus. He put his mother to death, because she wished his brother Alexander to succeed to the throne. Alexander, to avenge the death of his mother, solicited the assistance of Demetrius; but peace was re-established between the two brothers by the advice of Lysimachus; and soon afterwards Demetrius killed Antipater, and made himself king of Macedonia, 294. B.C. *Justin.* 21. c. 1.——A king of Macedonia, who reigned only 45 days, 277. B.C.——A king of Cilicia.——A powerful prince, the father of Herod. He was appointed governor of Judæa by Cæsar, whom he had assisted in the Alexandrine war. *Joseph.*——One of Alexander's soldiers, who conspired with Hermolaus against his life. *Curt.* 8. c. 6.——A celebrated sophist of Hieropolis, preceptor to the children of the emperor Severus. *Philostr.*——A Stoic philosopher of Tarsus, 144 B.C. *Strab.* 14.——A poet of Sidon, who could compose a number of verses *ex tempore*, upon any subject. In one of his epigrams, he ranked Sappho among the Muses. He had a fever every year, on the day of his birth, of which he at last died. He flourished about 80. B.C. Some of his epigrams are preserved in the Anthologia. He was preceptor of Cato Uticensis. *Plin.* 7. c. 51.—*Val. Max.* 1. c. 10.—*Cic. de Orat.* 3. *de Off.* 3. *de Quæst. Acad.* 4.—*Plut. in Cat.*——A Stoic philosopher, pupil of Diogenes of Babylon. He wrote two books on divination, and died at Athens. *Cic. de Div.* 1. c. 3. *Quæst. Acad.* 4. c. 6. *de Off.* 3. c. 12. ——A pupil of Aristotle, who wrote two books of letters.——A poet of Thessalonica, in the age of Augustus.——An archon at Athens. *Ol.* 97. *an.* 4.—*Jons. de Scrip. Hist. Phil.* 1. 1. c. 13.—*Voss. de Hist. Gr.* l. 3. p. 324.

ANTIPA'TRIA, a city of Macedonia, so called in honour of Antipater. *Liv.* Also Antipatri'a.

ANTIPAT'RIDAS, a governor of Telmessus. *Polyæn.* 5. c. 35.

ANTIP'ATRIS, a city of Palestine, so called by Herod in honour of his father Antipater.

ANTIPH'ANES, an ingenious statuary of Argos, whose statues were still seen and admired in the temple of Delphi, in the age of the Antonines. *Paus.* l. 5. 17, &c.——A comic poet before the age of Thespis whose poems are called 'Αντιφάνειος κωμωδία. *Voss. Hist. Gr.* l. 4. p. 504.—*Id. de Poet. Gr.* c. 6. ——A comic poet of Rhodes, or of Smyrna, who wrote 365 comedies, and died in the 74th year of his age, by the fall of an apple upon his head. Some of his verses are quoted by *Stobæus* and *Athenæus. Fabr. B. Gr.* 2. p. 414.—*Sax. Onom.* 1. p. 54.——A poet, a native of Athens, after the age of Panætius. *Suidas.*——A writer, of Thrace, who, according to *Stephanus*, composed some geographical treatises.——A poet of Colophon, to whose pen are attributed some heroic poems, especially one on the war of the Argives against Thebes.——A physician of Delus, who used to say that diseases originated from the variety of food that was eaten. *Suidas.*—*Clem. Alex. Strom.* 1.—*Iren. ad gent.* 2.—*Voss. de P. Gr. & de Hist. Gr.* 4.—*Gyrald. de P. Hist.* 6.—*Fabr. ibid.*

AN'TIPHAS and THYMBRÆUS, the two sons of Laocoon, called also Æthon and Melanthus. *Vid.* Laocoon. *Hygin.* fab. 135.—*Thessand. ap. Serv. Æn.* 2. v. 211.

ANTIPH'ATES, a king of the Læstrygones, descended from Lamus, who founded Formiæ. Ulysses returning from Troy, landed upon his coasts, and sent three men to examine the country. Antiphates devoured one of them, pursued the others, and sank the fleet of Ulysses with stones, except the ship in which Ulysses was. *Ovid. Met.* 14. v. 232. *Ex. Pont.* 4. ep. 10. v. 21.—*Fast.* 4. v. 69. *Ibin.* 390.—*Homer. Odyss.* 10.—*Tibul.* 4. el. 1. v. 59.—*Sil. Ital.* 8. v. 531.—*Hygin.* fab. 125.—*Plin.* 3. c. 5 & 8. ——A son of Sarpedon. *Virg. Æn.* 9. v. 696.——The grandfather of Amphiaraus. *Homer Odyss.* 15. v. 242.——A man killed in the Trojan war by Leonteus. *Homer. Il.* 12. v. 191.

ANTIPHEL'LUS, a place of Lycia. *Steph.*—*Plin.* 5. c. 27. & 31. c. 11.

ANTIPHE'MUS, a Rhodian, who, together with Entimus, a Cretan, founded Gela, in Sicily. *Thucyd.* 6. c. 4.

ANTIPH'ERON, a native of Oretum, who thought that he met his shadow everywhere. *Senec.* 1. *Nat. Quæst.* 3.—*Aristot.*

ANTIPH'ILI POR'TUS, now Vella, a harbour on the African side of the Red Sea. *Strab.* 16.

ANTIPH'ILUS, an Athenian, who succeeded Leosthenes in the command at the siege of Lamia, against Antipater. *Diod.* 18.——An architect employed in building the public treasury of Sicyon. *Paus.* 6. c. 19.——A celebrated painter, who represented a youth leaning over a fire and blowing it, from which the whole house seemed to be illuminated. He was an Ægyptian by birth, and pupil of Ctesidemus; but he successfully imitated the works of Apelles. *Plin.* 35. c. 10.

AN'TIPHON, a native of Rhamnusia, called Nestor, from his eloquence and prudence. The 16 orations, which are extant under his name, are supposed by some to be spurious. *Hermog. de form. Orat.* 2.—*Fabr. B. Gr.* 2. p. 750.——An orator, who promised Philip, king of Macedonia, that he would set on fire the citadel of Athens; for which he was put to death at the instigation of Demosthenes. *Cic. de Div.* 2. *Plut. in Alcib. & Demosth.*—*Thucyd.* 8.—*Arist.* 2. *Rhet.* 1.—*Soph. Elench.*—*Demosth. de Coron.*——A poet who wrote on agriculture. *Athen.*——An author who wrote a treatise on peacocks.——A rich man introduced by Xenophon as disputing with Socrates. ——A poet of Attica, who wrote tragedies, epic poems, and orations. Dionysius put him to death because he refused to praise his compositions. Being once asked by the tyrant what brass was the best, he answered, "that with which the statues of Harmodius and Aristogiton are made." *Plut. in Aristot.*——A foolish rhetorician. *Ionsius, in Hist. Phil. Script.* l. 4. enumerates 13 persons of that name. See also *Harles'* notes on *Fabricius*, 2. p. 750.

ANTIPH'ONUS, a son of Priam, who went with his father to the tent of Achilles, to redeem the body of Hector. *Homer. Il.* 24.

AN'TIPHRA, a town near Alexandria, not far from the sea. *Steph.*

AN'TIPHUS, a son of Priam, killed by Agamemnon during the Trojan war.——A son of Thessalus, grandson of Hercules. He went to the Trojan war with 30 ships. *Hom. Il.* 2. v. 185.——An intimate friend of Ulysses. *Homer. Odyss.* 17.——A son of Ganyctor the Naupactian. He, with the assistance of his brother, murdered the poet Hesiod. *Vid.* Hesiod. *Plut. de Solert. Anim.*——A son of Pilemenes, who conducted the Mæonians to the Trojan war. *Hom. Il.* 2.——A son of Myrmidon and Pisidice. *Apollod.* 1. c. 16.

ANTIPŒNUS, a noble Theban, whose daughters offered themselves as a sacrifice for the public safety. *Vid.* Androclea.

ANTIP'OLIS, a city of Gaul, built by the people of Marseilles, on the coast of the Mediterranean, nine miles west of Nice. *Tac.* 2. *Hist.* c. 15.—*Mela*, 2. c. 7.——The country on the other side of the Tiber, opposite Rome. *Plin.* 3. c. 5.—*Mart.* 13. epigr. 103.

ANTIPYR'GUS, a city of Marmarica. *Ptol.* It is called Tetrapyrgia by *Strabo*, and is now Luco.

ANTIR'RHIUM, a promontory of Ætolia, about a mile distant from the opposite shore of Rhium in Peloponnesus, whence the name. These two promontories form the Dardanelles of Lepanto, the modern name of the bay of Corinth. *Strab.* 8.—*Plin.* 2. c.90.

ANTIR'RHODUS, an island of Ægypt, near Pharus. *Strab.*

ANTIS'ARA, called also Tisara, a city and harbour of the Datini. *Steph.*

ANTIS'SA, a city at the north of Lesbus. It was the name also of an island near it. *Ovid. Met.* 15. v. 287.—*Plin.* 2. c. 89.

ANTIS'THENES, a Cynic philosopher, who taught rhetoric, and had among his pupils the celebrated Diogenes. When he had heard Socrates, he shut up his school, and told his pupils, "Go and seek for yourselves a master, I have found one." He sold all his property, and preserved only a very ragged coat, which drew the attention of Socrates, and tempted him to say to the Cynic, "Antisthenes, I can see thy vanity through the holes of thy coat." Antisthenes taught the unity of God, but recommended suicide. Some of his letters are extant. He flourished 396 B.C. His works were contained in 10 vols. *Laert.* 6. c. 15.—*Fabr. B. Gr.* 2. p. 698.—*Sax. Onom.* 1. p. 49.—*Cic. de Orat.* 3. c. 35. *Off.* 1. c. 35 & 41.—*Diog.* 6.—*Ælian.* 9. c. 35.—*Plut. in Lyc.* [The finest and most authentic bust of this philosopher is that in the Vatican. A sitting figure in the Farnese palace also bears his name.——An historian of Rhodes. *Diog.*—*Phleg. Trall. Mirab.* c. 3.—*Voss. de Hist. Gr.* l. 3. There were other persons of this name: one of whom was a disciple of Heraclitus; another, a physician; and a third, a native of Parus. *Schol. Aristoph. ad Eccles.*—*Philostr.*—*Fabr. ibid.*

ANTIS'TIA, the wife of Rubellius Plautus. *Tac. Ann.* 14. c. 22. It was also the name of a Roman family.

ANTISTIA'NA, a city of Hispania Citerior. *Antonin.*

ANTIS'TIUS, a noble Roman who repudiated his wife for talking with his freedman. *Alex. ab Alex.* 4.——An orator, one of those to whom M. Antonius delivered his son Commodus, to be educated. *Volaterr. anthrop.* 14.

ANTIS'TIUS C. REGI'NUS, a lieutenant in Cæsar's army in Gaul. *Cæs. B. G.* 6. & 7.

ANTIS'TIUS LA'BEO, an excellent lawyer, who ably defended the liberties of his country against the usurpation of Augustus, for which he was taxed with madness by the courtly muse of *Horace*, 1 *Sat.* 3. v. 82. *Suet. in Aug.* 54.

Antis'tius Pe'tro, of Gabii, was the author of a celebrated treaty between Rome and his country, in the age of Tarquinius Superbus. *Dion Hal.* 4.

Antis'tius Sosia'nus, a tribune of the people in the time of Nero. Being made prætor, he composed some satirical verses on the emperor, for which he was banished. *Tac. Ann.* 13. c. 28. & 14. c. 48.

Antis'tius Tur'pio, a soldier of Pompey's army, so confident of his valour, that he challenged all the adherents of Cæsar. *Hirt. Hisp. Bell.* 25.

Antis'tius Ve'tus, a triumvir, appointed for the purpose of coining money. *Plin.* 31. c. 2, &c.——A person accused of adultery and treason, and, in consequence, banished to an island. *Tac. Ann.* 3. c. 38. There were several other persons of this name, who are mentioned by *Cicero*, but were little known.

ANTITAU'RUS, one of the great branches of mount Taurus, which runs in a north-eastern direction, through Cappadocia, towards Armenia and the Euphrates.

ANTITH'EUS, an Athenion archon, Olymp. 166. *Paus.* 7. c. 17.

AN'TIUM, a maritime town of Italy, built by Ascanius, or, according to others, by a son of Ulysses and Circe upon a promontory 32 miles east of Ostium, was the capital of the Volsci. Camillus took it, and carried all the beaks of their ships to Rome, and placed them in the forum on a tribunal, which, from this circumstance, was called *Rostrum*. This town was dedicated to the goddess of Fortune, and the emperor Nero was born there. It is no longer in existence, but the promontory on which it stood is now called Capo d'Anzo. *Cluver.* 3. c. 27.—*Mela*, 2. c. 6.—*Cic. de Div.* 1.—*Horat.* 1. od. 35.—*Liv.* 8. c. 14.——A city of Thrace. *Cluver.* 4. c. 14.

ANTOBRO'GES, a people of Aquitania, not far from the Cadurci. *Plin.* 4. c. 19.

ANTOM'ENES, the last king of Corinth. After his death annual magistrates were chosen.

ANTO'NIA LEX, was enacted by M. Antony, the consul, A. U. C. 710. It abrogated the *lex Atia*, and renewed the *lex Cornelia*, by taking away from the people the privilege of choosing the priests, and restoring it to the college of priests. *Dio.* 44.—Another, by the same, A. U. C. 705. It ordained that a new decury of judges should be added to the two former, and that they should be chosen from the centurions. *Cic. in Philip.* 1 & 5.—Another, by the same. It allowed an appeal to the people, to those who were condemned *de majestate*, or of perfidious measures against the state.—Another, by the same, during his triumvirate. This law made it ever after a capital offence for any person to accept of the office, or even to propose the election, of a dictator, *Appian, de Bell. Civ.* 3.

ANTONIA, a daughter of M. Antony, by Octavia. She married Domitius Ænobarbus, and was mother of Nero and two daughters.——Another daughter of Antony and Octavia, who married Drusus, the son of Livia and brother of Tiberius. She was mother of Germanicus, Caligula's father; of Claudius the emperor; and the debauched Livia. Her husband died very early, and she would never marry again, but dedicated her time to the education of her children. Some suppose that her grandson Caligula ordered her to be poisoned, A. D. 38. *Val. Max.* 4. c. 3. [The finest bust of this Antonia is that at Rome, in the Museum of the Capitol.]——The daughter of Claudius and Ælia Petina, of the family of the Tuberones. She was repudiated by her husband for a slight cause. *Suet. Claud.* 1.—*Tac. Ann.* 1. 11. It was the name also of the sister of Germanicus.

Anto'nia, a castle at Jerusalem, which was so called in honor of M. Antony. *Joseph. B. J.* 5. c. 15.

ANTO'NII, a patrician and plebeian family, which were said to derive their origin from Antones, a son of Hercules, according to *Plutarch in Anton.*

ANTONI'NA, the wife of Belisarius.

ANTONI'NUS TI'TUS, surnamed *Pius*, was adopted by Adrian, whom he succeeded as emperor of Rome in his 52d year. This prince was remarkable for all the virtues that can form a perfect statesman, a judicious philosoper, and a benevolent king. Directing the whole of his attention to the happiness of his people, he rebuilt whatever cities had been destroyed by war in former reigns; and in cases of famine or inundation, he relieved the distressed, and supplied their wants with his own money. He suffered the governors of the provinces to remain long in their administration, that no opportunity of extortion might be given by new appointments. In his conduct towards his subjects he behaved with affability and humanity, and listened with patience to the complaints of all. When told of conquering heroes, he exclaimed with Scipio, "I prefer the preservation of the life of one citizen to the death of a hundred enemies." He did not prosecute the Christians like his predecessors; and his benevolence was universal, ever active to promote order, and to diffuse happiness and tranquillity over the whole earth. His last moments were easy, though preceded by a lingering illness. When consul of Asia, he lodged at Smyrna, in the house of a sophist, who capriciously obliged the governor to change his habitation at night. The sophist, when Antoninus became emperor, visited Rome, and was jocosely desired to use the palace as his own house, without any apprehension of being turned out at night. He extended the boundaries of the Roman province in Britain, and secured his possessions there by raising a rampart between the friths of Clyde and Forth; but he waged no wars during his reign, and only repulsed the enemies of the empire who appeared in the field. He died in the 75th year of his age, after a reign of 23 years, A. D. 161. [Of this emperor, there is a statue in the Villa Mattei at Rome, and two fine busts in the Vatican, and the Capitol.]

Antoni'nus M. Aure'lius, the adopted son of Titus, succeeded him on the throne. He was surnamed the philosopher; and was a prince as humane and beloved as his father, though his virtues were of a severer and more laborious kind. The son acquired, by penitent study and austere exercise, a high character for temperance, moderation, and goodness, which virtues were in the father the uncultivated fruits of nature and watchful experience. Like Titus, the benign Marcus detested war as the disgrace and calamity of humanity; but he disdained to stoop to the insults of an enemy, or not to resent the ambiguous conduct of a perfidious friend; and so highly finished a picture of moral excellence and universal benevolence do these two meritorious emperors afford to history, that they have drawn upon themselves the eyes and the admiration of posterity, as to point where every thing that is great, perfect, venerable, just, and amiable, is happilly centred. The 42 years during which they presided over the destinies of the empire, may be considered, therefore, as the most fortunate æra of Rome, where absolute power and uncontrolled dominion were directed by wisdom and virtue, to establish and to cement the happiness and the prosperity of a great nation. In conformity to the settlement recommended by Adrian, Marcus adopted and raised to the imperial dignity Verus, the son of Ælius Verus, a youth whose voluptuousness and dissipation were as conspicuous as the moderation of the philosopher. During their reign, the Quadi, Parthians, and Marcomanni were defeated. Antoninus wrote a book in Greek, entitled τὰ καθ' ἑαυτόν, concerning himself; the best editions of which are the 4to Cantab. 1652, and the 8vo Oxon. 1704. After the war with the Quadi had been finished, Verus died of an apoplexy, and Antoninus survived him eight years, and died in his 61st year, after a reign of nineteen years and ten days. *Dio. Cassius—Aurel. Victor.—Hist. August.* A Greek itinerary, and a book called *Iter Britannicum*, have been attributed to the emperor Antoninus. *Vid. Fabr. B. Gr.* 4. c. 20.—*Sax. Onom.* 1. p. 313.—*Harles. Not. Lit. Rom.* 1. p. 580. [A fine equestrian statue in bronze, exists in the Capitol. The finest bust is that of colossal size, in the Borghese collection at Paris.]

Antoni'nus Com'modus. *Vid.* Commodus.

Antoni'nus Bassia'nus Caracal'la, was son of the emperor Septimus Severus. He with his brother Geta succeeded to the empire; but the animosity of the two brothers against each other was so violent, that it was impossible to reconcile them. Geta at last fell a sacrifice to his brother's hatred, and was stabbed in his mother's arms, and not less than 20,000 were devoted to death for their pretended attachment to him. It is said that Caracalla attempted to destroy the writings of Aristotle, observing that Aristotle was one of those who sent poison to Alexander. He married his mother, and publicly lived with her, which gave occasion to the people of Alexandria to say, that he was an Œdipus, and his wife a Jocasta. This joke was fatal to them; for the emperor, to punish their severe reflections upon his conduct, ordered several thousands to be slaughtered. Caracalla was, at last, to the universal joy of the Roman people, assassinated at Edessa, by Macrinus, whom he had devoted to death, on the 8th of April in the 43d year of his age, A. D. 217. His body was sent to his wife, Julia, who stabbed herself at the sight. He was succeeded by his murderer. *Dio.* 77.—*Herodian.* 4.—*Hist. August.* [A statue of this tyrant is to be found at Naples, having been removed from the Palazzo Farnese; and the finest bust is in the British Museum.]

ANTONI'NUS LIBERA'LIS, was the author of a work entitled Μεταμορφώσεων συναγωγή, contained in 41 chapters, and collected from various writers. Very little is known respecting him or the time when he lived, though *Saxius* supposes him to have lived about the second century. *Fabr. B. Gr.* 4. p. 309. *Sax. Onom.* 1. p. 308. There were other persons of this name, but of little note. *Vid. Ionsius de Script. Hist. Phil.* 3. c. 10.

ANTONIOPOLIS, a city of Mesopotamia, so called in honor of Antony. *Marcell.* 8.

ANTO'NIUS M. GNI'PHO, a poet of Gaul, who taught rhetoric at Rome. Cicero, and other illustrious men, frequented his school. He never asked any remuneration for his lectures, whence he received more from the liberality of his pupils. *Suet. de Illustr. Gr.*

ANTO'NIUS M. an orator, grandfather to the triumvir of the same name. He was killed in the civil wars of Marius, and his head was fixed on the rostrum, where he had so often pleaded the cause of his country and of innocence. Cicero, who laments his fall, speaks as if ominously of the fate which awaited himself a few years after from the tyranny of this unfortunate man's grandson. *Cic. in Brut.* 36. *Orat.* 3. c. 8. *Ad Quir.post Red.* 5.—*Val. Max.* 9. c. 2.—*Lucan.* 2. v. 121.

ANTO'NIUS MAR'CUS, surnamed *Creticus* or *Cretensis*, the eldest son of the orator, obtained from the senate the office of managing the corn on the maritime coasts of the Mediterranean, with unlimited power. This gave him many opportunities of plundering the provinces, and enriching himself. He died of a broken heart, it is said, upon being defeated by the Cretans, against whom, actuated by avarice rather than ambition, he had made war. *Cic. Verr.* 2. c. 3.—*Liv.* 97.—*Plut in Ant.*—*Flor.* 3. c. 7.—*Sallust. Frag.*

ANTO'NIUS CA'IUS, another son of the orator, obtained a troop of horse from Sylla, and plundered Achaia. He was carried before the prætor M. Lucullus, and banished from the Senate by the censors, for pillaging a country in alliance with Rome, and for refusing to appear when summoned.

ANTO'NIUS CA'IUS, son of the preceding, was consul with Cicero, and assisted him to destroy the conspiracy of Catiline in Gaul, though he has been suspected by some authors of favouring the cause of the traitor, because he entrusted the command of the army to his lieutenant Petreius. He afterwards went to Macedonia, as his province, and fought unsuccessfully against the Dardani. He was accused on his return, by Cælius, of plundering the provinces; and, upon full conviction, was sentenced to perpetual exile. *Cic. Vat.* 11. *Cœl.* 31.—*Sallust Catil.* 24 & 59.—*Liv.* 103.

ANTO'NIUS MAR'CUS, the triumvir, was grandson of the orator, and son of Antonius, surnamed *Cretensis*. He was augur and tribune of the people, in which office he distinguished himself by his ambitious views. He always entertained resentment against Cicero, because Cicero had put to death Corn. Lentulus, who was concerned in Catiline's conspiracy. This Lentulus had married Antonius's mother after his father's death. When the Senate was divided between the factions of Pompey's and Cæsar's adherents, Antony proposed that both should lay aside the commands of their armies in the provinces; but, as this proposition met with no success, he privately retired to the camp of Cæsar, and advised him to march his army to Rome. His attachment to the cause of Cæsar is proved by his commanding the left wing of his army at Pharsalia; and, according to a premeditated scheme, he offered him a diadem at the Lupercalia, in the presence of the Roman people. When Cæsar was assassinated in the senate-house, Antony was apprehensive that the same fate awaited him also, but his life was spared by the moderation of Brutus. When the ferment occasioned by Cæsar's death was abated, Antony came forth from his concealment, and so prevailed upon the murderers by his artifice and dissimulation, that they permitted him to speak an oration over his friend's dead body. This permission proved a dangerous weapon in the hands of the crafty Antony; for, by exposing the bloody robe of the dictator to the public view, and recounting his many acts of kindness and munificence towards Rome, he so inflamed the populace, that they endeavoured to set on fire the houses of the conspirators, and even assassinated some of them. Under the plausible pretext of fighting for the public weal, he attacked and defeated the forces of his personal enemies. He besieged Mutina, which had been allotted to Brutus; and for this the senate, upon the remonstrance of Cicero, judged him an enemy to the republic. He was at last conquered by the consuls Hirtius and Pansa, and by young Cæsar; but Antony by persuading Octavius that their mutual enmity weakened instead of advancing their interests, rendered him devoted to his cause, and they formed, with Lepidus, the celebrated triumvirate, which was established with such cruel proscriptions, that Antony did not even spare his own uncle, that he might strike off the head of his enemy Cicero. The triumvirate divided the Roman empire among themselves; Lepidus was set over all Italy; Augustus had the west; and Antony afterwards returned into the east, where he changed his dominions by different conquests. He had married Fulvia, whom he repudiated to marry Octavia the sister of Augustus, thinking by this connection to strengthen the triumvirate. He assisted Augustus at the battle of Philippi against the murderers of J. Cæsar, and buried the body of M. Brutus, his enemy, in a most magnificent manner. During his residence in the east, he became enamoured of the fair Cleopatra, queen of Ægypt, and repudiated Octavia to marry her. This divorce incensed Augustus, who, pretending to avenge his sister's wrongs, meditated the ruin of his rival. Antony, in the mean time, assembled all the forces of the east, and with Cleopatra marched against Octavius. The two rivals met at Actium, where a naval engagement soon began, but Cleopatra, by fleeing with sixty ships, ruined the cause of Antony. After the battle of Actium, he followed Cleopatra, into Ægypt, where he was soon informed of the defection of all his allies and adherents, and, sensible that all hopes of reconciliation were lost, he stabbed himself. Antony died in the 56th year of his age, B. C. 30, leaving seven children by his three wives. He has been deservedly blamed for his great effeminacy, and so excessive was his fondness for drinking, that he is said to have written a book in praise of the pleasures of intoxication. He was fond of imitating Hercules, from whom, according to the account of his flatterers, he was descended; and he is often represented as Hercules, with Cleopatra as Omphale, dressed in the arms of her submissive lover, and beating him with her sandals. In his public character, Antony was brave and courageous; but, with the intrepidity of Cæsar, he possessed all his voluptuous inclinations; and, indeed his fondness for low company, and his licentiousness, form the subject of the best part of Cicero's Philippics. It is said, that on the night of Cæsar's murder, Cassius supped with Antony, and being asked whether he had a dagger with him, answered, "Yes, if you, Antony, aspire to sovereign power." *Plutarch* has written an account of his life. *Virg. Æn.* 8. v. 685.—*Horat.* ep. 9.—*Juv.* 10. v. 122.—*C Nep in Attic.*—*Cic. in Philip.*—*Justin.* 41 & 42. [A bust of Mark Antony is in the Gallery at Florence.]

ANTO'NIUS JU'LIUS, son of Antony the triumvir, by Fulvia, was consul with Paulus Fabius Maximus. He was surnamed *Africanus*, and was put to death by order of Augustus, for his criminal conversation with Julia, the emperor's daughter. Some say that he killed himself. He had married Marcella, daughter of Octavia, after her forced divorce from Agrippa. It is supposed that he wrote an heroic poem on Diomede, in 12 books. *Horace* dedicated od. 4. l. 2. to him. *Tac. Ann.* 4. c. 44.—*Dio*, 51. & 55. c. 10.—*Ovid Pont.* 1. el. 1. v. 23.——The triumvir's brother, was besieged in Pelusium by Augustus, and obliged by famine, to surrender himself with 300 men. The conqueror spared his life. Some say that he was sacrifised at the shrine of Cæsar.——A noble, but unfortunate youth, grandson of the triumvir. His father Julius, was put to death by Augustus, and he himself was removed to Marseilles, on pretence of finishing his education. *Tac. Ann.* 4. c. 44.

ANTO'NIUS FE'LIX, a freedman of Claudius, appointed governor of Judæa. He married Drusilla, the daughter of Antony and Cleopatra. *Id. Hist.* 5. c. 9.

ANTO'NIUS FLAM'MA, a Roman, condemned for extortion, under Vespasian. *Id. Hist.* 4. c. 45.

ANTO'NIUS MU'SA, a physician of Augustus. *Plin.* 29. c. 1.—*Sax Onom.* 1. p. 186.

ANTO'NIUS MEREN'DA, a decemvir at Rome. A.U.C. 304. *Liv.* 3. c. 35.

ANTO'NIUS Q. MEREN'DA, a military tribune, A.U.C. 332. *Liv.* 4. c. 42.

ANTO'NIUS PRI'MUS, was expelled from the senate under Nero, but was afterwards restored, and became notorious in the civil wars under Vespasian.

AN'TOR, one of the Centaurs. *Val. Flacc.* 1. v. 146.

ANTOR'IDES, a painter, pupil of Aristippus. *Plin.* 35. c. 10.

AN'TRO CORA'CIUS. *Vid.* Coracius.

ANTRO'NIA, a city of Messenia. It is called Antron by *Strabo*, and by *Stephanus*, who says that it is a city of Thessaly.

AN'TRUM, now St. Hermeland, an island at the mouth of the Ligeris in Gallia Celtica.

AN'TRUM SIBYL'LÆ, a place of Campania, now Grotta della Sibilla, the residence of the Cumæan Sibyl.

ANTYL'LA. *Vid.* Anthylla.

ANTYR'IUS, a general of Alexander the Great.

ANUBIN'GARA, a city of Taprobane. *Ptol.*

ANU'BIS, an Ægyptian deity, represented under the form of a man with the head of a dog, because when Osiris went on his expedition against India, Anubis accompanied him, and clothed himself in a sheep's skin. He is supposed by some authors to be the same as Mercury, because he is sometimes represented with a *caduceus*. Some make him brother of Osiris, others, his son by Nepthys, the wife of Typhon; and they say, that when Isis, the wife of Osiris heard of his birth, she sought him, and by means of her dogs, found him, and educated him with such tenderness that he became her guardian and faithful companion. His worship was also introduced into Greece and Italy; but when Mundus had corrupted the priests of Anubis at Rome, to offer violence to Paulina, the wife of Saturninus, the worship of the god was abolished, and the temple levelled with the ground. *Diod.* 1.—*Lucan.* 8. v. 331.—*Ovid. Met.* 9. v. 689.—*Plut. de Isid. & Osirid.*—*Herodot.* 4.—*Virg. Æn.* 8. v. 698.—*Propert.* 3. el. 9. v. 41.

ANUCH'THA, a city of Susiana. *Ptol.*

ANULI'NUS, a consul at the time when Caracalla massacred the Alexandrians.

ANU'LUS, a river of Mauritania.

ANUROGRAM'MI, a people of Taprobane. *Ptol.*

ANX'A, a town of Italy, formerly Gallipolis, and now Gallipoli. *Plin.* 3. c. 11.

ANXANTI'NI, a people of the Peligni. *Strab.*

ANXA'NUM, a town of the Ferentani, in Italy, now Lanciano or Lanzano. *Plin.* 3. c. 12.

ANX'IUS, a small river of Armenia, falling into the Euphrates.

ANX'UR, now Tarracina, a city of the Volsci, situate on the coast between Circeii and Amyclæ, taken by Romans, A.U.C. 348. It was sacred to Jupiter, who was called Jupiter Anxyrus, and represented there in his statues in the form of a beardless boy. *Liv.* 4. c. 59.—*Horat.* 1. sat. 5. v. 26.—*Lucan.* 3. v. 84. *Virg. Æn* .7. v. 799.——One of the auxiliaries of Perses against Æetes. *Val. Flacc.* 6. v. 68.

AN'YSIS, a king of Ægypt who was blind; he succeeded Asychis. *Herod.* 2. c. 141.——A city of Ægypt. *Id. Ibid.*

AN'YSUS, the father of Tetramnestus. *Id.* 7. c. 98.

AN'YTE, a poetess of Tegea. Sixteen of her epigrams are still extant, and may be found in Brunck's Analecta; they were also published by Wolf, Hamburgh, 1734, in Poetriarium octo Fragmentis et Elogiis. Reiske, in his Notit. poet. Anthol. p. 192. mentions another of this name. *Fabr. B. Gr.* 2. p. 106.—*Sax. Onom.* 1. p. 94.

AN'YTUS, an Athenian rhetorician, who, with Miletus and Lycon, accused Socrates of impiety, and was the cause of his condemnation. These false accusers were afterwards put to death by the Athenians. *Diog.*—*Ælian V. H.* 2. c 13.—*Horat.* 2. sat. 4. v. 3—*Plut. in Alcib.*——One of the Titans, whose statue was still seen in Arcadia in the age of *Pausanias*,8. c. 37.

ANZA'BE, a river of Asia, near the Tigris. *Marcel.* 18.

ANZE'TA, a city of Armenia Major. *Ptol.* The region is called Anætia by *Pliny*. 5. c. 24.

AOL'LIUS, afterwards called Abillius, a son of Romulus by Hersilia.

A'ON, a son of Neptune, who came to Eubœa and Bœotia, from Apulia. The inhabitants were called Aones, and the country Aonia, from him.

A'ONES, the inhabitants of Aonia, called afterwards Bœotia. The Muses have been called Aonides, because Aonia was more particularly frequented by them. *Paus.* 9. c. 5.—*Ovid. Met.* 3, 7, 10, 13. *Trist.* el. 5. v. 10. *Fast.* 3. v. 456, &c.—*Virg G.* 3. v. 11. *Ecl.* 6. v. 64.

AO'NIA, one of the ancient names of Bœotia. *Vid.* Aones. *Catull. Epith. Jul. & Mall.* 28.—*Propert.* 1. el. 2. v. 28. &c.—*Ovid Fast.* 1. v. 490. *Trist.* 4. el. 10. v. 39. *Met.* 1. v. 313, &c.

A'ORIS, a famous hunter, son of Aras, king of Corinth, who was so fond of his sister Arathyræa, that he called part of the country by her name. *Paus.* 2. c. 12.——The wife of Neleus, called more commonly Chloris. *Id.* 9. c. 36.

AOR'NUS or AOR'NIS, (ἄορνος, *avibus carens*) a rock taken by Alexander, supposed to be situated near the Ganges. It was so high, that birds were said to be unable to reach the top. Hercules had besieged it, but was never able to take it. *Dion. Per.* v. 1149. *Curt.* 8. c. 11.—*Arrian.* 4.—*Strab.* 15.—*Plut. in Alex.*

AOR'NUS or AVER'NUS, a lake near Baiæ and Puteoli. The exhalations which proceeded from it were fatal to birds. *Virg Æn.* 6. v. 242.

AOR'NUS, a lake near Tartessus.——A place of Epirus, where there was an oracle. *Paus.* 9. c. 80.

AOR'SI, a people of Salmatia; the country is now Severia.—*Strab.*—*Ptol.*

AO'RUS, a city of Crete. *Steph.*

AO'TI, a people of Thrace, near the Getæ, on the Ister. *Plin.* 4. c. 11.

APACH'NAS or PACH'NAN, the third of the shepherd kings of Ægypt; he reigned 36 years. *Joh. Marsham, Can. Chron.*

APAD'NA, a city of Mesopotamia. *Lib. Not.*

APAD'NAS, a place of Isauria. *Procop.* 5.

APÆ'I, a people of Upper Æthiopia. *Ptol.*

APÆ'SUS or PÆ'SUS, a city of Troas. *Steph.*

APA'ITÆ, a people of Asia Minor. They were formerly called Cercitæ. *Strab.*

APAL'Æ'I, a people of Scythia. *Solin.* c. 49.

APA'MA, a daughter of Artaxerxes, who married Pharnabazus, the satrap of Ionia.——A daughter of Antiochus. *Paus.* 1. 8. Also Ap'ama.

APA'ME, the mother of Nicomedes, by Prusias, king of Bithynia.——The mother of Antiochus Soter, by Seleucus Nicanor. Soter founded a city which he called by his mother's name.

APAME'A, a city of Phrygia, on the Marsyas, where it falls into the Mæander. Its ancient name was Celænæ, because it was enlarged and embellished from the ruins of that city. It was afterwards called Cibotus, which name it retained with that of Apamea. It is now Amphion Kar-Hissar. *Liv.* 38. c. 13. *Strab.* 12.—*Plin.* 5. c. 29.—*Çic. Att.* 5. ep. 16.——A city of Bithynia, situate on the Propontis, called Myrlea, by way of distinction, and now Moudania.——A city of Media.——A city of Mesopotamia, on the Euphrates, opposite Zeugma.——A city on the banks of the Tigris.——A city of Syria, on the Orontes, built by Seleucus Nicanor. *Vid.* Apame.

APAME'NE, a province of Syria, on the borders of the Orontes. Its capital was Apamea. *Ptol.*

APANES'TÆ, a town of Magna Græcia. *Plin.* 3. c. 11. The people were called Apanestini.

APANCHOM'ENE, an epithet of Diana among the Arcadians. *Clemens. in Protrept.*

APAP'PUS MAX'IMUS, the 20th of the Theban kings of Ægypt. *Joh. Marsham. Can. Chron.*

APAR'NI, a nation of shepherds near the Caspian Sea *Strab.* 11

APATU'RIA, a festival at Athens, which received its name from ἀπάτη, *deceit*, because it was instituted in memory of a stratagem, by which Xanthius, king of Bœotia, was killed by Melanthus, king of Athens. A war having arisen between the two nations about the boundaries of their territories, Xanthius proposed to the Athenian king to decide the matter by single combat. Thymœtes, who was then on the throne, refused the challenge, and his successor, Melanthus, accepted it. When they began the engagement, Melanthus exclaimed, that his antagonist had some person behind him to support him: upon which Xanthius looked behind, and was killed by Melanthus. From this success Jupiter was called ἀπατήνωρ, *deceiver*, and Bacchus, who was supposed to be behind Xanthius, was called Μελαναιγὶς, clothed in the skin of a *black goat*. Some derive the word from ἀπατορία, *i. e.* ὁμοπατορία, because on the day of the festival, the children accompanied their fathers to be registered among the citizens. The festival lasted three days. The first day was called δορπία, because *suppers*, δόρπος, were prepared for each separate tribe. The festival lasted three days. The second day was called ἀνάῤῥυσις ἀπὸ τοῦ ἄνω ἐρύειν, because sacrifices were offered to Jupiter and Minerva, and the head of the victims was generally turned up towards the heavens. The third was called Κουρεῶτις, from κοῦρος, a *youth*, or κουρὰ, *shaving*, because the young men had their hair cut off before they were registered, when their parents swore that they were freeborn Athenians. They generally sacrificed two ewes and a she-goat to Diana. This festival was adopted by the Greeks of Ionia, except the inhabitants of Ephesus and Colophon. *Athen.* l. 4. *Schol. Aristoph. Acharn.* 146.—*Xenoph. Hist. Gr.* lib. 1.—*Herod. Vit. Homer.*—*Polyæn.*—*Strab.* l. 19.——A surname of Minerva.——A surname of Venus.

APEAU'ROS, a mountain in Peloponnesus. *Polyb.* 4.

APEL'LAS, a geographer of Cyrene. He is probably the person called Apollas by *Athenæus*. *Voss. de Hist. Gr.* 3. &c.——A Chian, mentioned by *Cicero, ad Att.* 12. ep. 19.

APEL'LES, a son of Pithius, a celebrated painter, of Cos, or, as others say, of Ephesus, or of Colophon. He lived in the age of Alexander the Great, who forbade any other painter to draw his picture. He never spent a day without employing his pencil, whence the proverb of *Nulla dies sine lineâ*. His most perfect picture was that of Venus Anadyomene. He also made a painting of Alexander holding thunder in his hand, so much like life, that Pliny, who saw it, said that the hand of the king seemed to come out of the picture. This picture was placed in Diana's temple at Ephesus. With another picture of Alexander, that monarch was not much pleased, when a horse passing by at the moment, neighed at the horse represented in the piece; upon which Apelles remarked, that the horse was a much better judge of painting than the king. Alexander ordered him to draw the picture of Campaspe, one of his mistresses, when the painter became enamoured of her, and the king permitted him to marry her. He wrote three volumes upon painting, which were still extant in the age of Pliny. It is said that he was accused in Ægypt of conspiring against the life of Ptolemy, and that he would have been put to death, had not the real conspirator discovered himself, and saved the painter. Apelles never put his name to more than three pictures; a sleeping Venus, a Venus Anadyomene, and an Alexander. It is said that he used only four colours, white, yellow, red, and black, but with such skill and judgment, that none of the ancients ever surpassed him in delicacy of colouring, or sublimity of expression. The proverb of *Ne sutor ultra crepidam* is applied to him by some. *Plin.* 35. c. 10.—*Horat.* 2. ep. 1. v. 238.—*Cic. ad Fam* 1. ep. 9. *Off.* 3. c. 2.—*Ovid. de A. A.* 3. v. 401.—*Quintil.* 12. c. 10.—*Val. Max.* 8. c. 11.——A heretic of the second century, whose followers were called from him, Apellites, or Apellicians. *Euseb. Hist.* 5. c. 13.—*Epiph. Hær.* 44. &c.——A tragic poet of Ascalon, much esteemed by Caligula, according to *Dio. Cassius*, 59. c. 5.—*Fabr. B. Gr.* 2. p. 285.—*Suet. Calig.* 33.——A Macedonian general, &c.

APELLICON, a Peripatetic philosopher of Teus, whose fondness for books was so great, that he was accused of stealing them, when he could not obtain them with money. He greatly disfigured the works of Aristotle and Theophrastus, by his frequent interpolations. The extensive library which he had collected at Athens, was carried to Rome by Sylla, and among the valuable books was found the original manuscript of Aristotle. Apellicon died about 86 B. C. *Strab.* 13.

APENNI'NUS, a ridge of high mountains which runs through the middle of Italy, from Liguria to Ariminum and Ancona, and joins the Alps. Some have supposed that it ran across Sicily by Rhegium, before Italy was separated from Sicily. *Lucan.* 2. v. 306.—*Ovid. Met.* 2. v. 226.—*Ital.* 4. v. 743.—*Strab.* 2.—*Mela*, 2. c. 6.—*Plin.* 3. c. 5.

A'PER MAR'CUS, a Latin orator of Gaul, who distinguished himself as a politican as well as a writer. The dialogue of the orators, generally printed with works of Tacitus and Quintilian, is attributed to his pen. He died A. D. 85.

A'PER AR'RIUS, the murderer of the emperor Numerianus. *Vid.* Numerianus.

AP'ERA, a town of Galatia. *Antonin.*

APERAN'TIA, a city of Thessaly. Also Aperanti'a.

APERAN'TII, a people of Epirus, near the sources of the Achelous.

APERE'THES, a city of Arcadia. *Paus.* 8.

APERO'PIA, a small island on the coast of Argolis. *Paus.* 2. c. 34.

APER'RÆ, a city of Lycia. *Ptol.* It is called Apyre by *Pliny*, 5. c. 27., and is now Phinica.

AP'ESUS, AP'ESAS, or APESAN'TUS, a mountain of Peloponnesus, near Lerna. Jupiter received the epithet of Apesantius from being worshipped there. *Stat. Theb.* 3. v. 461.—*Plin.* 4. c. 5.

APET'UA, a city of Hispania Bætica, not far from Corduba. *Strab.*

APH'ACA, a town of Palestine, where Venus was worshipped, and where she had a temple and an oracle. *Selden, de Diis Syr.* 2. c. 3.—*Zosim* 1. c. 58. ——A city of Libya. *Steph.*

APHÆ'A, a name of Diana, who had a temple in Ægina. *Paus.* 2. c. 30.—*Virg. Cir.* 303.

APHÆR'IAS, the accuser of Lyncestes to Alexander. *Curt.* 7. c. 1.

APHAN'NE, an obscure region of Sicily; whence the proverb, *Ad Aphannas*, to signify obscurity. *Steph.*

A'PHAR, the capital city of Arabia, near the Red Sea. *Arrian in Peripl.*

APHARE'TUS, a person who carried off Marpessa, daughter of Œnomaus. *Plut in Parall.*

APH'AREUS, a king of Messenia, son of Perieres and Gorgophone, married Arene, daughter of Œbalus, by whom he had three sons, Idas, Pisus, and Lynceus. He reigned for some time conjointly with his brother Leucippus, but soon after seized upon the undivided sovereignty. He granted the maritime parts of his kingdom to Neleus, who settled there after he had been driven from Iolcus. *Apollod.* 1. c- 23. &c.—*Ovid. Met* 12. v. 341.—*Paus.* 3. c. 1.——An Athenian, son of Hippias, adopted by the orator Isocrates, wrote 37 tragedies, besides some orations. *Plut. in vit. Isocr.*—*Fabr. B. Gr.* 2. p. 285.——An Athenian son of Caletor, killed by Æneas during the Trojan war. *Homer Il.* 9. v. 83. &c.

A'PHAS, now Inacho, a small river of Greece, which falls into the bay of Ambracia. *Plin.* 4. c. 1.

APHEDAN'TES, a people of the Molossi. *Steph.*

APHE'DAS, a king of Athens, or, according to *Stephanus*, of the Molossi.

APHEL'LAS, a king of Cyrene, who endeavoured, with the aid of Agathocles, to reduce all Africa under his power. *Justin.* 22. c. 7.

APHE'SAS, a mountain in Peloponnesus, whence, as the poets have imagined, Perseus attempted to fly to heaven. *Stat. Theb.* 3. v. 461. *Vid.* Apesus.

APHE'TÆ, now Fetio, a city of Magnesia, on the Pagasæus, Sinus, where the ship Argo was launched. *Apollod.*

APHETE'RII, a surname of Castor and Pollux. *Paus. in Lacon.*

APHETE'RION, a harbour on the Ganges. *Ptol.*

APHE'TOR, a surname of Apollo, from his giving oracles. *Cæl. Rhod.* 8. c. 16.—*Lil. Gyrald. Syntag.* 7.—*Hesych.*

APHE'US or APHNE'US, a surname of Mars on mount Ctesius, in Arcadia. *Paus. in Arcad.* But see *Cæl. Rhod.* 20. c. 5.

APHI'DAS, a son of Arcas, inherited Tegea and the neighbouring country, which he divided with his brothers Azan and Elatus. His son Aleus succeeded him on the throne. *Paus.* 8. c. 4.——The fourteenth and last king of Athens, of the race of Erechtheus. *Paus.* 1. 7.——A famous sleeper. *Ovid. Met.* 12. v. 317.

APHID'NÆ, a part of the tribe Leontis, in Attica, which received its name from Aphidnus, one of the companions of Theseus. *Herodot.*——A city of Laconia. *Steph.*

APHID'NUS, a friend of Æneas, killed by Turnus. *Virg. Æn.* 9. v. 702.

APHNE'UM, a city of Phrygia and Lydia. *Steph.*

APHNE'US, *Vid.* Apheus.

APHŒBETUS, one of the conspirators against Alexander. *Curt.* 6. c. 7.

APHOPHIS, the fourth shepherd king of Ægypt, about the time of Moses. *Job. Marsham. Can. Chron.*

APHORMIUM, a lake of Thespia. *Steph.*

APHRICES, an Indian prince, who defended the rock Aornus with 20,000 foot and 15 elephants. He was killed by his troops, and his head sent to Alexander. *Diod. Sic.* 17.—*Curtius,* 8. c. 6. calls him Eryces.

APHRODISIA, an island in the Persian Gulph, where Venus was worshipped.——Festivals in honor of Venus, celebrated in different parts of Greece, but chiefly in Cyprus. They were first instituted by Cinyras, from whose family the priests of the goddess were always chosen. All the initiated offered a piece of money to Venus, and received as a mark of the favors of the goddess, a measure of salt and a φαλλός: the salt, because Venus arose from the sea; the φαλλός, because she was the goddess of wantonness. They were celebrated principally at Corinth, and in every part of Greece they were very much frequented. *Strab.* 14.—*Athen.* 13.—*Plaut. in Poen.* 1.—*Meurs. Gr. Fer.*

APHRODISIAS, a town of Caria, at the south of the Mæander, where Venus was worshipped. It is now Abodisia. *Tac. Ann.* 3. c. 62—*Plin.* 5. c. 29.——A city in Cilicia, also sacred to Venus. *Plin.* 5. c. 27.—*Liv.* 33. c. 20.

APHRODISIUM, a maritime city of Africa, now Mahometta.——A city and colony of Africa, near Hippo Regius, now Mabra.——A town of Cyprus, now Achaton.——A promontory and town of Hispania Citerior, now Capo de Cruz. *Plin.* 3. c. 3.—*Strab.*

APHRODITE, the Grecian name of Venus, from ἀφρός, *froth,* because she is said to have sprung from the froth of the ocean. *Hesiod. Theog.* 195.—*Auson. Ecl.* 9. v. 8.—*Plin.* 36. c. 5.

APHRODITES, a city of Æthiopia.——A city of Thrace. *Steph.*

APHRODITIA, a small region of Laconia. *Steph. ex Thucyd.*

APHTHONIUS, a sophist of the second century, who wrote a work on rhetoric, called προγυμνάσματα. It was published with Hermogenes and Longinus, by Crispinus, 1557; also in Greek and Latin, by Commelin, 1597. *Volaterran. Anthrop.* 1. 13.

APHYTE or APHYTIS, a city of Thrace, near Pallene, where Jupiter Ammon was worshipped. It was besieged by Lysander, but being warned by the god, in a dream, to raise the siege, he obeyed, and introduced the worship of the deity among his countrymen. *Herodot.* 7. c. 123.—*Paus.* 3. c. 18.

APIA, an ancient name of Peloponnesus, which it received from king Apis. *Homer. Il.* 1. v. 270.——A name of the earth under which she was worshipped by the Scythians. *Herodot.* 4. c. 59.

APIANUS or APION, was born at Oasis in Ægypt, whence he went to Alexandria, of which he was deemed a citizen. He succeeded Theus in the professorship of rhetoric in the reign of Tiberius; and wrote, among other works, a book against the Jews, which Josephus refuted. He was at the head of an embassy which the people of Alexandria sent to Caligula, to complain of the conduct of the Jews. Apion rendered himself ridiculous by his great vanity. He not only abused the learning which he possessed, in trifling and unprofitable researches, but he often made his page the vehicle of abusive language and intemperate satire; and he was not ashamed to boast that he bestowed immortality on those to whom he did the honor to dedicate his labors. *A Gell.* 1 & 5.—*Senec.* ep. 88.—*Plin. præf. Hist.*—*Bayle's Dict.*

APIATES, a people of Aquitania, conquered by P. Crassus. *Diod. Sic.* 39.

APICATA, married Sejanus, by whom she had three children. She was repudiated, that he might marry Livia. She destroyed herself after the death of Sejanus. *Tac. Ann.* 4. c. 3.

APICIUS. There were three persons of this name, all noted for their voracious appetite. The first lived about the age of Sylla; the second in the reign of Augustus and Tiberius; and the third, who had a particular method of preserving oysters, under Trajan. The second, who was the most famous wrote a book on the pleasures of, and incitements to, eating. He hanged himself after he had spent the greatest part of his estate, (*millies sestertium* above 807,290*l.*,) lest, after he had satisfied his creditors, nothing should remain to supply his extravagance; although, when all demands were paid, it was found that he left above 80,000*l.* (*centies sestertium.*) The best editions of Apicius Cælius *de arte coquinariâ,* are that of Amst. 12mo. 1709, and that of Bernhold, 1787, 8vo. *Tac. Ann.* 4. c. 1.—*Dio.* 57. p. 616.—*Senec. ad Helviam,* 10.—*Suidas in* Οςεια.—*Juv.* 11. v. 3.—*Mart.* 2. epigr. 69, &c.—*Sax. Onom.* 1. p. 360.—*Harles. Not. Lit. Rom.* 1. p. 538.

APIDANUS, now Epideno, one of the chief rivers of Thessaly, at the south of the Peneus, into which it flows a little above Larissa. *Lucan.* 6. v. 372.

APIDIUS MERULA, a senator, whose name was erased from the *Album senatorium. Tac. Ann.* 4. c. 42.

APPIENNATES, a people of Umbria. *Plin.* 3. c 14.

APILOCARIUM, a city of Lusitania. *Phleg. Trall.*

APINA or APINÆ, a small town of Apulia, destroyed, with Trica in its neighbourhood, by Diomedes; whence came the proverb of *Apina et Trica,* to express trifling things. *Mart.* 1. epigr. 114. v. 2. &c.—*Plin.* 3. c. 11.

APIOLA or APIOLÆ, an inconsiderable town of Italy, taken by Tarquinius Superbus. The Roman Capitol was begun with the spoils taken from it. *Plin.* 3. c. 5.

APION, a surname of Ptolemy, one of the descendants of Ptolemy Lagus.—*Vid.* Apianus.

APIS, one of the ancient kings of Peloponnesus, son of Phoroneus and Laodice. Some say that Apollo was his father, and that he was king of Argos; while others call him king of Sicyon, and fix the time of his reign about 200 years earlier. He was a native of Naupactum, and descended from Inachus, and received divine honors from his subjects after death, as he had been a beneficent and humane ruler. The country where he reigned was called Apia, and afterwards Peloponnesus. Some authors, amongst whom are *Varro* and *St. Augustine,* have imagined that Apis went to Ægypt with a colony of Greeks, and that he civilized the inhabitants, and polished their manners; for which they made him a god after death, under the name of Serapis. This tradition, according to some of the moderns, is without foundation. *Æschyl. in Suppl.*—*August, de Civ. Dei,* 18. c. 5.—*Paus.* 2. c. 5.—*Apollod.* 2. c. 1.—*Marsham. in Can. Chron.*——A son of Jason, killed by the horses of Ætolus. *Paus.* 5. c. 1.

APIS, a town of Ægypt, on the lake Mareotis.

APIS, a god of the Ægyptians, worshipped at Memphis, under the form of an ox. Some authors say that Isis and Osiris were the deities worshipped under this name, because, during their reign, they taught the Ægyptians agriculture. The Ægyptians believed that the soul of Osiris had really taken up its abode in the ox, where it wished to dwell, because that animal had been of the most essential service in agriculture, which Osiris had introduced into Ægypt. The ox that was regarded as the depositary of the soul of the god was always distinguished by particular marks; his body was black; he had a square white spot upon the forehead; the figure of an eagle upon the back; a knot under the tongue, like a beetle; the hairs of his tail were double; and his right side was marked with a whitish spot resembling the crescent of the moon. Without these an ox could not be selected as the representative of the god Apis; it is throught that the priests gave these distinguishing characteristics to the animal, on which their credit, and even the prosperity of their order, depended. The festival of Apis lasted seven days; the sacred ox was led in solemn procession by the priests, and every one was anxious to receive him into his house; and it was believed that the children who smelt his breath received the knowledge of futurity. The animal was conducted to the banks of the Nile with much ceremony; and if he had lived to the time which their sacred books allowed, they drowned him in the river, and embalmed his body, and buried it in solemn state in the city of Memphis. After his death, which sometimes was natural, the greatest cries and lamentations were heard in Ægypt, as if Osiris was just dead; and the priests shaved their heads, a sign of the deepest mourning. This general sorrow continued till another ox appeared, with the proper characteristics, and he was then followed with the greatest acclamations, as if Osiris were returned to life. This ox, which was found to represent Apis, was left 40 days in the city of the Nile before he was removed to Memphis, during which time none but women were permitted to appear before him, and this they performed, according to their superstitious notions, in a wanton and indecent manner. An ox was also worshipped at Heliopolis, under the name of Mnevis; and it is supposed that the Apis of Memphis was sacred to Osiris, and Mnevis to Isis. When Cambyses invaded Ægypt, the people were celebrating the festival of Apis, in the midst of the public calamity, with every mark of joy and triumph. When he saw that an ox was the object of their veneration, and the cause of such rejoicing, he wounded it in the thigh, and ordering the priests to be chastised, commanded his soldiers to slaughter such as were found celebrating such riotous festivals. The god Apis had generally two stables, or rather temples, for his habitation. If he ate from the hand it was a favourable omen; but if he refused the food that was offered him it was interpreted as unlucky. From this circumstance Germanicus, when he visited Ægypt, drew the omens of his approaching death. When his oracle was consulted, incense was burnt on an altar, and a piece of money placed upon it; after which, the people that wished to know futurity applied their ear to the mouth of the god, and immediately retired, stopping their ears till they had departed from the temple. The first sounds that were heard were regarded as the answer of the oracle to their questions. *Paus.* 7. c. 22.—*Herodot.* 2 & 3.—*Plin.* 8. c. 38. &c.—*Strab.* 7.—*Plut. in Isid. & Osir.*—*Apollod.* 1. c. 7. &c.—*Mela*, 1. c. 10.—*Plin.* 8. c. 39. &c.—*Ælian. V. H.* 4 & 6.—*Diod.* 1.

APISA'ON, son of Hippasus, was killed by Lycomedes, during the Trojan war. *Homer. Il.* 17. v. 348. ——Another warrior on the same side, killed by Eurypylus. *Id.* 11. v. 577.

APITA'MI, a people of Arabia. *Plin.* 6. c. 28.

APIT'IUS GAL'BA, a celebrated buffoon in the time of Tiberius. *Juv.* 5. v. 4.

APOBŒO'TI, a people of Ætolia. *Steph.*

APOC'OPI, mountains of India, within the Ganges. *Ptol.*

APOLLINA'RES LUDI, games celebrated at Rome in honour of Apollo, at which the people generally sat crowned with laurel. They were usually celebrated at the option of the prætor, till the year U.C. 545, when a law was passed to settle the celebration yearly on the same day, about the nones of July. *Liv.* 25. c. 12.—*Macrob. Sat.* 1. c. 17.

APOLLINA'RIS C. SULPITIUS, a grammarian of Carthage, in the second century, who is supposed to have been the author of the verses prefixed, as arguments, to Terence's plays. He was succeeded in his school by his pupil Pertinax, who afterwards became emperor of Rome. He had among his pupils Aulus Gellius, who speaks of his learning in the highest terms. *Jul. Capitol. in Pertin.*—*Aul. Gell.* 18. c. 4.

APOLLINA'RIS, a writer better known by the name of Sidonius. *Vid.* Sidonius.——An Alexandrian, who taught grammar at Laodicea, and was afterwards a presbyter of the Syrian Church.——A bishop of Loadicea, was son of the former, and was a grammarian, poet, rhetorician, and philosopher of great celebrity. He was the founder of the heretical sect of the Apollinaristæ. Fabricius mentions several other persons of this name, who are but little known. *Fabr. B. Gr.* 1. 5. c. 12. & 1. 2. c. 19.—*Sax. Onom.* 1. p. 417 & 424.

APOLLIN'IDES, a Greek engaged in the wars of Darius and Alexander. *Curt.* 4. c. 5.

APOL'LINIS ARX, a place at the entrance of the Sibyl's cave. *Virg. Æn.* 6.

APOL'LINIS PROMONTO'RIUM, a promontory of Africa, on the coast of the Mediterranean, and in the northern provinces of Mauritania. *Liv.* 30. c. 24.

APOL'LINIS TEMPLUM, a place in Thrace.——A place in Lycia. *Ælian. V. H.* 6. c. 9.

APOL'LO, a son of Jupiter and Latona, called also Phœbus. According to *Cicero*, 3. *de Nat. Deor.*, there were four persons of this name. The first was son of Vulcan, and the tutelary god of the Athenians. The second was son of Corybas, and was born in Crete, for the dominion of which he disputed even with Jupiter himself. The third was son of Jupiter and Latona, and came from the nations of the Hyperboreans to Delphi. The fourth was born in Arcadia, and called Nomion, because he gave laws to the inhabitants. To the son of Jupiter and Latona all the actions of the others seem to have been exclusively attributed. The Apollo, son of Vulcan, was the same as the Orus of the Ægyptians, and was the most ancient, from whom the actions of the others have been copied. The three other seem to be of Grecian origin. The tradition, that the son of Latona was born in the floating island of Delus, is derived from the Ægyptian mythology, which asserts that the son of Vulcan, which is supposed to be Orus, was saved by his mother Isis from the persecution of Typhon, and entrusted to the care of Latona, who concealed him in the island of Chemnis. Apollo was the god of all the fine arts, of medicine, music, poetry, and eloquence; of all which he was deemed the inventor. He had received from Jupiter the power of knowing futurity, and he was the only one of the gods whose oracles were in general repute over the world. His great dexterity in the management of the bow is celebrated; and in every part of the world he received homage as the president of the Muses, the oracles of poets and musicians, and the patron of the liberal arts and sciences. His amours with Leucothoe, Daphne, Issa, Bolina, Coronis, Clymene, Cyrene, Chione, Acacallis, Calliope, &c., are well known, as are also the various shapes he assumed to gratify his passion. He became father of Hyreus, Hyperenor, and Eleuthera, by Æthusa, daughter of Neptune; by Clymene, he had Phaethon; by Thya or Melene, Delphus; by Corycia, Lycoreus; and Phylacis, Philander, and Naxus, by Acacallis. The nymph Cyrene bore him Aristæus and Idmon; Coronis, Æsculapius; Chione, the musician, Philamnon; and by him Calliope, according to some, became mother of Orpheus; and Urania, of Linus. He was also father of Argeus, by Eubœa, daughter of Macareus; of Ilius, by Uræa, daughter of Neptune; and of Euripides, by Cleobula. Among his favourites he particularly distinguished young Hyacinthus, whom he accidentally killed with a quoit; as also Cyparissus, whom he changed into a cypress-tree. When his son Æsculapius had been destroyed by the thunder of Jupiter, for raising the dead to life, Apollo, in his resentment, killed the Cyclopes, who had fabricated the thunderbolts. Jupiter, incensed at this act of violence, banished Apollo from heaven, and deprived him of his dignity. The exiled deity retired to the court of Admetus, king of Thessaly, and became one of his shepherds, in which employment he remained nine years. From this circumstance Apollo was called the god of shepherds. During his residence in Thessaly, he rewarded the kindness of Admetus, by giving him a chariot, drawn by a lion and a bull, with which he was able to obtain in marriage Alceste, the daughter of Pelias. *Vid.* Admetus. He assisted Neptune in building the walls of Troy; but when Laomedon refused him the promised reward, he visited the country with a dreadful pestilence. He also assisted Alcathous, son of Pelops, in erecting the fortress of Megara in Attica; and the stone on which the god had placed his lyre, when employed in the work, was still shown in the age of Pausanias, and, when touched, sent forth a melodious sound. As soon as he was born, Apollo destroyed with his arrows the serpent Python, which Juno had sent to persecute Latona; hence he was called Pythius: and he afterwards vindicated the honour of his mother, by putting to death the children of Niobe. *Vid.* Niobe. He was not the inventor of the lyre, as some have imagined, but Mercury gave it to him, and received in return the famous *caduceus* with which Apollo was wont to drive the flocks of Admetus. His contest with Pan and Marsyas, and the punishment inflicted upon Midas, are well known. He received the surnames of Phœbus, Delius, Cynthius, Pæan, Delphicus, Nomius, Lycius, Clarius, Ismenius, Vulturis, Smintheus, &c. for reasons which are explained under those words. Apollo is generally represented with long hair, as a tall beardless young man, with a handsome shape, holding in his hand a bow, and sometimes a lyre; his head is generally surrounded with beams of light. His worship and power were universally acknowledged: temples and statues were raised to his honour in every country, particularly in Ægypt, Greece, and Italy. His statue, upon mount Actium, was seen from a great distance at sea; and, as a remarkable beacon to mariners to avoid the dangerous coast, was particularly famous. Augustus, before the battle of Actium, addressed himself to it for victory. The griffin, the cock, the grasshopper, the wolf, the crow, the swan, the hawk, the olive, the laurel, the palm-tree, &c. were sacred to Apollo; and, in his sacrifices, wolves and hawks were offered, as they were the natural enemies of the flocks over which he presided. Bullocks and lambs were also immolated on his altars. As he presided over poetry, he was often seen on mount Parnassus with the nine Muses. His most famous oracles were at Delphi, Delus, Clarus, Tenedus, Cyrrha, and Patara. His most splendid temple was at Delphi, where every nation and individual made valuable presents when they consulted the oracle. Augustus, after the battle of Actium, erected a temple in honour of the god on mount Palatine, which he enriched with a valuable library. The famous Colossus of Rhodes, which was one of the seven wonders of the world, was also a monument raised to celebrate the glory of the god. Apollo has been taken for the Sun: and though many passages in ancient writers might prove that Apollo, the Sun, Phœbus, and Hyperion, were sometimes regarded as different characters and deities; yet it is evident that the ancients considered the son of Latona as the god who guided the chariot of the Sun, and that he received, as that luminary, the homage of the various nations of the earth, though under different appellations, and in various characters. *Ovid. Met.* 1. fab. 9 & 10, &c.—*Schol. Apollon.* 1, 2, 3. *Argon.*—*Claudian. præf. in Ruf.*—*Orpheus. in Argon.* 991.—*Nonnus in Dionys.* 10.—*Schol. in Euripid.*—*Servius in* 7 *Æn.*—*Probus in* 3 *Georg.*—*Zenobius Cent.* 1. *Prov.* 18.—*Schol. Aristoph. in Nub.*—*Tzetzes in Chil. Hist.* 53.—*Athen.* 4. c. 4.—*Schol. Pind. in Olym. & Schol. in Arat.*—*Paus.* 2. c. 7. &c.—*Hygin.* fab. 9, 14, &c.—*Stat.* 1. *Theb.* 560. *Tibull.* 2. 1. 3.—*Plut. de Amor.*—*Homer. Il. & Hym. in Apol.*—*Virg. Æn.* 2, 3, &c. *G.* 4. v. 323.—*Horat.* 1. od. 10.—*Lucian. Dial. Mer. & Vulc.*—*Propert.* 2. el. 28.—*Callimach. in Apol.*—*Apollod.* 1. c. 3, 4 & 9, &c. Apollo had also a temple upon mount Leucas, which appeared at a great distance at sea; and served as a guard to mariners, and warned them to avoid the dangerous rocks that were along the coast. *Virg. Æn.* 3. v. 275. [The statues of Apollo are innumerable. By far the most celebrated is that of the Belvidere in the Vatican. The Apollino at Florence, and the Saurocthonon in the Vatican, are likewise very fine works of art. In the Gallery of the Giustiniani Palace, at Rome, there is a remarkably fine head of this deity.]

APOLLOCRATES, a friend of Dion at Syracuse, supposed by some to be the same as Dionysius. *Strab.* 6.

APOLLODO'RUS, a famous grammarian and mythologist of Athens, son of Asclepiades, and disciple of Panætius, the Rhodian philosopher, and of Aristarchus, the grammarian. He flourished about 115 B.C., and wrote a history extending from the destruction of Troy to his own age, beside other works. Of all his compositions, nothing is extant but three books of his *Bibliotheca*, an abridged history of the gods and ancient heroes, of whose actions and genealogy it gives a faithful and interesting account. The best edition is that of Heyne, Goett. in 2. vols. 8vo. 1782. & 1803. *Athen.*—*Plin* 7. c. 37.—*Diod.* 4 & 43.—*Fabr. B. Gr.* 3. c. 27.—*Sax. Onom.* 1. p. 136.——A tragic poet of Tarsus, who wrote several tragedies, entitled Ulysses, Thyestes, Supplices, &c.; some fragments of which are preserved in *Suidas* and *Athenæus, Deipnos.* 15.—*Fabr. ibid.* 1. 2. c. 19.——A comic poet of Gela, in Sicily, in the age of Menander, who wrote 47 plays, of which the Mysteries, Sisyphus, the Cheats, the Philadelphi, &c. are mentioned. Some imagine that Terence has borrowed his Phormio from the works of this writer. *Gyrald. de Poet. Gr.* 7.—*Donat. ad Terent.*—*Muntacutius ad Photii. Epist.* 156.—*Fabr. ibid.* 1. 2. c. 22.—*Sax. Onom.* 1. p. 87.——An architect of Damascus, who superintended the building of Trajan's famous pillar, and also of the celebrated bridge which the emperor built across the Danube. *Vid.* Pons Trajani. When Adrian proposed to equal his predecessors in the greatness of his designs, his plans for a temple were submitted to the judgment of Apollodorus, but the architect examined them with more freedom than became a subject. He told the emperor, that if the goddesses and other statues which were seated in the area of the temple, should take a fancy to rise, they would break their heads against the ceiling. This observation was cruelly punished by Adrian, who ordered the architect to be put to death. *Xiphil. in Aarian.*—*Fabr. ibid.* 3. c. 24.—*Sax. ibid.* 1. p. 297.——A disciple of Epicurus, the most learned of his school, and deservedly surnamed the Illustrious. He wrote about 40 volumes on different subjects. *Diog.* 7 & 10.——A highly distinguished painter of Athens, master of Zeuxis, to whom he not only confessed himself inferior, but to recommend whose pieces he wrote a poem. Two of his paintings, one a priest in a suppliant posture, another a representation of Ajax struck with lightning by Minerva, were seen and admired at Pergamus by Pliny. *Plin.* 35. c. 9.——A statuary in the age of Alexander, of such an irascible disposition that he destroyed his own pieces upon the least provocation. His friend Silanion cast a brazen statue of him, the features of which admirably pourtrayed the passionate dispositon of the artist. *Plin.* 34. c. 8.—*Hesych.*——A rhetorician of Pergamus, the preceptor and friend of Augustus, who wrote a book on rhetoric. *Strab.* 13.——A writer who composed a history of Parthia. *Id.* 2. c. 11.——A Lemnian, who wrote on husbandry.——A physician of Tarentum.——A physician of Cytium. A treatise, containing an account of all such persons as bore this name, was written by Scipio Testi of Naples, and printed at Rome, 1555. A work of the same kind was published by Dr. Gale, in 1675; and *Fabricius*, in the 27th chapter of his third book, enumerates upwards of fifty persons of this name.

APOLLO'NIA, a festival celebrated at Ægialea, in honor of Apollo and Diana, who came to that city after the conquest of the serpent Python. They were, however, disturbed, and fled to Crete. Ægialea was soon after visited by an epidemic distemper; and the inhabitants, by the advice of their soothsayers, sent seven chosen boys and as many virgins to entreat them to return. The deities granted their request; in honour of which a temple was raised to Πειθω, the goddess of persuasion, and the festival instituted. *Paus. in Corinth.*

APOLLO'NIA, a town on the coast of Thrace, part of which was built on a small island in the Euxine Sea. Apollo had a temple here, and it is now Sissipoli.——A town of Asia Minor, on the Mæander, now Seres.——A town of Macedonia, now Pollina, on the shores of the Adriatic, nearly opposite Brundusium.——A town of Sicily, on the Chydas.——A town of Crete.——A town on the coast of Asia Minor.——A town on mount Parnassus.——A town on the Rhyndacus, in Mysia.——A town of Assyria, at the east of Tigris. *Mela & Cluverius, passim.*

APOLLONI'ADES, a tyrant of Sicily, compelled to lay down his power by Timoleon.

APOLLO'NIAS, the wife of Attalus, king of Phrygia, to whom she bore four children.

APOLLONI'IDES, a tragic poet, some of whose verses are quoted by *Stobæus in florileg. serm.* 76.—*Fabr.* 2. p. 286.——A Stoic philosopher, and friend of Cato Uticensis, was present at his death. *Plut. in Cat. Min.*——A physician of Cos, at the court of Artaxerxes, who became enamoured of Amytis, the monarch's sister, and was some time after put to death for slighting her.——A governor of Chius, delivered up by his soldiers to the generals of Alexander. *Q. Curt.* 4. 21.——A physician of Cyprus, mentioned by *Galen*, 1. 1. *Meth. Med.* c. 7.——An historian of Nice.

APOLLO'NIUS, a Stoic philosopher of Chalcis, sent for by Antoninus Pius, to instruct Marcus Antoninus, his adopted son. When he arrived at Rome, he refused to wait upon his pupil, expecting his pupil to wait upon him. Upon this the emperor, laughing, said, "It was then easier for Apollonius to come from Chalcis to Rome, than from Rome to the palace." *Jul. Capit. in Vit. M. Antonin.*——A geometrician of Perga, in Pamphylia, who lived about 242 B.C. He composed a commentary upon Euclid, whose pupils he attended at Alexandria. He wrote a learned treatise on Conic Sections, part of which is now extant, and which has been translated and commented upon by many both of the ancients and moderns. Apollonius was the first who endeavoured to explain the apparent stopping and retrograde motion of the planets, by cycles and epicycles. The best edition is that of Dr. Halley, Oxon. fol. 1710. *Voss. de Hist. Gr.* 2.—*Fabr. B.*

Gr. 1. 3. c. 22.—*Sax. Onom.* 1. p. 108.——Son of Illeus or Silleus, was a poet of Naucratis in Ægypt, and is generally called Apollonius of *Rhodes*, because he lived there for some time. He was a pupil of Panætius and Callimachus, to the latter of whom he behaved with great ingratitude; and succeeded Eratosthenes as librarian to the famous library of Alexandria, under Ptolemy Evergetes. Of all his works nothing remains but his poem in four books, on the expedition of the Argonauts, a work valuable not only in itself, but from the labors of the Scholiast, which throws much light upon the history and mythology of the ancients. In this poem, the author, though greatly inferior to Homer in majesty and sublimity, yet displays many beauties and much variety. The passion of Medea is so exquisitely pourtrayed, that Virgil has incorporated the most pathetic parts in his interesting account of Dido. The best editions of Apollonius are those printed at Oxford, in 4to. by Shaw, 1777, in 2 vols.; and in 1 vol. 8vo. 1779; and that of Brunck, Argentorat. 12mo. 1780. *Quintil.* 10. c. 1.—*Voss. de Poet. Gr.*—*Gyrald. de Poet. Hist.* 3.——*Longin. de Sublim.*—*Fabr. ibid.* 3. c. 26.—*Sax. ibid.* 1. p. 120.

APOLLO'NIUS, surnamed *Molo*, a Greek orator, who was a native of Alabanda in Caria. He opened a school of rhetoric at Rhodes and Rome, and had J. Cæsar and Cicero among his pupils. He discouraged the attendance of those whom he supposed incapable of distinguishing themselves as orators, and recommended to them pursuits more congenial to their abilities. He wrote a history, in which he made some severe and uncandid reflections on the Jewish nation, according to the complaint of *Josephus, contra Apion. Cic. de Orat.* 1. c. 28. &c. *ad Famil* 3. ep. 16. *De Invent.* 1. c. 81.—*Quintil.* 3. c. 1, &c. —*Suet. in Cæs.* 4.—*Plut. in Cæs.*

APOLLO'NIUS TYANEN'SIS, a Pythagorean philosopher, well skilled in magic, and thoroughly acquainted with those arts which can captivate and astonish the vulgar. By renouncing the common indulgencies of age, and affecting singularity by letting his hair grow, wearing nothing but linen, and appearing barefooted, he aspired to the name of a reformer of mankind. He was courted by kings and princes, and commanded unusual attention by his numberless artifices. His friend and companion, Damis, wrote his life, which, 200 years after, also engaged the attention of Philostratus. His biographer, relates so many curious, extraordinary, and improbable anecdotes of his hero, that many have justly deemed it a romance; yet for all this, Hierocles had the presumption to compare the impostures of Apollonius, with the miracles of Jesus Christ. *Fabr. B. Gr.* 1. 2. c. 10.—*Sax. Onom.* 1. p. 247. [There is a bust of this philosopher in the Museum of the Capitol.]

APOLLO'NIUS, a sophist of Alexandria, pupil of Didymus, in the second century, was distinguished for his *Lexicon Græcum Iliadis & Odysseæ*, a book beautifully edited by Villoison, in 4to. 2 vols. Paris, 1773.

APOLLO'NIUS DYS'COLUS, a grammarian of Alexandria. *Sax. Onom.* 1. p. 302.

APOLLO'NIUS, a Greek historian, about the age of Augustus, who wrote upon the philosophy of Zeno and of his followers. *Strab.* 14.——A sculptor of Rhodes, who, with his countryman Tauriscus, executed a striking representation of Zethus and Amphion tying the revengeful Dirce to the tail of a mad bull. The celebrated antique, which is said to be still extant under the name of the Farnese bull, is notonly admired for the workmanship, but also for the size of the block of marble, out of which it must have been sculptured.——A native of Athens, son of Nestor, distinguished as a sculptor. Some have attributed the famous Torsus Belvidera to him.——An officer set over Ægypt by Alexander. *Curt.* 4. c. 8.——A wrestler. *Paus.* 5.——A physician of Pergamus, who wrote a work on agriculture. *Varro.*——A writer in the age of Antoninus Pius.——A physician.——A son of Sotades, at the court of Ptolemy Philadelphus.

APOLLO'NIUS SY'RUS, a Platonic philosopher.

APOLLO'NIUS HEROPHIL'IUS, a writer on ointments. For others of this name, see *Fabr. B. Gr.* 1. 3. c. 26.

APOLLOPH'ANES, a Stoic philosopher, a flatterer of king Antigonus. *Diog.*——A physician at the court of Antiochus. *Plin.* 22. c. 21.—*Cels.* 5. c. 18. —*Polyb.* 5.——A comic poet, in the 97th Olympiad. *Ælian. Anim.* 6.—*Suidas.*—*Athen.*—*Fabr. B. Gr.* 2. p. 422.

APOMY'IUS, an epithet of Jupiter at Elis, from his driving away flies, (ἀπὸ μυῖα). When Hercules was celebrating some mysterious ceremonies at Olympia, he was attacked by a number of flies, which he was unable to drive away; but when he had sacrificed to Jupiter, the whole swarm disappeared beyond the Alpheus. In commemoration of this event, a victim was yearly offered to Jupiter Apomyius. *Paus.* 5. c. 14.—*Plin.* 29. c. 6.

APONIA'NA, an island on the coast of Sicily, near Lilybæum. *Hirt. Afr.* 2.

APO'NIUS M., governor of Mœsia, rewarded with a triumphal statue by Otho, for defeating 9000 barbarians. *Tac. Hist.* 1. c. 79.

AP'ONUS, now Abano, a fountain, with a village of the same name, near Patavium. The waters of the fountain were hot, and supposed to have an oracular power. *Lucan.* 7. v. 194.—*Suet. in Tiber.* 14.—*Sil.* 12. v. 218.—*Cassiod. Var.* 2. 39.

APOSTRO'PHIA, a surname of Venus in Bœotia, where she was known by the names of Urania, Vulgaria, and Apostrophia. The first she received as patroness of pure and chaste love, the second as patroness of carnal and sensual desires, the third as patroness of illicit and unnatural gratifications. Under each of these names she had statues at Thebes, which were so ancient that they were reported to have been erected by Harmonia, the daughter of Cadmus, and made of the wood of the ship which conveyed Cadmus to Greece. This goddess was invoked by the Thebans to protect them againt all unlawful desires. She was honored by the Romans under the name of Verticordia; and her temple was without the Colline gate. *Ovid. Fast.* 4. v. 156.—*Paus.* 9. c. 16.—*Val. Max.* 8. c. 15.

APOTHEO'SIS, a ceremony observed by the ancients, when they raised their kings and heroes to the rank of deities. The nations of the east were the first who paid divine honors to their great men, and the Romans followed their example, and not only deified the most virtuous of their emperors, but also the most profligate. *Herodian*, 4. c. 2. has left a curious account of the apotheosis of a Roman emperor. After the body of the deceased was burnt, an ivory image was laid on a couch for seven days, representing the emperor under the agonies of disease. The city then exhibited universal sorrow, the senate visited the image, in mourning, and the physicians pronounced it every day in a more decaying state. When the death was announced, a band of young senators carried the couch and image to the Campus Martius, where it was deposited on an edifice in the form of a pyramid, and spices and combustible materials were thrown upon it. After this the knights walked round the pile in solemn procession, the images of the most illustrious Romans were drawn in state, and the new emperor, with a torch, set fire to the pile, in which he was assisted by the surrounding multitude. An eagle was then liberated from the middle of the pile, and was supposed to carry the soul of the deceased to heaven, where he was ranked among the gods. If the person was a female, a peacock, and not an eagle, was let loose. The Greeks observed ceremonies of nearly a similar nature. *Voss de Orig. Idol.* 1. 12.

APOTO'MIÆ, a nation of Marmarica. *Ptol.*

APOTROPÆ'I, a name of the gods Averrunci.

Apotro'phia, same as Apostrophia.

AP'PA, a city of Arabia Felix. *Ptol.*

APPADA'NA, a city of Persia. *Id.*

AP'PHA, a city of Parthia. *Id.*

APPHADA'NA, a city of Mesopotamia. *Id.*

AP'PHAR, a town of Mauritania Cæsariensis. *Id.*

AP'PIA VI'A. *Vid.* Via.

APPI'ADES, a name given to Venus and Pallas, because a temple was erected to their honour near the Appian road. The name was also applied to the courtezans who lived in a street near the temple of Venus, by the Appiæ Aquæ, and the forum of J. Cæsar. The word Appias in the singular is applied by Cicero to Venus, alone; and it expresses also the Appian aqueduct, which was near the temple of Venus. *Ovid. de Art. Am.* 1. v. 82, &c. *de Rem. A.* 660.—*Cœl. Rhod.* 12. c. 1.—*Sic. Fam.* 3. ep. 1.

APPA'NUS, a Greek historian of Alexandria, who flourished A.D. 123. He left his native city for Rome, where he distinguished himself at the bar of his eloquence, and gained the confidence of the emperor, by whom he was appointed governor of a province. His universal history, which consisted of 24 books, contained an account of all the nations which had been conquered by the Romans, in the order of time. This work the style of which is simple and unadorned, exhibits a great knowledge of military affairs, and the author has described his battles in a masterly manner. It is, however, greatly mutilated; and there is now extant only the account of the Punic, Syrian, Parthian, Mithridatic, and Spanish wars, with those of Illyricum, and the civil dissensions, and a fragment of the Celtic wars. The best editions of Appian are those of Tollius and the Variorum, 2 vols. 8vo. Amst. 1670, and that of Schweighauserus, 3 vols. 8vo. Lips. 1785. *Fabr. B. Gr.* 4. c. 14.—*Sax. Onom.* 1. p. 306.

APPI'ARA, a town of Lower Mysia. *Antonin.*

AP'PII FO'RUM, now Borgo Longo, a little village not far from Rome. It was situated on the Appia Via, and was built by Appius. *Horat.* 1. sat. 5.—*Cic. Att.*—*Act. Apost.* 28. v. 15.

AP'PIUS, the prænomen of an illustrious family at Rome.——A dictator, who conquered the Hernici.——A Roman, who, when he heard that he had been proscribed by the triumvirs, divided his riches among his servants, and embarked with them for Sicily. In their passage the vessel was shipwrecked and Appius alone saved his life. *Appian.* 4.

Ap'pius Appia'nus, a needy prodigal, whom Tiberius allowed to retire from the senate. *Tac. Ann.* 2. c. 48.

Appius Caudex, a son of Ap. Cl. Cæcus, defeated Hiero, king of Sicily.

Ap'pius Clau'dius, a Roman senator, was appointed one of the decemvirs, and persuaded his colleagues to retain their office after the time allotted for its duration had expired. *Vid.* Decemviri. He made a gross attempt upon the chastity of Virginia, (*vid.* Virginia), and destroyed himself, when cited to answer for his crime before the tribunals of his country. *Liv.* 3. c. 33.

Ap'pius Clau'dius Cæ'cus, a Roman orator who built the Appian way, and many aqueducts. He also distinguished himself in war; and in his second consulship, A. U. C. 458, he defeated the Samnites and Etrurians. When Pyrrhus demanded peace of the senators, Appius, grown old in the service of the republic, caused himself to be carried to the senate house, and disuaded his countrymen from granting a peace which would prove dishonourable to the Roman name. The Romans considered his blindness as a visitation from heaven, for his treatment of the family of the Potitii. *Vid.* Pinarius. *Liv.* 9. c. 42, &c.—*Senec.* 6. & 11.—*Ovid. Fast.* 6. v. 203.—*Cic. in Brut. & Tusc.* 4.

Ap'pius Clau'dius Cras'sus, a consul, who, with Sp. Naut. Rutulius, conquered the Celtiberians, and was afterwards defeated by Perseus, king of Macedonia. *Liv.* 2. *dec.* 5.

Ap'pius Clau'dius Len'tulus, a consul with M. Perpenna.

Ap'pius Clau'dius, Pul'cher, a grandson of Ap. Cl. Cæcus, consul in the age of Sylla, retired from grandeur to enjoy the pleasures of a private and domestic life. *Plut. in Lucull.*

Ap'pius Clau'sus, a general of the Sabines, who, being ill used by his countrymen, retired to Rome with 5000 of his friends, and become a senator. *Plut. in Poplic.*

Ap'pius Herdo'nius, seized the capitol with 4000 exiles, A.U.C. 292, and was soon after overthrown. *Liv.* 3. c. 15.—*Flor.* 3. c. 19.

Ap'pius Sila'nus, a person accused of treason, under Tiberius. *Tac. Ann.* 6. c. 9.——A censor, A.U.C. 442. *Horat.* 1. sat. 6. v. 20. This name was common to many consuls, whose history was not marked by any uncommon event. *Vid.* Claudius.

AP'PULA, an immodest woman, &c. *Juv.* 6. v. 64.

A'PRES, a leader of the auxiliaries of Æetes, slain by Colaxes. *Val. Flacc.* 6. v. 638.

A'PRIES or **A'PRIUS**, a king of Ægypt, in the age of Cyrus, supposed to be the Pharaoh Hophra of Scripture. He took Sidon, and lived in great prosperity till his subjects revolted to Amasis, by whom he was conquered and strangled. *Herodot.* 2. c. 161, &c.—*Diod.* 1.

APRO'NIA GENS, the name of a family at Rome. *Tacitus. Ann.* 4. c. 22. mentions a female of this name who was murdered by her husband.

APRONIA'NUS VIPSA'NUS, a proconsul of Africa, under Otho.

APROSCOLO'NIA, a town of Thrace. *Justin.*—*Plin.* 4. c. 11. It was called also Theodosiopolis, and is now Aprio.

APRUS'TUM, a town of the Brutii. *Plin.* 3. c. 11. It is called Abystrum by *Ptolemy*, but authors differ as to the name of the modern town.

AP'SALUS, an inland town of Macedonia, now Prespa. *Ptol.*

APSAN'DRUS, the sixth decennial archon at Athens.

AP'SARUS, a town of Cappadocia, on the confines of Chalcis. It is now Arcani.

AP'SILÆ, a nation of Scythia. *Steph.*—*Plin.* 6. c. 4.

AP'SINES, an Athenian sophist in the third century, author of a work called *Præceptor de Arte Rhetoricâ.* There were several rhetoricians of this name. *Vid. Fabr. B. Gr.* 1. 4. c. 33,—*Sax. Onom.* 1. p. 363.

APSIN'THES, a sophist of Gadara, who taught at Rome in the time of Maximilian.

APSIN'THII, a people of Thrace. They received their name from a small river called Apsinthus, which flowed through their territories. *Dion. Perieg.*

AP'SORUS or **AP'SARUS**, a city and river of Pontus, on the Euxine Sea. *Ptol.*—*Arrian.*——An island in the Adriatic, with a city of the same name. *Ptol. Stephanus.* calls it a city of Illyria.

AP'SUS, a small river of Illyricum, falling into the Ionian Sea, between Dyrrhachium and Apollonia. It is called Aous by *Strabo*, and *Pliny*, 3. c. 23. and Alores by *Appian. Lucan.* 5. v. 461.

AP'TA JU'LIA, a city of Gallia Narbonensis, now Apte. It afterwards became a colony, and was greatly ornamented by J. Cæsar, after whose name it was called. *Plin.* 3. c. 4.

AP'TERA, an inland town of Crete. *Ptol.*—*Plin.* 4. c. 12.

APTU'CHI FA'NUM, a city of Cyrenaica, now Langifarie. *Ptol.*

AP'UA, a city of Liguria, now Pontremoli. *Livy.* calls the inhabitants Apuani. *Cluver. Ital. Ant.* 1. c. 10.

APULE'IA LEX, was enacted by L. Apuleius, the tribune A.U.C. 652, for inflicting a punishment upon such as were guilty of exciting seditious commotions in the city.

Apule'ia Varil'ia, a grand-daughter of the sister of Augustus, convicted of adultery with a certain Manlius, in the reign of Tiberius. *Tac. Ann.* 2. c. 50.

APULE'IUS LU'CIUS, a learned man of the second century, born at Madaura in Africa. He studied successively at Carthage, Athens, and Rome, where he acquired a knowledge of the Latin language without the aid of a master. His apology for marrying Pudentilla, a rich widow, which is still extant, is a masterly composition. Most of his works have perished. There are, however, extant eleven books of Metamorphoses, or fables, concerning an ass, surnamed Golden, from their excellence, three books on the doctrine and life of Plato, &c. The best editions of Apuleius are the Delphin, 2 vols, 4to. Paris, 1688; and Pricæi, 8vo. Goudæ, 1650. *Sax. Onom.* 1. p. 323.—*Harles. Not. Lit. Rom.* 1. p. 498.—*Macrob.* 1. c. 2.—*August. de Civ. D.* 18. c. 18.—*Jul. Capitol. in Clodio.* [A bust of this poet is to be found in the Capitol.]

Apule'ius Saturni'nus, a tribune of the people, in the time of Marius, frequently mentioned by *Cicero.*

Apule'ius Cel'sus, a physician of Centuripa, in Sicily, in the age of Augustus or Tiberius. He wrote an herbarium, a work *De Re Rusticâ*, &c. *Harles, ibid.* 3. p. 161. *Livy* mentions several other persons of this name; they were, however, of no celebrity.

APU'LIA, now Puglia, a country of Italy between Daunia and Calabria, extending from the river Frento to Brundusium and Tarentum. It formed part of antient Daunia and Apulia Peucetia. It was famous for its wool; and some suppose that it was called after Apulus, an ancient king of the country before the Trojan war. Greek writers, and especially the poets, give it the name of Japygia; though Strabo confines the appellation of Japygia merely to Calabria. *Plin.* 3. c. 11.—*Cic. de Div.* 1. c. 43.—*Strab.* 6.—*Mela*, 2. c. 6.—*Martial. in Apophth.* 155.—*Cluver.* 3. c. 29.

AP'ULUM, a city of Dacia, now Alba Giulia. *Ptol.*

APUSCIDA'MUS, a lake of Africa. All bodies, however heavy, were said to swim on the surface of its waters. *Plin.* 31. c. 2.

APYRÆ, a city of Lycia, now Finica. *Plin.* 5. c. 27.

A'QUÆ AUGUSTÆ or TARBEL'LICÆ, now Acqs or Dax, a town of modern Gascony, in France, situated on the Aturus or Adour, before its fall into the bay of Biscay.

A'quæ Gratia'næ, a small town of modern Savoy, now called Aix.

A'quæ Helvet'icæ, a town of Switzerland, now Reichsbaden. *Cluver.* 2. c. 17.

A'quæ Ones'iæ, a small town at the foot of the Pyrenees, near the source of the Aturus; it is now called Bayèges.

A'quæ Sex'tiæ, now Aix, in Provence, a town at the east of the Rhone, a little above Marseilles, built by Sextius, A.U.C. 630, and famous for its warm baths. *Vid.* Sextiæ.

A'quæ So'lis or Cali'dæ, a town of Britain, now Bath.

A'quæ Tauri'næ, now Acqua Pendente, a town of Etruria, called Acqula by *Ptolemy*. *Plin.*

AQUA'RIUS, one of the signs of the Zodiac, rising in January and setting in February. Some suppose that Ganymede was changed into this sign, whilst others consider that Deucalion was represented by it. *Hygin. P. A.* 2. c. 29.—*Eratosth.* 26.—*Hegesian. apud Hyg.*—*Virg. G.* 3. v. 304.

Aq'uila Ponti'nus, one of the conspirators against Cæsar. *Cic. Phil.* 11. c. 6.

Aq'uila, a freedman of Mæcenas, employed by him as a short-hand writer, &c. *Dio.* 55. c. 7.——A native of Sinope, in Pontus, who, after apostatizing from Christianity to Judaism, translated the Bible into Greek. He is sometimes confounded with Onkelos, and lived about A.D. 123. *Fabr. B. Gr.* 3. p. 690.—*Sax. Onom.* 1. p. 296.——A rhetorician. *Sax. ibid.* 1. p. 372.——A civilian. *Sax. ibid.* 1. p. 400.——A river of Scythia. *Herodot.*——Two places of Mauritania Tingitana, called Major and Minor. *Antonin.*

AQUILA'RIA, a place of Africa, *Cæs.* 2. *Bell. Civ.* 23.

AQUILE'IA or AQUILE'GIA, a town founded by a Roman colony, called from its grandeur, *Roma secunda*, and situated at the north of the Adriatic Sea, on the confines of Italy. It is famous for the vigorous resistance which it made against the attacks of Attila, by whom, however, it was taken, A.D. 452. The Roman emperors often resided there. *Ital.* 8. v. 605.—*Martial.* 4. epigr. 25.—*Mela*, 2. c. 6.—*Herodian.* 8. c. 2.

AQUIL'IA or AQUIL'LIA, a patrician family at Rome, from which few illustrious men rose. They are supposed to have received their name from the dark colour of their complexion.

Aquil'ia, a Roman lady, exiled by Tiberius for adultery with Varius Ligur. *Tac. Ann.* 4. c. 42.

Aquil'ia Seve'ra, a vestal virgin, privately married by Heliogabalus. *Lamprid. & Dio. in Heliogab.*

A'QUILI'NUS. There were three consuls of this name; one the colleague of Julius Rusticus; another of Æmilianus; the third of Junius Maximus.

AQUIL'IUS GAL'LUS, an orator of eminence, mentioned by *Cicero*, *Brut.* 42. and author of a law *de dolo malo*. *Cic. N. D.* 3. c. 30. *Offic.* 3. c. 14.

Aquil'ius Mar'cus, a Roman consul, who had the government of Asia Minor, and was cruelly slain by Mithridates. *Justin.* 36. c. 4.

Aquil'ius Ma'rius, a Roman governor of Sicily, in the servile war. *Cic. in Verr.* 3. c. 54. *Brut.* 62, &c.

Aquil'ius Ni'ger, an historian mentioned by *Suetonius, in Aug.* 11.

Aquil'ius Reg'ulus, an informer, brother of Vipsanius Messala. *Tac. Hist.* 4. c. 42.—*Plin.* 6. ep. 2. 1. 2.

Aquil'ius Sabi'nus, a lawyer of Rome, surnamed the Cato of his age. He was father of Aquilia Severa, whom Heliogabalus married.

Aquil'ius Seve'rus, a poet and historian in the age of Valentinian.

AQ'UILO, a wind blowing from the north, so called from Aquila, on account of its keenness and velocity, so beautifully described by *Virgil*, *G.* 3. v. 196. & seq.—*Fest. de Verb. Sig.*

AQUILO'NIA, a city of the Hirpini in Italy, situated on the banks of the Aufidus. *Liv.* 10. c. 38.

AQUIN'CUM, a city of Lower Pannonia. It is said by *Lazius* to be now Cepol; by *Cluverius*, Buda.

AQUIN'IUS, a poet of moderate capacity. *Cic.* 5. *Tusc.*—*Catull.* 14. v. 18.

AQUI'NUM, now Aquino, a town of Latinum, on one of the branches of the Liris, near the borders of the Samnites, where Juvenal was born. A dye was invented there which greatly resembled the real purple. *Strab.*—*Ital.* 8. v. 404.—*Juv.* 3. v. 319.—*Horat.* 1. ep. 10. v. 27.

AQUI'NUS CORNE'LIUS, a lieutenant of a legion in Germany, who slew Fonteius Capito. *Tac. Hist.* 1. c. 7.

AQUITA'NIA, now Guienne and Gascony, one of the divisions of Gaul, bounded on the west by Spain, on the north by Gallia Lugdunensis, and on the south by Gallia Narbonensis. Its inhabitants were called Aquitani. *Tibull.* 1. el. 7. v. 3.—*Plin.* 4. c. 17.—*Strab.* 4.

A'RA, a constellation consisting of seven stars. near the tail of the scorpion. *Ovid. Met.* 2. v. 138.

A'ra Lugdunen'sis, a place in Gaul, at the confluence of. the Arar and Rhone, now called Lyons. *Juv.* 1. v. 44.

ARABAR'CHES, a vulgar person, among the Ægyptians, or, perhaps, a usual expression for the leaders of the Arabians, who resided in Rome. *Juv.* 1 v. 130. Some believe that *Cicero*, 2. ep. 17. *ad Attic*, alludes to Pompey under the name of Arabarches.

ARA'BIA, a large country of Asia, forming a peninsula between the Arabian and Persian Gulphs. It is generally divided into three different parts; Petræa, Deserta, and Felix. It is famous for the production of frankincense, and of Aromatic plants. The inhabitants formerly paid adoration to the sun, moon, and even serpents, had their wives in common, and circumcised their childreu. The country has often been invaded, but never totally subdued. Alexander the Great, it is said, expressed a wish to place the seat of his empire in their territories. We are indebted to the Arabians for the invention of algebra, and the numerical characters 1, 2, 3, &c. which were first used in Europe in 1253, in the Alphonsian tables, made by Alphonso, king of Castille. The Arabs had received these figures from the Indians in the year 900, and they were communicated to the rest of the western nations by the Spaniards. They were, however, universally used in England, according to Dr. Wallis, about the year 1130. *Herodot.* 1, 2, 3, &c.—*Diod.* 1 & 2.—*Plin.* 12 & 14.—*Strab.* 16.—*Xenoph.*—*Tibull.* 2. el. 2.—*Curt.* 5. c. 1.—*Virg. G.* 1. v. 57.——The wife of Ægyptus. *Apollod.*

ARAB'ICUS SINUS, a sea between Ægypt and Arabia, different, according to some authors, from the Red Sea, which they suppose to be between Æthiopia and India, and the Arabian Gulph further above, between Ægypt and Arabia. From Suez to the straits of Babelmandel, it is about 1,400 miles long; but its breadth varies greatly. The navigation is very difficult, on account of its sand-banks and hidden rocks, the position of which has not yet been accurately ascertained. *Plin.* 5. c. 11.—*Strab.*—*Cluver.* 1. c. 11 & 12.—*Mela*, 1. c. 2 & 3. c. 13.

AR'ABIS, ARA'BIUS, or AR'BIS, an Indian river. *Curt.* 9. c. 10. *Vid.* Arbis.

AR'ABO or NAR'ABO, according to *Ptolemy*, a river and city of Upper Pannonia. *Antonin.*

AR'ABS or AR'ABUS, a son of Apollo and Babylone, who first invented medicine, and taught it in Arabia, which is called after his name. *Plin.* 7. c. 56.

ARABY'ZA, a city of Cauconis, in Bithynia. *Steph.*

ARAC'CA or AREC'CA, a city of Susiana. *Tibull.* 4. el. 1.

ARACHNÆUM, a mountain of Argolis. *Steph.*

ARACH'NE, a woman of Colophon, daughter of Idmon, a dyer. She was so expert in working with the needle, that she challenged Minerva, the goddess of the art, but was defeated. The goddess was so jealous of the skill displayed by her rival, that she struck her through resentment; and when the unfortunate Arachne had hanged herself in despair, the goddess changed her into a spider. *Ovid. Met.* 6. fab. 1. &c.—*Juven. sat.* 2. 56.——A city of Thessaly. *Liv.*

ARACHO'SIA, a city of Asia, near the Massagetæ. It was built by Semiramis. *Steph.*——One of the Persian provinces, placed by geographers at the west of the Indus. *Plin.* 6. c. 23.—*Strab.* 11.

ARACHO'TÆ or ARACHO'TI, a people of India, who received their name from the river Arachotus. *Dionys. Perieg.*—*Curt.* 9. c. 7.

ARACH'THUS or AR'ETHON, one of the four capital rivers of Epirus, falling into the bay of Ambracia, near Nicopolis. *Strab.* 7.

ARACIL'LUM, now Araquil, a town of Hispania Tarraconensis. *Flor.* 4. c. 12.

ARACO'SII, an Indian nation. *Justin.* 13. c. 4. *Vid.* Arachoti.

ARACYN'THUS, a mountain of Acarnania, between the Achelous and Evenus. *Servius* places this mountain in Bœotia. *Plin.* 4. c. 2.—*Virg. Ecl.* 2. v. 24.

ARA'DIO, a very brave African, with whom the emperor Probus engaged in single combat, and slew him. *Vopisc. in Prob.* c. 9.

ARADU'CA, now Arzua, a city of Lusitania.—*Ptol.*

AR'ADUS, an island on the coast of Phœnicia, joined to the continent by a bridge. *Dionys. Perieg.*—*Mela*, 2. c. 7.—*Plin.* 2. c. 103.——An island near Crete.——An island in the Persian Gulph. *Bochart. Geogr. Sacr.* p. 346.—*Voss. ad Melam.* p. 202.

A'RÆ, rocks between Africa and Sardinia, where the Romans and Africans ratified a treaty. They are supposed to be the islands which are commonly called Ægates. *Virg. Æn.* 1. v. 109.

A'RÆ ALEXAN'DRI, or CÆSA'RIS, a place of European Sarmatia, near the Tanais. It is now Veliti Preuvos. *Ptol.*

A'RÆ FLA'VIÆ, a city of Germany, on the Danube, now Nordlingen. *Ptol.*

A'RÆ MU'TIÆ, a town of Etruria, now Aremuzze. *Plin.*

A'RÆ PHILÆNO'RUM, a maritime town of Africa, on the confines of Cyrene. *Sall. Bell. Jug.* 19.—*Val. Max.* 5. c. 6. It is now Nain, or, according to others, Porto di Sabia.

A'RÆ SABE'Æ, now Cataichi, a city of Media Atropatene, on the shores of the Caspian.

A'RÆ SESTIA'NÆ or TRES AUGUS'TI, now Capo di Pennas, a promontory of Spain. *Ptol.*

A'RÆ SO'LIS, a promontory of the Callaici in Spain, now Capo di Mongia. *Id.*

ARÆTHYR'EA, a small province of Achaia, afterwards called Asophis. The capital of the country bore the same name. *Homer. Il.* 2.—*Strab.* 8.

ARÆ'US, an epithet of Jupiter. *Cœl. Rhod.* l. 15. c. 18.

AR'AGA, a city of Arabia Felix. *Ptol.*

AR'AGUS, a river of the Molossi. *Strab.*——A river of Spain, now Arga.

ARAMÆ'I, a name of the Scythians. *Plin.* 6. c. 17.

ARAMA'VA, 'Αραμαύα, a city of Arabia. *Ptol.*

ARAM'BYS, a city of Africa, founded by Hanno. *Bochart. de Phœnic. col.* 1 c. 37.

ARAN'DIS, now Torre Vedra, a city of Lusitania. *Ptol.*

ARA'NIUM, a town in the Æthiopic Gulph. *Plin.* 6. c. 29.

ARAPHE'A, an island of Caria. *Steph.*—*Parthen. in Iphicl.*

AR'APHEN, a part of the tribe Ægeis. *Steph.*

A'RAR or **AR'ARIS**, now the Soane, a river of Gaul, flowing into the Rhone. Cæsar's soldiers made a bridge over it in one day. *Cæs. Bell. Gall.* 1. c. 12.—*Sil.* 3. v. 452.—*Virg. Ecl.* 1. v. 63.

ARARAUCE'LES, a people of Cyrenaica. *Plin.* 5. c. 5.

ARARE'NA, a region of the Nomades, of which Sabus was king. *Strab.* l. 10.

ARA'ROS, a comic poet, son of Aristophanes. He was so insipid a writer that the proverb ψυχρότερος 'Αράροτος, was used to denote a dull poet. *Fabr. B. Gr.* l. 2. c. 22.

AR'ARUS, a Scythian river flowing through Armenia. *Herodot.* 4. c. 48.

ARAS'PAS, a Mede, to whom Panthea was entrusted by Cyrus, &c. *Cœl. Rhod.* l. 13. c. 33.—*Xenoph. Cyrop.*

ARATI'A, an island opposite Persia, with a lofty mountain, sacred to Neptune. *Plin.* 6. c. 25.

ARA'TRII, a nation of India within the Ganges. *Arrian. in Peripl.*

ARA'TUS, a Greek poet of Soli in Cilicia, about 277 B.C. He was greatly esteemed by Antigonus Gonatas, king of Macedonia, at whose court he passed much of his time, and by whose desire he wrote a poem on Astronomy, called Phænomena, to which is subjoined another called Diosemea, commencing at the 722nd verse. Cicero represents him as unacquainted with astronomy, yet capable of writing upon it in elegant verses. Aratus wrote, besides, hymns and epigrams, &c., and had among his interpreters and commentators many of the learned men of Greece whose works are lost, besides Cicero, Claudius, and Germanicus Cæsar, who, in their youth, or moments of relaxation, translated the Phænomena into Latin verse. The best editions of Aratus are that of Grotius, 4to, apud Raphaleng. 1600; and that of Bishop Fell Oxon. 8vo. 1672. *Cic. de Nat. D.* 2. c. 41. *Div.* 2. c. 5.—*Orat.* 1. c. 16. *Acad.* 4. c. 20.—*Quintil.* 10. c. 1.—*Paus.* 1. c. 2.—*Ovid. Am.* 1. el. 15. v. 26.—*Plin.* ep. 5 & 6. *Fabr. B. Gr.* l. 3. c. 20.—*Sax. Onom.* 1. p. 103. [Of this poet a bust exists in the Capitol.]——The son of Clinias and Aristodama, was born at Sicyon, in Achaia, near the river Asopus. When he was but seven years of age, his father, who was at the head of the government of Sicyon, was assassinated by Abantidas, who made himself absolute. After some revolutions, the sovereignty came into the hands of Nicocles; whom Aratus murdered to restore his country to liberty. He prevailed upon his countrymen to join the Achæan league, which he strengthened by making a treaty of alliance with the Corinthians, and with Ptolemy king of Ægypt. He was chosen chief commander of the forces of the Achæans, and drove away the Macedonians from Athens and Corinth. He made war against the Spartans, but was conquered by their king Cleomenes. Upon this he solicited the assistance of king Antigonus, and drove away Cleomenes from Sparta. The Ætolians soon after attacked the Achæans; and Aratus called to his aid Philip, king of Macedonia. Philip, however, showed himself cruel and oppressive, put to death some of the noblest of the Achæans, and even seduced the wife of the son of Aratus. Aratus, therefore, withdrew himself from the society and friendship of Philip. But this rupture proved fatal to him; Philip dreaded the influence of Aratus, and caused him and his son to be poisoned. He was buried with great pomp by his grateful countrymen; and two solemn sacrifices called Aratea were anually offered in honour of his memory, the first on the day that he delivered Sicyon from tyranny, and the second on the day of his birth. Aratus died in the 62nd year of his age, B.C. 213. He wrote a history of the Achæan league, much commended by Polybius. *Plut. in Vita.*—*Paus.* 2. c. 8.—*Cic. de Offic.* 2. c. 23.—*Strab.* 14.—*Liv.* 27. c. 31.—*Polyb.* 2.——The son of the former, was also commander of the forces of the Achæans. *Polyb.* 4, 5.——A native of Cnidus, who wrote a history of Ægypt. *Voss. de Hist. Gr.*—*Fabr. B. Gr.* 3. c. 20

ARAVIS'CI or **ARABIS'CI**, a people of Pannonia. *Ptol.*—*Tac. Germ.* c. 28.

ARAURAC'IDES, a people of Pentapolis in Africa. *Ptol.*

ARAU'RIS, or **ARAU'RIUS** according to *Ptolemy*, a river of Gallia Narbonensis, called also Cyrta, from its meanderings. It is now the Erhau or Airau.

ARAU'SIO, a town of Gallia Narbonensis, situated in a fine plain on the eastern bank of the Rhone. It is now called Orange in Provence, and is famous for many valuable remains ofantiquity. It was a colony of the Secundani. *Plin.* 3. c. 4.—*Mela*, 2. c. 7.—*Cluver.* 2. c. 9.

ARAX'A, a city of Lycia.—*Steph.*

ARAX'E or **ARAX'I**, a people of Illyricum. *Id.*

ARAX'ES, now Arras, a celebrated river which separates Armenia from Mediai, and falls into the Caspian Sea. Alexander built a bridge over it, which was soon destroyed by the rapidity of the stream; but that built by Augustus in a later age remained uninjured; and to this probably the *pontem indignatus Araxes* of Virgil has a reference. *Mela*, 3. c. 6.—*Plin.* 6. c. 9 & 13.—*Ptol.* 5. c. 13.—*Propert.* 3. el. 11. v. 8.—*Lucan.* 1. v. 19. l. 7. v. 188.—*Strab.* 8.—*Virg. Æn.* 8. v. 728.—*Herodot.* 1. c. 202. &c.——A river which falls into the Euphrates, and is now called Bendemir. *Curt.* 5. c. 4 & 7.—*Strab* 15.——A river of Thessaly, the same as the Peneus.——A river in Europe, now called Volga.

ARAX'ES or ARO'SES, a river of Persia, flowing under the walls of Persepolis, and falling into the Persian Gulph.

ARAX'US, a promontory of Peloponnesus, which separates Elis from Achaia. *Steph. Byz.*—*Strab.* 11.*Paus.* 6. c. 24.

AR'BA or **SCARBO'NA**, an island and city of Illyricum. *Ptol.* 2. c. 17.—*Plin.* 3. c. 21.

ARBA'CE, a city of Celtiberia. *Steph.*

ARBA'CES, a Mede, who rebelled with Blocheus against Sardanapalus, and founded the empire of Media upon the ruins of the Assyrian power, 820 years B.C. He reigned 28 years. The great revolution which he effected in Asia seems to have been unknown to Herodotus; as the historian no where makes mention of him. *Diod.* 1.—*Justin.* 1. c. 3.—*Paterc.* 1. c. 6. Also Ar'baces.

ARBA'NIUM, a city near Pontus. *Steph.*

ARBAXA'NI, a people of Liguria. *Id.*

ARBE'LA, *(-orum,)* now Irbil, a town of Persia, on the river Lycus, famous for a battle fought there between Alexander and Darius, on the 2nd of October, B.C. 331. According, however, to some authors, the battle was not fought at Arbela, but near the small village of Gaugamela, in the neighbourhood, whose consequence from this occurrence has been lost in the fame of the more populous town of Arbela. *Strab.* 16.—*Ptol.* 6. c. 1.—*Curt.* 5. c. 1.—*Plut. in Alex.*——A town of Sicily, the inhabitants of which were very credulous; hence the proverb *Quid non fies, Arbelas profectus. Erasm. in. Adag.* Also Ar'bela.

ARBE'TIO, a Roman consul put to death by Constantine, upon suspicion of aiming at the sovereignty. *Amm. Marcel.* l. 15. c. 8.

AR'BII, AR'BIES or **ARBITÆ**, a people on the borders of India, so called from the river Arbis. *Plin.* 6. c. 23.—*Strab.*—*Steph.*

AR'BIS or **AR'ABIS**, a river on the western boundaries of India, which flows through Gedrosia. There is a town of the same name near its mouth. *Strab.*

AR'BITER PETRO'NIUS, a Latin writer. *Vid.* Petronius.

ARBOCA'LA or **ARBUCA'LE**, according to *Stephanus*, a city within the Iberus, taken by Annibal as he marched against Rome. *Plut. in Annib.*

AR'BON, a city of Illyria. *Steph.*

ARBO'NA or **ABNO'BA**, the name of a mountain. *Plin.* 4. c. 12.—*Ptol.*

ARBUS'CULA, an actress on the Roman stage, who laughed at the hisses of the populace, while she received the applauses of the knights. *Horat.* 1. *sat.* 10. v. 77.

AR'CA, a city of Cœlesyria. *Plin.* 7. c. 18.

ARCA'DIA, a country in the middle of Peloponnesus, surrounded by Achaia, Messenia, Elis, and Argolis. It received its name from Arcas, the son of Jupiter; and was anciently called Drymodes, (from δρυμός, *sylva querna*,) on account of the great number of oaks which it produced, and afterwards Lycaonia and Pelasgia. This country has been much celebrated by the poets, and was famous for its mountains, the most remarkable of which were Cyllene, Nonacris, Pholoe, and Lycæus abounding in excellent pastures, and serving for retreat not only to numerous herds of oxen, but to horses and to asses of peculiar beauty and strength; from which circumstance, these animals have proverbially been called the nightingales of Arcadia. The chief towns were Mantinea, Tegea, Mænalus, and Stymphalus. The inhabitants were for the most part shepherds, who lived upon acorns, were skilful warriors, fond of independence, and able musicians. They thought themselves more ancient than the moon. Pan, the god of shepherds, chiefly lived among them. *Strab.* 8.—*Plin.* 4. c. 5. —*Paus.* 8. c. 1, 2. &c.—*Athen.* 14.—*Eustath. ad Dionys. Per.* 415.—*Artemidor.* 2, *Oniroc.* 25.—*Dionys. Hal.* 1.—*Mela*, 2. c. 3.—*Ovid. Fast.* 1. v. 468. l. 2. v. 289.—*Apollon. Arg.* 4.—*Virg. Ecl.* 10. v. 30.—*Nonnus Bassaric.* 41.—*Seneca in Hippol.* —*Stat. Theb.* 4. v. 275.——A city of Ægypt. *Steph.* ——A fortified village of Zacynthus. *Diod. Sic.* l. 15.——The daughter of the emperor Arcadius, remarkable for her piety. *Sozom.* l. 9. c. 1 & 2.

ARCA'DIUS, the eldest son of Theodosius the Great, succeeded his father A.D. 395. Under him the Roman power was divided. He made the eastern empire his choice, and fixed his residence at Constantinople: while his brother Honorius was made emperor of the west, and lived in Rome. After this separation of the Roman empire, the powers looked upon one another with indifference; and, soon after, their indifference was changed into jealousy, and contributed to hasten their mutual ruin. In the reign of Arcadius, Alaricus attacked the western empire, and plundered Rome. Arcadius married Eudoxia, a bold ambitious woman, and died in the 31st year of his age, after a reign of thirteen years. He was an effeminate prince, who was governed by favorites, and abandoned himself to the pleasures of a voluptuous court.——A river of Cappadocia. *Ptol.*—*Salmas. ad Solin.* p. 888.

ARCA'NUM, a villa near Minturnæ, belonging to Cicero. *Cic.* 7. *Ep. ad Att.* 10.

AR'CAS, a son of Jupiter and Callisto. He nearly killed his mother, whom Juno had changed into a bear. He reigned in Pelasgia, which from him was called Arcadia, after his uncle Nyctimus, and communicated to his subjects the instruction he had received from Triptolemus and Aristæus. He taught them agriculture and the art of spinning wool. After his death, Jupiter made him a constellation with his mother. He married a nymph, by whom he had three sons, Azan, Aphidas, and Elatus, among whom he divided his kingdom. The descendants of Azan planted colonies on the coast of Phrygia. Aphidas received for his share Tegea, which, on that account, has been called the inheritance of Aphidas; and Elatus became master of mount Cyllene, and some time after passed into Phocis. *Paus.* 8. c. 4.—*Hygin.* fab. 155 & 176.—*Apollod.* 3. c. 8.—*Strab.* 8.—*Ovid. Fast.* 1. v. 470. ——A city of Armenia Minor. *Antonin.*—Also the name of one of Actæon's dogs.

AR'CE, a daughter of Thaumus, son of Pontus and Terra. She was born with wings; but was deprived of them by Jupiter, because she assisted the Titans against the gods. They were afterwards given to Achilles, who, was thence called ποδαρκης, the swift footed. *Ptol.*—*Hephæst.*

ARCELA'US or **ARCHELA'US**, a son of Ægyptus, who married Anaxibia, and was, like his brothers, murdered, *Apollod.* 2. c. 4.——A son Lycaon. *Id.* 3. c. 16.

AR'CENA, a town of Phœnicia, where Alexander Severus was born. *Lamprid. in Sever.* c. 1.

AR'CENS, a sicilian, whose son accompanied Æneas into Italy, where he was killed by Mezentius. *Virg. Æn.* 9. v. 581, &c.

ARCESILA'US, son of Battus, king of Cyrene, was driven from his kingdom in a sedition, and died B. C. 575. The second of that name died B. C. 560. *Polyæn.* 8. c. 41.—*Herodot.* 4. c. 159.——One of Alexander's generals, who obtained Mesopotamia at the general division of the provinces after the king's death.——*Diod. Sic.* 18.—— A chief of Catana, who betrayed his trust to Dionysius the elder. *Diod.* 14.——A philosopher of Pitane in Æolia, disciple of Polemon. He visited Sardes and Athens, and was the founder of the middle academy, as Socrates founded the ancient, and Carneades the new one. He had many pupils, was very fond of Homer, and generally divided his time among the pleasures of philosophy, love, reading, and the table. He died in his 75th year, B. C. 241. or 300, according to some. *Diog. in vitâ.*—*Persius* 3, v. 78.—*Cic. de Finib. In Acad.* 4. c. 6.——*Augustin. contra Acad.* 3.—*Lactant.* 3. c. 6.——The name of two painters.——A statuary. *Diog. Laert.* 4. *in Arces.*—*Plin.* 35. c. 11. l. 36. c. 5.—*Paus* 1. c. 1.——A leader of the Bœotians, killed by Hector, during the Trojan war. *Homer. Il.* 2 & 15. —*Hygin.* fab. 97.——An ancient comic poet, mentioned by *Laertius*, 4. c. 45.

ARCESI'NE, a city of Amorgus, one of the Cyclades. *Steph.*

ARCE'SIUS, son of Jupiter, married Chalcomedusa, by whom he had Laertes, the father of Ulysses. *Homer. Odyss.* 16.—*Eustath. in Il.* 2. & *Odyss.* 16 & 24.—*Ovid. Met.* 13. v. 144.

ARCHÆ'A, a city of Æolia. *Paus.* l. 2.

ARCHÆ'ANAX of Mitylene, was intimate with Pisistratus, tyrant of Athens, and fortified Sigeum with a wall, from the ruins of ancient Troy. *Strab.* 13.

ARCHÆATI'DIS, a country of Peloponnesus. *Polyb.*

ARCHAG'ATHUS, son of Archagathus, was slain in Africa by his soldiers, B.C. 285. He killed his grandfather Agathocles, tyrant of Syracuse. *Diod.* 20.—*Justin.* 22. c. 5. &c. says, that he was put to death by Archesilaus.——A Greek physician at Rome, B.C. 219. It is said that he introduced the use of the knife and cautery in his surgical operations; which so offended the ignorant Romans, that they banished him. *Plin.* 29. c. 1.

AR'CHAMA, a city of Cappadocia. *Ptol.*

ARCHAN'DER, father-in-law of Danaus. *Herodot.* 2. c. 98.

ARCHANDROP'OLIS, a town of Ægypt, so called after Archander. *Steph.*

AR'CHE, one of the Muses, according to *Cicero.*

ARCHE'BIUS, a native of Heraclea, who, when the enemy refused to fight, compelled them to engage by a stratagem, and routed them. *Polyæn.* 5.

ARCHEDE'MUS, a person ridiculed by the comic poets, because, though he had resided a long time at Athens, he could not obtain the rights of citizenship. *Schol. Ran Aristoph.* Also Archidamus.

ARCHED'ICUS, a Greek comic poet, mentioned by *Polybius. Athenæus* mentions two of his plays. *Fabr. B Gr.* l. 2. c. 22.

ARCHEG'ETES, a surname of Apollo. *Thucyd.* l. 6.

ARCHELA'IS, a colony of Cappadocia, founded by Claudius Cæsar.

ARCHELA'US, a person who married Berenice, and made himself king of Ægypt; a dignity which he enjoyed only six months, as he was killed by the soldiers of Gabinius, B.C. 56. He had been made priest of Comana by Pompey. His grandson was made king of Cappadocia by Antony, whom he assisted at the battle of Actium; and he maintained his independence under Augustus, till Tiberius perfidiously destroyed him. *Liv.* 76 & 82.

ARCHELA'US, a king of Macedonia, who succeeded his father Pediccas the Second. As he was but a natural child, he killed the legitimate heirs, to gain the kingdom. He was a great monarch; but was at last killed, after a reign of 23 years, by one of his favorites, because he had promised him his daughter, in marriage, and given her to another. He patronized the poet Euripides, *Diod.* 14.—*Justin* 7. c. 4.—*Ælian. V. H.* 2, 8, 12, 14.——A king of the Jews, surnamed Herod. He married Glaphyre, daughter of Archelaus, king of Macedonia, and widow of his brother Alexander. Cæsar banished him, for his cruelties, to Vienna, in Gaul, where he died. *Dio.*——A king of Lacedæmon, son of Agesilaus. He reigned 42 years with Charilaus, of the other branch of the family. *Herodot.* 7. c. 204.—*Paus.* 3. c. 2.——A general of Antigonus the younger, appointed governor of the Acrocorinthus, with the philosopher Persæus. *Polyæn.* 6. c. 5.——A celebrated general of Mithridates, against Sylla. *Id.* 8. c. 9.——A philosopher of Athens, or Messenia, son of Apollodorus, and successor to Anaxagoras. He was preceptor to Socrates, and was called *Physicus.* He supposed that heat and cold were the principles of all things. He first discovered the voice to be propagated by the vibration of the air. *Cic. Tusc.* 5.—*Diog. in vitâ.* —*Augustin. de Civ. Dei.* 8.——A man set over Susa by Alexander, with a garrison of 3000 men. *Curt.* 5. c. 2.——A Greek philosopher, who wrote a history of animals, and maintained that goats breathed not through the nostrils, but through the ears. *Plin.* 8. c. 50.——A son of Electryon and Anaxo. *Apollod.* 2.——A Greek poet, who wrote epigrams. *Varro de R. R.* 3. c. 16.——A sculptor of Priene, in the age of Claudius. He made an apotheosis of Homer; a piece of sculpture greatly admired, and said to have been discovered under ground A. D. 1658.——A tragedian of Abdera. *Luciân.* c. 1. tom. 3.——A writer of Thrace.

ARCHEM'ACHUS, a Greek writer, who published a history of Eubœa. *Athen.* 6.—*Voss. Hist. Gr.* 3. —*Clem. Alex. Strom.* 1.——A son of Hercules——A son of Priam. *Apollod.* 2 & 3.

ARCHEM'ORUS or OPHEL'TES, was son of Lycurgus, king of Nemæa, in Thrace, by Euridice. Hypsipyle, his nurse, was met by the army of Adrastus, and forced to show them a fountain where they might quench their thirst. To do this more expeditiously, she put down the child on the grass, and at her return found him killed by a serpent. The Greeks were so afflicted at this misfortune, that they instituted games in honor of Archemorus, which were called Nemæan. *Apollod.* 2 & 3. —*Paus.* 8. c. 48.—*Stat. Theb.* 6.—*Hygin.* fab. 74.

ARCHEN'NUS, an historian or grammarian, mentioned by the *Scholiast* on *Aristoph. in Avibus.*

ARCHEP'OLIS, a man in Alexander's army, who conspired with Dymnus against the king. *Curt.* 6. c. 7.

ARCHEPTOL'EMUS, son of Iphitus, king of Elis, went to the Trojan war, where he was killed by Ajax, son of Telamon. It is said that he re-established the Olympic games, *Homer. Il.* 8. v. 128.

ARCHES'TRATUS, a tragic poet, whose pieces were acted during the Peloponnesian war. *Voss. de Poet. Gr.—Plut. in Arist.*——A man so small and lean, that, according to some authors, when placed in a dish, he weighed no more than an obolus.——A follower of Epicurus, who wrote a poem in commendation of gluttony, and is supposed to have been the same as the last mentioned. *Athen.* 13.

ARCHETI'MUS, the first philosophical writer in the age of the seven wise men of Greece. *Diog. in Thalete* 1. c. 40.

ARCHE'TIUS, a Rutulian, killed by the Trojans. *Virg. Æn.* 12. v. 459.

AR'CHIA, one of the Oceanides, wife of Inachus. *Hygin.* fab. 143.

AR'CHIAS, a Corinthian descended from Hercules. He founded Syracuse, B.C. 732. Being told by an oracle to make choice either of health or riches, he chose the latter. *Dion. Hal.* 2.——A polemarch of Thebes, assassinated in the conspiracy of Pelopidas. He might have prevented this fatal insurrection, if he had not deferred to the morrow the reading of a letter, which he had received from Archias, the Athenian high-priest, which gave him information of his danger. *Plut. in Pelop.*——A high-priest of Athens, contemporary and intimate with the polemarch of the same name. *Id. ibid.*——A Theban taken in the act of adultery, and punished according to the law, by being tied to a post in the public place, for which punishment he abolished the oligarchy. *Aristot.*——A celebrated herald of Hybla. *Jul. Pollux.*——An archon at Athens, Olymp. 108. an. 3.

AR'CHIAS, AU'LUS LICIN'IUS, a poet of Antioch, intimate with Lucullus and other illustrious Romans. He obtained the rank and name of a Roman citizen by the means of Cicero, who ably defended him in an elegant oration, when his enemies had disputed his privileges and title to that distinction. He wrote a poem on the Cimbrian war, and began another concerning Cicero's consulship, which are now lost. Some of his epigrams are preserved in the Anthologia. *Cic. pro Arch.*

ARCHIBI'ADES, a philosopher of Athens, who affected the manners of the Spartans, and was very inimical to the views and measures of Phocion. *Plut. in Phoc.*——An ambassador of Byzantium. sent by Memnon to reconnoitre the strength of his enemy Leuco. *Polyæn.* 5. c. 44.

ARCHIB'IUS, a grammarian, son of Apollonius, illustrated the epigrams of Callimachus. *Suidas.* ——A grammarian who taught at Rome in the age of Trajan. *Id.*

ARCHIDA'MIA, a priestess of Ceres, who restored Aristomenes to liberty when he had been taken prisoner by her female attendants at the celebration of the festivals. *Paus.* 4. c. 17.——A daughter of Cleadas, who upon hearing that her countrymen the Spartans were debating whether they should send away their women to Crete, seized a sword, and ran to the senate house, exclaiming that the women would not survive the ruin of Sparta. Upon thist he proposed decree was rejected. *Plut. in Lycurg,—Polyæn.* 8. c. 49. Also Archidami'a.

ARCHIDA'MUS the First, son of Theopompus, king of Sparta, died before his father. *Paus.*

ARCHIDA'MUS the Second, king of Sparta, son of Anaxidamus, was succeeded on the throne by Agasicles.

ARCHIDA'MUS the Third, son of Agesilaus, of the family of the Proclidæ, reigned 42 years.

ARCHIDA'MUS the Fourth, grandson of Leotychidas, succeeded his grandfather, and reigned in conjunction with Plistoanax. He conquered the Argives and Arcadians, and privately assisted the Phocians in plundering the temple of Delphi. He was called to the aid of Tarentum against the Romans, and fell there in a battle, after a reign of 33 years. *Diod.* 16.—*Xenoph.*

ARCHIDA'MUS the Fifth, was son of Eudamidas the First, and father of Eudamidas the Second. *aPus. in Lacon.*

ARCHIDA'MUS, a king of Sparta, who conquered the Helots, after a violent earthquake. *Diod.* 11.——A son of Agesilaus, who led the Spartan auxiliaries to Cleombrotus at the battle of Leuctra. His assistance was implored against the Phocians, who had pillaged the temple of Apollo at Delphi; but he refused. He was killed in a battle against the Lucanians in Italy, B.C. 338, and his body was left without the honours of burial. He left two sons, Eudamidas and Agis, by Dinicha. *Paus.* 3. c. 10.——A son of Theopompus. *Paus.*——A Lacedæmonian prince, son of Telides. *Suidas.*

AR'CHIDAS, a tyrant of Athens, killed by his troops. *Plut. in Agesil.*

ARCHIDE'MIA, a fountain of Sicily. *Plin.* 3, c. 8.

ARCHIDE'MUS, a Stoic philosopher, who willingly exiled himself among the Parthians. *Plut. de Exil.*

ARCHIDE'US, a son of Amyntas, king of Macedonia. *Justin.* 7. c. 4.

ARCHIDI'UM, a city of Crete, named after Archidius, son of Tegeates. *Paus.* 8. c. 53.

ARCHIGAL'LUS, the high priest in the temple of Cybele. *Vid.* Galli.

ARCHIG'ENES, a physician born at Apamea, in Syria. He lived in the reigns of Domitian, Nerva, and Trajan, and died in the 73rd year of his age. He wrote a treatise on adorning the hair, as also ten books on fevers, which have perished. *Juv.* 6. v. 235.——A Sicilian, founder of Aricia.

ARCHIG'ETES, *Vid.* Archegetes.

AR'CHILE, a town of Pentapolis in Africa. *Ptol.*

ARCHIL'OCHUS, a poet of Parus, who wrote elegies, satires, odes, and epigrams, and was the first who introduced Iambics in his verses. He courted Neobule, the daughter of Lycambes, but the father gave her to another; upon which the disappointed Archilocus wrote a satire in so bitter and sarcastic a strain, that Lycambes hanged himself. The daughter also followed her father's example. His poems, from their licentiousness and indelicacy, were so offensive to the stern morals of the Spartans, that he was banished from their city. Archilochus did not greatly distinguish himself as a warrior. In a battle, he threw down his arms, and saved his life by a dishonourable flight; and thus drew upon him the ridicule and contempt of his contemporaries. He flourished 685 B.C. and it is said that he was assassinated. Some fragments of his poetry remain, which display great vigour and animation, boldness and vehemence; for which reason, perhaps, Cicero calls virulent edicts, *Archilochia edicta.* *Cic. Tusc.* 1. *Attis.* 2. ep. 21. l. 16. ep. 11.—*Quintil.* 10. c. 1.—*Herodot.* 1. c. 12.—*Horat. Art. Poet.* v. 79.—*Paus.* 10. c. 28.—*Ovid. in Ib.* 54.—*Stat.* 2. *Sylv.* 2. v. 115.—*Martial.* 7. epigr. 12.—*Athen.* 1, 3, 4, &c.—*Fabr. B. Gr.* 1. 2. c. 15.—*Sax. Onom.* 1. p. 14. [A bust of this poet is to be seen in the Vatican.——A son of Nestor, killed by Memnon in the Trojan war. *Homer. Il.* 2. 823.——A Greek historian who wrote a chronological table, and other works, about the time of the 20th or 30th Olympiad. *Clem. Alex.* 1. *Strom.* —*Euseb.* 10. *Prep. Ev.*——A Lacedæmonian poet, who flourished at Rome in the age of Tullus Hostilius.

ARCHIME'DES, a famous geometrician of Syracuse. When Marcellus, the Roman consul, besieged Syracuse, Archimedes constructed machines which greatly annoyed the enemy. When the town was taken, the Roman general offered a reward to him who should bring the philosopher alive and safe into his presence. All these precautions were, unhappily, useless. Archimedes was so deeply engaged in solving a problem, that he was even ignorant that the enemy were in possession of the town; and a soldier, without knowing who he was, killed him, because he refused to follow him, B.C. 212. Marcellus raised a monument over him, and placed upon it a cylinder and a sphere; but the place remained long unknown, till Cicero, during his quæstorship in Sicily, found it near one of the gates of Syracuse, surrounded with thorns and brambles. The manner in which Archimedes discovered how much brass a goldsmith had mixed with gold in making a golden crown for Hiero king of Syracuse, is well known to every one acquainted with hydrostatics, as well as the pumping screw which still bears its name. Many of his works are extant, especially his treatises *desphæra & cylindro, circuli dimensio, de lineis spiralibus, de quadratura paraboles, de numero arenæ,* &c.; the best edition of which is that of David Rivaltius, fol. Paris, 1615. An edition of Archimedes, founded on the basis of Torelli's edition, issued from the Clarendon press in 1793. *Cic. Tusc.* 1. c. 25. *De N. D.* 2. c. 34.—*Liv.* 24. c. 34.—*Quintil.* 1. c. 10.—*Vitruv.* 9. c. 3.—*Polyb.* 7.—*Plut. in Marcel.*—*Val. Max.* 8. c. 7.—*Lactant.* 2. c. 5.—*Fabr. B. Gr.* 1. 3. c. 22.—*Sax. Onom.* 1. p. 117. [Of Archimedes, a bust exists in the Capitol.]——A grammarian of Tralles, who published commentaries on Homer, and some works on mechanics. *Suidas.*

ARCHIN'ARA, a city of India within the Ganges. *Ptol.*

ARCHI'NUS, a man who, when he was appointed to distribute new arms among the populace of Argos, raised a mercenary band, and made himself absolute. *Polyæn* 3. c. 8.——A rhetorician of Athens. *Schol. in Aristoph. Ran.*

ARCHIPEL'AGUS, that part of any sea where a great number of islands are interspersed; such as that part of the Mediterranean which lies between Greece and Asia Minor, and is generally called Mare Ægæum.

ARCHIP'OLIS, a soldier who conspired against Alexander with Dymnus. *Curt.* 6. c. 7.

ARCHIP'PA, a courtezan who gained the affections of Sophocles in his old age. Her attachment to the poet excited the ridicule of her former lover, who observed that she was like owls which love to perch on tombs. *Athen.* 13.

ARCHIP'PE, a city of the Marsi, destroyed by an earthquake, and lost in the lake Fucinus. *Plin.* 3. c. 19.

ARCHIP'PUS, a king of Italy, from whom, perhaps, the town Archippe received its name. *Virg. Æn.* 7. v. 752.——A philosopher of Thebes, pupil to Pythagoras.—— The third perpetual Archon at Athens.——A comic poet of Athens, of whose eight comedies, only one obtained the prize. *Fabr. B. Gr.* 1. 2. c. 22.——A philosopher in the age of Trajan.

ARCHI'TIS, a name under which Venus was worshipped by the Assyrians. *Macrob Sat.* 1. c. 21.

AR'CHON, one of Alexander's generals, who received the province of Babylon, at the general division after the king's death. *Diod.* 18.

ARCHON'TES, the name of the chief magistrates of Athens. They were nine in number, and none were chosen but such as were descended from ancestors who had been free citizens of the republic for three generations. They were also to be without deformity in all the parts and members of their bodies; and were obliged to produce testimonials of their dutiful behaviour to their parents, of the services which they had rendered to their country, and of the competency of their fortune to support their dignity. They took a solemn oath, that they would observe the laws, administer justice with impartiality, and never suffer themselves to be corrupted. If they ever received bribes, they were compelled by the laws to dedicate to the god of Delphi a statue of gold of equal weight with their own body. They all had the power of punishing malefactors with death. The chief among them was called Archon. The year took its denomination from him; he determined all causes between man and wife, and took care of legacies and wills; he provided for orphans, protected the injured, and punished drunkenness with uncommon severity. If he suffered himself to be intoxicated during the time of his office, the misdemeanour was punished with death. The second of the archons was called Basileus. It was his office to keep good order, and to remove all causes of quarrel in the families of those who were dedicated to the service of the gods. The profane and the impious were brought before his tribunal; and he offered public sacrifices for the good of the state. He assisted at the celebratian of the Eleusinian festivals, and other religious ceremonies. It was required that his wife should be related to the whole people of Athens, and of a pure and unsullied life. He had a vote in the council of the Areopagus, but was obliged to sit among the members without his crown. The Polemarch was another archon of inferior dignity. He had the care of all foreigners, and provided a sufficient maintenance, from the public treasury, for the families of those who had lost their lives in the defence of their country. These three chief archons generally chose each of them two persons of respectable character, and of an advanced age, whose counsels and advice might assist and support them in their public capacity. The six other archons were indiscriminately called Thesmothetæ, and received complaints against persons accused of impiety, bribery, and ill behaviour. They settled all disputes between the citizens, redressed the wrongs of strangers, and forbade any laws to be enforced, but such as were conducive to the safety of the state. These officers were first appointed after the death of king Codrus. Their power was originally for life, but afterwards it was limited to ten years, and at last to one year. After some time, the qualifications which were required to be an archon were not strictly observed. Adrian, before he was elected emperor of Rome, was made archon at Athens, though a foreigner; and the same honours were conferred upon Plutarch. The perpetual archons, after the death of Codrus, were: Medon, whose office began B.C. 1070; Acastus, 1050; Archippus, 1014; Thersippus, 995; Phorbas, 954; Megacles, 923; Diognetus, 893: Pherecles, 865; Ariphron, 846; Thespieus, 826; Agamestor, 799; Æschylus, 778; Alcmæon, 756; after whose death the archons were decennial, the first of whom was Charops, who came into office 753; Æsimedes, 744; Clidicus, 734; Hippomenes, 724; Leocrates, 714; Apsander, 704; Eryxias, 694; after this the office became annual, and of these annual archons Creon was the first. *Aristoph. in Nub. & Avid.—Vell Paterc.* 1. 2.—*Justin.* 2. c. 6.—*Meursius de Arch.—Euseb. Chr.* 1.—*Pollux.* 8. c. 9.—*Sigon. de Rep. Athen.* 4. c. 3.—*Schol. Aristoph.—Plut. Sympos.* 1.—*Demosth.—Lysias.*

AR'CHYLUS, a general of Dionysius the elder. *Diod.* 14.

ARCHY'TAS, a musician of Mitylene. *Athen.* 13. 8.—*Laert.* 8. 82.——The son of Histiæus of Tarentum, was a follower of the Pythagorean philosophy, and an able astronomer and geometrician. He redeemed his master, Plato, from the power of ihe tyrant Dionysius; and for his virtues was seven times chosen, by his fellow citizens, governor of Tarentum. He was the reputed inventor of the screw and of the pulley. He perished in a shipwreck on the coast of Apulia, about 394 years B.C. A fragment of his writings has been preserved by Porphyry. *Horat.* 1. od. 28.—*Diog. in vit.—Cic. de Orat.* 3. c. 34. *Fin.* 2. c. 14. l. 5. c. 29. *Tusc.* 5. c. 22.—*Fabr. B. Gr.* 2. c. 13.—*Sax. Onom.* 1. p. 61.——A poet of Amphissa, who wrote epigrams. *Plut. Quæst. Gr.—Laert.* 8. 82.——A writer *de re rusticâ*, praised by *Laertius, Varro,* and *Columella.*

AR'CI, a town of Hispania Tarraconensis, called Arsi by *Ptolemy*, and now Harisa.

ARCIL'ACIS, a town of Hispania Bœtica, now Alcala Horra. *Ptol.*

ARCIROES'SA, a city of Heraclia, in Pontus. *Steph.*

ARCIT'ENENS, an epithet of Apollo, from his bearing a *bow. Virg. Æn.* 3. v. 75.

ARCI'VA, a town of Dacia. *Ptol.*

ARCOBRI'GA, a town of Lusitania, now Alcasor. *Id.* ——A town of Celtiberia, in Spain, now Arcoz. *Id.*

ARCONE'SUS, an island of Caria, called also Aspis. *Steph.* Also Arconne'sus.

ARC'TANES, a people of Epirus. *Id.*

ARCTI'NUS, a Milesian poet, said to be pupil to Homer. *Dionys. Hal.* 1.

ARC'TON, a name of the island of Cyzicus. *Steph.*

ARCTOPH'YLAX, a star near the great bear, called also Bootes. *Cic. de Nat. D.* 2. c. 42.

ARC'TOS, a mountain near the Propontis, said to have been inhabited by giants and monsters.—— The name of two celestial constellations near the north pole, commonly called Ursa Major and Minor; aupposed to be Arc s and his mother, who were made constellations by Jupiter. *Virg. G.* 1. —*Aratus.—Ovid. Fast.* 3. v. 107.

ARCTU'RUS, a star near the tail of the great bear, the rising and setting of which were generally supposed to portend great tempests. *Horat.* 3. od. 1. The name is derived from its situation, ἄρκτ® *ursus*, οὐρὰ *cauda. Pliny* tells us that it rose in his age on the 12th, or, according to *Columella*, on the 5th of September. It rises now about the beginning of October.

ARDABIG'ARA, a town and nation of Assyria. *Procopius.*

AR'DALUS, a son of Vulcan, said to have been the inventor of the pipe. He gave it to the Muses, who on that account have been called Ardalides and Ardaliotides. *Paus.* 2. c. 31.

ARDA'NIA, a country of Ægypt. *Strab.*

AR'DANIS, a promontory of Marmarica, now Capo Rameda. *Ptol.*

ARDAXA'NUS, a small river of Illyricum. *Polyb.*

AR'DEA, formerly Ardua, a town of Latium, built by Danae, or, according to some, by a son of Ulysses and Circe. It was the capital of Rutuli. Some soldiers set it on fire; and the inhabitants publicly reported, that their city had been changed into a bird, called by the Latins Ardea. It was rebuilt, and became a rich and magnificent city. A road called Ardeatina, branched from the Via Appia, and communicated to Ardea. *Cic. N. D.* 3. c. 47.—*Festus de V. Sig.—C. Nep. in Attic.* 14. —*Liv.* 1. c. 57. l. c. 71. l. 4. c. 9, &c.—*Virg. Æn.* 7. v. 412, &c.—*Ovid. Met.* 14. v. 573.—*Strab.* 5. —*Plin.* 5. c. 5. l. 35. c. 3. & 10.

ARDERIC'CA, a small town on the Euphrates, north of Babylon.

ARDIÆ'I, a people of Illyricum, whose capital was called Ardia. *Strab.* 7.

AR'DICES, a painter of Corinth. *Plin.* 35. c. 3.

ARDIN'IUM or ARDUN'IUM, a city in the plain of Thebes. *Steph.*

ARDISTAM'RA, a city of Galatia. *Ptol.*

ARDI'SUS, a king of Lydia, of the dynasty of the Heraclidæ, said by *Eusebius* to have lived in the first Olympiad.

AR'DIUS, a mountain running through the middle of Dalmatia. It is now Rosas. *Strab.*.

ARDO'NEA, a town of Apulia. *Liv.* 24. c. 20.

ARDO'TIUM, a town ot Illyricum, now Magonicha. *Ptol.*

AR'DUA. *Vid.* Ardea.

AR'DUBA, a town of Dalmatia, taken by Tiberius. *Diod.* 1. 56.

ARDUEN'NA, now Ardenne, a large forest of Belgic Gaul, which extended fifty miles from the Rhine to the borders of the Nervii, between the Meuse and the Moselle. *Tacit.* 8. *Ann.* c. 42.—*Cæs. Bell. Gall.* 6. c. 29.

ARDUI'NE, the goddess of hunting among the Gauls. She was represented with the same attributes as the Diana of Rome, and probably received her name from the forest Arduenna. *Gesner. Thes.—Erud. Ling. Lat.*

ARDYEN'SES, a nation near the Rhone. *Polyb.* 3.

AR'DYS, a son of Gyges, king of Lydia, who reigned 49 years, took Priene, and made war against Miletus. *Herodot.* 1. c. 15.

A'RE, a region of Arabia Felix.——An island in the Arabian Gulph. *Ptol.*

ARE'A, (from Ἄρης,) a surname of Minerva, from a temple which she had on Mars' hill, erected by Orestes, after he had been acquitted by the Areopagites. *Paus.* 1. c. 28.——An island of Pontus. ——A fountain of Thebes. *Steph.*

AREAC'IDÆ, a nation of Numidia. *Polyb.*

A'REAS, a general chosen by the Greeks against Ætolia. *Justin.* 24. c. 1.

AREC'CA, a city of Susiana, abounding in naphtha. *Plin.—Tibul.* 4. ep. 1. v. 283.—*Ptol.*

ARECOM'ICI, a people of Gallia Narbonensis, whose chief town was Nemausus, now Nismes. *Mela*, 2. c. 7.—*Cluver.* 2. c. 9.

ARE'FA, a city of Phœnicia. *Lib. Notit.*

ARE'GIA, a city of Hispania Tarraconensis, now Amaya. *Isador.*

ARE'GON, a painter of Corinth. *Strab.* l. 8.

AREG'ONIS, the mother of Mopsus by A.npyx. *Orph. in Argon.*

AREITH'OUS, a king of Arne in Peloponnesus, father of Menestius, who perished at the Trojan war, by the hand of Paris. *Hom. Il.* 7. v. 9.-——An attendant of Rigmus, son of Pircus of Thrace, who assisted Priam against the Greeks. *Id.* 20. v. 487.

ARE'IUS, one of the Argonauts. *Orpheus.*

ARELA'TUM or ARELA'TE, a town of Gallia Narbonensis, now Arles, on the Rhone. Its founder is said by some to have been Arulus, grandson of Priam, by others, Areli, the son of Gad; but it was most probably founded by the Phoceans. *Plin.* 10. c. 42.—*Strab.* 4.—*Mela*, 2. c. 5.

AREL'LIUS, a celebrated painter of Rome, in the age of Augustus. He painted the goddesses in the form of his mistresses. *Plin.* 35. c. 10.——A miser mentioned by *Horace.*

AREM'BUS, a town of India within the Ganges. *Ptol.*

AREMOR'ICA, a part of Gaul, situate at the north of the Loire, and now known by the name of Bretagne or Britany. *Cæs. B. G.* 7. c. 75.—*Plin.* 4. c. 17.

AREMPHÆI, or **ARGIMPÆI**, a people of Scythia, who lived upon berries, &c. *Mela*, 3. c. 5.—*Herod*.4.

ARE'NA or **ARE'NE**, a city of Messenia. *Hom. Il.* 2. v. 591.—*Strab*.—*Plin*. 4. c. 5. &c.

AREN'ACUM, a town of ancient Germany, now Arnhem. *Tacit. Hist*. 5. c. 20. Also Arena'cum.

AREN'DÆ, a city of Lycia. *Ptol.*

AREOPAGITÆ, the judges of the Areopagus. Its name was derived from ἄρεος πάγος, the hill of Mars, because Mars was the first who was tried there, for the murder of Hallirrhotius. Some say that the place received the name of Areopagus, because the Amazons pitched their camp there, and offered sacrifices to their progenitor Mars, when they besieged Athens; and others maintain, that the name was given to the spot, because Mars was the god of bloodshed, war, and murder, which were generally punished by that court. The precise time at which this celebrated seat of justice was instituted is unknown. Some suppose that Cecrops, the founder of Athens, first established it; while others give the credit of it to Cranaus, and others to Solon. The number of judges that composed this august assembly is not known. They were limited according to the opinions of different authors, to nine, to thirty-one, to fifty-one, and sometimes to a greater number. The most worthy and religious of the Athenians were admitted as members, and such archons as had discharged their duty with care and faithfulness. If any of them were convicted of immorality, or they were seen sitting at a tavern, they were expelled from the assembly; though the dignity of a judge of the Areopagus always was for life. The Areopagites took cognizance of murders, impiety, and immoral behaviour; and particularly of idleness, which they deemed the cause of all vice. They watched over the due execution of the laws, and had the management of the public treasury; they had also the liberty of rewarding the virtuous, and of inflicting severe punishment upon such as blasphemed against the gods, or slighted the celebration of the holy mysteries. They always sat in the open air, because they took cognizance of murder; and by the laws of Athens, it was not permitted for the murderer and accuser to be both under the same roof. This custom might also have originated from an idea that the persons of the judges were sacred, and they were consequently afraid of contracting pollution, by conversing in the same house with men who had been guilty of shedding innocent blood. Opposite to them were erected two stones, on which the accuser and the accused were seated; and on two columns near them were engraved the laws, according to the tenor of which they were to pass judgment. Their decision was delivered secretly; and two urns, one of brass and the other of wood, were placed to receive the pebbles, which, according as they were black or white, decreed condemnation or absolution. They always heard causes and passed sentence in the night, that they might not be prepossessed in favour of the plaintiff or of the defendant by seeing them. Whatever causes were pleaded before them, were to be divested of all oratory and elaborate speaking, lest eloquence should charm their ears, and corrupt their judgment. Hence arose the most just and impartial decisions; and their sentence was deemed sacred and inviolable, and the plaintiff and defendant departed equally convinced of its justice. The Areopagites generally sat on the 27th, 28th, and 29th days of every month. Their authority continued in its original state, till Pericles, who was refused admittance among them, resolved, in revenge, to lessen their consequence, and destroy their power. From that time, the morals of the Athenians gradually became corrupted, and the Areopagites were no longer conspicuous for their virtue and justice; and when they censured the debaucheries of Demetrius, one of the family at Phalereus, he plainly told them, that if they wished to make a reform at Athens, they must begin at home. *Juv*. 9. v. 102.—*Meursius, Areop*. 1,—*Xenoph*. 3. c. 5.—*Solin*. 13.—*Paus*. 1. c. 28.—*Lucian. de Gymn*.—*Lysias de Eratos*.—*Cic. de Off*. 1. c. 22. *ad Att*. 1. ep. 14.—*Suidas in Verbo*.—*Apollod*. 3.—*Ælian, V. H*. 5. c. 15 & 18.—*Pollux*, 8. c. 9 & 10.—*Scholiast. Æsch. in Eumen*. 561.—*Macrob. Sat*. 7. c. 1.—*Mitford's Hist. of Greece*. 1. p. 417.

AREOP'AGUS, a hill in the neighbourhood of Athens. *Vid*. Areopagitæ.

ARE'OS NE'SUS, an island of Pontus. *Steph.*

A'RES, a native of Cyzicus, slain with his brother Melanthus by Telamon, in a nocturnal conflict. *Val. Flac*. 3. v. 203.

A'res, *etis*, a region of Eubœa. *Steph.*

ARESCU'SA, a woman said to have been changed into a man, and to have received the name of Arescon. *Plin*. 7. c. 4.

AREST'Æ, a people of India, conquered by Alexander. *Justin*. 12. c. 8.

ARESTA'NUS, a countryman, whose goat suckled Æsculapius, when exposed by his mother. *Paus*. 2. c. 26.

ARESTOR'IDES, a patronymic given to the hundred-eyed Argus, as son of Arestor. *Ovid. Met*. 1. v. 584.

AR'ETA, the daughter, or according to others, mother to Aristippus, the philosopher. *Laert*. 2.—*Fabr*. 2. c. 2. *Art*. Aristippus.——A daughter of Dionysius, who married Dion. She was thrown into the sea. *Plut. in Dion*.——A female philosopher of Cyrene, B.C. 377.——A daughter of Rhexenor, descended from Neptune; she married her uncle Alcinous, by whom she had Nausica. *Homer. Od*. 7 & 8.—*Apollod*. 1.

ARETÆ'US, a celebrated physician of Cappadocia. The age in which he lived is not precisely ascertained: as some assert that he flourished in the time of Augustus; others, in the reign of Trajan or Adrian. His treatise on agues has been much and deservedly admired. The best editions of his works which are extant, are those of Boerhaave, L. Bat. fol. 1735, and of Wigan, Oxon, 1723, an edition highly commended by *Fabricius B. Gr*. 4. c. 4.—*Sax. Onom*. 1. p. 273.

ARETAPH'ILA, the wife of Melanippus, a priest of Cyrene. Nicocrates murdered her husband, to marry her; but she was so attached to the memory of Melanippus, that she endeavoured to poison him, and at last caused him to be assassinated by his brother Lysander, whom she married. Lysander proved as cruel as his brother, upon which Aretaphila ordered him to be thrown into the sea. After this, she retired to a private station. *Plut. de Virtut. Mulier*.—*Polyæn*. 8. c. 38.

ARETA'TES, a Cnidian, who wrote a history of Macedonia, besides a treatise on islands. *Plut. in par. Min*. c. 11.

ARE'TE or **AR'ETE**, *Vid*. Areta.

ARE'TES, one of Alexander's officers. *Curt*. 4. c. 15.

ARETHU'SA, a nymph of Elis, daughter of Oceanus, and one of Diana's attendants. The god of the river became enamoured of her, and pursued her over the mountains and the country. Arethusa implored the assistance of Diana, who changed her into a fonntain. The Alpheus immediately mingled his stream with hers; and Diana opened a secret passage under the earth and under the sea, through which the waters of Arethusa disappeared, and rose in the island of Ortygia, in Sicily. The river Alpheus followed her also under the sea, and rose likewise in Ortygia; so that, as mythologists relate, whatever is thrown into the Alpheus in Elis, rises again, after some time, in the fountain Arethusa, near Syracuse. *Vid*. Alpheus. *Ovid. Met*. 5. fab. 10.—*Athen*. 7.—*Virg. Æn* 3.—*Paus*.——One of the Hesperides. *Apollod*. 2. c. 5.——A daughter of Herileus, mother of Abas by Neptune. *Hygin*. fab. 157.——One of Actæon's dogs. *Hygin*. fab. 181.——A lake of Upper Armenia, near the fountains of the Tigris. Nothing, according to some authors, could sink under its waters. *Plin*. 2. c. 103.——A town of Macedonia, at a small distance from the mouth of the Strymon, now Tadino.——A town of Syria, on the borders of the Orontes. *Ptol*. 5. c. 13.—*Plin*. 5. c. 23. l. 6. c. 28.

ARETI'NUM, a Roman colony in Etruria, now Arezzo. *Ital*. 5. v. 123.—*Cluver*. 3. c. 3.

ARE'TIUM. *Vid*. Aretinum.

ARE'TUS, a son of Nestor and Anaxibia. *Hom. Od*. 3. v. 413.——A Trojan killed by Automedon, during the Trojan war. *Hom. Il*. 17. v. 494.——A famous warrior, whose only weapon was an iron club. He was treacherously killed by Lycurgus, king of Arcadia. *Paus*. 8. c. 11.—*Scholiast. Apollon*. 1. *Arg*.

AREV'ACÆ, a people of Hispania Tarraconensis. *Ptol*.—*Plin*. 3. c. 3.

A'REUS, a king of Sparta, preferred, in the succession, to Cleonymus, brother of Acrotatus, who had made an alliance with Pyrrhus. He rendered assistance to Athens when Antigonus besieged it, and died at Corinth. *Paus.* 3. c. 6.—*Plut.*——A king of Sparta, who succeeded his father Acrotatus the Second, and was succeeded by Leonidas, son of Cleonymus.——A philosopher of Alexandria, intimate with Augustus. *Sueton.*——A poet of Laconia.——An orator, mentioned by *Quintilian.* ——A river of Bithynia. *Plin.* 5. c. 32.

ARGADI'NA, a town of Margiana. *Ptol.*

ARGÆ'US, a son of Perdiccas, who succeeded his father in the kingdom of Macedonia. *Justin.* 7. c. 1. ——A mountain of Cappadocia, covered with perpetual snows. At the bottom of it was the capital of the country, called Maxara. *Claudian.*——A son of Ptolemy, killed by his brother. *Paus.* 1. ——A son of Licymnius. *Apollod.* 2.

ARGA'IS, an island near Lycia. *Steph.*——A small island near Canopus. *Id.*

AR'GALUS, a king of Sparta, son of Amyclas. *Paus.* 3. c. 1.

ARGA'NIA, a city of India. *Steph.*

ARGANTHO'NA, a huntress of Cios, in Bithynia, whom Rhesus married before he went to the Trojan war. When she heard of his death, she died in despair. *Parthen. Erotic.* c. 36.

ARGANTHO'NIUS, a mountain of Mysia, near Chius. *Strab.* The *Scholiast* on *Apollonius,* l. 1., calls it Arganthonïum.

ARGANTHO'NIUS, a king of Tartessus, near Cadiz; who reigned 80 years, and, according to *Pliny,* 7. c. 48. lived 120; according to *Anacreon,* mentioned by *Pliny,* (7. c. 48.) 150; and 300, according to *Silius Italicus,* 3. v. 396.

ARGARADAU'CA, a city of Media. *Ptol.*

ARGAR'ICUS SI'NUS, a bay of India, within the Ganges. *Id.* It is now the bay of Bengal.

AR'GAS, a name given to Demosthenes by Æschines from his uncouth deportment. *Hesych.*

AR'GE, a beautiful huntress changed into a stag by Apollo. *Hygin.* fab. 205.——One of the Cyclopes. *Hesiod.*——A daughter of Thespius, by whom Hercules had two sons. *Apollod.* 2. c. 35.——A nymph, daughter of Jupiter and Juno. *Apollod.* 1.

ARGEA'THÆ, a small village of Arcadia. *Paus.* 8 c. 23.

ARGE'I, a place at Rome where the bodies of certain Argives were buried, and where also some sacred ceremonies were observed in honor of the gods. *Varro de L. L.* 4. c. 8.—*Ovid. Fast.* 3. v. 791.—*Liv.* 1. c. 21.—*Festus de V. Sig.*

ARGE'LIA, a city of Germany. *Ptol.* It is now Torgaw, or, according to some, Erdfort.

ARGEN'NUM, a promontory of Ionia, now Capo Stellaro, or Capo Bianco.——A promontory of Sicily, now Capo di S. Alessio.——A promontory of Lesbus. *Strab.*

ARGENNU'SA, an island on the coast of Troas. *Steph.*

ARGENTA'NUM, an inland city of the Brutii, now S. Marco.

ARGENTA'RIUS, now Argentaro, a mountain of Tuscany.

ARGENTE'OLA, a city of Asturia, in Spain. *Ptol.* It is called Argentiolum by *Antoninus,* and is now Medules. Also Argente'olum.

ARGEN'TEUS, a river of Gallia Narbonensis, now Argenton. *Ptol.*

ARGEN'TEUS, MONS, a mountain of Hispania Tarraconensis, in which the Bætis rises. *Plin.* 3. c. 1.—*Bochart. de Phœn.* p. 666.

ARGENTI'NI, a people of Calabria. *Plin.* 3. c. 11.

ARGENTI'NUS, an imaginary deity at Rome, called the son of the goddess Pecunia, and invoked by those who were engaged in commercial affairs. *August. de Civ. D.* 4. c. 21.

ARGENTORA'TUM, an ancient town of Gaul, on the Rhine, now Strasburg, in Alsace, famous for its buildings and population.

AR'GES, a son of Cœlus and Terra, who is said to have had only one eye, in his forehead. *Apollod.* 1. c. 1.

ARGESTRATUS, a king of Lacedæmon, who reigned 35 years.

ARGE'US, a son of Perdiccas, king of Macedonia. *Justin.* 7. c. 2.—*Herodot.* 8. c. 139.——The father of Polymeles, killed by Patroclus. *Homer. Il.* 16. v. 417.——*Vid.* Argæus.

AR'GI (*plur. masc.*) *Vid.* Argos.

ARGI'A, daughter of Adrastus, married Polynices. When he was killed in the Theban war, she buried his body in the night, against the positive orders of Creon; for which action she was punished with death. Theseus revenged her death by killing Creon. *Hygin.* fab. 69 & 72.—*Stat. Theb.* 12. *Vid.* Antigone, & Creon.——A country of Peloponnesus, called also Argolis, of which Argos was the capital.——One of the Oceanides. *Hygin. Præf.*——The wife of Inachus, and mother of Io. *Id.* fab. 145.——The mother of Argos, by Polybus, *Id. ibid* A daughter of Autesion, wife of Aristodemus, and mother of Eurysthenes and Procles. *Apollod.* 2. —*Paus.* 4. c. 3.

AR'GIAS, a man who founded Chalcedon, A.U.C. 148.

ARGIDA'VA, a town of Dacia, now Argisch. *Ptol.*

AR'GILA, a city of Caria. *Steph.*——A town of Mauritania.

ARGILE'TUM, a place at Rome, near the Palatium, where the tradesmen generally kept their shops. The word is derived from *Argi letum,* because an Argive was said to have been slain there. *Virg. Æn.* 8. v. 345.—*Martial.* 1. epigr. 4.

ARGIL'IA, a village of Attica. *Hesych.*

ARGIL'II, a colony of the Andrii, in Thrace. *Thucyd.* 4. c. 103.

ARGIL'IUM, an inland town of Bithynia. *Ptol.*

ARGIL'IUS, a youth greatly beloved by Pausanias. He revealed his master's correspondence with the Persian king, to the ephori, and was put to death. *C. Nep. in Paus.*

ARGIL'LUS, a mountain of Ægypt, near the Nile. *Plut.*

AR'GILUS, a city of Emathia, not far from the mouth of the Strymon. *Herodot.* 7. c. 115.

ARGI'NA, a town of the Locri Ozoli. *Plin.* 4. c. 3.

ARGINU'SA, a city of Æolis, opposite Lesbus. *Schol. Aristoph. Ran.*

ARGINU'SÆ, three small islands near the shores of Asia Minor, between Mitylene and Methymna, where the Lacedæmonian fleet was conquered by Conon the Athenian. *Strab.* 13.—*Plin.* 5. c. 31.

ARGI'OPE, a nymph of mount Parnassus, by the musician Philammon, the son of Apollo, and mother of Thamyris. *Paus.* 4. c. 33.——A daughter of Teuthras, king of Mysia.

ARGIPHON'TES, a surname given to Mercury, because he killed the hundred-eyed Argus, by order of Jupiter. *Arnob.* 6.—*Macrob. Sat.* 1. c. 19.

ARGIPPÆ'I, a nation among the Sauromatians, who were said to have been born bald, and with flat noses. They lived upon trees. *Herodot.* 4. c. 23.

ARGI'RI, a city of India within the Ganges. *Ptol.*

ARGIRUN'TUM, now Pescha, a city of Liburnia, on the shores of the Adriatic. *Cluver.*

ARGITH'EA, a city of Epirus, on the borders of Thessaly.

ARGI'VA, a surname of Juno, under which she was worshipped at Argos. She had also a temple at Sparta, consecrated to her by Eurydice, daughter of Lacedæmon. *Paus.* 4. c. 13.—*Virg. Æn.* 3. v. 547.

ARGI'VI, the inhabitants of the city of Argos and the neighbouring country. The word is indiscriminately applied by the poets to all the inhabitants of Greece.

AR'GIUS, a steward of Galba, who privately interred the body of his master in his gardens. *Tac. Hist.* 1. c. 49. Also Argi'us.

ARGIZ'ALA, a city of Galatia. *Ptol.*

AR'GO, the name of the famous ship which carried Jason and his fifty-four companions to Colchis, when they engaged in the recovery of the golden fleece. The derivation of the word Argo has been the source of frequent disputes. Some derive it from Argos, the person who first proposed the expedition, and who built the ship. Others maintain that the vessel was built at Argos; whence its name. *Cicero, Tusc.* 1. c. 20. calls it Argo, because it carried Grecians, commonly called Argives, and *Diodorus,* 4. derives the word from ἀργός, which signifies *swift.* *Ptolemy* says, but falsely, that Hercules built the ship, and called it Argo, after a son of Jason, who bore the same name. The ship Argo had fifty oars. According to many authors, she had a beam on her prow, cut out of the forest of Dodona by Minerva, which, as it had the power of giving oracles to the Argonauts, warned them that they never should reach their country, till Jason had been purified of the murder of Absyrtus. This ship, according to the general opinion of ancient writers, was the first that ever sailed on the sea. After the expedition was finished, Jason ordered her to be drawn aground at the isthmus of Corinth, and consecrated to the god of tne sea. The poets have made her a constellation in heaven, and astronomers have adopted the name. Jason was killed by a beam which fell from the ship, as he slept on the ground near it. *Hygin.* fab. 14. *A. P.* 2. c. 37.—*Catul. de Nupt. Pel. & Thet.*—*Val. Flacc.* 1. v. 93, &c.—*Phædr.* 4. fab. 6.—*Seneca in Medeâ.*—*Apollon. Argon.*—*Apollod.* 1.—*Cic. de Nat.D. Tusc.* 1. c. 20.—*Claudian. in Pan.*—*Scholiast. Apollon. Arg.* 4.—*Ovid. Met.* 8. v. 302.—*Plin.* 7. c. 56.—*Manil.* 1.—*Diod.* 4.

ARGO'DA, a city of Taurica Chersonesus. *Ptol.*

ARGOLI'ICUS SI'NUS, a bay on the eastern coast of Peloponnesus.

AR'GOLIS or AR'GIA, now Romania, a country of Peloponnesus, between Arcadia and the Ægæan sea. Its chief city was called Argos.

AR'GON, one of the descendants of Hercules, who reigned in Lydia 505 years before Gyges. *Herodot.* 1. c. 7.

ARGONAU'TÆ a name given to those ancient heroes who accompanied Jason in his expedition on board the ship Argo to Colchis, about 79 years before the taking of Troy, or 1263. B.C. When Jason, the son of Æson, demanded of his uncle Pelias the crown which he had obtained by usurpation, (*vid.* Pelias, Jason, Æson,) Pelias said that he would restore it to him, provided he avenged the death of their common relation Phryxus, whom Æetes had basely murdered in Colchis. Jason, who was in the vigour of youth, and of an ambitious disposition, cheerfully undertook the expedition, and embarked with all the young princes of Greece in the ship Argo. In their way they stopped ut the island of Lemnus, where they remained two years, and raised a new race of men from the Lemnian women, who had murdered their husbands. *Vid.* Hipsipyle. After they had left Lemnus, they visited Samothrace, where they offered sacrifices to the gods, and thence passed to Troas and to Cyzicum. Here they met with a favourable reception from Cyzicus, the king of the country; but the night after their departure they were driven back by a storm on the coast of Cyzicum, and the inhabitants, supposing them to be their enemies the Pelasgi, furiously attacked them. In this nocturnal engagement the slaughter was great, and Cyzicus was killed by the hand of Jason, who, to expiate the murder which he had ignorantly committed, buried him in a magnificent manner, and offered a sacrifice to the mother of the gods, in whose honour he built a temple on mount Dindymus. From Cyzicum, the argonauts visited Bebrycia, otherwise called Bithynia, where Pollux accepted the challenge of Amycus, king of the country, in the combat of the cæstus, and slew him. They were driven from Bebrycia, by a storm, to Salmydessa, on the coast of Thrace, where they delivered Phineus, king of the place, from the dreadful persecution of the harpies. Phineus directed their course through the difficult passage of the Cyanean rocks, or the Symplegades, (*vid.* Cyaneæ,) and they safely entered the Euxine Sea. They visited the country of the Mariandynians, where Lycus reigned; and there lost two of their companions, Idmon, and Tiphys, their pilot. After they had left this coast, they were driven upon the island of Arecia, where they found the children of Phryxus, whom Æetes, their grandfather, had sent to Greece, to take possession of their father's kingdom. From this island they at last arrived safe in Æa, the capital of Colchis. When Jason had obtained the golden fleece, he immediately set sail with Medea. He was soon pursued by Absyrtus, the king's son, who overtook them in their flight, and was seized and murdered by Jason and Medea. After the murder of Absyrtus, the fugitives entered the Palus Mæotis, and by pursuing their course toward the left (according to the improbable accounts of poets, who were ignorant of geography,) they came to the island Peucestes, and to that of Circe. Here Circe informed Jason, that the murder of Absyrtus, from which she refused to purify him, was the cause of all his calamities. Soon after, they entered the Mediterranean by the columns of Hercules, and passed the straits of Charybdis and Scylla, where they must have perished, had not Tethys, the mistress of Peleus, one of the Argonauts, delivered them. They were preserved from the Sirens by the eloquence of Orpheus, and arrived in the island of the Phæacians, where they met the enemy's fleet, which had continued their pursuit by a different course. In the conference which here took place, it was resolved that Medea should be restored if she had not been actually married to Jason; but the wife of Alcinous, the king of the country, being appointed umpire between the Colchians and the Argonauts, had the marriage privately consummated by night, and declared that the claims of Æetes to Medea were now void. From Phæacia the Argonauts came to the bay of Ambracia, whence they were driven by a storm upon the coast of Africa, and after many disasters, they at last came in sight of the promontory of Malea in the Peloponnesus, where Jason was purified from the murder of Absyrtus, and soon after arrived safe in Thessaly. The impracticability of such a voyage is well known. *Apollonius Rhodius* gives another account equally improbable. He says that they sailed from the Euxine up one of the mouths of the Danube, and that Absyrtus pursued them by entering another mouth of the river. After they had continued their voyage for some leagues, the waters decreased, and they were obliged to carry the ship Argo across the country to the Adriatic, upwards of 150 miles. Here they met with Absyrtus, who had pursued the same measures, and conveyed his ships in like manner over the land. Absyrtus was immediately put to death; and soon after the beam of Dodona (*Vid.* Argo) gave an oracle, that Jason should never return home if he was not previously purified from the murder. Upon this they sailed to the island of Æa, where Circe, who was sister to Æetes, purified him without knowing who he was. There is a third traditlon, which maintains that they returned to Colchis a second time, and visited several places of Asia. This famous expedition was, on account of its importance, and the dangers which attended it, much celebrated in the ancient ages of the world. It has employed the pen of many writers; and among the historians, *Diodorus Siculus, Strabo, Apollodorus,* and *Justin;* and among the poets, *Onamacritus* (more generally called *Orpheus*) *Apollonius Rhodius, Pindar,* and *Valerius Flaccus,* have given interesting and particular accounts of its most remarkable particulars. The number of the Argonants is not exactly known. *Apollonius* and *Diodorus* say that they were 54, *Tzetzes* 50, but *Apollodorus* only 45. The following list is drawn from the various authors who have made mention of the Argonautic expedition: Jason, son of Æson, as is well known, was the chief of the expedition. His companions were Acastus son of Pelias, Actor son of Hippasus, Admetus son of Pheres, Æsculapius, son of Apollo, Ætalides son of Mercury and Eupoleme, Almenus son of Mars, Amphiaraus son of Œcleus, Amphidamus son of Aleus, Amphion son of Hyperasius, Anceus a son of Lycurgus, and another of the same name. Areus, Argus the builder of the ship Argo, Argus son of Phryxus, Armenus, Ascalaphas son of Mars, Asterion son of Cometes, Asterius son of Neleus, Augeas son of Sol, Atalanta daughter of Schœneus, disguised in male attire, Autolycus son of Mercury, Azorus, Buphagus, Butes son of Teleon, Calais son of Boreas, Canthus son of Abas, Castor son of Jupiter, Ceneus son of Elatus, Cepheus son of Aleus, Cius, Clytius and Iphitus son of Eurythus, Coronus, Deucalion son of Minos, Echion son of Mercury and Antianira, Ergynus son of Neptune, Euphemus son of Neptune and Macionassa, Eribotes, Euryaleus son of Cisteus, Eurydamas and Eurythion sons of Iras, Eurytus son of Mercury, Glaucus, Hercules son of Jupiter, Idas son of Aphareus, Ialmenus son of Mars, Idmon, son of Abas, Iolaus son of Iphiclus, Iphiclus son of Thestius, Iphiclus, son of Phyacus, Iphis son of Alector, Lynceus son of Aphareus, Iritus son of Naubolus, Laertes son Arcesius, Laocoon, Leodatus son of Bias, Leitus son of Alector, Meleager son of Œneus, Menœtius son of Actor, Mopsus son of Amphycus, Nauplius son of Neptune, Neleus the brother of Pelias, Nestor son of Neleus, Oileus, the father of Ajax, Orpheus son of Œager, Palemon son of Ætolus, Peleus and Telamon sons of Æacus, Periclymenes son of Neleus, Peneleus son of Hipalmus, Philoctetes son of Pœan, Philas, Pollux son of Jupiter, Polyphemus son of Elates, Pœas, son of Thaumacus, Phanus son of Bacchus, Phalerus son of Alcon, Phocas and Priasus sons of Ceneus one of the Lapithæ, Talaus, Tiphys, son of Aginus, Staphilus son of Bacchus, two of the name of Iphitus, Theseus son of Ægeus, with his friend Pirithous. Æsculapius was the physician, and Tiphys the pilot of the expedition. *Vid.* Phryxus, Helle, Jason, Medea, &c.

AR'GOS, *(sing. neut. & Argi, masc. plur.)* an ancient city, the capital of Argolis in Peloponnesus. Juno was the chief deity of the place. The kingdom of Argos was founded by Inachus, 1856 years B.C.; and after it had flourished for about 550 years, it was united to the crown of Mycenæ. Argos was built according to *Euripides, Iphig. in Aulid.*, by seven Cyclopes, who came from Syria. These Cyclopes were not Vulcan's workmen. The nine first kings of Argos were called Inachides, in honour of the founder of the monarchy. Their names were Inachus, Phoroneus, Apis, Argus, Criasus, Phorbas, Triopas, Sthenelus, and Gelanor. Gelanor gave a kind reception to Danaus, who drove him from his kingdom in return for his hospitality. The descendants of Danaus were called Belides. Agamemnon was king of Argos during the Trojan war; and eighty years after, the Heraclidæ seized the Peloponnesus, and deposed the monarchs. The inhabitants of Argos were called Argivi and Argolici; and this name has been often applied to all the Greeks, without distinction. *Flacc.* 6. v. 731. l. 8. v. 328.—*Lucan.* 10. v. 60.—*Plin.* 7. c. 56.—*Paus.* 2. c. 15. &c.—*Horat.* 1. od. 7. ep. 16. v. 57, &c.—*Ælian. V. H.* 9. c. 15.—*Strab.* 8.—*Mela*, 1. c. 13, &c. l. 2. c. 3.—*Virg. Æn.* 1. v. 40. &c.

AR'GOS AMPHILO'CHICUM, a town of Epirus. *Voss. ad Melam.* p. 158.

AR'GOS, a town of Thessaly, called Pelasgicon by the Pelasgians. *Lucan.* 6. v. 355.

AR'GOS HIP'PIUM, the ancient name of Arpi, a town of Apulia. *Cluver. Ital. Ant.* 4. c. 12.

AR'GUS, a son of Arestor; whence he is often called Arestorides. He married Ismene, the daughter of the Asopus, and distinguished himself so much by his strength that he killed a bull which laid waste Arcadia, destroyed a satyr equally terrible, and also the Æchidna, a dreadful monster, half a nymph and half a serpent. As he had a hundred eyes, of which only two were asleep at one time, Juno set him to watch Io, whom Jupiter had changed into a heifer; but Mercury, by order of Jupiter lulled all his eyes to sleep with the melodious sound of his lyre, and slew him. Juno placed the eyes of Argus after his death, in the tail of the peacock, a bird sacred to her divinity. *Moschus. Idyll.*—*Plaut. in Aulul.*—*Apollod.* 2. c. 1, &c.—*Ovid. Met.* 1. fab. 12 & 13.—*Propert.* 1. v. 585, &c. el. 3.—*Apollod.* 1. c. 9. l. 2. c. 1.——A son of Jupiter and Niobe, succeeded Phoronius on the throne of Argolis, and built the city of Argos, which became the capital of his dominions. He married Evadne, the daughter of Strymon and Nœera, by whom he had Jasus, Piranthus, Epidaurus, Criasus, &c. *Hygin.* 145 & 155.—*Apollod.* 2. c. 1.—*Paus.* 2. c. 16 & 22.—*Euseb. Præp. Ev.* 2.—*Scholiast. Theb.* 4. v. 589.——A son of Agenor. *Hygin.* fab. 145.——A son of Danaus, who built the ship Argo. *Id.* 14.——A son of Pyras and Callirhoe. *Hygin.* fab. 145.——A son of Phryxus. *Id.* 3.——A son of Polybus. *Id.* 14. One of Actæon's dogs. *Apollod.*——A dog of Ulysses, which knew his master after an absence of 20 years. *Hom. Od.* 17. v. 300.

ARGU'RA, a city of Thessaly, before called Argissa.——A place of Eubœa. *Steph.*

ARGY'NA, a town of the Locri Ozolæ. *Plin.* 4. c. 3.

ARGYN'NIS, a name of Venus, which she received from Argynnus, a youth who was greatly beloved by Agamemnon, and was drowned in the Cephisus. *Propert.* 3. el. 5. v. 52.—*Athen.* 13. c. 8.

AR'GYRA, a nymph greatly beloved by a shepherd called Selimnus. She was changed into a fountain, and the shepherd into a river of the same name, the waters of which were said to make lovers forget the object of their affections. *Vid.* Selimnus. *Paus.* 7. c. 23.

AR'GYRA, a city of Troas.——The native place of Diodorus Siculus, in Sicily. *Vid.* Agyrum.——A city and fountain of Achaia. *Steph.*——A region of India without the Ganges. *Ptol.*

ARGYRAS'PIDES, a Macedonian legion, which received this name from their silver shields. *Curt.* 4. c. 13.

AR'GYRE, an island beyond the mouth of the river Indus, abounding in metals. *Mela*, 3. c. 11.

ARGYRI'NI, a nation of Epirus. *Steph.*

ARGYRI'PA, a town of Apulia, built by Diomedes after the Trojan war, and called by *Polybius*, Argipana. The place still preserves the name of Arpi. *Virg. Æn.* 11. v. 246. Also Argyrip'pa.

ARGYRU'TUM, a city of Illyricum. *Ptol.* It is called Argyruntum by *Pliny*, 3. c. 21.

A'RIA, or ARI'A, a large country of ancient Asia, situate at the east of Parthia. *Mela*, 1. c. 2. l. 2. c. 7.——The wife of Pætus Cecinna, of Padua, a Roman senator, who was accused of being concerned with Scribonianus in his conspiracy against Claudius, and was, in consequence, carried to Rome by sea. She accompanied her husband, and in the boat she stabbed herself, and, with heroic courage, presented the sword to him, and he immediately followed her example. *Plin.* 7. 3. ep. 16.—*Mart.* 1. epigr. 14.—*Tac. Ann.* 16. c. 34.—*Dion.* 60.——Daughter of the preceding, wished to follow her example, when her husband Thrasea was pronounced guilty by Nero, but he prevailed upon her to live for the sake of her daughter. *Tac. ibid.*

ARIABIG'NES, a son of Darius, placed over the fleet of Xerxes, together with Prexaspes and Megabyzus. *Herodot.* 7. c. 97.

ARI'ACA, a city of Margiana. *Ptol.*

ARI'ACÆ, a people Scythia, on the borders of the Sogdiani. *Id.*

ARI'ACES, a town of India within the Ganges. *Id.*

ARI'ACOS, a town of Mysia, or of Troas. *Plin.* 5. c. 32.

ARIAD'NE, daughter of Minos the Second, king of Crete, by Pasiphae, fell in love with Theseus, who carried her away and married her; but when he arrived at the island of Naxus he forsook her, though she was already pregnant. Ariadne was so disconsolate upon being abandoned by Theseus, that she hanged herself, according to some authors, but *Plutarch* says, that she lived many years after, and had some children by Onarus, the priest of Bacchus. According to other writers, Bacchus loved her after Theseus had forsaken her, and gave her a crown of seven stars, which, after her death, was changed into a constellation. The Argives shewed Ariadne's tomb, and when one of their temples was repaired, her ashes were said to have been found in an earthen urn. *Homer. Odyss.* 11. v. 320., says, that Diana detained Ariadne at Naxus, in her temple. *Plut. in Thes.*—*Ovid. Met.* 8. fab. 2. *Heroid.* 10. *De Art. Am.* 2. *Fast.* 3. v. 462.—*Catull. de Nupt. Pel. & Thet.* ep. 61.—*Hygin.* fab. 14, 43, 270.—*Apollod.* 3. c. 1.—*Propert.* 3. el. 16.—*Philostr.* 1. c. 15.—*Nonnus. in Dionys.* 47. [A most exquisite statue of Ariadne is in the Vatican. It was ocen supposed to represent Cleopatra, but was decidedly meant for Ariadne.]

ARIÆ'US, an officer who succeeded to the command of the army of Cyrus the younger, after the battle of Cunaxa and the death of that prince. He made peace with Artaxerxes. *Xenoph.*

ARIALDU'NUM, a city of Spain. *Plin.*

ARIAM'NES, a king of Cappadocia, son of Ariarathes the Third.

ARIAN'DA, a city of Caria. *Mela*, 1. c. 16.—*Is. Vossius*, however, reads Carianda.

ARIA'NI or ARIE'NI, a people of Asia. *Dionys. Perieg.* 714.

ARIA'NIA, a nation near the Cadusii. *Steph.*

ARIAN'TAS, a king of Scythia, who yearly ordered every one of his subjects to present him with an arrow. *Herodot.* 4. c. 81.

ARIARATHE'A, a city near Cappadocia, so called from king Ariarathes. *Steph.*

ARIARA'THES the First, a king of Cappadocia, who joined Darius Ochus in his expedition against Ægypt, where he acquired much glory.

ARIARA'THES the Second, nephew of the preceding, defended his kingdom when invaded by the Macedonians, under Perdiccas, the general of Alexander; but he was defeated, and crucified in the 81st year of his age, 321 B.C.

ARIARA'THES the Third, son of the preceding, escaped the massacre which attended his father and his followers; and, after the death of Perdiccas, he recovered Cappadocia, by conquering Amyntas, the Macedonian general. He was succeeded by his son Ariamnes.

ARIARA'THES the Fourth, succeeded his father Ariamnes, and married Stratonice, daughter of Antiochus Theus. He died after a reign of 28 years, B.C. 220.

ARIARA'THES the Fifth, son of the preceding, married Antiochia, the daughter of king Antiochus, whom he assisted in his war against the Romans. Upon the fatal defeat of Antiochus, Ariarathes saved his kingdom from invasion, by paying the Romans a large sum of money remitted at the instance of the king of Pergamus.

ARIARA'THES the Sixth, called *Philopater*, from his piety, succeeded his father Ariarathes the Fifth, 166 B.C. An alliance with the Romans shielded him against the false claims that were laid to his crown by one of the favourites of Demetrius king of Syria. He was maintained on his throne by the friendship of Attalus, and assisted the Romans against Aristonicus, the usurper of Pergamus; but he was killed in the war B.C. 130, leaving six children, five of whom were murdered by his surviving wife Laodice.

ARIARA'THES the Seventh, the only surviving son of the preceding, was proclaimed king, and soon after married Laodice, the sister Mithridates Eupator, by whom he had two sons. He was murdered by an illegitimate brother; upon which his widow Laodice gave herself and the kingdom to Nicomedes king of Bithynia. Mithridates made war against the new king, and raised his nephew to the throne.

ARIARA'THES the Eighth, made war againt the tyrannical Mithridates, by whom he was assassinated in the presence of both armies, and the murderer's son, a child eight years old, was placed on the vacant throne.

ARIARA'THES the Ninth, brother of the preceding, was placed upon the throne by the Cappadocians, who revolted; but Mithridates expelled him, and restored his own son. The exiled prince died of a broken heart; and Nicomedes of Bithynia, dreading the power of the tyrant, interested the Romans in the affairs of Cappadocia. The arbiters wished to make the country free; but the Cappadocians demanded a king, and received Ariobarzanes, B.C. 91.

ARIARA'THES the Tenth, ascended the throne on the death of his brother Ariobarzanes, but his title was disputed by Sisenna, the eldest son of Glaphyra, by Archelaus priest of Comana. M. Antony, who was umpire between the contending parties, decided in favour of Sisenna; but Ariarathes recovered the kingdom for a while, though he was soon after obliged to yield in favour of Archelaus, the second son of Glaphyra, B.C. 36. *Diod.* 18.—*Liv.* 37 & 38,—*Justin.* 13 & 29.—*Strab.* 12.

ARIARA'THES, a king of Thrace, mentioned by *Livy*, 2. *Dec.* 5.

ARIAS'MENUS, one of the generals who assisted Perses against Æetes. *Val. Flacc.* 1. 6. *Arg.* v. 103.

ARIASPÆ, a people of Asia, near the source of the Arabis. Their chief town was called Ariaspe. Some geographers place them near the head of the Indus. *Plin.* 6. c. 17.—*Cluver.* 5. c. 13.

ARIBÆUS, a general mentioned by *Polyænus*, 7. c. 29.

ARIC'ADA, a city of Drangiana. *Ptol.*

ARI'CHUS, a grammarian. *Schol. in Aristoph Ran.*

ARIC'IA, an Athenian princess, niece of king Ægeus, whom Hyppolytus married after he had been raised from the dead by the art of Æsculapius. *Ovid. Met.* 15. v. 544.—*Virg. Æn.* 7. v. 762, &c.——A very ancient town of Italy, now Riccia, built by Hyppolytus, son of Theseus, after he had been transported into Italy by Diana. In a grove in the neigbourhood of Aricia, Theseus built a temple to Diana, where he established the same rites as were observed in the temple of that goddess in Tauris. The priest of this temple, called Rex was always a fugitive, and the murderer of his predecessor; and went constantly armed with a dagger, to prevent or resist whatever attempts might be made upon his life by one who wished to be his successor. The Arician forest, frequently called Nemorensis or Nemoralis Sylva, was very celebrated, and no horse would ever enter it, because Hyppolytus had been killed by them. Egeria, the favourite nymph and invisible protectress of Numa, generally resided in this famous grove, which was situated on the Appian way, beyond mount Albanus, about the middle of Latium. *Ovid. Met.* 15. *Fast.* 3. v. 263.—*Lucan.* 6. v. 74.—*Apollod.* 3. c. 20.—*Hygin.* fab. 49. 251.—*Scholiast. Eurip. in Alcest.*—*Lactant. Firm.* 1. c. 17.—*Cic. ad. Att.* 6. ep. 1.—*Sueton. in Cæs.* 46.—*Martial.* 9. epigr. 65. v. 3.—*Virg. Æn.* 7. v. 761, &c.

ARICI'NA, a surname of Diana, from her temple, near Aricia. *Vid.* Aricia.——The mother of Octavius. *Cic.* 3. *Phil.* c. 6.

ARIDÆUS, a companion of Cyrus the younger. After the death of his friend, he reconciled himself to Artaxerxes, by betraying to him the surviving Greeks in their return. *Diod.*——An illegitimate son of Philip, who, after the death of Alexander the Great, was made king of Macedonia, till Roxane should bring into the world a legitimate male successor. Aridæus had not the free enjoyment of his senses; and therefore Perdiccas, one of Alexander's generals, declared himself his protector, and even married his sister, to strengthen their connection. He was seven years in nominal possession of the sovereign power, and was put to death, with his wife Eurydice, by Olympias. *Justin.* 9. c. 8. l. 13. c. 2. l. 14. c. 5.—*Diod.*

ARIDI'CES, a philosopher mentioned by *Macrobius Sat.* l. 7. c. 3.

ARIE'TIS frons, or in Greek, Criumetopon, the most southern promontory of Taurica Chersonesus, opposite Paphlagonia.

ARIGÆUM, a town of India, which Alexander found burnt, and without inhabitants. *Arrian.* 4.

ARIGNO'TE, a learned woman, who is said to have written an account of the actions of Dionysius the tyrant. *Clem. Alex. Strom.* l. 4.

ARIGNO'TUS, a person ridiculed by *Aristophanes* as an unskilful musician, &c.

ARII, or ARI'I, a savage people of India.——A people of Arabia. *Plin.* 6. c. 20.——A people of Scythia. *Herodot.*——A people of Germany. *Tacit.*

AR'IMA, a place of Cilicia, or Syria, where it was said that Typhœus was overwhelmed by the earth. *Homer. Il.* 2. 782.

ARIMA'NIUS, a god of Persia and Media, who presided over the evils and disorders of human life, in the same manner as Oremasis, another divinity, presided over the moral and physical order of things. *Zoroast. in Plut. de Isid. & Osir.*—*Cœl. Rhod.* 7. c. 14.

ARIMAN'TIS, a city of the Pentapolis in Africa. *Ptol.*

ARIM'ARA, a city of Syria, on the Euphrates. *Id.*

ARIMASPES, a friend of Zoroaster. *Cœl. Rhod.* 1. 23. c. 4.

ARIMASPI, a people Scythia, conquered by Alexander the Great. They lived on the banks of a river, which was said to have golden sands. According to the mythologists, they had only one eye, in the middle of their foreheads, and waged continual war against the griffins, monstrous animals which collected the gold of the river. *Curt.* 7. c. 3.—*Mela*, 2. c. 1.—*Plin.* 7. c. 2.—*Lucan.* 3. v. 280.—*Strab.* 1 & 13.—*Herod.* 3. c. 116, &c.

ARIMASTHÆ, a wandering people, near the Euxine Sea. *Orpheus. Argon.*

ARIMA'ZES, a powerful prince of Sogdiana, who treated Alexander with much insolence. He, at last surrendered, and was cruelly exposed on the cross with his friends and relations. *Curt.* 7. c. 11.—*Polyæn.* 4. c. 3.

ARIM'ENES, the Vejovis or evil genius, or, according to *Hesychius*, the Pluto of the Persians.

ARIMI, a nation of Syria. *Strab.* 13.——Mountains and people of Mysia and Lydia. *Suidas.*

ARIMI'NUM, now Rimini, an ancient city of Italy, at the mouth of the Ariminus, below the Rubicon, on the borders of Gallia Cisalpina, on the Adriatic, founded by a colony of Umbrians, in the consulship of Sempronius and Appius Claudius. It was the cause of Cæsar's civil wars. Its harbour has been choaked up by the sand. *Horat.* epod. 5. v. 42.—*Lucan.* 1. v. 231.—*Plin.* 3. c. 15.—*Mela*, 2. c. 6.—*Cluver.* 3. c. 26.

ARIMI'NUS, now Marecchia, a river of Italy, rising in the Apennine mountains, and falling into the Adriatic. *Plin.* 3. c. 15.

ARIMPHÆI, a people of Scythia near the Riphæan mountains, who lived chiefly upon berries in the woods, and were remarkable for their innocence and mildness. *Plin.* 6. c. 7.—*Mela*, 1. c. 2.

AR'IMUS, a king of Mysia. *Varro.*

ARI'NA, a town of Mauritania Cæsariensis. *Ptol.* It is now Tezela.

AR'INES, an auxiliary of Æetes, slain in battle by Colaxes. *Val. Flacc.* 6. v. 638.

ARINIA'NUM, a colony planted on the banks of the Arnus, by Janus, according to *Cato;* it is now Arignano.——A town of the Falisci, now Rignano.

ARIN'THE, a city of the Œnotri. *Steph.* Some say it is Arianthe in Calabria.

ARIOBARZA'NES, a man made king of Cappadocia by the Romans, after the troubles which the false Ariarathes had raised, had subsided. Mithridates drove him from his kingdom, but the Romans restored him. He followed the interest of Pompey, and fought, in support of his cause, at Pharsalia, against J. Cæsar. He and his kingdom were preserved by means of Cicero. *Cic.* 5. *Manil.* 2. *ad Attic.* ep. 29.—*Horat.* ep. 6. v. 38.—*Flor.* 3.——A satrap of Phrygia, who, after the death of Mithridates, invaded the kingdom of Pontus, and kept it for 26 years. He was succeeded by the son of Mithridates. *Diod.* 17.——A general of Darius, who defended the passes of Susa against Alexander with 15,000 foot soldiers. After a bloody encounter with the Macedonians, he was killed as he attempted to seize the city of Persepolis. *Diod.* 17.—*Curt.* 4 & 5.——A Mede of elegant stature and great prudence, whom Tiberius appointed to settle the troubles of Armenia. *Tac. Ann.* 2. c. 4.——A satrap, who revolted from the Persian king. This name was common among the Persians and their Asiatic neighbours.——A mountain between Parthia and the country of the Massagetæ. *Orosius.*

ARI'OLA, a city of Gallia Belgica. *Antonin.*

ARIOMAN'DES, son of Gorybas, was general of the Athenians against the Persians. *Plut. in Cim.*

ARIOMAR'DUS, a son of Darius in the army of Xerxes when he invaded Greece. *Herodot.* 7. c. 78.

ARIOME'DES, a pilot of Xerxes. *Plut.*

ARI'ON, a famous lyric poet and musician of Methymna, in the island of Lesbus. He went into Italy with Periander, tyrant of Corinth, where he obtained celebrity, and acquired immense riches, by his profession. Some time after, he wished to revisit his country; and the sailors of the ship in which he embarked, resolved to murder him, that they might obtain possession of the riches which he was carrying to Lesbus. Arion, seeing that they were inflexible, begged that he might be permitted to play some melodious tune; and as soon as he had finished he threw himself into the sea. A number of dolphins had been attracted round the ship by the sweetness of his music; and it is said that one of them carried him safe on his back to Tænarus, whence he hastened to the court of Periander, who ordered the sailors, on their return, to be crucified. A hymn to Neptune has been preserved by *Ælian, H. A.* 12. 45. and is to be found in the 327th page of the third volume of Brunck's Analecta. *Fabr. B Gr.* 2. c. 15.—*Servius in Virg. Ecl.* 8. v. 56.—*Eustath. Od.* 3.—*Ovid. Fast.* 2. v. 93. *De Art. Am.* 3.—*Martial.* 8. epigr. 5.—*Plin.* 9. c. 8.—*A. Gell.* 16. c. 19.—*Hygin.* fab. 194.—*Herodot.* 1. c. 23 & 24.—*Ital.* 11.—*Propert.* 2. el. 26. v. 17.—*Plut. in Symp.*——A horse sprung from Ceres and Neptune, which had the power of speech, the feet on the right side like those of a man, and the rest of the body like a horse. Arion was brought up by the Nereides, who often harnessed him to his father's chariot, which he drew over the sea with great swiftness. Neptune gave him to Copreus, who presented him to Hercules. Adrastus, king of Argos, received him as a present from Hercules, and with him won the prize of the Nemæan games. Arion, therefore, is often called the horse of Adrastus. *Paus.* 8. c. 25.—*Propert.* 2. el. 34. v. 37.—*Apollod.* 3. c. 6.—*Stat. Theb.* 4. v. 43.——A horse of Polynices. *Stat. Theb.* l. 6. v. 501.

ARIOVIS'TUS, a king of the Germans, who professed himself the friend of Rome. When Cæsar was in Gaul, Ariovistus marched against him, but was vanquished with the loss of 80,000 men. *Cæs.* 1. *Bell. Gall.*—*Tacit.* 4. *Hist.*

ARIPH'RADES, a person ridiculed by *Aristophanes, Equit.* 4. for his filthiness.

ARI'PHRON, son of Pherecles, the 9th perpetual Archon of Athens, reigned 20 years.

ARIP'PARA, a city of India, within the Ganges. *Ptol.*

A'RIS, a small river of Messenia. *Paus.* 4. c. 31.

ARISA'BION, a city of India without the Ganges. *Ptol.*

ARIS'BA, a town of Lesbus, destroyed by an earthquake. *Plin.* 5. c. 31.——A town of Bœotia. *Suidas.*——A colony of the Mityleneans, in Troas, destroyed by the Trojans before the coming of the Greeks. *Virg. Æn.* 9. v. 264.—*Homer. Il.* 7.——Priam's first wife and mother of Æsacus, was divorced that the monarch might marry Hecuba. *Apollod.* 3. c. 23.

ARIS'BUS, a river of Thrace, according to *Stephanus;* but of Troas, according to *Strabo.*

ARISE'RIA, a city of Cyrrhestica, in Syria. *Ptol.*

ARIS'PÆ, a nation of India, near the Indus. *Arrian. in Indic.*

ARISTÆNE'TUS, an ancient author, under whose name are extant some Greek epistles on subjects of love and gallantry. Some writers suppose that this is a mere compilation from the finest passages of Plato, Lucian, Philostratus, &c. and that though they appear under the name of Aristænetus, no such person ever existed. He is supposed to have perished in an earthquake, A.D. 358, a circumstance mentioned both by *Libanius* and *Ammianus Marcellinus.* The epistles have been beautifully edited by Abreschius, Zwollæ, 1749. *Fabr. B. Gr.* 2. c. 10.—*Sax. Onom.* 1. p. 406.

ARISTÆ'NUS, a prætor of the Achæan league. *Liv.* 32. c. 19.

ARISTÆ'UM, a city of Thrace, at the foot of mount Hæmus. *Plin.* 4. c. 11.

ARISTÆ'US, a son of Apollo and the nymph Cyrene, was surnamed Nomius and Agreus, from his fondness for hunting. After he had travelled over the greatest part of the world, he came to settle in Greece, where he married Autonoe, the daughter of Cadmus, by whom he had a son called Actæon. The unfortunate death of this son rendered him inconsolable, and he passed into Sardinia, after which he visited Sicily, and the island of Cos, where some of his children settled. He, as Hyginus and Virgil relate, fell in love with Eurydice, the wife of Orpheus, and when she rejected his addresses, he pursued her into the fields. She was stung by a serpent that lay in the grass, and died in consequence; for which the gods punished Aristæus by destroying all his bees. In this calamity, he applied to his mother, who directed him to seize the sea-god Proteus, and consult him how he might repair the losses which he had sustained. Proteus advised him to appease the manes of Eurydice by the sacrifice of four bulls and four heifers; and as soon as he had done it, and left them exposed to the air, swarms of bees sprang from their rotten carcases, and restored Aristæus to his former prosperity. He was, after death, worshipped as a demi-god. Aristæus is said to have learned, from the nymphs, the cultivation of olives, and the management of bees, &c. which he afterwards communicated to the rest of mankind. *Nonnus,* 15 *Dionys.*—*Scholiast. Apollon.* 2. v. 502. & 4.—*Servius in Virg. G.* 1. v. 14. l. 4. v. 283 & 317.—*Virg. G.* 4. v. 317.—*Diod.* 4.—*Justin.* 13. c. 7.—*Ovid. Fast.* 1. v. 363.—*Cic. de Nat. D.* 3. c. 18.—*Paus.* 10. c. 17.—*Hygin.* fab. 161, 180, 247.—*Apollod.* 3. c. 4.—*Herodot.* 4. c. 4. &c.—*Polyæn.* 1. c. 24.

ARISTAG'ORAS, a writer who composed a history of Ægypt. *Plin.* 36. c. 12.——A son-in-law of Histiæus, tyrant of Miletus, who revolted from Darius, and incited the Athenians to take up arms against the Persians. He attacked the city of Sardes, which he reduced to ashes; but the Persian monarch was so exasperated at this act of hostility, that every evening before supper he ordered his servants to remind him of punishing the Athenians. Aristagoras was at last killed in Thrace, in a battle against the Persians B.C. 499. *Herodot.* 5. c. 30, &c. l. 7. c. 8.—*Polyæn.* 1. c. 24.——A man of Cyzicus. *Herodot.* 4. c. 138.——A man of Cumæ. *Id.* 5. c. 37.——The son of Hegesistratus, who fought against the barbarians at Mycale. *Id.* 9. c. 90.

ARISTAN'DER, a celebrated soothsayer, greatly esteemed by Alexander. *Plut. in Alex.*—*Plin.* 17. c. 25.——An Athenian, who wrote on Agriculture.

ARISTAN'DROS, a statuary of Sparta. *Paus.* 3. c. 18.

ARISTAR'CHE, a matron of Ephesus, who, by order of Diana, sailed to the coasts of Gaul with the Phocæans, and was made priestess of her temple. *Strab.* 4.

ARISTAR'CHUS, a celebrated grammarian of Samothrace, disciple of Aristophanes the grammarian. He lived the greatest part of his life at Alexandria in Ægypt, and Ptolemy Philometor entrusted him with the education of his sons. He was distinguished for his learning as well as for his critical powers; and he revised the poems of Homer with such severity, that, ever after, all severe critics were called Aristarchi. He wrote above 800 commentaries on different authors, much esteemed in his age. In his old age he became dropsical, upon which he starved himself, and died in his 72d year, B.C. 157. He left two sons called Aristarchus and Aristagoras, both noted for their stupidity. The first of these was sold for a slave, but out of respect for the merits of his father, the Athenians restored him to liberty. *Horat. de Art. Poet.* v. 449.—*Ovid.* 3. *ex Pont.* ep. 9. v. 24.—*Cic. ad Fam.* 3. ep. 11. *Ad Attic.* 1 ep. 14.—*Quintil.* 10. c. 1.—*Fabr. B. Gr.* l. 2. c. 2.—*Sax. Onom.* 1. p. 130.——A tragic poet of Tegea, in Arcadia, about 454 years B.C. He composed seventy tragedies, of which two only were rewarded with the prize. One of them, called Achilles, was translated into Latin verse by the poets Ennius and Plautus. *Suidas.—Euseb. Chron.—Gyrald. de Poet. Gr. Hist.* 7.—*Fabr. B. Gr.* 2. c. 19.——A physician to queen Berenice, the widow of Antiochus. *Polyæn.* 8. ——An orator of Ambracia. *Diod. Sic.* 17.——An astronomer of Samus, who first supposed that the earth turned daily round its axis, and revolved annually round the sun. This doctrine nearly proved fatal to him, as he was accused of disturbing the peace of the gods Lares; but he surmounted the prejudices of the age, and was permitted to pursue his studies undisturbed. He lived about 264 B.C. His treatise on the size and the distance of the sun and moon is extant, of which the best edition is that of Wallis, Oxon. 8vo, 1688. *Vitruv. de Archit.* 1. c. 3. l. 9. c. 9.—*Plut. in Facie in Orbe Lunæ.—Fabr. B. Gr.* 3. c. 18.—*Sax. Onom.* 1. p. 104.——A chronologer, who wrote an historical epistle upon the situation of Athens and the actions of its inhabitants, and a life of Dionysius the Areopagite. *Voss. de Hist. Gr.* p. 333.——An Athenian who betrayed Ænöe to the Bœotians. *Thucyd.* 8. c. 98.

ARISTAR'ETE, daughter of Nearchus, a celebrated painter. *Plin.* 35. c. 11.

ARISTAZA'NES, a noble Persian in favour with Artaxerxes Ochus. *Diod.* 16.

ARISTEAS, a poet of Proconnesus, who is reported to have appeared seven years after his death to his countrymen, and 540 years after to the people of Metapontum in Italy, and to have commanded them to raise him a statue near the temple of Apollo. He lived in the age of Crœsus, and wrote an epic poem on the Arimaspi in three books, and six of his verses are quoted by *Longinus. Herodot.* 4. c. 13.—*Suidas in Olymp.—Strab.* 14.—*Max. Tyr.* 22.—*Fabr. B. Gr.* 1. c. 2.——A physician of Rhodes.——A geometrician, intimate with Euclid. ——A poet, son of Demochares, in the age of Crœsus.——A comic poet. *Ælian.* 6. 51. *Anim.*——A general who commanded the Corinthian forces at the siege of Potidæa. He was taken by the Athenians, and put to death. *Herod.* 7. c. 137.

ARISTERÆ, an island on the coast of Peloponnesus. *Paus.* 2. c. 34.

ARIS'TEUS, a man of Argos, who excited king Pyrrhus to take up arms against his countrymen the Argives. *Polyæn.* 8. c. 68.——A sophist in the age of the emperor Antoninus.

ARIS'THENES, a shepherd who found Æsculapius when he had been exposed in the woods by his mother Corions.

ARIS'THUS, an historian of Arcadia. *Dionys. Hal.* 1.

ARISTI'BUS, a small river of Pæonia. *Polyæn.* 4. c. 12.

ARISTI'DES, a celebrated Athenian, son of Lysimachus. His great temperance and virtue procured him the surname of *Just.* He was the rival of Themistocles, by whose influence he was banished for ten years, B.C. 484; but before six years of his exile had elapsed, he was recalled by the Athenians. He was at the battle of Salamis, and was appointed chief commander of the combined armies of Athens and Lacedæmon with Pausanias against Mardonius, who was defeated at Platæa. He died so poor, that the expenses of his funeral were defrayed by the state; and his two daughters on account of their father's merits, received a dowry from the public treasury. The Athenians became more virtuous in imitating their great leader; and from the sense of his good qualities, at the representation of one of the tragedies of Æschylus, on the recitation of a sentence concerning moral goodness, the eyes of the audience were all at once turned from the actor to Aristides. It is said, that when he once sat as judge, the plaintiff, in his accusation, mentioned the injuries which his opponent had done ito Aristides. "Mention the wrongs you have received," replied the equitable Athenian, "I sit here as judge, and the lawsuit is yours and not mine." *C. Nep. & Plut in Vitâ.* [A bust of this philosopher remains in the Capitol.]——An historian of Miletus, fonder of stories and anecdotes than of truth. He wrote a history of Italy, of which the 40th volume has been quoted by *Plutarch, in Parall.*——An athlete, whose statue was seen at Olympia in the age of Antoninus, and on it was recorded that he had obtained a prize at the Olympian, Nemean, and Pythian games. *Paus.* 6. c. 16.——A painter of Thebes in Bœotia, in the age of Alexander, whose skill was displayed in the perfect representation of the passions. Pliny speaks of some of his paintings which were still extant in his age, and mentions that Attalus offered for one 6000 sesterces, *Plin.* 7. c. 38. l. 35. c. 10. & 11.

ARISTI'DES Æ'LIUS, a Greek orator of Adrianopolis, who wrote fifty-six orations, besides other tracts. When Smyrna was destroyed by an earthquake, he wrote so pathetic a letter to M. Aurelius, that the emperor ordered the city to be immediately rebuilt, and a statue was in consequence raised to the orator by the grateful inhabitants. His works consist of hymns in prose in honor of the gods, funeral orations, apologies, panegyrics, and harangues; the best edition of which is that of Jebb, 2 vols. 4to, Oxon 1722, and that in a smaller size in 12mo, 3 vols. of Canterus and P. Steph. 1604.—*Fabr. B. Gr.* 4. c. 32.—*Sax.* 1. p. 325. [A sitting figure, representing this Aristides, and probably one of the statues alluded to above, is now in the Vatican.]

ARISTI'DES, a man of Locris, who died from the bite of a weasel. *Ælian. V. H.* 14.——A philosopher of Mysia, intimate with M. Antoninus.——An Athenian, who wrote treatises on animals, trees, and agriculture.

ARISTI'DES QUINTILIA'NUS, a writer upon music, anterior to the age of Ptolemy. *Fabr. B. Gr.* 1. 3. c. 12.—*Sax.* 3. c. 10.——A native of Elea, who defended Caulonia against Dionysius. *Polyæn.* 6. c. 11. —*Fabricius,* 4. c. 32. enumerates several other persons of this name.

ARISTIL'LUS, a philosopher of the Alexandrian school, who, about 300 years B.C. attempted, with Timocharis, to determine the place of the different stars in the heavens, and to trace the course of the planets.

ARIS'TION, a sophist of Athens, who, assisted by Archelaus, the general of Mithridates, seized the government of his country, and made himself absolute. When driven from his ursurpation by the success of Sylla and the Roman armies, he destroyed himself by poison. *Liv.* 81 & 82.

ARISTIP'PUS, *the elder*, a philosopher of Cyrene; disciple of Socrates, and founder of the Cyrenaic sect. He was one of the flatterers of Dionysius of Sicily, and distinguished himself for his epicurean voluptuousness, in support of which he wrote a book, as likewise a history of Libya. When travelling in the deserts of Africa, he ordered his servants to throw away the money they carried, as too burdensome. On another occasion, discovering that the ship in which he sailed, belonged to pirates, he designedly threw his property into the sea, adding, that he chose rather to lose it than his life. Many of his sayings and maxims are recorded by *Diogenes,* in his life, and it evidently appears that he prostituted the noblest resources of a superior mind, to the meanest gratification of the senses. He courted the great and the opulent, that he might share their luxury and pleasures; and, by his wit and sarcasms, he reconciled the grossest misconduct to those rules of decorum and propriety, which, at other times, he wished to inculcate. *Horat.* 2 *Sat.* 3. v. 100.—*Fabr. B. Gr.* 2.

c. 24.—*Sax.* 1. p. 48.——His grandson, called *the younger*, was the pupil of his mother Arete, and hence called μητροδίδακτος. He was a warm defender of his opinions, and held that the principles of all things were pain and pleasure. He flourished about 363 years B. C. *Cic. Fin.* 2. c. 6. *Orat.* 3. c. 17.—*Horat.* 1. ep. 17. v. 14. 2 *Sat.* 3. v. 100.—*Fabr. ibid.*——A tyrant of Argos, whose life was one continued series of apprehension. He was killed by a Cretan, in a battle against Aratus, B.C. 242. *Diog.*——A man who wrote a history of Arcadia. *Diog.* 2.——A celebrated painter. *Plin.* 35. c. 4 & 10.

ARIS'TIUS M. a tribune of the soldiers in Cæsar's army. *Cæs. Bell. Gall.* 7. c. 42.——*Vid.* Fuscus. ——A satirist, who wrote a poem called Cyclops.

ARIS'TO. *Vid.* Ariston.

ARISTOBATH'RA, a town of India within the Ganges. *Ptol.*

ARISTOBU'LE, a name given by Themistocles to Diana, as the author of the best and most salutary counsels. *Cœl. Rhod.* 10. c. 5.

ARISTOBU'LUS, a name common to some of the high priests and kings of Judæa, &c. One of them was conquered and led in triumph by Pompey. *Plut. in Pomp.*—*Flor.* 3. c. 5.—*Eutrop.* 6. c. 16. —*Joseph.*——A king of Armenia. *Tacit.* 13. *Ann.* 17.——One of Alexander's attendants, who wrote the king's life, replete with adulation and untruth. Arrian has unguardedly followed his authority in several instances. *Plut. in Dem. &c.*——A philosopher of Judæa, B.C. 150.——A brother of Epicurus.

ARISTOCLE'A, a beautiful woman, passionately loved by Callisthenes, and equally admired by Strato. She died on the day of her nuptials, upon which Strato killed himself, and Callisthenes was never seen after. *Plut. in Amat.*

ARIS'TOCLES, a peripatetic philosopher of Messenia, who reviewed, in a treatise on philosophy, the various opinions of his predecessors. He also wrote on rhetoric, and likewise ten books on morals. *Fabr. B. Gr.* 3. c. 8.——A grammarian of Rhodes. ——A stoic of Lampsacus.——An historian. *Strab.* 4.——A musician. *Athen. &c.*——A prince of Tegea, &c. *Polyæn.*——A polemarch who was ejected from Sparta. *Thucyd.* 5. c. 72.——This name is common to many Greeks, of whom few or no particulars are recorded.

ARISTOCLI'DES, a tyrant of Orchomenus, who, because he could not win the affection of Stymphalis, killed her and her father; upon which all Arcadia took up arms, and destroyed the murderer.

ARISTOCLI'TUS, a musician, who traced his descent from Terpander, &c. *Schol. Aristoph. Nub.*

ARISTOC'RATES, a king of Arcadia, put to death by his subjects, for offering violence to the priestess of Diana's temple. *Paus.* 8. c. 5.——Grandson of the preceding, was stoned to death for taking bribes, during the second Messenian war, and being the cause of the defeat of his Messenian allies, B.C. 682. *Id. ibid.*——A man who endeavoured to abolish the democratical power at Athens. *Thucyd.* 8. c. 89.——An Athenian general, sent to the assistance of Corcyra, with twenty-five galleys. *Diod.* 15.——An Athenian, who was punished with death, for losing the battle of Arginusæ. *Schol. Aristoph. Ran.*——A Greek historian, son of Hyparchus. *Plut.*—*Athen.* 3.——A Rhodian, elected general by his fellow citizens. *Suidas.*

ARISTO'CREON, the writer of a book on geography. *Plin.* 5. c. 9.

ARISTOC'RITUS, wrote a treatise concerning Miletus. *Plin.* 5. c. 31.—*Schol. in Apollon.* 1. 2.

ARISTODE'ME, a daughter of Priam.

ARISTODE'MUS, son of Aristomachus, was one of the Heraclidæ. He, with his brothers Temenus and Chresphons, invaded and conquered Peloponnesus, and afterwards divided the country among themselves, 1104 years B. C. Aristodemus married Argia, daughter of Autesion, by whom he had the twins Procles and Eurysthenes, who married two twins. He was killed by a thunder-bolt at Naupactum; though some say that he died at Delphi in Phocis, and others, that he was murdered by the sons of Pylades and Electra. *Apollod.* 2. c. 37.—*Paus.* 2. c. 18. 1. 3. c. 1 & 16.—*Herodot.* 7. c. 204. 1. 6. c. 131.——A king of Messenia, who maintained a celebrated war against Sparta. He put his daughter to death for the good of his country; but being afterwards persecuted in a dream by her manes, he killed himself, after a reign of six years and some months, in which he had obtained much military glory, B.C. 724. *Paus. in Messen.*——A philosopher of Ægina.——A Spartan, entrusted with the education of the children of Pausanias——A tyrant of Arcadia.——A Carian, who wrote a history of painting.——The only Spartan who survived the battle of Thermopylæ. He afterwards sacrificed himself at the battle of Platæa. *Herodot.* 7. c. 229 & 230.——An archon at Athens. Ol. 107. an. 1.——A tyrant of Cumæ, surnamed Malacus or *effeminate.* He was slain by means of Xenocrites. *Paus. in Arcad.*—*Plut. de Virt. Mul.*——A philosopher of Nisa, mentioned by *Strabo.* 1. 14.——The instructor of the children of Pompey the Great. *Id.*——An Alexandrian, who wrote upon Pindar. *Athenæus*, 1. 10, cites his third book, and the *Scholiast* on *Pindar*, highly praises it. *Plutarch* speaks of a collection of fables by a person of this name, which of the above is not known. *Plut. Par. Min.* 35.

ARISTOD'ICUS, a Cumæan, who wished his countrymen not to follow the advice of the oracle, which had directed them to give up Pactya to the Persians. *Herodot.* 1. c. 158.

ARISTOG'ENES, a physician of Cnidus, who obtained great reputation by the cure of Antigonus Gonatas, king of Macedonia. He wrote 24 books on medicine, and lived in the 125th Olympiad.

ARISTOGI'TON and HARMO'DIUS, two celebrated friends of Athens, who, by their united efforts, delivered their country from the tyranny of the Pisistratidæ, B.C. 510. They received immortal honors from the Athenians. The statues, which were publicly erected by the people, in honor of these two heroes, were carried away by Xerxes, when he invaded Greece. The conspiracy of Aristogiton was so secretly planned, and so wisely carried into execution, that, it is said, a courtezan bit her tongue off, not to betray the trust reposed in her. *Paus.* 1. c. 29.—*Herodot.* 5. c. 55.—*Plut de* 10 *Orat.* ——An Athenian orator, surnamed *Canis*, from his impudence. He wrote orations against Timarchus, Timotheus, Hyperides, and Thrasyllus. *Fabr. B. Gr.* 1. 3. c. 9. *de Cynicis.*——A statuary. *Paus.*——An ambassador from the Athenians to Darius, taken upon the surrender of Damascus. *Q. Curt.* 3. c. 12.

ARISTOLA'US, a painter. *Plin.* 35. c. 11.

ARISTOL'OCHUS, a victor at the Olympic games. Ol. 109.

ARISTOM'ACHE, the wife of Dionysius of Syracuse. *Cic. Tusc.* 5. c. 20.——The wife of Dion. ——A poetess. *Plut. Symp.*——A daughter of Priam, who married Critolaus. *Paus* 10. c. 26.

ARISTOM'ACHUS, an Athenian, who wrote a treatise concerning the preparation of wine. *Plin.* 14. c. 9.——One of Hippodamia's suitors. *Paus.* 6. c. 21.——A son of Talaus and Lysimache, the daughter of Abas. *Apollod.* 1. c. 25.——The father of Hippomedon, one of the seven chiefs against Thebes. *Id.* 3. c. 11.——A chief of Crotona, who prevailed upon his party to deliver their city to Annibal. *Liv.* 24. c. 2 & 3.——A man of Soli, so excessively fond of bees, that he devoted fifty-eight years of his life in raising swarms of them. *Plin.* 11. c. 9. ——The son of Cleodæus, and grandson of Hyllus, whose three sons, Cresphons, Temenus, and Aristodemus, called Heraclidæ, conquered Peloponnesus. *Paus.* 2. c. 7. 1. 3, c. 15.—*Herodot.* 6, 7, & 8.——A man who laid aside the sovereign power at Argos, at the persuasion of Aratus, the Achæan chief. *Paus.* 2. c. 8.

ARISTOME'DES, a Thessalian general, in the interest of Darius the Third. *Curt.* 3. c. 9.——According to *Diodorus*, or Aristodemus, according to *Pausanias* and *Eusebius*, the 8th king of Corinth of the family of the Heraclidæ. *Joh. Marsham. Can. Chron. Sec.* 17.

ARISTOM'ENES, a commander of the fleet of Darius on the Hellespont, conquered by the Macedonians. *Curt.* 4. c. 1.——A Messenian general, who encouraged his countrymen to shake off the Lacedemonian yoke, under which they had groaned for above thirty years. He once defended the virtue of some Spartan women, whom his soldiers had insulted; and when he was taken prisoner and carried to Sparta, the women procured his liberty. He refused to assume the title of king, but was satisfied with that of commander, and acquired the surname of *Just*, from his equity. He often entered Sparta without being known, and twice escaped from the enemy, when taken captive. As he attempted to do it a third time, he was unfortunately killed. It is asserted, however, by some authors, that he died at Rhodes, about 671 years B.C. *Diod.* 15.—*Paus. in Messen.*——A Spartan, sent to the assistance of Dionysius. *Polyœan.* 2.——An Athenian comic poet, who flourished about the 87th Olympiad; the names of six of his plays are preserved. *Fabr. B. Gr.* l. 2. c. 22.

ARISTON, the son of Agasicles, king of Sparta, was the 14th king of the family of the Proclidæ. Being unable to raise children by two wives, he married another, famous for her beauty, by whom he had, after seven months, a son, Demaratus, whom he had the imprudence to call not his own. *Herodot.* 6. c. 61, &c.——A general of Ætolia.——A sculptor. *Plin.* 33. c. 12.——A Corinthian, who assisted the Syracusans against the Athenians. *Thucyd.* 7. c. 39.—*Polyæn* 5. c. 13.——An officer in Alexander's army. *Q. Curt.* 4. c, 38.——A philosopher of Chius, pupil of Zeno the stoic, and founder of a sect which continued but a little while. He maintained that the nature of the divinity is unintelligible. It is said that he died by the heat of the sun, which fell too powerfully upon his bald head. In his old age he was much given to sensuality. *Diog.*—*Fabr. B. Gr.* 3. c. 10. *de Stoicis.*——A lawyer in Trajan's reign, whose eulogium has been written by *Pliny*, ep. 22. l. 1.——A peripatetic philosopher of Alexandria, who wrote concerning the course of the Nile. *Strab.*—*Fabr. B. Gr.* 3. c. 8. *de Peripat.*——A wrestler of Argos, under whom Plato performed some exercises.——A musician of Athens. ——A tragic poet.——A peripatetic of Cos. *Fabr. ibid.*——A native of Pella, in the age of Adrian, who wrote on the rebellion of the Jews.——A tyrant of Byzantium, who espoused the side of Histiæus. *Herodot.* 4. c. 138.——A son of Autoleon, deprived of the kingdom of Pæonia by Lysimachus. ——A person sent by Ptolemy king of Ægypt, to explore the Sinus Arabicus, &c.

ARIS'TON JULIE'TES, a peripatetic of Julis, in the island of Cos. *Fabr. B. Gr.* 3. c. 8.

ARISTONAU'TA, the naval dock of Pellene. *Paus.* 2.

ARISTONI'CE, a Pythian priestess, whose answer to the Athenians is recorded by *Herodotus*, l. 7. c. 140.

ARISTONI'CUS, son of Eumenes, invaded Asia and the kingdom of Pergamus, which Attalus had left by his will to the Roman people. He was conquered by the consul Perpenna, and strangled in prison, 125 B.C. *Justin.* 36. c. 4.—*Flor.* 2. c. 20.—*Liv.* 69.—*Cic. Ph.* 11. c. 8. *Rull.* 2. c. 33.——A musician of Olynthus. *Polyæn.* l. 5.——A grammarian of Alexandria, who wrote a commentary on Hesiod and Homer, besides a treatise on the Museum established at Alexandria by the Ptolemies.——An historian of Tarentum. *Voss. Hist. Gr.* l. 4.—— A tyrant of Methymna, who, being ignorant that Chius had surrendered to the Macedonians, entered the harbour, and was taken and put to death. *Curt.* 4. c. 9.

ARISTON'IDES, a famous statuary. *Plin.* 34. c. 14.

ARISTON'OUS, son of Pisæus, one of the body guards of Alexander the Great.——A native of Gela, who, with Pystillus, founded Agrigentum. *Thucyd.* 6. c. 4.

ARIS'TONUS, a captain of Alexander's Pæonian cavalry. *Curt.* 9. c. 5.

ARISTON'YMUS, a comic poet, keeper of the library of Alexandria, under king Philadelphus. He died in his 77th year. *Athen*—*Fabr. B. Gr.* l. 2. c. 19. *de Trag.*——One of Alexander's musicians. *Plut. in Alex.*

ARISTOPH'ANES, a celebrated comic poet of Athens, son of Philippus of Rhodes. He wrote fifty-four comedies, of which only eleven are come down to us; the Plutus, Nubes, Ranæ, Equites, Archarnenses, Vespæ, Aves, Pax, Concionatrices, Cerealia Celebrantes, and Lysistrata. He lived in the age of Socrates, Demosthenes, Euripides, B.C. 434, and lashed the vices of his age with a masterly hand. The wit and excellence of his comedies are well known; but they abound sometimes too much with obscenity, and his attack upon the venerable characters of his age has been always censured, and with justice. As a reward for his abilities, the poet received a crown of olive in a public assembly; but if he deserved praise, he merited blame for his licentiousness, which was so offensive to his countrymen, that Alcibiades made a law which forbade the comic writers to introduce, on the stage, any living character by name. Aristophanes has been called the prince of ancient comedy, as Menander was of the new. His play called Nubes is pointedly against Socrates; and in it the philosopher and his precepts are very keenly ridiculed. It is said that St. Chrysostom so much admired the wit, the elegance, and the animation of the poet, that he always kept his comedies under his pillow. Madame Dacier, too, was equally struck with the beauties of his poetry, for she says that, after translating the "Nubes," she read the performance not less than 200 times, and always with increased pleasure, forgetting the ridicule which was hurled against the most respectable of the natives of Athens. The poet gave such a true and perfect delineation of the affairs of his country in his plays, that Plato sent his compositions to Dionysius of Syracuse, who wished to receive the most satisfactory account of the Athenian state. The best editions of the work of Aristophanes, are, Kuster's, fol. Amst. 1710, and the 12mo. L. Bat. 1670, and that of Brunck, 4 vols. 8vo. Argent. 1783, which would be still more perfect did it contain the valuable Scholia. *Quintil.* 10. c. 1.—*Paterc.* 1. c. 16.—*Horat.* l. sat. 4. v. 1.—*L. Gyrald. Poet. Hist.* 7.—*Fabr. B. Gr.* 2. c. 21.—*Sax. Onom.* 1. p. 46. [A bust, in the possession of the Grand Duke of Tuscany, at Florence, has the name of Aristophanes inscribed upon it.]——A grammarian of Byzantium, keeper of the library of Alexandria under Ptolemy Evergetes. He wrote a treatise on the harlots of Attica, and also a commentary on Homer. *Fabr. B. Gr.* l. 2. c. 2. art. 17.—*Diog. in Plat. & Epic.*—*Athen.* 9.——A Greek historian of Bœotia, quoted by *Plutarch, de Herod. Malig.* ——A writer on agriculture.——An archon of Athens. Ol. 112. an. 2. *Diod. Sic.* 17. c. 49.

ARISTOPHIL'IDES, a king of Tarentum in the reign of Darius son of Hystaspes. *Herodot.* 3. c. 136.

ARIS'TOPHON, a painter in the age of Socrates. Some of his pictures were very highly esteemed, especially one of Alcibiades, and another of Mars and Venus. *Plut. in Alc.*—*Athen.* 13.—*Plin.* 35. c. 11.——A comic poet in the age of Alexander, many of whose fragments are collected in Athenæus. *Stobæus.*—*Fabr. B. Gr.* l. 2. 22. *de Comic.* ——An archon at Athens. Ol. 112. an. 3.——One of the accusers of Iphicrates. *Polyæn.* 3.——A citizen of Athens, who, though accused 95 times, was always acquitted.——A pancratiast mentioned by *Pausanias, in Eliac.*

ARIS'TOR, the father of Argus, the hundred-eyed keeper of Io. *Ovid.* 1. *Met.* 264.

ARISTOR'IDES, the patronymic of Argus. *Ovid. Met.* 1. v. 624.

ARISTOTELE'A, festivals in honour of Aristotle, because he obtained the restitution of his country, Stagira, from Alexander.

ARISTOT'ELES, a famous philosopher, son of the physician Nicomachus, was born at Stagira, Ol. 99. The loss of his parents in his infancy, with the neglect of his relatives, caused him to disregard his education for foolish and dissipated pursuits. After spending his little patrimony, he, by the direction of the oracle at Delphi, came to Athens, where, as the pupil of Plato, he began to distinguish himself and display his great abilities. For nearly twenty years he was the diligent auditor of the philosopher, and he maintained himself by selling powders and receipts of pharmacy, the knowledge and preparation of which he had inherited from his father. From pupil he was now qualified to become master, and his school was soon frequented by those who admired his talents. Plato felt the rising power of the new philosopher, and accused him, it is said, of ingratitude and illiberality; but Aristotle grew in the public estimation. He was moderate in his meals, slept but little, and always had one arm out of his couch with a bullet in it, which, by falling into a brazen basin underneath, early awakened him. He was, according to some, ten years preceptor to Alexander, who received his instructions with the deference due to his learning and merits, and ever after respected him. Almost all his writings, which are composed on a variety of interesting subjects, are extant; he gave them to Theophrastus at his death, with strict injunctions not to publish them, and, therefore, after passing secretly through the possession of Neleus, and being buried 160 years, they fell into the hands of Apellicon, aud afterwards of Sylla, of Tyranion, and of Andronicus of Rhodes, who redeemed them from destruction, and with much labour and expense presented them to the public. According to Diogenes Laertius, who has preserved a catalogue, the whole of the treatises amount to above 400, on subjects highly important to literature and science. Aristotle had a deformed countenance, but his genius was a sufficient compensation for all his personal defects. He has been called by Plato the philosopher of truth; and Cicero compliments him with the title of a man of eloquence, universal knowledge, readiness, and acuteness of invention, and fecundity of thought. Aristotle neither worshipped nor cared for the divinity, concerning which his opinions were ever various and dissonant; and the more he disregarded the mythology of the ancients, the greater was the credit he acquired over his less philosophical predecessors. He was so authoritative in his opinions, that, as Bacon observes, he wished to establish the same dominion over men's minds, as his pupil over nations. Alexander, it is said, wished and encouraged his learned preceptor to write the history of animals; and, the more effectually to assist him, he supplied him with 800 talents, and, in his Asiatic expedition, employed above a thousand men to collect animals, either in fishing, hunting, or hawking, which were carefully transmitted to the philosopher. Aristotle's logic has long reigned in the schools, and been regarded as a perfect model for the imitation of all. As he expired, the philosopher is said to have uttered the following sentiment: *Fœde hunc mundum intravi, anxius vixi, perturbatus egredior; causa causarum, miserere mei.* The letter which Philip wrote to Aristotle has been preserved, and is in these words: "I inform you that I have a son; I thank the gods, not so much for making me a father, as for giving me a son in an age when he can have Aristotle for his instructor. I hope you will make him a successor worthy of me, and a king worthy of Macedonia. Aristotle married Pythias, the sister of Hermias the governor of Atarnea, a small city of Mysia; and he found himself so happy in this connexion, that he regarded his wife as more than mortal, and even offered sacrifices to her as to a protecting divinity. He died in the 63rd year of his age, B.C. 322. His treatises have been published separately; but the best edition of the works collectively is that of Duval, 2 vols. fol. Paris, 1629. Tyrrwhitt's edition of the Poetica, Oxon. 4to. 1794, is a valuable acquisition to literature. He had a son whom he called Nicomachus, by the courtezan Herpyllis. Some have improperly accused him of being accessary to the death of Alexander; and said that he drowned himself in the Euripus, because he could not find out the cause of its flux and reflux. There are, however, different reports as to the manner of his death; and some believe that he died at Athens, of a cholic, two years after Alexander's death. For a copious account of the life, writings, and editions of Aristotle, *vid. Fabr. B. Gr.* l. 3. c. 5. & *Sax. Onom.* 1. p. 76.—*Diog. in Vitâ.*—*Plut. in Alex. & de Alex. Fort.*, &c.—*Cic. Acad. Quæst.* 4. c. 38. *De Orat.* 3. c. 35. *De Finib.* 5. c. 4.—*Quintil.* l. c. 1. l. 2. c. 16. l. 5. c. 10. l. 10. c. 1.—*Ælian, V. H.* 4. c. 9.—*Justin.* 12. c. 6. & 16.—*Justin. Martyr*—*August. de Civ. Dei.* 8.—*Plin.* 2, 4, 5, &c.—*Athen.* 9.—*Val. Max.* 5. c. 6, &c. [A fine statue of Aristotle exists in the Palazzo Spada at Rome; and there is a bust in the Capitol.] ——A magistrate of Athens.——A commentator on Homer's Iliad.——An orator of Sicily, who answered the panegyric of Isocrates.——A friend of Æschines.——A man of Cyrene who wrote on poetry.——A schoolmaster mentioned in Plato's life written by Aristoxenus.——An obscure grammarian. *Diog. de Aristot.*——A governor of Antiochus, stationed at Chalcis. *Liv.* 36. c. 21.

ARISTOTI'MUS, a tyrant of Elis, 271 years B.C. *Paus.* 5. c. 5.

ARISTOX'ENUS, a celebrated musician, disciple of Aristotle, born at Tarentum. He wrote 453 different treatises on philosophy, history, &c. When disappointed in his expectations of succeeding to the school of Aristotle, he spoke with unbecoming ingratitude of his learned master. Of all his works, nothing remains but three books upon music, the most ancient on that subject extant. His treatise on harmonics may be found in the Antiquæ Musicæ Scriptores, 2 vols. 4to. Amst. 1652. *Fabr. B. Gr.* l. 3. c. 12.—*Sax. Onom.* 1. p. 85.—*Vossius.*—*Suidas*—*Cicero. de Orat.* 3. c. 33, *Ad. Att.* 8. ep. 4.——A philosopher of Cyrene, *Athen.*——A physician, whose writings are quoted by *Galen.*——A poet of Selinus. Ol. 29.——A Pythagorean philosopher.

ARIS'TUS, a Greek historian of Salamis, who wrote an account of Alexander's expedition. *Strab.* 14.—*Arrian.* 7.

ARISTYL'LUS, an obscure poet. *Aristoph. in Plut.*——An astronomer of Alexandria, 222. B.C.

ARIT'IUM, a city of Lusitania, now Benevente. *Ptol.*

ARI'US, or A'RIUS, a small river of Gaul, now lac de Burgian, and another of the same name in Asia. The inhabitants in the neighbourhood were called Arii. *Lucan.* 3. v. 281.——A celebrated writer, the head and founder of the Arian controversy, who denied the eternal divinity and consubstantiality of the Word. Though he was greatly persecuted for his opinions, he gained the favor of the emperor Constantine, and triumphed over his powerful antagonist Athanasius. He died on the night on which he was going to enter the church of Constantinople in triumph. Pressed by nature, he stepped aside to ease himself; but his bowels gushed out, and he expired on the spot. Arius was born in Africa, near Ægypt, and died A.D. 336. *Athanas.*

ARIU'SIUS. *Vid.* Arvisius.

ARIZAN'THI, a nation of Media. *Herod.* 1. c. 161.

ARMAG'ARA, a town of India within the Ganges. *Ptol.*

ARMA'IS, brother of Sesostris a king of Ægypt. *Joh. Marsham. Can. Chron. Sec.* 14.

ARMAMER'TES, or ARMAMITRES, the 7th king of Asyria from Ninus, A.M. 2229. *Euseb. Chron.*

AR'MATA, an epithet given to Venus by the Lacedæmonians.

ARMAVI'ARA or ARMAU'RIA, a town of Armenia Major. *Ptol.*

AR'MEDON, an island on the coast of Crete. *Plin.* 4. c. 12.

ARME'NA, a village of Paphlagonia. *Ptol.*—*Steph.*—*Pliny*, 6. c. 2. calls it a city, which was so cold that the inhabitants surrounded it with a wall, thinking to render it warmer. Hence the proverb, *Armenen muro cingere*, to express folly. It is now Carini.

AR'MENES, a son of Nabis, led in triumph at Rome. *Liv.* 34. c. 1.

ARME'NIA, a large country of Asia, divided into Upper and Lower Armenia. Upper Armenia, called also Major, has Media on the east, Iberia on the north, and Mesopotamia on the south. It was very mountainous, and gave rise to the rivers Tigris, Euphrates, Phasis, Cyrus, Araxes, and Lycus. Lower Armenia, or Minor, was bounded by Cappadocia, Armenia Major, Syria, Cilicia, and the Euphrates. The Armenians were a long time under the dominion of the Medes and Persians, till they were conquered, with the rest of Asia, by Alexander and his successors. The Romans made it one of their provinces, and, under some of the emperors the Armenians had the privilege of choosing their own kings; but they were afterwards reduced to a dependent state The country received its name from Armeus or Armenius, who was one of the Argonauts, and of Thessalian origin. It borrowed the names and attributes of its deities from the Persians. The Armenians paid adoration to Venus Anaitis. Armenia Major is now called Turcomania; and Minor, Anaduole. *Herodot.* 1. c. 194. l. 5. c. 49.—*Curt.* 4. c. 12. l. 5. c. 1.—*Strab.* 1 & 11.—*Mela*, 3. c. 5 & 8.—*Plin.* 6. c. 4, &c.—*Lucan.* 2.

ARMENI'ACUS, a name given to the emperors Marcus and Verus, from their military success in Armenia. *Jul. Cap. in Anton.* c. 9.

ARMEN'IDAS, an historian of Thebes. Some read, with greater probability, Antimenides.—*Apoll. Schol.* 1.—*Voss. H. Gr.* 3.—*Lil. Gyrald.* dial 9.

ARMENOCHAL'YBES, people of Cappadocia, near Armenia Major. *Plin.* 9. c. 4 & 9.

AR'MEUS, or ARME'IS, a king of Ægypt, supposed to be the same person as Danaus. *Euseb.*

AR'MIÆ, a people of the interior of Libya. *Ptol.*

ARMIA'NA, a town of Parthia. *Id.*

ARMIF'ERA, ARMIG'ERA, ARMIP'OTENS, and ARMIS'ONA, epithets applied to Minerva by the poets. *Ovid. Met.* 14. v. 475.—*Virg. Æn.* 2. v. 425, &c.

ARMILLA'TUS, one of Domitian's favorites. *Juv.* 4. v. 53.

ARMILUS'TRIUM, a festival at Rome, observed on the 19th of October, at which all the people appeared under arms. This festival has often been confounded with that of the Salii, though easily distinguished; because the latter was observed on the 2d of March, and at the celebration of the Armilustrium the people always played on a flute, but the Salii played upon the trumpet. It was instituted A.U.C. 543. *Varro de L. L.* 5. c. 3.—*Liv.* 27. c. 37.—*Fam. Nardi de Rom.* 7. c. 7.

ARMIN'IUS, a warlike general of the Germans, who for some time waged a bloody war against Rome. He was at last conquered by Germanicus in two great battles, and was poisoned by one of his friends, A.D. 19, in the 37th year of his age. *Dio.* 56.—*Tacit. Ann.* 1, &c.

ARMIS'TÆ, a people of Dalmatia. *Plin.* 3. c. 22.

AR'MITUS, a Syracusan, who, in a drunken fit, offered violence to his daughter. *Plut.*

ARMI'YSES, 13th king of Lower Ægypt, succeeded Achoreus, and reigned four years.

ARMORI'CÆ, cities of Celtic Gaul, famous for the warlike, rebellious, and inconstant disposition of the inhabitants, called Armorici. Armorica extended between the rivers Liger and Sequana, and comprehended those rich and populous provinces now called Britany and Normandy. *Cæs. Bell. G.*

ARMO'RUM PROMONTO'RIUM, now Capo dell' Armi, a promontory of Calabria.

ARMOS'ATA, or ARMOSA'TA. *Vid.* Arsamostata.

ARMO'ZON, a promontory of Carmania now called Cap. Jaquette, or, by many, Capo d'Ormus. *Ptol.*

ARMU'ZIA or ARMU'ZA, now Ormus, an island in the mouth of the Persian Gulph. *Id.*

AR'NE, a city of Lycia, called afterwards Xanthus. *Steph.*——A town of Umbria in Italy.——A daughter of Æolus, who gave her name to two towns, one in Thessaly, the other in Bœotia. Neptune assumed the shape of a bull to enjoy her company. *Strab.* 1 & 2.—*Paus.* 9. c. 40.—*Ovid. Met.* 6. fab. 4.—*Homer. Il.* 2. v. 507.

AR'NI, a people of Italy, probably the inhabitants of Arne, destroyed by Hercules.

ARNIEN'SIS, a tribe in Rome. *Liv.* 6. c. 5, &c.

ARNIS'SA, a Greek city in the country of the Taulantii, in Macedonia. *Ptol.*

ARNO'BIUS, a philosopher in Diocletian's reign, born at Sicca in Numidia. He became a convert to Christianity, but was refused ordination by the bishops till he gave them a proof of his sincerity, and of his faith. Upon this he wrote his celebrated treatise, in which he exposed the absurdity of irreligion, and ridiculed the heathen gods. He is called the Varro of ecclesiastical history. The book which he wrote, *De rhetorica institutione*, is not extant. The best edition of his treatise *Adversus gentes* is the 4to, printed L. Bat. 1651, and edited by Salmasius. *Harles. Not. Lit. Rom.* 1. p. 552. —*Sax. Onom.* 1. p. 382.

ARNO'BIUS MI'NOR, was a Gaul and Semipelagian: he wrote a commentary on the Psalms, edited by Erasmus, and lived about A.D. 460. *Harles. ibid.* —*Sax. Onom.* 1. p. 516.

AR'NUS, now Arno, a fine river of Etruria, rising in the Apennine mountains, and falling into the Mediterranean. *Liv.* 22. c. 2.—*Cluver.* 3. c. 31.

AR'OA, a town of Achaia. *Paus.* 7.

AROC'ELUM, a town of the Celtiberi in Spain: the people were called Arocelitani. *Plin.* 3. c. 3.

AR'OCHA, a river of the Locri in Italy. *Id.* 3. c. 10.

AROER'NI, a warlike nation of Gaul. *Steph.*

AR'OLUS, a city of Macedonia. *Ptol.*

ARO'MA, or AR'OMA, a town of Caria. *Strab.*—— A town of Cappadocia. *Capella. post. Plin.* 6.—— A city of the Æthiopians. *Steph.*

AROM'ATA, a promontory of Africa, now Capo de Gardafuni. *Ptol.*

A'RON, one of the leaders who assisted Æetes against Perses. *Val. Flacc.* 5. v. 590, &c.

ARON'CÆ, a people in the interior of Libya, the country is now probably Benin.

AROS'APES, a river of Ariana. *Plin.* 6. c. 23.

AR'OSIS. *Vid.* Araxes.

ARPA'NI, a people of Italy. *Plin.* 3. c. 11.

ARPES'SUS, a river of Thrace, falling into the Hebrus. *Appian.*

AR'PI, a city of Apulia, first called Argos Hippium, and afterwards Argyripa. It was built by Diomedes, after the Trojan war. *Justin.* 20. c. 1.—*Virg. Æn.* 10. 28, &c.

ARPI'NA, a city of Elis, so called from Arpina, daughter of Asopus. *Steph.*

ARPI'NUM, now Arpino, a town of the Volsci, famous for giving birth to Cicero and Marius. The words *Arpinæ chartæ* are sometimes applied to Cicero's works. *Mart.* 10. epigr. 19.—*Juv.* 8. v. 237.—*Cic. Rull.* 3.

ARPO'NIUM, a town of Magna Græcia. *Diod. Sic.*

AR'PUS, a prince of the Chatti, whose wife and daughter were taken by C. Silius, a lieutenant of Germanicus. *Tac. Ann.* 2. c. 7.

AR'RA, a town of Arabia Felix. *Ptol.*——A city of Illyria. *Steph.*

ARRÆ'I, a people of Thrace. *Plin.* 4. c. 11.

ARREB'ACI, a people of Spain. *Plin.* 3. c. 3.

ARREOMITH'RES, a Persian, slain, with 2,000 horse, at the Granicus.

ARRE'TUM or ARRE'TIUM, now Arezzo, a town of Etruria.

ARRHABÆ'US, the king of a nation in the neighbourhood of Macedonia, who greatly distressed Archelaus. *Aristot.* 5. *Polit.* c. 10.

AR'RHABON, a river of Iberia. *Steph.*

AR'RHADE, a city of Arabia Deserta. *Ptol.*

AR'RHAPA, a town of Assyria. *Id.* The country was called Arrhapachitis.

ARRHEPHO'RIA, a festival at Athens, in honor of Minerva. *Vid.* Hersephoria.

AR'RIA. *Vid.* Aria.

AR'RIA FADIL'LA, the mother of the emperor Antoninus Pius. *Jul. Cap. in Anton.*

AR'RIA GAL'LA, a beautiful, but immodest woman seduced by C. Piso. *Tacit.* 15. c. 59.

ARRIA'NUS FLA'VIUS, a Greek philosopher of Nicomedia, priest of Ceres and Proserpine, and disciple of Epictetus. He was called a second Xenophon from the elegance and sweetness of his diction, and distinguished for his acquaintance with military and political life. He wrote seven books on Alexander's expedition, a composition highly and deservedly valued; the periplus of the Euxine and Red Seas; eight books on the dissertations of Epictetus; besides an account of the Alani, Bithynians, and Parthians. He flourished about the 140th year of Christ, and for his learning and abilities were rewarded with the consulship, and government of Cappadocia by M. Antoninus. The best edition of Arrian's *Expeditio Alexandri*, is the fol. Gronovii. L. Bat. 1704, and the 8vo, à Raphelio, 2 vols. 1757, and the *Tactica*, 8vo, Amst. 1683. *Fabr. B. Gr.* 4. c. 10.—*Sax. Onom.* 1. p. 298.——A Greek historian, mentioned by *Julius Capitolinus* in his life of the emperor Gordian.——An Athenian who wrote a treatise on hunting, and the manner of keeping dogs.——A poet, who wrote an epic poem in twenty-four books on Alexander; also another poem, on Attalus king of Pergamus. He likewise translated Virgil's Georgics into Greek verse. *Sueton. in Tiber.* c. 69. *Fabricius* in a note to the chapter above quoted, enumerates nine persons of this name; but they were little known.

ARRIBAN'TIUM, a city of Dardania, in Upper Mysia. *Ptol.* It is now Wiczitterne or, perhaps, Novibazar.

AR'RIUS, a friend of Cicero, whose sumptuous feast *Horace* describes, 2 sat. 3. v. 86.

AR'RIUS OR A'RIUS, a philosopher of Alexandria in Ægypt, who so ingratiated himself with Augustus, after the battle of Actium, that the conqueror declared the people of Alexandria owed the preservation of their city to three causes; because Alexander was their founder, because of the beauty of the situation, and because Arrius was a native of the place. *Plut. in Anton.*

AR'RIUS AN'TONIN. the maternal grandfather of Antoninus Pius, was twice consul.

AR'RIUS AN'TONIN, a proconsul of Asia, put to death by Commodus, at the instigation of Cleander.

AR'RIUS A'PER, a Roman general who murdered the emperor Numerianus. *Vid.* Numerianus.

AR'RIUS VA'RUS, a præfect of horse in Armenia, under Corbulo. *Tac. Ann.* 13. 9.

ARRUN'TIUS, a Roman consul who was also a famous geographer. Upon being accused of adultery and treason, under Tiberius, he opened his veins, and bled to death. *Tacit. Ann.* 6. c. 47.

ARSA'BES, a satrap of Armenia.——A satrap of Persia. *Polyæn.* 4. 17. & 7. 28.

AR'SACE or ARSA'CIA, a celebrated city of Persia, so called from Arsaces.

AR'SACES, or ARSA'CES, a man of obscure origin, who, upon seeing Seleucus defeated by the Gauls, invaded and conquered Parthia, and laid the foundations of an empire, 250 B.C. He added the kingdom of the Hyrcani to his newly acquired possessions, and spent his time in establishing his power and revising the laws. After death he was made a god by his grateful subjects, and all his successors were called in honour of his name, *Arsacidæ.* *Justin.* 41. c. 5 & 6.—*Strab.* 11. & 12.

AR'SACES, the Second, his son and successor, waged war against Antiochus the son of Seleucus, who entered the field with 100,000 foot and 20,000 horse. He afterwards made peace with Antiochus, and died B.C. 217. *Justin.* 41. c. 5.

AR'SACES, the Third, king of Parthia, of the family of the Arsacidæ, was also called Priapatrus. He reigned twelve years, and left two sons, Mithridates and Phraates. Phraates succeeded him as being the elder, and at his death he left his kingdom to his brother, though he had many children; observing, that a monarch ought to have in view, not the dignity of his family, but the prosperity of his subjects. *Justin.* 31. c. 5.

AR'SACES, a king of Pontis and Armenia, in alliance with the Romans. He long fought with success against the Persians, till he was deceived by the snares of king Sapor, who put out his eyes, and soon after deprived him of life. *Marcellin.*——The eldest son of Artabanus, appointed over Armenia by his father, after the death of king Artaxias. *Tacit. Hist.* 6. 31.——A servant of Themistocles.——A commander sent by Alexander into Media to supplant Oxidates. *Curt.* 8. c. 3.

ARSACIDÆ, a name given to some of the monarchs of Parthia, in honour of Arsaces, the founder of the empire. The power subsisted till the 229th year of the Christian æra, when they were conquered by Artaxerxes king of Persia. *Justin.* 41.

AR'SACUS or AS'TACUS, an officer of Tisaphernes. *Thucyd.* 8. c. 108.

AR'SÆ, a people of Arabia Felix. *Ptol.*

ARSAGALI'TÆ, a people near the Indus. *Plin.* 6. c. 20.

ARSAM'ENES, the son of Darius, a satrap of Persia, and general of the Atii and Myci, in the invasion of Greece by Xerxes. *Herodot.* 7. c. 68.—*Diod. Sic.* 17.

ARSA'MES, the father of Hystaspes. *Herodot.* 1. c. 209, &c.——An illegitimate son of Artaxerxes Mnemon, was slain by Ochus, in conjunction with the son of Teribazus. *Mitford, H. Gr.* 9. p. 173.——A son of Darius and Artystone, the daughter of Cyrus, commanded the Æthiopians and Arabs in the expedition of Xerxes. *Herodot.* 7. c. 69.——A præfect of Cilicia, who surrendered to Alexander *Curt.* 3. c. 4. & 8. c. 8.

ARSAM'ETES, a river of Asia, near Parthia. *Tac. Ann.* 15. c. 15,

ARSA'MIA, a city of Germany. *Ptol.*

ARSAMOSA'TA, or ARSAMOS'ATA, a town of Armenia Major, 70 miles from the Euphrates, at the north of Edessa. *Tac. Ann.* 15. c. 10.

ARSA'NIAS, a river of Armenia, which, according to some, flows into the Tigris, and afterwards into the Euphrates. *Plin.* 5. c. 24, &c.

ARSATIA'NUM, a city of Pannonia, now Arsa. *Antonin.*

ARSE'A, a region of Armenia Major. *Cluver.* 5. c. 16.

ARSE'NE, a marsh of Armenia Major, the fishes of which are all of the same sort. *Strab.*

ARSENA'RIA, a colony of Mauritania Cæsariensis. *Mela*, 1. c. 6.

ARSE'NIUM, a town of Germany. *Ptol.*

AR'SES, the youngest son of Ochus, whom the eunuch Bagoas raised to the throne of Persia, and destroyed with his children, after a reign of three years. *Diod.* 17.

ARSE'SA, a region of Armenia Major. *Ptol.*

AR'SIA, a wood of Etruria, famous for a battle between the Romans and the Veientes. *Plut. in Popl.*—*Liv.* 2. c. 7.——A small river, now Arsa, which flows between Istria and Illyricum into the Adriatic, near the Absyrtides. *Cluver.* 4. c. 4.——A river of Italy, flowing through Campania. *Cluver.* 3. c. 24.

ARSIA'NA, a city of Susiana. *Amm. Marcell.*

AR'SICA, the name of Artaxerxes Mnemon, when a private person.

ARSICODA'NI, a people of Arabia Felix. *Plin.* 6. c. 28.

ARSICU'A, a city of Germany, now Brin. *Ptol.*

ARSIDÆ'US, a son of Datames, killed in a battle which he fought with the Pisidians. *Nep. in Dat.* 6.

ARSIE'TÆ, a people of European Sarmatia. *Ptol.*

ARSINA'RIUM, a promontory of Libya, now Capo Verde. *Id.*

ARSIN'OE, daughter of Leucippus and Philodice, was mother of Æsculapius by Apollo, according to some authors. She received divine honours at Sparta after death. *Apollod.* 3.—*Paus.* 2. c. 26. l. 3. c. 12.——A daughter of Phlegeus, promised in marriage to Alcmæon. *Apollod.* 3. c. 7.——A fountain of Peloponnesus. *Paus. Messen.*——The sister and wife of Ptolemy Philadelphus, worshipped after death under the name of Venus Zephyritis. Dinochares began to build a temple to her honor with loadstones, in which a statue of Arsinoe was to be suspended in the air by the power of the magnet; but the death both of the king and of the architect prevented the completion of the edifice. *Plin.* 34. c. 14.——A daughter of Ptolemy Lagus, who married Lysimachus, king of Macedonia. After her husband's death, Ceraunus, her own brother. married her, and ascended the throne of Macedonia. He previously murdered the sons of Arsinoe by Lysimachus, in their mother's arms. Arsinoe was some time after banished to Samothrace. *Justin.* 17. c. 1, &c.——A younger daughter of Ptolemy Auletes, sister of Cleopatra. Antony despatched her, to gain the good graces of her sister. *Hirt. Alex.* 4.—*Appian.*——The wife of Magas, king of Cyrene, committed adultery with her son-in-law. *Justin.* 26. c. 3.——A daughter of Lysimachus. *Paus.*

ARSIN'OE, a town of Ægypt, situated near the lake Mœris, on the west shore of the Nile, where the inhabitants paid the highest veneration to the crocodiles. They embalmed them after death, and buried them in the subterraneous cells of the Labyrinth. *Strab.*——A town called also Cleopatris, in honour of the Ægyptian queens, situate at the top of the Arabic Gulph, on the western side. It was the name also of towns in Cilicia, Æolia, Syria, Cyprus, Lycia, &c.—*Mela*, & *Cluver. passim.*

ARSIS'ACA, a city of Media. *Ptol.*

ARSI'TES, a satrap of the Paphlagonian cavalry. *Diod. Sic.* 17.

ARSI'TIS, a region of Hyrcania. *Id.*

ARSO'NIUM, a city of Germany.

AR'SOPÆ, a people near the Euxine sea. *Orph. in Argon.*

ARSYS'IA, a region of Chius. *Steph.*

ARTABA'NUS, son of Hystaspes, was brother to Darius the first king of Persia. He dissuaded his nephew Xerxes from making war against the Greeks, and at his return assassinated him with the hopes of ascending the throne. Darius, the son of Xerxes, was murdered in a similar manner; and Artaxerxes his brother, would have shared the same fate, had he not discovered the snares of the assassin, and punished him with immediate death. The assassin of Xerxes is supposed by some to have been the son of Artasyras, a favourite, and not the brother of Darius. *Ctesias. Hist.* 29.—*Diod.* 11.—*Justin.* 3. c. 1, &c.—*Herodot.* 4. c. 38. l. 7. c. 10, &c.

ARTABA'NUS the First, a king of Parthia, after the death of his nephew Phraates the Second. He undertook a war against a nation of Scythia, in which he perished. His son Mithridates succeeded him. *Justin.* 42. c. 2.

ARTABA'NUS the Second, a king of Media and afterwards of Parthia, after the expulsion of Vonones, whom Tiberius had made king there. He invaded Armenia, whence he was driven away by one of the generals of Tiberius. He was expelled from his throne, which Tiridates usurped; but some time after he was restored again to his ancient power, and died A.D. 48. *Tacit. Ann.* 5, &c.

ARTABA'NUS the Third, a king of Parthia, very inimical to the interests of Vespasian.

ARTABA'NUS the Fourth, a king of Parthia, who made war against the emperor Caracalla, who had attempted his life on pretence of courting his daughter. He was murdered, and the empire of Parthia abolished, and the crown transferred to the Persian monarchs. *Dio.*—*Herodian.*

ARTABA'NUS, the father of Artyphius. *Herod.* 7. c. 66.——The father of Bassaces. *Id.* 7. c. 75.

ARTABASTES, a king of Armenia. One of his letlers to Sapor is extant.

ARTABA'TES, the father of Pharnazathres. *Herodot.* 7. c. 65.

ARTABATITÆ, a wandering nation of Æthiopians. *Plin.* 6. c. 30.—*Solin.* c. 33.

ARTABAZA'NES or ARTOBARZA'NES, the eldest son of Darius when a private person. Xerxes, however, succeeded to the crown, because, though younger, he was the eldest of the children born to Darius when raised to the throne. *Justin.*—*Herodot.* 7. c. 1 & 2.

ARTABA'ZUS, a son of Pharnaces, general in the army of Xerxes. He fled from Greece upon the ill success of Mardonius. *Herodot.* 7, 8, & 9.——A general who made war against Artaxerxes, and was defeated. He was afterwards reconciled to his sovereign, and became the familiar friend of Darius the Third. After the murder of this prince, he surrendered himself with his sons to Alexander, who treated him with great humanity and confidence. *Curt.* 5. c. 9 & 12. l. 6. c. 5. l. 7. c. 3 & 5. l. 8. c. 1.——An officer of Artaxerxes employed against Datames. *Diod.* 15.

AR'TABRI or ARTABRI'TÆ, a people of Lusitania. The promontory at the western extremity of their territory was called Artabrum Celticum, or Nerium, and is now Cape Finisterre. *Sil.* 3. v. 362.

AR'TACHÆ'ES, an officer in the army of Xerxes, the tallest of all the troops, the king excepted. He was appointed, together with Bubares, to direct the labours of those whom Xerxes employed to dig round mount Athos. *Herodot.* 7. c. 21 & 117.

ARTACÆ'NA, a city of Asia, near Aria. *Curt.* 6. c. 6, &c.

AR'TACE, a town and seaport near Cyzicus. It did not exist in the age of Pliny. There was in its neighbourhood a fountain called Artacia. *Herodot.* c. 14.—*Procop. de Bell. Pers.* 1. c. 25.—*Strab.* 13.—*Plin.* 5. c. 32.——A city of Phrygia.——A fortified place of Bithynia.——A colony of the Milesians in Asia.

ARTACE'NE, a country of Assyria, near Arbela, where Alexander conquered Darius. *Strab.* 16.

AR'TACI, a people of Thrace. *Steph.*

ARTA'CIA, a fountain in the country of the Læstrygones. *Tibull.* 4. el. 1. v. 60.—*Od.* 10. 107.

ARTACI'NA, a city of Crete. *Ptol.*

ARTACOA'NA, a town of Ariana. *Plin.* 6. c. 23.

ART'ÆI, a name by which the Persians were called among their neighbours. *Herodot.* 7. c. 61.

ARTAG'ERAS, a town of Upper Armenia. *Strab.*

ARTAGER'SES, a general in the army of Artaxerxes, killed by Cyrus the younger. *Plut. in Artax.*

ARTAGIGAR'TA, a town of Armenia Major. *Ptol.*

ARTAGE'RA, a city of the interior of Libya. *Id.*

ARTAMIS, a city of the Pentapolis, in Africa. *Id.*

ARTA'NES, a king of the southern parts of Armenia. *Strab.* 11.——A brother of Darius, killed at Thermopylæ. *Herodot.* 7. c. 224.

ARTA'NES, a small river of Thrace which flows into the Ister. *Herodot.* 4. c. 49.——A river of Colchis. *Arrian.*

ARTANIS'SA, a town of Asiatic Iberia. *Ptol.*

ARTAPA'NUS, or, more probably, Artabanus, an author who wrote a work on the Jews. *Clem. Strom.* l. 1.

ARTAPHER'NES, a general whom Darius sent into Greece with Datis. He was conquered at the battle of Marathon by Miltiades. *Vid.* Datis. *C. Nep. in Milt.*—*Herodot.* 7. c. 74.——The father of the preceding, was brother of Darius, and præfect of Sardis. *Herodot.* 5. c. 25, &c.

ARTASY'RAS, a Persian counsellor, under Smerdis, privy to the conspiracy of the seven nobles. *Ctesias.*

ARTA'TUS, a river of Illyria, now Fiume della Istria. *Liv.* 43. c. 19.

ARTAVAS'DES, a son of Tigranes, king of Upper Armenia, who wrote tragedies, and was distinguished as an orator and historian. He was an ally of Rome, but Crassus was defeated partly on account of his delay. He betrayed M. Antony in his expedition against Parthia, for which Antony reduced his kingdom, and carried him to Ægypt, where he adorned the triumph of the conqueror led in golden chains. He was some time after put to death. *Appian. in Parth.*—*Strab.* 11.—*Plut. in Crass.*——A person to whom Tiberius gave the kingdom of Armenia, but he was expelled. *Tac. Ann.* 2. c. 3.

ARTAX'A or ARTAXIAS, a general of Antiochus the Great. When he was subdued, he became king of Armenia, and Tigranes was one of his successors. *Strab.* 11.

ARTAX'ATA, *orum*, now Ardesh, a strongly fortified town of Upper Armenia, said to have been built by Annibal for Artaxias, the king of the country. It was burnt by Corbulo, and rebuilt by Tiridates, who called it Neronea, in honour of Nero. *Strab.* 11.

ARTAXERX'ES the First, surnamed *Macrochir*, or *Longimanus*, succeded his father Xerxes. He cut off Artabanus (*vid.* Artabanus), made war against the Bactrians, and, with the assistance of the Athenians, reconquered Ægypt, which had revolted. In his private character Artaxerxes was humane and benevolent, and during his reign of 39 years, was greatly beloved by his subjects and respected by his allies. He died B.C. 425. He is supposed to be the Persian king Ahasuerus in the book of Esther. *C. Nep. in Reg.*—*Plut. in Artax.*—*Thucyd.* 1.—*Diod. Sic.* 11 & 12.—*Justin.* 3.—*Scaliger. de emend. temp.* 5.

ARTAXERX'ES the Second, king of Persia, was surnamed *Mnemon*, on account of his extensive memory. He was son of Darius the Second, by Parysatis, the daughter of Artaxerxes Longimanus, and had three brothers, Cyrus, Ostanes, and Oxathres. His original name was Arsaces, which he changed into Artaxerxes when he ascended the throne. His brother Cyrus was of such an ambitious disposition, that he resolved to make himself king, in opposition to Artaxerxes. Parysatis always favoured Cyrus; and when he had attempted the life of Artaxerxes, she obtained his pardon by her entreaties and influence. *Vid.* Cyrus. After he was delivered from the attacks of his brother, Artaxerxes, remembering the powerful assistance that had been brought against him by Grecian auxiliaries, excited dissensions among them, and prevailed upon them to declare war against Sparta. He married two of his own daughters, called Atossa and Amestris, and named his eldest son Darius to be his successor. Darius, however, conspired against his father, and was put to death. It is said that Artaxerxes died of a broken heart, in consequence of his son's infamous behaviour, in the 94th year of his age, after a reign of 46 years, B.C. 358. Artaxerxes had fifteen children by his concubines, and only four legitimate sons. *Plut. in Vitâ.*—*C. Nep. in Reg.*—*Justin.* 10. c. 1, &c.—*Diod.* 13, &c.

ARTAXERX'ES the Third, surnamed *Ochus*, succeeded his father Artaxerxes the Second, and established himself on his throne by murdering above eighty of his nearest relations. He recovered Ægypt, which had revolted, destroyed Sidon, and ravaged all Syria. He made war against the Cadusii, and greatly rewarded a private man called Codomanus for his uncommon valour. But his cruelty offended his subjects, and Bagoas at last obliged his physician to poison him, B.C. 337, and afterwards threw his flesh to be devoured by cats, and made handles for swords with his bones. *Justin.* 10. c. 3.—*Diod.* 17.—*Ælian, V. H.* 6. c. 8.

ARTAXERX'ES or ARTAXA'RES the First, a common soldier of Persia, who killed Artabanus A.D. 228, and again erected Persia into a kingdom, which had been extinct since the death of Darius. Severus the Roman emperor conquered him, and obliged him to remain within his own territories. *Herodian.* 5.

ARTAXERX'ES the Second, one of the successors of the preceding, reigned eleven years, during which he rendered himself odious by his cruelties.

ARTAXI'AS, son of Artavasdes, king of Armenia, was proclaimed king by his father's troops. He opposed Antony, by whom he was defeated, and became so odious to his subjects that the Romans raised Tigranes to the throne.——A son of Polemon, whose original name was Zeno. After the expulsion of Vonones from Armenia, he was made king by Germanicus. *Tacit. Ann.* 6. c. 31.——A general of Antiochus. *Vid.* Artaxa.

ARTAYC'TES, a Persian appointed governor of Sestus by Xerxes. He was suspended on a cross by the Athenians for his cruelties. *Herodot.* 7. c. 78, &c.

ARTAYN'TA, a Persian lady, whom Xerxes gave in

marriage to his son Darius. She was afterwards one of the mistresses of her father-in-law. *Herodot.* 9. c. 103. &c.

ARTAYN'TES, a Persian admiral, who sought safety in flight at the battle of Mycale. *Herodot.* 8. c. 130. l. 9. c. 107.

ARTEM'BARES, a celebrated Mede in the reign of Cyrus the Great. *Herodot.* 1. c. 114, &c.

ARTEMIDO'RUS, a native of Ephesus, who wrote a history and description of the earth in eleven books. He flourished about 104. B.C. The fragments of his works which remain may be found in Hudson's Geographi Græci Minores. They were also published by Hoeschelius under the title of *Artemidori et aliorum Geographica*, 4to. 1600. *Fabr. B. Gr.* 4. c. 15.——A physician in the age of Adrian.——A native of Ephesus, or rather of Daldis or Daldia, in Lydia, flourished in the reign of the emperor Antoninus Pius. He was naturally of a superstitious turn of mind, and published a work on dreams, which is still extant, divided into five books. The best edition is that of Rigaltius, in Greek and Latin, with notes printed at Paris, 4to. 1604, to which are annexed *Achmetis, Astrampsychi, et Nicephori Oneirocritica.*——A philosopher of Cnidus, son of the historian Theopompus. He established a school at Rome, and wrote a book on illustrious men, not extant. As he was a friend of J. Cæsar, he wrote down the particulars of the conspiracy which was formed against his life. He gave it to the dictator as he was going to the senate, but J. Cæsar put it with other papers which he held in his hand, thinking it to be of no immediate consequence. *Plut. in Cæs.*——A famous boxer. *Paus. El.* 2.—*Martial.* 6. epigr. 77. v. 3.——A pupil of Aristophanes, of Byzantium, wrote a work, *De re culinaria*, and another on Doris. *Athen.* 10 & 14.——A celebrated grammarian of Tarsus. *Strab.* l. 14. For a more copious account of these persons, and of others of this name, *vid. Fabr. B. Gr.* l. 4. c. 15. & *Voss. H. Gr.* c. 20. 22.

AR'TEMIS, the Greek name of Diana. Her festivals, called Artemisia, were celebrated in several parts of Greece, particularly at Delphi. There was a solemnity of the same name at Syracuse ; it lasted three days, which were spent in banqueting and diversions. *Athen.* 7.

ARTEMIS'IA, daughter of Lygdamus, reigned over Halicarnassus and the neighbouring country. She assisted Xerxes in his expedition against Greece with a fleet, and her valour was so remarkable, that the monarch, observed that all his men fought like women and all his women like men. The Athenians offered a reward of 10,000 drachms for her head. It is said that Artemisia was fond of a youth of Abydus, called Dardanus, and that to punish the disdain with which he received her licentious addresses, she put out his eyes while he was asleep, and afterwards leaped down the promontory of Leucas. *Ptolem. Hephæst.* 7.—*Herodot.* 7. c. 99. l. 8. c. 68.—*Justin.* 2. c. 12.——A queen of Caria, often confounded with the former. She was daughter of Hecatomnus, king of Caria, and was married to her own brother Mausolus, a prince famous for his personal beauty. She was so fond of her husband, that at his death she dissolved and drank his ashes after his body had been burned, and erected to his memory a monument, which, for its grandeur and magnificence, was deservedly called one of the seven wonders of the world. This monument she called *Mausoleum*, a name which has been given from that time to all monuments of unusual splendor. She invited all the literary men of her age to her court, and proposed rewards to him who should compose the best elegiac panegyric upon her husband. The prize was adjudged to Theopompus. She was so inconsolable for the death of her husband, that she died through grief two years after. *Vitruv.*—*Strab.* 14.—*Plin.* 25. c. 7. l. 36. c. 5.——*Vid.* Artemis.

ARTEMIS'IUM, a promontory of Eubœa. where Diana had a temple. The fleet of Xerxes had a partial engagement there with the Grecian ships. *Herodot.* 7. c. 175, &c.——A lake near the grove Aricia, with a temple sacred to Artemis, whence the name.——An inland city of the Oenotri.——A city of Eubœa.

ARTEMIS'IUS. a mountain of Arcadia, *Plin.* 4. c. 6.——The name of the month of May among the Macedonians. *Suidas.*

ARTEMI'TA, a city at the east of Seleucia in Syria. *Strab.* 15.——An island opposite the mouth of the Achelous, in the Ionian Sea. *Id.*

ARTEMON, an historian of Pergamus. *Voss. H. Gr.* c. 3.——A native of Clazomenæ, who was with Pericles at the siege of Samus, where it is said that he invented the battering ram, the *testudo*, and other equally valuable military engines. *Ælian. de Animal.* 12. c. 38.——A man who wrote a treatise on collecting books.——A native of Magnesia, who wrote the history of illustrious women.——A painter. *Plin.* 35. c. 11.——A Syrian, whose features bore a very strong resemblance to those of king Antiochus. *Vid.* Antiochus.

ARTE'NA, a city of Italy taken by the Romans. *Livy*, 4. c. ult. calls it a town of the Volsci.

ARTHABATICÆ. *Vid.* Artabatitæ.

ARTICAUD'NA, a city of Aria. *Ptol.*

ARTI'GIS, a city of Spain, now Althama. *Id.*

ARTIG'ULA, an island of Æthiopia. *Plin.* 6. c. 29.

ARTIMIRIPES, a king of Armenia, conquered by Antony.

ARTIM'PASA, a name of Venus among the Scythians. *Herodot.* 4. c. 59.

ARTI'NES, the 7th king of the Medes, reigned 22 years.

ARTOBARZA'NES. *Vid.* Artabazanes.

ARTOBRI'GA, a city of Vindelicia. *Ptol.* It is now Lebnary, according to *Cluverius.*

ARTOCH'MES, a general of Xerxes, who married one of the daughters of Darius. *Herodot.* 7. c. 73.

ARTO'NA or OR'TONA, a small town of the Latins, taken by the Æqui. *Liv.* 2. c. 43.

ARTONOSTRA, a daughter of Darius. *Herodot.* 6.43.

ARTON'TES, a son of Mardonius. *Paus. in Bœotic.*—*Herodot.* 9. 84.——The father of Bagæus, who was sent by Darius to assassinate Orœtes. *Id.* 3. 128.

ARTO'RIUS, a physician of Augustus, who, on the night previous to the battle of Philippi, saw Diana in a dream, who told him to assure Augustus of victory. *Val. Max.* 1. c. 7.

ARTOX'ARES, a eunuch of Paphlagonia, in the reign of Artaxerxes the First, cruelly put to death by Parysatis.

ARTU'RIUS, an obscure fellow, raised to honours and wealth by his flatteries, &c. *Juv.* 3. v. 29.

ARTYB'IUS, a Persian general, whom Darius commissioned to invade Cyprus. His horse was celebrated for the assistance which he afforded his master by standing on his hind legs, and fighting with his fore legs. They were, however, both slain. *Herodot.* 5. c. 108 & 111.

ARTYMNE'SUS, a city of Lycia. *Steph.*

ARTY'NES, a king of Media. *Diod. Sic.* 2. c. 34.

ARTYN'IA, a lake of Asia Minor, near Cyzicum *Plin.* 5. c. 32.—*Steph.*

ARTYPH'IUS, a son of Artabanus. *Herodot.* 7. c. 66.

ARTYSTO'NE, or ARTYS'TONE, a daughter of Cyrus. *Herodot.* 3. c. 88.

AR'UÆ, a people of Hyrcania, where Alexander kindly received the chief officers of Darius. *Curt.* 6. c. 9.

ARU'CIA, a town of Illyricum. *Id.*

ARUE'RIS, a god of the Ægyptians, son of Isis and Osiris. *Diod.* 1.—*Plut. de Is. & Osir.*

L. ARUNCULE'IUS COS'TA, an officer sent by J. Cæsar against the Gauls, by whom he was killed. *Cæs. Bell. Gall.* 5.

ARUN'DA, now Ronda, a city of Hispania Bætica. *Ptol.*

A'RUNS, an Etrurian soothsayer in the age of Marius. *Lucan.* 1. v. 586.——A soldier who slew Camilla in the Rutulian war, and was killed by Diana. *Virg. Æn.* 11. v. 759.——A brother of Tarquin the Proud. He married Tullia, who murdered him to espouse Tarquin, who had assassinated his wife.——A son of Tarquin the Proud, who, in the battle that was fought between the partisans of his father and the Romans, attacked Brutus the Roman consul, who wounded him, and threw him down from his horse. *Liv.* 2. c. 6.——A son of Porsenna, king of Etruria, sent by his father to take Aricia. *Liv.* 2. c. 14.——A native of Clusium, who, to resent the violence offered to his wife by Lucumo, one of his countrymen, invited the Gauls to invade Italy, by giving them the wine of the country, and alluring them by the most fascinating description of the richness and fertility of its soil. It is said that he conducted the invaders over the

Alps, and directed their attack against Clusium. *Liv.* 5. c. 33.

ARUN'TIUS, a Roman who ridiculed the rites of Bacchus, for which the god inebriated him to such a degree, that he offered violence to his own daughter Medullina, who murdered him. *Plut. in Parall.*——A man who wrote an account of the Punic wars, in the style of Sallust, in the reign of Augustus. *Tac. Ann.* 1.—*Senec.* ep. 14.——A Latin writer. *Senec. de Benef.* 6.

ARUN'TIUS PATER'CULUS, a man who gave Æmylius Censorinus, tyrant of Ægesta, a brazen horse as an instrument to torment criminals. The tyrant made the first experiment upon the body of the donor. *Plut. in Parall.*

ARUN'TIUS STEL'LA, a poet, in the age of Domitian, descended from a consular family.

ARUNU'II, a people of Gallia Lugdunensis. *Ptol.*

ARUPI'NUS, now Rovigno, a maritime town of Istria. *Tibull.* 4. el. 1. v. 110.

ARUSÆ'US, the accuser of L. Arruntius. *Tac. Ann.* 6. c. 7.

ARUSE'JUS LU'CIUS, a person put to death under Tiberius. *Id. ibid.* 6. c. 40.

ARUS'PEX. *Vid.* Harus'pex.

ARU'ZIS, a city of Media. *Ptol.*

ARVA'LES, a name given to twelve priests at Rome, who celebrated the festivals called Ambarvalia. According to some, they were descended from the twelve sons of Acca Laurentia, who was the nurse of Romulus. They wore a crown of ears of corn, and a white fillet. *Varro de L. L.* 4.—*Aul. G.* 6. c. 7.—*Plin.* 17. c. 2.—*Turneb.* 21. *Adv.* 1.—*Fab. Fulgent.* 1 *De Voc. Ant.*—*Massus. Sabinus in Mem.*—*Vid.* Ambarvalia.

ARVAL'TIS, a mountain of Libya. *Ptol.*

ARVA'RII, a people within the Ganges. *Id.*

ARVER'NI, now Auvergne, a powerful people of Gaul, near the Ligeris, who took up arms against J. Cæsar, and were conquered with great slaughter. Their chief town Arvernorum Civitas, or Augustonemetum, is now Clermont. They, as well as the Romans,, pretended to be descended from the Trojans. *Lucan.* 1. v. 427.—*Cæs. Bell. Gall.* 7.—*Strab.* 14.—*Plin.* 4. c. 19. l. 7. c. 50.

ARVI'NA A. COR. a dictator, who defeated the Samnites, A.U.C. 432. for which he was rewarded with a triumph. *Liv.* 8. c. 38.

ARVIR'AGUS, a king of Britain. *Juv.* 4. v. 127.

ARVIS'IUM or ARVI'SUS, a promontory of the island of Chius, famous for its wine. *Virg. Ecl.* 5. 71.

ARXA'NA, a region of Armenia. *Procrop.*

ARX'ATA, a town of Armenia, near the Araxes. *Strab.* 11. *Vid.* Artaxata.

ARXIP'PUS, the 21st archon of Athens. *Tzetzes. Proleg. in Hesiod.*

ARYAN'DES, a Persian appointed governor of Ægypt by Cambyses. He was put to death because he imitated Darius in whatever he did, and wished that immortal honours should be paid to himself. *Herodot.* 4. c. 166.

AR'YBAS, a native of Sidon, whose daughter was carried away by pirates *Homer. Od.* 15. v. 425. ——A king of the Molossi, who reigned ten years,

AR'YCA, a city of the Epicnemidian Locri. *Diod. Sic.* 14.

ARYCAN'DA, a city of Lycia. *Steph.*

ARYE'NIS, daughter of Alyattes, married Astyages king of Media. *Herodot.* 1. c. 74.

ARYMAG'DUS, a river of Cilicia, now Sequino. *Ptol.*

ARYMPHÆ'I, a people near the Mæotis. *Plin.* 6. c. 7.

AR'YPE, a city of Ægypt. *Steph.*

ARYPTÆ'US, a prince of the Molossi, who privately encouraged the Greeks against Macedonia, and afterwards embraced the party of the Macedonians.

AR'ZUS, a city and river of Thrace, now Chiaurlic. *Ptol.*

AS'ABO, huge mountains, and a promontory on the left of the Persian Gulph. *Ptol.*—*Auctor. Peripl.*

ASAB'ORUM, a promontory of Arabia Felix, now Mochandan. *Ptol.*

ASACHÆ'I, people in the mountains of Æthiopia. *Plin.* 8. c. 13.

AS'ACUS, a river washing the city of Heraclea, at the foot of mount Œta. *Liv.* 5. *Bell. Mac.*

A'SÆ, a village near Corinth.——A village of Thrace. *Steph.*

ASÆ'US, a Greek prince, slain by Hector. *Hom. Il.* 11.

ASALAMIN'IUS, an epithet of Bacchus in *Aristophanes.*

AS'AMA, a river of Mauritania Tingitana, now Omirabi. *Ptol.*

ASAMPA'TÆ, a people near the Mæotis. *Plin.* 6. c. 7.

AS'ANCA, a city of Germany, now Cleppern. *Ptol.*

ASAN'DER, a prince of the Bosporani, who separated Chersonesus Taurica from the continent by a wall. *Strab.* 7.

ASBES'TÆ or ASBYS'TÆ, a people of Libya above Cyrene, where the temple of Ammon was built. Jupiter is sometimes called on that account Abystius. *Herodot.* 4. c. 170.—*Ptol.* 4. c. 3.

AS'BOLUS, one of Actæon's dogs. *Ovid. Met.* 3. v. 218.

ASBO'TUS, a city of Thessaly. *Steph.*

AS'BYLUS, a man of Crotona. *Paus.*—*Plat. de Rep.*

ASBYS'TA, a city of Libya. *Steph. Vid.* Asbestæ.

ASCAL'APHUS, a son of Mars and Astyoche, who was among the Argonauts, and went to the Trojan war at the head of the Orchomenians, with his brother Ialmenus. He was killed by Deiphobus. *Homer. Il.* 2. v. 13. l. 9. v. 82. l. 13. v. 518.—*Apollod.* 3. c. 21.——A son of Acheron, who, being stationed by Pluto to watch over Proserpine in the Elysian fields, discovered that she had eaten some pomegranates from a tree. For this action Proserpine sprinkled water on his head, and turned him into an owl. *Apollod.* 1. c. 5. l. 2. c. 5.—*Ovid. Met.* 5. fab. 8.

ASCALIN'GIUM, a city of Germany. *Ptol.* It is supposed by some to be the modern Hildesheim.

AS'CALON, a town of Syria, near the Mediterranean; it is about 520 stadia from Jerusalem, and is still in existence. It was anciently famous for its onions. *Joseph. de Bell. Jud.* 3. c. 2.—*Theophrast. H. Pl.* 7. c. 4.

ASCA'NIA, an island of the Ægæan Sea.——A city of Troas, said to have been built by Ascanius.

ASCA'NIUS, called also Iulus, son of Æneas by Creusa, accompanied his father in his voyage to Italy. He behaved with great valour in the wars which his father carried on against the Latins, and succeeded Æneas in the kingdom of Latinus, and built Alba, to which he transferred the seat of his empire from Lavinium. The descendants of Ascanius reigned in Alba for above 420 years, under fourteen kfngs, till the age of Numitor. Ascanius reigned thirty-eight years; thirty at Lavinium, and eight at Alba; and was succeeded by Sylvius Posthumus, son of Æneas by Lavinia. Iulus, the son of Ascanius, disputed the crown with Sylvius; but the Latins gave it in favour of the latter, as he was descended from the family of Latinus, and Iulus was invested with the office of high-priest, which remained a long while in his family. *Liv.* 1. c. 3.—*Virg. Æn.* 1. &c. According to *Dionysius, Hal.* 1. c. 15, &c. the son of Æneas by Lavinia was also called Ascanius.——A river of Bithynia. *Virg. G.* 3. v. 270.

ASCANTI'CI, a people of Asiatic Sarmatia. *Plin.* 6. c. 7.

AS'CAPHUS, an island of the Ægean Sea. *Antonin.*

ASCAU'LIS, a city in the north of Germany. *Ptol.*

ASCHALI'TÆ, a people near the Indian Gulph. *Steph.*

ASCHE'ION, a city of Achaia. *Id.*

ASCHIL'ACÆ, a people of Troas. *Plin.* 5. c. 30.

AS'CII, a nation of India, in whose country objects at noon have no shadow. *Plin.* 2. c. 73.

ASCI'TÆ, Arabs mentioned by *Pliny*, 6. c. 29.

ASCLE'PIA, festivals in honour of Asclepius, or Æsculapius, celebrated all over Greece, when prizes for poetical and musical compositions were distributed. At Epidaurus they were called by a different name. *Meurs. Gr.*—*Pollux.* 1. c. 1.

ASCLEPI'ADES, a rhetorician in the age of Eumenes, who wrote an historical account of Alexander. *Arrian.* 7. p. 158.——A disciple of Plato.——A philosopher, disciple of Stilpo, and very intimate with Menedemus. The two friends lived together, and that they might not be separated when they married, Asclepiades took for his wife the daughter, and Menedemus, though much the younger, the mother. When the wife of Asclepiades was dead, Menedemus gave his wife to his friend, and married another. He was blind in his old age, and died in Eretria. *Plut.*—*Cic. Tusc.* 5. c. 39.——A native of Prusa in Bithynia, B.C. 90, who, after teaching rhetoric for some years, applied himself to the practice of medicine. He acquired such celebrity in his profession at Rome, that he became the head of a sect of physicians, and was accounted inferior only to the great Hippocrates. He relied so much upon his skill in the application of medicine, that he laid a wager he should never be sick; and he won it, as he died of a fall from a stair, at a very advanced age. None of his medical treatises are now extant. *Plin.* 26. c. 3. l. 7. c. 37.—*Apuleius Flor.* 19.—*Cic. Orat.* 1. c. 14. —*Galen. de Theriac.* c. 11. [A bust of Asclepiades is to be found in the Museum of the Capitol,] ——An Ægyptian who wrote hymns in honour of the gods of his country, and also a treatise on the coincidence of all religions.——A native of Alexandria, who wrote a history of the Athenian archons. ——The writer of a treatise on Demetrius Phalereus, ——A disciple of Isocrates, who composed six books on those events which had been the subject of tragedies. It is probable that he also wrote tragedies, and that he first made use of that sort of verse which from him has been called Asclepiadeum, of which the first ode of Horace is a beautiful specimen. *Plut. in Isocr.*—*Diomed.* 3 p. 408. ——A physician of Bithynia, under Trajan. He lived seventy years, and, by his skill and reputation, became a great favourite at the emperor's court.

ASCLEPIODO'RUS, a painter in the age of Apelles, twelve of whose pictures of the gods were sold to an African prince for 300 minæ each. *Plin.* 35. c. 10.——A sculptor. *Id.* 34. c. 8.——A soldier who conspired against Alexander with Hermolaus. *Curt.* 8. c. 21.——A mathematician of Alexandria. *Suidas.*

ASCLEPIOD'OTUS, or ASCLEPIODO'TUS, a general of Mithridates.——A musician, who was also a physician.

ASCLE'PIUS. *Vid.* Æsculapius.——A philosopher of Tralles, pupil of Ammonius. *Voss. de Math.* c. 10.

ASCLETA'RION, a mathematician in the age of Domitian, who said that he should be torn in pieces by dogs. The emperor ordered him to be put to death, and his body carefully secured; but as soon as it was placed on the burning pile, a sudden storm arose which put out the flames, and the dogs came and devoured the mathematician's body. *Sueton. in Domit.* 15.

AS'CLUS, a city of Italy. *Steph.*—*Sil. Ital.* 8. v. 439.

ASCO'LIA, a festival in honour of Bacchus, celebrated about December by the Athenian husbandmen, who generally sacrificed a goat to the god, because that animal is a great enemy to the vine. They made a bottle with the skin of the victim, which they filled with oil and wine, and afterwards leapt upon. He who could stand upon it first was pronounced victorious, and received the bottle as a reward. This was called ἀσκωλιάζειν παρὰ τὸ ἐπὶ τὸν ἀσκὸν ἅλλεσθαι, *leaping upon the bottle*, whence the name of the festival. This festival was also introduced into Italy, where the people besmeared their faces with the dregs of wine, and sang hymns in honour of the god. They always suspended some small images of the god on the tallest trees in their vineyards, and these images, which they called Oscilla, were supposed to convey fertility and abundance to whatever side of the country the wind turned them. *Virg. G.* 2. v. 384. & *Servius, ibid.*—*Pollux*, 9. c. 7.—*Natal. Com.* 5. c. 13.

ASCO'NIUS LA'BEO, a preceptor of Nero. *Tac. Ann.* 13. c. 10.

ASCO'NIUS PEDIA'NUS, a grammarian of Padua, said to have been intimate with Virgil and Livy. He wrote, besides learned historical treatises, some very valuable commentaries on Cicero's Orations, still extant. *Jerome* says, that he lived in the age of Vespasian, but the supposition is probably erroneous. His commentaries were published with the Orations of Cicero by Grævius. Also separately, Venet. 1563, and Lugd. Bat. 1698. *Harles. Lit. Rom.* 1. p. 365.—*Sax. Onom.* 1. p. 248.—*Fabr. Bib. Lat.* 2. c. 6.—*Quint.* 1. c. 7.

AS'CRA, a town of Bœotia, built, according to some, by the giants Otus and Ephialtes, at the foot of mount Helicon. Hesiod was born there, whence he is often called the *Ascræan* poet, and poems treating on agricultural subjects are, out of respect to his memory, called *Ascræum Carmen*. The town received its name from Ascra, a nymph, mother of Œoclus by Neptune. *Strab.* 9.—*Paus.* 9. c. 29.—*Paterc.* 1.—*Flor.* 1. c. 19. l. 3. c. 18.—*Plin.* 3. c. 13. l. 7. c. 43.—*Virg. G.* 2. v. 176.—*Ovid Fast.* 6. v. 14.

ASCRU'VIUM, a city of Illyricum, now Cataro, or, according to some authors, Castel Novo. *Ptol.*

AS'CULUM, now Ascoli, a town of Picenum, near the Truentus, which falls into the Adriatic, about sixty miles south of Ancona.——A town of Apulia, near the banks of the Aufidus. It is famous for the defeat of Pyrrhus by Curius and Fabricius. *Flor.* 3. c. 18.—*Cluver.* 3. c. 29.

ASCU'RA, a city of Armenia Major. *Ptol.*

ASCU'RIS, a small lake of Thessaly. *Liv.* 44. c. 2.

ASCU'RUS, a river of Colchis. *Arrian. in Peripl.*

AS'DARA, a town of Cappadocia. *Antonin.*

AS'DRUBAL, a Carthaginian, son-in-law of Hamilcar. He distinguished himself in the Numidian war, and was appointed general in chief on the death of his father-in-law, and for eight years presided with much prudence and valour over the Carthaginian affairs in Spain, where he laid the foundation of new Carthage on the shores of the Mediterranean. To stop his farther progress towards the east, the Romans, in a treaty with Carthage, forbade him to pass the Iberus, which was faithfully observed by the general. He was killed in the midst of his soldiers, B.C. 220, by a slave whose master he had put to death. The slave was caught, and executed after undergoing the greatest torments. Some say that he was killed in hunting. *Ital.* 1. v. 165.—*Appian. Iberic.*—*Polyb.* 2.—*Liv.* 21. c. 2, &c.——A son of Hamilcar, who came from Spain towards Italy, with a large reinforcement for his brother Annibal. He crossed the Alps, and entered Italy; but some of his letters to Annibal having fallen into the hands of the Romans, and divulged his plans, the consuls, M. Livius Salinator and Claudius Nero, attacking him suddenly near the Metaurus, totally routed him, B.C. 207. He was killed in the battle, but though 56,000 of his men shared his fate, and 5400 were taken prisoners, only 8000 Romans were slain. The head of Asdrubal was cut off, and some days after thrown into the camp of Annibal, who, at that moment, was in expectation of a promised reinforcement, and he exclaimed at the sight, "In losing Asdrubal, I lose all my happiness, and Carthage all her hopes." Asdrubal had before made an attempt to penetrate into Italy by sea, but had been intercepted and defeated by the governor of Sardinia. *Liv.* 21, 23, 27, &c.—*Polyb.*—*Horat.* 4. od. 4.——A Carthaginian general, surnamed *Calvus*, appointed governor of Sardinia, and taken prisoner by the Romans. *Liv.* 22. c. 20.——A son of Gisgon, appointed general of the Carthaginian forces in Spain, in the time of the great Annibal. He made head against the Romans in Africa, with the assistance of Syphax; but he was soon after defeated by Scipio. He died B.C. 206. *Liv.*——A Carthaginian, who advised his countrymen to make peace with Rome, and upbraided Annibal for laughing in the Carthaginian senate, while the calamities of the country moved the rest to tears. *Liv.*——A grandson of Masinissa, murdered in the senate-house by the Carthaginians.——A general, whose camp, though at the head of 20,000 men, was destroyed in Africa by Scipio, in the last Punic war. When all was lost, he fled to the enemy and begged his life. Scipio showed him to the Carthaginians, upon which his wife, with a thousand imprecations, threw herself and her two children into the flames of the temple of Æsculapius, which she, and others, had set on fire. This Asdrubal was not of the same family as Annibal. *Liv.* 51.——A Carthaginian general, conquered by L. Cæcilius Metellus in Sicily, in a battle in which he lost 120 elephants. These animals were led in triumph through Italy by the conquerors.

ASEL'LIO SEMPRO'NIUS, an historian and military tribune, who wrote an account of the actions in which he was present. *Dion. Hal.*—*Cic. Leg.* 1. c. 2.

ASEL'LIUS CLAUDIUS, a celebrated knight under Claudius Nero. *Liv.* 23. c. 47.

ASE'NA, a town of Spain. *Id.* 23. c. 27.

AS'ERUS, now Monreal, a city of Sicily. *Ptol.*

A'SIA, one of the three parts of the ancient world, separated from Europe by the Tanais, the Euxine, the Ægean, and Mediterranean Seas. The Nile and Ægypt divide it from Africa. It received its name from Asia, the daughter of Oceanus, or, according to *Herodotus*, 4. c. 45., from Asia the wife of Prometheus. This part of the globe has given birth to many of the greatest monarchies of the universe, and to the ancient inhabitants of Asia we are indebted for most of the arts and sciences. The soil is fruitful, and abounds with all the necessaries as well as luxuries of life. Asia was divided into many different empires, provinces, and states, of which the most conspicuous were the Assyrian and Persian monarchies. The Assyrian monarchy, according to *Eusebius*, lasted 1240 years, and according to *Justin*, 1300 years down to the year of the world 4380. The empire of Persia existed 228 years, till the death of Darius the Third, whom Alexander the Great conquered. The empire of the Medes lasted 259 years, according to *Eusebius*, or less, according to others, till the reign of Astyages, who was conquered by Cyrus the Great, who abolished the power of the Medes, and founded the Persian monarchy. Asia was generally divided into Major and Minor. Asia Major was the more extensive, and comprehended all the eastern parts. Asia Minor was a large country in the form of a peninsula, the boundaries of which may be known by drawing a line from the bay of Issus, in a northern direction, to the eastern part of the Euxine Sea. Asia Minor felt the shock of many revolutions. It was tributary to the Scythians for upwards of 1500 years, and was a long time under the power of the Lydians, Medes, &c. The western parts of Asia Minor were thickly peopled by Grecians colonies. The Romans generally and indiscriminately called Asia Minor by the name of Asia. *Cic. Flacc.* 27. *Ad Fam.* 2. ep. 15.—*Liv.* 9. c. 19. l. 37. c. 45. l. 38. c. 39.—*Strab.*—*Mela.*—*Justin.*—*Plin.* 5. c. 27.—*Tacit.* &c.

A'SIA, one of the Oceanides, who married Japetus, by whom she had Atlas, Prometheus, Epimetheus, and Menœtius, and gave her name to one of the three quarters of the ancient globe. *Apollod.* 1. c. 2.——One of the Nereides. *Hygin.*——A mountain of Laconia. *Paus.* 3. c. 24.

A'SIA PA'LUS, a lake in Mysia. *Virg. Æn.* 7, v. 701.

ASIA'NA, a city of Elis. *Steph.*

ASIATI'CUS, a Gaul, in the age of Vitellius. *Tacit. Hist.* 2.——The surname of one of the Scipios. Others also received the name from their conquests or campaigns in Asia. *Liv.* 37. c. 58.

ASI'BE, a city of Mesopotamia, called also Antiochia by the inhabitants. *Steph.*

ASI'DO, an inland town of Hispania Bætica. *Plin.* 3. c. 1.

ASILAS, an augur, who assisted Æneas against Turnus. *Virg. Æn.* 10. v. 175.

AS'INA, the surname of some of the Cornelian family. It is derived, as it is supposed by some authors, from one of the family, who, when required to produce sureties, brought into the forum an *Ass* loaded with money. *Macrob. Sat.* 1. c. 6.

AS'INA VIN'NIUS, a person to whom *Horace* inscribes the 13th epistle of his first book.

ASINÆ'US, a bay of Peloponnesus. *Plin.* 4. c. 5.

ASINA'RIA, a festival in Sicily, in commemoration of the victory obtained over Demosthenes and Nicias, at the river Asinarius. *Plut.*

ASINA'RIUS, according to *Plutarch* and *Diodorus*, Assinarus according to *Thucydides*, a small river on the eastern coast of Sicily, at the south of Syracuse, near which the Athenian generals, Demosthenes and Nicias were taken prisoners. *Thucyd.* 7. c. 84.

ASIN'DUM, a city of the Turditani in Spain, now Medina Sidonia. *Ptol.*

AS'INE, one of the Sporades.——An island of the Adriatic.——The name of three towns of Peloponnesus, viz. in Laconia, Argolis and Messenia. *Lucan.* 8.

AS'INES, a small river of Sicily, now Fiume Freddo. *Strab.* 8.

ASIN'IUS CAPITO, a learned grammarian. *A. Gell.* 5. c. 21.

ASIN'IUS GAL'LUS, son of Asinius Pollio the orator, married Vipsania, the daughter of Agrippa, after she had been divorced by Tiberius. This marriage gave rise to a secret enmity between the emperor and Asinius, who starved himself to death, either voluntarily, or by order of his imperial rival. He had six sons by his wife. He wrote a comparison between his father and Cicero, in which he ascribed the superiority to the former. He also wrote some epigrams, the wit and delicate humour of which were admired by the ancients. *Tacit.* 1 & 5. *Ann.*—*Dio.* 58.—*Plin.* 7. ep. 4.

ASIN'IUS MARCEL'LUS, grandson of Asinius Pollio, was accused of some misdemeanours, but acquitted, &c. *Tacit.* 14. *Ann.* 40.

ASIN'IUS POL'LIO. *Vid.* Pollio.

ASIN'IUS POL'LIO, a commander of Mauritania, under the first emperors, &c. *Tacit. Hist.* 2. c. 59.——An historian in the age of Pompey.

ASIN'IUS QUADRA'TUS, a man who published the history of Parthia, Greece, and Rome.

ASIN'IUS TORQUA'TUS, an historian in the third century.

ASIS'IUM, a town of Italy, now Assisi. *Ptol.* The inhabitants were called Asisinates. *Plin.* 3. c. 14.

A'SIUS, a son of Dymas, brother of Hecuba, killed by Idomeneus in the Trojan war. *Hom. Il.* 2. v. 342. l. 12. v. 95. l. 13. v. 384.——A poet of Samus, who wrote on the genealogy of ancient heroes and heroines. *Paus.* 7. c. 4.——A son of Imbracus, who accompanied Æneas into Italy. *Virg. Æn.* 10. v. 123.

A'SIUS CAM'PUS, a place near the Cayster. *Virg. Æn.* 1.

ASMU'RA, a city of Hyrcania, callad Asmorna by *Ammianus*. *Ptol.*

ASNA'US, a mountain of Macedonia, near which the river Aous flows, before it falls into the Adriatic. *Liv.* 32. c. 5.

ASO'PHIS, a small country of Peloponnesus, near the Asopus. It is called Arœthyrea by *Hom. Il.* 2. 575.

ASO'PIA, the ancient name of Sicyon. *Paus.* 2. c. 1.

ASOPI'ADES, a patronymic of Æacus, son of Ægina, the daughter of Asopus. *Ovid. Met.* 7. v. 484.

ASO'PIS, the daughter of Asopus.——A daughter of Thespius, mother of Mentor. *Apollod.* 2. c. 7.

ASO'PIUS, son of Phormio, an Athenian, sent with thirty ships against Peloponnesus, and slain in the expedition. *Thucyd.* 6. c. 7.

ASOPODO'RUS, son of Timander, a general of the Thebans, who defeated the Megarensians and Phliasians. *Herodot.* 9. c. 69.

ASO'PUS, a small river of Thessaly, falling into the bay of Malia at the north of Thermopylæ. *Strab.* 8.——A river of Bœotia, rising above Platæa, and flowing into the Euripus, after it has watered the territories of the Thebans and Platæans. The god of this river was son of Oceanus and Tethys, or, according to some, of Neptune, and Pero, or of Jupiter and Eurynome, and he married Merope, daughter of the Ladon, by whom he had two sons, Ismenus and Pelagon, and twenty daughters, the most known of whom are Ægina, Salamis, Sinope, Harpine, and Corcyra. When Jupiter had carried away Ægina to the island which afterwards bore her name, the father pursued the ravisher, but his attempts were defeated by the thunder of the god. *Stat. Theb.* 8.—*Apollod.* 1. c. 9. l. 3. c. 12.—*Paus.* 2. c. 5. This last author asserts, that Asopus was a Bœotian prince, who discovered the river which watered Thebes and the neighbouring country, to which he gave his own name. *Id.* 2. c. 12.——A river of Asia, flowing into the Lycus, near Laodicea.——A river of Peloponnesus, passing by Sicyon.——A river of Macedonia, flowing near Heraclea. *Strab. &c.*——A river of Phœnicia.——A town of Peloponnesus, now Esapo.

ASPAGO'NES, a people of India. *Plin.* 6. c. 21.

ASPALATHI'A, a city of the Taphii. *Steph.*

ASPAL'ATHIS, an island of Lycia. *Id.*

ASPAM'ITHRES, a favourite eunuch of Xerxes, who conspired with Artabanus to destroy the king and the royal family, &c. *Ctesias.*

ASPARA'GIUM, a small town near Dyrrhachium. *Cæs. Bell. Civ.* 3. c. 30.

ASPA'SIA, a daughter of Hermotimus, the Phocian, famous for her personal charms. She was priestess of the sun, and mistress to Cyrus, and afterwards to his brother Artaxerxes, from whom she passed to Darius. She was called *Milto, Vermilion*, on account of the remarkable beauty of her complexion. *Ælian. V. H.* 12. c. 1.—*Justin.* 10. c. 2.—*Plut. in Artax.*——A daughter of Axiochus, born at Miletus. She came to Athens, where she taught eloquence with such effect, that Socrates was proud to be among her scholars. She so captivated Pericles, by her mental and personal accomplishments, that he became her pupil, and at last took her for his mistress and wife. He was so fond of her, and so blind to her prejudices, that he made war against Samus at her instigation. The behaviour of Pericles towards Aspasia greatly corrupted the morals of the Athenians, and introduced lasciviousness and dissipation into the state. She however possessed superior excellence in mind as well as person, and Plato hesitates not to declare, that her instructions formed the greatest and most eloquent orators of her age. Some have confounded the mistress of Pericles with Aspasia the daughter of Hermotimus. *Vossius. in* 3 *Inst. Rhet.—Fabr. B. Gr.* 2. c. 23.—*Birman. ad.* 5 *Quint.* c. 11.—*Plut. in Pericl.—Quintil.* 11. [In the Vatican is a terminal head bearing the name of Aspasia.] ——The wife of Xenophon, if we follow the improper interpretation given by some to *Cic. de Inv.* 1. c. 31.—*Quint.* 5. c. 11.

ASPA'SIUS, a peripatetic philosopher in the second century, whose commentaries on different subjects were highly valued, especially those on the writings of Aristotle and Plato. *Fabr. B. Gr.* l. 3. c. 5. sec. 29. *in notâ.*——A sophist of Ravenna in the age of Alexander. *Philostrat.*——A sophist who wrote a panegyric on Adrian.——An historian of Tyre. *Suidas.*

ASPASTES, a satrap of Carmania, suspected of infidelity to his trust while Alexander was in the east. *Curt.* 9. c. 20.

ASPATH'ARÆ, a people of Serica. *Amm. Marcell.* l. 23.

ASPATHI'NES, one of the seven noblemen of Persia, who conspired against the usurper Smerdis. *Herodot.* 3. c. 70, &c. Also Aspath'ines.

ASPE'LIA, a name of the island of Cyprus. *Xenagor. ap. Plin.* 5. c. 31.

ASPEN'DIUS, a noted harper. *Asconius, in Orat. Cic. in Verr.*

ASPEN'DUS, a town of Pamphylia, at the mouth of the river Eurymedon. *Liv.* 37. c. 23. l. 38. c. 15.—*Cic. in Verr.* 1. c. 20. The inhabitants sacrificed swine to Venus.

AS'PERUM MA'RE, a part of the Æthiopic Ocean, called Barbaricum by *Ptolemy*, and Troglodyticum by *Pliny*. It is now Golfo de Melinde.

ASPHALEIUS, a name under which Neptune was worshipped, and entreated to render firm and unshaken the foundations of maritime cities. The god had temples at Tænarum and Rhodes under this appellation. *Scholiast. Aristoph. in Achar.*—*Servius. ad Virg. Æn.* 2. v. 610.—*Strab.* 1.—*Paus.* 7. c. 21. Also Aspha'lius.

ASPHALTI'TES, a lake. *Vid.* Mare Mortuum.

AS'PIS, a satrap of Cataonia, in Asia Minor, who revolted from Artaxerxes. He was reduced by Datames. *Cor. Nep. in Dat.*

As'pis, a city and mountain of Africa. *Sil. Ital.* 3. 244. ——One of the Cyclades.——A city of Macedonia.

ASPIS'II, a people of Scythia, whose country formed a part of modern Tartary. *Ptol.*

ASPITH'RA, a city of the Sinæ. *Id.* It is now Quan Cheu in the province of Canton.

ASPLE'DON, a son of Neptune by the nymph Midea. He gave his name to a city of Bœotia, the inhabitants of which went to the Trojan war. *Hom. Il.* 2. v. 511.—*Paus.* 9. c. 38.

ASPO'NA, a city of Galatia. *Antonin.*

ASPORE'NUS, a mountain of Asia Minor, near Pergamus, where the mother of the gods was worshipped, and called Asporena. *Strab.* 13.

ASPRE'NAS CALPUR'NIUS, a governor set over Galatia and Pamphylia by Galba. He slew the imposter Nero in the island of Cythnus. *Tac. Hist.* 2. c. 9.

Aspre'nas Lu'cius, a proconsul of Africa, under the emperors. *Tac. Ann.* 1. c. 53.

Aspre'nas C. No'nius, a young nobleman at Rome, lamed in the public diversions called *Lusus Trojæ. Suet. Aug.* 43. The family of the Asprenates enjoyed the consulship, though few particulars are recorded concerning their history. *Plin.* 33. c. 7.

ASPURGIA'NI, a people near the Palus Mæotis. *Steph.*

AS'SA, a town near mount Athos. *Herodot.* 7. c. 122.——A village of Scythia. *Steph.*

ASSABI'NUS, the Jupiter of the Arabians. *Plin.* 12. c. 19.

ASSACA'NI, a region of India, the capital of which was Magosa. *Strab.* 15. *Stephanus* calls the people Assaceni.

ASSACA'NUS, a king of the city of Massaga, in India. *Curt.* 8. c. 10.

AS'SARA, a river of Mauritania Cæsariensis, now Selsis. *Ptol.*

ASSAR'ACÆ, an inland nation of Libya, now, perhaps, the kingdom of Biafara. *Id.*

ASSAR'ACUS, a Trojan prince, son of Tros by Callirrhoe. He was father of Capys, the father of Anchises. The Trojans, especially the followers of Æneas, were frequently called the descendants of Asraracus, *gens. Assaraci. Homer. Il.* 20. v. 232.—*Virg. Æn.* 1. v. 284.——The name of two friends of Æneas, engaged in the Rutulian war. *Virg. Æn.* 10. v. 124.

ASSEC'OMA, a town of Spain. *Antonin.*

ASSE'RA, a city of the Chalcidenses. *Steph.*

ASSERIA'TES, people inhabiting the Alps. *Plin.* c. 19. Their country is now Val de Serra.

ASSERI'NI, a people of Sicily. *Diod. Sic.* 14.

ASSESIA'TES, a people of Illyria. *Plin* 3. c. 21.

ASSE'SUS, a city of Milesia. *Steph.*

ASSO'RUM, a mountain of Samus. *Id.*

ASSO'RUS, now Asaro, a town of Sicily, between Enna and Argyrium. *Cluver.* 3. c. 41.——A town of Macedonia, near the Echedorus.

AS'SOS, a maritime city of Lycia.——A city of Æolis.——A city of Mysia. *Plin.* 2. c. 96.

AS'SUM, a promontory of Tras, now Santiquaranti. *Ptol.*

ASSYR'IA, a large country of Asia, the boundaries of which have been different in its flourishing times. At first it was bounded by the Lycus and Caprus; but the name of Assyria, more generally speaking, is applied to all that territory which lies between Media, Mesopotamia, Armenia, and Babylon. The Assyrian empire was the most ancient in the world. It was founded by Ninus or Belus, B.C. 2059, according to some authors, and lasted till the reign of Sardanapalus, the thirty-first sovereign from Ninus, B.C. 820. According to Eusebius it flourished for 1240 years; according to Justin, 1300 years; but Herodotus says its duration was not above 500 or 600 years. Among the different monarchs of the Assyrian empire, Semiramis greatly distinguished herself, and extended the boundaries of her dominions as far as Æthiopia and Libya. In ancient authors, the Assyrians are often called Syrians, and the Syrians Assyrians, and the appellation is even applied to the Jews. The Assyrians assisted Priam in the Trojan war, and sent him Memnon with a powerful army. The king of Assyria generally styled himself king of kings, as a demonstration of his power and greatness. The country is now called Cusistan or Arziri. *Vid.* Syria. *Strab.* 16.—*Herodot.* 1 & 2.—*Justin.* 1.—*Plin.* 6. c. 13 & 26.—*Ptol.* 1. c. 2.—*Diod.* 2.—*Mela*, 1. c. 2.—*Virg. G.* 2. v. 465.—*Selden de Jure Nat. & Gent.* 1. c. 2.—*Cluver.* 5. c. 14.

AS'TA, a city of Spain, near the mouth of the Bætis, opposite Gades. *Mela*, 3. c. 1.—*Liv.* 39, c. 21.

As'ta Pompe'ia, a town of Liguria, on the river Tanarus. It is now called Aste or Asti. *Cluver.* 3. c. 35.

ASTABE'NI, a people of Hyrcania. *Ptol.*

ASTAB'ORAS, now Coror, a river of Æthiopia, which falls into the Nile. *Ptol.*

ASTACA'NI, a city of Bactriana. *Id.*

ASTACA'PRA, a city of India within the Ganges. *Id.* It is now probably, Janager.

ASTACE'NUM, an æstuary of Hispania Bætica. *Ptol.*

ASTACES. *Vid.* Mazaces.——A river of Pontus. *Plin.* 2. c. 103.

ASTACIL'ICIS, a city of Mauritania Cæsariensis. *Ptol.*

ASTACŒ'NI, a people of India, near the Indus. *Strab.* 15.

ASTACU'RES, a people of Africa Propria. *Ptol.*

ASTACU'BI, a people of Inner Libya. *Id.*

AS'TACUS, a town of Bithynia, built by Astacus, son of Neptune and Olbia, or rather by a colony from Megara and Athens. Lysimachus destroyed it, and carried the inhabitants to the town of Nicomedia, which was then lately built. *Paus.* 5. c. 12.—*Arrian.*—*Strab.* 17.——A city of Acarnania, near the mouth of the Achelous. *Plin.* 5. 32.

AS'TÆ, a nation of Thrace. *Steph.*

ASTAGE'NI, a nation of Arabia Felix. *Ptol.*

ASTAL'ICIS, now Tefezara, a town of Mauritania Cæsariensis. *Id.*

ASTAN'DA, a town of Aria. *Id.*

AS'TAPA, a town of Hispania Bætica, now Estepa la Vieja, in Andalusia. *Liv.* 38. c. 20.

ASTAPUS, a river of Æthiopia, falling into the Astoboras, and with it into the Nile. *Cluver.* 6. c. 3.

ASTARTE, a powerful divinity of Syria, the same as the Venus of the Greeks. She had a famous temple at Hierapolis in Syria, attended by 300 priests. She was represented in medals with a long habit, and a mantle over it, tucked up on the left arm. She had one hand stretched forward, and held in the other a crooked staff in the form of a cross. *Lucian. de Deâ. Syriâ.—Cic. de Nat. D.* 3. c. 23.—*Tertull. Ap.* 24 *Advers. Gen.* 3.

ASTASA'NA, a town of Aria. *Ptol.*

ASTEL'EBE, a city of Lydia. *Steph.*

ASTEL'EPHOS, a river of Colchis. *Arrian.* It is called Atelpos by *Pliny*, 6. c. 4.

ASTE'NAS, a town of Hispania Bætica. *Strab.*

ASTER, a dexterous archer of Amphipolis, or, according to *Justin*, of Methone, who offered his services to Philip king of Macedonia. Finding that his application was treated with neglect, he retired into the city, and aimed an arrow at Philip, who pressed it with a siege. The arrow, on which was written, "Aimed at Philip's right eye," struck the king's eye, and put it out; and Philip, to return the pleasantry, threw back the same arrow, with these words, "If Philip takes the town, Aster shall be hanged." The city yielded, and the conqueror kept his word. *Lucian. de Hist. Scrib.*—*Palmer. in Exercit.*

ASTE'RIA, a daughter of Cœus, one of the Titans, married Perses, son of Crius, by whom she had the celebrated Hecate. She enjoyed for a long time the favours of Jupiter, who had assumed the form of an eagle; but falling under his displeasure, she was changed into a quail, called *Ortyx* by the Greeks; whence the name of *Ortygia*, given to that island in the Archipelago, to which she retired. *Lactant. ad. Stat. Th.* 4. v. 796.—*Hesiod. Th.* v. 136, 376, 406.—*Servius. in Æn.* 3. v. 72.—*Scholiast. Stat.* 2. *Achil.* v. 9.—*Ovid. Met.* 6. fab. 4.—*Hygin.* fab. 58.—*Apollod.* 1. c. 2, &c.——One of the daughters of Danaus, who married Chætus, son of Ægyptus. *Apollod.* 2.——One of the daughters of Atlas, mother of Oenomaus, king of Pisa. She is called Sterope by some authors. *Hygin.* fab. 250.——A mistress of Gyges, to whom *Horace* wrote three odes, to comfort her during her lover's absence.

ASTE'RIA, a town of Greece, the inhabitants of which went with Agamemnon to the Trojan war. *Hom. Il.* 2. v. 782.

ASTE'RION or ASTE'RIUS, a river of Peloponnesus, which flowed through Argolis. The god of this river had three daughters, Eubœa, Prosymna, and Acræa, who nursed the goddess Juno, and of these, the first and the last gave their names to two hills on the borders of the river. At the foot of the first of these was a temple of Juno, attended only by women. *Stat. Theb.* 4. v. 122 & 714.—*Paus.* 2. c. 17.

ASTE'RION, a son of Cometes, who was one of the Argonauts. *Apollon.* 1.——A statuary, son of Æschylus. *Paus.*

ASTERIS, an island between Ithaca and Samus. *Homer. Od.* 4. c. 844.

ASTE'RIUM, a town of Macedonia, in the district of Pæonia. *Liv.* 40. c. 24.

ASTE'RIUS, a son of Minos the Second, king of Crete, by Pasiphæ. He was killed by Theseus, though he was thought the strongest man of his age. Apollodorus supposes him to be the same as the famous Minotaur. According to some authors, Asterion was son of Tectamus, one of the descendants of Æolus; and they add, that he was surnamed Jupiter, because he had carried away Europa, by whom he had Minos the First. *Diod.* 4.—*Apollod.* 3.—*Paus.* 2. c. 31.——A son of Neleus and Chloris. *Apollod.* 1. c. 12.

ASTERO'DIA, the wife of Endymion. *Paus.* 5. c. 1.——A nymph of Caucasus, first wife of Æetes. *Apollon.*

ASTER'OPE, or ASTEROPE'A, one of the Pleiades.

ASTER'OPE, a daughter of Pelias, king of Iolcus, who assisted her sister to kill her father, whom Medea promised to restore to the vigour of youth. Her grave was seen in Arcadia in the time of *Pausanias*, 8. c. 11.—*Apollod.* 1. c. 23.——A daughter of Deion by Diomede. *Apollod.* 1.——The wife of Æsacus. *Id.* 3.

ASTEROPÆUS, a king of Pæonia, son of Pelegon. He assisted Priam in the Trojan war, and was killed, after a brave resistance by Achilles. *Homer. Il.* 17. v. 217. l. 21. v. 140.—*Justin.* 7. c. 1.——A noble Spartan who assisted Lycurgus in forming his republic.

ASTERU'SIUS, a mountain at the south of Crete.——A town of Arabia Felix. *Diod. Sic.* 5.

ASTE'US, an archon at Athens. Ol. 101. an. 4.

ASTHÆ'A, an island of Gedrosia. *Ptol.*

ASTHAGU'RA, a city of India within the Ganges. *Id.*

AS'TIÆ, a promontory of Thrace. The people are called Asti by *Strabo*.

ASTI'CA, the territory of the Astici in Thrace, on the borders of the Euxine Sea. *Liv.* 38. c. 40.

ASTI'GI, a city of Hispania Bætica. *Mela*, 2. c. 6. It is now Ecija.——A city in the country of the Celtici in Lusitania. *Plin.* 3. c. 1.

ASTIN'OME, the wife of Hipponous.

ASTI'OCHUS, a general of Lacedæmon, who conquered the Athenians near Cnidus, and took Phocæa and Cumæ, B.C. 411.

ASTO'A, a village of Arabia Felix. *Ptol.*

AS'TOMI, a people of India. *Plin.* 7. c. 2.

ASTO'VIA or ASTUI'A, now Bedenhusen, a city of Germany. *Ptol.*

ASTRÆ'A, a daughter of Astræus, king of Arcadia, according to others, of Titan, Saturn's brother, by Aurora. Some make her daughter of Jupiter and Themis, and others consider her the same as Rhea the wife of Saturn. She was the goddess of Justice, and lived upon the earth, as the poets mentioned, during the golden age, which is often called the age of Astræa; but the wickedness and impiety of mankind drove her to heaven in the brazen and iron ages. She was, however, the last of the divinities who retired from the habitations of men, and after her return to heaven she was placed among the constellations of the zodiac, under the name of Virgo or Erigone. She is represented with a stern, but majestic countenance, holding a pair of scales in one hand, and a sword in the other. *Senec. in Octav.*—*Ovid. Met.* 1. v. 149.—*Arat.* 1. *Phænom.* v. 98.—*Hesiod. Theog.*—*Aul. Gell.* 14. c. 4.—*Manil.* 4. v. 542.——A city of Illyria. *Steph.*

ASTRÆUM, a town of Macedonia. *Ptol.*

ASTRÆ'US, one of the Titans who made war against Jupiter. He married Aurora, by whom he had the winds known by the names of Zephyr, Boreas, Notus, and Argestes. *Hesiod. in Theog.* 375 & seq.—*Apollod.* 1. c. 5.——A river of Macedonia, near Thermæ. *Ælian H. V.* 15. c. 1.

ASTRA'GOS, a fortified place of Caria, *Liv.* 33. c. 18.

ASTRAS'SUS, a city of India within the Ganges. *Ptol.*

ASTRA'TA, now Caiassa, an island of the Arabian Gulph. *Id.*

AS'TREUS, a person slain by Perseus at the court of Cepheus. *Ovid. Met.* 5. v. 144.

AS'TROBI, a nation of India. *Arrian.*

ASTU, a Greek word which signifies *city*, and was generally applied, by way of distinction, to Athens, which was the most capital city of Greece. The word *urbs* is applied with the same meaning of superiority to Rome, and πόλις to Alexandria, the capital of Ægypt, as also to Troy, and to Antioch, the capital of Syria. *C. Nep.* 7. c. 6. l. 9. c. 4.—*Cic. Leg.* 2. c. 2.

AS'TUR, an Etrurian, who assisted Æneas against Turnus. *Virg. Æn.* 10. v. 180.

AS'TURA, a small river of Latium, which rises near the groves of Aricia, and falls into the Tyrrhene Sea. There is at its mouth a small town of the same name, near which Cicero had a villa, where Antony's soldiers cut off the orator's head. *Cic. Fam.* 6. ep. 19. *Att.* 12. ep. 40.

AS'TURES, a people of Hispania Tarraconensis, who employed themselves in digging the valuable mines which were found in their country. Their chief towns were, Asturica Augusta, now Astorga, and Asturum Lucus, now Oviedo, at the north of Spain, near the shores of the Bay of Biscay, and their territories still retain the ancient name of Asturia. *Lucan.* 4. v. 298.—*Ital.* 1. v. 231.

ASTURICA'NI, a nation of Asiatic Sarmatia. *Ptol.*

ASTUSA'PES, a name of the Nile. *Plin.* 5. c. 9.

ASTY'AGE, a daughter of Hypseus, who married Periphas, by whom she had eight children, among whom was Antion, the father of Ixion. *Diod.* 4.

ASTY'AGES, son of Cyaxares, was the last king of Media. He was father of Mandane, whom he gave in marriage to Cambyses, a person of obscure birth in Persia, because he was told by a dream, that his daughter's son would dispossess him of his crown. From such a connexion he fondly hoped that none but mean and ignorant children could be raised; but he was disappointed, and though he had exposed his daughter's son in consequence of a second dream, he was deprived of his crown by his grandson, after he had reigned thirty-five years. Astyages was very cruel and oppressive; and Harpagus, one of his officers, whose son he had wantonly murdered, encouraged Mandane's son, who was called Cyrus, to take up arms against his grandfather, and he conquered him and took him prisoner, 559 B.C. *Xenophon*, in his *Cyropædia*, relates a different story, and asserts that Cyrus and Astyages lived together as the most sincere friends. *Justin.* 1. c. 4, &c. *Herodot.* 1. c. 74, 75, &c.—*Paus.* 5. c. 10.——A grammarian who wrote a commentary on Callimachus.——A man changed into a stone at the sight of Medusa's head. *Ovid. Met.* 5. fab. 6.

ASTY'ALUS, a Trojan killed by Neoptolemus. *Homer. Il.* 6.

ASTYANAS'SA, one of the attendants of Helen, represented as loose of manners. She wrote a book on a subject which has afforded matter to Aretinus for thirty-six sonnets. *Scaliger ad Catal.* p. 203. —*Suidas.*

ASTY'ANAX, a son of Hector and Andromache. He was very young when the Greeks besieged Troy; and when the city was taken, his mother saved him in her arms from the general conflagration. Ulysses, however, seized him, and barbarously threw him down from the walls of Troy. According to *Euripides*, he was killed by Menelaus; and *Seneca* says, that Pyrrhus, the son of Achilles, put him to death. Hector had given him the name of Scamandrius; but the Trojans, who hoped that he might prove as great as his father, called him Astyanax, or the bulwark of the city. *Homer Il.* 6. v. 400. l. 22. v. 500.—*Virg. Æn.* 2. v. 457. l. 3. v. 489.—*Ovid. Met.* 13. v. 415.—*Lescheus apud Paus.* 10. c. 25.——An Arcadian, who had a statue in the temple of Jupiter, on mount Lycæus. *Paus.* 8. c. 38.——A son of Hercules. *Apollod.* 2. c. 7.——A writer in the age of Gallienus. *Voss. H. Lat.* 2. c. 4.

ASTYCRATI'A, a daughter of Æolus. *Homer. Od.* 10.——A daughter of Amphion and Niobe.

ASTYD'AMAS, an Athenian, pupil of Isocrates, and son of the sister of Æschylus. He wrote, according to *Suidas*, 240 tragedies, of which only 15 obtained the prize. The success of one of his tragedies called Parthenopæus was so great, that he was honoured by his countrymen with a statue in the theatre, but the inscription which he placed upon it was so arrogant, that the Athenians removed it, and also fined him. Hence arose the proverb, *Astydamantis in morem se ipsum laudare. Fabr. B. Gr.* 2. c. 19. *de Trag.*——His son, who was also a tragic poet, *Suidas* ascribes eight tragedies to him. *Fabr. ibid.*——A Milesian, three times victorious at Olmypia. He was famous for his great bodily strength, as well as for his voracious appetite. He was once invited to a feast by king Ariobarzanes, and ate what had been prepared for nine persons. He exhibited the power of his arms by breaking a large bar of iron. *Athen.* 10. c. 1.

ASTYDAMI'A or ASTYADAMI'A, daughter of Amyntor, king of Orchomenus in Bœotia, married Acastus, son of Pelias, who was king of Iolcus. She became enamoured of Peleus, son of Æacus, who had visited her husband's court; and because he refused to gratify her passion, she accused him of attempting her virtue. *Vid.* Peleus. Peleus afterwards punished with death the cruel and false Astydamia. She is called by some Hippolyte, and by others Cretheis. *Apollod.* 3. c. 13.—*Pindar. Nem.* 4.——A daughter of Ormenus, carried away by Hercules, by whom she had Tlepolemus. *Ovid. Heroid.* 9. v. 50.

AS'TYLUS, or ASTY'LUS, one of the centaurs who was endowed with the knowledge of futurity. He advised his brothers not to make war against the Lapithæ. *Ovid. Met.* 12. v. 308.——A man of Crotona, who was victorious three successive times at the Olympic games. *Paus.* 6.

ASTYMEDU'SA, a woman whom Œdipus married after he had divorced Jocasta.

ASTYN'OME, the daughter af Chryses, the priest of Apollo, sometimes called Chryseis. She fell to the share of Achilles, at the division of the spoils of Lyrnessus.——A daughter of Amphion.——A daughter of Talaus. *Hygin.*

ASTYN'OUS, a Trojan prince, killed by Diomedes during the war. *Homer. Il.* 5. v. 144.——A Trojan, son of Protiaon. *Id. ib.* 15. v. 455.——A son of Phaethon, and father of Sandochus. *Apollod.* 3. c. 27.

ASTY'OCHE or ASTYOCHI'A, a daughter of Actor, who had by Mars, Ascalaphus and Ialmenus, who were at the Trojan war, and also in the number of the Argonauts, according to *Apollodorus*, 1. c. 47.—*Homer. Il.* 2. v. 20.—*Paus.* 9. c. 37.——A daughter of Laomedon by Strymo. *Apollod.* 3.——A daughter of Amphion and Niobe. *Id.* 3. c. 4.——A daughter of the Simois, who married Erichthonius. *Id.* 3. c., 12.——The wife of Strophius, sister to Agamemnon. *Hygin.*——A daughter of Amyntor, called also Astydamia.

ASTYOCHI'A, a daughter of Phylas, king of Ephyre, who had a son called Tlepolemus, by Hercules. *Hygin.* fab. 97. 162.

ASTY'OCHUS, a commander of the Lacedæmonian fleet. *Thucyd.* 8. 20, &c.

ASTYPALÆ'A, one of the Cyclades, between Cos and Carpathus, called after Astypalæa, the daughter of Phœnix, and mother of Ancæus, by Neptune. *Paus.* 7. c. 4.—*Ptol.* 5. c. 2.—*Strab.* 14.—*Plin.* 4. c. 12. l. 8. c. 39.

ASTYPH'ILUS, a soothsayer, well skilled in the knowledge of futurity. *Plut. in Cim.*

ASTYRA or ASTYRUM, a city of Mysia, near Troas. *Mela*, 1. c. 18.——A village near Adramyttium.——A city of Phœnicia, where Minerva Astyris was worshipped.——A city of Bœotia. *Steph.*

ASTYRON, a town built by the Argonauts on the coast of Illyricum. *Strab. ex Callimach.*

ASUCIAN'DÆ, a people of Asiatic Sarmatia. *Plin.* 6. c. 7.

ASU'RA, a town near Philiscus, on the Euphrates. *Id.* 5. c. 16.

AS'YCHIS, a king of Ægypt, who succeeded Mycerinus, and made a law that whoever borrowed money, should deposit his father's body in the hand of his creditors, as a pledge. He built a magnificent pyramid. *Herodot.* 2. c. 136.

ASY'LAS, a friend of Æneas, skilled in auguries. *Virg. Æn.* 9. v. 571. l. 10. v. 175.

ASYL'LUS, a gladiator. *Juv.* 6. v. 266.

AS'YPHUS, a fountain of Marmarica. *Ptol.*

ATAB'ICIS, a city in the Propontis. *Steph.*

ATAB'ULI, a nation of Lower Æthiopia. *Plin.* 6, c. 30.

ATAB'ULUS, a wind which frequently blew in Apulia. *Horat.* 1. sat. 5. v. 78.

ATABYR'TUM, a mountain in Rhodes, where Jupiter had a temple, whence he was surnamed Atabyrius. *Strab.* 14.—*Pindar. Olymp.* 7. v. 160.

AT'ACE. a town of Gaul, whence the adjective Atacinus. *Mela*, 2. 7.

ATACI'NUS P. Terentius Varro, a poet. *Vid.* Arroa.

ATÆ'A, a city of Laconia.——A city of Phœnicia. *Steph.*

ATALAN'TA, a daughter of Schœneus king of Scyrus. According to some she was the daughter of Jasus or Jasius, by Clymene: but others say that Menalion was her father. Some have maintained that there were two persons of that name. Atalanta was born in Arcadia, and determined to live in perpetual celibacy. Her beauty, however, gained her many admirers, and to free herself from their importunities, she, being very swiftfooted, proposed to run a race with them. Her suitors were to run without arms, and she was to carry a dart in her hand. Her lovers were to start first, and whoever arrived at the goal before her, was to be rewarded with her hand as the prize, but all those whom she overtook were to be killed with the dart with which she had armed herself. Many of her suitors perished in the dangerous contest, till Hippomenes proposed himself as her admirer. Venus had presented him with three golden apples from the garden of the Hesperides, or according to others, from an orchard in Cyprus, and as soon as he had started in the course, he artfully threw down the beautiful apples at some distance one from the other. While Atalanta stopped to pick up the tempting fruit, Hippomenes hastened on his course, and arriving first at the goal, obtained Atalanta in marriage. *Vid.* Hippomenes. According to Apollodorus. Atalanta was exposed to wild beasts as soon as born; but was suckled by a she-bear, and preserved by shepherds. She dedicated her time to hunting, and resolving to live in celibacy, she killed the two centaurs, Hyleus and Rhecus, who attempted her virtue. She was present at the hunting of the Calydonian boar, which she first wounded, and she received the head as a present from Meleager, who was enamoured of her. She was also at the games instituted in honor of Pelias, where she conquered Peleus. She had a son called Parthenopæus, by Hippomenes. Hyginus says, that that son was the fruit of her love with Meleager; and Apollodorus says, she had him by Milanion, or, according to others, by the god Mars. *Vid.* Meleager. *Apollod.* 1. c. 8. l. 3. c. 9, &c.—*Diod.* 4.—*Paus.* 1. c. 36, 45, &c.—*Hygin.* fab. 99, 174. 185, 270.—*Ælian. V. H.* 13. c. 1.—*Ovid. Met.* 8. fab. 4. l. 10. fab. 11. —*Euripid in Phœniss.*—*Propert.* 1. el. 1.—*Zenobius Cent.* 33.—*Palæphat. de Incr.* 14.—*Servius in Æn.* 3. v. 113.—*Heracl. Pont.* 12.—*Scholiast. Apollon.* 1. *Arg.*—*Lactant. in Theb. Stat.* 7. v. 267.—*Tzetzes Chil.* 13. v. 453. *Farnab. in Ovid. Met.* 10. fab. 11. [The finest representation of Atlanta, is that in the Barberini palace at Rome.] ——An island near Eubœa and Locris. *Paus.*—*Liv.* 35. c. 37.—*Thucyd.* 2. c. 32.

ATAPHER'NES, according to *Ctesias*, one of the seven noblemen who conspired against Smerdis.

ATAPHY'NI, a nation of Arabia. *Steph.*

ATARAN'TA, a nation of Libya. *Arrian.*

ATARAN'TES, a people of Africa, ten days' journey from the Garamantes. It is reported that there was in their country, a hill of salt. *Herodot.* 4. c. 184.

ATARBE'CHIS, a town in one of the islands of the Delta, in Ægypt, where Venus had a temple. *Herodot.* 2. c. 41.

ATAR'GATIS, a divinity among the Syrians, represented as a Siren, and called by the various names of Atergatis, Adargatis, Adergatis, Adergidis, Atargata, and Derceto. She is considered by Strabo, and others, to be the same as Venus, honoured by the Assyrians under the name of Astarte, but Lucian represents her as a different divinity. *Lucian de Deâ Syr.*—*Selden. de Diis Syr.* 2. c. 3. —*Strab.* 16.

ATAR'NA, a city of Mysia. *Steph.*

ATAR'NEA, a part of Mysia, opposite Lesbus, with a small town in the neighbourhood, of the same name. *Paus.* 4. c. 35.—*Herodot.* 7. c. 42.

ATAR'NES, a brother of Darius, king of Persia. *Herodot.* 7.

A'TAS or A'THAS, a youth of wonderful swiftness, who is said to have run 75 miles between noon and evening. *Martial.* 4. epigr. 19.—*Plin.* 7. c. 20.

A'TAX, now Aude, a river of Gallia Narbonensis, rising in the Pyrenean mountains, and falling into the Mediterranean Sea. *Lucan.* 1. v. 403.—*Mela*, 2. 7.

A'TE, the goddess of all evil, was the daughter of Jupiter. She raised such jealousy and sedition among the gods, that Jupiter banished her for ever from heaven, and sent her to dwell on earth, where she incited mankind to every species of wickedness, and sowed perpetual dissensions among them. *Homer. Il.* 19. She is the same as the Discord of the Latins.

ATEG'UA, a city of Hispania Bætica. *Dionys.* It is now Tebala Veia or Teivela.

C. ATE'IUS CAPI'TO, a tribune of the people, who endeavoured, by representing omens as unfavourable, to dissuade Crassus from going on his Parthian expedition. He was degraded by Appius for giving a false account of omens. *Cic. D.* 1. c. 16. —*Dio.* 39.

ATEL'LA or ATTEL'LA, now Aversa, a town of Campania, famous for a splendid amphitheatre, where farces and interludes, thence called *Atellanæ Fabulæ*, were first exhibited. *Liv.* 7. c. 2. —*Juv.* 6.—*Cluver.* 3. c. 29.

ATEL'LIUS P. HISTER., a governor of Pannonia. *Tac. Ann.* 12. c. 29.

ATE'NE, a part of the tribe Antiochis at Athens. *Steph.*

ATEPOM'ARUS, a chieftain of Gaul, who made war against the Romans. *Plut. in Parall.*

A'TER, a mountain of Cyrenaica. *Plin.* 5. c. 5.

ATE'RIA LEX, extended to all magistrates the power of imposing a fine: it had before been confined to the Consuls. *Dionys.* 10.—*A. Gell.* 11. c. 1.

ATE'RIUM, a city of Sicily. *Steph.*

ATER'NUS, a small river of Picenum, which rises in the Apennines, and falls into the Adriatic. The town at its mouth bears the name of Aternum, now Pescara. It is strong and well built, and is now subject to the king of Italy. *Mela*, 2. 6.—*Cluver.* 3. c. 39.

ATES'TE, a city of the Veneti. *Plin.* 17. c. 17.

ATETRO'NA, a city of Hispania Bætica. *Strab.*

ATHAMA'NES, an ancient people of Epirus, who existed long before the Trojan war, and still preserved the name and customs of their forefathers in the age of Alexander. *Ovid. Met.* 15. v. 311.—*Strab.* 7.—*Plin.* 2. c. 103.—*Mela*, 2. c. 3.—*Solin.* 12.

ATHAMA'NIA, a region of Illyria, or of Thessaly. *Steph.*

ATHAMANTI'ADES, a patronymic of Melicerta, Phryxus, or Helle, children of Athamas. *Ovid. Met.* 13. v. 319.—*Fast.* 4. v. 903.

ATH'AMAS, king of Thebes, in Bœotia, and son of Æolus, married Themisto, whom some call Nephele, and *Pindar*, Demotice, and by her he had Phryxus and Helle. Some time after, on pretence that Nephele was subject to fits of madness, he married Ino, the daughter of Cadmus, by whom he had two sons, Learchus and Melicerta. Ino became jealous of the children of Nephele; and they escaped to Colchis *Vid.* Ino, Phryxus & Argonautæ. According to the Greek scholiast of Lycophron, v. 22, Ino attempted to destroy the corn of the country; and as if it were the consequence of divine vengeance, the soothsayers, at her instigation, told Athamas, that before the earth would yield her usual increase, he must sacrifice one of the children of Nephele to the gods. The credulous father led Phryxus to the altar, where he was saved by Nephele. The prosperity of Ino was displeasing to Juno, and more particularly because she was descended from Venus. The goddess, therefore, sent Tisiphone, one of the furies, to the house of Athamas, who became inflamed with such sudden fury, that he took Ino to be a lioness, and her two children to be whelps, and killed Learchus, by dashing him against a wall; upon which Ino threw herself, with Melicerta, into the sea. Athamas afterwards adopted as his own, Coronus and Aliartis, the sons of Thersander his nephew. *Hygin.* fab. 1, 2, 5, 239.—*Apollod.* 1. c. 7 & 9.—*Ovid. Met.* 4. v. 467, &c. *Fast.* 6. v. 489.—*Paus.* 9. c. 34.——A servant of Atticus. *Cic. ad Attic.* 12. ep. 10.——A stage dancer. *Id. Pis.* 36. ——A tragic poet. *Id. Pis.* 20.——One of the Greeks, concealed in the wooden horse at the siege of Troy. *Virg. Æn.* 2. v. 263.

ATHAN'ADAS, an historian of the Ambraciotæ. *Voss. H. Gr.* 6. c. 3.

ATHANA'GIA, a city of the Ilergetes in Spain, now Ilerda. *Liv.* 21. c. 61.

ATH'ANAS, an historian of Syracuse, who wrote 13 books on the actions of Dion.——A rock in Scythia. *Eurip. in Cyclop.*

ATHANA'SIUS, a native of Alexandria, who, though born of heathen parents, was carefully educated in the Christian faith, and at the age of twenty-eight became bishop of Alexandria, on the death of Alexander. He was celebrated for his sufferings, and the determined opposition which he maintained against Arius and his doctrine. His writings, which were numerous, and some of which have perished, contain a defence of the mystery of the Trinity, the divinity of the Word and of the Holy Ghost, and an apology to Constantine. The creed which bears his name, is supposed by some not to be his composition. Athanasius died 2d May, A.D. 373, after filling the episcopal chair forty-seven years, and leading alternately a life of exile and of triumph. The latest edition of his works is that of the Benedictines, 3 vols. fol. Paris, 1698. *Sax. Onom.* 1. p. 395.—*Fabr. B. Gr.* 5. c. 2.

ATH'ANIS, a man who wrote an account of Sicily. *Athen.* 3.—*Plut. in Timol.*

ATH'ARE or ATH'ARA, the wife of a king of Damascus, worshipped by the Syrians after death. *Justin.* 36. c. 2.

ATHAR'RABIS, a city of Ægypt. *Steph.*

A'THEAS, a Scythian, king of Pontus, who implored the assistance of Philip of Macedonia against the Istrians, and ridiculed him when he had furnished him with an army. *Justin.* 9. c. 2.

ATHE'NA, the name of Minerva among the Greeks, and also among the Ægyptians, before Cecrops king of Athens had introduced the worship of the goddess into Greece. *Paus.* 1. c. 2.—*Plin.* 7. c. 56.—*Meursii Athen. Att.* Also Athe'ne.

ATHENÆ, a celebrated city of Attica, founded about 1556 years, B.C. by Cecrops, and an Ægyptian colony. It was called Cecropia from its founder, and afterwards Athenæ in honour of Minerva, who had obtained the right of giving it a name, in preference to Neptune. *Vid.* Minerva. It was governed by seventeen kings, in the following order: After a reign of 50 years, Cecrops was succeeded by Cranaus who began to reign 1506 B.C.; Amphictyon, 1497; Erichthonius, 1487; Pandion, 1437; Erechtheus, 1397; Cecrops the Second, 1347; Pandion the Second, 1307; Ægeus, 1283; Theseus, 1235; Menestheus, 1205; Demophoon, 1182; Oxyntes, 1149; Aphidas, 1137; Thymœtes, 1136; Melanthus, 1128; and Codrus, who was killed after a reign of 21 years, 1091. The history of the first twelve of these monarchs is most fabulous. After the death of Codrus, the monarchical power was abolished, and the state was governed by thirteen successive perpetual, and 317 years after, by seven decennial, and lastly, B.C. 684, after an anarchy of three years, by annual magistrates, called Archons. *Vid.* Archontes. Under this democratical form of government, the Athenians signalised themselves by their valour in the field, their munificence at home, and the successful cultivation of the fine arts. They were deemed so powerful by the Persians, that Xerxes, when he invaded Greece, chiefly directed his arms against Athens, which he took and burnt. Their military character was most conspicuously displayed in the battles of Marathon, of Salamis, of Platæa, and of Mycale. After these immortal victories, they rose in consequence and dignity among the neighbouring states, and boldly aspired to take the lead in the affairs of Greece. The town was rebuilt and embellished by Themistocles, and a new and magnificent harbour erected. Success in war made them arrogant, and they raised contentions among their neighbours, that they might aggrandize themselves by their fall. Luxury and intemperance, which had been long excluded from the city, by the severe but salutary laws of their countrymen, Draco and Solon, crept by degrees, however, among all ranks of people, and soon after all Greece united to destroy that city, which claimed a sovereign power over all the rest. The Peloponnesian war, though at first a private quarrel, was soon fomented into a universal war; and the arms of all the states of Peloponnesus (*Vid.* Peloponnesiacum bellum) were directed against Athens, which, after twenty-eight years of misfortunes and bloodshed, was totally ruined, on the 24th April, 404 B.C., by Lysander. After this, the Athenians were oppressed by thirty tyrants, and for a while laboured under the weight of their own calamities. They recovered, however, something of their usual spirit in the age of Philip, and boldly opposed his ambitious views; but their short-lived efforts were not of great service to the interest of Greece, and after submitting to the galling yoke of the successors of Alexander, they, at last, fell into the hands of the Romans, B.C. 86. The Athenians have been admired in all ages, for their love of liberty, and for the great men that were born among them. Public favour, however, was there attended with danger; and there are very few instances in the history of Athens, that can prove that the jealousy and frenzy of the people did not persecute and disturb the peace of the man who had fought their battles, and exposed his life in the defence of his country. Perhaps, not one city in the world can boast in such a short space of time, of such a number of truly illustrious citizens, equally celebrated for their humanity, their learning, and their military abilities. The Romans, in the more polished ages of their republic, sent their youth to finish their education at Athens, and respected the learning, while they despised the fallen military character of the inhabitants. The reputation which the Athenian schools had acquired under Socrates and Plato, was maintained by their degenerate and less learned successors; and they flourished with diminished lustre, till an edict of the emperor Justinian suppressed, with the Roman consulship, the philosophical meetings of the academy. It has been said by Plutarch, that the good men whom Athens produced, were the most just and equitable in the world; but that its bad citizens could not be surpassed in any age or country, for their impiety, perfidiousness, or cruelties. The reputation for learning, for military valour, and for polished elegance which Athens enjoyed during the splendid administration of Pericles, was tarnished by the corruption which this celebrated hero introduced. Prosperity was the forerunner of luxury and universal dissipation, every possible delicacy was drawn from distant nations, the wines of Cyprus, and the snows of Thrace, garlands of roses, perfumes, and all the effeminate customs which disgraced the Persian court, were introduced instead of the coarse meals, the herbs and plain bread which the laws of Solon had recommended, and which had nourished the heroes of Marathon and Salamis. The ancients, to distinguish Athens in a more peculiar manner, called it Astu, one of the eyes of Greece, the learned city, the school of the world, the common patroness of Greece. The Athenians thought themselves the most ancient nation of Greece, and supposed themselves the original inhabitants of Attica, for which reason they were called αὐτόχθονες, produced from the *same earth* which they inhabited, γηγενεῖς *sons of the earth, and* τέττιγες *grasshoppers.* They sometimes wore golden grasshoppers in their hair as badges of honour, to distinguish them from other people of later origin and less noble extraction, because those insects are supposed to spring from the ground. The number of men able to bear arms at Athens in the reign of Cecrops was computed at 20,000, and there appeared no considerable augmentation in the more civilized age of Pericles; but in the time of Demetrius Phalereus there were found 21,000 citizens, 10,000 foreigners, and 40,000 slaves. Among the numerous temples and public edifices of the city, none was more celebrated than that of Minerva, called the Parthenon, which, after being burnt by the Persians, was rebuilt by Pericles, with the finest marble, and would still have existed, a venerable monument of the hero's patriotism, and of the abilities of the architect, but for the rapacity of modern travellers, who have stripped it of its most valuable decorations. *Cic. ad Attic. in Verr. &c.—Thucyd.* 1, *&c.—Hygin.* fab. 164,—*Meursii Athenæ Att.—Æschin. contra Ctes.—Euseb. Chron —Justin.* 2. c. 6. &c.—*Diod.* 13, &c.—*Ælian. V. H.* 4. c. 6.—*Plin.* 7. c. 56.—*Xenoph. Memorab.—Fann. Palemon de Ponderibus,* 17 & 39.—*Plut. in Vitis, &c.—Strab.* 9, *&c.—Paus.* 1, *&c.—Val. Max. —Liv.* 31, &c.—*C. Nep. in Milt. &c.—Polyb.—Patercul.*

ATHENÆ'A, festivals celebrated at Athens in honour of Minerva. *Vid.* Panathenæa.

ATHENÆ'UM, a place at Athens sacred to Minerva, where the poets, philosophers, and rhetoricians generally declaimed and repeated their compositions. It was open for the use of all the professors of the liberal arts. Adrian, made a public building at Rome for the same laudable purposes.——A promontory of Italy, between the bay of Naples and the Sinus Pæstanus. It is called also Minervæ Promontorium, and is now Capo di Campanella. ——A fortified place between Ætolia and Macedonia. *Liv.* 38. c. 1. l. 39. c. 25.

ATHENÆ'US, a peripatetic philosopher of Cilicia in the time of Augustus. *Fabricius* suspects this to be the person whose history of Semiramis, *Diodorus Siculus* praises. *Fabr. B. Gr.* 4. c. 25.—*Diod.* 2. c. 20.—*Strab.* 14.——A Spartan sent by his countrymen to Athens, to negotiate a peace during the Peloponnesian war. *Thucyd.* 4. c. 119. ——A grammarian of Naucratis, who composed an elegant and miscellaneous work, called *Deipnosophistæ*, replete with very curious and interesting remarks and anecdotes of the manners of the ancients, and likewise valuable for the scattered pieces of ancient poetry which it preserves. The work consists of fifteen books, of which the two first, part of the third, and almost the whole of the last, are lost, and in many places the whole is dreadfully disfigured by the ignorance or officiousness of transcribers. Athenæus wrote, also, a history of Syria, and other works now lost. He died A.D. 194. The best edition of his works is that of Cassaubon, 2 vols. fol. Lugd. 1612, by far superior to the editions of 1595 and 1657. To this may be added, the later edition of Schweighaeuser, in 14 vols. 8vo. *Fabr. B. Gr.* 4. c. 25.—*Sax. Onom.* 1. p, 347.——An historian who wrote an account of Semiramis. *Diod.*——A brother of king Eumenes the Second, famous for his paternal affection.——A Roman general of Byzantium, in the age of Gallienus, who is supposed to have written a book on military engines. *Trebel. Pollio in vit. Gallieni.* c. 13.——A physician of Cilicia in the age of Pliny, who substituted other elements instead of the four commonly received.——A mathematician of Cyzicus, in the time of Archimedes. *Proclus.* l. 2. *in Eccl.* p. 19.——A stoic philosopher.——An epicurean philosopher.——A Greek cosmographer. *Fabr. ibid.*

ATHENAG'ORAS, a Greek in the time of Darius, to whom Pharnabazus entrusted the government of Chius, &c. *Curt.* 4. c. 21.——A writer on agriculture. *Varro.* l. 1. c. 1 & 5.——An Athenian philosopher, who was converted to Christianity in the age of Antoninus, and wrote a treatise on the resurrection, and an apology for the Christians, still extant. These writings prove him to have been a man of great erudition, extensive application, and a true master of the Attic style. He died A.D. 177. The best edition of his works is that of Dechair, 8vo, Oxon. 1706. The Romance of Theagenes and Charis is falsely ascribed to him. *Fabr. B. Gr.* l. 5. c. 1. v. 19.—*Sax.* 1. p. 319.——A person of Cumæ, mentioned by *Cicero, pro Flacco,* c. 7.——A præfect of king Philip of Macedon. *Liv.* 31. 27.——An inhabitant of Miletus. *Diod. Sic.* l. 20, &c.—*Fabr. ibid.*

ATHENA'IS, a Sibyl of Erythræa, in the age of Alexander the Great. *Strab.*——A daughter of the philosopher Leontius.

ATHE'NION, a peripatetic philosopher, 108 B.C.——A general of the Sicilian revolted slaves. Clodius is contemptuously called by Cicero an Athenion, as being the leader and associate of vulgar and infamous characters. *Cic. Att.* 2. ep. 12. *Varr.* 2. c. 54.—*Harus.* 72.——A tyrant of Athens, surnamed Ariston.——A comic poet, from one of whose plays *Athenæus,* l. 14. p. 660, quotes a long passage. *Fabr. B. Gr.* 2. c. 22. *de Com.*——A painter praised by *Pliny. Fabr. ibid.*

ATHEN'OCLES, a general skilful in the use of military engines. *Polyæn.* 6.——A turner of Mitylene. *Plin.* 34.——A writer on Assyria. *Agath.* 2.

ATHENODO'RUS, a philosopher of Tarsus, intimate with Augustus. The emperor often profited by his lessons, and was advised by him always to repeat the twenty-four letters of the Greek alphabet before he gave way to the impulse of anger. Athenodorus died in his 82d year, much lamented by his countrymen. *Suet.*——A poet who wrote comedy, tragedy, and elegiac poetry, in the age of Alexander. *Plut. in Alex.*——A philosopher, disciple to Zeno, and keeper of the royal library at Pergamus.——A statuary.——A man assassinated at Bactra for attempting to make himself absolute in the state. *Fabricius, B. Gr.* l. 3. c. 10. enumerates no less than thirteen persons of this name.

ATHENOP'OLIS, a town of Gallia Narbonensis. *Plin.* 3. c. 4. Some read Antipolis.

ATHE'RIUS or ATE'RIUS, a lawyer in the age of Cicero. *Cic. Fam.* 9. ep. 18.

ATH'ESIS, now Adige, a river of Cisalpine Gaul, at the north of the Po. It falls into the Adriatic Sea. *Virg. Æn.* 9. v. 680.

ATHE'US, a surname of Diagoras and Theodorus, because they denied the existence of a Deity. *Cic. de Nat. D.* 1. c. 1.

A'THIS, a city of Syria, on the Euphrates. *Ptol.*

ATH'LIBIS, a city of Ægypt.——A city of Arabia. *Steph.*

ATH'MONUM, a part of the tribe Cecropis at Athens. *Id.*

A'THOS, a mountain of Macedonia, projecting into the Ægean sea. It is so high that it overshadows the island of Lemnus, though at the distance of 87 miles; or, according to modern calculation, only eight leagues. When Xerxes invaded Greece, he made a trench of a mile and a half in length at the foot of the mountain, from Acanthus on the north, to Sane on the south, into which he brought the sea, and conveyed his fleet through it, so that two ships could pass one another. A sculptor, called Dinocrates, offered Alexander to cut mount Athos, and to make with it a statue representing the king holding a town in his left hand, and in the right a spacious basin, to receive all the waters which flowed from it. Alexander admired the boldness of the plan, and the ingenuity of the artist, but objected to the place; and he observed, that the neighbouring country was not sufficiently fruitful to produce corn and provisions for the inhabitants which were to dwell in the city in the hand of the statue. Athos is now called Monte Santo, and is famous for the monasteries erected there, which are said by modern travellers to contain many ancient and valuable manuscripts. *Herodot.* 6. c. 44. l. 7. c. 21, &c.—*Lucan.* 2. v. 672.—*Ælian. de Anim.* 13. c. 20, &c.—*Plin.* 4, c. 10.—*Æschin. contra Ctesiph.*

A'THRES, now Labus, a river of European Scythia. *Herodot.*

ATHRI'TÆ, a people of Arabia Felix. *Ptol.*

ATHRUL'LA, a town of Arabia. *Strab.*

ATHYM'BRA, a city of Caria, afterwards called Nyssa. *Strab.* 14.

A'THYR, the name of the month June among the Ægyptians. *Plut. in Isid. & Osir.*

ATH'YRAS, or ATH'YRUS, now Acqua Dolce, a river of Thrace, flowing into the Propontis. *Mela,* 2. c. 2.—*Cluver.* 4. c. 14

A'TIA, a city of Campania. *Diod. Sic.* 20.

A'TIA, the mother of Augustus, daughter of Atius Balbus, by Julia, Julius Cæsar's sister. The family of the Atii, to which she belonged, are represented, by the flattery of Virgil, as the lineal descendants of Atys, the companion of Ascanius. *Vid.* Accia.

A'TIA LEX, a law enacted A.U.C. 690, by T. Atius Labienus, tribune of the people. It abolished the Cornelian law, and put in full force the Lex Domitia, by transferring the right of electing priests from the college of priests to the people.

ATIL'IA LEX gave the præter and a majority of the tribunes the power of appointing guardians to those minors who were not previously provided for by their parents. It was enacted about A.U.C. 560.—Another A.U.C. 443, which gave the people the power of electing 16 tribunes of the soldiers in four legions *Liv.* 9. c. 30.

ATIL'IUS, a freedman, who exhibited combats of gladiators at Fidenæ. The amphitheatre, which contained the spectators, fell during the exhibition and about 50,000 persons were either killed or mutilated. *Tac. Ann.* 4. c. 62. The family of the Atilii was plebeian, but distinguished by the military conduct of some of its members. One of them, Marcus, is mentioned by *Livy,* 15, 17, & 19, and another by *Cicero, Fin.* 2. c. 35.

ATIL'IUS RU'FUS, a præfect of Syria, under Domitian. *Tac Agric.* c. 40.

ATIL'IUS VERGIL'IO, a standard bearer in a cohort which accompanied Galba. *Tac Hist.* 1. c. 41. *Plutarch,* however, reads Servilius.

ATIL'IUS VE'RUS, a centurion who nobly fought for the eagle of the seventh legion at Cremona. *Tac. Hist.* 3. c. 22.

ATIL'LA, the mother of the poet Lucan. She was unnaturally accused of conspiracy by her son, who expected by this means to clear himself of the charge. *Tac. Ann.* 15. c. 56.

ATI'NA, now Antino, an ancient town of the Volsci, one of the first cities which began hostilities against Æneas. *Virg. Æn.* 7. v. 630. l. 11. v. 869.—*Cic. de Div.* 1. c. 28.

ATI'NAS, a friend of Turnus, &c. *Virg. Æn.* 11. v. 869.

ATIN'IA LEX, was enacted by the tribune Atinius. It gave a tribune of the people the privileges of a senator, and the right of sitting in the senate. *A. Gell.* 14.—Another law which permitted the reclaiming of stolen goods, &c. *Cic. Varr.* 1. c. 42. —*Gellius,* 17. c. 7.

ATINTA'NIA, a part of Macedonia. *Steph.* The people were called Atintanes. *Polyb. Thucydides* places them among the Molossi.

ATI'SO, now Tosa, a river of the Insubres. *Plut. in Mar.*—*Cluver. Ital. Ant.* l. 1.

ATIZ'IES, a Persian nobleman, slain at the battle of Issus. *Curt.* 3. c. 11.—*Diodorus,* l. 17. calls him Antixyes.

ATLAN'TA or ATALAN'TA, a city of the Locri, made an island by an earthquake. *Euseb.*

ATLAN'TES, a people of Africa, in the neighbourhood of mount Atlas. They daily cursed the sun at his rising and at his setting. *Amm. Marcell.* 15. c. 4.—*Herodot.* 4. c. 184.—*Mela.* 1. c. 4.—*Plin.* 5. c. 8.—*Schol. Dionys. Peri.* 66.—*Solinus,* 34.

ATLANTI'ADES, a patronymic of Mercury, as grandson of Atlas. *Ovid. Met.* 1. v. 639.

ATLAN'TICA, a name given to the Fortunate Islands by some writers, who place there the Elysian Fields. They are the same as the Hesperides of *Pliny,* which he describes as situate in the Atlantic Ocean. *Plin.* 6. c. 31.

TLAN'TIDES, a people of Africa, near mount Atlas. They boasted that theirs was the country in which all the gods received their birth. Uranus was their first king, whom, on account of his knowledge of astronomy they enrolled in the number of their gods. *Diod.* 3.——The daughters of Atlas, seven in number; Maia, Electra, Taygeta, Asterope, Merope, Alcyone, and Celæno. They married some of the gods and most illustrious heroes, and their children founded various cities, and established several kingdoms in different parts of the world. The name of Hesperides was also given them, on account of their mother Hesperis. They were made constellations after death. *Vid.* Pleiades.

ATLAN'TIS, a celebrated island mentioned by the ancients. Its situation is not only unknown, but its very existence is doubted by modern writers, though some assert that it disappeared in some dreadful convulsion of nature, while others suppose that the description given of it is applicable to America, since Plato considers it as larger than both Africa and Asia. *Strab.* 1 & 2.—*Plin.* 2. c. 90. l. 6. c. 31.—*Plat. in Timæo.*—*Mela*, 1. c. 48. l. 2. c. 6. l. 3. c. 1 & 10.—*Keckerm. Contemp. de Terræ Motu Prob.* 4.—*Cluver.* 6. c. 11.

AT'LAS, one of the Titans, son of Japetus and Clymene, one of the Oceanides. According to Apollodorus, his mother's name was Asia. He married Pleione, daughter of Oceanus or Hesperis, according to others by whom he became father of seven daughters called Atlantides. *Vid.* Atlantides. He was king of Mauritania, and master of a thousand flocks of every kind, as also of beautiful gardens, abounding in every species of fruit, which he had entrusted to the care of a dragon. Perseus, after the conquest of the Gorgons, passed by the palace of Atlas, and claimed his hospitality. The king, who had been informed by an oracle of Themis that he should be dethroned by one of the descendants of Jupiter, refused to receive the illustrious stranger, and even offered him violence. Perseus, who was unequal in strength to his adversary, shewed him Medusa's head, and Atlas was instantly changed into a large mountain. This mountain which runs across the deserts of Africa east and west, is so high that the ancients have imagined that the heavens rested on its top, and that Atlas supported the world on his shoulders. Hyginus says that Atlas assisted the giants in their wars against the gods, for which Jupiter compelled him to bear the heavens on his shoulders. This fable arose from his fondness for astronomy, and his often frequenting elevated places, particularly mountains, whence he might observe the heavenly bodies. The daughters of Atlas were carried away by Busiris king of Ægypt, but recovered by Hercules, who received, as a reward from the father, the knowledge of astronomy, and a celestial globe. This knowledge Hercules communicated to the Greeks; whence the fable has farther said, that he eased for some time the labours of Atlas by taking upon his shoulders the weight of the heavens. According to some authors, there were two other persons of that name, a king of Italy, father of Electra, and a king of Arcadia, father of Maia, the mother of Mercury. *Virg. Æn.* 4. v. 481. l. 8. v. 186.—*Ovid. Met.* 4. fab. 17.—*Diod.* 3.—*Lucan.* 9. v. 667.—*Val. Flacc.* 5. v. 409, & seq.—*Hygin.* 83, 125, 155, 157, 192.—*Aratus in Astron.*—*Apollod.* 1.—*Hesiod. Theog.* v. 508, &c. [A fine statue of Atlas supporting the globe is in the Farnese collection at Naples. There is also a group of Hercules relieving him, in the Villa Mattei.]

AT'LAS, a river flowing from mount Hæmus into the Ister. *Herodot.* 4. c. 49.

ATMANIS'PHE, a village of Arabia Felix. *Ptol.*

ATOS'SA, a daughter of Cyrus, king of Persia, who was one of the wives of Cambyses, of Smerdis, and afterwards of Darius, by whom she had Xerxes. She was cured of a dangerous cancer by Democedes. She is supposed by some to be the Vashti of scripture. *Herodot.* 3. c. 68, &c.

AT'RACES, a people of Ætolia, who received their name from Atrax, son of Ætolus. Their country was called Atracia. *Ovid.* ep. 17. v. 247.

A'TRÆ, a city between the Euphrates and Tigris, besieged in vain by Septimus Severus. *Steph.*—*Dion.* 75.——A city of Arabia. *Zonaras.*

ATRAMI'TÆ, a people of Arabia Felix. *Steph.*

ATRAMYT'TIUM, a town of Mysia.

ATRA'NI, a people of the Hirpini in Italy. *Plin.* 3. c. 11.

AT'RAPES, an officer of Alexander, who, at the general division of the provinces, received Media. *Diod.* 18.

ATRATI'NUS A. SEM'PRON., a military tribune, A.U.C. 310. *Livy*, 4. c. 7. *Livy* mentions another of this name who was consul the following year.——The accuser of Cælius. *Cic. in Cæl.*

A'TRAX, a son of Ætolus, or, according to others, of the river Peneus. He was king of Thessaly, and built a town which he called Atrax, or Atracia. This town became so famous that the word *Atracii* has been applied to the inhabitants of Thessaly. Atrax was father of Hippodamia, who married Pirithous, and whom we must not confound with the wife of Pelops who bore the same name. *Propert.* l. el. 8. v. 25.—*Stat.* 1. *Theb.* v. 106.—*Ovid. Met.* 12. v. 209.—*Val. Flacc.* 6. v. 447.

A'TRAX, a city of Thessaly, whence the epithet of Atracius.——A river of Ætolia, which falls into the Ionian Sea. *Catull. Epigr.* 96. v. 5.

ATREB'ATES, or **ATREBA'TES**, now Artois, a people of Gaul, who, together with the Nervii, opposed J. Cæsar with 15,000 men. They were conquered, and Commius, a friend of the Roman general, was set over them as king. They were reinstated in their former liberty and independence on account of the services of Commius, and of his interest with Cæsar. *Cæs. Bell. Gall.* 2, &c.—*Plin.* 4. Also written Atreb'ati.

ATREBA'TII, a people of Britain, who were in possion of that part of the island which now forms the modern counties of Berks, Oxford, &c.

ATRE'NI, a people of Armenia. *Dion.* 75.

A'TREUS, son of Pelops by Hippodamia, was king of Mycenæ. Being suspected of the murder of Chrysippus (*Vid.* Chrysippus) he retired to the court of Eurystheus king of Argos, his nephew, and upon his death he succeeded him on the throne. He married, as some report, Ærope, his predecessor's daughter, by whom he had Plisthenes, Menelaus, and Agamemnon. Others affirm that Ærope was the wife of Plisthenes, by whom she had Agamemnon and Menelaus, who are the reputed sons of Atreus, because that prince took care of their education, and brought them up as his own. *Vid.* Plisthenes. Thyestes, the brother of Atreus, had followed him to Argos, where he seduced his wife, by whom he had two, or, according to some, three children. This incestuous commerce offended Atreus, and Thyestes was banished from his court. He was, however, soon after recalled by his brother, who determined cruelly to revenge the violence offered to his bed. He invited his brother to a sumptuous feast, where Thyestes was served with the flesh of the children he had had by his sister-in-law the queen. After the repast was finished, the arms and heads of the murdered children were produced, to inform Thyestes what he had feasted upon. This action appeared so cruel and impious that the sun is said to have shrunk back in his course with horror at the bloody sight. Thyestes immediately fled. *Vid.* Thyestes. Atreus afterwards married Pelopea, daughter of Thyestes, and adopted Ægisthus, her son, by her own father, and sent him to murder Thyestes, who had been seized at Delphi and imprisoned. Thyestes knew his son, and made himself known to him; he prevailed upon him to espouse his cause, and instead of becoming his father's murderer, he avenged his wrongs, and returned to Atreus, whom he assassinated. *Vid.* Thyestes, Ægisthus, Pelopea, Agamemnon & Menelaus. *Hygin.* fab. 83, 86, 87, 88, & 258.—*Euripid. in Orest. in Iphig. Taur.*—*Plut. in Parall.*—*Paus.* 9. c. 40.—*Apollod.* 3. c. 10.—*Senec. in Atr.*—*Pindar. Olymp.*—*Tzetzes in Lyc. & in Chil.* 1. *Hist.* 18.—*Schol. Eurip. in Orest.* 5. & 813.—*Lactant. in Arg. Thy. Senec.*—*Id. ad Theb. Statii.* 684.—*Servius in Æn.* l. v. 572. l. 11. v. 262.

ATRIANO'RUM PALU'DES, lakes called the seven seas. *Plin.* 3. c. 16.—*Strab.* 5.

ATRIA'NUS, a river of Italy, now Tataro. *Ptol.*

ATRICA'NI, a people of Italy. *Dion. Hal.* 5.

ATRI'DÆ, a patronymic given by Homer to Agamemnon and Menelaus, as being the son of Atreus. This according to Hesiod, Lactantius, Dictys of Crete, &c. is an erroneous opinion. They maintain that these princes were not the sons of Atreus, but of Plisthenes, and that they were brought up in the house under the eye of their grandfather. *Vid.* Plisthenes. *Schol. Homer. Il.* 2.—*Hesiod. apud Eustat.* 1 *Il.*—*Servius* 1 *Æn.* 462.—*Lactant. in* 1 *Ach.*—*Dictys. Cr.* 1.

ATRO'NIUS, a friend of Turnus, killed by the Trojans. *Virg. Æn.* 10.

ATROPA'TIA, a part of Media. *Strab.* 11.—*Steph.*—*Dionys.* v. 1019.

AT'ROPOS, one of the Parcæ. According to the derivation of her name (ἀ *non* τρέπω *verto*,) she was inexorable, and unmoved by the prayers of mortals. She was represented by the ancients in a black veil, with a pair of scissors in her hand. *Vid.* Parcæ. *Stat. Theb.* 3. v. 67. l. 4. *Sylv.* 8. v. 18.—*Hesiod. The.* 217.—*Hygin. Præf.*

AT'TA T. Q. a writer of merit in the Augustan age. His compositions were held in universal admiration, though Horace speaks of them with indifference. Only one verse is preserved of all his compositions. *Horat.* 2. ep. 1. v. 79.—*Voss. de poet. Lat.* c.——A city of Arabia Felix. *Ptol.*

ATTAC'ANA, a town of Armenia Major. *Id.*

AT'TACI, a nation of the Seræ. *Plin.* 7. c. 17.

AT'TACUM, a town of Hispania Tarraconensis, now Ateca, or, according to others, Daroca. *Ptol.*

AT'TALI, an Arabian nation addicted to plunder. *Plin.* 6. c. 26.

ATTALI'A, a city of Pamphylia, built by king Attalus. *Strab.* There were three other cities of this name in Asia Minor.

ATTAL'ICUS. *Vid.* Attalus the Third.

AT'TALIS, a tribe of Attica, so called from king Attalus. *Steph.*—*Liv. Dec.* 4. l. 1.

AT'TALUS the First, king of Pergamus, succeeded Eumenes the First. He not only defeated the Gauls who had invaded his dominions, but extended his conquests to mount Taurus, towards the east, and strengthened himself on the throne by obtaining the powerful assistance of the Romans against Antiochus. The Athenians rewarded his merit with great honours. He died at Pergamus after a reign of 44 years B.C. 197. *Liv.* 26, 27, 28, &c.—*Polyb.* 5.—*Strab.* 13.

AT'TALUS, the Second, was sent on an embassy to Rome by his brother Eumenes the Second, and at his return was appointed guardian to his nephew Attalus the Third, who was then an infant. Prusias waged a successful war against him, and seized his capital; but the conquest was stopped by the interference of the Romans, who restored Attalus to his throne. Attalus, who has received the name of *Philadelphus* from his fraternal love, was a munificent patron of learning, and the founder of several cities. He was poisoned by his nephew in the 82d year of his age, B.C 138. He had governed the nation with great prudence and moderation for twenty years. *Strab.* 13.—*Polyb.* 5.

AT'TALUS the Third, succeeded to the kingdom of Pergamus, by the murder of Attalus the Second, and made himself odious by his cruelty to his relations, and his wanton exercise of power. He was son of Eumenes the Second. and *Philopater.* He left the cares of government, to cultivate his garden, and to make experiments on the melting of metals. He lived in great amity with the Romans; and, as he died without issue by his wife Berenice, he left in his will the words, *P. R. meorum hæres esto,* which the Romans interpreted in their own favour, and therefore took possession of his kingdom, B.C. 133, and made it a Roman province. From this circumstance, whatever was valuable as an acquisition, or ample and magnificent as a fortune, was always called by an epithet of *Attalicus.* Attalus, as well as his predecessors, made themselves celebrated for the valuable libraries which they collected at Pergamus, and for the patronage which merit and virtue always found at their court. *Liv.* 24, &c.—*Plin.* 7, 8, 23, &c.—*Propert.* 3. el. 18. v. 19.—*Justin.* 39.—*Horat.* 1. od. 1.——

AT'TALUS, an officer in Alexander's army. *Curt.* 4. c. 13.——A Macedonian, very inimical to Alexander. He was put to death by Parmenio, and Alexander was justly accused of the murder. *Curt.* 6. c. 9. l. 8. c. 1.——A philosopher, preceptor to Seneca. *Senec.* ep. 108.——An astronomer of Rhodes.

ATTALY'DA, a city of Lydia. *Steph.*

ATTAR'RAS, an officer who seized those that had conspired with Dymnus against Alexander. *Curt.* 6. c. 8.

ATTASI'NI, a nation of the Massagetæ and Sacæ. *Strab.* Of Sogdiana, according to *Pliny,* 6. c. 16.

ATTE'IUS CAP'ITO. *Vid.* Ateius.

ATTE'IUS, an Athenian, who taught grammar and rhetoric at Rome, and is said to have assisted Sallust in the composition of his works. *Sueton. de illustr. Gramm.*

ATTE'IUS PRÆTEXTA'TUS, a Latin grammarian. *Sueton. Ibid.* c. 7.

ATTELEBUS'SA, an island of the Lycian Sea. *Ptol.*

ATTE'NA, a town of Upper Æthiopia. *Plin.* 6. c. 29.

ATTE'NE, a region of Arabia Felix. *Id.* 6. c. 28.

AT'TES, a son of Calaus of Phrygia, who introduced the worship of Cybele among the Lydians, and became a great favourite of the goddess. Jupiter was jealous of his success, and sent a wild boar to lay waste the country and destroy Attes. *Paus.* 7. c. 17.

AT'THIS, a daughter of Cranaus the Second, king of Athens, who gave her name to Attica, according to *Apollodorus,* 3. c. 14.—*Paus.* 1. c. 2.——A girl beloved by Sappho. *Ovid.* ep. 15. v. 18.

AT'TICA, a country of Achaia, or Hellas, at the south of Bœotia, west of the Ægean sea, north of the Saronicus Sinus, and east of Megara. It received its name, according to some authors, from Atthis, the daughter of Cranaus. It was originally called Ionia, from the Ionians, who settled there; and also from its situation near the sea, Acte, which signifies *shore;* and Cecropia, from Cecrops, the first of its kings. The most famous of its cities was and is still Athens, the inhabitants of which sometimes bear the name of *Attici.* Attica was famous for its gold and silver mines, which, at one time, constituted the best part of the public revenues. The face of the country was partly level, and partly mountainous, divided into the thirteen tribes of Acamantis, Æantis, Antiochus, Attalis, Ægeis, Erechtheis, Adrianis, Hippothoontis, Cecropis, Leontis, Æneis, Ptolemais, and Pandionis; the inhabitants of which were numbered in the 116th Olympiad, at 31.000 citizens, and 400,000 slaves, within 174 villages, some of which were of considerable extent. *Vid.* Athenæ. *Strab.* 9.—*Plin.* 4. c. 7. l. 7. c. 56.—*Eustath. ad Dionys. Per.*—*Paus.* 1. c. 2.—*Apollod.* 3. c. 26, &c.—*Lucan.* 3. v. 306.—*Ovid. Met.* 6. v. 70.—*Mart.* 11. epigr. 43.—*Horat.* 2. od 1. v. 12.—*Catull. de Nupt. P.* 79.

AT'TICUM, a place of Cyrenaica. *Antonin.*

AT'TICUS T. POMPO'NIUS, a celebrated Roman knight, to whom Cicero wrote a great number of letters, which contained the general history of the age. They are now extant, and are divided into seventeen books. In the time of Marius and Sylla, Atticus retired to Athens, where he so endeared himself to the citizens, by his kinduess and liberality, that his departure was the signal for general mourning, and statues were erected to his honour, in commemoration of his great munificence. He was such a perfect master of the Greek writers, and spoke their language with such ease and fluency, that he was surnamed *Atticus;* and, as a proof of his learning, he favoured the world with some valuable compositions. He behaved in such a disinterested manner, that he offended neither of the inimical parties at Rome, and both were equally anxious to court his approbation. He lived in the greatest intimacy with the illustrious men of his age; and was such a lover of truth, that he abstained from falsehood even in a joke. He not only protected, but also relieved Brutus in his distresses, when the whole empire had deserted his cause for that of his more successful rival; and he extended his regard and liberality with the same humane views to Cicero, as well as to Fulvia, the wife of his inveterate enemy. It is said that he refused to take aliments when unable to get the better of a fever, and died in his 77th year, B.C. 32. Atticus married in his 53rd year, and had an only daughter, who was afterwards married to Agrippa, the friend of Augustus, his grand-daughter, by this marriage, as soon as born, was betrothed by Augustus to Tiberius. *Cornelius Nepos,* one of his intimate friends, has written a minute account of his life, and, without doubt, in that circumstantial history, the character of Atticus appears, next to that of Socrates, the most humane, amiable, and benevolent amongst the records of the heathen ages. *Cic. ad Attic.* &c.

AT'TICUS JU'LIUS, one of Galba's servants, who entered his palace with a bloody sword, and declared that he had killed Otho. *Tacit. Hist.* 1. c. 35.

AT'TICUS HERO'DES, an Athenian in the age of the Antonines, descended from Miltiades, and celebrated for his munificence. His great riches arose from a marriage with a woman of opulence, as well as from an immense treasure which he discovered buried under an old house, and which the virtuous Nerva, rather than claim, as emperor of Rome, permitted him to use as he pleased.

AT'TICUS TI'BER. CLAUD. HERO'DES, son of the preceding, was a great orator, but of his orations only one, περὶ πολιτείας, is extant. It may be found in the Aldine edition of the Attic orators, Venet. 1513, and Paris, 1575; also in Reiske's Orat. Græc. vol. 8. Lips. 1773. He wrote also epistles and inscriptions; the best edition of the last is that of Visconti, Rome, 1794. In the year A.D. 143, he was honoured with the consulship, and generously erected an aqueduct at Troas, of which he had been made governor by the emperor Adrian, and raised in other parts of the empire several public buildings as useful as they were magnificent. *Fabr. B. Gr.* 1. 4. c. 32.—*Sax. Onom.* 1. p. 306.—*Philostrat. in Vit.* 2. p. 548.—*A. Gell. Noct, Att.*

AT'TICUS, a consul in the age of Nero, &c. *Tacit. Ann.* 15.

AT'TILA, a celebrated king of the Huns, a nation in the southern parts of Scythia, who invaded the Roman territories, in the reign of Valentinian, with an army of 500,000 men, and laid waste the fairest provinces of the empire. He took the town of Aquileia, and marched against Rome; but his retreat and peace were purchased with a large sum of money by the feeble emperor. Attila, who gloried in the appellation of *the scourge of God*, died A.D. 453. His body, deposited in a golden coffin, inclosed in another of silver, and in a third of iron, was buried in the midst of a large plain; and, like that of Alaric, his grave was filled with the most magnificent spoils obtained by conquest and war; and after the ceremony, the barbarous Huns, desirous of concealing the tomb of their monarch, slaughtered all those who had attended the funeral. *Jornand. de Reb. Get.*

ATTIL'IUS, a Roman consul in the first Punic war. *Vid.* Regulus.

ATTIL'IUS CALATI'NUS, a Roman consul, who came to an engagement with the Carthaginian fleet.

ATTIL'IUS MAR'CUS, a poet who translated the Electra of Sophocles into Latin verse, and wrote comedies, the unintelligible and unpolished language of which procured him the appellation of *Ferreus.*

ATTIL'IUS REG'ULUS, a Roman censor who built a temple to the goddess of concord. *Liv.* 23. c. 23, &c. The name of Attilius was common among the Romans, and many of the public magistrates were of this family; their lives, however, were not famous for any remarkable events.

ATTI'NAS, an officer set over Bactriana by Alexander. *Curt.* 8. c. 1.

AT'TIRI, a nation of Upper Æthiopia. *Ptol.*

AT'TIUM, a promontory of Corsica, now Punta di Laccivolo. *Ptol.*

AT'TIUS PELIG'NUS, an officer of Cæsar. *Cæs. Bell. Civ.* 1.

AT'TIUS TUL'LUS, the general of the Volsci, to whom Coriolanus fled when banished from Rome. *Liv.*

AT'TIUS VA'RUS, seized Auxinum in Pompey's name, whence he was expelled. After this he fled to Africa, which he alienated from J. Cæsar. *Cæs. Bell. Civ.* 1.

AT'TIUS, a poet. *Vid.* Accius. The family of the Attii was descended from Atys, one of the companions of Æneas, according to the opinion which *Virgil* has adopted in the fifth book of the *Æneid,* v. 568.

ATTU'BI, a town of Hispania Bætica, now Espejo. *Plin.* 3. c. 1.

ATU'RIA, a part of Assyria. *Strab.* 16.

AT'URUS, a small river of Gaul, now called Adour. It runs along the foot of the Pyrenean mountains, and falls into the Bay of Biscay. *Lucan.* 1. v. 420.

ATY'ADÆ, the descendants of Atys the Lydian.

ATYM'NUS or ATYM'NIUS, a son of Jupiter and Cassiopeia. *Schol. Apollon.*—*Salmas. ad Solin.* p. 172.

A'TYS, an ancient king of Lydia, who sent away his son Tyrrhenus, at the head of a colony of Lydians, who came to settle in Italy. *Strab.* 5.—*Herodot.* 1. c. 7.——A son of Crœsus king of Lydia. He was forbidden the use of all weapons by his father, who had dreamt that he was to perish by some military weapon. Some time after this, Atys prevailed on his father to permit him to go to hunt a wild boar which laid waste the country of Mysia, and he was killed in the attempt by Adrastus. *Herodot.* 1. c. 34, &c. *Vid.* Adrastus.——A Trojan, who came to Italy with Æneas, and is supposed to have been the progenitor of the family of the Atii at Rome. *Virg. Æn.* 5. v. 568.—*Servius in loco.*——A youth to whom Ismene, the daughter of Œdipus, was promised in marriage. He was killed by Tydeus before his nuptials. *Stat. Theb* 8. v. 598.——A son of Limniace, the daughter of the river Ganges, who assisted Cepheus in preventing the marriage of Andromeda, and was killed by Perseus with a burning log of wood. *Ovid. Met.* 5. v. 47.——A celebrated shepherd of Phrygia, beloved by Cybele. She entrusted him with the care of her temple, and made him promise that he would always live in celibacy. He violated his vow by an amour with the nymph Sangaris, upon which he became delirious, and mutilated himself with a sharp stone. This was afterwards intentionally done by his sacerdotal successors in the service of Cybele, to prevent their violating their vows of perpetual chastity. This account is the most general, and supported by the most respectable authorities. *Pausanias* relates, *in Achaic.* c. 17. that Atys was the son of the daughter of the river Sangaris. Atys, as soon as born, was exposed in the woods, but preserved by a she goat. The genius Agdistis saw him in the wood, and was captivated with his beauty. As Atys was going to celebrate his nuptials with the daughter of the king of Pessinus, Agdistis, who was jealous of his rival, inspired the king and his future son-in-law with such an uncommon fury, that they both attacked and mutilated one another in the struggle. *Ovid* says, *Met.* 10. fab. 2, &c. that Cybele changed Atys into a pine-tree as he was going to lay violent hands upon himself, and that tree was, ever after, sacred to the mother of the gods. After his death, Atys received divine honours, and temples were raised to his memory, particularly at Dymæ. *Catull. de Aty.* & *Berec.*—*Ovid. Met.* 10. fab. 3. *Fast.* 4. v. 223. &c.—*Lucian. in Deâ Syr.*—*Timoth. apud. Arnob.* 5. *Adv. Gentes.*—*Muretus. ad. Catull.* ep. 64.—*Hermesianax apud Paus.* 7. [There is a beautiful little statue of Atys in the Altieri palace at Rome. And there is another representation of him at a more advanced age, in the collection at Florence.]

A'TYS SYL'VIUS, son of Albius Sylvius, was king of Alba. *Liv.* 1. c. 3.

AUCHA'TÆ, a nation of Scythia, at the mouth of the Bosphorus. *Val. Flacc.* 6. v. 132.

AUCHI'SÆ, a people of Cyrene. *Diod. Sic.* 1. 3.

AUCHI'TÆ, a people of Africa, called Auchisæ by *Ptolemy*, and Auschitæ by *Stephanus. Herodot.* 4. c. 171.

AU'CHUS, a general of the Cimmerians, who assisted Perses against Æetes. *Val. Flacc.* v. 620.

AU'CULA, or AQU'ULÆ, a city of Etruria. *Ptol.*

AU'DATHA, a city of Arabia Deserta. *Id.*

AUDE'A, a city of Casiotis in Syria. *Id.*

AUDE'NA, a river of Italy, now Ula. *Liv.* 1. 41.

AUDIA'NI, a people of Japygia, or Messapia. *Strab.* 6.

AU'DON, a town of Mauritania Cæsariensis. *Ptol.*

AUFE'IA A'QUA, called afterwards Marcia, was the sweetest and most wholesome water in Rome, and was first conveyed into the city by Ancus Martius. *Plin.* 31. c. 3.

AUFIDE'NA, now Alfidena, a city of the Peligni, in Italy, situated on the river Sagrus, which rises in the Apennines, and falls into the Adriatic. Its inhabitants, called *Aufidenates*, were among the Sabines. *Liv.* 10. c. 12.—*Plin.* 3. c. 12.

AUFID'IA LEX, was enacted by the tribune Aufidius Lurco, A.U.C. 692. It ordained, that if any candidate, in canvassing for public office, promised money to the tribunes, and failed in the performance, he should be excused; but if he actually paid it, he should be compelled to pay every tribune 6000 sesterces.

AUFIDIE'NUS RUF'FUS, a centurion in the Pannonian legion, ridiculed by his soldiers for the strictness of his discipline. *Tac. Ann.* 1. c. 20.

AUFID'IUS, an effeminate person of Chius. *Juv.* 9. v. 25.

AUFID'IUS BAS'SUS, a famous historian in the age of Quintillian, who wrote an account of Germany, and of the civil wars.

AUFID'IUS CNE'IUS, a Roman senator, famous for his blindness and abilities. He wrote a Greek history. *Cic Tusc.* 5. c. 39. *Finib.* 19. *Dom.* 113.

AUFID'IUS M. LUR'CO, a man who enriched himself by fattening peacocks, and selling them for the tables of the luxurious Romans. *Varro. R. R.* 3. c. 6.—*Plin.* 10. c. 20.

AUFID'IUS LUS'CUS, a man obscurely born, and made a prætor of Fundi, in the age of Horace. *Hor.* 1. sat. 5. v. 34.

AU'FIDUS, a river of Apulia, falling into the Adriatic Sea, and now called Ofanto. It was on its banks that the Romans were defeated by Hannibal at Cannæ. *Vid.* Cannæ. *Liv.* 22. c. 43. l. 25. c. 12.—*Flor.* 2. c. 6.—*Val. Max.* 9. c. 2.—*Horat.* 3. od. 30. l. 4. od. 9.—*Virg Æn.* 11. v. 405.

AUFINA'TES, a people of Italy. *Plin.* 3. c. 12.

AU'GA, AU'GE, or AUGE'A, daughter of Aleus, king of Tegea, by Neæra, was violated by Hercules, and brought forth a son, called Telephus. Aleus was no sooner informed of his daughter's shame than he commissioned Nauplius to put her to death. Nauplius refused to perform the cruel office, and gave Auga to Teuthras, king of Mysia, who, being without issue, adopted her as his daughter. *Vid.* Teuthras. At his court she discovered her son Telephus, as he was going to unite himself to her, in consequence of the victory which he had obtained, and returned with him to Tegea. Pausanias says, that Auge was confined in a coffer with her infant son, and thrown into the sea, where, after being preserved and protected by Minerva, she was found by king Teuthras. *Apollod.* 2 & 3.—*Paus.* 8. c. 4.—*Hygin.* fab. 99 & 100.

AU'GARUS, an Arabian, who for his good offices, obtained the favour of Pompey, whom he afterwards perfidiously deceived. *Dio.*——A king of Osroene, whom Caracalla imprisoned, after he had given him solemn promises of friendship and support. *Dio.* 78.

AUGE'A a town of Laconia. *Paus.* 3. c. 21.——A town of Locris. *Homer.*

AUGE'AS or AUGI'AS, son of Elius, was one of the Argonauts, and afterwards king of Elis. He had an immense number of oxen and goats, and the stables in which they were kept had never been cleansed for 30 years. Hercules undertook to cleanse them, on condition that he received for a reward the tenth part of the herds of Augias, or something equivalent. The hero changed the course of the river Alpheus, or, according to others, of the Peneus, which immediately swept away all the dung and filth from the stables. Augias, however, refused the recompense promised, on pretence that Hercules had made use of artifice, and had not experienced any labour or trouble, and he further drove his own son Phyleus from his kingdom, because he supported the claims of the hero. This refusal was considered as a declaration of war, and Hercules in consequence not only conquered Elis, but put to death Augias, and gave the crown to Phyleus. *Pausanias*, 5. c. 2 & 3. says, that Hercules spared the life of Augias for the sake of his son, and that Phyleus went to settle in Dulichium; and that at the death of Augias, his other son, Agasthenes, succeeded to the throne. Augias has been called the son of Sol, because Elius signifies the sun. The proverb of Augean stable is now applied to an impossibility. *Hygin.* fab. 14, 30, 157.—*Plin.* 17. c. 9.—*Servius in Virg. Æn.* 8. v. 300.—*Strab.* 8.—*Apollod.* 2.

AU'GILA, a city of Libya. *Steph.*

AU'GILÆ, a people of Africa, who supposed that there were no gods, except the manes of the dead, of whom they sought oracles. *Mela*, 1 9.

AUGI'NUS, a mountain of Liguria. It is now Monte Codoro. *Liv.* 39. c. 2.

AU'GUR SEN'TIUS, a poet. *Vid.* Sentius.

AUG'URES, certain officers at Rome, who foretold future events, *ab avium garritu*, whence their name. They were first created by Romulus, to the number of three. Servius Tullius added a fourth, and the tribunes of the people, A.U.C. 454, increased the number to nine; and Sylla added six more during his dictatorship. They had a particular college, and their chief was called *magister collegii*. Their office was considered honourable; and if any one of them was convicted of any crime, he could not be deprived of his privileges; an indulgence granted to no other sacerdotal body at Rome. The augur generally sat on a high tower, to make his observations. His face was turned towards the east, and he had the north at his left and the south at his right. With a crooked staff he divided the face of the heavens into four different parts, and afterwards sacrificed to the gods, covering his head with his vestment. There were generally five things from which the augurs drew omens: the first consisted in observing the phænomena of the heavens, such as thunder, lightning, comets, meteors, &c. The second kind of omen was drawn from the chirping or flying of birds. The third was from the sacred chickens, the eagerness or indifference of which in eating the bread which was thrown to them, was looked upon as lucky or unlucky. The fourth was from quadrupeds, from their crossing the way, or appearing in some unaccustomed place. The fifth was from different casualties, which were called Dira, such as spilling salt on a table, or wine upon one's clothes, hearing strange noises, stumbling or sneezing, meeting a wolf, hare, fox, or pregnant bitch. The sight of birds on the left hand was always deemed a lucky omen; and the words *sinister & lævus*, though generally supposed to be terms of ill luck, were always used by the augurs in an auspicious sense. *Cic. de Div.*—*Liv.* 1, &c.—*Dionys. Hal.*—*Ovid. Fast.*

AUGUS'TA ASTU'RICA, a town of Asturia. *Vid.* Astures.

AUGUS'TA BO'NA, a town of Gaul, now Troyes on the Steyne in Champagne.

AUGUS'TA EMER'ITA, a town of Lusitania, built on the Anas by Roman soldiers, who had completed their years of service (*emeriti*) in the army. It is now called Merida, in Estramadura, and is famous for its remains of ancient magnificence.

AUGUS'TA PRÆTO'RIA, a town at the foot of the Alps, in modern Piedmont, now Aost. It contains many magnificent remains of antiquity.

AUGUS'TA RAURACO'RUM, a town on the Rhine, now Augst, near Basil and Huningen.

AUGUS'TA SUESSO'NUM, a town of Gaul, now Soissons, on the Aisne, at the east of Paris.

AUGUS'TA TAURINO'RUM, the capital of Piedmont, now Turin, on the Po.

AUGUS'TA TREVIRO'RUM, now Treves, on the Moselle.

AUGUS'TA VEROMANDUO'RUM, a town of Gaul, now St. Quintin, between the Somme and the Oyse in Picardy, about 100 miles from Paris.

AUGUS'TA VINDELICO'RUM, a town of Germany, now Augsburg, on the eastern extremity of Suabia, at the confluence of the Werdach and the Lech, which fall into the Danube below Donawert. The name of Augusta was given to no less than 70 different cities in the Roman provinces, in honour of Augustus and of the succeeding emperors. London, also, as capital of the country of the Trinobantes, was called Augusta Trinobantina. *Cluver. Geogr. Passim.*

AUGUS'TA MESSALI'NA, rendered infamous by her debaucheries, was called Augusta as wife of the emperor Claudius. *Juv.* 6. v. 118. The name of Augusta was first given to Livia, the wife of Augustus, and afterwards, the female relations of the emperors assumed the same appellation, in imitation of her. *Tac. Ann.* 12. c. 26. l. 15. c. 23. *Hist.* 2. c. 89.

AUGUS'TÆ, a city of Cilicia.——A city of Italy. *Steph.*

AUGUSTA'LIA, a festival at Rome, in commemoration of the day on which Augustus returned to Rome, after he had established peace in the different parts of the empire. *Dio.* l. 54.

AUGUSTI'NUS, a native of Tagaste in Africa, who became, from a heathen reprobate, a penitent convert to Christianity. He was ordained priest, in 391; and soon after became bishop of Hippo in Africa. Augustin was mild and humane; he betrayed no intemperate violence against heretics, but wisely considered that liberal allowance should be made for the failings and prejudices of mankind. His works, which are numerous, display the powers of a great genius, and an extensive acquaintance with the philosophy of Plato. He died in the 76th year of his age, A.D. 430. The best edition of his works is that of the Benedict. fol. Ant. 1700 to 1703, 12 vols. A full account of his life and writings, and of the editions of his works, is given by *Harles. Not. Lit. Rom.* 1. p. 652. See also *Sax. Onom.* 1. p. 446.

AUGUSTOBRI'GA, a city of Hispania Tarraconensis.——A city of Lusitania. *Ptol.* Its modern name is much disputed.

AUGUSTODU'NUM, now Autun, a town of Gaul, the capital of the ancient Ædui. It contains several valuable monuments of antiquity. *Mela*, 3. c. 2.—*Cluver.* 2. c. 11.

AUGUSTOM'AGUS, a town of Gaul, supposed to be Senlis, in the isle of France, at the north-east of Paris. *Cluver.* 2. c. 12.

AUGUSTORI'TUM, a town of Gallia Acquitanica, now Limoges on the Vienne, which falls into the Loire. *Cluver.* 2. c. 10.

AUGUS'TULUS, the last Roman emperor of the West, A.D. 475, conquered by Odoacer, king of the Heruli.

AUGUS'TUS OCTAVIA'NUS CÆ'SAR, second emperor of Rome, was son of Octavius, a senator, and Accia, daughter of Julius, and sister to Julius Cæsar. He was adopted by his uncle Cæsar, and inherited the greatest part of his fortune. He lost his father at the age of four; and though only 18 when his uncle was murdered, he hastened to Rome, where he ingratiated himself with the senate and people, and received the honours of the consulship two years after. He soon rose into consequence by his prudence and valour, and made war against his opponents, on pretence of avenging the death of his murdered uncle. But when he perceived, that by making him fight against Antony, the senate wished to debilitate both antagonists, he changed his views, and uniting himself with his former enemies, soon formed the second triumvirate, in which his cruel proscriptions shed the innocent blood of 300 senators and 200 knights, and did not even spare the life of his friend Cicero. Augustus retained for himself the more important provinces of the west, and banished, as it were, his colleagues, Lepidus and Antony, to more distant countries. But as long as the murderers of Cæsar were alive, the triumvirs had reason for apprehension, and therefore their forces were directed against the partisans of Brutus and the senate. The battle was fought at Philippi, where, it is said, the valour and conduct of Antony alone preserved the combined armies, and effected the defeat of the republican forces. The head of the unfortunate Brutus was carried in triumph to Rome, and thrown at the foot of Cæsar's statue. On his return to Italy, Augustus rewarded his soldiers with the lands of those unfortunate citizens, who, for their adherence to the interests of his rivals, had been proscribed; but, among the sufferers, were many who had never injured the conqueror of Philippi, especially Virgil, whose modest application procured the restitution of his property. The friendship which subsisted between Augustus and Antony was broken as soon as the fears of a third rival vanished away, and the aspiring heir of Cæsar was easily induced, by the little jealousies and insidious resentment of Fulvia, to take up arms. Her death, however, retarded hostilities: the two rivals were reconciled; their united forces were successfully directed against the younger Pompey; and, to strengthen their friendship, Antony agreed to marry Octavia, the sister of Augustus; but as this step was a political measure, and not dictated by affection, Octavia was slighted, and Antony resigned himself to the pleasures and company of the beautiful Cleopatra. Augustus immediately took up arms to avenge the wrongs of his sister, and to remove a man whose power and existence limited his ambitious views, and made him dependant. Both parties met at Actium, B.C. 31, to decide the fate of Rome. Antony was supported by all the powers of the east, and Augustus by the forces of Italy and the western world. Instead of braving danger, at a moment on which depended her honour and her life, Cleopatra fled in terror from the battle with 60 ships, and her flight ruined the interests of Antony, who followed her into Ægypt. The conqueror soon after passed into Ægypt, besieged Alexandria, and honoured with a magnificent funeral, the unfortunate Roman, and the celebrated queen, whom the fear of being led in the victor's triumph at Rome had driven to commit suicide. After he had established peace over all the world, Augustus shut up the gates of the temple of Janus, about the time that our Saviour was born. It is said that he twice resolved to lay down the supreme power, once immediately after the victory obtained over Antony, and afterwards on account of his ill health; but that his friend Mecænas dissuaded him from it by observing that he would leave the empire to be the prey of the most powerful, and expose himself to ingratitude and to danger. He died at Nola in the 76th year of his age, on the 18th of August, A.D. 14, after he had held the sovereign power 44 years. Augustus was an active prince, and when secure in the possession of absolute power, he consulted the good of the Romans with the most anxious care. He visited all the provinces except Africa and Sardinia, and his consummate prudence and experience gave rise to many salutary laws; but it may be said that he finished with a good grace, what he had begun with cruelty. While making himself absolute, he took care to leave his countrymen the shadow of liberty; and while under the character of perpetual tribune, of priest and imperator, he was invested with all the power of sovereignty, he guarded against offending the jealousy of the Romans, by not assuming the regal title. His refusal to read the letters which he found after Pompey's defeat, arose, perhaps, more from fear than from genuine sentiments of magnanimity, and he dreaded the discovery of names which, if known, would have, perhaps, united to sacrifice his ambition. His good qualities and many virtues which he probably never possessed, have been transmitted to posterity by the pen of adulation or gratitude, in the poems of Virgil, Horace, and Ovid. To distinguish himself from the obscurity of the family of the Octavii, and, if possible, to suppress the remembrance of his uncle's violent fate, he aspired after a new title; and the submissive senate yielded to his ambition by giving him the honourable appellation of *Augustus*. He has been accused of licentiousness and adultery, by his biographers; but the goodness of heart, and the fidelity of friendship, which he, in some instances, displayed, made in the opinion of partial and interested men, some amends for his natural foible. He was ambitious of being thought handsome; and as he was publicly reported to be the son of Apollo, according to his mother's declaration, he wished his flatterers to represent him with the figure and attributes of that god. Like Apollo, his eyes were clear, and he affected to have it thought that they possessed some divine irradiation: and was well pleased, if, when he fixed his looks upon any body, they held down their eyes as if overcome by the glaring brightness of the sun. Augustus distinguished himself by his learning; he was a perfect master of the Greek language, and wrote some tragedies, besides memoirs of his life, and other works, all now lost. He was married three times; to Claudia, to Scribonia, and to Livia; but he was unhappy in his matrimonial connections, and his only daughter Julia, by Scribonia, disgraced herself and her father by the debauchery and licentiousness of her manners. He recommended, at his death, his adopted son Tiberius as his successor, and left in his papers, as a solemn advice to future emperors, either through fear or envy, that they should not attempt to extend the boundaries of the empire beyond its present state. He left his fortune partly to Tiberius and partly to Drusus, and made donations to the army and Roman people. Virgil wrote his heroic poem at the desire of Augustus, whom he represented under the amiable and perfect character of Æneas. *Sueton in Vitâ.—Horat.—Virgil.—Paus.—Tacit.—Patercul.—Dio. Cass.—Ovid.* [There are a great many representations of Augustus. One of the finest statues of him is that in the Villa Albani; and of the busts, that in the Vatican.] The name of Augustus was afterwards given to the successors of Octavianus in the Roman empire, as a personal, and the name of Cæsar as a family distinction. Afterwards the title of Augustus was given only to the emperor, while that of Cæsar was bestowed on the second person in the state, who was considered as heir presumptive.

AU'LADIS, a city of Mesopotamia. *Ptol.*

AU'LÆ, a naval arsenal in Cilicia. *Steph.*

AULA'NIUS EVAN'DER, a sculptor. *Plin.* 36. c. 5.

AULER'CI, a people of Gaul, situate between the Seine and the Loire, or, according to some, comprehending the modern divisions of the Maine, Perche, and Evreux. *Cluver.* 2. 11.

AULES'TES, a king of the Etrurians when Æneas came into Italy. *Virg. Æn.* 12. v. 290.

AULE'TES, a general who assisted Æneas in Italy. with 100 ships. *Virg. Æn.* 10. v. 207.——The surname of one of the Ptolemean kings, father of Cleopatra.

AU'LI, a people of Macedonia, on the Ionian Sea. *Ptol.*

AU'LIS, a daughter of Oxyges. *Paus. Bœotic.*

Au'lis, a town of Bœotia, near Chalcis, on the sea-coast, now Megalo-Vathi, where all the Greeks met together, and entered into a solemn league against Troy. They were detained by contrary winds, by the anger of Diana, whose favourite stag had been killed by Agamemnon. To appease the resentment of the goddess, Agamemnon was obliged to sacrifice his own daughter Iphigenia, whom, however, Diana spared by substituting a ram. *Virg. Æn.* 4. v. 426.—*Ovid. Met.* 12. v. 9, &c.—*Homer. Il.* 2. v. 303.

AULOCRE'NE, a place of Asia Minor. *Plin.* 5. c 29, &c.—*Salmas. ad Solin.* 834.

AU'LON, a mountain of Calabria, opposite Tarentum, famous for its wine, which, according to *Horace*, 2. od. 6. v. 18. was superior to that of Falernum. *Martial.* 13. epigr. 125.—*Strab.* 6.——A place of Messenia. *Paus.*——A town of Illyricum, on the shores of the Adriatic, south of Apollonia.——A colony of the Corinthians in Macedonia. *Plin.* 4. c. 5.

AULO'NIUS, a surname of Æsculapius. *Paus. Mess.*

AU'LUS, a prænomen common among the Romans, and generally marked by the letter A.

Au'lus Gel'lius. *Vid.* Gellius.

AU'NUS, a Liguran, whose son was slain by Camilla in the wars of Æneas in Italy. *Virg. Æn.* 11. v. 700.

AU'RA, a mare celebrated at the Olympic games. Her master, Phidolas, having lost his seat at the beginning of the race, the animal continued her course, and after outstripping all the others, stood before the umpires, as if to claim the victory. The prize was consequently adjudged to Phidolas, whose statue and that of his faithful mare were erected at Olympia by the permission of the Eleans. *Paus.* 6. c. 13.

AU'RADIS, a sity of Media. *Ptol.*

AURA'NA, a city of Arabia Deserta. *Id.*——A city of Dalmatia, now Wrana.

AURANI'TIS, a tract of Babylonia. *Ptol.*

AU'RAS, a European river, flowing into the Ister from mount Hæmus. *Herodot.* 4. c. 49.

AURA'SIUS, a mountain in the south of Numidia, now Auraz. *Procrop.*

AURE'A CHERSONE'SUS, a peninsula of India beyond the Ganges, now supposed to be Malacca, or Malay.

AURE'LIA, a family at Rome descended from the Sabines. *Festus.*——The mother of J. Cæsar. *Suet. in Cæs.* 74.——A fish-woman. *Juv.* 5. v. 98.

Aure'lia, a town of Hispania Bætica. *Plin.* 3. c. 1.

Aure'lia Por'ta, a gate at Rome, now Porta S. Petri. *Procop.*

Aure'lia Lex, was enacted A.U.C. 653, by the prætor L. Aurelius Cotta, to invest the Senatorian and Equestrian orders, and the Tribuni Ærarii, with judicial power.—Another, A.U.C. 678. It abrogated a clause of the Lex Cornelia, and permitted the tribunes to hold other offices after the expiration of the tribuneship.

AURELIA'NUS, emperor of Rome after Flavius Claudius, A.D. 270, was famous for his military character; and his expedition against Zenobia, the celebrated queen of Palmyra, gained him great honours. He beautified Rome, was equally renowned for his cultivation of the useful arts of peace, was charitable to the poor, and became the author of many salutary laws. He was naturally brave; and in all the battles which he fought, it is said, that he killed no less than 800 men with his own hand. In his triumph he exhibited to the admiration of the Romans, people of fifteen different nations, all of which he had conquered. He was the first emperor who assumed a diadem. After a glorious reign, as he marched against the northern barbarians, he was assassinated near Byzantium, A.D. 275, on the 29th of January, by his soldiers, whom Mnestheus had incited to rebellion against their emperor. This Mnestheus had been threatened with death for some improper behaviour to the emperor, and therefore he secretly meditated his death. The soldiers, however, soon repented of their ingratitude and cruelty to Aurelian, and threw Mnestheus to be devoured by the wild beasts.——A physician of the fourth century. *Sax. Onom.* 1. p. 480. The English form is Aurelian.

AURE'LIUS, an emperor of Rome. *Vid.* Antoninus Bassianus.——A painter in the age of Augustus. *Plin.* 35. c. 10.

Aure'lius Vic'tor, an historian in the age of Constantius and Julian: two of his compositions are extant; an account of illustrious men, and a biography of all the Cæsars, extending to the age of Julian. The best editions of Aurelius are the 4to, of Artnzenius, Amst. 1733, and the 8vo, of Pitiscus Ultr. 1696. *Harles. Not. Lit. Rom.* 1. c. 7.

Aure'lius Antoni'nus, an emperor. *Vid.* Antoninus.

AURE'OLUS, a general who assumed the purple in the age of Gallienus. *Eutrop.* 1. 9.

AURIN'IA, a prophetess held in great veneration by the superstitious inhabitants of Germany. *Tacit. Germ.* 8. Some read Alteruna.

AURITI'NA, a city of the Pentapolis, in Africa. *Ptol.*

AURO'RA, a goddess, daughter of Hyperion and Thea, or, according to others, of Titan and Terra. Some say that Pallas, son of Crius, and brother to Perses, was her father; hence her surname of *Pallantias*. She married Astreus, by whom she had the winds, the stars, &c. Her amours with Tithonus and Cephalus are also famous; by the former she had Memnon and Æmathion, and by the latter Phaethon. *Vid.* Cephalus & Tithonus. She had also an intrigue with Orion, whom she carried away to the island of Delus, where he was killed by Diana's arrows. Aurora is generally represented by the poets, as drawn in a rose-coloured chariot, and opening with her rosy fingers the gates of the east, and pouring the dew upon the earth. Her chariot is generally drawn by white horses, and she is covered with a veil. Nox and Somnus fly before her, and the constellations of heaven disappear at her approach. She always sets out before the sun, and is the forerunner of his rising. The Greeks called her Eos. *Homer. Il.* 8. *Odyss.* 10. *Hymn. in Vener.*—*Ovid. Met.* 3. v. 184, 281, 600. 1. 9. v. 420. 1. 15. v. 189, &c.—*Theocrit. in Hyld.*—*Apuleius in Met.* 3.—*Apollod.* 1. 3.—*Virg. Æn.* 6. v. 535.—*Varro de L. L.* 5, 6, & 91.—*Hesiod. Theog.* v. 371.—*Hygin. Præf.* fab.—*Schol. Homer. Il.* 8. v. 480. —*Schol. Pindar. Isth.* 5.

AURUN'CA, an ancient town of Latium, built by Auson, the son of Ulysses by Calypso, on the east bank of the Liris. *Plin.* 3, c. 5.—*Virg. Æn.* 7. v. 727, &c.

AURUPI'NI, a people of the Japodes: their chief town was Aurupinum, now Aursperg. *Strab.*

AURUS'PI, a town of Upper Æthiopia. *Plin.* 6. c. 30.

AU'SA, now Vich, a city of Spain. *Ptol.*

AUSAN'CALI, a town of Liburnia. *Id.*

AU'SARA, the name of two cities in Arabia Felix. *Id.*

AUSCHI'SÆ. *Vid.* Auchitæ.

AUS'CI, a people of Gaul, between the rivers Aturus and Garumna. Their chief city was Augusta Auscorum, now Aux. *Cluver.* 2. c. 10.—*Mela,* 3. c. 2.

AU'SER, AU'SERIS, or AN'SER, now Serchio, a river of Etruria, which joins the Arnus below Pisa, just before it falls into the Tyrrhene Sea.

AU'SES or AUSEN'SES, a people of Africa, whose virgins yearly fought with sticks, in honour of Minerva. She who behaved with the greatest valour, received unusual honour, &c. *Herodot.* 4. c. 180.

AUSETA'NI, a people at the east of Spain, between the Iberus, and the Pyrenean mountains. *Liv.* 21. c. 23 & 61. l. 29. c. 2. l. 34. c. 20. l. 39. c. 56.

AUSIG'DA, a city of Libya, *Steph.*

AUSIN'GA, a city of Persia. *Ptol.*

AUSI'TIS, a town of Mauritania Cæsariensis. *Id.*

AU'SON, a son of Ulysses and Calypso, from whom the Ausones, a people of Italy, were descended.

AUSO'NIA, one of the ancient names of Italy, which it received from Auson, the son of Ulysses. The Ausones were defeated by the Romans; and the nation, together with the town, called Ausona, destroyed. *Liv.* 8. c. 16. l. 9. c. 25.—*Sil.* 9. v. 187.—*Ovid. Fast.* 2. v. 94.—*Virg. Æn.* 3. v. 171.

AUSO'NIUS DECIMUS MAG'NUS, a poet born at Bordeaux in Gaul, in the fourth century, son of Julius Ausonius, a physician, was preceptor to Gratian son of the emperor Valentinian, and made consul by the favour of his pupil. His compositions, which consist of epigrams partly translated from Greek authors, of epitaphs (*parentalia*) on his friends and relations, of idyllia, of epitaphs on the heroes of the Trojan war, of poetical epistles, &c. are written with spirit and elegance, and have been long admired. He wrote also the *consular fasti* of Rome, a useful performance, now lost. Some authors have supposed that he was a convert to Christianity; but the supposition is doubtful. His style is occasionally obscene; and his wanton verses, formed by a different arrangement of those of Virgil, fix an indelible stigma upon his memory. The best edition is that of Tollius, 8vo, L. Bat. 1671; or that of Jaubert, with a French translation. 4 vols. 12mo, Paris, 1769. *Harles. Not. Lit. Rom.* c. 8. *sec.* 9.—*Sax. Onom.* 1. p. 436.—*Voss. de poet. Lat.* c. 4.

AUS'PICES, a sacerdotal order at Rome, nearly the same as the augurs. *Vid.* Augures.

AUSTAGE'NA, a tract of Parthia which produced naptha. *Plin.* 2. c. 105.

AUSTANI'TIS, a region of Armenia Major. *Ptol.*

AUS'TER, one of the winds blowing from the south, whose breath was pernicious to flowers as well as to health. He was parent of rain. *Virg. Ecl.* 2. v. 58. *Vid.* Venti.

AUSTRA'NIA or AUSTRA'VIA, an island of the Northern Ocean, called Classaria by the Romans. *Plin.* 4. c. 13, &c.

AUS'TRI COR'NU, a promontory of Æthiopia. *Strab.* l. 16.

AU'SUM, a city of Mauritania Cæsariensis. *Ptol.*

AUTARIA'TÆ or AUTARTA'TÆ, a nation of Thesprotia. *Steph.*—*Strab.*—*Arrian.*—*Diod.*

AU'TARIS, a place of Arabia Felix. *Plin.* 6. c. 28.

AUTE'SION, a Theban, son of Tisamenus. *Vid.* Theras. *Herodot.* 4. c. 147.—*Paus.*

AU'THE, a daughter of the giant Alcyon.

AUTHETA'NI, a people of Hispania Tarraconensis. *Ptol.*

AU'TOBA, a village of Æthiopia, near the Nile. *Id.*

AUTOBU'LUS, a painter. *Plin.* 35. c. 11.

AUTOC'ANES, a mountain mentioned by *Homer. Hymn. in Apoll.* v. 35.

AUTOCH'THONES, the original inhabitants of a country who were the first possessors of it. The Athenians called themselves Autochthones, and boasted that they were as old as the country which they inhabited. *Paus.* 1. c. 14.—*Tacit. de Germ.* 2. c. 1.—*Cic. de Orat.* 3. c. 83.—*Censorin.* 4.

AU'TOCLES, an Athenian, sent by his countrymen with a fleet to the assistance of Alexander of Pheræ. *Diod. Sic.* 15.——An Athenian general sent against Cythera with 60 ships. *Thucyd.* 5. c. 53.

AUTOC'RATES, an historian mentioned by *Athenæus.* 9 & 11.——A poet who wrote both tragedies and comedies, according to *Suidas. Ælian.* 12. c. 9. *de Anim.* praises one his plays, called *Tympanistæ. Fabr. B. Gr.* 2. c. 19. *de Com.*

AUTO'LEON, a general of Crotona wounded when fighting against the Locri, &c. *Photius ex Conon.*—*Paus.* l. 3.

AUTOL'OLES, a people of Mauritania, descended from the Gætuli. They excelled all their neighbours in running and in manly exercises. *Lucan.* 4. v. 677.

AUTOL'YCUS, a son of Mercury by Chione, was one of the Argonauts. He was much celebrated for his expertness as a thief. He stole the flocks of his neighbours, and mingled them with his own after he had changed their marks. He did the same to Sisyphus, son of Æolus; but Sisyphus was as crafty as Autolycus, and he knew his own oxen by a mark which he had made under their feet. Autolycus was so pleased with the artifice of Sisyphus, that he formed an intimacy with him, and even permitted him freely to enjoy the company of his daughter Anticlea. *Vid.* Sisyphus, Laertes. *Hygin.* fab. 200, &c.—*Ovid. Met.* 1. fab. 8.—*Apollod.* 1.—*Homer. Odyss.* 14.——A son of Phryxus and Chalciope. *Hygin.* fab. 14.——A philosopher and mathematician of Pitane in Æolis. His book, περὶ κινουμένης σφαίρας was edited by Dasypodius, Argentorat, 1572. *Fabr. B. Gr.* l. 3. c. 18.—*Sax. Onom.* 1. p. 81.

AUTOM'ALAX, a city of Cyrene, now Altudia. *Ptol.*—*Strab.*

AUTOM'ATE, one of the Cyclades, called also Hiera. *Plin.* 2. c. 87.

AUTOM'ATE, a daughter of Danaus.

AUTOMA'TIA, a name of the goddess of fortune. Timoleon erected an altar to her in his house under this name. *Corp. Nep. in Timol.* 4.

AUTOM'EDON, a son of Dioreus, who accompanied the Greeks to the Trojan war with ten ships. He was the charioteer of Achilles, after whose death he served Pyrrhus in the same capacity, and from his dexterity in guiding a chariot, the word Automedon has been used as most expressive of superior skill and agility in the chariot race. *Ovid. Trist.* 5. el. 6. v. 10. *De Art. A.* 1. v. 5.—*Hygin.* fab. 97.—*Juv.* 1. v. 61.—*Homer. Il.* 9, 16, &c.—*Virg. Æn.* 2. v. 477.

AUTOMEDU'SA, daughter of Alcathous, killed by Tydeus, married Iphiclus the father of Protesilaus. *Apollod.* 2.

AUTOM'ENES, one of the Heraclidæ, king of Corinth. At his death, B.C. 779, annual magistrates, called Prytanes, invested with sovereign authority, were chosen, and their power continued 90 years, till Cypselus and his son Periander made themselves absolute.

AUTOM'OLI, a nation of Æthiopia. *Herodot.* 2. c. 30.—*Steph.*

AUTON'OE, a daughter of Cadmus, who married Aristæus, by whom she had Actæon, often called *Autonoeius heros*. The unfortunate death of her son, (*vid.* Actæon,) proved the source of so much sorrow to her that she retired from Bœotia to Megara, where she soon after died. *Paus.* 1. c. 44.—*Hygin.* fab. 179.—*Ovid. Met.* 3. v. 720.——One of the Danaides, who married Eucylochus. *Apollod.* 2.——One of the Nereides. *Hesiod. Theog.*——A female servant of Penelope. *Homer. Odyss.* 18. v. 181.

AUTOPHRADA'TES, a satrap of Lydia, who revolted from Artaxerxes. *Diod.* 15.

AUTOS'THENES, an archon of Athens. *Ol.* 27.

AUTRI'CUM, or AUT'RICUM, now Chartres, a town of Gaul, the capital of the Carnutes. *Ptol.*

AUTRIG'ONES, a people of Spain. *Mela*, 3. c. 1.

P. AUTRO'NIUS PÆ'TUS, a Roman, elected consul with Sylla, but accused of bribery, and declared incapable of holding any office. He joined Catiline in his conspiracy, and, after his death, fled into Greece. Cicero speaks of him as an orator, but only as having a good voice. *Cic. Att.* 3. ep. 2 & 7. *Brut.* 68.—*Sallust. Cat.* 17 & 18.—*Suet. Cæs.* 9.—*Dio.* 36.

AUTU'RA, the Eurre, a river of Gaul, which falls into the Seine.

AUXE'SIA and DA'MIA, two Cretan virgins who came from Crete to Troezene, where the inhabitants stoned them to death in a sedition. The Epidaurians raised them statues by order of the oracle, when their country was become barren. They were held in great veneration at Troezene; and festivals called Lithobolia were instituted in their honour. *Herodot.* 5. c. 82.—*Paus.* 2. c. 30.

AUX'IMUM, now Osimo, a town of Picenum, at the south-west of Ancona, not far from the Adriatic. *Lucan.* 2. v. 466.

AUXU'ME, a royal city of Æthiopia. *Ptol.* It is now, probably, Chazumo.

AU'ZA, a city of Africa Propria, not far from Utica. *Ptol.*

AUZA'CIA, a city of Scythia without the Imaus, now Acru. *Id.*

AVALI'TES, or ABALI'TES, a bay and emporium on the right of the Red Sea. It is now Zeila. *Steph.*

AV'ARA, a city of Arabia. *Id.*

AVARI'CUM, or AVAR'ICUM, a strong and fortified town of Gaul, in the country of the Bituriges, on the Avara, a small river at the south of the Loire, into which it falls. It is now called Bourges, the capital of Berry. *Cæs. Bell. G.* 7. c. 13.

AVA'RUM, a promontory of Hispania Tarraconensis, now Cabo de Viana. *Ptol.*

AVASTOM'ATHES, a people of Mauritania. *Ammian. Marcell.*

AV'ATHA, a town of Arabia. *Steph.*

AVAT'ICI, a people of Gallia Narbonensis. *Plin.*—*Mela*, 2. c. 5.
AVEL'LA. *Vid.* Abella.
AVENDO'NIS, a city of Liburnia, now Adelsberg. *Antonin.*
AVE'NIO, a town on the Rhone in Gaul, now Avignon in Provence.
A'VENS, a river of the Sabines, now Curese. *Varro.*
AVEN'TICUM, a town of the Helvetii, now Avances, at the north-east of the lake of Geneva. *Tacit. H.* 1. c. 68.
AVENTI'NUS, a son of Hercules, by Rhea, who assisted Turnus against Æneas, and distinguished himself by his valour. *Virg. Æn.* 7. v. 657.——A king of Alba, buried upon Mount Aventine. *Ovid. Fast.* 4. v. 51.——One of the seven hills on which part of the city of Rome was built. It was given to the people to build houses upon, by king Ancus Martius. It was not reckoned within the precincts of the city till the reign of the emperor Claudius, because the soothsayers looked upon it as a place of ill omen, because it was the burial place of Remus. The word is derived, according to some, *ab avibus*, because birds frequented the place in great numbers. Others suppose that it received its name from Aventinus, one of the Alban kings, who was buried upon it. Juno, the Moon, Diana, Bona Dea, Hercules, and the goddess of Victory and Liberty had each magnificent temples built upon it. *Varro de L. L.* 4.—*Virg. Æn.* 8. v. 235.—*Liv.* 1. c. 33.
AVER'NUS or AVER'NA, a lake of Campania, near Baiæ, the waters of which were so unwholesome and putrid, that no birds were seen on its banks; hence its original name was αορνος, *avibus carens.* The ancient poets regarded it as the entrance of the infernal regions, as also one of its rivers. All lakes, the waters of which were putrid and offensive to the smell, were indiscriminately called Averna. *Virg. Æn.* 4. v. 5. 12, &c. l. 6. v. 201, &c. l. 8. v. 442.—*Lucret.* 6. v. 740.—*Stat. Theb.* 11. v. 588.—*Sil. It.* 13. v. 601.—*Mela*, 2. c. 6.—*Strab.* 5.—*Diod.* 4,—*Aristot. de Adm.*
AVERRUN'CUS, a divinity whom the Romans invoked to avert all evils; and thence is derived the obsolete word *Averruncare*, which signified to avert or remove. *Aul. Gell.* 5. c. 12.—*Varro. de L. L.* 6. c. 5.
A'VIA, or rather Livia, a city of Spain. *Ptol.*
AVIDIE'NUS, a rich and sordid man, whom *Horace* styles happy. 2 *Ser.* 2. v. 55.
AVID'IUS, CAS'SIUS, a man saluted emperor by his army, A.D. 175. He reigned only three months, and was assassinated by a centurion. He was called a second Catiline, from his excessive love of bloodshed. *Diod.*
AVIE'NUS or AVIA'NUS FLA'VIUS, a poet who flourished in the age of the Antonines, A.D. 160. Of his works only 42 fables are left, and they are interpolated in many places. He was much inferior to Phædrus in genius and elegance of versification. His fables were published, together with those of Æsop, Lug. Bat. 1626. 8. also separately by Pulmann. Antw. 1602. 16. The best and latest edition is that of Cannegetier, Amstel. 1731. *Harles. Not. Lit. Rom.* 1. c. 8.—*Sax. Onom.* 1. p. 479.
AVIE'NUS RU'FUS FES'TUS, a poet who lived about the year 400 A.D. He translated into Latin heroic verse the Phænomena of Aratus, and the Periegesis of Dionysius. He also composed a description of the sea coast from Gades to Massilia, in Iambic verse, of which a short fragment is extant, and other pieces. His works were published by Melian, Madrit. 1634; also a Variorum edition, Amstelod. 1786. *Harles. ibid.*
AVINEN'SE, a town of Africa. *Plin.* 5. c. 4.
AVIT'TA, a town of Africa Propria. *Ptol.*
AVI'TUS, a governor of Britain under Nero. *Tac. Ann.* 14. c. 29.
AVI'TUS AL'PHIUS, a Latin poet, of whose poetry a few fragments, to the number of eight verses, are preserved in the Corpus Poetarum.
AVI'TUS AL'CIMUS ECDIC'IUS, a Christian poet who was bishop of Vienne, in ancient Gaul, and distinguished himself by his opposition to the Arian heresy. He wrote a heterogenous poem on original sin, in praise of celibacy, &c. divided into six books. *Harles. Not. Lit. Rom.* 1. p. 755.
A'VIUM, a city between Tyre and Sidon. *Strab.* 16.
A'VO or A'VUS, a river of Hispania Citerior, now Rio d'Avia. *Ptol.* There was another in the country of the Callaici.
A'VUS, a river of Thesprotia. *Steph.*——A river of Hispania Tarraconensis. *Ptol.* It is now Rio d'Avez.
AXATI'ARA, a town of Spain. *Plin.* 3. c. 1.
AX'ENUS, the ancient name of the Euxine Sea. The word, αξενος, signifies *inhospitable*, a name highly applicable to the manners of the ancient inhabitants of the coast. *Ovid.* 4. *Trist.* 4. v. 56.
AXI'ACÆ, people of European Sarmatia. *Mela*, 2. c. 1.—*Plin.* 4. c. 12.
AX'ICA, a city of India within the Ganges. *Ptol.*
AXIL'LA, a surname of the family of the Servilii. By dropping the letter *x*, the word was contracted into Ala. *Cic. Orat.* 45.
AX'IMA, a city of the Centrones, a people of the Alps, now Aime. *Ptol.*——A city of Persia. *Id.*
AXIN'IUM, a city of the Celtiberi. *Appian.*
AXI'OCHUS, a philosopher to whom Plato dedicated a treatise concerning death.
AXI'ON, brother of Alphesibœa, murdered Alcmæon, his sister's husband. *Vid.* Alcmæon & Alphesibœa.
AXIONI'CUS, a comic poet, four of whose plays are mentioned by *Athenæus.* He is also praised by *Stobæus. Grotius* and *Hertelius* have collected a few fragments of his works. *Fabr. B. Gr.* 2. c. 22. *de Com.*
AXIOP'OLIS, a city of Lower Mysia, now Colanamick. *Ptol.*
AXIO'TE, a nation of Troas. *Hesych.*
AXIO'THEA, the wife of Nicocles, king of Cyprus. *Polyæn.* 8. c. 48.——A woman who regularly attended the lectures of Plato in a man's dress. *Plut. & Laert.* 3. c. 46.
AX'IS, a town of Umbria. *Propert.* 4. el. 1. v. 125.
AX'IUS, a river of Macedonia, now Vardari. It flowed from mount Hæmus into the Sinus Thermaicus. *Liv.* 39. c. 54.—*Herodot.* 7. c. 123.
AX'IUS QUIN'TUS, a senator, intimate with Cicero, and spoken of by him as a usurer. *Sueton. Cæs.* 9.—*Cic. ad Att.* 1. ep. 12. l. 4. ep. 15.—*Varro. R. R.* 3.—*Gell.* 7. c. 3.
AX'O, one of the seasons, called Horæ by the moderns. *Hygin.* fab. 103.
AX'ON, a river of the Ionians in Asia Minor. *Plin.* 5. c. 7.——A river in Caria.
AX'ONA, a river of Belgic Gaul, now Aisne. The inhabitants of the neighbourhood were called Axones.
AX'UMIS, a city of India within the Ganges. *Ptol.*
AXUMI'TES, the metropolis of the Æthiopians. *Steph.*
AX'UR or ANX'UR, a surname of Jupiter, who had a temple at Trachis in Thessaly. He was represented as a beardless youth. *Virg. Æn.* 7. v. 699. l. 10. v. 545.
AX'US, a town about the middle of Crete. *Apollod.*—*Steph.*——A river of Macedonia.
AXY'LUS, a Phrygian of Arisbe, noted for his hospitality. *Homer Il.* 6.
A'ZA, a town of Armenia Minor. *Plin.* 6. c. 9.——A town of Cappadocia. *Ptol.*
AZABE'TIS TÆ'NIA, a city of Asiatic Sarmatia. *Id.*
AZAGA'RIUM, a town of European Sarmatia. *Id.*
AZAM'ORA, a castle of Armenia Minor, near Cataonia. *Strab.*
A'ZAN, a mountain of Arcadia, sacred to Cybele.
A'ZAN, a son of Arcas, king of Arcadia, by Erato, one of the Dryades. He divided his father's kingdom with his brothers Aphidas and Elatus, and called his share Azania. There was in Azania a fountain called Clitorius, the waters of which were said to give a dislike for wine to those who drank them. *Vitruv.* 8. c. 3.—*Ovid. Met.* 15. v. 322.—*Paus.* 8. c. 4.
AZA'NI, a people of Scythia within the Imaus. *Ptol.* ——A city of Phrygia. *Steph.*
A'ZAR, a mountain of Ægypt. *Ptol.*
AZ'ARA, a city of Armenia Major, near the Araxes. ——A temple in Persia, dedicated to Diana. *Strab.* ——A city of Asiatic Sarmatia. *Ptol.*
AZ'ATHA, a town of Armenia Major. *Id.*
AZEL'MICUS, a king of Tyre, under whom it was joined to the continent. *Arrian.* l. 2.
AZE'NIA, a part of the tribe Hippothoontis in Attica. *Steph.*

AZETE'NE, a region of Armenia Major. *Ptol.*

AZ'ICIS, a village of Marmarica. *Id.*

AZI'RIS, a place in Libya, surrounded on both sides by delightful hills covered with trees, and watered by a river, where Battus built a town. *Herodot.* 4. c. 157.——A town of Armenia Minor, now Arzichan. *Ptol.*

AZO'CHIS, a city of Mesepotamia. *Plin.* 6. c. 26.

AZ'ONAX, a man who taught Zoroaster the art of magic. *Plin.* 30. c. 1.

AZ'ONES, a name given to those divinities who had no fixed habitation assigned them in the heavens or in the zones, and who were worshipped by all nations promiscuously, such as the mother of the gods, Terra, Victory, &c. *Servius in Æn.* 12. v. 119.

AZ'ORUM, a town of Thessaly, near the Aliacmon. *Liv.* 42. c. 53. l. 44. c. 2.

AZO'RUS, one of the Argonauts.

AZO'TUS, the Azdod of Scripture, a large town of Syria, on the borders of the Mediterranean. *Joseph. Ant. Jud.* 15.

AZURITA'NUM, a town of Africa. *Plin.* 5. c. 4.

AZYL'IA, a town of Epirus. *Ptol.*

B.

BAAL'TIS or BEL'TIS, a goddess of the Phœnicians, the same as Dione, Venus, or the Moon. *Euseb. Præp. Evan.* l. 1.

BAAR'SA'TES, a river of Babylonia. *Ptol.*

BAB'BA, a town of Mauritania. It was a colony of Augustus, and also called Julia Campestris. *Plin.* 5. c. 1.

BABAC'TES, or BAC'TES, a name of Bacchus, *Hesych.*

BA'BÆ, a city of Libya. *Steph.*

BABANEN'SES, a people of Hispania Citerior. *Plin.* 3. c. 3.

BABIL'IUS, a Roman, who, by the help of a certain herb, is said to have passed in six days from the Sicilian Sea, to Alexandria, in Ægypt. *Plin. Proœm.* 19.

BAB'ILUS, an astrologer in Nero's age, who directed the emperor to avert the danger which seemed to hang over his head, from the threatening appearance of a comet, by putting all the leading men of Rome to death. His advice was faithfully followed. *Sueton. in Ner.* c. 36.

BAB'YLON, a son of Belus, who, as some suppose, founded the city which bears his name.

BAB'YLON, a celebrated city, the capital of the Assyrian empire, on the banks of the Euphrates. It had 100 brazen gates; and its walls, which were cemented with bitumen, and greatly enlarged and embellished by the activity of Semiramis, measured 385 stadia in circumference, 50 cubits in thickness, and 200 in height. It was taken by Cyrus, B.C. 538, after he had drained the waters of the Euphrates into a new channel, and marched his troops by night into the town, through the dried bed; and it is said that it was so extensive that its sudden capture by the Persian invader was unknown to the inhabitants of the distant suburbs till late in the evening. Babylon became famous for the death of Alexander, and for the new emperor which was afterwards established there under the Seleucidæ. *Vid.* Syria. Its greatness was so reduced in succeeding ages, according to Pliny's observations, that in his time it was but a desolate wilderness, and at present the place where it stood is unknown to travellers; so wonderfully fulfilled is the prophecy of Esaias, 13. v. 19, &c. 14. v. 22, &c. The inhabitants were early acquainted with astrology. They also first divided the year into twelve months, and the zodiac into twelve signs. *Plin.* 6. c. 26.—*Herodot.* 1, 2, 3.—*Justin.* 1, &c.—*Diod.* 2.—*Xenoph. Cyrop.* 7, &c.—*Propert.* 3. el. 11. v. 21.—*Ovid. Met.* 4. fab. 2.—*Martial.* 9. epigr. 77.——A town near the Bubastic branch of the Nile, at the vertex of the Delta, in Ægypt.

BABYLO'NIA, now Yerach, a large province of Assyria, of which Babylon was the capital. It was situated near the confluence of the Tigris and Euphrates. The inhabitants shook off the Assyrian yoke, and afterwards became very powerful. ——The surname of Seleucia, which arose from the ruins of Babylon, under the successors of Alexander. *Plin.* 6. c. 26.

BABYR'SA, a fortified castle near Artaxata, in Armenia. *Strab.* 11.

BABYSEN'GA, a market town of India without the Ganges. *Ptol.*

BABYT'ACE, a city of Armenia, the inhabitants of which were said to despise gold. *Plin.* 6. c. 27.

BACABA'SUS, betrayed the snares of Artabanus, brother of Darius, against Artaxerxes. *Justin.* 3. c. 1.

BAC'ALES, a people of Libya, near the sea. *Herod.* 4.

BACALI'TIS, a region of Upper Æthiopia. *Ptol.*

BAC'ARE, a maritime city of India without the Ganges. *Id.*

BACSACA'MI, a people of Arabia; their chief city was Riphearma. *Plin.* 6. c. 28.

BAC'ASIS, a town of the Jacetani, in Hispania Tarraconensis. *Ptol.*

BACA'TÆ, a people of Marmarica. *Id.*

BACCÆ'I, a nation of Spain. *Steph.*

BACCA'NÆ, a village of Etruria, now Baccano. *Antonin.*

BAC'CHÆ, the priestesses of Bacchus. *Paus.* 2. c. 7. *Vid.* Bacchantes.

BACCHANA'LIA, festivals in honour of Bacchus at Rome. When first introduced, women only assisted at the celebration, but afterwards both sexes were permitted to attend, and the disorders which arose from this promiscuous assemblage alarmed the senate, and the festival, which, by its repetition of four times annually, threatened the destruction of public morals, was suppressed. The Bacchanalia were the same as the Dionysia. *Vid.* Dionysia.

BACCHAN'TES, priestesses of Bacchus, who were represented, at the celebration of the orgies, covered with the skins of tigers or goats, and more often naked, with garlands of ivy, with a thyrsus or lighted torch in their hands, and with dishevelled hair. Their looks were wild; they uttered dreadful sounds, and clashing different musical instruments together, they threatened the affrighted spectators as if inspired with madness. They were also called Thyades, Mænades, and Mimallonides. *Natal. Com. Myth.* 5. c. 13.—*Pantheon. Mytic. de Bacc.*—*Plautus in Amph.* 2. sec. 2 —*Ovid. Met.* 6. v. 592.—*Horat.* 3. od. 25.—*Propert.* 3. el. 21.—*Lucan.* 1. v. 674.

BAC'CHI, a mountain of Thrace, near Philippi. *Appian.*

BAC'CHI and ANTIBAC'CHI, two islands in the Arabic Gulph. *Ptol.*—*Steph.*

BACCHI'A, a city of Albania. *Ptol.*

BACCHI'ADÆ or BACCHI'DÆ, a Corinthian family descended from Bacchia, daughter of Dionysius, or more probably from Bacchis, son of Prumnides. In their nocturnal orgies, they, as some report, tore to pieces Actæon, son of Melissus; which so enraged the father, that before the altar he solemnly entreated the Corinthians to revenge the death of his son, and then, in a fit of despair, threw himself into the sea. Upon this the Bacchiadæ were banished, and went to settle in Sicily, between Pachynum and Pelorus, where some suppose that they built Syracuse. *Ovid. Met.* 5. v. 407.—*Strab.* 8.—*Herodot.* 5. c. 92.

BAC'CHIDES, a general who betrayed the town of Sinope to Lucullus. *Strab.* 12.

BAC'CHIS or BA'LUS, king of Corinth, succeeded his father Prumnides. His successors were called Bacchidæ. They increased so much, that they chose one of their number to preside among them with regal authority; and as they contracted marriages only with the members of their own family, they preserved their dignity for nearly 200 years. Cypselus overturned this institution, by making himself absolute. *Strab.* 8.—*Paus.* 2. c. 4.—*Herodot.* 5. c. 92.—*Ovid. Met.* 5. v. 407.

BACCHI'UM, a small island in the Ægean Sea, opposite Smyrna. *Plin.* 5. c. 3.

BAC'CHIUS and BI'THUS, two celebrated gladiators of equal age and strength; whence arose the proverb, *Bithus contra Bacchium*, to express equality. *Suet. in Aug.*—*Horat.* 1. sat. 7. v. 20.

BACCHI'US, a musician who wrote a treatise called εἰσαγωγὴ μουσική, published by Morell, Paris, 1623. *Fabr. B. Gr.* l. 3. c. 12.——A writer *de re rustica*, mentioned by *Varro* and *Columella*. *Fabr. ibid.* ——A physician who wrote a work, in three books, explaining the difficult words of Hippocrates, &c. *Fabr. ibid.*——A person for whom Lysias wrote an oration. *Fabr. ibid.*

BAC'CHUS, was son of Jupiter and Semele, the daughter of Cadmus. After she had enjoyed the company of Jupiter, Semele was deceived, and perished by the artifice of Juno. *Vid.* Semele.

The child was with difficulty saved from the flames in which his mother perished, and put into his father's thigh, where he remained till the time of his birth. From this circumstance Bacchus has been called Bimater. According to some, Dirce, a nymph of the Achelous, saved him from the flames. There are different traditions concerning the manner of his education. Ovid says, that after his birth he was brought up by his aunt Ino, and afterwards entrusted to the care of the nymphs of Nysa. Lucian relates, that Mercury carried him, as soon as born, to the nymphs of Nysa; and Apollonius says, that he was conveyed by Mercury to a nymph in the island of Eubœa, whence he was driven by the power of the jealous Juno, who was the chief deity of the place. Some maintain, that the island of Naxus can boast of having been the place of his education, under the nymphs Philia, Coronis, and Clyda. Pausanias relates a tradition which prevailed in the town of Brasiæ in Peloponnesus, that Cadmus, as soon as he heard of his daughter's amours, shut her up, with her child, in a coffer, and exposed them on the sea. The coffer was carried by the waves to the coast of Brasiæ; but Semele was found dead, and the child alive. Semele was honoured with a magnificent funeral, and Bacchus properly educated. This diversity of opinion proves, without doubt, that there were many of the same name. Diodorus speaks of three, and Cicero of a greater number; but among them all, the son of Jupiter and Semele seems to have alone engrossed the celebrity due to the remarkable exploits of all the rest. Bacchus was the Osiris of the Ægyptians, and his history is drawn from the Ægyptian traditions concerning that ancient king. Bacchus assisted the gods in their wars against the giants, and was cut to pieces; but the son of Semele was not then born: this tradition, therefore, is taken from the history of Osiris, who was killed by his brother Typhon, and the worship of Osiris, under the name of Bacchus, was introduced by Orpheus into Greece. One of the first exploits of Bacchus was to redeem his mother from the infernal regions, and with the consent of Jupiter, she was raised to immortal honours under the name of Thyone. But of all the achievements of Bacchus, his expedition into the East is most celebrated. He marched at the head of an army, composed of men as well as of women, all inspired with divine fury, and armed with thyrsi, cymbals, and other musical instruments. The leader was drawn in a chariot by a lion and a tiger, and was accompanied by Pan, Silenus, and all the Satyrs. His conquests were easy, and without bloodshed; the people cheerfully submitted, and gratefully elevated to the rank of a god the hero who taught them the use of the vine, the cultivation of the earth, and the manner of making honey. Amidst his benevolence to mankind, Bacchus was relentless in punishing all want of respect to his divinity; and the punishment he inflicted on Pentheus, Agave, Lycurgus, the daughter of Minyas, Cyanippus, and others, is well known. He has received the names of Liber, Bromius, Lyæus, Evan, Thyoneus, Plilas, Dionysius, Bicornis, Brisæus, Iacchus, Dithyrambus, Messateus, Lampter, Ægobolus, Nyctelius, Polites, Melanegis, &c. which are mostly derived from the places where he was worshipped, or from the ceremonies observed in his festivals. He is generally represented crowned with vine and ivy leaves, with a thyrsus in his hand. His figure is that of an effeminate young man, to denote the joys which commonly prevail at feasts; and sometimes that of an old man, to teach us that wine taken immoderately will enervate us, and consume our health. The panther was sacred to him, because he went on his expedition covered with the skin of that beast. The magpye was also his favourite bird, because in triumphs people were permitted to speak wiih boldness and liberty. Bacchus is sometimes represented like an infant, holding a thyrsus and clusters of grapes with a horn. He often appears naked and riding upon the shoulders of Pan, or in the arms of Silenus, who was his foster-father. He also sits upon a celestial globe, bespangled with stars, and is then the same as the Sun or Osiris of Ægypt. The festivals of Bacchus generally called Orgies, Canephoria, Phallica, Bacchanalia, or Dionysia were introduced into Greece from Ægypt by Danaus and his daughters. *Vid.* Dionysia. His priestesses were called by the several names of Mænades, Thyades, Bacchantes, Mimallonides, and Bassarides, according to the peculiarity either of their dress or their gestures. Bacchus married Ariadne, after she had been forsaken by Theseus in the island of Naxus, and by her he had several children, among whom were Ceranus, Thoas, Œnopion, Tauropolis, and Evanthe. He was also father of Carmon by Alexirhea, of Philias by Clothonophyte, and of Narceus by Phiscoa of Elis. According to some, he was the father of Hymenæus, whom the Athenians regarded as the god of marriage. The Ægyptians sacrificed pigs to him, before the doors of their houses. The fir-tree, the yew-tree, the fig-tree, the ivy, and the vine, were sacred to him; and the goat was generally sacrificed to him on account of the great propensity of that animal to destroy the vine. According to Pliny, Bacchus was the first who ever wore a crown. His beauty is compared to that of Apollo, and, like him, he is represented with fine hair loosely flowing down his shoulders, and he was said to possess eternal youth. Sometimes he has horns, either because he taught the cultivation of the earth with oxen, or because Jupiter, his father appeared to him in the deserts of Libya under the shape of a ram, and supplied his thirsty army with water. The three persons of the name of Bacchus, whom *Diodorus* mentions, are, the one who conquered the Indies, and is surnamed the *bearded Bacchus;* a son of Jupiter and Proserpine, who was represented with horns; and the son of Jupiter and Semele, called the *Bacchus of Thebes.* Those mentioned by Cicero, and, a son of Proserpine; a son of Nisus, who built Nysa; a son of Caprius, who reigned in the Indies; a son of Jupiter and the Moon; and a son of Thyone and Nisus. *Cic. de Nat. D.* 2. c. 24. 1, 3, 23.—*Paus.* 2. c. 22. 37. l. 3. c. 24. l. 5. c. 19, &c.—*Herodot.* 1. c. 150. l. 2. c. 42, 48. 49.—*Plut. in Isid. & Osir.*—*Diod.* 1. 3. &c.—*Orpheus in Dionys.*—*Apollod.* 1. c. 9. l. 3, c. 4, &c.—*Ovid. Met.* 3. fab. 3, &c. *Amor.* 3. l. 3. *Fast.* 3. v. 715. l. 5. v. 166.—*Natal. Com.* 5. c. 13. —*Aratus in Ast.* 5.—*Hygin.* fab. 155, 157, &c. *P. A.* 2. c. 5 & 17.—*Servius in Æn.* 4. v. 469.—*Auson. Phyll.* 17.—*Plin.* 7. c. 56. l. 8. c. 2. l. 36. c. 5.—*Homer. Il.* 6.—*Lact. de Fals. Rel.* 1. c. 22.—*Virg. G.* 2, &c.—*Euripid. in Bacc.*—*Lucian. de Sacrif. de Baccho. in Dial. Deor.*—*Oppian. in Cyneg.*—*Philostrat.* 1. *Icon.* c. 50.—*Senec. in Chor. Oedip.*—*Martial.* 8. epigr. 26. l. 14. epigr. 107. [The statues of this deity are very numerous both in his Indian character and as a youth. Of the first, by far the finest is that in the Vatican, with the name Sardanapallos inscribed, which is supposed to be the name of the sculptor. And the finest of the innumerable busts of the bearded Bacchus, is in the possession of the earl of Egremont. As a youth, those which represent him leaning on a fawn, are far superior to the single figures, and are supposed to be copies of a celebrated groupe by Praxiteles, mentioned by Pliny. The finest are one in the Vatican, and another in the collection at Florence.]

BACCHYL'IDES, a lyric poet of Cos. nephew of Simonides, who, like Pindar, celebrated in his verses the praises of Hiero. Some of his poetry has been preserved, which proves him to have possessed a sublime genius, fertile powers of mind, and an elegant diction. He flourished about 452 B.C., and was the last of the nine lyric poets so deservedly celebrated in Greece. His writings are enumerated by *Meursius, B. Gr.* p. 1273.—*Marcel.*—*Fabricius in B. Gr.* 2. c. 15. s. 21.—*L. Gyrald. P. H. Dial.* 9.—*Euseb. Chron.*—*Sax Onom.* 1. p. 36.

BACE'LUS, an effeminate and luxurious person; whence the proverb *Bacelo similis. Hesych.*

BACE'NIS, a wood in Germany. *Cæs. Bell. Gall.* 6. c. 10.

BA'CIS, a famous soothsayer of Bœotia, said to be inspired by the sea nymphs, because his prophecies were regularly fulfilled. *Paus.* 10. c. 12.—*Suidas.*—*Cic.* l. *de Div.* c. 34.——A king of Corinth, called also Bacchis. *Vid.* Bacchis.——An Athlete of Troezene. *Paus.* 6. c. 8.——A famous bull, consecrated to the sun, and worshipped with divine honours in Ægypt. *Macrob. Sat.* 1. c. 21.

BAC'TRA (-*orum*), now Bagdasan or Budasan, the

capital of Bactriana, on the river Bactrus. *Virg. G.* 2. v. 138.—*Strab.* 2.

BAC'TRI or BACTRIA'NI, the inhabitants of Bactriana, who lived upon plunder, and, in consequence of their barbarous mode of life, always went armed. They were conquered by Alexander the Great. *Curt.* 4. c. 6. &c.—*Plin.* 6. c. 23.—*Plut. in Vitios. ad Infel. Suff.*—*Herodot.* 1 & 3.

BACTRIA'NA, a country of Asia, fruitful as well as extensive. It once formed part of the Persian empire, on the eastern parts of which it is situated. It is now Carassan or Corasan. *Diod.* 2.—*Justin.* 1. c. 1.

BAC'TRUS, now Buchian or Bacchara, a river on the borders of Asiatic Scythia, from which Bactriana received its name. *Lucan.* 3. v. 267.

BACUN'TIUS, a river of Pannonia, which falls into the Save, above Sirmium. It is now called Boszut. *Cluver.* 4. c. 1.

BAD'ACA, a town of Media. *Diod.* 19.

BAD'ACE, a town of Persia, in which Antigonus took refuge when conquered by Eumenes at the river Eulæus. *Salmas. ad Solin.* 702.

BA'DAS or BA'DA, a river of Syria, near which Memnon was buried. *Strab.* 15.

BA'DEOS, a city of Arabia Felix, near the Red Sea. *Steph.*

BADI'A, a town of Spain, on the river Anas. It was also called Pax Augusta. *Val. Max.* Also Ba'dia.

BA'DIUS, a Campanian, who challenged T. Q. Crispinus, one of his friends, by whom he was killed. *Liv.* 35. c. 18.

BADUHEN'NÆ, a grove in the country of the Frisii, or Friesland, in Holland, where 900 Romans were killed. *Tacit.* 4. *Ann.* c. 73.

BÆ'A, a mountain of Cephallenia, from Bæus or Baius, a pilot of Ulysses. *Steph.*

BÆ'ACA. a city of Chaonia. *Id.*

BÆ'BÆ, a town of Caria. *Id.*

BÆ'BIA LEX was enacted for the election of four prætors every other year. *Liv.* 40.—Another law by M. Bæbius, a tribune of the people, which forbade the division of the lands, whilst it substituted a yearly tax to be paid by the possessors, and to be divided among the people. *Appian.* 1.

BÆ'BIUS M., a Roman, in whose consulship the tomb of Numa was discovered. *Plut. in Num.*—*Val. Max.* 1. c. 1.

BÆ'BIUS LU'CIUS, a Roman prætor, who, being surprised by the Ligurians, fled to Marseilles, where he died of grief three days after. *Liv.* 37. c. 57. There were several persons of this name under the emperors, but they were little known.

BÆ'BRO, a town of Hispania Bætica. *Plin.* 3. c. 1.

BÆC'ULA, a town of the Ausetani, at the east of the Iberus in modern Catalonia. *Liv.* 27. c. 18. l. 28. c. 13.

BÆC'YLA, a town of Iberia, near the columns of Hercules. *Steph.*—*Casaubon ad Strab.* l. 3.

BÆ'NIS or MIN'IUS, a river of Lusitania. *Strab.*

BÆO'TIS, a name of Venus at Syracuse. *Hesych.*

BÆSIPPO. *Vid.* Besippo.

BÆTAR'RA, a city of Gallia Narbonensis, now Besiers. *Ptol.*—*Steph.*

BÆTARRE'NI, a people of Cœlesyria, near the Ithuræi. *Plin.* 5. c. 23.

BÆ'TICA, a division of Spain. *Vid.* Hispania.

BÆ'TIS a river of Spain, formerly called Tartessus, and now Guadalquiver. From this river the name of Bætica was given to that part of Spain, known in modern geography by the appellation of Andalusia and New Castile. The wool produced there was in high estimation for its fineness, so that Bæticus became an epithet applied to garments of superior quality. *Paus.* 6. c. 19.—*Plin.* 3. ep. 9.—*Liv.* 28. c. 30.—*Mela*, 3. c. 1.—*Strab.* 3.—*Claudian in Fesc.* 72.—*Senec. in Med.* 725.—*Ptol.* 2. c. 4.—*Sil.* 1. v. 146. l. 9. v. 234.—*Martial.* 8. epigr. 28. l. 12. ep. 100.

BÆ'TON, a Greek historian in the age of Alexander. *Plin.* 6. c. 17.—*Athen.* 10.

BÆ'TIUM, a city of Macedonia. *Steph.*

BÆ'TIUS, a river of Arabia Felix. *Ptol.*

BÆT'ULO or BETUL'LO, a town of Spain, now Badelona. *Mela*, 2. c. 6.

BÆTU'RIA, a country of Spain, now called Estramadura. *Cluver.* 2. c. 3.—*Liv.* 39. c. 30.

BAGA'CUM or BAG'ACUM, now Bavay, a town of the Nervii. *Ptolemy* calls it Baganum.

BAGIS'TAME, a delightful country of Media. *Diod.* 17.

BAGIS'TANES, a friend of Bessus whom he abandoned when he murdered Darius. *Curt.* 5. c. 13.

BAGIS'TANUS, a mountain of Media, on which was sculptured a figure of Semiramis. *Cœl. Rhod.* 1. 26. c. 24.

BAGO'AS or BAGO'SAS, an Ægyptian eunuch in the court of Artaxerxes Ochus, king of Persia, so powerful that nothing could be done without his consent. He led some troops against the Jews, and profaned their temple. He poisoned Ochus, gave his flesh to cats, and made knife handles with his bones, because he had killed the god Apis. He placed on the throne Arses, the youngest of the slaughtered prince's children, and four years after put him to death. He was at last killed, B.C. 335, by Darius, whom after raising to the crown, he had attempted to poison. *Diod.* 16 & 17.

BAGO'AS, a satrap in the Persian court, much esteemed by Alexander the Great. He was the cause that one of the satraps was put to death by the most excruciating torments. *Curt.* 10. c. 1.—*Plut. in Alex.* Most of the eunuchs of the monarchs of Persia were known by this appellation.—*Plin.* 13. c. 4.—*Quintil.* 5. c. 12.

BAGODA'RES, a friend of Bessus, whom he abandoned when he attempted the life of Darius. *Diod.* 17.

BAGOPH'ANES, a governor of Babylon, who, when Alexander approached the city, strewed all the streets with flowers, and burned incense on the altars, &c. *Curt.* 5. c. 1.

BAG'RADA, now Megrada, a river of Africa Propria running into the Mediterranean, between the towns of Utica and Carthage. It was on its banks that the Roman army under Regulus killed an enormous serpent, 120 feet long. *Plin.* 8. c. 14.—*Lucan.* 4. 588.——A river of Carmania, now Binimir. *Ptol.*

BA'IÆ, a city of Campania, near the sea, founded by Baius, one of the companions of Ulysses. It was famous for its baths and delightful situation, and many of the Roman senators had country houses there. Its ancient grandeur, however, has now disappeared, and Baiæ, with its magnificent villas, has yielded to the tremendous earthquakes which convulse Italy, and is no longer to be found. *Martial*, 14. epigr. 81.—*Horat.* 1. ep. 1.—*Strab.* 5.—*Propert.* 1. el. 11. l. 3. el. 17.—*Ovid. de A.A.* 1. v. 255.—*Juvenal.* 3.—*Cic pro Cœl.* ep. 1.—*Att.* 13.—*Senec.* epist. 52.—*Tacit.* 11. *Ann.* l. l. 15. c 52.

BAIOCAS'SES, a people of Gaul, probably the Viducasses of *Pliny*, 4. c. 18, and Biducasses of *Ptolemy*.

BAISAMP'SA, a city of Arabia. *Steph.*

BA'LA, a surname of Alexander, one of the kings of Syria. *Justin.* 35. c. 1.

BAL'ACRI, a people in the army of Alexander the Great. *Curt.* l. 4. c. 13.—*Arrian.* l. 3.

BAL'ACRUS, an officer in Alexander's army, who took Miletus. *Curt.* 4. c. 13.——A son of Amyntas, a præfect of some auxiliaries of Alexander. *Id.* 4. c. 5.

BAL'AGRUS, a Greek historian. *Steph.*

BALANA'GRÆ, a town of Cyrene. *Paus.* 2. c. 26.

BALANE'A, a town on the sea coast of Syria, at the south of the river Orontes. *Plin.* 5. c. 20.

BALANTIPYR'GON, a city of India within the Ganges; it is now Capilampa. *Ptol.*

BAL'ANUS, a prince of Gaul, who assisted the Romans in their Macedonian war, A.U.C. 581. *Liv.* 44. c. 14.

BAL'ARI or BALA'RI, a people of Sardinia. *Liv.* 41. c. 6.

BAL'ATRO, one of the attendants of Mecænas. *Horat.* 2. sat. 8. v. 21.

BAL'BIA, a city of the Brutii, famous for its wine, whence Vina Balbina. It is now Altmonte. *Plin.* 14. c. 6.

BALBIL'LUS C., a learned and benevolent Roman, made governor of Ægypt, of which he wrote the history, under Nero. *Tacit. Ann.* 13. c. 22.

BALBI'NUS, an admirer of Agna, mentioned by *Horace*, 1. sat. 3. v. 40.——A Roman, who, after governing several provinces with credit and honour, assassinated the Gordians, and seized the imperial purple. He was some time after murdered by his soldiers, A.D. 238. [There is a bust of this emperor in the Museum of the Vatican.]

BALBUR'RA, a city of Lycia. *Steph.*

BAL'BUS, a mountain in the interior of Africa, famous as the retreat of Masinissa after he had fought a battle against Syphax. *Liv.* 29. c. 31.

BAL'BUS L., a lawyer, &c., one of the pupils of Scævola

BAL'BUS, two Stoic philosophers at Rome, mentioned by *Cicero. de Orat.* 3. c. 21. *N.D.* 1. c. 7, &c.——A man killed by the assassins of the triumvirs.

BAL'BUS CORNE'LIUS, a native of Gades, who, on being made a citizen of Rome, took the name of Balbus, after L. Corn. Balbus, one of Julius Cæsar's friends. The influence of his friends, aided by his own merit, raised him to the consulship and to opulence, so that at his death he left each Roman citizen twenty-five denarii. *Vell* 2. c. 51.—*Dio.* 48. c. 52.—*Plin.* 7. c. 43.—*Sic. ad Att.* 7. c. 3. *In Balb.*——A nephew of the preceding by his sister; called *Minor*, to distinguish him from his uncle, called *Major.* He was engaged in the war against the Garamantes, as quæstor to Asinius Pollio, and built a theatre which bore his name. *Sueton. Aug.* 29.—*Plin.* 5. c. 5.—*Dio.* 54. c. 25. & l. 66. c. 24.

BAL'DUS, a city of Phœnicia. *Steph.*

BALEA'RES, three islands in the Mediterranean, on the coast of Spain, known in modern geography by the names of Majorca, Minorca, and Yvica. The word is derived from βάλλειν, *to throw*, because the inhabitants were expert archers and slingers. We are told by Florus, that the mothers never gave their children breakfast before they had struck with an arrow a certain mark in a tree. *Strab.* 14.—*Cæs. Bell. Gall.* 2. c. 7.—*Virg. G.* 1. v. 309.—*Ovid. Met.* 2. v. 72.—*Plin.* 3. c. 5.—*Flor.* 3. c. 8.—*Diod.* 5.

BALEPAT'NA, a town of India, supposed to be modern Pataxa.

BALE'SIUM, a maritime town of Italy, not far from Brundusium. *Plin.* 3. c. 11.

BALE'TUS, a son of Hippo, who is said to have founded Corinth. *Patercul.* 1. c. 3.

BALIS'TA, a mountain of Liguria. *Liv.* 40. c. 41.

BA'LIUS, a horse of Achilles. *Homer. Il.* 16. v. 149.—*Plaudian.* ep. 21. v. 9.

BAL'LA, a city of Macedonia. *Steph.*

BAL'LATHA, a city of Mesopotamia. *Ptol.* It was according to some, the Bathno of *Antoninus.*

BALLON'OTI, a people of European Sarmatia. *Flacc.* 6. v. 160.

BAL'NEÆ, (*baths*), private as well as public, were very numerous at Rome) They were used after walking, exercise, or labour, and were deemed more necessary than luxurious. Under the emperors it became so fashionable to bathe, that without this enjoyment, the meanest of the people seemed to be deprived of one of the necessaries of life. There were certain hours of the day appointed for bathing, and a small peice of money admitted the poorest as well as the most opulent. In the baths there were separate apartments for the people to dress and to undress; and, after they had bathed, they commonly covered themselves, the hair was plucked out of the skin, and the body rubbed over with a pumice stone, and perfumed to render it smooth and fair. The Roman emperors generally erected baths for their own use, and all endeavoured to eclipse each other in the magnificence of the building. It is said that Diocletian employed 40,000 of his soldiers in building his baths; and when they were finished, he cruelly put to death all the workmen. Alexander Severus first permitted the people to use them in the night, and he himself often bathed with the common people. Literary persons generally read while bathing, and we find many compositions written in the midst of this luxurious enjoyment.

BALOE'UM, a city of Macedonia. *Steph.*

BAL'SA, a town of Lusitania, now Tavila. *Ptol.*

BALVEN'TIUS, a centurion of great valour in Cæsar's army, killed by Ambiorix. *Cæs. Bell. Gall.* 5. c. 35.

BAL'YRAS, a small river of Peloponnesus. *Paus.* 4. c. 33.

BAMBA'LIO, a nick-name applied to Fadius. *Vid.* Fadius.

BAMBO'TUM, a river of Mauritania, filled with crocodiles. *Plin.* 5. c. 1.

BAMBY'CE, an ancient name of Hierapolis in Syria, called Magog by the inhabitants of the country. It is now Aleppo. *Cluver.* 5. c. 22. *Plin.* 5. c. 23.—*Strab.* 16.

BAMU'RÆ, a people of Libya. *Ital.* 3. v. 303.

BAN'ASA, called Valentia by *Pliny*, 5. c. 1., a city of Mauritania Tingitana. It is now Fanfara.

BANAU'RIDES, islands of Etruria. So called from Banaurus, son of Ajax. *Steph.*

BANDOB'ENA, a town of India, near the rivers Cophes and Coaspes. *Strab.*

BANI'SÆ or BASANI'SÆ, a people of Thrace. *Steph.*

BANNOMAN'NA, an island near Scythia. *Plin.* 4. c. 13.

BAN'TIA, now St, Maria de Vanse, a town of Apulia, in the midst of the Apennines, whence Bantinus. *Horat.* 3. od. 4. v. 15.

BAN'TII, a people of Thrace. *Steph.*

BAN'TIUS L., a gallant youth of Nola, whom Annibal found, after the battle of Cannæ, almost dead amongst the heaps of slain. He was sent home by the Carthaginian general with great humanity, upon which he resolved to betray his country to so generous an enemy. Marcellus, the Roman general, heard of it, and rebuked Bantius, who afterwards continued firm and faithful to the interests of Rome. *Liv.* 35. c. 15.

BANUR'RI, a people of Mauritania Tingitana. *Plin.* 3. c. 2.

BAPH'YRUS, a river of Macedonia, which runs by Olympus, and falls, after a short course, into the Sinus Thermaicus. *Liv.* 44. c. 6.

BAP'TÆ, the priests of Cotytto, the goddess of lasciviousness and debauchery at Athens. Her festivities were celebrated in the night; and so infamous and obscene was the behaviour of the priests, that they were said to disgust even Cotytto herself, though the goddess of obscenity. The name is derived from ϐάπτειν, *to wash*, because the priests bathed themselves in the most effeminate manner. *Juv.* 2. v. 92.

BAP'TÆ, a comedy of Cratinus, which gave such offence to the Baptæ, that they are said to have cast the poet into the sea.

BARA'CUM, a town of Cyrene. *Plin.* 5. c. 5.

BARACU'RA, a city of India without the Ganges, now Bengala. *Ptol.*

BARÆ'I, a people of Colchis and Iberia, who burnt the bodies of such of their friends as died by disease, but gave to the fowls of the air such as fell in war. *Ælian de Anim.* 10. c. 22.

BARAGA'ZA, a town of Æthiopia. *Plin.* 6. c. 29.

BARAMAL'ACUM, a town of the Nabathæi. *Id.* 6. l. 28.

BARA'THIA, a city of Africa Propria, now Brata. *Ptol.*

BAR'ATHRUM, a deep and obscure gulph at Athens, into which criminals were thrown. *Plaut. Rud.* 2. sc. 7. v, 12.—*Servius in Æn.* 3. v. 420.—*Suidas.*—*Cœl. Rhod.* 17. c. 19. The word is used for any dangerous abyss or gulph, and also for the infernal regions by *Valerius Floccus*, 2. v. 86 & 192.

BAR'BARI, a name originally applied to those who spoke inelegantly, or with harshness and difficulty. The Greeks and Romans generally called all nations except their own, by the name of Barbarians.

BAR'BARI, a city of Asia, near the mouth of the Indus. *Ptol.*

BARBARI'A or BARBA'RIA, a river of Macedonia. *Liv.* 44. c. 31.——A name given to Phrygia and the country round Troy. *Horat.* 1. ep. 2. v. 7.

BARBA'RIUM, a promontory of Spain, near the Tagus. *Strab.* 2.

BARBA'TIA, a town of Arabia.——A river of the Indian Ocean. *Plin.* 6. c. 28.

BARBA'TUS, the surname of a Roman family. *Sueton. Cl.* 21.

BARBOS'THENES, a mountain of Peloponnesus, ten miles from Sparta. *Civ.* 35. c. 27 & 30.

BARBYTH'ACE, a city of Persia. *Plin.* 6. c. 27.

BAR'CA, a friend of Cato the elder. *Plut. in Cat. Vid.* Barcha.

BARCÆ'I or BARCI'TÆ, a warlike nation of Africa near Carthage. *Virg. Æn.* 4. v. 43.

BARCA'NII, a people near the Hyrcani. *Steph.*

BAR'CE, the nurse of Sichæus. *Virg. Æn.* 4. v. 632.——A large country of Africa.——A city near Cyrene about nine miles from the sea, founded by the brothers of Arcesilaus king of Cyrene, 515 years B.C. Strabo says, that in his age it was called Ptolemais; but he is mistaken, having supposed it to be so called because most of the inhabitants retired to Ptolemais, which was on the seacoast, to enrich themselves by commerce. *Strab.* 17.—*Plin.* 5. c. 5.—*Ptol.* 4. c. 4.——A small village of Bactriana, where the people who had been taken prisoners by Darius in Africa, were confined. *Herodot.* 4. c. 204.——A city of Media. *Justin.* 1. c. 7.

BAR'CHA or BAR'CA, the surname of a noble family at Carthage, from which Annibal and Amilcar were descended. They created a powerful faction, known by the name of the *Barchinian faction*, and at last raised themselves to power, and disposed of all the offices of trust or emolument in the state. *Liv.* 21. c. 2 & 9. l. 28. c. 12. l. 30. c. 7 & 42.—*Cor. Nep.* 21. c. 1.

BARCHU'SA, a small city of Phœnicia. *Steph.*

BAR'CINO, a maritime town at the east of Spain, now Barcelona, the capital of Catalonia. It was founded by Hamilcar, and received its name from the family, Barca, to which it belonged, and was also called Faventia Colonia and Julia Augusta. It was recovered from the Moors A.D. 805. *Cluver.* 2. c. 6.

BARDÆ'I, a people of Illyricum, who were engaged in the factions of Marius. *Plut. in Mario.*

BARDESA'NES, an historian of Babylon, in the time of Alexander Severus. *Voss. de Hist. Gr.* 3. p. 483.

BAR'DI, a celebrated sacerdotal order among the ancient Gauls, which praised their heroes, and published their fame in their verses, or sang them to the sound of musical instruments. They were so highly esteemed and respected by the people, that at the sight of them, two armies, which were engaged in battle, were persuaded to lay down their arms, and to submit their fate to their absolute direction. *Lucan.* 1. v. 447.—*Strab.* 4.—*Marcell.* 15. c. 24. & *Vales in Loco.*—*Festus de Verb. Sig.*

BARDI'NES, a river near Damascus. *Steph.*

BAR'DO, a town of Spain. *Liv.* 33. c. 21.——A mountain of Italy. *Cluver. Ital. Ant.* 1. c. 10, &c.

BAR'DULI, a people of the Cantabri in Spain. *Plin.* 4. c. 22.

BAR'DUS CAS'SIUS, a Roman, intimate with J. Cæsar. *Cic. Ph.* 13. c. 2.

BARDYETÆ, a people of Spain on the Iberus. They are called Bardyali by *Strabo.*

BAR'DYLIS, an Illyrian prince, whose daughter Bercenna married king Pyrrhus. *Plut. in Pyrrh.*

BA'REAS SORA'NUS, a youth killed by his tutor Egnatius, a stoic philosopher. *Juv.* 3. v. 116.—*Tac. Ann.* 16. c. 23.

BARE'NE. a city of Media, near Ecbatana. *Steph.*

BA'RES, a naval officer of Persia, who wished to destroy Cyrene, but was opposed by Amasis. *Herodot.* 4. c. 203.

BAR'GASA, a city of Caria. *Steph.*

BARGA'TES, an attendant of Smerdis, privy to the plot of the seven nobles. *Ctesias.*

BARGE'NI, a people of the Troglodyti in Africa. *Plin.* 6. c. 29.

BAR'GUS, a river of Thrace, falling into the Hebrus. *Id.* 4. c. 11.

BARGU'SII, a people of Spain, at the east of the Iberus. *Liv.* 21. c. 19 & 23.

BARGYL'IA, a town of Caria, on the Sinus Bargylieticus. *Liv.* 32. c. 33. l. 37. c. 17.—*Plin.* 5. c. 20.

BARI'NE, a prostitute, whom *Horace*, 2. od. 8., accuses of perjury.

BAR'ISAS, a general who assisted Perses against Æetes. *Val. Flacc. Argon.* 6. v. 557.

BARIS'SES, one of the seven conspirators against the usurper Smerdis. *Ctesias.*

BA'RIUM, a town of Apulia, on the shores of the Adriatic, now Bari. It was remarkable for its fine fish. *Horat.* 1. sat. 5. v. 97.

BAR'NUUS, a town of Macedonia. near Heraclea. *Strab.* 7.

BAR'RA, a town of the Orobii in Italy. *Plin.* 3. c. 17.

BAR'RUS, a man ridiculed by *Horace*, 1. sat. 6. v. 30., as proud of his beauty.

BARSI'NE or BARSE'NE, a daughter of Darius, who married Alexander, by whom she had a son called Hercules. Cassander ordered her and her child to be put to death that they might not oppose his ambitious views. *Justin.* 13. c. 2. l. 15. c. 2.—*Arrian.*

BARTHAB'ACES, a priest of Cybele. *Plut in Mar.*

BAR'ULUM or BAR'OLUM, a town of Apulia Peucetia, now Barletta. *Strabo* calls it Baretum.

BARUS'SÆ, five islands in the Indian Sea. *Ptol.*

BARYG'ASA, a famous emporium of Gedrosia. *Steph.*——A city of India within the Ganges. *Ptol.*—*Arrian.*

BARZAEN'TES, a satrap of Persia and friend of Bessus. He revolted from Alexander. *Curt.* 8. c. 13.

BARZA'NES, a king of Assyria, tributary to Ninus. *Diod.* 2.

BASABOCA'TES, a people of Aquitania, near the Pictones. *Plin.* 4. c. 19.

BASCA'TIS, a rives of Sogdiana. *Ptol.*

BASE'RA, a city of Phœnicia. *Steph.*

BASILE'A, a daughter of Cœlus and Terra, who was mother of all the gods. *Diod.* 3.

Basile'a, An island at the north of Gaul, famous for its amber. *Diod.* 5.——An island in the Euxine Sea, *Plin.* 4. c. 13.——A town of Germany, supposed to be Basil on the Rhine, in Switzerland.

BASILE'I, a people of Sarmatia, who dwelt on each side of the Ister. *Strab.* 7.

BASILI'DÆ, European Sarmatians, descended from Hercules and Echidna. *Mela*, 2. c. 1.

BASILI'DES, the father of Herodotus, who, with others attempted to destroy Strattis, tyrant of Chius. *Herodot.* 8. c. 132.——A family which was possessed of an oligarchical power at Erythræ. *Strab.* 14.——A priest of mount Carmel, who foretold many momentous events to Vespasian, when he offered sacrifices. *Tacit.* 2 *Hist.* c. 87.—*Sueton. in Vesp.* 7.——A famons divine, born at Alexandria, in the second century, and founder of a sect which bore his name. Like Pythagoras, he enjoined five years of silence to his pupils, and particularly recommended to them great humility, and inward devotion. His writings are all lost. He died at Alexandria, A.D, 130.

BASILI'NA, the mother of Julian the apostate. She was noted for her piety. *Amm. Marcell.* 1. 22.

BASILIOPOT'AMOS, the ancient name of the Eurotas. *Strab.* 6.

BAS'ILIS, an historian who wrote concerning India. *Athen.*—*Plin.* 6. c. 39.

Bas'ilis, a city of Arcadia, built by Cypselus, near the river Alpheus. This town was in ruins in the age of Pausanias, and a temple of Ceres alone remained to point out its former consequence. *Paus.* 8. c. 29.

BASILI'US, a small river of Mesopotamia, falling into the Euphrates. *Strab.*

Basil'ius, a celebrated bishop of Neocæsarea, formerly Mazaca, in Cappadocia, was a zealous and able opposer of the Arians, whose tenets and doctrines he refuted with warmth, but great ability. He was eloquent as well as ingenious, and possessed of all those qualities which constitute the persuasive orator and the elegant writer. Erasmus has placed him in the number of the graatest orators of antiquity. He died in his 51st year, A.D. 379. The latest edition of his works is that of the Benedictines, fol. Paris, 1721. *Fabricius, B. Gr.* 5. c. 14. gives a very full account of Basil, his writings, and the best editions of his works. He enumerates, also, more than 30 other persons of this name. See also *Sax, Onom.* 1. p. 422.——A man, who, though patronised and esteemed by Cæsar, yet conspired against him *Cic. Fam.* 6. ep. 15.

BAS'ILUS, a general who assisted Antony. *Lucan.* 4. v. 416.——An insignificant lawyer. *Juv.* 7. v. 146.——A prætor, who plundered the provinces. *Id.* 10. v. 222.

BASIN'NI, a people of Arabia. *Steph.*

BAS'SA, a place of Arcadia, where Apollo had a temple. *Paus.* 8. c. 30 & 41.

BASSA'NIA, a town of Macedonia, on the borders of Illyricum. *Liv.* 44. c. 30.

BAS'SAREUS, a surname of Bacchus, from the dress or long Thracian robe, called *Bassaris*, which his priests wore. *Horat.* 1. od. 18. v. 11.

BASSAR'IDES, a name given to the votaries of Bacchus, and to Agave by Persius. It seems derived from Bassara, a town of Libya, sacred to the god, or from the Bassaris, a particular Thracian dress worn by his priestesses. *Persius*, 1. v. 101.

BASSIA'NA, a town of Pannonia, now Bossega. *Ptol.*

BAS'SUS AUFID'IUS, an historian in the age of Augustus, who wrote on the Germanic war. *Quintil.* 10. c. 1.

Bas'sus Cæ'sius, a poet in Nero's age, to whom Persius addressed his sixth satire. He distinguished himself by his lyric compositions, in the execution of which he proved so happy, that he has been ranked with Horace. Only two of his verses are extant. It is said that he was burnt in his villa by a sudden eruption of mount Vesuvius. *Paus.* 6.—*Persius*, 6. v. 1.

BAS'SUS JU'LIUS, an orator in the reign of Augustus, some of whose orations have been preserved by *Seneca.*

BAS'SUS SALE'IUS, an epic poet, who lived in the age of Vespasian. *Fabius*, 10. c. 1.

BAS'SUS, a man spoken of by *Horace*, 1. od. 36. c. 14. and described as fond of wine and women.

BAS'TA, a town of Italy, near the Japygian Acra. *Plin.* 3. c. 11.

BASTAN'ABUS, a harbour of Arabia. *Steph.*

BASTANÆ'I, a nation of Arabia Deserta. *Ptol.*

BASTAR'NÆ or BASTER'NÆ, a people of European Sarmatia, at the east of the Vistula, destroyed by a sudden storm as they pursued the Thracians. *Tacit. G.* 46.—*Liv.* 40. c. 5 & 58. l. 41. c. 19.—*Ovid. Trist.* 2. v. 198.—*Strab.* 7.

BASTERBI'NI, a people of Italy. *Plin.* 3. c. 11.

BAS'TIA, the wife of Metellus. *Liv. Epit.* 89.

BASTITA'NI or BASTU'LI, a people of Spain, near the Turduli. *Strab.* 3.

BA'TA, a sea-port of Asia, on the Euxine, opposite Sinope. *Strab.* 6.—*Ptol.* 5. c. 9.

BAT'ALA, an ancient town of the Sidicini in Italy. *Livy.*

BATANCÆS'ARA, a city of India within the Ganges now Baicadul. *Ptol.*

BAT'AVA CAS'TRA, a fortified place of Vindelicia, now Passau in Bavaria, where the Inn, (Ænus,) falls into the Danube. *Cluver.* 3. c. 4.

BATA'VI or BAT'AVI, a people of Germany, who inhabited that part of the continent known under the modern name of Holland, and called by the ancients, *Batavorum insula.* *Liv.* 4. c. 15.—*Sil. It.* 3. v. 608.—*Mart.* 6. epigr. 82. l. 14. epigr. 176.—*Cæsar, B. G.* 4. c. 10.—*Lucan.* 1. v. 431.

BA'TE, part of the tribe Ægeis. *Steph.*

BATE'A, a daughter of Teucer, wife of Dardanus. *Diod. Sic.* l. 5.

BATE'NI, a people of Mount Caucasus. *Plin.* 6. c. 16.

BA'THIS, now Jati, a river of Sicily. *Ptol.*

BA'THOS, a rives near the Alpheus. *Paus.* 8. c. 29.

BATH'YCLES, a celebrated artist of Magnesia. *Paus.* 3. c. 19.

BATHYL'LUS, a beautiful youth of Samus, greatly beloved by Polycrates the tyrant, and by the poet Anacreon. *Horat.* ep. 14. v. 9. Mecænas was also fond of a youth of Alexandria, of the same name. *Tacit.* 1.—*Ann.* 54.—*Juv.* 6. v. 63.——A poet who claimed, as his own, Virgil's distich, *Nocte pluit tota, &c.*

BATHYL'LUS, a fountain of Arcadia. *Paus.* 8. c. 31.

BATIA'TUS LENT, a man of Campania, who kept in his house a number of gladiators, who rebelled against him. *Plut in Cras.*

BATI'A, a naiad who married Œbalus. *Apollod.* 3. 10.

BATI'Æ, an inland city of Epirus. *Strab.* 7.

BATIE'IA, the tomb of Ilus, in Troas. *Id.* 3.

BATIE'NI, a town of Liguria, called Bacienni by *Paterculus.* *Ptol.*

BATI'NA or BANTI'NA. *Vid.* Bantia.

BA'TIS or BE'TIS, a eunuch, governor of Gaza, who boldly refused to submit to the Macedonian invaders, upon which he was seized and dragged round the city tied by the heels to Alexander's chariot. *Curt.* 4. c. 6.—*Arrian.* 2. c. 25.

BAT'NÆ, a city of Osrhoene. *Steph.*——A city of Mesopotamia, compared to Tempe. *Ammian.*—*Steph.*—*Zosim.*

BA'TO, a Dardanian, who revolted from king Philip to the Romans. *Liv.* 31. c. 28.

BA'TON, a native of Sinope, who wrote commentaries on the Persian affairs. *Strab.* 12.——A charioteer of Amphiaraus, swallowed up by the earth together with him. He was honoured with a consecrated place after death. *Paus.* 5. c. 17.

BATRACHOMYOMA'CHIA, a poem written by Homer, describing a *fight* between *frogs* and *mice.* It has been sometimes printed separately from the Iliad or Odyssey. The best edition of it is Mattaire's, 8vo. London, 1721. Some, however, among whom is *H. Stephanus*, doubt whether Homer was really the author of this poem.

BAT'RACHUS, a sculptor. *Plin.* 36. c. 5.

BATTI'ADES, a patronymic of Callimachus, from his father Battus. *Ovid. in Ib.* v. 53.——A name given to the people of Cyrene from king Battus. *Ital.* 3. v. 253.

BAT'TIS, a girl of Cos, whose person was admired and celebrated by Philetas the elegiac poet. *Ovid. Trist.* 1. el. 5. v. 2. *Pont.* 3. el. 1. v. 58.

BAT'TON, a comic writer, two of whose plays are mentioned by *Suidas.*

BAT'TUS the First, a Lacedæmonian who built the town of Cyrene, B.C. 630, with a colony from the island of Thera. He was son of Polymnestus and Phronime, and reigned in the town which he had founded, and after death received divine honours. The difficulty with which he spoke first procured him the name of Battus. *Herodot.* 4. c. 155, &c.—*Paus.* 3. c. 14. l. 10. c. 15.—*Strab.* 17.—*Justin.* 13. c. 7.

BAT'TUS the Second, was son of Arcesilaus, and grandson to Battus the First. He succeeded his father on the throne of Cyrene, and was surnamed Felix, and died 554 B.C. *Herodot.* 4. c. 159, &c.

BAT'TUS, a shepherd of Pylus, who promised Mercury that he would not discover his having stolen the flocks of Admetus, which Apollo tended. He violated his promise, and the god in revenge, turned him into a pumice stone. *Ovid. Met.* 2. v. 706.——A general of Corinth engaged in a war against Athens. *Thucyd.* 4. c. 43.——A buffoon of Cæsar's. *Plut. Symp.* 6.

BAT'ULUM, a town of Campania, the inhabitants of which assisted Turnus against Æneas. *Virg. Æn.* 7. v. 739.

BAT'ULUS, a surname of Demosthenes, from his effeminacy when young. *Plut. in Demosth.*

BA'TUM, a river of the Brutii. *Plin.* 3. c. 5.

BA'TUS, a Greek historian. *Pind. Schol. Od.* 4. *Isthm.*

BATYL'LUS, a celebrated dancer in Domitian's reign. *Juv.* 6. v. 63.

BAU'BO, a woman who hospitably received Ceres when she sought her daughter, and gave her some water to quench her thirst. *Ovid. Met.* 5. fab. 7. *Ovid*, however, 4. *Fast.* calls her Melanina.

BAU'CIS, an aged and infirm woman of Phrygia, who, with her husband Philemon, lived in a small cottage, when Jupiter and Mercury, in disguise, travelled over Asia. The gods came to the cottage, where they were treated with the best things which it afforded; and Jupiter was so pleased with the hospitality of the aged pair, that he metamorphosed their dwelling into a magnificent temple, of which Baucis and her husband were appointed priests. They both died at the same hour, according to their request to Jupiter, that one might not have the sorrow of following the other to the grave. Their bodies were changed, after their death, into trees before the doors of the temple. *Ovid. Met.* 8. v. 631, &c.

BAU'LI, a small town of Latium, near Baiæ. *Ital.* 12. v. 155.

BAU'MA, a town on the Æthiopic Gulph. *Plin.* 6. c. 29.

BAU'TIS, a river of Serica. *Ammian.* 23.

BA'VIUS and MÆ'VIUS, two stupid and malevolent poets in the age of Augustus. They attacked the superior talents of contemporary writers, and have therefore been immortalized by the satire and ridicule which they drew upon themselves from the pens of writers of reputation. *Virg. Ecl.* 3.

BAV'OTA, a town of the Salentini. *Ptol.*

BAZACA'TA, now Basse, an island of the Indian Sea. *Ptol.*

BAZAEN'TES, a conspirator with Bessus against Darius. He escaped into India. *Curt.* 6. c. 6.

BAZA'RIA, a country of Asia. *Id.* 8. c. 3.

BEBIA'NI, a people of Liguria. *Plin.* 3. 11.

BE'BIUS. *Vid.* Bæbius.

BEBRI'ACUM, now Labinta, or, according to others, Caneto, a village between Cremona and Verona. It is celebrated in history as the spot where Vitellius overcame Otho. *Juv.* 2. v. 106.—*Tacit. Hist.* 1. c. 15.

BEB'RYCE, a daughter of Danaus, who is said to have spared her husband. Most authors, however, assert that it was Hypermnestra. *Vid.* Danaides.

BEB'RYCES BEBRY'CES or BEBRYC'II, a nation of Asia, near Pontus, of Thracian origin, and, according to Arrian, descended from Bebryce. They were very expert in the combat of the Cæstus. In the time of the Argonauts Amycus, son of Neptune, was king of the country. *Virg. Æn.* 5. v. 373. & *Servius in Loco.*—*Solin.* 42.—*Tzetzes in Lycop.* 1305.—*Apollod.* 1.—*Strab.* 7 & 12.

BEBRYC'IA, an ancient name of Bithynia, from Bebryce, the daughter of Danaus. *Strab.* 13.—*Virg. Æn.* 5. v. 373.

BE'BRYX, a king of part of Spain. His daughter, Pyrene, is supposed to have given her name to the Pyrenean mountains, which formed part of her father's dominions. *Sil. It.* 3. v. 420, &c.

BECHI'RES or BECHI'RI, a nation of Scythia, which accompanied Attila into Italy. *Steph.*—*Dionys.* 765.—*Plin.* 6. c. 4.

BEDI'RUM, an inland city of Libya, the Debris of *Pliny*, 5. c. 5. *Ptol.*

BE'GIS, a city of the Tralliani. *Steph.*

BELE'GRA, a town of Picenum, now Civitella. *Ptol*

BELEMI'NA, a town of Laconia. *Paus.* 3. c. 21.

BELEN'DI, a people of Aquitania. *Plin.* 4. c. 19.

BELE'NUS or BEL'ENUS, a famous divinity, supposed to be the same as the Apollo of the Greeks, and the Orus of the Ægyptians, and highly venerated amongst the Gauls. Della Torre, a learned bishop, has written a dissertation to prove that this deity was first worshipped at Aquileia, and that his fame and votaries afterwards extended to Noricum and thence over part of Germany into Gaul. The ceremonies used in his worship are unknown. *Reinesius, Insc. Class.* 1. c. 51.—*Scalig. Aus. Lect.* 1. c. 9.—*Tertull. Adv. Gent. ap.* 24.

BELEPHAN'TES, a Chaldean, who from his knowledge of astronomy, told Alexander that his entering Babylon would be attended with fatal consequences to him. *Diod.* 17.

BELE'RIUM, a promontory of Britain, now called the Land's End.

BEL'ESES, a priest of Babylon, who told Arbaces, governor of Media, that he should one day reign in the place of Sardanapalus. His prophecy was verified, and he was rewarded by the gratitude of the new king with the government of Babylon, B.C. 826. *Diod.* 2.—*Paterc.* 1. c. 6.—*Justin.* 1. c. 3.

BEL'GÆ, a warlike people of ancient Gaul, separated from the Celtæ by the rivers Matrona and Sequana. Their country, according to Strabo, extended from the Rhine to the Loire. *Cæs. de Bell. Gall.* 1. c. 1. l. 2, &c —*Mela*, 3. c. 2.—*Strab.* 4. Some of the Britons were also called Belgæ, as, no doubt, descended from a Belgic colony. *Cæs. B. G.* 5. c. 12.

BEL'GICA, one of the four provinces of Gaul near the Rhine, according to the division made by Augustus, comprehending the modern territories called the Netherlands. According to the description given by Julius Cæsar, Belgica formed a third part of Gaul.

BELGI'TES, a people of Pannonia. *Plin.* 3. c. 25.

BEL'GIUM, the capital of Gallia Belgica. The word is often used to express the whole country. *Cæs. Bell. Gall.* 5. c. 24.

BEL'GIUS, a general of Gaul, who destroyed an army of Macedonians. *Justin.* 25. c. 2.—*Polyb.* 2. ——A river of Libya. *Hesych.*

BEL'IDES, a surname given to the daughters, or rather grand-daughters, of Belus. *Ovid Met.* 4. v. 463.

BELI'DES, a name applied to Palamedes, as descended from Belus. *Virg. Æn.* 2. v. 82.

BE'LION, a river of the Celtiberi. *Strab.*

BELIP'PO, a town of Hispania Bætica, *Plin.* 3. c. 1.

BELIS'AMA, the name of Minerva among the Gauls. The word signified queen of heaven. She was represented with a helmet on her head, but without either her ægis or her spear in her hand. *Cæs. Bell. Gall.* 6.

BELISA'RIUS, a celebrated general, who, in the degenerate age of Justinian, emperor of Constantinople, renewed all the glorious victories, battles, and triumphs which had rendered the first Romans so distinguished in the time of their republic. He died, after a life of military glory, and cruel experience of royal ingratitude, A.D. 555. Some historians have imagined that the account of his having been deprived of sight, and of his being obliged to beg for charity to support life, with the *Date obolum Belisario*, is a fabrication of modern times.

BELISTI'DA, a woman who obtained a prize at Olympia. *Paus.* 5. c. 8.

BELI'TÆ or BEL'ITÆ, a nation of Asia, present at the battle of Arbela. *Curt.* 4. c. 12.

BELLER'OPHON, son of Glaucus king of Ephyre, by Eurymede, was at first called Hipponomus. The murder of his brother, whom some call Alcimenus or Beller, procured him the name Bellerophon, or murderer of Beller. After this murder, Bellerophon fled to the court of Prœtus, king of Argos. Here the king's wife, called Antæa or Sthenobœa, fell in love with him; and as he slighted her passion, she accused him before her husband of attempts upon her virtue. Prœtus, instead of offering violence to the stranger, and unwilling to violate the laws of hospitality by punishing Bellerophon, sent him away to his father-in-law, Jobates, king of Lycia, and gave him a letter, in which he begged the king to punish with death a man who had treated his daughter so dishonourably. From that circumstance, all letters which are of an unfavourable tendency to the bearer are called letters of Bellerophon. Jobates, to satisfy his son-in-law, sent him to conquer a horrible monster, called Chimæra, in which dangerous expedition he hoped, and was even assured, that he must perish. *Vid.* Chimæra. But Minerva supported him, and, with the aid of the winged horse Pegasus, he conquered the monster, and returned victorious. After this, Jobates sent him against the Solymi, but he obtained another victory, and afterwards conquered the Amazons by the king's order. At his return from this third expedition, Bellerophon was attacked by a party sent against him by Jobates, but he destroyed all his assassins. Upon this, Jobates no longer sought his life, but gave him his daughter in marriage, and made him his successor on the throne of Lycia, as he was without male issue. Some authors have maintained that Bellerophon attempted to fly to heaven upon the horse Pegasus; and that Jupiter sent an insect, which stung the horse, and threw down the rider, who wandered upon the earth in the greatest melancholy and dejection till the day of his death, which happened one generation before the Trojan war. Bellerophon had two sons, Isander, who was killed in his war against the Solymi, and Hippolochus, who succeeded to the throne after his death, besides one daughter, called Laodamia. The wife of Bellerophon is called Philonoe, by Apollodorus, and Achemone by Homer. *Scholiast. Pind in Olymp.* 13.—*Homer. Il.* 6. v. 156, &c.—*Juv.* 10.—*Apollod.* 2. c. 3. l. 3. c. 1.—*Hygin.* fab. 157 & 243. *P.A.* 2. c. 18.—*Hesiod. Theog.* v. 325. —*Horat.* 4. od. 11. v. 26.—*Paus.* 9. c, 31.

BEL'LERUS, BELLE'RUS, or BEL'LER, a brother of Hipponomus. *Vid.* Bellerophon.

BELLETHA'NI, a people of Hispania Citerior, on the Iberus. *Plin.* 3. c. 3.

BELLIE'NUS, a Roman, whose house was set on fire at Cæsar's funeral, *Cic. Phil.* 2. c. 36.

BELLO'NA, the goddess of war, daughter of Phorcys and Ceto, was called by the Greeks Enyo, and often confounded with Minerva. She was anciently called Duelliona, and was the sister of Mars, or, according to others, his daughter, or his wife. She prepared the chariot of Mars when he was going to war; and she appeared in battles armed with a whip, to animate the combatants, with dishevelled hair, and a flaming torch in her hand. The Romans paid great adoration to this divinity; but she was held in the greatest veneration by the Cappadocians, and chiefly at Comana, where she had above 3,000 priests. Her temple at Rome was without the gates, near the Porta Carmentalis. In it the senators gave audience to foreign ambassadors, and to generals returned from war. At the gate was a small column, called *the column of war*, over which they threw a spear whenever war was declared against an enemy. The priests of this goddess consecrated themselves by great incisions in their body, and particularly in the thigh, of which they received the blood in their hands to offer as a sacrifice to the goddess. In their wild enthusiasm they often predicted bloodshed and wars, the defeat of enemies, or the besieging of towns. *Juv.* 4. v. 124.—*Varro de L. L.* 5.—*Hesiod. Theog.* v. 270. —*Paus.* 4. c. 30.—*Virg. Æn.* 8. v. 703.—*Stat. Theb.* 2. v. 718. l. 7. v. 73.—*Ital.* 5. v. 221.—*Lactant. de Fals. R.* 21.—*Alex.* 3. c. 12.—*Quint. Calab.* 8.—*Servius in Æn. loco cit.* & 12. v. 118.

BELLONA'RII, the priests of Bellona.

BELLOV'ACI or BELLOVA'CI, a people of Gaul, conquered by J. Cæsar. They inhabited the modern country of Beauvais in the isle of France, east of the Seine. *Cæs. Bell.* 2. c. 4 & 8.

BELLOVE'SUS, a king of the Celtæ, who, in the reign of Tarquinius Priscus, was sent at the head of a colony to Italy by his uncle Ambigatus. He is supposed to have been the first Gaul who crossed the Alps, and is considered the founder of Milan. *Liv.* 5. c. 34.

BEL'LUS, an orator of king Gentius. *Liv.* 44. c. 31.

BE'LON, a general in Alexander's army. *Curt.* 6. c. 11.——A city and river of Hispania Bætica. *Strab.* 3.

BELU'NUM, a town of the Veneti. *Cluver. It. Ant.* p. 118.

BE'LUS, one of the most ancient kings of Babylon, about 1800 years before the age of Semiramis, was made a god after death, and worshipped with much veneration by the Assyrians and Babylonians. He was supposed to be the son of the Osiris of the Ægyptians. The temple of Belus was regarded as the most ancient and most magnificent in the world. It had lofty towers, and was enriched by all the succeeding monarchs till the age of Xerxes, who, after his unfortunate expedition against Greece, plundered and demolished it. Among the riches which it contained, were many statues of massy gold, one of which was forty feet high. *Joseph. Ant. Jud.* 10.—*Herodot.* 1. c. 181, &c.—*Strab.* 16.—*Arrian.* 7.—*Diod.* 1, &c.—*Euseb. Chron.*—*Selden de Diis Syr.* 2. c. 1.—*Eustath. in Dionys. Per.*—*Stephan. Byz.*——A king of Ægypt, said to be the son of Epaphus and Libya, the father of Agenor.——The father of Danaus and Ægyptus, supposed by some to be Neptune, from whom the daughters of Danaus were called Belides. *Ovid. Met.* 4. v. 463.——A son of Phœnix the son of Agenor, who reigned in Phœnicia.

BE'LUS, one of his descendants, was the father of Dido who founded Carthage. *Virg. Æn.* 1. v. 621.

BE'LUS, a river of Syria, falling into the Mediterranean near Ptolemais. It abounds in sand proper for the manufacture of glass: and it was there that glass was first accidentally invented. *Plin.* 5. c. 19. l. 36. c. 26.

BENA'CUS, a lake of Italy, now Lago di Garda, through which the Mincius flows into the Po. *Virg. G.* 2. v. 160. *Æn.* 10. v. 205.—*Plin.* 9. c. 22.

BENDIDI'UM, a temple of Diana Bendis. *Liv.* 38. c. 41.

BEN'DIS, a name of Diana among the Thracians and their northern neighbours. *Strab.* 9.—*Suidas.* Her festivals, called *Bendidia*, were introduced into Athens, and celebrated on the 20th of the month called Thargelion. *Liv.* 38. c. 41.—*Procl. in Tim.* 1.

BE'NE, a city of Crete. *Steph.*

BENEVEN'TUM, a town of the Hirpini, built by Diomedes, 28 miles from Capua. Its original name was Maleventum, changed into the more auspicious word of Beneventum, when the Romans planted a colony there. It abounds in remains of ancient sculpture more than any other town in Italy. *Plin.* 3. c. 11.

BENLAU'NI, a people of Vindelicia. *Ptol.*

BENTHESICY'ME or BENTHESIC'YME, a daughter of Neptune, the nurse of Eumolpus. *Apollod.* 3. c. 15.

BEPOLITA'NUS, a youth whose life was saved by the delay of the executioner, who wished not to stain his fine clothes with blood. *Plut. de Virt. Mul.*

BER'ABÆ, a town of India without the Ganges. *Ptol.*

BERABON'NA, an emporium of India without the Ganges. *Id.*

BERAM'BE, a city of Babylonia. *Id.*

BER'BICÆ, a savage nation who are said to have destroyed their relations when arrived at a certain age. *Ælian. V. H.* 4. c. 1.

BERÆ'A, a town of Syria, at the north of the Orontes, 90 miles from the sea, and 100 from the Euphrates, now called Aleppo.——A town of some consequence in Macedonia, at the south of Pella near the bay of Therma, called also Berœa, or Berrhœa. It is the same which is mentioned in the Acts of the Apostles. c. 17. *Liv.* 44. c. 45. l. 45. c. 29.—*Thucyd.* 1. c. 61.

BER'BIS, a lake of Thessaly.——A town of Pannonia, now Berzenche. *Ptol.*

BERCERE'LIUS, a mountain of Macedonia. *Id.*

BERCORA'TES, a people of Gallia Aquitanica. *Plin.* 4. c. 19.

BER'DES, an officer of Alexander, sent by him to the Scythians. *Curt.* 8. c. 1.

BERECYN'THES, a people of Phrygia. *Strab.* 10.

BERECYN'THIA, a surname of Cybele, derived from mount Berecynthus in Phrygia, where she was particularly worshipped. She has been celebrated by Catullus in a poem entitled *De Berecynthiâ & Aty. Ovid. Fast.* 4. v. 355. *Met.* 11. v. 16.—*Catull.* 64.—*Plin.* 5. c. 29. l. 16. c. 15.—*Diod.* 5.—*Stat. Theb.* 4. v. 782.—*Virg. Æn.* 9. v. 82.

BERE'GRA, a town of the Prætuii in Italy. *Ptolemy* calls it erroneously Beretra. *Plin.* 3. c. 13.

BERENI'CE or BERONI'CE, a woman famous for her beauty, and mother of Ptolemy Philadelphus by Lagus. *Ælian. V. H.* 14. c. 43.—*Theocrit.*—*Paus.* 1. c. 7. [A fine bronze bust of this queen has been dug up at Herculaneum, and is in the collection of bronzes at Portici.

BERENI'CE, a daughter of Philadelphus who married Antiochus, king of Syria, after he had divorced Loadice, his former wife. After the death of Philadelphus, Loadice was recalled, and mindful of the cruel treatment which she had received, she poisoned her husband, placed her son on the vacant throne, and murdered Berenice and her child at Antioch, to which place she had fled, B.C. 248.——A daughter of Ptolemy Auletes, who usurped her father's throne for some time, and after strangling her husband Seleucus, married Archelaus, a priest of Bellona. Her father regained his power, and put her to death, B.C. 55.——The wife of Mithridates, who, when conquered by Lucullus, ordered all his wives to destroy themselves, for fear the conqueror should offer violence to their persons. She accordingly drank poison; but this not operating soon enough, she was strangled by a eunuch.——The mother of Agrippa, who shines in the history of the Jews, as daughter-in-law of Herod the Great.——A daughter of Agrippa, who married her uncle Herod, and afterwards Polemon, king of Cilicia. She was accused by Juvenal of committing incest with her brother Agrippa. It was said that she was passionately loved by Titus, who would have made her his wife, but for the prejudices entertained by the Romans against the Jews. *Juv.* 6. v. 157.—*Suet. Tit.* 7.—*Joseph. Ant.* 20. c. 5.—*Tacit. Hist.* 2. c. 2.——A daughter of Philadelphus and Arsinoe, who married her own brother Evergetes, whom she tenderly loved. When he went on a dangerous expedition, she vowed all the hair of her head to the goddess Venus, if he returned in safety. Some time after his victorious return, the locks which she had consecrated in the temple of Venus, disappeared; and Conon, an astronomer, to make his court to the queen, publicly reported that Jupiter had carried them away and made them a constellation. Berenice was put to death by her own son, B.C. 221. *Catull.* 67.—*Eratosth.* 12.—*Hygin. P. A.* 2. c. 24.—*Justin.* 26. c. 3. This name was common to many of the queens and princesses of the Ptolemean family in Ægypt.——A wife of king Attalus.——A woman who was the daughter, sister, and mother of persons who had been crowned at the Olympic games. In consequence of the honours thus obtained by the members of her family, she was the only woman allowed to be present at the games. *Val. Max.* 8. c. 15.—*Ælian. V. H.* 10. c. 1.

BERENI'CE, a city of Libya. *Strab.*—*Mela*, 3. c. 8.——The name of two towns in Arabia. *Strab.* 16. One in Ægypt, on the shores of the Red Sea, nearly under the tropic of Cancer, where the ships from India generally landed their cargoes. *Plin.* 6. c. 23. Another near the Syrtes, sometimes called Hesperis, as the gardens of the Hesperides were supposed by some authors to have been situated in the neighbourhood. *Plin.* 5. c. 5.—*Strab.* 17.

BERENIC'IDÆ, part of the tribe Ptolemais. *Steph.*

BERENI'CIS, a part of Africa near the town of Berenice, in the province of Cyrene. *Lucan.* 9. v. 523.

BERENTHE'ACES, a river of Arcadia. *Paus.* 1. 1.

BE'RES, a city of Thrace. *Steph.*

BERE'THIS, a village of Æthiopia, near the Nile. *Ptol.*

BE'REX, a nation between India and Æthiopia. *Steph.*

BER'GE, a city of Thrace. The inhabitants were called Bergæi. *Steph.*—*Hesych.*

BER'GIDUM, now Berdun, a city of Spain. *Ptol.*

BER'GION and AL'BION, two giants, sons of Neptune, who opposed Hercules as he attempted to cross the Rhone, and were killed with stones from Heaven. *Mela*, 2. c. 7.

BERGIS'TANI or BERGISTA'NI, a people of Spain, at the east of the Iberus. *Liv.* 34. c. 16.

BER'GIUM, a city of Germany. *Ptol.*

BER'GOS (or, *-i, -orum*), a town in the northern parts of Europe, supposed to be Bergen in Norway. *Plin.* 4. c. 16.

BER'GULA, a town of Thrace, called Bergulum, and also Arcadiapolis, by *Cedrenus.* It is now Bergas. *Ptol.*

BERGU'SIA, a city of Hispania Tarraconensis. *Livy*, 21. c. 19. and *Stephanus*, call the people Bargusii. ——A town of Gallia Narbonensis. *Antonin.*

BE'RIS or BI'RES, a small river in Cappadocia. *Arrian in Peripl.*——A mountain of Armenia.

BER'MIUS, a mountain of Macedonia. *Herodot.* 8. c. 138.

BER'NAMA, a town of the Hedetani, in Spain. *Ptol.*

BER'OE, an old woman of Epidaurus, nurse to Semele. Juno assumed her features, when she persuaded Semele not to grant her favours to Jupiter, if he did not appear before her in all the majesty of a god. *Hygin.* fab. 167 & 179.—*Ovid. Met.* 3. v. 278.——The wife of Doryclus, whose form was assumed by Iris at the instigation of Juno, when she advised the Trojan women to burn the fleet of Æneas in Sicily. *Virg. Æn.* 5. v. 620.——One of the Oceanides, attendant upon Cyrene. *Virg. G.* 4. v. 341.

BEROE'A. *Vid.* Beræa.

BERONI'CE. *Vid.* Berenice.

BERO'SUS, a native of Babylon, priest of Belus. He passed into Greece, for the purpose of acquiring information, and remained a long time at Athens. He composed a history of Chaldæa, signalized himself by his astrological predictions, and was rewarded for his learning with a statue in the Gymnasium at Athens. The age in which he lived is not precisely ascertained, though some fix it in the reign of Alexander, or 268 years B.C. Some fragments of his Chaldæan history are preserved by *Josephus contra Apion & in Antiq. Jud.* 105. The book which is now extant under his name, and which speaks of kings who never existed, is a suppositititious fabrication, imposed upon the world by Annius. Some suppose that there were two persons of this name, one who flourished about the 35th Olympiad, and another under Alexander the Great. *Fabr. B. Gr.* l. 3. c. 21, &c.—*Plin.* 7. c. 37.—*Vitruv.* 9. c. 7.

BERO'SUS, a hill on mount Taurus with three fountains.

BERRE'SA, a town of Æthiopia. *Plin.* 6. c. 29.

BERRHŒ'A, a town of Macedonia. *Thucyd.* 1. c. 61. *Vid.* Beræa.

BERSA'NE, a widow beloved by Alexander the Great. *Diod. Sic.*

BER'SIMA, a city of Mesopotamia. *Ptol.*

BER'TA, a city of Besantia in Macedonia. *Id.*

BERTIS'CAS, a mountain of Macedonia. *Id.*

BERU'NA, afterwards Verona, a city of Italy. *Steph.*

BERY'TUS or BER'YTUS, now Berut, an ancient town of Phœnicia, on the shores of the Mediterranean, famous in the age of Justinian for the study of the law. *Plin.* 5. c. 20.

BE'SA, a fountain in Thessaly. *Strab.* 8.——The name of a god worshipped at Abydus, in Ægypt. ——A city in Ægypt, in the Thebais, afterwards called Antinopolis by Adrian.

BES'ADÆ or PLA'DÆ, a people of India without the Ganges. *Ptol.*

BES'ARO, a city of Hispania Bætica. *Plin.* 3. c. 1.

BES'BICUS, a small island near Cyzicus. *Steph.*

BES'CIA, a city of the Ausones. *Id.* It is supposed to have been in Samnium, and that the inhabitants founded the city now called Vesciano, in its neighbourhood.

BESID'IÆ, a town of the Brutii. *Liv.* 30. c. 19.

BESIP'PO, a town of Hispania Bætica, where the geographer Mela was born. It is now Beier. *Mela*, 2. c. 6.

BES'SA, a city of Phocis.——A citadel in Peloponnesus. *Strab.*——A town in the country of the Opuntii, the inhabitants of which formed part of the forces of Ajax Oileus, during the Trojan war. *Steph.*

BES'SARA, a city of Assyria. *Ptol.*

BES'SI, a people of Thrace, on the left side of the Strymon, who maintained themselves by plunder. They were first attacked and defeated by Lucullus, and in after times they were described as yielding to the precepts of the Gospel, and exchanging a roughness that exceeded their inclement snows for the meekness and humility of lambs. *Strab.* 7.—*Ptol.* 3. c. 11.—*Liv.* 39. c. 53.—*Cic. Pis.* 14.—*Plin.* 4. c. 11.—*Eutrop.* 6.—*Claudian. de Cons. Mall.* 39.—*Flacc.* 2. v. 231.—*Paulinus ad Nicetam.*—*Ovid. Trist.* 4. el. 1. v. 67.—*Herodot.* 7. c. 111.

BES'SUS, a governor of Bactriana, who, after the battle of Arbela, seized Darius, his sovereign, and put him to death. After this murder, he assumed the title of king, but he was some time after brought before Alexander, who gave him to Oxatres, the brother of Darius. The prince ordered his hands and ears to be cut off, and his body to be exposed on a cross, and shot at by the soldiers. *Justin.* 12. c. 5.—*Curt.* 6 & 7.——A parricide, who confessed the murder which he had committed, upon destroying a nest of swallows, which, as he observed, reproached him with his crime. *Plut.*

BESSY'GA, a town of India, of which the people were called Bessygicæ. *Steph.*

BES'TIA L. a seditious Roman, who conspired with Catiline against his country. *Cic. Phil.* 2.

BE'TA, a city on the Arabian side of the Æthiopic Gulph. *Plin.* 6. c. 29.

BETAR'MONES, a name of the Corybantes. *Hom. Od.* 9. v. 250. &c.

BETHAR'GA, a town of Media. *Ptol.*

BE'TIS, a river in Spain. *Vid.* Bætis.

BE'TIS, a governor of Gaza. *Vid.* Batis.

BETUL'LO, a river and town of Spain. *Mela*, 2. c. 6. The river is now Beson. *Vid.* Bætulo.

BETU'NICA, a city of Spain, near Asturica. *Antonin.*

BETU'SA, a town of Mesopotamia, near the Tigris. *Ptol.*

BEU'DI, a city of the greater Phrygia. *Liv.* 38. c. 15.

BEZE'NI, a people of Galatia. *Ptol.*

BEZI'RA or BAZI'RA, according to *Arrian*, a town of India. *Curt.* 8. c. 10.

BI'A a daughter of Pallas by Styx. *Apollod.* 1. c. 2.

BIA'NA, a town of Arabia Felix. *Ptol.*

BIANDI'NA, a town of Laconia, now Prignico, or Rampano, according to others. *Id.*

BIA'NOR, a son of Tiberius, and Manto, the daughter of Tiresias, who received the surname of Œnus, and reigned over Etruria. He built a town, which he called Mantua, after his mother's name. His tomb was to be seen in the age of Virgil, on the road between Mantua and Andes. *Virg. Ecl.* 9. v. 60. *Æn.* 10. v. 198. *& Servius. locis cit.*——A Trojan chief killed by Agamemnon. *Homer. Il.* 11. v. 92.——A centaur killed by Theseus. *Ovid. Met.* 12. v. 345.

BI'AS, son of Amythaon, was king of Argos. He fell in love with Perone, daughter of Neleus, king of Pylus; but the father refused to give his daughter in marriage before he received the oxen of Iphiclus. Bias procured the oxen by means of his brother, Melampus, (*vid* Melampus,) and obliged Neleus to give his daughter in marriage. *Homer. Od.* 11.—*Paus.* 2. c. 6. & 18. l. 4. c. 34.—*Apollod.* 1. c. 9.——A Grecian prince, who went to the Trojan war. *Homer. Il.*

BI'AS, a river of Peloponnesus. *Paus.* 4. c. 34.

BI'AS, one of the seven wise men of Greece, son of Tautamidas, born at Priene, which by his counsels and influence, he long saved from ruin. He flourished B.C. 566, and died in the arms of his grandson. The words of *Omnia mea mecum porto*, which he is said to have uttered when his native city was taken, are attributed to him. *Diog.* 1.—*Plut. in Symp.*—*Val Max.* 7. c. 2.—*Paus.* 10. c. 24.—*Cic. Amic.* 16. *Parador*, 1.—*Auson. de 7 Sap.* —*Sidon. Carm.* 2. v. 161. [There is a fine terminal bust of this philosopher in the Vatican.]

BIA'TIA, now Baeza, a town of Spain. *Ptol.*

BIBAC'TA, an island at the mouth of the Indus. *Arrian. Indic.*

BIBAC'ULUS M. FU'RIUS, a Latin poet of Cremona in the age of Cicero, intimate with the poet Gallus, and Cato. He composed annals in Iambic verses, epigrams full of wit and humour, and other poems admired by the ancients for their ease, neatness, and elegance. Horace. however, has ridiculed his verses, of which only sixteen remain. *Horat.* 2. sat. 5. v. 41.—*Quintil.* 10.—*Euseb. Chron. Suet in Cæs.*—*Plin. in Præf. H. Nat.*—*Macrob. Sat.* 6. c. 1.——A prætor, &c. *Val. Max.* 1. c. 1.

BIB'ACUM, a city of Germany, now Bibrach. *Ptol.*

BIB'AGA, an island of India, famous for oysters. *Plin.* 6. c. 21.

BIB'ALI, a people of Hispania Tarraconensis. *Ptol.*

BIB'ASIS, a river of India. *Id.*

BIBE'SIA or POTI'NA, a goddess among the Romans, who presided over the liquors which were taken during meals. Another divinity, called Edesia, presided over the taking of the solid food. *Donat. in* 3 *Ec. Virg.*—*Aug. de Civ. D.* 4. c. 2.

BIB'LIA or BIL'LIA, a Roman lady famous for her chastity. She married Duillius.

BIB'LINA, a country of Thrace. *Suidas.*

BIB'LIS, a fountain of Lycia, into which Biblis, the sister of Caunus, was changed. *Ovid. Met.* 9. v. 662.

BIB'LUS or BYB'LUS. *Vid.* Byblus.

Bib'lus, a city of Phœnicia. *Curt.* 4.——A river of Naxus. *Steph.*

BIBRAC'TE, a large town of the Ædui in Gaul, where Cæsar often wintered. Under Augustus it received the name of Augustodunum, and is now Autun. *Cæs. Bell. G.* 7. c. 55, &c.

BI'BRAX, a town of the Remi, now Bievre. *Cæs. B. G.* 2. c. 6.

BIB'ROCI, a people of Britain, supposed to have inhabited the country in the neighbourhood of Bray, in Berkshire. *Cæs. B G.* 5. c. 21.

BIB'ULUS, a son of M. Calpurnius Bibulus by Portia, Cato's daughter. He was consul with Cæsar, but his services were so eclipsed by those of his more popular colleague, that he was regarded as of little consequence in the state, according to this distich mentioned by *Suetonius, in Jul.* c. 20.

Non Bibulo quicquam nuper, sed Cæsare factum est;
Nam Bibulo fieri consule nil memini.

Bib'ulus, one of the friends of *Horace*, 1 sat. 10. v. 86.——The surname of Bibulus belonged to the family of the Calpurnii.

BI'CES, a marsh near the Palus Mœotis. *Flacc.* 6. c. 68.

BI'CON, a Greek who assassinated Athenodorus, because he had made himself master of a colony which Alexander had made at Bactra. *Curt.* 9. c. 7.

BICOR'NIGER, a surname of Bacchus.

BICOR'NIS, the name of Alexander among the Arabians.

BICUR'GIUM, a city of Germany, now Erford. *Ptol.*

BI'DA, a city of Mauritania Cæsariensis. *Id.*

BID'ERIS, a city of India within the Ganges. *Id.*

BIDI'NE, a city of Scythia. *Suidas.*

BIDI'NI, a people of Sicily. *Plin.* 3. c. 8.

BIEN'DIUM, a harbour of Hispania Citerior. *Id.* 4. c. 20.

BIE'NOR, a noble person of Cyzicum, slain by the Argonauts. *Val. Flacc.* 3. v. 112.

BIE'PHI, a people of Dacia. *Ptol.*

BIFOR'MIS, a surname of Bacchus. He received it because he changed himself into an old woman, to fly from the persecution of Juno, or, perhaps, because he was represented sometimes as a young, and sometimes as an old man; or because wine, over which he presided, altered the feelings and character of men, and from sedate, sober, and grave, rendered them furious, intemperate, and disorderly. *Natal. Com.* 5. c. 13. The same name is applied, but not frequently, to Janus. *Ovid. Fast.* 1. v. 98.

BI'FRONS, a surname of Janus, because he was represented by the Romans with *two faces*, as acquainted with the past and future. *Virg. Æn.* 7. v. 180. l. 12. v. 198.—*Ovid. Fast.* 1. v. 65.—*Macrob. Sat.* 1. c. 9.

BIGER'RA, a city of Hispania Tarraconensis. *Ptol.*—*Plin.*

BIGERRIO'NES or BIGERRO'NES, called also Begerri by *Pliny*, 4. c. 19., a people of Gallia Aquitanica.

BI'GIS, a city of Drangiana. *Ptol.*

BI'I, a people of Upper Pannonia. *Id.*

BIL'BILIS, now Xiloca, a town of Celtiberia, where Martial was born. *Mart.* 1 epigr. 50.——A river of Spain. *Justin.* 44. c. 3.

BILBI'NA, a city of Persia. *Steph.*

BI'LIS, a river of Asia, not far from Heraclea. *Plin.* 6. c. 1.

BILLÆ'US, a river of Paphlagonia. *Arrian.*—*Apol. Argon.* l. 2.

BIMA'TER, a surname of Bacchus, which signifies that he had *two mothers*, because when he was taken from his mother's womb, he was placed till his second birth, in the thigh of his father Jupiter. *Ovid. Met.* 4. v. 12.—*Nat. Com.* 5. c. 13.

BIMA'TRA, a city of Mesopotamia. *Ptol.*

BINAG'ARA, a city of India within the Ganges. *Id.*

BIN'GIUM, a town of Germany on the Rhine. *Tac. Hist.* 4. c. 70.

BIN'NA, a city of Assyria. *Ptol.*

BINSIT'TA, a town of Mauritania Cæsariensis. *Id.*

BIN'THA, a city of the interior of Libya. *Id.*

BI'ON, a philosopher and sophist of Borysthenes, in Scythia, who rendered himself famous for his knowledge of poetry, music, and philosophy. He made the character and person of every body the object of his satire, and his compositions were distinguished for clearness of expression, facetiousness, wit, and pleasantry. He particularly imitated Archilochus and Hipponax in his compositions. He died 241 B.C. after atoning for the impious tenets of his younger years, by so firm a persuasion of the existence and power of Providence, that it even bordered upon superstition. *Cic. Tusc.* 3. c. 26.—*Horat.* 2. ep. 2. v. 60.—*Diog. in Vitâ.*——A Greek poet of Smyrna, who wrote pastorals in an elegant style. Moschus, his friend and disciple, mentions that he died by poison, but the precise time at which he lived is a subject of dispute among the learned. *Saxius* thinks that he lived about 145 B.C. Of his poems, besides some few fragments, these are now extant only six idyllia, written with elegance and simplicity, purity and ease. There are many good editions of this poet's works, generally printed with those of Moschus; the best of which are those of Heskin, 8vo, Oxon. 1748, of Schwebelius, 1746, of Harles, 1780. *Fabr. B. Gr.* l. 3. c. 16.——A soldier in Alexander's army, &c. *Curt.* 4. c. 13.——A native of Propontis, in the age of Pherecydes.——A man of Syracuse, who wrote a treatise on rhetoric.——A native of Abdera, disciple of Democritus. He first found out that there were certain parts of the earth where there were six months of perpetual light and darkness alternately.——A man of Soli, who composed a history of Æthiopia.——A person who wrote nine books on rhetoric, which he called by the names of the muses, and hence *Bionei sermones* mentioned by *Horace*, 2. ep. 2. v. 60.—*Diod.* 4.—*L. Gyrald. de P. Hist. Dial.* 3 & 6.——A tragic poet. *Fabr. B. Gr.* l. 2. c. 19.

BIPEDIM'NI, a people of Gallia Aquitanica. Their city is now Pamiers. *Plin.* 4. c. 19.

BIRAC'ELUM, a city of Etruria, now Vicarello. *Ptol.*

BIR'DAMA, a town of India within the Ganges. *Id.*

BIR'RHUS. *Vid.* Cœlius.

BI'SA, a city of Thrace. *Steph.*——A place of Attica, in the tribe Antiochus. *Strab.* 8.

BISAL'TÆ, a people of Scythia, or according to some, of Thrace or Macedonia. Their country was called Bisaltia. *Civ.* 44. c. 45. l. 45. c. 29.—*Plin.* 4. c. 10.—*Diod.* 4.—*Servius in Georg.* 3. v. 461.

BISAL'TES, a man of Abydus, &c. *Herodot.* 6. c. 26.

BISAL'TIS, a patronymic of Theophane, by whom Neptune, under the form of a ram, had the golden ram. Her father's name was Bisaltes. *Ovid. Met.* 6. v. 117.—*Hygin.* fab. 188.

BISAN'THE or BISA'TE, a town of Thrace, on the shores of the Propontis. It is now Rodostro. *Herodot.* 7. c. 137.

BISGARGITA'NI, a people of Hispania Citerior. *Plin.* 3. c. 3.—*Ptol.*

BISTI'ROS, a city of Thrace. *Steph*

BIS'TON, son of Mars and Callirhoe, built Bistonia in Thrace, whence the Thracians are often called *Bistones*. *Herodot.* 7. c. 11.—*Ovid. Trist.* 10. v. 2[illegible]. *Met.* 13. v. 430.—*Ital.* 2. v. 76.—*Seneca in Her. Oet.* 1042. *In Furent.* 226.—*Plin.* 4. c. 14.—*Lucan* 7. v. 569.

BIS'TONIS or BISTO'NIS, a lake of Thrace, near Abdera. *Herodot.* 7. c. 109.

BITH'IAS, a city of Mesopotamia. *Ptol.*

BI'THUS. *Vid.* Bacchius.

BITH'YÆ, a certain race of women in Scythia, whose eyes, as *Pliny*, l. 7. c. 2. reports, killed those who gazed upon them for some time.

BITHYN'IA, a country of Asia Minor, formerly called Bebrycia. It was bounded by the Euxine on the north, on the south by Phrygia and Mysia, on the west by the Propontis, and on the east by Paphlagonia. The country was first invaded by the Thracians, under Bithynus the son of Jupiter, who gave it the name of Bithynia. It was once a powerful kingdom. *Strab.* 12.—*Herodot.* 7. c. 75.—*Mela*, 1 & 2.—*Claud in Eutr.* 2. v. 247.—*Steph. Byzant.* According to *Pausanias*, 8. c. 9. the inhabitants came from Mantinea in Peloponnesus.

BIT'TIAS, a Trojan, son of Alcanor and Hiera, brought up in a wood sacred to Jupiter. He followed the fortunes of Æneas, and, with his brother, was killed by Rutuli, in Italy. *Virg. Æn.* 9. v. 672. l. 11. v. 396.——One of Dido's attendants, present when Æneas and the Trojans were introduced to the queen. *Virg. Æn.* 1. v. 742.

BITOA'NA, a city of Libya. *Ptol.*

BI'TON. *Vid.* Cleobis.——A writer on mechanics and warlike engines, who dedicated his book to king Attalus, which of that name is uncertain. Saxious supposes him to have lived in the 134th Olympiad. He also wrote on optics. *Fabr. B. Gr.* l. 3. c. 24.—*Sax. Onom.* 1. p. 108.—*Voss. de Math.* c. 48. sec. 22.

BITTI'GO, a mountain of India within the Ganges. *Ptol.*

BITUI'TUS or **BITU'ITUS**, a king of the Allobroges, conquered by a small number of Romans. *Val. Max.* 9. c. 6.—*Flor.* 3. c. 2.

BITUN'TUM, a town of Spain. *Mart.* 4. epigr. 55.

BITUR'GIA, a town of Etruria, probably founded by the Bituriges. *Ptol.*

BITU'RICUM, a town of Gaul, formerly the capital of the Belgæ. *Strab.* 4.

BITU'RIGES, a people of Gaul, divided from the Ædui by the river Ligeris. The country is now called Berry. *Cæs. Bell. G.* 7. c. 21.

BITU'RIS, a city of the Vascones in Spain. *Ptol.*

BITY'LA, an inland city of Laconia. *Id.*

BI'ULA, a city of Caria. *Strab.*

BIZ'ALA, an island near Taprobane. *Ptol.*

BIZ'IA, a citadel near Rhodope, belonging to the kings of Thrace. Tereus was born there. *Pausan.* 9.

BI'ZON, a city of Thrace swallowed up by the earth. *Plin.* 4. c. 11.

BIZO'NA, a city of Pontus. *Steph.*

BLAAN'DER, a city of Phrygia Major. *Ptol.*

BLAE'NE, a fruitful province of Pontus, where the general of Mithridates Eupator destroyed the forces of Nicomedes the Bithynian. *Strab.* 12.

BLÆ'SII, two Romans who killed themselves because Tiberius deprived them of the priesthood. *Tac. Ann.* 6. c. 40.

BLÆ'SUS JU'NIUS, a governor of Gaul. *Tacit. Hist.* 1. c. 59.——A surname given to Aristæus or Battus the founder of Cyrene, from his stammering. *Ovid. Ibin.* 541.—*Justin.* 13. c. 7.

BLAN'DA, a city of Italy, in the country of the Brutii, now Belvedere. *Mela*, 2. c. 4.——A city of Spain, now Blanes. *Id.* 2. c. 6.—*Plin.* 3. c. 3.

BLANDENO'NA, a place near Placentia. *Sic.* 2. ep. 15. *ad Quint.*

BLANDU'SIA, a fountain on the borders of the country of the Sabines, near Mandela, celebrated by Horace, who had there a country seat. *Horat.* 3. od. 13.

BLAS'CON, an island at the mouth of the Rhone, now Languillade. *Plin.* 3. c. 5.—*Strab.* 4.

BLASTOPHŒNI'CES, a people of Lusitania. *Appian. de Bell. Hisp.*

BLAU'DUS, a city of Phrygia. *Steph.*

BLEM'YES, a people of Africa, who, as is fabulously reported, had no heads, but had the eyes and mouth placed in the breast. *Mela*, 1. c. 4 & 9.

BLEMI'NA, a town of Arcadia. *Paus.* 8. c. 27.

BLE'RA, a city of Etruria, now Bieda. *Plin.* 3. c. 5.—*Ptol.*

BLESI'NON, a castle of the island of Corsica. *Strab.* 5.

BLIT'IUS CATULI'NUS, a Roman banished to an island of the Ægean sea after Piso's conspiracy, &c. *Tacit.* 15. *Ann.* c. 71.

BLIULÆ'I, a people of Arabia Felix. *Ptol.*

BLU'CIUM, a castle in Bithynia, where king Dejotarus kept his treasures. *Strab.* 12.

BOAC'TES, a river of Liguria. *Ptol.*

BOADICE'A or **BOADIC'EA**. *Vid.* Boudicea.

BO'Æ or **BOE'A**, a town of Laconia. *Paus.* 3. c. 21.

BOA'GRIUS, a river of Locris. *Strab.* 9.

BOA'RIUM, a market-place at Rome. *Plin.* 28. c. 2.

BOAU'LIA, a city of Scythia. *Steph.*

BOBO'NIA, a city of Italy, *Id.*

BOCA'LIAS, a small river in the island of Salamis. *Strab.* 9.

BOCA'LIUM, a town of Arcadia. *Plin.* 4. c. 6.

BOCA'NI, a people of Taprobane. *Ptol.*

BOCANUM HEM'ERUM, a city of Mauritania Tingitana, now Morocco. *Id.*

BOC'CAR or **BOC'CHAR**, a king of Mauritania. *Juvenal*, 5. v. 90, applies the word in a general sense to any native of Africa.

BOCCHO'RIS or **BOC'CHORIS**, a wise king and legislator of Ægypt. *Diod.* 1.

BOC'CHUS, a king of Gætulia, in alliance with Rome, who joined Jugurtha in his opposition to the Roman invades, and afterwards perfidiously delivered him to Sylla, the lieutenant of Marius. *Sallust. Jug.*—*Paterc.* 2. c. 12.

BOC'CORI, called also Concordienses, a people of Lusitania. *Plin.* 4. c. 22.

BODE'NI, a people of European Sarmatia. *Ptol.*

BODE'RIA or **BODO'TRIA**, the Frith of Forth in Scotland. *Ptol.*—*Tac. Agric.* 25.

BODINCOM'AGUM, a town near the Po, now Casal. *Plin.* 3. c. 16.

BODION'TII or **EBRODUN'TII**, a people of Sabaudia, whose town is now called Bonne. *Id.* 3. c. 20.

BODO'NA, a city of Thessaly. *Steph.*

BODU'NI, a people of Britain who surrendered to Claudius Cæsar. *Dio. Cass.* 60.

BODUOGNA'TUS, a leader of the Nervii, when Cæsar made war against them. *Cæs. Bell G.* 2. v. 23.

BOE'Æ, *Vid.* Boæ.

BŒ'BE, a town of Thessaly, near mount Ossa. *Ovid. Met.* 7. v. 231.——A lake of Crete. *Strab.* 9.

BŒBE'IS, a lake of Thessaly, near mount Ossa. *Lucan.* 7. v. 176.

BŒ'BIA LEX. *Vid.* Bæbia Lex.

BOEDRO'MIA, an Athenian festival instituted in commemoration of the assistance which the people of Athens received in the reign of Erechtheus, from Ion son of Xuthus, when their country was invaded by Eumolpus son of Neptune. The word is derived ἀπὸ τοῦ βοηδρομεῖν, *coming to help. Plutarch*, in his life of Theseus, says, that it was instituted in commemoration of the victory which Theseus obtained over the Amazons, in the month called at Athens Boedromion.

BOE'ON, a town of Taurica Chersonesus, now Czargati. *Ptol.*

BŒOTAR'CHÆ, the chief magistrates in Bœotia. *Liv.* 42. c. 43.

BŒO'TIA, a country of Greece, bounded on the north by Phocis, south by Attica, east by Eubœa, and west by the bay of Corinth. It was successively called Aonia, Messapia, Hyantis, Ogygia, and Cadmeis, and now forms a part of Livadia. It was called Bœotia, from Bœotus son of Itonus; or according to others, *a bove*, from a cow, by which Cadmus was led into the country where he laid the foundation of Thebes. The inhabitants were regarded as rude and illiterate, fonder of bodily strength than of mental excellence; yet their country produced many illustrious men, such as Pindar, Hesiod, Plutarch, &c. The mountains of Bæotia, particularly Helicon, were frequented by the Muses, to whom also many of their fountains and rivers were consecrated. *Herodot.* 2. c. 49. l. 5. c. 57.—*Ovid. Met.* 3. v. 10.—*Paus.* 9. c. 1, &c. —*C. Nep.* 7. c. 11.—*Strab.* 9.—*Justin.* 3, c. 6. l. 8. c. 4.—*Horat.* 2. ep. 1. v. 244.—*Diod.* 19.—*Liv.* 27. c. 30. l. 28. c. 8. l. 29. c. 12.

BŒO'TUS. *Vid.* Bootus.

BŒREBIS'TAS, a man who made himself absolute among the Getæ, by the strictness of his discipline. *Strab.* 7.

BOE'THIUS ANIC. MANL. TORQUA'TUS SEVERI'NUS, a celebrated Roman philosopher and poet, banished and afterwards punished with death, on suspicion of conspiracy, by Theodoric king of the Ostrogoths, A.D. 525. In his exile he was accompanied by his wife, Helpis, who shared and soothed his misfortunes, and who deserved his affection not less by her fondness for literature and poetry, than by her great mental fortitude. He left two sons. Patricius and Hypatius, who preserved their rank and consequence in the Roman state. It was during his imprisonment that he wrote his celebrated poetical treatise *De consolatione philosophiæ*, in five books. It may be said that with this respectable writer the Latin tongue, and the last remains of Roman dignity, sunk in the western world. The best edition of his works is that of Hagenau, 4to, 1491, or that of L. Bat. 1671, with the *notis variorum. Vossius de P. Latin.*—*Harles. Not. Lit. Rom.*. 1. p. 756.—*Sax. Onom.* 2. p. 15.

BOE'THUS, a stoic philosopher, mentioned by *Cicero, Div.* 1. c. 8. l. 2. c. 20.——A statuary. *Cic.*

in Verr. 4. c. 14.——A Carthaginian. *Paus.* 5. c. 17.——A foolish poet of Tarsus, who wrote a poem on the battle of Philippi. *Strab.* 14.

BŒ'US, one of the Heraclidæ.

BOGA'DIUM, a city of Germany, now Frislar. *Ptol.*

BOGDOMAN'TIS, a region of Asia Minor. *Id.*

BO'GES, a Persian, who destroyed himself and his family when besieged by the Athenians. *Herodot.* 7. c. 107.—*Paus.* 8. c. 8.

BO'GUD, a king of Mauritania in the interest of Cæsar. *Cæsar. Alex.* 59.

BOGUDIA'NA, a part of Mauritania Tingitana. *Plin.* 5. c. 2.

BO'GUS, a king of the Maurusii, present at the battle of Actium. *Strab.* 8.

BO'II, a people of Celtic Gaul, who, as is imagined, migrated into Cisalpine Gaul, and fixed their habitations in the northern provinces of Italy, on the banks of the Po. *Liv.* 5. c. 35.—*Plin.* 4. c. 18.—*Cæs. Bell. G.* 1. c. 28. l. 7. c. 17.—*Sil.* 4. v. 158.

BOIS'CUS, a poet of Cyzicus, who invented a peculiar Iambic metre. *Voss. de Re Poet.* l. 2. c. 25.

BOJA'NUM. *Vid.* Bovianum.

BOJOC'ALUS, a general of the Germans in the age of Tiberius. *Tacit. Ann.* 13. c. 55.

BOJODU'RUM, a city of Vindelicia, on the Danube, now Instat. *Ptol.*

BO'JON, a town of Cyrene. *Plin.* 5. c. 5.——A town of Doris in Greece. *Id.* 4. c. 7.

BO'LA, a town of the Æqui in Italy, of some consequence in the infancy of Rome. *Virg. Æn.* 6. v. 775.

BOL'ACA, a city of Triphylia in Peloponnesus. *Polyb.* 6.

BOLA'NUS, a man whom Horace represents as of the most irascible temper, and most inimical to loquacity. *Horat.* 1. sat. 9. v. 11.

BOLA'NUS MAR'CUS, a friend of Cicero. *Cic. ad. Fam.* 13. ep. 77.

BOL'BE, a marsh near Mygdonia, in Macedonia. *Thucyd.* 1. c. 58.

BOLBITI'NUM or BOLBIT'ICUM, one of the mouths of the Nile, with a town of the same name. *Herodot.* 2. c. 17. Also Bolbiti'ne.

BOL'BULÆ, a town and island in the Mediterranean. *Plin.* 5. c. 31.

BOLEN'TIUM, a city of Upper Pannonia. *Ptol.*

BOL'GIUS, a general of Gaul, in an expedition against Ptolemy, king of Macedonia. *Paus.* 10. c. 19.

BOLI'NA or BOL'INA, a virgin of Achaia, who rejected the addresses of Apollo, and threw herself into the sea to avoid his importunities. The god made her immortal. There was a city which bore her name in Achaia. *Paus.* 7. c. 23.—*Gyrald. H. D. Synt.* 5.

BOLINÆ'US, a river near Bolina. *Paus.* 7. c. 53.

BOLIN'GÆ, a people of Asia. *Plin.* 6. c. 20.

BOLIS'SUS, an island with a town of the same name, near Chius. *Thucyd.* 8. c. 24.

BOLOGE'SIA, a city near the Euphrates. *Steph.*

BOLOGESIPH'ORA, a city of Persia. *Id.*

BO'LUS, a king of the Cimbri, who killed a Roman ambassador. *Liv.* ep. 67.——A philosopher who wrote a book, *De Arte Medicâ*, and a history. *Suidas.*——A place not far from Cassandrea. *Polyæn.* 4. c. 6.

BOLU'TUS, a city of Illyria.——A city of Thesprotia. *Steph.*

BOM'BOS, a river of Cilicia. *Plin.* 5. c. 27.

BOMBYL'IA, a fountain of Bœotia. *Hesych.*

BOMIEN'SES, a people of Ætolia. *Thucyd.* 3. c. 96. —*Steph.*

BOMIL'CAR, a Carthaginian general, son of Amilcar, was suspected of conspiracy with Agathocles, and hanged in the forum, where he had received all his dignity. *Diod.* 26.—*Justin.* 22. c. 7.——An African, for some time the instrument of Jugurtha's cruelties. He at last conspired against him, and was put to death. *Sallust. Jug.* c. 35. 36. The name was common among the Carthaginians.

BOMI'TÆ, a town of Syria Antiochena. *Plin.* 5. c. 24.

BO'MO, an ancient name of Eubœa. *Hesych.*

BOMONI'CÆ, youths who were whipped at the altar of Diana Orthia, during the festival of the goddess. He who bore the lashes without uttering a groan, was declared victorious, and received a prize. *Paus.* 3. c. 16.—*Plut. in Lyc.*—*Hygin.* fab. 261.—*Servius in Æn.* 2. v. 116.

BO'NA DE'A, a name given to Ops, Vesta, Cybele, and Rhea, by the Greeks; and by the Latins to Fauna, or Fatua. This goddess was represented as so chaste, that no man but her husband saw her after her marriage; for which reason her festivals were celebrated only in the night by the Roman matrons in the houses of the highest officers of the state, and all the statues of men were carefully covered with a veil during their celebration. In the latter ages of the republic, however, the sanctity of these mysteries was profaned by the intrusion of men, and by the introduction of lasciviousness and debauchery. The celebration took place on the first of May. *Varro. apud Lact. de Fals. R.* 22. *Id apud Aug. de Civ.D* . 2. c. 4 & 5. —*Cic de Harusp. Resp.*—*Sueton. in Jul.* 6.—*Macrob. Sat.* 1. c. 12.—*L. Fenestella de Sacerd, R.* 1.—*Dion. Cass. Frag.* 57.—*Juv.* 6. v. 313.—*Propert.* 4. el. 10. v. 25.—*Ovid. de Art. Am.* 3. v. 637.

BON'CHÆ or BONCH'NÆ, a people between the rivers Euphrates and Cyrus. *Steph.*

BON'CHIS, a city of Æthiopia. *Id.*

BONDE'LIA, a town of Etruria, now Bagnone. *Ptol.*

BONIA'NUM, a town of Samnium. *Cic. pro Cluent.*

BON'NA, a town of Germany, on the Rhine, now Bona, in the Electorate of Cologne. *Tacit. H.* 4. c. 19.

BONO'NIA, called also Felsina, a town on the borders of the Rhine or Rheno, which flows from the Apennines into the Po. It is now called Bologna, and is famous for its public buildings, and for its paintings. *Val Max.* 8. c. 1. *Ital.* 8. v. 599.—*Tacit. Ann.* 12. c. 58.——A town of Gaul, now Boulogne. *Cluver.* 2. c. 12.

BONO'SUS, an officer of Probus, who assumed the imperial purple in Gaul. *Vopisc.* c. 15.——A bishop of Dacia, known in ecclesiastical history as the author of a heresy, which prevailed for upwards of 200 years. He died A.D. 410.

BO'NUS EVEN'TUS, a Roman deity, whose worship was first introduced into Italy by the peasants. He was represented holding a cup in his right hand, and in his left, ears of corn. His power was supposed to extend only over particular events, and not like that of Fortune, over the whole of human life. His statue, made by the hand of Praxiteles, was placed in the Capitol. *L. Gyrald. Hist. D.*—*Varro de R.R.* 1.—*Plin.* 34. c. 8.

BOOSCOE'TE, afterwards Germanicopolis, a city on the Hellespont. *Plin.* 5. c. *ult.*

BOOSU'RA, *(bovis cauda)*, a town of Cyprus, where Venus had a temple. *Strab.*

BOO'TES, a northern constellation, near the Ursa Major, also called Bubulcus and Arctophylax. Some suppose it to have been Icarus, the father of Erigone, who was killed by shepherds for inebriating them. Others maintain that it was Arcas, the son of Calisto, whom Jupiter placed in heaven, or else Erichthonius, king of Athens. *Hygin. P.A.* 2. c. 4.—*Dionys. Hal.* 1.—*Ovid. Fast.* 3. v. 405.—*Cic. de Nat. D.* 2. c. 42.

BOO'TUS or BŒO'TUS, a son of Neptune and Menalippa, exposed in the woods by his mother, but preserved by shepherds. *Hygin.* fab. 186.—*Paus.* 9. c. 1.

BO'RA, a mountain of Macedonia. *Liv.* 45. c. 29.

BORAM'MA, a retreat of robbers on mount Libanus. *Strab.* 16.

BORBETOM'AGUS, a town of the Vangiones on the western borders of the Rhine, now Worms, in the Palatinate, famous for the diets that have been held there.

BORCA'NI, a people of the Hirpini, in Italy. *Plin.* 3. c. 11.

BOR'COBE, a city of Thrace, near Lower Mœsia. *Id.* 4. c. 11.

BORCOVI'CUM, a town of Britain, now Berwick, at the mouth of the Tweed, in Scotland.

BO'REA, a town taken by Sextus Pompeius. *Cic.* 16. *ad Att.* ep. 4.

BORE'ADES, the descendants of Boreas, who long possessed the supreme power and the priesthood, in the island of the Hyperboreans. *Diod.* 1 & 2.

BO'REAS, the name of the north wind, represented as blowing with great violence from the Hyperborean mountains. According to the poets, he was son of Astræus and Aurora, but others make him son of the Strymon. He was passionately fond of Hyacinthus, (*vid.* Hyacinthus), and carried away

Orithyia, who had refused to receive his addresses, and by her he had Zetes and Calais, Cleopatra and Chione. He was worshipped as a deity, and represented with wings and white hair, and with distended mouth, blowing snow, storms, cold, hail, and all the inclement blasts of a northern climate. The Athenians dedicated altars to him, and to the winds, when Xerxes invaded Europe, and rewarded his supposed services by erecting him a temple on the banks of the Ilissus. He was also particularly honoured by the people of Megalopolis, and a large space of ground was set apart and consecrated to his divinity. Boreas changed himself into a horse, to unite himself with the mares of Dardanus, by which he had twelve mares so swift, that they ran, or rather flew over the sea, so as scarcely to wet their feet. *Homer. Il.* 20. v. 222.—*Hesiod. Theog.* v. 379.—*Apollod.* 3. c. 15.—*Herodot.* 7. c. 189.—*Ovid. Met.* 6. v. 700. *Trist.* 3. el. 10. v. 14. 45. *Ex. Pont.* 4. el. 10. v. 41.—*Hygin. Præf. Fab.*—*Aul. Gell.* 2. c. 22.—*Virg. Ec.* 7. v. 51. *G.* 1. v. 93, 370. l. 2. v. 316. l. 3. v. 278. *Æn.* 13. v. 350. l. 12. 365.—*Callim. in Delum.*—*Symonid. & Tyrtœus apud Stobœum.*—*Paus.* 1. c. 19. l. 8. c. 36.—*Natal. Comes*, 8. c. 11.—*Schol. Pind.* 4 *Pyth.*

BOREAS'MI, a festival at Athens, celebrated in honour of Boreas, who, as the Athenians supposed, was related to them on account of his marriage with Orithyia, the daughter of one of their kings. They attributed the overthrow of the fleet of Xerxes to the respect which he paid to his wife's native country. *Paus. Attic. & Arcad.*

BO'REUS, a Persian, &c. *Polyæn.* 7. c. 40.

BOR'GES, a Persian who burnt himself rather than submit to the enemy, &c. *Polyæn.* 7. c. 24.

BOR'GI, a people of Aria. *Ptol.*

BORGO'DI, a people of Asia. *Plin.* 6. c. 28.

BORMAN'ICO, a town of Gallia Narbonensis. *Id.* 3. c. 4.

BORMIS'CUS, a region of Macedonia, where the dogs tore Euripides in pieces. *Steph.*

BOR'NOS, a place of Thrace, near the shores of the Propontis. *C. Nep. in Alcib.* c. 7.

BO'RON, a town of the Troglodytæ. *Plin.* 6. c. 29.

BORSIP'PA or **BOROS'ITA**, a town of Babylonia, sacred to Apollo and Diana. The inhabitants were particularly fond of the flesh of bats. *Strab.* 16.—*Cluver.* 5. c. 21.

BO'RUS, a son of Perieres, who married Polydora, the daughter of Peleus. *Apollod.* 3. c. 13.—*Hom. Il* 16. v. 177.

BORUS'CI, a people of European Sarmatia. *Ptol.*

BORYS'THENES, a large river of Scythia, now the Dnieper, and inferior to no other European river but the Danube, according to *Herodotus*, 4. c. 45. &c. According to modern geography, it rises in Muscovy, and after passing through Poland, falls into the Black Sea, near Ockzakow. *Plin.* 4. c. 12.—*Dionys. Per.* 311.—*Strab.* 1 & 7.—*Propert.* 2. el. 7. v. 18.—*Ovid. de Pont.* 4. el. 10. v. 53.——**Borys'thenes**, a horse upon which the emperor Adrian used to hunt. After his death, the animal was honoured with a monument by his master. *Diod.*

BORYS'THENIS, a city of Scythia, near the mouth of the Borysthenes, built by a colony of Milesians 655 B.C. *Mela*, 2. c. 1.

BORY'ZA, a city of Pontus. *Steph.*

BO'SA, a town of Sardinia, now Buosa. *Ptol.*—*Plin.* 3. c. 7.

BO'SARA, a city of Arabia Felix. *Ptol.*

BOSIT'ARA, a city of Ægypt. *Steph.*

BOS'PHORUS or **BOS'PORUS**, two narrow straits, situate on the confines of Europe and Asia. One was called Cimmerian, and joined the Palus Mæotis to the Euxine, and is now known by the name of the straits of Cassa; and the other, which was called the Thracian Bosporus, and by the moderns the straits of Constantinople, opened a communication between the Euxine Sea and the Propontis. The Thracian Bosporus is sixteen miles long, and one and a half broad, and where narrowest, 500 paces, or four stadia, according to Herodotus. The word is derived from Βοὸς πόρος, *bovis meatus*, because, on account of its narrowness, an ox could easily swim across it. Cocks were heard to crow, and dogs to bark from the opposite banks, and in a calm day persons could talk one to the other. *Plin.* 4. c. 12. l. 6. c. 1.—*Ovid. Trist.* 3. el. 4. v. 49.—*Mela*, 1. c. 1.—*Strab.* 12.—*Varro. R.R.* 2. c. 1.—*Herodot.* 4. c. 85. The people who lived near it were called Bosporani, and Mithridates is thence called Bosporanus. *Tacit. Ann.* 12. c. 15.—*Ovid. Trist.* 2. v. 298.

BOS'TAR, a Carthaginian prophet, mentioned by *Silius Italicus*, 3. v. 647.

BOS'TRA, a maritime city of Phœnicia. *Strab.* 16.——A city of Arabia. *Steph.*

BOTACH'IDÆ, a place of Tagea, in Arcadia. *Id.*

BO'TER, a freedman of Claudius. *Suet. Claud.*

BOTIE'UM, a city of Phrygia, with a lake called Attæa, which produced salt. *Steph.*

BOTRO'DUS, a town of Spain, near Segobriga, destroyed by Tib. Gracchus. *Polyb.*—*Mart.* 1. ep. 50. v. 7.

BO'TRYS, a city of Syria, now Boteron. *Ptol.*

BOT'TIA, a colony of Macedonians, settled on the borders of Thrace. The people were called Bottiæi. *Plin.* 4. c. 1.—*Herodot.* 7. c. 185, &c.—*Thucyd.* 2. c. 99.

BOTTÆ'AS, a country at the north of Macedonia, on the Sinus Thermaicus. *Hrodot.* 7. c. 123, &c.

BOUDICE'A, **BOADIC'EA** or **BONDU'CA**, a queen of the Iceni in Britain, who rebelled upon being insulted by the Romans. Her revolt was so well planned, that it proved very destructive to the Roman forces in Britain; but at last the valour and superior experience of Suetonius prevailed over the undisciplined Britons, and Boudicea, after seeing 80,000 of her countrymen slaughtered in one battle, poisoned herself, A.D. 61. *Tacit. Ann.* 14. c. 31.

BOU'TA, a town of the interior of Libya. *Ptol.*

BOVIA'NUM, an ancient colony of the Samnites, at the foot of the Apennines, not far from Beneventum. It is now called Boiano. *Liv.* 9. c. 28.—*Plin.* 3. c. 12.

BOVIL'LÆ, a town of Latium, at the south-east of Rome. It is now Banco. *Ovid. Fast.* 3. v. 607.

BO'VIS AU'LA, a place of Eubœa. *Strab.*

BOX'US MACERIA'NUS, the person who slew Athenodorus by order of Bicon. *Curt.* 9. c. 7.

BRABAS'THENES, a mountain of Peloponnesus. *Liv.* 4. *Bell. Maced.*

BRACH'YLE, a city of the Ceretes, near the Iberi. *Steph.*

BRACHYL'LAS, a Bœotarch mentioned by *Livy*, 33. c. 27.

BRACHMA'NES, Indian philosophers, who derive their name from Brahma, one of the three Beings whom God, according to their theology, created, and with whose assistance he formed the world. They devoted themselves totally to the worship of the gods, and were accustomed from their youth to endure labour, and to live with frugality and abstinence. They never ate flesh, and abstained from the use of wine, and all carnal enjoyments. After they had spent 37 years in the greatest trials and privations, they were permitted to marry and indulge themselves more freely. According to modern authors, Brahma was the parent of all mankind, and he produced as many worlds as there are parts in the body, which they reckoned fourteen. They believed that there were seven seas, of water, milk, curds, butter, salt, sugar, and wine, each blessed with its particular paradise. *Strab.* 15.—*Diod.* 17.

BRAC'TIA, an island of Illyricum. *Plin.* 3. c. *ult.*

BRAE'SI, a people of Macedonia. *Steph.*

BRAE'SIA, a daughter of Cinyras and Metharme. *Apollod.* 3. c. 14.

BRAGODU'RUM, a town of Rhætia. *Ptol.*

BRAM'MA, a city of the Sinæ. *Id.*

BRA'NA, a town of the Turduli, in Spain. *Plin.* 3. c. 1.

BRANCHI'ADES, a surname of Apollo. *Strab.* 14.

BRAN'CHIDÆ, a people of Asia, near the river Oxus, put to the sword by Alexander. They were originally of Miletus, near the temple of Branchus, but had been removed thence by Xerxes. *Strab.* 11.—*Curt.* 7. c. 5.——The priests of Apollo Didymæus, who gave oracles in Caria. *Plin.* 5. c. 29.—*Amm. Marc.* 29. c. 1.

BRAN'CHUS, a youth of Miletus, son of Smicrus, beloved by Apollo, who bestowed upon him the power of prophecy. He gave oracles at Didyme, which were inferior to none of the Grecian oracles, except Delphi, and which exchanged the name of of Didymean for that of Branchidæ. The temple, according to Strabo, was set on fire by Xerxes, who took possession of the riches which it contained, and transported the people to Sogdiana, where they built a city, which was afterwards destroyed by Alexander. *Strab.* 15.—*Stat. Theb.* 3. v. 479. *& Schol in Loco.*—*Bocatius de Gen. D.* 5. c. 10.—*Lucian de Domo.*

BRANCHYL'LIDES, a chief of the Bœotians. *Paus.* 9. c. 13.

BRANCO'TII, a people of Asia. *Plin.* 6. c. 20.

BRA'SIÆ, a town of Laconia. *Paus.* 3. c 24.

BRAS'IDAS, a famous general of Lacedæmon, who, after many great victories over Athens and other Grecian states, died of a wound at Amphipolis, which Cleon, the Athenian, had besieged, B.C. 422. A superb monument was raised to his memory. *Paus.* 3. c. 24.—*Thucyd.* 4 & 5.—*Diod.* 5.

BRASIDI'A, festivals at Lacedæmon, in honour of Brasidas. None but freemen, born Spartans, were permitted to enter the lists, and such as were absent were fined.

BRAS'ILAS, a man of Cos. *Theocr.* 7.

BRATI'JA or BRAC'TIA, a province of Mœsia. *Plin.* 4. c. *ult.*

BRATUSPAN'TIUM, a town of the Bellovaci in Gaul.

BRAUCOM'AGUM, a city of the Alemanni, taken by Julian the apostate, and destroyed by Atilla. *Ptol.*

BRAU'RE, a woman who assisted in the murder of Pittacus, king of the Edoni. *Thucyd.* 4. c. 107.

BRAU'RON, a town of Attica, where Diana had a temple. The goddess had three festivals called *Brauronia*, celebrated once every fifth year, by ten men, who were called ἱεροποιοί. They sacrificed a goat to the goddess, and it was usual on this occasion to sing one of the books of Homer's Iliad. The most remarkable personages that attended, were young virgins in yellow gowns, consecrated to Diana. They were about ten years of age, and not under five, and therefore their consecration was called δεκατεύειν, from δέκα, *decem;* and sometimes ἀρκτεύειν, as the virgins themselves bore the name of ἄρκτοι, *bears*, from this circumstance. There was a bear in one of the villages of Attica so tame, that he ate familiarly with the inhabitants, and played harmlessly with their children. This familiarity lasted till a young virgin treated the animal too roughly, and was killed by it. The virgin's brothers killed the bear, and the country was soon after visited by a pestilence. The oracle was consulted, and the plague removed by consecrating virgins to the service of Diana. This was so faithfully observed, that no woman in Athens was ever married before a previous consecration to the service of the goddess. The statue of Diana of Tauris, which had been brought into Greece by Iphigenia, was preserved in the town of Brauron. Xerxes carried it away when he invaded Greece. *Paus.* 8. c. 46.—*Strab.* 9.—*Pollux.* 5 & 8. c. 9.—*Aristoph. in Lysist.* 644.—*Cœl. Rhod.* 14. c. 19.

BRE'A, a city of Thrace, founded by a colony from Athens. *Steph.*—*Hesych.*

BREGÆ'TIUM, a city of Upper Pannonia. *Ptol.*

BRE'GI or BRE'GES, a people of Phrygia. *Strab.* 12.

BREGMENTE'NI, a people of Troas. *Plin.* 5. c. 30 Some read Bregneni.

BREN'NI, BREN'CI or BREU'NI, a people of Rhœtia, dwelling near the rivers Ænus and Athesis. *Horat.* 4. od. 14.

BREN'NUS, a general of the Galli Senones, who invaded Italy, and after defeating the Romans at the river Allia, entered their city without opposition. The Romans, terrified by this sudden invasion, fled into the Capitol, and left the whole city in the possession of the enemy. The victorious Gauls climbed the Tarpeian rock in the night, and the Capitol would have been taken, had not the Romans been awakened by the noise of some geese which were before the doors, and immediately repelled the enemy. Camillus, who was in banishment, was recalled to the relief of his country, and so totally defeated the Gauls, that not one remained to carry back the news of their destruction. *Liv.* 5. c. 35. *Plut. in Camill.*——A Gaul, who made an irruption into Greece with 150,000 men and 15,000 horse, and endeavoured to plunder the temple of Apollo at Delphi. He was destroyed, with all his troops, by the god, or, more properly, he killed himself in a fit of intoxication, B. C. 278, after being defeated by the Delphians. *Paus.* 10. c. 22 & 23.—*Justin.* 24. c. 6, &c. Some authors maintain erroneously, that there was only one Brennus.

BREN'THE, a ruined city of Arcadia. *Paus.* 8. c. 28.—*Steph.*

BREN'THUS, a son of Hercules, after whom Brundusium, in Greek Βρεντήσιον, was called. *Steph.*

BRES'CIA. *Vid.* Brixia.

BRES'SUS, a city of Armenia Major. *Ptol.*

BRET'ENA, a city of the Veneti, in Italy. It is called Brinthium by *Pliny*, and is now Brignano. *Id.*

BRETI'NA, a town of Insubria, now Barlasina. *Id.*

BRETOLÆ'UM, a town of Lusitania, now Bretulla. *Id.*

BRET'TII, a people of Itusy. *Strab.* 6.

BRETTO'TIA, an island in the Adriatic Sea. *Steph.*

BRIAN'TICA, a region of Thrace, formerly Gallaica. *Herodot.* 7.

BRI'AREUS, or BRIA'REUS, a famous giant, son of Cœlus and Terra, who is said to have had 100 hands and 50 heads. He was called by men Ægæon and by the gods Briareus. When Juno, Neptune, and Minerva conspired to dethrone Jupiter, Briareus ascended the heavens, and seated himself next to him, and so terrified the conspirators with his fierce and threatening looks, that they desisted from their attempt. He assisted the giants in their war against the gods, and was thrown under mount Ætna, according to some accounts. *Hesiod. Theog.* v. 148.—*Apollod.* 1. c. 1.—*Homer. Il.* 1. v. 403.—*Virg. Æn.* 6. v. 287. l. 10. v. 565.——A Cyclops, made judge between Apollo and Neptune, in the dispute about the isthmus and promontory of Corinth. He adjudged the former to Neptune, and the latter to Apollo. *Paus.* 2. c. 1.

BRI'AS, a town of Pisidia. *Strab.*

BRI'CA or BRI'GA, a word used by the ancient inhabitants of Gaul and Germany, to signify a town.

BRICIN'NIA, a city of Thessaly. *Steph.*

BRIGÆ'CIUM, a city of Hispania Tarraconensis. *Ptol.* It is now Oviedo, or Braganza in Portugal, according to others.

BRIGAN'TES, a people in the northern parts of England, thought by some to have inhabited the county of York. *Juv.* 14. v. 196.—*Paus.* 8. c. 43.

BRIGANTI'NUS, a lake of Rhætia between the Alps, now the lake of Constance, through which the Rhine flows. The town on its eastern bank is now Bregentz in the Tyrol, anciently called Brigantium. *Plin.* 9. c. 17.

BRIGANTI'NUS POR'TUS, the ancient name of the seaport of Corunna in Spain.

BRI'GES, a people of Thrace. *Steph.*

BRIGIA'NI, a people dwelling among the Alps. *Plin.* 3. c. 21.

BRILES'SUS a mountain of Attica. *Thucyd.* 2. c. 23.—*Plin.* 4. c. 7.

BRILE'TUM, a mountain of Attica. *Plin.* 11. c. 37.

BRI'MO, (*terror*,) a name given to Proserpine or Hecate, because she was supposed to cause the terrors, which alarmed the weak and superstitious during the night. *Stat.* 2 *Sylv.* 3. v. 30.—*Cœl. Rhod.* 11. c. 16.—*Schol. Apollon.* 3. *Arg.*—*Propert.* 2. el. 2. v. 11.

BRIN'CI, a people of Thrace. *Suidas.*

BRINIA'TES, a people on the coast of Liguria. *Liv.* 39. c. 2. l. 41. c. 19.

BRI'SA, a promontory of Lesbus, where Bacchus, surnamed Briseus, was worshipped. *Steph.*

BRISABRI'TÆ, a people of India. *Plin.* 6. c. 20.

BRISE'IS, the prtronymic of Hippodamia, a woman of Lyrnessus. When her country was taken by the Greeks during the Trojan war, and her husband Mines, and her brother killed in the fight, she fell to the share of Achilles, in the division of the spoils. Agamemnon took her away some time after from Achilles, who, in consequence of this violent conduct, made a vow to absent himself from the field of battle. Briseis was very faithful to Achilles, and when Agamemnon restored her to him, he swore he had never offended her chastity. She is described by Dares as having been well proportioned in her figure, amiable in her manners, and fascinating in her looks. *Seneca in Troad. Act.* 2. *in Agam.* 2.—*Homer. Il.* l. 2, &c. —*Ovid. Heroid.* 3. *de Art. Am.* 2 & 3. *De Rem. A.* 2. *Trist.* 4. el. 1.—*Dares Phryg.*—*Propert.* 2. el. 8. 20 & 22.—*Paus.* 5. c. 24.—*Horat.* 2. od. 4.

BRI'SES, a man of Lyrnessus, brother to the priest Chryses. His daughter Hippodamia was called Briseis from him.

BRI'SEUS, a surname of Bacchus, from his nurse Brisa, or his temple at Brisa, a promontory of Lesbus, *Pantheon. Myt. in Bacc.* The poet Persius bestows the appellation of Briseus on Accius either on account of the tragedy of Bacchus which he had written, or because the god was supposed in a more particular manner to patronise the efforts of tragic writers. *Persius*, 1. v. 76.

BRITAN'NI, the inhabitants of Britain. *Vid.* Britannia.——A nation of Gallia Belgica. *Plin.* 4. c. 17.

BRITAN'NIA, an island in the Northern Ocean, the largest in Europe, conquered by J. Cæsar during his Gallic wars, B.C. 55, and first discovered to be an island by Agricola, who sailed round it. It continued to be a Roman province from the time of its conquest till A.D.448, and during that time, while it advanced in civilization by its intercourse with its polished conquerors, it was drained of its hardy youths to recruit the armies and fight the battles of Rome. The inhabitants in the age of Cæsar, used to paint their bodies, to render themselves more terrible in the eyes of their enemies. The name of Britain was unknown to the Romans before Cæsar invaded the island. *Cæs. Bell. G.* 4.—*Diod.* 5.—*Paus.* 1. c. 33.—*Tacit. in Agric.* 10.—*Plin.* 34. c. 17.

BRITAN'NICUS, a son of Claudius Cæsar by Messalina, so called because under that emperor part of Britain had been conquered by the Romans. Nero was raised to the throne in preference to him, by means of Agrippina, and caused him to be poisoned. His corpse was buried in the night; but it is said that a shower of rain washed away the white paint which the murderer had put over his face, so that it appeared quite black, and discovered the effects of poison. *Tacit. Ann.* 11, 12 & 13.—*Sueton in Ner.* c. 33. [There is a fine statue of Britannicus in the collection at Florence.]

BRIT'IUM, a town of Lusitania. *Plin.* 4. c. 21.

BRITOL'AGE, a people of Lower Mysia. *Ptol.*

BRITOMAR'TIS, a beautiful nymph of Crete, daughter of Jupiter and Charme, who devoted herself to hunting, and became a great favourite with Diana. She was loved by Minos, who pursued her so closely, that, to avoid his importunities, she threw herself into the sea. *Paus.* 2. c. 30. l. 3. c. 14.—*Callim. in Dian.* 199.—*Virg. in Cir.* 285.——A surname of Diana. *Solin.* 11.

BRITOMA'RUS or BRITOM'ARUS, a chief of the Galli Insubres, conquered by Æmilius. *Flor.* 2. c 4.

BRIT'ONES or BRITO'NES, the inhabitants of Britain. *Juv.* 15. v. 124.

BRIVA'TES, a capacious harbour at the north-west extremity of Gaul, now Brest. *Ptol.*

BRIX'ABA, a mountain near the Tanais. *Plut. de Flum.*

BRIXEL'LUM, now Bressello, a town at the north of Italy, near Mantua, where Otho slew himself when defeated. *Tacit. Hist.* 2. c. 32.

BRIXEN'TES, a people of Noricum. *Ptol.*

BRIX'IA, a town of Italy beyond the Po, at the north of Cremona, now Brescia. *Liv.* 21. c. 25.—*Jnstin.* 20. c. 5.——A river of Susiana. *Plin.* 6. c. 27.

BRIZ'ACA, a town of Armenia Major. *Ptol.*

BRI'ZO, the goddess of dreams, was worshipped by the women of Delus. She was invoked to protect the ships of the island, and to inspire her votaries with pleasant and propitious dreams? and, in her festivals, she was gratefully presented with offerings of fruits, and all other things except fish. *Athen.* 8. c. 3.

BRO'CHUS, a town of Phœnicia. *Polyb.* 1. 5.

BROCOM'AGUS, BROTOM'AGUS or BREUCOM'AGUS, a town of Germany, not far from Argentoratum. *Ptol.*

BRO'MIUS, a surname of Bacchus, [from Βρέμειν, *frendere*,] alluding to the groans which Semele uttered when consumed by Jupiter's fire, or, with equal probability, to the noise and shouts of the Bacchantes in the celebration of the orgies of the god. *Diod.* 4.—*Ovid. Met.* 4. v. 11.——A son of Ægyptus. *Apollod.* 2. c. 1.

BRO'MUS, one of the Centaurs. *Ovid. Met.* 12. v. 459.

BRON'GUS, a river falling into the Ister. *Herodot.* 4. c. 49.

BRON'TES, (*thunder*), one of the Cyclopes. *Virg. Æn.* 8. v. 425.—*Hesiod. Theog.* 142.

BRONTI'NUS, a Pythagorean philosopher. *Suidas* ——The father of Theano, the wife of Pythagoras. *Diog.*

BRO'TEAS and AM'MON, two men famous for their skill in the cæstus. *Ovid. Met.* 5. v. 107.

BRO'TEAS, one of the Lapithæ. *Id.* 12. v. 262.

BRO'TES, a native of Cyzicum, left half dead by Pollux in a nocturnal combat. *Val. Flacc.* 3. v. 152.

BRO'THEUS, a son of Vulcan and Minerva, who burned himself to avoid the ridicule to which his deformity subjected him. *Ovid. in Ib.* v. 517.

BRUC'TERI or BRUCTE'RI, a people of Germany, inhabiting the country which is now at the east of Holland. *Tacit. Ann.* 1. c. 51. *Hist.* 4. c. 21. *G.* 33.

BRUL'LITÆ, a people of Ephesus. *Plin.* 5. c. 29.

BRUMA'LIA, festivals celebrated at Rome in honour of Bacchus, about the month of December. They were first instituted by Romulus, and derived their name either from Bromius, one of the surnames of the god, or from an allusion to the cold season (*bruma*) during which they were celebrated. *Cæl. Rhod.* 28. c. 25.—*Rutgers. Lect. V.* 4. c. 8.—*Gyrald. Calend. Gr. & R.*

BRUN'DULUM, a harbour formed by the Athesis. *Plin.* 3. c. 16,

RUNDU'SIUM, now Brindisi, a city of Calabria, on the Adriatic Sea, where the Appian road terminated. It was founded by Diomedes after the Trojan war, or, according to Strabo by Theseus, with a Cretan colony. The Romans generally embarked at Brundusium for the opposite shores of Greece. Brundusium was famous for the birth of the poet Pacuvius, and the death of Virgil, as likewise for its harbour, which is capacious, and sheltered by the land and by a small island at the entrance against the fury of the winds and waves. Little remains of the ancient city, and even its harbour has now been choked up by the sand. *Justin.* 3. c. 4. l. 12. c 2.—*Strab.* 5.—*Cæs Bell. Civ.* 1. c. 24.—*Cic. ad. Att.* 4. ep. 1.—*Mela*, 2. c. 6 & 9.—*Lucan.* 2. v. 608. l. 5. v. 406.

BRUSIS, a part of Macedonia, so called from Brusus the son of Emathius. *Steph.*

BRUTID'IUS, a man dragged to prison in Juvenal's age, on suspicion of favouring the party of Sejanus. *Tacitus* and *Seneca* mention him as being a rhetorician and historian. *Juv.* 10. v. 82.

BRU'TII, a people in the farthest part of Italy, who were originally shepherds of the Lucanians, but revolted, and went in quest of a settlement. They received the name of Brutii, from their stupidity and cowardice in submitting, without opposition, to Annibal in the second Punic war. They were ever after held in the greatest disgrace, and employed in every servile work. Their country was called Brutiorum Ager. *Justin.* 23. c. 9.—*Strab.* 6.—*Diod.* 16. Also written Brut'tii.

BRU'TULUS PA'PIUS, a Samnite, who killed himself, upon being delivered to the Romans for violating a treaty. *Liv.* 8. c. 39.

BRU'TUS L. JU'NIUS, was the son of M. Junius and Tarquinia, second daughter of Tarquinius Priscus. The father, with his eldest son, were murdered by Tarquinius Superbus, and Lucius, unable to revenge their death, and dreading the power of the tyrant, pretended to be insane. This artifice saved his life; he was called *Brutus* for his stupidity, which he, however, soon after shewed to be feigned. When Lucretia killed herself, B.C. 509, in consequence of the brutality of Tarquin, Brutus snatched the dagger from the wound, and swore upon the reeking blade, immortal hatred to the royal family. His example animated the Romans. The Tarquins were proscribed by a decree of the senate, and the royal authority vested in the hands of consuls chosen from patrician families. Brutus, in his consular office, made the people swear that they would never again submit to kingly authority; but the first who violated their oath were in his own family. His sons Titus and Tiberius conspired with the Tuscan ambassador to restore the Tarquins; and when discovered, they were tried and condemned before their father, who was himself present at their execution. Some time after, in a combat which was fought between the Romans and the Tarquins, Brutus engaged with

Aruns, and so fierce was the attack that the two combatants pierced one another at the same time. The dead body was brought to Rome, and received as in triumph; a funeral oration was spoken over it, and the Roman matrons showed their grief by mourning a year for the father of the republic. *Flor.* 1. c. 9.—*Liv.* 1. c. 56. l. 2. c. 1, &c.—*Dion. Hal.* 4 & 5.—*C. Nep. in Attic.* 8.—*Ovid. Fast* 2. v. 717.—*Eutrop. de Tarq.*—*Virg. Æn.* 6. v. 818. *Plut. in Brut. & Cæs.* [A fine bronze bust of Lucius Junius Brutus, exists in the Museum of the Capitol.

BRU'TUS M. JUN., father of Cæsar's murderer, wrote three books on civil law. He followed the party of Marius, and was conquered by Pompey. After the death of Sylla, he was besieged in Mutina by Pompey, to whom he surrendered, and by whose orders he was put to death. He had married Servilia, Cato's sister, by whom he had a son and two daughters. *Cic de Orat.* c. 55.—*Plut. in Brut.*

BRU'TUS M. JUN., son of the preceding by Servilia, sometimes called Q. Cæpio, because adopted by his maternal uncle Q. Servilius Cæpio, was lineally descended from J. Brutus, who expelled the Tarquins from Rome. He seemed to inherit the republican principles of his great projenitor, and in the civil wars joined himself to the side of Pompey, though he was his father's murderer, and because he looked upon him as more just and patriotic. At the battle of Pharsalia, Cæsar not only spared the life of Brutus, but, by his kindness towards him, made him one of his most faithful friends. Brutus, however, forgot the favour, because Cæsar aspired to tyranny, and he did not hesitate to form a conspiracy with many of the most illustrious citizens of Rome against the tyrant, and stabbed him in Pompey's Basilica. The tumult which this murder occasioned was great; the conspirators fled to the Capitol, and, by proclaiming freedom and liberty to the populace, re-established tranquillity in the city. Antony, whom Brutus, contrary to the opinion of his associates, refused to seize, was active in avenging the death of the fallen Cæsar, and the murderers were obliged to leave Rome. Brutus retired into Greece, where he gained himself many friends by the influence of his character, and by his political conduct, as well as by persuasion, and he was soon after pursued thither by Antony, whom young Octavius accompanied. A battle was fought at Philippi. Brutus, who commanded the right wing of the republican army, defeated the enemy and even took the camp of Octavius; but Cassius, who had the care of the left, was overpowered by Antony. In another battle, the wing which Brutus commanded obtained a victory; but the other was defeated, and he found himself surrounded by the soldiers of Antony. He, however, made his escape, but hearing that many of his personal friends had deserted to the conquerors in despair, and that their attempts to seduce his soldiers were incessant and too successful, he at last fell upon his sword, B.C. 42, exclaiming, "O virtue, thou art but an empty name; I have worshipped thee as a goddess, but thou art the slave of fortune." Antony honoured the remains of this extraordinary man with a magnificent funeral, and sent his ashes to his mother Servilia; but Suetonius says, that Octavius sent his head to Rome, to be fixed below the statue of Cæsar; which mark of triumph, however, was never exhibited, as the head, according to Dio, was thrown into the sea in a storm, before the vessel reached Italy from Dyrrhachium. Brutus was not less celebrated for his literary talents, than his valour in the field. When he was in the midst of his camp, the greatest part of his time was employed in reading and writing; and on the day which preceded one of his most bloody battles, while the rest of his army was under continual apprehensions, Brutus calmly spent his hours till the evening in writing an epitome of Polybius. He was fond of imitating the austere virtues of Cato, and in reading the histories of nations, he imbibed those principles of freedom which were so eminently displayed in his political career. He was intimate with Cicero, to whom he would have communicated his conspiracy against Cæsar, had he not been apprehensive of his great timidity. He severely reprimanded him in his letters for joining the side of Octavius, who meditated the ruin of the republic. Plutarch mentions that Cæsar's ghost made its appearance to Brutus in his tent, and told him that he would meet him at Philippi. Brutus married Claudia, whom he afterwards divorced without assigning any reason, for which he was deservedly reprehended, and he immediately took for his second wife Porcia, the daughter of Cato, who killed herself by swallowing burning coals, when she heard the fate of her husband. It is said that both Brutus and Cassius fell upon those very swords which they had raised against the life of J. Cæsar. *C. Nep. in Attic.*—*Paterc.* 2. c. 48.—*Plut. in Brut. &c. Cæs.* 1.—*Flor.* 4. [There is a bust of this Brutus in the Museum of the Capitol.

BRU'TUS D. JUN. ALBI'NUS, also one of Cæsar's murderers, was distantly related to Marcus. It was he who prevailed upon the dictator to go to the senate-house, when he seemed doubtful, in consequence of the unfavourable appearance of omens, and of the alarming dreams of his wife. After the murder he went to Cisalpine Gaul, which he bravely defended against Anthony; and when besieged at Mutina, he boldly defied the attempts of the triumvirs, and might have triumphed in his opposition, had not the consuls Hirtius and Pansa, who came to his assistance been unfortunately defeated. Decimus, on this fatal occasion, endeavoured to fly into Greece to Brutus, but he was deserted by his soldiers, and, being betrayed into the hands of Antony, was, though consul elect, put to death by the conqueror's directions. *Appian.* 2 & 3.—*Val Max.* 9. c. 13.—*Vel. Pat.* 2. c. 64.—*Dio.* 46, 53.—*Plut. in Cæs. Brut.*

BRU'TUS JUN. one of the first tribunes of the people. *Plut.*——One of Carbo's generals.

BRYA'NIUM, a city of Thesprotia. *Steph.*

BRY'AS, a general of the Argives against Sparta, put to death by a woman to whom he had offered violence. *Paus.* 2. c. 20.

BRYAX'IS, a marble sculptor, who assisted in making the Mausoleum. *Paus.* 1. c. 40.

BRYA'ZON, a river of Bithynia. *Plin.* 5. c. 32.

BRY'CE, a daughter of Danaus by Polyxo. *Apollod.* 2. c. 1.

BRY'GES or BRY'GI, a people of Thrace, afterwards called Phryges. *Strab.* 7.—*Herodot.* 1. 6. c. 45.

BRYL'LION, a city of the Propontis. *Steph.*—*Pliny*, 5. c. 32, says that it is in Mysia.

BRYO'RUM LI'TUS, a part of Cyrenaica. *Ptol.*—*Mela*, 1. c. 7.

BRYSA'NI, a people in the north of Scythia. *Plin.* 6. c. 17.

BRYS'EA, a town of Laconia. *Paus.* 3. c. 20.——A city of Œonia. *Diod. Cic.* l. 5.

BRYS'IÆ or BRYSE'Æ, a city of Elis. *Steph.*

BRYSTA'CIA, a city of the Œnotri. now Briatico. *Id.*

BUA'NA, a town of Armenia Major. *Ptol.*

BU'BA, or BU'CA according to Strabo, a maritime town of the Frentani. *Id.*

BUBACE'NE, a country of Asia. *Curt.* 5. c. 11. & 8. c. 5.

BUBA'CES, a eunuch in the service of Darius, &c. *Curt.* 5. c. 11.

BU'BARIS, a Persian who married the daughter of Amyntas, king of Macedonia, against whom he had been sent with an army. *Justin.* 7. c. 13.

BUBASTI'ACUS, one of the mouths of the Nile.

BUBAS'TIS, a city of Ægypt, on the most easterly branch of the Nile, south of Pelusium. Cats were there held in great veneration, because Diana Bubastis, who was the chief deity of the place, is said to have transformed herself into a cat, when the gods fled into Ægypt. *Herodot.* 2. c. 59, 137 & 154.—*Gratian. Cyneg.* 42.—*Ovid. Met.* 9. v. 690. —*Strab.* 17.

BU'BASUS, a country of Caria, whence the appellation of Bubasides was applied to the natives. *Ovid. Met.* 9. v. 743.

BU'BEI, a people in the interior of Africa, conquered by Corn. Balbus. *Plin.* 5. c. 5.

BUBETA'NI, a people of Campania, near Corioli. *Plin.* 3. c. 5.

BU'BON, an inland city of Lydia, or according to *Strabo*, 13. of Lycia. *Plin.* 5. c. 27.

BUBO'NA, a goddess among the Romans, who was supposed to preside over oxen. *Aug. de Civ. D.* 6. c. 9.

BU'BULA, a city of Cyrene. *Plin.* 5. c. 5.

BUCEPH'ALA, a city of India, near the Hydaspes, built by Alexander, in honour of his favourite horse Bucephalus. *Curt.* 9. c. 3.—*Arrian.* 5. c. 19. —*Justin.* 12. c. 8.—*Diod.* 17.—*Plin.* 6. c. 20.

BUCEPH'ALUS, a favourite horse of Alexander, whose head resembled that of a bull, whence his name, (βουκεφαλὴ, *bovis, caput*). Alexander was the only one who could mount on his back, and he always knelt down to take up his master. He was present in an engagement in Asia, where he received a heavy wound, and hastened immediately out of the battle, and dropped down dead as soon as he had set down the king in a place of safety. He was thirty years old when he died, and Alexander built a city which, in gratitude for his faithful services, he called after his name. *Plut. in Alex.*—*Curt.*—*Arrian.* 5. c. 3.—*Plin.* 8. c. 42.—*Justin.* 12. c. 8.

BUCHÆ'TIUM, a city at the top of the Sinus Ambracius. *Strabo.*

BU'CIA, a city of Sicily, now Butera. *Ptol.*

BUCILIA'NUS, one of Cæsar's murderers. *Cic. ad Attic.* 14.

BUCIN'NA, an island of the Sicilian Sea. *Plin.* 3. c. 8.——A city of Sicily. *Steph.*

BUCOL'ICA, (from βουκολικὸς, *pastoralis,*) a sort of poem which treats of the care of flocks, and of the pleasures and occupations of the rural life. The most famous pastoral writers of antiquity were Moschus, Bion, Theocritus, and Virgil. The invention of Bucolics, or pastoral poetry, has been attributed to a shepherd of Sicily.

BUCOL'ICUM, one of the mouths of the Nile, situate between the Sebennytican and Mendesian mouths, and called by *Strabo*, Phatniticum. *Herodot.* 2. c. 17.

BUCO'LION, a king of Arcadia, after Laias. *Paus.* 8. c. 5.——A son of Laomedon, king of Troy, and the nymph Calybe.——A son of Hercules and Praxithea. He was also called Bucolus.——A son of Lycaon, king of Arcadia. *Apollod.* 2 & 3.

BU'COLUS, a son of Hercules and Marse.——A son of Hippocoon. *Apollod.* 2 & 3.

BU'CRA, a promontory of Sicily, now, probably, El Capo Longo. *Ptol.*

BUDÆ'A, a city of India within the Ganges. *Id.*

BUDA'RES, a Spanish general. *Liv.* 33. c. 30.

BUDE'A, a city of Magnesia.——A city of Phrygia. *Steph.*

BU'DII, a nation of Media. *Herodot.* 1. c. 101.

BUDI'NI, a people of Scythia. *Id.* 4. c. 21.

BUDI'NUM, a mountain of European Sarmatia. *Ptol.*

BUDO'RÆ, two islands near Crete. *Plin.* 4. c. 11.

BUDOR'GIS or BUDOR'IGUM, a city of Germany. *Ptol.* It is now Breslaw or Ratibor. Some suppose that Ratibor is the ancient Budorgis; and Budorigum, Breslaw.

BUDO'RIS, a city of Germany.

BUDO'RUM or BU'DORUM, a promontory of the island of Salamis. *Thucyd.* 2. c. 94.

BUDO'RUS, a river of Eubœa. *Ptol.*

BU'GEI, a people descended from the Parthenii. *Strab.* 6.

BU'GENES, a name under which Bacchus was worshipped at Argos. *Diod. Sic.* 5.

BU'GES or BY'CE, a river of European Scythia, flowing into the Mæotis. It is now Sessehan. *Ptol.*

BULA'NÆ, a people of European Sarmatia. *Id.*

BUL'BUS, a Roman senator, remarkable for his meanness. *Cic. in Ver.*

BULI'NI, a people of Illyria. *Steph.*

BU'LIS, a town of Phocis, built by a colony from Doris, near the sea-shore, at the north of the bay of Corinth. *Paus.* 10. c. 37.——A Spartan given up to Xerxes, to atone for the offence which his countrymen had committed in putting the king's messengers to death. *Herodot.* 7. c. 134, &c.

BUL'LA RE'GIA, a town of Numidia, called Bullaria by *Ptolemy*. *Plin.* 5. c. 3.

BULLAMIN'SA, a town of Africa Propria. *Ptol.*

BULLA'TIUS, a friend of *Horace*, to whom the poet addressed 1. ep. 11. in consequence of his having travelled over part of Asia.

BULLEN'SES or BULEN'SES, a people of the Locri. *Plin*, 4. c. 3.

BUL'LIS, a town of Illyricum, situate near the sea, at the south of Apollonia. The people were called Bullini. *Liv.* 36. c. 7. l. 44. c. 30.

BULLI'ONES, a barbarous people of Macedonia. *Plin.* 3. c. 23.

BU'LUA, a city of Liburnia, now Bedono. *Ptol.*

BUMATHA'NI, a people of Taprobane. *Id.*

BUME'LUS, a river of Assyria. *Curt.* 4. c. 9.

BUNAR'TIS, a city of Libya. *Steph.*

BUNE'A, a surname of Juno, at Corinth. *Vid.* Bunus.

BUNI'MA, a city of Epirus, founded by Ulysses. *Steph.*

BUNIT'IUM, a city of Germany, now Stralsund. *Ptol.*

BUN'NUS, a city of Illyria. *Steph.*

BUNOB'ORA, a town of Mauritania Cæsariensis, now Beni Arax. *Ptol.*

BUNO'MUS, a city of Macedonia, afterwards called Pella. *Steph.*

BU'NUS, a son of Mercury and Alcidamea, who obtained the government of Corinth when Æetes went to Colchis. He built a temple to Juno at Corinth, from which circumstance the goddess is often called Bunea. *Paus.* 2. c. 3 & 4.

BU'PALUS, a statuary of Clazomenæ, brother of Anthermus. *Vid.* Anthermus. He obtained great celebrity; and some golden statues of the Graces in the temple of Nemesis at Smyrna, and likewise those in the possession of Attalus, did credit to his taste and talents. *Paus.* 9. c. 35.—*Plin.* 36. c. 5.

BU'PHAGUS, a son of Japetus and Thornax, killed by Diana, whose virtue he had attempted. A river of Arcadia bears his name. *Paus.* 8. c. 24. ——A surname of Hercules, given him on account of his gluttony, of which he was accused by the Argonauts, and for which, as some assert, he was banished from their company. *Cæl. Rhod.* 14.

BUPHO'NIA a festival celebrated at Athens, in the month of June, in honour of Jupiter. According to Pausanias, some grains of barley and wheat were placed on the altar of the god, of which the intended victim was permitted to eat, soon after which one of the priests brought him to the ground with a blow of a hatchet, and ran out of sight. The assistants, as if they had not seen who gave the blow, immediately made a formal trial of the bloody instruments; a ceremony which originated in the high veneration in which the people of Attica held the ox, the shedding of the blood of which was regarded as a capital crime. The priest was called Buphonus. *Meurs. Att.* 6. c. 22.—*Cæl. Rhod.* 7. c. 6.—*Paus.* 1. c. 24.—*Ælian. V. H.* 8. c. .

BUPRA'SIUM, a city, country, and river of Elis. *Homer. Pliny*, 4. c. 15, places them in Achaia.

BU'RA, a daughter of Jupiter, or according to others, of Ion and Helice, from whom Bura or Buris, once a flourishing city in Peloponnesus, on the bay of Corinth, received its name. Ceres, Isis, Lucina, and Bacchus had each temples there, and Hercules was worshipped in a grotto in the neighbourhood, where he delivered oracles. This city was destroyed by the sea. *Ovid. Met.* 15. v. 293.—*Paus.* 7. c. 25.—*Strab.* 1 & 8.—*Diod.* 15.—*Plin.* 2. c. 92.

BURÆ'A, a city of Italy founded by Buræus. *Steph.*

BURA'ICUS, an epithet applied to Hercules, from his temple near Bura.——A river of Achaia. *Paus.* 7. c, 25.

BUR'CA, a town of Mauritania Cæsariensis. *Ptol.*

BURDIG'ALA, an ancient town of Gaul, at the mouth of the Garonne, now Bordeaux, famous for its population, opulence, and commerce. Ausonius. the poet, was born there. *Cluver.* 2. c. 15.

BUR'DO JU'LIUS, a præfect of the fleet under Vitellius. *Tac. Hist.* 1. c. 58.

BURGUNDIO'NES, a nation of Germany, part of the Vindileci, or Vandals. The place where they settled has been called, in modern geography, Burgundy.

BU'RII, a people of Germany. *Ptol.*

BUR'NUM or BUR'NIUM, a town of Illyricum, now Grachova. *Liv.*

BUR'RHUS AFRA'NIUS, a chief of the prætorian guards, put to death by Nero. *Tac. Ann.* 12. c. 42. l. 13 & 14.——A brother-in-law of the emperor Commodus

BUR'SA, the capital city of Bithynia, supposed to have been called Prusa, from its founder Prusias. *Strab.* 12.

BURSAONEN'SES, a people of Hispania Citerior. *Plin.* 3. c. 3.

BUR'SIA, a town of Babylonia. *Justin.* 12. c. 13.

BU'SA, a woman of Apulia, who entertained 10,000 Romans after the battle of Cannæ. *Val. Max.* 4. c. 8.

BU'SÆ, a nation of Media. *Herodot.* 1. c. 101.

BUSI'RIS, a king of Ægypt, son of Neptune and

Libya, or Lysianassa, who sacrificed all foreigners to Jupiter with the greatest cruelty. When Hercules visited Ægypt, Busiris carried him to the altar bound hand and foot. The hero soon disentangled himself, and offered the tyrant, his son Amphidamas, and the ministers of his cruelty. on the altar. Many Ægyptian princes have borne the same name. One of them built a town called Busiris, in the middle of the Delta, on that branch of the river which was called *Busiriticus fluvius*, where Isis had a famous temple. *Herodot.* 2. c. 59 & 61.—*Strab.* 17.—*Ovid. Met.* 9. v. 132. *Heroid.* 9 v. 69.—*Plut. in Thes.*—*Virg. G.* 3. v. 5.—*Apollod.* 2. c. 5.—*Stat.* 12 *Theb.* 155.

BUSMA'DIS, a city of Isauria. *Steph.*

BU'TA, a town of Achaia. *Diod.* 20.

BUTADÆ, a part of the Tribe Ægeis. *Steph.*——A family at Athens, from which the priests of Minerva were chosen. *Spon. Itin. Gr.* part. 3.—*Meurs. de pop. Att.*

BU'TEO, a surname of the Fabii, derived from *buteo* a hawk, a bird which is said to have perched on the ship of one of the Fabii during a naval expedition. *Plin.* 10. c. 8.—*Liv.* 30. c. 26.——A Roman orator. *Seneca.*

BU'TES, a person said by Virgil to be descended from Amycus king of the Hebryces, because, like them, he was very expert in the combat of the cæstus. He is mentioned by the poet as having appeared among the combatants at the funeral games given in honour of Hector, in which he was conquered and slain by Dares; but others assert that he came to Sicily, where he was received by Lycaste, a beautiful harlot, by whom he had a son called Eryx. Lycaste, on account of her beauty, was called Venus: hence Eryx is often called the son of Venus. *Servius in Æn.* 1. v. 574.—*Virg. Æn.* 5. v. 372.——A son of Teleon, one of the Argonauts. When he wished to swim to the island of the Sirens, whose songs had captivated him, Venus, who was enamoured of him, carried him away from the enchanted spot to Lilybæum, where she bore him Eryx. *Apollod.* 1. c. 9.—*Hygin.* fab. 14 & 260.——A Trojan slain by Camilla. *Virg. Æn.* 11. v. 690.——A son of Boreas, who built Naxus. *Diod.* 5.——A son of Pandion and Zeuxippe, priest of Minerva and Neptune. He married Chthonia, daughter of Erechtheus. *Apollod.* 3. c. 14. &c. ——An arm-bearer to Anchises, and afterwards to Ascanius. Apollo assumed his shape when he descended from heaven to encourage Ascanius to fight. Butes was killed by Turnus. *Virg Æn.* 9. v. 647. l. 12. v. 632.——A governor of Darius, besieged by Conon the Athenian.

BU'THIA, a city or region of Ionia. *Steph.*

BU'THOE, a city of Illyria, called by *Pliny*, 3. c. 22. Butua.

BUTHRO'TUM, now Butrinto, a sea-port town of Epirus, opposite Corcyra, visited by Æneas, in his voyage to Italy from Troy. *Virg. Æn.* 3. v. 293. —*Plin.* 4. c. 1.—*Cic. Att.* 16. ep. 16.

BUTHRO'TUS, a small river of Italy, near Locri.

BUTHYR'EUS, a noble statuary, disciple to Myron. *Plin.* 34. c. 8.

BU'TOA, an island in the Mediterranean, near Crete. *Plin.* 4. c. 12.

BUTOR'IDES, an historian who wrote concerning the pyramids. *Plin.* 36. c. 12.

BU'TRIUM, a city of Italy, now Butrio. *Steph.*

BUTUN'TUM, an inland town of Apulia. *Plin.* 3. c. 11.

BU'TUS or BU'TO, a town of the Delta in Ægypt, on the Sebennytican mouth of the Nile, where there was a temple of Apollo and Diana, and an oracle of Latona. *Herodot.* 2. c. 59 & 63.——A son of Pandion.

BUXEN'TUM, a town of Lucania in Italy, near the Tyrrhene Sea, now Policastro. *Liv.* 32. c. 39. l. 34. c. 45. l. 39. c. 23.

BU'ZA, a nation of India. *Plin.* 6. c. 20.

BU'ZARA, a mountain of Mauritania Cæsariensis. *Ptol.*

BUZE'RI, a people of Themiscyra, in Asia. *Plin.* 6. c. 3.

BU'ZES, a people of Marmarica. *Ptol.*

BUZY'GES or BU'ZYGES, an Athenian who first ploughed with harnessed oxen; a practice said by others to have been introduced by Triptolemus. Demophoon gave him the Palladium, with which Diomedes had entrusted him, to be carried to Athens. *Polyæn.* 1. c. 5.—*Plin.* 7. c. 56.—*Servius ad Virg. G.* 1. v. 19.

BUZYGE'US, a mountain of Thessaly. *Plin.* 4. c. 8.

BY'BE, a city of Thrace. The inhabitants were called Bybæ. *Steph.*

BYBLE'SIA or BYBAS'SIA, a country of Caria. *Herodot.* 1. c. 174.

BYB'LIA, a name of Venus. *Lucian in Deâ. Syr.*

BYB'LII, a people of Syria, whose capital was called Byblus. *Apollod.* 2. c. 1.——A nation of Scythia. *Steph.*

BYB'LIS, a daughter of Miletus and Cyane, or, according to some, of Eidotea, or Area. She fell in love with her brother Caunus, according to Ovid and Antoninus Liberalis, and when he refused to gratify her passion, she destroyed herself. Some say that Caunus became enamoured of her. and fled from his country to avoid incest. Others report that he fled from his sister's importunities, who sought him all over Lycia, and Caria, and was at last changed into a fountain of the same name. *Ovid. de Art. Am.* 1. v. 284. *Met.* 9. v. 451.—*Hygin.* fab. 243.—*Paus.* 7. c. 5.—*Parthen. Erot.* 11. —*Antonin. Lib.* 30.—*Apollod.* 3. c. 1.

BYB'LIS, a small island in the Mediterranean.

BYB'LUS, now Gibeletto, a town of Syria, at the north of Sidon, and not far from the sea, where Adonis had a temple. *Strab.* 16.

BYLAZO'RA, a place of Pæonia. *Liv.* 44. c. 26.

BYL'LIS, a maritime city of Illyria, founded by the Myrmidons who were with Neoptolemus. *Steph.*

BYR'CHANIS or BURCHA'NA, an island in the German Ocean. *Plin.* 4. c. 13.—*Strab.*

BYR'RHUS or BIR'RUS, a Roman, remarkable for his dishonesty and dissipation. *Horat.* 1. sat. 4. c. 69.

BYR'SA, a citadel in the middle of Carthage, in which the temple of Æsculapius was erected. Asdrubal's wife burnt it when the city was taken. When Dido came to Africa, she bought of the inhabitants as much land as could be encompassed by a bull's hide. After the agreement, she artfully cut the hide into small thongs, and inclosed a large piece of territory, on which she built a citadel which she called Byrsa, from Βύρσα, *a hide. Virg Æn.* 1. v. 371. & *Servius Loco.*—*Strab.* 17. —*Justin.* 18. c. 5.—*Flor.* 2. c. 15.—*Liv.* 34. c. 62.

BYS'ALAS, a country near the Syrtes. *Steph.*

BYS'NEI, a people of Bebrycia. *Id.*

BYZA'CIUM, a country of Africa. *Plin.* 5. c. 4. & 17. c. 5. Also written Byzace'na.

BYZAN'TIUM, a town situate on the Thracian Bosphorus, founded by a colony of Megara, under the conduct of Byzas, 658 years B.C. According to Paterculus it was founded by the Milesians, by the Lacedæmonians according to Justin, and according to Ammianus by the Athenians. The pleasantness and convenience of its situation were observed by Constantine the Great, who made it the site of a most magnificent and splendid city, which he destined to rival Rome, and to become the capital of the eastern Roman empire, A.D. 328, and which he called Constantinopolis. A number of Greek writers, who have deserved or usurped the name of *Byzantine historians*, flourished at Byzantium, after the seat of the empire had been transferred thither from Rome. Their works, which more particularly relate to the time in which they flourished, and are seldom read but by those who wish to form an acquaintance with the revolutions of the lower empire, were published in one large collection, in 36 vols. folio, 1648, &c. at Paris, and recommended themselves by the notes and supplement of Du Fresne du Cange. They were likewise printed at Venice, 1729, in 28 vols. though perhaps this edition is not so valuable as that of the French. *Strab.* 1.—*Plin.* 4. c. 11.—*Paterc.* 2. c. 15.—*C. Nep. in Paus. Alcib. Timoth*—*Justin.* 9. c. 1.—*Tacit.* 12. *Ann.* c. 62 & 63.—*Mela*, 2. c. 2. —*Marcell.* 22. c. 8.

BY'ZAS, a son of Neptune. His father and Apollo assisted him in the building of his capital, to which he gave the name of Byzantium. *Diod.* 4.

BYZE'A, a city of Scythia. *Steph.*

BYZE'RES, a people of Pontus, situated between Cappadocia and Colchis. *Dionys. Perieg.*—*Flacc.* 5. v. 153.

BY'ZES, a celebrated artist in the age of Astyages, king of Media. *Paus.* 5. c. 10.

BYZ'IA, a town in the possession of the kings of

Thrace, said to be hated by swallows on account of the horrible crimes of Tereus. *Plin.* 4. c. 11.

C.

CAAN'THUS, a son of Oceanus and Tethys. Apollo had carried away his sister Malia, and he burnt in revenge the ravisher's temple near the Isthmus. He was killed for this impiety by the god, and a monument was afterwards raised to his memory by the neighbouring people. *Paus.* 9. c. 10.

CAB'ADES, a king of Persia, who waged war with the emperors Anastasius and Justinian. He died A.D. 532, having reigned 41 years. *Agath.* l. 4.—*Procop. de Bell. Pers.*—*Niceph. Hist. Misc.* l. 16. c. 15.

CAB'ALA, a place of Sicily, where the Carthaginians were conquered by Dionysius. *Diod.* 15.

CABAL'ACA, a town of Albania. *Plin.* 6. c. 10.

CAB'ALES, a people of Africa. *Herodot.* 4. c. 171.

CABA'LII, a people of Asia Minor. *Id.* 3. c. 90.

CABA'LIS, a city near Cibyra, on the Mæander. *Steph.*

CABALLI'NUM, a town of the Ædui, now Chalons on the Saone. *Cæs. Bell. G.* 7. c. 42.

CABALLI'NUS, a clear fountain on mount Helicon, in Bœotia, sacred to the muses, and called also Hippocrene, because it was said to be raised from the ground by the foot of Pegasus. *Pers. Prol.* v. 1.

CABAL'LUS, the surname of a family at Rome. *Mart.* 1. epigr. 42. v. 17.

CABANDE'NA, a region of Susiana. *Ptol.*

CABAR'NI, the name of the priests of Ceres, at Parus. *Hesych.*—*Steph.*—*Suidas.*

CABAR'NUS, the name of the person who informed Ceres of the rape of Proserpine. *Steph.*

CABASI'TES, a province of Ægypt, with a town called Cabasa. *Ptol.*

CABAS'SUS, a town of Cappadocia. *Homer.*——A village near Tarsus. *Apion.*—*Steph.*

CABELEN'SES, a people of Mæonia, called also Lasonii. *Herodot.* 7. c. 77.

CABEL'LIO, a town of Gallia Narbonensis, now Cavaillon. *Plin.* 3. c. 4.

CABI'RA, a wife of Vulcan.——A town of Paphlagonia. *Strab.*

CABI'RI, certain deities held in the greatest veneration at Thebes, Lemnus, in Macedonia and Phrygia, but more particularly in the islands of Samothrace and Imbrus. The number of these deities is uncertain. It is unknown where their worship was first established; yet Phœnicia seems to be the place according to the authority of Sanchoniathon, and thence it was introduced into Greece by the Pelasgi. The festivals or mysteries of the Cabiri, were celebrated with the greatest solemnity at Samothrace. None but the consecrated priests were permitted to enter the temple, but so extensive was the influence of the deities, that all the ancient heroes and princes were generally initiated, that by this solemn act they might reconcile themselves to heaven, and have their persons and property protected against the accidents of shipwreck and storms. These deities are often confounded with the Corybantes, Anaces, Dioscuri, &c., and, according to Herodotus, Vulcan was their father. This author mentions the sacrilege which Cambyses committed in entering their temple, and turning to ridicule their sacred mysteries. They were supposed to preside over metals. *Herodot.* 2. c. 51.—*Strab.* 10, &c.—*Paus.* 9. c. 22, &c.—*Cic. de Nat. D.* 1.—*Normus. Dionys.* 27, 29, &c.—*Lactant. de Fals. R.* 1. c. 15.—*Scholia Argon Apoll.* 1.—*Cæl. Rhod.* 8. c. 52. 1. 9. c. 20.

CABIR'IA, a surname of Ceres.

CABIR'IA, the festivals of the Cabiri. *Vid.* Cabiri.

CABIR'IA, a city of Asia. *Steph.*

CABIR'II, a people of Bœotia. *Id.*

CABOLY'TÆ, a people of Paropanisum. *Ptol.*

CABUBATH'ARA, a mountain of Arabia Felix. *Id.*

CABU'RA, a fountain of Mesopotamia, where Juno bathed. *Plin.* 31. c. 3.

CAB'URUS, a chief of the Helvii, in the age of J. Cæsar. *Cæs.* l. 7. c. 65.

CAB'YLA, a city and small province of Thrace. *Steph.*—*Suidas.*

CA'CA, a goddess among the Romans, sister to Cacus, who is said to have discovered to Hercules where her brother had concealed his oxen. She presided over the excrement of the body. The vestals offered sacrifices in her temple. *Lactant.* 1. c. 10.—*Gyrald. in Hist. D.* 1.—*Servius. in Æn.* 8. v. 190.

CACA'GO, a fountain of Laconia. *Paus.* 3. c. 24.

CACH'ALES, a river of Phocis. *Paus.* 10. c. 32.

CA'CUS, a famous robber, son of Vulcan and Medusa, represented as a three-headed monster, and as vomiting flames. He resided in Italy, and plundered the neighbouring country. When Hercules returned from the conquest of Geryon, Cacus stole some of his cows, and dragged them backwards into his cave to prevent discovery. Hercules departed without perceiving the theft; but his oxen having lowed, were answered by the cows in the cave of Cacus, and the hero soon became acquainted with the loss which he had sustained. He ran to the place, tacked Cacus, and strangled him in his arms, though vomiting fire and smoke. Hercules erected an altar to Jupiter Servator, in commemoration of his victory, and an annual festival was instituted by the inhabitants in honour of the hero, who had delivered their country from such a public calamity. *Ovid.* 1. *Fast.* v. 551.—*Virg. Æn.* 8. v. 194.—*Propert.* 4. el. 10.—*Juv.* 5. e. 125.—*Liv.* 1. c. 7.—*Dionys. Hal.* 1. c. 9. *Aurel. Vict. de Rom.* 6.

CACU'THIS, a river of India flowing into the Ganges. *Arrian. Indic.* 4. c. 4.

CACYP'ARIS, a river at the east of Sicily, below *Syracuse. Thucyd.* l. 7.

CACY'RUM, a town of Sicily, at the west of Syracuse, now Cassaro. *Ptol.*

CAD'ARA, an island of the Red Sea. *Plin.* 9. c. 3.

CADE'NA, a place in the mountains of Lycaonia. *Strab.* 15.

CA'DI, a town of Phrygia. *Strab.* 12.——A town of Lydia. *Propert.* 4. el. 6. v. 7.

CADIS'CUS, a mountain af Crete, now Capo Busco. *Plin.* 4. c. 12.

CA'DIUS RUFUS, a person accused of bribery, under Claudius. *Tac. Ann.* 12. c. 22.

CADME'A, the citadel of Thebes, built by Cadmus. It is generally taken for Thebes itself, and the Thebans are often called Cadmeans. *Stat. Theb.* 8. v. 601.—*Paus.* 2. c. 5.—*C. Nepos,* 15.

CADME'IS, an ancient name of Bœotia.

CAD'MUS, son of Agenor king of Phœnicia, was ordered by his father to go in quest of his sister Europa, and he was never to return to Phœnicia if he did not bring her back. As his search proved fruitless, he consulted the oracle of Apollo about his future destinies, and was ordered to build a city where he should see a young heifer stop in the grass, and to call the country Bœotia. He found the heifer according to the directions of the oracle; and as he wished to thank the god by a sacrifice, he sent his companions to fetch water from a neighbouring grove. The waters were sacred to Mars, and guarded by a dragon, which destroyed all the Phœnician's attendants. Cadmus, tired with their seeming delay, went to the place, and saw the monster still feeding on their flesh. He attacked the dragon, and overcame it by the assistance of Minerva, and sowed the teech in a plain, upon which armed men suddenly rose up from the ground. He threw a stone in the midst of them, and they instantly turned their arms one against the other, till all perished except five, who assisted him in building his city. Soon after he married Hermione, the daughter of Venus, by whom he had a son Polydorus, and four daughters, Ino, Agave, Autone, and Semele. Juno persecuted these children, as being descended from Venus; and their misfortunes so distracted Cadmus and Hermione, that they retired to Illyricum, loaded with grief, and infirm with age. They intreated the gods to remove them from the misfortunes of life, and were immediately changed into serpents. Some explain the dragon's fable, by supposing that it was a king of the country whom Cadmus conquered by war; and that the armed men rising from the field, meant no more than men armed with brass, according to the ambigious signification of a Phœnician word. Cadmus was the first who introduced the use of letters into Greece; but some maintain, that the alphabet which he brought from Phœnicia, was only different from that which was used by the ancient inhabitants of Greece. This alphabet consisted only of sixteen letters, to which Palmedes afterwards added four, and Simonides of Melus the same number. The worship of many of the Ægyptian and Phœnician deities was also introduced into Europe by Cadmus, who is supposed to have come into Greece, 1493 B.C., and to have died at the age of 61 years. According to those who believe that Thebes was built at the sound of Amphion's lyre, Cadmus built only a small citadel which he called Cadmea, and laid the foundation of a city which was finished by one of his successors. *Ovid. Met.* 3. fab. 1, 2, &c.—*Herodot.* 1. c. 56. l. 2. c. 49. l. 4. c. 147.—*Hygin.* fab. 6. 76. 155. 179. 240. 275, &c.—*Diod.* 1, &c.—*Paus.* 9. c. 5, &c.—*Hesiod. Theog.* v. 937, &c.—*Pherecyd. Hist.* 4.—*Schol. Euripid. Chæniss.* 5.—*Schol. Apollon.* 3. v. 1185. *Marcellin.* 19.—*Conon. apud Phot.* 186. c. 37.—*Euseb. Chron.* 692. *Id. de Præp. Ev.* 10.—*Palæph. de Incr.* 6.——A son of Pandion of Miletus, celebrated as an historian in the age of Crœsus, and as the writer of an account of some cities of Ionia, in four books. *Voss. Hist. Gr.* 1. c. 1, &c. ——Another historian of Miletus, son of Archelaus, wrote a history of Attica in sixteen books, and a treatise on love in fourteen books. *Suidas. in Voce.*—*Diod.* 1.—*Dionys. Hal.* 2.—*Clement. Alex.* 3.—*Strab.* 1.—*Plin.* 5. c. 29.——A Roman executioner, mentioned by *Horace*, 1. sat. 6. v. 29.——A mountain of Asia Minor, at the north of Lycia. *Cluver.* 5. c. 18.

CADRA, a hill of Asia Minor. *Tacit. Ann.* 6. c. 2.

CAD'REMA, a city of Lycia. *Steph.*

CADRU'SI, a town founded by Alexander the Great, near Caucasus. *Plin.* 6. c. 23.

CADU'CEUS, a rod entwined at one end by two serpents, in the form of two equal semicircles. It was the ensign of Mercury, and the emblem of power; and was given him by Apollo in return for his lyre. Various interpretations have been put upon the two serpents round it. Some suppose them to be a symbol of Jupiter's amours with Rhea. Others say, that it originates from Mercury's having appeased the fury of two serpents that were fighting, by touching them with his rod. Prudence is generally supposed to be represented by the two serpents, and the wings are the symbol of diligence; both necessary in the pursuit of business and of commerce, which Mercury patronised. With the caduceus Mercury conducted to the infernal regions the souls of the dead, and by its powerful touch he could lull mortals to sleep, and even raise to life a dead person. *Virg. Æn.* 4. v. 242.—*Horat.* 1. od. 10.—*Macrob. Sat.* 1. c. 19.—*Plin.* 29. c. 3.—*Apul. Met.* 10.—*Servius. in Æn.* 8. v. 138.—*Hygin. P.A.* 2. c. 7.

CADUE'NI, a people of Caria. *Plin.* 5. c. 29.

CADUR'CI, a people of Gaul, at the east of the Garonne. Their country is now called Guienne. It was famous in ancient times for its fine linen, whence the word *Cadurcum* not only was used to express superior materials, but the covering of a bed, and even the bed itself, or whatever was made of linen. *Juv.* 6. v. 536. sat. 7. v. 221.—*Plin.* 19. c. 1.—*Cæs.*

CADU'SII, a people of Asia, on the south-west borders of the Caspian Sea. *Plut.*—*Steph.*

CAD'YTIS, a town of Syria. *Herodot.* 2. c. 159.

CÆ'A, an island of the Ægæn Sea among the Cyclades, opposite the promontory of Sunium. It was also called Ceus and Cea, from Ceus the son of Titan. *Ovid.* 20. *Heroid.*—*Virg. G.* 1. v. 14.

CÆ'CIAS, a wind blowing from the north. *Plin.* 2. c. 47.

CÆCIL'IA, the wife of Sylla. *Plut. in Syl.*——The mother of Lucullus. *Id. in Luc.*——A daughter of Atticus. *Cic. ad Att.* 6. ep. 2 & 4.

CÆCIL'IA CA'IA. *Vid.* Tanaquil.

CÆCIL'IA LEX, was proposed A.U.C. 693, by Cæcil. Metellus Nepos, to remove Taxes from all the Italian states, and to give them free exportation. —Another, called also Didia, A. U. C. 656, by the consul Q. Cæcilius Metellus and T. Didus. It required that no more than one single matter should be proposed to the people in one question, lest by one word they should inadvertently give their assent to a whole bill, which might contain some clauses worthy to be approved, and others unworthy. It required that every law before it was preferred, should be exposed to view on three market-days.—Another enacted by Cæcilius Metellus, the censor, concerning fullers. *Plin.* 35. c. 17.—Another, A.U.C. 701, to restore on the censors their original rights and privileges, which had been lessened by P. Clodius the tribune. Another called also Gabinia, A.U.C. 685 against usury.

CÆCILIA'NUS, a Latin writer before the age of Cicero.——A senator condemned for calumniating Messalinus. *Tac. Ann* 6. c. 7.

CÆCIL'II, a plebeian family at Rome, descended from Cæcas, one of the companions of Æneas, or from Cæculus the son of Vulcan, who built Præneste. The Cæcilii branched into other families, the best known of which are the Metelli. This family gave birth to many illustrious generals and patriots.

CÆCIL'IUS CLAU'DIUS ISIDO'RUS, a Roman who left in his will to his heirs, 4116 slaves, 3600 yokes of oxen, 257,000 small cattle, 600,000 pounds of silver. *Plin.* 33. c. 10.

CÆCIL'IUS, a native of Epirus and freedman of Atticus, who opened a school at Rome, and is said to have first taught reading to Virgil and some other growing poets.

CÆCIL'IUS LU'CIUS, a tribune of the people who wished to mitigate the penalties inflicted on such as were guilty of bribery.

CÆCIL'IUS LU'CIUS, a Sicilian orator in the age of Augustus, who wrote a treatise on the Servile wars, a comparison between Demosthenes and Cicero, and an account of the orations of Demosthenes.

CÆCIL'IUS METEL'LUS. *Vid.* Metellus.

CÆCIL'IUS QUIN'TUS, a Sicilian, surnamed Niger, quæstor to Verres. *Quintil.* 7. c. 2.

CÆCIL'IUS QUIN'TUS, the father-in-law of Pompey. *Cic. Fam.* 8. ep. 8.

CÆCIL'IUS QUIN'TUS, a name assumed by Atticus, when adopted into the family of the Cæcilii by his maternal uncle. *Cor. Nep. in Att.*—*Cic. Att.* 3. ep. 20.

CÆCIL'IUS STA'TIUS, a comic poet, originally a slave, but deservedly commended by Cicero and Quintilian for his wit and humour, though the orator, *ad Atticum*, calls him *Malus Latinitatis auctor*. He was intimate with the learned men of his age, and his abilities were so highly esteemed, that Terence submitted his compositions to his criticism as to a man of superior judgment. The names of thirty of his comedies are mentioned by ancient historians, among which are his Nauclerus, Plocius, Epiclerus, Syracusæ, Fœnerator, Fallacia, Pausimachus, Hypobolimæus, Cratinus, Hephæstion, Asotus, Andria, Subditivus, Annales Venatorium, Umbræ, Obolus, Synaristusæ, &c. He was a native of Gaul, and died at Rome 168 B.C. and was buried in the Janiculum. Only about 178 lines remain of his works, which may be found in the Fragmenta Comicorum, Amstel. 1686, or in Maittaire's Corpus Poet. Lat. London, 1713. *Harles. Not. Lit. Rom.* 1. p. 96.—*Sax. Onom.* 1. p. 125.—*Horat.* 2. ep. 1.—*Quintil.*—*Eusebius.*—*Gyrald. P.*

CÆCI'NA TUS'CUS, a son of Nero's nurse, made governor of Ægypt. *Suet. in Ner.*

CÆCI'NA, a Roman who wrote some physical treatises. ——A citizen of Volaterræ, defended by Cicero.

CÆC'UBUM, a town of Latium at the west of the Liris, near the bay of the Caieta. The neighbouring country, called Cæcubus Ager, was noted for the excellence and plenty of its wines. *Strab.* 5. —*Horat.* 1. od. 20. l. 2. od. 14, &c.—*Plin.* 3. c. 5. l. 14. c. 6.

CÆC'ULUS, a son of Vulcan, so called because his eyes were small. After a life spent in plunder, he built Præneste; but being unable to find inhabitants, he implored Vulcan to declare whether he really was his father. Upon this a flame suddenly shone among a multitude who were assembled to see some spectacle, and by this supernatural occurrence they were immediately persuaded to become the subjects of Cæculus. *Virg. Æn.* 7. v. 680, says, that he was found in fire by shepherds, and on that account called son of Vulcan, who is the god of fire. *Servius ad Virg. in loco.*

CÆ'CUS, a surname given to Appius Claudius, in consequence of his blindness.

CÆDIC'IUS Q., a consul, A.U.C. 498.——Another, A.U.C. 465.——A military tribune in Sicily, who bravely devoted himself to rescue the Roman army from the Carthaginians, B.C. 254. He escaped with his life.——A Roman centurion, appointed general by such of his countrymen as had fled to Veii, upon the invasion of Rome by the Gauls. *Liv.* 5. c. 45 & 46.——A severe judge in the reign of Vitellius. *Juv.* 13. v. 197.

CÆD'ICUS, a rich person. *Virg. Æn.* 9. v. 362. ——A friend of Turnus. *Id. ibid.* 10. 747.

CÆLESTI'NI, a people of Umbria. *Plin.* 3. c. 14.

CÆ'LIA LEX, was enacted A.U.C. 635. by Cæcilius, a tribune in the consulship of Q. Cælius Metellus. It ordained that in judicial proceedings before the people. in cases of treason the votes should be given upon tablets, contrary to the exception of the Cassian law.

CÆLI'NUM, a town and river of the Veneti. *Plin.* 3. c. 19.

CÆ'LIUM, a town of Calabria, near Brundusium, now Ceglie. *Id.* 3. c. 11.

CÆ'LIUS M. RU'FUS, an orator, pupil of Cicero, died very young. He accused Antony, Cciero's colleague in the consulship, of improper conduct in Macedonia, and obtained his condemnation. He afterwards brought charges of bribery against L. Atratinus, in consequence of which the son of Atratinus accused him of committing acts of public violence. Cicero defended him, when he was accused by Claudius of being accessary to Catalline's conspiracy, of having murdered some ambassadors from Alexandria, and of having carried on an illicit amour with Clodia, the wife of Metellus. *Orat. pro M. Cœl.—Quintil.* 10. c. 1.

CÆ'LIUS, a man of Tarracina, found murdered in his bed. His sons were suspected of the murder, but acquitted. *Val. Max.* 8. c. 1.

CÆ'LIUS L. ANTIP'ATER, wrote a history of Rome which M. Brutus epitomized, and which Adrian preferred to the historical works of Sallust. Cælius flourished 120 years B.C. *Val. Max.* 1. c. 7.—*Cic.* 13 *ad Attic.* ep. 8.

CÆ'LIUS AURELIA'NUS, a native of Sicca in Africa, distinguished as a physician. Though his style is very barbarous, being half Greek and half Latin, with harsh and obscure passages, yet his writings are valuable for the accurate history and description of diseases which he has preserved. The age in which he lived is not clearly ascertained, though some suppose him to have flourished before the time of Galen, since in his full catalogue of physicians he nowhere introduces the name of Galen. The only one of his works that has escaped the ravages of time is *De celeribus & tardis passionibus*, the best edition of which is that of Almeloveen, Amst. 1722 and 1755. *Sax. Onom.* 1. p. 480.

CÆ'LIUS, SABI'NUS, a writer in the age of Vespasian, who composed a treatise on the edicts of the curule ædiles.

CÆ'LIUS TU'BERO, a man who came to life after he had been carried to the burning pile. *Plin.* 7. c. 52.

CÆ'LIUS VIBE'NUS, a king of Etruria, who assisted Romulus against the Cæninenses, &c.

CÆ'LIUS, one of the seven hills on which Rome was built. Romulus surrounded it with a ditch and rampart, and it was enclosed by walls by the succeeding kings. It received its name from Cælius, who assisted Romulus against the Sabines.

CÆM'ARO, a Greek, who wrote an account of India. *Plut. de flum.*

CÆ'NE, a small island in the Sicilian Sea. *Plin.* 3. c. 8. ——A town of Mesopotamia, on the Tigris.——A town on the coast of Laconia, whence Jupiter is called Cæneus. *Plin.* 4. c. 5.—*Ovid. Met.* 9. v. 136.

CÆ'NEUS, one of the Argonauts. *Apollod.* 1. c. 9. ——A Trojan killed by Turnus. *Virg.*

CÆNI'DES or **CÆN'IDES**, a patronymic of Eetion, as descended from Cæneus. *Herodot.* 5. c. 92.

CÆNI'NA, a town of Latium, near Rome. The inhabitants, called Cæninenses, made war against the Romans when their virgins had been stolen away, soon after the foundation of the city. *Dionys, Hal.* 2. c. 9.—*Plut. in Rom.—Ovid. Fast.* 2. v. 135.—*Propert.* 4. el, 11. v. 9.—*Liv.* 1. c. 9.

CÆ'NIS or **CÆ'NYS**, a promontory of Italy, opposite to Pelorus in Sicily, a distance of about one mile and a half.

CÆ'NIS, a Thessalian woman, daughter of Elatus, to whom Neptune offered violence, and whom he afterwards permitted to change her sex, and to become invulnerable. She also changed her name, and was called Cæneus, In the wars of the Lapithæ against the Centaurs, she offended Jupiter; and when a thousand darts were directed against the invulnerable Cæneus, his enemies overwhelmed him with a huge pile of wood, from which, however, he escaped by being suddenly changed into a beautiful bird of yellow plumage. *Paus.* 5. c. 10.—*Ovid. Met.* 12. v. 172 & 479. l. 8. v. 305.—*Virgil, Æn.* 6. 448, says, that she again returned to her former sex. *Servius in Virg. citato,*

CÆNI'TES, a harbour of Achaia, not far from the Saronicus Sinus. *Plin.* 4. c. 5.

CÆNOMA'NI, a people of Cisalpine Gaul, at the north of Placentia on the Po, between the Addua and the Ollius.

CÆPA'RIUS, one of Catiline's associates in his conspiracy against the state. *Cic. Cat.* 3. c. 6.

CÆ'PIO Q. SERVIL'IUS, a Roman consul, A.U.C. 648, in the Cimbrian war. He plundered a temple at Tolosa, for which he was punished by divine vengeance, &c. *Justin.* 32. c. 3.—*Paterc.* 2. c. 12.

CÆ'PIO, a quæstor who opposed Saturninus, *Cic. ad Her.* The surname of Cæpio properly belonged to the family of the Servilii.

CÆRA'TUS, a town and river of Crete. *Strab.—Callim.*

CÆ'RE or **CÆ'RES**, anciently Agylla, now Cervetere, a city of Etruria, once the capital of the whole country, situate on a very small river east of Rome, called Cæretanus amnis. It was still in existence in the age of Strabo. When Æneas came to Italy, Mezentius was king over the inhabitans, called Cæretes or Cærites; but they banished their prince, and assisted the Trojans. The people of Cære hospitably received the Romans who fled with the fire of Vesta, when the city was besieged by the Gauls, and for this humanity they were made citizens of Rome, but witnout the privilege of voting in the public assemblies; whence *Cærites tabulæ* was applied to those who had no suffrage, and *Cærites cera* was considered a term of reproach. *Virg. Æn.* 8. v. 597. l. 10. v. 183.—*Liv.* 1. c. 2. l. 6. c. 5.—*Strab* 5.—*Gellius*, 16. c. 13.—*Horat.* 1. ep. 6. v. 62.—*Plin.* 3. c. 5.

CÆR'ESI, a people of Germany. *Cæs.* l. 2. c. 4.

CÆR'OBRYX, a city of Lusitania. It was called also Cezimbria. *Ptol.*

CÆ'SAR, a surname given to the Julian family at Rome, either because one of them kept an *elephant*, which bears that name in the Punic tongue, or because one was born with a thick head of hair, *Cæsaries*. This name, after it had been dignified in the person of Julius Cæsar, and of his successors, was given to the heir apparent of the empire in the age of the Roman emperors. The twelve first Roman emperors were distinguished by the surname of *Cæsar*. They reigned in the following order: Julius Cæsar, Augustus, Tiberius, Caligula, Claudius, Nero, Galba, Otho, Vitellius, Vespasian, Titus, and Domitian. In Domitian, or, perhaps with greater accuracy, in Nero, the family of Julius Cæsar was extinguished. But after such a lapse of time, the appellation of Cæsar seemed inseparable from the imperial dignity, and therefore it was assumed by the successors of the Julian family. *Suetonius* has written a minute account of these twelve princes, in an impartial manner.

CÆ'SAR CA'IUS JU'LIUS, the first emperor of Rome, was son of L. Cæsar, and Aurelia, the daughter of Cotta. He was descended, according to some accounts, from Iulus, the son of Æneas. When he reached his fifteenth year, he lost his father, and the year after he was made priest of Jupiter. Sylla was aware of his ambition, as well as of his superior abilities, and therefore endeavoured to destroy him; but Cæsar understood his intentions, and, to avoid discovery, artfully changed his lodgings every day. He afterwards ingratiated himself into Sylla's friendship, but the dictator, with great penetration, observed to those who solicited the advancement of young Cæsar, that they were warm in the interests of a man who would prove some day or other the ruin of their country and of their liberty. When Cæsar went to finish his studies at Rhodes, under Apollonius Molo, he was seized by pirates, who offered him his liberty for thirty talents. He indignantly gave them forty, and threatened to revenge their insults; and he was no sooner out of their power than he armed a ship, pursued them, and crucified them all. His eloquence procured him friends at Rome; and the generous manner in which he lived equally served to promote his interest with the populace. He obtained the office of high priest at the death of Metellus; and after he had passed through the inferior employments of the state, he was appointed over Spain, where he signalized himself by his valour and intrigues. On his return to Rome he was made consul, and he soon after effected a reconciliation between Crassus and Pompey, and formed the first celebrated triumvirate. Being appointed commander for the space of five years over the Gauls, by the interest of Pompey, to whom he had given his daughter Julia in marriage, he here enlarged the boundaries of the Roman empire by conquest, and invaded Britain, which was then unknown to the Roman people. He next checked the Germans, and soon after had his government over Gaul prolonged five years, by means of his friends at Rome. The death of Julia and of Crassus, the corrupted state of the Roman senate, and the ambition of Cæsar and Pompey, soon became the causes of a civil war. Neither of these celebrated Romans would suffer a superior, and the smallest matters were sufficient grounds for unsheathing the sword. Cæsar's petitions were received with coldness or indifference by the Roman senate; and by the influence of Pompey, a decree was passed to strip him of his overgrown power. Antony, who in vain opposed it as tribune, fled to Cæsar's camp with the news; and the ambitious general no sooner heard of the tumultuous proceedings at Rome, than he made it a plea of resistance. On pretence of avenging the violence which had been offered to the sacred office of tribune in the person of Antony, he crossed the Rubicon, which was the boundary of his province. This was a declaration of war, and Cæsar entered Italy sword in hand. Upon this, Pompey, with all the friends of liberty, left Rome, and retired to Dyrrachium; and Cæsar, after he had subdued all Italy in sixty days, entered Rome, and provided himself with money from the public treasury. He went to Spain, where he conquered the partisans of Pompey, under Petreius, Africanus, and Varro; and on his return to Rome was declared dictator, and soon after consul. Being without an open enemy in Italy, he left Rome, and went in quest of Pompey, observing that he was marching against a general without troops, after having defeated troops without a general in Spain. In the plains of Pharsalia, B.C. 48, the hostile generals engaged; but the fortune of Cæsar prevailed, and Pompey, being defeated, fled into Ægypt, where he was basely murdered. Cæsar, after he had made a noble use of his victory, pursued his adversary into Ægypt, where he for some time, forgot his fame and character in the arms of Cleopatra, by whom he had a son. His danger was great while at Alexandria; but he extricated himself with wonderful success, and made Ægypt tributary to his power. After several conquests in Africa, the defeat of Cato, Scipio, and Juba, and of Pompey's sons in Spain, he entered Rome, and triumphed over five different nations, Gaul, Alexandria, Pontus, Africa and Spain, and was created perpetual dictator. But now his glory was at an end, his uncommon success created him enemies, and the chief of the senators, among whom was Brutus, his most intimate friend, conspired against him, and stabbed him in the senate-house. He fell, pierced with twenty-three wounds, on the 15th of March, B.C. 44. in the 56th year of his age. Casca gave him the first blow, and he immediately attempted to make some resistance; but when he saw Brutus among the conspirators, he submitted to his fate, and fell down at their feet, muffling up his mantle, and exclaiming, *Et tu quoque Brute!* Cæsar might have escaped the sword of the conspirators, if he had listened to the entreaties of his wife Calpurnia, whose dreams, on the night previous to the day of his murder, were very extraordinary and alarming. He also received, as he went to the senate-house, a paper from Artemidorus, which discovered the whole conspiracy to him; but he unfortunately neglected the reading of what might have saved his life. When he was in his first campaign in Spain, Cæsar was observed to gaze at a statue of Alexander, and he even shed tears at the recollection that that hero had conquered the world at an age in which he himself had done nothing. The learning of Cæsar deserves commendation no less than his military character. He used the influence of his authority, and the assistance of men of science, for the reformation of the calendar, and well deserved the gratitude of mankind for this necessary and important regulation. He wrote his commentaries on the Gallic wars on the spot where he fought his battles, and the composition has been admired for the elegance, as well as correctness of his style. This valuable book was nearly lost; and when Cæsar saved his life in the bay of Alexandria, he was obliged to swim from his ship, with his arms in one hand and his commentaries in the other. Besides the Gallic and Civil wars, he wrote other pieces, which are now lost. The history of the war in Alexandria and Spain is attributed to him, and by others to Hirtius and Oppius. Cæsar has been blamed for his debaucheries and expenses; and the first year he held a public office, his debts were rated at 830 talents, which his friends discharged; yet, in his public character, he must be reckoned one of the few heroes that rarely make their appearance among mankind. His qualities were such that in every battle he could not but be conqueror, and in every republic, master; and to his sense of his superiority over the rest of the world, or to his restless ambition, we are to attribute his saying, that he wished rather to be first in a little village, than second at Rome. It was after his conquest over Pharnaces in one day, that he made use of these remarkable words, to express the celerity of his operations, *Veni, vidi, vici.* Conscious of the services of a man, who, in the intervals of peace, beautified and enriched the capital of his country with public buildings, libraries, and porticos, the senate permitted the dictator to wear a laurel crown upon his bald head; and it is said that they were going to give him the title or authority of king all over the Roman empire, except Italy, when he was murdered. In his private character, Cæsar has been accused of seducing one of the Vestal virgins, and suspected of being privy to Cataline's conspiracy; and it was his fondness for libidinous pleasures which made his contemporaries say, that he was the husband of all the women at Rome, and the woman of all the men. It is said that he conquered 300 nations, took 800 cities, and defeated three millions of men, one million of which fell in the field of battle. *Pliny*, 7. c. 25, says, that he could employ at the same time, his ears to listen, his eyes to read, and his hand to write, and his mind to dictate. His death was preceded, as many authors mention, by uncommon prodigies; and immediately after his death a large comet made its appearance. Cæsar when young was betrothed to Cossutia, a rich heiress, whom he dismissed to marry Cornelia, the daughter of Cinna, by whom he had Julia. His attachment to Cornelia was so great, that he never could be prevailed upon by the arts or threats of Sylla to divorce her; but her attachment he boldly preferred to his own personal safety. After her early death, which he lamented with great bitterness of grief, he married Pompeia, the grand-daughter of Sylla; and for his fourth wife he took Calpurnia, the daughter of the consul Piso, a connection formed from political motives. The best edition of Cæsar's Commentaries, are the magnificent one of Dr. Clarke, fol. Lond. 1712; that of Cambridge, with a Greek translation, 4to. 1727; that of Oudendorp, 2 vols, 4to., L. Bat. 1737; and that of Elzevir, 8vo. L. Bat. 1635. *Sueton. & Plut. in Vitâ.—Dio.—Appian.—Orosius.—Diod.* 16. & ccl. 31 & 37.—*Virg. G.* 1. v. 466.—*Ovid. Met.* 15. v. 782.—*Marcell.—Flor.* 3 & 4.—*Harles. Not. Lit. Rom.* 1. p. 166.—*Sax. Onom.* 1. p. 164. [The finest statue of Julius Cæsar is that in his character of high priest, existing in the Museum of the Capitol. It is sometimes mis-named Augustus. There is also a fine bust of him in the Vatican.]

Cæ'sar Lu'cius was father to the dictator. He died suddenly, when putting on his shoes.

Cæ'sar Octavia'nus. *Vid.* Augustus.

Cæ'sar Ca'ius, a tragic poet and orator, commended by *Cicero in Brut.* His brother C. Lucius was consul, and, in the civil wars of Marius, followed, as well as himself the party of Sylla. They were both put to death by order of Marius.

Cæ'sar Lu'cius, an uncle of M. Antony, who followed the interest of Pompey, and was proscribed by Augustus, for which Antony proscribed Cicero, the friend of Augustus. His son Lucius was put to death by J. Cæsar in his youth.

CÆ'SAR, the name of two sons of Agrippa, Caius and Lucius. *Vid.* Agrippa.

CÆ'SAR AUGUS'TA, a town of Spain, built by Augustus, on the Iberus, now called Saragossa. *Mela*, 2. c. 16.

CÆSARE'A, a city of Cappadocia.——A city of Bithynia.——A city of Mauritania.——A city of Palestine, so called by king Herod, in honour of Augustus. *Joseph. B. J.* 1. c. 16.—*Plin.* 5. c. 13 There were many small insignificant towns of that name, either built by the emperors, or called by their name, in compliment to them.

CÆSA'RION, the son of J. Cæsar, by Cleopatra, was at the age of thirteen, proclaimed by Antony and his mother, king of Cyprus, Ægypt, and Cœlesyria. He was put to death five years after by Augustus. *Suet. in Aug.* 17. & *Cæs.* 52.

CÆSA'RIUM, a town of Ægypt. *Strab.* 17.

CÆSAROBRICEN'SES, a people of Lusitania. *Ptol.* 4. c. 22.

CÆSARODU'NUM, a town of the Turones in Gaul, now Tours, on the Loire, in Tourraine.

CÆSAROM'AGUS or CÆSAROMA'GUS, a town of Gaul, called also Bratuspantium, now Beauvais. ——A town of Britain, now Chelmsford.

CÆSE'NA, a town of Umbria, on the river Sapis. *Plin.* 3. c. 15.

CÆSEN'NIUS. *Vid.* Cesennius.

CÆSE'TIUS, a Roman who protected his children against Cæsar. *Val. Max.* 5. c. 7.

CÆ'SIA, a surname of Minerva.

CÆ'SIA, a wood in Germany. *Tacit.* 1. *Ann.* c. 50.

CÆ'SIUS, a Latin poet, whose talents are described as scarcely above mediocrity. *Catull.* 14.

CÆ'SIUS BAS'SUS, a poet. *Vid.* Bassus.

CÆ'SIUS NAS'ICA, the commander of a legion in Britain. *Tacit.* 12. *Ann.* 40.

CÆ'SO QUIN'TIUS, a son of Q. Cincinnatus, who revolted to the Volsci. *Livy*, 3. c. 11. &c.

CÆSO'NIA, a lascivious woman who married Caligula, and was murdered at the same time with her daughter Julia. *Suet. in Calig.* c. 59.

CÆSO'NIUS MAX'IMUS, was banished from Italy by Nero, on account of his friendship with Seneca, &c. *Tacit.* 15. *Ann.* c. 71.

CÆT'ULUM, a town of Spain. *Strab.* 2.

CAICI'NUS, a river of Locris. *Thucyd.* 3. c. 103.

CAI'CUS, a companion of Æneas. *Virg. Æn.* 1. v. 187. l. 9. v. 35.——A general of Æetes. *Val. Flacc.* 6. v. 69.

CAI'CUS, a river of Mysia, falling into the Ægæan Sea, opposite Lesbus. It is now called Girmasti, and in ancient times it received, from its situation, the epithet of Mysus from Virgil, and of Teuthrantæus from Ovid. *Mela*, 1. c. 18.—*Ptol.* 5. c. 2.—*Strab.* 13.—*Virg. G.* 4. v. 370.—*Ovid. Met.* 2. v. 243.

CAIE'TA, a town, promontory, and harbour of Campania, which received its name from Caieta, the nurse of Æneas, whose ashes were deposited there in a marble tomb, by the piety of her illustrious protector. *Ovid. Met.* 14. v. 443.—*Virg. Æn.* 7. v. 2.

CA'IUS and CA'IA, prænomens very commonly given to individuals of both sexes, at Rome. C, in its natural position, denoted the man's name, and when reversed Ɔ it implied Caia. Every newly married woman, when entering her husband's house, was asked by him what her name was, and the general answer was, *Ubi tu Caius, ego Caia. Where you are the master in the house, I am the mistress.* This formality was said to be after the example of Tanaquil the wife of Tarquin, whose name was Caia Cæcilia. *Plin.* 8. c. 48.—*Quintil.* 1. c. 7.

CA'IUS, a lawyer who flourished about A D. 160. Of his Institutes there remains an epitome, though it is interpolated. A summary of them was published by Ægidius, 1517. The last impression of this edition is that of Paris, 1747. *Harles. Not. Lit. Rom.* 1. p. 508.—*Sax. Onom.* 1. p. 302.——A son of Agrippa by Julia. *Vid.* Agrippa.

CAL'ABER QUIN'TUS or COINTUS, so called because his works were discovered at Hydrus in Calabria, wrote a Greek poem in fourteen books, about the beginning of the third century. He was also called Smyrnæus. This poem is a continuation of Homer's Iliad, and after mentioning the several disasters which befel the Trojans after the death of their favourite hero, Hector, the untimely fate of Achilles, and the ruin of Priam's kingdom, the poet concludes by describing the return of the victorious Greeks to their native land, and their escape from the dangers of the sea, by which Ajax and other chiefs were overwhelmed. The best editions of this elegant and well written book are that of Rhodoman, 12mo. Hanover, 1604, with the notes of Dausqueius, and that of Pauw, 8 vo. L. Bat. 1734. *Fabr. B. Gr.* l. 2. c. 7.

CALA'BRIA, a country of Magna Græcia, in Italy. It has been called Messapia, Japygia, Salentinia, and Peucetia. The poet Ennius was born there. The country was fertile, and produced great variety of fruits, much cattle, and excellent honey. *Virg. G.* 3. v. 425.—*Horat.* 1. od. 31, *Epod.* 1. v. 27. l. 1. ep. 7. v. 14.—*Strab.* 6.—*Mela*, 2. c. 4.—*Plin.* 8. c. 48.—*Solin.* 8.—*Ital.* 1. v. 683.—*Val. Flacc.* 3. v. 581.—*Columell.* 7. c. 2.

CAL'ABRUS, a river of Calabria. *Paus.* 6.

CALACH'ANA, a region of Armenia Minor. *Strab.*

CALACHE'NE, a region of Assyria, called Calacina by *Ptolemy*. *Strab.* 16.

CALADU'NUM, a city of the Callaici, in Spain. *Ptol.*

CA'LÆ, a city of India.——An island near Taprobane. *Id.*

CALÆ'GIA, a town of Germany, now, probably, Wittenberg. *Id.*

CALÆ'I, islands in the mouth of the Persian Gulph. *Arrian. in Peripl.*

CALÆ'NUS or CAL'BIUS, a fountain of Lycia. *Steph.*

CALAGURITA'NI, a people of Calaguris, a town of Spain on the Iberus, who ate their wives and children rather than yield to Pompey. Calaguris is called Nascica, to distinguish it from another town of the same name more to the eastward, near the Pyrenees, called also Fibularia, *Liv.* 39. c. 21.—*Plin.* 3. c. 3.—*Val. Max.* 7. c. 6.

CAL'AIS and ZE'THES. *Vid.* Zethes.

CALAGU'TIS, a river of Spain. *Flor.* 8. c. 22.

CAL'AMÆ, a city of Messenia. *Steph. ex Polyb.*

CALAMEN'THÆ, a city of Libya, or of the Phœnicians. *Steph.*

CALA'MI, a place of Samus. *Herodot.* 9. c. 96.

CAL'AMIS, an excellent carver, whose works, especially a statue of Apollo, and some vases, are mentioned with high commendation, though he is considered far inferior to Praxiteles by *Cicero, de Clar.* 70.—*Paus.* 1. c. 3.—*Ovid. ex Pont.* 4. ep. 1. v. 33.—*Quintil.* 12. c. 10.—*Plin.* 34. c. 7 & 8.—*Propert.* 3. el. 9. v. 10.

CALAMIS'SUS, a town of the Locri. *Plin.* 4. c. 3.

CAL'AMOS, a town of Asia, near mount Libanus. *Plin.* 5. c. 20.——A town of Phœnicia. *Polyb.* ——Another of Babylonia. *Strab.*

CAL'AMUS, a son of the river Mæander, who was tenderly attached to Carpo the daughter of Zephyrus, and one of the Horæ. Their happiness was of short duration. Carpo was drowned in the Mæander, and Calamus, unable to bear her loss, entreated Jupiter to remove him from life, and he was consequently changed into a reed, *calamus*, which grows generally on the borders of rivers. *Servius in Ecl. Virg.* 5. v. 48.—*Paus.* 9. c. 35.

CALA'NUS, or CAL'ANUS, a philosopher, one of the gymnosophists. He followed Alexander in his Indian expedition, and being attacked by disease in his 83d year, he ordered a pile to be raised, upon which he mounted, decked with flowers and garlands, to the astonishment of the king and of the army. When the pile was set on fire, Alexander asked him whether he had any thing to say? "No," said he, "I shall meet you again in a very short time." Alexander died three months after in Babylon, and the recollection of what Calanus had said increased his reputation as a prophet. The real name of this philosopher, according to Plutarch, was Sphines, and he received that of Calanus from his saluting the Greeks in his own language with the word *Cale*, which signifies hail. *Strab.* 15.—*Cic. de Div.* 1. c. 23.—*Arrian. & Plut. in Alex.*—*Ælian.* 2. c. 41. l. 5. c. 6.—*Val. Max.* 1. c. 8.

CAL'AON, a river of Asia Minor, near Colophon. *Paus.* 7. c. 3.

CAL'ARIS, a city of Sardinia. *Flor.* 2. c. 6.

CALAR'NA, a city of Macedonia. *Steph.*

CALATA'RÆ, a people of Bactriana. *Ptol.*

CALATHA'NA, a town of Macedonia. *Liv.* 32. c. 13.

CALA'THIUS, a mountain of Laconia. *Paus.* 3. c. 26.

CAL'ATHUS, a son of Jupiter and Antiope. *Homer.*

CALATHU'SA, an island between the Chersonesus and Samothrace. *Plin.* 4. c. 12.——An island of Pontus. *Steph.*——A town of Arabia Deserta. *Ptol.*

CALA'TIA, a town of Campania, on the Appian way. It was made a Roman colony in the age of Julius Cæsar, and is now Gajatzo. *Sil.* 8. v. 543. —*Liv.* 9. c. 2. 28 & 43. l. 22. c. 13 & 61. l. 26. c. 16. l. 27. c. 31.

CALAT'IBUS, a city of Libya. *Steph.*

CALA'TIÆ, a people of India, who were said to eat the flesh of their parents. *Herodot.* 3. c. 38.

CAL'ATIS, a town of Thrace near Tomus, on the borders of the Euxine Sea. *Mela*, 2. c. 2.—*Strab.* 7.

CALA'VII, a people of Campania. *Liv.* 26. c. 27.

CALA'VIUS, a magistrate of Capua, who rescued some Roman senators from death, &c. *Liv.* 23. c. 2 & 3.

CALAURE'A or CALAURI'A, an island near Trœzene in the bay of Argos. Apollo, and afterwards Neptune, was the chief deity of the place, and his temple was served by a woman, whom nothing but marriage could remove from her sacred office. In the age of the Antonines there was still to be seen there the tomb of the orator Demosthenes, who poisoned himself there, to escape from the persecution of Antipater. *Ovid Met.* 7. v. 384.—*Plin.* 4. c. 12.—*Paus.* 1. c. 8. l. 2. c. 33.—*Strab.* 8.—*Mela*, 2. c. 9. Also Calau'ria.

CAL'BIS, a river of Caria. *Mela*, 1. c. 16.

CAL'CE, a city of Campania. *Strab.* 5.

CAL'CHAS, a celebrated soothsayer, son of Thestor. He accompanied the Greeks to Troy, in the office of high priest; and he informed them that that city could not be taken without the aid of Achilles, that their fleet could not sail from Aulis before Iphigenia was sacrificed to Diana, and that the plague could not be stopped in the Grecian army, before the restoration of Chryseis to her father. He told them also, that Troy could not be taken under ten years. He had received the power of divination from Apollo. Calchas was informed, that as soon as he found a man more skilled than himself in divination, he must perish; and this happened near Colophon, after the Trojan war. He was unable to tell how many figs were contained in the branches of a certain fig-tree; and when Mopsus mentioned the exact number, Calchas died through grief. *Vid.* Mopsus. *Homer. Il.* 1. v. 69.—*Æschyl. in Agam.*—*Euripid. in Iphig.* —*Paus.* 1. c. 43.—*Ital.* 13. v. 38.—*Apollod.* 3.

CALCHEDO'NIA. *Vid.* Chalcedon.

CALCHIN'IA, a daughter of Leucippus. She had a son by Neptune, who inherited his grandfather's kingdom of Sicyon. *Paus* 2. c. 5.

CAL'DIUS, a surname satirically applied to Claudius by his army, because he was very partial to warm *calidus*, drink. *Suet. Tib.* 42.

CAL'DUS CÆ'LIUS, a Roman who killed himself when detained as a prisoner by the Germans. *Paterc.* 2. c. 120. The appellation of Caldus is applied to men of rash and violent dispositions, *Cic. Inv.* 2. c. 9.

CA'LE, *-es*, or CA'LES, *-ium*, now Calvi, a town of Campania, in the Falernus Ager, the wines of which have been extolled by the ancient poets. *Horat.* 4. od. 12. v. 14.—*Juv.* 1. v. 69.—*Sil.* 8. v. 513.—*Virg. Æn.* 7. v. 728.

CALEDO'NIA, a country at the north of Britain, now, called Scotland. The reddish hair and lofty stature of its inhabitants seemed to indicate a German extraction, according to *Tacitus, in Vitâ Agric.* It was so little known to the Romans, and its inhabitants so little civilized, that they called it *Britannia Barbara*, and they never penetrated far into the country. *Martial.* 10. epigr. 44.—*Sil.* 3. v. 598.—*Ptol.* 2. c. 3.—*Flacc.* 1. v. 8.

CALEN'TUM, a place of Spain, where it is said that they made bricks so light that they swam on the surface of the water. *Plin.* 35. c. 14.

CALE'NUS, a famous soothsayer of Etruria, in the age of Tarquin. *Plin.* 28. c. 2.——A lieutenant of Cæsar's army. After Cæsar's murder, he concealed some persons who had been proscribed by the triumvirs, and behaved with great honour to them. *Plut. in Cæs.*

CALE'NUS Q. FU'SIUS, a tribune of the people at Rome, who, by a law, procured the acquittal of Clodius, who had insulted the religion of his country, in the violation of the rites of Bona Dea. *Cic. Att.* 1. ep. 14 & 16. *Phil.* 8. c. 3.

CALE'NUS JU'LIUS, a tribune in the army of Vitellius, sent into Gaul to announce a victory. *Tac. Hist.* 3, 35.

CA'LES. *Vid.* Cale.——A city of Bithynia, on the Euxine. *Arrian.*——A Roman colony near the Sidicini. *Liv.* 8. c. 16.

CALE'SIUS, a charioteer of Axylus, killed by Diomedes in the Trojan war. *Homer. Il.*

CAL'ETI, a people of Belgic Gaul, now Pays de Caux, in Normandy. *Cæs. Bell. G.* 2. c. 4. Their chief town was called Caletum, now Calais.

CAL'ETOR or CALE'TOR, a Trojan prince, slain by Ajax, as he was going to set fire to the ship of Protesilaus. *Homer. Il.* 15. v. 419.—*Paus.* 10. c. 14.

CAL'ETRA, a small town of Etruria.

CA'LEX, a small river of Asia Minor, falling into the Euxine Sea. *Thucyd.* 4. c. 75.

CALGUI'A, a city of Arabia Petræa. *Ptol.*

CALIAD'NE, the wife of Ægyptus. *Apollod.* 2. c. 1.

CALICAD'NUS, a river of Cilicia. *Plin.* 5. c. 27.

CALICE'NI, a people of Macedonia. *Polyb.* 3.

CALIC'ULA or CALUC'ULA, a city of Hispania Bætica, now Caliar. *Ptol.*—*Plin.* 3. c. 1.

CALID'IUS M., an orator and prætorian, who was killed in the civil wars, &c. *Cæs. Bell. Civ.* 1. c. 2.

CALID'IUS L. JU'LIUS, a man remarkable for his riches, the excellency of his character, his learning and poetical abilities. He was proscribed by Volumnius, but saved from destruction by the influence of Atticus. *C. Nep. in Attic.* 12.

CALIG'ULA C., the emperor, received this surname from his wearing in the camp, the *Caliga*, a military covering for the leg. He was son of Germanicus by Agrippina, and succeeded to the imperial purple on the death of Tiberius. During the first eight months of his reign, Rome experienced universal prosperity, the exiles were recalled, taxes were remitted, and profligates dismissed; but Caligula soon displayed his true character; he became proud, wanton, and cruel. He built a temple to himself as a divinity, and he not only ordered his head to be placed on the images of the gods, but he wished to imitate the thunders and power of Jupiter. The statues of all great and heroic characters were removed, as if Rome would sooner forget her virtues in their absence; and the emperor appeared in public places in the most indecent manner, encouraged roguery, committed incest with his three sisters, and established public places of prostitution. He often amused himself with putting innocent people to death; he attempted to famish Rome by a monopoly of corn; and as he took particular delight in the miseries of mankind, he often wished that the Romans had but one head, that he might have the gratification of striking it off. Wild beasts were constantly fed in his palace with human victims; and as if to outrage the feelings, and insult the dignity, of fallen Rome, a favourite horse was made high priest and consul, kept in marble apartments, and adorned with the most valuable trappings and pearls which the empire could furnish. Caligula built a bridge extending upwards of three miles into the sea; and would perhaps have shewn himself still more tyrannical, had not Chæreas, one of his servants, with others equally tired with the cruelties and the insults that were offered with impunity to the persons and character of the Romans, formed a conspiracy against his life. In consequence of this, the tyrant was murdered January 24th, in his 29th year, after a reign of three years and ten months, A. D. 41. It has been said, that Caligula wrote a treatise on rhetoric; but his opinion of learning and learned men may be gathered from his attempts to destroy the writings of Homer and of Virgil. *Dio.*—*Sueton. in Vitâ.*—*Tacit. Ann.* [There is no very celebrated statue of this emperor, but there are some fine busts, of which the best is that in the collection at the Villa Albani, near Rome.]

CALIN'DA, a city of Lycia, called Calymna by *Strabo*, and Calydua by *Pliny*, 5. c. 27 It is now Lagula.

CALIN'DRÆ, a city of Mygdonia in Asia.——A city of India within the Ganges. *Ptol.*

CALIN'GÆ, a nation of India. *Plin.* 6. c. 17.

CALIN'GII, a people of Arabia Felix. Their metropolis was Mariaba. *Plin.* 6. c. 28. 7. c. 2.

CALIN'GON, a promontory of India. *Id.* 6. c. 10.

CALINIPAX'A, a town of India. *Id.* 6. c. 17.

CALIOR'DI, a people of Taurica Chersonesus. *Id.* 4. c. 11.

CALIP'PUS, a mathematician of Cyzicus, B.C. 330.

CAL'IPUS, a river of Lusitania. *Ptol.*

CA'LIS, a man in Alexander's army, tortured for conspiring against the king. *Curt.* 6. c. 11.

CALIS'IA, a town of Germany, now Kalisch. *Ptol.*

CALI'TÆ, a people of the interior of Libya. *Id.*

CAL'IUR, a town of India within the Ganges. *Id.*

CALLÆS'CHRUS, the father of Critias. *Plut. in Alcib.*

CALLA'ICI, a people of Lusitania, now Gallicia, at the north-west of Spain. *Ovid.* 6. *Fast.* v. 461.

CALLANTIA'NI, a people of Pontus. *Diod. Sic.* l. 19.

CALLAN'TIS, a city of Sicily. *Suidas.*

CAL'LAS, a general of Alexander. *Diod.* 17.——A general of Cassander, employed against Polyperchon. *Id.* 19.

CAL'LAS, a small river of Eubœa. *Strab.*

CALLATE'BUS, a town of Caria. *Herodot.* 7. c. 31.

CALLA'TIA or CALLAN'TIA, a town of Lower Mœsia. *Ptol.*

CAL'LE, a town of ancient Spain, now Oporto, at the mouth of the Douro, in Portugal.

CALLATE'RIA, a town of Campania. *Strab.* 5.

CALLE'LI or CALE'NI, a people of Campania, who inhabited the town of Cale. *Vid.* Cale.

CALLE'TUM, a town of Spain. *Plin.* 3. c. 1.

CALLI'ADES, a magistrate of Athens when Xerxes invaded Greece. *Herodot.* 8. c. 51.

CAL'LIAS, an Athenian appointed to make peace between Artaxerxes and his country. *Diod.* 12.——A son of Temenus, who, with the assistance of his brothers, murdered his father. *Apollod.* 2. c. 6.——A Greek poet, son of Lysimachus. His compositions are lost, though the titles of some of his plays, such as Atalanta, the Cyclopes, the Frogs, &c., are mentioned by *Suidas.* He was surnamed *Schœnion*, because he was employed in twisting ropes [σχοῖνο,] through poverty. *Athen.* 10.—*Gyrald. de P. Gr. Dial.* 7.—*Fabr. B. Gr.* l. 2. c. 19 & 22.——A partial historian of Syracuse. He wrote an account of the Sicilian war, and was well rewarded by Agathocles, because he had represented him in a favourable light. *Athen.* 12.—*Dionys.*——An Athenian greatly revered for his patriotism. *Herodot.* 6. c. 121.——A soothsayer.——An Athenian, commander of a fleet against Philip of Macedon, whose ships he took, &c.——A rich Athenian, who liberated Cimon from prison, on condition of marrying his sister and wife Elpinice. *C. Nep. & Plut. in Cim.*——An historian, who wrote an explanation of the poems of Alcæus and Sappho. *Strab.* 13. p. 618.——A town of Arcadia. *Paus.* 8. c. 27.

CALLIB'IUS, a general in the war between Mantinea and Sparta. *Xenoph. Hist. G.*

CAL'LICA, an inland city of Bithynia. *Ptol.*

CALLIC'ATIS, a city of India within the Ganges. *Id.*

CALLICE'RUS, a Greek poet, some of whose epigrams are preserved in the Anthologia.

CALLICH'ORUS, a place of Phocis, where the orgies of Bacchus were annually celebrated.

CAL'LICLES, an Athenian, whose house was not searched, on account of his recent marriage, when an enquiry was made after the money given by Harpalus, &c. *Plut. in Demosth.*——A statuary of Megara.

CALLICOLO'NA, a place of Troy, near the Simois. *Homer.—Strab.*

CALLIC'RATES, an Athenian, who seized upon the sovereignty of Syracuse, by artfully imposing on the timidity of Dion when he had lost his popularity. He was expelled by the sons of Dionysius, after reigning 13 months. He is called Calippus by some authors. *C. Nep. in Dion.*——An officer entrusted with the care of the treasures of Susa by Alexander. *Curt.* 5. c. 2.——An artist of Lacedæmon, who made with ivory, ants and other insects, so small that they could scarcely be seen. It is said that he engraved some of Homer's verses upon a grain of millet. *Plin.* 7. c. 21. l. 36. c. 5.—*Ælian. V. H.* 1. c. 17.——An Achæan, who, by his perfidy constrained the Athenians to submit to the power of the Romans. *Paus.* 7. c. 10.——A Syrian who wrote an account of Aurelia's life.——A brave Athenian, killed at the battle of Platæa. *Herodot.* 9. c. 72.

CALLICRAT'IDAS, a Spartan, who succeeded Lysander in the command of the fleet. He took Methymna, and routed the Athenian fleet under Conon. He was afterwards defeated and killed near the Arginusæ, in a naval battle, B.C. 406. *Diod.* 13.—*Xenoph. Hist. G.*——One of the four ambassadors sent by the Lacedæmonians to Darius, upon the rupture of their alliance with Alexander. *Curt.* 3. c. 13.——A Pythagorean writer.

CALLIC'ULA, a hill of Campania, which served as boundary to the Falernian plains. *Liv.* 22. c. 15 & 16.

CALLIDE'MUS, a person, probably an historian, mentioned by *Pliny*, 4. c. 12.—*Voss. de Hist. Gr.* l. 3.

CALLID'IUS, a celebrated Roman, contemporary with Cicero, who speaks of his abilities both as an orator and as a statesman with the highest commendation. *Quintil.* 10. c. 1. l. 12. c. 6.—*Cic. in Brut.* 274.—*Paterc.* 2. c. 36.

CALLID'ROMUS, a place near Thermopylæ.

CALLI'GA, a town of India within the Ganges. *Ptol.*

CALLIGE'TUS, a man of Megara, received in his banishment by Pharnabazus. *Thucyd.* 8. c. 6.

CALLIM'ACHUS, an historian and poet of Cyrene, son of Battus and Mesalma, and pupil of Hermocrates the grammarian. He had, in the age of Ptolemy Philadelphus, kept a school at Alexandria, where Apollonius of Rhodes was one of his pupils. The bad conduct of this pupil highly offended Callimachus, who lashed him severely in a satirical poem called Ibis. *Vid.* Appollonius. The Ibis of Ovid is an imitation of this piece. He wrote a work, in 120 books, on famous men, besides treatises on birds; but of all his numerous compositions, which, according to *Suidas*, amounted to 800, only 74 epigrams, an elegy, and some hymns on the gods, are extant; the best editions of which are, that of Ernesti, 2 vols. 8vo. L. Bat. 1761, and that of Vulcanius, 12mo, Antwerp, 1584. Dr. Bloomfield, the editor of Æschylus, has also edited the works of this poet. Propertius admired the writings of this illustrious bard so much, that he styled himself the Roman Callimachus. and Catullus employed his pen in translating his poem on the hair of Berenice. The precise time of his death, as well as of his birth, is unknown. *Propert.* 4. el. 1. v. 65.—*Cic. Tusc.* 1. c. 84.—*Horat.* 2. ep. 2. v. 109.—*Quintil.* 10. c. 1.—*Fabr. B. Gr.* l. 3. c. 17.

CALLIMA'CHUS, the nephew of the preceding, was also a poet, and wrote an epic poem *de insulis*, according to *Suidas.*

CALLIMA'CHUS, an Athenian general, killed in the battle of Marathon. His body was found in an erect posture, covered with wounds. *Plut.*——A Colophonian, who wrote the life of Homer. *Plut.*——A statuary of Corinth, who spent the greater part of his life in beautifying the buildings of Athens. He is said to have been the inventor of the Corinthian chapter, which he used elegantly to adorn with the leaves of the acanthus. *Paus.* 1. c. 16.——A Greek painter whose ideas of beauty and perfection were so extravagant, that scarcely any of his pieces survived the severity of his criticism. *Plin.* 34. c. 1.——A physician. *Plin.* 21. c. 3.——An archon at Athens. Olymp. 107. an. 5.

CALLIME'DES, an Athenian general. *Diod. Sic.*——An archon at Athens. Ol. 105. an. 4.

CALLIM'EDON, a partisan of Phocion, at Athens, condemned by the populace.

CALLIM'ELES, a youth ordered to be killed and served up as meat by Apollodorus of Cassandrea. *Polyœn.* 6. c. 7.

CALLINI'CUM, a town of the Persians, on the banks of the Euphrates. *Procop.*——A city of Osrhoene. *Lib. Not.*——A city of Mesopotamia. *Amm. Marcell.*

CALLINI'CUS, a surname given to Hercules by *Pindar* and *Euripides*. *Jul. Cæs. Scalig. Poet.* l. 1. c. 18.

CALLINI'CUS SUTO'RIUS, a sophist of Syria or of Arabia, in the time of Antoninus Pius. *Voss. Hist. Gr.* 2. c. 13.

CALLI'NUS, an orator, who is said to have invented elegiac poetry, B.C. 776. Some of his verses are to be found in Stobæus. *Athen.—Strab.* 14. *Gyrald. de Poet. Gr.* 3.

CALLINU'SA, a promontory of Cyprus. *Ptol.*

CALLI'OPE, daughter of Jupiter and Mnemosyne, and one of the Muses, presided over eloquence and heroic poetry. She is said to have been the mother of Orpheus by Apollo, and also of Hymenæus and Ialemus by the same god, according to others. Some call her also mother of the Corybantes by Jupiter, and of the Syrens by the Achelous. She was represented with a trumpet in her right hand, and with books in the other, which signified that her office was to take notice of the illustrious actions of heroes, as her sister Clio was employed in celebrating them; she also held the three most famous epic poems of antiquity, and appeared generally crowned with laurel. It is said that she settled the dispute between Venus and Proserpine, concerning Adonis, whose company these two goddesses wished both perpetually to enjoy. *Hesiod. Theog.—Apollod.* 1. c. 3.—*Horat.* 3. od. 4.—*Ovid. Fast.* 5. v. 80. [The statues of this Muse are very numerous; the best is that in the Vatican.]

CALLI'OPE, a city of Parthia. *Steph.*

CALLIPATI'RA, wife of Callianax the athlete, went disguised in men's clothes with her son Pisidorus to the Olympic games. When Pisidorus was declared victor, she discovered her sex through excess of joy, and was arrested, as women were not permitted to appear there on pain of death. The glorious victory of her son obtained her release; but a law was instantly made obliging wrestlers to appear naked. *Paus.* 5. c. 6. l. 6. c. 7.

CAL'LIPHON, a painter of Samus, famous for his historical pieces. *Plin.* 10. c. 26.——A philosopher, who made the *summum bonum* to consist in pleasure joined to the love of honesty. This system was opposed by *Cicero, Quæst. Acad.* 4. c. 131 & 139. *De Offic.* 3. c. 119.

CAL'LIPHRON, a celebrated dancing master, who had Epaminondas in the number of his pupils. *C. Nep. in Epam.*

CALLIP'IA, a fountain of the Ephesians. *Plin.* 5. c. 29.

CALLIP'IDÆ, a people of European Scythia. *Solinus*, c. 14. calls them Callipodes, and *Herodotus*, 4. c. 17. Græcoscythæ.

CALLIP'IDES, a famous actor, called from Ionia to perform before Alexander. *Polyæn.* 6. c. 10.——A Greek historian mentioned by *Strabo*. He wrote a history of the Scythians.

CALLIP'OLIS, now Gallipoli, a city of Thrace on the Hellespont, at the north of the river Ægos. *Sil.* 14. v. 250.——A town of Sicily near Ætna.——A city of Calabria on the bay of Tarentum, on a rocky island, joined by a bridge to the continent. It is now called Gallipoli, and contains 6000 inhabitants, who trade in oil and cotton.

CAL'LIPUS or CALIP'PUS, an Athenian, disciple to Plato. He destroyed Dion, &c. He is called by some Callicrates. *Vid.* Callicrates. *C. Nep. in Dion.*

CAL'LIPUS, a Corinthian who wrote a history of Orchomenus. *Paus.* 6. c. 29.——A philosopher. *Diog. in Zen.*——A general of the Athenians, when the Gauls invaded Greece by Thermopylæ. *Paus.* 1. c. 3.

CALLIP'YGES or CALLIP'YGOS, a surname of Venus. *Cœl. Rhod.* 4. c. 8.

CALLIR'RHOE, a daughter of the Scamander, who married Tros, by whom she had Ilus, Ganymedes, and Assaracus. *Apollod.*——A daughter of Oceanus and Tethys, mother of Echidna, Orthos, and Cerberus, by Chrysaor. *Hesiod. Theog.—Apollod.* 2.—*Hygin.* Præf. Fab. 151.——A daughter of Lycus, tyrant of Libya, who kindly received Diomedes at his return from the Trojan war. He abandoned her, upon which she killed herself.——A daughter of the Achelous, who married Alcmæon. *Vid.* Alcmæon. *Paus.* 8. c. 24.——A daughter of Phocus, the Bœotian, whose beauty procured her many admirers. Her father behaved with such coldness to her lovers, that they murdered him. Callirhoe avenged his death with the assistance of the Bœotians. *Plut, Amat. Narr.*——A daughter of Piras and Niobe. *Hygin.* fab. 145.

CALLIR'RHOE, a fountain of Attica, where Callirhoe killed herself. *Vid.* Coresus. *Paus.* 7. c. 21.—*Stat.* 12. *Theb.* v. 629.—*Plin.* 4. c. 7.——A fountain of Judæa, the waters of which were possessed of medicinal properties. *Joseph. A.* 17. c. 8.—*Plin.* 5. c. 16.——A lake of Mesopotamia, near Antiochia. *Steph.*

CALLIS'TA, an island of the Sporades in the Ægæan Sea, called afterwards Thera. *Plin.* 4. c. 12.—*Paus.* 3. c. 1. Its chief town was founded 1150 years B C. by Theras.

CALLISTE'A, a festival at Lesbus, during which all the women presented themselves in the temple of Juno, and the fairest was rewarded in a public manner. There was also an institution of the same kind among the Parrhasians, first made by Cypselus, whose wife was honoured with the first prize. The Eleans had one also, in which the fairest man received as a prize a complete suit of armour which he dedicated to Minerva. *Meursius, Gr. Fer.—Athenæus.—Suidas.*

CALLIS'THENES, a Greek, who wrote a history of his own country in 10 books, beginning with the peace between Artaxerxes and Greece, and ending with the plundering of the temple at Delphi by Philomelus at the Phocian war.—*Diod.* 16.——A man who, with others, attempted to expel the garrison of Demetrius from Athens. *Polyæn.* 5. c. 17.——A philosopher of Olynthus, who accompanied Alexander in his oriental expedition as his preceptor, an office to which he had been recommended by his friend and master Aristotle. Calisthenes affected to look with contempt on the victories of Alexander, and asserted that his own fame, erected on the basis of philosophy and historical composition, would be far more durable. Alexander, accustomed to dictate, could not bear to be treated with such disrespect. When Calisthenes, therefore, refused to pay divine honours to his master, he was accused of conspiring against him. The philosopher, shamefully mutilated, and exposed to wild beasts, was dragged about in chains, till Lysimachus gave him poison, which ended together his tortures and his life, B.C. 328. None of his compositions are extant. *Curt.* 8. c. 6.—*Plut. in Alex.—Arrian.* 4.—*Justin.* 12. c. 6 & 7. l. 15. e 3.——A writer of Sybaris. *Plut. de flum.—Stobæus.*——A freedman of Lucullus. It is said that he gave poison to his master. *Plut. in Lucull.*

CALLIS'TO or CALIS'TO was daughter of Lycaon, king of Arcadia, and one of Diana's attendants. Jupiter was captivated by her beauty, and seduced her. Her crime was discovered as she bathed with Diana; but her child, called Arcas, was hid in the woods and preserved. Juno afterwards changed Calisto into a bear; but Jupiter made her a constellation, with her son Arcas under the name of the bear, which is also called Helice by the Greeks. *Ovid. Met.* 2. fab. 4, 5 & 6. *Fast.* 2. v. 155.—*Apollod.* 3. c. 8.—*Hygin.* fab 176 & 177. *P. A.* 2.—*Paus.* 8. c. 3.

CALLISTONI'CUS, a celebrated statuary at Thebes. *Paus.* 9. c. 16.

CALLISTRA'TIA, a town of Galatia. *Ptol.*

CALLIS'TRATUS, an Athenian, appointed general with Timotheus and Chabrias against the Lacedæmonian forces. *Diod.* 15.——A native of Aphidna, in the time of Epaminondas, said to have been the most eloquent orator of his age. *Nep. in Epam.—Xen. Hellen.* 6.——An Athenian orator, with whom Demosthenes made an intimate acquaintance, after he had heard him plead. *Meursius* conjectures that this is the same person who wrote ἐκφράσεις, or descriptions of fourteen statues, which were edited with the works of Philostratus, and of which Fred. Morell made a Latin version. *Fabr. B. Gr.* 4. c 22.—*Sax. Onom.* 1. p. 295.—*Xenophon.*——A Greek historian, praised by *Dionysius* of *Halicarnassus*.——A comic poet, the rival of Aristophanes. *Gyrald. P. Hist. Dial.* 7.——A statuary. *Plin.* 34. c. 8.——A secretary of Mithridates. *Plut. in Lucull.*——A grammarian, who made the alphabet of the Samians consist of twenty-four letters. *Fabricius*, l. 4. c. 22. enumerates 12 persons of this name. See also *Saxius*, 1. p. 349.

CALLITHY'IA, daughter of Peranthus, the first priestess of Juno at Argos. *Euseb.* num. 376.

CALLIX'ENUS, a general who perished by famine. *Xen. Hist.* l. 1.——An Athenian imprisoned for passing sentence of death upon some prisoners. *Diod.* 13.——A Rhodian, whose work, *de Alexandriâ*, is cited by *Athenæus*, 6. c. 11. and *Harpocration. Voss. Hist. Gr.* 3. p. 339.——A celebrated statuary in Olymp. 155. *Plin.* 34. c. 8.——A writer on painters and sculptors. *Photius in Bibl.*

CA'LON, a statuary. *Quintil.* 12. c. 10.—*Plin.* 34. c. 8.

CA'LON STO'MA, (καλὸν στόμα,) one of the mouths of the Danube. *Plin.* 4. c. 12.—*Ptol.*

CALON'DAS, called also Archias, the murderer of the poet Archilochus. *Salmas. ad Solin.* 52.

CA'LOR, now Calore, a river of Italy, near Beneventum. *Liv.* 24. c. 14.

CALOS-LIMEN, a harbour of the Euxine Sea. *Mela*, 2. c. 1.

CAL'PAS or **CAL'PE**, a river and harbour of Bithynia on the shores of the Euxine, at the east of the Bosphorus. It is now called Kirpe or Sarpah. *Xenoph. Anab.—Strab.* 11.

CAL'PE, a mountain in the most southern parts of Spain, opposite to Mount Abyla, on the African coast. It had a harbour of the same name near it, but it was afterwards called Carteia. These two mountains were called the pillars of Hercules. Calpe is now the celebrated fortress called Gebeltarik, or Gibraltar. *Cic. ad Fam.* 10. ep. 32.

CALPHUR'NIA or **CALPUR'NIA**, a noble family in Rome, said to be descended from Calpus, son of Numa. It branched out in the ages of the commonwealth, and assumed the different surnames of Pisones, Bibuli, Flammæ, Cæsennini, Asprenates, &c. The Pisones were again subdivided into the families of the Bestiæ, Frugi, and Cæsonii. *Vell. Pat.* 2. c. 57.—*Val. Max.* 4. c. 3.—*Plut. in Num. & Cæs.*

Calphur'nia or **Calpur'nia**, a daughter of L. Piso, who was Julius Cæsar's fourth wife. The night previous to her husband's murder, she dreamed that the roof of her house had fallen, and that he had been stabbed in her arms; and on that account she attempted to detain him. After Cæsar's murder, she placed herself under the protection of M. Antony. *Sueton. in Jul.*

Calphur'nia, a daughter of Marius, sacrificed to the gods by her father, who was advised to do it in a dream, if he wished to conquer the Cimbri. *Plut. in Parall.*——A woman who killed herself when she heard that her husband was murdered in the civil wars of Marius. *Paterc.* 2. c. 26. ——A favourite of the emperor Claudius, &c. *Tacit. Ann.* 11. c. 30.——A woman ruined by the jealousy of Agrippina, on account of her beauty, &c. *Tacit. Ann.* 12. c. 20.

Calphur'nia or **Calpur'nia Lex**, was enacted A.U.C. 604, to punish severely such as were guilty of using bribes, &c. *Cic. de Off.* 2.

CALPHURNIA'NA, a city of the Turduli in Hispania Bætica, now Carpio. *Ptol.*

CALPHUR'NIUS BESTIA, a Roman of noble birth, bribed by Jugurtha to espouse and defend his cause. It is said that he murdered his wives when asleep. *Plin.* 27. c. 2.

Calphur'nius Cras'sus, a patrician, who went with Regulus against the Massyli. He was seized by the enemy as he attempted to plunder one of their towns, and was ordered to be sacrificed to Neptune. Bisaltia, the king's daughter, fell in love with him and gave him an opportunity of escaping, and of conquering her father. Calphurnius returned victorious, and Bisaltia destroyed herself.——A man who conspired against the emperor Nerva. *Dion.* 68.

Calphur'nius Galeria'nus, son of Piso, put to death, &c. *Tacit. Hist.* 4. c. 11.

Calphur'nius Pi'so, a person condemned for using seditious words against Tiberius. *Tacit. Hist.* 4. c. 21.

Calphur'nius Pi'so, a person famous for his abstinence, *Val. Max.* 4. c. 3.

Calphur'nius Ti'tus, a Latin poet, born in Sicily, in the age of Diocletian. Seven of his eclogues are extant and generally found with the works of the poets who have written on hunting. Though abounding with many beautiful lines, they are however greatly inferior in elegance and simplicity to those of Virgil. The best edition is that of Kaempfer, 4to, L. Bat. 1728. The eclogues of Nemesian have sometimes been attributed to Calphurnius, and the edition published at Parma, about 1493, was the first which assigned seven only to Calphurnius, the rest to Nemesian. The latest edition is that of Burman, published at Mitau, 1774. Wernsdorf in his Poet. Lat. Min. has republished the works of these poets, and his preface and prolegomena contain much valuable information respecting them. *Harles. Not. Lit. Rom.* 1. p. 705.—*Sax.* 1. p. 377.

Calphur'nius Flac'cus, a rhetorician who lived under the emperors Adrian and Antoninus Pius. Some of his declamations remain, and may be found subjoined to the minor declamations of Quinctilian, edited by Pithoeus, Paris, 1580. Burnum has also published and illustrated them in the second volume of his Quinctilian. They possess neither eloquence nor elegance of diction. *Harles. ibid.* 1. p. 493.—*Sax. Onom.* 1. p. 308.——A Roman surnamed Frugi, who composed annals, B.C. 130.

CALTHÆ'I, a people of India, conquered by Alexander. *Polyæn.* 4. c. 3.

CALTIORIS'SA, a city of Armenia Minor. *Ptol.*

CALUCO'NES, a people of Rhætia. *Ptol.* They are called Collucones by *Pliny*, 3. c. 20.

CALUCU'LA, a town of Hispania Bætica. *Plin.* 3. c. 1.

CALUMAC'UMA, a town of Africa Propria, near the greater Syrtis. *Ptol.*

CALUM'NIA and **IMPUDEN'TIA**, two deities worshipped at Athens. Calumnia was ingeniously represented in a painting by Apelles.

CALUPE'NA a region of Armenia Minor. *Strab.* 11.

CA'LUS. *Vid.* Talus.

CALUSID'IUS, a soldier in the army of Germanicus. When his general wished to stab himself, Calusidius offered him his sword, observing that it was sharper than his own. *Tacit.* 1. *Ann.* c. 35.

CALU'SIUM, a town of Etruria. *Diod.* 1. 14.

CALVE'NA, a friend of Cæsar. *Cic. Att.* 14. ep. 5.

CAL'VIA, a female minister of Nero's lusts. *Tacit. Hist.* 1. c. 3.

CALVI'NA, a woman of loose character, mentioned by *Juvenal*, 3. v. 133.

CALVIS'IUS, a friend of Augustus. *Plut. in Anton.* ——An officer, whose wife disgraced herself by her intercourse with the soldiers of his camp. *Tacit. Hist.* c. 48.

CAL'VUS CORN. LICIN'IUS, a famous orator, equally known for writing iambics. As he was both factious and satirical, he did not fail to excite public attention by his severe animadversions upon Cæsar and Pompey, and he disputed the palm of eloquence with Cicero. His abilities were called into action by the death of his favourite Quintilia, whose sudden and untimely fate he deplored in verses, admired for their elegance, sublimity, and pathos. Calvus was of a diminutive stature, and of a feeble frame of body; yet his exertions in the forum were great and astonishing. He died in his youth. Only nine verses of his poetry are preserved in the collection of Latin poets. *Cic. Ep.—Horat.* 1. sat. 10. v. 19.—*Quint.—Senec.—Sueton.*——A name given to M. Crassus. *Cic. Att.* 1. ep. 16.

CAL'YBE, a town at the east of Thrace. *Strab.* 17.

Cal'ybe, the mother of Bucolion by Laomedon. *Apollod.* 3. c. 12.——An old woman, priestess in the temple which Juno had at Ardea. *Virg. Æn.* 7. v. 419.

CALYCAD'NUS, a river of Cilicia. *Plin.* 5. c. 27.

CAL'YCE, a daughter of Æolus, son of Helenus and Enaretta daughter of Deimachus. She had Endymion, king of Elis, by Æthlius the son of Jupiter. *Apollod.* 1. c. 7.—*Paus.* 5. c. 1.——A Grecian girl, who fell in love with a youth called Evathlus. As she was unable to gain the object of her love, she threw herself from a precipice, and thus perished. This tragical story was celebrated in verse by Stesichorus, and was still extant in the age of *Athenæus*, 14. c. 6.——A daughter of Hecaton, mother of Cycnus. *Hygin.* fab. 157.

CALYD'IUM, a town on the Appian way. *Strab.* 5.

CAL'YDON, a city of Ætolia, where Œneus, the father of Meleager, reigned. The Evenus flows through it, and it received its name from Calydon the son of Ætolus. During the reign of Œneus, Diana sent a wild boar to ravage the country, on account of the neglect which had been shown to her divinity by the king, at a public sacrifice. All the princes of the age assembled to hunt this boar, which event is greatly celebrated by the poets, under the name of the chace of Calydon, or of the Calydonian boar. Meleager killed the ferocious animal with his own hand, and presented the head to Atalanta, of whom he was enamoured. The skin of the boar was preserved, and was still seen in the age of Pausanias, in the temple of Minerva Alea. The tusks were also preserved by the Arcadians in Tegea, and Augustus carried them away to Rome, because the people of Tegea had followed the party of Antony. These tusks were shewn at Rome for a long time after. It is said that one was about half an ell long, but that the other was broken. The names of the princes who assembled on this famous occasion are mentioned by Ovid, Hyginus, Apollonius Rhodius, and Apollodorus; according to the last, whose opinion is more universally adopted, they were Meleager, Castor and Pollux, Dyras son of Mars, Idas and Lynceus sons of Aphareus, Admetus son of Pheres, Theseus, Jason son of Æson, Ancæus and Cepheus sons of Lycurgus of Arcadia, Pirithous son of Ixion, Iphiclus son of Amphitryon, Peleus and Telamon sons of Æacus, Atalanta, Eurytion son of Actor, Amphiaraus son of Oicleus, and all the sons of Thestius. *Vid.* Meleager & Atalanta. *Apollod.* 1. c. 8.—*Paus.* 8. c. 45.—*Strab.* 8.—*Homer. Il.* 9. v. 577.—*Hygin.* fab. 174.—*Ovid. Met.* 8. fab. 4. &c.

CAL'YDON, a son of Ætolus and Pronoe, daughter of Phorbas. He gave his name to a town of Ætolia.

CALYDO'NIS, a name of Deianira, as living in Calydon. *Ovid. Met.* 9. v. 112.

CALYDO'NIUS, a surname of Bacchus.

CALYM'NA or CALYM'NIA, one of the Sporades, situated between the islands Cos and Lebynthus. *Ovid. Art. Amm.* 2. v. 81.—*Mela*, 2. c. 9.

CALYN'DA, a town of the west of Lycia. *Ptol.* 5. c. 3.

CALYP'SO, one of the Oceanides, or one of the daughters of Atlas, according to some, reigned in the island of Ogygia, the situation and even existence of which is a matter of dispute. When Ulysses was shipwrecked on her coasts, she received him with great hospitality, and offered him immortality if he would remain with her as a husband. The hero refused, and after seven year's delay, he was permitted to depart from the island by order of Mercury, the messenger of Jupiter. During his stay, Ulysses had two sons by Calypso, Nausithous and Nausinous. Calypso was inconsolable at his departure, and her grief and mournful situation are beautifully and pathetically described by Propertius and Homer. *Apul. Miles.* 1.—*Homer. Od.* 1. v. 52. l. 7. v. 255. &c. & *Eustathius. locis.*—*Hesiod. Theog.* v. 360 & 1016.—*Ovid. de Pont.* 4. ep. 18. *Amor.* 2. el. 17. *De A.A.* 2.—*Propert.* 1. el. 15.

CALYP'SUS IN'SULA or OGYG'IA has been placed by geographers near the Lacinian promontory on the coast of the Brutii.

CAL'YTIS, a city of Syria. *Steph.*

CAM'ACÆ or CA'MÆ, a people of Scythia. *Plin.* 6. c. 17.

CAMALODU'NUM, a Roman colony, the first settled in Britain, supposed to be the modern Maldon or Colchester. *Dion.* 60.

CAMA'NE, a city of India within the Ganges. *Ptol.*

CAMAN'TIUM, a town of Asia Minor. *Athen.*

CAM'ARA, a town of India within the Ganges, now Comorin. *Arrian in Peripl.*——A city of Crete. *Ptol.* It was formerly Lato. *Steph.*

CAMARI'CA, a city of the Cantabri, called also Victoria. *Ptol.*

CAMARI'NA, a lake of Sicily, with a town of the same name, now Torre di Camarâna, built B.C. 552, at the south of the island. It was destroyed by the Syracusans, and rebuilt by Hipponous or by Psaumis. The lake was drained, contrary to the advice of Apollo, as the ancients supposed, and a pestilence was the consequence; but the lowness of the lake below the level of the sea prevents its being drained. The words *Camarinam movere* became proverbial to express an unsuccessful and dangerous attempt. *Virg. Æn.* 3. v. 701.—*Strab.* 6.—*Herodot.* 7. c. 154.—*Ital.* 14. v. 198.—*Pindar. Ol.* 5. 18.——A town of Italy. *Strab.* 6.

CAMATUL'LICI, a people of Gallia Narbonensis. *Plin.* 3. c. 4.

CAM BALA, *orum*, a place of Asia, which produced gold. *Strab.* 11.

CAMBAL'IDUS, a mountain of Persia, a branch of Caucasus. *Plin.* 6. c. 27.

CAMBAU'LES, a general of some Gauls who invaded Greece. *Paus.* 10. c. 19.

CAM'BEI, a nation of Illyricum. *Appian.*

CAMBERI'CHUM, one of the mouths of the Ganges. *Ptol.*

CAM'BES, a prince of Lydia, of such voracious appetite that he ate his wife, and afterwards destroyed himself through grief in the presence of his subjects. *Eustath. in* 1. *Od.*—*Ælian.* 1. *V. H.* c. 27.

CAMBE'TUM, a city of Hispania Tarraconensis. *Ptol.*

CAMBISE'NA, a region of Armenia. *Strab.* l. 12.

CAMBIS'THOLI, a people of India, near the Indus. *Arrian. in Indic.*

CAMBODU'NUM, a city of Vindelicia, now Munchen. *Ptol.*——A town of the Brigantes in Britain. *Id. Camden* supposees it to be Aldmonbury, in Yorkshire.

CAMBOLEC'TRI, a people of Gallia Narbonensis. *Plin.* 3. c. 4.

CAMBOR'ICUM or CAMBORI'TUM, a town of Britain, supposed to be the modern Cambridge. *Antonin.*

CAM'BRE, a place of Campania, near Puteoli. *Juv.* 7. v. 154.

CAMBU'NII, mountains of Macedonia. *Liv.* 42. c. 53.

CAMBU'SIS, a city of Æthiopia. *Plin.* 6. c. 29.

CAMBY'SES, king of Persia, was son of Cyrus the Great. He invaded and conquered Ægypt, where he killed the god Apis, and plundered the temples. When he marched against Pelusium, he placed at the head of his army a number of cats and dogs; and the Ægyptians refusing to kill animals which they reverenced as divinities, became an easy prey to their artful enemy. Cambyses afterwards sent an army of 50,000 men to destroy Jupiter Ammon's temple, and resolved to attack the Carthaginians and Æthiopians. He killed his brother Smerdis from mere suspicion, and flayed alive a partial judge, whose skin he nailed on the judgment seat, and appointed his son to succeed him, telling him to remember where he sat,. He died of a small wound in the thigh, which he had given himself with his sword, as he mounted on horseback; and the Ægyptians surreptitiously observed, that it was the same place in which he had wounded their god Apis, and that therefore he was visited by the hand of the gods. His death happened 521 years B.C. Cambyses left no issue to succeed him, and his throne, which was usurped by the magi, was ascended by Darius soon after. *Herodot.* 2, 3, &c.—*Justin.* 1. c. 9.—*Val. Max.* 6. c. 3.——A person of obscure origin, to whom Astyages gave his daughter Mandane in marriage. The king, who had been terrified by dreams which threatened the loss of his crown by the hand of his daughter's son, took this step in hopes that the children of so ignoble a marriage would ever remain in obscurity. He was disappointed. Cyrus, Mandane's son, when grown to manhood dethroned him. *Xenoph.* 1.—*Herodot.* 1. c. 46, 107, &c.—*Justin* 1. c. 4.

CAMBY'SES, a river of Asia, which flows from mount Caucasus into the Cyrus. *Mela*, 3. c. 6.

CAMBYSSE'NI, a people of Cyropolis. *Steph.*

CAME'CHIA, a town of Albania. *Ptol.*

CAMELA'NI, a people of Italy. *Plin.* 3. c. 14.

CAMELI'DÆ, two Islands upon the coast of Ionia. *Plin.* 5. c. 31.

CAMELI'TÆ, a people of Mesopotamia. *Strab.* 3.

CAME'LIUS, the physician of Augustus before Musa.

CAMELOBOS'CI, a people of Carmania. *Ptol.*

CAMELOC'ONI, a people of Arabia. *Steph.*

CAMELON'TIUM, a town of Ægypt. *Diod. Sic.* 18.

CAM'ERA, a field of Calabria. *Ovid. Fast.* 3. v. 582.

CAMER'ACUM or CAMERA'CUM, a town of ancient Gaul, now Cambray in Flanders. *Cluver.* 2. c. 19.

CAMERI'NUM or CAMER'TIUM, a town of Umbria, in the Apennines, very faithful to Rome during its various wars. The inhabitants were called Camertes. *Liv.* 9. c. 36.—*Cic. Syl.* 19. *Balb.* 22.

CAMERI'NUS, a Latin poet, who wrote a poem on the taking of Troy by Hercules. *Ovid. ex Pont.* el. 16. v. 19. Some of the family of the Camerini were distinguished for their zeal as citizens, as well as for their abilities as scholars. Among them was Sulpicius, who was commissioned by the Roman senate to go to Athens, to collect the best of Solon's laws. *Juv.* 7. v. 90.

CAME'RIUM or CAME'RIA, an ancient town of Italy, near Rome, taken by Romulus. *Plut. in Rom.*—*Liv.* 1. c. 38.—*Plin.* 3. c. 5.—*Dionys. Hal.* 2. c. 13.

CAMER'OPIS, a city of India. *Strab.*

CAMER'TES, a friend of Turnus, killed by Æneas. *Virg. Æn.* 10. v. 562. *Vid.* Camerinum.

CAME'SUS, a city of Thrace. *Ptol.*

CAMI'CUS, or CAM'ICUS, a river of Sicily, now Fiumedelle Canne, with a town of the same name, now Platanella, at the south of the island. *Strab.* 6.—*Cluver.*

CAMIG'ARA, a city of India within the Ganges. *Ptol.*

CAMILE'TÆ, a people beyond the Euphrates. *Strab.*

CAMIL'LA, queen of the Volsci, was the daughter

of Metabus and Casmilla. She was at an early age inured to the labours of hunting, and fed upon the milk of mares. Her father devoted her, when young, to the service of Diana. When she was declared queen, she marched at the head of an army, and accompanied by three youthful females of equal courage and dexterity with herself, to assist Turnus against Æneas, in which expedition she signalized herself by the numbers that perished by her hand. She was wounded by Aruns in the breast, as she was tearing the arms of Chloreus, the aged priest of Cybele, and she expired soon after. *Virg. Æn.* 7. v. 803. l. 11. v. 435.

CAMIL'LI and CAMIL'LÆ, priests instituted by Romulus for the service of the gods. *Dionys.* 2.

CAMIL'LUS L. FU'RIUS, a celebrated Roman, called a second Romulus, from his services to his country. He was banished by the people for distributing the spoils which he had obtained at Veii. During his exile, which he passed at Ardea, Rome was besieged by the Gauls under Brennus. In the midst of their misfortunes, the besieged Romans remembered with regret the abilities of the ill-treated Camillus, and elected him dictator. Camillus forgot the past ingratitude of his fellow-citizens in their present danger, and marched to the relief of his country, which he delivered after it had been in the possession of the enemy. He died in the 80th year of his age, B.C. 365, after he had been five times dictator, once censor, three times interrex, twice a military tribune, and had obtained four triumphs. He conquered the Hernici, Volsci, Latini, and Etrurians, and deserved the gratitude and veneration of the Roman people, by making them abandon their intention of leaving Rome to reside at Veii. When he besieged Falisci, he rejected, with proper indignation, the offers of a schoolmaster, who had betrayed into his hands the sons of the most worthy citizens of the place. *Plut. in Vitâ.*—*Liv.* 5.—*Flor.* 1. c. 13.—*Diod.* 14.—*Virg. Æn.* 6. v. 855.——A name of Mercury. *Servius in 2 Æn.* v. 543 & 558. The word Camillus was generally applied to the office of those who served as ministers or inferior servants in the temples of the gods. *Quintil.* 8. c. 3.——An intimate friend of Cicero.

CAMI'NA, an island of the Ægean Sea. *Plin.* 4. c. 12.

CAMI'RO and CLYT'IA, two daughters of Pandarus of Crete, left to the care of Venus, who educated them carefully, and loaded them with deserved favours. Juno also bestowed on them wisdom and beauty. Diana granted them grace and elegance of stature, and Minerva taught them the domestic arts and employments which adorn the female character. When they were grown up, the goddess, who had presided over their infancy, entreated Jupiter to give them kind husbands; but the father of the gods, to visit upon them the crime of their father, who was accessary to the impiety of Tantalus, ordered the harpies to carry them away, and deliver them to the furies. *Paus.* 10. c. 30.—*Homer. Odyss.* 20. v. 66.

CAMI'RUS or CAMI'RA, a town of Rhodes, which received its name from Camirus, a son of Hercules and Iole. The inhabitants were led to the Trojan war by Tlepolemus. *Mela*, 2. c. 9.—*Strab.* 14.—*Ptol.* 5. c. 2.—*Homer. Il.* 2. v. 163.

CAMISE'NA, a region of Parthia. *Strab.* 11.

CAMISSA'RES, a governor of part of Cilicia, father of the celebrated Datames. *C. Nep. in Dat.*

CAM'MA, a woman of Galatia, who avenged the death of her husband Sinetus upon his murderer Sinorix, by making him drink out of a cup the contents of which were poisoned, on pretence of marrying him according to the custom of the country, which required that the bridegroom and his bride should drink out of the same vessel. She escaped by refusing to drink on pretence of illness. *Polyæn.* 8. c. 39.

CAMMA'NIA, part of Thesprotia. *Steph.* It was afterwards called Cestrinia.

CAMŒ'NE, a name given to the muses, from the sweetness and melody of their songs, *a cantu camœno*, or, according to *Varro*, from Carmœnæ or Casmœnæ, by the rejection of *r* or *s*. *Vid.* Musæ. *Varro de L. L.* 5. c. 7.

CAM'PÆ, a town of Cilicia. *Ptol.*

CAMPA'NA LEX, or the Julian agrarian law, was enacted by J. Cæsar, A.U.C. 691. to divide some lands among the people. *Cic. ad Att.* 1. 2. ep. 18.

CAMPA'NIA, a country of Italy, of which Capua was the capital, and which was bounded by Latium, Samnium, Picenum, and part of the Mediterranean Sea. It was celebrated for its delightful views, and for its fertility. The air, though mild, was not generally considered wholesome. Capua is often called *Campana urbs*. As the inhabitants were ingenious, their earthen wares (*supelex.*) and their fine linen coverlets for beds (*peristromata*) were in high repute. Worts or excrescences in the face, because common in Campania, were called *Campanus morbus*. *Horat.* 1. sat. 5. v. 62. sat. 6. v. 118.—*Plaut. Ps.* 1. sc. 2. v. 12. *Stitch.* 2. sc. 3. v. 53.—*Strab.* 5.—*Cic. de Leg. Ag.* c. 35.—*Virg. Æn.* 10. v. 145.—*Justin.* 20. c. 1. l. 22. c. 1.—*Plin.* 3. c. 5.—*Mela*, 2. c. 4.—*Flor.* 1. c. 16.—*Liv.* 2. c. 52.—*Ptol.* 3. c. 1.

CAMPAS'PE or PANCAS'TE, a beautiful concubine of Alexander the Great. The king gave her to Apelles who had fallen in love with her, as he drew her picture. It is said that it was from her beauty that the painter copied the thousand charms with which he represented Venus as rising from the sea. *Plin.* 35 c. 10.

CAM'PE, a woman who kept the 100 handed monsters confined in Tartarus. Jupiter killed her, because she refused to give them their liberty to come to his assistance against the Titans. *Hesiod. Theog.* 500.—*Apollod.* 1. c. 2.

CAM'PESUS, one of the generals who assisted Æetes against Perses. *Val. Flacc.* l. 5. *Argon.* 593.

CAM'PI DIOME'DIS, a plain situate in Apulia. *Mart.* 13. epigr. 93.

CAMPO'NI, a people of Gallia Aquitanica. *Plin.* 4. c. 19.

CAMP'SA, a town near Pallene. *Herodot.* 7. c. 123.

CAMP'SARI, a people of Africa Propria. *Ptol.*

CAMPSEONY'SIS, a river of Themiscyra, near the Heniochi. *Plin.* 6. c. 4.

CAMPSIA'NI, a poor people of Germany. *Strab.* 1. 7.

CAM'PUS MAR'TIUS, a large plain at Rome, without the walls of the city, where the Roman youths performed their exercises, and learnt to wrestle and box, to throw the discus, hurl the javelin, ride a horse, drive a chariot, &c. In this plain the public assemblies of the people were held, and the officers of state chosen, and audience was here also given to foreign ambassadors. This celebrated spot was adorned with statues, columns, arches, and porticoes; and its pleasant situation caused it to be very much frequented. It was called Martius, because dedicated to Mars; and festivals, called Equiria, were there annually celebrated in honour of the god, on the 27th of February and the 14th of March, when exhibitions of horse-races and chariots took place. It was sometimes called Tibernius, from its closeness to the river Tiber. It was given the Roman people by a vestal virgin; but they were deprived of it by Tarquin the Proud, who appropriated it to his own use as a private field, and sowed corn in it. When Tarquin was driven from Rome, the people recovered possession of it, and threw away, into the Tiber, the corn which had grown there, deeming it unlawful for any man to eat of the produce of that land. The sheaves which were thrown into the river stopped in a shallow ford, and by the accumulated collection of mud at last became firm ground and formed an island, which was called the Holy Island, or the island of Æsculapius. Dead bodies were generally burnt in the Campus Martius. *Strab.* 5.—*Liv.* 2. c. 5. l. 6. c. 20.—*Ovid. Fast.* 2. v. 857.

CAMULOGI'NUS, a Gaul, raised to great honours by Cæsar, for his military abilities. *Cæs. Bell. G.* 7. c. 57.

CAM'ULUS, a surname of Mars among the Sabines and Etrurians. He was represented with a buckler in one hand and a spear in the other.

CAMU'NI or CAMU'LI, a people of Italy. *Plin.* 3. c. 20.—*Strab.*—*Dion.* 54.

CAMURISAR'BUM, a town of the Cappadocian Pontus. *Ptol.*

CAMU'RIUS, a soldier of the 15th legion, said to have been the person who slew Galba. *Tac. Hist.* 1. c. 41.

CA'MUS, a city of Cœlesyria. *Polyb.*

CA'NA, a city and promontory of Æolia. *Mela*, 1. c. 18.—*Plin.* 5. 30.

CAN'ACA, a city of the Turdetani, in Spain. *Ptol.*

CAN'ACE, a daughter of Æolus, who became enamoured of her brother Macareus, to whom she bore a child, whom she afterwards exposed. The cries of the child discovered the mother's crime; and Æolus sent his daughter a sword, and obliged her to kill herself. Some say that Neptune offered violence to Canace, and that by him she had many children. *Apollod.* 1.—*Hygin.* fab. 238 & 242.—*Ovid. Heroid.* 11. *Trist.* 2. v. 384. & *Ibin.* 457.

CAN'ACHE, one of Actæon's dogs. The word καναχή, expresses the noise of barking. *Ovid. Met.* 3. v. 217.—*Hygin.* fab. 181.

CAN'ACHUS, a statuary of Sicyon, the pupil of Polycletus of Argos, among the works of his chissel, an Apollo for Thebes in Bœotia, and another for the Milesians of Ionia, are mentioned with commendation. *Plin.* 34. c. 8.—*Paus.* 6. c. 9.

CA'NÆ or CA'NA, a city of Locris.——A city of Æolia. *Vid.* Cana.

CANA'RII, a people near mount Atlas in Africa, who received this name because they fed in common with their dogs. The islands which they inhabited were called Fortunate by the ancients, and are now known by the name of the Canaries. *Plin.* 5. c. 1. l. 6. c. 32

CA'NAS, a town of Lycia. *Plin.* 5. c, 27.

CANAS'IDA, a city of India. *Arrian. in Indic.*

CANASTRÆ'UM, a promontory of Macedonia, now Capo Canistro. *Plin.* 4. c. 10.

CAN'ATHA, a town of the Decapolis, near Syria. *Plin.* 5. c. 18.——A city of Media. *Ptol.*——A city near Bostra, in Arabia. *Steph.*

CANA'THRA, an island near Taprobane. *Ptol.*

CANA'THUS or CAN'ATHUS, a fountain of Nauplia, where Juno is said yearly to have washed herself to recover her infant purity. *Paus.* 2. c. 38.

CANAU'NA, a region of Arabia Felix. *Plin.* 6. c. 23.

CANCHLÆ'I, Arabs mentioned by *Pliny*, 5. c. 11.

CAN'DACE, a queen of Æthiopia, in the age of Augustus, so prudent and popular in her government that her successors always bore her name. She was blind of one eye. *Plin.* 6. c. 29. Also Canda'ce.

CAN'DALI, a people of India within the Ganges *Ptol.*

CANDA'NUM, a city of the Iazyges Metanastæ. *Id.*

CAN'DARA, a city of Paphlagonia, where was a temple of Juno. *Steph.*

CANDA'RI, a people of Sogdiana. *Plin.* 6. c. 16.—*Ptol.*

CANDA'VIA, a mountain of Epirus, which separates Illyricum from Macedonia. *Lucan.* 6. v. 331.

CADAU'LES or MYRSIL'US, son of Myrsus, was the last of the Heraclidæ who sat on the throne of Lydia. Not satified himself to enjoy the company of his wife, he boasted of her incomparable beauties to his favourite minister Gyges, and even introduced him secretly into his chamber, that he might view her charms to more advantage. The queen discovered the weakness of her husband, and was so incensed, that she commanded Gyges either to prepare for death, or to destroy his master and succeed to his bed and throne. Candaules was accordingly murdered, 718 years B.C., and Gyges married the queen, and ascended the throne. *Justin.* 1. 3. 7.—*Herodot.* 1. c. 7 &c.—*Plut. Symp.* ——The father of Damasithymus, a naval commander of Xerxes. *Herodot.* 7. c. 98.

CAN'DEI, a people of Arabia who fed on serpents. *Plin* 6. c. 29.

CANDI'OPE, a daughter of Œnopion, to whom violence was offered by her own brother.

CANDIPAR'NA, a town of India within the Ganges. *Ptol.*

CANDROG'ARI, a town Upper Æthiopia. *Plin.* 6. c. 30.

CAN'DYBA, a town of Lycia. *Id.* 5. c. 27.

CAN'DYS, a city of Media. *Ptol.*

CA'NE, a promontory of Elis, formerly Ægeates. *Steph.*

CANELA'TE, a city of Corsica, now St. Forenzio. *Ptol.*

CA'NENS, a nymph called also Venilia, daughter of Janus and wife of Picus king of Laurentes. When Circe had changed her husband into a bird, she lamented him so much, that she pined away, and was changed into a voice. She was regarded as a deity by the inhabitants. *Ovid. Met.* 14. 433 & 337.

CANEN'TULUM, a river of Gallia Acquitanica, now Charente. *Ptol.*

CANEPHO'RIA, festivals at Athens, in honour of Bacchus, or, according to others, of Diana, in which all marriageable women offered small baskets to the deity, and received the name of Canephoræ, whence statues representing women in that attitude were called by the same appellation. *Cic. in Verr.* 4.—*Symmach.* 1. ep. 29.—*Nat. Comes,* 5. c. 13.

CAN'ETHUM, a place of Eubœa. *Strab.*——A mountain of Bœotia. *Apollon.*

CANICULA'RES DI'ES, certain days in the summer in which the star Canis was said to influence the season, and to make the days warmer. *Manilius.* l. 5.

CANID'IA, a certain woman of Neapolis, against whom Horace inveighed as a sorceress. *Horat. epod.*

CANID'IUS, a tribune, who proposed a law to empower Pompey to go with two lictors only, to reconcile Ptolemy and the Alexandrians. *Plut. in Pomp.*

CANINDAS'TA, a town of Isauria. *Steph.*

CANINEFA'TES, a people of ancient Germany, near the Batavi, where Holland is now situate. *Tacit. Hist.* 4. c. 15.—*Plin.* 4. c. 15.

C. CANIN'IUS REB'ILUS, a consul with J. Cæsar. He was consul only for seven hours, because his predecessor died the last day of the year, and he was chosen only for the remaining part of the day: whence Cicero observed sarcastically, that Rome was greatly indebted to him for his vigilance as he had not slept during the whole time of his consulship. *Cic.* 7 *ad Fam.* ep. 33.—*Plut. in Cæs.* —*Macrob.* 2. sat. 3.—*Plin.* 7. c. 53.—*Suet. in Cæs.* 76.

CANIN'IUS LU'CIUS, a lieutenant of Cæsar's army in Gaul. *Cæs. Bell G.* 7. c. 83.

CANIN'IUS RU'FUS, a friend of Pliny the younger. *Plin.* 1. ep. 3.

CANIN'IUS GAL'LUS, an intimate friend of Cicero.

CANIP'SA, a city of Arabia Felix. *Ptol.*

CA'NIS, a river of Arabia Felix. *Id.*

CANIS'TIUS, a Lacedæmonian courier, who ran 1200 stadia in one day. *Plin.* 7. c. 20.

CA'NIUS, a poet of Gades, contemporary with Martial. He was so naturally merry, that he always laughed. *Mart.* 1. epigr. 62.——A Roman knight, who went to Sicily for his amusement, where he bought of Pythius gardens and ponds well stocked with fish, which disappeared on the morrow. *Cic.* 3. *de Offic.* 14.

CAN'NA, a town of Æolis. *Mela,* 1. c. 18.——A city of Lycaonia. *Ptol.*

CAN'NÆ, a small village of Apulia near the river Aufidus, where Hannibal conquered the Roman consuls, P. Æmylius and Terentius Varro, and slaughtered 40,000 Romans, on the 21st of May, B.C. 216. The spot where this famous battle was fought is still pointed out to the inquiring traveller by the natives, and denominated the field of blood. *Liv.* 23. c. 44, &c.—*Flor.* 2. c. 6. l. 3. c. 3.—*Plut. in Annib.*—*Plin.* 15. c. 18.

CANOGI'ZA, a city of India, without the Ganges. *Ptol.*

CANOP'ICUM OS'TIUM, the most westerly of the mouths of the Nile, twelve miles from Alexandria. *Paus.* 5. c. 21.

CANO'PUS, now Maadie, a city of Ægypt, twelve miles from Alexandria. celebrated for the temple of Serapis. It was founded by the Spartans, and therefore called Amyclæa, and it received its name from Canopus, the pilot of the vessel of Menelaus, who was buried in this place. The inhabitants were so dissolute in their manners, that Juvenal used the word Canopus as most strongly expressive effeminacy and debauchery. Virgil bestows upon it the epithet of Pellæus, because Alexander, who was born at Pella, built Alexandria in the neighbourhood. *Ital* 11. v. 433.—*Mela,* 1. c 9. l. 2. c. 7.—*Strab.* 17.—*Juv.* 6. v. 84. l. 15. v. 46.—*Quintil.* 1. c. 5.—*Tacit.* 2 *An.* c. 60.—*Statius,* 3 *Sylv.* 2. v. 3.—*Seneca,* ep. 51.—*Plin.* 5. c. 31.—*Virg. G.* 4. v. 287.

CANO'PUS, the pilot of the ship Menelaus, who died in his youth on the coast of Ægypt, from a wound caused by the bite of a serpent, and was honoured with a monument by his master, on the spot where a town of the same name was afterwards built. *Conon. Nar.* 8.—*Eustath. apud Diog. Per.*—*Mela* 2. c. 9. Also Cano'bus.

CAN'TABRA, a river falling into the Indus. *Plin.* 6. c. 20.

CAN'TABRI, a fierce and warlike people of Spain, who rebelled against Augustus, by whom they were conquered. Their country is now called Biscay, and the *Cantabricus Oceanus*, which washed their coast, the bay of Biscay. *Ptol.* 2. c. 6.—*Horat.* 2. od. 6 & 11.—*Strab.* 2 & 3. *Cæs. B. G.* 3. *Civ.* 1.—*Mela*, 3. c. 1 & 2.—*Plin.* 25. c. 8.—*Ital.* 3. v. 326.

CANTA'BRIÆ LACUS, a lake in Spain. *Suet. in Galb.* 8.

CANTABRIG'IA, the ancient name of the town of Cambridge. *Cluver.* 2. c. 23.

CANTE'RIUS, a mountain of the Sabines. *Varro de R. R.* c. 1.

CANTHA'RIUM, a promontory of Samus. *Strab.* 14.

CAN'THARUS, a famous sculptor of Sicyon, pupil of Eutycides. Some of his statues were preserved at Olympia, but Pliny speaks of them with great indifference. *Plin.* 34. c. 8.—*Paus.* 6. c. 17.——A comic poet of Athens, whose compositions are lost, though the names of some of his plays are preserved.—*Suidas.*—*Gyrald. de P. Hist. Dial.* 7.—*Fabr. B. Gr.* l. 2. c. 22.——An Athenian, whose artifice, and great dishonesty gave rise to the proverb *Cantharo astutior. Zenodotus.*—*Erasm. Adag.*

CAN'THI, a bay at the mouth of the Indus. *Ptol.*

CAN'THUS, a son of Abas, who was in the number of the Argonauts.

CAN'TIUM, a country in the south-eastern parts of Britain, now called Kent. *Cæs. Bell. G.* 5. c. 13 & 14.

CANUC'CIS, a town of Mauritania Cæsariensis. *Ptol.*

CAN'UCHA, a river of India flowing into the Ganges. *Plin.* 6. c. 18.

CANULE'IA, one of the first four vestals appointed by Numa. *Plut.*

CANULE'IA, LEX. *Vid.* Canuleius.

CANULE'IUS C., a tribune of the people, A. U. C. 310, who made a law to render it lawful for the patricians and plebeians to intermarry. It ordained also, that one of the consuls should be yearly chosen from the plebeians. *Liv.* 4. c. 3. &c.—*Flor.* 1. c. 17.

CANU'SIUM, now Canosa, a town of Apulia, whither the Romans fled after the battle of Cannæ. It was built by Diomedes, on the banks of the Aufidus, and its inhabitants have been called *Bilingues*, because they retained the language of their founder, and likewise adopted that of their neighbours. Horace complained of the grittiness of their bread. The wools of the place, as well as the dark red coloured cloths manufactured with them, were in high estimation, so that *Canusina vestis* became expressive of excellence. *Strab.* 6.—*Liv.* 9. c. 20. l. 22. c. 50.—*Cæs. Civ. B.* 1.—*Ptol.* 3. c. 1.—*Sueton. Ner.* 30.—*Martial.* 9. epigr. 23. l. 14. epigr. 127.—*Horat.* 1. sat. 5. v. 92. sat. 10. v. 30. —*Mela*, 2. c. 6.—*Plin.* 8. c. 11.

CANU'SIUS or GANU'SIUS, a Greek historian under Ptolemy Auletes. *Plut. in Cæsar.*

CANU'TIUS TIBERI'NUS, a tribune of the people, who violently attacked Antony when declared an enemy to the state. His satire cost him his life. *Patercul.* 2. c. 64.

CANU'TIUS, a Roman actor. *Plut. in Brut.*——An eloquent orator. *Cic. Brut.* 56.

CANY'TIS, a city of Syria. *Steph.*

CA'PÆ, a city on the Hellespont. *Id.*

CAP'ANEUS, a noble Argive, son of Hipponous and Astinome, and husband of Evadne, the daughter of Iphicles. Euripides agrees with the other poets in praising his military valour, but instead of painting him with Æschylus and Statius, as an odious tyrant, and an arrogant and impious blasphemer, he represents him as mild in his manners, faithful in his friendship, true to his engagements, and the enemy only of pride and perfidy. He went to the Theban war with the naked figure of a man painted on his shield, with the words *I will burn Thebes*, in golden letters, declaring that he would take and destroy the besieged city even in spite of Jupiter. Such daring guilt offended the gods, and the offender was immediately struck dead with a thunderbolt. When Theseus compelled the Thebans to grant funeral honours to the slaughtered Argives, his body was burnt separately from the others who had fallen in war, and his wife threw herself on the burning pile to mingle her ashes with his. It is said that Æsculapius restored him to life. A statue was erected to his honour at Delphi: and some of the ancients have recorded, that he first practised the taking of besieged towns by assault. *Ovid. Met.* 9. v. 404. *Trist.* 4. el. 3. l. 5. el. 6.—*Hom. Il.* 5.—*Apollod.* 3.—*Propert.* 1. el. 15.—*Veget.* 4. c. 21.—*Paus.* 10 c. 10.—*Stat. Theb.* 3, &c.—*Hygin.* fab. 68 & 70.—*Euripid. in Phœniss. & Suppl.*—*Æschyl. Sept. Ante Theb.*

CAP'ARA or CAP'ERA, a city of Lusitania. *Ptol.*

CAPAR'CELIS, a town of Armenia Minor. *Id.*

CARPASTI'TE, a province of Asia. *Plin.* 5. c. 9.

CAPEDU'NUM, a town of the Scordisci. *Strab.* 7.

CAPEL'LA, an elegiac poet at Rome in the age of J. Cæsar. *Ovid. de Pont.* 4. el. 16. v. 36.

CAPEL'LA MARTIA'NUS MIN'EUS FE'LIX, a native of Carthage, or, according to others, of Madaura, A.D. 490, who wrote a work, partly in poetry and partly in prose, called *Satyricon*, containing nine books, on the marriage of Mercury and Philology, and in praise of the liberal arts. Grotius, when only fourteen, published an edition of this poet, with great judgment and critical accuracy. The best edition is that of Walthardus, 8vo, Bernæ, 1763. *Vossius de P. Latin*—*Sax. Onom.* 1. p. 517. —*Harles. Not. Lit. Rom.* 1. p. 752.—*Voss. Hist. Lat.* l. 3. p. 712.

CAPEL'LA, a gladiator mentioned by *Juvenal*, 5. v. 155.

CAPE'NA, a gate at Rome, so called because the road through it led to a small town of the same name on the western banks of the Tiber, east of Veii. The Porta Capena was also called Appia, as the Appian road passes through it, and Madida, because one of the acqueducts which supplied Rome with water was built over it. *Liv.* 5. c. 10.—*Virg. Æn.* 7. v. 697.—*Martial.* 1. epigr. 47.—*Juv.* 3. v. 11.—*Ovid. Fast.* 5. v. 192.

CAPE'NAS, a small river of Italy. *Stat. Theb.* 13. v. 85.

CAPE'NI, a people of Etruria, in whose territory Feronia had a grove and a temple. *Virg. Æn.* 7. v. 697.—*Liv.* 5. c. 8. l. 22. c. 1. l. 27. c. 4. *Servius in loco cit.*

CA'PER or CA'PRUS, a river of Asia. *Vid.* Caprus.

CAPERTI'NI, fields near Massilia. *Justin.* l. 43. c. 3 & 4.

CAPE'TUS or CAP'ETUS, a king of Alba, who reigned 26 years. *Dionys.*——A suitor of Hippodamia. *Paus.* 6. c. 21,

CAP'EUS, a bay of Arabia Felix. *Plin.* 6. c. 28.

CAPHA'REUS or CAPHEREUS, a lofty mountain and promontory of Eubœa, where Nauplius king of the country to revenge the death of his son Palamedes, slain by Ulysses, set a burning torch in the darkness of night, which caused the Greeks to approach the coasts, and to be shipwrecked on the rocks. *Virg. Æn.* 11. v. 260.—*Ovid. Met.* 14. v. 481.—*Propert.* 4. el. 1. v. 115.

CA'PHAS, a mountain in the interior of Libya. *Ptol.*

CAPHE'RIS, an island between Chersonesus and Samothrace. *Plin.* 4. c. 12.

CA'PHO. a soldier mentioned by *Cicero*, *Ph.* 10. c. 10, l. 11. c. 5.——A centurion in Antony's army. *Id.* 8. c. 3.

CA'PHYÆ, a town of Arcadia. *Paus.* 8. c. 23.

CAPILLA'TI, a people inhabiting the Alps. *Plin.* 3. c. 20.

CA'PIO, a Roman famous for his friendship with Cato. *Plut de Patr Am.*

CAPI'SA, a town of Paropanisus. *Ptol.* The people were called Capissenæ. *Plin.* 6. c. 23.—*Arrian. in Indic.*

CAPITA'LIA, the highest mountain of India. *Plin.* 6. c. 20.

CAPIT'IUM, a city of Sicily. now Capizzi. *Cicer. Verr.* 2.

CAP'ITO, the uncle of Paterculus the historian, who joined Agrippa against Cassius. *Patercul.* 2. c. 69.

CAP'ITO FONTE'IUS, a man of great abilities and elegant manners, sent by Antony to settle his political disputes with Augustus. *Horat.* 1. sat. 5. v. 32.——A man accused of extortion in Cilicia, and severely punished by the senate. *Juv.* 8. v. 93. ——An epic poet of Alexandria, who wrote on love. ——An historian of Lycia, who wrote an account of Isauria in eight books. *Voss H. Gr.* 3. p. 339. ——A poet, who wrote on illustrious men. *Plin.* 8. ep. 12. The family of the Ateii was called by this name.

CAPITO'LIAS, a city of Cœlesyria. *Ptol.*

CAPITOLI'NI LU'DI, games yearly celebrated at Rome in honour of Jupiter, who had miraculously preserved the Capitol from the Gauls. *Liv.* 5. c. 30.

CAPITOLI'NUS, a surname of Jupiter, from his temple on mount Capitolinus, which was considered by the Romans as the centre of the destinies of their empire.——A surname of M. Manlius, who for his ambition, was thrown down the Tarpeian rock, which he had so nobly defended against the invading Gauls.

CAPITOLI'NUS, a mountain of Rome, called also Mons Tarpeius, and Mons Saturni. The Capitol was built upon it.

CAPITOLI'NUS, a man of lascivious morals, consul with Marcellus. *Plut. in Marcell.*

CAPITOLI'NUS JU'LIUS, an auther in Diocletian's reign, who wrote an account of the life of Verus, Antoninus Pius, the Gordians, &c. most of which are now lost. *Harles. Not. Lit. Rom.* 1. p. 571.—*Sax. Onom.* 1. p. 379.

CAPITO'LIUM, a celebrated temple and citadel at Rome, on the Tarpeian rock, the plan of which was made by Tarquinius Priscus. The splendid edifice was begun by Servius Tullius, finished by Tarquinius Superbus, and consecrated by the consul Horatius, after the expulsion of the Tarquins from Rome. It was built upon four acres of ground; the front was adorned with three rows of pillars, and the other sides with two. The ascent to it from the ground was by a hundred steps. The magnificence and richness of this temple are almost incredible. All the consuls successively made donations to it; and Augustus bestowed upon it at one time 2,000 pounds weight of gold. Its thresholds were made of brass, and its roof of gold. It was adorned with vessels and shields of solid silver, with golden chariots, &c. It was burnt during the civil wars of Marius, and Sylla rebuilt it, but died before the dedication which was performed by Q. Catulus. It was again destroyed in the troubles under Vitellius; and Vespasian, who endeavoured to repair it, saw it again in ruins before his death. Domitian raised it again for the last time, and made it more grand and magnificent than any of his predecessors; and spent 12.000 talents in gilding it. When the Romans first dug for the foundation of the building, they found the head of a man called Tolius, sound and entire in the ground, and thence drew an omen of the future greatness of the Roman empire. The hill was from that circumstance called Capitolium, *a capite Toli.* The consuls and magistrates offered sacrifices there, when they first entered upon their offices, and the triumphal processions were always conducted to the Capitol. *Virg. Æn.* 6. v. 136. l. 8. v. 347.—*Tacit.* 3 *Hist.* c. 72.—*Plut. in Poplic.*—*Liv.* l. 10, &c.—*Plin.* 33, &c.—*Sueton. in Aug.* c. 30. & *Domit.* 5.—*Stat.* 4 *Sylv.* 3.—*Juv.* 6. v. 386. 14. v. 91.

CAP'NIAS, a Greek poet, whose works have perished. *Suidas.*—*Voss. Poet Gr.* p. 82.

CAPOTA'NA, a city of Asia. *Ptol.*

CAPO'TES, a mountain of Asia. *Plin.* 5. c. 24.

CAPPADO'CIA, a country of Asia Minor, between the Halys, the Euphrates, and the Euxine. Crete, Cilicia, and Cappadocia, were the three bad kappas, or three provinces, beginning with the letter K or C, a popular distinction which was afterwards applied to mark the infamous conduct of the three Cornelii, Sylla, Cinna, and Lentulus. Cappadocia received its name from the river Cappadox, which separated it from Gallatia. The inhabitants were called Syrians and Leuco-Syrians by the Greeks. They were mean and perfidious in their character, and addicted to every vice, according to the ancients, who wrote this virulent epigram against them:

Vipera Cappadocem nocitura momordit; at illa
Gustato periit sanguine Cappadocis.

Their powers in eloquence were also so contemptible, that another epigram in Greek was pointed against them, and declared that a flying tortoise or a white crow were more common than an orator of Cappadocia. Their ideas of national independence were equally gross; and when offered their freedom by the Romans, they refused it, and begged of them a king, and they received Ariobarzanes. The country was some time after governed by a Roman proconsul. This country can boast of the birth of the geographer Strabo, of St. Basil, and of Gregory Nazianzen, among other illustrious characters. The horses of this country were in general esteem, and with these they paid their tribute to the king of Persia, while under his power, for want of money. Most of the slaves employed by the Romans were of Cappadocian origin; and as the country was occasionally called Syria, the word Syrus is frequently applied to slaves. The kings of Cappadocia mostly bore the name of Ariarathes. *Horat.* 1. ep. 6. v. 39 & 72.—*Plin.* 6. c. 3. l. 8. c. 44.—*Curt.* 3 & 4.—*Strab.* 11 & 16.—*Herodot.* 1. c. 73. l. 5. c. 49. l. 7. c. 72.—*Nepos* 14. c. 1.—*Justin.* 2. c. 4. l. 8. c. 3 l. 37. c. 3.—*Paterc.* 2. c. 39.—*Solin.* 3.—*Mela*, 1. c. 2. l. 3. c. 8.

CAP'PADOX, a small river of Cappadocia. *Plin.* 6. c. 3.

CAP'PAGUM, a town of Hispania Bætica. *Id.* 3. c. 1.

CAPRA'RIA, now Cabrera, a mountainous island in the Mediterranean, on the coast of Spain, about twelve miles south of Majorca, famous for its goats. *Plin.* 3. c. 6.——One of the Canary isles, now Gomera. *Plin.* 6. c. 32.

CAPRA'SIA, one of the mouths of the Po. *Plin.* 3. c. 16.

CA'PREÆ, now Capri, an island on the coast of Campania, abounding in quails, and rendered infamous by the residence and horrid debaucheries of the emperor Tiberius, during the last seven years of his life. The island in which, even now, medals are dug up, descriptive of the licentious conduct of the emperor, is about forty miles in circumference, surrounded by steep rocks, and accessible only in one place. The watch-tower, or pharos, erected there, was destroyed by an earthquake a few days before the death of Tiberius. *Ovid. Met.* 15. v. 709.—*Suet. in Tib.*—*Stat. Sylv.* 3. v. 5.

CA'PREÆ PA'LUS, a place near Rome, where Romulus disappeared from the midst of his senators. *Plut. in Rom.*—*Ovid. Fast.* 2. v. 491.—*Liv.* 1. c. 16.

CAPRE'TÆ, a people of Asia, in whose country Seleucus afterwards founded Apamia. *Plin.* 5. c. 30.

CA'PRIA, a lake of Pamphylia. *Strab.* 14.

CAPRIA'NUS, a mountain of Sicily, near Heraclea. *Diod. in Fragm.*

CAPRICOR'NUS, a sign of the Zodiac, in which appears 28 stars in the form of a goat, supposed by the ancients to be the goat Amalthæa, which fed Jupiter with her milk. Some maintain that it is Pan, who changed himself into a goat when frightened at the approach of Typhon. When the sun enters this sign, it is the winter solstice, or the longest night in the year. *Manil.* 2 & 4.—*Horat.* 2. od. 17. v. 19.—*Hygin.* fab. 196. *P. A.* 2. 28.

CAPRIFICIA'LIS, a day sacred to Vulcan, on which the Athenians made him offerings of money. *Plin.* 11. c. 15.

CAPRI'MA, a town of Caria. *Diod. Sic.* 19.

CAPRIPEDES, *Græc.* Αιγίποδες & Αιγιβάται, a surname of Pan, the Fauni, and the Satyrs, from their having goat's feet.

CA'PRIUS, a great informer in Horace's age. *Horat.* 1. sat. 4. v. 66.

CAPROTI'NA, a festival celebrated at Rome in the month of July, in honour of Juno, at which women only officiated. *Vid.* Philotis. *Varro. de L.L.* 5.—*Macrob.* 1. *Sat.* 11.

CA'PRUS, a harbour near mount Athos. *Mela*, 2. c. 2.——A river of Asia, falling into the Tigris. *Cluver.* 5. c. 14.

CAP'SA, a town of Libya, surrounded by vast deserts full of snakes. It was a place of consequence under Jugurtha, but was taken and destroyed by Marius. *Flor.* 3. c. 1.—*Sal. Bel. Jug.* 89.——A city of Chalcidice near Pallene. *Steph.*

CAP'SAGÆ, a town of Syria. *Curt.* 10.

CAPSITA'NI, a people of Zeugitana, or Africa Minor. *Plin.* 5. c. 15.

CAP'UA, the chief city of Campania in Italy, was supposed to have been founded by Capys, the father, or rather the companion of Anchises. This city was very ancient, and so opulent and powerful that it was called *altera Roma.* The soldiers of Annibal, after the battle of Cannæ, were enervated by the pleasures and luxuries which prevailed uncontrolled in this voluptuous city, under a soft climate; and thence Capua was truly said to have been a Cannæ to Annibal. The revolt of Capua to the Carthaginians proved its ruin. When taken by the Consuls Fulvius and Claudius, the inhabitants were punished for their perfidy; and, after a gradual decay, Capua now exhibits a mournful monument of devastation. In the plain where it once stood, a late king of Naples erected a magnificent palace called Casserta. *Virg. Æn.* 10. v. 145.—*Liv.* 4. c. 37. l. 7. c. 29. l. 8. c. 1. l. 22 & 23. c. 1. l. 24. c. 8.—*C. Nepos. in. Ann.* &c. —*Paterc.* l. c. 7. l. 2. c. 44.—*Flor.* l. c. 16.—*Cic. in Philip.* 12. c. 3.—*Plut. in Ann.*

CA'PYS, a Trojan, who came with Æneas into Italy, and, according to some authors, founded Capua. He was one of those who, against the advice of Thymœtes, wished to destroy the wooden horse, which proved the destruction of Troy. *Virg. Æn.* 10. v. 145.——A son of Assaracus, by a daughter of the Simois. He was father of Anchises by Themis. *Ovid. Fast.* 4. v. 33.—*Homer. Il.* 20. v. 239. —*Servius in. Æn.* 2. v. 35.

CA'PYS SYL'VIUS, a king of Alba, who reigned 28 years. *Dionys. Hal.* 1. c. 15.—*Virg. Æn.* 6. v. 768.

CAPYT'IUM, a city of Sicily. *Ptol.*

CAR, a son of Phoroneus, king of Megara, in whose reign his subjects first erected temples to Ceres. His tomb was seen in the age of the Antonines, on the road which leads from Megara to Corinth. *Paus.* 1. c. 39 & 40.——A son of Manes, who married Callirhoe, daughter of the Mæander. Caria received its name from him. *Vid.* Caria. *Herodot.* 1. c. 171.

CAR'ABI, a river of Scythia. *Plin.* 6. c. 17. Some read Cambari,

CARA'BIA, a town of Mygdonis in Macedonia. *Ptol.*

CAR'ABIS, a town of Spain. *Appian.*

CARACAL'LA BASSIA'NUS ANTONI'NUS, a Roman emperor. *Vid.* Antoninus.

CARAC'ATES or CARACA'TES, people of Germany. *Tacit.* 4. *Hist.* c. 70.

CARAC'CA, a town of the Carpetani, in Hispania Tarraconensis. *Ptol.*—*Plut. in Sertor.*

CARACE'NI, a people of Italy. *Ptol.*

CARAC'TACUS, a brave but unfortunate king of the Britons, conquered by Ostorius, A.D. 47, and sent in chains to Rome. His manly and independent conduct gained the friendship and regard of the emperor Claudius. *Tacit. Ann.* 12. c. 33 & 37.

CA'RÆ. certain places in Asia, between Susa and the Tigris, where Alexander pitched his camp. *Diod. Sic.* 17.

CARÆ'I, a people of Arabia Felix. *Ptol.*

CARÆ'US, a surname of Jupiter in Bœotia.

CAR'AGA, a town of Africa Propria. *Ptol.*

CARA'LIA, a city of Libya. *Steph.*

CAR'ALIS, the chief city of Sardinia, supposed to have been built by the Carthaginians. It is now Cagliari. *Mela,* 2. c. 7.—*Ptol.* 3. c. 3.—*Strab.* 5. —*Flor.* 2. c. 6.—*Plin.* 27. c. 6.—*Paus.* 10. c. 17.

CARAL'LIS or CARAL'LIA, a city of Isauria. *Steph.*

CARAM'BIS, now Kerempi, a promontory of Paphlagonia, projecting far northward into the Euxine Sea. *Mela,* 1. c. 20.—*Plin.* 4. c. 12. l. 6. c. 2.

CARAM'BUCIS, a river of Scythia, near the Riphæan mountains. *Plin.* 6. c. 13.

CARA'NA, a town of Pontus. *Strabo.* 12.

CARANI'TIS, a province of Armenia. *Plin.* 5. c. 24.

CAR'ANUS, or CARA'NUS, one of the Heraclidæ, who laid the foundation of the Macedonian empire, B.C. 814. He took Edessa, and reigned 28 years, which he spent in establishing and strengthing the government of his newly founded kingdom. He was succeeded by Perdiccas. *Justin.* 7. c. 1.—*Paterc.* 1. c. 6.—*Liv.* 45. c. 9.—*Paus.* 9. c. 40.

CARA'NUS, a general of Alexander. *Curt.* 7.

CARA'NUS, a harbour of Phœnicia. *Strab.* 16.

CAR'APE, a city of Armenia Minor. *Ptol.*

CAR'AROS, a town of Africa Propria. *Id.*

CARASE'NI, a people of Taurica Chersonesus. *Plin.* 4. c. 12.

CARASTA'CI, a people near the Mætos. *Id.* 6. c. 7.

CARA'TÆ, a nation of the Sacæ. *Ptol.*

CARAU'SIUS, a tyrant of Britain. He retained his power for seven years, A.D. 293. *Eutrop.* l. 9.

CAR'BACA, a city of Paropanisus. *Ptol.*

CAR'BANA, a city of Lycia. *Steph.*

CARBA'NIA, a small island near Italy, called by *Pliny* Barpana. *Mela,* 2. c. 7.

CAR'BI, a people of Arabia Felix. *Diod. Sic.* 3.

CARBILE'SI, a people of Thrace. *Plin.* 4. c. 11.

CARBIL'IUS. *Vid.* Carvilius.

CARBI'NA, a city of the Iapyges. *Athen.* 12. c. 7.

CAR'BO, a surname of the family of the Papirii at Rome. The only one of this family, who deserved the name of a respectable man, was an orator, who killed himself because he could not curb the licentious manners of his countrymen. *Cic. in Brut.* ——An orator, son of Carbo the orator, killed by the army, when desirous of re-establishing the ancient military discipline. *Cic. in Brut.*

CAR'BO CNE'US, a son of the orator Carbo, who embraced the party of Marius, and after the death of Cinna succeeded to the government. He was killed in Spain, in his third consulship, by order of Pompey. *Val. Max.* 9. c. 13.

CARCHE'DON, the Greek name of Carthage. *Dionys.* v. 195.

CAR'CINE, a town on the isthmus of the Taurica Chersonesus. A bay of the Euxine Sea, in the neighbourhood, bore the name of Carcinitis. *Mela,* 2. c. 1. Also Car'cina.

CARCI'NUM, a promontory of Magna Grœcia. *Plin.* 4. c. 12.——A city near Petilia. *Mela,* 2. c. 4.

CARCI'NUS or CAR'CINUS, a Greek tragic poet of Athens, in the age of Philip of Macedon. None of his plays remain, though *Athenœus* quotes verses from his Achilles and his Semele. He is said to have written 160 pieces, of which only one was rewarded with the prize. *Gyrald. P. Hist. Dial.* 7.—*Fabr. B. Gr.* l. 2. c. 19.——A poet of Agrigentum, distinguished as a tragic, and, according to others, as a comic writer in the age of Æschines, the disciple of Socrates, with whom he frequented the court of Dionysius of Syracuse. *Gyrald et supra.*—*Laert.* 2, *in Æschin.*—*Fabr. Ibid.*——A poet of Naupactus. said to be the inventor of those poetical compositions called Naupactian among the Greeks. *Pausan.* 10. c. 38.——A man of Rhegium, who exposed his son Agathocles, on account of some uncommon dreams during his wife's pregnancy. Agathocles was preserved. *Diod.* 19.——An Athenian general, who laid waste Peloponnesus in the time of Pericles. *Id.* 12.——A sophist mentioned by *Plato.*——A rhetorician. *Fabr. B. Gr.* l. 2. c. 19.

CAR'CINUS, a constellation, the same as Cancer. *Lucan.* 4. v. 536.

CAR'COME, a town of Mauritania Cæsariensis. *Ptol.*

CARDA'CES, a people of Asia Minor. *Strab.* 15.

CARDALE'NA, a region of Arabia Felix. *Plin.* 6. c. 28.

CARDAMI'NE, an island in the Arabian Gulph. *Id.* 6. c. 29.

CARDAM'YLE, a town of Argolis. *Homer. Il.* 9. —*Herodot.* 8. &c.

CAR'DAVA. a city of Arabia Felix. *Plin.*

CARDE'SUS, a city of Scythia. *Steph.*

CAR'DIA, a town in the Thracian Chersonesus, which was afterwards called Lysimachia, and now Hexamili, because the isthmus there is considered as only six miles broad. Eumenes, the celebrated general of Alexander the Great, was a native of the place. *C. Nep. in Eum.*—*Plin.* 4. c. 11.

CAR'DO or CARDIN'EA, a divinity at Rome, who was said to preside over hinges, She is the same as Carna. *Vid.* Carna.

CARDU'CHI or CAR'DUCHI, a warlike nation of Media, along the borders of the Tigris, now the Kurdes or Curds. *Diod.* 14.—*Cluver.* 5. c. 15.

CARDYTEN'SES, a people of Cyrrhestica in Syria. *Plin.* 5. c. 23.

CARDY'TUS, a large city of Syria. *Steph.*

CARECAR'DAMA, a town of India within the Ganges.—*Ptol.*

CARE'NE, a town of Mysia. *Steph.*

CAREN'SES, a people of Spain, near the Complutenses. *Plin.* 3. c. 3.

CARENTI'NI, a people of Italy, near the Ferentani. *Id.* 3. c 12.

CA'REON, a city of Spain. *Appian.*

CAREO'TÆ, a nation of European Sarmatia. *Ptol.*

CA'RES, a nation of Asia Minor, which inhabited Caria. They became so populous and powerful, that their country was not sufficiently extensive to contain them, upon which they seized upon the neighbouring island of the Ægæan sea. These islands were afterwards conquered by Minos, king of Crete. Nileus, son of Codrus, invaded their country, and slaughtered many of the inhabitants. In this calamity, the Carians, surrounded on every side by enemies, fortified themselves in the mountainous and inaccessible parts of the country, and, soon after, made themselves formidable by sea. They were anciently called Leleges. *Herodot.* 1. c. 146 & 171.—*Paus.* 1. c. 40.—*Strab.* 13.—*Curt.* 6. c. 3. —*Justin.* 13. c. 4.—*Virg. Æn.* 8. v. 725.

CAR'ESA, a small island of the Ægæan sea, opposite Attica. *Plin.*

CARE'SUS, a river of Troas. *Hom. Il.* 12.—*Plin.* 5. c. 30.

CAR'ETHA, an island in the Lycian Sea, afterwards Dionysia. *Plin.* 5. c. 31.

CARFIN'IA, an immodest woman mentioned by *Juvenal*, 2. v. 69.

CA'RIA, now Aldinelli, a country of Asia Minor, the boundaries of which have varied in different ages. Generally speaking, it was at the south of Iona, at the east and north of the Icarian Sea, and at the west of Phrygia Major and Lycia. It has been called Phœnicia, because a Phœnician colony first settled there; and afterwards it received the name of Caria, from Car, one of their kings, who first practised augury. The chief towns were called Halicarnassus, where Jupiter was the chief deity, Heraclea, Antioch, Myndus, Laodicea, Alabanda, &c. As Caria probably abounded in figs, a particular sort has been called Carica, and the words *In Care periculum facere*, having been proverbially used to signify the encountering of danger in the pursuit of a thing of trifling value. *Plin.* 5. c. 29. l. 13. c. 5.—*Ptol.* 5. c. 3.—*Mela*, l. c. 2 & 16. l. 2. c. 7.—*Cic. Flacc.* 27. *Div.* 1. c. 42. l. 2. c. 40.—*Zenob. Cent.* 3. 59. *Vid.* Cares.——A port of Thrace. *Mela*, 2. c. 2.

CARI'APA, a promontory of Parthia. *Ptol.*

CA'RIAS, a town of Peloponnesus. *Vitruv.* l. 1.

CA'RIAS, a general. *Vid.* Laches.

CARIA'TÆ, a town of Bactriana, where Alexander imprisoned Calisthenes. *Strab.* 11.

CARICON'TICHUS a city of Libya. *Steph.*

CAR'IDES, a city of Phrygia. *Id.*

CARIE'TES, a people of Spain. *Plin.* 3. c. 3.

CAR'IGE, a city of India within the Ganges. *Ptol.*

CARIL'LA, a town of the Piceni, destroyed by Annibal for its great attachment to Rome. *Sil. Ital.* 8.

CAR'IMA, a town of Galatia. *Ptol.*

CARI'NA, a virgin of Caria, &c. *Polyæn.* 8. c. 64.

CARI'NA, a mountain of Crete. *Plin.* 5. c. 32.

CARI'NÆ, a street at Rome, near the temple of Tellus. The houses of Pompey and Cicero were situated in this street, which, according to *Servius*, received its name from the resemblance which the roofs of the houses bore to keels of ships. *Cic.* 2. *ad Fratr.* 3.—*Virg. Æn.* v. 361.—*Horat.* 1. ep. 7. *Patercul.* 2. 77.

CAR'INE or CARI'NE, a town near the Caicus, in Asia Minor. *Herodot.* 7. c. 42.

CARI'NI, a people of Germany. *Plin.* 4. c. 14.

CARIN'II, a people of Illyricum. *Appian.*

CARIN'SII, a people of Sardinia. *Ptol.*

CARI'NUS M. AURE'LIUS, a Roman who attempted to succeed his father Carus as emperor. He disgraced himself by his debaucheries and cruelties. Diocletian defeated him in Dalmatia, and he was killed by a soldier whose wife he had debauched, A.D. 268.

CARIOSUELLI'TES, a people of Gallia Lugdunensis. *Plin.* 4. c. 18.

CARIOVAL'DA, a leader of the Batavi, in the service of Germanicus. *Tac. Ann.* 2. c. 11.

CARIPE'TA, a town of Arabia Felix. *Plin.* 6. c. 28.

CA'RIS, an ancient name of the island of Cos. *Steph.*

CARIS'IA AURE'LIA, a city of Spain, on the river Bætis. *Plin.* 3. c. 1.

CARISI'ACUM, a town of ancient Gaul, now Cressy in Picardy.

CARIS'SA, a town of Paphlagonia. *Plin.* 6. c. 3.

CARIS'SANUM, a place of Italy, near which Milo was killed. *Id.* 2. c. 56.

CARIS'TI, a nation of Hispania Tarraconensis. *Ptol.*

CARIS'TUM, a town of Liguria. *Liv.* 42.

CARIT'NI, a people of Germany. *Ptol.*

CA'RIUS, a surname of Jupiter in Caria. *Herodot.* 1. 171, &c.

CAR'MACÆ, a people of Asia near the Mæotis. *Plin.* 6. c. 7.

CAR'MALAS, a river of Asia Minor. *Strab.*

CARMAN'DE, a town on the Euphrates. near the Arabian Desert.

CARMA'NIA, a large country of Asia, between Persia and the river Arbis. The capital was called Carmana, now Kerman; and the inhabitants of the sea coast received the appellation of Ichthyophagi, (ἰχθῦς φαγεῖν,) because they lived on fish. *Plin.* 6. c. 23. l. 7. c. 34.—*Lucan.* 3. v. 250.—*Mela*, 3, c. 8.—*Arrian.*

CARMA'NOR, a Cretan, who purified Apollo of murder. *Paus.* 2. c. 30.

CAR'MARA, a city of India within the Ganges. *Ptol.*

CAR'ME, a nymph, mother of Britomartis by Jupiter. She was one of Diana's attendants. *Paus.* 2. c. 30.

CARME'JUS, a general who assisted Æetes against Perses. *Val. Flacc. Argon.* 5. v. 582.

CAR'MELIS, a city of Spain, the winter quarters of Servilius Galba. *Appian.*

CARME'LUS, a god among the inhabitants of mount Carmel, situate between Syria and Judæa. Neither temples nor statues were erected to his honour, but merely an altar on which sacrifices were regularly offered. Vespasian was one of those who paid homage to this divinity; and he was informed by the priest called Basilides, that he would one day rise to the sovereignty of a powerful state, a prophecy, which his elevation to the imperial purple soon after fulfilled. *Tacit.* 2 *Hist.* 78.—*Sueton. Vesp.* 5.—*Strab.* 16.

CARMEN'TA or CARMEN'TIS, a prophetess of Arcadia, mother of Evander, with whom she came as a fugitive to Italy, and was received by king Faunus about 60 years before the Trojan war. Her name was Nicostrata, and she received that of Carmentis from the wildness of her looks when giving oracles, as if *carens mentis*. She was regarded as the general oracle of the people of Italy during her life, and after death she received divine honours. She had a temple at Rome, and is supposed to be the divinity to whom the Greeks offered sacrifices under the name of Themis. *Ovid. Fast.* 1. v. 467. l. 6. v. 530.—*Plut. in Romul.*—*Virg. Æn.* 8. v. 339.—*Liv.* 5. c. 47.

CARMENTA'LES, festivals at Rome in honour of Carmenta, celebrated on the 11th of January, near the Porta Carmentalis, below the Capitol. This goddess was entreated to render the Roman matrons prolific, and their labours easy. *Liv.* 1. c. 7. —*Ovid. Fast.* 1. v. 464.—*Solin.* 2.—*Victorin. de Or. R.* 5.

CARMENTA'LIS POR'TA, one of the gates of Rome. It was afterwards called Scelerata, because the Fabii passed through it in going to that fatal expedition in which they perished. *Virg. Æn.* 8. v. 338.

CAR'MIDES, a Greek, gifted with an uncommon memory. *Plin.* 7. c. 24.

CARMI'NA, an island of India. *Steph.*

CAR'MON, a place of Messenia.——A temple of Apollo in Laconia.——A river of Achaia.——A mountain of Peloponnesus.

CARMYLES'SUS, a place in Anticragus, a mountain of Lycia. *Strab.* 14.

CAR'NA or CARDIN'EA, a goddess at Rome, who presided over hinges, as also over the entrails and secret parts of the human body. She was originally a nymph called Grane, who employed herself in hunting, and deserved, by her chastity and the simplicity of her life, the surname of Diana, which she obtained among the inhabitants of the country. Janus offered violence to her person, and, to make atonement for the insult, he granted her the power of presiding over the exterior of houses, and of removing all noxious birds from the habitations of men. Junius Brutus erected a temple to her honour on mount Cœlius; and, at a feast which was celebrated annually in June, the Romans offered her beans. bacon, and vegetables, to represent the rural simplicity of their ancestors. *Ovid. Sast.* 6. v. 101, &c.—*Macrob. Sat.* 1. c. 12.—*August de Civ.* 4. c. 8.—*Gyrald de Hist. D. Synt.* 1.—*Tertull. de Idol.* 15.

CARNA'NA, a city of the Minæi, near the Red Sea. *Steph.*

CAR'NAPÆ, a people near the Mæotis. *Plin.* 6. c. 7.

CAR'NASA, a city of India within the Ganges. *Ptol.*

CARNA'SIUS SAL'TUS, a village of Messenia in Peloponnesus. *Paus.* 4. c. 33.

CAR'NE, a town of Phœnicia, near mount Libanus. *Plin.* 5. c. 20.

CARNE'A, a festival observed in most of the Grecian cities, but more particularly at Sparta, where it was first instituted, about 675 B.C. in honour of Apollo, surnamed Carneus. It lasted nine days. *Paus.* 2. c. 11. l. 3. c. 24.—*Athen* 4. c. 4.

CARNE'ADES, a philosopher of Cyrene in Africa, founder of a sect called the third or new academy. The Athenians sent him, with Diogenes the stoic and Critolaus the peripatetic, on a public embassy to Rome, B. C. 155. The Roman youth were extremely fond of the company of these learned philosophers; but when Carneades in a speech had delivered an accurate and judicious dissertation upon justice, and in another speech had confuted all the arguments which he had advanced, and, apparently given no existence to the virtues which he had so much commended, a report prevailed over Rome, that a Grecian was come, who had so captivated the rising generation by his eloquence, that they forgot their usual amusements, and ran mad after philosophy. When this reached the ears of Cato the censor, he gave immediate audience to the Athenian ambassadors in the senate, and dismissed them in haste, expressing his apprehensions of their corrupting the Roman people, whose only profession, he sternly observed, was arms and war. One of his maxims with respect to the asp, against whose bite a person should warn even his greatest enemy, even with the certain loss of advantage to himself, so much resembles the pure precept of Christianity, to do to another what we would wish to be done to ourselves, that Carneades must for ever be considered as humane, benevolent, and pious. He died in the 90th year of his age, B.C. 128. He intended to leave his school to his pupil Mentor; but his intrigues with Melissa, the wife or concubine of the philosopher, produced an inveterate quarrel between the master and the scholar. *Cic. ad Attic.* 12. ep. 23. *De Orat.* 1. c. 45. l. 2. c. 155.—*Aul. Gell.* 17. c. 15.—*Fabric. B. Gr.* 3. c. 3.—*Plin.* 7. c. 30.—*Lactantius.* 5. c. 14.—*Val. Max.* 8. c. 8. [There is a curious bust of this philosopher in the Farnese collection at Naples.]

CARNE'ADES, another Athenian philosopher, pupil of Anaxagoras. *Suidas.*——An obscure elegiac poet. *Diog.*

CAR'NI, a warlike people who inhabited the country situated between the Alps and the north of the Adriatic, now Carniola. *Mela,* 2. c. 6.

CAR'NIA, a city of Ionia. *Steph.*

CAR'NICUM JU'LIUM, a town of Noricum. *Ptol.*

CARNI'ON, a town of Laconia. *Polyb.*——A river of Arcadia. *Paus.* 8. c. 34.

CAR'NON, a town of Arabia Felix. *Plin.*

CAR'NUS, a prophet of Acarnania, son of Jupiter and Europa. He was a great favourite with Apollo, from which circumstance that god was called Carneus. *Paus.* 3. c. 13.

CARNU'TES, a people of Gaul, between the Seine and the Loire, now Chartrain. Their capital Autricum Carnutum, is modern Chartres. *Cæs Bell. G.* 6. c. 4.

CARNU'TI, a people of Germany. *Plin.* 4. c. 12.

CARO'EA, a town of European Sarmatia. *Ptol.*

CAROP'OLIS, a city of Caria. *Steph.*

CARPA'SIA or **CARPA'SIUM**, a town of Cyprus. *Plin.* 5. c. 31.

CAR'PATES or **CARPA'TES**, a ridge of high mountains at the north of the Danube, between the modern countries of Poland, Hungary, and Transylvania. They are now called Krapac or Carpathian mountains.

CAR'PATHUS, an island in the Mediterranean, between Rhodes and Crete, now called Scapanto. It has given its name to a part of the neighbouring sea, between Rhodes and Crete, thence called the Carpathian Sea. Carpathus was at first inhabited by some Cretan soldiers of Minos. It was twenty miles in circumference, and was sometimes called Tetrapolis, from its four capital cities. *Plin.* 4. c. 12.—*Herodot.* 3. c. 45.—*Diod.* 5.—*Strab.* 10.—*Virg. G.* 4. v. 387.

CARPENTORAC'TE, a city of Gallia Narbonensis, now Carpentras. *Plin.* 3. c. 4.

CARPE'SII, a nation within the Iberus. *Steph.*

CARPETA'NI, a people of Hispania Tarraconensis; the country is now La Mancha. *Plin.* 3. c. 3.

CAR'PI, a people of Zeugitana. *Id.*

CARPI'A, an ancient name of Tartessus, in Spain. *Paus.* 6. c. 19.

CAR'PIS, a river of Mysia. *Herodot.* 4. c. 49.——A city of Africa, now Carpi. *Ptol.*

CAR'PO, a daughter of Zephyrus, and one of the Seasons. She was loved by Calamus, the son of Mæander, whose attachment she tenderly requitted. She was drowned in the Mæander, and was changed by Jupiter into all sorts of fruit. *Paus.* 9. c. 35.—*Servius in Ecl.* 5. c. 48.

CARPOPH'ORI, a name given to Ceres and Proserpine in Tegea, from the influence which they possessed over the fertility and productions of the earth. *Paus.* 8. c. 53.

CARPOPH'ORUS, an actor at Rome greatly esteemed by Domitian. *Martial.*—*Juv* 6. v. 198.

CARPUDE'MUM, an inland city of Thrace, now Cappa or Capsia. *Ptol.*

CAR'RA, a river of Syria. *Steph.*——A town of Arabia, on the shores of the Red Sea. *Mela,* 3. c. 14.

CAR'RÆ or **CAR'RHÆ**, a town of Mesopotamia, near which Crassus was killed. *Lucan.* 1. v. 105.—*Plin.* 5. c. 14.

CAR'REI, a people of Arabia Felix. *Plin.* 6. c. 28.

CAR'RHENES, an illustrious Parthian, who espoused the cause of Meherdates. *Tac. Ann.* 12. c. 12.

CARRINA'TES SECUN'DUS, a rhetorician, who came from Athens to Rome, where the boldness of his expressions, especially against tyrannical power, exposed him to the resentment of Caligula, by whom he was banished. *Juv.* 7. v. 205.

CARRODU'NUM, a town of Germany, now Cracow. *Ptol.*——A city in Vindelicia, now Cramburg. *Id.*——A city of Upper Pannonia, now Kornburg.

CARRU'CA, a town of Spain. *Hirt. Hisp.* 27.

CAR'SEÆ, a people of Asia Minor. *Polyb.*

CARSE'OLI, now Arsoli, a town of the Æqui, at the west of the lake Fucinus. The inhabitants were called Carseolani. *Ovid. Fast.* 4. v. 683 & seq.—*Cluver.* 3. c. 27.

CARSIDA'VA, a city of Dacia, now Kuryma. *Ptol.*

CARSITA'NI, a people of Italy, near Præneste. *Macrob. Saturn.* 3. c. 18.

CAR'SIUS, a priest accused, but acquitted, of supplying the enemy with corn under Tiberius. *Tac. Ann.* 4. c. 13.

CAR'SULI, a town of Umbria, now destroyed. *Plin.* 1. ep. 4.—*Strab.* 5.

CAR'SUM, a town of Lower Mysia. *Ptol.*

CAR'TA, a town of Hyrcania, at the south-east of the Caspian Sea. *Strab.*

CARTA'LIAS, a town of Spain. *Strab.* 3.

CARTAS'INA, a city of India within the Ganges. *Ptol.*

CARTE'IA, a town at the southern extremity of Spain, near the sea of Gades, or at the entrance of the Mediterranean, supposed to be the same as Calpe. *Mela,* 2. c. 8.

CARTEN'AGA, a town of India within the Ganges. *Ptol.*

CARTEN'NA, a town of Mauritania, on the shores of the Mediterranean, now Mostagan. *Cluver.* 6. c. 5.—*Mela,* 1. c. 6.

CAR'TENUS, a river of Mauritania Cæsariensis. *Ptol.*

CARTE'RIA, an island near Smyrna. *Id.*

CARTHÆ'A, a town in the island of Cea, whence the epithet of Cartheius. *Ovid. Met.* 7. v. 368.

CARTHAGINIEN'SES, the inhabitants of Carthage. *Vid.* Carthago.

CARTHA'GO, a celebrated city of Africa, the rival of Rome, and long the capital of the country, and mistress of Spain, Sicily, and Sardinia. Most writers seem to agree that it was built by Dido, about 869 years B.C. According to Paterculus, it was built 65, according to Justin 72, and according to Livy 94 years before the foundation of Rome. This city and republic flourished for 737 years, and the time of its greatest glory was under Annibal and Amilcar, whose valour and sagacity so directed its forces as to equal and nearly overturn its proud rival. During the first punic war it contained no less than 700,000 inhabitants, and exercised absolute sovereignty over 300 dependent cities in Africa. It maintained three famous wars against Rome, called the Punic wars (*vid.* Punicum Bellum), in the third of which Carthage with more perfidy than justice, was totally destroyed by Scipio, the second Africanus, B.C. 147, and only 5000 persons were found within the walls. It was 23 miles in circumference; and when it was set on fire by the Romans, it burned incessantly during 17 days. After the destruction of Carthage, the neighbouring town of Utica became powerful, and the Romans thought themselves secure; and as they had no rival who could contend with them in the field, they fell into indolence and inactivity. Cæsar planted a small colony on the ruins of Carthage. Augustus sent 3000 men; and Adrian, after the example of his imperial predecessors, rebuilt part of it, which he called Adrianopolis. Carthage was wrested from the Romans by the arms of Genseric, A.D. 439; and it was for more than a century the seat of the Vandal empire in Africa, and at last fell into the hands of the Saracens in the seventh century. The Carthaginians, in the flourishing times of their history, had two persons yearly chosen among them with regal authority. They were very superstitious, and generally offered human victims to their gods; an unnatural custom, which their allies wished them to abolish, but in vain. According to the Roman historians, who probably were not impartial judges, the Carthaginians bore the character of a faithless and treacherous people, and thence arose the censorious proverb, *Punica fides*. *Strab.* 17.—*Virg. Æn.* 1, &c.—*Mela*, 1, &c.—*Ptol.* 4. c. 3.—*Justin.* 4. c. 2.—*Liv.* 4. c. 29, &c.—*Paterc.* 1. c. 6.—*Plut. in Annib.* &c.—*Cic. in Agr.* 2. c. 35. *Rull.* 2. c. 94.—*Aug. de Civ.*—*Tertull. in Apol.*

CARTHA'GO NO'VA, a town built in Spain, on the coasts of the Mediterranean, by Asdrubal, the Carthaginian general. It was taken by Scipio when Hanno surrendered himself, after a heavy loss. It is now Carthagena in Murcia. *Solin.* 30.—*Mela*, 1. c. 7.—*Ptol.* 2. c. 6.—*Polyb.* 10.—*Liv.* 26. c. 43, &c.—*Sil.* 15. v. 220, &c.

CARTHA'GO, a daughter of Hercules.

CAR'THARA, a city of Mesopotamia. *Ptol.*

CAR'THASIS, a Scythian, &c. *Curt.* 7. c. 7.

CAR'TII, a people of Persia. *Strab.* 1. 11.

CARTISMAN'DUA, a queen of the Brigantes, who delivered Caractacus into the hands of Ostorius. *Tacit. Ann.* 12. c. 36.

CAR'TRIS, a peninsula of the Cimbri. *Plin.* 4. c. 13.

CARUAN'CAS, a mountain of Noricum. *Ptol.*

CAR'VANIS, a city of Pontus Polemoniacus, in Cappadocia. *Id.*

CARUEN'TUS, a city of the Latini. *Steph.*

CARVIL'IUS, one of the chieftains of Britain, who attacked Cæsar's naval station, by order of Cassivelaunus, &c. *Cæs. Bell. G.* 5. c. 22.——The first Roman who divorced his wife, during the space of above 600 years. This was for barrenness, B.C. 231. *Dionys. Hal.* 2.—*Val. Max.* 2. c. 1.

CARVIL'IUS SPU'RIUS, a Roman who made a large image with the breast-plates taken from the Samnites, and placed it in the Capitol. *Plin.* 34. c. 7.

CARU'RA, called Ortospanum by *Pliny*, a town of Phrygia Major, now Kare. *Cluver.* 5. c. 13.——A city of India within the Ganges. *Ptol.*

CA'RUS M. AURE'L., a Roman emperor who succeeded Probus. He was a prudent and active general, conquered the Sarmatians, and continued the Persian war which his predecessor had commenced. He reigned two years, and died on the banks of the Tigris, as he was going on an expedition against Persia, A.D. 283. He made his two sons, Carinus and Numerianus, Cæsars; and as his many virtues had flattered the Roman people with the hopes of national happiness, he was made a god after death. *Eutrop.*

CA'RUS, one of those who attempted to scale the rock Aornus, by order of Alexander. *Curt.* 8. c. 11.

CA'RYÆ, a town of Arcadia. *Vid.* Caryatæ. *Liv.* 34. c. 16.——A city of Laconia. *Paus.* 3. c. 10. A festival was observed here in honour of Diana Caryatis. It was then usual for virgins to meet at the celebration, and join in a certain dance, said to have been first instituted by Castor and Pollux. When Greece was invaded by Xerxes, the Laconians did not appear before the enemy, for fear of displeasing the goddess by not celebrating her festival. At that time the peasants assembled at the usual place, and sang pastorals, called Βουκολισμοί, from Βουκόλος, *a neat-herd*. From this circumstance some suppose that the name of Bucolics originated. *Stat.* 4. *Theb.* v. 225.

CARYAN'DA, an island with a town of the same name, on the coast of Caria, now Karacoion. *Mela*, 1. c. 16.

CARYA'TÆ, the inhabitants of Carya in Arcadia. Statues representing women in long robes were called *Caryatides columnæ*, either from the dress worn at the festivals of Diana Caryatis or some other unknown circumstance. *Vitruv.* 1. c 1.

CARYN'IA, a city of Achaia. *Plin.* 14. c. 18.

CARY'ONES, a nation of European Sarmatia. *Ptol.*

CARYS'TIUS ANTIG'ONUS, an historian, &c. B.C. 248.

CARYS'TUS, a maritime town at the south-eastern corner of Eubœa, still in existence. It was famous for its marble, and for the particular worship which the inhabitants paid to Apollo. *Strab.* 10. —*Plin.* 4. c. 12. l. 36. c. 6.—*Liv.* 31. c. 45. l. 32. c. 16.—*Mela*, 2. c. 9.—*Solin.* 17.—*Tibull.* 3. el. 3. v. 13.—*Ovid. Fast.* 4. v. 282.—*Lucan.* 5. v. 232.—*Plin.* 5. ep. 6 & 36.—*Stat.* 2. v. 93.—*Martial.* 9. epigr. 76.

CA'RYUM or CA'RYA, a place of Laconia, where Aristomenes preserved some virgins, &c. *Paus.* 4. c. 16.

CA'SÆ, a city of Cilicia. *Ptol.*

CAS'ALUS, a bay of Corsica, now probably Golfo di Calvi. *Id.*

CAS'AMA, a city of Palmyrene. *Id.*

CASAMAR'RI, a people of Upper Æthiopia. *Plin.* 6. c. 30.

CASAN'DRA, an island opposite Persia. *Id.* 6. c. 25.

CAS'CA SERVIL'IUS, a Roman who joined in the conspiracy formed by Brutus against Cæsar. He gave the first blow to the unhappy dictator. *Plut. in Cæs.*—*Appian. B.C.* 2.

CASCAN'DRUS, a desert island in the Indian Ocean. *Plin.* 6. c. 25.

CASCAN'TUM, now Cascante, a town of Spain on the western banks of the Iberus. *Id.* 3. l. 3.

CASCEL'LIUS AU'LUS, a lawyer of great merit in the Augustan age. *Horat. Art. Poet.* 371.

CA'SIA, a region of Scythia, beyond Imaus. *Ptol.*

CASILI'NUM, now Casilino, a town of Campania. When it was besieged by Hannibal, a mouse sold for 200 denarii, though Strabo says this price was given for a medimnus of corn, and that the avaricious seller perished, and the purchaser survived. The place was defended by 540 or 570 natives of Præneste, who, when half their number had perished either by war or famine, were obliged reluctantly to surrender to the conqueror. *Val. Max.* 7. c. 6.—*Liv.* 23. c. 19.—*Strab.* 5.—*Cic. de Inv.* 2. c. 57.—*Plin.* 3. c. 5.—*Ptol.* 3. c. 1.

CAS'INA, CASI'NA, or CASI'NUM, a small town of Campania. *Sil.* 4. v. 227.—*Varr. L.L.* 6.—*Liv.* 9. c. 28. l. 22. c. 13.

CASI'OPE, a city of Chaonia, in Epirus. *Ptol.*

CA'SIUS, a mountain near the Euphrates. *Suidas.* A mountain at the east of Pelusium, projecting into the sea, and resembling at a distance large heaps of sand, now called Cape del Kas, or Chisel. Pompey was slain near it, and there afterwards his tomb was raised by Adrian. Jupiter, surnamed Casius, had a temple there. The country round was called Casiotis, and a small town near the mountain, Casium, now Catich. *Strab.* 16.—*Plin.* 5. c. 12.—*Lucan.* 8. v. 858.——A mountain in Syria, from the top of which the sun can be seen rising, according to Pliny, three hours before it makes its appearance above the horizon, or to those who dwell at the bottom of the mountain. *Plin.* 5. c. 22. l. 6. c. 12.—*Strab.* 16.—*Mela*, 1. c. 11. l. 3. c. 13.—*Lucan.* 8. v. 857.

CAS'MARE, a town of Mauritania Cæsariensis. *Ptol.*

CAS'MENE, now Comiso, a town built by the Syracusans, on the sea coast, at the south of Sicily. *Thucyd.* 6. c. 5.

CASMIL'LA, the mother of Camilla. *Virg. Æn.* 11. v. 543.

CASMONA'TES, a people of Liguria. *Plin.* 3. c. 5.

CA'SUS, one of the Sporades. *Id.* 4. c. 12.

CA'SOS, an island and city of Persia. *Steph.*

CASPA'SIUM, a river of Asiatic Scythia. *Plin.* 6. c. 17.

CASPE'RIA, wife of Rhœtus, king of the Marubii, disgraced herself by her adulterous intercourse with her son-in-law. *Virg Æn.* 10. v. 388.

CASPE'RIA, a town of the Sabines, now Aspra. *Virg. Æn.* 7. v. 714.——A region of India within the Ganges. *Ptol.*

CASPER'ULA, a town of the Sabines. *Sil.* 8. v. 416.

CAS'PIÆ PORTÆ, certain passes of Asia, which some place about Caucasus and the Caspian Sea, or near Mount Taurus, or Armenia, or Cilicia. The neighbouring country was called Caspiana, or Caspia Regna, and the inhabitants Caspiani. *Diod.* 1.—*Plin.* 5. c. 37, l. 6. c. 13.—*Strab.* 2 & 11.—*Stat.* 4. *Sylv.* 4. v. 64.—*Virg. Æn.* 6. v. 798.—*Curt.* 4. c. 12.—*Nepos*, 14. c. 8.—*Ptol.* 6. c. 2.—*Dionys. Per.* 881.—*Tacit.* 1. *Hist.* 6, *Ann.* 6. c. 33.—*Mela*, 1. c. 15.

CASPIA'NA, a country of Armenia, at the south-west of the Caspian Sea. *Mela*, 1. c. 2. *Vid.* Caspiæ Portiæ.

CAS'PII, a Scythian nation near the Caspian Sea. Such as had lived beyond their 70th year were starved to death. The dogs of the country were remarkable for their fierceness. *Herodot.* 3. c. 92. &c. l. 7. c. 67, &c.—*C. Nep.* 14. c. 8.—*Curt.* 4. c. 12.—*Mela*, 3. c. 6.—*Virg. Æn.* 6. v. 798.

CASPI'RUS or CASPI'RA, a city of the Parthians, near India. *Steph.*

CAS'PIUM or HYRCA'NUM MA'RE, a large sea of Asia, in the form of a lake, which has no communication with other seas, and lies between the Caspian and Hyrcanian mountains, at the north of Parthia, receiving in its capacious bed the tribute of several large rivers. Ancient authors assure us, that it produced enormous serpents and fishes, different in colour and kind from those of all other waters. The eastern parts were more particularly called the Hyrcanian Sea, and the western the Caspian. It is now called the Sea of Sala, or Baku, and abounds in fish of great excellence. The Caspian is about 680 miles long, and in no part more than 260 in breadth. There are no tides in it, and on account of its numerous shoals it is navigable only to vessels drawing nine or ten feet of water. It has strong currents, and, like inland seas, is liable to violent storms. Some navigators examined it in 1708, by order of the Czar Peter; and after the labour of three years, a map of its extent was published. *Herodot.* 1. c. 202, &c.—*Curt.* 3. c. 2. l. 6. c. 4. l. 7. c. 3.—*Strab.* 11.—*Mela*, 1. c. 2. l. 3. c. 5 & 6.—*Plin.* 6. c. 13.—*Dionys. ePrieg.* v. 50.—*Pellarius. in Notit. Orb.*

CAS'PIUS MONS, a branch of Mount Taurus, between Media and Armenia, at the east of the Euphrates. The Caspiæ Portæ are placed in the defiles of the mountain by some geographers. *Cluver.* 5. c. 14. *Vid.* Caspiæ Portæ.

CASSANDA'NE, the mother of Cambyses. *Herodot.* 2. c. 1. l. 3. c. 2.

CASSAN'DER, son of Antipater, made himself master of Macedonia, after his father's death, where he reigned for 11 years. He married Thessalonica, the sister of Alexander the Great, to strengthen himself on his throne. He besieged Olympias in the town of Pydna, and put her to death; and Roxane, with her son Alexander, and Barsena, the mother of Hercules, both wives of Alexander, shared her fate. Antigonus, who had been for some time upon friendly terms with Cassander, declared war against him; and Cassander, to make head against his powerful adversary, concluded a treaty with Lysimachus and Seleucus, and obtained a memorable victory at Ipsus, B C. 301. He died of dropsy three years after his victory. *Paus.* 1. c. 25.—*Diod.* 19.—*Justin.* 12, 13, &c.

CASSAN'DRA, daughter of Priam and Hecuba, was passionately loved by Apollo, who promised to grant her whatever she asked, if she gratified his passion. She asked the power of knowing futurity; and as soon as she had received it, she refused to perform her promise, and slighted Apollo. The god, upon this, wetted her lips with his tongue, and by this action affected that no credit or reliance should ever be put upon her predictions, however true or faithful they might be. Some maintain that she received the gift of prophecy with her brother Helenus, by being placed one night, when young, in the temple of Apollo, where serpents were found wreathed round their bodies, and licking their ears, which circumstance gave them the knowledge of futurity. Cassandra was looked upon by the Trojans as insane, and was even confined, so that her predictions were universally disregarded. Her beauty, however, procured her many admirers; and among them Corœbus son of Mygdon, and Othryneus, are mentioned as urging their suit by the powerful assistance they gave to Priam during the Trojan war. When Troy was taken, Cassandra fled for shelter to the temple of Minerva, where Ajax found her, and offered her violence at the foot of Minerva's statue. In the division of the spoils of Troy, Agamemnon, who was enamoured of her, took her as his wife, and returned with her to Greece. She repeatedly foretold him the sudden calamities that awaited his return; but he gave no credit to her, and was assassinated by Clytemnestra. Cassandra shared his fate, and saw all her prophecies but too truly fulfilled. *Vid.* Agamemnon. *Æschyl. in Agam.*—*Homer. Il.* 13. v. 363. *Odyss.* 4.—*Hygin.* fab. 117.—*Q. Calab.* 13. v. 421. *Eurip. in Troad.*—*Paus.* 1. c. 16. l. 3. c. 19.—*Tzetzes in ycop.*—*Schol. Eurip. in Hecub.*—*Virg. Æn. et Servius in Æn.* 1. v. 45. *in* l. 2. v. 414. *in* l. 6. v. 842. *in* l. 11. v. 259.——A daughter of Jobates, who married Belerophon. *Homer.*

CASSANDRI'A, a large town of the peninsula of Pallene in Macedonia called also Potidæa. *Paus.* 5. c. 28.—*Mela*, 2. c. 3.

CASSANI'TÆ, a maritime people near the Red Sea. *Steph.* According to *Ptolemy* they were a people of Arabia Felix.

CASSANO'RUS, a city of Ægypt. *Steph.*

CAS'SERA, a town of Macedonia. *Plin.* 4. c. 10.

CAS'SIA LEX, was enacted by Cassius Longinus, A.U.C. 649. By it no man condemned, or deprived of military power, was permitted to enter the senate house.—Another, enacted by C. Cassius, the prætor, to chuse some of the plebeians to be admitted into the number of the patricians.—Another, A.U.C. 616, to make the suffrages of the Roman people free and independent. It ordained that they should be received upon tablets. *Cic. ad Læl.*—Another, A.U.C. 267, to make a division of the territories taken from the Hernici, half to the Roman people, and half to the Latins.—Another, enacted A.U.C. 596, to grant a consular power to P. Anicius and Octavius on the day they triumphed over Macedonia. *Liv.*

CAS SIDA, a town of India within the Ganges. *Ptol.*

CAS'SII, mountains of Scythia beyond Imaus. *Ptol.*

CASSIODO'RUS M. AURE'LIUS, a great statesman and popular writer in the sixth century. He recommended himself, by his prudence and abilities, to Theodoric king of the Goths in Italy, by whom he was made governor of Sicily, and afterwards entrusted with the highest offices of the state. Athalaric, the son and successor of Theodoric, equally respected his talents; but Cassiodorus was disgraced under Vitigez, and retired into Calabria to a monastery which he had founded and there devoted himself to literature and science. He was also fond of mechanics, and employed himself occasionally in the construction of sun-dials, water hour-glasses, lamps, and other curious things. He wrote, besides letters, two books *De divinis lectionibus*, a treatise on orthography, and twelve books *De rebus gestis Gothorum*, preserved only in the mutilated abridgment of Jornandes. He died A.D. 562, at the great age of 100. His works were edited by Chandler, 8vo, London, 1722. The best edition of his works is that of Garetius, Rotomag. 1679; reprinted at Venice, 1729. *Harles. Not. Lit. Rom.* 1. p. 766.—*Sax. Onom.* 2. p. 17.

CASSI'OPE or CASSIOPE'A, married Cepheus, king of Æthiopia, by whom she had Andromeda. She boasted herself to be fairer than the Nereides; upon which Neptune at the request of these despised nymphs, sent a huge sea monster to ravage Æthiopia. The wrath of Neptune could be appeased only by exposing Andromeda, whom Cassiope tenderly loved, to the fury of a sea monster; and just as she was going to be devoured, Perseus delivered her. *Vid.* Andromeda. Cassiope was made a southern constellation, consisting of thirteen stars called Cassiope. *Sic. de Nat. D.* 2. c. 43.—*Apollod.* 2. c. 4.—*Ovid. Met.* 4. v. 738.—*Hygin.* fab. 64. *P. A.* 2. c. 10. l. 3. c. 9.—*Manil.* 1. v. 354.—*Propert.* 1. el. 17. v. 3.

CASSI'OPE, a city of Epirus, near Thesprotia. *Ptol.* 3. c. 14.——A city in the island of Corcyra. *Plin.* 4. c. 12.

CASSI'OPE, the wife of Epaphus. *Stat. Sylv.*

CASSITER'IDES, islands in the western ocean, near the western shores of Britain, where tin (*cassiteron*) was found, supposed to be the Scilly islands, Land's

End, and Lizard Point of the moderns. *Plin.* 4. c. 22.

CASSIT'IRA, an island in the Indian Ocean. *Steph.*

CASSIVELAU'NUS, a Briton unanimously invested with sovereign authority by his countrymen, when J. Cæsar made a descent upon Britain. *Cæs. Bel. G.* 5. c. 19, &c.

C. CAS'SIUS LONGI'NUS, a celebrated Roman, who made himself known first by being quæstor to Crassus in his unfortunate expedition against Parthia. He followed the interest of Pompey; and when Cæsar had obtained a decisive victory in the plains of Pharsalia, Cassius was one of those who owed their lives to the mercy of the conqueror. He married Junia the sister of Brutus, and with this stern republican, he resolved to murder the man to whom he was indebted for his life, on account of his oppressive ambition. Full of his bloody purpose, before he stabbed Cæsar, he addressed himself to the statue of Pompey, who had fallen by the intrigues of him whom he was going to assassinate. When the provinces were divided among Cæsar's murderers, Cassius received Africa; and when his party had lost ground at Rome, by the superior influence of Augustus and M. Antony, he retired to Philippi, with his friend Brutus and their adherents. In the battle that was fought there, the wing which Cassius commanded was defeated, and the camp was plundered. In this unsuccessful moment, he suddenly gave up all hopes of recovering his losses, and concluded that Brutus was conquered and ruined as well as himself. Fearful of falling into the enemy's hands, he ordered one of his freedmen to run him through, and perished by that very sword which had inflicted the fatal wound on Cæsar. His body was honoured with a magnificent funeral by Brutus, who declared that he deserved to be called the last of the Romans. If Cassius was brave, he was equally learned, and some of his letters are still extant among Cicero's epistles. He was a strict follower of the doctrine of Epicurus. He was often too rash and violent in his opinions, and many of the wrong steps which Brutus took are to be ascribed to the prevailing advice of Cassius. He is allowed by Paterculus to have been a better commander than Brutus, though a less sincere friend. The day after Cæsar's murder, he dined at the house of Antony, who asked him whether he had then a dagger concealed in his bosom; yes, replied he, if you aspire to tyranny. Cassius had been even from his youth remarkable for his republican spirit and independent sentiments. When at school, he gave Faustus, Sylla's son, a violent box on the ear, for boasting of the greatness and absolute power of his father; and when called to account for this before Pompey, he with undaunted boldness declared that if Faustus still dared to repeat the same words, he would repeat his blows. Though in his late years attached to the doctrines of Epicurus, yet he always adhered to the temperance of the stoics, and drank nothing but water; whence Cæsar, when advised to beware of Antony and Dolabella, exclaimed, that he feared not the fat and the sleek, but rather the pale and the lean, alluding to Brutus and Cassius. *Suet. in Cæs. & Aug.—Plut. in Brut. & Cæs.—Patercul.* 2. c. 46.—*Dio.* 40.

CAS'SIUS LU'CIUS, brother to Caius, was made tribune and presided at the games exhibited by his brother and Brutus after Cæsar's murder. *Cic. Fam.* 12. ep. 2. *Att.* 14. ep. 2.

CAS'SIUS L., a person who joined Catiline's conspiracy, and was engaged to set Rome on fire. He fled from the city before the conspirators were discovered. *Sall. in Cat.* 44.

CAS'SIUS, a Roman citizen who condemned his son to death, on pretence that he had raised commotions in the state. *Val. Max.* 5. c. 8.——A tribune of the people tending to diminish the influence of the Roman nobility. He was competitor with Cicero for the consulship.——One of Pompey's officers, who, during the civil wars, revolted to Cæsar with ten ships, though he might have secured his person, and thus for ever ruined his cause, when he crossed the Hellespont, after the battle of Pharsalia. Some suppose him to be the same as Caius, which is improbable, as Caius was at the time on the coast of Sicily. This man was also among Cicero's murderers, according to some authors; and it is said that he first stabbed the dictator on the breast a little below the throat, though *Appian* relates that he struck him on the face, and that Casca was really the person who gave the first wound.——A poet of Parma, of great genius, who espoused the cause of Brutus. According to the scholiast on Horace, after the death of Brutus, he retired to Athens, where he was put to death by Varus, by the order of Augustus. His tragedies and other poems were much admired, and were edited by the poet Statius some time after. Some authors imagine this Cassius to be the same as Cassius Etruscus, who wrote in so voluminous a manner, that his papers and books were sufficient to form his funeral pile; but it is an erroneous conclusion. *Horat.* 1. sat. 10. v. 62. l. 1. ep. 4. v. 3.

SPU'RIUS CAS'SIUS VISCELLI'NUS, a Roman, put to death on suspicion of his aspiring to tyranny, after he had been three times consul, B.C. 485. The cause of his condemnation probably was his proposing an agrarian law, so offensive to the patricians, that they attributed his popularity to ambitious views against the independence of his country. Cassius was the first who was made master of the horse to a dictator. *Diod.* 11.—*Val. Max.* 6. c. 3.

CAS'SIUS BRU'TUS, a Roman who betrayed his country to the Latins, and fled to the temple of Pallas, where his father confined him, and he was starved to death.

Q. CAS'SIUS LONGI'NUS, an officer in the army of Cæsar. He had first sided with Pompey in the civil wars, but revolted to Cæsar, by whom he was made commander of the southern parts of Spain. His severity was so great and his exactions so cruelly levied, that the Spaniards attempted to murder him; and he at last left the province in disgrace, and was drowned on his return at the mouth of the Iberus. *Dio.* 41. c. 24. l. 42. c. 16.—*Cæs Alex.* c. 48.

L. CAS'SIUS LONGI'NUS, a consul to whom Tiberius married Drusilla, daughter of Germanicus. *Suet. in Cal.* c. 57.——A lawyer whom Nero wantonly put to death because he bore the name of J. Cæsar's murderer. *Suet. in Ner.* 37.

L. CAS'SIUS HEMI'NA, the most ancient writer of annals at Rome. He lived A.U.C, 608.

L. CAS'SIUS LONGI'NUS, a Roman tribune, whose severity in the execution of the law has rendered the words *Cassiani judices* applicable to rigid judges. He made a law to cause the votes of the people at the Comitia to be given by ballot, and not *vivâ voce* as before, in all public trials except for treason. *Cic. pro Rosc.* c. 30.

CAS'SIUS LONGI'NUS, a critic. *Vid.* Longinus.

CAS'SIUS LU'CIUS, a consul with C. Marius, slain with his army by the Tigurini, a people of Helvetia. It is generally supposed that he is the person who brought Jugurtha to Rome, on a public promise of safety, and induced him to depend upon his integrity as on the most solemn pledges of the state. *Cæs. B. G.* 1. c. 12 & 17.—*Liv.* 65.—*Oros.* 16. 17. —*Sallust. Jug.* 33.—*Appian. in Celt.*

M. CAS'SIUS SCÆ'VA, a soldier of uncommon valour in Cæsar's army. *Val. Max.* 3. c. 2.— An officer under Aurelius, made emperor by his soldiers, and murdered three months after.

CAS'SIUS PEDU'CEUS, a tribune who appealed from the decision of Metellus upon the acquittal of some Vestal virgins for incest, and who caused them on a second trial to be condemned to death. *Liv.* 63. *Asconius, Phil.* 9.

C. CAS'SIUS VA'RUS, a man who favoured the Manilian law, and was consul with Ter. Varro when Verres was prætor in Sicily. *Cic. Verr.* 1. c. 23. l. 3. c. 41.

CAS'SIUS FE'LIX, a physician in the age of Tiberius, who wrote on animals.

CAS'SIUS SEVE'RUS, an orator who wrote a severe treatise on illustrious men and women. He died in exile in his 25th year. *Vid.* Severus.

CAS'SIUS DI'O. *Vid.* Dio. The family of the Cassii branched, in process of time, into the surnames of Longinus, Viscellinus, Brutus, &c.

CASSO'PE, a city of the Molossi. *Steph.*

CAS'SOTIS, a nymph and fountain of Phocis. *Paus.* 10. c. 24.

CASTAB'ALA, a city of Cilicia, the inhabitants of which were assisted by their dogs in the wars which they waged against their neighbours. *Plin.* 8. c 40.

CAS'TABUS, a town of Chersonesus.

CASTA'LIA, a town near Phocis.

CASTA'LIA, a daughter of the Aschelous.

CASTA'LIUS, a son of Terra, father of Thyas, who became mother of Delphus by Apollo. *Paus.* 10. c. 6.

CASTA'LIUS FONS or CASTA'LIA, a fountain of mount Parnassus, in Phocis, sacred to the muses. The waters of this fountain were cool and excellent, and they were said to have the power of inspiring those that drank of them, with the true fire of poetry. The muses have received the surname of Castalides from this fountain. *Virg. G.* 3. v. 293.—*Martial* 7. epigr. 11. l. 12. epigr. 3.

CAS'TALO, a city of Oretania; the people were called Castalonites. *Steph.*

CASTANE'A a town of Macedonia near the Peneus, whence the *nuces Castaneæ* received their name. *Plin.* 4. c. 9.—*Mela*, 2. c. 3.

CASTA'NIA or CASTELLANA'TA, a city of Lucania. *Steph.*

CAS'TAX, a city of Iberia; the gentile name was Castacæus. *Id.*

CASTEL'LUM MENAPIO'RUM, a town of Belgium, on the Maese, now Kessel.

CASTEL'LUM MORINO'RUM, now mount Cassel, in Flanders.

CASTEL'LUM CATTO'RUM, now Hesse Cassel.

CAS'THENES or CASTHE'NES, a bay of Thrace, near Byzantium. *Plin.* 4. c. 11.

CASTIN'IUM, a mountain of Pamphylia. *Steph.*

CASTIANI'RA, a Thracian mistress of Priam, and mother of Gorgythion. *Homer. Il.* 8.

CASTOL'OGI, a people of Gallia Belgica. *Plin.* 4. c. 17.

CASTO'LUS, a city of Lydia. *Steph.—Xenoph.*

CASTOR and POLLUX were twin sons of Jupiter, by Leda. According to mythologists Leda brought forth two eggs, from one of which sprang Pollux and Helena; and from the other, Castor and Clytemnestra. The two former were the offspring of Jupiter, and the latter were believed to be the children of Tyndarus. Some suppose that Leda brought forth only one egg, from which Castor and Pollux were born. Mercury, immediately after their birth, carried the two brothers to Pallene, where they were educated; and as soon as they had arrived at years of maturity, they embarked with Jason in quest of the golden fleece. In this expedition Pollux conquered and slew Amycus, in the combat of the cæstus, and was ever after reckoned the god and patron of boxing and wrestling. Castor distinguished himself in the management of horses. The two brothers also cleared the Hellespont and the neighbouring seas from pirates, after their return from Colchis; from which circumstance they have always been deemed the friends of navigation. During the Argonautic expedition, in a violent storm, two flames of fire were seen to play around the heads of the sons of Leda, and immediately the tempest ceased, and the sea became calm. The above-mentioned fires, which are very common in storms, have since been known by the name of Castor and Pollux; and when they both appeared, it was a sign of fair weather; but if only one was seen, it prognosticated storms, and the aid of Castor and Pollux was consequently solicited. Castor and Pollux made war against the Athenians to recover their sister Helen, whom Theseus had carried away. They were initiated into the sacred mysteries of the Cabiri, and into those of Ceres of Eleusis. They were invited to a feast when Lynceus and Idas were going to celebrate their marriage with Phœbe and Talaira, the daughters of Leucippus, who was brother to Tyndarus. But their behaviour on this occasion was cruel and unmanly. They became enamoured of the two women whose nuptials they were to celebrate, and resolved to carry them away and marry them. This violent step provoked Lynceus and Idas: a battle ensued, and Castor killed Lynceus, and was himself killed by Idas. Pollux revenged the death of his brother, by killing Idas; and as he was immortal, and tenderly attached to his brother, he entreated Jupiter either to restore him to life, or to be deprived himself of immortality. Jupiter permitted Castor to share the immortality of his brother; and consequently, as long as the one was upon the earth, so long was the other detained in the infernal regions, and they alternately lived and died every day, or according to others, every six months. This act of fraternal love was rewarded by Jupiter, and he, made the two brothers constellations in heaven, under the name of Gemini, which never appear together, but when one rises the other sets, and so on alternately. Castor, according to some authors, made Talaira mother of Anogon, and Phœbe had Mnesileus by Pollux. The two brothers received divine honours after death. White lambs were more particularly offered on their altars, and the ancients were fond of swearing by their divinity, by the expressions of Ædepol and Æcastor. Among the ancients, and especially among the Romans, there prevailed many public reports at different times, that Castor and Pollux had made their appearance to their armies, and mounted on white steeds, had marched at the head of their troops, and furiously attacked the enemy. Their surnames were many, and they were generally represented mounted on two white horses, armed with spears, and riding side by side, with their heads covered with bonnets, on the top of which glittered stars. They were also called Dioscuri, as sons of Jupiter, Anaces, or Anactes for their clemency and benevolence to the Athenians, Ambulii from the extended duration of their life, Apheterii because they presided over boundaries, and Œbalii, Therapnæi, and Amyclæi fratres, from their residence in Laconia. *Servius in* 3. *Georg.* 89. *in Æn.* 3. v. 328.—*Tzetzes in Lycop.* 546.—*Theocr. Id. in Diosc.*—*Pind.* od. 10. *Nem*—*Val. Max.* 1. c. 8.—*Gyrald. Hist. P.*—*Ovid. Met.* 6. v. 109. *Fast.* 5. v. 701. *Am.* 3. el. 2. v. 54.—*Hygin.* fab. 77 & 78.—*Homer. Hymn. in Jov. Puer.* 2.—*Eurip. in Helen. In Orest.*—*Plut. in Thes.*—*Virg. Æn.* 6. v. 121.—*Manil.* 1. v. 337.—*Liv.* 2. *Dionys. Hal.* 6.—*Justin.* 20. c. 3.—*Horat.* 2. sat. 1. v. 27.—*Flor.* 2. c. 12.—*Cic. de Nat D.* 2. c. 2. l. 3. c. 21.—*Apollon.* 1.—*Apollod.* 1. c. 8. 9. l. 2. c. 4. l. 3. c. 11.—*Paus.* 3. c. 13, 14 & 24. l. 4. c. 3 & 27. [The finest representations of these brothers, are the two colossal statues on Monte Cavallo at Rome, one supposed to be the work of Phidias, and the other of Praxiteles. They have been falsely called Alexander and Bucephalus; probably on account of their having been brought from Alexandria.]

CAS'TOR, an ancient physician. *Plin.* 20. c, 17.——A swift runner. *Paus.* l. 3.——A friend of Æneas, who accompanied him into Italy. *Virg. Æn.* 10. v. 124.——An historian of Rhodes, said to be grandson to king Deiotarus, whom he accused before Cæsar of having conspired against his life. He wrote two books on Babylon and one on the Nile. *Cic. in Dej.* 1.—*Apollod.*—*Plut.*——A gladiator. *Horat.* 1. ep. 18. v. 19.

CAS'TRA ALEXAN'DRI, a place of Ægypt in the neighbourhood of Pelusium. *Curt.* 4. c. 7.

CAS'TRA ANNIB'ALIS, a town of the Brutii, now Roccella. *Plin.* 3. c. 10.

CAS'TRA CÆCILIA'NA, a fortified place of Spain, between the rivers Tagus and Anas. *Plin.* 4. c. 22.

CAS'TRA CORNE'LIA, a maritime town of Africa, between Carthage and Utica. *Mela*, 1. c. 7.

CAS'TRA CY'RI, a place of Cilicia, where Cyrus encamped when he marched against Crœsus. *Curt.* 3. c. 4.

CAS'TRA JU'LIA, a town of Spain, now Trugillo. *Plin.* 4. c. 22.

CAS'TRA POSTHUMIA'NA, a place of Spain. *Hist. Hisp.* 8,

CASTRA'TIUS, a governor of Placentia during the civil wars of Marius. *Val. Max.* 6. c. 2.

CAS'TRUM NO'VUM, a place of Etruria, on the shores of the Mediterranean. *Liv.* 36 c. 3.

CAS'TRUM TRUENTI'NUM, a town of Picenum. *Cic. de Attic.* 8. ep. 12.

CAS'TRUM IN'UI. *Vid.* Inui Castrum.

CAS'TULO, a town of Spain, one of the natives of which Annibal married. *Plut. in Sert.*—*Liv.* 24. c. 41.—*Ital.* 3. v. 99 & 391—*Plin.* 3. c. 3.

CASUEN'TUM, a river flowing into the bay of Tarentum. *Plin.* 3. c. 11. It is now Vasento.

CAS'ULA, a city of Africa Propria. *Ptol.*

CATABATH'MUS MAG'NUS, a great declivity near Cyrene, towards Ægypt on the east, fixed by Sallust as the boundary of Africa. There was another called Parvus, a little more to the east. *Sallust. Jug.* 17 & 19.—*Plin.* 5. c. 5.—*Mela*, 1. c. 8.

CATABE'NI, a people of Arabia Deserta. *Plin.* 12. c. 14.

CATACETI, a people of Asia, near the Mæotis. *Id.* 6. c. 7.

CAT'ADA, a river of Africa Propria. *Ptol.*

CATADU'PA, the name of the large cataracts of the Nile, the immense noise of which is said to stun the ears of travellers for a short space of time, and totally to deprive the neighbouring inhabitants of the power of hearing. *Cic. de Somn. Scip.* 5.—*Herodot.* 2. c. 17.—*Plin.* 5. c. 9.

CATÆ'A, an island of Persia. *Arrian.*

CATÆB'ATES, a name under which Jupiter had an altar at Olympia. *Paus. in Eliac.*

CATÆO'NIUM, a promontory of Marmarica. *Ptol.*

CATAGO'GIA, festivals in honour of Venus, celebrated by the people of Eryx, in Sicily. *Vid.* Anagogia.

CATAMA'NA, a city of Comagene, in Syria. *Ptol.*

CATAMEN'TELES, a king of the Sequani, in alliance with Rome, &c. *Cæs. Bel. G.* 1. c. 3.

CAT'ANA, a town of Sicily at the foot of mount Ætna, founded by a colony from Chalcis, 753 years B.C. Ceres had there a temple, in which none but women were permitted to appear. The town was large and opulent, and it is rendered remarkable for the dreadful overthrows to which it has been subjected from its vicinity to Ætna. Catana contains now about 30,000 inhabitants. *Mela*, 2. c. 7.—*Ptol.* 3. c. 4.—*Plin.* 3. c. 5.—*Max. Val.* 5. c. 4.—*Solin.* 11.—*Senecca de Ben.* 3. c. 37.—*Cic. in Ver* 4. c. 53. l. 5. c. 84.—*Diod.* 11 & 14.—*Strab.* 6.—*Thucyd.* 6. c. 3.

CATA'NII, a people near the Caspian Sea. *Steph.*

CATAO'NIA, a country of Asia Minor, above Cilicia, and at the south of Cappadocia, above mount Taurus. *C. Nep. in Dat.* 4.

CATAPLYS'TUM, one of the mouths of the Nile, according to *Mela*, 1. c. 10.

CATARACTA, a town of Italy, in the country of the Samnites.

CATARI'TÆ, a people of Arabia Felix. *Ptol.*

CATARAC'TES, a river of Pamphylia, now Dodensoui. *Mela*, 1. c. 4.—*Herodot.* 7. c. 26.

CAT'ARI, a people of Panonia. *Plin.* 3. c. 25.

CATAR'RYTHUM, a name of Hippo in Africa. *Plin.* 5. c. 4.

CAT'ATHRÆ, two islands of the Red Sea. *Ptol.*

CATENA'TES, a people of Vindelicia. *Plin.* 3. c. 20.

CAT'ENES, a Persian, by whose means Bessus was seized. *Curt.* 7. c. 43.

CATHÆ'A, a country of India. *Strab.* 15.

CATH'ARI, certain gods of the Arcadians. *Paus. in Arcad.*.

CATH'ARI, an Indian nation, where the wives accompanied their husbands to the burning pile, and were burnt with them. *Diod.* 17.

CATHA'RUM, a promontory of Libya. *Ptol.*

CATH'EI, mountains of Asiatic Sarmatia. *Plin.* 6. c. 7.

CATH'RAPS, a river of Asia. *Id.* 6. c. 25.

CATHU'LII, a people of Germany, conquered by Germanicus. *Ptol.*—*Strab.*

CA'TIA, an immodest woman, mentioned by *Horace*, 1. sat 2. v. 95.

CATICARDAM'NA, a city of India within the Ganges, now Chiromandel. *Ptol.*

CATIE'NA, a courtezan in Juvenal's age.—*Juv.* 3. v. 133.

CATIE'NUS, an actor in Rome in *Horace's* age, 2 sat. 3. v. 61.

P. CATIE'NUS PLOTI'NUS, a freedman, so attached to his patron, that he threw himself on his funeral pile, though appointed his heir by his will. *Plin.* 7. c. 30.

CATILI, inhabitants of the Alps, between Pola and Sergestus. *Plin.* 3. c. 20.

L. SER'GIUS CATILI'NA, a celebrated Roman, descended from a noble family. When he had squandered away his fortune, and been refused the consulship, he secretly meditated the ruin of his country, and conspired with others, as dissolute and depraved as himself, to extirpate the senate, plunder the treasury, and set Rome on fire. This conspiracy was timely discovered by the consul Cicero, whom he had resolved to murder; and Catiline, after he had declared his hostile intentions in the full senate, and attempted to vindicate himself, on seeing five of his accomplices arrested, retired to Gaul, where his partisans were assembling an army; while Cicero, at Rome, punished the condemned conspirators. Petreius, the other consul's lieutenant, attacked Catiline's ill-disciplined troops, near Fæsulæ, and routed them. Catiline was killed in the engagement, about the middle of December, B.C. 63. His character has been deservedly branded with the foulest infamy; and to the violence which he offered to a vestal, he added the more atrocious murder of his own brother, for which he would have suffered death, had not his friends and bribes prevailed over justice. It has been reported that Catiline and his associates drank human blood, to make their oaths more firm and inviolable. *Sallust* has written an account of the conspiracy. *Cic. in Catil.*—*Virg. Æn.* 8. v. 668.

CATIL'IUS, a pirate of Dalmatia. *Cic. Ep.* 5. c. 10.

CATIL'LI, a people of Latium, near the river Anio. *Sil.* 4. v. 225.

CATIL'LUS or CAT'ILUS, a son of Amphiaraus, who came to Italy with his brothers Coras and Tiburtus, where he built Tibur, frequently called Mænia Catili, and assisted Turnus against Æneas. *Virg. Æn.* 7. c. 672.—*Horat.* 1. od. 18. v. 2.

CAT'INA or CATI'NA, a town of Sicily called also Catana. *Vid.* Catana.——A town of Arcadia. *Plin.* 4. c. 6.

CA'TIUS M., an epicurean philosopher of Insubria, who wrote a treatise in four books, on the nature of things, and the *summum bonum*, and an account of the doctrines and tenets of Epicurus. He has been ridiculed by *Horace*, 2. sat. 4.—*Quintil.* 10. c. 1.

CA'TIUS VESTI'NUS, a military tribune in M. Antony's army. *Cic. Div.* 10. c. 23.

CATIVUL'CUS, a king of the Eburones, who poisoned himself that he might not fall into Cæsar's power. *Cæs. Com.* 5. 24, &c.

CATI'ZI, a tribe among the Pygmæans, supposed to have been driven from their country by cranes. *Plin.* 4. c. 11.

CA'TO, a surname of the Porcian family, rendered illustrious by the two Catos, Censorius and Uticensis. M. Porcius was born at Tusculum, and called *Censorius*, from having exercised the office of censor, and *Major*, to distinguish him from his great grandson of the same name. He rose to all the honours of the state, and the first battle which he ever saw was against Annibal, in which, though only in his seventeenth year, he behaved with remarkable valour. In his quæstorship, under Africanus against Carthage, and in his expedition in Spain against the Celtiberians, and in Greece, he displayed equal proofs of his courage and prudence. He was remarkable for his love of temperance; he drank nothing but water, and was always satisfied with whatever meats were laid upon his table by his servants, whom he never reproved with an angry word. During his censorship, which he obtained, though he had made many declarations of his future severity, if ever in office, he behaved with the greatest rigour, but with the strictest impartiality; and not only showed himself an enemy to the luxury and dissipation of his countrymen, but even accused his colleague of embezzling the public money. He afterwards drew upon himself much of the public attention by the violent opposition which he made against the introduction of the finer arts of Greece into Italy, and his treatment of Carneades is well known. This extraordinary prejudice arose from an apprehension that the learning and luxury of Athens would destroy the valour and simplicity of the Roman people; and he often observed to his son, that the Romans would be certainly ruined whenever they began to be infected with Greek. It appears, however, that he changed his opinion, and made himself remarkable for the knowledge of Greek which he acquired in his old age. He himself educated his son, and instructed him in writing, grammar, and other useful accomplishments. He was deemed so strict in his morals, that Virgil makes him one of the judges of hell. His implacable enmity towards Carthage, however, may be deservedly censured. When commissioned by the senate to settle the disputes between Masinissa and the capital of Africa, he viewed with a jealous eye the greatness and prosperity of the rival city. In every speech he inveighed against Africa, and at every opportunity, in the senate and out of the senate, *delenda est Carthago* was his most emphatic expression

Rome at last yielded to prejudice, and, as Cato wished, Carthage was reduced to ruin; but she left to her conquerors with her empire, to inherit her pride, her insolence, and her luxuries. It is said that Cato repented only of three things during his life; to have gone by sea when he could have gone by land, to have passed a day in inactivity, and to have revealed a secret to his wife. A statue was raised to his memory, by his grateful countrymen. In Cicero's age there were 150 of his orations extant, besides letters, and a celebrated work called Origines, of which the first book gave a history of the Roman monarchy; the second and third contained an account of the neighbouring cities of Italy; the fourth a detail of the first, and the fifth, of the second Punic war; and in the others the Roman history was brought down to the war of the Lusitanians, carried on by Servius Galba, Some fragments of the Origines remain, but they are thought by some to be supposititious. Cato's treatise, *De re rustica*, was edited by Auson. Pompna, 8vo. Ant. Plant. 1590; but the best edition of Cato, &c. seems to be Gesner's, 2 vols. 4to. Lips. 1735. Cato died in an extreme old age, about 150 B.C.; and Cicero, to show his respect for his merits and his virtues, has introduced him in his treatise on old age, as the principal character. Besides his son Marcus, whose early death he feelingly deplores in *Cicero de Senectute*, Cato had, after his 80th year, by the daughter of his client Salonius, a son called Marcus Salonius, whose son Marcus was the father of Cato of Utica. *Plutarch* and *C. Nepos* have written an account of his life. *Plin.* 7. c. 14.—*Cic. Acad. & de Senect.* &c.—*Harles. Not. Lit. Rom.* 1. p. 85.—*Sax. Onom.* 1. p. 119.

CA'TO MAR'CUS, the son of the censor, married the daughter of P. Æmylius. He lost his sword in a battle, and though fatigued and wounded, he went to his friends, and, with their assistance, renewed the battle, and recovered his sword. *Plut. in Cat.*

CA'TO, a courageous Roman, grandfather of Cato the censor. He had five horses killed under him in various battles. *Plut. in Cat.*

CA'TO VALE'RIUS, a grammarian of Gallia Narbonensis, in the time of Sylla, who instructed many noble pupils at Rome, and wrote some poems, one of which only remains, called Diræ, consisting of 183 heroic lines, in which the author laments, in pathetic language, the time when he bid adieu to his native country and his favourite Lydia. This poem, which has been falsely ascribed to Virgil, may be found in the third volume of the poet. Lat. Min. *Suet. de Ill. G.* 11.—*Ovid.* 2. *Trist.* 1. v. 436.

CA'TO MAR'CUS, surnamed *Uticensis*, from his death at Utica, was great grandson to the censor of the same name. The many virtues and the eager fondness for liberty which appeared in his childhood, seemed to promise a great character; and at the age of fourteen he earnestly asked his preceptor Sarpedo for a sword, to stab the tyrant Sylla. He was austere in his morals, and a strict follower of the tenets of the Stoics: he was careless of his dress, often appeared barefooted in public, and never travelled but on foot He was such a lover of discipline, that in whatever office he was employed he always reformed its abuses. After he had been set over the troops in the capacity of commander, his removal was universally lamented, and deemed almost a public loss by his affectionate soldiers. His fondness for candour was so great, that the veracity of Cato became proverbial. In his visits to his friends, he wished to give as little molestation as possible; and the importuning civilities of king Dejotarus so displeased him, when he was at his court, that he quitted his territories in disgust. He was very jealous of the safety and liberties of the republic, and watched carefully over the conduct of Pompey, whose power and influence were great, and therefore suspected. He often expressed his dislike to serve the office of tribune; but when he saw Metellus Nepos, a man of corrupt principles apply for it, he offered himself as a candidate, and obtained the tribuneship. In the conspiracy of Catiline, he supported the measures of Cicero with all his influence, and was the chief cause that the conspirators were capitally punished. When the provinces of Gaul were decreed to Cæsar for five years, Cato observed to the senators, that they had introduced a tyrant into the Capitol. His enemies, at the head of whom was Clodius the tribune, sent him to Cyprus against Ptolemy, who had rebelled, hoping that the difficulties of the expedition would injure his character in the public estimation. But his prudence surmounted all obstacles. Ptolemy submitted, and after a successful campaign, Cato was received at Rome with the most distinguished honours, which he, however, declined with becoming modesty. When the first triumvirate was formed between Cæsar, Pompey, and Crassus, Cato opposed them with all his might, and foretold the Roman people all the misfortunes which soon after followed. After repeated applications he was made prætor, but, in the opinion of some, he seemed rather to disgrace than support the dignity of that office, by the meanness of his dress. He applied for the consulship, but could never obtain it. When Cæsar had passed the Rubicon, Cato advised the senate to deliver the care of the republic into the hands of Pompey; for, though he was far from approving his general conduct, he nevertheless considered his motives as less dangerous and more patriotic than those of Cæsar. Eager to show his attachment to his country, he with his son followed Pompey, as soon as he was invested with the chief command, to Dyrrachium, where, after a small victory, he was entrusted with the care of the ammunition and fifteen cohorts. After the battle of Pharsalia, Cato took the command of the Corcyrean fleet; but when he heard of Pompey's death he traversed the deserts of Libya, to join himself to Scipio. He refused to take the command of the army in Africa, a circumstance of which he afterwards repented, when he saw the weakness and imprudence of young Scipio. The fatal battle of Thapsus, in which Juba and Scipio were defeated, added to his misfortunes, and he fled to Utica, where he hoped to collect the remains of the conquered army, and to withstand by a bold and active defence, the rapidity of the victor. The people of the town, however, were unwilling to expose themselves to Cæsar's vengeance; and Cato, when his enemy approached near the city, disdained to fly, and rather than fall alive into the conqueror's hands, he stabbed himself after he had read Plato's treatise on the immortality of the soul, B.C. 46, in the 49th year of his age. It is said that his friends foresaw his intended suicide, and endeavoured in vain to withdraw his sword from him; but his resolution was formed, and when he was discovered bleeding on the ground, with his bowels gushing out, he quietly permitted the physician to apply remedies and bandages to the part, that he might, in their absence, and with greater certainty, remove them, and finish the fatal blow, by tearing open the wounds with his nails, like a ferocious beast. His first wife was Attilia, the daughter of Soranus, a woman whose licentious conduct so offended him, that he divorced her. He afterwards united himself to Martia, daughter of of Philip. Hortensius, his friend, wished to raise children by Martia, and therefore obtained her from Cato. After the death of Hortensius, Cato took her again. This conduct was ridiculed by the Romans, who observed, that Martia had entered the house of Hortensius very poor, but returned to the bed of Cato loaded with treasures. It was observed that Cato appeared in mourning, and never laid himself down at his meals, after the defeat of Pompey, but always sat down, contrary to the custom of the Romans, as if depressed with the recollection that the supporters of republican liberty were decaying. *Plutarch* has written an account of his life. *Lucan.* 1. v. 128. &c.—*Val. Max.* 2. c. 10.—*Horat.* 3. od. 21.—*Virg. Æn.* 6. v. 841. l. 8. v. 670. [There is a bust thus designated in the Rondinini collection at Rome.]

CA'TO, a son of Cato of Utica, who was pardoned by Cæsar, and fell in the battle of Philippi, after he had acquired much honour. *Plut. in Cat. Min.*

CA'TO CA'IUS, the grandson of the censor and of Paulus Æmylius, was consul, and distinguished himself as an orator. He was accused of extortion, and being condemned by the Mamilian law, retired in exile to Tarraco in Spain. *Cic. Verr.* 4. c. 10. *Br.* 28 & 34. *Balb.* 11.

CA'TO, another of the same family, made tribune A.U.C. 697. He opposed the restoration of Ptolemy to the kingdom of Ægypt, and at the instigation of Pompey and Crassus, attempted to resist the election of magistrates, because the consuls withstood his innovations with respect to the laws. *Cic. Q. Fr.* 2. ep. 6.—*Liv.* 105.

CA'TO DIONYS'IUS, a philosopher of the second century. He wrote *Disticha de moribus*, addressed to his son. The best edition is that of Daumius, Cyneæ, 1662. Berolin. 1715.—*Harles. Not. Lit. Rom.* 1. p. 697.—*Sax. Onom.* 1. p. 330.

CAT'ONI, a people of Scythia near the Mæotis. *Plin.* 6. c. 7. Some read Caroni.

CATRALEU'COS, a city of Lusitania, now Guimaranes.

CATRE'A, a town of Crete, so called after king Catreus. *Paus.* 1. 8.

CA'TREUS, a king of Crete, inadvertently killed by his son at Rhodes. *Diod.* 5.

CATTA, a woman who had the gift of prophecy. *Suet. in Vitell.* 14.

CAT'TI, a powerful people of Germany, who inhabited the country situated between the Weser and the Rhine. *Tacit. Ann.* 13. v. 57.

CATTIG'ARA, a town of the Sinæ, now Canton. *Ptol.*

CATUAL'DA, a noble youth of the Gothones. *Tac. Ann.* 2. c. 6.

CATULIA'NA, a surname of Minerva from L. Catulus, who dedicated a standard to her. *Plin.* 34. c. 8.

CATUL'LUS C. or Q. VALE'RIUS, a poet of Verona. He was descended from an illustrious family, and came to Rome with Manlius in his youth, to improve himself. His abilities recommended him to the notice of Cicero, whose friendship and hospitality he celebrated, and he gradually became acquainted with the most distinguished characters of his age. But whilst he sang the praises of his favonrite Ipsitilla, or Clodia, to whom he paid his adoration, under the feigned appellation of Lesbia, he also ridiculed the follies of the age, and, as it is reported, did not scruple to direct his satire against the profligacy of Cæsar, under the name of Romulus, whose only revenge was to invite the poet, and hospitably entertain him at his table. Catullus was the first Roman who imitated with success the Greek writers, and introduced their numbers among the Latins. in iambics and verses of eleven syllables. Though the pages of the poet are occasionally disfigured with licentious expressions, and all the bitterness of satire, yet his composition is remarkable for great purity of style. Catullus died in the 46th year of his age, B.C. 40. His compositions were numerous, and those which have survived the ravages of time have been divided by some commentators into three books; the first of lyrics, the second of elegiacs, and the third of epigrams, though more generally comprehended under the general appellation of epigrams, 113 in number, but of very unequal length. The ancients esteemed his poem on the death of Lesbia's sparrow the most finished production of his muse. The best editions are that of Vulpius, 4to, Patavii, 1737, and that of Barbou, 12mo, Paris, 1754. *Martial.* 1. epigr. 62.—*Ovid. Trist.* 2. v. 427.—*Harles. Not. Lit. Rom.*. 1. p. 213.—*Sax. Onom.* 1. p. 148.

CATUL'LUS, a mimographer. *Juv.* 13. v. 111.

Q. LUTA'TIUS CAT'ULUS, went with 300 ships during the first Punic war against the Carthaginians, and destroyed 600 of their ships under Hamilcar, near the Ægates. This celebrated victory put an end to the war. *Liv.* 19.

CAT'ULUS, an orator, distinguished also as a writer of epigrams, and admired for the neatness, elegance, and polished style of his compositions. Some suppose that he is the person who was consul with Marius, and who shared in his victory and his triumph over the Cimbri. He espoused the party of Sylla, against Marius, and the boldness of his opposition incited his victorious enemy to destroy him, even against the powerful intercession of his numerous friends. He put an end to his life by shutting himself up in a room newly plastered, where he was suffocated with the smoke of burning coals. He left behind him well-written memoirs of his consulship after the manner of Xenophon, besides several elaborate orations, but only ten verses are preserved of the fragments of the poet's compositions. *Lucan.* 2. v. 174.—*Plut. in Mario.*——His son, became known by his patriotic attachment to the glories and liberties of Rome. He was consul and censor, and in every office studied the happiness of the people, and the prosperity of the state. He dedicated the temple of Jupiter in the Capitol, after it had been burnt; and after Catiline's conspiracy was suppressed, he hailed Cicero as the father of his country. He died in an advanced old age. *Cic. Fam.* 9. ep. 15. & *passim.*—*Dio.* 36. c. 13.—*Suet. Aug.* 94.—*Liv.* 98. —*Plut. in Pomp.*——A Roman sent by his countrymen to carry a present to the god of Delphi, from the spoils taken from Asdrubal. *Liv.* 27.

CATU'RIGES, a people of Gaul. Their town is now Chorges, near the source of the Durance. *Cæs. B. G.* 1. c. 10.—*Plin.* 3. c. 20.

CA'TUS DECIA'NUS, a governor of Britain under Nero. *Tac. Ann.* 14. c. 32.

CATYEUCHLA'NI, a people of Britain. *Ptol.*—According to *Camden* they inhabited the counties of Buckingham, Hertford, and Bedford.

CAUCABE'NI, a people of Arabia Deserta. *Ptol.*

CAU'CADÆ, a people on the river Lagous, near the Mæotis. *Plin.* 6. c. 7.

CAUCA'NA, a harbour of Sicily, near Syracuse. *Ptol.*

CAU'CASUS, a celebrated mountain of great height, extending between the Euxine and the Caspian Seas, which may be considered as a continuation of the ridge of mount Taurus. It was inhabited anciently by various savage nations who lived upon the wild fruits of the earth; was covered with snow in some parts, and in others was variegated with fruitful orchards and plantations. The inhabitants were supposed formerly to gather gold on the shores of their rivulets in sheep skins, but now they live without making use of money. The passes near this mountain called *Caucasiæ portæ*, bear now the name of Derbent; and it is supposed that through them the Sarmatians, called Huns, made their way when they invaded the provinces of Rome. *Plin.* 6. c. 11.—*Strab.* 11.—*Herodot.* 4. c. 203, &c.—*Virg. Ecl.* 6. *G.* 2. v. 440. *Æn.* 4. v. 366.—*Flacc.* 5. v. 155.—*Mela*, 1. c. 15 & 19.—*Ptol.* 5. c. 9. 1. 6. c. 12.

CAU'CHÆ, plains near Ctesiphon, through which the Tigris flows. *Plin.* 6. c. 27.

CAU'CON, a son of Clinus, who first introduced the Orgies into Messenia from Eleusis. *Paus.* 4. c. 1.

CAUCO'NES, a people of Paphlagonia, originally inhabitants of Arcadia, or of Scythia, according to some accounts. Some of them made a settlement near Dymæ in Elis. *Herodot.* 1. c. 147 & 4. c. 148.—*Strab.* 8, &c.

CAU'DI or CAU'DIUM, a town of the Samnites, near which, in a place called Caudinæ Furcæ, now Forchia d'Arpaia, the Roman army under T. Veturius Calvinus and Sp. Posthumius was obliged to surrender to the Samnites, and pass under the yoke. *Liv.* 9. c. 1. &c.—*Lucan.* 2. v. 138. *Vid.* Pontius Herennius.

CAULE'I, a people of Germany, near the Ocean. *Strab.*

CAU'LICI or CAULI'ACI, a people near the Ionian Gulph. *Steph.*—*Apollon.*

CAULO'NIA or CAU'LON, a town of Italy, in the country of the Brutii, on the eastern shores, founded by a colony of Achæans, and destroyed in the wars between Pyrrhus and the Romans. *Paus.* 6. c. 3.—*Virg. Æn.* 3. v. 553.

CAUMA'NA, a bay of the Indus, near its mouth. *Arrian. in Indic.*

CAU'MAS, one of the Centaurs, son of Ixion. *Boccat.*

CAU'NIUS, a man raised to affluence from poverty by Artaxerxes. *Plut. in Artax.*

CAU'NUS, a son of Miletus and Cyane. He was passionately fond of, or, according to others, he was tenderly loved by, his sister Byblis, and prudently retired to Caria. Here he was informed of the fate of his sister, (*Vid.* Byblis) by a Hamadryad, whom he married, and by whom he had a son called Ægialus, who succeeded him in the sovereignty of the country. He built a town there to which he gave his name. *Hygin.* fab. 243.—*Anton. Liber.* 30.—*Aristocrit, & Apoll. Rhod. apud Parthen.* 11.—*Ovid. Met.* 9. fab. 11.

CAU'NUS, a city of Caria, opposite Rhodes. The climate was considered as unwholesome, especially in summer, so that Cicero mentions the cry of a person who sold Caunian figs, (*qui Cauneas clamitabat*), which were very famous, at Brundusium, as a bad omen (*cave ne eas*) for Crassus who was going to attack the Parthians. *Cic. Div.* 2. c. 4.—*Strab.* 14. —*Herodot.* 1. c. 176.—*Liv.* 33. c. 20. l. 45. c. 25.—*Ptol.* 5. c. 2. —*Mela*, 1. c. 16.

CAUPHI'ACA, a city of Persia. *Ptol.*

CAURA'SIÆ, a people of Hispania Bætica. *Plin.* 3. c. 1.

CAURATA'NI, a people of Arabia Felix. *Id.* 6. c. 28.

CAU'RIUM or CAU'RA, a town of Lusitania, now Coria. *Ptol.*

CAU'RUS, an island with a small town, formerly called Andrus, in the Ægean Sea. *Plin.* 4. c. 12. ——A wind blowing from the north-west. *Virg. G.* 3. v. 356.

CA'US (*untis*), a small village of Arcadia. *Paus.* 8. c. 25.

CAVA'NA, a people of Mauritania Tingitana. *Ptol.*

CAV'ANA, a city of Arabia Felix. *Ptol.*

CAV'ARES, a people of Gaul, between the Rhone and the Druentia, who inhabited the present province of Comtat in Provence. *Plin.* 3. c. 4.

CAVARIL'LUS, a commander of some troops of the Ædui in Cæsar's army. *Cæs. Bell. G.* 7. c. 67.

CAVARI'NUS, a Gaul, made king of the Senones by Cæsar, and banished by his subjects. *Cæs. Bell. G.* 5. c. 54.

CA'VE, a town of Bithynia. *Xenoph. Hist.* 2.

CA'VII, a people of Illyricum. *Liv.* 44. c. 30.

CAY'CI or CHAU'CI, a nation of Germany, who inhabited the country now occupied by the people of Friesland and Groningen. *Lucan.* 1. v. 463.

CAY'CUS, a river of Mysia. *Vid.* Caicus.

CAYS'TER or CAYS'TRUS, now Kitcheck-Meinder, a rapid river in Asia, rising in Lydia, and falling into the Ægean Sea, near Ephesus. According to the poets, the banks and neighbourhood of this river were generally frequented by swans. *Strab.* 13.—*Mela*, 1. c. 17.—*Ptol.* 5. c. 2.—*Plin.* 5. c. 29. —*Ovid. Met.* 2. v. 253. l. 5. v. 386.—*Mart.* 1. epigr. 54.—*Homer. Il.* 2. v. 461.—*Virg. G.* 1. v. 384.

CAZ'ECA, a town of the Taurica Chersonesus. *Arrian. in Peripl.*

CE'A or CE'OS, an island near Eubœa, called also Co. *Vid.* Co.

CE'ADES, a Thracian, whose son Euphemus was engaged in the Trojan war. *Homer. Il.* 2.

CE'BA, now Ceva, a town of Liguria, now modern Piedmont. It was famous for cheese. *Plin.* 11. c. 42.

CEBALLI'NUS, a man who gave information of the snares laid against Alexander. *Diod.* 17.—*Curt.* 6. c. 7.

CEBAREN'SES, a people of Gaul. *Paus.* 1. c. 36.

CEBA'RES, a groom of Darius, who obtained the kingdom for his master by a stratagem. *Herodot.* 3.

CEBEN'NA, a mountain, now the Cevennes in Languedoc, separating the Arverni from the Helvii, and extending from the Garonne to the Rhone. *Cæsar, B. G.* 7. c. 8.—*Mela*, 2. c. 7.

CE'BES, a Theban philosopher, one of the disciples of Socrates, B.C. 405. He attended his learned preceptor in his last moments, and distinguished himself by three dialogues which he wrote; the first two are lost, but the third, called Tabula, presents a beautiful and affecting picture of human life. Little is known of the character of Cebes from history. Plato has mentioned his name only once, and Xenophon, the same, but both in such a manner as to prove only the goodness of his heart, and the purity of his morals. The best editions of Cebes are, that of Gronovius, 8vo. 1689; and that of Glasgow, 12mo, 1747. *Plato. in Phæd.* —*Xenoph. Memor.*—*Fabr. B. Gr.* l. 2. c. 24.—*Sax. Onom.* 1. p. 49.

CE'BREN, the father of Asterope. *Apollod.* 3. c. 12.

CEBRE'NIA, a country of Troas, with a town of the same name, called after the river Cebrenus, which is in the neighbourhood. Œnone, the daughter of the Cebrenus, received the patronymic of Cebrenis. *Apollod.* 3.—*Ovid. Met.* 11. v. 769.—*Stat.* 1 *Sylv.* 5. v. 21.

CEBRI'ONES, one of the giants conquered by Venus. ——An illegitimate son of Priam, killed with a stone by Patroclus. *Homer. Il.* 16. v. 727.—*Apollod.* 3.

CE'BRUS, now Zebris, a small river falling in a northern direction into the Danube, and dividing Lower from Upper Mœsia.

CECI'DES, an ancient dithyrambic poet. *Cratinus* ἐν πανόπταις.—*Aristoph. in Nub.*

CECIL'IA, a city of Syria, on the Euphrates. *Ptol.*

CECILIONI'CUM, a city of Lusitania. *Id.*

CECIL'IUS. *Vid.* Cæcilius.

CECI'NA, or rather Cecinna, a small river near Volaterra, in Etruria, which falls into the Tyrrhene Sea. *Mela*, 2. c. 4.

CECIN'NA A., a Roman knight in the interest of Pompey, who used to breed up young swallows, and send them, as messengers to carry news to his friends. He was particularly intimate with Cicero, with whom he corresponded. Some of his letters are still extant among those of Cicero. *Plin.* 10. c. 24.—*Cic.* 15. ep. 66. *Orat.* 29.

CECIN'NA, a scribe in the service of Octavius Cæsar. *Cic.* 16. *ad. Attic* ep. 8.——A man of consular dignity, sus pected of conspiracy, and murdered by Titus after an invitation to supper. *Suet. in Tit.* c. 6.

CECRO'PIA, the original name of Athens, in honour of Cecrops, its first founder. The ancients often use this word for Attica, and the Athenians are consequently called Cecropidæ. *Virg. Æn.* 6. v. 21.—*Ovid. Met.* 7. v. 671. *Fast.* 2. v. 81. *De A. A.* 1. v. 172. l. 3. v. 457.—*Lactant.* 1. c. 17.—*Martial.* 11. epigr. 43.—*Lucan.* 3. v. 306.—*Plin.* 7. c. 56.—*Catull.* 62. v. 79.—*Juv.* 6. v. 186.

CEC'ROPIS, the first and most ancient tribe of Athens. *Paus. in Attic.*

CE'CROPS, a native of Sais, in Ægypt, who led a colony to Attica about 1556 years B.C., and reigned over part of the country, which was called from him Cecropia. He softened and polished the rude and uncultivated manners of the inhabitants, and drew them from the country to inhabit 12 small villages which he had founded. He gave them wise laws and regulations for their government, and introduced among them the worship of those deities which were held in veneration in Ægypt. He married the daughter of Actæus, a Grecian prince, and was deemed the founder of Athens. He taught his subjects to cultivate the olive, and instructed them to look upon Minerva as the patroness of their city. It is said that he was the first who raised an altar to Jupiter, and offered him sacrifices in Greece. After a reign of fifty years, spent in regulating his newly formed kingdom, and in enlightening the minds of his subjects, Cecrops died, leaving three daughters, Aglaurus, Herse, and Pandrosus. He was succeeded by Cranaus, a native of the country. Some authors have described Cecrops as a monster, half a man and half a serpent; and this fable is explained by the recollection that he was acquainted with two languages, the Greek and Ægyptian; or that he had the command over two countries, Ægypt and Greece. Others explain it by an allusion to the salutary regulations which Cecrops made amongst the inhabitants concerning marriage and the intercourse between the two sexes. *Paus.* 1. c. 2. 5. l. 8. c. 2.—*Strab.* 9.—*Justin.* 2. c. 6.—*Herodot.* 8. c. 44.—*Apollod.* 3. c. 14. —*Ovid. Met.* 2. v. 561.—*Euseb. in Præm.* 2 *Chr. & No.* 463.—*Antonin. Lib.* 6.—*Hygin.* fab. 166.

CE'CROPS the Second, was the seventh king of Athens, and the son and successor of Erechtheus. He married Metiadusa the sister of Dædalus, by whom he had Pandion. He reigned 40 years, and died 1307 B.C. *Apollod*, 3. c. 15.—*Paus.* 1. c. 5.—*Euseb. Chr.*

CECRYPHALE'A, a place of Greece, near which the Athenians defeated the fleet of the Peloponnesians. *Thucyd.* 1. c. 105. Also Cecryphali'a.

CECYRI'NA, a city of Achaia, in Peloponnesus. *Paus.* 1. 7.

CE'DIAS, a village near Sinuessa. *Plin.* 3. c. 5.

CE'DON, an Athenan general killed in an engagement against the Spartans. *Diod.* 15.

CE'DREÆ or CEDRE'Æ, a city of Caria. *Steph.*

CEDREANI'TÆ, a people of Arabia Felix. *Id.*

CEDREA'TIS, the name of Diana, given her by the Orchomenians, because her images were hung on lofty cedars. *Paus.* l. 8.

CED'REI, a people of Arabia Petræa. *Plin.* 5. c. 11.

CE'DRIS, a river of Sardinia. *Ptol.*

CEDROS'SI, a people near the Red Sea. *Steph.*—*Mela*, 3. c. 13 & 1. c. 2.

CEDRU'SII, an Indian nation. *Curt.* 9. c. 11.
CEG'LUSA or CEGLU'SA, the mother of Asopus by Neptune. *Paus.* 2. c. 12.
CE'I, the inhabitants of the island of Cea.
CEL'ADON, a man killed by Perseus, at the marriage of Andromeda. *Ovid. Met.* 5. v. 144.——One of the Lapithæ, killed by Amycus, son of Ophion, at the marriage of Pirithous. *Ovid. Met.* 12. v. 250.
CEL'ADON, a river of Peloponnesus, flowing into the Alpheus. *Strab.* 8.—*Homer. Il.* 7. v. 133.
CELAD'ONE, a city of Locris. *Steph.*
CEL'ADUS, a small river of Arcadia. *Paus.* 8. c. 38.
CELADU'SA, an island in the Adriatic Sea. *Mela*, 3. c. 1.—*Plin.* 3. c. 26.
CE'LÆ, an island near Troas. *Plin.* 5. c. 31.
CELÆ'NA, a place of Campania, sacred to Juno. *Virg Æn.* 7. v. 739.
CELÆ'NÆ or CELE'NE, a city of Phrygia, once the capital of the country. Cyrus the younger had a palace there, with a park filled with wild beasts, where he exercised himself in hunting. The sources of the Mæander were in this park. Xerxes built a famous citadel there after his unfortunate expedition against Greece. The inhabitants of Celænæ were carried by Antiochus Soter to people the newly founded city of Apamea, in its neighbourhood. Marsyas is said to have contended there against Apollo. *Herodot.* 7. c. 26.—*Strab.* 12.—*Liv.* 38. c. 13.—*Xenoph. Anab.* 1.—*Curt.* 3. c. 1.—*Ovid. Fast.* 4. v. 172.—*Lucan.* 3. v. 206.—*Stat.* 2 *Theb.* 666.
CELÆ'NO, one of the daughters of Atlas, mother of Lycus by Neptune, and placed among the stars after death. *Apollod.* 3.—*Ovid.* 4 *Fast.* v. 173.——One of the harpies, daughter of Neptune, and Terra, who foretold the misfortunes which should befal the Trojans because they had destroyed the oxen of the islands called Strophades. *Virg. Æn.* 3. v. 245.——One of the Danaides. *Apollod.* 2. c. 1.——A daughter of Neptune and Ergea. *Hygin.* fab. 157.——A daughter of Hyamus, mother of Delphus by Apollo. *Paus.* 10. c. 6.
CELÆ'NUS, a mountain of Galatia. *Ptol.*
CELÆ'THI, a mountain of Thesprotia. *Steph.*
CEL'AMA, a town of Mauritania Cæsariensis. *Ptol.*
CE'LEÆ, a town of Peloponnesus. *Paus.* 2. c. 14.
CELEG'ERI, a people of Mœsia. *Plin.* 3. c. 26.
CELE'IA or CE'LIA, a town of Noricum, now Cilio. *Plin.* 3. c. 24.
CELELA'TES, a people of Liguria. *Liv.* 32. c. 29.
CELEN'DRÆ, CELEN'DRIS, or CELEN'DERIS, a colony of the Samians in Cilicia, with a harbour of the same name at the mouth of the Selinus. *Lucan.* 8. v. 259.—*Mela*, 1. c. 13.
CELE'NEUS, a Cimmerian who first taught with what ceremonies persons guilty of murder might be purified. *Flacc.* 3. v. 406.
CELEN'NA. *Vid.* Celæna.
CE'LER, a man who, with Severus, undertook to rebuild Nero's palace after the burning of Rome. *Tac. Ann.* 15. c. 42.
CE'LER FA'BIUS, a man who, by order of Romulus, killed Remus when he leaped over the walls of Rome. It is said that Romulus pursued him for so hastily shedding his brother's blood, but that he escaped his vengeance, and in consequence of this, his name was afterwards adopted in the Roman language to express quickness. *Ovid. Fast.* 4. v. 837.—*Plut. in Romul.*
CE'LER ME'TIUS, a noble youth, to whom Statius dedicated a poem.
CE'LER PUB'LIUS, a Roman, who slew the proconsul Silanus, in the reign of Nero. *Tac. Ann.* 13. c. 33.
CEL'ERES, 300 of the noblest and strongest youths of Rome, chosen by Romulus to be his body guards. They were supposed to receive their name from the quickness and dexterity of their evolutions, or probably from Celer, who had sacrificed Remus to the hasty orders of his brother. Their chief or captain was called Tribunus Celerum. *Liv.* 1. c. 15.
CELERI'NI, a people of Hispania Citerior. *Plin.* 3. c. 3.
CELE'TES, a people of Thesprotia. *Steph.*
CEL'ETRUM, a town of Macedonia. *Liv.* 31. c. 40.
CE'LEUS, a king of Eleusis, father of Triptolemus. He gave a kind reception to Ceres, when she wandered over the earth in quest of Proserpine, and the goddess in return, taught his son the cultivation of the earth. *Vid.* Triptolemus. His rustic dress became a proverb. The invention of several agricultural instruments, made of osier, is attributed to him. *Nicand. in Ther.*—*Ovid. Fast.* 4. v. 508. l. 5. v. 269.—*Virg. G.* 1. v. 165.—*Apollod.* 1. c. 5.—*Paus.* 1. c. 14. l. 7. c. 18.——A king of Cephallenia,
CE'LIA, a city of Noricum. *Plin.* 3. c. 24.——A city of Apulia Peucetia.——A city of Campania. *Diod.*
CEL'IDA, a town of the Pentapolis in Africa. *Ptol.*
CELID'NUS, a river of Macedonia, now Salnich, in Albania.
CEL'MUS, a man who is said to have nursed Jupiter, by whom he was greatly esteemed. He was changed into a stone for saying that Jupiter was mortal. *Ovid. Met.* 4. v. 281.
CEL'ONÆ, a place of Mesopotamia. *Diod.* 17.
CELO'TES, a painter of Teus, mentioned by *Quintilian*, 2. c. 13.
CEL'SA, a city of the Ilergetes in Spain. *Ptol.*—*Casaub. ad Strab.* l. 3. The gentile name was Celsenses. *Plin.* 3. c. 3.
CEL'SUS, an Epicurean philosopher in the second century, to whom Lucian dedicated one of his compositions. He wrote a treatise against the Christians, to which an answer was returned by Origen.
CEL'SUS A. CORNE'LIUS, a physician in the age of Tiberius, who wrote eight books on medicine beside treatises on agriculture, rhetoric, and military affairs. Some authors suppose that he was not a physician by profession, but that he studied medicine as a part of general science, and that he drew his information from respectable authors; whence he is sometimes called the Latin Hippocrates, and the medical Cicero, from the elegance of his style. He is universally admired for his extensive erudition, and the great purity of his Latin. The best edition of Celsus *de medicinâ*, are the 8vo. L. Bat. 1746, and that of Valart. Paris, apud Didot, 1772. This last edition is, however, full of typographical errors. Perhaps the best edition is that of Krause, Leipz. 1765. *Quintil.* 10. c. 1. l. 12. c. 11.—*Harles. Not. Lit. Rom.* 1. p. 337.—*Sax. Onom.* 1. p. 237.
CEL'SUS ALBINOVA'NUS, a friend of Horace, warned against plagiarism, 1. ep. 3. v. 15. and pleasantly ridiculed, in the 8th epistle. for his foibles. Some of his elegies have been preserved. He accompanied Tib. Cl. Naro in his eastern expedition.
CEL'SUS JUVEN'TIUS, a lawyer who conspired against Domitian. *Harles. Not. Lit. Rom.* 2. p. 165.—*Sax. Onom.* 1. p. 300.
CEL'SUS TI'TUS, a man proclaimed emperor by his soldiers, A.D. 265, against his will, and murdered seven days after.
CEL'TÆ, a name given to the nation that originally inhabited the country between the Ocean and the Palus Mæotis, according to some authors mentioned by *Plutarch*, *in Mario*.—This name, though anciently applied to the wandering hordes which settled at various times in Gaul, as well as in Germany and Spain, was more particularly given to those Gauls, whose country, called Gallia Celtica, was situated between the rivers Sequana and Garumna, modernly called la Seine and la Garonne. The Celtæ seem to have received their name from Celtus a son of Hercules or of Polyphemus. The promontory which bore the name of Celticum, is now called Cape Finisterre. *Cæs. Bell. G.* 1. c. 1, &c.—*Mela*, 3. c. 2.—*Herodot.* 4. c. 49.
CELTIBE'RI, a people of Spain, descended from the ancient Celtæ. They settled near the Iberus, and added the name of the river to that of their nation, and were afterwards called Celtiberi. They made strong head against the Romans and Carthaginians, when they invaded their country. Their country, called Celtiberia, is now known by the name of Arragon. *Diod.* 6.—*Flor.* 2. c. 17.—*Strab.* 4.—*Lucan.* 4. v. 10.—*Sil. It.* 3. v. 339.
CEL'TICA, a well-populated part of Gaul, inhabited by the Celtæ. *Vid.* Celtæ,
CEL'TICI, a people of Spain. *Strab.* 3. The promontory which bore their name, is now Cape Finisterre.
CELTIL'LUS, the father of Vercingetorix. *Cæs. Bell. G.* 7. c. 4.
CELTO'RII, a people of Gaul, near the Senones. *Plut. in Cam.*
CELTOS'CYTHÆ, a nation in the northern parts of Scythia. *Strab.* 10.

CEMBA'NI, a people of Arabia Felix. *Plin.* 6, c. 28.

CEMENE'LEON, a town of Liguria, called Cemeleon by *Pliny*, 3. c. 5.

CEM'MENUS, a lofty mountain of Gaul, now Les Sevennes. *Strab.*

CEMP'SI, a people at the east of Spain, at the bottom of the Pyrenean mountains. *Dionys. Perieg.* v. 358.

CEN'ABUM, a city of the Carnutæ, in Gaul, now Gian. *Ptol.*

CENÆ'UM, a promontory of Eubœa, where Jupiter Cenæus had an altar raised by Hercules. It is now Capo Litar. *Ovid. Met.* 9. v. 136.—*Thucyd.* 3. c. 93.

CEN'CHREÆ, now Kenkri, a town of Peloponnesus on the Isthmus of Corinth, with a harbour on the Sinus Saronicus. *Ovid. Trist.* 1. el. 9. v. 9.—*Plin.* 4. c. 4.

CENCHRE'US, a son of Neptune and Salamis, or, as some say, of Pyrene. He killed a large serpent at Salamis. *Paus.* 2. c. 2.—*Diod.* 4.

CEN'CHRIS, the wife Cinyras king of Cyprus, or, as others say, of Assyria. *Hygin.* fab. 58.

CEN'CHRIUS, a river of Ionia near Ephesus, where some suppose that Latona was washed after she had given birth to Apollo and Diana. *Tacit. Ann.* 3. c. 1.

CENES'POLIS, a town of Spain, the same as Carthago Nova. *Polyb.*

CENES'TUM, a city of Corsica, now S. Lucia, *Ptol.*

CENE'TIUM, a town of Peloponnesus. *Strab.*

CE'NEUS. *Vid.* Cænis.

CENICEN'SES, a people of Gallia Narbonensis. *Plin.* 3. c. 4.

CENIMAG'NI, a people in the eastern parts of Britain. *Cæs. Com.* 5. c. 21.

CENI'NA. *Vid.* Cænina.

CEN'NABA, a mountain of Mauritania Cæsariensis. *Ptol.* 1. 5.

CE'NON, a town of Italy. *Liv.* 2. c. 63.

CENSO'RES, two magistrates at Rome, created B.C. 443. Their office was to ascertain the population of the state, whence their name, to estimate the possession of every citizen, to reform and watch over the manners of the people, and to regulate the taxes. Their power also extended over the conduct of private families; they punished irregularity, and inspected the management and education of the Roman youth. They could inquire into the expenses of every citizen, and even degrade a senator from all his privileges and honours, if guilty of any extravagance. This punishment was generally executed by the omission of the offender's name in calling over the list of the senators. The office of censor was originally exercised by the kings. Servius Tullius, the sixth king of Rome, first established a *census*, by which every man was obliged to come to be registered, and to give in writing the place of his residence, his name and quality, the number of his children, and of his tenants, estates, domestics, &c. The institution of the census was very salutary to the Roman republic, and while it gratified the pride of the great in proclaiming the number of their clients and dependents, it infused a spirit of public liberty, and of national independence into the whole. By means of these regular musters, the Romans also became acquainted with their own strength, their ability to support a war, to make a levy of troops, or raise a tribute. It was required that every knight should be possessed of 400,000 sesterces, to enjoy the rights and privileges of his order; and a senator was entitled to sit in the senate, if his property amounted to 800,000 sesterces. This laborious and important task of numbering and reviewing the people, was, after the expulsion of the Tarquins, one of the duties and privileges of the consuls. But when the republic became more powerful, and when the number of the citizens was increased, the consuls were found unable to make the census, on account of the multiplicity of their engagements. After it had been neglected for 16 years, two new magistrates called censors were elected. They remained in office for five years, and every fifth year they made a census of all the citizens in the Campus Marius, and offered a solemn sacrifice, and made a lustration in the name of all the Roman people. This space of time was called a *lustrum*, and ten or twenty years were commonly expressed by two or four lustra. After the office of the censors had remained for some time unaltered, the people were jealous of their power, abridged the duration of their office, and a law was made, A.U.C. 420, by Mamercius Æmilius, to limit the time of the censorship to 18 months. After the second Punic war they were always chosen from such persons as had served the office of consul. This office was more honourable though less powerful, than that of the consuls; the badges of their office were indeed the same, but the censors were not allowed to have lictors to walk before them as the consuls. When one of the censors died, no one was elected in his room till the five years were expired, and his colleague immediately resigned. This circumstance originated from the death of a censor before the sacking of Rome by Brennus, and was ever after deemed an unfortunate occurrence in the annals of the republic. The emperors abolished the censors, and took upon themselves to execute their office.

CENSORI'NUS, AP. CL. was compelled, after many services to the state, to assume the imperial purple by the soldiers by whom he was murdered some days after, A D. 270.

CENSORI'NUS MAR'TIUS, a consul, to whom, as a particular friend, *Horace* addressed his 4 od. 8.

CENSORI'NUS, a very learned and ingenious grammarian of the third century, whose book *De die natali* is extant, being edited in 8vo, by Haverkamp, L. Bat. 1767. It treats of the birth of man, of years, months, and days. *Harles. Not. Lit. Rom.* 1. p. 528.—*Sax. Onom.* 1. p. 363.

CEN'SUS, the numbering of the people at Rome, performed by the censors; *a censeo*, to value. *Vid.* Censores.

CEN'SUS, a god worshipped at Rome, the same as Consus.

CEN'TA, an inland city of Mauritania Tingitana, now Benibahalud. *Ptol.*

CENTARE'TUS, a Galatian, who, when Antiochus was killed, mounted his horse in the greatest exultation. The horse, as if conscious of disgrace, immediately leaped down a precipice, and both perished by the fall. *Plin.* 8. c. 42.

CENTAU'RI, a people of Thessaly, represented by mythologists as half men and half horses. They were the offspring of Centaurus, son of Apollo, by Stilbia, the daughter of the Peneus. According to some, the Centaurs were the fruit of Ixion's adventure with the cloud, in the shape of Juno, or, as others assert, of the union of Centaurus with the mares of Magnesia. This fable of the existence of the Centaurs, arose from the ancient people of Thessaly having first tamed horses, and then having appeared to their neighbours mounted on them, a sight very uncommon at that time, and when at a distance, the horse and his rider certainly seem to possess only one body, and consequently to be one creature. Some derive the name ἀπὸ τοῦ κέντειν ταύρους, *goading bulls*, because they went on horseback in pursuit of their bulls which had strayed, or because they hunted wild bulls with horses. The battle of the Centaurs with the Lapithæ is famous in history. Ovid has elegantly described it, and it has also employed the pen of Hesiod, Valerius Flaccus, &c.; and *Pausanias in Eliac.* says that it was represented in the temple of Jupiter at Olympia, and also at Athens by Phidias and Parrhasius, according to *Pliny*, 36. c. 5. The origin of this battle was a quarrel at the marriage of Hippodamia with Pirithous. *Vid.* Pirithous. After the battle the Centaurs retired to Arcadia. Here their insolence was a second time punished by Hercules, who when he was going to hunt the boar Erymanthus, was kindly entertained by the Centaur Pholus, who presented him with wine which belonged to the rest of the Centaurs, but had been given them on condition of their treating Hercules with it, whenever he passed through their territory. They resented the liberty which Hercules took with their wine, and attacked him with the utmost fury. The hero defended himself with his arrows, and defeated his adversaries, who fled for safety to the Centaur Chiron. In the midst of the engagement Chiron was wounded in the knee, and died of the wound. The death of Chiron irritated Hercules the more, and the Centaurs that were present were all extirpated by his hand, and but few escaped the common destruction. The most celebrated of the Centaurs were Chiron, Eurytus, Amycus, Gryneus, Caumas, Lycidas, Arneus, Medon, Rhœtus, Pisenor, Mermeros, Pholus, &c. *Diod.* 4.—*Tzetzes. Chil.* 9. *Hist.* 237.—*Palœphat. de Inc.* 1.—*Servius in* 3. *Georg.*—*Lucret.* 5.—*Phleg. de Reb. Mir.*—*Hieronym. in vit. Paul. Erem.*—*Hesiod. in Scut. Hercul.*—*Homer. Il. & Odys.*—*Ovid. Met.* 12.—*Strab.* 9.—*Paus.* 5. c. 10, &c.—*Ælian. V. H.* 11. c. 2.—*Apollod.* 2. c. 5. l. 3.—*Virg. Æn.* 6. v. 286.—*Hygin.* fab. 33 & 62.—*Pindar. Pyth.* 2.

CENTI'NUM, a city of Umbria, now Sentinum. *Steph.*

CENTOBRI'CA, a town of Celtiberia in Spain. *Val. Max.* 5. c. 1.

CEN'TORES, a people of Scythia. *Flacc.* 6. v. 150.

CENTOR'IPA or CENTUR'IPA. *Vid.* Centuripa.

CENTRI'TES, a river between Armenia and Media, on the borders of the country of the Carduchi. *Xenoph.*—*Diod.*

CENTRO'NES, a people of Gaul, routed with great loss by J. Cæsar, when they attempted to obstruct his passage. They inhabited the country now called Tarantaise, in Savoy. There was a horde of Gauls of the same name subject to the Nervii, supposed to have lived near Courtray, in Flanders. *Cæs. G. B.* 1 c. 10. l. 5. c. 38.—*Plin.* 3. c. 20.

CENTRO'NIUS, a man who squandered away his immense riches on useless and whimsical buildings. *Juv.* 14. v. 86.

CENTUM'VIRI, the members of a court of justice at Rome. Three were originally chosen from each of the 35 tribes of the people, and though 105, they were always called Centumvirs. They were afterwards increased to 180, and still kept their original name. The prætor referred to their tribunal causes of the greatest importance, as their knowledge of the law was extensive. They were generally summoned by the Decemviri, who seemed to be the chief among them; and they assembled in the basilica, or public court, and had their tribunal distinguished by a spear with an iron head, whence a decree of their court was called *Hastæ judicium;* their sentences were regarded as impartial, and were consequently without appeal. *Cic. de Orat.* 1. c. 38.—*Quintil.* 4. 5 & 11.—*Plin.* 6. ep. 33.

CEN'TUM CEL'LÆ, a sea-port town of Etruria, built by Trajan, who had there a villa. It is now Civitia Vecchia. *Plin.* 6. ep. 31.

CENTU'RIA, a division of the people among the Romans, consisting of a hundred. The Roman people were originally divided into three tribes, and each tribe into ten Curiæ. Servius Tullius made a census; and when he had registered the place of habitation, name, and profession of the citizens, who amounted to 80,000 men able to bear arms, he divided them into six classes, and each class into several centuries, or companies of 100 men. The first class consisted of 80 centuries, 40 of which were composed of men from the age of 45 and upwards, appointed to guard the city. The 40 others were from 17 to 45 years of age, and therefore appointed to go to war and fight the enemies of Rome. Their arms were all the same, that is, a buckler, a cuiras, a helmet, cuishes of brass, with a sword, a lance, and a javelin; and as they were of the most illustrious citizens, they were called by way of eminence *Classici*, and their inferiors, *infra classem.* They were to be worth 1,100,000 *asses*, a sum equivalent to £1800 of English money. The second, third, and fourth classes, consisted each of twenty centuries, ten of which were composed of the more aged, and the others of the younger people. Their arms were a large spear, a sword, and a javelin; those in the second class were to be worth 75,000 *asses*, or about £121. In the third 50,000 *asses*, or about £80; and in the fourth, 25,000 *asses*, or about £40. The fifth class consisted of 30 centuries, three of which were carpenters by trade, and the others of different professions such as were necessary in a camp. They were all armed with slings and stones. They were to be worth 11,000 *asses*, or about £18. The sixth class contained only one centuria, comprising the whole body of the poorest citizens, who were called *Proletarii.* They were also called *capite censi*, as the censor took notice of their persons only, not of their estate. In the public assemblies in the Campus Martius, at the election of public magistrates, or upon trials for capital crimes, the people gave their votes by centuries, whence the assembly was called *comitia centuriata.* In these public assemblies, which were never convened but by the consuls, by permission of the senate, or by the dictator in the absence of the consuls, some of the people appeared under arms, for fear of a sudden attack from some foreign enemy. When a law was proposed in the public assemblies, its necessity was explained, and the advantages which it would produce to the state were enlarged upon; after which it was exposed in the most conspicuous parts of the city three market days, that the people might see it, and consider of its propriety. Exposing it to public view was called *proponere legem*, and explaining it *promulgare legem.* The person who merely proposed it, was called *lator legis;* and he who dwelt upon its importance and utility, and wished it to be enforced, was called *auctor legis.* When the assembly was to be held, the auguries were consulted by the consul, who, after haranguing the people, and reminding them to have in view the good and the glory of the republic, dismissed them to their respective centuries, that their votes might be gathered. They gave their votes *vivâ voce*, till the year of Rome, A.U.C. 615, when they changed the custom, and signified their approbation or disapprobation by ballots thrown into an urn. If the first class were unanimous, the others were not consulted, as the first were superior to all the others in number; but if they were not unanimous, they proceeded to consult the rest, and the majority decided the question. The advantages possessed by the first class over the others gave offence to the rest; and it was afterwards settled, that one class of the six should be drawn by lot, to give its votes first, without regard to rank or priority. After all the votes had been gathered, the consul, according to the number of the suffrages, declared aloud, either that the law which had been proposed was duly and constitutionally approved, or that it had been rejected. The same ceremonies were observed in the election of consuls, prætors, &c. The word *Centuria* is also applied to a subdivision of one of the Roman legions which consisted of a hundred men, and was the half of a manipulus, the sixth part of a cohort, and the sixtieth part of a legion. The commander of a centuria was called *Centurion*, and he was distinguished from the rest of his fellow soldiers by the branch of a vine which he carried in his hand.

CENTU'RIPA or CENTU'RIPI, *arum*, now Centorui, a town of some celebrity in Sicily, at the foot of mount Ætna. *Cic. in Verr.* 4. c. 23.—*Ital.* 14. v. 205.—*Plin.* 3. c. 8.

CE'OS or CE'A, an island. *Vid.* Co.

CEPA'RIUS, a Roman who joined in Catiline's conspiracy against his country. *Cic.* 3. *Cat.* 6.

CEPH'ALAS, a lofty promontory of Africa, near the Syrtis Major. *Strab.*

CEPHALE'NE or CEPHALLE'NIA, an island in the Ionian sea, below Corcyra, the inhabitants of which went with Ulysses to the Trojan war. It was anciently divided into four different districts, from which circumstance it received the name of Tetrapolis. Its plains abound in oil and in wines of excellent flavour, and it is about 93 miles in circumference, and from its capital Samo or Samos, it was frequently called Same. *Strab.* 10—*Plin.* 4. c. 12.—*Mela*, 2. c. 9.—*Ptol.* 3. c. 14.—*Homer. Il.* 2. v. 631.—*Thucyd.* 2. c. 30.—*Paus.* 6. c. 15.

CEPHAL'LEN, a noble musician, son of Lampus. *Paus.* 10. c. 7.

CEPH'ALO, an officer of Eumenes. *Diod.* 19.

CEPHALOE'DIS or CEPHALU'DIUM, now Cefalu, a town at the north of Sicily. *Sil.* 14. v. 253.—*Cic.* 2 *in Verr.* 51.

CEPH'ALON, a Greek of Ionia, who wrote a history of Troy, besides an epitome of universal history from the age of Ninus to the time of Alexander the Great; which he divided into nine books, inscribed with the names of the nine muses. He affected not to know the place of his birth, expecting that it would, like Homer's, become a subject of dispute among the learned. He lived in the reign of Adrian. *Euseb. Chron.* 1.—*Phot. Bibl.* 68—*Voss. de Hist. Græc.* 1. c. 3, &c.

CEPHALOT'OMI, a people near the Euxine Sea. *Plin.* 6. c. 5.

CEPH'ALUS, son of Deioneus, king of Thessaly,

married Procis, daughter of Erechtheus king of Athens. Aurora fell in love with him, and carried him away; but he refused to listen to her criminal addresses, and was impatient to return to Procris. The goddess sent him back; but to try the fidelity of his wife, she made him put on a different form, and he arrived at the house of Procris in the habit of a merchant. Procris suffered herself to be seduced by the gold of the stranger, who then discovered himself. This circumstance so ashamed Procris, that she fled from her husband, and devoted herself to hunting in the island of Eubœa. She here became one of the attendants of Diana, who presented her with a dog always sure of his prey, and a dart which never missed its aim, and always returned to the hands of its mistress of its own accord. Some say that the dog was a present from Minos, because Procris had cured his wounds. After this, Procris, willing to try her husband's virtue, returned in disguise to Cephalus, who yielded to the embraces of Procris, from a desire to possess the dog and the dart. Procris discovered herself, and a reconciliation was easily made between them. They loved one another with greater tenderness than before, and Cephalus received from his wife the presents of Diana. As he was particularly fond of hunting, he every morning early repaired to the woods, and when tired with excessive toil, and fatigued with the chase, he laid himself down in the cool shade, earnestly calling for *Aura*, or the refreshing breeze. This word was mistaken for the name of a mistress, and it was reported to Procris, that Cephalus daily paid a visit to a mistress whose name was Aura. Procris too readily believed the information, and secretly followed her husband into the woods. According to his daily custom, Cephalus retired to enjoy the cooling shade, and again called upon Aura. At the name of Aura, the unhappy Procris eagerly lifted up her head to see her expected rival. Her motion occasioned a rustling among the leaves of the bush that concealed her; and as Cephalus listened, he conceived it to be a wild beast, and immediately let fly his unerring dart. Procris was struck to the heart, and instantly expired in the arms of her husband. According to Apollodorus, there were two persons of the name of Cephalus; one, son of Mercury and Herse, carried away by Aurora, with whom he dwelt in Syria, and by whom he had a son called Tithonus. The other married Procris, and was the cause of the tragical events mentioned above. Cephalus was father of Arcesius by Procris, and of Phaethon, according to Hesiod, by Aurora. *Antonin.* l. 41.—*Tzetzes. Chil.* 1. c. 20.—*Hesiog. Theog.* 936.—*Ovid. Met.* 7. fab. 26.—*Hygin.* fab. 189.—*Apollod.* 3. c. 15.

CEPH'ALUS, a Corinthian lawyer, who assisted Timoleon in regulating the republic of Syracuse. *Diod.* 16.—*Plut. in Tim.*——A king of Epirus. *Liv.* 43. c. 18.——An orator, frequently mentioned by *Demosthenes.*

CEPHE'IS, a patronymic of Andromeda, as daughter of Cepheus. *Ovid. A.A.* 1. v. 193.

CEPHE'NES, an ancient name of the Persians. *Herodot.* 7. c. 61.——A name of the Æthiopians, from Cepheus, one of their kings. *Ovid. Met.* 5. v. 1.

CEPHEUS, a king of Æthiopia, father of Andromeda, by Cassiope. He was one of the Argonauts, and was changed into a constellation after his death. *Vid.* Andromeda. *Ovid. Met.* 4. v. 669. l. 5. v. 12.—*Hygin.* fab. 14 & 64. *P. A.* 2. c. 9.—*Cic. Tusc.* 5. c. 3.—*Colum.* 11. v. 2.—*Paus.* 4. c. 35. l. 8. c. 4.—*Apollodorus*, 1. c. 9. l. 2. c. 1. 4 & 7. l. 3. c. 9. mentions one, son of Aleus, and another, son of Belus. The former he makes king of Tegea, and father of Sterope; and says, that he, with his twelve sons, assisted Hercules in a war against Hippocoon, in which they were killed. The latter he calls king of Æthiopia, and father of Andromeda.——A son of Lycurgus, present at the chase of the Calydonian boar. *Apollod.* 1. c. 8.

CE'PHIS, a celebrated statuary. *Plin.* 34. c. 8.

CEPHIS'IA, a part of Attica, through which the river Cepheus flows. *Id.* 4. c. 7.

CEPHISI'ADES, a patronymic of Eteocles, son of Andreus and Evippe, from the supposition of his being the son of Cephisus. *Paus.* 9. c. 34.

CEPHISIDO'RUS, a tragic poet of Athens in the age of Æschylus. Suidas has preserved the titles of some of his plays. According to *Pollux* and *Athenæus*, he was a comic poet. *Fabric. B. Gr.* l. 2. c. 22.——An historian who wrote an account of the Phocian war. *Gyrald. P. Hist.*

CEPHIS'ION, the commander of some troops sent by the Thebans to assist Megalopolis, &c. *Diod.* 16.

CEPHISOD'OTUS, an archon at Athens. Ol. 105. an. 3.——A disciple of Isocrates, who inveighed with great bitterness against the writings of Aristotle. He wrote a book of proverbs. *Athen.* 2.

CEPHI'SUS or CEPHIS'SUS, a celebrated river of Greece, that rose at Lilæa in Phocis, and after passing at the north of Delphi and mount Parnassus, entered Bœotia, where it flowed into the lake Copais. The Graces were said to be particularly fond of this river, whence they are called the goddesses of the Cephisus. There was a small river of the same name in Attica, and another in Argolis. *Strab.* 9.—*Plin.* 4. c. 7.—*Paus.* 9. c. 24.—*Hom. Il.* 2. v. 29.—*Pind.* 14 *Olymp.*—*Lucan.* 3. v. 175.—*Ovid. Met.* 1. v. 369. l. 3. v. 19. l. 7. v. 439.

CEPHI'SUS a man changed into a sea monster by Apollo, when lamenting the death of his grandson. *Ovid. Met.* 7. v. 388.

CEPHREN, a king of Ægypt, who built one of the pyramids. *Diod.* 1.

CEPIA'NA, a city of the Celtici, in Lusitania. *Ptol.*

CE'PIO or CÆPIO, a man who by a quarrel with Drusus, caused a civil war at Rome, &c. *Val. Max.* 8. c. 5.

CE'PIO SERVIL'IUS, a Roman consul, who put an end to the war in Spain. He took gold from one of the temples of the gods of the country, and, in consequence of that sacrilege, the rest of his life proved a series of misfortunes. He was conquered by the Cimbrians, his goods were afterwards publicly confiscated, and he died at last in prison. *Liv.* 67.—*Val. Max.*

CE'PION, a musician. *Plut. de Mus.*

CEPOB'ROTAS or CEPROB'OTAS, a king of Muziris in India. *Plin.* 6. c. 23.—*Arrian. in Peripl.*—*Salmas. ad Solin.* p. 1185.

CEP'OE, a town of the Cimmerian Bosporus, now Copa. *Plin.* 6. c. 6.

CE'PUS, a town near the Euxine Sea. *Strab.*—*Diod.*

CER'ACA, a town of Macedonia. *Polyb.* 5.

CERAC'ATES, a people of Germany. *Tac.* 4. *Hist.* c. 70.

CERAM'BUS, a man changed by the nymphs into a beetle, or, according to others, into a bird, on mount Parnassus, before the deluge. *Ovid. Met.* 7. v. 353.

CERAM'ICA POR'TA, a gate at Athens, so called from its neighbourhood to the Ceramicus.

CERAMI'CUS, now Keramo, a bay of Caria, nea Halicarnassus, opposite Cos, which received it name from Ceramus. *Plin.* 5. c. 29.—*Mela*, 1. c 16.——The name of two places at Athens; the first used generally as a market, and for the holding of the assemblies of the people, was within the city, and formed a most beautiful public walk, adorned with magnificent porticoes; and the second was in the suburbs, without the walls, where the funeral eulogies of those who had honourably fallen in the service of their country were solemnly pronounced, and where their ashes were permitted to repose. In this place also the gratitude of Athens erected statues to her brave men, with suitable inscriptions, which, while they recalled the memory of the dead, at the same time excited their survivors to imitate their noble deeds, and share their laurels. *Plin.* 35. c. 12.—*Cic. de Finib.* 1. c. 11. *Ad. Att.* 1. ep 10.—*Paus.* 1. c. 3.

CERA'MIUM, a place of Rome, where Cicero and Milo had houses. *Cic. ad Attic.* l. 4.

CERAM'NUS, a general who assisted Perses. *Val. Flacc.* 6. v. 550.

CER'AMUS, a town at the west of Asia Minor, on a bay of the same name, near Halicarnassus. *Plin.* 5. c. 31.

CERAN'GE, a city of India within the Ganges. *Ptol.*

CERAS'TÆ, islands near Syene. *Plin.* 5. c. 9.

CERAS'TIS, a name given to Cyprus, from its many promontories protruding like horns. *Steph.*

CER'ASUS, *untis*, now Keresoun, a city of Pontus, on the shores of the Euxine Sea, from which cherries were first brought to Rome by Lucullus. *Marcell.* 22. c. 13.—*Plin.* 15. c. 25. l. 16. c. 18. l. 17. c. 14.—*Mela*, 1. c. 19.——A town built by a Greek colony from Sinope. *Diod.* 14.

CER'ATA, a place near Megara. *Plut. in Parall.*

CERA'TE, CERA'TÆ, or CEREA'TÆ, a city of Italy, near the lake Fucinus. It is now Cereto. *Strab.*

CERA'TE, a town of the Turones, in Gaul, now Ceray.

CERA'TON, a celebrated altar in the temple of Apollo at Delus. It was erected wholly with the horns of stags, without the assistance of cement; and as it was said to be the work of the god who presided over the temple, it not only commanded the attention of worshippers, but passed for one of the wonders of the world. It was said still to exist in the time of Plutarch. Theseus, on his victorious return from Crete, visited Delus, and offered sacrifices on the Ceraton, round which he led in solemn dance the band of Athenians who had accompanied him in his expedition. *Ovid. Heroid.* 20. v. 99. *Plut. de Inâ. Anim. & in Thes.—Callimac in Apoll.*

CERA'TUS, a river near Gnossus in Crete.

CERAU'NIA, a town of Achaia. *Polyb.* l. 2.

CERAU'NIA or CERAU'NII, large mountains of Epirus, extending far into the sea, and forming a promontory which divides the Ionian and Adriatic Seas. They were so called from being frequently struck by thunder. They are the same as the Acroceraunia. *Vid.* Acroceraunium.—Mount Taurus is also called Ceraunius. *Plin.* 5. c. 27.

CERAU'NIA or CERO'NIA, a town of Cyprus, now Cerines. *Cluver.* 5. c. 26.

CERAU'NIUS, a surname of Jupiter.

CERAU'NII, mountains of Asia, opposite the Caspian Sea. *Mela*, 1. c. 19.

CERAU'NUS, a river of Cappadocia. *Plin.* 6. c. 3.

CERAU'NUS a surname of Ptolemy the Second, from his boldness. *C. Nep. Reg.* c. 3.——A surname given by Clearchus, tyrant of Heraclea in Pontus, to his son, in contempt of Jupiter's thunder. *Justin.* 16. c 5.

CERAU'SIUS, a mountain of Arcadia. *Paus.* 8. c. 41.

CER'BALUS, now Cervaro, a river of Apulia, which falls into the Adriatic near Sipuntum. *Plin.* 3. c. 11.

CERBA'NI, a people of Arabia Felix. *Plin.* 6. c. 28.

CERBE'RION, a town of the Cimmerian Bosporus. *Plin.* 6 c. 6.

CER'BERUS, a dog of Pluto, the fruit of Echidna's union with Typhon. He had 50 heads, according to Hesiod, andthree according to other mythologists. He was stationed at the entrance of hell, to prevent the living from entering the infernal regions, and the dead from escaping from their confinement. It was usual for those heroes, who were in their life-time permitted to visit Pluto's kingdom, to appease the barking mouths of Cerberus with a cake. Orpheus lulled him to sleep with his lyre; but Hercules dragged him from hell, when he went to to redeem Alceste. Homer speaks of this animal, but does not mention either his name or the nature of his form; Hesiod, therefore, is the first who calls him Cerberus. *Cic. Tusc.* 1. c. 5. *De N. D.* 3. c. 17.—*Servius in. Æn* 6. v. 395. l. 8. v. 295 & 297.—*Virg. Æn.* 5. v. 134. l. 6. v. 417.—*Homer. Odyss.* 11. v. 622.—*Paus.* 2. c. 31. l. 3. c. 25.—*Hesiod. Theog.* 312.—*Tibull.* 1. el. 10, v. 35.

CER'CAPHUS, a son of Æolus. *Strab.* 1. 9.——A son of Sol, of great power at Rhodes. The Rhodian women were called Cercaphides from him. *Diod.* 5.

CERCASO'RUM, a town of Ægypt, at the top of the Delta, where the Nile divides itself into the Pelusian and Canopic mouths. *Herodot.* 2. c. 15.

CERCE'IS, one of the Oceanides. *Hesiod. Theog.* v. 355.

CERCE'NE, a country of Africa. *Diod.* 3.

CERCES'TES, a son of Ægyptus and Phœnissa. *Apollod.* 2. c. 1.

CER'CETÆ or CERCE'TII, now Circassia, a nation of Sarmatia on the northern borders of the Euxine Sea. *Plin.* 6. c. 5.—A bay of this sea was called Cerceticus, and is now Golfo de Susaco.

CERCE'TIUS, a mountain of Samus. Some mountains in Thessaly were also called Cercetii. *Plin.* 4. c. 8.

CER'CIDAS, a legislator of Megalopolis. *Steph.*——A native of Megalopolis, who wrote iambics. *Athen.* 10.—*Ælian. V. H.* 13.

CER'CII, a people of Italy. *Diod.* 14.

CERCI'NA or CERCIN'NA, a small island in the Mediterranean, near the smaller Syrtis, on the coast of Africa. *Tacit.* 1. *Ann.* 53.—*Strab.* 17.—*Liv.* 33. c. 48.—*Plin.* 5. c. 7.——A mountain of Thrace towards Macedonia. *Thucyd.* 2. c. 98.

CERCIN'IUM, a small town of Macedonia. *Liv.* 31. c. 41.

CER'CIUS or RHE'TIUS, and AM'PHITUS, charioteers of Castor and Pollux. *Ammian.* l. 22.

CERCO'PES, a people of Ephesus, made prisoners by Hercules. *Apollod.* 2. c. 6.——The inhabitants of the island Pithecusa, on the coast of Etruria, changed into monkeys on accouut of their dishonesty. *Ovid. Met.* 14. v. 91.

CERCO'PIA, a town of Phrygia Major. *Ptol.*

CER'COPS, a Milesian author of a fabulous history, praised by *Apollodorus*, 1. 2.——A Pythagorean philosopher. *Voss. Hist. Gr.* l. 4.

CER'CYON or CERCY'ONES, a king of Eleusis, son of Neptune, or, according to others, of Vulcan. He obliged all strangers to wrestle with him; and as he was a dexterous wrestler, they were easily vanquished by his superior skill and put to death. After many cruelties, he challenged Theseus in wrestling, and was defeated and put to death by his antagonist. His daughter Alope was loved by Neptune, to whom she bore a son. Cercyon exposed the child, called Hippothoon; but he was preserved by a mare, and afterward's placed upou his grandfather's throne by Theseus. *Ovid. Met.* 7. v. 439 —*Hygin.* fab. 187.—*Plut. in Thes.*—*Paus.* 1. c. 5 & 39.

CERCY'RA or CORCY'RA, an island in the Ionian Sea, which received its name from Cercyra, daughter of Asopus. *Vid.* Corcyra. *Diod.* 4.

CER'DIAS, a town taken by Lysander. *Xenoph. Hist.* 1 2.

CERDO'US, a surname of Apollo, and also of Mercury, from κέρδος, *lucrum. Suidas.*

CERDYL'IUM, a place near Amphipolis, in Thrace. *Thucyd.* 5. c. 6.

CEREA'LIS, the uncle of the emperor Gratian, proclaimed Valentinian his son emperor, in the 10th year of his age. *Socr.* l. 14. c. 26.——A city of Spain, otherwise Ebura. *Plin.* 3. c. 1.

CEREA'LES LU'DI, festivals in honour of Ceres, first instituted at Rome by Memmius the ædile, and annually celebrated on the 19th of April. Persons in mourniug were not permitted to appear at the celebration; therefore they were not observed after the fatal battle of Cannæ. They were the same as the Thesmophoria of the Greeks. *Vid.* Thesmophoria.

CEREL'LIA or CÆREL'LIA, a Roman matron, unusually fond of philosophy and literature. Her intimacy with Cicero, as a literary character, has been improperly imputed, by Calenus, to unchaste motives. *Cic. ad Fam.* 13. ep. 72.—*Attic.* 13. ep. 21, &c.—*Quintil.* 6. c. 3.

CEREL'LIA, the name of a Roman family, of which Macrinus, Faustinianus, and Julianus were slain by order of Severus, without any reason being assigned. *Spartian. in Sever.* c. 13.

CE'RES, the goddess of corn, was daughter of Saturn and Vesta. She had a daughter by Jupiter, whom she called Pherephata, *fruit-bearing*, and afterwards Proserpine. This daughter, while gathering flowers in the plains near Enna in Sicily was carried off by Pluto. The rape of Proserpine was grievous to Ceres, who sought her over all Sicily; and when night came, lighted two torches in the flames of mount Ætna, to continue her search by night all over the world. After many fruitless inquiries the goddess at last found her veil near the fountain Cyane; but no intelligence could be received of the place of her concealment, till the nymph Arethusa informed the distressed mother that her daughter had been carried away by Pluto. Ceres no sooner heard this, than she demanded of Jupiter the immediate restoration of her daughter. The endeavours of Jupiter to soften her resentment and mitigate her grief by representing Pluto as a powerful god, and his entreaties that she would allow him to become her son-in-law, proved fruitless; and the restoration was granted, provided Proserpine had not eaten any thing in the kingdom of Pluto. Ceres upon this repaired hastily to Pluto, but Proserpine had eaten the grains of a Pomegranate which she had gathered as she walked over the Elysian fields. *Vid.* Ascalaphus. The grief of Ceres for the loss of her daughter was so great, that Jupiter granted Proserpine permission to pass six months with her mother, and the rest of the year with Pluto. During the inquiries of Ceres for her daughter, the cultivation of the earth was neglected, and the ground became barren; to repair, therefore, in particular, the loss which mankind had suffered during her absence, the goddess went to Attica, which was become the most desolate country in the world, and instructed Triptolemus of Eleusis in every thing which concerned agriculture. *Vid.* Triptolemus. Her beneficence to mankind made Ceres respected. Sicily was supposed to be the favourite retreat of the goddess; and Diodorus says, that she and her daughter made their first appearance to mankind in Sicily, an island which Pluto received as a nuptial dowry from Jupiter when he married Proserpine. The Sicilians, in gratitude for the fertility bestowed upon their fields, made a yearly sacrifice to Ceres, every man according to his abilities; and the fountain of Cyane, through which Pluto opened himself a passage with his trident, when carrying away Proserpine, was publicly honoured with an offering of bulls, and the blood of the victims was permitted to flow into the waters of the fountain. Besides these, other ceremonies were observed in honour of the goddesses who had so peculiarly favoured the island. The commemoration of the rape of Proserpine was celebrated about the beginning of the harvest, and that of the search of Ceres at the time that corn is sown in the earth. The latter festival continued six successive days; and during the celebration the votaries of Ceres made use of some free and wanton expressions, as that language had made the goddess smile while bewailing the loss of her daughter. Attica also, which had been so eminently distinguished by the goddess, gratefully remembered her favours in the celebration of the Eleusinian mysteries. *Vid.* Eleusinia. Ceres also performed the duties of a legislator, and the Sicilians experienced the advantages of her salutary laws; hence her surname of Thesmophora. Ceres is the same as the Isis of the Ægyptians; and her worship, it is said, was first brought into Greece by Erechtheus. She met with different adventures when she travelled over the earth; and the impudence of Stellio was severely punished. To avoid the importunities of Neptune, she changed herself into a mare. *Vid.* Arion. The birth of Arion so offended Ceres, that she withdrew hersef from the sight of mankind; and the earth would have perished for want of her assistance, had not Pan discovered her in Arcadia, and given information of it to Jupiter. The Parcæ were sent by the god to comfort her, and at their persuasion she returned to Sicily, where her statues represented her veiled in black, with the head of a horse, and holding a dove in one hand, and in the other a dolphin. In their sacrifices, the ancients generally offered Ceres a pregnant sow, as that animal often injures and destroys the productions of the earth. While the corn was yet in grass, they offered her a ram, after the victim had been led three times round the fields. Ceres was occasionally represented with a garland of ears of corn on her head, holding in one hand a lighted torch, and in the other a poppy, which was sacred to her. She at other times appears as a countrywoman mounted on the back of an ox, and carrying a basket on her left arm, and holding a hoe; and sometimes she rides in a chariot drawn by winged dragons. She was supposed to be the same as Rhea, Tellus, and the Cybele, Bona Dea, Berecynthia, of the Phrygians, the Isis of the Ægyptians, the Atergatis of the Syrians, the Hera of the Arcadians, &c. She was said to be the mother of Plutus the god of riches, whom she bore to Jasius the son of Jupiter and Electra, in Arcadia. The people of Italy paid her great adoration, and her festivals were yearly celebrated by the Roman matrons in the month of April, during eight days. They always bore lighted torches in commemoration of the torches borne by the goddess; and whoever came to these festivals without a previous initiation was punished with death. Ceres is metaphorically called *bread* and *corn*, as the word *Bacchus* is frequently used to signify *wine*. *Apollod.* 1. c. 5. l. 2. c. l. l. 3. c. 12 & 14.—*Paus.* 1. c. 31. l. 2. c. 34. l. 3. c. 23. l. 8. c. 25, &c.—*Diod.* 1, &c.—*Ovid. Fast.* 4. v. 400, &c. *Met.* 5. fab. 7, 8, &c.—*Claudian. de Rapt. Pros.*—*Cic. in Verr.* 7.—*Callimach. in Cer.*—*Liv.* 29 & 31.—*Stat. Theb.* 12.—*Dionys. Hal.* 1. c. 33.—*Hygin. P. A.* 2.—*Hesiod. Theog.* 454, 912 & 970.—*Virg. G.* 1. v. 147 & 343. & *Servius loc.*—*Nat. Com.* 5. c. 14.—*Lactant. de Fals. R.* 21.—*Liv.* 29 & 31.—*Festus de Verb. Sig.*—*Meurs. Gr. Fer.*—*Theocrit. in Cer.* [There is no very celebrated statue of this goddess. That which should, perhaps, be considered the best, is in the garden of the Vatican.]

CERES'SUS, a place of Bœotia. *Paus.* 9. c. 14. ——A town of Hispania Tarraconensis. *Ptol.*

CER'ETÆ, a people of Crete. *Polyb.*

CERETA'NI, the inhabitants of Cerete, in Umbria.

CERE'VIA, a city of Gallia Togata.

CERIA'LIS ANIC'IUS, a consul elect, who wished a temple to be raised to Nero, as to a god, after the discovery of the Pisonian conspiracy. *Tacit. Ann.* 15. c. 74.

CE'RII, a people of Etruria. *Diod.* l. 14. It was probably the gentile name for the people of Cære.

CERIL'LI or CARIL'LÆ, now Cirella, a town in the country of the Brutii, south of the Laus. *Strab.* 6.—*Sil.* 8. 580.

CERIN'THUS, now Zero, a town of Eubœa, the inhabitants of which went to the Trojan war, headed by Elephenor son of Chalcodon. *Homer. Il.* 2. v. 54.—*Plin.* 4. c. 12.—*Ptol.* 3. c. 15.—*Strab.* 10.

CERIN'THUS, a beautiful youth long the favourite of the Roman ladies, and especially of Sulpitia. *Horat.* 1. sat. 2. v. 81.——One of the early heretics, against whose particular opinion, St. John wrote his Gospel.

CE'RIUS SEVE'RUS, a tribune of the prætorian cohort, in the time of Galba. *Tac. Hist.* 1. c. 31.

CER'MALA or GER'MALUS, a place where Romulus was exposed by one of the servants of Amulius. *Plut. in Romul.*—*Varro de L. L.* l. 4.

CERMO'RUM, a town of Macedonia. *Plin.* 4. c. 10.

CER'NAS, a priest of Cybele. *Epigr. Aleman. ap Plut.* l. περὶ φυγῆς.

CER'NE, an island without the pillars of Hercules, on the African coast. *Strab.* 1.—*Plin.* 5 & 6.

CERNE'TUM, a town of Italy. The inhabitants were called Cernetani. *Plin.* 3. c. 5.

CE'RON, a fountain of Hestiæotis, the waters of which were said to render black all the sheep that drank of them. *Plin.* 31. c. 2.

CEROPAS'ADES or CEROS'PADES, a son of Phraates king of Persia, given as a hostage to Augustus. *Strab.*

CEROPHÆ'I, a nation of Africa Propria. *Ptol.*

CEROS'SUS, a place of the Ionian Sea, or rather an island between Melite and Macedonia. *Apollon.* l. 4.

CER'PHERES, a king of Ægypt, who is supposed to have built the smallest of the pyramids. *Herodotus* l. 2. c. 127. calls him Chephren.

CERRHÆ'I, a people of Greece, who profaned the temple of Delphi. *Plut. in Sol.*

CERRETA'NI, a people of Spain that inhabited the modern district of Cerdana in Catalonia. *Plin.* 3. c. 3.

CERSOBLEP'TES, a king of Thrace, conquered by Philip king of Macedonia. *Polyæn.* 7. c. 31.

CERSU'NUM, an inland of Corsica. *Ptol.* Its ruins bear the name of Rosoli.

CER'TIMA, a town of the province of Celtiberia, in Spain. *Liv.* 40. c. 47.

CERTIS'SA, a town of Lower Pannonia. *Ptol.*

CERTO'NIUM, a town of Asia Minor. *Xenophon.*

CERVA'RIA, the last place in Gallia Aquitanica, near the temple of Venus, at the foot of the Pyrenees. *Mela,* 2. c. 5 & 6.——A town of the Oretani, in Spain. *Ptol.*

CEVA'RIUS PROC'ULUS, a Roman knight, who conspired with Piso against Nero. *Tacit. Ann.* 15. c. 50.

CER'VIUS P., an officer under Verres in Sicily. *Cic. in Verr.* 5. c. 44.

CERY'CES, certain priests at Athens. *Thucyd.* 8. c. 53.

CERYC'IUS, a mountain of Bœotia. *Paus.* 9. c. 20.
CERYMI'CA, a town of Cyprus. *Diod.*
CERYNE'A, a town of Achaia.——A mountain of Arcadia. *Paus.* 7. c. 25.
CERYNI'TES, a river of Arcadia. *Paus.* 7. c. 25.
CESA'TA or CESA'DA, a city of Spain, between Emerita and Cæsar Augusta. *Ptol.*
CES'CUS, a city of Pamphylia, or, according to *Suidas*, of Cilicia. *Plin.* 31. c. 2.
CESEL'LIUS BAS'SUS, a turbulent Carthaginian, who dreamt of money, and persuaded Nero, that immense treasures had been deposited by Dido in a certain place which he described. Enquiry was made, and when no money was found, Cesellius destroyed himself. *Tac. Ann.* 16. c. 1, &c.
CESEN'NIA, an infamous prostitute, born of an illustrious family at Rome. *Juv.* 6. v. 135.
CESEN'NIUS PÆ'TUS, a general sent by Nero to Armenia. *Tacit.* 15. *Ann.* 6 & 25.
CESEN'NIUS PRIS'CUS, a prætor of Syria, A.C. 47.
CESSE'LIUS, a celebrated lawyer, who could not be induced to insert the Triumviral statutes in his Sylloge of the laws. *Val. Max.* 6. c. 2.
CES'TIUS, an epicurean of Smyrna, who taught rhetoric at Rhodes, in the age of Cicero.——A governor of Syria. *Tacit. H.* 5.
CES'TIUS PROC'ULUS, a man acquitted of an accusation of embezzling the public money. *Id. Ann.* 13. c. 30.
CES'TIUS SEVE'RUS, an informer under Nero. *Tacit. H.* 4.
CES'TIUS, a bridge at Rome, now St. Bartholomæo.
CESTRI'NA, a part of Epirus. *Paus.* 2. c. 23.
CESTRI'NUS, son of Helenus and Andromache. After his father's death, he obtained possession of a part of Epirus, above the river Thyamis, and called the country Cestrina. *Paus.* 1. c. 11.
CES'TRUS, a river of Pamphylia. *Mela*, 1. c. 14.
CETA'RIA, a city of Sicily. *Ptol.*
CE'TES or CE'TEUS, a king of Ægypt, the same as Proteus. *Diod.* 1.
CETHE'GUS, the surname of one of the branches of the Roman family of the Cornelii, the most known of whom were,
CETHE'GUS MAR'CUS, an eloquent orator, called from his persuasive powers, *Suadæ medulla.* He was consul in the second Punic war. *Cic. in Brut.* 15.
CETHE'GUS, a tribune at Rome, of the most corrupt morals, who joined Catiline in his conspiracy against the state, and was commissioned to murder Cicero. *Plut. in Cic.* &c.
CETHE'GUS P. CORNE'LIUS, a powerful Roman, who embraced the party of Marius against Sylla. His mistress had obtained such an ascendancy over him, that she distributed his favours in the most profuse manner; and Lucullus was not ashamed to court her smiles, when he wished to be appointed general against Mithridates.
CETHE'GUS, a senator put to death for adultery, under Valentinian.——A Trojan killed by Turnus. *Virg. Æn.* 12. v. 513.
CE'TII, a people of Cilicia. *Strab.* 13.
CE'TIUS, a river of Mysia. *Plin.* 5. c. 30.——A mountain which separates Noricum from Pannonia. It is now Kalemberg.
CE'TO, a daughter of Pontus and Terra, who married Phorcys, by whom she had the three Gorgons. *Hesiod. Theog.* v. 237.—*Lucan*, 9. v. 646.
CETOBRI'CA or CET'OBRIX, a city of Lusitania. *Ptol.*
CETRIB'ONI, a people of India. *Plin.* 6. c. 20.
CETRO'NIUS CA'IUS, a lieutenant of the first legion. *Tac. Ann.* 1. c. 44.
CETRO'NIUS PISA'NUS, a præfect of the camp, bound on suspicion of being acquainted with Piso's conspiracy. *Id. Hist.* 4. c. 50.
CEU'CI, a people of Spain. *Plin.* 4. c. 20.
CE'US or CÆ'US, a son of Cœleus and Terra, who married Phœbe, by whom he had Latona and Asteria. *Hesiod. Theog.* v. 135.—*Virg. Æn.* 4. v. 179.
CE'YX, a king of Trachinia, son of Lucifer, and husband of Alcyone. He was unfortunately drowned as he went to consult the oracle of Clarus; and his wife, who was apprised of his misfortune in a dream, found his dead body washed on the sea shore. They were both changed into birds called Alcyones. *Vid.* Alcyone. *Ovid. Met.* 11. v. 587. *Heroid.* 18. v. 81.—*Hygin.* fab. 65.—*Paus.* 1. c. 32. According to *Apollodorus*, 1. c. 7. l. 2. c. 7. the husband of Alcyone and the king of Trachinia were two different persons.
CHA'A, a town of Peloponnesus. *Strab.* 17.
CHABI'NUS, a mountain of Arabia Felix. *Diod.* 3.
CHA'BOR or CHABO'RA, a river and mountain of Asia. *Ptol.*
CHA'BRIA or CHA'BRIÆ CAS'TRA, a village of Ægypt, near Pelusium, so called after Chabrias, who fixed his camp there. *Strab.* 17.
CHA'BRIAS, an Athenian general and philosopher, who chiefly signalized himself when he assisted the Bœotians against Agesilaus. In this celebrated campaign he ordered his soldiers to put one knee upon the ground, and firmly to rest their spears upon the other, and cover themselves with their shields, by which means he checked the enemy; and to commemorate this successful stratagem his countrymen raised a statue to his honour in that posture. He assisted also Nectanebus, king of Ægypt, and conquered the whole island of Cyprus; but he at last fell a sacrifice to his excessive courage, and disdaining to flee when he had it in his power to save his life, like his companions, he sank, together with his ship, B.C. 376. *C. Nep. in Vita.*—*Diod.* 16.—*Plut. in Phoc.*
CHA'BRIUS, a small river of Macedonia which flows into the Sinus Thermaicus. *Ptol.*
CHA'BRYIS, a king of Ægypt. *Diod.* 1.
CHÆANI'TÆ, a people at the foot of mount Caucasus. *Strab.* l. 11.
CHÆ'REA, the name of one of the characters in the Eunuch of Terence.
CHÆ'REAS, an Athenian, who wrote on agriculture. ——An officer at Rome, who murdered Caligula, A.D. 41, to prevent the violent death which was prepared for himself. In destroying the tyrant, Chæreas hoped to rouse his countrymen to assert their ancient liberties; but his efforts were vain, and the elevation of Claudius to the throne was followed by the death of the murderer and of his associates.——An Athenian mentioned by *Thucydides.* 8. c. 74.
CHÆREDE'MUS, a brother of Epicurus. *Diog.*
CHÆRE'MON, a comic, or, according to *Fabricius*, *B. Gr.* 2. c. 19. a tragic poet.——A Stoic who wrote on the Ægyptian priests. *Voss. Hist. Gr.* 2. c. 1.
CHÆR'EPHON, a comic poet of Athens, in the age of Philip of Macedonia. *Fabr. B. Gr.* l. 2. c. 19.
CHÆRESTRATA, the mother of Epicurus, descended from a noble family.
CHÆRIN'THUS, a beautiful youth. *Horat.* 1. *Serm.* 2. v. 81. *Tibullus*, l. 2. el. 2. v. 9. has also mentioned a person of this name.
CHÆRIP'PUS, an extortioner. *Juv.* 8. v. 96.
CHÆ'RO, the supposed founder of the town of Chæronea. *Plut. in Syll.*
CHÆRONI'A, CHÆRONE'A, or CHERRONE'A, a city of Bœotia, on the Cephisus, celebrated for the defeat of the Athenians by the Bœotians, B.C. 447, and for the victory which Philip of Macedonia obtained there with 32,000 men, over the confederate army of the Thebans and the Athenians, consisting of 30,000 men, on the 2nd of August B.C. 338. Archelaus, the lieutenant of Mithridates, was also defeated here by Sylla with an inferior force. Plutarch was born there. The town was anciently called Arne. *Paus.* 9. c. 40.—*Plut. in Pelop.* &c.—*Strab.* 9.
CHA'LA. *Vid.* Chalonitis.
CHALÆ'ON, a city of Locris, situate on the bay of Corinth. *Thucyd.* 3.——A port of Bœotia. *Plin.* 4. c. 3.
CHALAS'TRA or CHALES'TRA, a city of Macedonia, at the mouth of the Axius. *Plin.* 31. c. 10. —*Herod.* 7. c. 123.
CHALCÆ'A, a town of Caria.——A town of Phœnicia.
CHAL'CE, an island near Rhodes. *Plin.* 5. c. 31.
CHALCE'A, a festival at Athens. *Vid.* Panathenæa.
CHALCE'DON or CHALCEDO'NIA, now Kadi-Kemi, an ancient city of Bithynia, on the shores of the Propontis, opposite Byzantium, built by a colony from Megara, headed by Argias, B.C. 685. It was first called Procerastis, and afterwards Colpusa. *Strab.* 7.—*Plin.* 5. c. 32.—*Mela*, 1. c. 19.—*Ptol.* 5. c. 1.
CHAL'CIA, one of the Cyclades. *Plin.* 4. c. 12.—*Mela*, 2. c. 9.
CHALCIDE'NE, a part of Syria, between the Orontes and the Euphrates. It was very fruitful, and its chief city was Chalcis. *Plin.* 5. c. 23.

CHALCI'DES, a philosopher of the new academy, who wrote a commentary on the Timæus of Plato. *Voss. de Sect. Phil.* c. 16. sec. 12.

CHALCIDEN'SES, the inhabitants of the isthmus between Teus and Erythræ. *Strab.*——A people near the Phasis. *Diod.* 14.

CHAL'CIDEUS, a commander of the Lacedæmonian fleet, killed by the Athenians. *Thucyd.* 8. c. 8.

CHALCID'ICA, a country of Thrace.——A country of Syria.——A country of Macedonia.

CHALCID'ICUS, a mountain of Sicily. *Steph.*

CHALCIŒ'CUS, a surname of Minerva, because she had a temple at Chalcis in Eubœa, or because she had an altar of brass (χαλκός), in one of her temples. She was also called Chalciotis and Chalcidica; and some of her festivals celebrated at Sparta also bore the same name. *C. Nepos.* 4.—*Meurs. Misc. Lacon.* l. c. 3.—*Ælian. V. H.* 9 c. 12.—*Liv.* 35. c. 36.—*Virg. Æn.* 6. v. 17.

CHALCI'OPE, a daughter of Æetes, king of Colchis, who married Phryxus, son of Athamas, who had fled to her father's court for protection. She had some children by Phryxus, and she preserved her life from the avarice and cruelty of her father, who had murdered her husband to obtain possession of the golden fleece. *Vid.* Phryxus. *Ovid. Heroid.* 17. v. 232.—*Val. Flacc.* 1. 6. v. 479.—*Apollon.* 2.—*Hygin.* fab. 3. 14 & 21.——The mother of Thessalus by Hercules. *Apollod.* 2. c. 7.——The daughter of Rhexenor, who married Ægeus. *Id.* 3. c. 1.

CHAL'CIS, now Egripo, the chief city of Eubœa, situated in that part of the island which is nearest to Bœotia. It was founded by an Athenian colony. The island was said to have been anciently joined to the continent in the neighbourhood of Chalcis. There were three other towns of the same name in Macedonia near Olynthus, in Acarnania, and Sicily, all belonging to the Corinthians. *Plin.* 4. c. 12. —*Strab.* 10.—*Paus.* 5. c. 23.—*Cic. N. D.* 3. c. 10. ——A city of Ætolia, at the mouth of the Evenus. ——A city of Messapia, in Italy.——A town of Syria. *Vid.* Chalcidene.

CHALCI'TIS, a country of Ionia. *Paus.* 7. c. 5. ——A country of India.——An island opposite the mouth of the Rhyndacus in Mysia. *Plin.* 6. c. *ult.*

CHALCO'DON, a son of Ægyptus, by Arabia. *Apollod.* 2. c. 1.——A man of Cos, who wounded Hercules. *Id.* 2. c. 7.——The father of Elphenor, one of the Grecian chiefs in the Trojan war. He was killed by Amphitryon, in a war which he, at the head of the Eubœans, waged against the Thebans. *Apollod.* 3.—*Homer. Il.* 2. v. 48.—*Paus.* 8. c. 15. ——A man who assisted Hercules in his war against Augias. *Paus.* 8. c. 15.

CHALCOMEDU'SA, the wife of Arcesius, mother of Laertes, king of Ithaca. *Eustathius*, Od. 16, is the only author who has mentioned her name.

CHAL'CON, a Messenian, who cautioned Antilochus, son of Nestor, to beware of the Æthiopians by whom he was to perish. He was engaged in the Trojan war, but left the Grecian camp to espouse the cause of Priam, that he might solicit the affections of Penthesilea of whom he was enamoured. He was afterwards killed by Achilles, and his body exposed in derision on a cross. *Ptolem. Hephæst. apud Phot.*—*Asclep. apud Eustath.* od. 11.

CHAL'CUS, a man made governer of Cyzicus by Alexander. *Polyæn.* 5. c. 44.

CHALDÆ'A, a couutry of Asia, between Arabia and the Euphrates, after its confluence with the Tigris. Its capital was Babylon, the inhabitants of which were famous, in ancient times for their knowledge of astrology. *Cic. de Div.* 1. c. 1.—*Diod.* 2.—*Strab.* 2:—*Plin.* 6. c. 28.

CHALDÆ'I, the inhabitants of Chaldæa.——A people near Colchis. *Steph.*

CHAL'DIA, a region of Armenia. *Id.*

CHALDO'NE, a promontory of Arabia Felix. *Plin.* 6 c. 28.

CHALE'OS, a city of Achaia, on the Sinus Corinthiacus. *Ptol.*

CHA'LES, a herald of Busiris, put to death by Hercules. *Apollod.* 2. c. 5.

CHALES'TRA. *Vid.* Chalastra.

CHA'LIA, a city of Bœotia. *Steph.*

CHALINI'TIS, a surname of Minerva, ἀπὸ τοῦ χαλινοῦ, because she *bridled* and presented the horse Pegasus to Bellerophon.

CHALIS'TA, a city of Libya.——A city of the Amazons. *Steph.*

CHALONI'TIS, a country of Asia, at the east of Babylon. The chief town was Chala. *Plin.* 6. c. 27.

CHA'LUS, a river of Syria, according to *Xenophon*, the Syrians thought the fishes of this river to be gods, and would not suffer them to be injured.

CHALU'SUS, a river of Germany, discharging itself into the Sinus Codanus. *Ptol.*

CHAL'YBES or **CAL'YBES**, a people of Asia Minor, near Pontus, once very powerful, and possessed of a great extent of country, abounding in iron mines, in which the inhabitants worked naked. The Calybes attacked the ten thousand Greeks, in their retreat from the battle of Cunaxa, and behaved with much courage. They were partly conquered by Crœsus, king of Lydia. Some authors imagine that the Calybes were a nation of Spain. *Virg. Æn.* 8. v. 421.—*Strab.* 12, &c.—*Apollon.* 2. v. 375, —*Xenoph. Anab.* 4, &c.—*Herodot.* 1. c. 28.—*Justin.* 44. c. 3.

CHAL'YBON, a town of Syria, now supposed to be Aleppo, which gave the name of Chalybonitis to the neighbouring country.

CHALYBONI'TIS, a country of Syria between the Euphrates and the Orontes. Its chief town was Chalybon. The soil was so productive of luxurious wines that the kings of Persia drank no other. *Strab.* l. 15.

CHA'LYBS, a small river of Spain, near which *Justin.* 44. c. 3, places the people called Calybes. ——A river flowing from mount Taurus into the Euxine Sea.

CHAMA'NI or **CHAMA'VI**, one of the wandering hordes of Germany. *Tacit. in Germ.* 33.

CHANDAN'ACE, a city of Persia. *Steph.*

CHANDA'NE, a city of Apulia. *Id.*

CHA'NE, a river between Armenia and Albania, falling into the Caspian Sea. *Strab.* 11.

CHA'ON, a mountain of Peloponnesus.

CHA'ON, a son of Priam. *Vid.* Chaonia.

CHA'ONES, a people of Epirus, who inhabited Chaonia.

CHAO'NIA, a mountainous part of Epirus, near the Ionian Sea. It received its name from Chaon, a son of Priam, inadvertently killed by his brother Helenus, who established a kingdom there. There was a wood near, where doves (*Chaoniæ aves*) were said to deliver oracles. The words *Chaonius victus* are by ancient authors applied to acorns, the food of the first inhabitants. *Lucan.* 6. v. 426. *Claudian. de Pros. Rapt.* 3. v. 47.—*Virg. Æn.* 3. v. 335.—*Propert.* 1. el. 9.—*Ovid. A. A.* 1.

CHAONI'TIS, a country of Assyria. *Strab.*

CHA'OS, a rude and shapeless mass of matter, and confused assemblage of inactive elements, which, as the poets suppose, existed before the formation of the world, and from which the universe was formed by the hand and power of a superior being. This doctrine was first maintained by Hesiod, from whom succeeding poets have copied it; and it is probable that it was obscurely drawn from the account of Moses, by being copied from the annals of Sanchoniathon, who is said to have lived antecedent to the siege of Troy. Chaos was deemed by some, one of the oldest of the gods, and invoked as one of the infernal deities. *Virg. Æn.* 4. v. 510.—*Ovid. Met.* 1. fab. 1.—*Lucret.* 5.—*Diod.* 1.—*Hesiod. Theog.*—*Euripid.*

CHAR'ACA, a place of Phrygia. *Strab.*

CHAR'ACE, a city of Chersonesus Taurica. The inhabitants were called Characeni. *Ptol.*

CHARA'DRA or **CHAR'ADRA**, a town of Phocis. *Herodot.* 8. c. 33.

CHAR'ADRUS, a river of Peloponnesus, flowing near Neris in Messenia. *Stat. Theb* 4. v. 46.—*Paus. Mess.*—*Steph.*——A town and river of Cilicia, in Asia Minor.——A river of Phocis, flowing near Charadra, and falling into the Cephisus. *Stat. Theb.* 4. v. 712.——A place at Argos, where military causes were tried. *Thucyd.* 5. c. 60.

CHARÆ'ADAS, an Athenian general, sent with twenty ships to Sicily during the Peloponnesian war. He died 426 B.C. *Thucyd.* 3. c. 86.

CHARANDÆ'I, a people of Asia, near Pontus. *Orpheus in Argon.*

CHARAN'DRA, a bay of the Arabian Sea, near Arsinoe. *Plin.* 6. c. 29.

CHARAU'NI, a people of Scythia *extra Imaum. Ptol.*

CHA'RAX, a town of Armenia.——A city of Asia, the capital of Characene, a province at the north of the Persian Gulph, between the Tigris and the Eulæus.

CHA'RAX, a philosopher of Pergamus, who wrote a history of Greece in forty books.

CHA'RAX, a town of Parthia.——A promontory of Crete.——A promontory of Caria, now Trallis. *Steph.*

CHARAX'ES or CHARAX'US, a Mitylenean, brother of Sappho, who became passionately fond of the courtezan Rhodope, upon whom he squandered all his possessions, and reduced himself to poverty, and to the necessity of supporting himself by piratical excursions. *Ovid. Heroid.* 15. v. 117.—*Herodot.* 2. c. 135, *&c.*

CHARAX'US, one of the Centaurs, who was present at the marriage of Pirithous, and also took part in the quarrels of that memorable day. He was attacked by Rhœtus, who struck his head with a burning brand, and set his hair on fire, so that he died in the most excruciating torments. *Ovid. Met.* 12. v. 272.

CHARBA'NUS, a mountain of Media. *Plin.* 6. c. 27.

CHA'RES, an Athenian general. He was for some time the friend and coadjutor of Demosthenes in the government of Athens, and spent the last years of his life at Sigæum. *C. Nepos.*——A statuary of Lindus, who was twelve years employed in making the famous Colossus at Rhodes. *Plin.* 34. c. 7. ——A man who wounded Cyrus when fighting against his brother Artaxerxes.——An historian of Mitylene, who wrote a life of Alexander the Great, quoted by *Plutarch*, *Athenæus*, and *A. Gellius.* ——An Athenian who fought with Darius against Alexander. *Curt.* 4. c. 5.——A river of Peloponnesus. *Plut. in Arat.*

CHARE'TES, a river of Peloponnesus, near Argias. *Plut. in Arat.*

CHARIAN'DER, an archon at Athens, Ol, 101. an. 1.

CHARIA'TA, a town of Arabia Felix. *Ptol.*

CHARIA'TUM or CARIA'TUM, a small town of Calabria.

CHAR'ICLES, one of the thirty tyrants set over Athens by the Lacedæmonians. *Xenoph. Memor.* 1.—*Arist.* 5. *Polit.* c. 6.——A famous physician under Tiberius. *Tacit. Ann.* 6. c. 50.

CHARICLI'DES, an officer of Dionysius the younger, whom Dion gained over to his party in his conspiracy to dethrone the tyrant. *Diod.* 16. ——An archon at Athens, Ol. 104. an. 2.

CHARICLI'TUS, an officer who had the command of the Rhodian fleet. *Liv.* 37. c. 23.

CHAR'ICLO or CHARI'CLO, the mother of Tiresias, greatly favoured by Minerva. *Apollod.* 3. c. 6.——A daughter of Apollo, who married the centaur Chiron, or, according to others, Sciron, and became mother of Endeis. *Plut. in Thes.*—*Ovid. Met.* 2. v. 635.

CHARIDE'MUM, a promontory of Hispania Tarraconensis.

CHARIDE'MUS, a Roman exposed to wild beasts. *Martial.* 1. epigr. 44.——An Athenian banished by Alexander, and killed by Darius.

CHARID'OTUS, a surname under which Mercury was worshipped among the people of Samus, because he was considered as heaping riches upon those whom he protected.

CHAR'ILA, a festival observed once in nine years by the people of Delphi. It owed its origin to this circumstance. In a great famine the Delphians assembled and applied to their king to relieve their wants. He accordingly distributed the little corn which he had, amongst the noblest of his subjects; but as a poor little girl, called Charila, requested relief of the king with more than common earnestness, he beat her with his shoe, and the girl, unable to bear his treatment, hanged herself in her girdle. The famine increased; and the oracle being consulted informed the king, that to relieve his people, he must atone for the murder of Charila. Upon this a festival was instituted with expiatory rites. The king presided over this institution, and distributed pulse and corn to such as attended. Charila's image was brought before the king, who struck it with his shoe; after which it was carried to a desolate place, where the people put a halter round its neck, and buried it near the spot where Charila was buried. *Plut. in Quæst. Græc.*

CHARILA'US or CHARIL'LUS, a son of Polydectes, king of Sparta, educated and protected by his uncle Lycurgus. He made war against Argos, and attacked the people of Tegea. He was taken prisoner, and released on promising that he would cease from war, an engagement which he soon after broke. He died in the 64th year of his age. *Paus.* 2. c. 36. l. 6. c. 48.——A Spartan who changed the monarchical power into an aristocracy. *Aristot. Polit.* 5. c. 12.——A man of Palæopolis, who betrayed his native city into the hand of Publ. Philo, the Roman general. *Liv.* 8. c. 25.

CHARIL'LUS, one of the ancestors of Leutichydes, at Lacedæmon. *Herodot.* 8. c. 131.

CHARIM'ENES, a Milesian, &c. *Polyæn.* 5. c. 42.

CHARIN'DA, a river of Media. *Ptol.*

CHARI'NI or CARI'NI, a people of Germany. *Plin.* 4. c. 14.

CHARIOP'OLIS, a city of Laconia.

CHAR'IPHRON, one of the mouths of the Indus. *Ptol.*

CHA'RIS, a goddess among the Greeks represented as surrounded with pleasures, graces, and delights, over which she presided. She was the wife of Vulcan. *Vid.* Charites. *Homer. Il.* 18. v. 382.

CHARIS'IA, a town of Arcadia. *Paus.* 8. c. 3.

CHARIS'IA, a festival in honour of the Graces, celebrated with dances which continued all night. He who continued awake the longest was rewarded with a cake.

CHARIS'IUS, an orator at Athens. *Cic. in B.* 83.

CHARIS'IUS FLA'VIUS SOSIP'ATER, a grammarian mentioned by *Priscian.* His *Institutiones* may be found in the Corp. Vet. Grammat. published by Putschius. *Sax. Onom.* 1. p. 48.—*Harles. Not. Lit. Rom.* 1, p. 755.

CHARISTAS or CHARIS'TUS, a river of Colchis, called Charus, by *Strabo*, and Charien by *Pliny*, 6. c. 4.

CHARIS'THA, a town of Arabia.

CHARIS'TIA, festivals at Rome, annually celebrated on the 20th of Feburary, with the intention of reconciling friends and relations. *Val. Max.* 2. c. 1.—*Ovid. Fast.* 2. v. 617.

CHAR'ITES (sing. *Charis*,) or GRATIÆ, the Graces, daughters of Venus by Jupiter or Bacchus, were three in number, Aglaia, Thalia, and Euphrosyne. They were the constant attendants of Venus, and were represented as three young, beautiful, and modest virgins, holding one another by the hand. They presided over kindness, and all the good offices of private and domestic life, and their worship was the same as that of the nine Muses, with whom they had a temple in common. They were generally represented naked, because kindnesses ought to be conferred with sincerity and candor. The moderns explain the allegory of their holding their hands joined, by observing that they ought to be a perpetual and never-ceasing intercourse of kindness and benevolence among friends. Their youth denotes the constant remembrance that we ought ever to have of kindnesses received; and their virgin purity and innocence teach us that acts of benevolence ought to be done without any expectations of a requital, and that we ought never to suffer others or ourselves to be guilty of base or dishonourable actions. Homer speaks only of two Graces, one of them he calls the wife of Vulcan, and the other Pasithae; and the Lacedæmonians also worshipped only two, Clita and Phænna. Eteocles of Orchomenus was the first who offered them sacrifices. The goddess of persuasion was placed in the number of the Graces by Hermesianax the poet. *Theocr. Id. in Ch.*—*Paus.* 9. c. 35. —*Hesiod. Th.* 64 & 907.—*Orpheus, Hymn.*—*Apollod.* 1.—*Hygin.* præf. fab —*Homer. Il.* 14.—*Servius in Æn.* 1. v. 724.—*Lastant. in Theb.* 1. v. 286.—*Nonnus Dionys.* 8.—*Euripid. in Herc. Fur.* 673.—*Horat.* 1. od. 30. v. 5.—*Seneca de Benef.* 1. c. 4. | *Phurnutus de Nat. D.* 15.—*Fulgent.* 2.—*Aul. Gell.* 13. c. 11.—*Macrob. Sat.* 1. c. 7.

CHAR'ITON, a writer of Aphrodisium, at the latter end of the fourth century. He composed a Greek romance, called "The Loves of Chæreas and Callirhoe," which has been much admired for its elegance, and the originality of the characters which it so beautifully describes. There is a very learned edition of Chariton, by D'Orville, 2 vols. 4to, Amsterdam, 1750. This edition has since been republished with additions by Beckius. Lips. 1783. *Fabr. B. Gr.* 5. c. 6.—*Sax. Onom.* 1. p. 473.——A mountain of Africa, in which the Cinyps rises. *Herodot*. 4. c. 175.

CHARIX'ENA, a poetess mentioned by *Aristophanes*.

CHARMA'DAS, a philosopher of uncommon memory. *Plin*. 7. c. 24.—*Cicer. Tuscul*. 1, &c.——A painter mentioned by *Pliny*, 35. c. 8.

CHAR'ME or CAR'ME, the mother of Britomartis by Jupiter. *Diod*. 5.

CHAR'MIDES, a Lacedæmonian, sent by his king to quell seditions in Cyprus. *Paus*. 3. c. 2.——A boxer. *Id*. 6. c. 7.——A writer of Massilia.

CHARMI'NUS, an Athenian general, who defeated the Peloponnesians. *Thucyd*. 8. c. 42.

CHARMI'ONE, a female attendant upon Cleopatra, who stabbed herself after the example of her mistress. *Plut. in Anton.*

CHAR'MIS, a physician of Marseilles, in Nero's age, who used cold baths for his patients, and prescribed medicines contrary to the practice of his contemporaries. *Plin*. 29. c. 1.

CHAR'MIS, a city of Sardinia, founded by the Carthaginians. *Steph.*

CHARMO'NIA or CAR'MON, a city of Spain. *Ptol.*

CHARMOS'YNA, a festival observed in Ægypt. *Plut. de Isid.*

CHAR'MOTAS, a poet of Syracuse. His compositions were collected by Clearchus the disciple of Aristotle, but only a few scattered fragments are to be found in Athenæus. *Gyrald. Poet. H*. 3.

CHA'RON, son of Pythocles, an historian of Lampsacus, according to *Dionysius*, wrote a history before Herodotus. *Suidas*, *Plutarch* and *Athenæus*, mention his two books, *De Rebus Persicis*, and *Suidas* mentions others of his works. He lived between the 75th and 79th Olympiads. *Strab*. 1. 12.—*Voss. Hist. Gr*. 1. c. 1, &c.——Junior, lived in the time of Ptolemy Evergetes, and explained the Argonautica of his friend Apollonius. *Apollon. Schol*. 1. 2.——A Theban, who secreted Pelopidas and his friends in his house, when they delivered Thebes from tyranny. *Plut. in Pelop.*——An historian of Naucratis, who wrote a history of his native city, and of Ægypt. *Voss. Hist. Gr*. 3. p. 342, &c.——A Carthaginian writer. *Suidas.*

CHA'RON, a god of hell, son of Erebus and Nox. He conducted the souls of the dead in a boat over the rivers Styx and Acheron to the infernal regions, and received for his trouble an obolus. Such as had not been honoured with a funeral were not permitted to enter his boat, without previously wandering on the opposite shore for one hundred years. If any living person presented himself to cross the Stygian lake, he could not be admitted before he shewed Charon a golden bough, which he had received from the Sibyl; and Charon was imprisoned for one year, because he had ferried over, against his own will, Hercules, without this passport. Charon is represented as a robust old man with a hideous countenance, long white beard, and piercing eyes. His garment is ragged and filthy, and his forehead is covered with wrinkles. As all the dead were obliged to pay a small piece of money for their admission into Charon's boat, it was always usual among the ancients to place, under the tongue of the deceased, an obolus to pay the ferryman. This fable of Charon and his boat is borrowed from the Ægyptians, whose dead were carried across a lake, where sentence was passed on them, and according to their good or bad actions, they were honoured with a splendid burial, or left unnoticed in the open air. *Vid*. Acherusia. *Diod*. 1.—*Senec. in Herc. Fur. act*. 3. v. 765.—*Virg. Æn*. 6. v. 298, &c., *& Servius loco.*

CHARON'DAS, a man of Catana, in Sicily, who was the legislator of the people of Thurium. He made a law that no man should be permitted to come armed into the public assembly. He inadvertently broke this law, and when told of it, fell upon his sword, B.C. 446. *Val. Max*. 6. c. 5. *Diogenes Laertius* makes him a pupil of Pythagoras.——An archon at Athens, Ol. 11. an. 3.

CHARONE'A, a place of Asia. *Strab*. l. 12.

CHARONE'A SCROBS, a place of Italy near Naples, emitting deadly vapours. *Plin*. 2. c. 93.

CHARONI'UM, a cave near Nysa, where the sick were supposed to be delivered from their disorders by certain superstitious solemnities. *Strab*. l. 12.

CHA'ROPS or CHARO'PUS, a Trojan killed by Ulysses. *Homer. Il.*

CHA'ROPS, a powerful Epirot, who assisted Flaminius when making war against Philip the king of Macedonia, and sent his son to Rome to finish his education. *Liv*. 32. c. 6 & 11. l. 43. c. 5.—*Plut. in Flam.*——The first decennial archon at Athens. *Paterc*. 1. c. 8.

CHARTE'JA or CARTHE'JA, a town of the island of Cea. *Plin*. 3. c. 1.

CHARYB'DIS, a dangerous whirlpool on the coast of Sicily, opposite Scylla, on the Italian shore. It was regarded as very dangerous to sailors, and proved fatal to part of the fleet of Ulysses. The exact situation of the Charybdis is not known to the moderns, as no whirlpool sufficiently tremendous is now found to correspond to the alarming descriptions of the ancients. The words

Incidit in Scyllam qui vult vitare Charybdim,

became a proverb, to shew, that in our eagerness to avoid one evil, we often fall into a greater. The name of Charybdis was properly bestowed on mistresses who repaid affection and tenderness with ingratitude. It is supposed that Charybdis was an avaricious woman, who stole the oxen of Hercules, for which theft she was struck with thunder by Jupiter, and changed into a whirlpool. A signal tower, or Pharos, was erected near this dangerous place, which now bears the name of the Pharos of Messina. *Lycophr. in Cass. & Tzetzes in Lyc*. 45 & 248.—*Homer. Odyss*. 12.—*Propert*. 3. el. 11.—*Ital*. 14.—*Ovid in Ibin. De Ponto*. 4. el. 10. *Amor*. 2. el. 16.—*Virg. Æn*. 3. v. 420. *& Servius ibid.*

CHASUA'RII, or Casuarii, according to *Ptolemy*, or Chatuarii, according to *Strabo*, a people of Germany. *Cluver*. 3. c. 3.

CHAU'BI, a people of Germany. *Strab*. 7.

CHAU'CI according to *Pliny & Tacitus*, Cauchi or Cauci, according to *Ptolemy & Strabo*, a people of Germany. They are supposed to have inhabited the country, now called Friesland and Bremen. *Claud. de Laud. Stilich*. 1. v. 225.

CHAU'LA, a small town of Ægypt. *Strab*. 16.

CHAUM, a mountain of Argolis. *Paus*. 5.

CHAU'NI, a people of Thesprotia. *Steph.*

CHAU'RUS. *Vid*. Caurus.

CHE'LÆ, a Greek word (χηλή) signifying *claws*, which is applied to the Scorpion, one of the twelve signs of the zodiac, and lies, according to the ancients, contiguous to Virgo. *Virg. G*. 1. v. 33.——A place between the island of Apollonia and the river Sangarius. *Arrian.*

CHE'LES, a Satrap of Seleucus. *Polyæn*. 7. c. 30.

CHELI'DON, a mistress of Verres, the Sicilian quæstor. *Cic. in Verr*. 1. c. 40. Also Chel'idon.

CHELIDO'NI, a people of Illyria. *Steph.*

CHELIDO'NIA, a festival at Rhodes, in which it was customary for boys to go begging from door to door, singing certain songs. *Athen.*——A name of the wind Favonius, from the sixth of the ides of February to the seventh of the calends of March, the time when swallows first made their appearance. *Plin*. 2. c. 47.

CHELIDO'NIÆ, now Kelidoni, small islands in the Mediterranean, near the shores of Asia Minor, opposite the promontory of mount Taurus, very dangerous to sailors. *Dionys. Perieg*. v. 506.—*Plin*. 5. c. 27 & 31.—*Liv*. 33. c. 41.

CHELIDO'NIS, a daughter of king Leotychides, who married Cleonymus, and disgraced herself by her adulterous intrigues with Acrotatus. *Plut. in Pyrr.* Also Chelid'onis.

CHELIDONI'UM, a promontory of mount Taurus, projecting into the Mediterranean at the west of the Pamphylian Sea. *Plin*. 5 c 27.

CHELONA'TES or CHELONI'TES, a promontory and town of Peloponnesus. *Ptol*.—*Paus*. l. 1.

CHELO'NE, a nymph changed into a tortoise by Mercury, for not being present at the nuptials of Jupiter and Juno. Her house was on the side of a river; and the god, in precipitating her into the stream, added to her punishment by making her always carry her habitation with her; as she had derided the majesty of the father of the gods, she was condemned to perpetual silence, of which the tortoise became the emblem. *Servius in Æn*. 1. v. 509.

CHELO'NE, a promontory of Cos. *Paus*. 8.

CHELO'NIS, a daughter of Leonidas, king of Sparta, who married Cleombrotus. She accompanied her father, whom her husband had expelled, and soon after went into banishment with her husband, who had, in his turn, been expelled by Leonidas. *Plut. in Algid. & Cleom.*

CHELONOPH'AGI, a people of Carmania, in Asia, near the Indian Ocean, who fed upon tortoises, and covered their habitations with the shells of that animal. *Plin.* 6. c. 24.—*Strabo*, however, places them on the shores of the Sinus Arabicus, as do also *Agatharcides* and *Diodorus*. Probably there were people so called in both these places.

CHELYDO'NIUS, a mountain of Arcadia, near mount Cellenius. *Paus. in Arcad.*

CHELYDO'REUS, a mountain of Bœotia. *Paus. in Bœot.*

CHEM'MIS, an island in a deep lake in Ægypt. *Herodot.* 2. c. 156.

CHE'NA, a town of Laconia. *Steph.—Diod.*

CHE'NÆ, a village on mount Œta. *Paus.* 10. c. 24.

CHE'NIUS, a mountain near Colchis. *Diod.* 14

CHE'OPS or CHEOS'PES, a king of Ægypt, after Rhampsinitus, who built some remarkable pyramids. One thousand and sixty talents were expended during their construction, in supplying the workmen with leeks, parsley, garlick, and other vegetables. *Herodot.* 2. c. 124.

CHE'PHREN, a brother of Cheops, who also built a pyramid. The Ægyptians hated these two royal brothers so inveterately, that they publicly reported that the pyramids which they had built, had been erected by a shepherd. *Herodot.* 2. c. 127.

CHEP'TA, a river of Asia. *Plin.* 6. c. 17.

CHEREMOC'RATES, an artist, who built Diana's temple at Ephesus. *Strab.* 14.

CHE'RIAS, an athlete, slain by Hercules.——An Athenian physician. *Plin.*

CHERIS'OPHUS, a commander of 800 Spartans in the expedition which Cyrus undertook against his brother Artaxerxes. *Diod.* 14.

CHE'RON, son of Apollo and Thero, gave his name to Cheronæa. *Paus.* 9. c. 40.

CHERONÆ'A. *Vid.* Chæronea.

CHERRONE'SUS. *Vid.* Chersonesus.

CHERSE'US, a river of Phœnicia.

CHER'SIAS, an Orchomenian, reconciled to Periander upon the intercession of Chilo. *Pausanias*, 9. c. 38. praises some of his poetry. It is said that he wrote the epitaph on the tomb of Hesiod.

CHERSID'AMAS, a Trojan killed by Ulysses in the Trojan war. *Ovid. Met.* 13. v. 259.

CHER'SIPHRON, an architect, whose abilities were employed in the construction of Diana's temple at Ephesus. *Plin.* 36. c. 14. Also Ctesiphon,

CHERSONE'SUS, a Greek word, rendered by the Latins *peninsula*. Several are mentioned by the ancients, of which these five are the most celebrated; one called Peloponnesus; another called Thracian, at the south of Thrace, and west of the Hellespont, to which Miltiades led a colony of Athenians, and built a wall across the isthmus. From the isthmus to its further shores, it measured 420 stadia, extending between the bay of Melas and the Hellespont. The third, called Taurica, now Crim Tartary, was situate near the Palus Mæotis. The fourth, called Cimbrica, now Jutland, is in the northern parts of Germany; and the fifth, surnamed Aurea, lies in India beyond the Ganges. *Herodot.* 6. c. 33. l. 7. c. 58.—*Liv.* 31. c. 16.—*Cic. ad Br.* 2.——A city near Alexandria in Ægypt. *Hist. Alex.* 10.——A city of Spain. ——A city of the Taurica Chersonesus.——A city of Crete, now Chirroniso.——A city of Marmarica, on the sea coast, on the borders of Cyrenaica.

CHERUS'CI, a people of Germany, who long maintained an obstinate war against Rome. They inhabited the country between the Weser and the Elbe. *Tacit.—Cæs. B. G.* 6. c. 9.

CHESI'NUS or CHESSI'NUS, a river of European Sarmatia, now Lowat. *Cluver.*

CHE'SIUS, a river of Samus. *Plin.* 5. c. 31.

CHETÆ'US, a place of Ægypt, near Canopus. *Procop.*

CHETTÆ'A, a town of Marmarica in Africa. *Ptol.*

CHIDNÆ'I, a people near Pontus. *Orpheus in Argonaut.*

CHIDO'RUS, a river of Macedonia which falls into the Sinus Thermaicus, near Thessalonica. It was said not to have been sufficiently large to supply the army of Xerxes with water. *Herodot.* 7. c. 127.

CHILIAR'CHUS, a great officer of state at the court of Persia. *C. Nep. in Conon.* 3.

CHIL'IUS or CHIL'EUS, an Arcadian, who advised the Lacedæmonions, when Greece was invaded by Xerxes, not to desert the common cause of their country. *Herodot.* 9. c. 9.—*Polyæn.* 5. c. 30.

CHI'LO, a Spartan philosopher, son of Damagetus. He was called one of the seven wise men of Greece, and distinguished himself not only by the delivery of excellent moral precepts, but by a temperate and exemplary life. He was concise in his manner of speaking, whence the epithet Chilonian is applied to short, laconic expressions. The elegies which he wrote did not amount to 200 verses; and none of his works are extant beside his moral sentences, and a letter to Periander, preserved by Diogenes Laertius. Three of his maxims, as conveying the purest morality, were inscribed in golden letters in the temple at Delphi, and fully deserved immortality. They were, Know thyself;—Desire nothing too much;—and Misery is the sure companion of debt and strife. He died through excess of joy, in the arms of his son, who had obtained a victory at Olympia, B.C. 597; and the crowded assembly which assisted at the celebration, honoured the memory of the philosopher by attending his funeral. *Laert.* 1. c. 72.—*A. Gell.* 1. c. 3.—*Ausonius, Lud. Sept. Sap.*—*Plin.* 7. c. 33. ——A grammarian, the slave of Cato.

CHILO'NIS, the wife of Theopompus king of Sparta. *Polyæn.* 8. c. 34.

CHIMÆ'RA, a celebrated monster, sprung from Echidna and Typhon. It was represented as having three heads, those of a lion, a goat, and a dragon. It generally lived in Lycia, about the reign of Jobates, by whose orders Bellerophon, mounted on the horse Pegasus, attacked and overcame it. This fabulous tradition is explained by the recollection that there was a burning mountain in Lycia, called Chimæra, the top of which was the resort of lions, on account of its desolate wilderness; the middle, which was fruitful, was covered with goats; and at the bottom, the marshy ground abounded with serpents. Bellerophon is said to have conquered the Chimæra, because he first fixed his habitation on that mountain. *Plutarch* says, that the fable derived its origin from the captain of some pirates, who adorned his ship with the images of a lion, a goat, and a dragon. From the union of the Chimæra with Orthos sprang the Sphinx and the lion of Nemæa. *Homer. Il.* 6. v. 181.—*Solin.* 42.—*Plin.* 2. c. 109. l. 5. c. 27.—*Hesiod. Theog.* v. 322.—*Apollod.* 1. c. 9. l. 2. c. 3.—*Lucret.* 5. v. 903.—*Ovid.* 9. *Met.* v. 646.—*Trist.* 4. el. 7. v. 13. *Fast.* 2. v. 397.—*Virg. Æn.* 5. v. 118. l. 6. v, 288. & *Servius in. Æn. locis. cit.*

CHIMÆ'RA, a town of Chaonia in Epirus, at the south of the Acroceraunian mountains.——A town of Sicily. *Steph.*

CHIM'ARUS, a river of Argolis. *Paus.* 2. c. 36.

CHIME'RIUM, a mountain of Phthiotis in Thessaly. It is placed by some authors in Thesprotia, opposite the island of Corcyra. *Steph.—Plin.* 4. c. 8.

CHIN'NA, a city of Dalmatia. *Ptol.*

CHIOM'ARA, a woman who cut off the head of a Roman tribune when she had been taken prisoner. *Plut. de Virt. Mul.*

CHI'ON, a Greek writer, whose epistles were edited *cum notis* Cobergi, 8vo, Leipsic, 1765. *Vid.* Theognis.——An Archon at Athens. Ol. 103. an. 4.

CHI'ONE, a daughter of Dædalion, of whom Apollo and Mercury became enamoured. From her intercourse with the gods, Chione became mother of Philammon and Autolycus, the former of whom, as being the son of Apollo, became an excellent musician; and the latter was equally notorious for his robberies, of which his father Mercury was the patron. Chione grew so proud of her commerce with the gods, that she presumed to prefer her personal charms to those of Diana, for which impiety she was killed by the goddess, and changed into a hawk. *Ovid. Met.* 11. fab. 8.—*Hygin.* fab. 200.——A daughter of Boreas and Orithyia, who became mother of Eumolpus by Neptune. She threw her son into the sea, but he was preserved by his father. *Apollod.* 3. c. 15.—*Paus.* 1. c. 38. ——A noted prostitute. *Martial*, 3. epigr. 34.—*Juven.* 3. 136.

CHION'IDES, an Athenian poet, supposed by some to have been the inventor of comedy. *Fabr. B. Gr.* l. 2. c. 22.—*Voss. de Poet. Gr.*

CHI'ONIS, a victor at Olympia. *Paus.* 6. c. 13.

CHIONI'TÆ, a nation near Persia. *Amm. Marcell.*

CHIROC'RATES. *Vid.* Dinocrates.

CHIROGO'NIA, a surname of Proserpine. *Hesych.*

CHI'RON, a centaur, son of Phillyra and Saturn, who had changed himself into a horse to escape the inquiries of his wife Rhea. Chiron was famous for his knowledge of music, medicine, and shooting. He taught mankind the use of plants and medicinal herbs; and he instructed in all the polite arts the greatest heroes of his age; such as Achilles, Æsculapius, Jason, Peleus, Æneas, &c. He was wounded in the knee by a poisoned arrow, by Hercules, in the dreadful fight between the Lapithæ and the centaurs. Hercules ran to his assistance; but as the wound was incurable, and the cause of the most excruciating pains, Chiron begged Jupiter to deprive him of immortality. His prayers were heard, and he was placed by the god among the constellations, under the name of Sagittarius. *Hesiod. in Scuto.—Homer. Il.* 11.—*Paus.* 3, c. 18. l. 5. c. 19. l. 9. c. 31.—*Ovid. Met.* 2. v. 676.—*Apollod.* 2. c. 5. l. 3. c. 13.—*Horat. epod.* 13.—*Seneca in Thyest.—Catull.* 65.

CHITO'NE or CHITO'NIA, a name of Diana. *Steph.*

CHI'US, now Scio, an island in the Ægean sea, between Lesbus and Samus, on the coast of Asia Minor, which received its name, as some suppose, from Chione, or from χιών, *snow*, which was very frequent there. This land was well inhabited, and could once equip a hundred ships; and its chief town, called Chius, had a beautiful harbour capable of containing 80 ships. The wine of this island, so much celebrated by the ancients, is still in general esteem. Chius was anciently called Æthalia, Macris, and Pityusa. The inhabitants were so correct in their morals, that there was no adultery committed among them for the space of 700 years. *Plut. de Virt. Mul.—Horat.* 3. od. 19. v. 5. l. sat. 10. v. 24.—*Paus.* 7. c. 4.—*Mela,* 2. c. 2.—*Strab.* 2.—*Plin.* 36. c. 16.—*Ptol.* 5. c. 2.—*Athen.* 1. c. 4. Also written Chios.

CHLO'E, a surname of Ceres at Athens. Her yearly festivals, called Chloea, were celebrated with much mirth and rejoicing, and a ram was always sacrificed to her. The name Chloe is supposed to bear the same signification as *Flava,* so often applied to the goddess of corn. It has, from its signification, (χλόη, *herba virens*) being generally applied to women whose personal charms were rendered more attractive by the innocence and simplicity of their manners. *Paus.* 1. c. 22.—*Meursius, Gr. Fer.*

CHLO'REUS, a priest of Cybele, who came with Æneas into Italy, and was killed by Turnus. *Virg. Æn.* 11. v. 768. l. 12. v. 363.

CHLO'RIS, the goddess of flowers, who married Zephyrus. She is the same as Flora. *Ovid. Fast.* 5.——A daughter of Amphion, son of Jasus and Persephone, who married Neleus king of Pylus, by whom she had one daughter and twelve sons, who were all, except Nestor, killed by Hercules. *Homer. Odyss.* 11. v. 280. *& Scholiast in loco.—Diod.* 4.—*Paus.* 2. c. 21. l. 9. c. 36. It is to be observed, that Chloris is called the youngest of Amphion's children by *Homer*, and the eldest by *Apollodorus;* but the apparent contradiction is removed by the recollection that the latter writer has confounded Amphion son of Jupiter, with the Amphion of Orchomenus, two persons who have been carefully distinguished by Homer.——A prostitute, &c. *Horat.* 3. od. 15.

CHLO'RUS, a river of Cilicia. *Plin.* 5. c. 27.

CHLO'RUS CON'STANTINE, one of the Cæsars in Diocletian's age, who reigned two years after the emperor's abdication, and died July 25, A.D. 306.

CHO'ANA, a city of Media.——A city of Parthia.——A city of Bactriana. *Ptol.*

CHO'AR, the 16th king of the Sicyonians, reigned 30 years.

CHOARAX'ES, the boundary between Colchis and Armenia. *Strab.*

CHOARI'NA, a country near India, reduced by Craterus. *Strab.* 15.

CHOAS'PA, a city of Arachosia *Ptol.*

CHOASPES, a son of the Phasis. *Flacc.* 5. v. 585.

CHOAS'PES, an Indian river, one of the western branches of the Indus. *Curt.* 5. c. 2.——A river of Media, flowing into the Persian Gulph, a little at the east of the mouths of the Euphrates, and now called Karun. Its waters were so sweet that the kings of Persia drank no other; and in their expeditions always had some with them, which had been previously boiled. *Herodot.* 1. c. 188.—*Ælian. V. H.* 12. c. 40.—*Tibull.* 4. el. 1. v. 141.—*Plin.* 6. c. 37.

CHOAS'TES, a general of the Choatræ. *Flacc. Argon.* 6. v. 155.

CHO'ATRAS, a mountain of Asia; the inhabitants of the neighbourhood were called Choatræ. *Plin.* 5. c. 27.

CHO'BUS, a river of Colchis. *Arrian.—Plin.* 6. c. 4.

CHOD'DA, a city of Carmania. *Ptol.*

CHŒR'ADES and PHAROS, two islands opposite Alexandria in Ægypt. *Plin.*——Islands in the Euxine Sea. *Theocr. Id.* 13.——Islands in the Ionian Sea, near the promontory of Japygium, according to *Thucydides*, 7. c. 33.

CHŒR'ILUS, a tragic poet of Athens, who is said to have written 150 tragedies, of which only 13 obtained the prize. Of all these only the title of one, Alope, is preserved, a subject which also engaged the pen of Euripides and of Carcinus, but their compositions are lost. *Fabr. B. Gr.* 2. c. 19.—*Suidas.*——A poet of Samus, very intimate with Herodotus. He wrote a poem on the victory which the Athenians had obtained over Xerxes, and, on account of the excellence of the composition, he received a piece of gold for each verse from the Athenians, and was publicly ranked with Homer as a poet. The reward, though great, does not appear too extravagant, if we may judge from the elegant lines preserved by *Aristotle* in his *Rhetor.* and by *Josephus contra Apion. Gyrald. de P, Hist.* 3.—*Fabr. Ibid.*——One of Alexander's flatterers and friends. It is said that the prince promised him as many pieces of gold as there should be good verses in his poetry, and as many slaps on the forehead as there were bad; and that upon trial, scarcely six of his verses in each poem were entitled to the gold, while the rest were rewarded with the castigation. *Plut. in Alex.—Horat.* 2. ep. 1. v. 232.—*Curt.* 8. c. 5.—A sculptor of Olynthus. *Paus.* 6. c. 17.——An historian of the deeds of Lysander. *Plut. in vit. Lysandr.*

CHOLÆ'BUS, a tyrant of the Mapharitæ, a nation near the Euphrates. *Arrian. Peripl.*

CHOLIM'MA, a city of Armenia Major. *Ptol.*

CHOL'LE, a town of Palmyrene. *Id.*

CHOLMAD'ARA, a town near the Euphrates. *Id.*

CHOLOBETE'NE, a part of Armenia, of which Tigranes was præfect. *Steph.*

CHOL'OE, a town of the Galatian Pontus, in Cappadocia. *Ptol.*

CHOL'UA, the name of two cities in Armenia Major. *Id.*

CHO'MA, a city of Lycia. *Id.*

CHOMA'RI, a people near Bactriana. *Plin.* 6. c. 16.—*Ptol.*

CHOMP'SO, an island in the Nile, between Æthiopia and Ægypt. *Herodot.—Steph.*

CHON, the Ægyptian name of Hercules. *Steph.*

CHO'NE, a city of the Œnotri. *Aristot, Polit.* 7. c. 10.—*Strab.* 7. *Hesychius* says that it was the ancient name of Italy.

CHO'NIA or CHO'NIS, a town of Calabria. *Strab.*

CHON'NIDAS, a man appointed preceptor to Theseus, by his grandfather Pittheus king of Trœzene. The Athenians rewarded the good precepts which he had instilled into his pupil, by offering him a yearly sacrifice of a ram; from which circumstance arose the proverb of κριὸς τεῦφειὰ ἀπέτισεν, the ram has paid for the deucation. *Plut. in Thes.*

CHONDOMA'RIUS, a king of the Alemani, taken by Julian, in the reign of Constantius. *Amm. Marcell.* 16.

CHONU'PHIS, an Ægyptian prophet. *Plut. de Socrat. Gen.*

CHORAS'MI, a people of Asia, near the Oxus, at the east of the Caspian Sea. *Herodot.* 3. c. 93.

CHO'RAX, the 15th king of Sicyon.

CHORDIRAX'A a city of Mesopotamia. *Strab.*

CHORIEN'SIS PE'TRA, called by *Curtius* Dotinis,

a rock situated in the country of the Paratacæ, in India. *Arrian.*

CHORINE'US, a man killed in the Rutulian war. *Virg. Æn.* 9. v. 571. 12. v. 298.

CHOROD'NA, a city of Persis. *Ptol.*

CHORŒ'BUS, a man of Elis, who obtained a prize in the first Olympiad. *Vid.* Corœbus.——A youth of Mygdonia, who was enamoured of Cassandra. He perished during the Trojan war. *Virg. Æn.* 2. v. 341.——A man, who voluntarily devoted himself to death to free his native country, Thebes, from a pestilence. *Stat. Theb.* 2. v. 221. l. 6. v. 286.

CHOROMAN'DÆ, a disgusting people mentioned by *Pliny*, 7. c. 2.

CHOROMITHRE'NE, a region of Media. *Ptol.*

CHOROMNÆ'I, a people of Asia subdued by Ninus. *Diod.* 1.

CHOR'SA, a city of Armenia Major. *Ptol.*

CHOR'SIA, a town of Bœotia. *Paus.* 9.

CHORTAC'ANA, a city of Asia, taken by Alexander. *Diod. Sic.* 17.

CHORTA'ZO, a city of Ægypt.

CHORZE'NE, a region of Armenia Major. *Strab.*

CHORZIA'NI, a nation of Asia, near Persis. *Procop.*

CHOS'ROES, the name of two kings of Persia.

CHRE'MES, a sordid old man, mentioned in *Terence's Andria. Horat. in Art.* v. 94.——An archon at Athens, Ol. 113. an. 2.

CHREM'ETES, a river of Libya. *Aristot. in Meteor. &c.*

CHREMON'IDES, a naval commander of Ptolemy, conquered by Agathostratus the Rhodian. *Polyæn.* 5. c. 18

CHREN'DI, a nation of Hyrcania. *Ptol.*

CHRESPHON'TES, a son of Aristomachus. *Vid.* Aristodemus.

CHRES'TUS, an approved writer of Athens. *Colum.* 1. *de R. R.* c. 1.——A man who encouraged the Jews to make disturbances at Rome in the reign of Claudius, which was the cause of their expulsion from the city. *Suet. Cl.* 25.

CHRETI'NA, a city of Lusitania. *Ptol.*

CHRISTUS, the name of our blessed Saviour, derived from a Greek word signifying annointed. The heathen historians have repeatedly mentioned Him and the character of his religion. His followers were first called Christians at Antioch, A.D. 40, and the appellation then seemed to convey more of reproach than respectability. *Plin.* 10. ep. 97.—*Acts*, 11. v. 26.—*Sueton.*—*Tacit. Ann.*

CHRO'MIA, the daughter of Itonus, was, according to some, wife of Endymion, king of Elis. *Paus.* 5. c. 1.

CHRO'MII, mountains of Peloponnesus, in which the Asopus rises. *Steph.*

CHRO'MIOS, a son of Neleus and Chloris, who, with ten brothers, was killed in a battle by Hercules.——A son of Priam, killed by Diomedes. *Apollod* 3. c. 12.

CHRO'MIS, a leader of the Mysians in the Trojan war. *Homer Il.* 2. v. 365.——A young shepherd. *Virg. Ecl.* 6.——A Phrygian killed in Italy by Camilla. *Id. Æn.* 11. v. 675.——A son of Hercules. *Stat.* 6. v. 346.——One of the Centaurs killed by Pirithous. *Ovid Met.* 12. v. 333.——One of those who opposed the nuptials of Perseus and Andromeda. He killed Æmathion, respectable for his years as well as his virtues. *Id.* 5. v. 100.

CHRO'MIUS, a son of Pterilaus. *Apollod.* 2. c. 4.——An Argive, who, with Alcenor, survived a battle fought between 300 of his countrymen and 300 Spartans. *Herodot.* 1. c. 82.

CHRO'NIUM MA'RE, part of the Frozen Ocean. *Plin.* 4. c. 16.

CHRO'NIUS, a man who built a temple in honour of Diana at Orchomenus. *Paus.* 8. c. 48.

CHRO'NUS, the Greek name of Saturn or time, in whose honour festivals called Chronia were yearly celebrated by the Rhodians and some of the Greeks.

CHRY'ASUS, a king of Argos, descended from Inachus.

CHRY'SA or CHRY'SE, a town of Cilicia, famous for a temple of Apollo Smintheus, and equally known for being the birth place of Chryseis the wife of Eetion. *Homer. Il.* 1. v. 37 & 431.—*Strab.* 13.—*Ovid. Met.* 13. v. 174.

CHRY'SA, a daughter of Halmus, mother of Phlegias by Mars. *Paus.* 9. c. 36.

CHRY'SÆ FA'NUM, a place of Sicily, between Euna and Assorus.

CHRYSAMAX'US, a Laconian, victor at Olympia.

CHRYS'AME, a Thessalian, priestess of Diana Trivia. She fed a bull with poison, which she sent to the enemies of her country, who, after eating the flesh, became delirious, and were an easy conquest. *Polyæn.* 8. 43.

CHRYSAN'TAS, an officer in the army of Cyrus, who refrained from killing another, upon hearing the sudden barking of a dog. *Plut. Quæst. Rom.*

CHRYSAN'THIUS, a philosopher in the age of Julian, known for the great number of volumes which he wrote.

CHRYSAN'TIS, a nymph who told Ceres, when she was at Argos with Pelasgus, that her daughter had been carried away. *Paus.* 1. c. 14.

CHRYSA'OR, a son of Medusa by Neptune. Some report, that he sprang from the blood of Medusa, armed with a *golden sword*, whence his name. χρυσὸς ἄορ. He married Callirhoe, one of the Oceanides, by whom he had Geryon, Echidna, and the Chimæra. *Hesiod. Theog.* v. 295.——A rich king of Iberia. *Diod.* 4.——A son of Glaucus, from whom the town of Stratonice received the name Chrysaoris. *Steph. Byz.*—*Paus.* 5. c. 21.

CHRYSA'OREUS, a surname of Jupiter, from his temple at Stratonice, where all the Carians assembled upon any public emergency. *Strab.* 4.

CHRYSA'ORIS, a town of Caria, the same as Stratonice. *Paus.* 5. c. 21.

CHRYSA'ORUS, a river of Libya. *Steph.*

CHRY'SAS, a river of Sicily, which fell into the Simæthus at the east of the island. It was worshipped as a deity. *Cic. in Verr.* 4. c. 44.

CHRY'SE, an island and bay of the Eastern Ocean. *Ptol.*—*Steph.*

CHRYSE'I, a nation of India. *Ptol.*

CHRYSE'IS, the daughter of Chryses. *Vid.* Chryses.

CHRYSER'MUS, a Corinthian, who wrote a history of Peloponnesus, and of India, besides a treatise on rivers. *Plut. in Parall.*

CHRYS'ERUS or CHRYS'ORUS, a Greek historian, who compiled a list of the consuls from the expulsion of the kings. *Theoph. Antioch.* 3.

CHRY'SES, the priest of Apollo, father of Astynome, called from him Chryseis. When Lyrnessus was taken by the Greeks, and the spoils divided among the conquerors, Chryseis, who was the wife of Eetion, the sovereign of the place, fell to the share of Agamemnon. Chryses, upon this, went to the Grecian camp to solicit his daughter's restoration; and when his entreaties were scornfully rejected by Agamemnon, he implored the aid of Apollo, who visited the Greeks with a plague, and obliged them to restore Chryseis. It is with this pathetic story that the Iliad opens, and the manner in which Agamemnon resents the restitution and provokes the indignation and enmity of Achilles, gives an interest to the poem, and produces the dreadful catastrophe which decides the fate of Troy. *Homer. Il.* 1. v. 11, &c.—*Eustath. in Homer.*—*Tzetzes in Chil.* 8. *Hist.* 175.——A daughter of Minos. *Apollod.* 3. c. 1.

CHRYSIP'PA, a city of Cilicia, founded by Chrysippus. *Steph.*

CHRYSIP'PE, a daughter of Danaus. *Apollod.* 2. c. 1.

CHRYSIP'PUS, a natural son of Pelops, so highly favoured by his father, that Hippodamia, his stepmother, urged by jealousy, ordered her own sons, Atreus and Thyestes, to kill him, and to throw his body into a well, for which atrocious action they were banished. Some say that Hippodamia's sons refused to murder Chrysippus, and that she imbrued her own hands in his blood. *Plut. in Parall.*—*Hygin.* fab. 85.—*Plato de Leg.* 6.—*Apollod.* 3. c. 5.—*Paus.* 6. c. 20.——A stoic philosopher of Tarsus, or Soli, in Cilicia, who wrote about 311 treatises on various subjects. He died 207 B.C. in the 80th year of his age, through excess of wine, or, as others say, from laughing too much on seeing an ass eating figs out of a silver plate. Though very learned, yet he was absurd and ridiculous in his conduct and opinions, and he may be reckoned in the number of those ancient philosophers who upheld science, but did not adorn it with new discoveries, or more rapid advances towards perfection and correctness. *Val. Max.* 8. c. 7.—*Diog.*—*Horat.* 2. sat. 3, v. 40.—*Fabr. B. Gr.* 1.3. c. 10.—*Sax. Onom.* 1. p. 111.——A freedman of Cicero, reduced again to servitude in consequence of his improper conduct. *Cic. ad Att.* 7. ep. 2. l. 11. ep. 2. There were several other persons of this name. *Plin.* 26. c. 2. *Voss. Hist. Gr.* 1. c. 17, &c.

CHRY'SIS, a mistress of Demetrius. *Plut. in Demet.*——A priestess of Juno at Mycenæ. The temple of the goddess was burnt by the negligence of Chrysis, who fled to Phlius. *Paus.* 2. c. 17.—*Plut.*—*Thucyd.* 4. 133.——A courtezan introduced in *Terence's* plays.

CHRYSI'TES, a place of of Macedonia. *Liv.*

CHRYS'IUS, a river of Hispania Tarraconensis. ——A river of Dacia.

CHRYSOA'NA, a city of India without the Ganges. *Ptol.*

CHRYSOAS'PIDES, soldiers in the armies of Persia, whose arms were covered gold, to display the opulence of the prince whom they served, whence the name. *Justin.* 12. c. 7.

CHRYSOC'ERAS, a promontory of Thrace. on the Bosporus. *Plin.* 4. c. 11.

CHRYSOG'ONUS, a freedman of Sylla. *Cic. pro Ros.*——A celebrated singer in Domitian's reign. *Juv.* 6. v. 74.

CHRYSOLA'US, a tyrant of Methymna, &c. *Curt.* 4. c. 8.

CHRYSON'DIUM, a town of Macedonia. *Polyb.* 5.

CHRYSOP'OLIS, a promontory and port of Asia, opposite Byzantium, now Scutari. *Steph.*——A city of Cilicia. *Id.*

CHRY'SOR, the name of Vulcan, according to Sanchoniathon. *Euseb. prep. Evang.* 1.

CHRYSOR'RHAPIS, an epithet of Mercury.

CHRYSOR'RHOÆ, a people in whose country were golden streams. *Strab.*

CHRYSOR'RHOAS, a river of Peloponnesus. *Paus.* 2. c. 31.——A river of Syria, the Hebrew Pharpar. ——A river of Bithynia.——A river of Cappadocia.

CHRYSOS'TOMUS, a celebrated bishop of Constantinople, who died A.D. 407, in his 53rd year. He was a great disciplinarian, and by severely lashing the vices of his age, he procured himself many enemies. After having displayed his abilities as an elegant preacher, a sound theologian, and a faithful interpreter of scripture, he was banished for opposing the raising of a statue in honour of the empress Eudoxia, the wife of Arcadius. Chrysostom's works were nobly and correctly edited, without a Latin version, by Saville, 8 vols. fol. Etonæ, 1613. They have appeared, with a translation at Paris, edit. Benedict. Montfaucon, 13 vols. fol. 1718. *Fabr. B. G.* 5. c. 11.

CHRYSOTH'EMIS, a name which is given by *Homer* to Iphigenia, daughter of Agamemnon and Clytæmnestra. *Il.* 9. v. 145.——A Cretan, who first obtained the poetical prize at the Pythian games. *Paus.* 10. c. 7.

CHRY'SUM, one of the mouths of the Indus. *Ptol.*

CHRY'SUS, a river of Hispania Bætica.

CHRYX'US, a leader of the Boii, the grandson of Brennus, who took Rome. *Sil.* 4. v. 148.

CHTHO'NIA, a daughter of Erechtheus, who married Butes. *Apollod.* 3. c. 15.——A surname of Ceres, from a temple built to her honour by Chthonia, at Hermione. She had a festival there, called by the same name, and celebrated every summer. During the celebration, the priests of the goddess marched in solemn procession, accompanied by the magistrates, and a crowd of women and boys in white apparel, with garlands of flowers on their heads. Behind the procession an untamed heifer, just taken from the herd, was dragged. When they came to the temple, the victim was let loose, and four old women armed with scythes, sacrificed the heifer, and killed her by cutting her throat. A second, a third, and a fourth victim were in a like manner dispatched by the old women; and it was observable that they all fell on the same side. *Paus.* 2. c. 35.

CHTHO'NIA, a name of the island of Crete. *Steph.*

CHTHO'NIUS, a centaur killed by Nestor at the nuptials of Pirithous. *Ovid. Met.* 12. v. 441.——One of the soldiers who sprang from the dragon's teeth sown by Cadmus. *Hygin.* fab. 178.——A son of Ægyptus and Caliadne. *Apollod.* 2. c. 1.

CHTHO'NIUS, a name of the island of Crete. *Steph.*

CHUDU'CA, a city of Babylonia. *Ptol.*

CHU'NI, a people of Sarmatia. *Ptol.*—*Auson.* ep 1. v. 8.

CHURI'TÆ, a nation in the interior of Libya.

CHUSA'RIS, a river of Libya. *Ptol.*

CHUSISTA'NIA, a province of Persia.

CHU'TA, a region of Persia. The inhabitants were called Chutæi. *Joseph. Jud. Ant.* 9.—2 *Kings*, 17. v. 25.

CHU'ZIS, a city of Africa Propria. *Ptol.*

CHY'DAS, a small river at the north of Sicily, called by *Diodorus* Chrysa.

CHYRET'IÆ, a city of Macedonia. *Ptol.*

CHY'TOS, a harbour of Cyzicus. *Apollon. Scholiast.*

CHY'TRI or CHY'TRUS, a city of Cyprus *Steph.* —*Plin.* 5. c. 31.

CHY'TRI, a festival at Athens, properly part of the Anthesteria.

CHYTRI'UM, a place of Ionia, where Clazomenæ formerly stood. *Strab.*

CIA'BRUS or CIAM'BRUS, a river of Dacia. *Ptol.*

CI'ACIS, a city of Armenia Minor. *Id.*

CIÆ'NA, a city of Galatia. *Id.*

CI'AMUM, a promontory of Crete, now Capo Spada.

CIANI'CA, a town of Armenia. *Ptol.*

CI'ASA, a town of Babylonia. *Id.*

CIB'ALÆ or CIB'ALIS, now Swilei, a town of Pannonia, a little at the west of the Danube, where Licinius was defeated by Constantine. It was the birth-place of the emperor Gratian. *Eutrop.* 10. c. 4.—*Marcell.* 30. c. 24.

CIBAR'CI, a people of Spain. *Plin.* 4. c. 20.

CIBARI'TIS, a country of Asia Minor, near the Mæander. *Strab.*

CIBILITA'NI, a people of Bætica. *Plin.* 1. 4.

CIBO'TUS, a name of Apamea, as the emporium, κιβωτὸς, of all Asia. *Id.* 5. c. 29.

CIB'YRA, now Burun, a town of Phrygia, or of Caria, called by *Tacitus*, *Cybaritica civitas*, of which the inhabitants were dexterous hunters. *Horat.* 1. ep. 6. v. 33.—*Cic. in Ver.* 4. c. 13.—*Attic.* 5. ep. 2.

CICERE'IUS C., a secretary of Scipio Africanus, who was promoted to offices in the state, and obtained a triumph over the Corsicans. *Liv.* 41 & 42.

CIC'ERO M. T., a celebrated orator, born at Arpinum, was the son of a Roman knight, and lineally descended from the ancient kings of the Sabines. His mother's name was Helvia. After displaying promising abilities at school, he was taught philosophy by Philo, and law by Mutius Scævola. He acquired and perfected a taste for military knowledge under Sylla, in the Marsian war, and retired from Rome, which was divided into factions, to indulge his philosophic propensities. He was naturally of a weak and delicate constitution, and visited Greece on account of his health; though, perhaps, the true cause of his absence from Rome might be attributed to his fear of the tyranny of Sylla. His friends, who were well acquainted with his superior abilities, were anxious for his return; and when at last he obeyed their solicitations, he applied himself with uncommon diligence to oratory, and was soon distinguished above all the speakers of his age in the Roman forum. When he went to Sicily in the capacity of a quæstor, he behaved with great justice and moderation; and the Sicilians long remembered with gratitude the eloquence of Cicero, their common patron, which had been exerted to deliver them from the tyranny and avarice of Verres. After he had passed through the inferior offices of ædile and prætor, Cicero declared himself a candidate for the consulship, A.U.C. 691; and the patricians and the plebeians were equally anxious to raise him to that dignity, against the intrigues and bribery of Catiline. His new situation was critical, and required vigilance, wisdom, and circumspection. Catiline, with many dissolute and desperate Romans, had conspired against their country, and combined to murder Cicero himself. In this dilemma, Cicero, in full senate, accused Catiline of treason against the state; but as his evidence was not clear, his efforts to fix the guilt of treason upon the abandoned conspirators were then unavailing. He, however, stood upon his guard, and by the information of his friends, and the discovery of Fulvia, his life was saved from the daggers of Marcius and Cethegus, whom Catiline had sent to assassinate him. After this, Cicero commanded Catiline, in the senate, to leave the city; and this desperate conspirator marched out in triumph to meet the 20,000 men who were assembled to support his cause. The lieutenant of C. Antony, the other consul, attacked and defeated them in Gaul; and Cicero, at Rome, punished the rest of the conspirators with death. This capital punishment, though inveighed against by J. Cæsar as too severe, was supported by the opinions of Lutatius Catulus and Cato, and confirmed as just by the whole senate. After this memorable deliverance, Cicero received the thanks of the people, and was styled "the father of his country, and a second founder of Rome." The vehemence with which he had attacked Clodius, proved injurious to him; and when his enemy was made tribune, by the influence of Cæsar and Pompey, he began to be apprehensive for his personal safety. Legal forms, however, and not immediate violence, were the arms which Clodius wished to use against Cicero; and accordingly a law was passed by means of the tribune, which enacted that whosoever had put to death a Roman citizen uncondemned, should be interdicted the use of fire and water. Cicero, though not named, saw that his measures against Catiline were called in question, and therefore, though the Roman knights, to the number of 20,000, and the senate, put on mourning on his account, and espoused his cause as their own, he, after much hesitation, determined to go into voluntary exile. His departure from Rome to Macedonia was followed by the plunder of his property, the destruction of his house, the ill treatment of his wife and family, and the disgraceful promulgation of a law which forbad him, on pain of death, to approach within 468 miles of the city. He was not, however, neglected or despised in his banishment. Wherever he went he was received with the highest marks of approbation and reverence; a circumstance which, when he considered the unmerited treatment which he had received from his countrymen, might, perhaps, have led to that dejection of mind so unworthy the greatness of his former character. The storm of adversity, however, which had thus burst upon him was but momentary; and when the faction had subsided at Rome, and Pompey had exerted himself in his favor, the whole senate and people were unanimous for his return. After sixteen months' absence, he entered Rome with universal satisfaction; and in the fulness of his gratitude thanked the senate and people in two orations still extant. Though now frequently engaged in the defence of his clients and friends as an orator, he did not display that vigor of mind and independence of conduct which might have rendered him the terror of faction and conspiracy. He still knew that Clodius was his enemy, and while he attempted to flatter and conciliate the overgrown power of Cæsar and Pompey, and timidly to accommodate his opinions and measures to the necessities of the times, he contributed, by the respectability of his name, to forge those fetters which soon fatally shackled the liberties and independence of his country. When the vacant provinces were divided by lot among the senators, according to a law enacted by Pompey, Cicero received as his share Cilicia, with some of the neighbouring districts, and he conducted himself with so much integrity in his administration, and displayed so much prudence against the enemy, that, on his return, he was honoured with a triumph, which, however, the violence of the party prevented him from enjoying. During the civil commotions which arose between Cæsar and Pompey, he, after much hesitation, joined himself to the latter, and followed him to Greece. When victory had declared in favour of Cæsar at the battle of Pharsalia, Cicero went to Brundusium, and was reconciled to the conqueror, who treated him with great kindness and humanity. Prom this time Cicero retired into the country, and seldom visited Rome, but particularly devoted himself to study and the composition of his philosophical books. When Cæsar had been stabbed in the senate, Cicero, who was present, recommended a general amnesty, and was the most earnest to decree the provinces to Brutus and Cassius. But when he saw the interest of Cæsar's murderers decrease through their indolence and want of resolution, and the crafty Antony by his intrigues and dissimulation, rise into power, he determined to retire to Athens, but went no farther than Syracuse. On his return to Rome, he discovered that the country was more than usually distracted by private and public dissensions; but whilst he boldly opposed the views of Antony, he was not sufficiently circumspect against the schemes of young Octavius, afterwards called Augustus. The age, influence, and respectability of the orator were powerful associates in courting popularity, and therefore it is not surprising to find Augustus eager to obtain the approbation of Cicero, and expressing his wish to become his colleague in the consulship. That wish was not sincere; all former professions of friendship and of confidence were quickly forgotten at the secret call of ambition, and while Cicero hoped for the firm re-establishment of the consular government and the independence of the senate, Augustus was silently making rapid strides towards the sovereign power. The death of the two consuls at Mutina, which Antony had besieged, exhibited the views of the different parties, and the danger of the state. Augustus, without hesitation, without regard for the opinions of his friends, joined his interest to that of Antony, and the second triumvirate was soon after formed. The great enmity which Cicero bore to Antony was fatal to him; and Augustus, Antony, and Lepidus, the triumvirs, to destroy all cause of future quarrel, and each to dispatch his enemies, produced their list of proscription. About 200 were doomed to death, and Cicero was among the number upon the list of Antony. Augustus, without remorse, gave up to the sword of the assassin the man to whom he partly owed his greatness, and Cicero was pursued by the emissaries of Antony, among whom was Popilius, whom he had formerly defended upon an accusation of parricide. He had fled in a litter towards the sea of Caieta; and when the assassins came up to him, he put his head out of the litter, and it was severed from the body by Herenius. This memorable event happened on the 7th of December, 43 B.C., in the 64th year of his age. The head and right hand of the orator were carried to Rome, and hung up in the Roman forum; and so inveterate was Antony's hatred against the unfortunate man, that even Fulvia, the triumvir's wife, wreaked her vengeance upon his head, and drawing the tongue out of the mouth, bored it through repeatedly with a golden bodkin, verifying, in this act of inhumanity, what Cicero had once observed, that "no animal is more revengeful than a woman." Cicero has acquired more real fame by his literary compositions, than by his spirited exertions in the Roman senate. The learning and abilities which he possessed have been the admiration of every age and country, and his style has always been accounted the true standard of pure latinity. The words *nascitur poeta* have been verified in his attempts to write poetry: and the satire of Martial, *Carmina quod scribit musis et Apolline nullo*, though severe, is perfectly true. Cicero once formed a design to write the history of his country, but did not pursue the plan. He translated many of the Greek writers, poets as well as historians, for his own improvement. When he travelled into Asia, he was attended by most of the learned men of his age; and his stay at Rhodes, in the school of the famous Molo, conduced not a little to perfect his judgment. Like his countrymen, he was not destitute of ambition, and the arrogant expectations with which he returned from his quæstorship in Sicily, are well known. He was of a timid disposition, and he who shone as the father of Roman eloquence, never ascended the rostrum without feeling a secret emotion of dread. His conduct during the civil wars was far removed from that of a true patriot; and when we view him dubious and irresolute, sorry not to follow Pompey, and yet afraid to oppose Cæsar, the judgment would almost brand him with the disgraceful name of coward. In his private character, however, Cicero was of an amiable disposition; and though he was too elated with prosperity, and debased by adversity, the affability of the friend, and the benevolence of the man, conciliated the good graces of all. He married Terentia, whom he afterwards divorced, and by whom he had a son and a daughter. He afterwards married Publilia, a young woman of great beauty, to whom he was guardian; and because she seemed elated at the death of his favourite daughter Tullia, he repudiated her. The works of this celebrated man, of which, according to some, scarcely the tenth part is extant, have been edited by the best scholars in every country. His two books on Glory were extant in the middle of the 14th century, and given as a present to the celebrated Petrarch by Raimond Soranzo, a lawyer of the papal court. This poet lent them to a man of letters, formerly his preceptor, who, through extreme indigence, pawned them for bread. His sudden death, soon after, prevented his revealing in whose hands he had left them, and the valuable manuscripts were thus for ever lost to the world. A treatise of Cicero, *de republicâ*, has been lately found in the Vatican Library, and been published in this country. The most valuable editions of his works complete, are that of Verburgius, 2 vols. fol. Amst. 1724; that of Olivet, 9 vols. 4to. Geneva, 1753; the Oxford edition, in 10 vols. 4to. 1782; that of Lallemand, 12mo. 14 vols. Paris apud Barbou, 1768; and that of Ernesti, Halæ Sax. 1777. *Plutarch. in Vitâ.—Quintil.—Dio. Cass.—Appian.—Florus.—C. Nep. in Attic.—Eutrop.—Cic., &c.—Harles. Not. Lit. Rom.* 1. p. 124.—*Sax. Onom.* 1. p. 153. [The finest bust of Cicero is in the possession of the duke of Wellington.]

CIC'ERO MAR'CUS, the son of Cicero, was taken by Augustus as his colleague in the consulship. He endeavoured to revenge his father's death, by throwing public dishonour upon the memory of Antony, but his own conduct was entitled to little respect. He disgraced his father's virtues, and was so fond of drinking, that, as *Pliny* observes, he wished to deprive Antony of the honour of being the greatest drunkard in the Roman empire. He is said to have possessed nothing of his father's genius except his wit and his politeness. As a military man, he distinguished himself at the battle of Pharsalia, on the side of Pompey, and afterwards defeated C. Antonius in Macedonia. *Plut. in Cic.*

CIC'ERO QUIN'TUS, the brother of the orator, was Cæsar's lieutenant in Gaul, and proconsul of Asia for three years. He was proscribed with his son, at the same time as his brother Tully, but he might have escaped if he had fled with sufficient speed. When overtaken by Antony's emissaries, the son nobly offered himself to the sword of the assassins, refusing to discover his father; but the father rescued his affectionate son from torture by betraying his hiding-place, and they enjoyed the mutual satisfaction of perishing both at the same moment by the hand of their merciless executioners. *Plut. in Cic.—Appian.*

CICERO'NIS A'QUÆ, a place of Campania. *Plin.* 31. c. 2.

CICERO'NIS VIL'LA, a place near Puteoli, in Campania, where Cicero resided for some time. *Plin.* 31. c. 2.

CICER'RUS, a buffoon, ridiculed by *Horace*, 1. sat. 5. u. 52.

CICH'YRUS, a town of Epirus, near the mouth of the river Acheron, on the eastern side. *Strab.*

CICIAN'THI, a people of Asiatic Scythia. *Plin.* 6. c. 13.

CICILIA'NA, a city of Spain. *Antonin.*

CICIME'NI, a people near the Palus Mæotis. *Plin.* 6. c. 7.

CICO'NES, a people of Thrace, near the Hebrus. Ulysses, at his return from Troy, conquered them; and plundered their chief city Ismarus, because they had assisted Priam against the Greeks. The Ciconian women tore Orpheus to pieces for his obscene indulgences. *Ovid. Met.* 10. v. 83. l. 15, v. 313.—*Virg. G.* 4. v. 520, &c.—*Mela*, 2. c. 2.—*Homer. Il.* 2. v. 353.

CICU'TA, an old avaricious usurer, mentioned by *Horace*. 2. *Ser.* 3. v. 69.

CICYNE'THUS an island in the Pagasæus Sinus. *Plin.* 4. c. 12.—*Mela*, 2. c. 9.

CIE'RIUM or ARNE, a town of Bœotia. *Steph.*

CILBIA'NUM, a city of Lydia, near the Cayster. *Plin.* 5. c. 29.

CILE'NI, a people of Hispania Tarraconensis. *Id.* 4. c. 20.

CILICE'NE, a city of Lower Pannonia. *Antonin.*

CILIC'IA, a country of Asia Minor, on the sea coast, at the north of Cyprus, the south of Mount Taurus, and the west of the Euphrates. The inhabitants were bold and enterprising, and enriched themselves by piratical excursions, till they were conquered by Pompey. The country was opulent, and was governed by kings, under some of the Roman emperors; but reduced into a province by Vespasian. Cicero presided over it for some time as proconsul. It received its name from Cilix, the son of Agenor. *Apollod.* 3. c. 1.—*Ptol.* 5. c. 5, 6, 8.—*Paterc.* 2. c. 39.—*Varro, R. R.* 2. c. 11.—*Sueton. in Vesp.* 8.—*Herodot.* 2. c. 17. 34.—*Justin.* 11. c. 11.—*Curt.* 3. c. 4.—*Plin.* 5. c. 27.——Part of the country between Æolia and Troas, opposite Lesbus, in which was the town of Lyrnessus. *Strabo.* 13, calls it Trojan, to distinguish it from the other Cilicia. *Plin.* 5. c. 27.

CILIMBE'SII, people of the island of Corsica. *Ptol.*

CILIS'SA, a town of Phrygia. *Xenophon.*

CI'LIX, a son of Phœnix, or, according to *Herodotus*, of Agenor, was directed by his father to go in quest of his sister Europa. His inquiries proved fruitless, and, therefore, as he was not permitted to return home, he settled in a country to which he gave the name of Cilicia. *Apollod.* 3. c. 1.—*Herodot.* 7. c. 91.—*Hygin.* fab. 178.

CIL'LA, a town of Africa Propria. *Diod.* 20.——A town of Æolia. *Herodot.* 1. c. 149.——A town of Troas, which received its name, according to *Theopompus*, from a certain Cillus, who was one of Hippodamia's suitors, and killed by Œnomaus. *Hom. Il.* 1. v. 38.—*Ovid. Met.* 13. v. 174.

CIL'LABA, a city of Africa, near the Syrtus Major. *Plin.* 5. c. 5.

CIL'LES, a general of king Ptolemy, conquered by Demetrius. *Diod.* 19.

CIL'LUS, a charioteer of Pelops, in whose honour the city of Cilla was built. *Strab.* 13.

CIL'MA, a city of Africa Propria. *Ptol.*

CIL'NII, a people of Etruria. *Liv.* 10. c. 3.—*Silius.* 7. v. 29.

CIL'NIUS, the surname of the family of Mæcenas, originally from Etruria. *Liv.* 10. c. 3.

CI'LO, JUN., a tyrannical governor of Bithynia and Pontus. The provinces, irritated by his oppressive conduct, carried their complaints against him to Rome; but such was the clamour of the flatterers that attended the emperor Claudius, that he was unable to hear them; and when he asked what they had said, he was artfully told by one of Cilo's friends, that they returned thanks for the beneficent administration of their governor; upon which the emperor said, "Let Cilo be continued two years longer in his province." *Dio.* 60.—*Tacit. Ann.* 12. c. 21.

CIMÆ'US, a mountain of Asia, near Troas. *Ptol.*

CIM'ARA, a city of India without the Ganges. *Id.*

CIM'BER TUL'LIUS, one of Cæsar's murderers. He laid hold of the dictator's robe, which was the signal for the conspirators to strike. *Plut. in Cæs.—Cic. Phil.* 2. c. 11.

CIM'BRIUS, a chief of the Suevi. *Cæs. Com.* 1. 37.

CIMBI'NA, a city of Media. *Ptol.*

CIM'BRI, a people of ancient Germany, who at one time inhabited that part of the country which now forms the modern kingdom of Denmark. They were very powerful, and in their invasion of the Roman empire were so courageous, and even desperate, that they fastened their ranks each to the other with cords. In the first battle they destroyed 80,000 Romans, under the consuls Manlius and Servilius Cæpio. When Marius, however, in his second consulship, was chosen to carry on the war, the Teutones were stopped at Aquæ Sextiæ, and, after a bloody engagement, 20,000 were left dead on the field of battle, and 90,000 were taken prisoners, B.C. 102. The Cimbri, who had formed another army, had already penetrated into Italy, but were met at the river Athesis, by Marius and his colleague Catulus, a year after. An engagement ensued, and 140,000 of them were slain. This last battle put an end to this dreadful war, and the two consuls entered Rome in triumph. *Flor.* 3. c. 3.—*Plin.* 7. c. 22. l. 17. c. 1.—*Mela*, 3. c. 3.—*Paterc.* 2. c. 12.—*Plut. in Mario.*

CIM'BRICA CHERSONE'SUS. *Vid.* Chersonesus.

CIM'INUS, now Viterbe, a lake and mountain of Etruria. *Virg. Æn.* 7. v. 697.—*Liv.* 9. c. 36.

CIMME'RII, a people of Asia, dwelling near the Bosporus, called Cimmerius from them. Their country was involved in perpetual clouds, and hence arose the proverb of *tenebræ Cimmeriæ.* Some of them invaded Asia Minor and seized upon the kingdom of Cyaxares, which they held for 28 years, when they were driven back by Alyattes king of Lydia. *Strab.* 3.—*Plin.* 6. c. 6.—*Herodot.* 1. c. 6. &c. According to *Servius* on *Virgil, Æn.* 6. v. 107, there was a people of this name on the coast of Campania.

CIM'MERIS, a town of Troas, formerly called Edonis. *Plin.* 5. c. 30.

CIM'MERIS, the name of the mother of the gods among the Cimmerii. *Hesych.*

CIMME'RIUM, now Crim, a town of Taurica Chersonesus, the inhabitants of which were called Cimmerii. *Mela,* 1. c. 19.

CIMO'LIS or CINO'LIS, a town of Paphlagonia, on the shores of the Euxine Sea.

CIMO'LUS, now Argentiera, an island at the north of the Cretan Sea, between the islands of Parus and Melus, producing chalk and fuller's earth. *Ovid. Met.* 7. v. 463.—*Plin.* 35. c. 16.

CI'MON, an Athenian, son of Miltiades and Hegisipyle, noted for his debaucheries in his youth, and for the reformation of his morals when arrived at years of discretion. When his father died, he was imprisoned because unable to pay the fine laid upon him by the Athenians; but he was released from this unjust confinement by his sister and wife Elpinice. *Vid.* Elpinice. He behaved with remarkable courage at the battle of Salamis, and rendered himself popular by his munificence and valour. When placed at the head of the Athenian fleet, he defeated the Persians, took 200 ships, and totally routed their army by land on the very same day. The money which he obtained by his victories was not applied to his own private use; but with it he fortified and embellished the city. The greatness and goodness of his character, however, could not shield him against the jealousy and the illiberal suspicions of a fickle multitude; he was accused of treason, and though his life and general conduct were his best defence, he was, by the artifice and influence of his rival Pericles, banished from his country, and war was declared against Lacedæmon, that a foreign quarrel, and not the contemplation of national dissensions and of civil oppression, might engage the attention of the Athenians. After some time Cimon was recalled from his exile, and effected a reconciliation between Lacedæmon and his countrymen. He was afterwards appointed to carry on the war against Persia in Ægypt, and Cyprus, with a fleet of 200 ships; and on the coast of Asia he gave battle to the enemy, and totally ruined their fleet. He died as he was besieging the town of Citium in Cyprus, B.C. 449, in the 51st year of his age. He may be called the last of the Greeks, whose spirit and boldness defeated the armies of the barbarians. He was such an inveterate enemy to the Persian power, that he formed a plan for its total destruction; and in his wars he had so reduced that nation, that the king promised in a treaty not to pass the Chelidonian islands with his fleet, or to approach within a day's sail of the Grecian Seas. The munificence of Cimon has been deservedly praised for his leaving his gardens open to the public. *Thucyd.* 1. c. 100 & 112.—*Justin.* 2. c. 15.—*Diod.* 11.—*Plut. & C. Nep. in Vita.*—*Cic. Off.* 2. c. 18.——An Athenian, father of Miltiades. *Herodot.* 6. c. 34.——A Roman, supported in prison by the milk of his own daughter.——An Athenian, who wrote an account of the war waged by the Amazons against his country. *Arrian.* 1. 7.——A painter, mentioned by *Pliny,* 35. c. 8.

CINÆDOP'OLIS, an island off the coast of Doris, in Asia Minor. *Plin.* 5. c. 31.

CINÆ'THON. *Vid.* Cinethon.

CINÆ'THUS, a Chian, who is said to have composed the hymn to Apollo, usually attributed to *Homer,* and was the first who recited in public the verses of that poet. *Schol. Pind. Nem.* 2.—*Fabr. B. Gr.* 2. c. 5.

CINÆ'TIUS, according to *Ptolemy* Onugnathos, a promontory of Laconia.

CINAM'BRI, a people of Illyricum. *Appian.*

CINAR'ADAS, one of the descendants of Cinyras, who presided over the ceremonies of Venus at Paphus. *Tacit.* 2 *Hist.* c. 3.

CINCEN'SES, a people of Hispania Tarraconensis. *Plin.* 3. c. 3.

CIN'CIA LEX, was enacted by M. Cincius, a tribune of the people, A.U.C. 549. It decreed that no man should take any money from a client as a gift or fee in judging a cause. *Liv.* 34. c. 4.—*Cic. Sen.* 4.—*Tacit.* 11. *Ann.* 5.

CINCINNA'TUS L. Q., a celebrated Roman, who was informed, as he ploughed the field, that the senate had chosen him dictator. Upon this he left his agricultural pursuits with regret, and repaired to the field of battle, to oppose the Volsci and Æqui. He attacked and defeated the enemy, and returned to Rome in triumph; and 16 days after his appointment he laid down his office, and returned to complete the cultivation of his fields. In his 80th year he was again summoned against Præneste as dictator; and after a successful campaign, he resigned the absolute power, which he had enjoyed only 21 days, refusing to accept the rewards offered him by the senate. He flourished about 460 years B.C. *Liv.* 3. c. 26,—*Flor.* 1. c. 11. —*Cic. de Finib.* 4.—*Plin.* 18. c. 3.

CIN'CIUS, a senator who wrote *De re militari.* *Macrob.* 3. *Saturn.* c. 13.

L. CIN'CIUS ALIMEN'TIUS, a prætor of Sicily in the second Punic war, who wrote annals in Greek. *Dionys. Hal.* 1.

CIN'CIUS MAR'CUS, a tribune of the people, A.U.C. 549, author of the *Cincia lex.*

CIN'CIUS SEX'TUS, a Roman governor of the province of Syria. *Tac. Ann.* 15. c. 25.

CIN'DIA, a town of India within the Ganges. *Ptol.*

CIN'EAS, a Thessalian, minister and friend of Pyrrhus king of Epirus. He was sent to Rome by his master during the Tarentine war, to sue for a cessation of hostilities; but the Romans, though vanquished, refused to listen to the proposal whilst their enemy remained in possession of any part of the Italian territory. Cineas was a man of deep penetration, and he informed his master, who was inquisitive about the state of the hostile republic, that the Roman senate appeared like a vast assembly of kings; and he observed further, that to fight with them was to fight against another Hydra. He was said to be of such a retentive memory, that the day after his arrival at Rome he could salute every senator and knight by his name. *Plin.* 7. c. 24.—*Cic. Tusc.* 1. c. 24. *Ad Fan.* 9. ep. 25.——A king of Thessaly. *Herodot.* 5. c. 63. ——An Athenian, &c. *Polyæn.* 2, c. 32.

CINE'SIAS, a Greek poet of Thebes in Bœotia, who composed dithyrambic verses, some of which are quoted by *Athenæus.* He was from his great leanness surnamed Philyrinus, (φιλύρινος, *tiliaceus*). *Athen.* 12. c. 29.

CIN'ETHON, a Spartan, who wrote genealogical poems, in one of which he asserts that Medea had a son by Jason, called Medus, and a daughter called Eriopis. *Paus.* 2. c. 18.

CIN'GA, now Cinea, a river of Spain, flowing from the Pyrenean mountains into the Iberus. *Lucan.* 4. v. 21.—*Cæs. B. C.* 1. c. 48.

CINGET'ORIX, a prince of Gaul, who, when J. Cæsar invaded the country, formed an alliance with Rome. *Cæs. Bell. G.* 5. c. 3.——A prince of Britain, who attacked Cæsar's camp, by order of Cassivelaunus. *Id. ib.* c. 22.

CINGO'NIUS VAR'RO, a consul elect, slain by Galba. *Tac. Ann.* 14, c. 45. *Hist.* 1. c. 6.

CIN'GULUM, now Cingoli, a town of Picenum, in Italy, the inhabitants of which were called Cingulani. *Plin.* 3. c. 13.—*Cæs. Bell. Civ.* 1. c. 15.—*Sil. It.* 10. v. 34.—*Cic. Att.* 7. ep. 11.

CINIA'TA, a fortified castle of Galatia. *Strab.* 12.

CINITH'II, a people of Africa, near the mouths of the Triton, which falls into the Mediterranean, at the south of the Syrtis Minor. *Tac. Ann.* 2. c. 52.

CINTUM, a town of the island of Majorca. *Plin.* 3. c. 5.

CIN'NA, L. CORN., a Roman who distinguished himself by his enmity against Sylla, when engaged in the Mithridatic wars. The violence of his conduct armed the Romans against him, and he was forcibly expelled from the city by Octavius and the patricians. This disgrace, however, did not subdue his hatred against his enemies; he recalled Marius from banishment, and joining himself to Sertorius and Carbo, he raised a large force in Italy, and with his partisans approached Rome in four divisions. The entrance of these pretended friends into the city was the signal for slaughter. Rome exhibited the appearance of a town taken by storm, her citizens were butchered with indiscriminating fury, property was plundered, and the tyrannical Cinna and Marius appointed themselves consuls without the regular formalities of election. The death of Marius, though it weakened, did not destroy the power of Cinna; his oppressions and cruelties were continued till Sylla, returned victorious from the conquest of Mithridates, and encouraged and inflamed by the complaints of the Romans who fled from the persecution of his enemy, threatened the most formidable opposition. Cinna and his friend Carbo prepared the most vigorous defence; but private revenge prevented public punishment, and Cinna perished at Ancona by the secret dagger of an offended soldier. The name of Cinna became deservedly odious to the Romans, as conveying an idea of every thing that was cruel, arbitrary, and perfidious. Cinna's daughter, called Cornelia, married Julius Cæsar, by whom she became mother of Julia. *Plut. in Mar. Pomp. & Syll.—Lucan.* 4. v. 822.—*Apppian. Bell. Civ.* 1.—*Flor.* 3. c. 21.—*Paterc.* 2. c. 20. &c.—*Plut. in Cæs.*

CIN'NA, one of Cæsar's murderers. *Suet. Cæs.* 85.—*Val Max.* 9. c. 9.

CIN'NA, C. HEL'VIUS, a poet intimate with Cæsar, and acquainted with the great wits and poets of the age. He went to attend the obsequies of Cæsar, and being mistaken by the populace for the other Cinna, who had been one of the dictator's murderers, he was torn to pieces. He has been praised for his abilities and for the elegance of his verses; and it is said that he employed nine years in composing a poem called Smyrna. *Gyrald.—Plut. in Cæs.*

CIN'NA, a learned poet, contemporary with Virgil. *Virg. Ecl.* 9. v. 35.—*Mart.* 10. epigr. 21.——A grandson of Pompey. He conspired against Augustus, who generously pardoned him, and made him one of his most intimate friends. He was consul, and by his will appointed Augustus his heir. *Dio.—Seneca. de Clem.* c. 9.

CIN'NA, a town of Italy taken by the Romans from the Samnites. *Diod.*——A town of Macedonia. *Antonin.*——A town of Hispania Tarraconensis. *Ptol.*——A town of Persia. *Id.*——A town of Thessaly, so called from Cinnus, the brother of Coeus.

CIN'NADON, a Lacedæmonian youth, who resolved to put the Ephori to death, and to seize upon the sovereign power. His conspiracy was discovered, and he was sentenced to suffer death. *Aristot. Polit.* 5. c. 7.

CIN'NAMUS, a hair-dresser at Rome, raised to the rank of knight by the intrigues of his mistress. He ruined himself by his extravagance and folly. He is ridiculed by *Martial*, 7. epigr. 63.

CIN'NARUS, a man of Selinus, of infamous character.

CINNIA'NA, a town of Lusitania, famous for the valour of its citizens. *Val. Max.* 6. c. 4.——A town of Spain, at the foot of the Pyrenees.

CINO'TUS, a city of Doris, on the Sinus Bubesias. *Ptol.*

CINSTER'NÆ, a city of Africa Propria. *Id.*

CINTHYL'IA, a town of Hispania Tarraconensis.

CINX'IA, a surname given to Juno, because she presided over marriages, and was supposed to untie the girdle of new brides. *Arnob.* 4.—*Festus. de Verb. Sig.*

CIN'YPS or CIN'YPHUS, a river of Africa, which falls into the Mediterranean, a little at the west of the greater Syrtis. There was a town of the same name on the banks of the river, and the country in the neighbourhood also bears the name of Cinyps. *Virg. G.* 3. v. 312.—*Herodot.* 3. c. 198.—*Plin.* 5. c. 4.—*Martial.* 7. ep. 94.—*Ovid. Met.* 7. v. 272. l. 15. v. 755.—*Lucan.* 9. v. 787.

CIN'YRAS, a king of Cyprus, son of Paphus, who married Cenchreis, by whom he had a daughter called Myrrha. Myrrha fell in love with her father; and, in the absence of her mother at the celebration of the festival of Ceres, she introduced herself into his bed by means of her nurse. Cinyras had by her a son called Adonis; and when he knew the incest which he had committed, he attempted to stab his daughter, who escaped his pursuit, and fled to Arabia, where, after she had brought forth, she was changed into a tree, which still bears her name. Cinyras, according to Hyginus, stabbed himself in despair; but *Eustathius*, 10. *Il.* asserts that he was slain by Agamemnon. He was so rich, that his opulence, like that of Crœsus, became proverbial. *Lactant. in* 10. *Met.—Servius in* 9. *Ecl. Virg.—Plin.* 7. c. 4.—*Ovid. Met.* 10. fab. 9.—*Plut. in Parall.—Hygin.* fab. 242, 248. 251, 270, 271.——A son of Laodice. *Apollod.* 3. c. 9.——A man who conducted a colony from Syria to Cyprus. *Id.* 3. c. 14.——A Ligurian who assisted Æneas against Turnus. *Virg. Æn.* 10. v. 186.

CIP'PUS, a noble Roman, who as he returned home victorious, is said to have found two horns suddenly growing on his head, a prodigy which a soothsayer explained by informing him that if he entered the city he must reign there. Unwilling to enslave his country, he assembled the senate without the walls, banished himself for ever from the city, and retired to live upon a single acre of ground. *Ovid. Met.* 15. v. 565.

CIRCÆ'UM, now Circello, a promontory of Latium near a small town called Circeii, at the south of the Pontine marshes. The people were called Circenses. *Ovid. Met.* 14. v. 248.—*Virg. Æn.* 7. v. 799. —*Liv.* 6. c. 17.—*Cic. N. D.* 3. c. 19.

CIR'CE, a daughter of Sol and Perseis, celebrated for her knowledge of magic and venomous herbs. She was sister of Æetes king of Colchis, and of Pasiphae the wife of Minos. She married a Sarmatian prince of Colchis, whom she murdered to obtain his kingdom. She was expelled by her subjects, and conveyed by her father to the coast of Italy, where she fixed her residence in an island called Ææa. Ulysses, at his return from the Trojan war, visited the place, where all his companions, who ran headlong into pleasure and voluptuousness, were changed by Circe's potions into filthy swine. Ulysses, who was fortified against all enchantments by a herb called *moly*, which he had received from Mercury, went to Circe, and demanded, sword in hand, the restoration of his companions to their former state. She complied with his request, and loaded the hero with pleasures and honors. In this voluptuous retreat, Ulysses is said to have had by Circe one son called Telegonus, or two according to Hesiod, called Agrius and Latinus. For one whole year, Ulysses forgot his glory in Circe's arms, and at his departure the nymph advised him to descend to hell, and consult the manes of Tiresias, concerning the fates that attended him. Circe shewed herself cruel to Scylla her rival, and to Picus. *Vid.* Scylla & Picus. *Ovid. Met.* 14. fab. 1 & 5.—*Horat.* 1. ep. 2. l. 2. od. 17.—*Virg. Ecl.* 8. v. 70. *Æn.* 3. v. 386. l. 7. v. 10, &c.—*Hygin.* fab. 125, 199.—*Apollon.* 4. *Arg.—Homer. Odyss.* 10. v. 136, &c.—*Apollod.* 1. c. 9. *Hesiod. Theog.* 956.—*Strab.* 5.

CIRCEN'SES LU'DI, games performed in the circus at Rome. They were celebrated in honour of the god Consus, and were first established by Romulus at the rape of the Sabines. They were in imitation of the Olympian games among the Greeks, and by way of eminence, were often called the great games. Their original name was Consualia, and they were first called Circenses by Tarquin the elder after he had built the Circus. They were not appropriated to one particular exhibition; but were equally celebrated for leaping, wrestling, throwing the quoit and javelin, races on foot as well as in chariots, and boxing. Like the Greeks, the Romans gave the name of Pentathlum or Quinquertium to these five exercises. The celebration continued five days, beginning on the 15th of September. All games in general that were exhibited in the Circus, were soon after called Circensian games. Some sea-fights and skirmishes, called by the Romans Naumachiæ, were also afterwards exhibited in the Circus. *Virg. Æn.* 8. v. 636.—*Dion. Hal.* 7.—*Solin.* c. 45.

CIRCE'SIUM, a town of Mesopotamia, where the tomb of the emperor Gordian was situated. *Eutrop.* 9. c. 2.

CIRCID'IUS, a river of Corsica. *Ptol.*

CIR'CIUS, a part of mount Taurus. *Plin.* 5. c. 27. ——A rapid and tempestuous wind, frequent in Gallia Narbonensis, and said to be unknown in any other country. *Lucan.* 1. v. 408.

CIRCUMPADA'NI A'GRI, the country round the river Po, at the north of Italy. *Liv.* 21. c. 35.

CIR'CUS, a large and elegant building at Rome, where plays and shows were exhibited. There were eight of these buildings at Rome; the first, called Circus Maximus, raised and embellished by Tarquinius Priscus, was the grandest. Its figure was oblong, and it was filled all round with benches, and could contain, as some report, 300,000 spectators. It was about 2187 feet long, and 960 broad. All the emperors vied in beautifying it, after the example of J. Cæsar, who introduced large canals of water into it, which on a sudden could be covered with an infinite number of vessels, and represent a sea-fight.

CI'RIS, the name of Scylla daughter of Nissus, who was changed into a bird of the same name. *Ovid Met.* 8. v. 151.

CIR'NA, a mountain of Africa Propria. *Ptol.*

CIR'PHIS, a city, or rather a mountain of Phocis. *Strab.—Pindar. Scholiast.*

CIRRÆ'ATUM, a place near Arpinum, in Italy, where C. Marius lived when young. *Plut. in Mar.*

CIR'RHA or CYR'RHA, a town of Phocis, at the foot of mount Parnassus, where Apollo was worshipped. *Lucan.* 3. v. 172.

CIRRHA'DIA, a region of India without the Ganges. *Ptol.*

CIRRHÆ'I, a people near Athens. *Æschin. contra Ctesiph.*

CIR'THA or CIR'TA, a large and opulent town of Numidia, at the west of Carthage. *Strab.* 5—*Plin.* 5. c. 3.

CISALPI'NA GAL'LIA, a part of Gaul, called also Citerior and Togata. Its farthest boundary was near the Rubicon, and it touched the Alps on the Italian side. The chief divisions of Cisalpine Gaul were Liguria, Taurini, Insubres, Cenomanni, Euganei, Veneti, Histria, Lingones and Boii. *Vid.* Gallia.

CIS'AMUS, a city of Crete, now Chisamo. *Ptol.*

CISERUS'SA, an island not far from Cnidus. *Plin.* 5. c. 31.

CIS'IA, the mother of Memnon. *Steph.*

CISIAN'THI or CICIAN'THI, a people near Scythia. *Plin.* 6. c. 13.

CISIP'ADES, a people of Africa Propria. *Id.* 5. c. 4.

CISPADA'NA GAL'LIA, a part of ancient Gaul south of the Po.

CIS'PII, a people of Æthiopia. *Plin.* 6. c. 30.

CIS'PIUS, a man who permitted his wife to indulge her licentious inclinations by pretending to be asleep. When a slave, taking advantage of his supposed slumber, stole a goblet from his table, the angry master stopped him, exclaiming, *Non omnibus dormio.* *Cic.* 7. *Fam.* 24.—*Festus in Non.*

CIS'PIUS, a hill at Rome, part of mount Esquilinus. *Varro. de L.L.* 1.

CISRHENA'NI, part of the Germans who lived nearest Rome, on the west of the Rhine. *Cæs. B. G.* 6. c. 2.

CIS'SA, a river of Pontus. *Ptol.*——A small island near Istria. *Plin.* 3. c. 26.——A city of the Thracian Chersonesus.

CIS'SE, a city of Mauritania Cæsariensis. *Ptol.*

CISSE'IS, a patronymic given to Hecuba as daughter of Cisseus.

CISSE'NE, a mountain of Thrace. *Suidas.*

CIS'SEUS, a king of Thrace, father of Hecuba, according to some authors. *Virg. Æn.* 7. v. 320. & *Servius loco,* & l. 5. v. 537.——A son of Melampus, killed by Æneas. *Id. Æn.* 10. v. 317.——A son of Ægyptus. *Apollod.* 2. c. 1.

CIS'SI, a people of Cappadocia, near Trapezus. *Ptol.*

CIS'SIA, a country of Susiana, of which Susa was the capital. *Herodot.* 5. c. 49.

CIS'SIÆ, one of the gates of Babylon. *Id.* 3. c. 155.

CIS'SIDAS, a general of Dionysius, king of Sicily, sent with nine gallies to assist the Spartans, *Diod.* 15.

CISSOES'SA, a fountain of Bœotia. *Plut.*

CIS'SUS, a mountain of Macedonia.——A city of Thrace. *Lycoph.—Hesych.*

CIS'SUS, a man who acquainted Alexander with the flight of Harpalus. *Plut. in Alex.*

CISSU'SA, a fountain where Bacchus was washed when young. *Plut. in Lys.*

CISTHE'NE, a town of Æolia. *Mela,* 1. c. 18.——A town of Lycia. *Strabo. Salmasius,* however, reads Meciste.

CISTOBO'CI, a people of Dacia. *Ptol.*

CIT'AMUM, a town of Armenia Major. *Id.*

CITA'NUS, one of the Cyclades.

CITA'RII, a people of Sicily. *Plin.* 3. c. 8.

CITA'RIUS, a mountain of Macedonia. *Ptol.*

CITHÆ'RON, a king of Bœotia, gave his name to a mountain of the country situate at the south of the river Asopus, and sacred to Jupiter and the Muses, and also frequented by the priestesses of Bacchus in the celebration of their famous orgies. Actæon was torn to pieces by his own dogs on this mountain, and Hercules killed there an immense lion. *Virg. Æn.* 4. v. 303.—*Apollod.* 2. c. 4.—*Mela,* 2. c. 3.—*Strab.* 9.—*Paus.* 9. c. 1, &c.—*Plin.* 4. c. 7,—*Ptol.* 3 c. 15.

CITHARIS'TA, a promontory af Gaul. *Plin.* 3. c. 4.—*Mela,* 2. c. 5.

CITH'RUM or CIT'RON, according to *Strabo,* a town of Thessaly.

CITH'RUM, a town of Macedonia.

CIT'IUM, now Chiti, a sea-port town at the south of the island of Cyprus, where Cimon died in his expedition against Ægypt. *Plut. in Cim.—Thucyd.* 1. c. 112.

CITUO'RUM, a large island in the Danube. *Ptol.*

CI'US, a town of Mysia, on the shores of the Propontis. *Apollod.* 1. c. 9.——A river of Bulgaria, rising in Mount Rhodope.——A river of Thrace. *Plin.* 5. c. 32.——A commercial place of Phrygia. It was the name also of three cities in Bithynia.

CIV'ICA, the uncle of the Emperor Verus. *Casaub. ad Hist. Aug*——A proconsul of Africa, put to death by Domitian *Tac. Agric.* c. 42.

CIVI'LIS J., a powerful Batavian, who raised a sedition against Galba. *Tacit. Hist.* 1. c. 59.

CIVIL'IUS or CLIV'IUS, a leader of the Volsci, vanquished by Geganius, A.U.C. 312.

CIVIL'IUS TUL'LUS, a military tribune, A.U.C. 348.

CIZ'ARI, a castle of Paphlagonia, near Amisus. *Strab.* 12.

CIZ'YA, a city of Thrace. *Sozomen.* 6. c. 13.

CIZYCE'NUS, a celebrated Athenian geometrician. *Voss. de Scient. Math.* c. 13. sec. 4.

CIZ'YCUM, a city of Asia, on the Propontis. *Vid.* Cyzicus.

CLAAMET'IDUS, a son of Hercules by Astybia daughter of Thestius. *Apollod.* 2.

CLA'DEUS, a river of Elis, passing near Olympia, and honoured next to the Alpheus. *Paus.* 5. c. 7.

CLÆ'ON, a fountain of Phrygia, near Celænæ. *Plin.* 31. c. 2.

CLAMPE'TIA, a place in the country of the Brutii. *Id.* 3. c. 5.—*Mela,* 2. c. 4. In the 40th book of *Livy* for Dampetia read Clampetia.

CLA'NES, a river falling into the Ister. *Strab.* 4.

CLA'NIS, a centaur killed by Theseus. *Ovid. Met.* 12. v. 373.

CLA'NIS, a river of Gaul, now le Clain.

CLA'NIUS or CLA'NIS, a river of Campania at the south of Capua. It falls into the Tyrrhene Sea. *Virg. G.* 2. v. 225.

CLA'NUS or CLA'NIS, a river of Etruria, now Chiana. *Sil.* 8 v. 454.—*Tac. Ann.* 1. c. 79.——An island in the Ægean Sea.

CLARA'NUS, a grammarian of eminence mentioned by *Seneca,* ep. 66.—*Martial.* 10. epigr. 21.

CLAR'IÆ, a people of Thrace. *Plin.* 4. c. 11.

CLA'RIUS, a river of Cyprus. *Plut. in Solon.*

CLA'RUS, a town of Ionia famous for an oracle of Apollo. It was built by Manto, daughter of Tiresias, who fled from Thebes, after it had been destroyed by the Epigoni. Manto was so afflicted with her misfortunes, that a lake was formed from her tears on the spot where she first found the oracle. Apollo was thence surnamed *Clarius.* *Strab.* 14. —*Paus.* 7. c. 3.—*Servius. in Æn.* 3. v. 360.—*Mela,* 1. c 7.—*Ovid. Met.* 1. v. 516.——An island of the Ægean between Tenedius and Scius. *Thucyd.* 3. c. 33.

CLA'RUS, one of the companions of Æneas. *Virg. Æn.* 10. v. 126.

CLAS'SICUS, a commander of the cavalry of the Treveri, of an illustrious family. *Tac. Hist.* 4. c. 55.

CLASSIT'Æ, a people of Assyria. *Ptol.*

CLASTID'IUM, now Schiatezzo, a town of Liguria near the confluence of the Ticinus and the Po. *Strab.* 5.—*Plut. in Marcell.*—*Liv.* 21. c. 48, &c.—*Polyb.* 3.

CLATER'NA or CLITER'NA, a town of Æmilia, in Italy. *Plin.* 3. c. 15.

CLATER'NA, a town of Apulia, now Campo Marino.

CLA'TOS, a city in the interior of Crete. *Plin.* 4. c. 12.

CLAU'DIA, a patrician family at Rome, descended from Atta Clausus a chief of the Sabines, who is said to have removed to Rome soon after the expulsion of the Tarquins, with adherents to the number of 5000, according to some writers. The Claudian family gave birth to many illustrious patriots: and there were not less than twenty-eight of the family who were invested with the consulship, five with the office of dictator, and seven with that of censor, besides the honour of six triumphs and two ovations. The word is sometimes spelt Clodia; and, according to Virgil, the family were descended from Clausus, a Sabine chieftain, who supported Turnus against Æneas. The Claudii, were considered as very friendly to the patrician power; and only one, Claudius, the bitter enemy of Cicero's fame, is mentioned, who sacrificed the dignity and privileges of his rank for the acquisition of dangerous popularity. The emperor Tiberius was descended from this family. *Virg. Æn.* 7. v. 708.—*Sueton. in Tib.*—*Liv.* 6. c. 41. There was also a plebeian family of this name.

CLAU'DIA ANTO'NIA, a daughter of the emperor Claudius, married Cn, Pompey, whom Messalina caused to be put to death. Her second husband, Sylla Faustus, by whom she had a son, was killed by Nero, and she shared his fate, when she refused to marry his murderer.

CLAU'DIA PUL'CRA, a cousin of Agrippina, falsely accused of adultery and criminal designs against Tiberius. She was the wife of Varus, whose legions were destroyed in Germany, and after an honourable and virtuous widowhood of 27 years, she fell by the intrigues of the infamous Sejanus. *Tacit. Ann.* 4. c. 52.

CLAU'DIA, a vestal virgin, grand-daughter of Appius Cæcus, accused of incontinence. To show her innocence she offered to remove a ship which had brought the image of Vesta to Rome, and which had stuck in one of the shallow places of the river. This had already baffled the efforts of a number of men; and Claudia, after addressing her prayers to the goddess, untied her girdle, and with it easily dragged after her the ship to shore, and by this action was honourably acquitted. It is said, that to commemorate this remarkable event, a statue was erected to Claudia in the vestibule of Cybele's temple, which remained unhurt, though the edifice was twice burnt down. *Val. Max.* 1. c. 8. l. 5. c. 4.—*Propert.* 4. el. 12. v. 52.—*Ital.* 17. v. 34. —*Ovid. Fast.* 4. v. 315. *ex Ponto.* 1. ep. 2. v. 144. —*Herodian.* 1. c. 11.—*Tacit.* 4 *Ann.* 64.——A step-daughter of M. Antony, whom Augustus married. He dismissed her undefiled, immediately after the contract of marriage, on account of a sudden quarrel with her mother Fulvia. *Sueton. in Aug.* 62.——The wife of the poet Statius. *Stat.* 3. *Sylv.* 5.——A daughter of Appius Claudius, betrothed to Tib. Gracchus.——A daughter of Appius Cæcus, who, when incommoded in her carriage by the populace in the streets, on her return from the public games, expressed a wish that her brother Pulcher were alive again to lose another fleet, that the crowd might be less at Rome. She was tried for this expression, and deservedly fined. *Suet. Tib.* 2.—*Val. Max.* 8. c. 1.—*Gell.* 10. c. 6. ——The wife of Metellus Celer, sister of of P. Clodius and Appius Claudius.

CLAU'DIA, an inconsiderable town of Noricum. *Plin.* 3. c. 14.——A Roman road, which led from the Milvian bridge to the Flaminian way. *Ovid.* 1. *ex. Pont.* el. 8. v. 44.

CLAU'DIA, a tribe which received its name from Appius Claudius, who came to settle at Rome with a large body of attendants. It must, however, be considered as the Claudian family, descended from Clausus. *Vid.* Claudia. *Liv.* 2. c. 16.—*Halic.* 5.

CLAU'DIA LEX, *de comitiis*, was enacted by M. Cl. Marcellus, A.U.C. 702. It ordained, that at the public election of the magistrates, no notice should be taken of the votes of such as were absent. *Suet. in Cæs.* c. 28.—Another, *de usurâ*, which forbade people to lend money to minors on condition of payment after the decease of their parents. *Tac. Ann.* 11. c. 13.—Another, *de negotiatione*, by Q. Claudius the tribune, A.U.C. 535. It forbade any senator, or father of a senator, to have any vessel containing above 300 amphoræ, for fear of their engaging in commercial schemes. The same law also forbade the same thing to the scribes and attendants of the quæstors, as it was naturally supposed the people who had any commercial connections could not be faithful to their trust, or promote the interest of the state.—Another, A.U.C. 576, to permit the allies to return to their respective cities, after their names were enrolled. *Liv.* 41. c. 9.—Another, to take away the freedom of the city of Rome from the colonists, whom Cæsar had carried to Novicomum. *Sueton. in Jul.* 28.

CLAU'DIÆ A'QUÆ, the first water brought to Rome by means of an aqueduct of eleven miles in length, erected by the censor Appius Claudius, A.U.C. 441, *Eutrop.* 2. c. 4.—*Liv.* 9. c. 29.

CLAUDIA'NUS, a celebrated Latin poet, born at Alexandria in Ægypt, in the age of Honorius and Arcadius. He seems to possess all the majesty of Virgil, without being a slave to the corrupted style which prevailed in his age. Scaliger observes that he has compensated for the poverty of his matter by the purity of his language, the happiness of his expressions, and the melody of his numbers. As he was the favourite of Stilicho, he removed from the court when his patron was disgraced, and passed the rest of his life in retirement and learned ease; though some have maintained that he shared for a while the misfortunes of his friend, and was long exposed to the cruel persecution and jealousy of Hadrian the emperor's new minister. His poems, which are numerous, consist of Panegyrics on the consulship of Honorius and other illustrious men of that age, an account of the war against the Getæ, the Gildonic war, the praises of Stilicho, verses on Eutropius and Rufinus, on the rape of Proserpine, some idyllia and epigrams, &c. The poems on Rufinus and Eutropius have been considered as the best and most finished of his compositions. The best editions of his works are that of Burmann, 4to, 2 vols Amst. 1760, and that of Gesner, 2 vols. 8vo, Lips. 1758 The latest and most correct edition is the Bipontine, 1784. *Suidas.*—*Sidon. Apollin.*—*Gyrald. de L. Poet.* 4. —*Aug. de Civ. D.*—*Orosius.*—*Harles. Not. Lit. Rom.* 1. p. 723.—*Sax. Onom.* 1. p. 455.

CLAUDIA'NUS MAMER'CUS, a poet, philosopher, and theologian of Vienna, A.D. 460. *Sidon. Apollin.* 4. ep. 3. 11.

CLAUDIOME'RIUM, a city of the Artabri, in Spain. *Plin.*

CLAUDIOP'OLIS, a town of Cappadocia. *Plin.* 5. c. 24.——A town of Bithynia, near the river Elatus.——A town of Dacia.——A town of Cilicia, at the foot of mount Taurus.

CLAU'DIUS TIBER. DRUSUS NERO, son of Drusus, Livia's second son, and Antonia, and brother of the great Germanicus, succeeded as emperor of Rome, after the murder of Caligula, whose memory he endeavoured to annihilate. He made himself popular for a while, by taking particular care of the city, and by adorning and beautifying it with buildings; but these promising appearances soon vanished. He passed over into Britain, and was honoured with a triumph for victories which his generals had won, while he suffered himself to be governed by favourites, whose licentiousness and avarice plundered the state, and distracted the provinces. He married four wives, one of whom, called Messalina, he put to death on account of her lust and debauchery. He was at last poisoned by another called Agrippina, daughter of Germanicus, who wished to raise to the throne Nero, her son by her former husband Domitius. The poison was conveyed in mushrooms, of which he was particularly fond; but as it did not operate speedily, his physician, by order of the empress, made him swallow a poisoned feather. He died in the 63d year of his age, October 13, A.D. 54, after a reign of thirteen years, distinguished neither by humanity nor courage, but debased by weakness and irresolution. He was succeeded by Nero. *Tacit. Ann.* 11, &c —*Dio.* 60.—*Juv.* 6. v. 619.—*Suet. in Vitâ.* [The finest bust of Claudius is that in the Museum of the Vatican.]

CLAU'DIUS M. AUREL. or FLAV. VALER., the second emperor of that name, who succeeded Gallienus, was a Dalmatian by birth. He conquered the Goths, Scythians, and Heruli, and killed no less than 300,000 in a battle, A.D. 269; and after a reign of about two years, died of the plague in Pannonia. The excellence of his character, marked by personal bravery, and tempered with justice and benevolence, is well known by these words of the senate, addressed to him: *Claudi Auguste, tu frater, tu pater, tu amicus, tu bonus senator. tu vere princeps. Eutrop.* 9.—*Trebel. Pol. in Claud.*—*Orosius, &c.*

CLAU'DIUS AP'PIUS, an orator. *Cic. in Brut. Vid.* Appius.

CLAU'DIUS AP'PIUS, a consul, A.U.C. 259. He was a zealous supporter of the privileges of the patricians against the encroachments of the plebeians; and when the tribunes were elected, he advised the senators to control their great power by bribery and secret influence. *Liv.* 2. c. 21, &c.

CLAU'DIUS AP'PIUS, his son, inherited the prejudices of his father against the common people, and became so unpopular, and behaved with such severity to his soldiers, that in a war, which, as consul, he conducted against the Volsci, the Roman army, A.U.C. 283, suffered themselves to be defeated to show their contempt of their general. He was accused by the tribunes, but defended himself with energy and success; but before his appearance at another trial, he was found dead. *Liv.* 2. c. 56.

CLAU'DIUS AP'PIUS, the chief of the Decemviri, was also called Regillanus, and became odious for his attack upon Virginia. *Vid.* Appius.

CLAU'DIUS AP'PIUS CÆ'CUS, a Roman censor, who built an aqueduct A.U.C. 441, which brought water to Rome from Tusculum, a distance of seven or eight miles. The water was called Appia, and it was the first that was brought to the city from the country. Before his age, the Romans were satisfied with the waters of the Tiber, or of the fountains and wells in the city. *Vid.* Appius. *Liv.* 9. c. 29.—*Ovid. Fast.* 6. v. 203.—*Cic. de Sen.* 6.

CLAU'DIUS AP'PIUS PUL'CHER, besieged Capua in his consulship, A U C. 512, and died of the wound which he received, after the surrender of the town. *Liv.* 25 & 26.

CLAU'DIUS AP'PIUS PUL'CHER, a consul, A U.C. 611, who conquered the Salassi, a nation of Gaul, after having first suffered from them a severe defeat. He obtained a triumph, against the authority of the senate and people, by means of his daughter or sister, who as a vestal virgin accompanied him in his chariot, and thus by the sacredness of her character, prevented the interruption of his procession. *Cic. Cœl.* 14.—*Val. Max.* 5. c. 4.—*Oros.* 5. c. 4.—*Dio.* 34. c. 79.—*Suet. Tib.* 2.

CLAU'DIUS CA'IUS, was consul, A.U.C. 294; and on the death of his colleague Valerius, he shared the dignified office with the famous Cincinnatus. He was a man of great moderation; though, like his family, he boldly resisted the encroachments of the people, and even recommended the use of arms to oppose the claims of the plebeians to appoint a consul from their own body. This question was laid aside by choosing military tribunes indiscriminately from both the patricians and plebeians. *Liv.* 3 & 4.

CLAU'DIUS CA'IUS, son of Ap. Pulcher, was consul, A.U.C. 577, and triumphed over the Istrians and Ligurians. *Liv.* 41 & 43.

CLAU'DIUS CAU'DEX, the brother of Cæcus, first persuaded his countrymen to equip a fleet against Carthage, and instead of small open boats, to build capacious vessels. He transported his army over to Sicily, subdued Hiero, and obliged the Carthaginians to fly from Messana, and was thus the first Roman who triumphed over a transmarine enemy. *Liv.* 31. c. 1.—*Polyb.* 1. c. 20.—*Seneca de Brev.* 13. —*Sil.* 6. v. 660.—*Eutrop.*

CLAU'DIUS COS'SUS, an ambassador from the Helvetii to Vitellius. *Tac. Hist.* 1. c. 69.

CLAU'DIUS CRAS'SUS, was one of the military tribunes appointed with consular authority, A.U.C. 330; and he displayed the firmness of his family in support of the patrician power. *Liv.* 4. c. 35.

CLAU'DIUS, the son of Crassus, was military tribune, 351, A.U.C., and by a manly harangue dissuaded the Romans from abandoning the siege of Veii during the winter. When that city was taken, he in vain wished the money and the plunder to be lodged in the public treasury, and not divided among the army. He was dictator, and died in his consulship with Camillus, A.U.C. 405. *Liv.* 4, 5, 6 & 7.

CLAU'DIUS DEMIA'NUS, a person bound for his crimes by the pro-consul of Asia. *Tac. Ann.* 16. c. 10.

CLAU'DIUS FAVEN'TIUS, a centurion, who, being dismissed by Galba, persuaded the fleet at Misneum to revolt. *Id. Hist.* 3. c. 57.

CLAU'DIUS HERMINIA'NUS, a governor of Cappadocia, a great persecutor of the Christians. *Tertullian. in l. ad Scapulam.*

CLAU'DIUS MARCEL'LUS. *Vid.* Marcellus.

CLAU'DIUS MA'RIUS VIC'TOR, or VICTORI'NUS, a rhetorician and poet of Massilia, in the 5th century.

CLAU'DIUS NE'RO, a consul with Liv. Salinator, who defeated and killed Asdrubal, near the river Metaurum, as he was passing from Spain into Italy, with a reinforcement for his brother Annibal. *Liv.* 27, &c.—*Horat.* 4. od. 4. v. 37.—*Sueton. in Tib.*

CLAU'DIUS PETIL'IUS, a dictator, A.U.C. 442.

CLAU'DIUS PHIR'RICUS, a naval commander, slain by Decimus Pacarius, because he would not espouse the cause of Vitelius. *Tac. Hist.* 2. c. 16.

CLAU'DIUS POL'LIO, an historian *Plin.* 7. ep. 51.

CLAU'DIUS PON'TIUS, a general of the Samnites, who conquered the Romans at the Furcæ Caudinæ, and made them pass under the yoke. *Liv.* 9. c. 1, &c.

CLAU'DIUS PUB'LIUS, a great enemy to Cicero. *Vid.* Clodius.

CLAU'DIUS P. PUL'CHER, a consul, A.U.C. 595, who, when consulting the sacred chickens, ordered them to be dipped in water, because they would not eat. He was unsuccessful in his expedition against the Carthaginians in Sicily, and was, in consequence, disgraced on his return to Rome. *Liv.* 19.—*Polyb.* 1. c. 51.—*Cic. de N. D.* 2 c. 3. *Div.* 1. c. 16.—*Flor.* 2. c. 2.—*Gell* 10. c. 6.

CLAU'DIUS QUADRIGA'RIUS, an historian in the age of Sylla. Some suppose him to be the same as the translator of Acilius. He is quoted by Livy. *Vell. Pat.* 2. c. 9.—*Liv.* 8. c. 19. l. 9. c. 5. l. 25. c. 39. l. 33. c. 10. l. 35. c. 14.

CLAU'DIUS RU'FUS, a noble Roman slain by order of the Emperor Severus. *Spart. in Vit. Sever.* c. 13.

CLAU'DIUS SANC'TUS, a general of the Gauls. *Tac, Hist.* 4. c. 62.

CLAU'DIUS SEVE'RUS, a person chosen general by the Helvetii, to oppose the violence of Cæcina. *Id. Hist.* 1. c. 67.

CLAU'DIUS SULPIC'IUS LON'GUS, was consul, A.U.C. 431.

CLAU'DIUS THE'ON, a Greek historian. *Hieronym. in Dan. Præf.*

CLAU'DIUS TIBE'RIUS NE'RO, was the elder brother of Drusus, and son of Livia Drusilla, who married Augustus after his divorce of Scribonia. He married Livia, the emperor's daughter by Scribonia, and succeeded to the empire by the name of Tiberius. *Vid.* Tiberius. *Horat.* 1. ep. 3. v. 2.

CLAU'DIUS, a consul, accused of extortion in his province of Cilicia by Dolabella, but acquitted by means of Hortensius and Pompey. He was severe as a censor; and as an augur, supported the divine origin of the profession. He perished in the civil wars of Cæsar. *Cic.* 3. *Fam.* 4.—*Div.* 1. c. 47 & 58.—*Dio.* 40

CLAU'DIUS, the father of the emperor Tiberius, quæstor to Cæsar in the wars of Alexandria.

CLAU'DIUS, a prætor of Sicily. The name of Claudius was common to many Roman consuls, and other officers of state; but nothing remarkable is recorded of them, and their name is but barely mentioned. *Liv.*

CLAU'DUS, an island of the Cretan Sea. *Ptol.*

CLAU'SIUS or CLU'SIUS, a surname of Janus. *Macrob. Sat.* 1. c. 9.—*Ovid. Fast.* 1. v. 130.

CLAU'SUS or CLAU'DIUS, a king of the Sabines, who assisted Turnus against Æneas. He was the progenitor of that Ap. Claudius who migrated to Rome, and there became the founder of the Claudian family. *Virg. Æn.* 7. v. 707. l. 10. v. 345.

CLAVETINA'TII, a people of Vindelicia, probably the Catenates of *Pliny. Strab.*

CLAV'IGER, a surname given to Janus, from his being represented with a *key*. *Ovid. Fast.* 1. v. 228. Hercules also received that surname, as he was armed with a *club*. *Ovid. Met.* 15. v. 284. *Fast.* 1. v. 544.—*Sil. Ital.* 3. v. 14.

CLAZOM'ENÆ or CLAZOM'ENA, now Vourla, a

large city of Ionia, advantageously situated on the coast of the Ægæan Sea, between Smyrna and Chius. It was founded A.U.C. 98, by the Ionians, and gave birth to Anaxagoras and other illustrious men. *Cic. Orat.* 3. c. 34. *Tusc.* 1. c. 43.—*Paus.* 7. c. 3.—*Ælian. V. H.* 2. c. 25.—*Paterc.* 1. c. 4.—*Mela*, 1. c. 17.—*Plin.* 5. c. 29.—*Strab.* 14.—*Liv.* 38. c. 39. The English form is Clement.

CLE'ADAS, a man of Platæa, who raised tombs over those who had honourably fallen in the battle against Mardonius. *Herodot.* 9. c. 85.——The father of Chilonides. *Polyæn.* 1. 8. c. 34.

CLEAN'DER, one of Alexander's officers, who killed Parmenio by the king's command. He was punished with death for offering violence to a noble virgin, and afterwards assigning her as a prostitute to his servants. *Curt.* 7. c. 2. l. 10. c. 1.——The first tyrant of Gela. *Aristot.* 5. *Polit.* c. 12.——A soothsayer of Arcadia. *Herodot.* 6. c. 83.——A favourite of the emperor Commodus, who was put to death, A.D. 190, after abusing public justice and his master's confidence.

CLEAN'DRIA, a place of Troas whence the river Rhodius flows. *Strab.*

CLEAN'DRIDAS, a Spartan general. *Polyæn.* 2. c. 10.——A man punished with death for bribing two of the Ephori.

CLEAN'THES, a Stoic philosopher of Assos in Troas, successor of Zeno. He was said to be so poor, that, to maintain himself, he used to draw water for a gardener in the night, and study in the daytime. He affected to despise riches, and therefore, when cited to appear before the Areopagus at Athens, to declare how he obtained his livelihood, he produced his friend the gardener, for whom he drew the water, and a countrywoman for whom he occasionally kneaded dough. This disregard of money drew upon him not the censures but the admiration of his judges; but when they wished liberally to reward his merits with presents, he rejected them, observing that his labour was an inexhaustible treasure. Cicero calls him the father of the stoics; and, out of respect to his virtues, the Roman senate raised a statue to his honour in Assos. It is said that he starved himself to death in his 90th year, B.C. 240. *Strab.* 13.—*Cic. de Finib.* 2. c. 69. l. 4. c. 7.—*Seneca*, ep. 44 & 107.—*Aug. de Civ. D.* 5. c. 7.—*Lactant.* 1. c. 5.——An historian praised by the *Scholiast* on the *Equites* of *Aristophanes*.

CLEAR'CHUS, a tyrant of Heraclea in Pontus, who was killed by Chion and Leonidas, Plato's pupils, during the celebration of the festivals of Bacchus, after the enjoyment of the sovereign power for twelve years, 353. B.C. *Justin.* 16. c 4.—*Diod.* 15.——The second tyrant of Heraclea of that name, died B.C. 288.——A Lacedæmonian, sent by his countrymen to restore tranquillity among the people of Byzantium. He was recalled, but refused to obey, and fled to Cyrus the younger, who made him captain of his Greek auxiliaries. He directed the retreat of the 10,000, and obtained a victory over Artaxerxes, who was so enraged at the defeat, that when Clearchus fell into his hands, by the treachery of Tissaphernes, he immediately put him to death. *Diod.* 14.—*Xenoph. Anab.*—*Frontin. Str.* 4. c. 1.——A disciple of Aristotle, mentioned by *Josephus*, l. 1. *contra Apion.* The same historian quotes a beautiful fragment of his book *de somno.* *Voss. Hist. Gr.* 1. c. 9.

CLEAR'IDAS, a son of Cleonymus, governor of Amphipolis. *Thucyd.* 4. c. 132. l. 5. c. 10.

CLE'MENS ROMA'NUS, one of the fathers of the church, said to have been contemporary with St. Paul, and bishop of Rome. Several spurious compositions are ascribed to him, but the only thing extant is his epistle to the Corinthians, written to quiet the disturbances that had arisen there. It has been much admired for the spirit of meekness, forbearance, and conciliation which it uniformly breathes. The best edition is that of Wotton, 8vo, Cantab. 1718. *Fabr. B. Gr* 1. 5. c. 1.

CLE'MENS TI'TUS FLA'VIUS, another ecclesiastical father of Alexandria, called from that circumstance Alexandrinus, flourished 206 A.D. During the persecution of Severus, he fled from Ægypt to Jerusalem and Antioch, where, by his example, his eloquence, and his writings, he powerfully recommended and enforced the genuine precepts of Christianity. His works are various, elegant, and full of erudition; the best edition is Potter's 2 vols. folio, Oxon. 1715. *Fabr. Ibid.*

CLE'MENS, a senator, who favoured the party of Niger against Severus.——A slave of Posthumous Agrippa, slain by order of Tiberius for personating his master, whom he had murdered. *Tac. Ann.* 2. c. 39.

CLEMEN'TIA, one of the virtues worshipped by the Romans as a divinity. *Plut. in Cæs.*

CLE'O, a Sicilian among Alexander's flatterers. *Curt.* 8. c. 5.

CLE'OBIS and BI'TON, two youths, sons of Cydippe the priestess of Juno at Argos. When oxen could not be procured to draw their mother's chariot to the temple of Juno, they put themselves under the yoke, and drew it 45 stadia to the temple, amidst the acclamations of the multitude, who congratulated the happy mother on account of the filial affection of her sons. Cydippe entreated the goddess to reward the piety of her sons with the best gift that could be granted to a mortal. They went to rest and awoke no more; and by this, according to the opinion of ancient historians, the goddess shewed, that death is the only truly happy event that can happen to man. The Argives raised statues to their honour at Delphi. *Cic. Tusc.* 1. c. 47.—*Val. Max.* 5. c. 4.—*Herodot.* 1. c. 31.—*Plut. de Cons. ad Apol.*

CLEOBU'LA, the wife of Amyntor, by whom she had Phœnix. *Tzetz. in Lycop* ——A daughter of Boreas and Orithyia, called also Cleopatra. She married Phineus son of Agenor, by whom she had Plexippus and Pandion. Phineus repudiated her to marry a daughter of Dardanus. *Apollod.* 3. c. 15.——A woman, mother of a son, called Euripides, by Apollo.——Mother of Cepheus and Amphidamus by Ægus.——The mother of Pithus. *Hygin.* fab. 14. 97, &c.

CLEOBULI'NA, a daughter of Cleobulus, remarkable for her genius, learning, judgment, and courage. She composed enigmas, some of which have been preserved. One of them runs thus: "A father had twelve children, and these twelve children had each thirty white sons and thirty black daughters, who are immortal, though they die every day." In this there is no need of an Œdipus, to discover that there are 12 months in the year, and that every month consists of thirty days, and of the same number of nights. *Laert.*—*Athen.* 10. c. 15. Also Cleobule'ne and Cleobu'le.

CLEOBU'LUS, one of the seven wise men of Greece, son of Evagoras of Lindus, was famous for the beautiful shape of his body. He wrote some few verses, and died in the 70th year of his age, B.C. 564. *Diog. in Vitâ.*—*Plut. in Symp.*——An historian. *Plin.* 5. c. 31.——One of the Ephori. *Thucyd.* 5. c. 36.

CLEOCH'ARES, a man sent by Alexander the Great, to command Porus to surrender. *Curt.* 8. c. 13.

CLEOCHARI'A, the mother of Eurotas by Lelex. *Apollod.* 3. c. 10.

CLEOC'RITUS, a man of licentious character. *Suidas.*—*Schol. in Ran. Aristoph.* &c.

CLEODÆ'US, a son of Hyllus. He endeavoured to recover Peloponnesus after his father's death, but to no purpose. The Greeks honored his memory by a magnificent monument. *Herodot.* 6. c. 52. l. 7. c. 204. l. 8. c. 131.—*Paus.* 3. c. 15.

CLEOD'AMAS, a philosopher and geometrician of Thasus, in the time of Plato.——A native of Ache in Thessaly, who wrote *de cura equorum.* *Steph.*

CLEODA'MUS, a Roman general under Gallienus, *Treb. Ptol.*

CLEODE'MUS, a physician. *Plut. de Symp.*

CLEODO'RA, a nymph, mother of Parnassus. *Paus.* 2. c. 6.——One of the Danaides, who married Lyxus. *Apollod.* 2. 1.

CLEODOX'A, a daughter of Niobe and Amphion, changed into a stone by Apollo, as a punishment for her mother's pride. *Apollod.* 3. c. 5.—*Tzetzes in Lyc.*

CLEOG'ENES, a son of Silenus. *Paus.* 6. c. 1.

CLEOLA'US, a son of Hercules by Argele, daughter of Thestius, who, upon the ill success of the Heraclidæ in Peloponnesus, retired to Rhodes with his wife and children. *Apollod.* 2. According to *Diodorus Siculus*, l. 4. his mother was a female slave of Jardanus the Lydian.

CLEOM'ACHUS, a boxer of Magnesia. *Strab.*

CLEOMAN'TES, a Lacedæmonian soothsayer. *Plut. in Alex.*

CLEOM'BROTUS, a king of Sparta, son of Anaxandridas. He was deterred by an eclipse of the sun from finishing a wall across the isthmus of Corinth, as a protection against the Persian invaders. *Herodot.* 9. c. 7.——Son of Pausanias. was king of Sparta, after his brother Agesipolis the First. He made war against the Bœotians, and, that he might not be suspected of treacherous communication with Epaminondas, he, with unpardonable rashness, gave that general battle at Leuctra, in a very disadvantageous place. He was killed in the engagement, and his army was destroyed, B.C. 371. *Diod.* 15.—*Paus.* 9. c. 13.—*Xenoph.* ——A son-in-law of Leonidas king of Sparta, who for a while usurped the kingdom, after the expulsion of his father-in-law. When Leonidas was re-called, Cleombrotus was banished; and his wife, Chelonis, who had accompanied her father, now accompanied her husband in his exile. *Paus.* 3, c. 6.—*Plut. in Ag. & Cleom.*——A youth of Ambracia, who threw himself into the sea, after reading Plato's treatise on the immortality of the soul. *Cic. in Tusc.* 1. c. 34.—*Ovid. in Ib.* 493.—*Callim. Epigr.* 28.

CLEOMEDES, a famous athlete of Astypalæa, an island above Crete. In a combat at Olympia he killed one of his antagonists by a blow with his fist, and being, on account of this accidental murder, deprived of the victory, he became delirious. On his return to Astypalæa, he entered a school, and pulled down the pillars which supported the roof, and crushed to death sixty boys. He was pursued with stones, and fled for shelter into a tomb, the doors of which he so strongly secured, that his pursuers were obliged to break them for access. When the tomb was opened, Cleomedes could not be found either dead or alive. The oracle of Delphi was consulted with respect to his fate, and gave in answer, *Ultimus heroum Cleomedes Astypalæus.* Upon this the people offered sacrifices to him as a god. *Paus.* 6. c. 9.—*Plut. in Rom.*

CLEOM'ENES the First, king of Sparta, conquered the Argives, and burnt 5,000 of them, by setting fire to a grove, to which they had fled for refuge. He afterwards assisted in restoring them to liberty, after the tyranny of the Pisistratidæ. By bribing the oracle, he caused Demaratus, his colleague on the throne, to be pronounced illegitimate, because he refused to punish the people of Ægina, who had deserted the Greeks. He killed himself in a fit of madness, 491 B.C. *Herodot.* 5, 6 & 7.—*Paus.* 8. c. 3, &c.

CLEOM'ENES the Second, succeeded his brother Agesipolis the Second. He reigned 61 years in the greatest tranquillity, and was father of Acrotatus and Cleonymus, and was succeeded by Areus the First, son of Acrotatus. *Paus.* 3. c. 6.

CLEOM'ENES the Third, succeeded his father Leonidas. He was of an enterprising spirit, and resolved to restore the virtuous discipline of ancient Sparta, and the salutary laws of Lycurgus in their full force, by banishing luxury and intemperance. He killed the Ephori, and removed by poison, his royal colleague Eurydamides, and made his own brother, Epiclides, king, against the laws of the state, which forbade more than one of the same family to sit on the throne. He afterwards made war against the Achæans, and attempted to destroy their league. Aratus, the general of the Achæans, who supposed himself inferior to his enemy, called Antigonus to his assistance; and Cleomenes, when he had fought the unfortunate battle of Sellasia, B.C. 222, retired into Ægypt, to the court of Ptolemy Evergetes, where his wife and children had fled before him. Ptolemy received him with great cordiality; but his successor, weak and suspicious, soon expressed his jealousy of this noble stranger, and imprisoned him. Cleomenes killed himself, and his body was flayed and exposed on a cross, B.C. 219. *Polyb.* 6.—*Plut. in Vitâ.*—*Justin.* 28. c. 4.

CLEOM'ENES, a man appointed by Alexander the Great to receive the tributes of Ægypt and Africa. *Curt.* 4. c. 8.——A man appointed arbitrator between the Athenians and the people of Megara. ——A dithyrambic poet of Rhegium.——An historian.——A Sicilian, contemporary with Verres, whose licentiousness and avarice he was fond of gratifying. *Cic. in Verr.* 4. c. 12.——A Lacedæmonian general.——A son of Apollodorus of Athens, who is said to have been the sculptor of the beautiful antique statue of Venus de Medicis, long preserved at Florence in the gallery of the grand duke.

CLE'ON, an Athenian, who, though originally a tanner, became general of the armies of the state, by his intrigues and eloquence. He took Thoron in Thrace, and, after distinguishing himself in several engagements, was killed at Amphipolis in a battle with Brasidas the Spartan general, 422 B.C. *Thucyd.* 3, 4, &c.—*Plut. in Vitâ.*—*Diod.* 12.——A general of Messsenia, who disputed with Aristodemus for the sovereignty. *Paus.* 1. 4.——A statuary of Sicyon. *Paus.* 2. c. 8.——A poet who wrote a poem on the Argonauts.——An orator of Halicarnassus, who composed an oration for Lysander. *C. Nep. & Plut. in Lys.*—*Suidas.*——A Magnesian, who wrote some commentaries, in which he speaks of portentous events, &c. *Paus.* 10. c. 4. ——A Sicilian, one of Alexander's flatterers. *Curt.* 8. c. 5.——A tyrant of Sicyon.——A friend of Phocion.

CLEO'NÆ or CLEO'NA, a village of Peloponnesus, between Corinth and Argos. Hercules killed the lion of Nemæa in its neighbourhood, and thence the animal was called Cleonæus, and the games established there Cleonæan. The lion was made a constellation. Minerva had at Cleonæ a temple, in which her statue, made by Scyllis and Dipœnus, was preserved. *Stat.* 4. *Sylv.* 4. v. 28.—*Ovid. Met.* 6. v. 417.—*Sil.* 3. v. 32.—*Paus.* 2. c. 15.—*Auson. Id.* 19. v. 1.—*Plin.* 36. c. 5.—*Pind. Nem.* 4. c. 27.——A town of Phocis.

CLEO'NE, a daughter of Asopus. *Diod.* 4.

CLEONI'CA, a young woman of Byzantium, whom Pausanias king of Sparta, invited to his bed. She was introduced into his room when he was asleep, and unluckily overturned a lamp which was by the side of the bed. Pausanias was awakened at the sudden noise, and thinking it to be some assassin, seized his sword, and killed Cleonica before he knew who she was. *Paus.* 7. c. 17.—*Plut. in Cim.* &c.

CLEONI'CUS, a freedman of Seneca. *Tacit.* 15 *Ann.* c. 45.

CLEON'NIS, a Messenian, who disputed with Aristodemus for the sovereign power of his country. *Paus.* 4. c. 10.

CLEON'YMUS, a king of Sparta, who liberated Troezene from the power of Craterus. *Polyæn.* 2. c. 29.——A son of Cleomenes the second, who called Pyrrhus to his assistance, because Areus, his brother's son, had been preferred before him in the succession. *Plut. in Pyrrh.*—*Paus.* 1. c. 3. ——A general who assisted the Tarentines against the Romans, and was conquered by Æmylius the consul. *Strab.* 6.—*Diod.* 20.——A person of so cowardly a disposition, that *Cleonymo timidor* became a proverb. *Suidas.*——An Athenian, father of Cleon, according to some; but *Thucydides*, 1. 3. 36, calls him Cleænetus.

CLEOP'ATER, an officer of Aratus.

CLEOPA'TRA, the grand-daughter of Attalus, was betrothed to Philip of Macedonia, after he had divorced Olympias. When Philip was murdered by Pausanias, Cleopatra was seized by order of the resentful Olympias, and put to death. *Diod.* 16.—*Justin.* 9. c. 7.—*Plut. in Pyrrh.*——A sister of Alexander the Great, who married Perdiccas, and was killed by Antigonus, as she attempted to flee into Ægypt to Ptolemy. *Diod.* 16 & 20.—*Justin.* 9. c. 6, l. 13. c. 6.——A mistress of Claudius Cæsar. *Tac. Ann.* 11. c. 30.——A daughter of Boreas. *Vid.* Cleobula.——A daughter of Idas and Marpessa, the daughter of Evenus, king of Ætolia. She married Meleager, son of king Œneus. *Homer. Il.* 9. v. 552.—*Paus.* 4. c. 2.——One of the Danaides. *Apollod.* 2. c. 1.——A daughter of Amyntas of Ephesus. *Paus.* 1. c. 44.——A wife of Tigranes, king of Armenia, sister of Mithridates. *Justin.* 38. c. 3.——A daughter of Tros and Calirhoe. *Apollod.* 3. c. 12.——A daughter of Ptolemy Philometor, who married Alexander Bala, and afterwards Nicanor. She killed Seleucus, Nicanor's son, because he ascended the throne without her consent. She was suspected of preparing poison for her son Antiochus, and compelled to drink it herself, B.C. 120.——A wife and sister of Ptolemy Evergetes, who raised her son Alexander, a minor, to the throne of Ægypt, in preference to his elder brother, Ptolemy Lathurus, whose interest the people favoured. As Alexander became odious to the people, Cleopatra suffered Lathurus to ascend the throne, on condition, however, that he should repudiate his sister and wife, called Cleopatra, and marry Seleuca, his younger sister. She afterwards raised her favourite, Alexander, to the throne; but her character was so capricious, and her cruelty so offensive, that he fled to avoid her tyranny. Cleopatra laid snares for him; and when Alexander heard it he put her to death. *Justin.* 39. c. 3 & 4.

CLEOPA'TRA, a queen of Ægypt, daughter of Ptolemy Auletes, and sister and wife of Ptolemy Dionysius, celebrated for her beauty and her intrigues. She admitted Cæsar to her arms, to influence him to confer upon her the kingdom in preference to her brother, who had expelled her, and she had a son by him called Cæsarion. As she had supported the cause of Brutus, Antony, in his expedition to Parthia, summoned her to appear before him at Tarsus in Cilicia. Cleopatra obeyed; but mindful of the charms which she possessed, and which had subdued the heart of Cæsar, she appeared before her judge in the most captivating attire. Her artifice succeeded; Antony became enamoured of her, and publicly married her, forgetful of his connection with Octavia, the sister of Augustus. He gave her the greatest part of the eastern provinces of the Roman empire. This behaviour was the cause of a rupture between Augustus and Antony, and these two celebrated Romans met at Actium, where Cleopatra, by fleeing with sixty sail, ruined the interests of Antony, and he was defeated. Cleopatra had retired to Ægypt, whither Antony soon after followed her. Antony killed himself upon the false information that Cleopatra was dead; and as his wound was not mortal, he was carried to the queen, who drew him up by a cord from one of the windows of the monument, where she had retired to conceal herself. Antony soon after died of his wounds; and Cleopatra, after she had received pressing invitations from Augustus, and even pretended declarations of love, destroyed herself by the bite of an asp, not to fall into the conqueror's hands. In her character Cleopatra was artful, voluptuous, and extravagant. At one of the feasts which she gave to Antony at Alexandria, she melted pearls in her drink to render her entertainment more sumptuous and expensive. She was fond of appearing dressed as the goddess Isis; and she persuaded the weak Antony to make war against the richest nations to support her debaucheries. Her mental acquirements were so great, that she has been described as capable of giving audience to the ambassadors of seven different nations, and of speaking their various languages as fluently as her own. In Antony's absence, she improved the public library of Alexandria with the addition of that of Pergamus. Two treatises, *De medicamine faciei epistolæ eroticæ*, and *De morbis mulierum*, have been falsely attributed to her. She died B.C. 30, after a reign of 24 years, in the 39th year of her age. Ægypt became a Roman province after her death. *Flor.* 4. c. 11.—*Appian.* 5. *Bell. Civ.*—*Plut. in Pomp. & Ant.*—*Horat.* 1. od. 37. v. 21, &c.—*Strab.* 17. [There is a bust of Cleopatra in the Museum of the Capitol. A recumbent figure in the Vatican was also supposed to represent her, but it is decided to be Ariadne.]

CLEOPA'TRA, a daughter of Ptolemy Epiphanes, who married Philometor, and afterwards Physcon of Cyrene.

CLEOP'ATRIS or ARSIN'OE, a fortified town of Ægypt, near the top of the Arabian Gulph. *Strab* 16.

CLEOP'ATRUS, a præfect of the Corinthians. *Plut. in Arat.*

CLEOPH'ANES, an orator of Myrlea. *Strab.* 12.

CLEOPHAN'THUS, a son of Themistocles, famous for his skill in riding. *Plut. in Menon.*——A physician. *Plin.* 20. c. 5.——A painter of Corinth. *Id.* 35 c. 3.

CLE'OPHES, a queen of India, who submitted to Alexander the Great, by whom, as some suppose, she had a son. *Curt.* 8. c. 10.

CLEOPH'OLUS, a Samian, who wrote an account of Hercules.

CLE'OPHON, a tragic poet of Athens, ten of whose tragedies are mentioned by *Suidas. Aristot. Poet.* c. 22.—*Fabr. B. Gr.* 2. c. 19.

CLEOPHY'LUS, a man whose posterity are said to have saved the poems of Homer. *Plut.*

CLEOPOM'PUS, an Athenian, who took Thronium, and conquered the Locrians. *Thucyd.* 2. c. 26. & 58.——A man wdo married the nymph Cleodora, by whom he had Parnassus. *Paus.* 10. c. 6.

CLEOPTOL'EMUS, a man of Chalcis, whose daughter was given in marriage to Antiochus. *Liv.* 36. c. 11.

CLE'OPUS, a son of Codrus. *Paus.* 7. c. 3.

CLEO'RA, the wife of Agesilaus, king of Sparta.

CLEOS'TRATUS, a youth devoted to be sacrificed to a serpent among the Thespians. *Paus.* 9. c. 26.——An ancient philosopher and astronomer of Tenedus, about 536 B.C. He first settled the places of the constellations of the zodiac, and reformed the Greek calendar. *Plin.* 2. c. 8.—*Hygin in Poet. Astron* —*Voss. de scient. Math.* c. 33. sec. 11.

CLEOX'ENUS, wrote a history of Persia. *Suidas.* —*Voss. de Hist. Gr.* 4.

CLEP'SYDRA or CLEPSY'DRA, a fountain of Messenia. *Paus.* 4. c. 31.

CLEP'SYDRA, a town of Argos.

CLE'RI, a people of Attica. *Diod. Sic.* 13.

CLES'IDES, a Greek painter, about 276 B.C., who revenged the injuries which he had received from queen Stratonice, by representing her in the arms of a fisherman. She was, however, drawn with such personal beauty that she preserved the piece, and liberally rewarded the artist.

CLE'TA and PHAEN'NA, two of the Graces, according to some authors. *Paus.* 3. c. 18.

CLETH'ARRO, a town of Arabia Petræa. *Ptol.*

CLE'THUS, the husband of Pallene, who gave her name to a city of Thrace. *Steph.*

CLIB'ANUS, a mountain of Italy, near the promontory Lacinium. *Plin.* 3. c. 10.——A town of Isauria. *Id.* 5. c. 27.

CLIDEM'IDES, according to *Callistratus*, was the son of Sophocles, but *Appollonius* makes him an actor. *Schol in. Ran.*

CLIDE'MUS, a Greek, who wrote the history of Attica, and a work upon the unexpected return of men who had been a long time absent from their country. *Vossius, H. Gr.* 3.——A writer on the Amazonian war.

CLID'ICHUS, the third decennial archon at Athens.

CLIG'ENES, an Athenian, who was hated by his countrymen for oppressing the poor, *Schol. Aristoph. Ran.*

CLIM'ACHUS, a Thurian, who wrote a work *De decem elementis*, &c.

CLI'MAX, a pass of mount Taurus, formed by the projection of a hill into the Mediterranean Sea. *Strab.* c. 14.——A mountain of Phœnicia, near Byblus.——A mountain of Pamphylia. *Strab.* 4.——A maritime town of Galatia. *Ptol.*——A mountain of Arabia Felix. *Id.*

CLIM'ENUS, a son of Arcas, descended from Hercules. *Paus.* 1. 5.

CLIN'IAS, a Pythagorean philosopher and musician, who flourished 520 B.C. *Plut. Symp.*—*Ælian. V. H.* 14. c. 23.——A son of Alcibiades, the bravest man in the Grecian fleet which fought against Xerxes. *Herodot.* 8. c. 17.——The father of Alcibiades, killed at the battle of Coronea. *Plut. in Alc.*——The father of Aratus, killed by Abantidas, B.C. 263. *Plut. in Arat.*——A friend of Solon. *Id. in Sol.*——A person, probably an historian, mentioned by *Agatharcides* in his book *De mari Erythræo. Voss. Hist. Gr.* 3.

CLINIP'PIDES, an Athenian general in Lesbus. *Diod.* 12.

CLIN'IUS of Cos, was general of 7000 Greeks, in the pay of Nectanebus, king of Ægypt. He was killed with some of his troops, by Nicostratus and the Argives as he passed the Nile. *Diod.* 16.

CLI'O, the eldest of the Muses, was daughter of Jupiter and Mnemosyne, and presided over history. She is represented crowned with laurel, holding a trumpet in one hand and a book in the other. Sometimes she holds a *plec'rum* or quill with a lute. Her name signifies honour and reputation (κλέ❀, *gloria*); and it was her office faithfully to record the actions of brave and illustrious heroes. She had Hyacintha by Pierus son of Magnes, and was also mother of Hymenæus and Ialemus, according to others. *Cæl. Rhod. Ant.* 28. c. 24.—*Hesiod. Theog.* v. 75.—*Apollod.* 1. c. 3. —*Strab.* 14. [The finest representation of this Muse is in the Vatican.]——One of Cyrene's nymphs. *Virg. G.* 4. v. 341.

CLISITHE'RA, a daughter of Idomeneus, promised in marriage to Leucus, by whom she was murdered.

CLIS'THENES, the last tyrant of Sicyon. *Aristot. Polit.* 5. c. 12.——An Athenian of the family of Alcmæon. It is said that he established ostracism, and that he was the first who was banished by that institution. He banished Isagoras, and was himself soon after restored. *Plut. in Arist.*—*Herodot.* 5. c. 66, &c.——A person censured as effeminate and incontinent. *Aristoph.*——An orator. *Cic. in Brut.* c. 7.

CLI'TÆ, a people of Cilicia. *Tacit. Ann.* 12. c. 55. ——A place near mount Athos. *Liv.* 44. c. 11. ——A city of Bithynia. *Ptol.*

CLITAGO'RA, a Thessalian poetess. *Schol. Aristoph. Vesp.* 519.

CLITAR'CHUS, a man who made himself absolute at Eretria, by means of Philip of Macedon. He was ejected by Phocion. *Diod. Sic.* 16.——An historian, who accompanied Alexander the Great, of whose life he wrote the history. *Curt.* 9. c. 5.

CLI'TE the wife of Cyzicus, who hanged herself when she saw her husband dead.—*Apollon.* 1.—*Orpheus.*

CLITER'NIA or CLITER'NUM, according to *Ptolemy*, a town of Italy, now Celano. *Mela*, 2. c. 4.

CLITODE'MUS, an ancient writer. *Paus.* 10. c. 15.

CLITOM'ACHUS, a Carthaginian philosopher of the third academy, who was pupil and successor to Carneades at Athens, B.C. 128. *Diog. in Vitâ.* ——An athlete of a modest countenance and behaviour. *Ælian. V. H.* 3. c. 30.——A Thurian, a pupil of Euclid.

CLITON'YMUS, wrote a treatise on Sybaris and Italy. *Plut. Par. Min.* c. 10.—*Voss. Hist. Gr.* 3.

CLIT'OPHON, a man of Rhodes, who wrote a history of India, &c. *Voss. Ibid.*——An Athenian ridiculed by the comic poets. *Schol. in Ran. Aristoph.*

CLI'TOR, a son of Lycaon.——A son of Azan, who founded a city in Arcadia, called after his name. *Paus.* 8. c. 4.—*Apollod.* 3. c. 8. Ceres, Æsculapius, Ilythia the Dioscuri, and other deities, had temples in that city. There was also in the town a fountain called Clitorius, the waters of which were said to give a dislike for wine. *Ovid. Met.* 15. v. 322.—*Plin.* 32. c. 2.—*Liv.* 39. c. 35.—*Ptol.* 5. c. 16.

CLI'TOR, a river of Arcadia. *Paus.* 8. c. 12.

CLITO'RIA, the wife of Cimon the Athenian.

CLITUM'NUS, a river of Italy, the waters of which, when drunk, were said to render oxen white. *Propert.* 2. el. 10. v. 25.—*Virg. G.* 2. v. 146.—*Plin.* 2. c. 103.

CLI'TUS, a familiar friend and foster-brother of Alexander the Great, whom he accompanied in his Asiatic expedition, and to whose esteem he recommended himself by his courage and military experience. In a severe battle, the life of Alexander, who was generally foremost in danger, was saved by the timely and valorous interference of Clitus; but this friendly act was forgotten in the hour of drunkenness and debauchery. Clitus, though the friend of Alexander, would not demean himself to become his flatterer, and when he presumed at a feast, with the boldness and freedom of a blunt soldier, to extol the exploits of Philip above those of his son, the king's fury was kindled, and with a javelin he meanly stabbed to the heart the honest and unsuspecting veteran. When too late, Alexander became sensible of his atrocious conduct, and inconsolable for the loss of this valued friend. *Justin.* 12. c. 6.—*Plut. in Alex.*—*Curt.* 4. c. 13. l. 8. c. 1, 2, 18.——A commander of Polyperchon's ships, defeated by Antigonus. *Diod.* 18.——An officer sent by Antipater, with 240 ships, against the Athenians, whom he conquered near the Echinades. *Diod.* 18.——A Trojan prince son of Pisenor, and charioteer to Polydamas. He was killed by Teucer. *Homer. Il.* 15. v. 445.——A disciple of Aristotle, who wrote a book on Miletus. *Vos. Hist. Gr.* 1. c. 10.

CLOACI'NA, a goddess at Rome, who presided over the Cloacæ. Some suppose her to be Venus, whose statue was found in the Cloacæ, whence the name. The Cloacæ were large receptacles for the filth of the whole city, began by Tarquin the Elder, and finished by Tarquin the Proud. They were built all under the city; and the building was so strong and so firmly cemented, and the stones so large, that though they were continually washed by impetuous torrents, they remained in a perfect state during above 700 years. There were public officers chosen to take care of the Cloacæ, called *Curatores Cloacarum urbis.* *Liv.* 3. c. 48.—*Plin.* 5. c. 29.—*Aug. de Civ. D.* 4. c. 8 & 23.—*Prudent. de Anop.* 265.—*Tertull. de Pall.* 4.

CLOAN'THUS, one of the companions of Æneas, in his voyage from Troy to Italy. The family of the Cluentii at Rome were descended from him. *Virg. Æn.* 5. v. 122.

CLO'DIA, a noble patrician family at Rome, the same as the Claudia.

CLO'DIA, the wife of Lucullus, repudiated for her lasciviousness. *Plut. in Lucull.*——An opulent matron of Rome, mother of D. Brutus. *Cic. ad Attic.*——A vestal virgin. *Vid.* Claudia. ——A vestal virgin of the same family, who successfully repressed the rudenes of a tribune who attempted to stop the procession of her father in his triumph through the streets of Rome. *Cic. pro M. Cæl.*——A woman who married Q. Metellus, and afterwards disgraced herself by her amours with Cœlius, and her incest with her brother Publius, for which he is severely and eloquently arraigned by *Cicero, Ibid.* It is said by Cicero that she poisoned her husband.

CLO'DIA LEX, *de Cypro*, was enacted by the tribune Clodius, A.U.C. 695, to reduce Cyprus into a Roman province, and to expose Ptolemy, king of Ægypt, to sale in his regal ornaments. It empowered Cato to go with the prætorian power, and preside at the auction of the king's goods, and commissioned him to return the money to Rome. —Another, *de Magistratibus* A.U.C. 695, by Clodius, the tribune. It forbade the censors to put a stigma or mark of infamy upon any person who had not been actually accused and condemned by both the censors.—Another, *de Religione*, by the same, A.U.C. 696, to deprive the priest of Cybele, a native of Pessinus, of his office, and confer the priesthood upon Brotigonus, a Gallogrecian.—Another, *de Provinciis*, A.U.C. 696, which allotted the provinces of Syria, Babylon, and Persia, to the consul Gabinus; and Achaia, Thessaly, Macedon, and Greece, to his colleague Piso, with proconsular power. It also empowered these two officers to defray the expenses of their march from the public treasury.—Another, A.U.C. 695, which required the same distribution of corn among the people gratis, as had been given them before at six *asses* and a *triens* the bushel.—Another, A.U.C. 695, by the same, *de Judiciis*; to call to account such as had executed a Roman citizen without a judgment of the people, and all the formalities of a trial. This law was particularly directed against Cicero, for his conduct during Cataline's conspiracy.——Another, by the same, to pay no attention to the appearances of the heavens, while any affair was before the people.—Another, to make the power of the tribunes free, in making and proposing laws.—Another, to reestablish the companies of artists, which had been instituted by Numa, but since his time abolished.

CLODIA'NUS, a river of Hispania Tarraconensis. *Ptol.*—*Mela*, 2. c. 6.

CLO'DII FO'RUM, a town of Italy. *Plin.* 3. c. 15.

CLO'DIUS MA'CER, a turbulent Roman, put to death by order of Galba. *Tacit. Hist.* 1. c. 7.

CLO'DIUS PUB'LIUS, a Roman descended from an illustrious family, and remarkable for his licentiousness, avarice, and ambition. He introduced himself in women's clothes into the house of J. Cæsar, whilst Pompeia, Cæsar's wife, of whom he was enamoured, was celebrating the mysteries of Ceres, at which no man was permitted to be present. He was accused for this violation of human and divine laws; but he corrupted his judges, and by that means screened himself from justice. Seditious in his conduct, and eager for power, he descended from a patrician into a plebeian family to become a tribune. He was such an enemy to Cato, that he enacted a law to compel him to go with prætorian power on an expedition against Ptolemy, king of Cyprus, that, by the difficulty of the campaign he might ruin his reputation, and at the same destroy his interest at Rome during his absence. Cato, however, by his prudence and uncommon success, frustrated the views of Clodius. He was also an inveterate enemy to Cicero, who had appeared against him at his trial, and at the same time endeavoured to draw down the execration and vengeance of the populace upon his enormities. By his influence and intrigues, the orator was banished from Rome, partly on pretence that he had punished with death and without trial, the adherents of Catiline. Not satisfied with this seeming disgrace of his enemy, Clodius wreaked his vengeance upon Cicero's house, which he burnt, and exposed all his goods for sale; which, however, to his great mortification, no one offered to buy. In spite of Clodius, Cicero was recalled, and all his property was restored to him by the decree of the people. Baffled and disappointed in one instance, Clodius soon found another to give vent to his enmity; and Milo, Cicero's friend, was attacked with all the virulence of party. From accusation, Milo and Clodius had recourse to open violence; and accidentally meeting on the Appian road near Bovillæ, a quarrel ensued between their respective attendants, in which the masters soon eagerly joined. Clodius was wounded in the affray, and carried to a neighbouring house, where Milo, with unjustifiable resentment, pursued his enemy, and ordered him to be dragged out and put to death. The body of the murdered Clodius was left exposed in the public road, till Tedius, a senator, brought it to Rome, where the fatal catastrophe inflamed the passions of the populace. Milo was summoned to a trial, and though defended by all the powers and eloquence of Cicero, he was condemned and banished. Clodius had by Fulvia a son, who bore his name and was step-son of Antony. *Plut. in Cic.—Appian. de Civ.* 2.—*Cic. pro. Milon. & pro. Domo.—Dio.*

CLO'DIUS LICIN'IUS, wrote a history of Rome. *Liv.* 29. c. 22.—*Tacit.* 1. *Hist.* c. 7.

CLO'DIUS PUL'CHER, a Roman orator. *Ascon. Pædian.*

CLO'DIUS QUIRINA'LIS, a rhetorician in Nero's age. *Tacit. Ann.* 13. c. 30.

CLO'DIUS SEX'TUS, a rhetorician of Sicily, intimate with M. Antony, whose preceptor he was. *Suet. de Clar. Orat.—Cic. in Philip.*——A kinsman of Publius. He brought the body of his relation naked, and with all the wounds exposed, into the senate, where he inflamed the mob by his speeches, and tearing up the seats and tables of the edifice, made with them a funeral pile. The senate-house was destroyed in the conflagration, and Clodius, accused for this seditious conduct, was banished, but recalled afterwards by M. Antony. *Cic.* 14. *Att.* 13.—*Ascon. in Cic. Arg.*

CLŒ'LIA, a Roman virgin, given, with other maidens, as hostages to Porsenna, king of Etruria. She escaped from her confinement, and swam across the Tiber to Rome. Her unprecedented virtue was rewarded by her countrymen with an equestrian statue in the Via Sacra. *Liv.* 2. c. 13.—*Virg. Æn.* 8. v. 651.—*Dionys. Hal.* 5.—*Juv.* 8. v. 265.——A patrician family descended from Clœlius, one of the companions of Æneas. *Dionys.*

CLŒ'LIÆ FOS'SÆ, a place near Rome. *Plut. in Coriol.*

CLŒ'LIUS GRAC'CHUS, a general of the Volsci and Sabines in their wars against Rome. He was conquered by Q. Cincinnatus, the dictator.

CLŒ'LIUS TI'TUS SIC'ULUS, one of the first tribunes appointed with consular power. *Liv.* 4. c. 7.

CLŒ'LIUS TUL'LUS, a Roman ambassador put to death by Tolumnius, king of the Veientes. A statue was erected to his honour. *Liv.* 4. c. 17.

CLO'NAS, a musician. *Plut. de Music.*

CLO'NIA, the mother of Nycteus. *Apollod.* 3. c. 10.

CLO'NIA, a lake in the interior of Libya. *Ptol.*

CLO'NIUS, a Bœotian, who went with 50 ships to the Trojan war. *Homer. Il.* 2.——A Trojan killed by Messapus in Italy. *Virg. Æn.* 10. v. 749.——A Trojan killed by Turnus. *Id.* 9. v. 574.

CLO'TA or **GLO'TA**, the ancient name of the Clyde. *Tac. Agric.* c. 23.

CLO'THO, the youngest of the three Parcæ, was supposed to preside over the moment when men enter into life. She was represented as holding a distaff in her hand, and spinning the thread of life, whence her name κλώθειν to spin). She was also represented as wearing a crown with seven stars, and covered with a variegated robe. *Vid.* Parcæ. *Hesiod. Theog.* v. 218.—*Apollod.* 1. c. 3.

CLU'ACA, a city of Media. *Ptol.*

CLUACI'NA, a name of Venus, whose statue was erected in that place where peace was made between the Romans and Sabines, after the rape of the virgins. *Vid.* Cloacina.

CLUA'NA, a city of Picenum, in Italy. *Plin.* 3. c. 13.

CLUEN'TIUS, a Roman citizen, accused by his mother Sassia of having murdered his father-in-law, Oppianicus, 54 B.C. He was ably defended by Cicero, in an oration still extant. The family of the Cluentii was descended from Cloanthus, one of the companions of Æneas. *Virg. Æn.* 5. v. 122.—*Cic. pro Cluent.*

CLUIL'IA FOS'SA, a place five miles distant from Rome. *Liv.* 1. c. 23.

CLU'NIUM, a city of Corsica. *Ptol.*

CLU'PEA or **CLYP'EA**, now Aklibia, a maritime town of Africa Propria, 22 miles east of Carthage. It was situated near the promontory of Mercury, and received its name from its exact resemblance to a shield, *clypeus*. *Lucan.* 4. v. 586.—*Strab.* 17. *Liv.* 27. c. 29.—*Cæs. Cir.* 2. c. 23.

CLU'SIA, a daughter of an Etrurian king, of whom Val. Torquatus, the Roman general, became enamoured. He asked her in marriage of her father, who slighted his addresses; upon which he besieged and destroyed his town. Clusia threw herself down from a high tower, and fell to the ground unhurt. *Plut. in Parall.*

CLUSI'NI FON'TES, baths in Etruria. *Horat.* 1. ep. 15. v. 9.

CLUSI'NI, a people of Etruria. *Plin.* 3. c. 5.

CLUSI'NUS or **CLU'SIUS**, a surname of Janus, when his temple was shut. *Ovid. Fast.* 1. v. 130.

CLUSI'OLUM, a town of Umbria. *Plin.* 3. c. 14.

CLU'SIUM, now Chiusi, a town of Etruria, on the Clanis, taken by the Gauls under Brennus. Porsenna was buried there. At the north of Clusium there was a lake called Clusina Palus, which extended northward as far as Arretium, and had a communication with the Arnus, which falls into the sea at Pisæ. *Diod.* 14.—*Virg. Æn.* 10. v. 167 & 655.

CLU'SIUS, a small river of Cisalpine Gaul. It forms one of the tributary streams which fall into the Po. *Polyb.* 2.

CLUSTIME'NA, the wife of Dryas, mother of Lycurgus, according to some. *Stat. Theb.* 9. v. 842.—*Boccac. Gen. Deor.* 11. c. 21.

CLU'VIA, a noted debauchee, &c. *Juv.* 2. v. 49.——A courtezan of Campania, whose generosity towards the Roman captives was liberally rewarded by the senate. *Liv.* 26. c. 33 & 34.

CLU'VIA, a place of Samnium. *Liv.* 9. c. 31.

CLUVIDIE'NUS QUIE'TUS, a person sent to an island in the Ægean Sea, after the discovery of Piso's conspiracy. *Tac. Ann.* 15. c. 71.

CLUVIE'NUS, an obscure poet, mentioned by *Juvenal*, 1. v. 8.

CLU'VIUS RU'FUS, a quæstor, A.U.C. 693. *Cic. ad Fam.* 13. ep. 56.——A consul placed over Spain in the time of Galba. He wrote *res sub imperio Neronis gestas*. *Tac. Hist.* 1. c. 8.—*Ann.* 13. c. 20.

CLU'VIUS, a man of Puteoli, appointed by Cæsar to divide the lands of Gaul. *Cic. Liv.* 13. c. 7.——The father of Helvidius Priscus. *Tac. Hist.* 4. c. 5.

CLYM'ENE, a daughter of Oceanus and Tethys, who married Japetus, by whom she had Atlas, Prometheus, Menœtius, and Epimetheus. *Hesiod. Theog.* 508, &c.——One of the Nereides, mother of Mnemosyne, by Jupiter. *Hygin.* præf. fab. & fab. 152.—*Homer. Il.* 18. v. 47.—*Virg. G.* 4. v. 345.——The mother of Thesimenus, by Parthenopæus. *Hygin.* fab. 71.——A daughter of Mynias, mother of Atalanta, by Jasus. *Apollod.* 3.—*Paus.* 9. c. 36.

l. 10. c. 29.——A daughter of Cratus, who married Nauplius. *Apollod.* 2.——The mother of Phæthon, by Apollo. Hyginus asserts, however, that Phæthon was son of Clymenus and Merope, but other mythologists maintain a different opinion. *Hygin.* 154.—*Ovid. Met.* 1. v. 756.——A Trojan woman. *Paus.* 10. c. 26.——The mother of Homer, according to a report mentioned by Pausanias, who adds that he was shown her monument in the island of Ios, and by its side that of her illustrious son. *Paus.* 10. c. 24.——A female servant of Helen, who accompanied her mistress to Troy when she eloped with Paris. *Ovid. Heroid.* 17. v. 267.—*Homer. Il.* 3. v. 144.

CLYMENE'IDES, a patronymic given to Phaethon's sisters, as daughters of Clymene.

CLYM'ENUS, a king of Orchomenus, son of Presbon, and father of Erginus, Stratius, Arrhon, and Axius. He received a wound from a stone thrown by a Theban, of which he died. His son, Erginus, who succeeded him, made war against the Thebans, to revenge his death. *Apollod.* 2.—*Paus.* 9. c. 37.——One of the descendants of Hercules, who built a temple in honour of Minerva of Cydonia. *Id.* 6. c. 21.——A son of Phoroneus. *Id.* 2. c. 35.——A king of Elis. *Plin.*——A son of Œneus, king of Calydon.——A surname of Pluto. *Ovid. Fast.* 6. v. 757.

CLYPE'NUS, a bay of the German Ocean. *Plin.* 4. c. 13.

CLYSON'YMUS, a son of Amphidamas, killed by Patroclus during the Trojan war. *Apollod.* 3. c. 13.

CLYS'TRUS, a town of Silicia. *Ptol.*

CLY'TÆ, a people of Macedonia. *Plin.*

CLYTÆMNES'TRA, a daughter of Tyndarus king of Sparta, by Leda. She was born, together with her brother Castor, from one of the eggs which her mother brought forth. Clytæmnestra married Agamemnon king of Argos. She had before married Tantalus, son of Thyestes, according to Euripides, Pausanias, and Diodorus, but the opinion is rejected by Eustathius, who observes that Homer does not mention it, but on the other hand declares that her marriage with Agamemnon was celebrated as soon as she came to nubile years. When Agamemnon went to the Trojan war, he entrusted to his cousin Ægisthus the care of his wife and family, and of all his domestic affairs. Besides this, a certain favourite musician was appointed by Agamemnon to watch over the conduct of the guardian, as well as that of Clytæmnestra. In the absence of Agamemnon, Ægisthus paid his addresses to Clytæmnestra, and after he had criminally alienated her heart from her husband, he publicly lived with her. Her infidelity reached the ears of Agamemnon before the walls of Troy, and he resolved to take full revenge upon the adulterers at his return. He was prevented, however, from putting his schemes into execution. Clytæmnestra, with her adulterer, murdered him at his arrival, as he came out of the bath; or, according to other accounts, as he sat down at a feast prepared to celebrate his happy return. Cassandra, whom Agamemnon had brought from Troy, shared his fate; and Orestes would also have been deprived of life, like his father, had not his sister Electra removed him from the reach of the cruel Clytæmnestra. After this murder, Clytæmnestra publicly married Ægisthus, who ascended the throne of Argos. Orestes, after an absence of seven years, returned to Mycenæ, resolved to revenge his father's murder. He concealed himself in the house of his sister Electra, who had been married by the adulterers to a person of mean extraction and indigent circumstances. His death was publicly announced; and when Ægisthus and Clytæmnestra repaired to the temple of Apollo to return thanks to the god for the death of the surviving son of Agamemnon, Orestes, who with his faithful friend Pylades had concealed himself in the temple, rushed upon the adulterers, and killed them both with his own hand. They were buried without the walls of the city, as their remains were deemed unworthy to be laid in the sepulchre of Agamemnon. *Vid.* Ægisthus, Agamemnon, Orestes, Electra. *Diod.* 4.—*Homer. Odyss.* 11.—*Apollod.* 3. c. 10.—*Paus.* 2. c. 18 & 22.—*Euripid. in Orest.*—*Sophocl. in Electrā.*—*Hygin.* fab. 117 & 140.—*Propert.* 3. el. 19.—*Virg. Æn.* 4. v. 471.—*Philostr. Icon.* 2. c. 9.—*Eustath. in Odyss.* 11.—*Lycophr. in Cass.*—*Athenæus. in Deip.* 13.

CLYT'IA or CLYT'IE, a daughter of Oceanus and Tethys, beloved by Apollo She was deserted by her lover, who paid his addresses to Leucothoe; and this so irritated her, that she discovered the whole intrigue to her rival's father. Apollo despised her the more for this conduct, and she pined away and was changed into a flower, commonly called a sun-flower, which still turns its head towards the sun in his course, as in pledge of her unaltered love. *Ovid. Met.* 4. fab. 3, &c.

Clyt'ia, a daughter of Amphidamas, mother of Pelops by Tantalus. *Schol. Euripid.*——A concubine of Amyntor, son of Phrastor. She was the cause, by her calumny, that Amyntor put out the eyes of his falsely accused son Phœnix. *Pherecyd. apud Sch.*—*Euripid. in Orest.*—*Homer. Il.* 9.—*Apollod.* 3.——A daughter of Pandarus. *Paus.*

CLYT'IUS, a son of Laomedon by Strymo. *Homer. Il.* 10.——A youth in the army of Turnus, beloved by Cydon. *Virg. Æn.* 10. v. 325.——A giant killed by Vulcan in the war waged against the gods. *Apollod.* 1. c. 6.——The father of Pireus, who faithfully attended Telemachus. *Homer. Odyss.* 15. v. 251.——A man who followed Æneas into Italy, where he was killed by Turnus. *Virg. Æn.* 9. v. 774. l. 10. v. 129. l. 11. v. 666.——A son of Alcmæon, the son of Amphiaraus. *Paus.* 6. c. 17.

CLY'TUS, a centaur present at the contest occasioned by the nuptials of Pirithous. *Ovid. Met.* l. 6.—*Val. Flacc.* 8, *Argon.* v. 314.

CLYZÆ'I people between the Ænianæ and the Dolopes. *Diod. Sic.* 18. Some read Cyzæi.

CLYZOM'ENE, a town of Bithynia.

CNACA'DIUM, a mountain of Laconia. *Paus.* 3. c. 24.

CNAC'ALUS, a mountain of Arcadia, where festivals were celebrated in honour of Diana, who was called from this circumstance Cnacalysia. *Pausan.* 8. c. 23.

CNA'GIA, a surname of Diana, from Cnagius, a Spartan who carried off her image. *Pausanias, Lacon.* 3, relates the matter differently.

CNE'MUS, a Macedonian general, unsuccessful in an expedition against the Acarnanians. *Diod.* 12.—*Thucyd.* 2. c 66, &c.

CNE'US or CNÆ'US, a prænomen common to many Romans.

CNIDIN'IUM, a name given to a monument near Ephesus. *Diod. Sic.* 14.

CNI'DUS or GNI'DUS, a town on a promontory of the same name in Doris in Caria, which successively bore the names of Triopia, Pegusa, and Stadia. It was founded by Triopas the son of Abas. Venus, surnamed the Cnidian, was the chief deity of the place, and had there a temple rendered famous for a marble statue of the goddess. This beautiful image was the master-piece of Praxiteles, who had infused into it all the soft graces and attractions of the accomplished Phryne, or his favourite Cratina; and it became so deservedly celebrated that travellers visited the spot with eagerness and admiration, and Nicomedes king of Bithynia offered to pay all the debts with which the Cnidians were oppressed, that he might obtain possession of that elegant piece of statuary. *Lucian. Dial. Amor.*—*Horat.* 1. od. 30.—*Plin.* 36. c. 15.—*Strab.* 14.—*Ptol.* 5. c. 2.—*Mela,* 1. c. 16.—*Paus.* 1. c. 1.

CNO'PUS, one of the descendants of Codrus, was leader of the Ionian colonists. *Polyæn.* 8.——A name of the river Ismenus.

CNOS'SIA, a mistress of Menelaus. *Apollod.* 3. c. 11.

CNOS'SUS or GNOS'SUS, a celebrated town of Crete, about 25 stadia from the sea. It was built by Minos, and had a famous labyrinth. *Paus.* 1. c. 27.

Cnos'sus, a writer quoted by the *Scholiast* on *Apollonius,* l. 4.—*Voss. Hist. Gr.* 3. p. 346.

CO, CO'OS, or COS, now Zia, one of the Cyclades, situate near the coasts of Asia, about 15 miles from Halicarnassus. Its chief town was called Cos, and anciently bore the name of Astypalæa. It gave birth to Hippocrates, Apelles, and Simonides, and was famous for its fertility, for the wine and silk-worms which it produced, and for the manufacture of silk and cotton of a beautiful and delicate texture. The women of the island always dressed in white; and their garments were so thin and transparent, that their bodies could be seen through, according to *Ovid. Met.* 7. fab. 9. The women of Cos were changed into cows by Venus or Juno; because they reproached her for suffering Hercules to lead Geryon's flock through their territories. *Tibull.* 2. el. 4. v. 29.—*Isidor.* 14. c. 6.—*Horat.* 4. od. 12. v. 9. l. 1. *Sat.* 2. v. 101.—*Strab.* 14.—*Plin.* 11. c. 23.—*Propert.* 1. el. 2. v. 2. l. 2. el. 1. v. 5. l. 4. el. 2. v. 23.—*Ovid. A. A.* 2. v. 298.

Co, a city of Ægypt.

CO'A, a town of Arabia Felix. *Ptol.*

COAMA'NI, a people of Asia. *Mela*, 1. c. 2.

COAN'CA, a city of India within the Ganges. *Ptol.*

COAS'TRÆ or COAC'TRÆ, a people of Asia, near the Palus Mæotis. *Lucan.* 3. v. 246.

COB'ALI, certain dæmons, attendants upon Bacchus. *Aristoph. Schol. in Plut.*

COBAN'DI, a nation of Germany. *Ptol.*

COB'ARES, a celebrated magician of Media, in the age of Alexander. *Curt.* 7. c. 4.

COB'ILUS, a river of Bithynia. *Val. Flacc. Argon.* 5. v. 102. *Apollonius* is thought to call it Crobialus. It is probably the Cobulatus of *Livy*.

COB'ORIS, an island of the Arabic Gulph. *Plin.* 6. c. 28.

CO'BRYS, a city of Thrace. *Steph.*

CO'BUM or CO'BUS, a river of Colchis, rising in mount Caucasus. Its sands abound with gold, whence arose the fable of the golden fleece.

COC'ALA. a city of India within the Genges. *Ptol.* ——A place of Carmania. *Arrian.*

COCA'LIA, a city of Cappadocian Pontus. *Ptol.*

COC'ALUS, a king of Sicily, who hospitably received Dædalus, when he fled from the hands of Minos. When Minos arrived in Sicily, the daughters of Cocalus destroyed him while he was in the bath, bribed, it is said, by the beautiful and curious automata which Dædalus gave them. Some say Cocalus himself destroyed Minos, after he had privately invited him to a meeting; as he was unable to face him in the field. *Hygin.* fab. 44.—*Conon* 25 *apud Phot.*—*Schol. Pindar.* 4. *Nem.*—*Ovid Met.* 8. v. 261.—*Diod.* 4.

COCAN'ICUS, a lake of Sicily. *Plin.* 31. c. 7.

COCCE'IUS NER'VA, a friend of Horace and Mecænas, and grandfather of the emperor Nerva. He was one of those to whose prudence and moderation was referred the settlements of the disputes between Augustus and Antony. He afterwards accompanied Tiberius in his retreat in Campania, and starved himself to death. *Tacit. Ann.* 4. c. 58. l. 6. c. 26.—*Horat.* 1. sat. 5. v. 27.—*Appian. B. C.* 5.—*Cic.* 12. *Att.* 13 & 18. [There is a bust of Nerva in the collection of the Villa Pamfili, near Rome.

COCCE'IUS NER'VA, an architect of Rome in the age of Augustus, one of whose buildings, the present cathedral of Naples is still in existence.

COCCE'IUS, a nephew of Otho. *Plut.*——A man to whom Nero granted the honours of a triumph, after the discovery of the Pisonian conspiracy. *Tacit.* 15 *Ann.* c. 72.

COCCE'IUS PROC'ULUS, a man bribed by Otho. *Tac. Hist.* 1. c. 24.

COCCON'AGÆ, a people of India within the Ganges. *Ptol.*

COCCYG'IUS, called Coccyx by *Pausanias*, 1. 2, a mountain of Peloponnesus, near the river Inachus. Jupiter was surnamed Coccygius from this mountain.

CO'CHE or CHO'CHE, a town of Arabia Deserta. *Ptol.*

COCHLU'SA, an island near Lycia. *Steph.*

COCIL'LUM, a town of Mysia. *Plin.* 5. c. 30.

COCIN'THUS, a town and promontory of the Brutii, now cape Stilo, projecting into the Ionian Sea, at the north of Locri. *Plin.* 3. c. 5.—*Polyb.* 2.

CO'CLES PUB. HORAT., a celebrated Roman, who, alone, opposed the whole army of Porsenna at the head of a bridge, while his companions behind him were cutting off the communication with the other shore. When the bridge was destroyed, Cocles, though severely wounded in the leg by the darts of the enemy, leapt into the Tiber, and swam across with his arms. A brazen statue was raised to him in the temple of Vulcan, by the consul Publicola, for his eminent services. He had the use of only *one eye*, from which circumstance he received the name of Cocles. *Liv.* 2. c. 10.—*Val. Max.* 3. c. 2.—*Virg. Æn.* 8. v. 650.

COCOS'SII, a people of Mauritania Tingitana. *Ptol.*

COC'TIÆ or COT'TIÆ, certain parts of the Alps, called after Coctius, the conqueror of the Gauls, who was in alliance with Augustus. They were situated between the head of the Po, and the west of the river Duria. The inhabitants were called Cottii. *Tacit. Hist.* 4. c. 68.

COCUN'DÆ, a people of India. *Plin.* 6. c. 20.

COCY'TUS, a river of Epirus. The word is derived from κωκύειν, *to weep or lament.* Its etymology, the unwholesomeness of its water, and above all, its vicinity to the Acheron, have made the poets call it one of the rivers of hell, hence *Cocytia virgo* is applied to Alecto one of the furies. *Virg, G.* 3. v. 38. l. 4. v. 479. *Æn.* 6. v. 297. 323. l. 7. v. 479, *& Serius locis.*—*Paus.* 1. c. 17.——A small river of Campania, flowing into the Lucrine lake.

CODA'NUS SINUS, one of the ancient names of the Baltic Sea. *Plin.* 4. c. 13.

CODDU'RA, a city of India within the Ganges. *Ptol.*

CODOMAN'NUS, a surname of Darius the Third, king of Persia.

CODRA'VA, a city of India within the Ganges. *Ptol.*

COD'RIDÆ, the descendants of Codrus, who went from Athens at the head of several colonies. *Paus.* 7. c. 2.

CODROP'OLIS, a town of Illyricum. *Appian.*

CO'DRUS, the 17th and last king of Athens, was son of Melanthus. When the Heraclidæ made war against Athens, the oracle declared that the victory would be granted to that nation whose king was killed in battle. The Heraclidæ upon this gave strict orders to spare the life of Codrus; but the patriotic king disguised himself, and attacked one of the enemy, by whom he was killed. The Athenians in consequence, obtained the victory, and Codrus was deservedly called the father of his country. He reigned 21 years, and was killed 1070, B.C. To pay great honour to his memory, and to reward his patriotism, the Athenians made a resolution, that no man was worthy to reign after Codrus, and that no one should be permitted to hold the sovereign power of Athens, under the name of king, and the government was therefore entrusted to the care of perpetual archons. *Paterc.* 1. c. 2.—*Justin.* 2. c. 6 & 7.—*Conon. Narr.* 39.—*Paus.* 1. c. 19. l. 7. c. 25.—*Val. Max.* 5. c. 6.——A man who with his brothers, killed Hegesias, tyrant of Ephesus. *Polyæn.* 6. c. 49.——A Latin poet, contempory with Virgil. *Virg. Ecl.* 7. ——Another, in the reign of Domitian. whose poverty became a proverb. *Juv.* 3. v. 203. l. 1. v. 2.—*Mart.* 3. epigr. 15.

CODU'TÆ, a people of India without the Ganges. *Ptol.*

CŒC'ILE, a town of Hispania Bœtica. *Ptol.*

CŒCIL'IUS, a Roman centurion. *Cæs. Civ. Bell.* 1. c. 46.

CŒDAMU'SII, a people of Mauritania Cæsariensis. *Ptol.*

CŒ'LA, a place in the bay of Eubœa. *Liv.* 31. c. 47. ——A part of Attica, ennobled by the tombs of Miltiades and Thucydides. *Strab.* 10.

CŒLALE'TÆ, a people of Thrace. *Tac. Hist.* 3. c. 38.

CŒ'LE, passes in some mountains of Thessaly and Epirus, near Pindus and Œta. *Livy*, 32. c. 4.

CŒLEM'BA CŒLAM'BE or CŒAM'BE, a city of Gedrosia. *Ptol.*

CŒLERI'NI, a people of Hispania Tarraconensis. *Id.*

CŒLESYR'IA or CŒLOSYR'IA, a country of Syria, extending between mount Libanus and Antilibanus, where the Orontes takes its rise. Its capital was Damascus.—This name was given by Antiochus Cyzicenus to that part of Syria which he obtained as his share, when he divided his father's dominions with Grypus, B.C. 112. *Dionys. Perieg.*

CŒ'LI, the wife of Sylla. *Plut. in Syll.* The Cœlian family, which was plebeian, but, in later times, honoured with the consulship, was descended from Vibenna Cœles, an Etrurian, who came to settle at Rome in the age of Romulus.

CŒ'LIS, part of Attica. *Hesychius.* Some read Cœla. *Vid.* Cœla.

CŒ'LIUS, a Roman defended by Cicero. *Vid.* Cælius.——The name of two brothers of Tarracina, accused of having murdered their father in his bed. They were acquitted when it was proved that they were both asleep at the time of the murder. *Val. Max.* 8. c. 1.—*Plut. in Cic.*——A general of Carbo.——An orator. *Plut. in Pomp.*——A lieutenant of Antony.——A man who, after spending all his property in dissipation and luxury, became a public robber with his friend Birrhus. *Horat.* 1. sat. 4. v. 60. *Virgil* is supposed to allude to him in the following enigma,

Dic quibus in terris, et eris mihi magnus Apollo,
Tres pateat Cœli *spatium non amplius ulnas.*

——A Roman historian, who flourished B.C. 121.

CŒ'LIUS CUR'SOR, a Roman knight, in the age of the emperor Tiberius. *Tacit. Ann.* 3. c. 35.

CŒ'LIUS CAL'DUS, a quæstor under Cicero in Cilicia, into whose hands the care of the province was entrusted after the departure of the pro-consul. *Cic.* 6. *Att.* 5 & 6. *Fam.* 2. ep. 15.

CŒ'LIUS RU'FUS, a young patrician, who accused Antony, Cicero's colleague, of misconduct in Macedonia. He also raised an accusation against Atratinus for bribery; but the son of Atratinus retorted the charge, and accused Cœlius of attempting to poison Clodia. Cicero defended him, and obtained his acquittal. *Cic. Brut.* 79. *Cœl.* 1.

CŒ'LIUS, a hill of Rome. *Vid.* Cælius.

CŒ'LIUS POL'LIO, the commander of a castle in Armenia. *Tac. Ann.* 12. c. 45.

CŒ'LIUS SABI'NUS, a consul with Flavius Sabinus. *Id. Hist.* 1. c. 77.

CŒLOS'SA, a mountain not far from Phlius. *Strab.* 8.

CŒ'LUS or U'RANUS, an ancient deity, supposed to be the father of Saturn, Oceanus, Hyperion, &c. He was son of Terra, whom he afterwards married. The number of his children, according to some, amounted to forty-five. They were called Titans, and were so closely confined by the jealousy of their father, that they conspired against him, and were supported in the unnatural attempt by their mother, who provided them with a scythe. Saturn armed himself with this scythe, and mutilated his father as he was going to unite himself to Terra. From the blood which issued from the wound, sprang the giants, furies, and nymphs. The mutilated parts were thrown into the sea, and from them and the foam which they occasioned, arose Venus the goddess of beauty. *Hesiod. Theog.*—*Apollod.* 1. c. 1.—*Hygin.* præf. fab.

CŒNOMA'NI or CENOMA'NI AULER'CI, a people of Gaul. *Cæs. Com.* 7. c. 75.

CŒ'NUS, an officer in Alexander's army, son-in-law to Parmenio. He died of a distemper, in his return from India. *Curt.* 9. c. 3.—*Diod.* 17.——The second king of Macedonia, reigned 12 years, A.U.C. 385.

CŒR'ANUS, a Stoic philosopher. *Tacit. Ann.* 14. c. 52.——A person slain by Ulysses. *Ovid. Met.* 13. v. 257.——A Greek, charioteer to Merion. He was killed by Hector. *Homer. Il.* 17. v. 611.

CO'ES, a man of Mitylene, made sovereign of his country by Darius. His countrymen stoned him to death. *Herodot.* 5. c. 11 & 38.

COESTOB'OCI, a people of European Sarmatia. *Ptol.*

CŒS'YRA, a woman of Eretria, who married Pisistratus. *Schol. Aristoph. Acharn.*

CŒ'TI, a people of Asia near the Euxine Sea. *Xenoph.*

CŒ'US, a son of Cœlus and Terra. He was father of Latona, Asteria, &c. by Phœbe. *Hesiod. Theog.* 135 & 405.—*Apollod.* 1. c. 1.—*Virg. G.* 1. v. 279.

CŒ'US, a river of Messenia flowing by Electra. *Paus.* 4. c. 33.

COG'AMUS, a small river of Lydia. *Plin.* 5. c. 29.

COGIDU'NUS, a king of Britain, faithful to Rome. *Tacit. Agric.* c. 14.

COGNABAN'DA and COGNAB'ARA, cities of India within the Ganges. *Ptol.*

CO'HIBUS, a river of Asia, near Pontus. *Tacit. Hist.* 3. c. 48. It was perhaps the Cobus of *Pliny,* 6. c. 4.

CO'HORS, a division in the Roman armies, consisting of about 600 men. It was the tenth part of a legion, and cousequently its number was subject to the same fluctuation as that of the legions, being sometimes more and sometimes less.

COL'ADA, a city of India within the Ganges. *Ptol.*

COLŒ'NE, the name of Diana at Sardis. *Strab.*

COLÆ'NUS, a king of Attica, before the age of Cecrops, according to some accounts. *Paus.* 1. c. 31.

COLA'ICUM, a promontory of Taprobane. *Plin.* 6. c. 22.

COLA'NA, a town of Armenia Major. *Ptol.*

COLAPIA'NI, a people of Pannonia, so called from the river Colapis. *Plin.* 3. c. 25.

COLAR'NI, a people of Lusitania. *Plin* 4. c. 22.

COLAS'SIS, a pupil of the statuary Lysippus.

COLAX'AIS, one of the remote ancestors of the Scythians. *Herodot.* 4. c. 5, &c.

COLAX'ES, a son of Jupiter and Ora. *Flacc.* 6. v. 48.

COL'BI, a people of Æthiopia. *Ptol.*

COL'CHI, the inhabitants of Colchis.

COLCHIN'IUM, a town of Dalmatia, afterwards Olchinium. *Plin.* 3. c. 22.

COL'CHIS, *idis*, a country of Asia, at the south of Asiatic Sarmatia, east of the Euxine Sea, north of Armenia, and west of Iberia. It is now called Mingrelia, and was once famous for the expedition of the Argonauts, and as the birth-place of Medea. It was fruitful in poisonous herbs, and produced excellent flax. The inhabitants were originally Ægyptians, who settled there when Sesostris, king of Ægypt extended his conquests in the north. From the country arise the epithets Colchus, Colchicus, and Colchiacus, and Medea receives the name of Colchis. *Juv.* 6. v. 640.—*Flacc.* 5. v. 418.—*Horat.* 2. od. 13. v. 8.—*Strab.* 11.—*Ptol.* 5. c. 10.—*Ovid. Met.* 13. v. 24. *Amor.* 2. el. 14. v. 28.—*Mela,* 1. c. 19. 2. c. 3.

COLEN'DA, a town of Spain. *Appian.*

COLEN'TIUM, an island of Illyricum, called Scardona by *Ptolemy.* The people were called Colentini. *Plin.* 3. c. 22.

COLETIA'NI or COLETA'NI, a people of Pannonia. *Ptol.*

CO'LI, a people near Caucasus. The lower parts of this mountain were called Colici Montes, and the country Colica. *Steph.*

COLI'ACI, a people of India within the Ganges.

CO'LIAS, now Agio Nicolo, a promontory of Attica, where Venus had a temple. *Herodot.* 8. c. 96.

COLIP'PO, a town of Lusitania. *Plin.* 4. c. 21.

CO'LIS, the most southern promontory of India. *Mela,* 3. c. 7.

COLLA'CIA, a lascivious woman, &c. *Juv.* 6. v. 306.

COLLA'TIA, a town of Italy, on the Anio, built by the people of Alba. It was there that Sext. Tarquin offered violence to the virtuous Lucretia. *Liv.* 1. 37, &c.—*Strab.* 3.—*Virg. Æn.* 6. v. 774.—*Festus de Verb. Sig.*

COLLATI'NUS L. TARQUIN'IUS, a nephew of Tarquin the Proud, who married Lucretia, to whom Sext. Tarquin offered violence. He united with Brutus to drive the Tarquins from Rome, and for their service they were made the first consuls. As Collatinus was one of the family of the Tarquins, so much abominated by all the Roman people, he yielded to the prejudices of his countrymen, and laying down his office of consul, retired to Alba in voluntary banishment. *Liv.* 1. c. 57. l. 2. c. 2.—*Flor.* 1. c. 9.

COLLATI'NUS, one of the seven hills of Rome.

COLLI'NA, one of the gates of Rome, on mount Quirinalis. *Ovid.* 4. *Fast.* v. 871.

COLLI'NA, a goddess at Rome, who presided over hills.——One of the original tribes established by Romulus.

COLLO'DIS, an island adjacent to Sardinia. *Plin.* 3. c. 7.

CO'LO JUN., a governor of Pontus, who brought Mithridates to the emperor Claudius. *Tacit.* 12 *Ann.* c. 21.

COL'OA, a city and lake of Æthiopia. *Ptol.*

COL'OBI, a promontory of Africa, on the Arabic Gulph. *Mela,* 3. c. 8.

COL'OBON, a promontory of Æthiopia. *Ptol.*

COLOBO'NA, a city of Hispania Bætica. *Plin.* 3. c. 1.

COLOBROS'SUS, a city of Cilicia Trachea. *Ptol.*

COLOCASI'RIS, an island in the Azanian Sea. *Plin.* 6. c. 29.

COLOCAU'RUM, a city of Germany, *Ptol.*

COL'OE, a lake of Æthiopia, where there were also three cities of the same name. *Id.—Arrian.*——A place of Lydia, near Sardis. *Strab.* 13.

COLŒ'PHRYX, a mountain of Bœotia. *Hesychius.—Steph.*

COLO'NÆ, a place of Troas. *Nepos.* 4. c. 3.——A city of Phocis.——A city of Thessaly.——A city of Messenia.——A city of Erythræa. *Strab.—Ptol.*——A rock of Asia, on the Thracian Bosporus.

COLO'NIA AGRIPPI'NA, a city of Germany, on the Rhine, now Cologne.

COLO'NIA EQUES'TRIS, a town on the lake of Geneva, now Noyon.

COLO'NIA MORINO'RUM, a town of Belgic Gaul, now Terrouen, in Artois.

COLO'NIA NORBEN'SIS, a town of Spain, now Alcantara.

COLO'NIA TRAJA'NA, or Ulpia, a town of Germany, now Kellen, near Cleves.

COLO'NIA VALEN'TIA, a town of Spain, which now bears the same name.

COLO'NIS, an island in the Argolic Gulph. *Plin.* 4. c. 12.

COLO'NUS, an eminence near Athens, to which Œdipus retired during his banishment to Thebes, from which Sophocles has given the title of Œdipus Coloneus to one of his finest tragedies. According to *Pollux*, there were two places at Athens respectively known by the name of *Equestris* and *Agorœus Colonnus.*

COLOPE'NA, part of Cappadocia. *Plin.* 6. c. 3.——A city of Æolis, in Asia Minor. *Ptol.*

COL'OPHON, a celebrated town of Ionia, built by Mopsus, the son of Manto, and colonized by the sons of Codrus. It was the native country of Mimnermus, Nicander, and Xenophanes, and one of the cities which disputed for the honour of having given birth to Homer. Apollo had a temple there. *Strab.* 14.—*Plin.* 14. c. 20.—*Paus.* 7. c. 3.—*Tacit. Ann.* 2. c. 54.—*Cic. pro Arch. Poet.* 8.—*Ovid. Met.* 6. v. 8.

COLOS'SE or COLOS'SIS, a large town of Phrygia, near Laodicea, of which the government was democratical, and the first ruler called archon. One of the first Christian churches was established there, and one of St. Paul's epistles was addressed to the Christian converts there. *Plin.* 21. c. 9.

COLOS'SUS, a celebrated brazen image at Rhodes, which passed for one of the seven wonders of the world. Its feet rested upon the two moles which formed the entrance of the harbour, and ships passed in full sail between the legs. It was 70 cubits, or 105 feet high, and every part of the body was formed in the most exact proportion, so that few could clasp round its thumb. It was the work of Chares, the pupil of Lysippus, and the artist was employed 12 years in completing it. It was begun 300 years B.C., and after it had remained unhurt during 56 years, or, according to some writers, 88 years, it was partly demolished by an earthquake, 224 B.C. A winding staircase ran to the top, from which, by the help of glasses which were hung on the neck of the statue, the shores of Syria, and the ships that sailed on the coast of Ægypt, could also be discerned. This extraordinary monument remained in ruins for the space of 894 years; and the Rhodians, who had received several large contributions to repair it, divided the money among themselves, and frustrated the expectation of the donors by saying, that the oracle of Delphi forbade them to raise it up again from its ruins. In the year 672 A.D. it was sold by the Saracens, who had obtained possession of the island, to a Jewish merchant of Edessa, who loaded 900 camels with the brass, the value of which has been estimated at £36,000 English money. *Plin.* 34. c. 7 & 18.—*Festus de Verb. Sig.*

COLO'TES, a Teian painter, pupil of Phidias. *Plin.* 35. c. 8.——A disciple of Epictetus.——A follower of Epicurus, accused of ignorance by *Plutarch.*——A sculptor who made a statue of Æsculapius. *Strab.* 8. Also Col'otes.

COL'PE, a city of Ionia. *Plin.* 5. c. 29.

COL'SA, a city of Armenia Major. *Ptol.*

COL'TA, a place of Carmania, on the Red Sea. *Arrian.*

COLTHE'NE, a region and city of Armenia Major, near the Araxes. *Ptol.*

COL'UBÆ, a people of India. *Plin.* 6. c. 19.

COLUBRA'RIA, now Monte Colubre, a small island at the east of Spain, supposed to be the same as Ophiusa, at the south of Yvica. *Plin.* 3. c. 5.

COLUM'BA, a dove, the symbol of Venus among the poets. This bird was sacred to Venus, and received divine honours in Syria. Doves disappeared once every year from Eryx, in Sicily, where Venus had a temple; and they were said to accompany the goddess to Libya, whither she went to pass nine days, after which they returned. Doves were supposed to deliver oracles from the oaks of the forest of Dodona. *Tibull.* 1. el. 7. v. 17.—*Ælian. V. H.* 1. c. 15.

COLUMEL'LA L. JUN. MODERA'TUS, a native of Gades, in Spain, who wrote, among other works, twelve books on agriculture, of which the tenth is still extant. The style is elegant, and the work displays the genius of a naturalist, and the labours of an accurate observer. The age in which Columella lived is not accurately ascertained, though the majority of commentators maintain, that he flourished in the reign of the emperor Claudius. His works may be found among the writers *de re rustica*, the best edition of which is that of Gesner, 2 vols. 4to, Lips, 1735, and reprinted there 1772. *Sax. Onom.* 1. p. 246.—*Harles. Not. Lit. Rom.* 1. 366.

COLUM'NA RE'GIA, a city of the Brutii, now la Cothona. *Mela,* 2, c. 4.

COLUM'NÆ HER'CULIS, a name given to two mountains at the entrance into the Mediterranean Sea. They were called Calpe and Abyla, the former on the coast of Spain, and the latter on the coast of Africa, at the distance of only 18 miles. They were considered as the boundaries of the labours of Hercules, and were supposed to have been joined together till the hero's arms separated them, and opened a communication between the Mediterranean and Atlantic Seas.

COLUM'NÆ PRO'TEI, the boundaries of Ægypt, or the extent of the kingdom of Proteus. Alexandria was supposed to be built near them, though *Homer* places them in the island of Pharus. *Odyss.* 4. v. 351.—*Virg. Æn.* 11. v. 262.

COLUM'NÆ, small islands in the Red Sea. *Plin.* 6. c. 11.

COLU'THUS, a native of Lycopolis in Ægypt, who wrote a short poem on the rape of Helen, in imitation of Homer, in 384 verses. The composition remained long unknown, till it was discovered at Lycopolis, in the 15th century, by the learned cardinal Bessarion. Coluthus was, as some suppose, a contemporary of Tryphiodorus, who flourished about the beginning of the 6th century. The poem was first edited by Aldus, afterwards by H. Stephanus in his Poet. Princ. Paris, 1566. *Fabr. B. Gr.* 2. c. 7.—*Sax. Onom.* 2. p. 20.

COLYT'TUS, one of the tribes of Athens. *Strab.* 1.

COMAGE'NA, one of the five districts into which Syria was divided. It was near Cilicia, extending towards the east, as far as the Euphrates. Its chief towns were Antiochia ad Taurum and Samosata, known as the birth place of Lucian. *Strab.* 11 *&* 17.

COMA'NA (*-æ, & orum*), a town of Pontus. *Hirt. Alex.* 34.

COMA'NA, a town of Cappadocia, famous for a temple of Bellona, where there were above 6000 ministers of both sexes. They were consecrated to the service of the divinity by making deep incisions in the arm, and in their frantic zeal they ran through the streets with swords in their hands, prophesying the calamities and wars which attended the neighbouring states. The chief priest among them was very powerful, and knew no superior but the king of the country. This high office was generally conferred upon one of the royal family. *Hirt. Alex.* 66.—*Flacc.* 7. v. 636.—*Strab.* 12.—*Lamprid. in Vit. Com.* 9.—*Lactant.* 1. c. 21.—*Ptol.* 5. c. 7.——A town of Taprobane. *Ptol.*——A town of Phrygia. *Id.*——A town of Pisidia. *Id.*

COMA'NI, a people near Margiana. *Plin.* 6. c. 16.

COMA'NIA, a country of Asia. *Xenophon.*

COMARE'A, the ancient name of Cape Comorin in India.

COM'ARI, a people of Asia. *Mela*, 1. c. 2.

COM'ARUS, a port in the bay of Ambracia, near Nicopolis. *Strab.* 17.

COMAS'TUS, a place of Persia. *Polyæn.* 7. c. 40.

COMA'TA, a name of Gallia Celtica. *Lucan.* 1. v. 443.

COM'BA, an inland city of Lycia. *Ptol.*

COMBA'BUS, a favourite of Stratonice, wife of Antiochus.

COMBA'NA, a city of Carmania. *Ptol.*

COM'BE, a woman of Chalcis, daughter of Ophius, who first invented a brazen suit of armour. She was changed into a bird, and escaped from her children who had conspired to murder her. It is said that she gave birth to 100 children; whence the proverb ὥσπερ Χαλκιδικὴ τέτοκεν ἡμῖν γυνή, to denote a prolific mother. *Ovid. Met.* 7. v. 382. *& Farnab. loco.*

COM'BI or OM'BI, a city of Ægypt on the Nile. *Juv.* 15. v. 35.

COMBRE'A, a town near Pallene. *Herodot.* 7. c. 123.

COM'BUTIS, a general under Brennus. *Paus.* 10. c. 22.

COME'DÆ, a people of the Sacæ. *Ptol.*

COME'NII, a people of Illyria. *Id.*

COME'RUS, a Gaul, who led colonies into Italy. *Berosus*, 1. 3.

COME'TES, the father of Asterion, and one of the Argonauts. He married Antigone daughter of Pheres. *Apollod.* 1.—*Flacc.* 1. v. 356.——One of the Centaurs, killed at the nuptials of Pirithous. *Ovid. Met.* 12. v. 284.——A son of Thestius, killed at the chase of the Calydonian boar. *Paus.* 8. c. 45.——One of the Magi, intimate with Cambyses king of Persia. *Justin.* 1. c. 9.——An adulterer of Ægiale.——A son of Orestes.

COM'ETHO, a daughter of Pterilaus, who deprived her father of a golden hair in his head, upon which his life depended. She was put to death by Amphitryon for her perfidy. *Apollod.* 2. c. 4.

CO'MI. a people of Bactriana. *Ptol.*

COMIDA'VA, a town of Dacia. *Id.*

COMI'NI, a people of the Æquicolæ. *Plin.* 3. c. 12.

COMIN'IUM, a city of the Samnites.

COMIN'IUS Q. a Roman knight, who wrote some illiberal verses against Tiberius. *Tacit.* 4 *Ann.* c. 31.

COMISE'NE, a province of Armenia Major. *Strab.* 11.—*Ptol.*

COMIT'IA, (*-orum*), an assembly of the Roman people. The word is derived from *Comitium*, the place where they were convened, *quasi a comeundo*. The Comitium was a large hall, which was open at the top in the first ages of the republic, so that the assembly was often dissolved in rainy weather. The Comitia were called, some *consularia*, for the election of the consuls; others *prætoria*, for the election of prætors, &c. These assemblies were more generally known by the name of *Comitia Curiata*, *Centuriata*, and *Tributa*. The *Curiata* were when the people gave their votes by curiæ. The *Centuriata* were not convened in the later ages of the republic. *Vid.* Centuria. In the *Comitia tributa*, the votes were received from the whole tribes together. At first the Roman people were divided only into three tribes; but as their numbers increased, the tribes were at last enlarged to 35. The object of these assemblies was the election of magistrates and all the public officers of state; but they could be dissolved by one of the tribunes, if he differed in opinion from the rest of his colleagues. If one among the people was taken with the falling sickness, the whole assembly was immediately dissolved; whence that disease was called *morbus comitialis*. After the custom of giving their votes *vivâ voce* had been abolished, every one of the assembly, in the enacting of a law, was presented with two ballots, on one of which were the letters U. R. that is, *uti rogas*, be it as it is required; on the other was an A that is *antiquo* which bears the same meaning as *antiquam volo*, I forbid it, the old law is preferable. If the ballots inscribed with U. R. were more numerous than those inscribed with A. the law was approved constitutionally; if not, it was rejected. Only the chief magistrates, and sometimes the pontifices, had the privilege of convening these assemblies. Only eight of the magistrates had the power of proposing a law, *viz.* the consuls, the dictator, and prætor, the interrex, the decemvirs, the military tribunes, the kings, and the triumvirs. These were called *majores magistratus;* to whom one of the *minores magistratus* was added, the tribune of the people.

CO'MIUS. a man appointed king over the Attrebates, by J. Cæsar, for his services. *Cæs. Bell. G.* 4 c. 21.

COMMAGE'NE, *Vid.* Comagena.

COMMENA'SES, a river of India, flowing into the Indus. *Arrian.*

COM'MODUS L. AURELIUS ANTONI'NUS, son of M. Antoninus, succeeded his father in the Roman empire; and disgraced himself and his family by the most flagitious crimes. He was naturally of a licentious disposition, and was so desirous of being called Hercules, that he, like that hero, adorned his shoulders with a lion's skin, and armed his hand with a knotted club. He exhibited himself in public, and fought with the gladiators and wild beasts in the amphitheatre. He required divine honours from the senate, and was wont to put such an immense quantity of gold dust in his hair, that when he appeared bare-headed in the sunshine, his head glittered as if surrounded with sun-beams. Martia, one of his concubines, whose death he meditated, poisoned him; but as the poison did not operate quickly, he was strangled by a wrestler. This unprincipled emperor died in the 31st year of his age, and the 13th of his reign, A.D. 192. It has been observed, that he never trusted himself to a barber, but always burnt his beard, in imitation of Dionysius. *Herodian.* [There is a fine statue of Commodus, in the character of Hercules, with a child on his left arm, in the Museum of the Vatican, and a bust in the Albani collection at Rome.]

COM'MONE, an island near the city of Ephesus. *Plin.* 5. c. 31.

COMMO'NI, a people of Gallia Narbonensis. *Ptol.*

COM'MORIS, a village of Cilicia. *Cic. Fam.* 15. ep. 4.

CO'MON, a general of Messenia. *Paus.* 4. c. 26.

COMOP'OLIS, a town of Assyria. *Ptol.*

COMPITA'LIA, festivals celebrated by the Romans on the 12th of January and the 6th of March, in the cross ways, in honour of the household gods called Lares. On this festive occasion, small images of men and women were placed on tables in the public roads, to represent the protecting gods, lamps were burned in their honour, and the doors of houses were gaily decked with the branches of trees, whilst, within, the master of the family offered sacrifices at the feet of his Lares. Tarquin the Proud, or, according to some, Servius Tullius, instituted them, on account of an oracle which ordered him to offer heads to the Lares. He sacrificed to them human victims; but J. Brutus, after the expulsion of the Tarquins, thought it sufficient to offer them only poppy heads, and men of straw. The slaves were generally the ministers, and, during the celebration, they enjoyed their freedom. *Varro de L. L.* 5. c. 3.—*Ovid. Fast.* 5. v. 140.—*Dionys. Hal.* 4.—*Festus de Verb. Sig.*—*Servius in Georg.* 2. v. 382.—*Plin.* 36. c. 27.

COMPLU'TUM, a city of the Carpetani, in Hispania Tarraconensis, now Alcala de Henares. It is celebrated as the place which produced the Complutensian Polyglot Bible, A. D. 1515. *Cluver.* 2. c. 6.

COMP'SA, now Consa, a town of the Hirpini in Italy, at the east of Vesuvius, near the head of the Aufidus. The people were called Compsani. *Plin.* 3. c. 11.

COMP'SATUS, a small river of Thrace, falling into the lake Bistonis. *Herodot.* 7. c. 109.

COMPU'SA, a town of Bithynia. *Plin.* 5. c. *ult.*

CO'MUM, now Como, a town of Cisalpine Gaul, at the north of Insubria, and at the bottom of the lake Como, in the modern duchy of Milan. It was afterwards called Novo Comum by J. Cæsar, who transplanted a colony there, though it afterwards resumed its ancient name. It was the birth-place of the younger Pliny. *Plin.* 3. c. 18.—*Liv.* 33. c. 36 & 37.—*Suet. in Jul.* 28.—*Plin.* 1. ep. 3.—*Cic. Fam.* 13. ep. 35.

CO'MUS, the god of revelry, feasting, and nocturnal entertainments among the ancients. During the celebration of his festivals, men and women exchanged each other's dresses. He was represented as a young and drunken man, with a garland of flowers on his head, and a torch in his hand, which seemed falling. He is more generally seen sleeping upon his legs, and turning himself when the heat of the falling torch has scorched his side. *Philostrat.* 2. *Icon.—Plut. Quæst. Rom.* 55.—*Athen.* 12.

CONADIP'SAS, a region of Scythia, within Imaus. *Ptol.*

CONAPSE'NI, a people of Asiatic Sarmatia. *Id.*

CON'CANI, a people at the north of Spain, who lived chiefly on milk mixed with horses' blood. Their chief town, Concana, is now called Santilana, or Cangas de Onis. *Virg. G.* 3. v. 463.—*Sil.* 3. v. 361.—*Horat.* 3. od. 4. v. 34.—*Mela*, 3. c. 1.

CONCOR'DIA, the goddess of peace and concord, was particularly worshipped at Rome. Camillus first raised a temple to her honour in the Capitol where the magistrates often assembled for the transaction of public business. She had, besides this, other temples, especially one erected by a contribution raised from the public, and she was entreated by her votaries to promote the peace and union of families and citizens. The goddess of concord was generally represented as young, crowned with garlands, holding a cup in one hand, and in the other a cornucopia, or a sceptre, from which appeared to issue forth all sorts of fruits. Sometimes she appears holding a bundle of small sticks, to intimate that these when separated are weak and useless, but when united, powerful and difficult to be broken. The most ordinary symbol, however, of concord, is two hands joined together holding a caduceus, or a pomegranate. *Plut. in Camill.—Plin.* 33. c. 1.—*Cic. pro Domo.—Ovid. Fast.* 1. v. 639. l. 6. v. 637.—*Liv.* 9 & 22.—*Dio.* 50.

CONCOR'DIA, a town of Italy at the top of the Adriatic. *Hadr. Vales.*——A town of Germany.——A town of Hispania Bætica. *Ptol.* The people were called Concordienses. *Plin.* 4. c. 22.

CONCUBIEN'SES, a people of Umbria. *Id.* 3. c. 14.

CONDABO'RA, a town of the Celtiberi, in Spain.

CON'DALUS, an avaricious officer of Mausolus, king of Caria, &c. *Aristot. Polit.*

CONDA'TE, a town at the west of Gaul, now Rennes (*Rhedonum urbs*), in Britany.

CONDIGRAM'MA, a town of Carmania. *Plin.* 6. c. 23.

CONDIVIN'CUM, a town of Gaul, on the river Ligeris, now Nantes, in Britany. *Ptol.—Cæsar.*

CONDOCHA'TES, a river of India, flowing into the Ganges. *Arrian.*

CONDRU'SI, a people of Belgium, now Condrotz, in Liege. *Cæs. B. G.* 4. c. 6.

CON'DYBA, a city of Lycia. *Ptol.*

CONDYL'EA, a town of Arcadia. *Paus.* 8. c. 23.

CO'NE, a small island in the Euxine Sea, at the mouth of the Ister, supposed to be the same as the Insula Conopon of *Pliny*, 4. c. 12.—*Lucan.* 3. v. 200.

CONETODU'NUS and COTUA'TUS, two desperate Gauls, who excited their countrymen to rebel against Rome. *Cæs. B. G.* 7. c. 3.

CONFLUEN'TIA, a town of Germany, at the confluence of the Moselle and Rhine, now Coblentz.

CONFU'CIUS, a Chinese philosopher and legislator, deservedly celebrated for his great learning, the purity of his morals, and his patriotism. He was descended from a family allied to the throne; and had the happiness to see his services acknowledged and rewarded by his countrymen, as he was as much honoured among them as their monarch. He died about 479 B.C. His writings, in six books, are valuable for the directions which they contain on government, on the regulation of life, and the several duties of man, &c. They have been translated by Noel, one of the most ancient missionaries to China, and were printed at Prague in 1711. *Sax. Onom.* 1. p. 23.—*Scriptores in Catal. Bunav.* vol. 2. p. 1172.

CON'GA, a city of India within the Ganges. *Ptol.*

CONGE'DUS or CON'GEDUS, a small river of Spain. *Martial*, 1. ep. 50. v. 9.

CONGUS'TUS, a city of Galatia. *Ptol.*

CONI'ACI, a people of Spain at the head of the Iberus. *Strab.* 3. They were probably the same as the Conii of *Polybius*, and the Cunei of *Appian*.

CONI'ADES, a Greek writer, whose work, *De vini apparatu*, is cited by *Pliny*, 14. c. 19.

CON'ICA, a city of Paphlagonia. *Ptol.*

CONIMBRI'CA, a town of Spain, on the river Monda, now Coimbra, in Portugal.

CONIS'ALUS, a god worshipped at Athens, with the same ceremonies as Priapus at Lampsacus. *Strab.* 3.

CONIS'CI, a people of Spain. *Strab.*

CONISTOR'SIS, a city of Hispania Citerior. *Strab.*

CONI'SUM, a town of Mysia. *Plin.* 5. c. 30.

CON'NA, a city of Phrygia Major. *Ptol.*

CON'NIDAS or CONNI'DAS. *Vid.* Chonnidas.

CON'NAS, a musician, who is said to have instruted Socrates. *Cic.* 9 *Fam.* 22.

CO'NON, a famous Athenian general appointed governor of all the islands of the Athenians, but unfortunately defeated in a naval battle by Lysander, near the Egispotamos. He retired in voluntary banishment to Evagoras, king of Cyprus, and afterwards to Artaxerxes, king of Persia, by whose assistance he returned to Greece, and was enabled to free his country from slavery. He next defeated the Spartans near Cnidus, in an engagement where Pisander, the enemy's admiral, was killed. Encouraged by his advice and assistance, the Athenians fortified their city with a strong wall, and attempted to recover Iona and Æolia. Conon was perfidiously betrayed by a Persian, and died in prison in Asia, B.C. 393. *C. Nep. in Vitâ.—Plut. in Lys. & Artax.—Isocrates.*——A Greek astronomer of Samus, who wrote an account of all the eclipses which had been observed by the Ægyptians. To ingratiate himself with Ptolemy Evergetes, king of Ægypt, he declared that the queen's locks were become a constellation in the heavens, to which he gave the name of Berenice's crown. He was intimate with Archimedes, and flourished 247 B.C. *Catull.* 67.—*Hygin. P.A.* 2. c. 24.—*Propert.* 4. el. 1.—*Voss. de Mathem.* 33 & 54.—*Virg. Ecl.* 3. v. 40.——A Grecian mythologist, in the age of Julius Cæsar, who wrote a book which contained 40 fables, still extant, preserved by Photius. There was a treatise on Italy written by a man of the same name. *Voss. de Hist. Græc.* 1. c. 24.

CONONIEN'SES, a people of Gallia Narbonensis. *Plin.* 3. c. 4.

CONO'PAS, a dwarf, a great favourite with Julia the grand-daughter of Augustus. *Plin.* 17. c. 16.

CONSABUREN'SES, a people of Hispania Citerior. *Plin.* 3. c. 3. Their town Consaburum is now Consuegra.

CONSEN'TES, the name which the Romans gave to the twelve superior gods or *Dii majorum gentium.* The word signifies as much as *consentientes*, that is, who consented to the deliberations of Jupiter's council. They were twelve in number, and their names are briefly comprised by *Ennius* in these lines:

Juno, Vesta, Minerva, Ceres, Diana, Venus, Mars,
Mercurius, Jovis, Neptunus, Vulcanus, Apollo.
Varro de R.R.

CONSEN'TIA, now Cosenza, a town of Italy in the country of the Brutii. *Liv.* 8. c. 24. l. 28. c. 11.—*Cic. Fin.* 1. c. 3.

CONSID'IUS Æ'QUUS, a Roman knight, &c. *Tacit. Ann.* 3. c. 37.

CONSID'IUS CA'IUS, one of Pompey's adherents, &c. *Cæs. Bell. Civ.* 2. c. 23.

CONSID'IUS, a man who was governor of Africa before the civil wars of Pompey. *Cic. Leg.*

CONSID'IUS PROC'ULUS, a man executed for treason, on his birth-day. *Tacit. Ann.* 6. c. 18.

CONSILI'NUM, a town of Italy. *Mela*, 2. c. 4.

CONSI'VUS, a surname of Janus, as the god who protected the seed of the husbandmen, and presided over generation. *Macrob. Sat.* 1. c. 9.

CONSORA'NI, a people of Gallia Aquitanica. *Plin.* 4. c. 19.

CON'STANS, a son of Constantine the Great. *Vid.* Constantinus.

CONSTAN'TIA, a grand-daughter of Constantine the Great, who married the emperor Gratian.

CONSTANTI'NA, a princess, wife of the emperor Gallus.——A princess of the imperial family.

CONSTANTINOP'OLIS, now Stamboul, or by way of eminence, the Porte, formerly Byzantium, the capital of Thrace, a noble and magnificent city, built by Constantine the Great, and solemnly dedicated A.D. 333. It was the capital of the eastern Roman empire, and was called after its foundation, *Roma Nova*, on account of its greatness and magnificence, which seemed to rival Rome. The beauty of its prospects, the excellence of its harbour, and the many conveniences of its situation have deservedly been the admiration of every age, and reflect great honour on the judicious choice of the imperial founder. Constantinople was long the asylum of science and of learned men; but upon its conquest by Mahomet II. on the 28th of May, 1453, the professors retired from the barbarity of the victors, and found in Italy the protection which their learning and their misfortunes deserved. This migration was highly favourable to the cause of science, and whilst the pope, the head of the house of Medicis, and the emperor, munificently supported the fugitives, other princes imitated their example, and equally contributed to the gradual revival of literature in Europe.

CONSTANTI'NUS, son of Constantius, by Helena, surnamed the *Great*, from the greatness of his exploits, was born at Naissus, in Dacia, though some historians consider Britain as the place of his nativity. On the death of his father, he succeeded to the title of Cæsar, the lower rank of the imperial dignity; but being rendered illustrious by his victories over the Germans and Barbarians, he soon after assumed the nobler appellation of Augustus, though Gallienus, his colleague on the throne viewed with jealousy his elevation and promising talents. He marched with 40,000 men against his colleague Maxentius, whose cruelties in Italy deserved the severest chastisement. Before the battle which he fought with him, a luminous body of light, say historians, presented itself in the sky, in the form of a cross, to the astonished eyes of Constantine; and the inscription which it bore, *τουτῳ νικα*, *in hoc vince*, reminded the monarch of his superstitious adherence to the heathen religion, and he immediately became a convert to Christianity. The enemy was defeated, and the grateful emperor for ever after displayed at the head of his army a *labarum* or cross, the holy standard under the auspices of which he had obtained the victory. Yet, though Constantine thus embraced the Christian faith, he rejected the purity of its practice; and unable to endure a rival in his brother-in-law Licinius, he made war against him, and compelled him to abdicate the imperial power, and acknowledge him sole sovereign of the Roman world. Constantine, now without a rival, devoted himself to advance and establish the public and private welfare. Abuses in the state were removed, and if the emperor had done nothing beside affording protection and toleration to the thousands of meek and inoffensive individuals who had embraced the religion of Christ, his memory would deserve the noblest panegyrics of the historian. The views which he formed of the greatness of his empire were extensive and magnificent; and either to a secret jealousy of the antiquity and independent spirit of Rome, or to the contemplation of the superior advantages and more centrical position of Byzantium as a capital, we are to ascribe the foundation of Constantinople. The plan was in the conception sublime; but while Constantine plundered the capital of Italy of her fairest honours, and transported her senate, her magistrates, and her ensigns of dignity to her new rival, he laid the foundation of jealousy and mutual hatred. Rome and Constantinople, now equal in population and magnificence, by turns or accident occasionally honored with the residence of the imperial family, began to look upon each other with an eye of envy; and soon after the age of Constantine, a separation was made of the two empires, and Rome was called the capital of the western, and Constantinople of the eastern dominions of Rome. Constantine has been distinguished for personal courage, and liberally praised for the protection which he extended to the Christians. Though he at first persecuted the Arians, he afterwards inclined to their opinions, and favoured their cause. His murder of his son Crispus has been deservedly censured; for whatever were the provocations either in temper or conduct which he might have received, the imputation of cruelty and of enormous guilt must attach to him, who, while he pretended to profess and practise the many virtues of Christianity, did not hesitate to imbrue his hands in the blood of his family. By removing the Roman legions from the garrisons on the rivers at the extremities of the empire, Constantine opened an easy passage to the barbarians, and rendered his soldiers unwarlike. He however defeated 100,000 Goths, and received into his territories 300,000 Sarmatians who had been banished by their slaves, and allowed them land to cultivate. Constantine was learned, and preached as well as composed many sermons, one of which remains. He died A.D. 337, and after a reign of thirty-one years of the greatest glory and success. He left three sons, Constantinus, Constans, and Constantius, among whom he divided his vast empire. The eldest son, who had Gaul, Spain, and Britain, for his portion, was conquered by the armies of his brother, Constans, and killed in the 25th year of his age, A.D. 340. Magnentius, the governor of the province of Rhætia, murdered Constans in his bed, after a reign of thirteen years over Italy, Africa, and Illyricum; and Constantius, the only surviving brother, now become the sole emperor, A.D. 353, punished his brother's murderer, and being now without a rival, gave way to cruelty and oppression. He visited Rome, where he displayed a triumph, and died A.D. 361, in his march against Julian, who had been proclaimed emperor by his soldiers. *Zosim.*—*Eusebius.*—*Am. Marcell.*—*Julian.* [There is a colossal statue of Constantine the Great, in bronze, at Barletta, in Puglia.

CONSTANTI'NUS, a private soldier in Britain, raised on account of his name, to the imperial dignity.——A general of Belisarius.—The name of Constantine was very common to the emperors of the east in a later period.

CONSTAN'TIUS CHLO'RUS, son of Eutropius, and father of the great Constantine, merited the title of Cæsar, which he obtained by his victories in Britain and Germany. He became the colleague of Galerius, on the abdication of Diocletian; and after maintaining the character of a humane and benevolent prince, he died at York in England, after having appointed his son his successor, A.D. 306.

CONSTAN'TIUS, the second son of Constantine the Great. *Vid.* Constantinus.

CONSTAN'TIUS, the father of Julian and Gallus, was son of Constantius by Theodora, and died A.D. 337.——A Roman general of Nyssa, who married Placidia, the sister of Honorius, and was proclaimed emperor; an honour which he enjoyed only seven months. He died universally regretted, 421 A.D., and was succeeded in the west by his son Valentinian.——One of the servants of Attilla.

CONSUA'LES LU'DI or CONSUA'LIA, festivals at Rome in honour of Consus, the god of counsel, whose altar Romulus is said to have discovered under the ground. This altar was always covered except at the festival, when a mule was sacrificed, and games and horse races exhibited in honour of Neptune. It was during these festivals that Romulus and his new subjects carried away the Sabine women, who had assembled to be spectators of the games. They were first instituted by Romulus; though some say that he only regulated and re-instituted them, after they had been before established by Evander, and observed among the Greeks under the name of Hippocrasia. During the celebration, which happened about the middle of August, horses, mules, and asses were exempted from all labour, and were led through the streets adorned with garlands and flowers. *Auson.* 69. v. 9.—*Ovid. Fast.* 3. v. 199.—*Liv.* 1. c. 9.—*Dionys. Hal.* 1.

CONSUANE'TES, a people of the Alps called Consuantæ by *Ptolemy*. *Plin.* 3. c. 20.

CONSUARA'NI, a people of Gallia Narbonensis. *Id.* 3. c. 4.

CON'SUL (*a consulendo*), a magistrate appointed at Rome with regal authority for the space of one year. There were two consuls annually chosen by the people in the Campus Martius. The two first consuls were L. Jun. Brutus and L. Tarquinius Collatinus, chosen A.U.C. 244, after the expulsion of the Tarquins. In the first ages of the republic, the two consuls were always chosen from patrician families, or noblemen; but the people obtained the privilege, A.U.C. 388, of electing one of the consuls from their own body, and sometimes both were plebeians. The first consnl chosen from the plebeians was L. Sextius. It was required that every candidate for the consulship should be 43 years of age, which was called *ligitimum tempus.* He was always to appear at the election as a private man, without a retinue; and it was requisite, before he canvassed for the office, to have discharged the inferior functions of quæstor, ædile, and prætor. Sometimes, however, these qualifications were disregarded, as we find that Val. Corvinus was made consul in his 23d year, and Scipio in his 24th. Young Marius, Pompey, and Augustus, were also under the legal age when they were invested with the office; and Pompey had never been either quæstor or prætor. The power of the consuls was unbounded, and they knew no superior but the gods and the laws; but after the expiration of their office, their conduct was minutely scrutinized by the people, and their misbehaviour was often punished by the decisions of the public assemblies. The badge of their office was the *prætexta*, a robe fringed with purple; afterwards exchanged for the *toga picta* or *palmata.* They were preceded by twelve lictors, carrying the *fasees*, or bundles of sticks, in the middle of which appeared an axe. The axe, as being the characteristic rather of tyranny than of freedom, was taken away from the *fasces* by Valerius Poplicola, but it was restored by his successor. The consuls took it by turns, monthly, to be preceded by the lictors while at Rome, lest the appearance of two persons with the badges of royal authority should raise apprehensions in the multitude. While only one appeared thus publicly in state, a crier walked before the other, and the lictors followed behind without the fasces. The authority of the consuls was equal; yet the Valerian law gave the right of priority to the elder, and the Julian law, to him who had the greatest number of children, and he was generally called *consul major* or *prior*. As their power was absolute, they presided over the senate, and could convene and dismiss that assembly at pleasure. The senators were their counsellors; and, among the Romans, the manner of reckoning their years was by the name of the consuls; and by *M. Tull. Cicerone & Lucio Antonio Consulibus*, for instance, the year of Rome 691 was always understood. This custom lasted from the year of Rome 244 till the year 1294, or 541st year of the Christian æra, when the cousular office was totally suppressed by Justinian. In public assemblies the consuls sat in ivory chairs, and held in their hands an ivory wand, called *scipio eburneus*, which had an eagle on its top as a sign of dignity and power. When they had drawn by lot the provinces over which they were to preside during their continuance in office, they went to the Capitol to offer their prayers to the gods, and entreat them to protect the republic; after which they departed from the city, arrayed in their military dress, and preceded by the lictors. Sometimes the provinces were assigned them, without drawing by lot, by the will and appointment of the senators. At their departure, they were provided at the public expense, with whatever was requisite during their expedition. In their provinces they were both attended by the twelve lictors, and equally invested with regal authority. They were not permitted to return to Rome without the special command of the senate, and they always continued in the province till the arrival of their successor. At their return they harangued the people, and solemnly protested that they had done nothing against the laws or interests of their country, but had faithfully and diligently endeavoured to promote the greatness and welfare of the state. No man could be consul two following years; yet this regulation was sometimes broken, and we find Marius re-elected consul, after the expiration of his office, during the Cimbrian war. The office of consul, so dignified during the times of the commonwealth, became a mere title under the emperors, and retained nothing of its original authority but the useless ensigns of dignity. Even the office of consul, which was originally annual, was reduced to the space of two or three months by J. Cæsar. They who, after being elected on the 24th of October, the usual day of election, were admitted on the 1st of January, gave their names to the year, and were called *ordinarii.* Before they assumed the reins of government, between October and the 1st of January, they were called *consules designati*, and their sucessors during the year, whether appointed in consequence of death or abdication, were distinguished by the appellation of *suffecti;* but the year in the consular Fasti was never called after their name. Tiberius and Claudius abridged the time of holding the consulship, and the emperor Commodus made no less than twenty-five consuls in one year. Constantine the Great renewed the original institution, and permitted them to continue a whole year in office.

Here is annexed a list of the Consuls from the establishment of the consular power to the year of Rome 1059, and of Christ 306. After that time it is difficult to ascertain the real names of the consuls, on account of the various portions and occasionally independent districts into which the empire was divided, under discordant and hostile leaders. Even after the battle of Actium, when the independence of the republic was destroyed, the exhibition of the names of these shadows of imperial authority is more curious than useful.

The two first consuls, chosen about the middle of June, A.U.C. 244, were L. Jun. Brutus, and L. Tarq. Collatinus. Collatinus retired from Rome as being of the family of the Tarquins, and Pub. Valerius was chosen in his room. When Brutus was killed in battle, Sp. Lucretius Tricipitinus was elected to succeed him; and after the death of Lucretius, Marcus Horatius Pulvillus was chosen for the rest of the year with Valerius Poplicola. The first consulship lasted about sixteen months, during which the Romans fought against the Tarquins, and the Capitol was dedicated.

A.U.C. 246. Pub. Valerius Poplicola 2; Tit. Lucretius Tricipitinus. Porsenna supported the claims of Tarquin. The noble actions of Cocles, Scævola, and Clœlia.

——— 247. P. Lucretius, or M. Horatius Pulvillus; P. Valer. Poplicola 3. The vain efforts of Porsenna continued.

——— 248. Sp. Lartius Flavus; T. Herminius Aquilinus. Victories obtained over the Sabines.

——— 249. M. Valerius Volesus; P. Postumius Tubertus. Wars with the Sabines continued.

——— 250. P. Valerius Poplicola 4; T. Lucretius Tricipitinus, 2.

——— 251. Agrippa Menenius Lanatus; P. Postumius Tubertus 2. The death of Poplicola.

——— 252. Opiter Virginius Tricostus; Sp. Cassius Viscellinus. Sabine war.

——— 253. T. Postumius Cominius Aruncus; T. Lartius Flavus. A conspiracy of slaves at Rome.

——— 254. Serv. Sulpicius Camerinus; M. Tullius Longus.

——— 255. P. Veturius Geminus; T. Æbutius Elva.

——— 256. T. Lartius Flavus 2; Q. Clœlius Siculus. War with the Latins,

——— 257. A. Sempronius Atratinus; M. Minucius Augurinus.

——— 258. Aulus Postumius Albus Regillensis; Tit. Virginius Tricostus Cœlimontanus. The battle of Regillæ.

——— 259. Ap. Claudius Sabinus; P. Servilius Priscus. War with the Volsci.

——— 260. A. Virginius Tricostus; T. Veturius Geminus Cicurinus, The dissatisfied people retire to Mons. Sacer.

——— 261. Postumius Cominius Aruncus 2; Sp. Cassius Viscellinus 2. A reconciliation between the senate and people, and the election of the tribunes.

——— 262. T. Geganius Macerinus; P. Minucius Augurinus. A famine at Rome.

——— 263. M. Minucius Augurinus 2; Aul. Sempronius Atratinus 2. The haughty behaviour of Coriolanus to the populace.

——— 264. Q. Sulpitius Camerinus; Sp. Lartius Flavus 2. Coriolanus retires to the Volsci.

——— 265. C. Julius Iulus; P. Pinarius Rufus

Mamercinus. The Volsci make declarations of war.

A.U.C. 266. Sp. Nautius Rutilus; Sex. Furius Fusus. Coriolanus besieges Rome. He retires at the entreaties of his mother and wife, and dies.

——— 267. T. Sicinius Sabinus; C. Aquilius Tuscus. The Volsci defeated.

——— 268. Sp. Cassius Viscellinus 3; Proclus Virginius Tricostus. Cassius aspires to tyranny.

——— 269. Serv. Cornelius Cossus Maluginensis; Q. Fabius Vibulanus. Cassius is condemned, and thrown down the Tarpeian rock.

——— 270. L. Æmilius Mamercinus; Q. Fabius Vibulanus 2. The Æqui and Volsci defeated.

——— 271. M. Fabius Vibulanus; L. Valerius Poplicola Potitus.

——— 272. Q. Fabius Vibulanus 3; C. Julius Iulus. War with the Æqui.

——— 273. Cæso Fabius Vibulanus; Sp. Furius Fusus. War continued with the Æqui and Veientes.

——— 274. M. Fabius Vibulanus 2; Cn. Manlius Cincinnatus. Victory over the Hernici.

——— 275. Cæso Fabius Vibulanus 2; A. Virginius Tricostus Rutilus. The march of the Fabii to the river Cremera.

——— 276. L. Æmilius Mamercinus 2; C. Servilius Structus Ahala. The latter died, and C. Corn. Lentulus succeeded him. The wars continued against the neighbouring states.

——— 277. C. Horatius Pulvillus; T. Menenius Lanatus. The defeat and death of the 300 Fabii.

——— 278. Sp. Servilius Structus; Aul. Virginius Tricostus Rutilus. Menenius brought to his trial for the defeat of the armies under him.

——— 279. C. Nautius Rutilus; P. Valerius Poplicola.

——— 280. L. Furius Medullinus Fusus; C. Manlius Vulso. A truce of forty years granted to the Veientes.

——— 281. L. Æmilius Mamercinus 3; Opiter Virginius, or Vopiscus Julius Iulus. The tribune Genutius murdered in his bed for his seditions.

——— 282. P. Pinarius Rufus Mamercinus; P. Furius Fusus.

——— 283. Ap. Claudius Sabinus; T. Quintius Capitolinus Barbatus. The Roman army suffer themselves to be defeated by the Volsci, on account of their hatred to Appius, while his colleague is boldly and cheerfully obeyed against the Æqui.

——— 284. L. Valerius Poplicola Potitus 2; L. Æmilius Mamercinus 4. Appius is cited to take his trial before the people, and dies before the day of trial.

——— 285. T. Numicius Priscus; A. Virginius Tricostus Cœlimontanus.

——— 286. T. Quintius Capitolinus Barbatus 2; Q. Servilius Priscus.

——— 287. Tib. Æmilius Mamercinus 2; Q. Fabius Vibulanus 4.

——— 288. Q. Servilius Priscus 2; Sp. Postumius Albus Regillensis.

——— 289. Q. Fabius Vibulanus 5; T. Quintius Capitolinus Barbatus 3. In the census made this year, which was the ninth, there were found 124,214 citizens in Rome.

——— 290. Aul. Postumius Albus Regillensis; Sp. Furius Medullinus Fusus.

——— 291. L. Æbutius Elva; P. Servilius Priscus. A plague at Rome.

——— 292. T. Lucretius Tricipitinus; T. Veturius Geminus Cicurinus.

——— 293. P. Volumnius Amintinus Gallus; Serv. Sulpicius Camerinus. Dreadful prodigies at Rome and seditions.

——— 294. C. Claudius Sabinus Regillensis; P. Valerius Poplicola 2. A Sabine seizes the Capitol, and is defeated and killed. Valerius is killed in an engagement, and Cincinnatus is taken from the plough, and made dictator; he quelled the dissensions at Rome, and returned to his farm.

——— 295. Q. Fabius Vibulanus 6; L. Cornelius Maluginensis Cossus. The census made the Romans amount to 132,049.

——— 296. L. Minucius; C. Nautius Rutilus. Minucius is besieged in his camp by the Æqui; and Cincinnatus, being elected dictator, delivers him, obtains a victory, and lays down his power 16 days after his election.

A.U.C. 297. Q. Minucius Augurinus; C. Horatius Pulvillus. War with the Æqui and Sabines. Ten tribunes elected instead of five.

——— 298. M. Valerius Maximus; Sp. Virginius Tricostus Cœlimontanus.

——— 299. T. Romilius Rocus Vaticanus; C. Veturius Cicurinus.

——— 300. Sp. Tarpeius Montanus Capitolinus; A. Aterius Fontinalis.

——— 301. P. Curiatius or Horatius Tergeminus; Sex. Quintilius Varus.

——— 302. C. Menenius Lanatus; P. Cestius Capitolinus. The Decemvirs reduce the laws into twelve tables.

——— 303. Ap. Claudius Crassinus; T. Genutins Augurinus; P. Cestius Capitolinus; P. Postumius Albus Regillensis; Sex. Sulpicius Camerinus; A. Manlius Vulso; T. Romilius Rocus Vaticanus; C. Julius Iulus; T. Veturius Crassus Cicurinus; P. Horatius (or Curiatius) Tergeminus. The Decemvirs assume the reins of government, and preside with consular power.

——— 304 & 305. Ap. Claudius Crassinus; Q. Fabius Vibulanus; M. Cornelius Maluginensis; M. Sergius; L. Mincius; Q. Pœtilius; T. Antonius Merenda; C. Duillius; Sp. Oppius Cornicensis; M. Rabuleius. The Decemvirs continued. They act with violence. Appius endeavours to take possession of Virginia, who is killed by her father. The Decemvirs abolished; and L. Valerius Poplicola Potitus, and M. Horat. Barbatus chosen consuls for the rest of the year. Appius is summoned to take his trial. He dies in prison, and the rest of the Decemvirs are banished.

——— 306. Lart. Herminius Aquilinus; T. Virginius Tricostus Cœlimontanus.

——— 307. M. Geganius Macerinus; C. Julius Iulus. Domestic troubles.

——— 308. T. Quintius Capitolinus Barbatus 4; Agrippa Furius Fusus; or according to Dionysius Halicarn. M. Minutius, C. Quintius. The Æqui and Volsci advance to the gates of Rome and are defeated.

——— 309. M. Genucius Augurinus; C. Curtius Philo. A law passed to permit the patrician and plebeian families to intermarry.

——— 310. Military tribunes are chosen instead of consuls. The plebeians admitted among them. The first were A. Sempronius Atratinus; L. Atilius Longus; T. Clœlius Siculus. They abdicated their power three months after their election, and consuls were again chosen, L. Papirius Mugillanus; L. Sempronius Atratinus.

——— 311. M. Geganius Macerinus 2; T. Quintius Capitolinus Barbatus 5. The censorship instituted.

——— 312. M. Fabius Vibulanus; Postumius Æbutius Elva Cornicensis.

——— 313. C. Furius Pacilus Fusus; M. Papirius Crassus.

——— 314. Proculus Geganius Macerinus; L. Menenius Lanatus. A famine at Rome. Mælius attempts to make himself king.

——— 315. T. Quintius Capitolinus Barbatus 6; Agrippa Menenius Lanatus.

——— 316. Mamercus Æmilius Mamercinus; T. Quintius Cincinnatus; L. Julius Iulus. Military tribunes.

——— 317. M. Geganius Macerinus, L. Sergius Fidenas. Tolumnius, king of the Veientes, killed by Cossus, who takes the second royal spoils called *Opima*.

——— 318. M. Cornelius Maluginensis; L. Papirius Crassus.

——— 319. C. Julius Iulus; L. Virginius Tricostus.

——— 320. C. Julius Iulus 2; L. Virginius Tricostus 2. The duration of the censorship limited to 18 months.

——— 321. M. Fabius Vibulanus; M. Fossius Flaccinator; L. Sergius Fidenas. Military tribunes.

——— 322. L. Pinarius Rufus Mamercinus; L. Furius Medullinus; Sp. Postumius Albus Regillensis. Military tribunes.

——— 323. T. Quintius Pennus Cincinnatus; C. Julius Manto. Consuls. A victory over the Veientes and Fidenates by the dictator Posthumius.

——— 324. C. Papirius Crassus; L. Julius Iulus.

A.U.C. 325. L. Sergius Fidenas 2; Host. Lucret. Tricipitinus.

——— 326. A. Cornelius Cossus; T. Quintius Pennus Cincinnatus 2.

——— 327. C. Servilius Structus Ahala; L. Papirius Mugillanus 2.

——— 328. T. Quintius Pennus Cincinnatus; C. Furius Pacilus; M. Posthumus Albus Regillensis; A. Corn. Cossus. Military tribunes, all of patrician families. Victory over the Veientes.

——— 329. A Sempronius Atratinus; L. Quintius Cincinnatus; L. Furius Medullinus; L. Horat Barbatus.

——— 330. A Claudius Crassus Regillensis; Sp. Nautius Rutilus; L. Sergius Fidenas; Sex. Julius Iulus. Military tribunes.

——— 331. C. Sempronius Atratinus; Q. Fabius Vibulanus. Consuls who gave much dissatisfaction to the people.

——— 332. M. Manlius Vulso Capitolinus; Q. Antonius Merenda; L. Papirius Mugillanus; L. Servilius Strictus. Military tribunes.

——— 333. Numerius Fabius Vibulanus; T. Q. Capitolinus Barbatus.

——— 334. L. Q. Pennus Cincinnatus 3; L. Furius Medullinus 2; M. Manlius Vulso Capitolinus; A. Sempronius Atratinus. Military tribunes.

——— 335. A. Menenius Lanatus; Sp. Nautius Rutilus; P. Lucretius Tricipitinus; C. Servilius Ahala 2. Military tribunes.

——— 336. L. Sergius Fidenas; M. Papirius Mugillanus; C. Servilius Ahala 3.

——— 337. A. Menenius Lanatus 2; P. Lucret. Tricipitinus; L. Servil. Structus; Sp. Vetur. Crassus Cicurinus.

——— 338. A. Sempronius Atratinus 3; M. Papir. Mugillanus; Sp. Nautius Rutilus; Q. Fabius Vibulanus.

——— 339. P. Cornelius Cossus; Q. Cincinnatus; C. Valer. Pennus. Volusus; Q. Fabius Vibulanus.

——— 340. Cn. Corn. Cossus; Q. Fabius Vibulanus; P. Postumius Albus Regillensis; L. Valerius Potitus. Postumius stoned to death by the army.

——— 341. M. Corn. Cossus; L. Furius Medullinus. Consuls. Domestic seditions.

——— 342. Q. Fabius Ambustus; C. Furius Pacilus.

——— 343. M. Papirius Atratinus, or Mugillanus; C. Nautius Rutilus.

——— 344. Mamercus Æmilius Mamercinus; C. Valerius Potitus Volusus.

——— 345. Cn. Corn. Cossus; L. Furius Medullinus 2. Plebeians for the first time quæstors.

——— 346. C. Julius Iulus; P. Cornel. Cossus; C. Servil. Ahala. Military tribunes.

——— 347. L. Furius Medullinus; N. Fabius Vibulanus; C. Servilius Ahala; C. Valer. Potitus Volusus. Military tribunes.

——— 348. P. Cornelius Rutilus Cossus. L. Valer. Potitus; Cn. Corn. Cossus; N. Fabius Ambustus. Military tribunes. This year the Roman soldiers first received pay.

——— 349. T. Quintius Capitolinus Barbatus; C. Julius Iulus; M. Æmyl. Mamercinus; L. Fur. Medullinus; T. Q. Cincinnatus; A Manlius Vulso Capitolinus. Military tribunes. The siege of Veii begun.

——— 350. C. Valerius Potitus; P. Corn. Maluginensis; Sp. Nautius Rutilus; Cn. Corn. Cossus; C. Fabius Ambustus; M. Sergius Fidenas. Military tribunes.

——— 351. Manlius Æmilius Mamercius; M. Furius Fusus; Ap. Claudius Crassus; L. J. Iulus; M. Q. Varus; L. Val. Potitus; M. Fur. Camillus; Postumius Albinus. The Roman cavalry begin to receive pay.

——— 352. C. Servilius Ahala; Q. Sulp. Camerinus; Q. Serv. Priscus Fidenas; A. Manl. Vulso; L. Virgin. Tricostus; M. Serg. Fidenas. A defeat at Veii, occasioned by a quarrel between two of the military tribunes.

——— 353. L. Valerius Potitus 4; M. Furius Camillus 2; L. Julius Iulus; M. Æmil. Mamercinus; Cn. Corn. Cossus; C. Fabius Ambustus. A military tribune chosen from among the plebeians.

A.U.C. 354. P. Licinius Calvus; P. Mælius Capitolinus; P. Mænius; Sp. Furius Medullinus; L. Titinius; L. Publius Philo.

——— 355. C. Duillius; L. Atilius Longus: Cn. Genusius Aventinensis; M. Pomponius; Volero Publil. Philo; M. Vetur. Crassus Cicurinus.

——— 356. L. Valerius Potitus 5; M. Furius Camillus 3; L. Furius Medullinus; M. Valer. Maximus; Q. Servil. Priscus; Q. Sulpitius Camerinus.

——— 357. L. Julius Iulus; L. Furius Medullinus; L. Serg. Fidenas; A. Postum. Albinus; A. Manl. Vulso; P. Corn. Maluginensis.

——— 358. P. Licin. Calvus; L. Attil. Longus; P. Mælius Capitolinus; L. Titinius; P. Mænius; C. Genucius Aventinensis. Camillus declared dictator. The city of Veii taken by means of a mine. Camillus obtains a triumph.

——— 359. P. Corn. Cossus; P. Corn. Scipio; M. Val. Maximus; C. Fabius Ambustus; L. Furius Medullinus; Q. Servil. Priscus Fidenas. The people wish to remove to Veii.

——— 360. M. Furius Camillus; L. Fur. Medullinus; C. Æmil. Mamercinus; Sp. Postumius Albin. Regillensis; P. Corn. Scipio; L. Val. Poplicola. Falisci surrendered to the Romans.

——— 361. L. Lucret. Flavus; Serv. Sulpicius Camerinus, Consuls, after Rome had been governed by military tribunes for 15 successive years. Camillus strongly opposes the removing to Veii, and it is rejected.

——— 362. L. Valerius Potitus; M. Manlius Capitolinus. One of the censors dies.

——— 363. L. Lucretius Flavus; Ser. Sulp. Camerinus; M. Æmil. Mamercinus; L. Furius Medullinus; Agrippa Furius Fusus; C. Æmil. Mamercinus. Military tribunes. A strange voice heard, which foretold the approach of the Gauls. Camillus goes into banishment to Ardea. The Gauls besiege Clusium, and soon after march towards Rome.

——— 364. Q. Fabius Ambustus; C. Fab. Ambustus; Q. Sulp. Longus; Q. Servil. Priscus Fidenas; Serv. Corn. Maluginensis. Military tribunes. The Romans defeated at Allia by the Gauls. The Gauls enter Rome, and set it on fire. Camillus declared dictator by the senate, who had retired into the Capitol. The geese save the Capitol, and Camillus suddenly comes and defeats the Gauls.

——— 365. L. Valerius Poplicola 3; L. Virginius Tricostus; P. Corn. Cossus; A. Manl. Capitolinus; L. Æmil. Mamercinus; L. Postumius Albinus Regillensis. Camillus declared dictator, defeats the Volsci, Æqui, and Tuscans.

——— 366. T. Q. Cincinnatus; Q. Servilius Priscus Fidenas; L. Julius Iulus; L. Aquilin. Corvus; L. Lucret. Tricipitinus; Ser. Sulp. Rusus.

——— 367. L. Papirius Cursor; Cn. Sergius Fidenas; L. Æmilius Mamercinus; L. Menenius Lanatus; L. Val. Poplicola; Cn. Corn. Cossus.

——— 368. M. Furius Camillus; Q. Serv. Priscus Fidenas; L. Q. Cincinnatus; L. Horat. Pulvillus; P. Valer. Potitus Poplicola; Ser. Corn. Maluginensis.

——— 369. A. Manlius Capitolinus; P. Cornelius Cossus; T. Q. Capitolinus; L. Q. Capitolinus; L. Papir. Cursor; C. Serg. Fidenas. The Volsci defeated. Manlius aims at royalty.

——— 370. Ser. Corn, Maluginensis; P. Valerius Potitus Poplicola; M. Furius Camillus; Ser. Snlp. Rufus; C. Papir. Crassus; T. Q. Cincinnatus. Manlius is condemned, and thrown down the Tarpeian rock.

——— 371. L. Valerius Poplicola; A. Manlius Capitolinus; Ser. Sulpicius Rufus; L. Lucret. Tricipitinus; L. Æmil. Mamercinus; M. Trebonius Flavus.

——— 372. Sp. Papir. Crassus; L. Pap. Crassus; Ser. Corn. Maluginensis; Q. Serv. Priscus Fidenas; S. Sulp. Prætextatus; L. Æmil. Mamercinus.

——— 373. M. Furius Camillus; L. Furius Medullinus; A. Postumius Albin. Regillensis; L. Postumius Alb. Regillensis; L. Lucret. Tricipitinus; M. Fabius Ambustus.

——— 374. L. Valer. Poplicola; P. Val. Potitus Poplicola; L. Menen. Lanatus; C. Serg. Fidenas; Sp. Papir. Cursor; Ser. Corn. Maluginensis.

——— 375. C. Manlius Capitolinus; P. Manl.

Capitolinus: C. Julius Iulus; C. Sextilius; M. Albinius; L. Antistius.

A.U.C. 376. Sp. Furius Medullinus; Q. Servil. Priscus Fidenas; C. Licin. Calvus; P. Clœlius Siculus; M. Horat. Pulvillus; L. Geganius Macerinus.

——— 377. L. Æmilius Mamercinus; Ser. Sulp. Prætextatus; P. Val. Potitus Poplicola; L. Q. Cincinnatus; C. Vetur. Crassus Cicurinus; C. Q. Cincinnatus.

——— 378
——— 379
——— 380
——— 381
——— 382 } For five years anarchy at Rome. No consuls or military tribunes were elected. The only magistrates were L. Sextius Sextinus Lateranus, and C. Licinius Calvus Stolo, tribunes of the people.

——— 383. L. Furius Medullinus; P. Val Potitus Poplicola; A. Man. Capitolanus; Ser. Sulpit. Prætextatus; C. Val. Potitus; Ser. Corn. Maluginensis.

——— 384. Q. Servilius Priscus Fidenas; C. Veturius Crassus Cicurinus; M. Corn. Maluginensis; Q. Q. Cincinnatus; A. Corn. Cossus; M. Fabius Ambustus. Ten magistrates are chosen to take care of the Sibylline books.

——— 385. L. Q. Capitolinus; Sp. Servil. Structus; Ser. Corn. Maluginensis; L. Papir. Crassus; Ser. Sulp. Prætextatus; L. Vetur. Crassus Cicurinus.

——— 386. According to some writers, Camillus this year was sole dictator, without either consuls or tribunes.

——— 387. A. Corn. Cossus; L. Vet. Crassus Cicurinus; M. Corn. Maluginensis; P. Val. Potitus Poplicola; M. Geganius Macerinus; P. Manl. Capitolinus. The Gauls defeated by Camillus. One of the consuls for the future to be elected from among the plebeians.

——— 388. L. Æmilius Mamercinus, the patrician; L. Sextius Sextinus Lateranus, the plebeian, are created consuls. The offices of prætor and curule ædile, granted to the senate by the people.

——— 389. L. Genucius Aventinensis; Q. Servilius Ahala. Camillus died.

——— 390. C. Sulpitius Peticus; C. Licinius Stolo, or Calvus.

——— 391. Cn. Genutius Aventinensis; L. Æmilius Mamercinus.

——— 392. Q. Serv. Ahala 2; L. Genutius Aventinensis 2. Curtius devotes himself to the *Dii manes.*

——— 393. C. Sulpicius Peticus 2; C. Licinius Calvus 2. Manlius conquers a Gaul in single combat.

——— 394. C. Petilius Balbus, or Libo Visolus; M. Fabius Ambustus.

——— 395. M. Popilius Lænas; C. Manlius Capitolinus Imperiosus.

——— 396. C. Fabius Ambustus; C. Plautius Proculus. The Gauls defeated.

——— 397. C. Manlius Rutilus; Cn. Manlius Capit. Imperiosus 2.

——— 398. M. Fabius Ambustus 2; M Popilius Lænas 2. A dictator elected from the plebeians for the first time.

——— 399. C. Sulpicius Peticus 3; M. Valerius Poplicola 2; both of patrician families.

——— 400. M. Fabius Ambustus 3; T. Quintius Pennus Capitolinus.

——— 401. C. Sulpitius Peticus 4; M. Valerius Poplicola 3.

——— 402. M. Valerius Poplicola 4; C. Marcius Rutilus.

——— 403. C. Sulpicius Peticus 5; T. Q. Pennus Cincinnatus. A censor elected for the first time from the plebeians.

——— 404. M. Popilius Lænas 3; L. Corn. Scipio.

——— 405. L. Furius Camillus; Ap. Claudius Crassus. Valerius surnamed Corvinus, after conquering a Gaul.

——— 406. M. Valer. Corvus; M. Popilius Lænas 4. Corvus was elected at 33 years of age against the standing law. A treaty of amity concluded with Carthage.

——— 407. T. Manlius Imperiosus Torquatus; C. Plautius Hypsæus.

——— 408. M. Valerius Corvus 2; C. Pætilius Libo Visolus.

——— 409. M. Fabius Dorso; Ser. Sulpicius Camerinus.

A.U.C. 410. C. Marcius Rutilus; T. Manlius Imperiosus Torquatus.

——— 411. M. Valerius Corvus 3; A. Corn. Cossus Arvina. The Romans begin to make war against the Samnites, at the request of the Campanians. They obtain a victory.

——— 412. C. Marcius Rutilus 4; Q. Servilius Ahala.

——— 413. C. Plautinus Hypsæus; L. Æmilius Mamercinus.

——— 414. T. Manlius Imperiosus Torquatus 3; P. Decius Mus. The victories of Alexander the Great in Asia. Manlius puts his son to death for fighting against his order. Decius devotes himself for the army, which obtains a great victory over the Latins.

——— 415. T. Æmilius Mamercinus; Q. Publilius Philo.

——— 416, L. Furius Camillus; C. Mænius. The Latins conquered.

——— 417. C. Sulpicius Longus; P. Ælius Pætus. The prætorship granted to a plebeian.

——— 418. L. Papirius Crassus; Cæso Duillius.

——— 419. M. Valerius Corvus; M. Atilius Regulus.

——— 420. T. Veturius Calvinus; Sp. Posthumius Albinus.

——— 421. L. Papir. Cursor; C. Petil. Libo Visolus.

——— 422. A. Corn. Cossus Arvina 2; Cn. Domit. Calvinus.

——— 423. M. Claud. Marcellus; C. Valer. Potitus Flaccus.

——— 424. L. Papirius Crassus; C. Plautius Venno.

——— 425. L. Æmilius Mamercinus 2; C. Plautius Decianus.

——— 426. C. Plautius Proculus; P. Corn. Scapula.

——— 427. L. Corn. Lentulus; Publilius Philo 2.

——— 428. C. Pætilius Libo Visolus; L. Papirius Mugillanus. A law was made that no one should be imprisoned for debt.

——— 429. L. Furius Camillus 2; D. Jun. Brutus Scæva. The dictator Papirius Cursor desires to put to death Fabius, his master of the horse, because he fought in his absence, and obtained a famous victory. He pardons him.

——— 430. According to some authors there were no consuls elected this year, but only a dictator, L. Papirius Cursor.

——— 431. Luc. Sulpitius Longus; Q. Aulius Cerretanus.

——— 432. Q. Fabius Maximus Rullianus; L. Fulvius Corvus.

——— 433. T. Veturius Calvinus 2; Sp. Posthumius Albinus 2. C. Pontius, the Samnite, takes the Roman consuls in an ambuscade at Caudium.

——— 434. L. Papirius Cursor 2; Q. Publilius Philo 3.

——— 435. L. Papirius Cursor 3; Q. Aulius, or Æmilius Cerretanus 2.

——— 436. M. Fossius Flaccinator; L. Plautius Venno.

——— 437. C. Jun. Bubulcus Brutus; Q. Æmilius Barbula.

——— 438. Sp. Nautius Rutilus; M. Popilius Lænas.

——— 439. L. Papirius Cursor 4; Q. Publilius Philo 4.

——— 440. M. Pætilius Libo; C. Sulpicius Longus.

——— 441. L. Papirius Cursor 5; C. Jun. Bubulcus Brutus 2.

——— 442. M. Valerius Maximus: P. Decius Mus. The censor Appius makes the Appian way and aqueducts. The family of the Potitii extinct.

——— 443. C. Jun. Bubulcus Brutus 4; Q. Æmilius Barbula 2.

——— 444. Q. Fabius Maximus Rullianus 2; C. Martius Rutilus.

——— 445. According to some authors there were no consuls elected this year, but only a dictator, L. Papirius Cursor.

——— 446. P. Decius Mus 2; Q. Fabius Maximus Rullianus 3.

——— 447. Appius Claudius Cæcus; L. Volumnius Flamma Violens.

——— 448. P. Corn. Arvina; Q. Marcius Tremulus.

A.U.C. 449. L. Postumius Megellus: and T. Minucius Augurinus, in whose room was appointed M. Fulvius Corvus Pætinus.
——— 450. P. Sulpicius Saverrio; P. Sempronius Sophus. The Æqui conquered.
——— 451. L. Genucius Aventinensis; Ser. Cornelius Lentulus.
——— 452. M. Livius Dexter; M. Æmilius Paulus.
——— 453. Q. Fabius Maximus Rullianus; M. Valer. Corvus, not consuls, but dictators, according to some authors.
——— 455. M. Valerius Corvus; Q. Apuleius Pansa. The priesthood made common to the plebeians.
——— 455. M. Fulvius Pætinus; T. Manlius Torquatus, in whose room M. Valer. Corvus was appointed.
——— 456. L. Cornelius Scipio; Cn. Fulvius Centumalus.
——— 457. Q. Fabius Maximus Rullianus 4; P. Decius Mus 3. Wars against the Samnites.
——— 458. L. Volumrius Flamma Violens 2; Ap. Claudius Cæcus 2. Conquest over the Etrurians and Samnites.
——— 459. Q. Fabius Maximus Rullianus 5; P. Decius Mus 4. Decius devotes himself in a battle against the Samnites and the Gauls, and the Romans obtain a victory.
——— 460. L. Postumius Megellus; M. Atilius Regulus.
——— 461. L. Papirius Cursor; Sp. Carvilius Maximus. Victories over the Samnites.
——— 462. Q. Fabius Maximus Gurges; D. Jun. Brutus Sœva. Victory over the Samnites.
——— 463. L. Postumius Megellus 3; C. Jun. Brutus Bubulcus. Æsculapius brought to Rome in the form of a serpent from Epidaurus.
——— 464. P. Corn. Rufinus; M. Curius Dentatus.
——— 465. M. Valerius Maximus Corvinus; Q. Cædicius Noctua.
——— 466. Q. Marcius Tremulus; P. Corn. Arvina.
——— 467. M. Claudius Marcellus; C. Nautius Rutilus.
——— 468. M. Valerius Maximus Potitus; C. Ælius Pætus.
——— 469. C. Claudius Cænina; M. Æmilius Lepidus, or Barbula.
——— 470. C. Servilius Tucca; L. Cæcilius Metellus, or Dexter. War with the Senones.
——— 471, P. Corn. Dolabella Maximus; C. Domitius Caivins. The Senones defeated.
——— 472. Q. Æmilius Papus; C. Fabricius Luscinus. War with Tarentum.
——— 473. L. Æmilius Barbula; Q. Marcius Philippus. Pyrrhus comes to the assistance of the people of Tarentum.
——— 474. P. Valerius Lævinus; Tib. Cornucianus Nepos. Pyrrhus conquers the consul Lævinus, and though victorius, sues for peace, which is refused by the Roman senate. The census was made, and 272, 222 citizens were found.
——— 475. P. Sulpicius Saverrio; P. Decius Mus. A battle with Pyrrhus.
——— 476. C. Fabricius Luscinus 2; Q. Æmilius Papus 2. Pyrrhus goes to Sicily. The treaty between Rome and Carthage renewed.
——— 477. P. Corn. Rufinus 2; C. Jun. Brutus Bubulcus 2. Crotona and Locri taken.
——— 478. Q. Fabius Maximus Gurges 2; C. Genucius Clepsina. Pyrrhus returns from Sicily to Italy.
——— 479. M. Curius Dentatus 2; L. Corn. Lentulus Caudinus. Pyrrhus finally defeated by Curius.
——— 480. M. Curius Dentatus 3; Ser. Corn. Merenda.
——— 481. C. Fabius Dorso Licinus; C. Claudius Cænina 2. An embassy from Philadelphus, to conclude an alliance with the Romans.
——— 482. L. Papirius Cursor 2; Sp. Carvilius Maximus 2. Tarentum surrenders.
——— 483. L. Genucius Clepsina; C. Quintilius Claudius.
——— 484. C. Genucius Clepsina 2; Cn. Cornelius Blasio.
——— 485. Q. Ogulnius Gallus; C. Fabius Pictor. Silver money coined at Rome for the first time.

A.U.C. 486. P. Sempronius Sophus; Ap. Claudius Crassus.
——— 487. M. Atilius Regulus; L. Julius Libo. Italy enjoys peace universally.
——— 488. Numerius Fabius Pictor; D. Junius Pera.
——— 489. Q. Fabius Maximus Gurges 3; L. Mamilius Vitulus. The number of the quæstors increased to eight.
——— 490. Ap. Claudius Caudex; M. Fulvius Flaccus. The Romans aid the Mamertines, which occasions the first Punic war. Appius defeats the Carthaginians in Sicily. The combats of gladiators first instituted.
——— 491. M. Valerius Maximus Messala; M. Otacilius Crassus. An alliance between Rome and Hiero, king of Syracuse. A sun-dial, brought from Catana, first put up at Rome.
——— 492. L. Postumius Gemellus; Q. Mamilius Vitulus. The siege and taking of Agrigentum. The total defeat of the Carthaginians.
——— 493. L. Valerius Flaccus; T. Otacilius Crassus.
——— 494. Cn. Corn. Scipio Asina; C. Duilius Nepos. In two months the Romans build and equip a fleet of 120 gallies. The naval victory and triumph of Duillius.
——— 495. L. Corn. Scipio; C. Aquilius Florus. Expedition against Sardinia and Corsica.
——— 496. A. Atilius Calatinus; C. Sulpicius Paterculus. The Carthaginians defeated in a naval battle.
——— 497. C. Attilius Regulus; Cn. Corn. Blasio.
——— 498. L. Manlius Vulso; Q. Cædicius. At the death of Cædicius, Marcus Atilius Regulus 2, was elected for the rest of the year. The famous battle of Ecnoma. The victorious consuls land in Africa.
——— 499. Serv. Fulvius Pætinus Nobilior; M. Æmilius Paulus. Regulus, after many victories in Africa, is defeated and taken prisoner by Xanthippus. Agrigentum retaken by the Carthaginians.
——— 500. Cn. Corn. Scipio Asina 2; A. Atilius Calatinus 2. Panormus taken by the Romans.
——— 501. Cn. Servilius Cæpio; C. Sempronius Blæsus. The Romans, discouraged by shipwrecks, renounce the sovereignty of the seas.
——— 502. C. Aurelius Cotta; P. Servilius Geminus.
——— 503. L. Cæcilius Metellus 2; C. Furius Pacilus. The Romans begin to recover their power by sea.
——— 504. C. Atilius Regulus 2; L. Manlius Volso 2. The Carthaginians defeated near Panormus in Sicily. One hundred and forty-two elephants taken and sent to Rome. Regulus advises the Romans not to exchange prisoners. He is put to death with the most excruciating torments.
——— 505. P. Claudius Pulcher; L. Jun. Pullus. The Romans defeated in a naval battle. The Roman fleet lost in a storm.
——— 506. C. Aurelius Cotta; P. Servilius Geminus 2.
——— 507. L. Cæcilius Metellus 3; Num. Fabius Buteo. The number of citizens 252,222.
——— 508. M. Otacilius Crassus; M. Fabius Licinus.
——— 509. M. Fabius Buteo; C. Atilius Balbus.
——— 510. A. Manlius Torquatus Atticus; C. Sempronius Blæsus 2.
——— 511. C. Fundanius Fundulus; C. Sulpicius Gallus. A fleet built by individuals at Rome.
——— 512. C. Lutatius Catulus; A. Postumius Albinus. The Carthaginian fleet defeated near the islands Ægates. Peace made between Rome and Carthage. The Carthaginians evacuate Sicily.
——— 513. Q. Lutatius Cerco; A. Manlius Torquatus Atticus. Sicily is made a Roman province. The 39th census taken. The citizens amount to 260,000.
——— 514. C. Claudius Centho; M. Sempronius Tuditanus.
——— 515. C. Mamilius Turinus; Q. Valerius Falto.
——— 516. T. Sempronius Gracchus; P. Valerius

Falto. The Carthaginians give up Sardinia to Rome.
A.U.C. 517. L. Corn. Lentulus Caudinus; Q. Fulvius. Flaccus. The Romans offer Ptolemy Evergetes assistance against Antiochus Theos.
——— 518. P. Corn. Lentulus Caudinus; C. Licinius Varus. Revolt of Corsica and Sardinia.
——— 519. C. Atilius Balbus 2; T. Manlius Torquatus. The temple of Janus shut for the first time since the reign of Numa, about 440 years. A universal peace.
——— 520, L. Postumius Albinus; Sp. Carvilius Maximus.
——— 521. Q. Fabius Maximus Verrucosus; M. Pomponius Matho. Differences and jealousy between Rome and Carthage.
——— 522. M. Æmilius Lepidus; M. Publicius Malleolus.
——— 523. M. Pomponius Matho 2; C. Papirius Maso. The first divorce known at Rome.
——— 524. M. Æmilius Barbula; M. Junius Pera. War with the Illyrians.
——— 525. L. Postumius Albinus 2; Cn. Fulvius Centumalus. The building of New Carthage.
——— 526. Sp. Carvilius Maximus 2; Q. Fabius Maximus Verrucosus 2.
——— 527. P. Valerius Flaccus; M. Atilius Regulus. Two new prætors added to the other prætors.
——— 528. M. Valerius Messala; L. Apullius Fullo. Italy invaded by the Gauls. The Romans could now lead into the field of battle 770,000 men.
——— 529. L. Æmilius Papus; C. Atilius Regulus. The Gauls defeat the Romans near Clusium. The Romans gain a victory near Telamon.
——— 530. T. Manlius Torquatus 2; Q. Fulvius Flaccus 2. The Boii, part of the Gauls, surrender.
——— 531. C. Flaminius Nepos; P. Furius Philus.
——— 532. M. Claudius Marcellus; Cn. Corn. Scipio Calvinus. A new war with the Gauls. Marcellus gains the spoil called *opima*.
——— 533. P. Cornelius Scipio Asina; M. Minucius Rufus. Annibal takes the command of the Carthaginian armies in Spain.
——— 534. L. Veturius Philo; C. Lutatius Catulus. The Via Flaminia built.
——— 535. M. Livius Salinator; L. Æmilius Paulus. War with Illyricum.
——— 536. P. Corn. Scipio; T. Sempronius Longus. Siege of Saguntum, by Annibal, the cause of the second Punic war. Annibal marches towards Italy, and crosses the Alps. The Carthaginian fleet defeated near Sicily. Sempronius defeated near Trebia, by Annibal.
——— 537. Cn. Servilius Geminus; C. Flaminius Nepos, 2, in whose room was substituted M. Atil. Regulus 2. A famous battle near the lake Thrasymenus. Fabius is appointed dictator. Success of Cn. Scipio in Spain.
——— 538. C. Terentius Varro; L. Æmilius Paulus 2. The famous battle of Cannæ. Annibal marches to Capua. Marcellus beats Annibal near Nola. Asdrubal begins his march towards Italy, and his army is totally defeated by the Scipios.
——— 539. T. Sempronius Gracchus; and L. Posthumius Albinus, in whose room M. Claud. Marcellus was appointed; and aftewards Q. Fabius Maximus Verrucosus. Philip of Macedonia enters into alliance with Annibal. Sardinia revolts, and is reconquered by Manlius. The Carthaginians twice beaten in Spain by Scipio.
——— 540. Q. Fabius Maximus Verrucosus 3; M. Claudius Marcellus 3. Marcellus besieges Syracuse by Sea and land.
——— 541. Q. Fabius Maximus Verrucosus 4; T. Sempronius Gracchus 2. The siege of Syracuse continued.
——— 542. Q. Fulvius Flaccus 2; Ap. Claudius Pulcher. Syracuse taken and plundered. Sicily made a Roman province. Tarentum treacherously delivered to Annibal. The two Scipios conquered in Spain.
——— 543. Cn. Fulvius Centumalus; P. Sulpicius Galba Maximus. Capua besieged and taken by the Romans. P. Scipio sent to Spain with proconsular power.
A.U.C. 544. M. Claudius Marcellus 4; M. Valerius Lævinus 2. The Carthaginians driven from Sicily. Carthagena taken by young Scipio.
——— 545. Q. Fabius Maximus Verrucosus 5; Q. Fulvius Flaccus 3. Annibal defeated by Marcellus. Fabius takes Tarentum. Asdrubal defeated by Scipio.
——— 546. M. Claudius Marcellus 5; T. Quintius Crispinus. Marcellus killed in an ambuscade by Annibal. The Carthaginian fleet defeated.
——— 547. M. Claudius Nero; M. Livius Salinator 2. Asdrubal passes the Alps. Nero obtains some advantage over Annibal. The two consuls defeat Asdrubal, who is killed, and his head thrown into Annibal's Camp. The Romans make war against Philip.
——— 548. L, Veturius Philo; Q. Cæcilius Metellus. Scipio obtains a victory in Spain over Asdrubal, the son of Gisgo. Masinissa sides with the Romans.
——— 549. P. Cornelius Scipio; P. Licinius Crassus. Scipio is empowered to invade Africa.
——— 550. M. Cornelius Cethegus; P. Sempronius Tuditanus. Scipio lands in Africa. The census taken, and 215,000 heads of families found in Rome.
——— 551. Cn. Servilius Cæpio; C. Servilius Geminus. Scipio spreads general consternation in Africa. Annibal is recalled from Italy by the Carthaginian senate.
——— 552. M. Servilius Pulex Geminus; Ti. Claudius Nero. Annibal and Scipio come to a parley; they prepare for battle. Annibal is defeated at Zama. Scipio prepares to besiege Carthage.
——— 553. Cn. Corn. Lentulus; P. Ælius Pætus. Peace granted to the Carthaginians. Scipio triumphs.
——— 554. P. Sulpicius Galba Maximus 2; C. Aurelius Cotta. War with the Macedonians.
——— 555. L. Corn Lentulus; P. Vilius Tapulus. The Macedonian war continued.
——— 556. Sex. Ælius Pætus Catus; T. Quintius Flaminius. Philip defeated by Quintius.
——— 557. C. Corn. Cethegus; Q. Minicius Rufus. Philip is defeated. Quintius grants him peace.
——— 558. L. Furius Purpureo; M. Claudius Marcellus. The independence of Greece proclaimed by Flaminius at the Isthmian games.
——— 559. L. Valerius Flaccus; M. Porcius Cato. Quintius regulates the affairs of Greece. Cato's victories in Spain, and triumph. The Romans demand Annibal from the Carthaginians.
——— 560. P. Corn. Scipio Africanus 2; T. Sempronius Longus. Annibal flies to Antiochus.
——— 561. L. Cornelius Merula; Q. Minucius Thermus. Antiochus prepares to make war against Rome, and Annibal endeavours in vain to stir up the Carthaginians to take up arms.
——— 562. L. Quintius Flaminius; Cn. Domitius Ahenobarbus. The Greeks call Antiochus to deliver them.
——— 563. P. Corn. Scipio Nasica; M. Acilius Glabrio. The success of Acilius in Greece against Antiochus.
——— 564. L. Corn. Scipio; C. Lælius Nepos. The fleet of Antiochus under Annibal defeated by the Romans, Antiochus defeated by Scipio.
——— 565. M. Fulvius Nobilior; Cn. Manlius Vulso. War with the Gallogrecians.
——— 566. M. Valerius Messala; C. Livius Salinator. Antiochus dies.
——— 567. M. Æmilius Lepidus; C. Flaminius Nepos. The Ligurians reduced.
——— 568. Sp. Postumius Albinus; Q. Marcius Philippus. The Bacchanalia abolished at Rome.
——— 569. Ap. Claudius Pulcher; M. Sempronius Tuditanus. Victories in Spain and Liguria.
——— 570. P. Claudius Pulcher; L. Porcius Licinius. Philip of Macedon sends his son Demetrius to Rome.
——— 571. M. Claudius Marcellus; Q. Fabius Labeo. Death of Annibal, Scipio, and Philopœmen. The Gauls invade Italy.
——— 572. M. Bæbius Tamphilus; L. Æmilius Paulus. Death of Philip.
——— 573. P. Cornelius Cethegus; M. Bæbius Tamphilus. Expeditions against Liguria. The first gilt statue raised at Rome.

A.U.C. 574. A. Posthumius Albinus Lucus; C. Calpurnius Piso, in whose room Q. Fulvius Flaccus was appointed. The Celtiberians defeated.
——— 575. Q. Fulvius Flaccus; L. Manlius Acidinus Fulvianus. Alliance renewed with Perseus the son of Philip.
——— 576. M. Junius Brutus; A. Manlius Vulso.
——— 577. C. Claudius Pulcher; T. Sempronius Gracchus. The Istrians defeated.
——— 578. Cn. Corn. Scipio Hispalus, in whose room C. Val. Lævinus was appointed; Q. Petillius Spurinus.
——— 579. P. Mucius Scævola; M. Æmilius Lepidus 2.
——— 580. Sp. Postumius Albinus; Q. Mucius Scævola.
——— 581. L. Postumius Albinus; M. Popilius Lænas.
——— 582. C. Popilius Lænas; P. Ælius Ligur, both plebeians. War declared against Perseus.
——— 583. P. Licinius Crassus; C. Cassius Longinus. Perseus gains some advantage over the Romans.
——— 584. A. Hostilius Mancinus; A. Atilius Seranus.
——— 585. Q. Marcius Philippus 2; Cn. Servilius Cæpio. The campaign in Macedonia.
——— 586. L. Æmilius Paulus 2; C. Licinius Crassus. Perseus is defeated and taken prisoner by Paulus.
——— 587. Q. Ælius Pætus; M. Junius Pennus.
——— 588. M. Claudius Marcellus; C. Sulpicius Gallus.
——— 589. Cn. Octavius Nepos; T. Manlius Torquatus.
——— 590. Aulus Manlius Torquatus; Q. Cassius Longus.
——— 591. Ti. Sempronins Gracchus 2; M. Juvencius Phalna.
——— 592. P. Corn. Scipio Nasica; C. Marcius Figulus. Demetrius flies from Rome, and is made king of Syria.
——— 593. M. Valerius Messala; C. Fannius Strabo.
——— 594. L. Anicius Gallus: M. Corn. Cethegus.
——— 595. C. Cornelius Dolabella; M. Fulvius Nobilior.
——— 596. M. Æmilius Lepidus; C. Popilius Lænas.
——— 597. Sex. Jul. Cæsar: L. Aurelius Orestes. War against the Dalmatians.
——— 598. L. Corn. Lentulus Lupus; C. Marcius Figulus 2.
——— 599. P. Corn. Scipio Nasica 2; M. Claudius Marcellus 2.
——— 600. Q. Opimius Nepos; L. Postumius Albinus, in whose room M. Acil. Glabrio was appointed.
——— 601. Q. Fulvius Nobilior; T. Annius Luscus. The false Philip. Wars in Spain.
——— 602. M. Claudius Marcellus 3; L. Valerius Flaccus.
——— 603. L. Licinius Lucullus; A. Posthumius Albinus.
——— 604. T. Quintius Flaminius; M' Acilius Balbus. War between the Carthaginians and Masinissa.
——— 605. L. Marcinus Censorinus; M. Manlius Nepos. The Romans declare war against Carthage. The Carthagiaians wish to accept the hard conditions which are imposed upon them; but the Romans say that Carthage must be destroyed.
——— 606. Sp. Postumius Albinus; L. Calpurnius Piso Cæsonius. Carthage besieged.
——— 607. P. Corn. Scipio Africanus Æmilianus; C. Livius Mamilianus Drusus. The siege of Carthage continued with vigor by Scipio.
——— 608. Cn. Cornelius Lentulus; L. Mummius Achaicus. Carthage surrenders, and is destroyed. Mummius takes and burns Corinth.
——— 609. Q. Fabius Maximus Æmilianus; L. Hostilius Mancinus.
——— 610. Ser. Sulpicius Galba; L. Aurelius Cotta.
——— 611. Ap. Claudius Pulcher; Q. Cæcilius Metellus Macedonicus. War against the Celtiberians.
——— 612. L. Cæcilius Metellus Calvus; Q. Fabius Maximus Servilianus.

A.U.C. 613. Q. Pompeius Nepos; C. Servilius Nepos.
——— 614. C. Lælius Sapiens; Q. Servilius Cæpio. The wars with Viriatus.
——— 615. M. Popilius Lænas; Cn. Calpurnius Piso.
——— 616. P. Corn. Scipio Nasica Serapio; D. Junius Brutus Callaicus. The two consuls imprisoned by the tribunes.
——— 617. M. Æmilius Lepidus; C. Hostilius Mancinus. Wars against Numantia.
——— 618. P. Furius Philus; Sex. Atilius Serranus.
——— 619. Ser. Fulvius Flaccus; Q. Calpurnius Piso.
——— 620. P. Corn. Scipio 2; C. Fulvius Flaccus.
——— 621. P. Mucius Scævola; L. Calpurnius Piso Frugi. Numantia surrenders to Scipio, and is entirely demolished. The seditions of Ti. Gracchus at Rome.
——— 622. P. Popilius Lænas; P. Rupilius Nepos.
——— 623. P. Licinius Crassus Mucianus; L. Valerius Flaccus.
——— 624. C. Claudius Pulcher; M. Perpenna. In the census are found 313,823 citizens.
——— 625. C. Sempronius Tuditanus; M. Aquilius Nepos.
——— 626. Cn. Octavius Nepos; T. Annius Luscus Rufus.
——— 627. L. Cassius Longus; L. Cornelius Cinna. A revolt of slaves in Sicily.
——— 628. L. Æmilius Lepidus; L. Aurelius Orestes.
——— 629. M. Plautius Hypsæus; M. Fulvius Flaccus.
——— 630. C. Cassius Longinus; L. Sextius Calvinus.
——— 631. Q. Cæcilius Metellus Balearicus; T. Quintius Flaminius.
——— 632. C. Fannius Strabo; Cn. Domitius Ahenobarbus. The seditions of Caius Gracchus.
——— 633. Lucius Opimius Nepos; Q. Fabius Maximus Allobrogicus. The unfortunate end of Caius Gracchus. The Allobroges defeated.
——— 634. P. Manlius Nepos; C. Papirius Carbo.
——— 635. L. Cæcilius Metellus Calvus; L. Aurelius Cotta.
——— 636. M. Portius Cato; Q. Marcius Rex. Cato died, and was succeeded by Q. Ælius Tubero.
——— 637. L. Cæcilius Metellus; Q. Mutius Scævola.
——— 638. C. Licinius Geta; Q. Fabius Maximus Eburnus.
——— 639. M. Cæcilius Metellus; M. Æmilius Scaurus.
——— 640. M. Acilius Balbus; C. Portius Cato.
——— 641. C. Cæcilius Metellus Caprarius; Cn. Papirius Carbo.
——— 642. M. Livius Drusus; L. Calpurnius Piso. The Romans declare war against Jugurtha.
——— 643. P. Corn. Scipio Nasica; L. Calpurnius Piso Bestia. Calpurnius bribed and defeated by Jugurtha.
——— 644. M. Mincius Rufus; Sp. Postumius Albinus.
——— 645. Q. Cæcilius Metellus Numidicus; M. Junius Silanus. Success of Metellus against Jugurtha.
——— 646. Servius Sulpicius Galba; Q. Hortensius Nepos, in whose room was substituted M. Aurelius Scaurus. Metellus continues the war.
——— 647. C. Marius Nepos; L. Cassius Longinus, in whose room M. Æmil. Scaurus 2 is appointed. The war against Jugurtha continued with vigour by Marius.
——— 648. M. Atilius Serranus; Q. Servilius Cæpio. Jugurtha betrayed by Bocchus into the hands of Sylla, the lieutenant of Marius.
——— 649. P. Rutilius Rufus; Corn. Manlius Maximus. Marius triumphs over Jugurtha. Two Roman armies defeated by the Cimbri and Teutones.
——— 650. C. Marius Nepos 2; C. Flavius Fimbria. The Cimbri march towards Spain.
——— 651. C. Marius Nepos 3; L. Aurelius Orestes. The Cimbri defeated in Spain.
——— 652. C. Marius Nepos 4: Q. Lutatius Catulus. The Teutones totally defeated by Marius.

A.U.C. 653. C. Marius Nepos 5; M. Aquilius Nepos. The Cimbri enter Italy, and are defeated by Marius and Catulus.

——— 654. C. Marius Nepos 6; L. Valerius Flaccus. Factions against Metellus.

——— 655. M. Antonius Nepos; A. Postumius Albinus. Metellus is gloriously recalled.

——— 656. Q. Cæcilius Metellus Nepos; T. Didius Nepos.

——— 657. Cn. Corn. Lentulus; P. Licinius Crassus.

——— 658. Cn. Domitius Ahenobarbus; C. Cassius Longinus. The kingdom of Cyrene left by will to the Roman people.

——— 659. L. Licinius Crassus; Q. Mucius Scævola. Seditions of Norbanus.

——— 660. C. Cœlius Caldus; L. Domitius Ahenobarbus. The Mithridatic war.

——— 661. C. Valerius Flaccus; M. Herennius Nepos. Sylla exhibited a combat of 100 lions with men in the Circus.

——— 662. C. Claudius Pulcher; M. Perpenna Nepos. The allies wish to be admitted citizens of Rome.

——— 663. L. Marcius Philippus; Sex. Julius Cæsar. The allies prepare to revolt.

——— 664. Sex. M. Julius Cæsar; P. Rutilius Rufus. Wars with the Marsi.

——— 665. Cn. Pompeius Strabo; L. Porcius Cato. The great valour of Sylla, surnamed the Fortunate.

——— 666. L. Cornelius Sylla Felix; Q. Pompeius Rufus. Sylla appointed to conduct the Mithridatic war. Marius is empowered to supersede him; upon which Sylla returns to Rome with his army, and takes it, and has Marius and his adherents judged as enemies.

——— 667. Cn. Octavius; L. Cornelius Cinna, in whose room L. Corn. Merula is appointed. Cinna endeavours to recall Marius, and is expelled. Marius returns, and, with Cinna, marches against Rome. Civil wars and slaughter.

——— 668. C. Marius 7; L. Cornelius Cinna 2. Marius died, and L. Valerius Flaccus was chosen in his room. The Mithridatic war.

——— 669. L. Cornelius Cinna 3; Cn. Papirius Carbo. The Mithridatic war continued by Sylla.

——— 670. L. Cornelius Cinna 4; Cn. Papirius Carbo 2. Peace with Mithridates.

——— 671. L. Corn. Scipio Asiaticus; C. Junius Norbanus. The Capitol burnt. Pompey joins Sylla.

——— 672. C. Marius; Cn. Papirius Carbo 3. Civil wars at Rome between Marius and Sylla. Murder of the citizens by order of Sylla, who makes himself dictator.

——— 673. M. Tullius Decula; Cn. Cornelius Dolabella. Sylla weakens and circumscribes the power of the tribunes. Pompey triumphs over Africa.

——— 674. L. Corn. Sylla Felix 2; Q. Cæcilius Metellus Pius. War against Mithridates.

——— 675. P. Servilius Vatia Isauricus; Ap. Claudius Pulcher. Sylla abdicates the dictatorship.

——— 676. M. Æmilius Lepidus; Q. Lutatius Catulus. Sylla dies.

——— 677. D. Junius Brutus Lepidus; Mamercus Æmilius Livianus. A civil war between Lepidus and Catulus. Pompey goes against Sertorius in Spain.

——— 678. Cn. Octavius; M. Scribonius Curio. Sertorius defeated.

——— 679. L. Octavius; C. Aurelius Cotta. Mithridates and Sertorius make a treaty of alliance together. Sertorius murdered by Perpenna.

——— 680. L. Lucinius Lucullus; M. Aurelius Cotta. Lucullus conducts the Mithridatic war.

——— 681. M. Terentius Varro Lucullus; C. Cassius Varus Spartacus. The gladiators make head against the Romans with much success.

——— 682. L. Gellius Poplicola; Cn. Corn Lentulus Clodianus. Victories of Spartacus over three Roman generals.

——— 683. Cn. Aufidius Orestes; P. Corn. Lentulus Sura. Crassus defeats and kills Spartacus near Apulia.

——— 684. M. Licinius Crassus; Cn. Pompeius Magnus. Successes of Lucullus against Mithridates. The census amounts to above 900,000.

A.U.C. 685. Q. Hortensius 2; Q. Cæcilius Metellus. Lucullus defeats Tigranes king of Armenia, and meditates the invasion of Parthia.

——— 686. Q. Marcius Rex; L. Cæcilius Metellus. Lucullus defeats the united forces of Mithridates and Tigranes.

——— 687. M. Acilius Glabrio; C. Calpurnius Piso. Lucullus falls under the displeasure of his troops, who partly desert him. Pompey goes against the pirates.

——— 688. M. Æmilius Lepidus; L. Volcatus Tullus. Pompey succeeds Lucullus to finish the Mithridatic war, and defeats the enemy.

——— 689. L. Aurelius Cotta; L. Manlius Torquatus. Success of Pompey in Asia.

——— 690. L. Julius Cæsar; C. Marcius Figulus. Pompey goes to Syria. His conquests there.

——— 691. M. Tullius Cicero; C. Antonius Nepos. Mithridates poisons himself. Catiline conspires against the state. Cicero discovers the conspiracy, and punishes the adherents.

——— 692. D. Junius Silanus; L. Licinius Muræna. Pompey triumphs over the pirates, and over Mithridates, Tigranes, and Aristobulus.

——— 693. M. Puppius Piso; M. Valerius Messala Niger.

——— 694. L. Afranius Nepos; Q. Cæcilius Metellus Celer. A reconciliation between Crassus, Pompey, and Cæsar.

——— 695. C. Jul. Cæsar; M. Calpurnius Bibulus. Cæsar breaks the fasces of his colleague, and is sole consul. He obtains the government of Gaul for five years.

——— 696. L. Calpurnius Piso; A. Gabinius Nepos. Cicero banished by means of Clodius. Cato goes against Ptolemy king of Cyprus. Successes of Cæsar in Gaul.

——— 697. P. Corn. Lentulus Spinther; Q. Cæcilius Metellus Nepos. Cicero recalled. Cæsar's success and victories.

——— 698. Cn. Corn. Lentulus Marcellinus; L. Marcius Philippus. The triumvirate of Cæsar, Pompey, and Crassus.

——— 699. Cn. Pompeius Magnus 2; M. Licinius Crassus 2; Crassus goes against Parthia. Cæsar continued for five years more in the administration of Gaul. His conquest of Britain.

——— 700. L. Domitius Ahenobarbus; Ap. Claudius Pulcher. Great victories of Cœsar.

——— 701. Cn. Domitius Calvinus; M. Valerius Messala. Crassus defeated and slain in Parthia. Milo kills Clodius.

——— 702. Cn. Pompeius Magnus 3; the only consul. After the expiration of seven months he took for colleague Q. Cæcilius Metellus Pius Scipio. Revolts of the Gauls crushed by Cæsar.

——— 703. Ser. Sulpicius Rufus; M. Claudius Marcellus. Rise of the jealousy between Cæsar and Pompey.

——— 704. L. Æmilius Paulus; C. Claudius Marcellus. Cicero proconsul of Cilicia. Increase of the differences between Cæsar and Pompey.

——— 705. C. Claudius Marcellus 2; L. Cornelius Lentulus Crus. Cæsar begins the civil war. Pompey flees from Rome. Cæsar made dictator.

——— 706. C. Julius Cæsar 2; P. Servilius Vatia Isauricus. Cæsar defeats Pompey at Pharsalia. Pompey murdered in Ægypt. The wars of Cæsar in Ægypt.

——— 707. Q. Fusius Calenus; P. Vatinius. Power and influence of Cæsar at Rome. He reduces Pontus.

——— 708. C. Julius Cæsar 3; M. Æmilius Lepidus. Cæsar defeats Pompey's partisans in Africa, and takes Utica.

——— 709. C. Julius Cæsar 4; consul alone, and dictator, having for his master of horse M. Lepidus. Q. Fabius Maximus and C. Trebonius were elected consuls for about three months; and on the sudden death of Fabius, Caninius Rebilus was appointed. He conquered the partizans of Pompey in Spain, and was declared perpetual Dictator and Imperator, &c.

——— 710. C. Julius Cæsar 5; M. Antonius. Cæsar meditates a war against Parthia, and appoints M. Æmil. Lepidus consul in his room. Brutus and his adherents conspire against Cæsar, and murder him in the senate house. Antony raises himself to power. The rise of Octavius.

A.U.C. 711. C. Vibius Pansa; A. Hirtius. Antony judged a public enemy. He is opposed by the consuls and Augustus. He joins Augustus. Triumvirate of Antony, Augustus and Lepidus.

——— 712. L. Minutius Plancus; M. Æmilius Lepidus 2. Great honours paid to the memory of J. Cæsar. Brutus and Cassius join their forces against Augustus and Antony.

——— 713. L. Antonius; P. Servilius Vatia Isauricus 2. Battle of Philipi, and the defeat of Brutus and Cassius.

——— 714. Cn. Domitius Calvinus 2; C. Asinius Pollio, in whose room were appointed L. Corn. Balbus, and F. Caninius Crassus. Antony joins the son of Pompey against Augustus. The alliance of short duration.

——— 515. L. Marcus Censorinus; C. Calvisius Sabinus. Antony marries Octavia, the sister of Augustus, to strengthen their mutual alliance.

——— 716. Ap. Claudius Pulcher; C. Norbanus Flaccus; in whose stead were substituted C. Octavianus and Q. Pedius Cæsar; and afterwards C. Carrinas and Pub. Ventidius. Sext. Pompey, the son of Pompey the Great, makes himself powerful by sea, to oppose Augustus.

——— 717. M. Vipsanius Agrippa; L. Caninius Gallus. Agrippa is appointed by Augustus to oppose Sext. Pompey with a fleet. He builds the famous harbour of Misenum.

——— 718. L. Gellius Poplicola; M Cocceius Nerva. Agrippa obtains a naval victory over Pompey, who delivers himself to Antony, by whom he is put to death.

——— 719. L. Cornificius Nepos; Sex. Pompeius Nepos. Lentulus removed from power by Augustus.

——— 720. L. Scribonius Libo; M. Antonius Nepos. Augustus and Antony, being sole masters of the Roman empire, make another division of the provinces. Cæsar obtains the west, and Antony the east.

——— 721. C. Cæsar Octavianus 2; L. Volcatius Tullus. Octavia divorced by Antony, who marries Cleopatra.

——— 722. Cn. Domitius Ahenobarbus; C. Sosius. Dissension between Augustus and Antony.

——— 723. C. Cæsar Octavianus 3; M. Valer. Messala Corvinus. The battle of Actium, which, according to some authors, happened the year of Rome 721. The end of the commonwealth.

——— 724. C. Cæsar Octavianus 4; and M Licinius Crassus, in whose room was substituted Caius Antistius, afterwards Marcus Tullius, and again Lucius Sænius.

——— 725. C. Cæsar Octavianus 5; and Sext. Apuleius, in whose room Potit. Valer. Messala was appointed.

——— 726. C. Cæsar Octavianus 6; M. Vipsan. Agrippa 2.

——— 727. C. Cæsar Octavianus Augustus 7; M. Vips. Agrippa 3.

——— 728. C. C. Octav. Augustus 8; T. Statilius Taurus.

——— 729. C. C. Octav. Augustus 9; M. Junius Silanus.

——— 730. C. C. Octav. Augustus 10; C. Norbanus Flaccus.

——— 731. C. C. Octav. Augustus 11; Aul. Terent. Varro. Augustus divests himself of the consulship, and names P. Sestius, and Cn. Calpurn. Piso.

——— 732 M. Claud. Marcellus Æserninus: L. Aruntius Nepos.

——— 733. M. Lollius; Q Æmilius Lepidus.

——— 734. M. Apuleius Nepos; P. Silius Nerva.

——— 735. C. Sentius Saturninus; Q. Lucret. Vespillo.

——— 736. P. Corn. Lentulus; Cn. Corn. Lentulus.

——— 737. C. Furnius; C. Julius Silanus.

——— 738. L. Domit. Ahenobarbus; P. Corn. Scipio.

——— 739. M. L Drusus Libo; L. Capurn. Piso.

——— 740. Cn. Corn. Lentulus; M. Licinius Crassus.

——— 741. Tiber. Claud. Nero; P. Quintil. Varus.

——— 742. M. Valer. Messala; P. Sulpic. Quirinus. In Messala's room C. Valgius was appointed, and afterwards Canus Caninus Rebilus.

A.U.C. 743. Q. Ælius Tubero; Paul. Fabius Maximus.

——— 744. Jul. Anton Africanus; Q. Fabius Maximus.

——— 745. Nero Claud. Drusus; L. Quinctius; Crispinus.

——— 746. C. Asin. Gallus; C. Marcius Censorinus.

——— 747. Tib. Claudius Nero; Cl. Capurnius Piso.

——— 748. C. Antistius Vetus; Decimus Lælius Balbus.

——— 749. C. C. Octav. Augustus 12; L. Corn. Sylla.

——— 750. C. Calvisius Sabinus; L. Passienus Rufus.

——— 751. Cn. Corn. Lentulus; M. Valer. Messalinus.

——— 752. C. C. Octav. Augustus 13; M. Plaut. Silvanus, in whose room C. Caninius Gallus was substituted.

——— 753. Coss. Corn. Lentulus; L. Calp. Piso.

——— 754. C. Julius Cæsar; L. Æmilius Paulus.

——— 755. P. Alfinius or Afranius Varus; P. Vinucius Nepos.

——— 756. L. Ælius Lamia; M. Servilius Geminus.

——— 757. Sex. Ælius Catus; C. Sentius Saturninus.

——— 758. Cn. Corn. Cinna; L. Valerius Messala.

——— 759. M. Æmilius Lepidus; L. Arruntius Nepos. In their room C. Ateius Capito, C. Vibius Postumus.

——— 760. Q. Cæcilius Metellus Creticus; A. Licinius Nerva. In their room P. Corn. Lentulus, Scipio, T. Quinct. Crispinus Valerianus.

——— 761. M. Furius Camillus; Sex. Nonnius Quinctilianus. In their room L. Apronius, and A. Vibius Habitus.

——— 762. Q Sulpicius Camerinus; C. Poppæus Sabinus, and in their room M. Papius Mutilus, and Q. Poppæus Secundus.

——— 763. P. Corn. Dolabella; C. Julius Silanus.

——— 764. M. Æmilius Lepidus; T. Statilius Taurus.

——— 765. T. Germanicus Cæsar; C. Fonteius Capito. In Capito's room Caius Vitellius Varro was appointed.

——— 766. C. Silius Nepos; L. Munacius Plancus.

——— 767. Sext. Pompeius; Sext. Apuleius.

——— 768. Drusus Cæsar; C. Norbanus Flaccus.

——— 769. T. Statilius Sisena Taurus; L. Scribonius Libo; and in the room of one of them, Julius Pomponius Græcinus.

——— 770. C. Cæcilius Rufus; L. Pomponius Flaccus.

——— 771. Cl. Tiberius Nero Cæsar Augustus 2; Germanicus Cæsar 2.

——— 772. M. Julius Silanus; L. Norbanus Flaccus.

——— 773. M. Valerius Messala; M. Aurelius Cotta.

——— 774. Cl. Tiberius Nero; Drusus Cæsar 2.

——— 775. Decim. Haterius Agrippa; L. Sulpic. Galba.

——— 776. C. Asinius Pollio; C. Antistius Vetus.

——— 777. Servil. Corn. Cethegus; L. Vitellius Varro.

——— 778. Coss. Corn. Lentulus Isauricus; M. Asinius Agrippa.

——— 779. C. Calvisius Sabinus; Cn. Corn. Lent. Cossus Gætulicus.

——— 780. L. Calpurn. Piso; M. Licinius Crassus.

——— 781. Ap. Junius Silanus; P. Silius Nerva.

——— 782. C. Rubellius Geminus; C. Fusius Geminus.

——— 783. M. Vinucius Nepos; C. Cassius Longinus.

——— 784. Cl. Tiber. Nero Cæsar Augustus 3; and L. Ælius Sejanus, in whose room were successively appointed C. Memmius Regulus; Faustus Corn. Sylla; Sextidius Catulinus; L. Fulcin Tiro; L. Pompon. Secundus.

A.U.C.785. C. Domitius Ahenobarbus; A. Vitellius, in the room of M. Furius Camillus.
——— 786. Ser. Sulpic. Galba; C. Corn. Sylla, in the room of L. Salvius Otho, and Vibius Marsus.
——— 787. L. Vitellius Nepos; Paul Fabius Persicus.
——— 788. C. Gestius Gallus; M. Servil. Geminus.
——— 789. Sext. Papirius Gallianus; Q. Plautius Plautianus.
——— 790. Cn. Acerronius Proculus; C. Pontius Nigrinus.
——— 791. M. Aquilius Julianus; P. Nonius Asprenas.
——— 792. C. Cæsar Caligula 2; L. Apronius.
——— 793. C. Cæsar Caligula 3; L. Gellius Poplicola.
——— 794. C. C. Caligula 4; Cn. Sentus Saturninus.
——— 795. Claudius Imperator 2. Licinius Largus.
——— 796. Claudius Imper. 3; L. Vitellius.
——— 797. C. Quinctius Crispinus; T. Statilius Taurus.
——— 798. M. Vinucius Quartinus; M. Statilius Corvinus.
——— 799. C. Valerius Asiaticus 2; M. Valer. Messala.
——— 800. Claudius Imper. 4; L. Vitellius.
——— 801. A. Vitellius; L. Vipsanius Poplicola.
——— 802. C. Pomp. Longinus Gallus; Q. Veranius Lætus.
——— 803. C. Antistius Vetus; M. Suislius Rufus Nervilianus.
——— 804. Claudius Imp. 5; Ser. Corn. Scipio Orfitus.
——— 805. P. Corn. Sulla Faustus; L. Salvius Otho.
——— 806. D. Julius Silanus; Q. Hatirius Antoninus.
——— 807. Q. Asinius Marcellus; M. Acilius Aviola.
——— 808. Claud. Nero Cæsar, L. Antistius Vetus.
——— 809. Q. Volusius Saturninis; P. Corn. Scipio.
——— 810. Claud. Nero Cæsar 2; L. Calpurn Piso.
——— 811. Claud, Nero Cæsar 3; Valerius Messala.
——— 812. C. Vispan. Poplicola; L. Fonteius Capito.
——— 813. Cl. Nero Cæsar 4; Cossus Corn. Leutulus.
——— 814. C. Cæsonius Pætus; C. Petronius Sabinus.
——— 815. P. Marius Celsus; L. Asinius Gallus.
——— 816. L. Memmius Regulus; Paul. Virgilius Rufus.
——— 817. C. Lecanius Bassus; M. Licinius Crassus.
——— 818. P. Silius Nerva; C. Julius Atticus Vestinus.
——— 819. D. Seutonius Paulinus; L. Pontius Telesinus.
——— 820. L. Fonteius Capito; C. Julius Rufus.
——— 821. C, Silius Italicus; M. Celerius Trachalus.
——— 822. C. Sulp. Galba Cæsar; T. Vicinius Crispinianus.
——— 823. T. Flavius Vespasianus Cæsar 2; T. Vespasianus.
——— 824. T. Fl. Vespasianus Cæsar 3; M. Cocceius Nerva.
——— 825. T. Fl. Vesp. Cæsar 4; Tit, Vespas. Cæsar 2.
——— 826. T. Flav. Domitianus 2; M, Valerius Messalinus.
——— 827. T. Fl. Vespas. Cæsar 5; T. Vesp. Cæsar 3; to whom succeeded T. Fl. Domitianus 2.
——— 828. Fl. Vespas, Cæsar 6; T. Vespasianus Cæsar 4, succeeded by Domitianus 4.
——— 829. Fl. Vespas. Cæsar 7; T. Vespas. Cæsar 5, succeeded by Domitianus 5.
——— 830. Fl. Vespas Cæsar 8; T. Vespas. Cæsar 6, succeeded by Domitianus 6.
——— 831. L. Cæsonius Commodus Verus; C. Corn. Priscus.

A.U.C. 832. Fl. Vespas. Augustus 9; T. Vespas. Cæsar 7.
——— 833. T. Vespas. Augustus 8; Fl. Domitianus 7.
——— 834. M. Plautius Sylvanus; M. Asinius Pollio Verrucosus.
——— 835. Fl. Domitianus 8; T. Flav. Sabinus.
——— 836. Fl. Domit. Augustus 9; T. Virginius Rufus.
——— 837. Fl. Domit. Augustus 10; Ap. Junius Sabinus.
——— 838. Fl. Domit. Augustus 11; T. Aurelius Fulvius.
——— 839. Fl. Domitianus Aug. 12; Ser. Corn. Dolabella.
——— 840. Fl. Domitianus Aug. 13; A. Volusius Saturninus.
A.U.C. 841. Fl. Domitianus Aug. 14; L. Minucius Rufus.
——— 842. T. Aurelius Fulvius; A. Sempronius Atratinus.
——— 843. Fl. Domitianus Aug. 15; M. Cocceius Nerva 2.
——— 844. M. Ulpius Trajanus; M. Acilius Glabrio.
——— 845. Fl. Domitianus Aug. 16; A. Volusius Saturninus.
——— 846. Sex. Pompeius Collega; Corn. Priscus.
——— 847. L. Nonius Asprenas Torquatus; M. Aricius Clemens.
——— 848. F. Domitianus Aug. 17; T. Flavius Clemens.
——— 849. C. Fulvius Valens; C. Antistius Vetus.
——— 850. Cocceius Nerva 3; T. Virginius Rufus.
——— 851. Cocc. Nerva Augustus 4; Ulpius Trajanus 2.
——— 852. C. Socius Senecio 2; A. Corn. Palma.
——— 853. Ulp. Trajan. Aug. 3; M. Corn. Fronto 3.
——— 854. Ulp. Trajan. Aug. 4; Sex. Articulus Prætus.
——— 855. C. Socius Senecio 3; L. Licinius Sura.
——— 856. Ulp. Trajan, Aug. 5; L. Appius Maximus.
——— 857. —.—. Suranus 2; P. Neracius Marcellus.
——— 858. T. Julius Candidus; A. Julius Quadratus.
——— 859. C. Socius Senecio 4; L. Tutius Cerealis.
——— 860. C. Socius Senecio 5; S. Licinius Sura 3.
——— 861. Ap. Annius Trebonius; M. Atilius Bradua.
——— 862. A. Corn. Palma 3; C. Calvisius Tullus.
——— 863. Claudius Crispinus; Solenus Orfitus.
——— 864. C. Calpurnius Piso; M. Vettius Bolanus.
——— 865. Ulp. Trajan, August. 6; C. Julius Africanus.
——— 866. L. Publius Celsus 2; C. Claudius Crispinus.
——— 867. Q. Ninnius Hasta; P. Manlius Vopiscus.
——— 868. M. Valerius Messala; C. Pompilius Carus Pedo.
——— 869. Æmilius Ælianus; L. Antistius Vetus.
——— 870. Quinctius Niger; T. Vipsanius Apronianus.
——— 871. Ælius Adrianus Augustus; Tib. Claud. Fusus Salinator.
——— 872. Æl, Adr. Augustus 2; Q. Junius Rusticus.
——— 873. L. Catilius Severus; T. Aurelius Fulvus.
——— 874. M. Anuius Verres 2; L. Augurinus.
——— 875. M. Acilius Aviola; C. Corn. Pansa.
——— 876. Q. Arrius Pætinus; C. Veranius Apronianus.
——— 877. M. Acilius Glabrio; C. Bellitius Torquatus.
——— 878. P. Corn. Asiaticus 2; Q. Vettius Aquilinus.
——— 879. M. Lollius Pedius Verus; Q. Jun. Lepidus Bibulbus.
——— 880. —.—. Gallicanus; D. Cœlius Titianus.

A.U.C.881. L. Nonius Asprenas Torquatus; M. Annius Libo 2.
——— 882. P. Juventius Celsus 2; M. Annius Libo 2.
——— 883. Q. Fabius Catulinus; Q. Julius Balbus.
——— 884. Sp. Octavius Pontianus; M. Antonius Rufinus.
——— 885. Sentius Augurinus; Arrius Severianus.
——— 886. —.—, Hiberus; Jun. Silanus Sisenna.
——— 887. C. Julius Servilius; C. Vibius Juv. Verus.
——— 888. Pompeianus Lupercus; L. Junius Atticus Acilianus.
——— 889. L. Cæsonius Commodus; Sex. Vetulenus Civica Pompeianus.
——— 890. L. Ælius Cæsar Verus 2; P. Cœlius Barbinus Vibullius Pius.
——— 891. Sulpic. Camerinus; Quint. Niger Balbus.
——— 892. Antoninus Aug. Pius 2; Bruttius Præsens.
——— 893. Anton. Aug. Pius 3; M. Aurelius Cæsar.
——— 894. M. Peduceus Priscinus; T. Hæmius Severus.
——— 895. L. Cuspius Rufinus; L. Statius Quadratus.
——— 896. T. Bellicius Torquatus; T. Claud. Atticus Herodes.
——— 897. Lollianus Avitus; C. Gavius Maximus.
——— 898. Antoninus Pius Augustus 4; M. Aurelius Cæsar 2.
——— 899. Sex. Erucius Clarus; Cn. Claud. Severus.
——— 900. M. Valer. Largus; M. Valer. Messalinus.
——— 901. T. Bellicius Torquatus 2; M. Salvius Julianus Vetus.
——— 902. Serg. Corn. Scipio Orfitus; Q. Nonius Priscus.
——— 903. Romulus Gallicanus; Antistius Vetus.
——— 904, Sext. Quintilius Gorgianus Candianus; Sex. Quintil. Maximus.
——— 905. M. V. Acilius Glabrio; M. Valer. Verianus Homullus.
——— 906. C. Bruttius Præsens 2; M. Antonius Rufinus.
——— 907. L. Ælius Aurel. Junius Commodus; T. Sextilius Lateranus.
——— 908. C. Julius Severus; M. Rufinus Sabinianus.
——— 909. M. Sejonius Sylvanus; C. Serius Augurinus.
——— 910. —.—. Barbatus, or Barbarus; —.—, Regulus.
——— 911. Q. Flavius Tetullus; Claud. Sacerdos.
——— 912. Plautius Quintillus; Statius Priscus.
——— 913. T. Clodius Vibius Varus; Ap. Ann. Atilius Bradua.
——— 914. M. Aurel. Antonin. Cæsar 3; L. Ælius Aurel. Verus Cæsar 2.
——— 915. Q. Junius Rusticus; C. Vettius Aquilinus.
——— 916. L. Papirius Ælianus; Junius Pastor.
——— 917. M. Julius Pompeius Macrinus; L. Corn. Juventius Celsus.
——— 918. L. Arrius Pudens; M. Gavius Orfitus.
——— 919. Q. Servilius Pudens; L. Aufidius Pollio.
——— 920. L. Aurelius Verus 3; T. Numidius Quadratus.
——— 921. T. Junius Montanus: T. Vettius Paulus.
——— 922. Q. Socius Priscus; P. Cœlius Apollinaris.
——— 923. M. Corn. Cethegus; C. Erucius Clarus.
——— 924. L. Septimius Severus 2; L. Aufidius Herennianus.
——— 925. Claudius Maximus; Corn. Scipio Orfitus.
——— 926. M. Aurelius Severus 2; T. Claudius Pompeianus.
——— 927. Ap. Annius Trebonius Gallus; Fulvius Flaccus.

A.U.C. 928. Calpurnius Piso; M. Salvius Julianus.
——— 229. T. Vitrasius Pollio 2; M. Flavius Aper 2.
——— 930. L. Aurelius Commodus Augustus; Plautius Quinctillus.
——— 931. Julianus Vettius Rufus; Gavius Orfitus.
——— 932. L. Aur. Commodus Aug. 2; T. Annius Aurel. Verus: and on the 1st of July, P. Helvius Pertinax; M. Didius Severus Julianus.
——— 933. L. Fulvius Bruttius Præsens 2; Sext Quintil. Cordianus.
——— 934. L. Aur. Commodus Aug. 3; L. Antistius Burrhus.
——— 935. C. Petronius Mamertinus; Corn. Trebellius Rufus.
——— 936. L. Aurel. Commodus Aug. 4; M. Aufidius Victorinus.
——— 937. L. Eggius Marcellus; Cn. Papirius Ælianns.
——— 938. Triarius Maternus; M. Atilius Bradua.
——— 939. L, Aurel. Commodus Aug, 5; M. Acilius Glabrio 2.
——— 940. Claudius Crispinus; Papirius Ælianus.
——— 941. C. Allius Fuscianus 2; Duillius Silanus.
——— 942. Junius Silanus 2; Q. Servilius Silanus, in whose room was appointed Severus and Vitellius.
——— 943. L. Aurel. Commodus Aug. 6; M- Petronius Septimianus.
——— 944. Cassius Apronianus; M. Atilius Metilius Bradua.
——— 945. L, Aurel. Commodus Aug. 7; P. Helvius Pertinax.
——— 946. Q. Sosius Falco; C. Julius Erucius Clarus; and on the 1st of March, Fl. Claud. Sulpitianus; Fabius Cilo Septimianus; and on the 1st of July, Ælius and Probus.
——— 947. L. Septimius Severus 2; Clod. Albinus Cæsar 2.
——— 948, Q. Flavius Scopula Tertulius; Tincius Flav. Clemens.
——— 949. Cn. Domitius Dexter 2; L. Valer. Messala Priscus.
——— 950. Ap. Cl. Lateranus; M Marius Rufinus.
——— 951. T. Auturius Saturninus; C. Annius Trebonius Gallus.
——— 952. P. Corn. Anulinus 2; M. Aufidus Fronto.
——— 953. C. Claud. Severus; C. Aufidus Victorinus.
——— 954. L. Annius Fabianus; M. Nonius Mucianus.
——— 955. L, Septim. Severus Augustus 3; M. Aurel. Antoninus Augustus.
——— 956. P. Septim. Geta Cæsar; L. Fulvius Plautianus 2.
——— 957. L. Fabius Septimianus Cilo 2; M. Flavius Libo.
——— 958. M. Aurel. Anton. Augustus 2; P. Septimus Geta Cæsar.
——— 959. M. Nummius Annius Albinus; Fulvius Æmilianus.
——— 960. M. Flavius Aper; Q. Albius Maximus.
——— 961. M. Aurel. Anton. Augustus 3; P. Septim. Geta Cæsar.
——— 962. T. Claudianus Civica Pompeianus; Lollianus Avitus.
——— 963. Mar. Acilius Faustinus; C. Cæsonius Macer. Triarinus Rufinus.
——— 964. Q. Elpidius Rufus Lollianus Gentianus; Pomponius Bassus.
——— 965. C. Julius Asper; P. Asper; or C. Julius Asper 2; C. Julius Asper.
——— 966. M- Aurel. Anton. Augustus 4; D. Cæcilius Balbinus 2; afterwards M. Antonius Gordianus; and Helvius Pertinax.
——— 967. Silius Messala; Q. Aquilius Sabinus.
——— 968. Æmilius Lætus 2; Anicius Cerealis.
——— 969. A. Atius Sabinus 2; Sext. Corn. Anulinus.
——— 970. C. Bruttius Præsens; T. Messius Extricatus; and afterwards were appointed Macrinus Augustus; and Diadumenianus Cæsar.

A.U.C. 971. Anton. Augustus; Q. M. Coclatinus Adventus 2.
——— 972. M. Aurel. Antonin. Augustus; Licinius Sacerdos 2.
——— 973. M. Aurel. Antonin. Augustus 2; M. Aurel. Eutychianus Comazon.
——— 974. Annius Gratius Sabinianus; Claudius Seleucus.
——— 975. M. Aurel. Anton. Augustus 4; M. Aurelius Severus; and Alexander Cæsar.
——— 976. L. Marius Maximus; L. Roscius Ælianus.
——— 977. Claudius Julianus 2; Claudius Crispinus.
——— 978. M. Mætius Fuscus, or Rufus, or Priscianus; and L. Turpilius Dexter.
——— 979. M. Aurel. Severus Alexander Augustus 2; C. Marcellus Quinctilius 2.
——— 980. L. Cæcilius Balbinus; M. Æmilius Æmilianus, or M. Nummius Albinus.
——— 981. T. Manil. Modestus, or Vettius Modestus; Sergius Calpurn Probus.
——— 982. M. Aurel. Severus Alex. Aug. 3; Cassius Dio 3; in whose room succeeded M. Antonin. Gordianus.
——— 983. L. Calpurnius Virius Agricola; Sex. Catius Clementinus.
——— 984. M. Aurel. Claud. Civica Pompeianus; Polignianus, or Pelignus, or Felicianus.
——— 985. P. Julius Lupus; —. —. Maximus.
——— 986. —. —. Maximus 2; Ovinius Paternus.
——— 987. —. —. Maximus 3; C. Cælius Urbanus, or Maximus, or Urinatius Urbanus.
——— 988. L. Catilius Severus; L. Ragonius Urinatius Quintianus.
——— 989. C. Julius Maximinus Augustus; C. Julius Africanus.
——— 990. P. Titius Perpetuus; L. Ovinius Rusticus Cornelianus: 1st May, Julianus Silanus; and Ennius Messius Gallicanus; and afterwards, in the room of Ennius, L. Septim. Valerianus, and in July, T. Claud. Julianus; Celsus Ælianus.
——— 991. M. Ulpius, or Pius Crinitus; Proculus Pontianus.
——— 992. M. Antonin. Gordianus Augustus; M. Acilius Aviola.
——— 993. Vettius Balbinus 2; —. Venustus.
——— 994. M. Anton. Gordian. Augustus 2; T. Claud. Civica Pompeianus 2.
——— 995. C. Vettius Aufidius Atticus; C. Asinius Prætextatus.
——— 996. C. Julius (Julianus) Arrianus; Æmilius Papus.
——— 997. —. —. Peregrinus; A. Fulvius Æmilianus.
——— 998. M. Jul. Philippus Augustus; T. Fabius Jun. Titianus.
——— 999. Bruttius Præsens; Nummius Albinus 2.
——— 1000. M. J. Philip. Augustus 2; M. J. Philippus Cæsar.
——— 1001. M. J. Philippus Aug. 3; M. J. Philippus Cæsar 2.
——— 1002. M. Fulv. Æmilianus 2; Junius (or Vettius) Aquilinus.
——— 1003. C. Messius Quintius Trajanus Decius Aug. 2; Annius Maximus Gratus.
——— 1004. C. Mess. Quinct. Trajan. Dec. Aug. 3; Q. Herenn. Etruscus Mess. Decius Cæsar.
——— 1005. C. Vibius Trebonianus Augustus 2; C. Vibius Volusianus Cæsar.
——— 1006. C. Vibius Volusianus Aug. 2; M. Valer. Maximus.
——— 1007. P. Licin. Valerianus Augustus 2; M. Valer. Maximus.
——— 1008. P. Licin. Valerian Aug. 3; P. Licin. Gallienus. Aug. 2.
——— 1009. M. Valer. Maximus 2; M. Acilius Glabrio; afterwards Antonius and Galbus.
——— 1010. P. Licin. Valerian. Aug. 4; P. Licin. Gallienus Aug. 3; and on the 1st of July M. Ulpius Crinitus 2; L. Domitius Aurelianus.
——— 1011. M. Aurel. Memmius Tuscus; Pomponus Bassus.
——— 1012. Fulvius Æmilianus; Pomponius Bassus 2.
——— 1013. L. Cornelius Sæcularis 2; Junius Donatus.

A.U.C. 1014. P. Licin. Gallienus Aug. 4; L. Petronius Taurus Volusianus.
——— 1015. P. Licin. Gallienus Aug. 5; Ap. Pompeius Faustinus.
——— 1016. M. Nummius Albinus 2; Maximus Dexter.
——— 1017. P. Licin. Gallienus Aug. 6; Ann. or Amulius Saturninus.
——— 1018. P. Licin. Valerianus Cæsar 2; L. Cæsonius Macer. Lucillus (or Lucianus or Licinius) Rufinianus.
——— 1019. P. Licin. Galienus Aug. 7; —. —. Sabinillus.
——— 1020. Ovinius Paternus; —. —. Arcesilaus.
——— 1021. Ovinius Paternus 2; —. —. Marinianus.
——— 1022. M. Aurel. Claudius Aug. 2; —. —. Paternus.
——— 1023. Flavius Antiochianus; Furius Orfitus.
——— 1024. —. L. Domit. Valer. Aurelian. Aug. 2; M. Cejonius Virius Bassus 2, or Pomponius Bassus.
——— 1025. —. —. Quietus; —. —. Voldumianus; and 1st. of July, Q. Falson, or Nao Falconius, or Nicomachus.
——— 1026. M. Claud. Tacitus; M. Mæius Furius Placidianus.
——— 1027. L. Val. Domitius Aurelian. Aug. 3; C. Jul. Capitolinus.
——— 1028. L. Val. Domit. Aurelian. Aug. 4; T. Nonius (or Avonius) Marcellinus, and in his room, February 1st, M. Aurelian. Gordianus; and 1st of July, Vettius Cornificius Gordianus.
——— 1029. M. Claud. Tacitus Aug. 2; Fulvius Æmilianus; and in his room, 1st of February, Ælius Corpianus.
——— 1030. M. Aurel. Valer. Probus Aug.; M. Aurel. Paulinus.
——— 1031. M. Aurel. Valer. Probus Aug. 2; M. Furius Lupus.
——— 1032. M. Aurel Val. Probus Aug. 3; Ovinius Paternus.
——— 1033. Junius Messala; —. —. Gratus.
——— 1034. M. Aur. Val. Probus Aug. 4; C. Junius Tiberianus.
——— 1035. M. Aur. Valer. Probus Aug. 5; Pomponius Victorius.
——— 1036. M. Aur. Carus Aug. 2; M. Aurel. Carinus Cæsar; and in his room, 1st of July, M. Aurel. Numerianus; Cæsar Matronianus.
——— 1037. M. Aur. Carinus 2; M. Aurel, Numerian 2; and in their room, 1st of May, Dioclетianus and Annius Bassus; and 1st of September or November, M. Aur. Val. Maximinianus, and M. Junius Maximus.
——— 1038. C. Aurel. Valer. Diocletianus 2; —. —. Aristobulus.
——— 1039. M. Junius Maximus 2; Vettius Aquilinus.
——— 1040. C. Aur. Valer. Diocletian. Aug. 3. M. Aurel. Valer. Maximian. Herculius Aug.
——— 1041. M. Aur. Valer. Maximian. Hercul. Aug. 2; Pomponius Januarius.
——— 1042. Annius Bassus 2; L. Ragonius Quintianus.
——— 1043. C. Aurel. Valet. Diocletian. Aug. 4; M. Aur. Val. Maximian. Aug. 3.
——— 1044. C. Junius Tiberianus; Cassius Dio.
——— 1045. Afranius Hannibalianus; M. Aurelianus Asclepiodotus.
——— 1046. C. Aur. Val. Diocletian. Aug. 5; M. Aur. Val. Maximian. Hercul. Aug. 3.
——— 1047. Fl. Valerius Constantius Chlorus Cæsar; C. Galerius Valer. Maximianus Cæsar.
——— 1048. Numericus Tuscus; Annius Corn. Anulinus.
——— 1049. C. Aurel. Valer. Diocletian. Aug. 6; Fl. Valer. Constantius Chlorus Cæsar 2.
——— 1050. M. Aurel. Val. Maximian. Aug. 5; C. Galerius Maximianus Cæsar 2.
——— 1051. Anicius Faustus 2; Severus Gallus.
——— 1052. C. Aurel. Valer. Diocletian. Aug. 7; M. Aurel. Valer. Maximian. Aug. 6.
——— 1053. Fl. Valer. Constant. Chlorus Cæsar 3; C. Galerius Val. Maximian. Cæsar. 3.
——— 1054. Posthumius Titianus 2; Fl. Popilius Nepotianus.

A.U.C. 1055. Fl. Valer. Constant. Chlorus Cæsar 4; C. Galer. Maximian. Cæsar 4.
——— 1056. C. Aur. Val. Diocletian. Aug. 8; M. Aur. Val. Maximian. Aug. 7.
——— 1057. C. Aur. Val. Diocletian. Aug. 9; M. Aur. Val. Maximian. Aug. 8.

CON'SUS, a deity at Rome, who presided over counsels. Some suppose that he was the same as Neptunus Equestris. *Vid.* Consuales Ludi. *Plut. in Rom.—Aus.* ep. 69. & *Eleg. de fer. R.* 19.—*Dionys. Hal.* 1.—*Liv.* 1. c. 9.

CONSYG'NE, the wife of Nicomedes, king of Bithynia, was torn in pieces by dogs, for her lascivious deportment. *Plin.* 8. c. 40. Some read Consingis.

CONTADES'DUS, a small river of Thrace. *Herodot.* 4. c. 90.

CONTESTA'NIA, a region of Hispania Citerior; now, probably, Concentayna. *Plin.* 3. c. 3.

CONTRIBU'TA JU'LIA, a town of Beturia. *Id.* 3. c. 1. It is probably the Contrebia of *Livy*, 40. c. 33.

CONTU'BIA, a town in Spain. *Flor.* 2. c. 17.

CONU'PHIS, an Ægyptian, preceptor of Eudoxus. *Clem. Strom.*

CONVEN'NOS, an island at the mouth of the Thames. *Ptol.* It is now Sheppey.

CONVICTOLITA'NIS, a magistrate of the Ædui. *Cæs. Com.* 7. c. 32.

CO'ON, the eldest son of Antenor, killed by Agamemnon, during the Trojan war. *Homer. Il.*

CO'OS, COS, CE'A, or CO, an island of the Ægæan Sea. *Vid.* Co.

CO'PÆ, a place of Greece, near the Cephisus, *Plin.* 4. c. 7.

COPA'IS LA'CUS, now Limne, a lake of Bœotia, into which the Cephisus and other rivers empty themselves. It was famous for its excellent eels. *Paus.* 9. c. 24.

CO'PAR, a town of Arabia Felix. *Ptol.*

COPHAN'TA, a harbour of Carmania. *Id.*

COPHAN'TIS, a burning mountain of Bactriana. *Plin.* 2. c. 106.

CO'PHES, a son of Artabazus. *Curt.* 7. c. 14.

Co'phes, a river of India. *Dionys. Perieg.*

CO'PIA, the goddess of plenty, among the Romans, was represented as bearing in one hand a horn, from which dropped fruits, raisins, flowers, pearls, and pieces of gold and silver, and in the other she held a bundle of different ears of corn. Her figure was that of a young blooming virgin of tall stature, and her head was crowned with flowers. The horn of plenty (*cornucopia*) was the horn of the goat Amalthæa, and it was presented to the nymphs who had nursed Jupiter, when the favorite animal was placed among the constellations of heaven by the gratitude of the god. The statues of some of the gods, as Bacchus, Hercules, Apollo, Ceres, &c. and of some of the greatest heroes of antiquity, are often represented with this celebrated horn, in allusion to the services which they are supposed to have rendered to mankind. *Servius in Virg. G.* 1. v. 205.—*Hygin. P. A.* 2. c. 13.

COPIL'LUS, a general of the Tectosagæ, taken by the Romans. *Plut. in Syll.*

COPO'NIUS, C., a commander of the fleet of the Rhodians at Dyrrachium, in the interest of Pompey. *Cic.* 1. *de Div.* c. 38. *Attic.* 8. ep. 12. *Fam.* 1. ep. 31.—*Paterc.* 2. c. 83.

COP'RATES or COPRA'TES, a river of Asia, falling into the Tigris. *Diod.* 19.—*Strab.*

CO'PREUS, a son of Pelops, who fled to Mycenæ on the death of Iphitus. *Apollod.* 2. c. 5.

COP'TUS, now Kypt, a town of Ægypt, about 100 leagues from Alexandria, on a canal which communicates with the Nile. *Plin.* 5. c. 9. l. 6. c. 23. —*Strab.* 16.—*Juv.* 15. v. 28.

CO'RA, a town of Latium, on the confines of the Volsci, built by a colony of Dardanians before the foundation of Rome. *Lucan.* 7. v. 392.—*Virg. Æn.* 6. v. 775.

COR'ACA. a town of Arabia Petræa. *Ptol.*

CORACE'SIUM or CORACEN'SIUM, a town of Pamphylia, now Scandeloro *Liv.* 33. c. 20.

CORACE'SIUS, a part of mount Taurus. *Plin.* 5. c. 27.

CORA'CII, a region of Upper Æthiopia, abounding in reeds. *Strab.*

CORA'CIUS AN'TRO, a Sabine, who was informed by a soothsayer, that whoever sacrificed to Diana on mount Aventine a large and beautiful heifer which he had, would procure for his country the empire of Italy. He went to Rome for the purpose, but king Servius, informed of the importance of the sacrifice, told him to bathe in the Tiber before he approached the altar, and whilst he was gone, the monarch offered the victim. In consequence of this sacrifice, as some suppose, the horns of a bull were hung on the doors of the temple of Diana, whilst the horns of a stag appeared on the doors of the temples of the other gods. *Plut. Quæst. Rom.* 4.

CORACIN'SII, a people of Sardinia. *Ptol.*

CORAC'ODES, a harbour of Corsica. *Id.*

CORACONA'SUS, a town of Arcadia, near which the Ladon flowed into the Alpheus. *Paus.* 8. c. 25.

CORACONNE'SUS, an island near Libya. *Steph.*

CORAL'ETÆ, one of the wandering hordes of Scythia. *Flacc.* 6. c. 81.

CORAN'CALI, a people of India without the Ganges. *Ptol.*

CORA'LIUS, a name of the Sangarius, in Phrygia. *Plin.* 6 c. 1.

CORANI'TÆ, a people of Arabia Felix. *Plin.* 6. c. 21.

CORAL'LI, a savage people of Pontus. *Ovid. ex Pont.* 4. el. 2. v. 37.

CORA'NUS, a miser. *Vid.* Nasica.

CO'RAS, a brother of Catillus and Tiburtius, from whom the mountain Coras, and the city Cora, received their names. *Virg. Æn.* 7. v. 762, &c.

CORASE'NI, a people of Asia. *Herodot.* 2.

CORAS'PHI, a nation of Scythia, within Imaus. *Ptol.*

CO'RAX, an ancient rhetorician of Sicily, who first demanded a salary from his pupils. *Cic. in Brut.* 12. *de Orat.* 1. c. 20.—*Aul. Gell.* 5. c. 10.—*Quintil.* 3. c. 1.——A king of Sicyon.

Co'rax, a mountain of Ætolia. *Liv.* 36. c. 30.——A city of Taurica Chersonesus. *Ptol.*

CORAX'I, a people of Colchis. *Plin.* 6. c. 5.

COR'BASA, a city of Pamphylia. *Ptol.*

COR'BEUS, a Gaul who waged war against Rome for eight years. *Hirt. Bell. G.* 8. c. 6.

CORBIA'NA, a province of the Elymæi. *Strab.*

COR'BIS and OR'SUA, two brothers, who fought for the dominion of a city of Spain, in the presence of Scipio. *Liv.* 28. c. 21.—*Val. Max.* 9. c. 11.

COR'BULO DOMIT'IUS, a præfect of Belgium, who when governor of Syria, routed the Parthians, destroyed Artaxata, and established Tigranes in the kingdom of Armenia. Nero, jealous of his many virtues, ordered him to be murdered; and Corbulo hearing this, fell upon his sword, A.D. 66. His name was given to a place (*Monumentum*) in Germany, which some suppose to be modern Groningen. *Tacit. Ann.* 11. c. 18. [A bust of Corbulo exists at Paris, probably that which was in the Rondinini palace at Rome.]

COR'COBA, a city of Taprobane. *Ptol.*

CORCY'RA, an island in the Ionian sea, about 12 miles from Buthrotum, on the coast of Epirus; famous for the shipwreck of Ulysses, and for the gardens of Alcinous. It has been successively called Drepane, Sicheria, and Phæacia, and now bears the name of Corfu. It is about 97 miles long. A colony of Colchians settled there 1349 B.C., and afterwards the island was occupied by a number of Corinthians, who had been banished with Chersicrates at their head, about 703 years before the Christian era. The war which was carried on by the Athenians against the Corcyreans, and was called Corcyrean, was but a prelude to the more fatal events of the Peloponnesian war. Corcyra, when in the possession of the Romans, after the conquest of Greece, became a valuable station for their ships of war in their hostilities against the cities of Asia. *Ovid. Ib.* 512.—*Homer. Odyss.* 5. &c.—*Lucan.* 9. v. 32.—*Mela*, 2. c. 7.—*Plin.* 4. c. 12.—*Strab.* 6.—*Ptol.* 3. c. 14.

Corcy'ra Ni'gra, one of the small islands of the Adriatic on the coast of Illyricum.

CORCY'RIS, a city of Ægypt. *Steph.*

COR'DUBA, a famous city of Hispania Bætica, the native place of both the Senecas, and of Lucan. It is now called Cordova, in Andalusia on the Guadalquivir. *Martial.* 1. epigr. 72.—*Mela*, 2. c. 6.—*Cæs. Bell. Alex.* 57.—*Plin.* 3. c. 1

COR'DULÆ, a port of Pontus, supposed to give its name to a peculiar sort of fishes (Cordylæ) caught there. *Plin.* 9. c. 15.—*Martial.* 13. epigr. 1.

COR'DUS JU'LIUS, a præfect of Aquitania, in the time of Otho. *Tac. Hist.* 1. c. 76.

COR'DYLUS, a city of Pamphylia. *Steph.*

CORDYLU'SA, an island near Rhodes. *Plin.* 5. c. 31.

CO'RE, the daughter of Ceres, the same as Proserpine. Festivals called Corea were instituted to her honour in Greece *Schol. Pind. Olymp. Od.* 7.

CORE'SIA, a name of Minerva, in Arcadia. *Cic. de N. D.* 3. c. 23.

CORES'SUS, a hill near Ephesus. *Herodot.* 5. c. 100.

COR'ESUS, a priest of Bacchus at Calydon in Bœotia, who was deeply enamoured of the nymph Calirhoe, who treated his addresses with disdain. He complained to Bacchus, who visited the country with a pestilence. The Calydonians were directed by the oracle to appease the god by sacrificing Calirhoe on his altar. The nymph was led to the altar, and Coresus, who was to sacrifice her, forgot his resentment, and stabbed himself. Calirhoe afterwards killed herself on the brink of a fountain, which thenceforth bore her name. *Paus.* 7. c. 21.

CORE'TAS, a man who first gave oracles at Delphi. *Plut. de Orac. Def.*

CORFID'IUS, a Roman knight, among the friends of Ligarius, at whose trial, through mistake, he was supposed to have been present, as he was then dead. *Cic. Att.* 13. ep. 44. *Lig.* 11.—*Plin.* 7. c. 52.

CORFIN'IUM, now Pentinia, or Campo di Santo Pelino, the capital of the Peligni, near the middle of Italy, three miles from the river Aternus. *Cæs. Civ.* 1. c. 16.—*Lucan.* 2. v. 478.—*Sil.* 5. v. 522.

COR'ICÆ, two islands near Peloponnesus. *Plin.* 4. c. 12.

CORINÆ'UM, a promontory of mount Mimas in India. *Ptol.*

CORIN'DIUS, a city of India within the Ganges. *Id.*

CORIN'EA, a region of Armenia Major. *Id.*

CORIN'NA, a celebrated woman of Tanagra, near Thebes, disciple of Myrtis. It is said, that she obtained seven times a poetical prize, when Pindar was her competitor; but it must be acknowledged her beauty influenced the judges, and contributed to the defeat of her rivals. She composed 50 books of epigrams and odes, of which only some few verses remain. Her countrymen honoured her memory by erecting her statue in the most conspicuous part of the city. *Ælian.* 13. c. 25.—*Propert.* 2. el. 3.—*Paus.* 9. c. 22.—*Stat.* 5. *Sylv.* 3. v. 158.—*Sax. Onom.* 1. p. 34.—*Fabr. B. Gr.* 1. 2. c. 15.——A woman of Thespis, celebrated for her beauty, and called also by some, Corinthia. ——The name of Ovid's mistress; probably Julia was thus designated. *Amor.* 2. el. 6. *Trist.* 4. el. 9.—*Martial.* 8. epigr. 72.

CORIN'NUS, an ancient poet in the time of the Trojan war, on which he wrote a poem. *Homer*, as some suppose, borrowed his subject from Corinnus. *Suidas.*—*Meursius.*

CORINTHI'ACUS SI'NUS, a deep bay at the west of Corinth, called also Crisseus, and now known by the name of the Gulph of Lepanto.

CORIN'THUS, an ancient city of Greece, now called Corintho or Coranto, situated on the middle of the Isthmus of Corinth, at the distance of about sixty stadia on either side from the sea. It was first founded by Sisyphus, the son of Æolus, A.M. 2616, and received its name from Corinthus, the son of Peleus. Its original name was Ephyre; and it is called Bimaris, because it was situated between the Saronicus Sinus and Crisseus Sinus. The inhabitants were once very powerful; and the fear which merchants felt in sailing round the stormy capes of Malea and Tænara, tended to increase the consequence of this city, as by transporting their merchandise across the isthmus they rendered Corinth the emporium of the produce of Europe and Asia. Syracuse in Sicily, among other places, was founded by a Corinthian colony, and so anxious was the parent state for the prosperity of this infant city, that her citizens took up arms in its defence, and by the wise conduct of Timoleon, delivered it from the tyranny of its opressors. Corinth was totally destroyed by L. Mummius, the Roman consul, and burnt to the ground 146 B.C. The riches which the Romans found there were immense. During the conflagration, all the metals which were in the city melted and mixed together, and formed that valuable composition which has since been known by the name of Corinthium Æs. This, however, appears improbable, especially when it is remembered that the artists of Corinth made a mixture of copper with small quantities of gold and silver, and so brilliant was the composition, that the appellation of Corinthian brass afterwards stamped an extraordinary value on pieces of inferior worth. The citadel called Acrocorinthus was very lofty and difficult of access; whence the proverb of

Non culvis homini contingit adire Corinthum,

applied to an arduous undertaking. J. Cæsar planted a colony at Corinth, and endeavoured to raise it from its ruins, and restore it to its former grandeur. The government of Corinth was monarchical till 779 years B.C. when officers called Prytanes were instituted. The war which has received the name of the Corinthian war, because the battles were fought in the neighbourhood of Corinth, was begun B.C. 395, by the combination of the Athenians, Thebans, Corinthians, and Argives, against Lacedæmon. Pisander, and Agesilaus distinguished themselves in that war; the former, in the first year of hostilities, was defeated with the Lacedæmonian fleet, by Conon near Cnidus; while a few days after Agesilaus slaughtered 10,000 of the enemy. The most famous battles in that war were fought at Coronea and Leuctra; but Agesilaus refused to besiege Corinth, lamenting that the Greeks, instead of destroying one another did not turn their arms against the Persian power. *Martial.* 9. epigr. 58.—*Lycoph. in Cass.*—*Ptol.* 3. c. 16.—*Isidor.* 16. c. 19.—*Suet. Aug.* 70.—*Liv.* 45. c. 28.—*Flor.* 2. c. 16.—*Ovid. Met.* 2. v. 240.—*Horat.* 1. ep. 17. v. 36.—*Plin.* 34. c. 2 & 8.—*Stat. Theb.* 7. v. 106.—*Paus.* 2. c. 1, &c.—*Strab.* 8, &c. —*Homer. Il.* 15.—*Cic. Tusc.* 4. c. 14. *in Verr.* 4. c. 44. *de N.D.* 3.

CORIN'THUS, an actor at Rome. *Juv.* 8. v. 197.

CORIOLA'NUS, the surname of C. Martius, which he obtained after his victory over Corioli, where, though formerly only a private soldier, he gained the amplest honours. When master of the place, he accepted, as the only reward, the surname of Coriolanus, a horse and prisoners, and his ancient host, to whom he immediately gave his liberty. After a number of military exploits, and many services to his conntry, he was refused the consulship by the people, when his scars had for a while influenced them in his favour. This unworthy treatment raised his resentment; and when the Romans had received a present of corn from Gelo king of Sicily, Coriolanus insisted that it should be sold for money, and not be given gratis to the public. Upon this, the tribunes excited the people against him for his imprudent advice, and even wished him to be put to death. The popular tumult, however, was for a while checked by the influence of the senators, and Coriolanus was summoned to appear before a prejudiced tribunal. His refusal to appear on the appointed day, irritated his persecutors still more; he was banished, without a trial, by a majority of three tribes, and immediately retired among the Volsci, to Attius Tullus, his greatest enemy, from whom he experienced a most friendly reception. Full of resentment against his country, he advised Attius to make war against Rome, and marched himself at the head of the Volsci as general. The approach of Coriolanus greatly alarmed the Romans, who sent several embassies to endeavour to reconcile him to his country. He was, however, deaf to all proposals, and bade them prepare for unconditional submission. He pitched his camp at the distance of five miles only from the city; and his enmity against his country would have proved fatal, had not his wife Volumnia, and his mother Veturia, been prevailed upon by the Roman matrons to go and appease his resentment. The meeting of Coriolanus with his family was tender and affecting. He remained long inexorable; but at last the authority of a mother and the tears and entreaties of a wife prevailed, and Coriolanus withdrew the Volsci from the neighbourhood of Rome. To show their sense of Veturia's merit and patriotism, the Romans dedicated a temple to Female Fortune. The behaviour of Coriolanus, however, displeased the Volsci. He was summoned to answer for his conduct before the people of Antium; but the clamours which his enemies raised, were so prevalent, that he was murdered at the place appointed for his trial, B.C. 488. His body was honoured with a magnificent funeral by the Volsci, and the Roman matrons put on mourning for his loss. Some historians, however, say, that he died in exile, at an advanced age. *Plut. in Vitâ.* —*Flor.* 2. c. 22.—*Liv.* 2. c. 34. 41.—*Dionys. Hal.* 7 & 8.

CORI'OLI or **CORIOL'LA**, a small town of Latium on the borders of the Volsci. *Plin.* 3. c. 5.—*Plut.* —*Liv.* 2. c. 33.

CORIS'SIA or **CORIS'SUS**, a town of Cos. *Steph.*

CORIS'SUS, a town of Ionia. *Strab.* 14.

COR'ITUS. *Vid.* Corytus.

CO'RIUM, a place of Crete. *Steph.*

COR'MA, a river near Assyria. *Tacit.* 12. *Ann.* c. 14.

COR'MALOS, a river of Troas. *Plin.* 5, c. 30.

CORMA'NUM, a city of the Jazyges. *Ptol.*

COR'MASA, a town of Pamphylia. *Liv.* 38. c. 15.

COR'NA, a city of Cappadocia. *Ptol.*

CORNA'VII, a people of Britain. *Id.* They dwelt in the modern counties of Warwick, Stafford, &c.

COR'NE, a hill in Etruria, with a grove consecrated to Diana. *Plin.* 3. c. 5.——A city of Armenia Minor. *Ptol.*

CORNEA'TES, a people of Pannonia. *Plin.* 3. c. 35.

CORNE'LIA LEX, *de Civitate*, was enacted A.U.C. 670, by L Corn. Sylla. It confirmed the Sulpician law, and required that the citizens of the eight newly elected tribes should be divided among the 35 ancient tribes.—Another, *de Judiciis*, A.U.C. 673, by the same. It ordained that the prætor should always observe the same invariable method in judicial proceedings, and that the process should not depend upon his arbitrary will.—Another, *de Sumptibus*, by the same. It limited the expenses of funerals.—Another, *de Religione*, by the same, A.U.C. 677. It restored to the college of priests, the privilege of chusing the priests, which, by the Domitian law, had been lodged in the hands of the people.—Another, *de Municipiis*, by the same, which revoked all the privileges which had been sometime before granted to the several towns of Italy which had assisted Marius and Cinna in the civil wars.—Another, *de Magistratibus*, by the same, which gave the power of bearing honors and being promoted before the legal age, to those who had followed the interest of Sylla, while the sons and partisans of his enemies, who had been proscribed, were deprived of the privilege of offering themselves candidates for any office in the state.—Another, *de Magistratibus*, by the same, A.U.C. 673. It ordained that no person should exercise the same office within ten years' distance, or be invested with two different magistracies in one year. Another, *de Magistratibus*, by the same, A.U.C. 673. It divested the tribunes of the privileges of making laws, holding assemblies, and receiving appeals. All such as had been tribunes were incapable of holding any other office in the state by that law. —Another, *de Majestate*, by the same, A.U.C. 670. It made it treason to send an army out of a province, or engage in a war without the orders of the senate, to influence the soldiers to spare or ransom a captive general of the enemy, to pardon the leaders of robbers or pirates, or for a Roman citizen to visit a foreign court, without previous leave. The punishment was *aquæ et ignis interdictio.* Another, by the same, which gave the power to a man accused of murder, either by poison, weapons, or false accusations, and the setting fire to buildings, to choose whether the jury that tried him should give their verdict *clam* or *palam*, *viva voce*, or by *ballot*.—Another, by the same, which made it *aquæ et ignis interdictio* to such as were guilty of forgery, concealing and altering of wills, corruption, false accusations, and the debasing or counterfeiting of the public coin; all such as were accessary to this offence, were deemed as guilty as the offender.—Another, *de pecuniis repetundis*, by which a man convicted of peculation or extortion in the provinces, was condemned to suffer the punishment *aquæ et ignis interdictio.*—Another, by the same, which gave the power to such as were sent into the provinces with any government, of retaining their command and appointment, without of a renewal it by the senate, as was before observed.—Another, by the same, which ordained that the lands of proscribed persons should be common, except those about Volaterræ aud Fesulæ in Etruria, which Sylla divided among his soldiers.—Another by C. Cornelius tribune of the people, A.U.C. 686; which ordained that no person should be exempted from any law, according to the general custom, unless 200 senators were present in the senate at the time of deliberation; and no person thus exempted could hinder the bill of his exemption from being carried to the people for their concurrence.—Another, by Nasica, A.U.C. 582, to make war against Perseus, son of Philip, king of Macedonia, if he did not give proper satisfaction to the Roman people.

CORNE'LIA, a daughter of Cinna, who was the first wife of J. Cæsar. She became mother of Julia, Pompey's wife, and was so affectionately loved by her husband, that, at her death, he, as the greatest mark of respect to her memory and her virtues, pronounced a funeral oration over her body. *Plut. in Cæs.*——A daughter of Metellus Scipio, who married Pompey, after the death of her husband P. Crassus. She has been praised for her great virtues. When her husband left her in the bay of Alexandria, to go on shore in a small boat, she saw him stabbed by Achillas, and heard his dying groans without the possibility of aiding him. She attributed all his misfortunes to his connection with her. *Plut. in Pomp.*——A daughter of Scipio Africanus, who married Sempronius Gracchus, and was the mother of Tiberius and Caius Gracchus. She was courted by a king; but she preferred becoming the wife of a Roman citizen to the splendours of royalty. When a Campanian lady once exhibited her jewels at Cornelia's house, and entreated her to favour her with a sight of her own, Cornelia produced her two sons saying, "These are the only jewels of which I can boast." In her life-time, a statue was raised to her with this inscription, *Cornelia mater Gracchorum.* Some of her epistles, remarkable for great purity of diction, are preserved. *Plut. in Gracch.*—*Juv.* 6. v. 167.—*Val. Max.* 4. c. 4.—*Cic. in Brut.* 27 & 58. *de Claris. Orat.* 58. *Inv.* 1. c. 49.—*Patercul.* 2.—*Quintil.* 1. c 1.——A vestal virgin, buried alive in Domitian's age, for being guilty of incontinence. *Sueton. in Dom.* The Cornelian family was patrician, and was divided into the illustrious branches of the Lentuli, Scipiones, Syllæ, Cethegi, Balbi, &c.

CORNE'LIUS AUR. CEL'SUS, wrote eight books on medicine, still extant, and highly valued. *Vid.* Celsus.

Corne'lius Bal'bus, a man who hindered J. Cæsar from rising up at the arrival of the senators.

Corne'lius Bal'bus, a man of Gades, intimate with Cicero, by whom he was ably defended when accused.

Corne'lius, a freedman of Sylla the dictator.

Corne'lius Ca'ius, a soothsayer of Padua, who foretold the beginning and issue of the battle of Pharsalia.

Corne'lius Cethe'gus, a priest, degraded from his office for want of attention.

Corne'lius Cne'us. *Vid.* Scipio.

Corne'lius Cne'us, a man chosen by Marcellus to be his colleague in the consulship.

Corne'lius Cos'sus, a military tribune during the time that there were no consuls in the republic. He offered to Jupiter the spoils called *opima.*

Corne'lius Dolabel'la, a friend and admirer of Cleopatra. He told her that Augustus intended to remove her from the monument where she had retired and convey her to Rome.

Corne'lius Gal'lus, an elegiac poet. *Vid.* Gallus.

Corne'lius Len'tulus, a high priest, &c.

Corne'lius Len'tulus Cethe'gus, a consul.

Corne'lius Marcel'lus, a man killed in Spain by Galba.

Corne'lius Mer'ula, was made consul by Augustus, in the room of Cinna.

Corne'lius Mer'ula, a consul, sent againt the Boii in Gaul. He killed 1400 of them. His grandson followed the intrest of Sylla; and when Marius entered the city, he killed himself by opening his veins.

Corne'lius Ne'pos, an historian. *Vid.* Nepos.

Corne'lius Pub'lius. *Vid.* Scipio.

Corne'lius Seve'rus, an epic poet of great genius, in the age of Augustus. He wrote a poem on monnt Ætna, and on the death of Cicero.

Corne'lius Scip'io, a man appointed master of the horse by Camillus, when dictator.

Corne'lius Thus'cus, a mischievous person.

Corne'lius, an officer of Sylla, whom J. Cæsar bribed to escape the proscription which threatened his life. *Liv.* 4. c. 19.—*Quintil.* 10. c. 1.—*Plut.*—*Val. Max.*—*Tacit.*—*Suet.*—*Polyb.*—*C. Nep. &c.*

CORNEN'SES, a people of Sardinia. *Ptol.*

CORNIC'ULUM, a town of Latium in the country of the Sabines, not far from Rome. *Dionys. Hal.*

CORNIFIC'IUS, a poet and general in the age of Augustus, employed to accuse Brutus, &c. His compositions were highly valued for their ease and elegance, but nothing remains of them except a few letters inserted with those of his friend Cicero. His sister Cornificia was also gifted with a poetical genius. *Plut. in Brut.*—*Cœl. Rh.* 14. c. 1. ——A lieutenant of J. Cæsar. *Plut. in Cæs.*——A friend of Cicero, his colleague in the office of augur and his competitor for the consulship. *Cic. Att.* 1. ep. 1.

COR'NIGER, a surname of Bacchus.

CORNUCO'PIA. *Vid.* Copia.

COR'NUS, an inland city of Sardinia, now Corneto. *Ptol.*

CORNU'TUS, a stoic philosopher of Africa, preceptor to Persius the satyrist. He wrote some treatises on philosophy and rhetoric. It is said that he was banished by Nero for censuring with too much freedom the plan of writing some historical treatise which that tyrant had submitted to his opinion and revision. *Dio.* 62. 69.—*Pers.* 5. v. 36. ——A prætor of Rome, in the age of Cicero. *Cic. Fam.* 10. ep. 12.——A Roman saved from the proscription of Marius, by his servants, who hung up a dead man in his room, and said that it was their master. The assassins of Marius believed the story, especially when they saw the golden ring of Cornutus on the dead man's hand, and Cornutus escaped into Gaul. *Plut. in Mario*,

CORODA'MUM, a promontory of Arabia Felix, now Capo Razalgate.

CORŒ'BUS, a Phrygian, son of Mygdon and Anaximena. He assisted Priam in the Trojan war, with the hopes of being rewarded with the hand of Cassandra for his services. Cassandra advised him in vain to retire from the war. He was killed by Peneleus, or, according to others, by Pyrrhus or Diomedes. *Paus.* 10. c. 27—*Virg. Æn.* 2. v. 341, &c. *& Servius in loco.*——A courser of Elis, killed by Neoptolemus. He obtained a prize at Olympia, B.C. 776, in the 28th Olympiad from the institution of Iphitus; but this year has generally been called the first Olympiad. *Paus.* 5. c. 8.——A hero of Argolis, who killed a serpent called Pœne, sent by Apollo to avenge Argos, and placed by some authors in the number of the Furies. His country was afflicted with a plague, and he consulted the oracle of Delphi, which commanded him to build a temple, where a tripod which was given him should fall from his hand. This was on a hill in Megaris, where he accordingly erected a temple to Apollo, and built a small village, which, from the accident, was called Tripodisca. After his death the people of Megara raised him a monument, on which the principal events of his life were recorded in elegiac verses. *Stat. Theb.* v. 570.—*Paus.* 1. v. 43. The invention of pottery is attributed by *Pliny*, 7. c. 56. to an Athenian of the same name.

CORO'NA, a town of Messenia. *Plin.* 4. c. 5.

CORO'NE, a city of Bithynia. *Steph.*

CORONE'A, a town of Bœotia, built by Coronus, son of Thersander. Juno, as the chief goddess of the place, had there a temple; and, in the age of Pausanias, her statue, made by Pythodorus of Thebes, was still to be seen. In the public place there were two altars, of which one was sacred to the winds, and the other to Mercury, as the god who presided over the flocks. Coronea was famous as the spot near which, in the first year of the Corinthian war, Agesilaus defeated the allied forces of Athens, Thebes, Corinth and Argos, B.C. 394. *C. Nep. in Ages.*—*Paus.* 9. c. 34.—*Ptol* 3. c. 15.—*Diod.* 12.——A town of Peloponnesus.——A town of Corinth.——A town of Cyprus.——A town of Ambracia.——A town of Phthiotis. *Plin.* 4. c. 7.—*Strab.* 9.

CORON'IDES or **CORONI'DES**, a surname of the god Æsculapius, as son of Coronis, *Ovid. Fast.* 6. v. 746.

CORO'NIS, a daughter of Phlegias, who was loved by Apollo, who killed her on account of her criminal partiality for Ischis the Thessalian. According to some, Diana killed her for her infidelity to her brother, and Mercury saved the child, as she was on the burning pile. Others say, that she brought forth her son, and exposed him near Epidaurus, and they farther mention, that Apollo, suspicious of her fidelity, had set a crow to watch her behaviour. The child was preserved, and called Æsculapius; and the mother, after death, received divine honours, and had a statue at Sicyon, in her son's temple, which was never exposed to public view, and therefore when her votaries wished to pay her honours the image was always carried into the neighbouring temple of Minerva *Paus.* 2. c. 26.——The daughter of Coronæus, king of Phocis, changed into a crow by Minerva, when fleeting before Neptune. *Ovid. Met.* 2. v. 543.——One of the daughters of Atlas and Pleione.

CORON'TA, a town of Acarnania. *Thucyd.* 2. c. 102.

CORO'NUS, a son of Apollo. *Paus.* 2. c. 5.——A son of Phoroneus, king of the Lapithæ. *Diod.* 4. ——A son of Thersander.

Coro'nus, a mountain of Asia, now Basarasi. *Ptol.*

COROPAS'SUS, a town of Lycaonia. *Strab.*

CORPICEN'SII, a people of Sardinia. *Ptol.*

CORPIL'LI, a people of Thrace. *Plin.* 4. c. 11.

COR'RHA, a town of Armenia Major.——A city of Persia. *Ptol.*

CORRHA'GIUM, a town of Macedonia. *Liv.* 31. c. 27.

COR'SÆ, a place of Cilicia. *Hesych.*

COR'SEÆ, an island of Ionia, opposite Samus. *Steph. Herodian* has Corsia.

COR'SI, a people of Sardinia, descended from the Corsicans. They are called Corsii by *Ptolemy*, *Paus.* 10.

CORSI'A, a town of Bœotia. *Paus.* 9. c. 24.

COR'SICA, a mountainous island in the Mediterranean Sea, on the coast of Italy, about 150 miles long, and 50 bring broad. The inhabitants were savage, and bore the character of robbers, liars, and atheists, according to these verses of *Seneca*, who lived in exile among them:

Lex prima ulcisci, lex altera vivere rapto,
Tertia mentiri, quarta negare Deos.

They lived to a great age, and fed on honey, which was produced there in great abundance, though bitter in taste, from the number of yew trees and hemlock which grew in the island. Corsica was in the possession of the Carthaginians, and was conquered by the Romans, B.C. 231. The Greeks called it Cyrnus. In the age of Pliny, it was considered as in a flourishing state, as it contained no less than 33 towns. *Dio. Cass.* 110.—*Seneca Consol. ad Helv.* 8.—*Strab.*—*Martial.* 9. epigr. 27.—*Plin.* 3. c. 6. l. 7. c. 2.—*Ovid* 1 *Amor.* el. 12. v. 10.—*Virg, Ecl.* 9. v. 30.

CORSO'TE, a town of Armenia Major. *Xenoph.*

CORSU'RA, an island in the bay of Carthage. *Strab.*

COR'THACA or **COR'GATHA**, a city of India without the Ganges. *Ptol.*

CORTICA'TA, an island of Spain. *Plin.* 4. c. 20. ——A city of the Turditani, in Bætica, now Cortegana. *Ptol.*

CORTO'NA, an ancient town of Etruria, called Corytum by *Virgil*. It was at the north of the Thrasymene lake. *Dionys. H.* 1. c. 20 & 26.—*Liv.* 9. c. 37. l, 22. c. 4.

CORTONEN'SES, a people of Hispania Tarraconensis. *Plin.* 3. c. 3.

CÒTUO'SA, a city of Etruria. *Liv.*
CORTY'RA, a small region of Laconia. *Steph.*
COR'ULA, a city of India within the Ganges. *Ptol.*
CORUN'CALA, a city of India within the Ganges. *Id.*
CORUNCA'NIUS T., the first plebeian who was made high-priest at Rome. He was put to death when ambassador to Teucer, king of Illyricum, A.U.C. 522. *Plin.* 34. c. 6. The family of the Coruncanii was famous for the number of great men it produced for the service and honour of the Roman republic. *Cic. pro Domo.*
CO'RUS, a river of Arabia, falling into the Red Sea. *Herodot.* 3. c. 9.
CORU'SIA, a city of Asiatic Sarmatia. *Ptol.*
CORVI'NUS, a name given to M. Valerius, from a *crow*, which assisted him when he was fighting against a Gaul.
Corvi'nus, an orator. *Paterc.* 2. c. 36.
Corvi'nus Messa'la, an eloquent orator, in the Augustan age, distinguished for integrity and patriotism, yet ridiculed for his frequent quotations of Greek in his addresses to the Roman people. In his old age he became so forgetful, as not even to remember his own name.
Corvi'nus, a person of this family who became so poor, that he was obliged, to maintain himself, to become a shepherd. *Juv.* 1. v. 108.
CORYBAN'TES, the priests of Cybele, also called Galli. In the celebration of their festivals, they beat their cymbals, and behaved as if delirious. They first inhabited mount Ida in Phrygia, and thence passed into Crete, and secretly brought up Jupiter. Some suppose that they received their name from Corybas. *Vid.* Corybas. There was a festival at Cnossus in Crete, called Corybantica, in commemoration of the Corybantes, who were said to have educated Jupiter there. *Catull.* 64.—*Tibull.* 1. el. 4.—*Stat. Theb.* 8. v. 303.—*Paus.* 8. c. 37.—*Diod.* 5.—*Horat.* 1. od. 16.—*Virg. Æn.* 3. v. 111. l. 9. v. 617. l. 10. v. 250.
COR'YBAS, a son of Jasus and Cybele. He introduced the worship of his mother into Phrygia, when he accompanied Dardanus into Asia, and he afterwards married Thebe, daughter of Cilix. *Strab.* 10.—*Martial* 1. epigr. 71. *Diod.* 5.——A painter, a pupil of Nicomachus. *Plin.* 35. c. 11.
CORYBIS'SA, a city of Mysia. *Strab.* 10.
COR'YBUS, a promontory of Crete. *Id.* 8.
CORYC'IA, a nymph, mother of Lycorus by Apollo. *Paus.* 10. c. 6.
Coryc'ia, a promontory of Crete.——A harbour of Æthiopia. *Steph.*
CORYC'IDES, the nymphs who inhabited the foot of Parnassus. This name is often applied to the muses themselves. *Ovid. Met.* 1. v. 320.
CORYCIUS, an old man of Tarentum, whose time was happily employed in the care and management of his bees. *Virg. G.* 4. v. 127. Some suppose that the word Corycius implies not a person of that name, but a native of Corycus, who had settled in Italy.
COR'YCUS, now Churco, a lofty mountain of Cilicia, with a town of the same name, and also a cave, with groves which produced excellent saffron, superior to that of Sicily, or of Lycia, or Cyrene. The saffron plant was in high estimation among the ancients, who not only perfumed their theatres, but likewise their persons, with a juice extracted from it. *Dioscorid.* 1. c. 25.—*Solin.* 41.—*Lucret.* 2. v. 417.—*Martial.* 9. epigr. 39.—*Propert.* 4. el. 6.—*Horat.* 2. sat. 4. v. 68.—*Lucan.* 9. v. 809.—*Plin.* 5. c. 27.—*Cic. ad Fam.* 12. ep. 13.—*Strab.* 14.——A mountain of Ionia, long the noted retreat of robbers. *Strab.* 13.——A hill, at the foot of Parnassus, sacred to the muses. *Stat. Theb.* 7.—*Strab.* 9.
CORYDAL'LA, a city of Rhodes. *Steph.*
CORYDAL'LUS, a village of Attica in the tribe Hippothoontis. *Steph.*——A town of Lycia. *Ptol.*
COR'YDON, the name of a shepherd, often occurring in the pastorals of Theocritus and Virgil.
COR'YLA or CORYLE'UM, a village of Paphlagonia. *Xenoph.*
CORYM'BIFER, a surname of Lacchus, from his wearing a crown of *corymbi*, certain berries that grow on the ivy. *Ovid. Fast.* v. 393.—*Virg. Ec.* 3. v. 39.—*Propert.* 4. el. 6. v. 3.
COR'YNA, a town of Ionia. *Mela*, 1. c. 17.
COR'YNE, a city of Elis. *Ptol.*
CORYNE'TA or CORYNE'TES, a famous robber, son of Vulcan. He for a while lived near Epidaurus, where he plundered and terrified the inhabitants, till he was killed by Theseus. *Plut. in Thes.* He is also called Periphatus. *Vid.* Periphatus.
CORYPHÆ'UM, a mountain of Epidaurus, where Diana, surnamed *Coryphea* was worshipped. *Steph.*
COR'YPHAS, a town of Troas *Plin.* 5. c. 30.
CORYPHA'SIUM, a promontory of Peloponnesus. *Paus.* 4. c. 36.
COR'YPHE, a daughter of Oceanus. *Cic. de Nat. D.* 3. c. 23.
Cor'yphe, a mountain near the Ganges. *Plut.*
CORYPHEN'SES, a place of Tegea. *Paus.* 8. c. 45.
COR'YTHUS, a king of Corinth. *Diod.* 4.
CORY'TUS or COR'YTUS, an ancient king of Etruria, father to Jasius, whom Dardanus is said to have put to death, to obtain the kingdom. He gave his name to a town and mountain of Etruria, now Cortona, near which Dardanus was born. *Virg. Æn.* 3. v. 170. l. 7. v. 209.—*Sil.* 3. v. 123. l. 4. v. 721.
COS, an island. *Vid.* Co.
CO'SA, COS'SA, or CO'SÆ, a town of Etruria, near the sea coast. *Virg. Æn.* 10. v. 168.—*Liv.* 22. c. 11.—*Cic.* 9. *Att.* 6.—*Cæs. Bell. Civ.* 1. c. 34.
ÇOSAM'BA, a city of India within the Ganges. *Ptol.*
CO'SAS, a river of Latium, near Frusio. *Strab.* l. 5.
COSCI'NUS, a town of Apamea. *Plin.* 5. c. 29.
COSCO'NIUS, a Latin writer. *Varro. de L. L.* 5. ——A writer of wretched epigrams. *Martial.* 2. epigr. 77.
COSE'NUS, a river of Mauritania. *Plin.* 5. c. 1.
COSIN'GAS, a Thracian priest in Juno's temple, &c. *Polyæn.* 7. c. 22.
CO'SIS, a brother to the king of Albania, killed by Pompey. *Plut. in Pomp.*
COSMAÑA'TES, a people of Liguria. *Plin.* 3. c. 5.
COS'MUS, an effeminate Roman. *Juv.* 8.
COS'SAGUS, a river flowing into the Ganges. *Plin.* 6. c. 18.
COS'SEA, a part of Persia. *Diod.* 17.——A town of Thrace. *Steph.*
COSSETA'NIA, a region of Hispania Tarraconensis. *Plin.* 3. c. 3.
COSSINI'TES, a river of Thrace. *Ælian. de Animal.* 15. c. 25.
COS'SIUM, a town of Gallia Aquitanica, *Ptol.*—*Ausou.*
COSSOA'NUS, a river of India, flowing into the Ganges. *Arrian.*
COS'SUS, a surname given to the family of the Cornelii.
Cos'sus A. Cornel. a Roman, who killed Lar. Tolumnius, king of Veii, in a battle, and was the second who obtained the *Spolia Opima*, A.U.C. 317. *Virg. Æn.* 6. v. 841.
COSSU'TIA, was the first wife of Jul. Cæsar. *Suet. in Cæs.* 1.
COSSUTIA'NUS, an informer under Claudius. *Tacit. Ann.* 11. c. 6.
COSSU'TII, a family at Rome, from which Cossutia, Cæsar's wife was descended. *Suet. in Cæs.* 1. One of the family was distinguished as an architect about 200 B.C. and first introduced into Italy the more perfect models of the Grecian artists.
COSTOBŒ'I, robbers in Galatia. *Paus.* 10. c. 34.
COSY'RA, a barren island in the African Sea, half way between Melita and the African shores. *Ovid. Fast.* 3. v. 567.
COSY'RI, a people of India. *Plin.* 6. c. 17.
COS'YRUS, an island near Selinus.——A river and city of Sicily. *Steph.*
COTÆ'A, a region of Armenia Minor. *Ptol.*
COTÆNA, a city of Armenia Minor. *Id.*
COTAM'BA, a town of Persia. *Id.*
COTEN'SII, a people of Dacia. *Id.*
CO'TES or COT'TES, a promontory of Mauritania. *Strab.*
CO'THON, a small island near the citadel at Carthage, with a convenient bay, which served for a dockyard. *Servius in Virg. Æn.* 1. v. 431.—*Diod.* 3.
COTHO'NEA or COTHONE'A, the mother of Triptolemus. *Hygin.* fab. 147.
COT'INÆ, a place near the Bætis in Spain, where gold and brass were found. *Strab.*

COTINU'SA, an island near Spain. *Plin.* 4. c. 22.

COT'ISO, a king of the Daci, whose army invaded Pannonia, and was defeated by Corn. Lentulus, the lieutenant of Augustus. It is said that Augustus solicited his daughter in marriage. *Suet. in Aug.* 63.—*Horat.* 3. od. 8. v. 18.—*Plin.* 4. c. 12. —*Dio.* 51. c. 22.

COTO'NIS, an island near the Echinades, *Plin.* 4. c. 12.

COT'RADES, a city of Isauria. *Steph.*

COT'TA M. AURE'LIUS, a Roman, who opposed Marius. He was consul with Lucullus; and when appointed commander of the Roman forces in Asia, was defeated by sea and land by Mithridates. He was surnamed *Ponticus*, because he took Heraclea of Pontus by treachery. *Plut. in Lucull.*

COT'TA, an orator, greatly commended by *Cicero de Orat.*——A governor of Paphlagonia, very faithful to Sardanapalus. *Diod.* 2.——A spendthrift in the age of Nero, &c. *Tacit.*——An officer in Cæsar's army in Gaul.——A poet mentioned by *Ovid.* in *Ep. de Pont.*

COT'TIE AL'PES. *Vid.* Cottiæ.

COTTI'ARA, a city of India within the Ganges. *Ptol.*

COTTI'ARIS, a river of the Sinæ. *Id.*

COTTIS, a town of India within the Ganges. *Id.*

COT'TIUM, a place of Gallia Narbonensis, near the Alpes Cottiæ. *Strab.*

COT'TON, a city of Asia. *Liv.* 9. c. 37.

COT'TUS, a giant, son of Cœlus and Terra, who had 100 hands and 50 heads. *Hesiod. Theog.* v. 147.

COT'TUS a man among the Ædui, &c. *Cæs. Bell.*

COTTÆ'UM, a town of Galatia. *Plin.* 5. c. 32. ——A town of Phrygia, near the Sangaris.

COTYLÆ'UM, a mountain of Eubœa. *Steph.*

COTYLÆ'US, a surname of Æsculapius, under which appellation he was worshipped on the borders of the Eurotas. His temple was raised by Hercules. *Paus.* 3. c. 19.

COTYL'IUS, a mountain of Arcadia. *Paus.* 8. c. 41.

COTYO'RA, a city of Pontus in Asia Minor, on the Euxine Sea, founded by a colony from Sinope. *Diod.* 14.

COTYR'GA, an inland city of Sicily. *Ptol.*

CO'TYS, the father of Asia. *Herodot.* 4. c. 45. ——A son of Manes by Calirhoe, who succeeded his father on the throne of Mæonia.——A king of Thrace. *C. Nep. in Iphic.*——A king of Thrace, who favoured the interests of Pompey during the civil wars. He was of irascible temper. *Cæs. B. C.* 3. c. 4.—*Lucan.* 5. v. 54.——A king of Thrace, who divided the kingdom with his uncle, by whom he was killed. It is the same to whom Ovid writes from the place of his banishment. *Tacit.* 2. *Ann.* 64.—*Ovid.* 2. *de Pont.* ep. 9.——A king of the Odrysæ in Thrace. *Liv.* 42. c. 29.——A king of Armenia Minor, who fought against Mithridates, in the age of Claudius. *Tacit. Ann.* 11 & 13. ——A king who imagined that he should marry Minerva. He murdered some of his servants who wished to dissuade him from indulging such frivolous expectations. *Athen.* 12.

COTYT'TO, the goddess of debauchery, whose festivals, called Cotyttia, were celebrated by the Athenians, Corinthians, Thracians, &c. during the night. Her priests were called Baptæ, and nothing but debauchery and wantonness prevailed at the celebration. A festival of the same name was observed in Sicily, where the votaries of the goddess carried about boughs hung with cakes and fruit, which it was lawful for any person to pluck off. It was a capital punishment to reveal whatever was seen or done at these sacred festivals, and it cost Eupolis his life for an unseasonable reflection upon them. Yet though the priests were regarded as contemptible, and dishonoured among their fellow citizens, Alcibiades was one of those who was initiated into their mysterious secrets. The goddess Cotytto is supposed to be the same as Proserpine or Ceres, *Horat.* epod. 17. v. 58.—*Juv.* 2. v. 91.—*Strab.* 10.—*Synesius in Ep.*

COU'GIUM, a city of the Vaccæi, in Hispania Tarraconensis. *Ptol.*

COYMASE'NI, a people of Corsica. *Id.*

COZA'LA, a town of Armenia Major. *Id.*

COZIS'TRA, a city of Cappadocia. *Id.*

CRABA'SIA, a city of the Iberii. *Id.*

CRA'GUS, a woody mountain of Cilicia, which forms one of the extremities of mount Taurus. It was sacred to Apollo. *Ovid. Met.* 9. v. 645.—*Horat.* 1. od. 21.

CRAMBU'SA, a town of Lycia, *Strab.*——An island of Cilicia. *Steph.*

CRAMBU'TIS, a city of Ægypt. *Steph.* It is called Crambotis by *Herodotus.*

CRAN'AI, a surname of the Athenians, from their king Cranaus. *Herodot.* 8. c. 44.

CRAN'APES, a Persian, &c. *Herodot.*

CRAN'AUS, the second king of Athens, who succeeded Cecrops, and reigned nine years, B.C. 1497. *Paus.* 1. c. 2.——A city of Caria. *Plin* 5. c. 29.

CRAN'DA, a city of Upper Æthiopia. *Plin.* 6. c. 29.

CRA'NE, a nymph. *Vid.* Carna.

CRA'NE, a town of Arcadia. *Theophrast.*

CRANE'A, a small region of the Ambraciotæ. *Steph.*

CRANE'UM, a gymnastic school at Corinth. *Diog.*

CRANI'A, an ancient name of Tarsus. *Steph.*

CRA'NII, a town of Cephallenia. *Thucyd.* 2. c. 30. —*Strab.* 10.—*Palmer. Ant. Gr.* p. 530.

CRA'NON or CRAN'NON, a town of Thessaly, on the borders of Macedonia, at the south of Tempe. It was there that Antipater and Craterus defeated the Athenians after Alexander's death. *Liv.* 26. c. 10. l. 42. c. 64.

CRAN'TOR, a philosopher of Soli, among the pupils of Plato, B.C. 310. He wrote a treatise on grief, called *Consolatio*, so valuable, that Cicero recommends every word of it should be learnt by heart. *Horat.* 1. ep. 2. v. 4.—*Cic. Acad.* 4. c. 44. *Tusc.* 1. c. 48. *Acad.* 1. c. 10.—*Diog.*——An armour-bearer of Peleus, killed by Demoleon. *Ovid. Met.* 12. v. 361.

CRASE'RIUM, a region of Sicily. *Steph.*

CRASPEDI'TES, a bay of Phrygia. *Plin.* 5. c. *ult.*

CRAS'SIPES, a surname of the family of the Furii, one of whom married Tullia, Cicero's daughter, whom he soon after divorced. *Cic. Att.* 4. ep. 5. *Ad. Q. Fr.* 2. ep. 5 & 6.—*Liv.* 38. c. 42.

CRASSIT'IUS L., a philosopher who opened a school at Rome. *Suet. de Gram.* 18.

CRAS'SUS L. LICIN'IUS, a celebrated Roman orator deservedly commended by Cicero, and introduced in his book *De Oratore* as the principal speaker. Besides his great abilities as an orator and as a man of letters, Crassus possessed the wisdom of the senator, the intrepidity of the soldier, and the integrity of the magistrate. He passed through all the public offices of the state, in which he had his friend Scævola for colleague, except in the tribuneship and censorship; and as the governor of Gaul, he gained popularity by his justice and vigilance, and merited the honours of a triumph, which, however, were refused to his services through the intrigues of his enemies. During a vehement debate in the senate with Phillippus, Crassus was suddenly seized with a pain in his side, which in seven days terminated his life; and he was happy, as Cicero observes, in not being a witness of the many calamities which soon after afflicted Rome. *Cic. passim.*—*Paterc.* 2. c. 9.—*Quintil.* 6. c. 3.—*Val. Max.* 6. c. 2.

CRAS'SUS M., a grandfather of Crassus the triumvir, who, it is said, never laughed. *Plin.* 7. c. 19.—*Cic. Fin.* 5. c. 30.

CRAS'SUS M. LICIN'IUS, a celebrated Roman surnamed *Dives*, like the rest of his family. He was at first very circumscribed in his circumstances; but by educating slaves, and selling them at a high price, by purchasing the lands of those who were proscribed, and by many unjustifiable means, he grew rapidly into power and opulence. The cruelties of Marius and Cinna, however, obliged him to leave Rome, and he retired to Spain, where he remained concealed for eight months. After Cinna's death he passed into Africa, and thence into Italy, where he devoted himself to the interests of Sylla. When the gladiators, with Spartacus at their head had spread universal alarm in Italy, and defeated some of the Roman generals, Crassus was sent against them, a battle was fought in which Crassus slaughtered 12,000 of the slaves, and by this decisive blow soon put an end to the war, and was honoured with an ovation at his return. He was soon after made consul with Pompey; and in this high office he displayed his opulence by entertaining the populace at 10,000 tables. He was afterwards censor, and formed the first triumvirate with Pompey and Cæsar. As his love of riches was more predominant than that of glory, Crassus never imitated the ambitious conduct of his colleagues, but was satisfied with the province of Syria, which seemed to promise to his avarice an inexhaustible source of wealth. With the hope of enlarging his possessions, he, though the omens proved unfavourable, and though his friends deprecated his departure, and his enemies openly threatened his ruin, set off from Rome and embarked at Brundusium for Syria. He crossed the Euphrates, and, forgetful of the rich cities of Babylon and Seleucia, hastened to make himself master of Parthia, but he was delayed in his march by the delay of Artavasdes, king of Armenia, and the perfidy of Ariamnes. He was met in a large plain by Surena, the general of the forces of Orodes king of Parthia; and a battle was fought, in which 20,000 Romans were killed, and 10,000 taken prisoners. The darkness of the night favoured the escape of the rest, and Crassus, forced by the mutiny and turbulence of his disappointed soldiers, and the treachery of the guides, trusted himself to the general of the enemy, on pretence of proposing terms of accommodation, and he was put to death, B.C. 53. His head was cut off, and sent to Orodes, who, to insult his misfortunes, and to decide his avarice, poured melted gold down his throat. The firmness with which Crassus received the news of his son's death, who perished in that expedition, has been deservedly commended; and the words that he uttered when he surrendered himself into the hands of Surena, equally claim our admiration. He was wont often to say, that no man ought to be accounted rich, if he could not maintain an army. Though he has been called avaricious, yet he was liberal and generous in his intercourse with his friends, and the hospitality with which he treated the Romans could not always be attributed to sordid or interested motives. Eager at all times to relieve distress, he shewed himself willing to lend money unsolicited to his friends, and without interest. He was fond of philosophy and literature, and his knowledge of history was great and extensive. The standards which fell into the hands of the Parthians by the defeat of Crassus became the cause of new wars, and the wounds which the pride of Rome received by this calamitous event were never healed till Augustus had recovered the long-dishonoured trophies. *Appian. Parth.* 154.—*Justin.* 42, c. 4. —*Flor*, 3. c. 11.—*Dio*, 40, c. 27.—*Plin*, 2. c. 56.—*Val. Max.* 3. c. 4. 5.—*Ovid. Fast.* 5. v. 583, &c.—*Propert.* 2 el. 10. v. 13, &c.—*Cic. Div.* 1. c. 16. l. 2. c. 40.—*Plutarch in vitâ.*—*Flor.* 3. c. 11.

CRAS'SUS, PUB'LIUS, son of the rich Crassus, possessed great powers of mind, with a highly cultivated understanding, but military glory, the passion of the times, was his favourite pursuit. After displaying his valor in Gaul in the armies of Cæsar, he accompanied his father into Parthia at the head of a chosen troop of a thousand horse. When he saw himself in the fatal battle surrounded by the enemy, and without any hope of escape, he ordered one of his men to run him through. His head was cut off, and, fixed on a spear, was shown with insulting triumph to his father and his army by the Parthians. *Plut. in Crass.*—*Dio.* 39. c. 31.—*Cic. Brut.* 81. *Fam.* 5. ep. 8. l. 13. ep. 16. —*Appian. Parth.* 136.

CRAS'SUS, P. LICIN'IUS, a Roman, of the family of the triumvir, probably his great grandfather. He was consul with Scipio, the conqueror of Annibal, A.U.C. 549, and had the province of the Brutii allotted to him. A severe distemper which raged in his army prevented the exertion of his capabilities; but the next year he, in company with Sempronius, attacked and defeated Annibal near Crotona. His funeral, A.U.C. 571, was honoured by exhibition of games, and a shew of 120 gladiators. *Liv.* 28. c. 38. l. 29. c. 10. l. 39. c. 46.—*Cic. Brut.* 19.——A consul defeated by Perseus in Macedonia. He was afterwards victorious, and behaved with great tyranny towards the Grecian states. *Liv.* 41, 42, &c.

CRAS'SUS PUBL. LICIN'IUS MUCIA'NUS, a Roman high-priest, about 131 years B.C. consul with L. Valer. Flaccus, A.U.C. 623. He went to Asia with an army against Aristonicus, where he was killed, and was buried at Smyrna. *Paterc.* 2. c. 4.—*Liv.* 59.—*Cic. Phil.* 11. c. 8.

CRAS'SUS PUB'LIUS, a lieutenant of L. Cæsar in Italy, consul with Lentulus, A.U.C. 657. He slew himself to escape the cruelty of Marius. *Plut. Quæst. R.*—*Cic. Font.* 15. *In Arch.* 5. *Orat.* 3. c. 3.

CRAS'SUS, a son of Crassus the rich, killed in the civil wars after Cæsar's death.

CRASTI'NUS or CRAS'TINUS, a man in Cæsar's army, killed at the battle of Pharsalia. *Cæs. Bell. Civ.* 3. c. 99.

CRAS'TUS, a city of the Sicani, in Sicily. It is called by *Herodotus* Crastis.

CRAT'AIS, the mother of Scylla, supposed by some to be the same as Hecate. *Homer. Odyss.* 12. v. 124.

CRATÆ'US, a person who conspired against Archelaus. *Aristot. Pol.* 5. c. 10.

CRA'TER, a bay of Campania, near Misenus. It is now Golfo di Napoli. *Strab.* 5.

CRAT'ERUS, one of the generals of Alexander the Great. He rendered himself conspicuous by his literary fame, as well as by his valor in the field, and wrote the history of Alexander's life. He was greatly respected and loved by the Macedonian soldiers, and Alexander always trusted him with marked confidence. After Alexander's death, he with Antipater, subdued Greece, and passed with his colleague into Asia, where he was killed in a battle against Eumenes, B. C. 321. He had received for his share of Alexander's kingdoms, Greece and Epirus. *Nep. in Eumen.* 2.—*Justin.* 12 & 13. —*Curt.* 3.—*Arrian.*—*Plut. in Alex.*——An eminent physician intimate with Cicero and Atticus. *Cic.* 12. *ad Attic.* ep. 13.—*Horat.* 2. sat. 3. v. 161. —*Persius*, 3. v. 65.——A painter, whose pieces adorned the public buildings at Athens. *Plin.* 35. c. 11.——A famous sculptor. *Id.* 36. c. 5.——An Athenian, who collected into one body, all the decrees which had passed in the public assemblies at Athens.

CRA'TES, a philosopher of Bœotia, son of Ascondus, and disciple of Diogenes the cynic, B.C. 324. He sold his estates, and distributed the money among his fellow-citizens. He was naturally deformed, and rendered himself more hideous, by sewing sheep skins to his mantle, and by the singularity of his manners. He clothed himself as warmly as possible in the summer; but in the winter, his garments were uncommonly thin, and incapable of resisting the inclemency of the season. Hipparchia, the sister of a philosopher, became enamoured of him; and as he could not overcome her partiality for him by representing himself as poor and deformed, he married her. Some of his letters are extant. *Diog. in vitâ.*—*Sax. Onom.* 1 p. 82. —*Fabr. B. Gr.* 3. c. 13.——A stoic, son of Timocrates, who opened a school at Rome, where he taught grammar. *Sueton.*——A native of Pergamus, who wrote an account of the most striking events of every age, B.C. 165. *Ælian. de Anim.* 17. c. 9.——A philosopher of Athens, who succeeded to the school of his master Polemon.——An Athenian comic poet. *Suidas.*

CRATESICLE'A, the mother of Cleomenes, king of Sparta, who went to Ægypt in hopes of serving her country, &c. *Plut in Cleom.*

CRATESIP'OLIS, a queen of Sicyon, who severely punished some of her subjects, who had revolted at the death of Alexander, her husband, &c. *Polyæn.* 8. c. 58.

CRATESIP'PIDAS, a commander of the Lacedæmonian fleet, employed against the Athenians *Diod.* 13.

CRATE'VAS, a general of Cassander. *Diod.* 19. ——A physician mentioned by *Pliny*, 24. c. 17.

CRA'TEUS, a son of Minos, king of Crete.

CRA'THIS, a river of Achaia, falling into the bay of Corinth. *Strab.*——A river in Magna Græcia, falling into the bay of Tarentum, near Thurii. Its waters were supposed to give a yellow colour to the hair and beard of those who drank them. *Ovid.* 14. *Met.* v. 315.—*Paus.* 7. c. 25.—*Plin.* 31. c. 2.

CRATI'NUS, a native of Athens, celebrated for the

satirical severity of his comic writings, and for his fondness for drinking. He died at the age of 97' B.C. 431 years. Quintillian greatly commends his comedies, which the little remains of his poetry do not seem fully to justify. *Sax. Onom.* 1. p. 35.—*Fabr. B. Gr.* 1. 2. c. 22.—*Horat.* 1. sat. 4. 1. 1. ep. 20.—*Quintil.*—*Pers.* 1. v. 123.——A celebrated wrestler. *Paus.* 6. c. 3.——A statuary of uncommon beauty. *Id.*

CRATI'NUS, a river of Asia. *Plin.*

CRATIP'PUS, a philosopher of Mitylene, who taught among others, Cicero's son at Athens. After the battle of Pharsalia, Pompey visited the house of Cratippus, where their discourse chiefly turned upon Providence, which the warrior, overwhelmed with his misfortunes, blamed, and the philosopher defended. *Plut in Pomp.*—*Cic. in Offic.* 1. *Div.* 1. c. 3.——An historian, contemporary with Thucydides. *Dionys. Hal.*

CRAT'YLUS, a philosopher, preceptor to Plato after Socrates. *Diog. Laert. in Plat.* 3.

CRAU'GIÆ two small islands on the coast of Peloponnesus. *Plin.* 4. c. 12.

CRAU'SIS, the father of Philopœmen.

CRAVAL'IDÆ or CRAVAGAL'IDÆ, a region of Phocis, near Cirrha. *Suidas.*

CRAUX'IDAS, a man who obtained an Olympic crown at a horse race. *Paus.* 5. c. 8.

CRE'MA or CRE'ME, a city of Pontus. *Steph.*

CREM'ERA, a small river of Tuscany, falling into the Tiber, a little to the north of Rome. It is famous in Roman history for the death of the 300 Fabii, who were killed there in a battle against the Veientes, A.U.C. 277. It is now La Varca or La Valca. *Ovid. Fast.* 2. v. 205.—*Juv.* 2. v. 15ç.

CREM'IDES, a place of Bithynia. *Diod.* 14.

CREM'MA, a town of Lycia. *Strab.* 12.

CREM'MIA, a city of Crete, afterwards called Cortyn. *Steph.*

CREM'MYON or CROM'MYON, a town near Corinth, where Theseus killed a sow of uncommon size. *Ovid. Met.* 7. v. 435.

CREM'NI or CREM'NOS, a commercial place on the Palus Mœotis. *Herodot.* 4. c. 2.

CREMNIS'CUS, a town of Sarmatia, near the Ister. *Plin.* 4. c. 12.

CREMO'NA, a celebrated town of Cisalpine Gaul, on the Po, at the west of Mantua. It was a Roman colony, and suffered much when Annibal first passed into Italy. The wretched inhabitants were robbed of their lands and possessions during the second triumvirate, and with the spoils Augustus rewarded those veterans who had assisted him in enslaving his country, and in making himself absolute. Virgil has alluded to these events, and lamented the violence and robbery which extended from Cremona to Mantua and the neighbouring towns. *Virg, Ecl.* 9. v. 28.—*Liv.* 21. c. 56 —*Tacit. Hist.* 3. c. 4 & 19.

CREMO'NIS JU'GUM, a part of the Alps, over which, as some suppose, Annibal passed to enter Italy. *Liv.* 21. c. 38.

CREMU'TIUS COR'DUS, an historian who wrote an account of Augustus, and of the civil wars, in the shape of annals. He starved himself for fear of the resentment of Tiberius, whom he had offended, by calling Cassius the last of the Romans. His annals were destroyed by order of the jealous tyrant, but some copies, which have now perished, were preserved by Marcia, the historian's daughter. *Seneca.*—*Tacit. Ann.* 55. c. 34, 35.—*Suet. in Aug.* 35. *In Tib.* 60. *In Calig.* 16.

CREN'IDES, a city of Sicily, afterwards called Philippi. *Steph.*——A place of Bithynia, on the Euxine. *Arrian. in Peripl.*——A place near Heraclea in Pontus. *Steph.*

CRE'NIS, a nymph mentioned by *Ovid, Met.* 12. v. 313.

CRE'ON, king of Corinth, was son of Sisyphus. He promised his daughter to Jason, who repudiated Medea after he had lived ten years with her in perfect felicity, under the protection and in the house of the Corinthian king. Creon and his family shared his daughter's unhappy fate. *Vid.* Creusa. *Apollod.* 1. c. 9. 1. 3. c. 7.—*Eurip. in Med.*—*Hygin.* fab. 25.—*Diod.* 4.——A son of Menœtius, father to Jocasta, the mother and wife of Œdipus. At the death of Laius, who had married Jocasta, Creon ascended the vacant throne of Thebes; and when the ravages of the Sphinx (*Vid.* Sphinx) spread desolation and terror through the country of Bœotia, he offered his crown and daughter in marriage to him who could explain the ænigmas which the monster proposed. Œdipus was happy in his explanations, and he ascended the throne of Thebes, and married Jocasta, without knowing that she was his mother. When Eteocles and Polynices slew each other, Creon commanded that the bodies of the Argives, and more particularly the body of Polynices should remain unburied. If this was in any manner disobeyed, the officers were to be buried alive. Antigone the sister of Polynices, transgressed, and was accordingly punished. Hæmon, the son of Creon, who passionately loved Antigone, killed himself on her grave, when his father refused to grant her pardon. Creon was afterwards killed by Theseus, who had made war against him at the request of Adrastus, because he refused burial to the Argives. *Vid.* Eteocles, Polynices, Adrastus Œdipus. *Apollod.* 3. c. 56, &c.—*Paus.* 1. c. 39. 1. 9. c. 5, &c.—*Stat. in Theb.*—*Sophocl. in Antig.*—*Æschyl. Sept. contra Theb.*—*Euripid. in Phœn.* —*Seneca in Theb.*—*Hygin.* fab. 67 & 76.—*Diod.* 1 & 4.——The first annual archon at Athens, 684 B. C. *Pater.* 1. c. 8.

CREONTI'ADES, a son of Hercules by Megara, daughter of Creon, killed by his father, because he had slain Lycus.

CREOPH'AGI, a people of Upper Æthiopia. *Strab.*

CREOPH'ILUS, a Samian, who is said to have hospitably entertained Homer, from whom he received a poem in return. Some say that he was that poet's master, &c. *Strab.* 14.——An historian. *Athen.* 8.

CREPE'RIUS POL'LIO, a Roman, who spent all his property in the most extravagant debauchery *Juv.* 9. v. 6.

CRES, an inhabitant of Crete.——The first king of Crete. *Paus* 8. c. 53.

CRE'SA or CRES'SA, a town of Caria, now Porto Malfetan. *Plin.* 5. c. 28.

CRES'CENS, a freedman of Nero. *Tac. Hist.* 1. c. 76

CRE'SIUM, a city of Cyprus. *Steph.*

CRE'SIUS, a hill of Arcadia. *Paus,* 8. c. 44.

CRES'PA, a city of Liburnia. *Ptol.* It is called Crexa by *Pliny,* 5. c. 28.

CRESPHON'TES, a son of Aristomachus, who, with his brothers Temenus and Aristodemus, attempted to recover the Peloponnesus. He married Merope daughter of Cypselus king of Sicyon, by whom he had three sons, and he was at last murdered by Polyphontes, who usurped his crown and married his queen. *Paus.* 2. c. 18. 1. 4, c. 3. 1. 8. c. 5.—*Apollod.* 2,—*Hygin.* fab. 137 & 184. *Euripides* wrote a tragedy which he called *Cresphontes* descriptive of the fortunes of this renowned hero. *Cic Tusc* . 1. c. 48. *Her.* 2. c. 24.

CRES'SA, a city of Paphlagonia, founded by Meriones. *Steph.*

CRESSE'A, a region near Pallene. *Herodot.* 7.

CRES'SIUS, belonging to Crete. *Virg. Æn.* 4. v. 70. 1. 8. v. 294.

CRES'TON, a town of Thrace, capital of a part of the country called Crestonia. The inhabitants had each many wives; and when the husband died, she who had received the greatest share of his affection, was immolated on his grave. *Herodot.* 5. c, 5.

CRE'TA, now Candia, one of the largest islands of the Mediterranean Sea, at the south of all the Cyclades, extends from east to west 270 miles, and is about 50 miles in breadth. It is very mountainous and woody, was once famous for its hundred cities, and for the laws which the wisdom of Minos had established there. The inhabitants were infamously noted for their unnatural loves, their falsehoods, their piracies, and their robberies. Jupiter, as some authors report, was educated here by the Corybantes, and the Cretans boasted that they could show his tomb. There were different colonies from Phrygia, Doris, Achaia, &c. that established themselves there. The island, after groaning under the tyranny of democratical usurpation, and feeling the scourge of frequent sedition, was made a Roman province, B.C. 66, after a war of three years in which the inhabitants were so distressed, that they were even compelled to drink the water of their cattle. Chalk was produced there, and thence called Creta, and with it the Romans marked the lucky days in their calendar. *Horat.* 1. od. 36. v. 10. *Epod.* 9.—*Ovid. Fast.* 3. v. 444. *Epist.* 10. v. 106. *Met.* 9. v. 664. *De A. A.* 1. v. 298.—*Ptol.* 3. c. 17.—*Seneca in Med.*—*Servius in Æn.* 10. v. 325. —*Athen.* 13.—*Hesych.*—*Val. Max.* 7. c. 6.—*Strab.* 10.—*Lucan.* 3. v. 184.—*Virg. Æn.* 3. v. 104.—*Mela,* 2. c. 7.—*Plin.* 4. c. 12.

CRETÆ'US, a poet mentioned by *Propertius,* 2. el. 34. v. 29.

CRE'TE, the wife of Minos. *Apollod.* 3. c. 1.——A daughter of Deucalion. *Id.* 3. c. 3.

CRE'TEA, a country of Arcadia, where Jupiter was educated, according to some traditions. *Paus.* 8. c. 38.

CRETE'NIA, a town of Rhodes. *Steph.*

CRE'TES, the inhabitants of Crete. *Virg. Æn.* 4. v. 146.

CRE'TEUS, a Trojan, distinguished as a poet and musician. He followed the fortunes of Æneas, and was killed by Turnus in Italy. *Virg. Æn.* 9. v. 774.——A Trojan, killed by Turnus. *Id.* 12. v. 538.——A son of Minos, killed by one of his children as he had been forewarned by the oracle.

CRE'THEIS, the wife of Acastus, king of Iolcus, fell in love with Peleus, son of Æcus, and accused him of attempts upon her virtue, because he refused to gratify her criminal desires, &c. She is called by some Hippolyte, or Astyadamia. *Pindar. Nem.* 4.

CRE'THEUS, a son of Æolus, was the founder and sovereign of Iolcus. He married Tyro, his brother's daughter, after her amour with Neptune, and was father of three sons, Amythaon, Pheres, and Æson. *Propert.* 1. el. 13.—*Apollod.* 1. c. 7, &c.

CRE'THON, a son of Diocles, engaged in the Trojan war on the side of Greece. He was slain, with his brother Orsilochus, by Æneas. *Homer. Il,* 5. v. 540.

CRET'ICUS, a certain orator. *Juv.* 2. v. 67——A surname of M, Antony's father, from his expedition against Crete.

CREU'GA, a famous boxer. *Paus,* 2.

CREU'SA, a daughter of Creon, king of Corinth. When she was going to celebrate her nuptials with Jason, who had divorced Medea, she put on a poisoned garment, which immediately set her body on fire, and she expired in the most excruciating torments. She had received this dress as a gift from Medea, who wished thus to revenge herself upon Jason for his infidelity. Some call her Glauce. *Ovid. de Art. Am.* 1. v. 335. *Met.* 7. v. 395.—*Euripid. in Med.*——A daughter of Priam, king of Troy, by Hecuba. She married Æneas, by whom she had some children, among which was Ascanius. When Troy was taken, she fled in the night, with her husband; but they were separated in the midst of the tumult, and Æneas could not recover her, nor after the most laborious search could he ascertain where she was. Cybele saved her, and carried her to her temple, of which she became priestess; according to the relation of Virgil, who represented Creusa as appearing to her husband in a vision, while he was anxiously seeking her in the noise and tumultuous confusion of the fight. She predicted to Æneas the calamities that attended him, the fame which he should acquire when he came to Italy, and his consequent marriage with a princess of the country. *Paus.* 10. c. 16.—*Virg. Æn.* 2. v. 562, &c. ——A daughter of Erechtheus king of Athens. She was mother of Janus by Apollo.

CREU'SA, a town of Bœotia. *Strab.* 9.—*Paus.* 6. c. 32

CREU'SIS, a naval station of the Thespians, in the bay of Corinth. *Paus,* 9. c. 32.

CRI'ASUS, the fifth king of Argos, reigned 54 years *Apollod.* 2. c. 1.

CRI'NAS, a physician of Massilia, in the age of Nero. *Plin.* 29. c. 11.

CRINIP'PUS, a general of Dionysius the elder in Sicily. *Diod.* 15.—*Polyæn.* 3. c. 9.

CRI'NIS, a stoic philosopher. *Laert.*——A priest of Apollo.

CRINI'SUS or CRIMI'SUS, now Caltabellota, a river on the western parts of Sicily falling into the Mediterranean Sea, near Selinus. Near this river Timoleon defeated the Carthaginian forces. *C. Nep. in Tim.*—*Virg. Æn.* 5. v. 38. The word in the various editions of Virgil, is spelt Cremissus, Crimissus, Crimisus, Crimesus, Crinisus, Crimnisus. The Crinisus was a Trojan prince, who exposed his daughter on the sea, rather than suffer her to be devoured by the sea-monster which Neptune sent to punish the infidelity of Laomedon. *Vid.* Laomedon. The daughter was safely carried to the shores of Sicily. Crinisus some time after went in quest of his daughter, and was so disconsolate for her loss, that the gods changed him into a river in Sicily, and granted him the power of metamorphosing himself into whatever shape he pleased. He made use of this privilege to seduce the neighbouring nymphs, and among others, he paid court to his own daughter, by whom he had a son called Acestes, who afterwards became the king of that part of the country. *Servius in* 5 *Æn.* 554.

CRI'NO, a daughter of Antenor. *Paus.* 10. c. 27. ——One of the Danaides. *Apollod.*

CRIO'A, a village in the tribe Antiochis at Athens. *Steph.*

CRIS'IPHON, the architect of the temple at Ephesus. *Plin.* 7. c. 37. *Vitruvius* calls him Cresiphon. *Salmas. ad Solin.* p. 812.

CRI'SON, a man of Himera, who obtained a prize at Olympia, &c. *Paus.* 5. c. 23.

CRISPI'NA, a Roman matron, &c. *Tacit.* 1. *Hist.* 47.

CRISPI'NUS, a prætorian, who, though originally a slave in Ægypt, was, after the acquisition of riches raised to the honours of knighthood by Domitian. *Juv.* 1. v. 26.——A stoic philosopher, as remarkable for his loquacity, as for the foolish poem which he wrote to explain the tenets of his own sect, to which *Horace* alludes in the last verses of 1. sat. 1. l. 2. sat. 7. v. 45.——A centurion slain by his soldiers for putting Capito to death. *Tac. Hist.* 1. c. 58.

CRIS'PUS, the surname of the family of the Sallustii. *Vid.* Sallustius.

CRIS'PUS VIB'IO, a famous orator. *Quintil.* 10. c. 1. ——The second husband of Agrippina.

CRIS'PUS FLA'VIUS JU'LIUS, a son of the Great Constantine, made Cæsar by his father, and distinguished for his valour and extensive knowledge. Fausta, his step-mother, wished to seduce him; and when he resisted her criminal passion, she accused him before Constantine, who believed the accusation, and caused his son to be poisoned, A.D. 326.

CRISSÆ'US SI'NUS, a bay on the coasts of Peloponnesus, near Corinth, called also Corinthiacus Sinus, now the bay of Salona. It received its name from Crissa, a town of Phocis, situate on the bay, and near Delphi.

CRIT'ALA, a town of Cappadocia. *Herodot.* 7. c. 26.

CRITEN'SI, a people of Asia. *Plin.* 6. c. 30.

CRITH'EIS or CRITHE'IS, the mother of Homer, according to some authors. She married Phemius, a grammarian of Smyrna. *Plut. in vit. Hom.*

CRITHO'TE, a town of the Thracian Chersonesus. *C. Nep.*

CRIT'IAS, one of the 30 tyrants set over Athens by the Spartans, after the fatal battle of Ægospotamos. He was eloquent and well-bred, but of dangerous principles, and he cruelly persecuted his enemies, and put them to death. He was killed in a battle against those citizens whom his opression had banished. He had been among the disciples of Socrates, and had written elegies and other compositions, of which some fragments remain. *Cic.* 2 *De Orat.* *Tusc.* 1. c. 40.——An author, who wrote on republics. *Athen.* 11.——A writer, who addressed an elegy to Alcibiades. *Id.* 1. c. 10. 13.

CRI'TO, one of the disciples of Socrates, who attended his learned preceptor in his last moments, and composed some dialogues, now lost. *Cic. Div.* 1. c. 25. Tusc. 1. c. 43.—*Diog.*——A physician in the age of Artaxerxes Longimanus.——An historian of Naxus, who wrote an account of all that had happened during eight particular years of his life. *Suidas.*——A Macedonian historian, who wrote an account of Pallene, of Persia, of the foundation of Syracuse, of the Getæ, &c.——A

Greek physician in the service of Trajan. *Sax. Onom.* 1. p. 293.—*Fabr. B. Gr.* 6. c. 7.

CRITOBU'LUS, a general of Phocis, engaged at the battle of Thermopylæ, between Antiochus and the Romans. *Paus.* 10. c. 20.——A physician in the age of Philip king of Macedonia. He extracted the arrow which had been so dexterously shot into Philip's eye by Aster. As the physician of Alexander, he attended him in his Asiatic expedition, and cured him of the wound received from a dart during a battle. *Curt.* 9. c. 5. 25.—*Plin.* 7. c. 37.——A son of Crito, disciple to Socrates. *Diog. in Crit.*

CRITODE'MUS, an ancient historian. *Plin.* 7. c. 56.

CRITOGNA'TUS, a celebrated warrior of Alesia, when Cæsar was in Gaul. *Cæs. Bell. Gall.* 7, c. 77.

CRITOLA'US, a citizen of Tegea in Arcadia, who, with two brother, fought against the three sons of Demostratus of Pheneus, to put an end to a long war between their respective nations. The brothers of Critolaus were both killed, and he alone remained to withstand his three bold antagonists. He, however, conquered them; and when at his return, his sister deplored the death of one of his antagonists, to whom she was betrothed, he killed her in a fit of resentment. The offence deserved capital punishment; but he was pardoned on account of the services which he had rendered to his country. He was afterwards general of the Achæans, and it is said that he poisoned himself because he had been conquered at Thermopylæ by the Romans. *Cic.* 3. *de Nat. D.* 3. c. 38. *Tusc.* &c.——A peripatetic philosopher of Athens, sent ambassador to Rome, &c. 130 B.C. *Cic.* 2. *De Orat. Fin.* 5. c. 5.——An historian who wrote about Epirus. *Voss. de Hist. Gr.* p. 349.

CRI'U METO'PON, a promontory of Crete, now Capo Crio. *Dionys.* 87.——A promontory of Taurica Chersonesus, now Im Kermen. *Id.* v. 150.

CRI'US, a soothsayer, son of Theocles. *Paus.* 3. c. 13.——A man of Ægina, &c. *Herodot.* 6. c. 50.——A son of Cœlus and Terra, who married Eurybia, daughter of Tellus. by whom he had three sons, Astreus, the husband of Aurora, Pallas the husband of Styx, and Perses the father of Asteria by Hecate. *Hesiod Theog.* 375 *& seq.*—*Apollod.* 1.

CRI'US, a river of Achaia, called after a giant of the same name. *Paus.* 7. c. 27.

CROBI'ALUS, a town of Paphlagonia. *Apollon.* 2.

CROB'YZI or CROBY'ZI, a people of Thrace. *Herodot.*——A people near the Ister. *Steph.*——A people of Lower Mysia. *Ptol.*

CROC'ALA, an island at the mouth of the Indus. *Plin.* 6. c. 21.

CROC'ALE, one of Diana's attendants, daughter of the Ismenus. *Ovid. Met.* 3. v. 169.

CRO'CEÆ, a town of Laconia. *Paus.* 3. c. 21.

CROCIAT'ONUM, a city of Gallia Lugdunensis, now, probably, Carentan. *Ptol.*

CROCODILOP'OLIS, a town of Ægypt, near the Nile, above Memphis. The crocodiles were held there in the greatest veneration; and they were so tame, that they came to take food from the hand of their feeders. It was afterwards called Arsinoe. *Herodot.* 2. c. 69.—*Strab.* 17.

CROCODI'LUS, a mountain of Cilicia. *Plin.* 5. c. 27.

CROC'ORUS, a plain near Thessaly, on the Amphrysus. *Steph.*

CRO'CUS, a beautiful youth, enamoured of the nymph Smilax. He was changed into a flower of the same name, on account of the impatience of his love, and Smilax was metamorphosed into a yew-tree. *Ovid.* 4. *Met.* v. 283.

CROCYLE'UM or CROCYLI'UM, a city of Æolia. *Steph. in* Δῆμος.

CRŒ'SUS, the fifth and last of the Mermnadæ, who reigned in Lydia, was son of Alyattes, and passed for the richest of mankind. He was the first who made the Greeks of Asia tributary to the Lydians. His court was the asylum of learning; and Æsop among others, lived under his patronage. In a conversation with Solon, Crœsus wished to be thought the happiest of mankind; but the philosopher apprised him of his mistake, and gave the preference to virtuous poverty and domestic contentment. Crœsus undertook a war against Cyrus the king of Persia, and marched to meet him with an army of 420,000 men, and 60,000 horse. After a reign of fourteen years, he was defeated B.C. 548; his capital was soon after besieged, and he fell into the conqueror's hands, who ordered him to be burnt alive. The pile was already on fire, when Cyrus deard the conquered monarch three times exclaim, Solon! with lamentable energy. He asked him the reason of his exclamation, and Crœsus repeated the conversation which he had once held with Solon on human happiness. Cyrus was moved at the affecting recital, and at this proof of the inconstancy of human affairs, he ordered Crœsus to be taken from the burning pile, and became one of his most intimate friends. The kingdom of Lydia became extinct in his person, and the power was transferred to Persia. Crœsus survived Cyrus, but the time or the manner of his death is unknown. He was celebrated for the immensely rich presents which he made to the temple of Delphi, from which he received an obscure and ambiguous oracle, which he interpreted in his favour, and which was fulfilled in the destruction of his empire. *Herodot.* 1. c. 26, &c.—*Plut. in Solon.* 8. c. 24.—*Justin.* 1. c. 7.

CRO'MI, a people of Arcadia. Their country was called Cromitis.

CROMI'TIS. *Vid.* Cromi.

CROM'MYON. *Vid.* Cremmyon. *Ovid. Met.* 7.—*Xenoph.*——A town near Corinth. *Paus.* 2. c. 1.

CROMMYONE'SUS, an island near Smyrna. *Plin.* 5. c. 31.

CROM'NA, a town of Bithynia. *Strab.* 12.—*Val. Flacc.* 5. v. 105.

CRO'MUS, a son of Neptune. *Paus.* 2. c. 1.——A son of Lycaon. *Id.* 8. c. 3.

CRONE'A, a promontory near the Caspian Sea. *Plin.* 4. c. 5.

CRO'NIA, a festival at Athens, in honour of Saturn. The Rhodians observed the same festival, and generally sacrificed to the god a condemned malefactor.

CRO'NIUM, a town of Elis. *Diod.* 15.——A town of Sicily. *Polyæn.*——A mountain of Peloponnesus. *Ptol.*

CRO'PIA, a village in the tribe Leontis. *Steph.*

CRO'PHI, a mountain of Ægypt, near which were the sources of the Nile, according to some traditions, in the city of Sais. *Herodot.* 2. c. 28.

CROS, a city of Ægypt. *Steph.*

CROS'SA, a city near Pontus. *Id.*

CROSSÆ'A, a country situate partly in Thrace, and partly in Macedonia. *Herodot.* 7. c. 123.

CROT'ALUS, a navigable river of Italy, now Corace. *Plin.* 3. c. 10.

CRO'TON, a man killed by Hercules, by whom he was afterwards greatly honoured. *Diod.* 4.

CROTO'NA, a town of Italy, still known by the same name at the south of the bay of Tarentum, founded 759 years before the Augustan age, by Myscellus, at the head of a colony from Achaia. The inhabitants were excellent warriors, and great wrestlers; so that it was proverbially said, that the last of the Crotoniates was the first of the Greeks. Democedes, Alcmæon, Milo, &c., were natives of this place. Crotona was surrounded by a wall twelve miles in circumference, before the arrival of Pyrrhus in Italy. Its citizens acquired lasting fame in their battles against the Sybarites, but they struggled in vain against the attacks of Dionysius of Sicily, who reduced them under his power. It suffered likewise in the wars of Pyrrhus and Annibal, but it received ample glory in being the place where the celebrated Pythagoras established his school. *Ptol.* 3. c. 1.—*Herodot.* 8. c. 47.—*Strab.* 6.—*Plin.* 2. c. 96.—*Liv.* 1. c. 18. l. 24. c. 3.—*Justin.* 20. c. 2.

CROTONIA'TÆ, the inhabitants of Crotona. *Cic. de Inv.* 2. c. 1.

CROTONIA'TIS, a part of Italy, of which Crotona was the capital. *Thucyd.* 7. c. 35.

CROTOPI'ADES or CROTO'PIAS, a patronymic of Linus, as grandson of Crotopus. *Ovid in Ib.* 480.

CROTO'PUS, a king of Argos, son of Agenor, and father to Psamathe, the mother of Linus by Apollo. *Ovid. in Ib.* 480.—*Stat.* 1. *Theb.* 570.

CRO'TUS, a son of Eupheme, the nurse of the Muses. His infancy was protected by these goddesses, and after a life spent in the labours of the chase, and in paying due honours to his patronesses, he was placed by Jupiter among the stars, under the name of Sagittarius. *Hygin. P. A.* 2. c. 27.—*Paus.* 9. c. 29.—*Eratosthen. in Cat.* 28.

CRU'NOS, a town of Peloponnesus. *Mela*, 2. c. 2.

CRU'SA, an island in the Sinus Ceramicus. *Plin.* 5. c. 31.

CRU'SIS, a place near Olynthus, in Macedonia.

CRUSTUME'RIUM or CRUSTUME'RIA, a town of the Sabines, on the Tiber, north of Rome. *Liv.* 4. c. 9. l. 42. c. 34.—*Virg. Æn.* 7. v. 631.

CRUSTUMI'NUM, a town of Etruria, near Veii, famous for pears; whence the adjective *Crustumia. Virg. G.* 2. v. 88.

CRUSTU'MIUM, CRUSTU'NUS, or CRUSTUME'NIUS, now Conca, a small river flowing from the Apennines, by Ariminum. *Lucan.* 2. v. 406.

CRY'A, a city of Lycia. *Steph.*

CRY'ASSUS, a city of Caria. *Id.*

CRY'NIS, a river of Bithynia. *Plin.* 5. c. 32.

CRY'ON, a river of Asia Minor, flowing through Lydia. *Plin.* 5. c. 29.

CRYP'TA, a passage through mount Pausilypus. *Vid.* Pausilypus.

CRYP'TUS, a harbour of Arabia Felix. *Ptol.*——A harbour of Ægina. *Paus.* 2.

CRYS'SA, a river of Troas. *Plin.*

CTE'ATUS, one of the Grecian chiefs before Troy, *Paus.* 5. c. 4.——A son of Actor and Molione. called by some of the poets son of Neptune. He assisted Augias against Hercules, and was afterwards killed by him at the Isthmian games. *Apollod.* 2.—*Paus.* 6. c. 20.—*Homer. Il.* 13. v. 185.

CTEM'ENE, a town of Thessaly.

CTE'NOS, a harbour of Chersonesus Taurica. *Strab.*

CTE'SIAS, son of Ctesiochus, was a native of Cnidus. He was at the battle of Cunaxa, as physician to the Grecian army, and he was there taken prisoner by Artaxerxes. He became physician to the Persian king, whose wounds he cured, and he continued to enjoy his favour and protection for 17 years. He wrote a history of the Assyrians and Persians, which Justin and Diodorus have partially preferred to that of Herodotus. It consisted of 23 books, and began with the reign of Ninus, and continued in a general plan to the third year of the 95th Olympiad, or about 398 years B.C. Some fragments of this composition have been preserved by Photius, and are to be found in Wesseling's edition of Herodotus. *Strab.* 1.—*Athen.* 12.—*Diod.* 1.—*Plut. in Artax.*—*Sax. Onom.* 1. p. 59.—*Fabr. B. Gr.* 2. c. 25, &c.——A sycophant of Athens. *Aristoph. Acharn.*——An historian of Ephesus.

CTESIB'IUS, a mathematician of Alexandria, who flourished 135 years B.C. He was the inventor of the pump, and other hydraulic instruments. He also invented a clepsydra, or water clock. This invention of measuring time by water was very ingenious. Water was made to drop upon wheels it turned. The wheels communicated their regular motion to a small wooden image, which by a gradual rise, pointed with a stick to the proper hours and months, which were engraved on a column near the machine. This successful invention gave rise to many improvemeuts; and the modern manner of measuring time with an hourglass is an imitation of the clepsydra of Ctesibius. *Vitruv. de Archit.* 9. c. 9. l. 10. c. 12. *Plin.* 7. c. 37.

CTESIB'IUS, a cynic philosopher.——An historian who flourished 254 years B.C. and died in his 104th year. *Plut. in Dem.*—*Lucian. in Macr.*

CTES'ICLES, a general of Zacynthus. *Diod. Sic.* 15.——An archon at Athens. Ol. 110. an. 3.

CTESIDE'MUS, a painter who had Antiphilus among the number of his pupils. *Plin.* 35. c. 10.

CTESIL'LA, a daughter of Alcidamas, changed into a dove. *Ovid. Met.* 7. fab. 12.

CTESIL'OCHUS, an eminent painter, who represented Jupiter as bringing forth Bacchus. *Plin.* 35. c. 11.

CTES'IPHON, an Athenian, son of Leosthenes, who advised his fellow-citizens publicly to present Demosthenes with a golden crown for his great public services, and for his probity and virtue. This was opposed by the orator Æschines, the great rival of Demosthenes, who accused Ctesiphon of seditious views. Demosthenes undertook the defence of his friend, and delivered that celebrated oration which is still extant, and Æschines was banished. *Demost. & Æsch. de Coronâ.*—*Cic. Orat.* 3. c. 56.——A Greek architect, who made the plan of Diana's temple at Ephesus. He was also called Chresipheon, Chrisippon, and Cresiphon.——An elegiac poet, whom king Attalus placed over his possessions in Æolia. *Athen.* 13.——A Greek historian, who wrote a history of Bœotia, besides a treatise on trees and plants. *Plut. in Thes.*

CTES'IPHON, a large village of Assyria, now Elmodain, on the banks of the Tigris, at the east of Babylon, where the kings of Parthia originally resided in winter, on account of the mildness of the climate. *Strab.* 15.—*Ptol.* 6. c. 1.—*Plin.* 6. c. 26.

CTESIP'PUS, a son of Chabrias. After his father's death he was received into the house of Phocion, the friend of Chabrias. Phocion attempted to correct his natural foibles and extravagances, but in vain. *Plut. in Phoc.*——A man who wrote a history of Scythia. *Id. de flum.*——One of the descendants of Hercules.

CTIM'ENE, the youngest daughter of Laertes by Anticlea. *Homer. Odyss.* 15. v. 334.

CTIM'ENUS, the murderer of Hesiod. *Vid.* Antiphus.

CTYLINDRI'NE, a place of India within the Ganges. *Ptol.*

CU'BA, a city of India within the Ganges. *Id.*

CU'BI, a people of Gallia Celtica. *Plin.* 4. c. 19.

CUBULTERI'NI, a people of Italy. *Plin.* 3. c. 5.

CUCAD'MA, a town of Asiatic Sarmatia. *Ptol.*

CU'DUM, a promontory or town of India. *Mela*, 3. c. 7.

CU'LARO, a town of the Allobroges in Gaul, called afterwards Gratianopolis, now Grenoble. *Cic. Ep.*

CUL'CUA, a colony of Numidia. *Ptol.*

CU'MA or CU'MÆ, a town of Æolia, in Asia Minor, advantageously situated on the bay opposite the Arginusæ. The inhabitants were called Cumani. *Strab.* 13.—*Paterc.* 1. c. 4.——A city of Campania, near Puteoli, founded by a colony from Chalcis, aud the Æolian Cumæ, before the Trojan war. The inhabitants were called Cumæi, and Cumani. One of the sibyls, who fixed her residence in a cave in the neighbourhood, was called the Cumæan Sibyl. *Vid.* Sibyllæ. It was here also that Dædalus, after he had escaped from the prisons of Crete. and the resentment of Minos, erected a magnificent temple in honour of Apollo. Cumæ, on account of its delightful situation, became the favourite resort and residence of many of the Romans, who here passed their hours of relaxation from the severer duties of the state. *Mela*, 2. c. 4.—*Liv.* 4. c. 44.—*Ptol.* 3. c. 1.—*Ovid. Met.* 15. v. 712. *Fast.* 4. v. 158. *Pont.* 2. el. 8. v. 41.—*Cic. Rull.* 2. c. 26. *Attic.* 4. ep. 10. *Fam.* 9. ep. 23. *Acad.* 4. c. 25, &c.—*Paterc.* 1. c. 4.—*Virg. Æn.* 3. v. 441. & *Servius in loco.*—*Strab.* 5.

CUMA'NUM, a country house of Pompey, near Cumæ, in Campania. *Cic. ad Attic.* 4. ep. 10.——A country house of Varro. *Id. Acad.* 1. c. 1.

CU'MI, a town of Upper Æthiopia, on the banks of the Nile. *Plin.* 6. c. 30.

CUNAX'A, a place of Assyria, 500 stadia from Babylon, famous for a battle fought there between Artaxerxes and his brother, Cyprus the younger, about the 7th of September, B.C. 401. *Plut. in Artax.*—*Ctesias.*

CU'NEUS, a cape of Spain, now St. Vincent in the kingdom of Algarve, extending into the sea in the form of a wedge. *Mela*, 3. c. 1.—*Plin.* 4. c. 22.

CU'NI, a town of Gedrosia. *Ptol.*

CU'NICI, a city of Majorca. *Plin.* 3. c. 5.

CUNI'NA or CUNA'RIA, a diviuity, who, according to the Romans, presided over children when in the cradle; whence her name. *Varro apud Lactant.* 1. c. 20.

CUNUSITA'NI, a people of Sardinia. *Ptol.*

CUPA'VO, a son of Cycnus, who assisted Æneas against Turnus. *Virg Æn.* 10. v. 186.

CUPEN'TUS, a friend of Turnus, killed by Æneas. *Virg. Æn.* 12. v. 539

CU'PHE, an inland city of Libya. *Plin.*

CUPI'DO, the god of love, among the ancients. There are different traditions concerning his parents. *Cicero* mentions three Cupids; one, son of Mercury and Diana; another, son of Mercury and Venus; and the third, son of Mars and Venus. *Plato* mentions two. *Hesiod*, the most ancient theologist, speaks only of one, who, as he says, was produced at the same time as Chaos and the Earth. There were, according to the more received opinions, two Cupids, one of whom was the son of Jupiter and Venus; the other, son of Nox and Erebus, was distinguished by his wantonness and riotous disposition. Cupid is represented as a winged infant, naked, armed with a bow and a quiver full of arrows. On gems, and other pieces of antiquity, he is represented as amusing himself with some childish diversion. Sometimes he appears driving a hoop, throwing a quoit, playing with a nymph, catching a butterfly, or trying to burn with a torch; at other times he plays upon a horn before his mother, or closely embraces a swan, or with one foot raised in the air, he, in a musing posture, seems to meditate some playful trick. Sometimes like a conqueror he marches with a helmet on his head, a spear on his shoulder, and a buckler ou his arm; intimating that even Mars himself owns the superiority of love. His power was generally known by his riding on the back of a lion, or on a dolphin, or breaking to pieces the thunderbolts of Jupiter. Among the ancients Cupid was worshipped with the same solemnity as his mother Venus, and as his influence extended over the heavens, the sea, and the earth. and even the empire of the dead, his divinity was universally acknowledged, and vows, prayers, and sacrifices were daily offered to him. According to some accounts the union of Cupid with Chaos gave birth to men, and all the animals which inhabit the earth, and even the gods themselves, were the offspring of love before the foundation of the world. Cupid, like the rest of the gods, assumed different shapes; and we find him in the Æneid putting on at the request of his mother, the form of Ascanius, and appearing as a child in Dido's court, where he inspired the queen with love. *Virg. Æn.* 1. v. 693, &c.—*Cic de Nat. D.* 3.—*Ovid.* 1 *Met.* fab. 10.—*Hesiod. Theog.* v. 121, &c.—*Oppian. Hali.* 4.—*Cyneg.* 2.—*Bion. Idyll* 3.—*Moschus.*—*Eurip. in Hippol.*—*Theocrit. Idyll.* 3, 11, &c. [The most deservedly celebrated statue of Cupid is that in the Museum of the Capitol, supposed to be a copy of the celebrated figure by Praxiteles. There is also a beautiful group, of Cupid and Psyche, in the same Museum.

CUPIEN'NIUS, a friend of Augustus, who made himself ridiculous by the effeminacy of his dress. *Horat.* 1. sat. 2. v. 36.

CU'PRA, a town of Picenum. *Ptol.*—*Plin.* 3. c. 13.

CUQUE'NI or CUCUE'NI, a people of Gallia Aquitanica. *Ptol.*

CURAPORI'NA, a town of India within the Ganges. *Id.*

CUR'CUM, an inland town of Liburnia, now Cruck. *Id.*

CURE'NA, a city of Media. *Ptol.*

CUREN'SES, a people of Italy. *Plin*, 3. c. 12.

CU'RES, a town of the Sabines, of which Tatius was king. The inhabitants, called Quirites, were carried to Rome soon after the foundation of the city, and were admitted to all the rights and privileges of citizens. *Virg. Æn.* 1. v. 292. 8. v. 638. —*Liv.* 1. c. 13.—*Macrob.* 1. c. 9,—*Ovid. Fast.* 2. v. 477 & 480. 1. 3, v. 94.

CURE'TES, a people of Crete, called also Corybantes. Their knowledge of all the arts was extensive, and they communicated it to many parts of ancient Greece. They were entrusted with the education of Jupiter, and to prevent his being discovered by his father, they invented a kind of dance, and drowned his cries in the harsh sonnds of their shields and cymbals. As a reward for their attention, they were made priests and favourite ministers of Rhea, called also Cybele, who had committed to them the care of Jupiter. *Dion. Hal.* 2.—*Virg. G.* 4. v. 151,—*Strab.* 10.—*Paus.* 4. c. 33.—*Ovid. Met.* 4. v. 282. *Fast.* 4. v. 210.—*Servius in Virg. loco cit. & Æn.* 2. v. 104. 1. 3. v. 131.

CURE'TIS, a name given to Crete, as being the residence of the Curetes. *Ovid. Met.* 8. v. 136.

CU'RIA, a division of the Roman tribes. Romulus originally divided his subjects into three tribes, and each tribe into ten Curiæ. Over each Curia, was appointed a priest, who officiated at the sacrifices of his respective assembly. The sacrifices were called *Curionia*, and the priest *Curio*. To be eligible to this office he was to be above the age of fifty. His morals were to be pure and unexceptionable, and his body free from all natural defects. The *Curiones* were elected by their respective Curiæ, and above them was a superior priest called *Curio maximus*, chosen by all the Curiæ in a public assembly. The word *Curia* was also applied to public edifices among the Romans. These were generally of two sorts, religious and civil. In the former were held the assemblies of the priests, and of every consecrated order, for the regulation of religious sacrifices, and ceremonies. In the other the senate assembled for the dispatch of public business. The Curia was solemnly consecrated by the augurs, before a lawful assembly could be convened there. There were three at Rome, which more particularly claim our attention; *Curia Hostilia*, built by Tullus Hostilius; *Curia Pompeii*, where Julius Cæsar was murdered; and *Curia Augusti*, the palace and court of the emperor Augustus.

CU'RIA, a town of the Rhœti, on the river Rhine, now Coire, the capital of the Grisons in Switzerland.

CU'RIA LEX, *de Comitiis*, was enacted by M. Curius Dentatus the tribune. It forbade the convening of the *Comitia*, for the election of magistrates, without a previous permission from the senate.

CURIAN'DRA, a town of Bactriana. *Ptol.*

CURIA'NUM, a promontory of Gallia Aquitanica, now Cap de Buch.

CU'RIAS. *Vid.* Curium.

CURIA'TII, a family of Alba, which was carried to Rome by Tullus Hostilius, and entered among the Patricians. The three Curiatii, who engaged the Horatii, and lost the victory in the war with the Albans, were of this family. *Flor.* 1. c. 3.—*Dionys. Hal.* 3.—*Liv.* 1. c. 24.

CURIA'TIUS MATER'NUS, a Latin poet, in the age of Vespasian. A tragedy called Medea is the only remnant of his works. *Voss. de Poet. Lat.* c. 3.

CURIC'TA, an island off Illyria. *Plin.* 3. c. 21.—*Ptol.*

CU'RIO, the surname of the family of the Scribonii. There were three of this family in succession who distinguished themselves as orators at Rome.

CU'RIO CA'IUS, the grandfather ,is mentioned with great commendation by *Cicero*, *Brut.* 32.

CU'RIO CA'IUS SCRIBO'NIUS, his son, was consul 678, and gained great praise by his conquest of the Dardani, when governor of the province of Macedonia. He shone as an orator, though the awkward agitation into which he threw his body from side to side when speaking, procured him the surname of *Burbuleius*, from an obscure actor, who was ridiculed for such gestures. *Val. Max.* 9. c. 14.—*Plin.* 7. c. 12.—*Cic. Pis.* 19, 24. *Brut.* 16, 59, 60.—*Quintil.* 11· c. 3.

CU'RIO CA'IUS, his son, though possessed of great natural abilities, showed himself more eager in the pursuit of profligate pleasures, than of military fame or oratorical distinction. Cicero for a while interposed his friendship, his entreaties, and his authority, and roused him to deeds and pursuits worthy of his family; but extravagance and prodigality were so deeply rooted in the character of Curio, that he was prepared for public plunder, or for civil war. Cæsar, more wise and more intriguing, attached him to his party by discharging his debts, which, it is said, amounted to £500,000 English money, and Curio showed his gratitude, by embracing all the plans of agrandizement, of rapacity, and ambition, which might place his friend at the head of the state. During the civil war between Pompey and Cæsar, Curio, who had hitherto favoured the senate, artfully showed his enmity to Pompey, by pleading the cause of Cæsar, and by seizing Sicily for him. From Sicily, Curio passed into Africa, where he defeated Varus, and laid siege to Utica; but the efforts of Cato, and the speedy arrival of Juba, whom Curio, in his tribuneship, had attempted to deprive of his kingdom, turned the fortune of the war, and Curio, surrounded on all sides, and unwilling to fly, rushed boldly into the midst of the combatants, and fell on heaps of slain. *Lucan.* 4. v. 797, &c.—*Cæsar, B. C.* 2. c. 34.—*Appian.*—*Dio.* 40. 61.—*Val. Max.* 9. c. 1.—*Cic. Fam.* 2. ep. 1, &c. *Brut.* 81. *Phil.* 2. c. 18.—*Plin.* 36. c. 15.—*Plut in Cæs.*—*Flor.* 4. c. 2.

CURIO'NES, a people of Germany. *Ptol.*

CURIOP'OLIS, a city of Caria. *Steph.*

CURIOSOLI'TÆ or CURIOSOL'ITÆ, a people among the Gauls, who inhabited the country which now forms the most western part of Britany. *Cæs. Bell. G.* 2. c. 34, l. 3. c. 11.

CU'RIUM, a town of Cyprus, at a small distance from which, on the most southern part of the island, there is a cape which bears the name of Curias. *Herodot.* 5. c. 113.—*Plin.* 5. c. 31.

CU'RIUS DENTA'TUS MAR'CUS AN'NIUS, a Roman, celebrated for his fortitude and frugality. He was three times consul, and was twice honoured with a triumph. He obtained decisive victories over the Samnites, the Sabines, and the Lucanians, and defeated Pyrrhus near Tarentum. The ambassadors of the Samnites visited his cottage, while he was boiling some vegetables in an earthen pot, and deeming his poverty as easily assailable, they attempted to bribe him by the offer of large presents. The virtuous Roman refused their offers with contempt, nobly and indignantly exclaiming, "I prefer my earthen pots to all your vessels of gold and silver, and it is my wish to command those who are in possession of money, while I am deprived of it, and live in poverty." *Juv.* sat. 2. v. 3. 11. v. 78.—*Cic. Orat.* 1. c. 39.—*Plut. in Cat. Cens.*—*Horat.* 1. od. 12. v. 41.—*Flor.* 1. c. 15.——A lieutenant of Cæsar's cavalry, to whom six cohorts of Pompey revolted. *Cæs.* 1. *Bell. Cic.* 24.

CUR'TIA, a patrician family, which migrated with Tatius to Rome.

CURTIL'LUS, a celebrated epicure. *Horat.* 2. sat. 8. v. 52.

CURTIS'IUS TI'TUS, a soldier of the prætorian cohort, who revolted in the 10th year of the emperor Tiberius. *Tacit. Ann.* 4 c. 27.

CUR'TIUS AT'TICUS, a Roman knight, who accompanied Tiberius in his retreat into Campania. *Tacit. An.* 4

CUR'TIUS MONTA'NUS, an orator and poet under Vespasian. *Tacit. Ann.* 4.

CUR'TIUS M. a Roman youth, who nobly devoted himself to the gods Manes for the safety of his country, about 360 years B.C. A wide gap, called afterwards Curtius Lacus, had suddenly opened in the forum, and the oracle had said that it never would close before Rome threw into it whatever it had most precious. Curtius immediately perceived that no less than a human sacrifice was required, and arming himself, he mounted his horse, and solemnly threw himself into the gulph, which is said to have instantly closed over his head. *Liv.* 7. c. 6.—*Val. Max.* 5. c. 6.

CUR'TIUS NIC'IAS, a grammarian intimate with Pompey. *Suet. de Gr.*

CUR'TIUS Q. RU'FUS. *Vid.* Quintus.

CUR'TIUS FONS, a stream which conveyed water to Rome from the distance of 40 miles, by an aqueduct so elevated as to distribute the water through all the hills of the city. *Plin.* 36. c. 15.

CUR'TIUS LA'CUS, the gulph into which Curtius leaped.

CURU'LIS MAGISTRA'TUS, an officer at Rome, who had the privilege of sitting in an ivory chair in the public assemblies. The dictators, the consuls, the censors, the prætors, and the ædiles, claimed that privilege, and therefore were called *curules magistratus.* The senators who had passed through the above-mentioned offices, were generally carried to the senate-house in ivory chairs, as all generals in their triumphant procession to the Capitol. When appellations descriptive of distinction began to be used among the Romans, descendants of curule magistrates were called *nobiles*, the first of a family who discharged that office were known by the name of *noti* and those that had never been in office were called *ignobiles.*

CUR'ZOLA, an island in the Adriatic Sea. *Ptol.*—*Plin.* 3. c. 26.

CU'SA, a river of Mauritania Tingitana, now Omirabi. *Ptol.*

CUSSÆ'I, a nation of Asia destroyed by Alexander to appease the manes of his friend Hephæstion. *Plut. in Alex.*

CUSUETA'NI, a people of Italy. *Plin.* 3. c. 5.

CU'SUS, now the Wag, a river of Hungary, falling into the Danube.

CUTELE'TOS, an island near the Syrtis Major. *Mela.*

CUTIL'IUM, a small town of the Sabines, near a lake which contained a floating island, and of which the water was of an unusually cold quality. *Plin.* 3. c. 12. l. 31. c. 2.—*Senec. Q. N.* 3. c. 25.—*Liv.* 26. c. 11.

CY'ALUS, a city of Lydia, founded by Jupiter. *Steph.*

CYAMOSO'RUS, a river of Sicily. *Polyb.*

CY'ANE, a nymph of Syracuse, to whom her father offered violence in a fit of drunkenness. She dragged him to the altar, where she sacrificed him, and killed herself to stop a pestilence, which, as if sent as a punishment from heaven, had already begun to afflict the country. *Plut. in Parall.*——A nymph of Sicily, who endeavoured to assist Proserpine when she was carried away by Pluto. The god changed her into a fountain, now called Pisma, a few miles from Syracuse. *Ovid.* 5 *Met.* v. 112.

CY'ANE, a town of Lycia. *Plin.* 5. c. 27.

CY'ANE, an inn-keeper, &c. *Juv.* 8. v. 162.

CYA'NEÆ, now the Pavorane, two rugged islands at the entrance of the Euxine Sea, about twenty stadia from the mouth of the Thracian Bosporus. One of them is on the side of Asia, and the other on the European coast, and, according to Strabo, there is only a space of twenty furlongs between them. The waves of the sea, which continually break against them with a violent noise, fill the air with a darkening foam, and render the passage extremely dangerous to navigators. The ancients supposed that these islands floated, and even sometimes united to crush vessels into pieces when they passed through the straits. This tradition arose from their appearing, like all other objects, to draw nearer when navigators approached them. They were sometimes called *Symplegades* and *Planetæ.* It was reported that they were to continue to float till some bold pirate had steered his vessel through the dangerous strait, and when this was happily effected by Jason, in the Argonautic expedition, the islands became fixed and immoveable, and their situation and form was then fully explained and ascertained. *Orpheus, Arg.* 680 & 707.—*Homer. Odyss.* 12. v. 69.—*Plin.* 6. c. 12.—*Herodot.* 4. c. 85.—*Apollon.* 2. v. 317 & 600.—*Ovid. Trist.* 1. el. 9. v. 34.—*Lycoph.* 1285.—*Strab.* 1 & 3.—*Mela*, 2. c. 7.—*Juv.* 15. v. 19.—*Lucan.* 2. v. 718.—*Sch. Euripid. ad Med.* 2. & *Iphig.* 889 & 1388.—*Tzetzes ad Lyc. loco cit.*—*Sch. Apollon. loco cit.* &. l. 4. v. 786.

CYA'NEE or CYA'NEA, a daughter of the Mæander, mother of Byblis and Caunus, by Miletus, Apollo's son. *Ovid. Met.* 9. v. 451.

CYA'NEUS, a large river of Colchis. *Plin.* 6. c. 4.

CYANIP'PE, a daughter of Adrastus.

CYANNIP'PUS, a Syracusan who derided the orgies of Bacchus, for which impiety the god so inebriated him, that he offered violence to his own daughter Cyane, who sacrificed him on the altar. *Vid.* Cyane. *Plut. in Parall.*

CYARAX'ES or CYAX'ARES, son of Phraortes, was king of Media and Persia. He bravely defended his kingdom, which the Scythians had invaded, and afterwards made war against Alyattes. king of Lydia, and subjected to his power all Asia beyond the river Halys. He died after a reign of 40 years, B.C. 585. *Diod.* 2.—*Herodot.* 1. c. 73 & 103.

CYARAX'ES, another prince, supposed by some to be the same as Darius the Mede. He was son of Astyages, king of Media. He added seven provinces to his father's dominions, and made war against the Assyrians, whom Cyrus favoured. *Xen. Cyrop.* 1.

CYAR'DA, a city of Caria. *Steph.*

CYBAS'SUS or CABAS'SUS, a city of Caria. *Id.*

CYBE'BE, a name of Cybele, from κυβήβειν, because in the celebration of her festivals men were driven to madness. *Hesych.*

CYB'ELE, a goddess, daughter of Cœlus and Terra, and wife of Saturn. She is supposed by the most approved authors to be the same as Ceres, Rhea, Ops, Vesta, Bona Mater, Magna Mater, Berecynthia, Dindymene, &c., but she was particularly known and worshipped by the name of Cybele in Phrygia. According to Diodorus, she was the daughter of a Lydian prince called Menos, by his wife Dindymene, and he adds, that as soon as she was born, she was exposed on a mountain. She was preserved and suckled by some of the wild beasts of the forest, and received the name of Cybele from the mountain where she had been exposed, and happily saved from destruction. When she returned to her father's court, she had an intrigue with Atys, a beautiful youth. All the mythologists are unanimous in mentioning the amours of Atys and Cybele. The partiality of the goddess for Atys seems to have arisen from his having first introduced her worship into Phrygia. In Phrygia the festivals of Cybele were observed with the greatest solemnity, and her priests were called Corybantes, Galli, Curetes, &c. In the celebration of the festivals, they imitated the manners of madmen, and filled the air with dreadful shrieks, and repeated howlings, mixed with the confused noise of drums, tabrets, bucklers, and spears. This was in commemoration of the sorrows of Cybele for the loss of her favourite Atys. Cybele was generally represented as a robust woman, far advanced in pregnancy, to intimate the fecundity of the earth. She held keys in her hand, and her head was crowned with rising turrets, and sometimes with the leaves of the oak. She sometimes appears riding in a chariot drawn by two tame lions; Atys follows by her side, carrying a ball in his hand, and supporting himself on a firtree, which was sacred to the goddess. Sometimes Cybele is represented with a sceptre in her hand, and with her head covered with a tower. She also appears with many breasts, to shew that the earth gives aliments to all living creatures; and she at other times carries two lions under her arms. From Phrygia the worship of Cybele passed into Greece, and was solemnly established at Eleusis, under the name of the Eleusinian mysteries of Ceres. The Romans, by order of the Sibylline books, brought the statue of the goddess from Pessinus into Italy; and when the ship which carried it had run on a shallow bank of the Tiber, the virtue and innocence of Claudia were vindicated in removing it with her girdle. It is supposed that the mysteries of Cybele were first known about 1580 years, B.C. The Romans were particularly superstitious in washing every year, on the 6th of the calends of April, the shrine of this goddess in the sacred waters of the river Almon. *Vid.* Atys, Eleusis, Rhea, Corybantes, Galli, &c. *Augustin. de Civit. D.* 2. c. 4 & 5.—*Lucian. in Deâ Syr*—*Diod.* 3.—*Virg. Æn.* 9. v. 617. l. 10. v. 262.—*Lucan.* 1. v. 566.—*Ovid. Trist.* 4. v. 210 & 361. *Fast.* 4. v. 215 & 305.—*Plut. de Loquac.*—*Cic. ad Attic.*—*Cæl Rhod.* 8. c. 17, &c.—*Apollon. Arg.* 3.—*Catull.* 64.—*Lucret.* 2. v. 629, &c.—*Lactant. de Fals. R.* 13 & 14. *De Fals. Sap.* 20.—*Tibull.* 1. el. 4.—*Stat. Theb.* 8. v. 303.—*Juv.* 2. v. 88 & 100.—*Minut. Felix. in Oct.*—*Macrob. in Sat.* 1. c. 23. [There is no celebrated statue which goes by this name, but probably that called the Ceres of Eleusis, in the collection at Paris, is intended for Cybele. A fine head of this goddess will be found in the Museum of the Capitol.]

CYB'ELE or **CYB'ALA**, a town of Phrygia, so called after the goddess Cybele. *Apollod.* 3. c. 5.

CYB'ELUS, a mountain of Phrygia, where Cybele was worshipped.

CYB'IRA, a town of Lycaonia, whence the epithet Cybiraticus. *Horat.* 1, ep. 6. v. 33.

CYBIS'TRA, a town of Cappadocia, or, according to *Ptolemy*, of Armenia Minor. *Cic. Div.* 15

CYCE'SIUM, a town of Peloponnesus near Pisa, *Strab.*

CYCH'REUS or **CYCHRE'US**, a son of Neptune and Salamis. After death he was honoured as a god in Salamis and Attica. As he left no children to inherit the throne, he appointed Telamon his successor, because he had freed the country from a monstrous serpent. *Paus.* 1. c. 35.—*Plut. in Thes.*—*Apollod.* 3. c. 2.

CYCH'RI, a people of Thrace. *Plin.* 31. c. 2.

CYC'LADES, a name given to certain islands in the Ægæan Sea, those particularly that surround Delus as with a circle; whence the name (κύκλος, *circulus*). They were about 53 in number, the principal of which were Ceus, Naxus, Andrus, Parus, Melus, Seriphus, Gyarus, Tenedus, &c. The Cyclades were reduced under the power of Athens by Miltiades; but during the invasion of Greece by the Persians, several of them revolted from their ancient and natural allies. *C. Nep. in Mil.* 2.—*Plin.* 4. c. 12.—*Mela*, 2. c. 7.—*Ptol.* 3. c. 15.—*Strab* 10.—*Dionys. Perieg.*—*Ovid. Met.* 2. v. 64.—*Virg. Æn.* 3. v. 127. l. 8. v. 692.—*Sil.* 4. v. 247.

CYCLOB'ORUS, a river of Attica. *Steph.*

CYCLO'PES, a certain race of men of gigantic stature, supposed to be the sons of Cœlus and Terra. They are represented as having had but one eye in the middle of their forehead; whence their name (κύκλος, *circulus*; ὤψ, *oculus*). They were three in number, according to Hesiod, and were called Arges, Brontes, and Steropes. Their number was greater according to other mythologists, and in the age of Ulysses, Polyphemus was their king. *Vid.* Polyphemus. They inhabited the western parts of the island of Sicily. The tradition of their having only one eye, originated from their custom of wearing small bucklers of steel, which covered their faces, and had a small aperture in the middle, which corresponded exactly to the eye. From their vicinity to mount Ætna, they have been supposed to be the workmen of Vulcan, and to have fabricated the thunderbolts of Jupiter. The most solid walls and impregnable fortresses were said, among the ancients, to be the work of the Cyclopes; and we find that Jupiter himself was armed with what they had fabricated, and that the shield of Pluto, and the trident of Neptune, were the produce of their labour. The Cyclopes were reckoned among the gods, and a temple was dedicated to their service at Corinth. Apollo destroyed them all, because they had made the thunderbolts of Jupiter, with which his son Æsculapius had been killed. Different accounts have been given of the Cyclopes by the ancients, which cannot be reconciled without the aid of fiction or mythology. *Apollod.* 1. c. 1 & 2.—*Homer. Odyss.* 1. v. 71. l. 9. v. 106 & 188.—*Hesiod. Theog.* v. 140.—*Theocrit. Id.* 1, &c.—*Strab.* 8—*Virg. G.* 4. v. 170. *Æn.* 6. v. 630. l. 8. v. 418, &c. l. 11. v. 263.—*Ovid. Met.* 13. v. 780. l. 14. v. 249.—*Callimach. in Del.*—*Servius in Virg. loco cit.*——A people of Asia Minor.

CYC'NUS, a son of Mars by Pelopea, killed by Hercules. The manner of his death provoked Mars to such a degree, that he resolved severely to punish his murderer, but he was prevented by the thunderbolts of Jupiter. *Hygin.* fab. 31 & 281.—*Hesiod. in Scut. Herc.*—*Apollod.* 2.——A son of Neptune by Calyce, said to have been invulnerable in every part of his body. Achilles fought against him; but when he saw that his darts were of no effect, he threw him on the ground and smothered him. He then stripped him of his armour, and then saw him suddenly changed into a bird of the same name. *Ovid. Met.* 12. fab. 3.——A Bœotian, son of Hyrie, by Apollo. He was beloved by Phyllius, who refused to give him a favourite bull, in consequence of which he, in a fit of resentment, threw himself down a precipice on the top of mount Teumessus in Bœotia, and was changed into a swan. *Ovid. Met.* 7. v. 371, &c.——A son of Sthenelus, king of Liguria. He was deeply afflicted at the death of his friend and relation Phaethon, and was metamorphosed into a swan. *Hygin.* fab. 154.—*Ovid. Met.* 2. v. 367.—*Virg. Æn.* 10. v. 189.—*Paus.* 1. c. 30.——The name of a horse mentioned by *Statius* 6 *Theb.* v. 524

CYCO'NÆ, a people in the north of India. *Plin.* 6. c. 17.

CY'DA, a profligate Cretan, made judge at Rome by Antony. *Cic. in Phil.* 5 & 8.

CYD'ARAS, a river of Taprobane. *Plin.* 6. c. 22.

CYDATHENÆ'UM, a village of the tribe Pandionis. *Steph*—*Spon. Itin. Gr.* part. 3. p. 150.

CYD'DESIS, a people of Bithynia. *Ptol.*

CYD'IAS, an Athenian of great valor, &c. *Paus.* 10. c. 21.——A painter, who made a painting of the Argonauts. This celebrated piece was bought by the Roman orator Hortensius, for 164 talents. *Plin.* 34.

CYDIP'PE, the wife of Anaxilaus, &c. *Herodot.* 7. c. 165.——The mother of Cleobis and Biton. *Vid.* Cleobis.——A girl beloved by Acontius. *Vid.* Acontius.——One of Cyrene's attendant nymphs. *Virg. G.* 4. v. 339.——A priestess of Juno at Argos. *Joh. Marsh. Can. Chron. Sec.* 9.

CYDIP'PUS, an historian of Mantinea. *Clem. Alex. Strom.* l. 1.

CYD'NA, a city of Macedonia. *Steph.*

CYD'NUS, a river of Cilicia, near Tarsus, in which Alexander the Great bathed when covered with sweat. This imprudent action almost proved fatal to the monarch. *Curt.* 3. c. 4.—*Justin.* 11. c. 8.

CY'DON, a friend of Turnus against Æneas. *Virg. Æn.* 10. v. 335.

CY'DON or CYDO'NIA, now Canea, a town in the western parts of Crete, built by a colony from Samus. It was supposed that Minos generally resided there. Hence *Cydoneus.* *Ovid. Met.* 8. v. 22.—*Virg. Æn.* 12. v. 858.—*Sil.* 2. v. 109.—*Liv.* 37. c. 60.—*Lucan.* 7. v. 229.

CYDO'NIA, a small island opposite Lesbus. *Plin.* 2 & 4.

CY'DRA, a city of the Byrsi. *Steph.*—*Strabo*, l. 17 calls it Cydriæ.

CYD'RARA or CYDRA'RA, a city of Phrygia. *Herodot.* 7. c. 30.

CYDRI'NE, a city of Armenia. *Steph.*

CYDROLA'US, a man who led a colony to Samus. *Diod.* 5.

CY'DRUS, a native of Cyzicus, slain by Pollux. *Flacc.* 3. v. 192.

CYG'NUS. *Vid.* Cycnus.

CYL'ABUS, a place near Argos. *Plut. in Pyrrh.*

CYLAN'DUS, a city of Caria. *Steph. ex. Hecatæo.*

CYLBIA'NI, mountains of Phrygia where the Cayster takes its rise. *Plin.* 5. c. 29.

CYL'ICES, a people among the Illyrians. There was in their country a monument in honour of Cadmus. *Athen.*

CYLIN'DUS, a son of Phryxus and Calliope.

CYLLAB'ARIS, a public place for exercises at Argos, where was a statue of Minerva. *Paus. in Cor.*

CYLLAB'ARUS, a favourite of the wife of Diomedes, &c.

CYL'LARUS, the most beautiful of all the Centaurs was passionately fond of Hylonome. He was killed at the marriage of Pirithous; and Hylonome, inconsolable for his loss, stabbed herself in despair with the dart which had caused his death. *Ovid.* 12. *Met.* 408.——A celebrated horse of Pollux, or of Castor, according to *Seneca.* *Virg. G.* 3. v. 90.

CYL'LEN, a son of Elatus. *Paus.* 8. c. 4.

CYLLE'NE, the mother of Lycaon by Pelasgus. *Apollod.* 3. c. 8.

CYLLE'NE, a naval station of Elis, in Peloponnesus. *Paus* 4. c. 23.——A mountain of Arcadia, with a small town on its declivity, which received its name from Cyllen. Mercury was born there; hence his surname of Cyllenius, an epithet which is indiscriminately applied to any thing which he invented, or over which he presided. *Lucan.* 1. v. 663.—*Horat.* ep. 13. v. 13.—*Paus.* 8. c. 17.—*Virg. Æn.* 8. v. 139.—*Ovid. Met.* 13. v. 146. *A. A.* 3. v. 147.

CYLLE'NIUS, a surname of Mercury, from his being born on mount Cyllene. *Ovid. Met.* 13. v. 146.

CYLLYR'II, certain slaves at Syracuse. *Herodot.* 7. c. 155.

CY'LON, an Athenian, who aspired to tyranny. *Herodot.* 5. c. 71.

CY'MA or CY'MÆ, the largest and most beautiful town of Æolia, called also Phriconis, and Phricontis, and Cumæ. *Vid.* Cumæ. *Liv.* 37. c. 11.—*Cic. Flacc.* 20.—*Herodot.* 1. c. 149.

CYMOD'OCE, CY'ME, or CY'MO, one of the Nereides. *Hesiod. Theog.* v. 255.—*Virg. G.* 4. v. 338.—*Homer. Il.* 18. v. 39.—*Stat.* 2. *Sylv.* 2. v. 20.

CYM'OLUS and CYMO'LUS, or CIMO'LUS, an island of the Cretan Sea, between Melus and Parus. *Ovid.* 7. *Met.* v. 463.

CYMOTH'OE, one of the Nereides, represented by *Virgil, Æn.* 1. v. 141, as assisting the Trojans with Triton after the storm which Æolus, at the request of Juno, had raised against the fleet. *Servius in loco.*

CYN'ARA, one of *Horace's* favourites. 4. *Od.* 1. v. 4.

CYNÆGI'RUS, an Athenian, celebrated for his extraordinary courage. He was son of Euphorion, and brother of the poet Æschylus. After the battle of Marathon, he pursued the fleeing Persians to their ships, and seized one of the vessels with his right hand, which was immediately cut off by the enemy. Upon this he seized the vessel with his left hand, and when he had lost that also, he still, undaunted, kept his hold with his teeth. *Herodot.* 6. c. 114.—*Justin.* 2. c. 9.

CYNÆ'THA, a city of Thrace. *Steph.*

CYNÆ'THIUM, a town of Arcadia founded by one of the companions of Æneas, or, according to others, by Cynæthus, son of Lycaon. *Dionys. Hal.*—*Strab.*—*Plin.* 4. c. 6.—*Steph.*

CYNAMOL'GI, a barbarous people of Æthiopia. *Strab.*—*Plin.* 6. c. 30.

CYNA'NE, a daughter of Philip king of Macedonia, who married Amyntas son of Perdiccas, by whom she had Eurydice. *Polyæn.* 8.

CYNA'PES, a river falling into the Euxine Sea. *Ovid.* 4. *Pont.* el. 10. v. 49.

CYN'ARA, an island of the Ægean Sea, now Zenara. *Plin.* 4. c. 12.

CYNAX'A. *Vid.* Cunaxa.

CYN'DON, a river of Peloponnesus. *Hesych.*

CY'NE, a city of Libya. *Steph.*

CYN'EAS. *Vid.* Cineas.

CYNE'SII or CYNE'TÆ, a nation described as situated on the remotest shores of Europe, towards the ocean. *Herodot.* 2. c. 33.

CYNE'THUS or CYNÆ'THUS, a Greek poet of Chius, who first publicly recited the verses of *Homer*, at Syracuse. *Meurs. de Archont.* 2. c. 1.

CYNETHUS'SA, a small island in the Ægæan Sea. *Plin.* 4. c. 12.

CYN'IA, a lake of Acarnania. *Strab.* 10.

CYN'ICI, a sect of philosophers founded by Antisthenes the Athenian. They received this name from their canine (κυνικὸς) propensity to criticise the lives and actions of men. They were remarkable for their contempt of riches, for the negligence of their dress, and the length of their beards. Diogenes was one of their sect. *Dio.* 6. c. 13.—*Cic.* 1 *Off.* 35 & 41.

CYNIS'CA, a daughter of Archidamus king of Sparta, who obtained the first prize in the chariot races at the Olympic games. *Paus.* 3. c. 8.

CYN'NA, a town near Heraclea. *Steph.*

CY'NO, a woman who preserved the life of Cyrus the elder. *Herodot.* 1. c. 110.

CYNOCEPH'ALÆ, a town of Thessaly, where the proconsul Quintius conquered Philip of Macedon, and put an end to the first Macedonian war, B.C. 197. *Liv.* 33. c. 7.

CYNOCEPH'ALI, a nation in India, who, according to some traditions, had the heads of dogs. *Plin.* 7. c. 2.

CYNONNE'SUS, an island of Libya. *Steph.*

CYNOPHON'TIS, a festival at Argos, observed during the dog-days. It received its name ἀπὸ τοῦ κύνας φόνειν, because they used to kill all the dogs which they met.

CYNOP'OLIS, a city of Ægypt, where Anubis was worshipped. *Steph.*

CYNOR'TAS, one of the ancient kings of Sparta, son of Amyclas and Diomede. *Paus.* 3. c. 1.—*Apollod.* 3.—*Tzetzes. in Lycoph.*

CYNOR'TION, a mountain of Peloponnesus. *Paus.* 2. c. 27.

CY'NOS, a town of Locris. *Livy.*—*Steph.*——A town in Thessaly, where Pyrrha, Deucalion's wife was buried. *Strab.* 1. 9.

CYNOSAR'GES, a surname of Hercules.——A place near Athens, appropriated to the public exercises of the Athenian youths. It was here also that the Cynic philosophers established their school. *Herodot.* 5 & 6.—*Liv.* 31. c. 24.—*Paus.* 1. c. 19.—*Hesych.*

CYNOSSE'MA, (α κυνὸς σῆμα), a promontory of the Thracian Chersonesus, where Hecuba was changed into a dog, and buried. *Ovid.* 13. *Met.* 569.

CYNOSU'RA, a nymph of mount Ida in Crete. She nursed Jupiter, who in gratitude for her attention changed her into a star which bears the same name. It is the same as the Ursa Minor. *Ovid.*

Fast. 3. v. 107.—*Hygin. P. A.* 2. c. 2.—*Sil.* 3. v. 665. The English form is Cyn'osure.

CYNOSU'RA, a promontory of Arcadia. *Steph.*——A promontory of Achaia. *Ptol.*——A promontory of Marathon towards Eubœa. *Hesych.*——A town of Arcadia. *Lactant.*

CYN'THIA, a beautiful woman, who was mistress to. *Propertius*, 1. el. 1, &c.—*Martial.* 14. v. 187. ——A surname of Diana, from mount Cynthus, where she was born.

CYN'THIUS, a surname of Apollo, from mount Cynthus.

CYN'THUS, a mountain of Delus, so high that it is said to overshadow the whole island. Apollo was surnamed Cynthius, and Diana Cynthia, as they were born on the mountain, which, on that account, was considered sacred to them. *Virg, G.* 3. v. 36. —*Ovid.* 6. *Met*, v. 304. *Fast.* 3. v. 346.

CYNU'RA, a city of Argolis. *Steph.*

CYNUREN'SES, a people of Arcadia. *Paus.* 8. c. 27.

CY'NUS, a naval station of the Opuntii on the Euripus. *Id.* 10. c. 1.

CYONE'SUS, an island in the Nile, not far from the greater Delta. *Ptol.*

CYPÆ'RA, a city of Thessaly. *Ptol.*

CYPÆ'THA, a city of Libya. *Steph.*

CYPARIS'SI or CYPARIS'SIA, a town of Peloponnesus, near Messenia. *Liv.* 32. c. 31.—*Plin.* 4. c. 5.

CYPARIS'SUS, a youth, son of Telephus of Cea, beloved by Apollo. He killed a favourite stag of Apollo, for which he was so sorry that he pined away, and was changed by the god into a cypress tree. *Virg. Æn.* 3. v. 680.—*Ovid. Met.* 10. v. 121.

CYPARIS'SUS, a town near Delphi. *Mela*, 2. c. 3.

CYP'ASIS, a city near the Hellespont. *Steph.*

CYPHAN'TA, a harbour of the Argolic bay, now Stilo. *Ptol.*

CYPH'ARA, a fortified place of Thessaly. *Liv.* 32. c. 13.

CYP'RIÆ, three barren islands near Cyprus. *Plin.* 5. c. 31.

CYPRIA'NUS, a native of Carthage, who, though born of heathen parents, became a convert to Christianity, and was at last raised to the dignity of bishop of his country. He wrote 81 letters, besides several treatises, *De Dei gratiâ*, *De virginum habitu*, &c., and his compositions are valuable for the information which he furnishes concerning the discipline of the ancient church, and for the soundness and purity of his theology. He died a martyr, Sept. 14, A.D. 258, after he had been a convert to Christianity twelve years, and ten a bishop. The best editions of Cyprian are that of Fell, fol. Oxon, 1682. and that reprinted Amst. 1700. *Sax. Onom.* 1. p. 368.—*Fabr. B. Lat.* 1. 4. c. 2, &c.

CY'PRIS, a name applied to Venus as the goddess of Cyprus. Her statue represented her, under this name, in a female habit, in the gait and beard of a man. *Macrob. Sat.* 3. c. 8.—*Festus de Verb. Sig.*

CY'PRUS, a daughter of Antony and Cleopatra, who married Agrippa.

CY'PRUS, a large island in the Mediteranean Sea, at the south of Cilicia, and at the west of Syria, about 150 miles long and 70 broad, said, according to Pliny to have been formerly joined to the continent near Syria. It was anciently called Acamantis, Amathusia, Aspelia, Cerastis, Colonia or Colinia, Macaria, and Spechia. It has been celebrated for giving birth to Venus, surnamed *Cypris*, who was the chief deity of the place, and to whose service many places and temples were consecrated. It was anciently divided into nine small kingdoms, and was for some time under the power of Ægypt, and afterwards of the Persians. The Greeks made themselves masters of it, and it was taken from them by the Romans. There were three celebrated temples there, two sacred to Venus and the other to Jupiter. In ancient times the people of Cyprus were much given to pleasure and dissipation. The chief cities were Paphus, Citium, Amathus, Soli, Salamis, Idalium, Lapithus, Arsinoe, &c. *Strab.* 15.—*Ptol.* 5. c. 14.—*Flor.* 3. c. 9.—*Justin.* 18. c. 5.—*Plin.* 12. c. 24. l. 33. c. 5. l. 36. c. 26.—*Mela*, 2. c. 7.

CYPSEL'IDÆ, the name of three princes, descendants of Cypselus, who reigned at Corinth during 75 years. Cypselus was succeeded by his son Periander, who left his kingdom, after a reign of 40 years to Cypselus the Second. *Paus.* 2. c. 4. l. 5. c. 17.

CYP'SELUS, a king of Arcadia, who married his daughter to Cresphontes, son of Aristomachus, to strengthen himself against the Heraclidæ. *Paus.* 4. c. 3.——A man of Corinth, son of Eetion, and father of Periander. He destroyed the Bacchiadæ, and seized upon the sovereign power, about 659 years B.C. He reigned 30 years, and was succeeded by his son. He was so called from κυψέλος, *a coffer*, in which he was concealed by his mother Labda. *Paus.* 5. c. 17.—*Cic. Tusc.* 5. c. 37.—*Herodot.* 1. c. 114. l. 5. c. 92, &c.—*Aristot. Polit.* ——A son of Periander, and grandson of Cypselus, was an idiot.——The father of Miltiades. *Herodot.* 6. c. 35.

CYPTA'SIA, a town of Galatia, now Carosa. *Ptol.*

CY'RA, an island in the Persian Gulph. *Steph.*

CYRAU'NIS, an island of Libya. *Herodot.* 4. c. 195..

CYRBIA'NA, a province of the Elymæans, in Asia: *Strab.* 16.

CY'RE, a fountain near Cyrene. *Steph. Callimach. Hymn. Apoll.*

CYRENA'ICA, a country of Africa, of which Cyrene was the capital. *Vid.* Cyrene.

CYRENA'ICI, a sect of philosophers who followed the doctrine of Aristippus. They were so called because they formerly resided at Cyrene. They placed their *summum bonum* in pleasure, and said that virtue ought to be commended because it gave pleasure. *Laert. in Arist.*—*Cic. de Nat*, 2. 3.

CYRE'NE, the daughter of the river Peneus, of whom Apollo became enamoured. He carried her to that part of Africa which is called Cyrenaica, where she brought forth Aristæus. She is called by some daughter of Hypseus king of the Lapithæ, and son of the Peneus. *Virg. G.* 4. v. 321.—*Justin.* 13. c. 7.—*Pindar, Pyth.* 9.

CYRE'NE, a celebrated city of Libya, to which Aristæus, who was the chief of the colonists settled there, gave his mother's name. Cyrene was situated in a beautiful plain, about eleven miles from the Mediterranean Sea, at the east of the Syrtes, and it became the capital of the country, which was called Pentapolis, on account of the five celebrated cities which it contained. It gave birth to many great men, among whom were Calimachus, Eratosthenes, Anniceris, Carneades, Aristippus, &c. The town of Cyrene was built by Battus, B.C. 630, and the kingdom was bequeathed to the Romans B.C. 97, by king Ptolemy Apion. *Herodot.* 3 & 4. —*Paus.* 10. c. 13.—*Strab.* 17.—*Mela*, 1. c. 8.—*Plin.* 5. c. 5.—*Tacit. A.* 3. c. 70.

CYRI'ADES, one of the 30 tyrants, who, by their ambitious and seditious conduct, harassed the Roman empire, in the reign of Gallienus. He died A.D. 259.

CYRIL'LUS, a bishop of Jerusalem, who died A.D. 386. Of his writings, composed in Greek, there remain 23 *catacheses*, and a letter to the emperor Constantine; the best edition of which is by Miller, fol. Oxon. 1703. *Sax. Onom.* 1. p. 403.—*Fabr. B. Gr.* 5. c. 13, &c.——A bishop of Alexandria, who, for the best part of his life was engaged in quarrels with his contemporaries about heretical opinions, in which he displayed great zeal, and often unchristian violence. He died A.D. 444. The best editions of his writings, which are mostly controversial, and written in Greek, is that of Paris, fol. 7. vols. 1638. *Sax. Onom.* 1. p. 482.—*Fabr. B. Gr.* The English form is Cyril.

CY'RIS, a son of Sol, king of the Hyrcani, assisted Perses against Æetes. *Val. Flacc. Argon.* 6. v. 79.

CYRIZOBOR'CA, a town of India. *Plin.* 6. c. 19.

CYRMIA'NÆ, a nation of Thrace. *Herodot.*

CYR'NABA, a river of Scythia. *Plin.* 6. c. 17.

CYR'NE, a place of Eubœa.

CYR'NUS, a charioteer in the games which Scipio exhibited in Africa, &c. *Ital.* 16. v. 342.——A man of Argos, who founded a city in Chersonesus *Diod.* 5.

CYR'NUS, a river that falls into the Caspian Sea. *Plut. in Pomp.*——An island on the coast of Liguria, the same in Greek, as Corsica; and called after Cyrnus, the son of Hercules. *Virg. Ecl.* 9. v. 30.—*Paus.* 10. c. 17.

CYROP'OLIS, a large city of Asia, called also Cyrechata. *Steph.*

CYRRÆ'I, a people of Æthiopia. *Claud de Nilo.*

CYR'RHADÆ, an Indian nation. *Arrian in Peripl.*

CYR'RHES, a people of Macedonia, near Pella. *Plin.* 4. c. 10.

CYRRHES'TICA, a country of Syria, at the east of Cilicia, of which the capital was called Cyrrhum or Cyrrhus. *Plin.* 5. c. 23.—*Cic. Att.* 5. ep. 13.

CYR'RHUS, or CY'RUS, now Korr, a river of Iberia in Asia, falling into the Caspian Sea.

CYRSI'LUS or CYR'SILUS, an Athenian stoned to death by his countrymen, because he advised them to receive the army of Xerxes, and to submit to the power of Persia. *Demosthen. de Coron.*—*Cic.* 3. *de Offic.* c. 11.

CYRTÆ'SIS, a people of Africa Propria. *Ptol.*

CYRTE'A, a town on the Red Sea. *Steph.*

CYRTI'ADÆ, a place of Africa in the tribe Acamantis. *Hesych.*

CYRTO'NES, a people of Bœotia. *Steph.*

CYR'TUS, an inland city of Ægypt. *Id.*

CY'RUS, a king of Persia, son of Cambyses and Mandane, daughter of Astyages, king of Media. His father was of an obscure family, and his marriage with Mandane had been consummated on account of the apprehensions of Astyages. *Vid.* Astyages. Cyrus was exposed as soon as born: but he was preserved by a shepherdess, who educated him as her own son. As he was playing with his equals in years, he was elected king in a certain diversion, and exercised his power with such an independence of spirit, that he ordered one of his companions to be severely whipped for disobedience. The father of the youth, who was a nobleman, complained to the king of the ill treatment which his son had received from an obscure shepherd's son. Astyages ordered Cyrus before him, and discovered that he was Mandane's son, from whom he had so much to apprehend. He treated him at first with great coldness, and afterwards with marked severity, but Cyrus, unable to bear his tyranny, escaped from his confinement, and began to levy troops to dethrone his grandfather. He was encouraged and secretly assisted by the ministers of Astyages, who were displeased with the king's oppression. He marched against him, and Astyages was defeated and taken prisoner, B.C. 559. After this victory, the empire of Media became tributary to the Persians. Cyrus afterwards subdued the eastern part of Asia, and made war against Crœsus, king of Lydia, whom he conquered B.C. 598. He next invaded the kingdom of Assyria, and took the city of Babylon, by drying the channels of the Euphrates, and marching his troops through the bed of the river, while the people were celebrating a grand festival. He afterwards marched against Tomyris, the queen of the Massagetæ, a Scythian nation, and was defeated in a bloody battle, B. C. 530. The victorious queen, who had lost her son in a previous encounter, was so incensed against Cyrus, that she cut off his head, and threw it into a vessel filled with human blood, exclaiming "*Satia te sanguine quem sitisti!*" Xenophon has written the life of Cyrus; but his history is not to be considered as perfectly authentic. In the character of Cyrus, he has delineated the character of a brave and virtuous prince, and often puts into his mouth many of the sayings of Socrates. The chronology of the historian is moreover often false; and Xenophon, in his narration, has given existence to persons whom no other historian ever mentioned. The *Cyropædia*, therefore, is not to be looked upon as an authentic history of Cyrus the Great, but we must regard it as a philosophical treatise, valuable for its morality, and the soundness of its precepts, and particularly as displaying in an elegant and fascinating style, the character which every good and virtuous prince ought to bear. *Diod.* 1.—*Herodot.* 1. c. 75, &c.—*Justin.* 1. c. 5 & 7.

CY'RUS the Younger, was the younger son of Darius Nothus, and the brother of Artaxerxes. He was sent by his father, at the age of sixteen, to assist the Lacedæmonians against Athens, either that he might enlarge his mind by observation and travelling, or acquire the military discipline of the Greeks. When Artaxerxes succeeded to the crown at the death of Nothus, Cyrus, who was of an aspiring soul, attempted to assassinate him, and seat himself on his father's throne. His design was discovered and frustrated, and he would have been punished with death, had not his mother Parysatis, by her tears and entreaties, saved him from the hands of the executioner. This circumstance did not operate as a check on the ambitious views of Cyrus; but, when appointed governor over Lydia and the sea-coasts, he there secretly fomented rebellion, and levied troops against his sovereign under various pretences. When fully prepared, he threw off the mask, and took the field with an army of 100,000 barbarians, and 13,000 Greeks under the command of Clearchus. Artaxerxes met him with 900,000 men near Cunaxa. The battle was long and bloody, and Cyrus might have obtained the victory, had not his uncommon rashness proved his ruin. It is said that the two royal brothers met in person, and fought with the most inveterate fury, and their engagement unfortunately ended in the death of Cyrus, 401 years B.C., and thus prevented the final success and elevation to the throne of a prince, who, for his bravery in the field, his prudence in the cabinet, and a thousand amiable qualities in his private character, seemed to promise a new era of national glory and public prosperity to the Persian monarchy. Artaxerxes was so desirous that it should be universally reported that his brother had fallen by his hand, that he put to death two of his subjects for boasting that they had killed Cyrus. The Greeks, who were engaged in the expedition, obtained immortal glory in the battle; and after the death of Cyrus, they remained victorious in the field, though surrounded by enemies ten times more numerous than themselves. They were not, however. discouraged, though at a great distance from their country, and watched on every side by a powerful and harassing foe. They unanimously united in the election of commanders, and traversed all Asia, in spite of the continual attacks of the Persians; and nothing is more truly celebrated in ancent history than the bold and successful retreat of the ten thousand. The extent of their march, from Sardis to Cotyora, has been calculated at 1155 parasangs or leagues, performed in the space of thirteen months and a half, including the time which was devoted to take rest and refreshment. This retreat has been celebrated by the pen of Xenophon, who was one of the leaders, and among the personal friends and supporters of Cyrus. It is said, that in the letter which he wrote to Lacedæmon, to solicit auxiliaries, Cyrus boasted of his philosophy, his royal blood, and his ability to drink more wine than his brother, without being intoxicated; a strange recommendation with a nation which esteemed temperance as the greatest of virtues. *Plut. in Artax.*—*Diod.* 14—*Justin.* 5. c. 11.——A rival of *Horace*, in the affections of one of his mistresses. 1. *Od.* 17. v. 24.——A poet of Panepolis in the age of Theodosius.——An architect, whence *Cyrea opera* applied to the edifices, &c. which he raised. *Cic. Att.* 2. ep. 3. 1. 4. ep. 10.

CY'RUS, a river of Armenia, falling into the western parts of the Caspian Sea, and now called Kur.

CY'RUS or CYROP'OLIS, a city of Syria, built by the Jews in honour of Cyrus the Great, whose humanity in relieving them from their captivity they wished thus to commemorate. *Procop.*——A town of Media, on the southern borders of the Caspian Sea. *Ptol.*

CY'SA, a village of Carmania. *Arrian.*

CYS'TEN, a town of Upper Æthiopia. *Plin.* 6. c. 29.

CY'TÆ, a town of Colchis, on the shores of the Euxine Sea, well known for the poisonous herb which it produced, and for the birth of Medea. *Flacc.* 6. v. 693.—*Propert.* 2. el. 1. v. 73.

CYTÆ'IS, a surname of Medea, from her being an inhabitant of Cyta. *Propert.* 2. el. 4. v. 7.

CYTÆ'UM, a city of Crete. *Ptol.*

CYT'AIS, a region of Carmania. *Arrian.*

CYTEO'RUM, *Ptol.*; COTYO'RUM, *Plin.*; a city of Cappadocia, now Cocine.

CYTHE'RA, now Cerigo, an island on the coast of Laconia. It was particularly sacred to Venus, who was thence surnamed Cytheræa, and who rose as some authors suppose, from the sea, near its coasts. It was for some time under the power of the Argives, but always considered of the highest importance to maritime powers, as from its neighbourhood to the Peloponnesian coast it could harass an enemy by perpetual alarms; and from that circumstance Xerxes, on his invasion of Greece, was advised by Demaratus to seize it and convert it into a harbour for the reception of his fleets. The Phœnicians had built there a famous temple to Venus. *Virg. Æn.* 1. v. 262. l. 10. v. 5.—*Paus.* 3. c. 33.—*Ovid. Met.* 4. v. 288. l. 15. v. 386. *Fast.* 4. v. 15.—*Herodot.* 1. c. 29. l. 7. c. 235. —*Diog. Laert.* 1. c. 71.—*Strab.* 2.—*Mela*, 2. c. 7.

CYTHERÆ'A, a surname of Venus.

CYTHE'RUS or CYTHE'RIS, a courtezan in great favour with Antony. According to Servius, she is the same as Lycoris, the person beloved by Gallus, and celebrated by Virgil; but the supposition is apparently false. As the freedwoman of Volumnius Eutrapelus, Cytheris, was called Volumnia. *Virg. Ecl.* 10. v. 2. & *Servius in loco.* —*Cic. ad Att.* 10. ep. 10 & 16. *Phil.* 2, c. 24 & 25. *Fam.* 9. ep. 26.

CYTHE'RON. *Vid.* Cithæron.

CYTHE'RUM, a place of Attica, in the tribe Pandionis. *Strab.*—*Steph.*—*Diod. Sic.* 14.

CYTHE'RIUS or CYTHE'RUS, a river of Elis. *Paus.* 6. c. 22.

CYTHI'NA, a city of Thessaly. *Steph.*

CYTH'NUS, now Thermia, an island in the Ægæan Sea, east of Attica, famous for its cheese. It has been called Ophiusa and Dryopis. *Ovid. Met.* 5. v. 252

CYTIN'IUM, one of the four cities called Tetrapolis, in Doris, in Asia Minor. *Strab.* 9.—*Thucyd.* 1. c. 107.

CYTIS, an island of Arabia. *Plin.* 6. c. 29.

CYTISSO'RUS, a son of Phryxus, &c. *Herodot.* 7. c. 197.

CYTO'RUS, now Kudros, a mountain and town of Galatia, built by Cytorus, son of Phryxus, and abounding in box wood. *Catull.* 4. v. 13.—*Ovid. Met.* 4. v. 311.—*Strab.* 11.—*Virg. G.* 2. v. 437.

CYT'NI, a people of Pannonia. *Ptol.*

CYTO'NIUM, a city between Mysia and Lydia. *Steph.*

CYTO'RUM, a city of Paphlagonia, now Castelle. *Ptol.*

CYZ'ICUM or CYZ'ICUS, an island of the Propontis, about 530 stadia in circumference, with a town called Cyzicus. Alexander the Great joined it to the continent by two bridges, and from that time it was called a peninsula. It had two capacious harbours called Panormus and Chytus, the first natural and the other artificial. It became afterwards, from its advantageous situation one of the most considerable cities of Asia. It was besieged by Mithridates, and relieved by Lucullus. *Flor.* 3. c. 5.—*Plin.* 5 c. 32.—*Diod.* 18.

CYZ'ICUS, a son of Œneus and Stilba, who reigned in Cyzicus, and hospitably received the Argonauts in their expedition against Colchis. After their departure from the court of Cyzicus, they were driven back in the night, by a storm, upon the coast; and the inhabitants seeing such an unexpected number of men, furiously attacked them, supposing them to be the Pelasgi, their ancient enemies. In this nocturnal engagement many were killed on both sides, and Cyzicus perished by the hand of Jason himself, who honoured his remains with a splendid funeral, and raised a stately monument over his grave. *Apollod.* 1. c. 9.—*Flacc.*—*Apollon.*—*Orpheus.*

CYZ'ICUS, the chief town of the island of Cyzicum, built where the island is joined by the bridges to the continent. The town is situate partly on a mountain, and partly in a plain. The Argonauts built a temple to Cybele in the neighbourhood. It derived its name from Cyzicus, who was killed there by Jason. The Athenians, assisted by Pharnabazus, defeated, near this place, their enemies of Lacedæmon, B.C. 410. *Flor.* 3. c. 5, &c.—*Strab.*—*Apollon.* 1.—*Propert.* 3. el. 22.—*Flacc.* 2. v. 636.

D.

DA'Æ, DA'HÆ, or DA'I, now the Dahistan, a people of Scythia, who dwelt on the borders of the Caspian Sea. *Sil.* 13. v. 764.—*Lucan.* 7. v. 429.—*Virg. Æn.* 1. v. 728.

DABANEG'ARIS, a region of Arabia. *Plin.*

DA'CI or DA'CÆ, a warlike nation of Germany, beyond the Danube, whose country, called Dacia, was conquered by the Romans under Trajan after a desperate resistance during a war of 15 years, A.D. 103. The emperor joined the country to Mœsia, by erecting a magnificent bridge across the Danube, considered as the best of his works, which, however, his successor Adrian, demolished. Dacia, extending between the river Tibiscus and Hierasus, and bounded on the north by the Carpathian mountains, now forms the modern countries of Wallachia, Transylvania, and Moldavia. *Lucan.* 2. v. 53.—*Dio.* 58. c. 13.

DA'CICUS, a surname assumed by Domitian on his pretended victory over the Dacians. *Juv.* 6. v. 204.

DAC'TYLI, a name given to the priests of Cybele which some derive from δάκτυλος, *finger*, because they were ten, the same number as the fingers of the hand. They were successively called Curetes, Corybantes, and Idæi; it is, however, to be observed that neither *Homer* nor *Hesiod* speak of them, under the name of Dactyli. Strabo and Pausanias have made mention of five of them, and have attributed to them the discovery of iron mines, and the different operations of working that metal. *Strab.* 10.—*Paus*, 1. c. 8, l. 5. c. 7.

DAC'TYLIS, a famous sculptor. *Plin.* 36. c. 3.

DA'DA, a city of Pisidia, called Adada by *Ptolemy;* Adadata by *Strabo.*

DADASTA'NA, a city of Bithynia. *Ptol.*

DA'DES, a promontory of Cyprus. *Id.*

DAD'ICÆ, a people of Asiatic Scythia. *Herodot.* 3. c. 91.

DADU'CHUS, a minister of Ceres, who, at the celebration of the Eleusinian mysteries, carried a torch, whence the name (δᾳδοῦχος, *facem gestans*).

DÆD'ALA, a mountain and city of Lycia, where Dædalus was buried, according to *Pliny*, 5. c. 27 ——A city of Rhodes.——A city of India.——A city of Crete. *Ptol.*—*Steph.*

DÆD'ALA, a name given to Circe, from her being cunning, (δαιδαλος,) and like Dædalus, well skilled in all manner of deceit and artifice. *Virg. Æn.* 7. v. 282.

DÆD'ALA, the name of two festivals in Bœotia. One of these was observed at Alalcomenos, by the Platæans, in a large grove, where they exposed pieces of boiled flesh, and carefully observed whither the crows that came to prey upon them directed their flight. All the trees, upon which any of these birds alighted, were immediately cut down, and with them statues were made, called Dædala, in honour of Dædalus. The other festival was of a more solemn kind. It was celebrated every 60 years, by all the cities in Bœotia, as a compensation for the intermission of the smaller festivals, for that number of years, during the exile of the Platæans. Fourteen of the statues called Dædala, were distributed by lot among the Platæans, Lebadæans, Coroneans, Orchomenians, Thespians, Thebans, Tanagræans, and Chæroneans, because they had effected a reconciliation among the Platæans, and caused them to be recalled from exile, about the time that Thebes was restored by Cassander, the son of Antipater. During this festival, a woman in the habit of a bridemaid accompanied a statue, which was dressed in female garments to the banks of the Eurotas. This procession was attended to the top of Mount Cithæron, by many of the Bœotians. Here an altar of square pieces of wood, cemented together like stones, was erected, and upon it were thrown large quantities of combustible materials. Afterwards a bull was sacrificed to Jupiter, and an ox or heifer to Juno, by every one of the cities of Bœotia, and by the most opulent persons who attended the ceremony. The poorest citizens offered small cattle; and all these oblations, together with the Dædala, were then thrown into the common heap, and set on fire, and totally reduced to ashes. These festivals originated from this circumstance: when Juno, after a quarrel with Jupiter, had retired to Eubœa, and refused to be reconciled to him, the god, anxious for her return, went to consult Cithæron, king of Platæa, to find some effectual measure to overcome her obstinacy. Cithæron advised him to dress a statue in woman's apparel, and carry it in a chariot, and publicly report that it was Platæa, the daughter of Asopus whom he was going to marry. The advice was followed, and Juno, informed of her husband's intended marriage, repaired in haste to meet the chariot, and was easily reconciled to him, when she discovered the artful measures which he had made use of to effect a re-union. *Paus. & Plut.*

DÆDALE'A, a city of Italy, founded by Dædalus. *Steph.*

DÆDAL'IDE, a village of the tribe Cecropis. *Id.*

DÆDA'LION, a son of Lucifer, brother to Ceyx, and father of Philonis. He was so afflicted at the death of Philonis, whom Diana had put to death, that he threw himself down from the top of mount Parnassus and was immediately changed into a falcon by Apollo. *Ovid. Met.* 11. v. 295.

DÆD'ALUS, an Athenian, descended from Erechtheus, king of Athens. He was the most ingenious artist of his age, and to him mankind are indebted for the invention of the wedge, the axe, the wimble, the level, and many other mechanical instruments, and also for the sails of ships. He made statues, which, by moving of themselves, seemed to be endowed with life. When Talus, his sister's son, promised to rival him in the ingenuity of his inventions, he, moved with envy, threw him down from a window and killed him. After the murder of this youth, Dædalus, with his son Icarus, fled from Athens to Crete, where Minos, king of the country, gave him a cordial reception Dædalus made a famous labyrinth for Minos, and, according to mythologists, he assisted Pasiphae, the queen, to gratify her unnatural passion. For this action Dædalus incurred the displeasure of Minos, who ordered him to be confined in the labyrinth which he had constructed. Here he made himself wings with feathers and wax, and carefully fitted them to his body, and to that of his son, who was the companion of his confinement. The father and the son then boldly took their flight from Crete; but the heat of the sun melted the wax on the wings of Icarus, who soared too high, and he fell into that part of the ocean, which from him has been called the Icarian Sea. The father alighted at Cumæ, where he built a temple to Apollo, and thence directed his course to Sicily, where he was kindly received by Cocalus, who reigned over that part of the country. He left many monuments of his ingenuity in Sicily, which still existed in the age of Diodorus Siculus. It is said that he was dispatched by Cocalus, who was afraid of the power of Minos, who had declared war against him, because he had given an asylum to Dædalus. The flight of Dædalus from Crete, with wings, is explained by observing that he was the inventor of sails, which in his age might pass at a distance for wings. *Paus.* 1. c. 21. l. 7. c. 4. l. 9. c. 40.—*Plat. in Memn.*—*Aristot. in Pol.* 1.—*Plin.* 7. c. 56. l. 36. c. 3.—*Tzetzes, Ch.* 1. c. 19. *Ch.* 9. c. 394.—*Sidon.* 4. ep. 3.—*Diod.* 4.—*Palæphat. de Inc.* 2 & 13.—*Vossius de Inst. Orat.* 2.—*Diod.* 4.—*Ovid. Met.* 8. fab. 3. *Heroid.* 4. *De Art. Am.* 2. *Trist.* 3. el. 4.—*Hygin.* fab. 40. 244, &c.—*Virg. Æn.* 6. v. 14, *& Servius loco.*—*Apollod.* 3. c. 1, &c. —*Herodot.* 7. c. 170.

DÆD'ALUS, a statuary of Sicyon, son of Patroclus.

DÆD'ALUS, a statuary of Bithynia. *Paus.* 7. c. 14.—*Arrian.*

DÆ'MON, a kind of spirit which, as the ancients supposed, presided over the actions of mankind, gave them private counsels, and carefully watched over their most secret intentions. Some of the ancient philosophers maintained that every man had two of these accompanying dæmons; the one bad, and the other good. These dæmons had the power of changing themselves into whatever form they pleased. At the moment of death, the dæmon delivered up to judgment the person with whose care he had been entrusted; and according to the evidence which he delivered, sentence was passed upon the body. The dæmon of Socrates is famous in history. That great philosopher asserted, that the kind genius informed him when any of his friends were going to engage in some unfortunate enterprize, and stopped him from the commission of all crimes and impiety. These genii, or dæmons, though at first reckoned only as the subordinate ministers of the superior deities, at length received divine honour, so that we find altars and statues erected to a *Genio loci, Genio. Augusti, Junonibus*, &c. *Cic. Tusc.* 1. *De Div.* 1. c. 54.—*Plut. & Apul. de Gen. Socr.*—*Plotin. in Enn.* 8. c. 3.

DÆ'TAS, father of Machereus, who slew Pyrrhus. *Pind. Schol.*

DÆ'TOR, a Trojan mentioned by *Homer. Il.*

DAGASI'RA, a place of Carmania. *Arrian.*

DAGO'NIA, a town of Armenia Minor. *Ptol.*

DA'GRÆ, a town of Tyanitis, in Cappadocia. *Id.*

DAGU'SA, a city of Armenia Minor. *Id.*—*Plin.* 5. c. 32.

DA'HÆ. *Vid.* Daæ.

DA'I, a nation of Persia, who were all shepherds. *Herodot.* 1. c. 125.

DA'ICLES, a victor at Olympia, B.C. 753.

DA'IDIS, a solemnity observed by the Greeks. It lasted three days. The first was in commemoration of Latona's labour; the second in memory of Apollo's birth; and the third in honour of the marriage of Podalirius, and the mother of Alexander. Torches were always carried at the celebration; whence the name (ἀ δαΐς *fax.*)

DAIM'ACHUS, a master of horse at Syracuse, &c. *Polyæn.* 1.——A king of India, who wrote a history of his country. *Strab.* 1.—*Voss. de Hist. Gr.* l. 1. c. 12.

DAIM'ENES, a general of the Achæans. *Paus.* 7. c. 6.——An officer exposed on a cross, by Dionysius of Syracuse. *Diod.* 44.

DA'IPHRON, a son of Ægyptus, killed by his wife, &c. *Apollod.* 2. c. 1.

DAIP'PUS, a statuary. *Paus.*

DAI'RA, one of the Oceanides, mother of Eleusis by Mercury. *Paus.* 1. c. 38.

DALAN'DA, a city of Armenia Minor. *Ptol.*

DAL'ASIS, a region of Cilicia. *Id.*

DAL'DIS, a town of Lydia. *Suidas.*

DA'LE, a town of Teuthrania. *Plin.* 5. c. 30.

DA'LION or DAL'LON, a writer who was also a physician. *Plin.* 6. c. 30, &c.—*Voss. de Hist. Gr.* l. 3. p. 350.

DALMA'TIA, a part of Illyricum, at the east of the Adriatic Sea, near Liburnia on the west, the inhabitants of which, called Dalmatæ, were conquered by Metellus, B.C. 118. They chiefly lived upon plunder, and from their warlike and rebellious spirit were troublesome to the Roman emperors. They wore a peculiar garment called Dalmatica, afterwards introduced at Rome. Their chief town was called Salona, afterwards famous as the residence of the emperor Diocletian after his resignation of the purple. *Horat.* 2. od. 1. v. 16.—*Lamprid. in Commod.* 8.—*Strab.* 7.—*Ptol.* 2.

DALMA'TIUS, one of the Cæsars, in the age of Constantine, who died A.D. 337.

DAL'MIUM, one of the chief towns of Dalmatia. *Strab.* 7. Also Dalmin'ium and Delmin'ium.

DALOME'NA, a region of Assyria. *Strab.*

DA'MA, a town of Arabia Felix. *Ptol.*

DAMAGE'TUS, a man of Rhodes, who enquired of the oracle what wife he ought to marry? when he received for answer the daughter of the bravest of the Greeks. He applied to Aristomenes and obtained his daughter in marriage, B.C. 670. *Paus.* 4. c. 24.

DAM'ALIS, a courtezan at Rome, in the age of *Horace.* 1. od. 36. v. 13.

DAMA'NIA, a city of the Hedetani in Spain. *Ptol.*

DA'MAS, a Syracusan in the interest of Agathocles. *Diod.* 19.—*Voss. de Hist. Gr.* 3. p. 350.

DAMASCE'NE, a part of Syria near mount Libanus, of which Damascus was the capital.

DAMASCE'NUS JOH. *Vid.* Johannes.

DAMAS'CIUS, a stoic of Damascus, who wrote a philosophical history, the life of his master Isidorus, and four books on extraordinary events, in the age of Justinian. His works, which are now lost, were greatly esteemed according to *Photius. Bibl. cod.* 130.—*Suidas.*

DAMAS'CUS, a rich and ancient city of Damascene situate at the east of Tyre in Syria, where Demetrius Nicanor was defeated by Alexander Zebina. It is the modern Damas, or Sham. *Lucan.* 3. v. 215.—*Justin.* 36. c. 2.—*Mela*, 1. c. 11.

DAMA'SIA, a town of ancient Germany, called also Augusta, now Ausburg, in Swabia, on the Leck.

DAMA'SIAS, a magistrate at Athens. *Dion. Hal.* l. 3.

DAMASICH'THON, a king of Thebes. *Paus.* 9. c. 5.

DAMASIP'PUS, a captain in Philip's army.——A senator who accompanied Juba when he entered Utica in triumph. *Cæs. Bell. C.* 2.

DAMASIP'PUS L. JUN. BRU'TUS, a prætor at Rome, who favoured the party of Marius, and cruelly put to death a number of senators because they were friendly to Sylla's cause. He was slain afterwards by order of Sylla. *Sall. Cat.* 51.—*Liv.* 86.—*Cic. Fam.* 9. ep. 21.—*Appian. B. C.*1.—*Paterc.* 2. c. 22.

DAMASIP'PUS, a man, who, after he had spent all his patrimony, maintained himself by acting on the stage. *Juv.* 3. v. 185.——A dealer in old seals and curious vessels, who, after losing his all in unfortunate schemes in commerce, assumed the name and habit of a stoic philosopher. *Horat.* 2. sat. 3.——One of Niobe's sons.

DAMASIS'TRATUS, a king of Platæa, who buried Laius. *Apollod.* 3. c. 5.

DAMASITHY'NUS or **DAMASITH'YNUS**, a son of Candaules, general in the army of Xerxes. *Herodot.* 7. c. 98.——A king of Calyndæ, in Lycia, sunk in his ship by Artemisia. *Id.* 8. c. 87.

DAMAS'TES, a man of Sigæum, disciple of Hellanicus, about the age of Herodotus, &c. *Dionys.*—*Strab.* 14.—*Val. Max.* 8. c. 13.——A famous robber. *Vid.* Procrustes.

DAMAS'TOR, a Trojan chief, killed by Patroclus in the siege of Troy. *Homer Il.* 16. v. 416,

DAM'ASUS, a Spaniard, who distinguished himself at Rome, by writing hymns and other poems in Latin verse, and also other works in prose. He was so much esteemed that he was raised to the highest dignities in the church, and died at the advanced age of 80, in the time of the Emperor Theodosius. *Sax. Onom.* 1. p. 423.—*Voss. de Hist. Lat.* c. 8. p. 187, &c.

DA'MIA, a surname of Cybele.——A woman in whose honour the Epidaurians raised a statue. *Herodot.* 5. c. 82.

DA'MEAS, an eminent statuary of Clitor in Arcadia, in the age of Lysander. After the ruin of Athens by the Lacedæmonians, the conquerors made in the temple of Delphi an offering of nine beautiful statues, three of which, those of Diana, Neptune, and Lysander, were sculptured by Damias. They were still to be seen at Delphi in the age of Pausanias. *Paus.* 10. c. 9.—*Plin.* 34. c. 8.

DAMIP'PUS, a Spartan taken by Marcellus as he sailed out of the port of Syracuse. He discovered to the enemy that a certain part of the city was negligently guarded, and in consequence of this discovery Syracuse was taken by the Roman army. *Polyæn.* 8.

DA'MIS, a man who disputed with Aristodemus for the right of reigning over the Messenians. *Paus.* 4. c. 10.

DA'MIUM, a festival at Rome in honour of Damia or Cybele. It was celebrated on the first of May. *Festus. de Verb. Sig.*

DAM'NÆ, a nation of the Seræ; their chief city was Damna. *Ptol.*

DAMNANITA'NI. a people of Hispania Tarraconensis. *Plin.*

DAM'NIA, a region of Arabia Felix. *Id*,

DAM'NII, a people at the north of Britain, now Westmoreland. *Ptol.*

DAMNO'NII, a people of Britain, supposed to have inhabited the counties of Devon and Cornwall. *Ptol.*—*Camden.*

DAM'NORIX or **DAMNO'RIX**, a celebrated Gaul, in the interest of Julius Cæsar, &c.

DA'MO, a daughter of Pythagoras, who, by order of her father, devoted herself to perpetual celibacy, and induced others to follow her example. Pythagoras at his death, entrusted her with all the secrets of his philosophy, and gave her the unlimited care of his compositions, under the promise that she never would part with them. She faithfully obeyed her father's injunctions; and, though in extreme poverty, she refused to obtain money by the violation of her solemn promise. *Laert. in Pythag.*

DAM'OCLES, one of the flatterers of Dionysius the elder, of Sicily. When he admired the tyrant's wealth, and pronounced him the happiest man on earth, Dionysius prevailed upon him to undertake for a while the charge of royalty, and be convinced of the felicity which a sovereign enjoyed. Damocles ascended the throne, but while he gazed upon the wealth and splendour that surrounded him, he perceived a sword hanging over his head by a horse hair. This so terrified him that all his imaginary felicity vanished at once, and he begged Dionysius to semove him from a situation which exposed his life to such dangers. *Cic. in Tusc.* 5. c. 21.—*Hor.* 3. od. 1. v. 17.

DAMOC'RITA, a Spartan matron, wife of Alcippus who severely punished her enemies who had banished her husband, &c. *Plut. in Parall.* c. 5.

DAMOC'RITUS, a timid general of the Achæans, &c. *Paus.* 7. c. 13.——A Greek writer, who composed two treatises, one upon the art of drawing up an army in battle array, and the other concerning the Jews, in which he asserts that they worshipped the head of an ass, and yearly made a sacrifice of a pilgrim. The age in which he lived is not known. *Voss. de Hist. Gr.* 1. 3. p. 350.——A man who wrote a poetical treatise upon medicine. *Galen.*—*Plin.* 14. c. 2, &c.

DA'MON, a victor at Olympia, in the 102d Olympiad. *Paus.* 4. c. 27.——A poet and musician at Athens, intimate with Pericles, and distinguished for his knowledge of government and fondness for discipline. He was banished for his intrigues about 430 years B.C. *C. Nep.* 15. c. 2.——*Plut. in Pericl.*——A Pythagorean philosopher, very intimate with Pythias. When he had been condemned to death by Dionysius of Sicily, he obtained from the tyrant leave to go and settle his domestic affairs, on promise of returning at a stated hour to the place of execution. Pythias pledged himself to undergo the punishment which was to be inflicted on Damon, should he not return at the proper time, and he, consequently, delivered himself into the hands of the tyrant. Damon returned at the appointed moment, and Dionysius was so struck with the fidelity of the two friends, that he nobly remitted the punishment, and entreated them to permit him to share their friendship, and enjoy their confidence. *Val. Max.* 4. c. 7.—*Cic. Off.* 3. c. 10.——A man of Cheronæa, surnamed Peripoltas, of severe manners, but of an heroic mind. He was grossly insulted by a Roman officer in his native town, and he, accompanied by fifteen of his countrymen, revenged the affront by assassinating his enemy. The authors of this murder remained unknown, as they had all besmeared their faces to prevent discovery; but when they were condemned to death by the magistrates who wished to give the Romans satisfaction, they rose against their persecutors, and after putting to death the judges, retired from the town. Damon was afterwards invited to return to Cheronæa on pretence of forgiveness, and he was murdered in a bath, on his arrival, by his perfidious countrymen. *Plut. in Cim.*——A Cyrenean, who wrote a history of philosophy. *Laert.*—*Plin.* 7. c. 2.—*Voss. de H. Gr.* 3. p. 351.

DAMOPHAN'TUS, a general of Elis, in the age of Philopœmen. *Plut. in Phil.*

DAMOPH'ILA, a poetess of Lesbus, wife of Pamphilus. She was intimate with Sappho, and not only wrote hymns in honor of Diana and of the gods, but opened a school, where the younger persons of her sex were taught music and poetry. *Philostr. in Apol.*

DAMOPH'ILUS, an historian. *Diod.*——A Rhodian general engaged against the fleet of Demetrius. *Diod.* 20. —— A Greek painter. *Plin.* 35. c. 12.

DAM'OPHON, a sculptor of Messenia. *Paus*, 7. c. 23.

DAMOS'TRATUS, a philosopher who wrote a treatise concerning fishes. *Ælian V.H.* 13. c. 21.

DAMOX'ENUS, a comic writer of Athens. *Athen.* 3.——A boxer of Syracuse, banished for killing his adversary. *Paus.* 8. c. 40.

DAMYR'IAS, a river of Sicily. *Plut in Timol.*

DA'NA, a town of Taprobane, sacred to the Moon. *Ptol.*——A large town of Cappadocia. *Xenoph* 1. *de Exped. Cyri.*

DAN'ABA, a city of Palmyrene. *Ptol.*

DAN'ACE, a name given to the piece of money the ancients supposed Charon demanded of the dead to convey them over the Styx. *Suidas.*

DAN'AE, the daughter of Acrisius, king of Argos, by Eurydice. She was confined in a brazen tower by her father, who had been informed by an oracle, that his daughter's son would put him to death. His endeavours to prevent Danae from becoming a mother proved, however, fruitless; and Jupiter, who was enamoured of her, introduced himself to her bed by changing himself into a golden shower. Danae brought forth a son, with whom she was exposed on the sea by her father. The wind drove the bark which carried her to the coast of the island of Seriphus, where she was saved by some fishermen, and carried to Polydectes, king of the place, whose brother, Dictys, educated the child called Perseus, and tenderly treated the mother, with whom Polydictes fell in love. Perseus, after his expedition against the Gorgons, retired to Argos with Danae, to the house of Acrisius, whom he inadvertently killed. Some suppose that it was Prœtus the brother of Acrisius, who introduced himself to Danae in the brazen tower; and instead of a golden shower, it was maintained that the keepers of Danae were bribed by the gold of her seducer. Virgil mentions that Danae came to Italy with some fugitives of Argos, and that she founded a city called Ardea. *Ovid, Met.* 4. v. 611. *Art. Am.* 3. v. 415. *Amor.* 2. el. 19. v. 27.—*Horat.* 3. od. 16.—*Prop.* 2. el. 31.—*Mart.* 14. ep. 176.—*Hom. Il.* 14. v. 319.—*Terent. in Eun.* act. 3. sc. 5.—*Apollod.* 2. c. 2 & 4.—*Stat. Theb.* 1. v. 255.—*Virg. Æn.* 7. v. 410.——A daughter of Leontium, mistress to Sophron, governor of Ephesus. The fidelity of her attachment proved at last fatal to her: she apprised Sophron that Laodices conspired against his life, and whilst he escaped to Corinth, she was seized by the successful traitor and thrown down a precipice. *Phylarch. apud Athen.* 13.——A daughter of Danaus, to whom Neptune offered violence.

DAN'AI, a name given to the people of Argos, and promiscuously to all the Greeks, from Danaus, one of their kings. *Virg, & Ovid. passim.*

DANA'IDES, the fifty daughters of Danaus, king of Argos. When their uncle Ægyptus came from Ægypt into Greece with his fifty sons, they were promised in marriage to their cousins; but before the celebration of their nuptials, Danaus, who had been informed by an oracle that he was to be killed by the hands of one of his sons-in-law, made his daughters solemnly promise that they would destroy their husbands. They were provided with daggers by their father, and all, except Hypermnestra, stained their hands with the blood of their cousins, the first night of their nuptials, and as a a pledge of their obedience to their father's injunctions, they each presented him with a head of a murdered son of Ægyptus. The sisters were purified of this murder by Mercury and Minerva, by order of Jupiter; but according to the more received opinion, they were condemned to severe punishment in the infernal regions, and were compelled to fill with water a vessel full of holes, so that the water ran out as soon as poured into it, and therefore their labour proved infinite, and their punishment eternal. The names of the Danaides and of their husbands, were as follows, according to Apollodorus: Amymone married Enceladus; Automate, Busiris; Agave, Lycus; Scea, Dayphron; Hippodamia, Ister; Rhodia, Chalcedon; Calyce, another Lynceus; Gorgophone, Proteus; Cleopatra, Agenor; Asteria, Chætus; Glauce, Aleis; Hippodamia, Diacorytes; Hippomedusa, Alcmenon; Gorge, Hippothous; Iphimedusa, Euchenor; Rhode, Hippolitus; Pirea, Agoptolemus; Cercestes, Dorion; Pharte, Eurydamas; Mnestra, Ægius; Evippe, Arigius; Anaxibia, Archelaus; Nelo, Melachus; Clite, Clitus; Stenele, Stenelus; Chrysippe, Chrysippus; Antonoe, Eurylochus; Theane, Phantes; Electra, Peristenes; Eurydice, Dryas; Glaucippe, Potamon; Autholea, Cisseus; Cleodora, Lixus; Evippe, Imbrus; Erata, Bromius; Stygne, Polyctor; Bryce, Chthonius; Actea, Periphas; Podarce, Œneus; Dioxippe, Ægyptus; Adyte, Menalces; Ocipete, Lampus; Pilarge, Idmon; Hippodice, Idas; Adiante, Diaphron; Callidia, Pandion; Œme, Arbelus; Celena, Hixibius; Hyperia, Hippocoristes. The heads of the sons of Ægyptus were buried at Argos; but their bodies were left at Lerna, where the murder had been committed. *Apollod.* 2. c. 1.—*Horat.* 3. od. 11. *Phlegon. Tral. Mer.* 31.—*Tzetzes, Chil.* 7. c. 136.—*Strab.* 8.—*Paus.* 2. c. 16.—*Hygin.* fab. 168, &c. [There is a statue of one of the Danaides, holding the perforated vessel in her hand, in the Museum of the Vatican]

DAN'ALA, a city of Galatia. *Strab.* l. 12.

DAN'APRIS, now the Nieper, a name given in the middle ages to the Borysthenes, as Danaster the Niester, was applied to the Tyras.

DAN'AUS, a son of Belus and Anchinoe, who, after his father's death, reigned conjointly with his brother Ægyptus on the throne of Ægypt. Some time after, a difference arose between the brothers, and Danaus set sail with his fifty daughters in quest of a settlement. He visited Rhodes, were he consecrated a statue to Minerva, and arrived safely on the coast of Peloponnesus, where he was hospitably received by Gelanor, king of Argos. Gelanor had lately ascended the throne, and the first years of his reign were marked with dissensions with his subjects. Danaus took advantage of Gelanor's unpopularity, and obliged him to abdicate the crown. In Gelanor, the race of the Inachidæ was extinguished, and the Belides began to reign at Argos in Danaus. Some authors say, that Gelanor voluntarily resigned the crown to Danaus, on account of the wrath of Neptune, who had dried up all the waters at Argolis, to punish the impiety of Inachus. The successful settlement of Danaus invited the fifty sons of Ægyptus to embark for Greece. Their uncle however, caused his daughters to murder them the first night of their nuptials. His fatal orders were executed, but Hypermnestra alone spared the life of Lynceus. *Vid.* Danaides. Danaus, at first, persecuted Lynceus, but he was afterwards reconciled to him, and acknowledged him for his son-in-law, and successor, after a reign of fifty years. He died about 1425 years B.C., and after death, he was honoured with a splendid monument in the town of Argos, which still existed in the age of Pausanias. According to Æschylus, Danaus left Ægypt, not to be present at the marriage of his daughters with the sons of his brother, a connection which he deemed unlawful and impious. The ship in which Danaus came to Greece, was called Armais, and was the first that had ever appeared in that part of the world. It is said that the use of pumps was first introduced into Greece by Danaus. The fifty daughters of Danaus were not by the same mother; four were daughters of Europa, two of Elephantis, ten of Atlantea, of Phœbe, and the Hamadryads, seven of Æthiopis, twelve of one of the Dryads, and the rest of Crino *Apollod.* 2. c. 1.—*Paus.* 2. c. 19. l. 10. c. 10.—*Hygin.* fab. 168, &c.—*Herodot.* 2. c. 91, &c. 7. c 94.—*Æsch. in Supp.*

DAN'DACE, a city of Taurica Chersonesus. *Ptol.*

DANDAG'ULA, a people of India within the Ganges. *Plin.*

DAN'DARI or **DANDAR'IDÆ**, certain people dwelling near mount Caucasus. *Tacit.* 12. *Ann.* c. 15.

DAN'DON, a man of Illyricum, who, as *Pliny*, 7, c. 48, reports, lived 500 years.

DANDU'TI, a people of Germany. *Ptol.*

DAN'GULÆ, a people near Arachosia. *Plin.*

DANTHELIT'ICA, a province of Thrace. *Ptol.* *Pliny* calls the people Denselitæ; *Stephanus*, Dantheletæ.

DANU'BIUS, a celebrated river, the greatest in Europe, which rises, according to Herodotus, near the town of Pyrene, in the country of the Celtæ, and, after flowing through the greatest part of Europe, falls into the Euxine Sea. The Greeks called it Ister: but the Romans distinguished it by the appellation of the Danube, from its source till the middle of its course; and thence to its mouth he called it Ister, like the Greeks. It falls into the Euxine through seven months, or six according to others. Herodotus mentions five, but modern travellers discover only two. The Danube was generally supposed to be the northern boundary of the Roman empire in Europe; and, therefore, several castles were erected on its banks, to check the incursions of the neighbouring barbarians. It was worshipped as a deity by the Scythians. According to modern geographers, the Danube rises in the Black forest in Suabia, and after receiving by the way about forty navigable rivers, it finishes a course of 1600 miles by emptying itself into the Black Sea, the waters of which, according to Pliny, it sweetens for a distance of forty miles from the shore. The more considerable rivers which discharge themselves into the Danube, are called by the moderns, on the north, the Regen, Nab, Theysse, Alauta, Pruth; and on the south, the Iser, Lech, Inn, Ens, Drave, Save, Morava. *Dionys. Perieg.—Herodot* 2. c. 33. l. 4. c. 48, &c.—*Strab.* 4.—*Plin.* 4. c. 12 & 24.—*Ammian.* 23.

DA'OCHUS, an officer of Philip, king of Macedon, &c. *Plut. in Demosth.*

DAO'NA, a city of India without the Ganges. *Steph.*

DAORI'ZI, a people of Illyricum. *Plin.* 3. c. 22.

DA'PHA, a city of Arabia Deserta. *Ptol.*

DAPH'IDAS, a sophist, thrown from a rock by order of king Attalus. *Voss. de Poet. Gr.* p 88.

DAPH'NÆ, a town of Ægypt, on one of the mouths of the Nile, sixteen miles south of Pelusium. *Herodot.* 2. c. 30.

DAPHNÆ'US, a general of Syracuse, employed against Carthage. *Polyæn.* 5.

DAPH'NE, a daughter of the river Peneus, or of the Ladon, by the goddess Terra, of whom Apollo became enamoured. This passion had been raised by Cupid, with whom Apollo, proud of his late conquest over the serpent Python, had disputed the power of his darts. Daphne received with distrust and horror the addresses of the god, and fled from him. Apollo pursued her; but Daphne intreated the assistance of the gods, who changed her into a laurel. Apollo crowned his head with the leaves of the laurel, and ordered that that tree should be for ever sacred to his divinity. Some say that Daphne was admired by Leucippus, son of Œnomaus king of Pisa, who, to be in her company, disguised his sex, and attended her in the woods, in the habit of a huntress. Leucippus gained Daphne's esteem and love; but Apollo, who was his rival, discovered his sex, and Leucippus was immediately killed by the companions of Diana. *Ovid. Met.* 1. v. 452, &c.—*Parthen. Erotic.* c. 15.—*Paus.* 8. c. 20.—*Palæph. de Inc.* 50. ——A daughter of Tiresias, priestess of Apollo, in the temple of Delphi, and supposed by some to be the same as Manto. She was called Sibyl, on account of the wildness of her looks and expressions when she delivered oracles. Her oracles were generally given in verse, and Homer, according to some accounts, has introduced much of her poetry into his compositions. *Diod.* 4.—*Paus.* 10. c. 5.

DAPH'NE, a famous grove near Antioch, on the borders of the river Orontes, in which was a temple of Apollo. It was devoted to voluptuousness, and few besides the dissipated frequented it; whence the proverb of *Daphnicis moribus vivere* applied to an effeminate life. *Liv.* 33. c. 49.—*Strab.* 16.—*Eutrop.* 6. c. 11.—*Vulcat Gallic in Ovid.* 5.

DAPHNEPHO'RIA, a festival in honour of Apollo, celebrated every ninth year by the people of Bœotia. It was then usual to adorn an olive bough with garlands of laurel and other flowers, and to place on the top a brazen globe, on which were suspended smaller ones. In the middle was placed a number of crowns, and a globe of inferior size, and the bottom was adorned with a saffron-colored garment. The globe on the top represented the Sun, or Apollo; that in the middle was an emblem of the moon, and the others of the stars. The crowns, which were 65 in number, represented the sun's annual revolutions. This bough was carried in solemn procession by a beautiful youth of an illustrious family, and whose parents were both living. The youth was dressed in rich garments which reached to the ground, his hair hung loose and dishevelled, his head was covered with a golden crown, and he wore on his feet shoes called *Iphicratidæ*, from Iphicrates, an Athenian, who first invented them. He was called Δαφνηφόρος, *laurel-bearer*, and at that time he executed the office of priest of Apollo. He was preceded by one of his nearest relations, bearing a rod adorned with garlands, and behind him followed a train of virgins with branches in their hands. In this order the procession advanced as far as the temple of Apollo, surnamed *Ismenius*, were supplicatory hymns were sung to the god. This festival owed its origin to the following circumstance. When an oracle advised the Ætolians, who inhabited Arne and the adjacent country, to abandon their ancient possessions, and go in quest of a settlement, they invaded the Theban territories, which at that time were pillaged by an army of Pelasgians. As the celebration of Apollo's festival was near, both nations, who religiously observed it, laid aside all hostilities, and, according to custom, cut down laurel boughs from mount Helicon, and in the neighbourhood of the river Melas, and walked in procession in honour of the divinity. The day that this solemnity was observed, Polemates, the general of the Bœotian army, saw a youth in a dream that presented him with a complete suit of armour, and commanded the Bœotians to offer solemn prayers to Apollo, and walk in procession with laurel boughs in their hands every ninth year. Three days after this dream, the Bœotian general made a sally, and cut off the greatest part of the besiegers, who were compelled by this blow to relinquish their enterprise. Polemates immediately instituted a novennial festival in honour of the god who seemed to be the patron of the Bœotians. *Paus. Bœotic*, &c.

DAPH'NIS, a shepherd of Sicily, son of Mercury by a Sicilian nymph. He was educated by the nymphs, Pan taught him to play upon the pipe, and the muses inspired him with the love of poetry. It is supposed that he was the first who wrote pastoral poetry, in which his successor Theocritus so happily excelled. He was extremely fond of hunting: and at his death, five of his dogs from their attachment to him, refused all aliment, and pined away. The name of Daphnis has been appropriated by the poets, ancient and modern, to express a person fond of rural employments, and of the peaceful innocence which accompanies the tending of flocks. *Theocr. Id.* 1. & *Scholiast. ib.* —*Servius ad Ecl.*—*Virg.* 8. v. 68. & *Ecl.* 5. v. 25. —*Ælian. V. H.* 10. c. 18.—*Diod.* 4.——A shepherd of mount Ida, changed into a rock, according to *Ovid. Met.* 4. v. 275.——A servant of Nicocrates, tyrant of Cyrene, &c. *Polyæn.* 8.——A grammarian. *Suet. de Gr.*——A son of Paris and Œnone.

DAPH'NIS, a region of Lycia.——A town of Ægypt, near Pelusium. *Herod.*

DAPH'NUS, a small river of Locris, into which the body of Hesiod was thrown after his murder. *Plut. de Symp.*

DAPH'NUS, a physician who was said to prefer supper to dinner, because he supposed that the moon assisted digestion. *Athen.* 7.

DA'RA, a city founded by Arsaces. *Justin.* 41. c. 5.——A river of Carmania. *Ptol.*

DAR'ABA, a town of Arabia. *Strab.*

DAR'ABES, a people of Bactriana. *Val. Flacc. Argon.* 6. v. 66.

DARA'DI, an inland city of Libya. *Plin.* 5. c. 1.

DAR'ADUS, a river of Libya, now Senega. *Ptol.*

DARANIS'SA, a town of Armenia Major. *Id.*

DARANTA'SIA, a town of Belgic Gaul, called also *Forum Claudii*, and now Motier.

DA'RAPS, a king of the Gangaridæ, &c. *Flacc.* 6. v. 67.

DARAP'SA, a city of the Bactri. *Steph.*

DA'RAS, a town of Parthia. *Etym. Mag.*

DAR'DÆ, a people of India. *Steph.*

DAR'DANI, the inhabitants of Dardania.——A people of Mœsia on the south of the Danube, for some time very inimical to the neighbouring power of Macedonia. *Liv.* 26. c. 25. l. 27. c. 33. l. 31. c. 28. l. 40. c. 57.—*Plin.* 4. c. 1.

DARDA'NIA, a town or country of Troas, from which the Trojans were called *Dardani* and *Dardanidæ*. There was also a country of the same name at the east of Illyricum on the south of the Danube. This appellation is also applied to the island of Samothrace. *Virg. & Ovid. passim.*—*Strab.* 7.—*Ptol.* 3. c. 9.

DARDAN'IDES, a name given to Æneas, as descended from Dardanus. The word, in the plural number, is also applied to the Trojan women. *Virg. Æn.* 3. v. 94. l. 5. v. 45. l. 10. v. 545.—*Ovid. Met.* 13. v. 412.

DARDA'NIUM, a promontory of Troas, which received its name from the small town of Dardanus, about seven miles from Abydus. The two castle built on each side of the strait, by the emperos Mahomet IV. A.D. 1659, caused the modernr name of Dardanelles to be given to the place. *Strab.* 13.

DAR'DANUM, a promontory of India. *Strab.*

DAR'DANUS, a son of Jupiter and Electra. He killed his brother Jasius to obtain the kingdom of Etruria after the death of his reputed father Corytus, and afterwards fled to Samothrace, and thence to Asia Minor, where he married Batia, the daughter of Teucer, king of Teucria. After the death of his father-in-law he ascended the throne of the country, and reigned 62 years. He built the city of Dardania, and was reckoned the founder of the kingdom of Troy. He was succeeded by Erichthonius. Dardanus taught his subjects the worship of the goddess Minerva; and gave them two statues of that divinity, one of which was well known by the uame of Palladium. *Virg, Æn.* 3. v. 167 & 503. l. 4. v, 365. l. 8. v. 37. l. 10. v. 718.—*Servius in locis cit.*—*Dionys.* l. c. 53.—*Paus.* 7. c. 4.—*Hygin.* fab. 155 & 275.—*Apollod.* 3.—*Homer. Il.* 20. v. 215.——A Trojan killed by Achilles. *Homer. Il.* 20. v. 460.

DARDA'RII, a nation near the Palus Mæotis. *Plut. in Lucull.*

DAR'EMÆ, a nation of the Troglodytæ in Æthiopia. *Plin.* 4. c. 12.

DA'RES, a Phrygian, who lived during the Trojan war, in which he was engaged, and of which he wrote the history in Greek. This history was extant in the age of Ælian; but the Latin translation, now extant, is universally believed to be spurious, though it is attributed by some to Cornelius Nepos. Tho best edition is that of Smids cum notis var. 4to, & 8vo, Amst. 1702. *Homer. Il.* 5. v. 10 & 27.—*Sax. Onom.* 1. p. 8—*Fabr. B. Gr.* l. c. 5.——One of the companions of Æneas, descended from Amycus, and celebrated as a pugilist at the funeral games in honour of Hector, where he killed Butes. He was killed by Turnus in Italy. *Virg. Æn.* 5. v. 369. l. 12. v. 363.

DARE'TIS, a country of Macedonia. *Polyb.*——A country of Media. *Ptol.*

DAR'GIDUS, a river of Bactriana. *Ptol.*

DARI'A, a town of Mesopotamia. *Procop.*

DARI'AVES, the name of Darius in Persian. *Strab.* 16.

DARIDÆ'US, a king of Persia, in the reigns of Tiberius and Claudius. *Philostr. in vit. Apollon. Tyan.*

DARID'NA, a city of Paphlagonia. *Steph.*

DARIOR'IGUM, a town of Gaul on the shores of the Atlantic, now Vannes in Britany.

DARISTA'NE, a city or Persia. *Steph.*

DARI'TÆ, a people of Persia. *Herodot.* 3. c. 92.

DARI'UM, a town of Phrygia. *Steph.*

DARI'US, a noble satrap of Persia, son of Hytaspes, who conspired with six other noblemen to destroy Smerdis, who had usurped the crown of Persia after the death of Cambyses. On the murder of the usurper, the seven conspirators universally agreed, that he among them whose horse neighed first should be appointed king. In consequence of this resolution, the groom of Darius previously led his master's horse to a favourite mare, at a place near which the seven noblemen were to pass. On the morrow before sun-rise, when they proceeded all together, the horse recollecting the mare, suddenly neighed; and at the same moment, it is said, that a clap of thunder was heard, as if in approbation of the choice. The noblemen dismounted from their horses, and saluted Darius king; and a resolution was made among them that the king's wives and concubines should be taken from no other families but those of the conspirators, and that they should for ever enjoy the unlimited privilege of being admitted into the king's presence without previous introduction. Darius was 29 years old when he ascended the throne, and he soon distinguished himself by his activity and military accomplishments. He besieged Babylon; which he took after a siege of 20 months, by the artifice of Zopyrus. He next marched against the Scythians, and in his way conquered Thrace. This expedition was finally unsuccessful; and after several losses and disasters in the wilds of Scythia, the king retired in disgrace, and soon after turned his arms against the Indians, whom he subdued. But Darius had now a more powerful enemy to encounter. The Grecian cities of Asia still remembered the freedom and independence which their ancestors had enjoyed, therefore they submitted with reluctance to the Persian yoke. To assert their liberties they applied for assistance to the states of Greece and Athens, who warmly espoused their cause, and sent to their support a fleet of 25 ships. The combined forces advanced into Asia Minor, and laid siege to Sardes, the capital of Lydia, which they reduced to ashes. Darius saw with indignation the designs of the Greeks to foment war in his kingdom, and he was so exasperated against the Athenians in consequence of the burning of Sardes, that a servant every evening, by his order, reminded him of the vengeance which he had vowed against the invaders by repeating these words: "Remember, O king, to punish the Athenians." Mardonius, the king's son-in-law, was now entrusted, not only with the defence of the kingdom, but with a powerful force which was to carry war and devastation into the heart of Greece. This army, however, was on its march attacked and defeated by the Thracians; but the king, regardless of this defeat, collected a more numerous force, the command of which he entrusted to Datus and Artaphernes. They were conquered at the celebrated battle of Marathon, by 10,000 Athenians; and the Persians lost in that fatal expedition no less than 206,000 men. Darius was not disheartened by this severe blow, but he resolved to carry on the war in person, and immediately ordered a still larger army to be levied. He died in the midst of his preparations, B.C 485, after a reign of 36 years, in the 65th year of his age. *Herodot.* 1, 2, &c.—*Diod.* 1.—*Justin.* 1, c. 9.—*Plut. in Arist.*—*C. Nep, in Miltiad.*

DARI'US the Second, king of Persia, was also called *Ochus*, or *Nothus*, because he was the illegitimate son of Artaxerxes by a concubine. Soon after the murder of Xerxes he ascended the throne of Persia, and married Parysatis his sister, a cruel and ambitious woman, by whom he had Artaxerxes Mnemon, Amestris, and Cyrus the younger. He carried on many wars with success, under the conduct of his generals and of his son Cyrus. He died B.C. 404, after a reign of 19 years, and was succeeded by his son Artaxerxes, who asked him on his death-bed, what had been the guide of his conduct in the management of the empire, that he might imitate him? "The dictates of justice and of religion," replied the expiring monarch. *Justin.* 5. c. 11.—*Diod.* 12.

DARI'US the Third, surnamed *Codomanus*, was the last king of Persia. He was the son of Arsames and Sysigambis, and descended from Darius Nothus. The eunuch Bagoas raised him to the throne, though not nearly allied to the royal family, in hopes that he would be subservient to his will; but he prepared to poison him, when he saw him inclined to despise his advice, and to aim at independence. Darius discovered the perfidious intentions of this dangerous minister, and made him drink the poison which he had prepared against his life. The peace of Darius was early disturbed by the ambitious views of Alexander, king of Macedonia, who invaded Persia to avenge the injuries which the Greeks had suffered from the predecessors of Darius. The king of Persia met his adversary in person, at the head of 600,000 men. This army was remarkable, more for its display of opulence and luxury, than for the military courage of its soldiers; and Athenæus mentions, that the camp of Darius was crowded with 277 cooks, 29 waiters, 87 cup-bearers, 40 servants to perfume the king, and 66 to prepare garlands and flowers to deck the dishes and meats which appeared on the royal table. With such forces Darius could scarcely promise himself victory against the veterans of Macedonia; but he relied on the numbers, not on the valor of his army. His hopes were, however, soon disappointed at the battle of the Granicus, where his thousands fled with precipitation and dismay before a handful of Alexander's soldiers, Another battle was fought near Issus, but with the same result. The impetuosity of the Macedonians proved irresistible, and Alexander left 110,000 of the enemy dead on the field of battle, and took among the prisoners of war, the mother, wife, and children of Darius: he assembled another more powerful army, and the last decisive battle was fought at Arbela. The victory was long doubtful; but the intrepidity of Alexander, and the valor of the Macedonians, prevailed over the effeminate Persians; and Darius, sensible of his disgrace, and of the ruin of his affairs, fled towards Media. His misfortunes were now completed. Bessus, the governor of Bactriana, took away his life, in hopes of succeeding him on the throne; and Darius was found by the Macedonians, in his chariot, covered with wounds, and almost expiring, B.C. 331. He asked for water, and exclaimed when he received it from the hand of a Macedonian soldier, "It is the greatest of my misfortunes that I cannot reward thy humanity. Beg of Alexander to accept my warmest thanks, for the tenderness with which he has treated my wretched family, whilst I am doomed to perish by the hand of a man, whom I have loaded with kindness." These words of the dying monarch were reported to Alexander, who covered the dead body with his own mantle, and honoured it with a most magnificent funeral. The traitor Bessus met with a due punishment from the conqueror, who continued his kindness to the unfortunate family of Darius. In him the empire of Persia was extinguished, 228 years after it had been first founded by Cyrus the Great. *Diod.* 17.—*Plut. in Alex.*—*Just.* 10, 11, &c.—*Curtius.*

DARI'US, a son of Xerxes, king of Persia, who married Artaynta, and was killed by Artabanus, *Herodot.* 9. c. 108.—*Diod.* 11.——A son of Artaxerxes, declared successor to the throne, as being the eldest prince. He conspired against his father's life, and was capitally punished. *Plut. in Artax.*

DAR'NA, a city of Assyria. *Ptol.*

DAROCA'NA, a city of Paropanisus. *Id.*

DA'RON, a town of Ægypt. *Plin.* 6. c. 30.

DAR'RHÆ, a people near the Red Sea. *Steph.*

DARSA'NIA, a city of India. *Id.*

DAR'SII, a people of Thrace. *Id.*

DARVE'NUM. *Vid.* Durovernum.

DAS'CÆ, a city of Arcadia. *Steph.*

DAS'CON, a man who founded Camarina, in Sicily. *Thucyd.* 6. c. 5.

DASCYLI'TIS, a province of Persia. *Id.* 1. c. 129.

DASCYL'IUM, a town of Caria.——A town of Ionia. ——A town of Æolis. *Steph.*

DAS'CYLUS, the father of Gyges. *Herodot.* 1. c. 8.

DA'SEÆ, a small town of Arcadia. *Paus.* 8. c. 27.

DA'SIUS, a chief city of Salapia, who favoured Annibal. *Liv.* 26. c. 38.

DASSARE'TÆ, DASSARI'TÆ, DASSARE'NI, or, DASSARIT'II, a people between Illyricum and Macedonia, near the sources of the river Aliacmon. *Ptol.*—*Liv.* 27. c. 34.

DAT'AMES, a son of Camissares, governor of Caria and general of the armies of Artaxerxes. His great abilities as a general, and as a negociator were displayed in the service of the king, and in every expedition which he undertook he increased his own fame and the military glory of his country. The popularity which he deservedly acquired, however, procured him enemies; the courtiers of the monarch were soon engaged to deprecate the meritorious actions which, as they could not imitate, they affected to despise, and Artaxerxes was induced to persecute a man whom it was his duty to reward. Datames, unable now to live in safety as a peaceful subject, declared himself no longer the vassal of the Persian monarch, and established himself as the independent prince of a distant province. Every attempt to reduce him to obedience proved unsuccessful, but he at last fell by the dagger of a treacherous friend. He was assassinated by Mithridates, who had invited him to a parley, under pretence of entering into the most inviolable connection and friendship with him, 362. B.C. *C. Nep. in Datam.*—*Diod.* 15.

DATAPHER'NES, one of the friends of Bessus. After the murder of Darius, he betrayed Bessus into Alexander's hands. He afterwards revolted from the conqueror, and was delivered up by the Dahæ. *Curt.* 7. c. 5 & 8.

DA'THUS or DA'TUS, a town of Thrace near the Strymon. The city was so rich that the ancients generally made use of the proverb, *Dathus bonorum*, to express abundance. When Philip, the king of Macedonia, conquered it, he called it Philippi after his own name, an appellation by which it is best known among ancient authors. *Appian. de Civ.*

DA'TIS, a general of Darius the First, sent in conjunction with Artaphernes, with an army of 200,000 foot, and 10,000 horse, against the Greeks. He was defeated at the celebrated battle of Marathon, by Miltiades, and soon after was put to death by the Spartans. *C. Nep. in Milt.*—*Herodot.* 8.——A lieutenant of Daraps, king of the Gangaridæ. *Val. Flacc. Argon.* 6. v. 67.

DAT'THA, a town of Media. *Ptol.*

DATYLEP'TI, a people of Thrace. *Steph.*

DAU'CHILÆ, an inland people of Libya. *Ptol.*

DAU'CHIS, a mountain of Æthiopia. *Id.*

DAUDIA'NA, a town of Armenia Major. *Id.*

DAU'LIS, a nymph, daughter of the god of the Cephisus, from whom the city of Daulis in Phocis, anciently called Anachris, received its name. It at Daulis that Philomela and Procne made Tereus eat the flesh of his son, and hence the nightingale, into which Philomela was changed, is often called *Daulias avis.* *Ovid.* ep. 15. v. 154.—*Strab.* 9.—*Paus.* 10. c. 4.—*Ptol.* 3. c. 15.—*Liv.* 32. c. 18.—*Plin.* 4. c. 3.

DAU'NI, a people on the eastern part of Italy, near the river Aufidus, conquered by Daunus, from whom they received their name. *Plin.* 3. c. 11.

DAU'NIA, a name given to the northern parts of Apulia, on the coast of the Adriatic Sea. It received its name from Daunus, who settled there, and it is now called Capitanata. *Virg. Æn.* 8. v. 146.—*Sil.* 2. v. 500. l. 12. v. 429.—*Horat.* 4. od. 6. v. 27.

DAU'NIA JUTUR'NA, the sister of Turnus, was so called, after she had been made a goddess by Jupiter. *Virg. Æn.* 12. v. 139 & 785.

DAU'NUS, a son of Pilumnus and Danae. He came from Illyricum into Apulia, where he reigned over part of the country, and he was still on the throne when Diomedes came to Italy. *Ptol.* 3. c. 1.—*Festus de Verb. Sig.*—*Sil. It.* 8. v. 358. l. 12. v. 429.—*Servius in Æn.* 8. v. 9 —*Mela*, 2. c. 4. —*Strab.* 5.

DAU'NUS, a river of Apulia, now Carapelle. *Horat.* 3. od. 30.

DAU'RIFER, or DAU'RISES, a brave general of Darius, treacherously killed by the Carians. *Herodot.* 5. c. 116, &c.

DAU'SARA, a city near Edessa. *Steph.*

DAV'ARA, a hill near mount Taurus, in Asia Minor. *Tacit. Ann.* 6. c. 41.

DA'VE, a city of Arabia. *Steph.*

DAVEL'LI, a people of Upper Æthiopia. *Plin.* 6. c. 30.

DA'VUS, a comic character in the Andria of Terence. *Horat.* 1. sat. 10. v. 40.

DAXARE'NI, a nation of Arabia. *Steph.*

DAX'ATA, a city of the Seræ. *Ptol.*

DE'ABUS, called also Geryon, a monarch of the Celtiberi. *Berosus.*

DE'BA, a city of Commagena, in Syria. *Ptol.* ——A city of Mesopotamia. *Id.*

DE'BÆ, a nation of Arabia. *Diod.* 3.

DEB'OMA, a town of Macedonia. *Ptol.*

DEB'ORUS, a city of Pæonia. *Id.*

DE'BRIS, a town of the Garamantes. *Id.*—*Plin.*

DECADU'CHI or DECADAR'CHI, the name of magistrates appointed by Lysander after the battle of Ægospotamos, in the cities which were before under the dominion of Athens. *Corn. Nep. in Lys.* c. 1.

DECAP'OLIS, a district of Judea, so called from its ten cities. *Plin.* 5. c. 18.

DECEB'ALUS, a warlike king of the Daci, who carried on a successful war against Domitian. He was conquered by Trajan, Domitian's successor, but still left in possession of his throne. His active spirit again kindled rebellion, and the Roman emperor marched against him, and defeated him. He destroyed himself that he might not fall into the hands of the enemy, and his head was brought to Rome, and Dacia became a Roman province, A.D. 103. *Dio.* 68.

DECE'LEUM, or DECELE'UM or -EA, now Biala Castro, a small village of Attica, north of Athens. The Spartans, by the advice of Alcibiades, seized it and fortified it, which circumstance proved very disastrous to the Athenians, as they could be easily harassed by the sallies of the garrison. The Peloponnesian war has occasionally been called Decelean, because for some time hostilities were carried on in the neighbourhood of this town. *C. Nep.* 7. c. 4.

DECELUS, a man who informed Castor and Pollux that their sister Helen, whom Theseus had carried away, was concealed at Aphidnæ. *Herodot.* 9. c. 73.

DECEMVIRI, ten magistrates appointed with absolute authority among the Romans. The privileges of the patricians had raised dissatisfaction among the plebeians; who, though freed from the power of the Tarquins, still saw that the administration of justice depended upon the will and caprice of their superiors, without any written statute to direct them, and convince them that they were governed with equity and impartiality. The tribunes complained to the senate, and demanded that a code of laws might be framed for the use and benefit of the Roman people. This petition was complied with, and three ambassadors were dispatched to Athens, and to the other Grecian states, to collect the laws of Solon, and other celebrated legislators. Upon the return of the commissioners, it was universally agreed, that ten new magistrates called *Decemviri*, should be elected from the senate, to put the project into execution. Their power was made absolute; all other offices ceased after their election, and they presided over the city with regal authority. They were invested with the badges of the consul, to the enjoyment of which they had succeeded by turns, and one only was preceded by the fasces, and had the power of assembling the senate, and of confirming its decrees. The first decemvirs were Appius Claudius, T. Genutius, P. Sextus, Sp. Veturius, C. Julius, A. Manlius, Ser. Sulpitius, P. Curiatius, T. Romulus, Sp. Posthumius, A.U.C. 303. Under them, the laws, which had been exposed to public view, that every citizen might openly speak his sentiments, were publicly approved of as constitutional, and ratified by the priests and augurs in the most solemn manner. These laws were ten in number, and were engraved on tables of brass; two were afterwards added, and they were called the laws o. the twelve tables, *leges duodecim tabularum*, and *leges decemvirales*. The decemviral power which was beheld by all ranks of people with the greatest satisfaction, was continued; but in the third year after their creation, the decemvirs became odious on account of the tyranny of their conduct, and the attempt of Ap. Claudius to ravish Virginia, was followed by the total abolition of the office. The people were so exasperated against them, that they clamorously demanded them from the senate, to burn them alive. Consuls were again appointed, and tranquillity re-established in the state. There were other officers in Rome, called *decemvirs*, who were originally appointed, in the absence of the prætor, to administer justice. Their appointment became afterwards necessary, and they generally assisted at sales called *subhastationes*, because a spear, *hasta*, was fixed at the door of the place where the goods were exposed to sale. They were called *decemviri litibus judicandis*. The officers whom Tarquin appointed to guard the Sibylline books were also called decemviri. They were originally two in number, called *duumviri*, till the year of Rome 388, when their number was increased to ten, five of them being chosen from the plebeians, and five from the patricians. Sylla increased their number to fifteen, called *quindecemviri*.

DECENTII, a people of Pannonia. *Steph.*

DECENTIUS MAGNUS was made Cæsar by his brother Magnentius. He hanged himself A.D. 373 *Euseb. in Chron.* &c.

DECETIA, a town of Gaul, now Decise. *Cæs.*

DECIA LEX, was enacted by M. Decius the tribune, A.U.C. 442, to empower the people to appoint two proper persons to fit out and repair the Roman fleets.

DECIANA, a city of the Endigeti, in Hispania Tarraconensis. *Ptol.*

DECIANI, a people of Calabria. *Plin.* 3. c. 11.

DECIATUM, a region of Gallia Narbonensis. *Id.* 3. c. 4.

L. DECIDIUS SAXA, a Celtiberian in Cæsar's camp. *Cæs. Bell. Civ.* 1.

DECIETUM, a city of Italy. *Steph.*

DECINEUS, a celebrated soothsayer. *Strab.* 16.

DECIUS BRUTUS conducted Cæsar to the senate-house the day that he was murdered.

DECIUS CALPURNIANUS, a person put to death as an accomplice in the adulteries of Messalina. *Tac. Ann.* 11. c. 35.

DECIUS MESSIUS Q. TRAJANUS, a native of Pannonia, sent by the emperor Philip to appease a sedition in Mœsia. Instead of obeying his master's command, he assumed the imperial purple, and soon after marched against him, and, at his death, became the only emperor. He afterwards signalized himself against the Persians, but when he marched against the Goths, he pushed his horse into a deep marsh, from which he could not extricate himself, and he perished with all his army by the darts of the barbarians, A D. 251, after a reign of two years. This monarch enjoyed the character of a brave man, and of a great disciplinarian; and by his justice and exemplary life, merited the title of Optimus, which a servile senate lavished upon him.

DECIUS MUS, a celebrated Roman consul, who devoted himself to the gods Manes for the safety of his country, in a battle against the Latins, 338 years B.C.

DECIUS, his son, imitated his example, and devoted himself in like manner, for the good of his country, in his fourth consulship, when fighting against the Samnites, B.C. 296.——Son of the last-mentioned, also performed the same patriotic exploit in the war against Pyrrhus and the Tarentines, B.C, 280. These acts of self-devotion were of infinite service to the state. The soldiers were animated by this extraordinary example of bravery, and induced to follow with intrepidity a commander who, arrayed in an unusual dress, and addressing himself to the gods with solemn invocation, rushed into the thickest part of the enemy to meet his fate. *Liv.* 8, 9, &c.—*Val. Max.* 5. c. 6.—*Polyæ.* 2.—*Virg. Æn.* 6. v. 824.—*Cic. Tusc.* 1. c. 37.—*Juv.* 9. v. 254, &c. *Sat.* 14. v. 239.

DECTADES, an historian praised by *Parthenius, Erot.* c. 13.

DECULANI, a people of Italy. *Plin.* 3. c. 11.

DECUMANI, a people of Gaul. *Plin.*—*Mela.*

DECUMATES AGRI, lands in Germany, which paid a tenth part of their value to the Romans. *Tacit. G.* 29.

DECUNI, a people of Dalmatia. *Plin.* 3. c. 22.

DECURIO, a subaltern officer in the Roman armies. He commanded a *decuria*, which consisted of ten men, and was the third part of a *turma*, or the 30th part of a *legio* of horse, which was composed of 300 men. The badge of the Decuriones was a vine rod or sapling, and each had a deputy called *optio*.—There were also certain magistrates in the provinces called *decuriones municipales*, who formed a body to represent the Roman senate in free and corporate towns. They consisted of ten, whence their name; and their duty was to watch over the interests of their fellow-citizens, and to increase the revenues of the commonwealth. Their court was called *curia decurionum*, and *minor senatus;* and their decrees, called *decreta decurionum*, were marked with the letters D.D. at the top. They generally styled themselves *civitatum patres curiales*, and *honorati municipiorum senatores*. They were elected with the same ceremonies as the Roman senators; they were to be at least 25 years of age, and to be possessed of a certain sum of money. The election always took place on the calends of March.

DEDITAMENES, a friend of Alexander, made governor of Babylonia. *Curt.* 8. c 3.

DEERA, a plain of Susiana. *Ptol.*

DEES, a town of Arabia Felix. *Id.*

DEGIA, a city of Assyria. *Id.*

DEGIS, a brother of Decebalus king of the Daci. He came to Rome as ambassador to the court of Domitian. *Martial.* 5. epigr. 3.

DEICOON, a Trojan prince, son of Pergasus, intimate with Æneas. He was killed by Agamemnon. *Homer. Il.* 5. v. 534.——A son of Hercules and Megara. *Apollod.* 2. c. 7.

DEIDAMIA, a daughter of Lycomedes, king of Scyrus. She bore a son called Pyrrhus, or Neoptolemus, to Achilles, who lived in disguise at her father's court in woman's clothes, under the name of Pyrrha. *Propert.* 2. el. 9.—*Statius in Ach.*—*Apollod.* 3. c. 13.——A daughter of Pyrrhus, killed by the Epirots. *Polyæn.* 8.——A daughter of Adrastus, king of Argos, called also Hippodamia.

DEIL'EON, a companion of Hercules in his expedition against the Amazons. *Flacc.* 5. v. 115.

DEIL'OCHUS, a son of Hercules, by Megara, daughter of Creon, king of Thebes. *Homer. Od.*

DEIM'ACHUS, son of Neleus and Chloris, was killed with all his brothers, except Nestor, by Hercules. The names of his brothers were Taurus, Asterius, Pylaon, Eurybius, Epidaus, Eurymenes, Evagoras, Alastor, Periclymenus, and Nestor. *Apollod.* 1. c. 9.——The father of Enarette. *Id.* 1. c. 7.

DEI'OCES, a son of Arbianes, by whose means the Medes delivered themselves from the yoke of the Assyrians. He filled the office of judge over his countrymen, and his great popularity and love of equity raised him to the throne B.C. 700. He was succeeded by his son Phraortes, after a reign of 53 years. He built Ecbatana, according to Herodotus, and surrounded it with seven concentric walls, in the middle of which was the royal palace. *Herodot.* 1. c. 96, &c.—*Polyæn.*

DEI'OCHUS, a Greek, killed by Paris in the Trojan war. *Homer Il.* 15. v. 341.

DEI'ONE, the mother of Miletus by Apollo. Miletus is often called Deionides, on account of his mother. *Ovid. Met.* 9. v. 542.

DEI'ONEUS, or DEIONE'US, a king of Phocis, who married Diomede daughter of Xuthus, by whom he had Dia. He gave his daughter Dia in marriage to Ixion, who had promised to make apresent to his father-in-law. Deioneus accordingly visited the house of Ixion, but instead of receiving the promised favour, he was thrown into a large hole filled with burning coals by his son-in-law, and there stifled. *Hygin.* fab. 48 & 241.—*Diod.* 4.—*Ovid. Met.* 6.—*Apollod.* 1. c. 7 & 9. l. 2. c. 4.

DEIOPE'A, a nymph, the fairest of all the fourteen nymphs that attended upon Juno. The goddess promised her in marriage to Æolus, the god of the winds, if he would let loose the winds and destroy the fleet of Æneas, which was sailing for Italy. *Virg. Æn.* 1. v. 76.——One of the attendant nymphs of Cyrene. *Virg. G.* 4. v. 343.

DEIOT'ARUS, a governor of Galatia, made king of that province by the Roman people. In the civil wars of Pompey and Cæsar, Deiotarus followed the interest of the former. After the battle of Pharsalia, Cæsar severely reprimanded Deiotarus for his attachment to Pompey, and deprived him of part of his kingdom, leaving him only the bare title of royalty. When Deiotarus was accused by his grandson with attempts upon Cæsar's life, Cicero ably defended him in the Roman senate. He afterwards joined Brutus with a large army, and faithfully supported the republican cause. Deiotarus died in an advanced old age. *Strab.* 12.—*Lucan.* 5. v. 55.—*Cic. in Deiot.*

DEIPH'ILA. *Vid.* Deipyle.

DEIPH'OBE, a sibyl of Cumæ, daughter of Glaucus. It is supposed that she was the sibyl who conducted Æneas to the infernal regions. *Vid.* Sibyllæ. *Virg. Æn.* 6. v. 36.

DEIPH'OBUS, a son of Priam and Hecuba, who, after the death of his brother Paris, married Helen. His wife cruelly betrayed him, and introduced into his chamber Menelaus, to whom by this act of treachery she hoped to reconcile herself. The unfortunate prince was shamefully mutilated and killed by Menelaus. He had highly distinguished himself during the war, especially in his two combats with Merion, and that in which he slew Ascaphus son of Mars. *Dictys.* 2. *Virg. Æn.* 6. v. 495.—*Homer. Il.* 43.——A son of Hippolytus, who purified Hercules after the murder of Iphitus. *Apollod.* 2. c. 6.

DE'IPHON, a brother of Triptolemus, son of Celeus and Metanira. When Ceres travelled over the world, she stopped at his father's court, and undertook to nurse him and bring him up. To reward the hospitality of Celeus, the goddess began to make his son immortal; and every evening she placed him on burning coals, to purify him from whatever mortal particles he still possessed. The uncommon growth of Deiphon astonished Metanira, who wished to know what method Ceres took to make him so vigorous. She was so alarmed at seeing her son seated on burning coals, that the shrieks which she uttered disturbed the mysterious operations of the goddess, and Deiphon perished in the flames. *Apollod.* 1. c. 5.——The husband of Hyrnetho, daughter of Teneus, king of Argos. *Id.* 2. c 71.

DEIPHON'TES, a general of Temenus, who took Epidauria, &c. *Paus.* 2. c. 12.——A general of the Dorians, &c. *Polyæn.*

DEIP'NIAS, a town of Thessaly, near Larissa. *Steph.*

DEIP'YLE, daughter of Adrastus, who married Tydeus, by whom she became mother of Diomedes. *Apollod.* 1. c. 8.—*Diod.* 4.

DEIP'YLUS, a son of Sthenelus, engaged in the Trojan war. *Homer. Il.* 5.

DEIP'YRUS, a Grecian chief during the Trojan war. *Homer. Il.* 8.

DEIR'ADES, a village of the tribe Leontis. *Steph.*

DEITA'NIA, a region of Spain, near Carthago Nova. *Plin.* 3. c. 3.

DEJANI'RA, a daughter of Œneus, king of Ætolia. Her beauty procured her many admirers, but her father promised to give her in marriage only to him who proved to be the strongest of all his competitors. Hercules obtained the prize, and married Dejanira, by whom he had three children, the most known of whom is Hyllus. As Dejanira was once travelling with her husband, they were stopped by the swollen streams of the Evenus, upon which the centaur Nessus offered Hercules to convey her safe to the opposite shore. The hero consented, but no sooner had Nessus gained the opposite bank, than he attempted to offer violence to Dejanira, and to carry her away in the sight of her husband. Hercules, upon this, aimed a poisoned arrow at the seducer, and mortally wounded him. Nessus, as he expired, wished to avenge his death upon his murderer; and he gave Dejanira his tunic, which was covered with blood poisoned and infected by the arrow, observing, that it would have the power of reclaiming a husband from unlawful loves. Dejanira accepted the present, and when Hercules proved faithless to her bed, she sent him the centaur's tunic, which instantly caused his death. *Vid.* Hercules. Dejanira was so disconsolate at the death of her husband, which she had so inadvertently occasioned that she destroyed herself. *Ovid. Met.* 8 & 9.—*Apollod.* 2.—*Diod.* 4.—*Senec. in Hercul.*—*Hygin.* fab. 34 & 36.

DE'LA, a city of Arabia Felix. *Ptol.*

DEL'DON, a king of Mysia, defeated by the Romans under Crassus.

DE'LIA, a festival celebrated every fifth year in the island of Delus, in honour of Apollo. It was first instituted by Theseus, who, at his return from Crete, placed a statue of Venus there which he had received from Ariadne. At the celebration, they crowned this statue with garlands, appointed a choir of music, and exhibited horse races. They afterwards led a dance called γέρανος, in which they imitated by their motions, the various windings of the Cretan labyrinth, from which Theseus had extricated himself by Ariadne's assistance. *Thucyd.* 1. 3.—*Callim Hymn. in Delum.*—*Plut. Thes.* There was also another festival of the same name, yearly celebrated by the Athenians. It was also instituted by Theseus, who, when he was going to Crete, made a vow that if he returned victorious, he would yearly visit, in a solemn manner, the temple of Delus. The persons employed in this annual processsion were called Deliastæ and Theori. The ship, the same which conveyed Theseus, and had been carefully preserved by the Athenians, was called Theoris and Delias. When the ship was ready for the voyage, the priest of Apollo solemnly adorned the stern with garlands, and a universal lustration was made over the city. The Theori were crowned with laurels, and men armed with axes, preceded them in commemoration of Theseus, who had cleared the way from Trœzene to Athens, and delivered the country from robbers. When the ship arrived at Delus, the crew offered solemn sacrifices to the god of the island, and celebrated a festival in his honor. After this, they retired to their ship, and sailed back to Athens, where all the people of the city ran in crowds to meet them. Every appearance of festivity prevailed at their approach, and the citizens opened their doors, and prostrated themselves before the Deliastæ, as they walked in procession. During this festival, it was unlawful to put to death any malefactor, and on that account the life of Socrates was prolonged for thirty days after his condemnation. *Xenophon. Memor. & in Conv.—Plut. in Phæd.—Senec.* ep. 70.

De'lia, a surname of Diana, because she was born in Delus. *Virg. Ecl.* 3. v. 67. *Id. Culex.* 109.

De'lia, a city of Caria. *Steph.*

DELI'ADES, a son of Glaucus, killed by his brother Bellerophon. *Apollod.* 2. c. 3.——The priestesses in Apollo's temple. *Homer. Hymn. ad Ap.*

DELIAS'TÆ, the name of the deputies whom the people of Athens sent in solemn embassy to Delus. *Vid.* Delia.

DE'LIUM, a temple sacred to Apollo.——A town of Bœotia opposite Chalcis, famous for a battle fought there, B.C. 424, &c. *Liv.* 31. c. 45. l. 35. c. 51.

DE'LIUS, a surname of Apollo, because he was born in Delus.

De'lius Quin'tus, an officer in the service of Antony, who, when he was sent to cite Cleopatra before his master, advised her to make her appearance in the most captivating attire. He afterwards abandoned his friend, and fled to Augustus, who received him with great kindness. *Horace* has addressed 2 od. 3. to him. *Plut. in Anton.*

DELMA'TIUS FL. JUL., a nephew of Constantine the Great, honoured with the title of Cæsar, and put in possession of Thrace, Macedonia, and Achaia. His great virtues were unable to save him from a violent death, and he was assassinated by his own soldiers.

DELMIN'IUM or **DAL'MIUM**, a town of Dalmatia. *Flor*, 4. c. 12.

DELPHA'CIA, an island of the Propontis. *Plin.* 5. c. 32.

DEL'PHI, now Castri, a town of Phocis, situate in a valley at the south-west side of mount Parnassus. It was anciently called Pytho, because the serpent Python was killed there; and it received the name of Delphi, from Delphus, the son of Apollo. Some have also called it Parnassia Nape, the *valley* of Parnassus. Delphi was famous as the place where the Amphicyonic council assembled, but more particularly for a temple of Apollo and for an oracle celebrated in every age and country. The origin of the oracle, though fabulous, is described as something wonderful. A number of goats that were feeding on mount Parnassus, came to a place where there was a deep and long perforation in the earth. The steam which issued from the aperture seemed to inspire the goats, and they played and frisked about in such an uncommon manner, that the goatherd was tempted to look into the hole to see what mysteries the place contained. He was himself immediately seized with a fit of enthusiasm, and his expressions which were wild and extravagant, passed for prophecies. This circumstance was soon known about the country, and many experienced the same enthusiastic inspiration. The place was consequently regarded with reverence, and a temple was soon after erected in honour of Apollo, and a city built. According to some accounts, Apollo was not the first who gave oracles there; but Terra, Neptune, Themis, and Phœbe, were thought to preside over the place before the son of Latona. The oracles were generally given in verse; but when it had been sarcastically observed, that the god and patron of poetry was the most incorrect poet in the world, the priestess delivered her answers in prose. The oracles were always delivered by a priestess called Pythia. *Vid.* Pythia. The temple was destroyed and rebuilt several times. It was customary for those who consulted the oracle to make rich presents to the god; and no monarch distinguished himself more by the splendour of his donations than Crœsus. This sacred repository of opulence was often the object of plunder; but the attempts of Xerxes and afterwards of Brennus, to rob it of its treasures, were, it is said, defeated by the supernatural interference of the gods. During the sacred war, the people of Phocis carried off from it 10,000 talents, nearly £2,250,000 English money, to maintain their armies against their powerful opponents: and Nero carried away no less than 500 statues of brass, partly of the gods, and partly of the most illustrious heroes. In another age, Constantine the Great removed its most splendid ornaments to his new capital. It was universally believed, and supposed, by the ancients, that Delphi was in the middle of the earth; and on that account it was called *terræ umbilicus*. This, according to mythologists, was first found out by two doves, which Jupiter had let loose from the two extremities of the earth, and which met upon the spot where the temple of Delphi was built. *Cic. Div.* 2. c. 57. *Inv.* 2. c. 23.—*Sueton. Ner.* 40.—*Strab.* 9.—*Ptol.* 3. c. 15.—*Claudian. de Cons. Mallii. Theod. Paneg.—Apollon.* 2. v. 706.—*Diod.* 16.—*Plut. de Defect. Orac. &c.—Paus.* 10. c. 6. &c.—*Ovid. Met.* 10. v. 168.

DEL'PHICUS, a surname of Apollo, from the worship paid to him at Delphi.

DELPHIN'IA, festivals observed in Ægina, in honour of Apollo.

DELPHIN'IUM, a place in Bœotia, opposite Eubœa. *Strab.*

DELPHIN'IUS, a surname of Apollo, because he destroyed the serpent Python, called also Delphine, or because he guided, by means of a dolphin, a Cretan colony, which at last arrived at Cyrrha, and built, in gratitude, an altar to the god under that name. *Hom. Hymn. in Apoll.—Heliodor. Lariss. de Opt.—Plut. de Ind. Anim.*

DEL'PHIS, the priestess of the oracle of Apollo at Delphi. *Martial.* 2. epigr. 43.

DEL'PHUS, a son of Apollo, who built Delphi, and consecrated it to his father. His mother is called by some Celæno, by others Melæne, daughter of Cephis, and by others Thyas, daughter of Castalius, the first priestess of Bacchus. *Hygin.* 161.—*Paus.* 10. c. 6.

DELPHU'SA, a fountain of Delphi, *Steph.*

DELPHU'SIA, a city of Arcadia. *Id.*

DELPHY'NE, a serpent which watched over Jupiter. *Apollod.* 1. c. 6.

DEL'TA, a part of Ægypt, which received that name from its great resemblance to the form of the fourth letter of the Greek alphabet. It lies between the Canopian and Pelusian mouths of the Nile, extending at its base on the sea coast 160 miles, and it begins to be formed about ninety miles from the sea, where the river divides itself into several streams. It has been formed totally by the mud and sand, which, in the lapse of ages, have been washed down from the upper parts of Ægypt by the Nile, according to ancient tradition. *Cæs. Alex.* c. 27.—*Strab.* 15 & 17.—*Herodot.* 2. c. 13, &c.—*Plin.* 3. c. 16.

DELTHA'NII, a people of Peloponnesus. *Steph.*

DE'LUS, one of the Cyclades, at the north of Naxus was severally called Lagia, Ortygia, Asteria, Chlamydia, Pelasgia, Pyrpile, Cynthus, and Cynæthus, and now bears the name of Sdille. It was called Delus, from δῆλος, because it suddenly made its *appearance* on the surface of the sea. *Vid.* Apollo. The island was celebrated for the nativity of Apollo and Diana; and the solemnity with which the festivals of these deities were celebrated there, by the inhabitants of the neighbouring island and of the continent, is well known. One of the altars of Apollo, in the island, was reckoned among the seven wonders of the world. It had been erected, according to the mythologists, by Apollo, when only four years old, and made with the horns of goats, killed by Diana on mount Cynthus. It was unlawful to sacrifice any living creature upon that altar, which was religiously kept pure from blood and every pollution. The whole island of Delus was held in such veneration that the Persians, who had pillaged and profaned all the temples of Greece, never offered violence to the temple of Apollo, but regarded it with the utmost reverence. Apollo, whose image represented him in the shape of a dragon, delivered oracles there during the summer. No dogs, as Thucydides mentions, were permitted to enter the island. It was unlawful for a man to die, or for a child to be born there; and when the Athenians were ordered to purify the place, they dug up all the dead bodies that had been interred there, and transported them to the neighbouring islands. An edict was also issued, which commanded all persons labouring under any mortal or dangerous disease, to be instantly removed to the adjacent island called Rhane. Some mythologists suppose that Asteria, who was changed into a quail, to avoid the importuning addresses of Jupiter, was metamorphosed into this island, originally called Ortygia, from ὄρτυξ, *a quail*. The people of Delus are described by *Cicero, Acad.* 2. c. 16 & 18. l. 4. c. 18. as famous for rearing hens. *Strab.* 8 & 10.—*Ovid. Met.* 5. v. 329. l. 6. v. 333.—*Mela*, 2. c. 7.—*Plin.* 4. c. 12.—*Plut. de Solert. Anim. &c.*—*Thucyd.* 3, 4, &c.—*Virg. Æn.* 3, v. 73. & *Servius loco.*—*Lactant in* 4 *Theb.* 796.—*Ptol.* 3. c. 15.—*Petronius in Sat.*—*Callim ad Del.*—*Claudian. de* 4. *Cons. Hon.*

DEMA'DES, an Athenian, who, from a sailor, became an eloquent orator, and obtained much influence in the state. He was taken prisoner at the battle of Cheronæa, by Philip, and ingratiated himself into the favour of that prince, by whom he was greatly esteemed. He was afterwards put to death, with his son, on suspicion of treason, B.C. 322. One of his orations is extant. *Diod.* 16 & 17.—*Quintil.* 2. c. 17.—*Cic. Orat.* 26. *Br.* 9.—*Plut. in Dem.*

DEMÆN'ETUS, a rhetorician of Syracuse, the enemy of Timolean. *C. Nep. in Tim.* 5.

DEMAG'ORAS, one of Alexander's flatterers.——An historian, who wrote an account of the foundation of Rome. *Dionys. Hal.* 1.

DEMARA'TA, a daughter of Hiero of Sicily, &c. *Liv.* 24. c. 22.

DEMARA'TUS, the son and successor of Ariston on the throne of Sparta, B.C. 526. He was banished by the intrigues of Cleomenes, his royal colleague, on the pretext that he was illegitimate. He retired into Asia, and was kindly received by Darius son of Hystaspes king of Persia. When the Persian monarch made preparations to invade Greece, Demaratus, though persecuted by the Lacedæmonians, informed them of the hostilities which hung over their head. *Herodot.* 5. c. 75, &c. l. 6. c. 50, &c.—*Justin.* 2. c. 10 & 13.—*Plut. in Alex.*——A rich citizen of Corinth, of the family of the Bacchiadæ. When Cypselus had usurped the sovereign power, Demaratus, with all his family, migrated to Italy, and settled at Tarquinii, 658 years before Christ. His son, Lucumon, became king of Rome, under the name of Tarquinius Priscus. *Dionys. Hal.*—*Liv.* 1 c. 34.—*Cic. Tusc.* 5. c. 37.——A writer on Phrygia and on rivers. *Plut.*—*Voss. H. Gr.* p. 352.

DEMAR'CHUS, a Syracusan put to death by Dionysius.

DEMAR'ETE, the wife of Gelon of Sicily. *Diod.* 15.

DEMARIS'TE, the mother of Timoleon.

DEMA'TRIA, a Spartan mother, who killed her son because he returned from a battle without glory. *Plut. Lac. Inst.*

DE'MEA, the character of an old man in the Adelphi of *Terence*.

DEME'TRIA, a festival in honour of Ceres, called by the Greeks Demeter. It was then customary for the votaries of the goddess to lash themselves with whips made of the bark of trees. The Athenians had a solemnity of the same name, in honor of Demetrius Poliorcetes.

DEME'TRIAS, a considerable town at the east of Thessaly, on the bay of Pagasæ. The name was common to other places, so called in compliment to Demetrius. *Steph.*

DEME'TRIUM, a city of Æolis. *Steph.*

DEME'TRIUS, a son of Antigonus and Stratonice, surnamed Poliorcetes, *destroyer of towns.* At the age of 22, he was sent by his father against Ptolemy, king of Ægypt, who had invaded Syria. He was defeated near Gaza: but he soon repaired his loss, by a victory over one of the generals of the enemy. He afterwards sailed with a fleet of 250 ships to Athens, and restored the Athenians to liberty, by freeing them from the power of Cassander and Ptolemy, and expelling the garrison which had been stationed there under Demetrius Phalereus. After this successful expedition, he besieged and took Munychia, and defeated Cassander at Thermopylæ. His reception, at Athens, after these victories, was attended with the greatest servility, and the Athenians were not ashamed to raise altars to him as to a god, and to consult his oracles. This uncommon success raised the jealousy of the successors of Alexander; and Seleucus, Cassander, and Lysimachus, united to destroy Antigonus and his son. Their hostile armies met at Ipsus, B.C. 301. Antigonus was killed in the battle; and Demetrius, after a severe oss, retired to Ephesus. This unfortunate event encouraged his enemies; and the Athenians, who had lately adored him as a god, now refused to admit him into their city. He soon after, ravaged the territories of Lysimachus, and reconciled himself to Seleucus, to whom he gave his daughter Stratonice in marriage. Athens now laboured under tyranny, and Demetrius relieved it, and pardoned the inhabitants. The loss of his possessions in Asia recalled him from Greece, and he established himself on the throne of Macedonia, by the murder of Alexander the son of Cassander. Here he was continually at war with the neighbouring states; and the superior power of his adversaries obliged him at last to leave Macedonia, after he had been seated on the throne for seven years. He passed into Asia, and attacked some of the provinces of Lysimachus with various success; but famine and pestilence destroyed the greatest part of his army, and he retired to the court of Seleucus for support and assistance. He met with a kind reception, but this treatment was in a short time succeeded by distrust, and hostilities soon began; but after he had gained some advantage over his son-in-law, Demetrius was totally forsaken by his troops in the field of battle, and became an easy prey to the enemy. Though he was kept in confinement by his son-in-law, yet he maintained himself like a prince, and passed his time in hunting and laborious exercises. His son Antigonus offered Seleucus all his possessions, and even his person, to procure his father's liberty; but all proved unavailing, and Demetrius died in the 54th year of his age, after a confinement of three years, 286 B.C. His remains were delivered to Antigonus, honored with a splendid funeral procession at Corinth, and thence conveyed to Demetrias. The posterity of Demetrius remained in possession of the Macedonian throne till the age of Perseus, who was conquered by the Romans. Demetrius has rendered himself famous for his fondness of dissipation when among the dissolute, and his love of virtue and military glory in the field of battle. He has been commended as a great warrior; and his ingenious inventions, his warlike engines, and stupendous machines in his war with the Rhodians, justify his claims to that honorable character. He has been blamed indeed for his voluptuous indulgences; and his biographer has observed, that no Grecian prince had more wives and concubines than Poliorcetes. His obedience and reverence to his father have been justly admired; and it has been recorded that Antigonus ordered the ambassadors of a foreign prince to remark particularly the cordiality and friendship which subsisted between him and his son. *Plut. in Vitâ.*—*Diod.* 17.—*Justin.* 1. c. 17, &c.—*Cic. Off.* 2. c. 7. [A bronze statue of Demetrius Poliorcetes has been discovered at Palermo, and is to be seen in the Museum at that place.]——A son of Philip of Macedonia, delivered as a hostage to the Romans, and led in triumph by T. Q. Flaminius. When he afterwards apeared at Rome as the ambassador of his father, his great modesty and diffidence drew upon him the attention of the senate, and the father, though accused of hostile views against the republic, was pardoned on account of the innocence and integrity of the son. The popularity thus acquired at Rome, raised suspicions and jealousies in Macedonia; and Demetrius, falsely accused by his brother Perseus, who envied him his fame and meritorious services, was cruelly put to death, B.C. 180, by Philip, who acknowledging too late the innocence of his murdered son, and the perfidy of his surviving brother, at last fell a prey to lingering sorrow and unavailing remorse. *Liv.* 33. c. 30. l. 34. c. 52. l. 39. c. 47. &c. l. 40. c. 5, &c.—*Justin.* 32. c. 2.——A servant of Cassius.——A freedman of Pompey.——A son of Demetrius of Cyrene.——A son of Demetrius, surnamed Slender.——A Cynic philosopher, disciple of Apollonius Thyanæus, in the age of Caligula. The emperor wished to gain the philosopher to his interest by a large present, but Demetrius refused it with indignation, and said, if Caligula wishes to bribe me, let him send me his crown. Vespasian was displeased with his insolence, and banished him. The Cynic derided the punishment, and inveighed bitterly against the emperor. He died at a very advanced age, and Seneca observes, that "Nature had brought him forth, to show mankind that an exalted genius can live securely without being corrupted by the vices of the surrounding world." *Senec. Philostr. in Apoll.*——One of Alexander's flatterers. *Curt.* 6. c. 7.——A native of Byzantium who wrote on the Greek poets.——An Athenian killed at Mantinea, when fighting against the Thebans. *Polyæn.* 2.——A writer, who published a history of the irruptions of the Gauls into Asia. *Diog. Laert.*——A philological writer in the age of Cicero. *Cic. ad Attic.* 8. ep. 11.——A stage player. *Juv.* 3. v. 99.——A geographer, surnamed the *Calatian. Strab.* 1.——An architect, who assisted in finishing the temple of Diana at Ephesus. *Vitruv.* l. 7. *Præfat.*

Deme'trius Gona'tus, a prince who succeeded his father Antigonus on the throne of Macedonia. He reigned 11 years, and was succeeded by Antigonus Doson. *Justin.* 26. c. 2.—*Polyb.* 2.

Deme'trius the First, surnamed *Soter*, was son of Seleucus Philopater, the son of Antiochus the Great, king of Syria. His father gave him as a hostage to the Romans. After the death of Seleucus, Antiochus Epiphanes, the deceased monarch's brother, usurped the kingdom of Syria, and was succeeded by his son Antiochus Eupator. This usurpation displeased Demetrius, who was detained at Rome; he procured his liberty on pretence of going to hunt, and having made his escape, quickly passed into Syria, where the troops received him as their lawful sovereign, B.C. 162 He put to death Eupator and Lysias, and established himself on his throne by cruelty and oppression. Alexander Bala, the son of Antiochus Epiphanes, laid claim to the crown of Syria, and defeated Demetrius in a battle, in the 12th year of his reign. *Strab.* 16.—*Appian.*—*Justin.* 34. c. 3.

Deme'trius the Second, surnamed *Nicanor* or *Conqueror*, was son of Soter, to whom he succeeded by the assistance of Ptolemy Philometer, after he had driven from the throne the usurper Alexander Bala, B.C. 146. He married Cleopatra, the daughter of Ptolemy; who was, before, the wife of the expelled monarch. Demetrius gave himself up to luxury and voluptuousness, and suffered his kingdom to be governed by his favorites. At that time a pretended son of Bala, called Diodorus Tryphon, seized a part of Syria, and Demetrius, to oppose his antagonist, made an alliance with the Jews, and marched into the east, where he was taken by the Parthians. Phraates, king of Parthia, gave him his daughter Rhodogyne in marriage; and Cleopatra was so incensed at this new connexion, that she gave herself up to Antiochus Sidetes, her brother-in-law, and married him. Sidetes was killed in battle against the Parthians, and Demetrius regained possession of his kingdom. His pride and oppression rendered him now more odious, and his subjects asked a king of the house of Seleucus, from Ptolemy Physcon, king of Ægypt; and Demetrius unable, to resist the power of his enemies, fled to Ptolemais, which was then in the hands of his wife Cleopatra. The gates were shut against him by Cleopatra; and he was afterwards killed by order of the governor of Tyre, to which place he had fled for protection. He was succeeded by Alexander Zebina, whom Ptolemy had raised to the throne, B.C. 127. *Justin.* 36, &c.—*Appian. de Bell. Syr.*—*Joseph.*

Deme'trius the Third, surnamed *Eucerus*, was son of Antiochus Gryphus. After the example of his brother Philip, who had seized Syria, he made himself master of Damascus, B.C. 93, and soon after obtained a victory over his brother. He was taken in a battle against the Parthians, and died in captivity. *Joseph.* 1.

Deme'trius Phale'reus, a disciple of Theophrastus, who gained such an influence over the Athenians, by his eloquence, and the purity of his manners, that he was elected by them decennial archon, B.C. 317. He so embellished the city, and rendered himself so popular by his munificence, that the Athenians raised 360 brazen statues to his honor. Yet in the midst of all this popularity, his enemies raised a sedition against him, and he was condemned to death, and all his statues were thrown down, after enjoying the sovereign power for ten years. He fled to the court of Ptolemy Lagus, where he was received with kindness and cordiality. The Ægyptian monarch consulted him concerning the succession of his children: and Demetrius advised him to raise to the throne the children of Eurydice in preference to the offspring of Berenice. This advice so irritated Philadelphus, the son of Berenice, that, after his father's death, he sent the philosopher into Upper Ægypt, and there detained him in strict confinement. Demetrius, tired with his situation, put an end to his life by the bite of an asp, 284 B.C. According to some, Demetrius enjoyed the confidence of Philadelphus, and enriched his library at Alexandra with 200,000 volumes. All the works of Demetrius, on rhetoric, history, and eloquence, are lost, and the treatise on rhetoric, falsely attributed to him, is by some supposed to be the composition of Dionysius of Halicarnassus. The last edition of this treatise is that of Glasgow, 8vo. 1743. *Diog. in Vitâ.*—*Cic. in Brut. De Offic.* 1, *Finib.* 5. c. 9.—*Plut. in Exil.*—*Voss. Hist. Gr.* 1. c. 12.—*Sax. Onom.* 1. p. 89.—*Fabr. B. Gr.* 3. c. 11.

Deme'trius Sy'rus, a rhetorician at Athens, who had Cicero among his pupils. *Cic. in Brut.* c. 174.

DEMIN'SII, a people of Lower Mysia. *Ptol.*

DEMIUR'GUS, a name given to the first magistrate of some of the cities of Peloponnesus. *Liv.* 38. c. 30.—*Cic. ad Fam.* 9. ep 22.

DE'MO, the name of the Sibyl of Cumæ.

DEMOANAS'SA, the mother of Ægialeus.

DEMOCE'DES, a celebrated physician of Crotona, son of Calliphon, and intimate with Polycrates. He was carried as a prisoner from Samus to Darius, king of Persia, at whose court he acquired great riches and much reputation, especially by curing the king's foot, and the breast of Atossa. He was sent to Greece as a spy by the king, and, ashamed of his dishonourable employment, fled to Crotona, where he married the daughter of the wrestler Milo. *Ælian. V. H.* 8. c. 18.—*Herodot.* 3. c. 124, &c.

DEMOCH'ARES, an Athenian, sent with some of his countrymen with an embassy to Philip, king of Macedonia. The monarch gave them audience; and when he asked them what he could do to please the people of Athens? Demochares replied, "Hang yourself." This insolent answer raised the indignation of all the hearers; but Philip mildly dismissed them, and bade them ask their countrymen, which deserved most the appellation of wise and moderate, they who could use such ill language, or he who received it without any signs of resentment. *Senec. de Irâ.* 3. c. 23.—*Ælian. V. H.* 3, 7, 8, 12.—*Cic. in Brut.* 3. *De Orat.* 2. c. 23.——A poet of Soli, who composed a comedy on Demetrius Poliorcetes. *Plut. in Dem.*——A statuary, who wished to make a statue of mount Athos for Alexander the Great. *Vitruv. in præf.* l. 2.——A general of Pompey the younger, who died B.C. 36.

DEM'OCLES, a man accused off disaffection towards Dionysius, &c. *Polyæn.* 5.——A beautiful youth, passionately loved by Demetrius Poliorcetes. He threw himself into a cauldron of boiling water, rather than submit to the unnatural lusts of the tyrant. *Plut. in Dem.*

DEMOCLI'DES, a physician who cured Polycrates, tyrant of Samus, and wrote a book on medicine. *Suidas.*

DEMOC'OON, a natural son of Priam, who came from his residence at Abydus, to assist his country against the Greeks. He was, after a glorious defence, killed by Ulysses. *Homer. Il.* 4. v. 499.

DEMOC'RATES, an architect of Alexandria.——A wrestler. *Ælian. V. H.* 4. c. 15.——An Athenian who fought on the side of Darius, against the Macedonians. *Curt.* 6. c. 5.——A physician. *Plin.* 25. c. 2.

DEMOC'RITUS, a celebrated philosopher of Abdera, disciple of Leucippus. He travelled over the greatest part of Europe, Asia, and Africa, in quest of knowledge, and returned home in the greatest poverty. There was a law at Abdera, which deprived of the honor of a funeral, the man who had rduced himself to indigence; but Democritus, to avoid ignominy, repeated before his countrymen one of his compositions called *Diacosmus.* It was received with such uncommon applause, that he was not only presented with 500 talents, but statues were erected to his honor; and a decree passed that the expenses of his funeral should be paid from the public treasury. The philosopher retired to a garden near the city, where he dedicated his time to study and solitude; and, according to some authors, he put out his eyes, in order that he might apply himself more closely to philosophical enquiries. He was accused of insanity, and Hippocrates was ordered to enquire into the nature of his disorder. The physician held a conference with the philosopher, and declared that not Democritus, but his enemies were insane. He continually laughed at the follies and vanity of mankind, who distract themselves with care, and are at once a prey to hope and anxiety. He told Darius, who was inconsolable for the loss of his wife, that he would raise her from the dead, if he could find three persons who had gone through life without adversity, whose names he might engrave on the queen's monument. The king's enquiries to find such persons proved unavailing, and the philosopher in some manner soothed the sorrow of his sovereign. He taught his disciples that the soul died with the body; and therefore, as he gave no credit to the existence of ghosts, some youths, to try his fortitude, disguised themselves in a hideous habit, and approached his cave in the dead of night, with whatever noises could create astonishment and terror. The philosopher received them unmoved; and, without even looking at them, desired them to cease making themselves such objects of ridicule and folly. He died in the 109th year of his age, B.C. 361. His father was so rich that he entertained Xerxes, with all his army, as he was marching against Greece. All the works of Democritus are now lost. He was the author of the doctrine of atoms, and first taught that the milky way was occasioned by a confused light arising from a multitude of stars, an opinion still supported by modern astronomers. He may be considered as the parent of experimental philosophy, in the prosecution of which, he showed himself so ardent, that he declared he would prefer the discovery of one of the causes of the works of nature, to the diadem of Persia. It is said that he could make artificial emeralds, and tinge them with various colors, and that he could likewise dissolve stones and soften ivory. *Euseb.* 14. c. 27.—*Diog. in Vitâ.*—*Ælian. V. H.* 4. c. 20.—*Cic. de Finib.* 5. c. 19. *Tusc.* 1. c. 11.—*Plut. de Curios.*—*Val. Max.* 8. c. 7.—*Strab.* 1 & 15.—*Sax. Onom.* 1. p. 37.—*Fabr. B. Gr.* 1. 2. c. 23.——An Ephesian, who wrote a book on Diana's temple, &c. *Diog.*—*Athen.* 1. 12.——A powerful man of Naxus. *Herodot.* 7. c. 46.

DEMOD'ICE, the wife of Cretheus, king of Iolcus. She, according to Hyginus, endeavoured to corrupt the virtue of Phryxus, the son of Athamas, her husband's brother, and when slighted, she accused him of the criminal intentions which she herself had formed. Her guilt was afterwards discovered, and she was punished with death. Some call her Biadice, but the majority of mythologists give the name of Tyro, to the only wife whom Cretheus married. *Hygin. P. A.* 2. c. 20.

DEMOD'OCUS, a musician at the court of Alcinous, who sang in the presence of Ulysses the secret amours of Mars and Venus, and other poetical subjects. The gods, according to the poets, bestowed upon him the power of song, but denied him the blessing of sight. *Athen.* 1.—*Ovid. in Ib.* 272.—*Virg. Æn.* 10. v. 413.—*Eustath in Il.* 1.—*Gyrald. de P. Hist.* 2.—*Homer. Odyss.* 8. v. 44.—*Plut. de Mus.*——A Trojan chief, who came with Æneas into Italy, where he was killed. *Virg. Æn.* 10. v. 413.——An historian. *Plut. de Flum.*

DEMO'LEUS, a Greek, killed by Æneas in the Trojan war. *Virg. Æn.* 5. v. 260.

DEMO'LEON, a centaur, killed by Theseus at the nuptials of Pirithous. *Ovid. Met.* 12. v. 356.——A son of Antenor, killed by Achilles. *Homer. Il.* 20. v. 395.

DE'MON, an Athenian, nephew to Demosthenes. He was placed at the head of the government during the absence of his uncle, and obtained a decree that Demosthenes should be recalled, and that a ship should be sent to bring him back from the place of his exile.

DEMONAC'TES, a præfect of Armenia, routed by Mithridates. *Tac.* 11. c. 9.

DEMONAS'SA, a daughter of Amphiaraus, who married Thersander. *Paus.* 9. c. 5.

DEMO'NAX, a celebrated philosopher of Cyprus, in the reign of Adrian. He shewed no concern about the necessaries of life; but when hungry, he entered the first house he came to, and there satisfied his appetite. Practising virtue, without ostentation, and reproving the vicious without bitterness, he imitated the character of Socrates in the integrity of his conduct, and that of Diogenes in his disregard for the follies and vanities of life. He died in his 100th year, addressing those who attended his last moments with these words, "You may depart, the farce is over;" an expression likewise attributed to Augustus at his death. *Lucian.*——A man of Mantinea, sent to settle the goverment of Cyrene. *Herodot.* 4. c. 161.

DEMONE'SUS, an island of the Propontis. *Steph.*

DEMONI'CA, a woman who betrayed Ephesus to Brennus. *Plut. in Parall.*

DEMONI'CE, a daughter of Agenor, son of Pleuron by Epicaste. She became mother of Evenus, Thestius, and others by Mars. *Apollod.* 1.

DEMOPHAN'TUS, a general, killed by Antigonus. *Paus.* 8. c. 49.

DEMOPH'ILA, a name given to the Sibyl of Cumæ, who, as it is supposed by some authors, sold the Sibylline books to Tarquin. *Varro. apud Lact.* 1. c. 6.

DEMOPH'ILUS, an Athenian archon. Ol. 99. an. 4.——An officer of Agathocles of Sicily. *Diod.* 19.——A sophist who wrote on the lives of the ancients.——A painter. *Plin.* 35. c. 8.——A son of Ephorus the historian, wrote an account of the sacred war which had been omitted by his father. *Diod.* 1. 16.

DEM'OPHON, an Athenian who assisted the Thebans in recovering Cadmea, &c. *Diod.* 15.

DEMOPH'OON, son of Theseus and Phædra, was king of Athens, B.C. 1182, and reigned 33 years. He was engaged with the Greeks at the Trojan war, and, at his return, visited Thrace, where he was tenderly received and treated by Phyllis. He retired to Athens, and forgot the kindness and love of Phyllis, who hanged herself in despair. *Ælian. V. H.* 4. c. 5.—*Ovid. Heroid.* 2. *De A. A.* 2.—*Paus.* 10. c. 25.——A friend of Æneas, killed by Camilla. *Virg. Æn.* 11. v. 675.

DEMOP'OLIS, a son of Themistocles. *Plut. in Them.*

DE'MOS, a place of Ithaca, called also Crocyleum by *Stephanus. Thucyd.* 1. 3.—*Homer. Il.* 2.

DEMOS'THENES, a celebrated Athenian, son of a rich blacksmith, called Demosthenes, and of Cleobule. He was but seven years of age when his father died, and, consequently, little care was bestowed upon him by his guardians, who negligently managed his affairs, and embezzled the greatest part of his property. His education was totally neglected; and, for whatever advances he made in learning, he was indebted to his own industry and application. He became the pupil of Isæus and Plato, and applied himself to study the orations of Isocrates. At the age of 17 he gave an early proof of his eloquence and abilities against his guardians, from whom he obtained the restoration of the greatest part of his estate. His rising talents were, however, impeded by weak lungs, and a difficulty of pronunciation, especially of the letter *ρ*, but these obstacles were gradually overcome by unwearied application. To correct the stammering of his voice, he spoke with pebbles in his mouth; and he removed the distortion of his features, which accompanied his utterance, by watching the motions of his countenance in a looking-glass. That his pronunciation might be loud and full of emphasis, he frequently ran up the steepest and most uneven walks, where his voice acquired force and energy; and, on the sea-shore, when the waves were violently agitated, he declaimed aloud, to accustom himself to the noise and tumults of a public assembly. He also retired to the solitude of a subterraneous cave, to devote himself more closely to studious pursuits; and to eradicate all desire of appearing in public, he shaved one half of his head. In this silent retirement, by the help of a glimmering lamp, he composed a great part of his orations, which have been the admiration of every age, though his contemporaries and rivals severely inveighed against them, and observed that they smelt of oil. His abilities, as an orator, raised him to consequence at Athens, and he was soon placed at the head of the government. In this public capacity, he roused his countrymen from their habitual indolence, and animated them to resist the ambition and encroachments of Philip of Macedon. In the battle of Cheronæa, however, Demosthenes betrayed pusillanimity, and saved his life by dishonourable flight. After the death of Philip, he declared himself warmly against his son and successor, Alexander, whom he branded with the appellation of boy; and, when the Macedonian prince demanded of the Athenians their orators, Demosthenes reminded his countrymen of the fable of the sheep which delivered their dogs to the wolves. Though he had frequently boasted that all the gold of Macedonia would not be sufficient to tempt him, yet he suffered himself to be bribed by a small golden cup from Harpalus. The dissatisfaction which this occasioned, forced him to retire from Athens; and, during the time of his banishment, which was passed at Trœzene and Ægina, the orator lived with more effeminacy than true heroism. When Antipater made war against Greece, after the death of Alexander, Demosthenes was recalled from his exile, and a galley was sent to fetch him from Ægina. His return was attended with much triumph, and all the citizens crowded to the Piræus to see him land. His popularity, however, was short. Antipater and Craterus were near Athens, and demanded all the orators to be delivered into their hands. Demosthenes, with all his adherents, fled to the temple of Neptune in Calauria; and, when he saw that all hopes of safety were vanished, he took a dose of poison, which he always carried about him in a quill, and expired on the day that the Thesmophoria were celebrated, in the 60th year of his age, B.C. 322. The Athenians raised a brazen statue to his honor, with this inscription:

Εἴπερ ἴσην γνώμη ῥώμην Δημόσθενες εἶχες,
Οὔ ποτ' ἂν Ἑλλήνων ἦρξεν Ἄρης Μακέδων.

Demosthenes has been deservedly called the prince of orators, and Cicero, his successful rival among the Romans, calls him a perfect model, and such as he wished himself to be. These two great princes of eloquence have often been compared together; but the judgment hesitates to which to give the preference. They both arrived at perfection; but the measures by which they obtained it were diametrically opposite. Demosthenes has been compared, and with propriety, by his rival Æschines, to a Siren, from the melody of his expressions. The times in which he lived were times of public danger and national depravity, and therefore all the powers of his great genius were called forth to arouse the Athenians to a sense of their inactivity and threatened ruin. No orator indeed can be said to have expressed the various passions of hatred, of resentment, and of indignation, with more vehemence than he; for even now, the breast is warmed and agitated by those bold and energetic appeals, which converted a nation of indolent and effeminate citizens into a band of patriots, eager to defend the liberties of their country, to avenge her wrongs, and to emulate the heroic deeds which had immortalized the name of their forefathers. As a proof of the uncommon application of this celebrated orator, it need only be mentioned, that he transcribed eight or even ten times the history of Thucydides, that he might not only imitate, but possess the force and energy of the great historian. The best editions of his works are that of Wolfius, fol. Frankof. 1604; that left unfinished by Taylor, Cantab. 4to. and that published in 12 vols. 8vo. 1720, &c. Lips. by Reiske and his widow. Many of the orations have been published separately, and been enriched with many valuable notes. *Plut. in Vitâ.—Diod.* 16.—*Cic. in Orat.* &c.—*Paus.* 1. c. 8. l. 2. c. 33.—*Sax. Onom.* 1. p. 70.—*Fabr. B. Gr.* l. 2. c. 26. [An exceedingly fine statue of this orator is in the collection at Knowle, in Kent, and the finest of many busts of him is in the Musée Royale, at Paris.]——An Athenian general, sent to succeed Alcibiades, in Sicily. He attacked Syracuse with Nicias, but his efforts were ineffectual, and after many calamities, he fell into the enemy's hands, and his army was confined to hard labor. The accounts of the death of this Demosthenes are various; some believe that, according to the barbarous opinion of those times which esteemed suicide a proof of valor, he destroyed himself, whilst others suppose he was put to death by the Syracusans, B.C. 413. *Plut. in Nic.—Thucid.* 4, &c.—*Diod.* 12.——The father of the orator Demosthenes. He was very rich, and employed an immense number of slaves in the business of a sword-cutler. *Plut. in Dem.*——A governor of Cæsarea, under the Roman emperors.——A grammarian of Thrace, who rendered Homer's Iliad and Hesiod's Theogonia into prose. *Suidas.*——An historian of Bithynia. *Steph.—Voss. Hist. Gr.* l. 3. p. 354.

DEMOS'TRATUS, an archon at Athens. Ol. 96. an. 4.——A writer mentioned by *Pliny*, 37. c. 6.

DEMOT'ELES, one of the twelve writers on the Ægyptian pyramids. *Id.* 36. c. 12.

DEMOTI'MUS, a Sicyonian, sent in the eighth year of the Peloponesian war to reconcile the Athenians and Lacedæmonians. *Schol. in Aristoph. Eq.*

DEMU'CHUS, a Trojan, son of Philetor, killed by Achilles, during the Trojan war. *Hom. Il.* 20. v. 457.

DEM'YLUS, a tyrant, who tortured the philosopher Zeno. *Plut. de. Stoic. Rep.*

DEN'DA, a Roman municipal town in Macedonia. *Plin.* 3. c. 23.

DEN'NA, a town of Upper Æthiopia. *Plin.* 6. c. 29.

DENTHELE'TÆ, a people of Thrace. *Cic. Pis.* 34.

DENTA'TUS, the surname of M. Curius, because it was reported he was born with teeth. *Plin.* 7. c. 16.

DEN'TER ROMU'LIUS, or, more properly, Dentrix Romilius, a person made governor of Rome by Romulus. *Tac.* 6. c. 11.

DEOBRI'GA, a town on the Iberus, in Spain, now Miranda de Ebro.

DEOBRIG'ULA, a town of the Murbogi, in Hispania Tarraconensis. *Ptol.*

DEOD'ATUS, an Athenian who boldly opposed the cruel resolutions of Cleon against the captive prisoners of Mitylene.

DEO'IS, a name given to Proserpine from her mother Ceres, who was called Deo. Ceres received this name, *a δήω, invenio*, because she sought her daughter all over the world. *Ovid. Met.* 6. v. 114.

DEOP'ALE, a city of India within the Ganges. *Ptol.*

DE'RA, a city or region of Iberia. *Steph.*

DER'ADRÆ, a town of India within the Ganges. *Ptol.*

DE'RÆ, a place of Messenia.

DERANOB'ILA, a town of Carmania. *Ptol.*

DERAS'IDÆ, islands near Magnesia. *Plin.* 2. c. 89.

DER'BE, a town of Lycaonia, at the north of mount Taurus, in Asia Minor, now Alah-Dag. *Cic. Fam.* 13. ep. 73.

DER'BICES or **DERBI'CES**, a people near Caucasus, who killed all who had reached their 70th year. They buried such as died a natural death. *Strab.*

DER'CE, a fountain in Spain, the waters of which were said to be uncommonly cold.

DERCEN'NUS, an ancient king of Latium. *Virg. Æn.* 11. v. 850.

DER'CETO or **DER'CETIS**, a goddess of Syria, called also Atergatis. Some authors have supposed her to be the same as Astarte, and the Ashtaroth mentioned in Scripture. She was represented as a beautiful woman above the waist, and the lower part terminated in a fish's tail. As she was chiefly worshipped in Syria, and represented like a fish, the Syrians anciently abstained from eating fish. *Lucian de Dea Syr.—Plin.* 5. c. 13. —*Ovid. Met.* 4. v. 44.—*Diod.* 2.

DERCYL'IUS, one of the præfects of Pyrrhus. *Plut.*

DERCYL'LIDAS, an active general of Sparta, celebrated for his military exploits. He took nine different cities in eight days, and freed Chersonesus from the inroads of the Thracians by building a wall across the isthmus. He lived B.C. 399. *Diod.* 14.—*Xenoph. Hist. Græc.* l, &c.

DERCYL'LUS, a man appointed over Attica by Antipater. *C. Nep. in Phoc.* 2.

DER'CYNUS, a son of Neptune, killed by Hercules. *Apollod.* 2. c. 5.

DER'IDAS, a youth put to death by Amyntas the younger. *Arist.* l. 5. *Pol.* 10.

DE'RE, called also Dire, a market town of Æthiopia, on the Arabian Gulph. *Strab.*

DERE'A, a city of Arcadia. *Steph.*

DEREM'MA, a town of Mesopotamia. *Ptol.*

DERETI'NI, a people of Dalmatia. *Plin.* 3. c. 22.

DER'MONES, an inland nation of Libya. *Ptol.*

DER'RA, a place of Laconia. *Steph.*——A city of Macedonia. *Plin.* 5. c. 10.

DER'RHÆ or **DERSÆ'I**, a people of Thrace. *Steph.*

Der'rhæ, a people of Arabia Felix. *Ptol.*

DER'RHIS, a promontory of Marmorica. *Id.*

DERTO'NA, now Tortona, a town of Liguria, between Genoa and Placentia, where a Roman colony was settled. *Cic. Div.* 11.—*Plin.* 3. c. 5.

DERTO'SA, now Tortosa, a town of Spain, near the mouth of the Iberus.

DERUSI'CI, a people of Persia. *Steph.*

DESARE'NA, a region of India within the Ganges. *Arrian. in Peripl.*

DESER'TA BOJO'RUM, a tract of Noricum, now Wienerwald. *Strab.*

DESIDIA'TES or **DESITIA'TES**, a people of Liburnia. *Plin.* 3. c. 22. *Strabo.*, l. 7. calls them Dæsitiotæ.

DES'ILI, a people of Thrace. *Steph.*

DES'TICO, a small island near Thrace, not far from the Chersonesus. *Plin.* 4. c. 12.

DESU'DABA, a town of Media. *Liv.* 44. c. 26.

DESUVIA'RII, a people of Gallia Narbonensis. *Plin.* 3. c. 4.

DETUN'DA, a town of the Turduli, in Hispania Bætica. *Ptol.*

DEUCA'LION, a son of Prometheus, who married Pyrrha, the daughter of Epimetheus. He reigned over part of Thessaly, and the poets relate, that in his age, the whole earth was overwhelmed with a deluge. The impiety of mankind had irritated Jupiter, who resolved to destroy them, and immediately the earth exhibited a boundless scene of waters. The highest mountains were climbed up by the terrified inhabitants of the country; but this seeming place of security was soon overtopped by the rising waters, and no hope was left of escaping the universal calamity. Prometheus advised his son to make himself a ship, and by this means he saved himself and his wife Pyrrha from the general destruction. The vessel was tossed about nine successive days, and at last stopped on the top of mount Parnassus, where Deucalion remained till the waters had subsided. Pindar and Ovid make no mention of a vessel built by the advice of Prometheus; but, according to their relation, Deucalion saved his life by taking refuge on the top of mount Parnassus, or, according to Hyginus, of Ætna, in Sicily. As soon as the waters had retired from the surface of the earth, Deucalion and his wife went to consult the oracle of Themis, and were directed to repair the loss of mankind, by throwing behind them the bones of their grandmother. This expression meant only the stones of the earth; and after some hesitation about the meaning of this obscure oracle, they obeyed. The stones thrown by Deucalion immediately became men, and those of Pyrrha women. According to Justin, Deucalion was not the only one who escaped from the universal calamity; but many saved their lives by ascending the highest mountains, or trusting themselves in small vessels to the mercy of the waters. This deluge, which chiefly happened in Thessaly, according to the rerelation of some writers, was produced by the inundation of the waters of the river Peneus, the regular course of which was stopped by an earthquake near mounts Ossa and Olympus. Accord- cording to *Xenophon*, there were no less than five deluges. The first happened under Ogyges, and lasted three months. The second, which was in the age of Hercules and Prometheus, continued but one month. During the third, which happened in the reign of another Ogyges, all Attica was laid waste by the water. Thessaly was totally covered by the waters during the fourth, which happened in the age of Deucalion. The last was before the Trojan war, and its effects were severely felt by the inhabitants of Ægypt. There prevailed a report in Attica, that the waters of Deucalion's deluge had disappeared through a small aperture about a cubit wide, near the temple of Jupiter Olympius; and Pausanias, who saw it, further adds, that a yearly offering of flour and honey was thrown into it with religious ceremony. The deluge of Deucalion, so much celebrated in ancient history, is supposed to have happened 1503 years B.C. Deucalion had two sons by Pyrrha, Hellen, called by some, son of Jupiter, and Amphictyon, king of Attica, and also a daughter, Protogenea, who became mother of Æthlius by Jupiter. *Pind.* 9 *Olymp.*—*Ovid. Met.* 1. fab. 8. *Heroid.* 45. v. 167.—*Apollod.* 1. c. 7.—*Paus.* 1. c. 10. l. 5. c. 8. —*Juv.* 1. v. 81.—*Hygin.* fab. 153.—*Justin.* 2. c. 6.—*Diod.* 5. —*Lucian. de Deâ Syriâ.*—*Virg. G.* 1. v. 62.——One of the argonauts. *Val. Flacc. Argon.* l. v. 366.——A son of Minos. *Apollod.* 3. c. 1. ——A son of Abas.

DEUCE'TIUS, a Sicilian general. *Diod.* 11.

DEU'DORIX, a chief of the Cherusci, conquered and led in triumph by Germanicus. *Strab.*

DEUNA'NA, a town of the Cornavii, in Britain, now Doncaster. *Ptol.*

DEURI'OPUS or **-UM**, a region and town of Macedonia. *Strab.*—*Steph.*

DE'VA, a town of Britain, supposed to be Chester, on the Dee.——The river Dee.

DEV'ADÆ, an island of Arabia Felix, in the Indian Sea. *Plin.* 6. c. 28.

DEVEL'TUM or **DEUL'TUM**, a town of Thrace, with a lake of the same name. *Ptol.*—*Plin.* 4. c. 11.

DEXAM'ENE, one of the Nereides. *Homer. Il.* 18. v. 44.——A part of Ambracia. *Steph.*

DEXAM'ENUS, a man delivered by Hercules from the hands of his daughter's suitors. *Apollod.* 2. c. 5.——A king of Olenus, in Achaia, whose two daughters married the sons of Actor. *Paus.* 5. c. 3.

DEX'ARI, a people of Chaonia. *Steph.*

DEXIC'RATES, a comic poet, of whose works *Athenæus* and *Suidas* have preserved a fragment.

DEXIMONTA'NI, a people of Carmania. *Plin.* 6. c. 23.

DEXIPH'ANES, the father of Sostratus, the architect. *Steph.*

DEXIP'PUS, a Spartan, who assisted the people of Agrigentum, &c. *Diod.* 13.——A physician of Cos, pupil of Hippocrates. He wrote a book on medicine, &c. *Suidas.*——A peripatetic philosopher about A.D. 335. *Sax. Onom.* 1. p. 398.—*Fabr. B. Gr.* 4. c. 26.

Dexip'pus Heren'nius, an Athenian orator. He was also a philosopher and historian, and wrote four books, *de rebus post Alex. Magn. Gestis. Sax. Onom.* 1. p. 372.—*Fabr. B. Gr.* l. 5. c. 5.

DEXITH'EA, the wife of Minos. *Apollod.* 3. c. 1.

DEXITH'EUS, an archon at Athens. Ol. 98, an. 4. ——A harper, victor at the Pythian games. *Aristoph. Achor.*

DEX'IUS, a Greek, the father of Iphinous, killed by Glaucus in the Trojan war. *Homer. Il.* 7. v. 15.

DI'A a daughter of Deion, mother of Pirithous by Ixion. *Diod.* 4.

Di'a, an island in the Ægæan Sea, 17 miles from Delus. It is the same as Naxus. *Vid.* Naxus. *Ovid. Met.* 8. v. 157.——An island on the northern coast of Crete, now Stan Dia.——A city of Thrace.——A city of Eubœa, called also Dium. *Vid.* Dium.——A city of Peloponnesus.——A city of Lusitania.——A city of Italy, near the Alps. ——A city of Scythia, near the Phasis.——A city of Caria.——A city of Bithynia.——A city of Thessaly.

DIABA'TE, a small island near Sardinia, now Faluga. *Ptol.*

DIABE'TÆ, islands near Syme. *Steph.*

DIABE'TE, an island to the west of Sardinia and Corsica. *Id.*

DIABLIN'TES or **DIABLIN'DI**, called Diautæ by *Ptolemy*, a people of Gallia Celtica, now Diableres. *Plin.* 4. c. 18.

DIACECAU'MENE, a region near Æthiopia. *Hygin.*—*Strab.*

DIACHARE'NI, a people of Arabia. *Steph.*

DIACHER'SIS, a town of Cyrenaica, now Carcora. *Ptol.*

DIACTORI'DES, one of Agarista's suitors. *Herodot.* 6. c. 127.——The father of Eurydame, the wife of Leutychides. *Id.* 6. c. 71.

DIACUIS'TA, a famous city between Placentia and Genua. *Strab.* l. 5.

DI'ACUM, a town of Lower Mysia. *Ptol.*

DIADEMA'TUS, a cognomen of L. Metellus, from

his wearing a bandage on his forehead, to hide an ulcer. *Plut. de cognom.*

DIADO'CHUM, a city of Persia, not far from Ctesiphon. *Steph.*

DIADUMENIA'NUS, a son of Macrinus, who enjoyed the title of Cæsar during his father's lifetime, &c. *Jul. Capitol. in vit. Macrini.* [A bust of Diadumenianus may be found in the Capitoline Museum; and a fine statue in the Vatican.]

DIÆ'US of Megalopolis, a general of the Achæans, who killed himself when his affairs became desperate. *Paus.* 7. c. 16.

DI'AGON or -UM, a river of Peloponnesus, flowing into the Alpheus, and separating Pisa from Arcadia. *Paus.* 6. c. 21.

DIAGON'DAS, a Theban who abolished all nocturnal sacrifices. *Cic. de Leg.* 2. c. 15.

DIAG'ORAS, an Athenian philosopher. His father's name was Teleclytus, and he had for his instructor Democritus of Abdera, who ransomed him from slavery, and, by his kindness and instruction, rendered him one of his most zealous disciples and intimate friends. From a bigot he became a most unconquerable atheist; because he saw a man who laid a false claim to one of his poems, and who perjured himself in asserting that claim, go unpunished. His great impiety and blasphemies at last provoked his countrymen, and the Areopagites promised one talent to him who brought his head before their tribunal, and two if he were produced alive. He, however, escaped from his pursuers, though the whole of Greece was engaged to seize and bring to condign punishment a man whose opinions were so subversive of religion and of providence. He lived about 416 years B.C. *Cic. de Nat. D.* 1. c. 23. *l.* 3. c. 37, &c.—*Lactant. de Irâ Dei.* 4.—*Val. Max.* 1. c. 1.——An athlete of Rhodes, 460 years B.C. Pindar celebrated his merit in a beautiful ode still extant, which was written in golden letters in a temple of Minerva. He saw his three sons crowned the same day at Olympia, and died through excess of joy. *Cic. Tusc.* 1. c. 46.—*Plut. in Pel.*—*Paus.* 6. c. 7.—*Gell.* 3. c. 15.

DIA'LIS, a priest of Jupiter at Rome, first appointed by Numa. He was regarded with such veneration that he was never permitted to swear, even upon public trials. *Varro. L. L.* 4. c. 15.—*Servius in Æn.* 8. v. 663.—*Dionys.* 2. c. 65.—*Liv.* 1. c. 20.

DIAL'LUS, an Athenian who wrote a history of all the memorable occurrences of his age, in Ol. 120. *Diod. Sic. Frag.* c. 5.

DIAMASTIGO'SIS, a festival at Sparta in honor of Diana Orthia, which received that name ἀπὸ τοῦ μαςιγοῦν *from whipping*, because boys were at that time whipped before the altar of the goddess. These boys, called Bomonicæ, were originally freeborn Spartans; but afterwards they were of mean birth, and generally of a slavish origin. This operation was performed by an officer in a severe and unfeeling manner; and that no compassion should be raised, the priest stood near the altar with a small light statue of the goddess, which was said suddenly to become heavy and insupportable if the lash of the whip was too leniently applied. The parents of the children attended the solemnity, and exhorted them not to commit anything either by by fear or groans that might be unworthy of Laconian education. These flagellations were so severe, that many expired under the lash. Such a death was reckoned very honorable, and the corpse of the sufferer was buried with much solemnity, with a garland of flowers on its head. The origin of this festival is unknown. Some suppose that Lycurgus first instituted it to insure the youths of Lacedæmon to bear labour and fatigue. Others maintain, that it was a mitigation of the penalties imposed by an oracle, which ordered that human blood should be shed on Diana's altar; and according to their opinion, Orestes first introduced that barbarous custom, after he had brought the statue of Diana Taurica into Greece. There is another tradition, which mentions, that Pausanias, as he was offering prayers and sacrifices to the gods, before he engaged with Mardonius, was suddenly attacked by a number of Lydians who disturbed the sacrifice, and were at last repelled with staves and stones, the only weapons with which the Lacedæmonians were provided at that moment. In commemoration of this, therefore, that whipping of boys was instituted at Sparta, and after that the Lydian procession. *Plutarch. Lacon. Inst. et Aristid.*—*Pausan. Lacon.*—*Cicer. Tusc. Quæst.* 2.

DIAMU'NA, a river of India flowing into the Ganges. *Ptol.*

DIA'NA was the goddess of hunting. According to Cicero, there were three divinities of this name: a daughter of Jupiter and Proserpine, who became mother of Cupid; a daughter of Jupiter and Latona; and a daughter of Upis and Glauce. The second was the most celebrated of these three personages, and to her all the ancients allude. She was born at the same birth as Apollo, and had such an aversion to marriage, that she obtained from her father the privilege of living in perpetual celibacy, and of presiding over the travails of women. To shun the society of men, she devoted herself to hunting, and obtained the permission of Jupiter to have for her attendants 60 of the Oceanides, and 20 other nymphs, all of whom like herself, firmly abjured marriage. She is represented with a bent bow and quiver, and attended by dogs, and sometimes drawn in a chariot by two white stags. Sometimes she appears with wings, holding a lion in one hand, and a panther in the other, with a chariot drawn by two heifers, or two horses of different colors. She is represented taller by the head than her attendant nymphs, her face has something manly, her legs are bare, well shaped, and strong, and her feet are covered with a buskin worn by huntresses among the ancients. Her flowing hair is negligently collected in a knot on her shoulder, her robe is tucked up on one side, and decently fastened to her girdle, and often a crescent appears glittering upon her forehead, though sometimes she is represented without the crescent, but clothed with a large veil bespangled with shining stars. Diana received many surnames, particularly from the places where her worship was established, and from the functions over which she presided. She was called Lucina, Ilithyia, or Juno Pronuba, when invoked by women in childbed, and Trivia when worshipped in the cross-ways where her statues were generally erected. She was supposed to be the same as the moon, and as Proserpine or Hecate, and from that circumstance she was called Priformis; and some of her statues represented her with three heads, those of a horse, a dog, and a boar. Her power and functions, under these three different characters, have been beautifully expressed in these two verses:

Terret, lustrat, agit, Proserpina, Luna, Diana,
Ima, suprema, feras, sceptro, fulgore, sagittâ.

She was also called Agrotera, Dictynna, Britomartis, Epipyrgidia, Alphea, Speculatrix, Anaitis, Militta, Tunicata, Lucifera, Orthia, Taurica, Delia, Cynthia, Aricia, &c. She was supposed to be the same as the Isis of the Egyptians, whose worship was introduced into Greece with that of Osiris under the name of Apollo. When Typhon waged war against the gods, Diana is said to have metamorphosed herself into a cat, to avoid his fury. The most famous of her temples was that of Ephesus, which was regarded as one of the seven wonders of the world. *Vid.* Ephesus. She was there represented with a great number of breasts, and other symbols which signified that she occasionally appeared under the same emblems as Terra or Cybele. Though she was the patroness of chastity, yet she forgot her dignity to enjoy the company of Endymion, and the favours which she granted to Pan and to Orion are well known. *Vid.* Endymion, Pan, & Orion. The severity, however with which she resented intrusion or neglect, is marked in the melancholy fate of Actæon, who was torn to pieces by his dogs. (*Vid.* Actæon,) and in the distress which she caused in Calydon, when she punished the impiety of Œneus by sending a wild boar to depopulate his country, (*Vid.* Calydon,) and likewise in the punishment of Menalippe and of Cometho. The inhabitants of Taurica were particularly attached to the worship of this goddess, and they cruelly offered on her altar, all the strangers that were shipwrecked on their coasts. Her temple in Africa was served by a priest who had always murdered his predecessor and the Lacedæmonians yearly offered human victims to her till the age of Lycurgus, who changed this barbarous custom for the sacrifice of

flagellation. The Athenians generally offered her goats, and others a white kid, and sometimes a boar pig or an ox. Among plants the poppy and the ditamy were sacred to Diana. She, as well as her brother Apollo, had some oracles, among which those of Ægypt, Cilicia, and Ephesus are the most known. *Ovid. Fast.* 2. v. 155. *Met.* 3. v. 156. l. 7. v. 94. & 194, &c.—*Catull.* ep. 35.—*Hesiod. Theog.* 918.—*Callim. in Hym. de Insul.* 1.—*Homer. in Apoll. Scholiast. Apollon.* 1. *Arg.*—*Flac.* 8.—*Nicand. Col. in Reb. Ætol.*—*Manlius.* 1.—*Agathias in Anthol.*—*Plin.* 36.—*Cic. de Nat. D.* 3.—*Horat.* 3. od. 22.—*Virg. G.* 3. v. 392. *Æn.* 1. v. 505. l. 4. v. 511. l. 7. v. 774.—*Euripid. in Iph. Taur. & Orest.*—*Plut. in Thes.*—*Paus.* 2. c. 30. l. 8. c. 31 & 37.—*Stat.* 3. *Silv.* 1. v. 57.—*Apollod.* 1. c. 4, &c. l. 3 c. 5, &c. [The finest representation of this goddess is the companion to the Belvidere Apollo, in the Musée Royale, at Paris. But there are also two very fine statues, one in the British Museum, and another in the Borghese collection, which is now removed to Paris. In her Ephesian character the statues are very numerous. The best are those in the Vatican and at Florence.

DIA'NA, a river of Hispania Tarraconensis. *Ptol.*

DIA'NÆ FA'NUM, a promontory of Bithynia. *Ptol.*

DIA'NÆ ORAC'ULUM, a city of Arabia Felix. *Id.*

DIA'NÆ POR'TUS, a place on the eastern shore of Corsica. *Id.*

DIAN'ASA, the mother of Lycurgus. *Plut. in Lyc.*

DIANEN'SES, a people of Hispania Citerior. *Plin.* 3. c. 3.

DIA'NES, a people of Galatia. *Steph.*

DIA'NIUM, a town and promontory of Spain, opposite the island of Ophiusa in the Mediterranean, now Cape Martin, where Diana was worshipped. *Ptol.*—*Plin.*

DIAPH'ANES, a river of Cilicia, so called from the clearness of its waters. *Plin.* 5. c. 27.

DIARREU'SA, an island near Chius. *Id.* 5. c. 31.

DIARRHOE'A, a harbour of Cyrenaica, now Zanara. *Ptol.*

DI'AS, a sophist of Ephesus in the time of Philip. *Philost.*

DI'AS, a city of Lycia founded by Dyades. *Steph.*

DIA'SIA, festivals in honour of Jupiter at Athens. They received their name ἀπὸ τοῦ Διὸς καὶ τῆς ἄτης *from Jupiter and misfortune,* because, by making application to Jupiter, men obtained relief from their misfortunes, and were delivered from dangers. During this festival, things of all kinds were exposed to sale. *Aristoph. Nub.*—*Plut.*—*Phocion.*

DIBIC'TUS, a brother of Artabazus. *Polyæn.* 7.

DIB'IO, a town of France at the west of the river Arar, now Dijon in Burgundy.

DIBUTA'DES or DIBU'TADES, a Sicyonian, a potter at Corinth. *Plin.* 35. c. 12.

DICÆ'A or DICÆAR'CHIA, a town of Italy, now Puteoli. *Ital.* 13. v. 385.

DICÆOG'ENES, a poet who wrote tragedies and dithyrambic verses *Suidas.*—*Harpocrat.*

DICÆ'US, an Athenian, who was supernaturally apprised of the defeat of the Persians in Greece. *Herodot.* 8 c. 65.

DICÆAR'CHUS, a Messenian, famous for his knowledge of philosophy, history, and mathematics. He was one of Aristotle's disciples. He had composed a valuable history of the Spartan republic, which was publicly read over every year by order of the magistrates, for the improvement and instruction of youth. Besides other works, and maps mentioned by Cicero, he had written also three books upon the manners and customs of the Greeks, all which have unfortunately perished. *Cic.* 2. *Attic.* 2, 8 & 16. l. 6. ep. 2. l. 7. ep. 3. l. 8. ep. 4. l. 13. ep. 30 & 31. *Tusc.* 1. c. 21. *Acad. Quæst.* 4. c. 124. *Divin.* 1. c. 5. l. 2. c. 105. *Offic.* 2. c. 16.—*Plut.*—*Sax. Onom.* 1. p. 85.—*Fabr. B. Gr.* l. 2 c. 26. ——A general of the Ætolians. *Liv.* 35, &c.

DI'CE, one of the Horæ, daughters of Jupiter. *Apollod.* 1. c. 3.

DICE'NEUS, an Ægyptian philosopher in the age of Augustus, who travelled into Scythia, where he ingratiated himself with the king of the country, and by his instructions softened the wildness and rusticity of his manners. He also gained such an influence over the multitude, that they destroyed all the vines which grew in their country, to prevent the riot and dissipation, which the wine occasioned among them. He wrote all his maxims and laws in a book, that they might not lose the benefit of them after his death. *Jornandes.*

DIC'OMAS, a king of the Getæ. *Plut. in Anton.*

DIC'TÆ or DICTÆ'US MONS, a mountain in the eastern parts of Crete. The island is often known by the name of *Dictæa arva.* *Virg. Ecl.* 6. *Æn.* 3. v. 171.—Jupiter was called *Dictæus,* because worshipped there, and the same epithet was also applied to Minos. *Virg. G.* 2. v. 536.—*Ovid. Met.* 8. v. 43.—*Strab.* 10.—*Ptol.* 3. c. 17.

DICTAM'NUM or DICTYN'NA, now Dictamo, a town of Crete, where the herb called *dictamnus* chiefly grew. *Virg. Æn.* 12. v. 412.—*Cic. de Nat. D.* 2. c. 50.

DICTA'TOR, a magistrate at Rome invested with regal authority. This officer, whose name and magistracy seem to have been borrowed from the customs of the Albans or Latins was first chosen during the Roman war against the Latins. The consuls being unable to raise the requisite forces for the defence of the state, because the plebeians refused to enlist, if they were not discharged from all the debts which they contracted with the patricians, the senate found it necessary to elect a new magistrate with absolute and incontrollable power to take care of the state. The dictator remained in office for six months, after which he was to be again elected, if the affairs of the state seemed to be desperate; but if tranquillity was re-established, he generally laid down his power before the time was expired. In the exercise of his authority, he knew no superior in the republic, and even the laws were subjected to him. He was called dictator, because *dictus,* named by the consul, or *quoniam dictis ejus parebat populus,* because the people implicitly obeyed his command. He was named by the consul in the night, *vivâ voce,* and his election was confirmed by the auguries, though sometimes he was nominated or recommended by the voice of the people. As his power was absolute, he could proclaim war, levy forces, conduct them against an enemy, and disband them at pleasure. He punished as he pleased; and from his decision there was no appeal, at least till later times. He was preceded by twenty-four lictors, with the fasces; during his administration, all other magistrates, except the tribunes of the people, were suspended from their offices, and he was the absolute master of the republic. But amidst all this independence, the dictator was not permitted to go beyond the borders of Italy, and he was always obliged to march on foot in his expeditions; and he never could ride in difficult and laborious marches, without previously obtaining a formal leave from the people. He was chosen only when the state was in imminent danger either from foreign enemies or inward seditions. In the time of a pestilence a dictator was sometimes elected, as also to hold the *comitia,* or celebrate public festivals, to hold trials, to chose senators, or drive a nail in the Capitol, by which superstitious ceremony the Romans believed that a plague could be averted or the progress of an enemy stopped. This office, so respectable and illustrious in the first ages of the republic, became odious by the perpetual usurpations of Sylla and Jul. Cæsar; and after the death of the latter, the Roman senate, on the motion of the consul Antony, passed a decree, which for ever forbade a dictator to exist in Rome. The dictator, as soon as elected, chose a subordinate officer, called his master of the horse *magister equitum.* This appointment was highly respectable, but the master of the horse was totally subservient to the will of the dictator, and could do nothing without his express orders, though he enjoyed the privilege of using a horse, and had the same insignia as the prætors. This subordination, however, was some time after removed; and during the second Punic war, the master of the horse was invested with a power equal to that of the dictator. A second dictator was also chosen for the election of magistrates at Rome, after the battle of Cannæ. The dictatorship was originally confined to the patricians, but the plebeians, when admitted to share the consulship, were also permitted to become candidates for this superior dignity. Titus Lartius Flavius was the first dictator, A.U.C. 253. *Dionys. Hal.*—*Cic. de Leg.* 3.—*Dio.*—*Plut. in Fab.*—*Appian.* 3.—*Po-*

lyh. 3.—*Paterc.* 2. c. 28.—*Liv.* 1. c. 23. l. 2. c. 18. l. 4. c. 57. l. 9. c. 38.

DICTIDIEN'SES, certain inhabitants of mount Athos. *Thucyd.* 5. c. 82.

DIC'TIS, a city of Galatia. *Ptol.*

DICTYN'NA, a nymph of Crete, who first invented hunting nets. She was one of Diana's attendants, and for that reason the goddess is often called Dictynna. Some have supposed that Minos pursued her, and that to avoid his importunities, she threw herself into the sea, and was caught in fishermen's nets, δίκτυα, whence her name. There was a festival at Sparta in honor of Diana, called Dictynnia. *Paus.* 2. c. 30. l. 3. c. 12.—*Diod.* 5.—*Stat. Theb.* 9. v. 632.

DICTYN'NIA, a city of Crete.

DIC'TYS, a Cretan, who went with Idomeneus to the Trojan war. It is supposed that he wrote a history of this celebrated war, and that at his death he ordered it to be laid in his tomb, where it remained till a violent earthquake in the reign of Nero opened the monument where he had been buried. This convulsion of the earth threw out his history of the Trojan war, which was found by some shepherds, and afterwards carried to Rome. This mysterious tradition is deservedly deemed fabulous; and the Latin history of the Trojan war, which is now extant, and considered as the composition of Dictys of Crete, was composed in the 15th century, or according to others, in the age of Constantine, and falsely attributed to one of the followers of Idumeneus. The edition of Dictys is by Masellus, 4to, Mediol. 1477. *Sax. Onom.* 1. p. 8.—*Fabr. B. Gr.* 1. c. 5.——A king of of the island of Seriphus, son of Magnus and Nais. He married the nymph Clymene, and was made king of Seriphus by Perseus, who deposed Polydectes, because he behaved with wanton insolence to Danae. *Vid.* Polydectes. *Apollod.* 1. c. 9. l. 2. c. 4.——A centaur killed at the nuptials of Pirithous. *Ovid. Met.* 12. 334.

DI'DA, a celebrated pugilist. *Pausan.*

DI'DAS, a Macedonian, whose intrigues were basely employed by Perseus to render Demetrius unpopular and suspected by his father Philip. He became afterwards one of Philip's favourite generals. *Liv.* 40. c. 23, 24. l. 42. c. 51 & 58.

DIDAS'CÆ, a people of Upper Æthiopia. *Ptol.*

DIDAUCA'NA, a town of Bithynia. *Id.*

DID'IA LEX, *de Sumptibus*, by Didius, A.U.C. 606, to restrain the expenses that attended public festivals and entertainments, and limit the number of guests which generally attended them, not only at Rome, but in all the provinces of Italy. By it, not only those who received guests in these festive meetings, but the guests themselves, were liable to be fined. It was a wise and salutary extension of the Oppian and Fannian laws. *Macrob. Sat.* 3. c. 57.

DID'IUS, a governor of Spain, conquered by Sertorius. *Plut. in Sert.*——A man who brought to J. Cæsar the head of Pompey's eldest son. *Plut.*——A governor of Macedonia, who triumphed over the Scordisci. *Cic. Planc.* 25. *Pis.* 25.——A governor of Britain, in the reign of the Emperor Claudius. *Tac. Ann.* 12. c. 40.

DID'IUS JULIA'NUS, a rich Roman, who, after the murder of Pertinax, bought the empire which the Prætorians had exposed to sale, A.D. 192 His great luxury and extravagance rendered him odious; and when he refused to pay the money which he had promised for the imperial purple, the soldiers revolted against him, and put him to death, after a short reign. Severus was made emperor after him. *Spartian.*—*Dio. in Julian.* [A very fine head of Didius Julianus is to be found in the Museum of the Vatican.]

DI'DO, called also Elissa, a daughter of Belus king of Tyre, who married Sichæus, or Sicharbas, her uncle, who was priest of Hercules. Pygmalion, who succeeded to the throne of Tyre after Belus, murdered Sichæus, to get possession of the immense riches which he possessed; and Dido, disconsolate for the loss of her husband, set sail in quest of a settlement, with a number of Tyrians, to whom the cruelty of the tyrant had likewise become odious. According to some accounts, she threw into the sea the riches of her husband, which Pygmalion so greatly desired; and by that artifice prevailed upon the crews of the ships which had come by order of the tyrant to obtain the riches of Sichæus to share her fortunes. During her voyage, Dido visited the coast of Cyprus, where she carried away 50 women, and gave them as wives to her Tyrian followers. A storm drove her fleet on the African coast, and she bought of the inhabitants as much land as could be covered by a bull's hide, cut into thongs. Upon this piece of land she built a citadel, called Byrsa. (*Vid.* Byrsa,) and the increase of population, and the rising commerce among her subjects soon obliged her to enlarge her city, and the boundaries of her dominions. Her beauty, as well as the fame of her enterprize, gained her many admirers; and her subjects wished to persuade her to marry Iarbas, king of Mauritania, who threatened them with a dreadful war. Dido begged three months to give a decisive answer; and during that time, she erected a funeral pile, as if wishing, by a solemn sacrifice, to appease the manes of Sichæus, to whom she had promised eternal fidelity. When all was prepared, she stabbed herself on the pile in presence of her people, and by this uncommon action obtained the name of Dido, *valiant woman*, instead of Elissa. According to Virgil, Ovid, and other Roman writers, the death of Dido was caused by the sudden departure of Æneas, of whom she was deeply enamoured. This poetical fiction represents Æneas as living in the age of Dido, and introduces an anachronism of nearly 300 years. Dido left Phœnicia 247 years after the Trojan war, or the age of Æneas, that is, about 937 years B.C. This chronological error proceeds not from the ignorance of the poets, but is supported by the authority of *Horace*,

"*Aut famam sequere. aut sibi convenientia finge.*"

While Virgil describes, in a beautiful episode, the desperate love of Dido, and the submission of Æneas to the will of the gods, he at the same time gives an explanation of the inveterate hatred which existed between the republics of Rome and Carthage. Dido, after her death, was honoured as a deity by her subjects. *Justin.* 18. c. 4. &c.—*Paterc.* 1. c. 6.—*Virg. Æn.* 1, &c. & *Servius locis.*—*Eustathius in Dionys.*—*Ovid. Met.* 14. fab. 2. *Heroid.* 7. *Appian. Alex.*—*Oros.* 4. c 6.—*Herodian.*—*Dionys. Hal.* [There is a sitting figure of Dido in the Museum of the Vatican.]

DIDU'GUA, a city of Babylonia. *Ptol.*

DIDU'RI, a people on the confines of Albania. *Plin.* 6. c. 10.

DID'YMA, a place of Miletus. *Paus.* 2. c. 9.——An island in the Sicilian Sea. *Paus.* 10. c. 11. *Vid.* Didyme.

DID'YMÆ, a city of Libya. *Steph.*

DIDYMÆ'US, a surname of Apollo. *Macrob.* 1. 1. c. 17.

DIDYMA'ON, an artist, skilled in making suits of armour. *Virg. Æn.* 5. v. 359.

DID'YME, one of the Cyclades. *Ovid. Met.* 7. v. 469.——A city of Sicily *Id. Fast.* 4. v. 473.——One of the Lipari isles, now Saline.——A place near Miletus, where the Branchidæ had their famous oracle.

DIDYME'UM, a temple dedicated to Apollo at Miletus. *Plin.* 5. c. 31 —*Strab.*

DID'YMI, a mountain of Asia Minor. *Ptol. Strabo* calls it Dindymus.

DIDYMOT'ICOS, a place of Caria. *Suidas.*——A place of Asia Minor, near Æolia. *Polyb.*

DID'YMUS, a freedman of Tiberius. *Tac. Ann.* 6. c. 24.——A scholiast on Homer, surnamed Χαλκέντερος, was born at Alexandria, and flourished B.C. 40. He wrote a number of books, which are now lost. The best editions of the commentaries, falsely attributed to him, are that in 2 vols, 8vo. Venet. apud Ald. 1528, and that of Paris, 8vo. 1530. *Sax. Onom.* 1. p. 180.—*Fabr. B. Gr.* l. 2. c. 3 & 1. 5. c. 7. ——An ecclesiastical writer of Alexandria, in Ægypt. Though he had lost his eyesight at the age of five, he made such proficiency in the study of divinity, that he was chosen to fill the theological chair of Alexandria. In this office the number of his pupils bespoke the high character which was entertained of his abilities, and the books which he wrote evinced the extent of his learning, and the powers of his mind. Nothing of his compositions remains, except a treatise upon the Holy Spirit, to be found in Jerome's works, who translated it. Didymus died 395 A.D., in his 85th year. *Sax. Onom.* 1. p. 398.—*Fabr. B. Gr.*

l. 5. c. 24.—For other persons of this name, see the works of *Fabricius and Jonsius*.

DID'YMUS, a town of Argolis. *Pausan.*

DIEN'ECES, a Spartan, who, upon hearing, before the battle of Thermopylæ, that the Persians were so numerous that their arrows would darken the light of the sun, observed that it would be a great convenience, for they then should fight in the shade. *Herodot.* 7. c. 226.

DIEN'SES, a people of Macedonia. *Plin.* 4. c. 10.

DIER'NA, a city of Dacia, now Torrenburg. *Ptol.*

DIESPITER, a surname of Jupiter, as being the father of light. *A. Gell.* 5. c. 12.—*Hor. Od.* 34.

DIETHU'SA, an island near the Thracian Chersonesus. *Plin.* 4. c. 12.

DIEU'CHES, a physician mentioned by *Pliny*, l. 20. c. 5.

DIEU'CHIDAS, an historian of Megara. *Harpocrat.—Clem. Strom.* 1 & 6.

DIGE'NA, a city of Arabia Felix. *Ptol.*

DIGEN'TIA, a small river which watered Horace's farm, in the country of the Sabines. *Horat.* 1. ep. 18. v. 104.

DIGITIUS SEX., a sailor, who, at the taking of New Carthage, claimed of Scipio the prize of valor in opposition to Trebellius, a centurion. The general, to avoid a dissension between his army and his fleet, commended them both, and rewarded them with a mural crown. *Liv.* 26. c. 48.

DIG'MA, a part of the Piræus at Athens. *Xenoph. Hellen.* 5.—*Polyæn.* 1. 6.

DI'I, the divinities of the ancient inhabitants of the earth, were very numerous. Every object which caused terror, inspired gratitude, or contributed to the affluence of man, received the tribute of veneration. Man saw a superior agent in the stars, the elements, or the trees, and supposed that the waters which communicated fertility to his fields and possessions, were under the influence and direction of some invisible power, inclined to favour and to benefit mankind. Thus arose a train of divinities, which imagination arrayed in different forms, or armed with different powers. They were endowed with understanding, and were actuated by the same possessions which daily afflict the human race, and these phantoms of superstition were appeased and provoked as the imperfect being which gave them birth. Their wrath was mitigated by sacrifices and incense, and sometimes human victims bled to expiate a crime which superstition alone supposed to exist. The sun, from his powerful influence and animating nature first attracted the notice and claimed the adoration of the uncivilized inhabitants of the earth. The moon also was honoured with sacrifices, and addressed in prayers; and after immortality had been liberally bestowed on all the heavenly bodies, mankind classed among their deities the brute creation; and the cat and the sow shared equally with Jupiter himself, the father of gods and men, the devout veneration of their votaries. This immense number of deities has been divided into different classes, according to the fancy or caprice of the mythologists. The Romans, generally speaking, reckoned two classes of the gods, the *dii majorum gentium*, or *dii consentes*, and the *dii minorum gentium*. The former were twelve in number, six males and six females. *Vid.* Consentes. In the class of the latter were ranked all the gods who were worshipped in different parts of the earth. Besides these, there were some called *dii selecti*, sometimes classed with the twelve greater gods; these were Janus, Saturn, the Genius, the Moon, Pluto, and Bacchus. There were also some called demi-gods, that is, who had deserved immortality by the greatness of their exploits, and for their uncommon services to mankind. Among these were Priapus, Vertumnus, and those whose parents were some of the immortal gods. Besides these, there were some called *topici*, or national gods, whose worship was established at particular places, such as Isis in Ægypt, Astarte in Syria, Uranus at Carthage, &c. In process of time also, all the passions and the mortal virtues were regarded as powerful deities, and temples were raised to a goddess of concord, of peace, &c. According to the authority of *Hesiod*, there were no less than 30,000 gods that inhabited the earth, and were guardians of men, all subservient to the power of Jupiter. To these succeeding ages have added an almost equal number; and indeed they were so numerous, and their functions so various, that we find temples erected, and sacrifices offered to unknown gods. It is observable, that all the gods of the ancients had lived upon earth as mere mortals; and even Jupiter, who was ruler of heaven, is represented by the mythologists as a helpless child; and we are acquainted with all the particulars that attended the birth and education of Juno. In process of time, not only good and virtuous men, who had been the patrons of learning, and supporters of liberty, but also thieves and pirates were admitted among the gods; and the Roman senate courteously granted immortality to the most cruel, the most profligate, and the most abandoned of their emperors. *Voss. de Orig. & Prog. Idol.* l. 7. c. 1 & 8.——A people of Thrace, on mount Rhodope. *Thucyd.* l. 2.—*Tac. Ann.* 3. c. 38.

DIL'LIUS APONIA'NUS, a tribune of the third legion, in the interest of Vespasian. *Tac. Hist.* 3. c. 9.

DIL'LIUS VOC'ULA, a lieutenant of the 18th legion, in the German army. *Id. Ibid.* 4. c. 24.

DIM'ALOS, a city of Illyria, taken by Æmilius, A.U.C. 535.

DIMAS'SUS, a small island near Rhodes. *Plin.* 5. c. 31.——A mountain in the island Myconus, in the Ægean Sea. *Id.*

DIMU'RI, a people of India, near the Indus, *Plin.* 6. c. 20.

DINAR'CHUS, a Greek orator, son of Sostratus, and disciple to Theophrastus at Athens. He acquired both money and reputation by his compositions, and suffered himself to be bribed by the enemies of the Athenians, 307 B.C. Of sixty-four of his orations only three remain, and are to be found in the collection of Stephens, fol. 1575, or in that of Venice, 3 vols. fol. 1513. *Cic. de Orat.* 2. c. 53. *In Brut.* 17.—*Demost. de Coron.—Sax. Onom.* 1. p. 88.—*Fabr. B. Gr.* l. 2. c. 26.——A Corinthian ambassador, put to death by Polyperchon. *Plut. in Phoc.*——A native of Delus, who collected some fables in Crete, &c. *Dionys. Hal.*

DINARE'TUM, a promontory at the east of Cyprus. *Plin.* 5. c. 31.

DIN'DARI, a people of Dalmatia. *Id.* 3. c. 22.

DIN'DLOCHUS, a comic poet of Syracuse or Agrigentum, about the 72nd Olympiad. *Ælian. de Animal.* l. 6. c. 51.—*Suidas.*

DIN'DRYME, a city of Macedonia. *Steph.*

DINDYME'NE, a surname of Cybele. *Vid.* Dindymus.

DIN'DYMUS or -A (*orum*), a mountain of Phrygia, near a town of the same name in the neighbourhood of Cyzicus. It was from this place that Cybele was called Dindymene, as her worship was established there by Jason. *Strab.* 12.—*Stat.* 1. *Sylv.* 1. v. 9.—*Ovid. Met.* 2. v. 223. *Fast.* 4. v. 234 & 249.—*Paus.* 7. c. 17. & 20.—*Martial.* 8. epigr. 81.—*Horat.* 1. od. 16. v. 5.—*Virgil. Æn.* 9. v. 617.

DI'NE, a place of Arcadia, near the sea. *Paus.*

DIN'IA, DIG'NA, or DI'NA, a city of Gallia Narbonensis, now Digne sur la Bleone. *Plin*, 3. c. 4.

DIN'IÆ, a place of Phrygia. *Liv.* 38. c. 5.

DIN'IAS, a general of Cassander. *Diod.* 19.——A man of Pheræ, who seized the supreme power at Cranon. *Polyæn.* 2.——A man who wrote a history of Argos. *Plut. in Arat.*

DIN'ICHE, the wife of Archidamus. *Paus.* 3. c. 10.

DI'NIS, a Thracian general who rebelled against Tiberius. *Tacit. Ann.* 4. c. 50.

DI'NO or DI'NON. *Vid.* Dinon.

DINOCH'ARES, an architect who finished the rebuilding of the temple of Diana at Ephesus, after it had been burnt by Erostratus.

DINOC'RATES, an architect of Macedonia, who proposed to Alexander to cut mount Athos into the form of a statue, holding a city in one hand, and in the other a basin, into which all the waters of the mountain should empty themselves. This extraordinary project Alexander wisely rejected as too chimerical; but he employed the talents of the artist in building and beautifying Alexandria. Under the patronage and direction of Ptolemy Philadelphus, Dinocrates began to build a temple in honor of Arsinöe, in which he intended to suspend a statue of the queen by means of loadstones.

His death, and that of his royal patron, prevented the execution of a work which would have been the admiration of future ages. *Plin.* 5. c. 10. l. 7. c. 37. l. 34. c. 14.—*Auson. Id.* 3. v. 313.—*Solin.* 45 & 53.—*Marcell.* 22. c. 40.—*Plut. in Alex.*——A general of Agathocles. *Polyæn.* 5. *Com.* 2.——A Messenian, who behaved with great effeminacy and wantonness. He defeated Philopœmen, and put him to death, B.C. 183. *Plut. in Flamm.*—*Liv.* 39. c. 49.

DINOGETI'A, a city of Mœsia, or Lower Scythia, now Drimago. *Ptol.*

DINOL'OCHUS, a swift runner. *Paus.* 6. c. 1.——A Syracusan who composed 14 comedies. *Ælian. de Anim.* 6. c. 52.

DINOM'ENES, a man who conspired against Hieronymus, king of Sicily, and afterwards was made governor of Syracuse. *Liv.* 24. c. 7 & 23.—*Paus.* 8. c. 42.

DI'NON, a governor of Damascus, under Ptolemy, &c. *Polyæn.* 4.——A chief man among the Rhodians. *Liv.* 44. c. 23.——The father of Clitarchus, who wrote a history of Persia, in Alexander's age. He is esteemed a very authentic historian by *Cornelius Nepos in Conon. Plut. in Alex.* & *Isid.*—*Diog.*—*Ælian. H. A.* 17. c. 10. *V. H.* 7. c. 1.—*Plin.* 10. c. 49.——A statuary. *Plin.* 34. c. 8.

DINOS'THENES, an Olympian victor, who made a statue for himself. *Paus.* 6. c. 16.

DINOS'TRATUS, a celebrated geometrician, in the age of Plato.

DI'O or DI'ON. *Vid.* Dion.

DIOBE'SI, a people of Thrace. *Plin.* 4. c. 11.

DIOBU'LIUM, a town near Pontus. *Steph.*

DIOCÆSARE'A, a city of Cappadocia. *Plin.*

DIOCH'ARES, a freedman of Cæsar. *Cic. ad Attic.*

DIOCHI'TES, a town of Ægypt, where Osiris was buried. *Steph.*

DIOCLE'A, festivals celebrated in the spring at Megara, in honor of Diocles, who died in defence of a certain youth, to whom he was tenderly attached. *Theocritus* has described them in his 12th *Idyll.* v. 27.

DIO'CLEA, a town on the coast of Dalmatia, celebrated as the birth-place of the emperor Diocletian. *Plin.* 3. c. 23.

DI'OCLES, a general of Athens, &c. *Polyæn.* 5.—*Liv.* 35. c. 34.——A comic poet of Athens. *Athen.*——An historian, the first Grecian who ever wrote concerning the origin of the Romans, and the fabulous history of Romulus. *Plut. in Rom.*——One of the four brothers placed over the citadel of Corinth, by Archelaus, &c. *Polyæn.* 6.——A rich man of Messenia, son of Orsilochus the son of the Alpheus. His twin sons, Orsilochus and Creton went to the Trojan war, where they were both slain by Æneas. *Homer. Il.* 5. v. 541.—*Paus.* 4. c. 2.——A general of Syracuse. *Diod.* 13.——A physician of Carystus, in the age of Darius Hytaspes. He wrote some commentaries. *Suidas.*—*Sax. Onom.* 1. p. 107.—*Fabr. B. Gr.* l. 6. c. 7.—*Voss de Math. Poet. & Hist. Gr.* p. 355.

DIOCLETIANOP'OLIS, a town of Thessaly. so called in honour of Diocletian. *Polyb.*—*Antonin.*

DIOCLETIA'NUS CA'IUS VALE'RIUS JO'VIUS, a celebrated Roman emperor, born of an obscure family in Dalmatia. He was at first a common soldier, but by his merit and success, gradually rose to the office of a general, and at the death of Numerian, he was deemed worthy to be invested with the imperial purple. In his high station, he rewarded the virtues and fidelity of Maximian, who had shared with him all the subordinate offices in the army, by making him his colleague on the throne. He created also two subordinate emperors, Constantius and Galerius, whom he called Cæsars, whilst he reserved for himself and his colleague the superior title of Augustus. Diocletian has been celebrated for his military virtues, and was the friend and patron of learning and true genius. He was bold and resolute, active and diligent, and well acquainted with the arts which endear a sovereign to his people, and make him respectable even in the eyes of his enemies. His cruelty, however, against the Christians has been deservedly censured. After he had reigned 21 years, in the greatest prosperity, he exhibited to his astonished subjects an example of unusual moderation, by publicly abdicating the crown in the plains of Nicomedia, May 1, A.D. 304. Maximian, his colleague, followed his example, but not from choice; and when he some time after endeavoured to rouse the ambition of Diocletian, and persuade him to reassume the imperial purple, he received for answer that his illustrious colleague took now more delight in cultivating his little garden, in his retirement at Salona, than he formerly enjoyed when his power was extended over all the earth. Diocletian lived nine years after his abdication, in the greatest security and enjoyment at Salona, and died in the 68th year of his age. He was the first sovereign who voluntarily resigned his power. *Aurel. Vict.* 39.—*Eutrop.* 9. c. 19. [A bust of Diocletian exists in the Vatican.]

DIODO'RI, an island in the mouth of the Arabian Gulph. *Plin.* 6. c. 29.—*Arrian. in Peripl.* &c.

DIODO'RUS, an historian, surnamed *Siculus*, because he was born at Argyra, in Sicily. He wrote a history of Ægypt, Persia, Syria, Media, Greece, Rome, and Carthage, which was divided into 40 books, of which only 15 are extant, with some few fragments. This valuable composition was the fruit of the labour of 30 years, though the greater part may be considered as nothing more than a judicious compilation from Berosus, Timæus, Theopompus, Callisthenes, and others. The author, however, is too credulous in some of his narrations, and often wanders far from the truth. His style, which is neither elegant nor labored, contains great simplicity and unaffected correctness. He occasionally dwells too long upon fabulous reports and trifling incidents, while events of the greatest importance to history are treated with brevity, and sometimes passed over in silence. His manner of reckoning, by the Olympiads and the Roman consuls will be found very erroneous. Diodorous flourished about 44 years B.C. He spent much time at Rome to procure information, and authenticate his historical narrations. The best edition of his work is that of Wesseling, 2 vols. fol. Amst. 1746. *Sax. Onom.* 1. p. 198.—*Fabr. B. Gr.* l. c. 31.——A disciple of Euclid, in the age of Plato. *Diog. in Vitâ.*——A comic poet, whose plays are mentioned by *Athenæus.*——A son of Echeanax, who, with his brothers, Codrus and Anaxagorus, murdered Hegesias the tyrant of Ephesus, &c. *Polyæn.* 6.——An Ephesian, who wrote the life of Anaximander. *Diog.*——An orator of Sardes, in the time of the Mithridatic war. *Strab.* l. 13.——A stoic philosopher, preceptor to Cicero, called by some Diodotus. He lived and died in the house of his pupil, whom he had instructed in the various branches of Greek literature. *Cic. in Brut.* 90. *Fam.* 13. ep. 16.——A general of Demetrius.——An African, &c. *Plut.*——A writer, surnamed *Periegetes*, who wrote a description of the earth. *Plut. in Them.*

DIOD'OTUS, the preceptor of Cicero, called also Diodorus. *Vid.* Diodorus.

DIŒ'TAS, a general of Achaia, &c. *Polyæn.* 2.

DIOG'ENES, a celebrated Cynic philosopher of Sinope, banished from his country for coining false money. From Sinope, he retired to Athens, where he became the disciple of Antisthenes, who was at the head of the Cynics. Antisthenes, indeed, at first refused to admit him into his house, and even struck him with a stick; but Diogenes calmly bore the rebuke, and exclaimed, "Strike me, Antisthenes, but never shall you find a stick sufficiently hard to remove me from your presence, whilst there is any information to be gained from your conversation and acquaintance." Such firmness recommended him to Antisthenes, and he became his most devoted pupil. Dressing himself in the garment which distinguished the Cynics, he walked about the streets with a tub on his head, which served him as a house and a place of repose. Such singularity, joined to the greatest contempt for riches, soon gained him universal reputation, and Alexander the Great condescended to visit the philosopher in his tub. He asked Diogenes if there was anything in which he could gratify or oblige him. "Get out of my sunshine," was the only answer which the philosopher deigned to return to his illustrious visitor. This independence of mind so pleased the monarch, that he turned to his courtiers, and said, "Were I not Alexander, I should wish to be Diogenes." He was once sold as a slave, but the magnanimity of his character so pleased his master, that he appointed him preceptor to his children, and guardian of his estates. After a life spent in the greatest misery and indigence, he died B.C. 324, and in the 96th year of his age. He ordered his body to be carelessly thrown into a ditch, and some dust to be sprinkled over it. His orders were, however, disobeyed, and his friends honoured his remains with a magnificent funeral at Corinth. The inhabitants of Sinope raised statues to his memory, and the marble figure of a dog was placed on a high column erected on his tomb. His biographer has transmitted to posterity a number of sayings, remarkable for their simplicity and moral tendency. The life of Diogenes, however, will not bear a strict examination; he boasted so much of his poverty, and was so arrogant, that many have observed that the virtues of Diogenes arose from pride and vanity, not from wisdom or sound philosophy. His morals were corrupt and licentious, which has given occasion to some to observe, that the bottom of his tub would not bear too close an examination. *Diog. in Vita.—Plut. in Apoph.—Cic. de Nat. D.* 3. c. 36, &c. *Tusc.* 1. c. 104. l. 5. c. 92.—*Sax. Onom.* 1. p. 80.—*Fabr. B. Gr.* l. 3. c. 12. [There is a small statue of Diogenes in the Villa Albani at Rome.]——A stoic of Babylon, disciple of Chrysippus. He went to Athens, and was sent as ambassador to Rome, with Carneades and Critolaus, 155 years B.C. He died in the 88th year of his age, after a life of the most exemplary virtue. Some suppose that he was strangled by order of Antiochus, king of Syria, for speaking disrespectfully of his family in one of his treatises. *Cic. de Off.* 3. c. 51. *De Div.* l. c. 6. *De N. D.* l. c. 41.—*Quintil.* l. c. 1.—*Athen.* 5. c. 11.——A native of Apollonia in Crete, celebrated for his knowledge of philosophy and physic. He was pupil to Anaxagoras, and he often exercised his superior abilities in the service of the great men of his time, who employed him either in the framing of new laws, or in the drawing up of treaties. *Diog. in Vita.—Cic. de N.D.* 1. c. 29.——A Macedonian who betrayed Salamis to Aratus. *Paus.* 2. c. 8.

DIOG'ENES LAER'TIUS, an Epicurean philosopher, born in Cilicia. He wrote the lives of the philosophers in ten books still extant. This interesting work contains an accurate account of the ancient philosophers, and is replete with all their anecdotes, and particular opinions. It is compiled, however, without any plan, method, or precision, though much neatness and conciseness are observable through the whole. In this multifarious biography, the author does not seem particularly attached to any sect, except perhaps it be that of Potamon of Alexandria. Diogenes died A.D. 222. The best editions of his works are that of Meibomius, 2 vols. 4to, Amst. 1692, and that of Lips. 8vo, 1759. *Sax. Onom.* 1. p. 348.—*Fabr. B. Gr.* l. 4. c. 19.

DIOGENI'A, a daughter of Celeus. *Paus.* 1. c. 38. ——A daughter of the god of the river Cephisus, who married Erechtheus. *Apollod.*

DIOGENIA'NUS, a grammarian of Heraclea, under Adrian, wrote a dictionary and other works. His proverbs were first edited by A. Schott. *Sax. Onom.* 1. p. 339.—*Fabr. B. Gr.* l. 4. c. 9, &c.

DIOG'ENIS, a promontory of Æthiopia, on the Arabian Gulph. *Ptol.*

DIOG'ENUS, a man who conspired with Dymnus against Alexander the Great. *Curt.* 6. c. 7.

DIOGNE'TUS, a philosopher, who instructed the emperor Marcus Aurelius in Philosophy, and in writing dialogues. There is extant, among the works of St. Justin, a letter to Diognetus, supposed to be this person, on the false gods worshipped in those times. This letter is considered by historians as one of the most valuable remains of ecclesiastical antiquity, containing an interesting account of the life and manners of the primitive Christians.——The seventh archon of Athens, in whose time Homer flourished. *Marsh. Can. Chron ad sec.* 15.——A person who accompanied Alexander, to measure his line of march. *Plin.* 6. c. 17.——A celebrated painter, in the time of Antoninus.——The father of Clitomachus, the Carthaginian, who succeeded Carneades, and was before called Asdrubal.——A prince of Megara, subdued by Gelo. *Polyæn.* l. 1.——A general of the Erythæi, preserved from destruction by Polycreta, a captive. *Id.* 8. 608.——A pugilist, much honoured by the Cretans. *Vos. de Idolol.* 1. c. 14.

DIOME'DE, a daughter of Phorbas, whom Achilles brought from Lemnus, to be his mistress, after the loss of Briseis. *Homer. Il.* 9. v. 661.——The wife of Deion of Amyclæ.

DIOMEDE'A, a city of the Daunii, founded by Diomedes. *Steph.*

DIOME'DES, a son of Tydeus and Deiphyle, was king of Ætolia, and one of the bravest of the Grecian chiefs engaged in the Trojan war. He fought Hector and Æneas, and by repeated deeds of valor obtained much military glory. He went with Ulysses to carry away the Palladium from the temple of Minerva at Troy; and he also assisted in murdering Rhesus king of Thrace, and in plundering his camp and seizing his horses. At his return from the siege of Troy, he lost his way in the darkness of the night, and landed in Attica, where his companions plundered the country, and lost the Trojan Palladium. During his long absence, his wife Ægiale prostituted herself to Cometes, one of her domestics. This infamous conduct of the queen was attributed by some to the resentment of Venus, whom Diomedes had severely wounded in the arm in a battle before Troy. The infidelity of Ægiale proved highly displeasing to Diomedes. He resolved to abandon his native country, and the attempts of his wife to take away his life did not a little contribute to hasten his departure. He came to that part of Italy which has been called Magna Græcia, where he laid the foundations of a city, called Argyripa, and married the daughter of Daunus, the king of the country. He died there in extreme old age, or, according to a certain tradition, he perished by the hand of his father-in-law. His death was greatly lamented by his companions, who, in the excess of their grief were, as mythologists report, changed into birds resembling swans. These birds took flight into some neighbouring islands in the Adriatic, called *Diomedeæ insulæ*, and became remarkable for the tameness with which they approached the Greeks, and for the horror with which they shunned all other nations. They were called the birds of Diomedes. Altars were raised to Diomedes, as to a god, one of which *Strabo* mentions, as being at Timavus. *Homer. Il.* 2. 4, 5, 8, 9, 10, 11 & 14.—*Ital.* 13.—*Virg. Æn.* 1. v. 756. l. 11. v. 243, &c. *& Servius in loc.—Ovid. Met.* 14. fab. 10. —*Apollod.* 1. c. 8. l. 3. c. 7.—*Hygin.* fab. 97. 112 & 113.—*Paus.* 2. c. 30.——A king of Thrace, son of Mars and Cyrene, who is said to have fed his horses upon human flesh. It was one of the labours of Hercules to destroy him; and accordingly the hero attacked the inhuman tyrant, and gave him to be devoured by his own horses, which he had fed so barbarously. The names of these horses were Podarges, Lampon, Xanthus, and Dine, and they were killed afterwards by the hero with his club, when they had devoured his favourite Abderus, whom he had placed to guard them. *Hygin.* fab. 30.—*Ovid. in Ib.* v. 381.—*Lucret.* 2.—*Diod.* 4.—*Paus.* 3. c. 18.—*Apollod.* 2. c. 5. ——A friend of Alcibiades. *Plut. in Alcib.* ——A grammarian.

DIOM'EDON or DIOME'DON, an Athenian general put to death for his negligence at Arginusæ. *Thucyd.* 8. c. 19.——A man of Cyzicus, in the interest of Artaxerxes, king of Persia. *C. Nep. in Ep.*

DIO'MIA, a part of the tribe Ægeis. *Steph.*

DI'ON, a Syracusan, son of Hipparinus, was related to Dionysius the tyrant, and in conjunction with the philosopher Plato, who at his request had come to reside at the court of Syracuse, often advised him to lay aside the supreme power. His great popularity soon rendered him odious in the eyes of the tyrant, who, through fear or jealousy, banished him to Greece. To avenge his own and his coutry's wrongs, he there collected a numerous force, and resolved to free Sicily from tyranny. He entered the port of Syracuse with two ships only, and in three days reduced under his power an empire which had already subsisted for 50 years, and which was guarded by 500 ships of war, 100,000 foot, and 10,000 horse. The tyrant fled to Corinth, and Dion, fearful of the ambition or rivalship of the Sicilian nobles, kept the sovereign power in his own hands. When his mild government, however, seemed to promise the Sicilians the revival of liberty and of public confidence, he was shamefully betrayed and murdered by one of his familiar friends, called Callicrates, or Callipus, 354 years B.C., in the 55th year of his age, and four years after his return from Peloponnesus. His death was universally lamented by the Syracusans, who had witnessed his virtues, and who respected his character, and a monument was raised to his memory. *Diod.* 16.—*C. Nep. in Vitâ.*

Di'on Cas'sius, a native of Nicæa in Bithynia. His father's name was Apronianus. He was raised to the greatest offices of state in the Roman empire by Pertinax and his three successors. He was ten years in collecting materials for a history of Rome, which he made public in 80 books, after having been laboriously employed twelve years in its composition. This valuable history began with the arrival of Æneas in Italy, and was continued down to the eighth year of the reign of the emperor Alexander Severus, when Dion was a second time consul. The 34 first books are totally lost, the 20 following are mutilated, and we only possess fragments of the last 20. In the compilation of his extensive history, Dion took Thucydides for his model; but he is not perfectly happy in his imitation. His style is pure and elegant, and his narrations are judiciously managed, and his reflections learned; but upon the whole he is credulous, and occasionally the slave of partiality, satire, and flattery. He inveighs against the republican principles of Brutus and Cicero, and extols the cause of Cæsar. Seneca is the object of his satire, and he represents him as debauched and licentious in his morals. Dion flourished about 230, B.C. Xiphilinus of Trebizond, brother to the Patriarch of Constantinople, in the 11th century abridged the works of Dion, from the 35th to the 80th book. The best edition of Dion Cassius is that of Reimarus, 2 vols. fol. Hamb. 1750. His works have also been illustrated by the notes of Xylander. *Sax. Onom.* 1. p. 357.—*Fabr. B. Gr.* 5. c. 10.

Di'on, a famous Christian writer, surnamed Chrysostom, &c. *Vid.* Chrysostom.

Di'on, a promontory of the island of Crete, now Capo Sassoso. *Ptol.*——A town of Macedonia. *Paus.* 9. c. 36.

Dionæ'a, a surname of Venus as the supposed daughter of Jupiter and Dione.

Dio'ne, a nymph, daughter of Nereus and Doris. She was mother of Venus, by Jupiter, according to Homer and other authors. *Hesiod*, however, gives Venus a different origin. *Vid.* Venus. Venus is herself sometimes called Dione. *Virg.* 3. *Æn.* v. 19.—*Homer. Il.* 5. v. 381.—*Stat.* 1 *Sylv.* 1. v. 86.

Dio'nia, a city of Cyprus. *Steph.*

Dionys'ia, festivals in honour of Bacchus among the Greeks. These solemnities were first introduced into Greece from Ægypt by a certain Melampus, and if we admit that Bacchus is the same as the Isis of Ægypt, the Dionysia of the Greeks are the same as the festivals celebrated by the Ægyptians in honour of Isis. They were observed at Athens with more splendour and superstition than in any other part of Greece. The years were numbered by their celebration, the archon assisted at the solemnity, and the priests that officiated were honoured with the most dignified seats at the public games. At first they were celebrated with great simplicity, and the time was dedicated to innocent mirth. It was then usual to bring a vessel of wine, adorned with a vine branch, after which followed a goat, a basket of figs, and the φαλλοί. The worshippers imitated in their dress and actions, the poetical fictions recorded concerning Bacchus. They clothed themselves in fawns' skins, fine linen, and mitres, carried thyrsi, drums, pipes, and flutes, and crowned themselves with garlands of ivy, vine, fir, &c. Some imitated Silenus, Pan, and the Satyrs in the uncouth manner of their dress and their fantastical motions. Some rode upon asses, and others drove the goats to slaughter for the sacrifice. In this manner both sexes joined in the solemnity, and ran about the hills and country, nodding their heads, dancing in ridiculous postures, and filling the air with hideous shrieks and shouts, and crying aloud, Evoe Bacche! Io! Io! Evoe! Iacche! Io Bacche! Evohe! These were followed by a number of persons carrying sacred vessels, one of which contained pure water. Afterwards came a select number of noble virgins carrying little baskets of gold filled with all sorts of fruits. This was the most mysterious part of the solemnity. Serpents were sometimes put into baskets, and by their wreathing and crawling out, amused and astonished the beholders. After the virgins, followed a company of men carrying poles at the end of which were fastened φαλλοί. The heads of these men, who were called φάλλοφόροι, were crowned with ivy and violets, and their faces covered with other herbs. They marched singing songs upon the occasion of the festivals, called φαλλικὰ ἄσματα. Next to the φαλλοφόροι followed the ἰθύφαλλοι in women's apparel, with white striped garments reaching to the ground; their heads were decked with garlands, and on their hands they wore gloves composed of flowers. Their gestures and actions were like those of a drunken man. Besides these, there were a number of persons called λικνοφόροι who carried the λικνον or *mystical van* of Bacchus; without their attendance none of the festivals of Bacchus were celebrated with due solemnity, and, on that account the god is often called λικνίτης. The festivals of Bacchus were almost innumerable. The name of the most celebrated were the Dionysia ἀρχαιότερα, observed chiefly at Limnæ in Attica. The chief persons who officiated were fourteen women called γεραιαὶ *venerable*. They were appointed by one of the archons, and, before their appointment, they solemnly took an oath before the archon or his wife, that their body was free from all pollution. The greater Dionysia, sometimes called ἀστικὰ or τὰ κατ' ἄστυ, as being celebrated *within the city*, were the most famous. They were supposed to be the same as the preceding.—The lesser Dionysia, sometimes called τὰ κατ' ἀγρούς, because celebrated *in the country*, or λήναια from ληνός *a wine-press*, were to all appearance a preparation for the greater festivals. They were celebrated in autumn. The Dionysia, βραυρώνια observed at *Brauron* in Attica were a scene of lewdness, extravagance, and debauchery.—The Dionysia νυκτήλια were observed by the Athenians in honour of Bacchus Nyctelius. It was unlawful to reveal whatever was seen or done during the celebration.—The Dionysia, called ὠμοφαγια because human victims were offered to the god, or because the priests imitated the *eating of raw flesh*, were celebrated with much solemnity. The priests put serpents in their hair, and by the wildness of their looks and eccentricity of their actions feigned insanity.—The Dionysia ἀρκάδικα were yearly observed in Arcadia, and the children who had been instructed in the music of Philoxenus and Timotheus were introduced in a theatre, where they celebrated the festivals of Bacchus by entertaining the spectators with songs, dances, and different exhibitions. There were besides these, others of inferior note. There was also one observed every three years, called Dionysia τριετηρικά, and, it is said, that Bacchus instituted it himself, in commemoration of his Indian expedition, in which he was engaged for three years. There was also another, celebrated every fifth year, as mentioned by the scholiast of Aristophanes.—All these festivals in honour of the god of wine, were celebrated by the Greeks with great licentiousness, and they contributed much to the corruption of morals among all ranks of people. They were also introduced into Etruria, and were thence carried to Rome. Among the Romans both sexes promiscuously joined in the celebration during the darkness of night. The drunkenness, the debauchery, the impure actions and indulgencies, which soon prevailed at the solemnity, called aloud for the interference of the senate, and the consuls Sp. Posthumius Albinus and Q. Martius Philippus made a strict examination concerning the propriety and superstitious forms of the Bacchanalia. The disorder and pollution which were practised with impunity by no less than 7,000 votaries of either sex, were beheld with horror and astonishment by the consuls, and the Bacchanalia were abolished by a decree of the senate. They were, after some time, reinstituted, but not with such licentiousness as before. *Euripid. in Bacc.* v. 80, 81, 106, 125, 127, 160, &c.—*Virg. Æn.* 11. v. 737.—*Catull.* 61. v. 261.—*Schol. Aristoph. in Ran.* 299.—*Philost. Icon.* 1. c. 18.—*Diod.* 4.—*Ovid. Met.* 3. v 533. l. 4. v. 391. l. 6. v. 587.—*Ulpian. ad Demosth. contra Lept.*—*Meurs. Gr. feriat.*

DIONYSI'ADES, two small islands near Crete. ——Festivals in honour of Bacchus. *Paus.* 3. c. 13.

DIONYS'IAS, a fountain so called in honour of Bacchus. *Paus.* 4. c. 36.

DIONYS'IDES, a tragic poet of Tarsus. *Strab.* l. 14.

DIONYSIODO'RUS, a famous geometrician. *Plin.* 2. c. 109.——A Bœotian historian. *Diod.* 15.——A Tarentine who obtained a prize at Olympia in the 100th Olympiad.

DIONYSE'UM, a temple of Bacchus in Attica. *Paus.* 1. c. 43.

DIONYSIP'OLIS, a town of Thrace. *Mela*, 2. c. 2.

DIONYS'IUS, the First, or the elder, king of Sicily, was son of Hermocrates. He signalized himself in the wars which the Syracusans carried on against the Carthaginians, and, taking advantage of the power lodged in his hands, he made himself absolute at Syracuse. To strengthen himself in his usurpation he increased the pay of the soldiers, and recalled those who had been banished. Vowing eternal enmity against Carthage, he engaged in long wars against that republic, in which he experienced various success. Not satisfied with the honours of royalty, he was ambitious of being thought a poet, and his brother Theodorus was commissioned to go to Olympia, and repeat there some verses in his name, with other competitors, for the poetical prizes. His expectations were frustrated, and his poetry was received with groans and hisses. He was not, however, so unsuccessful at Athens, where a poetical prize was publicly adjudged to one of his compositions. This victory gave him more pleasure than all the triumphs which he had ever obtained in the field of battle But while distinction and poetical fame were courted abroad, tyranny and cruelty at home rendered Dionysius odious in the eyes of his subjects, and he became so suspicious that he never admitted even his wife or children to his private apartments without a previous examination of their garments. Afraid also of his domestics, he never ventured to trust his head to the hand of a barber but always burnt his beard. He made a subterraneous cave in the rock, said to be still extant, in the form of a human ear, which measured 80 feet in height and 250 in length. It was called the ear of Dionysius. This cave had a communication with an adjoining room where Dionysius spent the greatest part of his time to hear whatever was said by those whom his suspicions and cruelty had confined in the apartments above. The artists who had been employed in constructing this curious cave, were all put to death by order of the tyrant, for fear they should reveal to what purposes this building was to be appropriated. His impiety and sacrilege were as conspicuous as his suspicious credulity. He took a golden mantle from the statue of Jupiter, observing sarcastically, that the son of Saturn had too warm a covering for the summer, and too cold for the winter, and he substituted one of wool in its stead. He also robbed the statue of Æsculapius of its golden beard, and plundered the temple of Proserpine of its riches. He died of indigestion in the 63d year of his age, B.C. 368, after a reign of 38 years. Authors, however, are divided about the manner of his decease, and some are of opinion that he died a violent death. Some suppose that this tyrant invented the *catapulta*, an engine used for discharging showers of darts and stones in the time of a siege. *Diod.* 13, 14, &c.—*Justin.* 20, c. 1, &c.—*Xenophon. Hist. Græc.*—*C. Nep. Timol.*—*Plut. in Dion.*

DIONYS'IUS, the Second, surnamed the younger, was son of Dionysius the First, by Doris. He succeeded his father as tyrant of Sicily, and by the advice of Dion, his brother-in-law, he invited the philosopher Plato to his court, and under his tuition he devoted himself for a while to studious pursuits. The philosopher, enlarging on the virtues of justice and moderation, advised him to lay aside the supreme power, and he was warmly seconded in his admonitions by Dion. Dionysius, whose character was violent and irritable, not only rejected the exhortations of the philosopher, but cruelly ordered him to be seized and publicly sold as a slave. Dion, likewise, on account of his great popularity, soon became suspected by the tyrant; he was unfeelingly abused and insulted in his family, and his wife was given in marriage to another. This violent conduct was highly resented; Dion, who had been dishonorably banished, collected some forces in Greece, rendered himself master of Syracuse, and expelled the tyrant B.C. 357. *Vid.* Dion. Dionysius retired to Locri, where he behaved with the greatest oppression, and was consequently ejected by the citizens. He recovered Syracuse ten years after his expulsion, but his triumph was of short duration, and the Corinthians, under the conduct of Timoleon, obliged him to abandon the city. He fled to Corinth, where to support himself he kept a school, that he might as Cicero observes, still continue to possess absolute authority, and as he could not domineer over men, might still exercise his power over boys. It is said that he died from excess of joy when he heard that a tragedy of his own composition had been rewarded with a poetical prize. Dionysius was as cruel as his father, but he did not, like him, possess the art of conciliating the affections of his subjects, and of retaining his power. *Justin.* 21. c. 1, 2, &c.—*Diod.* 15, &c.—*Ælian. V, H.* 9. c. 8.—*Quintil.* 8. c. 6.—*C. Nep. in Dion.*—*Cic. Tusc.* 5. c. 2.

DIONYS'IUS, an historian of Halicarnassus, who left his country and came to reside at Rome, that he might carefully consult and examine all the Greek and Latin writers, whose compositions treated of the Roman history. He formed an acquaintance with all the learned of the age, and derived both important and genuine information from their company and conversation. After unremitted application for 24 years, he gave to the world his Roman antiquities in 20 books, of which only the 11 first are now extant, containing the account of nearly 312 years. His composition has been greatly valued by the ancients as well as the moderns for the easiness of his style, the fidelity of his chronology, and the judiciousness of his remarks and criticism. Like a faithful historian, he never mentioned any thing but what was properly authenticated, and he totally disregarded the fabulous traditions which fill and disgrace the pages both of his predecessors and followers. Dionysius was also an eloquent orator, a critic, and a politician. He lived during the Augustan age, and came to Rome about 30 years B.C. The best editions of his works are that of Oxford, 2 vols. fol. 1704, and that of Reiske, 6 vols. 8vo. Lips. 1774. *Sax. Onom.* 1. p. 195.—*Fabr. B. Gr.* l. 3. c. 32. ——A tyrant of Heraclea, in Pontus, in the age of Alexander the Great. After the death of the conqueror and of Perdiccas, he married Amestris, the niece of king Darius, and assumed the title of king. He is said to have been so corpulent, that he never exposed his person in public, and when he gave audience to foreign ambassadors he always placed himself in a chair which was conveniently made to hide his face and person from the eyes of the spectators. When he was asleep it was impossible to awake him without boring his flesh with pins. He died in the 55th year of his age, and as his reign had been remarkable for mildness and popularity, his death was long and sincerely lamented by his subjects. He left two sons and a daughter, and appointed his widow queen-regent. ——A surname of Bacchus, supposed to be derived from ἀπὸ τοῦ Διὸς and Νύσης, because he was son of Jupiter, and educated at Nysa. Others imagine that Jupiter was lame whilst Bacchus was in his thigh, and that his surname was derived from νύσσω *ferio*, or νύσος *claudus*. *Diod.* 4.—*Macrob. Sat.* 1. c. 18.—*Natal. Com.* 5. c. 13. ——A disciple of Chæremon.——A native of Chalcis, who wrote a book entitled κτίσεις, or *the origins of cities*. *Voss. de Hist. Gr.* 3. p. 358.——A commander of the Ionian fleet against the Persians, who went to plunder Phœnicia. *Herodot.* 6. c. 17.——A general of Antiochus Hierax.——A philosopher of Heraclea, disciple to Zeno. He starved himself to death, B.C, 279, in the 81st year of his age. *Diog.*—*Athen.* 7 & 10.——An epic poet of Mitylene.——A sophist of Pergamus.

Strab. 13.——A writer called Periegetes He lived as some authors suppose, in the Augustan age, and wrote, besides other pieces, now lost, a very valuable geographical treatise in Greek hexameters, which is still extant. This poem, though useful from the geographical information which it conveys, displays very little of the genius or fire of the poetical muse. The best editions of his treatise is that of Henry Stephens, 4to, 1577, with the scholia, and that of Hill, 8vo. Lond. 1688, *Sax. Onom*. 1. p. 202.—*Fabr. B. Gr*. l. 4. c. 2, &c. ——A Christian writer, A.D. 492, called Areopagita. The best edition of his works is that of Antwerp, 2 vols. fol. 1634.——The music master of Epaminondas. *C. Nep*.——A celebrated critic. *Vid*. Longinus.——A rhetorician of Magnesia, intimate with Cicero. *Cic. Br*. 91.——An Athenian who travelled to Heliopolis in Ægypt, and became one of the members of the Areopagus. He was one of those whom the preaching of St. Paul converted to Christianity at Athens, as it is mentioned in the Acts of the Apostles.——A Messenian madman, &c. *Plut. in Alex*.——A native of Thrace, generally called the Rhodian, because he lived for some time in the island of Rhods. He wrote some grammatical treatises and commentaries, B.C. 64. *Strab*. 14.—*Voss. de Hist. Gr*. l. c. 23.——A painter of Colophon.——A slave of Cicero, who plundered his master's library of several books, &c. *Cic. Fam*. 5. ep. 10. l. 13. ep. 77.——A slave of Atticus, employed as a librarian. *Cic*. 4. *Att*. 7, &c.——A learned man, who from a heathen became a convert to Christianity, and was made bishop of Alexandria. He died, A.D. 267. Of the few things which he wrote, some fragments are preserved in *Eusebius*. *Sax. Onom*. 1. p 366.—*Fabr. B. Gr*. l. 5. c. 11. For other persons of this name, see ***Hofmann's Lexicon Universale*** and *Fabricius*.

DI'OPE, a city of Arcadia. *Steph*.

DIOPI'THES, a person mentioned by ***Aristotle, Rh***. 2. c. 10.

DIOPH'ANES, a man who prevailed upon the Peloponnesians to join the Achæan league. *Paus*. 8. c. 30.——A rhetorician of Mitylene, intimate with Tib. Gracchus, whom he instructed in the art of oratory. *Cic. Br*. 27.—*Plut. in Gracch*.

DIOPHAN'TUS, an Athenian general of the Greek mercenary troops in the service of Nectanebus, king of Ægypt. *Diod*. 16.——A learned native of Alexandria, who wrote 13 books of arithmetical questions, of which six are still extant, the best edition of which is that in folio, Tolosæ, 1670. He died in his 84th year, but the age in which he lived is uncertain, as some authors place him in the reign of Augustus, and others under Nero or the Antonines. *Sax. Onom*. 1. p. 417.—*Fabr. B. Gr*. l. 4. c. 22.——A rhetorician. *Vid*. Diophanes. ——A Lacedæmonian, who wrote 14 books of antiquities. *Voss. de Hist. Gr*. l. 3.——A Pythagorean philosopher of Syracuse. *Id. ibid*.

DIOPŒ'NUS, a noble sculptor of Crete. *Plin*. 36. c. 4.

DIOP'OLIS, a name given to Cabira, a town of Armenia Minor, by Pompey. *Strab*. 12.

DIOR'DULI, a people of Taprobane. *Ptol*.

DIO'RES, a friend of Æneas, killed by Turnus. He had engaged in the games exhibited by Æneas, on his father's tomb in Sicily. *Virg. Æn*. 5. v. 297. l. 12. v. 509.——A Grecian chief, son of Amarynceus, killed before Troy, by Pirus, son of Imbrasus. *Homer. Il*. 2. v. 129. l. 4. v. 517.

DIORYC'TUS, a place of Acarnania, where a canal was cut, (διὰ ὀρύσσω) to make Leucadia an island. *Plin*. 4. c. 1.

DIOSCOR'IDES, a native of Anazarba in Cilicia, who lived, as some authors suppose, in the age of Nero. He was originally a soldier, but he afterwards applied himself to literature, and wrote a book upon medicinal herbs, of which the best edition is that of Saracenus, fol. Francof. 1598. *Sax. Onom*. 1. p. 255.—*Fabr. B. Gr*. l. 4. c. 3.——A man who wrote an account of the republic of Lacedæmon. *Athen*. l. 4.——A nephew of Antigonus. *Diod*. 19.——A Cyprian, in the age of Ptolemy Philadelphus, blind of one eye. *Laert*. 9.——A disciple of Isocrates.——An astrologer, sent ambassador by J. Cæsar, to Achillas, &c. *Cæs. Bell. Civ*. 3. c. 109.——An engraver in the age of Augustus. *Plin*. 37. c. 1.——A physician, surnamed Phacas or Lentinus, in the age of Antony and Cleopatra. *Suidas, &c*.

DIOSCOR'IDIS IN'SULA, an island situate at the south of the entrance of the Arabic Gulph, and now called Zocotora. *Plin*. 6. c. 28.

DIOS'CORON, an island of Italy, opposite the promontory Lacinium. *Plin*. 3. c. 10.

DIOSCU'RI, or *sons of Jupiter*, a name given to Castor and Pollux. There were festivals in their honor, called Dioscuria, celebrated by the people of Corcyra, and by the Lacedæmonians. They were observed with much festivity. The people, during these festivals, made a free use of the gifts of Bacchus, and diverted themselves with sports, of which wrestling matches always made a part. *Cic. N. D*. 3. c. 21.

DIOSCU'RIAS, a town of Colchis. *Plin*. 6. c. 28.

DIOS'PAGE, a town of Mesopotamia. *Id*. 6. c. 26.

DIOS'POLIS or THE'BÆ, a famous city of Ægypt, formerly called Hecatompylos. *Vid*. Thebæ.

DIOSTECNO'SIA, a fountain in the island of Andrus. *Plin*. 2. c. 103.

DIOTI'ME, a woman at Athens, of great literary eminence. She gave lectures upon philosophy, which Socrates attended. *Plut. in Symp*.

DIOTI'MUS, an Athenian skilled in maritime affairs, &c. *Polyæn*. 5.——A stoic who flourished 85 B.C.——An archon at Athens. Ol. 106. ann. 3.

DIOT'REPHES, an Athenian officer, &c. *Thucyd*. 3. c. 75.

DIOXIP'PE, one of the Danaides. *Apollod*. 2. c. 1.

DIOXIP'PUS, a soldier of Alexandria, who killed one of his fellow soldiers in a rage, &c. *Ælian*. ——An Athenian boxer, &c. *Diod*. 17.—*Plin*. 35. c. 11.——A Trojan killed by Turnus. *Virg. Æn*. 9. v. 574.——An Athenian comic poet. *Suidas*.—*Voss.de Hist. Gr*. p. 359.

DIPÆ'A, a place of Peloponnesus, where a battle was fought between the Arcadians and the Spartans. *Herodot*. 9. c. 35.

DIPH'ILAS, a man sent to Rhodes by the Spartans to destroy the Athenian faction there. *Diod*. 14. ——A governor of Babylon in the interest of Antigonus.——An historian.

DIPH'ILUS, an Athenian general, A.U.C. 311. ——An architect so slow in finishing his works that *Diphilo tardior* became a proverb. *Cic. ad Fratr*. 3. ep. 1.——A comic writer of Sinope, posterior to Menander. *Voss. de Poet. Gr*. l. 8. p. 60. *De Hist. Gr*. 3. p. 360.

DIPHOR'IDAS, one of the Ephori at Sparta, *Plut. in Ages*.

DIPH'RI, a city of Phœnicia. *Steph*.

DIP'NIAS, a city of Thessaly. *Id*.

DIPŒ'NA, a town of Arcadia. *Paus*. 8. c. 31.

DIPŒ'NUS, a famous sculptor. *Plin*. 35. c. 4.

DIP'OLIS, a name given to Lemnus, as having two cities, Hephæstia and Myrina. *Strab*. l. 3.

DIP'SAS (*-antis*), a river of Cilicia flowing from mount Taurus. *Lucan* 8. v. 255.

DIP'SAS, (*-adis*), a profligate and incontinent woman mentioned by *Ovid. Am*. l. v. 8.

DIP'SAS, a kind of serpent. *Lucan*, 9.

DIP'SON, a barren place of Arabia. *Plin*. 4. c. 5.

DIP'YLON, one of the gates of Athens. *Iac. Spon. Itin. Gr*. part 2. p. 195.

DIR'ADES, a part of the tribe Leontis. *Steph*.

DIRADIO'TES, an epithet of Apollo *Pausan*.

DI'RÆ, the daughters of Acheron and Nox, persecuted the souls of the guilty. They were the same as the Furies, and some suppose that they were called Furies in hell, Harpies on earth, and Diræ in heaven. They were represented as standing near the throne of Jupiter, in an attitude which expressed their eagerness to receive his orders, and to torment the guilty on earth by the most excruciating punishments. *Virg. Æn*. 4. v. 473 & 610. l. 8. v. 701. l. 12. v. 845.

DI'RÆ, a city of Upper Æthiopia, on the banks of the Nile. *Plin*. 6. c. 29.

DIR'CE, a woman whom Lycus, king of Thebes, married after he had divorced Antiope. When Antiope became pregnant by Jupiter, Dirce suspected her husband of infidelity to her bed, and imprisoned Antiope, whom she tormented with the greatest cruelty. Antiope escaped from her confinement, and brought forth Amphion and Zethus on mount Cithæron. When these children were informed of the cruelties to which their mother had been exposed, they besieged Thebes, put

Lycus to death, and tied the cruel Dirce to the tail of a wild bull, which dragged her over rocks and mountains, and exposed her to the greatest tortures, till the gods pitying her miserable fate, changed her into a fountain in the neighbourhood of Thebes. According to some accounts, Antiope became mother of Amphion and Zethus, before she was confined and exposed to the tyranny of Dirce. *Vid.* Amphion, & Antiope. *Propert.* 3. el. 15. v. 37.—*Paus.* 9. c. 26.—*Ælian. V. H.* 12. c. 57.—*Lucan.* 3. v. 175. l. 4. v. 550.—*Plaut. in Pseud.* 1. sc. 2. v. 65.—*Ovid. Ibis,* 537. [Dirce forms a prominent character in the celebrated group called "Il Toro Farnese," now at Naples.] ——A woman changed into a fish, for comparing her beauty to that of Pallas. *Ovid. Met.* 4. v. 726.——A fountain of Bœotia, sacred to the muses, whence Pindar, the Theban poet is called *Dircæus. Cygnus. Horat.* 4. od. 2. v. 25.

DIRCEN'NA, a cold fountain of Spain, near Bilbilis. *Martial.* 1. epigr. 50. v. 17.

DI'RE, a promontory and city near Æthiopia. *Steph.*

DIRI'NI, a people of Italy. *Plin.* 3. c. 11.

DIR'PHYA, a surname of Juno, from Dirphys, a mountain of Eubœa, where a temple was erected in honor of the goddess. *Steph.*

DIS, the god of riches among the Gauls, supposed to be the same as Pluto the god of hell. The inhabitants of Gaul considered themselves descended from this deity. *Cæs. Bell. G.* 6.—*Tacit.* 4. *Hist.* c. 84.

DIS'CERA, a nation of Cyrene, led in triumph by Corn. Balbus. *Plin.* 5. c. 5.

DISCOR'DIA, a malevolent deity, daughter of Nox, and sister to Nemesis, the Parcæ, and Death. She was driven from heaven by Jupiter, because she excited continual quarrels and dissensions among the gods. When the nuptials of Peleus and Thetis were celebrated, the goddess of discord was not invited, and this seeming neglect so irritated her, that she threw an apple into the midst of the assembly of the gods, with the inscription of *detur pulchriori.* This apple proved the cause of the ruin of Troy, and of infinite misfortune to the Greeks. *Vid.* Paris. The goddess of discord is represented with a pale ghastly look, her garment is torn, her eyes sparkle with fire, and in her bosom she holds a dagger concealed. Her head is generally entwined with wreaths of serpents, and she is attended by Bellona. She was supposed to be the cause of all the dissensions, murders, wars, and quarrels, public as well as private, which arose upon earth. *Virg. Æn.* 8. v. 702.—*Hesiod. Theog.* 225.—*Petronius.*—*Horat.* 1. sat. 4. v. 60.

DIS'ORÆ, a people of Thrace. *Steph.*

DIS'TA, a town of Aria. *Ptol.*

DITHYRAM'BUS, a surname of Bacchus, given to him either because he was twice born, or because Ceres collected and restored life to his limbs, which had been cut to pieces in the wars of the giants, or because the cave in which he was brought up had two entrances. The hymns sung in his honor were called Dithyrambics, and expressed in irregular numbers an enthusiastic poetical fury, similar to that caused by intoxication. *Horat.* 4. od. 2. v. 10.—*Scaliger. Poet.* 1. c. 44.

DITIO'NES, a people of Dalmatia. *Plin.* 3. c. 22.

DITTA'NI, a people of Spain. *Strab.*

DITTA'TIUM, a town of the Sequani. *Ptol.*

DI'VI, a name chiefly appropriated to those who were made gods after death, such as heroes and warriors, or the Lares, and Penates, and other domestic gods. *Arnob.* 1. 1.

DIV'ICO, an Helvetian sent ambassador to Cæsar. *Cæs. Bell. Gal.* 1. 1. c. 13.

DIVITI'ACUS, one of the leading men among the Ædui. He went to Rome to solicit assistance against Ariovistus, and during his residence there he was universally esteemed, and was honored with the friendship of Cæsar and Cicero. *Cæs. B. G.* 1. c. 3 & 19. 1. 6. c. 11.—*Cic. de Div.* 1. c. 41.

DI'UM, a town on the northern shores of Eubœa, where there were hot baths. *Plin.* 31. c. 2.——A promontory of Crete.——A town of Macedonia. *Liv.* 44. c. 7.

DI'UR, a river of Mauritania Tingitania, now Teculet. *Ptol.*

DIVODO'RUM, or DIVODU'RUM, a town of Gaul, now Metz, on the river Moselle in Lorrain.

DI'VUS FID'IUS, a god of the Sabines, worshipped also at Rome. *Dionys.* 2.

DIYL'LUS, an Athenian historian. *Diod.* 16. ——A statuary. *Paus.* 10. c. 13.

DIZE'RUS, a city of Illyria. *Steph.*

DIZOA'TRA, a town of Armenia Minor. *Ptol.*

DOA'NUS, a river India without the Ganges. *Ptol.*

DOBE'RES, a people of Pæonia, in the northern parts of Macedonia. *Herodot.* 5. c. 16.

DOBU'NI, a people of Britain inhabiting the country now Gloucestershire and part of Oxfordshire. *Ptol.*

DO'CHI, a people of Upper Æthiopia. *Plin.* 6. c. 30.

DOC'ILIS, a gladiator at Rome, mentioned by *Horace,* 1 ep. 18. v. 19.

DOCIMÆ'UM, a city of Phrygia. *Steph.*

DOC'IMUS, a man of Tarentum, deprived of his military dignity by Philip, son of Amyntus, for indulging himself with hot baths. *Polyæn.* 4. ——An officer of Antigonus. *Diod.* 19.——An officer of Perdiccas, taken by Antigonus. *Id.* 18.

DO'CLEA, a city of Dalmatia, now Antivari. The people were called Docleatæ. *Plin.* 3. c. 22.

DODO'NA, a town of Thesprotia in Epirus, or according to others, on the borders of Thessaly. There was in its neighbourhood, upon a small hill called Tmarus, a celebrated oracle of Jupiter. The town and the temple of the god were built by Deucalion, after the universal deluge, or by Pelasgus, according to others. The oracle was supposed to be the most ancient in Greece, and according to the traditions of the Ægyptians, mentioned by Herodotus, it was founded by a dove. Two black doves, as the historian relates, took their flight from the city of Thebes in Ægypt, one of which flew to the temple of Jupiter Ammon, and the other to Dodona, where, with a human voice, they acquainted the inhabitants that Jupiter had consecrated the ground, and that oracles would in future be delivered there. The extensive grove which surrounded Jupiter's temple at Dordona, was endowed with the gift of prophecy, and oracles were frequently delivered by the sacred oaks, and by the doves which inhabited the place. This fabulous tradition of the oracular power of the doves, is explained by Herodotus, who observes, that some Phœnicians carried away two priestesses from Ægypt, one of whom fixed her residence at Dodona, where the oracle was established. It may further be observed, that the fable may have arisen from the ambiguous meaning of the word πέλειαι, which signifies *doves,* in most parts of Greece, while in the dialect of the Epirots, it implies *old women.* In ancient times the oracles were delivered by the murmuring of a neighbouring fountain, but the custom was afterwards changed. Large kettles were suspended in the air near a brazen statue which held a lash in its hand. When a strong wind blew, the statue was agitated, and struck against one of the kettles, which communicated the motion to all the rest, and raised a clattering and discordant din, which continued for some time, and from which the artful priests drew their predictions. Some suppose that the noise was occasioned by the shaking of the leaves and boughs of an old oak, which the superstition of the people frequently consulted, and from which they pretended to receive oracles. It may be observed, with more probability, that the oracles were delivered by the priests, who, by artfully concealing themselves behind the oaks, gave occasion to the superstitious multitude to believe that the trees were supernaturally endowed with the power of prophecy. As the ship Argo was built with some of the oaks of the forest of Dodona, there were some beams in the vessel which gave oracles to the Argonauts, and warned them against the approach of calamity. Within the forest of Dodona there was a stream and a fountain of cool water, which was said to have the property of lighting a torch as soon as it touched it. This fountain was totally dry at noon-day, but full at midnight, from which time till the following noon it began to decrease, and at the usual hour was again deprived of its waters. The oracles of Dodona were originally delivered by men, but afterwards by women. *Vid.* Dodonides. *Plin.* 2. c. 103.—*Herodot.* 2. c. 57 —*Mela,* 2. c. 3.—*Homer Odyss.* 14. *Il.*—*Paus.* 7. c. 21.—*Strab.* 9 & 17.—*Plut. in Pyrrh.*—*Apollod.* 1. c. 9.—*Lucan.* 6. v. 427.—*Ovid. Trist.* 4. el. 8. v.

23.—*Lucret.* 6.—*Sch. Sophoc. in Trach.—Nat. Com.* 6. c. 20.

DODONÆ'US, a surname of Jupiter from his temple at Dodona. His statue, under this appellation, always represented him crowned with oak-leaves.

DODO'NE, a daughter of Jupiter and Europa.

DODO'NE, a fountain in the forest of Dodona. *Vid.* Dodona.

DODON'IDES, the priestesses who gave oracles in the temple of Jupiter in Dodona. According to some traditions, the temple was originally inhabited by seven daughters of Atlas, who nursed Bacchus. Their names were Ambrosia, Eudora, Pasithoe, Pytho, Plexaure, Coronis, and Tythe or Tyche. In later ages the oracles were always delivered by three old women, which custom was first established when Jupiter enjoyed the company of Dione, whom he permitted to receive divine honours in his temple at Dodona. The Bœotians were the only people among the Greeks who received their oracles at Dodona from men, for reasons which *Strabo*, l. 9. fully explains. *Hygin.* fab. 182.

DOEAN'TES, a plain and city of Phrygia. *Steph.*

DO'II, a people of Arabia Felix. *Diod.*

DOLABEL'LA CNE'US, a city prætor, afterwards made governor of Cilicia, where Verres was quæstor. *Cic. Verr.* 1. c. 15, &c.

DOLABEL'LA P. CORN., a Roman who married the daughter of Cicero, from whom he was afterwards divorced by mutual agreement. During the civil wars he warmly espoused the interests of J. Cæsar, whom he accompanied at the famous battle of Pharsalia, in Africa, and at Munda. He was made consul by the influence of his patron, though M. Antony his colleague opposed it. After the death of J. Cæsar, he seemed inclined to support the party of Brutus, but the intrigues of Antony gained him over, and the hopes of paying the immense debts which he had imprudently contracted made him desirous of encouraging innovation, and of effecting the ruin of the commonwealth for his private advantage. Antony procured him the government of Syria, which had been before promised to Cassius. Dolabella departed for this distant province, but the violence of his character proved his ruin. At Smyrna he put to death with great cruelty, Trebonius, one of Cæsar's murderers, for which he was declared an enemy to the republic by the Roman senate. In consequence of this he was pursued and besieged by Cassius in Laodicea, and when he saw that all hopes of safety had vanished, he killed himself, in the 27th year of his age. He was of small stature, which gave occasion to his father-in-law to ask him once when he entered his house, who had tied him so cleverly to his sword. *Cic. Fam.* 2. ep. 15. l. 3. ep. 10, &c. *Att.* 6. ep. 6, &c.—*Flor.* 4. c. 2.—*Dio.* 41. c. 40. l. 43. c. 51. l. 44. c. 53.—*Sueton. Aug.* 36.—*Liv.* 113.—*Plut. in Cic.*—*Vel. Pat.* 2. c. 28. —*Appian.* 4. ep. 625.

DOLABEL'LA P. CORNE'LIUS, conquered the Gauls, Etrurians, and Boii at the lake Vadimonis, B.C 283.

DOLABEL'LA CN. CORN., a consul with Decula, A.U C. 673. He triumphed over the Thracians, and was accused by Cæsar of extortion; but was ably defended by Cotta and Hortensius, and acquitted. *Cic. Br.* 92. *Pis.* 19.—*Suet. Cæs.* 4.

DOLABEL'LA P. CORN., a proconsul of Africa.—The family of the Dolabellæ distinguished themselves in the service of Rome, and one of them, L. Corn. conquered Lusitania, B.C. 99.

DOLA'TES, a people of Umbria, called also Salentini. *Plin.* 3. c. 14.

DOL'BA, a city of Adiabene. *Steph.*

DOL'ICÆ, islands of Arabia Felix, in the Indian Sea. *Plin.* 6. c. 28.

DOLICHA'ON, the father of Hebrus, who was killed by Mezentius in the Rutulian war. *Virg. Æn.* 10. v. 696.

DOL'ICHE, an island in the Ægean Sea. *Apollod.* 2, c. 6.——A town of Thessaly at the north east of the bay of Ambracia. *Liv.* 42. c. 53.——A town of Syria.

DOLICHIS'TE, an island opposite mount Chimæra, in Lycia. *Plin.* 5. c. 31. *Strabo* calls it Mechiste.

DOLI'ONES, the inhabitants of Cyzicus, called also Dolici or Dolionii. *Steph.*

DO'LIUS, a faithful servant, whom Penelope brought with her when she married Ulysses. *Homer. Od.* 4. v. 675.

DOLOME'NE, a country of Assyria. *Strab.* 16.

DO'LON, the son of Eumedes, was a Trojan chief, famed for his swiftness. Being sent by Hector to reconnoitre the Grecian camp by night, he was seized by Diomedes and Ulysses, to whom he revealed the situation, schemes, and resolutions of his countrymen, with the hopes of escaping with his life. He was immediately put to death by Diomedes, that he might not carry back any information to the Trojans. *Homer. Il.* 10. v. 314. —*Ovid. Met.* 13. v. 98.—*Virg. Æn.* 12. v. 349, &c. ——A poet. *Vid.* Susarion.

DOLON'CI, a people of Thrace. *Herodot.* 6. c. 34.

DOL'OPES, a people of Thessaly, near mount Pindus. Peleus reigned there, and sent a powerful force to the Trojan war under Phœnix. The Dolopes became masters of Scyrus, and, like the rest of the ancient Greeks, were fond of migration. *Virg. Æn.* 2. v. 7.—*Flacc.* 2. v. 10.—*Homer. Il.* 9. v. 480.—*Ptol.* 3. c. 14.—*Liv.* 36. c. 33.—*Strab.* 9.—*Plut. in Cimon.*

DOLO'PIA, the country of the Dolopes, near Pindus, through which the Achelous flowed.

DO'LOPS, a Trojan, son of Lampus, killed by Menelaus. *Homer. Il.* 15. v. 525.

DO'LUS, a writer of Mendes, in Ægypt. *Columell.* l. 7.

DOM'ADA, a town of Arabia. *Plin.* 6. c. 28.

DOMA'NA, a city of Armenia Minor. *Antonin.*——A city of Arabia Felix. *Ptol.*

DOMANET'ICA, a region of Pontus. *Strab.* 12.

DOMAZA'NES, a people of Arabia. *Plin.* 6. c. 29.

DOMETIOP'OLIS, a city of Isauria, now Domezopoli. *Steph.*

DOMIDU'CUS, a god who presided over marriage. Juno also was called Domiduca, from the power which she was supposed to possess, as the protectress of marriage. *August. de Civit. D.* 12. c. 3.

DOMIN'ICA, a daughter of Petronius, who married the emperor Valens.

DOMIT'IA, an illustrious family at Rome, subdivided into the branches of the Calvini, Ahenobarbi, Afri, Labeones, Marsi, &c. The Ahenobarbi had no other prænomen but Cneius and Lucius. *Sueton. Ner.* 1.

DOMIT'IA VI'A, a public road built by C. Domitius.

DOMIT'IA LEX *de Religione*, was enacted by Domitius Ahenobarbus the tribune, A.U C. 650. It transferred the right of electing priests from the college of priests to the assemblies of the people.

DOMIT'IA LONGI'NA, a Roman lady, who boasted of her debaucheries. She was the wife of the emperor Domitian. [There is a statue of this lady in the Guistiniani collection at Rome, and a bust in the Capitol.]

DOMITIA'NUS TI'TUS FLA'VIUS, son of Vespasian and Flavia Domitilla, made himself emperor of Rome, at the death of his brother Titus, whom, according to some accounts, he destroyed by poison. The beginning of his reign promised happiness to the people, but this expectation was soon frustrated. Domitian became cruel, capricious, and vindictive, and gave way to incestuous and unnatural indulgencies. He commanded himself to be called God and Lord in all the papers which were presented to him. He passed the greatest part of the day in catching flies and killing them with a bodkin, so that it was wittily answered by Vibius, to a person who asked him who was with the emperor, "Nobody, not even a fly." In the latter part of his reign Domitian became suspicious, and his anxieties were increased by the predictions of astrologers, but still more poignantly by the stings of remorse. He was so distrustful, even when alone, that he built a wall with shining stones round the terrace where he usually walked for pleasure or exercise, that in them he might perceive, as in a looking glass, whether any body followed him. All these precautions were unavailing, he perished by the hand of an assassin, the 18th of September, A.D. 96, in the 45th year of his age and the 15th of his reign. He was the last of the 12 Cæsars. Though so abandoned in character, he shewed some respect for learning, and in a little treatise, which he wrote upon the great care which ought to be taken of the hair to prevent baldness, he displayed much taste and elegance according to the observations of his biographers. After his death he was publicly deprived by the senate of all the honours which had been profusely heaped upon him, and even his body was left in the open air without the honours of a funeral. This contumelious treatment proceeded no doubt from the resentment ol the senators, whom he had exposed to terror as well as to ridicule. He once assembled that august body to know in what vessel a turbot might be most conveniently dressed. At another time they received a formal invitation to a feast, and when they arrived at the palace, they were introduced into a large gloomy hall hung with black, and lighted with a few glimmering tapers. In the middle were placed coffins, on each of which was inscribed the name of one of the invited senators. On a sudden a number of men burst into the room, clothed in black, with drawn swords, and flaming torches, who, after they had for some time terrified the guests, permitted them to retire in security. *Suet. in Vitâ.—Eutrop.* 7. [A statue of Domitian is in the Guistiniani collection, and a bust in the palace of the Conservators at Rome.]

DOMITIL'LA FLA'VIA, a woman who married Vespasian, by whom she had Titus, a year after her marriage, and, 11 years after, Domitian.——A niece of the emperor Domitian, by whom she was banished.

DOMIT'IUS DOMITIA'NUS, a general of the emperor Diocletian, employed in Ægypt. He assumed the imperial purple at Alexandria, A.D. 288, and supported the dignity of emperor for about two years. He died a violent death.

DOMIT'IUS A'FER, an orator, was preceptor to Quintilian, and endowed with superior talents. He disgraced himself, however, by his adulation, and by practising the arts of an informer under Tiberius and his successors. He was made consul by Nero, and died A.D. 59.

DOMIT'IUS CN. AHENOBAR'BUS, a Roman consul, who conquered Bituitus the Gaul in a dreadful battle, leaving 20,000 of the enemy on the field of battle, and taking 3000 prisoners. *Liv.* 33. c. 42. l. 34. c. 42. l. 36. c. 37.

DOMIT'IUS CNE'US CALVI'NUS, a consul, A.U. 700. He espoused the cause of Cæsar against Pompey, and was commissioned to oppose Scipio, over whom, after being himself defeated, he obtained a victory. In the battle of Pharsalia he had the command of the centre of Cæsar's army. He was rewarded for his bravery and attachment with the province of Asia, and though defeated by the superior forces of Pharnaces, he however maintained his situation, and accompanied his friend into Africa. He was afterwards governor of Spain, where he decimated some of his soldiers for their ill conduct. *Cic. Flacc.* 13. *Sext.* 53,—*Dio.* 40. c. 17, &c.—*Cæs. in B. C.* 3. &c. *Hirt. B. Alex.* 9. &c.—*Vell. Pat.* 2. c. 78.

DOMIT'IUS CNE'US AHENOBAR'BUS, his son, was known for his integrity as a magistrate, and his firmness as a senator. Though not naturally eloquent, he exerted his oratorical powers in the accusation of Jul. Silanus, and of M. Scaurus, and displayed great uprightness of conduct when he not only refused to see, but even imprisoned, a slave of Scaurus, who privately promised him intelligence by which his master might be more fatally criminated and condemned. *Val. Max.* 6. c. 5. l. 9. c. 1.—*Vell.* 2. c. 12.—*Cic. Rull.* 2. c. 7. *In Deiot.* 11. *Orat.* 2. c, 56. *Brut.* 45.—*Plin.* 17. c. 1.—*Asconius in Cic.*

DOMIT'IUS LU'CIUS AHENOBAR'BUS, son of Cneus, early distinguished himself as the rival and enemy of Cæsar. By the influence of Pompey he presided at the celebrated trial of Milo. When appointed by the senate to succeed Cæsar in Cisalpine Gaul, he shewed his ignorance of military manœuvres, by throwing himself into Corfinium, instead of uniting his forces to those of Pompey, and so apprehensive was he of the resentment of his victorious enemy, that he took poison to destroy himself. The clemency of Cæsar towards his adversaries, made him soon after repent his rashness, and he was greatly rejoiced to find that his slave had not given him, as he desired, a dose of poison, but a soporific potion. Cæsar's kindness, however, had no great weight with Domitius, as he soon after defended Marseilles against his lieutenants, and headed one of the wings of Pompey's army at the battle of Pharsalia. The ruin of Pompey proved fatal to his friend, who, as he fled from the field of battle, was slain by some horsemen; or, as Cicero says, by Antony. Lucan, who makes Domitius fall in the battle, varies much in his account of his conduct and character, and wishes to represent him as brave, virtuous, and heroic; while others, with more probability, describe him as cruel and insolent, possessed of a weak understanding, and inconstant in his opinions. *Plut. in Cæs.*—*Seneca de Benef.* 3.—*Appian.* p. 451, &c.—*Cic. Att.* 9. ep. 6, &c. *Ad. Fr. Ad Fam.*—*Sueton. Cæs & Ner.*—*Lucan.*—*Dio.* 41.—*Ascon. in Cic.*

DOMIT'IUS CNE'US, son of Lucius by Marcia the sister of Cato of Utica, was present with his father at the battle of Pharsalia, and shewed his attachment to the republican cause by becoming one of Cæsar's assassins; a fact which is, however, denied by Suetonius. He was entrusted by Brutus with the command of fifty ships to intercept the supplies of Antony and Augustus in Greece, and in the fatal battle of Philippi he had the good fortune to be the only one of the conspirators who escaped. He afterwards joined himself to Antony, by whose influence he was restored to the honours of the state; but when the triumvirate was dissolved by the ambition of the two rivals, Domitius, who despised the connection with Cleopatra, and foresaw the ruin of Antony, joined himself to Augustus, and thus ensured his personal safety. He died soon after of a fever, brought on, according to *Plutarch*, by remorse for his perfidy. *Sueton. Aug. & Ner.*—*Cic. Fam.* 6. ep. 22. *Phil.* 2. c. 11.—*Appian.*—*Paterc.* 2. c. 72 & 76.—*Dio.* 48. c. 16.

DOMIT'IUS LU'CIUS, son of Cneus just mentioned, was engaged as an officer in the German wars under Tiberius, and was notorious for his cruelty, insolence, and perfidy. He married Antonia, the daughter of Antony and Octavia, by whom he had Cneus, the father of Nero by Agrippina, the daughter of Germanicus.

DOMIT'IUS CNE'US the son, was equally as cruel and as profligate as his father, and the vices of this unfortunate family seemed still to acquire greater strength and more dreadful features in the bloody character of Nero. *Paterculus*, however, with unpardonable flattery, has endeavoured to represent the character of these Domitii as respectable and praiseworthy. *Sueton. Ner. Cal.*—*Tacit. Ann.* 1. c. 63. l. 4. c. 44. l. 11. c. 11. l. 12. c. 64.—*Dio.* 48. c. 54.

DOMIT'IUS, a consul with C. Fannius, A.U. 632. He conquered the Arverni and Allobroges, and erected a trophy of his victory, and travelled through his province in great military parade, mounted on an elephant. *Flor.* 3. c. 2.—*Suet. Ner.* 2.—*Liv.* 61. ——A Roman high-priest, engaged as ambassader in Macedonia, where he settled, with nine others, the affairs of the province after the defeat of Perseus by Paulus. *Liv.* 42. c. 28. l. 44. c. 18. l. 45. c. 17.——A grammarian in the reign of Adrian. He was remarkable for his virtues and his melancholy disposition.——A consul, during whose consulship peace was concluded with Alexander king of Epirus. *Liv.* 8. c. 17.——A consul under Caligula. He wrote some few things now lost.——A Latin poet in the age of Horace, called also Marsus. He wrote epigrams, remarkable for little besides their indelicacy, and also a poem called Amazonis, on the wars of Hercules against the Amazons. Like Catullus and other poets of his age, he sang the beauty of his mistress called Melenis. Only three of his verses remain. *Ovid. de Pont.* 4. el. 16. v. 5.—*Martial. Epigr.*

DONACE'SA, a mountain of Phthiotis. *Plin.* 4. c 8.

DONA'TUS ÆLIUS, a Latin grammarian, who flourished A.D. 353. Besides his grammar, some have attributed to him the lives of Terence and Virgil, an opinion to which *Vossius* does not assent. *Sax. Onom.* 1. p. 408.—*Harles. Not. Lit. Rom.* 1. p. 577.——A bishop of Numidia, promoter of a sect called Donatists. A.D. 311.

DONA'TUS, a bishop of Africa, of great learning and abilities. He was a zealous friend of the Donatists, who may be said to have received their name from him rather than from the preceding. He was banished from Carthage by his opponents, A. D. 356, and died in exile.

DONETTI'NI, a people of the Molossi. *Steph.*

DONILA'US, a prince of Gallogræcia, who assisted Pompey with 300 horsemen against J. Cæsar. *Cæs. B. Civ.* 3. c. 1.

DONU'CA, a mountain of Thrace. *Liv.* 40. c. 57.

DONY'SA, one of the Cyclades in the Ægæan Sea, between Patmus and Myconus. Green marble was found here in great abundance. *Virg. Æn.* 3. v. 125.

DO'RA, an island in the Persian Gulph. *Steph.* ——A fountain of Arabia. *Plin.* 6. c. 28.

DORACTE, an island in the Persian Gulph. *Strab.* 16.

DO'RATH, a town of Mauritania. *Ptol.*

DOR'CEUS, a man well skilled in music. *Val. Flacc.* 3. v. 159.——One of Actæon's dogs. *Ovid. Met.* 3. v. 210.

DO'RES, the inhabitants of Doris. *Vid.* Doris.

DO'RIA or **DOR'ICA**, a part of Achaia, near Athens.

DO'RIAS, a river of India without the Ganges. *Ptol.*

DOR'ICUS, an epithet applied not only to the inhabitants of Doris, but to all the Greeks in general. *Virg. Æn.* 2. v. 27.

DORIEN'SES, a people of Crete.——A people of Cyrene. *Callimach.*

DORIE'UM, a city of Phrygia. *Steph.*

DO'RIEUS, a son of Anaxandridas, who went to settle with a colony in Sicily, because he could not bear to submit to the authority of his brother at home. *Herodot.* 5. c. 42, &c.—*Paus.* 3. c. 3 & 16, &c.——A son of Diagoras of Rhodes. *Paus.* 6. c. 7.

DOR'ILAS, a rich Libyan prince, killed in the court of Cepheus, at the nuptials of Andromeda. *Ovid. Met.* 5. fab. 4.

DORILA'US, a general of the great Mithridates.

DO'RION, a town of Messenia, where Thamyras the musician is said to have challenged the muses to a trial of skill. *Stat. Theb.* 4. v. 182.—*Propert.* 2. el. 22. v. 19.—*Lucan.* 6. v. 352.

DO'RIS, a county of Greece between Phocis, Thessaly, and Acarnania. It received its name from Dorus, the son of Deucalion, who made a settlement there. It was called Tetrapolis, from its four cities, Pindus or Dryopis, Eripeum, Cytinium, Boium. To these four some add Lilæum and Carphia, and therefore call it Hexapolis. The name of Doris has been given to many parts of Greece, from the unsettled character of the Dorians, who emigrated to various places, as convenience or caprice dictated. The Dorians in the age of Deucalion, inhabited Phthiotis, which they exchanged for Histiæotis, in the age of Dorus. Thence they were driven by the Cadmeans, and came to settle near the town of Pindus; after which they passed into Dryopis, and thence into Peloponnesus. Hercules having re-established Æginius king of Phthiotis or Doris, who had been driven from his country by the Lapithæ, the grateful king appointed Hyllus, the son of his patron, to be his successor, and the Heraclidæ marched from that part of the country to go to recover Peloponnesus. The Dorians sent many colonies in different places, which bore the same name as their native country. The most famous of these is Doris in Asia Minor, of which Halicarnassus was once the capital. This part of Asia Minor was called Hexapolis, and afterwards Pentapolis, after the exclusion of Halicarnassus. *Ptol.* 3. c. 15. l. 5. c. 2.—*Strab.* 9, &c.—*Virg. Æn* 2. v. 27.—*Plin.* 4. c. 7. l. 5. c. 29.—*Apollod.* 2.—*Herodot.* 1. c. 144. l. 8. c. 31.

DO'RIS, a goddess of the sea, daughter of Oceanus and Tethys. She married her brother Nereus, to whom she bore fifty daughters called Nereides. Her name is often used to express the sea itself. *Propert.* 1. el. 17. v. 25.—*Virg. Ecl.* 10.—*Hesiod. Theog.* 240.——A woman of Locri, daughter of Xenetus, whom Dionysius the elder, of Sicily, married the same day with Aristomache. *Cic. Tusc.* 5.——One of the fifty Nereides. *Hesiod. Theog.* 250.—*Homer. Il.* 18. v. 45.

DORIS'CI, a nation near the source of the Indus. *Plin.* 6. c. 23.

DORIS'CUS, a place of Thrace, near the sea, on the western banks of the Hebrus, where Xerxes numbered his forces. *Herodot.* 7. c. 59. 108.—*Plin.* 4. c. 11.—*Mela*, 2. c. 2.

DO'RIUM, a town of Peloponnesus. *Paus.* 4. c. 33.

DO'RIUM, one of the Danaides. *Apollod.*

DO'RIUS a mountain of Asia Minor. *Paus.* 6. c. 2. ——A river of Lusitania. *Ptol.*

DOROCOT'TOROS, a city of Gallatia. *Steph.*

DO'RON, a city of Cilicia. *Plin.* 5. c. 27.

DO'ROS, a city of Caria. *Steph.*

DORO'THEUS, a painter of eminence in the age of Nero. *Plin.* 35. c. 10.

DORSEN'NUS, a comic poet of great merit in the Augustan age. *Plin.* 14. c. 13.—*Horat.* 2. ep. 10. 173.

DOR'SO C. FA'BIUS, a Roman, who, when Rome was in the possession of the Gauls, issued from the Capitol, which was then besieged, to go to a sacrifice, which was to be offered on mount Quirinalis. He dressed himself in the sacerdotal robes, and carrying on his shoulders the statues of the gods of his country, passed through the guards of the enemy, without betraying the least signs of fear. When he had finished his sacrifice, he returned to the Capitol unmolested by the Gauls, who were astonished at his boldness, and did not attempt to obstruct his passage, or interfere with his sacrifice. *Liv.* 5. c. 46.

DORTI'CUM, a city of Mœsia, near the Danube *Ptol.*

DO'RUS, a son of Hellen and Orseis, or, according to others, of Deucalion, who left Phthiotis, where his father reigned, and went to make a settlement with some of his companions near mount Ossa. The country was called Doris from him, and the inhabitants Dorians. *Herodot.* 1. c. 56, &c.—*Apollod.* 1.

DO'RUS, a city of Phœnicia, the inhabitants of which are called Dorienses. *Paus.* 10. c. 24.

DORY'AGUS, a Spartan, father to Agesilaus. *Herod.* 7.

DOR'YCLUS, or **DORY'CLUS**, an illegitimate son of Priam, killed by Ajax in the Trojan war. *Homer. Il.* 11.——A brother of Phineus, king of Thrace, who married Beroe. *Virg. Æn.* 5. v. 620.

DORYCTETA, a region of Asia Minor. *Diod.*

DORYLÆ'UM or **DORYLÆ'US**, a city of Phrygia, now Eski Shehr. *Plin.* 5. c. 29.—*Cic. Flacc.* 17.

DOR'YLAS, one the centaurs killed by Theseus, at the nuptials of Pirithous. *Ovid. Met.* 12. v. 180. ——A man killed by Alcyoneus, at the marriage of Andromeda. *Ovid. Met.* 12. v. 380. l. 5 v. 129.

DORYLA'US, a warlike person intimate with Mithridates Evergetes, and General of the Gnossians, B.C. 125. *Strab.* 10.

DORYS'SUS, a king of Lacedæmon, killed in a tumult. *Paus.* 3. c. 2.

DO'SA, a city of Assyria.——A city of India within the Ganges. *Ptol.*

DOSARE'NI, a nation of Arabia Felix. *Id.*.

DOS'ARON, a river of India within the Ganges. *Id.*

DOS'CI, a people near the Euxine Sea. *Strab.*

DOSI'ADAS, a poet who wrote a piece of poetry called Βωμὸς, which has been edited with learned notes by Salmasius.

DOSI'ADES, a Greek, who wrote a history of Crete. *Diod.* 5.—*Plin.* 4. c. 12.

DOSITH'EUS, an historian mentioned by *Plutarch* in *Par. Min.* ——An astrologer mentioned by *Pliny*, 18. c. 31.——A grammarian. *Sax. Onom.* 1. p. 346. *Fabr. B. Gr.* l. 5. c. 7.

DO'SON, a surname of Antigonus, because he was very liberal in his promises, which he never performed. *Plut. in Coriol.*

DOSSE'NUS. *Vid.* Dorsennus.

DOT'IDAS, a king of Messenia, &c. *Paus.* 4. c. 3.

DO'TIUM, a city of Thessaly. *Steph.*

DO'TO, one of the Nereides. *Virg. Æn.* 9. v. 102.

DO'TUS, a general of the Paphlagonians in the army of Xerxes. *Herodot.* 7. c. 72.

DOVEO'NA or **DEVEO'NA**, a city of the Cadurci, in Gaul. *Ptol.*

DOXAN'DER, a man mmentioned by *Aristotle*, 5, *Polit.*

DOX'IUS, a son of Cœlus, who first built a house with mud. *Plin.* 7. c. 56.

DRABES'CUS, a region of Thrace. *Steph.*

DRAC'ANUS, or **DRACA'NUS**, a mountain where Jupiter is said to have drawn Bacchus from his thigh. *Theocrit.*

DRACHI'NÆ, a people of Aria. *Ptol.*

DRA'CO, a celebrated lawgiver of Athens. When he exercised the office of Archon, he made a code of laws, B.C. 623, for the government of the city, which, on account of their severity, were said to be written in letters of blood. By them idleness was punished with as much severity as murder, the penalty of death being denounced against the one as well as the other. The rigor of these enactments gave occasion to a certain Athenian to ask of the legislator, why he was so severe in his punishments, and Draco gave for answer, that as the smallest transgression had appeared to him deserving death, he could not find any punishment more rigorous for more atrocious crimes. These laws were at first enforced, but they were often suspended on account of their extreme severity, and Solon abolished them, with the exception of that one which punished a murderer with death. The popularity of Draco was uncommon, but the gratitude of his admiring countrymen proved fatal to him. When he appeared once in the theatre, he was received with repeated applause, and the people, according to the custom of the Athenians, showed their respect to their lawgiver, by throwing garments upon him. This was done in such profusion, that Draco was soon covered by them, and, it is said, smothered by this extraordinary but fatal mark of the excessive veneration of his fellow-citizens. *Plut. in Sol.—Aristot. Pol.* 2. c. 10. *Rhet.* 2. c. 23.—*Ælian. V. H.* 8. c. 10.——A man who instructed Plato in music. *Plut. de Music.*——A physician, son of Hippocrates.——A mountain of Asia Minor. *Plin.* 5. c. 29.

DRAC'ONIS, an island of Libya. *Steph.*

DRACON'TIDES, a profligate citizen of Athens. *Plut. in Soph.*

DRAC'ONUM, a town and mountain of the island Icaria. *Steph.* According to *Pliny*, 4. c. 12, it is a desert island of the Ægean Sea.

DRACUN'TEUS or DRACUN'TUS, an island near Africa Propria. *Ptol.*

DRA'CUS, a general of the Achæans, conquered by Mummius. *Liv.* l. 52.

DRAG'MUS, a city of Crete. *Steph.*

DBAG'OGI, a people of Asia. *Arrian. de gest. Alex.* l. 3.

DRAN'CES, a friend of Latinus, remarkable for his weakness and eloquence. He showed himself an obstinate opponent of the violent measures which Turnus pursued against the Trojans. Some have imagined that the poet, in drawing this character, had an eye to the conduct and eloquence of Cicero. *Virg. Æn.* 11. v. 122, 220 & 336. l. 12. v. 644. & *Servius locis cit.*

DRANGIA'NA, a province of Persia. *Diod.* 17.

DRA'PES, a seditious Gaul, &c. *Cæs. Bell. Gall.* 8. c. 30.

DRAP'SACA, a city of Bactriani. *Arrian. Hist.* l. 3.

DRAS'OCA, a town of Paropanisus.——A town of India within the Ganges. *Ptol.*

DRA'VUS, a large river of Noricum, which falls into the Danube, near Mursa. It is now Dra. *Ptol.*

DRAUDACUM, a fortified place of Penestia. *Liv.* 43. c. 19.

DREC'ANUM, a village of Cos. *Strab.*

DREP'ANA or DREP'ANUM, now Trapani, a town on the western shores of Sicily, near mount Eryx, in the form of a scythe, whence its name, (δρέπανον *falx*). Anchises died there, in his voyage to Italy with his son Æneas. The Romans under Cl. Pulcher were defeated near the coast, B.C. 249, by the Carthaginian general Adherbal. *Ptol.* 3. c. 4.—*Virg. Æn.* 3. v. 707.—*Cic. Verr.* 2. c. 57.—*Ovid. Fast.* 4. v. 474.——A promontory of Peloponnesus, said likewise to derive its name from a scythe, because, as some mythologists observe, Saturn there mutilated his father Uranus with that instrument. *Strab.* 8.—*Ptol.* 3. c. 16.—*Paus.* 7. c. 23.

DREP'SA, the metropolis of Sogdiana. *Ptol.*

DRE'SIA, a city of Phrygia. *Steph.*

DRI'LÆ, a people of Cappadocia, on the shores of the Euxine Sea. *Arrian. in Peripl.*

DRI'LO, a river between Illyricum and Macedonia, which flows from mount Hæmus, and falls into the Adriatic at Lissus.

DRILO'NIUS, a city of Gallia Celtica. *Steph.*

DRILOPHYLI'TÆ, a people of India within the Ganges. *Ptol.*

DRIM'ACHUS, a famous robber of Chius. When a price was set upon his head, he ordered a young man to cut it off, and go and receive the money. Such an uncommon instance of generosity so pleased the Chians, that they raised a temple to his memory, and honored him as a god. *Athen.* 13.

DRIM'ATI, a people of Arabia Felix. *Plin* 6. c. 28.

DRI'NUS, a small river which falls into the Save, and with it into the Danube.

DRIOPI'DES, an Athenian ambassador sent to Darius when the peace with Alexander had been violated. *Curt.* 3. c. 13.

DRI'OS, a mountain of Arcadia. *Diod.*

DRO'I, a people of Thrace. *Thucyd.* 2. c. 101.

DROMÆ'US, a surname of Apollo, in Crete, and at Lacedæmon. *Plut. Symp.* 6. c. 4.

DROMICHÆ'TES a leader of the Thracians, in the interest of Antiochus. *Polyæn.* 4.

DROMIS'COS, an island near Miletus. *Plin.* 2. c. 89.

DRON'GILUM, a region of Thessaly. *Steph.*

DROP'ICI, a people of Persia. *Herodot.* 1. c. 125.

DROPI'DES, a poet, brother of Solon. *Voss. de P. Gr.* c. 3.

DRO'PION, a king of Pæonia. *Paus.* 10. c. 13.

DROS'ACHE, a city of the Seræ. *Ptol.*

DROS'ICA, a province of Thrace. *Id.*

DRUEN'TIUS or DRUEN'TIA, now Durance, a rapid river of Gaul which falls into the Rhone, between Arles and Avignon. *Sil. Ital.* 3. v. 468.—*Strab.* 4.

DRU'GERI or DRUGE'RI, a people of Thrace.

DRU'IDÆ, the ministers of religion among the ancient Gauls and Britons. They were divided into different classes, called the Bardi, Euhages, the Vates, the Semnothei, the Saronidæ, and the Samothei. From the sanctity of their office, as well as from the integrity of their conduct, they were held in the greatest veneration by the people. Their life was austere and recluse from the world, their dress was peculiar to themselves, and they generally appeared with a tunic which reached a little below the knee. As the chief power was lodged in their hands, they punished as they pleased, and could declare war and make peace at their option. Their authority extended not only over private families, but they could depose magistrates and even kings, if their actions in any manner deviated from the established laws of the estate. They had the privilege of naming the magistrates who annually presided over the cities of the country, and the kings themselves were created only with their approbation. They were entrusted with the education of youth, and all religious ceremonies, festivals, and sacrifices were under their peculiar care. They taught the doctrine of the metempsychosis, and believed the immortality of the soul. They were professionally acquainted with the art of magic, and from their knowledge of astrology, they drew omens, and persuaded their followers that they saw futurity revealed before their eyes. In their sacrifices they often immolated human victims to their gods, a barbarous custom, which long continued among them, and which the Roman emperors attempted to abolish to little purpose. The power and privileges which they enjoyed were beheld with admiration by their countrymen, and as their office was open to every rank and every station, there were many who daily proposed themselves as candidates to enter upon this important profession. The rigor, however, and severity of a long noviciate deterred many, and few were willing to attempt a labour, which enjoined them during 15 or 20 years to load their memory with the long and tedious maxims of the druidical religion. Their name is derived from the Greek word δρῦς *an oak*, because woods and solitary retreats were generally the favourite places of their residence. *Cæs. Bell. G.* 6. c. 13.—*Plin.* 16. c. 44.—*Diod.* 5.—*Vossius de Idol.* 1. c. 35.—*Cœl. Rhod.* 18. c. 21.—*Cluver. Ant. Ger.* 1. c. 24.

DRU'NA, the Drome, a small river of Gaul, falling into the Rhone.

DRUSIL'LA LIV'IA, a daughter of Germanicus and Agrippina, rendered herself infamous by her debaucheries and licentiousness. She committed incest with her brother Caligula, who was so tenderly attached to her, that, in a dangerous illness, he made her heiress of all his possessions, and commanded that she should succeed him in the Roman empire. She died A.D. 38, in the 23rd year of her age, and was deified by her brother Caligula, who survived her for some time.

DRUSIL'LA, a daughter of Agrippa, king of Judea, &c *Act. Apost.* 24. v. 14.

DRUSILLA'NUS, a slave of the emperor Claudius, &c. *Plin.* 33. c. 11.

DRUSIP'ARA, a city of Thrace. *Ptol.*

DRU'SO, an unskilful historian and mean usurer, who obliged his debtors, when they could not pay him, to hear him read his tedious compositions, to draw from them praises and flattery. *Horat.* 1. sat 3. v. 86.

DRUSOM'AGUS, a city of Rhætia. *Ptol.*

DRU'SUS, a son of Tiberius and Vipsania. He was born a few months after the marriage of his mother with Asinius Gallus, but, though seemingly withdrawn from the protection of his father, who, in compliance with the commands of Augustus, had unwillingly married his daughter Julia, he continued the object of his most tender care. He made himself famous by his intrepidity and courage in the Provinces of Illyricum and Pannonia, and was raised to the greatest honors of the state by his father; a blow, however, which he gave to Sejanus, an audacious libertine, proved his ruin. Sejanus corrupted Livia, the wife of Drusus, and in conjunction with her he caused the unsuspecting husband to be poisoned by a eunuch, A.D. 23. ——A son of Germanicus and Agrippina, who enjoyed offices of the greatest trust under Tiberius. His enemy Sejanus, however, after treating him with confidence, debauched his wife, and effected his ruin. Drusus was cruelly confined by Tiberius, and deprived of all aliment. He was found dead nine days after his confinement. A.D. 33.——A son of the emperor Claudius, whose death was caused by his catching in his mouth and swallowing a pear thrown into the air.——An ambitious Roman, grandfather to Cato. He was killed for his seditious conduct. *Paterc.* 1. c. 13.

DRU'SUS LIV'IUS, father of Livia, the wife of Augustus, was intimate with Brutus, and killed himself with him, after the battle of Philippi. *Paterc.* 2. c. 71. *Dio.* 48. c. 44.

DRU'SUS M. LIV'IUS, a celebrated Roman, who attempted to renew the Agrarian laws, which had proved fatal to the Gracchi. He was murdered as he entered his house, though he was attended by a number of clients and Latins, whom he wished to admit to the privileges of Roman citizens, B.C. 190. His assassin was supposed to be Q. Varius, who afterwards died a most miserable death. Author's however, differ about the manner of Drusus' death. His father, Marcus, was tribune with C. Gracchus, and so numerous and important were his services to the senate in opposition to the Gracchi, that he was called the patron of the senate. *Paterc.* 2. c. 13 & 14.—*Cic. Mil.* 7. *N.D.* 3. c. 33. *Br.* 28.—*Plut. in Gracch.*—*Suet. Tib.* 3.—*Cic. ad Her.* 4. c. 12.

DRU'SUS NE'RO or DEC'IMUS CLAU'DIUS, a son of Tiberius Nero and Livia, adopted by Augustus. He was brother to Tiberius, who was afterwards made emperor. He greatly signalized himself in his wars in Germany and Gaul against the Rhæti and Vindelici, and was honored with a triumph. He is said to have been the first Roman general who entered the Northern Ocean, with which he made a communication by transporting his troops along a canal of eight miles, which he cut between the Danube and the Issel, called after him *Fossa Drusiana.* Drusus, whose successes and popularity promised the greatest services to Rome, died, it is said, of a fall from his horse in the 30th year of his age, B.C. 9. His death was sincerely lamented by the Romans, and especially by his brother Tiberius, who travelled 200 miles in one day, to attend him in his last moments. The body being conveyd to Rome was received with military honors, and a funeral eulogy was pronounced by the emperor and by Tiberius, whilst the honorable appellation of Germanicus was conferred on his family. He left three children, the illustrious Germanicus, father of Caligula, Livia, and Claudius the successor of Caligula, by his wife Antonia the younger daughter of Antony and Octavia. *Dion.*—*Horat.* 4. od. 4.—*Tac. Ann,* 2. c. 8. l. 3. c. 5.—*Suet. Tib.*—*Plin.* 7 c. 20.—*Dio.* 55. c. 1, &c. [There is a fine bust of Drusus in the Museum of the Vatican.]

DRU'SUS M, LIV'IUS SALINA'TOR, a consul, who, with his colleague, Claudius Nero, conquered Asdrubal. *Horat.* 4. od. 4.—*Virg. Æn.* 6. v. 824.

DRU'SUS CA'IUS, an historian, who being one day missed from his cradle, was found the next day on the highest part of the house, with his face turned towards the sun. *Suet. in Aug.*

DRU'SUS MAR'CUS, a prætor, &c. *Cic. ad Her.* 2. c. 13.—The plebeian family of the Drusi produced eight consuls, two censors, and one dictator. The surname of Drusus was given to the family of the Livii, as some suppose, because one of them killed a Gaulish leader of the name of Drausus. *Paterc.* 2. c. 13 & 14.—*Suet. Tib.* 3.—*Aur. Vict. de Ill.* 6.—*Diod.* 36.—*Tacit. Ann.* 1. c. 3. 33. & 56. l. 2. c. 7. 8. 41, & 82. *De Mor. Ger.* 34 & 37.—*Virgil. Æn.* 6.v. 824, mentions the Drusi among the illustrious Romans, and that perhaps more particularly because the wife of Augustus was of that family.

DRU'ZON, a town of Phrygia Major. *Ptol.*

DRY'ADES, nymphs that presided over the woods. Oblations of milk, oil, and honey were offered to them, and sometimes the votaries sacrificed a goat. The Dryads were not generally considered immortal, but semi-goddesses, whose life and power terminated with the existence of the tree over which they were supposed to preside. Some of them were called Hamadryades, as patronizing particular trees. *Ovid. Heroid.* 4. v. 49. *Met.* 8. v. 758.—*Stat.* 1. *Sylv.* 3. v. 63.—*Propert.* 1. el. 20. v. 32.—*Chæron. Lampsac.*—*Apollon. Arg.* 2.—*Virg. G.* 1. v. 11.

DRYÆ'NA, a city of Cilicia, afterwards called Chrysopolis. *Steph.*

DRYANTI'DES, a patronymic of Lycurgus, king of Thrace, as son of Dryas. *Ovid. in Ib.* v. 345.

DRY'AS, a son of Hippolochus or of Orion, according to some, who was father to Lycurgus. He went with Eteocles to the Theban war, where he perished by an invisible weapon. *Stat. Theb.* 8. v. 355.——A son of Mars, who went to the chase of the Calydonian boar. *Apollod.* 1. c. 8.——A centaur who killed Rhætus at the nuptials of Pirithous. *Ovid. Met.* 12. v. 296.——A daughter of Faunus, who so hated the sight of men, that she always refused to appear in public.——A son of Lycurgus, killed by his father in a passion. *Servius ad Virg. Æn.* 3. v. 14.—*Apollod.* 3. c. 5.——A son of Ægyptus, murdered by his wife Eurydice. *Id.* 2. c. 1.

DRYBAC'TÆ, a people of Sogdiana. *Ptol.*

DRY'LÆ, a town not far from Trapezus. *Id.*

DRY'MÆ, a city of Libya. *Steph.*

DRYMÆ'A a town of Phocis. *Paus.* 10. c. 33.

DRY'MO, a sea nymph, one of the attendants of Cyrene. *Virg. G.* 4. v. 536.

DRY'MUS, a town between Attica and Bœotia. *Suidas.*

DRYMU'SA, an island of Ionia. *Steph.*

DRYNÆM'ETUM, a place of Galatia. *Strab.*

DRY'OPE, a woman of Lemnus, whose features Venus assumed to persuade all the females of the island to murder the men. *Flacc.* 2. v. 174.——A virgin of Œchalia, daughter of Eurytus, and sister to Iole. Andræmon married her after Apollo had offered violence to her. She became mother of Amphisus, who, when scarce a year old, was with his mother changed into a lotus. *Ovid. Met.* 10. v. 331.——A nymph, mother of Tarquitus by Faunus. *Virg. Æn.* 10. v. 551.——A nymph of Arcadia, nother of Pan, by Mercury, according to *Homer. Hym. in Pan.*

DRY'OPE, a city near Hermione. *Steph.*

DRYOPE'IA, a day observed annually at Asine in Argolis, in honour of Dryops, the son of Apollo.

DRY'OPES, a people of Macedonia, near mount Œta. They afterwards passed into the Peloponnesus, where they inhabited the towns of Asine and Hermione, in Argolis. When they were driven from Asine by the prople of Argos, they settled among the Messenians, and called a town of the country by the name of their ancient habitation Asine. Some of their descendants went, together with the Ionians, to settle in Asia Minor. *Herodot.* 1. c. 146. l. 8. c. 31.—*Paus.* 4. c. 34.—*Strab.* 7. 8. 13.—*Plin.* 4. c. 1.—*Virg. Æn.* 4. v. 146.—*Lucan.* 3. v. 179.

DRY'OPIS or DRYOPI'DA, a small country at the foot of mount Œta in Thessaly. Its true situation is not well ascertained. According to *Pliny*, it bordered on Epirus. It was for some time in the possession of the Hellenes, after they were driven from Histiæotis by the Cadmeans. *Herodot.* 1. c. 56.

DRY'OPS, a son Priam, killed by Achilles during the Trojan war. *Homer. Il.* 20. v. 455.——A son of Apollo. *Paus.* 4. c 34.——A friend of Æneas, killed by Clausus in Italy. *Virg. Æn.* 10. v. 346.

DRYPE'TIS or **DRYPE'TIS**, the younger daughter of Darius, given in marriage to Hephæstion by Alexander the Great. *Diod.* 18.

DRYS, a city of Thrace. *Steph.*——A city of Epirus. *Suidas.*

DRYU'SA, an ancient name of Samus. *Steph.*

DU'ARUS, a gulph of Arabia Felix. *Plin.* 6. c. 28.

DU'BIS or **ALDU'ABIS**, the Doubs or Doux, a small river of Gaul, falling into the Saone. *Cæs. B. G.* l. 2.

DU'BRIS POR'TUS, a town of Britain, supposed to be the modern Dover.

DU'CÆ, a region of Mauritania Cæsariensis. *Ptol.*

DUCE'TIUS, a Sicilian general, who died B.C. 440.

DU'DUA, a city of Galatia. *Ptol.*

DU'DUM, an inland town of Libya. *Id.*

DUIL'LIA LEX was enacted by M. Duillius, a tribune, A.U.C. 304. It made it a capital crime to deprive the Roman people of the power of electing the tribunes, or to create any new magistrate without a sufficient cause. *Liv.* 3. c. 55.—Ano- A.U.C. 392, to regulate what interest ought to be paid for money lent.

C. DUIL'LIUS NE'POS, a Roman consul, the first who obtained a signal victory over the naval power of Carthage, B.C. 260. He took 50 of the enemy's ships, and was, for his meritorious conduct, honoured with a naval triumph, the first that ever appeared at Rome. The senate permitted him, as the reward of his valour, to have music playing and torches lighted, at the public expense, every day while he was at supper. There were some medals struck in commemoration of this victory, and there still exists a column at Rome, which was erected on the occasion. *Cic. de Senec.* 13.—*Tacit. An.* 1. c. 12.

DULICH'IUM, an island of the Ionian Sea, the largest of the Echinades, opposite the Achelous. It was part of the kingdom of Ulysses, and accordingly some of the inhabitants accompanied their monarch to the Trojan war. It is said by some modern travellers to have been overwhelmed by the sea. *Strab.* 8.—*Paus.* 5. c. 3.—*Mela*, 2. c. 7.—*Ovid. Trist.* 1. el. 4. c. 67. *Met.* 14. v. 226. *R. A.* 272.—*Martial.* 11. epigr. 70. v. 8.—*Virg. Ecl.* 6. v. 76.

DULOP'OLIS, a town of Asia Minor, near Rhodes. *Plin.*——A small region of Ægypt. *Steph.*

DUMA'NA, a city of Asia, towards Arabia. *Plin.* 6. c. 29.

DU'MATHA, a city of Arabia. *Steph.*

DUM'NACUS, a leader of the Andes, who besieged Lemovicum. *Hirt.* l. 8. c. 44.

DUM'NORIX, a powerful chief among the Ædui. *Cæs. Bell. G.* 1. c. 9.

DU'NAX, a mountain of Thrace. *Strab.* It is called Donuca by *Livy.*

DUN'GA, a city of India within the Ganges. *Ptol.*

DU'RA, a city of Mesopotamia. *Steph.*

DU'RABA, a city of Babylonia. *Ptol.*

DURA'TIUS PIC'TO, a Gaul, who remained in perpetual friendship with the Roman people. *Cæs. Bell. G.* 8. c. 26.

DURBE'TA, a city of Mesopotamia, near the Tigris.

DUR'DUM, a mountain of Mauritania. *Ptol.*

DUR'GA, a city of Africa Propria. *Id.*

DU'RIA, a river of Italy falling into the Po.

DURI'NE, a town of Susiana. *Plin.* 6. c. 27.

DU'RIS, an historian of Samus, who flourished B.C. 257. He wrote the life of Agathocles of Syracuse, a treatise on tragedy, a history of Macedonia, and other works, often quoted with approbation by ancient writers, but now lost. *Cic. ad Att.* 6. ep. 1. —*Plut. in Per.*—*Strab.* 1.

DURI'OPUS, a city and region of Macedonia.

DU'RIUS, a large river of ancient Spain, now called the Douro, which falls into the ocean near Oporto in Portugal, after a course of nearly 300 miles. *Sil.* 1. v. 234.

DURO'A, a mountain of Mauritania Tingitana. *Ptol.*

DUROBRI'VÆ, a town of the Cantii, in Britain, now Rochester.

DUROCAS'SES, the chief residence of the Druids in Gaul, now Dreux. *Cæs. Bell. G.* 6. c. 13.

DUROCOR'TORUM, a town of Gallia Belgica, now Rheims. *Ptol.*—*Cæs.* 1. 6. c. 8.

DURO'NIA, a town of the Samnites. *Livy.*

DUROT'RIGES, a people of the West of Britain, their chief town was Dunium, now Dorchester.

DUROSTE'NA, a city of Lower Mysia. *Ptol.*

DUROVER'NUM or **DARVER'NUM**, the ancient name of Canterbury.

DU'SARE, a rock, the highest ground in Arabia.

DU'SII, a name applied by the Gauls to some divinities, whose attributes resembled those of the Fauns and Satyrs in the theogony of the Latins. *August. de C. D.* 15. c. 23.—*Cæl. Rh.* 2. c. 6.

DUUM'VIRI, two noble patricians at Rome, first appointed by Tarquin to keep the Sibylline books. which were supposed to contain the destinies of the Roman empire. These sacred books were placed in the Capitol, and carefully secured in a chest under the ground. They were consulted but seldom, and only by an order of the senate, on solemn occasions, either when the armies had been defeated in war, or when Rome seemed to be threatened by an invasion, or by sedition. These priests continued according to their original institution till the year U.C. 388, when a law was proposed by the tribunes to increase the number to ten, to be chosen promiscuously from patrician and plebeian families. They were from their number called Decemviri, and some time after Sylla increased them to fifteen, known by the name of Quindecemviri. *Duumviri perduelliones sive capitales.* They were first created by Tullus Hostilius, for trying such persons as were accused of treason. This office was afterwards abolished as unnecessary, but Cicero complains of their revival by Labienus the tribune. *Orat. pro Rabir.* Some of the commanders of the Roman ships were also called Duumviri, especially when there were two together. They were first created, A.U.C. 542.—There were also in the municipal towns in the provinces two magistrates called *Duumviri municipales.* They were chosen from the centurions, and their office was much the same as that of the two consuls at Rome. They were sometimes preceded by two lictors with fasces. Their magistracy continued for five years, on which account they have been called *Quinquennales magistrates.*

DYAGON'DAS, a Theban legislator, who abolished all nocturnal sacrifices. *Cic. de Leg.* 2. c. 15.

DYARDA'NES, a river in the extremities of India. *Curt.* 8. c. 9.

DY'MÆ, a town of Achaia on the western shores of the Peloponnesus. *Liv.* 27. c. 31. l. 32. c. 22.—*Paus.* 7. c. 17.

DYMÆ'I, a people of Ætolia. *Diod.* 19.

DY'MAS, a Trojan, who joined himself to Æneas when Troy was taken, and was at last unfortunately killed by his countrymen, who took him to be an enemy because he had dressed himself in the armour of one of the Greeks whom he had slain. *Virg. Æn.* 2. v. 340 & 428.——The father of Hecuba, who from him is called Dymantis. *Hygin.* fab. 91. 111 & 243.—*Apollod.* 3.—*Homer. Il.* 16. v. 718.—*Virg. Æn.* 2. v. 394.—*Ovid. Met.* 11. v. 761.

DYME'THUS, an inland town of Sicily, now Torre de l'Oliveto. *Ptol.*

DYM'NUS, one of Alexander's officers. He conspired in Asia with many of his fellow soldiers against his master's life. The conspiracy was discovered in time, and Dymnus stabbed himself before he was brought into the presence of the king. *Curt.* 6. c. 7.

DY'MUS, a river of Sogdiana. *Ptol.*

DYNAM'ENE, one of the Nereides. *Homer. Il.* 18. v. 43.

DYNAS'TE, a daughter of Thespius. *Apollod.*

DYN'DASUM, a city of Caria. *Steph.*

DY'OS, a river of Mauritania Tingitana. *Ptol.*

DY'RAS, a small river of Trachinia. It rises at the foot of mount Œta, and falls into the bay of Malia. *Herodot.* 7. c. 198.—*Strab.*

DYRASPES, a small river of Scythia. *Ovid. Pont.* 4. el. 10. v. 53.

DYRBÆ'I, a people of India. *Steph.*

DY'RIS, the name given to mount Atlas by the inhabitants of the neighbouring country. *Strab.*

DYRRA'CHIUM or **DYRRHA'CHIUM**, now Durazzo, a large city of Macedonia, bordering on the Adriatic Sea, founded by a colony from Corcyra, B.C. 623. It was the common landingplace from Brundusium, and on that account it was frequently called *Hadriæ taberna.* Cicero met with a favourable reception rom the inhabitants of this place during his exile. Its ancient name was Epidamnus, which the Romans considering ominous, changed into Dyrrachium. *Ælian.* 13. c. 16.—*Thucyd.* 1. c. 24.—*Plin.* 2. c. 106.—*Mela*, 2. c. 3.—*Paus.* 6. c. 10.—*Plut.*—*Cic.* 3. *Att.* 22.

DYRRODO'TIS, a river near the Caucasiæ Portæ. *Plin.* 6. c. 11.

DYR'SELA, a town of Pamphylia. *Ptol.*

DYR'TA, a city of the Assacani, in India. *Arrian. in Indic.*

DYSAU'LES, a brother of Celeus, who instituted the mysteries of Ceres at Celeæ. *Paus.* 2. c. 14.

DYSNICE'TUS, an Athenian archon. Ol. 102. an. 2.—*Paus* 4. c. 27.

DYSO'RUM, a mountain of Thrace. *Herodot.* 5. c. 22,

DYSPON'TII. a people of Elis. *Paus.* 6. c. 22.

DYSTUS, a city of Eubœa. *Steph. ex Theopompo.*

E.

E'ANES or Æ'ANES, a man supposed by some authors to have killed Patroclus, and to have fled to Peleus in Thessaly. *Strab.* 9.

EA'NUS, the name of Janus among the ancient Latins. The word seems to be derived *ab eundo*, because Janus was considered by some as the representative of the sun and of time, the motion of which is constant and regular. *Macrob. Sat.* 1. c. 9.—*Cic. de Nat.D.* 2.—*Gyrald. Synt.* 4.—*Quintil.* 5. c. 6.

E'ARES, a people of India. *Steph.*

EAR'INUS, a beautiful boy, eunuch to the emperor Domitian. *Stat.* 3. *Sylv.* 4,—*Mart.* 9. epigr. 12.

E'ASIS, the metropolis of Gedrosia. *Ptol.*

EA'SIUM, a town of Achaia in Peloponnesus. *Paus.* 7. c. 6.

E'BA, a city of Etruria. *Ptol.*

EB'DOME, a festival in honour of Apollo at Athens observed on the seventh day of every lunar month. The seventh day was sacred to him because it was his birthday, whence he was sometimes called ἑβδομαγενής. It was usual to sing hymns in honour of the god, and to carry about boughs of laurel. *Suidas,*—*Plut. Symp.* 1. 8. *Quæst.* 1.—*Hesiod. Dieb.*—There was also another of the same name, celebrated by private families the seventh day after the birth of every child.

EBLÆ'Æ, a city of Albania. *Ptol.*

EBLA'NA, the chief town of Hibernia, now Dublin. *Ptol.*

EBLITÆ'I, mountains of Arabia Felix. *Plin.* 6. c. 28.

EB'ODE, a town of Arabia Felix. *Id.*——A town of Arabia Petræa. *Ptol.*

EBODU'RUM, a city of Rhætia. *Id.*

E'BON, a name given to Bacchus by the people of Neapolis. *Macrob. Sat.* 1. c. 18.

EB'ORA, a town of Lusitania, now Evora, in Portugal.

EBOR'ACUM, EBORA'CUM, EBUR'ACUM or EBURA'CUM, the ancient name of York in England.

EBRI'ETAS, a daughter of Venus, of whom Praxiteles made a brazen statue. *Plin.* 34. c. 8.

EBRODU'NUM, a town of Gallia Narbonensis, now Ambrun.——A town of the Helvetii, now Yverdon.

EBU'DÆ or HEBU'DÆ, the western isles of Britain, now the Hebrides. *Plin.* 4. c. 16.

EB'URA, a city of Hispania Tarraconensis, now Talavera la Reyna.

EBURI'ACI EBRO'ICÆ or EBUROVI'CES, a people of Gallia Celtica. Their city is now Evreux. *Cæs.* 3. c. 17.—*Plin.* 4. c. 9.

EBURO'NES, a people of ancient Belgium, now the county of Liege. *Cæs. B. G.* 2. c. 4. 1. 6. c. 5.

EBU'RUM, a town of Germany, now, probably Olmutz. *Ptol.*

EB'USUS or EBU'SUS, one of the ancient Baleares, 100 miles in circumference, which was said to produce no hurtful animals. It is near the coast of Spain in the Mediterranean, and now bears the name of Yvica, and is famous for pasturage and for figs. *Plin.* 3. c. 5.

EB'USUS, a man engaged in the Rutulian war. *Virg. Æn.* 12. v. 299.

EBU'TIUS TIT. ELVA, master of the horse to the dictator A. Posthumius.

ECBAT'ANA, (-orum), now Hamedan, the capital of Media, and the palace of Deioces king of Media. It was surrounded with seven walls, which rose in gradual ascent one above the other, and were painted in seven different colors. The most distant was the lowest, and the innermost, which was the most celebrated, contained the royal palace. Parmenio was put to death there by order of Alexander the Great; there also Hephæstion died, and received a most magnificent burial. *Herodot.* 1. c. 98.—*Strab.* 11.—*Curt.* 4. c. 5. 1. 5. c. 8. 1. 7. c. 10.—*Diod.* 17——A town of Syra, where Cambyses gave himself a mortal wound when hunting on horseback. *Herodot.* 3—*Ptol.* 6. c. 2.—*Curt.* 5. c. 8.

ECDAM'NA, a city of Galatia. *Ptol.*

ECDIP'PA or ECDIP'POS, a city of Phœnicia, formerly Ace. *Plin.* 5. c. 19.

ECDYS'IA, festivals in Crete, observed in honor of Latona. *Ovid. Met.* 17.

ECECHIR'IA, the wife of Iphitus. *Paus.* 5. c. 10.

ECESTIEN'SES, a people of Sicily. *Plin.* 3. c. 8.

EC'ETRA, a town of the Volsci. *Liv.* 2. c. 25. 1. 3. c. 4.

ECHE'ANAX, an Ephesian, father of Anaxagoras, &c. *Polyæn.* 1. 6.

ECHEC'RATES, a Thessalian, who offered violence to Phœbas, the priestess of Apollo's temple at Delphi. From this circumstance a decree was made by which no woman was afterwards admitted to the office of priestess before the age of fifty. *Diod.* 4.——A Pythagorean philosopher of Locri, in the age of Plato. *Cic. Fin.* 5. c. 29.

ECH'EDÆ, a village of Attica. *Steph.*

ECHEDA'MIA or ECHEDAMI'A, a town of Phocis. *Paus.* 10 c. 3.

ECHEDO'RUS. *Vid.* Chidorus.

ECHEL'ATUS, a man who led a colony to Africa. *Strab.* 8.

ECHEL'IDÆ, a village of Attica, so called from a hero named Echelus. *Steph.*

ECH'ELUS, a Trojan chief killed by Patroclus, in the Trojan war.——A son of Agenor, killed by Achilles. *Homer. Il.* 16. v. 694. 1. 20. 474.

ECHEM'BRO'TUS, an Arcadian, who obtained the prize at the Pythian games. *Paus.* 10. c. 7.

ECHEM'ENES, an historian mentioned by *Athenæus*, 1. 13.

ECHE'MON, a son of Priam, killed by Diomedes. *Homer. Il.* 5. v. 160. Also Ech'emon.

ECH'EMUS, an Arcadian who conquered the Dorians when, under the command of Hyllus, they endeavoured to recover Peloponnesus. *Paus.* 8. c. 5.——A king of Arcadia, who joined Aristomenes against the Spartans. *Pausan. in Arcad.*

ECHENE'US, a Phæacian, remarkable for his age and for his mental accomplishments, when Ulysses visited the country. *Homer. Odyss.* 7. v. 155. 1. 11. v. 341.

ECH'EPHRON, one of Nestor's sons. *Apollod.* 1. c. 9.——A son of Priam. *Id.*——A son of Hercules. *Paus.* 8. c. 24.

ECHEP'OLIS, a Trojan, son of Thasius, killed by Antilochus. *Homer. Il.* 4. v. 458.

ECHES'TRATUS, a son of Agis, the first king of Sparta, who succeeded his father, B.C. 1058. *Herodot.* 7. c. 204.

ECHE'TIA, a city of Italy. *Steph.*

ECH'ETLA, a fortified town in Sicily, a few leagues at the west of Syracuse. *Polyb.* 1. 1.

ECHEVEREN'SES or ECHEVETHEN'SES, a people of Tegea, in Arcadia. *Paus.* 8. c. 45.

ECHID'NA, a celebrated monster sprung from the union of Chrysaor with Calirhoe, the daughter of Oceanus. She is represented by ancient writers to have been a beautiful woman in the upper parts of her body, but a serpent below the waist. She was mother, by Typhon, of Orthos, Geryon, Cerberus, the Hydra, &c. According to Herodotus, Hercules had three children by her, Agathyrsus, Gelonus, and Scytha. *Herodot.* 3. c. 108 —*Hesiod. Theog.* 295.—*Apollod.* 2.—*Paus.* 8. c. 18,—*Ovid. Met.* 9. v. 158.

ECHIN'ADES or ECHI'NÆ, five small islands near Acarnania, at the mouth of the river Achelous. They have been gradually formed by the inundations of that river, and by the sand and mud which its waters carry down, and they now bear the name of Curzolari. The mythologists supposed that they were five nymphs changed by the Achelous into as many islands. *Dionys. Per.* 433.—*Avienus. Per.* 594.—*Plin.* 2. c. 85.—*Herodot.* 2. c. 10.—*Ovid. Met.* 8. v. 588.—*Strab.* 2.

ECHI'NON, a city of Thrace. *Mela*, 2. c. 3.

ECHI'NUS, an island in the Ægæan Sea. *Cic. in Arat.*——A town of Acarnania. *Plin.* 4. c. 12.——A city of Phthiotis, on the sea shore opposite Eubœa. *Strab.—Liv.* 32. c. 33.——A city of Pentapolis in Africa. *Ptol.*

ECHINUS'SA, an island near Eubœa, called afterwards Cimolus. *Plin.* 4. c. 12.

ECHI'ON, one of the five brothers who assisted Cadmus in building the city of Thebes. Cadmus rewarded his services by giving him his daughter Agave in marriage. He was father of Pentheus by Agave, and succeeded his father-in-law on the throne of Thebes, as some have imagined, and, from that circumstance, Thebes has been called *Echioniæ*, and the inhabitants *Echionidœ*. *Ovid. Met.* 3. v. 311. *Trist.* 5. el. 5. v. 53.—*Horat.* 4. od. 3. v. 64.—*Virg. Æn.* 12. v. 515.—*Stat Theb.* 2. v. 310. l. 4. v. 509.—*Hygin.* fab. 178.—*Apollod.* 3.—*Paus.* 9. c. 5.——A son of Mercury and Antianira, who was the herald of the Argonauts. *Flacc.* 1. v. 400. *Hygin.* fab. 14 & 160.——A man remarkable for his great swiftness in running. He was at the chase of the Calydonian boar. *Ovid. Met.* 8. v. 292.——A musician at Rome in Domitian's age. *Juv.* 6. v. 76.——A statuary.——A painter, *Cic. Parad.* 5.—*Plin.* 34. c. 8. l. 37. c. 7.

ECHION'IDES, a patronymic given to Pentheus as descended from Echion. *Ovid. Met.* 3.

ECHIO'NIUS, an epithet applied to a person born in Thebes, which was founded with the assistance of Echion. *Virg. Æn.* 12. v. 515.

E'CHO or **ECH'O** a daughter of Aer and Tellus, who chiefly resided in the vicinity of the Cephisus. She was once one of Juno's attendants, and became the confidant of Jupiter's amours. Her loquacity, however, displeased Jupiter; and she was deprived of the power of speech by Juno, and only permitted to answer the questions that were put to her. Pan was one of her admirers. Echo, after she had been punished by Juno, fell in love with Narcissus, and, on being despised by him, she pined away, and was changed into a stone, which was still permitted to retain the power of voice. *Ovid. Met.* 3. v. 358 & 494.

EC'NOMOS, a mountain of Sicily, now Licata.

ECO'NIA, a city of Greece. *Plin.* 4. c. 7.

ECPHAN'TUS, a Syracusan philosopher, according to *Origen*.

ECTE'NÆ or **ECTE'NI**, a people of Greece who first inhabited Thebes in Bœotia. *Paus.* 9.—*Lycoph.*

ECTI'NI, a people of the Alps, conquered by Augustus. *Plin.* 3. c. 20.

E'CUR, a town of India within the Ganges. *Ptol.*

E'DA, a river of Messenia. *Suidas.*

ED'ANA, a city near the Euphrates, inhabited by the Phœnicians. *Steph.*

ED'DARA, a city of Arabia Deserta. *Ptol.*

EDES'SA or **EDE'SA** a town of Syria, afterwards Justinopolis.

EDES'SÆ POR'TUS or **ODYSSE'UM**, a harbour of Sicily, near Pachynus. *Vid.* Odysseia. *Cic. in Verr.* 5. c. 54.

EDE'TA or **LE'RIA**, a town of Spain, on the banks of the river Turias. *Plin.* 3. c. 3.—*Liv.* 28. c. 24.—*Sil.* 3. v. 371.

EDETA'NI, a people of Spain.

E'DI, a people of Scythia. *Steph. ex Hecat.*

EDIS'SA or **ÆDES'SA**, a town of Macedonia, taken by Caranus, and called Ægæ, or Ægeas. *Vid.* Ædessa.

EDO'IA, a city of Arabia Felix. *Diod.*

E'DON, mountain of Thrace, called also Edonus. From this mountain that part of Thrace which lies between the Strymon and the Nessus, is often called *Edonia*, and the epithet is generally applied not only to Thrace, but to any cold northern climate. The people in the neighbourhood were called Edoni or Edones. *Apollod.* 3.—*Herodot.* 7. c. 110.—*Virg. Æn.* 12. v. 325. *& Servius in loco.*—*Plin.* 4. c. 11.—*Lucan.* 1. v. 674.

EDON'IDES, a name given to the priestesses of Bacchus, because they celebrated the festivals of the god on mount Edon. *Ovid Met.* 11. v. 69.

EDO'NIS, a city of Phrygia, afterwards called Antandrus. *Steph.*

EDO'SA, a city in the bay of the Troglodytic Sea. *Plin.* 6. c. 29.

E'DRON, a harbour on the Po, *Id.* 3. c. 16.

EDU'LIUS, a mountain of Hispania Tarraconensis. *Ptol.*

EDUMÆ'I, a people of Arabia. *Steph.*

EDU'SA (*ab edere*), a goddess whose office was to watch over the aliments of young children, after they were weaned by their mothers. *Varro apud Rom.* 1. c. 237.—*Aug. de Civ. D.* 4. c. 2.

EDYL'IUS, a mountain which Scylla seized to attack the people of Cheronæa. *Plut. in Syll.*

ED'YME, a city of Caria. *Steph.*

EE'TION, the father of Andromache, and of seven sons, was king of Thebes in Cilicia. He was killed by Achilles, at the beginning of the Trojan war. The epithet *Eetioneus* is applied to his relations or descendants. *Homer. Il.* 1. v. 366. l. 6. v. 416.—*Strab.* 13.—*Hygin.* fab. 123.—*Apollod.* 4.——A son of Melas, father of Cypselus. *Paus.* 2. c. 4.——The commander of the Athenian fleet conquered near the Echinades, by the Macedonians under Clitus. *Diod.* 18.

EGELAS'TE or **EGELAS'TA**, a town of Hispania Citerior. *Plin.* 3. c. 3.—*Strab.*

EGEL'IDUS, a small river of Etruria. *Virg. Æn.* 8. v. 610.

EGE'RIA, a nymph of Aricia in Italy, where Diana was particularly worshipped. It is said that Numa paid particular attention to this nymph, and according to Ovid she beame his wife. *Vid.* Numa. Ovid says that Ægeria was so disconsolate at the death of Numa, that she melted into tears and was changed into a fountain by Diana. She was regarded by many as a goddess who presided over the pregnancy of women, and some authors maintain that she was the same as Lucina or Diana. *Liv.* 1. c. 19.—*Ovid. Met.* 15. v. 547. *Amor.* 2. el. 17. v. 18.—*Festus de Verb. Sig.*—*Virg. Æn.* 7. v. 775.—*Martial*, 2. epigr. 6. v. 16.—*Juv.* 6. v. 11. [There is a statue of this nymph in the cave of Egeria, near Rome; and also another in the Giustiniani collection in that city.]

EGE'RIUS, the grandson of Demaratus was so called from his poverty. *Liv.* 1. c. 34.

EGESARE'TUS, a Thessalian of Larissa, who favored the interests of Pompey during the civil wars. *Cœs.* 3. *Cic.* c. 35.

EGESIDE'MUS, a writer mentioned by *Pliny*, 9. c. 8.—*Solin.* c. 18.

EGESI'NUS, a philosopher, pupil of Evadner. *Cic. Acad.* 4. c. 6.

EGESTA, a daughter of Hippotes of Troy. Her father exposed her on the sea, for fear of being devoured by a marine monster which laid waste the country. She was carried safe to Sicily, where the god of the river Crinisus offered her violence.

EGES'TA, a town of Sicily. *Vid.* Ægesta.

E'GION, a city between Ætolia and Peloponnesus. *Mela.*

EGNA'TIA MAXIMIL'LA, a woman who accompanied her husband into banishment in the reign of Nero, &c.—*Tacit. Ann.* 15. c. 71.

EGNA'TIA, a town. *Vid.* Gnatia.

EGNA'TIUS P., a crafty and Perfidious Roman in the reign of Nero, who committed the greatest crimes for the sake of money. *Tacit. Hist.* 4. c. 10.

EGNA'TIUS, a senator mentioned by Cicero. *Cluent.* 48. Other persons of that name are noticed *ad Att.* 6. ep. 1. l. 7, ep. 18. l. 13. ep. 4. *Fam.* 13. ep. 34.

EGNATULE'IUS, a quæstor who revolted at the head of the Martian legion, from Antony to Augustus. *Cic. Ph.* 3. c. 3.

EGUR'RI or **EVOGAR'RI**, a people of Hispania Tarraconensis. *Ptol.*

EIDOM'ENE, a city of Macedonia. *Steph.*

EILEITHY'IA, a city of Ægypt.

EIMINA'TIUM, a city of Dalmatia. *Ptol.*

EIN'ATUS, a city, or, according to some, a river or mountain of Crete.

EI'ON, a commercial place at the mouth of the Strymon, at the east of Amphipolis. *Paus.* 8. c. 8.

EI'ONE, a promontory of Coroconda, between Pontus and the Palus Mæotis. *Plin.* 6. c. 6.

EI'ONES, a village of Peloponnesus on the sea coast. *Strab.*

EI'ONEUS, a Greek killed by Hector in the Trojan war. *Homer. Il.* 8.——A Thracian, father to Rhesus. *Id.* 10

EI'RAS, a mountain of Messenia, in which Aristomenes defended himself 11 years against the Lacedæmonians. *Pausan. in Mess.*

EIRES'IDE, a village of the tribe Acamantis. *Steph.*

EIZE'LOS, a fortified place of Sicily. *Id.*

ELABAC'ARE, a people of India near the Ganges. *Arrian. in Peripl.*

ELABON'TAS, a river near Antioch. *Strab.* 26.

ELACATÆ'UM, a mountain of Thessaly. *Steph.*

ELÆ'A, a town of Æolia in Asia Minor. *Liv.* 36. c. 43.—*Paus* 9. c. 5.——An island in the Propontis. ——A city of Phœnicia, between Tyre and Sidon. *Steph.*——A promontory of Cyprus, now Riso Carpasso.——A city and harbour of Æthiopia. *Strab.*

ELÆ'US, a part of Epirus.——A town of the Thracian Chersonesus. *Liv.* 31. c. 16. l. 37. c. 9.

ELÆ'US, a surname of Jupiter.

ELAGABA'LUS or HELIOGABA'LUS, ELAGAB'-ALUS and HELIOGAB'ALUS, the surname of the sun at Emessa. *Vid.* Heliogabalus.

ELAI'TES, a grove near Canopus in Ægypt. *Strab.*

ELA'IUS, a mountain of Arcadia. *Paus.* 8. c. 41.

ELA'NA, a city of Arabia Petræa, now Aila or Eylan. *Ptol.*

ELANCO'RUM, a market town of India within the Ganges. *Id.*

ELAPHEBO'LIA, a festival in honour of Diana, the Huntress, to whom a cake in the form of a deer, ἔλαφ☉, was offered. The festival owed its institution to the following circumstance: When the Phocians had been beaten by the Thessalians in a severe battle, they resolved, by the persuasiou of a certain Deiphantus, to raise a pile of combustible materials, and burn their wives, children, and effects, rather than submit to the enemy. This resolution was unanimously approved by the women, who decreed Deiphantus a crown for his magnanimity. When every thing was prepared, before they set fire to the pile, they engaged their enemies, and fought with such desperate fury, that they obtained a complete victory. One of the months of the year, March, was called Elaphebolion from this festival. *Gyrald. Calend. R. & Gr.* —*Athen.* δειπνοσοφ, 14.—*Plut. de virt. Mul.*

ELAPHIÆ'A, a surname of Diana in Elis, because she presided over the hunting of stags. *Paus.* 6. c. 22.

ELAPHI'TIS, an island of the Adriatic Sea. *Plin.* 5. c. 31.

ELAPHONNE'SUS, one of the Sporades. *Steph.*

EL'APHUS, a river of Arcadia. *Paus.* 8. c. 36.

ELAPHU'SA, an island of the Adriatic Sea. *Plin.* 4. c. 12.

ELAPTO'NIUS, a youth who conspired against Alexander. *Curt,* 8. c. 6.

ELA'RA or EL'ARA, a daughter of Orchomenus king of Arcadia, mother of the giant Tityus killed by Apollo. *Apollod.* 1.—*Strab.* 9.

EL'ATAS or ELA'TAS, a river of Bithynia. *Ptol.*

ELATI'A, the largest town of Phocis, near the Cephisus. *Paus.* 10. c. 34.—*Liv.* 28. c. 7.——A town of Thessaly. *Id.* 42. c. 54.

ELA'TUS or EL'ATUS, one of the first Ephori of Sparta, B.C. 760. *Plut. in Lyc.*

EL'ATUS, the father of Cæneus. *Vid.* Cænis. *Ovid. Met.* 12. v. 497.

EL'ATUS, a mountain of Asia.——A mountain of Zacynthus. *Plin.* 4. c. 12.

EL'ATUS, the father of Polyphemus the Argonaut, by Hipseia. *Apollod.* 3. c. 9.——The son of Arcas, king of Arcadia and Erato, who retired to Phocis, and left five sons, Epytus, Pereus, Cyllen, Ischys, and Stymphalus. *Id. ib.*—*Paus.* 8. c. 4.——A king in the army of Priam, killed by Agamemnon. *Homer. Il.* 6. v. 33.——One of Penelope's suitors, killed by Eumeus. *Homer. Odyss.* 22. v. 267.

ELA'VER or EL'AVER, a river in Gaul, falling into the Loire, now the Allier. *Cæs. Bell. Gall.* 1. 7.

ELA'VIA, a fortified place of Sicily. *Steph.*

ELBES'TII, a people of Libya. *Id.*

ELBON'THIS, a city between Ægypt and Cyrene. *Id.*

ELCETHI'UM, a city of Sicily. *Ptol.*

ELCOB'ORIS, a town of Lusitania. *Id.*

ELDAMA'RII, Arabs near Mesopotamia. *Plin.* 6. c. 26.

ELDA'NA, a city of Spain, now Duennas. *Ptol.* ——A city of India without the Ganges.

E'LEA or HE'LIA, a town of Lucania, on the Tyrrhene shore, opposite the Œnotrides, whence the followers of Zeno were called the Eleatic sect. *Cic. Acad.* 4. c. 42. *Tusc.* 2. c. 21 & 22. *N. D.* 3. c. 33.——A town of Æolia.

ELEC'TRA, one of the Oceanides, who married Thaumas son of Pontus, and became mother of the Harpies, and of Isis, the messenger of Juno. *Hesiod. Th.* 265.—*Homer. in Cerer.*——A daughter of Atlas and Pleione. She was mother of Jasion and Dardanus by Jupiter, who placed her after death in the constellation called Pleiades. *Paus.* 4. c. 33.—*Hygin.* fab. 193.—*Virg. Æn.* 8. v. 135.—*Ovid. Fast.* 4. v. 31 & 175.—*Apollod.* 3. c. 10 & 12.——One of the Danaides, who married Peristenes, according to *Apollodorus*, 2. c. 1. or Hyperantes, according to *Hyginus*, fab. 170.——A daughter of Agamemnon king of Argos. She preserved the life of her brother Orestes, by sending him to king Strophius, to escape from the dagger of Clytæmnestra and Ægisthus, and she afterwards assisted him in avenging upon these infamous adulterers, the death of their murdered father. Some have imagined that Ægisthus had married her to a man of obscure birth; but the more probable account is, that, as a proof of his gratitude and affection, Orestes gave her in marriage to his friend Pylades, by whom she became mother of two sons, Strophius and Medon. Her adventures and misfortunes form the subject of an interesting tragedy of the poet Sophocles. Her name was originally Laodice, which she is said to have exchanged for that of Electra, on account of the lateness of her marriage. *Hygin.* fab. 117. 122.—*Servius. in Æn.* 4. v. 471.—*Euripid. in Orest.*—*Eustath. & Scholiast. in Homer,* 9. *Il.*—*Paus.* 2. c. 16.—*Ælian. V, H.* 4. c. 26, &c.——A sister of Cadmus, who gave her name to one of the seven gates of Thebes. *Paus.* 9. c. 8.

ELEC'TRA, a city and river of Messenia in Peloponnesus, *Paus.* 4. c. 33.

ELEC'TRA, one of Helen's female attendants. *Id.* 10. c. 25.

ELEC'TRÆ, a gate of Thebes. *Paus.* 9. c. 8.

ELEC'TRIDES, islands in the Adriatic Sea, which received their name from the quantity of amber (*electrum*) which they produced. They were at the mouth of the Po, according to the statement of *Apollonius* of Rhodes, but some historians doubt of their existence. *Plin.* 2. c. 26. l. 37. c. 2.—*Mela,* 2. c. 7.

ELEC'TRYON, a king of Argos, son of Perseus and Andromeda. He was brother of Alcæus, whose daughter Anaxo he married, and by whom he had several sons and one daughter, Alcmena. He sent his sons against the Teleboans, a neighbouring horde which had ravaged his country, and they were killed, except Licymnius. Upon this Electryon promised his crown and daughter in marriage to him who should undertake to punish the Teleboans for the death of his sons. Amphitryon offered himself, and succeeded. Electryon inadvertently perished by the hand of his son-in-law. *Vid.* Amphitryon & Alcmena. *Apollod.* 2. c. 4.—*Paus.*—*Hygin.* fab. 244.

ELEGAR'DA, a city of Armenia Major. *Ptol.*

ELEGE'IA, the goddess of elegiac poetry, invoked, among others, by *Ovid. Am.* 3. el. 1. v. 7.

ELEGI'A, a city of Armenia, near which the Euphrates flows. *Plin.* 5. c. 24.

ELE'I, the inhabitants of Elis in Peleponnesus. They were anciently called Epei. In their country was the temple of Jupiter, and there also were celebrated the Olympic games, of which they had the superintendence. Their horses were in great repute, hence *Elei equi,* and *Elea palma. Propert.* 3. el. 9. v. 18.—*Paus.* 5.—*Lucan.* 4. v. 293.

EL'ELEUS, a surname of Bacchus, from the word ἐλελεῦς. which the Bacchanals loudly repeated during his festivals. His priestesses were in consequence called Eleleides. *Ovid. Met.* 4. v. 15. *Ep.* 4. v. 47.

E'LEON, a village of Bœotia.——A village in Phocis.

ELEON'TUM, a town of the Thracian Chersonesus.

ELEPHAN'TIS, a poetess who wrote a lascivious poem. *Martial.* 12. epigr. 43.——A princess by whom Danaus had two daughters, Gorgophone and Hypermnestra. *Apollod.* 2.

ELEPHAN'TIS, an island in the river Nile, in Upper Ægypt, with a town of the same name, which is often called Elephantina, by some authors. *Strab.* 17.—*Herodot.* 2. c. 9, &c.

ELEPHANTOPH'AGI, a people of Æthiopia, so called because they fed upon the flesh of elephants. *Strab.*

ELEPHE'NOR, son of Chalcodon, was one of Helen's suitors, and conducted an army of the Abantes of Eubœa to the Trojan war. *Apollod.* 3.—*Homer. Il.* 2. v. 47.

ELEPO'RUS, a river of Magna Græcia. *Polyæn.* 5.

EL'ETE, a city of Cœlesyria. *Ptol.*

ELEU'CHIA or ELEUCHI'A, a daughter of Thespius. *Apollod.*

E'LEUS, a city of Thrace. *Thucyd.* 8.

E'LEUS, a surname of Jupiter, from his temple at Elis. *Plin.* 4. c. 5.

E'LEUS, a river of Media.

E'LEUS, a king of Elis. *Paus.* 5. c. 3.

ELEU'SA, an inland town of Cilicia. *Plin.*

ELEU'SIN, a city of the island of Thera. *Ptol.*

ELEUSIN'IA, a great festival observed every fourth year by the Celeans, Phliasians, as also by the Pheneatæ, Lacedæmonians, Parrhasians, and Cretans, but more particularly by the people of Athens, every fith year, at Eleusis in Attica, where it was introduced by Eumolpus, B.C. 1356. It was the most celebrated of all the religious ceremonies of Greece, whence it is often called by way of eminence, μυστήρια, *the mysteries.* It was so religiously observed, that if any one ever revealed its secret mysteries, it was supposed that he had called down divine vengeance upon his head, and it was unsafe to live in the same house with him, and he was therefore publicly put to an ignominious death. This festival was sacred to Ceres and Proserpine, everything contained a mystery, and Ceres herself was known only by the name of ἀχθεία, from the *sorrow* and *grief* (ἄχθος) which she suffered for the loss of her daughter. This mysterious secrecy was solemnly observed, and enjoined to all the votaries of the goddess; and if any one ever appeared at the celebration, either intentionally, or through ignorance, without proper introduction, he was immediately punished with death. Persons of both sexes and all ages were initiated at this solemnity, and it was looked upon as so heinous a crime to neglect or depreciate this sacred office of religion, that it was one of the heaviest accusations which contributed to the condemnation of Socrates. The initiated were under the more particular care of the deities, and therefore their life was supposed to be attended with more happiness and real security than that of other men. This benefit was not only granted during life, but it extended even beyond the grave, and they were honored with the most distinguished places in the Elysian fields, while others were left to wallow in perpetual degradation and ignominy. Particular care was taken in examining the character of such as were presented for initiation. Such as were guilty of murder, though against their will, and such as were convicted of witchcraft, or any heinous crime, were not admitted, and the Athenians suffered none to be initiated but such as were members or inhabitants of their city. This regulation, which compelled Hercules, Castor, and Pollux to become citizens of Athens, was strictly observed during the first ages of the institution, but afterwards all persons, barbarians excepted, were freely initiated. The Eleusian festivals were divided into great and less mysteries. The less were instituted from the following circumstance. Hercules passed near Eleusis while the Athenians were celebrating the mysteries, and desired to be initiated. As this could not be done, because he was a stranger, and as Eumolpus was unwilling to displease him on account of his great power, and the many services which he had rendered to the Athenians, another festival was instituted without violating the laws. It was called μικρὰ, and Hercules was solemnly admitted to the celebration and initiated. These lesser mysteries were observed at Agræ near the Ilissus; the greater were celebrated at Eleusis, from which place Ceres has been called Eleusinia. In later times the smaller festivals were preparatory to the greater, and no person could be initiated at Eleusis without a previous purification at Agræ. This purification the votaries performed by keeping themselves pure, chaste, and unpolluted during nine preceding days, after which they came and offered sacrifices and prayers, wearing garlands of flowers, and having under their feet Διὸς κώδιον, *Jupiter's skin,* which was the skin of a victim offered to that god. The person who assisted was called ὑδρανὸς, from ὕδωρ, *water,* which was used at the purification, and they themselves were then called μύσται, *the initiated.* A year after the initiation at the less mysteries they sacrificed a sow to Ceres, and were admitted to the greater, and the secrets of the festival were solemnly revealed to them, from which they were called ἔφοροι and ἐπόπται, *inspectors.* The initiation was performed in the following manner: The candidates, crowned with myrtle, were admitted by night into a place called μυστικὸς σηκός, *the mystical temple,* a vast and stupendous building. As they entered the temple, they purified themselves by washing their hands in holy water, and were admonished to come with a mind pure and undefiled, without which the cleanness of the body would be unacceptable to the divinity. After this the holy mysteries were read to them from a large book called πέτρωμα, because made of *two stones,* πέτραι, fitly cemented together. After this the priest called Ἱεροφάντης, proposed to them certain questions, to which they were expected to give ready answers. After this, strange and amazing objects presented themselves to their sight, the place often seemed to quake, and to appear suddenly resplendent with fire, and immediately after to be enveloped in gloomy darkness. Sometimes thunders were heard, or flashes of lightning appeared on every side. At other times hideous noises and howlings were heard, and the trembling spectators were alarmed by sudden and dreadful apparitions. This was called αὐτοψία, *intuition.* After this the initiated were dismissed with the barbarous words of κόγξ, ὄμπαξ. The garments in which they were initiated were regarded as sacred, and of no less efficacy to avert evils than charms and incantations. From this circumstance, therefore, they were never left off before they were totally unfit for wear, after which they were appropriated for children, or reverently dedicated to the goddess. The chief person that attended at the initiation was called Ἱεροφάντης, *the revealer of sacred things.* He was a citizen of Athens, and held his office during life, though among the Celeans and Phliasians it was limited to the period of four years. He was obliged to devote himself totally to the service of the deities; his life was chaste and single, and he usually anointed his body with the juice of hemlock, which was said, by its extreme coldness, to extinguish, in a great degree, the natural heat. The Hierophantes had three attendants; the first was called δᾳδοῦχος, *torch-bearer,* and was permitted to marry; the second was called κήρυξ, *a cryer;* the third administered at the altar, and was called ὁ ἐπὶ βωμῷ The Hierophantes is said to have been a type of the powerful Creator of all things, Δᾳδοῦχος of the sun, Κῆρυξ of Mercury, and ὁ ἐπὶ βωμῷ of the moon. There were, besides these, other inferior officers who took particular care that everything was performed according to established custom. The first of these, called βασιλεύς, was one of the archons of Athens; he offered prayers and sacrifices, and took care that no indecency or irregularity prevailed during the celebration. Besides him there were four others called ἐπιμεληταί, *curators,* elected by the people. One of them was chosen from the sacred family of the Eumolpidæ, another from the Ceryces, and the rest from among the citizens. There were also ten persons who assisted at this and every other festival, called Ἱεροποιοί, because they *offered sacrifices.* This festival was observed in the month Boedromion or September, and continued nine days, from the 15th till the 23rd. During that time it was unlawful to arrest any man, or present any petition, on pain of forfeiting a thousand drachmas, or, according to others, on pain of death. It was also unlawful for those who were initiated to sit upon the cover of a well, to eat beans, mullets, or weasels. If any woman rode to Eleusis in a chariot during the solemnity, she was obliged, by an edict of Lycurgus, to pay 6,000 drachmas. The design of this law was to destroy all distinction between the richer and poorer sort of citizens. The first day of the celebration was called ἀγυρμός, *assembly,* as it may be said that the worshippers then first met together. The second day was called ἅλαδε, μύσται, *to the sea, you that are initiated,* because they were commanded to purify themselves by bathing in the sea. On the third day sacrifices, and chiefly a mullet, in

Greek, τρίγλη, were offered, as also barley, from a certain field of Eleusis. These oblations were called Θύα, and held so sacred that the priests themselves were not, as in other sacrifices, permitted to partake of them. On the fourth day the votaries made a solemn procession, in which the καλάθιον, *holy basket of Ceres*, was carried about in a consecrated cart, while on every side the people shouted χαῖρε Δημῆτερ, *Hail, Ceres!* Aftes these followed women, called κισοφόροι, who *carried baskets*, in which were sesamum, carded wool, grains of salt, a serpent, pomegranates, reeds, ivy boughs, certain cakes, &c. The fifth was called Ἡ τῶν λαμπάδων ἡμέρα, *the torch day*, because on the following night the people ran about with torches in their hands. It was usual on the occasion to dedicate torches to Ceres, and contend which should offer the biggest in commemoration of the travels of the goddess, and of her lighting a torch in the flames of mount Ætna. The sixth day was called Ἴακχος, from Iacchus, the son of Jupiter and Ceres who accompanied his mother in her search after Proserpine with a torch in his hand. From that circumstance, his statue represented him with a torch in his hand, and it was carried in solemn procession from the Ceramicus to Eleusis. The statue, with those that accompanied it, called Ιακχαγωγοί, were at that time crowned with myrtle. In the way, nothing was heard but singing and the noise of brazen kettles, as the votaries danced along. The way through which they issued from the city was called Ἱερὰ ὁδὸς, *the sacred way*; the resting place, Ἱερὰ συκῆ, from a *fig-tree*, which grew in the neighbourhood. They also stopped on a bridge over the Cephisus, where it was customary to deride those that passed by. After they had crossed this bridge, they entered Eleusis by a place called μυστικὴ εἴσοδος, *the mystical entrance*. On the seventh day were sports, in which the victors were rewarded with a measure of barley, as that grain had been first sown in Eleusis. The eighth day was called Ἐπιδαυρίων ἡμέρα, because Æsculapius, at his return from Epidaurus to Athens, was initiated by the repetition of the less mysteries. It became customary, therefore, from this occurrence to celebrate them a second time, that such as had not hitherto been initiated might be lawfully admitted. The ninth and last day of the festival was called πλημοχόαι, *earthen vessels*, because it was usual to fill two such vessels with wine, one of which being placed towards the east, and the other towards the west, they, after the repetition of some mystical words, were both thrown down, and the wine being spilt on the ground, was offered as a libation to the gods. Such was the manner of celebrating the Eleusinian mysteries, which have been deemed the most sacred and solemn of all the festivals observed by the ancient Greeks. Some have supposed that they were obscene and abominable, and that from this circumstance proceeded all the mysterious secrecy. They were introduced at Rome in the reign of Adrian, where they were observed with the same ceremonies, though perhaps with more freedom and licentiousness. These mysteries continued to be celebrated about 1800 years, and were at last abolished by Theodosius the Great. *Ælian. V.H.* 12. c. 24 —*Cic. de Leg.* 2. c. 14.—*Paus.* 10. c. 31, &c.—*Plut—Clem. Alex. Str.* 5.—*Schol. Aristoph. ad Plut.* v. 846 & 1014. *Ad. Nub.* 302. *Ad. Ran.* 333.—*Meursius, Eleus.—Demosth. in Mid.—Phurnut. de Nat. D.* 28.

ELEU'SIS or ELEU'SIN, now Lepsina, a town of Attica, equally distant from Megara and the Piræus, celebrated for the festivals of Ceres. *Vid.* Eleusinia. It was founded by Triptolemus, and received its name, according to some, from Eleusis, the founder's father, or from the residence which Ceres made there (ἔλευσις) when she left Enna in Sicily in quest of her daughter Proserpine. *Hygin.* fab. 147 & 275.—*Ovid. Fast.* 5. v. 507.—*Paus.* 9. c. 24.

ELEU'THER, a son of Apollo.——One of the Curetes, from whom a town of Bœotia and another in Crete received their names. *Paus.* 9. c. 2 & 19.

ELEU'THERÆ, a village of Bœotia, between Megara and Thebes, near which Mardonius was defeated with 300,000 men. *Plin.* 4. c. 7. l. 34. c. 8.

ELEUTHE'RIA, a festival celebrated at Platæa in honor of Jupiter Eleutherius, or the assertor of liberty, by delegates from almost all the cities of Greece. Its institution originated in this: After the victory obtained by the Greeks, under Pausanias, over Mardonius, the Persian general, in the country of Platæa, an altar and statue were erected to Jupiter Eleutherius, who had freed the country from the invasion of the barbarians. It was further agreed upon in a general assembly, by the advice of Aristides the Athenian, that deputies should be sent every fifth year from the different cities of Greece to celebrate Eleutheria, *festivals of liberty*. The Platæans celebrated also an anniversary festival in memory of those who had lost their lives in that famous battle. The celebration was thus: At break of day a procession was made with a trumpeter at the head, sounding a signal for battle. After him followed chariots loaded with myrrh, garlands, and a black bull, and certain free young men, as no signs of servility were to appear during the solemnity; because they in whose honor the festival was instituted, had nobly died in the defence of their country. They carried libations of wine and milk in large eared vessels, with jars of oil and precious ointments. Last of all appeared the chief magistrate of the city, who, though not permitted at other times to touch iron, or wear garments of any color but white, yet appeared clad in purple; and taking a water pot out of the city chamber, proceeded through the middle of the town with a sword in his hand, towards the sepulchres. There he drew water from a neighbouring spring, and washed and anointed the monuments; after which ,he sacrificed a bull upon a pile of wood invoking Jupiter and Mercury, and inviting to the entertainment the souls of those happy heroes who had perished in the defence of their country. After this he filled a bowl with wine, saying, "I drink to those who lost their lives in the defence of the liberties of Greece."—There was also a festival of the same name observed by the Samians in honor of the god of Love.—Slaves also, when they obtained their liberty, kept a holiday, which they called Eleutheria. *Paus.* 9. c. 2.—*Meurs. Gr. feri.—Plaut. in Pers.* act. 1. sc. 1. v. 29. & *Schol. in loco.*

ELEU'THERIS, a city of Bœotia. *Steph.*

ELEUTHERIS'CUS, a city of Macedonia. *Id.*

ELEUTHE'RIUM, a town of Mysia. *Id.*

ELEUTHE'RIUS, a surname of Jupiter, from his delivering mankind from various distresses incident to human life. *Meurs. Gr. feriatâ.*

ELEUTHEROCIL'ICES, a people of Cilicia, who preserved their national independence, and were never subject to a foreign prince. *Cic. ad Fam.* ep. 4. l. 5. *ad Att.* 20.

ELEU'THERUS, a river of Syria, falling into the Mediterranean a few leagues north of Tyre. Some authors suppose that the river properly called by that name is much higher up, nearer the river Orontes. *Plin.* 9. c. 10.

ELEU'THO, a surname of Juno Lucina from her presiding over the delivery of pregnant women. *Pindar, Olym.* 6. & *Schol.*

EL'GOS, a town of Lycia. *Steph.*

ELIBYR'GE, a city of Tartessus. *Id.*

ELIC'IUS, a surname of Jupiter (*ab eliciendo,*) worshipped on mount Aventine, because he had been drawn upon earth by the prayers and devotions of the Romans, and especially of Numa, to whom he gave an undoubted pledge of the duration, prosperity, and greatness of the Roman empire. *Ovid. Fast.* 3. v. 328.

ELICO'CI, a people of Gallia Narbonensis. *Ptol.*

ELICRA'NUM, a city of Illyria. *Polyb.*

ELIEN'SIS or ELI'ACA, a sect of philosophers founded by Phædon of Elis, who was originally a slave, but restored to liberty by Alcibiades. *Diog.* 2.—*Strab.* 9.

ELIME'A or ELIMIO'TIS, a district of Macedonia, or of Illyricum according to others. It is generally placed between Illyricum and Thessaly, and near the river Aous. The chief town was called Elyma or Elimea. *Liv.* 42. c. 53. l, 45. c. 30.

ELI'NI, a nation of Thesprotia.——A city of Sicily. *Steph.*

ELI'ONES, a people of Africa Propria. *Ptol.*

E'LIS, a country of Peloponnesus at the west of Arcadia, and the north of Messenia, extending along the coast, and watered by the river Alpheus. The capital of the country, called Elis, now Belvidere, became large and populous in the age of Demosthenes, though in the age of Homer it did not exist. The other towns of importance were Ephyra, Cyllene, Pisa, Olympia, and Pylus. Elis was originally governed by kings, and received its name from one of its monarchs. It was famous for the horses it produced, the celerity of which was so often tried and known at the Olympic games. *Strab.* 8.—*Plin.* 4. c. 5.—*Paus.* 5. c. 1.—*Ovid. Met.* 5. v. 494.—*Cic. Fam.* 13. ep. 26. *De Div.* 2. c. 12. —*Liv.* 27. c. 32.—*Virg. G.* 1. v. 59. l. 3. v. 202.

ELIS'ARI, a nation of Arabia Felix. *Ptol.*

ELISPHA'SII, a people of Peloponnesus. *Polyb.* 11.

ELIS'SA, a queen of Tyre, more commonly known by the name of Dido. *Vid.* Dido.

ELIS'SUS, a river of Elis. *Strab.*——A city of Arcadia. *Paus.*

E'LIUS, a freedman in great favour with Nero. *Dio.*

ELIX'OTA, an island of the Hyperboreans, near the river Cerambicus. *Steph.*

ELIX'US, a river of the island of Ceus. *Strab.*

ELLO'PIA, a region of Eubœa.——An ancient name of that island.

ELLO'PIUM, a city of Ætolia. *Steph.*

ELLO'TIA, a festival at Crete, in honour of Europa. ἀπὸ τοῦ ἑλέσθαι αὐτὴν ὑπὸ ταύρου. *Hesych. Athen.* l. 15 ——A festival celebrated by the Corinthians in honour of Minerva.

ELMAN'TICA, a city of Iberia. *Steph.* Perhaps the Salmantica of *Ptolemy.*

ELO'NE, a city of Perrhœbia, called also Limona. *Steph.*

ELORI'NI, a people of Sicily. Their town is now Olorino. *Cic.* 1 5. *Verr.*

ELO'RUS or HELO'RUS, a river of Sicily, on the eastern coast, between Syracuse and Pachynum, called after a king of the same name. The town at its mouth was called Elorum. *Herodot.* 7. c. 145.

E'LOS, a city of Achaia, called after a servant maid of Athamas of the same name.

ELOTÆ. *Vid.* Helotæ.

ELPE'NOR, one of the companions of Ulysses, changed into a hog by Circe's potions, and afterwards restored to his former shape. He fell from the top of a house where he was sleeping, and was killed. *Ovid. Met.* 14. v. 252, *Trist.* 3. el. 4. v. 19.—*Homer. Odyss.* 10. v. 552. l. 11. v. 51.

EL'PIA, a city of the Daunii, built by the Rhodians. *Steph.*

ELPINI'CE, a daughter of Miltiades, who nobly offered to marry Callias, a man that promised to release from confinement Cimon, her brother and husband, whom the laws of Athens had made responsible for the fine imposed on his father. *C. Nep. in Cim.*

ELPI'NUS, an archon at Athens. Ol. 106. an. 1.

EL'UI, a people of Gallia Aquitanica, between the Garumna and the Ligeris. *Strab.* l. 4.

ELUI'A, a city of Paphlagonia. *Ptol.*

ELUI'NA, a surname of Ceres. *Juv.* 3. v. 320.

ELU'RI, a people of Scythia. *Steph.*

EL'USA or ELU'SA, a city of Arabia. *Ptol. Salmas. ad Solin.* p. 488.

ELUSABE'TRIS, the chief city of the Ausci, in Gaul, now Aux. *Mela*, 3. c. 2.

ELUSA'TES, a people of Aquitania. *Plin.* 4. c. 19.

ELU'SII, a people of Mauritania Cæsariensis. *Ptol.*

EL'YCES, a man killed by Perseus, at the court of Cepheus. *Ovid. Met.* 5. fab. 3.

ELYCO'CI. *Vid.* Elicoci.

ELYD'NA, a city of India without the Ganges.

EL'YMA, a city of Macedonia, now Cannina. *Id.* ——A city of Sicily, founded by Æneas, now Palymite. *Diod. Hal.*—*Thucyd.*

ELYMA'IS, a country of Persia, between the Persian Gulph and Media. The capital of the country was called Elymais, and was famous for a rich temple of Diana, which Antiochus Epiphanes attempted to plunder. The Elymeans assisted Antiochus the Great in his wars against the Romans. *Strab.*

EL'YMI, a nation descended from the Trojans, in alliance with the people of Carthage. *Paus.* 10. c. 8.—*Thucyd.*

ELYMIO'TÆ, a people of Macedonia; their country is now called Placani. *Ptol.*

ELYM'NIUM, an island, with a city of the same name, near Eubœa. *Steph.*

EL'YMUS, a man at the court of king Acestes, in Sicily. *Virg. Æn.* 5. v. 73.——A hero, who gave his name to the city of Elyma, in Macedonia.

EL'YRUS, a town of Crete. *Id.* 10 c. 16.

ELYS'IUM or ELYS'II CAM'PI, a place or island in the infernal regions, where, according to the mythology of the ancients, the souls of the virtuous were placed after death. The employments of the heroes who dwelt in these regions of bliss were various; the manes of Achilles are represented as waging war with the wild beasts, while the Trojan chiefs are innocently exercising themselves in managing horses, or in handling arms. To these innocent amusements some poets have added continual feasting and revelry, and supposed that the Elysian fields were filled with all kinds of voluptuous enjoyment. The Elysian fields were, according to some, in the Fortunate Islands on the coast of Africa, in the Atlantic. Others place them in the island of Leuce; and, according to the authority of Virgil, they were situate in Italy. According to Lucian, they were near the moon; or in the centre of the earth, if we rely upon the authority of Plutarch. *Virg. Æn.* 6. v. 638.—*Claudian.*—*Homer Odyss.* 4.—*Pindar.*—*Tibull.* 1. el. 3. v. 57.—*Lucian.*—*Plut. de Consol.*

EMA'THIA, a name given anciently, and particularly by the poets, to the countries which formed the empires of Macedonia and Thessaly. *Virg. G.* 1. v. 492. l. 4. v. 390.—*Lucan.* 1. v. l. l. 10. v. 50. l. 6. v. 620. l. 7. v. 427.—*Ovid. Met.* 5. v. 314.

EMA'THION, a son of Titan and Aurora, who reigned in Macedonia. The country was called Emathia from him. Some suppose that he was a famous robber destroyed by Hercules. *Ovid. Met.* 5. v. 313.—*Justin.* 7. c. 1.——A man killed at the nuptials of Perseus and Andromeda. *Ovid. Met.* 5. v. 100.——A man killed in the wars of Turnus. *Virg. Æn.* 9. v. 571.

EM'BATUM, a place of Asia, opposite the island of Chios.—*Steph.*—*Thuc.*—*Polyb.* 3.

EMBOLI'MA or ECBOLI'MA, or EMBOL'IMA and ECBOL'IMA, a town of India, near the branches of the Indus. *Curt.* 8. c. 12.

EMER'ITA a town of Spain, situate on the river Anas, famous for dyeing wool. *Plin.* 9. c. 41.

EME'UM, a place of Upper Æthiopia. *Plin.* 6. c. 29.

EM'ESA or EMIS'SA, a town of Phœnicia.

EMMEN'IDÆ, a family at Agrigentum, which traced its origin to Polynices.

EM'NI, a people of Taprobane. *Ptol.*

EMO'DA, a mountain of India. *Strab.*—*Plin.* 5. c. 27.

EMO'DI MON'TES, the Himalaya mountains

EMPED'OCLES, a philosopher, poet, and historian of Agrigentum, in Sicily, who flourished 444 B.C. He was the disciple of Telauges the Pythagorean, and warmly adopted the doctrine of transmigration. He wrote a poem upon the opinions of Pythagoras, very much commended, in which he spoke of the various bodies which nature had given him. His poetry was bold and animated, and so universally esteemed, that it was publicly recited at the Olympic games, with that of Homer and Hesiod. Empedocles was an inveterate enemy to tyranny, and refused to become the sovereign of his native city. He taught rhetoric in Sicily, and often alleviated the anxieties of his mind as well as the pains of his body with music. It is reported that his curiosity to visit the flames of the crater of Ætna proved fatal to him. Some maintain that he wished it to be believed that he was a god, and, that the manner of his death might be unknown, it is said that he threw himself into the crater, and perished in the flames. His expectations, however, were frustrated, for the volcano threw up one of his sandals. Others report that he lived to an extreme old age, and that he was drowned in the sea about the year 440 B.C. *Horat.* 1. ep. 12. v. 20. *Art. P.*—*Cic. de Orat.* 1. c. 50, &c.—*Diog. in Vitâ.*—*Athen.* 1 & 4.—*Lucret.* 1. v. 731.—*Fabr. B. Gr.* 2. c. 12.—*Sax. Onom.* 1. p 39.

EMPEL'ATHRA, a city of India within the Ganges. *Ptol.*

EMPLO'CIA, a festival at Athens. *Hesych.*—*Meurs. Gr. Fer.* p. 108.

EMPO'CLUS, an historian. *Athen.* 9. *Casaubon*, however, proposes to read Posidonius.

EMPO'RIA PU'NICA, certain places near the Syrtes. *Polyb.—Liv.*

EMPO'RIÆ or **EMPO'RIUM**, a town of Spain in Catalonia, now Ampurias, at the foot of the Pyrennees. *Liv.* 34. c. 9 & 16. l. 26. c. 19.

EMPU'SA, A monstrous spectre, which was believed to devour human beings. It was sent by Hecate to frighten travellers, and could assume various forms.

EM'PYLUS, a rhetorician, intimate with M. Brutus. He wrote a book on the death of Cæsar. *Plut. in Brut.*

ENAG'ORA, an island of Asia. *Plin.* 5. c. 31.

ENAREPH'ORUS, a son of Hippocoon, one of Helen's suitors.

ENARET'TA or **ENAR'ETE**, a nymph who bore seven sons and five daughters to Hellen.

ENCEL'ADUS, a son of Titan and Terra, the most powerful of all the giants who conspired against Jupiter. He was struck by Jupiter's lightning, and overwhelmed by the god under mount Ætna. Some suppose that he is the same as Typhon. According to the poets, the flames of Ætna proceeded from the breath of Enceladus; and as often as he turned his weary side, the whole island of Sicily felt the motion, and shook from its very foundations. *Virg. Æn.* 3. v. 578.—*Qu. Smyrn.* 5. v. 640. l. 12. v. 581.—*Claudian. de Pros. Rap.* 1. v. 154.—*Hesiod. Theog.* 820.—*Philost. Icon.* 2. c. 17.—*Hygin. in Præf. Fab.*——A son of Ægyptus.

ENCHE'LEÆ or **ENCHEL'EÆ**, a town of Illyricum, where Cadmus was changed into a serpent. *Lucan.* 3. v. 189.—*Strab.* 7.

ENDE'IS or **EN'DEIS**, a nymph, daughter of Chiron. She married Æacus, king of Ægina, by whom she had Peleus and Telamon. *Paus.* 2. c. 29.—*Apollod.* 3. c. 12.—*Diod.* 4.

EN'DERA or **ENDE'RA**, a place of Upper Æthiopia. *Strab.* 16.

ENDE'RUM, a town of Illyricum, now Endero. *Ptol.*

ENDYM'ION, a shepherd, son of Æthlius and Calyce. It is said that he required Jupiter to grant him the privilege of being always young, and of sleeping as much as he would; whence the proverb of *Endymionis somnum dormire*, to express a long sleep. Diana saw him naked as he slept on mount Latmus, and was so struck with his beauty, that she came down from heaven every night to enjoy his company. Endymion married Chromia, called also Asterodia, daughter of Itonus, or, according to some, Hyperipne, daughter of Arcas, by whom he had three sons, Pæon, Epeus, and Ætolus, and a daughter called Eurydice; and so little ambitious did he show himself of sovereignty, that he proposed his crown as a prize to his sons, an honorable distinction which was gained by Epeus. The fable of Endymion's amours with Diana, or the moon, arises from his knowledge of astronomy, and as he passed the night on some high mountain, to observe the heavenly bodies, it has been reported that he was courted by the moon. Some suppose that there were two of that name, the son of a king of Elis, and the shepherd or astronomer of Caria. The people of Heraclea maintained that Endymion died on mount Latmus, and the Eleans pretended to show his tomb at Olympia in Peloponnesus. *Apollod.* 1.—*Ovid. de A.A.* 3. v. 83. *Heroid.* 17. *Am.* 1. el. 13.—*Flac.* 8.—*Auson. Id.* 6. v. 40.—*Propert.* 2. el. 15.—*Cic. Tusc.* 1.—*Juv.* 10.—*Theocrit.* 3. *& Scholiast. ib.*—*Paus.* 5. c. 1. l. 6. c. 20. [There is a sleeping figure representing Endymion, at Florence].

ENE'TI or **HENE'TI**, or **EN'ETI** and **HEN'ETI**, a people near Paphlagonia. *Steph.*

ENGON'ASIS, a name applied to the constellation of Hercules, because he is represented as resting on his knees (*in genibus*). *Cic. N. D.* 2. c. 42.

ENGY'UM or **EN'GYUM**, now Gangi, a town about the middle of Sicily, near the sources of the river Himera. It was freed from tyranny by Timoleon. *Cic. Verr.* 3. c. 43. l. c. 44.—*Ital.* 14. v. 250.

ENIEN'SES, a people of Greece. *Herod.*

ENI'OCHE, a nurse of Medea. *Val. Flacc.* 5. *Argon.* v. 357.

ENI'OPEUS, a charioteer of Hector, killed by Diomede. *Homer. Il.* 8. v. 120.

ENI'PEUS, a river of Thessaly, which flows near Pharsalia before it falls into the Peneus, and afterwards discharges itself through the vale of Tempe into the Gulph of Therma. *Lucan.* 6. v. 373.—*Liv.* 44. c. 20.——A river of Elis Peloponnesus, of which Tyro, the daughter of Salmoneus, became enamoured. Neptune assumed the shape of the god of that river, to enjoy the company of Tyro. *Ovid. Am.* 3. el. 5.—*Strab.* 1.

ENIS'PE, a town of Arcadia. *Paus.* 8. c. 25.

EN'NA, now Castro Janni, a town near the middle of Sicily, with a beautiful plain from which Proserpine was carried away by Pluto. *Mela*, 2. c. 7.—*Diod.* 2.—*Strab.* 6.—*Ptol.* 3. c. 4.—*Sil. It.* 13. v. 431. l. 14. v. 246.—*Cic. Ver.* 3 c. 49 l. 4. c. 104.—*Ovid. Fast.* 4. v. 522.—*Liv.* 24. c. 37.

EN'NIA, the wife of Macro, and afterwards of the emperor Caligula. *Tacit. Ann.* 6. c. 45.

EN'NIUS Q., an ancient poet, born at Rudii, in Calabria, obtained the name and privileges of a Roman citizen by the friendship of M. Fulvius Nobilior. His style was rough and unpolished, but his defects, which are more particularly to be attributed to the age in which he lived, have been fully compensated for by the energy of his expressions and the fire of his poetry. Quintilian warmly commends him, and Virgil has shown his opinion of the excellence of his poetical merit by introducing many whole lines from his works into his own compositions, which he calls pearls gathered from the dunghill. Ennius wrote in heroic verse 18 books of the annals of the Roman republic, and displayed much knowledge of the world in some dramatical and satirical compositions. He died of the gout, contracted, it is said, by frequent intoxication, about 169 years B.C. in the 70th year of his age, and was buried on the Appian road, about one mile from Rome. Ennius was intimate with the great men of his age; he accompanied Cato in his quæstorship in Sardinia, and was esteemed by him of greater value than the honors of a triumph; and Scipio, on his death-bed, ordered his body to be buried by the side of his poetical friend. This epitaph was said to be written upon him:

> Aspicite, o cives, senis Enii imaginis formam!
> Hic vestrum pinxit maxima facta patrum.
> Nemo me lacrymis decoret, neque funera fletu
> Faxit: cur? volito vivus per ora virûm.

Conscious of his merit as the first epic poet of Rome, Ennius bestowed on himself the appellation of the Homer of Latium. Of the tragedies, comedies, annals and satires which he wrote, nothing remains but fragments to the number of 990 lines, collected from the quotations of ancient authors. The best edition of these is by Hesselius, 4to, Amst. 1707. *Ovid. Trist.* v. 424.—*Aul. Gell.* 11. c. 4. l. 12. c. 4. l. 15. c. 24. l. 17. c. 17.—*Stat.* 2. *Sylv.* 7. v. 75.—*Horat.* 4. *Od.* 7. v. 20. l. sat. 10. v. 54. *Ep. ep.* 21. v. 50.—*Italic.* 12. v. 293.—*Val. Max.* 8. c. 15.—*Aug. de Civ. D.* 2. c. 21.—*Macrob. Sat.* 6. c. 1. & 2.—*Cic. de Finib.* 1. c. 4. *De Offic.* 2. c. 18.—*Quintil.* 10. c. 1.—*Lucret.* 1. v. 117. &c.—*C. Nep. in Catone.*—*Sax. Onom.* 1. p. 121.—*Harles. Not. Lit. Rom.* 1. p. 83.

EN'NIUS LU'CIUS, a Roman knight accused of treason by Ateius Capito. *Tac. Ann.* 3. c. 70.

EN'NOMUS, a Trojan prince, who, with Chromis, commanded the Mysians. He was skilled in the knowledge of augury, and perished by the hands of Achilles. *Homer. Il.* 2. v. 365. l. 11. v. 422.

ENNOSIGÆ'US, *terræ concussor*, a surname of Neptune. *Juv.* 10. v. 182.—*Gell.* 2. c. 28.

ENO'DIA, an epithet of Hecate. *Steph.*—*Hesych.*

ENO'DIUS, an epithet of Mercury.

ENOM'IDES, a writer on the names, nature, and actions of the gods. *Etym. Magn.*

ENO'NA, a city of Dacia. *Ptol.*

EN'OPE, a town of Peloponnesus, near Pylus. *Paus.* 3. c. 26.

E'NOPS, a shepherd loved by the nymph Neis, by whom he had Satnius, who gave his name to the river Satnion. *Homer. Il.* 14. v. 443.——The father of Thestos.——A Trojan killed by Patroclus. *Il.* 16. v. 401.

E'NOS, a town of Thrace, near the mouth of the Hebrus, the foundation of which is improperly attributed to Æneas, as it existed before the Trojan war. *Ptol.* 3. c. 11.—*Homer. Il.* 4. v. 520.—*Apollod.* 2.—*Strab.* 11.—*Mela*, 2. c. 2.

ENOSICH'THON, a surname of Neptune, frequently used in the Greek poets.

ENO'SIS, an island near Sardinia. *Plin.* 3. c. 7.

ENOTOCŒ'TÆ, a nation whose ears are described as hanging down to their heels. *Strab.*

ENTEL'LA, a town of Sicily inhabited by Campanians. It was situated on the river Crinisus, a little at the north of Selinus. *Ital.* 14. v. 205.—*Cic. Ver.* 3. c. 43.

ENTEL'LUS, a famous athlete among the friends of Æneas. He was intimate with Eryx, and entered the lists against Dares, whom he conquered in the funeral games of Anchises, in Sicily. *Virg. Æn.* 5. v. 387, &c.

ENTRI'BÆ, a people of Thrace. *Steph.*

ENYA'LIUS, a surname of Mars.

ENY'DRA, a city of Casiotis, in Syra. *Strab.*

ENY'O, a sister of Mars, called by the Latins Bellona, supposed by some to be the daughter of Phorcys and Ceto. *Ital.* 10. v. 203.—*Martia. de Spect.* 24. l. 6. epigr. 31.—*Stat. Theb.* 8. v. 658.

EO'A, a city of Africa Propria. *Ptol. Mela* calls it Oea.

EODAN'DA, an island of Arabia Felix. *Plin.* 6. c. 28.

E'ONE, a daughter of Thespius. *Apollod.*

EORDÆ'A, a district at the west of Macedonia. *Liv.* 31. c. 39. l. 33 c. 8. l. 42. c. 53.

EOR'DI, a people of Thessaly. *Steph.*

EORI'TÆ, a people of Arachosia. *Ptol.*

E'OS, the name of Aurora among the Greeks, whence the epithet Eous is applied to all the eastern parts of the world. *Ovid. Fast.* 3. v. 406. *A. A.* 3. v. 537. l. 6. v. 478.—*Virg. G.* 1. v. 288. l. 2. v. 115.

E'os, a mountain of Ægypt. *Plin.* 6. c. 19.

EO'US, one of the horses of the sun. *Ovid. Met.* 2. v. 153, &c.

EPA'CRIA, a city of Attica. *Steph.*

EPA'GRIS, one of the Cyclades, called by *Aristotle* Hydrussa. *Plin.* 4. c. 12.

EPAMINON'DAS, son of Polymnus, a famous Theban, descended from the ancient kings of Bœotia. He has been celebrated for his private virtues as well as for his great military accomplishments. His love of truth was so great that he never disgraced himself by falsehood. He formed a most sacred and inviolable friendship with Pelopidas, whose life he saved in battle. By his advice Pelopidas delivered Thebes from the tyrannical power of Lacedæmon, and this became the signal for war. Epaminondas was placed at the head of the Theban armies, and defeated the Spartans at the celebrated battle of Leuctra, about 371 years B.C. Making a proper use of this victory, he entered the territories of Lacedæmon with 50,000 men. Here he gained many friends and partisans; but at his return to Thebes he was seized as a traitor for violating the laws of his country. While he was making the Theban arms victorious on every side, he neglected the law which forbade any citizen to retain in his hands the supreme power more than one month, and all his eminent services seemed unable to redeem him from death. He paid implicit obedience to the laws of his country, and only begged of his judges that it might be inscribed on his tomb that he had suffered death to save his country from ruin. This animated reproach was felt by the people, he was pardoned by the general voice, and again invested with the sovereign power. He was successful in a war in Thessaly, and assisted the Eleans against the Lacedæmonians. The hostile armies met near Mantinea, and while Epaminondas was bravely fighting in the thickest of the enemy, he received a fatal wound in the breast, and expired, when he heard that the Bœotians had obtained the victory, exclaiming, that he died unconquered, in the 48th year of his age, 363 years B.C. The Thebans sincerely lamented his death; in him their power was extinguished, for only during his life had they enjoyed freedom, and risen to eminence among the Grecian states. Epaminondas was frugal as well as virtuous, and he refused with indignation the rich presents which were offered to him by Artaxerxes the king of Persia. He is represented by his biographer as an elegant dancer and a skilful musician, accomplishments highly esteemed among his countrymen. *Plut. in Parall.*—*C. Nep. in Vitâ.*—*Xenoph. Quæst. Græc.*—*Diod.* 15.—*Polyb.* 1.—*Cic. Fam.* 5. ep. 12.

EPANTE'RII, a people of Italy. *Livy.*

EPAPHRODI'TUS, a freedman punished with death by Domitian, for assisting Nero to destroy himself. *Suet. in Ner.*—*Plin. Pan.* 53.——A freedman of Augustus sent to watch the conduct of Cleopatra. *Plut.*——A name assumed by Sylla.——A grammarian of Chæronea, who is said to have had a library of 30,000 choice books. *Suidas.*—*Schol. Aristoph.* [There is a statue of Epaphroditus, small sitting figure, in the Altieri palace at Rome.]

EP'APHUS, a son of Jupiter and Io, who founded a city in Ægypt, which he called Memphis, in honour of his wife, who was the daughter of the Nile. He had a daughter called Libya, and was worshipped as a god at Memphis. *Herodot.* 2. c. 153. l. 3. c. 27.—*Ovid. Met.* 1. v. 699, &c.—*Hygin.* 149, 155, 275.—*Apollod.* 2.

EPAR'DUS, a river flowing through the country of the Mardi. *Arrian.*

EPARI'TÆ, a people of Arcadia. *Steph.*

EPASNAC'TUS, a Gaul in alliance with Rome, &c. *Cæs. Bell. G.* 8. c. 44.

EPEB'OLUS, a soothsayer of Messenia, who prevented Aristodemus from obtaining the sovereignty. *Paus.* 4. c. 9, &c.

EPE'I or ELE'I, a people of Peloponnesus. *Plin.* 4. c. 5.

EPETI'NI, a people of Liburnia. *Id.* 3. c. 22.

EPE'TIUM, now Voscio, a town of Illyricum. *Ptol.*

EPE'US, a son of Endymion and Asterodia, who reigned in a part of Peloponnesus. At a race in Olympia where his brothers Pæon and Ætolus were his competitors, he obtained the prize, which was the succession to his father's kingdom, and he afterwards married Anaxirhoë, daughter of Coronus, by whom he had a daughter, called Hyrmine. As he died without male children, he was succeeded by Ætolus. His subjects were called from him Epei. *Paus.* 5. c. 1.——A son of Panopus, who distinguished himself at the games, celebrated before Troy by Achilles to honour the memory of Patroclus. He was the fabricator of the famous wooden horse which proved the ruin of Troy. *Virg. Æn.* 2. v. 264.—*Justin.* 20. c. 2.—*Paus.* 2. c. 29. l. 10. c. 26.—*Homer. Odyss.* 8. v. 493.—*Hygin.* fab. 108.—*Plin.* 5. c. 56.

EPH'ESUS, a celebrated city of Ionia, built, as Justin mentions, by the Amazons; or by Androchus son of Codrus, according to Strabo; or by Ephesus, a son of the river Cayster. It was famous for a temple of Diana, which was reckoned one of the seven wonders of the world. The temple was 425 feet long and 200 feet broad, and was adorned with the choicest paintings and statues. The roof was supported by 127 columns, sixty feet high, which had been placed there by so many kings. Of these columns, 36 were carved in the most beautiful manner, one of which was the work of the famous Scopas. This celebrated building was not totally completed till 220 years after its foundation. Ctesiphon was the chief architect. There was above the entrance a huge stone, which, according to Pliny, had been placed there by Diana herself. The riches which were deposited in the temple were immense, and the goddess who presided over it was worshipped with the most awful solemnity. In her statue, which was made of ebony, she was represented as crowned with turrets, and holding lions on her arms, whilst a number of breasts seemed to indicate the fecundity and resources of the earth or of nature. Pliny mentions that the stair-case which led to the top of the lofty edifice, was formed of the trunk of one single vine. This celebrated temple was burnt on the night that Alexander was born (*Vid.* Erostratus,) and soon after it rose again from its ruins with additional splendour and magnificence. Alexander offered to rebuild it at his own expense, if the Ephesians would place upon it an inscription which denoted the name of the benefactor. This generous offer was refused by the Ephesians, who observed, in the language of adulation, that it was improper that one deity should raise temples to the other. Lysimachus ordered the town of Ephesus to be called Arsinoe, in honour of his wife; but after his death the new appellation was lost and the town was again known by its ancient name. Though modern authors are not agreed about the ancient ruins of this once famed city, some have given the barbarous name of Ajasalouc to what they conjecture to be the remains of Ephesus. The words *literæ Ephesiæ* are applied to letters containing magical powers. *Plin.* 36. c. 14.—*Strab.* 12 & 14.—*Clem. Alex. Strom.* 1. c. 18.—*Mela,* 1. c. 17.—*Paus.* 7. c. 2.—*Plut. in Alex.*—

Justin. 2. c. 4.—*Callim. in Dian.*—*Ptol.* 5.—*Cic. de Nat. D.* 2.—*Ptol.* 5. c. 2.

EPH'ETÆ, a number of magistrates at Athens, first instituted by Demophoon, the son of Theseus. They were reduced to the number of fifty-one by Draco, who, according to some authors, first established them. They were superior to the Areopagites in authority, and their privileges were very numerous. Solon, however, lessened their power, and entrusted them only with the trial of manslaughter and conspiracy against the life of a citizen. They were all more than fifty years old, and it was required that their manners should be pure and innocent, and their behaviour strictly correct and full of gravity. *Plut. in Sol.*—*Suidas.*

EPHIAL'TES or EPHIAL'TUS, a giant, son of Neptune, who was said to grow nine inches every month. *Vid.* Aloeus.

EPHIAL'TES, an Athenian, famous for his courage and strength. He fought with the Persians against Alexander, and was killed at Halicarnassus. *Diod.* 17.——A Trachinian, who led a detachment of the army of Xerxes by a secret path to attack the Spartans at Thermopylæ. *Paus.* 1. c. 4.—*Herodot.* 7. c. 213.

EPHIALTI'UM, a promontory of the island Carpathus. *Ptol.*

EPH'ORI, powerful magistrates at Sparta, first created by Lycurgus, or, according to some by Theopompus, B.C. 760. They were five in number, could check and restrain the authority of the kings, and even imprison them, if guilty of irregularities. They fined Archidamus for marrying a wife of small stature, and imprisoned Agis for his unconstitutional behaviour. They were nearly the same as the tribunes of the people at Rome, created to watch with a jealous eye over the liberties and rights of the populace. They had the management of the public money and were the arbiters of peace and war. Their office was annual, and they had the privilege of convening, proroguing, and dissolving the greater and lesser assemblies of the people. The former was composed of 9000 Spartans, or inhabitants of the city; the latter of 30,000 Lacedæmonians, inhabitants of the inferior towns and villages in the immediate neighbourhood. *C. Nep. in Paus.* 3.—*Aristot. Pol.* 2. c. 7.

EPH'ORUS, an orator and historian of Cumæ in Æolia, about 352 years B.C. He was disciple of Isocrates, by whose advice he wrote a history which gave an account of all the actions and battles that had happened between the Greeks and barbarians for 750 years, from the return of the Heraclidæ to Peloponnesus, to the 20th year of the reign of Philip, Alexander's father. His work, now lost, was divided into thirty books, and was held in high esteem among the ancients, though some, especially *Diodorus Siculus*, accuse him of inaccuracy and falsehood. He left a son called Demophilus, who is said to have finished the incomplete history of his father. *Quintil.* 10. c. 1.—*Cic. Orat.* 2. c. 13 & 23. *Br.* 56. *Orat.* 51. 57.

EPH'YRA or EPH'YRE, the ancient name of Corinth, which it received from a nymph of the same name, and thence Ephyreus is applied to Dyrrachium, which was founded by a Corinthian colony. *Virg. G.* 2. v. 264.—*Ovid. Met.* 2. v. 239 —*Plin.* 4. c. 4.—*Claudian de G. Bell.* 629.—*Lucan.* 6. v. 17. —*Stat. Theb.* 4. v. 59.—*Ital.* 14. v. 181.——A city of Thesprotia in Epirus.——A city of Elis.——A city of Ætolia. *Homer. Il.* 2. v. 166. *Odyss.* 1. v. 259., l. 2. v. 328.—*Strab.* 7 & 8.—*Paterc.* 1. c. 1.—*Paus.* 9. c. 36.

EPH'YRA, one of Cyrene's attendants. *Virg. G.* 4. v. 343.—*Paus.* 2. c. 1.

EPH'YRIS, a town of Laconia. *Herodot.*

EPICA'DIUS CORN., a freedman of Sylla, who finished the annals left incomplete by his master. *Macrob. Sat.* 1. c. 11.—*Voss. de Hist. Lat.* 1. c. 9.

EPICA'RIA, a town of Dalmatia. *Ptol.*

EPICAS'TE, a name of Jocasta, the mother and wife of Œdipus. *Paus.* 9. c. 5.——A daughter of Ægeus, mother of Thestalus by Hercules. *Apollod.* 2.——A daughter of Calydon, son of Æolus. *Id.* 1.

EPICER'DES, a man of Cyrene, greatly esteemed by the Athenians for his beneficence. *Demosth. adv. Leptin.*

EPICH'ARIS, a woman accused of conspiracy against Nero. She firmly refused to discover the associates of her guilt, though exposed to the greatest torments, &c. *Tacit.* 15, *Ann.* c. 51 & 57.

EPICHAR'MUS, a poet and Pythagorean philosopher of Sicily, who introduced comedy at Syracuse, in the reign of Hiero. His compositions were imitated by Plautus. He wrote also some treatises upon philosophy and medicine. According to *Aristotle* and *Pliny*, he added the two letters χ and ϑ to the Greek alphabet. He flourished about 440 years B.C., and died in the 90th year of his age. *Horat.* 2 ep. 1. v. 58.—*Diog.* 3 & 8.—*Cic. ad Attic.* 1. ep. 19. *Tusc.* 1. c. 8.—*Stob.* 117.—*Theocr.* ep. 17.—*Sax. Onom.* 1. p. 33.—*Fabr. B. Gr.* 2. c. 19.

EP'ICLES, a Trojan prince, killed by Ajax. *Homer. Il.* 12. v. 378.

EPICLI'DES, a Lacedæmonian of the family of the Eurysthenidæ. He was raised to the throne by his brother Cleomenes the Third, in the place of Agis, against the laws and constitution of the state. *Paus,* 2. c. 9.

EPICNEMID'II. *Vid.* Locris.

EPICRA'TES, a Milesian, servant to J. Cæsar.——A man of some eminence at Athens. *Cic. Fam.* 16. ep. 21.—The name is applied to Pompey, as expressive of supreme authority. *Cic. Att.* 2 ep. 3. ——A poet of Ambracia. *Ælian.*—*Sax. Onom.* 1. p. 68.—*Fabr. B. Gr.* 2. c. 22.

EPICTE'TUS, a stoic philosopher of Hierapolis in Phrygia, originally the slave of Epaphroditus, the freedman of Nero. Though driven from Rome by Domitian, he, after residing some time at Nicopolis in Epirus, returned on the emperor's death, and gained the esteem of Adrian and Marcus Aurelius. Like the Stoics, he maintained the doctrine of the immortality of the soul, but declared himself strongly against suicide, which was so warmly adopted by his sect. He died at a very advanced age, and left behind him nothing but a character long and deservedly respected for humility and modesty, for patience and resignation, for greatness of soul, and contempt of riches. The earthen lamp which the philosopher used, was sold some time after his death for 3,000 drachmas. His Enchiridion is a faithful picture of the Stoic philosophy; and his dissertations, which were delivered to his pupils, were collected by Arrian. His style is concise and devoid of all ornament, full of energy, and abounding in useful maxims. The value of his compositions is well known from the saying of the emperor Antoninus, who thanked the gods that he could collect from the writings of Epictetus wherewith to conduct life with honor to himself and advantage to his country. There are several good editions of the works of Epictetus, with those of Cebes and others, the most valuable of which, perhaps, will be found to be that of Reland Traject. 4to, 1711; and Arrian's by Upton, 2 vols. 4to. Lond. 1739. An excellent translation of Epictetus into English has appeared from the pen of Mrs. Carter. *Sax. Onom.* 1. p. 272.—*Fabr. B. Gr.* 4. c. 7.—*A. Gell.*—*Arrian.*

EPICU'RIUS, a surname of Apollo, which he received from the assistance which he gave to the people of Phiglaia in Arcadia, when they were visited by a pestilence. The temple erected to his honor on the neighbouring hill of Cotylius, was built with freestone, and next to that of Tegea, was considered one of the most elegant and magnificent in Peloponnesus. *Paus.* 8. c. 42.

EPICU'RUS, a celebrated philosopher, son of Neocles and Cherecrata, born at Gargettus in Attica. Though his parents were poor and of an obscure origin, yet he was early sent to school, where he distinguished himself by the brilliancy of his genius, and at the age of twelve, when his preceptor repeated to him this verse from Hesiod,

Ἤτοι μὲν πρώτιστα χάος γένετ', &c.

In the beginning of things Chaos was created.

Epicurus earnestly asked him, who created it? To this the teacher answered that he knew not, but only philosophers. "Then," says the youth, "philosophers henceforth shall instruct me." After having improved himself, and enriched his mind by travelling, he visited Athens, which was then crowded by the followers of Plato, the Cynics, the Peripatetics, and the Stoics. Here he established himself, and soon attracted a number of followers by the sweetness and gravity of his manners, and by his social virtues. He taught them that the happiness of mankind consisted in pleasure, not indeed such as arises from sensual gratification, or from vice, but from the enjoyments of the mind, from sobriety, from temperance, and a due restraint of the tumultuous and disorderly passions, and from the sweets of virtue. This doctrine was warmly attacked by the philosophers of the different contemporary sects, and particularly by the Stoics. They observed that the author of this new doctrine disgraced the gods by representing them as inactive, given up to pleasure, and unconcerned with the affairs of mankind. The philosopher refuted all the arguments of his adversaries by the purity of his morals, and his frequent attendance on places of public worship. His health was at last impaired by continual labour, and he died of a retention of urine, which long subjected him to the most excruciating torments, which he bore with unparalleled fortitude. His death happened 270 years B.C., in the 72nd year of his age. His disciples shewed their respect for the memory of their learned preceptor, by the unanimity which prevailed among them. While philosophers in every sect were at war with mankind, and among themselves, the followers of Epicurus enjoyed perfect peace, and lived in the most solid friendship. The day of his birth was observed with universal festivity, and during a month all his admirers gave themselves up to mirth and innocent amusements. Of all the philosophers of antiquity, Epicurus is the only one whose writings deserve attention for their number. He wrote no less than 300 volumes, according to Diogenes Laertius; and Chrysippus was so jealous of the fecundity of his genius, that no sooner had Epicurus published one of his volumes, but he immediately composed one, that he might not be surpassed in the number of his productions. The followers of Epicurus have been numerous in every age and country, his doctrines were rapidly disseminated over the world, and when the gratification of the senses was substituted for the practice of virtue, the morals of mankind were gradually undermined and destroyed. Even Rome, whose austere simplicity had happily nurtured virtue and cradled heroism, felt the attack and was corrupted. When Cyneas spoke of the tenets of the Epicureans in the Roman senate, Fabricius indeed intreated the gods that all the enemies of the republic might become his followers. But those were the feeble efforts of expiring virtue; and when Lucretius introduced the popular doctrine in his poetical composition, the smoothness and beauty of the numbers contributed, together with the effeminacy of the Epicureans, to enervate imperceptibly the conqueror of the world. *Diog. in Vitâ.—Ælian V. H.* 4. c. 13.—*Cic. de Nat. D.* 1. c. 24 & 25. *Tusc.* 3. 49. *De Finib.* 2. c. 22.—*Seneca de Beat. Vit.* 13.—*Plin.* 25. c. 6.—*Lactant.* 3. c. 17.—*Sax. Onom.* 1. p. 93. —*Fabr. B. Gr.* l. 3. c. 33. [The finest bust of Epicurus is one in bronze at Naples. There is a double terminal head of Epicurus and Metrodorus in the Museum of the Capitol at Rome.]

EPICY'DES or EPIC'YDES, a tyrant of Syracuse, B.C. 213.

EPIDAM'NUS, a town of Macedonia on the Adriatic, nearly opposite Brundusium. The Romans settled a colony there which they called Dyrrachium, considering the ancient name (*ad damnum*) ominous. *Paus.* 6. c. 10.—*Plin.* 3. c. 23.—*Plautus, Men.* 2. act. 1. v. 42.

EPIDAPHNE, a town of Syria, called also Antiochia. The illustrious Germanicus, son of Drusus, died there. *Tac. Ann.* 2. c. 83.

EPIDAU'RIA, a festival at Athens in honor of Æsculapius. *Cic. de Nat. Deor.* l. 3.—*Paus.* l. 2.

EPIDAU'RIA, a district of Peloponnesus.

EPIDAU'RUS, a town of the north of Argolis in Peloponnesus, on the Sinus Saronicus, chiefly dedicated to the worship of Æsculapius, who had there a famous temple. It received its name from Epidaurus, a son of Argus and Evadne. It is now called Piduara.—*Strab.* 8.—*Ptol.* 3. c. 16.—*Virg. G.* 3. v. 44.—*Paus.* 3 c. 21.—*Mela*, 2. c. 3.——A town of Dalmatia on the sea shore opposite the island of Melita, now Ragusi Vecchio.——A town of Laconia, on the sea shore, called also Limera for the sake of distinction, and now Malvasia.

EPID'IUM, one of the western isles of Scotland, now the Mull of Cantyre, according to some. *Ptol.*

EPIDE'LIUM, a town of Laconia, where the image of Apollo, which was thrown into the sea at Delos, is said to have landed.

EPID'IUS, a man who wrote concerning unusual prodigies. *Plin.* 16. c. 25.

EPIDO'TÆ, certain deities who presided over the birth and growth of children, and were known among the Romans by the name of Dii Averrunci. They were also worshipped by the Lacedæmonians, and chiefly invoked by those who were persecuted by the ghosts of the dead, &c. *Paus.* 3. c. 17, &c.

EPIG'ENES, a Babylonian astrologer and historian. *Plin.* 7. c. 56.——An Athenian poet, B.C. 380.

EPI'GEUS, a Grecian prince who left his native country after the murder of a relation, and fled to Peleus, who engaged him to accompany his son Achilles to the Trojan war. He was, after many deeds of heroic bravery, killed by Hector. *Homer. Il.* 16. v. 570.

EPIG'ONI, the sons and descendants of those brave Grecian heroes who were killed in the first Theban war. The war of the Epigoni is famous in ancient history. It was undertaken ten years after the first. The sons of those who had perished in the first war, resolved to avenge the death of their fathers, and marched against Thebes, under the command of Thersander; or, according to others, of Alcmæon the son of Amphiaraus. They were assisted in their expedition by the Corinthians, the people of Messenia, Arcadia, and Megara. The Thebans had also engaged all their neighbours in their quarrel, as in one common cause, and the two hostile armies met and engaged on the banks of the Glissas. The fight was obstinate and bloody, but victory declared for the Epigoni, and some of the Thebans fled to Illyricum with Leodamas their general, while others retired into Thebes, where they were soon besieged, and forced to surrender. In this war Ægialeus was the only chief who was killed, and his father Adrastus was the only person who escaped alive the first war. This whole war, as Pausanias observes, was the subject of an epic poem; and Callinus, who quotes some of the verses, ascribes them to Homer, which opinion has been adopted by many writers. "For my part," continues the geographer, "I own that next to the Iliad and Odyssey of Homer, I have never seen a finer poem." Euripides called one of his tragedies by the name of Epigoni. *Cic. Offi.* 1. c. 31. *Tusc.* 2. c. 25.—*Paus.* 9. c. 9 & 25.—*Pindar. Pyth.* 8. 55.—*Apollod.* 1 & 3.—*Diod.* 4.——The sons of those Macedonian veterans who in the age of Alexander the Great formed connections with the women of Asia. *Justin.* 12. c. 4.

EPIG'ONUS, a mathematician of Ambracia. *Athen.* 4 & 14.—*Jul. Pollux. Onom.* 4. c. 9.——A poet. *Voss. de Hist. Gr.* l. 3.

EPIGRANE'A, a fountain of Bœotia. *Plin.* 4. c. 7.

EPI'I or EPE'I, a people of Elis. *Vid.* Epei.

EPIIE'IDÆ, a village in the tribe Cecropis. *Steph.*

EPIL'ARIS, a daughter of Thespius. *Apollod.*

EPIMARANI'TÆ, a people of Arabia Felix. *Plin.* 6. c. 28.

EPIMEL'IDES, the founder of Corone. *Paus.* 4. c. 34.

EPIM'ENES, a man who conspired against Alexander's life. *Curt.* 8. c. 6.

EPIMEN'IDES, son of Agiasarchus, an epic poet of Crete, contemporary with Solon. He is reckoned one of the seven wise men of Greece by those authors who exclude Periander from the number. While he was tending his flocks one day, he entered into a cave, where he fell asleep. His sleep continued for 40, or 47, or according to Pliny, 57 years, and when he awoke he found every object around him so considerably altered, that he scarcely knew where he was. His brother apprized him of the length of his sleep, to his great astonishment. It is supposed that he lived 157, or, according to others, 299 years. After death he was revered as a god, and greatly honoured by the Athenians, whom he had delivered from a plague, and to whom he had given much useful advice. He is said to have been the first who built temples in the Grecian communities. Besides his poems on the genealogy of the gods, on the Argonautic expedition, and on Minos and Rhadamanthus, he wrote several treatises on sacrifices, and on the commonwealth of Crete, all which have perished. *Cic. de Div.* 1. c. 18 & 34.—*Diog. in Vitâ.*—*Paus.*

1. c. 14.—*Plut. in Solon.*—*Val. Max.* 8. c. 13.—*Strab.* 10.—*Plin.* 7. c. 12.—*Tzetzes. Chil.* 5.—*Max Tyr.* 28. *Dis.*—*Suidas.*—*Meursius ad Ap. Hist. Mir.* 1. [The finest bust of Epimenides is one in the Vatican.]

EPIME'THEUS, a son of Japetus and Clymene, one of the Oceanides, who inconsiderately married Pandora, by whom he became father of Pyrrha the wife of Deucalion. *Vid.* Pandora. It is said that Epimetheus was changed into a monkey by the gods, and sent into the island of Pithecusa. *Apollod.* 1. c. 2 & 7.—*Ovid. Met.* 1. v. 390.—*Claudian. in Eutr.* 2. v. 490.—*Hygin.* fab. 142.—*Hesiod. Theog.* 512. *Vid.* Prometheus.

EPIME'THIS, a patronymic of Pyrrha, as the daughter of Epimetheus. *Ovid. Met.* 1. v. 390.

EPI'OCHUS, a son of Lycurgus, who received divine honours in Arcadia.

EPI'ONE, the wife of Æsculapius. *Paus.* 2. c. 29.

EPIPHANE'A, town of Cilicia, at the north-east of Issus, now called *Surpendkar*. *Plin.* 5. c. 27.—*Cic. ad Fam.* 15. ep. 4.——A town of Syria on the Euphrates. *Plin.* 5. c. 24.

EPIPHANI'A or EPIPHANE'A, a colony of the Phœnicians on the Orontes.——A city in Asia Minor, re-peopled with pirates by Pompey.

EPIPH'ANES, (*illustrious*), a surname given to the Antiochi, kings of Syria. *Tacit. Hist.* 2. c. 25.——A surname of one of the Ptolemies, the fifth of the house of Lagidæ. *Strab.* 17.—The surname of Epiphanes is also applied to Jupiter, because he appeared to mankind. *Plut. in Marc.*—*Cic. de Nat. D.* 2.——A king, in the interests of Otho. *Tac. Hist.* 2. c. 25.——A son of Carpocrates, worshipped by the Cephalenians. *Clem.* 1. *Strom.*

EPIPHA'NIUS, a bishop of Salamis in Cyprus, who was active in refuting the writings of Origen; but his compositions are more valuable for the fragments of other writers which they preserve than for their own intrinsic merit. The only edition is by Dionys. Petavius, 2 vols. Paris, 1622. The bishop died A.D. 403. *Sax. Onom.* 1. p. 424.—*Fabr. B. Gr.* 1. 5. c. 10.——A scholiast of the sixth century. the friend of Cassiodorus. He translated the Greek histories of Socrates, Sozomen, and Theodoret into Latin.

EPIPOLÆ, a district of Syracuse on the north side of the city, surrounded by a wall, by Dionysius, who, to complete the work expeditiously, employed 60,000 men upon it, so that in thirty days he finished a wall 4½ miles long, and of great height and proportionate thickness. *Steph.*

EPI'RUS, a country situate between Macedonia, Achaia, and the Ionian Sea, divided into the four districts of Acarnania, Thesprotia, Molossis, and Chaonia. It was formerly governed by kings, of whom Neoptolemus, son of Achilles, was one of the first. It was afterwards joined to the empire of Macedonia, and with it at last became a part of the Roman dominions. It is now called Larta. *Strab.* 7.—*Mela*, 2. c. 3.—*Ptol.* 3. c. 14.—*Plin.* 4. c. 1.—*Virg. G.* 3. v. 121.

EPIS'TROPHUS, a son of Iphitus king of Phocis, who went to the Trojan war at the head of the Phocian nation. *Homer. Il.* 2. v. 24.—*Apollod.* 3.—*Hygin.* fab. 97.——A prince who assisted the Trojans against the Greeks. *Homer. Il.* 2. v. 363.

EPIT'ADES, a man who first violated a law of Lycurgus, which forbade laws to be made. *Plut. in Agid.*

EPITA'LIUM, a city of Triphylia, called Thryon by *Homer*, and Thryoessa by *Strabo*. It is now Zunchio. *Steph.*

EPITAU'SA, a city of India within the Ganges. *Ptol.*

EPITRA'GIA, a surname given by Theseus to Venus, because she changed herself into a goat. There was a remarkable statue of this goddess in Elis, supposed to be the work of Scopas. *Plut. in Thes.*

EP'ITUS. *Vid.* Epytus.

E'PIUM or EPI'UM, a town of Peloponnesus on the borders of Arcadia. *Plin.* 4. c. 6.

EP'ONA, at Rome, the goddess and protector of horses.

EPO'PEUS, a son of Neptune and Canace, who came from Thessaly to Sicyon, where he seized the sovereign power after the death of Corax king of the country. He afterwards carried away Antiope daughter of Nycteus king of Thebes, which violent conduct was followed by a war, in which Nycteus and Epopeus were both killed. *Paus.* 2. c. 6.—*Apollod.* 1. c. 7, &c.——A son of Aloeus, grandson to Phœbus. He reigned at Corinth, after the death of Bunus. *Paus.* 2. c. 1 & 3.——One of the Tyrrhene sailors, who insulted and abused Bacchus. *Ovid. Met.* 3. v. 619.

EPORE'DIA, a city of the Salassii. *Ptol.*—*Plin.* 3. c. 17.

EPORED'ORIX, a powerful person among the Ædui in Gaul, who commanded his countrymen in their war against the Sequani. *Cæs. Bell. G.* 7. c. 67.

E'PRIUS MARCEL'LUS, a person accused of bribery by the Lycians, but acquitted. *Tac. Ann.* 13. c. 33.

EPUI'A, the ancient name of Ambracia. *Steph.*

EP'ULO, a Rutulian killed by Achates. *Virg. Æn.* 12. v. 459.

EPYT'IDES, a patronymic given to Periphas the son of Epitus, and the companion of Ascanius. *Virg. Æn.* 5. v. 547.

EP'YTUS, a king of Alba. *Ovid. Fast.* 4. v. 44.——A king of Arcadia, son of Elatus, the son of Arcas and Erato. *Paus.* 8. c. 7 & 14.——A king of Messenia, of the family of the Heraclidæ. He was son of Cresphontes, and his reign was so mild and equitable that his descendants exchanged the honourable name of Heraclidæ for that of Epytides. He was succeeded by Glaucus, who was equally as illustrious as his father. *Paus.* 4. c. 3.——The father of Periphas, a herald in the Trojan war. *Homer. Il.* 17. v. 324.

EQUAJUS'TA, a town of Thessaly. *Arist.* 11. *Polit.* c. 3.

EQUES'TER, a surname of Neptune, who created horses.

EQUIC'OLUS, a Rutulian engaged in the wars of Æneas. *Virg. Æn.* 9. v. 684.

EQUIR'IA, festivals first established at Rome by Romulus in honour of Mars, when horse-races and games were exhibited in the Campus Martius, on the 27th of February and the 14th of March. *Gyrald. Gal. Rom. & Gr.*—*Tertull. de Spect.* 5.—*Festus de Verb. Sig.*—*Varro de L. L.* 5. c. 3.—*Ovid. Fast.* 2. v. 859.

EQUOTU'TICUM, now Castel Franco, a little town on the borders of Apulia, to which, as some suppose, *Horace* alludes in this verse, 1. sat. 5. v. 87.

"*Mansuri oppidulo, quod versu dicere non est.*"

ER'ACON, an officer in the army of Alexander the Great, imprisoned for his cruelty. *Curt.* 10. c. 1.

ERAC'TUM or HERAC'TUM, a town of the Bastarnæ, now Rovv. *Ptol.*

ERÆ'A, a city of Greece, destroyed in the age of *Strabo*. 3.

ERA'NA, a small village of Cilicia on mount Amanus. *Cic. Fam.* 15. ep. 4.

ERANU'SA, an island near Locri, in Italy. *Plin.* 3. c. 10.

ERASIN'IDES, one of the six Athenian commanders put to death after the victory of Arginusæ, B.C. 406.

ERASIN'II, a people of Thrace. *Id.* 2. c. 103, &c.

ERASI'NUS, now Rasino, a river of Peloponnesus, flowing for a little space under the ground in Argolis. *Ovid. Met.* 15. v. 275.—*Plin.* 2. c. 13.

ERASIP'PUS, a son of Hercules and Lysippe.

ERASIS'TRATUS, a celebrated physician, grandson to the philosopher Aristotle. He perceived by the motion of the pulse the love which Antiochus had conceived for his mother-in-law Stratonice, and was, for this discovery rewarded with 100 talents by the father of the young Prince. He was a great enemy to bleeding and violent physic, but his name is rendered still more illustrious when he is considered as the first experimentalist in anatomy. He died B.C. 257. *Plin.* 25. c. 15.—*A. Gellius.* 16. c. 3.—*Val. Max.* 5. c. 7.—*Plut. in Demetr.*

ER'ATO, one of the Muses, who presided over lyric, tender, and amorous poetry. She is represented as crowned with roses and myrtle, holding in her right hand a lyre, and a lute in her left, musical instruments of which she was considered the inventress. Love is sometimes placed by her side holding a lighted flambeau, while she herself appears with a thoughtful, but oftener with a gay and animated look. She was invoked by lovers especially in the month of April, which, among the Romans was more particularly devoted to love. *Apollod.* 10.—*Virg. Æn.* 7. v. 37.—*Apollon. Arg.* 3.—*Ovid. de Art. Am.* 2. v. 425. [The statues of this Muse are very numerous. The best is one in the Vatican Museum at Rome.]——One of the Nereides. *Apollod.* 1. c. 2.——One of the Dryades, wife of Arcas king of Arcadia, and mother of Azan, Aphidas, and Elatus. *Paus.* 8. c. 4.——One of the Danaides, who married Bromius. *Apollod.* 2.——A queen of the Armenians after the death of Ariobarzanes, &c. *Tacit. Ann.* 2. c. 4.

ERATOS'THENES, son of Aglaus, was a native of Cyrene, and the second person entrusted with the care of the Alexandrian library. He dedicated his time to grammatical criticism and philosophy, but more particularly to poetry and mathematics. He has been called from his extensive knowledge a second Plato, the cosmographer, and the geometer of the world. He is supposed to have been the inventor of the armillary sphere. With the instruments with which the munificence of the Ptolemies supplied the library of Alexandria, he was enabled to measure the obliquity of the ecliptic, which he called 20½ degrees. He also measured a degree of the meridian, and determined the extent and circumference of the earth with great exactness, by those means afterwards adopted by the moderns. He starved himself after he had lived to his 82d year, B.C. 194. Some few fragments remain of his compositions. He collected the annals of the Ægyptian kings by order of one of the Ptolemies. *Cic. ad Attic.* 2. ep. 6.—*Varro de R. R.* 1. c. 2.—*Quintil.* 1. c. 1.—*Sax. Onom.* 1. p. 110.—*Fabr. B. Gr.* 3. c. 15.

ERATOS'TRATUS, an Ephesian, who burnt the famous temple of Diana the same night that Alexander the Great was born. Eratostratus is said to have committed this act merely to eternize his name; and the Ephesians, by making a law to forbid the mentioning of his name, rendered themselves instrumental in spreading his infamous celebrity. *Plut. in Alex.*—*Val. Max.* 8. c. 14.

ER'ATUS, a son of Hercules and Dynaste. *Apollod.*——A king of Sicyon, who died B.C. 1671.

ERBES'SUS, a town of Sicily at the north of Agrigentum, now Monte Bibino. *Liv.* 24. c. 30.

ERCHI'A, a small village of Attica, the birth-place of Xenophon. *Laert.* 2. c. 48.

EREB'IDÆ, a part of the country of the Lotophagi. *Steph.*

ER'EBUS, a deity of hell, son of Chaos and Caligo. He married Nox, by whom he had Lux and Dies. The poets often used the word Erebus to signify hell itself, and particularly that part where the souls of those who had lived a virtuous life resided, whence they passed into the more tranquil regions of the Elysian fields. *Claudian. de Rap. Pr.*—*Hygin. in præf. fab.*—*Hesiod. Th.* 124.—*Cic. de Nat. D.* 3. c. 17.—*Virg. Æn.* 4. v. 26.—*Servius in Æn.* 6. v. 404.

ERECHTHE'IS, a tribe of Athens.

ERECH'THEUS, son of Pandion the First, was the sixth king of Athens. He was father of Cecrops the Second, Metion, Pandorus, and four daughters, Creusa, Orithyia, Procris, and Chthonia, by Praxithea. In a war against Eleusis he sacrificed Chthonia, to obtain a victory which the oracle promised to his army for such an extraordinary sacrifice. In that war he killed Eumolpus, Neptune's son, who was the general of the enemy, for which he was struck with thunder by Jupiter at Neptune's request. Some say that he was drowned in the sea. After death he received divine honours at Athens. He reigned 50 years, and died B.C. 1347. According to some accounts he was the first person who introduced the mysteries of Ceres at Eleusis. *Ovid. Met.* 6. v. 877.—*Paus.* 2. c. 25.—*Hygin.* fab. 46, 47, 238.—*Apollod.* 3. c. 15.—*Cic. pro Sext.* 21. *Tusc.* 1. c. 48. *Nat. D.* 3. c. 15. *De Fin.* 5. c. 22.

ERECHTHI'DES or **EREC'THIDES**, a name given to the Athenians, from their king Erechtheus. *Ovid. Met.* 7. v. 430.

EREM'BI, a people of Arabia. *Dionys. de sit orbis.*

ERE'MUS, an island near Lemnus. *Steph.*——A region of Æthiopia. *Ælian. Hist. An.* 17. c. 40.

ERE'NE, an island near Taprobane. *Ptol.*

ERENE'A, a village of Megara. *Paus.* 1. c. 44.

ERE'SII, a people of Æolis. *Plin.* 5. c. 30.

ERES'SA, a town of Æolia. *Mela*, 1. c. 18.

ERE'SUS, ER'ESUS or **ERES'SUS**, a town of Lesbos, where Theophrastus was born. The barley which grew there yielded flour so beautiful and pure, that Mercury was said to procure it for the food of the gods. *Archistrat. in Gastrin.*

ERE'TRIA, a city of Eubœa on the Euripus, anciently called Meleneis and Arotria. It was destroyed by the Persians in their wars against Greece, and the ruins were hardly visible in the age of Strabo. It received its name from Eretrius, a son of Phaæthon, and was remarkable for the medicinal herbs produced in its neighbourhood. *Celsus.* 5. c. 15.—*Vitruv.* 7. c. 13.—*Dioscorid.* 5. c. 171.—*Paus.* 7. c. 8. &c.—*Mela*, 2. c. 7.—*Plin.* 4. c. 12.—*C. Nep. in Milt.* 4.——A town of Ionia bore the same name. *Paus.* 7. c. 10.

ERE'TUM, a town of the Sabines near the Tiber, whence came the adjective *Eretinus. Virg. Æn.* 7. v. 711.—*Tibull.* 4. el. 8. v. 4.

EREUTHA'LION, a friend and arm-bearer of Lycurgus king of Arcadia, from whom he inherited a famous iron club that had once been in the possession of Mars. He was conquered and slain by Nestor in a war between the Pylians and Arcadians. *Homer. Il.* 7.

EREV'ATIS, a city of Lycia. *Steph.*

ER'GA, a town of the Ilergetes in Spain. *Ptol.*

ER'GANE, a river, the waters of which were said to intoxicate like wine. *Athen.*

Er'gane, a surname of Minerva, under which she had an altar in the temple of Jupiter Olympia. *Ælian.* 1. c. 2.—*Paus.* 5. c. 14.

ERGAN'ICA, a city of Spain, now Erganicum. *Ptol.*

ERGAVI'CA, a town of the Vascones in Spain. *Ptol.*—*Plin.* 3. c. 3.

ERGEN'NA, a celebrated soothsayer of Etruria. *Pers.* 2. v. 26.

ERGE'TIUM, a city of Sicily. *Plin.* 3. c. 8.

ER'GIAS, a Rhodian, who wrote a history of his country. *Athen.* 8.

ERGI'NUS, a king of Orchomenus, who obliged the Thebans to pay him a yearly tribute of 100 oxen, because his father had been killed by a Theban. Hercules, indignant at the exaction of this disgraceful tribute, attacked his servants and mutilated them, and afterwards killed Erginus, who attempted to avenge their death by invading Bœotia with an army. *Apollod.* 2.—*Pindar. Olymp.* 4.—*Paus.* 9. c. 17.——A son of Neptune among the Argonauts. *Hygin.* 14.—*Apollod.* 1.——One of the four brothers who kept the Acrocorinthus, by order of Antigonus. *Polyæn.* 6.

Ergi'nus, a river of Thrace. *Mela*, 2. c. 2.

ERGIN'NUS, a man made pilot of the ship Argo by the Argonauts, after the death of Tiphys.

ERIBŒ'A, a surname of Juno. *Homer. Il.* 5.——The mother of Ajax Telamon. *Sophocl. in Ajac.*—*Diou.* 4.—*Hygin.* fab. 97.—*Pindar. Isth.* 6.

Eribœ'a, a city of Macedonia. *Ptol.*

ERIB'OTES or **ERIBO'TES**, a man skilled in medicine, &c. *Orpheus in Argon.*

ERICA'TES, a man of Lycaonia. killed by Messapus in Italy. *Virg. Æn.* 10. v. 749.

ERICE'A, a village in the tribe of Ægeis at Athens. *Steph.*

ERICH'THO, a Thessalian woman, famous for her knowledge of poisonous herbs and medicine. *Lucan.* 6. v. 507.—*Ovid. Heroid.* 15. v. 139.——One of the furies. *Ovid. Ep.* 21. v. 151.

ERICHTHO'NIUS, the fourth king of Athens, was son of Vulcan. He was very deformed, and had the tails of serpents instead of legs. Minerva placed him in a basket, which she entrusted to the care of the daughters of Cecrops, with strict injunctions not to examine its contents. Aglaurus, one of the sisters, had the curiosity to open the basket, for which the goddess punished her indiscretion by making her jealous of her sister Herse. *Vid.* Herse. Erichthonius was young when he ascended the throne of Athens, and he reigned 50 years, and died B.C. 1437. The invention of chariots, and the manner of harnessing horses to draw them, are attributed to him. He was made a constellation after death under the name of Bootes. *Arati. Phœn.* 11.—*Fulgent.* 2. *Myt.*—*Lactant.* 3. c. 17.—*Eratosth.* 13.—*Palephat. de Inc.* 13.—*Ovid. Met.* 2. v. 553.—*Hygin. P. A.* 2. c. 13. fab. 166.—*Apollod.* 3. c. 14.—*Paus.* 4. c. 2.—*Virg. G.*

1. v. 205. l. 3. v. 113.——A son of Dardanus, who reigned in Troy, aud died 1374 B.C. after a long reign of about 75 years. He married Astyoche, daughter of the Simois, by whom he had Tros. *Homer. Il.* 20. v. 219.—*Apollod.* 3. c. 10.

ERICIN'IUM, a town of Sardinia. *Ptol.*——A town of Macedonia. *Liv.* 36. c. 17.

ERICU'SA, one of the Lipari isles, now Alicur. ——An island of the Ionian Sea, now Pachsu. *Plin.* 4. c. 12.

ERID'ANUS, one of the largest rivers of Italy, rising in the Alps, and, after receiving several considerable tributary streams, falling into the Adriatic by several mouths now called the Po. It was in its neighbourhood that the Heliades, the sisters of Phaæthon were changed into poplars, according to Ovid. Virgil calls it the king of all rivers, and Lucan compares it to the Rhine and Danube. An Eridanus is mentioned among the constellations. *Stat. Theb.* 12. v. 413.—*Apollon.* 4. *Arg.*—*Nonn. in. Dionys.* 38.—*Cic. in Arat.* 145.—*Claudian. de Cons. Hon.* 6. v. 175.—*Ovid. Met.* 2. fab. 3.—*Paus* 1. c. 3.—*Strab.* 5.—*Lucan.* 2. v. 409.—*Virg. G.* 1. v. 482.—*Æn.* 6. v. 669.

ERIG'ONE, a daughter of Icarius, who hanged herself when she heard that her father had been killed by some shepherds whom he had intoxicated. She was made a constellation, under the name of Virgo, and her dog, called Mæra (*Erigoneius canis*), became also a constitution called Canicula. Bacchus deceived her by changing himself into a beautiful grape. *Ovid. Met.* 6. fab. 4. *Fast.* 5. v. 723.—*Stat.* 11 *Theb.* v. 644 —*Virg. G.* 1. v. 33.—*Apollod.* 3. c. 14.—*Hygin.* fab. 1 & 24. *P. A.* 2. c. 4.—*Minut. Felix.* 21. c. 16.—*Servius in Virg. loco. cit.*——A daughter of Ægisthus and Clytæmnestra, who had by her brother Orestes, Penthilus, who shared the regal power with Tisamenus, the legitimate son of Orestes and Hermione. *Paus.* 2. c. 18.—*Paterc.* 1. c. 1.—*Tzetzes in Lycoph.*

ERIGONE'IUS. *Vid.* Erigone.

ERIGO'NUS, a river of Macedonia, now Vistrizza, dischargingitself into the Sinus Thermaicus. *Strab.*

ERIG'ONUS, a painter. *Plin.* 35. c. 11.

ERIGY'IUS, a Mitylenean, one of Alexander's officers. *Curt.* 6. c. 4.

ERIL'LUS, a philosopher of Carthage, contemporary with Zeno. *Diog.*

ER'IMUM, an inland city of the Oenotri. *Steph.*

ERINÆ'I, a people of Asiatic Sarmatia. *Ptol.*

ERIN'DES, a river of Asia, near Parthia. *Tacit. Ann.* 11. c. 10.

ERINE'SES, river of India flowing into the Ganges. *Arrian.*

ERIN'EUS, a city of Doris. *Strab.*——A city of Italy.——A city of Achaia.——A small river of Sicily, now Noti. *Thucyd.*

ERINIA'TES, a village of Megaris. *Steph.*

ERIN'NA, a poetess of Lesbos, intimate with Sappho. The few fragments which are inscribed to and preserved in Stobæus under her name, belong probably to another of the same name in a more modern age, as she there bestows praises on the city of Rome. These fragments are among the *Carmina novem poetarum fœmiuarum.* Antwerp, 8vo, 1568. *Propert.* 2 el. 3. v. 22.—*Plin.* 34. c. 8. —*Fabr. B. Gr.* 1. 2. c. 15.

ERIN'NYES, the Greek name of the Eumenides. *Vid.* Eumenides. *Virg. Æn.* 2. v. 337.

ERIN'NYS, a surname of Ceres, on account of her amour with Neptune under the form of a horse. She had a temple under this name on the banks of the Ladon in Arcadia, with a statue which represented her as holding a basket in the left hand, and a flambeau in the right. At Phygalia, her statue represented her as dressed in black, with a horse's head, and having a dove in one hand, and a dolphin in the other. *Apollod,* 3.—*Paus.* 8. c. 25 & 42.

ERIO'NIA, a region near Sardes. *Steph.*

ERIO'PIS or ERI'OPIS, a daughter of Medæa. *Paus.* 2. c. 3.

ERIPH'ANIS, a Greek woman, famous for her poetical compositions. She was extremely attached to the hunter Melampus, and to enjoy his company she accustomed herself to live in the woods, and to share with him the labours of the chase. *Athen.* 14.

ERIPH'IDAS, a Lacedæmonian, who being sent to suppress a sedition at Heraclea, assembled the people, and beheaded 500 of the ringleaders. *Diod.* 14.

ERIPHRY'SA, one of the Æolian islands. *Strab.* 6.

ER'IPHUS, an Athenian poet.

ERIPHY'LE, a sister of Adrastus, king of Argos, and wife of Amphiaraus, was daughter of Talaus and Lysimache. When her husband concealed himself that he might not accompany the Argives in their expedition against Thebes, where he knew he was to perish, Eriphyle suffered herself to be bribed by Polynices with a golden necklace, and discovered where Amphiaraus was. For this treacherous deed, Eriphyle was murdered by the hands of her son. *Vid.* Amphiaraus. *Virg. Æn.* 6. v. 445.—*Homer. Odyss.* 11.—*Cic. in Verr.* 4. c. 18. *Inv.* 1. c. 50.—*Apollod.* 1. c. 9. l. 3. 6 & 7.—*Hygin.* fab. 73.—*Paus.* 5. c. 17.—*Parthen. in Erot.* 26.—*Lactant. in Theb.* 2. v. 272.—*Propert.* 3. el. 13.

E'RIS, the goddess of discord among the Greeks. She was the same as the Discordia among the Latins. *Vid.* Discordia. *Hygin.* 92.

ERISICH'THON, a Thessalian, son of Triops, who derided Ceres, and cut down her groves. The goddess, to punish his impiety, afflicted him with continual hunger. He squandered all his possessions to gratify the cravings of his appetite, and at last devoured his own limbs for want of food. His daughter Metra had the power of transforming herself into whatever animal she pleased, and she made use of that artifice to maintain her father, who sold her, after which she assumed another shape, and became again his property. *Callimac. in Cerer.*—*Athen.* 10.—*Tzetzes in Lycophr.*—*Ovid. Met.* 8 fab. 18.

ERITHI'NI or ERITHY'NI, rocks in the Euxine Sea, on the coast of Bithynia. *Arrian. in Peripl.* —*Steph.*

ER'ITHUS, a son of Actor, killed by Perseus. *Ovid. Met.* 5.

ERIX'O, a Roman knight condemned by the people for having whipped his son to death. *Senec.* 1. *De Clem.* 14.

ERIZE'LI, a people of Phrygia. *Ptol.*

ERMÆ'A or HERMÆ'A, an island near Sardinia, now la Tavolara. *Ptol.*

EROC'ADE, part of the tribe Hippothoontis. *Steph.*

ERO'CHUS, a town of Phocis. *Paus.* 10. c. 3.

EROPÆ'I, a people of Africa Propria. *Ptol.*

ERO'PUS or ÆR'OPAS, a king of Macedonia, who, when in the cradle, succeeded his father Philip the First, B.C. 602. He made war against the Illyrians, whom he conquered. *Justin.* 7. c. 2.

E'ROS, a servant, of whom Antony demanded a sword to kill himself. Eros produced the instrument, but instead of giving it to his master killed himself in his presence. *Plut. in Anton.*——A comedian. *Cic. pro Rosc.* 2.——A son of Chronus or Saturn, god of love. *Vid.* Cupido.

EROS'TRATUS. *Vid.* Eratostratus.

EROTID'IA or ERO'TIA, a festival in honor of Eros, the god of love. It was celebrated by the Thespians every fifth year with sports and games, when musicians and others contended. If any quarrels or seditions had arisen among the people, it was then usual to offer sacrifices and prayers to the god, and to intreat him that he would totally remove them. *Eustath. Il.* 10.—*Plut. Erotic.*—*Paus. Bœotic.*

ER'PIS or HER'PIS, a city of Mauritania Tingita *Ptol.*

ERRANOB'OA, a river of India, flowing into the Ganges. *Plin.* 6. c. 18.

ERRU'CA, a town of the Volsci, in Italy. *Diod. Sic.*

ER'SE. *Vid.* Herse.

ER'THA, a city of Parthia, near the Euphrates. *Steph.*

ERX'IAS, a man who wrote a history of Colophon. He is perhaps the same person as Ergias, who wrote a history of Rhodes. *Athen.* 13.

ERY'ALUS, a Trojan chief killed by Patroclus. *Homer. Il.* 16. v. 411.

ERYAN'NOS, a river of Troas, flowing from mount Ida. *Plin.* 5. c. 30.

ERYBTUM, a town at the foot of mount Parnassus. *Diod. Sic.*

ERYCI'NA, a surname of Venus from mount Eryx, in Sicily, where she had a temple. She was also worshipped at Rome under this appellation. *Horat.* 1. od. 2. v. 33.—*Ovid. Fast.* 4. v. 874.—*Sueton. Claud.* 55.

ERYMAN'THIS, a surname of Callisto, as an inhabitant of Erymanthus. Arcadia was also known by that name.

ERYMAN'THUS, a mountain of Arcadia, with a river and town of the same name. It was there that Hercules killed a prodigious boar, which he carried on his shoulders to Eurystheus, who was so terrified at the sight that he hid himself in a brazen vessel. *Paus.* 8. c. 24.—*Virg. Æn.* 6. v. 802.—*Plin.* 4. c. 6.—*Cic. Tusc.* 2. c. 8. l. 4. c. 22. *Ovid. Met.* 2. v. 499.

ER'YMAS, a Trojan killed by Turnus. *Virg. Æn.* 9. v. 702.

ERYM'NÆ, a town of Thessaly. *Paus.* 8. c. 24. ——A town of Magnesia. *Plin.* 4. c. 9.——A town of Lycia, afterwards Tralles. *Steph.*

ERYM'NEUS, a peripatetic philosopher, who flourished B.C. 126.

ER'YMUS, a huntsman of Cyzicus. *Val. Flacc. Arg.* 3.

ERYS'ICE, a city of Acarnania, afterwards called Œneadæ. *Steph.*

ERYSICH'THON. Vid. Erisicthon.

ERYSTHE'A, a city of Cyprus, in which Apollo, surnamed Hylates, was worshipped. *Id.*

ERYTHE'A, a small island between Gades and Spain, where Geryon reigned. *Plin.* 4. c. 22.—*Mela*, 3. c. 6.—*Propert.* 4. el. 10. v. 1.—*Sil.* 16. v. 195.—*Ovid. Fast.* 5. v. 649.

Erythe'a, a daughter of Geryon. *Paus.* 10. c. 37.

ERYTHI'NI, a town of Paphlagonia. *Steph.*—*Strab.* 12.

ER'YTHRA, a city of Ionia, called also Cnopupolis.——A city of Lybia.——A city of Locris.——A city of Bœotia.——A city of Cyprus. *Steph.*

ERYTHRABO'LOS, a promontory of Libya. *Id.*

ER'YTHRÆ, a town of Ionia, opposite Chius, once the residence of a Sibyl. It was built by Neleus, the son of Codrus. *Paus.* 10. c. 12.—*Liv.* 44. c. 28. l. 38. c. 39.

ERYTHRÆ'UM MA'RE, a part of the ocean on the coast of Arabia. As it has a communication with the Persian Gulph and with that of Arabia or the Red Sea, it has often been mistaken by ancient writers, who by the word Erythræan understood indiscriminately either the Red Sea or the Persian Gulph. It received this name either from Erythras, or from the redness (ἐρυθρὸς, *ruber*) of its sands or waters. *Paus.* 1. c. 5. l. 10. c. 12.—*Curt.* 8. c. 9.—*Plin.* 6. c. 23.—*Herodot.* 1. c. 180 & 189. l. 3. c. 93. l. 4. c. 37.—*Mela*, 3. c. 8.—*Stat.* 4. *Sylv.* 6. v. 88.—*Tibull.* 3. el. 3. v. 17.

ER'YTHRAS, a son of Hercules. *Apollod.*——A son of Perseus and Andromeda, drowned in the Red Sea, which from him, as some suppose, was called Erythræum. *Arrian. Ind.* 6. c. 19.—*Mela*, 3. c. 7.

ERYTH'RION, a son of Athamas and Themistone, *Apollod.*

ER'YTHRON or **ERYTH'RON**, a place of Pentapolis in Africa, now Furcelli. *Ptol.*

ER'YTHROS or **ERYTH'ROS**, a place of Latium. *Strab.*

E'RYX, a son of Butes and Venus, who relying upon his strength, challenged all strangers to fight with him in the combat of the cæstus. Hercules accepted his challenge, after many had yielded to his superior skill, and Eryx was killed in the combat and buried on a mountain in Sicily, which was called after his name, and on which he had built a temple to Venus. *Virg. Æn.* 5. v. 24. 402. 759. *& Servius loco.*—*Hygin.* fab. 16 & 260.—*Dionys. Hal.* 1.—*Diod.* 4.—*Liv.* 22. c. 9 & 10. ——An Indian killed by his subjects for opposing Alexander, &c. *Curt.* 8. c. 11.

E'ryx, a mountain of Sicily, now Giuliano, near Drepanum, which received its name from Eryx, who was buried there. This mountain is described as so steep, that the houses which were built upon it seemed every moment ready to fall. Dædalus had enlarged the top, and enclosed it with a strong wall. He also consecrated there to Venus Erycina a golden heifer, which so much resembled life, that it seemed to exceed the power of art. The magnificent temple of the goddess was plundered by Hamilcar, general of Carthage. There were some festivals celebrated there by the inhabitants. *Vid.* Anagogia. *Ælian. H. A.* 4. c. 2. *V. H.* 1. c. 15.—*Ovid. Fast.* 4. v. 478.—*Hygin.* fab. 16 & 260.—*Liv.* 22. c. 9.—*Mela*, 2. c. 7.—*Paus.* 3. c. 16.

ERYX'O, the mother of Battus, who artfully killed the tyrant Learchus, who courted her. *Herodot.* 4. c. 160.

E'SAR, a town of the Ægyptians in Æthiopia. *Plin.* 6. c. 30.

ESBONI'TÆ, a people of Arabia Petræa. *Id.* 5, c. 11.

ES'CAMUS, a river of Mœsia, now Ischar. *Id.* 26. c. 3.

ESER'NIUS, a famous gladiator. *Cic.*

ESIONEN'SES or **ESIONE'Æ**, a people of Asia. *Strab.*

ESO'PIS, a city of Locris. *Id.* 6.

ESQUIL'IÆ or **ESQUILI'NUS MONS**, one of the seven hills of Rome, which was joined to the city by king Tullus. Birds of prey generally came to devour the dead bodies of criminals who had been executed there, and thence they were called *Esquilinæ alites.* It is now called M. di S. Maria Maggiore. *Liv.* 2. c. 11.—*Horat.* 5. epod. v. 100.—*Tac. Ann.* 2. c. 32.

ESSED'ONES, a people of Asia, above the Palus Mæotis, who ate the flesh of their parents mixed with that of cattle. They gilded the head, and kept it in their houses as a sacred relic. *Mela*, 2. c. 1.—*Plin.* 4. c. 12.

ES'SUI, a people of Gaul. *Cæs. in Com.*

ES'SUS, a city of Locris. *Steph.*

ESTIÆO'TIS, a district of Thessaly, placed by most geographers on the banks of the Peneus, before it is joined by the Enipeus.

ESTIO'NES, a people of Vindelicia.

ESUBIA'NI, a people of the Alps. *Plin.* 3. c. 20.

ESUB'OPES, a king of the Colchi. *Id.* 33. c. 3.

ES'ULA or **ÆS'ULUM**, a town of Latium, near Tibur. *Horat.* 3. od. 29. v. 6.

ESTIÆ'A or **ES'TIA**, solemn sacrifices to Vesta, of which it was unlawful to carry away any thing or communicate it to any body. *Hesych.*—*Diogenian.*—*Tarrhœus*,

ETAE'IS, a city of Laconia. *Steph.*

ETAX'ALOS, an island of Arabia Felix. *Plin.* 6. c. 28.

ETEAR'CHUS, a king of Oaxus in Crete. After the death of his wife he married a woman who rendered herself odious for her tyranny over her step-daughter Phronima. Etearchus imprudently gave ear to all the accusations which were brought against his daughter, and at last cruelly ordered her to be thrown into the sea. She had a son called Battus, who led a colony to Cyrene. *Herodot.* 4. c. 154.

ETELES'TA, a city of the Carpetani, in Spain. *Ptol.*

ETEOCLE'A, a tribe in Bœotia, *Paus.*—*Stat. Theb.* 7. v. 688.

ETE'OCLES, a son of Œdipus and Jocasta. After his father's death, it was agreed between him and his brother Polynices, that they should reign alternately each a year. Eteocles, by right of seniority, first ascended the throne of Thebes, but after the first year of his reign was expired he refused to give up the crown according to his agreement. Polynices, upon this, went to implore the assistance of Adrastus, king of Argos. He received the king's daughter in marriage, and was soon after assisted by a numerous army, headed by seven famous generals. These hostile preparations were forseen by Eteocles, who on his part did not remain inactive, but collected a powerful force to resist the invaders. He chose seven brave chiefs to oppose the seven leaders of the Argives, and stationed them at the seven gates of the city. He placed himself against his brother Polynices, and he opposed Menalippus to Tydeus, Polyphontes to Capaneus, Megareus to Eteoclus, Hyperbius to Parthenopæus and Lasthenes to Amphiaraus. Much blood was shed in light and unavailing skirmishes, and it was at last agreed between the two brothers that the war should be decided by single combat. They both fell in an engagement conducted with the most inveterate fury on either side, and it is even said that the ashes of these two unnatural brothers, who had been so inimical one to the other, separated themselves on the burning pile, as if, even after death, sensible of resentment, and hostile reconciliation. *Stat. Theb.* 12.—*Aus.* ep. 131. —*Ovid. Trist.* 5. el. 6.—*Apollod.* 3. c. 5, &c.—*Æschyl. Sept. contra Theb.*—*Eurip. in Phœnis.*—*Paus.* 5. c. 9. l. 9. c. 6.——A Greek, son of Andreus by a daughter of Leucon, king of Orchomenus, the first who raised altars to the Graces. *Paus.* 9. c. 34.

ETE'OCLUS, one of the seven chiefs of the army of Adrastus, in his expedition against Thebes, celebrated for his valour, disinterestedness, and magnanimity. He was killed by Megareus, the son of Creon, under the walls of Thebes. *Eurip. in Supp—Apollod.* 3. c. 6.——A son of Iphis.

ETEOCRE'TÆ, an ancient people of Crete. *Diod.*

ETEO'NUS, a town of Bœotia on the Asopus. *Stat. Theb.* 7. v. 266.

ETEO'NEUS, an officer at the court of Menelaus when Telemachus visited Sparta. He was son of Boethus. *Homer. Odyss.* 4. v. 22.

ETEONI'CUS, a Lacedæmonian general, who upon hearing that Callicratidas was conquered at Arginusæ, ordered the messengers who brought the intelligence to be crowned and to enter Mitylene in triumph. This so terrified Conon, who was besieging the town, that he concluded that the enemy had obtained some advantageous victory, and he immediately raised the siege. *Diod.* 13.—*Polyæn.* 1.

ETE'SIÆ, periodical northern winds of a gentle and mild nature, very common in Italy for five or six weeks in the months of spring and autumn. They were generally preceded by winds, which the ancients called Prodromi. *Plin.* 2. c. 47.—*Aul. Gell.* 2. c. 22.—*Seneca, Quæst Nat.* 5. c. 10. l. 11. c. 18. —*Cic. N. D.* 2. c. 53.—*Lucret.* 5. v. 741.

ETE'TA, a city of Upper Mœsia, now Recana. *Ptol.*

ETHAG'ARI, a people of the Seræ. *Id.*

ETHA'LION, one of the Tyrrhene sailors changed into dolphins for carrying away Bacchus. *Ovid. Met.* 3. v. 647.

ETHECU'SA, an island on the coast of Caria. *Plin.* 5. c. 31. Some copies read Hierussa.

ETHE'LEUM, a river of Asia, forming the boundary between Troas and Mysia. *Strab.*

ETHE'LUS, a man of Cyzicum of immense stature. *Val Flacc. Argon.* 3. v. 138.

ETHE'MON, a person killed at the marriage of Andromeda. *Ovid. Met.* 5. v. 163.

ETHI'NI, a people of Africa Propria. *Plin.* 5. c. 5.

ETHNESTÆ, a people of Thessaly. *Steph.*

ETH'ODA, a daughter of Amphion and Niobe.

E'TIAS, a daughter of Æneas. *Paus.* 3. c. 22.

ETI'NI, a people of Sicily. *Plin.* 3. c. 8.

E'TIS or E'TIA, a town of Peloponnesus. *Paus.* 3. c. 22.

ETRU'RIA. *Vid.* Hetruria.

ETRUS'CI, the inhabitants of Etruria. *Vid.* Hetruria.

ETRUS'CUS CL., a man raised from a mean condition to the dignity of knighthood by Vespasian, for his service in the war against the Jews. When banished by Domitian, he was accompanied into exile by his son, whose sorrow for his father's death is celebrated by Statius in a poem called Lacrymæ Etrusci. Etruscus built a bath at Rome, called by his own name, and highly commended. *Mart.* 7. ep. 39. l. 6. ep. 42.—*Stat.* 1. *Sylv.* 5. l. 3. *Sylv.* 3.

ET'YLUS, the father of Theocles. *Paus.* 6. c. 19.

EU'BAGES, certain priests held in great veneration among the ancient Gauls and Britons. *Vid.* Druidæ. *Strab.* 4.—*Marcell.* 15. c. 9.

EUBA'TAS or EU'RATOS, an athlete of Cyrene, whom the courtezan Lais in vain endeavoured to seduce. His wife erected a beautiful statue to his honour in his native town. *Ælian. V. H.* 10. c. 2. —*Paus. Eliac.* 1. c. 8.

EU'BIUS, an obscene writer. *Ovid. Trist.* 2. v. 415.

EUBŒ'A, the largest island in the Ægean Sea after Crete, now called Negroponte. It is separated from the continent of Bœotia by the narrow straits of the Euripus and was anciently known by the different names of Macris, Oche, Ellopia, Chalcis, Abantis, Asopis. It is 150 miles long, and 37 broad in the widest part, and 365 in circumference. The principal town was Chalcis, and it was reported that in the neighbourhood of Chalcis the island had been formerly joined to the continent. Eubœa was contributory to the Greeks; some of its cities, however, remained for some time independent. *Stat.* 5. *Sylv.* 3. 136.—*Propert.* 2. el. 26. v. 38.—*Virg. Æn.* 6. v. 17.—*Sil. It.* 11. v. 293. —*Plin.* 2. c. 18. l. 4. c. 12.—*Strab.* 10.—*Ovid. Met* 14. v. 155.

EUBŒ'A, one of the three daughters of the river Asterion, who was one of the nurses of Juno. *Paus.* 2. c. 17.——One of Mercury's mistresses.——A daughter of Thespius. *Apollod.* 2

EUBŒ'A, a town of Sicily near Hybla.

EUBŒ'US, a son of Hercules and Anthippe daughter of Thestius. *Apollod.* 2.——A poet of Parus, in age of Philip of Macedon, who wrote *parodiarum Homericarum libri sex*, now lost.

EUBO'ICUS, belonging to Eubœa. The epithet is also applied to the country of Cumæ, in Italy, because that city was built by a colony from Chalcis, in Eubœa. *Ovid. Fast.* 4. v. 257.—*Virg. Æn.* 6. v. 2. l. 9. v. 710.

EU'BOTE or EUBO'TE, a daughter of Thespius. *Apollod.*

EU'BOTES or EUBO'TES, a son of Hercules. *Id.* 2.

EUBU'LE, an Athenian virgin, daughter of Leon, sacrificed with her sisters, by order of the oracle of Delphi, for the safety of her country, which had been visited by a dreadful famine. *Ælian. V. H.* 12. c. 18.—*Suidas. verb. Leocorion.*

EUBU'LIDES, a philosopher of Miletus, pupil and successor to Euclid. Demosthenes was one of his pupils, and by his advice and encouragement to perseverance, he was enabled to conquer the difficulty which he felt in pronouncing the letter R. He severely attacked the doctrines of Aristotle. *Diog. Laert. in Euclid.*—*Athen.* 8.—*Phot. Cod.* 265. ——An historian, who wrote an account of Socrates, and of Diogenes. *Laertius.*——A famous statuary of Athens. His son, called Euchir, was equally celebrated. *Paus.* 8. c. 14.——An archon at Athens. Ol. 96. an. 3.

EUBU'LUS, an Athenian orator, rival to Demosthenes.——An Athenian in the 101st Olympiad, who wrote plays, 50 of which are mentioned by *Athenæus*, 24 by *Suidas*, and more by *Meursius.*——An historian, who wrote a voluminous account of Mithras. *Porphyr. in Nymph. Antr.*——A son of Carmanor, father of Carme. *Paus.* 2. c. 30.——A philosopher of Alexandria, in Ægypt. *Diog. Laert. in Timon.* l. 9.

EUBURIA'TES, a people of Liguria, vanquished by Fulvius. *Plin.* 3. c. 5.

EUCE'RUS, a man of Alexandria, accused of adultery with Octavia, that Nero might have occasion to divorce her. *Tacit. Ann.* 14. c. 60.

EUCHE'NOR, a son of Ægyptus and Arabia. *Apollod.*——A son of Polyidus, who was told that he should either die of a lingering disease in his palace, or gloriously perish in war. He preferred an honorable death, and accompanied the Greeks to Troy, where he was slain. *Homer. Il.* 13. v. 663.

EU'CHIDES, an Athenian, who walked to Delphi and returned the same day, a journey of about 107 miles. The object of this extraordinary journey was to obtain some sacred fire.

EUCLI'DES, a native of Megara, disciple of Socrates, B.C. 404. When the Athenians had forbidden all the people of Megara on pain of death to enter their city, Euclides disguised himself in women's clothes that he might attend the lectures of Socrates. *Aul. Gell.* 6. c. 10.—*Diog. in Socrate.*——A mathematician of Alexandria, who flourished 300 B.C. He distinguished himself by his writings on music and geometry, but particularly by fifteen books of problems and theorems, with demonstrations on the elements of mathematics, in which he digests with great judgment and precision, into regularity and order, all the fundamental principles of the pure mathematics, taught by Thales, Pythagoras, Eudoxus, and other illustrious philosophers. This most valuable work has been greatly mutilated by commentators. Euclid was so respected in his lifetime that king Ptolemy became one of his pupils. He established a school at Alexandria, which attained such great celebrity that, from his age to the time of the Saracen conquest, no mathematician was found but what had studied at Alexandria. He was so respected that Plato, himself a mathematician, being asked concerning the building of an altar at Athens, referred his enquirers to the illustrious mathematician of Alexandria. The latest edition of Euclid's writings is that of Gregory, fol. Oxon. 1703. *Val. Max.* 8. c. 12.—*Cic. de Orat.* 3. c. 33. 72.—*Fabric. Bib. Gr.* 3. c. 4.—*Gell.* 6. c. 10.

EU'CLUS, a prophet of Cyprus, who is said to have foretold the birth and greatness of the poet Homer. *Paus.* 10. c. 12 & 25.

EU'CRATE, one of the Nereides. *Apollod.*

EU'CRATES, the father of Procles the historian. *Paus.* 2. c. 21.—*Athen.* 13.
EUCRATID'IA, a city of the Bactri. *Steph. ex Strab.* 1. 11.
EU'CRATIS, a king of Bactria, who basely conspired against his father's life, that he might enjoy the sovereign power alone. *Alex. ab Alex.* 2. c. 6.
EU'CRITUS. *Vid.* Evephenus.
EUCTE'MON, a Greek of Cumæ, exposed to great barbarities. *Curt.* 5. c. 5.——An astronomer, who flourished B.C. 431. He was contemporary with Meton, and assisted him in his solar observations *Ælian. Var. Hist.* 10. c. 7.—*Voss. de Math.* c. 33. sect. 11.
EUCTRE'SII, a people of Peloponnesus. *Xenoph.*
EUDÆ'MON, a general of Alexander the Great. ——A Greek poet of Pelusium, coeval with Libanius the rhetorician. *Suidas.*——A name of Arabia Felix. *Mela,* l. 2.
EUDAM'IDAS, a son of Archidamus the Fourth, brother to Agis the Fourth. He succeeded to the Spartan throne, after his brother's death, B.C. 330. *Paus.* 3. c. 10.——A son of Archidamus, king of Sparta, who succeeded to the throne B.C. 268. ——The commander of a garrison stationed at Trœzene by Craterus. *Polyæn.*
EU'DAMUS or EUDA'MUS, a son of Agelaus, of the family of the Heraclidæ. He succeeded his father as king of Corinth.——A learned naturalist and philosopher.
EUDE'MIA, an island of the Ægean Sea. *Plin.* 4. c. 12.
EUDE'MUS, the physician of Livia, the wife of Drusus. He was employed to administer poison to Drusus, and was afterwards put to death by order of Tiberius. *Tacit. Ann.* 4. c. 3.——An orator of Megalopolis, preceptor to Philopœmen. *Plut.*——An historian of Naxus. *Voss. de Hist. Gr.* l. 3. *De Math.* c. 32.——A philosopher of Cyprus, said to have been intimate with Aristotle. *Cic. Div.* 1. c. 25.——An archon at Athens, Ol. 106. an. 3.
EUDIP'NE, an island of Libya. *Steph.*
EUDI'PUS, a town of Cappadocia. *Ptol.*
EUDIX'ATA, a town of Armenia Major. *Id.*
EU'DO, a river of Caria. *Plin.* 5. c. 29.
EUDO'CIA, a daughter of the sophist Leontius of Athens, born about 400 A.D. She was so well versed in philosophy, that her father, as if foreboding her future greatness, left his property to his sons, reserving for her only a small portion. The injustice of this treatment made her appeal to the court for protection, and the friendship of Pulcheria, sister of Theodosius, raised her to eminence and distinction, so that from a heathen and a subject, she at last became a Christian and an empress. Her high rank did not draw her from literary pursuits, which at last unfortunately proved her misery. Theodosius gave her an apple of extraordinary size, which from pure regard, she presented to Paulinus the philosopher, who immediately considered it as a gift worthy of the emperor. This circumstance roused the suspicious of Theodosius, and Eudocia, on being questioned, had the weakness say she had eaten the apple, which being proved a falsehood by the production of the fruit, caused her disgrace. Some say, that after spending some time in exile in Palestine, she was reconciled to Theodosius, who was convinced of her innocence and virtue. She died A.D. 460, leaving behind her several pieces in prose and verse, on literary and theological subjects. *Sax. Onom.* 1. p. 486.—*Voss. de Poet. Gr.* c. 9.
EUDOC'IMUS, a man who appeased a mutiny among some soldiers by telling them that a hostile army was in sight. *Polyæn.* 5.
EUDO'RA, one of the Nereides. *Apollod.*——One of the Atlantides. *Hygin.* 192.
EUDO'RUS, a son of Mercury and Polymela, who went to the Trojan war with Achilles. *Homer. Il.* 16. v. 179.——A peripatetic philosopher of Alexandria, who wrote, among other things, a treatise on the Nile, mentioned by *Strabo.*
EUDO'SES, a people of Germany.
EUDOX'I SPEC'ULA, a place in Ægypt. *Strab.* l. 2.
EUDOX'IA, the wife of the emperor Arcadius.——A daughter of Theodosius the younger, who married the emperor Maximus, and invited Genseric the Vandal over into Italy. *Procop.* &c.
EUDOX'US, a son of Æschines of Cnidus, who studied under Plato, and distinguished himself by his knowledge of astrology, medicine, and geometry. He was the first who regulated the year among the Greeks, and first brought from Ægypt the celestial sphere and the knowledge of regular astronomy. He died in his 52nd year, B.C. 352. *Lucan.* 10. v. 187.—*Cic. Div.* 2. c. 42.—*Diog.*—*Petron.* 88.—*Sax. Onom.* 1. p. 69.—*Fabr. B. Gr.* 3. c. 5. ——A native of Cyzicus, who sailed all round the coast of Africa from the Red Sea, and after a long and perilous voyage, returned by the columns of Hercules into the Mediterranean. *Plin.* 2. c. 67.—*Strab.* 2 & 8.——A Sicilian, son of Agathocles.——A physician. *Diog.*
EU'DRAPA, a town of Macedonia. *Ptol.*
EU'ELPIS, an historian of Carystus. *Porph.* l. 2. *de abstinent.*
EUEMER'IDAS, an historian of Cnidus. *Plut. de Flum.*
EU'GAMON, an historian of Cyrene, who wrote a book on Thesprotion. *Clem. Strom.* 6. *Eusebius,* 10. *Præp. Evang.* calls him Eugrammon.
EUGA'NEI, a people of Italy, on the borders of the Adriatic, who, upon being expelled by the Trojans seized upon a part of the Alps. *Sil.* 8. v. 604.—*Liv.* 1. c. 1.
EUGE'NIUM, a city of Illyria. *Liv.* 1. c. 1.
EUGE'NIUS, a usurper of the imperial title after the death of Valentinian the Second. A.D. 392.
EU'GEON, an ancient historian of Greece before the Peloponnesian war. *Dion. Hal.*
EUGE'RIA, a goddess to whom the Romans sacrificed at the approach of child-birth. *Fest. de Verb. Sig.*—*Arnob. adv. gentes,* &c.
EUGI'A, a small region of Arcadia. *Steph.*
EUGO'A, a town of Upper Æthiopia. *Plin.* 6. c. 29.
EUHEM'ERUS. *Vid.* Evemerus.
EU'HYDRA, a city of Phœnicia. *Plin.* 5. c. 20.
EUHYD'RIUM, a city of Thessaly. *Livy,* 32. c. 13.
EULÆ'US, now Tritiri, a river of Asia, falling into the Persian Gulph. It is also called Choaspes. *Plin.* 6. c. 23.
EULIM'ENE, one of the Nereides.
EU'MACHUS, a Campanian who wrote a history of Annibal. *Athen.*—*Voss. de Hist. Gr.* l. 3.
EUMÆ'US, a herdsman and steward of Ulysses, who knew his master at his return home from the Trojan war after 20 years' absence, and assisted him in removing Penelope's suitors. He was originally the son of the king of Scyrus, and upon being carried away by pirates, was sold as a slave to Laertes. *Homer. Odyss.* 13. v. 403. l. 14. v. 3. l. 15. v. 288. l. 16. v. 1. l. 17, 18, &c.
EUMA'THIUS, the author of "the loves of Ismenus and Ismenia," which work has been attributed to Eustathius. *Voss. de Hist. Gr.* l. 4. c. 19.
EUME'DA, an auxiliary of Perses against Æetes. *Val. Flacc. Argon.* 6. v. 143.
EUME'DES, a Trojan, son of Dolon, who came to Italy with Æneas, where he was killed by Turnus. *Virg. Æn.* 12. v. 346.—*Ovid. Trist.* 3 el. 4. v. 27.
EUME'LIS, the patronymic of Parthenope as daughter of Eumelus. *Stat.* 4. *Sylv.* 8. v. 49.
EUME'LUS, a son of Admetus, king of Pheræ, in Thessaly. He went to the Trojan war in eleven ships at the head of the inhabitants of the neighbouring town, and he boasted in the possession of two of the fleetest horses in the Grecian army, which Apollo himself had fed in the mountain of Thessaly. He distinguished himself in the games exhibited by Achilles in honor of Patroclus. *Homer. Il.* 2. v. 221 & 270. l. 23. v. 288.——A man whose daughter was changed into a bird. *Ovid. Met.* 7. v. 390.——A man contemporary with Triptolemus, of whom he learned the art of agriculture. *Paus.* 7. c. 18.——One of the followers of Æneas, who first informed his friends that his fleet had been set on fire by the Trojan women. *Virg. Æn.* 5. v. 665.——One of the Bacchiadæ, who wrote among other things, a poetical history of Corinth, B.C. 750, of which a small fragment is still extant. *Athen.* 2.—*Varro. de R.R.* 2. c. 5.—*Paus.* 2. c. 1. *Voss. de Hist. Gr.* 1. l. c. 5, &c.——A king of the Cimmerian Bosporus, who died B.C. 304.
EU'MENES, a Greek officer in the army of Alexander, son of a charioteer. He was the best entitled, for military prudence and acknowledged abilities, of all the officers of Alexander, to succeed after the death of his master. He conquered Paphlagonia and Cappadocia, of which he obtained the government, till the power and jealousy of Antigonus obliged him to abandon his possessions. To sup-

port himself against his enemies he joined his forces to those of Perdiccas, and defeated Craterus and Neoptolemus. Neoptolemus perished by the hands of Eumenes. When Craterus had been killed during the war, his remains received an honorable funeral from the hand of the conqueror; and Eumenes, after weeping over the ashes of a man who once was his dearest friend, sent his remains to his relations in Macedonia. Eumenes afterwards fought against Antipater, and conquered him, and after the death of Perdiccas, his ally, his arms were directed against Antigonus, by whom he was conquered, chiefly by the treacherous conduct of some of his officers. This fatal battle obliged him to disband the greatest part of his army to secure himself a retreat, and he fled with only 700 faithful attendants to Nora, a fortified place on the confines of Cappadocia, where he was soon besieged by the conqueror. He supported the siege for a year with courage and resolution, but some disadvantageous skirmishes so reduced him, that his soldiers, grown desperate, and bribed by the offers of the enemy, had the infidelity to betray him into the hands of Antigonus. The conqueror, either from shame or remorse, had not the courage to visit the captive Eumenes; but when he was asked by his officers, in what manner he wished him to be kept, he answered, keep him carefully as you would keep a lion. This severe command was obeyed; but the asperity of Antigonus vanished in a few days, and Eumenes, delivered from the weight of chains, was permitted to enjoy the company of his friends. Antigonus even doubted whether he should not restore to his liberty a man with whom he had lived in the greatest intimacy while both were subservient to the command of Alexander, and these secret emotions of pity and humanity were not a little increased by the petitions of his son Demetrius for the release of Eumenes. But the calls of ambition unhappily prevailed; and when Antigonus recollected what an active enemy he then held in his power, he ordered Eumenes to be put to death in the prison, though some imagine that he was murdered without the knowledge of his conqueror, B.C. 315. Such was the end of a man who raised himself to eminence and to sovereign power by merit alone. His skill in public exercises first recommended him to the notice of Philip, and under Alexander his attachment and fidelity to the royal person, and particularly his military accomplishments, promoted him to the rank of a general. Even his enemies revered him; and Antigonus, by whose orders he perished, honored his remains with a splendid funeral, and conveyed his ashes to his wife and family in Cappadocia It has been observed, that Eumenes had such a universal influence over the successors of Alexander, that none during his lifetime presumed to assume the title of king: and it does not a little redound to his honor that the wars which he carried on were not from private or interested motives, but for the support and welfare of his deceased benefactor's children. *Plut. & C. Nep. in Vitâ.—Diod.* 29.—*Justin.* 13.—*Curt.* 16.—*Arrian.*——A king of Pergamus, who succeeded his uncle Philetærus on the throne, B.C. 263. He made war against Antiochus son of Seleucus, and enlarged his possessions by seizing upon many of the cities of the kings of Syria. He lived in alliance with the Romans, and made war against Prusias, king of Bithynia. He was a great patron of learning, but unfortunately much given to wine. He died of excess in drinking, after a reign of 22 years. He was succeeded by Attalus. *Strab.* 15.——A celebrated orator of Athens about the beginning of the fourth century. Some of his harangues and orations are extant.——An historical writer in Alexander's army. *Athen.—Ælian.* 3. c. 23.

EU'MENES the Second, succeeded his father Attalus on the throne of Asia and Pergamus. His kingdom was small and poor, but he rendered it powerful and opulent, and his alliance with the Romans did not a little contribute to the increase of his dominions after the victories obtained over Antiochus the Great. He carried his arms against Prusias and Antigonus, and died B.C. 159, after a reign of 38 years, leaving the kingdom to his son Attalus the Second. He has been admired for his benevolence and magnanimity, and his love of learning greatly enriched the famous library af Pergamus, which had been founded by his predecessors in imitation of the Alexandrian collection of the Ptolemies. His brothers were so attached to him and devoted to his interest, that they enlisted among his body guards to show their fidelity. *Strab.* 13. —*Justin.* 31 & 34.—*Polyb.*

EUME'NIA or EUMENI'A, a city of Phrygia, built by Attalus in honor of his brother Eumenes.——A city of Thrace. *Plin.* 4. c. 11.——A city of Caria. *Plin.* 5. c. 29.——A city of Hyrcania.

EUMEN'IDES, a man mentioned by *Ovid*, 3 *Trist.* el. 4. v. 27. Read Eumedes.——A name given to the Furies by the ancients, particularly by the Sicyonians. They sprang from the drops of blood which flowed from the wound which Cœlus received from a scythe by the hands of his son Saturn. According to others, they were daughters of the earth, and conceived from the blood of Saturn. Some make them daughters of Acheron and Night, or Pluto and Proserpine, or Chaos and Terra, according to Sophocles, or as Epimenides reports, of Saturn and Evonyme. According to the most received opinions, they were three in number, Tisiphone, Megara, and Alecto, to which some add Nemesis. *Plutarch* mentions only one called Adrasta, daughter of Jupiter and Necessity. They were supposed to be the ministers of the vengeance of the gods, always employed in punishing the guilty upon earth, as well as in the infernal regions. They inflicted their vengeance upon earth by wars, pestilence, and dissensions, and by the secret stings of conscience; and in hell they punished the guilty by continual flagellation and repeated torments. They were also called Furiæ, Erinyes, and Diræ, and they received the appellation of Eumenides, which signifies benevolence and compassion, after they had ceased to persecute Orestes, who in gratitude offered them sacrifices, and erected a temple in honor of their divinity. Their worship was almost universal, and the people presumed not to mention their names, or to fix their eyes upon their temples. They were honored with sacrifices and libations, and in Achaia they had a temple, which, when entered by any one guilty of crime, suddenly rendered him furious, and deprived him of the use of his reason. In their sacrifices, the votaries used branches of cedar and of alder, hawthorn, saffron, and juniper, and the victims were generally turtle-doves and sheep, with libations of wine and honey. The Eumenides were generally represented with a grim and frightful aspect, with a black aud bloody garment, and serpents wreathing round their head instead of hair. They held a burning torch in one hand, and a whip of scorpions in the other, and were always attended by terror, rage, paleness, and death. In hell they were seated around Pluto's throne, as the ministers of his vengeance. *Æschyl. in Eumen.—Sophocl. in Œdip. Col. & Schol. loca.—Lycoph. in Cass. & Tzetzes*, v. 406 & 1137.—*Hesiod Th.* 185.—*Apollod.* 1. c. 1.—*Orpheus, Hymn. in Eum.—Lactant. apud. Theb.* 1. v. 477.—*Servius in Æn.* 4. v. 609. l. 6. v. 250 & 375.—*Ælian. H. A.* 10. c. 33.—*Eustath. in Il.* 1.—*L. Gyrald. Hist. D.* 6.—*Nonnus Dionys.* 44.—*Ovid. Met.* 4 fab. 13. l. 10. fab. 10.—*Catull. de Nupt. Pel.—Seneca in Hercul. Fur.* 87. *In Medea*, 13.—*Stat. Theb.* 1. v. 91. l. 4. v. 486. l. 5. v. 67.—*Cic. in Pis.* 20. *Pro. Rosc.* 24. *De N. D.* 3. c. 18.—*Sueton. in Ner.* 34.—*Isidor.* 8 *Orig.* 2.—*Horat.* 2. od. 13.—*Virg. G.* 4. v. 481. *Æn.* 4. v. 469, &c.

EUMENID'IA festivals in honor of the Eumenides, called by the Athenians σεμναὶ θεαί, *venerable goddesses.* They were celebrated once every year with sacrifices of pregnant ewes, with offerings of cakes made by the most eminent youths, and with libations of honey and wine. At Athens none but free-born citizens, such as had led a life the most virtuous and unsullied, were admitted to the celebration, and such only were accepted by the goddesses who punished all sorts of wickedness in a very severe manner. *Philo.—Paus. Bæotic.*

EUME'NIUS, a Trojan killed by Camilla during the Rutulian war. *Virg. Æn.* 11. v. 666.——An orator at the court of Constantius Chlorus, author of a panegyric spoken before the emperor, still preserved among the "Panegyrici Veteres."

EUMOL'PE, one of the Nereides. *Apollod.*

EUMOL'PIDÆ, the priests of Ceres at the celebration of her festivals of Eleusis. All causes relating to impiety or profanation were referred to their judgment, and their decisions, though occasionally severe, were considered as generally impartial. The Eumolpidæ were descended from Eumolpus, a king of Thrace, who was made priest of Ceres by Erechtheus, king of Athens. He became so powerful after his appointment to the priesthood, that he maintained a war against Erechtheus. This war proved fatal to both; Erechtheus and Eumolpus were both killed, and peace was re-established between their descendants, on condition that the priesthood should ever remain in the family of Eumolpus, and the regal power in the house of Erechtheus. The priesthood continued in the family of Eumolpus for 1200 years; a remarkable circumstance, because he who was once appointed to the holy office was obliged to remain in perpetual celibacy. *Paus.* 2. c. 14.—*Alex. ad Alex.* 4. c. 6.—*Meurs. Gr. Fer.* 13.—*Schol. Persius*, 5.

EUMOL'PUS, a king of Thrace, son of Neptune and Chione. He was thrown into the sea by his mother, who wished to conceal her shame from her father. Neptune saved his life, and carried him into Æthiopia, where he was brought up by Amphitrite, and afterwards by a woman of the country, one of whose daughters he married. An act of violence offered to his sister-in-law obliged him to leave Æthiopia, and he fled, with his son Ismarus, to Thrace, where he married the daughter of Tegyrius, the king of the country. This connection with the royal family rendered him ambitious; he ungratefully conspired against his father-in-law, and fled, when the conspiracy was discovered, to Attica, where he was initiated into the mysteries of Ceres of Eleusis, and made hierophantes or high priest. He was afterwards reconciled to Tegyrius, and inherited his kingdom. He made war against Erechtheus, the king of Athens, and perished in battle. *Vid.* Eumolpidæ. *Apollod.* 2. c. 5, &c.—*Hygin.* fab. 73.—*Diod.* 5.—*Paus.* 2. c. 14. *Suidas* and the *Scholiast* of *Pindar* consider Eumolpus as the son of the poet Musæus, and attribute some poetical pieces to his pen, especially a work on the festivals of Ceres.

EUMON'IDES, a Theban, &c. *Plut.*

EU'NÆ, a city of Caria.——A city of Argolis. *Steph.*

EUNÆ'US, a son of Jason, by Hypsipyle, daughter of Thoas. *Homer. Il.* 7.—*Hygin.* 15 & 273.—*Stat. Theb.* 6. v. 340, &c.

EUNA'PIUS, a physician, sophist, and historian, born at Sardis. He flourished in the reign of Valentinian and his successors, and wrote a history of the Cæsars, of which few fragments remain. His life of the philosophers of his age is still extant. It is composed with fidelity and elegance, precision and correctness. It was edited by Commelin, 8vo, Heidelburg, 1596; reprinted at Geneva, 1616. *Sax Onom.* 1. p. 457.—*Fabr. B. Gr.* 5. c. 5.

EUNI'CUS, a statuary mentioned by *Pliny*, 34. c. 8.

EUNO'MIA, one of the Horæ, daughter of Juno. *Apollod.*

EU'NOMUS, a son of Pyrtanes, who succeeded his father on the throne of Sparta. *Paus.* 2. c. 36.——A famous musician of Locris, rival to Ariston, over whom he obtained a musical prize at Delphi, after he had been wonderfully assisted by a cicada, whose melodious voice is said to have supplied the loss of one of the seven strings of his lyre which he had broken. *Conon. Narratt.* 5.—*Strab.* 6.——A man killed by Hercules. *Apollod.*——A Thracian, who advised Demosthenes not to be discouraged by his ill success in his first attempts to speak in public. *Plut. in Dem.*——The father of Lycurgus, killed by a kitchen knife. *Plut in Lyc.*

EU'NON, a king of the Adorsi, in the time of Claudius. *Tac. Ann.* 12. c. 15. Also Euno'nes.

EUNOS'TI, a harbour of Ægypt, near Pharus. *Strab.*

EU'NUS, a Syrian slave, who inflamed the minds of the servile multitude, and incited them to rebellion by pretended inspiration and enthusiasm. Oppression and misery induced 2,000 slaves to join his cause, and such was the popularity of his opposition to Rome, that he soon saw himself at the head of 60,000 men. With such a force he defeated the Roman armies, till Perpenna obliged his famished forces to surrender, and exposed on a cross the greatest part of his followers, B.C. 132. *Plut. in Sert.*—*Flor.* 3. c. 19.

EUONYM'IA, a city of Caria.——A village of the tribe Erechtheis. *Steph.*

EUON'YMUS, one of the Lipari isles. *Plin.* 3. c. 9.

EU'ORAS, a grove of Laconia. *Paus.* 3. c. 10.

EUPA'GIUM, a town of Peloponnesus. *Diod.*

EUPAL'AMON, one of the hunters of the Calydonian boar. *Ovid. Met.* 8. v. 360.

EUPAL'AMUS, the father of Dædalus and of Mætiadusa. *Apollod.* 3. c. 15.—*Hygin.* fab. 244.

EUPA'LIA, EUPA'LION or EUPA'LIUM, a city of Locris. *Steph.*

EU'PATOR, a son of Antiochus. The surname of Eupator was given to many of the Asiatic princes, such as Mithridates, &c. *Strab.* 12.

EUPATO'RIA or EUPATO'RIUM, a town of Paphlagonia, built by Mithridates, and called afterwards Pompeiopolis, by Pompey. *Plin.* 6. c. 2.——A town called Magnopolis, in Pontus, on the river Iris, now Tchenikeh. *Strab.* 12.

EUPA'TRIA, a city of the Lydians, *Steph.*

EUPEI'THES, a prince of Ithaca, father of Antinous. In the former part of his life he had fled before the vengeance of the Thesprotians, whose territories he had laid waste in the pursuit of some pirates. During the absence of Ulysses he was one of the most importunate lovers of Penelope. *Homer Odyss.* 16.

EU'PHAES, succeeded Androcles on the throne of Messenia, and in his reign the first Messenian war began. He died B.C. 730. *Paus.* 4. c. 5 & 6.

EUPHAN'TUS, son of Eubulides, a poet and historian of Olynthus, preceptor to Antigonus, king of Macedonia. *Diog. in Eucl.* 1. 2.

EUPHE'ME, a woman who was nurse to the Muses, and mother of Crocus by Pan. *Paus.*—*Hygin.* 224. *P.A.* 2. c. 27.

EUPHE'MIUS, an author mentioned by *Stephanus* in 'Αφόρμιον. Probably he was the Euphemus mentioned by *Pollux*, 10. c. 27. *Voss.*

EUPHE'MUS, a son of Neptune and Europa, who was in the number of the Argonauts, and of the hunters of the Calydonian boar. He was so swift and light that he could run over the sea almost without wetting his feet. *Pindar. Pyth.* 4. & *Schol. loco.*—*Apollod.* 1. c. 9.—*Hygin.* fab. 14 & 157.—*Apollon. Arg.* 1. v. 179. & *Scholiast. loco.*—*Paus.* 5. c. 17.——One of the Greek captains before Troy. *Homer. Il.* 2. v. 323.

EUPHOR'BENI, a people of Phrygia Major. *Plin.* 5. c. 29.

EUPHOR'BUS, a famous Trojan, son of Panthous, as skilful in guiding the chariot as wielding the lance. He was the first who wounded Patroclus, whom Hector killed. He perished by the hand of Menelaus, who hung up his shield in the temple of Juno at Argos as a monument of his victory. Pythagoras, the founder of the doctrine of the metempsychosis, or transmigration of souls, affirmed that he had formerly been Euphorbus, and that his soul recollected many exploits which had been done while it animated the Trojan's body. As a further proof of his assertion, he, at first sight, pointed out the shield of Euphorbus in the temple of Juno. *Horat.* 1. od. 28. v. 11.—*Ovid. Met.* 15, v. 160.—*Paus.* 2. c. 17.—*Homer. Il.* 16. v. 808. l. 17. v. 9.—*Diog. Laert.* 8. c. 1.—*Lactant. de Fals. Sap.* 18.——A physician of Juba, king of Mauritania.

EUPHO'RION, son of Polymnestus, a Greek poet of Chalcis in Eubœa, in the age of Antiochus the Great. Tiberius took him for his model for correct writing, and was so partial to his works that he hung his pictures in all the public libraries of Rome, and Virgil himself did not disdain to imitate and copy him in his eclogues. He died in his 56th year, B.C. 220. *Cicero, de Nat. D.* 2. c. 64, calls him *Obscurum.*—*Columell. de R.R.*—*Parthen.*—*Erot.*—*Varr. de R.R.*—*Virg. Ec.* 10. v. 50.—*Servius in loco, & in Ecl.* 6. v. 72.—*Quintil.* 10, c. 1.——The name of the father and son of Æschylus. *Suidas.*

EUPHRA'NOR, a famous painter and sculptor of Corinth, who wrote on symmetry and the art of coloring. His most famous paintings were the 12 gods, the battle of Mantinea, and Theseus. *Paus.* 1. c. 3.—*Quintil.* 12. c. 10.—*Plin.* 34. c. 8.—This name was common to many Greeks.

EUPHRAN'TA, a city of Libya. *Steph.*

EUPHRA'TES, a disciple of Plato, who governed Macedonia with absolute authority in the reign of Perdiccas, but rendered himself odious by his cruelty and pedantry. After the death of Perdiccas, he was cruelly put to death by Parmenio.——A stoic philospher in the age of Adrian, who destroyed himself, with the emperor's permission, in order that he might escape the impending miseries of old age, A.D. 118. *Dio.*

Euphra'tes, a large and celebrated river of Mesopotamia, rising from mount Taurus in Armenia, and discharging itself with the Tigris into the Persian gulph after a course of about 500 miles. It is very rapid in its course, and passes through the middle of the city of Babylon. It inundates the country of Mesopotamia at a certain season of the year, rising about sixteen feet, and like the Nile, happily fertilises the adjacent fields. Cyrus changed the course of its waters, when he besieged Babylon, and marched through the dry channel into the midst of the terrified city. *Strab.* 11.—*Mela*, 1. c. 2. l. 3. c. 8.—*Plin.* 5. c. 24.—*Ptol.* 5. c. 13.—*Stat. Theb.* 8. v. 290.—*Virg. G.* 1. v. 509. l. 4. v. 560.

EU'PHRON, an aspiring man of Sicyon, who enslaved his country by bribery. *Diod.* 15.

EUPHROS'YNE, one of the Graces, sister to Aglaia and Thalia. *Paus.* 9. c. 35. [The finest group of these three sisters is at Sienna, in the Cathedral.]

EUPLÆ'A, a small island of the Tyrrhene Sea, near Neapolis. *Stat.* 3. *Sylv.* 1. Also Euplœ'a.

EU'POLIS, a comic poet of Athens, who flourished 435 years, B.C. and severely lashed the vices and immorality of his age. His poetical abilities early displayed themselves, for it is said that he had composed 17 dramatical pieces at the age of 17. Seven of his compositions were rewarded with the prize in the public theatres of Athens. Some suppose that Alcibiades put Eupolis to death because he had ridiculed him in a comedy which he had written against the Baptæ, the priests of the goddess Cotytto, and the impure ceremonies of their worship; but *Suidas* maintains that he perished in a sea-fight between the Athenians and the Lacedæmonians in the Hellespont, and that on that account his countrymen, lamenting his untimely fate, decreed, that no poet should ever after go to war. *Horat.* 1. sat. 4. l. 2. sat. 10.—*Cic. ad Attic.* 6. ep. 1.—*Ælian.*—*Aul. Gell.* 1. c. 15.—*Plin.* 1. ep. 20.—*Quintil.* 10. c. 1.—*Plato apud Gyrald. de P. Hist.* 6.——A native of Elis, victor at Olympia, in the 96th Olympiad.

EUPOM'PUS, a geometrician of Macedonia.——A painter. *Plin.* 34. c. 8.

EU'PORUS, a faithful servant of Gracchus. *Macrob. Sat.* 1. c. 11.

EUPYRID'Æ, a village of the tribe Leontis. *Steph.*

EURA'NIUM, a town of Caria. *Plin.* 5. c. 29.

EURIANAS'SA, a town near Chius. *Plin.* 5. c. 31.

EURIP'IDES, a celebrated tragic poet, born at Salamis the day on which the army of Xerxes was defeated by the Greeks. He was descended from a respectable family at Athens, though Aristophanes and Valerius Maximus report that his mother Clito was employed in the mean occupation of a cabbage-seller. Whatever might have been his parents' situation in life, it is certain that the greatest care was bestowed upon the cultivation of his infant genius, as he early studied eloquence under Prodicus, ethics under Socrates, and philosophy under Anaxagoras. His natural powers inclined to dramatical composition, and his writings became so much the admiration of his countrymen, that the unfortunate Greeks, who had accompanied Nicias in his expedition against Syracuse, were freed from slavery, only by repeating some verses from the pieces of Euripides. The poet often retired from the society of mankind, and confined himself in a solitary cave near Salamis, where he wrote and finished his most excellent tragedies. The talents of Sophocles were looked upon by Euripides with jealousy, and the great enmity which unhappily prevailed between the two poets, gave an opportunity to the comic muse of Aristophanes to ridicule them both on the stage with humour and success. During the representation of one of the tragedies of Euripides, the audience, displeased with some lines in the composition, desired the writer to strike them out; Euripides heard the reproof with marks of displeasure and indignation; he advanced on the stage, and told the spectators, that he came there to instruct them, and not to receive instruction. Another piece, in which he called riches the *summum bonum* and the admiration of gods and men, gave equal dissatisfaction, but the poet desired the audience to listen with silent attention, for the conclusion of the whole would show them the punishment which attended the lovers of opulence, acquired by guilty or dishonourable means. The ridicule and envy to which the severity of his muse, and the unbending tendency of his principles exposed him, obliged him at last to remove from Athens. He retired to the court of Archelaus, king of Macedonia, where he received the most conspicuous marks of royal munificence and friendship. His end was as deplorable as it was uncommon. It is said, that the dogs of Archelaus met him in his solitary walks, and that, animated by the encouragement of some of the envious courtiers, the enraged animals tore his body to pieces, 407 years B.C., in the 78th year of his age. Euripides wrote 75 tragedies, of which only 19 are extant; the Phœnissæ, Orestes, Medea, Andromache, Electra, Hippolytus, Iphigenia in Aulis, Iphigenia in Tauris, Hercules, the Troades, Hecuba, Alcestis, Supplices, Rhesus, Bacchæ, Cyclops, Heraclidæ, Helena, and Ion. Besides these a few verses remain of the fragment of Danae. He is peculiarly happy in expressing the more tender and animated passions. To pathos he has added sublimity, and the most common expressions have received dignity and the most perfect polish from his pen. In his person, as it is reported, he was noble and majestic, and his deportment was always grave and serious. He was slow in composing, and laboured with difficulty, from which circumstance Alcestes, a foolish and malevolent poet of his age, once observed, that he had written 100 verses in three days, while Euripides had written only three. "True," said Euripides, "but there is this difference between your poetry and mine; yours will expire in three days but mine shall live for ages to come." Euripide, was such an enemy to the fair sex that some have called him μισογύνης, *woman-hater*, and perhaps, from this deeply rooted aversion arise the impure and diabolical machinations which appear in his female characters, an observation, however, which he refuted, by saying that he had faithfully copied nature. In spite of all his antipathy he was married twice, but his connections were so injudicious, that he was compelled to divorce both his wives. The best editions of this great poet are that of Musgave, 4 vols. 4to, Oxon. 1778; that of Canter apud Commelin. 12mo, 2 vols. 1597; and that of Barnes, fol. Cantab. 1694. There are also several valuable editions of detached plays. Among these the Hecuba, Phœnissæ, Orestes, and Medea, edited by the late professor Porson, deservedly rank foremost. An extensive acquaintance with the learned languages, more particularly with the works of the Greek tragedians, and a critical acumen such as is rarely possessed by scholars, were applied by him to the correction of the text, and the explanation of the more difficult passages of this beautiful writer, and most deeply is it to be regretted that he did not live to finish the task which he had undertaken. Professor Hermann and other German scholars, and Doctors Monk and Elmsley have also published some very excellent editions of separate plays. The most correct text of the whole of the works of Euripides, is that of the edition of Matthiæ. *Diod.* 13.—*Val. Max.* 3. c. 7.—*Cic. In.* 1. c. 50. *Or.* 3. c. 7. *Acad.* 1, 4. *Offic.* 3. *Finib.* 2. *Tusc.* 1 & 4, &c.—*Aul. Gell.* 15. c. 20.—*Athen.* 13. c. 2.—*Quintil.* 10. c. 1. [The finest and most authentic bust of Euripides is that in the Neapolitan Museum.]

EURI'PUS, a narrow strait which separated the island of Eubœa from the coast of Bœotia. Its flux and reflux, which continued regular during 18 or 19 days, and were uncommonly irregular during the rest of the month, or which, according to others, varied seven different times in the daytime, and as often in the night, or more properly in 24 hours, was a matter of deep inquiry among ancient philosophers, and it was said that Aristotle threw himself into it because he was unable to find out the true causes of that phænomenon. From these circumstances the proverb of *Euripo mobilior* became proverbial to express fickleness, and the word Euripus was employed by Cicero in the same signification as *mobilis.* Canals or aqueducts were called *Euripi* by the Romans. *Seneca in Her. Œt.* 779. ep. 83 & 90.—*Lucan.* 5. v. 235.—*Vossius de Ins. Or.* 5.—*Justin. Martyr. ad Gent.*—*Cic. ad Att.* 14. ep. 5.—*Sueton. in Cæs.* 39.—*Liv.* 28. c. 6.—*Mela*, 2. c. 7.—*Plin.* 2. c. 95.—*Strab.* 9

EURI'PUS, a Greek author who wrote concerning the pupils of Socrates. *Meurs. in lect. Att.*

EURO'MUS, a city of Caria. *Liv.* 32. c. 33. l. 33. c. 30.

EURO'PA, one of the three grand divisions of the earth known among the ancients, extending, according to modern surveys, about 3,000 miles from north to south, and 2,500 from east to west. Though inferior in extent, yet Europe is superior to other parts of the world in the learning, power, and abilities of its inhabitants. It is bounded on the east by the Ægean Sea, Hellespont, Euxine, Palus Mæotis, and the Tanais, extending, in a northern direction to the Frozen Ocean. The Mediterranean divides it from Africa on the South, and on the west and north it is washed by the Atlantic and Northern Oceans. It is supposed by most authors to have received its name from Europa, who was carried there by Jupiter. *Mela*, 2 c. 1.—*Plin.* 3. c. 1, &c.—*Lucan.* 3. v. 275.—*Virg. Æn.* 7. v. 222.

EURO'PA, a daughter of Agenor king of Phœnicia, and Telephassa. She was so beautiful that Jupiter became enamoured of her, and the better to engage her affections, he assumed the shape of a bull, and mingled with the herds of Agenor, while Europa, and her female attendants, were gathering flowers in the meadows. Europa caressed the beautiful animal, and at last had the courage to mount upon his back. The god took advantage of her situation, and retiring towards the shore, crossed the sea with Europa on his back, and arrived safe in Crete. Here he assumed his original shape, and declared his love. The nymph, a stranger on an unknown shore, consented, though she had once made vows of perpetual celibacy, and became mother of Minos, Sarpedon, and Rhadamanthus. After this amour with Jupiter, she married Asterius king of Crete. This monarch, seeing himself without children by Europa, adopted the fruit of her amours with Jupiter, and always esteemed Minos, Sarpedon, and Rhadamanthus, as his own children. Some suppose that Europa lived about 1552 years B.C. *Ovid, Met.* 2. fab. 13. *Fast.* 5. v. 604.—*Mosch. Idyl.*—*Apollod.* 2. c. 5. l. 3. c. 1. ——One of the Oceanides. *Hesiod. Th.* 356.——A part of Thrace near mount Hæmus. *Justin.* 7. c. 1.

EUROPÆ'US, a patronymic of Minos the son of Europa. *Ovid. Met.* 8. v. 23.

EU'ROPS, a king of Sicyon, son of Ægialeus, who died B.C. 1993. *Paus.* 2. c. 5.

EU'ROPUS or EURO'PUS, a king of Macedonia, &c. *Justin.* 7. c. 1.

EURO'PUS or EU'ROPUS, a town of Macedonia, on the river Axius. *Plin.* 4. c. 10.——A city of Syria on the Euphrates, called also Amphipolis and Thapsacum. *Plin.* 5. c. 25.——A city of Media.——A city of Crete. *Steph.*

EURO'TAS, a son of Lelex, father of Sparta, who married Lacedæmon. He was one of the first kings of Laconia, and gave his name to the river which flows near Sparta. *Apollod.* 3. c. 16.—*Paus.* 3. c. 1.

EURO'TAS, a river of Laconia, which flows by Sparta and falls into the Laconic Gulph. It was called by way of eminence, Basilipotamos, *the king of rivers*, and worshipped by the Spartans as a powerful god. Laurels, reeds, myrtles, and olives grew on its banks in great abundance. *Ptol.* 3. c. 16. —*Catull.* 65.—*Strab.* 8.—*Paus.* 3. c. 1.—*Liv.* 35. c. 29.—*Virg. Ecl.* 6. v. 82.——A river in Thessaly near mount Olympus, called also Titaresus. It joined the river Peneus, but was not supposed to incorporate its waters with it. *Strab.* 6.—*Plin.* 4. c. 8.

EURO'TO, a daughter of Danaus by Polyxo. *Apollod.*

EU'RUS, a wind blowing from the eastern parts of the world. The Latins sometimes called it Vulturnus or Apeliotes. *Virg. G.* 2. v. 107, 339 & 441. —*Val. Flacc.* 1. v. 538.—*Ovid. Trist.* 1. el. 2. *Met.* 11, &c.

EURY'ALE, a queen of the Amazons, who assisted Æetes, &c. *Flacc.* 5. v. 6, 11.——A daughter of Minos, mother of Orion by Neptune.——A daughter of Prætus, king of Argos.——One of the Gorgons who was immortal. *Hesiod. Theog.* v. 207.

EURY'ALUS, one of the Peloponnesian chiefs who went to the Trojan war with 80 ships. *Homer. Il* 2. v. 72.——An illegitimate son of Ulysses and Evippe, killed by Telemachus according to *Sophocles*, as quoted by *Parthen. Erot.* 3.——A son of Melas, taken prisoner by Hercules, &c. *Apollod.* 1. c. 8.——A Trojan who went with Æneas into Italy, and distinguished himself by his valour, but more particularly by his friendship with Nisus, immortalized by the masterly pen of the Mantuan bard. *Vid.* Nisus. *Virg. Æn.* 9. v. 179.——A pleasant place of Sicily, near Syracuse. *Liv.* 25. c. 25.——A Lacedæmonian general in the second Messenian war.——An actor. *Juv.* 6. v. 81.

EURYAM'PUS, a city of Magnesia. *Steph.*

EURYANAS'SA, an island of the Ægæan Sea. *Plin.* 5. c. 31.

EURYB'ATES, a Grecian herald in the Trojan war, who conducted Briseis from the tent of Achilles by order of Agamemnon. *Homer. Il.* v. 32. *Odyss.* 19. v. 244.—*Ovid. Heroid.* 3.——A warrior of Argos, often victorious at the Nemean games, &c. *Paus.* 1. c. 29.——One of the Argonauts.

EURYB'ATUS, an Ephesian who, when sent with money by Crœsus to hire mercenaries, deserted to Cyrus; his name, in consequence, became proverbial among the Greeks for treachery.

EURYB'IA, the mother of Lucifer and all the stars. *Hesiod.*——A daughter of Pontus and Terra, mother of Astræus, Pallas, and Perses, by Crius. *Hesiod. Th.* 237, 375.—*Apollod.*——A daughter of Thespius. *Apollod.*

EURYBI'ADES, a Spartan, who had the command of the Grecian fleet, which engaged with Xerxes at the battle of Artemisium and Salamis. He has been charged by his enemies with want of courage, and also with the ambitious design of raising himself above the control of his countrymen. He offered to strike Themistocles when he wished to speak about the manner of attacking the Persians, upon which the Athenian said, "Strike, but hear me." A magnificent tomb, which still existed in the age of Pausanias, was raised over his remains, under the walls of Sparta. *Paus.* 3. c. 16.—*Herodot.* 8. c. 2, 74, &c.—*Plut. in Them.*—*C. Nep. in Them.*

EURYB'IUS, a son of Eurytus king of Argos, killed in a war between his countrymen and the Athenians. *Apollod.* 2. c. 8.——A son of Nereus and Chloris. *Id.* 1. c. 9.——A son of Hercules and Crate. *Id.* 1 & 2.

EURYCLE'A, a beautiful daughter of Ops of Ithaca. Laertes bought her for 20 oxen, and gave her his son Eulysses to nurse, and treated her with much tenderness and attention. She distinguished herself by her fidelity and attachment to the family of Laertes, and she was the first to discover and welcome the return of Ulysses to his palace. *Homer. Odyss.* 1. v. 428. l. 19. v. 287. l. 22. v. 318. l. 23. v. 1. Also Eurycli'a.

EU'RYCLES, an orator of Syracuse, who, when the Athenian invaders were defeated, proposed to put Nicias and Demosthenes, the generals, to death, and to confine all the Athenian soldiers to hard labor in the quarries. *Plut.*——A Lacedæmonian at the battle of Actium on the side of Augustus. *Id. in Anton.*——A soothsayer of Athens.

EURYC'RATES, a king of Sparta, descended from Hercules. *Herodot.* 7. c. 204.

EURYCRATI'DAS, a son of Alexander, &c. *Herodot.* 7. c. 204.

EURYD'AMAS, a Trojan skilled in the interpretation of dreams. His two sons were killed by Diomedes during the Trojan war. *Homer. Il.* 5. v. 148.——One of Penelope's suitors. *Odyss.* 22. v. 283.——A wrestler of Cyrene, who in a combat, had his teeth dashed to pieces by his antagonist. He swallowed them without showing any signs of pain, or discontinuing the fight. *Ælian V. H.* 10. c. 19.—*Cœl. Rh.* 11. c. 75.——A son of Ægyptus. *Apollod.*——A surname of Hercules, expressive of his great power. *Ovid. Ib.* 331.—*Sil.* 2. v. 186.

EURYD'AME, the wife of Leotychides, king of Sparta. *Herodot.* 6. c. 71.

EURYDAMI'DAS, a king of Lacedæmon, of the family of the Proclidæ. *Paus.* 3. c. 10.

EURYD'ICE, the wife of Amyntas, king of Macedonia. She had by her husband Alexander, Perdiccas and Philip, and one daughter called Euryone. A criminal partiality for her daughter's husband, to whom she offered her hand and the kingdom, engaged her in an unnatural conspiracy against Amyntas, who must have fallen a victim to her infidelity had not Euryone discovered it. Amyntas forgave her. Alexander ascended the throne after his father's death, and perished by the ambition of his mother. Perdiccas, who succeeded him, shared his fate; but Philip, who was the next in succession, secured himself against all attempts from his mother, and ascended the throne in peace and with universal satisfaction. Eurydice fled to Iphicrates, the Athenian general, for protection. The manner of her death is unknown. *Justin.* 7. c. 4.—*C. Nep. in Iphic.* 3.——A daughter of Amyntas, who married her uncle Aridæus, the illegitimate son of Philip. After the death of Alexander the Great, Aridæus ascended the throne of Macedonia, but he was totally governed by the intrigues of his wife, who called back Cassander, and joined her forces with his to march against Polyperchion and Olympias. Eurydice was forsaken by her troops, and Aridæus was pierced through with arrows by order of Olympias, who commanded Eurydice to destroy herself either by poison, the sword, or the halter. She chose the latter. *Diod. Sic.* 19.——A daughter of Nereus and Doris, wife of the poet Orpheus. As she fled before Aristæus, who wished to offer her violence, she was bitten by a serpent in the grass, and died in consequence of the wound. Orpheus was so disconsolate that he ventured to descend into the infernal regions, where, by the melody of his lyre, he obtained from Pluto the restoration of his wife to life, provided he did not look behind him before he came upon earth. He, however, unhappily violated the conditions, of which his eagerness to see his wife rendered him forgetful. He looked behind, and Eurydice eluding his eager embraces, vanished for ever from his sight. *Vid.* Orpheus. *Virg. G.* 4. v. 457, &c.—*Paus.* 9. c. 30.—*Ovid. Met.* 10. v. 30, &c. *Trist.* 4. el. 1. v. 17. *Hygin.* fab. 164.——A daughter of Adrastus, wife of Ilus. *Apollod.* 3. c. 12.——One of the Danaides, who married Dyas. *Id.* 2. c. 1.——The wife of Lycurgus, king of Nemea, in Peloponnesus. *Id.* 1. c. 9.——A daughter of Actor. *Id.*——A wife of Æneas. *Paus.* 10. c. 26.——A daughter of Amphiaraus. *Id.* 3. c. 17.——A daughter Antipater, who married one of the Ptolemies. *Id.* 1. c. 7.——A daughter of king Philip. *Id.* 5. c. 17.——A daughter of Lacedæmon. *Id.* 3. c. 13.——A daughter of Clymenus, who married Nestor. *Homer. Odyss.* 3. v. 452.——A wife of Demetrus, descended from Miltiades.—*Plut. in Demetr.*

EURYGA'NIA, or EURYGANI'A, a wife of Œdipus. *Apollod.*

EURYL'EON, a king of the Latins, called also Ascanius. *Dion. Hal.* 1.

EURYL'OCHUS, one of the companions of Ulysses, the only one who had resolution enough to taste the fatal potions of Circe. His prudence, however, forsook him in Sicily, where he carried away the flocks sacred to Apollo, for which sacrilegious crime he was shipwrecked. *Homer. Odyss.* 10. v. 205. l. 12. v. 195.—*Ovid. Met.* 14. v. 287.——A man who broke a conduit which conveyed water into Cyrrhæ, &c. *Polyæn.* 6.——A man who discovered the conspiracy which was made against Alexander the Great by Hermolaus and others. *Curt.* 8 c. 6.

EURYM'ACHUS, a powerful Theban, who seized Platæ by treachery. *Thucyd.*——One of Penelope's suitors, son of Polybus of Ithaca. He was killed by Ulysses. *Homer. Odyss.* 1. v. 339. l. 2. v. 177. l. 18 v. 63. l. 21. v. 186. l. 22. v. 44.—*Ovid. Heroid.* 1. v. 91.—*Paus.* 9. c. 41.——A son of Antenor.——A lover of Hippodamia. *Paus.*

EURYM'EDE, the wife of Glaucus king of Ephyra. *Apollod.*

EURYM'EDON, the father of Peribœa, by whom Neptune had Nausithous. *Homer. Odyss.* 7.——A son of Faunus, who was engaged in the Theban war. *Stat. Theb.* 11. v. 32.——A man who accused Aristotle of propagating profane doctrines in the Lyceum.

EURYM'EDON, a river of Pamphylia, which falls into the Pamphylian Sea. It was near this river that the Persians were defeated by the Athenians under Cimon, B C. 470. *Liv.* 33. c. 41. l. 37. c. 23.

EURYM'ENÆ, a city of Thessaly. *Steph.*

EURYM'ENES, a son of Neleus and Chloris. *Apollod.*

EUR'YMUS, the father of the augur Telemus, who is called in consequence Eurymides. *Ovid. Met.* 13. v. 771.

EURYN'OME, one of the Oceanides, mother of the Graces. *Hesiod. Theog.* 906.—*Ovid. Met.* 4. v. 210.—*Apollod.* 1.——The wife of Orchamus, an Arabian prince, mother of Leucothoe. *Ovid. Met.* 4. v. 210.——A daughter of Apollo, mother of Adrastus and Eriphyle.——A woman of Lemnus, daughter of Doryclus and wife of Codrus. *Flacc.* 2. v. 136.——The wife of Lycurgus, son of Aleus. *Apollod.* 3. c. 9.——The mother of Asopus by Jupiter. *Id.* 3. c. 12.——One of Penelope's female attendants. *Homer. Odyss.* 17. v. 515.——An Athenian sent with a reinforcement to Nicias in Sicily. *Plut. in Nic.*

EURYN'OMUS, one of the deities of hell. *Paus.* 10. c. 28.

EURY'ONE, a daughter of Amyntas, king of Macedonia, by Eurydice. *Vid.* Eurydice. *Just.* 7. c. 4.

EU'RYPHON, a celebrated physician of Cnidos, quoted by Galen.

EU'RYPON, a king of Sparta, son of Sous. His reign was so glorious that his descendants were called Eurypontidæ. *Paus.* 3. c. 7.

EURYP'YLE, a daughter of Thespius.

EURYP'YLUS, a son of Telephus and Astyoche, was killed in the Trojan war by Pyrrhus. He paid his addresses to Cassandra, and strongly recommended himself to her notice and affection by the valor with which he fought the enemies of his father's kingdom. *Quint. Sm.* 6. v. 120. 368. l. 7. v. 414. l. 9. v. 200.—*Paus.* 3. c. 26. l. 9. c. 6.—*Hygin.* fab. 112.—*Homer. Il.* 11. v. 510.——A Grecian, son of Evemon, who went to the Trojan war in 40 ships. *Homer. Il.* 2. v. 243.——A prince of Olenus, who went with Hercules against Laomedon. *Paus.* 7. c. 19.——A son of Mecisteus, who signalized himself in the war of the Epigoni against Thebes. *Apollod.* 3.——A son of Temenus, king of Messenia, who conspired against his father's life. *Id.* 3. c. 6.——A king of Cos, son of Neptune by Astyochea, was killed by Hercules. *Id.* 2. c. 7.——One of Penelope's suitors. *Id.* 3. c. 10.——A Thessalian who became delirious for looking into a box which fell to his share after the plunder of Troy. *Paus.* 7. c. 19.——A soothsayer in the Grecian camp before Troy, sent to consult the oracle of Apollo, how his countrymen could return home in safety. The result of his inquiries was the injunction to offer a human sacrifice to the gods. *Virg. Æn.* 2. v. 114.—*Ovid.*

EURYS'ACES, son of Ajax Telamon and Tecmessa. He and his brother Philæus gave the island of Salamis to the Athenians, and in return received the Attic franchise. Eurysaces was honoured with an altar at Athens.

EURYS'THENES, a son of Aristodemus, who lived in perpetual dissension with his twin-brother Procles, while they both sat on the Spartan throne. It was unknown which of the two was born first, the mother who wished to see both her sons raised to the throne, refused to declare it, and they were both appointed kings of Sparta by order of the oracle of Delphi, B.C. 1102. After the death of the two brothers, the Lacedæmonians, who knew not to what family the right of seniority and succession properly belonged, permitted two kings, one of each family, to sit together on the throne. The descendants of Eurysthenes were called Eurysthenidæ, and those of Procles, Proclidæ. It was therefore inconsistent with the laws of Sparta for two kings of the same family to ascend the throne together, yet that law was sometimes violated by oppression and tyranny. Eurysthenes had a son called Agis, who succeeded him. His descendants were called Agidæ. There sat on the throne of Sparta thirty-one kings of the family of Eurysthenes, and only twenty-four of the Proclidæ. The former were the more illustrious. *Vid.* Lacedæmon. *Herodot.* 4. c. 147. l. 6. c. 52.—*Paus.* 3. c. 1.—*C. Nep. in Ages.*

EURYSTHEN'IDÆ. *Vid.* Eurysthenes.

EURYS'THEUS, a king of Argos and Mycenæ, son of Sthenelus and Nicippe the daughter of Pelops, and husband to Antimache daughter of Amphidamas. Juno hastened his birth by two months, that he might come into the world before Hercules, the son of Alcmena, as the younger of the two children was doomed by the irrevocable order of Jupiter to be subservient to the will of the other.

Vid. Alcmena. This natural right was cruelly exercised by Eurystheus, who was jealous of the fame of Hercules, and who, to destroy so powerful a relation, imposed upon him the most dangerous and uncommon enterprises, well known by the name of the twelve labors of Hercules. The success of Hercules in achieving those perilous labors alarmed Eurystheus in a great degree, and he furnished himself with a brazen vessel, where he might secure himself a safe retreat in case of danger. After the death of Hercules, Eurystheus renewed his cruelties against his children, and made war against Ceyx, king of Trachinia, because he had given them support, and treated them with kindness and hospitality. He was killed in the prosecution of this war by Hyllus, the son of Hercules. His head was sent to Alcmena the mother of Hercules, who, mindful of the cruelties which her son had suffered, insulted it, and tore out the eyes with the most inveterate fury. Eurystheus was succeeded on the throne of Argos by Atreus his nephew. *Hygin.* fab. 30 & 32.—*Homer. Il.* 19. v. 91.—*Thucyd.* 1.—*Herodot.* 5. c. 39. l. 9. c. 26.— *Justin.* 2. c. 4.—*Apollod.* 2. c. 4, &c.—*Paus.* 1. c. 33. l. 3. c. 6.—*Ovid. Met.* 9. fab. 6.—*Heroid.* 9.—*Virg. Æn.* 8. v. 292.

EURYTA'NES, a people of Italy, or rather of Ætolia. *Steph.*—*Casaub. ex Strab.* l. 10.

EU'RYTE, a daughter of Hippodamus, who married Parthaon. *Apollod.*——The mother of Hallirhotius, by Neptune. *Id.*

EURYT'EÆ or EURYTE'Æ, a town of Achaia. *Paus.* 7. c. 18.

EURYT'ELE, a daughter of Thespius.——A daughter of Leucippus. *Apollod.*

EURYTH'EMIS, the wife of Thestius. *Apollod.*

EURYTH'ION or EURYT'ION, a centaur whose insolence to Hippodamia was the cause of the fatal quarrel between the Lapithæ and Centaurs at the nuptials of Pirithous. *Ovid. Met.* 12.—*Propert.* 2. el. 33.—*Homer. Il.* 12. *Odyss.* 21.—*Hygin.* fab. 31.—*Paus.* 5. c. 10.—*Hesiod. Theog.* [There are many fine representations of these poetical creations, especially two in the Museum of the Capitol; but there are none to which names can be given with certainty.]——A herdsman of Geryon killed by Hercules. *Apollod.* 2.——A king of Sparta who seized upon Mantinea by stratagem. *Polyæn.* 2.—— One of the Argonauts. *Ovid. Met.* 8. v. 311.——A son of Lycaon, who signalized himself during the funeral games exhibited in Sicily by Æneas. *Virg. Æn.* 5. v. 495.——A silversmith. *Id.* 10. v. 499.——A man of Heraclea convicted of adultery. His punishment was the cause of the abolition of the oligarchical power there. *Aristot.* 5. *Polit.*——A son of Actor, king of Phthia who purified Peleus of the murder of Phocus, and gave him his daughter Antigone in marriage. He was killed at the chase of the Calydonian boar. *Apollod.* 1 & 3.

EU'RYTIS, (*-idos*) a patronymic of Iole, the daughter of Eurytus. *Ovid. Met.* 9. fab. 11.

EU'RYTUS, a son of Mercury, among the Argonauts. *Flacc.* 1. v. 439.——A king of Œchalia, father to Iole. He offered his daughter as a prize to him who should shoot an arrow better than himself. Hercules presented himself to contend with him, and, after having conquered him, put him to death because he refused his daughter as the reward of his victory. *Apollod.* 2. c. 4 & 7.——A son of Actor, concerned in the wars between Augias and Hercules, and killed by the hero. *Paus.* 2. c. 15.—*Apollod.* 2.——A son of Augias, killed by Hercules as he was going to Corinth to celebrate the Isthmian games. *Apollod.*——A person killed in hunting the Calydonian boar.——A son of Hippocoon. *Id.* 3. c. 10.——A giant killed by Hercules or Bacchus for making war against the gods.——An eminent artist who made the armour of Pallas, the son of Evander. *Virg. Æn.* 10. v. 499.

EUSE'BIA AUREL., an empress, wife of Constantius. She was celebrated for her beauty, her genius, and the great chastity of her manners, as well as the humanity of her character. By her advice Constantius married his sister Helena to Julian. She died, A.D. 360, highly and deservedly regretted.

EUSE'BIUS, a bishop of Cæsarea, in great favour with the emperor Constantine. He was concerned in the theological disputes of Arius and Athanasius, and distinguished himself by his writings, which consisted of an ecclesiastical history, the life of Constantine, Chronicon, evangelical preparations, and other numerous treatises most of which are now lost. He died about the year of Christ 340, aged 73. The best edition of his *Præparatio* and *Demonstratio Evangelica*, is by Vigerus, 2 vols. folio, Rothomagi, 1628; and of his ecclesiastical history, by Reading, folio, Cantab 1720. *Sax. Onom.* 1. p. 392.—*Fabr. B. Gr.* 5. c. 4. There were several bishops and divines that bore the same name in the four first centuries of Christianity.——A surname of Bacchus.

EUSEM'ATA, a city of Armenia Minor. *Ptol.*

EUSTA'THIUS, a Greek commentator on the works of Homer, who flourished at Constantinople about the year of Christ 1170. The best edition of this very valuable author is that published at Basil, 3 vols. fol. 1560. It is to be lamented that the design of Alexander Politus, begun at Florence in 1735, and published in the first five books of the Iliad, is not executed, as a Latin translation of these excellent commentaries is among the desiderata of the present day. *Sax. Onom.* 2. p. 251.—*Fabr. B. Gr.* 2. c. 3.——A man who wrote a very foolish romance in Greek, entitled *De Ismeni et Ismenes amoribus*, edited by Gaulminus 8vo, Paris 1617. But see Eumathius.

EUSTE'PHIUS, a sophist of Aprodisium, who wrote declamations. *Suidas.*

EUSTRA'TIUS, a commentator on Aristotle, who flourished under Alexius Commenus. Only fragments of his writings are extant.

EUTÆ'A, a town of Arcadia. *Paus.* 8. c. 27.

EUTA'NE, a town of Caria. *Plin.* 5. c. 22.

EUTA'SUM, a city of Arcadia. *Paus.*

EUTEL'IDAS, a famous statuary of Argos. *Id.* 6. c. 10 & 15.

EUTER'PE, one of the muses who presided over music, and was looked upon as the inventress of the flute, and of all wind instruments. She is represented as crowned with flowers, and holding a flute in her hands. Some mythologists have attributed to her the invention of tragedy, more commonly supposed to be the production of her sister Melpomene. *Vid.* Musæ. [The best representation of this Muse is in the series at the Museum of the Vatican.]——The name of the mother of Themistocles according to some.

EUTHE'NÆ, a city of Asia. *Steph.*

EUTHYC'RATES, a sculptor of Sicyon, son of Lysippus. His statues of Hercules and Alexander were in general esteem; and that of Medea, in which she was represented as riding in a chariot, drawn by four horses, was much admired. *Plin.* 34. c. 8.——A man who betrayed Olynthus to Philip. *Diod.* l. 16.——A statuary. *Plin.* 4. c. 8.

EUTHYOR'ITUS, an archon at Athens. Ol. 113. an. 1.

EUTHYDE'MUS, a Greek orator and rhetorician, who greatly distinguished himself by his eloquence, &c. *Strab.* 15.

EUTHYME'DES, a painter mentioned by *Pliny*, 35 c. 11.

EUTHYM'ENES, a chronographer. *Clem. Alex. Strom.*

EUTHY'MUS, a celebrated boxer of Locri in Italy, &c. *Paus.* 6. c. 6.—*Plin.* 7. c. 47.

EU'TOCUS, a son of Apollo and Cyrene. *Boccat.* l. 5.

EUTRAP'ELUS, a man described as artful and fallacious by *Horace*, 1. ep. 18. v. 31.——A hairdresser. *Martial.* 7. epigr. 82.——A friend of M. Antony, so called from the politeness of his manners, and the raillery of his wit. *Cic. Fam.* ep. 32 & 33.

EUTRE'SII, the inhabitants of a district of Arcadia.

EUTRE'SIS, a village of Bœotia, where Apollo Eutresites had a celebrated temple and oracle. *Steph.*

EUTRE'SIUM, a city of Arcadia. *Id.*

EUTRO'PIUS FLA'VIUS, a Latin historian in the age of Julian, under whom he carried arms in the fatal expedition against the Persians. His origin as well as his dignity are unknown; yet some suppose, from the epithet of *Clarissimus* prefixed to his history that he was a Roman senator. He wrote an epitome of the history of Rome, from the age of Romulus to the reign of the emperor Valens, to whom the work was dedicated. He wrote also a treatise on medicine, without being acquainted with the art. Of all his works the Roman history alone is extant. It is an interesting work, divided into 10 books, composed with conciseness and precision, but without elegance. The best edition of Eutropius is that of Haverkamp, cum notis variorum, 8vo, L. Bat. 1729 and 1762. *Eutr.* 10. c. 16. *Sax Onom.* 1. p. 419.—*Harles. Not. Lit. Rom.* 1. p. 595.

EUTRO'PIUS, a famous eunuch at the court of Arcadius, the son of Theodosius the Great. After enjoying the highest offices of the state, he was beheaded, A.D. 399.

EUTYCH'IDE, a woman of Lydia who was thirty times brought to bed, and carried to the grave by twenty of her children, *Plin.* 7. c. 3.

EUTYCHI'A, an island near Thessaly. *Plin.* 4. c. 12.

EUTYCH'IDES, a learned servant in the family of Atticus, &c. *Cic.* 15. *ad Attic.*——A sculptor. Ol. 120. He made a famous statue of the god of the river Eurotas. *Plin.* 34. c. 8.

EUXAN'THIUS, a daughter of Minos and Dexithea. *Apollod.*

EUXEN'IDAS, a Greek painter, &c. *Plin.* 35. c. 10.

EUX'ENUS, a man who wrote a poetical history of the fabulous ages of Italy. *Dionys. Hal.* 1.

EUXI'NUS PON'TUS, a sea between Asia and Europe, partly at the north of Asia Minor, and at the West of Colchis, surrounded on all sides by high ridges of mountains. It was anciently called ἄξεινος, *inhospitable*, on account of the savage manners of the inhabitants who dwelt on its coasts. Commerce with foreign nations, however, and the plantation of colonies in their neighbourhood, gradually softened their ferocity, and the sea was no longer Axinus, but Euxinus, *hospitable.* The Euxine is supposed by Herodotus to be 1387 miles long, and 420 broad. Strabo calls it 1100 miles long, and in circumference 3125. It abounds with a variety of fish, and receives the tribute of about 40 rivers, many of which are very large. It is not of great depth, except in the eastern parts, whence some have imagined it had a subterraneous communication with the waters of the Caspian. It is now called the Black Sea, from the thick dark fogs which overspread its surface. *Ovid. Trist.* 3. el. 13. l. 4. el. 4. v. 54.—*Strab.* 2, &c.—*Mela*, 1. c. 1.—*Plin.* 9.—*Herodot.* 4. c. 85.

EUXIP'PE, a woman who killed herself, because the ambassadors of Sparta had offered violence to her. *Diod.* 1. 15.

EVAD'NE, a daughter of Iphis or Iphicles of Argos, who slighted the addresses of Apollo, and married Capaneus, one of the seven chiefs who went with Adrastus against Thebes. When her husband had been struck with lightning by Jupiter for his impiety, and his ashes had been separated from the rest of the Argives, she threw herself on his burning pile, and perished in the flames. *Euripid. Supp.* act. 5.—*Apollod.* 3.—*Ovid. Trist.* 5. el. 15. —*Virg. Æn.* 6. v. 447.—*Propert.* 1. el. 15. v. 21.—*Stat. Theb.* 12. v. 800.——A daughter of the Strymon and Neæra. She married Argus, by whom she had four children, Jasus, Piranthes, Epidaurus, and Criasus. *Apollod.* 2.

EVÆ'MON, the father of Eurypylus, went to the Trojan war with forty ships. *Homer. Il.* 2.——A city of the Orchomenians. *Steph.*

EVÆN'ETUS, an archon at Athens, Ol. 111. an. 2.

EV'AGES, a poet distinguished for his genius, but not for his learning. *Dionys. in Hist. illustr.*

EV'AGON, one of those natives of Cyprus, whom it is said that serpents did not injure by their bite. *Plin.* 28. c. 3.

EVAG'ORAS, a king of Cyprus who retook Salamis, of which his father had been deprived in a war against the Persians. He afterwards commenced hostilities against Artaxerxes, the king of Persia, with the assistance of the Ægyptians, Arabians, and Tyrians, and obtained some advantage over the fleet of his enemy. The Persians, however, soon repaired their losses, and Evagoras saw himself defeated both by sea and land, and obliged to become tributary to the power of Artaxerxes, and to be stripped of all his dominions except the town of Salamis. He was assassinated soon after this fatal change of fortune, by a eunuch, 374 B.C. He left two sons, Nicocles, who succeeded him, and Protagoras.——A grandson of the preceding, succeeded his father Nicocles. He showed himself oppressive, and his uncle Protagoras took advantage of his unpopularity to deprive him of his power. Evagoras fled to Artaxerxes Ochus, who gave him a government more extensive than that of Cyprus, but his oppression rendered him odious, and he was accused before his benefactor, and by his orders put to death. *C. Nep.* 12. c. 2.—*Diod.* 14.—*Paus.* 4. c. 3.—*Justin.* 5. c. 6.——A man of Elis, who obtained a prize at the Olympic games. *Paus.* 5. c. 8.—*Ælian. H. A.* 13. c. 40.——A Spartan, famous for his services to the people of Elis. *Paus.* 6. c. 10. ——A son of Neleus and Chloris. *Apollod.* 1. c. 9. ——A son of Priam. *Id.* 3. c. 12.——A king of Rhodes.——An historian of Lindus in the age of Augustus, author of a history of Ægypt, besides the life of Timagenes, a lexicon in *Thucydidem*, and other works. *Suidas.*——An historian of Thasus, whose works proved serviceable to Pliny in the composition of his natural history. *Plin.* 10.

EVAG'ORE, one of the Nereides. *Apollod.*

EVA'GRIUS, a Greek writer of the fifth century. *Sax. Onom.* 1. p. 441.—*Fabr. B. Gr.* 5. c. 24. ——A patriarch of Antioch, who succeeded Paulinus, A.D. 380. He wrote some works now lost. *Hieron. de Script. Eccles.* c. 125.——An ecclesiastical historian of Epiphania in Syria, born about A.D. 536. His history was last edited by Reading, in fol. Cambridge, 1720, with various notes. *Sax. Onom.* part. 2.

EVAL'CES, an historian who wrote a book called Ἐφεσιακά, according to *Athenæus.* l. 13.

E'VAN, a surname of Bacchus, which he received from the wild ejaculation of *Evan! Evan!* used by his priestesses; or, according to a less probable opinion, from a temple or mountain of the same name in Messenia. *Sil. It.* 1. v. 101.—*Ovid. Met.* 4. v. 15.—*Virg. Æn.* 6. v. 517.

EVAN'DER, a son of Mercury, by the prophetess Carmente, was king of Arcadia. An accidental murder obliged him to leave his country, and he retired to Italy, where he drove the aborigines from their ancient possessions, and reigned in that part of the country where Rome was afterwards founded. He kindly received Hercules when he returned from the conquest of Geryon; and he was the first who raised altars to him as a god. He afterwards assisted Æneas against the Rutuli, and distinguished himself by his hospitality. It is said that he first brought the Greek alphabet into Italy, and introduced there the worship of the Greek deities. He was honored as a god after death by his subjects, who raised him an altar on mount Aventine; and as his reign had been distinguished by mildness and hospitality, some have considered him as the Saturn of Latium, and described his as the golden age. Evander had a son named Pallas, who was slain by the Rutuli, and, to commemorate his virtues and his glorious death, he called the town, which he erected on the bank of the Tiber, for the capital of his kingdom, by the name of Pallantium, which appellation was afterwards lost in that of the Palatine Hill. Some authors call him Echemus, of Arcadia, and Timandra, a sister of Helen, the daughter of Tyndarus and Leda. The more received opinion, however, makes him son of Carmente by Mercury. *Paus.* 8. c. 43. *Liv.* 1. c. 7.—*Ital.* 7. v. 18.—*Dionys. Hal.* 1. c. 7.—*Ovid. Fast.* 1. v. 500. l. 5. v. 91.—*Virg. Æn.* 8. v. 100, &c. & *Servius loco.*—*Hygin.* fab. 277.—*Aurel. Vict. de Orig. R.* 6.—*Tacit. Ann.* 11. c. 14.——A philosopher of the second academy, who flourished B.C. 215.——A sculptor. *Plin.* 36. c. 5. ——A sculptor. *Acron. ad Horat.* 1. sat. 3 v. 91.

EVAN'DRIA, a town of Lusitania, now Olivenza. *Ptol.*

EVAN'GELUS, a Greek historian, who wrote *de re militari.* *Plut.*——A comic poet. *Athen.* 14, &c.

EVANOR'IDAS, a man of Elis, who wrote an account of all those who had obtained a prize at Olympia. He had himself been victorious in the games, and had also been appointed umpire. *Paus.* 6. c. 8.

EVAN'THES, a man who, at the head of some Locrians, planted a colony in Lucania. *Strab.* 6. ——A celebrated Greek poet. *Athen.* 7.—*Plin.* 8. c. 21.——An historian of Miletus. *Diog. in Thal.* ——A philosopher of Samus. *Plut. in Solon.* ——A writer of Cyzicus, highly commended by St.

Jerome. 2 *Contra Jov.*——A son of Œnopion of Crete, who left his country to settle at Chius. *Paus.* 7. c. 4.

EVAR'CHUS, a river of Asia Minor flowing into the Euxine on the confines of Cappadocia. *Flacc.* 6. v. 102.

E'VAS, *antis*, a native of Phrygia, who accompanied Æneas into Italy, where he was killed by Mezentius. *Virg. Æn.* 10. v. 702.

E'VAX, an Arabian prince of great learning and uncommon application. He studied medicine, and wrote a book *de simplicium effectibus*, which he dedicated to the emperor Nero. This is mentioned by *Pliny* 25. c. 2, though *Salmasius* and *Hardouin* declare that some manuscripts of that author do not contain the passage. *Voss. de Philos.* c. 12. sec. 9.

EVA'ZÆ, a people of Sarmatia, near the Tanais. *Plin.* 6. c. 7.

EVEL'THON, a king of Salamis in Cyprus. *Polyæn.* 8.

EVEM'ERUS or EUHEM'ERUS, an ancient historian of Messana, intimate with Cassander. He travelled over Greece and Arabia, and wrote a curious history of the gods, in which he proved, from the monuments and records which he found in the temples, especially that of Jupiter Triphylius, that they all had been upon earth, as mere mortal men. Ennius translated it into Latin. It is now lost, though it existed in the age of Athenæus. *Cic. de N. D.* 1. c. 42. *Varro de R.R.* 1. c. 48.—*Lactant. de Fals. C.* c. 11.—*Plut. de Isid. & Ot.*

EVE'NOR, a Grecian painter, father of Parrhasius. *Plin.* 35. c. 9.

EVE'NUM, a river of Troas. *Plin.* 4. c. 2.

EVE'NUS, a river running through Ætolia, and falling into the Ionian Sea. It received its name from Evenus, the son of Mars and Demonice, who was so disconsolate at the loss of his daughter Marpessa, whom Idas had carried away, and whom he pursued in vain, that he threw himself into the Lycormas, which afterwards retained his name. Plutarch calls the wife of Evenus, Ulcipe; his mother, Sterope, his daughter Marpessa; and her ravisher, Apharetus. *Plut. Parall.* 40.—*Hygin.* fab. 242.—*Ovid. Met.* 9. v. 104.—*Strab.* 7.——An elegiac poet of Parus, preceptor to the historian Philistus of Syracuse. He lived in the 93rd Olympiad. *Vossius Hist. Gr.*——A son of Jason and Hipsipile, queen of Lemnus, who supplied the Greeks with some provisions during the Trojan war, and fought himself bravely on their side. *Homer. Il.* 7. v. 467.

EVEPHE'NUS or EVEPH'ENUS, a Pythagorean philosopher, whom Dionysius condemned to death, because he had alienated the people of Metapontum from his power. The philosopher begged leave of the tyrant to go and give his sister in marriage, and promised to return in six months. Dionysius consented upon receiving Eucritus, who pledged himself to die if Evephenus did not return at the promised time. Evephenus returned at the appointed moment, to the astonishment of Dionsius, and delivered his friend Eucritus from the death which threatened him. The tyrant was so pleased with these two friends, that he pardoned Evephenus, and begged to share their friendship and confidence. *Polyæan.* 5.

EV'ERES or EVE'RES, a son of Pterelaus, the only one of his family who did not perish in a battle against Electryon. *Apollod.*

EV'ERES, a son of Hercules and Parthenope. *Id.* 2. ——The father of Tiresias. *Apollod.*

EVER'GETÆ, a people of Scythia, called also Arimaspi. *Curt.* 7. c. 3.

EVER'GETES, a surname, signifying benefactor, given to Philip of Macedonia, and also to Antigonus Doson, and Ptolemy of Ægypt. It was also commonly given to the kings of Syria and Pontus, and we often see among the former an Alexander Evergetes, and among the latter a Mithridates Evergetes. Some of the Roman emperors have also claimed, but little deserved, that epithet, so expressive of benevolence and humanity. *Curt.* 7. c. 3.—*Justin.* 12. c. 5.

EVESPER'IDES, a people of Africa. *Herodot.* 4. c. 171.

EVIA, a city of the Dassaretici, in Macedonia. *Ptol.*

E'VIAS, a female worshipper of Bacchus, so called from his surname of Evius. *Horat.* 3. od. 25. v. 9.

E'VII, a people of Liguria. *Steph.*

EVIP'PE, one of the Danaides, who married and murdered Imbras. *Apollod.* 2.——Another of the Danaides. *Id.* 2. c. 1.——The mother of the Pierides, who were changed into magpies. *Ovid. Met.* 5. v. 303.

EVIP'PE, a town of Caria. *Steph.*

EVIP'PUS, a son of Thestius, king of Pleuron, killed by his brother Iphiclus in the chase of the Calydonian boar. *Apollod* 1. c. 7.——A Trojan killed by Patroclus. *Homer. Il.* 16. v. 417.

E'VIUS, a surname of Bacchus, which he received from the exclamation of his father Jupiter in the war against the giants, Evie! courage, my son, and thence originated the Evohe! so loudly and so frequently repeated at the celebration of his festivals. *Colum. de R.R.* 10. c. 224.—*Horat.* 2. od. 11. v. 17.

EXA'DIUS, one of the Lapithæ present at the nuptials of Pirithous. *Homer. Il.* 1. v. 264.—*Ovid. Met.* 12. v. 266.

EXÆ'THRES, a Parthian, who cut off the head of Crassus, &c. *Polyæn.* 7.

EXAG'ONUS, the ambassador of a nation of Cyprus, who came to Rome and talked so much of the power of herbs, serpents, &c., that the consuls ordered him to be thrown into a vessel full of serpents. These venomous creatures, far from hurting him, caressed him, to the astonishment of the Roman people, and harmlessly licked him with their tongues. *Plin.* 28. c. 3.

EXAMPÆ'US, or ἱραὶ ὁδοί, a fountain of Scythia, the waters of which were said to render bitter the stream of the river Hypanis. *Herodot.* 4. c. 52.

EXCIPIN'IUS, a Macedonian, a favourite of Alexander. *Curt.* 7. c. 9.

EXECES'TUS, a tyrant of Phocis, who had two charmed rings. *Aristot. de Rep. Phoc.*—*Clem. Alex. Strom.* 1.

EXILA'NI, a people of Hispania Bœtica. *Strab.*

EXOBYGI'TÆ, a people of European Sarmatia. *Ptol.*

EXOM'ATÆ, a people of Asiatic Sarmatia. *Flacc.* 6. v. 144.—*Plin.* 6.—*Polyæn.* 8.

EXOP'OLIS, a nation of Asiatic Sarmatia, on the Tanais. *Ptol.*

F.

FABA'RIA, festivals celebrated at Rome on the 1st of June, in honor of the goddess Carna, the wife of Janus, when beans *(fabæ)* were presented as an oblation. From this circumstance the same name was sometimes applied to the calends of June. *Macrob. Sat.* 1. c. 12.—*Aug. de Civ. Dei*, 4. c. 8.

FAB'ARIS, now Farfa, a small river of Italy in the territories of the Sabines, called also Farfarus. It falls into the Tiber. *Ovid. Met.* 14. v. 330.—*Virg. Æn.* 7. v. 715. *& Servius loco.*

FABA'TUS CALPUR'NIUS, the grandfather of Calpurnia, wife of the younger Pliny, many of whose letters are addressed to him.

FABA'TUS L. ROS'CIUS, one of Cæsar's lieutenants in Gaul, who espoused Pompey's cause. He was killed at Mutina B.C. 43.

FA'BIA. *Vid.* Fabius Fabricanus.

FA'BIA LEX, *de ambitu*, was to circumscribe the number of Sectatores or attendants which were allowed to candidates in canvassing for some high office. It was proposed, but did not pass.

FA'BIA, a tribe at Rome. *Horat.* 1. ep. 7. v. 52. ——A vestal virgin, sister to Terentia, Cicero's wife. She was accused of incontinence with Catiline, but acquitted. *Ascon. in Cic. toga. Camd.* ——Two daughters of M. Fabius Ambustus. The elder married the patrician Ser. Sulpicius, the younger, the plebeian C. Licinius Stolo.

FABIA'NI, some of the Luperci at Rome, instituted in honor of the Fabian family.

FABIEN'SES, a people of Italy. *Plin.* 3. c. 5.

FA'BII, a noble and powerful family at Rome, who derived their name from *faba*, a bean, because some of their ancestors cultivated this pulse. They were said to be descended from Fabius, a supposed son of Hercules by an Italian nymph, and they were once so numerous and powerful, that they took upon themselves to wage a war against the Veientes. They came to a general engagement near the river Cremera, in which all the family, consisting of 306 men were slain, B.C. 477. One of the family, whose tender age had detained him at

Rome, alone remained, and from him arose the noble Fabii in the following ages. The family was divided into different branches, the Ambusti, the Maximi, the Vibulani, the Buteones, the Dorsones, and the Pictores, Labeones, and Gurgites, the three first of which are frequently mentioned in the Roman history, but the others seldom. *Dion.* 9. c. 5.—*Liv.* 2. c. 46, &c.—*Cic. in Cat. Maj.*—*Plut. in Fab.*—*Flor.* 1. c. 2.—*Ovid. Fast.* 2. v. 239. *Trist.* 2. v. 235.—*Virg. Æn.* 6. v. 845.

FA'BIUS, a Roman, chosen general against the Carthaginians in Italy. He lost all his forces in a battle, and fell wounded by the side of Annibal. *Plut. in Parall.*——A consul with J. Cæsar for the last three months of the year. He conquered Pompey's adherents in Spain. *Dio.* 43. c. 46. ——A high-priest who wrote some annals, and made war against Viriathus in Spain. *Liv.* 30. c. 26.—*Flor.* 3. c. 2.——A Roman sent to consult the oracle at Delphi, while Annibal was in Italy.——A person chosen dictator merely to create new senators.——A lieutenant of Lucullus, defeated by Mithridates.——A son of Paulus Æmilius, adopted into the family of the Fabii.——A Roman lawyer, whom *Horace* ridicules as having been caught in adultery ——A loquacious person mentioned by *Horace*, 1. sat. 1. v. 14.——A Roman consul, surnamed Ambustus, because he was struck with lightning.——A lieutenant of Cæsar in Gaul.

FA'BIUS Q. ÆMILIA'NUS, was descended from Æmilius, and was surnamed Allobrogicus from his victory over the Allobroges, &c. *Flor.* 2. c. 17.—*Vell.* 2. c. 10.—*Plin.* 33. c. 11.

FA'BIUS DORSEM'NUS or DOSSE'NUS, a poet of Atella. *Plin.* 14. c. 13.—*Horat.* 1. 2. *Ep.* v. 73.—*Senec. Epist.* 89.

FA'BIUS DOR'SO. *Vid.* Dorso.

FA'BIUS FABRICA'NUS, a Roman, assassinated by his wife Fabia, that she might more freely enjoy ths company of a favorite youth. His son was saved from his mother's unnatural fury, and when he came of age, he avenged his father's death by putting to death his mother and her adulterer. The senate took cognizance of the action, and patronized the parricide. *Plut. in Parall.*

FA'BIUS QUIN'TUS MAX'IMUS GUR'GES, son of Fabius Max. Rull. was defeated by the Samnites, and would have been disgraced by the senate, had not his venerable father interfered and promised to serve as his lieutenant, that thus he might wipe away the infamy thrown upon the Roman arms. In consequence of this offer the Samnites were conquered, and Pontius their general was cruelly beheaded. *Liv.* 11.

FA'BIUS LUPER'CUS, a priest of Pan at Rome. The priests were divided into two classes, called Fabiani, the friends of Remus, and Quintiliani, the friends of Romulus. *Ovid. Fast.* 2. v. 375.—*Propert.* 4. el. 1. v. 26.—*Fest.*

FA'BIUS Q. MAX'IMUS, a celebrated Roman, first surnamed Verrucosus, from a wart on his lip, and Agnellus, from his mild and inoffensive manners. Though dull and unpromising in his childhood, he afterwards became famous for deeds of valor and heroism, and was gradually raised to the highest offices of the state. As ambassador in Africa, he boldly supported the independence of the Roman character, and when the Carthaginian senate hesitated to choose between peace and war, and desired that he would give whichever he chose, he disdainfully threw open his robe, exclaiming, take war. In his first consulship he obtained a victory over Liguria, and the fatal battle of Thrasymenus occasioned his election to the dictatorship. In this important office he began to oppose the rapid progress of Annibal, not by fighting him in the open field, like his predecessors, but he continually harassed his army by countermarches and ambuscades, from which he received the surname of Cunctator, or *delayer*. Such operations gave offence to some of the senators, and Fabius was even accused of cowardice. He, however, still pursued the measures which prudence and reflection seemed to dictate as most salutary to Rome, and patiently bore to see his master of the horse raised to share the dictatorial dignity with himself, by means of his enemies at home. When he had laid down his office of dictator, his successors for a while wisely followed his plan, till the rashness of Varro, and his contempt for the cautious operations of Fabius, occasioned the fatal battle of Cannæ. Tarentum was obliged to surrender to his arms, after this disgraceful defeat, and on that occasion the Carthaginian enemy observed that Fabius was the Annibal of Rome. When he had made an agreement with Annibal for the ransom of the captives, which was altogether disapproved by the Roman senate, Fabius nobly sold all his estates to pay the money, rather than forfeit his word to the enemy. The bold proposal of young Scipio to go and carry the war from Italy to Africa, was rejected as chimerical and dangerous. He did not, however, live to see the success of the Roman arms under Scipio, and the conquest of Carthage, by measures which he had treated with contempt and heard proposed with indignation. He died in the the 100th year of his age, after he had been five times consul, and twice honored with a triumph. The Romans were so sensible of his great merit and services, that the expenses of his funeral were defrayed from the public treasury. Fabius was called the *shield*, as Marcellus deserved the appellation of the *sword*, of Rome. *Ovid. Fast.* 2. v. 242.—*Cic. Br.* 18. *Orat.* 2. c. 67.—*Plut. in Vitâ.*—*Flor.* 2. c. 6.—*Liv.* 21, &c.—*Sil.* 2. v. 384.—*Polyb.*

FA'BIUS Q. MAX'IMUS, his son, showed himself worthy of his noble father's virtues. During his consulship he received a visit from his father on horseback in the camp. The son ordered the father to dismount, and the old man cheerfully obeyed, embracing his son, and saying, I wished to know whether you knew what it was to be consul. He died before his father, and the Cunctator, with the moderation of a philosopher, delivered a funeral oration over the dead body of his son. *Plut. in Fabio.*

FA'BIUS NUME'RIUS, supposed to be son of Fabius Pictor, wrote the Roman annals in Greek. *Cic. Div.* 1. c. 21.

FA'BIUS PIC'TOR, the first Roman who wrote an historical account of his country, from the age of Romulus to the year of Rome 536. He flourished B.C. 225. The work, which is now extant, and which is attributed to him, is a spurious composition, imposed upon the world by Annius of Viterbum, according to Vossius. *Polyb.* 1.—*Liv.* 1. c. 44. 1. 2. c. 40. 1. 8. c. 30. 1. 10. c. 37 1. 22. c. 7 & 57.—*Voss. de Hist. Lat.* 1. c. 3.—*Harles. Not. Lit. Rom.* 1. p. 81.

FA'BIUS QUIN'TUS, was the only survivor of the Fabian family after the battle of Cremera. He was three times consul, and was at last banished. *Liv.* 3. c. 1, &c.

FA'BIUS MAX'IMUS RULLIA'NUS was the first of the Fabii who obtained the surname of Maximus, for curbing the power of the populace at elections. He was master of the horse to Papirius Cursor the dictator, and his victory over the Samnites in that capacity, nearly cost him his life, because he engaged the enemy without the command of the dictator. He was five times consul, twice dictator, and once censor. He triumphed over seven different nations in the neighbourhood of Rome, and rendered himself illustrious by his patriotism. *Liv.* 8. c. 29 & 38. 1. 9. c. 23.

FA'BIUS RUS'TICUS, an historian in the age of Claudius and Nero. He was intimate with Seneca, and the encomiums which Tacitus pssses upon his style, make us deeply regret the loss of his compositions. *Tac. Ann.* 13. c. 20.

FABRATE'RIA, a colony and town of the Volsci in Latium. *Ital.* 8. v. 398.—*Cic. Fam.* 9. ep. 24.

FABRICIUS, a Latin writer in the age of Nero, who employed his pen in satirizing and defaming the senators. His works were burnt by order of Nero.——A tribune who proposed the recalling of Cicero from exile. *Cic. Sext.* 35. *Red. in Sen.* 8.

FABRIC'IUS, a bridge at Rome, built by the consul Fabricius over the Tiber. *Horat.* 2. sat. 3. v. 36.

FABRIC'IUS CA'IUS LUSCI'NUS, a celebrated Roman who, in his first consulship, obtained several victories over the Samnites and Lucanians, and was honored with a triumph. The riches which were acquired in those battles were immense, the soldiers were liberally rewarded by the consul, and the treasury was enriched with 400 talents. Two years after Fabricius went as ambassador to Pyrrhus, where he rejected with contempt presents, and heard with indignation offers, which might have corrupted the fidelity of a less virtuous citizen. Pyrrhus admired the magnanimity of Fabricius, but his astonishment was more powerfully awakened when he opposed him in the field of battle, and saw him make a discovery of the perfidious offers of his physician, who pledged himself to the Roman general for a sum of money to poison his royal master. To this greatness of soul was added the most consummate knowledge of military affairs, and the greatest simplicity of manners. Fabricius never used silver plate at his table. A small salt-cellar, the feet of which were of horn, was the only silver vessel which appeared in his house. The contempt of luxury and useless ornaments Fabricius wished to inspire among the nobles of Rome, and during his censorship he banished from the senate Cornelius Rufinus, who had been twice consul and dictator, because he kept in his house more than ten pounds weight of silver plate. Such were the austere but simple manners of the conqueror of Pyrrhus, who observed, that he wished rather to command those who had money than possess it himself. He lived and died in the greatest poverty. His body was buried at the public charge, and the Roman people were obliged to give a dowry to his two daughters, when they had arrived at marriageable years. *Val. Max.* 2. c. 9. l. 4. c. 4.—*Flor.* 1. c. 18.—*Cic,* 3. *de Offic.*—*Justin.* 18. c. 2.—*Aul. Gell.* 4. c. 8. l. 17. c. 21.—*Eutrop.* 2. c. 8.—*Plut. in Pyrrh.*—*Virg. Æn.* 6. v. 844.

FABRIC'IUS VEIEN'TO. *Vid.* Veiento.

FABULI'NUS, a divinity worshipped among the Romans, who considered him as presiding over the first articulation of children. *Varro. apud Noni.*

FABUL'LA, a woman of loose character. *Juv.* 2. v. 68,

FACELI'NA or FASCEL'LINA, a small place on the sea shore at the north of Sicily, where Diana had a temple. *Servius ad Virg. Æn.* 2. 117.—*Hygin.* 261.—*Sil.* 14. v. 261.

FA'DIUS Q., a freedman, father of Fulvia, Antony's wife. He was called Bambalio from his stammering. *Cic. Phil.* 2. c. 2 & 36. l. 3. c. 6.

FA'DIUS TI'TUS, a quæstor in Cicero's consulship. He was unjustly banished. *Cic. Fam.* 5. ep. 18. *Ad Att.* 3. ep. 23.

FA'DUS, a Rutulian, killed in the night by Euryalus. *Virg. Æn.* 9. v. 344.

FÆS'ULÆ, now Fiesole, a town of Etruria, famous for its augurs. *Cic. Mur.* 24.—*Ital.* 8. v. 478.—*Sallust. Cat.* 27.

FAGUTA'LIS, a surname of Jupiter, either because the beech *(fagus)* was consecrated to him, or because one of his temples was surrounded with such trees. *Plin.* 16. c. 10.—*Festus de Verb. Sig.*

FALA'CRIUM, a promontory of Sicily, now Rasocolmo. *Ptol.*

FALA'NIUS, a Roman knight accused of treason under Tiberius. *Tac. Ann.* 1. c. 73.

FALCID'IA LEX was enacted by the tribune C. Falcidius, A.U.C. 713, concerning wills and the rights of heirs. *Cic. Man.* 19.

FALCO'NIA PRO'BA, a Roman poetess, A.D. 394, who composed a history of the Old and New Testaments from the verses of Virgil. Some suppose her to have been the same as Anicia Falconia Proba. *Sax. Onom.* 1. p. 438.—*Harles. Not. Lit. Rom.* 1. p. 721.

FALE'RIA, a town of Picenum, now Fallerona, of which the inhabitants were called Falerienses. *Plin.* 3. c. 13.

FALE'RII or -IUM, now Palari, a town of Etruria, near the shores of the Tiber, of which the inhabitants were called Falisci. The Romans borrowed some of their laws from Falerii. The place was famous for its pastures, and for a peculiar sort of sausage. *Vid.* Falisci. *Martial.* 4. epigr. 46.—*Justin.* 20. c. 1.—*Liv.* 10. c. 12 & 16.—*Ovid. Fast.* 1. v. 84. *Pont.* 4. el. 8. v. 41.—*Cato, R. R* 4 & 14.—*Servius in Virg. Æn.* 7. v. 695.—*Plin.* 3. c. 5.—*Strab.* 5.

FALERI'NA, a tribe at Rome. *Liv.* 9. c. 20.

FALER'NUS, a fertile mountain and plain of Campania, famous for its wine, which the Roman poets have greatly celebrated for its superior goodness and flavor. *Liv.* 22. c. 14.—*Plin.* 3. c. 5. l. 14. c. 6.—*Martial.* 12. epigr. 57.—*Virg. G.* 2. v. 96.—*Horat.* 1. od. 20. v. 10, 2. *Sat.* 4. v. 15.—*Strab.* 5. *Flor.* 1. c. 15.—*Varro apud Macrob.* 3. c. 16.

FALIS'CI, a people of Etruria, originally a Macedonian colony. When their town was besieged by Camillus, a schoolmaster went out of the gates with his pupils, and betrayed them into the hands of the Romans, that by possessing so valuable a part of the inhabitants he might easily oblige the place to surrender. Camillus heard the proposal with indignation, and ordered the man to be stripped naked and whipped back to the town by those whom his perfidy wished to betray. This instance of generosity operated upon the people so powerfully that they immediately surrendered to the Romans. *Plut. in Camil.*

FALIS'CUS GRA'TIUS. *Vid.* Gratius.

FA'MA, was worshipped by the ancients as a powerful goddess, and generally represented blowing a trumpet, &c. *Stat.* 3. *Theb.* 427. [There is a statue of this goddess in the collection at Florence.]

FAMISULA'NUS VECTONIA'NUS, a tribune of a legion in Armenia. *Tac. Ann.* 15. c. 7.

FAN'NIA, a woman of Minturnæ, who hospitably entertained Marius in his flight, though he had formerly sat in judgment upon her, and divorced her from her husband.

FAN'NIA LEX, *de Sumptibus*, was enacted by Fannius the consul, A.U.C. 593. It ordered that no person should spend more than 100 *asses* a day at the great festivals, 30 *asses* on other days, and 10 at all other times. *Paterc.* l. c. 17. l. 2. c. 9.—*Aul. Gell.* 2. c. 24.—*Macrob. Sat.* 3. c. 17.

FAN'NIUS CA'IUS, a writer of annals, son-in-law of Lælius. Brutus abridged an elegant history which he had composed *Cic. Br.* 21 & 26. 87. *Tusc.* 4. c. 17. *Att.* 12. ep. 5.

FAN'NIUS CA'IUS, an author in Trajan's reign, the loss of whose history of the cruelties of Nero, in three books, is greatly regretted. Pliny the younger describes him as polished and eloquent, and naturally endowed with great powers of mind, improved by study and exercise. *Plin.*

FAN'NIUS CE'PIO, a person who killed himself when apprehended in a conspiracy which he had formed against Augustus. *Mart.* 12. epigr. 80.

FAN'NIUS QUADRA'TUS, an inferior poet, ridiculed by Horace because his poems and pictures were consecrated in the library of Apollo's temple on mount Palatine, as it was then usual for such as possessed merit. *Horat.* 1. sat. 4. v. 21.

FAN'NIUS, a tribune who commanded in Sicily, during the civil wars. After Cæsar's death, he sided with Cn. Pompey, and advised him to relieve D. Brutus in Mutina. *Cic. Ph.* 13. c. 6. *Att.* 7. ep. 15.

FA'NUM FORTU'NÆ, a town of Umbria, with a celebrated temple to Fortune.

FA'NUM VACU'NÆ, now Vocone, a village in the country of the Sabines. *Horat.* 1. ep. 10. v. 49.

FAR'FARUS, a river of the Sabines, the same as Fabaris. *Vid.* Fabaris. *Ovid. Met.* 14. v. 330.

FAR'NUS or PHAR'NUS, a king of Media. *Diod.*

FASCEL'LINA. *Vid.* Facelina.

FAS'CELIS, a surname of Diana, because her statue was brought from Taurica by Iphigenia in a bundle *(fascis)* of sticks, and placed in the grove of Aricia. *Hygin.* fab. 261.—*Paus* 3. c. 16.—*Servius in Æn.* 2. v. 116.

FAS'CINUS, an early Latin divinity, worshipped as the protector from sorcery, witchcraft, and evil demons.

FAT'UA, a name of a goddess better known under the appellation of Fauna, which she assumed after her marriage with Faunus. *Vid.* Fauna.

FAU'CIUS M., a magistrate at Arpinum. *Cic. Fam.* 13. 11.

FAU'CULA, a prostitute who privately conveyed food to the Roman prisoners at Capua. *Liv.* 26. c. 33.

FAU'LA, a mistress of Hercules. *Verrius ap. Lactant.*

FAU'NA, a deity among the Romans, daughter of Picus, and originally called Marica. Her marriage with Faunus procured her the name of Fauna, and her knowledge of futurity that of *Fatua* and *Fatidica*. It is said that she never saw a man after her marriage with Faunus, and that her uncommon chastity occasioned her being ranked among the gods after death. She is the same, according to some as *Bona Mater*. Some mythologists, however, accuse her of drunkenness, and say that she expired under the blows of her husband, for an immoderate use of wine. *Virg. Æn.* 7. v. 47, &c.—*Varro apud Lact. de Fals. R.* 22. —*Macrob. Sat.* 1. c. 12.—*Justin.* 43. c. 1.

FAUNA'LIA, festivals at Rome, in honor of Faunus.

FAU'NI, certain deities of the country, represented as having the legs, feet, and ears of goats, and the rest of the body human. They were called satyrs by the Greeks. The peasants offered them a lamb or a kid with great solemnity. *Virg. G.* 1. v. 10.—*Ovid. Met.* 6. v. 392.—*Horat.* 1. od. 4. v. 11.—18. v. 2.

FAU'NUS, a son of Picus, who is said to have reigned in Italy about 1300 years B.C. His bravery as well as wisdom have given rise to the tradition that he was son of Mars. He raised a temple in honor of Pan, called by the Latins Lupercus, at the foot of the Palatine hill, and dispensed his hospitality to strangers with a liberal hand. His great popularity and fondness for agriculture, made his subjects revere him as one of their country deities after his death. He was consulted by his votaries, as he had the power of delivering oracles. *Dionys.* 1. c. 7.—*Virg. Æn.* 7. v. 47. l. 8. v. 314. l. 10. v. 55.—*Horat.* 1. od. 17.—*Justin.* 43. c. 1.—*Ovid. Fast.* 2. v. 424.

FAUS'TA, a daughter of Sylla, wife of Milo. *Horat.* 1. sat. 2. v. 64.—*Cic. Att.* 5. ep. 8.—*Plut. in Syll.* ——The wife of the emperor Constantine, daughter of Maximian, and sister of Maxentius. She prostituted herself to the meanest of the people, and caused her son-in-law Crispus to be put to death because he refused to gratify her guilty passion. Constantine soon became informed of her infidelity and licentiousness, and she expiated her crimes by being suffocated in a warm bath, A.D. 327. *Zosim.* l. 2.—*Amm. Marcell.* 14.

FAUSTI'NA, the wife of the emperor Antoninus Pius, rendered herself infamous by her debaucheries. She died A.D. 141, in her 37th year. [There is a statue of this empress in the Museum of the Capitol, and a bust in the Vatican.]——Daughter of the preceding, though blessed with beauty, liveliness, and wit, became the most abandoned of her sex. She married M. Aurelius the emperor, who pitied, but did not punish, her irregularities. She died A.D. 175, near mount Taurus in Asia, as she was attending her husband in his expedition against the rebellious Cassius. [There is a bust of this Faustina in the Capitol.]——The third wife of the emperor Heliogabalus, was grand-daughter to the preceding. She was happily unlike her predecessors in their licentious conduct, but not possessed of such personal charms. [A bust of this Faustina is also to be found in the Capitol.]

FAUS'TITAS, a goddess among the Romans, supposed to preside over cattle. *Horat.* 4. od. 5. v. 17.

FAUS'TULUS, a shepherd of Amulius, king of Alba, ordered to expose Romulus and Remus. He privately brought them up at home. *Liv.* 1. c. 4.—*Justin.* 43. c. 2.—*Plut. in Rom.*

FAUS'TUS, an obscure poet under the first Roman emperors, two of whose dramatic pieces, Thebæ and Tereus, are mentioned by *Juvenal*, 7. v. 12. ——A name given by Sylla to his son, born after his elevation to the dictatorship. *Plut. in Syll.*—*Cic. Sull.* 19. *Clu.* 34. *Att.* 4. ep. 10.

FAVEN'TIA, a town of Spain. *Plin.* 3. c. 1.——A town of Italy, now Faenza. *Ptol.* 2. c. 4. l. 3. c. 1. —*Ital.* 8. v. 597.—*Plin.* 14. c. 15.—*Martial.* 2. epigr. 74.

FAVE'RIA, a town of Istria. *Liv.* c. 11.

FA'VO, a Roman mimic, who, at the funeral of Vespasian, imitated the manners and gestures of the deceased emperor. *Suet. in Vesp.* 19.

FAVO'NIUS, the name of one of the winds. *Vid.* Venti.

Favo'nius, a man called the ape of Cato, because he imitated his manners. Augustus cruelly put him to death after the battle of Philippi. *Suet. Aug.* 13.—*Val. Max.* 2. c. 10.

FAVORI'NUS, a philosopher and eunuch at Rome, in the reign of Adrian. He was born at Arles in Gaul, and taught in the schools of Athens and Rome with reputation and success. The extent of his learning did not procure him the favor of the emperor, as Adrian wished to be considered first in science as well as in power. Among the works ascribed to his pen is a Greek miscellaneous history, often quoted by Diogenes Laertius. *A. Gell.* 1. c. 3.—*Ælian de Var. Hist.*

FEBIA'NA CAS'TRA, a town of Suevia, now Bebenhausen. *Ptol.*

FE'BRIS, the goddess or averter of fever at Rome.

FEB'RUUS, a god at Rome, who presided over purifications. Pluto was sometimes called by this name, as oblations of purification were offered to the manes of the dead. Juno was often invoked under the name of Februa, as she presided over parturition, and in that character influenced the evacuation of the secundines. The Feralia, sacrifices which the Romans offered to the gods Manes, were also called Februa, whence the name of the month of February, during which the oblations were made. *Varro. de L.L.* 5. c. 3.—*Macrob. Sat.* 1. c. 13 —*Ovid. Fast.* 2. v. 19.—*Marti. Capell.* 2. —*Servius in Georg.* 1. v. 43.—*Isidor.* 5. c. 33.

FECIA'LES, a number of priests at Rome, employed in declaring war against foreign nations, and in proclaiming peace. When the Romans thought themselves injured, one of this sacerdotal body was empowered to demand redress, and after the allowance of 33 days to consider the matter, war was declared if submissions were not made, and the Fecialis hurled a bloody spear into the territories of the enemy in proof of intended hostilities. *Liv.* 1. c. 3. l. 4. c. 30.—*Dionys. Hal.* 2. c. 19.—*Plut. in Num.*

FEL'GINAS, a Roman knight, killed by Pompey, at Dyrrachium. *Cæs.* 3. *Bell. Civ.*

FELIC'ITAS, a divinity at Rome, who presided over happiness, and to whom the Romans erected a temple in the age of Augustus. *Aug. Civ. D.* 4. c. 21. —*Plin.* 34. c. 8.

FELIGINA'TES, a people of Umbria. *Plin.* 3. c. 14.

FE'LIX M. ANTO'NIUS, a freedman of Claudius Cæsar, made governor of Judæa, Samaria, and Palestine. He is called by Suetonius the husband of three queens, as he married the two Drusillæ, one grand-daughter of Antony and Cleopatra, and the other a Jewish princess, sister of Agrippa. The name of his third wife is unknown.—*Suet. in Cl.* 18.—*Tacit. Ann.* 12. c. 14.

Fe'lix Minu'tius. *Vid.* Minutius.

FELSI'NA or FEL'SINA, a city of Italy, afterwards called Bononia. *Plin.* 3. c. 15.

FEL'TRIA, a town of Italy at the north of Venice.

FENESTEL'LA, a Roman historian, author of annals, and other works, quoted by *Pliny*, *Gellius*, and others. The work on the priesthood and magistracy of Rome, commonly attributed to him, is a forgery of Fiocchi or Flocco. The fragment of his annals has been edited by Haverkamp in the second volume of his Sallust. He died at Cumæ, A.D. 20. in his 70th year. *Harles. Not. Lit. Rom.* 1. p. 210.—*Voss. de H. Lat.* 1. c. 19.

Fenestel'la, one of the gates of Rome. *Ovid. Fast.* 6. v. 578.

FE'NIUS RU'FUS, a præfect of the prætorian cohort under Nero. *Tac. Ann.* 13. c. 22, &c.

FEN'NI or FIN'NI, the inhabitants of Finningia or Eningia, thought to be modern Finland. *Tacit. G.* 46.—*Plin.* 4. c. 13.

FERA'LIA, a festival in honor of the dead, observed at Rome on the 17th or 21st of February. It continued for 11 days, during which presents were carried to the graves of the deceased, marriages were forbidden, and the temples of the gods were shut. It was universally believed that the manes of their departed friends came and hovered over their graves and feasted upon the provisions. Their punishments in the infernal regions were also suspended, and during that time they were supposed to enjoy rest and liberty. *Val. Max.* 11.—*Ovid. Fast.* 11. v. 631.

FERENTI'NUM, a town of the Hernici, at the east of Rome. The inhabitants were called Ferentinates, or Ferentini. *Sil.* 8. v. 394.—*Liv.* 1. c. 50. l. 9. c. 43 & 44.

FEREN'TUM or FOREN'TUM, a town of Apulia, now Forenza. *Horat.* od. 4. v. 15.—*Liv.* 9. c. 16 & 20.

FERE'TRIUS, a surname of Jupiter, *a ferendis spoliis*, because he aided the Romans under Romulus. He had a temple at Rome, built by Romulus, where the spoils called *opima*, obtained from Acron, king of Cænina, were deposited by the victorious monarch. Only two generals obtained these celebrated spoils after the age of Romulus. *Liv.* 1. c. 10.—*Plut. in Rom.*— *C. Nep. in Att.* 20.—*Festus de Verb. Sig.*—*Propert.* 4. el. 11. v. 46.

FE'RIÆ LATI'NÆ, a festival at Rome instituted by Tarquinius Superbus. The principal magistrates of 47 towns in Latium usually assembled on a mount near Rome, where they, together with the Roman magistrates, offered a bull to Jupiter Latialis, of which they carried home some part, after they had sworn mutual friendship and alliance. This festival continued but one day originally, but in process of time four days were dedicated to its celebration. *Dionys. Hal.* 4. c. 49.—*Cic. ad Fam.* 8. ep. 6, *Pro. Planc.*—*Liv.* 21. c. 63. The Feriæ among the Romans were certain days set apart to celebrate festivals, and during that time it was unlawful for any person to work. These solemnities were either public or private. The public were of four different kinds. The *feriæ stativæ* were certain immoveable days always marked in the calendar, and observed by the whole city with much festivity and public rejoicing. The *feriæ conceptivæ* were moveable feasts, and the day appointed for the celebration was always previously fixed by the magistrates or priests. Among these were the *feriæ Latinæ*, which were first established by Tarquin, and regularly observed by the consuls before they set out for the provinces; the *Compitalitæ*, &c. The *feriæ imperativæ* were appointed only by command of the consul, dictator, or prætor, as a public rejoicing for some important victory gained over the enemies of Rome. The *feriæ nundinæ* were regular days in which the people of the country and neighbouring towns assembled together and exposed their respective commodities to sale. They were called *nundinæ* because kept every ninth day. The *feriæ privatæ* were observed only in families in commemoration of birthdays, marriages, funerals, and the like. The days on which the *feriæ* were observed were called by the Romans *festi dies*, because dedicated to mirth, relaxation, and festivity. *Liv.* 1. 55 & 6. 42.—*Tac. Ann.* 11. 82.—*Dio.* 52. 8, &c.

FERO'NIA, a nymph of Campania, who presided over the woods and groves, and was worshipped by the Romans as a goddess. The name was derived *a ferendo*, because she gave assistance to her votaries, or perhaps from the town of Feronia, near mount Soracte, where she had a temple. It was usual to make a yearly sacrifice to her, and to wash the face and hands of the votaries in the waters of the sacred fountain, which flowed near her temple. It is said that those who were inspired with the spirit of this goddess could walk barefooted over burning coals without receiving any injury from the flame. The goddess had a temple and grove about three miles from Anxur, which was plundered of all its riches by Annibal on his return from the neighbourhood of Rome. She had also another in the district of Capena. *Liv.* 22. c. 1. l. 26. c. 11. l. 33. c. 26.—*Virg. Æn.* 7. v. 697 & 800.—*Varro. de L.L.* 4. c. 10.—*Servius in Æn.* 8. v. 564.—*Alex. ab Alex.* 4. c. 10.—*Ital.* 13. v. 84.—*Strab.* 5.—*Horat.* 1. sat. 5. v. 24.

Fero'nia, a city at the bottom of mount Soracte. *Horat.* 1. *Serm.* 5. v. 24.

FERRA'RIA or DIA'NIUM, a promontory of Spain, now Cabo Martin. *Mela*, 2.

FERRA'TUS MONS, one of the principal mountains of Africa, on the borders of Mauritania.

FESCEN'NIUM or FESCEN'NIA (*-orum*), a town of Etruria, now Galese, where the *Fescennine verses* were first invented. These verses, the name of which conveys an idea of vulgar obscenity, were a sort of rustic dialogue spoken *ex tempore*, in which the actors exposed the failings and vices of their adversaries, and endeavoured to raise the laughter of the company. They were often repeated at nuptials, as also at harvest-home. They were proscribed by Augustus as of immoral tendency. *Plin.* 3. c. 5.—*Seneca, Contr.* 21.—*Festus de V. Sig.*—*Virg. Æn.* 7. v. 695 & *Servius loco.*—*Horat.* 2. ep. 1. v. 145.—*Macrob. Sat.* 2. c. 4.

FESSO'NIA, a goddess at Rome, supposed to aid the weary *(fessi)*, especially soldiers. *August. de Civ. Dei.* 1. 4.

FES'TUS, a friend of the emperor Domitian, who killed himself in an illness. *Martial.* 1. epigr. 79.

Fes'tus Pompe'ius, a grammarian who abridged the work of Verrius Flaccus *De significatione verborum*. Scaliger speaks of him with commendation. The best edition is that of Dacier, Paris, 1681; it was re-edited by Le Clerc, with the notes of Scaliger. Fulvius Ursinus, and A. Augustinus. Amstel. 1699. 4to. *Harles. Not. Lit. Rom.* 1. p. 576.

Fes'tus Por'cius, a pro-consul who succeeded Felix as governor of Judæa, under Claudius. His name is mentioned in the Acts of the Apostles.

FES'ULÆ. *Vid.* Fæsulæ.

FIBRE'NUS, a river of Italy, falling into the Liris, after passing through Cicero's farm at Arpinum. *Sil.* 8. v. 400.—*Cic. Leg.* 2. c. 1.

FICA'NA, a town of Latium, at the south of Rome, near the Tiber, and not far from Ostia. *Liv.* 1. c. 33.

FICA'RIA, a small island at the east of Sardinia, now Serpentaria. *Plin.* 3. c. 7.

FICOLEN'SES, a people of Italy, near the Samnites. *Plin.* 3. c. 5.

FICU'LEA or FICUL'NEA, a small town of Latium beyond mount Sacer at the north of Rome. Cicero had a villa there, and the road that led to the town was called Ficulnensis, afterwards Nometana Via. *Cic.* 12. *Att.* 34. *Div.* 1. c. 38. 3. c. 52.

FIDE'NA or FIDE'NÆ, an inland town of Latium, at the north of Rome on the banks of the Tiber: the inhabitants were called Fidenates. The place was conquered by the Romans, B.C. 435. *Virg. Æn.* 6. v. 773.—*Juv.* 1. v. 44. *Dionys. Hal.* 2. c. 13.—*Horat.* 1. ep. 11. v. 8.—*Ptol.* 3. c. 1.—*Liv.* 1. c. 14, 15 & 27. l. 2. c. 19. l. 4. c. 17 & 21.

FIDEN'TIA, a town of Cisalpine Gaul, on the south of the Po, between Placentia and Parma. *Vell.* 2. c. 28.—*Plin.* 3. c. 15.—*Cic. In.* 2. c. 54.

FIDEN'TIÆ, a city of Hispania Bætica, otherwise Julia. *Plin.* 3. c. 11.

FI'DES, the goddess of faith, oaths, and honesty, worshipped by the Romans. Numa was the first who paid her divine honors, and he directed that her worship should be maintained at the expense of the public. The temple raised in honor of the goddess gradually fell into decay, but was rebuilt by Att. Collatinus. It stood in the capitol, according to Pliny, though Cicero says that only the statue of the goddess was there. The only dress of this divinity was a white veil, expressive of frankness, candor, and modesty, and the heads and hands of her priests were likewise adorned with white, they were permitted to offer oblations only with the right hand. No animal was offered on her altars, as the goddess was an enemy to bloodshed. Sometimes she is represented with a cup in one hand, and in the other a cornucopia, sometimes sitting, and crowned with an olive branch; with a turtle, the symbol of peace, in one hand, and a military ensign in the other. The symbol of fidelity is represented by two hands strongly joined together. *Varr. de L.L.* 4. c. 10.—*Cic. de Off.* 3. *De N. D.* 2.—*Dion. Hal.* 2. c. 21.—*Plin.* 35. c. 10.—*Horat.* 1. od. 35.—*Plut. in Numâ.*

FIDIC'ULÆ, a place of Italy. *Val. Max.* 7. c. 6.

FIDICULA'NIUS FAL'CULA, a senator at Rome, mentioned by *Cicero, Cluent.* 37. *Cæcin.* 10.

FID'IUS DI'US, a divinity, the god of faith and truth, by whom the Romans generally swore. He was also called Sanctus Sabus, and Semipater, and he was solemnly addressed in prayers on the 5th of June, which was yearly consecrated to his service. Some suppose him to have been the same as Hercules, while others assert that he was the first king of the Sabines, whom either the gratitude or the adulation of his subjects, and of his son Sabus, who gave his name to the nation elevated to rank with the gods after his death. *Festus de V. Sig.*—*Lactant. Fals. R.* 15.—*Aug. de Civ D.* 18. c. 19.—*Plaut. Asin.* 1. v. 48.—*Ovid. Fast.* 6. v. 213.—*Varro de L.L.* 4. c. 10.—*Dionys. Hal.* 2 & 9.

FIDUS'TIUS M., a Roman senator, proscribed by Sylla, and 33 years after by Antony, by whom he was put to death. *Plin.* 7. c. 43.—*Dio.* 47.

FIG'ULUS, a consul with L. Cæsar, A.U. 690. His tomb is described as having been very sumptuous. *Cic. Leg.* 2. c. 25. *Att.* 1. ep. 2.

Fig'ulus C. Mar'cius, a consul with Nasica, A.U. 592. He resigned his office, through the informality of his election, and was six years after consul with Lentulus. *Cic. Br.* 20. *Div.* 2. c. 35.—*N.D.* 2. c. 4.

Fig'ulus Nigid'ius, a senator known for his great knowledge of astrology. *Lucan.* 1. v. 639.

FIM'BRIA C. FLA'VIUS, a Roman consul, A.U. 650. He served in Asia with the consul Valerius

Flaccus, whom he put to death, and after displaying great courage in his encounters with the armies of Pontus, he took their king, Mithridates, prisoner. The return of Sylla into Asia, and the consequent peace, put an end to the ambitious hopes of Fimbria, who, seeing the success of his rival, and the rapid desertion of his own troops to his party, killed himself. *Plut in Lucull.—Cic. Rab.* 7. *Off.* 3. c. 19.—*Liv.* 82. 83.

FIRÆ'SI, a people of Scandinavia; their country is now Fiering. *Ptol.*

FIRMA'NUS TARUTIUS, a mathematician and astrologer at Rome, who, from the horoscope of Romulus, determined the era of Rome.

FIRMIA'NUS SYMPO'SIUS CÆLIUS, author of 100 riddles for promoting the festivities of the Saturnalia. *Printed* in the *Poet. Lat. Min.* of Wernsdorf, vol. 6.

FIR'MICUS MATER'NUS JU'LIUS, a writer in the age of Constantine the Great; supposed author of a book in favour of Christianity, entitled, *De Errore profanarum religionum ad Constantium et Constantem.*

FIR'MIUS CA'TUS, a senator banished to an island, &c. *Tac. Ann.* 2. c. 27, &c.

FIR'MUM, now Fermo, a town of Picenum on the Adriatic, the part of which was called Castellum Firmanorum. *Cic.* 8 *Att.* 12.—*Plin.* 7. c. 8.—*Velleius.* 1. c. 14.

FIR'MUS M., a powerful native of Seleucia who proclaimed himself emperor of Rome, and was at last conquered by Aurelian.

FISCEL'LUS, a part of the Apennine mountains in Umbria, near which the Nar rises. *Ital.* 8. v. 518. —*Plin.* 3. c. 12.

FIS'ERA, a city of Corsica. *Ptol.*

FLACCIL'LA ANTO'NIA, a Roman matron in Nero's age, &c. *Tac. Ann.* 15. c. 7.

FLACIL'LA Æ'LIA, the mother of the emperor Arcadius and Honorius, was daughter of Antonius, a præfect of Gaul.

FLAC'CUS, a consul who marched against Sylla, and was assassinated by Fimbria. *Plut.*——A poet. *Vid.* Valerius.——A governor of Ægypt, who died A.D. 39.——A name of the poet Horace. *Vid.* Horatius. This surname was given to the families of the Fulvii and Valerii, from their broad and loose ears. *Plin.* 11. c. 87.

FLAC'CUS VER'RIUS, a grammarian, tutor to the two grandsons of Augustus, and the supposed author of the Capitoline marbles.

FLAMI'NES, priests at Rome, instituted by Numa. Of these Dialis was consecrated to the service of Jupiter, Martialis to Mars, Quirinalis to Quirinus. *Festus.—Priscian.*

FLAMIN'IA LEX, *agraria*, by C. Flaminius, the tribune, A.U.C. 525. It required that the lands of Picenum, from which the Galli Senones had been expelled, should be divided among the Roman people.

FLAMIN'IA VI'A, a celebrated road which led from Rome to Ariminum and Aquileia. It received its name from Flaminius, who built it, and was killed at the battle of Thrasymenus against Annibal. ——A gate of Rome opening to the Via Flaminia, now called del Popolo.

FLAMIN'IUS C., a Roman consul, of a turbulent disposition, who was drawn into a battle near the lake of Thrasymenus, by the artifice of Annibal. He was killed in the engagement, and an immense number of Romans shared his unhappy fate, B.C. 217. The conqueror wished to give a burial to his body, but it could not be found in the heaps of slain. While tribune of the people, Flaminius proposed an agrarian law against the advice of his friends, of the senate, and of his own father. *Cic. de Inv.* 2. c. 17. *N.D.* 2. c. 3. *Div.* 1. c. 35. l. 2. c. 33.—*Liv.* 22. c. 3, &c.—*Polyb.—Flor.* 2. c. 6.—*Val. Max.* 1. c. 6.

FLAMIN'IUS CALP. FLAM'MA, a tribune, who at the head of 300 men saved the Roman army in Sicily, B.C. 258, by engaging the Carthaginians and cutting them to pieces.

FLAMIN'IUS TI'TUS QUIN'TUS, called also Flaminius, a celebrated Roman raised to the consulship, A.U. C. 556, was trained in the art of war in the campaigns against Annibal. He was sent at the head of the Roman troops against Philip, king of Macedonia, and in his expedition he met with uncommon success. He totally defeated Philip on the confines of Epirus, and made all Locris, Phocis, and Thessaly, tributary to the Roman power. He granted peace to the conquered monarch, and proclaimed all Greece free and independent at the Isthmian games. He thus procured the name of patrons of Greece for the Romans, and insensibly paved their way to universal dominion. Flaminius by his ready compliance with their national customs and prejudices, gained uncommon popularity, and received the name of father and deliverer of Greece. He was afterwards sent ambassador to king Prusias, who had given refuge to Annibal, and his intrigues and artifice hastened out of the world a man who had long been a terror to the Romans. Flaminius was found dead in his bed, after a life spent in the greatest glory, in which he had imitated with success the virtues of his great model Scipio. *Cic. Mur.* 14.—*Liv.* 33. c. 7, &c. *Plut. in Vitâ.—Flor.*

FLAMIN'IUS LU'CIUS, the brother of the preceding, signalized himself in the wars of Greece. He was expelled by Cato, his brother's colleague in the censorship, for killing a Gaul; an action which was highly resented by his brother Titus. *Plut. in Flam.—Liv.* 32. c. 16. l. 39. c. 42. l. 43. c. 11.—*Cic. Sen.* 12.

FLAMMONIEN'SES, a people near the Veneti. *Plin.* 3. c. 19.

FLANAT'ICUS SI'NUS, a bay of the Flanates, in Liburnia, on the Adriatic, now the gulph of Quarnero. *Plin.* 3. c. 19 & 21.

FLA'VIA, a city of Palestine. *Plin.* 5. c. 3.——A city of Hispania Tarraconensis. *Ptol.*

FLA'VIA LEX, *agraria*, enacted by L. Flavius, A.U.C. 693, for the distribution of a certain quantity of land among Pompey's soldiers and the commons.

FLAVIN'IUM or FLAVI'NA, now Fojano, a town of Etruria, on the banks of the Tibur. The inhabitants assisted Turnus against Æneas. *Virg. Æn.* 7. 696.—*Sil.* 8. v. 492.

FLA'VIUM, a town of Noricum, now S. Andres. *Plin.* 3. c. 24.

FLA'VIUM BRIGAN'TIUM, a city of the Callaici, now Compostella. *Ptol.*

FLA'VIUS SCEVI'NUS, a senator who conspired with Piso against Nero, &c. *Tacit. Ann.* 15. c. 40.

FLA'VIUS, a Roman who informed Gracchus of the violent measures adopted by the senate against him. ——The name of the emperor Vespasian's family. Hence his partisans are called Flaviani, and Domitian his son, *Flavius ultimus. Suet. Vesp.* 1. *Dom.* 10 & 18.—*Tacit. Hist.* 3. c. 7 & 23.—*Juv.* 4. v. 37.——A tribune who wounded one of Annibal's elephants in an engagement.——A schoolmaster of great eminence at Rome in the age of *Horace.* 1. sat. 6. v. 72.

FLA'VIUS LU'CIUS, a tribune, who, to little purpose, proposed an agrarian law. He was prætor in the consulship of Cæsar and Bibulus, and warmly espoused the cause of the dictator in the civil war. *Cic. Att.* 1. ep. 18 & 19. l. 10. ep. 1. *Ad. Fr.* 1. ep. 2.—*Dio.* 37. c. 52.

FLA'VIUS MAR'CUS, a tribune, who wished the people of Tusculum to be punished, &c. *Liv.* 8. c. 37.

FLAVO'NA, a town of Illyricum. *Ptol.—Plin.* 3. c. 21. Some however read Flammona.

FLA'VUS L. CÆSE'TIUS, tribune of the people B.C. 44; was removed from office by Julius Cæsar, because he removed the crowns from his statues, and had imprisoned a man for saluting him as king.

FLA'VUS SU'BRIUS, a tribune in the prætorian guard; was the most active of the conspirators against Nero, A.D. 66: called Piso's conspiracy.

FLE'VUS, the right branch of the Rhine, which formed a large lake on its falling into the sea called Flevo, now Zuider-Zee. It was afterwards called Helium, now Ulie; when its breadth became more contracted, and a fort was erected there which obtained the name of Flevium Frisiorum. *Tacit. Ann.* 2. c. 6. l. 4. v. 72.—*Plin.* 4. c. 15.—*Mela*, 3. c. 2.

FLO'RA, the goddess of flowers and gardens among the Romans, was the same as the Chloris of the Greeks. Some suppose that she was originally a common courtezan, who left to the Romans the immense riches which she had acquired by her lasciviousness, in remembrance of which a yearly festival was instituted in her honour. She was worshipped even among the Sabines, long before the foundation of Rome, and likewise among the Phoceans, who built Marseilles, many years before the existence of the capital of Italy. Tatius was the first who raised her a temple in the city of Rome. It is said that Flora married Zephyrus, and that she received from him the privilege of presiding over flowers, and of enjoying perpetual youth. *Vid.* Floralia. She was generally represented as crowned with flowers, and holding in her hand the horn of plenty. *Ovid. Fast.* 5. v. 195, &c.—*Justin.* 43. c. 4.—*Plut. in Rom.*—*Varro de R. R.* 1. c. 13.—*Lactant.* 1. c. 20. [These is a colossal statue of this goddess in the Farnese collection, now removed to Naples; and another small one, of superior workmanship, in the Museum of the Capitol.]——A celebrated courtezan, passionately loved by Pompey the Great. She was so beautiful, that when the temple of Castor and Pollux at Rome, was adorned with paintings, her picture was placed among them.——Another courtezan, &c. *Juv.* 2. v. 49.

FLORA'LIA, games celebrated at Rome in honour of Flora. They began on the 28th of April, and continued for several days. They were instituted about the age of Romulus, but they were not celebrated with regularity till the year U.C. 580 They were observed yearly, and exhibited a scene of the most unbounded licentiousness. It is reported that Cato wished once to be present at the celebration, and that when he saw that the awe occasioned by his presence interrupted the festival, he retired, not chosing to be a spectator of the exhibition of naked women in a public theatre This behaviour so captivated the degenerate Romans, that the virtuous and venerable senator was treated with the most uncommon applause as he retired. *Val. Max.* 2. c. 10.—*Varro de L. L.* 1. c. 23.—*Paterc.* 1. c. 14.—*Plin.* 18. c. 29.—*Ovid. Fast.* 5. v. 195.—*Alex. ab Alex.* 6. c. 8.—*Lactant.* 1. c. 20.—*Seneca.* ep. 97.—*Mart.* 8. epigr. 67.

FLOREN'TIA, a town of Italy on the Arnus, now Florence, the rich and magnificent capital of Tuscany. It was originally called Fluentia, from its being situated on the streams (*fluentia*) of the Arnus. *Tacit. An.* 1. c. 79.—*Flor.* 3. c. 21.—*Plin.* 3. c. 5.

FLORIA'NUS, a man who wore the imperial purple at Rome for two months only, A.D. 276. *Aur. Vict. in vitâ.*

FLO'RUS L. ANNÆUS JU'LIUS, a Latin historian of the same family which produced Seneca and Lucan, A.D. 116. He wrote an abridgement of Roman annals in four books, composed in a florid and poetical style, and which is to be considered rather as a panegyric on many of the great actions of the Romans than a faithful and correct recital of their history. Florus also wrote poetry, and ventured to enter the lists against the emperor Adrian, who satirically reproached him with frequenting taverns and places of dissipation. The best editions of Florus are Duker's, 2 vols. 8vo, L. Bat. 1722 & 1744; and that of J. Frid. Fischer, 8vo, Lips. 1760. *Lactant. Inst. D.* 7, c. 15.—*Spartian.*—*Vossius.*—*Harles. Not. Lit. Rom.* 1. p. 427.

Flo'rus Ju'lius, a friend of Horace, who accompanied Claudius Nero in his military expeditions. The poet has addressed two epistles to him.——A noble person of the Treviri, who excited his countrymen to rebellion. *Tac. Ann.* 3. c. 42.

Flo'rus Ges'sius, also called Festus, and Cestius Florus, was a native of Clazomenæ. His cruel and oppressive conduct in his government of Judæa, drove the Jews into rebellion A.D. 65.

FLUO'NIA, a surname of Juno Lucina, who was invoked under that appellation by the Roman matrons, to stop excessive discharges of blood. *Mart. Cap.* 2.—*Festus. de V. Sig.*—*Arnobius*, 3.

FO'CAS, a Roman grammarian, author of a life of Virgil in verse. *Voss. de H. Lat.* p. 817.

FOCUNA'TES, a people of the Alps. *Plin.* 3. c. 20.

FO'LIA, a woman of Ariminum, remarkable for her knowledge of poisonous herbs, and for her petulance. *Horat.* ep. 5. v. 42.

FONS SO'LIS, a fountain in the province of Cyrene, which was said to be cool at mid-day and warm at the rising and setting of the sun. *Herodot.* 4. c. 181.

FONTA'NUS, a poet mentioned by *Ovid. Pont.* 4. el. 16.

FONTE'IA, a vestal virgin. *Cic. Font.* 17.——A plebeian family at Rome, into which Clodius was adopted. *Vid.* Fonteius.

FONTE'IUS CAPI'TO, an intimate friend of *Horace.* 1 sat. 5. v. 32.

Fonte'ius Ti'tus, a prætor who was for some time governor of Spain. *Liv.* 40 & 41.

Fonte'ius Mar'cus, a governor of Gaul, in whose defence Cicero exerted his oratorical powers. *Cic. Font.* 1. *Att.* 4. ep. 15.

Fonte'ius, a Roman, who raised commotions in Germany after the death of Nero. *Tacit. Hist.* 1. c. 7.——A man who conducted Cleopatra into Syria by order of Antony. *Plut. in Ant.*

FONTINA'LIA, a festival celebrated at the Porta Fontinalis of Rome, on the 13th of October, in honour of the nymphs who presided over fountains. During the ceremonies observed upon the occasion, wells and fountains were ornamented with garlands. *Festus de V. Sig.*—*Varro de L. L.* 5. c. 3.—*Liv.* 35. c. 10.

FON'TUS, a Roman divinity, son of Janus. He presided over flowing waters.

FOR'CULUS or **FORICULUS**, a deity at Rome, who presided over doors. *Tertull. de Id.* 15. *De Corn. Mil.* 13.—*Aug. de Civ. D.* 4. c. 8.

FORDICID'IA, a festival at Rome, on the 17th of the Calends of March, so called from the slaughter of pregnant cows, (*fordæ*). *Ovid. Fast.* 1. 4. v. 629.

FOREN'TUM, a town of Italy. *Vid.* Ferentum.

FORETA'NI or **FORE'TII**, a people of Italy, beyond the Po. *Plin.* 3. c. 5.

FOR'MIÆ, a maritime town of Campania, at the north-east of Caieta. It was anciently the abode of the Læstrygones, and it became known for the excellent wines which were produced on the neighbouring hills. It was occasionally called *Mamurrarum urbs*, from the *Mamurræ*, a family of consequence and opulence who lived there. *Liv.* 8. c 14. l. 38. c. 36.—*Horat.* 1. od. 20. v. 11. l. 3. od. 17. 1 sat. 5. v. 37.—*Plin.* 36. c. 6.

FORMIA'NUM, a villa of Cicero near Formiæ, in the neighbourhood of which the orator was assassinated. *Cic. Fam.* 11. ep. 27. l. 16. ep. 10.—*Tacit. Ann.* 16. c. 10.

FOR'MIO, now Risano, a river of Istria, the ancient boundary of Italy eastward, afterwards extended to the Arsia. *Plin.* 3. c. 18 & 19.

FOR'NAX, a goddess at Rome, who presided over the baking of bread. Her festivals, called *Fornacalia*, were first instituted by Numa. *Ovid Fast.* 2. v. 525.—*Plin.* 18. c. 2.

FO'RO AP'PII, a people of Italy, whose capital was called *Forum Appii.* *Vid.* Forum Appii. *Plin.* 3. c, 5.

Fo'ro Augusta'na, a city of Hispania Citerior, called also *Libisosona.* *Plin.* 3. c. 3.

Fo'ro Bremita'ni, a people of Umbria. *Id.* 3, c, 14.

FORTU'NA, a powerful deity among the ancients, daughter of Oceanus according to Homer, or one of the Parcæ according to Pindar. The goddess of Fortune was worshipped in different parts of Greece and in Achaia her statue held the horn of plenty in one hand, and had a winged Cupid at its feet. In Bœotia she had a statue which represented her as holding Plutus the god of riches in her arms, to intimate that fortune is the source whence wealth and honours flows. Bupalus was the first artist who made a statue of Fortune for the people of Smyrna, and he represented her with the polar star upon her head, and the horn of plenty in her hand. The Romans paid particular attention to the goddess of Fortune, to whose favour they were so much indebted, and they had no less than eight different temples erected to her honour in their city. Tullus Hostilius was the first who built her a temple. Her most famous temple in Italy was at Antium, in Latium, where presents and offerings were regularly sent from every part of the country. Fortune has been called Pherepolis, the protectress of cities, and Acrea from her temple at Corinth on an eminence, ἄκρον. She was called Prænestine at Præneste in Italy, where she had also a temple. Besides, she was worshipped among the Romans under different names, such as Female fortune, Virile fortune, Equestrian, Evil, Peaceful, Virgin, &c. On the first of April, which was consecrated to Venus among the Romans, the Italian widows and marriageable virgins assembled in the temple of Virile fortune, and, after burning incense and stripping themselves of their garments, they intreated the goddess to hide from the eyes of their husbands whatever defects there might be on their bodies. The goddess of Fortune is represented on ancient monuments with a horn of plenty, and sometimes two, in her hands. She is blind-folded, and generally holds a wheel in her hand as an emblem of her perpetual inconstancy. Sometimes she appears with wings, and treads upon the prow of a ship, and holds a rudder in her hands *Dionys. Hal.* 4.—*Ovid. Fast.* 6. v. 569.—*Plut. de Fort. Rom & in Cor.*——*Cic. de Div.* 2.—*Liv.* 10. —*Augustin. de Civ. D.* 4. c. 18.—*Flor.* 1.—*Val. Max.* 1. c. 5.—*Homer. Hym. in Cerer.*—*Pindar apud Paus.* 7. c. 26.—*Juv.* 10. v. 365. & 14. v. 315. —*Horat.* 1. od. 35. v. 1.—*Paus.* 1. 2. c. 7. 1. 4. c. 30. 1. 6. c. 25.—*Gyrald. H. Deor.* 16.—*Sil. Ital.* 8. v. 366.—*Stat.* 1. *Sylv.* 3. v. 80.—*Vitruv.* 3.—*Lactant. Fals. R.* 2. c. 8.—*Lucan.* 2. v. 193, [The best statue of this deity is that in the Vatican.]

FORTUNA'TÆ IN'SULÆ, islands in the Atlantic Sea, at the west of Mauritania, supposed to be the Canary Isles of the moderns. They were represented as the seats of the blessed, where the souls of the virtuous were placed after death. The air was wholesome and temperate, and the earth produced an immense number of various fruits without the labours of men. *Strab.* 1.—*Plut. in Sertor.*—*Horat.* 4. od. 8. v. 27. *Epod.* 16.—*Plin.* 6. c. 31 & 32.

FORTUNATIA'NUS ATIL'IUS, a Latin grammarian, who wrote on prosody.

FORTUNA'TUS, a freedman of L. Vetus, pro-consul of Asia. *Tac. Ann.* 16. c. 10.

FOR'ULI, a town of the Sabines, built on a stony place. *Strab.* 5.—*Virg. Æn.* 7. v. 714.

FO'RUM, an open space, in which the people met for the transaction of business. They were divided into *fora civilia*, in which justice was administered and public affairs discussed, and *fora venalia*, in which provisions and other things were sold.

FO'RUM AP'PII, a town of Latium on the Appia Via, at the west of the Pontine marshes. *Cic.* 1. *Att.* 10.—*Horat.* 1. sat. 5. v. 3.

Fo'rum, Alie'ni, a town of Italy, on one of the branches of the Po, now Ferrara. *Tacit. H.* 3. c. 6.

Fo'rum Augus'tum, a place at Rome. *Ovid.* 5. *Fast.* v. 552.

Fo'rum Aure'lii, a town of Etruria, now Montalto. *Cic. Cat.* 1. c. 9.

Fo'rum Clau'dii, another in Etruria, now Oriolo. *Plin.* 3. c. 15.

Fo'rum Corne'lii, another, now Imola, in the Pope's dominions, *Plin.* 3. c. 16.—*Cic. Fam.* 12. ep. 5.

Fo'rum De'cii, a town of the Sabines. *Plin.* 3. c. 12.

Fo'rum Domit'ii, a town of Gaul, now Frontignan, in Languedoc.

Fo'rum Egurro'rum, a town of Hispania Tarraconensis, now Medina de Rio Seco. *Ptol.*

Fo'rum Flamin'ii, a town of Umbria, now San Giavane. *Plin.* 3. c. 14.

Fo'rum Ful'vii, a town of Liguria, now Valenza. *Plin.* 3. c. 5.

Fo'rum Gallo'rum, a town of Gallia Togata, now Castel Franco. *Cic. Fam.* 10. ep. 30.

Fo'rum Ju'lii, a town of Venice, called also Forajuliensis urbs, now Friuli. *Cic. Fam.* 12. ep. 26.

Fo'rum Ju'lium, a town of Gallia Narbonensis, now Frejus, in Provence, on the shores of the Mediterranean. *Cic. Fam.* 10. ep. 17.—*Strab.* 4.

Fo'rum Lebuo'rum, a town of Insubria. *Polyb.*

Fo'rum Lep'idi, a town of ancient Gaul, south of the Po.

Fo'rum Licin'ii, a city of Insubria, now La Pieve d'Incino.

Fo'rum Liv'ii, a city of Gallia Togata, now Forli. *Plin.* 3. c, 15.

Fo'rum Narbaso'rum, a city of Hispania Tarraconensis, now Arvas. *Ptol*

Fo'rum Nero'nis, a city of Gallia Narbonensis. *Plin.* 3. c. 4.—*Ptol.*

Fo'rum No'vum, a city of the Sabines, now Vescovio. *Plin.* 3. c. 12.

Fo'rum Popil'ii, a town at the south of Ravenna, on the Adriatic, now Forlimpopoli. *Plin.* 3. c. 15.

Fo'rum Segusiano'rum, a town of Gallia Celtica, now Feurs. *Ptol.*

Fo'rum Sempro'nii, a town of Umbria, now Fossombrone. *Plin.* 3. c. 14.

Fo'rum Tibe'rii, a town of Helvetia on the Rhine, now Keyserstul. *Ptol.*

Fo'rum Voco'nii, a town of Gaul, now Gonsaron, between Antibes and Marseilles. *Cic. Fam.* 10. ep. 17. Many other places bore the name of Forum, such as those where there was a public market, or rather where the prætor held a court of justice (*forum vel conventus*), and thence they were called sometimes *conventus* as well as *fora*, into which provinces were generally divided under the administration of a separate governor. *Cic. Ver.* 2. c. 20. l. 4. c, 48. l. 5. c. 11. *Vatin.* 5. *Fam.* 3. ep. 6 & 8. *Attic.* 5. ep. 21.

FO'SI, a people of Germany, near the Elbe, considered as the Saxons of *Ptolemy*. *Tacit. G.* 36.

FOS'SA, the straits of Bonifacio between the islands of Corsica and Sardinia, called also Taphros. *Plin.* 3. c. 6.

Fos'sa Dru'si or Drusia'na, a canal eight miles in length, opened by Drusus from the Rhine to the Issel, below the separation of the Waal. *Suet. Claud.* 1.—*Tacit. Hist.* 5. c. 23.

Fos'sa Maria'na, a canal cut by Marius, during the Cimbrian war, from the Rhone to Marseilles, and now called Galejon. Sometimes the word is used in the plural, Fossæ, as if more than one canal had been formed by Marius. *Plin.* 3. c. 4. —*Strab.* 4.—*Mela*, 2. c. 5.

FOS'SÆ PHILISTI'NÆ, one of the mouths of the Po. *Tacit. Hist.* 3. c. 9.

Fos'sæ Papyria'næ, a city of Etruria, now Fosdinovo. *Ptol.*

FRAN'CI, a people of Germany and Gaul, whose country was called Francia. *Claudian.*

FRATE'RIA or PHRATE'RIA, a city of Dacia, now Brossa. *Ptol.*

FRA'US, a divinity, daughter of Orcus and Nox, worshipped among the Romans. She was represented under the form of a beautiful woman, whose deformities were concealed in the extremities of her body, which was terminated by a serpent spotted with various colours. *Capell.* 2.—*Gyrald. Hist. D.* 1.

FREGEL'LA, a famous town of the Volsci in Italy, on the river Liris, destroyed for revolting from the Romans. *Ital.* 5. v. 452.—*Liv.* 8. c. 22. l. 27. c. 10, &c.—*Cic. Fam.* 13. ep. 76.

FREGE'NÆ, a town of Etruria on the sea coast, a little to the west of the Tiber. The people were called Freginates. *Plin.* 3. c. 5.

FREN'ATRIX or FEN'ATRIX, a surname of Pallas, because she first was supposed to have tamed the horse, and rendered him useful to mankind. She had a temple at Corinth, in which her statue was made of wood, except the hands, face, and feet, which were of white marble. *Paus.* 2. c. 4. —*Gyrald. H. D.* 11.

FRENTA'NI, a people of Italy, near Apulia, who received their name from the river Frento, now Fortore, which runs through the eastern part of their country, and falls into the Adriatic opposite the islands of Diomedes. *Plin.* 3. c. 11.—*Liv.* 9. c. 45.—*Sil.* 8. v. 520.

FREN'TO, a river of Italy, which formed the boundary between the Frentani and Apulia.

FRE'TUM (*the sea*), a name sometimes given to the Sicilian Sea, or the Straits of Messina. *Cæs. C.* 1. c. 29.—*Flor.* 1. c. 26.—*Cic.* 2. *Att.* 1.

FRIG'IDUS, a river of Tuscany, now Freddo. *Tibul.* 4. *El.* 8. v. 4.

FRINIA'TES, a people in Liguria, who were transplanted to Samnium after being defeated by the Romans.

FRISIABO'NES, a people of Germany. *Plin.* 4. c. 15.

FRIS'II, a people of Germany near the Rhine, now the Frisons of Friesland. *Tacit. A.* 1. c. 60. *Hist.* 4. c. 15 & 72. *G.* 34.

FRONTI'NUS SEX. JUL., a celebrated geometrician, who made himself known by the military knowledge which he displayed at the head of the Roman armies in Britain, and in other provinces, as well as by the books which he wrote *de strategematibus* and *de aquæ ductibus urbis Romæ*, and which he dedicated to Trajan. He ordered at his death that no monument should be raised to his memory, saying, *memoria nostri durabit, si vitâ meruimus.* The best edition of the works of Frontinus is that of Oudendorp. 8vo, L. Bat. 1779. *Harles. Not. Lit. Rom.* 1. p. 418.

FRON'TO MAR'CUS CORNEL., a preceptor of the emperor M. Antoninus, by whom he was greatly esteemed. None of his works are extant, though his compositions are mentioned with high commendation by *Macrobius, St. Jerome, Ausonius,* and others.

FRON'TO JU'LIUS, a learned Roman, who was so partial to the company of poets, that he freely lent them his house and gardens, which continually re-echoed with the compositions of his numerous visitors. *Juv.* 1. *Sat.* v. 12.

FRU'SINO, a small town of the Volsci, on one of the branches of the Liris. *Juv.* 3. v. 223.—*Liv.* 10. c. 1.—*Sil.* 8. v. 399.—*Cic. Att.* 11. ep. 4 & 13.

FU'CINUS or **FUCI'NUS** a lake of Italy, in the country of the Marsi, at the north of the Liris. J. Cæsar attempted to drain it, and Claudius afterwards employed 30,000 men for eleven years to perforate a mountain to convey the water into the Liris, but with no permanent success. This lake, surrounded by a ridge of high mountains, is now called Celano, and is supposed to be 47 miles in circumference, and not more than 12 feet deep on an average. *Plin.* 36. c. 15.—*Tac. Ann.* 12. c. 56. —*Virg. Æn.* 7. v. 759.—*Sueton. Claud.* 20.—*Dio.* 60.

FUFFE'TIUS or **SUFFE'TIUS, ME'TUS** or **MET'TIUS**, a dictator at Alba, whose body was torn to pieces by carriages drawn different ways, by order of Tullus, king of Rome, towards whom he had behaved with great treachery in a battle. *Liv.* 1. c. 28.—*Virg. Æn.* 8. v. 642.

FUFID'IUS, a wretched usurer, &c. *Horat.* 1. sat. 2.——An orator. *Cic. Br.* 29.—*Plin.* 33. c. 1.

FU'FIUS GEM'INUS, a man greatly promoted at Rome by the interest of Livia, &c. *Tacit. Ann.* 5. c. 1 & 2.

FU'FIUS KALE'NUS QUIN'TUS, a lieutenant of C. Cæsar, employed in Spain against Petreius and Afranius.

FUGA'LIA, festivals at Rome celebrated on the 23d of February, to commemorate the expulsion and flight of the Tarquins. *Aug. de Civ. D.* 2. c. 6.—*Ovid. Fast.* 2. v. 685.

FULCIN'IUS TRI'O, a noted informer under Tiberius. *Tac. Ann.* 2. c. 28.

FULGINA'TES, (sing. *Fulginas*) a people of Umbria, whose chief town, Fulginum, now Foligno, was situated on one of the small streams which fall into the Tiber. *Sil. It.* 8. v. 462.—*Plin.* 1. c. 4. l. 3. c. 14.

FULGI'NUS Q., a brave officer in Cæsar's legions, &c. *Cæs. Bell. Civ.* c. 10.

FULGO'RA, a goddess at Rome who presided over lightning. She was invoked by her votaries to save them from the effects of violent storms of thunder. *Aug. de Civ. D.* 6. c. 10.

FULGIN'IUM, FUL'LINUM or **FUL'GINUM**, a small town of Umbria. *Vid.* Fulginates.

FULGEN'TIUS FA'BIUS PLANCI'ADES, a Latin grammarian, author of a collection of tales illustrating the exploits of the gods and heroes, and other works. The best edition is in the *Mythrographi Latini* of Muncker Auct. 1681, and of Van Staveren Lug. Bat. 1742.

FULGU'RIUS, an epithet of Jupiter, who had a temple erected to him at Rome under this name. *Virtruv.*

FULSINA'TES, a people of Illyricum. *Plin.* 3. c. 21.

FUL'VIA LEX, was proposed by Flaccus Fulvius, but rejected A.U.C. 628. It tended to make all the people of Italy citizens of Rome.

FUL'VIA, a bold and ambitious woman who married the tribune Clodius, and afterwards Curio, and at last M. Antony. She discovered to Cicero the designs of Catiline against his life, and afterwards took a part in all the intrigues of her husband's triumvirate and shewed herself cruel as well as revengeful. When Cicero's head had been cut off by order of Antony, Fulvia ordered it to be brought to her, and barbarously bored through the orators tongue with her golden bodkin. Antony divorced her to marry Cleopatra, upon which she attempted to avenge her wrongs, by persuading Augustus to take up arms against her husband. When this scheme did not succeed, she raised a faction against Augustus, in which she artfully engaged L. Antonius her brother-in-law, and when all her attempts proved fruitless, she retired into the east where her husband received her with great coldness and indifference. This unkindness totally broke her heart, and she died soon after, about 40 years B.C. *Plut. in Cic & Anton.*—*Flor.* 4. c. 5. —*Paterc.* 2. c. 74.

FUL'VIUS, a man who migrated to Rome from Tusculum, and became consul A.U.C. 432. It is said that he triumphed over his countrymen. *Plin.* 7. c. 43.—*Liv,* 8. c. 14, 37, &c.——A Roman senator, intimate with Augustus. He disclosed the emperor's secrets to his wife, who revealed them to all the Roman matrons, for which he received so severe a reprimand from Augustus, that he and his wife hanged themselves in despair.

FUL'VIUS AURE'LIUS, a lieutenant in Mœsia, under Otho. *Tac. Hist.* 1. c. 79.

FUL'VIUS FLAC'CUS CEN'SOR, a Roman who distinguished himself in his wars against the Spaniards. When censor, he plundered a marble temple of Lacinian Juno, to finish the building of one which he had erected to Fortune, in consequence of a vow. This was considered as sacrilege, and opposed by the Romans, upon which it was said that misfortunes overwhelmed the house of Fulvius, and that he was bereaved of his senses by the offended Juno, and that, on the death of his son, he strangled himself in despair. *Liv.* 39. c. 39, &c. l. 40. c. 1, &c. l. 42. c. 3 & 128.

FUL'VIUS MAR'CUS FLAC'CUS, a consul, A.U.C. 629. He assisted the people of Marseilles in war, and was the first who conquered the Ligurians. He espoused the party of the Gracchi, and strongly interested himself in the turbulent factions of the times, upon which he was killed by the consul Opimus, and his house levelled to the ground. His body was thrown into the river by the populace, and his widow was forbidden to put on mourning for his death. *Plut. in Gracch.*—*Liv.* 60.—*Appian. C. B.* 1. p. 360.—*Cic. Dom.* 48.

FUL'VIUS MAR'CUS NOBIL'IOR, a consul who triumphed over the Ætolians, and built a temple in honour of Hercules and of the Muses, which he adorned with a beautiful picture of these goddesses by Zeuxis from Ambracia. He was intimate with Ennius, who accompanied him in his Ætolian expedition. *Cic. Tusc.* 1. c. 2. *Arch.* 11.—*Plin.* 35. c. 10.—*Liv.* 37. c. 50.

FUL'VIUS Q. FLAC'CUS, a Roman engaged in the second Punic war. He took Capua from Annibal, and put to death eighty of the principal inhabitants, against the advice of his colleague App. Claudius. *Liv.* 26. c. 15. l. 27. c. 6.—*Sil.* 12. v. 571. —*Cic. Rull.* 2. c. 33.

FUL'VIUS SER. NOBIL'IOR, a Roman consul who went to Africa after the defeat of Regulus. After he had acquired much glory against the Carthaginians, he was shipwrecked on his return with 200 ships. His grandson Marcus was sent to Spain, where he greatly signalized himself. He was afterwards rewarded with the consulship.

FUNDA'NIUS C., the father-in-law of Varro, intimate with Cicero. *Varr. R. R.* 1. c. 2.—*Cic. ad Fr.* 1. ep. 2.

FUNDA'NIUS CAIUS, a comic poet in the age of Augustus, praised by Horace for the pleasing characters which he gave of artful slaves, &c. *Horat.* 1. sat. 10. v. 42. l. 2, sat. 8. v. 19.

FUNDA'NIUS MAR'CUS, a tribune who wished to abrogate the Appian law. *Liv.* 34. c. 1.

FUNDA'NUS, a lake near Fundi in Italy, which discharges itself into the Mediterranean. *Tacit. Hist.* 3. c. 69.

FUN'DI, a town of Italy, near Caieta on the Appian road, at the bottom of a small deep bay called Lacus Fundanus. *Horat.* 1. sat. 5. v. 34.—*Liv.* 8. c. 14 & 19. l. 38. c. 36.—*Plin.* 3. c. 5.—*Cic. Rull.* 2. c. 25 —*Tacit. Ann.* 4. c. 59.—*Strab.* 5.

FURCO'NIUM, a city of Vestini, now Forcone. *Ptol.* From the ruins of this city and Amiternum, the city of Aquila arose.

FU'RIÆ. *Vid.* Eumenides.

FU'RIA, a family which migrated from Medullia in Latium, and came to settle at Rome under Romulus, and was admitted among the patricians. Camillus was of this family, and it was he who first raised it to distinction. This illustrious family was supposed to be anciently the same as the Fusii. It branched into the families of Aculeones, Bibaculi, Crassipedes, Camilli, Lusci, Pacili, Phili, Purpureones and Medullini. *Liv.* 3, &c.—*Quintil.* 1. c. 4.—*Plut. in Camill.*

FU'RIA LEX, *de Testamentis*, was introduced by C.

Furius the Tribune. It forbade anybody to leave as a legacy more than a thousand*sas es*, except to the relations of the master who manumitted, and a few others. *Cic.* 1. *Verr.* 42.—*Liv.* 35.

FURI'NA, the goddess of robbers, was worshipped at Rome. Her festivals, called Furinalia, were celebrated in the month of July. C. Gracchus was put to death in her grove. *Plut. in Tib. & C. Gracc.*—*Fest. de V. Sig.*—*Cic. de Nat.* 3, c. 8.—*Varro de L. L.* 5. c. 3 & 15.

FU'RIUS, a Roman slave who obtained his freedom, and applied himself with unremitted attention to cultivate a small portion of land which he had purchased. The uncommon fruits which he reaped from his labors, rendered his neighbours jealous of his prosperity, and he was accused of witchcraft, but honorably acquitted.——A friend of Catullus, described as being in very indigent circumstances. ——the name of Camillus. *Vid.* Camillus.

Fu'rius Medulli'nus L., a military tribune.

Fu'rius M. Bibac'ulus, a Latin poet of Cremona, from whom Virgil is said to have borrowed some verses. *Vid.* Bibaculus.

Fu'rius An'tias, another Latin poet, who wrote annals, and other poems, praised for their elegance, polished style, and happy diction. Only seventeen verses are preserved of his poetry, collected in the Corpus Poetarum. *Macrob. Sat.* 18. c. 11.—*Aul. Gell.* 1. c. 13.

Fu'rius Lu'cius Camil'lus, a consul A.U.C. 405. He made war gainst the Gauls, and erected a temple to the goddess Moneta. *Liv.* 7. c. 24. l. 26. c. 28.

FUR'NIUS, a man accused of adultery with Claudia Pulchra, and condemned, &c. *Tacit. Hist.* 4. c. 52.——A friend of Horace, who was consul, and distinguished himself by his elegant historical writings. *Horat.* 1. sat. 10. v. 36.——A friend of Cicero, lieutenant of Plancus. *Cic. Fam.* 10. ep. 1.

FUS'CUS ARIST., a friend of Horace, as conspicuous for the integrity and propriety of his manners as for his extensive learning and great abilities. The poet addressed his 22 od. l. 1. and ep. 10. to him.

Fus'cus Corn., a prætor, sent by Domitian against the Daci, where he perished. *Juv.* 4. v. 112.

FU'SIA LEX, *de Comitiis*, A.U.C. 527, forbade any business to be transacted at the public assemblies on certain days, though among the *fasti*.—Another, A.U.C. 690, which ordained that the votes in a public assembly should be given separately.—Caninia, another by Camillus and C. Caninius Galbus, A.U.C. 751, to check the manumission of slaves.

FUSID'IUS, an orator mentioned by *Cicero in Brut.*

FU'SIUS, a Roman orator. *Cic.* 2 *de Orat.* c. 22. ——A Roman actor, whom *Horace* 2. sat. 3. v. 60. ridicules. He intoxicated himself; and when on the stage fell asleep while he personated Ilione, in which character he ought to have been roused by the cries of a ghost, but he still continued sleeping. Some authors read Furius, not Fusius. *Vid.* Fúria.

Fu'sius Cot'ta, a Roman killed in the wars of Gaul, while he presided there over one of the provinces. *Cæs. Bell. G.* 7. c. 3.

FUT or **PHTHUT**, according to *Ptolemy*, a river of Mauritania, not far from mount Atlas.

FYTER'NUS, a river of the Frentani. *Ptol.* Some read Tyfernus.

G.

GA'ANA, a city of Cœlesyria. *Ptol.* It is called Sinna by *Strabo*, l. 16. p. 755, according to *Simler.*

GAB'ALA, a small town of the isthmus of Corinth, where Doto, one of the Nereides, had a magnificent temple, in which was preserved the veil that Eriphyle received to engage her son Alcmæon to head an army against Thebes. *Paus.* 2. c. 1.——A name given to some small towns of Syria. *Ptol.* 5. c. 15.

GABALÆ'CA, a city of the Varduli in Spain. *Ptol.*

GAB'ALE, a city of Media. *Id.*

GAB'ALES, a people of Gallia Aquitanica. *Plin.* 4. c. 19.

GAB'AZA or **GABA'ZA**, a country of Asia, near Sogdiana, at the east of the Caspian Sea. *Curt.* 8. c. 4.

GAB'BA, a city of Syria. *Steph.*—*Plin.* 12. c. 17.

GABEL'LUS, now La Secchia, a small river falling in a northern direction into the Po, nearly opposite the Mincius. *Plin.* 3. c. 16.

GABE'NE, or **GABIE'NE**, a country of Persia, on the east of the entrance to the Persian Gulph. *Diod.* 19.—*Polyæn.* 4.

GABE'RIUS, a Roman knight mentioned by *Varro, de R.R.* 2. c. 3.

GA'BIA or **GABI'NA**. *Vid.* Gabina.

GABIE'NUS, a friend of Augustus, beheaded by order of Sext. Pompey. It is maintained that he spoke after death.

GA'BII, once a celebrated city of the Volsci, built by the kings of Alba, but now no longer in existence. It was taken by the artifice of Sextus, the son of Tarquin, who gained the confidence of the inhabitants, by deserting to them, and pretending that his father had ill treated him. Romulus and Remus were educated there. as it was the custom at that time to send there the youth of the neighbouring country. Juno was the chief deity of the place. The inhabitants had a peculiar mode of tucking up their dress, which was by throwing one of their skirts over the left shoulder, and tying it in a knot to the other under the right arm, whence the expression *Gabinus cinctus*. This mode of dress originated in their being suddenly attacked by their enemies while offering a sacrifice. *Isidor.* 19.—*Orig.* 24.—*Virg Æn.* 6. v. 773. l. 7. v 612 & 682. & *Servius in locis cit.*—*Liv.* 5. c. 46. l. 6. c. 29. l. 8. c. 9. l. 10. c. 7.—*Ovid. Fast.* 2. v. 709.—*Plut. in Romul. de fort. R.*

GABI'NA, a name given to Juno because she was particularly worshipped at Gabii. *Virg Æn.* 7. v. 682.

GABIN'IA LEX, *de Comitiis*, introduced by A. Gabinius the tribune, A.U.C. 614. It required that in the public assemblies for electing magistrates, the votes should be given by tablets and not *vivâ voce.* Another for convening the senate daily, from the calends of February to those of March.—Another *de Comitiis*, which made it a capital punishment to convene any clandestine assembly, agreeably to the old law of the twelve tables.—Another, *de Militiâ*, by A. Gabinius the tribune, A.U.C. 685. It granted to Pompey the power of carrying on the war against the pirates who infested the coasts of the Mediterranean, during three years, and of obliging all kings, governors, and states, to supply him with all the necessaries which he wanted, over all the Mediterranean Sea, and in the provinces, as far as 400 *stadia* from the sea.—Another, *de Usurâ*, by Aul. Gabinius, the tribune, A.U.C. 685. It ordained, that no action should be granted for the recovery of any money borrowed upon small interest, to be lent upon larger. This was at that time a usual practice at Rome, which obtained the name of *versuram facere.*—Another against fornication.

GABINIA'NUS, a rhetorician in the reign of Vespasian.

GABIN'IUS, an ancient Roman historian. *Strab.* l. 17.——A prætor accused of extortion in Achaia. *Cic. Cæc.* 20. *Arch.* 5.

Gabin'ius Au'lus, a Roman consul who made war in Judæa, and re-established tranquillity there. He suffered himself to be bribed, and as the commander of the Roman armies in the east replaced Ptolemy Auletes on the throne of Ægypt. He was accused, at his return, of receiving bribes; but Cicero, though formerly ill treated by him, at the request of Pompey, ably defended him. He was afterwards lieutenant to Cæsar during the civil wars, and died at Salona when besieged there by Octavius, 40 years B.C. *Appian Illy.* 762.—*Hirt. Alex.* 43.—*Cic. Dom.* 9. *Sext.* 25. *Manil.* 17.

Gabin'ius Au'lus, a lieutenant of Antony.

GA'BIUS BAS'SUS, an author in the age of Trajan. *Plin. Ep.*—*Macrob. Sat.* 1. c. 9, &c.

GA'BRI, a people of Asiatic Sarmatia. *Plin.* 6. c. 7.

GA'BRIS, the name of two towns in Media. *Ptol.*

GA'DES (*-ium*), **GADIS** (*-is*), or **GADI'RA**, a small island in the Atlantic, on the Spanish coast, 25 miles from the columns of Hercules. It was sometimes called Tartessus and Erythia, according to Pliny, and is now known by the name of Cadiz. Geryon, whom Hercules killed, fixed his residence there. Hercules, surnamed Gaditanus, had there a celebrated temple, in which all his labors were engraved with excellent workmanship. The inhabitants were called Gaditani, and their women were known for their agility of body, as well as for their incontinence. *Horat.* 2. od. 2. v. 11.—*Stat.* 3 *Sylv.* 1. v. 183.—*Paterc.* 1. c. 2.—*Ptol.* 2. c. 4.—*Liv.* 21. c. 21. l. 24. c. 49. l. 26. c. 43.—*Plin.* 4. c. 23.—*Strab.* 3.—*Cic. pro. Gab.*—*Justin.* 44. c. 4.—*Paus.* 1. c. 35.

GADITA'NUS, a surname of Hercules. *Vid.* Gades.

GÆ'A, a city of Arabia Felix. *Ptol.*——An island in the Syrtis Major. *Id.*

GÆSA'TÆ, a people on the borders of the Rhone, who assisted the Senones in taking and plundering Rome under Brennus. *Strab.* 5.

GÆTU'LIA, a province of Libya, in the inland parts of the country, near the Garamantes, which formed part of king Masinissa's kingdom. The country was the favorite retreat of wild beasts, and is now called Bildulgerid. *Sallust. in Jug.*—*Sil.* 3. v. 287.—*Plin.* 5. c. 4.

GÆTU'LICUS LEN'TULUS CN., an officer in the age of Tiberius, &c. *Tacit. Ann.* 4. c. 42.

GÆTU'LICUS, his son, was consul A.U.C. 778, and was put to death by Caius Caligula. *Diod. Cass.* l. 59. Some suppose that he is the same person that wrote some epigrams, in which he displayed great genius and wit, though he too often indulged in indelicate expressions. Only three of his numerous verses are preserved. *Sidonius.*

GA'GE or GA'GÆ, a city of Lycia. *Plin.* 5. c. 27.

GA'IA, a river of Hispania Tarraconensis. *Livy.*

GA'LA, father of Masinissa, was king of Numidia, and the determined ally of Carthage against Rome. *Liv.* 24. c. 48, &c l. 29. c. 29.

GALA'BRII, a nation near Thrace. *Strab.* 7.

GALACTOPH'AGI, a people of Asiatic Scythia. *Homer Il.* 3.

GAL'ADA, GALADE'NE, or GALADI'TIS, a region of Arabia. *Steph.*

GAL'ADRÆ, a city of the Macedonians, in Pieria. *Id.*

GAL'ADRUS, a mountain so called from a son of Emathius. *Id.*

GALÆ'SUS. *Vid.* Galesus.

GALAN'THIS, a servant-maid of Alcmena, whose sagacity eased the labors of her mistress. She was changed into a weasel by Lucina, and condemned to bring forth her young by the mouth. This fable arose from a vulgar notion of the ancients, who believed this of the weasel, because she carries her young in her mouth, and continually shifts her habitation from place to place. The Bœotians paid great veneration to the weasel, which, as they supposed, facilitated the labors of Alcmena. *Ælian. H. Anim.* 2.—*Ovid. Met.* 9. fab. 6.

GAL'APHA, a city of Mauritania Tangitana. *Ptol.*

GALARI'NA, a city of Sicily. *Steph.*—*Cluver. Sic. Ant.* 2. c. 8.

GAL'ATA, a town of Syria.——A small island near Sicily. *Plin.* 3. c. 8.——A town in the northern parts of Sicily, west of Ætna. *Cic.*——A mountain of Phocis. *Plut*

GAL'ATÆ, the inhabitants of Galatia. *Vid.* Galatia.

GALATE'A or GALATHE'A, a sea-nymph, daughter of Nereus and Doris. She was passionately loved by the Cyclops Polyphemus, whom she treated not only with coldness but disdain; while Acis, a shepherd of Sicily, enjoyed her unbounded affection. The happiness of these two lovers was disturbed by the jealousy of the Cyclops, who crushed his rival to pieces with a fragment of a broken rock, while he leaned on the bosom of Galatea. Galatea was inconsolable for the loss of Acis, and as she could not restore him to life, she changed him into a fountain. *Ovid. Met.* 13. v. 789.—*Virg. Æn.* 9. v. 103.—*Servius. in Ecl. Virg.* 9. v. 39. This story seems to be borrowed from the account of Philoxenus, who lived at the court of Dionysius of Sicily, and enjoyed the favors of a mistress of the tyrant. The poet was sent to the quarries, where he composed a poem, in which he satirized the tyrant under the name of Polyphemus, and spoke of his misfortunes and those of his mistress under the assumed appellation of Acis and Galatea. *Athen. Deip.* 1. c. 3.—*Nannius. Misc.* 6. c. 1.——The daughter of a Celtic king, from whom the Gauls were called Galatæ. *Ammian.* 15.——A country girl, &c. *Virg. Ecl.* 3.

GALA'TIA or GALLOGRÆ'CIA, a country of Asia Minor, between Phrygia, the Euxine, Cappadocia, and Bithynia. It received its name from the Gauls, who sent a colony there under Brennus, some time after the sacking of Rome. *Strab.* 12.—*Justin.* 37. c. 4.—*Liv.* 38. c. 12. 40.—*Lucan.* 7. v. 540.—*Cic.* 6. *Att.* 5.—*Plin.* 5. c. 32.—*Ptol.* 5. c. 4.

GALAU'RUS, a king of the Taulantii, conquered by Argæus. *Polyæn.* 4.

GALAX'IA, a festival in which the people boiled a mixture of barley, pulse, and milk, called Γαλαξία by the Greeks.

GALAX'IUS, a river of Bœotia, which derived its name from the milky colour of its water.

GAL'BA, a surname of the first of the Sulpicii, from the smallness of his stature. The word signifies a small worm, or, according to some, it implies, in the language of Gaul, fatness, for which the founder of the Sulpician family was particularly remarkable. ——A king among the Gauls, who made war against J. Cæsar. *Cæs. Bell. Gall.* 2. c. 4.——A brother of the emperor Galba, who killed himself. &c. *Tac. Ann.* 6. c. 40.—— A mean buffoon in the age of Tiberius. *Juv.* 5. v. 4. *& Scholiast.*—*Martial.* 1. epigr. 42. l. 10. epigr. 101.

GAL'BA SER'VIUS, a lawyer at Rome, who defended the cause of adulterers with great warmth, as being one of the fraternity. *Horace*, ridicules him, 1 sat. 2. v. 46.

GAL'BA SER'VIUS SULPIC'IUS, a Roman who rose gradually to the greatest offices of the state, and exercised his power in the provinces with equity and unremitting diligence. He dedicated the greatest part of his time to peaceful pursuits, and lived in retirement chiefly to avoid the suspicions of Nero. His disapprobation of the emperor's oppressive command in the provinces, was the cause of new disturbances, and when Nero ordered him to be put to death, he escaped from the hands of the executioner, and was publicly saluted emperor. When he was seated on the throne, he unfortunately suffered himself to be governed by favourites, who exposed the goods of the citizens to sale, to gratify their avarice. Exemptions were sold at a high price, and the crime of murder was blotted out, and impunity purchased with a large sum of money. Such irregularities in the ministers greatly displeased the people, and when Galba refused to pay the soldiers the money which he had promised them, when he was raised to the throne, they assassinated him in the 73d year of his age, and in the eighth month of his reign, and proclaimed Otho emperor in his room, January 16th, A.D. 69. The virtues which had shone so bright in Galba, when a private man, totally disappeared when he ascended the throne; and he who had formerly shown himself the most impartial judge, forgot when at the head of the government the duties of an emperor, and of a father of his people. *Sueton. & Plut. in Vitâ.*—*Tacit.* [The best head of Galba is that in the Capitol.]

GAL'BA SER'GIUS, a celebrated orator before the age of Cicero. During his command in the province of Spain, he with great perfidy cut off 7000, or, according to Suetonius, 30,000 Lusitanians, which gave rise to the war of Viriathus. On his return to Rome he was accused for this criminal conduct, but by showing his sons to the Roman people, and imploring their protection, he saved himself from the punishment which either his guilt or the persuasive eloquence of his adversaries, M. Cato and L. Scribonius, urged as due to him. *Cic. de Orat.* l. c. 53. *Ad. Her.* 4. c. 5.—*Val. Max.* 3. c. 6.—*Liv.* 49.—*Tacit. Ann.* 3. c 66.—*Suet. Galb.* 3.

GAL'BA CA'IUS his son, was the first of the college of priests condemned by public sentence. *Cic. Or.* 1. c. 56. *Br.* 26. 34.

GAL'BA SER'GIUS, his son, was great-grandfather to the emperor of that name. He was lieutenant to J. Cæsar in Gaul, and afterwards conspired against his life. *Cæs. B. G.* 3. c. 1, l. 4. c. 3.—*Suet. in Galb.* 3.—*Cic. Phil.* 13. c. 16.—*Pater.* 2. c. 56.

GAL'BA SULPIC'IUS, the son of Sergius, was grandfather to the emperor. He was prætor at Rome, but devoted himself particularly to literary pursuits, and wrote a history of Rome replete with much valuable information. *Suet. Galb.*

GALEA'GRA, a tower in Sicily. *Liv.* 25. c. 23.

GALE'NUS CLAU'DIUS, was son of Nicon, an architect of eminence, and was a celebrated physician in the age of M. Antoninus and his successors. He was born at Pergamus, and applied himself with unremitting assiduity to the study of philosophy, mathematics, and chiefly of physic. He visited the most learned seminaries of Greece and Ægypt;

and at last came to Rome, where he soon rendered himself famous in his profession. Many, however, astonished at the extraordinary cures which he performed, and jealous of his fame, attributed his success to magic. He was very intimate with Marcus Aurelius, the emperor, after whose death he returned to Pergamus, where he died, in his 90th year A.D. 193. He wrote no less than 200 volumes, the greatest part of which were burnt in the temple of Rome, where they had been deposited. Galenus confessed himself greatly indebted to the writings of Hippocrates for his medical knowledge, and bestowed well-deserved encomiums upon him. To the diligence, application, and expeiimeuts of those two celebrated physicians, the moderns are indebted for many useful discoveries; yet, for the little progress then made in experimental philosophy and science, their opinions are often ill-grounded, their conclusions hasty, and their reasoning false. What remains of the works of Galen, has been published, without a Latin translation, in 5 vols fol. Basil. 1538. Galen was likewise edited, together with Hippocrates, by Charterius, 13 vols, fol. Paris, 1679, but this edition is very incorrect. *Fabr. B. Gr.* 4. c. 19.—*Sax. Onom.* 1. p. 317.

GA'LEO, a Roman who so respected the character of Cicero, both as an orator and as a man, that he left all his property him. *Cic.* 11. *Att.* 11.

CALE'OLÆ, certain prophets in Sicily. *Cic.* 1. 1. *de Div.*

GALEO'THÆ, a people of Attica. *Steph.*

GALEP'SUS, a city of Thrace. *Id.*

GALE'RIA, one of the Roman tribes.——The wife of Vitellius. *Tacit. Hist.* 2. c. 60.

GALE'RIA FAUSTI'NA, the wife of the emperor Antoninus Pius.

GALE'RIUS, a native of Dacia made emperor of Rome by Diocletian. *Vid.* Maximianus.

GALE'RIUS TRACHA'LUS, an orator in favour with Otho. *Tac. Hist.* 1. c. 90.

GALE'SUS, now Galeso, a river of Calabria, which flows into the bay of Tarentum, near the city. The poets have celebrated it for the shady groves in its neighbourhood, and the fine sheep which fed on its fertile banks. *Martial.* 2. epigr. 43, l. 4. epigr. 28.—*Virg. G.* 4. v. 126.—*Horat.* 2. od. 6. v. 10.——A rich person of Latium, accidentally killed as he attempted to make a reconciliation between the Trojans and Rutulians, when Ascanius had killed the favourite stag of Tyrrheus. This melancholy event was the prelude to all the enmity which arose between the hostile nations. *Virg. Æn.* 7. v. 535.

GALILÆ'A, a celebrated country of Palestine, often mentioned in Scripture. Its principal towns were Cana, Chorazin, Tiberias, Capernaum, Bethlehem, Zabulon, Acon, &c.

GALINTHIA'DIA, a festival at Thebes, in honour of Galinthias a daughter of Prœtus. It was celebrated before the festival of Hercules, by whose orders it was first instituted. *Voss. de Idol.* 1. c. 13.

GAL'LA, the wife of Constantius, son of Constantius Chlorus, and mother of Gallus Cæsar.——Daughter of Valentinian, and wife of Theodosius the Great.

GALLÆ'CIA, a country in the N. of Spain. The inhabitants, who were the most uncivilized in Spain, were defeated with great slaughter by D. Brutus B.C. 138, who obtained in consequence the name of Gallæcus.

GALLE'SIUM, a city of Ephesus. *Steph.*

GAL'LI, a nation of Europe, naturally fierce, and inclined to war. They were very superstitious; and in their sacrifices often immolated human victims. In some places they had large idols made with twigs, which they filled with men, and reduced to ashes. They believed themselves descended from Pluto; and from that circumstance they always reckoned their time, not by the days, as other nations, but by the nights. Their obsequies were splendid; and not only the most precious things, but also slaves and oxen, were burnt on the funeral pile of the deceased. They were so fully persuaded of another life, that they considered the debts contracted on earth would be paid in the infernal regions, and therefore they frequently followed their departed friends by rushing into the flames, or sent them intelligence by throwing letters on the blazing pile. Children, among them, never appeared in the presence of their fathers, before they were able to bear arms in the defence of their country. The government, as in other countries, was aristocratical, and the people obeyed the Druids as supreme in religion and in laws. *Val. Max.* 2. c. 6.—*Marcell.* 15. c. 9.—*Mela*, 3. c. 2.—*Justin.* 6. c. 6. l. 12. c. 13. l. 20. c. 5.—*Cæs. Bell. G.*—*Strab.* 4.—*Tacit. Vid.* Gallia.

GAL'LI, the priests of Cybele, who received that name from the river Gallus in Phrygia, where they celebrated the festivals of the goddess. They mutilated themselves in imitation of Atys, the favourite of Cybele, before they were admitted to the priesthood, (*vid.* Atys,) and in the celebration of their festivals they exhibited all the gestures of madness, and amidst the confused noise of cymbals and drums made incisions in their arms and in their thighs, as an acceptable sacrifice to the divinity. The chief among them was called Archigallus; in his dress he resembled a woman, and carried suspended to his neck a large collar with two representations of the head of Atys. *Vid.* Corybantes, Dactyli, &c. *Diod.* 4.—*Ovid. Fast.* 4. v. 36.—*Lucan.* 1. v. 466.—*Lucian. de Deâ Syriâ.*—*Lucret.* 2.—*Lactant.* 1. c. 17.

GAL'LIA, a large country placed in a most commanding situation in Europe, and anciently called Galatia by the Greeks. The inhabitants were called Galli, Celtiberi, and Celtoscythæ, by themselves Celtæ, by the Greeks Galatæ. Ancient Gaul was divided into four different parts by the Romans, called Gallia Belgica, Narbonensis, Aquitanica, and Celtica. Gallia Belgica was the largest province, bounded by Gallia Narbonensis, and the German Ocean; and contained the modern country of Alsace, Lorraine, Picardy, with part of the Low Countries, of Champagne, and of the isle of France. Gallia Narbonensis, which contained the provinces now called Languedoc, Provence, Dauphiné, Savoy, le Gevaudan, le Vivarez, and le Pays de Foix, was bounded by the Alps and Pyrenean mountains, by Aquitania, Belgium, and the Mediterranean. Gallia Aquitanica, now comprehending the provinces of Poitou, Saintogne, Guienne, Berry, Perigord, Quercy, Limosin, Gascogny, Auvergne, &c. was situate between the Garumna, the Pyrenean mountains, and the ocean. Gallia Celtica, or Lugdunensis, was bounded by Belgium, Gallia Narbonensis, the Alps, and the ocean. It contained the country at present known by the name of Lyonnois, Touraine, Franche Comté, Senenois, Switzerland, and part of Normandy. Besides these grand divisions, there is often mention made of Gallia Cisalpina, or Citerior; Transalpina or Ulterior, which refers to that part of Italy which was conquered by some of the Gauls who crossed the Alps. By Gallia Cisalpina, the Romans understood that part of Gaul which lies in Italy; and by Transalpina, that which lies beyond the Alps, in regard only to the inhabitants of Rome. Gallia Cispadana, and Transpadana, is applied to a part of Italy, conquered by some of the Gauls, and then it means the country on this side of the Po, or beyond the Po, with respect to Rome. By Gallia Togata, the Romans understood Cisalpina Gaul, where the Roman gowns, *togæ*, were usually worn as the inhabitants had been admitted to the rank of citizenship at Rome. Gallia Narbonensis, was called Bracatta, on account of the peculiar covering which the inhabitants wore on their thighs. The epithet of Comata was applied to Gallia Celtica, because the people suffered their hair to grow to an uncommon length. The inhabitants of Gaul were naturally great warriors; and their valour overcame the Roman armies, took the cities of Rome, and even invaded Greece in different ages. They spread themselves over the greatest part of the world. They were very superstitious in their religious ceremonies, and revered the sacerdotal order, as if they had been gods. *Vid.* Druidæ. They long maintained a bloody war against the Romans; and Cæsar resided 10 years in their country before he could totally subdue them. *Cæs. Bell. Gall.*—*Paus.* 7. c. 6.—*Ptol.* 2. c. 7.—*Plin.* 11. c. 31.—*Solin.* 24.—*Mela*, 1. c. 3. l. 2. c. 5, 6, & 7. l. 3. c. 1, 2, 5, & 6.—*Strab.* 5, &c.

GAL'LICA FLA'VIA, a city of the Ilergetes in Spain. *Ptol.*

GALLICA'NUS MONS, a mountain of Campania. *Plut.*

GAL'LICUS A'GER, was applied to the country between Picenum and Ariminum, which, when the Galli Senones were banished from it, was divided among the Roman citizens. *Liv.* 23. c. 14. l. 39. c. 44.—*Cic. Cat.* 2.—*Cæs. Civ.* 1. c. 29.

GAL'LICUS SI'NUS, a part of the Mediterranean Sea on the coast of Gaul, now called the gulph of Lyons.

GALLIE'NUS PUBL. LICIN'IUS, a son of the emperor Valerian. He reigned conjointly with his father for seven years, and obtained possession of the throne as sole emperor A.D. 260. In his youth he showed the activity of his military character, in an expedition against the Germans and Sarmatæ; but when he came to the purple, he delivered himself up to pleasure and indolence. He often appeared with his hair powdered with gold dust; and was satisfied to enjoy tranquillity at home, while his provinces abroad were torn by civil quarrels and sedition. He heard of the loss of a rich province, and of the execution of a malefactor, with the same indifference; and when he was apprized that Ægypt, among other dependent states, had revolted, he only observed, that he could live without the produce of Ægypt. He was of a disposition naturally inclined to raillery and the ridicule of others. When his wife had been deceived by a jeweller, Gallienus ordered the malefactor to be placed in the circus, in expectation of being exposed to the ferocity of a lion. While the wretch trembled at the expectation of instant death, the executioner, by order of the emperor, let loose a capon upon him. An uncommon laugh was raised upon this, and the emperor observed, that he who had deceived others, should expect to be deceived himself. In the midst of these ridiculous diversions, Gallienus was alarmed by the revolt of two of his officers, who had assumed the imperial purple. This intelligence roused him from his lethargy; he marched against his antagonists, and put all the rebels to the sword, without showing the least favour to either rank, sex, or age. These cruelties irritated the people and the army; emperors were elected by different divisions of the army, and no less than thirty tyrants aspired to the imperial purple. Gallienus resolved boldly to oppose his adversaries; but in the midst of his preparations, he was assassinated at Milan by some of his officers in the 50th year of his age, A.D. 268. Though deservedly hated, Gallienus was nevertheless possessed of great abilities, and distinguished himself by his eloquence, his wit, his genius, and his poetical effusions. *Treb. Pollio, &c.* [There is a bust of Gallienus in the Capitol.]

GALLINA'RIA SYL'VA, a wood near Cumæ in Italy, famous as being the retreat of robbers. *Juv.* 3. v. 307.

GAL'LIO, a proconsul of Achaia. *Acts*, 18. v. 12. ——A brother of Seneca killed by Nero.

GAL'LIO JU'NIUS, a parasite at the court of Tiberius. *Tac. Ann.* 6. c. 3.

GALLIP'OLIS, a fortified town of the Salentines, on the Tarentine Gulph. *Plin.* 3. c. 11.

GALLITÆ, an Alpine nation conquered by Augustus. *Id. ibid.* c. 23.

GALLITALU'TÆ, a people of India near the Indus. *Id.* 6. c. 20.

GAL'LIUS Q., a candidate for the prætorship B.C. 64. He was accused of bribery, and defended by Cicero in an oration, a few fragments of which remain.

GALLOGRÆ'CIA, a country of Asia Minor. *Vid.* Galatia.

GALLO'NIUS C., a Roman knight appointed over Gades, &c. *Cæs.* 1. 2. *de Bell. Civ.* c. 4.

GALLO'NIUS PUB'LIUS, a luxurious Roman, who, as was observed, never dined well, because he was never hungry. *Cic. de Fin.* 2. c. 8 & 28.—*Horat.* 2 sat. 2. v. 47.

GAL'LUS. *Vid.* Alectryon.——A general of the emperor Otho, &c. *Plut.*——A lieutenant of Sylla. ——An officer of M. Antony, &c.——A Roman, who assassinated Decius, the emperor, and raised himself to the throne. He showed himself indolent and cruel, and beheld with the greatest indifference the revolt of his provinces, and the invasion of his empire by the barbarians. He was at last assassinated with his son Volucianus by his soldiers, A.D. 253, after a reign of nearly three years.

GAL'LUS, a small river of Phrygia, which falls into the Sangaris, and with it is discharged into the Euxine Sea. Its waters, if drunk in moderation, are said to be very efficacious in curing madness. *Plin.* 32. c. 2.—*Ovid. Fast.* 4. v. 361.

GAL'LUS Æ'LIUS, the third governor of Ægypt in the age of Augustus, who was the first Roman who made war against the Arabians. *Dio.* 53. c. 29.—*Plin.* 6. c. 28.—*Joseph. B. Jud.* 15. c. 12.

GAL'LUS CA'IUS, a friend of the great Scipio Africanus, famous for his knowledge of astronomy, and his exact calculations of eclipses. *Cic. de Senect.*

GAL'LUS CORNE'LIUS, a Roman knight born at Forum Julium, now Frejus in France, rendered himself famous by his poetical, as well as his military talents. He was passionately fond of the slave Lycoris, called also Cytheris, and celebrated her beauty in his poetry. She proved ungrateful, and forsook him to follow M. Antony, which gave occasion to Virgil to write his tenth eclogue. Gallus, as well as the other poets of his age, was in the favour of Augustus, by whom he was appointed governor of Ægypt. He became forgetful of the favours which he had received, and, either urged by avarice or actuated by revenge for supposed injuries, he pillaged the province, and then conspired against his benefactor, according to some accounts, for which he was banished by the emperor. This disgrace operated so powerfully upon him, that he killed himself in despair, A.D. 26. Some few fragments remain of his poetry, and it seems that he particularly excelled in elegiac composition. It is said, that Virgil wrote a eulogium on his poetical friend, and inserted it at the end of his Georgics; but that he totally suppressed it, for fear of offending his imperial patron, of whose favours Gallus had shown himself so undeserving, and, instead of that, substituted the beautiful episode about Aristæus and Eurydice. This eulogium, according to some, was suppressed at the particular desire of Augustus. The six elegies printed in fragments of his works by Manutius, are supposititious, and must be attributed to the pen of an Etrurian called Maximianus, in the age of the emperor Anastasius. *Quintil.* 10. c. 1.—*Virg. Ecl.* 6. v. 64 & 10. v. 2.—*Ovid. Amat.* 3. el. 15. v. 29. *Am.* 1. el. 15. v. 29. l. 3. el. 9. v. 64. *Trist.* 2. v. 445. l. 4. el. 10. v. 53. *Propert.* 5. el. 34.—*Gyrald. de Poet. Hist.* 4.—*Vossius.* —*Dio*, 53. c. 23.—*Suet. Aug.* 66.—*Harles. Not. Lit. Rom.* 1. p. 231.—*Sax. Onom.* 1. p. 181 & 563.

GAL'LUS VIB'IUS, a celebrated orator of Gaul, in the age of Augustus, of whose orations Seneca has preserved some fragments.

GAL'LUS FLA'VIUS CLAU'DIUS CONSTAN'TIUS, a brother of the emperor Julian, raised to the imperial throne under the title of Cæsar, by Constantius, his relation. He ungratefully conspired against his benefactor, and was condemned to be beheaded, A.D. 354.

GALMODROE'SI, a people of Asia beyond the Ganges. *Ptol.*

GAL'OPES, a people of Arabia Felix, *Plin.*

GALO'RUM, a city of Galatia, now Garipo. *Ptol.*

GAL'YBA, a city of Africa Propria. *Id.*

GAMAL'IBA, a city of India within the Ganges. *Id.*

GAMANODU'RUM, a city of Noricum. *Id.*

GAMAR'GA, a small region of Media. *Diod. Sic.*

GAMAX'US, an Indian prince, brought in chains before Alexander for revolting.

GAM'BREGUM, a city of Ionia. *Steph.*

GAMBRE'VES, a people of Upper Æthiopia. *Plin.* 6. c. 29.

GAMBRIV'II, a people of Germany. *Tac. Ger.* c. 2.

GAM'BUA, a city of Phrygia Major. *Ptol.*

GAME'LIA, a surname of Juno, as Gamelius was applied to Jupiter, on account of their presiding over marriages.

GAME'LIA, a festival privately observed at three different times. The first was at the celebration of a marriage; the second in commemoration of a birthday, and the third was the anniversary of the death of a person. As it was observed generally on the first of January, marriages on that day were considered as of good omen, and the month was called Gamelion among the Athenians. *Cic. de Fin.* 2. c. 31.—*Gyrald. de D. Hist.* 3, &c.—*Meursii. Gr. fer.*

GAM'MACE, a town of Arachosia. *Ptol.*

GAMPHASAN'TES, a people of Æthiopia. *Mela*, 1.

GAN'DARA, an Indian nation. *Steph.*

GANDAR'IDÆ or GANDARI'TÆ, a people of the Punjaub in India.

GAN'DRI, a people of Asia. *Plin.* 6. c. 16.

GAN'GA or GAN'GITA, a river of Thrace. *Appian. Civ.* 4.

GAN'GAMA, a place near the Palus Mæotis. *Strab.* 7.

GAN'GARA, a people of Albania. *Ptol.*

GANGARI'DÆ, a populous nation near the mouths of the Ganges. They were said to be so powerful that Alexander did not dare to attack their army, which consisted of 200,000 men and 4,000 elephants. Some attributed this to the exhausted state or indolence of his troops. They are placed by Valerius Flaccus among the deserts of Scythia. *Diod.* 1 & 4.—*Justin.* 12. c. 8.—*Curt.* 9. c. 2.—*Virg. Æn.* 3. v. 27. *& Servius in loco.*—*Flacc.* 6. v. 67.

GAN'GES, a large river of India, falling into the Indian Ocean, said by Lucan to have been the boundary of Alexander's victories in the east. Like the Nile, it inundates the adjacent country in the summer, and in some places rises about 32 feet above its common level. Like other rivers, it was held in the greatest veneration by the natives of India, and this superstition is said still to exist among the modern Hindoos. The Ganges is now discovered to rise in the mountains of Thibet, and to run upwards of 2,000 miles before it reaches the sea, receiving in its course the tribute of several large rivers, 11 of which are superior to the Thames, and often equal to the great body of the waters of the Rhine. *Lucan.* 3. v. 230.—*Strab.* 5.—*Plin.* 6. c. 87.—*Curt.* 8. c. 9.—*Mela,* 3. c. 7.—*Virg. Æn.* 9. v. 31.

GAN'GRA, a city of Paphlagonia.

GANNAS'CUS, an ally of Rome, put to death by Corbulo, the Roman general, &c. *Tacit. Ann.* 11. c. 18.

GANYME'DE, a name of Hebe, who was worshipped under this name at Philus in Peloponnesus. *Paus.* 2. c. 13,

GANYME'DES, a beautiful youth of Phrygia, son of Tros, and brother of Ilus and Assaracus. According to Lucian he was son of Dardanus. He was taken up to heaven by Jupiter, as he was hunting, or rather tending his father's flocks on mount Ida, and he became the cup-bearer of the gods in the place of Hebe. Some say that he was carried away by an eagle, to satisfy the unnatural desires of Jupiter. Ganymedes is generally represented sitting on the back of a flying eagle, whilst the bird embraces his limbs with his talons, with a gentleness and delicacy, which in providin g for his security, seems still afraid to hurt him. Such was the elegant attitude in which he was represented by the sculptor Leochares, in a beautiful statue which Nero is supposed to have plundered to adorn the temple of peace at Rome. *Athen.* 13.—*Martial.* 11 epigr. 27 & 44.—*Stat.* 1. *Theb.* v. 548.—*Val. Flacc. Arg.* 9. v. 972.—*Hygin.* 244 & 271.—*Apollod.* 2 & 3.—*Quint. Smyr.* 8. v. 427.—*Theocrit. Id.* 12. —*Plin.* 34. c. 8.—*Lucian. Dial. D.* 20.—*Paus.* 5. c. 24.—*Homer. Il.* 20. v. 231.—*Virg. Æn.* 5. v. 252. —*Ovid. Met.* 10. v. 155. *Fast.* 2. v. 145. l. 4. v. 943.—*Horat.* 4. od. 4.—*Cic.* 1. *Tusc.* 26. [The most beautiful representation of Ganymedes is a small group of the eagle carrying him off in the Vatican.]

GARAMAN'TES, (sing. *Garamas*), a people in the interior parts of Africa, now called the deserts of Zaara. They lived like the brute creation, in common, and acknowledged as their own, only such children as resembled them, and scarcely clothed themselves, on account of the warmth of their climate. *Virg. Æn.* 4. v. 198. l. 6. v. 795.—*Lucan.* 4. v. 334.—*Strab.* 2.—*Plin.* 5. c. 8.—*Sil. It.* 1. v. 142. l. 11. v. 181.—*Seneca in Hipp.* 65.—*Ptol.* 4. c. 6.

GARAMAN'TIS, a nymph who became mother of Iarbas, Phileus, and Pilumnus, by Jupiter. *Virg. Æn.* 4. v. 198.

GAR'AMAS, a king of Libya, whose daughter was mother of Ammon by Jupiter. It is supposed that he gave his name to the nation over which he reigned.

Gar'amas, a mountain of Asia from which the Phasis rises. *Vibius.*

GAR'APHA, a harbour of Africa Propria. *Ptol.*

GAR'APHI, mountains of Mauritania Cæsariensis. *Id.*

GAR'ATAS, a river of Arcadia, near Tegea, on the banks of which Pan had a temple. *Paus.* 8. c. 44.

GARBA'TA, a mountain of Upper Æthiopia. *Ptol.*

GAR'CUS, an island of Taprobane. *Id.*

GAR'DEI, a people of Asiatic Sarmatia. *Plin.* 6. c. 8.

GAREA'TÆ, a people of Arcadia. *Paus.* 8. c. 45.

GAREATHY'RA or **GAREATH'YRA**, a town of Cappadocia. *Strab.* 12.

GARGA'NUS, MONS. now St. Angelo, a lofty mountain of Apulia, which projected in the form of a promontory into the Adriatic Sea. *Virg. Æn.* 11. v. 257.—*Lucan.* 5. v. 880.

GARGA'PHIA, a valley near Platæa, with a fountain of the same name, where Actæon was torn to pieces by his dogs. *Ovid. Met.* 3. v. 156.

GAR'GARIS. *Vid.* Gargoris.

GARGA'RUM, a town of Lampsacus.——a town of Epirus.——A town of Italy, so called from Gargarus, son of Jupiter. *Steph.*

GAR'GARUS, (plu. *-a, -orum,*) a town and mountain of Troas, near mount Ida, famous for its fertility. *Virg. G.* 1. v. 103.—*Macrob.* 5. c. 20.—*Strab.* 13.—*Plin.* 5. c. 30.

GAR'GE, a city of Libya. *Steph.*

GARGET'TUS, a small village of Attica, celebrated as the birth-place of the philosopher Epicurus. *Cic. Fam.* 15. ep. 16.

GARGIL'IUS MARTIA'LIS, an historian. *Vopisc. in Prob.*

Gargil'ius, a hunter, who purchased game, and imposed it upon his friends and the public as the fruit of his great exertions in the chase. *Horat.* 1. ep. 6. v. 57.

GARGIT'TIUS, a dog which kept Geryon's flocks, and was killed by Hercules. *Pollux in fab.*

GAR'GORIS, an ancient king of the Curetes, who first discovered the method of collecting honey, and of feeding bees. He wished to destroy a child which his daughter had brought fourth, and which was the fruit of an improper connection, but when his repeated attempts failed, he left him his crown and kingdom. *Justin.* 44. c. 4.

GARI'TES, a people of Aquitain, in Gaul. *Cæs.* 3. c. 6.

GAROC'ELI, a people of the Alps. *Cæs. de Bell. Gal.* c. 3.

GARO'DES, an island of the Nile. *Plin.* 6. c. 30.

GAR'PHETI, a people of Arabia. *Id.* 6 c. 28.

GAR'RHA, a city of Mauritania Cæsariensis. *Ptol.*

GARUM'NA, a river of Gaul, now called Garonne, which rises in the Pyrenean mountains, at the southern extremity of Aquitania. It falls into the bay of Biscay near Bourdeaux, and has, by the persevering labors of Lewis the Fourteenth, a communication with the Mediterranean by the canal of Languedoc, carried upwards of 100 miles through hills and over vallies. *Mela,* 3. c. 2.—*Ptol.* 2. c. 7. —*Cæs. Gall.* 1.

GARUM'NI, the people dwelling near the Garumna. *Cæs. Com.* 3. c. 6.

GASAN'DÆ, a people of Arabia. *Diod. Sic.* l. 3.

GAS'TRON, a general of Lacedæmon, &c. *Polyæn.* 2.

GASTRO'NIA, a region of Macedonia. *Steph.*

GA'THEÆ, a town of Arcadia. *Paus.* 8. c. 34.

GATHE'ATAS or **GATHEA'TAS**, a river of Arcadia. *Id. ib.*

GAU'DARA, a village of Macedonia. *Steph.*

GAUGAME'LA, a village near Arbela, beyond the Tigris, where Alexander obtained his third and last victory over Darius. *Curt.* 4. c. 9.—*Strab.* 2 & 16.

GAULANI'TIS, a district in Palestine, on the east of the Lake of Tiberias.

GAU'LUS or **GAU'LEON**, now Gozat, an island in the Mediterranean Sea, at the west of Malta, opposite Libya. It produces no venomous creatures. *Plin.* 3. c. 8.

GAU'RIUM, a harbour of the island of Andrus. *Liv.* 31. c. 45. Also Gau'rion.

GAU'RUS, a mountain of Campania, famous for its wines. *Lucan.* 2. v. 667.—*Sil.* 12. v. 160.—*Stat.* 3. *Sylv.* 5. v. 99.

GA'US, a man who followed the interests of Artaxerxes, from whom he revolted, and by whom he was put to death. *Diod.* 15.

GA'VIUS L. FIRMA'NUS, a man made præfect of Cilicia by Cicero, for which favor he proved himself very ungrateful. *Cic.* 6. *Att.* 1 & 3.

GA'ZA, a famous town of Palestine, once well fortified as being the frontier place on the confines of Ægypt. Alexander the Great took it after a siege of two months. *Diod.* 17.

GAZ'ACA, a city of Media. *Steph.*

GAZE'TÆ, a people of Galatia. *Id.*

GAZIU'RA, a city of Pontus Galaticus, the ancient residence of the kings of Pontus.

GA'ZUS, the largest city of India. *Id.*

GE'A, a town near Petræ, in Arabia. *Id.*

GEB'ALA, a region of Arabia. *Id.*

GEBELE'ZIS, a deity, the same as Zamolxis. *Herod.* 4. c. 94.

GEBEN'NA, a town and mountain of Gaul, southwest of Lyons, now les Cevennes. *Lucan.* 1. v. 435,

GEDRO'SIA, a barren province of Persia, near India. *Strab.* 2.

GEGA'NII, a family of Alba, part of which migrated to Rome, under Romulus. One of the daughters, called Gegania, was the first of the vestal virgins created by Numa. *Plut. in Num.*——One of the family was consul, and triumphed over the Volsci. *Liv.* 3. c. 65. l. 4. c. 10.

GE'LA, a town at the south of Sicily, about ten miles from the sea, according to Ptolemy, which received its name from a small river in the neighbourhood called Gelas. It was built by a mixed colony from Rhodes and Crete, 713 years B.C. After it had continued in existence 404 years, Phintias, tyrant of Agrigentum, carried the inhabitants to Phintias, a town in the neighbourhood, which he had founded, and employed the stones of Gela to beautify his own city. Phintias was also called Gela. The inhabitants were called Gelenses, Geloi, and Gelani. *Virg. Æn.* 3. v. 702.—*Ptol.* 3. c. 4.—*Ovid. Fast.* 4. v. 470.—*Sil. It.* 14. v. 219.—*Strab.* 6.—*Paus.* 8. c. 46.

GELA'NOR, a king of Argos, who succeeded his father Sthenelus. His right to the sovereignty was disputed by Danaus, a foreign prince, who had lately arrived from Ægypt, and whilst the competitors were pleading their cause in the presence of the people, a wolf boldly attacked under the walls of the city, a herd of cows, and the bull that followed them. The incident was interpreted by the superstitious or prejudiced assembly as an extraordinary omen, and Gelanor, compared to the bull, was made to yield to the superior power and influence of his rival. *Paus.* 2. c. 16 & 19. *Vid.* Danaus.

GE'LAS. *Vid.* Gela.

GELASI'NUS, the god of laughter, from γελάω. *Mart.* 7. epigr. 24.

GEL'DUBA, a fortified place on the Rhine. *Tac. Hist.* 4. c. 26.

GEL'LIA CORNE'LIA LEX, *de Civitate*, introduced by L. Gellius and Cn. Cornel. Lentulus, A.U.C. 682. It enacted that all those who had been presented with the privilege of citizens of Rome by Pompey, should remain in the possession of that liberty. *Cic. pro. Balb.*

GELLIA'NUS, an historian mentioned by *Pliny*, 3. c 12.

GEL'LIAS, a native of Agrigentum, famous for his munificence and hospitality. *Diod.* 13.—*Val. Max.* 4. c. 8.

GEL'LIUS, a consul and censor, who bestowed the highest praise on Cicero for his vigilance and energy in crushing Catiline's conspiracy. *Cic. ad Quir.* 7. *Pis.* 3.—*Plut. in Pomp.*——A consul who defeated a party of Germans in the interest of Spartacus. *Plut.*——A Roman historian, of little reputation. *Cic. Div*, 1. c. 26.

GEL'LIUS AU'LUS, a Roman grammarian, who flourished in the age of M. Antonius, about 130. A.D. He published a work which he called *Noctes Atticæ*, because he composed it at Athens in the long nights of winter. It is a curious collection of incongruous matter, which contains many fragments from ancient writers, and often serves to explain antique monuments. It was originally composed by the author for the improvement of his children, and abounds with many gramatical remarks and ingenious reflections. The best editions of A. Gellius are that of Gronovius, 4to. L. Bat. 1706, and that of Conrad, 2. vols. 8vo. Lips. 1762. An elegant translation of this author, with valuable notes, has lately appeared from the pen of Mr. Beloe. *Harles. Not. Lit. Rom.* 1. p. 513.—*Sax. Onom.* 1. p. 311.

GE'LO or GE'LON, a son of Dinomenes, who made himself absolute at Syracuse, 491 years B.C. He conquered the Carthaginians at Himera, and rendered his government popular by his great equity and moderation. He reigned seventeen years, and his death was universally lamented at Syracuse. He was called the father of his people, and the patron of liberty, and honored as a demigod. His brother Hiero succeeded him. *Paus.* 8. c. 42.—*Herodot.* 7. c. 153, &c.—*Diod.* 11.—*Dionys. Hal.* 8.—*Plut. Apoph. & de his qui sero a Numine pun.*—*Justin.* 23. c. 4.——A man who attempted to poison Pyrrhus. *Plut. in Pyrrh.*——A governor of Bœotia.——A son of Hiero the younger, who revolted from the Romans to the side of Carthage. *Liv.* 23. c. 30. l. 24. c. 5.—*Paus.* 6. c. 9.——A general of Phocis, destroyed with his troops by the Thessalians. *Paus.* 10. c. 1.

GELO'I or GE'LOI, the inhabitants of Gela in Sicily. *Vid.* Gela. *Virg. Æn.* 3. v. 701.

GELO'NES or GELO'NI, a people of Scythia, situated on the banks of the Borysthenes on the east; they were inured from their youth to labor and fatigue, and painted themselves to appear more terrible in battle. They were descended from Gelonus, a son of Hercules. *Virg. G.* 2. v. 15. *Æn.* 8. v. 725.—*Mela*, 1. c. 1.—*Claudian. in Ruf.* 1. v. 315.

GE'LOS, a port of Caria. *Mela*, 1. c. 16.

GEM'INI, a sign of the Zodiac which represents Castor and Pollux, the twin sons of Leda. Some suppose that this sign represents Triptolemus and Jason. The sun enters Gemini in the latter part of the month of May. *Hygin. P.A.* 2. c. 22.—*Plin.* 18. c. 20.

GEMIN'IUS, a Roman, who acquainted M. Antony with the situation of his affairs at Rome, &c.——An inveterate enemy of Marius. He seized his person when he fled from his persecutors at Rome, and carried him to Minturnæ. *Plut. in Mario.*——A friend of Pompey, from whom he received a favorite mistress called Flora. *Plut.*——A Roman knight, and friend of Sejanus, put to death on suspicion of being concerned in a conspiracy, *Tac. Ann.* 6. c. 14.

GEM'INUS or GEMI'NUS, an astronomer and mathematician of Rhodes. *Voss. de Scient. Math.* l. 160.

GEMO'NIÆ, a place at Rome where the carcases of criminals were thrown. *Suet. Tib.* 53 & 61.—*Tacit. Hist.* 3. c. 74.

GENA'BUM or CENA'BUM, a town of Gaul, now Orleans, on the Loire. *Cæsar. B.C.* 7. c. 3.—*Lucan* 1. v. 440.

GENAU'NI, a people of Rhætia, placed by most geographers between the source of the Athesis and the Ænus. *Horat.* 4. od. 14. v. 10.

GEN'ESE, a city of Laconia. *Steph.*

GENE'SIUS JOSE'PHUS, an historian about A.D. 950, who wrote the history of Byzantium from A.D. 813 to 836.

GENETÆ'US, a surname of Jupiter, from Cape Genetus, where he was worshipped as "the hospitable."

GENE'TES, a promontory of Cappadocia, where Jupiter Xenus had a temple. *Val. Flacc.* 5. v. 147.—*Strab.* 12.—*Plin.* 6. c. 4.

GEN'ITRIX, a surname of Venus. She had a temple under that name at Rome, and her festivals were celebrated in September. *Appian.* 2 *De Bell. Civ.*

GENETYL'LIS, an epithet of Venus. *Aristoph. in Nub.*

GENE'VA, an ancient, populous, and well fortified city in the country of the Allobroges, on the lake Lemanus, now the lake of Geneva. The inhabitants were long celebrated for their love of freedom and independence, and for their learning. *Cæs. B. G.* 1. c. 2.

GENI'SUS or GEN'ISUS, a man of Cyzicus, killed by the Argonauts, &c. *Flacc.* 3. v. 45.

GE'NIUS, a spirit or dæmon, which, according to the ancients, presided over the birth and life of every man. Each person was supposed to have two of these aerial attendants, one good, the other evil; and according to their different influence his actions were guided. The genii which presided over females were called Junones, and those who protected towns and countries were ranked among the divinities of a higher order. *Apul. de Socr. Deo.*—*Servius in Æn.* 2. v. 351. l. 5. v. 85 & 95. l. 6. v. 743 & 12. 538.—*Horat.* 2. ep. 2. v. 187.—*Drak. ad Sil. Ital.* 2. v. 585.—*Senec.* ep. 110. *Vid.* Dæmon.

GENO'A, a people of Molossia. *Steph.*

GENSERI'CUS, a famous Vandal prince, who passed from Spain to Africa, where he took Carthage. He laid there the foundation of the Vandal kingdom, and in the course of his military expeditions, invaded Italy, and in July 455 A.D. took Rome, which he delivered up to the pillage and violence of his barbarous soldiers for 14 days. Genseric, so eminent for his presence of mind in the midst of dangers, and the strong energies of a bold undaunted spirit, died A.D. 477, and was succeeded by his son Huneric, who had married Eudoxia, the daughter of the Roman emperor. *Victor. Utic. de persec. Vandal.* 1 & 2.—*Procop. de B. V.* 1, &c.

GEN'TA, a city of India without the Ganges. *Steph.*

GENTI'NUS, a city of Troas founded, by a son of Æneas. *Id.*

GEN'TIUS, a king of Illyricum, who imprisoned the Roman ambassadors at the request of Perseus, king of Macedonia. This offence was highly resented by the Romans, and Gentius was conquered by Anicius and led in triumph with his family, B.C. 169. *Liv.* 43. c. 19, &c.

GEN'UA, now Genoa, a celebrated town of Liguria, on the sea shore. It was destroyed by Annibal, and rebuilt by the Romans. *Liv.* 21. c. 32. l. 28 c. 46. l. 30. c. 1.

GENU'SUS or GEN'USUS, now Semno, a river of Illyricum, falling into the Adriatic, at the north of Apollonia. *Lucan* 5. v. 462.

GENU'TIA LEX, *de magistratibus*, by L. Genutius the tribune, A.U.C. 411. It ordained that no person should exercise the same magistracy within ten years, or be invested with two offices in one year.—Another, enacted in the same year, to choose both consuls from the plebeians. *Liv.* 10. c. 9. Another against usury.

GENU'TIUS, a tribune of the people, cut off in his own house by the intrigues of his enemies. *Liv.* 2. c. 54.——A plebeian augur. *Liv.* 10. c. 9.——A consul.

GEOR'GICA, a poem of Virgil, in four books. The first treats of ploughing the ground; the second of sowing it; the third of the management of cattle, &c., and in the fourth, the poet gives an account of bees, and the manner of keeping them among the Romans. The word is derived from γέα *terra*, and ἔργον *opus*, because it particularly treats of husbandry. The work is dedicated to Mecœnas, the great patron of poetry in the age of Virgil. The author was seven years in writing and polishing it; and in the Georgics, by correctness of style, dignity of versification, and happiness of expression, has showed how much he excelled all other writers. The work is evidently an imitation of Hesiod, who wrote a poem called *Opera & Dies*, nearly on the same subject.

GEOR'GIUS PISI'DES. *Vid.* Pisides.

GEPHY'RA, one of the cities of the Seleucidæ in Syria. *Strab.* 9.——A city of Bœotia. *Steph.*

GEPHYR'ÆI or GEPHYRÆ'I, a people of Phœnicia, who passed with Cadmus into Bœotia, and thence into Attica. *Herodot.* 5. c. 57.

GEPHYRO'TE, a city of Libya. *Steph.*

GEP'IDÆ, a gothic people settled between the Oder and the Vistula. They were destroyed by the Lombards in the reign of Justinian.

GER, Γείρ, a great river of Libya. *Ptol.—Plin.* 5. c. 4.—*Solinus*, c. 24. calls it the Niger.

GERÆ'A, a city of Lusitania. *Ptol.*

GERÆS'TUS, a port of Eubœa. *Liv.* 31. c. 45.

GERA'NIA, a mountain between Megara and Corinth.——A city of Phrygia.——A city of Thrace, called also Cattuza. *Pliny* 4. c. 5. calls the people Catisi.

GERAN'THRÆ. *Vid.* Geronthræ.

GER'ASA, a city of Cœlesyria. *Steph.*

GERAS'TUS, a son of Mygdon. *Id.*

GERE'A, a city of India. *Id.*

GERELA'NUS, a tribune employed by Nero to slay Atticus Vestinus. *Tac. Ann.* 15. c. 69.

GE'REN, a city of Lesbus, so called from a son of Neptune. *Steph.*

GERE'NIA, a town of Apulia Daunia, now Gerione. *Liv.* 22. c. 18.——A town of Messenia, the birthplace of Nestor.

GERES'TICUS POR'TUS, a harbour of Teius, in Ionia. *Liv.* 37. c. 27.

GER'GIS or GERGI'THUS, a city of Troas. Hence Apollo Gergithius. *Steph.*

GERGITH'IUS, a writer on the arrival of Æneas in Italy. *Athen.* 6.

GERGI'THUM, a town near Cumæ in Æolia. *Plin.* 5. c. 30.

GERGO'VIA, a town of Gaul, near the sources of the Elaver, which falls into the Loire. *Cœs. B. G.* 7. c. 9.

GE'RION, an ancient augur.

GERMA'NIA, an extensive country of Europe, at the east of Gaul. Its inhabitants were warlike, fierce, and uncivilized, and proved watchful and indefatigable opposers of the power of Rome. Cæsar first entered their country, but he rather checked their fury than conquered them. His example was followed by his imperial successors or their generals, who sometimes invaded the country to chastise the insolence of the inhabitants. The ancient Germans were very superstitious, and, in many respects, their religion was the same as that of their neighbours the Gauls; whence some have concluded that these two nations were of the same origin. They paid uncommon respect to their women, who, as they believed, were endowed with something more than human. They built no temples to their gods, but paid great attention to the heroes and warriors which their country had produced. Tacitus, in whose age even letters were unknown among them, observed their customs with accuracy, and has delineated them with the genius of an historian, and the reflection of a philosopher. *Tacit. de Morib. Germ.—Mela*, l. c. 3. l. 3. c. 3.—*Cœs. Bell. G.—Strab.* 4.

GERMA'NI, the inhabitants of Germany. *Vid.* Germania.

GERMANICI'A, GERMANIC'IA or GERMANICE'A, a city of Comagene, now Adata. *Steph.*

GERMANICOP'OLIS, a city of Asia Minor, near the Hellespont. *Plin.* 5. c. 32. *Ammianus Marcellinus*, l. 27, says, that it was in Cilicia.

GERMAN'ICUM MA'RE, the German Ocean, washes the shores of Germany between the mouths of the Rhine and of the Albis. *Ptol.—Plin.* 4. c. 13.

GERMAN'ICUS CÆ'SAR, a son of Drusus and Antonia, the niece of Augustus. He was adopted by his uncle Tiberius, and raised to the most important offices of the state. When his grandfather Augustus died, he was employed in a war in Germany, and the affection of the soldiers unanimously saluted him emperor. He refused the unseasonable honour, and appeased the tumult which his indifference had occasioned. He continued his wars in Germany, and defeated the celebrated Arminius, and was rewarded with a triumph at his return from Rome. Tiberius declared him governor of the east, with unlimited power, and sent him to appease the seditions of the Armenians. But his success was soon looked upon with an envious eye by Tiberius, and his death was meditated. He was secretly poisoned, as it is supposed, by Piso and Plancina, at Daphne, near Antioch, A.D. 19, in the 34th year of his age. The news of his death was received with the greatest grief, and the most bitter lamentations, and Tiberius seemed to be the only one who rejoiced in the fall of Germanicus. He had married the virtuous Agrippina, by whom he had nine children, one of whom was Caligula. Germanicus has been commended, not only for his military accomplishments, but also for his learning humanity, and extensive benevolence. In the midst of war he devoted some moments to study, and he favoured the world with two Greek comedies, some epigrams, and a translation of Aratus into Latin verse. The works of Germanicus were edited by Schmid, Luneb. 1728. There are also other editions. *Harles. Not. Lit. Rom.* l. p. 301.—*Sax Onom.* l. p. 203.—*Sueton. Cal.* l. c. 2 & 7.—*Tacit. Ann.* l. c. 3, 7, 33, &c. [The finest bust of Germanicus is in the Capitol.]——This name was common in the age of the emperors, not only to those who had obtained victories over the Germans but even to those who had entered the borders of their country at the head of an army. Domitian applied the name of Germanicus, which he himself had vainly assumed, to the month of September, in honour of himself. *Suet. in Dom.* 13.—*Martial.* 8. epigr. 2. v. 4.

GERMA'NII, a people of Persia. *Herodot.* l. c. 125.

GERMANOP'OLIS, a city of Paphlagonia, now Ginopoli. *Ptol.*

GER'RHA, a city of Ægypt, now Maseli.

GER'RHÆ, a people of Scythia, in whose country the Borysthenes rises. The kings of Scythia were generally buried in their territories. *Herodot.* 4. c. 71.

GER'RHI, a people of Asiatic Sarmatia. *Ptol.*——A people of Arabia Felix.

GERON'THRÆ, a town of Laconia, where a yearly festival, called Geronthræa, was observed in honor of Mars. The god had there a temple, with a grove, into which no woman was permitted to enter during the time of the solemnity. *Paus. Lacon.*

GERUN'DA, a town of the Ausetani, in Hispania Tarraconensis.

GE'RUS or GER'RHUS, a river of Albania, falling into the Caspian Sea. *Plin.* 4. c. 12.——A river of Scythia. *Herodot.* 4. c. 19.

GERU'SA, a city of Asiatic Sarmatia, now S. Georgio. *Ptol.*

GE'RYON or **GERY'ONES**, a celebrated monster, born from the union of Chrysaor with Calirhoe, and represented by the poets as having three bodies and three heads. He lived in the island of Gades, in Spain, where he kept numerous flocks, which were guarded by a two-headed dog, called Orthos. and by Eurythion. Hercules, by order of Eurystheus, went to Gades, and destroyed Geryon, Orthos, and Eurythion, and carried away all his flocks to Tirynthus. According to Servius, Geryon was the sovereign of three provinces in Spain, or of the three islands of Majorca, Minorca, and Ivica ; from which circumstance the ancients have made him a three-headed monster. *Hesiod. Theog.* 187.—*Virg. Æn.* 7. v. 661. l. 8. v. 202.—*Ital.* l. v. 277.—*Apollod.* 2.—*Hygin.* in præf. fab. & fab. 30.—*Lucret.* 5. v. 28.—*Seneca in Agam.* v. 841.—*Servius, Æn.* 7. v. 662.—*Palæph. de incred.*

GESAN'DER, a leader of the Jazyges. *Val. Flacc. Argon.* 6. v. 280.

GESITH'OUS, an auxiliary of Æetes against Perses. *Id. ibid.* 6. v. 639.

GESSA'TÆ, a people of Gallia Togata. *Plut. in Marcell.*

GES'SIUS FLO'RUS, a governor of Judæa, slain in war. *Tac. Hist.* 5. c. 10,

GESSORI'ACUM, a town of Gaul, now Boulogne, in Picardy, on the British Channel.

GES'SUS, a river of Ionia. *Plin.* 5. c. 29.—*Strab.* 14.

GETA, a Roman expelled from the senate, and afterwards restored to his dignity, and made censor. *Cic. Clu.* 42.—*Val. Max.* 2. c. 9.——One of the characters of Terence's Adelphi and Phormio.——A man who raised seditions at Rome in Nero's reign, &c. *Tacit. Hist.* 2. c. 72.

GE'TA SEPTIM'IUS, a son of the emperor Severus, brother to Caracalla. In the eighth year of his age he was moved with compassion at the fate of some of the partisans of Niger and Albinus, who had been ordered to be executed ; and his father, struck with his humanity, retracted his sentence. After his father's death he reigned at Rome, conjointly with his brother ; but Caracalla, who envied his virtues, and was jealous of his popularity, ordered him to be poisoned ; and when this could not be effected, he murdered him in the arms of his mother Julia, who, in attempting to ward off the fatal blows from his body received a wound in her arm from the hand of her unnatural son, on the 28th of March, A.D. 212. Geta had not reached his 23d year. [There is a bust of Geta in the Capitol.]

GE'TÆ, (*Getes*, sing.) a people of European Scythia, near the Daci, on the borders of the Euxine Sea, on both sides of the mouths of the Danube. Ovid, the place of whose banishment was in their country, describes them as a savage and warlike nation. The word Geticus is frequently used for Thracian. *Ovid. de Pont. Trist.* 5. el. 7. v. 111. el. 12. v. 10. —*Mela*, 2, c. 2.—*Strab.* 7.—*Stat.* 2 *Sylv.* 2. v. 61. l. 3. s. 1. v. 17.—*Lucan.* 2. v. 54. l. 3. v. 95.

GETHOS'YNE, a female attendant of Berenice, widow of Antiochus. *Polyæn.* 7.

GETHUS'SA, a city of Libya. *Steph.*

GETU'LIA. *Vid.* Gætulia.

GICH'THIS, a city of Africa Propria, now probably Galfanagar. *Ptol.*

GIGANE'UM, a city of Colchis. *Id.*

GIGAN'TIS, an ancient name of Arcadia. *Steph.*

GIGAN'TES, the sons of Cœlus and Terra, sprang, according to Hesiod from the blood of the wound which Cœlus received from his son Saturn ; but Hyginus calls them sons of Tartarus and Terra. They are represented as having been men of uncommon stature, with strength proportioned to their gigantic size. Some of them, as Cottus, Briareus, and Gyges, had 50 heads and 100 arms, and serpents instead of legs. They were of a terrible aspect, their hair hung loose about their shoulders, and their beard was suffered to grow untouched. Pallene, and its neighbourhood, was the place of their residence. The defeat of the Titans, with whom they are often confounded, and to whom they were nearly related, incensed them against Jupiter, and they all conspired to dethrone him. The god was alarmed, and called all the deities to assist him against this powerful enemy, who hurled against him rocks of such magnitude, that those which fell into the sea became islands, and those on the earth huge mountains. Their other weapons were trees torn up by the roots, and burning woods, and their daring strength was so prodigious that they began to heap mount Ossa upon Pelion, to scale heaven with greater facility. At the sight of such dreadful adversaries, the gods fled with the greatest consternation into Ægypt, where they assumed the shape of different animals. Jupiter, however, remembered that they were not invincible, provided he called a mortal to his assistance ; and by the advice of Pallas, he armed his son Hercules in his cause. With the aid of this celebrated hero, the giants were soon attacked, put to flight, and signally defeated. Alcynœus and Eurytus were destroyed by the arm of Hercules, Porphyrion by Jupiter, Clytius perished under the stroke of Vulcan, Mercury killed Hippolitus, Diana Gration, Neptune Polybotes, and Minerva, after she had killed Enceladus, fleaed Pallas and adorned herself with his skin. All the rest of inferior note, were dispersed either by the thunderbolts of Jupiter, or by the club of Hercules, and some were crushed to pieces under mountains or buried in the sea. *Vid.* Enceladus, Aloides, Porphyrion, Typhon, Otus, Titanes, &c. The existence of giants has been asserted by all the writers of antiquity, and received as an undeniable truth. Homer tells us, that Tityus when extended on the ground covered nine acres ; and that Polyphemus ate two of the companions of Ulysses at once, and walked along the shores of Sicily, leaning on a staff, so huge that it might have served for the mast of a ship. Plutarch also mentions, in support of the existence of giants, that Sertorius opened the grave of Antæus in Africa, and found in it a skeleton which measured six cubits in length. *Apollod.* 1. c. 6.—*Hesiod. Th.* 150 & 185.—*Macrob. Sat.* 1. c. 20.—*Philost. in her.* 1.—*Horat.* 3. od. 4.—*Paus.* 8. c. 2, &c.—*Ovid. Met.* 1. v. 151. *Trist.* 4. el. 7. v. 17. *Fast.* 5. v. 35.—*Plut. in Sertor.*—*Hygin.* fab. 28, &c.—*Homer. Odyss.* 7 & 10.—*Virg. G.* 1. v. 280. *Æn.* 6. v. 580. & *Servius locis.*—*Schol. Apollon.* 2, v. 40.—*Claudian. in Fr. Gig.*

GIGAR'TUM, a town of Phœnicia. *Strab.* 16.—*Plin.* 5. c. 20.

GI'GIS, one of the female attendants of Parysatis, who was privy to the poisoning of Statira. *Plut. in Artax.*

GIGO'NUS, a city of Thrace. *Steph.*

GIL'DA, a city of Libya. *Id.*

GIL'DO or **GIL'DON**, a governor of Africa, in the reign of Arcadius. His character, and the war in which he was engaged, have been described by the poet Claudian. He died A.D. 398. *Amm. Marcell.* 29. c. 5, &c.

GILIGAM'BÆ, a people of Libya. *Steph.*

GIL'LO, an infamous adulterer in Juvenal's age. *Juv.* 1. v. 40.

GIL'LUS, a Tarentine exile, who ransomed some Persian spies who were taken by pirates. *Herod.* 3. c. 138.

GINDA'NES, a people of Libya, who fed on the leaves of the lotus. *Herodot.* 4. c. 176.

GIN'DARA, a village near Antiochia, the inhabitants of which were called Gindarenses or Gindari. *Plin.* 5. c. 23.—*Steph.*

GIN'DES, a river of Albania, which flows into the Cyrus, and with it into the Caspian Sea.——A river of Mesopotamia. *Tibull.* 4. el. 1. v. 141.

GIN'GE. *Vid.* Gigis.

GIN'GLA, a town of Commagene. *Plin.* 5. c. 24.

GINGLYMO'TE, a city of Phœnicia. *Steph.*

GIN'GRAS, a name of Adonis among the Phœnicians. *Pollux.* 4. c. 10.

GINGU'NUM, a mountain of Umbria, now Gergnone. *Strab.* l. 5.

GIP'PIUS, a Roman who pretended to sleep, that his wife might indulge her adulterous propensities, whence the proverb. *Non omnibus dormio. Lucil. apud Berould.*

GIR'BA, a city on the island of Meninx in Africa, celebrated for its manufacture of purple.

GIS'CO, son of Himilcon, the Carthaginian general, was banished from his country by the influence of his enemies. He was afterwards recalled, and empowered by the Carthaginians to punish, in what manner he pleased, those who had occasioned his banishment. He was satisfied to see them prostrate on the ground, and to place his foot on their neck, showing that independence and forgiveness are two of the most brilliant virtues of a great mind.

He was made a general soon after, in Sicily, against the Corinthians, about 309 years B.C., and after distinguishing himself by his success and intrepidity, he obliged the enemies of his country to sue for peace.

GIS'IRA, a city of Africa Propria. *Ptol.*

GIS'SA, an island of the Illyrian Sea, near Liburnia, now Gisse. *Plin.* 3. c. 21.

GITI'ADAS, a Lacedæmonian statuary and poet, about 516 B.C.

GIT'LUI, a town of Mauritania Cæsariensis. *Ptol.*

GLA'BRIO, a surname of the Acilian family.

Gla'brio Mar'cus, a prætor at the trial of Verres. *Cic. in Verr.*

GLADIATO'RII LUDI, combats originally exhibited on the grave of deceased persons at Rome. They were first introduced at Rome by the Bruti, upon the death of their father, A.U.C. 488. It was supposed that the ghosts of the dead were rendered propitious by the shedding of human blood; therefore at funerals it was usual to murder slaves in cool blood. In succeeding ages, it was reckoned less cruel to oblige them to kill one another like men, than to slaughter them like brutes, therefore the barbarity was covered by the specious show of pleasure and voluntary combat. Originally, only captives, criminals, or disobedient slaves, were trained up for combat; but when the diversion became more frequent, and was exhibited on the smallest occasion, to procure esteem and popularity, many of the Roman citizens enlisted themselves among the gladiators, and Nero, at one show, exhibited no less than 400 senators, and 600 knights. The people were treated with these combats, not only by the great, the opulent, and the ambitious; but the very priests had their *Ludi pontificales*, and *Ludi sacerdotales*. It is supposed that there were no more than three pair of gladiators exhibited by the Bruti. Their numbers, however, increased with the luxury and power of the city; and the gladiators became so formidable, that Spartacus, one of their body, had the courage to take up arms, and defeated the Roman armies, with a train of his fellow sufferers only. The more sagacious of the Romans were sensible of the dangers which threatened the state by keeping such a number of desperate men in arms, and therefore, many salutary laws were proposed to limit their number, as well as to settle the time in which the show could be exhibited with safety and convenience. Under the emperors, not only senators and knights, but even women engaged among the gladiators, and seemed to forget the delicacy, as well as the weakness of their sex. When there were to be any shows, hand-bills were circulated to give notice to the people, and to mention the place, number, time, and every circumstance requisite to be known. When the gladiators were first brought upon the *arena*, they walked round the place with great pomp and solemnity, and after that they were matched in equal pairs with great nicety. They first had a skirmish with wooden files, called *rudes* or *arma lusoria*. After this the more effective weapons, such as swords, daggers, &c. called *arma decretoria*, were given them, and the signal for the engagement was given by the sound of the trumpet. As they had all previously sworn to fight till death, or suffer death in the most excruciating torments, the fight was bloody and obstinate, and when one signified his submission by surrendering his arms, the victor was not permitted to grant him his life, without the leave and approbation of the surrounding multitude. This was done by clenching the fingers of both hands between each other, and holding the thumbs upright close together, or by bending back their thumbs. The first of these was called *pollicem premere*, and signified the wish of the people to spare the life of the conquered. The other sign, called *pollicem vertere*, signified their disapprobation, and ordered the victor to put his antagonist to death. The victor was generally rewarded with a palm, and other expressive marks of the people's favor. He was most commonly presented with a *pileus* and *rudis*. When one of the combatants received a remarkable wound, the people exclaimed *habet*, and expressed their exultation by repeated shouts. The combats of gladiators were sometimes different, either in weapons or dress, whence they were generally distinguished into the following orders: The *secutores* were armed with a sword and buckler, to keep off the net of their antagonists, the *retiarii*. These last endeavoured to throw their net over the head of their antagonist, and in that manner to entangle him, and prevent him from striking. If this did not succeed, they betook themselves to flight. Their dress was a short coat, with a hat tied under the chin with broad ribbon. They carried a trident in their left hand. The *Thraces*, originally Thracians, were armed with a faulchion and small round shield. The *Myrmillones*, called also *Galli*, from their Gallic dress, were much the same as the *secutores*. They were, like them, armed with a sword, and on the top of their head-piece, they wore the figure of a fish embossed, called μορμύρος, whence their name. The *Hoplomachi*, were completely armed from head to foot, as their name implies. The *Samnites*, armed after the manner of the Samnites, wore a large shield, broad at the top, and narrow at the bottom, in order more conveniently to defend the upper parts of the body. The *Essedarii*, generally fought from the *essedum*, or chariot used by the ancient Gauls and Britons. The *andabatæ* ἀναβάται, fought on horseback, with a helmet that covered and defended their faces and eyes The *andabatarum more pugnare*, is to fight blindfolded. The *meridiani* engaged in the afternoon. Hence *postulatitii*, were men of great skill and experienee, and such as were generally exhibited by the emperors. The *fiscales* were maintained out of the emperor's treasury, *fiscus*. The *dimachærii* fought with two swords in their hands, whence their name. These cruel exhibitions were wisely abolished by Constantine the Great, nearly 600 years after their first institution. They were, however, revived for a while, under Constantius and his two successors, but Honorius for ever put an end to these cruel barbarities. [Two of the most celebrated statues of antiquity, bear the names of gladiators; "the fighting gladiator" in the Borghese collection, now at Paris, and "the dying gladiator," in the Vatican, at Rome: but they are not either of them really representations of such characters; their proper designations being undecided.]

GLANDOMI'RUM, a city of Hispania Tarraconensis. *Ptol.* Also Glandima'rium.

GLA'NIS, a river of Cumæ.——A river of Iberia.——A river of Italy, called also Clanis. *Ital.* 8. v. 454.

GLA'NUM, a town of Gaul, now St. Remi, in Provence. *Ptol.*

GLAPH'YRE or **GLAPH'YRA**, wife of Archelaus the high-priest of Bellona's temple in Cappadocia, was celebrated for her beauty and intrigues. She obtained the kingdom of Cappadocia for her two sons from M. Antony, whom she corrupted by defiling the bed of her husband. This amour of Antony with Glaphyra highly displeased his wife Fulvia, who wished Augustus to avenge his infidelity, by receiving from her the same favors which Glaphyra had granted to Antony.

Glaph'yre, grand-daughter of the preceding. She was a daughter of Archelaus, king of Cappadocia, and married Alexander, a son of Herod, by whom she had two sons. After the death of Alexander she married her brother-in-law Archelaus. *Joseph.* 17. c. 15.

GLAPH'YRUS, a noted adulterer. *Juv.* 6. v. 77.

GLAU'CE, the wife of Actæus, daughter of Cychræus. *Apollod.*——A daughter of Cretheus, mother of Telamon.——One of the Nereides.——A daughter of Creon, who married Jason. She is also called Creusa. *Vid.* Creusa.——One of the Danaides, who married Alcis. *Apollod.*

GLAU'CIA, a surname of the Servilian family. *Cic. Orat.* 3. c. 41. l. 2. c. 61.

Glau'cia, a town of Ionia. *Steph.*

Glau'cia Ca'ius, a prætor put to death by the consuls Marius and Valerius. *Cic. Rab.* 7. *Cat.* 3. c. 6.

GLAU'CIAS, a freedman of Melior. *Mart.* 6. epigr. 28.

GLAUCIP'PE, one of the Danaides. *Apollod.*

GLAUCIP'PUS, a Greek, who wrote a treatise concerning the sacred rites observed at Athens. *Macrob. Sat.* 1. c. 13.

GLAU'CON, a writer of dialogues at Athens. *Diog. in Vit.*

GLAUCON'OME, one of the Nereides.

GLAUCO'PIS, a surname frequently given to Minerva, from the blueness of her eyes. *Homer.—Hesiod.*

GLAU'CUS, a son of Hippolochus, and father of Bellerophon. He assisted Priam in the Trojan war, and had the simplicity to exchange his golden suit of armour with Diomedes for an iron one, whence came the proverb of *Glauci et Diomedes permutatio*, to express a foolish purchase. He behaved with much courage in his encounters with the Greeks, and was killed by Ajax. *Virg. Æn.* 6. v. 483.—*Martial.* 9. epigr. 96.—*Homer. Il.* 6. v. 119. l. 12. v. 309. l. 16. v. 492. l. 17. v. 140.—*Herodot.* 1. c. 147.—*Plato. in Symp.*—*Aristot. Eth.* 5.——A fisherman of Anthedon in Bœotia, son of Neptune and Nais, or according to others, of Polybus, the son of Mercury. As he was fishing, he observed that all the fishes which he laid on the grass received fresh vigor as they touched the ground, and immediately escaped from him by leaping back into the sea. He attributed the cause of it to the grass, and by tasting it, he found himself suddenly moved with a desire of living in the sea. Upon this he leaped into the water, and was made a sea deity by Oceanus and Tethys, at the request of the gods. After this extraordinary transformation, he became enamoured of the Nereid Scylla, whose ingratitude was severely punished by Circe. *Vid.* Scylla. Theolytus, an author quoted by Athenæus, says that he carried away Ariadne from Naxus, for which Bacchus tied him with ignominy to a tree, and restored him to his liberty after he heard his name and situation. Glaucus is represented like the other sea deities with a long beard, dishevelled hair, and shaggy eyebrows, and with the tail of a fish. He received the gift of prophecy from Apollo, and according to some accounts he was the attendant and interpreter of Nereus. He assisted the Argonauts in their expedition, and foretold that Hercules, and the two sons of Leda, would one day receive immortal honors. The fable of his metamorphosis has been explained by some authors, who observe that he was an excellent diver, who was devoured by fishes as he was swimming in the sea. *Ovid. Met.* 13. v. 905, &c.—*Philostr. Icon.* 2. c. 15.—*Virg. G.* 1. v. 437.—*Tzetzes in Lyc.* 755. *Lactant. Argon.* 13.—*Eustath. in Il.* 2.—*Servius in Æn.* 5. v. 823. l. 6. v. 74.—*Eurip. in Orest.*—*Palœph. de Inc.* 28.—*Heraclit. Pont.* 10.—*Hygin.* fab. 199.—*Athen.* 7. c. 12.—*Apollon.* 1.—*Diod.* 4.—*Aristot. de Rep. Del.*—*Paus.* 9. c. 22.——A son of Sisyphus, king of Corinth, by Merope the daughter of Atlas, born at Potnia, a village of Bœotia. Venus, offended at his conduct towards her, inspired his mares with such fury, that they tore his body to pieces as he returned from the games which Adrastus had celebrated in honor of his father. He was buried at Potnia. *Hygin.* fab. 250 & 273.—*Virg. G.* 3. v. 367.—*Servius loco.*—*Palœph. de Inc.* 26.—*Apollod.* 1 & 2.——A son of Minos the Second, and Pasiphae, who was smothered in a cask of honey. His father, ignorant of his fate, consulted the oracle, to know where he was, and received for answer, that the soothsayer who best described him an ox, which was of three different colors among his flocks, would give him the most satisfactory intelligence of his son's situation. Polyidus was found superior to all the other soothsayers, and was commanded by the king to find the young prince. When he had found him, Minos confined him with the dead body, and told him that he never would restore him to liberty, if he did not restore him to life. Polyidus was struck with the king's severity, but while he stood in astonishment, a serpent suddenly came towards the body and touched it. Polyidus killed the serpent, and immediately a second came, which seeing the other without motion or signs of life, quickly disappeared, and soon after returned with a certain herb in his mouth. This herb he laid on the body of the dead serpent, which was immediately restored to life. Polyidus, who had attentively considered what passed, seized the herb, and with it he rubbed the body of the dead prince, who was instantly raised to life. Minos received Glaucus with gratitude, but he cruelly refused to restore Polyidus to liberty, before he taught his son the art of divination and prophecy. He consented with great reluctance, and when he was at last permitted to return to Argolis his native country, he desired his pupil to spit in his mouth. Glaucus willingly consented, and from that moment he forgot all the knowledge of divination and of the art of healing, which he had received from the instructions of Polyidus. Hyginus ascribes the recovery of Glaucus to Æsculapius. *Apollod.* 2. c. 3.—*Hygin.* 136 & 251, &c.—*Tzetzes in Lycoph.* 811.—*Palœph. de Inc.* 27.——A son of Epytus, who succeeded his father on the throne of Messenia, about ten centuries before the Augustan age. He introduced the worship of Jupiter among the Dorians, and was the first who offered sacrifices to Machaon the son of Æsculapius. *Paus.* 4. c. 3.——A son of Antenor, killed by Agamemnon during the Trojan war. *Dictys. Cret.* 4. c. 22.——A son of Imbrasus, killed by Turnus in the Rutulian war. *Virg. Æn.* 12. v. 343.——An Argonaut, the only one of the crew who was not wounded in a battle against the Tyrrhenians. *Athen.* 7. c. 12.——A son of Hippolytus, whose descendants reigned in Ionia. *Eustath. Il.* 2.——An athlete of Eubœa, son of Demylus, and descended from Glaucus of Anthedon. *Paus.* 6. c. 9.——A son of Priam. *Apollod.* 3.——A physician of Cleopatra. *Plut. in Anton.*——A warrior in the age of Phocion. *Id. in Phoc.*——A physician exposed on a cross, because Hephæstion died while under his care. *Id. in Alex.*——An artist of Chius. *Paus.*——A Spartan. *Id.*——An historian of Rhegium in Italy.

GLAU'CUS, a grove of Bœotia. *Id.*——A bay of Caria on the Mediterranean, now the gulph of Macri. *Id.*——A bay and river of Libya. *Plin.* 5. c. 27.——A small river of Peloponnesus, now Rio di Patrasso.——A river of Colchis, falling into the Phasis. It is the same as the Cyaneus. *Strab.* 11.

GLAU'TIAS, a king of Illyricum, who educated Pyrrhus. *Plut.*

GLESSA'RIA, an island in the German Ocean. *Plin.* 4. c. 13. It is now Sudau.

GLE'TES, a people of Iberia. *Steph.*

GLIC'IUS GAL'LUS, a friend of Quinctianus, banished by Nero. *Tac. Ann.* 15. c. 56.

GLI'CON. *Vid.* Glycon.

GLIS'SAS or GLI'SAS, a town of Bœotia, with a small river in the neighbourhood. *Paus.* 9. c. 19.

GLYC'ERA, a beautiful woman, celebrated by *Horace*, 1. od. 19. 30.——A courtezan of Sicyon, so skilful in making garlands, that some attributed to her the invention of them. *Plin.* 35. c. 11.——A famous courtezan whom Harpalus brought from Athens to Babylon. *Diod. Sic.* 17.

GLYCE'RIUM, a harlot of Thespis, who presented her countrymen with the beautiful painting of Cupid, which Praxiteles had given her.——The mistress of Pamphilus in Terence's Andria.

GLYCE'RIUS, Emperor of the West A.D. 473. He was dethroned A.D. 474 by Julius Nepos, and became bishop of Salona.

GLY'CON, a man remarkable for his strength. *Horat.* 1. ep. 1. v. 50.——A physician who attended the consul Pansa, and was accused of poisoning his patron's wound. *Suet. Aug.* 11.——A sculptor of Athens, to whose superior execution it is said that the moderns are indebted for the long-admired statue of the Farnese Hercules.

GLYM'PES, a town on the borders of the Lacedæmonians and Argives. *Polyb.* 4.

GNA'TIA, a town of Apulia, on the shores of the Adriatic, about thirty miles from Brundusium, badly supplied with water. *Horat.* 1. sat. 5.

GNI'DUS *Vid.* Cnidus.

GNOS'SIS or GNOS'SIA, an epithet given to Ariadne because she lived, or was born, at Gnossus. The crown which she received from Bacchus, and which was made a constellation, is called Gnossia Stella. *Virg. G.* 1. v. 222.—*Ovid.* ep. 15.

GNOS'SUS or GNO'SUS, a famous city of Crete, the residence of king Minos. It was originally called Ceratus, from the neighbouring stream, and the inhabitants boasted that they possessed the tomb where the remains of Jupiter had been deposited. The name of Gnossia Tellus is often applied to the whole island. *Virg. Æn.* 6. v. 23.—*Strab.* 10.—*Homer. Il.* 2. v. 153.—*Ptol.* 3. c. 17.—*Lactant.* 1. c. 11.

GOARE'NE, a region of Arabia, called also Goarea. *Steph.*

GOBANIT'IO, a chief of the Arverni, uncle to Vercingetorix. *Cæs. Bell. G.* 7. c. 4.

GO'BAR, a governor of Mesopotamia, who checked

the course of the Euphrates, that it might not run rapidly through Babylon. *Plin.* 6. c. 26.

GOB'ARES, GO'BRYAS or CHOB'ARIS, a Persian governor, who conspired with Darius against the usurper Smerdis. *Vid.* Darius. *Herodot.* 3. c. 70.—*Val. Max.* 3. c. 2.

GOGARE'NE, a region between the Colchi and Iberi. *Steph.*

GOL'GI, (*-orum*), a place of Cyprus sacred to Venus Golgia, and to Cupid. *Paus.* 8. c. 5.—*Catull.* 61. v. 96.

GOMOLI'TÆ, a people of Idumæa. *Steph.*

GOM'PHI, a town of Thessaly, near the springs of the Peneus, at the foot of Pindus. It was plundered by Cæsar in the civil wars. *Cæs. B.C.* 3. c. 80.

GONA'TAS, the surname of one of the Antigoni.

GON'DRÆ, a people of Thrace. *Herod.—Steph.*

GONE'IS, a city of Thrace. *Steph.*

GONI'ADES, nymphs in the neighbourhood of the river Cytherius. *Strab.* 8.

GONIP'PUS and PANOR'MUS, two youths of Andania, who disturbed the Lacedæmonians when celebrating the festivals of Pollux. *Paus.* 4. c 27.

GON'NI or GONOCON'DYLON, a town of Thessaly at the north of the Peneus, and near the entrance into Tempe. *Liv.* 36. c. 10. l. 42. c. 54.—*Strab.* 4.

GONOES'SA, a town of Ætolia. *Senec. in Troad.—Homer. Il.* 2.

GONUS'SA, a town of Sicyon. *Paus.*

GOR'AMA, a region of the Arabes Scenitæ. *Steph.*

GORDE'NE, called by *Strabo* Gorduena, a region of Armenia Major. *Ptol.*

GORDIA'NUS M. ANTO'NIUS AFRICA'NUS, a son of Metius Marcellus, descended from Trajan by his mother's side, and from the Gracchi by the side of his father. In the midst of the greatest affluence he cultivated learning, and though surrounded by vicious characters, was an example of piety and virtue. He applied himself to the study of poetry, and composed a poem in 30 books upon the virtues of Titus, Antoninus, and M. Aurelius. He was some time after elected consul, and went to take the government of Africa, in the capacity of proconsul. After he had attained his 80th year, in the enjoyment of the greatest splendour and domestic tranquillity, he was aroused from his peaceful occupations by the tyrannical reign of the Maximini, and he was proclaimed emperor by the rebellious troops of his province. He long declined to accept the imperial purple, but the threats of immediate death occasioned his compliance. Maximinus marched against him with the greatest indignation; and Gordian sent his son, with whom he shared the imperial dignity, to oppose the enemy. Young Gordian was killed; and the father, worn out with age, and rendered desperate by his misfortunes, strangled himself at Carthage, before he had been six weeks at the head of the empire, A.D. 236. He was universally lamented by the army and people. [There is a bust of Gordianus in the Capitol.]

GORDIA'NUS M. ANTO'NIUS AFRICA'NUS, son of the preceding, was instructed by Serenus Sammonicus, who left him his library, which consisted of 62,000 volumes. His enlightened understanding, and peaceful disposition, recommended him to the favour of the emperor Heliogabalus, and he was afterwards made præfect of Rome, and then consul by the emperor Alexander Severus. He passed into Africa, in the character of lieutenant to his father, who had obtained that province; and seven years after he was elected emperor in conjunction with him. He marched against the partisans of Maximinus, his antagonist, in Mauritania, and was killed, in his 46th year, in a bloody battle on the 25th of June. A.D. 236, after a reign of about six weeks.

GORDIA'NUS M. ANTO'NIUS PI'US, grandson of the first Gordian, was but 12 years old when he was honoured with the title of Cæsar. He was proclaimed emperor in the 16th year of his age, and his election was attended with universal marks of approbation. In the 18th year of his age, he married Furia Sabina Tranquillina, daughter of Misitheus, a man celebrated for his eloquence and public virtues. Misitheus was entrusted with the most important offices of the state by his son-in-law; and his administration proved how deserving he was of the confidence and affection of his imperial master. He corrected the various abuses which prevailed in the state, restored the ancient discipline among the soldiers, and by his prudence and political sagacity, all the chief towns in the empire were stored with provisions, which could, upon any emergency, maintain the emperor and a large army during 15 days. Gordian was not less active than his father-in-law; and when Sapor, the king of Persia, had invaded the Roman provinces in the east, he boldly marched to meet him, and in his way defeated a large body of Goths, in Mœsia. He conquered Sapor, and took many flourishing cities in the east, from his adversary. For this success the senate decreed him a triumph, and saluted Misitheus as the guardian of the republic. Gordian was assassinated in the east, A.D. 244, by the means of Philip, who had succeeded to the virtuous Misitheus, and who usurped the sovereign power by murdering this warlike and amiable prince. The senate, sensible of the merit of their deceased emperor, honoured his remains with a most splendid funeral on the confines of Persia, and ordered that the descendants of the Gordians should ever be free at Rome, from all the heavy taxes aud burdens of the state. During the reign of Gordianus, there happened an uncommon eclipse of the sun, during which the stars appeared in the middle of the day. [A bust of this emperor will be found in the Capitol.]

GORDIE'US, a mountain in Armenia where the Tigris rises, supposed to be the Ararat of Scripture. *Bochart. Geog. Sac.* 1. c. 3.—*Plin.* 6. c. 11.

GORDITA'NUM, a promontory of Sardinia. *Ptol.—Plin.* 3. c. 7.

GOR'DIUM, a town of Phrygia, near the sources of the river Sangaris. *Justin.* 11. c. 7.—*Liv.* 38. c. 18.—*Curt.* 3. c. 1.

GOR'DIUS, a Phrygian, who, though originally a peasant, was raised to the throne. During a sedition the Phrygians consulted the oracle, and were told that all their troubles would cease as soon as they chose for their king, the first man whom they met going to the temple of Jupiter mounted on a chariot. Gordius was the object of their choice, and, in gratitude for his sudden elevation, he immediately consecrated his chariot in the temple of Jupiter, at Gordium. The knot which tied the yoke to the draught tree, was made in such an artful manner, that the ends of the cord could not be perceived. From this circumstance, a report was soon spread that the empire of Asia was promised by the oracle to him that could untie the Gordian knot. Alexander, in his conquest of Asia, passed by Gordium; and, as he wished to leave nothing undone, which might inspire his soldiers with courage, and make his enemies believe that he was destined to conquer Asia, he cut the knot with his sword; and, from that circumstance, asserted that the oracle was really fulfilled, and that his claims to universal empire were fully justified. *Justin.* 11. c. 7.—*Curt.* 3. c. 1.—*Arrian.* 1.——A tyrant of Corinth. *Aristot.* 5. *Pol.* 12.

GORDU'NI, a people of Gallia Belgica. *Cæsar.*

GOR'DUS, a city of Phrygia, near Gordium. It is called Juliogordus by *Ptolemy*. See also *Pliny*, 5. c. 32.

GORDIUTI'CHOS, a town of Caria.

GORDYÆ'I MON'TES, the broad belt of mountains which divides Assyria from Media. *Strabo.*

GORDYE'NE or CORDUE'NE, a mountainous district of Armenia, which formed a constant object of contention between the Romans, Parthians, and Persians.

GORDYN'IA. *Vid.* Gortynia.

GORGA'SUS or GOR'GASUS, a man who received divine honours at Pheræ, in Messenia. *Paus.* 4. c. 30.

GOR'GE, a daughter of Œneus, king of Calydon, by Althæa, daughter of Thestius. She and Dejanira were the only two daughters of Œneus who were not changed into birds by Diana at the death of Meleager. She married Andremon, by whom she had Oxilus, who headed the Heraclidæ, when they made an attempt to recover the Peloponnesus. Her tomb was shown at Amphissa, in Locris. *Hygin.* fab. 174.—*Antonin.* l. 2.—*Paus.* 10. c. 38.—*Apollod.* 1 & 2.—*Ovid. Met.* 8. v. 542.——One of the Danaides. *Apollod.* 2. c. 1.

GOR'GIAS, son of Carmantides, a celebrated sophist and orator, was surnamed Leontinus, because born at Leontium in Sicily. He was sent by his countrymen to solicit the assistance of the Athenians against the Syracusans, and was successful in his embassy. He was the first who attempted to speak *ex tempore* on any subject proposed to him, and became so wealthy, that he was the first person who presented the temple of Apollo at Delphi with a golden statue. He lived to his 108th year, and died B.C. 400. Only two fragments of his compositions are extant, the one an apology for Helen, the other in praise of the Athenians who had bravely fallen in the service of their country. *Paus.* 6. c. 17.—*Cic. in Orat.* 22, 23 & 101. *De Orat.* 1. c. 51. *Inv.* 1. c. 5. *Senect.* 15. *In. Brut.* 15.—*Diod.* 12.—*Quintil.* 3. c. 1. l. 12. c. 11.—*Athen.* 12.—*Plin.* 33. c. 4.——An officer of Antiochus Epiphanes.——An Athenian who wrote an account of all the prostitutes of Athens. *Athen.* 13.——A Macedonian, forced to war with Amyntas, &c. *Curt.* 7. c. 1.——An Epirot, said to have been born after his mother's death, and to have been discovered in her coffin, as she was carried to the grave. *Val. Max.*

GORGIP'PIA, a city of India. *Steph.*

GORGIP'PUS, son of Satyrus, succeeded his father in the kingdom of Pontus. *Polyæn.* 8.

GOR'GO, the wife of Leonidas, king of Sparta, &c.

GOR'GO, the name of the ship in which Perseus embarked, after he had conquered Medusa.

GOR'GONES, three celebrated sisters, daughters of Phorcys and Ceto, whose names were Stheno, Euryale, and Medusa, all immortal except Medusa. According to the mythologists, their hair was entwined with serpents, their hands were of brass, their wings of the color of gold, their body was covered with impenetrable scales, and their teeth were as long as the tusks of a wild boar, and they turned to stones all those on whom they fixed their eyes. Æschylus says, that they had only one tooth and one eye between them, of which they had the use of each in their turn; and, accordingly, it was at the very moment in which they were exchanging the eye, that Perseus attacked them and cut off Medusa's head. According to some authors, Perseus, when he went to the conquest of the Gorgons, was armed with an instrument like a scythe by Mercury, and provided with a looking-glass by Minerva, besides winged shoes, and the helmet of Pluto, which rendered all objects clearly visible and open to the view, while the person who wore it remained totally invisible. With weapons like these, Perseus obtained an easy victory; and after his conquest, returned his arms to the different deities, whose favors and assistance he had so recently experienced. The head of Medusa remained in his hands, and after he had finished all his laborious expeditions, he gave it to Minerva, who placed it on her ægis, with which she turned into stones all such as fixed their eyes upon it. It is said, that after the conquest of the Gorgons, Perseus took his flight in the air towards Æthiopia; and that the drops of blood which fell to the ground from Medusa's head were changed into serpents, which have ever since infested Libya. The horse Pegasus also arose from the blood of Medusa, as well as Chrysaor with his golden sword. The residence of the Gorgones was beyond the ocean towards the west, according to Hesiod. Æschylus represents them as inhabiting the eastern part of Scythia, and Ovid, as the most received opinion, informs us that they lived in the inland parts of Libya, near the lake of Triton, or the gardens of the Hesperides. Diodorus and others explain the fable of the Gorgons, by supposing that they were a warlike race of women near the country of the Amazons, whom Perseus, with the help of a large army, totally destroyed. *Hesiod. Theog.* 270 & 280. *In Scuto*, 216.—*Ital.* 9. v. 442.—*Martial.* 9. epigr. 26.—*Homer Il.* 5. v. 733. l, 11. v. 36.—*Apollon.* 4.—*Apollod.* 2. c. 1 & 4, &c.—*Virg. Æs.* 6. v. 289.—*Diod.* 1 & 4.—*Paus.* 2. c. 20, &c.—*Æschyl. Prom. Act.* 4.—*Pindar Pyth.* 7 & 12. *Olymp.* 3.—*Ovid. Met.* 4. v. 618, &c.—*Palephat de Phorcyn.*—*Cœl. R ant. Le.* 18. c. 38.

GOR'GONES, islands in the Atlantic Ocean, called also Gorgades and Hesperides, and now Isole di Capo Verde. *Plin.* 6. c. 31.

GORGONIA, a surname of Minerva, because Perseus armed with her shield, had conquered the Gorgon Medusa.

GORGO'NIUS, a Roman, ridiculed by Horace for his ill smell. *Horat.* 1. sat. 2. v. 27.

GORGO'PAS, a general who conquered Eunomus, and was at last vanquished by Chabrias. *Xenoph.* l. 3.

GORGOPH'ONE, a daughter of Perseus and Andromeda, who married Perieres, king of Messenia, by whom she had Aphareus and Leucippus. After the death of Perieres, she married Œbalus, by whom she became mother of Icarus and Tyndarus. She is the first whom the mythologists mention as having had a second husband. *Paus.* 2. c. 21. l. 4. c. 2.—*Apollod.* 1, 2, & 3.——One of the Danaides. *Apollod.* 2. c. 1.

GORGOPH'ONUS, a son of Electryon and Anaxo. *Apollod.* 2. c. 4.

GORGOPH'ORA, a surname of Minerva, from her ægis, on which was placed the had of the Gorgon Medusa. *Cic.*

GOR'GUS, the son of Aristomenes the Messenian. He was married, when young, to a virgin, by his father, who had experienced the greatest kindnesses from her friendship and humanity, and had been enabled to conquer seven Cretans, who had attempted his life, &c. *Paus.* 4. c. 19.——A son of Theron, tyrant of Agrigentum. *Polyæn.* 6.——A man whose knowledge of metals proved very serviceable to Alexander the Great. *Strab.* 15.

GOR'GUS, a small river of Assyria, which falls into the Tigris. *Ptol.*

GORGYTH'ION, a son of Priam, killed by Teucer. *Homer. Il.* 1.

GOR'NEAS, a fortified place in Armenia. *Tac. Ann.* 12 c. 45.

GOR'TUÆ, a people of Eubœa, who fought with the Medes at the battle of Arbela. *Curt.* 4. c. 12.

GOR'TYN, GOR'TYS or GORTY'NA, an inland town of Crete. It was on the inhabitants of this place that Annibal, to save his money, practised an artifice recorded by *Cornelius Nepos, in Ann.* 9.—*Plin.* 4. c. 12.—*Lucan.* 6. v. 214. l. 7. v. 214.—*Virg. Æn.* 11. v. 773.

GORTYN'IA, a town of Arcadia, in Peloponnesus. *Paus.* 8. c. 28.——A town of Macedonia, west of Pella.

GO'THI or GOT'THI, a celebrated nation in the north of Germany, called also Gothones, Gutones, Gythones, and Guttones. They were warriors by profession, and like all their savage neighbours, they were fearless of danger, restless, and ambitious. They extended their power over all parts of the world, and chiefly directed their arms against the Roman empire. Their first attempt against the possessions of Rome, was on the provinces of Greece, whence they were driven by Constantine. They afterwards plundered Rome under Alaric, one of their most celebrated kings, A.D. 410. From enemies the Goths gradually became the mercenaries of the Romans, and as they were powerful and united, they soon dictated to their imperial masters, and introduced disorder, anarchy, and revolutions into the west of Europe. *Tacit. Ann.* 2. c. 2, &c. Also Gotho'nes and Gutto'nes.

GOTHI'NI, a Celtic people of Germany, subject to the Quadi.

GRACCHA'NUS M. JU'NIUS, author of a work *De Potestatibus*, which gave an account of the Roman constitution from the time of the kings. It is now lost, but fragments are cited by Joannes Lydus.

GRAC'CHUS, a general of the Sabines, taken by Q. Cincinnatus. *Plut. in Gracch.*—*Liv. Ep.* 41.—*Flor.* 3. c. 16.——A Roman consul, defeated by Annibal, &c. *C. Nep. in Ann.*

GRAC'CHUS TIB. SEMPRON., a master of the horse to the dictator Junius, after the battle of Cannæ. When consul, Gracchus conducted himself with great bravery and prudence. He took the camp of the Campanians, and obliged Annibal to raise the siege of Cumæ. After distinguishing himself in Lucania, and defeating a body of Carthaginians under Hanno, he at last was taken in an ambuscade, where he fell bravely fighting. *C. Nep.* 22. c. 5.—*Liv.* 22. c. 57. l. 23. c. 32, &c. l. 24. c. 10, &c.

GRAC'CHUS T. SEMPRO'NIUS, son of Publius, and father of Tiberius and Caius Gracchus, was twice consul and once censor, and was distinguished by his integrity as well as his prudence and superior abilities both in the senate and at the head of the armies. In his prætorship he waged a successful war against the Celtiberians, over whom at his return to Rome he triumphed, and his arms were equally prosperous against the Sardinians. His services were also very useful to the republic in the embassy which he undertook into Asia, to ascertain the power and intrigues of Antiochus and Eumenes. He married Sempronia, called by some Cornelia, of the family of the Scipios, a woman of great virtue, piety, and learning, and by her he had 12 children, all of whom, with the exception of Tiberius and Caius, and a daughter who married the younger Africanus, died before they arrived at the age of puberty. *Liv.* 38. c. 57, &c.—*Val. Max.* 1. c. 1. l. 4. c. 2 —*Polyb.* 105.—*Cic. de Orat* 1. c. 48. *Div.* 1. c. 18. l. 2. c. 29. *N.D.* 2. c. 4. *Fr.* 2. ep. 2.

GRAC'CHUS TIBE'RIUS, after distinguishing himself at the taking of Carthage and in the Numantine war, endeavoured to renew the Agrarian law, which had already caused such dissensions at Rome. *Vid.* Agraria. By the means of violence, his proposition passed into a law, and he was appointed commissioner with his father-in-law Appius Claudius, and his brother Caius, to make an equal division of the lands among the people, that no one should possess more than 500 acres of land. The riches of Attalus, which had been left to the Roman people by will, were next distributed without opposition: but Tiberius was assassinated in the midst of his adherents by P. Nasica, while the populace were all unanimous to re-elect him to serve the office of tribune the following year. Not less than 300 people were slain in this unfortunate sedition, and it was observed they were all slain with clubs or stones, and not by any military weapons. The bodies of the slain were thrown into the Tiber, and Caius in vain attempted to pay his brother the honors of a public funeral. *Cic. Brut.* 27. *Off.* 3. c. 30. *Acad.* 4. c. 5. *Am.* 12. *Cat.* 1. c. 1. *Phil.* 8. c. 4.—*Vell.* 2. c. 3.—*Val. Max.* 6. c. 3.—*Plut. in Gracc.*—*Appian. B.C.*

GRAC'CHUS CA'IUS, for some years after the death of his brother Tiberius, lived in literary retirement. His abilities and great virtues were, however, afterwards displayed in Sicily, as quæstor to the consul Orestes, but in the popular office of tribune, his endeavours to repress the exhorbitant powers of the senate, and of the nobles, and to raise the people to greater consequence in the state, created those violent dissensions, and that turbulence of faction which had proved so fatal to Tiberius. Caius supported the cause of the people with more vehemence, but less moderation than his brother; and his success served only to awaken his ambition, and animate his resentment against the nobles. Invested with the privileges of a tribune, he soon became the arbiter of the republic, and in the exercise of the duties of this popular office treated the patricians with contempt. This behaviour hastened his ruin. During his absence in Africa, his enemies, by secret machinations and by open intrigues, undermined his power, and in the tumult, which, after his return, accompanied the discussion of some of the laws which he had proposed, he fled to the temple of Diana, and unwilling to sacrifice either himself or his adherents to popular fury, he offered terms of accommodation. These were rejected by the arts of Opimius the consul, and Caius, now abandoned and grown desperate, ordered his slave Epicrates to kill him, B.C. 121. The head of the unfortunate tribune was cut off and carried to Opimius by Septimuleius, who received as a reward its weight in gold. Not less than 3,000 of his adherents are said to have perished in this unhappy quarrel, and their bodies were plunged into the Tiber. The memory of the Gracchi was held in the highest esteem by the people. Statues were erected to them, they were worshipped as gods, and their virtuous mother considered herself as the happiest of Roman matrons in having given birth to such illustrious sons. Caius has been accused of having stained his hands in the blood of Scipio Africanus the younger, who was found murdered in his bed. *Plut. in Vitâ.*—*Cic. Br.* 33. *Div.* 1. c. 26. *Fin.* 4. c. 24. *Off.* 2. c. 21. *Phil.* 8. c. 4.—*Victor. de V. Ill.*—*Seneca Cons. ad M.*—*Quintil.* 1. c. 10.—*Val. Max.* 1. c. 7.—*Vell.* 2. c. 6.—*Appian.*—*Liv.* 60, &c.—*Lucan.* 6. v. 796.—*Flor.* 2. c. 17. l. 3. c. 14, &c.

GRAC'CHUS SEMPRO'NIUS, a Roman banished to an island on the coast of Africa, for his adulteries with Julia the daughter of Augustus. He was assassinated by order of Tiberius, after he had been banished 14 years. Before he perished he penned a letter to his long neglected wife Alliaria. *Tacit. Ann.* 1. c. 53.

GRADI'VUS, a surname of Mars among the Romans, perhaps from κραδαίνειν, *brandishing a spear.* Though he had a temple without the walls of Rome, and though Numa had established the Salii in his honor, yet his most favorite residence was supposed to be among the fierce and savage Thracians and the Getæ, over whom he particularly presided. *Virg. Æn.* 3. v. 35.—*Seneca in Her. Oet.* act 4.—*Servius in Æn.* 3. v. 35.—*Vitruv.* 1. c. 7.—*Homer. Il.*—*Liv.* 1. c. 20. l. 2. c. 45.

GRÆ'Æ, winged monsters, daughters of Phorcys and Ceto. They were three in number, and received their name from the whiteness of their hair, which was long and bushy, and which served them like a veil for a covering to the head and back. According to some authors they had but one eye and one tooth between them both, which they reciprocally lent to each other; and from this circumstance, probably, they have been confounded with the Gorgons. Their names were Pephredo, Enyo, and Dino. *Æschyl. in Prom.*—*Apollod.* 2.—*Hesiod. Th.* 270.

GRÆ'CI, the inhabitante of Greece. *Vid.* Græcia.

GRÆ'CIA, a celebrated country of Europe, bounded on the west by the Ionian Sea, on the south by the Mediterranean Sea, on the east by the Ægæan, and on the north by Thrace and Dalmatia. It is generally divided into four large provinces, Macedonia, Epirus, Achaia or Hellas, and Peloponnesus. The Greeks have severally been called Achæans, Argians, Danai, Dolopes, Hellenians, Ionians, Myrmidons, and Pelasgians. The most celebrated of their cities were Athens, Sparta, Argos, Corinth, Thebes, Sicyon, Mycenæ, Delphi, Trœzene, Salamis, Megara, Pylus, Orchomenus, Eleusis, &c. Their chief rivers were the Peneus, the Eurotas, the Alpheus, the Achelous, and the Ilissus; and their mountains were Pindus, Ossa, Olympus, Cithæron, Helicon, Parnassus, &c, where not only the nymphs and the muses, but the gods themselves deigned to fix their residence. The inhabitants, whose early history is obscured by fabulous accounts, and improbable traditions, asserted that they were the original inhabitants of the country, and born from the earth where they dwelt; and they heard with contempt the probable conjectures which traced their origin among the first inhabitants of Asia, and the colonies of Ægypt. In the first periods of their history the Greeks were governed by monarchs; and there were then as many kings as there were cities. The monarchical power gradually decreased; the love of liberty established a republican government; and no part of Greece, except Macedonia, remained in the hands of an absolute sovereign. The expedition of the Argonauts first rendered the Greeks known and respected among their neighbours; and in the succeeding age, the wars of Thebes and Troy gave opportunity to their heroes and demi-gods to display their valor in the field of battle. The simplicity of the ancient Greeks rendered them virtuous, active, and enterprising; and the establishment of the Olympic games, in particular, contributed to their aggrandizement, and made them ambitious of fame. The austerity of their laws, and the education of their youth, particularly at Lacedæmon, rendered them brave and active, insensible to bodily pain, and fearless and intrepid in the time of danger. The celebrated battles of Marathon, Thermopylæ, Salamis, Platæa, and Mycale, sufficiently show what superiority the courage of a little army can obtain over millions of undisciplined barbarians. After many signal victories over the Persians, they became elated with their success; and when they found no one able to dispute their power abroad, they turned their arms one against the other, and leagued with foreign states to destroy the most flourishing and powerful of their cities. The Messenian and Peloponnesian wars are examples of the dreadful calamities which arise from civil discord; and the success with which the gold and the sword of Philip and of his son corrupted and enslaved Greece, fatally prove that when a nation becomes indolent and dissipated at home, it ceases to be respectable in the eyes of the neighbouring states. The annals of Greece, however, abound with singular proofs of heroism and resolution. The bold retreat of the 10,000 who had assisted the younger Cyrus against his brother Artaxerxes, reminded their countrymen of their superiority over all other nations; and taught Alexander that the conquest of the east might be effected by a handful of Grecian soldiers. While the Greeks rendered themselves so illustrious by their military exploits, the arts and sciences were assisted and fostered among them by conquest, and received fresh lustre from the application and industry of their professors. Their generals were also orators; and eloquence seemed to be so nearly connected with the military profession, that he was despised by his soldiers who could not address them upon any emergency with a spirited and well delivered oration. The language of Greece was universally studied; and the country was the receptacle of the youths of the neighbouring states, who there imbibed the principles of liberty and moral virtue. The Greeks planted several colonies, and totally peopled the western coasts of Asia Minor. This country, under the name of Asiatic Greece, contained the provinces of Æolia, Ionia, Caria, Doris, and the neighbouring islands, and the famous cities of Ephesus, Smyrna, Miletus, Colophon, Halicarnassus, Cnidus, Cumæ, &c. In the eastern parts of Italy, there were also many settlements made by them, and the country received from its Greek inhabitants the name of Magna Græcia. For some time Greece submitted to the yoke of Alexander and his successors, and at last, after a spirited though ineffectual struggle in the Achæan league, it fell under the power of Rome, and became one of its dependent provinces, being governed by a proconsul.

GRÆ'CIA MAG'NA, a part of Italy where the Greeks planted colonies, whence the name. Its boundaries are very uncertain; some say that it extended along the southern parts of Italy, and others suppose that Magna Græcia comprehended only Campania and Lucania. To these some add Sicily, which was likewise peopled by Greek colonies. *Ovid. Fast.* 4. v. 64.—*Strab.* &c.—*Plin.* 3. c. 5.

GRÆCI'NUS, a senator, put to death by Caligula, because he refused to accuse M. Silanus. He wrote a treatise *De re rusticâ*. *Columell.* 1. c. 1.—*Senec. de Benef.* 2.

GRÆ'CUS, a man from whom some suppose that Greece received its name. *Aristot.* 1 *Meteor.*

GRÆ'ES, an Æolian colony, dwelling in Parium. *Steph.*

GRA'IS, son of Echelatus, a descendant of Orestes, was a leader of the Æolians in their migrations, and occupied the country between Ionia and Mysia called Æolis. *Strab.* 13.—*Paus.* 3.

GRA'IUS, an inhabitant of Greece.

GRAM'MIUM, a city of Crete. *Steph.*

GRAMMI'TÆ, a people near Gallia Celtica. *Id.*

GRAM'PIUS MONS, the Grampian mountains in Scotland. *Tacit. Agric.* 29.

GRANI'ACUM or GRANIA'NUM, a promontory of Corsica, now Capo d'Erbicara. *Ptol.*

GRANI'CUS or GRAN'ICUS, a river of Bithynia, which falls into the Propontis. It is famous for the battle fought there between the armies of Alexander and Darius, on the 22d of May, B.C. 334, when 600,000 Persians were defeated by 30,000 Macedonians. *Diod.* 17.—*Plut. in. Alex.*—*Justin.*—*Curt.* 3. c. 1.

GRANIONA'RIUM or GRAVIONA'RIUM, a city of Germany, now Bamberg. *Ptol.*

GRA'NIUS PETRO'NIUS, an officer who, being taken by Pompey's generals, refused the life which was tendered to him; observing, that Cæsar's soldiers received not, but granted life. He killed himself. *Plut. in Cæs.*

GRA'NIUS MARCEL'LUS, a prætor of Bithynia, accused of treason under Tiberius. *Tac. Ann.* 1. c. 74.

GRA'NIUS MARTIA'NUS, a senator who, being accused by C. Gracchus of treason, slew himself in the consulship of C. Cestius and M. Servilius. *Id. An.* 6. c. 38.

GRA'NIUS SILVA'NUS, a tribune of the prætorian cohort, who conspired against Nero. *Tac. Ann.* 15. c. 50.

GRA'NIUS, GRA'NIS or GRU'NUS, according to *Arrian*, a river of Susiana, flowing into the Persian Gulph.

GRA'NIUS, a quæstor whom Sylla had ordered to be strangled, only one day before he died a natural death. *Plut.*——A son of the wife of Marius by a former husband.

GRA'NIUS QUIN'TUS, a man intimate with Crassus and other illustrious men of Rome, whose vices he lashed with an unsparing hand. *Cic. Brut.* 43 & 46. *Orat.* 2. c. 60.

GRAN'UA, a river of Germany, a tributary of the Danube in the land of the Quadi.

GRAP'TUS, a freedman of Nero. *Tac. Ann.* 13. c. 47.

GRASID'IUS, a minister of the debaucheries of Albucilla, banished by the senate to an island. *Id. ibid.* 6. c. 48.

GRASTIL'LUS, called by some Prastillus, a city of Macedonia. *Steph.*

GRA'TIÆ. *Vid.* Charites.

GRATIANOP'OLIS. *Vid.* Accusio Colonia.

GRATIA'NUS, a native of Pannonia, was son of the emperor Valentinian the First. He was raised to the throne, though only eight years old; and after he had reigned for some time conjointly with his father, he became sole emperor in the 16th year of his age. He soon after took Theodosius for his colleague, and appointed him over the eastern parts of the empire. His courage in the field was as remarkable as his love of learning, and fondness for philosophy. He slaughtered 30,000 Germans in a battle, and supported the tottering state by his wisdom, prudence, and intrepidity. His enmity to the Pagan superstition of his subjects proved his ruin; and Maximus who undertook the defence of the worship of Jupiter and of all the gods, was joined by an infinite number of discontented Romans, and met Gratian near Paris. Gratian was forsaken by his troops in the field of battle, and was murdered by the rebels, A.D. 383, in the 24th year of his age.

GRATIA'NUS, a Roman soldier, invested with the imperial purple by the rebellious army in Britain, in opposition to Honorius. He was assassinated, four months after, by those very troops to whom he owed his elevation, A.D. 407.——The father of Valentinian, celebrated for his bodily strength. *Aurel. Victor. in Valent.*——A son of Theodosius the Great.

GRATIA'RUM COL'LIS, a range of hills in Africa, in which rises the Cinyps.

GRATID'IA, a woman of Neapolis, called Canidia by *Horace*, and represented by him as an infamous sorceress. *Epod.* 3. od. 3. v. 8. &c.

GRA'TIUS FALIS'CUS, a Latin poet contemporary with Ovid, and mentioned only by him among the more ancient authors. He wrote a poem on coursing, called Cynegeticon. This work, without any elevation of sentiment, and possessing little of the true fire of poetry, is far inferior to the Greek poem of Oppian, though considered superior in merit to the similar compositions of Nemesianus. The best editions are, that of Lug. Bat. 4to, 1728, and a Variorum, Mitav. 1775. *Harles. Not. Lit. Rom.* 1. p. 291.—*Sax. Onom.* 1. p. 194.—*Ovid. Pont.* 4. el. 16. v. 34.

GRA'TUS JU'LIUS, a præfect of the camp, thrown into chains by the partisans of Vitellius. *Tacit. Hist.* 2. c. 26.

GRA'VII, a people of Spain at the south-east of the river Minius. *Ital.* 3. v. 366.

GRAVIS'CÆ, now Monte Alto, a maritime town of Ætruria, which assisted Æneas against Turnus. The air was unwholesome, on account of the marshes and stagnant waters in its neighbourhood. *Virg. Æn.* 10. v. 184.—*Liv.* 40. c. 29. l. 41. c. 16.

GRA'VIUS, a Roman knight of Puteoli, killed at Dyrrachium, &c. *Cæs. Bell. Civ.* 3.——An informer. *Tacit. Ann.* 4. c. 21.

GREG'ORAS NICEPH'ORUS, a Byzantine historian, born A.D. 1295, and died A.D. 1359. His history begins with the capture of Constantinople by the Latins A.D. 1204, and goes down to A.D. 1359.

GREGO'RIUS, a bishop of Nyssa, author of the Nicene creed. His style is represented as allegorical and affected; and he has been accused of mixing philosophy too much with theology. His writings consist of commentaries on Scripture, moral discourses, sermons on mysteries, dogmatical treatises, panegyrics on saints; the best edition of which is that of Morell, 2 vols. fol. Paris, 1615. The bishop died A.D. 396. *Sax. Onom.* 1. p. 433. *Fabr. B. Gr.* 5. c. 20.——Another Christian writer whose works were edited by the Benedictines, in 4 vols. fol. Paris, 1705.

GREGO'RIUS THEOD. THAUMATUR'GUS, a disciple of Origen, afterwards bishop of Neocæsarea, the place of his birth. He died A.D. 266; and if is said that he left only seventeen idolaters in his diocese, having found there only seventeen Christians. Of his works, there are extant his gratulatory oration to Origen, a canonical epistle, and other treatises in Greek, the best edition of which is that of Paris, fol. 1621. *Sax. Onom.* 1. p. 365.—*Fabr. B. Gr.* 5. c. 1.

GREGO'RIUS NAZIANZE'NUS, surnamed the *Divine*, was bishop of Constantinople, which he resigned when his election was disputed. His writings rival those of the most celebrated orators of Greece in eloquence, sublimity, and variety. His sermons are more for philosophers than common hearers, but replete with seriousness and devotion. Erasmus said that he was afraid to translate his works, from the apprehension of not transfusing into another language the smartness and acumen of his style, and the stateliness and happy diction of the whole. Gregory also wrote four odes in praise of the Divinity, containing 276 lines. He died A.D. 389. The best edition is that of the Benedictines, the first volume of which, in fol. was published at Paris 1778. *Sax. Onom.* 1. p. 420.—*Fabr. B. Gr.* 5. c. 13.

GRESTO'NIA, a region of Thrace. *Steph.*

GRIN'NES, a people among the Batavians. *Tacit. Hist.* 5. c. 20.

GROS'PHUS, a man distinguished as much for his probity as his riches, to whom *Horace* addressed 2 od. 16.

GRO'VII, a people of Spain. *Mela*, 3. c. 1.—*Ptol.*—*Sil.* 1. 235.

GRU'DII, a people tributary to the Nervii, supposed to have inhabited the country near Tournay or Bruges, in Flanders. *Cæs. G.* 5. c. 38.

GRUMEN'TUM, now Agromento, an inland town of Lucania on the river Aciris. *Liv.* 23. c. 37. l. 27. c. 41.

GRYL'LUS, a son of the historian Xenophon, who killed Epaminondas, and was himself slain at the battle of Mantinea, B.C. 363. His father was offering a sacrifice when he received the news of his death, and he threw down the garland which was on his head; but he replaced it when he heard that the enemy's general had fallen by his hands; and observed that his glorious death ought to be celebrated with demonstrations of joy rather than of lamentation. *Aristot.*—*Paus.* 8. c. 11, &c. ——One of those companions of Ulysses, who were changed into swine by the incantations of Circe It is said that he refused to be restored to his human shape, preferring the indolence and inactivity of these squalid animals. *Plut. Brut. Anim.*

GRYNI'A a city of Troas. *Steph.*

GRYNE'UM or GRYNI'UM, a town near Clazomenæ, on the coast of Asia Minor, where Apollo had a celebrated temple with an oracle, on account of which he is called Grynæus. *Strab.* 13.—*Virg. Ecl.* 6. v. 72. *Æn.* 4. v. 345.

GRYNE'US, one of the Centaurs, who fought against the Lapithæ, and was killed with the horns of a stag, after he had crushed to pieces Broteus and Orion with a ponderous altar. *Ovid. Met.* 12. v. 260.

GRYPS or GRY'PHUS, a griffin, a fabulous monster dwelling in the Riphæan mountains between the Hyperboreans and the Arimaspians, and guarding the gold of the former. Its body was that of a lion with the head and wings of an eagle.

GUGER'NI, a people of Germany, between the Ubii and Batavi. Also called Guberni.

GULUS'SA, a Numidian, second son of Masanissa, who, with his brothers Micipsa and Mastanabal, succeeded to his father's dominions B.C. 149.

GU'NAS, a place of Syria. *Steph.*

GUN'NUGI or CANUC'CIS, a town of Mauritania Cæsariensis, now Capo di Tenes. *Plin.* 5. c. 3.—*Ptol.*

GURÆ'US, a river of India.

GUR'GES, a surname of the son of Q. Fabius Rullianus, given him from his prodigality. *Macrob. Sat.* 1. 2. c. 9.

GY'ARUS, an island in the Ægæan Sea, at the east of Delus. The Romans were accustomed to send their most illustrious culprits into exile there. *Ovid.* 7. *Met.* v. 407.

GY'AS, one of the companions of Æneas, who distinguished himself at the games exhibited after the death of Anchises in Sicily, and obtained the third prize. *Hygin.* fab. 273.—*Ital.* 1. v. 440.—*Virg. Æn.* 1. v. 226 & 616. l. 5. v. 118, &c.——A part of the territories of Syracuse, in the possession of Dionysius. *Plut. in Dion.*——A Rutulian, son of Melampus, killed by Æneas in Italy. *Virg. Æn.* 10. v. 318.

GYGÆ'US, a lake of Lydia, 40 stadia from Sardes. *Propert.* 3. el. 11. v. 18.

GY'GE, a maid of Parysatis, queen of Persia. *Plut.*

GY'GES, a son of Cœlus and Terra, represented as having fifty heads and a hundred hands. He, with his brothers, made war against the gods, and was afterwards punished for this rebellion in Tartarus. Hesiod, however, mentions that Jupiter solicited his assistance against the Titans, and that by the aid of this powerful ally he was enabled to confine them in Tartarus. *Hesiod. Theog.* 148.—*Apollod.* 1.—*Horat.* 2. od. 14. v. 14.—*Ovid. Trist.* 4. el. 7. v. 18.——A Lydian to whom Candaules, king of the country, showed his wife naked. The queen was so incensed at this instance of imprudence in her husband, that she ordered Gyges either to prepare for death himself or to murder Candaules. He chose the latter, and marrying the queen ascended the vacant throne, about 718 years B.C. He was the first of the Mermnadæ who reigned in Lydia. He reigned 38 years, and distinguished himself by the immense sacrifices which he made to the oracle of Delphi. According to Plato, Gyges descended into a deep chasm of the earth, where he found a brazen horse, the sides of which he opened, and saw within the body the carcase of a man of uncommon size, from whose finger he took a famous brazen ring. This ring, when put on his own finger, rendered him invisible; and by means of its virtue, he introduced himself to the queen of Candaules, murdered her husband, and married her, and usurped the crown of Lydia. *Herodot.* 1. c. 8,—*Plato, Dial.* 10.—*De Rep.*—*Val. Max.* 7. c. 1.—*Justin.* 1. c. 7.—*Plin.* 7. c. 46.—*Tzetzes. Chil.* 1. c. 3.—*Solin.* 7.—*Plut. Quæst. Gr.* 45.—*Cic. Offic.* 3. c. 9.——A man killed by Turnus in his wars with Æneas. *Virg. Æn.* 7. v. 762.——A beautiful boy of Cnidus, in the age of Horace. *Horat.* 2. od. 5. v. 30.

GYLIP'PUS, a Lacedæmonian, sent B.C. 414, by his countrymen to assist Syracuse against the Athenians who had invaded Sicily. He obtained a decisive victory over Nicias and Demosthenes, the enemy's generals, and obliged them to surrender. He afterwards accompanied Lysander in his expedition against Athens. After the fall of the city he was entrusted by the conqueror with the money which had been taken in the plunder, which amounted to 1500 talents, but as he conveyed it to Sparta, he unsewed the bottoms of the bags which contained it, and secreted about 300 talents. His theft was discovered; and to avoid the punishment which he deserved, he fled from his country, and by this act of dishonesty tarnished the glory of his victorious actions. *Tibull.* 4. el. 1. v. 199.—*Plut. in Niciâ.*——An Arcadian in the Rutulian war. *Virg. Æn* 12. v. 272.

GYMNA'SIA, a large city near Colchis. *Diod.* 14.

GYMNA'SIUM, a place among the Greeks, where all the public exercises were performed, and where not only wrestlers and dancers exhibited their feats of agility, but also philosophers, poets, and rhetoricians repeated their compositions. The room was high and spacious, and could contain many thousand spectators. The exercises of the Gymnasium were running, leaping, throwing the quoit, wrestling and boxing, and they were called by the Greeks πένταθλον, and by the Romans *quinquertia.* In riding, the athlete led a horse, on which he sometimes was mounted, conducting another by the bridle, and jumping from the one upon the other. Whoever came first to the goal, and jumped with the greatest agility, obtained the prize. In running on foot the athletes were sometimes armed, and he who came first was declared victorious. In throwing the quoit, the prize was adjudged to him who threw it to the greatest distance. The quoits were made either with wood, stone, or metal. The wrestlers employed all their dexterity to bring their adversary to the ground; and the boxers had their hands armed with gauntlets, called also *cæstus.* Their blows were dangerous, and often ended in the death of one of the combatants. In wrestling and boxing, the athletes were generally naked, whence the word Gymnasium, γυμνός, *nudus.* They anointed themselves with oil to brace their limbs, and to render their bodies slippery, and more difficult to be grasped. *Plin.* 2. ep. 17.—*C. Nep.* 20. c. 5.

GYMNE'SIÆ, islands near the mouth of the Iberus

in the Mediterranean, called Baleares by the Greeks. *Plut.* 5. c. 8.—*Strab.* 2.

GYM'NETES or GYMNE'TES, a people of Æthiopia, who lived almost naked. *Plin.* 5. c. 8.

GYM'NIAS, a town of Colchis. *Xenoph. Anab.* 4.

GYMNOSOPHIS'TÆ, a certain sect of philosophers in India, who according to some, placed their *summum bonum* in pleasure, and their *summum malum* in pain. They were generally naked, as their name implies, and they exposed themselves for 37 years in the open air, to the heat of the sun, the inclemency of the seasons, and the coldness of the night. They were often seen in the fields fixing their eyes full upon the disc of the sun from the time of its rising till the hour of its setting, and sometimes they stood whole days upon one foot in burning sand without moving, or showing any concern for what surrounded them. Alexander was astonished at the sight of a sect of men who seemed to despise bodily pain, and who inured themselves to suffer the greatest torture without uttering a groan, or expressing any marks of fear. The conqueror condescended to visit them, and his astonishment was increased when he saw one of them ascend a burning pile with firmness and unconcern, to avoid the infirmities of old age, and stand upright on one leg and unmoved, while the flames gradually surrounded him on every side. *Vid.* Calanus. The Brachmans were a branch of the sect of the Gymnosophistæ. *Vid.* Brachmanes. *Strab.* 15. &c.—*Plin.* 7. c. 2.—*Cic. Tusc.* 5. *De Div.* 1. c. 23.—*Tertul. Apol.* 41.—*Clem. Alex. Str.* 5.—*Lucan.* 3. v. 240.—*Dion.*—*Curt.* 8. c. 9.

GYNÆ'CEAS, a woman said to have been the wife of Faunus, and the mother of Bacchus and of Midas.

GYNÆCOCRATUME'NI, a people of Sarmatia. *Plin.* 6. c. 7.

GYNÆCOP'OLIS, a city of Phœnicia.——A city of Ægypt. *Plin.* 5. c. 9.—*Steph.*

GYNÆCOTHŒ'NAS, a name of Mars at Tegea, on account of a sacrifice offered to him by women without the assistance of the men, who were not permitted to be present. *Paus.* 8. c. 48.

GYN'DES, now Zeindeh, a river of Assyria, which falls into the Tigris. When Cyrus marched against Babylon, the progress of the army was stopped by this river, in which one of his favorite horses was drowned. This so irritated the monarch that he ordered the river to be conveyed in 360 different channels by his soldiers, so that after this minute diversion of its waters it hardly reached the knee *Herodot.* 1. c. 189 & 202.

GYPSE'IS, an island of Æthiopia. *Steph.*

GY'RAS, a mountain of Tenus, an island in the Ægæan Sea. *Plin.* 5. c. 5.

GYR'EI, a people of Arabia Felix. *Id.* 6. c. 28.

GYR'TON, a city of Thessaly, called by *Homer* Gyrtona. *Steph.*—*Plin.* 4. c. 9.

GYTHEA'TES, a bay of Peloponnesus. *Plin.* 4. c. 5. *Vid.* Gytheum.

GYTHE'UM or GYTH'IUM, a sea-port town of Laconia, at the mouth of the Eurotas, in Peloponnesus, built by Hercules and Apollo, who were said there to have desisted from their quarrels. The inhabitants were called Gytheatæ. *Cic. Offic.* 3. c. 11.

GYZAN'TES, a people of Lybia.

H.

HABES'SUS, a city of Lycia, afterwards called Antiphellus. *Plin.* 5. c. 27.

HA'BIS, an illegitimate son of the daughter of Gargaris, king of the Curetes, in Spain, by an unknown person. He was exposed in the woods, where the goats of the desert fed him with their milk. Some shepherds having found him, brought him to the palace, when Gargaris, still unappeased, commanded him to be thrown to hungry swine; but he was still uninjured. He was afterwards precipitated into the sea, and miraculously preserved. When grown up he was dragged before the monarch, whose vengeance had now yielded to compassion, and he was adopted as successor to a throne for which the gods, by such supernatural interference seemed to have destined him. As king of Spain, Habis distinguished himself by his benevolence, his subjects were made happy under his mild government, salutary laws were enacted, and, together with subordination, agriculture and plenty flourished in the country. *Justin.* 44. c. 4.

HA'DA or A'DA, the Juno of the Babylonians. *Hesych.*—*Voss. de Idol.* 1. c. 22.

HADES. *Vid.* Ades.

HADRIANOP'OLIS, a town of Thrace, on the Hebrus.——A city of Bithynia, where Licinius was conquered by Constantine, A.D. 320.

HADRIA'NUS, a Roman emperor. *Vid.* Adrianus.

HADRIA'NUS C. FA'BIUS, a prætor in Africa, who was burnt by the people of Utica for conspiring with the slaves. *Cic. Verr.* 1. c. 27. l. 5. c. 26.

HADRIANUTHE'RÆ, a city of Mysia, founded by the emperor Hadrian.

HADRIAT'ICUM MA'RE. *Vid.* Adriaticum.

HADRUME'TUM. *Vid.* Adrumetum.

HÆ'DUI or HÆD'UI. *Vid.* Ædui.

HAG'ALUS, a woody mountain of Attica. *Paus.*

HÆMO'DES, a mountain of Lycia. *Mela.*

HÆ'MON, a Theban youth, son of Creon, who was so captivated with the beauty of Antigone, the daughter of Œdipus, that he killed himself on her tomb, when he heard that she had been put to death by his father's orders. *Sophocl. in Ant.*—*Ovid. Trist.* 3. el. 3. *In Ibin.* 561. *Propert.* 2. el. 8. v. 21. [There is a fine group of Hæmon and Antigone, at the Villa Ludovisi, near Rome.——A Rutulian engaged in the wars of Turnus. *Virg. Æn.* 9. v. 685.——A friend of Æneas against Turnus. He was a native of Lycia. *Id.* 10. v. 126.

HÆ'MON, a river of Bœotia, formerly the Thermodon, according to *Plutarch in Demosthen.*

HÆMO'NIA. *Vid.* Æmonia.

HÆ'MUS, a long ridge of mountains which separated Thrace from Thessaly, so high that the Euxine and Adriatic Seas were visible from the top, though this, however, is denied by Strabo. It received its name from Hæmus, son of Boreas and Orithyia, who married Rhodope, and was changed into this mountain for aspiring to divine honors. *Strab.* 7. p. 313.—*Plin.* 4. c. 11.—*Ovid. Met.* 6. v. 87.—*Servius in Æn.* 1. v. 321.—*Claudian in Prob. & Ol.* 120.—*Marcellin.* 14. c. 11. l. 27. c. 4. & l. 31. c. 8. ——A stage player. *Juv.* 3. v. 99.

HÆ'NA SEXTIL., a poet of Corduba, in Spain. He came to Rome, where he distinguished himself as a writer more by his genius than his learning. He had composed a poem in praise of Cicero, which he repeated in the house of Messala Corvinus, in the presence of a few select friends, in the number of whom was Asinius Pollio, who abruptly left the company on pretence of being offended with the poet's flattery to the deceased orator in this line:

Deflendus Cicero, Latiæque silentia linguæ.

Seneca.—*Quintil.*

HÆS'TÆ, a people of Sarmatia, probably the Æstyi of *Tacitus, Germ.* 45.—*Cassiod.* l. 5.

HA'GES, a brother of king Porus, who opposed Alexander, &c. *Curt.* 8. c. 5. & 14.——One of Alexander's flatterers. *Cœl. Rhod.*——A man of Cyzicus, killed by Pollux. *Flacc.* 3. v. 191.

HAG'NO, a nymph.——A fountain of Arcadia. *Paus.* 8. c. 38.

HAGNAG'ORA, a sister of Aristomenes. *Paus.*

HA'LÆ, a town of Bœotia.——A town of Cilicia. ——Part of the tribe Cecropis. *Steph.*

HALÆ'SUS or HALE'SUS, a son of Agamemnon by Briseis or Clytæmnestra. Some authors say that he conspired with Ægisthus against his father, for which he was deservedly banished; but others maintain that he was so afflicted at the misfortunes of his family that he retired into Italy. Here he settled on Mount Massicus, in Campania, where he built Falisci, and afterwards assisted Turnus against Æneas. He was killed by Pallas. *Virg. Æn.* 7. v. 724. l. 10. v. 352.—*Servius. in locis*—*Ovid. Am.* 3. el. 13. v. 32.

HALA'LA, a village at the foot of mount Taurus.

HALARO'DII, a people near Pontus. *Steph.*

HALCY'ONE. *Vid.* Alcyone.

HALEN'TUM, a town at the north of Sicily. *Cic. Verr.* 3. c. 43. l. 4. c. 23.

HALE'SA. or HAL'ESA. *Vid.* Alæsa.

HALE'SIUS, a mountain and river near Ætna, where Proserpine was gathering flowers when she was carried away by Pluto. *Colum.*

HALE'SUS, a chief of the Oscans, and an ally of Turnus, was slain by Evander. He is said to have founded the town of Falerii.

HALE'SUS, a small river near Colophon in Asia Minor. *Plin.* 5. c. 29.

HA'LIA, one of the Nereides. *Apollod.*

HA'LIA or HALI'A, a festival observed at Rhodes in honor of the sun. *Athen.* 13.

HALIAC'MON or **ALIAC'MON**, a river which separates Thessaly from Macedonia, and falls into the Sinus Thermaicus, near the town of Pydna. *Cæs. Civ.* 3. c. 36.—*Plin.* 31. c: 2.—*Herodot.* 7. c. 127.

HALIAR'TUS, a town of Bœotia, founded by Haliartus, the son of Thersander. The monuments of Pandion, king of Athens, and of Lysander, the Lacedæmonian general, were to be seen in that town. *Strab.* 9.—*Liv.* 42.c. 44 & 63.—*Paus.* 9. c. 32.——A town of Peloponnesus.

HA'LIAS, a district of Argolis, so called because fishing was the chief occupation of its inhabitants. Their chief town was called Haliæ.

HALICARNAS'SUS, now Boudron, a maritime city of Caria, with a bay of the same name. The mausoleum, in honor of king Mausolus, which was one of the seven wonders of the world, was erected there. It was the residence of the sovereigns of Caria, and was celebrated for having given birth to Herodotus, Dionysius, Heraclitus, &c. *Justin.* 2. c. 12.—*Maxim. Tyr.* 35.—*Vitruv. de Arch.*—*Diod.* 17.—*Herodot.* 2. c. 178.—*Strab.* 14.—*Liv.* 27. c. 10 & 16. l. 33. c. 20.—*Mela*, 1. c. 16,—*Ptol.* 5. c. 2.

HALIC'YÆ, an inland town of Sicily, near Lilybæum, now Saleme. *Plin.* 3. c. 8.—*Cic. Verr.* 2. c. 33.—*Diod.* 14.

HALICYR'NA, a city of Acarnania. *Steph.*

HALIE'IS, a town of Argolis, near Trœzene. *Thucyd.* 1.

HALIME'DE, a Nereid.

HALIRRHO'THIUS, a son of Neptune and Euryte, who offered violence to Alcippe, daughter of Mars, because she slighted his addresses. This conduct highly offended Mars, who killed the ravisher. Neptune cited Mars to appear before the tribunal of justice to answer for the murder of his son. The cause was tried at Athens, in a place which has been called from thence Areopagus, and the murderer was acquitted. Servius gives a different account, and says that Halirrhotius, incensed against Minerva for the defeat of her father, in the contest which arose from the giving of a name to the city of Athens, cut down all the olive trees in the neighbourhood, and that in this sacrilegious action he was mortally wounded by his own hatchet. His death was attributed by his irritated father to Mars, and the accusation was produced and debated before the Areopagites. *Servius in* 1 *Geor.* v. 18.—*Apollod.* 3. c. 14.—*Paus.* 1. c. 21.

HALITÆ'A, a fountain of Ephesus. *Plin.* 5. c. 29. —*Paus.*

HALITHER'SUS, an old man, who foretold to Penelope's suitors the approaching return of Ulysses, and their own destruction. *Homer. Odyss* 2. v. 157. l. 17. v. 68. l. 24. v. 450.

HA'LIOS, a son of Alcinous, famous for his skill in dancing. *Homer. Odyss.* 8. v. 120 & 370.——A Trojan, who came with Æneas into Italy, where he was killed by Turnus. *Virg. Æn.* 9. v, 767.

HALIUS'SA, an island in the Argolic Gulf.

HALIZO'NES, a people of Paphlagonia. *Strab.* 14. —*Herodot.* 4. c. 17.

HAL'MUS, a son of Sisiphus, father of Chrysogone. He reigned in Orchomenus. *Paus.* 9. c. 35.

HALMYDES'SUS or **SALMYDES'SUS**, a town of Thrace, on the coast of the Euxine Sea, now Stagnara. *Mela*, 2. c. 2.

HAL'MYRIS, a lake of Lower Mysia, made by the Danube. *Plin.* 4. c. 12.

HALOC'RATES, a son of Hercules and Olympusa. *Apollod.*

HALO'NE, an island of the Propontis, opposite Cyzicus. *Plin.* 5. c. 31.

HALONNE'SUS, **HALONE'SUS** or **ALONNE'SUS**, an island on the coast of Macedonia, at the bottom of the Sinus Thermaicus. It was said to be inhabited only by women, who had slaughtered all the males, and they defended themselves against an invasion. *Mela*, 2. c. 7.

HALOSYD'NE, the "sea-born," a surname of Amphitrite and Thetys,

HALO'TIA, a festival observed in Tegea. *Paus.*

HALO'TUS, a eunuch, who used to taste the meat of the emperor Claudius. He poisoned the emperor's food by order of Agrippina. *Tacit. Ann.* 2. c. 66.

HA'LUS, a city of Achaia.——A city of Thessaly. ——A city of Parthia. *Tac. Ann.* 6. c. 41.

HALYÆ'ETUS, a man changed into a bird of the same name. *Ovid. Met.* 3. v. 176.

HALYAT'TES. *Vid.* Alyattes.

HAL'YCUS, now Platani, a river on the southern coast of Sicily, not far from Lilybæum.

HA'LYS, now Kizil-ermark, a river of Asia Minor, rising in Cappadocia, and falling into the Euxine Sea. It received its name ἀπὸ τοῦ ἁλὸς, from *salt*, because its waters were of a salt and bitter taste, from the nature of the soil over which they flowed. It is famous for the defeat of Crœsus, king of Lydia, occasioned by his mistaking the ambiguous meaning of this oracle:

Χρῦσος Ἅλυν διαβὰς μεγάλην ἀρχὴν διαλύσει.

If Crœsus passes over the Halys he will destroy a great empire.

That empire was his own. *Ptol.* 5. c. 4.—*Mela*, 1. c. 19.—*Cic. de Div.* 2. c. 56.—*Curt.* 4. c. 11.—*Strab.* 12.—*Lucan.* 3. v. 272.—*Herodot.* 1. c. 28.——A man of Cyzicus, killed by Pollux. *Val. Fl.* 3. v. 157.

HALYZ'IA or **ALYZ'IA**, a maritime town of Epirus, near the mouth of the Achelous, where the Athenians obtained a naval victory over the Lacedæmonians. It is now Alcipo, or, according to others, Trigordon, where there are many valuable remains of antiquity, *Xenoph.*

HAMADRY'ADES, nymphs who lived in the country, and presided over trees, with which they were said to live and die. The word is derived from ἅμα, *simul*, and δρῦς *quercus*. *Virg. Ecl.* 10—*Ovid. Met.* The English form is Ham'adryads.

HA'MÆ, a town of Campania, near Cumæ. The wood on its site is still called Selva di Hami. *Liv.* 23. c. 25.

HAMAX'A, a region of Bithynia. *Steph.*——The name of a star. *A. Gell*, 2. c. 21.—*Hom. Od.*

HAMAXANTI'NA, a part of the tribe Hippothoon. *Steph.*

HAMAX'IA, a city of Cilicia. *Steph. ex Strab.* 14.

HAMAX'ITUS, a town near the promontory Lectum.

HAMAXOBI'TÆ or **HAMAXOB'II**, a people of European Sarmatia. *Horat.*—*Sil.* 3. v. 290.—*Plin.* 4. c. 12.

HAMIL'CAR. *Vid.* Amilcar.

HAMMÆ'UM or **AMMO'NIUM LI'TUS**, a promontory of Arabia Felix, now Capo d'Aden. *Plin.* 6. c. 29.—*Ptol.*

HAMMANIEN'SES, a people of Africa between the Nasamones and Troglodytæ. *Plin.* 5. c. 5.

HAMMOD'ARA, a town between Ægypt and Æthiopia. *Id.* 6. c. 29.

HAM'MON. *Vid.* Ammon.

HAN'APIS, a river of Scythia. *Herod.*

HAN'NIBAL *Vid.* Annibal.

HANNIBALLIA'NUS, a son of Constantine Chlorus and his second wife Theodora, and half brother of Constantine. He was put to death at the death of Constantine.

HAN'NO. *Vid.* Anno.

HAR'CALO, a man famous for his knowledge of poisonous herbs, &c. He touched the most venomous serpents and other reptiles without receiving the smallest injury. *Sil.* 1. v. 406.

HAR'MA, a city of Bœotia Tanagrica.——A village of Attica.

HARMAS'TIS, a city of Iberia, in Asia. *Plin.* 6. c. 10.

HAR'MATA, a city of India. *Steph.*

HARMATE'LIA, a town of the Brachmanes in India, taken by Alexander. *Diod.* 17.

HAR'MATUS, a town of Troas, on the confines of Æolis. The people were called Hermatapolitæ. *Plin.* 5. c. 30.

HARMIL'LUS, an infamous debauchee. *Juv.* 10. v. 224.

HARMO'DIUS, a noble Athenian, who, to avenge himself on Hipparchus, who had offered violence to his sister, formed a conspiracy with Aristogiton to cut off the tyrant's family, and to restore Athens to liberty. This celebrated conspiracy proved fatal to Harmodius, who was slain by the guards after the assassination of their master; but Aristogiton displayed in the midst of tortures, the most invincible courage, and after accusing the friends of Hippias, the brother of Hipparchus, as accomplices, and seeing them put to death before him for their pretended crimes, he resigned himself to his fate with the greatest composure, B.C. 510. *Vid.* Aristogiton. The Athenians, to reward the patriotism of these illustrious citizens, made a law that no one should ever bear the names of Aristogiton and Harmodius. *Herodot.* 5. c. 55.—*Meur-*

sius de Pis. 13.—*Thucyd.* 13.—*Vossius inst. Orat.* 1.—*Cic. Tusc.* 1. c. 49.—*Plin.* 34. c. 8.—*Gell.* 9. c. 2. —*Seneca. Ir.* 2. c. 25.—*Justin.* 2. c. 9.——A writer *de legibus*, cited by *Athenæus*, 1. 15.

HARMO'NIA or HERMIONE'A. *Vid.* Hermione.

HARMON'IDES, a Trojan beloved by Minerva. He built the ships in which Paris carried away Helen. *Homer. Il.* 5.

HARMO'ZON, a promontory of Carmania. The people in its neighbourhood were called Harmozæi. *Plin.* 6. c. 25.

HARPA'GIA or HARPA'GIUM, a town near Parium, whence Ganymedes was stolen. *Steph.*

HAR'PAGUS, a general of Cyrus. He conquered the interior of Asia, after he had revolted from Astyages, who had cruelly forced him to eat the flesh of his son, because he had disobeyed his orders in not putting to death the infant Cyrus. *Justin.* 1. c. 5 & 6.—*Herodot.* 1. c. 108.

HAR'PAGUS, a river near Colchis. *Diod.* 14.

HARPAL'ICE. *Vid.* Harpalyce.

HARPA'LION, a son of Pylæmenes, king of Paphlagonia, who assisted Priam during the Trojan war, and was killed by Merion. *Homer. Il.* 13. v. 643

HAR'PALUS, a man entrusted with the treasures of Babylon by Alexander. His hopes that Alexander would perish in his expedition in the east, rendered him dissipated, negligent, and vicious. When he heard that the conqueror was returning with great resentment, he fled to Athens, where, when brought to justice, he bribed the orators, among whom was Demosthenes. He escaped with impunity to Crete, where he was at last assassinated by Thimbro, B.C. 325. He had devoted himself to the courtezan Pythionice, whom, according to some, he married, and he erected to her memory when dead, one of the most magnificent monuments of which Greece could boast. Plutarch, however, says that only thirty talents were spent in the erection, and that it was by no means superior to other edifices of the like nature. It is said by some authors that Glycerium succeeded Pythionice in the affections of Harpalus, and that when dead she was honored with a brazen statue in Syria. *Athen.* 13.—*Paus.* 1. c. 37.—*Plut. in Phoc.*—*Diod.* 17.——A robber, who scorned the power of the gods. *Cic.* 3. *De Nat. D.*——A celebrated astronomer of Greece, 480 years B.C. He corrected the cycle of eight years invented by Cleostratus, and proposed a new one of nine years, when he supposed that the sun and moon returned to the same point. That was afterwards corrected by Meton, who added ten years to it. *Diod. Sic.* 12.—*Fest. Avien.*

HARPAL'YCE, the daughter of Harpalycus, king of Thrace. Her mother died when she was but a child, and her father fed her with the milk of cows and mares, and immured her early to sustain the fatigues of hunting. When her father's kingdom was invaded by Neoptolemus, the son of Achilles, she repelled and defeated the enemy with manly courage. The death of her father, which happened soon after in a sedition, rendered her disconsolate; and, flying from the society of mankind, she lived in the forests upon plunder and rapine. Every attempt to secure her and restore her to her subjects proved fruitless, till her great swiftness was overcome by intercepting her with a net. After her death the people of the country appeased her manes by proper oblations on her tomb. *Virg. Æn.* 1. v. 321. & *Servius in loco.*—*Hygin.* fab. 193 & 252.——A beautiful virgin, daughter of Clymenus and Epicaste of Argos. Her father becoming enamoured of her, enjoyed her company by means of her nurse, who introduced him as a stranger Some time after she married Alastor, but the father's passion became more violent in his daughter's absence, and he cruelly murdered her husband to bring her back to Argos. Harpalyce, to revenge her wrongs, killed her younger brother, or, according to some, the fruit of her incest, and served it up as meat before her father. After this atrocious action, she begged the gods to remove her from the world, and was changed into an owl. Clymenus killed himself. *Hygin.* fab. 253 & 255. *Parthen. in Erot.* 13.——A mistress of Iphiclus, son of Thestius. She died in despair on seeing herself despised by her lover. This mournful story has been celebrated in verse in the form of a dialogue called Harpalyce. *Athen.* 14.

HARPALYCE'A, a city of Phrygia. *Steph.*

HARPAL'YCUS, one of the companions of Æneas, killed by Camilla. *Virg. Æn.* 11. v. 675.——The father of Harpalyce, king of the Amymneans, a people of Thrace. *Servius in Æn.* 1. v. 321.

HAR'PASA, a town of Caria. *Plin.* 2. c. 96.

HAR'PASUS, a river of Caria. *Liv.* 38. c. 13.——A river of Armenia which falls into the Araxes, and with it into the Caspian Sea.

HARPEDOPH'ORUS, a surname of Mercury and of Perseus, because they were represented armed with the harpe, an instrument by which Argus and Medusa perished. *Lucan.* 9. v. 662 & 676.—*Ovid. Met.* 5. v. 69.

HAR'PIS, a city of Lower Mysia. *Ptol.*

HARPOC'RATES, a divinity of the Ægyptians, supposed to be the same as Orus the son of Isis, and considered as the god of silence. He is represented as holding one of his fingers on his mouth, with a hat on his head, as the symbol of liberty, and clothed with a wolf's skin, bespangled with eyes and ears, to intimate that every thing may be heard and seen, but that the mysteries of religion ought never to be revealed. Sometimes he appears upon the flower of the lotus, with his finger still on his mouth. The peach-tree was particularly consecrated to him. The Romans placed his statues at the entrance of their temples. Most probably Harpocrates was a philosopher, celebrated for enjoining silence upon his pupils, and hence *Harpocratum reddere* became proverbial to imply silence and secrecy. An image of Harpocrates was dug up among the ruins of Mutina. *Catull.* 75. *Varro de L.L.* 4. c. 10.—*Plut. de Isi. & Os.* —*Arcana. Arcaniss.* 1. p. 41.—*Ovid. Met.* 9. v. 691.—*Carter. de Imag. Deor.* [Statues of this deity are not uncommon, but there are none of great celebrity. That in the Capitol may be considered the best.]

HARPOCRA'TION, a Platonic philosopher of Argos, from whom Stobæus compiled his eclogues. *Phot. Bibl.*—*Suidas.*——A sophist, called also Ælius. ——A sophist, surnamed Caius. *Phot. Bibl.*

HARPOCRA'TION VALE'RIUS, a rhetorician of Alexandria in Ægypt, author of a valuable lexicon on the ten orators of Greece. It contains an exact description of the great men, &c. who flourished in their age. The best edition is that of J. Gronovius, in 4to. 1696. at Leyden. *Sax. Onom.* 1. p. 407. —*Maussac. in Harpocrat.*

HARPY'IÆ, winged monsters, who were represented as having the face of a woman, and the body of a vulture, and with their feet and fingers armed with sharp claws. They were three in number, Aello, Ocypete, and Celæno, and were daughters of Neptune and Terra, or, according to others, of Thaumas and Electra. They were sent by Juno to plunder the tables of Phineus, whence they were driven to the islands called Strophades by Zethes and Calais. They emitted an infectious smell, and spoiled whatever they touched by their filth and excrements. They plundered Æneas during his voyage towards Italy, and predicted many of the calamities which attended him. *Virg. Æn.* 3. v. 212. l. 6. v. 289. (Harpies.)

HARU'DES, a people of Germany. *Cæs. G.* 1. c. 31. —*Ptol.* 2. c. 11.

HARUS'PEX, a soothsayer at Rome, who drew omens by consulting the entrails of the victims which were sacrificed to the gods. He received the name of *Aruspex, ab aris inspiciendis*, and that of *Extispex, ab extis inspiciendis*. The order of Aruspices was first established at Rome by Romulus, and the first Aruspices were Tuscans by origin, as the natives of that country were particularly skilled in that branch of divination. They had received all their knowledge from a boy named Tages, who, as was commonly reported, sprang from a clod of earth. *Vid.* Tages. They were originally three, but the Roman senate yearly sent six noble youths, or, according to others, twelve, to Etruria, to be instructed in all the mysteries of the art. The office of the Haruspices consisted in observing these four particulars; the beast before it was sacrificed; its entrails; the flames which consumed the sacrifice; and the flour, frankincense, &c. which was used. If the beast was led up to the altar with difficulty, escaped from the conductor's hands, roared when it received the fatal blow, or died in agonies, the omen was considered unfortunate. But, on the contrary, if it followed without compulsion, received the blow without resistance, and died without groaning, and after much effusion of blood, the haruspex, from these circumstances, foretold prosperity. When the body of the victim was opened, each part was scrupulously examined ; if anything was wanting, if it had a double liver, or a lean heart, the omen was regarded as unfortunate. If the entrails fell from the hands of the haruspex, or seemed besmeared with too much blood, or if no heart appeared, as is said to have happened in the two victims which J. Cæsar offered a little before his death, the omen was equally unlucky. When the flame was quickly kindled, violently consumed the sacrifice, and arose pure and bright, and like a pyramid, without any paleness, smoke, crackling, the omen was favorable. But when the fire was kindled with difficulty, and was extinguished before the sacrifice was totally consumed, or when it rolled in circles round the victim with intermediate spaces between the flames, it was considered as an unfavorable omen. With regard to the frankincense, meal, water, and wine, if there was any deficiency in the quantity, if the color was different or the quality was changed, or if anything was done with irregularity, it was deemed inauspicious. This custom of consulting the entrails of victims did not originate in Tuscany, but was in use among the Chaldæans, Greeks, Ægyptians, &c., and the crafty as well as the more enlightened part of mankind well knew how to render it subservient to their wishes or tyranny. Agesilaus, when in Ægypt, raised the drooping spirits of his soldiers by a superstitious artifice. He secretly wrote in his hand the word νίκη, *victory*, in large characters, and holding the entrails of a victim in his hand till the impression was communicated to the flesh, he showed it to his soldiers, and animated them by observing, that the gods signified their approaching victories even by marking it in the body of the sacrificed animals. *Cic. de Div.*

HAS'DRUBAL. *Vid.* Asdrubal.

HATE'RIUS Q., a patrician and orator of Rome under the first emperors. He died in the 90th year of his age. *Tac. Ann.* 4. c. 61.

HATE'RIUS AGRIP'PA, a senator in the age of Tiberius, hated by the tyrant for the independence of his conduct and character. *Id. ibid.* 6. c. 4.

HATE'RIUS ANTONI'NUS, a dissipated senator, whose extravagance was supported by Nero. *Id. ibid.* 13. c. 34.

HAUSTANES, a man who conspired with Bessus against Darius, &c. *Curt.* 8. c. 5.

HEB'DOLE. *Vid.* Ebdome.

HE'BE, a daughter of Jupiter and Juno. According to some she was the daughter of Juno only, who, conceived her after eating lettuces. As she was fair, and always enjoyed the bloom of youth, she was called the goddess of youth, and made by her mother cup-bearer to the gods. She was afterwards, however, dismissed from her office by Jupiter, because she fell down in an indecent posture as she was pouring out nectar to the gods at a grand festival, and Ganymedes, the favorite of Jupiter, succeeded her as cup-bearer. She was employed by her mother to prepare her chariot, and to harness her peacocks whenever requisite. When Hercules was raised to the rank of a god, he wss reconciled to Juno by marrying her daughter Hebe, by whom he had two sons, Alexiares and Anicetus. As Hebe had the power of restoring gods and men to the vigor of youth, she, at the instance of her husband, performed that kind office for Iolas his friend. Hebe was worshipped at Sicyon, under the name of Dia, and at Rome under the name of Juventas. She is generally represented as a young virgin crowned with flowers, and arrayed in a variegated garment. *Homer. Il.* 4. v. 2. l. 5. v. 721. *Odyss.* 11. v. 602.—*Pindar. Nem.* 7 & 10.—*Hesiod. Th.* 923.—*Catull.* 69. v. 115.—*Philost. Icon.* 2. c. 20.—*Strab.* 8.—*Aug. de Civ. D.* 4. c. 2.—*Servius in Æn.* 1. v. 32. l. 5. v. 134. l. 6. v. 64.—*Gyrald. de Hist.* 10.—*Paus.* 1. c. 19. l. 2. c. 12.—*Ovid. Met.* 9. v. 400. *Fast.* 6. v. 76. *Trist.* 5. el. 3. v. 37. —*Apollod.* 1. c. 3. l. 2. c. 7.

HEBE'SUS, a Rutulian, killed in the night by Euryalus. *Virg. Æn.* 9. v. 344.

HE'BRUS, now Mirza, a river of Thrace, which was supposed to have golden sands. It falls into the Ægean Sea by two mouths, opposite the island of Samothrace. The head of Orpheus was thrown into its waters after it had been cut off by the Ciconian women. The river received its name from Hebrus, son of Cassander, a king of Thrace, who was said to have drowned himself there. *Mela*, 2. c. 2.—*Strab.* 7.—*Virg. G.* 4. v. 463. *Æn.* 12. v. 331.—*Horat.* 1. od. 25. v. 19. l. 1. ep. 3. v. 3.—*Timoth. de Fluv.* 11.—*Ovid. Met.* 11. v. 50.

HE'BRUS, a youth of Lipara, beloved by Neobule. *Horat.* 3. od. 12. ——A man of Cyzicus, killed by Pollux. *Flacc.* 3. v. 149.——An auxiliary of Perses killed by Jason. *Id.* 6. v. 620.——A friend of Æneas, son of Dolichaon, killed by Mezentius in the Rutulian war. *Virg. Æn.* 10. v. 696.

HECAER'GOS and HECAER'GE, surnames applied to Apollo and Diana, and expressive of the distance to which the rays of the beneficent luminaries over which they preside are darted. *Clem. Alex.* 5. *Strom.*

HEC'ALE, a poor old woman who kindly received Theseus as he was going against the bull of Marathon, or, according to others, against the Sarmatians. She died before his return, and the hero honored her memory by instituting a festival sacred to Jupiter, which she herself had vowed to the god. Her poverty and her great age became proverbial. *Ovid. de Rem. Am.* 747.—*Petron. Arb.* 135.—*Plin.* 22. c. 22.—*Plut. in Thes.*——A daughter of Minos, king of Crete. *Apollod.* 3.

HEC'ALE, a municipal town of the tribe Leontis. *Steph.*

HECALE'SIA, a festival in honor of Jupiter of Hecale, instituted by Theseus, in commemoration of the kindness of Hecale. *Vid.* Hecale. *Steph. Byzant.*—*Plut. Thes.*

HECA'LIUS, a surname of Jupiter. *Vid.* Hecale.

HECAME'DE, a daughter of Arsinous, who fell to the lot of Nestor after the plunder of Tenedus by the Greeks. *Homer. Il.* 11. v. 623.

HEC'ATÆ FA'NUM, a celebrated temple, sacred to Hecate at Strathonice in Caria. *Strab.* 14.

HECATÆ'US, a celebrated historian of Miletus, born 549 years B.C. in the reign of Darius Hystaspes. His works have unfortunately perished. *Herodot.* 2. c. 143.——A celebrated sculptor. *Plin.* 33. c. 12. l. 34. c. 8.——A Macedonian, intimate with Alexander. *Diod.* 17.——A Macedonian, brought to the army against his will by Amyntas, &c. *Curt.* 7. c. 1.——A philosopher and historian of Abdera, in the time of Alexander and Ptolemy Lagus. *Euseb.*—*Sax. Onom.* 1. p. 81.—*Fabr. B. Gr.* 3. c. 8.

HEC'ATE, a daughter of Perses and Asteria, according to Hesiod, or rather of Jupiter and Latona, was the same as Proserpine or Diana. She was called Luna in heaven, Diana on earth, and Hecate or Proserpine in hell, whence her name of *Diva triformis, tergemina, triceps.* She was supposed to preside over magic and enchantments, and was generally represented like a woman with three heads, that of a horse, a dog, or a boar, and sometimes she appeared with three different bodies, and three different faces. Dogs, lambs, and honey, were generally offered to her, especially in highways and cross-roads, whence she obtained the name of *Trivia.* Her power was extended over heaven, the earth, the sea, and hell, and to her influence kings and nations supposed themselves indebted for their prosperity. *Ovid.* 7. *Met.* v. 94. *Heroid.* 12.—*Val. Flacc.* 7. v. 182.—*Tibull.* 1. el. 2.—*Hesiod. Theog.* v. 410, &c.—*Apollod.*—*Apollon. Arg.* 3.—*Lycoph.* 1175.—*Theocrit. in Pharm.* —*Euripid. in Med.*—*Horat.* 3. od. 22.—*Paus.* 2. c. 22.—*Virg. Æn.* 4. v. 511.—*Diod.* 4.—*Lucan.* 6. v. 700.

HECATE'SIA, a yearly festival observed by the people of Stratonice in honor of Hecate. The Athenians paid also particular worship to this divinity, who was deemed the patroness of families and of children. From this circumstance the statues of the goddess were erected before the doors of the houses, and upon every new moon a public supper was provided at the expense of the richest people, and set in the streets, where the poorest of the citizens were permitted to retire and feast upon it, while they reported that Hecate had devoured it. There were also expiatory offerings presented to supplicate the goddess to remove whatever evils might impend over the head of the public, &c.

Strab. l. 14.—*Aristoph. Schol. in Vesp.*—*Schol. in Theocr. Idyl.* 2.—*Plutarch.*

HEC'ATIS NE'MUS, a promontory of European Sarmatia. *Ptol.*

HEC'ATO, a native of Rhodes, pupil of Panætius. He wrote a work on the duties of man, &c. *Cic.* 3. *Off.* 15.

HECATOMBŒ'A, a festival celebrated in honor of Juno by the Argives and the people of Ægina. It receives its name from ἑκατόν, and βοῦς, a sacrifice of a hundred oxen, which were always offered to the goddess, and the flesh distributed among the poorest citizens. There were also public games, first instituted by Archinous, a king of Argos, in which the prize was a shield of brass, with a crown of myrtle. *Pindar. Schol. Olymp.* 7, 8.—*Eustath. Il.* β.

HECATOMBŒ'UM, a place of Achaia, in Peloponnesus. *Polyb.*

HECATOMBŒ'US, a surname given to Jupiter, Neptune, and Apollo, as likewise that of Hecatombœa, to Juno, because hecatombs were particularly offered to their divinity. The festival in honor of Juno, was celebrated on the first of July, whence that month was called Hecatombœon. *Meurs. Gr. Fer.*

HECATOM'NUS, a præfect of Caria, entrusted by Artaxerxes with the command against Evagoras. *Diod. Sic.* 15.

HECATOMPHO'NIA, a solemn sacrifice offered by the Messenians to Jupiter when any of them had killed a hundred enemies in war. *Paus.* 4. c. 19.

HECATOM'POLIS, an epithet given to Crete, from its hundred cities. *Strab.* 11.

HECATOM'PYLOS, an epithet applied to Thebes, in Ægypt, on account of its hundred gates. *Ammian.* 22. c. 16.——The capital of Parthia in the reign of the Arsacidæ. This celebrated city was situated near the sources of the Araxes. *Ptol.* 6. c 5.—*Strab.* 11.—*Plin.* 6. c. 15 & 25.

HECA'TON, a stoic philosopher, native of Rhodes. He wrote several works, all of which are lost.

HECATONNE'SI, small islands between Lesbus and Asia. *Strab.* 13.

HECTODU'RUM, a town of Rhætia, now Echtal. *Ptol.*

HECTOR, son of king Priam and Hecuba, was the most valiant of all the Trojan chiefs. He married Andromache the daughter of Eetion, by whom he had Astyanax. He was appointed captain of all the Trojan forces, when Troy was besieged by the Greeks; and the valor with which he behaved showed how well qualified he was to discharge that important office. He engaged with the bravest of the Greeks, and according to Hyginus, no less than 31 of the most valiant of the enemy perished by his hand. When Achilles had driven back the Trojans towards the city, Hector, too great to flee, waited the approach of his enemy near the Scæan gates, though his father and mother, with tears in their eyes, blamed his rashness and entreated him to retire. The sight of Achilles terrified him, and instead of awaiting his approach, he fled before him in the plain. The Greek pursued him to the source of the Scamander, and perceiving an unprotected part in his cuirass, directed his spear to the vulnerable spot. Jupiter held, says Homer, in his hand the immortal balance which was to decide the destinies of Hector and Troy; the fate of Achilles preponderated, and the son of Priam received the fatal blow. The fallen hero was not only spoiled of his arms, but the conqueror, with a barbarity peculiar to the times, pierced his feet, tied him to his chariot with a thong, and with insulting triumph drove himself three times round the tomb of Patroclus and the walls of Troy. The body was preserved by the gods from putrefaction and from a mangled appearance, till it was ransomed by the aged Priam, and the Trojans obtained from the Greeks a truce of some days to pay the last offices to the greatest of their leaders. The Thebans boasted in the age of the geographer Pausanias that they had the ashes of Hector preserved in an urn, by order of an oracle; which promised them undisturbed felicity as long as they were in possession of that hero's remains. The epithet *Hectoreus* is applied by the poets to the Trojans, as expressive of valor and intrepidity. *Homer. Il.* 2. 3. 6. 8. 10. 11. 12, &c.—*Philost. in Her.* 13.—*Virg. Æn.* 1, &c.—*Ovid. Met.* 12 & 13.—*Dictys. Cret.*—*Dares. Phryg.*—*Hygin.* fab. 90 & 112.—*Paus.* 1, 3. & 9. c. 18.—*Quintil. Smyrn.* 1. v. 104. l. 3. v. 192. ——A son of Parmenio, drowned in the Nile. Alexander honored his remains with a magnificent funeral. *Curt.* 4. c. 8. l. 6. c. 9.

HEC'UBA, daughter of Dymas, a Phrygian prince, or, according to others, of Cisseus, a Thracian king, was the second wife of Priam, king of Troy, and proved the chastest of women, and the most tender and unfortunate of mothers. During the Trojan war she saw the greatest part of her children perish by the hands of the enemy. And when Troy was taken she fell to the lot of Ulysses, a man whom she hated for his perfidy and avarice, and she embarked with the conquerors for Greece. On their voyage the Greeks landed in the Thracian Chersonesus, where her daughter Polyxena was sacrificed to the manes of Achilles. Hecuba was inconsolable, and her grief was still more increased at the sight of the body of her son Polydorus, which was washed on shore. *Vid.* Polydorus. Determined to revenge the death of her son, she went to the house of his murderer, Polymnestor, tore out his eyes, and attempted to deprive him of his life. She was hindered from executing her bloody purpose by the arrival of some Thracians, and fled with the female companions of her captivity. She was immediately pursued, and, in her flight, suddenly changed into a bitch. After this metamorphosis she threw herself into the sea, according to Hyginus, and that place was from that circumstance, called Cyneum. Hecuba had a great number of children by Priam, among whom were Hector, Paris, Deiphobus, Pammon, Helenus, Polites, Antiphon, Hipponous, Polydorus, Troilus, and among the daughters, Creusa, Ilione, Laodice, Polyxena and Cassandra. *Homer. Il.* 16. v. 718. l. 22. v. 450.—*Tzetzes Chil.* 7. c. 135.—*Eustath. in Il.* 3.—*Euripid in Hec. & Troad.*—*Ennil. frag.* —*Quint. Smyr.* 14. v. 212 & 256.—*Seneca in Troad.*—*Plin.* 4. c. 11.—*Mela*, 2. c. 2.—*Ovid. Met.* 11. v. 761. l. 13. v. 515.—*Hygin.* fab. 111.—*Virg. Æn.* 3. v. 44.—*Servius in loco*, l. 7. v. 320. & l. 5. v. 535. l. 10. v. 705.—*Juv.* 10. v. 271.—*Strab.* 13.—*Dictys. Cret.* 4 & 5 —*Apollod.* 3. c. 12.

HEC'UBÆ SEPUL'CRUM or CYNOS'SEMA, a promontory of Thrace. *Ovid. Met.* 13. v. 550, &c.

HEDETA'NI, a people of Hispania Tarraconensis. *Ptol.*

HED'ILA, a poetess of Samus. *Athen.* 7. c. 19.

HEDON'ACUM, a village of Bœotia. *Paus.* 9. c. 31.

HED'YLUS, a poet, son of Melicertus, was a native of Athens. He was a contemporary and rival of Callimachus. Eleven of his epigrams are extant.

HEDYM'ELES, an admired musician in Domitian's age. *Juv.* 6. v. 381.

HED'YPHON, a river of Babylonia. *Strab.*

HEDYP'NUS, a river of Susiana, flowing into the Eulæus. *Plin.* 6. c. 27.

HEGEL'OCHUS, a general of 6000 Athenians sent to Mantinea to check the progress of Epaminondas. *Diod.* 15.——An Ægyptian general who flourished B.C. 128.

HEG'EMON or HEGE'MON, a Thracian poet in the age of Alcibiades. He wrote a poem called Gigantomachia, besides other works and parodies. *Athen.* 4. c. 16.—*Gyrald. P. Hist.* 3 —*Ælian. V.H.* 4. c. 11.——A poet who wrote a poem on the battle of Leuctra, &c. *Ælian. V.H.* 4. c. 11.—*Voss. de H. Gr.*——A friend of Phocion.

HEGEM'ONE, the name of one of the Athenian Charites or Graces.——A surname of Diana, at Sparta.

HEGESAG'ORAS, a writer praised by the *Scholiast* on *Apollonius*, l. 1.

HEGESAN'DER, an historian of Delphi. *Voss. de H. Gr.*

HEGESI'ANAX, an historian of Alexandria, who wrote an account of the Trojan war. *Athen.* l. 3. —*Voss. de Poet. Gr.*

HEGE'SIAS, a tyrant of Ephesus under the patronage of Alexander. *Polyæn.* 6.——A philosopher of Cyrene, who so eloquently convinced his auditors of their failings and follies, and persuaded them that there were no dangers after death, that many were guilty of suicide. Ptolemy forbade him to continue propagating his doctrines. *Diog. in Arist.* —*Val. Max.* 8. c. 9.—*Cic. Tusc.* 1. c. 34.——An historian of Magnesia, who was also admired as an orator, but he corrupted the elegant diction of Attica, by the introduction of Asiatic idioms. *Cic. Orat.* 67, 69. *Brut.* 83.—*Strab.* 9.—*Plut. in Alex.* ——An archon at Athens, Ol. 114.——A writer upon Cyprus. *Athen.* 11. c. 3.

HEGESIG'ONUS, a writer on the natives of India. *Tzetzes. Chil.* 1. *Hist.* 18.

HEGESIL'OCHUS, one of the chief magistrates of Rhodes in the age of Alexander and his father Philip.——A native of Rhodes, who lived 171 B.C. He engaged his countrymen to prepare a fleet of 40 ships to assist the Romans in their war against Perseus king of Macedonia.

HEGESIN'OUS, a man who wrote a poem on Attica. *Paus.* 2. c. 29.

HEGESI'NUS, a philosopher of Pergamus, of the 2d academy. He flourished B.C. 193.

HEGESIP'PUS, an historian who wrote a work on Pallene. *Dionys. Hal.* 1.—*Steph. in* Μηκύβερνα.—*Parthen. Erot.* c. 6. This latter writer mentions a work on the affairs of the Milesians, by an author of the same name.——A comic poet of Tarentum. *Suidas.*——A contemporary of Demosthenes, to whom is attributed the oration *de Haloneso*, commonly called the seventh Philippic. *Etymol. in Hegesip.*——An ecclesiastical historian, A.D. 178, fragments of whose works are preserved by Eusebius. They have been edited, with notes, by Haloixius. Some other works attributed to him were the productions of another person of this name, who flourished A.D. 375. *Sax. Onom.* 1. p. 329. *Voss. de H. Gr.* 2. c. 14.—*Gronov. in Script. Eccles.* c. 1.

HEGESIP'YLA or HEGESIP'YLE, a daughter of Olorus king of Thrace, who married Miltiades and became mother of Cimon. *Plut.*—*Herodot.* 6. c. 39.

HEGE'SIS, a Lacedæmonian, a descendant of Hercules. *Herodot.* 7. c. 204.

HEGESIS'TRATUS, an Ephesian, who consulted the oracle to know in what particular place he should fix his residence. He was directed to settle where he found peasants dancing with crowns of olives on their heads. This was in Asia, where he founded Elea, &c. *Plut.*——An illegitimate son of Pisistratus, made by him tyrant of Sigeum. *Herodot.* 5. c. 94.——A soothsayer, who, being taken by the Spartans, and fastened to a log, escaped by cutting off the foot to which it was chained. *Id.* 9. c. 37.——Son of Aristagoras, was sent on an embassy by the Samians. *Id. ibid.* c. 90 & 91.

HEGETHMA'TIA, a city of Germany, now Lignitz. *Ptol.*

HEGETOR'IDES, a Thasian, who, when his country was besieged by the Athenians, and a law forbade any one on pain of death to speak of peace, went to the market-place with a rope about his neck, and boldly told his countrymen to treat him as they pleased, provided they saved the city from the calamities which the continuation of the war seemed to threaten. The Thasians were awakened by the freedom and patriotism of their fellow citizen, the law was abrogated, and Hegetorides pardoned. *Polyæn.* 2.

HEGO'NIS, a promontory of Macedonia. *Ptol.*

HE'LA, a small region of Asia, the emporium of king Attalus. *Steph.*

HEL'ENA, the most beautiful woman of her age, sprung from one of the eggs which Leda, the wife of king Tyndarus brought forth. *Vid.* Leda. According to some authors, Helen was daughter of Nemesis by Jupiter, and Leda was only her nurse; and, to reconcile this variety of opinions, some imagine that Nemesis and Leda are the same persons. Her beauty was so universally admired even in her infancy, that Theseus, with his friend Pirithous, carried her away before she had attained her 10th year, and concealed her at Aphidnæ, under the care of his mother Æthra. Her brothers, Castor and Pollux, recovered her by force of arms, and she returned unpolluted to Sparta, her native country. There existed, however, a tradition recorded by Pausanias, that Helen was of nubile years when carried away by Theseus, and that she bore to him a daughter, who was entrusted to the care of Clytemnestra. This violence offered to her person, did not in the least diminish, but rather augmented the celebrity of her charms, and her hand was eagerly solicited by the young princes of Greece. The most celebrated of her suitors were Ulysses son of Laertes, Antilochus son of Nestor, Sthenelus son of Capaneus, Diomedes son of Tydeus, Amphilochus son of Cteatus, Meges son of Phileus, Agapenor son of Ancæus, Thalpius son of Eurytus, Mnestheus son of Peteus, Schedius son of Epistrophus, Polyxenus son of Agasthenes, Amphilochus son of Amphiaraus, Ascalaphus and Ialmus sons of the god Mars, Ajax son of Oileus, Eumelus son of Admetus, Polypætes son of Pirithous, Elphenor son of Chalcodon, Podalirius and Machaon sons of Æsculapius, Leonteus son of Coronus, Philoctetes son of Pæan, Protesilaus son of Iphiclus, Eurypylus son of Evemon, Ajax and Teucer sons of Telamon, Patroclus son of Menœtius, Menelaus son of Atreus, Thoas, Idomeneus, and Merion. Tyndarus was more alarmed than pleased at the sight of such a number of illustrious princes, who eagerly solicited each the honor of becoming his son-iu-law. He knew that he could not prefer one without displeasing all the rest, and from this perplexity he was at last liberated by the sagacious advice of Ulysses, who began to be already celebrated in Greece, by his superior knowledge and prudence. This prince, who clearly saw that his pretensions to Helen would not probably meet with success in opposition to so many rivals, proposed to extricate Tyndarus from all his difficulties if he would promise him his niece Penelope in marriage. Tyndarus consented, and Ulysses upon this advised the king to bind, by a solemn oath, all the suitors, that they would approve of the uninfluenced choice which Helen should make of one among them; and engage to unite together to defend her person and character, if ever any attempts were made to ravish her from the arms of her husband. The advice of Ulysses was cheerfully followed, the princes consented, and Helen fixed her choice upon Menelaus, and married him. Hermione was the early fruit of that union, which continued for three years with mutual happiness. After this Paris, son of Priam, king of Troy, came to Lacedæmon on pretence of offering a sacrifice to Apollo. He was kindly received by Menelaus, but shamefully abused his favors, and during his absence in Crete corrupted the fidelity of Helen, and persuaded her to follow him to Troy, B.C 1198. At his return, Menelaus, highly sensible of the injury which he had received, assembled the Grecian princes, and reminded them of their solemn promises. They resolved to make war against the Trojans; but they previously sent ambassadors to Priam to demand the restitution of Helen. The influence of Paris at his father's court prevented the restoration: and the Greeks returned home without receiving the satisfaction which they required. Soon after their return, their combined forces assembled and sailed for the coast of Asia. The behaviour of Helen during the Trojan war is not clearly known. Some assert that she had willingly followed Paris, and that she warmly supported the cause of the Trojans; while others believe that she never ceased to recollect with tears the kindness and affection of her former husband, and to curse the day in which she had proved faithless to his bed. Homer maintains the latter opinion: and some have added, that she often betrayed the schemes and resolutions of the Trojans, and secretly favored the cause of Greece. When Paris was killed in the ninth year of the war, she voluntarily married Deiphobus, one of Priam's sons, and when Troy was taken she made no scruple to betray him, and to introduce the Greeks into his chamber, to ingratiate herself with Menelaus. She returned to Sparta, and the love of Menelaus forgave her numerous errors. Some, however, say that she obtained her life with difficulty from her husband, whose resentment she had kindled by her infidelity. After she had lived for some years at Sparta, Menelaus died, and she was driven away from Peloponnesus by Megapenthes and Nicostratus, the illegitimate sons of her husband, and retired to Rhodes, where at that time Polyxo, a native of Argos, reigned over the country. Polyxo remembered that her widowhood originated in the frailties of Helen, her husband, Tlepolemus having been killed in the Trojan war, and she therefore, meditated revenge. When Helen one day retired to bathe in the river, Polyxo disguised her attendants in the habits of furies, and sent them with orders to murder her enemy. Helen was forcibly tied to a tree, and cruelly strangled, and her misfortunes were afterwards remembered, and the crimes of Polyxo expiated by the temple which the Rhodians raised to Helen Dendritis, or *tied to a tree*. There is a tradition mentioned by Herodotus, which says that Paris was driven, as he returned from Sparta, upon the coast of Ægypt, where Proteus, king of the country, expelled him from his dominions for his ingratitude to Menelaus, and confined Helen. From that circumstance, therefore, Priam informed the Grecian ambassadors that neither Helen nor her possessions were in Troy, but in the hands of the king of Ægypt. The Greeks, disbelieving this assertion, besieged the town, and took it after a ten years' siege, and Menelaus, by visiting Ægypt as he returned home, recovered Helen at the court of Proteus, and was convinced that the Trojan war had been undertaken upon very unjust and unpardonable grounds. Helen was honored after death as a goddess, and the Spartans built her a temple at Therapne, which was said to have the power of giving beauty to all the deformed women that entered it. Helen, according to some authors, was conveyed into the island of Leuce after her death, where she married Achilles, who had been once one of her warmest admirers. The age of Helen has been a matter of deep enquiry among the chronologists. If she was born at the same birth with Castor and Pollux, who accompanied the Argonauts in their expedition against Colchis about thirty-five years before the Trojan war, according to some, she was no less than thirty years old when Troy was reduced to ashes, supposing that her brothers were only fifteen when they embarked with the Argonauts. But she is represented by Homer as so incomparably beautiful during the siege of Troy, that, though seen at a distance, she influenced the counsellors of Priam by the superior brightness of her charms; therefore we must suppose with others, that her beauty remained long undiminished, and was extinguished only at her death. *Apollod.* 3. c. 10, &c.—*Hygin.* fab. 77.—*Herodot.* 2. c. 112.—*Plut. in Thes.* &c.—*Cic. de Offic.* 3.—*Horat.* 3. od. 3.—*Dictys. Cret.* 1, &c.—*Paus.* 1. c. 33. l. 2. c. 22, l. 3. c. 18.—*Virg. Æn.* 1. v. 654. l. 6. v. 495.—*Tzetzes. in Lyc.*—*Servius in Æn. loco. cit.* & l. 2. v. 166. & 310. l. 3. v. 328.—*Lactant.* l. c. 21.—*Pindar. Nem.* 10.—*Diod.* 4.—*Homer Il.* 2, 3, &c. *Odyss.* 4. 15.—*Eustath. in Il.*—*Eurip. in Hec. & Troad.*—*Coluthus. de Rapt. Hel.*—*Propert* 2. el. 15. v. 13.—*Quint. Smyr.* 10. v. 344 & 389. l. 13. v. 356 & 385. l. 14. v. 148.—*Seneca in Troad.*—*Max. Tyr.* 27.—*Philostr. in Her.*—*Plato. de Rep.* 9. ——A young woman of Sparta, often confounded with the daughter of Leda As she was going to be sacrificed for the good of her country, because the lot had fallen upon her, an eagle came and carried away the knife of the priest, upon which she was released, and the barbarous custom of offering human victims abolished. *Plut de Hist. Ro & Gr.* 35.——A daughter of the emperor Constantine, who married Julian.——The mother of Constantine the Great. She was born at Drepanum in Bithynia, where she was engaged in the obscure employment of inn-keeper. Constantius Chlorus saw and loved her, but his marriage with her was some time after followed by a divorce, when he was elevated to the imperial dignity. After the accession of her son to the purple, Helena was drawn from her obscurity, and merited the high rank which she held in the empire, by the liberality of her conduct, the humanity of her character, and the virtues of her private and public life. She died in her 80th year, A.D. 328.——A daughter of Musæus, an Athenian, who lived prior to Homer, and wrote a poem on the Trojan war, from which Homer is said to have derived the argument of his Iliad.—*Phot. Cod.* 190. l. 4.—*Ptol.* &c.

HEL'ENA, an island on the coast of Attica, to which Helen retired after the siege of Troy. It is now Macronisi. *Plin.* 4. 12.

HELE'NIA, a festival observed in Laconia in honor of Helen, who received there divine honours. It was celebrated by virgins riding upon mules, and in chariots made of reeds and bulrushes. *Hesych.*

HELENI'US, a small island near Canopus. *Steph.*

HELE'NOR, son of Licymnia, a Lydian prince who accompanied Æneas to Italy, and was killed by the Rutulians. *Virg. Æn.* 9. v. 444, &c.

HEL'ENUS, a celebrated soothsayer, son of Priam and Hecuba, greatly respected by all the Trojans. When Deiphobus, after the death of Paris, received Helen in marriage in preference to himself, he retired to mount Ida, where Ulysses, by the advice of Calchas, took him prisoner. As he was well acquainted with futurity, the Greeks made use of prayers, threats, and promises, to induce him to reveal the secrets of the Trojans, and either the fear of death or the gratification of resentment, unfortunately seduced him to disclose to the enemies of his country, that Troy could not be taken whilst it was in possession of the Palladium, nor before Polydectes came from his retreat at Lemnus, and assisted in conducting the siege. After the ruin of his country, he fell to the share of Pyrrhus the son of Achilles, and saved his life by warning him to avoid a dangerous tempest which in reality proved fatal to all those who set sail. This endeared him to Pyrrhus, and he received from his hand Andromache the widow of his brother Hector, by whom he had a son called Cestrinus. This marriage, according to some, was consummated after the death of Pyrrhus, who had lived with Andromache as his wife. Helenus was the only one of Priam's sons who survived the ruin of his country. After the death of Pyrrhus, he reigned over part of Epirus, which he called Chaonia, in memory of his brother Chaon, whom he had inadvertently killed in Troy. Helenus received Æneas as he voyaged towards Italy, and foretold to him some of the calamities which attended his fleet. The manner in which he received the gift of prophecy is doubtful. *Vid.* Cassandra. *Virg. Æn.* 3. v. 295, &c. & *Servius ib.*—*Paus.* 1. c. 11. l. 2. c. 33.—*Homer. Il.* 6. v. 76. l. 7. v. 47.—*Hygin.* 128.—*Sch. Eurip. in Hecub.* 87.—*Sophocl. in Philoct.* 2. sc. 2.—*Conon.* 34.—*Justin.* 17. c. 3.—*Dictys Cret.*—*Dares Phryg.*—*Ovid. Met.* 13. v. 99 & 723, l. 15. v. 437.——A Rutulian killed by Pallas. *Virg. Æn.* 10. v. 388.——A son of Diocles, king of Sicambri.

HELER'NI LU'CUS, a place near Rome. *Ovid. Fast.* 6. v. 105.

HE'LES or **HA'LES**, a river of Lucania, near Velia, falling into the Tyrrhene Sea. *Cic. ad Att.* 16. ep. 7. *Fam.* 7. ep. 20.

HE'LIA, a small island of Sicily, near Drepanum. *Plin.* 3. c. 5.

HELI'ADES, the daughters of Sol and Clymene. They were three in number, Lampetie, Phaetusa, and Lampethusa, or seven, according to Hyginus: Merope, Helie, Ægle, Lampetie, Phœbe, Ætheria, and Dioxippe. Germanicus mentions nine, of whom five bear the same names as those of Hyginus; and instead of Lampetie, and Ætheria, he substitutes Ægiale, Petre, Charie, and Arethusa. The Heliades were so afflicted at the death of their brother Phaethon (*vid.* Phaethon), that they were changed by the gods into poplars, and their tears into precious amber, on the banks of the river Po. *Ovid. Met.* 2. v. 340.—*Martial.* 4. epigr. 32.—*Senec. in Herc. Oet.* 187.—*Germanic. ad Arat.*—*Tzetzes Chil.* 4. c. 137.—*Apollon.* 4 *Arg.*—*Servius ad* 6 *Ecl.*—*Virg.* v. 62. *Æn.* 10. v. 189.—*Lactant. in Arg.*—*Ovid. Met.* 2.—*Hygin.* fab. 154.——The first inhabitants of Rhodes. This island being covered with mud when the world was first created was warmed by the cherishing beams of the sun, and from thence sprang seven men, who were called Heliades, ἀπὸ τοῦ ἡλίου. The eldest of these, called Ochimus, married Hegetoria, one of the nymphs of the island, and his brothers fled from the country for having put to death, through jealousy, one of their number. *Diod.* 5.—*Harduin. ad Plin.* 5. c. 9.

HELIAS'TÆ, a name given to the judges of the most numerous tribunal at Athens. They consisted of 1000, and sometimes 1500, they were seldom assembled, and only upon matters of the greatest importance to the public welfare. It was before this tribunal that Pisistratus presented himself with false complaints of ill treatment, by which means he enslaved his country; and here also Phryne was accused of impiety and corruption. The oath which each of the judges of this tribunal took is mentioned by Demosthenes. *Posidip. apud Athen.* 13. c. 22.—*Aristot. de Rep.* 2.—*Demosth. contr. Tim.*—*Diog. in Sol.*

HELICA'ON, a Trojan prince, son of Antenor. He married Laodice, the daughter of Priam, whose form Iris assumed to inform Helen of the state of the rival armies before Troy. Helicaon was wounded in a night engagement, but his life was spared by Ulysses, who remembered the hospitality which he had formerly received from his father Antenor.

Homer. Il. 2. v. 123.—*Servius in Æn.* 1. v. 246.—*Lescheus apud Paus.* 10. c. 26.

HEL'ICE, a star near the north pole, generally called Ursa Major. It is supposed to have received its name from the town of Helice, of which Calisto who was changed into the constellation of the Great Bear, was an inhabitant. *Lucan.* 2. c. 237. ——A town of Achaia, on the bay of Corinth, overwhelmed by the inundation of the sea. Neptune had there a magnificent temple, from which circumstance he was surnamed Heliconius. *Homer Il.* 2. v. 82. l. 8. v. 203.—*Strab.* 8.—*Ptol.* 3. c. 16. —*Plin.* 2. c. 92.—*Ovid. Met.* 15. v. 293.

HEL'ICE, a daughter of Silenus, king of Ægiale, who married Ion son of Xuthus. *Paus.* 7. c. 24.——A daughter of Lycaon, king of Arcadia.

HEL'ICON, now Zagaro Vouni, a mountain of Bœotia, on the borders of Phocis. It was sacred to the Muses, who had there a temple, and who were supposed to have selected this favoured spot for their residence. The fountain Hippocrene flowed from this mountain. *Strab.* 8.—*Ptol.* 3. c. 15.—*Servius ad Virg. Ecl.* 6. v. 64.—*Ovid. Met.* 2. v. 219.—*Paus.* 9. c. 28, &c.—*Virg. Æn.* 7. v. 641. l. 10. v. 163. *Georg.* 3. v. 11 & 291.——A river of Macedonia, near Dium. *Paus.* 9. c. 30.——A river of Sicily falling into the Tyrrhene Sea, opposite the Lipari isles. It is now Olivieri.

HELICONI'ADES, a name given to the muses because they lived upon mount Helicon. *Lucret.* 5. v. 1050.—*Pers. in Pr.* 10.—*Catull.* 62. v 1.

HELICO'NIS, a daughter of Thespius. *Apollod.*

HELICO'NIUS, a sophist of Byzantium, who wrote an epitome of Annals, extending to the age of Theodosius the Great. *Suidas.*——A celebrated mathematician. *Id.*

HELIN'GAS, a city of Hispania Tarraconensis. *Polyb.*

HELI'NI, a people of Thesprotia. *Steph.*

HELIODO'RUS, one of the favorites of Seleucus Philopator, king of Syria. He attempted to plunder the temple of Jerusalem, about 176 years B.C., by order of his master, &c. 2 *Mac.* c. 3. v. 7 ——A Greek mathematician of Larissa. ——A famous sophist, born at Emessa in Phœnicia, in the age of Theodosius, and made bishop of Tricca in Thessaly. He is particularly known for his romance in ten books, called Æthiopica, or the history of the loves of Theagenes and Chariclea. Some suppose that the author of the Æthiopica was not the bishop. The best editions of this entertaining work are by Commelin, 8vo, Lugd. 1611, and by Bourdelot, 8vo, Paris, 1619. *Sax. Onom.* 1. p. 450. —*Fabr. B. Gr.* 5. c. 6. ——A learned Greek rhetorician in the age of *Horace. Serm.* sat. 5. v. 2.——A man who wrote a treatise on tombs. *Plut. de* 10 *Orat.*——A poet.——A geographer.——A surgeon at Rome, in Juvenal's age. *Juv.* 6. v. 372.——A mathematician of Athens. *Plin.* 34. c. 8.——A native of Larissa, a writer on Optics ——A stoic, a commentator on Aratus. For others of the same name, see *Voss. H. Gr.* p. 372.—*Lil. Gyrald.* l. 3, &c.

HELIOGAB'ALUS, HELIOGABA'LUS, ALAGAB'ALUS or ALAGAB'ALUS, a surname given to the emperor M. Aurelius Antoninus, because he had been priest of that divinity in Phœnicia. After the death of Macrinus, he was invested with the imperial purple, and the senate, however unwilling to submit to a youth only fourteen years of age, reluctantly approved of his election, and bestowed upon him the title of Augustus. Heliogabalus made his grandmother Mœsa, and his mother Semis, his colleagues on the throne; and to bestow more dignity upon the sex, he chose a senate of women, over which his mother presided, and prescribed all the models and fashions which prevailed in the empire. Rome, however, soon displayed a scene of cruelty and debauchery, and the most infamous of the populace became the most approved favourites of the prince. To insult the feelings of his subjects, he even raised his horse to the honours of the consulship, and obliged his subjects to pay adoration to the god Heliogabalus, which was a large black stone, in shape like a cone. To this ridiculous deity temples were raised at Rome, and the altars of the gods were sacrilegiously plundered to deck those of the new divinity. Heliogabalus married four wives, and moreover professed himself to be a woman, and gave himself up to one of his officers, called Hierocles, who, by stooping to infamy, became the most powerful of the favorites, and enriched himself by selling all offices and all places of honour to the people. Such licentiousness soon displeased the populace, and Heliogabalus, unable to appease the seditions of the soldiers, hid himself in the filth and excrements of the camp, where he was found in the arms of his mother. His head was severed from his body the 10th of March, A.D. 222, in the 18th year of his age, after a reign of three years, nine months and four days. He was succeeded by Alexander Severus. The cruelties of this profligate youth were as conspicuous as his licentiousness. He burthened his subjects with the most oppressive taxes; his halls were covered with carpets of gold and silver tissue, and his mats were made with the down of hares, and with the soft feathers which were found under the wings of partridges. He was fond of covering his shoes with precious stones, to draw the admiration of the people as he walked along the streets, and he was the first Roman who ever wore a dress of silk. He often invited the most common of the people to share his banquets, and sometimes made them sit down on large bellows full of wind, which, by suddenly emptying themselves, threw the guests on the ground, and then left them a prey to wild beasts. He often tied some of his favorites to a large wheel, and was particularly delighted to see them whirled round like Ixion, and sometimes suspended in the air, or sunk beneath the water. [There is a bust of Heliogabalus in the Museum of the Capitol.]——A deity among the Phœnicians.

HELIOP'OLIS, now Matarea, a famous city of Lower Ægypt, in which was a temple sacred to the sun. The inhabitants worshipped a bull called Mnevis, with the same ceremonies as the Apis of Memphis. Apollo had an oracle there. *Cic. N. D.* 3. c. 21.—*Ptol.* 4. c. 5.—*Plin.* 36. c. 26.—*Strab.* 17.—*Diod.* 1.——A small village without the Delta, near the city of Babylon.——A town of Syria, at the east of mount Libanus. It is now Balbec. *Plin.* 5. c. 22.

HELIOTRO'PIUM, a city of Thessaly. *Polyb.*

HEL'ISOS, a river of Attica. *Stat. Theb.* 4. v. 52.

HELIS'SON, a town and river of Arcadia. *Paus.* 8. c. 29.

HELIS'YCI, a people of Lignria. *Steph.*

HE'LIUM, a name given to the mouth of the Maese in Germany. *Plin.* 4. c. 15.

HE'LIUS, a celebrated favorite of the emperor Nero, put to death by order of Galba, for his cruelties. *Dion. Cass. in Ner.*——A gladiator mentioned by *Martial*, l. 5. epigr. 25.

HE'LIX, a noble youth, slain by Nestor in the contest between Perses and Æetes.

HELIXOE'A, an island of the Hyperboreans, not less than Sicily. *Steph.*—*Hecat.*

HELIX'US, a river of Cos. *Strab.* 8.

HELLANI'CE, a sister of Clitus, nurse to Alexander the Great. *Curt.* 8. c. 1.

HELLAN'ICUS or HELLANI'CUS, a celebrated Greek historian, born at Mitylene. He wrote a history of the ancient kings of the earth, with an account of the founders of the most famous towns in every kingdom, and died B.C. 411, in the 85th year of his age. His works have unfortunately perished. *Paus.* 2. c. 3.—*Aul. Gell.* 15. c. 23.—*Cic. de Orat.* 2. c. 53.

HELLAN'ICUS, a brave officer rewarded by Alexander *Curt.* 5. c. 2.——An historian of Miletus, who wrote a description of the earth. *Voss. Hist. Gr.* 1. c. 1. l. 4. c. 5. Also Hellani'cus.

HELLANOC'RATES, a man of Larissa, abused by Archelaus. *Arist. Polit.* 5. c. 10.

HEL'LAS, a name anciently applied to the territories of Acarnania, Attica, Ætolia, Doris, Locris, Bœotia, and also to all Greece. It received this name from Hellen son of Deucalion, and now forms a part of Livadia. *Plin.* 4. c. 7.—*Strab.* 8. —*Mela*, 2. c. 3.—*Paus.* 2. c. 20.

HEL'LAS, a beautiful woman, mentioned by Horace as beloved of Marius. The lover killed her in a fit of passion, and afterwards destroyed himself. *Horat.* 2. sat. 3. v. 277.

HEL'LE, a daughter of Athamas and Nephele, sister to Phryxus. She fled from her father's house accompanied by her brother, to avoid the cruel oppression of her mother-in-law Ino. According to some accounts she was carried through the air on a golden ram, which her mother had received from Neptune, and in her passage she became giddy and fell from her seat into that part of the sea which from her received the name of Hellespont. Others say that she was carried on a cloud or rather upon a ship, from which she fell into the sea and was drowned. *Vid.* Phryxus. *Ovid. Heroid.* 13, &c. *Met.* 4. fab. 14.—*Pindar. Pyth.* 4.—*Hygin. P. A.* 2. c. 20.—*Diod.* 4.—*Paus.* 9. c. 34.

HEL'LEN, son of Deucalion and Pyrrha, reigned in Phthiotis about 1495 years, B.C., and gave the name of Hellenians to his subjects. He had, by his wife Orseis, three sons; Æolus, Dorus, and Xuthus, who gave their names to the three different nations, afterwards known by the names of Æolians, Dorians, and Ionians. These last derived their name from Ion, son of Xuthus, and from the difference either of expression, or pronunciation in their respective languages, arose the different dialects well known in the Greek language. *Paus.* 3. c. 20. l. 7. c. 1.—*Diod.* 5.—*Apollod.* 1.

HELLE'NES, the inhabitants of Greece. *Vid.* Hellen.

HELLE'NIUS, a surname of Jupiter as protector of the Greeks: he was particularly worshipped under this appellation at Ægina. *Pind. Nem.* 5. v. 19.

HELLESPON'TIAS, a wind blowing from the north-east. *Plin.* 2. c. 47.

HELLESPON'TUS, now the Dardanelles, a narrow strait between Asia and Europe, near the Propontis, which is said to have received its name from Helle. *Vid.* Helle. It is about 60 miles long, and in the broadest parts, the Asiatic coast is about three miles distant from the European, and only half a mile in the narrowest, according to modern investigation; so that people can converse one with the other from the opposite shores. It is celebrated for the love and death of Hero and Leander, and for the bridge of boats which Xerxes built over it when he invaded Greece. *Strab.* 13.—*Plin.* 8. c. 32.—*Herodot.* 7. c. 34.—*Polyb.*—*Mela*, 1. c. 1.—*Ptol.* 5. c. 2.—*Ovid. Met.* 13. v. 407.—*Liv.* 31. c. 15. l. 33. c. 33.—The country along the Hellespont on the Asiatic coast, bore the same name. *Cic. Verr.* 1. c. 24. *Fam.* 13. ep. 53.—*Strab.* 12.—*Plin.* 5. c. 30.

HELLEVIO'NES, HELUÆ'ONES or HELLU'SII, a people of Germany. *Ptol.*—*Tac. Germ.* c. 46.

HELLO'PIA, a small country of Epirus, near Dodona. The people were called Hellopes. *Strab.* 7.—*Plin.* 4. c. 12.

HELLO'TIA, two festivals, one of which was observed in Crete, in honor of Europa, whose bones were then carried in solemn procession with a myrtle garland called ἑλλωτις, no less than twenty cubits in circumference. The other festival was celebrated at Corinth with games and races, where young men entered the lists and generally ran, carrying burning torches in their hands. This festival was instituted in honor of Minerva, surnamed Hellotis, ἀπὸ τοῦ ἕλους, *from a certain pond* of Marathon, where one of her statues was erected, or ἀπὸ τοῦ ἑλεῖν τὸν ἵππον τὸν Πήγασον, because by her assistance Bellerophon took and managed the horse Pegasus, which was, according to some, the original cause of the institution of the festival. Others derive the name from Hellotis, a Corinthian woman, from the following circumstance; when the Dorians and the Heraclidæ invaded Peloponnesus, they took and burnt Corinth, whilst the terrified inhabitants, and particularly the women, escaped by flight, except Hellotis and her sister Eurytione, who took shelter in Minerva's temple, relying for safety upon the sanctity of the place. When this was known, the Dorians set fire to the temple, and the two sisters perished in the flames. This wanton act of cruelty was followed by a dreadful plague, and the Dorians, to alleviate the misfortunes which they suffered, were directed by the oracle to appease the manes of the two sisters, and therefore they raised a new temple to the goddess Minerva, and established the festivals which bore the name of one of the unfortunate women. *Sch. Pind. Ol.* 13.—*Gyrald. Hist. D.* 11.—*Athen.* Δειπνοσοφ. l. 15.

HEL'NES, an ancient king of Arcadia. *Polyæn.* 1.

HELO'RIS, a general of the people of Rhegium, sent to besiege Messana, which Dionysius the tyrant defended. He fell in battle, and his troops were defeated. *Diod.* 14.

HELO'RUM, HELO'RUS or ELO'RUS, now Muri Ucci, a town at the mouth of a river of the same name in Sicily, at the north of the promontory of Pachynum. *Vid.* Elorus. *Virg. Æn.* 3. v. 698.—*Ital.* 11. v. 270.——A small river of Magna Græcia. *Athen.* l. 8.

HE'LOS, a place of Arcadia. *Paus.* 8. c. 36.——A town of Laconia, taken and destroyed by the Lacedæmonians under Agis the Third, of the Heraclidæ, because they refused to pay the tribute which was imposed upon them. The Lacedæmonians carried their resentment so far, that, not satisfied with the ruin of the unfortunate city, they reduced the inhabitants to the lowest and most miserable slavery, and made a law which forbade their masters, upon any pretext whatever, either to give them their liberty, or to sell them in any other country. To complete their infamy, all the slaves of the state and the prisoners of war were called by the disgraceful appellation of Helotæ, and were obliged to wear peculiar garments, which exposed them to greater contempt and degradation. They were never instructed in the liberal arts, and their cruel masters often obliged them to drink to excess, to show the free-born citizens of Sparta the beastliness and disgrace of intoxication. They once every year received a number of stripes, that by this wanton flagellation they might recollect that they were born and died slaves. The Spartans even declared war against them; but Plutarch, who, from interested motives, endeavours to palliate the guilt and cruelty of the Lacedæmons, declares that it was because they had assisted the Messenians in their war against Sparta, after it had been overthrown by a violent earthquake. This earthquake was supposed by all the Greeks to be a punishment from heaven for the cruelties which the Lacedæmonians had exercised against the Helots. In the Peloponnesian war, these miserable slaves behaved with uncommon bravery, in consequence of which they were rewarded with their liberty by the Lacedæmonians, and appeared in the temples and public shows crowned with garlands. Their joy was not, however, of long continuance, and the sudden disappearance of the 2,000 manumitted slaves was attributed to the inhumanity of the Lacedæmonians. *Thucyd.* 4.—*Pollux.* 3, c. 8.—*Strab.* 8.—*Plut. in Lyc.* &c.—*Aristot. Polit.* 2.—*Paus. Lacon.* &c.——A city of Ægypt. *Steph.*—*Strab.*

HELO'TÆ or HELO'TES, the public slaves of Sparta. *Vid.* Helos.

HELVECO'NES or HELVECO'NÆ, a people of Germany. *Tacit. Germ.* c. 43.

HELVE'TIA, a vestal virgin, struck dead by lightning in Trajan's reign.

HELVE'TII, a warlike nation of Gaul conquered by J. Cæsar. Their country is the modern Switzerland. *Cæs. Bell. G.* 1, &c.—*Tacit. Hist.* l. c. 67 & 69.

HEL'VIA, the mother of Cicero.

HEL'VIA RESI'NA, a town of Picenum.

HELVID'IA, the name of a Roman family.

HEL'VII, the inhabitants of the modern country of Viviers, were a people of Gaul on the west of the Rhone. *Plin.* 3. c. 4. *Cæs. B. G.* c. 1.

HELVIL'LUM, a town of Umbria, supposed to be the same as Suillum, now Sigillo. *Plin.* 3. c. 14.

HELVI'NA, a fountain of Aquinum, where Ceres had a temple. *Juv.* 3. v. 320.

HELVI'NUM, a river of Picenum, now Salinelli.

HEL'VIUS CIN'NA, a Roman, who, at the instigation of Cæsar, proposed a law, which, however, was not passed, to permit every man to marry as many wives as he chose. *Suet. in Cæs.* c. 52.——A poet. *Vid.* Cinna.

HEL'VIUS SUCCES'SUS, a freedman, father of the emperor Pertinax.

HEL'YMUS and PAN'OPES, two hunters at the court of Acestes in Sicily. *Virg. Æn.* 5. v. 73, &c.

HEMASI'NI, a people of Dalmatia. *Plin.* 3. c. 22.

HEMA'THION, a son of Aurora and Cephalus or Tithonus *Apollod.* 3.

HEMERE'SIA, a surname of Diana, as "the soothing goddess."

HEMEROSCOPI'UM, a city of the Celtiberi, a colony of the Phocians. *Steph.*

HEM'ERTE, an island in the Ægean Sea. *Plin.* 5. c. 31.

HEMIC'YNES, a people near the Massagetæ. *Steph.*—*Apollod. in Argon.*

HEMITH'EA, a daughter of Cycnus and Proclea. She was so attached to her brother Tenes, that she refused to abandon him when his father Cycnus exposed him on the sea. They were carried by the wind to Tenedus, where Hemithea long enjoyed tranquillity, till Achilles, captivated by her charms, offered her violence. She was rescued from his embrace by her brother Tenes, who was instantly slaughtered by the offended hero. Hemithea could not have been rescued from the attempts of Achilles, had not the earth opened and swallowed her up, after she had fervently entreated the assistance of the gods. *Vid.* Tenes. *Paus.* 10. c. 14.—*Diod.* 4.—*Tzetzes. in Lyc.* 232.

HEMO'DES or HEMO'DUS, a name of mount Taurus. *Mela*, 1. c. 15.

HE'MON. *Vid.* Hæmon.

HE'MUS. *Vid.* Hæmus.——A Grecian actor. *Juv.* 6. v. 197.

HENESI'OTUS, a region of Asiatic Sarmatia, *Ptol.*

HEN'ETI, a people of Paphlagonia, who are said to have settled in Italy near the Adriatic, where they gave the name of Venetia to their new habitation. *Liv.* 1. c. 1.—*Eurip.*

HENI'OCHI, a people of Asiatic Sarmatia, on the shores of the Euxine, at the west of Colchis, descended from Amphytus and Telechius, the charioteers (ἡνιόχοι) of Castor and Pollux, and thence called Lacedæmonii. *Mela*, 1. c. 21.—*Paterc.* 2. c. 40.—*Flacc.* 3. v. 270. l. 6. v. 42.

HEN'NA. *Vid.* Enna.

HEPHÆSTI'A, a festival in honor of Vulcan, (Ἥφαιστος) at Athens. There was then a race with torches between three young men. Each in his turn ran a race with a lighted torch in his hand, and whoever could carry it to the end of the course before it was extinguished obtained the prize. They delivered it one to the other after they finished their course, and from that circumstance we see many allusions in ancient authors, who compare the vicissitudes of human affairs to this delivering of the torch; particularly in these lines of *Lucretius*, 2:

Inque brevi spatio mutantur sæcla animantum,
Et quasi cursores vitai lampada tradunt.

Paus.—*Hesych.*—*Persii. Vet. Schol.*—*Aristoph. Schol. in Ran.*

HEPHÆSTI'A, the capital town of Lemnus, now Cochio. *Steph.*

HEPHÆSTI'ADES, a name applied to the Lipari isles as sacred to Vulcan.

HEPHÆS'TII, mountains in Lycia, which were said to be set on fire by the lightest touch of a burning torch. *Plin.* 6. c. 106.

HEPHÆS'TION, a Greek grammarian of Alexandria in the age of the emperor Verus. There remains of his compositions a treatise entitled *Enchiridion de metris & poemate*, the best edition of which is that of Pauw, 4to. Ultraj. 1726. Professor Gaisford has since published a valuable edition of this author. *Sax. Onom.* 1. p. 309.—*Fabr. B. Gr.* 1. 5. c. 7.——A Macedonian, famous for his intimacy with Alexander the Great. He accompanied the conqueror in his Asiatic expedition, and was so faithfully attached to him, that Alexander often observed that Craterus was the friend of the king, but Hephæstion the friend of Alexander. He died at Ecbatana, 325 years B.C., according to some, from excess of drinking or eating. Alexander was so inconsolable at the death of this faithful subject, that he shed tears at the intelligence, and ordered the sacred fire to be extinguished, which was never done but at the death of a Persian monarch. The physician who attended Hephæstion in his illness was accused of negligence, and by the king's order inhumanly put to death, and the public games were interrupted. The body of the deceased favorite was entrusted to the care of Perdiccas, and honored with the most magnificent funeral at Babylon. Hephæstion was so like the king in features and stature, that he was often saluted by the name of Alexander. *Curt.*—*Arrian.* 7, &c.—*Plut. in Alex.*—*Ælian. V.H.* 7. c. 8.——A Theban who wrote on the horoscope. *Voss. de Scient. Math.* c. 37. sect. 11.

HEPHÆSTIUM or HEPHÆS'TION, a city of Lycia, near Chimæra. *Plin.* 5. c. 27.

HEPITA'LIUM, a city of Trypylia. *Steph.*

HEPTANE'SIA, a city of India within the Ganges. *Ptol.*

HEPTAPHO'NOS, a portico at Olympia, which received this name because the voice was re-echoed seven times in it. *Plin.* 36. c. 15.

HEPTAP'OLIS, a district of Ægypt, which contained seven cities.

HEPTAP'OROS, a river of Troas, flowing from mount Ida. *Plin.* 5. c. 30.

HEPTAP'YLOS, a surname of Thebes in Bœotia, from its seven gates.

HEPTAYD'ATON, called by *Cicero* Septem Aquæ, a place of Latium, near the lake Fucinus.

HE'RA, the name of Juno among the Greeks.——A daughter of Neptune and Ceres when transformed into a mare. *Apollod.* 3.

HE'RA, a town of Æolia.——A town of Arcadia. *Paus* 6. c. 7.——A town of Sicily, called also Hybla Minima. *Cic. ad Attic.* 2. c. 1.

HERACLE'A or HERACLI'A, a maritime town of Sicily, at the west of Agrigentum. Minos planted a colony there when he pursued Dædalus; and the town anciently known by the name of Macara, was called from him Minoa. It was called Heraclea after Hercules, when he obtained a victory over Eryx in the neighbourhood.——A town of Macedonia, on the river Erigon.——A town in Bithynia, on the shores of the Euxine, celebrated for its naval power, and its consequence among the Asiatic states. The inhabitants conveyed home in their ships the 10,000 at their return.——A town in Crete.——A town in Parthia.——A town in Pontus.——A town in Phthiotis, near Thermopylæ, called also Trachinea, to distinguish it from others.——A town in Lucania, near the river Aciris, on the bay of Tarentum. *Cic. Arch.* 4.——A town in Syria, on the Mediterranean, a little at the south of the mouth of the river Orontes.——A town in Chersonesus Taurica.——A town in Thrace, called also Perinthus, on the shores of the Propontis. There were also three cities of this name in Ægypt. There were no less than forty cities of this name in different parts of the world, all built in honor of Hercules, from whom the name is derived.

HERACLE'A, a festival at Athens celebrated every fifth year in honor of Hercules. The Thisbians and Thebans in Bœotia observed a festival of the same name, in which they offered apples to the god. This custom of offering apples arose from this circumstance. It was always usual to offer sheep, but the overflowing of the river Asopus prevented the votaries of the god from observing it with the ancient ceremony; and as the word μῆλον signifies both an *apple* and a *sheep*, some youths, acquainted with the ambiguity of the word, offered apples to the god with much sport and festivity. To represent the sheep they raised an apple upon four stick as the legs, and two more were placed at the top to represent the horns of the victim. Hercules was delighted with the ingenuity of the youths, and the festivals were ever after continued with the offering of apples instead of sheep. *Pollux*, 8. c. 9.—There was also a festival of the same name observed at Sicyon, in honor of Hercules. It continued two days, the first was called ὀνόμασας, the seond ἡράκλεια.—At a festival of the same name at Cos, the priest officiated with a mitre on his head, and in women's apparel.—At Lindus a solemnity of the same name was also observed, and at the celebration nothing was heard but execrations and profane words, and whosoever accidentally dropped any other words was accused of having profaned the sacred rites.

HERACLE'A, a daughter of Hiero, tyrant of Sicily, &c.

HERAC'LEON, a grammarian of Ægypt, who wrote commentaries on Homer and the lyric poets. *Steph.*

HERACLEO'TES, a surname of Dionysius the philosopher.——A philosopher of Heraclea, who, like his master Zeno, and all the Stoics, firmly believed that pain was not an evil. A severe illness, attended with acute pains, obliged him to renounce his principles, and at the same time the philosophy of the Stoics, about 264 years B.C. He became afterwards a strong supporter of the Cyrenaic sect, which placed the *summum bonum* in pleasure. He wrote some poetry, and chiefly treatises of philosophy. *Diog. in Vit.*

HERAC'LEUM or HERACLE'UM, a promontory

of Cappadocia, now Capo di Limon. *Strab.* l. 12. ——A town of Ægypt, near Canopus, on the western mouth of the Nile, to which it gave its name. *Diod.* 1.—*Tacit. Ann.* 2. c. 60.—*Strab.* 2 & 17. ——The port town of Gnossus in Crete.——A town of Thessaly on the Sinus Thermaicus, at the north of the mouth of the river Peneus.

HERACLIA'NUS, one of the officers of Honorius, put Stilicho to death A.D. 408, and received in reward the government of Africa. He afterwards revolted, and was put to death A D. 413.

HERACLI'DÆ, the descendants of Hercules, greatly celebrated in ancient history. Hercules at his death left to his son Hyllus all the rights and claims which he had upon the Peloponnesus, and permitted him to marry Iole, as soon as he came of age. The posterity of Hercules were not more kindly treated by Eurystheus than their father had been, and they were obliged to retire for refuge from his tyrannical persecution, to the court of Ceyx, king of Trachinia. Eurystheus pursued them thither; and Ceyx, afraid of his resentment, begged the Heraclidæ to depart from his dominions. From Trachinia they came to Athens, where Theseus, the king of the country, who had accompanied their father in some of his expeditions, received them with great humanity, and assisted them against their common enemy Eurystheus. In the invasion of the country, Eurystheus was killed by the hand of Hyllus himself, and his children perished with him, and all the cities of the Peloponnesus became the undisputed property of the Heraclidæ. Their triumph, however, was short, their numbers were lessened by a pestilence, and the oracle informed them that they had taken possession of the Peloponnesus before the gods permitted their return. Upon this they abandoned the Peloponnesus, and came to settle in the territories of the Athenians, where Hyllus, obedient to his father's commands, married Iole, the daughter of Eurytus. Soon after, still anxious to recover the Peloponnesus, he consulted the oracle, and the ambiguity of the answer determined him to make a second attempt. He challenged to single combat Atreus, the successor of Eurystheus on the throne of Mycenæ, and it was mutually agreed that the undisturbed possession of the Peloponnesus should be ceded to whosoever defeated his adversary. Echemus accepted the challenge for Atreus, and Hyllus was killed in the encounter, and the Heraclidæ a second time departed from Peloponnesus. Cleodæus, the son of Hyllus, made the third attempt, and was equally unsuccessful, and his son, Aristomachus, some time after, met with the same unfavorable reception, and perished in the field of battle. Afterwards Aristodemus, Temenus, and Chresphontes, the three sons of Aristomachus, encouraged by the more expressive and less ambiguous word of an oracle, and desirous to avenge the death of their progenitors,' assembled a numerous force, and with a fleet invaded Peloponnesus. Their expedition was attended with success, and, after some decisive battles, they became masters of the peninsula, which they divided among themselves two years after. The recovery of the Peloponnesus by the descendants of Hercules, forms an interesting epoch in ancient history, which is universally believed to have happened 80 years after the Trojan war, or 1104 B.C. This conquest was totally achieved about 120 years after the first attempt of Hyllus. *Apollod.* 2. c. 7. &c.—*Herodot.* 9. c. 26.—*Paus.* 1. c. 17.—*Paterc.* 1. c. 2.—*Clemen. Alex. Strom.* 1.—*Thucyd.* 1. c. 12, &c.—*Diod.* 1, &c.—*Aristot. de Rep.* 7. c. 17.

HERACLI'DES, a philosopher of Heraclea in Pontus, for some time disciple of Seusippus and Aristotle He wished it to be believed that he was carried into heaven the very day of his death, and, to render it the more credible, he begged one of his friends to put a serpent into his bed. The serpent, however, terrified at the noise made by the numerous visitors, escaped from his bed before the philosopher had expired. He lived about 335 years B.C. *Cic. Tusc.* 5. *Ad. Quint.* 3.—*Diog. in Pyth.* ——An historian of Pontus, surnamed *Lembus*, who flourished B.C. 177.——A man who, after the retreat of Dionysius the Younger from Sicily, raised cabals against Dion, in whose hands the sovereign power was lodged. He was put to death by Dion's order. *C. Nep. in Dion.*——A youth of Syracuse, engaged in the battle in which Nicias and the Athenians were defeated.——A son of Agathocles. *Polyæn.* 1. 5. *com.* 4.——A man placed over a garrison at Athens by Demetrius. *Idem.* l. 5.——A sophist of Lycia, who opened a school at Smyrna, in the age of the emperor Severus. *Philostrat.*——A painter of Macedonia, in the reign of king Perseus. *Plin.*——An architect of Tarentum, intimate with Philip king of Macedonia. He fled to Rhodes on pretence of a quarrel with Philip, and set fire to the Rhodian fleet. *Polyæn.* 5.——A celebrated grammarian of Mopsus in Cilicia. *Steph.* For an account of persons of this name, see *Voss. H. Gr.* l. 1. c. 9 & 20. l. 34.

HERACLI'TUS, a celebrated Greek philosopher of Ephesus, who flourished about 500 years before the Christian era. His father's name was Blyson or Heracion. Naturally of a melancholy disposition, he passed his time in a solitary and unsocial manner, and received the appellation of the obscure philosopher, (σκοτεινός,) and of the mourner, from his custom of weeping at the follies, frailty, and vicissitude of human affairs. He employed his time in writing different treatises, and one particularly, in which he supported that there was a fatal necessity, and that the world was created from fire, which he deemed a god omnipotent and omniscient. His opinions about the origin of things were adopted by the Stoics, and Hippocrates entertained the same notions of a supreme power. Heraclitus deserves the appellation of man-hater for the rusticity with which he answered the polite invitations of Darius king of Persia. To remove himself totally from the society of mankind, he retired to the mountains, where, for some time, he fed on grass, in common with the wild inhabitants of the place. Such a diet was soon productive of a dropsical complaint, and the philosopher, weakened by disease, condescended to revisit the town. The enigmatical manner in which he consulted the physicians made his applications unintelligible, and he was left at last to depend for cure upon himself. He fixed his residence in a dunghill, in hopes that the continual warmth which proceeded from it might remove his complaint, and restore him to the enjoyment of his former health. But the attempt proved ineffectual, and he died in the 60th year of his age. Some say that he was torn to pieces by dogs. *Diog. in Vitâ.*—*Clemens. Alex. Strom.* 5.—*Morer. Dict. Hist.* [There is a bust of this philosopher in the Capitol; and another, with his name inscribed, at Florence.]——A lyric poet.——A writer of Halicarnassus, intimate with Callimachus. He was remarkable for the elegance of his style.——A native of Lesbus, who wrote a history of Macedonia.——A writer of Sicyon, &c. *Plut. de flum.* A book, *de incredibilibus*, written by a person of this name, was edited by Leo Allatius, 1641. *Voss. H. Gr.* l. 4. p. 515.

HERACLI'US or HERACLEUS, a river of Greece. *Paus.* 10. c. 37.

HERAC'LIUS, a brother of Constantine the Fourth, &c. ——A Roman emperor, A.D. 610.

HERÆ'A, festivals at Argos in honor of Juno, who was the patroness of that city. They were also observed by the colonies of the Argives which had been planted at Samus and Ægina. There were always two processions made on the occasion to the temple of the goddess, without the city walls. The first was of the men in armour, the second of the women, among whom the priestess, a woman of the first quality, was drawn in a chariot by white oxen. Hence the sacrifice is often called ἑκατόμβαια, and sometimes λεχέρνα, from λέχος, *a bed*, because Juno presided over marriages, births, &c. There was a festival of the same name, in Elis, celebrated every fifth year, in which sixteen matrons wove a garment for the goddess. There were also others ininstituted by Hippodamia, who had received assistance from Juno when she married Pelops. Sixteen matrons, each attended by a maid, presided at the celebration. The candidates for the honors of the day were young virgins, who, being divided into classes, according to their age, ran races each in their order, beginning with the youngest. The habit of all was exactly the same, their hair was dishevelled, and their right shoulder bare to the breast, with coats reaching no lower than the knee. She who obtained the victory was rewarded with crowns of olive, and obtained a part of the ox that was offered in sacrifice, and was permitted to dedicate her picture to the goddess. There was also a solemn day of mourning at Corinth, which bore the same name, in commemoration of Medea's children, who were buried in Juno's temple. They had been slain by the Corinthians; who, as it is reported, to avert the scandal which accompanied so barbarous a murder, presented Euripides with a large sum of money to write a play, in which Medea is represented as the murderer of her own children. *Schol. in Lycoph.*—Another festival of the same name at Pallene, with games, in which the victor was rewarded with a garment called πελληνικὴ χλαῖνα.——A town of Arcadia.

HERÆ'I MON'TES, a chain of mountains about the middle of Sicily. *Diod.* 14.

HERÆ'UM, a temple and grove sacred to Juno, situate between Argos and Mycenæ.——A town of Thrace, near Perinthus. *Herod.*—*Steph.*——A town of Sardinia. *Ptol.*

HE'RAS, the name of a physician mentioned by *Martial*, l. 6. epigr. 78.

HERBES'SUS or ERBES'SUS, a town of Sicily at the north of Agrigentum, built by a Phœnician or Carthaginian colony. *Sil.* 14. v. 265.

HER'BITA, an inland town of Sicily, west of Ætna. *Diod. Sic.* l. 12.—*Cic. Verr.* 2. c. 64. l. 3. 32.

HERBULEN'SES. a people of Sicily. *Plin.* 3. c. 9.

HERCE'US, (*ab* ἕρκος), an epithet given to Jupiter, because he was worshipped in the *impluvium* or open court in the middle of the house. *Ovid. Ib.* 286.—*Lucan.* 9. v. 979.—*Athen.* 4. p. 189.

HERCULA'NEA VI'A, a mound raised between the Lucrine lake and the sea, called also *Herculeum iter*. *Sil.* 12. v. 118.

HERCULA'NEUM, HERCULA'NIUM, HERCULA'NUM, HERCULEN'SE OPPIDUM, and HERCULE'A URBS, a town of Campania swallowed up, with Pompeii, by an earthquake, produced from an eruption of mount Vesuvius, August 24th, A.D. 79, in the reign of Titus. After being buried under the lava for more than 1600 years, these famous cities were discovered in the beginning of the 18th century; Herculaneum in 1713, about 24 feet under ground, by laborers digging for a well, and Pompeii 40 years after, about 12 feet below the surface, and from the houses and the streets, which in a great measure remain still perfect, have been drawn busts, statues, manuscripts, paintings, and utensils, which do not a little contribute to enlarge our notions concerning the history, the architecture, and the particular arrangements of the ancients, and to develope many classical obscurities. The valuable antiquities so miraculously recovered, are preserved in the Museum of Portici, a small town in the neighbourhood, and the engravings, &c ably taken from them have been munificently presented to the different learned bodies of Europe. *Seneca, Nat. Q.* 6. c. 1 & 26.—*Cic. Att.* 7. ep. 3.—*Mela*, 2. c. 4.—*Paterc.* 2 c. 16.

HER'CULES, a celebrated hero, who, after death, was ranked among the gods, and received divine honors. According to the ancients there were many persons of the same name. Diodorus mentions three, Cicero six, and Varro extends the number to no less than forty-three. Of all these, the son of Jupiter and Alcmena, generally called the Theban, is the most celebrated, and to him, as may be easily imagined, the actions of all the others have been attributed. *Vid.* Alcmena. Hercules was brought up at Tirynthus; or, according to Diodorus, at Thebes, and before he had completed his eighth month, the jealousy of Juno, intent upon his destruction, sent two large snakes to devour him. The child, not terrified at the sight of the serpents, boldly seized them, one in each hand, and squeezed them to death, while his brother Iphiclus alarmed the house with his frightful shrieks. *Vid.* Iphiclus. Hercules was early instructed in the liberal arts, and Castor, the son of Tyndarus, taught him how to fight, Eurytus how to shoot with a bow and arrow, Autolycus to drive a chariot, Linus to play on the lyre, and Eumolpus to sing. He, like the rest of his illustrious contemporaries, soon after became the pupil of the centaur Chiron, and under him he perfected his education, and rendered himself the most valiant and accomplished of the age. In the 18th year of his age he resolved to deliver the neighbourhood of mount Cithæron from a huge lion which preyed on the flocks of Amphitryon, his supposed father; and which terrified the inhabitants and laid waste the adjacent country. He went to the court of Thespius, king of Thespis, who shared in the general calamity, and he received there the most hospitable treatment, and was entertained during fifty days. The fifty daughters of the king became all mothers by Hercules, during his stay at Thespis. After he had destroyed the lion of mount Cithæron, he delivered his country from the disgraceful tribute of a hundred oxen which it annually paid to Erginus. *Vid.* Erginus. Such public services became universally known, and Creon, who then sat on the throne of Thebes, rewarded the patriotic deeds of Hercules by giving him his daughter in marriage, and entrusting him with the government of his kingdom. As Hercules by the irrevocable decree of Jupiter was subjected to the power of Eurystheus, (*vid.* Eurystheus.) and obliged to obey him in every respect, Eurystheus, acquainted with his successes and rising power, ordered him to appear at Mycenæ and perform the labors which by priority of birth he was empowered to impose upon him. Hercules indignantly refused, and Juno, to punish his disobedience, rendered him so delirious that he killed his own children by Megara, supposing them to be the offspring of Eurystheus. *Vid.* Megara. When he recovered the use of his senses, he was so struck with the misfortunes that had proceeded from his insanity, that he concealed himself and retired from the society of men for some time. He afterwards consulted the oracle of Apollo, and was informed that he must be subservient for twelve years to the will of Eurystheus, in compliance with the commands of Jupiter; and that after he had achieved the most celebrated labors he should receive the reward due to his glorious actions, and be reckoned in the number of the gods. So plain and expressive an answer determined him to go to Mycenæ, and to bear with fortitude whatever gods or men imposed upon him. Eurystheus seeing so great a man totally subjected to him, and apprehensive of so powerful an enemy, commanded him to achieve a number of enterprizes the most difficult and arduous ever known, generally called the twelve labors of Hercules. The favor of the gods had completely armed him against every danger, when he undertook these remarkable labors. He had received a coat of arms and helmet from Minerva, a sword from Mercury, a horse from Neptune, a shield from Jupiter, a bow and arrows from Apollo, and from Vulcan a golden cuirass and brazen buskin, with a celebrated club of brass, according to the opinion of some writers, but more generally supposed to be of wood, and cut by the hero himself in the forest of Nemea.—The first labor imposed upon Hercules by Eurystheus, was to kill the lion of Nemea, which ravaged the country near Mycenæ. The hero, unable to destroy him with his arrows, boldly attacked him with his club, pursued him to his den, and after a close and sharp engagement choked him to death in his arms. He carried the dead beast on his shoulders to Mycenæ, and ever after clothed himself with the skin as a trophy of victory. Eurystheus was so astonished at the sight of the beast, and at the courage of Hercules, that he ordered him never to enter the city gates when he returned from his expeditions, but to wait for his orders without the walls. He even made himself a brazen vessel into which he retired for security whenever Hercules returned. The second labor of Hercules, was to destroy the Lernæan hydra, which had seven heads, according to Apollodorus, 50 according to Simonides, and 100 according to Diodorus. This celebrated monster he attacked with his arrows, and soon after he came to a close engagement, and by means of his heavy club he destroyed the heads of his enemy. But this was productive of no advantage, for as soon as one head was beaten to pieces with the club, immediately two sprang up, and the labor of Hercules would have remained unfinished had not he commanded his friend Iolas immediately to burn, with a hot iron, the root of the head which he had crushed to pieces. This succeeded (*vid.* Hydra), and Hercules became victorious, opened the belly of the monster, and dipped his arrows in the gall to render the wounds which he gave fatal and incurable.--He was ordered in his third labor, to bring alive and unhurt into the presence of Eurystheus a stag, famous for its incredible swiftness, its golden horns, and brazen feet. This celebrated animal frequented the neighbourhood of Œnoe, and Hercules was employed for a whole year in continually pursuing it and at last caught it in a trap, or when tired, or according to others, by slightly wounding it and lessening its swiftness. As he returned victorious, Diana snatched the stag from him, and severely reprimanded him for molesting an animal which was sacred to her, but Hercules pleaded necessity, and by representing the commands of Eurystheus, he appeased the goddess, and again obtained possession of the beast.—The fourth labor was to bring alive to Eurystheus a wild boar which ravaged the neighbourhood of Erymanthus. In this expedition he destroyed the centaurs (*vid.* Centauri), and caught the boar by closely pursuing him through the deep snow. Eurystheus was so frightened at the sight of the boar that, according to Diodorus, he hid himself in his brazen vessel for some days.—In the fifth labor Hercules was ordered to clean the stables of Augias, where 3000 oxen had been confined many years. *Vid* Augias.—For his sixth labour he was ordered to kill the carnivorous birds which ravaged the country near the lake Stymphalis in Arcadia. *Vid.* Stymphalis.—In his seventh labor he brought alive into Peloponnesus a prodigious wild bull which laid waste the island of Crete.—In his eighth labor he was employed in obtaining the mares of Diomedes, which fed upon human flesh. He killed Diomedes, and gave him to be eaten by his mares, which he brought to Eurystheus. These celebrated animals were sent to mount Olympus by the king of Mycenæ, where they were devoured by the wild beasts; or, according to others, they were consecrated to Jupiter, and their breed still existed in the time of Alexander the Great.—For his ninth labor, he was ordered to obtain the girdle of the queen of the Amazons. *Vid.* Hippolyte.—In his tenth labor he killed the monster Geryon, king of Gades, and brought to Argos his numerous flocks, which had been fed upon human flesh. *Vid.* Geryon.—The eleventh labor was to obtain apples from the garden of the Hesperides. *Vid.* Hesperides.—The twelfth and most dangerous of his labors, was to bring upon earth the three-headed dog Cerberus. This was cheerfully undertaken by Hercules, and he descended into hell by a cave on mount Tænarus. He was permitted by Pluto to carry away his friends Theseus and Pirithous, who were condemned to punishment in hell, and Cerberus also was granted to his prayers, provided he made use of no arms, but only force, to drag him away. Hercules, as some report, carried him back to hell after he had brought him into the presence of Eurystheus. — Besides these arduous labors, which the jealousy of of Eurystheus imposed upon him, Hercules also achieved others of his own accord, equally great and celebrated. *Vid.* Cacus, Antæus, Busiris, Eryx, &c. He accompanied the Argonauts to Colchis before he delivered himself up to the king of Mycenæ, and he also assisted the gods in their wars against the giants, and it was through his powerful support alone that Jupiter obtained a victory. *Vid.* Gigantes. He conquered Laomedon, and pillaged Troy. *Vid.* Laomedon. When Iole, the daughter of Eurytus, king of Œchalia, of whom he was deeply enamoured, was refused to his entreaties, he became the prey of a second fit of insanity, and murdered Iphitus, the only one of the sons of Eurytus who favored his addresses to Iole. *Vid.* Iphitus. He was some time after purified of the murder, and his insanity ceased, but the gods persecuted him the more, and he was visited by a disorder which obliged him to apply to the oracle of Delphi for relief. The coldness with which the Pythia received him, irritated him, and he resolved to plunder Apollo's temple and carry away the sacred tripod. Apollo opposed him, and a severe conflict was begun, which nothing but the interference of Jupiter with his thunderbolts could have prevented. He was upon this told by the oracle that he must be sold as a slave, and remain three years in the most abject servitude to recover from his disorder. He complied, and Mercury, by order of Jupiter, conducted him to Omphale, queen of Lydia, to whom he was sold as a slave. Here he cleared all the country from robbers, and Omphale, who was astonished at the greatness of his exploits, at last restored him to liberty, and married him. Hercules had Agelaus, and Lamon, according to others, by Omphale, from whom Crœsus, king of Lydia was descended. He became also enamoured of one of Omphale's servants, by whom he had Alceus. After he had completed the years of his slavery, he returned to Peloponnesus, where he re-established on the throne of Sparta, Tyndarus, who had been expelled by Hippocoon. He became one of Dejanira's suitors, and married her after he had overcome all his rivals. *Vid.* Achelous. He was obliged to leave Calydon, his father-in-law's kingdom, because he had inadvertently killed a man with a blow of his fist, and it was on account of this expulsion that he was not present at the hunting of the Calydonian boar. From Calydon he retired to the court of Ceyx, king of Trachinia. In his way he was stopped by the swollen stream of the Evenus, where the centaur Nessus attempted to offer violence to Dejanira, under the perfidious pretence of conveying her over the river. Hercules perceived the distress of his wife, and killed the centaur, who, as he expired, gave her a tunic, which, as he observed, had the power of recalling a husband from unlawful love. *Vid.* Dejanira. Ceyx, king of Trachinia, received him and his wife with great marks of friendship, and purified him of the murder which he had committed at Calydon. Hercules was still mindful that he had been refused the hand of Iole, he therefore made war against her father Eurytus, and killed him, with three of his sons. Iole fell into the hands of her father's murderer, and found that she was loved by Hercules with the same affection as before. She accompanied him to mount Œta, where he was going to raise an altar and offer a solemn sacrifice to Jupiter. As he had not then the tunic in which he arrayed himself to offer a sacrifice, he sent Lichas to Dejanira, in order to provide himself a proper dress. Dejanira, informed of her husband's attachment to Iole, sent him a philter, or more probably the fatal tunic which she had received from Nessus, and Hercules as soon as he had put it on fell into a desperate distemper, and found the poison of the Lernæan hydra penetrating through his bones. He attempted to pull off the poisoned garment, but it was too late, and in the midst of the pains and tortures which he experienced, he inveighed with the most bitter imprecations against the credulity of Dejanira, the cruelty of Eurystheus, and the jealousy and hatred of Juno. As the distemper was incurable, he implored the protection of Jupiter, gave his bow and arrows to Philoctetes, and erected a large burning pile on the top of mount Œta. He spread on the pile the skin of the Nemean lion, and laid himself down upon it as on a couch, leaning his head on his club. Philoctetes, or, according to others, Pæan or Hyllus, was ordered to set fire to the pile, and the hero saw himself on a sudden surrounded with the flames without betraying any marks of fear or astonishment. Jupiter saw this melancholy scene from heaven, and told the surrounding gods that he would raise to the skies the immortal parts of a hero who had cleared the earth from so many monsters and tyrants. The gods applauded Jupiter's resolution, the pile was suddenly surrounded with a dark smoke, and after the mortal parts of Hercules had been consumed by the fire, he was carried up to heaven in a chariot drawn by four horses. Some loud claps of thunder accompanied his elevation, and his friends, unable to find either his bones or his ashes, showed their gratitude to his memory, and their sense of his glorious services, by raising an altar on the spot where the burning pile had stood. Menœtius, the son of Actor, offered him a sacrifice of a bull, a wild boar, and a goat, and enjoined the people of Opus yearly to observe the same religious ceremonies. His worship soon became as universal as his fame, and Juno, who had once persecuted him with such inveterate fury, forgot her former resentment, and gave him her daughter Hebe in marriage. Hercules has received various surnames and epithets, either from the place where his worship was established, or from the labors which he achieved. His temples were numerous and magnificent, and his divinity universally revered. No dogs or flies ever entered his temple at Rome, and that of Gades, according to Strabo, was always forbidden to women and pigs. The Phœnicians offered quails on his altars, and as it was supposed that he presided over dreams, the sick and infirm were sent to sleep in his temples, that they might receive in their dreams the agreeable presages of their approaching recovery. Among trees, the white poplar was particularly dedicated to his honor. Hercules is generally represented naked, with strong and well-proportioned limbs; he is sometimes covered with the skin of the Nemean lion, and holds a knotted club in his hands, on which he often leans. Sometimes he appears crowned with the leaves of the poplar, and holding the horn of plenty under his arm. At other times he is represented standing with Cupid, who insolently breaks to pieces his arrows and his club, to intimate the degraded state to which the passion of love reduced the hero, who suffered himself to be beaten and ridiculed by Omphale, who dressed herself in his armour while he was sitting to spin with her female servants. The children of Hercules was as numerous as the labors and difficulties which he underwent, and indeed they became so powerful soon after his death, that they alone had the courage to invade all Peloponnesus. *Vid.* Heraclidæ. He was father of Deicoon and Therimachus, by Megara; of Ctesippus, by Astydamia; of Palemon, by Autonoe; of Everes, by Parthenope; of Glycisonetes, Gyneus, and Odites, by Dejanira; of Thessalus, by Chalciope; of Thestalus, by Epicaste; of Tlepolemus, by Astyoche; of Agathyrsus, Gelon, and Scytha, by Echidna, &c. Such are the most striking characteristics of the life of Hercules, who is said to have supported for a while the weight of the heavens upon his shoulders (*vid.* Atlas), and to have separated by the force of his mighty arm the celebrated mountains which were afterwards called the boundaries of his labors. *Vid.* Abyla. He is held out by the ancients as a true pattern of virtue and piety, and as his whole life had been employed for the common benefit of mankind, he was deservedly rewarded with immortality. His judicious choice of virtue in preference to pleasure, as described by Xenophon is well known. *Diod.* 1 & 4.—*Cic. de Nat. D.* 1. 3. c. 16, &c.—*Apollod.* 1 & 2. —*Paus.* 1. 3. 5, 9 & 10.—*Hesiod. in Scut. Herc. &c.* —*Hygin.* fab. 29, 32, &c. *P.A.* 2. c. 14.—*Ovid. Met.* 9. v. 236, &c. *Amor. Trist, &c.*—*Homer. Il.* 8, &c.—*Theocrit.* 24.—*Eurip. in Herc.*—*Virg. Æn.* 8. v. 294.—*Lucan.* 3 & 6.—*Apollon.* 2.—*Dionys. Hal.* 1.—*Sophocl. in Trachin.*—*Plut. in Amphit.*—*Senec. in Herc. Furent. & Œt.*—*Plin.* 4. c. 6. 1. 11, &c.—*Philostr. Icon.* 2. c. 5.—*Arnobius.* 4.—*Capell.* 2.—*Servius in Æn.* 6. v. 803, &c. 1. 8. v. 103 & 295, &c.—*Tzetzes in Lyc.*—*Schol. Hesiod. Th.* 56 & 329. —*Schol. Hom. ad Il.* 14. v. 323.—*Sch. Apollod.* 1. v. 143.—*Euseb. præp. Ev.* 2. c. 2.—*Pisander. apud Nat. Com.* 7.—*Auson. Id.* 19.—*Quint. Calab.* 6. v. 232.—*Herodot.* 1. c. 7. 1. 2. c. 42, &c.—*Quint. Smyrn.* 6. v. 207, &c.—*Callim. Hymn. in Dian.*—*Pindar. Olymp.* od. 3.—*Ital.* 1. v. 438.—*Stat.* 2. *Theb.* v. 564.—*Mela,* 2. c. 1.—*Lucian. Dial.*—*Lactant. de Fals. Rel. & in Theb.*—*Strab.* 3. &c.—*Horat. Od. Sat. &c.* [The finest and most celebrated statue of Hercules is that by Glycon the Athenian, called the Farnese Hercules, which is at Naples. The celebrated Belvidere Torso is supposed to be also a representation of this demigod. There is also an exquisite little bronze figure, attributed to Lysippus, in the British Museum; where will be found a head similar to the Farnese, but finer, and believed to be part of a statue from which that was copied by Glycon].——A son of Alexander the Great.——A surname of the emperor Commodus, &c. *Voss. de Orig. & Progr. Idol.* 1. 1 & 2. *passim.*

HERCU'LEUM, a promontory at the south eastern extremity of the country of the Brutii, now Capo di Spartivento. *Strab.* 1. 6.

Hercu'leum Fre'tum, a name given to the strait which forms a communication between the Atlantic and Mediterranean, now the strait of Gibraltar.

HERCU'LEUS, one of Agrippina's murderers. *Tacit. Ann.* 14. c. 8.

Hercu'leus La'cus, a lake of Sicily, now Lago di Leontini. *Strab.* 1. 6.

HER'CULIS COLUM'NÆ, two lofty mountains, situate one on the most southern extremities of Spain, and the other on the opposite part of Africa. They were called by the ancients, the latter Abyla and the former Calpe. They were reckoned the boundaries of the labours of Hercules, and according to ancient tradition they were joined together till they were severed by the arm of the hero, and a communication opened between the Mediterranean and Atlantic Seas. *Dionys. Perieg. Sil.* 1. v. 142.—*Mela,* 1. c. 5. 1. 2. c. 6.—*Plin.* 3. c. 1.

Her'culis Fa'num, a harbour of Melita. *Plin.* 1. 2. c. 97.

Her'culis In'sula, a small island on the coast of Spain, called also Scombraria, from the tunny fish (*scombros*) caught there. *Strab.* 3.

Her'culis In'sulæ, two islands near Sardinia. *Plin.* 3. c. 7.

Her'culis Labro'nis *vel* Libur'ni Por'tus, a sea-port town in Italy, on the Tyrrhene Sea, now Leghorn.

Her'culis Lu'cus, a wood in Germany, sacred to Hercules. *Tac. A.* 2. c. 12.

Her'culis Monœ'ci Por'tus, now Monaco, a sea-port town of Genoa. *Tac. H.* 3. c. 42.—*Lucan.* 1. v. 405.—*Virg. Æn.* 6. v. 830.

Her'culis Por'tus, a sea-port of the Brutii, on the western coast.

Her'culis Promonto'rium. *Vid.* Herculeum.

HERCUNIA'TES, a people of Pannonia. *Plin.* 3. c. 25.

HERCY'NA, a nymph who accompanied Ceres as she travelled over the world. She was the companion of Proserpine, who, to her astonishment, raised a fountain from under a stone where she had seen a goose, that had escaped from her hand, go and take shelter. The fountain grew into a river, and bore the name of Hercyna, on the banks of which a temple was erected, with the statue of a nymph holding a goose in her hands. *Liv.* 65. c. 27.—*Paus.* 9. c. 39.

HERCYN'IA SILVA, HERCYN'IUS SALTUS or **HERCYN'IUM JUGUM**, a celebrated forest of ancient Germany, which, according to Cæsar, required nine days' journey to cross it; and which in some parts was found without any boundaries, though travelled over for sixty days successively. It extended to the modern countries of Switzerland, Basil, Spires, Transylvania, and a great part of Russia. In length of time the trees were rooted up, and when population increased, the greatest part of it was made habitable. *Cæs. Bell. G.* 6. c. 24.—*Mela,* 3. c. 3.—*Paterc.* 2.—*Seneca in Medeâ.*—*Claudian. de Bell. Get.* 330.—*Strab.* 4.—*Liv.* 5. c. 54.—*Tacit. G.* 30. *An.* 2. c. 45.—*Cluver. Antiq. Ger.* 3. c. 47.—*Dalechamp. ad Plin.* 16. c. 2.

HERDO'NIA, a small inland town of Apulia between the rivers Aufidus and Cerbalus. *Ital.* 1. v. 568.—*Strab.* 1. 6.

HERDO'NIUS, a man put to death by Tarquin because he had boldly spoken against him in a public assembly, &c.

HERE'A, a town of Arcadia on an eminence, the bottom of which was watered by the Alpheus. It was built by Hereus son of Lycaon, and was said to produce a wine possessed of such unusual properties, as to give fecundity to women, and cause madness in men. *Ælian. V. H.* 13. c. 6.—*Plin.* 14. c. 18.—*Paus.* 8. c. 24,—*Ptol.* 3. c. 16.

HE'REN, a mountain of Mauritania Cæsariensis. *Ptol.*

HEREN'NIUS, an officer of Sertorius defeated by Pompey, &c. *Plut.*——A centurion sent in pursuit of Cicero by Antony. He overtook the orator, and cut off his head. *Plut. in Cic.*——A Samnite general, &c.——A tribune, by whom a law was proposed to adopt Clodius among the plebeians. *Cic.* 1. *Att.* 18.

Heren'nius Ca'ius, a man to whom Cicero dedicates his book *de Rhetorica*, a work attributed by some to Cornificius.

Heren'nius Gal'lus, a lieutenant of the first legion, ill treated by his soldiers, &c. *Tac. Hist.* 4. c. 19, &c.

Heren'nius Phi'lo, a Phœnician who wrote a book on Adrian's reign. He also composed a treatise divided into twelve parts, concerning the choice of books, &c.

Heren'nius Sene'cio, a Roman historian under Domitian. *Tacit. Agric.* 2, &c.—*Voss. de H. Lat.* p. 154.

HERES'IDES, the priestesses of Juno at Argos. *Joh. Marsh. Can. Chron.*

HE'REUS, a son of Lycaon, who founded a city in Arcadia called Herea. *Paus.* 8. c. 24

HERIL'LUS, a philosopher of Chalcedon, disciple of Zeno. *Diog. in Zen.—Cic. Acad.* 4. c. 42. *Fin.* 5. c. 25.

HER'ILUS, a king of Præneste, son of the nymph Feronia. As he is said to have received three lives from his mother, he was killed three times by Evander. *Virg. Æn.* 8. v. 563. & *Servius loco.*

HE'RIUS or **HERI'US**, a river of Gallia Lugdunensis. *Ptol.*

HERMAR'CHUS, a native of Mitylene, successor and disciple of Epicurus, B.C. 267. *Laert.* 10, c. 21.—*Cic. Fin.* 30. *Acad.* 4. c. 30.

HER'MÆ, statues of Mercury in the streets of the city of Athens. *C. Nep. in Alcib.—Cic. ad Att.* 1. ep. 4 & 8. [Many of these statues remain; there is one in the British Museum.]

Her'mæ, two youths who attended those who consulted the oracle of Trophonius. *Paus.* 9. c. 39.

HERMÆ'A, a festival in Crete in honor of Mercury, when the masters waited upon the servants. It was also observed at Athens and Babylon. *Paus.* 8. c. 14.—*Athen.* διπνοσοφ. 14.—*Æsch. in Timarch.*

HERMÆ'UM, a promontory at the east of Carthage; the most northern point of Africa, now Cape Bon. —*Liv.* 29. c. 27.—*Strab.* 17.

HERMAG'ORAS, a famous rhetorician of Æolis, who came to settle at Rome in the age of Augustus. *Cic. Br.* 76. *Inv.* 1. c. 6 & 51.——A philosopher of Amphipolis who wrote many dialogues. *Suidas.*——A famous orator and philosopher. *Cic. de clar. orator.*

HERMAN'DICA, a town of the Vaccæi in Spain. *Liv.* 21. c. 5.—*Polyb.* 3.

HERMANDU'RI. *Vid.* Hermunduri.

HERMAN'DUS, a river of Arachosia. It is called Erymanthus by *Polybius*, l. 2.

HERMAPHRODI'TUS, son of Venus and Mercury, educated on mount Ida by the Naiades. At the age of 15 he began to travel to acquire knowledge and to gratify his curiosity. When he came to Caria, he bathed himself in a fountain, and Salmacis, the nymph who presided over it, became enamoured of him and attempted to gain his affections. Hermaphroditus continued deaf to all entreaties, and Salmacis, endeavouring to obtain by force what was denied to prayers, closely embraced him, and entreated the gods to make them two but one body. Her prayers were heard, and Hermaphroditus begged the gods that all who bathed in that fountain might become effeminate. *Ovid. Met.* 4. v. 347.—*Hygin.* fab. 271.—*Martial.* 10. epigr. 4.—*Luciani Somn.—Plat. in Sympos.—Cæl. Rh.* 15. c. 10. [There are three very fine recumbent statues of Hermaphroditus. One at Florence, and two in the Borghese collection, now at Paris. That which was in the Palazzo Borghese is the best.]

HER'MAS, surnamed the Shepherd, was an ancient father of the church, who is supposed to have lived in the time of the Apostles.

HERMATHE'NA, a statue which represented Mercury and Minerva united in the same body. This statue was generally placed in schools where eloquence and philosophy were taught, because these two deities presided over the arts and sciences.

HERMATOT'ROPHI, a people near Margiana. *Plin.*

HERME'AS, a tyrant of Mysia, who revolted from Artaxerxes Ochus, B.C. 350. *Diod. Sic.* l. 6.—*Polyæn.* l. 6, &c.——A general of Antiochus, put to death by him on suspicion of treason. *Polyb.*

HERME'IAS, a native of Methymna, who wrote a history of Sicily. *Athen.* 10. c. 21. *Diodorus Siculus*, l. 15. calls him Ermæus.

HER'MES, the name of Mercury among the Greeks *Vid.* Mercurius.——A famous gladiator. *Martial.* 5. epigr. 25.——An Ægyptian philosopher. *Vid.* Mercurius Trismegistus.

HERMESI'ANAX, an elegiac poet of Colophon, son of Agoneus. He was so popular among his countrymen that they publicly honored him with a statue. He had written three books of elegies dedicated to Leontium, a woman celebrated for her learning as well as her beauty. Some fragments of his works are quoted by Athenæus. *Paus.* 6, c. 17.—*Athen.* 13.—*Gyrald. P H.* 3.——A native of Cyprus, who wrote a history of Phrygia. *Plut. de flum.*

HER'MIAS or **HERMI'AS**, a Galatian philosopher in the second century. His *irrisio philosophorum gentilium*, was printed with Justin Martyr's works, fol. Paris, 1615 and 1636, and with the Oxford edition of Tatian, 8vo, 1700.

HERMIN'IUS, a general of the Hermanni, who routed Varos with three legions. *Tac. Hist.* 3. c. 42. ——A Roman who bravely defended a bridge with Cocles against the army of Porsenna. *Liv.* 2. c. 10. ——A Trojan killed by Catillus in the Rutulian war. *Virg. Æn.* 11. v. 642.

Hermin'ius Mons, the chief mountain of Lusitania.

HERMI'ONE or **HARMO'NIA**, a daughter of Mars and Venus, who married Cadmus. The gods, except Juno, honored her nuptials with their presence, and she received, as a present, a rich veil and a splendid necklace which had been made by Vulcan. She was changed into a serpent with her husband Cadmus, and placed in the Elysian fields. *Apollod.* 3.—*Ovid. Met.* 4. fab. 13.—*Hygin.* fab. 6, 148 & 159.—*Diod.* 5.—*Paus.* 9. c. 16.

Hermi'one, a daughter of Menelaus and Helen. She was privately promised in marriage to Orestes the son of Agamemnon; but her father, ignorant of this pre-engagement, gave her hand to Pyrrhus the son of Achilles, whose great services he had experienced in the Trojan wnr. Pyrrhus, at his return from Troy, carried home Hermione, and married her. Hermione, tenderly attached to her cousin Orestes, looked with horror upon her forced conneetion with Pyrrhus. According to others, however, Hermione received the addresses of Pyrrhus with pleasure, and even reproached Andromache, his concubine, with stealing his affections from her. Her jealousy of Andromache, according to some, induced her to unite herself to Orestes, and to destroy Pyrrhus. She gave her hand to Orestes after this murder, and received the kingdom of Sparta as a dowry. *Homer. Odyss.* 4.—*Eurip. in Andr. & Orest.—Ovid. Heroid.* 8.—*Dictys. Cret.* 6.—*Coluthus de Rap. Hel.—Propert.* 1. el. 4.

Hermi'one, a town of Argolis, where Ceres had a famous temple. The inhabitants lived by fishing. The descent to hell from their country was considered so short that no money, according to the usual rite of burial, was put into the mouth of the dead to be paid to Charon for their passage. The sea on the neighbouring coast was called Hermonicus Sinus, now Golfo de Napoli de Romania. *Plin.* 4. c. 5.—*Ptol.* 3. c. 16.—*Virg. in Ciri.* 472.—*Strab.* 8.—*Mela*, 2. c. 3.—*Paus.* 2. c. 34.——A city near the Riphæan mountains. *Orph. in Arg.*

HERMION'ICUS SI'NUS. *Vid.* Hermione.

HERMIP'PUS, a freedman, disciple of Philo, in the reign of Adrian, by whom he was greatly esteemed. He wrote five books upon dreams, and other works. *Tertull. de Anim.* c. 48.—*Origen. cont. Cels.* l. 1, &c.——A man who accused Aspasia, the mistress of Pericles, of impiety and prostitution. He was son of Lysis, and distinguished himself as a poet by 40 theatrical pieces and other compositions, some of which are quoted by *Athenæus. Gyrald. Poet. Hist.* 7.—*Plut.*——A Peripatetic philosopher of Smyrna, who flourished B. C. 210. *Joseph. cont. Apion.—Diog. Laert.—Origen.—Suidas, &c.*

HERMOCHE'MIA, a name of Ægypt. *Hesych.—Voss. de Idol.* l. 1. c. 2.

HERMOC'RATES, a general of Syracuse, against Nicias the Athenian. His lenity towards the Athenian prisoners was looked upon by his countrymen as treacherous. He was in consequence banished from Sicily without even a trial, and he was murdered as he attempted to return back to his country, B.C. 408. *Plut. in Nic. &c.*——A sophist celebrated for his rising talents. He died in the 28th year of his age, in the reign of the emperor Severus. *Philostrat.*——The father-in-law of Dionysius, tyrant of Sicily. *Polyæn.* l. 5. ——A Rhodian employed by Artaxerxes to bribe the Grecian states, &c.——A sophist, preceptor to Pausanias the murderer of Philip. *Diod.* 16.

HERMODO'RUS, a Sicilian, pupil to Plato.——A philosopher of Ephesus, of great merit, who is said to have assisted, as interpretér, the Roman decemvirs in the composition of the ten tables of laws, which had been collected in Greece. *Cic. Tusc.* 5. c. 36.—*Plin.* 34. c. 5.——A native of Salamis, contemporary with Philo the Athenian architect. *Cic. in Orat.* 1. c. 14.——A poet who wrote a book called Νόμιμα, on the laws of different nations. *Athen*. l. 2. c. 16.——A poet mentioned by *Plutarch, in Apophthegm.*

HERMOG'ENES, an architect of Alabanda in Caria, employed in building the temple of Diana at Magnesia. He wrote a book of some merit, upon his profession. *Vitruv. præf.* l. 7.—*Fabr. B. Gr.* 4. c. 33.——A rhetorician of Tarsus in the second century, the best editions of whose *rhetorica* are that of Sturmius, 3 vols. 12mo, Argent. 1571, and that of Caspar Laurentius, Genev. 1614. He was a remarkable instance of early maturity, and early deficiency of talents, so that at the age of fifteen he excited the admiration of the learned, and at fifty-one, lost, with his memory, the faculties of speech, whence the saying *Hermogenes in pueritiâ senex, & in senectute puer.* He died A.D. 161, and it is said that his body was opened and his heart found hairy and of an extraordinary size. *Volaterran. Anthrop.* l. 15. *col.* 462.—*Sax. Onom.* l. p. 316.—*Fabr. B. Gr.* 4. c. 33 ——A lawyer in the age of Diocletian.——A musician. *Horat.* 1. sat. 3. v. 129. *Vid.* Tigellius.——A heretic of the second century. He was a native of Africa, and known as a painter and stoic philosopher. Tertullian was engaged in refuting his heretical doctrines. *Fabricius, in loco citato,* enumerates fourteen persons of this name.

HERMOG'ENES M. TIGEL'LIUS, a detractor of Horace.

HERMOGENIA'NUS, a Roman jurist who lived in the time of Constantine the Great.

HERMOLA'US, a young Macedonian among the attendants of Alexander. As he was one day hunting with the king, he killed a wild boar which was coming towards him. Alexander, who followed close behind him, was so disappointed because the beast had been killed before he could dart at it, that he ordered Hermolaus to be severely scourged. This treatment irritated Hermolaus so much, that he conspired to take away the king's life. The plot was discovered by one of the conspirators, and Alexander seized them, and asked what had impelled them to conspire to take his life. Hermolaus answered for the rest, and observed that it was unworthy of Alexander to treat his most faithful and attached friends like slaves, and to shed their blood without the least mercy. Alexander ordered him to be put to death. *Curt.* 8. c. 6.——A grammarian in the time of Justinian. *Voss. de H. Gr.* l. 2. c. 22. ——A statuary of some celebrity. *Plin.* 36. c. 5

HER'MON, a king of Lydia, who is supposed to have founded Adramythus, in Mysia, but little is known respecting him. *Plin.* 5. c. 30.—*Steph.*——A prince of the Pelasgi, &c. *Erasm in Chiliad.*

HERMONAS'SA, a city of Mysia.——A city of Asiatic Sarmatia. *Ptol.*——A city of Cappadocia. *Strab.* l. 11.

HERMON'THIS, a city of Ægypt, where Jupiter, Apollo, and Isis were worshipped. *Steph.*

HERMOP'OLIS, two towns of Ægypt, on the Nile, now Ashmunein and Demenhur. *Plin.* 5. c. 9.

HER'MOS, a village in the tribe Acamantis. *Steph.*

HERMOTI'MUS, a famous prophet of Clazomenæ. It is said that his soul separated itself from his body at particular times, and wandered in every part of the earth to explain futurity, after which it returned again and animated his frame. His wife, who was acquainted with the frequent absence of his soul, took advantage of it, and burnt his body, as if totally dead, and deprived the soul of its natural receptacle. Hermotimus received divine honors in a temple at Clazomenæ, into which it was unlawful for women to enter. *Plin.* 7. c. 52, &c.—*Lucian. in ene. Muscæ.*—*Tertull. de Anim.* 2. c. 28 & 44.—*Origen. contra. Cels.* 3.

HERMUN'DURI or HERMUNDU'RI, a people of Germany, subdued by Aurelius. Their country was situated at the north of the Danube, and they were considered by Tacitus as a tribe of the Suevi, but called, together with the Suevi, Herminones by *Pliny,* 4. c. 14. *Tacit. Ann.* 13, *extra.*—*Vell.* 2. c. 106.

HER'MUS, a river of Asia Minor, the sands of which, according to the poets, were covered with gold. It flows near Sardes, and receives the waters of the Pactolus, after which it falls into the Ægean Sea, at the north of Smyrna. It is now called Kedous or Sarabat. *Virg. G.* 2. v. 37.—*Servius ad Æn.* 7. 721.—*Ptol* 5. c. 2.—*Lucan.* 3. v. 210.—*Martial.* 8. epigr. 78.—*Sil.* 1. v. 159.—*Plin.* 5. c. 29.

HER'NICI, a people of Latium, on the banks of the Liris, celebrated for their inveterate enmity to the rising power of infant Rome. *Liv.* 9. c. 43 & 44.—*Sil.* 4. v. 226.—*Juv.* 14. v. 180.—*Dionys. Hal.* 8. c. 10.—*Virg. Æn.* 7. v. 684.—*Servius in loco.*—*Festus de V. Sig.*

HE'RO, a beautiful priestess of Nenus at Sestus, greatly enamoured of Leander, a youth of Abydus. These two lovers were so faithful to one another, that Leander in the night escaped from the vigilance of his family, and swam across the Hellespont, while Hero in Sestus directed his course across the stormy strait by holding a burning torch on the top of a high tower. Leander was at last drowned in a tempestuous night as he attempted his usual course, and Hero in despair threw herself down from her tower and perished in the sea. *Musæus. de Leand. & Hero.*—*Ovid. Heroid.* 17 & 18.—*Virg. G.* 3. v. 258.—*Lucan.* 9.—*Martial.*—*Ital.* 10.

HE'RO, a city of Ægypt, called also Hæmus, because Typhon was there killed by lightning. *Strab.* 2. p. 85, &c.

HERO'DES, son of Antipater, surnamed the Great, and Ascalonita, followed, during the civil wars of Rome, the interest of Brutus and Cassius, and afterwards that of Antony. He was made king of Judea by means of Antony, and, after the battle of Actium, he was continued in his power by his flattery and submission to Augustus. He rendered himself odious to his subjects by his cruelty, and, as he knew that the day of his death would become a day of mirth and festivity, he ordered the most illustrious of his people to be confined and murdered the very moment that he expired, that every eye in the kingdom might seem to shed tears at the death of Herod. He died in the 70th year of his age, after a reign of 40 years. *Josephus.*—*Horat.* 2. ep. 2. v. 184.

HERO'DES AN'TIPAS, a son of Herod the Great, governor of Galilæa, &c. *Joseph. Antiq.* l. 17 & 18. *de B. J.* c. 2.

HERO'DES, AGRIP'PA, a Jew, intimate with the emperor Caligula, &c. *Joseph. Antiq.* 18 & 19.—*Act. Apost.* c. 12. v. 19. This name was common to many of the Jews.

HERO'DES AT'TICUS. *Vid.* Atticus.

HERODIA'NUS, a Greek historian, who flourished A.D. 247, was born at Alexandria in Ægypt. He wrote a Roman history in eight books, from the death of Marcus Antoninus to Gordian. His style is peculiarly elegant, but it wants precision, and the work too plainly shows that the author was not a perfect master of geography, or sufficiently accurate in chronology. He is accused of being too partial to Maximinus, and too severe upon Alexander Severus. Of his works there have been several editions; that of Aldus, 1503; the Latin version of Politian, Rome, 1493, and many others. But that of Wolfius, Halæ, 1792, 8vo, is the latest and best. *Sax. Onom.* l. p. 316.—*Fabr. B. Gr.* 4. c. 39.

HERODIA'NUS Æ'LIUS, son of Apollonius Dyscolus, was a celebrated grammarian, born at Alexandria. He afterwards went to Rome, where he became a favorite with the emperor M. Antoninus, A.D. 163. He is called by *Ammianus Marcellinus,* l. 22, 16, *artium minutissimus sciscitator,* and by *Priscian, maximus auctor artis grammaticæ,* but, unfortunately, only a few fragments of his works remain. They are to be found in the Grammatici Veteres of Aldus. *Sax. Onom.* l. p. 316.—*Fabr. B. Gr.* 4. c. 39.

HEROD'ICUS, a grammarian mentioned by the *Scholiast.* on *Aristoph. Ran.*——The præceptor of Hippocrates. *Soran. in huj. vit.*—*Voss. H. Gr.* l. 1. c. 21, &c.

HEROD'ICUS CRATÆ'US, a disciple of Crates, author of many works. *Suidas.*

HERODO'RUS, a writer on the Macrones, a nation of Pontus. *Voss. H. Gr.* l. 3. p. 374.

HEROD'OTUS or EROD'OTUS, a celebrated historian of Harlicarnassus, son of Lyxus or Xylus, and Dryo. He fled to Samus when his country labored under the oppressive tyranny of Lygdamus, and travelled over Ægypt, Italy, and all Greece. He afterwards returned to Halicarnassus, and expelled the tyrant; but this patriotic deed, far from gaining the esteem and admiration of the populace, displeased and irritated them, so that Herodotus was obliged to fly to Greece from their resentment. Unable to attain honors at home, he sought for reputation in literature, and, in his 39th year, publicly repeated at the Olympic games, the history which he had composed, B.C. 445. It was received with such universal applause, that the names of the nine Muses were unanimously given to the nine books into which it is divided. This celebrated composition, which has procured its author the title of the father of history, is written in the Ionic dialect. Herodotus is among the historians what Homer is among the poets, and Demosthenes among the orators of ancient times. His style abounds with elegance, ease, and sweetness; and if there is any of the fabulous or incredible, the author candidly informs the reader that it is introduced upon the authority of others. The work is a history of the wars of the Persians against the Greeks, from the age of Cyrus to the battle of Mycale in the reign of Xerxes, and, besides this, it gives an account of the most celebrated nations in the then known world. Herodotus had written another history of Assyria and Arabia, which has unhappily perished. The life of Homer, generally attributed to him, is supposed by some not to be the production of his pen. Plutarch has accused him of malevolence towards the Greeks, an imputation which can easily be refuted. The two best editions of this great historian are that of Wesseling, fol. Amsterdam, 1763, and that of Glasgow, 9 vols. 12mo. 1761. Herodotus has appeared in an English translation by Littlebury, 2 vols.; by Beloe, 4 vols., and the three first books were also translated by the author of this work. Larcher's French translation is a valuable work. *Cic. de Leg*. 1. *De Orat*. 2. c. 30.—*Dionys. Hal*. 1.—*Quintil*. 10. c. 1. *Lucian. in Ætion*.—*Plut. de Mal. Herod*.—*Sax. Onom*. 1. p. 37.—*Fabr. B Gr*. 2. c. 20. [The finest and most authentic head of Herodotus, is a double terminus, with Thucydides, at Naples.] —— A man who wrote a treatise concerning Epicurus. *Diog*.——A Theban wrestler of Megara, in the age of Demetrius, son of Antigonus. He is said to have been six feet and a half in height, and to have eaten generally twenty pounds of flesh, with bread in proportion, at each of his meals. *Athen*. 10.——An athlete, whose victories are celebrated by *Pindar*. *Isthm*. 1.——An athlete of Clazomenæ, who obtained a victory at Olympia, for which he was honored with a statue. *Paus*. 6. c. 17. *Fabricius*, 2. c. 20. enumerates fifteen persons of this name.

HER'OES or HERO'ES, a name which was given by the ancients to such as were born from a god, or to such as had signalized themselves by their actions, and seemed to deserve immortality by the services which they had rendered to their country or to mankind. The heroes Homer describes, such as Ajax, Achilles, &c. were endowed with such prodigious strength, that they could lift up and throw stones, which the united force of four or five men of his age could not have moved. The heroes were supposed to be interested in the affairs of mankind after death, and they were invoked with much solemnity. As the altars of the gods were crowded with sacrifices and libations, so the heroes were often honored with a funeral solemnity, in which their great exploits were enumerated. The respect paid to heroes, might, perhaps, proceed from the opinions of some philosophers, who taught that the souls of great men were often raised to the stars, and introduced among the immortal gods. According to the notions of the Stoics, the ancient heroes inhabited a pure and serene climate, situate in a region above the moon. Besides those heroes, such as Bacchus, Hercules, Æsculapius, &c. who were raised to the dignity of gods, the Greeks have celebrated the names of Cadmus, Inachus, Jasius, Perseus, Theseus, Cecrops, Erichthon, Pandion, Triptolemus, Celeus, Hippolytus, Menelaus, Agamemnon, Castor and Pollux, Æacus, Peleus, and many others, all of whom had monuments erected to celebrate their memory, and groves consecrated around their tomb, where the vows of their descendants and admirers were frequently poured forth with all the fervor of devotion, accompanied by profuse gifts and oblations. *Cic. de Nat. D*. 3. c. 15 & 19.—*Tertull. de Anim*. 2. c. 28 & 44.—*Strab*. 6, &c.—*Paus*. 1. c. 30. l. 10. c. 8.—*Diod*. 4.

HERO'IS, a festival celebrated every ninth year by the Delphians, in honor of an unknown heroine. A great number of mysterious rites were introduced during the celebration of them, with a representation of something like Semele's resurrection. *Plut. Quæst. Gr.*

HE'RON, a mechanist of Alexandria, disciple of Ctesibus. Among his works are Χειροβαλλιστρας κατασκευὴ καὶ συμμετρία, edited by Baldus; *Barulcus sive de oneribus trahendis*; Βελοποιητικὰ, edited by Baldus, August. Vindel. 1616, 4to.; Πνευματικα, edited Commandine, Urbin. 1575, Paris, 1583, Amstelod. 1680; Περὶ αὐτοματοποιητικῶν, edited by Baldus. Venet. 1661, &c. *Sax. Onom*. 1. p. 116.—*Fabr. B. Gr*. 3. c. 24.——A mathematician of the fifth century, præceptor of the philosopher Proclus. *Eutocius ad. Archimed*. p. 28. Edit. Basil. —*Kuster ad Suidam. in* Ολυμπιόδωρος.——Another mechanist under Heraclius, &c. *Vid. Sax. Onom*. 2. p. 72.—*Fabr. B. Gr*. 3. c. 24.

HERO'NA, a city of Dalmatia. *Ptol.*

HERO'NE, a promontory of India within the Ganges. *Arrian.*

HEROPH'ILA, a Sybil, who as some suppose, came to Rome in the reign of Tarquin. Others suppose her to have been more ancient, and fix her age before the Trojan war, as she foretold that Helen should one day prove the destruction of Priam's kingdom. She composed several poems, some of which were said to be in the possession of the people of Delus, so late as the reign of the emperor Antoninus. She gave oracles at Samus, Delphi, Delus, and Clarus, and died in Troas, where her monument was to be seen in the age of Pausanias, in a grove sacred to Apollo Smintheus. *Varro & Eurip. apud. Lactant. de Fals. R*. 6. *& de Ira Dei*. 22.—*Suidas*.—*Paus*. 10. c. 12. *Vid*. Sibyllæ.

HEROPH'ILUS, an impostor in the reign of J. Cæsar, who pretended to be the grandson of Marius. He was banished from Rome by Cæsar for his seditious conduct, and was afterwards strangled in prison.——A Greek physician of Chalcedon, about 570 years B.C. He was one of the first who dissected human bodies, and discovered, as some report, the lacteals, the nerves, with their various uses, the glands, the pulse, &c., and gave to the different parts of the human frame, the names which they still bear. *Plin*. 11. c. 37, &c.—*Cic. Acad. Quæst*. 12.—*Plutarch de plac. Phil*. l. 4. c. 22, &c.

HEROP'OLIS, a town of Ægypt on the Arabic Gulph. *Ptol*. It is called by *Mela*, Heropoliticum.

HEROS'TRATUS. *Vid*. Erostratus.

HER'PA, a town of Cappadocia, on the river Carmalius. *Strab*. 12.

HERPEDETA'NI, a people of Mauritania Tingitana. *Ptol.*

HER'SE, a daughter of Cecrops, king of Athens, beloved by Mercury. The god disclosed his love to Aglaurus, Herse's sister, in hopes of procuring by her means, an easy admission to Herse: but Aglaurus, through jealousy, discovered the amour. Mercury was so offended at her behaviour, that he struck her with his caduceus and changed her into a stone. Herse became mother of Cephalus by Mercury, and, after death, she received divine honors at Athens. *Paus*. 1. c. 2 & 28.—*Apollod*. 3.—*Fulgent*. 2.—*Ovid. Met*. 2. v. 559, &c.——A wife of Danaus. *Apollod.*

HERSEPHO'RIA or ARRHEPHO'RIA, festivals celebrated at Athens in June, in honor of Minerva, or, more probably, of Herse, daughter of Cecrops. Young maidens between the age of seven and eleven, descended from the most illustrious families, were dressed in white habits, and carried in procession the sacred vases and other requisite utensils. Cakes, called ἀνάστατοι, were made for their entertainment. *Meursius, Gr. fer*.—*Castell. in Arrheph*.—*Harpocrat*.—*Suidas*.—*Etymolog*.—*Athen*. 3.—*Plut*.—*Isocr.*

HERSIL'IA, one of the Sabines, forcibly carried away by the Romans, at the celebration of the Consualia. She was given in marriage to Romulus, though, according to some, she married Hostus, a youth of Latium. After death she was made immortal by Juno, and received divine honors among the Romans, under the name of Ora or Horta, because she exhorted and invited her votaries to virtue and morality. *Liv*. 1. c. 11.—*Ovid. Met*. 14. v. 832.—*Plut. Qu. Rom*. 44.—*Ital*. 13. v 812.—*Macrob. Sat*. 1. c. 8.

HER'THA or HER'TA, a goddess among the Germans and Saxons who settled in Britain, supposed to have been the same as Terra, and from whose name the English words *hearth* and *earth* are supposed to be derived. She had a temple and a covered chariot dedicated to her service in a remote island, and was supposed to visit the earth at stated times. No persons, except her ministers, were permitted to touch her sacred chariot, but as soon as the priests declared that the goddess had entered into it, chosen heifers were harnessed to it, and it was conducted through the country, where rejoicings, and the acclamations of a venerating people marked the solemn procession. *Tacit. de Germ.* 40.—*Henr. Spelmann. in Gloss.*

HER'ULI, a savage nation in the northern parts of Europe, who successfully attacked the Roman empire in its decline. *H. Grot. Proleg. in Hist. Suecorum, Gothorum, et Vandalorum.*

HE'SA or **HÆ'SA**, a city of Sicily. *Sil. Pun. Bell.* 14. v. 219.

HESÆ'NUS, a mountain near Pæonia. *Aristot. Mirab. Hist. Anim.* l. 9. c. 45.

HESI'DRUM, a river of India. *Plin.* 6. c. 17.

HESI'ODUS, a celebrated poet born at Ascra in Bœotia. His father's name was Dius, and his mother's Pycimede. He lived in the age of Homer, and even obtained a poetical prize in competition with him, according to Varro and Plutarch. Quintilian, Philostratus, and others maintain that Hesiod lived before the age of Homer; but Vel. Paterculus and others maintain that he flourished about 100 years after him. Hesiod is the first who wrote a poem on agriculture. This poem is called *The Works and the Days;* and besides the instructions which are given to the cultivator of the field, the reader is pleased to find many moral reflections worthy of the refined precepts of a Socrates or a Plato. His *Theogony* is a miscellaneous narration executed without art, precision, choice, judgment, or connection, yet it is most valuable for the faithful and minute account which it gives of the gods of antiquity. His *Shield of Hercules* is but a fragment of a larger poem, in which it is supposed that he gave an account of the most celebrated heroines among the ancients. Hesiod, without being master of the fire and sublimity of Homer, is admired for the elegance of his diction, and the sweetness of his poetry. Besides these poems he wrote others, now unfortunately lost. Pausanias says, that in his age Hesiod's verses were still written on tablets in the temple of the Muses, of which the poet was a priest. If we believe Clemens of Alexandria, 6 *Strom.* the poet borrowed much from Musæus. One of Lucian's dialogues bears the name of *Hesiod*, and in it the poet is introduced as speaking of himself. Virgil, in his Georgics, has imitated the compositions of Hesiod, and taken the *opera* and *dies* of the Ascræan bard for the model of his more highly finished poem. Cicero strongly commends him, and the Greeks were so partial to his poetry and moral instructions, that they ordered their children to learn all his works by heart. Hesiod was murdered by the sons of Ganyctor of Naupactum, and his body was thrown into the sea. Some dolphins brought back the body to the shore, which was immediately known, and the murderers were discovered by the poet's dogs, and thrown into the sea. If Hesiod flourished in the age of Homer, he lived 907 B.C. The best editions of this poet are that of Robinson, 4to, Oxon. 1737, and London, 1756; that of Loesner, 8vo, Lips. 1778; and that of Parma, 4to, 1785. *Cic. N.D.* 1. c. 14. *Br.* 4. *Fam.* 6. ep. 18.—*Virg. Ec.* 6. v. 70.—*Paus.* 9. c. 3, &c.—*Quintil.* 10. c. 1.—*Plut. de* 7. *Sep. & de Anim. Sag.*—*Paterc.* 1. c. 7.—*Varro apud Gell.* 3. c. 11. l. 17. c. 21.—*Gyrald. Poet. H.* 2.—*Philostr. Heroic.* 2.—*Suidas.*—*Vossius de P. Gr.* 2.—*J. Scalig.* 1. *Poet.* 5.—*Sax. Onom.* 1. p. 12.—*Fabr. B. Gr.*2.c.8.—[There is a bust of Hesiod in the Capitol.]

HESI'ONE, a daughter of Laomedon king of Troy, by Strymo, the daughter of the Scamander. It fell to her lot to be exposed to a sea-monster, to whom the Trojans yearly presented a marriageable virgin, to appease the resentment of Apollo and Neptune, whom Laomedon had offended; but Hercules promised to deliver her from the impending danger, provided he received as a reward six beautiful horses. Laomedon consented, and Hercules attacked the monster just as he was going to devour Hesione, and killed him with his club. Laomedon, however, ungratefully refused to reward the hero's services; Hercules, incensed at his treachery, besieged Troy, and put the king and all his family to the sword, except Podarces or Priam, who had advised his father to give the promised horses to his sister's deliverer. The conqueror gave Hesione in marriage to his friend Telamon, who had assisted him during the war, and established Priam upon his father's throne. The removal of Hesione to Greece proved at last fatal to the Trojans; and Priam, who remembered that his sister had been forcibly given to a foreigner, encouraged his son Paris to go to Greece to reclaim the possessions of Hesione, or more probably to revenge his injuries upon the Greeks by carrying away Helen, which gave rise, soon after to the Trojan war. Lycophron mentions, that Hercules threw himself, armed from head to foot, into the mouth of the monster to which Hesione was exposed, and that he tore his belly to pieces, and came out safe with the loss of his hair only, after a confinement of three days within the body of the monster. *Homer. Il.* 5. v. 638.—*Apollod.* 2. c. 5, &c.—*Diod.* 4.—*Lycoph. in Alex.*—*Hygin.* fab. 31 & 89.—*Servius. in Æn.* 8. v. 3. l. 5. v. 30. l. 8. v. 91.—*Quint. Sm.* 1. v. 501.—*Ovid. Met.* 11. v. 212. ——The wife of Nauplius. *Apollod.*

HES'PERA, a large island on the western coast of Africa, once the residence of the Amazons. *Diod.* 3.

HESPE'RIA, a name common both to Italy and Spain. It is derived from Hesper or Vesper, the setting sun, or the evening, whence the Greeks called Italy Hesperi, because it was situate towards the setting sun, or in the west. The same name, for similar reasons, was applied to Spain by the Latins. *Virg. Æn.* 1. v. 634. l. 2. v. 580. l. 3. v. 163. l. 6. v. 6. l. 7. v. 3.—*Servius in locis.*—*Macrob. Sat.* 1. c. 3.—*Horat.* 1. od. 36. v. 4. l. 1. od. 27. v. 28.—*Sil.* 7.v.15.—*Ovid. Met.* 11.v. 258.——A daughter of the river Cebrenus. *Ovid. Met.* 11. v. 769.

HESPER'IDES, three celebrated nymphs, daughters of Hesperus. Apollodorus mentions four, Ægle, Erythia, Vesta, and Arethusa; and Diodorus confounds them with the Atlantides, and supposes that they were the same number. They were appointed to guard the golden apples which Juno gave to Jupiter on the day of their nuptials; and the place of their residence, said by Hesiod to have been beyond the ocean, is more universally believed to have been near mount Atlas, in Africa, according to Apollodorus. This celebrated place or garden abounded with fruits of the most delicious kind, and was carefully guarded by a dreadful dragon which never slept. It was one of the labors of Hercules to procure some of the golden apples of the Hesperides. The hero, ignorant of the situation of this celebrated garden, applied to the nymphs in the neighbourhood of the Po for information, and was told that Nereus the god of the sea, if properly managed (*vid.* Nereus), would direct him. Hercules seized Nereus as he was asleep, and the sea-god, unable to escape from the hero's grasp, answered all the questions which he proposed. Some say that Nereus sent Hercules to Prometheus, and that from him he received all his information. When Hercules came into Africa, he repaired to Atlas, and demanded of him three of the golden apples. Atlas unloaded himself, and placed the burden of the heavens on the shoulders of Hercules, while he went in quest of the apples. At his return Hercules expressed a wish to ease his burden by putting something on his head, and when Atlas assisted him to remove his inconvenience, Hercules artfully laid aside the burden from his shoulders, and seized the apples which Atlas had thrown on the ground. According to other accounts, Hercules himself gathered the apples, without the assistance of Atlas, and previously killed the watchful dragon which kept the tree. These apples were brought to Eurystheus, and afterwards carried back by Minerva into the garden of the Hesperides, as they could be preserved in no other place. Hercules is sometimes represented gathering the apples, and the dragon which guarded the tree appears bowing down his head, as having received a mortal wound. This monster, as it is supposed, was the offspring of

Typhon, and it had a hundred heads, and could utter as many different voices. This number, however, is reduced by some to only one head. According to *Palæphatus de Incredib.* the Hesperides were certain persons who had an immense number of flocks, and the ambiguous word μῆλον, which signifies both *an apple* and *a sheep*, gave rise to the fable of the golden apples of the Hesperides. *Diod.* 4.—*Quint. Sm.* 6. v. 256.—*Apollon. Ar.* 4. v. 139, 4. *& Scholiast. loco.*—*Philostr. Icon.* 2. c. 20 & 21.—*Virg. Ecl.* 6. v. 61.—*Stat.* 3. *Sylv.* 1. v. 158. —*Ovid. Met.* 4. v. 637, &c. l. 9. v. 90.—*Hygin* fab. 30.—*Apollod.* 3. c. 5.—*Hesiod. Theog.* v. 215, &c. *& Scholiast. loco.*

HESPER'IDES IN'SULÆ or HESPER'IDUM IN'SULÆ, islands in the Atlantic Ocean which Hanno saw in his voyage round the southern extremities of Africa. They are supposed to be the Cape Verd islands of the moderns.

HESPE'RION COR'NU, a promontory of Libya. *Ptol.*—*Plin.* 5. c. 1. Also Hespe'rium.

HES'PERIS. *Vid.* Hesperus.

HES'PERIS, a town of Cyrenaica, now Bernice or Bengazi, where most authors have placed the garden of the Hesperides.

HESPERI'TIS or HESPER'ITIS, a country at the west of Africa. *Diod.* 18.

HESPE'RIUS, a mountain of Æthiopia. *Plin.* 1. c. 106.

HES'PERUS, a son of Japetus, brother to Atlas. He is said to have ascended Mount Atlas to make observations on the stars, and, as he never returned, the evening star was called after his name. According to the report of some authors he came to settle in Italy, and the country received the name of Hesperia from him. He had a daughter called Hesperis, who married Atlas, and became mother of seven daughters, called Atlantides or Hesperides. *Diod.* 4.

HES'PERUS, the name applied to the planet Venus, when it appeared after the setting of the sun. It was called Phosphorus by the Greeks, and Lucifer by the Latins when it preceded the sun. *Cic. de Nat. D.* 2. c. 20.—*Senec. de Hippol.* 749. *Id. in Med.* 71.

HES'TIA, one of the Hesperides. *Apollod.*

HESTLÆ'A, a town of Eubœa. *Vid.* Histiæa.

HESTLÆ'A, a female writer of Alexandria, who wrote a dissertation on the subject of Homer's Iliad, whether it is to be considered as history or as a fable. *Strab.* l. 13.

HE'SUS, a deity among the Gauls, supposed to have been the same as the Mars of the Romans. *Lucan.* 1. v. 445.—*Lactant. Fals. R.* 21.—*Cæs. Bell. G.* 6.

HESYCH'IA, a daughter of Thespius. *Apollod.*

HESYCH'IUS, a celebrated grammarian of Alexandria, the most learned and instructive of all ancient critics, according to *Is. Casaubon.* The age in which he lived is not precisely known, though it is supposed to have been about the third century. His learned lexicon or vocabulary of Greek works, so valuable and so interesting to those who wish to study the Greek language, proves him to have been either a Christian, or well acquainted with the tenets of Christianity, as he mentions the names of the apostles. His lexicon has been learnedly edited by Albert, 2 vols. fol. L. Bat. 1746. *Sax. Onom.* 1. p. 464.—*Fabr. B. Gr.* 4. c. 37.

HETRIC'ULUM, now Lataraco, a small town in the country of the Brutii. *Liv.* 30. c. 19.

HETRU'RIA or ETRU'RIA, a celebrated country of Italy, extending along the shores of the Mediterranean, between the river Andenna on the west, and the Tiber on the east. It originally contained twelve different nations, which had each their respective monarch called Lucumon. Their names were Veientes, Clusini, Perusini, Cortonenses, Arretini, Vetuloni, Volaterrani, Rusellani, Volscinii, Tarquinii, Falisci, and Cæretani. The inhabitants were particularly noted for their superstition, and their great confidence in omens, dreams, auguries, &c. They proved powerful and resolute enemies to the rising empire of Rome, and were conquered only after much effusion of blood. *Plin.* 3. c. 5.—*Strab.* 5.—*Virg. Æn.*—*Plut. in Rom.*—*Mela,* 2. c. 4.

HEURIP'PA, a surname of Diana.

HEXAP'YLUM, a gate at Syracuse. The adjoining place of the city or the wall bore the same name. *Diod.* 11 & 14.—*Liv.* 24. c. 21. l. 25. c. 24. l. 32. c. 39.

HIAR'BAS, a king of Gætulia. *Vid.* Iarbas.——An African king, slain by Pompey. *Eutr.* 5. c. 6.—*Liv.* 89.

HI'BER, a name applied to a Spaniard as living near the river Hiberus or Iberus. *Vid.* Iberus.

HIBER'NIA or HYBER'NIA, a large island at the west of Britain, called Ireland. Some of the ancients have called it Ibernia, Juverna, Iris, Hierna, Ogygia, Ivernia. *Juv.* 2. v. 160.—*Mela,* 3. c. 6.—*Diod.* 4.—*Cæs. Bell. G.* 5. c. 13.—*Ptol.* 2. c. 2. —*Plut. de Facie in Lun.*—*Strab.* 4.—*Orpheus.*—*Aristot.*

HIBRIL'DES, an Athenian general. *Dionys. Hal.* 7. Read Hybrilides.

HICE'SIUS, an historian, who left a work on mysteries. *Clem. in Protrept. Pliny,* 14. c. 9, &c. mentions a physician of celebrity of this name, and asserts that he wrote on wine.

HICETA'ON, a son of Laomedon, brother to Priam, and father of Menalippus. *Homer. Il.* 3. v. 147. l. 15. v. 546. l. 20. v. 238.——The father of Thymetes, who came to Italy with Æneas. *Virg. Æn.* 10. v. 123.

HIC'ETAS, a philosopher of Syracuse, who believed that the earth moved, and that all the heavenly bodies were stationary. *Diog in Phil.*——A tyrant of Syracuse. *Vid.* Icetas.

HIEMP'SAL, a king of Numidia. *Cic. Vat.* 5. *Rull.* 1. c. 4.——A son of Micipsa, cruelly murdered by Jugurtha. *Sallust. in Jug.* 12.

HI'ERA, a woman who married Telephus, king of Mysia, and was said to surpass Helen in beauty. *Hyginus* calls her Laodice, the daughter of Priam. ——The mother of Pandarus and Bitias by Alcanor. *Virg. Æn.* 9. v. 673.——A name applied to Cybele, the mother of the gods.

HI'ERA, the most westerly island of the Ægates, opposite Lilybæum.——One of the Lipari islands, called also Therasia, now Vulcano. *Paus.* 10. c. 11.—*Mela.* 2. c. 7.—*Isidor.* 14. c. 6.—*Plin.* 2. c. 89 & 109.

HIERÆ'A, a small region of Cyrene in Africa. *Steph.*

HIER'AMÆ, a city of Caria. *Id.*

HIERANE'SUS, an island of the Cretan Sea, and of Ægypt. *Id.*

HIER'APHE, an island of Libya. *Id.*

HIERAP'OLIS or BAM'BYCE, a town of Syria, near the Euphrates. *Ptol.* 5. c. 15.—*Plin.* 5. c. 26. ——A town of Phrygia, famous for hot baths, now Bambouk-kalé. *Plin.* 4. c. 12. l. 2. c. 95.—*Ptol.* 5. c. 2.

HI'ERA-PYT'NA, a city of Crete, first called Cyrba and afterwards Camiros.

HIER'ASUS, a river of Dacia. *Ptol.*

HIER'ATIS, a town of Persia, on the Persian Gulph. *Arrian.*

HI'ERAX, a youth who awoke the hundred-eyed Argus, to inform him that Mercury was stealing Io. Mercury killed him, and changed him into a bird of prey, called a hawk. Some suppose that Hierax was a man of opulence in Mariandynia in Asia Minor, who was changed into a hawk by Neptune, because he supplied the people of Troy with corn during a famine with which the offended god of the sea had visited their country. *Antonin. Lib.* 3.—*Apollod.* 2. c. 1.——A surname of Antiochus, king of Syria, and brother to Seleucus, from his great rapacity. *Justin.* 37. c. 3.——An Ægyptian philosopher and heresiarch in the third century. *Epiphan. Hær.* 67.

HIER'ICHUS *(-untis)*. the name of Jericho in the Holy Land, called the city of palm-trees, from the great number of dates found in the neighbourhood. *Plin.* 5. c. 14.—*Tacit. H.* Also Hier'icus.

HI'ERO the First, a king of Syracuse, after his brother Gelon, rendered himself odious in the beginning of his reign by his cruelty and avarice. He made war against Theron, the tyrant of Agrigentum, and took Himera. He obtained three different crowns at the Olympic games, two in horse-races, and one at a chariot-race, and from these victories, immortalized by the pen of Pindar, he has obtained greater celebrity than from the administration of his government, or the successive defeats of his jealous neighbours. In the latter part of his reign the conversation of Simonides, Epicharmus, Pindar, Æschylus, Bacchylides, &c. softened in some measure the roughness of his morals, and the severity of his government, and rendered him the liberal patron of learning, genius, and merit. He died after a reign of 18 years B.C. 467, leaving the crown to his brother Thrasybulus, who disgraced himself by his vices and tyranny. *Herodot* 7.—*Athen.* 14. *Pluto. Ep. ad Dionys.*—*Cic. de Nat. D.* 1. c. 22.—*Plut. in Apoph.*—*Ælian. V. H.* 4. 15. l. 9. c. 1 & 5. l. 12. c. 25.—*Diod.* 11.

HI'ERO the Second, king of Syracuse, was descended from Gelon. He was unanimously elected king by all the states of the island of Sicily, and invested with power to carry on the war against the Carthaginians. He joined his enemies in besieging Messana, which had surrendered to the Romans, but though brave and at the head of a valorous army, he was beaten by Appius Claudius, the Roman consul, and obliged to retire in disgrace to Syracuse, where he was soon blocked up. Seeing all hopes of victory lost, he made peace with the Romans, and proved so faithful to his engagements during the fifty-nine years of his reign, that the Romans never had a more firm or more attached ally. He died in the 94th year of his age, about 225 B.C. He was universally regretted, and all the Sicilians showed, by their lamentations, that they had lost in him a common father and a friend. Hiero liberally patronized the learned, and employed the talents of his relation Archimedes for the good and the ornament of his country. He built a ship which in magnitude and workmanship, surpassed all the vessels of antiquity, but as it was too large to enter the harbours of Sicily, he presented it to his friend and ally, Philadelphus of Ægypt. He wrote a book on agriculture, now lost. He was succeeded by his unworthy grandson Hieronymus. It was reported of him that he was the son of Hierocles by a slave, and that his father, ashamed of his connection, exposed him to the wild beasts in in a forest, where he was fed for several days by bees, a circumstance which moved the heart of an unnatural parent to preserve a child whose infancy was attended with such promising omens. *Val. Max.* 4. c. 8.—*Ælian. V.H.* 4. 8.—*Justin.* 23. c. 4. —*Flor.* 2. c. 2.—*Liv.* 16. [An exceedingly fine head of Hiero, with his name inscribed in Greek letters, is to be found in the Museum of the Capitol.]

HI'ERO, an Athenian, intimate with Nicias the general. *Plut. in Nic.*——A Parthian, &c. *Tacit. Ann.* l. 6. c. 42, &c.

HIEROCÆSARE'A, a town of Lydia. *Tacit. Ann.* 2. c. 47. l. 3. c. 62.

HIEROCE'PIA, an island near Paphus, in Cyprus. *Strab.* 15.

HIER'OCLES, a prosecutor of the Christians under Diocletian, who pretended to find inconsistencies in Scripture, and preferred the miracles of Apollonius Thyaneus to those of Christ. His writings, which betrayed the furious bigot and the artful hypocrite, were ably and satisfactorily refuted by Lactantius and Eusebius. They were edited with a learned dissertation by Bp. Pearson, in 8vo. London, 1654. *Sax. Onom.* 1. p. 385.——A Platonic philosopher, who taught at Alexandria, and wrote a book on providence and fate, fragments of which are preserved by Photius, a commentary on the golden verses of Pythagoras; and facetious moral sentences, &c. He flourished A.D. 485. Like most of the Platonics, Hierocles took a wife only to raise children, and in his conduct and character displayed a total aversion to incontinence and licentious indulgences. The best edition of Hierocles is that of Asheton and Warren, 8vo. London, 1742. *Fabr. B. Gr.* 2. c. 12.—*Sax. Onom.* 1. p 385. Bp. Pearson, in his *Prolegomena ad Hierocl. de Provid. & fato*, enumerates 16 persons of this name. See also *Voss. H. Gr.* l. 3 & 4.——A general in the interest of Demetrius. *Polyæn.* 5.——A governor of Bithynia and Alexandria, under Diocletian.——An officer. *Vid.* Heligabalus.——The father of Hieron, descended from Gelon. *Just.* 23. c. 4.

HIERODU'LUM, a town of Libya. *Strab.* 14.

HIEROMI'ACE, a river of Syria, flowing near Gadara. *Plin.* 5. c. 18.

HI'ERON, a promontory of Hibernia, and also of European Sarmatia. *Ptol.*——A lake of Asia Minor, near the Euxine Sea. *Arrian.*

HI'ERON O'ROS, a maritime town of Crete. *Id.*

HIERON'ICA LEX was introduced by Hiero, tyrant of Sicily, to settle the quantity of corn, and the price and time of receiving it, between the farmers of Sicily and the collector of the corn tax at Rome. This law, on account of its justice and candor, was continued by the Romans when they became masters of Sicily. *Cic. Verr.* 2. c. 13 & 60.

HIERON'YMUS, a tyrant of Sicily, who, when only 15 years old, succeeded his grandfather Hiero. He rendered himself odious by his cruelty, oppression, and debauchery, and, as if to render his reign more unpopular, he abjured the alliance of Rome, which Hiero had cultivated with so much honor and advantage to himself and to his country. He was assassinated, and all his family was overwhelmed in his fall, and totally extirpated, B.C. 214. *Sil.* 14 v. 87.—*Liv.* 24. c. 4, &c.——An historian of Rhodes, who wrote an account of the actions of Demetrius Poliorcetes, by whom he was appointed governor of Bœotia, B.C. 254. He maintained that the absence of pain was the chief good. *Cic. Acad.* 4. c. 42. *Orat.* 57.—*Plut. in Dem.* ——An Athenian set over the fleet while Conon went to the king of Persia. *Diod. Sic.* l. 14.——A Christian writer, commonly called St. Jerome, born at Strido in Pannonia, and distinguished for his abilities and zeal against heretics. He travelled over various parts of the world, and enlarged his mind by all the information which a judicious and attentive observer could collect from the diversity of manners, of opinions, and of prejudices, and with commendable earnestness he devoted his studies to the improvement of mankind, and to the advancement of Christian charity. He wrote commentaries on the Prophets, St. Mathew's Gospel, &c. a Latin version known by the name of the Vulgate, polemical treatises, and an account of ecclesiastical writers before him. He died A.D. 420, in the 91st year of his age. Of his works, which are replete with great animation, striking sublimity, and extensive erudition, the best edition is that of Vallarsius, fol. Veronæ, 1734 to 1740, 10 vols. *Sax. Onom.* 1. p. 425.—*Fabr. B. Gr.* 5. c. 24. *Bibl. Lat.* l. 4. c. 3, &c.

HIEROPH'ILUS, a Greek physician. He instructed his daughter Agnodice in the art of midwifery, &c. *Vid.* Agnodice.

HIEROSOL'YMA, a celebrated city of Palestine, the capital of Judæa, taken by Pompey, who, on that account, was surnamed Hierosolymarius. Titus also took it and destroyed it on the 8th of September, A.D. 70, according to Josephus 2177 years after its foundation. In the siege of Jerusalem by Titus, 110,000 persons are said to have perished, and 97,000 to have been made prisoners, and afterwards either sold for slaves or wantonly exposed for the sport of their insolent victors to the fury of wild beasts. *Joseph. Bell. J.* 7. c. 16.—*Cic. ad Attic.* 2. ep. 9. *Flacc.* 28.—The new city built in the neighbourhood by the emperor Adrian, was called Ælia Capitolina.

HIGNA'TIA VI'A, called Egnatia by *Cicero*, a large road which led from the Ionian Sea to the Hellespont across Macedonia, a distance of about 530 miles. *Strab.* 7.

HILA'RIA, a daughter of Leucippus and Philodice. As she and her sister Phœbe were going to be united to their cousins Lynceus and Idas, they were forcibly carried off by Castor and Pollux, who married them. Hilaria had Anagon by Castor, and she, as well as her sister, obtained after death the honors which were generally paid to heroes. *Apollod.* 3.—*Propert.* 1. el. 2. v. 16.—*Meursius, Misc. Lac.* 15.—*Paus.* 2. c. 22. l. 3. c. 19.

HILA'RIA, festivals at Rome in honor of the mother of the gods, observed on the 25th of March, when nature, over which the goddess presided, seemed to resume the vigor of the returning year. The city was then filled for several days with gaiety and pleasure, the statue of the goddess was carried in procession through the streets, preceded by the most valuable possessions, which every votary was eager to produce on this solemn occasion. Every appearance of sorrow and mourning was suspended or banished from the city, and individuals were permitted to dress themselves in whatever attire they pleased, and even to assume the robes of magistrates. *Macrob. Sat.* 1. c. 21.—*Herodian. in Com.* 1.—*Turneb.* 24. *Adv.* 45. —*Vopiscus in Aurel.*—*Cœl. Rh.* 6. c. 16.

HILA'RIUS, a bishop of Poictiers in France, who wrote several treatises in favor of the Christian religion, the most famous of which is on the Trinity, in 12 books, and also a poem called Genesis, addressed to Pope Leo. The best edition is that of the Benedictine monks, fol. Paris, 1693. Hilary died A.D. 372, in his 80th year. *Sax. Onom.* 1. p.

403.—*Harles. Not. Lit. Rom.* 1 p. 586.—*Fabr. B. Lat.* 14. c. 3, &c.——Bishop of Arles was born A.D. 401, died A.D. 449. He wrote two orations, one pronounced at the funeral of St. Honoratus, the other on the miracles of St. Genesius, and a letter to Eucherius. These opuscula were published with the works of Leo the Great, by Pasch. Quesnel, Lugd. 1700. *Sax. Onom. Ibid.—Harles. Ibid.* 1. p. 685.

HIMANTOP'ODES, a people of Æthiopia. *Plin.* 5. c. 8.

HIMEL'LA, now Aia, a small river in the country of the Sabines. *Virg. Æn.* 7. v. 714.

HIM'ERA, a city of Sicily, built by the people of Zancle, and destroyed by the Carthaginians 240 years after. *Strab.* 6——A river of Sicily, now Fiumi de Termini, falling at the east of Panormus into the Tuscan Sea, with a town of the same name at its mouth, and also celebrated baths. *Cic Verr.* 4. c. 33.——A river of Sicily, now Fiume Salso, running in a southern direction, and dividing the south of the island almost into two parts. *Liv.* 24. c. 6. l. 25. c. 49.——The ancient name of the Eurotas. *Strab.* 6.—*Mela*, 2. c. 7.—*Polyb.*

HIME'RIUS, a Greek sophist of Prusias in Bithynia, in the reigns of the emperors Constantius and Julian. He employed himself in declamations, and chiefly directed the vehemence of his attacks against the Christians. His works have been edited by Wernsdorf, Erlang. 1785, and Gotting. 1790. *Sax. Onom.* 1. p. 413.—*Fabr. B. Gr.* 4. c. 32.

HIMIL'CO, a Carthaginian sent to explore the western parts of Europe. *Fest. Avien.*——A son of Amilcar, who succeeded his father in the command of the Carthaginian armies in Sicily. He was cut off, with his army, by a plague, B.C. 398. *Justin.* 19. c. 2.

HIPPAG'ORAS, a man who wrote an account of the republic of Carthage. *Athen.* 14.

HIPPAL'CIMUS or **HIPPAL'MUS**, a son of Pelops and Hippodamia, who was among the Argonauts. *Hygin.* fab. 14.—*Sch. Eurip. ad Orest.* 5.—*Apollod.* 1.

HIP'PALUS, the first person who is mentioned as having sailed in open sea from Arabia to India. *Arrian. in Perip.*

HIP'PANA, a town of Sicily, near Panormus.

HIPPAR'CHIA, a woman of Maronea in Thrace, in Alexander's age, who became enamoured of Crates the Cynic philosopher, because she heard him discourse. She married him, though he at first contemptuously rejected her addresses. She wrote some things, now lost. *Vid.* Crates. *Diog.* 6.—*Suidas.*

HIPPAR'CHUS, a son of Pisistratus, who, with his brother Hippias, succeeded his father as tyrant of Athens. He patronised some of the learned men of the age, and, by inviting Anacreon and Simonides to his court, he showed his fondness for literature, and softened the odium which attached itself to his usurped power. He first arranged in regular order the poems of Homer, according to the opinion of Plato, though Cicero attributes to his father this eminent service to literature and mankind. The seduction of a sister of Harmodius raised him many enemies, and he was at last assassinated by a desperate band of conspirators, with Harmodius and Aristogiton at their head, 513 B.C. *Cic. Orat.* 3. c. 33.—*Ælian. V.H.* 8. c. 2.——One of Antony's freedmen.——The first person who was banished by ostracism at Athens.——The father of Asclepiades.——An illustrious mathematician and astronomer of Nicæa in Bithynia. He first discovered that the interval between the vernal and the autumnal equinox is 186 days, seven days longer than between the autumnal and vernal, occasioned by the eccentricity of the earth's orbit. He divided the heavens into 49 constellations, 12 in the ecliptic, 21 in the northern, and 16 in the southern hemisphere, and gave names to all the stars. He makes no mention of comets. from viewing a tree on a plain from different situations, which changed its apparent position, he was led to the discovery of the parallax of the planets, or the distance between their real or apparent position, viewed from the centre, and from the surface of the earth. He also determined the longitude and latitude, and fixed the first degree of longitude at the Canaries. He likewise laid the first foundation of trigonometry, so essential to facilitate astronomical studies. He was the first who, after Thales and Sulpicius Gallus, found out the exact time of eclipses, of which he made a calculation for 600 years After a life of labor, honorably and usefully spent in the service of science and astronomy, and after publishing several treatises, and valuable observations on the appearance of the heavens, he died 125 years B.C. His commentary on Aratus' phænomena is still extant, edited and translated by Petavius. *Voss. de Sc. Math.* 160.—*Plin.* 2. c. 12 & 26. l. 7. c. 5.—*Sax. Onom.* 1, p. 130.—*Fabricius*, *B. Gr.* l. 3. c. 18. enumerates fifteen persons of this name.——An Athenian who conspired against Heraclides, who kept Athens for Demetrius, &c. *Polyæn.* 5.

HIPPARI'NUS, a son of Dionysius who ejected Callippus from Syracuse, and held the sovereign power for twenty-seven years. *Polyæn* 5.——The father of Dion.

HIPPA'RION, one of Dion's sons. *Polyæn.* l. 5. *in Dionys.*

HIP'PARIS, a river of Sicily, near Camarina. *Schol. Pindar. Olymp.* od. 5.

HIP'PASUS, a son of Ceyx of Trachinia, who assisted Hercules against Eurytus. *Apollod.* 2. c. 7.——A pupil of Pythagoras, born at Metapontum in Italy. He maintained that every thing was produced from fire. *Diog.* 8.——A centaur, killed at the nuptials of Pirithous. *Ovid. Met.* 12. v. 352.——One of the Argonauts, son of Eurytus and father of Actor. *Hygin.* fab. 14 & 173.——An illegitimate son of Priam. *Hygin.* fab. 90.

HIP'PEUS, a son of Hercules by Phorcis, the eldest of the fifty daughters of Thestius. *Apollod.* 2. c. 7.

HIP'PI, four small islands on the coast of Ionia, near Erythræ. *Strab.* l. 13.

HIP'PIA, a lascivious woman, &c. *Juv.* 6. v. 82.——A surname of the Minerva said to be daughter of Neptune, represented on horseback. Juno also bore the same name. *Paus.* 5. c. 15.

Hip'pia, a city of Perrhæbia, called also Phalanna. *Steph.*

HIP'PIAS, a philosopher of Elis, who maintained that virtue consisted in not being in want of the assistance of men. At the Olympic games he boasted that he was master of all the liberal and mechanical arts; and he said that the ring upon his finger, and the tunic, cloak, and shoes, which he then wore, were all the work of his own hands. *Cic. de Orat.* 3. c. 32. *Brut.* 81 & 185.—*Apul. in Flor.* 2.—*Quintil.* 12. c. 11.——A son of Pisistratus, who, with his brother Hipparchus, became tyrant of Athens after the death of his father. He attempted to revenge the death of his brother, who had been assassinated, and in consequence of the violent measures which he adopted, he was driven from his country. He fled to king Darius in Persia, and was killed at the battle of Marathon, fighting against the Athenians, B.C. 490. He had five children by Myrrhine, the daughter of Callias. *Herodot.* 6.—*Thucyd.* 7.—*Cic.* 9. *Att.* 11.——An historian of Erythræ. *Athen.*

HIP'PICI, mountains of Asiatic Sarmatia. *Ptol.*

HIP'PIS or more correctly **HIP'PYS**, an historian and poet of Rhegium, in the reign of Xerxes.

HIP'PIUS, a surname of Neptune, from his having raised a horse (ἵππος) from the earth in his contest with Minerva concerning the giving a name to Athens. He had a temple at Mantinea on the borders of Laconia, erected by Agamedes and Trophonius. *Paus Æliac* 15.——A surname of Mars. *Id.*—These two gods, with Juno and Minerva, were the only divinities represented by the ancients on horseback.

HIP'PO, a daughter of Scedasus, who, when the ambassadors of Sparta offered her violence, destroyed herself, cursing the city that gave birth to such men. *Paus.* 9. c. 13.

Hip'po, a celebrated town in Africa, on the Mediterranean, at the west of Carthage and Utica. *Ital.* 3. v. 252.—*Strabo*, 17, says that there were two cities of the name in Africa, one of which, situated more to the westward, by way of distinction is called Regius. *Plin.* 5. c. 3. l. 9. c. 8.—*Mela*, 1. c. 7.—*Liv.* 29. c. 3 & 32.——A town of Spain. *Liv.* 39. c. 30.——A town of the Brutii, now Monte Leone.

HIPPOB'OTES, a large meadow near the Caspian Sea, where 50,000 horses could graze. *Strab.* l. 11.

HIPPOB'OTUS, a Greek historian, who composed a treatise on philosophers. *Diog. & Porphyr. in Pyth.*

HIPPOCAM'PI, fabulous sea animals, supposed to have had the fore-feet of the horse, and the rest of the body like a fish. *Diosc.* 2. c. 3.—*Plin.* 32. c. 11.

HIPPOCENTAU'RI, a race of monsters who dwelt in Thessaly. *Vid.* Centauri.

HIPPOC'OON, a son of Œbalus, brother to Tyndarus. He was put to death by Hercules, because he had driven his brother from the kingdom of Lacedæmon. He was present at the chase of the Calydonian boar. *Diod.* 4.—*Apollod.* 1. 3. c. 10. *Paus. Lacon.*—*Hygin.* fab. 173 & 273.—*Ovid. Met.* 8. v. 314.——Son of Hyrtacus, a friend of Æneas, who distinguished himself in the funeral games celebrated in honor of Anchises in Sicily. *Virg. Æn.* 3. v. 492, &c.

HIPPOCORYS'TES, a son of Ægyptus, who married Hyperipte.——A son of Hippocoon, slain by Hercules. *Apollod.*

HIPPOC'RATE, a daughter of Thespius, mother of Hippozygus by Hercules. *Apollod.*

HIPPOC'RATES, a celebrated physician of Cos, of the particulars of whose life little is known but what is deemed fabulous. He studied physic, in which his grandfather Nebrus was so eminently distinguished; and he improved himself by reading the tablets hung up in the temples of the gods, where each individual had written down the diseases under which he had labored, and the means by which he had recovered. Skilful and diligent in his profession, he openly declared the measures which he had taken to cure a disease, and candidly confessed that in one instance of 42 patients which were entrusted to his care, only 17 had recovered, and the rest had fallen a prey to the distemper, in spite of his medical applications. He devoted all his time to the service of his country; and when Artaxerxes invited him, even by force of arms, to come to reside at his court, Hippocrates firmly and modestly answered, that he was born to serve his countrymen, and not a foreigner. He enjoyed the rewards to which his well-directed labors were entitled, and while he lived in the greatest popularity, he was carefully employed in observing the symptoms and the growth of every disorder, and from his judicious remarks, succeeding physicians have received the most valuable advantages. He died in the 99th year of his age, B.C. 361, free from all disorders of the mind and body; and after death he received, with the name of Great, the same honors as Hercules. His writings, few of which remain, have procured him the epithet of divine, and show that he was the Homer of his profession. The oath which he took to discharge his profession with honor and fidelity is happily preserved, and is particularly entitled to the admiration of the world. According to Galen, the opinion of Hippocrates is as respectable as the voice of an oracle. His works were all written in the Ionic dialect by the advice of Democritus, though he was a Dorian. His memory is still venerated at Cos, and the present inhabitants of the island show a small house, which he, as they assert, once inhabited. The works of Hippocrates which are accounted genuine are, 1, 'Επιδημιῶν, 1st and 3rd books; 2, προγνωστικόν; 3, προῤῥητικόν; 4, ἀφορισμοί; 5, περὶ διαίτης ὀξέων; 6, περὶ ἀέρων, ὑδάτων, τόπων; 7, περὶ τῶν ἐν κεφαλῇ τρωμάτων. The other compositions generally ascribed to him are spurious. The former have been edited separately by various persons; but the best editions of the whole are that of Fœsius, Genev. fol. 1657; of Linden, 2 vols. 8vo. Amst. 1665; and that of Mackius, 2 vols. fol. Viennæ, 1743. *Plin.* 7. 37.—*Cels. Præf.*—*Cic. de Orat.* 3, *N.D.* 3. c. 38.—*Sax. Onom.* 1. p. 44. *Fabricius, B. Gr.* 2. c. 23. has given a copious and elaborate account of this author and his works. [The finest head of Hippocrates is a terminus in the Museum at Naples.]——An Athenian general in the Peloponnesian war. *Plut.*——An officer of Chalcedon, killed by Alcibiades. *Plut in Alc.*——A Syracusan defeated by Marcellus.——A tyrant of Gela.——The father of Pisistratus.——A mathematician expelled by Pythagoras from his school for teaching for hire.

HIPPOCRA'TIA or HIPPOCRATI'A, a festival observed in Arcadia in honor of Neptune.

HIPPOCRE'NE, a fountain of Bœotia, near mount Helicon, sacred to the muses. It first rose from the ground, when struck by the feet of the horse Pegasus, whence the name (ἵππου κρήνη, *the horse's fountain.* *Ovid.* 5. *Met.* v. 256.

HIPPOCU'RÆ, two cities of India within the Ganges. *Ptol.*

HIPPOD'AMUS, a son of Priam. *Apollod.*

HIPPOD'AME or HIPPODAMI'A, a daughter of Œnomaus, king of Pisa, in Elis, who married Pelops, son of Tantalus. Her father, who is said to have been either enamoured of her himself, or afraid lest he should perish by one of his daughter's children, according to an oracle, refused to marry her, except to the person who could overcome him in a chariot race. His dexterity in driving and the swiftness of his horses ensured the defeat of his rivals; but to increase their danger, it is said, that he always compelled his daughter to mount the chariot of her lover, either to delay him by the charms of her person or to confound by her presence the probability of success. As the beauty of Hippodamia was universally celebrated, many courted her, and accepted her father's severe conditions, though death attended a defeat. Thirteen had already been conquered, and forfeited their lives, when Pelops came from Lydia and boldly entered the lists. Pelops previously bribed Myrtilus, the charioteer of Œnomaus, and by this artifice ensured himself the victory. Œnomaus, mounted on a broken chariot, which the corrupted Myrtilus had purposely provided for him, was easily overcome, and killed in the course. Pelops married Hippodamia, and avenged the death of Œnomaus, by throwing into the sea the perfidious Myrtilus, who claimed for the reward of his treachery, the favors which Hippodamia could grant only to her husband. Hippodamia became mother of Atreus and Thyestes, and it is said that she died of grief for the melancholy death of her father, which her guilty correspondence with Pelops and Myrtilus had occasioned. Others suppose that she destroyed herself when she was discovered to be guilty of the murder of Chrysippus son of Pelops, though it is more probable that she was expelled by her revengeful husband, and that she died at Argos. *Lucian. in Char.*—*Schol. Apollon.* 1. *Arg.*—*Propert.* 1. el. 2.—*Plut. in Parall.* 33.—*Virg. G.* 3. v. 7.—*Hygin.* fab. 84 &.253—*Paus.* 5. c. 14. l. 6. c. 21.—*Diod.* 4.—*Ovid. Heroid.* 8. & 17. ——A daughter of Adrastus, king of Argos, who married Pirithous, king of the Lapithæ. The festivity which prevailed on the day of her marriage was interrupted by the attempts of Eurytus to offer violence to her person. *Vid.* Pirithous. She is called Ischomache by some, and Deidamia by others. *Hygin.* fab. 33.—*Eustath.* 21. *Odyss.*—*Schol. Hom. ib.*—*Propert.* 2. el. 2.—*Ovid. Met.* 12. —*Plut. in Thes.*——A daughter of Danaus. *Apollod.* ——A daughter of Brises, mistress of Achilles. ——A daughter of Anchises, who married Alcathous. *Homer. Il.* 13. v. 429.

HIPPOD'AMUS, a man of Miletus, who is said to have settled a republic without any previous knowledge of government. *Aristot.* 2. *Polit.*——A Pythagorean philosopher.——An Athenian who gave his house to his country when he knew such a concession would improve the port of the Piræeus. *Schol. in Aristoph. Equit.*——An Athenian archon. ——A man famous for his voracious appetite.——A son of the Achelous. *Apollod.*

HIPPOD'ICE, one of the Danaides. *Apollod.*

HIPPOD'ROMUS, a son of Hercules by Anthippe. *Id.*——A Thessalian, who succeeded to a school at Athens, in the age of M. Antony. *Philostr.*——A place where horse races were exhibited. *Martial.* 12. epigr. 50.

HIP'POLA, a town of Peloponnessus. *Paus.* 3. c. 25.

HIPPOL'OCHUS, a son of Bellerophon, father to Glaucus, who commanded the Lycians during the Trojan war.—A son of Glaucus also bore the same name. *Homer. Il.* 6. v. 119.——A son of Antimachus slain in the Trojan war by Agamemnon. *Id.* 11. v. 122.

HIPPOLYTE, called also Antiope, a queen of the Amazons, given in marriage to Theseus by Hercules, who had conquered her and taken away her girdle to present it to Eurystheus. *Vid.* Hercules. She had a son by Theseus, called Hippolytus. *Plut. in Thes.*—*Propert.* 4. el. 3.—*Hygin.* fab. 30. —*Diod.* 4.—*Justin.* 2. c. 4.—*Ovid. Heroid.* 20. v. 119.—*Servius in* 11. *Æn.* v. 661.——The wife of

Acastus, who fell in love with Peleus, who was in exile at her husband's court. She accused him of incontinence, and of attempts upon her virtue, before Acastus, only because he refused to gratify her licentious desires. She is also called Astyochia and Astydamia. *Vid.* Acastus.——A daughter of Cretheus. *Apollod.*

HIPPOL'YTUS, a son of Theseus and Hippolyte, famous for his virtues and his misfortunes. His step-mother Phædra fell in love with him, and when he refused to pollute his father's bed, she accused him of offering violence to her person. Her accusation was unhappily credited, and Theseus entreated Neptune severely to punish the incontinence of his son. Hippolytus fled from the resentment of his father, and as he pursued his way along the sea-shore, his horses were so frightened at the noise of sea-calves, which Neptune had purposely sent there, that they ran among the rocks till his chariot was broken and his body torn to pieces. Temples were raised to his memory in several parts of Greece, particularly at Trœzene, where he received divine honors. According to some accounts, Diana restored him to life, and after this resuscitation, he assumed the name of Virbius. *Diod.* 4.—*Paus.* 1. c. 22. l. 2. c. 32. *Schol. Hom.* 16. *Sch. Eurip. in Hipp.*—*Senec. in Hipp.* 2. sc. 3.—*Ovid. Fast.* 3. v. 268. *Met.* 15. v. 469.—*Virg. Æn.* 7. v. 761, &c.——A son of Ropalus king of Sicyon, greatly beloved by Apollo. *Plut. in Num.*——A giant killed by Mercury.——A son of Ægyptus. *Apollod.* 1 & 2.——A Christian writer in the third century, whose works have been edited by Fabricius, Hamburgh, fol. 1716. *Sax. Onom.* 1. v. 353.—*Fabr. B. Gr.* l. 5. c. 1.

HIPPOM'ACHUS, a musician, who when he saw one of his unskilful pupils praised by the multitude, desired him to cease playing, and assigned the applause he received as a proof of his want of skill. *Ælian. V.H.* l. 2. c. 6.

HIPPOM'EDON, a son of Nisimachus and Mythidice, one of the seven chiefs who went against Thebes. He was killed by Ismarus, son of Acastus. *Æsch. Sept. cont. Theb.*—*Hygin.* fab. 70.—*Sch. Statii*, l. *Theb.* v. 44.—*Apollod.* 3. c. 6.—*Paus.* 2. c. 36. l. 10. c. 10.

HIPPOMEDU'SA, a daughter of Danaus. *Apollod.*

HIPPOM'ENES, an Athenian archon, who exposed his daughter Limone to be devoured by horses, because she had been guilty of adultery. *Ovid. in Ib.* 459.——A son of Macareus and Merope, who, with the assistance of Venus, married Atalanta. *Vid.* Atalanta. These two fond lovers were changed into lions by Cybele, whose temple they had profaned. *Ovid. Met.* 10. v. 585, &c.——The father of Megareus.

HIPPOMOL'GI, a people of Scythia, who, as the name implies, lived upon the milk of horses. Hippocrates has given an account of their manner of living, *De Aqua et Aer.* 44.—*Homer. Il.* 13. v. 5.—*Strab* 7. Also Hippemol'gi.

HIP'PON or HIP'PO, a town of Africa. *Vid.* Hippo.

HIPPO'NA, or rather Epona, a goddess who presided over horses, and whose statues were placed in horses' stables. It is said that she was the monstrous fruit of the passion of Fluxius Tellus for a mare. *Apul.* 3. *Met.*—*Prudent. Ap.* 197.—*Plut. in Par. De R. et Gr.* 29.—*Tertull. in Apol.* 16.—*Juv.* 8. v. 157.

HIP'PONAX or HIPPO'NAX, a Greek poet, born at Ephesus, 540 years B.C. He wrote poetry in the same style as Archilochus, and was not inferior to him in the vigor and beauty of his lines. His satirical raillery obliged him to flee from Ephesus. As he was naturally deformed, two brothers, Buphalus and Anthermus of Chius, made a statue of him, which, by representing the natural deformity of his features, exposed the poet to universal ridicule. Hipponax resolved to revenge the injury, by the bitterness of his invectives, and he wrote such keen and satirical lampoons against them, that they hanged themselves in despair. *Cic. Orat.* 56. *Ad. Famil.* 7. ep. 24.—*Athen.* 12.—*Plin.* 36. c. 5.

HIPPONE'SUS, a city of Caria, and another of Lydia. *Steph.*

HIPPONIA'TES or HIPPONI'ATES, a bay in the country of the Brutii, near Hipponium. *Ptol.*

HIPPONI'CUS, son of Callias, an Athenian, who wished to dedicate a statue to his country, &c. *Ælian. V.H.* l. 14. c. 16.

HIPPO'NIUM, a city in the country of the Brutii where Agathocles built a dock. *Strab.*

HIPPON'OUS, the father of Peribœa and Capaneus. He was killed by the thunderbolts of Jupiter before the walls of Thebes. *Apollod.* 1. c. 8. l. 3. c. 1.—*Paus.* 10. c. 10.—*Hygin.* fab. 70.——A son of Hercules, who burnt himself to death in consequence of an unfavourable answer which he had received from the oracle. *Hygin.* fab. 242.——The first name of Bellerophon.——A son of Priam.

HIPPOP'ODES, a people of Scythia, who were said to have horses' feet. *Solin.* 30.—*Mela*, 3. c. 6.—*Plin.* 4. c. 13.—*Dionys. Perieg.*

HIPPORE'Æ, a people of Upper Æthiopia. *Plin.*

HIP'POS, a city of Sicily. *Steph.*—*Plin.* 6. c. 4.

HIPPOS'TRATUS, a favorite of Lais.——A writer of Sicilian genealogies, according to the *Scholiast* on *Pindar*. He wrote also an account of the actions of Minos. *Voss. H. Gr.* p. 378.——An author who wrote on the extraordinary shapes of men in India. *Tzetz. Chil.* 7. *H.* 144.

HIPPOT'ADES, the patronymic of Æolus, son of Hippotas, by Segesta, as also of Amastrus, his son, who was killed in the Rutulian war. *Virg. Æn.* 11. v. 674.—*Ovid. Met.* 11. v. 431.

HIPPOTAM'ADA, a village in the tribe Oeneis. *Steph.*

HIP'POTAS or HIP'POTES, a Trojan prince, changed into a river. *Vid.* Crinisus.

HIP'POTAS, the father of Æolus, who from thence is called Hippotades. *Homer. Odyss.* 10. v. 2.—*Ovid. Heroid.* 18. v. 46. *Met.* 14. v. 224.

HIP'POTES, son of Phylas, one of the Heraclidæ, exiled for slaying a priest of Apollo. *Apollod.* 2. c. 8.

HIPPOTH'OE, a daughter of Mestor and Lysidice, carried away to the islands called Echinades by Neptune, by whom she had a son named Taphius. This son distinguished himself by his valor, and returned to Argos at the head of the Teleboans. *Apollod.* 2. c. 4.——One of the Nereides. *Id.* 1. c. 2.——A daughter of Pelias. *Id.*

HIPPOTH'OON, a son of Neptune and Alope (*vid.* Alope), preserved by mares, whence his name, and when grown up, placed on his grandfather's throne by the friendship of Theseus. *Perizon. ad Ælian. V.H.* 12. c. 42.—*Hygin.* fab. 117.—*Paus*, 1. c. 38.

HIPPOTHOON'TIS, one of the 12 Athenian tribes, which received its name from Hippothoon. *Paus. in Attic.* 4 & 5.

HIPPOTH'OUS, a son of Lethus, killed by Ajax in the Trojan war. *Homer. Il.* 2. v. 347. l. 17. v. 217 & 288.——A son of Priam. *Apollod.* 3. c. 12.——A son of Ægyptus. *Id.*——One of the hunters of the Calydonian boar. *Ovid. Met.* 1. v. 307.——A son of Hippocoon, slain by Hercules. *Apollod.*

HIPPO'TION, a prince who, accompanied by his three sons, Palmis, Ascanius, and Moris, assisted the Trojans, and was killed by Merion. *Homer. Il.* 13. v. 792. l. 14. v. 514.

HIPPUCO'ME, a small town of Lysia. *Steph.*

HIPPU'RIS, one of the Cyclades. *Mela*, 2. c. 7.—*Plin.* 4. c. 12.

HIPPURIS'CUS, an island of Caria. *Steph.*

HIPPU'ROS, a harbor of Taprobane. *Plin.* 4. c. 12.

HIP'PUS, a river falling into the Phasis. *Strab.* 11.

HIP'SIDES, a Macedonian, a friend of Menedemus, &c. *Curt.* 7. c. 7.

HI'RA, a maritime town of Peloponnesus. *Homer. Il.* 12. *Vid.* Abia.

HIR'ASA, a place of Libya, to which the Afri transported Battus. *Steph.*

HIRMIN'IUM, a river of Sicily. *Plin.* 3. c. 8.

HIRPI'NI, an inland people of Italy, situate between Campania and Apulia. *Sil.* 8. v. 570.

HIRPI'NUS Q., a Roman, to whom *Horace* dedicated his 2 *od.* 11. and also 1. *ep.* 16.

HIR'RIUS C., an ædile, &c. *Cæs. B. C.* 1. c. 15.—*Plin* 9. c. 55.—*Macrob. Sat.* 2. c. 11.

HIR'TIA LEX, *de magistratibus*, by A. Hirtius. It enacted that none of Pompey's adherents should be raised to any office or dignity in the state.

HIR'TIUS AU'LUS, a consul with Pansa, who assisted Decimus Brutus when besieged at Mutina by Antony. They defeated the forces of Antony, but were both killed in battle B.C. 43. *Suet. in Aug* 10. *In Cæs.* 56.—*Cic. Att.* 14. ep. 6. *Phil.* 7. c. 4. *Fam.* 10. ep. 3 & 33.——An historian to whom the eighth book of Cæsar's history of the Gallic wars, as also that of the Alexandrian and Spanish wars, have been attributed. The style is inferior to that of Cæsar's Commentaries. The author, who was Cæsar's friend, and Cicero's pupil, is supposed by most authors to have been no other than the consul before mentioned. *Sax. Onom.* 1. p. 168.—*Harles, Not. Lit. Rom.* 1. p. 174.

HIRTULE'IUS, a general of Sertorius, who was defeated and slain by Metellus, B.C. 78.

HIR'TUS, a debauched fellow, &c. *Juv.* 10. v. 222.

HIS'BON, a Rutulian, killed by Pallas. *Virg. Æn.* 10. v. 384.

HIS'PALIS, an ancient town of Spain, now called Seville. *Plin.* 3. c. 3.—*Cæs. Fam.* 10. ep. 32.

HISPA'NIA or **HISPA'NIÆ**, called by the poets Iberia, and Hesperia Ultima, a large country of Europe, separated from Gaul by the Pyrenean mountains, and bounded on every other side by the sea. Spain was first known to the merchants of Phœnicia, and was next invaded by the Carthaginians, to whose power it long continued in subjection. The Romans became sole masters of it at the end of the second Punic war, and divided it at first into Citerior and Ulterior, which last was afterwards separated into Bætica and Lusitania by Augustus. The Hispania Citerior was also called Tarraconensis. The inhabitants were naturally warlike, and the country, from its mountainous nature, as well as from the spirit of its people, presented a formidable obstacle to the ambitious views of Rome. The Spaniards are described by some writers as frequently destroying themselves when life was become useless, and even burdensome, by its infirmities. Spain was famous for its rich mines of silver, which employed 40,000 workmen, and daily yielded to the Romans no less than 20,000 drachms. These have long since failed, though in the flourishing times of Rome, Spain was said to contain more gold, silver, brass, and iron than the rest of the world. It gave birth to Quintilian, Lucan, Martial, Mela, Silius, Seneca, &c. *Justin.* 44.—*Strab.* 3.—*Mela*, 2. c. 6.—*Plin.* 3. c. 1 & 20.

HISPA'NUS, a native of Spain. The word Hispaniensis was also used, but generally applied to a person living in Spain and not born there. *Martial.* 12. *præf.*

HISPEL'LUM, a town of Umbria. *Plin.* 3. c. 14.

HIS'PO, a noted debauchee, &c. *Juv.* 2. v. 50. ——An informer under Tiberius. *Tacit. Ann.* 1. c. 74.

HISPUL'LA, a lascivious woman. *Juv.* 6. v. 74.

HISTAS'PES, a relation of Darius the Third, killed in a battle, &c. *Curt.* 4. c. 4.

HIS'TER, a river. *Vid.* Ister.

His'ter Pacu'vius, a man distinguished as much by his vices as by his immense riches. *Juv.* 2. v. 58.

HISTIÆ'A, a city of Eubœa, anciently called Talantia. It was near the promontory called Ceneum. *Homer. Il.* 2.

HISTIÆ'OTIS or **HISTIÆO'TIS**, a country of Thessaly, situate at the west of mount Olympus and mount Ossa, on both sides of the Peneus, anciently called Doris, from Dorus, the son of Deucalion, and inhabited by the Pelasgi. The Pelasgi were driven from the country by the Cadmeans, and these last were in their turn dispossessed by the Perrhæbeans, who gave to their newly acquired possessions the name of Histiæotis, or Estiæotis, from Histiæa, or Estiæa, a town of Eubœa, which they had then lately destroyed, and the inhabitants of which they had carried to Thessaly with them. *Strab.*—*Herodot.* 4.——A small country of Eubœa, of which Histiæa, or Estiæa, was the capital.

HISTIÆ'US, a tyrant of Miletus, who excited the Greeks to take up arms against Persia. *Herodot.* 5, &c.——An historian of Miletus. *Joseph. Antiq.* 1. c. 3.—*Euseb. Chron.* 1. 1.

HISTO'NIUM, a city of Italy near mount Garganus. *Mela*, 1. 2.—*Plin.* 3. c. 12.

HIS'TRIA. *Vid* Istria.

HO'DIUS, a herald in the Trojan war. *Homer. Il.* 9.

HODOMAN'TI, a people of Thrace. *Steph. ex Thucyd.* l. 2.

HOL'OCRON, a mountain of Macedon. *Plut. in Æmyl.*

HOLOPHYX'US, a city of Crete. *Plin.* 4. c. 12.

HOMERI'TÆ, a people of Arabia Felix.

HOMEROMAS'TIX, *(Homeri flagellator)*, a surname given to Zoilus, because he criticised Homer with unusual severity and bitterness. The appellation is applied to all illiberal critics. *Plin. Præf.* 11.

HOME'RUS, a celebrated Greek poet, the most ancient of all the profane writers. The age in which he lived is not exactly known, though some suppose it to have been about 168 years after the Trojan war, or according to others 160 years before the foundation of Rome. According to Paterculus, he flourished 968 years B.C., or 884 according to Herodotus, who supposes him to be contemporary with Hesiod. The Arundelian Marbles with great probability fix his era 907 years B.C., and make him also contemporary with Hesiod. This diversity of opinion proves the antiquity of Homer; and the same uncertainty prevails also concerning the place of his nativity. No less than seven illustrious cities disputed the right of having given birth to the poet, as is well expressed in these lines:

Smyrna, Chius, Colophon, Salamis, Rhodus, Argos, Athenæ,
Orbis de patriâ certat, Homere, tuâ.

Homer was called Melesigenes, because he was supposed to have been born on the borders of the river Meles. There prevailed a report that he had established a school at Chius in the latter part of his life; and, indeed, this opinion is favored by the present inhabitants of the island, who still glory in showing to travellers the seats where the venerable master and his pupils sat in the hollow of a rock, at the distance of about four miles from the modern capital of the island. These difficulties and doubts have not been removed, though Aristotle, Herodotus, Plutarch, and others have employed their pen in elucidating the history of his life. In his two celebrated poems, the Iliad and the Odyssey, Homer has displayed the most consummate knowledge of human nature, and rendered himself immortal by the sublimity, the fire, the sweetness, and the elegance of his poetry. He deserves a greater share of admiration when we consider that he wrote without a model, and that none of his poetical imitators have been able to surpass, or, perhaps, to equal their great master. If there are any faults found in his poetry, they are to be attributed rather to the age in which he lived, than to himself; and we must observe, that the world is indebted to Homer for his happy successor Virgil. In his Iliad, Homer has described the resentment of Achilles, and its fatal consequences in the Grecian army before the walls of Troy. These two poems are each divided into 24 books, the same number as the letters of the Greek alphabet, and, though the Iliad claims an uncontested superiority over the Odyssey, yet the same force, the same sublimity and the same elegance prevail in both poems, though in the latter the style of the poet is divested of its more powerful fire; and Longinus, a critic of the most refined taste and correct judgment, has beautifully compared the Iliad to the mid-day, and the Odyssey to the setting sun, observing that the latter still preserves its original splendor and majesty, though deprived of its meridian heat. The poetry of Homer was so universally admired in ancient times, that every man of learning could repeat with facility the most striking passages in the Iliad or Odyssey; and, indeed, it proved in after times a sufficient authority to settle disputed boundaries, or to support any argument. The poems of Homer are the compositions of a man who examined with the most crititical accuracy whatever deserved notice and claimed attention. Modern travellers are astonished to see the different scenes which the pen of Homer delineated about 3000 years ago, still existing in the same unvaried form; and the sailor who now steers his course along the Ægæan, views all the promontories and rocks which the poet describes as appearing to Nestor and Menelaus, when they returned victorious from the Trojan war. The ancients had such a veneration for Homer, that they not only raised temples and altars to him, but offered sacrifices to him, and worshipped him as a god. The inhabitants of Chius celebrated festivals every fifth year in his honor, and medals were struck, which reprepresented him sitting on a throne, holding in his hand his Iliad and Odyssey. In Egypt his memory was consecrated by Ptolemy Philopator, who erected a magnificent temple, within which was placed a statue of the poet beautifully surrounded with a representation of the seven cities which contended for the honor of his birth. The inhabitants of Cos boasted that Homer was buried in their island; and the Cyprians claimed the same honor, and said that he was born of Themisto, a female native of Cyprus. Alexander the Great was so fond of Homer, that he generally placed his compositions under his pillow, with his sword; and he carefully deposited the Iliad in one of the richest and most valuable caskets of Darius, observing, that the most perfect work of human genius ought to be preserved in a box the most valuable and costly in the world. It is said, that Pisistratus, tyrant of Athens, was the first who collected and arranged the Iliad and Odyssey in the manner in which they now appear to us; and that it is to the labors of Lycurgus that we are indebted for their preservation. Many of the ancients have written the life of Homer, yet their enquiries and labors have not much contributed to discover the native place, the parentage, or the connections, of a man whom several authors have represented as deprived of sight. Besides the Iliad and Odyssey, Homer wrote, according to the opinion of some authors, a poem upon Amphiaraus' expedition against Thebes, besides the Phoceis, the Cercopes, the small Iliad, the Epicichlides, and the Batrachomyomachia, and many hymns to some of the gods. The merit of originality is taken very improperly, perhaps, from Homer, by those who suppose, with Clemens Alex. 6. *Strom.* that he borrowed from Orpheus, or that, according to Suidas [*voce Corinnus*], he took his plan of the Iliad from Corinnus, an epic poet, who wrote on the Trojan war at the very time that the Greeks besieged that famed city. Agathon, an ancient painter, according to Ælian, represented the superior merit of the poet in a manner as bold as it was indelicate. Homer was represented as vomiting, and all the other poets as swallowing what he ejected. Of the numerous commentaries published on Homer, that of Eustathius, bishop of Thessalonica, is by far the most extensive and erudite. The best editions of Homer's Iliad and Odyssey may, perhaps, be found to be Barnes, 2 vols. 4to, Cantab. 1711; that of Glasgow, 2 vols. fol. 1758; that of Berglerus, 2 vols. 12mo, Amst. 1707; that of Dr. Clarke, of the Iliad, 2 vols. 4to, 1729, and of the Odyssey, 1740; and that of Oxford, 5 vols. 8vo. 1780, containing the scholia, hymns, and an index. But of all editions that of Heyne is entitled to a decided preference. *Herodot.* 2. c. 53. —*Theocrit.* 16.—*Aristot. Poet.*—*Strab.* 1.—*Dio. Chris.* 33 *Orat.*—*Paus.* 2. c. 33. l. 9. c. 30. l. 10. c. 24.—*Aul. Gell.* 3. c. 2.—*Heliodor.* 3.—*Ælian. V.H.* 13. c. 14 & 22.—*Val. Max.* 8. c. 8.—*Quintil.* 1. c. 5. l. 5. c. 11. l. 10. c. 1. l. 12. c. 10.—*Plin.* 7. c. 29.—*Paterc.* 1. c. 5.—*Dyonys. Hal.*—*Plut. in Alex. &c.*—*Sax. Onom.* 1. p. 11.—*Fabr. B. Gr.* 1. 2. c. 3. [The finest head of Homer is a bust in the British Museum. There is also a very fine bronze in the same collection; and a celebrated marble head in the possession of the late king of Naples.]

HOME'RUS, one of the Greek poets called Pleiades, born at Hierapolis, B.C. 263. He wrote 45 tragedies, all of which have unhappily perished. *Vossius. de P. Gr.* 2. There were seven other poets, of inferior note, who bore the name of Homer. *L. Gyrald. Poet. H.* 2.

HOMIL'IÆ, a city of Thessaly. *Ptol.*

HOM'OLE or HOMOLE'A, a lofty mountain of Thessaly, once the residence of the Centaurs. *Virg. Æn.* 7. v. 675.

HOM'OLE or HOMO'LIUM, a town in Magnesia, at the foot of Ossa.

HOMOLIP'PUS, a son of Hercules and Xanthis. *Apollod.*

HOMOLO'IDES, one of the seven gates of Thebes. *Stat. Theb.* 7. v. 252.—*Apollod.*

HOMONADEN'SES, a people of Cilicia. *Tac. Ann.* 3. c. 48.—*Strab.* l. 12.

HO'NOR, a virtue which received divine homage among the Romans. A temple was first erected to her at Rome by Scipio Africanus, and another was afterwards built by Claud. Marcellus, by the side of an edifice consecrated to virtue, through which it was necessary to pass before that of Honor could be approached: a lesson of great moral import, and highly becoming the first age of Roman greatness, when virtue alone was the guide to distinctions and to public rewards. A third temple was raised to Honor by Marius after the defeat of the Cimbri. *Cic. de Nat. D.* 2. c. 23.—*Val. Max.* 1. c. 1.—*Festus. de Verb. Sig.*—*Ovid. Fast.* 5. v. 474.—*Liv.* 29.

HONO'RIUS, an emperor of the western empire of Rome, who, with his brother Arcadius, succeeded his father Theodosius the Great. He was neither bold nor vicious, but he was of a modest and timid disposition, unfit for enterprise, and fearful of danger. He conquered his enemies by means of his generals, and suffered himself and his people to be governed by ministers who took advantage of their imperial master's indolence and inactivity to screen their acts of rapacity and oppression. He died of a dropsy in the 39th year of his age, on the 15th of August, A.D. 423. He left no issue, though he married two wives. Under him and his brother the Roman power was divided into two different empires. The successors of Honorius, who fixed their residence at Rome, were called the emperors of the west, and the successors of Arcadius, who sat on the throne of Constantinople, were distinguished by the name of emperors of the eastern Roman empire. This division of power in the lapse of time proved fatal to both empires, which soon began to look upon one another with indifference, contempt, and jealousy.——A Greek surname of Jupiter, the same as the Terminalis of the Latins. He was worshipped under the form of a stone, over which, as separating fields and boundaries, the ancients bound themselves by oaths in the most solemn manner. *Aul. Gell.* 12. c. 6.—*Apuleius de Deo. Socr.*—*Dionys. Hal.* 2.

HONO'RIUS VENAN'TIUS, a Christian writer. *Vid.* Venantius.

HONOS'CA, a maritime city of Hispania Tarraconensis, now Villa Joyosa, according to *Ortelius. Liv.* 22. c. 20.

HOP'LEUS, an Argive, slain by Æpytus. *Stat. Theb.* 10. 400.

HO'RA, a goddess at Rome, supposed to be Hersilia, one of the Sabine women, who married Romulus. She was said to preside over beauty. *Ovid. Met.* 14. v. 851.

HORACI'TÆ, a people near Illyricum. *Polyb.*

HORAPOL'LO or HO'RUS, a Greek writer, probably an Ægyptian, whose age is unknown. His Hieroglyphica, a curious and entertaining book, has been edited by Corn. de Pauw. 4to, Ultraj, 1727, and others. *Vid. Fabr. B. Gr.* l. 1. c. 13.—*Sax. Onom.* 1. p. 5.

HO'RÆ, three sisters, daughters of Jupiter and Themis, according to Hesiod, called Eunomia, Dice, and Irene. They were the same as the seasons who presided over the spring, summer, and winter, and were represented by the poets as opening the gates of heaven and of Olympus, and yoking the horses of Phœbus at the approach of morning. *Homer. Il.* 5. v. 749.—*Paus.* 5. c. 11.—*Hesiod. Theog.* 902.—*Ovid. Met.* 2. v. 26.—*Fast.* 1. v. 125. —*Horat.* 1. od. 12. v. 16.—*Martial.* 4. epigr. 8.

HORA'TIA, the sister of the Horatii, killed by her brother for mourning the death of the Curatii. *Cic. de Inv.* 2. c. 20.

HORA'TIA LEX, enacted by M. Horatius, to pay certain honors to Caia Tarratia, a vestal virgin. *A. Gell.* l. 6. c. 7. *Plutarch. in Publ.* calls her Tarquinia.—Another, enacted by M. Horatius Barbatus, consul with Valer. Poplicola, respecting the punishment of those persons and their families, who injured the ædiles or other magistrates. *Liv.* 3 c. 55.—*Dionys.* l. 5.—Another, called Horatia Valeria, enacted by the same, making the laws passed by the tribes binding on the people. *Liv.* l. 1.—*Dion. Hal.* l. 2, &c.

HORA'TII, three brave Romans, born at the same birth, who fought against the three Curiatii, about 667 B.C. This celebrated fight took place between the hostile camps of the people of Alba and Rome, and on their success depended the victory. In the first attack two of the Horatii were killed, and the only surviving brother, by joining artifice to valor, obtained an honorable trophy; by pretending to flee from the field of battle, he easily separated his antagonists, and, in attacking them one by one, he was enabled to conquer them all. As he returned victorious to Rome, his sister reproached him with the murder of the Curiatii, to one of whom she was promised in marriage. He was so incensed at the rebuke, that he killed his sister. This violence raised the indignation of the people;

He was tried and capitally condemned. His eminent services, however, pleaded in his favor, the sentence of death was exchanged for a more moderate, but more ignominious punishment, and a was only compelled to pass under the yoke. A trophy was raised in the Roman forum, on which he suspended the spoils of the conquered Curiah. *Cic. de Invent.* 2. c. 26.—*Liv.* 1. c. 24, &c.—*Dion. Hal.* 3. c. 3.

HORA'TIUS, a consul, who defeated the Sabines. ——A consul, who dedicated the temple of Jupiter Capitolinus. During the ceremony he was informed of the death of his son, but he did not forget the sacred character which he then bore for the feelings of a parent. and after ordering the body to be buried, continued the dedication. *Liv.* 2.

Hora'tius Co'cles. *Vid.* Cocles.

Hora'tius C. Flac'cus, a celebrated poet, born at Venusium. His father, who was a freedman, assumed the name of his master Horatius, who had granted him his liberty, and, though poor in his circumstances, liberally educated his son, and sent him to learn philosophy at Athens, after he had received the lessons of the best masters of Rome. Horace, enticed by the prospect of military glory, followed Brutus from Athens, but the timidity which he betrayed at the battle of Philippi so effectually discouraged him, that he for ever abandoned the profession of arms, and, on his return to Rome, applied himself to cultivate poetry. His rising talents claimed the attention of Virgil and of Varius, who recommended him to the protection of Mecænas and Augustus, two most deservedly celebrated patrons of literature. Under the fostering protection of the emperor and his minister, Horace gave himself up to indolence and refined pleasure. He was a follower of Epicurus, and while he liberally indulged his appetites, he neglected the calls of ambition, and never suffered himself to be carried away by the tide of popularity or by a desire to obtain public employments. He even refused to become the secretary of Augustus, and the emperor was not offended at his modest refusal. He lived at the tables of his illustrious patrons as if he were in his own house; and Augustus, while sitting at his meals with Virgil at his right hand, and Horace at his left, often ridiculed the short breath of the former, and the watery eyes of the latter, by observing that he sat between tears and sighs, *Ego sum inter suspiria et lacrymas.* Horace was warm in his friendship, and if ever any ill-judged reflection had caused offence, the poet immediately made every concession which could produce a reconciliation, and not destroy the pleasing intercourse of friendly society. Horace died in the 57th year of his age, B.C. 8. His gaiety was suitable to the liveliness and dissipation of a court, and his familiar intimacy with Mecænas, is, according to some commentators, too serious to be considered as a poetical rhapsody or an unmeaning effusion; and indeed it is remarkable, that the poet survived the patron only three weeks, and ordered his bones to be buried near friend. He left all his possessions to Augustus. The poetry of Horace, so much commended for its elegance and sweetness, is deservedly censured for the licentious expressions and indelicate thoughts which he too frequently introduces. In his odes he has imitated Pindar and Anacreon; and if he has confessed himself inferior to the former, he has shown that he bears the palm over the latter by the splendor of his genius and his more elegant and refined sentiments, by the ease and melody of his more elegant and refined sentiments, by the ease and melody of his expressions, and by the pleasing variety of his numbers. In his satires and epistles, Horace displays much wit, and much satirical humor, without much poetry, so that his style, simple and unadorned, differs little from prose. In his art of poetry he has shown great taste and judgment, and has rendered into Latin hexameter, what Aristotle had some ages before, delivered to his pupils in Greek prose. The poet gives in this excellent work judicious rules and useful precepts to the most powerful and opulent citizens of Rome, who, in the midst of peace and enjoyment, wished to cultivate poetry and court the muses. The best editions of Horace will be found to be that of Basil, 1580, illustrated by eighty commentators; that of Baxter, edited by Gesner, Lips. 1752; that of Glasgow, 12mo, 1744; that of the great Bentley, Cantabr. 1711, London, 1765; and that of Combe, London, 1792.—*Suet. in Aug.*—*Ovid. Trist.* 4. el. 10. v. 49.—*Harles. Not. Lit. Rom.* 1. p. 256.—*Sax. Onom.* 1. p. 186.

HOR'CIAS, the general of 3,000 Macedonians, who revolted from Antigonus in Cappadocia. *Polyæn.* 4.

HORDEO'NIUS FLAC'CUS, a lieutenant of the army in Germany, despised by his soldiers. *Tac. Hist.* 1. c. 9, &c.

HORDONIEN'SES, a people of Apulia. *Plin.* 3. c. 11. Their city was Hordonia or Erdonia.

HORES'TI, a people of Great Britain. According to *Camden*, they inhabited the country now called Eskdale. *Tac. Agr.* 38.

HOR'ICI, a people of Italy. *Steph.*

HOR'MA, a town of Macedonia. *Ptol.*

HORMIN'IUS, a mountain of Bithynia, called Hippius by *Pliny*, 5. c. 32.—*Ptol.*

HORMIS'DA, a name which some of the Persian kings bore in the reign of the later Roman emperors.

HOR'MUS, a freedman, a general of Vespasian, afterwards knighted. *Tac. Hist.* 3. c. 12.

HORRA'TUS, a Macedonian soldier, who fought with another private soldier in sight of the whole army of Alexander. *Curt.* 9. c. 7. *Diodorus Siculus*, l. 17. calls him Coragus.

HOR'TA, a town of the Sabines, on the confluence of the Nar and the Tiber. *Virg. Æn.* 7. v. 716.

Hor'ta. *Vid.* Hersilia.

HORTA'NUM, a city of Etruria. *Plin.* 3. c. 5.

HORTEN'SIA, a celebrated Roman lady, daughter of the orator Hortensius, whose eloquence she had inherited in the most eminent degree. When the triumvirs had obliged 14,000 women to give upon oath an account of their possessions, towards defraying the expenses of the state, Hortensia undertook to plead their cause, and was so successful in her attempt, that 1,000 of her female fellow-sufferers escaped from the avarice of the triumvirate. *Val. Max.* 8. c. 3.—*Quintil.* 1. c. 2.—*Appian. B. Civ.* l. 4.

Horten'sia Lex, by Q. Hortensius the dictator, A.U.C. 667. It ordered the whole body of the Romans to pay implicit obedience to whatever decrees were enacted by the commons. The nobility, before this law was enacted, had claimed an absolute exemption.

HORTEN'SIUS, a rich Roman, to whom Cato the elder, without reluctance, gave up his wife, and took her again after his death. This behaviour of Cato was highly censured at Rome, and it was observed that Cato's wife had entered the house very poor, but that she returned to the bed of Cato in the greatest opulence. *Plut. in Cat.*——A Roman slain by Antony on his brother's tomb. *Id.*——A prætor who gave up Macedonia to Brutus. *Id.*——A Roman, the first who introduced the eating of peacocks. This was at the feast which he gave when he was created augur.——One of Sylla's lieutenants. *Id.*——A poet. *Ovid. Trist.* 2. v. 441.

Horten'sius Q., a celebrated orator, who began to distinguish himself by his eloquence in the Roman forum at the age of nineteen. His friend and successor Cicero speaks with great approbation of his oratorical powers, and mentions the uncommon extent of his memory. The affected action of Hortensius at the bar procured him the ludicrous surname of Dionysia, a celebrated stage dancer at that time. He was prætor and consul, and died 50 B.C., in his 63rd year. None of his orations are extant, but it is remarkable that Quintilian mentions them as undeserving the great commendation which Cicero had so liberally bestowed upon them. Hortensius was very rich, and not less than 10,000 casks of Arvisian wine were found in his cellar after his death. He had written pieces of amorous poetry, and annals, all lost. *Cic. in Brut.* 64, 90 & 92. *Ad Attic. De Orat. &c. Pro Lege Man.* 17. *De Offic.* 2. c. 16. —*Quintil.* 4. c. 5. l. 10. c. 6. l. 12. c. 7.—*Varro de R.R.* 3. c. 5. [There is a head of Hortensius at the Villa Albani.]

Horten'sius Cor'bio, a grandson of the orator of the same name, noted for his lasciviousness.

HORTO'NA or ORTO'NA, a town of Italy, on the confines of the Æqui. *Liv.* 3. c. 30.

HO'RUS, a son of Isis, one of the deities of the Ægyptians.——A king of Assyria. *Plin.* 30. c. 5.

——A cynic philosopher mentioned by *Macrobius*, *Saturn*. 1. c. 7.—There were also grammarians of Miletus, of Thebes, and of Alexandria, of this name. *Vid. Fabr. B. Gr.* l. c. 13.

HO'SA, a river of Etruria, now Martha. *Ptol.*

HOSPITA'LIS, a surname given to Jupiter among the Romans, and which was the same as the Xenius of the Greeks. The god was so called because he presided over hospitality, and caused to be punished every violation of its most sacred laws. *Virg. Æn.* 1. v. 735.

HOSTIÆ'I or **HOSTI'ONES**, a people near the Western Ocean. *Steph.* They are called Cassini by *Artemidorus*.

HOSTIL'IA LEX was enacted by Aulus Hostilius A.U.C. 583. By it such as were among the enemies of the republic, or absent when the state required their assistance, were guilty of rapine.

Hostil'ia, a large town on the Po, nearly at the east of Mantua. *Tacit. Ann.* 2. c. 40.—*Plin.* 21. c. 12.

HOSTILIA'NUS PERPEN'NA, an emperor after Vibius Volusianus. He died of the plague shortly after his elevation, and was succeeded by C. Jul. Æmilianus. *Casaub. ad Hist. Aug.*

HOSTIL'IUS TUL'LUS, the third king of Rome. *Vid.* Tullus.

HOS'TIUS, a Latin poet, in the age of J. Cæsar, who composed a poem on the wars of Istria. *Macrob. Sat.* 6. c. 3 & 5.——A lawyer. *Cic. Orat.* 1. c. 57.

Hos'tius Hostil'ius, a warlike Roman presented with a crown of boughs by Romulus for his intrepid behaviour in a battle. *Dionys. Hal.*

Hos'tius Lucre'tius Tricipiti'nus, a consul, A.U.C. 327.

HOSTO'RIUS, a centurion, sent to receive hostages given by the præfect of Scythia to the king of Parthia. *Tac. Ann.* 13. c. 8.

HUNNERI'CUS, king of the Vandals A.D. 477, was the son of Genseric. He was a great persecutor of the Christians. The English form is Hun'neric.

HUN'NI, a warlike people of Sarmatia, who invaded the empire of Rome in the fifth century, and settled in Pannonia, to which they gave the name of Hungary.

HYACIN'THIA, an annual solemnity observed at Amyclæ, in Laconia, in honor of Hyacinthus and Apollo. It continued for three days, during which time the grief of the people was so great for the death of Hyacinthus, that they did not adorn their hair with garlands or eat bread, but fed only upon sweetmeats. They did not even sing pæans in honor of Apollo, or observe any of the solemnities which were usual at other sacrifices. On the second day of the festival there were a number of different exhibitions. Youths, with their garments girt about them, entertained the spectators, by playing sometimes upon the flute, or upon the harp, and by singing anapæstic songs, in loud echoing voices, in honor of Apollo. Others passed across the theatre mounted on horses richly adorned, and, at the same time, choirs of young men came upon the stage singing their uncouth rustic songs, and accompanied by persons who danced to the sound of vocal and instrumental music, according to the ancient custom. Some virgins were also introduced in chariots of wood, covered at the top, and magnificently adorned. Others appeared in race chariots. The city began then to be filled with altars of Apollo, and the votaries liberally entertained their friends and slaves. During this latter part of the festivity, all the people were particularly anxious to be present at the games, and the city was left, in consequence, almost without inhabitants. *Athen.* 4.—*Ovid. Met.* 10. v. 219.—*Paus.* 3. c. 1 & 19.—*Hesych.*

HYACIN'THUS, a son of Amyclas and Diomede, greatly beloved by Apollo and Zephyrus. He returned the former's affection, and Zephyrus, incensed at his coldness and indifference, resolved to punish his rival. As Apollo who was entrusted with the education of Hyacinthus once played at quoit with his pupil, Zephyrus blew the quoit, as soon as it was thrown by Apollo, upon the head of Hyacinthus, and the unfortunate youth was killed by the blow. Apollo was so disconsolate at the death of Hyacinthus, that he changed his blood into a flower, which bore his name, and also placed his body among the constellations. The Spartans at the same time established yearly festivals in honor of the nephew of their king. *Vid.* Hyacinthia. *Ovid. Met.* 10. v. 185, &c.—*Apollod.* 3, &c.—*Lucian. Dial. Deor.* 14 & 15.—*Palæph.* 47.

HY'ADES, five daughters of Atlas, king of Mauritania, who were so disconsolate at the death of their brother Hyas, who had been killed by a wild boar, that they pined away and died. They became stars after death, and were placed near Taurus, one of the twelve signs of the zodiac, and received the name of Hyades from their brother Hyas. Their names were Phaola, Ambrosia, Eudora, Coronis, and Polyxo. To these some have added Thione and Prodice, maintaining that they were daughters of Hyas and Æthra one of the Oceanides. Euripides calls them daughters of Erechtheus. The ancients supposed that the rising and setting of the Hyades were always attended with much rain, whence their name (ὕω *pluo.*) The seven other sisters did not long survive the death of the Hyades, and they also became a constellation called Pleiades. *Ovid. Fast.* 5. v. 165. *Met.* 3. v. 314.—*Eurip. in Ion.* 1155.—*Nonus Dion.* 31. c. 3.—*Hygin.* fab. 182 & 192. *P.A.* 2. c. 21.—*Schol. Theocr.* 13.—*Aul. Gell.* 13. c. 9.—*Proclus in Hesiod.*

HYÆ'A, a city of the Locri Ozoli. *Steph.*

HYAG'NIS, a Phrygian, father of Marsyas. He was considered by the ancients as the inventor of the flute, and of those beautiful airs known by the name of Phrygian. *Athen.* 14.—*Plut de Music.*

HY'ALA, a city at the mouth of the Indus, similar to Sparta in its government and political institutions. *Diod. Sic.* l. 17.

Hy'ala, one of Diana's attendant nymphs. *Ovid, Met.* 2. v. 171.

HYAMÆ'A or **HYAME'A**, a city of Messenia. *Steph.*

HYAMPE'A, one of the two peaks of Parnassus.

HYAMP'OLIS, a city between Locris, Thessaly, and Phocis, on the Cephisus. It was founded by the Hyanthes, after they had been driven from Thebes. *Strab.* 4, 7, & 9.—*Paus.* 3. c. 1. l. 10. c. 35.

HYAN'TES, the ancient name of the inhabitants of Bœotia, derived from king Hyas. Cadmus is sometimes called Hyanthius, because he was king of Bœotia. *Ovid. Met.* 3. v. 147.—*Plin.* 4. c. 7.

HYAN'THIS, an ancient name of Bœotia.

HYAN'TIA, a city of Locri. *Steph.*

HYAPE'A, a city of Phocis. *Id.*

HYARBI'TA, a man who endeavoured to imitate Timagenes, &c. *Horat.* 1. ep. 18. v. 15.

HY'AS, a son of Atlas, king of Mauritania, by Æthra. His extreme fondness for shooting proved fatal to him, and, in his attempts to rob a lioness of her whelps, he was killed by the enraged animal. Some say that he died by the bite of a serpent, and others that he was killed by a wild boar. His sisters mourned his death with such afflicting lamentations, that Jupiter, in compassion for their sorrow, changed them into stars. *Vid.* Hyades. *Hygin.* fab. 192.—*Schol. Homer. Il.* 18. v. 486.—*Ovid. Fast.* 5. v. 170.——A king of Bœotia, whence Hyantius or Hyanthius is applied to a native of the country. *Ovid. Met.* 3. v. 147.

HY'BA or **HYB'ADÆ**, a village in the tribe Leontis. *Steph.*

HYBAN'DA, an island on the coast of Ionia, afterwards joined to the continent. *Plin.* 2. c. 89.

HYB'ELE, a city near Carthage. *Steph.*

HYB'LA or **HY'BLA**, a mountain in Sicily, called afterwards Megara, where thyme and odoriferous flowers of all sorts grew in abundance. It was famous for its bees and its honey. There was at the foot of the mountain, on the sea shore, a little above Syracuse, a town of the same name. There was also another near mount Ætna, close to Catana. *Paus.* 5. c. 23.—*Strab.* 6.—*Mela*, 2. c. 7.—*Cic. Ver.* 3. c. 43. l. 5. c. 25.—*Sil.* 14. v. 26.—*Stat.* 14. v. 226.——A city of Attica. *Servius. ad Ecl. Virg.* 1. v. 55.

HYB'REAS, an orator of Caria, &c. *Strab.* 13.

HYBRIA'NES or **HYBRI'ANES**, a people near Thrace. *Id.* l. 7.

HYC'CARA, a town of Sicily, the native place of Lais. *Athen.* l. 13.—*Thucyd.* l. 6.—*Plut. in Nic.* It is now Muro Carini.

HY'DA or **HY'DE**, a town of Lydia, under mount Tmolus, which some suppose to have been the same as Sardes. *Homer. Il.* 2.—*Strab.* l. 13.

HYD'ARA, a town of Armenia Major. *Strab.* 12.

HYDAR'CÆ, a people of India who fought against Bacchus. *Steph.*

HYDAR'NES, one of the seven noble Persians who

conspired to destroy the usurper Smerdis, &c. *Herodot.* 3 & 6.—*Strab.* 11.

HYDAS'PES, a river of Asia, the situation of which is not satisfactorily explained by ancient writers, though some suppose it was the Choaspes, and others the Araxes, both of which rivers discharge themselves into the Persian Gulph. *Virg. G.* 4. v. 211.——A river in India, now Behut or Chelum, the boundary of Alexander's conquests in the east. It falls into the Indus. *Curt.* 5. c. 2.—*Lucan.* 8. v. 227.—*Horat.* 1. od. 22. v. 7.—*Strab.* 15.

Hydas'pes, a friend of Æneas, killed in the Rutulian war. *Virg. Æn.* 10. v. 747.

HYD'IA, a town of Sicily. *Ptol.* According to *Fazellus*, it is now Cabra.

HYDIS'SUS, a city of Caria. *Steph.*—*Plin.* 5. c. 29.

HY'DRA, a celebrated monster, which infested the neighbourhood of the lake Lerna in Peloponnesus. It was the fruit of Echidna's union with Typhon, or, according to Epimenides of Crete, it was the offspring of Styx, one of the Oceanides, by Piras, a person whose name is not mentioned by mythologists. This monster had a hundred heads, according to Diodorus; fifty, according to Simonides; and nine, according to the more received opinion of Apollodorus, Hyginus, &c. As soon as one of these heads was cut off, two immediately grew up. It was one of the labors of Hercules to destroy this dreadful monster, and this he easily effected with the assistance of Iolas, who applied a burning iron to the wounds as soon as one head was cut off. While Hercules was destroying the hydra, Juno, jealous of his glory, sent a sea-crab to bite his foot. This new enemy was soon dispatched; and Juno, unable to succeed in her attempts to lessen the fame of Hercules, placed the crab among the constellations, where it now bears the name of Cancer. The conqueror dipped his arrows in the gall of the hydra, and, from that circumstance, all the wounds which he gave proved incurable. *Hesiod. Theog.* 315.—*Apollod.* 2. c. 5.—*Paus.* 5. c. 17. l. 5. c. 17. l. 3. c. 18.—*Diod.* 4.—*Lucret.* 5. v. 26.—*Simonid. apud Sch. Hesiod. Th.* 313.—*Hygin.* fab. 30—*Alcæi Fragm.*—*Ovid. Met.* 9. v. 69.—*Horat.* 4. od. 4. v. 61.—*Virg. Æn.* 6. v. 276. l. 7. 658.

HYDRA'MIA, a city of Crete. *Steph.*

HYDRAO'TES, a river of India, crossed by Alexander in his Asiatic expedition.

HY'DRAX, a town of the Pentapolis in Africa. *Ptol.*

HYD'REA, an island near Trœzene. *Steph.*

HYDRE'LA, a city of Caria. *Id.*

HYDREU'MA, the name of various places in Upper Æthiopia and elsewhere. *Plin.* 6. c. 23.

HYDRI'ACUS, a river of Carmania. *Ptol.*

HYD'RIAS, a region of Asia Minor. *Herod.* l. 5. c.118.

HYDROCH'OUS, the Greek name of Aquarius.

HYDROPHO'RIA, a festival observed at Athens, so called ἀπὸ τοῦ φέρειν ὕδωρ, *from carrying water.* It was celebrated in commemoration of those who perished in the deluge of Deucalion and Ogyges. *Meursius Gr. Fer.*—*Etymol. Auct.*——A festival celebrated at Ægina, in honor of Apollo, in the month Delphinius. *Pind. Schol. Nem.* 5.

HYDRUN'TUM or **HY'DRUS**, a city of Calabria, 50 miles south of Brundusium. As the distance from thence to Greece was only 60 miles, Pyrrhus, and afterwards Varro, Pompey's lieutenant, meditated the building here a bridge across the Adriatic. Though so favorably situated, Hydrus, now called Otranto, is but an insignificant town, scarce containing 3000 inhabitants. *Plin.* 3. c. 11.—*Cic.* 15. *Att.* 21. l. 16. ep. 5.—*Lucan.* 5. v. 375.

HYDRU'SA, a town of Attica. *Strab.* 9.——A name of Andrus, one of the Cyclades.

HY'ELA, a town of Lucania. *Strab.* 6.

HYEMP'SAL, a son of Micipsa, brother to Adherbal, cruelly murdered by Jugurtha, after the death of his father. *Sallust de Jug. Bell.*

HYET'TUS, a town of Bœotia. *Paus.* 9. c. 24.

HYETUS'SA, an island on the coast of Caria. *Plin.* 5. c. 31.

HYGAS'SUS, a city of Caria. *Steph.*

HYGI'A or **HYGIE'A**, the goddess of health, daughter of Æsculapius, was held in great veneration among the ancients. Her statues represented her with a veil, and her matrons usually consecrated their locks to her divinity. She was also represented on monuments like a young woman holding a serpent in one hand, and in the other a cup, out of which the serpent sometimes drank. According to some authors, Hygeia is the same as Minerva, who is said to have received that name from Pericles, who erected her statue, because she had told him in a dream, the means of curing an architect, whose assistance he wanted to build a temple. *Plin.* 35. c. 11.—*Martial.* 11. epigr. 61.—*Plut. in Pericl.*—*Paus.* 1. c. 23.—*L. Gyrald. Hist. D.* 11. [Mr. J. Hope possessed a very pretty figure, representing this goddess. There is also a fine group of Æsculapius and Hygeia in the Vatican.]

HYGENNEN'SES, a people of Asia Minor. *Herod.* 3. c. 90.

HYGI'ANA, a town of Triphylia in Peloponnesus. *Polyb.*

HYGI'NUS C. JUL., surnamed Polyhistor, a Latin grammarian, one of the freedmen of Augustus. He was a native of Alexandria, or, according to some, he was a Spaniard, and very intimate with Ovid. He was appointed librarian to the library of mount Palatine, and was able to maintain himself by the liberality of C. Licinius. He wrote a mythological history, which he called fables, and *Poeticon Astronomicum*, besides treatises on the cities of Italy, and on such Roman families as were descended from the Trojans, a book on agriculture, commentaries on Virgil, the lives of great men, &c. now lost. The best edition of Hyginus is that of Muncker, contained in his *Mythographi Latini*, 2 vols. 8vo, Amst. 1681. These compositions have been greatly mutilated, and their incorrectness and bad Latinity have induced some authors to suppose that they are spurious. *Gell.* 1. c. 7 & 10.—*Sueton. de Gram.* 20.—*Scaliger. ad Euseb. Chr.*—*Harles. Not. Lit. Rom.* 1. p. 309.—*Saxius. Onom.* 1. p. 199, supposes that there were three persons of this name, Hyginus Polyhistor; Hyginus Gromaticus, who lived in the age of Trajan and of Adrian, and Hyginus Mythographus.

HY'GRIS, a city of European Sarmatia. *Ptol.*

HY'I, a people of Susiana. *Plin.* 6. c. 27.

HY'LA or **HY'LAS**, a small river of Mysia, where Hylas was drowned. *Virg. G.* 3. v. 6.

Hy'la, a colony of Phocis, afterwards Elæa. *Suidas.*—*Strab.*

HYLAC'TOR, one of Actæon's dogs, from his barking (ὑλακτῶ *latro*). *Ovid. Met.* 3.

HYLÆ'A or **HYLE'A**, a small region of Asiatic Sarmatia. *Val. Flacc. Argon.* 6. v. 74.

HYLÆ'US, a Centaur killed by Hercules on mount Pholoe. *Virg. Æn.* 8. v. 294.——A Centaur slain by Theseus at the nuptials of Pirithous. *Stat.* 7. *Theb.* 267.—*Ovid. Met.* 12. v. 378.——A Centaur killed by Bacchus. *Virg. G.* 2. v. 457.—*Stat. Theb.* 6. v. 530.——A Centaur slain by Atalanta. *Apollod.* 3.——One of the hunters of the Calydonian boar.——One of Actæon's dogs. *Ovid. Met.* 3. v. 213. l. 8. v. 312.

HYLA'MI, a city of Lycia. *Steph.*

HYLAS, a son of Theodamas, king of Mysia, by Menodice, stolen away by Hercules, and carried on board the ship Argo to Colchis. On the Asiatic coast the Argonauts landed to take a supply of fresh water, and Hylas., following the example of his companions went to the fountain with a pitcher and fell into the water and was drowned. The poets have embellished this tragical story, by saying, that the nymphs of the river, enamoured of the beautiful Hylas, carried him away; and that Hercules, disconsolate at the loss of his favorite youth, filled the woods and mountains with his complaints, and at last abandoned the Argonautic expedition to go and seek him. *Apollod.* 1. c. 9.—*Hygin.* fab. 14. 271.—*Virg. Ecl.* 6. v. 44. & *Servius loco.*—*Val. Flacc.* 1.—*Stat. Theb.* 5.—*Schol. Appollon.* 3. *Arg.* v. 1218 & 1236.—*Tzetzes. Chil.* 1. c, 43.—*Propert.* 1. el. 20.

Hy'las, a river of Bithynia. *Plin.* 5. c. 23.

HYLA'TÆ, a river of Bithynia. *Plin.* 5. c. 23.

HYL'ATUS, a name of Apollo in Cyprus. *Steph.*

HY'LAX, a dog mentioned in *Virgil*, *Ecl.* 8.

HY'LE, a city of Cyprus.——A city of the Locri Ozoli. *Steph.*——A small city of Bœotia. *Strab.* l. 9.—*Plin*, 4. c. 7.

HYL'IAS, a river of Magna Græcia. *Thucyd.* l. 7.

HYLLA'ICUS, a port of Peloponnesus, near Messenia.

HYLLAR'IMA, a town of Caria. *Steph.*

HYLLEN'SES, Ὑλλεῖς, a people of Illyricum. *Id.*

HYL'LIS, a peninsula or promontory of Liburnia, on the Adriatic Sea. *Plin.* l. 3. c. 22.

HYLLU'ALA, a village of Caria where Hyllus died. *Steph.*

HYL'LUS, a son of Hercules and Dejanira, who, soon after his father's death, married Iole. He was persecuted, as his father had been, by the envy of Eurystheus, and was at last obliged to flee from the Peloponnesus. The Athenians, pitying their misfortunes, gave a kind reception to Hyllus and the rest of the Heraclidæ, and marched against Eurystheus. Hyllus obtained a victory over his enemies, killed Eurystheus with his own hand, and sent his head to Alcmena, his grandmother. Some time after he attempted to recover the Peloponnesus with the Heraclidæ, but was slain in single combat by Echemus, king of Arcadia. *Vid.* Heraclidæ, Hercules, &c. *Herodot.* 7. c. 204, &c, —*Strab.* 9,—*Apollod.* 2.—*Hygin.* fab. 36 & 174 —*Sch. Thucyd.* 1.—*Diod.* 4.—*Ovid. Met.* 9. v. 279. *Heroid.* 9, v. 168.

Hyl'lus, a river of Lydia or of Phrygia, according to *Livy*, l. 37. c. 38, flowing into the Hermus. *Herodot.* 1. c. 180.—*Strab.* 12.

HYLON'OME, the wife of Cyllarus, who killed herself the moment that her husband was murdered by the Lapithæ. *Ovid. Met.* 12. v. 405.

HYLOPH'AGI, a people of Æthiopia. *Diod.* 3.

HYL'YCUS, a river of Argolis. *Athen.* l. 3.

HYMA'NI, a people of Liburnia. *Plin.* 3. c. 21.

HYMENÆ'US or **HY'MEN**, the god of marriage among the Greeks, was son of Bacchus and Venus, or according to others, of Apollo, and one of the Muses. Hymenæus, according to the more received opinions, was a young Athenian of extraordinary beauty, but ignoble origin. He became enamoured of the daughter of one of the richest and noblest of his countrymen, but as the rank and superior birth of his mistress removed him from her presence and conversation, he contented himself to follow her wherever she went. In a certain procession, in which all the matrons of Athens went to Eleusis, Hymenæus, to accompany his mistress, disguised himself in women's clothes, and joined the religious troop, his youth and the fairness of his features favoring his disguise. A great part of the females of the procession was seized by the sudden arrival of some pirates, and Hymenæus, who shared the captivity of his mistress, encouraged his female companions, and assassinated their ravishers while they were asleep. Immediately after this, Hymenæus repaired to Athens, and promised to restore to liberty the matrons who had been enslaved, provided he was allowed to marry one of them who was the object of his passion. The Athenians consented, and Hymenæus experienced so much felicity in the married state, that the people of Athens instituted festivals in his honor, and solemnly invoked him at their nuptials, as the Latins did their Thalassius. Hymen was generally represented as crowned with flowers, chiefly with marjoram or roses, and holding a burning torch in one hand, and in the other a vest of a purple color. It was supposed that he always attended at nuptials; for, if absent, matrimonial connections were fatal, and ended in the most dreadful calamities; and hence the people ran about, calling aloud, Hymen! Hymen! &c. *Ovid. Medea. Met.* 12. v. 215. *Heroid* 9. v. 134. *Ep.* 11. v. 101. ep. 12. v. 137.—*Virg. Æn.* 1. v. 651. l. 4. v. 100. l. 6. v. 623. l. 7. v. 555. l. 10. v. 720. l. 11. v. 217, &c.—*Servius ad Virg. Ecl.* 8. v. 30. *Æn.* 4. v. 99 & 127.—*Lactant. in Theb.* 3. v. 283.—*Schol. Homer. Il.* 18. v. 493.—*Donatus. in Adelph. Terent.* —*Claudian in Epith. Pallad.*—*Catull.* ep. 62. [The beautiful half figure known by the name of the Genius of the Vatican, is more frequently called Hymen.

HYMET'TUS, a mountain of Attica, about 22 miles in circumference, and about two miles from Athens, still famous, as it was in ancient times, for its bees and excellent honey. There was also a quarry of marble there. Jupiter had there a temple, whence he is called Hymettius. *Strab.* 9.—*Ital.* 2. v. 228. l. 14. v. 200.—*Plin.* 36. c. 3.—*Horat.* 2 od. 18. v. 3. 2 *Sat.* 2. v. 15.—*Cic.* 2 *Fin.* 34.—*Martial.* 7. epigr. 87.

HYN'IDOS, a town in Caria. *Plin.* 5. c. 29. Probably the Idymos of *Ptolemy*.

HYO'PE, a city of the Matieni. *Steph.*

HY'OPS, a city of Iberia, not far from the river Lesyrus. *Id.*

HYPÆ'A or **HYP'ATA**, now If, an island off Marseilles, one of the Stoechades. *Plin.* 3. c. 5.

HYPÆL'OCHI, a nation of the Molossi. *Steph.*

HYPÆ'PA or **IPE'PÆ**, now Berki, a town of Lydia, sacred to Venus, between mount Tmolus and the Caystrus. *Strab.* 13.—*Ovid. Met.* 11. v. 152.

HYPÆ'SIA, a district of Peloponnesus. *Strab.* 8.

HYP'ANA, a town of Peloponnesus, called Epina by *Strabo*, l. 8.

HYP'ANIS, a river of European Scythia, now called Bog, which falls into Borysthenes, and with it into the Euxine. Its waters, at the distance of about 40 miles from their source, lost their original sweetness, by the falling in of a little stream which was said to impart to them a brackish and unpleasant taste. *Mela*, 2. c. 1.—*Virg. G.* 4. v. 370.—*Strab.* 7.—*Herodot.* 4. c. 52, &c.—*Ovid. Met.* 15. v. 285.——A river of India. *Strab.* l. 15.—*Salmas. ad Solin.* p. 992.——A river near the Cimmerian Bosporus. *Aristot.* l. 5. *H. Anim.*—*Cic. Tusc.* 2. c. 39.

Hypa'nis, a Trojan who joined himself to Æneas, and was killed by his own countrymen, who took him for one of the enemy, in the night that Troy was burned by the Greeks. *Virg. Æn.* 2. v. 428.

HYPARI'NUS, a son of Dion, who reigned at Syracuse for two years after his father.——The father of Dion.

HYP'ATA, a city of Thessaly, on the Sinus Maliacus. *Steph.*—*Liv.* 41. c. 25.

HYPA'TES, a river of Sicily, near Camarina. *Ital.* 14, v. 231.

HYPA'TIA, a native of Alexandria, daughter of Theon, and his successor in the government of the Platonic school established there. She has been highly celebrated for her beauty, her virtues, and her great erudition, and, though a heathen, she deserved those many encomiums which have been bestowed upon her character. After a life of great public utility and exemplary virtue, she was attacked by a number of wild enthusiasts, who inhumanly assassinated her in March 415, A.D. *Socrates*, 7. c. 15.—*Suidas. Synes.* ep.

HYPATODO'RUS, a statuary of Thebes, who flourished 372 B.C.

HYP'ATUS, a mountain of Bœotia, with a temple to Jupiter the "supreme."

HYPE'NOR, a Trojan killed by Diomedes during the Trojan war. *Homer. Il.* 5. v. 144.

HYPER'BATUS, a prætor of the Achæans, B.C. 224.

HYPER'BIUS, a son of Ægyptus. *Apollod.*——A son of Mars, said to have been the first who slew animals. *Plin.* 7. c. 56.

HYPER'BOLUS, an Athenian demagogue, on whom Nicias and Alcibiades, when in danger of ostracism, combined to inflict that punishment, and thereby averted it from themselves.

HYPERBORE'I or **HYPERBO'REI**, a nation in the northern parts of Europe and Asia, who were said to live to an incredible old age, even to a thousand years, and in the enjoyment of all possible felicity. The sun was said to rise and set to them but once a year, and therefore, perhaps, they are placed by Virgil under the north pole. The word signifies *people who dwell beyond the wind Boreas.* Thrace was the residence of Boreas, according to the ancients. Whenever the Hyperboreans made offerings to the gods, they always sent them towards the south, and the people of Dodona were the first of the Greeks who received them. The word Hyperborean is applied in general, to all those who inhabit any cold climate. *Orpheus in Arg.*—*Pind. Pyth.* 10.—*Apollon. Arg.* 2.—*Æschyl in Sup.*—*Diod.* 2. —*Strab.* 1 & 7.—*Ptol.* 5. c. 9.—*Solin*, c. 31.—*Plin.* 4. c. 12. l. 6. c. 17.—*Mela*, 3. c. 5.—*Virg. G.* 1. v. 240. l. 3. v. 169 & 381 —*Herodot.* 4. c. 13, &c.—*Cic. N. D.* 3. c. 23. l. 4. c. 12.

HYPERDEX'ION, a region of Lesbus, where Jupiter Hyperdexius and Minerva Hyperdexia were worshipped. *Steph.*

HYPERE'A, **HYPERI'A**, **HYPE'REA** or **HYPE'RIA**, a fountain of Thessaly, with a town of the same name. *Strab.* 9.—*Plin.* 4. c. 8.

Hypere'a, A fountain in Messenia. *Flacc.* l. v. 375.

HYPERE'CHIUS, a grammarian of Alexandria, who wrote on grammar. *Suidas.*

HYPERE'SIA, a town of Achaia. *Strab.* 8.

HYPER'IDES or **HYPERI'DES**, son of Glaucippus,

an Athenian orator, disciple to Plato and Isocrates, and long the rival of Demosthenes. He distinguished himself by his eloquence, and the active part which he took in the management of the Athenian republic. After the unfortunate battle of Cranon, he was taken prisoner, and that he might not be compelled to betray the secrets of his country, he cut off his tongue. He was put to death by order of Antipater, B.C. 322. Only one of his numerous orations remains, admired for the sweetness and elegance of its style. *Plut. in Phoc. & Demost.—Cic. in Orat.* 1. c. 31. l. 2. c. 53. l. 3. c. 16.—*Quintil.* 10. c. 1. l. 12. c. 10.

HYPERI'ON, a son of Cœlus and Terra, who married Thea, by whom he had Aurora, Sol, and Luna. Hyperion is often taken by the poets for the sun itself. *Cic. N. D.* 3. c. 21.—*Sil.* 15. v. 214.—*Hesiod. Theog.—Apollod.* 1. c. 1 & 2.—*Homer. Hymn. ad Ap.*——A son of Priam. *Apollod.* 1. c. 2.

HYP'ERIS, a river of Persia. *Plin.* 6. c. 23. Some read Superis. *Salmas ad Solin.* p. 1181.

HYPERMNES'TRA, one of the fifty daughters of Danaus, who married Lynceus, son of Ægyptus. She disobeyed her father's inhuman command, and suffered Lynceus to escape unhurt from the bridal bed. Her father, enraged at her conduct, summoned her to appear before a public tribunal to answer for her disobedience, but the people acquitted her, and Danaus was reconciled to her and her husband, to whom he left his kingdom at his death. Some say that Lynceus returned to Argos with an army, and that he conquered and put to death his father-in-law, and took possession of his crown. *Vid.* Danaides. *Paus.* 2. c. 19.—*Apollod.* 2. c. 1.—*Ovid. Heroid.* 14.—*Lactant. ad. Theb.* 1. v. 324. l. 6. v. 290.—*Schol. Pind. Nem.* 10, v. 10.——A daughter of Thestius. *Apollod.*

HYPER'OCHUS, the father of Œnomaus of Pisa. *Tzetz. Lycoph.*——The father of Eurypilus. *Schol. Pind. Olymp.* 7.——A man who wrote a poetical history of Cumæ. *Paus.* 10. c. 12.—*Athen.* l. 13.

HYPHÆ'US, a mountain of Campania. *Plut. in Syll.*

HYPHANTE'IUM, a mountain of Phocis.

HYPH'ASIS or **HYP'ASIS**, a river of India, said, by some authors, to have been the boundary of Alexander's conquests. It is called by some writers Hypanis. *Salmas. ad Solin* p. 790.

HYPOTA'AN, a general who assisted Æetes, and was slain by Colaxes. *Val. Flacc.* 6. v. 639.

HYPOB'ARUS, a river of India. *Plin.* 37. c. 2.

HYPOCHAL'CIS, a city of Ætolia, under mount Chalcis. *Steph.*

HYPOD'ROMUS, a city of Æthiopia. *Ptol.*

HYP'SA, now Belici, a river of Sicily, falling into the Crinisus, and soon after into the Mediterranean, near Selinus. *Ital.* 14. v. 228.

HYPSAL'TÆ, a people of Thrace. *Plin.* 4. c. 11. *Stephanus* calls them Hypselitæ.

HYPSE'A, a Roman matron, of the family of the Plautii. She was blind, according to Horace; or, perhaps, was partial to some lover, who was recommended neither by personal nor mental excellence. *Horat.* 1. sat. 2. v. 91.

HYPSE'NOR, a priest of the Scamander, killed during the Trojan war. *Homer. Il.* 5.

HYP'SEUS or **HYPSE'US**, a son of the river Peneus, father of Astiagea, the wife of Periphas, and of Cyrene, the mother of Aristæus. *Diod.* 4.—*Pind. Pyth.* 9.

Hyp'seus, an eloquent pleader at the Roman bar before the age of Cicero. *Cic. de Orat.* 1. c. 36.

HYP'SICLES, a mountain of Phocis.

HYPSICRATE'A, the wife of Mithridates, who, disguised in male attire, accompanied her husband when he fled before Pompey. *Plut. in. Pomp.*

HYPSICRATES, a Phœnician, who wrote a history of his country in the Phœnician language. This history was saved from the flames of Carthage, when that city was taken by Scipio, and translated into Greek.——A grammarian. *Varro. L. L.* l. 4. —*Steph. in* Αἴσιοι.—*A. Gell.* 16. c. 12.

HYP'SILE, a city of Ægypt. *Ptol.* It is the Hysipis of *Antoninus*, according to *Simler*.

HYPSIPIDES, a Macedonian in Alexander's army, famous for his friendship for Menedemus, &c. *Curt.* 7. c. 7.

HYPSIP'YLE, a queen of Lemnus, daughter of Thoas and Myrine. During her reign, Venus, whose altars had been universally slighted, punished the Lemnian women, and rendered their mouths and breath so extremely offensive to the smell, that their husbands abandoned them, and gave themselves up to some female slaves, whom they had taken in a war against Thrace. This contemptuous treatment was highly resented by the women of Lemnus, they resolved on revenge, and all put to death their male relations, Hypsipyle alone excepted, who spared the life of her father Thoas. Soon after this cruel murder, the Argonauts landed at Lemnus, in their expedition to Colchis, and remained for some time in the island. During their stay the Argonauts rendered the Lemnian women mothers; and Jason, the chief of the Argonautic expedition, left Hypsipyle pregnant at his departure, and promised her eternal fidelity. Hypsipyle brought forth twins, Euneus and Nebrophonus, whom some have called Deiphilus or Thoas. Jason, however, forgot his vows and promises to Hypsipyle, and the unfortunate queen was soon after forced to leave her kingdom by the Lemnian women, who conspired against her life, still mindful that Thoas had been preserved by means of his daughter. Hypsipyle, in her flight, was seized by pirates, and sold to Lycurgus, king of Nemea. In her captivity, she was entrusted with the care of Archemorus (*vid.* Archemorus,) who was killed by a serpent. Lycurgus attempted to revenge the death of his son, but Hypsipyle was screened from his resentment by Adrastus, the leader of the Argives. *Ovid. Heroid.* 6.—*Apollon.* 1. v. 209.—*Propert.* 1. el. 15.—*Diod.* 4.—*Tzetzes in Lyc.—Schol. Eurip. in Hecub.—Sch. Hom. Il.* 7. v. 467.—*Lactant. in Theb.* 6. v. 342.—*Sch. Pind. in Nem.* 8. & *Pyth.* 4. v. 88.—*Stat.* 5. *Theb.* v. 29.—*Flacc.* 2. v. 113.—*Apollod.* 1. c. 9. l. 3. c. 6.—*Hygin.* fab. 15, 74, &c.

HYPSIZ'ORUS, a mountain near Pallene. *Plin.* 4. c. 10.

HYPSURA'NIUS, the founder of Tyre, according to *Sanchoniathon apud Euseb. Præp. Evang.* l. 1. See also *Joh. Marsham. Can. Chron. Sec.* 12.

HYP'SUS, *untis*, son of Lycaon, founded Thyræum, a city of Arcadia. *Steph. in* Θυραῖον.

HYRCA'NE, a city of Lydia, according to an ancient coin mentioned by *Jac. Spon. Itin.* part 3. p. 188 —*Liv.* 37. c. 38.

HYRCA'NIA, a large country of Asia, at the north of Parthia, and the west of Media, described as abounding in serpents, wild beasts, &c. It was very mountainous, and unfit for drawing up a body of cavalry in order of battle. *Virg. Æn.* 4. v. 367. —*Cic. Tusc.* 1. c. 45.—*Strab.* 2 & 11.

HYRCA'NUM MA'RE, a large sea, called also the Caspian. *Vid.* Caspium Mare.

HYRCA'NUS, a name common to some of the high priests of Judæa. *Josephus.*

HYR'IA, a country of Bœotia, near Aulis, with a lake, river, and town of the same name. It received its name from Hyrie, a woman, who wept so much for the loss of her son Cycnus, that she was changed into a fountain. *Ovid. Met.* 7. v. 372. —*Herodot.* 7. c. 170.——A town of Isauria, on the Calycadnus. *Plin.* 4. c. 7.

HYR'IEUS or **HYR'EUS**, a peasant, or as some say, a prince of Tanagra, son of Neptune and Alcyone, who kindly entertained Jupiter, Neptune, and Mercury, when travelling over Bœotia. Being childless, he asked of the gods to give him a son without his marrying, as he had promised his wife, who was lately dead, and whom he tenderly loved, that he never would marry again. The gods, to reward the hospitality of Hyreus, made water in the hide of a bull, which had been sacrificed the day before, and ordered him to bury it in the ground for nine months. At the expiration of the nine months, Hyreus opened the earth, and found a beautiful child in the bull's hide, whom he called Orion. *Vid.* Orion. *Ovid. Fast.* 5 v. 495 & 535. —*Lycop. in Cass.—Tzetzes, ib.—Hygin. A.P.* 2. c. 34. *Fab.* 195.—*Isidor. Or.* 3. c. 70.

HY'RIS, a promontory of Bithynia, near Chalcedon. *Steph.*

HYR'IUM, a town of Apulia Daunia, at the foot of mount Garganus. *Plin.* 3. c. 11.—*Dionys. Afer de Sit. Orb.*

HYRMI'NE, a town of Elis, so called by Actor, the founder, in honor of his mother Hermine. *Strab* 8.

HYRNE'THO or **HYR'NETHO**, a daughter of Temenus, king of Argos, who married Deiphon, son of

Celeus. She was the favorite of her father, who greatly enriched her husband. *Apollod.* 2. c. 6.—*Paus.* 2. c. 19.

HYRNITH'IUM, a plain of Argos, near Epidaurus, fertile in olives. *Strab.* 6.

HYR'TACUS, a Trojan of mount Ida, father to Nisus, one of the companions of Æneas. *Virg. Æn.* 9. v. 177 & 406. Hence the patronymic of Hyrtacides is applied to Nisus. It is also applied to Hippocoon. *Id.* 5. v. 492.

HYR'TACUS, a city of Crete. *Steph.*

HYSAE'IS, an island of the Æthiopians. *Id.*

HYS'BE, a city of Lydia. *Id.*

HYSCE'NA, a city of Illyricum. *Id.*

HYS'IA or HYS'IÆ, a town of Bœotia, built by Nycteus, Antiope's father. *Thucyd.* 5.

HYS'IA, a village of Argolis.——A city of Arcadia.——A city, the residence of the king of Parthia.

HYS'PA. *Vid.* Hypsa.

HYSPIR'ATIS, a region of Armenia. *Strab.*—*Salmas. ad Solin.* p. 1152.

HYS'SUS or HYS'SI, a port and river of Cappadocia, near the city Cerasus. *Arrian in Peripl.*—*Ptol.*

HYSTAS'PÆ, a people of Persia. *Steph.*

HYSTAS'PES, a noble Persian, of the family of the Achæmenides. His father's name was Arsames. His son Darius reigned in Persia after the murder of the usurper Smerdis. Hystaspes was the first who introduced the learning and mysteries of the Indian Brachmans into Persia, and to his researches in India the sciences were greatly indebted, particularly in Persia. Darius is called son of Hystaspes, to distinguish him from his royal successor of his own name. *Herodot.* 1. c. 209. 1. 5. c. 83.—*Ctesias, Fragm.*——A son of Darius by Atossa, daughter of Cyrus. *Herod.* 7. c. 64.

HYSTIE'US. *Vid.* Histiæus.

HYT'ANIS, a river of Carmania. *Plin.* 6. c. 23.

HYTEN'NA, a city of Lycia. *Steph.*

HYTHMI'TÆ, a people near Liburnia. *Id.*

I.

I'A, a daughter of Midas, who married Atys, &c.

IAC'CHUS, a surname of Bacchus, *ab* ἰάχειν, from the *noise* and *shouts* which the Bacchanals raised at the festivals of this deity. *Virg. Ecl.* 6. *G.* 1. v. 166.—*Ovid. Met.* 4. v. 15.—*Claudian Rap. Pros.* 1.—Some suppose that he was a son of Ceres, who accompanied his mother in her travels through the world, and assuaged her grief for the loss of Proserpine. In consequence of this, it is said, that in the celebration of the Eleusinian mysteries, the word Iacchus was frequently repeated. *Herodot.* 8. c. 65.—*Paus.* 1. c. 2.—*Salmas. ad Solin.* p. 750.

IA'DER, a small river of Dalmatia which falls into the Adriatic Sea. *Lucan. C.B.* 4. v. 405.

IAD'ERA or IA'DERA, a town of Illyricum, with a good harbour.

IALE'MUS or IAL'EMUS, a son of the muse Calliope, whose name, from his melancholy poems, and imperfect compositions, it is said, has been applied by the Greeks to such elegies as were expressive of sorrow and mourning, as were the Næniæ among the Latins. *Athen.* 14.—*Gyrald. de Musis*—*Hesychus.*

IAL'MENUS, a son of Mars and Astyoche, who went to the Trojan war with his brother Ascalaphus, with 30 ships, at the head of the inhabitants of Orchomenus and Aspledon in Bœotia. *Paus.* 9. c. 37.—*Hygin.* fab. 97.—*Homer. Il.* 2. v. 19.

IAL'YSUS, a town of Rhodes, built by Ialysus, son of Ochimus and grandson of the sun. It was of this prince that Protogenes was making a beautiful painting when Demetrius Poliorcetes took Rhodes. This celebrated picture, which had engaged the artist for seven years, and deserved the highest commendation of Apelles, was seized by the conqueror, and immediately reclaimed by the Rhodians. Demetrius, however, refused to yield it, but promised to preserve what he considered as superior to all the paintings of his ancestors. In process of time it was carried to Italy, where it still adorned the capital of the world in the age of Pliny. The Telchines were born at Ialysus. *Ovid. Met.* 7. fab. 9.—*Plin.* 35. c. 6.—*Cic.* 2. *ad Attic.* ep. 21.—*Plut. in Dem.*—*Ælian.* 12. c. 5.

IAM'BE, a daughter of Pan and Euche, servant-maid of Metanira, wife of Celeus, king of Eleusis. She tried to exhilarate Ceres, when she travelled over Attica in quest of Proserpine, and in memory of the jokes and stories which she made use of, it is said that free and satirical verses have been called *Iambics.* *Apollod.* 1. c. 5.—*Hesychius.*—*Nicander in Alexiph.*

IAM'BLICHUS, a Pythagorean philosopher of Chalcis in Cœlesyria, and disciple of Porphyry, lived in the age of Constantine. He wrote a book on the mysteries of the Ægyptians, published by Aldus, Venet. 1516, and at Oxford in 1678; a life of Pythagoras, edited by Arcerius Franck. 1598, and by Kuster, Amstel. 1707; exhortations to the study of philosophy, also edited by Arcerius; a book on Mathematics, never published, except some fragments which were edited by Scutellius at the end of the Mysteries of the Ægyptians, Rom, 1556. He wrote also other works, which have perished. *Sax. Onom.* 1. p. 391.—*Fabr. B. Gr.* 4. c. 31.—*Eunapius in Vitâ*, &c.——A writer of Apamea in Syria, to whom Julian addressed three epistles, &c. *Fabr. Ibid.*—*Sax. Onom.* 1. p. 326.——A Babylonian, author of "The loves of Rhodanus and Sinonis," &c. For an account of persons of this name, see *Fabricius, loc. citat.*—*Jonsius, de Script. H. Phil.* p. 174 & 292, &c.

IAM'ENUS, a Trojan, killed by Leonteus. *Homer. Il.* 12. v. 139 & 193.

IAM'IDÆ, certain prophets among the Greeks, descended from Iamus, a son of Apollo, who received the gift of prophecy from his father, a privilege which was also granted to his posterity. *Paus.* 6. c. 2.

IAMNI'A or IAM'NIA, a city of Palestine, the seat of the Sanhedrim after the destruction of Jerusalem.

IA'MUS, son of Apollo and Evadne.

IANI'RA, one of the Nereides. *Hesiod in Theog.*

IAN'THE, a girl of Crete, who married Iphis. *Vid.* Iphis. *Ovid. Met.* 9. v. 714, &c.

IAN'THE, one of the Oceanides.——One of the Nereides. *Paus.* 4. c. 30.—*Homer. Il.* 8. v. 47.

IAP'ETUS. *Vid.* Japetus.

IA'PIS, an Ætolian, who founded a city upon the banks of the Timavus. *Virg. G.* 3. v. 475.——A Trojan, son of Jasus and the favorite of Apollo, from whom he received the knowledge of the power of medicinal herbs, which he piously employed to lengthen the age of his father. *Id. Æn.* 12. v. 391 & 420.

IAP'YDES, a warlike people of Illyricum, who tattooed their bodies.

IAPYD'IA, a district in the western parts of Illyricum, now called Carniola. *Liv.* 43. c. 5.—*Tibull.* 4. v. 109.—*Cic. Balb.* 14.

IAPYG'IA, a country on the confines of Italy, situated between Tarentum, Barium, and Brundusium. It is called by some Messapia, Peucetia, or Salentinum. *Plin.* 3. c. 11.—*Strab.* 6.—*Solin.* 8.

IAPYG'IUM, a promontory of the Salentini, now Capo di S. Maria. *Ptol.*—*Strab.* 1. 2.

IA'PYX, a son of Dædalus, who conquered a part of Italy, which he called Iapygia. *Ovid. Met.* 14. v. 458.—*Plin.* 3, c. 11.

IA'PYX, a wind which blew from Apulia, and was favorable to such as sailed from Italy towards Greece. It was nearly the same as the Charus of the Greeks. *Horat.* 1. od. 3. v. 4, 1. 3. od. 7. v. 20.—*Aul. Gell.* 2. c. 22.—*Apuleius de Mundo.*

IAR'BAS, a son of Jupiter and Garamantis, king of Gætulia, from whom the Tyrians bought land to build Carthage. He courted Dido, but the arrival of Æneas prevented his success, and the queen, rather than marry Iarbas, destroyed herself. *Vid.* Dido. *Virg. Æn.* 4. v. 36, &c.—*Justin.* 18. c. 6.—*Ovid. Fast.* 3. v. 552.

IAR'CHAS or JAR'CAS, a celebrated Indian Philosopher. His seven rings were said to be famous for their power of restoring old men to the bloom and vigor of youth, according to the tradition of *Philostratus in Apoll. Tyan.*

IAR'DANES, a Lydian, father of Omphale, the mistress of Hercules. *Musæi Frag.*—*Apollod.* 2.—*Palæph. de Inc.* 45.—*Diod.* 4.—*Herodot.* 1. c. 7.

IAR'DANUS or IAR'DANES, a river of Arcadia.——A river of Crete. *Homer. Il.* 7. v. 135.—*Strab.* 8.—*Paus.* 6. c. 21.

IAS'IDES, a patronymic given to Palinurus as descended from a person of the name of Jasius. *Virg. Æn.* 5. v. 843.——A patronymic of Iapis, a son of Iasus. *Id.* 12. v. 392.

IA'SION or IA'SIUS, a son of Jupiter and Electra, one of the Atlantides, who reigned over part of Arcadia, where he diligently applied himself to agriculture. He married the goddess Cybele or Ceres; and all the gods honored the celebration of his nuptials with their presence. He had by Ceres two sons, Philomelus and Plutus, to whom some have added a third, Corybas, who introduced the worship and mysteries of his mother into Phrygia. He had also a daughter, whom he exposed as soon as born, saying that he would raise only male children. The child, who was suckled by a she-bear, and miraculously preserved, rendered herself famous afterwards under the name of Atalanta. Iasion was killed with a thunderbolt of Jupiter, and ranked among the gods after death by the inhabitants of Arcadia. *Hesiod. Theog.* 970.—*Virg. Æn.* 3. v. 168.—*Hygin. Poet.* 2. c. 4.—*Homer. Odyss.* 5. v. 125.—*Ovid. Am.* 3. el. 10. v. 25.—*Diod.* 3 & 6. —*Callim. in Dian.* 28.—*Dionys. Hal.* 1. c. 53.—*Propert.* 1. el. 1. v. 10.

I'ASIS, a name given to Atalanta as daughter of Iasius.

IA'SIUS, a son of Abas, king of Argos, brother of Dardanus. *Serv. ad Virg. Æn.* 3. v. 168.——A descendant of Janus, reigned over Italy in the age of Deucalion. *Beros.* l. 5.——The father of Palinurus. *Virg. Æn.* 5. v. 843.

I'ASUS, a king of Argos, who succeeded his father Triopas. *Paus.* 2. c. 16.——A son of Argus, father of Agenor. *Apollod.*——A son of Argus and Ismene. *Id.*——A son of Lycurgus of Arcadia, by Cleophile. *Id.*

I'ASUS, an island, with a town of the same name, on the coast of Caria. The bay adjoining was called Iasius Sinus. *Plin.* 5. c. 28.—*Liv.* 32. c. 33. l. 37. c. 17.

IAXAR'TES, now Sir or Sihon, a river of Sogdiana, mistaken by Alexander for the Tanais. It falls into the Caspian Sea at the east. *Curt.* 6 & 7.—*Plin.* 6. c. 16.—*Arrian.* 4. c. 15.——An auxiliary of Æetes against Perses. *Val. Flacc.* 5. v. 596.

IAZ'YGES, a people on the borders of the Palus Mæotis. *Tacit. Ann.* 12. c. 29.—*Ovid. Trist.* 2. v. 191. *Pont.* 4. el. 7. v. 9.

IBE'RIA, a country of Asia, situated between Colchis on the west, and Albania on the east. Pompey invaded it, and made great slaughter of the inhabitants, and obliged them to surrender by setting fire to the woods where they had fled for safety. It is now called Georgia. *Plut. in Luc. Anton. &c.* —*Dio.* 36.—*Flor.* 3.—*Flacc.* 5. v. 166.—*Appian. Parthic.*——An ancient name of Spain, derived from the Iberus. *Lucan.* 6. v. 258.—*Horat.* 4. od. 14. v. 50.

IBE'RUS, a river of Spain, now called Ebro, which rises in the north of that kingdom, and falls into the Mediterranean opposite Majorca. After the conclusion of the first Punic war it was regarded as the line of separation between the Roman and Carthaginian possessions in that country. *Lucan.* 4. v. 335.—*Plin.* 3. c. 3.—*Horat.* 4. od. 14. v. 50.—*Strab.* 3.—*Mela,* 1. c. 2. l. 2. c. 6. l. 3. c. 5.—*Ptol.* 5. c. 11.—*Liv.* 21. c. 2. 5. l. 23. c. 28.—*Virg. G.* 3. v. 428.—*Servius in Æn.* 7. v. 664.——A river of Iberia in Asia, flowing from mount Caucasus into the Cyrus. *Strab.* 3.—*Plin.* 3. c. 3.

IBE'RUS, a fabulous king of Spain.

I'BI, an Indian nation. *Diod. Sic.* l. 7.

I'BIS, a poem of the poet Callimachus, in which he bitterly satirizes the ingratitude of his pupil the poet Apollonius. Ovid has also written a poem which bears the same name, which inveighs bitterly against Hyginus, the supposed hero of the composition. *Suidas.*

IB'YCUS, a lyric poet of Rhegium, about 540 B.C. was murdered by robbers, who being some time after in the market-place, one of them observed some cranes in the air, and said to his companions, αἱ Ἰβύκου ἔκδικοι πάρεισιν, *there are the birds that are conscious of the death of Ibycus.* These words raised suspicions; the assassins were seized, and when tortured confessed their guilt. *Cic.* 4. *Tusc.* c. 43.—*Ælian. V. H.*—*Sax. Onom.* 1. p. 23. —*Fabr. B. Gr.* 2. c. 15.——The husband of Chloris, whom *Horace,* 3 od 15. ridicules.

IBYL'LA, a city of Tartessus. *Steph.*

ICA'DIUS, a robber killed by a stone, &c. *Cic. Fat.* 3.

ICA'RIA, a small island in the Ægean Sea, between Chio, Samus, Myconus, and Patmus, where the body of Icarus was thrown by the waves, and buried by Hercules. *Mela,* 2. c. 7.—*Ptol.* 5. c. 2.—*Strab.* 10 & 14.——A village of the tribe Ægeis, so called from Icarius, the father of Erigone. *Steph.*

IC'ARIS or ICARIO'TIS, a name given to Penelope, as daughter of Icarius. *Propert.* 3. el. 13. v. 10.

ICA'RIUM MA'RE, a part of the Ægean Sea between the islands of Patmus, Lerus, &c. and the Asiatic coast. *Vid.* Icarus.

ICA'RIUS, an Athenian, father of Erigone. He gave wine to some peasants, who drank it with the greatest avidity, ignorant of its intoxicating nature. They were soon deprived of their reason, and the resentment of their friends and neighbours was in consequence immediately turned upon Icarius, who perished by their hands. After death he was honoured with public festivals, and his daughter was led to discover the place of his burial by means of his faithful dog Mœra. Erigone hanged herself in despair, and was changed into a constellation called Virgo. Icarius was also changed into the star Bootes, and the dog Mœra into the star Canis. *Hygin.* fab. 130. *P. A.* 2. c. 4 & 40.—*Propert.* 2. el. 34. v. 29.—*Tibull.* 4. el. 1. v. 9.—*Ovid. in Ib.* v. 611. *Lucian. in Dial. Junon.*—*Paus.* 1. c. 2.—*Ælian. H. A.* 6. c. 28.—*Apollod.* 3. c. 14.——A son of Œbalus of Lacedæmon. He gave his daughter Penelope in marriage to Ulysses, king of Ithaca, but he was so tenderly attached to her, that he wished her husband to settle at Lacedæmon. Ulysses refused to abandon his native country, and when he saw the earnest petitions of Icarius, he told Penelope that she might either follow him to Ithaca, or remain with her father. Penelope blushed in the deepest silence, and covered her head with her veil. Icarius upon this permitted his daughter to go with her husband to Ithaca, and immediately erected a temple to the goddess of modesty, on the spot where Penelope had covered her blushes with her veil. *Homer. Odyss.* 16. v. 435.—*Apollod.* 1 & 3.—*Strab.* 10.—*Hygin.* fab. 256.—*Eustath. in Odyss.* 1.

ICA'RIUS, a mountain of Attica. *Plin.* 4. c. 7.

IC'ARUS, a son of Dædalus, who, with his father, fled with wings from Crete to escape from the resentment of Minos. He unfortunately directed his flight too high, the sun melted the wax which cemented his wings, and he fell into that part of the Ægean Sea which was called after his name. *Vid.* Dædalus. *Ovid. Met.* 8. v. 178. *Trist.* 4. v, 32. —*Servius in* 6. *Æn.* v. 14.—*Tzetzes Chil.* 12. *Hist.* 19.—*Philostr.* 1. *Ic.* 16.—*Hygin.* fab. 40.—*Palæph. de Inc.* 13.—*Diod.* 4.—*Paus.* 9. c. 11.—*Isidor.* 14. c. 6.——A victor at Olympia. *Paus.* 1. 4.

ICARU'SA, a river of Asiatic Sarmatia. *Plin.* 6, c. 5.

ICAT'ALÆ, a people of Asiatic Sarmatia. *Id. ibid.* c. 7.

ICAU'NA, now L'Yonne, a river of Gaul, falling into the Seine.

IC'CIUS, a lieutenant of Agrippa in Sicily. *Horace* addressed 1 od. 29. to him, and ridicules him for abandoning the pursuits of philosophy and the muses for military employments.——One of the Rhemi in Gaul, ambassador to Cæsar. *Cæs. B. G.* 2. c. 1.

IC'ELOS, one of the sons of Somnus, who had the power of changing himself into all sorts of animals, whence his name (εἴκελος, *similis.*) *Ovid. Met.* 11. v. 640.

ICE'NI, a people of Britain who submitted to the Roman power. They are supposed to have inhabited the modern counties of Suffolk, Norfolk, Cambridge, &c. *Tac. Ann.* 12. c. 31.—*Cæs. G.* 5. c. 21.

ICE'SIA, an island near Sicily, called Thermissa by *Strabo,* l. 6.

IC'ETAS, a man who obtained the supreme power at Syracuse after the death of Dion. He attempted to assassinate Timoleon, for which he was put to death, B.C. 340. *C. Nep. in Tim.*

ICH'ANA, a town of Sicily. *Steph.* The inhabitants were called Ichanenses.

ICH'ARA, an island of the Persian Gulph. *Plin.* 6. c. 28.

ICH'NÆ, a town of Macedonia, whence Themis and Nemesis are called Ichnæa. *Homer. Hym. in Apoll.* —*Lycoph. in Cass.*—*Plin.* 4. c. 10.

ICHNU'SA, an ancient name of Sardinia, given to it from its likeness to a human foot. *Paus.* 10. c. 17. —*Ital.* 12. v. 358.—*Plin.* 3. c. 7.

ICHONU'PHIS, a priest of Heliopolis, at whose house Eudoxus resided when he visited Ægypt with Plato. *Diog. Laert. in Eudoxo.*

ICHTHYOPH'AGI, a people of Æthiopia, who received this name from their eating fishes. There was also an Indian nation of the same name, who were said to build their houses with the bones of fishes. *Diod.* 3.—*Ptol.* 4. c. 5. l. 6. c. 7. l. 7. c. 3. —*Strab.* 2 & 15.—*Plin.* 6. c. 23. l. 15. c. 7.

ICH'THYS, a promontory of Elis. *Strab.* 15.—*Plin.* 4. c. 5.—*Athen.* l. 8.

ICILTUS L., a tribune of the people who proposed a law, A.U.C. 397, by which mount Aventine was given to the Roman people to build houses upon. *Liv.* 3. c. 54.

Icil'ius Sp, a tribune who made a law, A.U.C. 261, that forbade any man to oppose or interrupt a tribune while he was speaking in a public assembly. *Liv.* 2. c. 58.——A tribune, who signalized himself by his inveterate enmity against the Roman senate. He took an active part in the management of affairs after the murder of Virginia, &c.

IC'IUS, a harbour in Gaul on the modern straits of Dover, from which Cæsar crossed into Britain. *Cæs. B Gr.* l. 5, c 1.

ICHMA'LIUS, a turner, whose abilities were exerted in adorning the palace of Ulysses. *Homer. Odyss.* 19. v. 55.

ICO'NIUM, the capital of Lycaonia, now Koniech. *Plin.* 5. c. 27.

ICO'SIUM, a colony and town of Mauritania Cæsariensis. *Plin.* 5. c. 3.

ICTI'NUS, a celebrated architect 430 B.C. He built a famous temple to Apollo Epicurius at Phigalia, and to Minerva at Athens. This last extended 100 feet on all sides, and was remarkable for its magnificence. *Paus.* 8. c. 42.—*Plut. in Perr. & de Comm. Not.*—*Strab.* 9.

ICTIMU'LI or VICTIMU'LI, a place at the foot of the Alps, abounding in gold mines. *Strab.* l. 5.

ICULIS'MA, a town of Gaul, now Angoulesme, on the Charente. *Auson.* ep. 15, v. 22.

I'CUS, a small island near Eubæa. *Strab.* 9.

I'DA, a nymph of Crete who went into Phrygia, where she gave her name to a mountain of that country. *Virg. Æn.* 8. v. 177. *& Servius in loco.* ——The mother of Minos the Second.

I'da, a celebrated mountain, or more properly a ridge of mountains in Troas, chiefly in the neighbourhood of Troy. The abundance of its fountains made it the source of many rivers, and particularly of the Simois, Scamander, Æsepus, Granicus, &c. It was on mount Ida that the shepherd Paris adjudged the prize of beauty to the goddess Venus. Ida was covered with green wood, and from its top there was an extensive view of the Hellespont and the adjacent countries, from which reason the poets say that it was frequented by the gods during the Trojan war. *Strab.* 13.—*Mela*, 1. c. 18.—*Homer. Il.* 14. v. 283.—*Virg Æn.* 3. v. 6. 5. v. 449. 7. v. 303, &c.—*Ovid. Fast.* 4. v. 79.—*Horat.* 3. od. 11.—*Ptol.* 5. c. 2.—*Quint. Calab.* 3. v. 303.——A mountain of Crete, the highest in the island, where it is reported that Jupiter was educated by the Corybantes, who, on that account, were called Idæi. *Ptol.* 3. c. 17.—*Ovid Fast.* 4. v. 145.—*Virg. Æn.* 3. v. 105.—*Servius*, *Æn.* 3. v. 112. l. 5. v. 449. l. 9. v. 80.—*Strab.* 10.

IDÆ'A, a surname of Cybele because she was worshipped on mount Ida. When her worship was introduced into Italy, the Romans adopted the same ceremonies which were observed in Phrygia, and the goddess was served by a priest born at Troas. *Apollon.* 2 *Arg* 1127.—*Tibull.* 1. el. 4.—*Eurip. in Orest.*—*Virg. Æn.* 10. v. 252.—*Propert.* 4. el. 11.—*Dionys. Hal.* 1.—*Claud. de Rap. Pros.*—*Pollux.* 5. c. 13.—*Liv.* 29.—*Lactant* 2. c. 7.—*Lucret.* 2. v. 611.

IDÆ'US, a surname of Jupiter, from mount Ida. ——An arm-bearer and charioteer of king Priam, killed during the Trojan war. *Virg. Æn.* 6. v. 487. ——One of the attendants of Ascanius. *Id.* 9. v. 500.——A poet of Rhodes, who celebrated the actions of his countrymen in 3,000 verses. *Suidas.*

Idæ'us Si'nus, a bay of Troas, called by some Adramyttenus, now Golfo di Landramiti. *Strab.* 13.

ID'ALIS, the country round mount Ida. *Lucan.* 3. v. 204.

ID'ALUS, a mountain of Cyprus, at the foot of which is Idalium, a town with a grove sacred to Venus, who was in consequence called *Idalæa*. *Virg. Æn.* 1. v. 685. l. 10. v. 52.—*Flacc.* 8. v. 229.—*Ovid. de Art. A.* 3. v. 166.—*Catull.* 37 & 62.—*Propert.* 2. el. 13.

IDANTHYR'SUS, a powerful king of Scythia, who refused to give his daughter in marriage to Darius the First, king of Persia. This refusal was the cause of a war between the two nations, and Darius marched against Idanthyrsus at the head of 700,000 men. He was defeated, and retired to Persia, after an inglorious campaign. *Strab.* 13.

IDAR'NES, an officer of Darius, by whose negligence the Macedonians took Miletus. *Curt.* 4. c. 5.

I'DAS, a son of Aphareus and Arane, famous for his valor and military glory. He was among the Argonauts, and married Marpessa the daughter of Evenus king of Ætolia. Marpessa was carried away by Apollo, and Idas pursed the ravisher with bows and arrows, and obliged him to restore her. *Vid.* Marpessa. According to Apollodorus, Idas with his brother Lynceus associated with Pollux and Castor to carry away some flocks; but, when they had obtained a sufficient quantinty of plunder, they refused to divide it into equal shares. This provoked the sons of Leda, Lynceus was killed by Castor, and Idas, to revenge his brother's death, immediately killed Castor, and in his turn perished by the hand of Pollux. According to Ovid and Pausanias, the quarrel between the sons of Leda and those of Aphareus had a different origin: Idas and Lynceus, as they say, were going to celebrate their nuptials with Phœbe and Hilaria, the two daughters of Leucippus; but Castor and Pollux, who had been invited to partake of the common festivity, offered violence to the brides, and carried them away. Idas and Lynceus fell in the attempt to recover their wives. *Homer. Il.* 9. v. 549. —*Hygin.* fab. 14, 100, &c.—*Ovid. Fast.* 5. v. 700. —*Apollod.* 1 & 3.—*Paus.* 4. c. 2. l. 5, c. 18.——A son of Ægyptus. *Apollod.*——A Trojan killed by Turnus. *Virg. Æn.* 9. v. 575.

ID'EA or IDÆ'A, a daughter of Dardanus, who became the second wife of Phineus king of Bithynia, and abused the confidence reposed in her by her husband. *Vid.* Phineus. *Apollod.* 3.

Id'ea, the mother of Teucer by Scamander. *Apollod.*

Id'ea or Idæ'a, a town of Lydia near mount Sipylus. *Strab.*—*Plin.* 5. c. 29.

IDES'SA, a town of Iberia, on the confines of Colchis. *Strab.* 1.

IDE'TES, a people of Iberia. *Steph.*

I'DEX, a small river of Italy, now Idice, near Bononia.

ID'ICRA, a city of Mauritania Cæsariensis. *Antonin.*

IDISTAVI'SUS, a plain, now Hastenback, where Germanicus defeated Arminius, near Oldendorp, on the Weser, in Westphalia. *Tac. A.* 2. c. 16.

ID'MON, son of Apollo and Asteria, or, as some say, Cyrene, was the prophet of the Argonauts. He was killed in hunting a wild boar in Bithynia, where his body received a magnificent funeral. It is said that he had predicted the time and manner of his own death. *Apollod.* 1. c. 9.—*Orpheus.*—*Ovid. Ib.* 506.—*Val. Flacc.* 1. v. 228.—*Hygin.* fab. 14 & 18.—*Apollon.* 1 *Arg.* v. 139.—*Pherecyd. apud Sch. Apollon. loco.*——A dyer of Colophon, father of Arachne. *Ovid. Met.* 6. v. 8.——A man of Cyzicus, killed by Hercules, &c. *Flacc.* 3. v. 167. ——A son of Ægyptus, killed by his wife. *Vid.* Danaides.

IDOM'ENE, a daughter of Pheres, who married Amythaon, by whom she had Bias king of Argos, and the soothsayer Melampus. *Apollod.* 1. c. 9.

Idom'ene, a city of Macedonia. *Steph.*

IDOMENE'US or IDOM'ENEUS, succeeded his father Deucalion on the throne of Crete, and accompanied the Greeks to the Trojan war with a fleet of 90 ships. During this celebrated war he rendered himself famous by his valor, and slaughtered many of the enemy. At his return he made a rash vow to Neptune in a dangerous tempest, that if he escaped from the fury of the seas and storms, he would offer to the god whatever living creature first presented itself to his eye on the Cretan shore. This was no other than his own son, who came to congratulate his father on his safe return. Idomeneus performed his promise to the god, and the inhumanity of this sacrifice rendered him so odious in the eyes of his subjects, that he abandoned Crete, and migrated in quest of a new settlement. He came to Italy, and founded a city on the coast of Calabria, which he called Salentum, and he died in an extreme old age, after he had had the satisfaction of seeing his new kingdom flourish, and his subjects happy. According to the *Scholiast* of *Lycophron*, v. 1217, Idomeneus, during his absence in the Trojan war, entrusted the government of his kingdom to Leucos, to whom he promised his daughter Clisithere in marriage at his return. Leucos at first governed with moderation; but he was persuaded by Nauplius, king of Eubœa, to put to death Meda, the wife of his master, with her daughter Clisithere, and to seize the kingdom. Idomeneus, at his return, found it impossible to expel the usurper. *Ovid. Met.* 13. v. 358.—*Hygin.* 92.—*Homer. Il.* 11, &c. *Odyss.* 19.—*Paus.* 5. c. 25.—*Virg. Æn.* 3. v. 122.——A son of Priam.——A Greek historian of Lampsacus, in the age of Epicurus. He wrote a history of Samothrace, and the life of Socrates, besides other compositions now lost. *Athen.* 14.—*Strab.* 14.—*Diog.* 10.—*Plut. in Per.*

IDO'THEA, a daughter of Prœtus, king of Argos. When afflicted with madness, she, with her sisters, was restored to her senses by Melampus. *Vid.* Prœtides. *Homer. Odyss.* 11.——A daughter of Proteus, who informed Menelaus how to obtain from her father the knowledge of the means which might ensure his safe return to his country. *Homer. Odyss.* 4. v. 363.——A daughter of Oceanus, or, according to others, of Melissa, one of the nymphs who educated Jupiter.

ID'RIAS, a city of Caria, formerly Chrysaoris. *Steph.*

ID'RIEUS, the son of Euromus of Caria, brother to Artemisia, who succeeded to Mausolus, and invaded Cyprus. *Diod.* 16.—*Polyæn.* 7.

IDU'BEDA, a river and mountain of Spain, at the west of Saguntum. *Strab.* 3.—*Plin.* 3. c. 3.

IDU'ME or IDUME'A, a country of Syria, famous for palm-trees. Gaza was its capital, and there Cambyses deposited his riches, as he was going to invade Ægypt. *Lucan.* 3. v. 216.—*Sil.* 3. v. 600.—*Virg. G.* 3. v. 12.

IDY'IA, one of the Oceanides, who married Æetes king of Colchis, by whom she had Medea, &c. *Hygin.* præf. fab. & fab. 25.—*Hesiod. Th.* 960.—*Schol. Apollon.* 2. v. 242.—*Cic. de Nat. D.* 3. c. 19.

ID'YMA, a city of Caria, with a river called Idymus. *Steph.*

ID'YRUS, a city and river of Pamphylia. *Id.*

IE'TÆ or I'ETÆ, a place of Sicily. *Ital.* 14. v. 272.

IGE'NI or ICE'NI, a people of ancient Britain. *Tacit. Ann.* 12. c. 31, &c.

IGIL'GILI or IGILGIL'IUM, now Gigeri, a small city of Africa, on the shores of the Mediterranean. *Plin.* 5. c. 2.

IGIL'IUM, now Giglio, an island in the Mediterranean, on the coast of Tuscany. *Mela,* 2. c. 7.—*Cæs. B. G.* 1. c. 34. It is called Ægilium by *Pliny,* 3. c. 6.

IGNA'TIUS, an officer of Crassus in his Parthian expedition.——A bishop of Antioch, born at Nura, in Sardinia, and educated by the evangelist St. John. He appeared before Trajan when at Antioch, and vindicated the innocent lives of the Christian converts, but the emperor, though mild in character, considered his address an infringement of the laws, and therefore ordered him to be sent in chains to Rome, and there he was torn to pieces in the amphitheatre by lions, A.D. 107. His writings were seven letters to the Ephesians, Romans, &c. and he supported the divinity of Christ, and the propriety of the episcopal order, as superior to priests and deacons. The best edition of his works is that of Aldrich, Oxon, in 8vo, 1708, and that in the Patres Apostolici of Cotelier, 1672, Amstel., afterwards edited by Le Clerc, and enriched with the notes and Prolegomena of Archbp. Usher, and the Ignatii Vindiciæ of Bp. Pearson, 1698. *Sax. Onom.* 1. p. 290.—*Fabr. B. Gr.* 5. c. 1.

IGNIG'ENA, a surname applied to Bacchus, because he was saved from the flames which consumed his mother Semele. *Ovid. Met.* 4. v. 12.

IGU'VIUM, a town of Umbria, on the Via Flaminia, now Gubio. *Cic. ad Att.* 7. ep. 13.—*Sil.* 1. v. 460.

ILACU'RIS or ILARCU'RIS, a town of Hispania Tarraconensis, now Caros de los Infantes, according to *Moletius. Ptol.*

ILAI'RA, a daughter of Leucippus, carried away with her sister Phœbe, by the sons of Leda, as she was going to be married. *Apollod.*

IL'ARIS, a city of Lycia. *Steph.*

ILA'TRIA, a city of Crete, now Elbe. *Id.*

IL'BA. *Vid.* Ilva.

ILERCA'ONES or ILERCAONEN'SES, a people of Spain. *Liv.* 22. c. 21.

ILER'DA, now Lerida, a town of Hispania Tarraconensis, the capital of the Ilergetes, on an eminence on the right banks of the river Sicoris. *Liv.* 21. c. 23. l. 22. c. 21.—*Lucan.* 4. v. 13.—*Plin.* 3. c. 3.

ILERGE'TES. *Vid.* Ilerda.

IL'IA or RHE'A, a daughter of Numitor, king of Alba, consecrated by her uncle Amulius to the service of Vesta, which required perpetual chastity, that she might not become a mother to dispossess him of his crown. He was, however, disappointed in his expectations; violence was offered to Ilia by the god Mars, and she brought forth Romulus and Remus. *Vid.* Romulus. Ilia was buried alive by Amulius, for violating the laws of Vesta; and, because her tomb was near the Tiber, some suppose that she married the god of that river. *Horat.* 1. od. 2.—*Virg. Æn.* 1. v. 277.—*Ovid. Fast.* 2. v. 598.

IL'IA, a wife of Sylla.

ILI'ACI LU'DI, games instituted by Augustus, in commemoration of the victory which he had obtained over Antony and Cleopatra at Actium. They are supposed to be the same as the Trojani Ludi and the Actia; and Virgil says, that they were celebrated by Æneas, not only because they were instituted at the time when he wrote his poem, but because he wished to compliment Augustus, by making the founder of Lavinium solemnize games on the very spot, which was, many centuries after, to be immortalized by the trophies of his patron. During these games were exhibited horse races, and gymnastic exercises. *Virg. Æn.* 3. v. 280.

ILI'ACUS, an epithet applied to such persons as belonged to Troy. *Virg. Æn.* 1. v. 101.

ILI'ADES, a surname given to Romulus, as son of Ilia. *Ovid.*——A name given to the Trojan women. *Virg. Æn.* 1. v. 484.

IL'IAS, a celebrated poem composed by Homer, upon the Trojan war. It begins with a description of the wrath of Achilles, and delineates all the calamities which befell the Greeks, from the refusal of that hero to appear in the field of battle. It finishes with the death of Hector, whom Achilles sacrificed to the shades of his friend Patroclus. It is divided into twenty-four books. *Vid.* Homerus.

IL'IAS, a surname of Minerva, from a temple erected to her honor, at Daulis, in Phocis. This sacred spot was remarkable for some dogs kept by the priests, which were said to bark only at such persons as were not natives of the country. The temple was erected, as some suppose, after the return of Ulysses from his embassy to Troy, by the Greeks, who had made a vow which they thus fulfilled, in honor of the Trojan goddess. *Dio. Chrys. Bell. Tr.*—*Gyrald. Il. D.* 11.—*Xenoph. in Hell.*

IL'ICI or IL'ICE, a town of Hispania Tarraconensis.

ILIEN'SES, a people of Sardinia. *Liv.* 40. c. 19. l. 41 c. 6 & 12.

ILIN'GÆ, a people of Germany, called Elysii by *Tacitus, Ger.* c. 43. *Ptol.* Their city is now Leigneitz.

IL'ION, a town of Macedonia. *Liv.* 31. c. 27.

ILI'ONA or ILIO'NA, the eldest daughter of Priam, who married Polymnestor. *Virg. Æn.* 1. v. 653.

ILIO'NEUS or ILI'ONEUS, a Trojan, son of Phorbas, distinguished by his eloquence. He went into Italy with Æneas. *Virg. Æn.* 1. v. 521.

ILIO'NEUS, a son of Artabanus, made prisoner by Parmenio, near Damascus. *Curt.* 3. c. 13.——One of Niobe's sons. *Ovid. Met.* 6. fab. 6.

IL'IPA, a town of Hispania Bætica. *Liv.* 40. c. 1.

ILIS'SUS, a small river of Attica, falling into the sea near the Piræus. There was a temple on its banks, sacred to the Muses. *Stat. Theb.* 4. v. 52. [One of the finest statues of antiquity, brought from the pediment of the Parthenon at Athens, represents this river. It is now in the British Museum.]

ILITHY'IA, a goddess called also Juno Lucina. Some suppose her to be the same as Diana, though Hesiod and others call her daughter of Jupiter and Juno, and distinguish her from the daughter of Jupiter and Latona. She presided over the travails of women; and in her temple at Rome, it was usual for her votaries to carry a small piece of money as an offering. This custom was first established by Servius Tullius, who, by enforcing it, was enabled to know the exact number of the Roman people. *Hesiod. Th.* 450.—*Homer. Il.* 11. v. 269. *Odyss.* 19. v. 188.—*Diod.* 5.—*Orpheus in Di.*—*Callim. Hym. in Dian.*—*Plut. de reb. Rom.*—*Apollod.* 1 & 2.—*Horat. Carm. Sæcul.*—*Ovid. Met.* 9. v. 283.

IL'IUM or IL'ION, a citadel of Troy, built by Ilus, one of the Trojan kings, from whom it received its name. It is generally taken for Troy itself; and some authors have supposed that the town was called Ilium, and the adjacent country Troja. *Vid.* Troja. *Liv.* 35. c. 43. l. 37. c. 9 & 37.—*Virg. Æn.* 1, &c. *& Servius ib.*—*Strab.* 13.—*Ovid. Met.* 13. v. 505. l. 14. v. 467. *Fast.* 6. v. 422. *Ibin.* 498. —*Horat.* 3. od. 3.—*Justin.* 11. c. 5. l. 31. c. 8. Some writers imagine that after the fall of Troy, a small town was erected on the plain about 30 stadia or three miles from the site of the old city, and that it was in this city which still existed in the age of Marcus Aurelius, and the ruins of which modern travellers have visited, that Alexander offered a sacrifice to Minerva. *Tacit. Ann.* 4. c. 55. l. 6. c. 12.—*Justin.* 11. c. 5. l. 31. c. 8.—*Strab.* 13.—*Mela,* 1. c. 18. l. 2. c. 2.

ILLAR'CO, a town of Spain, now Alarco. *Plin.* 3. c. 1.

ILLIB'ERIS, a town of Gallia Narbonensis, through which Annibal passed, as he marched into Italy. *Plin.* 3. c. 1.—*Liv.* 21. c. 3.

Illib'eris or Ellib'eris, a city of Hispania Bætica, now Elvire. *Plin.* 3. c. 4.—*Liv.* 21. c. 61.

IL'LICE, now Elche, a town of Spain in the Mediterranean, at the east of Carthagena, with a harbour and bay, *Sinus et Portus Illicitanus,* now Alicant. *Plin.* 3. c. 3.—*Voss. ad Melam.* p. 191.

ILLIP'ULA, two towns of Spain, one of which was called Major, and the other Minor. *Plin.* 3. c. 1. —*Liv.* 40. c. 1.—*Strab.* 3.

ILLITUR'GIS, ILITUR'GIS, or ILUR'GIA, a city of Spain, near the modern Andujar, on the river Bætis, destroyed by Scipio, for having revolted to the Carthaginians. *Liv.* 23. c. 49. l. 24. c. 41. l. 26. c. 17.—*Plin.* 3. c. 1, &c.

ILLUR'CIS, a city of Iberia, afterwards called Gracchuris, from Sempronius Gracchus. *Steph.*

ILLYB'IRRIS, ILIB'ERIS or ILLIB'ERRIS, a river of Gallia Narbonensis, called Illeris by *Ptolemy,* and Illebernis by *Athenæus,* l. 8. c. 2.

ILLYR'ICUM, IL'LYRIS, or ILLYR'IA, a country bordering on the Adriatic Sea, opposite Italy, whose boundaries have been different at different times. It became a Roman province, after Gentius its king had been conquered by the prætor Anicius; and it now forms part of Croatia, Bosnia and Sclavonia. *Strab.* 2 & 7.—*Paus.* 4. c. 35.—*Mela,* 2. c. 2, &c.—*Flor.* 1. c. 18. l. 4. c. 2.—*Ptol.* 2. c. 17.

ILLYR'ICUS SI'NUS, that part of the Adriatic which lies on the coast of Illyricum.

ILLYR'IUS, a son of Cadmus and Hermione, from whom Illyricum received its name. *Apollod.*

ILOR'CI, now Lorca, a town of Hispania Tarraconensis. *Plin.* 3. c. 3.

IL'UA, now Elba, an island in the Tyrrhene Sea, between Italy and Corsica, celebrated for its iron mines. The people are called Iluates. *Liv.* 30. c. 39.—*Virg. Æn.* 10. v. 173.—*Plin.* 3. c. 6. l. 34. c. 14.

ILUMBERITA'NI, a people of Hispania Tarraconensis, whose town is now Lombier. *Plin.* 3. c. 3.

IL'URO, now Oleron, a town of Gascony in France.

I'LUS, the fourth king of Troy, was son of Tros by Calirhoe. He married Eurydice the daughter of Adrastus, by whom he had Themis, who married Capys, and Laomedon the father of Priam. He built, or rather improved and embellished, the city of Ilium, called also Troy, from his father Tros. Jupiter gave him the Palladium, a celebrated statue of Minerva, and promised that as long as it remained in Troy, so long would the town continue impregnable. When the temple of Minerva was in flames, Ilus rushed into the middle of the fire to save the Palladium, for which action it is said that he was deprived of his sight by the goddess; though he recovered it some time after. *Homer. Il.*—*Strab.* 13.—*Apollod.* 3. c. 12.—*Ovid. Fast.* 4. v. 33. l. 6. v. 419.—*Servius in Virg. Æn.* 8. v. 130.—*Tzetzes in Lyc.*—*Eustath in Il.* 8.——A name of Ascanius, while he was at Troy. *Virg. Æn.* 1. v. 272.——A friend of Turnus, killed by Pallas. *Virg. Æn.* 10. v. 400.

ILVA'TES, a people of Liguria.

IMACH'ARA, a town of Sicily. *Ptol.*—*Plin.* 3. c. 8.

IMANUEN'TIUS, a king of the Trinobantes, killed by Cassivelaunus. *Cæs. Bell. G.* 5.

IMA'US or IM'AUS, a large mountain of Scythia, which is part of mount Taurus. It divides Scythia, which is generally called *Intra Imaum,* and *Extra Imaum.* It extends, according to some, as far as the boundaries of the eastern ocean. *Plin.* 6. c. 17.—*Strab.* 1.

IM'BARUS, a part of mount Taurus, in Armenia, according to *Strabo,* l. 11., or in Cilicia, according to *Pliny,* 5. c. 27.

IMBRAC'IDES, a patronymic given to Asius, as son of Imbracus. *Virg. Æn.* 10. v. 123.

IMBRAS'IDES, a patronymic given to Glaucus and Lades, as son of Imbrasus. *Virg. Æn.* 12. v. 343.

IM'BRASUS or PARTHE'NIUS, a river of Samus. Juno, who was worshipped there, received the surname of Imbrasia, and the inhabitants boasted that the goddess was born on the banks under a willow-tree, which they still showed in the age of Pausanias. *Plin.* 5. c. 2.—*Paus.* 7. c. 4.

Im'brasus, the father of Pirus, the leader of the Thracians during the Trojan war. *Virg. Æn.* 10. v. 123. l. 12. v. 343.—*Homer. Il.* 4. v. 520.

IM'BREUS, one of the Centaurs, killed by Dryas at the nuptials of Pirithous. *Ovid. Met.* 12. v. 310.

IM'BREX CAI. LICIN'IUS, a poet. *Vid.* Licinius.

IM'BRIUS, a Trojan of Pedea, killed by Teucer, son of Mentor. He had married Medesicaste, Priam's daughter. *Homer. Il.* 13. v. 170.

IMBRIV'IUM, a place of Samnium. *Liv.* 8. c. 24.

IM'BRUS, now Embro, an island of the Ægean Sea, near Thrace, 32 miles from Samothrace, with a small river and town of the same name. Imbrus was governed for some time by its own laws, but afterwards became successively subject to the power of Persia, Athens, Macedonia, and the kings of Pergamus. It afterwards became a Roman province. The divinities particularly worshipped there were Ceres and Mercury. Antenodorus was born there. *Thucyd.* 8.—*Plin.* 4. c. 12.—*Homer. Il.* 13. v. 33.—*Strab.* 2.—*Mela,* 2, c. 7.—*Ovid. Trist.* 10. v. 18.

IMIL'CE, a heroine of Carthage. *Sil. Ital. Pun. Bell.* 3. v. 57.

IMIL'CO. *Vid.* Himilco.

IM'ME or I'ME, a town of Syria. *Ptol.*—*Salmas. ad Solin.* p. 631.

IM'OLA, a city of Æmilia, formerly Forum Cornelii. *Strab.* 5.—*Plin.* 3. c. 16.

IM'YRA, a city of Phœnicia. *Steph.*

IN'ACHI, a name given to the Greeks, particularly the Argives, from king Inachus.

INA'CHIA, a name given to Peloponnesus, from the river Inachus. *Steph.*—*Strab.* 7.

Ina'chia, a festival in Crete, observed in honor of Inachus; or, according to others, in commemoration of Ino's misfortunes. *Hesych.*

Ina'chia, a courtezan in the age of *Horace. Epod.* 11. v. 8. ep. 12. v. 14.

INACH'IDÆ, the name of the eight first successors of Inachus, on the throne of Argos.

INACH'IDES, a patronymic of Epaphus, as grandson of Inachus. *Ovid. Met.* 1. v. 704.——A patronymic of Perseus, as descended from Inachus. *Id.* 4. fab. 11.

IN'ACHIS, a patronymic of Io, as daughter of Inachus. *Ovid. Fast.* 1. v. 454.

INA'CHIUM, a town of Peloponnesus, called also Argos Hippium. *Plin.* 4. c. 5.

IN'ACHUS, a son of Oceanus and Tethys, father of Io, and also of Phoroneus and Ægialeus. He founded the kingdom of Argos, and was succeeded by Phoroneus, B.C. 1807, and gave his name to a river of Argos, of which he became the tutelary deity. He reigned 60 years. *Virg. G.* 3. v. 151. —*Apollod.* 2. c. 3.—*Paus.* 2. c. 15.

In'achus, a river of Argolis, now Planizza. *Virg. Æn.* 7. v. 372, &c.——A river of Acarnania. *Ovid. Met.* 1. v. 583.—*Mela,* 2. c. 3.—*Strab* 6, 7, 8.—*Plut de flum.*

INAM'AMES, a river in the east of Asia, as far as which Semiramis is said to have extended her empire. *Polyæn.* 8. According to *Casaubon,* it is the river called Iomanes by *Pliny,* 6. c. 19.

INAR'IME, an island on the coast of Campania, with a mountain, under which Jupiter confined the giant Typhœus. It is now called Ischia, and is remarkable for its fertility and population. There was formerly a volcano in the middle of the island *Virg. Æn.* 9. v. 716.

IN'ARUS, a town of Ægypt, in the neighbourhood of which the town of Naucratis was built by the Milesians. *Strab.* 17.—*Salmas. ad Solin.* p. 476.

In'arus or In'aros, a tyrant of Ægypt, who died B.C. 456.

IN'ATUS, a city of Crete. *Steph.*

INCITA'TUS, a horse of the emperor Caligula, made high priest. *Suet.* c. 55. *in Vit. Calig.*

IN'DARA, a city of the Sicani. *Steph.*

INDATHYR'SUS. *Vid.* Idanthyrsus.

IN'DIA, the most celebrated and opulent of all the countries of Asia, was bounded on one side by the Indus, from which it derives its name. It is situate at the south of the kingdoms of Persia, Parthia, &c. along the sea coast. It has always been reckoned famous for the riches which it contains; and so persuaded were the ancients of its wealth, that they supposed its very sands were gold. It contained 9000 different nations, and 5000 remarkable cities, according to geographers. Bacchus is regarded as the first who conquered it, and in the more recent ages part of it became tributary to the power of Persia. Alexander invaded it; but his conquest was checked by the valor of Porus, one of the kings of the country, and the Macedonian warrior was unwilling or afraid to engage another. Semiramis had some ages before extended her empire far in India. The Romans knew little of the country, yet their power was so universally dreaded, that the Indians paid homage by their ambassadors to the emperors Antoninus, Trajan, &c. India was divided into several provinces. There was an India *extra Gangem*, an India *intra Gangem*, and an India *Propria;* but these divisions are not particularly noticed by the ancients, who, even in the age of Augustus, gave the name of Indians to the Æthiopian nations. *Virg. G.* 4. v. 394.—*Solin.* c. 55.—*Ptol.* 7. c. 1 & 2.—*Diod.* 1.—*Strab.* 1, &c.—*Mela,* 3. c. 7.—*Plin.* 5. c. 28.—*Cart.* 8. c. 10.—*Justin.* 1. c. 2. l. 12, c. 7.

INDIB'ILIS and MANDO'NIUS, two chiefs of the Ilergetes, who were defeated by Scipio. The former was slain, and the latter taken prisoner, and soon afterwards put to death. *Vid.* Mandonius.

INDIG'ETES, a name given to those deities who were worshipped only in some particular places, or who were raised to the rank of gods from men, as Hercules, Bacchus, &c. Some derive the word from *in loco geniti*, born at the same place where they received their worship. *Virg. G.* 1. v. 498.—*Ovid. Met.* 14. v. 608.—*Festus de V. Sig.*—*Macrob. in Som. Scip.* 1. c. 9.—*Aul. Gell.* 2. c. 16.—*Servius in Virg. G.* 1. v. 498. *Æn.* 12. v. 794.—*Meursius, Gr. Fer.*

INDIGE'TES or INDIGE'TÆ, a people of Spain. *Plin.* 3. c. 3.—*Strab.* 3.

INDUCIOM'ARUS, a person who contended with Cingetorix for the government of the Treviri.

IN'DUS, now Sinde, a large river of Asia, from which the adjacent country has received the name of India. It falls into the Indian Ocean by two mouths. According to Plato, it was larger than the Nile; and Pliny says, that 19 considerable rivers discharge themselves into it, before it falls into the sea. *Cic. N. D.* 2. c. 52.—*Strab.* 15.—*Curt.* 8. c. 9.—*Diod.* 2.—*Ovid. Fast.* 3. v. 720. *Trist.* 5. el. 3. v. 24.—*Plin.* 6. c. 20.——A small river of Caria. *Liv.* 38. c. 14.—*Strab.* 15.—*Ptol.* 5. c. 2.

INDUS'TRIA, a town of Liguria, called also Bodincomagum. *Plin.* 3. c. 16.

IN'FERI, the gods of Hades. Poetically, the inhabitants generally of the nether world.

IN'FERUM MA'RE, a name given to the Tuscan Sea, as situated below Italy; as Superum was applied to the Adriatic above Italy.

INGÆV'ONES or INGÆVO'NES, a people of Germany, subdivided into the Sicambri, Teutones, and Cauchi. *Plin.* 4. c. 13 & 14.—*Tac. Ger.* c. 2.—*Hug. Grot. Proleg. in H. Goth.*

INGAU'NI, a people of Liguria. Their city was Albingaunum. *Plin.* 3. c. 5.

INGEN'UUS, governor of Pannonia, A.D, 258. He assumed the purple, but was defeated and slain by Gallienus.

I'NO, a daughter of Cadmus and Harmonia, who nursed Bacchus. She married Athamas, king of Thebes, after he had divorced Nephele, by whom he had had two children, Phryxus and Helle. Ino became mother of Melicerta and Learchus, and soon conceived an implacable hatred against the children of Nephele, because they were to ascend the throne in preference to her own. Phryxus and Helle were informed of Ino's machinations, and escaped to Colchis on a golden ram. *Vid.* Phryxus. Juno, jealous of Ino's prosperity, resolved to disturb her peace: and more particularly, because she was one of the descendants of her greatest enemy, Venus. Tisiphone was sent, by order of the goddess, to the house of Athamas; and she filled the whole palace with such fury, that Athamas taking Ino to be a lioness, and her children whelps, pursued her, and dashed her son Learchus against a wall. Ino escaped from the fury of her husband, and from a high rock threw herself into the sea, with Melicerta in her arms. The gods pitied her fate, and Neptune made her a sea deity, known afterwards by the name of Leucothoe. Melicerta became also a sea god, by the name of Palæmon. *Homer Odyss.* 5. v. 333.—*Paus.*. 1. c. 44. l. 2. c. l. l. 9. c. 5.—*Lactant. ad Theb.* l. v. 13 & 230. l. 7. v. 421.—*Servius ad Virg. G.* 1. v. 437.—*Cic. Tusc. de Nat. D.* 3. c. 48.—*Plut. Symp.* 5.—*Ovid. Met.* 4. fab. 13, &c.—*Apollod.* 2. c. 4.—*Hygin.* fab. 12, 14 & 15.

INO'A, festivals in memory of Ino, celebrated yearly with sports and sacrifices at Corinth. *Tzetz. in Lycoph.*—An anniversary sacrifice was also offered to Ino at Megara, where she was first worshipped under the name of Leucothoe. *Paus. Attic.*—Another in Laconia, in honor of the same. It was usual at the celebration, to throw cakes of flour into a pond, which, if they sank, were presages of prosperity; but if they swam on the surface, were considered as inauspicious and very unlucky. *Paus.*—*Lacon.*

INO'PUS, a river of Delus, which the inhabitants suppose to be the Nile, passing from Ægypt under the sea. It was near its banks that Apollo and Diana were born. *Plin.* 2. c. 103.—*Flacc.* 5. v. 105.—*Strab.* 6.—*Paus.* 2. c. 4.

INO'US, a patronymic given to the god Palæmon, as son of Ino. *Virg. Æn.* 5. v. 823.

IN'SUBRES, the inhabitants of Insubria, supposed to be of Gallic origin. They were conquered by the Romans, and their country became a province, where the modern towns of Milan and Pavia were built. *Strab.* 2.—*Tacit. A.* 11. c. 23.—*Plin.* 3. c. 17.—*Liv.* 5. c. 34.—*Ptol.* 3. c. 1.

INSU'BRIA, a country of Cisalpine Gaul, at the north of the Po, between the rivers Ticinus and Addua. *Vid.* Insubres.

INTAPHER'NES, one of the seven Persian noblemen who conspired against Smerdis, who had usurped the crown of Persia. He was so disappointed from not obtaining the crown, that he fomented sedition against Darius, who had been raised to the throne after the death of the usurper. When the king had ordered him and all his family to be put to death, his wife, by frequently visiting the palace, excited the compassion of Darius, who pardoned her, and permitted her to redeem from death any one of her relations whom she pleased. She claimed the preservation of her brother; and when the king expressed his astonishment, because she preferred him to her husband and children, she replied that she could procure another husband and children likewise; but that she could never have another brother, as her father and mother were dead. Intaphernes was put to death. *Herodot.* 3.

INTEME'LIUM, a town at the west of Liguria on the sea-shore, on the Ligusticus Sinus. *Cic. Div.* 8. c. 14.

INTERAM'NA, now Terni or Terani, an ancient city of Umbria, the birth-place of the historian Tacitus, and also of the emperor of the same name. It is situate between two branches of the Nar (*inter amnes)*, whence its name. *Varro. L.L.* 4. c. 5.—*Tacit. Hist.* 2. c. 64.——A colony on the confines of Samnium, on the Liris. *Liv.* 10. c. 36.

INTERCA'TIA, a town of Spain. *Strab.* 3.—*Polyb.*—*Plin.* 3. c. 3.

INTERCI'SA, a town in Umbria, where a road was cut through the rocks by Vespasian.

INTER'NUM MA'RE, the Mediterranean Sea.

INTEROCRE'A or INTEROCRE'UM, a town of the Sabines, now Interdoco. *Strab.* 5.

IN'TERREX, a supreme magistrate at Rome, who was entrusted with the care of the government after the death of a king, till the election of another. This office was exercised by the senators alone, and none continued in power longer than five days, or, according to *Plutarch*, twelve hours. The first interrex mentioned in Roman history, is after the death of Romulus, when the Romans quarrelled with the Sabines concerning the choice of a king. There was sometimes an interrex during the consular government; but this happened only to hold assemblies in the absence of the superior magistrates, or when the election of any of the acting officers was disputed. *Liv.* 1. c. 17.—*Dionys.* 2. c. 15.

INTON'SUS, *unshorn*, a surname of Apollo and Bacchus, in allusion to the eternal youth of those gods.

IN'UI CAS'TRUM, a city of Italy, at the east of Ostia, on the shores of the Mediterranean. It received its name from Inuus, a divinity supposed to be the same as the Faunus of the Latins, and worshipped in this city. *Virg. Æn.* 6. v. 775.

INUS'SUS, a city of Ægypt. *Steph.*

IN'UUS or IN'CUBUS, a name given by the Romans to Pan, Faunus, and the Satyrs. *Liv.* 1. c. 5.—*Virg. Æn.* 6. v. 775. & *Servius loco.*—*Macrob. Sat.* 1. c. 22.

IN'YCUS, INY'CUS, or IN'YCUM, a city of Sicily. *Pausan.*—*Steph. in* Κάμικος.

I'O, a daughter of Inachus, or, according to others, of Jasus or of Pirenes, was priestess of Juno at Argos. Jupiter became enamoured of her; but Juno, jealous of his intrigues, discovered the object of his affection, and surprised him in the company of Io, though he had shrouded himself in clouds and thick mists. Jupiter, to avoid intrusion, changed his mistress into a beautiful heifer; and the goddess, who well knew the fraud, obtained from her husband the animal, whose beauty she had condescended to commend. Juno commanded the hundred-eyed Argus to watch the heifer; but Jupiter, anxious for the situation of Io, sent Mercury to destroy Argus, and to restore her to liberty. *Vid.* Argus. Io, liberated from the importunate vigilance of Argus, was now persecuted by Juno; who sent one of the furies, or rather a malicious insect, to torment her. She wandered over the greatest part of the earth, and crossed over the sea, till at last she stopped on the banks of the Nile, still exposed to the unceasing torments of Juno's insect. Here she entreated Jupiter to restore her to her ancient form; and when the god had changed her from a heifer into a woman, she brought forth Epaphus. She afterwards married Telegonus king of Ægypt, or Osiris according to others, and treated her subjects with such mildness and humanity, that, after death, she received divine honors, and was worshipped under the name of Isis. According to Herodotus, Io was carried away by Phœnician merchants, who wished to make reprisals for Europa, who had been stolen from them by the Greeks. Some suppose that Io never came to Ægypt. She is sometimes called Phoronis from her brother Phoroneus. *Æschyl in Prom. Vinct.*—*Sophoc. in El.*—*Val. Flacc.* 7. v. 110.—*Ovid. Met.* 1. v. 748.—*Paus.* 1. c. 25. l. 3. c. 18.—*Moschus.*—*Apollod.* 2. c. 1.—*Virg. Æn.* 7. v. 789.—*Hygin.* fab. 145.—*Nonnus. Dion.* 1 & 3.—The word Io was used as an exclamation of joy among the Romans, and sometimes also of sorrow. *Virg. Æn.* 7. v. 400.—*Tibull,* 2. el. 4. v. 6.—*Ovid. A.A.* 2. v. 1.—*Horat.* 4. od. 2. *Epod.* 9.

IOB'ATES, JOB'ATES or JOBA'TES, a king of Lycia, father of Stenobœa, the wife of Prœtus, king of Argos. He was succeeded on the throne by Bellerophon, to whom he had given one of his daughters, called Philonoe, in marriage, *Vid.* Bellerophon. *Apollod.* 2. c. 2.—*Hygin.* fab. 57.—*Servius in Æn.* 5. v. 118.

I'OBES, a son of Hercules by a daughter of Thespius. He died in his youth. *Apollod.* 2. c. 7.

IOLA'IA, a festival observed at Thebes, the same as that called Heraclea. It was instituted in honor of Hercules and his friend Iolas, who assisted him in conquering the hydra. It continued during several days, on the first of which were offered solemn sacrifices. The next day horse races and athletic exercises were exhibited. The following day was set apart for wrestling, and the victors were then crowned with garlands of myrtle, generally used at funeral solemnities. They were sometimes rewarded with tripods of brass. The place where the exercises were exhibited was called Iolaion, and here were to be seen the monument of Amphitryon, and the Cenotaph of Iolas, who was buried in Sardinia. These monuments were adorned with garlands and flowers on the day of the festival. *Pindar. Schol. Ol.* 7. *Schol. in Isthm.*

I'OLAS or IOLA'US, a son of Iphiclus, king of Thessaly, who assisted Hercules in conquering the hydra. *Vid.* Hydra. He was restored to his youth and vigor by Hebe, at the request of his friend Hercules, and some time afterwards he assisted the Heraclidæ against Eurystheus, and killed the tyrant with his own hand. According to *Plutarch*, Iolas had a monument in Bœotia and Phocis, where lovers used to go and bind themselves by the most solemn oaths of fidelity, considering the place as sacred to love and friendship. According to Diodorus and Pausanias, Iolas died and was buried in Sardinia, where he had gone to make a settlement at the head of the sons of Hercules by the fifty daughters of Thespius. A grove in Sicily was particularly devoted to the honor of Iolas by Hercules himself, and not only festivals were celebrated in his honor at that place, but the inhabitants of Agyrium suffered their hair to grow till it became a suitable offering to their favorite hero. *Diod.* 4.—*Lucian. in Phalar.*—*Hygin.* fab. 14.—*Tzetzes in Lycoph.* 839.—*Ovid. Met.* 9. v. 399.—*Apollod* 2. c. 4.—*Paus.* 7. c. 2. l. 10. c. 17.——A compiler of a Phœnician history,——A friend of Æneas, killed by Catillus in the Rutulian wars. *Virg. Æn.* 11. v. 640.——A son of Antipater, cup-bearer to Alexander the Great. *Plut.*——A shepherd mentioned by *Virgil, Ecl.* 2. v. 57. Ecl. 3. v. 79.

IOL'CUS, a town of Magnesia, in Thessaly, a little above Demetrias, where Jason was born. It was founded by Cretheus, son of Æolus and Enaretta. Mela mentions it as being at some distance from the sea, though all the other ancient geographers place it on the sea shore.—*Paus.* 4. c. 2.—*Horat. Epod.* 5. v. 21.—*Apollod.* 1. c. 9.—*Strab.* 8.—*Mela,* 2. c. 3.—*Lucan.* 3. v. 192.

I'OLE, a daughter of Eurytus, king of Œchalia. Her father promised her in marriage to Hercules, but he afterwards refused to perform his engagements, and Iole was carried away by force. *Vid.* Eurytus. It was to extinguish the love of Hercules for Iole, that Dejanira sent him the poisoned tunic, which caused his death. *Vid.* Hercules and Dejanira. After the death of Hercules, Iole married Hyllus his son by Dejanira. *Apollod.* 2. c. 7.—*Ovid. Met.* 9. v. 279. *Heroid.* 9. v. 133.—*Diod.* 4. [There is a head of Iole decked with the skin of the Nemean lion, in the Villa Albani at Rome.

IOL'LAS or IOLA'US, son of Antipater, king of Macedonia. He was cup-bearer to Alexander, and is supposed to have poisoned him.

I'OLUM, a mountain of Perrhæbia. *Steph.*

I'ON, a son of Xuthus and Creusa, daughter of Erechtheus, who married Helice, the daughter of Selinus, king of Ægiale. He succeeded to the kingdom of his father-in-law, and built a city which he called Helice, on account of his wife. His subjects received the name of Ionians from him, and the country that of Ionia. *Vid.* Iones & Ionia. *Apollod.* 1. c. 7.—*Paus.* 7. c. 1.—*Strab.* 7.—*Herodot.* 7. c. 94. l. 8. c. 44.——A tragic poet of Chius, whose tragedies, when represented at Athens, met with universal applause. He is mentioned and greatly commended by Aristophanes, Athenæus, and others. *Athen.* 10, &c.——A native of Pisa, engaged in the Theban war. *Stat. Theb.* 8. v. 454.——A native of Ephesus introduced in Plato's dialogues as reasoning with Socrates.

ION'DA, a town of Asia, near Ephesus. *Diod. Sic.* l. 4.

I'ONE, one of the Nereides. *Apollod.*

IO'NES, a name originally given to the subjects of Ion, who dwelt at Helice. In the age of Ion, the Athenians made war against the people of Eleusis, and implored his aid. Ion conquered the Eleusinians and Eumolpus, who was at their head; and the Athenians, sensible of his services, invited him to come and settle among them; and the more strongly to show their attachment to him, they assumed the name of Ionians. Some suppose that after this victory, Ion passed into Asia Minor, at the head of a colony. When the Achæans were driven from Peloponnesus by the Heraclidæ, eighty years after the Trojan war, they came to settle among the Ionians, who were then masters of Ægialus. They were soon dispossessed of their territories by the Achæans, and went to Attica, where they met with a cordial reception. Their migration from Greece to Asia Minor was about 60 years after the return of the Heraclidæ, B.C. 1044, and 80 years after the departure of the Æolians; and they therefore finally settled themselves, after a wandering life of about 30 years.

IO'NIA, a country of Asia Minor, bounded on the

north by Æolia, on the west by the Ægæan and Icarian Seas, on the south by Caria, and on the east by Lydia and part of Caria. It was peopled by colonies from Greece, and particularly from Attica, by the Ionians, or subjects of Ion. Ionia was divided into twelve small states, which formed a celebrated confederacy, often mentioned by the ancients. These twelve states were Priene, Miletus, Colophon, Clazomenæ, Ephesus, Lebedus, Teus, Phocæa, Erythræ, Smyrna, and the capitals of Samus and Chius. The inhabitants of Ionia, in commemoration of this union, built a temple, which they called Pan Ionium, from the concourse of people that flocked there from every part of Ionia. After they had enjoyed for some time their freedom and independence, they were made tributary to the power of Lydia by Crœsus. The Athenians assisted them to shake off the slavery of the Asiatic monarchs; but they soon forgot their gratitude as well as their relation to their mother country, and joined Xerxes when he invaded Greece. They were afterwards delivered from the Persian yoke by Alexander, and restored to their original independence. They were reduced by the Romans under the dictator Sylla. Ionia has been always celebrated for the salubrity of the climate, the fruitfulness of the ground, and the genius of its inhabitants. *Herodot.* 1. c. 6 & 28.—*Plin.* 5. c. 17 & 28.—*Strab.* 14.—*Mela*, 1. c. 2 & 17. l. 2. c. 7.—*Ptol.* 5. c. 2.—*Paus.* 7. c. 1.——A name given to Hellas, or Achaia, because it was for some time the residence of the Ionians.

IO'NIUM MA'RE, a part of the Mediterranean Sea, at the bottom of the Adriatic, lying between Sicily and Greece. That part of the Ægean Sea which lies on the coasts of Ionia, in Asia, is called, in contradistinction, the Sea of Ionia, and not the Ionian Sea. According to some authors, the Ionian Sea received its names from Io, who swam across it, after she had been metamorphosed into a heifer. *Strab.* 7, &c.—*Dionys. Perieg.*—*Æsch. in Prom.*—*Lycop. in Cass.*

IO'PAS, an African chieftain, among the suitors of Dido. He was an excellent musician, poet, and philosopher, and exhibited his superior abilities at the entertainment which Dido gave to Æneas. *Virg. Æn.* 1. v. 744.

I'OPE or JOP'PA, now Jaffa, a famous town of Phœnicia, more ancient than the deluge, according to some traditions. It was about forty miles to the west of the capital of Judæa, and was remarkable for a seaport much frequented, though very dangerous, on account of the great rocks that lie before it. *Strab.* 16, &c.—*Propert.* 2. el. 28. v. 51.

I'OPE, a daughter of Iphicles, who married Theseus. *Plut.*

I'OPHON, a son of the poet Sophocles, who accused his father of imbecility in the management of his affairs. As a reply to the accusation, the old man repeated before his judges the tragedy of Œdipus Coloneus, which he had just finished. *Lucian. de Macrob.*—*Suidas.*—*L. Gyrald. de Poet. D.* 7.——A poet of Gnossus, in Crete. *Paus.* 1. c. 34.

I'OPIS, a region of Laconia. *Steph.*

I'OS, now Nido, an island in the Ægean Sea, at the south of Naxus, celebrated, as some say, for the tomb of Homer, and the birth of his mother. *Plin.* 4. c. 12. *Vitâ Homer.* 34.—*Paus.* 10. c. 24.—*Mela*, 2. c. 7.—*Strab.* 10.

IO'TÆ, a people of Scythia within Imaus. *Ptol.*

IOTAP'ATA, a city of Syria. *Vid.* Josephus.

IOT'APE, a city of Cilicia. *Ptol.*

IP'ANA. a city near Carthage. *Steph.*

IPASTUR'GI, a town of Spain. *Plin.* 3. c. 1.

IPHIANAS'SA, a daughter of Prœtus, king of Argos, who, with her sisters Iphinoe and Lysippe, ridiculed Juno, &c. *Vid.* Prætides.——The wife of Endymion. *Apollod.* Iphigenia is also called Iphianassa. *Lucr.* 1. v. 86.

IPH'IAS, or Evadne, a daughter of Iphis, and wife of Capaneus.

IPHIAS'TÆ, a people of the tribe Acamantis. *Hesych.*

IPH'ICLUS, IPHI'CLUS, IPH'ICLES and IPHI'CLES, a son of Amphitryon and Alcmena, born at the same birth with Hercules. As these two children were together in the cradle, Juno, jealous of the future greatness of Hercules, sent two large serpents to destroy him. At the sight of the serpents Iphicles alarmed the house, but Hercules, though not a year old, boldly seized them, one in each hand, and squeezed them to death. *Apollod.* 2. c. 4.—*Theocrit.*—*Servius ad Æn.* 8. v. 288.——A king of Phylace, in Phthiotis, son of Phylacus and Clymene. He had bulls of a remarkable size, which were kept by a monster of terrible appearance. Melampus, at the request of his brother (*vid.* Melampus), attempted to steal them away, but he was caught in the fact, and imprisoned. Iphiclus soon received some advantages from the prophetical knowledge of his prisoner, and not only restored him to liberty, but also presented him with the oxen. Iphiclus, who was childless, learned from the soothsayer how to become a father. He had married Automedusa, daughter of Alcathous, and afterwards a daughter of Creon, king of Thebes. He was father of Podarce and Protesilaus. *Homer. Odyss.* 11. *Il.* 13 & 23.—*Apollod.* 1. c. 9.—*Paus.* 4. c. 36.—*Hygin.* fab. 34.——A son of Thestius, king of Pleuron, who was among the Argonauts. *Apollod.* 2. c. 1.

IPHIC'RATES, a celebrated general of Athens, who, though son of a shoemaker, rose from the lowest station to the highest offices of the state. He made war against the Thracians, and after gaining some important victories over the Spartans, he went to the assistance of the Persian king against Ægypt. He changed the dress and arms of his soldiers, and rendered them more alert and expeditious in using their weapons. He married a daughter of Cotys king of Thrace, by whom he had a son called Mnestheus, and died 380 B.C. When he was once reproached with the meanness of his origin, he observed that he would be the first of his family, but that his dictator would be the last of his own. *C. Nep. in Iphic.*——A sculptor of Athens.——An Athenian, sent to Darius the Third, king of Persia, &c. *Curt.* 3. c. 13.

IPHID'AMAS, a son of Antenor and Theano, killed by Agamemnon. *Homer. Il.* 10. v. 222.

IPHIGENI'A, called also Iphianassa, a daughter of Agamemnon and Clytæmnestra. When the Greeks, going to the Trojan war, were detained by contrary winds at Aulis, they were informed by Calchas the priest of Apollo, and the soothsayer of the army, that to appease the gods, they must sacrifice to Diana, Iphigenia, Agamemnon's daughter. *Vid.* Agamemnon. The father, who had provoked the goddess by killing her favorite stag, heard this with the greatest horror, and unwilling to shed the blood of his daughter, he, as chief of the Grecian forces, commanded one of his heralds, to order all the assembly to depart, each to his respective home. Ulysses and the other generals interfered, and Agamemnon reluctantly consented to immolate his daughter for the common cause of Greece. As Iphigenia was tenderly loved by her mother, the Greeks sent for her, pretending that she was to be given in marriage to Achilles. Clytæmnestra gladly permitted her departure, and Iphigenia came to Aulis, where she saw the bloody preparations for her sacrifice. In her distress she implored the protection of her father, but tears and intreaties were unavailing. Calchas took the knife into his hand; but, as he was going to strike the fatal blow, Iphigenia suddenly disappeared, and a goat of uncommon size and beauty was found in her place. This supernatural change animated the Greeks, the wind suddenly became favorable, and the combined fleet set sail from Aulis. Iphigenia's innocence had excited the compassion of the goddess on whose altar she was going to be sacrificed, and she carried her to Taurica, where she entrusted her with the care of her temple. In this sacred office Iphigenia was obliged, by the command of Diana, to sacrifice all the strangers who came into that country. Many had already been offered as victims on the bloody altar, when Orestes and Pylades came to Taurica. Their mutual and unparalleled friendship (*vid.* Pylades and Orestes), disclosed to Iphigenia that one of the strangers whom she was going to sacrifice was her own brother; and upon this she conspired with the two friends to flee from the barbarous country, and to carry away the statue of the goddess. They successfully effected their enterprise, and murdered Thoas, who wished to enforce the human sacrifices. According to some authors, the Iphigenia who was sacrificed at Aulis was not a daughter of Agamemnon, but a daughter of Helen, by Theseus. Homer does not speak of the sacrifice of Iphigenia, though very minute in the description of the Grecian forces, adventures, &c. The statue of Diana, which Iphigenia brought away from Taurica, was afterwards placed in the grove of Aricia in Italy. *Paus.* 2. c. 22. l. 3. c. 16.—*Ovid. Met.* 12. v. 31.—*Virg. Æn.* 2. v. 116.—*Æschyl. in Agam.*—*Euripid. in Iphig Aul. & Taur.*—*Cic. Tusc.* 1. c. 48.—*Propert.* 3. el. 5. v. 53.—*Aul. Gell.*—*Macrob. Saturn.*

IPHIMEDI'A or IPHIM'EDE, a daughter of Triopas, who married the giant Alœus. She fled from her husband, and had two sons, Otus and Ephialtes, by Neptune, her father's father. *Homer Odyss.* 11. v. 124.—*Paus.* 9. c. 22.—*Apollod.* 1. c. 7.

IPHIM'EDON, a son of Eurystheus, killed in a war against the Athenians and the Heraclidæ. *Apollod.*

IPHIMEDU'SA, one of the daughters of Danaus, who married Echenor. *Id. Vid.* Danaides.

IPHIN'OE, one of the principal women of Lemnus, who conspired to destroy all the males of the island after their return from a Thracian expedition. *Flacc.* 2. v. 163.——One of the daughters of Prœtus. She died of a disease while under the care of Melampus. *Vid.* Prœtides. *Apollod.* 2.

IPHIN'OUS, one of the Centaurs. *Ovid. Met.* 12. v. 210.

I'PHIS, son of Alector, succeded his father on the throne of Argos. He advised Polynices, who wished to engage Amphiaraus in the Theban war, to bribe his wife Eriphyle, by giving her the golden collar of Harmonia. This succeeded, and Eriphyle betrayed her husband. Iphis is placed in the number of the Argonauts by Flaccus, though some imagine that Iphis was a son of Mercury. *Apollod.* 3.—*Flacc.* 1. v. 441. l. 3. v. 135. l. 7. v. 342.——A beautiful youth of Salamis, of ignoble birth. He became enamoured of Anaxarete, and the coldness and contempt which he experienced from her rendered him so desperate that he hanged himself. Anaxarete saw him carried to his grave without emotion, and was instantly changed into a stone. *Ovid. Met.* 14. v. 703.——An Argive killed in the Theban war by Athamas. *Stat. Theb.* 8. v. 445.——The father of Evadne, the wife of Capaneus. *Ovid. A.A.* 3. v. 22.——A daughter of Thespius. *Apollod.*——A mistress of Patroclus, given him by Achilles, to whose share she had fallen at the division of the spoils after the taking of Scyrus. *Homer. Il.* 9. v. 664.——A daughter of Ligdus and Telethusa, of Crete. When Telethusa was pregnant, Ligdus ordered her to destroy her child if it proved a daughter, because his poverty could not afford to maintain a useless charge. The unnatural conduct of her husband alarmed Telethusa, and she would have obeyed, had not Isis commanded her in a dream to spare the life of her child. Telethusa brought forth a daughter, who was given to a nurse, and passed for a boy, under the name of Iphis. Ligdus continued ignorant of the deceit, and, when Iphis was come to years of puberty, her father resolved to give her in marriage to Ianthe, the beautiful daughter of Telestes. A day to celebrate the nuptials was appointed, but Telethusa and her daughter were equally anxious to put off the marriage; and, when all was unavailing, they implored the assistance of Isis, by whose advice the life of Iphis had been preserved. The goddess was moved, she changed the sex of Ithis, and, on the morrow, the nuptials were consummated with the greatest rejoicings. *Ovid. Met.* 9. v. 666, &c.—*Antoninus, Liber.* 17, calls Iphis Leucippe, gives the name of Lamprus to her father, of Galatæa to her mother, and speaks of the goddess Latona, and not Isis.

IPHITHE'A, the mother of Orphe, Lyco, and Carya, by Dion king of Lycaonia. *Serv. ad Virg. Ecl.* 8.

IPHIT'ION, an ally of the Trojans, son of Otryntheus and Nais, killed by Achilles. *Homer. Il.* 20. v. 382.

IPH'ITUS, a son of Eurytus, king of Œchalia. When his father had promised his daughter Iole to the person who could overcome him or his sons in drawing the bow, Hercules accepted the challenge, and came off victorious. Eurytus, however, refused his daughter to the conqueror, observing, that Hercules had killed one of his wives in a fury, and that Iole might perhaps share the same fate. Some time after, Autolycus stole away the oxen of Eurytus, and Hercules was suspected of the theft. Iphitus was sent in quest of the oxen, and, in his search, he met with Hercules, whose good favors he had already gained by advising Eurytus to give Iole to the conqueror. Hercules assisted Iphitus in searching for the lost animals; but, when he recollected the ingratitude of Eurytus, he killed Iphitus by throwing him down from the walls of Tirynthus. *Homer. Odyss.* 21. v. 14.—*Hygin.* fab 35.—*Diod.* 4.—*Tzetzes. Chil.* 1. *Hist.* 36.—*Servius in Æn.* 8. v. 291.—*Apollod,* 2. c. 6.——A Trojan who survived the ruin of his country, and fled with Æneas to Italy. *Virg. Æn.* 2. v 340, &c.—*Homer. Il.* 8. v. 128.——A king of Elis in the age of Lycurgus. He re-established the Olympic games 338 years after their institution by Hercules, or about 884 years B.C. This epoch is famous in chronological history, as every thing previous to it seems involved in fabulous obscurity. *Paterc.* 1. c. 8 —*Paus.* 5. c. 4.—*Scalig. de Emend. Temp.* 1.—*Petav. de Doctr. Temp.* 9, &c.

IPH'THIME or IPHTHI'ME, a sister of Penelope, who married Eumelus. She appeared by the direction of Minerva, to her sister in a dream, to comfort her in the absence of her son Telemachus. *Homer. Odyss.* 4. v. 795.

IPSE'A, the mother of Medea. *Ovid. Heroid.* 17. v. 232. *Vid.* Idyia.

IP'NUS or IPNE'A, a city of the Locri Ozoli. *Steph.*

IP'NUS, a small region of Samus, where Juno had a temple. *Id.*

IP'PA, a town of Mauritania Cæsariensis. *Ptol.*

IPSICU'RI, a people of Liguria, called also Arbazani. *Steph.*

IP'SUS, a place of Phrygia, celebrated for a battle which was fought there about 301 B.C. between Antigonus and his son, and Seleucus, Ptolemy, Lysimachus, and Cassander. The former led into the field an army of above 70,000 foot and 10,000 horse, with 75 elephants. The latter's forces consisted of 64,000 infantry, besides 10,500 horse, 400 elephants, and 120 armed chariots. Antigonus and his son were defeated *Plut. in Demetr.*

I'RA, a city of Messenia which Agamemnon promised to Achilles, if he would resume his arms to fight against the Trojans. This place is famous in history as having supported a siege of eleven years against the Lacedæmonians. Its capture, B.C. 671, put an end to the second Messenian war. *Homer. Il.* 9. v. 150 & 292.—*Strab.* 7.—*Paus.* 4. c. 20.—*Eustath. in* 9 *Il.*

IR'ASA, a place of Libya. *Herodot.* 4. c. 116.

I'RATH, a town of Mauritania Cæsariensis. *Ptol.*

IRE'DÆ, a village of the tribe Acamantis. *Steph.*

IRENÆ'US, a native of Greece, disciple of Polycarp, and afterwards bishop of Lyons in France. He wrote on different subjects; but, as what remains is in Latin, some suppose that he composed in that language, and not in Greek. Fragments of his works in Greek are however preserved, which prove that his style was simple, though clear and often animated. His opinions concerning the soul are curious. He suffered martyrdom during the persecution which was raised against the Christians by the emperor Severus, A.D. 202. The best editions of his works are that of Grabe, Oxon. fol. 1702, and that of Massuetus, Paris. 1710. *Sax. Onom.* 1. p. 328.—*Fabr. B Gr.* 5. c. 1.

IRE'NE, a daughter of Cratinus the painter. *Plin.* 35. c. 11.

IRE'NE, one of the seasons among the Greeks, called by the moderns Horæ. Her two sisters were Dia and Eunomia, called by some authors Carpo and Thallo, all daughters of Jupiter and Themis. *Apollod.* 1. c. 3.—*Paus.* 5. c. 11 & 17. l. 9. c. 35.

IRENOP'OLIS, a city of Cilicia. *Ptol.*

IRE'SUS, a delightful spot in Libya, near Cyrene, where Battus fixed his residence. The Ægyptians were once defeated there by the inhabitants of Cyrene. *Herodot.* 4. c. 158, &c.

IR'IA FLA'VIA, a city of Hispania Tarraconensis. *Ptol.*

I'RIS, daughter of Thaumas and Electra, was one of the Oceanides and messenger of the gods, more particularly of Juno. Her office was to cut the thread which seemed to detain the soul in the body of those that were expiring. Iris was the goddess of the rainbow, and, from that circumstance, she is represented with wings, with all the variegated and beautiful colors of the rainbow, and appears sitting behind Juno ready to execute her commands. She is likewise described as supplying the clouds with water when Jupiter determined to deluge the world. *Hesiod. Theog.* v. 266.—*Ovid. Met.* l. v. 271 & *seq.* l. 4. v. 480. l. 11. v. 585.—*Virg. Æn.* 4. v. 694.—*Servius in Æn.* 4. v. 700. l. 5. v. 610. l. 9. v. 16. [There is a fine statue of Iris among the marbles brought from the Parthenon by Lord Elgin, and placed in the British Museum.]

I'RIS, a river of Asia Minor, which rises in Cappadocia, and after flowing through Pontus, falls into the Euxine Sea. *Flacc.* 5. v. 121.

I'RON, a Cyzicene, slain by the Argonauts. *Flacc. Argon.* 3. v. 111.

IRRHE'SIA, an island of the Ægean Sea. *Plin.* 4. c. 12.

I'RUS, a beggar of Ithaca, who executed the commissions of Penelope's suitors. When Ulysses returned home, disguised in a beggar's dress, Irus hindered him from entering the gates, and even challenged him to fight. Ulysses brought him to the ground with a blow, and dragged him out of the house. From his poverty originates the proverb *Iro pauperior.* *Hom. Odyss.* 8. v. 1 & 35.—*Propert.* 3. el. 3. v. 39.—*Martial.* 5. epigr. 41. l. 6. epigr. 77.—*Ovid. Trist.* 3. el. 7. v. 42. *In Ibin.* 419.

I'RUS, a mountain of India. *Ptol.*—*Arrian.*——A city of Thessaly. *Steph.*

IS, a small river falling into the Euphrates. Its waters abound with bitumen. *Herodot.* 1. c. 179. ——A small town on the river of the same name. *Id. ib.*

IS'ADAS, a Spartan, who, upon seeing the Thebans entering the city, stripped himself naked, and, with a spear and sword, engaged the enemy. He was rewarded with a crown for his valor, but was fined at the same time a thousand drachms. *Plut.*

ISÆ'A, one of the Nereides. *Apollod.* 1. c. 2. But read Nesæa, according to the emendation of Heyne.

ISÆ'US, an orator of Chalcis, in Eubœa, who came to Athens, and became there the pupil of Lysias, and soon after the master of Demosthenes. Some suppose that he atoned for the dissipation and imprudence of his early years by frugality and temperance. Demosthenes imitated him in preference to Isocrates, because he studied force and energy of expression rather than floridness of style. Ten of his sixty-four, or, according to *Meursius*, fifty, orations, are extant, which have been elegantly translated by Sir William Jones, 1779. Among the editions are those of Aldus, Stephens, and Reiske, in the 7th vol. of his *Oratores Græci. Sax. Onom.* l. 65.—*Fabr. B. Gr.* 2. c. 26.—*Plut. de* 10 *Orat, Dem*—*Quintil.* 12. c. 10.—*Biblioth. Photii.* ——A Greek orator, who came to Rome A.D. 17. He is greatly commended by Pliny the younger, who observes, that he always spoke *ex tempore*, and wrote with elegance, unlabored ease, and great correctness. *Plin.* 2. ep. 3.—*Juven.* 3. v. 74

ISAFLEN'TES, a people of Mauritania. *Amm. Marcell.* 29. c. 6.

ISAG'ORAS, a tragic poet, disciple of Chrestius. He flourished under Antoninus the philosopher.——An Athenian who made war with Clisthenes. *Herodot.* 5, c. 66, &c.

ISAG'URUS or **ITHAG'URUS**, a town of India within the Ganges. *Ptol.*

ISAL'ECUS, a city of Lusitania. *Id.*

ISAM'NIUM, a promontory of Ireland. *Ptol.* St. John's Foreland, according to *Camden.*

IS'AMUS, a river of India. *Strab.* 11.

ISAN'DER, a son of Bellerophon, killed in the war which his father waged against the Solymi. *Homer. Il.* 6.

ISA'PIS or **SA'PIS**, now Il Savio, a river of Umbria. *Lucan.* 2. c. 46.

I'SAR or **IS'ARA**, the Isore, a river of Gallia Narbonensis, near which Fabius routed the Allobroges. It rises at the east of Savoy, and falls into the Rhone near Valence. *Plin.* 3. c. 4.—*Lucan.* 1. v. 399.

I'SAR, a river of Gallia Celtica, now the Oyse, which falls into the Seine below Paris.

I'SAR or **ISÆ'US**, a river of Vindelicia, which, after a northern course, falls into the Danube. *Strab.* 4.

ISAR'CHUS, an Athenian archon, B.C. 424.

ISAR'CI, a people of the Alps, conquered by Augustus. *Plin.* 3. c. 20.

IS'ARI, a people of India. *Id.* 6. c. 17.

ISAU'RA, (*-æ* or *-orum*), the chief town of Isaura. *Plin.* 5. c. 27.

ISAU'RIA, a country of Asia Minor, near mount Taurus, the inhabitants of which were of a bold and warlike character. The Roman emperors, particularly Probus and Gallus, made war against them and conquered them. *Flor.* 3. c. 6.—*Mela,* 1. c. 2.—*Eutrop.* 6. c. 3.—*Marcell.* 14. c. 25.—*Ptol.* 5. c. 4.—*Strab.* 2.—*Cic.* 15. *Fam.* 2.

ISAU'RICUS, a surname of P. Servilius, from his conquests over the Isaurians. *Ovid.* 1 *Fast.* 594. —*Cic.* 5 *Att.* 21.

ISAU'RUS, now la Foglia, a river of Umbria, falling into the Adriatic.——A river in Magnia Græcia now Donato. *Lucan.* 2. v. 406.

ISBU'RUS, a river of Sicily, now Calatabellota. *Ptol.*

IS'BUS, a city of Isauria. *Steph.*

IS'CA DANMONIO'RUM, a city of Britain, now Exeter. *Ptol.*

IS'CHALIS, a town of Britain, now Ilchester. *Ptol.*

ISCHE'NIA, an annual festival observed at Olympia, in honour of Ischenus, the grandson of Mercury, and Hiera, who, in a time of famine, devoted himself for his country, and was honoured with a monument near Olympia. *Tzetz. in Lycoph. Cassandr,* v. 42.

IS'CHERA, an inland city of Libya. *Ptol.*

ISCHOLA'US, a brave and prudent general of Sparta, &c. *Polyæn.* 11.

ISCHOM'ACHUS, a noble athlete of Crotona, about the consulship of M. Valerius and P. Posthumius.

ISCHOP'OLIS, a town of Pontus, now Tripoli. *Ptol.* —*Strab.* 12.

IS'CIA. *Vid.* Œnotrides.

ISCI'NA, a city of Africa Propria. *Ptol.*

ISDEGER'DES, a king of Persia, appointed by the will of Arcadius, guardian to Thedosius the Second. He died after a reign of twenty-one years, A.D. 421.

ISDICÆ'A, a city of Thrace. *Ptol.*

ISE'PUS, a nation of Scythia. *Steph.*

ISE'A, certain festivals observed in honor of Isis, which continued nine days. It was usual to carry vessels full of wheat and barley, as the goddess was supposed to be the first who taught mankind the use of corn. These festivals were adopted by the Romans, among whom they soon degenerated into licentiousness. They were abolished by a decree of the senate, A.U.C. 696. They were introduced again, about 200 years after, by Commodus. *Juv.* 6. v. 487.—*Lud. Viv. ad Civ. Dei.* 18. c. 5.—*Diod. Sic.* 1.

ISE'UM, a city of Ægypt, so called in honor of Isis *Steph.*

ISI'ACI, the priests of Isis. Their life was tinctured with austerity, they passed the night in prayer before the statue of the goddess, and after singing hymns in her honor at the rising of the sun, they were permitted to wander in quest ef relief. Their heads were shaved, they clothed themselves in fine linen, and their feet were covered with the thin bark of the papyrus. They were not permitted to taste salt, or the flesh either of sheep or hogs, and they were likewise forbidden to eat certain fishes, such especially as were caught with a line, and also onions, because as they believed they only grew during the ill-omened wane of the moon. *Cic. de Div.* 1. c. 133.—*Val. Max.* 7. c. 3.—*Plut. de Isid. & Os.*

ISIACO'RUM POR'TUS, a harbour on the shore of the Euxine. *Arrian. in Peripl.*

ISIDO'RUS, a native of Charax, in the age of Ptolemy Lagus, who wrote some historical treatises, besides a description of Parthia. *Sax. Onom.* 1. p. 237.—*Voss. de H. Gr.* 3. p. 298.—*Fabr. B Gr.* 2. c. 10.——A disciple of Chrysostom, called Pelusiota, from his living in Ægypt. He died about the year 440 A.D,, after a laborious life of exemplary piety and practical virtue. Of his epistles 2013, divided into five books, remain, written in Greek, with conciseness and elegance. The best edition is that of Paris, fol. 1601. *Sax. ibid.* 1. p. 497.—*Fabr. ibid.* 2. c. 10.——A Christian Greek writer, who flourished in the seventh century. He is surnamed Hispalensis His works have been edited by de Breul, Paris 1601, and Colon. 1618.

ISIG'ONUS, a Greek writer before the time of Pliny, a few fragments of whose works are extant.

ISION'DA, a city of Asia Minor.

I'SIS, a celebrated deity of the Ægyptians, daughter of Saturn and Rhea, according to Diodorus of Sicily. Some authors suppose her to be the same as Io, who was changed into a cow, and restored by Jupiter to her human form in Ægypt, where she taught agriculture, and governed the people with mildness and equity, for which reasons she received divine honors after death. According to some traditions mentioned by Plutarch, Isis married her brother Osiris. These two ancient deities, as some authors observe, comprehended all nature and all the gods of the heathens. Isis was the Venus of Cyprus, the Minerva of Athens, the Cybele of the Phrygians, the Ceres of Eleusis, the Proserpine of Sicily, the Diana of Crete, the Bellona of the Romans, &c. Osiris and Isis reigned conjointly in Ægypt, but the rebellion of Typhon, the brother of Osiris, proved fatal to this sovereign. *Vid.* Osiris and Typhon. The ox and cow were the symbols of Osiris and Isis, because these deities, while on earth, had diligently applied themselves in cultivating the fields. *Vid.* Apis. Isis was supposed to be the moon, as Osiris the sun, and she was represented as holding a globe in her hand, with a vessel full of ears of corn. The Ægyptians believed that the yearly and regular inundations of the Nile proceeded from the abundant tears which Isis shed for the loss of Osiris, whom Typhon had basely murdered. The word *Isis*, according to some authors, signifies *ancient*, and, on that account, the inscriptions on the statues of the goddess were often in these words: *I am all that has been, that shall be, and none among mortals has hitherto taken off my veil.* The worship of Isis was universal in Ægypt; the priests were obliged to perpetual chastity, their heads were close shaved, and they always walked barefooted, and clothed themselves in linen garments. As the goddess was often represented with a sistrum in her right hand, with which she was supposed to inflict diseases; her priests also were adorned with the same instrument. In their meals they never ate onions, abstained from salt, and were forbidden to eat the flesh of sheep and of hogs. During the night they were employed in continual devotion near the statue of the goddess. Cleopatra, the beautiful queen of Ægypt, was wont to dress herself like this goddess, and affected to be called a second Isis. *Cic. de Div.* 1.—*Plut. de Isid. & Osirid.*—*Diod.* 1.—*Dyonys. Hal.* 1.—*Herodot.* 2. c. 59.—*Lucan.* 1. v. 831.—*Martial.* 12. epigr. 29. v. 19.—*Juv.* 13. v. 93.—*Pers.* 5. c. 186.—*Ovid.Met.* 9. v. 776.—*Suet. Oth.* 12. [The finest statue of Isis is in the Capitol; unless, as Mr. Townley supposed, the figure usually called a Canephora, in his collection, now at the British Museum, represents that deity].

ISMARA, a city of Armenia Major, near the Euphrates. *Ptol.*

IS'MARUS (IS'MARA, *plur.*) a rugged mountain of Thrace, covered with vines and olives, near the Hebrus, with a town of the same name. The wines which the country produced were esteemed of superior excellence. The word Ismarius is indiscriminately used for Thracian. *Homer. Odyss.* 9.—*Virg. G.* 2. v. 37. *Æn.* 10. v. 351.

Is'marus, a Theban, son of Astacus. *Apollod.*——A son of Eumolpus. *Id.*

Is'mara, a Lydian, who accompanied Æneas to Italy, and fought with great vigor against the Rutuli. *Virg Æn.* 10. v. 139.

ISME'NE, a daughter of Œdipus and Jocasta, who when her sister Antigone had been condemned to be buried alive by Creon, for giving burial to her brother Polynices, against the tyrant's positive orders, declared herself as guilty as her sister, and insisted upon being equally punished with her. This instance of generosity was strongly opposed by Antigone, who wished not to see her sister involved in her calamities. She was betrothed to Atys, a youth of Cyrrha, who was slain by Tydeus before the celebration of the nuptials. *Stat. Theb.* 8. v. 555.—*Sophocl. in Antig.*—*Apollod.* 3. c. 5. ——A daughter of the river Asopus, who married the hundred-eyed Argus, by whom she became mother of Jasus. *Apollod.* 2. c. 1.

ISME'NIAS, a celebrated musician of Thebes. When he was taken prisoner by the Scythians, Athias, the king of the country, observed that he could listen with greater pleasure to the neighing of a horse than to the music of Ismenias. *Plut. in Apoph.*—*Plin.* 37. c. 1.——A Theban, bribed by Timocrates of Rhodes, that he might use his influence to prevent the Athenians and some other Grecian states from assisting the Lacedæmonians, against whom Xerxes was engaged in war. *Paus.* 3. c. 9.——A Theban general, sent to Persia with an embassy by his countrymen. As none were admitted into the king's presence without prostrating themselves at his feet, Ismenias had recourse to artifice to avoid doing an action which would prove disgraceful to his country. When he was introduced he dropped his ring, and the motion he made to recover it from the ground was mistaken for the most submissive homage, and Ismenias had a satisfactory audience of the monarch.

Isme'nias, a river of Bœotia, falling into the Euripus. Apollo had a temple there, from which circumstance he was called Ismenius. *Paus.* 9. c. 10. —*Ovid. Met.* 2.—*Strab.* 9.

ISMEN'IDES, an epithet applied to the Theban women, as living near the Ismenus, a river of Bœotia. *Ovid. Met.* 4. v. 31.

ISME'NIUS, a surname of Apollo at Thebes, where he had a temple on the borders of the Ismenus. The statue of the god, made of cedar, was the work of Canachus, and was still admired in the age of Pausanias, as likewise one of Minerva, of marble, made by Scopas, and a Mercury, by Phidias. A youth of a respectable parentage and of an engaging appearance, was yearly chosen to officiate as priest of the god, in the ceremonies of the place, and it is said that Hercules was once invested with this sacred office. *Paus.* 9. c. 10.

ISME'NUS, a son of Apollo and Melia, one of the Nereides, who gave his name to the Ladon, a river of Bœotia, near Thebes, which falls into the Asopus, and afterwards into the Euripus. *Paus.* 9. c. 10.——A son of Asopus and Metope. *Apollod.* 3. c. 12.——A son of Amphion and Niobe, killed by Apollo. *Id.* 3. c. 5.—*Ovid. Met.* 6. fab. 6.

Isme'nus, a river of Bœotia, now Ismeno. *Plin.* 4. c. 7.

ISOC'RATES, a celebrated orator, son of Theodorus, a rich musical instrument maker at Athens. He was educated in the schools of Georgias, Tisias, Theramenes, and Prodicus, but his oratorical abilities were never displayed in public; and Isocrates was prevented by an unconquerable timidity, from speaking in the national assemblies of Athens. He opened a school of eloquence, where he was soon distinguished by the number, character, and fame of his pupils, and by the immense riches which he amassed. He was intimate with Philip of Macedon, and regularly corresponded with him; and to his familiarity with that monarch the Athenians were indebted for some of the few peaceful years which they passed. The aspiring ambition of Philip, however, displeased Isocrates, and the defeat of the Athenians at Cheronæa had such an effect upon his spirits, that he did not survive the disgrace of his country, but died, after he had been four days without taking any aliment, in the 99th year of his age, about 338 years B.C. Isocrates has always been much and deservedly admired for the sweetness and graceful simplicity of his style, for the harmony of his expressions, and the dignity of his language. The remains of his orations which are extant inspire the world with the highest veneration for his abilities, as a moralist, an orator, and, above all, as a man. His merit, however, is lessened by those who accuse him of plagiarism from the works of Thucydides, Lysias, and others, seen particularly in his panegyric. He was so remarkably studious of correctness that his sentences have all the music of poetry. The severe conduct of the Athenians against Socrates highly displeased him, and, in spite of the undeserved unpopularity of that great philosopher; he put on mourning the day of his death. About twenty-one of his orations are extant. Isocrates was honored after death with a brazen statue by Timotheus, one of his pupils, and Aphareus, his adopted son. The best editions of Isocrates are that of Battie, 2 vols. 8vo. Cantab, 1729, and London 1749, and that of Auger, 3 vols. 8vo. Paris 1782. *Plut. de* 10 *Orat.* &c.—*Cic. Orat.* 20 *de Inv.* 2. c. 126. *Sen.* 5 & 7. *In Brut.* c. 15. *De Orat.* 2. c. 7.—*Suidas.*—*Quintil.* 2. c. 9. l. 9. c. 4. l. 10. c. 1 & 4.—*Paterc.* 1. c. 16. —*Sax. Onom.* 1. p. 55.—*Fabr. B. Gr.* 2. c. 26. [The most authentic bust of this orator is in the Villa Albani at Rome.]——One of the officers of the Peloponnesian fleet, &c. *Thucyd.*——One of the disciples of Isocrates, who wrote five orations, and contended with other illustrious orators at the funeral of Mausolus. *Suidas.*——A rhetorician of Syria, an enemy to the Romans, &c.

ISOL'OCHUS, father of Pythodorus, who succeeded Laches in the command in Sicily. *Thucyd.*

ISO'NÆ, a town of Assyria. *Ptol.*
ISON'DÆ, a people of Asiatic Sarmatia. *Id.*
IS'PA, a city of Armenia Minor. *Ptol.*
IS'SA, now Lissa, an island in the Adriatic Sea, on the coast of Dalmatia.——A small town of Illyricum. *Mela*, 2. c. 7.—*Strab.* 1, &c.—*Marcel.* 26. c. 25.—*Ptol.* 2. c. 17.
IS'SATIS, a city of Parthia. *Plin.* 6. c. 15.
IS'SE, a daughter of Macareus, the son of Lycaon. She was beloved by Apollo, who, to obtain her confidence, changed himself into the form of a shepherd to whom she was attached. This metamorphosis of Apollo was represented on the web of Arachne. *Ovid. Met.* 6. v. 124.
ISSE'DON, a city of Scythia, beyond Imaus. *Steph.* ——A city of the Seres, now Cambalis.
ISSO'RIA, a surname of Diana.
ISSO'RIUM, a mountain of Laconia, from which Diana was called Isoria. *Steph.*
IS'SUS, now Aisse, a town of Cilicia, on the confines of Syria, famous for a battle fought there between Alexander the Great and the Persians under Darius, in October, B.C. 333, in consequence of which it was called Nicopolis. In this battle the Persians lost, in the field of battle, 100,000 foot, and 10,000 horse, and the Macedonians only 300 foot, and 150 horse, according to Diodorus Siculus. The Persian army, according to Justin, consisted of 400,000 foot, and 100,000 horse, and 61,000 of the former, and 10,000 of the latter were left dead on the spot, and 40,000 were taken prisoners. The loss of the Macedonians, as he further adds, was no more than 130 foot and 150 horse. According to Curtius, the Persian slain amounted to 100,000 foot and 10,000 horse; and those of Alexander to 32 foot, and 150 horse, killed, and 504 wounded. This spot is likewise famous for the defeat of Niger by the emperor Severus, A.D. 194. *Plut. in Alex.*—*Justin.* 11. c. 9.—*Curt.* 3. c. 7.—*Arrian.*—*Diod.* 17.—*Cic.* 5 *Att.* 20.—*Fam.* 2. ep. 10.—*Ptol.* 5. c. 8.
IS'TER or IS'TRUS, an historian, disciple to Callimachus. *Diog.*—*Athen.* 1. 9. c. 9.—*Harpocrat.*—*Plut.*—*Voss. de H. Gr.* 4. c. 12.
Is'ter, a large river of Europe, called also the Danube. *Vid.* Danubius.
Is'ter, a son of Ægyptus. *Apollod.*
IST'HMIA, sacred games among the Greeks, which received their name from the isthmus of Corinth, where they were observed. They were celebrated in commemoration of Melicerta, who was changed into a sea deity, when his mother Ino had thrown herself into the sea with him in her arms. The body of Melicerta, according to some traditions, when cast upon the sea-shore, received an honorable burial, in memory of which Isthmian games were instituted B.C. 1326. They were interrupted after they had been celebrated with great regularity during some years, and Theseus at last reinstituted them in honor of Neptune, whom he publicly called his father. These games were observed every third, or, according to the more received opinion, every fifth year, and held so sacred and inviolable, that even a public calamity could not prevent the celebration. When Corinth was destroyed by Mummius, they were observed with the usual solemnity, and the Sicyonians were intrusted with the superintendence of them, which had been before one of the privileges of the ruined Corinthians. Combats of every kind were exhibited on the occasion, and the victors were rewarded with garlands of pine leaves. Some time after the custom was changed, and the victor received a crown of dry and withered parsley. The years among the Greeks were reckoned by the celebration of the Isthmian games, as among the Romans from the consular government. *Paus.* 1. c. 44. 1. 2. c. 1 & 2.—*Ovid. Met.* 4. v. 531.—*Plin.* 4. c. 5.—*Schol. Aristoph. in Vesp. & in Equi.*—*Plut in Thes.*
IST'HMIUS, a king of Messenia, &c. *Paus.* 4. c. 3.
IST'HMUS, a small neck of land which joins one country to another, such as that of Corinth, which joins Peloponnesus to Greece, called often the Isthmus by way of eminence. Nero attempted to cut it across, and make a communication between the two seas, but in vain. It is now called Hexamili. *Strab.* 1.—*Mela*, 2. c. 2.—*Plin.* 4. c. 4.—*Lucan.* 1. v. 101.
ISTIÆO'TIS or ISTIÆ'OTIS. *Vid.* Histiæotis.
ISTO'NE, a mountain near Corcyra. *Steph.*
IS'TRIA, a small province at the west of Illyricum, at the top of the Adriatic Sea, the inhabitants of which were originally pirates, and lived chiefly on plunder. They were not subjected to Rome till six centuries after the foundation of that city. *Strab.* 1.—*Mela*, 2. c. 3.—*Liv.* 10. c. 2. l. 21. c. 16. l. 39. c. 55.—*Plin.* 3. c. 19.—*Justin.* 9. c. 2.—*Ptol.* 3. c. 1.
ISTRIA'NA, a city of Arabia Felix, on the Persian Gulph. *Steph.*
ISTRIA'NUS, a river of Taurica Chersonesus. *Ptol.*
ISTROP'OLIS, a city of Thrace, near the mouth of the Ister, founded by a Milesian colony. *Plin.* 4. c. 11.
IS'TUS, an island of Africa. *Steph.*—*Boch. Geo.* p. 824.
ISU'ELI, a people of Æthiopia. *Plin.* 6. c. 30.
ISU'RA, an island of the Arabic Gulph. *Id.* 6. c. 28.
ISU'RIUM, a town of the Brigantes, now Boroughbridge. *Ptol.*
I'SUS and AN'TIPHUS, sons of Priam, the latter by Hecuba, and the former by a concubine. They were seized by Achilles as they were tending their father's flocks on mount Ida, but they were redeemed by Priam, and fought against the Greeks. They were both killed by Agamemnon. *Homer. Il.* 11. v. 102.
I'sus, a city of Bœotia. *Strab.* 9.
ITA'LIA, a celebrated country of Europe, bounded by the Adriatic and Tyrrhene Seas, and by the Alpine mountains. Its figure has been compared with some truth, to a man's leg, extending in length 600 miles, and being about 400 miles in its greatest breadth. It has borne at different periods the different names of Saturnia, Œnotria, Hesperia, Ausonia, and Tyrrhenia, and, according to some authors, it received the name of Italy, either from Italus, a king of the country, or from Italos, a Greek word which signifies *an ox*, an animal very common in that part of Europe. The boundaries of Italy appear to have been formed by nature itself, which seems to have been particularly bountiful in supplying this country with whatever may contribute not only to support, but also to the pleasures and luxuries of life. It has been called the garden of Europe; and the beautiful panegyric which Pliny bestows upon it seems not to be in any degree exaggerated. The ancient inhabitants called themselves Aborigines, offspring of the soil, and the country was soon after peopled by various colonies from Greece. The Pelasgi and the Arcadians made settlements there, and the whole country was divided into as many different governments as there were towns, till the rapid increase of the Roman power (*vid.* Roma), changed the face of Italy, and united all its hitherto independent states in support of one common cause. Italy has been the mother of arts as well as of arms, and the immortal monuments which remain of the eloquence and poetical abilities of its inhabitants are universally known. It was divided into eleven small provinces or regions by Augustus, though sometimes known under the three greater divisions of Cisalpine Gaul, Italy, properly so called, and Magna Græcia. The sea above was called Superum and that at the south Inferum. *Ptol.* 3. c. 1.—*Dionys. Hal.* 1. c. 1.—*Diod.* 4.—*Strab.* 1. 2. 5.—*Mela*, 1. c. 3. l. 2. c. 4 & 7.—*Justin.* 4. c. 1. l. 12. c. 1. l. 28. c. 2. l. 43. c. 1.—*Virg. Æn.* 1. v. 534. l. 3. v. 166. l. 6. v. 6. l. 7. v. 3.—*Servius locis cit.*—*Columel. de R. R.* 5.—*Macrob. Sat.* 1. c. 3.—*Solin.* 7.—*C. Nep. in Dion. Alcib. &c.*—*Liv.* 1. c. 2. l. 5. c. 33.—*Varro de R. R.* 2. c. 1 & 5.—*Polyb.* 2.—*Flor.* 2.—*Ælian. V. H.* 1. c. 16.—*Lucan.* 2. v. 397, &c.—*Plin.* 3. c. 5 & 8.
ITAL'ICA, a town of Italy, called also Corfinium. *Strab.* 3.——A town of Spain, now Sevilla la Vieja, built by Scipio, for the accommodation of his wounded soldiers. *Gell.* 16. c. 13.—*Appian. Hisp.*
ITAL'ICUS, a poet. *Vid.* Silius.
IT'ALUS, a son of Telogonus. *Hygin.* fab. 127. ——An Arcadian prince, who is said to have come to Italy, where he established a kingdom called after him. It is supposed that he received divine honors after death, as Æneas invokes him among the deities to whom he paid his adoration when he invaded Italy. *Virg. Æn.* 7. v. 178.—*Serv. in Æn.* 1. v. 530.—*Dionys.* 1. c. 12.——A prince whose daughter Roma by his wife Leucaria is said to have married Æneas and Ascanius. *Plut in Rom.* ——A king of the Cherusci, &c. *Tacit. Ann.* 1. c. 16.
IT'AMUS, a harbour of Arabia Felix. *Ptol.*
ITA'NI, a people of Hispania Tarraconensis. *Plin.* 3. c. 3.

ITA'NUS, a town of Crete, near a promontory of the same name.

ITAR'GIS, a river of Germany.

ITE'A, a daughter of Danaus. *Hygin.* fab. 170.

IT'EA, a village in the tribe Acamantis. *Steph.*

ITEM'ALES, an old man, who exposed Œdipus on mount Cithæron. *Hygin.* fab. 65.

ITES'UI, a people of Gallia Lugdunensis. *Plin.* 4. c. 18.

ITH'ACA, a celebrated island in the Ionian Sea, on the western parts of Greece, with a city of the same name, famous for being part of the kingdom of Ulysses. It is very rocky and mountainous, measures about 25 miles in circumference, and is now known by the name of Isola del Compare, or Thiachi. *Homer. Il.* 2. v. 139. *Odyss.* 1. v. 186. l. 4. v. 601. l. 9. v. 20.—*Virg. Æn.* 3. v. 272.—*Strab.* 1 & 8.—*Mela*, 2. c. 7.

ITHACE'SIA, a name given to Baiæ, because built by Bajus, the pilot of Ulysses. *Sil.* 8. v. 540. l. 12. v. 113.

ITHACE'SIÆ, three small islands opposite Vibo, on the coast of the Brutii. *Plin.* 3. c. 7.

ITHOB'ALUS, a king of Tyre, who died B.C. 595. *Josephus.*

ITHO'ME, a town of Phthiotis. *Homer. Il.* 2.——A town of Messenia, which surrendered after ten years' siege, to Lacedæmon, 724 years B.C. Jupiter was called Ithomates, from a temple which he had there, where games were also celebrated, and the conqueror rewarded with an oaken crown. *Paus.* 4. c. 32.—*Stat. Theb.* 4. v. 179.—*Strab.* 8.

ITHOMA'IA, a festival in which musicians contended, observed at Ithome, in honor of Jupiter, who is said to have been nursed by the nymphs Ithome and Neda, the former of whom gave her name to a city, and the latter to a river.

ITHYPHAL'LUS, an obscene surname of Priapus. From this word obscene verses were called Ithyphallica, or Priapeia, such as were under this name attributed to Catullus, Virgil, Martial, and Petronius. *Diod.* 1. 5.—*Columell.* 10.—*Cœl. Rh.* 7. c. 16. *Scaliger. Poet.* 1.

IT'IUS POR'TUS, a town of Gaul, on the shores of the British Channel, now Wetsand, or Boulogne in Picardy. Cæsar set sail thence on his passage into Britain. *Cæs. G.* 4. c. 21. l. 5. c. 2 & 5.

ITO'NIA, a surname of Minerva, from a place in Bœotia, where she was worshipped. *Callimach.*

ITO'NUS, a king of Thessaly, son of Deucalion, who first invented the manner of polishing metals, and of coining money. *Lucan.* 6. v. 402.

ITUC'CI, a colony and city of Hispania Bætica; called also Virtus Julia. *Plin.* 3. c. 1.

ITU'NA or IT'UNA, a river of Britain, now Eden, in Cumberland.

ITURÆ'A, a country of Palestine, the inhabitants of which were very skilful in drawing the bow. *Lucan.* 7. v. 230 & 514.—*Virg. G.* 2. v. 448.—*Strab.* 17.

ITURICEN'SES, a people of Hispania Tarraconensis. *Plin* 3. c. 3.

ITURIS'SA, a city of the Vascones, in Spain. *Mela*, 3. c. 1.—*Ptol.*

ITU'RUM, a town of Umbria. *Strab.* 5.

IT'YLUS, a son of Zetheus, and Aedon, killed by his mother. *Vid.* Aedon. *Homer. Odyss.* 19. v. 462.

ITYMO'NEUS, son of Hyperochus, a brave warrior slain by Nestor.

ITYRÆ'I, a people of Palestine. *Vid.* Ituræa.

I'TYS, a son of Tereus, king of Thrace, by Procne, daughter of Pandion, king of Athens. He was killed by his mother when he was about six years old, and served up as meat before his father. He was changed into a pheasant, his mother into a swallow, and his father into an owl. *Vid.* Philomela. *Ovid. Met.* 6. v. 620. *Amor.* 2. el. 14. v. 29. —*Horat.* 4. od. 12.——A Trojan, who came to Italy with Æneas, and was killed by Turnus. *Virg. Æn.* 9. v. 574.——A man of Cyzicus, slain by Castor. *Flacc. Arg.* 3. v. 189.

IU'LUS. *Vid.* Ascanius.

IU'LUS, a son of Ascanius, born in Lavinium. In the succession to the kingdom of Alba, Æneas Sylvius, the son of Æneas and Lavinia, was preferred to him. He was, however, made chief priest. *Dionys.* 1.—*Virg. Æn.* 1. v. 271.——A son of Antony the triumvir, by Fulvia. *Vid.* Antonius Julius.

IXIB'ATÆ, a people of Pontus. *Juv.* 2. v. 160.

IXI'ON, a king of Thessaly, son of Phlegyas, or, according to Hyginus, of Leontes, or, according to Diodorus, of Antion, by Perimela, daughter of Amythaon. He married Dia, daughter of Eioneus or Deioneus, and promised his father-in-law a valuable present for the choice which he had made of him to be his daughter's husband. His unwillingness, however, to fulfil his promises obliged Deioneus to have recourse to violence to obtain it, and he stole away some of his horses. Ixion concealed his resentment under the mask of friendship; he invited his father-in-law to a feast at Larissa, the capital of his kingdom, and when the unsuspecting Deioneus came, according to the appointment, he threw him into a pit, which he had previously filled with wood and burning coals. This premeditated treachery so irritated the neighbouring princes, that all of them refused to perform the usual ceremony, by which a man was then purified of murder, and Ixion was deservedly shunned and despised by all mankind. Jupiter at last had compassion upon him, and carried him to heaven, and introduced him at the table of the gods. Here he became enamoured of Juno, and attempted to seduce her. Jupiter, however, deceived him, by substituting a cloud in the place of Juno. *Vid.* Centauri. The father of the gods, displeased with the insolence of Ixion, banished him from heaven, struck him with his thunder, and ordered Mercury to tie him to a wheel in hell. This wheel was perpetually in motion, and consequently the punishment of Ixion was eternal. *Diod.* 4.—*Hygin.* fab. 62.—*Pindar.* 2 *Pyth.* 2.—*Virg. G.* 4. v. 484. *Æn.* 6. v. 601.—*Servius in G.* 3. v. 38.—*Ovid. Met.* 12. v. 210 & 338.—*Philostr. Icon.* 2. c. 3.—*Lactant. in Theb.* 2.—*Tzetzes in Lyc.* 1200. & *Chil.* 7. *Hist.* 99. & l. 9. *Hist.* 237.—*Schol. Homer.* 1. *Il.* & *Odyss.* 21. —*Schol. Apollon.* 2. v. 1235. l. 3. v. 62.——One of the Heraclidæ, who reigned at Corinth for thirty-seven years. He was son of Alethes. *Diod. Sic. apud. Syncel.* p. 179.

IXION'IDES, the patronymic of Pirithous, as son of Ixion. *Propert.* 2. el. 1. v. 38.

IZ'ACHA, a town of Mauritania Cæsariensis. *Ptol.*

IZ'ALA, a mountain near Persia. *Amm. Marcell.*

IZ'ATHA, a town of Mauritania Cæsariensis. *Ptol.*

IZ'ELUS, a fortified place of Sicily. *Steph.*

IZ'GLI, a people of India. *Plin.* 6. c. 17.

J.

JAB'RUDA, a city of Syria. *Ptol.*

JACCETA'NI, a people of Hispania Tarraconensis.

JA'DES, a Greek writer on music. *Priscian. de Pond.* ——A statuary. *Plin.* 34. c. 8.

JÆ'TIA, a city of Sicily. *Steph.*

JA'GATH, a town of Mauritania Tingitana. *Ptol.*

JA'MÆ, a people of Scythia. *Steph.*

JA'MI, a people of Scythia. *Steph.*

JAM'NA, a city of Minorca. *Ptol.* It is now Cittadella.——A maritime city of Palestine, called Jamnis by *Pliny*, 5. c. 13, Jamnia by *Antoninus*, and Jamnetorum Portus by *Ptolemy.*

JAMNE'A, a town of Phœnice. *Ptol.*—*Salmas. ad Solin.* p. 569 & 576.

JANO'SUM, a city of the Celtæ, now Compostella. *Mela*, 2.

JANIC'ULUM or JANICULA'RIS MONS, one of the seven hills at Rome, joined to the city by Ancus Martius, and made a kind of citadel, to protect the place against invasion. This hill (*vid.* Janus), which was on the opposite shore of the Tiber, was joined to the city by the bridge Sublicius, the first ever built across that river, and perhaps in Italy. The Janiculum was more thinly inhabited than the other parts of the city on account of the grossness of the air, though from its top, the eye could have a commanding view of the whole city. It was famous for the burial of king Numa, and also of the poet Italicus. Porsenna, king of Etruria, pitched his camp on mount Janiculum, and the senators took refuge there in the civil wars, to avoid the resentment of Octavius. *Liv.* 1. c. 33, &c.—*Dio.* 47.—*Ovid.* 1. *Fast.* v. 246. —*Virg. Æn.* 8. v. 358.—*Mart.* 4. epigr. 64. l. 7. epigr. 16.

JANIS'CUS, a son of Æsculapius and Lampetie. *Schol. in Plut. Aristoph.*

JA'NUS, the most ancient king of Italy. He was a native of Thessaly, and son of Apollo, according to some authors; and he came to Italy, where he planted a colony and built a small town on the river Tiber, which he called Janiculum. Some authors make him son of Cœlus and Hecate; and others make him a native of Athens. During his reign, Saturn, driven from heaven by his son Jupiter, took refuge in Italy, where Janus received him with much hospitality, and made him his colleague on the throne. Janus is represented with two faces, because he was acquainted with the past and the future; or, according to others, because he was taken for the sun who opens the day at his rising, and shuts it at his setting. Some statues represented Janus with four heads. He sometimes appeared with a beard, and sometimes without. In religious ceremonies, his name was always invoked before all other deities, because he presided over all gates and avenues, and it was through him only that prayers could reach the immortal gods. From that circumstance he often appears with a key in his right hand, and a rod in his left. Sometimes he holds the number 300 in one hand, and in the other 65, to show that he presides over the year, of which the first month bears his name. Some suppose that he is the same as the world, or Cœlus; and from that word they call him Eanus, *ab eundo*, because of the revolution of the heavenly bodies. He was called by different names, such as *Consivius, a conserendo*, because he presided over generation: and *Quirinus* or *Martialis*, because he presided over war. He is also called *Patulcius* and *Clausius*, because the gates of his temple were open during the time of war, and shut in time of peace. He was chiefly worshipped at Rome, where he had many temples, some erected to him under the name of Janus Bifrons, and others of Janus Quadrifons. The temples of Quadrifons were built with four equal sides, with a door and three windows on each side. The four doors were the emblems of the four seasons of the year, and the three windows on each of the sides the three months of each season, and, all together the twelve months of the year. Janus was generally represented in statues as a young man. The first day of the year was particularly devoted to him, when incense and aromatic plants were burnt on his altars, young bullocks, fattened in the plains of Falisci, were also offered in sacrifice, and the votaries appeared at the Capitol, each attired in new garments. Janus was ranked among the gods, from the great popularity of his government, and the civilization which he had introduced among the wild inhabitants of Italy. His temple, which was always open in time of war, was shut only three times during above 700 years, under Numa, 234 B.C. and under Augustus, and during that long period of time, the Romans were continually employed in war. As the statue of the god looked both ways, the word Janus is used to express a passage or thoroughfare which has an opening at both ends. *Ovid. Fast.* 1. v. 65, &c.—*Virg. Æn.* 7. v. 607. *& Servius loco.—Berosius apud Tertull. in Apol.* 19. *& apud Vitruv.* 9. c. 9.—*Q. Fabius Pictor.—Varro. de L.L.* 1. *& apud Aug. de Civ.* 7. c. 2 & 4.—*Macrob. Sat.* 1. c. 9. [A statue of Janus will be found in the Museum of the Capitol.]

JA'NUS, a street at Rome, near the temple of Janus. It was generally frequented by usurers and money brokers, and booksellers also had their shops there. *Cic.* 2. *Off.* 25. *Phil.* 6. c. 5.—*Horat.* 1. ep. 1. v. 54. l. 2. *Sat.* 3. v. 18.

JANXU'ATIS, a city of Libya. *Steph.*

JAPET'IDES, a musician present at the nuptials of Perseus and Andromeda. *Ovid. Met.* 5. v. 111.

JAP'ETUS, a son of Cœlus or Titan, by Terra, who married Asia, or according to others, Clymene, by whom he had Atlas, Menœtius, Prometheus, and Epimetheus. The Greeks looked upon him as the father of all mankind, and therefore from his great antiquity, old men were frequently called Japeti. His sons received the patronymic of *Japetionides*. *Ovid. Met.* 4. v. 631.—*Hesiod. Theog.* 136. v. 508.—*Apollod.* 1. c. 1.

JARGA'NUM, a promontory of Phrygia Magna. *Ptol.*

JAR'SATH, a maritime city of Mauritania Cæsariensis. *Ptol.*

JA'SON, a celebrated hero, son of Alcimede, daughter of Phylacus, by Æson the son of Cretheus and Tyro, the daughter of Salmoneus. Tyro, before her connection with Cretheus, who was the son of Æolus, had two sons, Pelias and Neleus, by Neptune. Cretheus was king of Iolcus, and at his death the throne was usurped by Pelias, and Æson the lawful heir was cruelly driven into retirement and obscurity. The education of young Jason was entrusted to the care of the Centaur Chiron, and he was removed from the presence of the usurper who had been informed by an oracle that one of the sons of Æolus would dethrone him. After he had made the most rapid progress in every branch of science, Jason left the Centaur, and by his advice went to consult the oracle. He was ordered to visit Iolcus his native country, covered with the spoils of a leopard, and dressed in the garments of a Magnesian. In his journey he was stopped by the inundation of the river Evenus or Enipeus, over which he carried Juno, who had changed herinto an old woman. In crossing the stream he lost one of his sandals, and at his arrival at Iolcus, the singularity of his dress and the fairness of his complexion attracted the notice of the people, and drew a crowd around him in the market-place. Pelias came with the rest to gaze at him, and as he had been warned by the oracle to beware of a man who should come to Iolcus with one foot bare and the other shod, the appearance of Jason, who had lost one of his sandals, alarmed him. His apprehensions were soon found to be well founded. Jason, accompanied by his friends repaired to the palace of Pelias, and boldly demanded the kingdom which he had unjustly usurped. The boldness and popularity of Jason intimidated Pelias; he was unwilling to resign the crown, and at the same time he feared the resentment of his adversary. As Jason was young and ambitious of glory, Pelias at once to remove his immediate claims to the crown, reminded him that Æetes king of Colchis had severely treated and inhumanly murdered their common relation Phryxus. He observed that such a treatment called aloud for punishment, and that the undertaking would be attended with great glory and eternal fame. He farther added, that his old age had prevented him from avenging the death of Phryxus, and that if Jason would undertake the expedition, he would resign to him the crown of Iolcus when he returned victorious from Colchis. Jason readily accepted a proposal which seemed to promise such military fame. His intended expedition was made known in every part of Greece, and the youngest and bravest of the Greeks soon assembled from all parts to accompany him, and to share his toils and glory. They embarked on board a ship called Argo, and after a series of extraordinary adventures they arrived at Colchis. *Vid.* Argonautæ. Æetes, when informed of the demand of Jason, promised to restore the golden fleece, which was the cause of the death of Phryxus, and of the voyage of the Argonauts, provided they submitted to his conditions. Jason was to tame bulls which breathed flames, and which had feet and horns of brass, and to plough with them a field sacred to Mars. After this he was to sow in the ground the teeth of a serpent from which armed men would arise, whose fury would be converted against him who ventured to plough the field. He was also to kill a monstrous dragon which watched night and day at the foot of the tree on which the golden fleece was suspended. These conditions were severe, and the Colchians were alarmed for the fate of the Argonauts; but Juno, who watched with an anxious eye over the safety of Jason, extricated him from all these difficulties. Medea, the king's daughter, fell in love with the Grecian hero, and as her knowledge of herbs, enchantments, and incantations was very uncommon, she pledged herself to deliver her lover from all his danger if he promised her eternal fidelity. Jason, not insensible to her charms and to her promises, vowed eternal fidelity to her in the temple of Hecate, and received from her hand whatever herbs and instruments were necessary to protect him from the approaching dangers. He appeared in the field of Mars, tamed the fury of the oxen, ploughed the plain, and sowed the dragon's teeth. Immediately an army of men sprang from the furrowed field, and ran towards Jason. He threw a stone among them, and they fell one upon the other till their formidable ranks were destroyed. The vigilance of the dragon was lulled to sleep by the power of herbs, and Jason took from the tree the celebrated golden fleece, which was the sole object of his voyage. These actions were performed in the presence of Æetes and his people, who were all equally astonished at the boldness and success of Jason. After this celebrated conquest, Jason immediately set sail for Europe with Medea, who had been so instrumental to his preservation. Upon this Æetes, desirous to revenge the perfidy of his daughter Medea, sent his son Absyrtus to pursue the fugitives. Medea killed her brother, and strewed his limbs in her father's way, that she might more easily escape, while he was employed in collecting the mangled body of his son. *Vid.* Absyrtus. The return of the Argonauts into Thessaly was celebrated with universal festivity; but Æson, Jason's father, was unable to attend, on account of the infirmities of old age. This obstruction was, however, quickly removed, and Medea, at the request of her husband, restored Æson to the vigor and sprightliness of youth. *Vid.* Æson. Pelias wished also to see himself restored to the flower of youth, and his daughters, persuaded by Medea, who wished to avenge her husband's wrongs, cut his body to pieces, and placed his limbs in a cauldron of boiling water. Their credulity was severely punished. Medea suffered the flesh to be consumed to the bones, and Pelias was never restored to life. This inhuman action drew the resentment of the populace upon Medea, and she fled to Corinth with her husband Jason, where they lived in the enjoyment of undisturbed happiness during ten successive years. Jason's partiality for Glauce, the daughter of the king of the country, afterwards disturbed their matrimonial felicity, and Medea was divorced. This infidelity was severely avenged by Medea (*vid.* Glauce), who destroyed her children in the presence of their father. *Vid.* Medea. After his separation from Medea, Jason lived an unsettled and melancholy life. As he was one day reposing himself by the side of the ship which had carried him to Colchis, a beam fell upon his head, and he was crushed to death. This tragical event had been before predicted to him by Medea, according to the relations of some authors. Some say that he afterwards returned to Colchis, where he seized the kingdom of Æetes, and reigned in great security. *Hesiod. Th.* 993.—*Paus.* 2. c. 3, l. 8. c. 11. *Eurip. in Med.*—*Ovid.* 7. fab. 2, 3, &c.—*Diod.* 4.—*Apollod.* 1. c. 9.—*Cic. de Nat.* 3.—*Ovid. Trist.* 3. el. 9. *Heroid.* 6.—*Hygin.* fab. 5, 12, 13, 23, 24, 25 & 157.—*Servius in Virg. Ec.* 4. v. 34. *Æn.* 7. v. 207.—*Schol. Eurip. in Hec.*—*Isidor. Or.* 16. c. 14.—*Sch. Apollon.* 4. v. 412.—*Lactant. ad Theb.* 5, 402 & 455.—*Strab.* 7.—*Apoll. — Flac. — Pindar.* 3. *Nem.* 4. *Pyth.*—*Justin.* 42. c. 2, &c.—*Senec. in Med.*—*Tzetz. ad Lycophr.* 175, &c.—*Athen.* 13. [There is a fine statue of Jason in the Vatican.]——A native of Argos, who wrote a history of Greece in four books, which ended at the death of Alexander. He lived in the age of the emperor Adrian. *Athen.* l. 13.——A tyrant of Thessaly, who formed an alliance with the Spartans, and cultivated the friendship of Timotheus.——A native of Byzantium, who wrote on tragic authors. *Plut. de flum.*

JA'SON TRALLIA'NUS, a man who wrote tragedies, and gained the esteem of the kings of Parthia. *Polyæn.* 7.

JASON'IDÆ, the patronymic of Thoas and Euneus, as sons of Jason by Hypsipyle. *Stat, Theb.* 6. v. 340.

JASO'NIUM, a promontory of Cappadocia, now St. Thomas.——A mountain, part of Taurus. *Strab.* 11.——A city of Margiana. *Ptol.*

JAS'SII, a people of Pannonia. *Id.*

JAS'TUS, a river of Scythia, within Imaus. *Id.*

JATHRIP'PA, a city of Arabia. *Steph.*

JA'TII, a people near Margiana. *Plin.*

JATI'NA, a town of the largest of the Balearic Isles. *Id.*

JATI'NUM, a town of Gallia Belgica, on the Matrona. *Ptol.*

JAT'RUS, a river of Mysia, near Nicropolis. *Plin.* 3. c. 26.

JA'TUR, a city of India within the Ganges. *Ptol.*

JAVOLE'NUS PRIS'CUS, a Roman jurist, one of the council of Antoninus Pius.

JELLE'JA, a city between Genua and Placentia. *Strab.* 5

JEN'YSUS, a town of Syria. *Herodot.* 3. c. 5.

JE'RA, one of the Nereides. *Homer. Il.* 18. v. 42.

JER'ICHO, a city of Palestine, besieged and taken by the Romans under Vespasian and Titus. *Plin.*

JER'NA, a river of Spain. *Mela,* l. 3. *Strabo* mentions a mountain also of the same name.

JER'NE or JER'NIA, a name of Ireland. *Strab.* 1.

JERO'MUS or JERON'YMUS, a Greek of Cardia, who wrote a history of Alexander the Great.——A native of Rhodes, disciple of Aristotle, of whose compositions some few historical fragments remain *Dionys. Hal.* 1.—*Diod.* 5.—*Paus.* 1. c. 9 & 13.—*Athen.* 12 & 14.—*Suidas.*

JERU'SALEM. *Vid.* Hierosolyma.

JET'ERUS, a river of Mœsia, flowing from mount Rhodope. *Plin.* 3. c. 26.

JOAN'NES or JOHAN'NES DAMASCE'NUS, one of the Greek fathers, who wrote a hymn upon the birth of our Saviour, &c. His works were edited at Paris, in 2 vols. folio 1712.

JOCASTA or JOCAS'TE, a daughter of Menœceus, who married Laius, king of Thebes, by whom she had Œdipus. She afterwards married her son Œdipus, without knowing who he was, and had by him Eteocles, Polynices, &c. *Vid.* Liaus, Œdipus. When she discovered that she had committed incest by marrying her own son, she hanged herself in despair. She is called Epicasta by some mythologists. *Homer. Odyss.* 11. v. 270.—*Paus.* 9. c. 5 & 26.—*Schol. Eurip. in Phœniss.* 13.—*Stat. Theb.* 8. v. 42.—*Senec. & Sophocl. Œdip.*—*Apollod.* 3. c. 5.—*Hygin.* fab. 66, 67, & 242.

JOP'PA or JOP'PE, a maritime city of Palestine, called by Strabo the port of Jerusalem.

JOR'DANES or JORDA'NES, a river of Judæa, illustrious in sacred history. It rises near mount Libanus, and, after running in a southern direction through the lake Samachonitis, and that of Tiberias, it falls, after a course of 150 miles, into the Dead Sea. *Strab.* 16.

JORNAN'DES, an historian, who wrote a book on the Goths, among which nation he was born. His work *de rebus Gothicis* was translated by Maupertius, and is so much like the history of the Goths, by Cassiodorus, that some have thought it an abridgement of it. He wrote besides a book *de regnorum et temporum successione, &c.* in which he has largely borrowed from Florus, but without acknowledgment. He died A.D. 552. *Harles. Not. Lit. Rom.* 1. p. 765.—*Voss. de H. Lat.* 2. c. 20, &c.

JOSE'PHUS FLA'VIUS, a celebrated Jew, born in Jerusalem, who signalized his abilities in supporting an obstinate siege of forty-seven days against Vespasian and Titus, in Jotapat, a small town of Judæa. When the city surrendered, there were found not less than 40,000 Jews slain, and the number of captives amounted only to 1,200. Josephus saved his life by fleeing into a cave, where 40 of his countrymen had also taken refuge. He dissuaded them from committing suicide, and, when they had all drawn lots to kill one another, Josephus fortunately remained the last, and then surrendered himself to Vespasian. He gained the conqueror's notice and esteem, by fortelling that he would become one day the master of the Roman empire. Josephus was afterwards present at the siege of Jerusalem by Titus, and received, from the conqueror's hands, all the books which that unfortunate city contained. He came to Rome with Titus, where he was honored with the name and privileges of a Roman citizen. Here he was deservedly esteemed by the emperors Vespasian and Titus, and dedicated his time to study. He wrote the history of the wars of the Jews, first in Hebrew for the use of his countrymen, and afterwards translated it into Greek. This composition so pleased Titus, that he authenticated it by placing his signature upon it, and also preserved it carefully in one of the public libraries. Josephus finished another work, which he divided into 20 books, containing the history of the Jewish antiquities, in some places subversive of the authority and miracles mentioned in the Scriptures, beginning with the creation of the world, and ending about the 12th year of Nero's reign, when the Jews began to rebel against the Roman power. He also wrote two books to defend the Jews against Apion their greatest enemy; besides an account of his own life, &c. Josephus has been admired for his lively and animated style, the bold propriety of his expressions, the exactness of his descriptions, and the persuasive eloquence of his orations. He has been called the Livy of the Greeks. Though, in some cases, inimical to the Christians, yet he has commended our Saviour so strongly, that St. Jerome calls him a Christian writer. Josephus died A.D. 93, in the 56th year of his age. The best editions of his works are Hudson's, 2 vols. fol. Oxon. 1720, and Havercamp's 2 vols. fol. Amst. 1726. The best English translation is that of the celebrated Whiston. *Sueton. in Vesp. &c.—Josephus, Bell. Jud.* 3. c. 14.—*Sax. Onom.* 1. 270.—*Fabr. B. Gr.* 4. c. 8.

JOVIA'NUS or JOVINIA'NUS FLA'VIUS CLAU'DIUS, a native of Pannonia, elected emperor of Rome by his soldiers after the death of Julian. He at first refused to be invested with the imperial purple, because his subjects followed the religious principles of the late emperor; but they removed his groundless apprehensions, and, when they assured him that they were sincerely attached to Christianity, he accepted the crown. He concluded a disadvantageous treaty with the Persians, against whom Julian was marching with a victorious army. Jovian died seven months and twenty days after his elevation, and was found in his bed, suffocated by the vapors of charcoal, which had been lighted in his room, A.D. 364, though some attribute his death to intemperance. He burned a celebrated library at Antioch. *Hieron. in Chron.* —*Amm. Marcell.* 25. c. 10.—*Theodoret.* 4.—*Socr.* 3.—*Sozom. H.* 6.

JU'BA, a king of Numidia and Mauritania, who succeeded his father Hiempsal, and favored the cause of Pompey against J. Cæsar. He defeated Curio, whom Cæsar had sent to Africa, and after the battle of Pharsalia, he joined his forces to those of Scipio. He was conquered in a battle at Thapsus, and being totally abandoned by his subjects, he killed himself with Petreius, who had shared his good fortune and his adversity. His kingdom became a Roman province, of which Sallust was the first governor. *Plut. in Pomp. & Cæs.—Flor.* 4. c. 12.—*Suet. in Cæs.* c. 35.—*Dion.* 41.—*Mela*, 1. c. 6.—*Lucan.* 3, &c.—*Cæsar de Bell. Civ.* 2.—*Paterc.* 2. c. 54.

JU'BA the Second, was the son of Juba the First. He was led among the captives to Rome to adorn the triumph of Cæsar. His captivity was the source of the greatest honors, and his application to study procured him more glory than he could have obtained from the inheritance of a kingdom. He gained the heart of the Romans by the courteousness of his manners, and Augustus rewarded his fidelity by giving him in marriage Cleopatra, the daughter of Antony, and conferring upon him the title of king, and making him master of all the territories which his father had once possessed. His popularity was so great, that the Mauritanians rewarded his benevolence by making him one of their gods. The Athenians also raised a statue to his honor, and the Æthiopians worshipped him as a deity. Juba wrote a history of Rome in Greek, which is often quoted and commended by the ancients, but of which only few fragments remain. He also wrote on the history of Arabia, and the antiquities of Assyria, chiefly collected from Berosus. Besides these, he composed some treatises upon the drama, Roman antiquities, the nature of animals, painting, grammar, &c. now lost. *Strab.* 17.—*Suet. in Cal.* 26.—*Plin*, 5. c. 25 & 32. l. 6. c. 37.—*Athen.* 1 & 3.—*Paus.* 1. c. 17.—*Suidas.—Dion.* 51, &c.—*Voss. de H. Gr.* 1. 2. c. 4.

JUDACIL'IUS, a native of Asculum, celebrated for his patriotism, in the age of Pompey, &c.

JUDÆ'A, a famous country of Asia bounded by Arabia, Ægypt, Phœnicia, the Mediterranean Sea, and part of Syria. The inhabitants, whose history is best collected from the Holy Scriptures, were chiefly governed after the Babylonish captivity by the high priests, who raised themselves to the rank of princes, B.C. 153, and continued in the enjoyment of regal power till the age of Augustus. *Plut. de Osir.—Strab.* 16.—*Dion.* 36.—*Tacit. Hist.* 5. c. 6. —*Lucan.* 2. v. 593.

JUGA'LIS, a surname of Juno, because she presided over marriage, in the celebration of which it was usual for the husband and the wife to pass under the yoke (*jugum*). The goddess had an altar in one of the streets of the city of Rome, which, from this circumstance, received the name of Vicus Jugarius. *Festus de V. Sig —Servius in Æn.* 4. v. 16. —*Rosin. Ant. R.* 2. c. 6.

JUGAN'TES, a people of Britain. *Tacit. Ann.* 12. c. 32.

JUGA'RIUS, a street in Rome, below the Capitol.

JUGUN'THI, a people of Germany. It is uncertain whether they were Goths or Alemanni.

JUGUR'THA, the illegitimate son of Manastabal, the brother of Micipsa. Micipsa and Manastabal were the sons of Masinissa, king of Numidia. Micipsa, who had inherited his father's kingdom, educated his nephew with the same care and tenderness as his two sons Adherbal and Hiempsal; but, as he was of an aspiring disposition, he sent him with a body of troops to the assistance of Scipio, who was besieging Numantia, hoping to lose a youth whose restless ambition seemed to threaten, at some future time, destruction to the happiness of his children. His hopes, however, were frustrated; Jugurtha showed himself brave and active, and after endearing himself to the Roman general, he returned to Africa, loaded with military honors. Micipsa, now anxious to convert the abilities of this artful youth to the safety and protection of his family, appointed him successor to his kingdom conjointly with his two sons, hoping that gratitude would make him respect the memory of his benefactor. But Jugurtha, giving way to his ambitious projects, cut off Hiempsal, and stripping Adherbal of his possessions, obliged him to flee to Rome for safety. The Romans listened to the well grounded complaints of Adherbal, but Jugurtha's gold prevailed among the corrupt senators, and the suppliant monarch, forsaken in his distress, perished by the snares of his enemy. The Roman character, however, though obscured by the licentiousness of the times, reassumed its wonted dignity, the wrongs of Masinissa's wretched family were, though late, contemplated with compassion, and Cæcilius Metellus marched at the head of an army against Jugurtha, who, no longer secure in his artful evasions and proffered terms of submission, fled in dismay to solicit support among his savage neighbours. Marius and Sylla succeeded Metellus in the conduct of the war, and fought with equal success. Jugurtha was at last betrayed by his father-in-law Bocchus, from whom he had claimed assistance, and was delivered into the hands of Sylla, after carrying on a war of various success for five years, and displaying, in the cabinet and in the field, talents worthy better times and a better cause. He was exposed to the view of the Roman people, and dragged in chains to adorn the triumph of Marius. He was afterwards put into prison, where he died six days after of hunger, B.C. 106. The name and the wars of Jugurtha have been immortalized by the pen of Sallust. *Sallust. in Jug.—Flor.* 3. c. 1.—*Paterc.* 2. c. 10, &c.—*Plut. in Mar. & Sylla.—Eutrop.* 4. c. 3. —*Cic. Br.* 33. *N. D.* 3. c. 30.—*Horat.* ep. 9. v. 23.— *Ovid. Pont.* 4. el. 3. v. 45.—*Quintil.* 8. c. 3.

JU'LA, a city of Arabia Felix. *Ptol.*

JU'LIA LEX, *prima de provinciis*, by J. Cæsar, A. U. C. 691. It confirmed the freedom of all Greece. It further ordained that the Roman magistrates should act there as judges, and that the towns and villages through which the Roman magistrates and ambassadors passed should maintain them during their stay, and that the governors, at the expiration of their office should leave a scheme of their accounts in two cities in their province, and deliver a copy of it at the public treasury; that the provincial governors should not accept of a golden crown, unless they were honored by the senate; that no supreme commander should go out of his province, enter any dominions, lead an army, or engage in a war, without the previous approbation and command of the senate and the people. Another, *de sumptibus*, in the age of Augustus. It limited the expense of provisions on the *dies profesti*, or days appointed for the transaction of business, to 200 sesterces; on common calendar festivals to 300; and, on all extraordinary occasions, such as marriages, births, &c. to 1000.—Another *de provinciis*, by J. Cæsar, when dictator. It ordained that no prætorian province should be held more than one year, and a consular province more than two years. Another called also *Campania agraria*, by the same A.U.C. 691. It required that all the lands of Campania formerly rented according to the estimation of the state, should be fairly divided among the plebeians, and that all the members of the senate should bind themselves by an oath, to establish, confirm and protect that law. Another, *de civitate*, by L. J. Cæsar, A.U.C. 664. It rewarded with the name and privileges of citizens of Rome, all such as, during the civil wars, had remained the constant friends of the republican liberty. When that civil war was at an end, all the Italians were admitted as free denizens, and composed eight new tribes.—Another, *de judicibus*, by J. Cæsar. It confirmed the Pompeian law in a certain manner, requiring the judges to be chosen from the richest people in every century, allowing the senators and knights in the number, and excluding the *tribuni ærarii*. Another, *de ambitu*, by Augustus. It restrained the illicit measures used at elections, and restored to the *comitia* their ancient privileges, which had been destroyed by the ambition and bribery of J. Cæsar.—Another, by Augustus, *de adulterio & pudicitiâ*. It punished adultery with death. It was afterwards confirmed and enforced by Domitian. *Juvenal, Sat.* 2. v. 30. alludes to it.—Another, called also *Papia*, or *Papia Poppæa*, which was the same as the following, only enlarged by the consuls Papius and Poppæus, A.U.C. 762.—Another *de maritandis ordinibus*, by Augustus. It proposed to such as engaged in matrimony, rewards of a particular description. It inflicted punishment on celibacy, and permitted the patricians, the senators and sons of senators excepted, to intermarry with the *libertini*, or children of those who had been *liberti*, or servants manumitted. Horace alludes to it when he speaks of *lex marita*.—Another, *de majestate*, by J. Cæsar. It punished with *aquæ & ignis interdictio* all such as were found guilty of the *crimen majestatis*, or treason against the state.

Ju'lia, a daughter of J. Cæsar, by Cornelia, famous for her personal charms and for her virtues. She married Corn. Cæpio, whom her father obliged her to divorce to marry Pompey the Great. Her amiable disposition more strongly cemented the friendship of the father and of the son-in-law; but her sudden death in child-bed, B.C. 53. unhappily broke all ties of intimacy and relationship, and soon produced a civil war. *Plut.*—*Suet. Cæs.* 1, 21 & 26.—*Lucan.* 1. v. 125.—*Paterc.* c. 2. c. 47. [The finest bust of Julia is in the Vatican.]——The mother of M. Antony, whose humanity is greatly celebrated in saving her brother-in-law J. Cæsar, from the cruel prosecutions of her son.——An aunt of J. Cæsar, who married C. Marius. Her funeral oration was publicly pronounced by her nephew.——The only daughter of the emperor Augustus by Scribonia, was remarkable for her beauty, her genius, and her debaucheries. She was tenderly loved by her father, who gave her in marriage to Marcellus; after whose early death she was given to Agrippa, by whom she had five children. *Vid.* Agrippa. She became a second time a widow, and was married to Tiberius, after his divorce from his former wife Vipsania. Her lasciviousness and debaucheries so disgusted her husband, that he retired from the court of the emperor; and Augustus, informed of her lustful propensities and infamy, banished her from his sight, and confined her in a small island on the coast of Campania. She was starved to death, A.D. 14, by order of Tiberius. *Tac. Ann.* 1. c 53.—*Plut.*——A daughter of the emperor Titus, who married her relation Sabinus, and, after his murder, became the mistress of her brother Domitian. She died in consequence of his cruelty to her whilst pregnant. [There is a statue of this lady in the Barberini palace at Rome, and a bust in the Capitol.]——A daughter of Julia, the wife of Agrippa, who married Paul. Æmil. Lepidus, and was banished for her licentiousness to the island of Trimeta in the Adriatic, where she languished for many years, a prey to sorrow and solitary wretchedness, and died in her 41st year. *Tacit. Ann.* 4. c. 71.—*Suet. Aug.* 1. c. 101.——A daughter of Germanicus and Agrippina, born in the island of Lesbus, A.D. 17. She married a senator called M. Vinucius, at the age of 16, and enjoyed the most unbounded favours in the court of her brother Caligula, who is accused of being her first seducer. She was afterwards banished by Caligula, on suspicion of conspiracy. Claudius recalled her; but she was soon after banished by the powerful intrigues of Messalina, and put to death about the 24th year of her age. She was no stranger to the debaucheries of her age, and prostituted herself as freely to the meanest of the people, as to the nobler companions of her brother's extravagance. Seneca, as some suppose, was banished to Corsica for having seduced her.——A celebrated woman, born at Emesa in Syria. She is also called Domna. She applied herself to the study of geometry and philosophy, &c. and rendered herself conspicuous, as much by her mental as by her personal charms. She came to Rome, where her learning recommended her to all the literati of the age. She married Septimus Severus, who, twenty years after this matrimonial connection, was invested with the imperial purple. Severus was guided by the prudence and advice of Julia, but was blind to her foibles, and often punished with the greatest severity those crimes which were enormous in the empress. She is even said to have conspired against the emperor, but she resolved to blot out, by patronizing literature, the spots which her debauchery and extravagance had rendered indelible in the eyes of virtue. Her influence, after the death of Severus, was for some time productive of tranquillity and cordial union between his two sons and successors. Geta, at last, however, fell a sacrifice to his brother Caracalla, and Julia was even wounded in the arm while she attempted to screen her favorite son from his brother's dagger. According to some, Julia committed incest with her son Caracalla, and publicly married him. She starved herself when her ambitious views were defeated by Macrinus, who aspired to the empire in preference to her, after the death of Caracalla. *Æl. Spartian*, [A statue of Julia exists in the Villa Albani, and a bust in the Vatican.]

Ju'lia, a town of Gallia Togato, called Fidentia or Fidentiola, by *Antoninus*, and now Bergo di S. Domnino. *Plin.* 3. c. 1.——A city of Italy, founded by Dædalus. *Steph.*

Ju'lia Ap'ulum, a city of Dacia. *Ptol. Vid.* Alba Julia.

Ju'lia Cæsare'a, a city of Mauritania Cæsariensis, founded by Juba. *Plin.—Mela.*

Ju'lia Char'itas, a city of Hispania Bætica. *Plin.* 4. c. 22.

Ju'lia Fa'ma or Se'ria, a town of Hispania Bætica. *Id.* 3. c. 1.

JULI'ACUM, a town of Germany, now Juliers, near the Maese. *Tac.—Amm. Marcell.*

JULIA'NUS, a son of Julius Constantius, the brother of Constantine the Great, born at Constantinople. The massacre which attended the elevation of the sons of Constantine the Great to the throne, nearly proved fatal to Julian and to his brother Gallus. The two brothers were privately educated together, and taught the doctrines of the Christian religion. Gallus received the instructions of his pious teachers with deference and submission, but Julian showed his dislike for Christianity by secretly cherishing a desire to become one of the votaries of Paganism. He gave sufficient proofs of his propensity when he went to Athens in the 24th year of his age, where he applied himself to the study of magic and astrology. He was some time after appointed by Constans over Gaul, with the title of Cæsar, and there he showed himself worthy of the imperial dignity by his prudence and valor, and by the numerous victories which he obtained over the enemies of Rome, in Gaul and Germany. His mildness, as well as his condescension, gained him the hearts of his soldiers, and when Constans, to whom Julian was become suspected, ordered him to send him part of his forces to go into the east, the army immediately mutinied, and promised unshaken fidelity to their leader, by refusing to obey the orders of Constans. They even compelled Julian, by threats as well as by entreaties, to accept of the title of independent emperor and of Augustus; and the death of Constans, which soon after happened, left him sole master of the Roman empire, A.D. 361. Julian soon disclosed his religious sentiments, and, publicly disavowing the doctrines of Christianity, offered solemn sacrifices to all the gods of ancient Rome. This change of religious opinion was attributed by some to the austerity with which he had been taught the precepts of Christianity, or, according to others, to the literary conversation and persuasive eloquence of some of the Athenian philosophers. From this circumstance, therefore,

Julian has been called the Apostate. After he had made his public entry at Constantinople, he determined to continue the Persian war, and check those barbarians who had for sixty years derided the indolence of the emperors of Rome. When he had crossed the Tigris, he burned his fleet, and advanced with boldness into the enemy's country. His march was that of a conqueror, he met with no opposition from a weak and indigent enemy; but the country of Assyria had been left desolate by the Persians, and Julian, without corn or provisions, was obliged at last to retire. As he could not convey his army again over the streams of the Tigris, he took the resolution of marching up the sources of the river, and thus imitate the bold return of the 10,000 Greeks. As he advanced through the country he defeated the officers of Sapor, the king of Persia; but a second engagement proved fatal to him, and he received a deadly wound as he was animating his soldiers to battle. He expired the following night, the 27th of June, 363, in the 32nd year of his age. His last moments were spent in conversation with a philosopher about the immortality of the soul, and he breathed his last without expressing the least sorrow for his fate, or for the suddenness of his death. Julian's character has been admired by some, and censured by others, but the malevolence of his enemies chiefly arises from his apostacy. As a man and as a monarch he demands our warmest commendations; but we must blame his idolatry, and despise his bigoted principles. He was moderate in his successes, merciful to his enemies, and amiable in his character. He abolished the luxuries which reigned in the court of Constantinople, and dismissed with contempt the numerous officers who waited upon Constantius, to anoint his head or perfume his body. He was frugal in his meals, and slept little, often reposing himself on a skin spread on the ground. He awoke at midnight, and spent the rest of the night in reading or writing, and issued early from his tent to pay his daily visit to the guards around the camp. He was not fond of public amusements, but rather dedicated his time to study and solitude. When he passed through Antioch in his Persian expedition, the inhabitants of the place, offended at his religious sentiments, ridiculed his person, and lampooned him in satirical verses. The emperor made use of the same arms for his defence, and rather than destroy his enemies by the sword, he condescended to expose them to derision, and unveil their follies and debaucheries in a humorous work, which he called Misopogon, or *beard-hater*. He imitated the virtuous example of Scipio and Alexander, and laid no temptation for his virtue by visiting some female captives that had fallen into his hands. In his matrimonial connections, Julian rather consulted policy than inclination, and his marriage with the sister of Constantius arose from his unwillingness to offend his benefactor, rather than obey the laws of nature. He was buried at Tarsus, but his body was afterwards conveyed to Constantinople. Julian distinguished himself by his writings, as well as by his military character. Besides his Misopogon, he wrote the history of Gaul. He also wrote two letters to the Athenians; and, besides, there are now extant sixty-four of his letters on various subjects. His Cæsars, the most famous of all his compositions, is a satire upon all the Roman emperors from J. Cæsar to Constantine. It is written in the form of a dialogue, in which the author severely attacks the venerable character of M. Aurelius, whom he had proposed to himself as a pattern, and speaks in scurrilous and abusive language of his relation to Constantine. It has been observed of Julian, that like Cæsar, he could employ at the same time his hand to write, his ear to listen, his eyes to read, and his mind to dictate. The best edition of his works is that of Spanheim, fol. Lips. 1696; and of the Cæsars, that of Heusinger, 8vo. Gothæ, 1741. *Sax. Onom.* 1. p. 411.—*Fabr. B. Gr.* 5. c. 8.—*Julian.*—*Socrat.*—*Eutrop.*—*Amm.*—*Liban. &c.* [A bust of him will be found in the Capitol.]——A son of Constantine.——A maternal uncle of the emperor Julian——A Roman, who proclaimed himself emperor in Italy during the reign of Diocletian, &c.——A governor of Africa.——A general in Dacia in Domitian's reign.

JULIA'NUS SAL'VIUS, a counsellor of the emperor Adrian, who collected the edicts of the prætors into one code called *edictum perpetuum*. *Eutrop.* 8. c. 17.

JULIA'NUS DID'IUS, his grandson or great grandson, was raised to the imperial purple after the death of Commodus, an honor which he enjoyed only sixty-six days according to *Dio*, or seven months according to *Eutropius*. *Vid.* Didius.

JU'LIAS, a city of Palestine, so called by the tetrarch Philip, in honor of Julia, daughter of Augustus.

JU'LII, a patrician family of Alba, brought by Romulus or Tullus to Rome, where, by their merit and intrigues, they soon rose to the greatest honors of the state, J. Cæsar and Augustus were of this family; and it was said, perhaps through flattery, that they were lineally descended from Æneas, the founder of Lavinium. *Suet. in Cæs.* 6.—*Dio.* 41. c. 34. l. 43. c. 22.—*Liv.* 1. c. 30.—*Tacit.* 4. *Ann.* 9.—*Virg. Æn.* 1. v. 288.

JULIOB'ONA, a city of Gallia Celtica. *Ptol.*

JULIOBRI'GA, a city of Hispania Tarraconensis. *Id.*

JULIOM'AGUS, a city of Gaul, now Angers, in Anjou. *Plin.* 4. c. 18.—*Cæs. B. G.* 2. c. 8, &c.

JULIOP'OLIS, a town of Bithynia, supposed by some to be the same as Tarsus of Cilicia. *Strab.* 12.

JU'LIS, a town of the island of Cos, which gave birth to Simonides, &c. The walls of this city were composed of marble, and it is said that there are now some pieces remaining entire about twelve feet in height, which convey some idea of its ancient splendor. *Plin.* 4. c. 12.

JU'LIUM PRÆSID'IUM, a city of Lusitania, now Santaren. It is called Scalabis by *Pliny*, 4. c. 22, and Scalabiscus by *Ptolemy*.

JU'LIUS CÆ'SAR. *Vid.* Cæsar.

JU'LIUS AFRICA'NUS, a chronologer, who flourished A.D. 220. *Voss. de H. Gr.* p. 236.

JU'LIUS AGRIC'OLA. *Vid.* Agricola.

JU'LIUS AGRIP'PA, a person banished from Rome by Nero, after the discovery of the Pisonian conspiracy. *Tacit. Ann.* 15. c. 71.

JU'LIUS AQ'UILA, a Roman knight left by Didius, with a few cohorts on the shores of the Bosporus. *Tac. Ann.* 12. c. 15.

JU'LIUS ATERIA'NUS, a Latin historian cited by *Trebellius Pollio in Victor*.

JU'LIUS CA'NUS, a celebrated Roman, put to death by order of Caracalla. He bore the undeserved punishment inflicted on him with the greatest resignation, and even pleasure.

JU'LIUS L. CÆ'SAR, a Roman consul, uncle to Antony the triumvir, the father of Cæsar the dictator. He died as he was putting on his shoes. *Plin.* 7. c. 53.

JU'LIUS CEL'SUS, a tribune imprisoned for conspiring against Tiberius. *Tacit. Ann.* 6. c. 14.

JU'LIUS CLASSICA'NUS, a governor of Britain, successor to Catus Decianus. *Tac. Ann.* 14. c. 38.

JU'LIUS CONSTAN'TIUS, the father of the emperor Julian, was killed at the accession of the sons of Constantine to the throne, and his son nearly shared his fate.

JU'LIUS COR'DUS, an historian, who wrote lives of the emperors. *Tacit. Hist.* 1. c. 76.

JU'LIUS FLO'RUS. *Vid.* Florus.

JU'LIUS FIR'MICUS MATER'NUS, the author of a work on the mysteries and errors of the Gentiles, flourished under the sons of Constantine.

JU'LIUS MAR'ATHUS, a freedman of Augustus, who wrote on the actions of the emperor. *Suet. in Aug.* 79.

JU'LIUS MAXIM'INUS, a Thracian, who, from shepherd, became an emperor of Rome. *Vid.* Maximinus.

JU'LIUS OB'SEQUENS, a Latin writer, who flourished A.D. 214. The best edition of his book *de prodigiis* is that of Oudendorp, 8vo, L. Bat. 1720.

JU'LIUS POL'LUX. *Vid.* Pollux.

JU'LIUS POR'TUS, a harbour, built near Baiæ by Augustus, by the introduction of the sea into the lakes Avernus and Lucrinus. *Suet. Aug.* 16.—*Virg. G.* 2. v. 163.

JU'LIUS POS'TUMUS, a præfect of Damatia, an instrument of the crimes of Sejanus. *Tac. Ann.* 4. c. 12.

JU'LIUS PRIS'CUS, a centurion, promoted to the command of the prætorian cohort by Vitellius. *Id. Hist.* 2. c. 92.

JU'LIUS PROC'ULUS, a Roman, who solemnly declared to his countrymen, after Romulus had disappeared, or rather had been murdered by the senators, that he had appeared to him in a shape more than human, and had ordered him to tell the Romans to honor him as a god. Julius was believed. *Plut. in Rom.—Ovid.*

JU'LIUS S. a prætor, &c. *Cic. ad Her.* 2. c. 13.

JU'LIUS SILVA'NUS, a commander of the army in Gaul, proclaimed emperor by his legions, after the death of Gallus Cæsar. He reigned only twenty-eight days, being slain by his soldiers. *Ferron. in Consuet. Burdigal.* 2. p. 248.—*Du Fresne dissert. de inf. ævi Numism.* p. 59.

JU'LIUS SOLI'NUS. *Vid.* Solinus.

JU'LIUS TITIA'NUS, a writer in the age of Diocletian. His son became famous for his oratorical powers, and was made preceptor in the family of Maximinus. Julius wrote a history of all the provinces of the Roman empire, greatly commended by the ancients. He also wrote some letters, in which he happily imitated the style and elegance of Cicero, for which he was called the ape of his age.

JU'LIUS VIN'DEX, a præfect of Gaul, who conspired with Galba against Nero. *Tac. Ann.* 15. c. 74, &c. —*Suet. Ner. Claud.* c. 41.

JUNGA'RIA or JUNCA'RIA, an inland city of Hispania Tarraconensis. *Ptol.*

JU'NIA LEX, *Sacrata*, enacted by L. Junius Brutus, the first tribune of the people, A.U.C. 260. It ordained that the person of the tribune should be held sacred and inviolable; that an appeal might be made from the consuls to the tribunes; and that no senator should be able to exercise the office of a tribune.—Another, A.U.C. 627, which excluded all foreigners from enjoying the privileges or names of Roman citizens.—Another by Junius Brutus, enacted A.U.C. 244, to deprive Tarquin of the government, and elect two consuls in his stead. *Dionys.* l. 4. *Liv.* 2. c. 8, &c. See also *Thom. Dempster. in Joh. Rosin. Antiq Rom.* 8. c. 7, &c.

JU'NIA, a niece of Cato of Utica, who married Cassius, and died in the reign of Tiberius sixty-four years after her husband had killed himself at the battle of Philippi. *Tacit. Ann.* 3. c. 76.

JU'NIA CALVI'NA, a beautiful Roman lady, accused of incest with her brother Silanus. She was descended from Augustus. She was banished by Claudius, and recalled by Nero. *Tacit. Ann.* 2. c. 4.

JU'NIA SILA'NA, a noble lady, wife of C. Silius, divorced from her husband by Messalina. *Tac. Ann.* 11. c. 12, &c. The Junian family descended from Brutus, who expelled the Tarquins, were patricians, but some of the Bruti known in later times were plebeians. *Cic. Ver.* 1. 6, &c. *N.D.* 2. c. 3. *Leg.* 3. c. 20, &c.

JU'NIUS BLÆ'SUS, proconsul of Africa under the emperors. *Tacit. Ann.* 3. c. 35.

JU'NIUS BRU'TUS. *Vid.* Brutus.

JU'NIUS LU'PUS, a senator who accused Vitellius of aspiring to the sovereignty, &c. *Tacit. Ann.* 12. c. 42.

JU'NIUS RUS'TICUS, a senator in favor with Tiberius. *Tac. Ann.* 5. c. 4.

JU'NIUS D. SILA'NUS, a Roman who committed adultery with Julia the grand-daughter of Augustus, &c. *Tacit. Ann.* 3. c. 24.

JU'NO, a celebrated deity among the ancients, daughter of Saturn and Ops. She was sister to Jupiter, Pluto, Neptune, Vesta, Ceres, &c. She was born at Argos, or, according to others, in Samus, and was entrusted to the care of the Seasons, or, as Homer and Ovid mention, to Oceanus and Tethys. Some of the inhabitants of Argolis supposed, that she had been brought up by the three daughters of the river Asterion; but the inhabitants of Stymphalus in Arcadia, maintained, that she had been brought up under the care of Temenus, the son of Pelasgus. Juno was devoured by Saturn, according to some mythologists; and, according to Apollodorus, she was again restored to the world by means of a potion which Metis gave to Saturn, to make him discharge the stone which his wife had given him to swallow instead of Jupiter. *Vid.* Saturnus. The nuptials of Jupiter and Juno were celebrated with the greatest solemnity; the gods, all mankind, and all the brute creation, attended. Chelone, a young woman, was the only person who refused to come, and who derided the ceremony; for this impiety, Mercury changed her into a tortoise, and condemned her to perpetual silence; from which circumstance the tortoise has always been used as the symbol of silence among the ancients. By her marriage with Jupiter, Juno became the queen of all the gods, and mistress of heaven and earth. Her conjugal happiness, however, was frequently disturbed by the numerous amours of her husband, and she showed herself jealous and inexorable in the highest degree. Her severity to the mistresses and illegitimate children of Jupiter was unparalleled. She persecuted Hercules and his descendants with the most inveterate fury; and her resentment against Paris, who had given the golden apple to Venus in preference to herself, was the cause of the Trojan war, and of all the miseries which happened to the unfortunate house of Priam. Her severities to Alcmena, Ino, Athamas, Semele, &c. are also well known. Juno had some children by Jupiter. According to Hesiod, she was mother of Mars, Hebe, and Ilithyia, or Lucina; and besides these, she brought forth Vulcan, only by smelling a certain plant. According to others, it was not Vulcan, but Mars, or Hebe, whom she brought forth in this manner, and this was after eating some lettuces at the table of Apollo. The repeated infidelities of Jupiter at last provoked Juno to such a degree, that she retired to Eubœa, and resolved for ever to abandon him. Jupiter procured a reconciliation, after he had applied to Cithæron for advice, and after he had obtained forgiveness by fraud and artifice. *Vid.* Dædala. This reconciliation, however cordial it might appear, was soon dissolved by new offences; and, to stop the complaints of the jealous Juno, Jupiter had often recourse to violence, and even to blows. He punished the cruelties which she had exercised upon his son Hercules, by suspending her from the heavens by a golden chain, and tying a heavy anvil to her feet. Vulcan, for assisting his mother in this degrading situation, was kicked down from heaven by his father, and broke his leg in the fall. This punishment rather irritated than pacified Juno. She resolved to be revenged, and engaged some of the gods to conspire against Jupiter and to imprison him, but Thetis delivered him, by bringing to his assistance the famous Briareus. Apollo and Neptune were banished from heaven for joining in the conspiracy, though some attribute their exile to different causes. The worship of Juno was universal, and even more extensive than that of Jupiter, according to some authors. Her sacrifices were offered with the greatest solemnity. She was particularly worshipped at Argos, Samus, Carthage, and afterwards at Rome. The ancients generally offered on her altars a ewe lamb and a sow the first day of every month. No cows were ever immolated to her, because she assumed the form of that animal when the gods fled into Ægypt during their war with the giants. Among birds, the hawk, the goose, and particularly the peacock, often called *Junonia avis (vid.* Argus,) were sacred to her. The dittany, the poppy, and the lily, were her favorite flowers. The latter flower was said to have been originally of the color of the crocus; but when Jupiter placed Hercules to the breasts of Juno while asleep, some of her milk fell down upon earth, and changed the color of the liles from purple to a beautiful white. Some of the milk is also said to have dropped over that part of the heavens which, from its whiteness, still retains the name of the milky way, *lactea via.* As Juno's power was extended over all the gods, she often made use of the goddess Minerva as her messenger, and even had the privilege of hurling the thunder of Jupiter when she pleased. Her temples were numerous, the most famous of which were at Argos, Olympia, Carthage, &c. At Rome no woman of debauched character was permitted to enter into her temple, or even to touch it. The surnames of Juno are various; they are derived either from the functions or things over which she presided, or from the places where her worship was established. She was the queen of the heavens; she protected cleanliness, presided over marriage and child-birth, and particularly patronised the most faithful and virtuous of the sex, and severely punished incontinence in matrons. She was the goddess of all power and empire, and was also the patroness of riches. She is represented sitting on a throne with a diadem on her head, and a golden sceptre in her right hand. Some peacocks generally sat by her, and a cuckoo often perched on her sceptre, while Iris behind her displayed the thousand colours of her beautiful rainbow. She is sometimes represented as carried through the air in a rich chariot drawn by peacocks. The Roman consuls, when they entered office, were obliged to offer her a solemn sacrifice. The Juno of the Romans was called Matrona or Romana. She was generally represented as veiled from head to foot, and the Roman matrons always imitated this manner of dressing themselves, and deemed it indecent in any married woman to leave any part of her body, except her face, uncovered. She has received the surnames of Olympia, Samia, Lacedæmonia, Argiva, Telchinia, Candrena, Rescinthes, Prosymna, Imbrasia, Acrea, Cithæronia, Bunea, Ammonia, Fluonia, Anthea, Migale, Gemelia, Tropeia, Boopis, Parthenos, Teleia, Xera, Egophage, Hyperchinia, Juga, Ilithyia, Lucina, Pronuba, Caprotina, Mena, Populonia, Lacinia, Sospita, Moneta, Curis, Domiduca, Februa, Opigenia, &c. *Cic. de Nat. D.* 2.—*Paus.* 2, &c.—*Apollod.* 1. 2. 3.—*Apollon.* 1.—*Argon.*—*Homer. Il.* 1, &c.—*Virg. Æn.* 1, &c.—*Herodot.* 1. 2. 4, &c.—*Sil.* 1.—*Dionys. Hal.* 1.—*Liv.* 23. 24. 27, &c.—*Ovid. Met.* 1, &c.—*Fast.* 5.—*Plut. Quæst. Rom.*—*Tibull.* 4. el. 13.—*Athen.* 15.—*Plin.* 34. [The finest figure of Juno is an exceedingly grand naked figure, rather larger than life in the Vatican. There are also two very fine busts considerably larger than life, in the gardens of the Ludovisi palace at Rome; and at Mr. Coke's, at Holkham, in Norfolk.]

JUNONA'LIA or **JUNO'NIA**, festivals celebrated at Rome in honor of Juno, the same as the Heraea of the Greeks. *Vid.* Heræa. *Liv.* 27. c. 37.

JUNO'NES, a name of the protecting genii of women among the Romans. The Roman matrons generally swore by them, as the men by their genii. There were altars often erected to their honors. *Plin.* 2. c. 7.—*Seneca*, ep. 110.—*Turneb.* 16. c. 19.

JUNO'NIA, a name which Gracchus gave to Carthage, when he went with 6000 Romans to rebuild it.—The name of two of the Fortunate Isles, distinguished by the appellation of Major and Minor. *Plin.* 4. c. 22. The former is now Forteventura, the latter, Lancerotta.

JUNONIG'ENA, a surname of Vulcan, a son of Juno alone. *Ovid. Met.* 4. v. 173.

JUNO'NIS PROMONTO'RIUM, a promontory of Peloponnesus, now Capo Giallo. *Plin.* 3. c. 1.

Juno'nis Promonto'rium, a promontory of Spain, now Cape Trafalgar. *Id.* 2. c. 107.

Juno'nis Lacin'iæ Tem'plum, a temple of Juno in Italy between Crotona and the Lacinian promontory.

JU'PITER, the most powerful of all the gods of the ancients. According to Varro, there were no less than 300 persons of that name; Diodorus mentions two; and Cicero three, two of Arcadia, and one of Crete. To the Jupiter of Crete, who passed for the son of Saturn and Ops, the actions of the rest have been attributed. According to the opinion of the mythologists, Jupiter was saved from destruction by his mother, and entrusted to the care of the Corybantes. Saturn, who had received the kingdom of the world from his brother Titan on condition of not raising male children, devoured all his sons as soon as born; but Ops, offended at her husband's cruelty, secreted Jupiter, and gave a stone to Saturn, which he devoured on the supposition that it was a male child. Jupiter was secretly educated in a cave on mount Ida, in Crete, and fed upon the milk of the goat Amalthæa, or upon honey, according to others. He received the name of *Jupiter, quasi juvans pater*. His cries were drowned by the noise of cymbals and drums, which the Corybantes beat at the express command of Ops. *Vid.* Corybantes. As soon as he was a year old, Jupiter found himself sufficiently strong to make war against the Titans, who had imprisoned his father because he had brought up male children. The Titans were conquered, and Saturn set at liberty by the hands of his son. Saturn, however, soon after, apprehensive of the power of Jupiter, conspired against his life, and was, for his treachery, driven from his kingdom, and obliged to flee for safety into Latium. Jupiter now become the sole master of the empire of the world, divided it with his brothers. He reserved for himself the kingdom of heaven, and gave the empire of the sea to Neptune, and that of the infernal regions to Pluto. The peaceful beginning of his reign was soon interrupted by the rebellion of the giants, who were sons of the earth, and who wished to revenge the death of their relations the Titans. They were so powerful that they hurled rocks and heaped up mountain upon mountain, to scale heaven, so that all the gods to avoid their fury, fled to Ægypt, where they assumed the form of different animals. Jupiter, however, animated them, and, by the assistance of Hercules, totally overpowered the gigantic race, which had proved such formidable enemies. *Vid.* Gigantes. Jupiter, now freed from every apprehension, gave himself up to the pursuit of pleasure. He married Metis, Themis, Eurynome, Ceres, Mnemosyne, Latona, and Juno (*vid.* Juno,) and, in short, became a Proteus to gratify his illict passions. He introduced himself to Danae in a shower of gold, to Antiope in the form of a satyr, to Leda in the form of a swan, he became a bull to seduce Europa, and he enjoyed the company of Ægina in the form of a flame of fire. He assumed the habit of Diana, to corrupt Callisto, and became Amphitryon to gain the affections of Alcmena. His children were also numerous as well as his mistresses. According to *Apollodorus*, 1. c. 3. he was father of the Seasons, Irene, Eunomia, the Fates, Clotho, Lachesis, and Atropos, by Themis; of Venus, by Dione; of the Graces, Aglaia, Euphrosyne, and Thalia, by Eurynome, the daughter of Oceanus: of Proserpine, by Styx; of the nine Muses, by Mnemosyne, &c. *Vid.* Niobe, Laodamia, Pyrrha, Protogenia, Electra, Maia, Semele, &c. The worship of Jupiter was universal: he was the Ammon of the Africans, the Belus of Babylon, the Osiris of Ægypt, &c. His surnames were numerous, many of which he received from the place or functions over which he presided. He was called Feretrius, Inventor, Elicius, Capitolinus, Latialis, Pistor, Sponsor, Herceus, Anxurus, Victor, Maximus, Optimus, Olympius, Fluvialis, &c. The worship of Jupiter surpassed that of the other gods in solemnity. His altars were not, like those of Saturn and Diana, stained with the blood of human victims, but he was delighted with the sacrifice of goats, sheep, and white bulls. The oak was sacred to him, because he first taught mankind to live upon acorns. He is generally represented as sitting upon a golden or ivory throne, holding, in one hand, thunderbolts just ready to be hurled, and, in the other, a sceptre of cypress. His looks express majesty, his beard flows long and negligently, and the eagle stands with expanded wings at his feet. He is sometimes represented with the upper parts of his body naked, and these below the waist carefully covered, as if to show that he is visible to the gods above, but that he is concealed from the sight of the inhabitants of the earth. Jupiter had several oracles, the most celebrated of which were at Dodona, and Ammon in Libya. As Jupiter was the king and father of gods and men, his power was extended over the deities, and every thing was subservient to his will, except the Fates. From him mankind received their blessings and their miseries, and they looked upon him as acquainted with every thing, past, present, and future. He was represented at Olympia with a crown like olive branches, his mantle was variegated with different flowers, particularly the lily, and the eagle perched on the top of the sceptre which he held in his hands. The Cretans represented Jupiter without ears, to signify, that the sovereign master of the world ought not to give a partial ear to any particular person, but be equally candid and propitious to all. At Lacedæmon he appeared with four heads, that he might seem to hear with greater readiness the different prayers and solicitations which were daily poured out to him from every part of the earth. It is said that Minerva came armed from his brains after he had ordered Vulcan to open his head. *Paus.* 1, 2, &c.—*Liv.* 1. 4. 5, &c.—*Diod.* 1 & 3.—*Homer. Il.* 1. 5, &c. *Odyss.* 1. 4, &c. *Hymn. ad Jov.*—*Orpheus.*—*Callimac. Jov.*—*Pindar. Olymp.* 1. 3. 5.—*Apollon.* 1, &c.—*Hesiod. Theog. in Scut. Herc.*

Oper. & Dies.—Lycophron. in Cass.—Virg. Æn. 1, 2, &c. *G.* 3.—*Ovid. Met.* 1. fab. 1, &c.—*Horat.* 3. od. 1, &c. [The finest statue existing of Jupiter is in the Vatican, having been removed from the Verospi palace at Rome, and is supposed to be a copy of the celebrated statue by Phidas. There is also a very fine colossal bust in the same Museum]

JU'RA, a high ridge of mountains separating the Helvetii from the Sequani, or Switzerland from Burgundy. *Cæs. G.* 1. c. 2.

JUSTINIA'NA, a town of Illyria, the birth-place of Justinian.

JUSTINIA'NUS, emperor of the east, succeeded his uncle Justin the First, August 1, A.D. 527. He was happily seconded in his efforts to support the tottering power of the imperial throne at Constantinople, by the military abilities of the great Belisarius, and by the intrigues and spirited conduct of his consort Theodosia. His name is immortalized in history by the code of laws which, under his direction, was selected by the ablest lawyers of the age, and to which the name of Justinian's Pandects or Digests was given. Justinian is also known for finally abolishing the consulate, which still feebly presented to the degenerate Romans the shadow of their departed republican greatness. The church of St. Sophia at Constantinople, so much admired for its beauty and the magnificence of its architecture, was e ected under his patronage. He died in his 83d year, after a reign of thirty-nine years. *Procop. de Bell, Pers. &c.—Evagr.* 4.—*Agathias.—Nicephorus.—Paul. Diac. &c.*

JUSTI'NUS M. JUNIA'NUS or **FRONTI'NUS**, a Latin historian in the age of Antoninus, who epitomized the history of Trogus Pompeius in forty-four books. This epitome, according to some traditions, was the cause that the more extensive work of Trogus was lost. It comprehends the history of the Assyrian, Persian, Grecian, Macedonian, Roman empires, &c. in a neat and elegant style. The work is replete with many judicious reflections, and animated harangues: but the author is often too credulous, and sometimes examines events too minutely, while others are related only in a few words and often in obscure language. The indecency of many of his expressions is deservedly censured. The best editions of Justin are that of Ab. Gronovius, 8vo, L. Bat. 1719, that of Hearne, 8vo, Oxon. 1703, and that of Barbou, 12mo, Paris, 1770. *Harles. Not. Lit. Rom.* 1. p. 493.—*Sax. Onom.* 1. p. 309.

Justi'nus Mar'tyr, a Platonic philosopher, born in Palestine, and converted to Christianity, of which he became a most able and zealous advocate. He died in Ægypt, and wrote two apologies for the Christians, besides his dialogue with a Jew; two treatises, &c. in a plain and unadorned style. The best editions of Justin Martyr are that of Prudentius Maran, Paris, fol. 1636; that of his apologies, 2 vols. 8vo, 1700, and 1703; and of his dialogue with Trypho, that of Jebb, published in London 1722. *Sax. Onom.* 1. p. 304.—*Fabr. B. Gr.* 5. c. 1.

Justi'nus, an emperor of the east, who reigned nine years, and died A.D. 526. *Zonaras.—Evagr.* 4. ——An emperor, who died 517 A.D., after a reign of thirteen years. *Zonar. in Ann.—Evagr. H.* 5.—*Paul. Diac.—Du Fresne de Inf. Ævi. Numism.* n. 71.

JUS'TUS, a Jewish historian, cotemporary with Josephus.

JUTUR'NA, a sister of Turnus, king of the Rutuli. She received with contempt the addresses of Jupiter, but, according to others, she would not have been unfavourable to his passion, had the god consented to reward her love with immortality. She was afterwards changed into a fountain of the same name near the Numicus, falling into the Tiber. The waters of that fountain were used in sacrifices, and particularly in those of Vesta, and it was reported they had the power of healing diseases. *Varro de L. L.* 1. c. 10 —*Ovid. Fast.* 1. v. 708. 1. 2. 585.—*Virg. Æn.* 12. v. 139.—*Servius loco & Æn.* 6. v. 90.—*Cic. Cluent* 36.

JUVA'VUM or **JUVA'VIA**, now Salzburg, a town in Noricum.

JUVENA'LIS, DEC'IMUS JU'NIUS, an illustrious poet born at Aquinum in Italy. He came early to Rome, and was for some years engaged in the laborious but lucrative profession of the bar; after which he applied himself to write satires, sixteen of which are extant. He spoke with virulence against the partiality of Nero for the pantomime Paris, and although his satire and declamation were particularly pointed against this ruling favorite of the emperor, yet Juvenal lived in security during the reign of Nero. After the death of Nero, however, the effects of the resentment of Paris were severely felt, and the satirist was sent by Domitian as governor on the frontiers of Ægypt. Juvenal was then in the 80th year of his age, and he suffered much from the trouble which attended his office, or rather his exile. He returned, however, to Rome after the death of Paris, and died in the reign of Trajan, A.D. 128. His writings are fiery and animated, and abound with humor. He is particularly severe upon the vices and dissipation of the age in which he lived, but the gross and indecent manner in which he too often exposes to ridicule the follies of mankind, rather encourages than disarms the debauched and licentious. He wrote with acrimony against all his adversaries, either political or personal, and whatever displeased or offended him was exposed to his severest censure. It is to be acknowledged, that Juvenal is far more correct than his cotemporaries, a circumstance which some have attributed to his judgment and experience, which were uncommonly mature, as his satires were the production of old age. He may be called, and with reason perhaps, the last of the Roman poets. After him poetry rapidly decayed, and nothing more claims our attention as a perfect poetical composition. The best editions are that of Casaubon, 4to. L. Bat. 1695, with Persius, and of Hawkey, Dublin, 12mo, 1746, and of Grævis, *cum notis variorum*, 8vo, L. Bat. 1684; to which may be added the later edition of Ruperti, Leipz. 1802. *Lil. Girald. in Dial. poet.—Juv.* 3. v. 319.—*Martial.* 7. epigr. 23 & 90. 1. 12, epigr. 18.—*Sax. Onom.* 1. p. 274.—*Harles. Not. Lit. Rom.* 1. p. 482.

JUVEN'CUS CA'IUS VET'TIUS or **VES'TIUS AQUILI'NUS**, a Spaniard who distinguished himself in the reign of Constantius and Constans, as a champion of Christianity. He turned the Gospel history into heroic verse, in four books, if not with great elegance or superior genius, yet with matchless fidelity; and he also wrote hymns. The chief editions are, Paris, 1499; Venet. 1502; Colon 1537; and of Reusch. Franc. and Lips. 1710. His book on Genesis will be found in the 9th volume of the Nov. Collect. Veter. Monim. of Edm. Martene.—*Sax. Onom.* 1. p. 397.—*Harles. Not. Lit. Rom.* 1. p. 712.

JUVEN'TAS or **JUVEN'TUS**, a goddess at Rome, who presided over youth and vigor. She is the same as the Hebe of the Greeks, and is represented as a beautiful nymph, arrayed in variegated garments. *Cic. Tusc.* 1. c. 26 *Br.* 18. *Att.* 1. ep. 18.—*Liv.* 5. c. 54. 1. 21. c. 62. 1. 36. c. 36.—*Ovid. ex Pont.* 1. ep. 9. v. 12.—*August de Civ. Dei.* 4. c. 2 & 23.—*Horat.* 1. od. 30. v. 7.

JUVEN'TIUS, the first plebeian raised to the honor of curule ædile. *Cic. Planc.* 24.

JUVER'NA, a name of Ireland. *Juv.* v. 160.

L.

LAAN'DER, a youth, brother to Nicocrates, tyrant of Cyrene, &c. *Polyæn.* 8.

LAAR'CHUS, the guardian of Battus of Cyrene. He usurped the sovereign power for some time, and endeavoured to marry the mother of Battus, to establish his tyranny more firmly. The queen, to deceive him, gave him a friendly invitation, and caused him to be assassinated, and restored the power to Battus. *Id. Ibid.*

LAAT'THA, a city of Arabia Felix. *Ptol.*

LA'BA, a town of Arabia Felix, toward the Sinus Elaniticus. *Id.*

LAB'ACA, a city of India within the Ganges. *Id.*

LAB'ANIS, an island in the Arabian Gulph. *Plin.* 6. c. 28.

LAB'ARA, a city of Caria. *Steph.*

LAB'ARIS, a king of Ægypt after Sesostris.

LAB'ARUS, a river of the Insubres. *Pliny*, 3. c. 16, calls it Lambrus.

LAB'ASÆ, a people of India without the Ganges. *Ptol.*

LAB'DA, a daughter of Amphion, one of the Bacchiadæ was born lame. She married Eetion, by whom she had a son whom she called Cypselus, because she saved his life in a coffer. *Vid.* Cypselus. This coffer was said to be preserved at Olympia. *Herodot.* 5. c. 92.—*Arist. Polit.* 5.

LABAC'IDES, a name given to Œdipus, as descended from Labdacus.

LAB'DACUS, a son of Polydorus by Nycteis, the daughter of Nycteus, king of Thebes. His father and mother died during his childhood, and he was left to the care of Nycteus, who, at his death, left his kingdom in the hands of Lycus, with orders to restore it to Labdacus as soon as he reached the age of manhood. He was father to Laius. It is unknown whether he ever sat on the throne of Thebes. According to Statius, his father's name was Phœnix. His descendants were called Labdacidæ. *Stat. Theb.* 6. v. 451.—*Apollod.* 3. c. 5.—*Paus.* 2. c. 6. l. 9. c. 5.

LAB'DALON, a promontory at the east of Sicily, near Syracuse. *Diod.* 13.—*Liv.* 25. c. 24, &c.

LABEA'TIS, now Scutari, a lake in Dalmatia. The inhabitants of the neighbourhood were called Labeatæ. *Liv.* 44. c. 31. l. 45. c. 26.—*Plin.* 3. c. 22.

LABE'CIA, a town of Arabia destroyed by Ælius Gellus. *Plin.* 6. c. 28.

LA'BEO, a surname of the families of the Antistii, Asconii, Cethegi, &c., because one of them, it is said, had large lips. *Plin.* 11. c. 37.——One of Cæsar's murderers. After sharing the dangers of Brutus at the battle of Philippi, he caused himself to be slain by one of his freedmen, that he might not survive the destruction of the liberty of his country. *Appian. Alex.* 4.——A tribune of the people at Rome, who condemned the censer Metellus to be thrown down from the Tarpeian rock, because he had expelled him from the senate. The execution of this rigorous sentence was stopped by the interference of another of the tribunes.

LA'BEO ANTIS'TIUS, son of the preceding, a celebrated lawyer in the age of Augustus, whose ambitious views he boldly opposed, and whose offers of the consulship he refused. He was accustomed to devote himself to the company and conversation of the learned for six months, and the rest of the year was spent in writing and composing. His works were said to amount to 500 volumes, all of which are lost, though some were extant in the age of Justinian. *Horace*, 1. sat. 3. v. 82, has unjustly taxed Labeo with insanity, because, no doubt, he inveighed against his patron. Some fragments of his works are preserved in the Jurisprudentia Restituta of Wieling. *Sax. Onom.* 1. p. 202.—*Suet. in Aug.* 45.—*Tacit. Ann.* 3. c. 75.—*Dio.* 54.—*Gell.* 13. c. 12.

LA'BEO Q. FA'BIUS, a Roman consul, A.U.C. 571, who obtained a naval victory over the fleet of the Cretans. According to some accounts he assisted Terence in composing his comedies.

LA'BEO AC'CIUS, an obscure poet, who recommended himself to the favor of Nero by an incorrect translation of Homer into Latin verse. The work is lost, and only this curious line is preserved by an old scholiast, *Persius*, 1. v. 4. *Crudum manducus, Priamum, Priamique Pisinnos.*

LABE'RIUS J. DEC'IMUS, a Roman knight, famous for his poetical talents in writing pantomimes. J. Cæsar compelled him to act one of his characters on the stage. The poet consented with great reluctance, but he showed his resentment during the acting of the piece, by throwing severe aspersions upon J. Cæsar, by warning the audience against his tyranny, and by drawing upon him the eyes of the whole theatre. Cæsar, however, disregarded the severity of his reflections, and restored him to the rank of knight, which he had forfeited by appearing on the stage; but to his mortification when he went to take his seat among the knights, no one offered to make room for him, and even his friend Cicero said, *Recepissem te nisi angustè sederem.* Laberius was offended at the observation, and reflected upon his unsettled and pusillanimous behaviour during the civil wars of Cæsar and Pompey, by replying *Mirum si Angustè sedes, qui soles duabus sellis sedere.* Laberius died ten months after the murder of J. Cæsar. Some verses to the number of 116, remain of his plays, the titles of some of which are preserved. These fragments are to be found in the Fragmenta Vet. Poet. of Stephens, 1564, and of Mattaire, vol. 2. *Macrob. Sat.* 2. c. 3 & 7.—*Horat.* 1. sat. 10.—*Senec.* 2. *Controv.* 18.—*Suet. in Cæs.*—*Aul. Gell.* 3. c. 7. l. 10. c. 17.—*Sax. Onom.* 1. p. 560.—*Harles. Not. Lit. Rom.* 1. p. 296, &c.

LABE'RIUS Q. DU'RUS, a tribune of the soldiers in Cæsar's legions, killed in Britain. *Cæs. Bell. G.* 5. c. 5.

LABER'RIS, now Pennaflor, a town of Asturia, in Spain. *Ptol.*

LABE'RUS, a town of Ireland, now Killair, according to *Camden.* But geographers differ as to the name of the modern town. *Ptol.*

LABI'CUM, now Colonna, a small town of Italy, called also Lavicum, between Gabii and Tusculum which became a Roman colony about four centuries B.C. *Virg. Æn.* 7. v. 796.—*Liv.* 2. c. 39. l. 4. c. 47. l. 6. c. 21.—*Strab.* 5.—*Ital.* 8. v. 368.

LABIE'NUS T. AT'TIUS, a tribune who accused Rabirius of killing Saturninus. He was afterwards lieutenant to Julius Cæsar in the wars of Gaul, but he deserted his cause for that of Pompey. After sharing the dangers of the battle of Pharsalia, he fell in the service of the republic at the battle of Munda. *Cæs. Bell. G.* 6, &c.—*Cic.* 7. *Att.* 11 & 12. l. 8. ep. 2. *Fam.* 1. ep. 32.—*Rab.* 1 —*Lucan.* 5. v. 346.

LABIE'NUS, a Roman who followed the interest of Brutus and Cassius, and afterwards became general of the Parthians against Rome. He was conquered by the officers of Augustus. *Strab.* 12 & 14.—*Dio.* 48.

LABIE'NUS TI'TUS, an historian and orator at Rome, in the age of Augustus, a great admirer of his own compositions. The senate ordered his papers to be burnt on account of their seditious contents; and Labienus, unable to survive the loss of his writings, destroyed himself. *Seneca in Præf.* 5 *Contr.*—*Suet. in Calig.* 16.—*Voss. H. Lat.* 1. c. 23.

LABINE'TUS, or **LABYNE'TUS**, a king of Babylon, &c. *Herodot.* 1. c. 74.

LABIS'CO, a city of Gallia Narbonensis. *Antonin.*

LAB'OCLA, a city of India within the Ganges. *Ptol.*

LABO'RIÆ, fertile plains near Capua, Cales, &c. now Terra di Lavoro. *Plin.* 17. c. 4.

LABOSSARDA'CHUS, a king of Babylon. *Joh. Marsh, Can. Chron. Sec.* 18.

LAB'OTAS, a river near Antioch. *Strab.* 16.

LABO'TAS, a son of Echestratus, who made war against Argos, &c.

LABRAN'DEUS, a surname of Jupiter in Caria. The word is derived from *labrys*, which in the language of the country signify a hatchet, which Jupiter's statue held in its hand. This hatchet originally belonged to the queen of the Amazons, and from her conqueror Hercules, passed into the hands of Omphale, queen of Lydia, and her descendants on the throne till the age of Candaules, when it was given to the Carians, and exchanged for the sceptre in the hand of Jupiter's statue. Some, however, suppose that Jupiter is called Labradeus because rain proceeded from him. *Plut. in Thes.* —*Lactant*, 1. c. 22.—*Ælian. de Nat. A.* 12. c. 30. —*Plin.* 32. c. 2.

LABRAN'DUS, a town of Caria, called Labranda by *Pliny. Steph.*

LA'BRIS, a town of Arabia Felix. *Ptol.*

LA'BRO, a port of Italy on the Mediterranean, now Livorno. *Cic.* 2. *ad Fra.* 6.—*Plin.* 3. c. 5.

LABUL'LUS, a man whose meanness and avarice *Martial* has ridiculed, l. 11. epigr. 25. l. 12. epigr. 36.

LABYRIN'THUS, a building, the numerous passages and perplexing windings of which rendered escape from it difficult, and almost impracticable. There were four, very famous among the ancients, one near the city of Crocodiles or Assinoe, another in Crete, a third at Lemnus, and a fourth in Italy, built by Porsenna. That of Ægypt was the most ancient, and Herodotus, who saw it, declares that the beauty of the building, and the art with which it was constructed, were almost beyond belief. It was built by twelve kings who at one time reigned in Ægypt, and it was intended for the place of their burial, and to commemorate the actions of their reign. It was divided into 12 halls, or, according to Pliny, into 16, or, as Strabo mentions, into 27. The halls were vaulted according to the relation of Herodotus. They had each six doors opening to the north, and the same number to the south, all surrounded by one wall. The edifice contained 3000 chambers, 1500 in the upper part, and the same number below. The chambers above were seen by Herodotus, who was astonished beyond conception at their magnificence, but he was not permitted to see those below, where were buried the holy crocodiles and the monarchs whose united labors had raised the edifice. The roofs and walls were incrusted with marble, and adorned with sculptured figures. The halls were surrounded with stately and polished pillars of white stone and, according to some authors, the opening of the doors was attended with a terrible noise like peals of thunder. The labyrinth of Crete was built by Dædalus, in imitation of that of Ægygt, and is the best known of all those mentioned in classical history. It was the place of confinement for Dædalus himself, and the prison of the Minotaur. According to Pliny, the labyrinth of Lemnus surpassed the others in grandeur and magnificence. It was supported by forty columns of uncommon height and thickness, and equally admirable for their beauty and splendor. Modern travellers are still astonished at the noble and magnificent ruins which appear of the Ægyptian labyrinth, at the south of the lake Mœris, about 30 miles from the ruins of Arsinoe. *Mela*, 1. c. 9.—*Plin*. 36. c. 13. —*Strab*. 10.—*Diod*. 1.—*Herodot*. 2. c. 148.—*Virg. Æn*. 5. v. 588.—*Ovid. Met*. 8. v. 156.—*Plin*. 36. c. 13.—*Isidor*. 15. c. 2.—*Cœl. Rh*. 17. c. 9.

LACÆ'NA, an epithet applied to a female native of Laconia, and among others, to Helen. *Virg. Æn*. 6. v 511.

LACANI'TIS, a region of Cilicia. *Ptol.*

LAC'CI, a lake of Marmarica. *Id.*

LACCI'NI, a people of Italy. *Plin*. 3. c. 21.

LACCOBAR'DI, a people of Germany. *Ptol.*

LACCOBRI'GA. *Vid*. Lacobriga.

LACCOPLU'TI, a surname of the descendants of Callias, who was called Lacoplutus, from finding a treasure in the plains of Marathon. *Suidas.*

LACEDÆ'MON, a son of Jupiter and Taygeta, the daughter of Atlas, who married Sparta the daughter of Eurotas, by whom he had Amyclas and Eurydice the wife of Acrisius. He was the first who introduced the worship of the Graces into Laconia, and who built a temple to these divinities. From Lacedæmon and his wife, the capital of Laconia was called Lacedæmon and Sparta. *Apollod*. 3. c. 10.—*Schol. Eurip. in Orest*. 626.—*Schol. Pind*. 3 *Olymp*. 54.—*Hygin*. fab. 155.—*Paus*. 3. c. 1.

LACEDÆ'MON, a noble city of Peloponnesus, the capital of Laconia, called also Sparta. It has been severally known by the name of Lelegia, from the Leleges the first inhabitants of the country, or from Lelex one of their kings; and Œbalia from Œbalus the sixth king from Eurotas. It was also called Hecatompolis, from the hundred cities which the whole province contained at one period. Lelex is supposed to have been the first king. His descendants, 13 in number, reigned successively after him, till the reign of the sons of Orestes, when the Heraclidæ recovered the Peloponnesus, about 80 years after the Trojan war. Procles and Eurysthenes, the descendants of the Heraclidæ, enjoyed the crown together, and, it was decreed that, after their decease, the two families should always sit on the throne together. *Vid*. Eurysthenes. These two brothers began to reign B.C. 1102, their successors in the family of Procles were called Proclidæ, and afterwards Eurypontidæ, and those of Eurysthenes, Eurysthenidæ, and afterwards Agidæ.

THE PROCLIDÆ.	B.C.	THE AGIDÆ.	B.C.
Sous,	1060	Agis,	1059
Euryphon,	1028	Echestratus,	1058
Prytanis,	1021	Labotas,	1023
Eunomus,	986	Doryssus,	986
Polydectes,	907	Agesilaus,	957
Lycurgus,	898	Archelaus,	913
Charilaus,	873	Teleclus,	853
Nicander,	809	Alcamenes,	813
Theopompus,	770	Polydorus,	776
Zeuxidamus,	723	Eurycrates,	724
Anaxidamus,	690	Anaxander,	687
Archidamus,	651	Eurycrates 2d,	644
Agasicles,	605	Leon,	607
Ariston,	564	Anaxandrides,	563
Demaratus,	526	Cleomenes,	530
Leotychides,	491	Leonidas,	491
		Plistarchus, under the guardianship of Pausanias,	480
Archidamus 2d,	469	Plistoanax,	466
Agis,	427	Pausanias,	408
Agesilaus,	397	Agesipolis,	397
		Cleombrotus,	380
		Agesipolis 2d,	371
Archidamus 3d,	361	Cleomenes 2d,	370
Agis 2d,	338	Aretus or Areus	309
Eudamidas,	330	Acrotatus,	265
Archidamus 4th,	295	Areus 2d,	264
Eudamidas 2d,	268	Leonidas 2d,	257
Agis 3d,	244	Cleombrotus 2d,	243
Archidamus 5th,	230	Leonidas restored,	241
Euclidas,	225	Cleomenes 3d,	235
Lycurgus 2d,	219	Agesipolis 3d,	219

Under the two last kings, Lycurgus and Agesipolis, the monarchical power was abolished, though Machanidas the tyrant made himself absolute, B.C. 210, and Nabis, 206, for 14 years. In the year 191 B.C. Lacedæmon joined the Achæan league, and, about three years after, the walls were demolished by order of Philopœmen. The territories of Laconia shared the fate of the brave but unfortunate confederacy of the Achæans, and the whole was conquered by Mummius, 147 B.C. and converted into a Roman province. The inhabitants of Lacedæmon have rendered themselves illustrious for their courage and intrepidity, for their love of honor and liberty, and for their aversion to sloth and luxury. They were inured from their youth to labor, and their laws commanded them to regard war as their profession. They never applied themselves to any trade, as their only employment was arms, and they left every thing else to the care of their slaves. *Vid*. Helotæ. They hardened their body by stripes and other manly exercises, and accustomed themselves to undergo hardships, and even to die, without fear or regret. From their valor in the field, and their moderation and temperance at home, they were courted and respected by all the neighbouring princes, and their assistance was at different times implored to protect the Sicilians, Carthaginians, Thracians, Ægyptians, Cyreneans, &c. They were forbidden by the laws of their country, (*vid*. Lycurgus,) to visit foreign states, lest their morals should be corrupted by an intercourse with effeminate nations. The austere manner in which their children were educated, rendered them ambitious of glory, and fearful of dishonor, and therefore undaunted in the field of battle; and, from this circumstance, Leonidas, with a small band, was enabled to resist the millions of the army of Xerxes at Thermopylæ. The women were as courageous as the men, and many a mother celebrated with festivals the death of her son who had fallen in battle, or coolly put him to death if by a shameful flight, or the loss of his arms, he brought disgrace upon his country. As to domestic manners, the Lacedæmonians as widely differed from their neighbours as in political concerns, and their noblest women, contrary to the general habits of Greece, were not ashamed to appear on the stage hired for money. In the affairs of Greece, the interest of the Lacedæmonians was often powerful, and obtained a decided superiority for 500 years. Their jealousy of the power and greatness of the Athenians is well known. The authority of their monarchs was checked by the watchful eye of the Ephori, who had the power of imprisoning the kings themselves if guilty of misdemeanors. *Vid*. Ephori. Among other national virtues the Lacedæmonians were remarkable for the honor and reverence which they paid to old age. The names of Lacedæmon and Sparta are promiscuously applied to the capital of Laconia, and often confounded together. The latter was applied to the metropolis, and the former was reserved for the inhabitants of the suburbs, or rather of the country contiguous to the walls of the city. This propriety of distinction was originally observed, but in process of time it was totally disregarded, and both appellatives were soon synonymous and indiscriminately applied to the city and country. *Vid*. Sparta, Laconia. The place where the city stood is now called

Paleo Chori, (*the old town*), and the new one erected on its ruins at some distance on the west is called Misitra. *Liv.* 34. c. 33. l. 45. c. 28,—*Strab.* 8.—*Thucyd.* 1.—*Paus.* 3.—*Justin.* 2. 3, &c.—*Herodot.* 1, &c.—*Plut. in Lyc. &c.*—*Diod.*—*Mela*, 2. There were some festivals celebrated at Lacedæmon, the names of which are not known, It was customary, during the celebration, for the women to drag all the old bachelors round the altars, and beat them with their fists, that the shame and ignominy to which they were exposed might induce them to marry. *Athen.* 13.——An inland city of Cyprus. *Steph.*—*Strab.* 8.

LACEDÆMO'NII or **LACEDÆM'ONES**, the inhabitants of Lacedæmon. *Vid.* Lacedæmon.

LACEDÆMO'NIUS, a son of Cimon by Clitoria. He received this name from his father's regard for the Lacedæmonians. *Plut.*

LACER'TA, a soothsayer in Domitian's age, who acquired immense riches by his art. *Juv.* 7. v. 114.

LACETA'NIA, a district at the north of Spain. The inhabitants were called Lacetani. *Liv.* 21. c. 23.—*Plin.* 3. c. 3.

LACH'ARES, a man who seized the supreme power at Athens, when the city was distracted by civil discord, and was afterwards banished B.C. 296. *Polyæn.* 4.——An Athenian three times taken prisoner. He deceived his keepers, and escaped, &c. *Id.* 3.——A son of Mithridates, king of Bosporus. He was received into alliance by Lucullus, A.U.C. 685.——A robber condemned by M. Antony. ——An Ægyptian buried in the labyrinth near Arsinoe.——An Athenian sophist, disciple of Heracleon. *Suidas.*

LA'CHES, an Athenian general in the age of Epaminondas. *Diod.* 12.——An Athenian sent with Carias at the head of a fleet in the first expedition undertaken against Sicily in the Peloponnesian war. *Justin.* 4. c. 3.——An eminent artist who finished the Colossus of Rhodes.

LACH'ESIS, one of the Parcæ, whose name is derived ἀπὸ τοῦ λαγχάνειν, *to measure out by lot.* She presided over futurity, and was represented as spinning the thread of life, or, according to others, as holding the spindle. She generally appeared covered with a garment variegated with stars, and holding spindles in her hand. *Vid.* Parcæ. *Stat. Theb.* 2. v. 249.—*Martial.* 4. epigr. 54.—*Seneca. in Œdip.* 984.—*Juv.* 3. v. 27.

LA'CIA or **LACI'ADÆ**, a village of the tribe Œneis. *Steph.*

LAC'IDAS, a Greek philosopher of Cyrene who flourished B.C. 241. His father's name was Alexander. He was disciple of Arcesilaus, whom he succeeded in the government of the second academy. He was greatly esteemed by Attalus, king of Pergamus, who gave him a garden where he spent his hours in study, but he refused to visit the court, observing that the portraits of kings ought to be contemplated only at a distance. He taught his disciples to suspend their judgment, and never to speak decisively. He died through excess of drinking, about 212 B.C. *Diog.* 4.—*Cic. Acad.* 4. c. 6.

LACI'DES, a village near Athens, which derived its name from Lacius, an Athenian hero, whose exploits are not recorded. Here Zephyrus had an altar sacred to him, and likewise Ceres and Proserpine a temple. *Paus.* 1. c. 37.

LACI'NIA, a surname of Juno from her temple at Lacinium in Italy, which the Crotonians held in great veneration, and where there was a famous picture of Helen by Zeuxis. *Vid.* Zeuxis. On an altar near the door were ashes, which, it was said, the wind could not blow away. Fulvius Flaccus took away a marble piece from this sacred place to finish a temple that he was building at Rome to Fortuna Equestris; and it is said, that, in consequence of this sacrilege, he afterwards led a miserable life, and died in the greatest agonies after hearing of the death of one of his sons. The marble was sent back by order of the senate to the temple of the offended goddess. *Lucan.* 2. v. 434.—*Servius in Æn.* 3. v. 551.—*Mela*, 2. c. 4.—*Lactant.* 2. c. 7.—*Arnobius*, 6.—*Strab.* 6.—*Ovid.* 15. *Met.* v. 12 & 702.—*Liv.* 42. c. 3.—*Val. Max.* 1. c. 1.

LACINIEN'SES, a people of Liburnia. *Plin.* 3. c. 21.—*Athen.* 10.

LACIN'IUM, a promontory of Magna Græcia, now Cape Colonna, which, with the promontory of Salentum, forms the entrance of the Tarentine Gulph, about 70, or, according to some, 100 miles wide. Juno Lacinia had a temple there held in great veneration. The place is said to have received its name from Lacinius, a famous robber, killed there by Hercules. *Liv.* 24. c. 3. l. 27. c. 5. l. 30. c. 20.—*Virg. Æn.* 3. v. 552.—*Plin.* 3. c. 11.

LACIPE'A, a city of Spain, near Emerita. *Antonin.*

LACIP'PO, a city of Hispania Bætica. *Ptol.*—*Plin.* 3. c. 1.—*Mela*, 2. c. 5

LACIS'THENES, a Lacedæmonian, vanquished in battle by the Bœotians. *Diod. Sic.* l. 14.

LA'CIUS & ANTIPHE'MUS, two brothers, the former of whom founded Phaselis, in Pamphylia, the latter Gela, in Sicily. *Steph. in* Γέλα.—*Joh. Marsh. Can. Chron. Sec* 17.

LAC'MON, a part of mount Pindus, whence the Inachus flows. *Herodot.* 9. c. 93.

LA'CO CORNE'LIUS, a favourite of Galba, mean and cowardly in his character. He was put to death. *Tac. Hist.* 1. c. 6, &c.

LA'CO, an inhabitant of Laconia or Lacedæmon.

LACOB'RIGA or **LACOBRI'GA**, a city of Spain, a little at the west of Numantia, where Sertorius was besieged by Metellus. *Plin.* 3 c. 3.—*Mela*, 3. c. 1.

LA'CON, one of Actæon's dogs, so called from his Lacedæmonian origin. *Ovid. Met.* 3. v. 219.

LACO'NIA, LACON'ICA or **LACEDÆ'MON**, a country in the southern part of the Peloponnesus, having Argos and Arcadia on the north, Messenia on the west, the Mediterranean on the south, and the bay of Argos at the east Its extent from north to south was about fifty miles. It is watered by the river Eurotas; and in ancient times the capital was called Sparta, or Lacedæmon. The inhabitants never went on an expedition or engaged an enemy but at the full moon. *Vid.* Lacedæmon. The brevity with which they always expressed themselves is now become proverbial, and by the epithet of Laconic we understand whatever is concise and not loaded with unnecessary words. The word Laconicum is applied to some hot baths used among the ancients, supposed to have been first used at Lacedæmon. *Cic.* 4. *Att.* 10.—*Strab.* 8.—*Ptol.* 3. c. 16.—*Mela*, 2. c. 3.

LAC'RATES, a Theban, general of a detachment sent by Artaxerxes to the assistance of the Ægyptians. *Diod.* 16.

LACRATI'DES, an archon at Athens, in the time of Darius. *Schol. in Aristoph Acharn.*

LACRIAS'SUS, a city of Armenia Minor. *Ptol.*

LAC'RINES, a Lacedæmonian ambassador, sent to Cyprus. *Herodot.* 1. c. 152.

LACTAN'TIUS LU'CIUS CÆ'LIUS or **CÆCILIUS FIRMIA'NUS**, a celebrated writer, born in Africa, or, according to some authors, at Fermo, in the march of Ancona. His learning and virtues recommended him to the notice of Constantine, by whom he was appointed preceptor to his son Crispus. His principal works are *de opificio Dei;* his *Divinæ Institutiones*, in seven books; *de irâ Dei;* an Epitome of his Institutes; *de paschâ*, &c. The expressive purity, elegance, and energy of his style have gained him the name of the Christian Cicero. He died A.D. 325. The best editions of his work are that of Sparke, 8vo. Oxon. 1684, that of Biineman, 2 vols. 8vo, Lips. 1739, and that of Du Fresnoy, 2 vols. 4to, Paris, 1748. Several of his works have been published separately. Some suppose that he was not the author of the poem *de Phœnice. Harles. Not. Lit. Rom.* 1. p. 561.—*Sax. Onom.* 1. p 386.

LACTA'RIUS MONS or **LAC'TIS MONS**, a mountain in Campania, where Narses gained a victory over the Goths A.D. 553.

LAC'TER, a promontory of the island of Cos. *Strab.* 14.

LACU'RIS, now Loquera, a town of the Oretani, in Spain. *Ptol.*

LAC'YDES or **LACY'DES**. *Vid.* Lacidas.

LACY'DUS, an effeminate king of Argos. *Plutarch.*

LA'DAS a celebrated courier in the service of Alexander the Great, born at Sicyon. He obtained a crown at Olympia, and was honored with a brazen statue, which represented him in the attitude of a wrestler, full of confidence, and eager for victory. It was the work of Myron, and was still seen and admired on the banks of the Eurotus in the age of

Pausanias. *Catull.* 55.—*Paus.* 2. c. 19. l. 3. c. 21. l. 8. c. 12.—*Solin.* 6.—*Antholog.* 5.—*Martial.* 10. epigr. 10.—*Juv.* 13. v. 97.

LA'DE, an island of the Ægean Sea, on the coast of Asia Minor, where a naval battle was fought between the Persians and Ionians. *Herodot.* 6. c. 7. *Paus.* 1. c. 35.—*Strab.* 17.

LADEP'SI, a people of Bithynia. *Steph.*

LA'DES, a son of Imbrasus, killed by Turnus. *Virg. Æn.* 12. v. 343.

LADISAC'ITES, a bay of the Persian Sea. *Steph.*

LADOCE'A or LADOCI'A, a village of Arcadia.

LA'DON, a river of Arcadia, falling into the Alpheus. The metamorphosis of Daphne into a laurel, and of Syrinx into a reed, happened near its banks. *Strab.* 1.—*Mela,* 2. c. 3.—*Paus.* 8. c. 25.—*Ovid. Met.* 1. v. 659.

LA'DON, an Arcadian, who followed Æneas into Italy, where he was killed by Halesus. *Virg. Æn.* 10. v. 413.

LA'DON, one of Actæon's dogs. *Ovid. Met.* 3. v. 216.

LÆ'CA M. POR'CIUS, one of Catiline's accomplices in his conspiracy. He is called Lecca by *Cicero. Cat.* 1. c. 4.—*Sall. Cat.*

LÆ'LAPS, one of Actæon's dogs. *Ovid. Met.* 3. ——The dog of Cephalus, given him by Procris. *Vid.* Lelaps. *Id. Met.* 7.

LÆ'LIA, a vestal virgin.

LÆLIA'NUS, a general proclaimed emperor by his soldiers in Gaul, A.D. 268, after the death of Gallienus. His triumph was short; he was conquered and put to death after a few months' reign by another general called Posthumus, who aspired to the imperial purple as well as himself.

LÆ'LIUS C., a Roman consul, A.U.C. 614, surnamed *Sapiens*, so intimate with Africanus the younger, that Cicero represents him in his treatise *De Amicitiâ*, as explaining the real nature of friendship, with its attendant pleasures. Like the bravest of his contemporaries, he shone in war, and distinguished himself particularly in his expedition in Spain against Viriathus. It is said, that he assisted Terence in the composition of his comedies. His modesty, humanity, and the manner in which he patronised letters, are as celebrated as his greatness of mind and integrity as a statesman. *Cic. de Orat. Off.* 2. c. 11. l. 3. c. 4.—*Horat.* 2. sat. 1. v. 72.

LÆ'LIUS, the father of the preceding, commanded the Roman fleet in the second Punic war, and was rewarded for his valor with a golden crown and thirteen oxen. *Liv.* 26. c. 42. l. 27. c. 7. l. 29. c. 1, &c.——A consul, who accompanied Scipio Africanus the elder in his campaigns in Spain and Africa.

LÆ'LIUS ARCHELA'US, a famous grammarian. *Suet. de Illustr. Gramm.*

LÆ'NA or LEÆ'NA, the mistress of Harmodius and Aristogiton. Being tortured because she refused to discover their accomplices in the conspiracy against the Pisistratidæ, she bit off her tongue, in order that she might frustrate the cruel efforts of her executioners.

LÆ'NA, a man who was acquainted with the conspiracy formed against Cæsar.

LÆ'NAS, a surname of the Popilii which they received from Marcus Popilius, who once rushed from the altar where he was offering a sacrifice, in his sacerdotal robe (*læna*), to appease a sedition. *Cic. Br.* 14.

LÆ'NEUS, a river of Crete, to which Jupiter brought Europa, whom he had carried off from Phœnicia. *Strab.*

LÆ'NIUS. *Vid.* Lenius.

LÆ'PA MAG'NA, a town of Hispania Bætica, now Lepe. *Mela,* 3. c. 1.—*Plin.* 3. c. 1.

LAER'TES, a king of Ithaca, son of Arcesius and Chalcomedusa, who married Anticlea the daughter of Autolycus. Anticlea was pregnant by Sisyphus when she married Laertes, and eight months after her union with the king of Ithaca she brought forth a son called Ulysses. *Vid.* Anticlea. Ulysses was treated with paternal affection by Laertes, though not really his son, and Laertes ceded to him his crown and retired into the country, where he spent his time in gardening. He was found in this mean employment by his son at his return from the Trojan war, after 20 years' absence, and Ulysses, at the sight of his father, whose dress and melancholy looks declared his sorrow, long hesitated whether he should suddenly introduce himself as his son, or whether he should, as a stranger, gradually awaken the paternal feelings of Laertes, who had believed that his son was no more. This last measure was preferred, and when Laertes had burst into tears at the mention which was made of his son, Ulysses threw himself on his neck exclaiming, "*O father, I am here for whom you weep.*" This welcome declaration was followed by a recital of all the hardships which Ulysses had suffered, and immediately after the father and son repaired to the palace of Penelope the wife of Ulysses, whence all the suitors who had long importuned the princess, were forcibly removed. Laertes was one of the Argonauts, according to *Apollodorus,* 1. c. 9.—*Homer. Odyss.* 11 & 24.—*Ovid. Met.* 13. v. 32. *Heroid.* 1. v. 98.—*Tzetzes in Lyc.* 344.

LAER'TES, a city of Cilicia, which gave birth to Diogenes, surnamed Laertius, from the place of his birth. *Steph.*

LAER'TIUS DIOG'ENES. *Vid.* Diogenes.

LÆSTRYG'ONES, the most ancient inhabitants of Sicily. Some suppose them to be the same as the people of Leontium, and to have been neighbours to the Cyclopes. They are reported to have fed on human flesh, and when Ulysses came on their coasts, they sank his ships, and devoured many of his companions. *Vid.* Antiphates. They were of a gigantic stature, according to Homer, who, however, does not mention their country, but only speaks of Lamus as their capital. A colony of them, as some suppose, passed over into Italy, with Lamus at their head, where they built the town of Formiæ, whence the epithet of Læstrygonia is often used for that of Formiana. *Plin.* 3. c. 5.—*Ovid. Met.* 14. v. 233, &c. *Fast.* 4. *Ex Pont.* 4. ep. 10. v. 21—*Tzetz. in Lycophr.* v. 662 & 818.—*Homer. Odyss.* 10. v. 81. & *Eustathus in Odyss.* 9.—*Sil.* 7. v. 276.

LÆ'TA, the wife of the emperor Gratian, celebrated for her humanity and generous sentiments.

LÆTO'RIA LEX, enacted that proper persons should be appointed to provide for the security and the possessions of such as were insane, or squandered away their estates. It made it a high crime to abuse the weakness of persons under such circumstances. *Cic. de Offic.* 3.

LÆTRI'NA, a city of Elis, where Pelops was buried. *Tzetz. in Lycoph.*

LÆ'TUS, a Roman whom Commodus condemned to be put to death. This cruel sentence excited Lætus against Commodus; he conspired against him, and raised Pertinax to the throne. *Lamprid. in Comm.* —*Dio. in Pertin.*——A general of the emperor Severus, put to death for his treachery to the emperor; or, according to others, on account of his popularity.——A friend of Cicero, resident at Naples. *Cic. Att.* 4. ep. 9.——A writer on Phœnicia. *Clem. Alex. Strom.* l. 1.

LÆ'VI or LE'VI, the ancient inhabitants of Gallia Transpadana. *Plin.* 3. c. 17.

LÆVI'NUS P. VALE'RIUS, a Roman consul sent against Pyrrhus, A.U.C. 474. He informed the monarch that the Romans would not accept him as an arbitrator in the war with Tarentum, and feared him not as an enemy. He was defeated by Pyrrhus.

LÆVI'NUS MAR'CUS, a Roman general in the second Punic war. He behaved with great valour, and drove the Carthaginians from Sicily. *Liv.* 23. c. 24 & 30. l. 24. c. 40. &c.—*Cic. Verr.* 3. c. 54.

LÆVI'NUS P. VAL., a man deservedly despised at Rome because he was distinguished by no good quality. *Horat.* 1. sat. 6. v. 12.

LÆ'VIUS or LÆ'LIUS, an ancient Latin poet, before the age of Cicero. Two lines of his Eratopægnia, or love games, are preserved by *Gellius. Lil. Girald. dial.* 4.—*Voss. de poet. Lat.*

LÆ'VUS CRIS'PUS, a lieutenant under Plancus, &c. *Cic. Fam.* 10. ep. 18 & 20.

LAGA'RIA, a town of Lucania, now Lagara. *Plin.* —*Strab.* 6.

LA'GIA, a name of the island Delus. *Vid.* Delus.

LAG'IDES. *Vid.* Lagus.

LAGIN'IA or LAGINI'A, a town of Caria, called Lagina by *Strabo* l. 14.—*Steph.*

LAGNU'TUM, a town of Mauritania Cæsariensis. *Ptol.*

LAGO'US, a river of Asiatic Sarmatia. *Plin.* 5. c. 32.

LA'GUS, a Macedonian of mean extraction. He received in marriage Arsinoe the daughter of Meleager, who was then pregnant by Philip king of Macedonia, and being willing to hide the disgrace of his wife, he exposed the child in the woods. An eagle preserved the life of the infant, fed him with her prey, and sheltered him with her wings against the inclemency of the air. This uncommon preservation was divulged by Lagus, who adopted the child as his own, and called him Ptolemy, conjecturing that as his life had been so miraculously preserved, his days would be spent in grandeur and affluence. This Ptolemy became king of Ægypt after the death of Alexander. According to other accounts Arsinoe was nearly related to Philip king of Macedonia, and her marriage with Lagus was not considered as dishonourable, because he was opulent and powerful. The first of the Ptolemies is called *Lagus*, to distinguish him from his successors of the same name. Ptolemy, the first of the Macedonian kings of Ægypt, wished it to be believed that he was the legitimate son of Lagus, and he preferred the patronymic of *Lagides* to all other appellations. It is even said, that he established a military order in Alexandria, which was called Lageion. The surname of Lagides was transmitted to all his descendants on the Ægyptian throne till the reign of Cleopatra, Antony's mistress. Plutarch has mentioned an anecdote, which serves to show how far the legitimacy of Ptolemy was believed in his age. A pedantic grammarian, says the historian, once displaying his knowledge of antiquity in the presence of Ptolemy, the king suddenly interrupted him with the question of, *Pray, tell me, Sir, who was the father of Peleus? Tell me*, replied the grammarian without hesitation, *tell me, if you can, O king! who the father of Lagus was?* This reflection on the meanness of the monarch's birth did not in the least excite his resentment, though the courtiers all glowed with indignation. Ptolemy praised the humour of the grammarian, and showed his moderation by taking him under his patronage. *Paus. Attic.—Justin.* 13.—*Curt.* 4.—*Plut. de Irâ. Cohib.—Lucan.* 1. v. 684.—*Ital.* 1. v. 196.——A Rutulian, killed by Pallas son of Evander. *Virg. Æn.* 10. v. 381.

LAGU'SA, an island in the Pamphylian Sea.——An island near Crete. *Strab.* 10.—*Plin.* 5. c. 31.

LAG'YRA or LAGY'RA, a city of Taurica Chersonesus. *Ptol.*

LA'IAS, a king of Arcadia who succeeded his father Cypselus, &c. *Paus.* 8. c. 5.——A king of Elis, &c.

LA'IS, a celebrated courtezan, daughter of Timandra, the mistress of Alcibiades, born at Hyccara in Sicily. She was carried away from her native country into Greece, when Nicias the Athenian general invaded Sicily. Lais resided at Corinth, where she ridiculed the austerity of philosophers, and laughed at the weakness of those who pretended to have gained a superiority over their passions. The success with which her debaucheries met at Corinth encouraged Lais to pass into Thessaly, and more particularly to enjoy the company of a favorite youth called Hippostratus. She was, however, disappointed: the women of the place, jealous of her charms, and apprehensive lest her influence and the licentiousness of her character should corrupt the fidelity of their husbands, assassinated her in the temple of Venus, about 340 years B.C. Some suppose that there were two persons of this name, a mother and her daughter. *Cic. ad Fam.* 9. ep. 26.—*Ovid. Amor.* 1. el. 5.—*Plut. in Alcib.—Paus.* 2. c. 2.—*Aul. Gell.* 1. c. 8.—*Clem. Alex.* 2.—*Athen.* 12.

LAI'ADES, a patronymic of Œdipus son of Laius. *Ovid. Met.* 6. fab. 18.

LA'IUS, a son of Labdacus, who succeeded to the throne of Thebes, which his grandfather Nycteus had left to the care of his brother Lycus, till his grandson came of age. Laius was driven from his kingdom by Amphion and Zethus, who were incensed against Lycus for the indignities which Antiope had suffered from him. He was afterwards restored, and married Jocasta the daughter of Creon. An oracle informed him that he should perish by the hand of his son, and in consequence of this dreadful intelligence he resolved never to approach his wife. A day foolishly spent in debauch and intoxication made him violate his vow, and Jocasta brought forth a son. The child as soon as born was given to a servant with orders to put him to death. The servant was moved with compassion, and only exposed him on mount Cithæron where his life was preserved by a shepherd. The child called Œdipus was educated in the court of Polybus, but an unfortunate meeting with his father in a narrow road fulfilled but too fatally the words of the oracle. Œdipus without knowing who he was, ordered his father to make way for him; Laius refused, and was instantly murdered by his irritated son. His arm-bearer or charioteer shared his fate. *Vid.* Œdipus. *Sophocl. in Œdip.—Hygin.* fab. 9 & 66.—*Diod.* 4.—*Apollod.* 3. c. 5.—*Paus.* 9. c. 5 & 26.—*Plut. de Curios.—Stat. Theb.* 1. v. 296. l. 2. v. 66.

LA'LA, a city of Armenia Major. *Ptol.*

LAL'AGE, a woman at Rome, of great beauty, beloved by the poet Horace. *Horat* 1 od. 22, &c.—*Propert.* 4. el. 7.—*Martial.* 2. epigr. 62.——A woman censured for her cruelty. *Martial.* 2. epigr. 66.

LALAS'SIS, a river of Isauria. *Plin.* 5. c. 27.

LALENE'SIS, a town of Armenia Minor. *Ptol.*

LALETA'NI, a people of Hispania Tarraconensis. *Mart.* epigr. l. 1. 50. v. 22.—*Plin.* 14. c. 6.

LALISAN'DA or DALISAN'DA, a city of Isauria. *Steph.*

LA'MA, a city of Lusitania. *Ptol.* It is now Lamegal.

LAM'ACHUS, a son of Xenophanes, sent into Sicily with Nicias. He was killed B.C. 414, before Syracuse, where he displayed much courage and intrepidity. *Plut. in Alcib.*——A governor of Heraclea in Pontus, who betrayed his trust to Mithridates, after he had invited all the inhabitants to a sumptuous feast.

LAMAL'MON, a large mountain of Æthiopia.

LAMBA'NA, a town of Mesopotamia. *Ptol.*

LAM'BE, an island of the Arabic Gulph. *Plin.* 6. c. 29.

LAMBRA'NI, a people of Insubria, near the Lambrus. *Suet. in Cæs.* c. 9.

LAMBRI'ACA or LAMBRI'CA, a town of Spain, called Flavia Lambris by *Ptolemy*.

LAM'BRUS, a river of Cisalpine Gaul, falling into the Po. *Plin.* 3. c. 16, &c.

LAMFOCTEN'SE, (*oppidum*), a town of Mauritania. *Amm. Marcell.*

LAME'TUS, a river of the Bruttii, near Croton.

LA'MIA, a town of Thessaly, at the bottom of the Sinus Maliacus or Lamiacus, and north of the river Sperchius, famous for a siege which it supported after Alexander's death. *Vid.* Lamiacum. *Diod.* 16, &c.—*Paus.* 7. c. 6.——A small river of Greece, opposite mount Œta.

LA'MIA, a daughter of Neptune, mother of Hierophile, an ancient Sibyl, by Jupiter. *Paus.* 10. c. 12.——A famous Grecian courtezan, daughter of Cleanora, and mistress to Demetrius Poliorcetes, at whose court she became particularly known by her extravagance, her intrigues, and her ascendancy over her lover's affections. She also distinguished herself as a player on the flute, and the admiration which she gained was paid no less to her personal charms, than to her wit, to the accomplishments of her mind, and to her superior skill in music and poetry. *Plut. in Dem.—Athen*, 13.—*Ælian. V. H.* 13. c. 9.——A woman of Segesta in Sicily. *Cic.* 4. *Verr*, 26.——A Roman put to death during the reign of Domitian. The names of the most illustrious persons of this family are mentioned by *Tacitus*, 6. *Ann.* 27.—*Cic. post. Red.* 6. *Sext.* 13. *Fam.* 12. ep. 19. l. 11. ep. 16 & 17.—*Horat.* 1. od. 26. v. 8. l. 1. ep. 14. v. 6 —*Juv.* 6. v. 385

LA'MIA ÆL'IUS, a prætor placed on the funeral pile before he was dead. *Plin.* 7. c. 52.

LA'MIA ÆL'IUS, a governor of Syria under Tiberius. He was honoured with a public funeral by the senate; and *Horace* dedicated his 26 od. lib. 1. to his praises, as also 3 od. 17. *Tac. Ann.* 6. c. 27.

LA'MIA and EUXE'SIA, two deities of Crete, whose worship was the same as that established at Eleusis. The Epidaurians made them two statues of an olive tree, which was given them by the Athenians, provided they came to offer a sacrifice to Minerva at Athens. *Paus.* 2. c. 30, &c.—*Herodot.* 5.

LAMI'ACUM BEL'LUM happened after the death of Alexander the Great, when the Greeks, and particularly the Athenians, incited by their orators, resolved to liberate themselves from the garrisons of the Macedonians. Leosthenes was appointed commander of a numerous force, and marched against Antipater, who then presided over Macedonia. Antipater entered Thessaly at the head of 13,000 foot and 600 horse, and was beaten by the superior force of the Athenians and of their Greek confederates. Antipater after this defeat fled to Lamia, B.C. 323, where he resolved to maintain a siege with about 8,000 or 9,000 men that had escaped with him from the field of battle. Leosthenes, unable to take the city by storm, began a regular siege His operations were, however, delayed by the frequent sallies of Antipater; and Leosthenes being killed by the blow of a stone, Antipater made his escape out of Lamia, and soon after, with the assistance of the army of Craterus brought from Asia, he gave the Athenians battle near Cranon, and though only 500 of their men were slain, yet they became so dispirited, that they sued for peace to the conqueror. Antipater, though with difficulty, consented, provided they raised taxes in the usual manner, received a Macedonian garrison, defrayed the expenses of the war, and lastly, delivered into his hands Demosthenes and Hyperides, the two orators whose prevailing eloquence had excited their countrymen against him. These severe and disadvantageous terms were accepted by the Athenians, yet Demosthenes had time to escape and poison himself. Hyperides was carried before Antipater, who ordered his tongue to be cut off, and afterwards put him to death. *Plut. in Demosth.—Diod.* 17.—*Justin.* 11, &c.

LA'MIÆ, small islands of the Ægean Sea, opposite Troas. *Plin.* 5. c. 31.

LA'MIÆ, a celebrated family at Rome, said to be descended from Lamus the king of the Læstrygones. *Hor.* 3. od. 17. v. 1. *Vid.* Lamia.——Certain monsters of Africa, who were represented as having the face and breast of a woman, and the rest of the body like that of a serpent. They allured strangers to come to them, that they might devour them, and though they were not endowed with the faculty of speech, yet their hissings were said to be pleasing and agreeable. Some believed them to be witches, or rather evil spirits, which, under the form of a beautiful woman, enticed young children and devoured them. According to some, the fable of the Lamiæ is derived from the amours of Jupiter with a certain beautiful woman called Lamia, whom the jealousy of Juno rendered deformed, and whose children she destroyed: upon which Lamia became insane, and so desperate, that she devoured all the children that came in her way. They are also called Lemures. *Vid.* Lemures. *Philostr. in Ap.—Horat. Art. Poet.* v. 340. —*Plut. de Curios.—Dion. in Libyc.—Apul.* 5. *Met.* —*Dio. in Hist. Libyc,—Gyrald. Synt.* 15.

LAM'IDA, a city of Mauritania Cæsariensis. *Ptol.*

LAMIN'IUM, a town of Hispania Tarraconensis. *Plin.* 3. c. 1.

LAMI'RUS, a son of Hercules by Iole.

LAMO'TIS, a region of Cilicia. *Ptol.*

LAM'PA or **LAP'PA**, a town of Crete, said to have been built by Agamemnon, but called after Lampus.

LAM'PAGÆ, a people of India within the Ganges. *Ptol.*

LAMPE'A or **LAMPE'US MONS**, a mountain on the frontiers of Achaia and Elis.

LAM'PEDO, a woman of Lacedæmon, who was daughter, wife, sister, and mother of a king. She lived in the age of Alcibiades. Agrippina, the mother of Claudius, could boast the same honors. *Plato in* 1 *Alc.—Plin.* 7. c. 41.—*Plut in Ages.— Tacit. Ann.* 12. c. 22 & 37.

LAMPE'SA, a city of Africa Propria. *Ptol.*

LAMPE'TIA, a daughter of Apollo and Neæra. She, with her sister Phaethusa, guarded her father's flocks in Sicily when Ulysses arrived on the coasts of that island. These flocks were fourteen in number, seven herds of oxen and seven flocks of sheep, consisting each of fifty. They fed by night as well as by day, and it was deemed unlawful and even sacrilegious to touch them. The companions of Ulysses, impelled by hunger, paid no regard to their sanctity, or to the threats and intreaties of their chief; but they carried away and killed some of the oxen. The watchful keepers complained to their father, and Jupiter, at the request of Apollo, punished the offence of the Greeks. The hides of the oxen suddenly appeared to walk, and the flesh which was roasting began to bellow, and nothing was heard but dreadful noises and loud lowings. The companions of Ulysses embarked on board their ship, but here the resentment of Jupiter followed them. A storm arose, and they all perished except Ulysses, who saved himself on the broken piece of a mast. *Homer. Odyss.* 12. v. 119.—*Propert.* 3. el. 12.—According to *Ovid. Met.* 2. v. 349, Lampetia was one of the Heliades, who was changed into a poplar tree at the death of her brother Phaethon.

LAM'PETO or **LAM'PEDO**, a queen of the Amazons, who boasted herself to be the daughter of Mars. She made extensive conquests in Asia, where she founded several cities. She was surprised afterwards by a band of barbarians, and destroyed with her female attendants. *Justin.* 2. c. 4.

LAM'PEUS, LAM'PIA, LAMPE'US or **LAMPI'A**, a mountain of Arcadia. *Stat.* 8 —*Plin.* 4. c. 6.

LAM'PON, LAM'POS, or **LAM'PUS**, one of the horses of Diomedes.

LAM'PON, one of the horses of Hector.——One of the horses of Aurora. *Homer. Il.* 8. v. 185. *Odyss.* 23. v. 246.——A horse mentioned by Italicus as swifter than the wind. *Ital.* 16. v. 367.

LAM'PON, a son of Laomedon, father of Dolops. *Homer. Il.* 5. v. 525.——A soothsayer of Athens, in the age of Socrates. *Plut. in Pericl.*

LAMPO'NIA, LAMPONI'A, or **LAMPO'NIUM**, a small city of Troas. *Herodot.* 5. c. 26.

LAMPO'NIA, an island on the coast of Thrace. *Strab.* 13.—*Plin.* 4. c. 12.

LAMPO'NIUS, an Athenian general, sent to attempt the conquest of Sicily. *Justin.* 4. c. 3.

LAM'PRÆ two municipal towns of the tribe Erechtheis. *Suidas.* They now form a village called Lambrica, inhabited by Albanian Christians. *Spon. Itin.* part. 2.

LAMPRID'IUS ÆLIUS, a Latin historian in the fourth century, who wrote the lives of the emperors Commodus, Heliogabalus, and Alexander Severus. These lives, which are still extant, may be found in the works of the *Historiæ Augustæ Scriptores.* His style is inelegant, and his arrangement injudicious. *Sax. Onom.* 1. p. 378.—*Harles Not. Lit. Rom.* 1. p. 560.—*Voss. de Hist. Lat.* 1. 2.

LAM'PRUS, a celebrated musician, &c. *C. Nep. in Epam.*

LAMP'SACE, a daughter of Mandron. *Polyæn.* 8. *Vid.* Lampsacus.

LAMP'SACUS or **LAMP'SACUM**, now Lamsaki, a town of Asia Minor, on the borders of the Propontis, at the north of Abydus. Priapus was the chief deity of the place, of which he was regarded by some as the founder. His temple there was the asylum of lewdness and debauchery, hence the epithet *Lampsacius* is used to express wantonness. Alexander, in his Asiatic expedition, resolved to destroy the city on account of the vices of its inhabitants, or more probably for its firm adherence to the interests of Persia. It was however saved from destruction by the artifice of Anaximenes. *Vid.* Anaximenes. It was formerly called Pityusa, and received the name of Lampsacus, from Lampsace, a daughter of Mandron, a king of Phrygia, who gave information to some Phoceans who dwelt there, that the rest of the inhabitants had conspired against their lives. This timely information saved them from ruin, and the city afterwards bore the name of their preserver. The wine of Lampsacus was famous, and therefore the city was allotted by Xerxes to supply the table of Themistocles with wine. *Mela*, 1. c. 19.—*Strab.* 13.—*Paus.* 9. c. 31.—*Herodot.* 5. c. 117.—*C. Nep. in Themist.* c. 10.—*Ovid.* 1. *Trist.* 9. v. 26. *Fast.* 6. v. 345.—*Liv.* 33. c. 38. l. 35. c 42.—*Mart.* 11. epigr. 17. 52.

LAMPSEMAN'DUS, an island of Caria, in the Sinus Ceramicus. *Plin.* 5. c. 31.

LAMP'SUS, part of the region of the Clazomenians. *Steph.*

LAMP'TERA, a town near Phocea in Ionia. *Liv.* 37. c. 31.

LAMPTE'RIA, a festival at Pallene in Achaia, in honor of Bacchus, who was surnamed Lampter, from λάμπειν, *to shine*, because during this solemnity, which was observed in the night, the worshippers went to the temple of Bacchus bearing lighted torches in their hands. It was also customary to place vessels full of wine in every street of the city. *Paus.* 4. c. 21.

LAM'PUS, a son of Ægyptus.——A man of Elis. ——A son of Prolaus. The name was common to some horses. *Vid.* Lampon.

LAMPYREN'SES, a curia of Attica. *Strab.* 2.

LA'MUS, a king of the Læstrygones, who is supposed by some to have founded Formiæ in Italy. The family of the Lamiæ at Rome was, according to the opinion of some, descended from him. *Horat.* 3. od. 17.——A son of Hercules and Omphale, who succeeded his mother on the throne of Lydia, but was afterwards banished and retired to Caria. He is called Laomedes by Palæphatus, and Agelaus by Apollodorus. *Ovid. Heroid.* 9. v. 54.—*Apollod.* 2.—*Diod.* 4.—*Palæph. de Inc.* 45.——A Latian chief, killed by Nisus in the Rutulian war. *Virg. Æn.* 9. v. 334.——A Spartan general, hired by Nectanebus king of Ægypt. *Diod.* 16.——A son of Neptune, founder of Formiæ, according to *Eustathius on Homer, Od.* 10.

LA'MUS, a river of Bœotia, which flowed from mount Helicon. *Paus.* 9. c. 31.——A city of Cilicia, now Lamo. *Sil. Ital. P. Bell.* 1. 8. v. 530.——A river of Cilicia; the circumjacent region was called Lamusia. *Steph.*——A town near Formiæ, built by the Læstrygones.

LAMY'RA, a city of Lycia, where C. Cæsar, grandson of Augustus, died. *Velleius.*

LAM'YRUS, *buffoon*, a surname of one of the Ptolemies.——One of the auxiliaries of Turnus, killed by Nisus. *Virg. Æn.* 9. v. 334.

LANA'RIUM, a river of Sicily. *Antonin.*

LANAS'SA, a daughter of Cleodæus, who married Pyrrhus, the son of Achilles, by whom she had eight children.—*Plut. in Pyrr.*—*Justin.* 17. c. 3. ——A daughter of Agathocles, who married Pyrrhus, whom she soon after forsook for Demetrius. *Plut.*

LAN'CIA, a town of Lusitania. *Flor.* 4. c. 12.

LANCIA'TI, a people of Austria in Spain. *Ptol.*

LAN'DI, a people of Germany, conquered by Cæsar. *Strab.* 7.

LAN'GARUS, a king of the Agriani, an ally of Alexander. *Freinshem. suppl. in Curt.* 1. c. 12.

LAN'GIA or LANGI'A, a river of Peloponnesus, falling into the bay of Corinth. *Stat. Theb.* l. 4. v. 717.

LANGIEN'SES, a people of Liguria, whose town is now Langascho. *Plin.* 3. c. 3, &c.

LAN'GO, a city of the Elei in Peloponnesus. *Plut. in Cleom.*

LANGOBAR'DI or LONGOBAR'DI, a warlike nation of Germany, along the Sprhe, called improperly Lombards by some. *Tacit. Ann.*2.c.45. *G.*40.

LANGOBRI'GA, a town of Lusitania, near the mouth of the Durius.

LANI'CE, the nurse of Alexander the Great, and sister of Clytus.

LAN'ISE, an island of the Ægæan Sea. *Plin.* 4. c. 12.

LA'NOS, a river and promontory of the Seres. *Id.* 6. c. 17.

LANU'VIUM, a town of Latium, about sixteen miles from Rome, on the Appian Road. Juno had there a celebrated temple, in which the consuls, on first entering upon office, offered sacrifices to the goddess. *Cic. pro. Mur. de Nat. D.* 1. c. 29. *Pro Milon.* 10.—*Propert.* 4. el. 8. v. 3.—*Liv.* 8. c. 14. —*Ital.* 13. v. 364.

LAOBO'TAS or LABO'TAS, a Spartan king, of the family of the Agidæ, who succeeded his father Echestratus, B.C. 1023. During his reign war was declared against Argos, by Sparta. He sat on the throne for thirty-seven years, and was succeeded by Doryssus his son. *Paus.* 3. c. 2.

LAOC'OON, a son of Priam and Hecuba, or, according to others, of Antenor or of Capys. Being priest of Apollo, he was commissioned by his countrymen to offer a bullock to Neptune to render him propitious. During the sacrifice, two enormous serpents issued from the sea, and attacked Laocoon's two sons, who stood next to the altar. The father immediately attempted to defend his sons, but the serpents falling upon him squeezed him in their complicated wreaths, so that he died in the greatest agonies. This punishment was supposed to be inflicted upon him for his temerity in dissuading the Trojans to bring into the city the fatal wooden horse, as also for his impiety in hurling a javelin against its sides as it entered within the walls. Hyginus, however, attributes his punishment to his marriage against the consent of Apollo, or, according to others, he was slain for polluting the temple of the god. The sons of Laocoon are called Antiphatus and Thymbræus by Hyginus, and by Thessander quoted by Servius, Æthron, and Melanthus. This dreadful fate of the priest of Apollo, described in so masterly a style by Virgil and Petronius, is still more familiar to the moderns, by a celebrated marble group representing the death of Laocoon and his sons, the work of Polydorus, Athenodorus, and Agesander. This famous monument was rescued from the ruins of the palace of Titus in the beginning of the 16th century, and was preserved till lately at the Farnese palace. It represents Laocoon at the very moment when the two serpents writhe themselves around him, and destroy the power of life by their mortal venom. *Virg. Æn.* 2. v. 41 & 201.—*Hygin.* fab. 135.—*Plin.* 36. c. 5.—*Servius in Æn.* 2. v. 201 & 211.—*Tzetzes in Lycoph.* 347.—*Petrodius Arbit Sat.* [The abovementioned group is now in the Museum of the Vatican.]

LAODAMAN'TIA, an island of Libya. *Steph.*

LAOD'AMAS, a son of Alcinous, king of the Phæacians, who offered to wrestle with Ulysses, while at his father's court, Ulysses, grateful for the hospitality of Alcinous, refused the challenge. *Homer. Od.* 7. v. 170.——A son of Eteocles, king of Thebes. *Paus.* 9. c. 15.

LAODAMI'A or LAODA'MIA, a daughter of Acastus and Astydamia, married Protesilaus. The departure of her husband for the Trojan war was the source of grief to her, but when she heard that he had fallen by the hand of Hector, her sorrow was greatly increased. To keep alive his memory she ordered a wooden statue to be made and regularly placed in her bed. This was seen by one of the servants, who officiously informed Iphiclus, that his daughter's bed was daily defiled by a stranger. Iphiclus watched the conduct of his daughter, and ordered the wooden image to be burned, in hopes of dissipating his daughter's grief. But he did not succeed, for Laodamia threw herself into the flames with the image and perished. The poets have feigned, that Protesilaus was restored to life, and to Laodamia, for three hours, and that when he was obliged to return to the infernal regions, he persuaded his wife to accompany him. *Virg. Æn.* 6. v. 447.—*Ovid. Her.* ep. 13.—*Hygin.* fab. 104.—*Philostr.* 2. *Ic.* 9.—*Propert.* 1. el. 19.—*Servius in Virg. loco. cit.*——A daughter of Bellerophon by Achemænia, the daughter of king Iobates. She had a son by Jupiter, called Sarpedon. She dedicated herself to the service of Diana, and hunted in her company, but her haughtiness proved fatal to her, and she perished by the arrows of the goddess. *Homer. Il.* 6. v. 197. l. 12. v. 305. l. 16. v. 419.—*Servius. Æn.* 1. v. 104.——A daughter of Alexander, king of Epirus, by Olympias, the daughter of Pyrrhus. She was assassinated in the temple of Diana, to which she had fled for safety during a sedition. *Justin.* 28. c. 3.

LAOD'ICE, a daughter of Priam and Hecuba, who became enamoured of Acamas, son of Theseus, when he came, together with Diomedes, to demand the restoration of Helen. She obtained an interview with him at the house of Philebia, the wife of a governor of a small town of Troas which the Greek ambassador had visited, and bore him a son, which he called Munitus. She afterwards married Helicaon, son of Antenor, and then Telephus, king of Mysia. Some call her Astyoche. According to the Greek scholiast of Lycophron, Laodice threw herself from the top of a tower, and was killed when Troy was sacked by the Greeks. According to Pausanias, the famous painting of the fall of Troy by Polygnotus, represented her near an altar, at some distance from the captive princes of Troy. *Dictys. Cret.* 1.—*Paus.* 13. c. 26.—*Homer. Il.* 3 & 6.—*Eustath.* 1. *Hom. Il.*—*Schol. ad Odys.* 1. v. 520.—*Parthenias*, 16.—*Tzetzes, Lycoph.* 320.——A daughter of Cyclus, mentioned by the scholiast of *Homer, Il.* 1, as the mistress of Ulysses during the Trojan war.——One of the Oceanides. ——A daughter of Cinyras, by whom Elatus had some children. *Apollod.* 3. c. 14.——A daughter of Agamemnon, called also Electra. *Homer. Il.* 9. v. 145.——A sister of Mithridates who married Ariarathes, king of Cappadocia, and afterwards her own brother Mithridates. During the secret absence of Mithridates, she prostituted herself to her servants, expecting that her husband was dead; but when she saw her hopes frustrated she attempted to poison Mithridates, for which she was put to death.——A queen of Cappadocia, put to death by her subjects for poisoning five of her children.——A sister and wife of Antiochus the Second. She put to death Berenice, whom her husband had married. *Vid.* Antiochus the Second. She was murdered by order of Ptolemy Evergetes, B.C. 246.——A daughter of Demetrius, shamefully put to death by Ammonius, the tyrannical minister of the vicious Alexander Bala, king of Syria.——A daughter of Seleucus.——The mother of Seleucus. *Justin.*—*Appian. in Syr.*

LAODICE'A, a city of Cœlesyria, called Cabiosa, or ad Libanum, and now Laudicha. *Dionys.* v. 915.——Now Ladik, a city of Asia, on the borders of Caria, Phrygia, and Lydia, celebrated for its commerce, and the fine soft and black wool of its sheep. It was originally called Diospolis, and afterwards Rhoas; and received the name of Laodicea, in honour of Laodice, the wife of Antiochus. *Plin.* 5. c. 29.—*Strab.* 12.—*Mela,* 1. c. 12.—*Cic.* 5. *Att.* 15. *Pro Flacc.*—*Ptol.* 5. c. 2.—*Spanheim de usu num, &c.*——A city of Media destroyed by an earthquake in the age of Nero. *Coloss.* 4. v. 15.—*Plin.* 5. c. 20.—*Strab.* 11, &c.——A city of Syria, on the shores of the Phœnician Sea, founded by Seleucus. *Strab.* 11, &c.—*Tac. Ann.* 2. c. 79, &c.

LAODICE'NE, a province of Syria, which received its name from Laodicea, its capital.

LAOD'OCUS, a son of Antenor, whose form Minerva assumed to advise Pandarus to break the treaty which subsisted between the Greeks and Trojans. *Homer. Il.* 4, v. 87.——An attendant of Antilochus. *Homer. Il.* 17. v. 699.——A son of Priam. *Apollod.* 3. c. 12.——A son of Apollo and Phthia. *Id.* 1. c. 7.

LAOG'ONUS, a son of Bias, brother to Dardanus, killed by Achilles at the siege of Troy. *Homer. Il.* 20. v. 460.——A priest of Jupiter, killed by Merion in the Trojan war. *Homer. Il.* 16. v. 604.

LAOG'ORAS, a king of the Dryopes, who accustomed his subjects to live by rapine. He plundered the temple of Delphi, and was killed by Hercules. *Apollod.* 2. c. 7.—*Diod.* 4.

LAOG'ORE, a daughter of Cinyras and Metharme, daughter of Pygmalion. She died in Ægypt. *Apollod.* 3. c. 14.

LAOM'EDON, son of Ilus king of Troy, married Strymo, called by some Placia, or Leucippe, by whom he had Podarces, afterwards better known by the name of Priam, and Hesione. He built the walls of Troy, in which work he was assisted by Apollo and Neptune, whom Jupiter had banished from heaven, and condemned to serve Laomedon for one year. When the walls were finished, Laomedon refused to reward the labours of the gods, and his territories were soon after laid waste by the god of the sea, and his subjects were visited by a pestilence sent by Apollo. Sacrifices were offered to the offended divinities, but the calamities of the Trojans increased, and nothing could appease the gods, according to the words of the oracle, but annually to expose to a sea monster a Trojan virgin. Whenever the monster appeared the marriageable maidens were assembled, and the lot decided which of them was to be doomed to death for the good of her country. When this calamity had continued for five or six years, the lot fell upon Hesione, Laomedon's daughter. The king was unwilling to part with a daughter whom he loved with uncommon tenderness, but he was sensible that his refusal would excite more strongly the wrath of the gods. In the midst of his fears and hesitations, Hercules offered to deliver the country from this calamity, if Laomedon would promise to reward him with a number of fine horses. The king consented, but when the monster was destroyed, he refused to fulfil his engagements, and Hercules besieged Troy and took it. Laomedon was put to death, after a reign of 29 years, his daughter Hesione was given in marriage to Telamon, one of the conqueror's attendants, and Podarces, was ransomed by the Trojans, and placed upon his father's throne. According to Hyginus, the wrath of Neptune and Apollo was kindled against Laomedon, because he refused to offer on their altars, as a sacrifice, all the first born of his cattle, accoding to a vow which he had made. *Homer. Il.* 6. v. 23. l. 21, &c.—*Scholiast. ad Il.* 3. v. 250.—*Philostr.* 11. c. 3.—*Tzetzes. in Lyc.* 617.—*Servius, Æn.* 1. v. 554 & 623, &c.—*Virg. Æn.* 2 & 9.—*Ovid. Met.* 11. fab. 6.—*Apollod.* 2. c. 5.—*Paus.* 7. c. 20.—*Horat.* 3. od. 3.—*Hygin.* 89.——A turbulent demagogue, who, in the 2d year of the 95th Olympiad, excited his fellow citizens against Dionysius.——A satrap of Phœnicia, &c. *Curt.* 10. c. 10.——An Athenian, &c. *Plut.*——An Orchomenian. *Id.*

LAOMEDONTE'US or LAOMEDON'TEUS, an epithet applied to the Trojans from Laomedon. *Virg. Æn.* 4. v. 542. l. 7. v. 105. l. 8. v. 18.

LAOMEDON'TIA, the ancient name of Lampsacus. *Steph.*

LAOMEDONTI'ADÆ, a patronymic given to the Trojans from Laomedon their king. *Virg. Æn.* 2. v. 248.

LAON'OME, the wife of Polyphemus one of the Argonauts.

LAONOME'NE, a daughter of Thespius, by whom Hercules had two sons, Teles and Menippides, and two daughters, Lysidice and Stentedice. *Apollod.* 2. c. 7.

LAOR'IPA, a village in Libya. *Ptol.*

LAOS'THENES, a king of Assyria, A.M. 3029, reigned 45 years. *Euseb in Chron.*

LAOTH'OE, a daughter of Altes, a king of the Leleges, who married Priam, and became mother of Lycaon and Polydorus. *Homer Il.* 21. v. 85.——One of the daughters of Thespius, mother of Antidus, by Hercules. *Apollod.* 2. c. 7.

LAO'US, a river of Laconia.

LAP'ATHUS, a castle on the borders of Epirus and Thessaly. *Liv.* 42. c. 2.——A city of Crete, called Lapethus by *Pliny,* 5. c. 31.—*Strab.* 14.

LAPA'TIA CO'RI or TRILEU'CUM, a promontory of Hispania Tarraconensis. *Ptol.*

LAPER'SA, a mountain of Laconia. *Steph.*

LAPE'THUS, a mountain of Cyprus. *Id.*

LAPH'AES, a statuary who made a statue of Hercules for the people of Sicyon, and one of Apollo for the Ægirites. *Paus.* 7. c. 26.

LAPH'RIA or LA'PHRIA, a surname of Diana at Patræ in Achaia, where she had a temple with a statue of gold and ivory which represented her in the habit of a huntress. The statue was made by Menechmus and Soidas, two artists of great celebrity. This name was given to the goddess from Laphrius, the son of Delphus, who consecrated the statue to her. There was also a festival of the goddess celebrated there called Laphria, of which *Pausanias,* 7. c. 18, gives an account.

LAPH'YRA, an epithet of Minerva, from λάφυρα, *spoils.*

LAPHYS'TIUM or LAPHYS'TIUS, a mountain in Bœotia, where Jupiter had a temple, whence he was called *Laphystius.* Bacchus was also called *Laphystius* from the temple which he had on mount Laphystium, and his priestesses were in consequence often called Laphystides. *Paus.* 9. c. 34.—*Tzetzes. Lyc.* 1327.

LA'PIS, a surname of Jupiter among the Romans, either in allusion to the stone which Rhea gave to Saturn, and which he devoured instead of Jupiter, or from the stone which those who made an oath by Jupiter held in their hand. The god was on those occasions invoked with the greatest solemnity, and the person who swore entreated him to banish him from his possessions, in the same manner as he threw away the stone from his hand. *Aul. Gell.* 1. c. 21.—*Hygin.* fab. 139.—*Tzetzes ad Lyc.* 399.—*Festus de V. Sig.*——A king of Crete.

LAP'ITHÆ, a people of Thessaly. *Vid.* Lapithes.

LAP'ITHÆ, a mountain of Laconia. *Steph.*

LAPITHÆ'UM, a town on mount Taygetus. *Paus.* 3. c. 20.

LAP'ITHES, a son of Apollo, by Stilbe. He was brother to Centaurus, and married Orsinome, daughter of Euronymus, by whom he had Phorbas and Periphas. The name of Lapithæ was given to the numerous children of Phorbas and Periphas, or rather to the inhabitants of the country of which they had obtained the sovereignty. The chief of the Lapithæ assembled to celebrate the nuptials of Pirithous, one of their number, and among them were Theseus, Dryas, Hopleus, Mopsus, Phalerus, Exadius, Prolochus, Titaresius, Œneus, &c. The Centaurs were also invited to share in the common festivity, ond the meeting would have passed away in innocent mirth, had not one of the intoxicated Centaurs offered violence to Hippodamia, the betrothed wife of Pirithous. The Lapithæ resented the injury, and the Centaurs supported their companions, upon which the quarrel became universal, and ended in blows and mutual slaughter. Many of the Centaurs were slain, and they at last were obliged to retreat. Among the Lapithæ, Theseus and Nestor shewed themselves brave and intrepid in supporting the cause of their friends. This quarrel is said to have arisen from the resentment of Mars, whom Pirithous neglected to invite among the other gods, at the celebration of his nuptials, and, therefore, the divinity punished the insult by sowing dissension among the festive assembly. Hesiod has described the battle of the Centaurs and Lapithæ, as also Ovid, in a more copious manner. The invention of bits and bridles for horses is attributed to the Lapithæ. *Virg. G.* 3. v. 115. *Æn.* 6. v. 601. l. 7. v. 305.—*Ovid. Met.* 12. v. 530. l. 14. v. 670.—*Hesiod in Sout.*—*Diod.* 4.—*Pind.* 2 *Pyth.*—*Strab.* 9.—*Stat, Theb.* 7. v. 304.—*Hygin.* fab. 33. —*Scholiast Apollon. Arg.* 3.—*Servius ad Virg. locis cit.*

LAP'PA, an inland city of Crete. *Ptol.*

LAP'SIAS, a river of Bithynia. *Plin.* 5. c. 32.

LAR or **LARS**, a name applied to the kings of Etruria, probably to express their rank and dignity. *Liv.* 2. c. 9. l. 4. c. 17.—*Cic. Phil.* 9. c. 9.

LA'RA or **LARUN'DA**, one of the Naiads, daughter of the river Almon in Latium. She revealed to Juno the amours of her husband Jupiter with Juturna, for which the god cut off her tongue, and ordered Mercury to conduct her to the infernal regions. The messenger of the gods fell in love with her by the way, and gratified his passion. Lara became mother of two children, to whom the Romans paid divine honors, under the name of Lares. *Ovid. Fast.* 2. v. 599.—*Lactant.* 1. c. 20. 35.—*Varro, L. L.* 4. c. 10.

LARAN'DA, a city of Lycaonia. *Ptol.* 5. c. 6.

LARA'RIA, festivals in honor of the Lares, celebrated in December. *Macrob. Sat.* 1. c. 10.

LARAS'SA, a city of Media. *Ptol.*

LARENDA'NI, a people of Arabia Felix. *Plin.* 6. c. 28.

LAREN'TIA or **LAUREN'TIA**. *Vid.* Acca.

LA'RES, gods of inferior power at Rome, who presided over houses and families. They were two in number, sons of Mercury by Lara. *Vid.* Lara. In process of time their power was extended, not only over houses, but also over the country and the sea, and we find Lares *Urbani* to preside over the cities, *Familiares* over houses, *Rustici* over the country, *Compitales* over cross ways, *Marini* over the sea, *Viales* over the roads, *Patellarii, &c.* According to the opinion of some authors, the worship of the gods Lares, who are supposed to be the same as the Manes, arose from the ancient custom among the Romans and other nations, of burying their dead in their habitations, and from their belief that the departed spirit continually hovered over the houses, for the protection of its inhabitants. The statues of the Lares resembling monkeys, and covered with the skin of a dog, were placed in a niche behind the doors of the houses, or around the hearths. At the feet of the Lares was the figure of a dog in the act of barking, to intimate their care and vigilance. Incense was burnt on their altars, and a sow was also offered to them on particular days. Their festivals were observed at Rome in the month of May, when their statues were crowned with garlands of flowers, and offerings of fruit presented. The word Lares seems to be derived from the Etruscan word *Lars* which signifies conductor, or leader. *Ovid. Fast.* 5. v. 129 —*Juv.* 8. v. 8.—*Plut. in Quæst. Rom.*—*Varro de L. L.* 4. c. 10.—*Horat.* 3. od. 23.—*Plaut in Aul.*, *& Cist.* [There are innumerable representations of these deities; chiefly small bronze figures, of no peculiar merit in the workmanship. But there are also heads of better character. One of the best will be found in the possession of the Earl of Egremont.]

La'res, a city of Africa Propria. *Ptol.*

LAR'GA, a well-known prostitute at Rome in Juvenal's age. *Juv.* 4. v. 25.

LAR'GUS, a surname of the family of the Scribonii. *Cic. Fam.* 6. ep. 8. *Or.* 2. c. 59.——A Latin poet, who wrote a poem on the arrival of Antenor in Italy, where he built the town of Padua. *Ovid ex Pont.* 4. ep. 16. v. 17.—*Gyrald. de P. H.* 4.

LARIAG'ARA, a city of India without the Ganges. *Ptol.*

LARI'CES, a people of India within the Ganges. *Id.*

LARI'DES, a son of Daucus or Daunus, who assisted Turnus against Æneas, and had his hand cut off at one blow by Pallas the son of Evander. *Virg. Æn.* 10. v. 391.

LARI'NA, a virgin of Italy, who accompanied Camilla in her war against Æneas. *Virg. Æn.* 11. v. 655.

Lari'na, a fountain of Attica. *Plin.* 4. c. 7.

LARI'NUM or **LARI'NA**, now Larino, a town of the Frentani, on the Tifernus, before it falls into the Adriatic. The inhabitants were called Larinates. *Ital.* 15. v. 565.—*Cic. Clu.* 63. 4 *Att.* 12. l. 7. ep. 13.—*Liv.* 22. c. 18. l. 27. c. 40.—*Cæs, C.* 1. c. 23.

LAR'ISE, a city of Æolia. *Herod. in vit. Hom.* c. 11.

LARIS'SA, a daughter of Pelasgus, who gave her name to some cities in Greece. *Paus.* 2. c. 23.

Laris'sa, a city between Palestine and Ægypt, where Pompey was murdered and buried, according to some accounts.——A large city on the banks of the Tigris. It had a small pyramid near it, greatly inferior to those of Ægypt.——A city of Asia Minor, on the southern confines of Troas. *Strab.* 13.——A city in Æolia, seventy stadia from Cyme. It is surnamed Phriconis, by Strabo, by way of distinction. *Strab.* 13.—*Homer. Il.* 2. v. 640.——A city near Ephesus.——A city on the borders of the Peneus in Thessaly, also called Cremaste, from its situation (*Pensilis*), the most famous of all the cities of that name. It was here that Acrisius was inadvertently killed by his grandson Perseus. Jupiter had there a famous temple, on account of which he is called Larissæus. The same epithet is also applied to Achilles, who reigned there. It is still extant, and bears the same name. *Ovid. Met.* 2. v. 542.—*Virg. Æn.* 2. v. 197. —*Lucan.* 6.—*Liv.* 31. c. 46. l. 42. c. 56.——A city of Syria, on the river Orontes.——The citadel of Argos, built by Danaus. *Strab.* 9.

LARISSÆ'US. *Vid.* Larissa.

LARIS'SUS or **LARI'SUS**, a river of Peloponnesus, which flows between Elis and Achaia. *Strab.* 8.—*Liv.* 27. c. 33.—*Paus.* 8. c. 43.

LA'RIUS, a large lake of Cisalpine Gaul, at the north of Insubria, through which the Addua runs in its way into the Po, above Cremona. It is now Lago di Como. *Virg. G.* 2. v. 159.

LAR'NUM, a river of Hispania Tarraconensis, flowing from the Pyrenees, and now Larno. *Plin.* 3. c. 3.

LAR'NUS, a small desolate island on the coast of Thrace. *Id.* 4. c. 12.

LARO'NIA, a shameles courtezan in Juvenal's age. *Juv.* 2. v. 86.

LARS. *Vid.* Lar.

Lars Tolum'nius, a king of the Veientes, conquered by the Romans, and put to death, A.U.C. 329. *Liv.* 4. c. 17 & 19.

LARTID'IUS, a name expressive of cunning, and said to be derived from Ulysses son of Laertes, or from some noted knave of that name at Rome. *Cic.* 7. *Att* 1.

T. LAR'TIUS FLA'VUS, a consul who appeased a sedition raised by the poorer citizens, and was the first dictator ever chosen at Rome, B.C. 498. He made Spurius Cassius his master of the horse. *Liv.* 2. c. 18.

Lar'tius Spu'rius, one of the three brave Romans who withstood the fury of Porsenna's army at the head of a bridge, while the communication was cutting down behind them. His companions were Cocles and Herminius. *Vid.* Cocles. *Liv.* 2. c. 10 & 18.—*Dionys. Hal.* 5.—*Plut. in Par.* 8.—*Servius. in Æn.* 11. v. 642.—*Val. Max.* 3. c. 2. The name of Lartius was common to many Romans.

LARTOLÆÆ'TÆ or **LÆÆTA'NI**, a people of Hispania Tarraconensis. *Strab.* 3.

LARUNE'SIÆ, an island of the African Sea, now Mollicolno. *Ptol.*

LAR'VÆ, a name given to those spirits, which, according to the superstitious notions of the Romans, issued from their graves in the night, and came to terrify the world. The name is derived from *Larva*, a mask. Some call them Lemures. *Apuleius de Deo. Soc.*—*Aug. de Civ. Dei.* 9. c. 11.—*Servius in Virg. Æn.* 3. v. 64, &c.

LARYM'NA, a town of Bœotia, where Bacchus had a temple and a statue.——A town in Achaia. *Strab.* 9 & 16.—*Paus.* 9. c. 23.—*Mela.* 1. c. 16. l. 2. c. 3.

LARYS'IUM a mountain of Laconia. *Paus.* 3. c. 22.

LAS, a city of Laconia, now Lasa. *Schol. in Lycoph.* —*Paus.*

LASÆ'A, the name of a city, probably in Crete. *Plin.* 4. c. 12.—*Act. Apost.* 27. v. 8.

LASCORI'A, a city of Galatia. *Ptol.*

LAS'ICE, a city of Africa Propria. *Ptol.*

LA'SOS, an inland city of Crete. *Plin.* 4. c. 12.

LAS'SIA, an ancient name of the island of Andrus. *Plin.* 5. c. 12.

LAS'SIO, a city of Triphylia. *Diod. Sic.* 5.

LA'SION, a town in Elis, the constant source of dispute between the Elians and Arcadians.

LAS-IP'PA, a city of India. *Ptol.*

LAS'SUS or LA'SUS, a dithyrambic poet born at Hermione in Peloponnesus, about 500 B.C., and reckoned among the wise men of Greece by some authors. He was also acquainted with music. Some fragments of his poetry are to be found in Athenæus. He wrote an ode upon the Centaurs, and a hymn to Ceres without inserting the letter S in the composition. *Athen.* 8.—*Vossius. de P. Gr.* 4.—*Gyrald. P. Hist.* 9.

LASTHENES, a governor of Olynthus, corrupted by Philip king of Macedonia.——A Cretan demagogue conquered by Metellus the Roman general. ——A cruel minister at the court of the Seleucidæ. kings of Syria.

LASTHENI'A or LASTHE'NIA, a woman who disguised herself in male attire, that she might attend Plato's lectures. *Diog. Laert.* 3.

LASTI'GI, a town of Hispania Bætica. *Plin.* 3. c. 1.

LA'SUS, a Greek lyric poet, native of Hermione in Argolis.

LAT'AGUS, a king of Pontus who assisted Æetes against the Argonauts, and was killed by Darapes. *Flacc.* 5. v. 584. l 6. v. 573.——One of the companions of Æneas, killed by Mezentius. *Virg. Æn.* 10. v. 697.

LATAME'DA, a river of India without the Ganges. *Ptol.*

LATA'NIA, a town of Bithynia. *Id.*

LATERA'NUS PLAU'TUS, a Roman consul elect A.D. 65. A conspiracy with Piso against the emperor Nero proved fatal to him. He was led to execution, when he would not disclose the names of his associates. When the first blow did not sever his head from his body, he looked at the executioner, and shaking his head he replaced it on the block with the greatest composure, and it was cut off. There exists now a celebrated palace at Rome, which derives its name from its ancient possessors, the Laterani. *Tacit. Ann.* 15. c. 49 & 60.—*Juv.* 10. c. 17.—*Arrian.* 1. c. 1.

LAT'ERA STAG'NUM, a lake in Gallia Narbonensis, with a fortress of the same name.

LATEREN'SIS M., a friend of Cicero, of strong republican principles. He bore some of the offices of the state, and killed himself rather than join the party of Antony with Lepidus. *Cic. Fam.* 8. ep. 8. l. 10. ep. 21 & 23. *Att.* 2. ep. 18. *Planc.* 1. *Vat.* 11.

LATE'RIUM, a villa belonging to Q. Cicero at Arpinum. *Cic. ad Attic.* 10. ep. 1. l. 4. ep. 7. *Ad. fr.* 3. ep. 1.—*Plin.* 15. c. 15.

LA'THON, LE'THON, LE'THES or LETHÆ'US, a river in Africa, falling into the Lacus Hesperidum.

LATIA'LIS, a surname of Jupiter, who was worshipped by the inhabitants of Latium upon mount Albanus at stated times. The festivals, which were first instituted by Tarquin the Proud, lasted fifteen days. *Liv.* 21. c. 63.—*Dionys. Hal.* 4. c. 49.—— *Vid.* Feriæ Latinæ.

LATIA'RIS. *Vid.* Latinius.

LATI'NI, the inhabitants of Latium. *Vid.* Latium.

LATIN'IUS LATIA'RIS, a celebrated informer, at the court of Tiberius. To gratify the passions of Sejanus he procured the destruction of Sabinus, and on the fall of his patron, he met the punishment which his profligate conduct deserved. *Tac. Ann.* 4. c. 68. l. 6. c. 4.

LATI'NUS the First, a son of Faunus by Marica, king of the Aborigines in Italy, who from him were called Latini. He married Amata, by whom he had a son and a daughter. The son died in his infancy, and the daughter, called Lavinia, was secretly promised in marriage by her mother to Turnus king of the Rutuli. The gods opposed this meditated union, and the oracles declared that Lavinia must become the wife of a foreign prince. The arrival of Æneas in Italy seemed favorable to this prediction, and Latinus offered his daughter to the foreign prince. Turnus, however, claimed Lavinia as his lawful wife, and prepared to support his cause by arms. In the contest which ensued, Æneas obtained the victory, and married Lavinia. Latinus soon after died, and was succeeded by his son-in-law on the throne of Latium. *Virg. Æn.* 9, &c.—*Ovid. Met.* 13. v. 613. l. 14. v. 449. *Fast.* 2. v. 544. l. 6. v. 601.—*Dionys. Hal.* 1. c. 13.—*Liv.* 1. c. 1, &c.—*Justin.* 43. c. 1.

LATI'NUS the Second, was a son of Sylvius Æneas, and was also surnamed Sylvius. He was the fifth king of the Latins, and succeeded his father. *Dionys.* 1. c. 15.—*Liv.* 2. c. 3.

LATI'NUS, a son of Ulysses and Circe. *Serv. Æn.* 7. v. 47. l. 12. v. 164.

LATI'NUS PACA'TUS, an orator of Drepanum, A.D. 389.

LA'TIUM, a country of Italy on the east of the river Tiber. It originally extended from the Tiber to Circeii, but afterwards comprehended the territories of the Volsci, Æqui, Hernici, Ausones, Umbri, and Rutuli. The first inhabitants were called Aborigines, and received the name of Latini from Latinus, one of their kings. According to others, the word is derived from *lateo, to conceal*, because Saturn concealed himself there when he fled from the resentment of his son Jupiter. Laurentum was the capital of the country in the reign of Latinus; Lavinium under Æneas, and Alba under Ascanius. *Vid.* Alba. The Latins rose into consequence when Romulus had founded the city of Rome in their country. *Virg. Æn.* 7. v. 38. l. 8. v. 322.—*Strab.* 5.—*Dionys. Hal.* 3. c. 10. l. 4. c. 7. l. 6. c. 1. —*C. Nepos. in Att.* 4.—*Varro. de L. L.* 4. c. 5.—*Servius in Æn. locis. cit.*—*Justin.* 20. c. 1.—*Plut. in Romul.*—*Plin.* 3. c. 12.—*Tacit.* 4. *Ann.* 5.

LA'TIUS, a surname of Jupiter at Rome. *Stat.* 5. *Sylv.* 2. v. 292.

LAT'MICUS SI'NUS, a gulf of Ionia, into which the Mæander fell.—It is now an inland lake.

LAT'MUS, a mountain of Caria, near Miletus. It was the residence of Endymion, whence he is often called *Latmius Heros.* *Vid.* Endymion. *Mela,* 1. c. 17.—*Ovid. Trist.* 2. v. 299. *Art. Am.* 3. v. 83. —*Plin.* 5. c. 29.—*Strab.* 14.—*Cic.* 1. *Tus.* 28.—*Val. Flacc.* 8. v. 28.

LATO'BIUS, the god of health among the Corinthians.

LATOBRI'GI or LATOB'RIGI, a people of Belgic Gaul. *Cæs. B. G.* 1. c. 2 & 7.

LATO'IS, a name of Diana, as being the daughter of Latona.

LATO'IS, a country house near Ephesus. *Athen.* 1. c. 4.

LATO'MIÆ. *Vid.* Lautumiæ.——A place of Latium, between Rome and Præneste. *Liv.* 26. c. 27.

LATO'NA, a daughter of Cœus the Titan and Phœbe, or, according to Homer, of Saturn, was beloved by Jupiter. Juno, always jealous of her husband's amours, sent the serpent Python to persecute her. Latona wandered from place to place in the time of her pregnancy, continually alarmed for fear of Python. She was driven from heaven, and Terra, influenced by Juno, refused to give her a place where she might bring forth. Neptune, however, moved with compassion for her misfortunes, struck the island of Delus with his trident, and made it immoveable. Latona, changed into a quail by Jupiter, came to Delus, where she resumed her original shape, and leaning against the trunk of a palm or olive tree, gave birth to Apollo and Diana. Juno, however, soon discovered the place of her retreat, and obliged her to leave the island. She wandered over the greatest part of the world, and in Caria, where her fatigue compelled her to stop, she was insulted by some peasants of whom she asked for water, while they were weeding a marsh. Their refusal and insolence provoked her, and she entreated Jupiter to punish their barbarity, upon which they were all changed into frogs by the avenging god. She was afterwards exposed to repeated insults by Niobe, who boasted herself greater than the mother of Apollo and Diana, and ridiculed the presents which the piety of her neighbours had offered to Latona. *Vid.* Niobe. Her beauty proved fatal to the giant Tityus, whom Apollo and Diana put to death. *Vid.* Tityus. At last, Latona, though persecuted and exposed to the resentment of Juno, became a powerful deity, and saw her children receive divine honors. Her worship was generally established where her children received adoration, particularly at Argos, Delus, &c. where she had temples. She had an oracle in Ægypt, celebrated for the true and decisive answers which it gave. *Diod.* 5.—*Herodot.* 2. c. 155.—*Homer. Il.* 21. *Hymn. in Ap. & Dian.*—*Hesiod. Theog.* 405.—*Apollod.* 3. c. 5 & 10.—*Juv.* 6. v. 175. *Sat.* 10. v. 292.—*Athen.* 10.—*Lucian. Dial. Nept & Irid.*—*Serv. in Æn.* 3. v. 72 & 91.—*Horat.* 4. od. 6.—*Paus.* 2. c. 21. l. 8. c. 53,—*Herodot.* 2. c. 59 & 155.—*Ovid. Met.* 6. v. 160 & 185.—*Hygin.* fab. 140.

LATOP'OLIS. or LA'TO, a city of Ægypt. *Strab.*

LATO'RUM. a city of Ægypt. *Ptol.*

LATOVI'CI, a people of Pannonia. *Plin.* 3. c. 25.

LATO'US, a name given to Apollo as son of Latona. *Ovid. Met.* 6. fab. 9.—*Paus. in Achaic.*

LA'TREUS, one of the Centaurs, who, after killing Halesus, was himself slain by Cœneus. *Ovid. Met.* 12. v. 463.

LA'TRIS, an auxiliary of Perses against Æetes. *Flacc. Argon.* 6. v. 121.

La'tris, an island of Germany, at the mouth of the Vistula. *Plin.* 4. c. 13

LATU'RUS, a bay of the Libyan Sea. *Mela,* 1. c. 6.

LATUSA'TES, a people of Gallia Aquitanica. *Plin.* 4. c. 19.

LATYM'NUM, a mountain of Croton, or, according to others, of Laconia. It is now Monte di Crotone. *Schol. Theocr.*

LA'UD, a river of Mauritania Tingitana. *Plin.* 5. c. 2.

LAU'DA or LAU'DUM, a city of the Insubres. *Strab.* 5.

LAUDAMI'A, a daughter of Alexander king of Epirus and Olympias daughter of Pyrrhus, killed in the temple of Diana by the enraged populace. Her murderer, called Milon, soon after became so furious that he stabbed himself and died in 12 days. *Justin.* 28. c. 3.——The wife of Protesilaus. *Vid.* Laodamia.

LAU'DIA, a town of Mauritania Cæsariensis. *Ptol.*

LAUDI'CE. *Vid.* Laodice.

LAUFEL'LA, a wanton woman, &c. *Juv.* 6. v. 319.

LAU'GASA, a town of Armenia Minor. *Ptol.*

LAU'RA, a place near Alexandria in Ægypt. *Athen.* l. 12.——A city of Sicily. *Isac. in Lycoph.*

LAU'REA TUL'LIUS, a freedman of Cicero, who wrote epigrams and other trifling pieces, commended for their ease and elegance, and in which he celebrated the liberality and the praises of his patron. Only 10 verses are preserved of his compositions. *Cic. in Epist.*—*Plin.* 31. c. 2.

LAURENTA'LIA, certain festivals celebrated at Rome in honor of Laurentia on the last day of April, and on the 23d of December. They formed in process of time, part of the Saturnalia. *Ovid. Fast.* 3. v. 57.

LAUREN'TES A'GRI, the country in the neighbourhood of Laurentum. *Tibull.* 2. el. 5. v. 41.

LAUREN'TIA. *Vid.* Acca.

LAURENTI'NI, the inhabitants of Latium. They received this name from the great number of laurels which grew in the country. King Latinus found one of uncommon size and beauty, when he was going to build a temple to Apollo, and the tree was consecrated to the god, and preserved with the most religious care. *Virg. Æn.* 7. v. 59.—*Servius in Æn.* 1. v. 2. l. 7. v. 661 & 678.

LAUREN'TIUS, belonging to Laurentum or Latium. *Virg Æn.* 10. v. 709.

LAUREN'TUM, now S. Lorenzo, the capital of the kingdom of Latium in the reign of Latinus. It was situated on the sea coast, a few miles east of the mouth of the Tiber. *Vid.* Laurentini. *Strab.* 5.—*Mela,* 2. c. 4.—*Liv.* 1. c. 1.—*Virg. Æn.* 7. v. 171.

LAURE'OLUS, a noted robber, who was crucified and then devoured by wild beasts. *Mart. in Amphith.* epigr. 7.

LAURI'ACUM or LAURE'ACUM, a town at the confluence of the Ens and the Danube, now Lorch.

LAU'RIUM, a place of Attica, where there were gold mines, from which the Athenians drew considerable revenues, and which enabled them to build a fleet, according to the advice of Themistocles. These mines failed before the age of Strabo. *Thucyd.* 2.—*Paus.* 1. c. 1.—*Strab.* 9.

LAU'RON, a town of Spain, now Laurigi, where Pompey's son was conquered by Cæsar's army. *Plut. in Sertor.*

LA'US, a city of Lucania. *Plin.* 3. c. 5.——Now Laino, a town on a river of the same name, which forms the southern boundary of Lucania. *Strab.* 6.

La'us Pompe'ia, now Lodi, a town of Italy so called from a colony sent thither by Pompey. It was founded by the Boii. *Plin.* 17. c. 13.

LAU'SUS, a son of Numitor, and brother of Ilia. He was put to death by his uncle Amulius, who usurped his father's throne. *Ovid. Fast.* 4. v. 54.——A son of Mezentius, king of the Tyrrhenians, remarkable for the gentleness of his character, which formed a striking contrast with the violence of his father's, and for his skill and dexterity in the management of arms, and in all military evolutions. He was killed by Æneas. *Virg Æn.* 7. v. 649. l. 10. v. 426, &c.

LAU'TIUM, a city of Latium. *Dion. Hal. Hist. Rom.* 5.

LAUTU'MIÆ or LATO'MIÆ, a prison at Syracuse cut out of the solid rock by Dionysius the tyrant, and now converted into a subterraneous garden. *Cic. Ver.* 5. c. 27.—*Liv.* 26. c. 27. l. 32. c. 26.

LAV'ARA, a large town of Lusitania, now Aveiro, *Ptol.*

LAVER'NA, the goddess of thieves and dishonest persons at Rome. She not only presided over robbers, called from her Laverniones, but protected those who were guilty of fraud. Her worship was very popular, and she had an altar near one of the gates of the city, which, from that circumstance, was called the gate of Laverna. She was generally represented by a head without a body. *Horat.* 1. ep. 16. v. 66.—*Varro de L. L.* 4 —*Auson.* ep. 4.—*Plaut. Aul.* 2. act. v. 31. *In Frag. Cornic.*—*Festus de V. Sig.*—*Rosin. Antiq. R.* 2. c. 19.

Laver'na, a place mentioned by *Plutarch, in Sylla,* &c.

LAVER'NIUM, a temple of Laverna, near Formiæ. *Cic.* 7. *Att.* 8.

LAVIN'IA, a daughter of Latinus by Amata, was betrothed to her relation Turnus, but was given to Æneas after the death of Turnus. *Vid.* Latinus. At her husband's death she was left pregnant, and being apprehensive of ill treatment from Ascanius her son-in-law, she fled into the woods, where she brought forth a son called Æneas Sylvius. *Dionys. Hal.* 1.—*Virg. Æn.* 6. v. 760. l. 7. v. 51.—*Servius locis. & Æn.* 4. v. 236.—*Ovid. Met.* 14. v. 507. *Fast.* 3. v. 629.—*Liv.* 1. c. 1.

LAVIN'IUM or LAVI'NUM, a town of Italy, built by Æneas, and called by that name in honor of Lavinia. It was the capital of Latium during the reign of Æneas, and was situated on the coast of the Tyrrhene Sea, near the mouth of the Numicus. It is now Citta Lavinia. *Virg. Æn.* 1. v. 6, 262 & 274.—*Servius in locis.*—*Strab.* 5.—*Dionys. Hal.* 1.—*Liv.* 1. c. 2.—*Justin.* 43. c. 2.

LAX'TA, a city of the Celtiberi, in Spain. *Ptol.*

LA'ZI, a people of Scythia. *Plin.* 6. c. 4. *Stephanus* places them in Themiscyra, on the Euxine Sea.

LE'A, a town of Upper Æthiopia. *Plin.* 4. c. 12.

LE'ADES, a son of Astacus, who killed Eteoclus. *Apollod.*

LE'Æ, a city of Africa Propria. *Ptol.*

LEÆ'I, a nation of Pæonia in Macedonia. *Thucyd.* l. 2.

LEÆ'NA. *Vid.* Læna.

LEAN'DER, a youth of Abydus, celebrated for his unfortunate amours with Hero. *Vid.* Hero.

Lean'der or Lean'drius, a Milesian, who wrote an historical commentary upon his country. *Clem. Strom.* 1.—*Diog. Laert. in Thalet.*

Lean'der, a writer of Cyrene.—*Suidas.*—*Voss. H. Gr.* l. 2. c. 12,

LEAN'DIS, a city of Cataonia, in Armenia Minor. *Ptol.*

LEAN'DRE, a daughter of Amyclas, who married Arcas. *Apollod.*

LEAN'DRIAS, a Lacedæmonian refugee at Thebes, who declared, according to an ancient oracle, that Sparta would lose the superiority over Greece when conquered by the Thebans at Leuctra. *Diod.* 15.

LEANI'RA or LEAN'DRE. *Vid.* Leandre.

LEANI'TÆ, a people of Arabia Felix. *Ptol.*

LEAR'CHUS, a son of Athamas and Ino, crushed to death by his father. *Vid.* Athamas. *Ovid. Fast.* 6. v. 490.—*Flacc.* 1. v. 280.

LEBADE'A, now Livadia, a town of Bœotia, near

mount Helicon. It received this name from the mother of Aspledon, and became famous for the oracle and cave of the prophet Trophonius. No moles could live there, according to Pliny. *Strab.* 9.—*Plin.* 16. c. 36.—*Paus.* 9. c. 59. Also Lebadi'a.

LEB'ANON, a high mountain in Syria.

LEB'EDUS or **LEB'EDOS**, a town of Ionia, at the north of Colophon, where festivals were yearly observed in honor of Bacchus. Lysimachus destroyed it, and carried part of the inhabitants to Ephesus. It had been founded by an Athenian colony, under one of the sons of Codrus. *Strab.* 14.—*Horat.* 1. ep. 11. v. 7.—*Herodot.* 1. c. 142.—*Cic.* 1. *Div.* 33. —*Paterc.* 1. c. 4.—*Plin.* 5. c. 29.—*Mela*, 1. c. 17. —*Paus.* 7. c. 3 & 5.

LEBE'NA, a commercial town on the southern coast of Crete, with a temple sacred to Æsculapius, built upon the model of that of Balanagræ. This city gave birth to Leucocomas and Euxynthete, according to Theophrastus quoted by *Strabo*, 10. *Ptol.* 5. c. 17.—*Paus.* 2. c. 26.

LEBETHRA, *Vid.* Libethra.

LEBIN'THUS or **LEBYN'THUS**, now Levita, one of the Sporades a little at the north of Crete. *Strab.* 10.—*Mela*, 2. c. 7.—*Ovid. Met.* 8. v. 222.

LEBO'NIA, now Lavagna, a town on the coast of Liguria. *Ptol.*

LEBO'RIÆ or **LEBO'RIUS CAM'PUS**, a place of Italy. *Plin.* 18. c. 11.

LEBU'NI. a people of Hispania Citerior. *Plin.* 3. c. 4.

LECA'NIUS, the murderer of Galba. *Tac. Hist.* 1. c. 41.

LEC'CA. *Vid.* Laca.

LECHÆ'UM, now Pelago, a port of Corinth. *Stat. Theb.* 2. v. 381 —*Liv.* 32. c. 23.

LECTISTER'NIA, festivals at Rome observed in times of public calamity, to which the gods were solemnly invited, and their images were placed on beds round the tables, whence their name. This festival was first observed, A.U.C. 354. in consequence of a pestilential distemper which had visited Rome. It lasted eight days, and the gods particularly honored were Neptune, Mercury, Hercules, Apollo, Latona, and Diana. During the celebration the citizens kept open table, each according to his ability, and in the temples of the invited divinities a profusion of meats was served up at the expense of the republic, for the ministers and officers of the gods. *Liv.* 5. c. 13. l. 7. c. 2. l. 27. c. 4. l. 40. c. 19.—*Val. Max.* 2. c. 1.—*Turneb. Adv.* 30. c. 32.—*Servius in Æn.* 8. v. 130. l. 12. v. 199.

LEC'TUM, a promontory, now cape Baba, opposite the northern extremity of the island of Lesbus, separating Troas from Æolia. *Liv.* 37. c. 37 —*Plin.* 5. c. 30, &c,

LEC'YTHUS, a town of Eubœa. *Thucyd.* l. 4.

LE'DA, a daughter of king Thestius and Eurythemis, married Tyndarus, king of Sparta. She was seen bathing in the river Eurotas by Jupiter, who became enamoured of her, and assumed the shape of a swan to deceive her. In consequence of this amour she brought forth two eggs, from one of which sprang Pollux and Helena, and from the other Castor and Clytæmnestra. The two former were deemed the offspring of Jupiter, the latter of Tyndarus. Some mythologists attribute this amour to Nemesis, and not to Leda: and maintain that Leda was only entrusted with the education of the children; (*vid.* Helena :) while others assert that Leda received the name of Nemesis after death. Homer and Hesiod make no mention of the metamorphosis of Jupiter into a swan, whence some have concluded that the fable was unknown to them, and consequently invented since their age. *Apollod.* 1. c. 8. l. 3. c. 10.—*Ovid. Met.* 6. v. 109. *Heroid.* 17. v. 55.—*Hygin.* fab. 77.—*Isocr. in Hel.*—*Homer. Odyss.* 11.—*Eurip. in Hel.*—*Virg. in Cir.* 489.—*Eratosthen.* 25.—*Tzetzes in Lyc.* 87.—*Lactant. de Fals. R.* 21. & *ad Theb.* 4. v. 236. l. 10. v. 497.—*Servius in Æn.* 2. v. 601. l. 3. v. 328.—*Eustath. ad Dionys Per.* 687.—*Sch. Apollon.* 1. v. 146. [There are several representations of Leda. The finest is a statue in the Vatican.]——A famous dancer in the age of *Juvenal.* 6. v. 63.

LEDÆ'A, an epithet given to Hermione, as related to Leda. *Virg. Æn.* 3. v. 328.

LE'DUM, now Lez, a small river of Gaul near the modern Montferrier. *Mela*, 2. c. 5.

LE'GES, a people of Asia, on the Caspian Sea. *Plut. in Pomp.*

LE'GIO, a corps of soldiers in the Roman armies, the numbers of which were different at different periods of the republic. The legion, under Romulus, consisted of 3000 foot and 300 horse. and was soon after augmented to 4000, after the admission of the Sabines into the city, whence it was called *quadrata.* When Annibal was in Italy it consisted of 5000 soldiers, and afterwards it decreaed to 4000, or 4500. Marius made it consist of 6200, besides 700 horse. During the consular government it was usual tolevy four legions, which were divided between the two consuls. This number was, however, often increased, as time and occasion required, and *Livy* speaks of 10, 16, 18, and even more. Augustus maintained a standing army of twenty-three or twenty-five legions, and this number was seldom diminished. In the reign of Tiberius there were 27 legions, and the peace establishment of Adrian maintained no less than 30 of these formidable brigades. They were distributed over the various provinces of the Roman empire, and their stations were settled and permanent. The peace of Britain was protected by three legions; sixteen were stationed on the banks of the Rhine and Danube, viz. two in Lower, and three in Upper Germany: one in Noricum, one in Rhætia, three in Mœsia, four in Pannonia, and two in Dacia. Eight were stationed on the Euphrates, six of which remained in Syria, and two in Cappadocia, while the remote provinces of Ægypt, Africa, and Spain, were guarded each by a single legion. Besides these, the tranquillity of Rome was preserved by 20,000 soldiers, who under the titles of city cohorts and of prætorian guards, watched over the safety of the monarch and of the capital. The legions were distinguished by different appellations, and generally borrowed their name from the order in which they had been first raised, as *prima, secunda, tertia, quarta*, &c. Besides this distinction, another more expressive and often more honorable, was generally added, as from the name of the emperor who embodied them, as *Augusta, Claudiana, Galbiana, Flavia, Ulpia, Trajana, Antoniana*, &c.; from the provinces or quarters where they were stationed, as *Britannica, Cyrenaica, Gallica*, &c. from the provinces which had been subdued by their valor, as *Parthica, Scythica, Arabica, Africana*, &c.; from the names of the deities whom their generals particularly worshipped, as *Minervia, Apollinaris*, &c.; or from more trifling accidents, as *martia, fulminatrix, rapax, adjutrix*, &c. Each legion was divided into ten *cohorts*, each cohort into three *manipuli*, and every manipulus into two centuries or *ordines*. The chief commander of the legion was called *legatus*, lieutenant. The standards borne by the legions were various. In the first ages of Rome a wolf was the standard, in honor of Romulus: after that a hog, because that animal was generally sacrificed at the conclusion of a treaty, and therefore it indicated that war was undertaken for the purpose of obtaining peace. A minotaur was sometimes the standard, to intimate the secrecy with which the general was to act, in commemoration of the labyrinth. Sometimes a horse or a boar was used, till the age of Marius, who changed all these for an eagle, which was made of silver, and held sometimes a thunderbolt in its claws. The Roman eagle ever after remained in use, though Trajan, for some time, made use of the dragon.

LE'GIO GERMAN'ICA or SEP'TIMA, a city of Hispania Tarraconensis, now Leon. *Ptol.*—In Britain, one legion, Augusta Secunda, was stationed at Isca Silurum, now Caerleon, *the city of the legion*; another, Vigesima Victrix, at Deva, now Chester, called Legeacester by the Saxons.

LEG'NA, a city of Galatia. *Antonin.*

LE'GUM, a city of Sicily, near Lilybæum. *Ptol.*

LEI'NUM, a city of European Sarmatia, now Lutzko, according to *Niger.*

LE'ITUS or **LE'TUS**, a commander of the Bœotians at the siege of Troy. He was saved from the victorious hand of Hector, and from death, by Idomeneus. *Homer. Il.* 2, 6 & 17.

LE'ITUS, a son of Alector, who was one of the Argonauts. *Apollod.* 1.

LE'LAPS, a dog that never failed to seize and conquer whatever animal he was ordered to pursue. It was given to Procris by Diana. and Procris reconciled herself to her husband by presenting him with this valuable gift. According to some, Procris had received it from Minos, as a reward for the dangerous wounds of which she had cured him. This animal was particularly famous for having delivered Bœotia from the ravages of a dangerous fox, which had been sent to infest the country, because the inhabitants did not pay sufficient reverence to the oracle of the goddess Themis: *Hygin.* fab. 128.—*Ovid. Met.* 7. v. 771.—*Paus.* 9. c. 19.—*Anton. Liber.*——One of Actæon's dogs. *Ovid. Met.* 3. v. 211.

LELEGE'IS, a name applied to Miletus, because once possessed by the Leleges. *Plin.* 5. c. 29.

LEL'EGES, (*a* λέγω, *to gather*) a wandering people, composed of different unconnected nations. They were originally inhabitants of Caria, and went to the Trojan war with Altes their king. Achilles plundered their country, and obliged them to retire to Halicarnassus, where they fixed their habitation. The inhabitants of Laconia and Megara also bore this name for some time, from Lelex, one of their kings. *Strab.* 7 & 8.—*Homer Il.* 21. v. 85.—*Virg. Æn.* 8. v. 725.—*Plin.* 4. c. 7. l. 5. c. 30.—*Paus.* 3. c. 1.

LE'LEX, an Ægyptian, who came with a colony to settle at Megara, where he reigned about 200 years before the Trojan war. His subjects were called from him Leleges, and the place Lelegeia Mœnia. *Paus.* 3. c. 1.——A Greek, who was the first king of Laconia, in Peloponnesus. His subjects were also called Leleges, and the country where he reigned Lelegia. *Id.*——A native of Naryx, who was present at the chase of the Calydonian boar. *Ovid. Met.* 8. v. 312.——A Trœzenian, intimate with Theseus. *Ovid. Met.* 8. v. 566.

LEMAN'NUS or LEMAN'NIS, a place in Britain, where Cæsar is supposed to have first landed, and therefore placed by some writers at Lime, in Kent. *Ptol.*—*Camden, &c.*

LEMAN'NUS, a large lake in the country of the Allobroges, through which the Rhone flows by Geneva. It is now called the lake of Geneva or Lausanne, and is situated between the Pays de Vaud, Switzerland, and Savoy. Its trout and perch are famous. *Cæs. B. G.* 1. c. 2 & 8.—*Ptol.* 2. c. 10.—*Lucan.* 1. v. 396.—*Mela*, 2. c. 5.

LEM'BA, a town of Syria. *Joseph. Ann.* l. 13.

LEM'NOS or LEM'NUS, an island in the Ægæan Sea, between Tenedus, Imbrus, and Samothrace. It was sacred to Vulcan, called *Lemnius Pater*, because he fell there when kicked from heaven by Jupiter. *Vid.* Vulcanus. It was noted for two horrible massacres, that of the Lemnian women murdering their husbands (*vid.* Hypsipyle), and that of the Lemnians, or Pelasgi, in killing all the children which they had had by some Athenian women, whom they had carried away to become their wives. These two acts of cruelty have given rise to the proverb *Lemnian actions*, which is applied to all barbarous and inhuman deeds. The first inhabitants of Lemnus were the Pelasgi, or, more properly, the Thracians, who were murdered by their wives. After them came the children of the Lemnian widows by the Argonauts, whose descendants were at last expelled by the Pelasgi, about 1100 years B.C. Lemnus is about 112 miles in circumference, according to *Pliny*, who says, that it is often overshadowed by mount Athos, though at the distance of 87 miles. It has been called Hypsipyle, from queen Hypsipyle. It is famous for a certain kind of earth or chalk, called *terra Lemnia*, or *terra sigillata*, from the seal or impression which it can bear. As many of the inhabitants were blacksmiths, the poets have fixed the forges of Vulcan in that island. Lemnus was also celebrated for a labyrinth, which, according to some traditions, surpassed those of Crete and Ægypt. Some remains of it were still visible in the age of Pliny. The island of Lemnus, now called Statimene, was reduced under the power of Athens by Miltiades, and the Carians, who then inhabited it, were obliged to emigrate. *Virg. Æn.* 8. v. 454.—*Homer. Il.* 1. v. 593.—*C. Nep. in Milt.*—*Strab.* 1, 2, & 7.—*Herodot.* 6. c. 140.—*Mela*, 2, c. 7.—*Apollon.* 1. *Arg.*—*Flacc.* 2. v. 78.—*Ovid. Art. Am.* 3. v. 672.—*Stat.* 3. *Theb.* 274.—*Ptol.* 3. c. 13.—*Lactant. ad Theb.* 5. v. 29.—*Schol. Apollon.* 1. v. 209.—*Schol. Eurip. ad Hec.*—*Schol. Homer. Il* 7. v. 467.

LEMO'NIA, a tribe at Rome. *Cic. Phil.* 9.

LEMOVI'CES, a people of Gaul, south of the Loire: they inhabited the country now called Limosin and Limoges. *Cæs. G.* 7. c. 14.

LEMO'VII, a nation of Germany, placed by *Cellarius* on the borders of the Baltic Sea, at the west of the Vistula. *Tacit. de Germ.*

LEM'URES, a name given to the manes of the dead. The ancients supposed that the soul after death, wandered over the world, and disturbed the peace of its inhabitants. The good spirits were called *Lares familiares*, and the evil ones were known by the name of *Larvæ* or *Lemures*. They were said to terrify the good, and continually to haunt the wicked and impious. The Romans celebrated festivals in their honor, called *Lemuria* or *Lemuralia*, in the month of May. These festivals were first instituted by Romulus to appease the manes of his brother Remus, from whom they were called *Remuria*, and by corruption *Lemuria*, and they continued three nights, during which the temples of the gods were shut, and marriages prohibited. It was usual also, at this time, for the people to throw black beans on the graves of the deceased, or to burn them, as the smell was supposed to be disagreeable to them. They also muttered magical words, and by beating kettles and drums, they believed that the ghosts would depart, and no longer terrify their relations upon earth. *Ovid. Fast.* 5. v. 421, &c.—*Horat.* 2. ep. 2. v. 209.—*Persius*, 5. v. 185.—*Apuleius de Socr.*—*Servius in Æn.* 3. v. 63.

LEMU'RIA or LEMURA'LIA. *Vid.* Lemures.

LENÆ'US, a surname of Bacchus, from ληνός, *a winepress*. There was a festival called *Lenæa*, celebrated in his honor, in which the ceremonies observed at the other festivals of the god chiefly prevailed. There were, besides, poetical contentions, &c. *Paus.*—*Virg. G.* 2. v. 4.—*Æn.* 4. v. 207.—*Ovid. Met.* 4. v. 14.—*Tibull.* 3. el. 7. v. 6.—*Stat.* 4. *Sylv.* 6. v. 80.——A king of Pontus, said to have been left naked on the island of Leuce. *Ovid. Ib.* 331.

LENÆ'US POMPE'IUS, a learned grammarian at Rome, ordered by Pompey to translate into Latin some of the medical manuscripts of Mithridates, king of Pontus. *Plin.* 25. c. 2.

LE'NIUS, C. and M., two brothers, who hospitably received Cicero at Brundusium during his banishment. Marcus is supposed to have been the first who formed an aviary. *Varr. R.R.* 3. c. 5.—*Cic. Fam.* 13. ep 63. *Att.* 5. ep. 20 & 21. *Planc.* 41. *Sext.* 63.

LENTID'IUS, a partisan of Clodius. *Cic. Dom.* 33. *Sex.* 37.

LENTIEN'SES, a people of Vindelicia. *Amm. Marcell.* 37. c. 12.

LEN'TO CÆ'SEN., one of the seven persons appointed over Etruria by Antony. *Cic. Phil.* 12. c. 9.

LEN'TUDUM, a city of Upper Pannonia, now Lutenberg. *Ptol.*

LEN'TULUS, a celebrated family at Rome, a branch of the Cornelii, which produced many great men.

LEN'TULUS BATIA'TUS, a man who trained up some gladiators at Capua, who escaped from his school.

LEN'TULUS CN., surnamed Gætulicus, was made consul A.D. 26, and was some time after put to death by Caligula, who was jealous of his great popularity. He wrote a history mentioned by Suetonius, and also attempted poetry. *Tac. Ann.* 6. c. 30.—*Suet. in Calig. &c.*

LEN'TULUS CNE'US CORN., a tribune at the battle of Cannæ. On that fatal day, he observed in his flight the consul P. Æmylius, sitting on a stone, covered with blood, and offered him his horse, which that illustrious warrior refused, enjoining him to hasten his return to Rome, and charge the senators to make a vigorous resistance against the victorious enemy. Lentulus was afterwards engaged in Spain, where his services entitled him to the honor of an ovation. *Liv.* 22. c. 49. l. 25. c. 17. l. 31. c. 50. l. 33. c. 27.

LEN'TULUS CORN., surnamed Sura, joined in Catiline's conspiracy, and assisted in corrupting the Allobroges. He was convicted in full senate by Cicero, and put into prison, and afterwards executed by order of the senate. *Dio.* 37. c. 30. l. 46. c. 20.—*Plut. in Cic.*

Len'tulus L., a friend of Pompey put to death in Africa.

Len'tulus L. Corn., a consul, A.U.C. 427, who dispersed some robbers who invested Umbria. He was in the army at the disgraceful treaty of Caudium. *Liv.* 8. c. 22.*1. 9. c. 4.

Len'tulus Lu'cius, a Roman officer in Spain, afterwards made consul A.U. 555. *Liv.* 28, &c.

Len'tulus Pub'lius, a senator, wounded in the insurrection made by Caius Gracchus. He afterwards became unpopular and retired to Sicily, where he died. *Val. Max.* 5. c. 3.—*Cic. Ph.* 8. c. 4. *Cat.* 4. c. 6.

Len'tulus P., a friend of Brutus, mentioned by *Cicero* (*de Orat.* 1. c. 48.) as a great and consummate statesman.

Len'tulus P. Corn., a prætor, defeated by the rebellious slaves in Sicily.

Len'tulus Spin'ther, a senator who strongly promoted the recall of Cicero. He was set over the province of Cilicia, and endeavoured to restore Ptolemy to his throne. He was slain during the civil wars. *Cic. Off.* 2. c. 16. *Ad. Quir.* 5. *In Senat.* 4. *Fam.* 6. ep. 21.

Len'tulus, his son, was engaged in Asia in the service of the republic. Two of his letters are extant. *Cic. Fam.* 12. ep. 14 & 15.——A consul who triumphed over the Samnites.—Besides these, there are a few others, whose names are merely mentioned in history, but whose lives are not marked by any uncommon event. The consulship was in the family of the Lentuli in the years of Rome 427, 479, 517, 518, 553, 555, 598, &c. *Tacit. Ann.*—*Liv.*—*Flor*—*Plin.*—*Plut.*—*Eutrop.*

LE'O, a native of Byzantium, who flourished 350 years B.C. His philosophical and political talents endeared him to his countrymen, and he was sent upon every occasion as ambassador to Athens, or to the court of Philip, king of Macedonia. This monarch, well acquainted with the abilities of Leo, was sensible that his views and claims upon Byzantium would never succeed while it was protected by the vigilance of such a patriotic citizen. To remove him, therefore, he had recourse to artifice and perfidy. A letter was forged, in which Leo made solemn promises of betraying his kingdom to the king of Macedonia for money. This was no sooner known than the people ran enraged to the house of Leo, and the philosopher, to avoid their fury, and without attempting his justification, strangled himself. He had written some treatises upon physic, and also the history of his country, and of the wars of Philip, in seven books, which have unfortunately perished. *Plut. in Niciâ.*—*Athen.* 12.—*Suidas.*—*Philostr. in Heroic.*——A Corinthian at Syracuse, &c.——A king of Sparta.——A son of Eurycrates. *Athen.* 12. *Philostr.*——An emperor of the east, surnamed the Thracian. He reigned seventeen years, and died A.D. 474, being succeeded by Leo the Second for ten months, and afterwards by Zeno.——An orator of Alabanda, confounded by some with Leo of Byzantium.——An author of Pella, who wrote on the nature of the gods, &c. *Arnob. con. gent.* l. 4.—*Voss. H. Gr.* p. 500.

LEOB'ATES, a Spartan of the family of the Heraclidæ. *Herod.* 7. c. 65.

LEOCH'ARES, a sculptor, one of those employed upon the Mausoleum. *Plin.* 34. c. 8.

LEOCO'RIUM, a monument and temple erected by the Athenians to Pasithea, Theope, and Eubule, daughters of Leos, who immolated themselves for the public safety when an oracle had ordered that, to stop the raging pestilence, some of the blood of the citizens must be shed. *Ælian.* 12. c. 28.—*Cic. N.D.* 3. c. 19.—*Paus.* 1. c. 5.—*Suidas. voce.*

LEOC'RATES, an Athenian decennial archon, who flourished B.C. 460., and conquered the Corinthians and Epidamnians. *Diod.* 11.

LEOD'AMAS, a son of Eteocles, one of the seven Theban chiefs who defended the city against the Argives. He killed Ægialeus, and was himself killed by Alcmæon. *Apollod.* 3.—*Paus.* 1. c. 19.——A son of Hector and Andromache. *Dictys. Cret.* 6.

LEOD'OCUS, one of the Argonauts. *Flacc.* 1. v. 359.

LEOG'ORAS, an Athenian debauchee, who maintained the courtezan Myrrhina. *Thucyd.* 4.—*Aristoph. Nub &c. & Schol.*

LE'ON, a king of Sparta. *Herodot.* 7. c. 204.——A native of Phlius, to whom Pythagoras explained the reason of his assuming the appellation of philosopher. *Cic. Tusc.* 5. c. 3.——A native of Megara, &c. *Cic. Verr.* 5. c. 6.

Le'on, a town of Sicily, near Syracuse. *Liv.* 24. c. 25.——A promontory of Eubœa, now Cabo Mantello. *Ptol.*——A promontory of Crete, now Capo Leon.

LEO'NA. *Vid.* Læna.

LEON'ATUS or **LEONA'TUS**, one of Alexander's generals. He distinguished himself by his valor in Alexander's expedition into Asia, and once saved the king's life in a dangerous battle. At the general division of the provinces he received for his portion that part of Phrygia which borders on the Hellespont. He was empowered by Perdiccas to assist Eumenes in making himself master of Cappadocia, which had been allotted to him. Like the rest of the generals of Alexander, he was ambitious of power and dominion. He aspired to the sovereignty of Macedonia, and secretly communicated to Eumenes the different plans which he meant to pursue to execute his designs. He afterwards passed from Asia into Europe to assist Antipater against the Athenians, and was killed in a battle which was fought soon after his arrival. Historians have mentioned, as an instance of the luxury of Leonatus, that he employed a number of camels to procure some earth from Ægypt to wrestle upon, as, in his opinion, it seemed particularly calculated for that purpose. *Plut. in Alex.*—*Curt.* 3. c. 12. l. 6. c. 8.—*Justin.* 13. c. 2.—*Diod.* 18.—*C. Nep. in Eum.*——A Macedonian who accompanied Pyrrhus into Italy against the Romans.

LEONICEN'SES, a people of Hispania Citerior. *Plin.* 3. c. 3.

LEON'IDAS, a celebrated king of Lacedæmon, of the family of the Eurysthenidæ, sent by his countrymen to oppose Xerxes, king of Persia, who had invaded Greece with about five millions of souls. He was offered the kingdom of Greece by the enemy, if he would not oppose his views; but Leonidas received the proposal with indignation. Before the engagement Leonidas exhorted his soldiers to dine heartily, as they were to sup in the realms of Pluto. The battle was fought in the narrow pass of Thermopylæ, and 300 Spartans, who had refused to abandon the scene of action, withstood the enemy with such vigor, that they were obliged to retire during three successive days. Perfidy, however, prevailed over valor, and Ephialtes, a Trachinian, conducted a detachment of Persians by a secret path up the mountains, whence they suddenly fell upon the rear of the Spartans, and crushed them to pieces. Only one of the 300 escaped; he returned home, where he was treated with insults and reproaches, for fleeing ingloriously from a battle in which his brave companions, with their royal leader, had perished. This celebrated battle, which happened 480 B.C., taught the Greeks to despise the numbers of the Persians, and to rely on their own strength and intrepidity. Temples were raised in honor of the fallen hero, and festivals, called Leonidea, yearly celebrated at Sparta, in which only free-born youths were permitted to contend. *Herodot.* 7. c. 120, &c.—*C. Nep. in Them.*—*Justin.* 2.—*Val. Max.* 1. c. 6.—*Paus.* 3. c. 4.—*Plut. in Lyc. & Cleom.* [There is a bust of Leonidas in the collection at the Villa Albani, near Rome.]——A king of Sparta after Areus the Second, 257 years B.C. He was driven from his kingdom by Cleombrotus his son-in-law, but afterwards re-established.——A friend of Parmenio, appointed commander, by Alexander, of the soldiers who lamented the death of Parmenio, and who formed a separate cohort. *Curt.* 7. c. 2.——A learned man of Rhodes, greatly commended by *Strabo*, &c.

LEON'IDES, an Athenian intimate with Cicero. He gave the orator a favorable account of the progress of his son, &c. *Cic. Fam.* 15. ep. 21. *Att.* 15. ep. 16 & 18. 1. 16. ep. 16.——A preceptor of Alexander the Great. *Quintil.*—*Curt. Suppl.* 2. c. 7.

LEONTIS'CUS, a celebrated pugilist of Mamertina. *Suidas.*

LEON'TIUM or **LEONTI'NI**, a town at the east of Sicily, about five miles distant from the sea-shore, between Catana and Syracuse. It was built by a colony from Chalcis in Eubœa, and was, according to some accounts, once the habitation of the Læstrygones, for which reason the neighbouring fields are often called *Læstrygonii Campi*. The country was extremely fruitful, whence Cicero calls it the grand magazine of Sicily. The wine which it produced was the best of the island. The people implored the assistance of the Athenians against the Syracusans, B.C. 247. *Thucyd.* 6.—*Polyb.* 7.—*Ovid. Fast.* 4. v. 467.—*Ital.* 14. v. 126.—*Cic. in Verr.* 6.—*Plin.* 18. c. 10.—*Ptol.* 3. c. 4.—*Mela*, 2. c. 7.—*Cluver. Sicil.* 1. c. 10.

LEON'TIUM, a celebrated courtezan of Athens, who studied philosophy under Epicurus, and was one of his most renowned pupils. *Vid.* Epicurus. She had a son by Metrodorus, to whom Epicurus was so partial, that he recommended him to his executors on his death-bed. Leontium wrote a book in support of the doctrines of Epicurus against Theophrastus. This book was a valuable performance, if we believe the testimony of Cicero, who praises the purity and elegance of its style, and its truly Attic turn of expression. Leontium had also a daughter called Danae, who married Sophron. *Cic. de Nat. D.* 1. 33.

LEON'TIUS, a statuary of illustrious origin, whose works are enumerated by *Pliny*, 34. c. 8.

LEONTOCEPH'ALE, a strongly fortified city of Phrygia. *Plut.*

LEON'TON or LEONTOP'OLIS, a town of Ægypt, where lions are said to have been worshipped. *Ælian. H. An.* 12. c. 7.—*Plin.* 5. c. 10.

LEONTYCH'IDES. *Vid.* Leotychides.

LE'OS, a son of Orpheus. *Vid.* Leocorium.

LEOS'THENES, an Athenian general, who, after Alexander's death, drove Antipater to Thessaly, where he besieged him in the town of Lamia. The success which for a while attended his arms was of short duration; he received a fatal blow from a stone thrown by the besieged, B.C. 323. The death of Leosthenes was followed by the total defeat of the Athenian forces. His funeral orations was pronounced at Athens by the orator Hyperides, in the absence of Demosthenes. *Vid.* Lamiacum. *Diod.* 17 & 18.—*Strab.* 9. ——A general of Athens, condemned on account of the bad success which attended his arms against Peparethus. *Diod. Sic.* 15.

LEOSTHE'NIUM, a bay of the Thracian Bosporus. *Steph.*

LEOTROPHI'DES, a dithyrambic poet of Athens, who was so thin, that *Leotrophide macilentior* became a proverb.—*Suidas.*—*Erasmus.*

LEOTYCHI'DES, a king Sparta, son of Menares, of the family of the Proclidæ. He was appointed commander of the Grecian fleet, and put an end to the Persian war by the famous battle of Mycale. It is said that he cheered the spirits of his fellow soldiers at Mycale, by raising a report that a battle had been fought at Platæa, in which the barbarians had been defeated. This succeeded, and though the information was premature, yet the Greeks obtained a victory at Platæa, on the same day that the Persian fleet was destroyed at Mycale. Leotychides was accused of a capital crime by the Ephori, and fled to the temple of Minerva at Tegea, where he perished, B.C. 469, after a reign of 22 years. He was succeeded by his grandson Archidamus, *Paus.* 3. c. 7 & 8.—*Diod.* 11.——A son of Agis, king of Sparta, by Timæa. The legitimacy of his birth was disputed by some, as it was generally reported that he was the son of Alcibiades. He was prevented from ascending the throne of Sparta by the intrigues of Lysander, though Agis had declared him upon his death-bed his lawful son and heir, and Agesilaus was appointed in his place. —*C. Nep. in Ages.*—*Plut.*—*Paus.* 3. c. 8.

LEPETYM'NUS or LEPETH'YMUS, a mountain near Methymna in Lesbus. *Plin.* 5. c. 1.

LEPHYR'IUM, a city of Cilicia.

LEP'IDA, a noble woman, accused of attempts to poison her husband, from whom she had been separated for 20 years. She was condemned under Tiberius *Tac. Ann.* 3. c. 22.——A woman who married Scipio ——A wife of Galba, the emperor. ——A wife of Cassius, &c.

LEP'IDA DOMIT'IA, a daughter of Drusus and Antonia, great niece to Augustus, and aunt to the emperor Nero. She is described by Tacitus as dissolute in her morals, and violent in her temper, though celebrated for her beauty. She was put to death by means of her rival, Agrippina, Nero's mother. *Tacit. Ann.* 12. c. 64.

LEPIDO'TUM, a city of Ægypt. *Ptol.*

LEP'IDUS M. ÆMIL'IUS, a Roman, celebrated in history as being one of the triumvirs, with Augustus and Antony. He was of an illustrious family, but was remarkable for his ambition, his narrowness of mind, and his great want of military abilities. He was sent against Cæsar's murderers, and, some time after, he leagued with M. Antony, who had gained the heart of his soldiers by artifice, and that of their commander by his address. When his influence and power among the soldiers had made him one of the triumvirs, he showed his cruelty like his colleagues, by his proscriptions, and even suffered his own brother to be sacrificed to the dagger of the triumvirate. He received Africa as his portion in the division of the empire; but his indolence soon rendered him despicable in the eyes of his soldiers and of his colleagues; and Augustus, who was well acquainted with the unpopularity of Lepidus, went to his camp, and obliged him to resign his power, to which, as a triumvir, he was entitled. After this degrading event, Lepidus sank into obscurity, and retired, by order of Augustus, to Cereeii, a small town on the coast of Latium, where he was forgotten as soon as out of power, and where he ended his days in peace, B.C. 13. Lepidus married a sister of Brutus, and Cassius another. The son of Lepidus married one of Antony's daughters. *Cic. Phil.* 5. c. 14, &c. *Fam.* 10. ep. 20. l. 12. ep. 2 & 10.—*Dio.* 44. c. 33,—*Appian.*—*Plut. in Aug.*—*Flor.* 4. c. 6 & 7.——A Roman consul, sent to be the guardian of young Ptolemy Epiphanes, whom his father in his will had committed to the care of the Roman people. *Tacit. Ann.* 2. c. 67.—*Justin.* 30. c. 3. ——A son of Julia, the grand-daughter of Augustus. He was intended by Caius as his successor in the Roman empire. He committed adultery with Agrippina when young. *Dion.* 59 ——An orator, mentioned by *Cicero, in Brut.*——A censor, A.U.C. 73. ——A Greek author of an historical epitome. *Steph. in* Τεγέα.

LEPIL'IUS, a courier in the service of L. Metellus in Sicily. *Cic Verr.* 2. c. 26.

LEPI'NUS, a mountain of Italy, now Monte Segni. *Colum.* 10.

LEPON'TII, a people situated at the source of the Rhine between the Alps and the Po. *Plin.* 3. c. 20.

LEP'REA, a daughter of Pyrgeus, from whom the town of Lepreum derived its name.

LE'PREOS, a son of Pyrgeus, who built a town in Elis, which he called after his own name. He laid a wager that he would eat as much as Hercules; upon which he killed an ox and ate it up. He afterwards challenged Hercules to a trial of strength, and was killed in the contest. *Paus.* 5. c. 5.

LE'PRIA, an island of the Ægean Sea. *Plin.* 5. c. 31.

LE'PRIUM or LE'PREUM, a town of Elis. *Cic.* 6. *Att.* 2.—*Plin.* 4. c. 5.

LEP'TA Q., an officer under Cicero, when proconsul of Cilicia. *Cic. Fam* 3. ep. 7. His son bore the same name. *Cic. ibid.* 6. p. 18.

LEPTE'ACRA, a promontory of India, called by some Drepanum. *Solin.*——A promontory of Ægypt, on the Sinus Arabicus. *Plin* 3. c. 8.—*Ptol.*

LEP'TINES, a general of Demetrius, who ordered Cn. Octavius, one of the Roman ambassadors to Antiochus, to be put to death. *Cic. Phil.* 9. c. 7. ——A son of Hermocrates, of Syracuse, brother to Dionysius the tyrant. He was sent by his brother against the Carthaginians, and sank fifty of their ships. He was afterwards defeated by Mago, and banished by Dionysius. He always continued a faithful friend to the interests of his brother, though naturally an avowed enemy to tyranny and oppression. He was killed in a battle with the Carthaginians. *Diod.* 15.——A famous orator at Athens, who endeavoured to set the people free from oppressive taxes. He was opposed by Demosthenes. *Cic. Or.* 31.——A tyrant of Apollonia, in Sicily, who surrendered to Timoleon. *Diod* 16.

LEP'TIS, the name of two cities of Africa, on the sea-coast, one of which, called Major, now Lebeda, was between the two Syrtes, and had been built by a Tyrian or Sidonian colony. The other, called Minor, now Lempta, was about 18 Roman miles at the south of Adrumetum. It paid every day a talent to the republic of Carthage, by way of tribute. *Lucan.* 2. v. 251.—*Plin.* 5. c. 19.—*Sallust. in Jug.* 77.—*Mela*, 1. c. 8.—*Strab.* 3.—*Cæs. C.* 2. c. 38.—*Cic.* 5. *Verr.* 59.

LE'PUS, a constellation in the heavens. *Colum.* 11. c. 2.—*Cic. N. D.* 2. c. 44.

LEPYD'NUS, the husband of Methymna, the daughter of Macareus. *Steph. in* Μήθυμνα.

LE'RIA, an island in the Ægean Sea, on the coast of Caria, about 18 miles in circumference, peopled by a Milesian colony. Its inhabitants were said to be very dishonest. *Strab.* 10.—*Herodot.* 5. c. 125.——A town of Hispania Tarraconensis, called also Edeta, and now Liria. *Ortelius.* ——A river of the Boii, now Laire, which is called Sigmas by *Ptolemy.*

LERI'NA or **PLANA'SIA**, a small island in the Mediterranean, on the coast of Gaul. *Tacit. Ann.* 1. c. 3.

LER'NA or **LER'NE**, a country of Argolis, celebrated for a grove and a lake, into which, according to the poets, the Danaides threw the heads of their murdered husbands. It was there also that Hercules killed the famous hydra. *Virg. Æn.* 6. v. 803. l. 12. v. 517. & *Servius loc.*—*Strab.* 8.—*Mela*, 2. c. 3.—*Ovid. Met.* 1. v. 597.—*Lucret.* 5. v. 26.—*Stat. Theb.* 4. v. 638.—*Diod.* 4.—*Tzetzes Lycop.* 213.—*Schol. Pind. Oly.* 7. v. 60.—*Schol. Eurip. Phœnis.* 196.—*Lactant. ad Theb.* l. v. 384.—*Apollod.* 2. c. 15. There was a festival, called Lernæa, celebrated there in honour of Bacchus, Proserpine and Ceres. The Argives used to carry fire to this solemnity from a temple upon mount Crathis, dedicated to Diana. *Paus.*

LE'RO, a small island in the Mediterranean, on the coast of Gaul. *Strab.* 4.—*Plin.* 3. c. 5.

LE'ROS, an island. *Vid.* Leria.

LERTO'SA, a city of Spain, now Tortosa. *Ptol.*—*Strab.*

LESBO'NAX, a philosopher of Mitylene, in the first century. Of his works only two orations are preserved, published by Aldus, Venet. 1513, and H. Stephanus, 1575, with the orations of Æschines, Lysias, and others. *Sax. Onom.* 1. p. 236.—*Fabr. B. Gr.* 2. c. 26.——A Roman grammarian who wrote a treatise περὶ σχημάτων, published by Valckenaer with Ammonius. *Fabr. & Sax. ibid.*

LESBOTH'EMIS, a statuary, native of Lesbus.

LES'BUS or **LES'BOS**, a large island in the Ægean Sea, now known by the name of Metelin, 168 miles in circumference. It has been severally called Ægira, Lasia, Æthiope, Pelasgia, from the Pelasgi by whom it was first peopled, Macaria from Macareus who settled in it, and lastly Lesbus from the son-in-law and successor of Macareus, who bore the same name. The chief towns of Lesbus were Methymna and Mitylene. Lesbus was originally governed by kings, but it was afterwards subjected to the neighbouring powers. The wine which the island produced was greatly esteemed by the ancients, and is still in the same repute among the moderns. The Lesbians were celebrated for their skill in music, and their women for their beauty, but the general character of their people was so debauched and dissipated, that the epithet of *Lesbian* was often used to signify licentiousness and extravagance. Lesbus has given birth to many illustrious persons, such as Arion, Terpander, &c. The best verses were, by way of eminence, often called *Lesboum carmen*, from Alcæus, and Sappho, who distinguished themselves for their poetical compositions, and were also natives of the place. *Diod.* 5.—*Strab.* 13.—*Virg. G.* 2. v. 90.—*Horat.* 1. ep. 11. v. 1, l. 1. od. 26. v. 11.—*Athen.* 1. c. 30.—*Ptol.* 5. c. 2.—*Aul. Gell.* 13. c. 5.—*Servius in Æn.* 8. v. 55.—*Herodot.* 1. c. 160. ——A son of Lapithas grandson of Æolus, who married Methymna, daughter of Macareus. He succeeded his father-in-law, and gave his name to the island over which he reigned.

LES'CHES, a Greek poet of Lesbus, who flourished B.C. 600. Some suppose him to be the author of the little Iliad, of which only few verses remain quoted by *Pausanias*, 10. c. 25.—*Euseb. Chron.*—*Gyrald. P. H.* 3.—*Voss. de Poet. Gr.* 3.

LES'SA, a town of Argolis. *Paus.*

LESTO'RUM RE'GIO, Λῃστῶν χώρα, the country of pirates, a region of India without the Ganges. *Ptol.*

LESTRYG'ONES. *Vid.* Læstrygones.

LES'YRUS, a river of Iberia. *Steph.*

LETAN'DROS, an island of the Ægean Sea. *Plin.* 4. c. 12.

LETA'NUM, a town of Propontis, built by the Athenians. *Diod. Sic.*

LETHÆ'US, now Fiume de Mangresia, a river of Lydia flowing by Magnesia into the Mæander. *Strab.* 10, &c.——A river of Macedonia, near Tricca. *Solinus.*——A river of Crete.

LE'THE, one of the rivers of hell, the waters of which the souls of the dead drank after they had been confined for a certain space of time in the regions of Tartarus. It had the power of making them forget whatever they had done, seen, or heard before, as the name λήθη, *oblivion*, implies.

Le'the or **Le'thon**, a river of Africa, near the Syrtes, which ran under the ground, and some time after rose again, whence the origin of the fable.

Le'the, a river in Bœotia, the waters of which were drunk by those who consulted the oracle of Trophonius. *Ovid. Trist.* 4. el. 1. v. 47.—*Ex. Pont.* 4. el. 1. v. 17. *De A. A.* 3. v. 340.—*Lucan.* 3. v. 28. l. 5. v. 221. l. 6. v. 769.—*Virg. G.* 4. v. 545. *Æn.* 6. v. 714.—*Ital.* 1. v. 235. l. 10. v. 555.—*Paus.* 9. c. 39.—*Horat.* 4. od. 7. v. 27.

LE'THES, a river of Hispania Tarraconensis, now Lima. *Strab.* 3.——A river of Hispania Bætica, now Guadelete.

LETI'NI, a people of Sicily. *Cic. in Verr.*

LE'TO, a name of Latonia.

LETO'A, an island of the Libyan Sea, near Crete. *Ptol.*

LETRI'NI, a town of Elis. *Paus.*

LE'TUS, a mountain of Liguria, now monte S. Pelegrino *Liv.* 41. c. 18.——A Bœotian. *Vid.* Leitus.

LETU'POLIS, a city of Egypt.—*Ptol.*—*Steph.*

LEU'CA, a town of the Salentini, near a cape of the same name in Italy. *Lucan.* 5 v. 376.——A town of Ionia, between Cumæ and Clazomenæ. *Strab.*—*P. Mela.*——An island of Crete, opposite Cydonia. *Plin.* 5. c. 32.——A town of Argolis. *Strab.* 6, &c.—*Liv.* 26. c. 6.——An island of India, within the Ganges. *Ptol.*

LEUCA'DIUS, a surname of Apollo. *Vid.* Leucas.

LEU'CAS or **LEUCA'DIA**, an island of the Ionian Sea, now called St. Maura, near the coast of Epirus, famous for a promontory called Leucate, Leucas, or Leucates, whence desponding lovers threw themselves into the sea. Sappho had recourse to this leap to free herself from the violent passion which she entertained for Phaon. The word is derived from λευκὸς, *white*, on account of the white appearance of its rocks. Apollo had a temple on the promontory, whence he is often called Leucadius. The island was formerly joined to the continent by a narrow isthmus, which the inhabitants dug through after the Peloponnesian war. *Stat.* 5. *Sylv.* 3. v. 154.—*Auson. id.* 6. v. 24.—*Ovid. Heroid.* 15. v. 171.—*Strab.* 6, &c.—*Ital.* 15. v. 302.—*Virg. & Servius Æn.* 3. v. 274. l. 8. v. 59, 677.

Leu'cas, a town of Phœnicia.

LEUCA'SIUM, a village of Arcadia. *Paus.* 8. c. 25.

LEUCAS'PIS, a Lycian, one of the companions of Æneas, was drowned in the Tyrrhene Sea. *Virg. Æn.* 6. v. 334.

Leucas'pis, a harbour of Libya. *Ptol.*

LEUCA'TE. *Vid.* Leucas.

LEU'CE, a small island in the Euxine Sea, of a triangular form, between the mouths of the Danube and the Borysthenes. According to the poets, the souls of the ancient heroes were placed there after death, and there enjoyed perpetual felicity. From that circumstance it has often been called the island of the blessed. According to some accounts, Achilles celebrated there his nuptials with Iphigenia, or rather Helen, and shared the pleasures of the place with the manes of Ajax and other illustrious heroes. *Strab.* 2.—*Mela*, 2. c. 7.—*Ammian.* 22.—*Q. Calab.* 3. v. 773.—*Dionys. Per.*—*Paus.* 3 c. 19.—*Ptol. Hephæst.* 4.—*Conon. Narr.* 18.

Leu'ce, one of the Oceanides whom Pluto carried into his kingdom. She died there, and the god planted a poplar tree in the Elysian fields, to which he gave her name. *Servius ad Virg. Ecl.* 7. v. 61.

LEU'CI, a people of Gaul, between the Moselle and the Maese. Their capital is now called Toul. *Cæs. B. G.* 1. c. 40.

LEU'CI, mountains on the west of Crete, now monti di Sfachia, appearing at a distance like *white* clouds, whence the name. *Strab.* 4.

LEUCIM'NA, a promontory of Corcyra, now Capo Bianco. *Strab.* 7.

LEUCIP'PE, one of the Oceanides. *Paus.* 4. c. 30. ——The name of Laomedon's queen, according to some, who became mother of Priam. *Tzetzes in Lyc.* 14.——A daughter of Thestor. *Vid.* Theonoe.

LEUCIP'PIDES, the daughters of Leucippus. *Vid.* Leucippus.

LEUCIP'PUS, a celebrated philosopher of Abdera, about 428 years B.C. He was a disciple of Zeno, the first who broached the famous system of atoms and of a vacuum, which was afterwards more fully explained and improved upon by Democritus and Epicurus. Many of his hypotheses have been adopted by the moderns with advantage. *Diogenes* has written his life. *Cic. Acad.* 4. c. 37. *N. D.* 1. c. 24.——A son of Perieres and Gorgophone, and brother of Tyndarus king of Sparta, married Philodice daughter of Inachus, by whom he had two daughters, Hilaira and Phœbe, known by the patronymic of Leucippides. They were carried away by their cousins Castor and Pollux, as they were going to celebrate their nuptials with Lynceus and Idas. *Ovid. Fast.* 5. v. 701.—*Apollod.* 3. c. 10, &c. —*Paus.* 3. c. 17 & 26.——A son of Xanthus, descended from Bellerophon. He became deeply enamoured of one of his sisters, with whom he committed incest. Some time after the father resolved to give his daughter in marriage to a Lycian prince. The future husband was informed that the daughter of Xanthus secretly entertained a lover, and he communicated the intelligence to the father. Xanthus upon this watched in his daughter's chamber, and as she attempted to escape she received a mortal wound from her father, who took her to be the lover. Leucippus came to her assistance, and stabbed his father in the dark, without knowing who he was. This accidental parricide obliged Leucippus to flee from his country. He came to Crete, where the inhabitants refused to give him an asylum, when acquainted with the atrociousness of his crime, and he at last came to Ephesus, where he died in the greatest misery and remorse. *Hermesianax apud Parthen* c. 5.——A son of Œnomaus, who became enamoured of Daphne. To obtain her confidence he disguised himself in the dress of a female, and attended his mistress as a companion. He thus gained the affections of Daphne, but his artifice at last proved fatal through the influence and jealousy of his rival Apollo, for when Daphne and her attendants were bathing in the Ladon, the sex of Leucippus was discovered, and he perished by the darts of the females. *Parthen. Erotic.* c. 15.—*Paus.* 8. c. 20.——A son of Hercules by Marse, one of the daughters of Thespius. *Apollod.* 3. c. 7.

LEUCOGÆ'US COL'LIS, and LEUCOGÆ'I FON'TES, a place of Campania, between Neapolis and Puteoli, now la Lumera. *Plin.* 18. c. 11, &c.

LEUCOGÆ'US, a place of Marmarica, now Riva bianca. *Ptol.*

LEU'COLA, a harbour of Cyprus. *Strab.* 14.—*Plin.* 5. c. 31.

LEUCOLITH'I, a people of Lycaonia. *Plin* 5. c. 27.

LEU'CON, a tyrant of Bosporus, who lived in great intimacy with the Athenians. He was a patron of the useful arts, and greatly encouraged commerce. His father's name was Satyrus, and that of his son and successor Spartacus. *Strab.* 7.—*Demosth. in Sept.*—*Diod.* 14.——A king of Pontus, killed by his brother, whose bed he had defiled. *Ovid. in Ib.* 309.——A son of Athamas and Themisto. *Paus.* 6. c. 22.—*Apollod.* 1.

LEU'CON, a town of Africa, at the east of Cyrene. *Herodot.* 4. c. 160.

LEUCO'NE, a daughter of Aphidas, who gave her name to a fountain of Arcadia. *Paus.* 8. c. 44.—*Turneb. Adv.* 11. c. 28.

LEUCO'NES, a son of Hercules. *Apollod.*

LEUCO'NIUM, a place in the island of Chius.

LEUCO'NIUS, a fountain of Arcadia. *Paus.*

LEUCON'OE, a daughter of Lycambes. The Leuconoe, to whom *Horace* addresses his 1. od. 11. seems to be a fictitious name.——A nymph who relates to her companions the amours of Sol, &c. *Ovid. Met.* 4. v. 168.

LEU'CONON, a city of Pannonia. *Antonin.*

LEUCOP'ETRA, a place on the isthmus of Corinth, where the Achæans were defeated by the consul Mummius.——A promontory six miles east from Rhegium in Italy, where the Apennines terminate and sink into the sea. It is now Capo dell' Armi. ——A mountain of Asia which separates Parthia from Hyrcania. *Polyb.*——A place of Arabia. *Plin.* 3. c. 5. *Strab.* 6.

LEU'COPHRYS, a temple of Diana, with a city of the same name, near the Mæander. The goddess, surnamed Leucophryne, was represented under the figure of a woman with many breasts, and crowned with victory. *Xenoph.*—*Plin.* 5. c. 31. ——An ancient name of Tenedus. *Paus.* 10. c. 14. *Strab.* 13 & 14.

LEUCOPH'YRA, a people of the tribe Antiochis. *Hesych.*

LEUCOP'OLIS, a town of Caria. *Plin.* 5. c. 29.—*Polyæn.* 5 & 6.

LEU'COS, a river of Macedonia, near Pydna. It is now Fiume di Chitri. *Plutarch.*——*Vid.* Idomeneus.

LEUCO'SIA or LEUCA'SIA, a small island in the Tyrrhene Sea, at the south of the Sinus Pæstanus. It received its name either from one of the companions of Æneas, who was drowned there, or from one of the sirens, who was thrown there by the sea. —*Strab.* 5.—*Ovid. Met.* 15. v. 708.—*Plin.* 2. c. 90. —*Festus Verb Sig.*

LEUCO'SIA, the ancient name of Samothrace. *Aristot. de republ.*

LEUCOS'YRI or LEUCOSY'RI, a people of Asia Minor, called afterwards Cappadocians. *Strab.* 12. The same name is given to the inhabitants of Cilicia where it borders on Cappadocia. *C. Nep.* 14. c. 1.—*Eustath. Sch. in Dionys.*

LEUCOS'YRUS, a river of Cilicia, afterwards called Pyramus. *Steph.*

LEUCO'THEA, a daughter of king Orchamus by Eurynome. Apollo became enamoured of her, and to introduce himself to her with greater facility, he assumed the form and features of her mother. Their happiness was complete, when Clytia, who tenderly loved Apollo, and was jealous of his partiality for Leucothea, discovered the whole intrigue to her father, who ordered his daughter to be buried alive. The lover, unable to save her from death, sprinkled nectar and ambrosia on her tomb, which, penetrating as far as the body, changed it into a beautiful tree which bears the frankincense. *Ovid. Met.* 4. v. 196.

LEUCO'THEA, an island of the Tyrrhene Sea, near Capreæ. *Plin.* 3. c. 6.——A fountain of Samus. *Id.* ——A town of Ægypt.——A town of Arabia. *Id.*—*Mela*, 2. c. 7.——A part of Asia which produces frankincense. *Plin.* 5. c. 9.

LEUCOTH'OE or LEUCO'THEA, the name of Ino the wife of Athamas after she was changed into a sea deity. *Vid.* Ino. She was called Matuta by the Romans, who raised her a temple, where all the people, particularly women, offered vows for their brother's children. They did not intreat the deity to protect their own children, because Ino had been unfortunate in hers. No female slaves were permitted to enter the temple, or, if their curiosity tempted them to transgress this rule, they were beaten away with the greatest severity. To this supplicating for other people's children, Ovid seems to allude in these lines: *Fast.* 6.

Non tamen hanc pro stirpe suâ pia mater adorat,
Ipsa parum felix visa fuisse parens.

Her divinity was also implored by sailors to protect them against storms and perils of the sea. *Homer. Odyss* 5. v. 333.—*Cic. de Nat. D.* 3. c. 15 & 19.—*Tusc.* 1. c. 11.—*Ovid. Fast.* 6. v. 545.—*Lactant de Fals. R.* 21. & *ad Theb.* 2. v. 380 & 383.—*Plut. Symp.* 5. *Quæst.* 3.—*Servius in Virg. G.* 1. v. 437. *Æn.* 5. v. 241.—*Paus.* 1. c. 42.—*Aug. de Civ. dei.* 18. c. 14.—*Sch. Pind.* 3 *Pyth.* 173. & *Od.* 11. v. 51. [There is a fine statue of this deity at Paris, having been removed from the Villa Albani near Rome; it is remarkable as carrying an infant Bacchus on the left arm.]

LEUCOTH'OE, a name of Aurora. *Mart. Capell*, 2. *Phil.*

LEUC'TRA, a village of Bœotia, between Platæa and Thespia, famous for the victory which Epaminondas the Theban general obtained there over the superior force of Cleombrotus, king of Sparta, on the 8th of July, B.C. 371. In this famous battle 4000 Spartans were killed, with their king Cleombrotus, and no more than 300 Thebans. From that time the Spartans lost the sovereignty of Greece, which they had possessed for nearly 500 years. *Plut. in Pelop. & Ages.*—*C. Nep. in Epam.* 6 & 8. *In Ages.* 6. *In Pelop.* 2 & 4.—*Justin.* 6. c. 6.—*Xenophon. Hist. Græc.*—*Diod.* 15.—*Paus. Lacon.*—*Cic. de Offic.* 1. c. 18. *Tusc.* 1. c. 46. *Att.* 6. ep. 1.—*Strab.* 9.

LEUC'TRUM, a town of Laconia. *Strab.* 8.

LEU'CUS, one of the companions of Ulysses, killed before Troy by Antiphus son of Priam. *Hom. Il.* 4. v. 491.

LEUCYA'NIAS, a river of Peloponnesus, flowing into the Alpheus. *Paus.* 6. c. 21.

LEUGÆ'SA, a city of Armenia Minor. *Ptol.*

LEU'NI, a people of Vindelicia, called Genauni by *Horace*. *Plin.* 4. c. 20.

LEU'PAS, a harbour of Arabia Felix. *Plin.* 6. c. 28.

LEUPHITOR'GA, a city of Upper Æthiopia. *Ptol.*—*Plin.* 6. c. 29.

LEUSA'NA, a city of Pannonia. *Antonin.*

LEUSIN'IUM, a city of Dalmatia. *Id.*

LEUTYCH'IDES, a Lacedæmonian, made king of Sparta on the expulsion of Demaratus. *Herodot.* 6. c. 65, &c. *Vid.* Letychides.

LEVA'NA, a goddess of Rome, who presided over the action of the person who took up from the ground a newly born child, after it had been placed there by the midwife. This ceremony was generally performed by the father, and so religiously observed, that the legitimacy of the child could be disputed without it. *Aug. de Civ. D.* 4. c. 2.—*Herodian.* 7.—*Gyrald. H. Deor.* 1.

LE'VI, or, more properly, Lævi, a people of Liguria. *Plin.* 3. c. 17.

LEVI'NUS. *Vid.* Lævinus.

LEVUM'NE, a mountain of Macedonia, near Pallene. *Plin.* 4. c. 10.

LEXA'NOR, an auxiliary of Perses. *Flacc* 6. v. 688.

LEXIA'NÆ, a people of Arabia Felix. *Plin.* 6. c. 28.

LEXO'VII, a people of Gaul, at the mouth of the Seine, conquered with great slaughter by a lieutenant of J. Cæsar. *Cæs. Bell. G.*—*Plin.* 4. c. 18.

LI'BA, an island of the Indian Sea.——A town of Mesopotamia. *Polyb.*

LIB'ANA, a town of the Celtiberi in Spain. *Ptol.*

LIB'ANÆ, a city of Syria. *Steph.*

LIBA'NIUS, a celebrated sophist of Antioch in the age of the emperor Julian. He was educated at Athens, and opened a school at Antioch, which produced some of the best and most of the literary characters of the age. Libanius was naturally vain and arrogant, and contemptuously refused the offers of the emperor Julian, who wished to purchase his friendship and intimacy by raising him to offices of the greatest splendor and affluence in the empire. When Julian had imprisoned the senators of Antioch for their impertinence, Libanius undertook the defence of his fellow-citizens, and paid a visit to the emperor, in which he astonished him by the boldness and independence of his expressions. Some of his orations, and above 1600 of his letters are extant. They discover much affectation and obscurity of style, and we cannot perhaps much regret the loss of writings which afforded nothing but a display of pedantry, and frequent quotations from Homer. Julian submitted his writings to the judgment of Libanius with the greatest confidence, and the sophist freely rejected or approved them, showing that he was more attached to the person than to the fortune and greatness of the imperial writer. The time of his death is unknown. The best edition of Libanius seems to be that of Paris, fol. 1606, with a second volume published by Morell, 1627. The latest edition is that of Reiske, of which the 4th volume was published in 1797. His epistles have been edited by Wolf, fol. 1738. *Fabr. B Gr.* 5. c. 43.—*Sax. Onom.* 1. p. 405.

LIB'ANUS, a high mountain of Syria, famous for cedars. *Strab.* 6.

LIBAR'NA or LIBAR'NUM, a town of Liguria. *Cluver. Ital. Antiq.* 81.—*Plin.* 3. c. 5.

LIBENTI'NA, LUBENTI'NI or LUBEN'TIA, a surname of Venus, who had a temple at Rome, where it was the custom for young women when arrived at nubile years, to dedicate the toys which had furnished them with amusement in their youthful days. *Varro. de L.L.* 5. c. 6.—*Aug. de Civ. Dei.* 4. c. 8.

LI'BER, a surname of Bacchus, which signifies *free*. He received his name from his delivering some cities of Bœotia from slavery, or, according to others, because wine, of which he was the patron, delivered mankind from their cares. The word is often used for wine itself. *Senec. de Tranq. Anim.*—*Servius. in Æn.* 1. v. 175. l. 3. v. 20.—*Plin.* 7. c. 56.—*Festus de V. Sig.*—*Terent. Eun.* 4. sc. 5.

LIB'ERA, a goddess, the same as Proserpine. Cicero speaks of Liber and Libera as children of Ceres, to whom the Romans paid adoration. *Cic. in Verr.* 4. c. 48 & 53. & l. 5. c. 14. *N.D.* 2. c. 24.—*Aug. de Civ. Dei.* 7. c. 2 & 3.—*Minuc. Felix.* 21.——A name given by St. Augustin to the divinity who presided over the union of the sexes. *De Civ. D.* 6, c. 9.——A name given to Ariadne by Bacchus, or Liber, when he had married her. *Ovid. Fast.* 3. v. 513. [There is an exceedingly beautiful statue of her in the British Museum.]

LIBERA'LIA or LIBE'RIA, festivals yearly celebrated at Rome in honor of Bacchus, on the 17th of March. Young men then put on the toga virilis, and slaves were permitted to speak with freedom, and everything bore the appearance of independence. They were much the same as the Dionysia of the Greeks. *Cic.* 6. *Att.* ep. 1.—*Varro. de L.L.* 5.—*Ovid. Fast.* 3. v. 713 & 788.—*Servius in* 5. *Ecl. Virg. & Æn.* 7. v. 397.

LIBERA'LIS ANTONI'NUS, a writer of Metamorphoses. Some suppose that he is the person alluded to by *Seutonius* in his book *de claris Rhetoribus*, and that he lived in the time of Claudius; but *Scaliger* is of a different opinion, as he wrote in Greek, and M. Antonius Liberalis wrote in Latin. *Hieron. in Chron. Euseb.* The latest edition of his "Transformationum Congeries" is that of Teucher, Leipz. 1791.—*Fabr. B. Gr.* 3. c. 27.—*Sax. Onom.* 1. p. 308.

LIBERAL'ITAS, one of the virtues honored as a divinity among the Romans. She had no temple, but was represented under a female form, holding in one hand a cornucopia, from which appeared ears of corn, jewels, gold and silver, toys, &c. and with the other she was in the act of distributing pieces of money, to reward merit and industry. *Spanh. Diss.* 14.

LIBER'TAS, a goddess of Rome, who had a temple on mount Aventine, raised by T. Gracchus, and enlarged and adorned by Pollio with many elegant statues and brazen columns, and a gallery, in which were deposited the public acts of the state. She was represented in a light dress, holding a rod in one hand, and a cap in the other, both signs of independence, as the former was used by the magistrates in the manumission of slaves, and the latter was worn by slaves, who were soon to be set at liberty. Sometimes a cat was placed at her feet, as this animal is very fond of liberty, and impatient when confined. *Liv.* 24. c. 16, l. 25. c. 7. l. 43. c. 6.—*Ovid. Trist.* 3. el. 1. v. 72.—*Plut. in Grac.*—*Dio. Cas.* 44.—*Sueton in Aug.* 31.—*Cic. Dom.* 35.

LIBE'THRA, a fountain of Magnesia in Thessaly, or of Bœotia, according to some authors, sacred to the Muses, from which they are called Libethrides. *Virg. Ecl.* 7. v. 21.—*Plin.* 4. c. 9.—*Mela*, 2. c. 3.—*Strab.* 9 & 10.—*Solin.* 8.—*Gyrald. de Musis.*

LIBE'THRIDES, a name given to the Muses from the fountain of Libethra, or from mount Libethrus in Thrace. *Strab.* 9 & 10.

LIBE'THRIUS MONS, a mountain of Bœotia, a branch of Mount Helicon.

LIB'ICI, LIBE'CII, or LI'BRI, a people of Gaul, who passed into Italy, and settled there, A.U.C. 364. *Liv.* 5. c. 35. l. 21. c. 38.—*Plin.* 3. c. 17.—*Polyb.* 2.

LIBIS'OSA or LIBIS'OCA, a town of Hispania Taraconensis, called Libisosona by *Pliny*, 3. c. 3.—*Ptol.*

LIBIS'SONIS or BIS'SONIS TUR'RIS, a town of Sardinia. *Plin.* 3. c. 7.—*Ptol.*

LIBIS'TUS, a city of Thrace, near Lower Mœsia. *Plin.* 4. c. 11.

LIBITI'NA, a goddess at Rome who presided over funerals. According to some, she is the same as

Venus, or, more properly, Proserpine. Servius Tullius first raised her a temple at Rome, in which everything necessary for funerals was exposed to sale, and where the registers of the dead were usually kept. *Dionys. Hal.* 4.—*Liv.* 40. c. 19.—*Val. Max.* 5. c. 2.—*Plut. Quæst. Rom.*—*Rhod.* 19. c. 18.

LI'BO, a friend of Pompey, who watched over the fleet, &c. *Plut.*——A Roman citizen, &c. *Horat.* 1. ep. 19.——A friend of the first triumvirate, who killed himself and was condemned after death. ——A writer of annals, &c. *Cic. Att.* 18. ep. 31 & 32. The name of Libo belonged to the family of the Scribonii.

LI'BON, a Greek architect who built the famous temple of Jupiter Olympius in Elis. He florished about 450 B.C.

LIBOPHŒNI'CES, the inhabitants of the country near Carthage. *Plin.* 5. c. 4.—*Ptol.*—*Strab.* 17.

LIB'UI, a people of Gallia Cispadama.

LI'BUM, a town of Bithynia. *Antonin.*

LIBUR'NA, a town of Dalmatia. *Strab.* 7.

LIBUR'NIA, now Croatia, a country of Illyricum, between Istria and Dalmatia, whence a colony came to settle in Apulia in Italy. There were at Rome a number of men whom the magistrates employed as public heralds, who were called Liburni, probably from being originally of Liburnian extraction. Certain ships of a light construction but with strong beaks were also called Liburnian. *Propert.* 2. el. 11. v. 44.—*Juv.* 4. v. 75.—*Martial.* 1. epigr. 50. v. 33.—*Horat.* 1. od. 37. v. 30. *Epod.* 1. v. 1.—*Lucan.* 3. v. 534.—*Plin.* 6. ep. 16.—*Mela*, 2. c. 3.—*Strab.* 7.—*Ptol.* 2. c. 17.

LIBUR'NIDES, islands on the coast of Liburnia, in the Adriatic. *Strab.* 5.

LIBUR'NUM MA'RE, that part of the Adriatic Sea which borders on the coast of Liburnia.

LIBUR'NUS, a mountain of Campania *Polyb.*——A harbour of Etruria. *Ptol.*

LIB'YA, a daughter of Epaphus and Cassiopea, who became mother of Agenor and Belus by Neptune. *Apollod.* 2. c. 1. l. 3. c. 1.—*Paus.* 1. 44.

LIB'YA, a name given to Africa, one of the three grand divisions of the ancient globe. Libya, properly speaking, formed only a part of Africa, bounded on the east by Ægypt, and on the west by that part called by the moderns the kingdom of Tripoli. The ancients, according to some traditions mentioned by *Herodotus*, and others, sailed round Africa, by steering westward from the Red Sea, and entered the Mediterranean by the columns of Hercules, after a perilous navigation of three years. From the word Libya are derived the epithets of Libys, Libyssa, Libysis, Libystis, Lybicus, Libysticus, Libystinus, Libystæus. *Virg. Æn.* 4. v. 106. l. 5. v. 37.—*Lucan.* 4.—*Sallust.* &c

LIB'YCI, a people of Italy. *Plin.* 3. c. 16.

LIB'YCI MON'TES, a range of mountains in Ægypt.

LIB'YCUM MA'RE, that part of the Mediterranean which lies on the coast of Cyrene. *Strab.* 2.

LIB'YCUS or **LIBYS'TIS**. *Vid* Libya.

LIBYPHŒNI'CES, a name applied to the inhabitants of the Phœnician cities of Carthage.

LIBYS'SA, a small river of Bithynia, with a town of the same name, where the tomb of Annibal was still extant in the age of Pliny. *Appian. Alex.*—*Plin.* 5. c. 32.

LIBYSTI'NI, a people near the Colchi. *Steph.*

LICA'TII, a people of Vindelicia. *Ptol.*—*Strab.* 4. They are called Licates by *Pliny*, 3. c. 20.

LI'CHA, a city near Lycia. *Thucyd.* 8.

LICH'ADES, small islands near Cæneum, a promontory of Eubœa, so called from Lichas. *Vid.* Lichas. *Ovid Met.* 9. v. 155, 218.—*Strab.* 9.

LI'CHAS, a servant of Hercules who brought him the poisoned tunic from Dejanira. He was thrown by his master into the Eubœan Sea with great violence, and changed into a rock by the gods. *Ovid. Met.* 9. v. 211.—*Diod.* 4.—*Apollod.* 2.

LICHE'NI, a people of Arabia Felix *Plin.* 6. c. 28

LI'CHES, an Arcadian who found the bones of Orestes buried at Tegea, &c. *Herodot.*

LICHIN'DUS, a city of Sicily. *Steph.*

LICIN'IA LEX. was enacted by L. Licinius Crassus, and Q. Mutius, consuls, A.U.C. 659. It ordered all the inhabitants of Italy to be enrolled on the list of citizens in their respective cities.—Another by C. Licinius Crassus, the tribune, A.U.C. 608. It transferred the right of chusing priests from the college to the people. It was proposed but did not pass. Another by C. Licinius Stolo, the tribune. It forbad any person to possess 500 acres of land, or keep more than 100 head of large cattle, or 500 of small.—Another by P. Licinius Varus, A.U.C. 545, to settle the day for the celebration of the Ludi Apollinares, which was before uncertain.——Another by P. Licinius Crassus Dives, B.C. 110. It was the same as the Fannian law, and farther required that no more than 30 *asses* should be spent at any table on the calends, nones, and nundinæ, and allowed only three pounds of fresh and one of salt meat on ordinary days. None of the fruits of the earth were forbidden.—Another, *de sodalitiis*, by L. Licinius, the consul, A.U.C. 692. It imposed a severe penalty on party clubs, or societies assembled or frequented for election purposes, as coming under the definition of *ambitus*, and of offering violence, in some degree, to the freedom and independence of the people.—Another, called also Æbutia, by Licinius and Æbutius, the tribunes. It enacted, that when any law was presented with respect to any office or power, the person who proposed the bill, as well as his colleagues, in office, his friends and relations, should be declared incapable of being invested with the said office or power.

LICIN'IA, the wife of C. Gracchus, who attempted to dissuade her husband from his violent measures by a pathetic speech. She was deprived of her dowry after the death of Caius.——A vestal virgin accused of incontinence, but acquitted, A.U.C. 636 ——A vestal put to death for her lasciviousness under Trajan.——The wife of Mecænas, distinguished for conjugal tenderness. She was sister to Proculeius, and bore also the name of Terentia. *Horat.* 2. od. 12. v. 13.—The family of the Licinii branched into the families of the Crassi, Luculli, Murænæ, Nervæ, Stolones, &c.

LICIN'IUS C. VALE'RIUS LICINIA'NUS, a celebrated Roman emperor. His father was a poor peasant of Dalmatia, and he was himself for some time a common soldier in the Roman armies. His valour recommended him to the notice of Galerius Maximinus, who had once shared with him the inferior and subordinate offices of the army, and had lately been invested with the imperial purple by Diocletian. Galerius loved him for his friendly services, particularly during the Persian war, and showed his regard for his merit by taking him as a colleague in the empire, and appointing him over the provinces of Pannonia and Rhætia. Constantine, who was also one of the emperors, courted the favour of Licinius, and, sensible of his great abilities, made his intimacy more durable by giving him his sister Constantia in marriage, A.D. 313. The continual successes of Licinius, particularly against Maximinus, increased his pride, and rendered him jealous of the greatness of his brother-in-law. The persecutions of the Christians, whose doctrines Constantine followed, soon caused a rupture, and Licinius had the mortification to lose two battles, one in Pannonia, and the other near Adrianopolis. Treaties of peace were made between the contending rivals, but the restless ambition of Licinius soon broke them; and, after many engagements, a decisive battle was fought near Chalcedonia. Ill fortune again attended Licinius, he was conquered and fled to Nicodemia, where the conqueror soon obliged him to surrender, and to resign the imperial purple. The tears of Constantia obtained a doubtful forgiveness for her husband, but Constantine knew what a turbulent and active enemy had fallen into his hands, therefore he ordered him to be strangled at Thessalonica A.D. 324. His wretched family shared his fate. The avarice, licentiousness and cruelty of Licinius were as conspicuous as his misfortunes. He was an enemy to learning, and this aversion is said to have proceeded from his ignorance of letters, and the rusticity of his education. *Socr.* l. 1.—*Eutrop.* 10,—*Euseb. Chron.* &c —*Zosim.* l. 2.

LICIN'IUS FLA'VIUS VALE'RIUS LICINIA'NUS, was son of the preceding by Constantia. He was honored with the title of Cæsar when scarcely twenty months old, but he was involved in his father's ruin, and put to death by order of Constantine. *Idacius in Fast. Chron. Alex.* &c.

LICIN'IUS OR LICINIA'NUS C. JUL. VA'LENS, was proclaimed emperor in the time of Decius, but enjoyed the dignity only for a short time. *Victor, in Decio.*

LICIN'IUS CA'IUS IM'BREX, a comic poet in the age of Africanus, preferred by some in merit to Ennius and Terence. His Nævia and Neæra are quoted by ancient authors, but of all his poetry only two verses are now preserved. *Aul. Gell.*

C. LICIN'IUS CAL'VUS, a tribune of the people celebrated for the consequence of his family, as well as for his intrigues and abilities. He was a plebeian, and was the first of that body who was raised to the important office of master of the horse to the dictator. He was surnamed Stolo, or *useless sprout*, on account of the law which he had enacted during his tribuneship. *Vid.* Licinia Lex, by Stolo. He afterwards made a law which permitted the plebeians to share the consular dignity with the patricians, A.U.C. 388. He himself reaped the benefits of this law, and was one of the first plebeian consuls. This law was proposed and passed by Licinius, as it is reported, at the instigation of his ambitious wife, daughter of M. Fabius Ambustus, who was jealous of her sister, who had married a patrician, and who seemed, in the eyes of her plebeian family, to be of a higher dignity, from being the wife of a consul. *Liv.* 6. c. 34, &c.—*Plut.*

LICIN'IUS C. CAL'VUS. a celebrated orator and poet in the age of Cicero He distinguished himself by his eloquence in the forum, and his poetry, which some of the ancients have compared to the effusions of Catullus. His orations are greatly commended by Quintilian. Some believe that he wrote annals quoted by Dionysius of Halicarnassus. He died in the 30th year of his age. *Quintil.—Cic. in Brut.* 81.

LICIN'IUS CRAS'SUS. *Vid.* Crassus.

LICIN'IUS P. CRAS'SUS, a Roman sent against Perseus, king of Macedonia. He was at first defeated, but afterwards repaired his losses, and obtained a complete victory, &c.

LICIN'IUS LUCUL'LUS. *Vid.* Lucullus.

LICIN'IUS MA'CER, a Roman accused by Cicero when prætor. He derided the power of his accuser, but when he saw himself condemned, he grew so desperate that he killed himself. *Plut.*

LICIN'IUS MUCIA'NUS, a Roman who wrote a work upon the history and geography of the eastern countries, often quoted by *Pliny*. He lived in the reign of Vespasian.

LICIN'IUS P. TEG'ULA, a comic poet at Rome, about 200 B.C. He is ranked by *Gellius* as the fourth of the best comic poets which Rome produced. Few lines of his compositions are now extant. He wrote an ode which was sung all over the city of Rome by nine virgins, during the Macedonian war. *Liv.* 31. c. 12.—*Lil. Gyrald. dial.* 8. *poet.—Glandorp. in Onom. &c.*

LICIN'IUS VAR'RO MURÆ'NA, a brother of Proculeius, who conspired against Augustus with Fannius Cæpio, and suffered death for his crime. *Horace* addressed his 2 od. 10. to him, and recommended equanimity in every situation. *Dio.* 54.

LICIN'IUS, a consul sent against Annibal.——A consul who defeated the robbers that infested the Alps.——A high priest.

LIC'INUS or LICI'NUS, a barber and freedman of Augustus, raised by his master to the rank and dignity of a senator, merely because he hated Pompey's family. *Horat. Art. P.* 301.

LICOR'NUS, a mountain of Arcadia. *Stat. Theb.* 1. v. 356. *Pliny*, 4. c. 6, calls it Lyceum. See *Barth. Animadv. ad Stat. loc. citat.*

LICNE'NI, a people of Corsica. *Ptol.* Their country is now Val di Nicolo.

LI'CUS or LYC'IAS, now Lech, a river of Vindelicia. *Ptol.*

LICYM'NIUS, a son of Electryon and brother of Alcmena. He became so infirm in his old age, that when he walked, he was always supported by a slave. Tlepolemus, son of Hercules, observing the slave inattentive to his duty, threw a stick at him, which unfortunately missed its aim, and killed Licymnius. The murderer fled to Rhodes. *Apollod.* 2. c. 7.—*Diod.* 5.—*Homer. Il.* 2. v. 170.—*Pind. Olymp.* 7.

LI'DE, a mountain of Caria. *Herodot.* 1. c. 175.

LIE'BRIS, a city of Phœnicia. *Steph.*

LIGANI'RA, a city of India within the Ganges. *Ptol.*

LIGA'RIUS Q., a Roman, deservedly held in high estimation as pro-consul of Africa, after Confidius. In the civil wars he followed the more popular interest of Pompey, but by the influence of his friends he was pardoned when the cause of Cæsar triumphed. Cæsar, however, and his adherents were determined upon the ruin of Ligarius, and Tubero was engaged to criminate him, but Cicero, by an eloquent oration, still extant, defeated his accusers, and procured his acquittal. He became afterwards, one of Cæsar's murderers. *Cic. pro Lig.—Plut. in Cæsar.*

LIGAU'NIA, a nation of Gallia Narbonensis. *Plin.* 3. c. 4.

LIGE'A, one of the Nereides. *Virg. G.* 4.

LI'GER, a Rutulian killed by Æneas. *Virg. Æn.* 10. v. 576.

LI'GER or LIG'ERIS, now La Loire, one of the largest rivers of Gaul, falling into the Atlantic Ocean near Nantes. *Strab.* 4.—*Plin.* 4. c. 18.—*Cæs. B. G.* 7. c. 55 & 75.

LI'GIR, a river of Bœotia, near Plateæ. *Steph.*

LIG'ORAS, an officer of Antiochus, king of Syria, who took the town of Sardis by stratagem, &c.

LI'GUR, a surname of the Ælian family. *Cic. Cluent.* 26.

LIG'URES, the inhabitants of Liguria. *Vid.* Liguria.

LIGU'RIA, a country at the west of Italy, bounded on the east by the river Macra, on the south by part of the Mediterranean called the Ligustic Sea, on the west by the Varus, and on the north by the Po. The commercial town of Genoa was anciently, and is now, the capital of the country. The origin of the inhabitants is not known, though in their character they are represented by the ancients as vain, unpolished, and addicted to falsehood. According to some they were descended from the ancient Gauls or Germans, or, as others assert, they were of Greek origin, perhaps the posterity of the Ligyes mentioned by Herodotus. Liguria was subdued by the Romans, and its chief harbour, after Genoa, now bears the name of Leghorn. *Lucan.* 1. v. 442.—*Mela*, 2. c. 1.—*Strab.* 4, &c.—*Ptol.* 3. c. 1.—*Dionys. Hal.* 1. c. 10.—*Virg. Æn.* 11. v. 715.—*Cato apud Servium. Æn.* 11. v. 700.—*Cic. Agr.* 2. c. 35.—*Tacit. Hist.* 2. c. 15.—*Plin.* 2. c. 5, &c.—*Liv.* 5. c. 35. l. 22. c. 33. l. 39. c. 6, &c.—*C. Nep. in Ann.—Flor.* 2. c. 8.

LIGURI'NUS, a Latin poet. *Martial.* 3. epigr. 44.——A beautiful youth in the age of Horace, 4. od. 1. v. 33.

LIGU'RIUS, a friend of Cæsar. *Cic. Fam.* 16. ep. 18. *Ad. Att.* 11. ep. 9.

LI'GUS, a woman who inhabited the Alps. She concealed her daughter from the pursuit of Otho's soldiers. &c. *Tacit. Hist.* 2. c. 13.

LIGUS'TICÆ AL'PES, a part of the Alps, which borders on Liguria. This portion of the Alps is sometimes called Maritimæ.

LIGUS'TICUM MA'RE, the north part of the Tyrrhene Sea, on the coast of Liguria, now the Gulph of Genoa *Plin.* 2. c. 47.

LIG'YES, a people of Asia who inhabited the country between Caucasus and the river Phasis. Some suppose them to have been a colony of the Ligyes of Europe, more commonly called Ligures. *Herodot.* 7. c. 72.—*Dionys. Hal.* 1. c. 10.—*Strab.* 4.—*Diod.* 4.

LIGYR'GUM, a mountain of Arcadia. *Polyb.*

LIGYS'TUS, a son of Phaethon. *Fab. Pictor.*

LILÆ'A, a town of Achaia near the Cephisus. *Stat. Theb.* 7. v. 348.—*Plin.* 4. c. 3.—*Strab* 1.

LILÆ'US, a river of Bithynia, called Lillius by *Arrian. Plin.—Salmas. ad Solin.* p. 880.

LILYBÆ'UM or LILYBÆ'ON, now Coco, a promontory at the south west corner of Sicily, opposite the Ægates, with a town of the same name, now called Marsala. The town was large and well fortified, and maintained long sieges against the Carthaginians, &c., particularly one of ten years against Rome in the first Punic war. It had a large and capacious port, which the Romans, in the wars with Carthage, endeavoured in vain to stop and fill up with stones, on account of its convenience and vicinity to the coast of Africa. Nothing now remains of this once-powerful city but the ruins of temples and aqueducts. *Virg. Æn.* 3. v. 706.—*Mela*, 2. c. 7.—*Strab.* 6.—*Cic. in Verr.* 5.—*Cæs. Bell. Afric.—Diod.* 22.

LIMÆ'A, LIM'IA or LIM'IUS, a river of Lusitania

Strab. 3.—*Plin.* 4 c. 22. It was called also Lethe, and the river of Oblivion. *Sil. Pun. Bell.* 1. v. 236.

LIME'NIA, a town of Cyprus, now Limnat. *Strab.* 14.

LIM'ICI, a people of Hispania Tarraconensis. *Ptol.*

LIMIN'IUM, a town between Emerita and Cæsar-Augusta. *Antonin.*

LIM'ITES ROMA'NI, fortifications built by the Romans on the Rhine and Danube to protect their possessions from the attacks of the Germans.

LIM'NÆ, a fortified place on the borders of Laconia and Messenia. *Paus.* 3. c. 14.——A town of the Thracian Chersonesus. *Strab.* 8.

LIMNÆ'UM, the name of the temple of Diana at Limnæ, from which the goddess was called Limnæa, under which appellation she was worshipped at Sparta and in Achaia. The Spartans wished to seize her temple in the age of Tiberius, but the emperor interfered, and gave it to the lawful possessors, the Messenians. *Paus.* 3. c. 14. l. 7. c. 20. *Tac. Ann.* 4. c. 43.

LIMNATID'IA. a festival in honor of Diana, surnamed Limnatis, from Limnæ, a school of exercise at Trœzen, where she was worshipped, or from λιμναι, *ponds*, because she presided over fishermen. *Paus. Achaic.*—*Artemid.*

LIMNI'ACE, the daughter of the Ganges, mother of Atys. *Ovid. Met.* 5. v. 48.

LIMNI'ADES, certain nymphs who presided over stagnant waters and pools. *Nat. Com.* 5. c 12.

LIMNO'NIA, one of the Nereides. *Homer. Il.* 18. v. 41.

LIMNOTHALAS'SA, an island near Spain. *Strab.* 4.

LIM'NUS, an island of the British Sea. *Ptol.* It is now Ramsey, according to *Camden.*

LI'MON, a place of Campania. between Neapolis and Puteoli. *Stat.* 3. *Sylv.* 1. v. 149.

LIMO'NE, a city of Perrhæbia. *Steph.* in Ἠλώνη.

LIM'ONUM or LIMO'NUM, a town of Gaul, afterwards Pictavium, now Poictiers. *Cæs. G.* 8. c. 26.

LIMU'SA, a city of Lower Pannonia *Anton.*

LIM'YRA, a town of Lycia. *Ovid. Met.* 9. v. 645. —*Vell.* 2. c. 102.

LIMYR'ICA, a region of India, within the Ganges. *Ptol.*—*Plin.* 31. c. 2.

LIM'YRUS, a river of Lycia.

LINCA'SII, a people of Gallia Narbonensis. *Strab.* 4.

LIN'DUM, a colony of Britain, supposed to be that part of the island now comprising the county of Lincoln.

LIN'DUS, a city on the south-east part of Rhodes, built by Cercaphus son of Sol and Cydippe. Hercules had there a celebrated temple, and likewise Minerva, which last had been built by the Danaides. Lindus is not only famed for the foundation of Gela in Sicily, by one of its colonies, but it gave birth to Cleobulus, one of the seven wise men, and to Chares and Laches, who were employed in making and finishing the famous Colossus of Rhodes. *Strab.* 14.—*Homer, Il.* 2. v. 163.—*Mela,* 2. c. 7.—*Plin.* 34.—*Herodot.* 7. c. 153.—*Lactant. de Fals. R.* 21.——A grandson of Apollo. *Cic. de Nat. D.* 3. c. 21.

LIN'GONES, now Langrois, a people of Gallia Belgica, between the rivers Mosa, Arar, and Matrona, made tributary to Rome by J. Cæsar. Their town Lingonæ is now Langres. They passed into Italy, where they made a settlement near the Alps, at the head of the Adriatic. *Tacit. H.* 4. c. 55.—*Martial.* 11. epigr. 57. v. 9. l. 14. epigr. 159.—*Lucan* 1. v. 398.—*Cæs. Bell. G.* 1. c. 26.

LINIT'IMA, a town of Upper Æthiopia. *Plin.* 6. c. 29.

LI'NON, a small region near the Hellespont. The inhabitants were called Linusii. *Steph. ex Strab.* 1. 13.

LINTER'NA PA'LUS, now Lago di Patria, a lake of Campania, near Linternum. *Ital.* 7. v. 278.

LINTER'NUM, a town of Campania, at the mouth of the river Clanis, known as the country residence of Scipio Africanus, who died and was buried there, ordering this inscription to be placed over his remains, *Ingrata patria, nec ossa mea habebis. Liv.* 34. c. 45.—*Sil.* 6. v. 654. l. 7. v. 278.—*Cic.* 10. *Att.* 13.—*Ovid. Met.* 15. v. 713.

LI'NUS, a name common to different persons, who are often taken one for the other, and the history of whom is involved in obscurity. One was son of Urania, and Amphimarus, the son of Neptune. Another was son of Apollo by Psammathe daughter of Crotopus king of Argos. Martial mentions him in his 78 epigr. l. 9. The third son of Ismenius, and born at Thebes in Bœotia, taught music to Hercules, who, in a fit of anger, struck him on the head with his lyre and killed him. He was son of Mercury and Urania, according to Diogenes, who mentions some of his philosophical compositions, in which he asserted that the world had been created in an instant. He was killed by Apollo, for presuming to compare himself to him. Apollodorus, however, and Pausanias maintain that his ridicule of Hercules for his awkwardness in holding the lyre was fatal to him, *Apollod.* 2. c. 4.—*Diog.* 1.—*Virg. Ecl.* 4.—*Paus.* 2. c. 15. l. 9. c. 20.—*Martial.* 9. epigr. 88. v. 4.—*Tacit. Ann.* 11. c. 14.

LI'NUS, a fountain in Arcadia, the waters of which were said to prevent abortion. *Plin.* 31. c. 2.

LIP'ARA, the largest of the Æolian islands on the northern coast of Sicily, now called the Lipari. It had a city of the same name, which, according to Diodorus, it received from Liparus the son of Auson, king of these islands, whose daughter Cyane was married by his successor Æolus, according to Pliny. The inhabitants of this island were at one time powerful by sea, and long withstood the attacks of the Etrurians. From the large tribute which they paid to Dionysius, the tyrant of Syracuse, they must have been very opulent. The island was celebrated for the variety of its fruits, and its raisins are still in great repute. It had some convenient harbours, and a fountain, the waters of which were much frequented on account of their medicinal powers. According to Diodorus, Æolus reigned at Lipara before Liparus. *Liv.* 5. c. 28.—*Plin.* 3. c. 9.—*Ital.* 14. v. 57.—*Virg. Æn.* 1. v. 56. l. 8. v. 417.—*Mela,* 2. c. 7.—*Strab.* 6.—*Diod.* 5.—*Schol. Callim. in Delum.*—*Schol. Theocr. in Id.*——A town of Etruria.

LIP'ARIS, a river of Cilicia, so called ἀπὸ τοῦ λιπαροῦ, because its waters were said to be as smooth as oil. *Plin.* 5. c. 27.—*Vitruv.* 8. c. 3.

LIP'ARUS. *Vid.* Lipara.

LIPAX'US, a city of Thrace. *Steph.*

LIPH'LUM, a town of the Æqui, taken by the Romans.

LIPHOEC'UA, a city the Æqui, taken by the Romans. *Diod. Sic.* 14.

LIPODO'RUS, one of the Greeks settled in Asia by Alexander, &c.

LIQUEN'TIA, now Livenza, a river of Cisalpine Gaul, falling into the Adriatic Sea. *Plin.* 3. c. 18.

LIRCÆ'US, fountain near Nemea. *Stat. Theb.* 4. v. 711. The more approved reading is Lyrcius. *Priscian.* 1. 2.—*Barth. ad Stat. loc. cit.*

LIR'IA, a river of Gallia Narbonensis, now le Lez. *Plin.* 3. c. 4.

LIRI'OPE, one of the Oceanides, mother of Narcissus, by the god of the river Cephisus. She was so fond of her son, whose beauty was of a superior nature, that she consulted Tiresias with respect to his future life. The prophet answered that Narcissus might attain a great length of years if he never saw himself, and the words, though disregarded by Liriope, proved fatally true. *Ovid. Met.* 3. v. 341.

LIRI'OPE, a fountain of Bœotia, on the borders of Thespis, where Narcissus was drowned according to some accounts. *Paus.*

LI'RIS, now Gariliano, a river of Campania, which it separates from Latium. It falls into the Mediterranean Sea, after watering the towns of Sora, Fregellæ, and Minturnæ, and receiving the tributary streams of the Trerus, the Fibrenus, the Cosa, and the Melpes. *Liv.* 10. c. 21.—*Virg. Æn.* 7. v. 47. —*Horat.* 1. od. 32. v. 7. l. 3. od. 17. v. 4.—*Mela,* 2. c. 4.—*Lucan.* 2. v. 424.

LI'RIS, a warrior killed by Camilla, &c. *Virg. Æn.* 11. v. 670.

LIRNYT'IA, a city of Pamphylia. *Steph. ex Hecatæo.*

LIS'CUS, a magistrate of the Ædui. *Mela,* 2. c. 4. —*Cæs. B. G.* 1. c. 16.

LIS'INAS, a town of Thessaly. *Liv.* 32. c. 14.

LIS'SA, the name of a fury whom Euripides introduces on the stage, as conducted by Iris at the command of Juno to inspire Hercules with that fatal rage which ended in his death.

LIS'SA, an island of the Illyrian Sea, now Isola di Fara. *Plin.* 3. c. 26.——A town of the Acetani, in Spain. *Ptol.*

LIS'SIA, an island on the coast of Britain. *Anton.*

LIS'SON, a river of Sicily, flowing by Leontium, and now Fiume de Lentini. *Liv.* 43. c. 30.

LIS'SUS, now Alessio, a town at the mouth of the Drilo, on the shores of the Adriatic, between the provinces of Macedonia and Illyricum. *Plin.* 3. c. 22.—*Liv.* 44. c. 10.—*Lucan.* 5. v. 719——A small river of Thrace, falling into the Ægæan Sea, between Thasus and Samothrace. It was dried up by the numerous armies of Xerxes, when he invaded Greece. *Strab* 7.—*Herodot.* 7. c. 109.—*Juv.* 10. v. 177.

LIS'TA, a town of the Sabines, the inhabitants of which were called Listini. *Dion. Hal.*

LIT'ABRUM, now Buitrago, a town of Hispania Tarraconensis. *Liv.* 32. c. 14. l. 35. c. 22.

LITÆ'Æ, a city of Laconia. *Steph.*

LITA'NA, a wood in Gallia Togata, now Selva di Lugo. *Liv.* 23. c. 24.

LITAV'ICUS, one of the Ædui, who assisted Cæsar with 10,000 men. *Cæs. B. G.* 7. c. 37.

LI'TA, a city of Macedonia.

LITER'NUM. *Vid.* Linernum.

LITHE'SIUS, a surname of Apollo. *Steph.*—*Suidas.*

LITHOBO'LIA, a festival celebrated at Trœzene in honor of Limia and Auxesia, who came from Crete, and were stoned to death by the fury of the seditious populace. Hence the name of the solemnity, λιθοβολία, *lapidation.* *Pausan. Corinth.*

LI'THRUS, a town of Armenia Minor. *Strab.* 12.

LIT'TAMUM, now Lutach, a city of Noricum. *Antonin.*

LITU'BIUM, now Ritorbio, a town of Liguria, at the south of the Po. *Liv.* 32. c. 29.

LITYER'SAS, an illegitimate son of Midas king of Phrygia, who made strangers prepare his harvest, and afterwards put them to death. He is said to have had such a gluttonous appetite, that he daily devoured as much meat as might have been a sufficient load for a beast of burden. He was at last killed by Hercules. *Theocr. Id.*—*Sosith apud. Athen.* 10.

LITYER'SES, the songs of reapers, either in honor of Ceres, who presided over corn, or in remembrance of the son of Midas. Pollux considers the Lityerses as songs expressive of sorrow and mourning, and that they were first composed for the purpose of consoling Midas for the loss of his favourite son. The name was afterwards borrowed by the Greeks, and, without allusion to the history of the Phrygian prince, applied to the songs which reapers sing during the time of harvest. *Athen.* 14.—*Pollux.* 1. c. 3.—*Servius in Ecl. Virg.* 8. v. 68.—*Schol. Theocr. Idyll.* 10.

LIV'IA LEX, *de sociis*, proposed to make all the inhabitants of Italy free citizens of Rome. It was so unpopular, that M. Livius Drusus, who framed it, was found murdered in his house before it passed.—Another, by M. Livius Drusus the tribune, A.U.C. 662, which required that the judicial power should be lodged in the hands of an equal number of knights and senators.

LIV'IA DRUSIL'LA, a celebrated Roman lady, daughter of L. Drusus Calidianus. She married Tiberius Claudius Nero, by whom she had the emperor Tiberius and Drusus Germanicus. The attachment of her husband to the cause of Antony was the beginning of her greatness. Augustus saw her as she fled from the danger which threatened her family, and when she fell at his feet imploring his pardon, he was captivated with her beauty. Divorcing his wife Scribonia, he, with the approbation of the augurs, celebrated his nuptials with Livia, though she was then pregnant. Raised to the imperial dignity, Livia took advantage of the passion of Augustus, which she made subservient to her ambitious views. Her children by Claudius were adopted by the complying emperor; and, that she might make the succession of her son Tiberius more certain, Livia is accused of secretly involving in one common ruin the heirs and nearest relations of Augustus. Her cruelty and ingratitude are still more strongly marked, when she is charged with having murdered her own husband to hasten the elevation of Tiberius. If she was anxious for the aggrandizement of her son, Tiberius proved ungrateful, and unnaturally hated a woman to whom he owed his life, his elevation, and his greatness. Livia died in the 86th year of her age, A.D. 29. Tiberius showed himself as undutiful after her death as before, for he neglected her funeral, and expressly commanded that no honors, either private or public, should be paid to her memory. *Tacit. Ann.* 1. c. 3.—*Suet. in Aug. Tib. & Claud.*—*Dion. Cass.*—*Plin.* 7. c. 45. l. 15. c. 30. [A representation of Livia Drusilla, in the character of Pity, is in the Vatican at Rome.]

LIV'IA. *Vid.* Drusilla.

LIV'IA HORESTIL'LA, a Roman lady debauched by Caligula on the day on which she was going to marry Piso. *Suet in Calig.* 25.

LIV'IA OCELLI'NA, was Galba's stepmother, and committed adultery with him. *Suet. in Gal.* 3.

LIV'IA, a daughter of Drusus. She was the wife of Drusus, son of Tiberius, and bore him two sons; but afterwards murdered him, at the instigation of Sejanus, whom she married. *Tac. Ann.* 4. c. 39.—*Suet. Claud.* c. 1. *Tib.* 44.

LIV'II, a people of Gallia Narbonensis. *Plin.*

LIVIL'LA, a sister of Caligula. *Vid.* Julia.

LIVINE'IUS REG'ULUS, a senator, who, being degraded from his dignity, gave an exhibition of gladiators at Pompeii, at which a fierce quarrel arose between the inhabitants and the people of Nuceria. For this conduct he was banished. *Tac. Ann.* 3. c. 11, &c.

LIVIOP'OLIS, a town of Cappadocia. *Plin.* 6. c. 4.

LIV'IUS ANDRONI'CUS, a dramatic poet who flourished at Rome about 240 B.C. He was the first who turned the personal satires and fescennine verses, so long the admiration of the Romans, into the form of a dialogue and regular play. Though the character of a player, so valued and applauded in Greece, was reckoned vile and despicable among the Romans, Andronicus acted a part in his dramatical compositions, and engaged the attention of his audience, by repeating what he had laboriously formed after the manner of the Greeks. Andronicus was the freedman of M. Livius Salinator, whose children he educated, and whose name he assumed. His poetry was grown obsolete in the age of Cicero, whose nicety and judgment would not even recommend the reading of it Some few of his verses, about 105 in number, are preserved in the Corpus Poetarum. *Cic. Tusc.* 1. c. 1. *Br.* 18. *Sen.* 14. *Leg.* 2. c. 15.—*Horat.* 2. ep. 1. v. 89.—*Sax Onom.* 1. p. 108.

LIV'IUS DRU'SUS, a tribune who joined the patricians in opposing the ambitious views of C. Gracchus. *Plut. in Gracc.*

LIV'IUS M. SALINA'TOR, a Roman consul sent against the Illyrians. The success with which he finished his campaign, and the victory which some years after he obtained over Asdrubal, who was passing into Italy, with a reinforcement for his brother Annibal, show how deserving he was to be placed at the head of the Roman armies His surname of Salinator arose from his imposing an odious tax on salt while censor. *Liv.* 27. c. 46, &c.

LIV'IUS, an uncle of Cato of Utica. *Plut.*

LIV'IUS TI'TUS, a native of Padua, celebrated for his writings. He passed the greatest part of his life at Naples, but more particularly at Rome, at the court of Augustus, who liberally patronized the learned. Few particulars of his private life are known, yet his fame was so universally spread even in his lifetime, that an inhabitant of Gades traversed Spain, Gaul, and Italy, merely to see the man whose writings had given him such pleasure and satisfaction in the perusal. Livy died at Padua, in his 67th year, and according to some, on that same day Rome was also deprived of another of its brightest ornaments by the death of the poet Ovid, A.D. 17. It is said that Livia had appointed Livy to be preceptor to young Claudius, the brother of Germanicus, but death prevented the historian from enjoying an honour to which he was particularly entitled by his learning and his universal knowledge. The name of Livy is rendered immortal by his most valuable history of the Roman empire. Besides this, he wrote some philosophical treatises and dialogues, with a letter, addressed to his son, on the merits of authors, which ought to be read by young men. This letter is greatly commended by Quintilian, who expatiates with great warmth on the judgment and candour of the author. His Roman history was comprehended in 140 or 142 books, of which, unfortunately, only thirty-five are extant. It began with the foundation of Rome, and was continued till the death of Drusus in Germany. The merit of this history is well known, and the high rank which Livy holds among historians will never be disputed. He is always great, his style is clear and intelligible, labored without affectation, diffusive without tediousness, and argumentative without pedantry. In his harangues he is bold and animated, and in his narrations and descriptions he claims a decided superiority for vigour, clearness, and perspicuity. He is always elegant, and though many have branded his provincial words with the name of Patavinity, yet the expressions, or rather the orthography of words, which in Livy are supposed to distinguish a native of a province of Italy from a native of Rome, are not loaded with obscurity, and the perfect classic is as familiarly acquainted with the one as with the other. Livy has been censured, and perhaps with justice, for being too credulous, and for burdening his history with vulgar prejudices and superstitious tales. He may disgust when he mentions that milk and blood were rained from heaven, or that an ox spoke, or a woman changed her sex, yet he candidly confesses that he recorded what had made an indelible impression upon the minds of a credulous age. His candour has also been called in question, and he has sometimes shewn himself too partial to his countrymen, but he is every where an indefatigable supporter of the cause of justice and virtue. The works of Livy have been divided by some of the moderns into fourteen decades, each consisting of ten books. The first decade comprehends the history of 460 years. The second decade is lost, and the third comprehends the history of the second Punic war, which includes about eighteen years. In the fourth decade Livy treats of the wars with Macedonia and Antiochus, which contain about twenty-three years. For the first five books of the fifth decade, we are indebted to the researches of the moderns. They were found at Worms, A.D. 1431. These are the books that remain of Livy's history, and the loss which the celebrated work has sustained by the ravages of time, has in some measure been compensated by the labours of J. Freinshemius, who with great attention and industry has made an epitome of the Roman history, which is now incorporated with the remaining books of Livy. The third decade seems to be superior to the others, yet the author has not scrupled to copy from his contemporaries and predecessors, and we find many passages taken word for word from Polybius, in which the latter has shewn himself more informed in military affairs and superior to his imitator. The best editions of Livy will be found to be those of Maittaire, 6 vols. 12mo, London, 1722; of Drakenborch, 7 vols 4to, Amst. 1738; of Ruddiman, 4 vols 12mo, Edin. 1751; of Crevier, Paris, 1768: and of Walker, Dublin, the first two volumes of which appeared in 1797—1799, and the remaining five in 1809—1813. *Euseb. Chron.—Quintil.* 2. c. 5. l. 8. c. 1. l. 10. c. 1, &c.—*Tacit. Ann.* 3. c. 34.—*Suet. Cl.* 41. —*Plin.* 2. ep. 3 & 8.—*Harles. Not. Lit. Rom.* 1. p. 192.—*Sax. Onom.* 1. p. 196.——A governor of Tarentum, who delivered up his trust to Annibal, &c.——A high-priest who devoted Decius to the Dii Manes.——A commander of a Roman fleet sent against Antiochus in the Hellespont.

LIX, LIX'A or LIX'US a small river of Mauritania, with a city of the same name, on the Atlantic Ocean. Antæus had a palace there, and, according to some accounts, it was in the neighbourhood that Hercules conquered him. *Ital.* 3. v. 258.—*Mela*, 3. c. 10.—*Strab.* 2.

LIX'US, a son of Ægyptus. *Apollod.*

LOBE'TUM, a city of Hispania Tarraconensis, now Albaracin. The people were called Lobetani. *Plin.* 3. c. 3.

LO'BON, a native of Argos, who wrote a book concerning poets. *Diog. Laert. in Epimen. & Thalet.*

LOCA'NUS, a river of Calabria, flowing from the Apennines. *Ptol.*

LOCAR'ICUM, a town of Sicily. *Antonin.*

LOCA'RIE, one of the horses of the Sun. *Hygin.* fab. 183.

LOCAS'TRA, a city of Media. *Ptol.* Some read Choastra.

LO'CEUS, a man who conspired against Alexander the Great with Dymnus. *Curt.* 6. c. 7.

LO'CHA, a large city of Africa, taken and plundered by Scipio's soldiers. *Appian. Alex.*

LOCHAR'NA, a town of Peloponnesus. *Ptol.*

LO'CHIAS, a promontory and citadel of Ægypt near Alexandria. *Strab.* 17.

LO'CHIS, a city of Asiatic Sarmatia. *Ptol.*

LOCOBORMAN'NUM, a town of Liguria. *Antonin.*

LOCO'ZUS, a city of Phrygia. *Steph.*

LO'CRA, a river of Corsica, now Capitello. *Ptol.*

LO'CRI, a town of Magna Græcia in Italy, on the Adriatic, about seventy-five miles from Rhegium. It was founded by a Grecian colony about 757 B.C. as some suppose. The inhabitants were called Locri or Locrenses. *Virg Æn.* 3. v. 399.—*Strab.* —*Plin.—Liv.* 22. c. 6. l 23. c. 30.

LO'CRIS, a country of Greece, the inhabitants of which were known by the names of Ozolæ, Epicnemidii, and Opuntii. The country of the Ozolæ, called also Epizephyrii, from their westerly situation, was at the north of the bay of Corinth, and extended above twelve miles northward. On the west it was separated from Ætolia by the Evenus, and it had Phocis at the east. The chief city of this division was called Naupactus. The Epicnemidii were at the north of the Ozolæ, and had the bay of Malia at the east, and mount Œta on the north. They received their name from their situation, which was near a mountain called Cnemis. They alone, of all the Locrians, had the privilege of sending members to the council of the Amphictyons. The Opuntii, who received their name from their chief city called Opus, were situated on the borders of Euripus, and near Phocis and Eubœa. *Plin.* 3. c. 5.—*Strab.* 6, &c.—*Ptol.—Mela,—Liv.* 26. c. 26, l. 28. c. 6.—*Paus. Ach. & Phoc.*

LOCUS'TA, a woman in Rome in favour with Nero. She was well skilled in the knowledge of poisonous herbs, and was therefore employed to poison Claudius and Britannicus. She at last attempted to destroy Nero himself, for which she was executed. *Tacit. Ann.* 12. c. 66, &c.—*Suet. in Ner.* 33. —*Juv.* 1. v. 71.

LOCU'TIUS. *Vid.* Aius.

LOL'LIA PAULI'NA, a beautiful woman, daughter of M. Lollius, who married C. Memmius Regulus, and afterwards, after being forcibly divorced, Caligula. She was again divorced by the capricious monarch, and when proposed for wife to the emperer Claudius, she was through envy put to death by means of Agrippina. *Tac. Ann.* 12. c. 1, &c.—*Plin.* 9. c. 35.

LOLLIA'NUS SPU'RIUS, a Roman general proclaimed emperor by his soldiers in Gaul, and soon after murdered. *Trebell. in* 30 *Tyran.*

LOL'LIUS M., a companion and tutor of C. Cæsar, the son-in-law of Tiberius. He was consul A.U.C. 733, and offended Augustus by his misconduct and rapacity in the provinces. Horace has addressed two of his epistles to him, but the partiality and regard of the poet seem to have been ill-bestowed on a man, who, to a great violence of temper, added traitorous designs against the honour of his country. Lollius died a natural death, though Pliny mentions that he poisoned himself. *Hor. Ep.—Dio.* 54. c. 20.—*Paterc.* 2. c. 97 & 102.—*Plin.* 9. c. 35.—*Tac. Ann.* 3.—Other members of the family of the Lollii are mentioned among others, by *Cicero, Att.* 2. ep. 2. l. 12. ep. 21. *Verr.* 3. c. 25.

LOL'LIUS UR'BICUS, a Latin historian who composed a history of his own time. *Lamprid. in Diadumen.* —*Jul. Capit. in Antonin. Pio.*

LON'CIUM, a town of Noricum. *Antonin.*

LONDI'NUM, the capital of Britain, was founded, as some suppose, between the ages of Julius Cæsar and Nero. It has been severally called Londinium, Lundinium, &c. Ammianus calls it *vetustum oppidum.* It is represented as having been a considerable, opulent, and commercial town in the age of Nero. *Tac. Ann.* 14. c. 33.—*Ammian.* 27. c. 8.

LON'DOBRIS, a small island near Lusitania. *Ptol.*

LONGAN'ICUM or LONGAT'ICUM, a town of Noricum, now Logitsch. *Antonin.*

LONGA'NUS, a river of Sicily, now Fiume di Castro Reale. *Ptol.*

LONGARE'NUS, a man guilty of adultery with Fausta, Sylla's daughter. *Horat.* 1. sat. 2. v. 67.

LON'GATIS. a region of Bœotia. *Lycoph.*

LONGIM'ANUS, a surname of Artaxerxes, from his having one hand longer than the other. The Greeks called him Macrochir. *C. Nep. in Reg.*

LONGI'NUS, a governor of Judæa.——A proconsul.——A lawyer, whom, though blind and respected, Nero ordered to be put to death, because he had in his possession a picture of Cassius, one of Cæsar's murderers. *Juv.* 10. v. 16.——A friend of the orator Antonius, well skilled in the history, politics, and jurisprudence of his country. *Cic. Orat.* 1. c. 60.

Longi'nus Dionys'ius Cas'sius, a celebrated philosopher and critic of Athens. After residing for some time in this seat of literature, he was invited to assume the honorable office of preceptor of the Greek language to the children of Zenobia, the famous queen of Palmyra, whose secretary and confidential minister he soon became, but his ardent zeal and spirited activity in her cause proved at last fatal to him. When the emperor Aurelian approached the gates of Palmyra with a victorious army, Longinus returned to his summons a spirited letter, which roused his severest indignation. The fortune of Rome prevailed, but when the city at last opened her gates, Zenobia and her secretary endeavoured to escape, but in vain. Dragged into the presence of the conqueror, the unfortunate queen forgot the heroism of her former character, and revealed that Longinus was the author of the letter which had derided the attempts of the Roman arms. Aurelian could conquer, but not forgive, and Longinus was immediately led to execution, and shamefully sacrificed to the fury of the Roman soldiers, A.D. 273. At the moment of death he showed himself great and resolute, and with a philosophical and unparalleled firmness of mind, he even repressed the tears and sighs of the spectators who pitied his miserable end. Longinus has rendered his name immortal by his critical remarks on ancient authors. His treatise on the sublime gives the world reason to lament the loss of his other valuable compositions, which amounted, according to Dr. Pearce, altogether to twenty-five treatises. The best editions of that author are that of Tollius, 4to Traj. ad Rhen. 1694, and that of Toup. 8vo, Oxon. 1778. *Fabr. B. Gr.* 4. c. 33. —*Sax. Onom.* 1. p. 370.

Longi'nus Cas'sius, a tribune driven out of the senate, for favouring the interest of J. Cæsar. He was made governor of Spain, by Cæsar, &c.——The husband of Tiberius' grand-daughter. *Tac. Ann.* 6. c. 45.

LONGOBAR'DI, a nation of Germany. *Tacit. de Germ.*

LON'GULA, a town of Latium, on the borders of the Volsci. *Liv.* 2. c. 33 & 39. l. 9. c. 39.—*Plin.* 3. c. 5.

LON'GUM, a promontory of Sicily, now Lognina. *Ptol.*

LONGUN'TICA, a maritime city of Hispania Tarraconensis. *Liv.* 22. c. 20.

LON'GUS T., a Roman, consul with Africanus, A.U.C. 560, when the seats of the people were separated from those of the senators in the public theatres. *Cic. Corn.* 1.

Lon'gus, a Greek author who wrote a novel called the amours of Daphnis and Chloe. The age in which he lived is not precisely known, as no author among the ancients has made mention of him. The best editions of this pleasing writer are that of Paris, 4to, 1754, and that of Villoison, 8vo, Paris, 1778. *Voss. H. Gr.* 4.—*Simler. in Bibl. Gesn.*

LOPADU'SA, a small island of Africa, *Plin.* 3. c. 8. —*Strab.* 17.

LO'PHIS, a river of Bœotia. *Paus.*

LOP'SI, a people of Liburnia. *Plin.* 3. c. 21.

LOP'SICA, a maritime town of Liburnia. *Ptol.*

LOR'DI, a people of Illyricum, according to *Strabo*, 7: but this is a corrupt reading for 'Εόρδοι.

LORE'NI, a people of Lydia. *Plin.* 5. c. 29.

LO'RIUM or **LAU'RIUM**, a place of Etruria. *Antonin.*

LOR'YMA, a town of Doris. *Liv.* 37. c. 17.—*Diod. Sic.* 14. It is called Larymna by *Pliny*, 5. c. 28.

LOS, an island near Thessaly. *Steph.*

LO'SA, a city of Gallia Aquitanica. *Antonin.*

LO'TIS or **LO'TOS**, a beautiful nymph, daughter of Neptune. Priapus attempted to offer her violence, and to save herself from his importunities, she implored the assistance of the gods, who changed her into a tree called Lotus, consecrated to Venus and to Apollo. *Ovid. Met.* 9. v. 348.—*Servius*, 2. *Georg.* v. 81.

LOTO'A or **LETO'JA**, a small island of the Ionian Sea, near Cephallenia. *Plin.* 4 c. 12.

LOTOPH'AGI, a people on the coast of Africa near the Syrtes. They received this name from their living upon the lotus. Ulysses visited their country when he returned from the Trojan war. *Herodot.* 4. c. 177.—*Homer. Odyss.* 9.—*Ital.* 3. v. 310. —*Ovid. Trist.* 4. el. 1. v. 31 —*Plin.* 5. c. 7. l. 13. c. 17.—*Ptol.* 4. c. 3.—*Strab.* 17.—*Mela*, 1. c. 7.

LO'US or **A'OUS**, a river of Macedonia, near Apollonia. *Strab.* 7.—*Liv.* 32. c. 5, &c.

LO'VIA, a city of Pannonia. *Antonin.*

LOX'IAS, a surname of Apollo. *Macrob. Sat.* 1. c. 17.—*Senec. in Œdip.*

LOX'O, a daughter of Boreas, who brought the worship of Diana to Delos. The name is often used for Diana herself.

LU'A, a goddess at Rome, who presided over things which were purified by lustrations, whence the name (*a luendo*). She is supposed to be the same as the Ops or the Rhea of the Greeks. *Liv.* 8. c. 1. l. 45. c. 33.

LUAN'GI, a people of Hispania Tarraconensis. *Ptol.*

LU'CA, now Lucca, a city of Etruria, at the west of the river Arnus. *Liv.* 21. c. 5. l. 41. c. 13.—*Cic.* 13. *Fam.* 13.

LU'CAGUS, one of the friends of Turnus, killed by Æneas. *Virg. Æn.* 10. v. 575.

LUCA'NI, a people of Italy, descended from the Samnites, or from the Brutii. *Plin.* 3. c. 5.—*Dion.* v. 362.

LUCA'NIA, a country of Italy, between the Tyrrhene and Sicilian Seas, and bounded by Peucetia, the Picentini, and the country of the Brutii. The country was famous for its grapes. Its chief cities were Velia, Posidonia, Heraclea, Lybaris, &c. *Strab.* 6.—*Plin.* 3. c. 5.—*Mela*, 2. c. 4.—*Stat.* 3. *Syl.* 1. v. 85 —*Virg. Æn.* 7. v. 563.—*Festus de V. Sig.*—*Liv.* 8. c. 17. l. 9. c. 20. l. 10. c. 11.—*Horat.* 2. ep. 2. v. 178.

LUCA'NIUS Q., a centurion in Cæsar's army, &c. *Cæs. B. G.* 5. c. 10.

LUCA'NUS M. ANNÆ'US, a native of Corduba in Spain. He was early removed to Rome, where his rising talents, and, more particularly, the praises and panegyrics which he lavished on the characters of the great, recommended him to the emperor Nero. This intimacy was soon productive of honor, and Lucan was raised to the dignity of augur and quæstor, before he had attained the proper age. The poet had the imprudence to enter the lists against his imperial patron; he chose for his subject Orpheus, and Nero took the tragical story of Niobe. Lucan obtained an easy victory, but Nero became jealous of his poetical reputation, and resolved upon revenge. The insults to which Lucan was now daily exposed, provoked at last his resentment, and he joined Piso in a conspiracy against the emperor. The whole was discovered, and the poet had nothing left but to choose the manner of his execution. He had his veins opened in a warm bath, and as he expired he pronounced with great energy the lines which, in his Pharsalia, l. 3. v. 639—642, he had put into the mouth of a soldier, who died in the same manner as himself. Some have accused him of pusilanimity at the moment of his death, and say that, to free himself from the punishment which threatened him, he accused his own mother Attilla, and involved her in the crime of which he was guilty. This circumstance, which throws an indelible blot upon the character of Lucan, is not mentioned by some writers, who observe that he expired with all the firmness of a philosopher. He died in his 26th year, A.D. 65. Of all his compositions none but his Pharsalia remains. This poem, which is divided into ten books, contains an account of the civil wars of Cæsar and Pompey, but is unfinished. Opinions are various as to the merit of the poetry. It possesses neither the fire of Homer nor the melodious numbers of Virgil. If Lucan had lived to a greater age, his judgment and genius would have become more matured, and he might have claimed a more exalted rank among the poets of the Augustan age. His expressions, however, are bold and animated, his poetry correct, and his narrative interesting, though his irregularities are numerous, and to use the words of Quintilian, he is more an orator than a poet. He also wrote a poem upon the burning of Rome, now lost. It is said that his wife Polla Argentaria, not only assisted him in the composition of his poem, but even corrected it after his death. *Scaliger*, more severe than just in his criticism, says, that Lucan rather barks than sings. The best editions of Lucan are those of Oudendorp, 4to, L. Bat. 1728; of Bentley, 4to, printed at Strawberry-hill, 1760; and of Barbou, 12mo, Paris, 1767. *Quintil.* 10.—*Suet.*—*Tac. Ann.* 15. c. 49, &c.—*Martial.* 7. epigr. 20.—*Sax. Onom.* 1. p. 253.—*Harles. Not. Lit. Rom.* 1. p. 451.

Luca'nus Ocel'lus or Ucel'lus, an ancient Pythagorean philosopher, whose age is unknown. He wrote, in the Attic dialect, a book on the nature of the universe, which he deemed eternal; and from his work were drawn the systems adopted by Aristotle, Plato, and Philo Judæus. The work was first translated into Latin by Nogarola. Another book of Ocellus, on laws, written in the Doric dialect, was greatly esteemed by Archytas and Plato, a fragment of which has been preserved by Stobæus, of which, however, it is doubted whether Ocellus was the author. There is an edition of Ocellus with a learned commentary, by C. Emman. Vizzanius Bononiæ, 1646, in 4to.

LUCA'RIA or LUCE'RIA, festivals at Rome, celebrated in a large grove, between the Via Salaria and the Tiber, where the Romans hid themselves when besieged by the Gauls. It was observed on the 1st of February, or in July according to others, and on that day the comedians received their salary, which was always paid by the public treasury. *Tacit. Ann.* 1. c. 77.—*Festus de V. Sig.*—*Varro de L.L.* 5. c. 3.—*Ovid. Fast.* 2.—*Gyrald. Calend. R. & Gr.*—*Plut. in Quæst. R.* 88.

LUCCE'IUS L., a celebrated historian, author of a history of the Marsic war, and of the civil wars of Marius and Sylla. Cicero, who knew and admired his abilities, requested him to give to the world a history of his consulship. He favored the cause of Pompey, but was afterwards pardoned by J. Cæsar. Nothing of his compositions remain besides a consolatory letter to Cicero on the death of his daughter.—*Cæs. B. G.* 3. c. 18.—*Cic. ad Fam.* 5. ep. 12. &c.

Lucce'ius Albi'nus, a governor of Mauritania after Galba's death. *Tac. Hist.* 2. c. 58.

LUCEN'TIA, a city of Hispania Citerior. *Mela*, 2. c. 6. *& Voss. ad eund.* p. 192.

LUCEN'TUM, a town of Spain, now Alicant. *Plin.* 3. c. 3.

LU'CERES, a body of horse composed of Roman knights, first established by Romulus and Tatius. It received its name either from Lucumo, an Etrurian, who assisted the Romans against the Sabines, or from *lucus*, a grove where Romulus had erected an asylum, as a place of refuge for all fugitives, slaves, homicides, &c. that he might people his city. The Luceres were some of these men, and they were afterwards incorporated with the legions. *Propert.* 4. el. 1. v. 31.

LUCE'RIA, a town of Apulia, at the foot of the Apennines, on the north of the river Cerbalus. It was famous for its wool. *Liv.* 9. c. 2 & 12. 1. 10. c. 35.—*Horat.* 3. od. 15. v. 14.—*Lucan.* 2. v. 473.

LUCE'RIUS, a surname of Jupiter as father of light.

LUCETIUS, a Rutulian killed by Ilioneus. *Virg. Æn.* 9. v. 570.

LUCIA'NUS, a celebrated Greek writer of Samosata. His father was poor in his circumstances, and Lucian was early bound to one of his uncles, who was a sculptor. This employment highly displeased him; he made no proficiency in the art, and resolved, at last, to seek his livelihood by means more congenial to his inclinations. A dream, in which Learning seemed to draw him to her, and to promise fame and immortality, confirmed this resolution, and he began to write. The artifices and unfair dealings of the lawyers, whose profession he had next embraced, disgusted him, and he began to study philosophy and eloquence. He visited different places; and Antioch, Ionia, Greece, Italy, Gaul, and more particularly Athens, became successively acquainted with the depth of his learning, and the power of his eloquence. The emperor M. Aurelius was sensible of his merit, and as a mark of his favor appointed him registrar to the Roman governor of Ægypt. He died of the gout, A.D. 180, in his 90th year, and some of the moderns have asserted that he was torn to pieces by dogs for his impiety, particularly for ridiculing the religion of Christ. The works of Lucian, which are numerous, and written in the Attic dialect, consist partly of dialogues, in which he introduces different characters with much dramatic propriety. His style is easy, simple, elegant, and animated, and he has enriched his compositions with many lively sentiments, and much true Attic wit. His frequent obscenities, however, and his manner of exposing to ridicule not only the religion of his country, but also that of all other nations, have deservedly drawn upon him the censure of every age, and branded him with the appellation of atheist and blasphemer. He wrote the life of Sostrates, a philosopher of Bœotia; as also that of the philosopher Demonax. Some have also attributed to him, with great impropriety, the life of Apollonius Thyaneus. The best editions of Lucian are that of Grævius, 2 vols. 8vo, Amst. 1687; that of Grævius, 2 vols. 8vo, Amst. 1687; that of Reitzius, 4 vols. 4to. Amst. 1743; and that of Bourdelot, Paris, 1615. Among the English versions are that of Spence, London, 1684. and that of Franklin, London, 1780. *Suidas.*—*Fabr. B. Gr.* 4. c. 18.—*Sax. Onom.* 1. p. 322.

LU'CIFER, the name of the planet Venus, or morning star. It is called Lucifer, when it appears in the morning before the sun; but when it follows it, and appears some time after its setting, it is called Hesperus. According to some mythologists, Lucifer was son of Jupiter and Aurora, and had the care of harnessing the horses of Apollo. *Hesiod. Th.* 381.—*Virg. Æn.* 2. v. 801.—*Ovid. Heroid.* 18. v, 112. *Trist.* 3 & 5. v. 56.—*Lucan.* 1. v. 232. l. 2. v. 725. l. 10. v. 434.—*Plaut. in Menæch.* 1. sc. 2. v. 62.—*Seneca, Hippol.* 751. *In Œdip.* 506.

Lu'cifer, a Christian writer, whose work was edited by the Coleti, fol. Venet. 1778. *Harles. Not. Lit. Rom.* 1. p. 593.

LUCIF'ERA, a name applied to Diana as the moon. She was represented as dressed in a veil bespangled with stars, with a crescent on her head, and a torch in her hand. *Hygin.* fab. 261.—*Lactant. ad Theb.* 8.

LUCIF'ERI FA'NUM, a town of Spain. *Strab.* 13.

LUCIL'IUS C., a Roman knight born at Aurunca, illustrious not only for the respectability of his ancestors, but more deservedly for the uprightness and innocence of his character. He lived in the greatest intimacy with Scipio the first Africanus, and even attended him in his war against Numantia. He is looked upon as the founder of Satire, and as the first successful satirical writer among the Romans. He was superior to his poetical predecessors at Rome, and though he wrote with great roughness and inelegance, but with much facility, he gained many admirers, whose praises have perhaps been lavished with too liberal a hand. Horace compares him to a river which rolls upon its waters precious sand, accompanied with mire and dirt; but though the criticism is severe, yet the judgment of posterity has been in favour of the satirist, and not only the emperor Adrian, whose name is as respectable in literature as it is in war, but Quintilian himself, have spoken with admiration and with applause of the labours of the father of Roman satire. Of the thirty satires which he wrote, only about 937 scattered verses remain. He died at Naples, in the 46th year of his age, B.C. 103, and was magnificently buried at the public expense. His fragments have been collected and published with notes by Fr. Dousa, 4to, L. Bat. 1597, and lastly by the Vulpii 8vo, Patav. 1735. *Quintil.* 1. c. 9. l. 10. c. 1.—*Horat.* 1. sat. 4. v. 6. sat. 10. v. 1. l. 2. sat. 1. v. 70.—*Cic. Fam.* 12. ep. 16. *De Orac.* 2. c. 9. *Ad Heren.* 2. c. 53.—*Juv.* 1. v. 165.—*Plin. Præf. Hist.*—*Persius*, 1. v. 114 & 128.—*Martial.* 12. epigr. 96. v. 7.—*Varro, R. R.* 3. c. 2, 17.—*Sax. Onom.* 1. p. 141.

Lucil'ius Bal'bus, the preceptor of Serv. Sulpicius *Cic. Br.* 42.

Lucil'ius Bas'sus, the admiral of Vitellius' fleet, which he betrayed to Vespasian. *Tacit. Hist.* 2. c. 100.

Lucil'ius Cap'ito, a governor of Asia under Tiberius. *Tac. Ann.* 4. c. 15.

Lucil'ius Lon'gus, a friend of Tiberius, to whom a statue was decreed. *Id. ibid.*

Lucil'ius Luci'nus, a famous Roman, who fled with Brutus after the battle of Philippi. They were soon after overtaken by a party of horse, and Lucilius suffered himself to be severely wounded by the darts of the enemy, exclaiming that he was Brutus. He was taken and carried to the conquerors, whose clemency spared his life. *Plut.*

Lucil'ius, a poet of mean capacity. *Cic. Att.* 12. ep. 3.——A tribune who attempted in vain to procure the election of Pompey to the dictatorship. *Cic. Att.* 5. ep, 20.——A centurion, slain by his soldiers for his severity. *Tac. Ann.* 1. c. 23.

LUCIL'LA, a daughter of M Aurelius, celebrated for the virtues of her youth, her beauty, her debaucheries, and her misfortunes. At the age of sixteen her father sent her to Syria to marry the emperor Verus, who was then employed in the war against the Parthians and Armenians. The conjugal virtues of Lucilla were highly commendable at first, but when she saw Verus plunge himself into every species of debauchery and dissipation, she followed his example and prostituted herself. At her return to Rome she saw the incestuous commerce of her husband with her mother, &c. and disgusted with his conduct, at last poisoned him. She afterwards married an old but virtuous senator, by order of her father, and was not ashamed soon after to gratify the criminal sensualities of her brother Commodus. The coldness and indifference with which Commodus treated her afterwards determined her on revenge, and she with many illustrious senators conspired against his life, A.D. 185. The plot was discovered, Lucilla was banished, and soon after put to death by her brother in the 38th year of her age. [A statue of Lucilla will be found in the Vatican, in the character of Venus Victrix.]——The mother of M. Aurelius. *Jul. Capitol. in vit. hujus.*

LUCIL'LUS TARRHÆ'US, an historian who wrote a history of Thessalonica, the Scholia on the Argonautica of Apollonius, and other works. *Steph. in* Θεσσαλονικη.—*Tzetz. Chil.* 8. *Hist.* 159, &c.

LUCI'NA, a goddess, daughter of Jupiter and Juno, or, according to others, of Latona. As it was said that her mother brought her into the world without pain, she was invoked by women in labor, and presided over the birth of children. She received this name either from *lucus*, a grove in which was her temple, or from *lux*, as Ovid explains it:

Gratia Lucinæ, dedit hæc tibi nomine lucus;
Aut quia principium tu, Dea, lucis habes.

Some suppose her with great probability to be the same as Diana or Juno, because these two goddesses were also sometimes called Lucina, and presided over the labours of women. She was called Ilithya by the Greeks, and Opigena by the Latins. She had a famous temple at Rome, raised A.U.C. 396. *Varr. de L. L.* 4.—*Cic. de Nat. D.* 2. c. 27. —*Ovid. Fast.* 2. v. 449.—*Plin.* 16. c. 44.—*Homer. Il.* 11.—*Apollod.* 1.—*Paus.* 1. c. 18.—*Diod.* 5.— *Plut de Rebus. R.* 77.—*Catull.* 35. v. 13.—*Orpheus in Dian.*—*Callimach. in Dian.*—*Terent. Andr.* 3. sc. 1. v. 15.—*Horat. Carm. Sec.*

LU'CIUS, a Roman soldier killed at the siege of Jerusalem, by saving in his arms a man who jumped down from one of the walls. *Joseph.*——A brother of M. Antony. *Vid.* L. Antonius.——A Roman general, who defeated the Etrurians, &c. ——A relation of J. Cæsar.——A Roman ambassador, murdered by the Illyrians.——A writer, called by some Saturantius Apuleius. *Vid.* Apuleius.——A brother of Vitellius, &c.——A son of Agrippa, adopted by Augustus. *Vid.* Agrippa. ——A man put to death for his incontinence, &c. The word Lucius was a prænomen common to many Romans, of whom an account is given under their family names.

LUCOPIB'IA, a city of Albion. *Ptol.*

LUCOTE'TIA, the ancient name of Paris, according to *Ptolemy.*

LUCRE'TIA, a celebrated Roman lady, daughter of Lucretius, and wife of Tarquinius Collatinus. Her accomplishments unhappily proved fatal to her happiness, and to her life, and the praises which a number of young nobles at Ardea, among whom were Collatinus and the sons of Tarquin, bestowed upon the domestic virtues of their wives at home, were productive of a revolution in the state. While every one was warm with the idea, it was universally agreed to leave the camp and go to Rome, to ascertain the veracity of their respective assertions. Collatinus had the pleasure to see his expectations fulfilled in the highest degree, and, while the wives of other Romans were involved in the riot and dissipation of a feast, Lucretia was found at home, diligently employed in the midst of her female servants, and easing their labour by sharing it herself. The beauty and innocence of Lucretia inflamed the passion of Sextus, the son of Tarquin, who was a witness of her virtues and industry. He cherished his criminal desires, secretly retired from the camp, and came to the house of Lucretia, where, as the friend of her husband he met with a kind reception. In the dead of night, he introduced himself to Lucretia, who refused to his intreaties what her fear of shame at last granted to his threats. She yielded to her ravisher, when he threatened to murder her, and to slay one of her slaves, and put him in her bed, that this apparent adultery might seem to have met with the punishment which it deserved. Lucretia, thus dishonoured, in the morning sent for her husband and her father from the camp, and, after she had revealed to them the indignities she had suffered from the son of Tarquin, and entreated them to avenge her wrongs, she stabbed herself with a dagger which she had previously concealed under her clothes. This fatal blow was the signal for rebellion. The body of the virtuous Lucretia was exposed to the eyes of the senate and of the people, and the violence and barbarity of Sextus, joined to the unpopularity and oppression of his father, so irritated the Roman populace, that they from that moment expelled the Tarquins for ever from Rome. Brutus, who was present at the tragical death of Lucretia, kindled the flames of rebellion, and the republican consular government was established A.U.C. 244. *Liv.* 1. c. 57, &c.—*Dionys. Hal.* 4. c. 15.—*Cic.* 2. *Fin.* 20. *Leg.* 2. c. 4.—*Ovid. Fast.* 2. v. 741.—*Val. Max.* 6. c. 1.—*Plut.*—*Aug. de Civ. D.* 1. c. 19.— *Martial.* 1. epigr. 91. v. 5.——The wife of Numa. *Plut.*

LUCRET'ILIS, now Libretti, a mountain in the country of the Sabines, hanging over a pleasant valley near which the house and farm of Horace were situated. *Horat.* 1. od. 17. v. 1.—*Cic.* 7. *Att.* 11.

T. LUCRE'TIUS CA'RUS, a celebrated Roman poet and philosopher, who was early sent to Athens, where he studied under Zeno and Phædrus. The tenets of Epicurus and Empedocles, which then prevailed at Athens,, were warmly embraced by him, and when united with the doctrines of Anaximander and Democritus, they were explained and elucidated in a poem in six books, which is called *De rerum naturâ*. In this poem the masterly genius and unaffected elegance of the poet are every where conspicuous; but the opinions of the philosopher are justly censured, who denies the existence of a Supreme Being, and is the advocate of atheism and impiety, and earnestly endeavours to establish the mortality of the soul. This composition, which, notwithstanding many incomparable beauties, has, according to some critics, little claim to be called an heroic poem, was written and finished while the poet labored under a violent delirium, occasioned by a philtre, which the jealousy of his mistress, or his wife Lucilla, had administered. It is said that Lucretius destroyed himself in the 44th year of his age, about 54 B.C. Cicero, after his death revised and corrected his poems, which had been partly written in the lucid intervals of reason and of sense. Lucretius, whose poem shows that he wrote Latin better than any other man ever did, would have proved no mean rival to Virgil, had he lived in the more polished age of Augustus. The best editions of his works are that of Creech, 8vo, Oxon. 1695; that of Havercamp 2 vols. 4to, Lug. Bat. 1745; that of Glasgow, 12mo, 1759; that of Gil. Wakefield, London; and that of Baskerville. Birmingham, 1772. *Ovid. Am.* 1. el. 15. v. 23.—*Paterc.* 2. c. 36.—*Quintil.* 3.

c. 1. l. 10. c. 1.—*Cic. ad Fr.* 2. ep. 11.—*Gyrald. de P. Hist.* 4.—*Lucret.* 1. v. 26.—*Harles. Not. Lit. Rom.* l. p. 111.

LUCRE'TIUS QUIN'TUS, a Roman, who killed himself because the inhabitants of Sulmo, over which he was appointed with a garrison, were inclined to favour the cause of J. Cæsar. *Cæs. B. Civ.* 1. c. 18. He is also called Vespillo.

SP. LUCRE'TIUS TRICIPITI'NUS, father of Lucretia, wife of Collatinus, was made consul after the death of Brutus, and soon after died himself. Horatius Pulvillus succeeded him. *Liv.* 1. c. 58.—*Plut. in Pub.*

LUCRE'TIUS, an inter-rex at Rome.

LUCRE'TIUS OSEL'LA, a Roman put to death by Sylla because he had applied for the consulship without his permission. *Plut.*

LUCRI'NUM, a town of Apulia. *Strab.* 5.

LUCRI'NUS, a small lake of Campania, opposite Puteoli. Some believed that it was formed by Hercules, when he passed through Italy with the bulls of Geryon. It abounded with excellent oysters, and was united by Augustus to the Avernus, and a communication formed with the sea, near a harbour called Julius Portus. The Lucrine lake disappeared on the 30th of September, 1538, in a violent earthquake, which raised on the spot a mountain four miles in circumference, and about 1000 feet high, with a crater in the middle. *Cic.* 4. *Att.* 10.—*Strab.* 5 & 6.—*Mela*, 2. c. 4.—*Propert.* 1. el. 11. v. 10.—*Horat.* 2. od. 15. v. 3. l. 5. od. 2. v. 49. l. 1. sat. 4. v. 32.—*Virg. Georg.* 2. v. 161.—*Festus de V. Sig.*—*Servius in Æn.* 3. v. 386 & 442.

C. LUCTA'TIUS CAT'ULUS, a Roman, consul with Marius. He assisted his colleague in the dreadful war which the Cimbri waged against Rome, and shared in his triumph over that fierce and barbarous people. *Vid.* Cimbricum Bellum. He was eloquent as well as valiant, and the history of his consulship, which he wrote with great veracity, convinces us of his literary talents. That history is now unfortunately lost. *Cic. de Orat.*—*Varro de L.L.*—*Flor.* 2. c. 2.—*Voss. H. Lact.* c. 12.

LUCTA'TIUS C. CAT'ULUS, a Roman consul. *Vid.* Catulus.

LUCTE'RIUS CADUR'CUS, a general of great boldness, sent by Vercingetorix against the Rutheni, &c. *Cæs. B. G.* 7. c. 2.

LUCUL'LEA, a festival established by the Greeks in honor of Lucullus, who had behaved with great prudence and propriety in his Asiatic province. *Plut. in Luc.*

LUCUL'LI HOR'TI, gardens of Lucullus, situate near Neapolis, &c. *Tacit. Ann.* 11. c. 1.

LUCUL'LI VIL'LA, a country seat near mount Misenus, where Tiberius died. *Tacit. Ann.* 6. c. 50.

LUCUL'LUS, a consul, who went to Spain, &c.——A Roman put to death by Domitian.——A brother of Lucius Lucullus, a lieutenant under Sylla.——A prætor of Macedonia.

LUCUL'LUS LU'CIUS LICIN'IUS, a Roman celebrated for his luxury and military talents. He was born about 115 years B.C., and soon distinguished himself by his proficiency in the liberal arts, particularly eloquence and philosophy. His first military campaign was in the Marsian war, where his valor and cool intrepidity recommended him to the notice of his general and the public. His mildness and constancy gained him the admiration and confidence of Sylla, and during his quæstorship in Asia, and prætorship in Africa, he rendered himself conspicuous by his justice, moderation, and humanity. He was raised to the consulship A.U.C. 680, and entrusted with the care of the Mithridatic war, and in this expedition first displayed his military talents in rescuing his colleague Cotta, whom the enemy had besieged in Chalcedonia. This was soon followed by a victory over the force of Mithridates, on the borders of the Granicus, and by the conquest of all Bithynia. His victories by sea were as great as those by land, and Mithridates lost a powerful fleet near Lemnus. Such considerable losses weakened the enemy, and Mithridates retired with precipitation towards Armenia, to the court of king Tigranes, his father-in-law. His flight was perceived, and Lucullus crossed the Euphrates with great expedition, and gave battle to the numerous forces which Tigranes had already assembled to support the cause of his son-in-law. According to the probably exaggerated account of Plutarch, no less than 100,000 foot, and nearly 55,000 horse, of the Armenians, lost their lives in that celebrated battle. All this carnage was made by a Roman army amounting to no more than 18,000 men, of whom, as the historian asserts, only five were killed, and 100 wounded during the combat. The taking of Tigranocerta, the capital of Armenia, was the consequence of this important victory, and Lucullus there obtained possession of the greatest part of the royal treasures. This continual success, however, was attended with serious consequences. The severity of Lucullus, and the haughtiness of his commands, offended his soldiers, and soon tended to alienate his wavering adherents at Rome. Pompey was soon after sent to succeed him, and to continue the Mithridatic war, and the interview which he had with Lucullus began with acts of mutual kindness, and ended in the most inveterate reproaches and open enmity. Lucullus was permitted to retire to Rome, and only 1600 of the soldiers who had shared his fortunes and his glory were suffered to accompany him. He was received with coldness at Rome, and, with difficulty obtained a triumph, which was certainly due to his fame, his successes, and his victories. In this ended the days of his glory; he retired to the enjoyment of ease and peaceful society, and no longer interested himself in the commotions which disturbed the tranquillity of Rome. He dedicated his time to studious pursuits, and to literary conversation. His house was enriched with a valuable library, which was opened for the service of the curious and the learned. Lucullus fell into a delirium in the last part of his life, and died in the 67th or 68th year of his age. The people showed their respect for his memory, by their wish to give him an honorable burial in the Campus Martius; but their offers were rejected, and he was privately buried, by his brother, on his estate at Tusculum. Lucullus has been admired for his many accomplishments, but he has been censured for his severity and his extravagance. The expenses of his meals are described as having been immoderate, his halls were distinguished by the different names of the gods; and when Cicero and Pompey attempted to surprise him, they were astonished at the costliness of a supper which had been prepared upon the word of Lucullus, who had merely said to his servant that he would sup in the hall of Apollo. In his retirement Lucullus was fond of artificial variety; subterraneous caves and passages were dug under the hills on the coast of Campania, and the sea water was conveyed round the house and pleasure grounds, where the fishes flocked in such abundance, that, it is said, not less than 25,000 pounds worth were sold at his death. In his public character Lucullus was humane and compassionate, and he showed his sense of the vicissitudes of human affairs by shedding tears at the sight of one of the unfortunate cities of Armenia, which his soldiers had reduced to ashes. He was a perfect master of the Greek and Latin languages, and employed himself for some time in writing a concise history of the Marsic wars in Greek hexameters. Such were the striking characteristics of a man who meditated the conquest of Parthia, and, for a while, gained the admiration of all the inhabitants of the East by his justice and moderation, and who might have disputed the empire of the world with a Cæsar or a Pompey, had not, at last, his fondness for retirement, happily for himself and for Rome, withdrawn him from the reach and from the pursuit of ambition. *Cic. pro Arch.* 4. *Quæst. Acad.* 2. c. 1. *Leg.* 3. c. 13. *Off.* 1. c. 39. *Att.* 1. ep. 19.—*Plin.* 36. c. 6.—*Tacit. Ann.* 6. c. 50.—*Plut. in Vitâ.*—*Flor.* 3. c. 5.—*Strab.*—*Appian. in Mithr. &c.*—*Orosius*, 6. *&c.*

LU'CUMO, the first name of Tarquinius Priscus, afterwards changed into Lucius. The word is Etrurian; it signifies prince or chief, and was at one time generally applied to the twelve kings or rulers who presided over the twelve cities of Etruria. One of them, who had offered violence to the wife of Aruns, assisted Romulus against the Samnites. *Plut. in Rom.*—*Servius in Æn.* 2. v. 278. l. 5. v. 560. l. 8. v 65 & 475.—*Liv.* 1. c. 34

LU'CUS, a king of ancient Gaul. *Ptol.* 2. c. 8.—*Strab.* 4.—*Cæs.* 6 & 7.

Lu'cus a town of Gaul, at the foot of the Alps.

LUGDUNEN'SIS GAL'LIA. *Vid.* Gallia.

LUGDU'NUM, a large and ancient town of Gallia Celtica, built at the confluence of the Rhone and the Arar, or Saone, by Manutius Plancus, when he was governor of the province. This town, now called Lyons, is the second city in France in point of population. *Juv.* 1. v. 44.—*Strab.* 4.

Lugdu'num Batavo'rum, a town on the Rhine, just as it falls into the German Ocean. It is now called Leyden, and is famous for its university.

Lugdu'num Convena'rum, a town at the foot of the Pyrenees, now St. Bertrand in Gascony.

LUGIO'NUM, a city of Lower Pannonia. *Ptol.*

LU'MA, a town of Arabia Deserta. *Ptol.*——A city near Mæander. *Nicet.*

LU'NA, daughter of Hyperion and Terra, was the same, according to ancient mythologists, as Diana. She was worshipped by the ancient inhabitants of the earth with many superstitious ceremonies. It was supposed that magicians and enchanters, particularly those of Thessaly, had an uncontrollable power over the moon, and that they could draw her down from heaven at pleasure by the mere force of their incantations. Her eclipses, according to this preposterous opinion, proceeded from this extraordinary influence of magical power; and on that account, it was usual to beat drums and cymbals to ease her labors. The Arcadians believed that they were older than the moon. Among the people of Carrhæ in Mesopotamia, those husbands were said to be subservient to their wives, who considered the moon as a female deity, but those who paid their worship to her as to a male god under the name of Lunus, possessed the freedom and the authority of masters. *Spartian in Carac.* 7.—*Ovid. Met.* 12. v. 263, &c.—*Tibull.* 1. el. 8. v. 21.—*Hesiod Theog.*—*Apollod.* 1. c. 2.—*Liv.* 40. c. 2. *Virg. Ecl.* 8. v. 69.

Lu'na, a maritime town of Etruria, famous for the white marble which it produced, and called also *Lunensis portus.* It contained a fine capacious harbour, and abounded in wine, cheese, &c. The inhabitants were naturally given to augury, and to the observation of uncommon phænomena. *Mela,* 2. c. 4.—*Lucan.* 1. v. 586.—*Plin.* 14. c. 6.—*Liv.* 34. c. 8.—*Sil.* 8. v. 481.

LU'NA MONS, a promontory of Lusitania, now Panta di Luna, called *Promontorium magnum* by *Pliny.*——A mountain of Æthiopia, whence the Nile rises, according to *Ptolemy.*

LUNA'RIUM, a promontory of Hispania Citerior. *Ptol.*

LU'PA, *(a she-wolf)*, was held in great veneration at Rome, because Romulus and Remus, according to an ancient tradition, were suckled and preserved by one of these animals. This fabulous story arises from the surname of Lupa, a *prostitute*, which was given to the wife of the shepherd Faustulus, to whose care and humanity these illustrious children owed their preservation. *Ovid. Fast.* 2. v. 415.—*Plut. in Romul.*

LUPER'CAL, a place at the foot of mount Aventine, sacred to Pan, where festivals called Lupercalia were yearly celebrated, and where the she-wolf was said to have brought up Romulus and Remus. *Virg. Æn.* 8. v. 343.—*Ovid. Fast.* 2. v. 381.—*Servius. in Virg. loco cit.*

LUPERCA'LIA, a yearly festival observed at Rome on the 15th of February, in honor of the god Pan. It was usual on the occasion, first to sacrifice two goats and a dog, and to touch with a bloody knife the forehead of two illustrious youths, who were always obliged to smile while they were touched. The blood was then wiped away from the forehead with soft wool dipped in milk. After this the skins of the victims were cut into thongs, with which whips were made for the youths. With these whips the youths ran about the streets, and whipped freely all those whom they met in their way. Women in particular were fond of receiving lashes from them on these occasions, as they superstitiously believed that they removed barrenness, and eased the pains of child-birth. This excursion in the streets of Rome was performed by naked youths, because Pan is always represented naked, and a goat was sacrificed because that deity was supposed to have the feet of a goat. A dog was also added, as a necessary and useful guardian of the sheepfold. This festival, as Plutarch mentions, was first instituted by the Romans in honor of the she-wolf which suckled Romulus and Remus. This opinion is controverted by others, and Livy observes, with Dionysius of Halicarnassus, that they were introduced into Italy from Arcadia. by Evander. The name seems to be borrowed from the Greek name of Pan, *Lyceus* from λύκος, *a wolf*, not only because these ceremonies were like the Lycean festivals observed in Arcadia, but from the rapacity of the wolves. The priests who officiated at the Lupercalia were called Luperci. Augustus forbade any person above the age of fourteen to appear naked, or to run about the streets during the Lupercalia. Cicero, in his Philippics, reproaches Antony for having disgraced the dignity of the consulship by running naked, and armed with a whip, about the streets. It was during the celebration of these festivals that Antony offered a crown to J. Cæsar, which the indignation of the populace obliged him to refuse. *Ovid. Fast.* 2. v. 427.—*Varro. L.L.* 5. c. 3.—*Dionysius. Hal.* 1.—*Liv.* 1. c. 5.—*Plut. de Rom.*—*Justin.* 43. c. 1. —*Cic. in Phil.*—*Val. Max.* 2. c. 2.—*Juv.* 2. v. 142.

LUPER'CI, a number of priests at Rome, who assisted at the celebration of the Lupercalia, in honor of the god Pan, to whose services they were dedicated. This order of priests was the most ancient and respectable of all the sacerdotal offices. It was divided into two separate colleges, called Fabiani and Quintiliani, from Fabius and Quintilius, two of their original high priests. The former were instituted in honor of Romulus, and the latter of Remus. To these sacerdotal bodies J. Cæsar added a third, called from himself, the Julii, and this action contributed not a little to render his cause unpopular, and to betray his ambitious and aspiring views. *Vid.* Lupercalia. *Plut. in Rom.*—*Cic. Phil.* 2. c. 34.—*Dio. Cas.* 45.—*Virg. Æn.* 8. v. 663.

LUPER'CUS, a grammarian in the reign of the emperor Gallienus. He wrote some grammatical pieces, which have been preferred by some writers to Herodian's compositions. *Suidas.*—*Voss. H. Gr.* 2. c. 16.——A writer to whom Martial addressed many of his epigrams. *Martial.* 11. epigr. 118.

LU'PIAS, LUP'PIA or LU'PIA, now Lippe, a town of Germany with a small river of the same name, falling into the Rhine. *Tacit. Ann.* 1, &c.

LUPODU'NUM, a town of Germany on the Neckar.

LU'PUS, a general of the emperor Severus. *Casaub. ad Leo. Spartian.*——A governor of Britain.——A tribune, &c. *Cic. Fam.* 1. ep. 1. *Att.* 8. ep. 12. ——A quæstor in the reign of Tiberius, &c. *Tac. Ann.* 4 c. 27.——A comic writer of Sicily, who wrote a poem on the return of Menelaus and Helen to Sparta, after the destruction of Troy. *Ovid. ex Pont.* 4. ep. 16. v. 26.—*Harles. Not. Lit. Rom.* 1. p. 305.

Lu'pus P. Rut., a Roman, who contrary to the omens, marched against the Marsi with his army, and was killed. He has been taxed with impiety, and was severely censured in the Augustan age. *Horat.* 2. sat. 1. v. 68.—*Cic. N. D.* 1. c. 23.

LUR'CO, a surname of the Aufidian family.

Lur'co Mar'cus, a Roman, intimate with Cicero. It is supposed that he became opulent by feeding peacocks. *Cic. Flac.* 4. *Att.* 1. ep. 16. *Varro, R. R.* 3. c. 6.—*Plin.* 10. c. 20.

LURI'NUM, now Luri, an inland town of Corsica. *Ptol.*

LUS'CIUS, a comic writer, contemporary with Terence. *Voss. Poet. Lat.* c. 1.

LU'SIA, a village of the tribe Œneis. *Steph.*

LUSITA'NIA, a part of ancient Spain, the extent and situation of which have not been accurately defined by the ancients. According to the more correct descriptions, it extended from the Tagus to the sea of Cantabria, and comprehended the modern kingdom of Portugal. The inhabitants were warlike, and were conquered by the Roman army under Dolabella, B.C. 99, with great difficulty. Their early history represents them as living generally upon plunder, and as being rude and unpolished in their manners. It was usual among them to expose their sick in the high roads, that their diseases might be cured by the casual directions and advice of travellers. They were very moderate in their meals, and never ate but of one dish. Their clothes were commonly black, and they generally warmed themselves by means of stones heated in the fire. *Strab.* 3.—*Mela*, 2. c. 6. l. 3. c. 1.—*Liv.* 21. c. 43. l. 27. c. 20.

LU'SIUS, a river of Arcadia. *Cic. de Nat. D.* 3. c. 22.—*Paus. Arc.* 28.

Lu'sius, a grandson of Marius, slain by Trebonius. *Plut. in Mar.*——A præfect of the prætorian cohort, under Claudius. *Tac. Ann.* 11. c. 31.

Lu'sius Quie'tus, a brave general of Trajan. *Amm. Marcell.* 29. c. 5.

LUSO'NES, a people of Spain, near the Iberus. *Strab.* 3.

LUS'SI or LU'SI, a city of Arcadia. *Steph.*

LUSSO'NIUM, a city of Lower Pannonia. *Ptol.*

LUS'TRICUS BRUTIA'NUS, a Roman poet. *Martial.* 4. epigr. 23.—*Plin. Jun.* l. 6. ep. 22.

LUTA'TIUS CAT'ULUS, a Roman who shut the temple of Janus after peace had been made with Carthage. *Vid.* Luctatius.

Luta'tius Plac'idus, a Scholiast on Statius, in the age of Theodosius. *Barth. animadv. ad Stat. Theb.* 6. v. 360.

LUTE'RIUS, a general of the Gauls, defeated by Cæsar, &c.

LUTE'TIA, a town of Belgic Gaul, on the confluence of the rivers Sequana and Matrona, which received its name, as some suppose, from the quantity of clay, *lutum*, which was found in its neighbourhood. J. Cæsar fortified and embellished it, from which circumstance some authors call it *Julii Civitas.* Julian the apostate resided there some time. It is now called Paris, the capital of France *Cæsar. de Bell. G.* 6 & 7.—*Strab.* 4 —*Ammian.* 20.

LUTE'VA or LUTA'VA, called by *Pliny*, 3. c. 4, *Forum Neronis*, and now Lodesue, a city of Gallia Narbonensis.

C. LUTO'RIUS PRIS'CUS, a Roman knight who celebrated the virtues and services of Germanicus in a beautiful elegy. He was put to death by order of Tiberius. *Tacit. Ann.* 3. c. 49, &c.

LUX'IA, a river of Hispania Bætica. *Plin.* 3. c. 1.

LYÆ'US, a surname of Bacchus. It is derived from λύειν *solvere*, because wine, over which Bacchus presides, gives freedom to the mind, and delivers it from all cares and melancholy. The word is often used for wine. *Horat.* 1. od. 8. v. 8. l. 3. od. 21. v. 14. l. 5. od. 9. v. 38.—*Virg. Æn.* 1. v. 690.—*Seneca in Œd.* 508.—*Propert.* 2. el. 24. v. 35. l. 3. el. 3. v. 43.—*Ovid. Fast.* 2. v. 401. l. 5. v. 521. *Amor.* 2. el. 11. v. 49. l. 3. el. 15. v. 17. *A. A.* 3. v. 765. *Pont.* 1. ep. 10. v. 29.—*Terent. in Eun.* 4. sc. 5.—*Ital.* 6. v. 183.—*Lucan.* 1. v. 675.

LY'BAS, one of the companions of Ulysses, &c.

LYB'IA, a town of Hispania Tarraconensis. *Antonin.*

LY'BUM, a city of Cælesyria, between Damascus and Laodicea. *Id.*

LYB'YA or LYBIS'SA, a small village of Bithynia, where Annibal was buried.

LYC'ABAS, an Etrurian, who had been banished from his country for murder. He was one of those who offered violence to Bacchus, and who were changed into dolphins. *Ovid. Met.* 4. v. 624.——One of the Lapithæ, who ran away from the battle which took place at the nuptials of Pirithous. *Id Met.* 12. v. 302.——An Assyrian, killed by Perseus. *Ovid. Met.* 5. v. 60.

LYCABE'TUS or LYCABET'TUS, a mountain of Attica, near Athens. *Stat. Theb.* 12, v. 621.—*Plin.* 4. c. 7, &c.

LYCÆ'A, festivals in Arcadia, in honor of Pan, the god of shepherds. They were the same as the Lupercalia of the Romans. Some authors assert that they were first observed by Lycaon, in honor of Jupiter.—*Plut. Cæs. & Arcad.*—*Meurs. Gr. Fer.*

LYCÆ'UM, a celebrated place near the banks of the Ilissus, in Attica. It was in this pleasant and salubrious spot that Aristotle taught philosophy, and as he generally instructed his pupils while walking, they were called Peripatetics, *a* περιπατέω, *ambulo.* The philosopher continued his instructions in this favourite spot for twelve years, till terrified by the false accusations of Eurymedon, he was obliged to flee to Chalcis. *Strab.* 10 & 12.—*Cic. Acad.* 1. c. 4. *Fin.* 3. c. 2, 12, &c.—*Diog.*—*Ælian. V. H.* 9. c. 10.—*Paus.* 1. c. 19.

LYCÆ'US, a mountain of Arcadia, sacred to Jupiter, where a temple was built in honor of the god, by Lycaon, the son of Pelasgus. It was also sacred to Pan, whose festivals, called Lycæa, were celebrated there. *Virg. G.* 1. v. 16. *Æn.* 8. v. 343. —*Paus.* 8. c. 8.—*Strab.* 8.—*Horat.* 1. od. 17. v. 2. *Ovid. Met.* 1. v. 698. The grove which surrounded the temple of Jupiter, surnamed Lycæus from the situation, was considered so sacred that no person was permitted to enter it, or to molest the animals which had taken refuge there, and it was even supposed that neither the trees nor any other object had any shadow, when opposed to the rays of the sun. *Paus.* 8. c. 2, 30, 37 & 38.

LYCAM'BES, the father of Neobule. He promised his daughter in marriage to the poet Archilochus, and afterwards refused to fulfil his engagement after she had been courted by a man of superior opulence. This irritated Archilochus : he wrote a bitter invective against Lycambes and his daughter, and the satire rendered them both so desperate that they hanged themselves. *Aristot. Rhet.* 3.—*Horat.* ep. 6. v. 13. l. 1. ep. 19. v. 23 & 27.—*Ovid. in Ib.* 52.—*Martial.* 7. epigr. 12.

LYCA'ON, the first king of Arcadia, was son of Pelasgus and Melibœa. He built a town called Lycosura on the top of mount Lycæus, in honor of Jupiter. He had several wives, by whom he had a daughter called Calisto, and fifty sons, of whom the most illustrious were Nyctimus, Mænalus, Pallas, Thesprotus, Macareus, Menelæus, Helix, Hycus, Bucolion, Acacus, Clitor, Stymphalus, and Orchomenus, who mostly built cities in various parts of Greece, to which they gave their own names. He was succeeded on the throne by Nyctimus, who was himself succeeded by Arcas the son of Calisto. He lived about 1820 B.C. *Apollod.* 3.—*Hygin.* fab. 176.—*Catul.* ep. 76. v. 66.—*Paus.* 8. c. 2, &c.

Lyca'on, a king of Arcadia, celebrated for his cruelties. He, according to mythologists, was changed into a wolf by Jupiter, because he offered human victims on the altar of the god Pan. Some attribute his metamorphosis to a very different cause. The sins of mankind, as they relate, were becoming so enormous, that Jupiter visited the earth to punish their wickedness and impiety. He came to Arcadia, where he was announced as a god, and the people, awed by his presence, began to pay proper adoration to his divinity. Lycaon, however, who used to sacrifice all strangers to his wanton cruelty, laughed at the pious prayers of his subjects, and to try the divinity of the god, he served up human flesh on his table. This impiety so irritated Jupiter, that he immediately destroyed the house of Lycaon, and changed him into a wolf. *Ovid. Met.* 1. v. 198, &c.—*Servius in Æn.* 1. v. 735. & *Ecl.* 6. v. 41.—*Natal. Comes.* 9. c. 9.—These two monarchs are often confounded together, though it appears that they were two different characters, and that not less than an age elapsed between their reigns.——A son of Priam and Laothoe. He was taken by Achilles and carried to Lemnus, whence he escaped. He was afterwards killed by Achilles in the Trojan war. *Hom. Il.* 21. v. 34. l. 23. v. 746.—*Apollod.* 3.——The father of Pandarus, killed by Diomedes before Troy. *Hom. Il.* 2. v. 333. l. 5. v. 276.—*Servius in Æn.* 5. v. 496.——A Gnossian artist, who made the sword which Ascanius gave to Euryalus. *Virg. Æn.* 9. v. 304.

LYCAO'NIA, an inland country of Asia, between Cappadocia, Pisidia, Pamphylia, and Phrygia, made a Roman province under Augustus, Iconium was the capital. *Ptol.* 5. c. 6.—*Strab.* 10.—*Mela*, 1. c. 2.—*Liv.* 27.—c. 54. l. 38. c. 39.—Arcadia bore also that name from Lycaon, one of its kings. *Dionys. Hal.*

Lycao'nia, an island in the Tiber, now Isola di S. Bartholomeo. *Liv.* 37. c. 56.——A city of Phrygia Minor.

LYCAP'SUS, a small town near Lydia. *Steph.*

LY'CAS, a priest of Apollo, in the interest of Turnus. He was killed by Æneas. *Virg. Æn.* 10. v. 315.——An officer of Turnus. *Id.* 10. v. 561.

LYCAS'TE, a daughter of Priam by a concubine. She married Polydamas, the son of Antenor.——A famous courtezan of Drepanum, called Venus on account of her great beauty. She had a son called Eryx by Butes, son of Amycus.

LYCAS'TUM, a town of Cappadocia. *Plin.* 6. c. 3.

LYCAS'TUS, an ancient town of Crete, the inhabitants of which accompanied Idomeneus to the Trojan war. *Homer. Il.* 2. *Enum.* 154.—*Mela*, 2. c. 7.

LYCAS'TUS, a son of Minos the First, king of Crete. He was father of Minos the Second, by Ida, the daughter of Corybas. *Diod.* 4.——A son of Minos and Philonome, daughter of Nyctimus. He succeeded his father on the throne of Arcadia. *Paus.* 8. c. 3 & 4.

LY'CE, one of the Amazons, &c. *Flacc.* 6. v. 374.

LYCE'A, a festival celebrated at Argos in honor of Apollo, surnamed Lyceus, from his delivering the country of Argolis from wolves. It is said that a human sacrifice was offered at this festival. *Pindar. Schol. in Pyth.—Sophocl. Schol. in Electr.*

LYC'EAS, a native of Naucratis, who wrote a work on Ægypt. *Athen.* 11.—*Plin.* l. 36.

LY'CES, a town of Macedonia. *Liv.* 31. c. 33.

LYCE'UM. *Vid.* Lycæum.

LYCE'US, a surname of Apollo, derived from λύκος, *lupus*, either because the wolf was offered in sacrifice on his altars, as he presided over sheep, or because Latona, before the birth of Apollo, changed herself into that animal to avoid the persecutions of Juno. The god had a temple erected to his honor in Argolis by Danaus under this name, when that ambitious prince, in his contention for the crown of Argos against Gelanor, persuaded the inhabitants when they saw a bull attacked and defeated by a wolf, that Apollo wished to convince them, that as the wolf, a stranger to the country, had obtained the victory, so they ought to declare in his favor against the less favored pretensions of his rival. His arguments prevailed with the superstitious natives, and the new monarch shewed his gratitude by erecting a temple to Apollo Lyceus. *Paus.* 2. c. 19.—*Ælian. H, H.*

LYCH'NIDUS, now Ochrida, a city with a lake of the same name, in Illyricum, near the sources of the river Aliacmon. *Liv.* 27. c. 32. l. 44. c. 2.

LYCHNI'TIS, a lake of Armenia Major. *Steph.*

LYC'IA, a country of Asia Minor, bounded by the Mediterranean on the south, Caria on the west, Pamphylia on the east, and Phrygia on the north. It was anciently called Mylias and Tremilis, from the Myliæ or Solymi, a people of Crete, who came to settle there. The country afterwards received the name of Lycia from Lycus, the son of Pandion, who established himself there. The inhabitants have been greatly commended by all the ancients, not only for their sobriety and justice, but for their great dexterity in the management of the bow. They were conquered by Crœsus, king of Lydia, and afterwards by Cyrus. Though they were subject to the power of Persia, yet they were governed by their own kings, and only paid a yearly tribute to the Persian monarch. They became part of the Macedonian empire when Alexander came into the east, and were afterwards ceded to the house of the Seleucidæ. The country was reduced into a Roman province by the emperor Claudius. Apollo had there his celebrated oracle at Patara, and the epithet *hyberna* was applied to the country, because the god, on account of the mildness of the climate, was said to pass the winter in his temple there. *Virg. Æn.* 4. v. 143 & 446. l. 7. v. 816. l. 8. v. 166.—*Stat. Theb* 6 v. 686.—*Herodot.* 1. c. 173.—*Strab.* 13.—*Liv.* 37. c. 16. l. 38. l. c. 39.

LYC'IDAS, a centaur, killed by the Lapithæ at the nuptials of Pirithous. *Ovid. Met.* 12. v. 310.——A shepherd's name. *Virg. Ecl.*——A beautiful youth the admiration of Rome in the age of Horace. *Horat.* 1. od. 4. v. 19.

LYC'IDE, a town of Mysia. *Plin.* 5. c. 30.

LYCIM'NA, a town of Peloponnesus. *Strab.* 8.

LYCIM'NIA, a slave, mother of Helenor by a Lydian prince. *Virg. Æn.* 9. v. 446.

LYCIS'CUS, an Athenian archon. Olpmp. 109. an. 1.——A Messenian of the family of the Epytidæ. When his daughters were doomed by lot to be sacrificed for the good of their country, he, to save them from death, fled with them to Sparta, and Aristodemus upon this cheerfully gave up his own children, and soon after succeeded to the throne. *Paus.* 4. c. 9.——A youth who enjoyed the friendship and affectionate regard of the poet Horace. *Horat.* ep. 11. v. 36.

LYC'IUS, a son of Hercules and Toxicreta.——A son of Lycaon.

LYC'IUS or LYCI'US, an epithet given to Apollo from his temple in Lycia, where he gave oracles, particularly at Patara, whence the appellation of *Lyciæ sortes* was applied to his answers, and even to the will of the Fates. *Virg. Æn.* 4. v. 346.

LY'CO. *Vid.* Lycon.

LYC'OA, a city of Arcadia, from which Diana was called Lycoanitis. *Steph.*—*Plin.* 5. c. 9.

LYCOME'DES, a king of Scyrus, son of Apollo and Parthenope. He was secretly entrusted with the care of young Achilles, whom his mother Thetis had disguised in woman's clothes, to remove him from the Trojan war, where she knew that he must unavoidably perish. Lycomedes has rendered himself infamously celebrated for his treachery to Theseus, who had implored his protection when driven from the throne of Athens by the usurper Mnestheus. Lycomedes, as it is reported, either envious of the fame of his illustrious guest, or bribed by the emissaries of Mnestheus, led Theseus to an elevated place, on pretence of showing him the extent of his dominions, and perfidiously threw him down a precipice, where he was killed. *Plut. in Thes.—Paus.* 1. c. 17. l. 7. c. 4.—*Apollod* 3. c. 13.—*Stat. Ach.* 1.——An Arcadian, who, with 500 chosen men, put to flight 1,000 Spartans, and 500 Argives, &c. *Diod.* 15.——A person of Tegea, who occasioned commotions among the Arcadians. *Id. ibid.*——An Athenian, the first who took one of the enemy's ships at the battle of Salamis. *Plut.*—*Herodot.* 8. c. 11.

LY'CON, son of Astyanax, a philosopher of Troas, in the age of Aristotle. He was greatly esteemed by Eumenes, Antiochus, &c. and distinguished himself so much by his eloquence that he received the surname of Glycon, expressive of the sweetness and powerful influence of his works. He died in the 74th year of his age. Of all his writings nothing remains but his will, which is curious from its antiquity, as well as from the nature of its contents. *Diog. in Vit.—Cic. Tusc.* 3. c. 32. [There is a bust of Lycon in the Albani collection, near Rome.]——A man who wrote the life of Pythagoras. *Athen.* 10.——A writer of epigrams.——A player greatly esteemed by Alexander.——A Syracusan who assisted in murdering Dion.——An orator in the number of those who vented their spleen and malice in their accusation of the innocent Socrates. *Diog.* 2.

LY'CON, a city of Ægypt, called also Lycopolis.——A town of Lusitania. *Plin.* 5. c. 9.

LYCO'NE, a city of Thrace. *Steph.*——A mountain of Argolis. *Paus.* 2. c. 24.

LYC'OPHRON, a son of Periander, king of Corinth. The murder of his mother Melissa by his father had such an effect upon him, that he resolved never to speak to a man who had been so wantonly cruel against his relations. This resolution was strengthened by the advice of Procles, his maternal uncle, and Periander at last banished to Corcyra a son whose disobedience and obstinacy had rendered him odious in his sight. Cypselus, the eldest son of Periander, being incapable of reigning from natural infirmities, Lycophron was the only surviving child who could urge any claim to the crown of Corinth. But when the infirmities of Periander obliged him to look for a successor, Lycophron refused to come to Corinth while his father was there, and he was only induced to leave Corcyra, on condition that Periander would come and dwell there while he remained master of Corinth. This exchange, however, was prevented, as the Corcyreans, who were apprehensive of the tyranny of Periander, perfidiously murdered Lycophron before he left that island. *Herodot.* 3.—*Aristot.*

LYC'OPHRON, a tyrant of Pheræ in Thessaly. *Diod. Sic.* 14.——A brother of Thebe, the wife of Alexander tyrant of Pheræ. He assisted his sister in murdering her husband, and afterwards seized the sovereignty. He was dispossessed by Philip of Macedonia. *Plut.—Diod.* 16.——A general of Corinth, killed by Nicias. *Plut. in Nyc.*——A native of Cythera, son of Mastor. He went to the Trojan war with Ajax, the son of Telamon, after the accidental murder of one of his fellow-citizens, and was there killed. *Hom. Il.* 15, v. 450.——A famous Greek poet and grammarian, born at Chalcis in Eubœa. He was one of the poets who flourished under Ptolemy Philadelphus, and who, from their number, obtained the name of Pleiades. Lycophron died of a wound inflicted by an arrow which was wantonly shot at him. He wrote several tragedies, the titles of twenty of which have been preserved by Suidas. The only remaining composition of this poet is called Cassandra or Alexandra. Its obscurity has procured the epithet of *Tenebrosus* for its author. It is a mixture of prophetical effusions which, as he supposes, were uttered by Cassandra during the Trojan war. The best editions of Lycophron are that of Basil, 1546, fol. enriched with the Greek commentary of Tzetzes, a writer of eminence, learning, and judgment, who flourished in the 12th century; that of Canter, 8vo, apud Commelin, 1596; and that of Potter, fol. Oxon, 1702. *Ovid. in Ib.* 533.—*Stat.* 5. *Sylv.* 3. v. 157.—*Suidas.*—*Fabr. B. Gr.* 3. c. 15. —*Sax. Onom.* 1. p. 96.

LYCOP'OLIS, now Siut, a town of Ægypt. It received this name on account of the number of wolves, λύκοι, which were said to have repelled an army of Æthiopians, who had invaded Ægypt. *Diod.* 1.—*Strab.* 17.

LYCO'PUS, an Ætolian, who assisted the Cyreneans against Ptolemy. *Polyæn.* 8.

LYCORE'A, a town of Phocis, at the top of Parnassus, where the people of Delphi took refuge during Deucalion's deluge, and to which spot they were said to have been directed by the howlings of wolves. The top of this mountain is still called Liacoura by the inhabitants. *Jac. Spon. Itin.* part. 2.—*Paus. Phoc.* 6.

LYCO'REUS, the supposed founder of Lycorea, was son of Apollo and Corycia. *Schol. Apollon.* 11. v. 713.—*Hygin.* fab. 161.

LYCO'RIAS, one of the attendant nymphs of Cyrene. *Virg. G.* 4. v. 449.

LYCO'RIS, a freedwoman of the senator Volumnius, also called Cytheris, and Volumnia from her master. She was celebrated for her beauty, her intrigues, and her inconstancy. The poet Gallus was greatly enamoured of her, and his friend Virgil comforts him in his 10th eclogue for the loss of the favors of Cytheris, who had followed M. Antony's camp, and was become the Aspasia of Rome. The charms of Cleopatra, however, prevailed over those of Cytheris, and the unfortunate courtezan lost the favors of Antony and of all the world at the same time. Lycoris was originally a comedian. *Virg. Ecl.* 10.—*Ovid. Art. A.* 3. v. 537. *Trist.* 2. v. 445.—*Martial.* 8. epigr. 73. v. 5.——A beautiful woman frequently celebrated by *Martial.*

LYCOR'MAS, a river of Ætolia, the sands of which were said to be of a golden color. It was afterwards called Evenus from king Evenus who threw himself into it. *Ovid. Met.* 2. v. 245.

LYCOR'TAS, the father of the historian Polybius, flourished B.C. 184. He was chosen general of the Achæan league, and revenged the death of Philopœmen, &c. *Plut.*

LYCOS'THENE, a city of Lydia. *Steph.*

LYCOSU'RA, a city built by Lycaon on mount Lycæus, in Arcadia. *Id.*

LYCOZI'A, a city of Thrace. *Id.*

LYC'TUS or **LYT'TUS**, a town of Crete, the country of Idomeneus, whence he is often called Lyctius. *Virg. Æn.* 3. v. 401.

LYCURGE'A, a festival celebrated at Sparta in honor of the renowned lawgiver Lycurgus. *Plut. Lycurg.* —*Strab.* 8.

LYCUR'GIDES or **LYCURGI'DES**, the patronymic of a son of Lycurgus. *Ovid. in Ib.* v. 503.

LYCUR'GUS, a king of Nemea, in Peloponnesus. He was raised from the dead by Æsculapius. *Stat. Theb.* 5. v. 638.—*Apollod.* 3. c. 6.——A giant killed by Osiris in Thrace. *Diod.* 1.——A king of Thrace, son of Dryas. He has been represented as cruel and impious, on account of the violence which he offered to Bacchus. He, according to the opinion of the mythologists, drove Bacchus out of his kingdom, and abolished his worship, for which impiety he was severely punished by the gods. He put his own son Dryas to death, in a moment of frenzy, and cut off his own legs, mistaking them for vine boughs. He was put to death in the greatest torments by his subjects, who had been informed by the oracle, that they should not taste wine till Lycurgus was no more. This fable is explained by observing, that the aversion of Lycurgus for wine, over which Bacchus presided, arose from the offence which the vice of intoxication gave him, and, therefore, the monarch ordered all the vines of his dominions to be cut down, that himself and his subjects might be preserved from the extravagance and debauchery which are produced by too free a use of wine. *Hygin.* fab. 132.—*Homer. Il.* 6. v. 180.—*Apollod.* 3. c. 5.—*Plut. in Com. de Aud. P.*—*Paus.* 8. c. 4. —*Nonnus Dionys.* 20.—*Ovid. Met.* 4. v. 22. *In Ibin.* 347. *Fast.* 3. v. 721. *Trist.* 5. el. 3. v. 39.—*Propert.* 3. el. 16. v. 22.—*Val. Flacc.* 1.—*Lucan.* 1. v. 574.—*Virg. Æn.* 3. v. 14.—*Horat.* 2. od. 19. ——A son of Hercules and Praxithea, daughter of Thespius. *Apollod.* 2. c. 7.——A son of Pheres, the son of Cretheus. *Id.* 1. c. 9.——An orator of Athens, in the age of Demosthenes, surnamed Ibis, famous for the justice and impartiality of his administration when at the head of affairs. He was one of the thirty orators whom the Athenians refused to deliver up to Alexander. Some of his orations are extant. He died about 330 B.C. *Diod.* 16.——A king of Tegea, son of Aleus, by Neæra, the daughter of Pereus. He married Cleophile, called also Eurynome, by whom he had Amphidamas, &c. *Apollod.* 3. c. 9.—*Cic. ad Br.* 9 & 34. *Att.* 1. ep. 13.—*Homer. Il.* 7. c. 142.——A celebrated lawgiver of Sparta, son of king Eunomus, and brother to Polydectes. He succeeded his brother on the Spartan throne; but when he was informed that the widow of Polydectes was pregnant he kept the kingdom not for himself, but till Charilaus, the child that was born, was arrived at years of maturity. He had previously refused to marry his brother's widow, who wished to strengthen him on his throne by destroying her own son Charilaus, and to leave him in peaceful possession of the crown. The integrity with which he acted, when guardian of his nephew Charilaus, united with the disappointment and the resentment of the queen, raised him many enemies, and he at last yielded to their satire and malevolence, and retired to Crete. He travelled, like a philosopher, for information and improvement, and visited Asia and Ægypt without suffering himself to be corrupted by the licentiousness and luxury which prevailed there. The confusion which followed his departure from Sparta, had rendered his presence absolutely necessary, and he returned home at the earnest solicitations of his countrymen. The disorder which reigned at Sparta, induced him to reform the government; and the more effectually to execute his undertaking, he had recourse to the oracle of Delphi. He was received by the priestess of the god with every mark of honor, his intentions were warmly approved by the divinity, and he was called the friend of gods, and himself rather a god than a man. After so flattering a reception from the most celebrated oracle of Greece, Lycurgus found no difficulty in reforming the abuses of the state, and all were equally anxious in promoting a revolution which had received the sanction of heaven. This memorable event happened 884 B.C. Lycurgus first established a senate, which was composed of 28 senators, whose authority preserved the tranquility of the state, and maintained a due and just equilibrium between the kings and the people, by watching over the intrusions of the former, and checking the seditious turbulence of the latter. All distinction was destroyed, and, by making an equal and impartial division of the land among the various members of the commonwealth, Lycurgus banished luxury, and encouraged the useful arts. The use of money, both of gold and silver, was totally forbidden, and the introduction of heavy brass and iron coin brought no temptations to the dishonest, and left every individual in the possession of his effects without any fear of robbery or violence. All the citizens dined in common, and no one had greater claims to indulgence and luxury than another. The intercourse of Sparta with other nations was forbidden, and few were permitted to travel. The youths were entrusted to the public instructor, as soon as they had attained their seventh year, and their education was left to the wisdom of the laws. They were taught early to think, to answer in a short and laconic manner, and to excel in sharp repartee. They were instructed and encouraged to carry off things by surprise, but if ever the theft was discovered, they were subjected to severe punishment. Lycurgus was happy and successful in establishing and enforcing these laws, and by his prejudice and the wisdom of his administration, the face of Lacedæmon was totally changed, and, in process of time, produced a set of men distinguished for their intrepidity, their fortitude, and their magnanimity. After this, Lycurgus retired from Sparta to Delphi, or, according to others, to Crete, but, before his departure, he bound all the citizens of Lacedæmon by a solemn oath, that neither they nor their posterity, would alter, violate, or abolish the laws which he had established before his return. He soon after, as it is reported, put himself to death, and ordered his ashes to be thrown into the sea, fearful lest if they were carried to Sparta the citizens should consider themselves freed from the oath which they had taken, and empowered to make a revolution. The wisdom and salutary effect of the laws of Lycurgus were plainly demonstrated at Sparta, where for 700 years they remained in full force, but the legislator has been censured as cruel and impolitic. He showed himself inhuman in ordering mothers to destroy those of their children, whose feebleness or deformity in their youth seemed to promise incapability of action in maturer years, and that they would become a burden to the state. His regulations about marriage must necessarily be censured, and no lasting conjugal felicity can be expected from the union of a man with a person whom he perhaps never knew before, and whom he was compelled to choose in a dark room, where all the marriageable women in the state assembled on stated occasions. The peculiar dress which was appointed for the females might be termed improper; and the law must, for ever, be called injudicious and immoral, which ordered them to appear naked on certain days of festivity, and wrestle in a public assembly promiscuously with boys of equal age with themselves. These things indeed contributed as much to corrupt the morals of the Lacedæmonians, as the other regulations seemed to be calculated to banish dissipation, riot, and debauchery. Lycurgus has been compared to Solon, the celebrated legislator of Athens, and it has been judiciously observed, that the former gave his citizens morals conformable to the laws which he had established, and that the latter had given the Athenians laws which coincided with their custom, and manners. The office of Lycurgus demanded resolution, and he, in the establishment of his code, showed himself inexorable and severe. In Solon artifice was requisite, and he shewed himself mild and even voluptuous. The moderation of Lycurgus has been greatly commended, particularly when we recollect that he treated with the greatest humanity and confidence Alcander, a youth who had put out one of his eyes in a seditious tumult. Lycurgus had a son called Antiorus, who left no issue. The Lacedæmonians shewed their respect for the memory of their great legislator by yearly celebrating a festival in his honor. The introduction of money into Sparta in the reign of Agis, the son of Archidamus, was one of the principal causes which corrupted the innocence of the Lacedæmonians, and rendered them the prey of intrigue and of faction. The laws of Lycurgus were abrogated by Philopœmen B.C. 188, but only for a little time, as they were soon after re-established by the Romans. *Plut. in Vitâ.—Justin.* 3. c. 2, &c.—*Strab.* 8, 10, 15, &c.—*Dionys. Hal.* 2.—*Paus.* 3. c. 2. [There is a statue of Lycurgus in the Vatican; and a bust in the Farnese collection at Naples.]

LY'CUS, a king of Bœotia, successor to his brother Nycteus, who left no male issue. He was entrusted with the government only during the minority of Labdacus, the son of the daughter of Nycteus. He was farther enjoined to make war against Epopeus, who had carried away by force Antiope, the daughter of Nycteus. He was successful in this expedition, Epopeus was killed, and Lycus recovered her, and married Antiope, though she was his own niece. This new connection highly displeased his first wife Dirce, and Antiope was delivered to the jealous and unfeeling queen, and tortured in the most cruel manner. Antiope at last escaped, and entreated her sons, Zethus and Amphion to avenge her wrongs. The children, incensed on account of the cruelties which their mother had suffered, besieged Thebes, killed Lycus, and tied Dirce to the tail of a wild bull, which dragged her about till she died. *Paus.* 9. c. 5.—*Apollod.* 3. c. 5. [Lycus, of course, forms a part of the celebrated group before alluded to, called "Il Toro Farnese," at Naples.]——A king of Libya, who sacrificed whatever strangers came upon his coast. When Diomedes, at his return from the Trojan war, had been shipwrecked there, the tyrant seized him and confined him. He, however, escaped by means of Calirhoe, the tyrant's daughter, who was enamoured of the illustrious stranger, and who hanged herself when she saw herself deserted by him. *Plut. Paral.*——A son of Neptune by Celæno, made king of a part of Mysia by Hercules. He offered violence to Megara, the wife of Hercules, for which he was killed by the incensed hero. Lycus gave a kind reception to the Argonauts. *Hygin.* fab. 18, 31, 32 & 137.—*Apollod.* 3. c. 10. ——A son of Ægyptus, married Agave. *Apollod.*——A son of Mars.——A son of Lycaon, king of Arcadia.——A son of Pandion, king of Athens. *Aristoph.*——The father of Arcesilaus. ——One of the companions of Æneas, drowned in the storm which drove the Trojan fleet on the coast of Carthage. *Apollod.* 2. c. 3.—*Paus.* 1, &c. —*Virg. Æn.* 1. v. 222.—*Hygin.* fab. 97 & 159.——An officer of Alexander in the interest of Lysimachus. He made himself master of Ephesus by the treachery of Andron, &c. *Polyæn.* 5.——One of the Centaurs.——A son of Priam.——An historian who wrote a history of Libya and Sicily in the age of Ptolemy Lagus. *Suidas.—Voss. H. Gr.* 1. c. 12. ——A celebrated physician of Neapolis. *Plin.* 20. c. 20.——One of the friends of Æneas, who fell with Helenor from the ramparts of a tower on fire, and was killed by Turnus. *Virg. Æn.* 9. v. 545, &c. ——A youth beloved by Alcæus. *Horat.* 1. od. 32.

LY'CUS, a river of Phrygia, which disappears near Colossæ, and rises again at the distance of about four stadia, and at last falls into the Mæander. *Ovid. Met.* 15. v. 273.——A river of Sarmatia, falling into the Palus Mœotis.——A river in Paphlagonia, near Heraclea. *Ovid.* 4. *Ex. Pont.* el. 1. v. 47.——A river in Assyria. *Curt.* 3. c. 1.—*Arrian.* 3.——A river in Armenia, falling into the Euxine near the Phasis. *Virg. G.* 4. v. 367.——A town of Crete.

LY'DA, a town of Lycia. *Ptol.* It is called Chyda by some authors. *Curt. in Suppl.* 1. 2. c. 2.

LY'DE, the wife of the poet Callimachus, &c. *Ovid. Trist.* 1. el. 5.——A woman in Domitian's reign, who pretended that her medicines could remove barrenness. *Juv.* 2. v. 141.

LYD'IA, a celebrated kingdom of Asia Minor, the boundaries of which were different at different times. It was first bounded by Mysia Major, Caria, Phrygia Major, and Ionia, but in its more flourishing times it contained the whole country which lies between the Halys and the Ægæan Sea. It was anciently called Mæonia, and received the name of Lydia from Lydus, one of its kings. It was governed by monarchs, who after the fabulous period of their history, reigned for 249 years in the following order: Ardysus began to reign 797 B.C.; Alyattes, 761; Meles, 747; Candaules, 735; Gyges, 718; Ardysus the Second, 680; Sadyattes, 631; Alyattes the Second, 619; and Crœsus, 562, who was conquered by Cyrus, B.C. 548, when the kingdom became a province of the Persian empire. There were three different races that reigned in Lydia, the Atyadæ, Heraclidæ, and Mermnadæ. The history of the first is obscure and fabulous, the Heraclidæ began to reign about the time of the Trojan war, and the crown remained in their family about 505 years, and was always transmitted regularly from father to son. Candaules was the last of the Heraclidæ; and Gyges the first, and Crœsus the last of the Mermnadæ. The Lidyans were great warriors in the time of the Mermnadæ. They invented the art of coining gold and silver, and were the first who exhibited public sports, &c. *Herodot.* 1. c. 6 1. 3. c. 90. 1. 7. c. 74.—*Euseb. Chron.*—*Ptol.* 5. c. 2.—*Strab.* 2, 5 & 13.—*Mela*, 1. c. 2.—*Plin.* 3. c. 5.—*Dionys. Hal.* 1.—*Diod.* 4.— *Justin.* 13. c. 4.

LYD'IA, a mistress of *Horace*, &c. 1. od. 8.

LYD'IUS, a river of Macedonia, which falls below Pella into the bay of Therma. *Ptol.* It is now

Castoro.——An epithet applied to the Tiber, because it passed along the borders of Etruria, the inhabitants of which were originally a Lydian colony. *Virg. Æn.* 2. v. 781. l. 8. v. 479.

LY'DUS, a son of Atys, and Callithea, king of Mæonia, which from him received the name of Lydia. His brother Tyrrhenus led a colony to Italy, and gave the name of Tyrrhenia to the settlement which he made on the coast of the Mediterranean. *Herodot.* 7. c. 74.—*Serv. in Æn.* 8. v. 479.

LYG'DAMIS or LYG'DAMUS, a man who made himself absolute at Naxus. *Polyæn.—Hymn. in Dian.*

Lyg'damis, a general of the Cimmerians who passed into Asia Minor, and took Sardis in the reign of Ardys, king of Lydia. *Callim.*——An athlete of Syracuse, celebrated for his great strength, which was said to be equal to that of Hercules. *Paus.* 5. c. 9.——A prince, father of Artemisia, the celebrated queen of Halicarnassus. *Herodot.* 7. c. 99. —*Paus.* 3. c. 11.

LYG'DAMUM, a town of Mysia. *Plin.* 5. c. 31.

LYG'DAMUS, a servant of the poet Propertius, or of his mistress Cynthia.

LYG'DUS, a eunuch employed by Sejanus to administer poison to Drusus, son of Tiberius. *Tac. Ann.* 4. c. 8, &c.

LYG'II, a nation of Germany. *Tacit. de Germ.* 42.

LYG'IUS, a river of Thrace. *Arrian.* l. 1.

LYGODES'MA, a surname of Diana at Sparta, because her statue was brought by Orestes from Tauris, shielded round with Osiers. *Paus.* 3. c. 16

LY'GUS. *Vid.* Ligus.

LYLÆ'US, a river of Bithynia. *Plin.* 5. c. 32.

LY'LE, a city of Arcadia.

LY'MAX, a river of Arcadia. *Paus.* 8. c. 41.

LYM'INIS, a town of Cappadocia. *Marcell.*

LYMTRE or LYMI'RE, a town of Lycia. *Ovid. Met.* fab. 12.—*Plin.* 5. c. 27.

LYMPHOR'TA, a town near Gedrosia. *Plin.* 6. c. 23.

LYNCÆ'E, a city of Macedonia. *Hesych.*

LYNCES'TÆ, a noble family of Macedonia, connected with the royal family. *Justin.* 11. c. 2, &c.

LYNCES'TES, a son of Amyntas, in the army of Alexander the Great. *Curt.* 5. c. 2.

Lynces'tes Alexan'der, a son-in-law of Antipater, who conspired against Alexander, and was put to death. *Id.* 7. c. 1, &c.

LYNCES'TIUS, a river of Macedonia, the waters of which were said to be of an intoxicating quality. *Ovid. Met.* 17. v. 329.

LYNCE'US, son of Aphareus, was among the hunters of the Calydonian boar, and one of the Argonauts. He was so sharp-sighted that, as it is reported, he could see through the earth, and distinguish objects at the distance of above nine miles. He stole some oxen with his brother Idas, and they were both killed by Castor and Pollux, when they were going to celebrate their nuptials with the daughters of Leucippus. *Pindar. Nem.* 10. v. 115, &c. —*Apollod.* 1 & 3.—*Hygin.* fab. 4.—*Paus.* 4. c. 2.—*Ovid. Met.* 3. v. 303. *Fast.* 5. v. 709. *Seneca. Med.* 228.—*Cic. Fam.* 9. ep. 2.—*Horat.* 1. ep. 1. v. 28.—*Plin.* 2. c. 17.—*Val. Flac.* 1. v. 462.—*Tzetzes ad Lyc.* 512.—*Apollon. Arg.* 1.——A son of Ægyptus, who married Hypermnestra, the daughter of Danaus. His life was spared by the love and humanity of his wife. *Vid* Danaides. He made war against his father-in-law, dethroned him, and seized his crown. Some say that Lynceus was reconciled to Danaus, and that he succeeded him after his death, and reigned forty-one years. *Apollod.* 2. c. 1.—*Paus.* 2. c. 16, 19 & 25.—*Ovid. Heroid.* 14.—*Hygin.* fab. 168 & 273.—*Servius in Æn.* 10. v. 497.—*Sch. Pind.* 10. *Nem.* v. 10.—*Lactant. ad Theb.* 1. v. 324. l. 6. v. 290.——One of the companions of Æneas, killed by Turnus. *Virg. Æn.* 9. v. 768.——A son of Hercules by Tiphysa. *Apollod.*

LYNCI'DES, the patronymic of the son of Lynceus, or, according to some, the name of a person. *Ovid. Met.* 4. v. 768. l. 5. v. 99 & 185.

LYN'CUS, LYNCÆ'US, or LYNX, a cruel king of Scythia, or, according to others, of Sicily. He received, with feigned hospitality, Triptolemus, whom Ceres had sent all over the world to teach mankind agriculture, and as he was jealous of his commission he resolved to murder this favorite of the gods in his sleep. As he was going to give the deadly blow to Triptolemus, he was snddenly changed by the gods into a lynx, an animal which is the emblem of perfidy and of ingratitude. *Ovid. Met.* 5. v. 650.—*Serv. Æn.* 1. v. 323

Lyn'cus, an inland town of Macedonia, at the west of Pella, of which the inhabitants were called Lyncestæ. *Plin.* 2. c. 103. l. 4. c. 10.

LYN'DUS, a town of Sicily.

LY'RA, the name of one of the constellations in the heavens. *Varr. R.R.* 2. c. 3.—*Col.* 10. v. 79.—*Ovid. Fast.* 2. v. 75.

LYR'CÆ, a people of Scythia, who lived by hunting.

LYRCÆ'US, a mountain of Arcadia. *Vid.* Lycæus. ——A fountain. *Stat. Theb.* 4. v. 711.

LYRCE'A, a town of Peloponnesus, formerly called Lyncea. *Paus.* 2. c 35.

LYR'CUS, a son of Phoroneus, the son of Inachus. He was sent in quest of Ino, whom Jupiter had carried away, and after unsuccessful enquiries, he returned to Caunus in Caria, where Ebialus the king of the country gave him his daughter in marriage, and part of his dominions. As he was childless he consulted the oracle of Apollo, how he might raise a successor, and received for answer, that the first woman to whom he should be united, would make him a father. On his return home, he was forcibly stopped by Staphilus, by whose daughter Hemithea he had Basiles, who succeeded him. *Nicænet. & Apoll. Rhod. apud Parthen.* 1.

LYRNES'SUS, a city of Troas, the native country of Briseis, called from that circumstance Lyrnessis. It was taken and plundered by Achilles and the Greeks, at the time of the Trojan war, and the booty divided among the conquerors. *Homer Il.* 2. v. 197.—*Ovid. Met.* 12. v. 108. *Heroid.* 3. v. 5. *Trist.* 4. el. 1. v. 15.—*Strab.* 13.—*Servius. in Æn.* 10. v. 128. l. 12. v. 547.——A city of Cilicia, called also Homala, or rather Mallos.—*Strab.* 13.—*Curt.* 3. c. 4. ——An island opposite the promontory of Sigæum. *Plin.* 5. c. 27.

LYR'OPE, a town of Pamphylia. *Ptol.*

LY'SA, a city of Arabia Petræa. *Id.*

LYSAN'DER, a celebrated general of Sparta, in the last years of the Peloponnesian war. He drew Ephesus from the interest of Athens, and gained the friendship of Cyrus the Younger. He gave battle to the Athenian fleet consisting of 124 ships, at Ægospotamos, and destroyed it all, except three ships, with which the enemy's general fled to Evagoras king of Cyprus. In this celebrated battle, which happened 405 B.C., the Athenians lost 3,000 men, and with them their influence among the neighbouring states. Lysander well knew how to take advantage of this important victory, and in the following year, Athens, worn out by a long war of twenty-seven years, and discouraged by repeated misfortunes, gave itself up to the power of the enemy, and consented to destroy the Piræus, to deliver up all its ships, except twelve, to recall all those who had been banished, and, in short, to be submissive in every degree to the power of Lacedæmon. Besides these humiliating conditions, the government of Athens was totally changed, and thirty tyrants were set over it by Lysander. This glorious success, and the honor of having put an end to the Peloponnesian war, increased the pride of Lysander. He had already begun to pave his way to universal power, by establishing aristocracy in the Grecian cities of Asia, and now he attempted to make the crown of Sparta elective. In the pursuit of his ambition, he used prudence and artifice; and as he could not easily abolish a form of government which ages and popularity had confirmed, he had recourse to the assistance of the gods. His attempt, however, to corrupt the oracles of Delphi, Dodona, and Jupiter Ammon, proved ineffectual, and he was even accused by the priests of the Libyan temple of attempting to bribe them. The sudden declaration of war against the Thebans, saved him from the accusations of his adversaries, and he was sent by the Lacedæmonians, together with Pausanias, against the enemy. The plan of his military operations was discovered; the Haliartians, whose ruin he secretly meditated, attacked him unexpectedly, and he was killed in a bloody battle, which ended in the defeat of his troops, 394 B.C. His body was recovered by his colleague Pausanias, and honored with a magnificent funeral. Lysander has been commended for his bravery and great presence of mind, but his ambition deserves the severest censure, and his cruelty and his duplicity have greatly stained his character. He was arrogant and vain in his public as well as private conduct, and he received and heard with the greatest avidity the hymns which his courtiers and flatterers sang to his honor. Yet in the midst of all his pomp, his ambition, and his intrigues, he died extremely poor, and his daughters were rejected by two opulent citizens of Sparta, to whom they had been betrothed during the life of their father. This behaviour of the lovers was severely punished by the Lacedæmonians, who generously protected from injury the innocent children of a man whom they hated for his sacrilege, his contempt of religion, and his perfidy. The father of Lysander, whose name was Aristoclites, or Aristocrates, was descended from Hercules, though not reckoned of the race of the Heraclidæ. *Plut. & C. Nep. in Vitâ.—Diod.* 13. ——A Trojan chief, wounded by Ajax, son of Telamon, before Troy. *Homer. Il.* 11. v. 491.——One of the Ephori in the reign of Agis, &c. *Plut.*——A grandson of the great Lysander. *Paus.*

LYSAN'DRA, a daughter of Ptolemy Lagus, who married Agathocles the son of Lysimachus. She was exposed to the jealousy and persecution of Arsinoe, and fled to Seleucus for protection. *Paus.* 1. c. 9, &c.

LYSA'NIAS, a writer cited by *Athenæus*, l. 7.

LYSA'NIAS, a Greek orator.——An Arcadian who expelled Lycaon from his kingdom.

LYSA'NIAX, a man made king of Ituræa, by Antony, &c.

LY'SE, a daughter of Thespius. *Apollod.*

LYSI'ADES, an Athenian, son of Phærus the philosopher, &c. *Cic. Philip.* 5.——An Athenian archon. Olymp. 95. an. 4.——A tyrant of Megalopolis, who died B.C. 226. *Plut.*

LYSIANAS'SA, one of the Nereides. *Apollod.* 1. c. 2.——A daughter of Epaphus, mother of Busiris. *Id.* 2. c. 5.

LYS'IAS, a celebrated orator, son of Cephalus, a native of Syracuse. His father left Sicily and went to settle at Athens, where Lysias was born and carefully educated. In his fifteenth year he accompanied the colony which the Athenians sent to Thurium, and after a long residence in Italy, he returned home in his forty-seventh year. Though possessed of great abilities, he was not engaged in the service of the state through the hatred or jealousy of the thirty tyrants, but his powers of oratory rendered him truly illustrious. As the friend and companion of Socrates, he attended him in his imprisonment, and wrote an elegant oration in his defence, which the philosopher read with satisfaction, but declined to use, nobly sensible that if his public services and innocence of manners could not defend his honor and his life, no efforts of art or persuasion would prevail. Lysias, known to the Grecian states by his eloquence, by the simplicity, correctness, and purity of his diction, wrote no less than 425 orations according to Plutarch, though the number may with more probability be reduced to 230. Of these thirty-three are extant, the best editions of which are that of Taylor, 8vo, Cantab. 1740, and that of Auger, 2 vols. 8vo, Paris, 1783. He died in the seventy-third year of his age, 378 B.C. An English translation was published by Dr. Gillies, London, 1778, and a French translation by Auger, Paris, 1781. *Fabr. B. Gr.* 2. c. 26.—*Sax. Onom.* 1. p. 52.—*Plut. de Orat.—Cic. de Orat* 2. c. 52. *In Brut.* 17.—*Quintil.* 3. c. 8. l. 10. c. 1.—*Diog.* 2. [A bust of Lysias is in the Farnese collection at Naples.]——An Athenian general, &c. ——A tyrant of Tarsus, B.C. 267.

LYS'IAS, a city of Syria, near Apamea, now Berziech.

LYS'ICLES, an Athenian sent with Chares into Bœotia, to stop the conquests of Philip of Macedonia. He was defeated at Chæronea, and sentenced to death for his ill conduct there.

LYSID'ICE, a daughter of Pelops and Hippodamia, who married Mastor, the son of Perseus and Andromeda. *Apollod.* 2. c. 4.—*Paus.* 8. c. 14.——A daughter of Thespius. *Apollod.*

LYSID'ICUS, a partisan of Antony, whom Cicero, alluding to the Greek derivation of the name (λύσις & δίκη), denominates the destroyer of law and justice. *Cic. Phil.* 11. c. 6.

LYSIM'ACHE, a daughter of Abas the son of Melampus. *Apollod.* 1. c. 9.——A daughter of Priam. *Id.* 3. c. 12.

LYSIMA'CHIA or **LYSIMACHI'A**, now Hexamili, a city of the Thracian Chersonesus, on the shores of the Propontis, built in a very eligible situation by Lysimachus after the destruction of Cardia. *Polyb.* 5. c. 34. l. 34. c. 57, &c.—*Paus.* 1. c. 9.——A town of Ætolia, built by Lysimachus. *Strab.* 7 & 10. ——A city in Æolia. *Mela*, 2. c. 2.

LYSIMACH'IDES, an archon at Athens. Olymp. 110. an. 2.

LYSIM'ACHUS, son of Agathocles, was one of the favorite generals of Alexander. After the death of that monarch, he made himself master of part of Thrace, where he built a town which he called Lysimachia. He sided with Cassander and Seleucus against Antigonus and Demetrius, and fought with them at the celebrated battle of Ipsus. He afterwards seized Macedonia, after expelling Pyrrhus from the throne, B.C. 286; but his cruelty rendered him odious to the people, and the murder of his son Agathocles so offended his subjects, that the most opulent and powerful revolted from him and abandoned the kingdom. He pursued them to Asia, and declared war against Seleucus, who had given them a kind reception. He was killed in a bloody battle 281 B.C. in the eightieth year of his age, and his body was found among the heaps of slain only by the fidelity of a little dog, which had carefully watched near it. It is said that the love and respect of Lysimachus for his learned master Callisthenes proved nearly fatal to him. He, as Justin mentions, was thrown into the den of a hungry lion, by order of Alexander, for having given Callisthenes poison, to save his life from farther ignominy and insult; and when the furious animal darted upon him, he wrapped his hand in his mantle, and boldly thrust it into the lion's mouth, and by twisting his tongue, killed the animal which was ready to devour him. This extraordinary act of courage in his self-defence recommended him to Alexander, who pardoned him, and ever after honored him with his particular esteem. *Justin.* 15. c. 3, &c. *Diod.* 10, &c.—*Paus.* 1. c. 10.—*Plin.* 8. c. 16.—*Seneca de Irâ.* 3. c. 17. *Clem.* 1. c. 25.—*Val. Max.* 9. c. 3.—*Plut. in Demet.* [There is a bust of Lysimachus in the Vatican.]——An Acarnanian, preceptor to Alexander the Great. He used to call himself Phœnix, his pupil Achilles, and Philip, Peleus. *Plut. in Alex.—Justin.* 15. c. 3.——An historian of Alexandria, who had written a history of Ægypt, quoted by Josephus, another of Thebes, and a treatise on agriculture, quoted by Varro, all now lost. *Varro de R. R.* 1.—*Joseph. contra. Ap.* 1.—*Voss. H. Gr.* l. 3.——A son of Aristides, rewarded by the Athenians on account of the virtue of his father. *Plutarch. in Arist.*——A chief priest among the Jews, about 204 B.C. &c. *Josephus.*——A physician who was particularly attached to the system adopted by Hippocrates. *Schol. Nicandri in Alexipharm.*——A governor of Heraclea in Pontus, &c.

LYSIME'LIA or **LYSIMELI'A**, a marsh of Sicily, near Syracuse, now Pantanella. *Thucyd.* 7.—*Theocr. Idyll.* 16.

LYSIN'OE, now Aglasson, a city of Asia near Pamphylia. *Liv.* 38. c. 15.

LYSIP'PE, a daughter of Prœtus. *Apollod.* 2. *Vid.* Prœtides.——A daughter of Thespius, mother of Erasippus by Hercules. *Id.*

LYSIP'PUS, a famous statuary of Sicyon. He was originally a white-smith, and afterwards applied himself to painting, till his talents and inclination taught him that he was born to excel in sculpture. He flourished about 325 B.C. Alexander the Great not only patronised him, but showed himself so partial to him, that he forbade any other sculptor to make his statue. Lysippus excelled in the execution of the hair, and was the first who made the head of his statues smaller that they might appear taller. This was observed by one of his friends, and the artist gave for answer, that his predecessors had represented men in their natural form, but that he represented them such as they appeared. Lysippus made no less than 600 statues, the most admired of which were those of Alexander; one of Apollo of Tarentum forty cubits high; one of a man coming out of a bath, with which Agrippa adorned his baths at Rome, and one of Socrates.

He also, at the request of Alexander, made statues of the twenty-five horsemen who were drowned in the Granicus, which were afterwards brought to Rome by Metellus after the conquest of Macedonia. All these were so valued, that, in the age of Augustus, they were bought for their weight in gold. Lysippus had three sons who were equally eminent in the art of sculpture. *Plut. in Alex.—Cic. in Brut.* c. 164. *Ad. Her.* 4. c. 148.—*Plin.* 34. c. 8. l. 37. c. 7,—*Paus.* 9. c. 27.—*Propert.* 3 el. 7. v. 9.—*Stat.* 1. *Sylv.* 1. v. 86.—*Paterc.* 1. c. 11.—*Horat.* 2. ep. 1. v. 240.——A comic poet, some of whose plays are mentioned by *Athenæus. Plin.* 7. c. 37.——A general engaged in the Achæan league.

LY'SIS, a Pythagorean philosopher, preceptor to Epaminondas. He flourished about 388 B.C. He is supposed by some to have been the author of the golden verses which are attributed to Pythagoras. *C. Nep. in Epam.* 2.—*Cic. Orat.* 3. c. 34. *Off.* 1. c. 44.

LYSIS'TRATUS, an Athenian parasite. *Aristoph. Equit.*——A brother of Lysippus. He was the first artist who ever made a statue with gypsum and potter's clay. *Plin.* 34. c. 8. l. 35. c. 12.——An Archon at Athens. Olymp. 102. an. 4.

LYSITH'OUS, a son of Priam. *Apollod.*

LYSIZO'NA, a surname of Diana from her presiding over, and unloosening the girdles of pregnant women. She was worshipped under that name at Athens. *Theocr. in Ptol. Laud. Id.* 17. v. 60.—*Schol. Apollon.* 1.

LY'SO, a friend of Cicero, deservedly commended for his kindness and hospitality. He was born at Patræ, in Achaia. *Cic.* 13. *Fam.* 19.——A native of Lilybæum. *Cic. Fam.* 13. ep. 34.

LYS'TRA, a town of Lycaonia. *Act. Apost.* 14. v. 6.—*Plin.* 5. c. 32.

LY'TÆ, a small region of Thessaly. *Steph.*

LYTÆ'A, a daughter of Hyacinthus, put to death by the Athenians. *Apollod.*

LYTAR'MIS, a promontory on the Scythian Ocean. *Plin.*

LYTIER'SAS. *Vid.* Lityersas.

LYXE'A, a city of Acarnania. *Steph.*

LYZA'NIAS, a king of Chalcis, &c.

M.

MA'CÆ, a people of Arabia Felix. *Mela,* 3. c. 8. They are placed in Africa at the south of the larger Syrtis by *Herodotus*, 4. c. 175, and other writers. *Sil.* 3. v. 275. l. 5. v. 194.

MACANI'TÆ, a people of Mauritania Tingitana. *Ptol.*

MA'CAR, a son of Criasius or Crinacus, the first Greek who led a colony to Lesbus. He had two daughters, Mitylene and Methymna, who gave their names to the two chief cities of Lesbus, and his four sons took possession of the four neighbouring islands, Chius, Samus, Cos, and Rhodes, which were called the seats of the Macares or the blessed. *Dionys. Hal.* 1.—*Diod.* 5.—*Mela,* 2. c. 7.—*Homer. Il.* 24.

MAC'ARA, an island of Lycia. *Steph.*——A city of Sicily, now Citadella.

MACA'REA, a city of Arcadia, called *Beata* by the Romans. *Steph.*

MACARE'ON and SI'DES, famous surgeons mentioned by *Galen. Method.* 5 & l. 2, γενικῶν, c. 12.—*Æginet.* 17. c. 17.

MACA'REUS or MAC'AREUS, an ancient historian of the island of Cos. *Athen.* 6, &c.——A son of Æolus, who debauched his sister Canace, and had a son by her. The father ordered the child to be exposed, and sent a sword to his daughter, and commanded her to destroy herself. Macareus fled to Delphi, where he became priest of Apollo. *Hygin.* 242.—*Ovid. Met. Heroid.* 11 *In Ib.* 563.——One of the companions of Ulysses, left at Caieta in Italy, where Æneas found him. *Ovid. Met.* 14. v. 159.——A son of Lycaon.—*Apollod.* 3. c. 8.—*Paus.* 8. c. 3.——A priest of Bacchus. *Ælian. V. H.* 13. c. 2.

MACA'RIA, a daughter of Hercules and Dejanira. After the death of Hercules, Eurystheus made war against the Heraclidæ, whom the Athenians supported, and the oracle declared, that the descendants of Hercules should obtain the victory, if any of them devoted himself to death. This was cheerfully done by Macaria, who refused to endanger the life of the children of Hercules by suffering the victim to be drawn by lot, and the Athenians in consequence obtained a victory. Great honors were paid to the patriotic Macaria, and a fountain of Marathon was called by that name. *Paus.* 1. c. 32.—*Euripid. Heracl.* 2.—*Cœl. Rhod.* 13. c. 7.

MACA'RIA, an ancient name of Cyprus.——A lake near Marathon, in which many of the Persians were drowned, from which circumstance arose the proverb, *in Macariam abi. Pausan.*

MAC'ARIS, an ancient name of Crete.

MACATU'TÆ, a people of the Pentapolis in Africa. *Ptol.*

MACCABÆ'I, the descendants of Judas Maccabeus, who obtained his name from his glorious victories against Antiochus IV. king of Lyria, B.C. 167.

MAC'CARA, a region above Pharsalus. *Steph.*

MAC'CI, a people in the interior of Libya. *Ptol.*

MAC'CO, a woman represented as so stupid, that her name became proverbial among the Greeks to intimate a want of common sense. *Apuleius in Apol.*—*Turneb. Adv.* 17. c. 21.

MACCOCALIN'GÆ, a nation of the Brachmanes in India. *Plin.* 6. c. 17.

MACCU'RÆ, a people of Mauritania Cæsariensis. *Ptol.*

MACED'NON, a small region near Pindus. *Steph.*

MACED'NUS, a son of Lycaon. *Apollod.*

MAC'EDO, a son of Osiris, who had a share in the divine honors which were paid to his father. He was represented clothed in a wolf's skin, for which reason the Ægyptians held that animal in great veneration. *Diod.* 1.—*Plut. in Isid. & Os.*——A man who gave his name to Macedonia. Some authors suppose him to be the same as the son or general of Osiris, whilst others consider him as grandson of Deucalion by the mother's side. *Diod* 1.—*Solin.* 15.—*Steph. Byzant.*——A philosopher, mentioned by *Gellius*, 13. c. 18.

MACEDO'NIA, a celebrated country, situated between Thrace, Epirus, and Greece. Its boundaries have been different at different periods of its history. Philip increased it by the conquest of Thessaly and part of Thrace, and, according to Pliny, it contained no less than 150 different nations. The kingdom of Macedonia, first founded B.C. 814, by Caranus, a descendant of Hercules, and a native of Argos, continued in existence 646 years, till the battle of Pydna. The family of Caranus remained in possession of the crown until the death of Alexander the Great, and began to reign in the following order: Caranus, after a reign of 28 years, was succeeded by Cœnus, who ascended the throne 786 B.C.; Thurimas 774; Perdiccas 729; Argæus 678; Philip 640; Æropas 602; Alcetas or Alectas 576; Amyntas 547; Alexander 497; Perdiccas the Second 454; Archelaus 413; Amyntas the Second 399; Pausanias 398; Amyntas the Third 397; Argæus the tyrant 390; Amyntas restored 390; Alexander the Second 371; Ptolemy Alorites 370; Perdiccas the Third 366; Philip son of Amyntas 360; Alexander the Great 336; Philip Aridæus 323; Cassander 316; Antipater and Alexander 298; Demetrius king of Asia 294; Pyrrhus 287; Lysimachus 286; Ptolemy Ceraunus 280; Meleager two months: Antipater the Etesian 45 days Antigonus Gonatas 277; Demetrius 243; Antigonus Doson 232; Philip 221: Perseus 179; who was conquered by the Romans 168 B.C. at Pydna. Macedonia has been at different times known by the several names of Æmonia, Mygdonia, Pæonia Edonia, Æmathia, &c. The inhabitants of Macedonia were naturally warlike, and though in the infancy of their empire they were little known beyond the borders of their country, yet they signalized themselves greatly in the reign of Philip, and the valor of Alexander added the kingdom of Asia to their dominions. The Macedonian Phalanx, or body of soldiers, was always held in the highest repute, and it resisted and generally subdued the repeated attacks of the bravest and most courageous enemies. *Liv.* 44.—*Just.* 6. c. 9. l. 7. c. 1, &c.—*Strab.* 7.—*Mela,* 1. c. 3, &c.—*Plin.* 4. c. 10, &c.—*Solin.* 15.—*Aul. Gell.* 9. c. 3.—*Isidor.* 14. c. 4.—*Scalig. ad Auson. de. Cl. Urb.* 3.—*Curt.* 3 & 4.—*Paus.* 8. c. 7.

MACEDON'ICUM BEL'LUM was undertaken by the Romans against Philip king of Macedonia some few months after the second Punic war, B.C. 200. The war originated in the hostilities which Philip had exercised against the Achæans, the friends and allies of Rome. The consul Flaminius, was entrusted with the management of this war, and he conquered Philip on the confines of Epirus, and afterwards in Thessaly. The Macedonian fleets were also defeated; Eubœa was taken; and Philip, disheartened by repeated losses, sued for peace, which was granted him in the fourth year of the war. The ambition and cruelty of Perseus, the son and successor of Philip, afterwards offended and irritated the Romans. Another war was undertaken, in which the Romans at first suffered two defeats. This, however, did not discourage them; Paulus Æmylius was chosen consul in the 60th year of his age, and empowered to carry on the war with vigour. He came to a general engagement near the city of Pydna. The victory sided with the Romans, and 20,000 of the Macedonian soldiers were left on the field of battle. This decisive blow put an end to the war, which had already continued for three years, 168 B.C. Perseus and his sons Philip and Alexander were taken prisoners, and carried to Rome to adorn the triumph of the conqueror. About fifteen years after, new seditions were fomented in Macedonia, and the false pretensions of Andriscus, who called himself the son of Perseus, obliged the Romans to send an army to quell these commotions, which threatened the immediate ruin of their power in that province. Andriscus at first obtained many considerable advantages over the Roman forces, till at last he was conquered and delivered up to the consul Metellus, who carried him to Rome, After these commotions, which are sometimes called the third Macedonian war, Macedonia was finally reduced into a Roman province, and governed by a proconsul, about 148 B.C.

MACEDON'ICUS, a surname given to Metellus, from his important conquests in Macedonia. It was also given to such as had obtained any victory in that province.

MACEL'LA, a town at the west of Sicily, taken by the consul Duillius. *Liv.* 26. c. 21.

MA'CER ÆMYL'IUS, a Latin poet of Verona, intimate with Tibullus and Ovid, and commended for his genius and learning, and the elegance of his poetry. He wrote in a pleasing and familiar style, some poems upon serpents, plants, and birds, mentioned by Ovid, in which he imitated the Greek poet Nicander. He also composed a poem upon the ruins of Troy, to serve as a supplement to Homer's Iliad. His compositions are now lost, except ten scattered verses preserved in the Corpus Poetarum. The book which is extant on the virtues of herbs, and which bears his name, is supposititious, and, as Scaliger observes, is the production neither of a great poet nor a learned physician. Macer was accompanied by his friend Ovid in his visits to Asia and Sicily. He died B.C. 16 *Ovid. Trist.* 4. el. 10. v. 44. *Ex Pont.* 2. epigr. 10.—*Quintil.* 10. c. 1.—*Voss. de P. L.*—*Fabricius, Bibl. L.* 4. c. 12. *Gyrald. de P. H.* 4.—*Harles. Not. Lit. Rom.* 1. p. 303.

MA'CER C. LICIN'IUS, an orator condemned for extortion during Cicero's prætorship. It is supposed that he destroyed himself on hearing the result of his trial, though various accounts are given of the manner of his death. *Val. Max.* 9. c. 12.—*Cic. Att.* 1. epigr. 4. *Leg.* 1. c. 2.—*Liv.* 4, &c.—*Plut. in Cic.*

MA'CER L. CLO'DIUS, a proprætor of Africa in the reign of Nero. He assumed the title of emperor, and was put to death by order of Galba.

MA'CER, the paternal grandfather of the emperor Severus. *Spartian.*

MACERI'NUS. *Vid.* Geganius.

MACHÆRA, a river of Africa, near Carthage. *Polyb.*

MACHÆ'RA, a common crier at Rome. *Juv.* 7. v. 9.

MACHÆTE'GI or MACHAGE'NI, a nation of Scythia, within Imaus. *Ptol.*

MACHAN'IDAS, a man who made himself absolute at Sparta. He was killed by Philopœmen, after being defeated at Mantinea, B.C. 208. Nabis succeeded him. *Plut.*—*Liv.* 27. c. 30. l. 28. c. 5 & 7.

MACHA'ON, a celebrated physician, son of Æsculapius and brother of Podalirius. He went to the Trojan war with the inhabitants of Trica, Ithome, and Œchalia. According to some he was king of Messenia. As physician to the Grecian forces, he healed the wounds which they had received during the Trojan war, and was one of those concealed in the wooden horse. Some suppose that he was killed before Troy, by Eurypylus, the son of Telephus. He received divine honors after death, and had a temple in Messenia. *Homer. Il.* 2. v. 239. l. 4. v. 192.—*Propert.* 2. el. 1. v. 61.—*Dictys Cret.* 1. c. 14.—*Paus.* 3. c. 26.—*Orph. de Lapid.* 11. v. 5.—*Tzetzes ad Lycoph.* 905 & 1046.—*Ovid. ex Pont.* 3. ep. 4.—*Quint. Smyr.* 6. v. 409.—*Virg. Æn.* 2. v. 263 & 426.

MACHÆ'REUS, a son of Dætas, priest of Apollo's temple at Delphi. According to Strabo, Pausanius, and other writers, he murdered Neoptolemus, either because he had insulted the god, or because he meditated the plunder of his temple. Others, especially Virgil and Paterculus, consider Orestes as the murderer of Neoptolemus. *Hygin.* fab. 123. —*Strab.* 9.—*Pherecyd. apud Sch. Euripid. Orest.* 1657.—*Paus.* 1. c. 11.—*Asclepiad. apud. Sch. Pind.* 7. *Nem.*—*Virg. Æn.* 3. v. 331.—*Patercul.* 1. c. 1.

MACHELO'NES, a people near Pontus. *Arrian. in Peripl*

MACHOR'BÆ, a harbour of Arabia Felix. *Plin.* 6. c. 28.

MACHURE'BI or MACURE'BI, a people of Mauritania Cæsariensis. *Ptol.*—*Plin.* 5. c. 3.

MACHU'SII, a people of Mauritania Cæsariensis. *Ptol.*

MA'CI, a people near Arachosia. *Plin.* 6. 23.

MACIC'RATIS, a city of Ægypt, founded by the Athenians. *Euseb.*

MAC'IDOS, a city of Thrace, called Madi by *Ptolemy*, and Madytos by *Xenophon;* and now Maiton.

MACIS'TOS, a city of Triphylia. *Steph. in* Μάκιςος.

MAC'NA, a city of Arabia Felix. *Ptol.*

MACOD'AMA, a maritime city of Africa Propria, called Macomades by *Antoninus*, and now Macros. *Ptol.*

MACOM'ADÆ, a town of Africa, near the greater Syrtis. *Antonin.* It is called Calumacuma by Ptolemy.

MACOPSI'SA, a city of Sardinia. *Ptol.*

MACORA'BA or MACOR'ABA, a town of Arabia Felix. *Id.*

MA'CRA, a river flowing from the Apennines into the Mediterranean, and dividing Liguria from Etruria. *Lucan.* 2. v. 426.—*Liv.* 39. c. 32.—*Plin.* 3. c. 5.

MA'CRAS, a plain of Cœlesyria. *Strabo.* It is now Marzi.

MACRE'NIS, a nation of Corsica. *Ptol.*

MA'CRI CAM'PI, a plain in Cisalpine Gaul, near the river Gabellus. *Liv.* 41, c. 18. l. 45. c. 12.

MA'CRI CAM'PI, a plain near Mutina. *Col.* 7. c. 2.

MA'CRIA, a small island near Rhodes. *Plin.* 5. c. 31. ——A promontory near Teos in Ionia. *Pausan. Achaic.* l. 7.

MACRIA'NUS M. FUL'VIUS JU'LIUS, an Ægyptian of obscure birth, who, from a private soldier, rose to the highest command in the army, and proclaimed himself emperor of Rome, when Valerian had been made prisoner by the Persians, A.D. 260. His liberality to his troops supported his usurpation; his two sons Macrianus and Quietus were invested with the imperial purple, and the enemies of Rome were severally defeated either by the emperors or their generals. When he had supported his dignity for a year in the eastern parts of the world, Macrianus marched towards Rome, to crush Gallienus, who had been proclaimed emperor. He was defeated in Illyricum by the lieutenant of Gallienus, and put to death with his son, A.D. 262. *Trebell. Pollio de* 30 *Tyrann.* c. 15.

MACRI'NUS M. OPIL'IUS SEVE'RUS, a native of Africa, who rose from the most ignominious condition to the rank of præfect of the prætorian guards, and at last of emperor, after the death of Caracalla, whom he inhumanly sacrificed to his ambition, A.D. 217. The beginning of his reign was popular; the abolition of the taxes, and an affable and complaisant behaviour, endeared him to his subjects. These promising appearances did not, however, long continue, and the timidity which Macrinus betrayed in buying the peace of the Persians by a large sum of money, soon rendered him odious; and while he affected to imitate the virtuous Aurelius, without possessing the good qualities of his heart, he became contemptible and insignificant, This affectation irritated the minds of the populace, and when severe punishments had been inflicted on some of the disorderly soldiers, the whole army mutinied; and their tumult was increased by their consciousness of their power and numbers, which Macrinus had the imprudence to betray, by keeping almost all the military force of Rome encamped together on the plains of Syria. Heliogabalus was proclaimed emperor by the rebellious troops, and Macrinus, who attempted to save his life by flight, was seized in Cappadocia, and his head was cut off and sent to his successor, June 7th, A.D. 218. Macrinus reigned about two months and three days. His son, called Diadumenus, shared his father's fate. *Jul. Capitol. in vit.—Aur. Victor. in Macrin.—Æl. Lamprid. in Diadum.* [There are several busts of Macrinus; that in the Vatican is the best. There is also a statue of him in the Vatican.]——A friend of the poet Persius, to whom his second satire is inscribed.

MACRIT'IUS or **CRITIUS**, a native of Cos, the founder of Sinope in Pontus. *Steph.*

MA'CRO, a favourite of the emperor Tiberius, celebrated for his intrigues, perfidy, and cruelty. He destroyed Sejanus, and raised himself upon the ruins of that unfortunate favorite. He was accessary to the murder of Tiberius, and conciliated the good opinion of Caligula, by prostituting to him his own wife called Ennia. He soon after became unpopular, and was obliged by Caligula to kill himself, together with his wife, A.D. 38. *Tacit. Ann.* 6. c. 15 & 23, &c.—*Sueton. Tib.* 73. *Cal.* 26.

MACRO'BII, a people of Æthiopia, celebrated for their justice and the innocence of their manners. They generally lived to their 120th year, some say to a thousand, and, indeed, from their longevity they have obtained their name (μακρὸς βίος, *long life*), to distinguish them more particularly from the other inhabitants of Æthiopia. After so long a period spent in virtuous actions, and happily exempt from the indulgences of vice, and from maladies, they dropped into the grave as to sleep without pain, and without terror. *Orph. Argon.* 1105.—*Herodot.* 3. c. 17.—*Mela*, 3. c. 9.—*Plin.* 7. c. 48.—*Val. Max.* 8. c. 3.—*Solin.* 33.

MACRO'BIUS AUREL. AMBRO'SIUS THEODO'-TIUS, a Latin writer, who died A.D. 415. Some suppose that he was chamberlain to the emperor Theodosius the Second, but this appears to be groundless, when we observe that Macrobius was a follower of paganism, and that none were admitted to the confidence of the emperor, or to the enjoyment of high stations, except such as were of the Christian religion. Macrobius has rendered himself famous for a composition called *Saturnalia*, a miscellaneous collection of antiquities and criticisms, supposed to have been the result of a conversation of some of the learned Romans during the celebration of the Saturnalia. This work was written for the use of his son, and the bad latinity which the author has often introduced, proves that he was not born in a part of the Roman empire where the Latin tongue was spoken, as he himself candidly confesses. The *Saturnalia* are useful for the learned reflections which they contain, and particularly for some curious observations on the two greatest epic poets of antiquity. Besides this composition, Macrobius wrote a commentary on *Cicero's Somnium Scipionis*, which was composed for the improvement of the author's son, and dedicated to him. The best editions are that of Gronovius, 8vo, L. Bat. 1670, and that of Zeune, Lips. 8vo, 1774. *Harles. Not. Lit. Rom.* 1. p. 677.—*Sax. Onom.* 1. p. 478.

MACROCEPH'ALI, a people of the Bosporus. *Mela*, 1. c. 19. *Stephanus*, however, places them near the Colchi, and *Pliny*, 6. c. 4, near Cersus, in Cappadocia.

MAC'ROCHIR, a Greek name of Artaxerxes, the same as *Longimanus*. This surname was given him from his having one *hand longer* than the other. *C. Nep. in Reg.*

MACROCREM'NII, mountains near the Ister and the Tyra. *Plin.* 4. c. 12.

MA'CRON, a town of Thrace, not far from the Chersonesus. *Id.* 4. c. 11.

MACRO'NES, a nation of Pontus, on the confines of Colchis and Armenia. *Flacc.* 5. v. 152.—*Herodot.*

MACRONTI'CHOS, a town of Thrace. *Suidas.*

MACROPOGO'NES, a people near the Euxine Sea. *Strab.*

MA'CRYES, a people of Libya. *Steph.*

MACRYNE'A, a city of Ætolia. *Id.*

MACTO'RIUM, a town at the south of Sicily, near Gela. *Id.*

MAC'ULA, a man who hospitably offered Cicero the use of his villa in the Falernian country. *Cic. Fam.* 6. ep. 19.

MACULO'NUS, a rich but penurious Roman, &c. *Juv.* 7. v. 40.

MA'CUM, a city of upper Æthiopia. *Plin.* 6. c. 29.

MACYN'IA or **MACYN'IUM**, a town of Ætolia.

MADAS'ARA, a city of Arabia Felix. *Ptol.*

MADASUM'MA, a city of Africa Propria. *Antonin.*

MAD'ATES or **MAD'ETAS**, a general of Darius, who bravely defended a place against Alexander. The emperor was so indignant at the bold resistance which he made that he resolved to put him to death, though thirty orators pleaded for his life. Sisygambis prevailed over the almost inexorable Alexander, and Madates was pardoned. *Curt.* 5. c. 3.

MADAU'RA or **MADU'RUS**, a town of Numidia, at the south-west of Carthage. The inhabitants were called *Madurenses*. It was the native place of Apuleius. *Apul. Met.* 11.—*Plin.* 5. c. 4.

MADES'TES, a town of Thrace.

MADISAN'TES SI'NUS, part of the Persian Gulph, now Golfo di Saudra. *Ptol. Stephanus* calls it Mesanites.

MAD'OCE, a town of Arabia Felix. *Ptol.*

MADUATE'NI, a people of Thrace. *Liv.* 38. c. 40.

MA'DYES, or **MAD'YES**, a Scythian prince who pursued the Cimmerians in Asia, and conquered Cyaxares, B.C. 623. He retained the supreme power of Asia Minor in his hands for some time. *Herodot.* 8. c. 103.

MAD'YRUS, a city of the Hellespont. *Steph.*

MAD'YTUS, a sea-port of the Thracian Chersonesus.

MÆ'A, a city of the Hellespont. *Id.*

MÆAN'DER, a son of Oceanus and Tethys.

MÆAN'DER, a celebrated river of Asia Minor, rising near Celænæ, and flowing through Caria and Ionia into the Ægæan Sea between Miletus and Priene. after it has been increased by the waters of the Marsyas, Lycus, Eudon, Lethæus, &c. It is celebrated among ancient writers, for its various windings, which amount to no less than 600, and from which all obliquities have received the name of Mæanders. It forms in its course, according to the observations of some travellers, the Greek letters ι ζ ξ ς & ω, and from its windings Dædalus, it is said, formed the first idea of his famous labyrinth. *Ovid. Met.* 8. v. 145, &c.—*Virg. Æn.* 5. v. 254.—*Lucan*, 3. v. 208. l. 6. v. 475.—*Homer. Il.* v. 376.—*Herodot.* 2. c. 29.—*Cic. Pis.* 22.—*Strab.* 12, &c.—*Mela*, 1. c. 17.—*Paus.* 8. c. 41.—*Liv.* 37. c. 45. l. 38. c. 13.—*Solin.* 43.—*Plut. de Flum.—Qu Calab.* 1. v. 262.—*Propert.* 2. el. 23. v. 85.—*Seneca in Herc. Fur.* 684. *In Phœn.* 606.—*Ital.* v. 139.

MÆAN'DRIA, a city of Epirus.

MÆAN'DRIUS, a scribe in the service of Polycrates tyrant of Samus, &c. *Herod.* 3. c. 123.

MÆA'TÆ, a people in the southern parts of Scotland. *Dio.* 76. c. 12.

MÆCE'NAS. *Vid.* Mecænus.

MÆ'CIUS or **ME'TIUS TAR'PA.** *Vid.* Tarpa.

MÆ'DI, a people of Mædica, a district of Thrace, between the rivers Strymon and Nestus. *Liv.* 26. c. 25. l. 40. c. 21.

MÆ'LIUS. *Vid.* Melius.

MÆMACTE'RIA, sacrifices offered to Jupiter at Athens in the winter month Memacterion. The god, surnamed Mæmactes, was then intreated to send mild and temperate weather, as he presided over the seasons, and was the god of the air. *Harpocration.—Suidas.—Hesych.—Plut.* περὶ ἀοργησίας.

MÆN'ACA, a town of Hispania Bætica.

MÆN'ADES, a name of the Bacchantes or priestesses of Bacchus. The word is derived from μαίνομαι, *to be furious*, because, in the celebration of the festivals, their gestures and actions resembled those of mad women. *Ovid. Fast.* 4. v. 458. *Met.* 9. v. 573. l. 11. v. 22.—*Catull. de Aty.* 64. v. 23.—*Martial.* 11. epigr. 85.—*Juv.* 6. v. 316.—*Seneca in Med.* 382. *In Phœniss.* 365. *In Œdip.* 486.

MÆN'ALA, a town of Spain near Malaca. *Strab.—Avienus.*

MÆNA'LIA, a city of Galatia. *Steph.*

MÆN'ALUS, (*plur.* Mænala,) a mountain of Arcadia, sacred to the god Pan, and greatly frequented by shepherds. It received its name from Mænalus, a son of Lycaon. It was covered with pine trees, the echoes and shady retreats of which have been greatly celebrated by all the ancient poets. *Ovid. Met.* 1. v. 216.—*Virg. G.* 1. v. 17. *Ecl.* 8. v. 24.—*Paus.* 8. c. 3.—*Strab.* 8.—*Mela*, 2. c. 3.——A town of Arcadia. *Steph.*

Mæn'alus, a son of Lycaon.——The father of Atalenta.

MÆNA'RIA, an island of the Balearic Sea. *Plin.* 3. c. 5.

MÆ'NIUS, a prætor who was employed in making inquiries concerning poisonings, &c. *Liv.* 40. c. 35 & 43.——A dictator accused and honorably acquitted, &c.——A spendthrift at Rome. *Horat.* 1. ep. 15. v. 26.

Mæ'nius Ca'ius, a Roman consul who conquered the Antiates, Aricini, and Lavinii, and was honored with a column to commemorate his important services to the state. Near this column, thieves and disorderly slaves were generally punished. From the spoils of Antium some beaks of ships *(rostra)* were brought to Rome, which were placed in the forum, to adorn the pulpit whence the orators addressed the people, and hence *rostrum* has been generally used to signify a pulpit. *Liv.* 2. c. 56. l. 3. c. 17. l. 8. c. 13.—*Plin.* 34. c. 5.—*Cic. Cœc.* 16.

Mæ'nius Lu'cius, a tribune at Rome, who proposed to reduce the interest of money to one per cent. *Liv.* 7. c. 16.

Mæ'nius Mar'cus, the author of an agrarian law. *Liv.* 4. c. 53.

MÆN'OBA, a town of Hispania Bætica.

MÆNOBO'RA, a city of the Mastieni, near the columns of Hercules. *Steph.*

MÆNOM'ENA or MÆNOM'ENI, mountains of Sardinia. *Ptol.* They are called *Insani* by *Livy*, 30. c. 39, and *Florus*, 2. c. 6.

MÆ'NON, a tyrant of Sicily, B.C. 285.

MÆ'NUS, a river of Germany, now called the Mayne, falling into the Rhine at Mayence.

MÆ'ON, a Theban, son of Hæmon. He, with 50 companions, attacked Tydeus, who had declared war against Thebes, and who was returning in security to his own camp from the hostile city, and the whole number were defeated by the hero, who only spared the life of Mæon, that he might carry back the news of the fate of his countrymen. *Homer. Il.* 4. v. 391.

MÆO'NIA, a country of Asia Minor, the same as Lydia. It is to be observed, that only part of Lydia was known by the name of Mæonia, that is, the neighbourhood of mount Tmolus, and the country watered by the Pactolus. The rest of the province on the sea coast was called Lydia. *Strab.* 12.—*Ovid. Met.* 6. v. 103. *Ex Pont.* 4. ep. 16. v. 27.—*Virg. Æn.* 4. v. 216. The Etrurians, as being descended from a Lydian colony, are often called *Mæonidæ*, (*Virg. Æn.* 11. v. 759.) and even the lake Thrasymenus, in their country, received the appellation of *Mæonius lacus. Sil. Ital.* 15. v. 35.

MÆON'IDÆ, a name given to the Muses, because Homer, their greatest and worthiest favorite, was supposed to be a native of Mæonia. *Met.* 5.

MÆON'IDES, a surname of Homer, because, according to the opinion of some writers, he was born in Mæonia, or, because his father's name was Mæon. *Martial.* 5. epigr. 10.—*Ovid.* The surname is also applied to Bacchus, as he was worshipped in Mæonia.

MÆ'ONIS, an epithet applied to Omphale as queen of Lydia or Mæonia. *Ovid.* The epithet is also applied to Arachne as a native of Lydia. *Id. Met.* 6.

MÆO'TÆ, a people of Asiatic Sarmatia. *Strab.*—*Polyb.*

MÆO'TIS PA'LUS, a large lake, or rather part of the sea between Europe and Asia, at the north of the Euxine, with which it communicates by the Cimmerian Bosporus, now called the Sea of Azoph or Zaback. It was worshipped as a deity by the Massagetæ. It extends about 390 miles from south-west to north-east, and is about 600 miles in circumference. The Amazons were called *Mæotides*, because they lived in the neighbourhood. *Strab.* 1 & 11.—*Mela*, 1. c. 1, &c.—*Justin* 2. c. 1.—*Curt.* 5. c. 4.—*Ovid. Fast.* 3. el. 12. *Ep. Sab.* 2. v. 9.—*Virg. Æn* 6, v. 739.—*Lucan.* 2. v. 641. l. 3. v. 277. l. 5. 440. l. 8. v. 318—*Seneca in Herc. Fur.* 1327. *In Œdip.* 474—*Ptol.* 5. c. 9.

MÆ'PA, a city of Armenia Major. *Ptol.*

MÆ'PHA, the metropolis of Arabia Felix. *Id.*

MÆ'RA, a woman changed into a dog. *Ovid. Met.* 7. v. 362.——The dog of Icarius. *Vid.* Mera.

MÆRO'NA, a city of Persia. *Ptol.*

MÆ'SIA. *Vid.* Mœsia.

Mæ'sia Syl'va, a wood in Etruria, near the mouth of the Tiber. *Liv.* 1. c. 33. It is now Bosco di Baccano.

MÆSO'LIA, a region of India within the Ganges. *Ptol.*—*Arrian.*

MÆTO'NIUM, a town of European Sarmatia. *Ptol.*

MÆ'VIA, an immodest woman. *Juv.* 1. v. 22.

MÆ'VIUS, a poet of inferior note in the Augustan age, who made himself known by his illiberal attacks on the character of the first writers of his time, as well as by his affected compositions. His name would have sunk into oblivion if *Virgil* had not ridiculed him in his third eclogue, v. 90, and *Horace* in his tenth epode, v. 2.

MAG'ABA, a mountain in Galatia.

MAG'DOLUM or MAGDO'LUM, a town of Ægypt where Pharaoh Necho defeated the Assyrians.

MAGÆ'A, a fountain of Sicily, not far from Plemmyrium *Plin.* 3. c. 8. It is now Maddalena.

MAG'ARIS, a town of India within the Ganges. *Ptol.*

MA'GAS, a king of Cyrene, in the age of Ptolemy Philadelphus. He reigned 50 years, and died B.C. 257. *Polyæn.* 2. c. 28.

MAGDO'JUS, a town of Ægypt. *Steph.*

MAGEL'LA, a town of Sicily, near Enna, about the middle of the island. *Polyb.* 1. c. 24.

MAGEL'LI, a people of Liguria. *Plin.* 3. c. 5.

MAG'ETÆ, a people of Africa. *Stat. Achill.* 2. v. 417.

MAGETO'BRIA, a town of the Sequani near which the Gauls were defeated by the Germans shortly before Cæsar's arrival in Gaul.

MA'GI, a religious sect among the eastern nations of the world, and particularly in Persia. They had great influence in the political as well as religious affairs of the state, and the monarch was seldom permitted to ascend the throne without their previous approbation. Zoroaster was founder of their sect. They paid particular homage to fire, which they deemed a deity, as pure in itself, and the purifier of all things. In their religious tenets they had two principles, one good, the source of every thing good; ard the other evil, from which sprang all manner of ills. Their professional skill in the mathematics and philosophy rendered every thing familiar to them, and, from their knowledge of the phænomena of the heavens, the word Magi was applied to all learned men; and, in process of time, the Magi, from their superior experience and profession, were confounded by the ignorant with the magicians, who impose upon the superstitious and credulous. Hence the word *Magi* and *magicians* became synonymous among the vulgar. Smerdis, one of the Magi, seized upon the crown of Persia after the death of Cambyses, and the fraud was not discovered till the seven noble Persians conspired against the usurper and elected Darius king. From this circumstance, there was a certain day on which none of the Magi were permitted to appear in public, as the populace had the privilege of murdering any of them whom they met. *Strab.*—*Cic. de Div.* 1. c. 23 & 41.—*Apul. in Apol.*—*Porphyr.* 4.—*Herodot.* 3. c. 62, &c.——A people near Media, whose city was Pasagarda. *Steph.*—*Plin.* 6. c. 26.—*Solin.* c. 55.

MA'GIA, a city of Illyria. *Steph.*——A city of Carmania. *Ptol.*

MAGI'TÆ, a people of Arabia Felix. *Ptol.*

P. MA'GIUS CHI'LO, a Roman who murdered his friend Marcellus at Athens, and afterwards destroyed himself, in a fit of insanity. *Cic. Att.* 13. ep. 10. *Fam.* 4. ep. 12.

Ma'gius De'cius, a man of consequence at Capua, known for his strong and unshaken attachment to the Romans during the second Punic war. *Liv.* 23. c. 7 & 10.—*Cic. Rull.* 2. c. 34. *Pis.* 11.

Ma'gius Lu'cius, an adherent of Marius, who revolted to Mithridates, and was again reconciled to the Romans and then settled at Myndus. *Cic. Verr.* 1. c. 34.

Ma'gius, a man in the interest of Pompey, grandfather to the historian Velleius Paterculus. *Paterc.* 2. c. 115.

MAG'NA GRÆ'CIA, a part of Italy. *Vid.* Græcia Magna.

MAG'NA MA'TER, a name given to Cybele.

MAGNEN'TIUS, a usurper, who distinguished himself by his cruelty and perfidy. He conspired against the life of the emperor Constans, and murdered him in his bed. This cruelty was highly resented by Constantius, the brother of the murdered prince; and the assassin, unable to escape the fury of his antagonist, murdered his own mother and the rest of his relations, and afterwards killed himself by falling upon a sword, which he had thrust against a wall, A.D. 353. He was the first Christian who ever murdered his lawful sovereign. *Idacius & Marcellin. in Chron.—Julian Orat.* 1 & 2.—*Socr.* 2. c. 10, &c.—*Sozom.* 4. c. 1.—*Zosim.* l. 2.

MAG'NES, a shepherd of mount Ida, who found himself detained by the iron nails which were under his shoes, as he walked over a stone mine. From him the magnet received its name, as being the person who had been first sensible of its extraordinary properties. Some say that Magnes was a slave of Medea, whom that enchantress changed into a magnet. *Orpheus de Lapid.* 10. v. 7.—*Plin.* 36. c. 16.——A son of Æolus and Anaretta, who married Nais, by whom he had Pierus, &c. *Apollod.* 1. c. 7.—*Antonin. Liber.* 23.——A poet and musician of Smyrna, in the age of Gyges king of Lydia. *Suidas.*——The surname of Demetrius the friend of Atticus and Cicero. *Cic. ad Att.* 4. ep. 11. l. 8. ep. 11.——The surname of another Demetrius, who studied with Cicero in Asia. *Cic. Br.* 91. ——The father of Glaphyra. *Steph.*——An Athenian comic poet in the age of Epicharmus. *Schol. in Aristoph. Equit.*

MAGNE'SIA, a town of Asia Minor on the Mæander, about fifteen miles from Ephesus, now called Guzelhizar. It is celebrated for the death of Themistocles, and also for a battle which was fought there 187 B.C., between the Romans and Antiochus king of Syria. The forces of Antiochus amounted to 70,000 men, according to Appian, or 70,000 foot and 12 000 horse, according to Livy, which have been exaggerated by Florus to 300,000 men; the Roman army consisted of about 28,000 or 30,000 men, 2,000 of which were employed in guarding the camp. The Syrians lost 50,000 foot and 4,000 horse, and the Romans only 300 killed, with 25 horse. Magnesia was founded by a colony from Magnesia in Thessaly, and was commonly called *Magnesia ad Mæandrum*, to distinguish it from another city called *Magnesia ad Sipylum* in Lydia, at the foot of mount Sipylus. This last was destroyed by an earthquake in the reign of Tiberius *Plin.* 5. c. 29.——A country at the east of Thessaly, and at the south of Ossa. It was sometimes called Æmonia and Magnes Campus. The capital was also called Magnesia.——A promontory of Magnesia in Thessaly. *Liv.* 33. c. 32. l. 35. c. 31.—*Ovid. Met.* 11. 408.—*Strab.* 12 & 13.—*Lucan.* 6. v. 385.—*Ptol.* 5. c. 2.—*Cor. Nep. in Them.* 10.—*Mela*, 2. c. 3.—*Flor.* 2.—*Appian.*

MAGNOP'OLIS, or EUPATO'RIA MAGNOP'OLIS, a city of Pontus.

MAG'NUS CLAU'DIUS, a brother of Piso, adopted by Galba, and killed by Claudius. *Tac. H.* 1. c. 48.

MA'GO, a Carthaginian general sent against Dionysius tyrant of Sicily. He obtained a victory, and granted peace to the conquered; but in a battle, which soon after followed this treaty of peace, he was unfortunately killed.——His son, succeeded to the command of the Carthaginian army, but he disgraced himself by fleeing at the approach of Timoleon, who had come to assist the Syracusans. He was accused in the Carthaginian senate for this cowardly conduct, but he prevented by suicide the execution of the sentence justly pronounced against him. His body was exposed on a gibbet.——A brother of Annibal the Great. He was present at the battle of Cannæ, and was deputed by his brother to convey to Carthage the news of the celebrated victory which had been obtained over the Roman armies. His arrival at Carthage was unexpected; but more powerfully to astonish his countrymen on account of the victory of Cannæ, he emptied in the senate-house the three bushels of golden rings which had been taken from the Roman knights slain in the battle. He was afterwards sent to Spain, where he defeated the two Scipios, and was himself, in another engagement, totally ruined. He afterwards retired to the Baleares, which he conquered; and one of the cities there still bears his name, and is called Port Magonis, *Port Mahon.* After this he landed in Italy with an army, and took possession of part of Insubria. He was defeated in a battle by Quintilius Varus, and died of a wound received 203 B.C. *Liv.* 22. c. 46. l. 23. c. 12. l. 30. c. 18. *Cornelius Nepos. in Ann.* 8, gives a very different account of his death, and says, that he either perished in a shipwreck or was murdered by his servants. Perhaps Annibal had two brothers of that name. [There is a bust of Mago in the Capitol.]——A Carthaginian, more known by the excellence of his writings than by his military exploits. He wrote twenty-eight volumes upon husbandry; these were preserved by Scipio at the taking of Carthage, and presented by him to the Roman senate. They were translated into Greek by Cassius Dionysius of Utica, and into Latin by order of the Roman senate, though Cato had already written so copiously upon the subject; and the Romans, as it has been observed, consulted the writings of Mago with greater earnestness than the books of the Sibylline verses. *Cic. Or.* 1. c. 58.—*Varr. R. R.* 1. c. 1.—*Plin.* 18. c. 3.—*Columella.* ——A Carthaginian, sent by his countrymen to assist the Romans against Pyrrhus and the Tarentines, with a fleet of 120 sail. This offer was politely refused by the Roman senate. This Mago was father of Asdrubal and Amilcar. *Val. Max.* —*Justin.* 18 & 19.

MAGO'A, a town of Persia, near Susiana. *Plin.* 6. c. 27.

MA'GON, a river of India falling into the Ganges. *Arrian.*

MAGONTI'ACUM or MAGONTE'A, a large city of Germany, now called Mentz. *Tacit. Hist.* 4, 15 & 23.

MAG'UDA, a city of Mesopotamia. *Ptol.*

MAGUL'ABA, a town of Arabia Felix. *Id.*

MAGU'RA, an inland town of Libya.

MA'GUS, an officer of Turnus, killed by Æneas. *Virg. Æn.* 10. v. 522.

MAGU'SA, a town of Arabia Felix. *Plin.* 6. c. 28.

MAGUSTA'NA, a city of Armenia Major. *Ptol.*

MAHAR'BAL or MAHER'BAL, a Carthaginian, who was at the siege of Saguntum, and who commanded the army of Annibal at the battle of Cannæ. He advised the conqueror immediately to march to Rome, but Annibal required time to consider on so bold a measure; upon which Maherbal shrewdly observed, that Annibal knew how to conquer, but not to make a proper use of his victory. *Liv.* 21. c. 12. l 22. c. 51. l. 23. c. 18.

MA'IA, a daughter of Atlas and Pleione, mother of Mercury by Jupiter. She was one of the Pleiades, and the most luminous of the seven sisters. *Vid.* Pleiades. *Apollod.* 3. c. 10.—*Macrob. Sat.* 1. c. 12. —*Ovid. Fast.* 5. v. 85.—*Virg. Æn.* 1. v. 301.——A surname of Cybele.

MAI'AMA, festivals in honor of Maia, celebrated on the first of May among the Romans. The day was devoted to diversion and pleasure, and the principal inhabitants frequented Ostia to spend their time in greater festivity, and were adorned with garlands of flowers, and the very doors of the houses were decked with branches, from which were suspended fruits and cakes. *Varro, de Vitâ. R. R.* 1. —*Macrob.* 1. c. 12.

MAJES'TAS, a goddess among the Romans, daughter of Honor and Reverentia. *Ovid. Fast.* 5. v. 25.

AJOR'CA, the greatest of the islands called Baleares, situated on the coast of Spain, in the Mediterranean. *Strab*

MAJORIA'NUS JUL. VALE'RIUS, an emperor of the western Roman empire raised to the imperial throne. A.D. 457. He signalized himself by his private as well as public virtues. He was massacred after a reign of thirty-seven years, by one of his generals. *Idac. & Marcell. in Chron. &c.*

MA'IS, a river between the Ganges and Indus *Arrian.*

MA'LA FORTU'NA, the goddess of evil fortune, was worshipped among the Romans. *Cic. de Nat. D.* 3.—*Plin.* 2. c. 7.

MAL'ACHA or MAL'ACHATH, an inland town of Libya. *Ptol.*

MAL'ACHUS or MAR'ACHUS, a poet of Syracuse. *Aristot. Quæst.*

MALA'CIA, a city founded by Philoctetes. *Cœl. Rhod.* 6. c. 1.

MAL'ACUS, an ancient author, who wrote concerning the borders of the Siphnii. *Athen.* 6.

MALÆ'A, a city of Arcadia. *Paus.* 8.

MALAMAN'TUS, a river of India. *Arrian. apud Salmas. ad Solin.* p. 993.

MALAN'GA, a city of India, supposed to be the modern Madras.

MALA'NIUS, an inland city of the Œnotri, now Maida. *Steph.*

MAL'CECA, a town of Spain, between Corduba and Emerita. *Antonin.*

MAL'CHUS, an historian, who wrote an account of some of the emperors. *Phot. in Bibl. Cod.* 78.—*Voss. H.Gr.* 2. c. 21, &c.

MAL'COÆ, a people of the interior of Libya. *Ptol.*

MALE'A or MA'LEA, a promontory of Lesbus. *Thucyd.*

MALE'A or MA'LEA, a promontory in Peloponnesus, at the south of Laconia. The sea is so rough and boisterous there, that among the ancients, who were little acquainted with the art of navigation, the dangers which attended a voyage round it gave rise to the proverb of *Cum ad Maleam deflexeris, obliviscere quæ sunt domi. Strab.* 8 & 9.—*Lucan.* 6. v. 58 —*Plut. in Arat.*—*Virg. Æn.* 5. v. 193.—*Mela*, 2. c. 3.—*Liv.* 21. c. 44.—*Ovid. Am.* 2. el. 16. v. 24. el. 11. v. 20.—*Seneca in Medeâ*, 149.—*Paus.* 3. c. 23.

MALECE'NA, a city of Armenia Minor. *Antonin.*

MAL'ELAS JOAN'NES, a native of Antioch, and a Byzantine historian. He lived shortly after Justinian the Great.

MALE'OS or MA'LEOS, one of the Eubudes, now Mul. *Ptol.*

MALETHUBA'LUS, a mountain of Mauritania Cæsariensis. *Id.*

MALEVEN'TUM, the ancient name of Beneventum. *Liv.* 9. c. 27.—*Plin.* 3. c. 11.

MALE'US or MA'LEUS, a mountain of India. *Plin.* 6. c. 19.—*Solin.* c. 55.

MAL'HO or MA'THO, a general of an army of Carthaginian mercenaries, 258 B.C.

MA'LIA, a city of Phthiotis, near mount Œta and Thermopylæ. There were in its neighbourhood some hot mineral waters, which the poet *Catullus* has mentioned. From Malia, a gulph or small bay in the neighbourhood at the western extremities of the island of Eubœa, has received the name of the Gulph of Malia, Maliacum Fretum, or Maliacus Sinus. Some call it the Gulph of Lamia. It is often taken for the Sinus Pelasgicus of the ancients. *Paus.* 1. c. 4.—*Herodot.*

MA'LIA, a daughter of Oceanus. *Vid.* Caanthus.

MALI'ACA, a city of Hispania Tarraconensis, now Malgrado. *Ptol.*

MALIA'NE, a town of Arachosia. *Id.*

MA'LIAS, a town of Spain. *Appian.*

MALIAT'THA, a city of Arabia Petræa. *Ptol.*

MAL'IBA, a city of India without the Ganges. *Id.*

MA'LII, a people of Mesopotamia. *Strab.* 16.

MALIP'PALA, a city of India within the Ganges. *Ptol.*

MA'LIS, a servant maid of Omphale, beloved by Hercules.

MAL'LABA, a city of Arabia Felix. *Ptol.*

MALLÆ'TA, a city of India within the Ganges. *Id.*

MAL'LEA or MAL'LIA A'QUA. *Vid.* Malia.

MALLE'NE, or MALE'NE, a city of Mysia.

MALLE'OLUS, a man who murdered his mother, for which crime he was tied in a sack and thrown into the sea, a punishment first inflicted upon him. *Oros.* 5. c. 16.—*Liv.* 68.—*Cic. ad Heren.* 1. c. 13.

MALLE'OLUS CNE'US, the quæstor of Dolabella in Asia. His son was plundered by his guardian Verres. *Cic. Verr.* 1. c. 15 & 36.

MAL'LI, a people of India who opposed Bacchus. *Steph.*

MAL'LIA, a town of the Brutii, the remains of which are now called Mallea. *Antonin.*

MAL'LIUS, a Roman consul defeated by the Gauls, &c.

MAL'LIUS GLAU'CIA, a freedman, client to T. Roscius Magnus, &c. *Cic. pro Rosc.*

MALLOPH'ORA, (*lanam ferens*), a surname under which Ceres had a temple at Megara, because she had taught the inhabitants the utility of wool, and the means of tending sheep to advantage. This temple was represented as so old in the age of Pausanias that it was falling to decay. *Paus.* 1. c. 44. —*Cœl. Rhod.* 25. c. 1.

MAL'LOS, a town of Cilicia. *Lucan.* 3. v. 227.

MAL'LUS, a mountain of India within the Ganges. *Plin.* 6. c. 17.

MALOR'IGES, a general of the Frisii. *Tac. Ann.* 13. c. 54.

MALTA'NUS, a harbour of Etruria. *Antonin.*

MALTECO'RÆ, a people of India. *Plin.* 6. c. 20.

MAL'THACE, an island not far from Corcyra. *Id.* 4. c. 2.

MALTHI'NUS, a fictitious name under which *Horace* has lashed some of his friends or enemies. 1. sat. 2. v. 27.

MAL'UA, a river of Africa, rising in mount Atlas, and dividing Mauritania Tingitana from Cæsariensis. *Ptol.*

MAMM'ALA, a town of Arabia Felix. *Id.*

MAMARCI'NA, a city of Ausonia. *Steph.*

MAMA'US, a river of Peloponnesus, formerly called Amathus. *Strab.* 8.

MAM'BLIA, a town of Æthiopia, looking towards Africa. *Plin.* 9. c. 26.

MAMBU'TA, a town of Mesopotamia. *Ptol.*

MAMERCI'NUS LUC. ÆM., a Roman, twice appointed consul and dictator. *Liv.* 8. c. 1, 16, 20. l. 9. c. 21.

MAMER'CUS, a tyrant of Catana, who surrendered to Timoleon. His attempts to speak in a public assembly at Syracuse, were received with groans and hisses, upon which he dashed his head against a wall, and endeavoured to destroy himself. The blows were not fatal, and Mamercus was soon after put to death as a robber, B.C. 340. *Polyæn.* 5.—*C. Nep. in Tim.*——A dictator at Rome, B.C. 437. ——A rich man who was refused the consulship at Rome, because to avoid expense, he would not solicit the place of ædile.—*Cic. Off.* 2. c. 17.——A consul with D. Brutus. *Id Br.* 47.

MAMER'THES, a Corinthian who killed his brother's son in hopes of reigning, upon which he was cruelly mutilated by his brother. *Ovid. in Ib.* 549.

MAMERTI'NA, a town of Campania, famous for its wines.——A name of Messana, in Sicily. *Martial.* 13. epigr. 117.—*Strab.* 6 & 7.—*Cic. Verr.* 2. c. 5. l. 3. c. 6.—*Liv.* 28. c. 28.—*Plin.* 3. c. 8. l. 14. c. 6.—*Festus de V. Sig.*

MAMERTI'NI, a mercenary band of soldiers which passed from Campania into Sicily, at the request of Agathocles. When they were thus engaged in the service of their new master, they claimed the privilege of voting at the election of magistrates at Syracuse, and had recourse to arms to support their unlawful demands. This sedition was, with difficulty, appeased by the authority of some leading men, and the Campanians were ordered to leave Sicily. In their way to the coast they were received with great kindness by the people of Messana, and soon returned perfidy for hospitality. They conspired against the inhabitants, murdered all the males in the city, and married their wives and daughters, and rendered themselves masters of the place. After this violence they assumed the name of Mamertini, and called their city *Mamertina*, from a provincial word which in their language signified *martial* or *warlike*. The Mamertines were afterwards defeated by Hiero. *Plut. in Pyrrh. &c.*

MAMER'TIUM, a town of the Bruttii.

MAM'ILAS, the 14th king of Assyria, A.M. 2465. *Euseb. in Chron.*

MAMIL'IA LEX, *de limitibus*, enacted by the tribune Mamilius. It ordained, that in the boundaries of the lands five or six feet of land should be left uncultivated, which no person could convert into private property. It also appointed commissioners to see it carried into execution *Cic in Br.*

MAMIL'II, a plebeian family at Rome, descended from the Aborigines. They first lived at Tusculum, from whence they came to settle at Rome. *Liv.* 2. c. 20.—*Cic. N.D.* 2. c. 2.

MAMIL'IUS C. LIMETA'NUS, a tribune who proposed to punish those Romans who had been bribed by Jugurtha. *Sall. J.* 40.—*Cic. Br.* 33.

MAMIL'IUS LU'CIUS, a dictator of Tusculum, honored with the freedom of the city of Rome, for assisting the Romans when Herdonius seized the Capitol. *Liv.* 3. c. 18 & 29.

MAMIL'IUS MANCI'NUS a tribune who proposed to appoint Marius to supersede Metellus in the conduct of the Jugurthine war. *Sallust. J.* 73.

MAMIL'IUS MA'RIUS, a consul A.U. 604, who composed forms for the more regular arrangement and settlement of sales and bargains. He is frequently called Manilius. *Vid.* Manilius. *Varr. R.R.* 2. c. 3. 11.—*Cic. Orat.* c. 58.

MAMIL'IUS OCTA'VIUS, was dictator of Tusculum, and was slain at the battle of Regillus, in his attempts to restore Tarquin, his father-in-law, to the throne.

MAMIL'IUS C. VIT'ULUS, the first plebeian made Curio Maximus. *Liv.* 27. c. 8.—The Mamilii are sometimes called Manilii.

MAMITUS, the 13th king of Assyria, A.M. 2385, reigned 30 years, and was a formidable enemy of the Ægyptians and Syrians. *Berosus.—August. C. D.* 18. c. 7.

MAMMÆ'A, the mother of the emperor Severus, who died A.D. 235. *Aurel. Vict.—Euseb.* 1. 6. c. 15.

MAM'MIDA, a city of Persia. *Ptol.*

MAMMISÆ'A, a region of Syria. *Plin.* 5. c. 23.

MAMORTHA, a city of Samaria. *Plin.* 5. c. 13.

MAMP'SARUS, a mountain of Africa Propria. *Ptol.*

MAMU'DA, a city of Upper Æthiopia. *Plin.* 6. c. 29.

MAMU'GA, an inland city of Syria. *Ptol.*

MAMU'RIUS VETU'RIUS, a worker in brass in Numa's reign. He was ordered by the monarch to make a number of ancylia or shields, like that one which had fallen from heaven, that it might be difficult to distinguish the true one from the others. He was very successful in the execution of his undertaking, and asked for no other reward, but that his name might by frequently mentioned in the hymns which were sung by the Salii in the feast of the Ancylia. This request was granted. *Ovid. Fast.* 3. v. 392.—*Varro de L.L.* 5. c. 6.—*Servius in Æn.* 2. v. 166. l. 7. v. 188.

MAMUR'RA, a Roman knight born at Formiæ. He followed the fortunes of J. Cæsar in Gaul, where he greatly enriched himself. He built a magnificent palace on mount Cœlius, and was the first who incrusted his walls with marble. Catullus has severely attacked him in his epigrams. Formiæ is sometimes called Mamurrarum Urbs. *Plin* 36. c. 6.—*Cic. Att.* 7. ep. 7. l. 13. ep. 52.—*Catul.* 55.—*Horat.* 1. sat. 5. v. 37.

MANÆ'ANA, a town of Mauritania Cæsariensis *Ptol.*

MANA'PIA, a city of Hibernia. *Ptol.* It is now Wexford, according to *Camden.*

MANARMA'NIS, a harbour of Germany. *Ptol.*

MANAS'TABAL, son of Masinissa, who was father to the celebrated Jugurtha. *Sallust. Jug. Bell.*

MANA'TES, a people of Italy. *Plin.* 3. c. 5.

MANCHA'NE, a town of Mesopotamia. *Ptol.*

MAN'CIA HEL'VIUS, a Roman orator, B.C. 90. He was so remarkably ugly that he was laughed at for his deformity.

MANCI'NUS C., a Roman general, who, though at the head of an army of 30,000 men, was defeated by 4,000 Numantians, B.C. 138 He made a truce with the enemy which was disapproved at Rome, in consequence of which he was at his own request delivered up to the Numantians, who refused to receive him. *Cic. in Orat.* 1. c. 40. *Off.* 3. c. 30. *Cæc.* 34.

MANCU'NIUM, a town of Britain. *Antonin.* It is now Manchester, according to *Camden.*

MAN'DA, the greatest river of India within the Ganges. *Ptol.* It is now Menan, according to *Mercator.*

MANDA'ETH, a town of Æthiopia, on the Sinus Adulicus. *Ptol.*

MANDAGANDE'NI, a people of Troas. *Plin.* 5. c. 30.

MANDAG'ARA, a town of India within the Ganges. *Ptol.*

MANDAGAR'SIS, a town of Media. *Id.*

MANDAGRÆ'UM, a river of Asiatic Scythia. *Plin.* 6. c. 17.

MANDALUM, a lake of Æthiopia. *Id.* 6. c. 29.

MANDA'NE or MAN'DANE, a daughter of king Astyages, married by her father to Cambyses, an ignoble person of Persia. A dream of the monarch had been interpreted unfavorably by the soothsayers, who assured him that his daughter's son would dethrone him. The marriage of Mandane with Cambyses would, in the monarch's opinion, prevent the effects of the dream, and the children of this connection would, like their father, be poor and unnoticed. The expectations of Astyages were eventually frustrated, as he was dethroned by his grandson. *Vid.* Cyrus. *Herodot.* 1. c. 107.

MANDA'NES, an Indian prince and philosopher, whom Alexander invited by his ambassadors, on pain of death, to come to his banquet, as being the son of Jupiter. The philosopher ridiculed both the threats and promises of Alexander, &c. *Strab.* 15.

MANDA'REI, a people of Asiatic Sarmatia. *Plin.* 6. c. 7.

MAN'DEI, a people of India on the Ganges. *Id.* 6. c. 17.

MANDE'LA, a small village in the country of the Sabines, near Horace's country seat. It is now Poggio. *Horat.* 1. ep. 18. v. 105.

MANDIACLI'NI, a people of India. *Arrian. in Indic.*

MANDIANI'TÆ, a people of Arabia. *Steph.*

MANDO'NIUS, a prince in Spain, who for some time favored the cause of the Romans. When he heard that Scipio the Roman commander, was ill, he raised commotions in the provinces, for which he was severely reprimanded, and at last, after repeated provocations, he destroyed himself. *Liv.* 22. c. 21. l. 26. c. 49. l. 27. c. 19. l. 28. c. 24. l. 29. c. 2 & 3.

MAN'DORI, a people of the interior of Libya. *Ptol.*

MAN'DROCLES, a general of Artaxerxes, &c. *C. Nep. in Dat.*

MAN'DRON, a king of the Bebryces, &c. *Polyæn.* 8.

MANDROP'OLIS, a city of Phrygia, called Mandropus by *Livy.* *Steph.*

MANDRUE'NI or MADRYE'NI, a people near Margiana. *Plin.* 6. c. 16.

MAN'DRUS, a river near Sogdiana. *Id. ibid.*——A mountain in the interior of Libya.——A river of India within the Ganges. *Ptol.*

MANDU'BII, a people of Gaul inhabiting the country now called Burgundy. *Cæs. Bell. G.* 7. c. 8.

MANDUBRA'TIUS, a young Briton, who went over to Cæsar in Gaul. His father Immanuentius was one of the kings of Britain, and had been put to death by order of Cassivelaunus. *Cæs. Bell. G.* 5. c. 20.

MANDU'RIA, a city of Calabria, a little at the east of Tarentum, the inhabitants of which were wont to eat dogs' flesh. *Plin.* 2. c. 103.—*Liv.* 27. c. 15.

MANDU'RIUS LA'CUS, now Andorio, a lake of Daunian Apulia. *Leander a Plin.* 2. c. 103.

MAN'EROS, the name of a ceremony observed among the Ægyptians, when in their festivals the head of a dead person was produced to all those who were present, and an invitation made to enjoy the present time while life permitted.—The same name was given to a song in which mankind were exhorted to improve the shortness of life by a proper use of it, in commemoration of the son of one of the Ægyptian kings who died prematurely. *Plut. in Isid. & Os.—Herodot.* 2.

MA'NES, a son of Jupiter and Tellus, who reigned in Mæonia. He was father of Cotys by Callirrhoe, the daughter of Oceanus. *Dion. Hal.* 1. 11.

MA'NES, a name generally applied by the ancients to the souls of men when separated from the body. They were reckoned among the infernal deities, and were generally supposed to preside over the burying places and monuments of the dead. They were worshipped with great solemnity, particularly by the Romans, and the number three was considered as sacred to them, in consequence of which all invocations to them were repeated three times, with becoming solemnity. The augurs always invoked them when they proceeded to exercise their sacerdotal offices. Virgil introduces his hero as sacrificing to the infernal deities, and to the Manes, a victim whose blood was received in a ditch. The word *manes* is supposed to be derived from Mania, who was by some regarded as the mother of those tremendous deities. Others derive it from *manare, quod per omnia ætherea terranaque manabant*, because they filled the air, particularly in the night, and were intent upon molesting and disturbing the peace of mankind. Some say, that *manes* comes from *manis*, an old Latin word, which signified *good* or *propitious*. The word *manes* is differently used by ancient authors; sometimes it is taken for the infernal regions, and sometimes it is applied to the deities of Pluto's kingdom, whence the epitaphs of the Romans were always superscribed with the letters D. M. *Dis Manibus*, to warn the sacrilegious and profane, not to molest the monuments of the dead. *Propert.* 1. el. 19.—*Virg.* 4. *G.* v. 469. *Æn.* 3, &c.—*Horat.* 1. sat. 8. v. 28.—*Festus de V. Sig.—Nonnius*, 1. c. 337.—*Ovid. Heroid.* 3. v. 105.—*Sil. Ital.* 6. v. 113.—*Mart. Capell.* 2.—*Homer. Odyss.* 9. v. 65.—*Servius ad Virg. pass.—Auson. in Parent.—Macrob.* 1. c. 3.—*Varro de L. L.* 8.—*Apuleius de Socrat.*

MA'NES, a river of the Epicnemidian Locri, called also Boagrius. *Strab.* 9.

MANE'SIUM, a town of Phrygia. *Steph.*

MAN'ETHO or **MANE'THO**, surnamed the Mendesian, a celebrated priest of Heliopolis in Ægypt, B.C. 261. He wrote in Greek, a history of Ægypt, which has been often quoted and commended by the ancients, particularly by Josephus. It was chiefly collected from the writings of Hermes, and from various journals and annals, which were preserved in the Ægyptian temples. This history was greatly interpolated and disfigured by the Greeks. The author maintained that all the gods of the Ægyptians had been mere mortals, and had all lived upon earth. This history, which is now lost, had been epitomized, and some fragments are still extant. There is also extant a Greek poem ascribed to Manetho, in which the power of the stars, which preside over the birth and fate of mankind, is explained. The Apotelesmata of this author were edited in 4to, by Gronovius, L. Bat. 1698.—*Suidas.*—*Plut. de Is. & Os.*—*Hieronym. contra Jov.* 2.—*Fabr. B. Gr.* 3. c. 21.—*Sax. Onom.* 1. p. 105.—*Voss. H. Gr.* 1. c. 14.—*Marsh. Can. Chron.*

MANETHU'SA, a city of Crete. *Mela*, 2. c. 7.

MANEZAR'DUM, a town of Galatia *Antonin.*

MANGA'NUR, a city of India within the Ganges. *Ptol.*

MAN'GON, an island of the Arabian Gulph. *Ptol.*

MA'NIA, a goddess, supposed to have been the mother of the Lares and the Manes. She was called Lara by some, was invoked at the festivals of the Lares, and appeased by oblations of poppy heads or garlick. *Varro de L.L.* 8 c. 38.—*Macrob.* 1. c. 7.—*Arnob.* 4.——A female servant of queen Berenice, the daughter of Ptolemy. *Polyæn.* 8.——A mistress of Demetrius Poliorcetes, so named from her folly. She was also called Demo. *Plut. in Dem.*——A wife of Zenis, a prince of Dardania. *Polyæn.*—*Xenoph.*

Ma'nia, a city of Parthia. *Plin.* 6. c. 25——A promontory of Lesbus. *Ptol.*

MANIÆ'NA, a city of India within the Ganges. *Ptol.*

MANIL'IA LEX, by Manilius the tribune, A.U.C. 678. It required that all the forces of Lucullus and his province, together with Bithynia, which was then under the command of Glabrio, should be resigned into the hands of Pompey, and that this general should, without any delay, declare war against Mithridates, and still retain the command of the Roman fleet, and of the Mediterranean, as before. *Cicer. pro leg. Manil.*—Another which permitted all those whose fathers had not been invested with public offices, to be employed in the management of affairs.

Manil'ia, a woman rendered infamous by her debaucheries. *Juv.* 6. v. 242.

MANIL'IUS, a Roman who married the daughter of the last Tarquin. He lived at Tusculum, and received his father-in-law into his house, when banished from Rome, &c. *Liv.* 2. c. 15.

Manil'ius Ca'ius, a tribune who proposed Pompey to prosecute the Mithridatic war. *Cic. Man.* 14.

Manil'ius Ca'ius or **Mar'cus**, a celebrated mathematician and poet of Antioch, who wrote a poetical treatise on astronomy, of which five books are extant, treating of the fixed stars. The style of this composition is neither pleasing nor elegant. The age in which he lived is not known, though some suppose that he flourished in the Augustan age. No author, however, in the age of Augustus has made mention of Manilius, and even Quintilian himself has, much to the surprise of the learned, passed over his name and his labors in silence, though he has trealed of Lucretius, of Macer, and other writers on the same subject. Pliny, however, is supposed to speak of him when he mentions a Manlius who was distinguished for his knowledge of astronomy, and who placed a perpendicular golden rod at the top of the obelisk erected by Augustus in the Campus Martius, that thus he might distinguish the progress of time, and the proper division of days and nights by the inclination of the shadow. The best editions of Manilius, are those of Bentley 4to, London, 1739, and Stoebern 8vo, Argentor. 1767. *Vossius de P. L.* 2.—*Plin.* 36. c. 10.—*Gyrald. de P. H.* 4.—*Harles. Not. Lit. Rom.* 1. p. 298.—*Sax. Onom.* 1. p. 203.

Manil'ius Mar'cus, another mentioned by Cicero, as supporting the character of a great lawyer, and of an eloquent and powerful orator. He was consul with Censorinus, A.U. 605. *Cic. Br.* 27. *Acad.* 4. c. 32. *Cic. Or.* 33. c. 3. *De Orat.* 1. c. 48.

Manil'ius Ti'tus, a learned historian at Rome in the age of Sylla and Marius. He is greatly commended by *Cicero, pro Roscio.*—*Plin.* 10. c. 11.—*Voss. de L. Hist.* 1. c. 9.

MAN'IMI, a people in Germany. *Tacit. G.* 43.

MANI'OLÆ, islands off the coast of India without the Ganges, now Islas de Pracel. *Ptol.*

MA'NIS, a very ancient king of Phrygia, called by some Masdes. *Cœl. Rhod.* 21. c. 7.

MA'NIUS MAR'CIUS, an ædile who enacted a law which ordered that corn should be distributed to the Roman people at an *as* the bushel. *Plin.* 18. c. 3.

MAN'LIA LEX, enacted by the tribune P. Manlius, A.U.C. 557, received the office of *treviri epulones*, first instituted by Numa. The *epulones* were priests, who prepared banquets for Jupiter and the gods at public festivals, &c.

MAN'LIUS ATIL'IUS, a general who defeated a Carthaginian fleet, &c.

Man'lius Ca'ius or **Au'lus**, a senator sent to Athens to collect the best and wisest laws of Solon, A.U.C. 300. He opposed the Agrarian law, for which he was accused before the people by Genucius, but on the day appointed for his trial, his accuser was found dead in his bed. *Liv.* 2. c. 54. l. 3. c. 31 & 33.

Man'lius Cincinna'tus, made war against the Etrurians and Veientes with great success. He died of a wound which he received in battle.

Man'lius Imperio'sus, so called from the haughtiness of his character, was father of Manlius Torquatus, and was made dictator. He was accused for detaining his son at home. *Vid.* Manlius Torquatus. *Liv.* 7. c. 3, 4 & 5.—*Cic. Off.* 3. c. 31.

Man'lius Mar'cus, a celebrated Roman, whose valor was displayed in the field of battle, even at the early age of sixteen. When Rome was taken by the Gauls, Manlius with a body of his countrymen retired into the Capitol, which he defended when it was suddenly surprised in the night by the enemy. This action gained him the surname of *Capitolinus*, and the geese, which by their clamor had awakened him to arm himself in his own defence were ever after held sacred among the Romans. A law which Manlius proposed, to abolish the taxes on the common people, some time afterwards, roused the indignation of the senators against him, and the dictator Corn. Cossus, seized him as a rebel, but the populace put on mourning, and delivered from prison their common father. This did not in the least check his ambition; he continued to raise factions, and even secretly to attempt to make himself absolute, till at last the tribunes of the people themselves became his accusers He was tried in the Campus Martius; but when the distant view of the Capitol, which Manlius had so bravely defended, seemed to influence the people in his favor, the court of justice was removed, and Manlius was condemned. He was thrown down from the Tarpeian rock, A.U.C. 371, and to render his ignominy still greater, none of his family were afterwards permitted to bear the surname of *Marcus*, and the place where his house had stood was deemed unworthy to be inhabited. *Liv.* 5. c. 31 & 47. l. 6. c. 5 & 20.—*Cic. Dom.* 38. *Phil.* 1. c. 13.—*Plin.* 7. c. 28.—*Flor.* 1. c. 13 & 26.—*Val. Max.* 6. c. 3.—*Virg. Æn.* 6. v. 825.

Man'lius Torqua'tus, a celebrated Roman, who was distinguished in his youth by a lively and cheerful disposition. His promising talents were, however, impeded by a difficulty of speaking; and the father, unwilling to expose the son's rusticity at Rome, detained him in the country. The behaviour of the father was publicly censured, and Marius Pomponius the tribune, cited him to answer for his unfatherly behaviour to his son. Young Manlius was informed of this, and with a dagger in his hand he entered the house of the tribune, and made him solemnly promise that he would drop the accusation. This action of young Manlius endeared him to the people, aud he was soon after chosen military tribune. In a war against the Gauls, he accepted the challenge of one of the enemy, whose gigantic stature and ponderous arms had rendered him terrible and almost invincible in the eyes of the Romans. The Gaul was conquered, and Manlius stripped him of his arms, and, from the collar (*torques*), which he took from the enemy's neck, he was ever after surnamed *Torquatus*. Manlius was the first Roman who was raised to the dictatorship, without having been previously consul. The severity of Torquatus to his son has been deservedly censured. He most unfeelingly put to death his son because he had engaged one of the enemy, and obtained an honorable victory without his previous permission. This uncommon rigor displeased many of the Romans; and though Torquatus was honored with a triumph, and commended by the senate for his services, yet the Roman youth showed their disapprobation of the consul's severity, by refusing him at his return the homage which every other conqueror received. Some time after, the censorship was offered to him, but he refused it, observing, that the people could not bear his severity, nor he the vices of the people. From the rigor of Torquatus, all edicts and actions of severity and justice have been called *Manliana edicta*. *Liv.* 7. c. 5 & 10. l. 8. c. 7.—*Cic. Fin.* 2. c. 32.—*Val. Max.* 6. c. 9.—*Plut. in Par.* 22.—*Flor.* 1. c. 13 & 14.

MAN'LIUS TORQUA'TUS, a learned man in the age of Cicero.

MAN'LIUS VA'LENS, the præfect of a legion in Britain, &c. *Tacit. Ann.* 12. c. 40.

MAN'LIUS VOL'SO a Roman consul who received an army of Scipio in Asia, and made war against the Gallogrecians, whom he conquered. He was honored with a triumph at his return, though it was at first strongly opposed by the senate. *Flor.* 3. c. 11.—*Liv.* 38. c. 12, &c.

MAN'LIUS, a prætor who reduced Sardinia. He was afterwards made dictator.——A general who was defeated by a rebel army of slaves in Sicily.——A prætor in Gaul, who fought against the Boii, with very little success.——A conspirator with Catiline against the Roman republic, and was slain in the battle against Petreius. *Cic. Cat.* 3. c. 6.—*Sall. Cat.* 27, 32, 59 & 60.——A Roman, in whose consulship the temple of Janus was shut after the second Punic war. *Liv.* 1. c. 19.——A person banished under Tiberius for his adultery.——A Roman appointed judge between Silanus and the commissioners from the province of Macedonia. When all parties had been patiently heard, the father said, "It is evident that my son has suffered himself to be bribed, therefore I deem him unworthy of the republic and of my house, and I order him to depart from my presence." Silanus was so struck at the rigor of his father's sentence, that he hanged himself. *Val. Max.* 5. c. 5.

MANNACAR'TA, a city of Arabia. *Steph.*

MAN'NUS. the son of Tuisco, both regarded as powerful divinities among the Germans. *Tacit. de Germ.* c. 2.——A slave who gave information about a fire caused at Rome by the villany of some Campanians. *Liv.* 26. c. 27.

MAN'OBA, a town of Hispania Bætica, with a river of the same name. It is called Menoba by *Pliny*, 3. c. 1.

MAN'RALI, a people of Colchis. *Ptol.*

MANSUE'TUS J., a friend of Vitellius, who entered the Roman armies, and left his son, then very young, at home. The son was promoted by Galba, and soon after met a detachment of the partisans of Vitellius, among whom his father was. A battle was fought, and Mansuetus was inadvertently wounded by the hand of his son, &c. *Tacit. Hist.* 3. c. 25.

MAN'TALUS, a city of Phrygia. *Steph.*

MANTHYRE'A, a town of Arcadia. *Id.*

MAN'TIAS, a general of Athens, sent with 3,000 men to reduce Argæum. *Diod. Sic.* 16.

MANTINE'A, a town of Arcadia. It was taken by Aratus and Antigonus, and in compliment to the latter it was afterwards called Antigonia. The emperor Adrian built there a temple in honor of his favorite Alcinous. It was famous for the battle which was fought there between Epaminondas, at the head of the Thebans, and the combined forces of Lacedæmon, Achaia, Elis, Athens, and Arcadia, about 363 B.C. *Strab.* 8.—*Ptol.* 3. c. 16.—*C. Nepos. in Epam.*—*Diod.* 15.

MANTINE'US or **MAN'TINEUS**, the father of Ocalea, who married Abas the son of Lynceus and Hypermnestra. *Apollod* 2. c. 9.

MANTINO'RUM OP'PIDUM, a town of Corsica, supposed to be the modern Bastia.

MAN'TIT'TUR, a city of India within the Ganges. *Ptol.*

MAN'TIUS, a son of Melampus by Iphianassa, daughter of Proteus. *Homer. Odyss* 5.

MAN'TO, a daughter of the prophet Tiresias, endowed with the gift of prophecy. She was made prisoner by the Argives when the city of Thebes fell into their hands, and as she was regarded the worthiest part of the booty, the conquerors sent her to Apollo, the god of Delphi, where she officiated as priestess, and where she gave oracles. From Delphi she came to Clarus in Ionia, where she established an oracle of Apollo. Here she married Rhadius the sovereign of the country, by whom she had a son called Mopsus. Manto afterwards visited Italy, where she married Tiberinus, king of Alba, or, as the poets mention, the god of the river Tiber. From this marriage sprang Ocnus, who built a town in the north of Italy, which, in honor of his mother, he called Mantua. Manta, according to a certain tradition, was so struck at the misfortunes which afflicted Thebes, her native country, that she gave way to her sorrow, and was changed by the gods into a fountain. Some suppose her to be the same personage who conducted Æneas into hell, and who sold the Sibylline books to Tarquin the proud. She received divine honors after death. *Virg. Æn.* 1. v. 199. l. 10. v. 199. & *Servius locis.*—*Mela*, 1. c. 17.—*Ovid. Met.* 6. v. 157.—*Diod.* 4.—*Apollod.* 3. c. 7.—*Strab.* 14 & 16.—*Paus.* 9. c. 10 & 33. l. 7. c. 3.

MAN'TUA, a town of Italy, on the Mincius, at the north of the Po, founded about 300 years before Rome by Bianor or Ocnus, the son of Manto. It was anciently the capital of Etruria. When Cremona, which had followed the interest of Brutus, was given to the soldiers of Octavius, Mantua also, which was in the neighbourhood, shared the common calamity, though it had favored the party of Augustus, and many of the inhabitants were tyrannically deprived of their possessions. Virgil, who was among them, and a native of the town, and from thence often called *Mantuanus*, applied for redress to Augustus, and obtained it by means of his poetical talents. *Strab.* 5.—*Virg. Ecl.* 1, &c. *G.* 3. v. 12. *Æn.* 10. v. 180.—*Ptol.* 3. c. 1.—*Servius ad Virg. loc. cit.*—*Ovid. Am.* 3. el. 15. v. 7.—*Stat.* 4. *Sylv.* 2. v. 9.—*Ital.* 8. v. 595.

MANTUR'NA, one of the deities who presided over marriage among the Romans. *Aug. de Civ. Dei.* 6. c. 9.

MAPE'TA, a city of Sarmatia, now Copa. *Ptol.*

MAPU'RA, a city of India within the Ganges. *Id.*

MARABI'NA, a town of the Pentapolis in Africa. *Id.*

MARACAN'DA, a town of Sogdiana. *Arrian.*—*Curt.* 8. c. 1. It is now Samarcand.

MAR'ACHE, a city of India. *Steph.*

MAR'ACHES, a people of Ætolia. *Plin.* 4. c. 2.

MARACO'DRA, a city of Bactriana. *Ptol.*

MAR'AGA, a city of Arabia Felix. *Id.*

MARA'NE, a town of Arabia Felix. *Plin.* 6. c. 28.

MA'RAS. a rich person of Beroe, in Syria. *Suidas.*

MAR'ATHA, a village of Arcadia. *Paus.* 8. c. 28.

MARATHE'SIUM, a city of Caria. *Steph.*

MAR'ATHI, a nation beyond the Tanais. *Athen.*

MAR'ATHON, a village of Attica, ten miles from Athens, celebrated for the victory which the 10,000 Athenians and 1000 Platæans, under the command of Miltiades, gained over the Persian army, consisting of 100,000 foot and 10,000 horse, or, according to Val. Maximus, 300,000, or, as Justin says, of 600,000, under the command of Datis and Artaphernes, on the 28th of September, 490, B.C. In this battle, according to Herodotus, the Athenians lost only 192 men, and the Persians 6,300. Justin has estimated the loss of the Persians, in this expedition and in the battle, at 200,000 men. To commemorate this immortal victory of their countrymen, the Greeks raised small columns, with the names inscribed on the tombs of the fallen heroes. It was also in the plains of Marathon that Theseus overcame a celebrated bull, which ravaged the neighbouring country. Erigone is called *Marathonia virgo*, as being born at Marathon. *Stat.* 5. *Sylv.* 3. v. 74.—*C. Nep. in Milt.*—*Herodot.* 6, &c. *Justin.* 2. c. 9.—*Val. Max.* 5. c. 3.—*Plut. in Parall.*

MAR'ATHON, a king of Attica, son of Epopeus, who gave his name to a small village there. *Paus.* 2. c. 1.——A king of Sicyon.

MARATHO'NIA, a city of Thrace, not far from Abdera. *Steph.*

MAR'ATHOS, a town of Phœnicia. *Mela*, 1. c. 12.

MAR'ATHUS, a city of Acarnania. *Steph.*

MARATHUS'SA, an island near Clazomenia. *Steph. Plin.* 4. c. 12, &c.

MARCÆ'UM, a mountain of Troas, near Gergithe. *Steph.*

MAR'CALA, a city of Armenia Minor. *Ptol.*

MARCEL'LA, a daughter of Octavia, the sister of Augustus by Marcellus. She married Agrippa.

MARCELLE'A, a festival at Syracuse, in honor of Marcellus. *Cicer.* 4. *in Verr.—Cœl. Rhod.* 18. c. 12.

MARCELLI'NUS AMMIA'NUS, a celebrated historian who carried arms under Constantius, Julian, and Valens, and wrote a history of Rome from the reign of Domitian, where Suetonius stops, to the emperor Valens. His style is neither elegant nor labored, but his work is greatly valued for its veracity, and in many of the actions which he mentions, the author was nearly concerned. This history was composed at Rome, whither Ammianus retired from the noise and troubles of the camp, and it is remarkable that he does not betray that severity against the Christians which other writers have manifested, though the author was warm in favour of Paganism, the religion which for a while was seated on the throne. It was divided into 31 books, of which only the eighteen last remain, beginning at the death of Magnentius. Ammianus has been liberal in his encomiums upon Julian, whose favours he enjoyed, and who patronised his religion. The negligence with which some facts are stated has induced many to believe that the history of Ammianus has suffered much from the ravages of time, and that it has descended to us mutilated and imperfect. The best editions of Ammianus, are that of Gronovius, fol. and 4to. L. Bat. 1693, and of Ernesti, 8vo, Lips, 1773. *Harles. Not. Lit. Rom.* 1. p. 621.—*Sax. Onom.* 1. p. 437.

MARCEL'LUS CORN., a Roman knight accused of incest with Lepida. *Tac. An.* 16. c. 8.

Marcel'lus Mar'cus Clau'dius, a famous Roman general, who, after the first Punic war, had the management of an expedition against the Gauls of Insubria, where he obtained the *Spolia opima*, by killing with his own hand Viridomarus the king of the enemy. Such extraordinary success rendered him popular at Rome, and he was soon after entrusted to oppose Annibal in Italy. He was the first Roman who obtained some advantage over this celebrated Carthaginian, and showed his countrymen that Annibal was not invincible. The troubles which were raised in Sicily by the Carthaginians at the death of Hieronymus, alarmed the Romans, and Marcellus, in his third consulship, was sent with a powerful force against Syracuse. He attacked it by sea and land, but his most skilful operations proved ineffectual, and the invention and industry of a philosopher (*vid.* Archimedes), were able to baffle all his efforts, and to destroy the great and stupendous machines and military engines of the Romans, during three successive years. The perseverance of Marcellus, however, obtained the victory. The inattention of the inhabitants during their nocturnal celebration of the festivals of Diana, favoured his operations; he forcibly entered the town, and by a rapid manœuvre made himself master of it. The conqueror enriched the capital of Italy with the spoils of Syracuse, and when he was accused of rapacity, for stripping the conquered city of all its paintings and ornaments, he confessed that he had done it to adorn the buildings at Rome, and to introduce a taste for the fine arts and elegance of the Greeks among his less polished countrymen. After the conquest of Syracuse, Marcellus was called upon by his country to oppose the victorious Annibal a second time. In this campaign he behaved with greater vigor than before; the greatest part of the towns of the Samnites, which had revolted, were recovered by force of arms, and 3000 of the soldiers of Annibal made prisoners. Some time after, an engagement with the Carthaginian general proved unfavourable; Marcellus had the disadvantage: but on the morrow a more successful skirmish vindicated his military character, and the honor of the Roman soldiers. Marcellus, however, was not sufficiently vigilant, against the snares of his artful adversary. He imprudently separated himself from his camp, and was killed in an ambuscade in the 60th year of his age, in his 5th consulship, A.U.C. 546. His body was honored with a magnificent funeral by the conqueror, and his ashes were conveyed in a silver urn to his son. Marcellus claims our commendation for his private as well as public virtues; and the humanity of the general will ever be remembered with admiration, who, at the surrender of Syracuse, wept at the thought that many were going to be exposed to the avarice and rapacity of an incensed soldiery, which the policy of Rome and the laws of war rendered inevitable. *Virg. Æn.* 6. v. 855.—*Paterc.* 2. c. 38.—*Cor. Nep. in Ann.—Liv.* 22, &c.—*Plut. in Vitâ*, &c. [A statue of the consul Marcellus is to be found in the Giustiniani palace at Rome; and a bust in the Capitol.]

Marcel'lus M.C., son of the preceding, was caught in the ambuscade which proved fatal to his father, but he forced his way through the midst of the enemy and escaped. He received the ashes of his father from the conqueror. He rose gradually through all the offices of the state, and in his consulship triumphed over the Insubres. He dedicated the temple to Virtue, which his father had, 17 years before, vowed to erect. *Liv.* 27, &c.—*Plut. in Marcell.*——One of the descendants of the great Marcellus, signallized himself in the civil wars of Cæsar and Pompey, by his firm attachment to the latter. He was banished by Cæsar, but he was afterwards recalled at the pressing solicitations of the senate, when Cicero had undertaken his defence in an oration which is still extant. He was assassinated on his return at Athens, by Magius Chilo, an event communicated to Cicero with great feeling by Sulpicius.——The grandson of Pompey's friend, rendered himself popular by his universal benevolence and affability. He was son of Marcellus by Octavia the sister of Augustus, and was early betrothed to Pompeia the daughter of Sex. Pompey. He, however, married Julia, the emperor's daughter, and was publicly intended as his successor. The suddenness of his death, which was accelerated, if not caused, by the injudicious application of the cold bath, under the direction of Antonius Musa, at the early age of 18, was the cause of much lamentation at Rome, particularly in the family of Augustus, and Virgil procured himself great favors by celebrating the virtues of this amiable prince. *Vid.* Octavia. The body of Marcellus, as a national tribute to his many virtues, was buried at the public expense. *Virg. Æn.* 6. v. 883.—*Suet. in Aug.—Tacit. Ann.* 1. c. 3. 1. 41. *Hist.* 1. c. 15.—*Suet. Aug.* 29 & 43.—*Dio.* 53. c. 33. 1. 54. c. 26.—*Plin.* 25. c. 7.—*Propert.* 3. el. 16. v. 7.—*Plut. in Marcell.—Senec. Consol. ad Marc.* 2—*Paterc.* 2. c. 93.

Marcel'lus, a man who conspired against Vespasian.——The husband of Octavia, the sister of Augustus.——A conqueror of Britain.——An officer under the emperor Julian. *Cassiodor.*——A man put to death by Galba.——A man who gave Cicero information of Catiline's conspiracy.——A colleague of Cato in the quæstorship.——A native of Side in Pamphylia, who wrote an heroic poem on physic, divided into 42 books. He lived in the reign of Marcus Aurelius.——A Roman, sent as ambassador to Masinissa after being honored with the consulship. He perished in a shipwreck, an event which it is said he had foretold. *Liv.* 43. c. 11, &c. —*Cic. Pis.* 19.—*Div.* 2. c 5.—*Fat.* 14.

MAR'CHADÆ, a nation of the Troglodytæ, near the Arabic Gulph. *Plin.* 6. c. 29.

MARCHU'BII, a people of Africa Propria. *Plin.* 5. c. 4.

MAR'CIA LEX, enacted by Marcus Censorinus, forbade any man to be invested with the office of censor more than once. *Plut. in Coriol.*—Another, enacted by L. Marcus Philippus, tribune of the people, similar to that introduced by Gracchus. *Cic. in Off.*—Another, proposed by L. Marcius, tribune of the people, A.U.C. 557, respecting peace with king Philip. *Liv.* 33.

Mar'cia, the wife of Regulus. When she heard that her husband had been put to death at Carthage in the most excruciating manner, she retorted the punishment upon some Carthaginian prisoners whom she shut up in a barrel, which she had previously filled with sharp nails. The senate interfered, and put an end to her wanton cruelty. Gellius reports that not Marcia, but her children, avenged the tortures of Regulus on the Carthaginian captives. *Diod.* 24.—*Gell.* 6. c. 4.——A favourite of the emperor Commodus, whom she poisoned. *Lamprid. in Comm.* c. 8.——A vestal virgin, punished for her incontinence.——A daughter of Philip, who married Cato the censor. Her husband gave her his friend Hortensius for the sake of procreating children, and after his death he took her again. ——A daughter of Cato of Utica.——A daughter of Cremutius. *Vid.* Cremutius.

MAR'CIA, a stream of water at Rome. *Vid.* Martia Aqua.——An ancient name of the island of Rhodes.

MARCIA'NA, a sister of the emperor Trajan, who, on account of her public and private virtues and her amiable disposition, was declared Augusta and empress by her brother. She died A.D. 113. [There is a bust of Marciana in the Capitol.]

MARCIANOP'OLIS, the capital of Lower Mœsia, at the south of the Danube, on the borders of the Euxine. It receives its name in honor of the empress Marciana, and is now called Breslaw. *Amm. Marcell.*

MARCIA'NUS, a native of Thrace, born of an obscure family. After he had served for some time in the Roman army as a common soldier, he was made private secretary to one of the officers of Theodosius. His winning address and uncommon talents raised him to higher stations; and on the death of Theodosius the Second, A.D. 450, he was invested with the imperial purple in the East. The subjects of the Roman empire had reason to be satisfied with their choice. Marcianus showed himself active and resolute, and when Attila, the barbarous king of the Huns, asked of the emperor the annual tribute, which the indolence and cowardice of his predecessors had regularly paid, the successor of Theodosius firmly replied, that he kept his gold for his friends, but that iron was the metal which he had prepared for his enemies. In the midst of universal popularity Marcianus died, after a reign of six years, in the 69th year of his age, as he was making warlike preparations to repel the barbarians that had invaded Africa. His death was universally lamented, and his merit deserved it, since his reign has been distinguished by the appellation of the golden age. Marcianus married Pulcheria, the sister of his predecessor. *Marcell. Chron.—Evagr.* 1 2. *Niceph.* 14, &c.——A geographer of Heraclea, who wrote a *Periplus maris externi*, also composed an Epitome of the geographical works of Artemidorus of Ephesus. His works were first edited by Hœschelius, August, 1600, and afterwards by Hudson, in the 1st volume of the Geographical Minores, Oxon. 1698. *Fabr. B. Gr.* 4. c. 2.—*Sax. Onom.* 1. p. 479.

MARCIA'NUS CAPEL'LA, a writer. *Vid.* Capella

MAR'CIUM or MAR'CIUS MONS, a mountain of Latium, near Lanuvium. *Diod.—Plut.*

H. MAR'CIUS SABI'NUS, was the progenitor of the Marcian family at Rome. He came to Rome with Numa, and it was he who advised Numa to accept of the crown, which the Romans after the death of Romulus offered to him. He attempted to make himself king of Rome, in opposition to Tullius Hostilius, and when his efforts proved unsuccessful, he killed himself. His son, who married a daughter of Numa, was made high priest by his father-in-law. He was father of Ancus Martius. *Plut. Numă.—Liv.* 1. c. 32.

MAR'CIUS, a Roman who accused Ptolemy Auletes, king of Ægypt, in the Roman senate of misdemeanor against the republic.——A Roman consul defeated by the Samnites. He was more successful against the Carthaginians, and obtained a victory, &c.——A prætor, who built a famous aqueduct called *Aqua Marcia*, which conveyed excellent water to the city from the mountains of the Peligni, about sixty miles from Rome. From Tibur to the city this celebrated aqueduct was raised on arches for nine miles, and long remained a monument of Roman ingenuity and national perseverance. *Plin.* 31. c. 3. l. 36. c. 15.—*Dio.* 49. c. 42.—*Stat.* 1. *Sylv.* 5. v. 25.——A general who defeated the Hernici. ——A man whom Catiline hired to assassinate Cicero.

MAR'CIUS C. RU'TILUS, a consul who obtained a victory over the Etrurians, and triumphed without the authority of the senate. He was the first plebeian dictator, and was four times consul. *Liv.* 7. c. 17, &c.

MAR'CIUS LU'CIUS, a Roman knight, who, after the death of the Scipios, took the command of the armies in Spain, and distinguished himself by his valor and great presence of mind. Scipio the younger, who superseded him, highly esteemed him, though the Romans were jealous of his success, and the influence which his services procured him in the state. *Liv.* 25 & 26, &c.

MAR'CIUS Q. REX, a consul with Metellus, A.U.C. 686, who married the sister of Clodius. He was appointed over Cilicia, but either through resentment or disaffection he did not second the efforts of Lucullus in the Mithridatic war, and in vain claimed a triumph on his return to Rome. During Catiline's conspiracy he went to Fesulæ to support the authority of the senate. *Dio.* 35. c. 4, &c. *Cic. Pis.* 4.—*Sallust. Cat.* 30, &c.

MAR'CIUS SAL'TUS, a place of Liguria. *Liv.*

MARCODA'VA, a town of Dacia, now Marcozech. *Ptol.*

MARCODU'RUM, a town of the Vibii, now Duren. *Tac. Hist.* 4. c. 28.

MARCOL'ICA, a celebrated city of Spain. *Liv.*

MARCOMAN'NI, or MARCOM'ANI, a people of Germany, who originally dwelt on the banks of the Rhine and the Danube. They proved powerful enemies to the Roman emperors. Augustus granted them peace, but they were afterwards subdued by Antoninus and Trajan, &c. *Paterc.* c. 109.—*Tacit. An.* 2. c. 46 & 62. *G.* 42.

MAR'CUS, a prænomon common to many of the Romans. *Vid.* Æmilius, Lepidus, &c.——A son of Cato, killed at Philippi, &c.

MAR'CUS CARYNEN'SIS, a general of the Achæan league, 255. B.C.

MARDE'NE, or MARDYE'NE, a part of ancient Persia which took its name from the Mardi or Amardi.

MAR'DI, a people of Persia, on the confines of Media. They were very poor, and generally lived upon the flesh of wild beasts. Their country, in later times, became the residence of the famous assassins destroyed by Hulakou the grandson of Zingis Khan. *Herodot.* 1 & 3.—*Plin.* 6. c. 16.

MAR'DIA, a place of Thrace, famous for a battle between Constantine and Licinus, A.D. 315.

MAR'DONES, a people of Epirus. *Steph.*

MARDO'NIUS, a general of Xerxes, who, after the defeat of his master at Thermopylæ and Salamis, was left in Greece at the head of an army of 300,000 chosen men, to subdue the country, and reduce it under the power of Persia. His operations were rendered useless by the courage and vigilance of the Greeks; and in a battle at Platæa Mardonius was defeated and left among the slain, B.C. 479. He had formerly been commander of the armies of Darius in Europe, and it was chiefly by his advice that Xerxes invaded Greece. He was son-in-law of Darius. *Plut. in Arist.—Herodot.* 6, 7 & 8.—*Diod.* 11.—*Justin.* 2. c. 13, &c.

MAR'DUS or AMAR'DUS, a river of Medea, falling into the Caspian Sea.

MA'RE MOR'TUUM, called also, from the bitumen which it throws up, the lake Asphaltites, is situate in Judæa, and is nearly 100 miles long and 25 broad. Its waters are more impregnated with salt than those of the sea, but the vapors exhaled from them are not so pestilential as has been generally represented. It is supposed that the thirteen cities, of which Sodom and Gomorrah, as mentioned in the Scriptures, were the capital, were destroyed by a volcano, on the site of which this immense lake was formed. Volcanic appearances now mark the face of the country, and earthquakes are frequent there. *Plin.* 5. c. 6.—*Joseph. J. Bell.* 4. c. 27.—*Strab.* 16. p. 764.—*Justin.* 36. c. 3.

MARE'A or MA'REA, a city in Ægypt. *Steph.*

MAREO'TIS or MARI'A, now Siwan, a lake in Ægypt, at the north of Alexandria. Its neighbourhood is famous for wine, though some authors make the *Marioticum vinum* grow in Epirus, or in a certain part of Libya, called also Mareotis, near Ægypt. *Virg. G.* 2. v. 81.—*Servius in loco.*—*Ptol.* 6. c. 5.—*Curt.* 4. c. 7.—*Lucan.* 9. v. 154. l. 10. v. 117 & 161.—*Horat.* 1. od. 38. v. 14.—*Strab.* 17.

MA'RES, the ninth Theban king of Ægypt, reigned 26 years. *Joh. Marsh. Can. Chron.*

MA'RES, a people of Asia who served in the armies of Xerxes. Their armour was of wicker work, with leather shields and javelins.

MARE'CRA, a city of India within the Ganges. *Ptol.*

MARE'SA or MARES'CHA, an ancient fortress of Palestine.

MARGÆ'A, a city of Elis. *Steph.* *Casaubon* supposes that it is the Margaiæ of *Strabo.*

MAR'GANA or MAR'GALÆ, a city of India. *Steph.*

MAR'GARA, a city of India within the Ganges. *Ptol.*

MAR'GASI, a people of Media. *Ptol.*

MARGASTA'NA, a small island of the Persian Gulph. *Arrian. in Indic.*

MARGIN'IA or MARGIA'NA, a town and country near the river Oxus, at the east of Hyrcania, celebrated for its wines. The vines were said to be so uncommonly large that two men could scarcely clasp the trunk of one of them. *Curt.* 7. c. 10.—*Ptol.* 5.

MARGI'TES, a man against whom, as some authors suppose, Homer wrote a poem, to ridicule his superficial knowledge, and to expose his affectation. When Demosthenes wished to prove Alexander an inveterate enemy to Athens, he called him another Margites. *Plut. in Demost.—Suidas.*

MAR'GIUM, a city of Phrygia, afterwards called Apollonia. *Steph.*

MARGU'NIUS MAX'IM., one of the Greek fathers, bishop of Cythera, who wrote, among other things, nine hymns on sacred subjects, in the manner of Anacreon.

MAR'GUS, a large river of Mœsia falling into the Danube, with a town of the same name, now Kastolatz.——A river of Margiana which falls into the Oxus, and with it, into the Caspian.

MARI'A, the Virgin—Mother of our blessed Lord Jesus Christ.

MA'RIA LEX, enacted by C. Marius, the tribune, A.U.C. 634. It ordered the planks called *pontes*, on which the people stood up to give their votes in the *comitia*, to be narrower, that no others might stand there to interrupt the proceedings of the assembly by appeal, or to create other disturbances. Another, called also Porcia, by L. Marius and Porcius, tribunes, A.U.C. 691. It fined such commanders as gave a false account to the Roman senate of the number of slain in a battle, a certain sum of money. It obliged them to swear to the truth of their return when they entered the city, according to the best computation.

MARI'ABA, a city of Arabia, near the Red Sea. *Strab.* 15.

MARIAM'NE, the wife of Herod, put to death by him. *Joseph. J. A.* 15. c. 3.

MARIAM'NIA, a city of Phœnicia. *Steph. ex Paus.* 9.

MARIA'NA COLO'NIA, a city of Corsica, so called from Marius. *Plin.* 3. c. 6.

MARIA'NÆ FOS'SÆ, a town of Gallia Narbonensis, which received its name from the dyke *(fossa)*, which Marius opened thence into the sea. *Plin.* 3. c. 4.—*Strab.* 4.

MARIANDY'NUM, a district of Bithynia, whence the poets feign that Hercules dragged Cerberus out of hell. *Ptol.* 5. c. 1.—*Mela*, 1. c. 2 & 19. l. 2. c. 7.—*Eustath. ad Dionys. Per.*

MARIANDY'NUS SI'NUS, part of the Euxine Sea, near Bithynia. *Plin.* 6. c. 1.

MARIA'NE, a lake of Asia, probably the Mantiana of *Strabo*. *Ptol.*

MARIA'NI MON'TES, now Sierra Morena, mountains of Hispania Tarraconensis. *Ptol.*

MARIA'NUS, a surname given to Jupiter, from a temple built to his honor by Marius, at Rome. It was in this temple that the Roman senate assembled to recall Cicero, a circumstance said to have been communicated to him in a dream. *Val. Max.* 1. c. 7.

MARIA'NUS MONS, a mountain in Hispania Bœtica. The modern Sierra Morena.

MARI'CA, a nymph of the river Liris, near Minturnæ. She married king Faunus, by whom she had Latinus, and was afterwards called Fauna and Fatua, and honored as a goddess. A city of Campania bore her name. Some suppose her to have been the same as Circe. *Virg. Æn.* 7. v. 47.—*Lucan.* 4. v. 424.—*Servius ad Virg. Æn.* 12. v. 164.

MARI'CA, a wood on the borders of Campania, sacred to the nymph Marica. *Liv.* 27. c. 37.—*Horat.* 3. od. 17. v. 4.

MARI'CI, a people of Liguria. *Plin.* 3. c. 17.

MAR'ICUS, a Gaul thrown to lions, in the reign of Vitellius. It is said that the animals refused to devour him. *Tacit. Hist.* 2. c. 61.

MARIG'ERI a people of Upper Æthiopia. *Plin.* 6. c. 30.

MARIM'ATHA, a town of Arabia Felix. *Ptol.*

MARI'NA, a daughter of Arcadius, &c.

MARINIA'NA, a city of Pannonia. *Antonin.*

MARI'NUM or MARI'NI FA'NUM, now St. Marino, a city of Umbria. *Strab.*

MARI'NUS, a friend of Tiberius, put to death, &c. *Tac. Ann.* 6. c. 10.

MARI'NUS LA'CUS, a lake of Etruria, now Lago d'Orbitello. *Strab.* 3.

MA'RIO, a slave in Cicero's family. *Cic. Fam.* 16. ep. 1.

MA'RION, a king of Tyre, in the age of Alexander the Great.

MA'RIS, a river of Scythia.

MA'RIS, a son of Armisodares, who assisted Priam against the Greeks, and was killed by Antilochus. *Homer. Il.* 16. v. 317.

MARIS'SA, an opulent town of Judæa.

MAR'ISUS or MA'RUS, according to *Tacitus. Ann.* 2. c. 63. a river of Dacia.

MAR'ISUS a large river of Thrace, flowing from mount Hæmus. *Virg. G.* 4. v. 524.

MARI'TA LEX. *Vid.* Julia de Maritandis.

MARI'THI MON'TES, mountains of Arabia Felix. *Ptol.*

MARIT'IMA COLO'NIA, a city of Gallia Narbonensis, now Martegues. *Id.*

MA'RIUM, a town of Cyprus. *Steph.—Catull. Epigr.* 37. v. 12.

MA'RIUS, C., a celebrated Roman, who from a peasant, became one of the most powerful and cruel tyrants that Rome ever beheld during her consular government. He was born at Arpinum, of obscure and illiterate parents. His father bore the same name as himself, and his mother was called Fulcinia. He early forsook the meaner occupations of the country for the camp, and signalized himself under Scipio at the siege of Numantia. The Roman general saw and admired the courage and intrepidity of young Marius, and foretold his future greatness. By his seditions and intrigues at Rome, while he exercised the inferior offices of the state, Marius rendered himself known; and his marriage with Julia, who was of the family of the Cæsars, contributed in some measure to raise him to consequence. He passed into Africa as lieutenant to the consul Metellus against Jugurtha, and, after he had there ingratiated himself with the soldiers, and raised enemies to his friend and benefactor, he returned to Rome and canvassed for the consulship. The extravagant promises which he made, and the malevolent insinuations about the conduct of Metellus proved successful. He was elected, and appointed to finish the war against Jugurtha. He showed himself capable in every respect of succeeding Metellus. Jugurtha was defeated, and afterwards betrayed into the hands of the Romans by the perfidy of Bocchus. No sooner was Jugurtha conquered, than new honors and fresh trophies awaited Marius. The provinces of Rome were suddenly invaded by an army of 300,000 barbarians, and Marius was regarded as the only man whose activity and boldness could resist so powerful an enemy. He was again elected consul, and sent against the Teutones. The war was prolonged, and Marius was a third and fourth time invested with the consulship. At last two engagements were fought, and not less than 200,000 of the barbarian forces of the Ambrones and Teutones were slain in the field of battle, and 90,000 made prisoners. The following year was also marked by a total overthrow of the Cimbri, another horde of barbarians, in which 140,000 were slaughtered by the Romans, and 60,000 taken prisoners. After such honorable victories, Marius, with his colleague, Catulus, entered Rome in triumph, and, for his eminent services, he deserved and received the appellation of the third founder of Rome. He was elected consul a sixth time; and, as his intrepidity had delivered his country from its foreign enemies, he now sought employment at home, and his restless ambition began to raise seditions, and to oppose the growing power of Sylla. This proved the cause of a civil war. Sylla refused to deliver up the command of the forces with which he was empowered to prosecute the Mithridatic war, and he resolved to oppose the author of a demand which he considered arbitrary and oppressive. He advanced to Rome, and Marius was obliged to save his life by flight. The unfavourable winds prevented him from seeking a safer retreat in Africa, and he was left on the coasts of Campania, where the emissaries of his enemy discovered him in a marsh, where he had plunged in the mud to conceal himself, and left only his mouth above the surface for respiration. He was violently dragged to the neighbouring town of Minturnæ, and the magistrates, all devoted to the interests of Sylla, passed sentence of immediate death upon their magnanimous prisoner. A Gaul was commanded to cut off his head in the dungeon, but the stern countenance of Marius disarmed the courage of the executioner, and when he heard the exclamation of *Tune, homo, audes occidere Caium Marium*, the dagger dropped from his hand. Such an uncommon adventure awakened the compassion of the inhabitants of Minturnæ. They released Marius from prison, and favored his escape to Africa, where he joined his son Marius, who had been rousing to arms the princes of the country in his cause. Marius landed near the walls of Carthage, and received no small consolation at the sight of the venerable ruins of that once powerful city, which, like himself, had been exposed to calamity, and felt the cruel vicissitude of fortune. The place of his retreat was soon known, and the governor of Africa, to conciliate the favour of Sylla, compelled Marius to flee for safety to a neighbouring island. He soon after learned that Cinna had embraced his cause at Rome, when the Roman senate had stripped him of his consular dignity and bestowed it upon one of his enemies. This intelligence animated Marius; he set sail to assist his friend at the head of only a thousand men. His army, however, gradually increased as he advanced, and he entered Rome like a ferocious conqueror. His enemies were inhumanly sacrificed to his fury, Rome was filled with blood, and he who had once been called the father of his country, marched through the streets of the city, attended by a number of assassins, who immediately slaughtered all those whose salutations were not answered by their leader. When Marius and Cinna had sufficiently gratified their resentment, they made themselves consuls; but Marius, already worn out with old age and infirmities, died sixteen days after he had been honored with the consular dignity for the seventh time, B.C. 86. His end was probably hastened with the uncommon quantities of wine which he drank when laboring under a dangerous disease, to remove, by intoxication, the stings of a guilty conscience. Such was the melancholy end of Marius, who had rendered himself conspicuous by his victories, and odious by his cruelty. As he was brought up in the midst of poverty and among peasants, it will not appear wonderful that he always betrayed rusticity in his behaviour, and despised in others those polished manners and that studied address which education had denied him. He despised the conversation of the learned, only because he was illiterate, and if he occasionally appeared an example of sobriety and temperance, he owed those advantages to the years of obscurity which he had passed at Arpinum. His countenance was stern, his voice firm and imperious, and his disposition unyielding and untractable. He always betrayed the greatest timidity in the public assemblies, as he had not been early taught to make eloquence and oratory his pursuit. He was in the 70th year of his age when he died, and Rome seemed to rejoice at the fall of a man whose ambition had proved fatal to so many of her citizens. His only qualifications were those of a great general, and with these he rendered himself the most illustrious and powerful of the Romans, because he was the only one whose undaunted fierceness seemed capable of opposing the barbarians of the north. The manner of his death, according to some opinions, remains doubtful, though some have charged him with the crime of suicide. Among the instances which are mentioned of his firmness, this may be recorded. A swelling in the leg obliged him to apply to a physician, who urged the necessity of cutting it off. Marius gave it, and saw the operation performed without a distortion of the face, and without a groan. The physician asked the other, and Marius gave it with equal composure. *Plut. in Vitâ.—Paterc.* 2. c. 9.—*Flor.* 3. c. 1, 3, 16 & 21.—*Juv.* 8. v. 245, &c.—*Lucan.* 2. v. 69. [A fine statue of Marius will be found in the Museum of the Capitol.]

MA'RIUS CA'IUS, the son of the great Marius, was as cruel and vindictive as his father, and shared his good and his adverse fortune. He made himself consul in the 25th year of his age, and murdered all the senators who opposed his ambitious views. He was at last defeated by Sylla, and fled to Præneste, where he was slain in attempting to escape, or, as others say, he killed himself. *Plut. in Mario.—Paterc.* 2. c. 26.—*Cic. N. D.* 3. c. 32.—*Appian. B. C.* 1.

MA'RIUS CEL'SUS, a friend of Galba, saved from death by Otho, &c.—*Tac. Hist.* 1. c. 45.

MA'RIUS MAX'IMUS, a Latin writer, who published an account of the Roman emperors from Trajan to Alexander, now lost. His compositions were entertaining, and executed with great exactness and fidelity. Some, however, have complained that his writings abounded with many fabulous and insignificant stories. *Voss. Hist. Lat.* 2. c. 3.

MA'RIUS M. AURE'LIUS, a native of Gaul, who, from the mean employment of a blacksmith, became one of the generals of Gallienus, and at last caused himself to be saluted emperor. Three days after this elevation, a man who had shared his poverty without partaking of his more prosperous fortune, publicly assassinated him, and it is said that he was killed by a sword which he himself had made in the time of his obscurity. Marius has been often celebrated for his great strength, and it is confidently reported that he could stop with one of his fingers only, the wheel of a chariot in its most rapid course.

MA'RIUS M. GRATIDIA'NUS, a prætor scourged and cruelly put to death by Catiline, or, according to others, by Sylla, at the tomb of Catulus. He was brother or uncle to the great Marius. *Cic. de Pet. Cons.* 3.—*Plut. in Syll.*—*Val. Max.* 9. c. 2.—*Lucan.* 2. v. 175, &c.

MA'RIUS PRIS'CUS, a governor of Africa, accused of extortion in his province by Pliny the younger, and banished from Italy. *Plin.* 2. ep. 11.—*Juv.* 1. v. 48.

MA'RIUS SEX'TUS, a rich Spaniard, thrown down from the Tarpeian rock on account of his riches, &c. *Tacit. Ann.* 6. c. 19.

MA'RIUS, a lover, &c. *Vid.* Hellas.——One of the Greek fathers of the fifth century, whose works were edited by Garner, 2 vols. fol. Paris, 1673; and Baluzius, ib. 1684.—The family of the Marii was plebeian. Some are mentioned by various authors without any remarkable event to excite particular enquiry with respect to their history. *Liv.* 23. c. 7 & 35. l. 22. c. 42.—*Cic. Verr.* 5. c. 16. *Att.* 12. ep. 49. *Fam.* 12. ep. 15. *Fr.* 5. ep. 1. *Sex. Ross.* 32. *Brut.* 45.

MAR'MA a city of Arabia Felix. *Plin.* 6. c. 28.——A city of Phœnicia. *Steph.*

MAR'MACES, a people of Æthiopia. *Id.*

MAR'MACUS, the father of Pythagoras. *Diog. Laert.* 8. c. 1.

MAR'MARES, a nation and city of Lycia. *Diod. Sic.* l. 17.

MARMAR'ICA. *Vid.* Marmaridæ.

MARMAR'IDÆ, the inhabitants of that part of Libya called Marmarica, which was situated between Cyrene and Ægypt. They were swift in running, and pretended to possess some drugs or secret power to destroy the poisonous effects of the bite of serpents. *Sil. It.* 3. v. 300. l. 11. v. 182.—*Lucan.* 4. v. 680. l. 9. v. 894.

MARMAR'IDUS, the name of a magician. *Plin.* 31. c. 1.

MARMA'RION or MARMA'RIUM, a town of Eubœa, whence Apollo is called Marmarinus and Marmarius. *Strab.* 10.—*Steph.*

MAR'MAX, a river of Elis. *Paus.* 6.

MA'RO. *Vid.* Virgilius.——The surname of the Papirian family of patrician rank at Rome. *Cic. Fam.* 11. ep. 21.

MAROBOD'UI, a nation of ancient Germany. *Tacit. de Germ.*

MAROBOD'UUS, a king of the Marcomanni, B.C. 18. His power excited the jealousy of Augustus, who was only prevented by the revolt of the Dalmatians, from sending a powerful army against him. Maroboduus was eventually expelled his kingdom by the other German tribes, and died at Ravenna, A.D. 35, aged 53 years.

MA'RON, a son of Evanthes, high-priest of Apollo in Africa, when Ulysses touched upon the coast. *Homer. Odyss.* 9. v. 179.——An Ægyptian who accompanied Osiris in his conquest, and built a city in Thrace, called from him Maronea. *Mela*, 2. c. 2.—*Diod.* 1.

MARONE'A, a city of the Cicones, in Thrace, near the Hebrus, of which Bacchus was the chief deity. The wine of the country was reckoned excellent, and with it, as it is supposed, Ulysses intoxicated the Cyclops Polyphemus.—*Plin.* 14 c. 4.—*Herodot.* —*Mela.* 2. c. 2.—*Tibull.* 4. el. 1. v. 57.

MARO'NIAS, a city of Chalcidice in Syria. *Ptol.*

MARO'RA, a city of Cappadocia. *Ptol.*

MARPE'SIA, a celebrated queen of the Amazons, who waged a successful war against the inhabitants of Mount Caucasus. The mountain was called *Marpesius Mons* from her. *Justin.* 2. c. 4.—*Virg. Æn.* 6. v. 471 *& Servius loco.*

MARPES'SA, a daughter of the Evenus who married Idas, by whom she had Cleopatra the wife of Meleager. Marpessa was tenderly loved by her husband; and when Apollo endeavoured to carry her away, Idas pursued the ravisher with a bow and arrows, resolved on revenge. Apollo and Idas were separated by Jupiter, who permitted Marpessa to accompany which of the two lovers she most regarded. She gladly returned to her husband. *Homer. Il.* 9. v. 549.—*Ovid. Met.* 8. v. 305.—*Apollod.* 1. c. 7.—*Paus.* 4. c. 2. l. 5. c. 18.

MARPES'SUS, a town of Mysia. *Lactant.* 1. c. 6. ——A mountain of Parus, abounding in white marble, whence *Marpessia cautes.* The quarries are still visited with admiration by modern travellers. *Virg. Æn.* 6. v. 471.—*Plin.* 4. c. 12. l. 36. c. 5.

MARRA'SIUM, a town of Persia, now Marazu. *Ptol.*

MAR'RES, a king of Ægypt, who had a crow which conveyed his letters wherever he pleased. It is said that he raised a celebrated monument to this faithful bird near the city of Crocodiles. *Ælian. An.* 6. c. 7,

MAR'RICHE, a city of Parthia. *Ptol.*

MARRU'BII, a people of Italy, near the lake Fucinus.

MARRUCI'NI, a people of Picenum. *Sil. It.* 15. v. 564.

MARRU'VIUM or **MARRU'BIUM**, now San Benedetto, a place near the lake Fucinus in Italy. *Virg. Æn.* 7. v. 750.—*Sil. It.* 8. v. 497.

MARS, the god of war amongst the ancients, was the son of Jupiter and Juno according to Hesiod, Homer, and all the Greek poets, or of Juno alone, according to Ovid. The education of Mars was entrusted by Juno to the god Priapus, who instructed him in dancing and in every manly exercise. His trial before the celebrated court ot the Areopagus, according to the authority of some authors, for the murder of Hallirhotius, forms an interesting epoch in history. *Vid.* Areopagitæ. The amours of Mars and Venus are well known. The god of war gained the affections of Venus; but Apollo informed Vulcan of his wife's infidelity, and awakened his suspicions. Vulcan secretly laid a net round the bed, and the two lovers were exposed to the ridicule of all the gods, till Neptune prevailed upon the husband to set them at liberty. This disgraceful discovery so provoked Mars that he changed into a cock his favorite Alectryon, whom he had stationed at the door to watch against the approach of the sun, (*vid.* Alectryon,) and Venus also showed her resentment by persecuting, with the most inveterate fury, the children of Apollo. In the wars of Jupiter and the Titans, Mars was seized by Otus and Ephialtes, and confined for fifteen months till Mercury procured him his liberty. During the Trojan war Mars interested himself zealously on the side of the Trojans, but whilst he defended these favorites of Venus with uncommon activity, he was wounded by Diomedes, and hastily retreated to heaven to conceal his confusion and his resentment, and to complain to Jupiter that Minerva had directed the unerring weapon of his antagonist. The worship of Mars was not very universal among the ancients; his temples were not numerous in Greece, but in Rome he received the most unbounded honors, and the warlike Romans were proud of paying homage to a deity whom they esteemed as the patron of their city, and the father of the first of their monarchs. His most celebrated temple at Rome was built by Augustus after the battle of Philippi. It was dedicated to Mars Ultor, or the *avenger.* His priests among the Romans were called Salii: they were first instituted by Numa, and their chief office was to guard the sacred Ancylia, one of which, as was supposed, had fallen down from heaven. Mars was generally represented under the figure of a naked old man, armed with a helmet, a pike, and a shield. Sometimes he appeared in a military dress, and with a long flowing beard, and sometimes without. He generally rode in a chariot drawn by furious horses, which the poets called Flight and Terror. His altars were stained with the blood of the horse, on account of his warlike spirit, and of the wolf, on account of his ferocity. Magpies and vultures were also offered to him on account of their greediness and voracity. The Scythians generally offered him asses, and the people of Caria dogs. The weed called dog-grass was sacred to him, because it grows as, it is commonly reported, in places where the ground has been stained with the effusion of human blood. The surnames of Mars are not numerous. He was called Gradivus, Mavors, Quirinus, Salisubsulus, among the Romans. The Greeks called him Ares, and he was the Enyalus of the Sabines, the Camulus of the Gauls, and the Mamers of Carthage. Mars was the father of Cupid, Anteros, and Harmonia, by the goddess Venus. He had Ascalaphus and Ialmenus by Astyoche; Alcippe by Argaulus; Cycnus by Pelopeia; Tereus by Bostonis; Molus, Pylus, Evenus, and Thestius by Demonice, the daughter of Agenor. Besides these, he was the reputed father of Romulus, Œnomaus, Bythis, Thrax, Diomedes of Thrace, Lycus, &c. He presided over gladiators, and was the god of hunting, and of whatever exercises or amusements required exertions of a manly and warlike nature. Among the Romans it was usual for the consul, before he went on an expedition, to visit the temple of Mars, where he offered his prayers, and in a solemn manner shook the spear which was in the hand of the statue of the god, at the same time exclaiming, "*Mars vigila!* god of war, watch over the welfare and safety of this city." *Ovid. Fast.* 5. v. 231. *Trist.* 2. v. 925. *Met.* 4. fab. 5.—*Hygin.* fab. 148. *P.A.* 2. c. 17.—*Virg. G.* 4. v. 346. *Æn.* 8. v. 701.—*Lucian in Alectr.*—*Varro de L.L.* 4. c. 10.—*Homer. Odyss.* 1, &c. *Il.* 5.—*Flacc.* 6.—*Apollod.* 1, &c.—*Hesiod. Theog.*—*Pindar.* od. 4. *Pyth.*—*Quint. Smyr.* 14.—*Paus.* 1. c. 21 & 28.—*Juv.* 9. v. 102.—*Servius in Æn.* 1. v. 100. l. 2. v. 163. l. 6. v. 778. l. 8. v. 1. l. 12. v. 118.—*Gyrald. Synt.* 10.—*Schol. Eurip in Orest.*—*Solin.* 13. —*Meursius in Areop.*—*Festus de V. Sig.* [The finest of the few representations of this deity will be found in the Villa Ludovisi near Rome. It is a sitting figure.] The planet Mars was supposed to portend wars and tumults, and it ruled the winds and thunders, according to ancient writers. *Cic. N. D.* 2. c. 2.—*Lucan.* 1. v. 660. l. 10. v. 206.

MARSÆ'US, a Roman ridiculed by *Horace*, 1. sat. 2. v. 55, for his prodigality to courtezans.

MAR'SALA, a town of Sicily.

MARSA'TII, a people of the Batavi. *Plin.* 4. c. 15. —*Tac. Hist.* 4. c. 56.

MARSE, a daughter of Thespius. *Apollod.*

MAR'SI, a nation of Germany, which afterwards came to settle near the lake Fucinus in Italy, in a country chequered with forests, and abounding with wild boars and other ferocious animals. They at first proved very inimical to the Roman power, but in process of time, they became its firmest supporters. They are particularly celebrated for the civil war in which they were engaged, and which from them has received the name of the *Marsian war.* The large contributions which they made to support the interest of Rome, and the number of men which they continually supplied to the republic, rendered them bold and aspiring, and they claimed with the rest of the Italian states a share of the honor and privileges which were enjoyed by the citizens at Rome, B.C. 91. This petition, though supported by the interest, the eloquence, and the integrity of the tribune Drusus, was received with feelings of jealousy, and at last rejected, by the Roman senate; and the Marsi, with their allies, showed their dissatisfaction by taking up arms. Their resentment was increased, when Drusus, their friend at Rome, had been basely murdered by means of the nobles; and they erected themselves into a republic, and Corfinium was made the capital of their new empire. A regular army was now begun, and the Romans led into the field an army of 100,000 men, and were opposed by a superior force

Some battles were fought in which the Roman generals were defeated, and the allies reaped no inconsiderable advantages from their victories. A battle, however, near Asculum, proved fatal to their cause, 4,000 of them were left dead on the spot, their general, Francus, a man of uncommon experience and superior abilities, was slain, and such as escaped from the field perished by hunger in the Apennines, where they had fled for shelter. After many defeats, and the loss of Asculum, one their principal cities, the allies, grown dejected and tired of hostilities which had already continued for three pears, sued for peace one by one, and tranquillity was at last re-established in the republic, and all the states of Italy were admitted to the rights and privileges of citizens of Rome. The armies of the allies consisted of the Marsi, the Peligni, the Vestini, the Hirpini, Pompeiani, Marcini, Picentes. Venusini, Ferentanæ, Apuli, Lucani, and Samnites. The Marsi were greatly addicted to magic. *Horat.* ep. 5. v. 76. ep. 17. v. 29.—*Appian.*—*Val. Max.* 8.—*Paterc.* 2. *Plut. in Sert. Mario, &c.*—*Cic. pro Balb.*—*Strab.*—*Tacit. Ann.* 1. c. 50 & 56. *G.* 2.

MARSIG'NI, a people of Germany. *Tacit. G.* 43. They are, probably, the Marvigni of *Ptolemy.*

MARSIP'PUS, a city of Phœnicia. *Steph.*

MARSONI'CA, a city of Lower Pannonia. *Ptol.*

MAR'SUS DOMIT'IUS, a Latin poet. *Vid.* Domitius.

MAR'SYA, a city of Phœnicia. *Steph.*

MARSY'ABÆ, a town of Arabia Felix. *Strab.* 16.

MAR'SYAS, a celebrated piper of Celænæ, in Phrygia, son of Olympus, or of Hyagnis, or, according to others, of Œagrus. He was so skilful in playing on the flute, that he is generally considered the inventor of it. According to the opinion of some. he found it when Minerva had thrown it aside on account of the distortion of her face when she played upon it. Marsyas became enamoured of Cybele, and travelled with her as far as Nysa, where he had the imprudence to challenge Apollo to a trial of his skill as a musician. The god accepted the challenge, and it was mutually agreed that he who was defeated should be flead alive by the conqueror. The muses, or according to Diodorus, the inhabitants of Nysa, were appointed umpires. Each exerted his utmost skill, and the victory, with much difficulty, was adjudged to Apollo. The god, upon this, tied his antagonist to a tree, and flayed him alive. The death of Marsyas was universally lamented; the Fauns, Satyrs, and Dryads wept at his fate, and from their abundant tears, a river of Phrygia, well known by the name of Marsyas, is said to have arisen. The unfortunate Marsyas is often represented on monuments as tied, his hands behind his back, to a tree, while Apollo stands before him with his lyre in his hands, and a youth, supposed to be Olympus, the unfortunate musician's pupil, in a supplicating posture eager to save the life of his friend, or to honor his remains with funereal rites. In independent cities among the ancients, the statue of Marsyas was generally erected in the forum, to represent the intimacy which subsisted between Bacchus and Marsyas, as the emblems of liberty. It was also erected at the entrance of the Roman forum, as a spot to which usurers and merchants resorted to transact business, being principally intended *in terrorem litigatorum;* a circumstance to which *Horace* seems to allude, 1 sat. 6. v. 120. At Celænæ, the skin of Marsyas was shown to travellers for some time; it was suspended in the public place in the form of a bladder or a foot-ball. *Hygin.* fab. 165.—*Ovid. Fast.* 6. v. 707. *Ex Ponto,* 3. el. 3. *Met.* 6. fab. 7.—*Diod,* 3.—*Ital.* 8. v. 503.—*Paus.* 10. c. 30.—*Apollod* 1. c. 4.—*Apul. in Met.* 11.—*Plut. de Irat. Coh.*—*Plin.* 5. c. 29. l. 7. c. 56.—*Philostr. Icon.* 1. c. 20 & 21.—*Lucian. Dial. Jun. & Lat.*—*Palæphat. Inc.* 48.—*Servius. in Æn.* 3. v, 20. [A representation of Marsyas tied to the tree, is in the possession of the Grand Duke of Tuscany, at Florence.]

MAR'SYAS, a river, the sources of which were near those of the Mæander, and these two rivers had their confluence a little below the town of Celænæ. *Liv.* 38. c. 13.—*Ovid. Met.* 2. v. 265.—*Lucan.* 3. v. 208.

MAR'SYAS, a writer who published a history of Macedonia, from the first origin and foundation of that empire till the reign of Alexander, in which he lived. *Suidas.*—*Voss. H. Gr.* 1. c. 10, &c.——An Ægyptian who commanded the armies of Cleopatra against her brother Ptolemy Physcon, whom she attempted to dethrone.——A man put to death by Dionysius, the tyrant of Sicily.

MAR'THA, a celebrated prophetess of Syria, whose arts and religious frauds proved of the greatest service to C. Marius in the numerous expeditions which he undertook. *Plut. in Mario.*

MAR'THAMA, a town of Africa Propria. *Appian.*

MAR'THULA, a city of the Cappadocian Pontus. *Ptol.*

MAR'TIA, a vestal virgin put to death for her incontinence.——A daughter of Cato. *Vid.* Marcia.

MAR'TIA A'QUA, a stream of water at Rome, celebrated for its clearness and salubrity. It was conveyed to Rome by means of an aqueduct from the lake Fucinus, a distance of above thirty miles, by Ancus Martius, whence it received its name. *Tibull.* 3. el. 7. v. 26.—*Plin.* 31. c. 3. l. 36. c. 15.

MARTIA'LES LU'DI, games celebrated at Rome in honor of Mars. *Dio.* l. 56.

MARTIA'LIS MAR'CUS VALE'RIUS, a native of Bilbilis, in Spain, who came to Rome about the twentieth year of his age, where he recommended himself to the notice of the great by his poetical genius. As he was the panegyrist of the emperors, he gained the highest honors in the state, and was rewarded in the most liberal manner. Domitian gave him the tribuneship; but the poet, unmindful of the favors which he had received, after the death of his benefactor, exposed to ridicule the vices and cruelties of a monster, whom in his lifetime he had extolled as the pattern of virtue, goodness, and moral excellence. Trajan treated the poet with coldness; and Martial after he had passed thirty-five years in the capital of the world, in the greatest splendour and affluence, retired to his native country, where he had the mortification to be the object of malevolence, satire, and ridicule. He received some favors from his friends, and his poverty was alleviated by the liberality of Pliny the younger, whom he had panegyrized in his poems. Some however, imagine, that his retirement in Spain was accompanied with comfortable ease and domestic happiness. Martial died about 104 A.D. in the seventy-fifth year of his age. He is now well known by the fourteen books of epigrams which he wrote, and the merit of which is best described by the candid confession of the author in this line,

Sunt bona, sunt quædam mediocra, sunt mala plura.

But the genius which he displays in some of his epigrams deserves commendation, though many critics are liberal in their censure upon his style, his thoughts, and particularly upon his puns, which are often low and despicable. In many of his epigrams the poet has unhappily shown himself a declared enemy to decency, and the book is to be read with caution, since it may corrupt the purest morals. It has been observed of Martial, that his talent was epigrams. Every thing which he did was the subject of an epigram. He wrote inscriptions upon monuments in the epigrammatic style, and even a new-year's gift was accompanied with a distich, and his poetical pen was employed in begging a favor as well as in satirizing a fault. The best editions of Martial are those of Rader. fol. Mogunt. 1627; of Schrevelius, 12mo, L. Bat. 1619; and of Smids, 8vo, Amst 1701. *Harles. Not. Lit. Rom.* 1. p. 475.—*Sax. Onom.* 1. p. 276 & 579.

MARTIA'LIS CORNE'LIUS, a person praised for his bravery by *Tacitus. Hist.* 3. c. 70.

MARTIA'LIS, a friend of Otho.——A man who conspired against Caracalla.

MARTIA'NUS. *Vid.* Marcianus.

MAR'TIE, a place of Spain, between Bracara and Asturica. *Antonin.*

MARTI'NA, a woman skilled in the knowledge of poisonous herbs, &c. *Tacit. Ann.* 2. c. 74, &c,

MARTI'NI, a people of Arabia Deserta. *Ptol.*

MARTINIA'NUS. an officer, made Cæsar by Licinius to oppose Constantine. He was put to death by order of Constantine.

MAR'TION, a native of Smyrna, who wrote a book *de simplicibus effectibus.* *Plin.* 28. c. 4.

MAR'TIUS, a surname of Jupiter in Attica, expressive of his power and valour. *Paus.* 5, c. 14.—*Festus de V. Sig.*——A consul sent against Perseus, &c.——A consul employed against the Dalmatians

&c.——A consul who defeated the Carthaginians in Spain.——A consul who defeated the Privernates, &c.

MAR'TIUS FES'TUS, a Roman knight, engaged in Piso's conspiracy against Nero. *Tac. Ann.* 15. c. 50.

MAR'TIUS MA'CER, a captain in the army of Otho. *Id Hist.* 2. c. 23.

MARUL'LUS EPID'IUS, a tribune of the people, who tore the garlands with which Cæsar's statues had been adorned, and who ordered those that had saluted him to be imprisoned. He was, in consequence of this violent conduct, deprived of his office by J. Cæsar. *Plut.—Cic. Phil.* 13. c. 15.—*Paterc.* 2. c. 68.—*Suet. Cæs.* 79.

MARUL'LUS, a governor of Judæa.——A Latin poet in the age of Antoninus the philosopher. He satirized the emperor with great licentiousness, but his invectives were wisely disregarded, and himself despised. *Hieron. contra Ruffin.*

MARUL'LUS TAC'ITUS, a poet of Calabria in the fifth century. He flattered Attila after the taking of Aquileia, and the invasion of Italy, but the rude barbarian, offended with the adulation of the poet, who described him as descended from heaven, ordered him to be burnt. *Philip. Callimach. in Attila.*

MARUL'LUS, a rhetorician, preceptor of *Seneca. Controvers.* 1.

MARUN'DÆ, a people of Media.

MARUN'DÆ, a people of India within the Ganges. *Ptol.*

MA'RUS, a river of Germany, which separates modern Hungary and Moravia. It is now the Morava and falls into the Danube. *Tacit. Ann.* 2. c. 63.

MARYANDY'NI, an ancient people of Asia Minor.

MAS'ADA, a town of Palestine, on the lake Asphaltites. *Plin.* 5, c. 17. It is called Moasada by *Strabo*, Massada by *Josephus*, and is now Massa.

MASÆSYL'II, a people of Libya, where Syphax reigned. *Vid.* Massyla.

MASANOR'ADA, a city of Caria. *Steph.*

MAS'ARA, a city of Armenia Minor. *Ptol.*

MASA'TI, a people of the interior of Libya. *Plin.* 5. c. 1.

MAS'CA, a city of the Celtiberi. *Strabo.*——A river of Arabia Deserta. *Xenoph. Exped. Cyri.* l. 1.

MASCHA'NE, a city of the Arabes Scenitæ. *Steph.*

MAS'COTUS, a city of Libya. *Steph.*

MAS'CULA, a city of Numidia. *Antonin.—Augustin.*

MASDORA'NI, a people of Asia, near Parthia. *Ptol.*

MASDORA'NUS, a mountain which separated the Parthians from Aria. *Ptol.*

MA'SES, a city of the Argives, called also Masetus, and the people Masetii. *Steph.*

MAS'ICES, a people of Mauritania Tingitana. *Ptol.*

MASIC'YTUS, a mountain dividing Pamphylia and Lycia. *Ptol.—Pliny*, 5. c. 27., calls it Massycites. *Q. Calab.* l. 3.

MASINIS'SA, a son of Gala, king of a small part of Africa, who assisted the Carthaginians in their wars against Rome. He proved a most indefatigable and courageous enemy, but an act of generosity rendered him at last friendly to the interests of Rome. After the defeat of Asdrubal, Scipio, the first Africanus, who had obtained the victory, found, among the prisoners of war, one of the nephews of Masinissa. Scipio, with great disinterestedness, sent him back to his uncle loaded with presents, and escorted him with a detachment for the safety and protection of his person. Masinissa was struck with the liberal conduct of the Roman general, forgot all former hostilities, and joined his troops to those of Scipio. This change of sentiments was not the effect of a wavering or unsettled mind, for Masinissa showed himself the most attached and the firmest ally which the Romans ever had. It was to his exertions that they owed many of their victories in Africa, and particularly in that battle which proved fatal to Asdrubal and Syphax. The Numidian conqueror, charmed with the beauty of Sophonisba, the captive wife of Syphax, carried her to his camp and married her; but when he percived that this new connection displeased Scipio, he sent poison to the ill-fated queen, and recommended her to destroy herself, since he could not preserve her life in a manner which became her rank, dignity, and fortune, without offending his Roman allies. In the battle of Zama, Masinissa greatly contributed to the defeat of the great Annibal, and the Romans, who had been so often spectators of his courage and valor, rewarded his fidelity with the addition of the kingdom of Syphax, and of some of the Carthaginian territories. At his death Masinissa showed the confidence which he placed in the Romans, and the esteem which he entertained for the rising talents of Scipio Æmilianus, by entrusting him with the care of his kingdom, and by empowering him to divide it among his sons. Masinissa died in the 97th year of his age, after a reign of above sixty years, 149 B.C. In the first years of his reign Masinissa was exposed to the greatest danger, and was often obliged to save his life by seeking a retreat among his savage neighbours. But his alliance with the Romans proved the beginning of his greatness. He was remarkable for the health which he long enjoyed. In the last years of his life he was seen at the head of his armies, showing the most indefatigable activity, and he often remained for many successive days on horseback, without a saddle under him, or a covering upon his head, and without manifesting any marks of fatigue. This strength of mind and body he chiefly owed to the temperance which he observed. He was seen eating brown bread at the door of his tent like a common soldier the day after he had obtained an immortal victory over the armies of Carthage. He left fifty-four sons, three of whom were legitimate, Micipsa, Gulussa, and Manstabal. His kingdom was fairly divided among them by Scipio and the illegitimate children received as their portion very valuable presents. The death of Gulussa, and Manastabal soon after left Micipsa sole master of the large possessions of Masinissa. *Strab.* 17.—*Polyb.—Appian. Lybic.—Cic. de Senect.* 10.—*Val. Max.* 8.—*Sallust. in Jug.—Liv.* 25. c. 34. l. 28. c. 16. l. 29. c. 4. l. 30. c. 5. l. 31. c. 19. l. 34. c. 61. l. 42. c. 23. l. 45. c. 13.—*Ovid. Fast.* 6. v. 769.—*Justin.* 33. c. l. l. 38. c. 6. [There are two heads of Masinissa in the Capitol, and a third in the Borghese collection, now at Paris. One of the former is the best.]

MASITH'OLUS, a river in the interior of Libya. *Ptol.*

MA'SO, a name common to several persons mentioned by *Cicero, Fam.* 9. ep. 21, &c. *Balb.* 23. *N.D.* 3. c. 20.

MAS'PII, a people of Persia. *Steph.*

MAS'SA, a river of Libya. *Ptol.*

MAS'SA BÆB., an informer at the court of Domitian. *Juv.* l. v. 35.

MAS'SACA, a town of India, taken by Alexander the Great. *Steph.*

MASSÆSY'LI, a people of Africa Propria. *Strab.*

MAS'SAGA, a city of India. *Arrian. in Indic.* It is called Mazaga by *Curtius*, 8. c. 10.

MASSAG'ETÆ, a people of Scythia who had their wives in common, and dwelt in tents. They had no temples, but worshipped the sun, to which they offered horses, on account of their swiftness. When their parents had come to a certain age, they generally put them to death, and ate their flesh, mixed with that of cattle. Authors are divided with respect to the particular spot in which they resided. Some place them near the Caspian Sea, others at the north of the Danube, and some confound them with the Getæ and the Scythians. *Horat.* l. od. 25. v. 40.—*Dionys. Per.* 738.—*Herodot.* l. c. 204. l. 4. c. 172.—*Ptol.* 6. c. 19.—*Isidor.* 9. c. 2.—*Strab.* l.—*Mela*, l. c. 2,—*Lucan.* 2. v. 50. l. 3. v. 283.—*Claudian. in Ruf.* l. v. 312.—*Justin.* l. c. 8.

MAS'SALA, a city of the Homeritæ in Arabia Felix. *Plin.* 6. c. 28.

MASSA'LIA, a river of Crete. *Ptol.*

MASSA'NA. *Vid.* Messana.

MASSA'NI, a people who dwelt at the mouth of the Indus. *Diog. Sic.* 17.

MAS'SIA, a town of Hispania Bætica. *Plin.* 3. c. 1.

MAS'SICUS, a mountain of Campania, near Minturnæ, famous for its wine, which even now preserves its ancient character of superior excellence. It is now Monte Marisco. *Plin.* 14. c. 6.—*Horat.* l. od. l. v. 19.—*Virg. G.* 2. v. 143.—*Liv.* 22. c. 14.—*Columel.* c. 3. 8.—*Martial.* l. epigr. 27. l. 13. epigr. 108.

MAS'SICUS, an Etrurian prince, who assisted Æneas against Turnus with 1000 men. *Virg. Æn.* 10. v. 166, &c.

MASSIL'IA, a town of Gallia Narbonensis, on the shores of the Mediterranean, now called Marseilles, founded B.C. 539, by the people of Phocæa, in Asia, who quitted their country to avoid the tyranny of the Persians. It was celebrated for its laws, its fidelity to the Romans, and for its being long the seat of literature and of science. It acquired great consequence by its commercial pursuits during its infancy; and even waged war against Carthage. By becoming the ally of Rome, its power was establish ed; but in warmly espousing the cause of Pompey against Cæsar, its desire of attaining greater political consequence was frustrated, and it was so much reduced by the insolence and resentment of the conqueror, that it never after recovered its independence and warlike spirit. *Herodot*. 1. c. 164. *Plin*. 3. c. 4.—*Justin*. 37. c. 1. l. 43. c. 3.—*Mela*, 2. c. 5 & 7.—*Solin*. 8.—*Cæs. de Civ*. 1.—*Lucan*. 3, v. 307, 341. l. 4. v. 257. l. 5. v. 53.—*Strab*. 1 & 4.—*Liv*. 5. c. 3.—*Horat*. ep. 16. v. 17.—*Flor*. 4. c. 2.——*Cic. Flacc*. 26. *Off*. 2. 8.—*Tacit. A*. 4. c. 44. *Agr*. 4.—*Seneca ad Helv*. 8.

MASSI'VA, a son of Gulussa, and grandson of Masinissa. He was put to death at Rome, by Bomilcar.

MASSY'LA, an inland part of Mauritania, near mount Atlas. When the inhabitants, called Massyli, went on horseback, they never used saddles or bridles, but only sticks. Their character was warlike, their manners simple, but their love of liberty unconquerable. Some suppose them to be the same as the Masæsylii, though others say that only half the country belonged to this last-mentioned people. *Liv*. 24. c. 48. l. 28. c. 17. l. 29. c. 32.—*Sil*. 3. v. 282. l. 16. v. 171.—*Lucan*. 4. v. 682.—*Virg. Æn*. 4. v. 132.

MAS'TA, a mountain and city of Upper Æthiopia. *Ptol*. It is now Grari.

MASTAN'ABAL, *vide* Manastabal.

MASTANESO'SUS, a king Mauritania. *Cic. Vat*. 5.

MASTAU'RA, a city of Lydia. *Steph*.

MAS'THALA, a city of Arabia Felix. *Ptol*.

MASTIA'NI, the inhabitants of Mastia, near the columns of Hercules. *Steph*.

MASTIN'IUS, a man mentioned by *Cicero*, *Fam*. 2. ep. 15. *Verr*. 3. c. 24.

MASTI'TÆ, a people of Upper Æthiopia. *Ptol*. They were probably the Mathitæ of *Pliny*, 6. c. 30.

MAS'TOR, a king of Mycenæ, succeeded on the throne by Electryon. *Joh. Marsham. Can. Chron. Sec*. 11.

MASTRAM'ELA, a lake near Marseilles, now Lac de Martegue. *Plin*. 3. c. 4.

MASTU'SIA, a promontory of the Thracian Chersonesus. *Ptol*.—*Plin*. 4. c. 11. It is now Capo Griego.

MAS'TYA, a town of the Milesians, in Paphlagonia. *Plin*. 6. c. 2.

MASU'RIUS SABI'NUS, a Roman knight under Tiberius, learned, but poor. *Pers*. 5. v. 90.—*Athen*. 14.—*Voss. Hist. Lat*. 1. c. 21, &c.

MATA'LIA, a town of Crete. *Ptol*. It is now Matala.

MATAU'RUS, a city of Sicily, founded by the Locrians. *Steph*.

MATEL'GÆ, a town of the Garamantes. *Plin*. 5. c. 5.

MATE'NI, a people of Asiatic Sarmatia. *Ptol*.

MATER'NUS, a poet in the age of Vespasian, whose tragedy, called Cato, gave great offence to the government, He was put to death by Domitian. *Dio*. 67. c. 12.

Mater'nus Ju'lius Fir'micus, a Sicilian convert to Christianity in the middle of the fourth century. He wrote a work in eight books, called Astronomica, edited by Aldus, Venet. 1499: also a work *de errore profanarum religionum*, edited by Flaccius, Argentor. 1562, 8vo, and by Wower. 1603, and published with Minucins Felix and Cyprian, Roterdam. 1743. He was a learned and eloquent writer, and his style was much superior to that of the age in which he lived. *Harles. Not. Lit. Rom*. 1. p. 574.—*Sax. Onom*. 1. p. 401.

MATHATHÆ'I, a people of Arabia Felix. *Plin*. 6. c. 28.

MA'THO, an infamous informer, patronised by Domitian. *Juv*. 1. v. 32.——A seditious African. *Cœl. Rhod*. 29. c. 2.

MATIA'NA, a part of Media. *Steph. ex Strab*.

MATIE'NI, a people in the neighbourhood of Armenia. *Dion*. v. 1002.

MATIN'IUS P., a merchant engaged in a dispute with the people of Salamis for money lent to them, &c. *Cic. ad Att*. 5. ep. 21.

MATI'NUS, a mountain of Apulia, abounding in yew trees and bees. *Lucan*. 9. v. 184.—*Horat*. 4. od. 2. v. 27. *Epod*. 16. v. 28.

MATIS'CO, a town of the Ædui, in Gaul, now called Mascon. *Cæs. B. G*. 7. c. 90.

MATIS'SA, a town of Corsica. *Ptol*. It is now Matagi.

MA'TIUM, a city of Themiscyra, near Colchis. *Plin*. 4. c. 12.

MATRA'LIA, a festival at Rome, observed in honor of Matuta or Ino. Only matrons and free-born women were allowed to be present at the celebration. They made offerings of flowers and carried their relation's children in their arms, recommending them to the care and patronage of the goddess in preference to their own, in remembrance of the history of Ino and Melicerta, a custom which indirectly tended to introduce harmony and friendship into private families. *Varro de L.L*. 5. c. 22.—*Ovid. Fast*. 6. v. 47.—*Plut. in Cam. & Quæst. R*. 16 & 17.—*Resin. Ant. R*. 4. c. 10.

MAT'RICA, a town of Lower Pannonia. *Antonin*. It is now Thelen, according to *Simler*.

MATRI'NUS, a river of Picenum, near Adria. *Strab*. 5.—*Ptol*. It is thought by some to be now la Piomba.

MAT'RONA, a river of Gaul, now called the Marne, falling into the Seine. *Auson. Mos*. 462.

Matro'na, one of the surnames of Juno, because she presided over marriage and over child-birth.

MATRONA'LIA, festivals at Rome in honor of Mars, celebrated on the first of March by married women, in commemoration of the rape of the Sabines, and of the reconciliation which their intreaties had effected between their fathers and husbands. Flowers were then offered in the temples of Juno. *Ovid. Fast*. 3. v. 229.—*Plut. in Rom*.

MATTI'ACI, a nation of Germany, inhabiting the modern territory of Marpurg, in Hesse. The *Mattiacæ aquæ* was a small town, now Wissbaden, opposite Mentz. *Tacit. de Germ*. 29. *Ann*. 1. c. 56.

MAT'TIUS CN., a Latin poet, who wrote farces which were highly applauded for their wit and humor. He wrote also a poem in heroic verse, which he called the Iliad, but of all these compositions, which were once so much honored with public approbation, only fourteen lines have been preserved, collected in the Corpus Poetarum. It is said that he was intimate with Augustus, and that he discovered the method of cutting trees and groves into regular forms, and of innoculating and propagating trees. His three books on laying out a table are mentioned by *Columella*, 12. v. 144.—*Gellius*, 6. c. 6. l. 15. c. 25. l. 20. c. 9.—*Plin*. 15. c. 14.—*Cic. Att*. 15. ep. 2.—*Tacit. An*. 12. c. 60.—*Suet. Cæs*. 52.

MATUSA'RUM, a city of Lusitania. *Antonin*. It is now Puente de Sor.

MATU'TA, a deity among the Romans, the same as the Leucothoe of the Greeks. She was originally Ino, who was changed into a sea deity, (*vid*. Ino and Leucothoe), and was worshipped by sailors as such at Corinth, in a temple sacred to Neptune. Only married women and freeborn matrons were permitted to enter her temples at Rome. *Vid*. Matralia. *Liv*. 5. c. 23. l. 6. c. 33. l. 15. c. 7.—*Paus*. 2. c. 1.—*Ovid. Fast*. 6 v. 455, 480 & 545.—*Cic. de Nat. D*. 3. v. 19. *Tusc*. 1. c. 12.

MATYCE'TÆ, a nation of Scythia. *Steph*.

MAT'YLUS, a city of Pamphylia. *Ptol*.

MAU'MA, a city of Upper Æthiopia. *Plin*. 6. c. 29.

MAUREN'SII, a people of Mauritania Tingitana. *Ptol*.

MAU'RI, the inhabitants of Mauritania. This name was derived, according to some authors, from their black complexion (μαῦροι.) Every thing among them grew in greater abundance and greater perfection than in other countries. *Strab*. 17.—*Mart*. 5. epigr. 29. l. 12. epigr. 67.—*Sil. Ital*. 4. v. 569. l. 10. v. 402.—*Mela*, 1. c. 5. l. 3. c. 10.—*Justin*. 19. c. 2.—*Sallust. Jug*.—*Virg. Æn*. 4. v. 206.—*Lucan*. 3. v. 294. l. 4. v. 679. l. 9. v. 300. l. 10. v. 455.—*Manil*. 4. v. 720.

MAURICIUS JU'NIUS, a senator in the age of Domitian, by whom he was banished. *Tac. Hist*. 4. c. 40.—*Plin*. 4. ep. 22. & l. 1. ep. 5.

MAURITA'NIA or **MAURETA'NIA** a country

in the Western part of Africa, which forms the modern kingdoms of Fez and Morocco. It was bounded on the west by the Atlantic, on the south by Gætulia, and on the north by the Mediterranean, and is sometimes called Marusia. It became a province in the reign of the emperor Claudius. *Vid.* Mauri.

MAU'RUS ÆLIUS, a freedman of Phlegon Trallianus, wrote some works mentioned by *Spartian, in Severo.* c. 20.—*Voss. Hist. Lat.* 2. c. 2.

MAU'RUS TERENTIA'NUS. *Vid.* Terentianus.

MAURU'SII, the people of Maurusia, a country near the columns of Hercules. It is also called Mauritania. *Vid.* Mauritania. *Virg. Æn.* 4. v. 206.

MAU'SOCA, a city of Hyrcania. *Ptol.*

MAUSO'LI, a nation of the interior of Libya. *Id.*

MAUSO'LUS the First, a king of Caria. His wife Artemisia was so disconsolate at his death, which happened B.C. 353, that she drank up his ashes, and resolved to erect one of the grandest and noblest monuments ever known in ancient times, to celebrate the memory of a husband whom she tenderly loved. This famous monument, which passed for one of the seven wonders of the world, was called Mausoleum, and from it all other magnificent sepulchres and tombs have received the same name. It was built by four different architects. Scopas erected the side which faced the east, Timotheus finished the south, Leochares the west, and Bruxis the north. Pithis was also employed in raising a pyramid over this stately monument, and the top was adorned by a chariot drawn by four horses. The expenses of this edifice were immense, and this gave occasion to the philosopher Anaxagoras to exclaim, when he saw it "how much money changed into stones!" *Vid.* Artemisia. *Herodot.* 7. v. 99.—*Strab.* 14.—*Diod.* 16.—*Paus.* 8. c. 16.—*Flor.* 4. c. 11.—*Gell.* 10. c. 18.—*Propert.* 3. el. 2. v. 21.—*Suet. Aug.* 100.—*Plin.* 36. c. 5.—*Cic. Tusc.* 3. c. 31.

MAUSO'LUS the Second, joined the people of Byzantium, Rhodes, Cos, &c. against the Athenians.

MAU'SOS, a small town near Corinth. *Steph.*

MA'VORS, a name of Mars. *Vid.* Mars.

MAVOR'TIA, an epithet applied to every country the inhabitants of which were warlike, but especially to Rome, founded by Romulus, the reputed son of Mavors. *Virg. Æn.* 1. v. 280, and to Thrace, *Id.* 3. v. 13.

MAX'ALA, a city in the interior of Africa, taken by Corn. Balbus. *Plin.* 5. c. 5.

MAXEN'TIUS MAR'CUS AURE'LIUS VE'RUS, a son of the emperor Maximianus Hercules. The voluntary abdication of Diocletian, and of his father, raised him in the state, and he declared himself independent emperor or Augustus, A.D. 306. He afterwards incited his father to reassume the imperial authority, and in a perfidious manner destroyed Severus, who had delivered himself into his hands, and relied upon his honor for the safety of his person. His victories and successes were impeded by Galerius Maximianus, who opposed him with a powerful force. The defeat and voluntary death of Galerius soon restored peace to Italy, and Maxentius passed into Africa, where he rendered himself odious by his cruelty and oppression. He soon after returned to Rome, and was informed that Constantine was marching with an army to dethrone him. He gave his adversary battle near Rome, and after he had lost the victory, he fled back to the city The bridge over which he crossed the Tiber was in a decayed condition, and he fell into the river and was drowned, on the 24th September, A.D. 312. The cowardice and luxuries of Maxentius were as conspicuous as his cruelties. He oppressed his subjects with heavy taxes to gratify the cravings of his pleasures, or the avarice of his favorites. He was debauched in his manners, and neither virtue nor innocence were safe whenever he was inclined to voluptuous pursuits. He was naturally deformed, and of an unwieldy body. To visit a pleasure ground, or to exercise himself under a marble portico, or to walk on a shady terrace, was to him an Herculean task, which required the exertion of the greatest resolution. *Euseb. in Hist. & Vit. Constantin.*—*Zosin.* 2 & 3.—*Eutrop.* 1. 10, &c.

MAXE'RA, a river of Hyrcania. *Ptol.* It is now Firi.

MAXILU'A, a city of the Turdetani, in Bætica. *Ptol.*

MAXIMIA'NUS MAR'CUS AURE'LIUS VALE'RIUS HER'CULES, a native of Sirmium, in Pannonia, who served as a common soldier in the Roman armies. When Diocletian had been raised to the imperial throne, he remembered the valor and courage of his fellow soldier Maximianus, and rewarded his fidelity by making him his colleague in the empire, and by ceding to him the command of the provinces of Italy, Africa, and Spain, and the rest of the western territories of Rome. Maximianus showed the propriety of the choice of Diocletian, by his wisdom and his repeated victories over the barbarians. In Britain, however, success did not attend his arms; but in Africa he defeated and put to death Aurelius Julianus, who had proclaimed himself emperor. Soon after Diocletian abdicated the imperial purple, and obliged Maximianus to follow his example, on the 1st of April A.D. 304. Maximianus reluctantly complied with the command of a man to whom he owed his greatness; but before the first year of his resignation had elapsed, he was roused from his indolence and retirement by the ambition of his son Maxentius. He reassumed the imperial dignity, and showed his ingratitude to his son by wishing him to resign the sovereignty, and to retire to private life. This proposal was not only rejected with the contempt which it deserved, but the troops mutinied against Maximianus, and he fled for safety to Gaul, to the court of Constantine, to whom he gave his daughter Faustina in marriage. Here he again acted a perfidious character, and reassumed the imperial power, which his misfortunes had obliged him but a short time before to relinquish. This offended Constantine; and when nothing seemed capable of checking the ambitious views of Maximianus, he had recourse to artifice. He prevailed upon his daughter Faustina to leave the doors of her chamber open in the dead of night; and when she promised faithfully to execute his commands, he secretly introduced himself into a chamber, where he stabbed to the heart the man who slept by the side of his daughter. This was not Constantine: Faustina, faithful to her husband, had apprized him of her father's machinations, and a eunuch had been placed in his bed. Constantine watched the motions of his father-in-law, and, when he heard the fatal blow given to the eunuch, he rushed in with a band of soldiers, and secured the assassin. Constantine resolved to destroy a man who was so hostile to him, and nothing was left to Maximianus but to choose his own death. He strangled himself at Marseilles, A.D. 310, in the 60th year of his age. His body was found fresh and entire in a leaden coffin about the middle of the eleventh century. *Euseb.* l. 8.—*Eutrop.* l. 9.—*Oros.* l. 7.—*Amm. Marcell.* 16.—*Zosim.* l. 2.—*Socr.* l. 1.—*Theodoret.* l. 5, &c.

MAXIMIA'NUS GALE'RIUS VALE'RIUS, a native of Dacia, who, in the first years of his life, was employed in keeping his father's flocks. He afterwards entered the Roman armies, where his valor and bodily strength recommended him to the notice of his superiors, and particularly to Diocletian, who invested him with the imperial purple in the east, and gave him his daughter Valeria in marriage. Galerius deserved and enjoyed the confidence of his benefactor. He conquered the Goths and Dalmatians, and checked the insolence of the Persians. In a battle, however, with the king of Persia, Galerius was defeated; and, to complete his ignominy, and render him more sensible of his disgrace, Diocletian obliged him to walk behind his chariot arrayed in his imperial robes. This humiliation stung Galerius to the quick; he assembled another army, and marching against the Persians, he gained a complete victory, and took the wives and children of his enemy. This success elated Galerius to such a degree, that he claimed the most dignified appellations, and ordered himself to be called the son of Mars. Diocletian himself dreaded his power, and it is said that he was even induced to abdicate the imperial dignity by his threats. This resignation, however, is attributed by some to a voluntary act of the mind, and to a desire of enjoying solitude and retirement. As soon as Diocletian had abdicated, Galerius was proclaimed Augustus, A.D. 304, but his cruelty rendered him odious, and the Roman people offended at his oppression, raised Maxentius to the imperial dignity the following year, and Galerius was obliged to yield to the torrent of his unpopularity, and to flee before his more fortunate adversary. He died in the greatest agonies, A.D. 311. The bodily pains and sufferings which preceded his death, were, according to the Christian writers, the effects of the vengeance of an offended Providence for the cruelty which he had wantonly exercised against the followers of Christ. In his character Galerius was capricious and tyrannical, and he often feasted his eyes with the sight of dying wretches, whom his barbarity had delivered to bears and other wild beasts. His aversion to learned men arose from his ignorance of letters; and as he was deprived of the benefits of education, he proved the more cruel and inexorable. *Lactant. de M. P.* 33.—*Eusebius*, 8. c. 16.

MAXIMILIA'NA CORN., a vestal virgin, buried alive for incontinence, A.D. 92.

MAXIMI'NUS CA'IUS JU'LIUS, the son of a peasant of Thrace. He was originally a shepherd, but by heading his countrymen against the frequent attacks of the neighbouring barbarians and robbers, he inured himself to the labors and to the fatigues of a camp. He entered the Roman armies where he gradually rose to the first offices; and on the death of Alexander Severus he caused himself to be proclaimed emperor, A.D. 235. The popularity which he had gained when general of the armies, was unfortunately at an end when he ascended the throne. He was now delighted with acts of the greatest barbarity, and no less than 400 persons lost their lives on suspicion of having conspired against the emperor's life. They died in the greatest torments, and, that the tyrant might the better entertain himself with their sufferings, some were exposed to wild beasts, others expired by blows, some were nailed on crosses, while others were shut up in the bellies of animals just killed. The noblest of the Roman citizens were daily the objects of his cruelty; and, as if they were more conscious than others of his mean origin, he resolved to spare no means to remove from his presence a number of men whom he looked upon with an eye of envy, and who, as he imagined, hated him for his oppression, and despised him for the poverty and obscurity of his early years: so detestable was the character of the suspicious and tyrannical Maximinus. In his military capacity he acted with the same ferocity; and, in an expedition in Germany, he not only cut down the corn, but set fire to the whole country to the extent of 450 miles, and totally destroyed it. Such a monster of tyranny at last provoked the people of Rome. The Gordians were proclaimed emperors, but their innocence and pacific virtues were unable to resist the fury of Maximinus. After their fall, the Roman senate invested twenty men of their number with the imperial dignity, and entrusted the care of the republic to their hands. These measures so highly irritated Maximinus that, at the first intelligence he howled like a wild beast, and almost destroyed himself by knocking his head against the walls of his palace. When his fury was abated, he marched to Rome, resolved on revenge and indiscriminate slaughter. His bloody machinations were, however, stopped, and his soldiers, ashamed of accompanying a tyrant whose cruelties had procured him the name of Busiris, Cyclops, and Phalaris, assassinated him in his tent before the walls of Aquileia, A.D. 238, in the 65th year of his age. The news of his death was received with the greatest rejoicings at Rome, public thanksgivings were offered to the gods, and whole hecatombs flamed on the altars. Maximinus has been represented by historians as of a gigantic stature, he was eight feet high, and the bracelets of his wife served as rings to adorn the fingers of his hand. His voracity was as remarkable as his corpulence, and he is said generally to have eaten forty pounds of flesh every day, and to have drunk eighteen bottles of wine. His strength was proportionable to his gigantic shape; he could alone draw a loaded waggon, and with a blow of his fist he often broke the teeth in a horse's mouth; he also crushed the hardest stones between his fingers, and cleft trees with his hands. *Herodianus.*—*Jornand. de Reb. Get.*—*Capitol. in Maximin.*—*Euseb.* l. 6.—*Oros.* l. 7.—*Aurel. Victor. de Cæsar.* c. 41. [A bust of Maximinus will be found in the Capitol.]—Maximinus made his son, of the same name, emperor as soon as he was invested with the purple, and his choice was unanimously approved by the senate, by the people, and by the army.

MAXIMI'NUS C. VALE'RIUS, surnamed *Daza*, a shepherd of Thrace, was raised to the imperial dignity by Diocletian, A.D. 305. He was nephew to Galerius Maximianus, by his mother's side, and to him he was indebted for his rise and consequence in the Roman armies. As Maximinus was ambitious and fond of power, he looked with an eye of jealousy upon those who shared the dignity of emperor with himself. He declared war against Licinius, his colleague on the throne, but a defeat which soon after followed on the 30th of April, A.D. 313, between Heraclea and Adrianopolis, left him without resources and without friends. His victorious enemy pursued him, and he fled in terror beyond Mount Taurus, forsaken and almost unknown. He attempted to put an end to his miserable existence, but his efforts were ineffectual, and though his death is attributed by some to despair, it is more universally believed that he expired in the greatest agonies, worn out by a dreadful distemper which consumed him day and night with inexpressible pains, and reduced his body to a mere skeleton. This miserable end, according to the ecclesiastical writers, was the visible punishment of heaven, for the barbarities which Maximinus had exercised against the followers of Christianity, and for the many blasphemies which he had uttered. *Victor. de Cæsar.* c. 55 & 57.—*Eutrop.*—*Euseb.*—*Zosim. &c.* [There is a bust of him also, in the Capitoline Museum, which is called Maximus son of Maximinus the giant.]

MAXIMI'NUS, a minister of the emperor Valerian.

MAXIMI'NUS, one of the ambassadors sent by young Theodosius to Attila, king of the Huns.

MAX'IMUS FLA'VIUS MAG'NUS CLE'MENS, a native of Spain, who proclaimed himself emperor, A.D. 383. The unpopularity of Gratian favored his usurpation, and he was acknowledged by his troops. Gratian marched against him, but he was defeated, and soon after assassinated. Maximus refused the honors of a burial to the remains of the unhappy Gratian: and, when he had made himself master of Britain, Gaul, and Spain, he sent ambassadors into the East, and insolently demanded of the emperor Theodosius to acknowledge him as his associate on the throne. Theodosius endeavoured to amuse and delay him, but Maximus resolved to support his claim by arms, and crossed the Alps. Italy was laid desolate, and Rome opened her gates to the conqueror. Theodosius now determined to revenge the audacity of Maximus, and had recourse to artifice. He began to prepare a naval armament, and Maximus, not to appear inferior to his adversary, had already embarked his troops, when Theodosius, by secret and forced marches, fell upon him, and besieged him in Aquileia. Maximus was betrayed by his soldiers, and the conqueror, moved with compassion at the sight of his fallen and dejected enemy, granted him his life; but the multitude refused him mercy, and instantly struck off his head, A.D. 388. His son Victor, who had shared the imperial dignity with him, was soon after sacrificed to the fury of the soldiers. *Zosim.* l. 4.—*Theodoret.* l. 5.—*Socr.* l. 5.—*Pacat. in Paneg.*—*Paulin. in Ambros.*

MAX'IMUS PETRO'NIUS, a Roman, descended from an illustrious family. He caused Valentinian the Third to be assassinated, and ascended the imperial throne; and, to strengthen his usurpation he married the empress, to whom he had the weakness and imprudence to betray that he had sacrificed her husband to his love for her person. This declaration, instead of gaining the affections of the empress, excited her to revenge. She had recourse to the barbarians to aid her in punishing the murderer of Valentinian, and Maximus was stoned to death by his soldiers, and his body thrown into the Tiber, A.D. 455. He reigned only 77 days. *Procop. de Bell. Vandal.* l. 1.—*Evagr.* l. 2.—*Sidon. Apollin.* l. 2. ep. 23. *ad Sarran.*—*Nicephor.* l. 15, &c.

MAX'IMUS PUPIA'NUS. *Vid.* Pupianus.

MAX'IMUS, a celebrated cynic philosopher and magician of Ephesus. He instructed the emperor Julian in magic; and, according to the opinion of some historians, it was in the conversation and company of Maximus that the apostacy of Julian originated. The emperor not only visited the philosopher, but even submitted his writings to his inspection and censure. Maximus refused to live in the court of Julian, and the emperor, not dissatisfied with the refusal, appointed him high pontiff in the province of Lydia, an office which he discharged with the greatest moderation and justice. When Julian marched with his army into the East, the philosopher promised him success, and even said that his conquests would be more numerous and extensive than those of the son of Philip. He persuaded his imperial pupil that, according to the doctrine of metampsychosis, his body was animated by the soul which once animated the hero whose greatness and victories he was going to eclipse. After the death of Julian, Maximus was almost sacrificed to the fury of the soldiers, but the interposition of his friends saved his life, and he was permitted to retire to Constantinople. He was soon after accused of magical practices before the emperor Valens, and beheaded at Ephesus, A.D. 366. He wrote some philosophical and rhetorical treatises, some of which were dedicated to Julian. They are all now lost. *Ammian. Marcell.* 22. c. 29.—*Eunap. in vit. Philos.*—*Sozom.* l. 6.—*Socr.* l. 4.—*Zosim.* l. 4.—*Baron. in Annal.*

MAX'IMUS TYR'IUS, a Platonic philosopher, in the reign of M. Aurelius, of whose history but few authentic particulars are known. This emperor, who was naturally fond of study, became one of the pupils of Maximus, and paid great deference to his instructions. There are extant forty-one curious and instructive dissertations of Maximus on moral and philosophical subjects, in Greek, written in an easy and plain style. This valuable work was first brought into Italy from Greece by Janus Lascaris, and presented to Lorenzo de Medicis. The best editions are that of Davis, 8vo, Cantab. 1703; and that of Reiske, 2 vols. 8vo. Lips. 1774. *Volaterran.* l. 7. *Anthr. &c.*—*Fabr. B. Gr.* 4. c. 20.

MAX'IMUS, one of the Greek fathers of the 7th century, whose works were edited by Combesis, 2 vols. fol. Paris, 1675.

MAX'IMUS PAU'LUS FA'BIUS, a consul with M. Antony's son. *Horace* speaks of him, 4. od. 1. v. 10, as a gay, handsome youth, fond of pleasure, yet industrious and indefatigable.

MAX'IMUS, an epithet applied to Jupiter, as being the greatest and most powerful of all the gods.

MAX'IMUS, a native of Sirmium, in Pannonia. He was originally a gardener, but, by enlisting in the Roman armies, he became one of the military tribunes, and his marriage with a woman of rank and opulence soon rendered him independent. He was father to the emperor Probus.——A general of Trajan, killed in the eastern provinces.——One of the murderers of Domitian, &c.——A philosopher, native of Byzantium, in the age of Julian the emperor.——A sophist of Alexandria, author of some declamations. *Phot. cod.* 135.——A writer on the actions of Apollonius Tyanensis. *Philostr. in vit. huj.* l. c. 5.—*Tzetz. Chil.* 2. *Hist.* 291.——A grammarian of Madaura, who wrote to Augustine the epistle numbered 43, in that father's works.

MAXU'LA, a colony and town of Africa, now Marsa. *Antonin.*—*Plin.* 5. c. 4.

MAYL'LES, a son of Æneas, by Lavinia. *Apollod. in Euxen.*

MAZ'ACA, a large city of Cappadocia, the capital of the province. It was called Cæsarea by Tiberius, in honor of Augustus. It is now Tisaria.

MAZ'ACÆ, a people of Asiatic Sarmatia. *Plin.* 6. c. 7.

MAZ'ACES, a Persian governor of Memphis. He made a sally against the Grecian soldiers of Alexander, and killed great numbers of them. *Curt.* 4. c. 1.

MAZACY'LA, a city of Marmarica. *Ptol.*

MAZÆ'UM, a city of Bithynia. *Steph.*

MAZÆ'US, a satrap of Cilicia, under Artaxerxes Ochus. *Diod. Sic.* 16.——A governor of Babylon, son-in-law to Darius. He surrendered to Alexander, &c. *Curt* 5. c. 1.

MAZA'NÆ, a city of Palestine. *Steph.*

MAZ'ARA, a river of Sicily. *Diod.*

MAZ'ARA, a fortified place of the Selinuntii. *Steph.* ——A city of Armenia Major. *Ptol.*

MAZ'ARES, or MAZA'RES, a satrap of Media, who reduced Priene under the power of Cyrus. *Herodot.* 1. c. 161.

MAZ'ARIS, a city of Sicily. *Antonin.*

MAZAX'ES, (*sing. Mazax*), a people of Africa, famous for shooting arrows. *Lucan.* 4. v. 681.

MAZ'ERAS, a river of Hyrcania, falling into the Caspian Sea. *Plut.* 6. c. 78.—*Plin.* 6. c. 16.

MAZ'ICES, MAZI'CES, MAZY'GES, or MAZ'YGES, a people of Libya, very expert in the use of missile weapons. The Romans made use of them as couriers, on account of their great swiftness. *Suet. in Ner.* 30.—*Lucan.* 4. v. 684.

MAZORA'NI, a people of Aria, on the confines of Parthia and Carmania *Ptol.*

ME'ARUS or MET'ARUS, a river of Hispania Tarraconensis, now Rio Major. *Mela*, 3. c. 1.—*Ptol.*

MECHA'NEUS, or MECH'ANEUS, a surname of Jupiter, from his patronizing undertakings. He had a statue near the temple of Ceres at Argos, and there the Greeks swore, before they went to the Trojan war, either to conquer or perish in the expedition. *Paus.* 2. c. 22.

MECÆ'NAS or MECŒ'NAS C. CIL'NIUS, a celebrated Roman knight, descended from the ancient kings of Etruria. He has rendered himself immortal by his liberal patronage of learned men and of letters; and to his prudence and advice Augustus acknowledged himself indebted for the security which he enjoyed. His fondness for pleasure and ease removed him far from the reach of ambition, and he preferred living, as he was born, a Roman knight, to all the honors and dignities which either the friendship of Augustus or his own popularity could heap upon him. It was from the result of his advice, against the opinion of Agrippa, that Augustus resolved to keep the supreme power in his hands, and not plunge, by a voluntary resignation, Rome into civil commotions. The emperor received the private admonitions of Mecœnas in the same friendly manner as they were given, and he was not displeased with the liberty of his friend, who threw a paper to him with these words, *Descend from the tribunal, thou butcher!* while he sat in the judgment-seat, and betrayed revenge and impatience in his countenance. He was struck with the admonition, and abruptly left the tribunal without passing sentence of death on the criminals. To the interference of Mecœnas, Virgil owed the restitution of his lands, and Horace was proud to boast that his learned friend had obtained his forgiveness from the emperor, for joining the cause of Brutus at the battle of Philippi. Mecœnas was himself fond of literature, and, according to the most received opinion, he wrote a history of animals, a journal of the life of Augustus, a treatise on the different natures and kinds of precious stones, besides the two tragedies of Octavia and Prometheus, and other things, all now lost. He died eight years before Christ; and, on his deathbed, he particularly recommended his poetical friend Horace to the care and confidence of Augustus. Seneca, who has liberally commended the genius and abilities of Mecœnas, has not withheld his severest censure from his dissipation, indolence and effeminate luxury. From the patronage and encouragement which the princes of heroic and lyric poetry among the Latins deservedly received from the favorite of Augustus, all patrons of literature have ever since been called *Mecœnates.* Virgil dedicated to him his Georgics, and Horace his Odes. *Suet. in Aug.* 66, &c.—*Plut. in Aug.*—*Herodian.* 7.—*Senec.* ep. 19 & 92.

MECIS'TEUS, a son of Echius, or Talaus, was one of the companions of Ajax. He was killed by Polydamas. *Homer. Il.* 8. v. 333. l. 15. v. 339.—*Paus.* 2. c. 30.—*Apollod.* 1.——A son of Lycaon. *Apollod.*

ME'CON, a city of Peloponnesus, afterwards called Sicyon. *Strab.* 8.

MEC'RIDA, the wife of Lysimachus. *Polyæn.* 6.

MECYBER'NA, a town of Macedonia, in the peninsula of Pallene. *Plin.* 4. c. 10.

MECY'RA, a place of Marmarica. *Antonin.*

ME'DA, a city of Arabia Felix. *Ptol.*

MED'ABA, a city of the Nebathæi. *Steph.*

MED'AMA, a river and city of the Brutii. *Voss. ad Melam*, p. 168.

MEDE'A, a celebrated musician, daughter of Æetes, king of Colchis. Her mother's name, according to the more received opinion of Hesiod and Hyginus, was Idyia, or, according to others, Ephyre or Hecate, Asterodia, Antiope, or Neæra. She was the niece of Circe. When Jason came to Colchis in quest of the golden fleece, Medea became enamoured of him, and it was to her that the Argonauts owed their preservation. *Vid.* Jason & Argonautæ. Medea had a secret interview with her lover in the temple of Hecate, where they bound themselves by the most solemn oaths and mutually promised eternal fidelity to each other. No sooner had Jason overcome all the difficulties which Æetes had placed in his way, than Medea embarked with the conquerors for Greece. To stop the pursuit of her father, she tore to pieces her brother Absyrtus, and left his mangled limbs in the way through which Æetes was to pass. This act of barbarity some have attributed to Jason, and not to her. When Jason, reached Iolcus, his native country, the return and victories of the Argonauts were celebrated with universal rejoicings: but Æson, the father of Jason was unable to assist at the solemnity, on account of the infirmities of his age. Medea, at her husband's request, removed the weakness of Æson, and by drawing away the blood from his veins, and filling them again with the juice of certain herbs, she restored him to the vigor and sprightliness of youth. This sudden change in Æson, astonished the inhabitants of Iolcus, and the daughters of Pelias were also desirous to see their father restored, by the same extraordinary power, to the vigor of youth. Medea, willing to revenge the injuries which her husband's family had suffered from Pelias, increased their curiosity, and by cutting to pieces an old ram, and making it, in their presence a young lamb, she prevailed upon them to try the same experiment upon their father's body. They accordingly killed him of their own accord, and boiled the flesh in a cauldron, but Medea refused to perform the same friendly offices for Pelias which she had done for Æson, and his limbs were consumed by the heat of the fire, and even deprived of the honors of a burial. This action greatly irritated the people of Iolcus, and Medea, with her husband, fled to Corinth to avoid the just resentment of an offended populace. Here they lived for ten years with much conjugal tenderness; but the love of Jason for Glauce, the king's daughter, at last interrupted their mutual harmony, and Medea was divorced. Medea revenged the infidelity of Jason by causing the death of Glauce, and the destruction of her family. *Vid.* Glauce. This action was followed by another still more atrocious. Medea killed two of her children in her father's presence, and, when Jason attempted to punish the barbarity of the mother, she escaped from his vengeance through the air upon a chariot drawn by winged dragons. From Corinth Medea came to Athens, where, after she had undergone the necessary purification for the murder, she married king Ægeus, or, according to others, lived in an adulterous manner with him. From her connection with Ægeus Medea had a son, who was called Medus. Soon after, when Theseus wished to make himself known to his father (*vid.* Ægeus), Medea, jealous of his fame, and fearful of his influence, attempted to poison him at a feast which had been prepared for his entertainment. Her attempts, however, failed of success, and the sight of the sword which Theseus wore by his side, convinced Ægeus that the illustrious stranger against whose life he had so basely conspired, was no other than his own son. The father and the son were reconciled, and Medea, to avoid the punishment which her wickedness deserved, mounted her fiery chariot and disappeared through the air. She came to Colchis, where, according to some, she was reconciled to Jason, who had sought her in her native country after her sudden departure from Corinth. She died at Colchis, as *Justin* asserts, after she had been restored to the confidence of her family. After death, she married Achilles in the Elysian fields, according to the traditions mentioned by *Simonides*. The murder of Mermerus and Pheres, the youngest of Jason's children by Medea, is not attributed to their mother, according to Ælian, but the Corinthians themselves assassinated them in the temple of Juno Acræa. To avoid the resentment of the gods, and to deliver themselves from the pestilence which had visited their country after so horrid a massacre, they engaged the poet Euripides, for five talents, to write a tragedy, which cleared them of the imputation, and represented Medea as the cruel assassin of her own children. And besides, that this opinion might be the better credited, festivals were appointed, in which the mother was represented with all the barbarity of a fury murdering her own sons *Vid.* Heræa. *Apollod.* 1. c. 9.—*Hygin.* fab. 21, 22, 23, 26, &c.—*Plut. in Thes.*—*Dionys. Perieg.*—*Ælian. V.H.* 5. c. 21.—*Paus.* 2. c. 3. l. 8. c. 11.—*Eurip. in Med.*—*Diod.* 4.—*Ovid. Met.* 7. fab. 1. *in Med. Heriod.* 6 & 12. *Trist.* 3. el. 9. v. 25. *Fast.* 2. v. 41.—*Strab.* 7.—*Cic. de Nat. D.* 3. c. 19 & 26.—*Apollon. Argon.* 3, &c.—*Orpheus, Arg.* v. 864.—*Hesiod. Th.* 956 & 994.—*Homer. Odyss.* 12. v. 70.—*Tzetzes in Lyc.* 174.—*Servius in Ecl.* 8. v. 47. l. 2, *Georg.* 140. *Æn.* 2. v. 490.—*Schol. Apollon.* 3. v. 242. l. 4. v. 412, 460, &c.—*Schol. Eurip. in Med.* 117.—*Flacc.*—*Lucan.* 4. v. 556.

MEDE'NI, a people of Africa Propria. *Ptol.*

ME'DEON, or ME'DION, a city of Bœotia.——A city of Phocis, so called from Medeon, son of Pylades and Electra.——A city of Epirus. *Steph.*

MEDESICAS'TE, a daughter of Priam, who married Imbrius, son of Mentor, who was killed by Teucer, during the Trojan war. *Homer. Il.* 13. v. 172.—*Apollod.* 3.

ME'DIA, a celebrated country of Asia, bounded on the north by the Caspian Sea, west by Armenia, south by Persia, and east by Parthia and Hyrcania. It was originally called Aria till the age of Medus, the son of Medea, who gave it the name of Media. The province of Media was first raised into an independent kingdom by its revolt from the Assyrian monarchy, B.C. 820; and, after it had for some time enjoyed a kind of republican government, Deioces, by his wisdom and artifice, procured himself to be called king, 700 B.C. After a reign of 53 years he was succeeded by Phraortes, B.C. 647; who was succeeded by Cyaxares, B.C. 625. His successor was Astyages, B.C. 585, in whose reign Cyrus became master of Media, B.C. 551; and ever after the sovereignty was transferred to the Persians. The Medes were of a bold and warlike spirit in the primitive ages of their power; they encouraged polygamy, and were remarkable for the homage which they paid to their sovereigns, who were styled King of Kings. This pompous title was afterwards adopted by their conquerors, the Persians, and was still in use in the age of the Roman emperors. *Justin.* 1. c. 5.—*Herodot.* 1, &c.—*Polyb.* 5 & 10.—*Curt.* 5, &c.—*Diod. Sic.* 13.—*Ctesias.*

ME'DIAS, a tyrant of Scepsis, in Mysia Minor. *Xenoph. Hellen,* 1. 3.—*Polyæn.* 1. 2.

MEDIC'CARA, a town of Africa Propria. *Ptol.*

MEDIM'NI, a people of Æthiopia. *Plin.* 6. c. 30.

MEDIOLA'NUM, now Milan, the capital of Insubria, at the north of the Po. *Liv.* 5. c. 34. l. 34. c. 46.——A town of Britain. *Id.* It is now Lancaster. *Burton. in Antonin. Itin.* p. 132.

MEDIOLA'NUM AULERCO'RUM, a town of Gaul, now Evreux, in Normandy. *Ptol.*

MEDIOLA'NUM SANTO'NUM, a town of Gallia Aquitanica. *Id.* It is now Saintes, in Guienne.

MEDI'OLUM, a city of the Celtiberi, in Spain. *Ptol.*

MEDIOMAT'RICI, or MEDIOMAT'RICES, a nation that lived on the borders of the Rhine. Their chief town is Metz. *Strab.* 4.—*Cæs. Bell. G.* 4. c. 10.

ME'DION, a city near Ætolia. *Steph.*

MEDITERRA'NEUM MA'RE, a sea which divides Europe and Asia Minor from Africa. It receives its name from its situation, *medio terræ, in the middle of the land.* It has a communication with the Atlantic by the columns of Hercules, and with the Euxine through the Ægean. The word Mediterraneum does not occur in the classics; but the sea now so called is sometimes denominated *internum nostrum* or *medius liquor*, and frequently bears in Scripture the appellation of the *Great* Sea. The first naval power that ever obtained the command of it, as recorded in the fabulous pages of the writer Castor, was Crete, under Minos. Afterwards it passed into the hands of the Lydians, B.C. 1179; of the Pelasgi, 1058; of the Thracians, 1000; of the Rhodians, 916; of the Phrygians, 893; of the Cyprians, 868; of the Phœnicians, 826; of the Ægyptians, 787; of the Milesians, 753; of the Carians, 734; and of the Lesbians, 676, who retained it for 69 years. *Horat.* 3. od. 3. v. 46.—*Plin.* 2. c. 68.—*Sallust. Jug.* 17.—*Cæs. B. G.* 5. c. 1.—*Liv.* 26. c. 42.

MEDITRI'NA, the goddess of medicines, whose festivals, called *Meditrinalia*, were celebrated at Rome on the last day of September. *Varro de L.L.* 5. c. 3.

MEDITRINA'LIA, festivals at Rome, in honor of the goddess Meditrina, who was supposed to preside over the cure of disorders They were celebrated on the last day of September, when the first fruits of the vintage were offered as an oblation. *Varro de L.L.* 5. c. 3.—*Festus de V. Sig.*—*Voss. Orat. Inst.* 5.

ME'DIUS, a prince of Larissa, in Thessaly, who made war against Lycophron, tyrant of Pheræ. *Diod.* 14.

MED'MA, or MES'MA, a town of the Brutii. *Steph.*—*Plin.* 3. c. 5.

MED'MASUS, a city of Caria. *Steph.* It is called Medmassa by *Pliny*, 5. c. 29.

MED'ME a city of Italy, the citizens of which were called Medmæi.——A city of Liguria. *Steph.*

MEDO'ACUS or MEDU'ACUS, a river in the country of the Veneti, falling into the Adriatic Sea. *Liv.* 10. c. 2.—*Plin.* 3. c. 16. *Vid.* Meduacus.

MEDOBITHY'NI, a people of Thrace. *Casaubon. ad Strab.* l. 7.

MEDOBRI'GA, a town of Lusitania, between the rivers Anas and Tagus, now destroyed. *Hirtius*, 48.

ME'DON, son of Codrus, the 17th and last king of Athens, was the first archon that was appointed with regal authority, B.C. 1070. In the election Medon was preferred to his brother Neleus, by the oracle of Delphi, and he rendered himself popular by the justice and moderation of his administration. His successors were called from him *Medontidæ*, and the office of archon remained for above 200 years in the family of Codrus under 12 perpetual archons. *Paus.* 4. c. 5. l. 7. c. 2.—*Paterc.* 1. c. 2.——A man killed in the Trojan war. Æneas saw him in the infernal regions. *Virg. Æn.* 6. v. 483.——A statuary of Lacedæmon, who made a famous statue of Minerva, preserved in the temple of Juno at Olympia. *Paus.* 5. c. 17.——One of the Centaurs. *Ovid. Met.* 12. v. 303.——One of the Tyrrhene sailors changed into dolphins by Bacchus. *Id. Met.* 3. v. 671.——An illegitimate son of Ajax Oileus. *Homer.* 2. v. 727.——One of Penelope's suitors, whose life was spared by Ulysses, at the intercession of Telemachus. *Homer. Odyss.* 22. v. 356. l. 24. v. 438.—*Ovid. Heroid.* 1.——A man of Cyzicus, killed by the Argonauts. *Val. Flacc.* 3. v. 118.——A king of Argos, who died about 990 years B.C.——A son of Pylades and Electra. *Paus.* 2. c. 16.

ME'DON, a river of Peloponnesus. *Strab.*

MEDON'TIAS, a woman of Abydus, with whom Alcibiades cohabited. *Lysias.*

MEDOSAC'CUS, a king of the Sarmatæ. *Polyæn.* 8.

MEDU'ACUS, the name of two rivers, Major, now Brenta, and Minor, now Bachilione, near Venice, falling into the Adriatic Sea. *Plin.* 3. c. 16.—*Liv.* 10. c. 2. Also Medo'acus.

MEDUA'NA, a river of Gaul, flowing into the Ligeris, and now called the Mayne. *Lucan.* l. v. 438.

MEDUBRICEN'SES, a people of Spain, called also Plumberii. *Plin.* 4. c. 22.

MED'ULI, a people of Gallia Aquitanica. Their country is now Medoquins or Medoc. *Strab.*—*Plin.* 3. c. 20.

MEDUL'LIA, a town of Latium, built by the Albini. *Steph.*

MEDULLI'NA, a Roman virgin, to whom her father offered violence, &c. *Plut. in Parall.*——An infamous courtezan in the Juvenal's age. *Juv.* 6. v. 321.

MEDUL'LUM, a city of Vindelicia. *Ptol.*

ME'DUS, now Kur, a river of Media, falling into the Araxes. Some take Medus adjectively as applying to any of the great rivers of Media. *Strab.* 15. —*Horat.* 2. od. 9. v. 21.

ME'DUS, a son of Ægeus and Medea, who gave his name to a country of Asia. Medus, when arrived at years of maturity, went to seek his mother, whom the arrival of Theseus in Athens had driven away. *Vid.* Medea. He came to Colchis, where he was seized by his uncle Perses, who had usurped the throne of Æetes. Medus assumed another name, and called himself Hippotes, son of Creon. Meanwhile Medea arrived in Colchis, disguised in the habit of a priestess of Diana, and when she heard that one of Creon's children was imprisoned, she resolved to hasten the destruction of a person whose family she detested. To effect this with greater certainty, she told the usurper, that Hippotes was really a son of Medea, sent by his mother to murder him. She begged Perses to give her Hippotes, that she might sacrifice him to her resentment. Perses consented. Medea discovered that it was her own son, and she instantly armed him with the dagger which she had prepared against his life, and ordered him to stab the usurper. He obeyed, upon which Medea discovered who she was, and placed her son Medus on his grandfather's throne. *Hesiod. Theog.* v. 994.—*Hygin.* fab. 27.—*Paus.* 2. c. 3.—*Tzetzes. in Lyc.* 175.—*Eustath. in Dionys. Per.* 1017.—*Apollod.* 1.—*Justin.* 42. c. 2 & 3.—*Senec. in Med.*—*Diod*

ME'DUS, a tragedy written by Pacuvius. *Cic. Off.* 1. c. 31.

MEDU'SA, one of the three Gorgons, daughter of Phorcys and Ceto. She was the only one of the Gorgons who was subject to mortality. She was celebrated for her personal charms and the beauty of her locks. Neptune became enamoured of her, and obtained her favours in the temple of Minerva. This violation of the sanctity of the temple provoked Minerva, who changed the beautiful locks of Medusa, which had inspired Neptune's love, into serpents. According to Apollodorus and others, Medusa and her sisters came into the world with snakes on their heads instead of hair, and with yellow wings and brazen hands. Their bodies were also covered with impenetrable scales, and their very looks had the power of killing or turning to stones. Perseus rendered his name immortal by the conquest of Medusa. He cut off her head, and the blood that dropped from the wound produced the innumerable serpents that have ever since infested Africa. The conqueror placed Medusa's head on the ægis of Minerva, which he had used in his expedition. The head still retained the same petrifying power as before, as was fatally known in the court of Cepheus. *Vid.* Andromeda. Some suppose that the Gorgons were a nation of women, whom Perseus conquered. *Vid.* Gorgones. *Apollod.* 2. c. 4.—*Hesiod. Theog.* v. 278. *In Scuto.* 225.—*Æschyl. in Prom.* 4.—*Pind. Pyth.* 7 & 12.—*Stat. Theb.* 1. v. 594.—*Martial.* 9. epigr. 26.—*Hygin.* fab. 151 & 164. *A. P.* 2. c. 12.—*Servius in Æn.* 2. v. 616. l. 6. v. 289.—*Schol. Apollon.* 4. v. 1090.—*Palæphat. de Inc.* 1.—*Plin.* 6. c. 31.—*Cœl. Rhod.* 18. c. 38.—*Tzetzes in Lyc.* 838.—*Ovid. Met.* 4. v. 618.—*Lucan.* 9 v. 624.—*Apollon.* 4.—[There is a fine head of Medusa in the Palace of the Conservators at Rome.] ——A daughter of Priam. *Apollod.*——A daughter of Sthenelus. *Id.*

MEDYL'LAI, a colony of the Romans, founded by the Albini. *Steph.*

ME'GA, a promontory of Mauritania Cæsariensis. *Ptol.*

MEGABY'ZI or MEGALOBY'ZI, certain priests who attended in Diana's temple at Ephesus. They were all eunuchs. *Quintil.* 5. c. 12.—*Plin.* 35. c. 10.—*Strab.* 14,—*Meurs. Gr. Fer.*

MEGABY'ZUS or MEGABA'ZUS, one of the noble Persians who conspired against the usurper Smerdis. He was placed at the head of an army in Europe by king Darius, where he took Perinthus and conquered all Thrace. He was greatly esteemed by his sovereign. *Herodot.* 3, &c.——A son of Zopyrus, a satrap of Darius. He conquered Ægypt, &c. *Herodot.* 3. c. 160 —*Thucyd.* l. 1.—*Schol. Aristoph. in Av.*——A satrap of Artaxerxes. He revolted from his king, and defeated two large armies that had been sent against him. The interference of his friends restored him to the king's favor, and he showed his attachment to Artaxerxes by killing a lion which threatened his life in hunting. This act of affection in Megabyzus was looked upon with envy by the king. He was discarded from his favor, though afterwards reconciled to the monarch by means of his mother. He died in the 76th year of his age, B.C. 447, greatly regretted. *Ctesias.*

MEG'ACLES, an Athenian archon, who involved the greatest part of the Athenians in the sacrilege which was committed in the conspiracy of Cylon. *Plut. in Sol.*——The sixth perpetual archon of Athens, who reigned 30 years in the age of Sesostris. *Joh. Marsham. Can. Chron. Sec.* 15.——A brother of Dion, who assisted his brother against Dionysius, &c.——A son of Alcmæon, who revolted with some Athenians after the departure of Solon from Athens. He was ejected by Pisistratus, *Polyæn. in Pisistr.*——A man who exchanged dress with Pyrrhus when assisting the Tarentines in Italy. He was killed in that disguise.——A native of Messana in Sicily, famous for his inveterate enmity to Agathocles, tyrant of Syracuse. *Polyæn.* 5. c. 2.——A man who destroyed the leading men of Mitylene, because he had been punished by them. *Aristot. Pol.* 5 c. 10.——A man who wrote an account of the lives of illustrious persons. *Athen.* 1. 10.——The maternal grandfather of Alcibiades.

MEGACLI'DES, a peripatetic philosopher in the age of Protagoras. *Laertius.*

MEGÆ'RA, one of the furies, daughter of Nox and Acheron. The word is derived from μεγαίρειν, *invidere, odisse*, and she is represented as employed by the gods, like her sisters, to punish the crimes of mankind, by visiting them with diseases, with inward torments, and with death. *Virg. Æn.* 12. v. 846. *Vid.* Eumenides.

MEGA'LIA, a small island opposite Smyrna. *Plin.* 5. c. 31.

MEGALAR'TUS, a name under which Ceres was worshipped. *Cœl. Rhod.* 9. c. 16.

MEG'ALE, the Greek name of Cybele, the mother of the gods, whose festivals were celebrated with great solemnity. *Vid.* Megalesia.

MEGA'LEAS, a seditious person of Corinth. He was seized in consequence of his treachery to Philip, king of Macedonia, upon which he destroyed himself to avoid punishment.

MEGALE'SIA, games in honor of Cybele, instituted by the Phrygians, and introduced at Rome during the second Punic war, when the statue of the goddess was brought from Pessinus, in obedience to the Sibylline books, which promised victory when Cybele's image had reached the city. It was deposited, on the 12th of April, in the temple of Victory on the Palatine hill, where the festivals were solemnly celebrated in the midst of a great concourse of people. *Varro. de L.L.* 5. c. 3.—*Cic. de Arusp.* 12.—*Liv.* 29. c. 14.—*Ovid. Fast.* 4. v. 337.

MEGA'LIA, a small island on the coast of Campania, near Neapolis. *Stat.* 2. *Sylv.* v. 80.

MEGALOBY'SÆ. *Vid.* Megabyzi.

MEGALOP'OLIS, a town of Arcadia in Peloponnesus, built by Epaminondas. It joined the Achæan league, B.C. 232, and was taken and ruined by Cleomenes, king of Sparta. The inhabitants were called *Megalopolitæ*, or *Megalopolitani*. *Strab.* 8. —*Paus.* 9. c. 14.—*Liv.* 28. c. 8.——A city of Caria. ——A city of Iberia. *Steph.*

MEGALOS'TRATA, a poetess, intimate with Alcman. *Athen.*

MEGAME'DE, the wife of Thestius, mother, by him, of 50 daughters. *Apollod.* 2.

MEGANI'RA, the wife of Celeus, king of Eleusis in Attica. She was mother of Triptolemus, to whom Ceres, as she travelled over Attica, taught agriculture. She received divine honors after death, and had an altar raised to her honor, near the fountain where Ceres had first been seen when she arrived in Attica. *Paus.* 1. c. 39.——The wife of Arcas. *Apollod.*

MEGAPEN'THES, an illegitimate son of Menelaus, who, after his father's return from the Trojan war, was married to a daughter of Alector, a native of Sparta. His mother's name was Teridae, a slave in the family of Menelaus. *Homer. Odyss.* 4. v. 8.—*Apollod.* 3.——A son of Prœtus king of Tirynthus. He succeeded his father, and afterwards reigned at Argos. *Apollod.* 2.—*Tzetzes in Lyc.* 838.

MEG'ARA, a daughter of Creon, king of Thebes, given in marriage to Hercules, because he had delivered the Thebans from the Orchomenians. *Vid.* Erginus. When Hercules visited the infernal regions by order of Eurystheus, violence was offered to Megara by Lycus, a Theban exile, and she would have yielded to her ravisher, had not Hercules returned that moment and punished him with death. This murder highly displeased Juno, and she rendered Hercules so delirious, that he, in a fit of madness, killed Megara and the three children whom he had by her, thinking them to be wild beasts. Some say that Megara did not perish by the hand of her husband, but that he afterwards married her to his friend Iolas. The names of Megara's children by Hercules were Creontiades, Therimachus, and Deicoon. *Pindar. Isthm.* 4. v. 109.—*Hygin.* fab. 32.—*Senec. in Herc.* —*Apollod.* 2. c. 6.—*Diod.* 4.

MEG'ARA, (-æ, and *pl.*-orum) a city of Achaia, the capital of a country called Megaris, founded about 1131 B.C. It is situate nearly at an equal distance from Corinth and Athens, on the Sinus Saronicus. It was built upon two rocks, and is still in being, and preserves its ancient name. It received its name from Megareus a son of Neptune, who was buried there, or from Megareus, a sôn of Apollo. It was originally governed by twelve kings, but became afterwards a republic, and fell into the hands of the Athenians, from whom it was rescued by the Heraclidæ. At the battle of Salamis the people of Megara furnished twenty ships for the defence of Greece, and at Platæa they had 300 men in the army of Pausanias. There was here a sect of philosophers called the Megaric, who regarded the world as eternal. *Cic. Acad.* 4. c. 42. *Orat.* 3. c. 17. *Att.* 1. ep. 8.—*Paterc.* 1. c. 2.—*Ptol.* 3. c. 15. *Paus.* 1. c. 39.—*Strab.* 6.—*Mela*, 2. c. 3.—*Voss. de Philos. sect.* c. 11.

MEG'ARA, a town of Sicily, at the mouth of the river Alabus, on the sea coast at the north of Syracuse, founded by a colony from Megara in Greece, about 728 B.C. It was destroyed by Gelon king of Syracuse. Before the arrival of the Megarean colony it was called *Hybla parva*. *Strab.* 26, &c.—*Virg. Æn.* 3. v. 689.

MEGARE'US, or MEG'AREUS, the father of Hippomenes, was son of Onchestus. According to Hyginus he was son of Neptune and Œnope, and married Merope. *Ovid. Met.* 10. v. 605.—*Hygin.* fab. 157 & 185.——A son of Creon, who defended Thebes against Adrastus and the Argives. *Æsch. Sept. contra. Theb.*——A son of Apollo.

MEGAR'ICUM, a small town of Bithynia. *Steph.*

MEG'ARIS, a small country of Greece, between Phocis on the west and Attica on the east. Its capital city was called Megara. *Vid.* Megara. *Strab.* 8.—*Plin.* 3. c. 8.—*Mela*, 2. c. 3 & 7.

MEG'ARIS, the sister of Theagenes, and wife of Cylon *Schol. Aristoph. Equit.*

MEGAR'SUS, a town of Sicily. *Lycoph.*——A town of Cilicia, at the mouth of the Pyramis.——A river of India. *Dionys.*

MEGA'SA, a city of Libya. *Steph.*

MEGAS'THENES, a Greek historian in the age of Seleucus Nicanor, who lived about 300 B.C. He wrote about the oriental nations, and particularly the Indians. His history is often quoted by the ancients. What now passes as his composition is spurious. *Voss Hist Gr.* 11. p. 54.—*Sax. Onom.* 1. p. 92.

MEGATI'CHOS, a town on a mountain between Ægypt and Æthiopia. *Plin.* 6. c. 29.

ME'GES, one of Helen's suitors, governor of Dulichium and of the Echinades. He went with forty ships to the Trojan war. *Homer. Il.* 2. 627. l. 5. v. 69. l. 15. v 302.—*Hygin.* fab. 97.—*Euripid. in Iphig. Aul.* 284.—*Dictys. Cret.* 1. c. 13 & 17.—*Apollod.* 3. ——A Trojan chief wounded by Admetus of Argos, on the night when Troy was taken. *Paus.* 10. c. 25.

MEGIL'LA, a native of Locris, remarkable for beauty, and mentioned by *Horace*, 1. od. 27. v. 11.

MEGIS'BA, a lake of the island of Taprobane. *Plin.* 6. c. 22.

MEGIS'TA, an island of Lycia, with a harbour of the same name. *Liv.* 37. c. 22. It is now Strongallo, according to some authors.

MEGIS'TIAS, a soothsayer who told the Spartans who defended Thermopylæ, that they should all perish, &c. *Herodot.* 7. c. 219, &c.

MEGIS'TIAS, a river. *Vid.* Mella.

ME'LA POMPO'NIUS, a Spaniard, born at Tingentera, or at Carteia, according to others, flourished about 45 A.D. and distinguished himself as the author of a geography divided into three books, and written with elegance, great perspicuity, and brevity. The best editions of this book called *De Situ Orbis*, are those of Jac. Gronovius, 8vo, L. Bat. 1683; republished by his son with important additions in 1748; of Is. Vossius, Hagæ Com. 1658; and of Reynolds, 4to, Eton, 1761. *Mela*, 2. c. 6.—*Harles. Not. Lit. Rom.* 1. p. 347,—*Sax. Onom.* 1. p. 243.

MEʹLA, a Roman, intimate with Antony. *Cic. Plin.* 13. c. 2.

MELÆʹCA, a village of Attica. *Stat. Theb.* 12. v. 619.

MELÆʹNA, an island of the Ionian Sea, called also Corcyra. *Plin.* 3. c. 26.

MELÆʹNE, an ancient name of Cephallenia. *Plin.* 4. c. 12.

MELÆʹNE, a town of Arcadia, so called from Melenæus, son of Lycaon. *Steph.—Plin.* 4. c. 6.

MELÆNEʹIS, a village of the tribe Antiochis. *Steph.*

MELAMPEʹA, a city of Lydia. *Id.*

MELAMʹPUS, a celebrated soothsayer and physician of Argos, son of Amythaon and Idomenea, or Dorippe. He lived at Pylus in Peloponnesus. His servants once killed two large serpents, which had made their nests at the bottom of an oak, and Melampus paid so much regard to these two reptiles, that he raised a funeral pile and burned them upon it. He also took particular care of their young ones, and fed them with milk. Some time after this the young serpents crept to Melampus as he slept on the grass, near the oak, and, as if sensible of the kindness of their benefactor, wantonly played round him, and softly licked his ears. This awoke Melampus, who was astonished at the sudden change which his senses had undergone. He found himself acquainted with the chirping of the birds, and with all their rude notes, as they flew around him. He took advantage of this supernatural gift, and soon made himself perfect in the knowledge of futurity, and Apollo also instructed him in the art of medicine. He had soon after the happiness of curing the daughters of Prœtus, by giving them ellebore, which from this circumstance has been called *melampodium*, and, as a reward for his skill, he received the eldest of these princesses in marriage. *Vid.* Prœtides. The tyranny of his uncle Neleus, king of Pylus, obliged him to leave his native country, and Prœtus, to show himself more sensible of his services, gave him part of his kingdom, over which he established himself. About this time the personal charms of Pero, the daughter of Neleus, had gained many admirers, but the father promised his daughter to him only who should deliver into his hands the oxen of Iphiclus. This condition displeased many of the suitors, but Bias, who was also one of her admirers, engaged his brother Melampus to steal the oxen, and to deliver them to him. Melampus was caught in the attempt, and imprisoned, and nothing but his services to Iphiclus as a soothsayer and physician would have saved him from instant death. All this pleaded in favour of Melampus, but when he had taught the childless Iphiclus how to become a father, he not only obtained his liberty, but also the oxen, and with them he compelled Neleus to give Pero in marriage to Bias. A severe distemper, which had rendered the women of Argos insane, was afterwards happily removed by Melampus; and Anaxagoras, who then sat on the throne, rewarded his services by giving him part of his kingdom, where he established himself, and where his posterity reigned during six successive generations. He received divine honors after death and temples were raised to his memory. *Homer. Odyss.* 11. v. 287. l. 15. v. 225.—*Lactant. ad Theb.* 1. v. 670. l. 3. v. 453.—*Propert.* 2. el. 2. v. 15.—*Herodot.* 2 & 9.—*Apollod.* 2. c. 2.—*Paus.* 2. c. 18. l. 4. c. 3.—*Virg. Ecl.* 6. v. 48. *G.* 3. v. 550.—*Servius ad Virg. loc. cit.*—*Sax. Onom.* 1. p. 6 & 103.—*Fabr. B. Gr.* 1. c. 15.——The father of Cisseus and Gyas. *Virg. Æn.* 10.——A son of Priam. *Apollod.* 3.

MELAMʹPUS, one of Actæon's dogs. *Ovid. Met.* 3. v. 207.

MELAMʹPYGES, a surname of Hercules, from the black and hairy appearance of his back, &c.

MELAʹNA, a promontory of Chius. *Strab.*

MELANCHÆʹTES, one of Actæon's dogs, so called from his *black hair*. *Ovid. Met.* 3.

MELANCHLÆʹNI, a people near the Cimmerian Bosporus. *Mela*, 2, c. 1.

MELANʹCHRUS, a tyrant of Lesbus, who died about 612 B.C.

MELANʹDIA, a region of Sicyonia. *Steph.*

MELʹANE, one of the ancient names of Samothrace. *Plin.* 4. c. 12.

MELANEʹA, a town of Arcadia. *Id.* 4. c. 6.

MELANEʹIS, a city of Eubœa. *Steph.* It was also called Eretria and Arotria, according to *Strabo*.

MELʹANES, black mountains, near the deserts of Arabia. *Ptol.*

MELʹANEUS, or MELAʹNEUS, the father of Eurytus, from whom Eretria has been called Melaneïs.

MELʹANEUS, a Centaur. *Ovid. Met.* 12. v. 306.——One of Actæon's dogs. *Id.* 3. v. 223.——An Æthiopian, killed at the nuptials of Perseus. *Id.* 5. v. 128.

MELANGEʹA, a town of Arcadia. *Pausan.* l. 8.

MELANGIʹTÆ, a nation of Arabia Felix. *Ptol.*

MELAʹNIA, a town of Cilicia. *Strab.*

MELAʹNION, the same as Hippomenes, who married Atalanta, according to some mythologists. *Apollod.* 3.—*Paus.* 3. c. 12.—*Palæphat.* 14.

MELANIPʹPE, a daughter of Desmontes, or Æolus, who had two children by Neptune, for which criminal conduct her father put out both her eyes, and confined her in a prison. Her children, called Bœotus and Æolus, who had been exposed and preserved, delivered her from confinement, and Neptune restored to her her eye-sight. She afterwards married Metapontus, whose wife Theano had wished to adopt her two sons, and then attempted to murder them. This story employed the pen of *Euripides*, and likewise that of *Accius*, who both made it the subject of a tragedy. *Hygin.* 186.—*Cic. Off.* 1. c. 31.—*Varro R. R.* 2. c. 5.—*Dionys. Hal. Rh.* 57.——A nymph who married Itonus, son of Amphictyon, by whom she had Bœotus, who gave his name to Bœotia. *Paus.* 9. c. 1.

MELANIPʹPIDES, a Greek poet who flourished about 520 B.C. He was son of Crito and wrote epigrams, elegies, hymns, and two poems, the one upon Marsyas, and the other on the Danaides. His grandson, of the same name, flourished about sixty years after, at the court of Perdiccas the Second, of Macedonia, and wrote some tragedies, one of which was called Proserpine. Some fragments of their poetry are extant, quoted by *Athenæus*, 14., by *Clem. Alex. Stromat.*—*Suidas.*—*Gyrald. de P. Hist.* 9.—*Grotius.*

MELANIPʹPUS, a priest of Apollo, at Cyrene, killed by the tyrant Nicocrates. *Polyæn.* 8.——A son of Astacus, one of the Theban chiefs who defended the gates of Thebes against the army of Adrastus king of Argos. He was opposed by Tydeus, whom he slightly wounded, and was at last killed by Amphiaraus, who carried his head to Tydeus as a trophy. Tydeus, to take revenge for the wound which he had received, bit the head with such barbarity that he swallowed the brains, and Minerva, offended with his conduct, took away the herb which she had given to him to cure his wound, and he, in consequence, died. *Apollod.* 1. c. 8.—*Æschyl. Sept. contra Theb.*—*Paus.* 9. c. 18.——A son of Mars, who became enamoured of Cometho, a priestess of Diana Triclaria. He concealed himself in the temple, and offered violence to his mistress, for which offence against the sanctity of the place, the two lovers soon after perished by a sudden death, and the country was visited by a pestilence, which was stopped only after the offering of a human sacrifice by the direction of the oracle. *Paus.* 7. c. 19.——A Trojan killed by Antilochus in the Trojan war. *Homer. Il.* 15. v. 545.——A Trojan killed by Patroclus. *Homer. Il.* 16. v. 694.——A Trojan killed by Teucer. *Ib.* 8. v. 276.——A son of Agrius.——A son of Priam.——A son of Theseus.

MELANIPʹPUS, a river of Pamphylia. *Steph.*

MELAʹNO, an island of Doris, in the Sinus Ceramicus. *Plin.* 5. c. 31.

MELANOGÆTUʹLI, a nation of Æthiopia, in the interior of Libya. *Ptol.*

MELANOSʹYRI, a people of Syria. *Strab.*

MELANʹTHII, rocks near the island of Samus. *Strab.* But read Melantii. *Apollon. Argon.* l. 4.

MELANʹTHIUS, a river of Cappadocia, discharging itself into the Euxine Sea. *Plin.* 6. c. 4.

MELANʹTHIUS, a man who wrote a history of Attica. *Harpocrat.*—*Athen.* l. 7.——A famous painter of Sicyon, who wrote on his art. *Plin.* 35. c. 7.—*Diog. Laert. in Polem.*——A tragic poet in the age of Phocion, of a very malevolent disposition. *Plut. in Cimon.*—*Suidas.*—*Voss. Hist.* l. 3. p. 385. *Poet. Gr.* c. 7. p. 46.——A Trojan killed by Eurypylus in the Trojan war. *Homer. Odyss.*——A goatherd of Ulysses, who assisted Penelope's suitors in the plunder of his master's property. He shared the fate of the suitors, but as he had wantonly insulted Ulysses, he was the last put to death, after enduring several indignities. *Homer. Odyss.* 17. v. 212. l. 20. v. 174. l. 22, v. 135.—*Paus.* 10. c. 25.—*Tzetzes in Lyc.* 775.—*Ovid.* 1 *Heroid.* v. 95.

MELAN'THO, a daughter of Proteus, to whom Neptune, under the form of a dolphin, offered violence. *Ovid. Met.* 6. v. 12.——One of Penelope's women, sister to Melanthius. She followed the example of her brother in her abuse of the confidence of her mistress and the plunder of her property, and she was likewise put to death. *Homer. Odyss.* 18. v. 320. l. 19. v. 65. *Homer. Il.* 18, &c.

MELAN'THUS, a son of Andropompus, whose ancestors were kings of Pylus. He was driven from his paternal kingdom by the Heraclidæ, and came to Athens, where king Thymœtes resigned the crown in his favor, on condition that he should fight a battle against Xanthius, a general of the Bœotians, who had made war against him. He fought and conquered (*vid.* Apaturia,) and his family, surnamed the Neleidæ, sat on the throne of Athens, till the age of Codrus. He succeeded to the crown of Athens 1128 years B.C. and reigned 37 years. *Paus.* 2. c. 18.—*Conon. Narr.* 39.——A man of Cyzicus, slain in a nocturnal engagement. *Flacc.* 3. v. 203.——A river of European Sarmatia, falling into the Borysthenes. *Ovid. Pont.* 4. ep. 10. v. 55.

MELAN'TIAS, now Melitias, a city of Thrace, on the Propontis. It is called Athyra by *Suidas* and *Procopius*; Melancia, by *Antoninus*; and *villa Cæsariana*, by *Ammianus Marcellinus.*

ME'LAS, a son of Neptune, by a nymph of Chius. *Paus.* 7. c. 4.——A son of Proteus. *Homer. Il.* 14. v. 117.——A Greek, son of Antasus of Gonusa. *Paus.* 2. c. 4.——A son of Phryxus, who was among the Argonauts, and was drowned in a part of the sea which bore his name. *Apollod.* 1.—*Eustath. ad Dionys. Per.* 536.—*Schol. Apollon.* 1. v. 922.

ME'LAS, a river of Mygdonia. *Ovid. Met.* 1. 2.——A river of Asia Minor, near Smyrna. *Solin.* c. 43. ——A river which divides Cilicia from Pamphylia. *Plin.* 5. c. 27. It is now Crionero.——A river of Bœotia, the waters of which were said to possess the property of turning black the color of the wool of such sheep as drank there. *Plin.* 2. c. 103.—*Virg. G.* 1. 4.—*Dionys.* 415.——A river of Thrace, which was not large enough to supply the army of Xerxes with water. *Herod.*——A river in Sicily, at the north of the island, west of Pelorum. *Ovid. Fast.* 4.—*Cluver. Sicil. Antiq.* 2. c. 5.——A river of Cappadocia, near Cæsarea. *Paus.* 9. c. 38.—*Ptol.* 3. c. 11.—*Herodot.* 7. c. 58 & 198.—*Strab.* 8, 9 & 12.—*Mela*, 1. c. 14. l. 2. c. 2.—*Liv.* 36, c. 22. l. 38. c. 40.

MELCOMA'NI, a people of Dalmatia. *Plin.* 3. c. 22.

MEL'DÆ or MELDO'RUM URBS, a city and people of Gallia Lugdunensis, now Meaux, in Champagne. *Ptol.*

MEL'DITA, a town of Africa Propria. *Id.*

MELEA'GER, a celebrated hero of antiquity, son of Œneus, king of Ætolia, by Althæa, daughter of Thestius. The Parcæ were present at the moment of his birth, and predicted his future greatness. Clotho said, that he would be enterprising and courageous; Lachesis foretold his uncommon strength; and Atropos declared that he should live as long as the fire-brand, which was then on the fire, remained entire and unconsumed. Althæa no sooner heard this than she snatched the stick from the fire, and kept it with the most jealous care, as the life of her son was destined to depend upon its preservation. The fame of Meleager increased with his years; he signalized himself in the Argonautic expedition, and afterwards delivered his country from the incursions of the neighbouring inhabitants, who made war against his father at the instigation of Diana, whose altars Œneus had neglected. *Vid.* Œneus. No sooner were these destroyed than Diana punished the negligence of Œneus by a greater calamity. She sent a huge wild boar, which laid waste all the country, and seemed invincible on account of its immense size and great ferocity. It became soon a public concern, all the neighbouring princes assembled to destroy this terrible animal, and nothing became more famous in mythological history than the hunting of the Calydonian boar. The princes and chiefs that assembled, and who are mentioned by mythologists, were Meleager son of Œneus, Idas and Lynceus sons of Aphareus, Dryas son of Mars, Castor and Pollux sons of Jupiter and Leda, Pirithous son of Ixion, Theseus son of Ægeus, Anceus and Cepheus sons of Lycurgus, Admetus son of Pheres, Jason son of Æson, Peleus and Telamon sons of Æacus, Iphicles son of Amphitryon, Eurytrion son of Actor, Atalanta daughter of Schœneus, Iolas the friend of Hercules, the sons of Thestius, Amphiaraus son of Oileus, Protheus, Cometes, the brothers of Althæa, Hippothous son of Cercyon, Leucippus, Adrastus, Ceneus, Phileus, Echeon, Lelex, Phœnix son of Amyntor, Panopeus, Hyleus, Hippasus, Nestor, Menœtius the father of Patroclus, Amphicides, Laertes the father of Ulysses, and the four sons of Hippocoon. This troop of armed men attacked the boar with great and determined bravery, and it was at last killed by Meleager. The conqueror gave the skin and the head to Atalanta, who had first wounded the animal. This partiality to a woman, irritated the others, and particularly Toxeus and Plexippus, the brothers of Althæa, and they endeavoured to deprive Atalanta of the honorable present. Meleager defended a woman of whom he was enamoured, and whom he had thus honorably distinguished, and killed his uncles in the attempt. Meantime the news of this celebrated conquest had already reached Calydon, and Althæa went to the temple of the gods to return thanks for the glorious victory which her son had gained. As she went she met the corpses of her brothers that were brought from the chase, and at this mournful spectacle she filled the whole city with her lamentations. She was upon this informed that they had been killed by Meleager, and in the moment of resentment, to revenge the death of her brothers, she threw into the fire the fatal stick, on which her son's life depended, and Meleager died as soon as it was consumed. Homer does not mention the fire-brand, whence some have imagined that this fable is posterior to that poet's age. He, however, says, that the death of Toxeus and Plexippus so irritated Althæa, that she uttered the most horrible curses and called down imprecations upon the head of her son. Meleager had married Cleopatra, the daughter of Idas and Marpessa, as also Atalanta, according to some accounts. *Apollod.* 1. c. 8.—*Antonin.* 1. *Arg.* 1. v. 997. l. 3, v. 518.—*Paus.* 10. c. 31.—*Hygin.* 14.—*Ovid. Met.* 8. v. 452.—*Homer. Il.* 9. v. 539 & 562.—*Nicander. apud. Anton. Liber.* 2.—*Val. Flacc.* 1. v. 435. l. 6. v. 719.—*Tzetzes. in Lyc.* 493. [The finest statue of Meleager is in the Museum of the Capitol.]——A general, who supported Aridæus when he had been made king of Macedonia, after the death of his brother Alexander the Great. *Curt.* 3. c. 9.—*Justin.* 13. c. 2.——A brother of Ptolemy, made king of Macedonia B.C. 280 years. He was invested with the regal authority only two months. *Pausan. in Peoc.*—*Justin.* 24. c. 5.——A Greek poet in the reign of Seleucus, the last of the Seleucidæ, about 150 years B.C. He was born at Gadara, a town of Syria, and died at Cos. It is to his well-directed labors, that we are indebted for the Anthologia, or collection of Greek epigrams, which he selected from forty-six of the best and most esteemed poets. The original collection of Meleager has been greatly altered and improved by succeeding editors. The best edition of the Anthologia is that of Brunck in three vols. 4to, and 8vo, Angentor. 1772, in which the poems of Meleager, mostly epigrams, amounting to 129, display great elegance and genuine wit. *Fabr. B Gr.* 3 c. 32.—*Sax. Onom.* 1. p. 142.

MELEA'GRIDES, the sisters of Meleager, daughters of Œneus and Althæa. They were so disconsolate at the death of their brother Meleager, that they refused all aliments, and were at the point of death, changed into birds called Meleagrides, guinea-hens, the feathers and eggs of which, as it is supposed, are of a different color. The youngest of the sisters Gorge and Dejanira, who had been married, escaped this metamorphosis. *Apollod.* 1. c. 8.—*Ovid. Met.* 8. v. 540.—*Plin.* 10. c. 26.—*Lactant. ad Theb.* 8. v. 483.—*Anton. Liber.* 2.

MELEGE'NE, an island in the Adriatic Sea, near Dalmatia. *Ptol.*

MELEN'DA, a city of India within the Ganges. *Ptol.*

ME'LES, a king of Lydia, who succeeded his father Alyattes on the throne, about 747 B.C. He was father of Candaules. *Herodot.* 1. c. 84.——A beautiful Athenian youth, greatly beloved by Timagoras, whose affections he repaid with the greatest coldness and indifference. He even ordered Timagoras to leap down a precipice, from the top of the citadel of Athens, and Timagoras, not to disoblige him, obeyed, and was killed in the fall. This token of true friendship and devoted affection had such an effect upon Meles, that he threw himself down from the same place, to atone by his death for the ingratitude which he had shown to Timagoras. *Paus.* 1. c. 30.—*Suidas.*—*Gyrald. de P. Hist.* 7.

Me'les (-ētis,) a river of Asia Minor, in Ionia, near Smyrna. Some of the ancients supposed that Homer was born on the banks of that river, from which circumstance they call him *Melesigenes*, and his compositions *Meletææ chartæ*. It is even asserted by some authors that he composed his poems in a cave near the source of that river. *Strab.* 12. —*Stat.* 2 *Sylv.* 7. v. 34.—*Tibull* 4. el. 1. v. 201.—*Paus.* 7. c. 5.—*Plin.* 5. c. 20.—*Homeri Vita*, 3.

MELESAN'DER, an Athenian general, who died B.C. 414.

MELESIG'ENES or MELESIG'ENA, a name given to Homer. The poet, it is said, was blind, and he begged for support from the people of Cumæ, promising that in return he would render their city the most illustrious of all the colonies of Greece. His petition was disdainfully rejected by the magistrates of the place, and the poet from that time was no longer called Melisegenes, by those who admired his talents and pitied his poverty, but Homer, which, in the language of Cumæ, signified the blind man. *Herodot.*—*Dionys. et Plut. in Vitâ.*—*Strab.* 12. *Vid* Meles.

MEL'ETE, one of the four Muses, daughter of the second Jupiter, mentioned by *Cicero. N. D.* 3. c. 21.

ME'LIA, a daughter of Oceanus, who married Inachus. *Apollod.* 2. c. 1.——A nymph, mother of Pholus by Silenus. *Id.* 2. c. 5.——A daughter of Oceanus, sister to Caanthus. She became mother of Ismarus and Tenerus by Apollo. Tenerus was endowed with the gift of prophecy, and the river Ladon, in Bœotia, received the name of Ismarus. *Schol. Apollon.* 1. v. 537.—*Sch. Sophoc. in Œdip. Ty.* 20.—*Paus.* 9. c. 10.——One of the Nereides. ——A daughter of Agenor.

MELIBŒ'A, a daughter of Oceanus, who married Pelasgus. *Apollod.* 3. c. 8.——A daughter of Amphion and Niobe. *Id.* 3. c. 5.

Melibœ'a, a maritime town of Magnesia in Thessaly, at the mouth of the Peneus, and at the foot of mount Ossa, famous for dying wool. The epithet of *Melibœus* is applied to Philoctetes, because he reigned there. *Virg. Æn.* 3. v. 401. l. 5. v. 251.—*Herodot.* 7. c. 188.—*Homer. Il.* 2. *enum.* 224.—*Strab.* 6.—*Lucan.* 6. v. 354.—*Plin.* 4. c. 9.——A small island at the mouth of the Orontes in Syria, whence *Melibœa purpura*. *Mel.* 2. c. 3.

MELIBŒ'US, a shepherd introduced in *Virgil's* Eclogues.

Melibœ'us, a mountain of Italy. *Isac. in Lycoph.*

MELICER'TES, a son of Athamas and Ino. He was saved by his mother from the fury of his father, who prepared to dash him against a wall as he had done his brother Learchus. The mother was so terrified at the inhuman conduct of her husband, that she threw herself into thesea, with Melicerta in her arms. Neptune had compassion on the misfortunes of Ino and her son, and changed them both into sea deities. Ino was called Leucothoe or Matuta, and Melicerta was known among the Greeks by the name of Palæmon, and among the Latins by that of Portumnus. Some suppose that the Isthmian games were instituted in honor of Melicerta. *Vid.* Isthmia. *Apollod.* 1. c. 9. l. 3. c. 4.—*Paus.* 1. c. 44.—*Hygin.* fab. 1 & 2.—*Ovid. Met.* 4. v. 529, &c. *Fast.* 6. v. 494 & 547.—*Schol. Pind. Pyth.* 4.—*Lactant. de Fals. R.* 21.—*Plut. Symp.* 5. *Quæst.* 5. [Melicerta is represented in the arms of Ino, in a group in the Villa Albani, near Rome. It has been called Leucothea with an infant Bacchus, but Ino and Leucothea being the same, it is evident that it is intended for Ino and Melicerta.]

MELIE'I or MELIEN'SES, a people of Thessaly. *Steph.*

MELIGU'NIS, one of the Æolian islands near Sicily the same as Lipara. *Callim. Hymn. in Dian.*—*Bochart. de Phœnic.* *Colon.* 1. c. 27.

MELI'NA or MELI'NE, a daughter of Thespius, mother of Laomedon, by Hercules. *Apollod.* 2. c. 7.

Meli'na, a city of Argolis, whence Venus was called Melinea. *Steph.*

MELINOPH'AGI, a people of Thrace. *Steph.*

MELIODU'NUM, a city of Germany. *Ptol.* According to *Lazias* it is now Mileusko.

MELIP'IA, a town of Mœsia. *Antonin.*

MELISAN'DER, a Milesian who wrote a poem on the battle of the Centaurs and Lapithæ. *Ælian. V. H.* 11. c. 2.—*Joh. Marsham. Can. Chron.* sec. 15.

MEL'ISA, or MEL'ISE, a town of Magna Græcia. *Ovid. Met.* 15. fab. 1.

MELIS'SA, a daughter of Melissus, king of Crete, who, with her sister Amalthæa, is said to have fed Jupiter with the milk of goats. She first found out the means of collecting honey; whence some have imagined that she was changed into a bee, as her name is the Greek word for that insect. *Columell.* 100.——One of the Oceanides, who married Inachus by whom she had Phoroneus and Ægialus. *Apollod.* 2.——A daughter of Procles, who married Periander, the son of Cypselus, by whom, in her pregnancy, she was killed with a blow of his foot, in consequence of the false accusation of his concubines. *Diog. Laert.*—*Paus.* 1. c. 28.——A woman of Corinth, who refused to initiate others into the festivals of Ceres, after she had received admission. She was torn to pieces upon this disobedience, and the goddess made a swarm of bees rise from her body. *Servius in Æn.* 1. v. 430.

MELIS'SUS, a king of Crete, father of Melissa and Amalthæa. *Hygin. P. A.* 2. c. 13.—*Lactant.* 1. c. 22.—*Columella*, 2. c. 2.——A philosopher, who was also an admiral of the Samian fleet, B.C. 441. He was defeated by Pericles. He maintained that the world was infinite, immoveable, and without a vacuum. According to his doctrines, no one could advance any argument upon the power or attributes of providence, as all human knowledge was weak and imperfect. Themistocles was among his pupils. He flourished about 440 B.C. *Euseb. in Chron.*—*Diog. Laert.* l. 9.—*vit. Philos.*—*Cic. Acad* 4. c. 37.——A freedman of Mecænas, appointed librarian to Augustus. He wrote some comedies, now lost. *Ovid. Pont.* 4. ep. 16. v. 30.—*Sueton. de Gram.*

MEL'ITA, an island in the Mediterranean Sea, between Sicily and Africa, now called Malta. The soil was fertile, and the country famous for its wool. It was first peopled by the Phœnicians, and after the fall of their power it was possessed by the Carthaginians, and was at last conquered by the Romans during the second Punic war, by Sempronius the consul. St. Paul was shipwrecked there and cursed all venomous creatures, which are not now to be found in the whole island. Some, however, and perhaps with greater probability, from the account of the accident given in the Acts of the Apostles, suppose that the island on which the apostle was shipwrecked was the island of the same name in the Adriatic on the coast of Illyricum, now called Medele. Malta was the residence of the knights of Malta, formerly of St. John of Jerusalem, who settled there A.D. 1530, by the permission of Charles V., after their expulsion from Rhodes by the Turks. *Strab.* 6.—*Mela*, 2. c. 7.—*Cic. in Ver.* 4. c. 46.—*Liv.* 21. c. 57. —*Ovid. Fast.* 3. v. 567.—*Ital.* 14. v. 252.——An island on the coast of Illyricum, in the Adriatic, now Melede. *Plin.* 3. c. 26.——A town of the Brutii, now Mileto. *Cic. Ver.* 6.

Mel'ita, an ancient name of Samothrace. *Strab.* 10.

MELITÆEN'SES, a people of Phthiotis. Their town is called Melitara by *Ptolemy*, Melitea by *Strabo*.

MEL'ITE, a village of the tribe Œneis. *Steph.*—*Plin.* 4. c. 7.—*Plut. in Solon.* *Harpocration*, however, assigns it to the tribe Cecropis. *Jac. Spon. Itin. Gr. Part.* 3. p. 168.

Mel'ite, one of the Nereides. *Virg. Æn.* 5. v. 825. —*Hom. Il.* 18. v. 42.

MELITE'NE, a province of Susiana, on the river Tigris. *Ptol.*——A city of Cappadocia. *Steph.*

MEL'ITO, a bishop of Sardes, in the second century. He presented an excellent apology for the Christians to the emperor M. Aur. Antoninus. He wrote also various other works which have perished. *Euseb. in Chron. A. C.* 170.—*Hieron. de Script. Eccles.* c. 24.—*Sax. Onom.* 1. p. 319.—*Fabr. B. Gr.* l. 5. c. 1, &c.

MELITOP'OLIS, a city of Bithynia. *Strab.*

MELIT'TA, a city built by Hanno on the Atlantic Sea. *Arrian. in Peripl.*

MELITTÆ'A, a city of Thessaly. *Steph.*

MELI'TUS, a poet and orator of Athens, who, urged by malice and envy, became one of the principal accusers of Socrates. After his eloquence had prevailed, and Socrates had been put ignominiously to death, the Athenians repented, though too late, of their severity to the philosopher, and condemned his accusers. Melitus perished among them. His character was mean and insidious, and his poems had nothing great or sublime. *Diog.* 2 *in Socr.* & 6 *in Anth.—Suidas.—Gyrald. de P. H.* 7.—*Voss. de Poet. Gr.* c. 7.——A son of Jupiter and the nymph Othreis, exposed by his mother for fear of the resentment of Juno. He was miraculously fed by bees, and saved by a shepherd, and when grown up he signalized himself, and built in Thessaly a city to which he gave his name. *Nicander apud Anton. Liber.* 13.

MELITUS'SA, a city of Illyria. *Steph.*

ME'LIUS SP., a Roman knight accused of aspiring to the sovereign power, on account of his uncommon liberality to the populace. He was summoned to appear before the dictator L. Q. Cincinnatus, and when he refused to obey, he was put to death by Ahala, the master of horse, A.U.C. 314. *Varro de L. L.* 4.—*Val. Max.* 6. c. 3.—*Liv.* 4. c. 13.—*Cic. Cat.* 1. c. 1. *Dom.* 38. *Sen.* 16.

MELIXAN'DRUS. *Vid.* Melisander.

MELIZIG'ARA, a town of India within the Ganges. *Arrian. in Peripl.*

MEL'LA or ME'LA, a small river of Cisalpine Gaul, falling into the Ollius, and with it into the Po. *Catull.* 68. v. 33.—*Virg. G.* 4. v. 278.

MEL'LA ANNÆ'US, the father of Lucan. He was accused of being privy to Piso's conspiracy against Nero, upon which he opened his veins and bled to death. *Tacit.* 16. *Ann.* c. 17.

MELLISUR'GIS, a town of Macedonia between Thessalonica and Apollonia. *Antonin.*

MELLO'NA, a rural deity worshipped by the Romans, because she was supposed to preside over bees and honey, *Aug. de Civ. Dei.* 4. c. 44.—*Arnob.* 4.—*Gyrald. de Hist. D.* 1.

MELOB'OSIS, or MELOB'OTE, one of the Oceanides. *Hesiod. L. Theog.* v. 354.

MELOC'ABUS, a city of Germany. *Ptol.* It is now Coburg.

ME'LON, an astrologer, who feigned madness and burnt his house that he might not go upon an expedition, which he knew would be attended with great calamities. *Plut. in Niciâ.*——An interpreter of King Darius. *Curt.* 5. c. 13.

MEL'PES, now Molpa, a small river of Lucania, falling into the Tyrrhene Sea. *Plin.* 3. c. 5.

MELPI'A, a village of Arcadia. *Paus.* 3. c. 38.

MELPOM'ENE, one of the Muses, daughter of Jupiter and Mnemosyne. She presided over tragedy. The ode of Horace, addressed to her, as the patroness of lyric poetry, was considered so beautiful by Scaliger, that he wished rather to be the author of it than king of Arragon. Melpomene was generally represented as a young woman with a serious countenance. Her garments were splendid; she wore a buskin, and held a dagger in one hand, and in the other a sceptre and crowns. *Horat.* 3. od. 4.—*Hesiod. Theog.* 52 & 915. [The finest statues of Melpomene are in the Vatican. One is of colossal size, but is inferior in beauty to the smaller.]

ME'LUS, now Milo, an island at the east of Argolis, about twenty-four miles from Scyllæum, about sixty miles in circumference, and of an oblong figure. It enjoyed its independence for above 700 years before the time of the Peloponnesian war. This island was originally peopled by a Lacedæmonian colony, 1116 B.C.; and for this reason the inhabitants refused to join the rest of the islands and the Athenians against the Peloponnesians. This refusal, though so honorable to them, was severely punished. The Athenians took Melus, and put to the sword all such as were able to bear arms. The women and children were made slaves, and the island left desolate. An Athenian colony repeopled it, till Lysander reconquered it, and re-established the original inhabitants in their possessions. The island produced a kind of earth successfully employed in painting and medicine. *Strab.* 7.—*Mela*, 2. c. 7.—*Plin.* 4. c. 12. l. 35. c. 6. —*Thucyd.* 2. &c.—*Festus de V. Sig.*

ME'LUS, a son of Manto. *Steph.*

MELZITA'NUM, a town of Africa Propria. *Plin.* 5, c. 5.

MEMAC'ENI, a powerful nation of Asia, &c. *Curt.* 7. c. 6.

MEMBRE'SA, a city of Africa Propria. *Antonin.*

MEM'MIA SULPIT'IA, a woman who married the emperor Alexander Severus. She died when young. *Lamprid. in Alexandr.* c. 20.

MEM'MIA LEX, ordained that no one should be entered on the calendar of criminals who was absent on the public account. *Cic. in Vatin.—Val. Max.* 3. c. 7.

MEM'MIUS, a Roman citizen, accused of *ambitus*. *Cic. ad Fratrem.* 3.——A tribune who severely inveighed against the pride and corruption of the nobility during the Jugurthine war. When a candidate for the consulship against Glaucia, he was shamefully assassinated by the partisans of his competitor. *Sallust. Jug.* 27, 30, 31.—*Cic. Br.* 36. *Orat.* 2. c. 70. *Cat.* 4. c. 2. *Appian. B. C.* 1. p. 369. ——A Roman who accused Jugurtha before the Roman people——A lieutenant of Pompey, &c. —The family of the Memmii were plebeians. They were descended, according to some accounts, from Mnestheus the friend of Æneas. *Virg. Æn.* 5. v. 117.

MEM'MIUS CA'IUS GEMEL'LUS, a Roman knight, who rendered himself illustrious by his eloquence and poetical talents. He was accused of improper intrigues during his canvassing for the consulship, for which he was condemned and banished to Athens. It is supposed that he had an improper intercourse with the wives of Lucullus and Pompey. Lucretius dedicated his poem to him. *Cic. in Brut.* 70. *Att.* 1. c. 18. l. 4. ep. 16 & 18. l. 6. ep. 1.

MEM'MIUS REG'ULUS, a Roman of whom Nero observed, that he was the firmest support and safeguard of the empire. *Tac. Ann.* 14. c. 47.

MEM'NON, a king of Æthiopia, son of Tithonus and Aurora. He came with a body of 10,000 men to assist his uncle Priam, during the Trojan war, where he behaved with great courage, and killed Antilochus, Nestor's son. The aged father challenged the Æthiopian monarch, but Memnon refused it on account of the venerable age of Nestor, and accepted that of Achilles. He was killed in the combat in the sight of the Grecian and Trojan armies. Aurora was so disconsolate at the death of her son, that she flew to Jupiter, bathed in tears, and begged the god to grant her son such honors as might distinguish him from other mortals. Jupiter consented, and immediately a numerous flight of birds issued from the burning pile on which the body was laid, and, after they had flown three times round the flames, they divided themselves into two separate parties, and fought with such acrimony that above half of them fell down into the fire, as victims to appease the manes of Memnon. These birds were called *Memnonides;* and it was observed by some of the ancients, that they never failed to return yearly to the tomb of Memnon in Troas, and repeat the same bloody engagement, in honor of the hero from whom they received their name. The Æthiopians or Ægyptians, over whom Memnon reigned, erected a celebrated statue to honor the memory of their monarch. This statue had the wonderful property of uttering a melodious sound every day, at sun-rising, like that which is heard at the breaking of the string of a harp when it is wound up. This was effected, as it is conjectured, by the rays of the sun when they fell upon it. At the setting of the sun, and in the night, the sound was lugubrious. The existence of this phenomenon is asserted by the testimony of the geographer Strabo, who professes himself ignorant whether it proceeded from the basis of the statue, or from the people that were then around it. This celebrated statue was dismantled by order of Cambyses, when he conquered Ægypt, and its ruins still astonish modern travellers by their imposing grandeur and beauty. Memnon was the inventor of the alphabet, according to *Anticlides*, a writer mentioned by *Pliny*, 7. c. 56.—*Mosch. in Bion.—Ovid. Met.* 13. v. 578, &c.—*Ælian.* 5. c. 1. —*Paus.* 1. c. 42. l. 10. c. 31.—*Strab.* 13 & 17. *Juv.* 15. v. 5.—*Plin.* 36. c. 7.—*Quint. Calab.* 2. v. 99, 120, 234, 308, 570 & 646.—*Philostr. in Icon.* 1. c. 7. —*Hygin.* fab. 112.—*Hesiod. Theog.* 984.—*Homer. Odyss.* 4. v. 186.—*Solin.* 43.—*Tacit.* 2. *Ann.* 61. [A colossal head is placed in the British Museum, which was imported from Ægypt, under the care of the celebrated Belzoni, as the head of the famous statue of Memnon.]——A general of the Persian forces, when Alexander invaded Asia. He distinguished himself for his attachment to Darius, for his valor in the field, the soundness of his counsels, and his great sagacity. He defended Miletus against Alexander, and died in the midst of his successful enterprises, B.C. 333. His wife Barsine was taken prisoner with the wife of Darius. *Diod.* 16.——A governor of Cœlesyria. *Curt.* 4. c. 8.——A man appointed governor of Thrace by Alexander. *Diod. Sic.* 17. c. 7.——A man who wrote a history of Heraclea in Pontus, in the age of Augustus. *Phot. Cod.* 224.—*Voss. Hist. Gr.* c. 5. p. 182.—*Sax. Onom.* 1. p. 181. *Fabr. B. Gr.* c. 38.

MEMNO'NES, a people of Æthiopia. *Plin.* 6. c. 30.

MEM'PHIS, a celebrated town of Ægypt, on the western banks of the Nile, above the Delta. It once contained many beautiful temples, particularly those of the god Apis, (*bos Memphites*), whose worship was observed by the Ægyptians with the greatest solemnity. *Vid.* Apis. It was in the neighbourhood of Memphis that those famous pyramids were erected, the grandeur and beauty of which still astonish the modern traveller. These noble monuments of Ægyptian vanity, which pass for one of the wonders of the world, are about 20 in number, three of which, by their superior size, particularly claim attention. The largest of these is 481 feet in height measured perpendicularly, and its base covers 480,249 square feet, or something more than 11 English acres of ground. It has steps all round, with massy and polished stones, so large that the breadth and depth is formed of one single stone. The smallest stone used in the building, according to an ancient historian, is not less than 30 feet in length. The number of steps, according to modern observation, amounts to 208, a number which is not always assented to as correct by travellers. The place where Memphis formerly stood is not now known, the ruins of its fallen grandeur were from time to time conveyed to Alexandria, to beautify its palaces, or adorn the neighbouring cities. *Tibull.* 1. el. 7. v. 28. *Sil. It.* 14. v. 660.—*Strab.* 17.—*Mela*, 1. c. 9.—*Diod.* 1.—*Plut. in Isid.* —*Herodot.* 2. c. 10, &c.—*Joseph. Ant. Jud.* 8. c. 6. *Lucan.* 1. v. 640. l. 3. v. 222. l. 4, &c.

MEM'PHIS, a nymph, daughter of the Nile, who married Epaphus, by whom she had Libya. She gave her name to the celebrated city of Memphis. *Apollod* 2. c. 1.—*Hygin.* fab. 149.——The wife of Danaus. *Apollod.* 2. c. 1.

MEMPHI'TIS, a son of Ptolemy Physcon, king of Ægypt. He was put to death by his father.

MEMP'SIS, a person against whom Arrhibæus made war. *Polyæn.* 7. c. 30.

ME'NA or ME'NES, the first king of Ægypt, according to some accounts, A.M. 1251. *Diod. Sic.*

ME'NA, a goddess worshipped at Rome, and supposed to preside over the monthly infirmities of women. She was supposed by some authors to be the same as Juno. The sacrifices offered to her were young puppies that still sucked their mother. *Aug. de Civ. Dei.* 4. c. 2.—*Plin.* 29. c. 4.

MEN'ACHUS, a son of Ægyptus, who married Nelo. *Apollod.* 2. c. 1.

MENÆ'NUM or ME'NÆ, an inland town of Sicily. *Plin.* 4. c. 10.—*Diod. Sic.*—*Cluver. Sic. Ant.* 2. c. 9. The people are called Menenii by *Cicero*, *Verr.* 3.

MENÆCH'MUS, a Platonic philosopher, pupil of Eudoxus.——An historian of Sicyon. *Voss. Hist. Gr.* 1. c. 11.

MENAL'CAS, a shepherd, frequently introduced in Virgil's eclogues.

MENAL'CIDAS, an intriguing Lacedæmonian in the time of the Achæan league. He was accused before the Romans, and killed himself.

MENALIP'PE, a sister of Antiope, queen of the Amazons, taken by Hercules, when that hero made war against this celebrated nation. She was ransomed, and Hercules received in exchange the arms and belt of the queen. *Juv.* 8. v. 229.——A daughter of the Centaur Chiron, beloved by Æolus, son of Hellen, who offered violence to her. She retired into the woods to hide her disgrace from the eyes of her father, and when she had brought forth, she entreated the gods to remove her totally from the pursuit of Chiron. She was changed into a mare, and called Ocyroe. Some suppose that she assumed the name of Menalippe, and lost that of Ocyroe. She became a constellation called the horse, after death. Some authors call her Hippe or Evipper *Hygin P.A.* 2. c. 18.—*Pollux*, 4.—*Eratosth. Catast.* 18.—*Sch. Juv.* 8. v. 229.——Menalippe is a name common to other persons, but it is generally spelt *Melanippe* by the best authors. *Vid.* Melanippe.

MENALIP'PUS. *Vid.* Melanippus.

MENAN'DER, a celebrated comic poet of Athens, educated under Theophrastus. He was universally esteemed by the Greeks, and received the appellation of Prince of the New Comedy. He did not disgrace his compositions, like Aristophanes, by mean and indecent reflections and illiberal satire, but his writings were replete with elegance, refined wit, and judicious observations. So favorable was the public opinion with regard to his poetical merit, that not only Greece honored the productions of his genius, but the kings of Ægypt and Macedonia, with a liberality which reflects honor on their memory, sent ambassadors to invite him to their courts. Of 108 comedies which he wrote, nothing remains but a few fragments. It is said that Terence translated all these, and indeed we have cause to lament the loss of such valuable writings, when we are told by the ancients that the elegant Terence, so much and so deservedly admired at Rome, was, in the opinion of his countrymen reckoned inferior to Menander. It is said that Menander drowned himself in the 52nd year of his age. B.C. 293, because the compositions of his rival Philemon obtained more applause than his own. Only eight of his numerous comedies were rewarded with a prize. The name of his father was Diopythus, and that of his mother Hegistrata. His fragments, with those of Philemon, were published by Clericus, 8vo. 1709. Much information with respect to this poet and his works may be gathered from the "Emendationes" of Dr. Bentley, Cantab. 1714, the "Infamiæ emendationum, &c." of Jac. Gronovius, Lug. Bat. 1710, and the "Philargirii Cantabrigiensis emendationes, &c." of Corn. de Pauw. Amstel. 1711. *Fabr. B. Gr.* 2. c. 22.—*Sax. Onom.* 1. p. 87.—*Quintil.* 10. c. 1.—*Paterc.* 1. c. 16.—*Aul. Gell.* 17. c. 4.—*Suidas.*—*Gyrald. de P. Hist.* 7.—*Plin.* 7. c. 39.—*Sueton. in Ter.*—*Phœd.* 5. fab. 1.—*Hor.* 2. sat. 3. v. 11.—*Propert.* 3. el. 21. v. 28.—*Ovid. Trist.* 2. v. 309. [There is a fine statue, a sitting figure, in the Museum of the Vatican; and a double terminus of Menander and Posidippus in the Neapolitan Museum.]——A man who wrote an account of embassies, &c.——A king of Bactria, whose ashes were divided among his subjects, &c. ——An historian of Ephesus. *Voss. Hist. Gr.* 3. p. 386.——An historian of Pergamus. *Tatian. adv. gent.*—*Clem. Alex. Strom.* 2.——An Athenian general defeated at Ægospotamos by Lysander.——An Athenian sent to Sicily with the troops under the command of Nicias.——A man put to death by Alexander, for deserting a fortress of which he had the command.——An officer under Mithridates, sent against Lucullus.—For other persons of this name see *Harles'* note on *Fabricius B. Gr.* 2. c. 22.

MENA'PIA, a city of Bactriana. *Ptol.*

MENA'PII, a people of Belgic Gaul, near the river Mosa. *Cæs. B. Gell.*

MEN'APIS, a Persian exile, made satrap of Hyrcania, by Alexander. *Curt.* 6. c. 4.

ME'NAS, a freedman of Pompey the Great, who distinguished himself by the active and perfidious part which he took in the civil wars which were kindled between the younger Pompey and Augustus. When Pompey invited Augustus to his galley, Menas advised his master to seize the person of his enemy, and, at the same time, the Roman empire, by cutting the cables of his ship. "No," replied Pompey, "I should have approved of the measure if you had done it without consulting me; but I scorn to break my word." Horace has ridiculed the pride of Menas with great virulence and animosity, and recalled to his mind his former meanness and obscurity. It is said that Menas revolted from Pompey to Augustus, and from Augustus to Pompey, and that he again, a second time, betrayed his master carrying with him part of his fleet. Augustus acknowledged his services, and admitted him with every mark of cordiality to his table, an honor which was never bestowed on any other freedman. *Suet. Aug.* 74.—*Plut. in Ant.* —*Appian.B. C.* 5. p. 714.—*Horat.* 4. *Epod.*—*Paterc.* 2. c. 73.

MENCHE'RES, the twelfth king of Memphis, called Mucerinus by *Herodotus*, 2. c. 134. *Joh. Marsham. Can. Chron. Sec.* 5.

MENDÆ'I a people of Thrace, near the city of Ænus. *Steph.*

MEN'DE, a city of Sicily. *Id.*

MEN'DELE, a city of India within the Ganges. *Ptol.*

MEN'DES, a city of Ægypt, near Lycopolis, on one of the mouths of the Nile, called from it, the Mendesian mouth. Pan was worshipped there with the greatest solemnity under the form of a goat. *Herodot.* 2. c. 42 & 46.—*Strab.* 17.—*Diod.* 1.—*Plut. in Gryllo.*—*Clem. Alex. Coh. ad Gent.* 1.

MENDICULE'A, a town of Lusitania. *Ptol.*

MENECI'NA, a town of the Brutii. *Steph.* It is now Mendicino.

MEN'ECLES, an orator of Alabanda in Caria, who settled at Rhodes, and had Cicero, Crassus, and other celebrated Romans in the number of his pupils. *Cic. de Orat.* 2. c. 53. *Br.* 95. *Or.* 69.—*Strab.* 15.—*Tzetzes in Lyc.* 885.

MEN'ECLES, BAC'ALEUS, an historian mentioned by *Athenæus.*

MENECLI'DES, a detractor of the character of Epaminondas. *Corn. Nep. in Epam.*

MENEC'RATES, a physican of Syracuse, famous for his vanity and arrogance. He was so elated with his successful practice, that he was generally accompanied by some of his patients, whose disorders he had cured. He disguised one in the habit of Apollo, and the other in that of Æsculapius, while he reserved for himself the title and name of Jupiter, whose power was extended over those inferior deities. He crowned himself like the master of the gods, and, in a letter which he wrote to Philip, king of Macedon, he styled himself, in these words, *Menecrates Jupiter, to king Philip, greeting.* The Macedonian monarch answered, *Philip to Menecrates greeting, and better sense.* Philip also invited him to one of his feasts, but when the meats were served up, a separate table was put for the physician, on which he was served only with perfumes and frankincense, like the father of the gods. This entertainment displeased and disconcerted Menecrates, and, remembering that he was a mortal, he hurried away from the company. He lived about 360 B.C. The book which he wrote on cures is lost. *Ælian. V.H.* 10. c. 51.—*Athen.* 7. c. 13.—*Suidas.*——One of the generals of Seleucus.——A physician under Tiberius.——A Greek historian of Nysa, disciple to Aristarchus, B.C. 119. *Strab.* 16.——An historian of Xanthus. *Dion. Hal.* 1.—*Voss. H. Gr.* p. 387.——A man appointed to settle the disputes of the Athenians and Lacedæmonians in the 8th year of the Peloponnesian war. His father's name was Amphidorus.——An officer in the fleet of Pompey, the son of Pompey the Great.——A comic poet of Athens. *Suidas.*

MENEDE'MIUM, a city of Lycia. *Steph.*

MENEDE'MUS, an officer of Alexander, killed by the Danæ. *Curt.* 7. c. 6.——A Socratic philosopher of Eretria, who was originally a tent-maker, an employment which he left for the profession of arms Being once told that it is great happiness to possess what we wish for, he answered yes, but it is greater to desire nothing but what we possess. The persuasive eloquence and philosophical lectures of Plato had such an influence over him, that he gave up his offices in the state to have more frequent opportunities of cultivating literature. It is said that he died through melancholy, when Antigonus one of Alexander's generals, had made himself master of his country, B.C. 301, in the 74th year of his age. Some attribute his death to a different cause, and say, that he was falsely accused of treason, upon which he became so desperate that he died, after he had passed seven days without taking any aliments. He was called the *Eretrian Bull*, on account of his sternness and gravity *Strab.* 9.—*Diog. Laert.* 2. *de vit. Phil.*—*Athen.* 10.—*Strab.* 9.——A Cynic philosopher of Lampsacus, who said that he was come from the infernal regions to observe the sins and wickedness of mankind. His habit was that of the furies, and his behaviour was a proof of his insanity. He was disciple of Colotes of Lampsacus. *Laert.* 6. *de vit. Phil.*——An officer of Lucullus.——A philosopher of Athens. *Cic. de Orat.* 1. c. 19.——An old man introduced among the characters of Terence's plays. *Heaut.* 1. *Sc.* 1.

MENEG'ERE, a city of Africa Propria. *Antonin.*

MENEG'ETAS, a boxer or wrestler in Philip of Macedon's army, &c. *Polyæn.* 4. c. 2.

MENELAE'A or MENELAI'A, a festival celebrated at Therapnæ in Laconia, in honor of Menelaus. He had there a temple, where he was worshipped with his wife Helen as one of the supreme gods. *Isocr. in Helen Encom.*—*Paus. Lacon.*

MENELA'I POR'TUS, a harbour on the coast of Africa, between Cyrene and Ægypt. *C. Nep. in Ages.* 8.—*Strab.* 1.

MENELA'I MONS, a hill near Sparta, with a fortification, called *Menelaium.* *Liv.* 34. c. 28.—*Steph.*

MENELA'US, a king of Sparta, brother of Agamemnon. His father's name was Atreus, according to Homer, or, according to the more probable opinion of Hesiod, Apollodorus, &c. he was the son of Plisthenes and Ærope. *Vid.* Plisthenes. He was educated with his brother Agamemnon in the house of Atreus, but soon after the death of this monarch, Thyestes, his brother, usurped the kingdom, and banished the two children of Plisthenes. Menelaus and Agamemnon thus abandoned, retired to the court of Œneas king of Calydonia, who treated them with tenderness and paternal care. From Calydonia they went to Sparta, where, like the rest of the Grecian princes, they solicited the hand of Helen, the daughter of king Tyndarus. By the artifice and advice of Ulysses, Helen was permitted to choose a husband, and she fixed her eyes upon Menelaus, and married him, after her numerous suitors had solemnly bound themselves by an oath to defend her, and protect her person against the violence or assault of every intruder. *Vid.* Helena. As soon as the nuptials were celebrated, Tyndarus resigned the crown to his son-in-law. The happiness of the young monarch was, however, of short duration; Helen was the fairest woman of the age, and Venus had promised Paris the son of Priam, to reward him with such a beauty. *Vid.* Paris. The arrival of Paris in Sparta was, consequently, the cause of extraordinary events. The absence of Menelaus in Crete gave opportunities to the Trojan prince to assail and finally to corrupt the fidelity of Helen, and to carry away home what the goddess of beauty had promised to him as his due. This perfidious action was highly resented by Menelaus; he reminded the Greek princes of their oath and solemn engagements when they courted the daughter of Tyndarus, and immediately all Greece took up arms to defend his cause. The combined forces assembled at Aulis in Bœotia, where they chose Agamemnon for their general, and Chalcis for their high priest; and, after their applications to the court of Priam for the recovery of Helen had proved fruitless, they set sail for the coast of Asia, to meet their enemies in the field. During the Trojan war, Menelaus behaved with great spirit and courage, and Paris must have fallen by his hand, had not Venus interposed and saved him from certain death. He also expressed a wish to engage Hector, but Agamemnon interfered, and prevented him from fighting with so powerful an adversary. In the tenth year of the Trojan war, Helen, as it is reported, obtained the forgiveness and the good graces of Menelaus, by introducing him with Ulysses, the night that Troy was reduced to ashes, into the chamber of Deiphobus, whom she had married after the death of Paris. This perfidious conduct reconciled her to her first husband, and she returned with him to Sparta, after a voyage of eight years' duration. Menelaus died some time after his return. He had a daughter called Hermione, and Nicostratus, according to some, by Helen, and a son called Megapenthes by a concubine. Some say that Menelaus went to Ægypt on his return from the Trojan war, to obtain Helen, who had been detained there by the king of the country. *Vid.* Helena. The place which Menelaus once inhabited was still entire in the days of Pausanias, as well as the temple which had been raised to his memory by the people of Sparta. *Homer. Odyss.* 4, *&c. Il.* 1. *&c.*—*Apollod.* 3. c. 10.—*Paus.* 3. c. 14 & 19.—*Dictys Cret.* 2, *&c.*

—*Virg. Æn.* 2, *&c.*—*Quintil. Smyrn.* 14 & 147.—*Ovid. Heroid.* 5. v. 105. ep. 13. v. 47. *De A. A.* 2. v. 360. *De Rem. A.* 773. *Met.* 13. v. 203.—*Hygin.* fab. 79.—*Eurip. in Iphig.*—*Sophocles.*—*Eustath in Il.*—*Scholiast. in Il.*—*Propert.* 2. el. 2. v. 43. el. 12. v. 13. el. 25. v. 7.—*Servius Æn.* 2. v. 166 & 310. l. 5. v. 496. l. 10. v. 91. [A fragment of a celebrated group of Menelaus rescuing the dead body of Patroclus, is preserved at Rome, where it is denominated Pasquin, and is made the vehicle of lampoons against the government, &c. Two copies of the group, nearly entire, are in the possession of the Grand Duke of Tuscany, at Florence; and a copy of the head of Menelaus will be found in the Museum of the Vatican, at Rome.]——A lieutenant of Ptolemy, placed over Salamis. *Polyæn.* 4. c. 7.—*Paus.*——A mathematician in the age of the emperor Trajan. He wrote three books on the Sphere.——A Greek rhetorician of Marathos in Phœnicia, who settled at Rome, and, as is supposed assisted C. Gracchus in the composition of his orations. *Cic. Br.* 26.——A native of Anæa, in Caria, an historian of celebrity. *Steph. in* Ἀναία.——A poet who wrote a poem called Thebias in 12 books. *Suidas.*

MENELA'US, a city of Ægypt. *Strab.* 14.

MENE'NIA, a tribe and family at Rome.

MENE'NIUS AGRIP'PA, a celebrated Roman who appeased the Roman populace in the infancy of the consular government by repeating to them the well-known and interesting fable of the belly and the limbs. He flourished 495 B.C., and is said to have died so poor that the expenses of his funeral were defrayed by the public. *Liv.* 2. c. 16, 32 & 33.

MENE'NIUS, a Roman consul, A.U.C. 250.——An insane person in the age of *Horace.*

MEN'EPHRON, a man who attempted to offer violence to his own mother. He was changed into a wild beast. *Diod.* 4.—*Hygin.* 253.—*Ovid. Met.* 7. v. 387.

ME'NES, the first king of Ægypt. He built the town of Memphis, as it is generally supposed, and deserved, by his meritorious services to his country and his popularity, to be called a god after death. *Herodot.* 2. c. 1 & 90.—*Diod.* 1.—*Joh. Marsham. Can. Chron.*

MENESAR'DUS, a son of Pythagoras. *Euseb. Chron.*

MENES'THEI POR'TUS, a town of Hispania Bætica. Some suppose it to be the Besippo of *Pliny*, 3. c. 1.—*Ptol.*—*Strab.* It is now Puerto de S. Maria.

MENES'TEUS, MENES'THEUS or MNES'THEUS, a son of Peteus, who so insinuated himself into the favor of the people of Athens, that, during the long absence of Theseus, he was elected king. The lawful monarch at his return home was expelled, and Mnestheus established his usurpation by the popularity and great moderation of his government. As he had been one of Helen's suitors, he went to the Trojan war at the head of the people of Athens, and died in his return in the island of Melus. He reigned 23 years B.C. 1205, and was succeeded by Demophoon the son of Theseus. *Plut. in Thes.*—*Homer. Il.* 2, 11, 12 & 13.—*Paus.* 2. c. 25. l. 3. c. 18.—*Apollod.* 3.——A son of Iphicrates, who distinguished himself in the Athenian armies. *C. Nep. in Tim.*

MENES'THIUS, a Greek killed by Paris during the Trojan war. *Homer. Il.* 7. v. 8.——A son of the Sperchius and Polydora, who accompanied Achilles to the Trojan war. *Homer. Il.* 16. v. 173.

MENES'TRATUS, a statuary who executed a beautiful statue of Hecate, which was placed in the temple of Diana at Ephesus. *Plin.* 36. c. 5.

MEN'ETAS, a man made governor of Babylon by Alexander. *Curt.* 5. c. 1.

MENE'TOR, an ancient author mentioned by *Athenæus.*

MEN'IDAS, or, according to *Diodorus Siculus*, l. 17, Minidas, the præfect of the Scythian cavalry in the army of Alexander.

ME'NINX or LOTOPHAGI'TIS IN'SULA, now Zerbi, an island on the coast of Africa near the Syrtis Minor. It was peopled by the people of Neritus, and thence called Neritia. *Plin.* 5. c. 7.—*Strab.* 17.—*Sil. It.* 3. v. 318.

MENIP'PE, one of the Amazons who assisted Æetes, &c. *Val. Flacc.* 6. v. 377.

MENIP'PIDES, a son of Hercules. *Apollod.*

MENIP'PUS, a Cynic philosopher of Phœnicia. He was originally a slave, and obtained his liberty with a sum of money, and became one of the greatest usurers at Thebes. He grew so desperate from the continual reproaches and insults to which he was daily exposed on account of the meanness of his character, that he destroyed himself. He wrote 13 books of satires which have been lost. *M. Varro* composed satires in imitation of his style, and called them Menippean. Menippus was so severe in his satires that Lucian has in some of his dialogues, selected him as a character under whose name he could successfully convey the ridicule and virulence of his witty reflections on men and manners. *Macrob.* 1. c. 11. *Cic. Acad.* 1. c. 2.—*Gell.* 13. c. 30.——A native of Stratonice in Caria, who was preceptor to Cicero for some time. *Cic. Br.* 91.——A celebrated geographer of Pergamus. *Salmas. ad Solin.* p. 850.——A comic poet. *Suidas.*—*Voss. H. Gr.* p. 388.

MENIS'CUS, a citizen of consequence at Entella in Sicily, who appeared as a witness against Verres. *Cic. Verr.* 3. c. 87.

ME'NIUS, a plebeian consul at Rome. He was the first who formed the rostrum in the forum at Rome with the beaks *(rostra)* of the enemy's ships. *Liv.* 8. c. 14.—*Plin.* 34. c. 5.——A son of Lycaon, killed by the same thunder-bolt which destroyed his father. *Ovid. Ibin.* 472.

ME'NIUS, a river of Peloponnesus, falling into the Ionian Sea. *Strab.*

MENLA'RIA, a city of Spain. *Ptol.* It is now Marcia.

MENLAS'CUS, a small river of Hispania Tarraconensis, called Magrada by *Mela*, 3. c. 1. It is now Oria, or, according to others, Rio Menlasco.

MENNEIA'NA, a city of Upper Pannonia. *Antonin.*

MEN'NIS, a town of Assyria, abounding in bitumen. *Curt.* 5. c. 1.

MEN'NIUS RUFFI'NUS, a præfect of cavalry, who bound Lucilius Bassus. *Tac. Hist.* 3. c. 12.

MENOBAR'DI, a people of Armenia Major. *Plin.* 6. c. 9.

MENOCALE'NI, some inhabitants of the Alps. *Plin.* 3. c. 20.

MENOC'RITUS, a Greek, who was freedman to Lentulus Spinther. *Cic.* l. *Fam.* 9.

MENOD'OTUS, a physician in the age of Serapion. *Galen. in Therapeut.*——A Samian historian. *Athen.* 15.

MENŒ'CEUS, a Theban, father of Hipponome, Jocasta, and Creon.——A young Theban, son of Creon. He voluntarily offered himself to death when Tiresias, to ensure victory on the side of Thebes against the Argive forces, ordered the Thebans to sacrifice one of the descendants of those who sprang from the dragon's teeth, and he killed himself near the cave where the dragon of Mars had formerly resided. The gods required this sacrifice because the dragon had been killed by Cadmus, and no sooner was Creon dead than his countrymen obtained the victory. *Hygin.* fab. 25.—*Philstor*, 1. *Icon.* 4.—*Stat. Theb.* 10. v. 6 & 14.—*Lactant. ad Theb.* 7. v. 250.—*Schol. ad Eurip. Phœn.* 949.—*Apollod.* 3. c. 6.—*Cic. Tusc.* 1. c. 98.—*Sophocl. in Antig.* 162.

MENŒCI'NA or MENECI'NA, an inland city of Œnotria. *Steph.*

MENŒ'TES, the pilot of the ship of Gyas, at the naval games exhibited by Æneas on the anniversary of his father's death. He was thrown into the sea by Gyas for his inattention, and saved himself by swimming to a rock. *Virg. Æn.* 5. v. 161, &c.——An Arcadian killed by Turnus in the wars of Æneas. *Id.* 12. v. 517.

MENŒTI'ADES. *Vid.* Menœtius.

MENŒ'TIUS, a son of Actor and Ægina after her amour with Jupiter. He left his mother and went to Opus, where he had, by Sthenele, or according to others by Philomela, or by Polymela, Patroclus, often called from him Menœtiades. Menœtius was one of the Argonauts. *Apollod.* 3. c. 14.—*Homer. Il.* 1. v. 307.—*Hygin.* fab. 97.—*Eustath. in Il.* 1. v. 337. *Sch. Apollon.* 4. v. 816.—*Ovid. A.A.* 1. v. 743.—*Servius in Æn.* 1. v. 104.—*Sch. Homer. ad* 17. *Il.* 134.—*Sch. Pind. ad Olymp.* 9. v. 104.——A son of Ceuthonymus, keeper of Pluto's flocks. He apprised Geryon of the intended attack of Hercules against his property, and as he was a noted boxer, he assaulted the hero, who defeated him, but at the request of Proserpine, spared his life. *Apollod.* 2.——A son of Japetus and Asia, who was struck with lightning by Jupiter in the war of the Titans. *Id. Hesiod Theog.* 513. calls him son of Japetus and Clymene.

ME'NON, a Thessalian commander in the expedition of Cyrus the younger against his brother Artaxerxes.—He was disgraced on the suspicion that he had betrayed his fellow-soldiers. *Diod.* 14.—*Polyæn.* 7. c. 18.——A Thessalian, refused the freedom of Athens, though he furnished a number of auxiliaries to the people.——The husband of Semiramis.——A sophist in the age of Socrates. *Plut.* περὶ Πολυφιλ.——One of the first kings of Phrygia, said to be son of Jupiter, and father of Cybele by Callirrhoe, or Dindyme. *Dionys. Hal.* 1.—*Diod.* 3.——A Trojan chief killed by Leontheus. *Homer. Il.* 12. v. 193.——A scholar of Phidias, &c.——The name of one of Plato's compositions. *Cic. Tusc.* 1. c. 24.

MENOPH'ILUS, a eunuch to whom Mithridates, when conquered by Pompey, entrusted the care of his daughter. Menophilus murdered the princess for fear of her falling into the hands of the enemy. *Ammian.* 16.——A slave in the house of Atticus, employed by Cicero in setting his books in order, *Cic.* 4. *Att.* 7.——A Jew ridiculed by *Martial*, ep. 7. v. 51.

MENOS'GADA, a town of Germany. *Ptol.*

MEN'TA or MIN'THE. *Vid.* Minthe.

MEN'TES, a king of the Taphians in Ætolia, son of Anchialus, in the time of the Trojan war. Minerva borrowed his form when she introduced herself as the friend and adviser of young Telemachus. This man, according to some commentators, was a rich merchant of Leucas intimate with Homer, and thus the poet has immortalized the name of his friend, *Eustath. & Schol. in Odyss.*——A Ciconian chief whose form Apollo borrowed to prevent Menelaus from carrying off the dead body of Panthous. *Homer. Il.* 17. v. 70.

MENTIS'SA, a town of Spain. *Liv.* 26. c. 17. It is called Mentessa by *Ptolemy*, and Mentisa by *Antoninus*, and is now Montizon.

MENTONO'MON, an æstuary of the German Ocean. *Plin.* 37. c. 2.

MEN'TOR, a faithful friend of Ulysses. Some of the moderns have supposed that Mentor was a native of Ithaca, who received Homer during his travels with so much hospitality, and such tenderness, that the poet out of gratitude has introduced him in his Odyssey, and thus immortalized his name. *Homer. Odyss.* 2. v. 224.——A Trojan prince killed by Teucer. *Homer. Il.* 13. v. 170.——A son of Hercules. *Apollod.* 2. c. 14.——A king of Sidonia who revolted against Artaxerxes Ochus, and was afterwards restored to his favor by his treachery to his allies, &c. *Diod.* 16.——A son of Eurystheus. *Apoll.* 2. c. 8.——An excellent artist particularly skilful in polishing cups and engraving flowers on them. *Plin.* 33. c. 11.—*Mart.* 9. epigr. 63. v. 16.

MEN'TORES, a people of Illyricum. *Plin.* 3. c. 21.

MENTYR'NA, a city of the Samnites. *Steph.*

MENU'THIAS, a town of Ægypt, near Canopus. *Steph.*

MENYL'LUS, a Macedonian placed over the garrison which Antipater had stationed at Athens. He attempted in vain to corrupt the integrity of Phocion. *Plut.*

MEPHI'TIS, a goddess supposed to preside over the public cloacæ, and all infected places. In the general destruction of Cremona, her temple was the only building preserved. *Plin.* 2. c. 93.—*Virg.* 7. *Æn.* v. 84.—*Pers.* 3. v. 99.—*Tacit. Hist.* 3. c. 33.

MEPHRES, the 42nd Theban king of Ægypt, reigned 12 years. *Joh. Marsham Can. Chron.*

ME'RA, a priest of Venus. *Stat. Theb.* 8. v. 478.

ME'RA, a dog of Icarius, which by his cries showed Erigone where the body of her murdered father had been thrown. Immediately after this discovery, the daughter hanged herself in despair, and the dog pined away, and was made a constellation in the heavens known by the name of Canis. *Ovid. Met.* 7. v. 363.—*Hygin.* fab. 130. *P.A.* 2. c. 4 & 40—*Apollod.* 3.—*Schol. Hom. Il.* 10. v. 29.—*Ælian. Hist. An.* 7. c. 28.

ME'RA or MŒ'RA, one of the Atlantides who married Tegeates son of Lycaon. She had a monument erected to her memory at Tegea in Arcadia. *Homer. Odyss.* 11. v. 325.—*Paus.* 8. c. 48.

MER'CIMEN, a city of Africa Propria. *Antonin.*

MERCU'RII PROMONTO'RIUM, a cape of Africa, near Clypea. *Liv.* 26. c. 44. l. 29. c. 27.—*Plin.* 5. c. 4.

MERCU'RIUS, a celebrated god of antiquity, called Hermes by the Greeks. There were no less than five persons of this name according to Cicero; a son of Cœlus and Lux; a son of Valens and Coronis; a son of the Nile; a son of Jupiter and Maia; and another called by the Ægyptians Thoth. Some add a sixth, a son of Bacchus and Proserpine. To the son of Jupiter and Maia, the actions of all the others have been probably attributed, as he is the most famous, and the best known in mythological history. Mercury was the messenger of the gods, and of Jupiter in particular; he was the patron of travellers and of shepherds; he conducted the souls of the dead into the infernal regions, and not only presided over orators, merchants, and declaimers, but was also the god of thieves, pick-pockets, and all dishonest persons. His name is derived *a merce*, because he was the god of merchandise among the Latins, or, more probably, from the Hebrew. He was born, according to the more received opinion, in Arcadia, on mount Cyllene, and in his infancy he was entrusted to the care of the Horæ or Seasons. The day that he was born, or more probably the following day, he gave an early proof of his craftiness and dishonesty, in stealing away the oxen of Admetus, which Apollo tended. He gave another proof of his thievish propensity, by secreting the quiver and arrows of the divine shepherd, and he increased his fame by robbing Neptune of his trident, Venus of her girdle, Mars of his sword, Jupiter of his sceptre, and Vulcan of many of his mechanical instruments. These specimens of his art recommended him to the notice of the gods, and Jupiter took him as his messenger, interpreter, and cup-bearer in the assembly of the gods. This last office he discharged till the promotion of Ganymedes. He was presented by the king of heaven with a winged cap, called *petasus*, and with wings for his feet called *talaria*. He had also a short sword called *herpe*, which he lent to Perseus. With these he was enabled to transport himself with the greatest celerity into whatever part of the universe he pleased. As messenger of Jupiter, he was entrusted with all his secrets. He was the ambassador and plenipotentiary of the gods, and he was concerned in all alliances and treaties. He was the confidant of Jupiter's amours, and he was often set to watch against the jealousy and intrigues of Juno. The invention of the lyre and its seven strings is ascribed to him. This he gave to Apollo, and received in exchange the celebrated *caduceus*, with which the god of poetry used to drive the flocks of king Admetus. *Vid.* Caduceus. In the wars of the giants against the gods, Mercury showed himself brave, spirited, and active. He delivered Mars from the long confinement which he suffered from the superior power of the Aloides. He purified the Danaides of the murder of their husbands, he tied Ixion to his wheel in the infernal regions, he destroyed the hundred-eyed Argus, he sold Hercules to Omphale the queen of Lydia, he conducted Priam to the tent of Achilles, to redeem the body of his son Hector, and he carried the infant Bacchus to the nymphs of Nysa. Mercury had many surnames and epithets. He was called Cyllenius, Caduceator, Acacetos, from Acacus, an Arcadian; Acacesius, Tricephalus, Triplex, Chthonius, Camillus, Argiphontes, Agoneus, Dolius, Arcas, &c. His children are also numerous as well as his amours. He was father of Autolycus, by Chione; Myrtillus, by Cleobula; Libys, by Libya; Echion and Eurytus, by Antianira; Cephalus by Creusa; Prylis, by Issa; and of Priapus, according to some. He was also father of Hermaphroditus, by Venus; of Eudorus, by Polimela; of Pan, by Dryope, or Penelope. His worship was well established, particularly in Greece, Ægypt, and Italy. He was worshipped at Tanagra in Bœotia, under the name of Criophorus, and represented as carrying a ram on his shoulders, because he had delivered the inhabitants from a pestilence by telling them to carry a ram in that manner round the walls of their city. The Roman merchants yearly celebrated a festival on the fifteenth of May in honor of Mercury, in a temple near the Circus Maximus. A pregnant sow was then sacrificed, and sometimes a calf, and particularly the tongues of animals were offered to him, as the divinity who presided over eloquence. After the votaries had sprinkled themselves with water with laurel leaves, they offered prayers to the god, and intreated him to be favourable to them, and to forgive whatever artful measures, false oaths, or falsehoods they had uttered in the pursuit of gain. The chief ensigns of his power and offices are his *caduceus*, his *petasus*, and his *talaria*. Sometimes he is represented sitting upon a cray fish, holding in one hand his caduceus, and in the other the claws of the fish. At other times he appears like a young man without a beard, holding in one hand a purse, as being the tutelary god of merchants, with a cock on his wrists, as an emblem of vigilance, and at his feet a goat, a scorpion, and a fly. Some of his statues represent him resting his foot upon a tortoise. In Ægypt his statues represented him with the head of a dog whence he was often confounded with Anubis, and received the sacrifice of a stork. Offerings of milk and honey were made to him because he was the god of eloquence, the powers of which are sweet and persuasive. Sometimes his statues represented him without arms, because, according to some, the power of speech can prevail over every thing even without the assistance of arms. *Homer Odyss.* 1, &c. *Il.* 1, &c. *Hymn. in Merc.*—*Lucian. in Mort. Dial.*—*Ovid. Fast.* 5. v. 667. *Met.* 1, 4, 11, 14.—*Martial.* 9. epigr. 35.—*Stat. Theb.* 4.—*Paus.* l. 7, 8 & 9.—*Orpheus.*—*Plut. in Num.*—*Varro de L. L.* 6.—*Plato in Phæd*—*Liv.* 36.—*Virg. G.* 1. *Æn.* 1. v. 48.—*Diod.* 4 & 5.—*Apollod.* 1, 2, & 3.—*Apollon. Arg.* 1.—*Horat.* 1. od. 10.—*Hygin.* fab. *P. A.* 2.—*Tzetz. in Lyc.* 219 & 680.—*Cic. de Nat. D.* 3. c. 22.—*Servius in Æn.* 1. v. 301. l. 4. v. 577. l. 8. v. 138. l. 11. v. 543 & 558.—*Lactant. ad Theb.* 4. v. 483.—*Festus de V. Sig.*—*Aug. de Civ.* 7. c. 14. —*Isidor.* 8. c. 11.—*Nat. Comes.* 5. c. 6.—*Arnob.* 4. —*Apul.* 6. c. 8.—*Manil.* 1. v. 30.—*Petron.* 100.—*Martian. Capell.* 2.—*Phurnut. de N. D.* c. 16.—*Gyrald. Hist. D.* 9.—*Lactantius* l. c. 10.—*Philostr.* l. *Icon.* c. 27.—*Macrob.* 1. *Sat.* c. 12 & 19. [The finest statue of Mercury is in the Vatican, and was formerly called Antinous. There is another very fine one at Florence.] The planet Mercury which is nearest to the sun, was supposed by the ancients to influence the waters of rivers, and particularly the inundation of the Nile. *Lucan*, 1. v. 662. l. 10. v. 209, &c.—*Cic. N. D.* 2. c. 20.—*Plin.* 2. c. 8.

Mercu'rius Trismegis'tus, a priest and philosopher of Ægypt who taught his countrymen how to cultivate the olive, and measure their lands, and to understand hieroglyphics. He lived in the age of Osiris, and wrote forty-two books on theology, medicine, and geography, from which Sanchoniathon, the Phœnician historian, has taken his theogonia. In one of his compositions he compared providence to a circle, the centre of which is every where, and the circumference no where, a curious idea which has been adopted in modern times by Pascal. *Aug. de Civ. D.* 8. c. 23.—*Lactant.* 1. c. 6.—*Am. Marcel.* 21.—*Isidor.* 8. c. 11.—*Diod.* 1 & 5.—*Plut. de Isid. & Os.*—*Cic.* 3. *de Nat. D.*—*Clemens. Alex. Strom.* 6.—*Fabr. B. Gr.* 1. c. 7.—*Sax. Onom.* 1. p. 5.

MER'ETRIX, a name under which Venus was worshipped at Abydus and Samus, because both those places had been benefited by the intrigues or the influence of courtezans. *Athen.* 13.

ME'RI, a city of Mesopotamia, near Edessa. *Simler. ex MS. Antonin.*

MERIBRI'GA, a city of Lusitania. *Ptol.* It is now Abnedara.

MER'ICUS, a Spaniard, who betrayed Syracuse to Marcellus the Roman general. In the triumph exhibited at Rome, he appeared adorned with a golden crown, &c. *Liv.* 36. c. 21.

MERI'ONES, a charioteer of Idomeneus, king of Crete, during the Trojan war, was son of Molus, a Cretan prince, and Melphidis. He signalized himself before Troy, and fought with Deiphobus the son of Priam, whom he wounded. He was greatly admired for his services and humanity by the Cretans, who even paid him divine honors after death. *Horat.* 1. od. 6. v. 15.—*Homer. Il.* 2. *enum.* v. 158. l. 10. v. 260. l. 13. v. 93 & 156. l. 23. v. 528.—*Hygin.* fab. 97.—*Dictys. Cret.* 1, &c.—*Ovid. Met.* 13. fab. 1.——A brother of Jason, son of Æson, famous for his great opulence and for his avarice. *Polyæn.* 6. c. 1.

MER'MERUS or **MER'MEROS**, a centaur, wounded in the battle against the Lapithæ. *Ovid. Met.* 12. v. 305.

Mer'merus, a Trojan, killed by Antilochus. *Homer. Il.* 14. v. 513.——A son of Jason and Medea, who was father to Ilus of Corinth. *Paus.* 2. c. 3.

MERMES'SOS, a city of Troas. *Steph.*

MERM'NADÆ, a race of kings in Lydia, in which Gyges was the first. They sat on the Lydian throne in uninterrupted succession till the reign of Crœsus, who was conquered by Cyrus king of Persia. They were descendants of the Heraclidæ, and probably received the name of Mermnadæ from Mermnas, one of their own family. They were descended from Lemnos, or, according to others, from Agelaus, the son of Omphale by Hercules. *Heredot.* 1. c. 7 & 14.

MEROBRI'GA. *Vid.* Medobriga.

MER'OE, an island of Æthiopia with a town of the same name, on the Nile, celebrated for its wines. Its original name was Saba, and Cambyses gave it that of Meroe from his sister. Some have imagined that the queen who came to hear and who admired the wisdom of Solomon reigned here. The place abounded in mines of silver and gold, and other metals, and the inhabitants were celebrated for their social virtues and innocent manners. The breasts of their women are described by Juvenal as of a very unusual size. *Mela*, 1. c. 9. l. 3. c. 9.—*Paus.* 1. c. 33.—*Juv.* 13. v. 163.—*Strab.* 17.—*Herodot.* 2. c. 31.—*Plin.* 2. c. 173.—*Lucan.* 4. c. 333. l. 10. v. 163, 237 & 303.—*Claudian. de tertio Hon.* 20.

MER'OPE, one of the Atlantides. She married Sisyphus son of Molus, and like her sisters, was changed into a constellation after death. *Vid.* Pleiades It is said that in the constellations of the Pleiades the star of Merope appears more dim and obscure than the rest, because she, as the poets observe, married a mortal, while her sisters, whose stars glitter with great lustre, married some of the gods, or their descendants. *Ovid. Fast.* 4. v. 175.—*Diod* 4.—*Hygin.* fab. 192. *P. A.* 2. c. 21.—*Apollod.* 1. c. 9.—*Servius in Virg. G.* 1. v. 138.——A daughter of Cypselus, who married Cresphontes, king of Messenia, by whom she had three children. Her husband and two of her children were cruelly murdered by Polyphontes The murderer wished her to marry him, and she would have been forced to comply had not Epytus, or Telephontes, her third son, revenged his father's death by assassinating Polyphontes. *Apollod.* 2. c. 6.—*Paus.* 4, c. 3.—*Hygin.* fab. 137 & 184.—*Sch. Soph. in Aj.* 1302. ——A daughter of Œnopion beloved by Orion. *Apollod.* 1. c. 4.—*Hygin. P. A.* 2. c. 34.——A daughter of the Cebrenus, who married Æsacus the son of Priam. *Tzetzes in Lyc.* 228.——A daughter of Erechtheus, mother of Dædalus. *Plut. in Thes.* ——A daughter of Pandarus.——A daughter of the river Sangarius, who married king Priam. *Apollod.* 3. c. 23.

MERO'PIA, one of the Cyclades, called also Siphnus and Acis. *Plin.* 4. c. 12.

ME'ROPS, a king of the island of Cos, who married Clymene, one of the Oceanides. He was changed into an eagle by the gods, and placed among the constellations. *Ovid. Met.* 1. v. 763.—*Apollod.* 3. —*Hygin. P. A.* 2. c. 16.—*Sch. Apollon.* 1. v. 977. ——A celebrated soothsayer of Percosus in Troas, who foretold the death of his sons Adrastus and Amphius, who were engaged in the Trojan war. They slighted their father's advice, and were killed by Diomedes. *Homer. Il.* 2. *enum.* 336. l. 11. v. 328.——One of the companions of Æneas, killed by Turnus. *Virg. Æn.* 9. v. 702.

ME'ROS, a mountain of India, sacred to Jupiter. It is called by Pliny, 6. c. 21, Nysa. Bacchus was educated upon it, whence arose the fable that Bacchus was confined in the thigh (μηρός) of his father. *Mela*, 2. c. 7.—*Plin.* 8. c. 13.—*Curt.* 8. c. 10.—*Diod.* 1.

MER'ULA CORN., a Roman who fought against the Gauls, and was made consul by Octavius in the place of Cinna. He some time after destroyed himself in despair before the altar of Jupiter in the Capitol. *Paterc.* 2. c. 20 & 22.—*Appian. B. C.* 1. p. 390.—*Plut.*

MESAB'ATES, a Persian eunuch, flayed alive by order of Parysatis, because he declared that he had cut off the head and right hand of Cyrus. *Plut. in Artax.*

MESA'BIUS, a mountain of Bœotia hanging over the Euripus. *Paus.* 9. c. 22.

MES'ADA, a city of Arabia Petræa. *Ptol.*

MESAM'BRIA, a tract of land and peninsula in Persia. *Arrian. in Indic.*

MESA'PIA, an ancient name of Bœotia.

MESAU'BIUS, a servant of Eumæus, the steward of Ulysses. *Homer. Odyss.* 14. v. 449.

L. MESCIN'IUS RU'FUS, a quæstor under Cicero during his consulship. *Cic. Fam.* 5. ep. 19 & 20. l. 13. ep. 26 & 28, &c. *Att.* 6. ep. 3.

ME'SE, an island of Gallia Narbonensis, called also Pomponiana. *Plin.* 3. c. 5.

MESEM'BRIA, now Miseuria, a city of Thrace, on the borders of the Euxine Sea. Hence Mesembriacus. *Ovid.* 1. *Trist.* 6. v. 37.—*Herodot.* 4. c. 93. l. 6. c. 33.—*Strab.* 7.—*Mela*, 2. c. 2.——A city of Thrace at the mouth of the Lissus.

MESE'NE, an island in the river Tigris, where Apamea was built, now Disel. *Plin.* 6. c. 27.

MES'OLA, a city of Laconia. *Steph.*

MESOME'DES, a lyric poet in the age of the emperor Antoninus. *Capitol. in Anton. Pio.* c. 7. & *Salmas. in loco.*

MESOPOTA'MIA, a fertile country of Asia, which received its name from its situation (μέσος ποταμός) *between* the *rivers* Tigris and Euphrates. It is yearly inundated by the Euphrates, and the water properly conveyed over the country by canals. It is now called Diarbec. *Strab.* 2.—*Mela*, 1. c. 11.—*Cic. de Nat. D.* 2. c. 52.—*Diod.* 1.—*Ptol.* 5. c. 18.

MES'SA, a town of Laconia. *Paus.* 3.

MES'SABA, a city of Caria. *Steph.*

MESSAB'ATÆ or MASSAB'ATÆ, a people of Persia. *Steph.*—*Ptol.*

MESSA'LA, a name of Valerius Corvinus, from his having conquered Messana in Sicily, the *n* being gradually lost in the letter *t*. It is said that he first brought a clock to Rome from Catana, in Sicily, A.U.C. 490. *Plin.* 7. c. 60.—*Senec. de Brev. Vitæ*, 13.——A friend of Brutus, who seized the camp of Augustus at the battle of Philippi. He was afterwards reconciled to Augustus, whom he faithfully served in the battle of Actium, and on other occasions. His eloquence and knowledge of jurisprudence have rendered him known no less than his favor with the emperor, but more probably he owes his celebrity to the praises and flattery of poetical friendship. Horace has immortalized his name and his great qualities, and Tibullus has paid also particular honors to him as his friend and liberal patron. *Horat.* 1. sat. 6. v. 42. sat. 10. v. 85. l. 3. od. 21. *Art.* 371.—*Quintil.* 10. c. 1.—*Tibull* 1. el. 1, &c.—*Tacit. Ann.* 11. c. 6 & 7. l. 13. c. 34. —*Appian. B. C.* 5. p. 736.—*Paterc.* 2. c. 71.—*Dio.* 50.——A consul with Piso, A.U.C. 693. *Cic.* 1. *ad Att.* ep. 13.——The father of Valeria who married the dictator Sylla.——A great flatterer at the court of Tiberius.——A governor of Syria.——A tribune in one of the Roman legions during the civil war between Vespasian and Vitellius, of which he wrote an historical account mentioned by *Tacitus, Orat.* 14.——A consul with Domitius, &c.——A painter at Rome who flourished, B.C. 235.

MESSA'LA CORVI'NUS, a writer, whose book *de Augusti progenie* was edited 12mo, L. Bat. 1648. *Harles. Not. Lit. Rom.* 1. p. 598.

MESSALI'NA VALE'RIA, a daughter of Messala Barbatus. She married the emperor Claudius, and disgraced herself by her cruelties and incontinence. Her husband's palace was not the only seat of her lasciviousness, but she prostituted herself in the public streets, and there were few men at Rome who could not boast of having enjoyed the favors of the impure Messalina. Her extravagance and profligate conduct at last irritated her husband; he commanded her to appear before him to answer all these accusations which were brought against her, upon which she attempted to destroy herself, and when her courage failed, one of the tribunes, who had been sent to her, despatched her with his sword, A.D. 48. *Juv.* 6. v. 118. *Sat.* 10. v. 333.—*Tacit. Ann.* 11. c. 37.—*Suet. in Claud.* 26.—*Dio.* [There are several busts of Messalina; one of the best is in the Townley collection at the British Museum.]

MESSALI'NA STATIL'IA, was descended from a consular family, and married the consul Atticus Vistinus, whom Nero murdered. She received her husband's murderer with great marks of complacency and affection, and married him. She had married four husbands before she came to the imperial throne; and after the death of Nero she retired to literary pursuits and peaceful occupations. Otho courted her, and would have married her had he not destroyed himself. In his last moments he wrote her a very pathetic and consolatory letter. *Tacit. Ann.*

MESSALI'NUS M. VALER., a Roman officer in the reign of Tiberius. He was appointed governor of Dalmatia, and rendered himself known at Rome by his opposition to Piso, and by his attempts to persuade the Romans of the necessity of suffering women to accompany the camps on their different expeditions. *Tacit. Ann.* 3.

MESSALI'NUS, one of Domitian's informers.——A flatterer of the emperor Tiberius.

MESSA'NA or MESSE'NE, an ancient and celebrated town of Sicily, on the straits which separate Italy from Sicily. It was anciently called Zancle, and was founded 1600 years B.C. The inhabitants, being continually exposed to the depredations of the people of Cumæ, implored the assistance of the Messenians of Peloponnesus, and with their assistance repelled the enemy. After this victorious campaign, the Messenians entered Zancle, and lived in such intimacy with the inhabitants that they changed their name, and assumed that of their auxiliaries the Messenians, and called their city Messana. Another account says, that Anaxilaus, tyrant of Rhegium, made war against the Zancleans with the assistance of the Messenians of Peloponnesus, and that after he had obtained a decisive victory over them, he called the conquered city Messana in compliment to his allies, about 494 years B.C. After this revolution at Zancle, the Mamertini took possession of it, and made it the capital of the neighbouring country. *Vid.* Mamertini. It afterwards fell into the hands of the Romans, and was for some time the chief of their possessions in Sicily. The inhabitants were called Messenii, Messanienses, and Mamertini. The straits of Messana have always been looked upon as very dangerous, especially by the ancients, on account of the rapidity of the currents, and the irregular and violent flowing and ebbing of the sea. *Strab.* 6.—*Mela*, 2. c. 7.—*Paus.* 4. c. 23.—*Diod.* 4.—*Thucyd.* 1, &c.—*Herodot.* 6. c. 23. l. 7. c. 28.—*Ptol.* 3 c. 4.—*Liv.* 31. c. 49.—*Ital.* 14. v. 194.—*Martial.* 13. epigr. 117.

MESSA'PIA, a country of Italy between Tarentum and Brundusium. It is the same as Calabria. It received this name from Messapus, the son of Neptune, who left a part of Bœotia called Messapia, and came to settle in Italy, where he assisted the Rutulians against Æneas. *Ovid. Met.* 14. v. 513. —*Virg. Æn.* 7. v. 691. l. 8. v. 6. l. 9. v. 27. l. 10, &c.

MESSA'PUS, a son of Neptune. *Vid.* Messapia.

MES'SATIS, a town of Achaia. *Paus.* 7. c. 18.

MES'SE, a town in the island of Cythera. *Stat, Theb.* 4. c. 226.

MESSE'IS, a fountain of Thessaly. *Strab.* 9.—*Plin.* 4. c. 8.

MESSE'NE, a daughter of Triopas, king of Argos, who married Polycaon, son of Lelex, king of Laconia. She encouraged her husband to levy troops, and to seize a part of Peloponnesus, which, after it had been conquered received her name. She received divine honors after her death, and had a magnificent temple at Ithome, where her statue was made half of gold and half of Parian marble. *Paus.* 4. c. 1 & 3.

MESSE'NE or MESSE'NA, now Maura-Matra, a city in the Peloponnesus, the capital of the country called Messenia. The inhabitants have rendered themselves famous by the war which they carried on against the Spartans, and which received the apelation of the *Messenian war*. The first Messenian war arose from the following circumstances; the Messenians offered violence to some Spartan women who had assembled to offer sacrifices in a temple, which was common to both nations, and which stood on the borders of their respective territories, and they, moreover, killed Teleclus, the Spartan king, who had attempted to defend the innocence of these unprotected females. This account, according to the Spartan traditions is contradicted by the Messenians, who observe that Teleclus, with a chosen body of Spartans, assembled at the temple before mentioned, disguised in women's clothes, and all secretly armed with daggers. This hostile preparation was to surprise some of the neighbouring inhabitants; and in a quarrel which soon after arose, Teleclus and his associates were all killed. These quarrels were the cause of the first Messenian war, which began B.C. 743 years. It was carried on with vigor and spirit on both sides, and after many obstinate and bloody battles had been fought, and it had continued for 19 years, it was at last finished by the taking of Ithome by the Spartans. This place stood a siege of ten years, and was defended with all the power and resources of the Messenians, but in the conquest the inveterate hatred of Sparta was manifested in the solemn oath by which her soldiers bound themselves not to return home till they had reduced the last strong hold of their rivals. The insults to which the common Messenians were generally exposed, by their haughty masters at last excited their resentment, and they resolved to shake off the yoke. They suddenly revolted, and the second Messenian war was begun 685 B.C. and continued 14 years. The Messenians at first gained some advantages, but a fatal battle in the third year of the war so totally disheartened them that they fled to Ira, where they resolved to maintain an obstinate siege against their victorious pursuers. The Spartans were assisted by the Samians in besieging Ira, and the Messenians were at last obliged to submit to the superior power of their adversaries. The taking of Ira by the Lacedæmonians, after an obstinate siege of 11 years, put an end to the second Messenian war. Peace was re-established for some time in Peloponnesus, but after the expiration of 200 years, the Messenians attempted a third time to free themselves from the tyranny of Lacedæmon, B.C. 464. At that time the Helots had revolted from the Spartans, and the Messenians by joining their forces to these wretched slaves, looked upon their respective calamities as common, and thought themselves interested in each other's welfare. The Lacedæmonians were assisted by the Athenians, but they soon grew jealous of one another's power, and their political connection produced the most inveterate enmity, and at last ended in open war. Ithome was the place in which the Athenians had a second time gathered all their forces, and though ten years had already elapsed, both parties seemed equally confident of victory. The Spartans were afraid of storming Ithome, as the oracle of Delphi had threatened them with the greatest calamities, if they offered any violence to a place which had been solemnly dedicated to the service of Apollo. The Messenians, however, were soon obliged to submit to the terms imposed by their victorious adversaries, B.C. 453, and they consented to leave their native country, and totally to depart from the Peloponnesus, solemnly promising that if they ever returned into Messenia, they would suffer themselves to be sold as slaves. The Messenians upon this, miserably exiled, applied to the Athenians for protection, and were permitted to inhabit Naupactus, whence some of them were afterwards removed to take possession of their ancient territories in Messenia, during the Peloponnesian war. The third Messenian war was productive of great revolutions, and though originally merely a private quarrel, it soon engaged the attention of all the neighbouring states, and kindled the flames of dissension in every part of Greece. Every state took up arms as if in its own defence, or to prevent additional power and dominion from being lodged in the hands of its rivals. The descendants of the Messenians at last returned to Peloponnesus, B.C. 370, after a long banishment of 300 years. *Paus. Mess.* &c.—*Justin.* 3. c. 4, &c.—*Strab.* 6, &c.—*Thucyd.* 1, &c.—*Diod.* 11, &c.—*Plut. in Cim.* &c.—*Polyæn.* 3.—*Polyb.* 4, &c.

MESSE'NIA, a province of Peloponnesus, situate between Laconia, Elis, Arcadia, and the sea. Its chief city was Messena. *Vid.* Messene.

MES'SOA or MES'OA, a city and tribe of Laconia. *Steph.* It was more probably a part of the city of Sparta. *Vid. Salmas ad Solin.* p. 825.

MESSO'GIS, a mountain of Lydia, famous for its wine *Steph.*

MES'TOR, a son of Perseus and Andromeda, who married Lysidice, daughter of Pelops, by whom he had Hippothoe. *Apollod.* 2.——A son of Pterelaus. *Id.*——A son of Priam. *Id.* 2 & 3.

MESU'LA, a small town of Italy, in the country of the Sabines.

MET'ABUS, a king of the Privernates. He was father of Camilla, whom he consecrated to the service of Diana, when he had been banished from his kingdom by his subjects for his cruelty and tyrannical disposition. *Virg. Æn.* 11. v. 540.—*Hygin.* fab. 252.—*Servius in Virg. loco. cit.*——A son of Sisyphus, grandson of Æolus, who founded Metapontum. *Steph.*

METACHOE'UM, a fortified place of Bœotia, between Coronea and Orchomenus.

METACOMP'SO or TACOMP'SON, a city of Ægypt, near Syene. *Plin.* 6. c. 29. It is called Tachempso by *Mela*, 1. c. 9.

MET'ACUM, a city of Arabia Felix. *Ptol.*

METADU'LA, a city of Cappadocia. *Id.* Some read Megaluda.

METAGIT'NIA, a festival in honor of Apollo, celebrated by the inhabitants of Melite, who migrated to Attica. It received its name from its being observed in the month called Metageitnion. *Suidas.* —*Harpocrat. Plutarch. de Exil.*

METALAS'SUS, a city of Cappadocia. *Ptol.*

METANI'RA, the wife of Celeus, king of Eleusis, who first taught mankind agriculture. She is also called Meganira. *Apollod.* 1. c. 5.—*Nicander. in Ther. & Alex.*

MET'APA, a city of Acarnania. *Steph.*

METAPI'NUM, one of the mouths of the Rhone. *Plin.* 3. c 4.

METAPON'TUM, a town of Lucania in Italy on the bay of Tarentum, founded about 1269 years B.C. by Metabus, the father of Camilla, or Epeus, one of the companions of Nestor. Pythagoras retired thither for some time, and perished in a sedition. Annibal made it his head quarters when in that part of Italy, and its attachment to Carthage was afterwards severely punished by the Roman conquerors, who destroyed its liberties and independence. It is now Torre di Mare, and a few broken pillars of marble are the only vestiges of the once famed city of Metapontum. *Strab.* 5.—*Ptol.* 3. c. 1.—*Mela*, 2. c. 4.—*Justin.* 12. c. 2.—*Liv.* 1, 8, 25, 27, &c. Also written Metapon'tium.

METAPON'TUS, a son of Sisyphus, who married Theana. *Vid.* Theana. *Hygin.* fab. 186.

MET'ARIS, a river or æstuary on the eastern shore of Britain. *Ptol.* According to *Camden* it is now the Wash.

MET'ARUS, a river of Hispania Tarraconensis. *Ptol.* It is called Mearus by *Mela*, 3. c. 1.

METAU'RUS, now Metaro, a river in Umbria. It falls into the Adriatic Sea, and was famous for the defeat of Asdrubal, by the consuls Livius and Nero. *Horat.* 4. od. 4. v. 38.—*Mela*, 2. c. 4.—*Lucan.* 2. v. 495.——A small river in the country of the Brutii, now Marro fiume. It falls into the Tyrrhene Sea. The town at its mouth was called Metaurum. *Plin.* 3. c. 5.

METEL'LA, the wife of Sylla.

METEL'LI, the surname of the illustrious family of the Cæcilii at Rome, who, as *Paterculus*, 2. c. 8, observes, obtained in the short space of twelve years the honors of twelve consulships or censorships, or triumphs.

METEL'LUS, a general, who defeated the Achæans, took Thebes, and invaded Macedonia, &c.

METEL'LUS Q. CÆCIL'IUS, rendered himself illustrious by his successes against Jugurtha the Numidian king, from which he was surnamed *Numidicus*. He took, in this expedition, the celebrated Marius, and he had soon cause to repent of the confidence which he had placed in him. Marius raised himself to power by defaming the character of his benefactor, and Metellus was recalled to Rome and accused of extortion and ill-management. Marius was appointed his successor to finish the Numidian war, and Metellus was acquitted of the crime laid to his charge before the tribunal of the Roman knights, who observed that the probity of his whole life and the greatness of his exploits were stronger proofs of his innocence, than the most powerful arguments. Metellus showed himself as much the patron of literature and of learned men as he was distinguished for integrity and unshaken virtue. His father Lucius Calvus was brother to Metellus Macedonicus. *Plut. in Mario.—Cic. Br.* 35. *Cluent.* 35. *Dom.* 31. *Ad. Quir.* 3. *In. Scn.* 15. *Balb.* 5. *Att.* 1. ep. 16. *Verr.* 4. c. 66.—*Sallust. de Bell. Jug.—Val. Max.* 3. c. 8.—*Gellius,* 17. c. 2.—*Paterc.* 2. c. 9.

Metel'lus L. Cæcil'ius, saved the palladium from the flames, when Vesta's temple was on fire. He was then high priest. He lost his sight and one of his arms in doing it, and the senate, to reward his zeal and piety, permitted him always to be drawn to the senate house in a chariot, a distinguished honour which no Roman had ever before enjoyed. He also gained a great victory over the Carthaginians in the first Punic war, and led in his triumph thirteen generals and 120 elephants taken from the enemy. Besides being twice consul he was honored with the dictatorship, and the office of master of the horse, &c. *Val. Max.* 1. c. 4.—*Plin.* 7. c. 44. l. 8. c. 3.—*Appian. in Mithri.—Juv.* 3. v. 139.—*Ovid. Fast.* 6. v. 437.—*Senec. Controv.* 4.

Metel'lus Q. Cæcil'ius Ce'ler, distinguished himself by his spirited exertions against Cataline. He married Clodia the sister of Clodius, who disgraced him by her incontinence and lasciviousness. He died fifty-seven years B.C. He was greatly lamented by Cicero, who shed tears at the loss of one of his most faithful and valuable friends. *Cic. de Cœl* 14. *Fam.* 5. ep. 1.

Metel'lus L. Cæcil'ius, a tribune of the people in the civil wars of J. Cæsar and Pompey. He favored the cause of Pompey, and opposed Cæsar when he entered Rome with a victorious army. He refused to open the gates of Saturn's temple in which were deposited great treasures, upon which they were broken open by Cæsar, and Metellus retired, when threatened with death. *Cæs. B. C.* 1. c. 33.—*Lucan.* 3. v. 102, &c.—*Plut. Cæs.—Cic. Att.* 10. ep. 4.

Metel'lus Q. Cæcil'ius, the grandson of the high priest who saved the palladium from the flames, was a warlike general, and from his conquest of Crete and Macedonia received the surname of *Macedonicus.* He had six sons, of whom four are only particularly mentioned by Plutarch. *Val. Max.* 2. c. 7. l. 5. c. 1. l. 9. c. 3.—*Paterc.* 1. c. 12. l. 2. c. 8.—*Plin.* 7. c. 13 & 44.—*Plut. de Garrul.—Paus.* 7. c. 8 & 13.

Metel'lus Q. Cæcil'ius, one of the sons of the preceding, surnamed *Balearicus,* from his conquest of the Beleares.

Metel'lus L. Cæcil'ius, surnamed *Diadematus,* is supposed to be the same as that called Lucius with the surname of *Dalmaticus,* from a victory obtained over the Dalmatians, during his consulship with Mutius Scævola. *Val. Max.* 8. c. 5.—*Plin.* 7. c. 44. l. 34. c. 8.

Metel'lus Ca'ius Cæcil'ius, surned *Caprarius,* was consul with Carbo, A.U.C. 641.

Metel'lus Mar'cus, was the fourth son of Q. Cæcil. Metellus; and of these four brothers it is remarkable, that two of them triumphed in one day, but over what nation is not mentioned by *Eutropius,* 4.

Metel'lus Ne'pos, a consul, who, though originally inimical to Cicero, became the chief promoter of his recall from exile. Metellus afterwards opposed for a time the power of the senate and fled to Pompey, who had married his sister. *Suet. Cæs.* 16 & 55.—*Cic. Att.* 1. ep. *Quint.* 3. c. 9.—*Dio.* 37, 38.

Metel'lus, a consul who accused C. Curio his father's detractor.

Metel'lus, a general of the Roman armies in an expedition against the Sicilians and Carthaginians Before he marched he offered sacrifices to all the gods, except Vesta, for which neglect the goddess was so incensed that she demanded the blood of his daughter Metella. When Metella was going to be immolated, the goddess is said to have substituted a heifer in her place, and to have carried her to her temple at Lanuvium, of which she became the priestess.——A consul who commanded in Africa, &c. *Val. Max.—Plin.—Plut.—Liv.—Paterc.* 2.—*Elor.* 3. c. 8.—*Paus.* 7. c. 8 & 13. *Cic in Tusc.* &c.—*Juv.* 3. v. 138.—*Appian. Civ.—Cæs. Bell. Civ.—Sallust. in Jug.*

Metel'lus Luc'ius Cæcil'ius or Quin'tus, surnamed *Creticus,* from his conquest in Crete, B.C. 66, is supposed by some to have been the son of Metellus Macedonicus.

Metel'lus Cim'ber, one of the conspirators against J. Cæsar. It was he who was employed to give the conspirators the signal to attack and murder the dictator in the senate-house.

Metel'lus Pi'us, a general in Spain, against Sertorius, on whose head he set a price of 100 talents and 20,000 acres of land. He distinguished himself also in the Marsian war, and was high priest. He obtained the name of *Pius* from the sorrow which he showed during the banishment of his father Metellus Numidicus, whom he caused to be recalled. *Paterc.* 2. c. 15.—*Sallust. Jug.* 44.—*Val. Max.* 5. c. 2.—*Plut. in Sert. & Syll.—Cic. Balb.* 2 & 17. *Planc.* 28 & 29.

METHAR'MA or METHAR'ME, a daughter of Pygmalion, king of Cyprus, and mother of Adonis by Cinyras, &c. *Apollod.* 3. c. 14.

METHI'ON, the father of Phorbas, &c. *Ovid. Met.* 5. fab. 3.

METHO'DIUS, surnamed Eubulius, a bishop of Tyre, who maintained a spirited controversy against Porphyry, and suffered martyrdom at Chalcis in Greece, in the last years of Diocletian's persecution, about 303 A.D. He was esteemed for his learning and virtues, and his zeal in support of the Christion faith gave rise to many valuable and elaborate treatises. The best edition of his works is that of Paris, fol. 1657. *Sax. Onom.* 1. p. 390.—*Fabr. B. Gr.* 1. 5. c. 1.

METHO'NE, a town of Messenia in Peloponnesus, where king Philip gained his first victory over the Athenians, B.C. 360.——A town of Macedonia, south of Pella, in the siege of which, according to *Justin,* 7. c. 6, Philip lost his right eye.——A city of Magnesia. *Homer. Il.* 2. v. 71.—*Steph. in* Μεθώνη.

METHU'RIDES, four small islands in the Sinus Megaricus. *Steph.—Plin.* 4. c. 12.

METHU'RION, a city of Arcadia.——A city of Thessaly. *Steph.*

METHYD'RIUM, a town of Peloponnesus, near Megalopolis. *Val. Flacc.—Xenoph.*

METHYM'NA, a town in the island of Lesbus, which received its name from a daughter of Macareus. It was the second city of the island in size, population, and opulence, and its territory is fruitful, and the wines it produces excellent. It was the native place of Arion. When the island of Lesbus revolted from the power of the Athenians, Methymna alone remained firm to its ancient allies. *Diod.* 5.—*Thucyd.* 3.—*Horat.* 2. sat. 8. v. 50.—*Virg. G.* 3. v. 90.—*Ovid. Met.* 11. v. 5. *A.A.* 1. v. 57. *Heroid.* 15. v. 15.—*Propert.* 4. el. 8. v. 38.—*Ital.* 7. v. 200.

METIADU'SA, a daughter of Eupalamus, who married Cecrops, by whom she had Pandion. *Apollod.* 3. c. 15.

METIL'IA LEX, was enacted A.U.C. 536, to settle the power of the dictator, and of his master of the horse, within certain bounds. *Liv.* 22. c. 25.

METIL'II, a patrician family brought from Alba, to Rome, by Tullus Hostilius. *Dionys. Hal.*

METI'LIS or METE'LIS, a city of Ægypt, near Alexandria. *Steph.* It is now Bechis.

METIL'IUS, a man who accused Fabius Maximus before the senate, &c.

METI'NA, the name of a goddess at Rome, whose festival was celebrated on the 30th of September.

Meti'na, an island of Gallia Narbonensis. *Plin.* 8. c. 5. It is now le Brescon.

METI'OCHUS, a son of Miltiades, who was taken prisoner by the Phœnicians, and given to Darius, king of Persia. He was treated with great kindness and liberality by the monarch, though his father had conquered the Persian armies in the plains of Marathon. *Plut.—Herodot.* 6. c. 41.——An Athenian entrusted with the care of the public roads, &c. *Plut.*

METI'ON or ME'TION, son of Erectheus, king of Athens, and Praxithea. He married Alcippe, daughter of Mars and Agraulus. His sons drove

Pandion from the throne of Athens, and were afterwards expelled by Pandion's children. *Apollod.* 3. c. 15.—*Paus.* 2. c. 6.

METIOSE'DUM, a town of France, now Meudon. *Cæs. B. Gall.* 7. c. 58.

ME'TIS, one of the Oceanides. She was Jupiter's first wife, and became celebrated for her great prudence and sagacity above the rest of the gods. Jupiter, who was afraid lest he should bring into the world a child more cunning and greater than himself, devoured her in the first month of her pregnancy. Some time after this adventure, the god caused his head to be opened by Vulcan, from which issued Minerva, armed from head to foot. According to Apollodorus, 1. c. 2. Metis gave a potion to Saturn, and obliged him to throw up the children which he had devoured. *Hesiod. Theog.* v. 890.—*Apollod.* 1. c. 3.—*Hygin. Præf. Fab.*

METIS'CUS, a charioteer to Turnus. *Virg. Æn.* 12. v. 469.

METI'TA, a town of Armenia Minor. *Ptol.*

ME'TIUS, a critic. *Vid.* Tarpa.

ME'TIUS CA'RUS, a celebrated informer under Domitian, who enriched himself with the plunder of those who were sacrificed to the emperor's caprice and suspicions. *Plin.* 1. ep. 5, &c.

ME'TIUS CUR'TIUS, one of the Sabines, who fought against the Romans on account of the virgins whom Romulus had urged his subjects to carry off.

ME'TIUS SUFFE'TIUS, a dictator of Alba, in the reign of Tullus Hostilius. He fought against the Romans, and, at last, to finally settle their disputes, he proposed a single combat between the Horatii and Curiatii. The Albans were conquered, and Metius promised to assist the Romans against their enemies. In a battle against the Veientes and Fidenates, Metius showed his infidelity by forsaking the Romans at the first onset, and retired to a neighbouring eminence, to wait for the event of the battle, and to fall upon whatever side proved victorious. The Romans obtained the victory with difficulty, and Tullus, upon this, ordered him to be tied between two chariots, which were drawn by four horses two different ways, and his limbs were torn away from his body, about 669 years B.C. *Liv.* 1. c. 23, &c.—*Flor.* 1. c. 3.—*Virg. Æn.* 8. v. 642.

METŒ'CIA, festivals instituted by Theseus in commemoration of the people of Attica having removed to Athens. *Plut. in Thes.*

ME'TON, an astrologer and mathematician of Athens. His father's name was Pausanias. He refused to go to Sicily with his countrymen, and pretended to be insane, because he foresaw the calamities that would attend that expedition. In a book called *Enneadecaeteris*, or the cycle of 19 years, he endeavoured to adjust the course of the sun and of the moon, and maintained that the solar and lunar years regularly begin from the same point in the heavens, every nineteenth year, which, however, the more accurate observations of the moderns have shown to differ about 1 hour, 27 minutes, and 32 seconds. This system is called by the moderns *the golden number*. Meton flourished B.C. 432. *Vitruv.* 1.—*Plut in Niciâ.*—*Hygin. P.A. Præf.*—*Servius, Æn.* 3. v. 284.—*Auson.* 2. ep. 12. ——A native of Tarentum, who pretended to be intoxicated, that he might attract the notice of his countrymen, when he wished to dissuade them from making an alliance with king Pyrrhus. *Plut. in Pyrr.*——A man who was in Cicero's debt, &c. *Cic. Att.* ep. 51.

METO'PE, the wife of the river Sangarius. She was the mother of Hecuba. *Apollod.*——The daughter of the Ladon, who married the Asopus. *Id.*

METO'PE, a river of Arcadia. *Callimach. Hymn.* 1.

ME'TRA, a daughter of Erisichthon, a Thessalian prince, beloved by Neptune. When her father had spent all his property to gratify the canine hunger under which he unhappily labored, she, from motives of filial affection, prostituted herself to her neighbours, and received for reward oxen, goats, and sheep, which she presented to Erisichthon. Some say that she had received from Neptune the power of changing herself into whatever animal she pleased, and that her father sold her continually to gratify his hunger, and that she instantly assumed a different shape, and became again his property. *Callimach. in Cerer.*—*Tzetzes in Lyc.* 1395.—*Ovid. Met.* 8. fab. 21.——A favorite of king Ariobarzanes. *Cic. Fam.* 13. ep. 4.

METRAGYR'TE, one of the names of Tellus, or Cybele.

METRO'BIUS, a player at Rome, greatly favoured by Sylla. *Plut.*

MET'ROCLES, a pupil of Theophrastus, who undertook the care of the education of Cleombrotus, and Cleomenes. He suffocated himself when grown old and infirm. *Diod. Laert. in vit. ejus.* l. 6.

METRODO'RUS, a physician of Chius, B.C. 444. He was disciple of Democritus, and had Hippocrates among his pupils. His compositions on medicine, &c. are lost. Among other opinions he maintained that the world was eternal and infinite, and denied the existence of motion. *Diog.*—*Euseb. præp. Evang.* 17. c. 14.—*Plin.* 7. c. 24.——A painter and philosopher of Stratonice, B.C. 171. He was sent to Paulus Æmylius, who, after the conquest of Perseus, demanded of the Athenians a philosopher and a painter, the former to instruct his children, and the latter to make a painting of his triumphs. Metrodorus was sent, as in him alone were united the philosopher and the painter. *Plin.* 35. c. 11. —*Cic.* 5. *De Finib.* 1. *De Orat.* 4. *Acad. Tusc.* 1. c. 24.—*Diog. in Epic.*——A friend of Mithridates, sent as ambassador to Tigranes, king of Armenia. He was remarkable for his learning, moderation, humanity, and justice. He was put to death by his royal master for his infidelity, B.C. 72. *Strab.* —*Plut.*——A person of a very retentive memory. *Plin.* 7. c. 24.——A philosopher of Athens, intimate with Epicurus, whose pupil he was. *Cic. Fin.* 2. c. 3. *Tusc.* 2. c. 3. For other persons of this name, *vid. Voss. H. Gr.* p. 389, *& Jonsium. de Script. Hist. Phil.* 1. c. 20.

ME'TRON, a noble Macedonian, in the army of Alexander the Great. *Curt.* 6. c. 7.

METROPH'ANES, an officer of Mithridates, who invaded Eubœa, &c.——A sophist, who wrote commentaries on Hermogenes and Aristides, and two books on Phrygia. *Steph.*—*Suidas.*—*Voss. H. Gr.* p. 389.

METROP'OLIS, a town of Phrygia on the Mæander. ——A city of Thessaly. *Cæs.* 3. *Bell. Civ.* c. 80. ——A city of Lydia, on the Cayster. *Plin.* 5. c. 29. *Stephanus* enumerates 10 cities of this name.

MET'TIUS M., a prince of the Gauls, sent by J. Cæsar as ambassador to Ariovistus. *Cæs. Bell. G.* 1. c. 47.——*Vid.* Metius.

METU'LUM, a town of Liburnia, at the siege of which Augustus was wounded. *Dio.* 49.

METUSCIL'IUS, a friend of Pompey, &c. *Cic. Att.* 8. ep. 12.

MEVA'NIA, now Bevagna, a town of Umbria, on the Clitumnus, the birth-place of the poet Propertius. *Lucan.* 1. v. 473.—*Propert.* 4. l. 1. v. 124.

ME'VIUS, a wretched poet. *Vid.* Mævius.

ME'VIUS PU'DENS, a person who bribed the prætorian cohorts against Galba. *Tac.* 1. c. 24.

MEZEN'TIUS, a king of the Tyrrhenians when Æneas came into Italy. He was remarkable for his cruelties, and wantonly put his subjects to death by slow tortures, or sometimes tied a man to a dead corpse face to face, and suffered him to die in that condition. He was expelled by his subjects, and fled to Turnus, who employed him in his war against the Trojans. He was killed by Æneas, with his son Lausus. *Dionys. Hal.* 1. c. 15.—*Justin.* 43. c. 1.—*Liv.* 1. c. 2. *Virg. Æn.* 7. v. 648. l. 8. v. 482. l. 9. v. 522. l. 10. v. 150. l. 11. v. 6.—*Ovid. Fast.* v. 881.

MEZETU'LUS, a Numidian who opposed Masinissa's claims to the empire of Numidia. He took refuge among the Carthaginians. *Liv.* 29. c. 29, &c.

MIACO'RUS, a city of Chalcis. *Steph.*

MI'ACUM, a town of Hispania Tarraconensis. *Antonin.*

MIASE'NA, a city of Armenia, towards Syria. *Id.*

MIC'CA, a virgin of Elis, a daughter of Philodemus, murdered by a soldier called Lucius, &c. *Plut. de Cl. Mul.*

MICCI'ADES, a famous sculptor. *Plin.* 36. c. 5.

MICIP'SA, a king of Numidia, son of Masinissa, who at his death, B.C. 119, left his kindom between his sons Adherbal and Hiempsal, and his nephew Jugurtha. Jugurtha abused his uncle's favors by murdering his two sons, and seizing upon the whole kingdom. *Sallust. de Jug.—Flor.* 3. c. 1.—*Plut. in Gracc.*

MICTION or MIC'TIO, a Eubœan, greatly attached to the interest of Rome. *Liv.* 35. c. 38, &c.

MIC'TIS, an island six days' sail beyond Britain, according to *Pliny*, 4. c. 16.

MICYBER'NA, a town of the Hellespont, taken by Philip of Macedon. *Diod. Sic.* 16.

MIC'YTHUS, a youth, through whom Diomedon, by order of the Persian king, made an attempt to bribe Epaminondas. *C. Nep. in Epa.* 2.——A servant of Anaxilaus of Rhegum, son of Chœrus. After the death of his master he retired to Tegea, in Arcadia, and as his riches were considerable he distinguished his residence by valuable presents of statues of gods and heroes to the temple and grove of Jupiter at Olympia. *Paus.* 5. c. 26.—*Herodot.* 7. c. 170.

MI'DAS, a king of Phrygia, son of Gordius or Gorgias. In his infancy, according to a Phrygian tradition, as he was asleep, a number of ants entered into his mouth, and made there a large deposit of their treasures, as in a place of the greatest security. This was considered as a sign of his future prosperity, which seemed to be verified when he accidentally found a large treasure, which proved the origin of his greatness and opulence. The hospitality which he showed to Silenus, the preceptor of Bacchus, who had been brought to him by some peasants, was liberally rewarded; and Midas, when he conducted back the old man to the god, was permitted to choose whatever recompense he pleased. He had the imprudence and avarice to demand of the god that whatever he touched might be turned into gold. His prayer was granted, but he was soon convinced of his injudicious choice; and when the very meats which he attempted to eat became gold in his mouth, he begged Bacchus to take away a present which must soon prove fatal to the receiver. He was ordered to wash himself in the river Pactolus, the sands of which were said to have been turned into gold by the touch of Midas. Some time after this adventure Midas had the imprudence to assert that Pan was superior to Apollo in singing and in playing on the flute, for which rash opinion the offended god changed his ears into those of an ass, to show his ignorance and stupidity. This Midas attempted to conceal from the knowledge of his subjects, but one of his servants saw the length of his ears, and being unable to keep the secret, and afraid to reveal it, apprehensive of the king's resentment, he opened a hole in the earth, and after he had whispered there that Midas had the ears of an ass, he covered the place as before, as if he had buried his words in the ground. On that spot, as the poets mention, grew a number of reeds, which, when agitated by the wind, uttered the same sound that had been buried beneath, and published to the world that Midas had the ears of an ass. Some explain the fable of the long ears of Midas, by the supposition that he kept a number of informers and spies, who were continually employed in collecting every seditious word that dropped from the mouths of his subjects. Midas, according to Strabo, died by drinking hot bull's blood. This he did, according to Plutarch, to free himself from the numerous unpleasant dreams which continually tormented and affrighted him. Midas, according to some, was son of Cybele. He built a town, which he called Ancyræ *Ovid. Met.* 11. fab. 5.—*Plut. de Superst.*—*Strab.* 1.—*Hygin.* fab. 191 & 274.—*Max. Tyr.* 30.—*Paus.* 1. c. 4.—*Val. Max.* 1. c. 6.—*Herodot.* 1. c. 14.—*Ælian. V. H.* 4. c. 17. l. 12. c. 45. *H. A.* 3. c. 1.—*Curt.* 3. c. 1.—*Justin.* 11. c. 7.—*Conon. Narr.* 1.—*Tzetzes in Lyc.* 1403.—*Athen.* 2.—*Philostr. in Vit.*—*Apollod.* 6. c. 27.—*Cic. de Div.* 1. c, 36. l. 2. c. 31.

MIDE'A or MID'EA, a town of Argolis. *Paus.* 6. c. 20.

MIDE'A, a town of Lycia. *Stat. Theb.* 4. v. 45.——A town of Bœotia, deluged by the inundations of the lake Copais. *Strab.* 8.—*Paus.* 9. c. 38.

MIDE'A, a nymph who had Aspledon by Neptune. *Paus.* 9. c. 38.——A mistress of Electryon. *Apollod.*

MID'ILA, a city of Africa Propria. *Augustin.*—*Cyprian, &c.*

MIE'ZA, a town of Macedonia, formerly called Strymonium. *Steph.*

MILA'NION, a youth who became enamoured of Atalanta. He is supposed by some to be the same as Meleager or Hippomenes. *Propert.* 1. el. 1. v. 9.—*Ovid. Art. Am.* 2. v. 188.——A son of Amphidamas.

MILE'SII, the inhabitants of Miletus. *Vid.* Miletus.

MILESIO'RUM MU'RUS, a place of Ægypt at the entrance of one of the mouths of the Nile. *Strab.* 171.

MILE'SIUS, a surname of Apollo. *Strab.*—*Lactant* 4. *de verâ sap.* 13,

MILE'TIA, one of the daughters of Scedasus, to whom, as well as her sister, some young Spartans offered violence. *Plut. & Paus.*

MILETOP'OLIS, a city of Mysia, now Melitopoli.——A city of Persia. *Steph. ex Strab.* l. 12.

MILE'TUM, a town of Calabria, built by the people of Miletus of Asia.——A town of Crete. *Hom. Il.* 2. v. 154.

MILE'TUS, a son of Apollo, by Aria, or Acacallis, who fled from Crete to avoid the resentment of Minos, whom he meditated to dethrone. He came to Caria, where he built a city which he called by his own name, and where he married Eidothea the daughter of Eurytus, a prince of the country by whom he had Caunus and Byblis. Some suppose that he only conquered a city there, called Anactoria, which, on account of his services assumed his name. They farther say, that he put the inhabitants to the sword, and divided the women among his soldiers. Cyanea, daughter of the Mæander, fell to his share. *Strab.* 14.—*Ovid. Met.* 9. v. 446.—*Paus.* 7. c. 2.—*Apollod.* 3. c. 1.—*Parthen. Er.* 10—*Antonin. Lib.* 30.

MILE'TUS, a celebrated town of Asia Minor, the capital of all Ionia, situate about ten stadia south of the mouth of the river Mæander, near the sea coast on the confines of Ionia and Caria. It was founded by a Cretan colony under Miletus, or, according to others, by Neleus, the son of Codrus, or by Sarpedon, Jupiter's son. It has successively been called Lelegeis, Pithyusa, and Anactoria. The inhabitants, called Milesii, were warlike and powerful, and long maintained an obstinate war against the kings of Lydia. They early applied themselves to navigation, and planted no less than eighty colonies, or according to Seneca, 380, in different parts of the world. Miletus gave birth to Thales, Anaximenes, Anaximander, Hecatæus, Timotheus the musician, Pittacus, one of the seven wise men, &c. Miletus was also famous for a temple and oracle of Apollo Didymæus, and for its excellent wool, with which were made stuffs and garments held in the highest reputation among the ancients both for softness, elegance, and beauty. The words *Milesiæ fabulæ*, or *Milesiaca*, were used to express wanton and ludicrous plays. *Ovid. Trist* 2. v. 413,—*Capitolin. in Alb.* 11.—*Virg. G.* 3. v. 306.—*Strab.* 15.—*Paus.* 7. c. 2.—*Mela*, 1. c. 17.—*Plin.* 5. c. 29.—*Herodot.* 1, &c.—*Senec. de Consol. ad Alb.*

MIL'IAS. *Vid.* Milyas.

MILICH'IE, a fountain near Syracuse. *Plin.* 3. c. 8.

MIL'ICHUS, a freedman who discovered Piso's conspiracy against Nero. *Tac.* 15. *Ann.* c. 54.

MILI'NUS, a certain pirate killed by the Libyan Hercules. *Berosus.*

MILIO'NIA, a town of the Samnites, taken by the Romans.

MIL'LUS, a son of Æneas by Lavinia. *Apollod. in Euxen.*

MI'LO, a celebrated athlete of Crotona in Italy. His father's name was Diotimus. He early accustomed himself to carry the greatest burdens, and by degrees became a monster in strength. It is said that he carried on his shoulders a young bullock four years old, for above 40 yards, and afterwards killed it with one blow of his fist, and ate it up in one day. He was seven timss crowned at the Pythian games, and six at Olympia. He presented himself a seventh time, but no one had the boldness to enter the lists against him. He was one of the disciples of Pythagoras, and to his uncommon strength the learned preceptor and his pupils owed their life. The pillar on which the roof of the school rested suddenly gave way, but Milo supported the whole weight of the building, and gave the philosopher and his auditors time to escape. In his old age Milo attempted to pull up a tree by the roots and break it. He partly effected it, but his strength being gradually exhausted, the trunk, when half cleft, re-united, and his hands remained pinched in the body of the tree. Milo was then alone, and being unable to disentangle himself, he was eaten up by the wild beasts of the place about 500 years B.C. *Ovid. Met.* 15.—*Cic. de Senect.*—*Val. Max.* 9. c. 12.—*Strab.* 16.—*Paus.* 6. c. 11.—*Ælian. V.H.* 2. c. 24.—*Plin.* 37. c. 10.—*Athen.* 10.—*Aul. Gell.* 15. c. 16.—*Solin.* 3.——A general of the forces of Pyrrhus in Italy. He was made governor of Tarentum, and that he might be reminded of his duties to his sovereign, Pyrrhus sent him as a present a chain, which was covered with the skin of Nicias the physician, who had perfidiously offered the Romans to poison his royal master for a sum of money. *Polyæn.* 8. &c.——A tyrant of Pisa in Elis, thrown into the river Alpheus by his subjects for his oppression. *Ovid. in Ib.* v. 325.

MI'LO, a mountain of India. *Solinus.* c. 55.

MI'LO T. AN'NIUS, a native of Lanuvium, who attempted to obtain the consulship of Rome by intrigue and seditious tumults. Clodius the tribune opposed his views with great warmth, yet Milo would have succeeded, had not an unfortunate event totally frustrated his hopes. As he was going into the country, attended by his wife and a numerous retinue of gladiators and servants, he met on the Appian road his enemy Clodius, who was returning to Rome with three of his friends and some domestics completely armed. A quarrel arose between the servants. Milo supported his attendants, and the dispute became general. Clodius in the struggle received many severe wounds, and was obliged to retire to a neighbouring cottage. Milo pursued his enemy in his retreat, and ordered his servants to dispatch him. Eleven of the servants of Clodius, as also the owner of the house who had given them reception, shared his fate. The body of the murdered tribune was carried to Rome, and exposed to public view. The enemies of Milo inveighed bitterly against the violence and barbarity with which the sacred person of a tribune had been treated. Cicero undertook the defence of Milo, but the continual clamours of the friends of Clodius, and the sight of an armed soldiery, which surrounded the seat of judgment, so terrified the orator, that he forgot the greatest part of his arguments, and the defence which he made was weak and injudicious. Milo was consequently condemned, and banished to Masilia. Cicero soon after sent his exiled friend a copy of the oration which he had delivered in his defence, in the form in which we have it now; and Milo, after he had read it, exclaimed, *O Cicero, hadst thou spoken before my accusers in these terms, Milo would not be now eating figs at Marseilles.* The friendship and cordiality of Cicero and Milo were the fruits of long intimacy and familiar intercourse. It was by the successful labors of the orator that Milo was recalled from banishment and restored to his country. *Cic. pro Milon.*—*Paterc.* 2. c. 47 & 68.—*Dio.* 40.

MILO'NIA, a famous city of the Samnites. *Steph.*

MILO'NIUS, a drunken buffoon at Rome, accustomed to dance when intoxicated. *Horat.* 2. sat. 1. v. 24.

MILTAS, a soothsayer who assisted Dion in explaining prodigies, &c. *Plut. in Cimon.*

MILTIADE'A, sacrifices, accompanied with horse races, in honor of Miltiades. *Herod.* 1. 4.

MILTI'ADES, an Athenian, son of Cypselus, who obtained a victory in a chariot race at the Olympic games, and led a colony of his countrymen to the Chersonesus. The causes of this appointment are striking and singular. The Dolonci, a nation of Thrace harassed by a long war with the Absynthians, were directed by the oracle of Delphi to take for their king the first man whom they met on their return home, who invited them to come under his roof and partake of his entertainments. This was Miltiades, whose attention, the appearance of the Dolonci, with their strange arms and garments, had excited. He invited them to his house, and in return for his kindness, was made acquainted with the commands of the oracle. He obeyed, and when the oracle of Delphi had approved a second time the choice of the Dolonci, he departed for the Chersonesus, and was invested by the inhabitants with sovereign power. The first measure which he took was to stop the further incursions of the Absynthians, by building a strong wall across the Isthmus. When he had established himself at home, and fortified his dominions against foreign invasion, he turned his arms against Lampsacus. His expedition was unsuccessful; he was taken in an ambuscade and made prisoner. His friend Crœsus, king of Lydia, was informed of his captivity, and procured his release by threatening the people of Lampsacus with his severest displeasure. He lived a few years after he had recovered his liberty. As he had no issue, he left his kingdom and all his possessions to Stesagoras the son of Cimon, who was his brother by the same mother. The memory of Miltiades was greatly honored by the Dolonci, and they regularly celebrated festivals and exhibited shows in commemoration of a man to whom they owed their preservation and national independence.

MILTI'ADES, the son of Cimon, was sent by the Athenians with one ship to take possession of the Chersonesus. The principal inhabitants of the country visited the new governor to condole with him; but their confidence in his sincerity proved fatal to their freedom. Miltiades seized their persons, and made himself absolute in Chersonesus; and to strengthen himself he married Hegesipyla, the daughter of Olorus the king of the Thracians. His prosperity, however, was of short duration. In the third year of his government his dominions were threatened with an invasion by the Scythian Nomades, whom Darius had some time before irritated by entering their country. He fled before them, but as their hostilities were but momentary, he was quickly restored to his kingdom. Three years after he left Chersonesus and set sail for Athens, where he was received, with great applause. He was present at the celebrated battle of Marathon, in which all the chief officers ceded their power to him, and left the event of the battle to depend upon his superior abilities. He obtained an important victory (*vid.* Marathon), over the more numerous forces of his adversaries; and when he had demanded of his fellow citizens an olive crown as the reward of his valor in the field of battle, he was not only refused, but severely reprimanded for his presumption. The only reward, therefore, that he received for a victory which proved so beneficial to the interests of universal Greece, was in itself simple and inconsiderable, though truly great in the opinion of that age. He was represented in the foreground of a picture among the rest of the commanders who fought at the battle of Marathon, and he seemed to exhort and animate his soldiers to fight with courage and intrepidity. Some time after Miltiades was entrusted with a fleet of 70 ships, and ordered to punish those islands which had revolted to the Persians. He was successful at first, but a sudden report that the Persian fleet was coming to attack him, changed his operations as he was besieging Parus. He raised the siege and returned to Athens, where he was accused of treason, and particularly of holding correspondence with the enemy. The falsity of these accusations might have appeared if Miltiades had been able to appear in the assembly. A wound which he had received before Parus detained him at home, and his enemies, taking advantage of his absence, became more eager in their accusations and louder in their clamors. He was condemned to death, but the sentence was retracted on the recollection of his great services to the Athenians, and he was put into prison till he had paid a fine of 50 talents into the treasury. His inability to discharge so great a sum detained him in confinement, and soon after his wounds became incurable, and he died about 489 years B.C. His body was ransomed by his son Cimon, who was obliged to borrow and pay the 50 talents, to give his father a decent burial. The supposed crimes of Miltiades were probably aggravated in the eyes of his countrymen, when they remembered how he had made himself absolute in Chersonesus; and in condemning the barbarity of the Athenians towards a general, who was the source of their military prosperity, we must remember the jealousy which ever reigns among a free and independent people, and how watchful they are in defence of the natural rights which they see wrested from others by violence and oppression. Cornelius Nepos has written the life of Miltiades the son of Cimon, but his history is incongruous and incorrect; and the author by confounding the actions of the son of Cimon with those of the son of Cypselus, has made the whole obscure and unintelligible. Greater reliance in reading the accounts of both the Miltiades is to be placed on the narration of Herodotus, whose veracity is undoubted, and who was better informed and more capable of giving an account of the life and exploits of men who flourished in his own age, and of which he could see the living monuments. Herodotus was born about six years after the famous battle of Marathon, and C. Nepos, who was a writer of the Augustan age, flourished about 450 years after the age of the father of history. *C. Nep. in Vitâ.—Herodot.* 4. c. 137. l. 6. c. 34, &c.—*Plut. in Cim —Val. Max.* 5. c. 3.—*Justin.* 2.—*Paus.* [The finest representation of Miltiades is in the Museum at Naples.]——An archon at Athens.

MIL'TO, a favorite mistress of Cyrus the younger. *Vid.* Aspasia.

MIL'VIUS, a parasite at Rome, &c. *Horat.* 2. sat. 7.

MIL'VIUS, a bridge at Rome over the Tiber, now called Ponte Molle. *Cic. ad Att.* 13. ep. 33.—*Sall. Cat.* 45.—*Tacit. A.* 13. c. 47.

MIL'YAS, a country of Asia Minor, better known by the name of Lycia. Its inhabitants, called Milyades, and afterwards Solymi, were among the numerous nations which formed the army of Xerxes in his invasion of Greece. *Herodot.—Cic. Verr.* 1. c. 38.

MIMAL'LIS, the name given by *Callimachus* to an island called Melus by some, and Zephyria by others. *Plin.* 4. c. 12.

MIMAL'LONES, the Bacchanals, who, when they celebrated the orgies of Bacchus, put horns on their heads. They are also called Mimallonides, and some derive their name from the mountain Mimas, on which they celebrated their orgies. *Pers.* 1. v. 99.—*Ovid. A.A.* v. 541. *Stat. Theb.* 4. v. 660.

MI'MAS, a giant whom Jupiter in the wars of the giants destroyed with thunder, or overwhelmed under the island Prochyte. *Sil. It.* 12. v. 147. —*Horat.* 3. od. 4.——A Trojan, son of Theano and Amycus, born on the same night as Paris, with whom he lived in great intimacy. He followed the fortunes of Æneas, and was killed by Mezentius in Italy. *Virg. Æn.* 10. v. 702.

MI'MAS, a mountain of Thrace. *Suidas.—Solin.* c. 43.—*Ovid. Met.* 2. fab. 1, &c.

MIMNE'DUS, a city of the Lydians. *Steph. ex Hecatæo.*

MIMNER'MUS, a Greek poet and musician of Colophon, in the age of Solon, who devoted the labors of his muse to the service of love and pleasure, and regarded the business, and the anxieties of human life, with the unconcern of a philosopher and the contempt of a satirist. He chiefly excelled in elegiac poetry, whence some have attributed the invention of it to him, and indeed he was the first poet who made elegy an amorous poem, instead of a mournful and melancholy tale. In the expression of the tender passions, Propertius prefers him to Homer, as this verse shows:

Plus in amore valet Mimnermi versus Homero.

In his old age Mimnermus became enamoured of a young musician called Nanno, who, as his friend and favorite has acquired immortality in his poetry. Some few fragments of his works remain, collected by Stobæus, to the number of about 51 lines, on old age, on the shortness of life, on valor, &c. He is supposed by some to be the inventor of the pentameter verse, which others attribute to Callinus, or Archilochus. The surname of Ligustiades, (λιγύς, *shrill-voiced*), has been applied to him, though some imagine the word to be the name of his father. *Strab.* 1 & 14.—*Paus.* 9. c. 29.—*Diog.* 1.—*Suidas.—Propert.* 1. el. 9. v. 11.—*Horat.* 1. ep. 6. v. 65. l. 2. ep. 2. v. 101.—*Athen.* 13.—*Stobæus*, 46 & 61.—*Fabr. B. Gr.* l. 2. c. 11.—*Sax. Onom.* 1. p. 20.

MINAG'ARA, a city of India within the Ganges. *Ptol. Castaldus* calls it Maciquapatan.

MIN'CIUS, now Mincio, a river of Venetia, flowing through the lake Benacus, and falling into the Po. Virgil, who has immortalized it in one of his poems was born on its banks. *Virg. Ecl.* 7. v. 13. *G.* 3. v. 15. *Æn.* 10. v. 206.

MIN'DARUS, a commander of the Spartan fleet during the Peloponnesian war. He was defeated by the Athenians, and died 410 B.C. *Plut.—Voss. ad Justin.* 5. c. 4.

MINE'IDES, the daughters of Minyas or Mineus, king of Orchomenus, in Bœotia. They were three in number, Leuconoe, Leucippe, and Alcithoe. Ovid calls the two first Clymene and Iris. They derided the orgies of Bacchus, for which impiety the god inspired them with an unconquerable desire of eating human flesh. Under the influence of this dreadful appetite, they drew lots which of them should give up her son as food for the rest. The lot fell upon Leucippe, and she gave up her son Hippasus, who was instantly devoured by the three sisters. They were afterwards changed into bats. In commemoration of this bloody crime, it was usual among the Orchomenians for the high priest, as soon as the sacrifice was finished, to pursue with a drawn sword, all the women who had entered the temple, and even to kill the first he came up to. *Ovid. Met.* 4. fab. 12.—*Plut. Quæst. Gr.* 38.

MINER'VA, the goddess of wisdom, war, and all the liberal arts, was produced from Jupiter's brain, without a mother. The god, as it is reported, married Metis, whose superior prudence and sagacity above the rest of the gods, made him apprehend that the children of such a union would be of a more exalted nature, and more intelligent than their father. To prevent this, Jupiter devoured Metis in her pregnancy, and, some time after, to relieve the pains which he suffered in his head, he ordered Vulcan to cleave it open. As soon as the blow was given, Minerva issued forth, all armed and grown up, from her father's brain, and was immediately admitted into the assembly of the gods, and made one of the most faithful counsellors of her father. The power of Minerva in heaven was very extensive; she could hurl the thunders of Jupiter, prolong the lives of men, bestow the gift of prophecy, and, indeed, she was the only one of all the divinities whose authority and consequence were equal to those of Jupiter. The exploits of Minerva were numerous, as well as the kindnesses by which she endeared herself to mankind. Her quarrel with Neptune concerning the right of giving a name to the capital of Cecropia deserves attention. The assembly of the gods settled the dispute by promising the preference to whichever of the two gave the most valuable present to the inhabitants of the earth. Neptune, upon this, struck the ground with his trident, and immediately a horse issued from the earth. Minerva produced the olive, and obtained the victory by the unanimous vote of the gods, who observed that the olive, as the emblem of peace, is far preferable to the horse, the symbol of war and bloodshed. The victorious deity called the capital Athenæ, and became the tutelary goddess of the place. Minerva was always jealous of her power, and the manner in which she punished the presumption of Arachne is well known. *Vid.* Arachne. The attempts of Vulcan to offer her violence, showed, in an honorable light, the estimation in which she held her virtue. Jupiter had sworn by the Styx to give to Vulcan, who had made him a complete suit of armour, whatever he desired. Vulcan demanded Minerva, and the father of the gods, who had granted permission to Minerva to live in perpetual celibacy, consented, but privately advised his daughter to make all the resistance which she could to frustrate the attempts of her lover. The prayers and the force of Vulcan, however, proved ineffectual, and from his fruitless efforts sprang the extraordinary monster Erichthonius. *Vid.* Erichthonius. Minerva is said to have been the first who built a ship, and it was her zeal for navigation and her care for the Argonauts, which placed the prophetic tree of Dodona behind the ship Argo when going to Colchis. She was known among the ancients by various appellations. She was called Athena, Pallas, (*vid.* Pallas,) Parthenos, from her remaining in perpetual celibacy; Tritonia, because worshipped near the lake Tritonis; Glaucopis, from the blueness of her eyes; Agorea, from her presiding over markets; Hippia, because she first taught mankind how to manage the horse; Stratea and Area, from her martial character; Coryphagenes, because born from Jupiter's brain; Sais, because worshipped at Sais, &c. Some authors have attributed to her the invention of the flute, whence she was surnamed Aedon, Luscinia, Musica, Salpiga, &c. She, as it is reported, once amused herself in playing upon her favorite flute before Juno and Venus, but the goddess ridiculed the distortion of her face in blowing the instrument. Minerva, convinced of the justness of their remarks, by looking at herself in a fountain near mount Ida, threw away the instrument, and denounced a melancholy death against him who found it. Marsyas found it, and afforded a miserable proof of the veracity of prediction. The worship of Minerva was universally established; she had magnificent temples in Ægypt, Phœnicia, all parts of Greece, Italy, Gaul, and Sicily. Sais, Rhodes, and Athens particularly claimed her protection, and it is even said, that Jupiter rained a shower of gold upon Rhodes, which had paid so much veneration and such an early reverence to his daughter. The festivals celebrated in her honor were solemn and magnificent. *Vid.* Panathenæa. She was invoked by every artist, and particularly such as worked in wool, embroidery, painting, and sculpture. It was the duty of almost every member of society to implore the assistance and patronage of a deity who presided over sense, taste, and reason. Hence the poets have taken occasion to say,

Tu nihil invitâ dices, faciesve Minervâ,

and,

Qui bene placârit Pallada, doctus erit.

Minerva was represented in different ways, according to the different characters in which she appeared with a countenance expressive rather of masculine firmness and composure than softness and grace. Most usually she was represented with a helmet on her head, and with a large plume nodding in the air. In one hand she held a spear, and and in the other a shield, with the dying head of Medusa upon it. Sometimes this Gorgon's head was on her breast-plate, with living serpents writhing round it, as well as round her shield and helmet. In most of her statues she is represented as sitting, and sometimes she holds in one hand a distaff, instead of a spear. When she appeared as the goddess of the liberal arts, she was arrayed in a variegated veil, which the ancients called *peplum*. Sometimes Minerva's helmet was covered at the top with the figure of a cock, a bird, which, on account of its great courage is properly sacred to the goddess of war. Some of her statues represented her helmet adorned with a sphinx in the middle, and supported on either side by griffins. In some medals, a chariot drawn by four horses, or sometimes a dragon or a serpent, with winding spires, appears at the top of her helmet. She was partial to the olive tree; the owl and the cock were her favorite birds, and the dragon among reptiles was sacred to her divinity. The functions, offices, and actions of Minerva seem so numerous that they undoubtedly originate in more than one person. Cicero speaks of five personages of that name; a Minerva, mother of Apollo, daughter of the Nile, who was worshipped at Sais in Ægypt; a third, born from Jupiter's brain; a fourth, daughter of Jupiter and Coryphe; and a fifth, daughter of Pallas, generally represented with winged shoes. This last put her father to death, because he attempted to offer violence to her virtue. *Paus.* 1, 2, 3, &c. —*Horat.* 1. od. 16. l. 3. od. 4.—*Virg. Æn.* 2, &c. —*Strab.* 6, 9, & 13.—*Philost. Icon.* 2.—*Ovid. Fast.* 3, &c. *Met.* 6.—*Cic. de Nat. D.* 1. c. 15, l. 3. c. 23, &c.—*Apollod.* 1, &c.—*Pindar. Olymp.* 7.—*Lucan.* 9. v. 354.—*Sophocl. Œdip.*—*Homer. Il. &c. Odyss. Hymn. ad Pall*—*Diod.* 5.—*Hesiod. Theog. Æschyl. in Eum.*—*Lucian. Dial.*—*Clem. Alex. Strom.* 2.—*Orpheus. Hymn.* 31.—*Q. Smyrn.* 14. v. 448.—*Apollon.* 1.—*Hygin.* fab. 198.—*Stat. Theb.* 2. v. 721. l. 7, &c.—*Callim. in Cerer.*—*Ælian. V.H.* 12.—*C. Nep. in Paus.*—*Plut. in Lyc.* &c.—*Thucyd.* 1.—*Herodot.* 5.—*Servius in Æn.* 2. v. 615. l. 4. v. 201. l. 1. 8v. 435.—*Festus de V. Sig.*—*Schol. Apollon.* 2. v. 615.—*Phurnut. de Nat. D.* 20.—*Gyrald. H.D.* 11.—*Meursius. in Misc.*—*Arnob.* 3.—*Tzetzes. in Lyc.* 1417.—*Hesychius.*—*Suidas. Isid. Orig.* 8. c. 11. l. 19. c. 20. [The finest statues of this goddess are the celebrated Giustiniani Minerva in that palace at Rome, and that in the collection of Mr. T. Hope, in London. There is also a very fine head in the British Museum, the helmet and ægis of which are of bronze.]

MINER'VÆ CAS'TRUM, a town of Calabria, in Italy, on the shores of the Adriatic Sea. It is now Castro.

MINER'VÆ PROMONTO'RIUM, a cape at the most southern extremity of Campania. *Plin.* 3. c. 5.

MINERVA'LIA, festivals at Rome in honor of Minerva, celebrated in the months of March and June. During the solemnity scholars obtained some relaxation from their studious pursuits, and the present, which it was usual for them to offer to their masters on the occasion, was called *Minerval*, in honor of the goddess Minerva, who patronised literature. *Varro de R. R.* 3. c. 2.—*Ovid. Trist.* 3. v. 809.—*Liv.* 9. c. 30.—*Macrob. Sat.* 1. c. 12.—*Tertull. de Idol.* 10.

MIN'ICA, a city of Syria, near Emessa. *Antonin.*

MIN'IO, now Mignone, a small river of Etruria, falling into the Tyrrhene Sea. *Virg. Æn.* 10. v. 83.

MIN'IO, one of the favorites of Antiochus, king of Syria.

MINNÆI, a people of Arabia, on the Red Sea. *Plin.* 12. c. 14.—*Dionys.* v. 958.

MINNODU'NUM, a town of Gallia Lugdunensis. *Antonin.* It is now Moudon,

MINO'A, a town of Sicily built by Minos, when he was pursuing Dœdalus, and called also Heraclea. *Diod. Sic.* 16.——A town of Peloponnesus. *Ptol.* ——A town of Crete.——A city of Amorgus, one of the Cyclades. *Steph.*——An ancient name of Parus. *Id.*

MINO'IS, belonging to Minos. Crete is called *Minoia regna*, as being that legislator's kingdom. *Virg. Æn.* 6. v. 14.——A patronymic of Ariadne. *Ovid. Met.* 8. v. 157.

MI'NOS, the First, a king of Crete, son of Jupiter and Europa, who gave laws to his subjects, B.C. 1406, which still remained in full force in the age of the philosopher Plato. His justice and moderation procured him the appellation of the favorite of the gods, the confident of Jupiter, and the wise legislator, in every city of Greece; and, according to the poets, he was rewarded for his equity, after death, with the office of supreme and absolute judge in the infernal regions. In this capacity he is represented sitting in the midst of the shades, and holding a sceptre in his hand, as the emblem of his authority. The dead plead their different causes before him, and the impartial judge shakes the fatal urn, which is filled with the destinies of mankind. He married Ithona, by whom he had Lycastus, who was the father of Minos the Second. *Homer. Odyss.* 19. v. 178.—*Virg. Æn.* 6. v. 432.—*Apollod.* 3. c. 1.—*Hygin.* fab. 41—*Diod.* 4.—*Horat.* 1. od. 28.—*Ovid.* 3. *Am.* el. 10. v. 4. *De A. A.* 2. v. 25.—*Conon. Narr.* 25.—*Lactant. ad Theb.* 4. v. 531 & 187.—*Schol. Eurip. in Hipp.* 683.—*Vossius de Idol.* 1. c. 14.

MI'NOS the Second, was a son of Lycastus, the son of Minos the First, and king of Crete. He married Pasiphae, the daughter of Sol and Perseis, and by her he had several children. He increased his paternal dominions by the conquest of the neighbouring islands, but he showed himself cruel in the vindictive war which he carried on against the Athenians, who had put to death his son Androgeus. *Vid.* Androgeus. He took Megara by the treachery of Scylla, (*vid.* Scylla), and not satisfied with a victory, he obliged the vanquished to bring him to Crete, seven chosen boys and the same number of virgins, to be devoured by the Minotaur. *Vid.* Minotaurus. This bloody tribute was at last abolished, when Theseus had succeeded in destroying the monster. *Vid.* Theseus. When Dædalus, whose industry and invention had fabricated the labyrinth, and whose imprudence, in assisting Pasiphae in the gratification of her unnatural desires, had offended Minos, fled from the place of his confinement with wings, (*vid.* Dædalus), and arrived safe in Sicily, the incensed monarch pursued the offender, resolved to punish his infidelity. Cocalus, king of Sicily, who had hospitably received Dædalus, entertained his royal guest with dissembled friendship; and, that he might not deliver to him a man whose well known ingenuity and abilities he wished to employ for the benefit of his subjects, put Minos to death. Some say that the daughters of Cocalus put the king of Crete to death by detaining him so long in a bath that he fainted, after which they suffocated him. Minos died about 35 years before the Trojan war. He was father of Androgeus, Glaucus, and Deucalion, and two daughters, Phædra and Ariadne. Many authors have confounded the two monarchs of this name, the grandfather and the grandson, but Homer, Plutarch, and Diodorus prove plainly that they were two different persons. *Paus. in Ach.* 4.—*Plut. in Thes.*—*Hygin.* fab. 41.—*Ovid. Met.* 8. v. 141.—*Diod.* 4.—*Virg. Æn.* 6. v. 21.—*Plut. in Min.*—*Athen.* 1.—*Flacc.* 14. v. 40.—*Conon. Narr.* 25.—*Schol. Pind. Nem.* 4.—*Sch. Homer. Il.* 2. v. 145.

MINOTAU'RUS, a celebrated monster, half a man, and half a bull, according to this verse of Ovid, *A. A.* 2. v. 24.

Semibovemque virum, semivirumque bovem.

It was the fruit of Pasiphae's unnatural amour with a bull. Minos refused to sacrifice a white bull to Neptune, an animal which he had received from the god for that purpose. This offended Neptune, and he made Pasiphae, the wife of Minos, enamoured of this beautiful animal, which had been refused to his altars. Dædalus prostituted his talents in being subservient to the queen's unnatural desires, and, by his means, Pasiphae's horrible passions were gratified, and the Minotaur came into the world. Minos confined in the labyrinth a monster which convinced the world of his wife's lasciviousness and indecency, and reflected disgrace upon his family. The Minotaur usually devoured the chosen young men and maidens, whom the tyranny of Minos yearly exacted from the Athenians. Theseus delivered his country from this shameful tribute, when it had fallen to his lot to be sacrificed to the voracity of the Minotaur, and, by means of Ariadne, the king's daughter, destroyed the monster, and then made his escape from the windings of the labyrinth. The fabulous tradition of the Minotaur, and of the infamous commerce of Pasiphae with a favourite bull, has been often explained. Some suppose that Pasiphae was enamoured of one of her husband's courtiers, called Taurus, and that Dædalus favoured the passion of the queen, by suffering his house to become the retreat of the two lovers. Pasiphae, some time after, brought twins into the world, one of whom greatly resembled Minos, and the other Taurus. From the natural resemblance of their countenances with that of their supposed fathers, originated their name, and, consequently, the fable of the Minotaur. *Ovid. Met.* 8. fab. 2.—*Hygin.* fab. 40.—*Plut. in Thes.*—*Palæphat.*—*Virg. Æn.* 6 v. 26.—*Servius loco.*—*Lactant. ad Achill. Stat.* 1. v. 192. & *Theb.* 5. v. 441.—*Tzetzes. Chil.* 1. c. 18. [There is a fine fragment representing the head and breast of the Minotaur, in the hall of animals, in the Museum of the Vatican.]

MIN'THE, a daughter of Cocytus, loved by Pluto. Proserpine discovered her husband's infidelity, and changed his mistress into an herb, called by the same name, *mint*. *Ovid. Met.* 10. v. 729.

Min'the, a mountain of Peloponnesus. *Paus.* l. 4.

MINTUR'NÆ, a town of Campania, between Sinuessa and Formiæ, near the mouth of the Liris. It was in the marshes, in its neighbourhood, that the great Marius concealed himself in the mud, to avoid the partisans of Sylla. Marica was worshipped there, hence *Maricæ regna* applied to the place. *Strab.* 2.—*Mela*, 2. c. 4.—*Liv.* 8. c. 10. l. 10. c. 21. l. 27. c. 38.—*Horat.* 1. ep. 5, v. 5.—*Paterc.* 2. c. 14 —*Lucan.* 2. v. 424.

MINU'CIA, a vestal virgin, accused of debauchery on account of the beauty and elegance of her dress. She was condemned to be buried alive, because a female supported the false accusation, A.U.C. 418. *Liv.* 8. c. 15.

Minu'cia, a public road leading from Rome to Brundusium, by a different direction from the Appian. *Vid.* Via.

MINU'CIUS AUGURI'NUS, a Roman consul slain in a battle against the Samnites.

Minu'cius Lu'cius, a tribune of the people, who accused Mælius of aspiring to the sovereignty of Rome. He was honored with a brazen statue for causing the corn collected by Mælius to be sold at a reduced price to the people. *Liv.* 4. c. 12 & 16.—*Plin.* 18. c. 3.

Minu'cius M. Ru'fus, a master of the horse to the dictator Fabius Maximus. His disobedience to the commands of the dictator was productive of an extension of his prerogative, and the master of the horse was declared equal in power to the dictator. Minucius, soon after this, fought with ill success against Annibal, and was saved by the interference of Fabius; which circumstance had such an effect upon him that he laid down his power at the feet of his deliverer, and swore that he would never act but by his directions. He was killed at the battle of Cannæ. *Liv.* 22. c. 8, &c.—*C. Nep. in Ann.*

Minu'cius, a Roman consul who defended Coriolanus from the insults of the people, &c.

Minu'cius Lu'cius, a consul, defeated by the Æqui, and disgraced by the dictator Cincinnatus, who liberated his army. *Liv.* 3. c. 26. 29.

Minu'cius, an officer under Cæsar, in Gaul, who afterwards became one of the conspirators against his patron. *Cæs. B. G.* 6. c. 29.——A tribune who warmly opposed the views of C. Gracchus.

Minu'cius Q. Ru'fus, a consul, who, when refused the honors of a triumph by the senate for his conquests in Gaul, exhibited a triumphal procession on mount Albanus. *Liv.* 33. c. 22, &c.

Minu'cius Q. Ther'mus, a prætor in Spain. He was afterwards engaged against the Ligurians, and was slain in a battle against the Thracians. *Liv.* 34. c. 10, &c.

Minu'cius, a Roman, chosen dictator, and obliged to lay down his office, because, during the time of his election, the sudden cry of a rat was heard.——A Roman, one of the first who were chosen quæstors.

Minu'cius M. Fe'lix, an African lawyer, who flourished 207 A.D. He has written an elegant dialogue in defence of the Christian religion, called *Octavius*, from the principal speaker in it. This book was long attributed to Arnobius, and even printed with his works as an eighth book, (*Octavus*), till Balduinus discovered the imposition in his edition of Felix, 1560. The two last editions are that of Davies, 8vo, Cantab. 1712; and of Gronovius, 8vo. L. Bat. 1709. An English translation with critical notes, was published by Lord Hailes, Edinburgh. 1781, 8vo. *Sax. Onom.* 1. p. 361.—*Harles. Not. Lit. Rom* 1. p. 522.

MIN'YA, a city of Thessaly, anciently called Almonia.——A city of Elis, near Pylus.——A city of Phrygia. *Steph.*

MIN'YÆ, a name given to the inhabitants of Orchomenus in Bœotia, from Minyas king of the country. Orchomenus the son of Minyas, gave his name to the capital of the country, and its inhabitants still retained their original appellation in contradistinction to the Orchomenians of Arcadia. A colony of Orchomenians passed from Bœotia into Thessaly and settled in Iolcus; from which circumstance the people of the place, and particularly the Argonauts, were called Minyæ. This name they received, according to the opinion of some, not because a number of Orchomenians had settled among them, but because the chief and noblest among them were said to be descended from the daughters of Minyas. Part of the Orchomenians accompanied the sons of Codrus when they migrated to Ionia. The descendants of the Argonauts, as well as the Argonauts themselves, received the name of Minyæ. They first inhabited Lemnus, where they had been born from the Lemnian women who had murdered their husbands. They were driven from Lemnus by the Pelasgi about 1160 years B.C., and came to settle in Laconia, whence they passed into Calliste with a colony of Lacedæmonians. *Hygin.* fab. 14.—*Paus.* 9. c. 6.—*Apollon.* 1. *Arg.*—*Herodot.* 4. c. 145.—*Festus de V. Sig.*—*Sch. Pind. in Pyth.* 4.—*Tzetzes in Lyc.*—*Servius ad Virg. Ec.* 4. v. 34.

MIN'YAS, a king of Bœotia, son of Neptune and Tritogenia, the daughter of Æolus. Some make him the son of Neptune and Callirrhoe, or of Chryses, Neptune's son, and Chrysogenia, the daughter of Halmus. He married Clytodora, by whom he had Presbon, Periclymenus, and Eteoclymenus. He was father of Orchomenus, Diochithondes, and Athamas, by a second marriage with Phanasora, the daughter of Paon. According to Plutarch and

Ovid, he had three daughters, called Leuconoe, Alcithoe, and Leucippe. They were changed into bats. *Vid.* Mineides. *Paus.* 9. c. 36.—*Plut. Quæst. Græc.* 38.—*Ovid. Met.* 4. v. 1 & 468.—*Sch. Pind. Isth.* 1.—*Sch. Apollon.* 1 & 3.

MINYE'A, a festival observed at Orchomenus in honour of Minyas, the king of the place. The Orchomenians were called Minyæ, and the river upon the banks of which their town was built, Minya. *Pindar. Schol. Isthm.* od. 1.

MINYE'IDES. *Vid.* Mineides.

MINYE'IUS or **MINYE'JUS**, a river of Thessaly, called afterwards Orchomenus, falling into the sea near Arene. *Homer. Il.* 11.—*Strab.* 8.

MINYI'A, a country of Amorgus, one of the Cyclades. *Steph.* According to *Ptolemy*, it is a city in an island of the Icarian Sea, between Cos and Samus.

MIN'YTUS, one of Niobe's sons. *Apollod.*

MIR'ACES, a eunuch of Parthia, &c. *Flacc.* 6. v. 690.

MIROBRI'GA, a city of Spain. *Ptol.* It is now Villa de Capilla.

MI'RUS, a river of Phrygia. *Suidas.*

MISAG'ENES, a son of Masinissa, engaged in the Roman armies. *Liv.* 42. c. 29 & 62. l. 45. c. 14.

MIS'ARIS, a promontory of European Sarmatia. *Ptol.*

MIS'CERA, a city of Sicily. *Steph.*

MISE'NUM. *Vid.* Misenus.

MISE'NUS, a son of Æolus, who was piper to Hector. After Hector's death he followed Æneas to Italy, and was drowned on the coast of Campania, because he had challenged one of the Tritons to a trial of skill. Æneas afterwards found his body on the sea shore, and buried it on a promontory which bore his name, now Miseno.

Mise'nus, a town on the promontory at the west of the bay of Naples, with a capacious harbour where Augustus and some of the Roman emperors generally stationed one of their fleets. *Virg. Æn.* 3. v. 239. l. 6. v. 164 & 234.—*Strab.* 5.—*Mela*, 2. c. 4. —*Liv.* 24. c. 13.—*Tacit. H.* 2. c. 9, *An.* 15. c. 51.— —*Plin.* 6. ep. 16 & 20.—*Ital.* 12. v. 155.—*Flor.* 1. c. 16.

MISE'TUS, a city of Macedonia. *Steph.*

MISGE'TES, a people of the Iberi. *Id.*

MISITH'EUS or **MIS'ITHEUS**, a Roman, of Greek extraction, celebrated for his virtues and his misfortunes. He was father-in-law to the emperor Gordian, whose counsels and actions in the government of the state he guided by his prudence and moderation. He was sacrificed to the ambition of Philip, a wicked senator, who succeeded him as præfect of the prætorian guards. He died A.D. 243, and left all his possessions to be appropriated for the good of the public. *Jul. Capitol. in vit. Gordian.* 111. c. 23.

MIS'NA, a naval station of the Carthaginians. *Cœl. Rhod.* 18. c. 38.

MIS'PILA, a city of the Medes. *Steph.*

MIS'THIUM, a city of Galatia. *Id.*

MIS'TIA, a city of Magna Græcia, on the borders of the Locri. *Mela*, 2. c. 4. It is called Mystia by *Pliny*, 3. c. 10, and Mistræ by others.

MIS'UA, a city of Africa, called Nisua by *Ptolemy*, and now Nuchia or Nubia. *Antonin.*

MIS'YNOS, an island of the Libyan Sea, near Cyrenaica. *Ptol.*

MI'THRAS, a god of Persia, supposed to be the Sun, or, according to others, Venus Urania. His worship was, in process of time, introduced at Rome, and the Romans raised him altars, on which was this inscription,

Deo Soli Mithræ, or *Soli Deo invicto Mithræ.*

He is generally represented as a young man whose head is covered with a turban, after the manner of the Persians. He supports his knee upon a bull that lies on the ground, and one of whose horns he holds in one hand, while with the other he plunges a dagger into its neck. *Stat. Theb.* 1. v. 720.— *Curt.* 4. c. 13.—*Claudian. de Laud. Stil.* 1. [One of the best representations of Mithra will be found in the British Museum.]

MITHRACE'NES, a Persian who fled to Alexander after the murder of Darius by Bessus. *Curt.* 5.

MITHRADA'TES, a herdsman of Astyages, ordered by Harpagus to put young Cyrus to death. He refused, and educated him at home as his own son, &c. *Herodot.*—*Justin.*

MITHRE'NES, a Persian who betrayed Sardes, &c. *Curt.* 3. c. 12.

MITHRIDA'TES the First, was the third king of Pontus. He was tributary to the crown of Persia, and his attempts to render his country independent proved fruitless. He was conquered in a battle, and obtained peace with difficulty. Xenophon calls him merely a governor of Cappadocia. He was succeeded by Ariobarzanes, B.C. 363. *Diod.* —*Xenoph.*

Mithrida'tes the Second, king of Pontus, was grandson to Mithridates the First. He made himself master of Pontus, which had been conquered by Alexander, and had been ceded to Antigonus at the general division of the Macedonian empire among the conqueror's generals. He reigned about twenty-six years, and died at the advanced age of eighty-four years, B.C. 302. He was succeeded by his son Mithridates the Third. Some say that Antigonus put him to death, because he favored the cause of Cassander. *Appian. Mith.*— *Diod.*

Mithrida'tes the Third, was son of the preceding monarch. He enlarged his paternal possessions by the conquest of the provinces of Cappadocia and Paphlagonia, and died after a reign of thirty-six years. *Diod.*

Mithrida'tes the Fourth, succeeded his father Ariobarzanes, who was the son of Mithridates the Third.

Mithrida'tes the Fifth, succeeded his father Mithridates the Fourth, and strengthened himself on his throne by an alliance with Antiochus the Great, whose daugter Laodice he married. He was succeeded by his son Pharnaces.

Mithrida'tes the Sixth, succeeded his father Pharnaces. He was the first of the kings of Pontus who formed an alliance with the Romans. He furnished them with a fleet in the third Punic war, and assisted them against Aristonicus, who had laid claim to the kingdom of Pergamus. This fidelity was liberally rewarded; he was called *Evergetes*, and received from the Roman people the province of Phrygia Major, and was honored with the title of friend and ally of Rome. He was murdered B.C. 123. *Appian. Mithr.*—*Justin.* 37, &c.

Mithrida'tes the Seventh, surnamed *Eupator* and *The Great*, succeeded his father Mithridates the Sixth, though only eleven years of age. The beginning of his reign was marked by cruelty, ambition, and artifice. He murdered his own mother, who had been left by his father co-heiress of the kingdom, and fortified his constitution by drinking antidotes against the poison with which his enemies at court attempted to destroy him. He early inured his body to hardship, and employed himself in every manly exercise, often remaining whole months in the country, and making the frozen snow and the bare earth the place of his repose. Naturally ambitious and cruel, he spared no pains in the acquisition of power and dominion. He murdered the two sons whom his sister Laodice had had by Ariarathes, king of Cappadocia, and placed one of his own children, eight years old, on the vacant throne. These violent proceedings alarmed Nicomedes, king of Bithynia, who had married Laodice, the widow of Ariarathes. He suborned a youth to be king of Cappadocia, as the third son of Ariarathes, and Laodice was sent to Rome to impose upon the senate, and assure them that her third son was still alive, and that his pretensions to the kingdom of Cappadocia were just and well grounded. Mithridates used the same arms of dissimulation. He also sent to Rome Gordius, the governor of his son, who solemnly declared before the Roman people, that the youth who sat on the throne of Cappadocia was the third son and lawful heir of Ariarathes, and that he was supported as such by Mithridates. This intricate affair excited the attention of the Roman senate, and, to finally settle the dispute between the two monarchs, the powerful arbiters took away the kingdom of Cappadocia from Mithridates, and Paphlagonia from Nicomedes. These two kingdoms being thus separated from their original possessors, were presented with their freedom and independence; but the Cappadocians refused it, and received Ariobarzanes for king. Such were the first seeds of enmity between Rome and the king of Pontus. *Vid.* Mithdaticum bellum. Mithridates never lost an opportunity by which he might lessen the influence of his adversaries; and, the more effectually to destroy their power in Asia, he ordered all the Romans that were in his dominions to be massacred. This execrable deed was carried into execution in the course of one night, and no less than 150,000, according to Plutarch, or 80,000 Romans, as Appian mentions, were made, at one blow, the victims of his cruelty. This universal massacre called aloud for revenge. Aquilius, and, soon after, Sylla, marched against Mithridates with a large army. The former was made prisoner, but Sylla obtained a victory over the king's generals, and another decisive engagement rendered him master of all Greece, Macedonia, Ionia, and Asia Minor, which had submitted a short time before to the victorious arms of the monarch of Pontus. This ill fortune was aggravated by the loss of about 200,000 men, who were killed in the several engagements that had been fought; and Mithridates, weakened by repeated disasters both by sea and land, sued for peace from the conqueror, which he obtained on condition of defraying the expenses which the Romans had incurred by the war, and of remaining satisfied with the possessions which he had inherited from his ancestors. While these negociations for peace were carried on, Mithridates was not unmindful of his real interest. His poverty, and the exhausted resources of his kingdom, not his inclinations, obliged him to wish for peace. Soon after these events he took the field with 140,000 infantry and 16,000 horse, which consisted of his own forces and those of his son-in-law, Tigranes, king of Armenia. With such a numerous army, he soon made himself master of the Roman provinces in Asia; none dared to oppose his conquests, as the Romans, relying on his fidelity, had withdrawn the greatest part of their armies from the country. Intelligence of his warlike preparation was no sooner received at Rome than Lucullus, the consul, marched into Asia, and, without delay, blocked up the camp of Mithridates, who was then besieging Cyzicus. The Asiatic monarch escaped from his attack, and fled into the heart of his kingdom. Lucullus pursued him with the utmost celerity, and would have taken him prisoner after a battle, had not the avidity of his soldiers preferred the plundering of a mule loaded with gold to the taking of a monarch who had exercised such cruelties against their countrymen, and shown himself so faithless to the most solemn engagements. After this escape, Mithridates was more careful about the safety of his person, and he even ordered his wives and sisters to destroy themselves, fearful of their falling into the enemy's hands. The appointment of Glabrio to the command of the Roman forces, instead of Lucullus, was favorable to the cause of Mithridates, and by the injudicious operations of this general he recovered the greatest part of his dominions. The sudden arrival of Pompey, however, soon put an end to his victories. A battle was fought near the Euphrates in the night, in which the troops of Pontus labored under every disadvantage. The engagement was by moonlight, and as the moon then shone in the face of the enemy, the lengthened shadows of the arms of the Romans having induced Mithridates to believe that the two armies were close together, the arrows of his soldiers were darted from a great distance, and their efforts rendered ineffectual. A universal overthrow ensued, and Mithridates, undaunted in the midst of his misfortunes, rushed through the thick ranks of the enemy, at the head of 800 horsemen, 500 of whom perished in the attempt to follow him. He fled to Tigranes, but that monarch, terrified at the name and power of the Romans, refused an asylum to his father-in-law, whom he had before supported with all the collected forces of his kingdom. Mithridates found a safe retreat among the Scythians, and, though destitute of friends, power, and resources, yet he meditated the destruction of the Roman empire, by penetrating into the heart of Italy by land. These wild projects were rejected by his followers, and he sued for peace. It was denied to his ambassadors, and the victorious Pompey declared, that, to obtain it, Mithridates must ask it in person. He scorned to trust himself into the hands of his enemy, and resolved to conquer or to die. His subjects, however, whose spirits were broken by repeated disasters, refused to listen to him any longer, they revolted from him, and made his son Pharnaces king. The son showed himself ungrateful to his father, and, according to some writers, even ordered him to be put to death. This unnatural treatment broke the heart of Mithridates; he obliged his wife to poison herself, and attempted to do the same himself. It was in vain; the frequent antidotes which he had taken in the early part of his life, strengthened his constitution against the poison, and, when this was unavailing, he attempted to stab himself. The blow was not mortal; and a Gaul, who was then present, at his own request, gave him the fatal stroke, about sixty-three years B.C. in the seventy-second year of his age. Such were the misfortunes, abilities, and miserable end of a man, who supported himself so long against the power of Rome, and who, according to the declaration of the Roman authors, proved a more powerful and indefatigable adversary to the capital of Italy than Annibal, Pyrrhus, Perseus, or Antiochus. Mithridates has been commended for his eminent virtues, and equally censured for his vices. As a commander and a king he deserves the most unbounded applause, and it may create admiration to see him waging war with such success during so many years against the most powerful people upon earth, led into the field by a Sylla, a Lucullus, and a Pompey. He was the greatest monarch that ever sat on a throne, according to the opinion of Cicero; and, indeed, no better proof of his military character and the powerful resources of his mind can be produced, than the great rejoicings which happened in the Roman armies and in the capital at the news of his death. No less than twelve days were appointed for public thanksgiving to the immortal gods, and Pompey, who had sent the first intelligence of his death to Rome, and who had partly hastened his fall, was rewarded with the most uncommon honors. *Vid.* Ampia Lex. It is said that Mithridates conquered twenty-four nations, whose different languages he knew, and spoke with the same ease and fluency as his own. As a man of letters he also deserves attention. He was acquainted with the Greek language, in which he even wrote a treatise on botany. His skill in physic is well known, and even now there is a celebrated antidote which bears his name, and is called *Mithridate.* Superstition, as well as nature, had united to render him great; and, if we rely upon the authority of Justin, his birth was accompanied by the appearance of two large comets, which were seen for seventy days successively, the splendor of which esclipsed the mid-day sun, and covered the fourth part of the heavens. *Justin.* 37. c. 1. &c.—*Strab.—Diod.* 14.—*Flor.* 3. c. 5, &c.—*Plut. in Syll. Luc. Mar. & Pomp.—Val. Max.* 4. c. 6, &c.—*Dio.* 30, &c.—*Appian. Mithrid.—Plin.* 2. c. 97. l. 7. c. 24. l. 25. c. 2. l. 33. c. 3, &c.—*Cic. pro Man.* &c.—*Paterc.* 2. c. 18.—*Eutrop.* 5.—*Joseph.* 14.—*—Oros.* 6, &c.

MITHRIDA'TES, a king of Parthia who took Demetrius prisoner.——A king of Armenia.——A king of Pergamus, who warmly embraced the cause of J. Cæsar, and was made king of Bosporus by him. Some suppose him to have been the son of the great Mithridates by a concubine. He was murdered, &c.——A king of Iberia.——A king of Comagena.——A celebrated king of Parthia, who enlarged his possessions by the conquest of some of the neighbouring countries. He examined with a careful eye the constitution and particular regulations of the nations which he had conquered, and framed from them a code of laws for the benefit of his own subjects. *Justin.—Orosius.*——A king of Parthia, who murdered his father, and made himself master of the crown.——A king of Pontus, put to death by order of Galba, &c.

MITHRIDA'TES, a man made king of Armenia by Tiberius. He was afterwards imprisoned by Caligula, and set at liberty by Claudius. He was murdered by one of his nephews, and his family were involved in his ruin. *Tacit. Ann.*——A man in the armies of Artaxerxes. He was rewarded by the monarch for having wounded Cyrus the younger; but when he boasted that he had killed him, he was cruelly put to death. *Plut. in Artax.*——A son of Ariobarzanes, who basely murdered Datames. *C. Nep. in Dat.*

MITHRIDAT'ICUM BEL'LUM, begun eighty-nine years B.C., was one of the longest and most celebrated wars ever carried on by the Romans against a foreign power. The ambition of Mithridates, from whom it received its name, may be called the primary origin of it. His views upon the kingdom of Cappadocia, of which he was stripped by the Romans, first engaged him to take up arms against the republic. Three Roman officers, L. Cassius the proconsul, M. Aquilius, and Q. Oppius, opposed Mithridates with the troops of Bithynia, Cappadocia, Paphlagonia, and Gallo-græcia. The army of these provinces, together with the Roman soldiers in Asia, amounted to 70,000 men, and 6,000 horse. The forces of the king of Pontus were greatly superior to these; he led 250,000 foot, 40,000 horse, and 130 armed chariots into the field of battle, under the command of Neoptolemus and Archelaus. His fleet consisted of 400 ships of war, well manned and provisioned. In the first engagement the king of Pontus obtained the victory, and dispersed the Roman forces in Asia. He became master of the greatest part of Asia, and the Hellespont submitted to his power. Two of the Roman generals were taken, and M. Aquilius, who had been entrusted with the conduct of the war, was carried about in Asia, and exposed to the ridicule and insults of the populace, and at last put to death by Mithridates, who ordered melted gold to be poured down his throat, as a slur upon the avidity of the Romans. The conqueror took every possible advantage of his victory; he rapidly subdued all the islands of the Ægæan Sea, and though Rhodes refused to submit to his power, yet all Greece was soon over-run by his general Archelaus, and made tributary to the kingdom of Pontus. Meanwhile, the Romans, incensed against Mithridates on account of his perfidy, and of his cruelty in massacreing 80,000 of their countrymen in one day, appointed Sylla to march into the east. Sylla landed in Greece, where the inhabitants readily acknowledged his power; but Athens shut her gates against the Roman commander, and Archelaus, who defended it with the greatest courage, baffled for a while all the efforts and operations of the enemy. This spirited defence was of short duration. Archelaus retreated into Bœotia, where Sylla soon followed him. The two hostile armies drew up in line of battle near Chæronea, and the Romans obtained the victory, and of the almost innumerable forces of the Asiatics, no more than 10,000 escaped. Another battle in Thessaly, near Orchomenus, proved equally fatal to the king of Pontus. Dorylaus, one of his generals, was defeated, and he was soon after obliged to sue for peace. Sylla listened to the terms of accommodation, as his presence at Rome was now become necessary to quell the commotions and cabals which his enemies had raised against him. He pledged himself to the king of Pontus to confirm him in the possession of his dominions, and to procure him the title of friend and ally of Rome; and Mithridates consented to relinquish Asia and Paphlagonia, to deliver Cappadocia to Ariobarzanes, and Bythynia to Nicomedes, and to pay to the Romans 2,000 talents to defray the expenses of the war, and to deliver into their hands seventy gallies with all their rigging. Though Mithridates seemed to have re-established peace in his dominions, yet Fimbria, whose sentiments were contrary to those of Sylla, and who made himself master of the Roman army in Asia by intrigue and oppression, kept him under continual alarms, and rendered the existence of his power precarious. Sylla, who had returned from Greece to ratify the treaty which had been made with Mithridates, rid the world of the tyrannical Fimbria; and the king of Pontus, awed by the resolution and the determined firmness of his adversary, at last agreed, though with reluctance, to the conditions. The hostile preparations of Mithridates, which had been continued in the time of peace, became suspected by the Romans, and Muræna, who was left as governor of Asia in Sylla's absence, and who wished to make himself known by some conspicuous action, began hostilities by taking Comana and plundering the temple of Bellona. Mithridates did not oppose him, but, assuming the character of a friendly but injured monarch, complained of the breach of peace before the Roman Senate. Muræna was publicly reprimanded; but, as he did not cease from hostilities, it was easily understood that he acted by the direction of the Roman people. The king upon this marched against him, and a battle was fought, in which both the adversaries claimed the victory. This was the last blow which the king of Pontus received in this war, which is called the second Mithridatic war, and which continued for about three years. Sylla at that time was nominated perpetual dictator at Rome, and he commanded Muræna to retire from the kingdom of Mithridates. The retirement of Sylla from power changed the face of affairs; the treaty of peace between the king of Pontus and the Romans, which had never been committed to writing, demanded frequent explanations, and Mithridates at last threw off the mask of friendship, and openly declared war. Nicomedes, at his death, left his kingdom to the Romans, but Mithridates disputed their right to the possessions of the deceased monarch, and entered the field with 120,000 men, besides a fleet of 400 ships in his ports, 16,000 horsemen to follow him, and 100 chariots armed with scythes. Lucullus was appointed over Asia, and entrusted with the care of the Mithridatic war. His valor and prudence showed his merit; and Mithridates, in his vain attempts to take Cyzicum, lost no less than 300,000 men. Success continually attended the Roman arms. The king of Pontus was defeated in several bloody engagements, and with difficulty saved his life, and retired into the territories of his son-in-law Tigranes king of Armenia. Lucullus pursued him, and, when his application for the person of the fugitive monarch had been rejected by Tigranes, he marched to the capital of Armenia, and terrified, by his sudden approach, the numerous forces of the enemy. A battle ensued. The Romans obtained an easy victory, and no less than 100,000 foot of the Armenians perished, and it is said that only five men of the Romans were killed. Tigranocerta, the rich capital of the country, fell into the conqueror's hands. After such signal victories, Lucullus had the mortification to see his own troops mutiny, and to be dispossessed of the command by the arrival of Pompey. The new general showed himself worthy to succeed Lucullus, by pursuing the same vigorous measures. He defeated Mithridates, and rendered his affairs so desperate, that the monarch fled for safety into the country of the Scythians, where, for a while, he meditated the ruin of the Roman empire, and, with more wildness than prudence, secretly resolved to invade Italy by land, and march an army across the northern wilds of Asia and Europe to the Apennines. Not only the kingdom of Mithridates had fallen into the enemy's hands, but also all the neighbouring kings and princes were subdued, and Pompey saw prostrate at his feet Tigranes himself, that king of kings who had lately treated the Romans with such contempt. Meantime the wild projects of Mithridates terrified his subjects; and fearful to accompany him in a march of above 2000 miles across a barren and uncultivated country, they at last revolted and made his son king. The monarch, forsaken in his old age even by his own children, and overwhelmed with misfortunes, put an end to his life (*vid.* Mithridates the Seventh), and gave the Romans cause to rejoice, as the third Mithridatic war was ended in his fall, B.C. 63. Such were the unsuccessful struggles of Mithridates against the power of Rome. He was always full of resources, and the Romans had never a greater or more dangerous war to sustain. The duration of the Mithridatic war is not precisely known. According to Justin, Orosius, Florus, and Europius, it lasted for forty years; but the opinion of others, who limit its duration to thirty years, is far more credible; and, indeed, by proper calculation, there elapsed scarcely more than twenty-six years from the time that Mithridates first entered the field against the Romans till the time of his death. *Appian. in Mithrid.—Justin.* 37, &c.—*Flor.* 2, &c.—*Liv.—Plut. in Luc. &c.—Orosius.—Paterc.—Dion.*

MITHRIDA'TIS, a daughter of Mithrodates the Great. She was poisoned by her father that she might not fall into the hands of the Romans.

MITHROBARZA'NES, a king of Armenia, &c. ——An officer sent by Tigranes against Lucullus, &c. *Plut.*——The father-in-law of Datames.

MITYLE'NE or MITYLE'NÆ, the capital city of the island of Lesbus, which received its name from Mitylene, the daughter of Macareus, a king of the country. It was greatly commended by the ancients for the stateliness of its buildings and the fruitfulness of its soil, but more particularly for the great men whom it produced at different times. Pittacus, Alcæus, Sappho, Terpander, Theophanes, Hellenicus, &c. were all natives of Mitylene. It was long a seat of learning, and, with Rhodes and Athens, it had the honor of having educated many of the great men of Greece and Rome. In the Peloponnesian war the Mityleneans suffered greatly for their revolt from the power of Athens; and in the Mithridatic wars they had the boldness to resist the Romans, and disdained to regard the treaties which had been made between Mithridates and Sylla. *Cic. de Leg. Ag.—Strab.* 13.—*Mela*, 2. c. 7. —*Diod.* 3 & 12.—*Paterc.* 1. c. 4.—*Horat.* .1 od. 7. v. 1. l. 1. ep. 11. v. 17.—*Lucan.* 7. v. 786. l. 8. v. 109.—*Thucyd.* 3, &c.—*Plut. in Pomp. &c.* A festival was celebrated by the inhabitants in honor of Apollo Μαλλοεις. *Hesych.—Thucyd.* 1. 3.

MI'TYS, a man whose statue fell upon his murderer and crushed him to death, &c. *Aristot.* 10. *de Poet.*

Mi'tys, a small river of Macedonia. *Liv.*

MIZÆ'I, a people of Elymais, on the borders of Persia.

MNASAL'CAS, a Greek poet, who wrote epigrams. *Athen.—Strab.*

MNA'SEAS, an historian of Phœnicia. ——An historian of Colophon.

Mna'seas, an historian of Patræ, in Achaia, who flourished 141 B.C. *Vossius, H. Gr.* 1. c. 21.—*Gesner. in Bibl.—Suid.*

MNAS'ICLES, a general of Thymbro, who being indignant at the unequal division of some booty, fled to the Cyreneans. *Diod.* 58

MNAS'ILUS, a youth who assisted Chromis in binding the old Silenus whom they found asleep in a cave. Some commentators imagine that Virgil spoke of his friend Varus under the name of Mnasilus. *Virg. Ec.* 6. v. 13.—*Servius in loco.*

MNASIN'OUS and ANAX'IS, the sons of Pollux and Phœbe, and of Castor and Hilaira, whose statues were erected in the temples sacred to the Dioscuri at Argos and Amyclæ. *Paus.* 2. c. 22, l. 3. c. 18.

MNASIPPI'DAS, a Lacedæmonian, who imposed upon the credulity of the people, &c. *Polyæn.* 2. c. 23.

MNASIP'PUS, a Lacedæmonian sent with a fleet of 65 ships and 1500 men to Corcyra, where he was killed, &c. *Diod.* 15.

MNASIS'TRATUS, a man who farmed some of the public lands in Sicily. *Cic. Verr.* 3. c. 46.

MNASITH'EUS, a friend of Aratus

Mnasith'eus, a celebrated painter of Sicyon. *Plin.* 35. c. 11.

MNA'SON, a tyrant of Elatia, who gave 3600 minæ of gold for twelve pictures of twelve gods to Asclepiodorus, and 1200 minæ, for as many goddesses to Theomnestus. *Plin.* 35. c. 10.

MNASYR'IUM, a place in Rhodes. *Strab.* 14.

MNEMI'UM, a promontory of Æthiopia, on the Arabic Gulph. *Ptol.*

MNE'MON, a surname given to Artaxerxes the Second, on account of his retentive memory. *C. Nep in Reg.*

MNEMOS'YNE, a daughter of Cœlus and Terra, mother of the nine Muses, by Jupiter, who assumed the form of a shepherd to enjoy her company. The word *Mnemosyne* signifies *memory*, and therefore the poets have rightly called memory the mother of the Muses, because it is to that mental endowment that mankind are indebted for their progress in science. *Ovid. Met.* 6. fab. 4.—*Pindar. Isth.* 6. v. 110.—*Hesiod. Theog.* v. 915.—*Phædrus*, 3. fab. prol.—*Plut. de Liber. Educ.—Anton. Liber.* 9.—*Apollod.* 1. c. 1, &c. [There is a statue of Mnemosyne in the Vatican, at Rome.]

Mnemos'yne, a fountain of Bœotia, the waters of which were generally drunk by those who consulted the oracle of Trophonius. *Paus.* 9. c. 39.

MNESAR'CHUS, a celebrated Stoic of Greece, pupil to Panætius. He considered philosophy as the foundation of oratory. *Cic. de Orat.* 1. c. 11 & 17. *Fin.* 2. *Acad.* 4. c. 22.

MNESIDA'MUS or MNESIDE'MUS, an officer who conspired against the lieutenant of Demetrius. *Polyæn.* 5. c. 17.

MNESILA'US, a son of Pollux and Phœbe. He was also called Mnasinous. *Apollod.*

MNESIL'OCHUS, an Acarnanian who wished to persuade his countrymen to assist Antiochus against Rome. *Liv.* 36. c. 11 & 12.

Mnesil'ochus, a comic poet. *Schol. Aristoph. in Aves.*

MNESIM'ACHE, a daughter of Dexamenus, king of Olenus, courted by Eurytion whom Hercules killed. *Apollod.* 2.

MNESIM'ACHUS, a comic poet, three of whose plays are mentioned by *Suidas*. *Athen.* 8, 9, &c.—*Voss. Poet. Gr.* c. 7. p. 50.

Mnesim'achus, a poet mentioned by the *Scholiast* on *Apollonius*, l. 4.

MNESITH'EUS, a physician author of several works. *Galen. l. de alim. facult.*

MNES'TER, a freedman of Agrippina, who murdered himself on the death of his mistress. *Tacit. Ann.* 14. c. 9.

Mnes'ter, a pantomime, a favorite with Messalina. *Id. ibid.* 11. c. 36.

MNESTHEUS, a Trojan, descended from Assaracus. He obtained the prize given to the best sailing vessel by Æneas, at the funeral games of Anchises, in Sicily, and became the progenitor of the family of the Memmii at Rome. *Virg. Æn.* 4. v. 116, &c.——A son of Peteus. *Vid.* Menestheus. ——A freedman of Aurelian, &c. *Eutrop.* 9.—*Aur. Vict.*——A physician, mentioned by *Pliny*, 21. c. 3.

MNES'TRA, a daughter of Danaus. *Apollod.*——A mistress of Cimon.

MNE'VIS, a celebrated bull, sacred to the sun in the town of Heliopolis. He was worshipped with the same superstitious ceremonies as Apis, and, at his death, he received the most magnificent funeral. He was the emblem of Osiris. *Diod.* 1.—*Plut. de Isid.—Plin.* 8. c. 48.

MNI'ARA, a town of Mauritania Cæsariensis, called Mina by *Antoninus.—Ptol.*

MOAPHER'NES, the uncle of Strabo's mother, &c. *Strab.* 12.

MO'CA, a town of Arabia Petræa. *Ptol.*

MOCAR'SUS, a small region of Thrace. *Steph.*

MOCA'TA, a city of Bithynia. *Id.*

MOCHU'RA, an inland city of Arabia Felix. *Ptol.*

MO'CHUS, a Phœnician, who wrote a history of his country in his native tongue. *Athen.* 3.—*Voss. H Gr.* 3, p. 390.

MO'CLE, a city of Phrygia. *Steph.*

MODES'TUS, a Latin writer, under the emperor Tacitus, A.D. 275, whose book *De re militari* was elegantly edited in 2 vols. 8vo, Vesaliæ, 1670. *Harles. Not. Lit. Rom.* 1. p. 546.

Modes'tus Ju'lius, a grammarian. *Suet. de illustr. Gramm.* c. 20.—*Harles. ibid.—Sax. Onom.* 1. p. 374.

Modes'tus Aufid'ius, a commentator on Virgil. *Philargyr. Georg.* l. 2, &c.

MO'DIA, a rich widow at Rome. *Juv.* 3. v. 130.

MODIA'NA, a city of Arabia Felix. *Ptol.*

MODI'RIS, a town of India within the Ganges. *Id.*

MO'DIUS, a Roman knight, mentioned by *Cicero. Verr.* 2. c. 48. [There is a bust of Modius in the Musée Royale, at Paris.]

MODOGAL'LA, a city of India within the Ganges. *Ptol.*

MO'DRON, a place of Phrygia Major. *Strab.*

MODUN'GA, a city of Mauritania Cæsariensis. *Ptol.*

MODU'RA, a city of India within the Ganges. *Id.*

MODUT'TI, a city of Taprobane. *Ptol.* It is now Pinder.

MŒ'CIA, one of the tribes at Rome. *Liv.* 8. c. 17.

MŒ'DI, a people of Thrace, conquered by Philip of Macedonia.

MŒ'NUS, now the Mayne, a river of Germany which falls into the Rhine near Mentz. *Tacit. de Germ.* 28.

MŒ'ON, a Sicilian, who poisoned Agathocles, &c.

MŒ'RA, a dog. *Vid.* Mera.

MŒRAG'ENES, a native of Asia whose dispute with Atticus about a slave is mentioned by *Cicero. Att.* 5. ep. 15. l. 6. ep. 1.

Mœrag'enes, an author, who wrote four books on Apollonius. *Philostratus*, l. c. 4. declares him unworthy of credit, and he is mentioned by *Tzetzes, Chil.* 2. *Hist.* 60.

MŒRAGETES, (*fatorum ductor,*) a surname of Jupiter, and also of Apollo. *Paus.* 5. c. 15.

MŒ'RIS, a king of India, who fled at the approach of Alexander. *Curt.* 9. c. 8.——A steward of the shepherd Menalcas in *Virgil's Ecl.* 9.——A king of Ægypt. He was the last of the 300 kings who are said to have reigned from Menes to Sesostris, and he reigned 68 years. *Herodot.* 2. c. 13.

MŒ'RIS, a celebrated lake in Ægypt, supposed to have been dug by the king of the same name. It is about 220 miles in circumference, and intended as a reservoir for the superfluous water during the inundation of the Nile. There were two pyramids in it, 600 feet high, half of which lay under the water, and the other appeared above the surface. *Herodot.* 2. c. 4, &c.—*Mela,* 1. c. 6.—*Plin.* 36. c. 12.—*Strab.* 17.

MŒ'SIA, a country of Europe, bounded on the south by the mountains of Dalmatia, and on the north by mount Hæmus, extending from the confluence of the Savus and the Danube to the shores of the Euxine. It was divided into Upper and Lower Mœsia. Lower Mœsia was on the borders of the Euxine, and contained that tract of country which received the name of Pontus from its vicinity to the sea, and which is now part of Bulgaria. Upper Mœsia was situated beyond the other, in the inland country, and is now called Servia. *Plin.* 3. c. 26.—*Virg. G.* 1. v. 102.—*Paus.* 1. c. 4.—*Eustath. ad Diog. Per.* 322 & 830.—*Servius ad Virg. loco cit. & in Ecl.* 6. v. 43.—*Sch. Apollon.* 1. *Arg.* v. 1115.

MOG'ARA, a town of Galatia. *Antonin.*

MO'GRUS, a river of Pontus. *Arrian.*—*Pliny,* 6. c. 4. calls it Nogrus.

MO'LÆ, daughters of Mars, said to have been changed into millstones. They were worshipped by millers, and according to some authors, were called daughters of Mars, because this god as presiding over war, destroys men as the millstone crushes the corn. *Gellius,* 13. c. 22.—*Turneb. Adv.* 19. c. 11.

MOLE'A or MOLI'A, a festival in Arcadia, in commemoration of a battle in which Lycurgus slew Ereuthalion, and obtained the victory. The name is derived from μωλοςα, *a fight. Apoll. Rhod. Schol,* 1. 1. v. 164.

MO'LION or MOLI'ON, a Trojan prince, who distinguished himself during the defence of his country against the Greeks, as the friend or companion of Thymbræus. They were both slain by Ulysses and Diomedes. *Homer. Il.* 11. v. 320.

MOLI'ONE, the wife of Actor, son of Phorbas. She became mother of Cteatus and Eurytus, who, from her are called Molionides. These two heroes, who are represented by some as only forming one body, with two heads, four legs, and four arms, were invited to assist Augeas against Hercules, and their united efforts proved successful against their powerful enemy, till he attacked them unexpectedly as they were going to Corinth, and slew them. *Paus.* 2. c. 15. l. 5. c. 2. l. 6. c. 20.—*Homer. Il.* 11. v. 706.—*Ovid. Met.* 8. v. 387.—*Schol. Pindar. Olymp.* 10. v. 30 —*Apollod.* 2. c. 7.

MO'LO, an eminent philosopher of Rhodes, called also Apollonius. Some are of opinion that Apollonius and Molo are two different persons, who were both natives of Alabanda, and disciples of Menecles, of the same place. They both visited Rhodes, and there opened a school, but Molo flourished some time after Apollonius. Molo had Cicero and J. Cæsar among his pupils. *Vid.* Apollonius. *Cic. de Orat.* 1. c. 17 & 28. *Br.* 90. *Att.* 2. ep. 1, &c.—*Val. Max.* 2. c. 2.

MO'LO, a prince of Syria, who revolted against Antiochus, and killed himself when his rebellion was attended with ill success.

MOLŒ'IS, a small river of Bœotia, near Cithæron. *Herodot.*

MO'LON, an archon at Athens, Olymp. 104. an. 3.

MOLOR'CHUS, an old shepherd near Cleonæ, who received Hercules with great hospitality. The hero to repay the kindness which he had received, destroyed the Nemean lion, which laid waste the neighbouring country. There were two festivals instituted in his honour called Molorchea. Some imagine that Hercules received his famous club from this hospitable old man. *Paus.* 2. c. 15.—*Martial.* 9. epigr. 44. l. 14. epigr. 44.—*Apollod.* 2. c. 5.—*Virg. G.* 3. v. 19.—*Stat. Theb.* 4. v. 160. l. 3 *Sylv.* 1. v. 29.—*Lactant. Theb. loco.*—*Servius ad Virg.* 3. *Georg.* 19.—*Gyrald. in Vit. Herc.*

MOLOS'SI, a people of Epirus, who inhabited that part of the country which was called Molossia or Molossis from king Molossus. The country, extending between the rivers Acheron and Arethon, had the bay of Ambracia on the south, and the country of the Perrhæbeans on the east. The dogs of the place were famous, and received the name of Molossi among the Romans. Dodona was the capital of the country according to some writers. Others, however, reckon Dodona the chief city of Thesprotia. *Lucret.* 5, v. 10, 62.—*Lucan.* 4. v. 440.—*Strab.* 7.—*Liv.* 8. c. 24.—*Propert.* 4. el. 8. v. 24.—*Ovid. Met.* 1. v. 226. l. 13. v. 717.—*Justin.* 7. c. 6.—*C. Nep.* 2. c. 8.—*Virg. G.* 3. v. 495.—*Horat.* 2. sat. 6. v. 114. *Epod.* 6. v. 5.

MOLOS'SIA or MOLOS'SIS. *Vid.* Molossi.

MOLOS'SUS, a son of Pyrrhus and Andromache. He reigned in Epirus after the death of Helenus, and part of his dominions received the name of Molossia from him. *Paus.* 1. c. 11.—*Apollod.* 3.

MOLOS'SUS, a surname of Jupiter in Epirus. *Stat. Theb.* 8. v. 201.——An Athenian general, &c. ——The father of Meriones of Crete. *Vid.* Molus. *Homer. Odyss.* 6.

MOLPA'DIA, one of the Amazons, &c. *Plut.*

MOL'PIS, an author who wrote a history of Lacedæmon. *Athen.* l. 4.

MO'LUS, a Cretan, father of Meriones by Melphidis. *Homer. Il.* 2. *enum.* v. 158. l. 10. v. 269.—*Hygin.* fab. 97.—*Dictys. Cret.* l. c. l.——A son of Deucalion. *Apollod.*——A son of Mars and Demonice. *Id* l & 2.

MOLYBDA'NA, a city of the Mastieni. *Steph.*

MOLYC'RIA or MOLYC'RION, a town of Ætolia between the Evenus and Naupactum. *Paus.* 5. c. 3. It is still Molicria.

MOLYN'DIA, a city of Lycia. *Steph.*

MO'LYS, a city of Libya. *Id.*

MOMEMPHIS, a town of Ægypt, on the west side of the Canopic branch of the Nile. *Strab.* 17.

MO'MUS, the god of pleasantry among the ancients, was son of Nox, according to Hesiod. He was continually employed in satirizing the gods, and whatever they did was freely turned into ridicule. He blamed Vulcan, because in the human form which he had made of clay, he had not placed a window in the breast, by which whatever was done or thought there, might be easily brought to light. He censured the house which Minerva had built, because the goddess had not made it moveable, by which means a bad neighbourhood might be avoided. In the bull which Neptune had produced, he observed that his blows might have been surer if his eyes had been placed nearer the horns. Venus herself was also exposed to his satire; and when the sneering god had found no fault either in the features or in the body of the goddess, he observed, as she retired, that the noise of her feet was too loud, and excessively ungraceful in the goddess of beauty. These illiberal reflections upon the gods were the cause that Momus was driven from heaven. He is generally represented raising a mask from his face, and holding a small figure in his hand. *Hesiod in Theog.* 215.—*Vitruv. in Præf.* 2.—*Tzetzes. ad Hesiod. loc. cit.*—*Sch. Pindar.* 6. *Olymp.*—*Lucian. in Herm.*

MO'NA, an island between Britain and Hibernia, anciently inhabited by Druids. It is supposed by some authors to be the modern island of Anglesey, and by others the island of Man. *Tacit.* 14. *Ann.* c. 18 & 19.—*Plin.* 4. c. 16.—*Ptol.*

MON'ABÆ, a city of Isauria. *Steph.*

MONÆ'SES, a Parthian general, who favored the cause of M. Antony against Augustus. He abandoned Phraates after his murder of his father Orodes, but he afterwards displayed his abilities against the Romans. *Plut. in Ant.*—*Dio.* 40. c. 24. *Appian. de Bell. Parth.* p. 157.—*Horat.* 3. od. 6. v. 9.——A Parthian in the age of Mithridates, &c.

MONA'LUS, a river of Sicily, between Cephalœdis and Alæsa. *Ptol.* It is now Pollina.

MON'DA or MUN'DA, a river of Lusitania, falling into the Atlantic between the Durius and Tagus. *Plin.* 4. c. 22. It is now Mondego.

MONE'SI or MENEO'SI, a people of Aquitania. Their country is now probably Moneins or Monins. *Plin.* 4. c. 19.

MONE'SUS, a general killed by Jason at Colchis. *Val. Flacc.* 6. v. 651.

MONE'TA, a surname of Juno among the Romans. She is said to have received it because she advised them to sacrifice a pregnant sow to Cybele, to avert an earthquake. *Cic. de Div.* 1. c. 15.—*Livy*, 7. c. 28, says, that a temple was vowed to Juno, under this name, by the dictator Furius, when the Romans waged war against the Aurunci, and that the temple was raised to the goddess by the senate, on the spot where the house of Manlius Capitolinus formerly stood. *Ovid. Fast.* 1. v. 642. l. 6. v. 184. —*Suidas*, however, says, that Juno was surnamed Moneta, from assuring the Romans, when in the war against Pyrrhus they complained of want of pecuniary resources, that money could never fail to those who cultivated justice.

MON'IMA, a beautiful woman of Miletus, whom Mithridates the Great married. When his affairs grew desperate, Mithridates ordered his wives to destroy themselves; and Monima, in consequence, attempted to strangle herself, but when her efforts were unavailing, she ordered one of her attendants to stab her. *Plut. in Luc.*

MON'IMUS, a philosopher of Syracuse.

MONODAC'TYLUS, a mountain of Æthiopia. *Ptol. Pliny*, 6. c. 29. calls it Pentadactylus.

MON'ODUS, a son of king Prusias. He had one continued bone instead of a row of teeth, whence his name (μόνος ὀδούς.) *Plin.* 7. c. 16.—*Val. Max.* 1. c. 8.—*Festus.*

MONŒ'CUS, now Monaco, a town and port of Liguria, where Hercules had a temple, whence he is called *Monœcius;* and the harbour *Herculis portus. Strab.* 4.—*Tacit. H.* 3. c. 42.—*Virg. Æn.* 6. v. 830.—*Lucan.* 1. v. 405.—*Ital.* 1. v. 184.

MONŒ'TIUS, one of the Argonauts. *Val. Flacc.* 6. v. 343.

MONOGLOS'SUM, a town of India within the Ganges. *Ptol.*

MONO'LEUS, a lake of Æthiopia, from which the river Astaboras flows. *Strab.*

MONOPH'AGE, sacrifices in Ægina. *Plut. in Quæst. Gr.*—*Athen.*

MONOPH'ILUS, a eunuch of Mithridates. The king entrusted him with the care of one of his daughters; and the eunuch, when he saw the affairs of his master in a desperate situation, stabbed her, lest she should fall into the enemy's hands, &c.

MONS SA'CER, a mountain near Rome, celebrated as the spot to which the Roman populace retired in a tumult, which was the cause of the election of the tribunes of the people.

MONS SEVE'RUS, a mountain near Rome, &c.

MONTA'NUS JU'LIUS, a poet who wrote hexameter and elegiac verses. *Ovid. ex Pont.* 4.—*Voss de Poet. Lat.* p. 36.

MONTA'NUS CUR'TIUS, an orator under Vespasian. *Tac. Ann.* 16. c. 28.

MONTA'NUS, a favorite of Messalina.——One of the senators whom Domitian consulted about boiling a turbot. *Juv.* 4.——A Phrygian in the second century, the founder of a new sect, which from him were called *Montanists.* By severity of discipline, and a studied zeal and imposing address, assisted by the gold and the prophecies of Priscilla and Maximilla, two females of wealth and distinction who espoused his tenets, he prevailed upon several churches to adopt his wild views, and to consider him as a messenger peculiarly favored by the immediate inspiration of God. It is said, that he at last hanged himself, and thus proved himself to be rather an enthusiastic madman than a religious impostor. *Euseb. Hist.* 5. c. 15.—*Epiphan. hær.* 48. —*Philastr. de hær.* c. 50.—*Theodor. hær. fab.* 1. 3.—*August. de hær.* c. 26.

MON'YCHUS, a powerful giant, who is said to have been able to root up trees and hurl them like a javelin. He received his name from having the feet of a horse, as the word implies. *Juv.* 1. v. 11. *Val. Flacc.* 1. v. 145, &c.

MON'YMA. *Vid.* Monima.

MON'YMUS, a servant of Corinth, who, not being permitted by his master to follow Diogenes, the cynic, whose doctrines he highly admired, pretended madness, and obtained his liberty. He became a great admirer of the philosopher, and also of Crates, and even wrote something in the form of facetious stories. *Diog. Laert.* 6. c. 82.

MO'PHIS, an Indian prince conquered by Alexander. *Diod. Sic.* 13.

MOP'SIUM, a hill and town of Thessaly, between Tempe and Larissa. *Liv.* 42. c. 61.

MOPSO'PIA, an ancient name of Athens, from Mopsus, one of its kings, and thence the epithet of *Mopsopius* is often applied to an Athenian. *Ovid.* ep. 8. v. 72.

MOPSUES'TIA or MOP'SUS, a town of Cilicia, not far from the sea. *Cic. Fam.* 3. c. 8.

MOP'SUS, a celebrated prophet during the Trojan war, son of Manto and Apollo. He was consulted by Amphimachus, king of Colophon, who wished to know what success would attend his arms in a war which he was going to undertake. He predicted the greatest calamities; but Calchas, who had been a soothsayer of the Greeks during the Trojan war, promised the most brilliant success. Amphimachus followed the opinion of Calchas, but the prediction of Mopsus was fully verified. This had such an effect upon Calchas that he died soon after. His death is attributed to another mortification of the same nature. The two soothsayers, jealous of each other's fame, came to a trial of their skill in divination. Calchas first asked his antagonist how many figs a neighbouring tree bore; ten thousand except one, replied Mopsus, and one single vessel can contain them all. The figs were carefully gathered, and his conjectures were true. Mopsus, now, to try his adversary, asked him how many young ones a certain pregnant sow would bring forth. Calchas confessed his ignorance, and Mopsus immediately said, that the sow would bring forth on the morrow ten young ones, of which only one should be a male, all black, and that the females should all be known by their white streaks. The morrow proved the veracity of his prediction, and Calchas died from excessive grief produced by this defeat. Mopsus, after death, was ranked among the gods; and had an oracle at Malia, celebrated for the true and decisive answers which it gave. *Strab.* 9.—*Paus.* 7. c. 3.—*Ammian.* 14.—*Plut. de Orac. Defect.*—*Tertull. de An.* 46.—*Origen. contra Cels.* 3.—*Clem. Alex.* 1 *Strom.*—*Tzetzes in Lyc.* 426 & 980.—*Servius in Ecl. Virg.* 6. v. 72.——A son of Ampyx and Chloris, born at Titaressa in Thessaly. He accompanied the Argonauts in the character of their prophet and soothsayer, and died in Libya, on his return from Colchis, from the bite of a serpent. Jason erected him a monument on the sea-shore, where the Africans afterwards built him a temple where he gave oracles. He has often been confounded with the son of Manto, as their professions and names were alike. *Hesiod. in Scut.* 181.—*Apollon.* 1. v. 65.—*Orpheus, Arg.* 127.—*Stat. Theb.* 3. v. 521.—*Tzetzes. in Lycop.* 980.—*Athen.* 2. c. 15.—*Am. Marcel.* 14. c. 8.—*Apul. de Deo. Socr.*—*Hygin.* fab. 14, 128, 173.—*Strab.* 9. ——A shepherd in *Virgil's Eclogues.*

MO'RA, a town of Corsica. *Ptol.* It is now Villa de Mori.

MORDIÆ'UM, a city of Pisidia, afterwards called Apollonia.—*Steph.*—*Athen.*

MO'REI or MORIEN'SES, a people of India. *Steph.*

MORGAN'TIUM, a town in the eastern parts of Sicily, near the mouth of the Symethus below Catana. *Cic. in Ver.* 3. c 18. *Livy*, 24. c. 27, calls it Murgantia.

MORGEN'TIUM, a city of Calabria in Italy. *Steph.* It is now S. Georgio.

MORGI'NA, a city of Sicily. *Steph.*

MOR'GUS, a river of the Salassi. *Plin.* 3. c. 16. It is now Orcho.

MOR'INI, a people of Belgic Gaul, on the shores of the British Ocean. The shortest passage to Britain was from their territories. They were called *extremi hominum* by the Romans, because situate on the extremities of Gaul. Their city, called *Morinorum Castellum*, is now Mount Cassel, in Artois; and *Morinorum civitas*, is Terouenne, on the Lis. *Virg. Æn.* 8. v. 726. *Cæs.* 2. *Bell. G.* 21.

MORISE'NI, a people of Thrace. *Plin.* 4. c. 11.

MORITAS'GUS, a king of the Senones on the arrival of Cæsar in Gaul. *Cæs. B. G.* c. 54.

MO'RIUS, a river of Bœotia. *Plut.*

MOROS'GI, a people of the Varduli in Spain. *Plin.* 4. c. 20.

MOR'PHEUS, the son and minister of the god Somnus, who very naturally imitated the grimaces, gestures, words, and manners of mankind. He is sometimes called the god of sleep. He is generally represented as a sleeping child of great corpulence, and with wings. He holds a vase in one hand, and in the other are some poppies. He is represented by Ovid as sent to inform, by a dream and vision, the unhappy Halcyone of the melancholy fate of her husband Ceyx. *Ovid. Met.* 11. fab. 10.

MORS, one of the infernal deities, born of Night, without a father. She was worshipped by the ancients, particularly the Lacedæmonians, with great solemnity, and represented not as an actually existing power, but as an imaginary being, but the nature of their ceremonies and offerings to her is now unknown. Euripides introduces her on the stage in one of his tragedies, and the painters and sculptors of Greece and Rome were frequently engaged in making a representation of this divinity, but not in ghastly but symbolic forms. Sometimes a Cupid appeared overturning a flambeau, or a child was represented asleep, or a withered rose was placed on a tomb. The moderns represent her as a skeleton armed with a scythe and with a scymetar. *Eurip. Alc.—Homer. Il.* 16. v. 672.—*Virg. Æn.* 6. v. 278.—*Ælian. V.H.* 2. c. 35.—*Cic. de Senect.—Paus.* 3. c. 18. l. 5. c. 18.

MOR'SIMUS, a frigid tragic poet, who was also a clever oculist. *Aristoph. Equit.*

MOR'TUUM MARE. *Vid.* Mare Mortuum.

MORU'NI, a people inhabiting the mountains of India. *Plin.* 6. c. 20.—*Solin.* c. 22.

MORYCH'IDUS, an archon at Athens, in whose time it was decreed that no one should be ridiculed on the stage by name. *Schol. Aristoph. Acharn.*

MOR'YCHUS, a surname of Bacchus in Sicily.——A tragic poet ridiculed by Aristophanes. His stupidity gave rise to the proverb *Morycho stultior. Erasm. in Adag.*

MORYL'II, a people of Macedonia. *Plin.* 4. c. 10.

MO'RYS, a Trojan, son of Hippotion, killed by Meriones during the Trojan war. *Homer. Il.* 13. v. 792. l. 14. v. 514.

MO'SA, a river of Belgic Gaul falling into the German Ocean, and now called the Maese or Meuse. The bridge over it, *Mosæ pons*, is supposed to have been situated near the modern town of Maestricht. *Tacit. H.* 4. c. 66.

MOSÆ'US, a river of Susiana, flowing into the Persian Gulph. It is called Museus by *Marcellinus.*

MOS'CHA, now Mascat, a port of Arabia on the Red Sea.

MOS'CHI, a people of Asia, at the west of the Caspian Sea, and on the north of Armenia. The mountains at the south of their country were called *Moschici montes. Mela*, 1. c. 2. l. 3. c. 5.—*Lucan.* 3. v. 270.

MOS'CHION, a name common to four different writers, whose compositions, character, and native place are unknown. Some fragments of their writings remain, some few verses, and a treatise *de morbis mulierum*, edited by Gesner, 4to, Basil. 1566. [There are several representations of one of these men. One is a bust at Naples.]

MOS'CHUS, a Phœnician who wrote the history of his country in his mother tongue.——A philosopher of Sidon. He is regarded by some authors as the founder of anatomical philosophy. *Strab.*——A Greek Bucolic poet in the age of Ptolemy Philadelphus. The sweetness and elegance of his eight eclogues, which are still extant, make the world regret the loss of poetical pieces by no means inferior to the most beautiful of the productions of Theocritus. The best editions of Moschus with Bion are that of Heskin, 8vo, Oxon. 1748; of Harles, Erlang, 1780, &c. The works of this delicate writer have been translated by Politian into Latin verse with great success. *Suidas.—Gyrald. de P.H.* 3. *Fabr. B. Gr.* 3. c. 16.—*Sax. Onom.* 1. p. 132.——A Greek rhetorician of Pergamus in the age of Horace, defended by Torquatus when he was accused of having poisoned some of his friends. *Horat.* 1. ep. 5. v. 9. *Fabricius* mentions several other persons of this name.

MOSEL'LA, a river of Belgic Gaul falling into the Rhine, at Coblentz, and now called the Moselle. *Flor.* 3. c. 10.—*Tacit. An.* 13. c. 53.

MO'SES, a celebrated legislator and general among the Hebrews, well known in sacred history. He was born in Ægypt 1571 B.C. and after he had performed his miracles before Pharaoh, conducted the Israelites through the Red Sea, and given them laws and ordinances, during their peregrination of forty years in the wilderness of Arabia, he died at the age of 120. His writings have been quoted and commended by several of the heathen authors, who have occasionally divested themselves of their prejudices against his countrymen and extolled his learning and the effects of his superior wisdom. *Longinus.—Diod.* 1.—*Juv.* 14. v. 102.—*Tacit. Hist.* 5. c. 2.—9.—*Plin.* 30. c. 1.—*Justin.* 36. c. 2.

MO'SON, a city of Galatia. *Ptol.*

MOSSI'NI, a people of Mysia, near Pergamus. *Plin.* 5. c. 30.

MOSSI'NUS, a river of Caria. *Id.* 5. c. 29.

MOSTE'NI, a city of Lydia. *Ptol.*

MOSY'CHLUS, a mountain of Lemnus. *Nicand. in Theriac.* v. 472.

MOSY'LON, a promontory and town of Æthiopia. *Steph.* It is now Omgauli. The people in the neighbourhood were called Mosyli. *Ptol.*

MOSYNŒ'CI, a nation on the Euxine Sea, in whose territories the 10,000 Greeks stayed on their return from Cunaxa. *Xenoph.*

MOTE'NE, a region of Armenia Major. *Ptol.*

MOTE'NUM, a city of Upper Pannonia. *Antonin.*

MO'THO, a village of Arabia in which Antigonus was slain by Rhabilus. *Steph.*

MOTHO'NE, a town of Magnesia where Philip lost one of his eyes. *Justin.* 7. c. 6. The word is oftener spelt Methone.

MOTIE'NI, a small region of Iberia, a colony of the Romans. *Steph.*

MO'TYA or MOTY'A, a town at the south of Sicily, situate a little at the north of Agrigentum. It was besieged and taken by Dionysius, tyrant of Syracuse. *Diod. Sic.* 14, &c.

MOTYCH'ANUS, a river of Sicily. *Ptol.*

MOTYLÆ, a fortified place of Sicily, near Motye. *Steph*

MU'CIA, sister of Metellus Celer, married Cn. Pompey, by whom she was divorced on suspicion of a criminal intercourse with J. Cæsar during the Mithridatic war. *Plut. in Pomp.—Suet. Cæs.* 50,—*Cic. Att.* 1. ep. 12. *Fam.* 5. ep. 2.

MUCIA'NUS, a facetious and intriguing general under Otho and Vitellius, &c. *Plin.* 12. c. 11.

MUCIS'SUS, a city of Cappadocia. *Steph.*

MU'CIUS. *Vid.* Mutius.

MU'CRÆ, a village of Samnium. *Ital.* 8. v. 565.

MUL'CIBER, a surname of Vulcan (*a mulcendo ferrum,*) from his occupation. *Ovid. Met.* 2. v. 5. *Vid.* Vulcanus.

MULI'ADAS, a river of Spain. *Strab.* 3. *Casaubon* however reads Μούνδας.

MU'LIUS, a Grecian prince who married Agamede the eldest daughter of Augeas, and bravely fought in the war of the Epei against the people of Pylus, till he was overpowered by the arms of Nestor and slain. *Hom. Il.* 11. v. 738.——A servant of Amphinomus, one of Penelope's suitors. *Homer. Odyss.* 18. v. 422.

MULLI'NUS, a scribe of Alexander the Great. *Curt.* 8. c. 11.

MULO'NA, a town of Æthiopia. *Plin.* 6. c. 29.

MU'LUCHA or MULU'CHA, a river of Africa, which divides Numidia from Mauritania. *Plin.* 5. c. 2. *Strab.*

MUL'VIUS PONS, a bridge on the Flaminian way, about one mile distant from Rome. *Mart.* 3. epigr. 14.

MUMAS'TIS, a city of Caria. *Steph.*

MUM'MIUS L., a Roman consul sent against the Achæans, whom he conquered, B.C. 147. He destroyed Corinth, Thebes, and Chalcis, by order of the senate, and obtained the surname of *Achaicus* from his victories. He did not enrich himself with the spoils of the enemy, like too many of his countrymen, but returned home without any increase of fortune. He was so unacquainted with the value of the paintings and works of the most celebrated artists of Greece, which were found in the plunder of Corinth, that he said to those who conveyed them to Rome, that if they lost them or injured them, they should make others in their stead. His services were deservedly rewarded on his return, with a magnificent triumph. He was afterwards censor with Africanus the younger, A.U.C. 611. *Cic. Br.* 22. *Off.* 2. c. 22. *Verr.* 1. c. 21.—*Virg. Æn.* 6. v. 836.—*Paterc.* 1. c. 13.—*Strab.* 8.—*Plin.* 34. c. 7. l. 37. c. 1.—*Flor.* 2. c. 6.—*Paus.* 5. c. 24.

MUM'MIUS PUB'LIUS, a man commended by C. Publicius for the versatility and propriety of his manners. *Cic. de Orat.* 2.

MUM'MIUS, a Latin poet. *Macrobius,* 1. *Satur.* 10. ——A lieutenant of Crassus, defeated, &c. *Plut. in Crass.*

MUM'MIUS M., a prætor. *Cic. in Verr.*

MUM'MIUS SPU'RIUS, a brother of Achaicus before mentioned, and his lieutenant in the Corinthian expedition, was distinguished as an orator, and for his fondness for the Stoic philosophy. *Cic. ad Brut.* 25. *Ad. Att.* 13. ep. 5, 6 & 7. *Orat.* 2. c. 67.

MUM'MIUS LU'CIUS QUADRA'TUS, a tribune of the people with Clodius. He was the friend of Cicero. He is by some authors called Ninnius. *Cic. Dom.* 48. *Sext.* 11.

MUNA'TIUS PLAN'CUS, a consul sent to the rebellious army of Germanicus. He was almost killed by the incensed soldiery, who suspected that it was through him that they had not all been pardoned and indemnified by a decree of the senate. Calpurnius rescued him from their fury.

L. MUNA'TIUS PLAN'CUS, an orator and disciple of Cicero. His father, grandfather, and great grandfather bore the same name. He was with Cæsar in Gaul, and was made consul with Brutus. He promised to favor the republican cause for some time, but he deserted again to Cæsar. He was long Antony's favorite, but he abandoned him at the battle of Actium to conciliate the favors of Octavius. His services were great in the senate; for, through his influence and persuasion, that venerable body flattered the conqueror of Antony with the appellation of Augustus. He was rewarded by Augustus with the office of censor. *Plut. in Ant.*

MUNA'TIUS GRA'TUS, a Roman knight who conspired with Piso against Nero. *Tacit. Ann.* 15. c. 50.—*Suet. in Aug.* 29.

MUNA'TIUS, a friend of *Horace.* 1. ep. 3. v. 31.

MUNA'TIUS T. PLAN'CUS BUR'SA, an associate of Catiline, and a great enemy to Cicero and Milo. *Cic. Fam.* 7. ep.—*Dio.* 40. c. 35.

MUN'DA, a small town of Hispania Bætica, near the sea-coast, celebrated for a battle which was fought there on the 17th of March, B C. 45, between Cæsar and the republican forces of Rome, under Labienus and the sons of Pompey. Cæsar obtained the victory after an obstinate and bloody battle, and by this blow put an end to the Roman republic. Pompey lost 30,000 men, and Cæsar only 1,000, and 500 wounded. *Sil. Ital.* 3. v. 400.—*Hirt. Bell. Hisp.* 27.—*Lucan.* 1.

MUNICHIA'TES, a city of Arabia Petræa. *Ptol.*

MUNI'TUS, a son of Laodice, the daughter of Priam by Acamas. He was entrusted to the care of Æthra as soon as born, and at the taking of Troy he was made known to his father, who saved his life, and carried him to Thrace, where he was afterwards killed by the bite of a serpent. *Parthen.* 16.

MUNYCH'IA, a port of Attica, between the Piræeus and the promontory of Sunium, called after king Munychus, who built there a temple to Diana, in whose honor he also instituted festivals called Munychia. The temple was held so sacred that whatever criminals fled thither for refuge were pardoned. During the festival it was customary to offer small cakes called *amphiphontes,* ἀπὸ τοῦ ἀμφιφάειν, *from shining all round,* because there were lighted torches hung round when they were carried to the temple, or because they were offered at the full moon, because it was full moon when Themistocles conquered the Persian fleet at Salamis. The port of Munychia was well fortified, and of great importance to the Athenian power, therefore the Lacedæmonians, when sovereigns of Greece, always kept a regular garrison there. *Plut.*—*Ovid. Met.* 2. v. 709.—*Ptol.* 3. c. 15.—*Cor. Nepos. in Thras.* 2. —*Strab.* 9.—*Paus.* 1. c. 1.—*Gyrald. de An. & Mens.* —*Plut. de glor. Athen.*—*Harpocrat.*—*Etymol. Auct.*—*Suidas.*—*Eustath. Il.* σ'.

MURÆ'NA L. LICIN., a celebrated Roman left at the head of the armies of the republic in Asia by Sylla. He invaded the dominions of Mithridates at first with success, but soon after met with a defeat, and was recalled by Sylla with marks of displeasure. He was, however, honored with a triumph at his return to Rome, and afterwards commanded one of the wings of Sylla's army at the battle against Archelaus near Chæronea. He was ably defended in an oration by Cicero, when his character was attacked. It is supposed that he was killed during the civil commotion soon after. *Cic. pro Mur. Manil. Br.* 90.—*Appian. de Mithrid.*

MURÆ'NA, a son of the preceding, was lieutenant to Lucullus in Asia, &c. *Cic. Mur.* 1.—*Dio.* 37.——A man put to death for conspiring against Augustus, B.C. 22.

MUR'BOGI, a people of Hispania Tarraconensis; their chief town was Burgi. *Ptol.*

MUR'CIA. *Vid.* Murtia.

MUR'CUS L. STA'TIUS, a proconsul of Asia, who, after the murder of Cæsar, commanded the republican fleet. After the death of Cassius he joined the younger Pompey, by whom he was unjustly put to death. *Paterc.* 2. c. 77.—*Dio.* 48. c. 19.—*Cic. Phil.* 11. c. 12.

MUR'CUS STA'TIUS, a man who murdered Piso in Vesta's temple in Nero's reign. *Tacit. H.* 1. c. 43.

MURGAN'TIA, a town of Samnium. *Liv.* 25. c. 27.

MUR'GIS, a town of Hispania Tarraconensis, now Muxacra.——A town of Hispania Bætica, now Murga. *Antonin.*

MUROE'LA, a city of Upper Panonia.

MURRHE'NUS, a friend of Turnus killed by Æneas, &c. *Virg. Æn.* 12. v. 529.

MUR'SA, now Essek, a town of Hungary, near which the Drave falls into the Danube.——A city of Ionia, founded by Adrian. *Steph.*

MUR'TIA or MYR'TIA (*a* μύρτος), a supposed surname of Venus, because she presided over the *myrtle.* The goddess, worshipped under this name, had a temple at the foot of mount Aventine, and as she patronized indolence, laziness, and cowardice, her statues were generally covered with moss to represent inactivity more forcibly. *Plin.* 15. c. 29.—*Festus de V. Sig.*—*Aug. de Civ. Dei.* 4. c. 16. —*Arnob.* 4.—*Varro de L.L.* 4. c. 32.

MURO'IS, a town of Africa Propria. *Ptol.*

MUS, a Roman consul. *Vid.* Decius.

MU'SA ANTO'NIUS, a freedman and physician of Augustus. He cured his imperial master of a dangerous disease under which he labored, by recommending him to the use of the cold bath, and the eating of lettuces. He was magnificently rewarded for this celebrated cure. He was honored with a brazen statue by the Roman senate, which was placed near that of Æsculapius, and Augustus permitted him to wear a golden ring, and to be exempted from all taxes. He was not so successful in recommending the cold bath to Marcellus, as he had been to Augustus, and his illustrious patient died under his care. The cold bath was for a long time discontinued, till Charmis of Marceilles introduced it again, and convinced the world of its great benefits in various disorders. Musa was brother to Euphorbus, the physician of king Juba. Two small treatises, *De Herbâ Botanicâ,* and *De tuendâ Valetudine,* are supposed to be the productions of his pen. *Sueton.* 59.—*Horat.* 1. ep. 15. v. 3.—*Scholiast. Plin.* 19. c. 8.—*Dio* 53. c. 30.—*Sax. Onom.* 1. p. 186.—*Fabr. B. Gr.* 6. c. 9, &c.——A daughter of Nicomedes, king of Bithynia. She attempted to recover her father's kingdom from the Romans, but to no purpose, though Cæsar seemed to favor her cause. *Paterc.*—*Suet. in Cæs.*

MU'SÆ, certain goddesses who presided over poetry, music, dancing, and all the liberal arts. They were daughters of Jupiter and Mnemosyne, and were nine in number, Clio, Euterpe, Thalia, Melpomene, Terpsichore, Erato, Polyhymnia, Calliope, and Urania; or, in verse,

> Κλειώ τ', Εὐτέρπη τε, Θαλειά τε, Μελπομένη τε,
> Τερψιχόρη τ', Ἐρατώ τε, Πολύμνιά τ', Οὐρανίη τε,
> Καλλιόπη θ', ἣ καὶ προφερεςάτη ἐςὶν ἁπασῶν.

Some suppose that there were in ancient times only three muses, Melete, Mneme, and Aœde, and, according to *Varro,* the people of Sicyon directed three artists to make each their statues to place in the temple of Apollo, that out of them the most finished might be selected. The nine, when executed, appeared in such unequalled perfection, that they were all erected in the temple, and it is said that from that time the muses have beeen considered nine in number. Cicero, however, the friend and contemporary of Varro, speaks only of four muses, Telxiope, Aœde, Arche, Melete, and afterwards he mentions nine, according to the more received opinion. The muses were, according to others, daughters of Pierus and Antiope from which circumstance they are called Pierides., The name of Pierides might probably be derived from mount Pierus where they were born, or where they resided. They have been severally called Castalides, Aganippedes, Lebethrides, Aonides, Heliconides, &c., from the places where they were worshipped, or over which they presided. Apollo, who was the patron and the conductor of the muses, has received the name of Musagetes, or leader of the muses. The same surname was also given to Hercules. The palm tree, the laurel, and all the fountains of Pindus, Helicon, Parnassus, &c., were sacred to the muses. They were generally represented as young, beautiful, and modest virgins. They were fond of solitude, and commonly appeared in different attire, according to the arts and sciences over which they respectively presided. *Vid.* Clio, Euterpe, Thalia, Melpomene, &c. Sometimes they were represented as dancing in a chorus, to intimate the near and indissoluble connexion which exists between the liberal arts and sciences. The muses sometimes appear with wings, because by the assistance of wings they freed themselves from the violence of Pyrenæus. Their contest with the daughters of Pierus is well known. *Vid.* Pierides. The worship of the muses was universally established, particularly in the enlightened parts of Greece, Thessaly, and Italy. No sacrifices were ever offered to their honor, though no poet ever began a poem without a solemn invocation to the goddesses who presided over verse. There were festivals instituted in their honor in several parts of Greece, especially among the Thespians, every fifth year. The Macedonians observed also a festival in honor of Jupiter and the muses. It had been instituted by king Archelaus, and it was celebrated with stage plays, games, and different exhibitions, which continued nine days, according to the number of the muses. *Plut. Erot.—Pollux.—Æschin. in Tim.—Paus.* 9. c. 29.—*Apollod.* 1. c. 3.—*Cic. de Nat. D.* 3. c. 21.—*Hesiod. Theog.* v. 52 & 915.—*Virg. Ec.* 3. v. 85. *Ec.* 6. v. 63, *Ec.* 8. v. 63. *Ec.* 9. v. 33. *Ec.* 10. v. 12. *Georg.* 3. v. 11, *& Servius locis. cit.—Ovid. Met.* 4. v. 310. *Fast.* 5. v. 7.—*Hom. Hymn. Mus. Odyss.* 24. v. 61.—*Festus de V. Sig.—Juv.* 7. v. 58.—*Diod.* 1.—*Martial.* 4. epigr. 14. [The finest representations of the Muses altogether, are those in the Vatican, but there are one or two single statues superior to them, which have been mentioned under their respective titles.]

MUSÆ'UM, a place near Olympus in Macedonia. *Steph.*

MUSÆ'US, an ancient Greek poet, supposed to have been son or disciple of Linus or Orpheus, and to have lived about 1410 years B.C. Virgil has paid particular honor to his memory by placing him in the Elysian fields attended by a great and attentive multitude, and taller by the head than his followers. None of the poet's compositions are extant. The elegant poem of the loves of Leander and Hero, comprehended in 341 lines, was written by a poet of this name, who flourished in the fourth century according to the more received opinions. Among the editions of Musæus two may be selected as the best, that of Rover, 8vo, Leovard. 1743. *Virg. Æn.* 6. v. 677.—*Diog.—Servius ad Virg. loco.—Gyrald. de P. H.* 2.—*Fabr. B. Gr.* 1. c. 16.—*Sax. Onom.* 1. p. 8. ——A Latin poet, whose compositions were offensively obscene. *Martial.* 12. epigr. 96.——A poet of Thebes who lived during the Trojan war. *Voss. H. Gr.* 4. p. 519, &c.

MUSAG'ORES, three rocks near Crete. *Plin* 4. c. 12.—*Mela*, 2. c. 7.

MUS'CA, a freedman of Atticus. *Cic.* 6. *Att.* 1. ——A lyric poet, who wrote odes and epigrams. *Cœl. Rhod.* 14. c. 1.

MUSCAN'DA, a city of Antiochana in Cappadocia. *Ptol.*

MUSCA'RIA, a city of the Vascones in Hispania Tarraconensis. *Id.*

MUSCA'RIUS, a surname of Jupiter among the Eleans. The word signifies to drive away flies.

MUSO'NIUS RU'FUS, a stoic philosopher of Etruria, in the reign of Vespasian. *Tacit. Hist.* 3. c. 81.—*Jons. Script. Hist.* 3. c. 7.

MUS'SE, a city of Africa Propria, on the river Cinyphus. *Ptol.*

MUSTE'LA, a man greatly esteemed by *Cicero. Ad Attic.* 12.——A gladiator. *Cic. Philip.* 2.

MUS'THIS, the eighteenth king of the Thebais in Ægypt. *Joh. Marsham. Can. Chron. ex. Eratosth.*

MUS'TIUS C., a Roman knight. *Cic. Verr.* 1. c. 51.

MU'TA or TAC'ITA, a goddess who is represented as presiding over silence among the Romans. She is supposed by some to have been the same as Lara or Larunda, daughter of the Almon, who was punished by Jupiter, and to whom Mercury offered violence *Vid.* Lara. *Ovid. Fast.* 2. v. 580.—*Lactant.* 1. c. 20.

MU'THI, a city of the Thebais in Ægypt. *Antonin.*

MUTHUL'LUS, a river of Numidia. *Sallust. Jug.* 48.

MU'TIA, a daughter of Q. Mutius Scævola, and sister of Metellus Celer. She was Pompey's third wife, but her incontinent behaviour so disgusted her husband that at his return from the Mithridatic war, he divorced her, though she had borne him three children. She afterwards married M. Scaurus. Augustus greatly esteemed her. *Plut. in Pomp.*——A wife of Julius Cæsar, beloved by Clodias the tribune. *Suet. in Cæs.* 50.——The mother of Augustus.

Mu'tia Lex, the same as that which was enacted by Licinius Crassus, and Q. Mutius, A.U.C. 657. *Vid.* Licinia Lex.

MUTI'CA or MU'TYCE, an inland town of Sicily, west of the cape Pachynus. *Cic. in Verr.* 3. c. 43.

MUTIL'IA PRIS'CA, a woman intimate with Livia Augusta. *Tac. Ann.* 4. c. 12.

MU'TINA, a Roman colony of Cisalpine Gaul, situate between the Appennines and the Po, where M. Antony besieged D. Brutus, whom the consuls Pansa and Hirtius delivered. Two battles were fought there on the fifteenth of April B.C. 43, in which Antony was defeated, and at last obliged to retire. Mutina is now called Modena. *Lucan.* 1. v. 41. 1, 7. v. 872.—*Sil.* 8. v. 592.—*Ovid. Met.* 15. 822.—*Cic. Fam.* 10. ep. 14. *Brut.* ep. 5.—*Strab.* 5.—*Ptol.* 3. c. 1.—*Liv.* 21. c. 25.—*Propert.* 2 el. 1. v. 27.

MUTI'NES or MU'TINES, one of Annibal's generals, who was honoured with the freedom of Rome, on delivering up Agrigentum to the Roman army. *Liv.* 25. c. 41. l. 27. c. 5.

MUTI'NUS. *Vid.* Mutunus.

MU'TIUS, the father-in-law of C. Marius.——A Roman who saved the life of young Marius, by conveying him away from the pursuit of his enemies in a load of straw.——A friend of Tiberius Gracchus, by whose influence he was raised to the office of tribune.

Mu'tius C. Scæv'ola, surnamed *Cordus*, is famous in Roman history for his courage and intrepidity. When Porsenna, king of Etruria, had besieged Rome to reinstate Tarquin in all his rights and privileges, Mutius determined to deliver his country from so dangerous an enemy. He disguised himself in the habit of a Tuscan, and as he could fluently speak the language, he gained an easy introduction into the camp of the enemy, and soon into the royal tent. Porsenna sat alone with his secretary, when Mutius entered. The Roman immediately rushed upon the secretary, mistaking him for his royal master. This occasioned a noise; and Mutius, unable to escape, was seized and brought before the king. He disdained to answer the enquiries of the courtiers, but told them he was a Roman, and to give them a proof of his fortitude, he laid his right hand on an altar of burning coals, and sternly looking at the king, and without uttering a groan, he boldly informed him, that 300 young Romans like himself had conspired against his life, and entered his camp in disguise, determined either to destroy him, or perish in the attempt. This extraordinary confession astonished and alarmed Porsenna, he made peace with the Romans, and retired from their city. Mutius obtained the surname of *Scævola*, because he had lost the use of his right hand by burning it in the presence of the Etrurian king. *Plut. in Par.—Flor.* 1. c. 10.—*Liv.* 2. c. 12.—*Aurel. Vict. de Vir. Ill.* 12.—*Aug. de Civ. Dei.* 2. c. 18.—*Martial.* 1. epigr. 22. l. 8. epigr. 25.

Mu'tius Q. Scæv'ola, a Roman consul, son-in-law

of Lælius. He obtained a victory over the Dalmatians, and signalized himself greatly in the Marsian war. He is highly commended by Cicero, whom he instructed in the study of the civil law. *Cic. Am.* 1. *Phil.* 8. c. 10.—*Plut.*

Mu'tius, a proconsul of Asia, which he governed with so much justice and popularity, that he was generally proposed to others as a pattern of equity and moderation. Cicero speaks of him as eloquent, learned, and ingenious, equally eminent as an orator and a lawyer. He was murdered in the temple of Vesta, by Damasippus, during the civil wars of Marius and Sylla, eighty-two years B.C. *Plut.*—*Cic. de Orat.* 1. c. 48. *S. Rosc.* 12. *N.D.* 3. c. 32. *Verr.* 2. c. 21. *Off.* 3. c. 11.—*Paterc.* 2. c. 22.

MUTU'NUS or **MUTI'NUS**, a deity among the Romans, much the same as the Priapus of the Greeks. The Roman matrons, and particularly newly married women, disgraced themselves by the obscene ceremonies which custom obliged them to observe before the statue of this impure deity. *August. de Civ. D.* 4. c. 9. l. 6. c. 9.—*Lactant.* 1. c. 20.

MUTUS'CÆ, a town of Umbria, famous for its olives. *Virg. Æn.* 7. v. 711.

MUTUSTRATI'NI, a people of Sicily. *Plin.* 3. c. 8. Their city was Mutustrata, now Mistretta.

MUZA'NA, a city of Armenia Minor. *Antonin.*

MUZI'RIS, a town of India. *Plin.* 6. c. 23.—*Salmas. ad Solin.* p. 1285.

MYAG'RUS or **MY'ODES**, a divinity among the Ægyptians called also Achor. He was entreated by the inhabitants to protect them against flies and serpents. His worship afterwards passed into Greece and Italy. *Plin.* 10. c. 28.—*Paus.* 8. c. 26.

MYAR'IDA, an inland city of Cilicia. *Plin.* 5. c. 27.

MYC'ALE, a celebrated magician, who boasted that she could draw down the moon from her orb. She was mother of Broteas and Orion, who were present at the battle of the Lapithæ. *Ovid. Met.* 12. v. 203.

Myc'ale, a city and promontory of Asia Minor, opposite the island of Samus, celebrated for a battle which was fought there between the Greeks and Persians on the 22d of September, 479 B.C. the same day that Mardonius was defeated at Platæa. The Persians were about 100,000 men, that had just returned from the unsuccessful expedition of Xerxes in Greece. They had drawn their ships to the shore, and fortified themselves, as if determined to support a siege. They suffered the Greeks to disembark from their fleet without the least molestation, but were soon obliged to give way before the cool and resolute intrepidity of an inferior number of men. The Greeks obtained a complete victory, slaughtered some thousands of the enemy, burned their camp, and sailed back to Samus with an immense booty, in which, among other very valuable things, were seventy chests of money. *Herodot.*—*Justin.* 2. c. 14.—*Diod.*

Myc'ale, a woman, mentioned by *Juvenal*, 4. v. 141.

MYCALES'SUS, an inland town of Bœotia, where Ceres had a temple. It is now Malacasa. *Paus.* 9. c. 19.—*Homer. Il.* 2. en. 5.—*Thucyd.* 7.—*Strab.* 9.——A city of Caria.——A mountain opposite Samus. *Steph.*

MYCE'NÆ, an ancient town of Argolis, built by Perseus, son of Danae. It was situate on a small river at the east of the Inachus, about 50 stadia from Argos, and received its name from Mycene, a nymph of Laconia. It was once the capital of a kingdom, the monarchs of which reigned in the following order; Acrisius, 1344 B.C. Perseus, Electryon, Mæstor and Sthenelus alone for eight years; Atreus and Thyestes, Agamemnon, Ægisthus, Orestes, Æyptus, who was dispossessed 1104 B.C. on the return of the Heraclidæ. The town of Mycenæ was taken and laid in ruins by the Argives, B.C. 568; and, in the age of the geographer Strabo, the place where it stood was scarcely known. *Homer. Il.* 2. v. 76. l. 4. v. 52. *Odyss.* 2. v. 12.—*Ovid. Met.* 6. v. 414.—*Lucan.* 2. v. 544.—*Paus.* 2. c. 16.—*Strab.* 8.—*Virg. Æn.* 6. v. 839.—*Mela*, 2. c. 3. The epithet *Mycenæus* is applied to Agamemnon, as he was one of the kings of Mycenæ.

MYCE'NIS (*-idis*), a name applied to Iphigenia, the daughter of Agamemnon, as residing at Mycenæ. *Ovid. Met.* 12. v. 34.

MYCERI'NUS, a son of Cheops, king of Ægypt. After the death of his father he reigned with great justice and moderation. *Herodot.* 2. c. 129.

MYCIBER'NA, a town of the Hellespont taken by Philip of Macedon. *Diod.* 12.

MYC'ITHUS, a servant of Anaxilaus, tyrant of Rhegium. He was entrusted with the care of the kingdom, and of the children of the deceased prince, and he exercised his power with such fidelity and moderation, that he acquired the esteem of all the citizens, and, at last, restored the kingdom to his master's children when come to years of maturity, and retired, respected and beloved, to peace and solitude with a small portion. He is called by some Micalus. *Justin.* 4. c. 2.—*Macrob. Sat.* 1. c. 11.

MY'CON, a celebrated painter, who, with others, assisted in making and perfecting the Pœcile of Athens. He was the rival of Polygnotus. *Plin.* 33. c. 13. l. 35. c. 6.——A youth of Athens, changed into a poppy by Ceres. *Servius in Georg.* 1. v. 212.——A shepherd mentioned by *Virgil*, *Ecl.* 3. v. 10. *Ecl.* 7. v. 30.——A physician, who wrote on the remedies to be used for the bites of serpents. *Cœl. Rhod.* 13. c. 29.

MYC'ONE, **MYC'ONOS** or **MIC'ONE**, one of the Cyclades, between Delus and Icaria, which is supposed to have received its name from Myconus, an unknown person. It is about three miles at the east of Delus, and is thirty-six miles in circumference. It remained long uninhabited on account of the frequent earthquakes to which it was subject. Some suppose that the giants whom Hercules killed were buried under that island, whence arose the ancient proverb of *everything is under Mycone*, applied to those who treat of different subjects under one and the same title. Strabo observes, and his testimony is supported by that of modern travellers, that the inhabitants of Mycone became bald very early, even at the age of 20 or 25, from which circumstance they were called by way of contempt, *the bald heads of Mycone*. Pliny says that the children of the place were always born without hair. The island was poor, and the inhabitants are said to have been very avaricious; whence Archilochus reproached a certain Pericles, that he came to a feast like a Myconian, that is, without previous invitation. *Virg. Æn.* 3. v. 76.—*Strab.* 10.—*Plin.* 11. c. 37. l. 12. c. 7. l. 14. c. 1.—*Athen.* 1.—*Thucyd.* 3. c. 29.—*Mela*, 2. c. 7.—*Ovid. Met.* 7. v. 463. *Epist.* 21. v. 81.

MY'DON, one of the Trojan chiefs who defended Troy against the Greeks. He was killed by Antilochus. *Homer. Il.* 5. v. 580.——A Trojan slain by Achilles. *Id. Il.* φ. v. 209.

MYEC'PHORIS or **MYCEPH'ORIS**, a town in Ægypt, in a small island near Bubastis, on the Tanitic branch of the Nile.

MYE'NUS, a mountain of Ætolia. *Plut. de Flum.*

MY'ES or **MYEN'TIS**, a city of Ionia. *Steph.*

MYE'ZA, a town of Æmathia. *Plin.*—*Ptol.* It is now Lagovischio.

MYG'DON, a brother of Amycus, killed in a war against Hercules. *Apollod.*——A brother of Hecuba. *Vid.* Mygdonus.

MYGDO'NIA, a small province of Macedonia, at the west of Thrace, between the rivers Axius and Strymon. The inhabitants, called *Mygdones*, migrated into Asia, and settled near Troas, where the country received the name of their ancient habitation. Cybele was called *Mygdonia*, from the worship which she received in Mygdonia in Phrygia. *Horat.* 2. od. 12. v. 22. l. 3. od. 16. v. 41.—*Ovid. Met.* 6. v. 45.—*Flacc.* 3. v. 47. l. 8. v. 228.—*Claudian. de Cons. Mall.* 299.——A small province of Mesopotamia; it was probably peopled by a Macedonian colony. *Plin.* 4. c. 10.—*Ovid. Heroid.* 20. v. 106.—*Horat.* 2. od. 12. v. 22.

MYGDO'NIUS, a river of Macedonia flowing by Nisibis. *Strab.*

MYG'DONUS or **MYG'DON**, a brother of Hecuba, Priam's wife, who reigned in part of Thrace. His son Corœbus was called *Mygdonides* from him. *Virg. Æn.* 2. v. 341.—*Servius. ad Virg. loco.*—*Homer. Il.* 3. v. 186.

Myg'donus, a small river running through Mesopotamia into the Tigris.

MYGI'SI, a city of Caria from which Minerva was called Mygisia. *Steph.*

MY'IAGRUS, a celebrated statuary. *Plin.* 34. c. 8.

MY'LA or MY'LAS, a small river in the east of Sicily, with a town of the same name. *Liv.* 24. c. 30 & 31.—*Suet. Aug.* 16.

MY'LA, a town of Thessaly, now Mulazzo. *Liv.* 42. c. 54.

MYL'ACES, a nation of Epirus. *Lycophr.*

MYL'ASA, (*-orum*), a town of Caria at the south of Miletus. *Liv.* 38. c. 39.

MY'LES, a son of Lelex, king of Laconia.

MYL'IAS, a part of Phrygia Major, or of Lycia, according to *Arrian. in Indic.* and *Ptolemy.*

MYLIT'TA, a surname of Venus among the Assyrians. *Herodot.* 1. c. 131 & 199.—*Strab.* 16.—*Selden. de diis Syr.*

MYLO'IS, a river of Arcadia. *Hesych.*

MY'LON, a city of Ægypt. *Steph.*

MY'LON, a comic poet. *Hesych.*

MYN'DONES, a people of Libya. *Steph.*

MYN'DUS, a maritime town of Caria, near Halicarnassus. *Cic. Fam.* 3. ep. 8.—*Mela*, 1. c. 16.—*Plin.* 5. c. 89.

MY'NES, a prince of Lyrnessus, who married Briseis. He was killed by Achilles, and his wife became the property of the conqueror. *Homer. Il.* 3.

MYN'IÆ. *Vid.* Minyæ.

MY'ON, a city of the Locri in Epirus. *Steph.*

MYO'NIA, a town of Phocis. *Paus.* 10.

MYONNE'SUS, a town and promontory of Ionia, now Jalanghi-Liman. *Liv.* 37. c. 13 & 27.

MY'RA (*-orum*), a town of Lycia on a high hill, two miles from the sea. *Plin.* 5. c. 27.—*Strab.* 14.

MYRÆ'UM, an inland city of Africa. *Ptol.*

MYRCI'NUS, a town on the borders of Macedonia, on the Strymon, near Philippi. *Stephanus* calls it Myrcinnus.

MYRE'NE, a beautiful woman of Greece, who, after her father, mother, and brothers had been murdered by robbers, and their house plundered of its property, was carried away as the most valuable part of the booty. She was confined in a cave, whence she escaped, and on her return, was made priestess of Venus by her countrymen. On the day of a festival she perceived, among the multitude, one of the ferocious assassins of her family, who was immediately seized and confessed where the place of his concealment was. A youth who admired the virtues of Myrene promised, if he was rewarded with her hand, to discover and bring to punishment the rest of the robbers, and after a successful enterprise he received the expected prize, but Venus, offended that she was deprived of her favorite priestess, destroyed by a sudden death the bridegroom, and changed the bride into a plant called myrtle, which she ordered, as a proof of her affection, to continue green and odoriferous throughout the year. *Servius in Æn.* 3. v. 23.

MYR'GETÆ, a people of Scythia. *Steph.*

MYRIAN'DRUS, a town of Seleucia at the north of Syria, on the bay of Issus, which is sometimes called Sinus Myriandricus. *Liv.* 2. c. 108.

MYRI'CUS, a city of Troas, opposite Tenedus and Lesbus. *Steph.*

MYRI'NA, a maritime town of Æolia, called also Sebastopolis, and now Sanderlic. *Tacit. Ann.* 2. c. 47.—*Liv.* 33. c. 30.—*Strab.* 13.—*Mela*, 1. c. 18.—*Paterc.* 1. c. 4.——A town of Lemnus, now Palio Castro. *Plin.* 4. c. 12.——A town of Asia, destroyed by an earthquake in Trajan's reign.

MYRI'NA, a queen of the Amazons, &c. *Dion.* 4. ——The wife of Thoas king of Lemnus, by whom she had Hipsipyle. *Schol. Apollon.* 1. v 604.

MYR'INUS, a surname of Apollo, from Myrina in Æolia, where he was worshipped.

MYRI'NUS, a gladiator. *Mart.* 12. epigr. 29.

MYR'ICE, a town of Arcadia, called also Megalopolis. *Demosth. de fals. legat.*

MYRION'YMA, a name applied to Isis, as having a thousand names.

MYRLE'A or APAME'A, a town of Bithynia. *Plin.* 5. c. 32.

MYRMEC'IDES, an artist of Miletus mentioned as making chariots so small that they could be covered by the wing of a fly. It is said also that he inscribed an elegiac distich on a grain of Indian sesamum. *Cic.* 4. *Acad.* 38.—*Ælian. V.H.* 1. c. 17. *Plin.* 36. c. 5.

MYRME'CIUM, a town of Taurica. *Steph.*——A promontory on the Cimmerian Bosporus. *Ptol.*—*Plin.* 4. c. 12.

MER'MEX, a philosopher of Henetus in Paphlagonia. *Steph. ex Diog. Laert. Hist. Phil.* 2. c. 13.——*Salmas. ad Solin.* p. 889.

MYRMID'ONES, a people on the southern borders of Thessaly, who accompanied Achilles to the Trojan war. They received their name from Myrmidon, a son of Jupiter and Eurymedusa, who married one of the daughters of Æolus, son of Hellen. His son Actor married Ægina, the daughter of the Asopus. He gave his name to his subjects, who dwelt near the river Peneus in Thessaly. According to some, the Myrmidons received their name from their having been originally ants, μύρμηκες, changed by Jupiter into men. *Vid.* Æacus. According to Strabo, they received it from their industry, because they imitated the diligence of the ants, and like them were indefatigable, and continually employed in cultivating the earth. *Ovid. Met.* 7. v. 654.—*Strab.*—*Hygin.* fab. 52.—*Apollod.* 1.—*Virg. Æn.* 2. v. 7.—*Servius. ad Virg. Æn.* 4. v. 402 & l. 11. v. 403. *Lactant. ad Theb.* 7. v. 310.—*Isid. Orig.* 9. c. 2.

MYRMIS'SUS, a city near Lampsacus. *Steph.*

MY'RON, a tyrant of Sicyon, successor, and, probably, son of Orthagoras. *Aristot. Pol.* 5. c. 11 & 12.——A man of Priene, who wrote a history of Messenia. *Paus.* 4. c. 6.—*Athen.* 6 & 16.——A celebrated statuary of Eleutheræ in Bœotia, peculiarly happy in his imitations of nature. He made a cow so much resembling life, that even bulls were deceived and approached her as if alive, a circumstance frequently noticed in many epigrams in the Anthologia. He flourished about 442 years B C. *Ovid. Art. Am.* 3. v. 319.—*Paus.*—*Juv.* 8. v. 102. —*Cic. Verr.* 4. c. 60.—*Orat.* 3. c. 7.—*Her.* 4. c. 6. —*Plin.* 34. c. 7.—*Propert.* 2. el. 23. v. 7. el. 41 — *Stat.* 1. *Sylv.* 2. v. 50. l. 4. *Sylv.* 6. v. 25.

MYRONIA'NUS, an historian. *Diog.*

MYRON'IDES, an Athenian general, who conquered the Thebans. *Polyæn.* 1. c. 35.

MYRO'NOS, an island in the Arabic Gulph. *Steph.*

MYR'RHA, a daughter of Cinyras, king of Cyprus. She became enamoured of her father, and under the influence of this unnatural passion, secretly introduced herself into his bed. She had a son by him, called Adonis. When Cinyras was apprised of the incest which he had committed, he attempted to stab his daughter, but Myrrha fled into Arabia, where she was changed into the herb myrrh. *Hygin.* fab. 58 & 275.—*Ovid. Met.* 16. v. 298.—*Plut. in Par.*—*Apollod.* 3.—*Antonin. Lib.* 34.—*Servius. ad Virg. Ec.* 10. v. 8. *Æn.* 5. v. 72. l. 6. v. 623.—*Stobæus.* 62.

MYR'RHINUS or MYRRHI'NUS, a part of the tribe Pandionis at Athens. *Strab.*—*Schol. Arist. in Plut.*

MYR'SILUS, a son of Myrsus, the last of the Heraclidæ who reigned in Lydia. He is also called Candaules. *Vid.* Candaules.——A Lesbian, who wrote on Italy. The work edited by Annius under his name is supposed to be a forgery. *Voss. Hist. Gr.* 3. p. 391.

MYR'SINUS, a city of Elis, afterwards called Myrtuntium. *Steph.*

MYR'SUS, the father of Candaules. *Herodot.* 1. c. 7.——A Greek historian in the age of Solon.

MYR'TALE, a courtezan of Rome, mistress to the poet *Horace.* 1. od. 33.

MYR'TEA, a surname of Venus. *Vid.* Murtia.

MYR'TILUS, son of Mercury and Phaethusa, or Cleobule or Clymene, was arm-bearer to Œnomaus, king of Pisa. He was so experienced in riding and in the management of horses, that he rendered those of Œnomaus the swiftest in all Greece. His infidelity proved at last fatal to him. Œnomaus had been informed by an oracle, that his daughter Hippodamia's husband would cause his death, and on that account he resolved to marry her only to him who should overcome him in a chariot race. This seemed totally impossible, and to render it more terrible, Œnomaus declared to the suitors, that death would be the inevitable consequence of a defeat. The charms of Hippodamia were so great that many sacrificed their life in the fruitless endeavour to obtain her hand. Pelops, at last, presented himself, undaunted at the melancholy fate of those who had gone before him, but before he entered the course he bribed Myrtilus, who was himself enamoured of Hippodamia, gave an old chariot to Œnomaus, which broke in the course and caused his death. Pelops, in consequence of this act of treachery, gained the victory, and married Hippodamia; and when Myrtilus had the audacity to claim the reward promised to his perfidy, Pelops threw him headlong into the sea, where he perished. The body of Myrtilus, according to some, was carried by the waves to the sea-shore, where it received an honorable burial, and as he was the son of Mercury he was made a constellation. *Diod.* 4. —*Hygin.* fab. 84 & 224.—*Paus.* 8. c. 14.—*Apollon.* 1. v. 752.—*Schol. Eurip. Orest.* 1002.—*Lactant. ad Theb.* 4. v. 306. l. 6. v. 336.—*Servius ad Virg.* 1. *G.* 205. l. 3. v. 7.—*Tzetzes Lyc.* 156.

MYR'TIS, a Greek woman who distinguished herself by her poetical talents. She flourished about 500 years B.C., and instructed the celebrated Corinna in versification. Pindar, also, as some report, was for some time one of her pupils.

MYRTO'UM MA'RE, a part of the Ægæan Sea, which lies between Eubœa, Attica, and Peloponnesus, as far as Cape Malea. It received this name from Myrto, a woman, or from Myrtus, a small island opposite to Carystus in Eubœa; or, according to some, from Myrtilus, the son of Mercury, who was drowned there, &c. *Paus.* 8. c. 14.—*Hygin.* fab. 84.—*Plin.* 4. c. 11.—*Servius. ad Virg. G.* 3. v. 7.—*Schol. Apollon.* 3. v. 12 & 13.—*Schol. Eurip. in Orest.* v. 982 & 990.—*Sch. Aristoph. in. Equit.* 558 & 993.—*Tzetzes in Lyc.* 156.

MYRTUN'TIUM, a name given to that part of the sea which lies on the coast of Epirus between the bay of Ambracia and Leucas. *Strab.*

MYR'TUS. *Vid.* MYRTOUM MARE.

MYRTU'SA, a mountain of Libya. *Callim. in Apoll.*

MYS, *gen.* Myos, an artist skilful in the art of working and polishing silver. He beautifully represented the battle of the Centaurs and Lapithæ, on a shield in the hands of Minerva's statue made by Phidias. *Paus.* 1. c. 28.—*Martial.* 8. epigr. 34 & 51. l. 14. epigr. 93.—*Propert.* 3. el. 9. v. 14.

MYSCEL'LUS or MISCEL'LUS, a native of Rhypæ in Achaia, who founded Crotona in Italy, according to the order of an oracle, which told him to build a city where he found rain with fine weather. The meaning of the oracle long perplexed him, till he found a beautiful woman all in tears in Italy, which circumstance he interpreted in his favor. According to some, Myscellus, who was the son of Hercules, went out of Argos, without the permission of the magistrates, for which he was condemned to death. The judges had put each a black ball as a sign of condemnation, but Hercules changed them all and made them white, and had his son acquitted, upon which Myscellus left Greece and came to Italy, where he built Crotona. *Ovid. Met.* 15. v. 19.—*Strab.* 6 & 8.—*Suidas.*—*Sch. Aristoph. in Nub.*

MYS'IA, a country of Asia Minor, generally divided into Major and Minor. Mysia Minor was bounded on the north and west by the Propontis and Bithynia, and by Phrygia on the southern and eastern borders. Mysia Major had Æolia on the south, the Ægæan on the west, and Phrygia on the north and east. Its chief cities were Cyzicum, Lampsacus, &c. The inhabitants were once very warlike, but they greatly degenerated from the virtues of their forefathers; and the words *Mysorum ultimus* were emphatically used to signify a person of no merit. The ancients generally hired them to attend their funerals as mourners, because they were naturally melancholy and inclined to shed tears. They were once governed by monarchs. They are supposed to have been descendants of the Mysians of Europe, a nation which inhabited that part of Thrace which was situate between mount Hæmus and the Danube. *Strab.*—*Herodot.* 1, &c.—*Cic. in Ver. Flacc.* 27.—*Flor.* 3. c. 5.—*Appian in Mithrid.*

MYS'IA, a festival in honour of Ceres, who was surnamed Mysia from Mysius, an Argive, who raised her a temple near Pallene in Achaia. Some derive the word ἀπὸ τοῦ μυσιᾶν, to *cloy* or *satisfy*, because Ceres was the first who satisfied the wants of men by giving them corn. The festival continued during seven days, &c. *Pausan. Achaic.*

MYS'IUS, a river of Æolis. *Strab.* Some read Mœsius.

MYSOC'ARAS, a harbour of Mauritania Tingitana. *Ptol.*

MYSOMACED'ONES, a people of Mysia Major, descended from the Macedonians, whence the name. *Plin.* 5. c. 29.

MY'SON, a native of Sparta, accounted one of the seven wise men of Greece. When Anacharsis consulted the oracle of Apollo, to know which was the wisest man in Greece, he received for answer, he who is now ploughing his fields. This was Myson. *Diog. in Vit.*

MYS'TES, a son of the Roman poet Valgius, whose early death was so lamented by the father, that Horace wrote an ode to allay the grief of his friend. *Horat.* 2. od. 9.

MYSTICH'IDES, an archon at Athens. Olymp. 98. an. 3.

MYTH'ECUS, a sophist of Syracuse. He studied cookery, and when he thought himself sufficiently skilled in dressing meat, he went to Sparta, where he gained much practice, especially among the younger citizens. He was soon after expelled the city by the magistrates, who observed with their accustomed simplicity, that the aid of Mythecus was unnecessary, as hunger was the best seasoning.

MYTILE'NE. *Vid* Mitylene.

MY'US, *gen.* Myuntis, a town of Ionia on the confines of Caria, founded by a Grecian colony. It was one of the 12 capital cities of Ionia, situate at the distance of about 30 stadia from the mouth of Mæander on the south. Artaxerxes king of Persia, gave it to Themistocles to supply his table with meat. Magnesia was to support him in bread, and Lampsacus in wine. *C. Nep. in Themis.*—*Strab.* 14.—*Herodot.* 1. c. 142.—*Diod.* 11.

N.

NAÆ'RA, one of the attendants of Cleopatra, who followed the example of her mistress, by putting herself to death. *Plut. in Anton.*

NAAG'RAMMA, a city of India within the Ganges. *Ptol.*

NAAG'RAMMUM, or as it is in some MSS. Maagrammum, the metropolis of Taprobane. *Id.*

NAAR'DA, a city of Syria, near the Euphrates. *Steph.* *Ptolemy* places it in Mesopatamia.

NABABU'RUM, a town of Mauritania Cæsariensis. *Ptol.*

NABARZA'NES, an officer of Darius the Third, at the battle of Issus. He afterwards conspired with Bessus to murder his royal master, either to obtain the favor of Alexander, or to seize the kingdom. He was pardoned by Alexander. *Curt.* 3, &c. *Diodorus*, 17. calls him Nabarnes.

NABATHÆ'A, a country of Arabia, of which the capital was called Petra. The word is often applied to any of the eastern countries of the world by the poets, and seems to have been derived from Nabath, the son of Ismael. *Ovid. Met.* 1. v. 61. l. 5. v. 163.—*Strab.* 16.—*Lucan.* 4. v. 63. —*Juv.* 11. v. 126.—*Seneca. in Herc. Œt.* 160. *In Agam.* 483.—*Isid.* 9. *Orig.* 2.

NABDAL'SA, a Numidian put to death by Jugurtha, against whose life he had conspired, together with Bomilcar. *Sallust. Jug.* 70, &c.

NA'BIS, a well known tyrant of Lacedæmon, who, in all acts of cruelty and oppression, surpassed the infamous deeds of a Phalaris or a Dionysius. His house was filled with flatterers and spies, who were continually employed in watching the words and the actions of his subjects. When he had exercised every art of terror and of persecution to plunder the citizens of Sparta, he made a statue, which in resemblance was like his wife, and was clothed in the most magnificent apparel, and whenever any one refused to deliver up his riches, the tyrant led him to the statue, which immediately, by means of secret springs, seized the unhappy victim in its arms, and tormented him in the most excruciating manner with sharp-bearded points which were hidden under the clothes. To render his tyranny more popular, Nabis made an alliance with Flaminius, the Roman general, and pursued with the most inveterate enmity the war which he had undertaken against the Achæans. He besieged Gythium, and defeated Philopœmen in a naval battle. His triumph was however of short duration; the general of the Achæans soon repaired his losses, and Nabis was defeated in an engagement, and treacherously murdered by Alexander the Ætolian, as he attempted to save his life by flight, B.C. 192, after a usurpation of 14 years. *Polyb.* 13.—*Justin.* 30 & 31.—*Plut. in. Phil.*—*Paus.* 7. c. 8.—*Flor.* 2. c. 7.—*Liv.* 29. c. 12. l. 32. c. 39. l. 33, &c.——A priest of Jupiter Ammon, killed in the second Punic war, as he fought against the Romans. *Sil.* 15. v. 672.

NA'BIUS, NA'VIUS, NA'BUS, NA'VUS or NA'-BLIS, a river of Hispania Tarraconensis. *Ptol.* It is called Narius by *Mela*, 2. c. 3.

NA'BLA, a city of Asiatic Sarmatia. *Ptol.*

NAB'OLUS, the son of Hippasus, the charioteer of Laius. *Stat. Theb.* 7. v. 355.

NABONAS'SAR, a king of Babylon, after the division of the Assyrian monarchy. From him the Nabonassarean epoch received its name, agreeing with the year of the world 3306, or 706 B.C.

NACH'ABA, a city of Arabia Deserta. *Ptol.*

NACO'LIA, a city of Phrygia Major, so called from the nymph Nacole, or Nacolus, son of Dascylus. *Stephanus* calls it Nacolia, and the Turks, Einagiol.

NAC'ONE or NACO'NA, a city of Sicily. *Steph.*

NAC'RASA, a city of Lycia. *Ptol.*

NAC'RI CAM'PI, a place of Gallia Togata, near Mutina. *Liv.* 41. c. 18. Some read Macri. It is now Val di Montirone, according to *Leander*.

NADAG'ARA. *Vid.* Nargara.

NÆNIA, the goddess of funerals at Rome, whose temple was without the gates of the city. The songs which were sung at funerals were also called *nænia* from her. They were generally filled with the praises of the deceased, but sometimes they were so unmeaning and so inapplicable to the purpose for which they were intended, that the word became proverbial to signify nonsense. *Varro de Vit. P.R.*—*Quint* 8. c. 2—*Festus. de V. Sig.*—*Arnob.* 7.—*Plaut. Asin.* 41. c. 1. v. 63.—*Rosin. A. R.* 2. c. 19.

NÆ'VIA, a female mentioned by Martial, 1. epigr. 72.

NÆ'VIA, a gate of the city of Rome. *Festus.*

NÆ'VIUS CN., a Latin poet in the first Punic war. He originally served in the Roman armies, but afterwards applied himself to study, and wrote comedies, besides a poetical account of the first Punic war, in which he had been engaged. His satirical disposition and the severity and ridicule with which he treated his fellow citizens displeased the leading men of the state, and he was imprisoned. When at last liberated from a confinement which had afforded him opportunity to add to the number of his plays, and not to correct the satirical propensity of his muse, the poet continued his offensive virulence, till he was driven away from Rome by the influence of the consul Metellus. He passed the rest of his life in Utica, where he died, about 203 years B.C. Some fragments of his poetry are extant, to the number of 308 lines, and may be found in the Corpus Poetarum. Among his plays the *Hariolus*, *Hector*, and *Leon* are mentioned. *Cic. Tus.* l. c. 1. *Br.* 15, &c. *Leg* 2. c. 15. *De Senect.*—*Horat.* 2. ep. 1. c. 53.—*Aul. Gell.* 1. c. 24. l. 3. c. 3. l. 27. c. 21.—*Harles. Not. Lit. Rom.* 1. p. 80.

NÆ'VIUS, a tribune of the people at Rome, who accused Scipio Africanus of extortion.

NÆ'VIUS SEX'TUS, a public crier who revolted from Marius to Sylla. He was defended against an accusation by the eloquence of Cicero. *Cic. Quint.* 1.

NÆ'VIUS, an augur in the reign of Tarquin. To convince the king and the Romans of his power, as an augur, he cut a flint with a razor, and by this extraordinary action, turned the ridicule of the populace into admiration. Tarquin rewarded his merit by erecting him a statue in the comitium, which was still in being in the age of Augustus. The razor and flint were buried near it under an altar, and it was usual among the Romans to make witnesses in civil causes swear near it. This miraculous event of cutting a flint with a razor, though believed by some writers, is treated as fabulous and improbable by Cicero, who himself had been an augur. *Dionys. Hal.*—*Liv.* 1. c. 36.—*Cic. de Divin.* 1. c. 17. *De Nat. D.* 2. c. 3. l. 3. c. 6.

NÆV'OLUS, an infamous pimp in Domitian's reign. *Juv.* 9. v. 1.

NAGAD'IBA, a city of Taprobane. *Ptol.*

NAGARU'RIS, a city of India within the Ganges. *Id.*

NA'GIA, a town of the Gebanitæ, in Arabia Felix. *Plin.* 6. c. 28.

NAG'IDOS or NAT'IDOS, a city of Pamphylia on the borders of Cilicia. *Mela*, l. c. 13.

NAHANARVA'LI, NAHAR'VALI or NAHAR-VA'LI, a people of Germany. *Tacit. Germ.* 43.

NAI'ADES or NAI'DES, certain inferior deities who presided over rivers, springs, wells, and fountains. The Naiades generally inhabited the country, and resorted to the woods or meadows near the stream over which they presided, whence the name (νάειν *to flow*).) They are represented as young and beautiful virgins, often leaning upon an urn, from which flows a stream of water. Ægle was the fairest of the Naiades, according to Virgil. They were held in great veneration by the ancients, and sacrifices of goats and lambs were often offered to them, with libations of wine, honey, and oil. Sometimes they only received from their votaries offerings of milk, fruit, and flowers. *Vid.* Nymphæ. *Virg. Ecl.* 6. v. 20.—*Ovid. Met.* 14. v. 328.—*Homer. Odyss.* 13. v. 103. [There are several representations of these nymphs, which have for the most part been designated Venus. The celebrated crouching Venus in the Vatican, is probably one of these nymphs.]

NA'IS, one of the Oceanides, mother of Chiron or Glaucus by Magnes. *Apollod.* 1. c. 9.—*Virg. Ec.* 2. v. 46.—*Stat.* 3. *Sylv.* 4. v. 42.——A nymph, mother by Bucolion of Æsepus and Pedasus. *Homer. Il.* 6. v. 22.——A nymph in an island of the Red Sea, who was said by her incantations to turn to fishes all those who approached her residence after she had admitted them to her embraces. She was herself changed into a fish by Apollo. *Ovid. Met.* 4. v. 49, &c. The word is used for water, by *Tibullus*, 3. 7.

NAIS'SUS or NÆS'SUS, now Nissa, a town of Mœsia, at the south of the Danube, the birth-place of Constantine. It is placed by some in Illyricum or Thrace. *Steph.*

NAL'CUA, a city of Britain. *Ptol.*

NAMA'DUS, a river of India within the Ganges. *Ptol. Arrian in Indic.* calls it Lamnæus.

NAMNE'TES or NANNE'TES, a people of Gallia Celtica, at the mouth of the Ligeris. *Id.* 2. c. 8. Their chief city is now Nantes.

NANAGU'NA, a river of India within the Ganges. *Ptol.*

NANIG'ERIS, an island of the Indian Ocean. *Id.*

NANTUA'TES or NANTUA'TÆ, a people of Gaul, near the Alps. *Cæs. B. G.* 3. c. 1.

NAPÆ'Æ, certain divinities among the ancients who presided over the hills and woods of the country. Some suppose that they were tutelary deities of the fountains, while the Naiades presided more immediately over the sea. Their name is derived from νάπος, *a grove*. *Virg. G.* 4. v. 535.—*Servius loco.*—*Stat.* 4. *Theb.* 255.

NAP'ARIS, the ancient name of the Dniester. *Herodot.*

NAPA'TA or NAP'ATA, a town of Upper Æthopia. *Strab.*—*Steph.*

NA'PE, one of Actæon's dogs. *Ovid. Met.* 3. v. 212.—*Hygin.* fab. 181.

NAPH'ILUS, a river of Peloponnesus falling into the Alpheus. *Paus.* 8.

NA'PIS, a town of Scythia. *Steph.*

NAPO'CA, a town of Dacia. *Ptol.*

NAR, now Nera, a river of Umbria, the waters of which, famous for their sulphureous properties, pass through the lake Velinus, and issuing thence with great rapidity fall into the Tiber. *Ovid. Met.* 14. v. 330.—*Virg. Æn.* 7. v. 517.—*Cic. ad Attic.* 4. ep. 15.—*Tacit. An.* 1. c. 79. l, 3. c. 9.

NA'RA, a city of Byzacene in Africa. *Antonin.*

NARACUSTO'MA or NARRACUSTO'MA, one of the mouths of the Ister. *Arrian.*

NAR'BIS, a city of Illyria. *Steph.*

NAR'BO MAR'TIUS, now Narbonne, a town of Gaul, founded by the consul Marcius. A. U. C. 636. It became the capital of a large province of Gaul, which obtained the name of Gallia Narbonensis. *Paterc.* l. c. 15. l. 2. c. 8.—*Plin.* 3.

NARBONEN'SIS GAL'LIA, called also Braccata by *Pliny*, 5. c. 4, one of the four great divisions of ancient Gaul, was bounded by the Alps, the Pyrenean mountains, Aquitania, Belgicum, and the Mediterranean, and contained the modern provinces of Languedoc, Provence, Dauphiné, and Savoy.

NARCÆ'A, a surname of Minerva in Elis, from her temple there, erected by Narcæus.

NARCÆ'US, a son of Bacchus and Physcoa, who defeated his enemies in war, and built a temple to Minerva in Elis, and established the religious ceremonies observed in other places in honor of his father. The sixteen matrons who had the care of Juno's festivals in Elis, were also appointed to preside over the musicians whom Narcæus selected to honor the memory of his mother Physcoa. *Paus.* 5. c. 15.

NAR'CASUS, a city of Caria. *Steph.*

NAR'CES, a city of Numidia. *Polyb.—Appian.*

NARCIS'SUS, a beautiful youth, son of the god of the river Cephisus and the nymph Liriope, was born at Thespis in Bœotia. He saw the reflection of his image in the clear waters of a fountain, and became enamoured of it, thinking it to be the nymph of the place. His fruitless attempts to approach this beautiful object so provoked him that he grew desperate and killed himself. His blood was changed into a flower, which still bears his name. The nymphs raised a funeral pile to burn his body, according to Ovid, but they found nothing but a beautiful flower. Pausanias says, that Narcissus had a sister as beautiful as himself, of whom he became deeply enamoured. He often hunted in the woods in her company, but his pleasure was soon interrupted by her death, and still to keep afresh her memory, he frequented the groves, where he had often attended her, or reposed himself on the brim of a fountain, where the sight of his own reflected image still awakened sentiments of affection and tenderness. The fountain was called Narcissus, and was in the territory of Thespia. *Paus.* 9. c. 21.—*Hygin.* fab. 271.—*Ovid. Met.* 3. v. 346, &c.—*Plut. in Symp.* 6. —*Lactant. ad Theb.* 7. v. 340.—*Conon. Nar.* 24.—*Philostrat.* 1. *Icon.* 23. [There is a fine statue of Narcissus in the collection of the Grand Duke of Tuscany, at Florence.]——A freedman and secretary of Claudius, who abused his trust and the infirmities of his imperial master, and plundered the citizens of Rome to enrich himself. Messalina, the emperor's wife, endeavoured to remove him, but Narcissus sacrificed her to his avarice and resentment. Aggrippina, who succeeded in the place of Messalina, was more successful. Narcissus was banished by her intrigues, and compelled to destroy himself, A. D. 54. Nero greatly regretted his loss, as he had found him subservient to his most criminal and extravagant pleasures. *Tacit. Ann.* 11. c. 33 & 38. l. 12. c. 53. l. 13. c. 1.—*Juv.* 14. v. 328.—*Dio.* 60. c. 34.—*Suet. Cl.* 28.——A favorite of the emperor Nero, put to death by Galba.——A wretch who strangled the emperor Commodus. He was thrown to lions to be devoured. *Casaubon ad Spart. in Sever.* c. 14.

NARDIN'IUM, a town of the Selini, in Hispania Tarraconensis. *Ptol.*

NAR'GARA, a town of Africa, where Annibal and Scipio came to a parley. *Liv.* 30. c. 29. It is called Margarum by *Polybius*, 15. c. 5.

NARIS'CI, a nation of Germany, in the upper Palatinate. *Tacit. de Germ.* 42.

NARMA'LIS, a city of Pisidia. *Steph.*

NAR'NIA or NAR'NA, anciently Nequinum, now Narni, a town of Umbria, washed by the river Nar, from which it received its name. There are still visible in its neighbourhood the remains of an aqueduct, and of a bridge erected over the river by Augustus. One of the arches is still entire, measuring above 100 feet in height and 150 in width. *Liv.* 10. c. 9.

NA'RO, now Narenta, a small river of Dalmatia, falling into the Adriatic, and having the town of Narona, now called Narenza, on its banks, a little above the mouth.

NAR'SES, a king of Persia, A.D. 294, defeated and taken prisoner by Maximianus Galerius, after a reign of seven years. *Euseb. in Chron.—Eutrop.* 9. ——A eunuch in the court of Justinian, who was deemed worthy to succeed Belisarius, &c. *Procop. de Bell. Goth.* 3.—*Evagr.* 4.—*Niceph, &c.*

NAR'TES, a people of Umbria, called also Interamnates. *Plin.* 3. c. 4.

NARTHE'CIS, a small island near Samus. *Strab.—Steph.* It is called Narthex by *Suidas.*

NARYC'IA, NARYC'IUM, NAR'YCUS or NA'RYX, a name applied to Locri a town of Magna Græcia, built by a colony of Locrians after the fall of Troy. The place in Greece from which they came bore the same name, and was the country of Ajax Oileus. The word Narycian is more universally understood, as applying to the Italian colony, near which pines and other trees grow in abundance. *Virg. G.* 2. v. 438. *Æn.* 3. v. 399.—*Ovid. Met.* 15. v. 705.

NASAMO'NES, a savage people of Libya, near the Syrtes, who generally lived upon plunder. *Curt.* 4. c. 7.—*Lucan.* 9. v. 439.—*Herodot.* 2. c. 165.—*Sil. It.* 2. v. 116. l. 11. v. 180.

NAS'CIO or NA'TIO, a goddess at Rome, who presided over the birth of children. She had a temple at Ardea. *Cic. de Nat. D.* 3. c. 18.

NAS'CUS or NAS'CUM, a city of Arabia Felix. *Plin.* 3. c. 3.—*Ammian.* It is now Magiaraba.

NASI'CA, the surname of one of the Scipios. His integrity was considered to be so great, that the senate adjudged his house to be the holiest receptacle for the image of Cybele when brought to Rome. Nasica was the first who invented the measuring of time by water, B. C. 159, about 134 years after the introduction of sun dials at Rome. *Vid.* Scipio. *Liv.* 29. c. 11. 14.—*Cic. Harusp.* 13.—*Ovid. Fast.* 4. v. 347.—*Plin.* 7. c. 34.—*Val. Max.* 8. c. 15.——An avaricious Roman, who married his daughter to Coranus, a man as mean as himself, that he might not only not repay the money which he had borrowed, but moreover become his creditor's heir. Coranus, understanding his meaning, purposely alienated his property from him and his daughter, and exposed him to ridicule. *Horat.* 2. sat. 5. v. 64, &c.

NASIDIE'NUS, a Roman knight, whose luxury, arrogance, and ostentation, exhibited at an entertainment which he gave to Macænas, were ridiculed in the happiest manner by *Horace*, 2. sat. 8.

NASID'IUS L., a man sent by Pompey to assist the people of Massilia. After the battle of Pharsalia, he followed the interests of Pompey's children, and afterwards revolted to Antony. *Appian.* 5.

NA'SO, one of the murderers of J. Cæsar.

NASO CN. OCTAV., a Roman knight. *Cic. Fam.* 13. ep. 31.

NASO, one of Ovid's names *Vid.* Ovidius.

NASSU'NIA, a city of Asiatic Sarmatia. *Ptol.*

NAS'SUS or NA'SUS, a town of Acarnania, near the mouth of the Achelous. *Liv.* 26. c. 24.

NAS'SUS, a part of the town of Syracuse.

NAS'UA, a general of the Suevi, when Cæsar was at the head of the Roman armies in Gaul.

NATA'LIS ANTO'NIUS, a Roman knight who conspired with Piso against Nero. He was pardoned for discovering the conspiracy. *Tacit. Ann.* 15. c. 50.

NA'TIO. *Vid.* Nascio.

NATI'SO, now Natisone, a river rising in the Alps, and falling into the Adriatic Sea, a little to the east of Aquileia. *Plin.* 3. c. 18.—*Cluver. Ital. Ant.* 1. p. 183.

NAT'TA, a man whose manner of living was so mean that his name became almost proverbial at Rome. *Horat.* 1. od. 6. v. 124.

NAUBA'RUM, a city of European Sarmatia, on the Palus Mæotis. *Plin.* 4. c. 12.—*Ptol.*

NAU'BOLUS, *Vid.* Nabolus.

NAU'BOLUS, a Phocean, father of Iphitus. The sons of Iphitus were called Naubolides from their grandfather. *Apollod.*——A son of Lernus, one of the Argonauts, and father of Clytonas. *Flacc.* 1. v. 362. l. 3. v. 480.—*Homer. Il.* 2. v. 517.—*Apollon.* 1. v. 86. l. 135 & 207.—*Paus.* 10. c. 33.—*Apollod.* 2.—*Diod.* 4.—*Hygin.* fab. 14.

NAU'CLES, a general of the mercenary troops of Lacedæmon against Thebes, &c. *Xenoph.*

NAU'CRATES, a Greek poet, who was employed by Artemisia to write a panegyric upon Mausolus. ——A comic poet confounded by *Giraldus* with Nausicrates. *Athen.* 9.——An orator who endeavoured to alienate the cities of Lycia from the interest of Brutus.——An historian of Erythræ. *Cic. Orat.* 2. c. 23.

NAU'CRATIS, a city of Ægypt, on the left side of the Canopic mouth of the Nile. It was in ancient times celebrated for its commerce, and no ship was permitted to land at any other place, but was obliged to sail directly to the city, there to deposit its cargo. It gave birth to Athenæus. The inhabitants were called Naucratitæ or Naucratiotæ. *Herodot*. 2. c. 97 & 179.—*Plin*. 5. c. 9.

NAU'LOCHUS, a maritime town of Sicily, at the west of the promontory of Pelorum. *Suet. in Aug*. c. 16.——A town of Thrace on the Euxine Sea. *Plin*. 4. c. 11.——A promontory of the island of Imbrus.——A town of the Locri. *Plin*. 4. c. 3.

NAUMA'CHIUS, a Greek poet, some of whose verses are quoted by ancient writers. About seventy-four of these are preserved in the collection of Greek poets, and they contain useful directions to a woman that has entered into the marriage state, that she may conduct herself with propriety and decorum, and ensure, not only the propriety of her household, but the good graces and the affections of her husband. *Stobœus*, c. 68, 74 & 83.

NAUPAC'TUS or NAUPAC'TUM, a maritime city of Ætolia on the north of the Corinthian Gulph, now called Lepanto. The word is derived from ναῦς and πήγνυμι, because it was there that the Heraclidæ *built* the first *ship*, which carried them to Peloponnesus. It first belonged to the Locri Ozolæ, and afterwards fell into the hands of the Athenians, who gave it to the Messenians, who had been driven from Peloponnesus by the Lacedæmonians. It became the property of the Lacedæmonians after the battle of Ægospotamos, and was restored to the Locri. Philip of Macedonia afterwards took it and gave it to the Ætolians, from which circumstance it has generally been called one of the chief cities of their country. *Strab*. 4.—*Paus*. 4. c. 25.—*Mela*, 2. c. 3.—*Ovid. Fast*. 2. v. 43.

NAU'PLIA, a maritime city of Peloponnesus near Argos, the naval station of the Argives. The famous mountain of Canathos was in its neighbourhood. *Paus*. 2. c. 38.—*Strab*. 8. It is now Napoli di Romania.

NAUPLI'ADES, a patronymic of Palamedes son of Nauplius. *Ovid. Met*. 13. v. 39.

NAU'PLIUS, a son of Neptune and Amymone, king of Eubœa. He married Clymene, daughter of Crateus of Crete, called by some Hesione or Philyra, and by her he was father to the celebrated Palamedes, who was so unjustly sacrificed to the artifice and resentment of Ulysses by the Greeks during the Trojan war. The death of Palamedes highly irritated Nauplius, and to revenge the injustice of the Grecian princes, he attempted to debauch their wives and ruin their characters. When the Greeks returned from the Trojan war, Nauplius saw them with pleasure distressed in a storm on the coasts of Eubœa, and to make their disasters still more universal, he lighted fires on such places as were surrounded with the most dangerous rocks, that the fleet might be shipwrecked upon the coast. This contrivance succeeded to his wishes, but Nauplius was so disappointed when he saw Ulysses and Diomedes escape from the general calamity, that he threw himself into the sea. According to some mythologists there were two persons of this name, a native of Argos, who went to Colchis with Jason, and who was son of Neptune and Amymone. The other was king of Eubœa, and lived during the Trojan war. He was, according to some, son of Clytonas, one of the descendants of Nauplius the Argonaut. The Argonaut was remarkable for his knowledge of navigation, and so well versed in astronomy that he acurately described and gave a name to the constellation of the Ursa Minor. He built the town of Nauplia, and sold Auge, daughter of Aleus, to king Teuthras, to withdraw her from her father's resentment. *Orph. Argon*. v. 200.—*Apollod*. 2. c. 7.—*Apollon*. 1, &c.—*Flacc*. 1. v. 372. l. 5. v. 65.—*Virg Æn*. 2. v. 82.—*Servius ad Æn*. 11. v. 260.—*Strab*. 8.—*Paus*. 2. c. 38. l. 4. c. 35.—*Hygin*. fab. 14 & 116.—*Schol. Eurip. in Orest*. 54.—*Schol. Apollon*. 1. v. 133 & 138.—*Lactant. ad Theb*. 2. v. 432. l. 6. v. 288.

NAUPORTUS, a town of Pannonia, on a river of the same name, now called Ober or Upper Laybach. *Vell. Pat*. 2. c. 110.—*Plin*. 3. c. 18.—*Tacit. Ann*. l. c. 20.

NAU'RA, a district of Scythia in Asia. *Curt*. 8. c. 2.——A promontory of India within the Ganges. *Arrian. in Peripl*.

NAUSIC'AA, a daughter of Alcinous, king of the Phæacians. While she was washing the garments of her father, attended by a number of female servants, she met Ulysses shipwrecked on the coast, and it was to her humanity that he owed the kind reception which he experienced from the king her father. She married, according to Aristotle and Dictys, Telemachus the son of Ulysses, by whom she had a son called Perseptolis or Ptoliporthus. *Hom. Odyss*. 6.—*Paus*. 5. c. 19.—*Hygin*. fab. 126.—*Aristot apud Eustath*. 16.—*Odyss*.—*Dictys. Cret*. 6. c. 6.—*Martial*. 12. epigr. 31.—*Tzetzes. in Lyc*. 818.

NAU'SICLES, an Athenian sent to assist the Phocians with an army of 5,000 foot and 300 horse. Olymp. 107. an. 1.

NAUSIG'ENES, an archon at Athens, Olymp. 103. an. 4.

NAUSIM'ENES, an Athenian whose wife lost her voice from the shock which she received upon seeing her son guilty of incest.

NAUSINI'CUS, an archon at Athens, Olymp. 100. an. 3.

NAUSIPH'ANES, a scholar of Democritus, the instructor of Epicurus, &c. *Cic. N.D*. 1. c. 26 & 33.

NAUSIS'TRATUS, an admiral of the Rhodians. *Polyæn*. 5. c. 27.

NAUSITH'OE, one of the Nereides. *Apollod*. 1.

NAUSITH'OUS, a king of the Phæacians, father to Alcinous. He was son of Neptune and Peribœa, though Hesiod calls him son of Ulysses and Calypso. *Hesiod Theog*. 1016.—*Eustath. in Odyss*. 16. ——The pilot of the vessel which carried Theseus into Crete. *Philoch. apud Plut. in Thes*.——A man who left Hesperia to avoid the neighbourhood of the Cyclopes, and who went to settle in a desert island. *Plut. de Exilio*.

NAUSTATH'MUS, a port of Phocæa in Ionia. *Liv*. 37. c. 31.——A port of Cyrenaica, now Porto di Bonandria. *Strab*. 17.

NAU'TACA, a city of Sogdiana. *Arrian*.

NAU'TES, a Trojan soothsayer, who comforted Æneas when his fleet had been burnt in Sicily, and who afterwards received from the hands of Diomedes the Palladium which had been stolen from Troy. He was the progenitor of the Nautii at Rome, a family to whom the Palladium of Troy was, in consequence of the service of their ancestors, entrusted. *Virg*.

NA'VA, now Nape, a river of Germany, falling into the Rhine at Bingen, below Mentz. *Tacit. Hist*. 4. c. 70.

NAVA'LIA or NABA'LIA, a city of Germany. *Ptol*. It is now Suoll.

NA'VIUS AC'TIUS, a famous augur. *Vid*. Nævius. *Æn*. 5. v. 794.—*Dionys. Hal*. 1.—*Servius. ad Virg. Æn*. 2. v. 166. l. 3. v. 407. l. 5. v. 704.

NAX'IA, a city of Caria. *Steph*.

NAXUA'NA, a city of Armenia Major. *Ptol*.

NAX'US or NAX'OS, now Naxia, a celebrated island in the Ægean Sea, the largest and most fertile of all the Cyclades, about 105 miles in circumference, and 30 broad. It was formerly called Strongyle, Dia, Dionysius, and Callipolis, and received the name of Naxus, from Naxus, who was at the head of a Carian colony, which settled in the island. Naxus abounds with all sorts of fruits, and its wines are still in the same repute as formerly. The Naxians were formerly governed by kings, but they afterwards exchanged this form of government for a republic, and enjoyed their liberty till the age of Pisistratus, who appointed a tyrant over them. They were reduced to submission by the Persians, but in the expedition of Darius and Xerxes against Greece, they revolted and fought on the side of the Greeks. During the Peloponnesian war they supported the interest of Athens. Bacchus was the chief deity of the island, as it was there that he celebrated his triumph over India, and that he espoused the forsaken Ariadne; and there also he punished the insolence of those sailors who had offered violence to his person and to his liberty. The capital of the island was also called Naxus, and near it, on the 20th of Sept. B.C. 377, the Lacedæmonians were defeated by Chabrias. *Thucyd*. 1, &c.—*Herodot*.—*Pindar. Pyth*. 4. v. 156.—*Hygin*. fab. 28 & 43.—*Diod*. 5, &c.—*Ovid Met*. 3. v. 636.—*Virg. Æn*. 3. v. 125.—*Paus*. 6. c. 16.—*Tzetzes. in Lyc*. 115.—*Servius. ad Georg*. 1. v. 222. *Æn*. 1. v. 71. l. 3. v. 125.—*Sch. Apollon*. 3. v. 234 & 996. l. 4. v. 426 & 761.—*Eustath. ad Dionys. Per*. 525.—*Lactant. ad Theb*. 6. v. 357.——An ancient town on the eastern side of Sicily, founded 759 years B.C. There was also another town at the distance of five miles from Naxus, which bore the same name, and was often called by contradistinction Taurominium. *Plin.* 3.—*Diod.* 13.——A town of Crete noted for hones. *Plin.* 36. c. 7.

NAX'US, a Carian who gave his name to the largest island of the Cyclades.

NAZ'ADA, a city of Media. *Ptol.*

NAZ'AMA, a town of Apemene in Syria. *Ptol.*

NAZIAN'ZUS, a town of Cappadocia, where St. Gregory was born, and hence he is called Nazianzenus.

NE'A or NO'VA IN'SULA, a small island between Lemnus and the Hellespont, which rose out of the sea during an earthquake. *Plin.* 2. c. 87. It is now Nio.——A town and fortified place of Mysia. *Steph.*

NEÆ'RA, a nymph of Sicily, mother of Phaethusa and Lampetia by the Sun. *Hom Odyss.* 12. v. 133. ——A woman mentioned in *Virgil's Ecl.* 3.——A mistress of the poet *Tibullus.* el. 3.——A favorite of *Horace.* 3. od. 14. v. 21. l. 5. od. 15. v. 11.——A daughter of Pereus, who married Aleus, by whom she had Cepheus, Lycurgus, and Auge, to whom Hercules offered violence. *Apollod.* 3. c. 9.—*Paus.* 8. c. 4.——The wife of Autolycus. *Paus.*——A daughter of Niobe and Amphion. *Apollod.*——The wife of the Strymon. *Id.*

NEÆ'THUS, now Neto, a river of Magna Græcia which falls into the Ionian Sea a little at the north of Crotona. *Ovid Met.* 15. v. 51.

NEAL'CES, a friend of Turnus in his war against Æneas. *Virg. Æn.* 10. v. 753.——A native of Cyzicum, killed by Pollux *Val. Flacc.* 3. v. 191.——A painter, amongst whose capital pieces are mentioned a painting of Venus, a sea-fight between the Persians and Ægyptians, and an ass drinking on the shore, with a crocodile preparing to attack it.

NEANDRI'A or NEAN'DRUS, a town of Troas. *Plin.* 5. c. 30.

NEAN'THES, an orator and historian of Cyzicum, disciple of Philiscus the Milesian. He flourished under Ptolemy Philadelphus, and wrote several valuable works. *Porphyr.* 4. *de abstin.*—*Athen.* 4, 9 & 13.—*Clem. Strom.* 5.—*Voss. Hist. Gr.* 1. c. 16, &c.

NEAP'OLIS, a city of Campania, anciently called Parthenope, and now better known by the name of Naples, rising like an amphitheatre at the back of a beautiful bay 30 miles in circumference. As the capital of that part of Italy, it is now inhabited by above 400,000 souls, who exhibit the opposite marks of extravagant magnificence and extreme poverty. Augustus called it Neapolis. *Suet. in Aug.* 98.——A town of Africa, near the promontry of Mercury, now Nabel.——A town of Africa, near the Syrtis Minor, and the mouth of the Cinyphius. It is now Napoli di Barbaria. *Dionys.* 204.——A city of Macedonia, now Christopoli.——A town of Ægypt. ——A city of Palestine, called also Sichem.——A city of Ionia on the borders of Caria, between Ephesus and Samus. *Ptol.*—*Strab.*——A part of Syracuse. *Liv.* 95. c. 24.—*Cic. in Verr.* 5.——A town of Sardinia, now Napoli.

NEAR'CHUS, an officer of Alexander in his Indian expedition. He was ordered to sail upon the Indian Ocean with Onesicritus, and to survey it. He wrote a curious account of this voyage and of the king's life, but his veracity has been called in question by *Arrian.* After the king's death he was appointed over Lycia and Pamphylia. *Curt.* 9. c. 10.—*Polyæn.* 9.—*Justin.* 13. c. 4.—*Strab.* 2, &c.—*Voss. Hist. Gr.* 1. c. 10.——A beautiful youth, &c. *Horat.* 3. od. 20. v. 6.——An old man mentioned by *Cicero de Senect.*

NE'BIS, a river of Hispania Tarraconensis. *Ptol.* It is called Næbis by *Strabo*, and is now Neiva.

NE'BO, a high mountain near Palestine, beyond Jordan, from the top of which Moses was permitted to view the promised land.

NEBRIS'SA, a town of Spain near the mouth of the Bætis, now Lebrixa.

NEBRO'DES, a mountain of Sicily, in which the river Himera rises. *Sil.* 14. v. 237.

NEBROPH'ONUS, a son of Jason and Hipsipyle. *Apollod.*

NEBROPH'ONUS, one of Actæon's dogs. *Ovid. Met.* 3. v. 211.

NEB'ULA, a name given to Nephele, the wife of Athamas. *Lactant. ad Achill. Stat.* l. v. 65.—*Hygin.* fab. 1.

NECES'SITAS, a divinity who presided over the fates and destinies of mankind, and who was regarded as the mother of the Parcæ. Her temple at Corinth was held so sacred, that only her priests were permitted to enter within its precincts. *Paus.* 2. c. 4. —*Plut. in Symp.* 9.—*Quæst.* 14.

NE'CHOS, a king of Ægypt, who attempted to make a communication between the Mediterranean and the Red Seas, B.C. 610. No less than 12,000 men perished in the attempt. It was discovered in his reign that Africa was circumnavigable. *Herodot.* 2. c. 158. l. 4. c. 42.

NE'CLAS, a city of Arabia Petræa. *Ptol.*

NECRET'ICE, a region of Colchis, *Ptol.* It is called Nitice by *Arrian.*

NECROP'OLIS, a city of Ægypt, 30 stadia from Alexandria, where Cleopatra destroyed herself.

NECTAN'EBUS, NECTAN'ABIS or NECTAN'EBES, a king of Ægypt, who defended his country against the Persians, and was succeeded on the throne by Tachus, B.C. 363. *Euseb.*

NECTAN'EBUS, his grandson, made an alliance with Agesilaus, king of Sparta, and, with his assistance, quelled a rebel lion of his subjects. Some time after he was joined by the Sidonians, Phœnicians, and inhabitants of Cyprus, who had revolted from the king of Persia. This powerful confederacy was soon attacked by Darius the king of Persia, who marched in person at the head of a formidable army. Nectanebus, to defend his frontiers against so powerful an enemy, levied 20,000 mercenary soldiers in Greece, the same number in Libya, and 60,000 were furnished in Ægypt. This numerous body proved unequal to the Persian forces; and Nectanebus, defeated in a battle, gave up all hopes of resistance, and fled into Æthiopia, B.C. 350, where he found a safe asylum. His kingdom of Ægypt became from that time tributary to the king of Persia. *Plut. Ages.*—*Diod.* 16, &c.—*Polyæn.* 2.—*C. Nep. in Ages.* —*Plin.* 36. c. 9.

NECTIBE'RES, a people of Mauritania Tingitana. *Ptol.*

NECYI'A, a city of Umbria. *Steph.*

NECYS'IA, a solemnity observed by the Greeks in memory of their dead. *Suidas.*—*Harpocrat.*

NE'DA, a nymph of Messenia, supposed to have been one of the nurses of the infant Jupiter. She gave her name to the river Neda, which flowed through Messenia. *Paus.* 4. c. 33.—*Cœl Rhod.* 18. c. 9, &c.

NEDI'NUM, a town of Illyricum. *Ptol.* It is now Nadin.

NE'DON, a city of Laconia, from which, according to *Stephanus*, Minerva was called Nedusia.

NEDU'SIA, a surname of Minerva, from the worship which she received at Nedus in Laconia. She had a temple in another part of Laconia erected to her, under that name, by Nestor after his return from Troy. *Strab.* 8 & 11.

NE'GRA, a town of Arabia Felix. *Steph.*

NE'IS, the wife of Endymion. *Apollod.*

NE'ITH, the Minerva of the Ægyptians. *Plut. in Timæo.*

NEI'TIS, one of the seven gates of Thebes, called after Neis, son of Zethus. *Paus.* 9. c. 9.

NELAX'A, a town of Syria. *Ptol.*

NELCYN'DA, a region of Carmania, on the shores the Indian Sea. *Arrian.*

NE'LEUS or NELE'US, a son of Neptune and Tyro. He was brother to Peleus, with whom he was exposed by his mother, who wished to conceal her incontinence from her offended father. They were preserved and brought to Tyro, who had then married Cretheus, king of Iolcus. After the death of Cretheus, Pelias and Neleus seized the kingdom of Iolcus, which belonged to Æson, the lawful son of Tyro by the deceased monarch. After they had reigned for some time conjointly, Pelias expelled Neleus from the throne, and kept the sovereign power in his hands. Neleus came to Aphareus, king of Messenia, who treated him with kindness, and permitted him to build a city, which he called Pylus. Neleus married Chloris, the daughter of Amph ion, by whom he had a daughter and twelve sons, who were all, except Nestor, killed by Hercules, together with their father. Neleus promised his daughter in marriage only to the suitor who brought him the bulls of Iphiclus. Bias was the successful lover. *Vid.* Melampus. *Ovid. Met.* 6. v. 418. *Heriod.* 1. v. 63. —*Paus.* 4. c. 36. l. 9. c. 36.—*Apollod.* 1. c. 9. l. 2.

c. 6.—*Homer. Odyss.* 11. v. 253 & 279. l. 15. v. 212. —*Pind. Pyth.* 4.—*Eustath. in Hom. Od.* 3.—*Hygin.* fab. 10, 14 & 31.——A son of Codrus who founded Miletus. *Perizon. ad Ælian. V.H.* 8. c. 5.

NE'LEUS or NELE'US, a river of Eubœa. *Antigon. in mirab.*

NE'LIA a city of Thessaly on the Sinus Pelasgicus. *Strab.*

NE'LO, one of the Danaides, who married Menachus. *Apollod.* 2.

NEMANTURIS'TA, a city of the Vascones, in Spain. *Ptol.*

NEMAU'SUS, a town of Gaul, in Languedoc, on the western side, and near the mouth of the Rhone, now called Nismes. It still contains some valuable remains of antiquity. *Ptol.* 2. c. 10.—*Mela*, 2. c. 5.—*Plin.* 3. c. 4.—*Sueton. in Tiber.* c. 13.—*Strab.* 14, &c.

NE'MEA, a town of Argolis between Cleonæ and Phlius with a wood, where Hercules, in the 16th year of his age, killed the celebrated Nemean lion. This animal, the off-spring of the hundred-headed Typhon, infested the neighbourhood of Nemea, and kept the inhabitants under continual alarms. It was the first labor of Hercules to destroy it; and the hero, when he found that his arrows and his club were useless against an animal whose skin was hard and impenetrable, seized him in his arms and squeezed him to death. The conqueror clothed himself in the skin, and games were instituted by the inhabitants to commemorate so great an event. The Nemean games were originally instituted by the Argives in honour of Archemorus, who died by the bite of a serpent (*vid.* Archemorus), and Hercules, in consequence of the destruction of the lion, some time after renewed them. They were one of the four great and solemn games which were observed in Greece. The Argives, Corinthians, and inhabitants of Cleonæ, generally presided by turns at the celebration, in which were exhibited foot, horse, and chariot races, boxing, wrestling, and other manly and athletic trials of skill. The conqueror was rewarded with a crown of olive, afterwards of green parsley, in memory of the adventure of Archemorus, whom his nurse laid down on a sprig of that plant. The Nemean games were celebrated every third, or, according to others, every fifth year, or more properly on the first and third year of every Olympiad, on the 12th day of the Corinthian month *Panemos*, which corresponds to our August. They served as an era to the Argives, and to the inhabitants of the neighbouring country. It was always usual, at these games, for an orator to pronounce a funeral oration in memory of the death of Archemorus, and those who distributed the prizes were always dressed in mourning. *Liv.* 27. c. 30 & 31. l. 34. c. 41,—*Ovid. Met.* 9. v. 97. *Ep.* 9. v. 61.—*Clem. Alex.*—*Athen.*—*Polyæn.*—*Strab.* 8.—*Hygin.* fab. 30 & 273.—*Apollod.* 3. c. 6.—*Plin.* 4. c. 6.—*Virg. Æn.* 8. v. 295.—*Paus.* 2. c. 15. l. 8. c. 48.—*Lucian. de Gymnas.*—*Stat.* 1. *Sylv.* 3.—*Schol. Pindar, in Isth.* 2. ——A river of Peloponnesus falling into the bay of Corinth. *Liv.* 33. c. 15. It is now Langra.——A fountain of the Celtiberi in Spain. *Mart.* 1. epigr. 50. v. 18.

NEMER'TES, one of the Nereides. *Hesiod. Theog.* 261.

NEMESE'A, a solemnity in memory of deceased persons; so called from the goddess Nemesis, who was thought to defend the relics and memory of the dead from injuries. *Soph. Elec.*—*Demosth. orat. adv. Spud.*—*Suidas.*

NEMESIA'NUS M. AUREL. OLYM'PIUS, a Latin poet born at Carthage in the third century. He wrote a poem on hunting, called Cynegeticon, and four eclogues, according to some; but Wernsdorf, and other learned men, have satisfactorily proved that the eclogues were the production of Calpurnius. The chief edition is Burman's, Mitau, 1774. His works may also be found in the Poetæ Latinæ Minores of Wernsdorf. *Harles. Not. Lit. Rom.* 1. p. 703.—*Sax. Onom.* 1. p. 377.

NEM'ESIS, one of the infernal deities, daughter of Nox. She was the goddess of vengeance, and represented always prepared to punish impiety, and at the same time liberally to reward the good and virtuous. She is made one of the Parcæ by some mythologists, and is represented with a helm and a wheel. The people of Smyrna were the first who erected statues to her honor with wings, to show with what celerity she is prepared to punish the crimes of the wicked both by sea and land, as the helm and the wheel in her hands intimate. Her power was supposed not only to exist in this life, but she was also employed after death to find out the most rigorous and effectual means of correction. Nemesis was particularly worshipped at Rhamnus in Attica, where she had a celebrated statue ten cubits long, made of Parian marble by Phidias, or, according to others, by one of his pupils. The Romans were also particularly attentive to the adoration of a deity whom they solemnly invoked, and to whom they offered sacrifices, before they declared war against their enemies, to show the world that their wars were undertaken upon the most just grounds. Her statue at Rome was in the Capitol. Some authors suppose that Nemesis was the person whom Jupiter deceived in the form of a swan, and that Leda was entrusted with the care of the children which sprang from the two eggs. Others, however, observe, that Leda obtained the name of Nemesis after death. According to Pausanias there was more than one Nemesis. The goddess Nemesis was surnamed *Rhamnusia*, because worshipped at Rhamnus, and *Adrastia* from the temple which Adrastus, king of Argos, erected to her honor when he went against Thebes, to revenge the indignities which his son-in-law Polynices had suffered in being unjustly driven from his kingdom by Eteocles. The Greeks celebrated a festival called *Nemesea* in memory of deceased persons, as the goddess Nemesis was supposed to defend the relics and the memory of the dead from insult and profanation. *Hygin. P.A.* 2. c. 8.—*Paus.* 1. c. 33.—*Apollod.* 3. c. 10.—*Hesiod. Theog.* 224.—*In Oper.* 199.—*Sophoc. in El.* 1.—*Eurip. in Phœniss.* 189.—*Callim. in Cerer.* 56.—*Marcell*, 14. c. 11 & 39.—*Auson. Id.* 5. v. 66. *Id.* 8. v. 40.—*Lactant. de Fals. R.* 21.—*Plin.* 11. c. 28. l. 36. c. 5. [A statue of Nemesis is to be found in the Vatican, and another in the collection of the late Grand Duke of Tuscany, at Florence. There is also a head in the British Museum, much mutilated, which was brought from the above-mentioned temple at Rhamnus.——A mistress of *Tibullus.* 2. el. 3. v. 55.—*Martial.* epig. 73. v. 7.

NEME'SIUM, a city of Marmarica. *Ptol.*

NEME'SIUS, a Greek writer, whose elegant and useful treatise "De Naturâ Hominis," was edited in 12mo. Ant. apud. Plant. 1565, and in 8vo, Oxon. 1671.—*Fabr. B. Gr.* 5. c. 14.—*Sax. Onom.* 1. p. 428.

NEMESTRI'NUS, a god who presided over the feasts celebrated at Rome under the name Nemora. Arnobius is the only ancient author who mentions this divinity. *Arnob.* 4.—*Voss. de Idol.* 2. c. 62.

NEMET'ACUM, a town of Gaul, called also Nemetocerna or Atrebatum. It is now Arras. *Antonin.*

NEMETA'TÆ, a people of Hispania Tarraconensis. *Ptol.*

NEME'TES, a nation of Germany at the west of the Rhine. Their town is now Spire, which was formerly called Noviomagus. *Tacit. de Germ.* 28.

NEMETOBRI'GA, a city of Hispania Tarraconensis. *Ptol.* It is now Val de Nebro.

NEMORA'LIA, festivals observed in the woods of Africa, in honor of Diana, who presided over the country and the forests, on which account that part of Italy was sometimes denominated Nemorensis Ager. *Ovid. de A.A.* 1. v. 259.

NEMOS'SUS (or -um), the capital of Arverni in Gaul, now Clermont. *Lucan.* 1. v. 419.—*Strab.* 4.

NEN'SIA, a city of Africa Propria. *Ptol.*

NEOBU'LE, a daughter of Lycambes betrothed to the poet Archilochus. *Vid.* Lycambes. *Horat. Epod.* 6. v. 13. l. 1. ep. 3. v. 79.—*Ovid. in Ib.* 54.—*Martial.* 7. epigr. 11.—*Arist.* 3. *Rhet.*——A beautiful woman to whom Horace addressed 3. od. 12.

NEOCÆSARE'A, a town of Cappadocia, on the river Lycus. *Steph.*

NEOCH'ABIS, a king of Ægypt. *Athen. Deipnos.* l. 10.

NE'OCLES an Athenian philosopher, father, or, according to Cicero, brother to the philosopher Epicurus. *Cic.* 1. *De Nat. D.* c. 21.—*Diog.* 10. c. 1. ——The father of Themistocles. *Ælian. V.H.* 2. &c.—*C. Nep. in Them.*

NEOCLI'DES, a rhetorician of Athens, ridiculed by *Aristophanes. in Plut.*

NEOG'ENES, a man who made himself absolute, &c. *Diod.* 15.

NEOM'AGUS, a city of the Regni in Britain. *Ptol.* Some suppose that it is the Noviomagus of *Antoninus*, and that it is now Croydon. *Burton. in Antonin. Itin.* p. 175.——A town of Gallia Celtica. *Ptol.* It is now Lisieux.

NEOME'NIA, festivals observed by the ancients at the time of the new moon, in honor of all the gods, but especially of Apollo and Diana. The Athenians, on the day of the solemnity, spread tables in the streets, at which the poor were abundantly supplied, and the Romans also honored the divinities by a public assembly, at which all the senators were expected to attend. *Horat.* 3. od. 17.—*Isidor.* 6. c. 8.—*Tertull. de Idol.* 14. & *Adv. Max.* 1. c. 20.—*Demosth. in Aristogit.*—*Hesych.*

NEOME'RIS, one of the Nereides. *Apollod.* 1.

NE'ON, a town of Phocis. There was also another of the same name, in the same country, on the top of Parnassus. It was afterwards called Tithorea. *Plut. in Syll.*—*Paus. Phoc.*—*Herodot.* 8. c. 32.

NE'ON, one of the commanders of the ten thousand Greeks who assisted Cyrus against Artaxerxes.

NEONTI'CHOS, a town of Æolia, near the Hermus. *Herodot.*—*Plin.* 5. c. 30.

NE'OPHON or **NE'OPHRON**, a Greek poet, who wrote several tragedies. He was intimate with Callisthenes, and slain, together with him, by order of Alexander. *Suidas.*

NEOPTOL'EMUS, a king of Epirus, son of Achilles and Deidamia, called *Pyrrhus*, from the *yellow* color of his hair. He was carefully educated under the eye of his mother, and gave early proofs of his valor. After the death of Achilles, Calchas declared in the assembly of the Greeks, that Troy could not be taken without the assistance of the son of the deceased hero. Upon this, Ulysses and Phœnix were commissioned to bring Pyrrhus to the war. He returned with them with pleasure, and received the name of Neoptolemus (*new soldier*), because he had come into the field later than the rest of the Greeks. On his arrival before Troy, he paid a visit to the tomb of his father, and wept over his ashes. He afterwards, according to some authors, accompanied Ulysses to Lemnus, to engage Philoctetes to come to the Trojan war. He greatly signalized himself during the remaining time of the siege, and he was the first who entered the wooden horse. He was inferior to none of the Grecian warriors in valor, and Ulysses and Nestor alone could claim a superiority over him in eloquence, wisdom, and address. His cruelty, however, was as great as that of his father. Not satisfied with breaking down the gates of Priam's palace, he exercised the greatest barbarity upon the remaining members of his family, and, without any regard to the sanctity of the place where Priam had taken refuge, he slaughtered him without mercy; or, according to others, dragged him by the hair to the tomb of his father, where he sacrified him, and where he cut off his head, and carried it in exultation through the streets of Troy, fixed on the point of a spear. He also sacrificed Astyanax to his fury, and immolated Polyxena on the tomb of Achilles, according to those who deny that that sacrifice was voluntary. When Troy was at last taken, the captives were divided among the conquerors, and Pyrrhus received for his share Andromache the widow of Hector, and Helenus the son of Priam. With these he departed for Greece, and he probably escaped from destruction by giving credit to the words of Helenus, who foretold him that, if he sailed with the rest of the Greeks, his voyage would be attended with fatal consequences, and perhaps with death. This obliged him to take a different course from the rest of the Greeks, and he travelled over the greatest part of Thrace, where he had a severe encounter with queen Harpalyce. *Vid.* Harpalyce. The place of his retirement after the Trojan war is not accurately known. Some authors maintain that he went to Thessaly, where his grandfather still reigned; but this is confuted by others, who observe, perhaps with more reason, that he went to Epirus, where he laid the foundations of a new kingdom, because his grandfather Peleus had been deprived of his sceptre by Acastus, the son of Pelias. Neoptolemus lived with Andromache after his arrival in Greece, but it is unknown whether he treated her as a lawful wife or as a concubine. He had a son called Molossus, by this unfortunate princess, and two others, if we rely on the authority of Pausanias. Besides Andromache, he married Hermione the daughter of Menelaus, as also Lanassa the daughter of Cleodæus, one of the descendants of Hercules. The cause of his death is variously related. Menelaus, before the Trojan war, had promised his daughter Hermione to Orestes, but the services which he experienced from the valor and the courage of Neoptolemus during the siege of Troy, induced him to reward his merit by making him his son-in-law. The nuptials were accordingly celebrated, but Hermione became jealous of Andromache, and, because she had no children, resolved to destroy her Trojan rival, who seemed to steal away the affections of their common husband. In the absence of Neoptolemus at Delphi, Hermione attempted to murder Andromache, but she was prevented by the sudden interference of Peleus, or, according to others, of the populace. When she saw her schemes defeated, she determined to lay violent hands upon herself, to avoid the resentment of Neoptolemus. The unexpected arrival of Orestes, however, changed her resolutions, and she consented to elope with her lover to Sparta. Orestes, at the same time, to revenge and to punish his rival, caused him to be assassinated in the temple of Delphi, and he was murdered at the foot of the altar by Machareus the priest, or, by the hand of Orestes himself, according to Virgil, Paterculus, and Hyginus. Some say that he was murdered by the Delphians, who had been bribed by the presents of Orestes. It is unknown for what reason Neoptolemus went to Delphi. Some assert that he wished to consult the oracle, to know how he might have children by the barren Hermione; others say, that he went thither to offer the spoils which he had obtained during the Trojan war, to appease the resentment of Apollo, whom he had provoked by calling him the cause of the death of Achilles. The plunder of the rich temple of Delphi, if we believe others, was the real object of the journey of Neoptolemus, and, it cannot but be observed, that he suffered the same death, and the same barbarities which he had inflicted in the temple of Minerva upon the aged Priam and his wretched family. From this circumstance, the ancients have made use of the proverb of *Neoptolemic revenge*, when a person had suffered the same savage treatment which others had received from his hand. The Delphians celebrated a festival, called *Neoptolemea*, with great pomp and solemnity in memory of Neoptolemus, who had been slain in his attempt to plunder their temple, because, as they said, Apollo, the patron of the place, had been in some manner accessory to the death of Achilles. *Paterc.* 1. c. 1.—*Virg. Æn.* 2 & 3.—*Paus.* 10. c. 24.—*Ovid. Met.* 13. v. 334, 455, &c. *Heroid.* 8.—*Strab.* 9.—*Pind. Nem.* 7.—*Eurip. Androm. & Orest. &c.*—*Plut. in Pyrr.*—*Justin.* 17. c. 3.—*Dictys Cret.* 4, 5 & 6.—*Homer. Odyss.* 11. v. 504. *Il.* 19. v. 326.—*Lycop. in Cass.* 314.—*Sophocl. Philoct.*—*Apollod.* 3. c. 13.—*Hygin.* fab. 97, 102, 123.—*Eustath. in Odyss.* 11.—*Servius. in Æn.* 2. v. 166. l. 3. v. 297. & 322. l. 11. v. 264.—*Schol. Eurip. in Orest.* 1657.—*Philostr. Her.* 19, &c.—*Dares Phryg.*—*Q. Smyrn.* 14, 303.—*Heliodor. Æthiop.* l. 3.——A king of the Molossi, father of Olympias the mother of Alexander. *Justin.* 17. c. 3.——Another king of Epirus.——An uncle of the celebrated Pyrrhus, who assisted the Tarentines against Rome. He was made king of Epirus by the Epirots, who had revolted from their lawful sovereign, and was put to death when he attempted to poison his nephew, &c. *Plut. in Pyrrh.*——A tragic poet of Athens, greatly favored by Philip king of Macedonia. When Cleopatra, the monarch's daughter, was married to Alexander of Epirus, he wrote some verses, which proved to be too prophetic of the tragical death of Philip. *Diod.* 16.——A relation of Alexander the Great. He accompanied him in his Asiatic expedition,

and was the first who climbed the walls of Gaza, when that city was taken After the king's death, he received Armenia as his province, and made war against Eumenes. He was supported by Craterus, but an engagement with Eumenes proved fatal to his cause. Craterus was killed, and himself mortally wounded by Eumenes, B.C. 321. *C. Nep. in Eumen.*——One of the officers of Mithridates the Great, beaten by Lucullus in a naval battle. *Plut. in. Luc.*——A tragic writer. *Sueton. in Calig.* c. 57.

NE'ORIS, a large country of Asia, near Gedrosia, almost destitute of water. The inhabitants were called Neoritæ, and it was said to be usual among them to suspend their dead bodies from the boughs of trees. *Diod.* 17.——A town of Iberia, near the river Harmastis. *Plin.* 6. c. 10.

NE'PE, a constellation in the heavens, the same as Scorpio.——An inland town of Etruria, at the west of mount Soracte. It was called also Nepete, and the inhabitants were called Nepesini. *Ital.* 8. v. 490.—*Liv.* 5. c. 18. l. 26. c. 34.

NEPHA'LIA, festivals in Greece in honor of Mnemosyne the mother of the Muses, and of Aurora, Venus, &c. No wine was used during the ceremony, but merely a mixture of water and honey. *Pollux*, 6. c. 3.—*Athen.* 15.—*Suidas.*—*Plut. in Symp.* 4.

NEPH'ELE, the first wife of Athamas king of Thebes, was mother of Phryxus and Helle. She was repudiated by her husband on pretence of being subject to fits of insanity, and Athamas married Ino the daughter of Cadmus, by whom he had several children. Ino became jealous of Nephele, because her children would succeed to their father's throne before her own, by right of seniority, and she resolved to destroy them. Nephele was apprized of her wicked intentions, and removed her children from the reach of Ino, by giving them a celebrated ram sprung from the union of Neptune and Theophane, on the back of which they escaped to Colchis. *Vid.* Phryxus. Nephele was afterwards changed into a cloud, whence her name is given by the Greeks to the clouds. Some call her Nebula, which word is the Latin translation of Nephele. The fleece of the ram, which saved the life of Nephele's children, is often called the Nephelian fleece. *Apollod.* 1. c, 9. *Hygin.* fab. 2, 3, 4.—*Ovid. Met.* 11. v. 195.—*Flacc.* 11. v. 56.—*Auson. Id.* 3. v. 187.

Neph'ele, a mountain of Thessaly, once the residence of the Centaurs.

NEPH'ELIS, a cape of Cilicia. *Liv.* 33. c. 20. According to *Ptolemy* it was a city, about ten miles from Antioch.

NEPHEONI'TÆ, a people of Asiatic Sarmatia. *Plin.* 6. c. 7.

NEPH'ERIS, a town of Africa Propria. *Antonin. Strab.*

NEPHERI'TES, a king of Ægypt, who assisted the Spartans against Persia, when Agesilaus was in Asia. He sent them a fleet of 100 ships, which were intercepted by Conon, as they were sailing towards Rhodes, &c. *Diod.* 14.

NE'PHUS, a son of Hercules, by Praxithea. *Apollod.*

NEPI'A, a daughter of Jasus, who married Olympus king of Mysia, whence the plains of Mysia are sometimes called *Nepiæ campi. Callimach.*

NE'POS CORN., a celebrated historian in the reign of Augustus. He was born at Hostilia, and, like the rest of his learned contemporaries, shared the favors and enjoyed the patronage of the emperor. He was the intimate friend of Cicero and Atticus, and recommended himself to the notice of the great and opulent by delicacy of sentiment and a lively disposition. According to some writers he composed three books of chronicles, as also a biographical account of all the most celebrated kings, generals, and authors of antiquity. Of all his valuable compositions nothing remains but his lives of illustrious Greek and Roman generals, which have often been attributed to Æmylius Probus, who published them in his own name in the age of Theodosius, to conciliate the favor and friendship of that emperor. The language of Cornelius has always been admired, and he is entitled to many commendations for the delicacy of his expressions, the elegance of his style, and the clearness and precision of his narrations. Some assert that he translated "Dares Phrygius," from the Greek original; but the inelegance of the diction, and its many incorrect expressions, plainly prove that it is the production, not of a writer of the Augustan age, but the spurious composition of a more modern pen. Cornelius speaks of his account of the Greek historians *in Dion.* c. 3. Among the many good editions of Cornelius Nepos, two may be selected as the best, that of Verheyk, 8vo, L. Bat. 1773, and that of Glasgow, 12mo, 1761. *Harles. Not. Lit. Rom.* 1. p. 174.—*Sax. Onom.* 1. p. 150.

Ne'pos Ju'lius, an emperor of the West, A.D. 474, who deposed Glycerius, and was afterwards slain by his soldiers, whom Glycerius had corrupted. *Jornand. in Chron.*—*Cassiodor.*—*Evagr. &c.*

NEPOTIA'NUS FLA'VIUS POPIL'IUS, a son of Eutropia, the sister of the emperor Constantine. He proclaimed himself emperor after the death of his cousin Constans, and rendered himself odious by his cruelty and oppression. He was murdered by Anicetus, after one month's reign, and his family were involved in his ruin, A.D. 350. *Zozim.* 1. 1.—*Victor. in Epist. Histor.*—*Socrat.* 1. 2, &c.

NEP'THYS, wife of Typhon, became enamoured of Osiris her brother-in-law, and introduced herself to his bed. She had a son by him called Anubis. *Plut. de Isid.*

NEPTU'NI A'RÆ, a maritime city of Africa Propria. *Ptol.*

Neptu'ni Fa'num, a place near Cenchreæ. *Mela*, 1. c. 19. According to *Ptolemy* it is near Patræ. ——A place in the island of Calauria. *Plut. in Demosth.*——A place near Mantinea. *Plin.* 4. c. 5.

Neptu'ni Promonto'rium, a promontory of Campania, and of Arabia Felix. *Eustathius in Dionys.* calls it Ποσειδονιὰς ἀκρα.

NEPTU'NIA, a town and colony of Magna Græcia. *Paterc.* 1. c. 15.

NEPTU'NIUM, a promontory of Arabia, at the entrance of the gulph. *Ptol.*—*Diod. Sic.*

NEPTU'NIUS, an epithet applied to Sext. Pompeius, because he believed himself to be descended from the god of the sea, on account of his father's great exploits on the ocean. Agrippa, the grandson of Augustus by Julia, assumed the same appellation. *Horat. Epod.* 9.—*Dion.* 48 & 55.

NEPTU'NUS, a god, son of Saturn and Ops, and brother to Jupiter, Plato, and Juno. He was devoured by his father the day of his birth, and again restored to life by means of Metis, who gave Saturn a certain potion. Pausanius says that his mother concealed him in a sheepfold in Arcadia, and that she imposed upon her husband, telling him that she had brought a colt into the world, which was instantly devoured by Saturn. Neptune shared with his brethren in the division of the empire of Saturn, and received as his portion the kingdom of the sea. This, however, did not seem equivalent to the empire of heaven and earth, which Jupiter had claimed, and he therefore conspired to dethrone him with the rest of the gods. This conspiracy was discovered, and Jupiter condemned Neptune to build the walls of Troy. *Vid.* Laomedon. A reconciliation was soon after effected, and Neptune was reinstated in all his rights and privileges. Neptune disputed with Minerva the right of giving a name to the capital of Cecropia, but he was defeated, and the olive which the goddess suddenly raised from the earth was deemed, in the opinion of the gods, more serviceable to mankind than the horse which Neptune had produced by striking the ground with his trident, as that animal is the emblem of war and slaughter. This decision highly offended Neptune, he renewed the combat by fighting for Trœzene, but Jupiter settled their disputes by permitting them to be conjointly worshipped there, and by giving the name of Polias, or the *protectress of the city*, to Minerva, and that of king of Trœzene to the god of the sea. Neptune also disputed his right to the isthmus of Corinth with Apollo; and Briareus the Cyclops, who was mutually chosen umpire, gave the isthmus to Neptune, and the promontory to Apollo. Neptune, as being god of the sea, was invested with more extensive power than any of the other gods, except Jupiter. Not only the oceans, rivers, and fountains were subjected to him, but he could also cause earthquakes at his pleasure, and raise islands from the bottom of the sea with a blow of his trident. The worship of Neptune was established in almost every part of the earth, and the Libyans, in particular, venerated him above all other nations, and looked upon him as the first and greatest of the gods. The Greeks and Romans were also attached to his worship, and celebrated their Isthmian games and Consualia with the greatest solemnity. He was generally represented sitting in a chariot made of a shell, and drawn by sea horses or dolphins. Sometimes he is drawn by winged horses, and holds his trident in his hand, and stands up as his chariot flies rapidly over the surface of the sea. Homer represents him as issuing from the sea, and in three steps crossing the whole horizon. The mountains and the forests, says the poet, trembled as he walked; the whales, and all the fishes of the sea, appear round him, and even the sea itself seems to feel the presence of its god. The ancients generally sacrificed a bull and a horse on his altars, and the Roman soothsayers always offered to him the gall of the victims, which in taste resembles the bitterness of the sea water. The amours of Neptune were numerous. He obtained, by means of a dolphin, the favors of Amphitrite, who had made a vow of perpetual celibacy, and he placed among the constellations the fish which had persuaded the goddess to become his wife. He also married Venilia and Salacia, which are only names of Amphitrite, according to some authors, who observe, that the former word is derived from *venire*, alluding to the continual motion of the sea. Salacia is derived from *salum*, which signifies the sea, and is properly applicable to Amphitrite. Neptune became a horse to enjoy the company of Ceres (*vid.* Arion), and to deceive Theophane he changed himself into a ram. *Vid.* Theophane. He assumed the form of the river Enipeus, to gain the confidence of Tyro, the daughter of Salmoneus, by whom he had Pelias and Neleus. He was also father of Phorcus and Polyphemus by Thoosa; of Lycus, Nycteus, and Euphemus, by Celeno; of Chryses by Chrysogenia; of Ancæus by Astypalea; of Bœotus and Hellen by Antiope; of Leuconoe by Themisto; of Agenor and Bellerophon by Eurynome the daughter of Nysus; of Antas by Alcyone the daughter of Atlas; of Abas by Arethusa; of Actor and Dictys by Agamede the daughter of Augias; of Megareus by Œnope daughter of Epopeus; of Cycnus by Harpalyce; of Taras, Otus, Ephialtes, Dorus, Alesus, &c. The word *Neptunus* is often used metaphorically by the poets, to signify *sea water*. In the Consualia of the Romans, horses were led through the streets of the city finely equipped and crowned with garlands, as the god, in whose honor the festivals were instituted, had produced the horse, an animal so beneficial for the use of mankind. *Paus.* 1, 2, &c.—*Hom. Il.* 7, &c.—*Varro. de. L. L.* 4.—*Cic. de Nat. D.* 2. c. 26. l. 2. c. 25.—*Hesiod. Theog.*—*Virg. Æn.* 1. v. 12, &c. l. 2, 3, &c.—*Apollod.* 1, 2, &c.—*Ovid. Met.* 6. v. 117, &c.—*Herodot.* 2. c. 50. l. 4. c. 188.—*Macrob. Saturn.* 1. c. 17.—*Aug. de Civ. D.* 18.—*Plut. in Them.*—*Hygin.* fab. 157.—*Eurip. in Phœniss.*—*Flacc.*—*Apollon. Rhod.* [The finest remaining statue, and a grand colossal bust of this divinity, are to be found in the Vatican, though inferior in style to the fragment in the Elgin collection, in the British Museum.

NER'ABUS, a city of Syria. *Steph.*

NERA'TIUS PRIS'CUS, a celebrated lawyer, very intimate with Trajan. Some of his writings are extant in the Pandects, and Gellius mentions a work, "de Nuptiis," written by him. *Gell.* 4. c. 4.—*Gesner. in Biblioth.*—*Sax. Onom.* 1. p. 300—*Harles. Not. Lit. Rom.* 1. p. 532.

NERE'IDES, nymphs of the sea, daughters of Nereus and Doris. They were fifty in number, according to some mythologists, and their names were as follows: Sao, Amphitrite, Proto, Galatea, Thoe, Eucrate, Eudora, Galena, Glauce, Thetis, Spio, Cymothoe, Melita, Thalia, Agave, Eulimene, Erato, Pasithea, Doto, Eunice, Nesea, Dynamene, Pherusa, Protomelia, Actea, Panope, Doris, Cymatolege, Hippothoe, Cymo, Eione, Hipponoe, Cymodoce, Neso, Eupompe, Pronoe, Themisto, Glauconome, Halimede, Pontoporia, Evagora, Liagora, Polynome, Laomedia, Lysianassa, Autonoe, Menippe, Evarne, Psamathe, Nemertes. In those which Homer mentions, to the number of thirty, we find the following names different from those spoken of by Hesiod: Halia, Limnoria, Iera, Amphitroe, Dexamene, Amphinome, Callianira, Apseudes, Callanassa, Clymene, Janira, Nassa, Mera, Orithya, Amathea. Apollodorus, who enumerates forty-five, mentions the following names different from the others: Glaucothoe, Protomedusa, Pione, Plesaura, Calypso, Cranto, Neomeris, Dejanira, Polynoe, Melia, Dione, Isea, Dero, Eumolpe, Ione, Ceto. Hyginus, and others, differ from the preceeding authors in the following names: Drymo, Xantho, Ligea, Phyllodoce, Cydippe, Lycorias, Cleio, Beroe, Ephira, Opis, Asia, Deopea, Arethusa, Crenis, Eurydice, and Leucothoe. The Nereides were implored as the rest of the deities; they had altars erected to their honor chiefly on the coasts of the sea, where the piety of mankind made offerings of milk, oil, and honey, and often of the flesh of goats. When they were on the sea shore they generally resided in grottos and caves, which were adorned with shells, and shaded by the branches of vines. Their duty was to attend upon the more powerful deities of the sea, and to be subservient to the will of Neptune. They were particularly fond of Alcyons, and as they had the power of ruffling or calming the waters, they were always addressed by sailors, who implored their protection, that they might grant them a favorable voyage and a prosperous return. They are represented as young and handsome virgins, sitting on Dolphins, and holding Neptune's trident in their hand, or sometimes garlands of flowers, &c. *Orpheus, Hymn.* 23.—*Catull. de Rapt. Pel.*—*Ovid. Met.* 11. v. 361, &c.—*Stat.* 2. *Sylv.* 2. l. 3. *Sylv.* l.—*Paus.* 2. c. 1.—*Apollod.* 1. c. 2 & 9.—*Hesiod. Theog.*—*Homer. Il.* 18. v. 39.—*Plin.* 36. c. 5.—*Hygin*, &c.

NERE'IUS, a name given to Achilles, as son of Thetis, who was one of the Nereides. *Horat.* ep. 17. v. 8.

NERES'SUS, a town of the island of Cea. *Æschines*, ep. 1. *ad Philocr.*

NE'REUS, a deity of the sea, son of Oceanus and Terra. He married Doris, by whom he had 50 daughters, called the Nereides. *Vid.* Nereides. Nereus was generally represented as an old man with a long flowing beard, and hair of an azure colour. The chief place of his residence was in the Ægean sea, where he was surrounded by his daughters, who often danced in chorusses round him. He was endowed with the gift of prophecy in a remarkable degree, and informed those that consulted him of the different fates that attended them. He acquainted Paris with the consequences of his elopement with Helen; and it was by his directions that Hercules obtained the golden apples of the Hesperides, but the sea god often evaded the troublesome importunities of inquirers by assuming different shapes, and totally escaping from their grasp. The word Nereus is often taken for the sea itself. Nereus is sometimes called the most ancient of all the gods. *Hesiod. Theog.* 240.—*Servius in Æn.* 3. v. 73.—*Hygin.*—*Homer. Il.* 18.—*Apollod.*—*Orpheus, Argon.*—*Horat.* 1. od. 13.—*Eurip. in Iphig.*

NER'ICUS, a city of Acarnania. *Hom. Il.* v. 213.

NE'RII, a people of Hispania Tarraconensis. *Mela*, 3. c. 1.

NE'RIO, NERIE'NE or NERIE'NIS, the wife of Mars, mentioned by *Gellius*, 13. c. 21.—*Plaut. Truc.* 2. sc. 6. v. 34.

NER'IPHUS, a desert island near the Thracian Chersonesus. *Plin.* 4. c. 11.

NERI'PI, a people of Asiatic Sarmatia. *Id.* 6. c. 7.

NE'RIS, a city of Messenia. *Steph.*—*Stat. Theb.* 4.

NER'ITUM, a town of Calabria, now called Nardo, on the bay of Tarentum.

NER'ITUS or NER'ITOS, a mountain in the island of Ithaca, as also a small island in the Ionian Sea, according to Mela. The word Neritus is often applied by ancient writers to the whole island of Ithaca, and Ulysses the king of it, is called *Neritius dux*, and his ship *Neritia navis*. The people of Saguntum are called *Neritia proles*, as descended from a Neritian colony. *Sil. It.* 2. v. 317.

—*Virg. Æn.* 3. v. 271. *Plin.* 4. c. 12.—*Mela*, 2. c. 7.—*Ovid. Met.* 13. v. 712. *Rem. A.* 263.

NE'RIUM or ARTA'BRUM, a promontory in the north-west of Spain, on the Atlantic, now Cape Finisterre. *Strab.* 3.

NE'RIUS, an eminent silversmith at Rome, in the age of *Horace.* 2. sat. 3. v. 69.——A usurer in Nero's age, who was so eager to get money, that he married as fast as he could, and then destroyed his wives by poison, to possess himself of their estates. *Pers.* 2. v. 14.

NE'RO CLAU'DIUS DOMITIUS, a celebrated Roman emperor, son of Caius Domitius Ahenobarbus and Agrippina the daughter of Germanicus. He was adopted by the emperor Claudius, A.D. 50, and four years after he succeeded him on the throne. The beginning of his reign was marked by acts of the greatest kindness and condescension, by affability, complaisance, and popularity. The object of his administration seemed to be the good of his people; and when he was desired to sign his name to a list of malefactors that were to be executed, he exclaimed, *I wish to heaven I could not write.* He was an enemy to flattery, and when the senate had liberally commended the wisdom of his government, Nero desired them to withhold their praises till he deserved them. These promising virtues were soon discovered to be artificial, and Nero displaying the flagitious propensities of his nature, soon delivered himself from the sway of his mother, and at last ordered her to be assassinated. This unnatural act of barbarity might astonish some of the Romans, but Nero had his devoted adherents, and when he declared that he had taken away his mother's life to save himself from ruin, the degenerate senators applauded his measures, and the people re-echoed their approbation. Many of his courtiers shared the unhappy fate of Agrippina, and Nero sacrificed to his fury or caprice all such as obstructed his pleasure, or diverted his inclination. In the night he generally sallied out from his palace to visit the meanest taverns, and all the scenes of debauchery which Rome contained. In this nocturnal riot he was fond of insulting the people in the streets, and his attempts on one occasion to offer violence to the wife of a Roman senator, nearly cost him his life. He also turned actor, and publicly appeared on the Roman stage in the meanest characters. In his attempts to excel in music, and to conquer the disadvantages of a hoarse rough voice, he moderated his meals, and often passed the day without eating. The celebrity of the Olympian games next attracted his notice. He passed into Greece, and presented himself as a candidate for the public honors. He was defeated in wrestling, but the flattery of the spectators adjudged him the victory, and Nero returned to Rome with all the pomp and splendour of an eastern conqueror, drawn in the chariot of Augustus, and attended by a band of musicians, actors, and stage dancers, from every part of the empire. These private and public amusements of the emperor were indeed innocent; his character was injured, but the national liberty remained inviolate, and the persons of his subjects were respected. But his conduct soon became more abominable; he disguised himself in the habit of a woman, and was publicly married to one of his eunuchs. This violence to nature and decency was soon exchanged for another; Nero resumed his sex, and celebrated his nuptials with one of his meanest catamites, and it was on this occasion that one of the Romans observed that the world would have been happy if Nero's father had had such a wife. But now his cruelty was displayed in a more superlative degree, and he sacrificed to his wantonness his wife Octavia Poppæa, and the celebrated writers, Seneca, Lucan, Petronius, &c. The Christians also did not escape his barbarity. He had heard of the burning of Troy, and as he wished to renew that dismal scene, he caused Rome to be set on fire in different places. The conflagration soon became universal, and raged during nine successive days. All was desolation, nothing was heard but the lamentations of the mothers whose children had perished in the flames, the groans of the dying, and the continual fall of palaces and buildings. Nero was the only one who seemed to enjoy the general consternation. He placed himself on the top of a high tower, and sang on his lyre the destruction of Troy, a dreadful scene, which his barbarity had realized before his eyes. He attempted to avert the public odium from his head, by a feigned commiseration of the miseries of his subjects, and began with marks of apparent sorrow to repair the streets and the public buildings at his own expense. He built himself a celebrated palace, which he called his golden house. It was profusely adorned with gold, with precious stones, and with whatever was rare and exquisite. It contained spacious fields, artificial lakes, woods, gardens, orchards, and whatever could exhibit beauty and grandeur. The entrance of this edifice could admit a large Colossus of the emperor 120 feet high, the galleries were each a mile long, and the whole was covered with gold. The roofs of the dining halls represented the firmament, in motion as well as in figure, and continually turned round night and day, incessantly showering down all sorts of sweet waters and perfumes. When this grand edifice, which, according to Pliny, extended all round the city, was finished, Nero in exultation exclaimed, that now he could lodge like a man. His profusion was not less remarkable in all his other actions. When he went a fishing, his nets were made with gold and silk. He never appeared twice in the same garment, and when he undertook a voyage there were thousands of servants to attend his person and take care of his wardrobe. This continuation of debauchery and extravagance at last roused the resentment of the people. Many conspiracies were formed against the emperor, but they were generally discovered, and such as were accessary suffered the greatest punishments. The most dangerous conspiracy formed against Nero's life was that of Piso, from which he was delivered by the confession of a slave. The conspiracy of Galba proved, however, more successful, and the conspirator, when he was told that his plot was known to Nero, declared himself emperor. The unpopularity of Nero favored his cause, he was acknowledged by all the Roman empire, and the senate had the courage and virtue to condemn the tyrant that sat on the throne to be dragged naked through the streets of Rome, and whipped to death, and afterwards to be thrown down from the Tarpeian rock like the meanest malefactor. This, however, was not done; and Nero, by a voluntary death, prevented the execution of the ignominious sentence. He killed himself A.D. 68, in the thirty-second year of his age, after a reign of thirteen years and eight months. Rome was filled with acclamations at the intelligence, and the citizens, more strongly to indicate their joy, wore caps such as were generally used by slaves, who had received their freedom. Their vengeance was now not only exercised against the statues of the deceased tyrant, but his friends were the object of the public resentment, and many were crushed to pieces in such a violent manner, that one of the senators amid the universal joy, said that he was afraid, they should soon have cause to wish for Nero. The tyrant, as he expired, begged that his head might not be cut off from his body, and exposed to the insolence of an enraged populace, but that the whole might be burnt on the funeral pile. His request was granted by one of Galba's freedmen, and his obsequies were performed with the usual ceremonies. Though his death seemed to be the source of universal gladness, yet many of his favorites lamented his fall, and were grieved to see that their pleasures and amusements were stopped by the death of the patron of debauchery and extravagance. Even the king of Parthia sent ambassadors to Rome to condole with the Romans, and to beg that they would honor and revere the memory of Nero. His statues were also crowned with garlands of flowers, and many believed that he was not dead, but that he would soon make his appearance, and take due vengeance upon his enemies. It will be sufficient to observe, in finishing the character of this tyrannical emperor, that the name of *Nero* is even now used emphatically to express a barbarous and unfeeling oppressor. *Pliny* calls him the common enemy and the fury of mankind, and in this description he has been followed by all writers, who exhibit Nero as a pattern of the most execrable barbarity and unpardonable wantonness. *Plut. in Galb.—Suet. in Vitâ.—Plin.* 7. c. 8, &c.—*Dio.* 64.—*Aurel. Victor.*—*Tacit. Ann.* [The finest statue of Nero is that in the character of Apollo Musagetes, in the Vatican; and of the busts that in the Capitol may be considered the best.]

Ne'ro Clau'dius, a Roman general, who after distinguishing himself in the taking of Capua was sent into Spain to succeed the two Scipios. He suffered himself to be imposed upon by Asdrubal, who was passing from Spain into Italy with a large reinforcement for his brother Annibal. A dreadful engagement was fought near the river Metaurus in Umbria, in which 56,000 of the Carthaginians were left on the field of battle, and great numbers taken prisoners, 207 B.C. Asdrubal, the Carthaginian general, was also killed, and his head was cut off and thrown into his brother's camp, by the conquerors. *Appian. in Han.—Oros.* 4.—*Liv.* 27, &c.—*Hovat.* 4. od. 4. v. 37.—*Flor.* 2. c. 6.—*Val. Max.* 4. c. 1.

Ne'ro Tib. Claud., the husband of Livia. He had previously paid his addresses to Tullia, Cicero's daughter, but her engagement with Dolabella prevented the union. During the civil wars of Pompey, Nero favored the party of Cæsar, but after the dictator's death he for a while supported the interests of Brutus, and the republic. In the disputes between Antony and Augustus, he professed himself the warm friend of Antony, but he was reconciled to his victorious rival Augustus, to whom either for interested or political reasons, he yielded up his wife Livia. Nero died soon after, leaving by Livia two sons, Tiberius, afterwards emperor, and Drusus, born three months after Livia's union with the emperor. *Suet. Aug.* 62. *Tib.* 4, *&c. Cl.* 1.—*Tacit. Ann.* 1. c. 10. l. 5. c. 1.—*Paterc.* 2. c. 75.—*Dio.* 48. c. 15.—*Cic. Fam.* 13. ep. 64. *Att.* 6. ep. 6.—*Horat.* 4. od. 4.

Ne'ro, a Roman who opposed Cicero when he wished to punish with death such as were accesary to Catiline's conspiracy.——A son of Germanicus, who was ruined by Sejanus, and banished from Rome to Pontia by Tiberius. He died in the place of his exile. His death was voluntary, according to some. *Sueton. in Tiber.*——A name of Domitian, because his cruelties surpassed those of his predecessors, and also *Calvus*, from the baldness of his head. *Juv.* 4. v. 37. The Neros were of the Claudian family, which, during the republican times of Rome, was honored with twenty-eight consulships, five dictatorships, six triumphs, seven censorships, and two ovations. They assumed the surname of Nero, which in the language of the Sabines, signifies *strong* and *warlike.* *Sueton. in Tib.* 1.

NE'RON, an island of the Red Sea. *Plin.* 38. c. 2.

NERO'NIA, a name given to Artaxata, the capital of Armenia, by Tiridates, who had been restored to his kingdom by Nero, which favor he acknowledged by calling the capital of his dominions after the name of his benefactor.

NERONIA'NÆ THER'MÆ, baths at Rome, erected by the emperor Nero. *Mart.* 7. epigr. 33. v. 4.

NERO'NIAS, an inland city of Cilicia, called also Irenopolis. *Ptol.*——A name given to Cæsarea Philippi, in Cœlesyria. *Joseph.*

NERTOBRI'GA or **NERTOBRI'CA**, a town of Hispania Bætica, on the river Bilbilis, which falls into the Iberus. *Appian.* It is now Valera.

NERULI'NUS, a son of P. Suilius, accused of bribery by his father, but protected by Nero. *Tac. Ann.* 13. c. 43.

NER'ULUM, an inland town of Lucania, now Lagonero, taken by storm by Æmilius. *Liv.* 9. c. 20.

NERU'SII, a people of the Alps. *Plin.* 3. c. 20. They are called Nerusii by *Ptolemy.* Their town Vintium, is now Venza or Vence.

NER'VA COCCE'IUS, a Roman emperor after the death of Domitian, A.D. 96. He rendered himself popular by his mildness, generosity, and the active part which he took in the management of affairs. He suffered no statues to be raised to his honor, and applied to the use of the government all the gold and silver images which flattery had erected to his predecessor. In his civil character he was the pattern of good manners, sobriety, and temperance. He forbade the mutilation of male children, and gave no countenance to the law which permitted the marriage of an uncle with his niece. He made a solemn declaration that no senator should suffer death during his reign; and this he observed with such sanctity that, when two members of the senate had conspired against his life, he was satisfied to tell them that he was informed of their wicked machinations. He also conducted them to the public spectacles, and seated himself between them, and, when a sword was offered to him, according to the usual custom, he magnanimously desired the conspirators to try it upon his body. Such goodness of heart, such confidence of the self-conviction of the human mind, and such reliance upon the consequence of his lenity and indulgence, deservedly conciliated the affection of all his subjects. Yet, as envy and danger are the constant companions of greatness, the prætorian guards at last mutinied, and Nerva nearly yielded to their fury. He uncovered his aged neck in the presence of the incensed soldiery, and bade them wreak their vengeance upon him, provided they spared the lives of those to whom he was indebted for the empire, and whom his honor commanded him to defend. His seeming submission was unavailing, and he was at last compelled to surrender to the fury of his soldiers, some of his friends and supporters. The infirmities of his age, and his natural timidity, at last obliged him to provide against any future mutiny or tumult, by choosing a successor. He had many friends and relations, but he did not consider the aggrandisement of his family, and he chose for his son and successor, Trajan, a man of whose virtues and greatness of mind he was fully convinced. This voluntary choice was approved by the acclamations of the people, and the wisdom and prudence which marked the reign of Trajan showed how discerning was the judgment, and how affectionate were the intentions of Nerva, for the good of Rome. Nerva died on the 27th of July, A.D. 98, in his 72nd year, and his successor showed his respect for his merit and for his character by raising him altars and temples in Rome, and in the provinces, and by ranking him in the number of the gods. Nerva was the first Roman emperor who was of foreign extraction, his father having been a native of Crete. *Suet in Dom.—Martial.* 11. epigr. 6.—*Tacit.* 1. *Hist.* 1. *Agric.* 3.—*Plin. Paneg.—Diod.* 69. [There is a colossal statue of Nerva in the Vatican; and the bust in the Capitol may be considered the finest.]

Ner'va M. Cocce'ius, a consul in the reign of Tiberius. He starved himself because he would not be concerned in the extravagance of the emperor.

Ner'va, a celebrated lawyer, consul with the emperor Vespasian. He was father to the emperor of that name.

Ner'va, a river in the country of the Cantabri in Spain. *Ptol. Mela,* 3. c. 1. calls it Nesua. It is now Nervio.

NERVES'IÆ, a small town of the Æquicoli, in Latium. *Plin.* 25. c. 8.

NER'VII, a warlike people of Belgic Gaul, who continually upbraided the neighbouring nations for submitting to the power of the Romans. They attacked J. Cæsar, and were totally defeated. Their country forms the modern province of Hainault. *Lucan.* 1. v. 428.—*Cæs. Bell. G.* 2. c. 15.

NESAC'TIUM, a town of Istria. *Plin.* 3. c. 19. It is called Nesactum by *Ptolemy,* and Nesattium by *Livy,* and is now Castello Novo.

NESÆ'A, one of the Nereides. *Virg. G.* 4. v. 338. *Æn.* 5. v. 826.—*Hesiod. Th.* 250. *Hygin.* fab. præf.—*Tzetzes. ad Lyc.* 399.

Nesæ'a, a part of Hyrcania through which the Ochus flows. *Strab.*

NE'SI, a people of European Scythia, whose horses were formerly much celebrated. *Plin.* 6. c. 20.

NESIM'ACHUS, the father of Hippomedon, a native of Argos, who was one of the seven chiefs who made war against Thebes. *Hygin.* fab. 70.—*Schol. Stat.* 1. *Theb.* 44.

NE'SIS (*-is* or *-idis*), now Nesita, an island on the coast of Campania, within the bay of Naples, famous for its asparagus. Lucan and Statius speak of its air as unwholesome and dangerous. *Plin.* 19. c. 8.—*Lucan.* 6. v. 90.—*Cic. ad Att.* 16. ep. 1 & 2.—*Stat.* 3. *Sylv.* 1. v. 148.

NESSO'NIS, a lake of Thessaly, near Larissa. *Strabo. Suidas* calls it *Nesonium Stagnum.*

NES'SON, a city of Thessaly. The inhabitants were called Nessonites. *Steph.*

NES'SUS, a celebrated Centaur, son of Ixion and the Cloud. He offered violence to Dejanira, whom Hercules had entrusted to his care, with orders to carry her across the river Evenus. *Vid.* Dejanira. Hercules saw the distress of his wife from the opposite bank of the river, and immediately let fly one of his poisoned arrows, which struck the Centaur to the heart. Nessus, as he expired, gave the tunic he then wore to Dejanira, assuring her that, from the poisoned blood which had flowed from his wounds, it had received the power of calling a husband away from unlawful loves. Dejanira received it with pleasure, and this deadly present afterwards caused the death of Hercules. *Vid.* Hercules. *Apollod.* 2. c. 7.—*Ovid. Ep.* 9.—*Senec. in. Herc. Fur.*—*Paus.* 3. c. 28.—*Diod.* 4.—*Sophoc. in Trach.* 564.—*Hygin.* fab. 34.—*Eustath. ad Dionys. Per.* 426.—*Lactant. ad Theb.* 4. v. 833. l. 11. v. 225.

NES'TOCLES, a famous statuary of Greece, rival to Phidias. *Plin.* 34. c. 8.

NES'TOR, a son of Neleus and Chloris, nephew to Pelias, and grandson to Neptune. He had eleven brothers, who were all killed, with his father, by Hercules. His tender age detained him at home, and was happily the cause of his preservation. The conqueror spared his life, and placed him on the throne of Pylus. Nestor married Eurydice, the daughter of Clymenes, or, according to others, Anaxibia, the daughter of Atreus. He early distinguished himself in the field of battle, and was present at the nuptials of Pirithous, when a bloody battle was fought between the Lapithæ and Centaurs. As king of Pylus and Messenia, he afterwards led his subjects to the Trojan war, where he distinguished himself among the rest of the Grecian chiefs by eloquence, address, wisdom, justice, and an uncommon prudence of mind. Homer describes his character as the most perfect of all his heroes; and makes Agamemnon exclaim, that, if he had ten generals like Nestor, he should soon see the walls of Troy reduced to ashes. After the Trojan war, Nestor retired to Greece, where he enjoyed, in the bosom of his family, the peace and tranquillity which were due to his wisdom, his services, and his old age. The manner and the time of his death are unknown: the ancients are all agreed that he lived three generations of men, which length of time some suppose to be 300 years, though, more probably, only 90, allowing 30 years for each generation. From that circumstance, therefore, it was usual among the Greeks and the Latins, when they wished a long and happy life to their friends, to wish them to see the years of Nestor. He had two daughters, Pisidice and Polycaste; and seven sons, Perseus, Straticus. Aretus, Echephron, Pisistratus, Antilochus, and Trasimedes. Nestor was one of the Argonauts, according to *Valerius Flaccus,* 1. v. 380, &c.—*Dictys. Cret.* 1. c. 13, &c.—*Homer. Il.* 1, &c. *Od.* 3 & 11.—*Hygin.* fab. 10 & 273.—*Paus.* 3. c. 26. l. 4. c. 3 & 31.—*Apollod.* 1. c. 9. l. 2. c. 7.—*Ovid. Met.* 12. v. 169, &c.—*Horat.* 1. od. 15.—*Cic. ad Fam.* ep. 14.—*Aul. Gell.* 19. c. 7.—*Italic.* 1. v. 145. l. 6. v. 569.—*Juv.* 10. v. 240.—*Q. Smyrn.* 2. v. 260. l. 3. v. 513. l. 4. v. 118, 309. l. 5. v. 139, &c.—*Schol. Homer. Il.* 1. v. 250. & *Horat.* 2. od. 9. v. 13.——A poet of Lycaonia, in the age of the emperor Severus. He was father to Pisander, a poet who flourished under the emperor Severus. *Hesych.*—*Suidas.*——One of the body guards of Alexander, sent by the people of Epirus to carry off Deidamia, the daughter of Pyrrhus. *Polyæn.* 8. c. 52.——A grammarian of Alexandria, the instructor of Marcellus, the nephew of Augustus. *Strab.* 14.—*Athen.* 10.—*Voss. H. Gr.* 2. c. 4.

NESTO'RIUS, a bishop of Constantinople, who flourished A.D. 431. He was condemned and degraded from his episcopal dignity for his heretical opinions. *Hist. Trip.* 12. c. 4 & 5.—*Cassian. de Incarn.*—*Cyrill. contra Nestor.*—*Socr.* l. 7.—*Evagr.* l. 1, &c,——A man intimate with Cicero. *Cic.* 6. *Fam.* 11.

NE'SUS, a small river of Thrace, rising in mount Rhodope, and falling into the Ægean Sea above the island of Thasus. It was for some time the boundary of Macedonia on the east. It is called Nestus by *Herodotus* and *Pliny,* 4. c. 11., Nastus by *Stephanus,* and Nessus by others. It is now Nesto, but it is called by the Turks Charason.——A town and river of Upper Mysia. *Steph.*—*Ptol.* It is now Nissava.——A city of Iberia. *Steph.*

NE'TIUM. a town of Peucetia. *Strab.*

NE'TON, an image of Mars, religiously worshipped by the Accitani, a people of Hispania Tarraconensis. *Macrob. Sat.* 1. c. 19.

NE'TUM or **NEE'TUM**, a town of Sicily, now called Noto, on the eastern coast, south of Syracuse. The inhabitants were called Netini and Netinenses. *Plin.* 3. c. 8.—*Sil.* 14. v. 269.—*Cic. in Ver.* 4. c. 26. l. 5. c. 51.

NE'VA, a city of Cœlesyria between Capitolia and Damascus. *Antonin.*

NEU'RI, a people of Sarmatia. *Mela,* 2. c. 1.

NI'A, a river in the interior of Libya. *Ptol.*

NIACUR'RA, a city of Commagene. *Antonin.*

NI'BAS, a district of the town of Thessalonica, in Macedonia, where, as Pliny says, cocks never crowed, whence the proverb, *Cum Nibas coccysaverit,* to express an event not at all to be expected. *Plin.* 29. c. 4.—*Erasm. Adagia.*

NI'BIS, a city of Ægypt. *Steph.*

NICÆ'A, a widow of Alexander, who married Demetrius.——A daughter of Antipater, who married Perdiccas. *Diod. Sic.* 18.

Nicæ'a, a city of India, built by Alexander on the very spot where he had obtained a victory over king Porus.——A town of Achaia, near Thermopylæ, on the bay of Malia.——A town of Illyricum. ——A town of Corsica.——A town of Thrace. ——A town of Bœotia.——A town of Bithynia, now Nice or Is-nik, built by Antigonus, the son of Philip, king of Macedonia. It was originally called, Antigonia, and afterwards Nicæa by Lysimachus, who gave it the name of his wife, who was daughter of Antipater. It is chiefly celebrated for the ecclesiastical council held there A.D. 324. *Strab.* 12.—*Mela,* 2. c. 5.—*Catull.* 47. v. 5.—*Curt.* 9. c. 3.—*Steph. Byzant.*——A town of Liguria, built by the people of Massilia, in commemoration of a victory. *Plin.* 3. c. 5. It is now Nizza.

NICÆN'ETUS, an historian of Abdera, or of Samus. He is mentioned by *Athenæus,* l. 13 & 15. *Lil. Gyrald. poet. Hist.* l. 3.

NICAG'ORAS, a sophist of Athens, who flourished in the reign of the emperor Philip, about 246 A.D. He wrote the lives of illustrious men, and was reckoned one of the greatest and most learned men of his age. Authors speak of four writers of this name frequently confounded together; one of Athens, the second of Rhodes, the third of Cyprus, and the fourth of Locri. *Jonsius Hist. Phil.* 3. c. 14.—*Arnob.* l. 4.—*Fulgent.* l. 2.—*Voss. H. Gr.* l. 4. p. 519.

NIC'AMA, the metropolis of India within the Ganges. *Ptol.*

NICAN'DER. a king of Sparta, son of Charillus, of the family of the Proclidæ. He reigned thirty-nine years, and died B.C. 770. *Paus.* 2. c. 36.——A writer of Chalcedon.——A leader of Ætolia, very inimical to the Romans. *Liv.* 35. c. 12, l. 36. c. 29. l. 38. c. 1, &c.——A pirate. *Liv.* 37. c. 11.——A Greek grammarian, poet, and physician, of Colophon, 137 B.C. His writings were held in estimation, but his judgment cannot be highly commended, since, without any knowledge of agriculture, he ventured to compose a book on that intricate subject. Two of his poems, entitled "Theriaca," on venomous beasts, and the remedies to be used to cure the wounds inflicted by them, and "Alexipharmaca," on antidotes against poison, are still extant, the best editions of which are those of Gorræus, with a translation in Latin verse by Grevinus, a physician at Paris, 4to, Paris, 1557; and Baudinius, 8vo, with an Italian version by Ant. Mar. Salvinius, Florent. 1764. The Alexipharmaca has been also edited by Schneider, Hal. 1792. *Fabr. B. Gr.* 3. c. 29.—*Sax. Onom.* 1. p. 135.—*Cic.* 1. *Orat.* c. 16.—*Plut. de. Aud. Poet.*—*Anthol. Gr.* 1. c. 39.—*Strab.* 17.—*Voss. de H. Gr.* 4. c. 14.——An athlete of Elis, who obtained the prize, and was twice crowned at Olympia, where his statue made by Daippus was erected. *Paus.* 6. c. 16.

NICAN'DRA, a priestess of Dodona. *Herodot.* 2. c. 55.

NICA'NOR, a man who conspired against the life of Alexander. *Curt.* 6.——A son of Parmenio, who died in Hyrcania, &c. *Id.* 3. c. 9, &c.——A surname of Demetrius. *Vid.* Demetrius the Second. ——An unskilful pilot of Antigonus. *Polyæn.* 4. c. 6.——A servant of Atticus. *Cic.* 5. ep. 3. ——A Samian, who wrote a treatise on rivers, &c. *Suidas.*——A governor of Media, conquered by Seleucus. He had been governor of the Athenians under Cassander, by whose orders he was put to death.——A general of the emperor Titus, wounded at the siege of Jerusalem.——A man of Stagira, by whom Alexander the Great sent a letter to recall the Grecian exiles. *Diod.* 18.——A governor of Munychia, who seized the Piræus, and was at last put to death by Cassander, because he wished to make himself absolute over Attica. *Diod.* 18. ——A brother of Cassander, destroyed by Olympias. *Id.* 19.——A general of Antiochus, king of Syria. He made war against the Jews, and shewed himself uncommonly cruel.

NICAR'CHUS, a Corinthian philosopher in the age of Periander. *Plut. in Sympos.* 7. *Sapient.*——An Arcadian chief, who deserted to the Persians, at the return of the ten thousand Greeks. *Xenophon.*

NICARTHI'DES, a man set over Persepolis by Alexander, with 3000 Macedonians. *Curt.* 5. c. 6.

NICA'SIA, a small island near Naxus. *Steph.*

NICA'SIO, a senator of the town of Enna. *Cic. Ver.* 4. c. 51.

NICA'TES, a mountain of Italy, mentioned by *Livy.* It is now Majella.

NICA'TOR, a surname given to Seleucus, king of Syria, from his having been unconquered. *Appian.*

NICAT'ORIS, a city of Syria. *Steph.*

NICATO'RIUM, a mountain of Assyria, near Arbela. *Strab.*

NI'CE, a daughter of Thestius. *Apollod.*——A favorite of Verres, wife to Cleomenes of Syracuse, &c. *Cic. Ver.* 5. c. 30.

NIC'EA, a city of Macedonia, near Heraclea. *Antonin.*

NICEAR'CHUS, a painter. *Plin.* 35. c. 11.

NICEPHO'RIUM, a town of Mesopotamia, on the Euphrates, where Venus had a temple. *Plin.* 6. c. 26.—*Liv.* 32. c. 33.—*Tacit. An.* 6. c. 41.——A city near Edessa, called also Constantina. *Steph.* It is now Nasivancasi.

NICEPHO'RIUS, now Khabour, a river which flowed by the walls of Tigranocerta. *Tacit. An.* 15. c. 4.

Nicepho'rius, a name of Jupiter, from Nicephorium, where he had a temple. *Spart. in vit. Adrian.* c. 2.

NICEPH'ORUS CÆ'SAR, a Byzantine historian, whose works were edited, fol. Paris, 1661.

Niceph'orus Grego'ras, another, edited in fol. Paris, 1702.

Niceph'orus, a Greek ecclesiastical historian, whose works were edited by Ducæus, 2 vols. Paris, 1630.

NI'CER, now the Necker, a river of Germany, falling into the Rhine near the modern town of Manheim. *Auson. Mos.* 423.

NICER'ATUS, a poet who wrote a poem in praise of Lysander.——The father of Nicias, who perished in Sicily. *Schol. in Aristoph.*——An archon at Athens, Olymp. 12. an. 1.

NIC'EROS, a celebrated painter. *Plin.* 35. c. 10.

NICER'TÆ, a large village of Apamea. *Strab.*

NICE'TAS, one of the Byzantine historians, whose works were edited, fol. Paris, 1647. *Voss. H. Gr.* 2. c. 28, &c.——A Pythagorean philosopher of Syracuse, who maintained that the earth moved round its axis, and that the sun and the stars were stationary. *Cic.* 4. *Acad.* 39

NICETE'RIA, a festival at Athens, in memory of the victory which Minerva obtained over Neptune, in their dispute about giving a name to the capital of the country. *Proclus, in Timæum, Comm.* 1. The same name was applied to contests about drinking; and among these the one which Alexander gave is mentioned as remarkable. The monarch wished to honor the memory of Calanus the gymnosophist, and therefore, to please his Indian subjects, he proposed rewards to the best drinkers; one talent to the first, thirty minæ for the second, and ten for the third. Promachus obtained the first prize by drinking four measures of wine, about twenty-four pints; but he survived his victory only three or four days; and thirty-five of his competitors likewise fell a sacrifice to their intemperance. *Ælian. V. H.* 2. c. 41.—*Athen.* 10. c. 12.—*Plut. in Alex.*—*Perizonius ad Ælian. loc. cit.*—*Schol. Juv.* 3. v. 68.

NICE'TES, a sophist of Smyrna, in great favor with Adrian. *Philostr.*

NIC'IA or **NICÆ'A**, a city. *Vid.* Nicæa.

Nic'ia, a river falling into the Po at Brixellum. It is now called Lenza, and separates the duchy of Modena from that of Parma.

NIC'IAS, an Athenian general, celebrated for his valor and his misfortunes. He early conciliated the good will of the people by his liberality, and established his military character by taking the island of Cythera from the power of Lacedæmon. When Athens determined to make war against Sicily, Nicias was appointed, with Alcibiades and Lamachus, to conduct the expedition, which he reprobated as impolitic, and as the cause of future calamities to the Athenian power. In Sicily he behaved with great firmness, but often blamed the quick and inconsiderate measures of his colleagues. The success of the Athenians remained long doubtful. Alcibiades was recalled by his enemies to take his trial, and Nicias was left at the head of affairs. Syracuse was surrounded by a wall, and, though the operations of the siege were carried on slowly, yet the city would have surrendered, had not the sudden appearance of Gylippus, the Corinthian ally of the Sicilians, cheered up the courage of the besieged at that critical moment. Gylippus proposed terms of accommodation to the Athenian general, but they were refused. Some battles were fought, in which the Sicilians obtained the advantage; and Nicias at last, tired of his ill success, and grown desponding, demanded of the Athenians a reinforcement or a successor. Demosthenes was, upon this, sent to his assistance with a powerful fleet; but the advice of Nicias was despised, and the admiral, by his eagerness to come to a decisive engagement, ruined his fleet and the interests of his country. The fear of his enemies at home prevented Nicias from leaving Sicily; and when at last a continued series of ill success obliged him to adopt defensive measures, he found himself surrounded on every side by the enemy, without hope of escaping. He gave himself up to the conquerors with all his army, but the assurances of safety which he had received soon proved vain and false, and he was no sooner in the hands of the enemy than he was shamefully put to death with Demosthenes. His troops were sent to the quarries, where the plague and hard labor diminished their numbers and aggravated their misfortunes. Some suppose that the death of Nicias was not violent. He perished about 413 years B.C., and the Athenians lamented in him a great and valiant but unfortunate general. *Plut. in Vitâ.*—*C. Nep. in Alcib.*—*Thucyd.* 4, &c.—*Diod.* 15.——A grammarian of Rome, intimate with Cicero. *Cic. ad Att.* 7. epist. 3, &c.——A man of Nicæa, who wrote a history of philosophers. *Athen.* 4, 6, 10 & 13.—*Jons. de Hist. Phil. Script.* p. 340.——A physician of Pyrrhus, king of Epirus, who made an offer to the Romans of poisoning his master for a sum of money. The Roman general disdained his offers, and acquainted Pyrrhus with his treachery. He is oftener called Cineas. *Eutrop.* 2. c. 1.—*Marcell.* 30. c. 1.—*Val. Max.* 6. c. 5.—*Liv.* 13.——A painter of Athens, in the age of Alexander. He was chiefly happy in his pictures of women. *Ælian. V.H.* 2. c. 31.—*Plin.* 35. c. 6.—*Paus.* 1. c. 29.

NICIP'PE, a daughter of Pelops, who married Sthenelus. *Apollod.*——A daughter of Thespius, mother of Antimachus by Hercules. *Id.*

NICIP'PUS, a tyrant of Cos, one of whose sheep is said to have brought forth a lion, which was considered as portending his future greatness, and his elevation to the sovereignty. *Ælian. V. H.* 1. c. 29.

NI'CO one of the Tarentine chiefs who conspired against the life of Annibal. *Liv. Dec.* 3. l. 26. c. 39.——A celebrated architect and geometrician. He was father of Galen, the prince of physicians. ——One of the slaves of Craterus.

Ni'co, the name of an ass which Augustus met before the battle of Actium, a circumstance which he considered as a favorable omen. *Suet. Aug.* 96. ——The name of an elephant remarkable for his fidelity to king Pyrrhus.

NICOCH'ARES, a Greek comic poet in the age of Aristophanes. *Athen.—Suidas.*

NIC'OCLES, a familiar friend of Phocion, condemned to death. *Plut.*——A king of Salamis, celebrated for his contest with a king of Phœnicia, to prove which of the two was most effeminate.——A king of Paphus, who reigned under the protection of Ptolemy, king of Ægypt. He revolted from his friend to the king of Persia, upon which Ptolemy ordered one of his servants to put him to death, to strike terror into the other dependent princes. The servant, unwilling to murder the monarch, advised him to kill himself. Nicocles obeyed, and all his family followed his example, 310 years B.C. ——An ancient Greek poet, who called physicians a happy race of men, because light published their good deeds to the world, and the earth hid all their faults and imperfections.——A king of Cyprus, who succeeded his father Evagoras on the throne, 374 years B.C. It was with him that the philosopher Isocrates contended. *Isocrat. ad Nic.—Athen.* 8.—*Ælian. V.H.* 7. c. 2.—*Plut. in Isocr.*——A tyrant of Sicyon, deposed by means of Aratus, the chief of the Achæan league. *Plut. in Arat.—Cic. Off.* 2. c. 23.

NICOC'RATES, a tyrant of Cyrene. *Polyæn.* 8. c. 38.——An archon at Athens, Olymp. 111. an. 4. ——A king of Salamis in Cyprus, who made himself known by the valuable collection of books which he made. *Athen.* 1.

NICO'CREON, a tyrant of Salamis in Cyprus, in the age of Alexander the Great. He ordered the philosopher Anaxarchus to be pounded to pieces in a mortar. *Cic. Tusc.* 2. c. 22.

NICODE'MUS, an Athenian appointed by Conon over the fleet which was going to the assistance of Artaxerxes. *Diod.* 14.——A tyrant of Centuripa, in Sicily, expelled by Timoleon, Olymp. 110. an. 2. *Diod. Sic.* 16.——An ambassador sent to Pompey by Aristobulus.

NICODO'RUS, a wrestler of Mantinea, who studied philosophy in his old age. *Ælian. V.H.* 2. c. 23.—*Suidas.*——An Athenian archon, Olymp. 117. an. 4. *Dion. Hal. in Dinarch.*

NICOD'ROMUS, a son of Hercules and Nice. *Apollod.*——An Athenian who invaded Ægina, &c.

NICOLA'US, a celebrated Syracusan, who endeavoured, in a pathetic speech, to dissuade his countrymen from offering violence to the Athenian prisoners who had been taken with Nicias their general. His eloquence was unavailing.——An officer of Ptolemy, employed against Antigonus. ——A peripatetic philosopher and historian of Damascus, intimate with Augustus, to whom he made frequent presents of the finest dates of his country, which the emperor called Nicolai. *Suet.* —*Plin.* 13. c. 4.—*Athen.* 14. p. 852.—*Fabr. B. Gr.* 3. c. 8.—*Sax. Onom.* 1. p. 200.

NICOM'ACHA, a daughter of Themistocles.

NICOM'ACHUS, the father of Aristotle, whose son also bore the same name. The philosopher also composed his ten books of morals for the use and improvement of his son, and hence they are called Nicomachea. *Suidas.* — *Gesner. Thes. Erud.* ——One of Alexander's friends, who discovered the conspiracy of Dymnus. *Curt.* 6.——An excellent painter. *Cic. Br.* 18.—*Plin.* 35. c. 10.——A Pythagorean philosopher, who wrote the life of Apollonius Thyanæus. *Sidon. Apoll.* 1. 8. ep. 3. *Voss. H. Gr.* 2. c. 16.——A tragic poet of Alexandria, in Troas, who wrote eleven tragedies. *Suidas.* ——A poet who obtained a prize in a contest, in which he had Euripides and Theognis for his competitors. *Gyrald. Hist. P.* 7.——A Lacedæmonian general conquered by Timotheus. *Polyæn.* 3. c. 10.——A writer in the fifth century, &c.——A musician, contemporary with Ismenias and Dionysiodorus. *Plin.* 37. c. 1.——A writer on Ægyptian festivals. *Athen.* 10.——An archon at Athens, Olymp. 109. an 4.

NICOME'DES the First, a king of Bithynia, about 278 years B.C. It was by his exertions that this part of Asia became a monarchy. He behaved with great cruelty to his brothers, and built a town, which he called by his own name, Nicomedia. *Justin.* 34. c. 4. &c.—*Paus. &c.*

NICOME'DES the Second, was ironically surnamed *Philopater*, because he drove his father Prusias from the kingdom of Bithynia, and caused him to be assassinated B.C. 149. He reigned 59 years. Mithridates laid claim to his kingdom, but all their disputes were decided by the Romans, who deprived Nicomedes of Paphlagonia, and his ambitious rival of Cappadocia. Nicomedes gained the affections of his subjects by a courteous behaviour, and by a mild and peaceful government. *Justin.* —*Paterc.* 2. c. 4, &c.

NICOME'DES the Third, son and successor of the preceding, was dethroned by his brother Socrates, and afterwards, by the ambitious Mithridates. The Romans re-established him on his throne, and encouraged him to make reprisals upon the king of Pontus. He followed their advice, but was again expelled from his dominions, till Sylla came into Asia, and restored him to his former power and independence. *Strab.—Appian.*

NICOME'DES the Fourth, was son and successor of Nicomedes the Third. He passed his life in an easy and indolent manner, and enjoyed the peace which his alliance with the Romans had procured him. He died B.C. 75, without issue, and left his kingdom, with all his possessions to the Roman people. *Strab.* 12.—*Appian. Mithrid. Justin.* 38. c. 2, &c.—*Flor.* 3. c. 5.

NICOME'DES, a celebrated geometrician in the age of the philosopher Eratosthenes. He made himself known by his useful machines, &c.——An engineer in the army of Mithridates.——One of the preceptors of the emperor M. Antonius. *Dio.*——An historian who wrote περὶ Ορφέως. *Athen.* 14.

NICOMEDI'A or NICOME'DIA, now Is-nikmid, a town of Bithynia, founded by Nicomedes the First. It was the capital of the country, and has been compared, for its beauty and greatness, to Rome, Antioch, or Alexandria. It became celebrated for being, for some time, the residence of the emperor Constantine, and of many of his imperial successors. Some suppose that it was originally called Astacus and Olbia, though it is generally believed that these were all different cities. *Ammian.* 17.—*Paus.* 5. c. 12.—*Plin.* 5. c. 32. sec. 10. ep. 42.—*Mela*, 2. c. 1 & 5.—*Strab.* 12, &c.

NI'CON, a pirate of Pheræ in Peloponnesus, who betrayed his country to the Messenians. *Polyæn.* 2. c. 35.——An athlete of Thasus, who obtained the victory 14 times at the Olympic games. The statue which his countrymen had erected to his honor, was insulted after his death by one of his rivals; and, as if it were to avenge his wrongs, it fell upon the intruder, and crushed him to pieces. The friends of the dead man complained of the accident; and, as the laws of Draco were very severe, even against inanimate things which caused murder, the offending statue was ignominiously thrown into the sea, till the people, visited by a famine and warned by the oracle, restored it again to its place with veneration. *Suidas. Fabric. B. Gr.* 5. c. 42.——A native of Tarentum. *Vid.* Nico. ——A Samian pilot, whose stratagem in escaping from the enemy's fleet is recorded by *Polyænus*, 5. c. 34.——An archon at Athens, Olymp. 100. an. 2.

NICO'NIA, a town of Pontus. *Strab.* 7.—*Suidas.*

NICOPH'ANES, an elegant painter of Greece, whose pieces are mentioned with commendation by *Pliny*, 35. c. 10.

NICOPHE'MUS, an archon at Athens, Olymp. 104. an. 3.

NIC'OPHON, a writer mentioned by the *Scholiast* on *Aristoph. Aves.*

NIC'OPHRON, a comic poet of Athens, contemporary with Aristophanes. Some of his verses are quoted by *Athenæus. Gyrald. de P. Hist.* 7.—*Suidas.*

NICOP'OLIS, a city of Lower Ægypt.——A town of Armenia Minor, built by Pompey the Great in memory of a victory which he had there obtained over the forces of Mithridates. *Strab.* 12.——A city of Thrace, built on the banks of the Nestus by Trajan, in memory of a victory which he obtained there over the barbarians.——A town of Epirus, built by Augustus after the battle of Actium. *Paus.* 7. c. 18.—*Suet. in Aug.*—*Plin.* 4. c. 1.—*Strab.* 17.——A town near Jerusalem founded by the emperor Vespasian.——A town of Mœsia.——A town in Dacia, built by Trajan, to perpetuate the memory of a celebrated battle.——A town near the bay of Issus, built by Alexander, or more properly, called by this name, in consequence of his victory over Darius. *Strab.* 14.

NICOSTRATA, a courtezan who left all her possessions to Sylla.

Nicos'trata, the same as Carmenta, mother of Evander. *Ovid. Fast.* 1. v. 468. l. 6. v. 530.—*Gyrald. P. Hist.* 2.

NICOS'TRATUS, a man of Argos, of great strength. He was fond of imitating Hercules, by clothing himself in a lion's skin, and carrying a club in his hand. *Diod.* 16.——One of Alexander's soldiers. He conspired against the king's life with Hermolaus. *Curt.* 8. c. 6.——A painter who expressed great admiration at the sight of Helen's picture by Zeuxis, and said to a person who enquired into the cause of his great surprise, "You would not ask if you had my eyes." *Ælian.* 14. c. 47.——An actor of Ionia. *Polyæn.* 6. c. 10.——A comic poet of Argos, surnamed Clytæmnestra. He lived after the age of Aristophanes, and not only wrote with success, but supported with applause the best character of some of his plays, whence the proverb *ut Nicostratus omnia faciam*, to imply a successful undertaking. *Diog. in Polem.*—*Gyrald. de P. Hist.* 7.——An orator of Macedonia, in the reign of the emperor M. Antoninus. *Suidas.*—*Hermogen.*—*Ælian. V. H.* 4. c. 2.——A son of Menolaus and Helen. *Paus.* 2. c. 18.——A general of the Achæans, who defeated the Macedonians.——A slave of Oppianicus, &c. *Cic. Clu.* 62.——A sophist of Trapezus, in the age of Claudius and Valerian. He wrote a history of Philip, Gordian, Decius, &c. *Evagr. Hist.* 5. c. ult.—*Voss. H. Gr.* 4. c. 20.

NICOTELE'A, a woman of Messenia, who said that she became pregnant of Aristomenes by a Genius, in the shape of a dragon. *Paus.* 4. c. 14.

NICOT'ELES, a Corinthian drunkard, &c. *Ælian. V. H.* 2. c. 41.——An archon at Athens, Olymp. 97. an. 2.

NIGDE'NI, a people of Africa Propria. *Ptol.*

NI'GER, a friend of M. Antony. sent to him by Octavia.——A surname of Clitus, whom Alexander killed in a fit of drunkenness. This name was given to him to distinguish him from another Clytus called Λευκός, or *Candidus*. *Athen.* 12. c. 9.—*Diod.* 17. c. 20.—*Plut. Alex.* c. 20.

Ni'ger C. Pescen'nius Justus, a celebrated governor in Syria, well known by his valor in the Roman armies, while yet a private man. At the death of Pertinax, he was declared emperor of Rome, and his claims to that elevated situation were supported by a sound understanding, prudence of mind, moderation, courage, and virtue. He proposed to imitate the actions of the venerable Antoninus, of Trajan, of Titus, aud of M. Aurelius. He was remarkable for his fondness for ancient discipline, and never suffered his soldiers to drink wine, but obliged them to quench their thirst with water and vinegar. He forbad the use of silver or gold utensils in his camp, all the bakers and cooks were driven away, and the soldiers ordered to live, during the expedition they undertook, merely upon biscuits and the plainest food. In his punishments Niger was inexorable: he condemned ten of his soldiers to be beheaded in the presence of the army, because they had stolen and eaten a fowl. The sentence was heard with groans: the army interfered: and, when Niger consented to diminish the punishment for fear of kindling rebellion, he yet ordered the criminals to make each a restoration of ten fowls to the person whose property they had stolen: they were, besides, ordered not to light a fire the rest of the campaign, but to live upon cold aliments, and to drink nothing but water. Such great qualifications in a general seemed to promise the restoration of ancient discipline in the Roman armies, but the death of Niger frustrated every hope of reform. Severus, who had also been invested with the imperial purple, marched against him; some battles were fought, and Niger was, at last, defeated, A.D. 194. His head was cut off, fixed on a long spear, and carried in triumph through the streets of Rome. He reigned about one year. *Herodian.* 3.—*Eutrop.* l. 8. [There is a statue of Niger in the Altieri palace at Rome.]

Ni'ger or Ni'gris, (*-itis*), a river of Africa, which rises in Æthiopia, and is said to fall by three mouths into the Atlantic Ocean. It was but little known to the ancients, and has not yet been satisfactorily explored by the moderns. *Plin.* 5. c. 1 & 8.—*Mela*, l. c. 4. l. 3. c. 10.—*Ptol.* 4. c. 6.

P. NIGID'IUS FIG'ULUS, a celebrated philosopher at Rome, one of the most learned men of his age, after Varro. He foretold the future greatness of Augustus at his birth, and acquired so much celebrity by his knowledge of astrology, and his calculation of the celestial phœnomena, that the ignorance or superstition of his contemporaries gave him the degrading appellation of magician and necromancer. He was intimate with Cicero, and gave him his most unbiassed opinions concerning the conspirators who had leagued with Catiline to destroy Rome. He was made prætor, and honored with a seat in the senate. In the civil wars he followed the interests of Pompey, for which he was banished by the conqueror. He died in the place of his banishment, 47 years B.C. All his works on augury, grammar, animals, &c. have perished. *Cic. ad Fam.* 4. ep. 13.—*Lucan.* l. v. 639.—*Macrob. Sat.* l. c. 9. l. 3. c. 4. l. 6. c. 8.—*Plin.* 29. c. 4 & 6.—*Aul. Gell.* 4. c. 9. l. 5. c. 2. l. 13. c. 24. l. 16. c. 3. l. 19. c. 14.—*Suet. Aug.* 94.

NIGIL'PIA, a town of Mauritania Cæsariensis. *Ptol.*

NIGI'RA, an inland city of Libya, capital of the Nigritæ. *Id.* It is now Guber, or, according to some geographers, Cano.

NIGIUTI'MI, a people of Africa Propria. *Id.* According to *Villanovanus*, they were the Cinitii of *Tacitus, Ann.* 2. c. 52. and the Ethini of *Pliny*, 5. c. 4.

NIGRAM'MA, a city of India within the Ganges. *Ptol.*

NIGRI'NUS, a Platonic philosopher. *Lucian. in Nigrin.*

NIGRI'TÆ or NIGRE'TES, a people in the interior of Africa, who dwelt on the banks of the Niger. *Mela*, l. c. 4. *Plin.* 5. c. 1.

NI'LEUS, a son of Codrus, who conducted a colony of Ionians to Asia, where he is said to have built Ephesus, Miletus, Priene, Colophon, Myus, Teos, Lebedus, Clazomenæ, &c. *Paus.* 7. c. 2, &c.——A philosopher who had in his possession all the writings of Aristotle. *Athen.* l. He is not mentioned, however, by *Laertius*.

NI'LIS, a lake of Mauritania. *Plin.* 5. c. 9.

NILOP'OLIS, a city of Ægypt. *Ptol.*

NI'LUS, a Theban king of Ægypt, who gave his name to the river which flows through the middle of Ægypt and falls into the Mediterranean Sea. *Joh. Marsham. Can. Chron.* sec. 10.

Ni'lus, anciently called Ægyptus, one of the most celebrated rivers in the world. Its sources were unknown to the ancients, and the moderns are equally ignorant of their exact situation, whence an impossibility is generally expressed by the proverb of *Nili caput quærere*. It flows through the middle of Ægypt in a northern direction, and when it comes to the town of Cercasorum, it then divides itself into several streams, and falls into the Mediterranean by seven mouths. The most eastern canal is called the Pelusian, and the most western is called the Canopic mouth. The other intermediate canals are the Sebennytican, that of the Sais, the Mendesian, Bolbitinic, and Bucolic. They have all been formed by nature, except the two last, which have been dug by the labors of men. The island formed by the division of the Nile into several streams is called Delta, from its resemblance to the fourth letter of the Greek alphabet. The Nile yearly overflows the country, and it is to those regular inundations that the Ægyptians are indebted for the fertile produce of their lands. The waters begin to rise in the month of May, continue rising for 100 successive days, and then decrease gradually the same number of days. If the river does not rise as high as 16 cubits, a famine is generally expected; but if it exceeds this by many cubits, it produces most dangerous consequences: houses are overturned, the cattle are drowned, and a great number of insects are produced from the mud, which destroy the fruits of the earth. The river, therefore, proves a blessing or a calamity to Ægypt, and the prosperity of the nation depends so much upon it, that the tributes of the inhabitants were in ancient times, and are still, under the present government, proportioned to the rise of the waters. The overflowings of the Nile, the causes of which remained unknown to the ancients, though they were indefatigable in endeavouring to discover them, are owing to the heavy rains which regularly fall in Æthiopia, in the months of April and May, and which rush down like torrents upon the country, and lay it all under water. These causes, as some people suppose, were well known to Homer, as indeed he seems to declare, by saying, that the Nile flowed down from heaven. The inhabitants of Ægypt, near the banks of the river, were called Niliaci, Niligenæ, &c., and large canals were also from this river denominated Nili or Euripi. *Cic. Leg.* 2. c. 1. *Ad. Q. Fr.* 3. ep. 9. *Ad. Att.* 11. ep. 12.—*Strab.* 17.—*Ovid. Met.* 5. v. 187. l. 15. v. 753.—*Mela,* 1. c. 9. l. 3. c. 9.—*Seneca, Quæst. Nat.* 4. c. 2.—*Lucan,* 1, 2, &c.—*Claudian. Ep. de Nilo.*—*Virg. G.* 4. v. 288. *Æn.* 6. v. 800. l. 9. v. 31.—*Diod.* 1, &c.—*Herodot.* 2.—*Lucret.* 6. v. 712.—*Ammian.* 22.—*Paus.* 10. c. 32.—*Plin.* 5. c. 10.—*Is. Vossius de Nil.* &c. 15. [The finest representation of the river Nile is in the Vatican. There is also a fine statue, in Ægyptian stone, at the Villa Pamfili, near Rome.]

NI'LUS. one of the Greek fathers who flourished A.D. 440. His works were edited at Rome, fol. 2 vols. 1668 & 1678.

NINÆ'A, an inland city of the Œnotri. *Steph.* It is now S. Donato.

NIN'IAS. *Vid.* Ninyas.

NIN'NIUS, a tribune who opposed Clodius the enemy of Cicero.

NIN'NIUS QUADRAT. *Vid.* Mummius.

NIN'OE, a city of Caria, called also Amphrodisias. It was founded by the Leleges, and received the name of Ninoe, from Ninus. *Steph.*

NI'NUS, a son of Belus who built a city on the banks of the Tigris, to which he gave his own name, and founded the Assyrian monarchy, of which he was the first sovereign, B.C. 2059. He was very warlike, and extended his conquests from Ægypt to the extremities of India and Bactriana. He became enamoured of Semiramis the wife of one of his officers, and married her after her husband had destroyed himself through fear of his powerful rival. Ninus reigned 52 years, and at his death left his kingdom to the care of his wife Semiramis, by whom he had a son. The history of Ninus is very obscure, and even fabulous according to the opinion of some authors. Ctesias is the principal historian from whom it is derived, but little reliance is to be placed upon a writer whom Aristotle deems unworthy to be believed. Ninus after death received divine honors, and became the Jupiter of the Assyrians, and the Hercules of the Chaldeans. *Ctesias.*—*Diod.* 2.—*Justin.* 1. c. 1.—*Herodot.* 2.

NI'NUS, a celebrated city, now Nino, the capital of Assyria, built on the banks of the Tigris by Ninus, and called Nineveh in Scripture. It was, according to the relation of Diodorus Siculus, fifteen miles long, nine broad, and forty-eight in circumference. It was surrounded by large walls 100 feet high, on the top of which three chariots could pass together abreast, and was defended by 1500 towers, each 200 feet high. Ninus was taken by the united armies of Cyaxares and Nabopolassar king of Babylon, B.C. 606. *Strab.* 1.—*Diod.* 2.—*Herodot.* l. c. 185, &c.—*Paus.* 8. c. 33.—*Lucian. in Charon.*—*Lucan.* 3. v. 215.—*Plin.* 6. c. 26.

NIN'YAS, a son of Ninus and Semiramis king of Assyria, who succeeded his mother, who had voluntarily abdicated the crown. Some suppose that Semiramis was put to death by her own son, because she had encouraged him to commit incest. The reign of Ninyas was remarkable for its luxury and extravagance. The prince left the care of the government to his favorites and ministers, and gave himself up to pleasure, riot, and debauchery, and never appeared in public. His successors imitated the example of his voluptuousness, and therefore their names and their history are little known till the age of Sardanapulus. *Justin.* 1. c. 2.—*Diod.* 1, &c.

NI'OBE, a daughter of Tantalus, king of Lydia, by Euryanassa or Dione. She married Amphion, the son of Jasus, by whom she had ten sons and ten daughters according to *Hesiod,* or two sons and three daughters according to *Herodotus.* Homer and Propertius say, that she had six daughters and as many sons; and Ovid, Apollodorus, &c., according to the more received opinion, maintain that she had seven sons and seven daughters. The sons were Sipylus, Minytus, Tantalus, Agenor, Phædimus, Damasichthon, and Ismenus; and the daughters Cleodoxa, Ethodæa or Thera, Astyoche, Phthia, Pelopia or Chloris, Asticratea, and Ogygia. Prosperity and the number of her children increased her pride, and she had the imprudence not only to prefer herself to Latona who had only two children, but even insulted her, and ridiculed the worship which was paid to her, observing, that she had a better claim to altars and sacrifices than the mother of Apollo and Diana. This insolence provoked Latona, who entreated her children to punish the arrogant Niobe. Her prayers were heard, and all the sons of Niobe were slain immediately by the darts of Apollo, and all the daughters, except Chloris, who had married Neleus, king of Pylus, were destroyed by Diana; and Niobe, struck at the suddenness of her misfortunes, was changed into a stone. The carcases of Niobe's children, according to Homer, were left unburied in the plains for nine successive days, because Jupiter changed into stones all such as attempted to inter them. On the tenth day they were honored with a funeral by the gods. *Homer. Il.* 24.—*Ælian. V.H.* 12. c. 36. *Apollod.* 3. c. 5.—*Ovid. Met.* 6. fab. 5.—*Hygin.* fab. 9.—*Horat.* 4. od. 6.—*Propert.* 2. el. 16.—*Lactant. ad Theb.* 6. v. 124. l. 7. v. 250 & 353.—*Schol. Eurip. in Phœniss.* 162.—*Sch. Sophoc. in Electr.* 152.—*Eustath. ad Homer. Il.* 24. v. 609. [The finest statues of Niobe and her children are in the Capitol at Rome,]——A daughter of Phoroneus, king of Peloponnesus, by Laodice. She was beloved by Jupiter, by whom she had a son called Argus, who gave his name to Argia or Argolis, a country of Peloponnesus. *Paus.* 2. c. 22.—*Apollod.* 2. c. 1. l. 3. c. 8.—*Schol. Theb. Stat.* 4. v. 589.—*Euseb. Præp. Ev.* 2.—*Joh. Voss. de Idolol.* 1. c. 14.——A daughter of Assaon, and wife of Philotus, who committed incest with her father. *Parthen Erot.* 33.——A fountain of Laconia. *Plin.* 4. c. 5.

NIOS'SUM, a city of European Sarmatia. *Ptol.*

NIPHÆ'US, an Italian leader killed by his horses, &c. *Virg. Æn.* 10. v. 570.

NIPHAN'DA, a city of Paropansius. *Ptol.*

NIPHA'TES, now Curdo, a large ridge of mountains in Asia, which divides Armenia from Assyria, and from which the Tigris takes its rise. *Virg. G.* 3. v. 30.—*Strab.* 11.—*Ptol,* 6.—*Mela,* 1. c. 15.——A small river flowing from the mountains of the same name into the Tigris. *Horat.* 2. od. 9. v. 20.—*Lucan.* 3. v. 245.—*Claudian. de Rap. Pros.* 3. v. 263.

NIPHAVAN'DRA, a city of Media. *Ptol.*

NI'PHE, one of Diana's companions, so called from her *snowy* whiteness. *Ovid. Met.* 3. v. 245.

NIP'SA, a city of Thrace. *Steph.*

NI'REUS, a king of Naxus, son of Charopus and Algaia, much celebrated for his beauty. He was one of the Grecian chiefs during the Trojan war. *Homer. Il.* 2. v. 673.—*Horat.* 2. od. 20.—*Q. Calab.* 6. v. 372. l. 7. v. 7.

NI'SA, a town of Greece. *Homer. Il.* 2. v. 508.——A city. *Vid.* Nysa.——A celebrated plain of Media, near the Caspian Sea, famous for its horses. *Herodot.* 3. c. 106.—*Strab.* 11.—*Aristot. de H. Anim.* 9.—*Marcell.* 23. c. 21.—*Eustath. ad Dionys. Per.*—*Oppian.* 1.

NI'SA, a countrywoman. *Virg. Ecl.* 8.

NISÆ'A, a naval station on the coasts of Megaris, so called from Nisus, son of Pandion. *Strab.* 9.——A town of Parthia, called also Nisa.

NISÆ'E, a sea nymph. *Virg. G.* 4. v. 338. But according to *Homer. Il.* 18. v. 40. we ought to read *Nesæa.*

NISE'IA. *Vid.* Nisus.

NISER'GE, a city of Persia. *Ptol.*

NI'SEUS, a native of Cyzicus, slain by Telamon. *Val. Flacc.* 3. v. 198.

NIS'IBIS, a town of Mesopotamia, built by a colony of Macedonians on the river Tigris, and celebrated as being a barrier between the provinces of Rome and the Persian empire during the reign of the Roman emperors. It was sometimes called Antiochia Mygdonica, and is now Nisibin. *Joseph.* 20. c. 2.—*Strab.* 11.—*Ammian.* 25. c. 31 & 38.—*Philostr.* 8. c. 13.—*Plin.* 6. c. 13.——A city of Aria. *Ptol.*

NISICA'TES or NISI'TÆ, a people of Upper Æthiopia, fabulously said to have three or four eyes. This report probably arose from their expertness in aiming arrows. *Plin.* 6. c. 30.

NISO'PE, a small island near Lesbus, *Steph.*

NIS'SOS, a town of Macedonia, near Pallene. *Plin.* 4. c. 10.

NIS'UA, a maritime city of Africa Propria. *Ptol.*

NI'SUS, a son of Hyrtacus, born on mount Ida near Troy. He went to Italy with Æneas, and signalized himself by his valor against the Rutulians. He was united in the closest friendship with Euryalus, a young Trojan, with whom he entered, in the dead of night, the enemy's camp. As they were returning victorious, after much bloodshed, they were perceived by the Rutulians, who attacked Euryalus. Nisus, in endeavouring to rescue his friend from the darts of the enemy, perished with him, and their heads were cut off and fixed on a spear, and carried in triumph to the camp. Their death was greatly lamented by all the Trojans, and their great friendship, like that of Pylades and Orestes, or of Theseus and Pirithous, is become proverbial. *Virg. Æn.* 9. v. 176, &c.——A king of Dulichium, remarkable for his probity and virtue. *Homer. Odyss.* 18. v. 126.——The father of the fifth Bacchus mentioned by Cicero. His wife was the nymph Thione. *Cic. de Nat. D.* 3. c. 23. ——A king of Megara, son of Mars, or more probably of Pandion. He inherited and divided his father's kingdom with his brothers, and received as his portion the kingdom of Megaris. The peace of the brothers was interrupted by the hostilities of Minos, who wished to avenge the death of his son Androgeus, who had been murdered by the Athenians. Megara was therefore besieged, and Attica laid waste. The fate of Nisus depended upon a yellow lock, which as long as it continued on his head, according to the words of an oracle, promised him life and success to his affairs. His daughter Scylla, often called *Niseia Virgo*, saw from the walls of Megara the royal besieger, and became desperately enamoured of him. To obtain a more immediate interview with the object of her passion, she stole away the fatal hair from her father's head as he was asleep; the town was immediately taken, but Minos disregarded the services of Scylla, and she, in despair, threw herself into the sea. The gods changed her into a lark, and Nisus assumed the nature of the hawk, at the very moment that he destroyed himself not to fall into the enemy's hands. These two birds have continually been at variance with each other, and Scylla by flying with apprehension from the sight of her father, seems to suffer the punishment which her perfidy deserved. Some say that Scylla was changed into a fish, and her father into a sea-bird, the chief food of which is fish. *Apollod.* 3. c. 15.—*Paus.* 1. c. 19.—*Strab.* 9.—*Ovid. Met.* 8. v. 6, &c. *Virg. G.* 1. 404, &c.—*Hygin.* 198 & 242.—*Propert.* 3. el. 17. v. 21.—*Lactant. ad Arg.* 8.—*Servius ad Virg. Ec.* 6. v. 74. *G.* 1. v. 404. *Æn.* 1. 239. l. 6. v. 286.—*Tzetzes in Lyc.* 650.—*Schol. Theocr. Id.* 12. v. 27.—*Schol. Eurip. Hipp.* 35 & 1200.

NISY'RUS, an island in the Ægean Sea, at the west of Rhodes, with a town of the same name. It was originally joined to the island of Cos, according to *Pliny*, and bore the name of Porphyris. Neptune, who was supposed to have separated them with a blow of his trident, and to have there overwhelmed the giant Polybotes, was worshipped there, and called Nisyreus. *Apollod.* 1. c. 6.—*Strab.* 10.—*Mela.* 2. c. 7. It is now Nisaro.

NITA'ZUM, a city of Galatia. *Antonin.*

NIT'ERIS, a nation in the interior of Africa, conquered by Corn. Balbus. *Plin.* 5. c. 5.

NITE'TIS, a daughter of Apries, king of Ægypt, married by his successor Amasis to Cyrus. *Polyæn.* 8. c. 29.

NITI'BRUM, a town of Africa, capital of Niteris. *Plin.* 5. c. 5.

NITIOBRI'GES or NITIOB'RIGES, a people of Gaul, supposed to have occupied that part of the country now called l'Agenois, in Guienne. *Cæs. B. G.* 7. c. 7.

NITO'CRIS, a celebrated queen of Babylon, who built a bridge across the Euphrates, in the middle of that city, and dug a number of reservoirs to receive the superfluous waters of that river. She ordered herself to be buried over one of the gates of the city, and placed an inscription on her tomb, which signified that her successor would find great treasures within, if ever they were in need of money, but that their labors would be but ill repaid if ever they ventured to open it without necessity. Cyrus opened it through curiosity, and was struck upon finding within, these words, "If thy avarice had not been insatiable, thou never wouldst have violated the monuments of the dead." *Herodot.* 1. c. 185.——A queen of Ægypt who built a third pyramid. *Jon. Marsham. Can Chron.* sec. 7.

NIT'RIA, a country of Ægypt, with two towns of the same name, above Memphis. *Strab.* 17.——An emporium of India within the Ganges. *Ptol.*

NIVA'RIA, an Island at the west of Africa, supposed to be the modern Teneriffe, one of the Canaries. *Plin.* 6. c. 32.

NIX'II, a name given by the Romans to such divinities as presided over the delivery of women, &c. There were three statues sacred to them in the Capitol, in a bending posture, which had been brought to Rome after the victory obtained over Antiochus of Syria, by M. Acilius. *Festus de V. Sig.*—*Rosin. A.R.* 2. c. 19.

NIX'US, one of the signs of the Zodiac, called by the Greeks *Engonasis*, represented in a bending posture. Some suppose that it is a representation of Hercules, whilst others suppose it to be Theseus. *Eustath. Catas.* 4.—*Cic. in Arato*, 373 & 400.—*Hygin. P.A.* 2. c. 6.—*Avienus in Arat.* 2107.

NO'Æ, a city of Sicily. *Steph.*

NO'AS, a river of Thrace, rising in mount Hæmus, and falling into the Ister. *Herodot.* 4. c. 49.—*Val. Flacc.* 4. v. 719.

NOBIL'IA, a town of the Oretani, in Spain, on the Tagus. *Liv.* 35. c. 2. Some, however, read Noliba.

NOBIL'IOR Q. FUL'VIUS, a Roman known for his learning, and more particularly for having granted the privileges of a citizen to the poet Ennius, &c. *Cic. Br.* 20.

NOCTIFER, a name applied to the evening star. *Catull.* 63. v. 7.

NOCTILU'CA, a surname of Diana. She had a temple at Rome, on mount Palatine, where torches were generally lighted in the night. *Festus de V. Sig.*—*Rosin. A.R.* 2. c. 8.—*Varro de L.L.* 4.—*Horat.* 4. od. 6. v. 38.

NOCTUR'NUS, a god, supposed to be the same as Vesper or Nox, and who was said to preside over the night. *Virg. G.* 3. v. 538.—*Stat. Theb.* 6. v. 240.—*Turneb. Adv.* 24. c. 27.

NODI'NUS, a divinity said to preside over the knots which are found in barley as it ripens. *Varro de R.R.* 1. *apud. Aug. de Civ. D.* 4. c. 8.—*Plin.* 18.

NODI'NUS, a small river near Rome. *Cic. de Nat. D.* 3. c. 20.

NO'EGA or NOEGAUCE'SIA, a town of Hispania Tarraconensis. *Mela*, 3. c. 1. *Ptol.*

NOE'LA, a town of Hispania Tarraconensis. *Plin.* 4. c. 20. It is now Noya.

NOEM'AGUS, a city of Gallia Narbonensis, near Gebenna. *Ptol.*

NŒ'MON, a servant of Achilles, whose office it was to warn his master not to kill a son of Apollo. He was killed by Achilles for inattention. *Homer. Il.* 23. *Odyss.* 4.—*Ptol Heph.* 4.

NOE'MON, a Trojan killed by Turnus. *Virg. Æn.* 9. v. 767.

NOE'SIA, one of the Sporades near Rhodes. *Eustath.*

NO'LA, an ancient town of Campania, which became a Roman colony before the first Punic war. It was founded by a Tuscan, or, according to others, by a Eubœan colony. It is said that Virgil had introduced the name of Nola into his Georgics, but that, when he was refused a glass of water by the inhabitants as he passed through the city, he totally blotted it out of his poem, and substituted the word *ora*, in the 225th line of the second book. Nola was besieged by Annibal in the second Punic war, and bravely defended by Marcellus. Augustus died there on his return from Neapolis to Rome. Bells were first invented there in the beginning of the fifth century, from which reason they have been called *Nolæ* or *Campanæ* in Latin. The inventor was St. Paulinus, the bishop of the place, who died A.D. 431, though many imagine that bells were known long before, and only introduced into churches by that prelate. Before his time, congregations were called to the church by the noise of wooden rattles (*sacra ligna*) *Paterc*. 1. c. 7.—*Suet. in Aug.*—*Sil.* 8. v. 517. l. 12. v. 161.—*A. Gellius*. 7. c. 20.—*Liv.* 23. c. 14 & 39. l. 24. c. 13. —*Servius*. *Æn.* 7. v. 740.—*Georg.* 2. v. 225.— *Mantuan. Alph.* 6. v. 125.

NOM'ADES, a name given to all those uncivilized people who had no fixed habitation, and who continually changed the place of their residence, to go in quest of fresh pasture for the numerous cattle which they tended. There were Nomades in Scythia, India, Arabia, and Africa. Those of Africa were afterwards called Numidians, by a small change in the letters which composed their name. *Ital.* 1. v. 215.—*Plin.* 5. c. 3.—*Herodot.* 1. c. 15. l. 4. c. 187.—*Strab.* 7.—*Mela,* 2. c. 1. l. 3. c. 4.—*Virg. G.* 3. v. 343.—*Paus.* 8. c. 43. —*Dionys. Per.* 186.—*Marcell.* 31. c. 6.—*Sallust. de Jug.*

NO'MÆ, a town of Sicily, on the north-west, between the rivers Alæsus and Monalus. *Diod.* 11. —*Sil.* 14. v. 266.

NOMAS'TÆ, a people of Scythia within Imaus. *Ptol.*

NOM'BA, a city of Judæa. *Steph. ex Joseph.*

NOMENTA'NUS, an epithet applied to L. Cassius as a native of Nomentum. He is mentioned by Horace as a worthless character, debased by luxury and dissipation. *Horat.* 1. sat. 1. v. 102, *& alibi.*

NOMEN'TUM, a town of the Sabines in Italy, famous for wine, and now called Lamentana. The dictator Q. Servilius Priscus gave the Veientes and Fidenates battle there A.U.C. 312, and totally defeated them. *Ovid. Fast.* 4. v. 905.—*Martial.* 13. epigr. 15 & 119.—*Liv.* 1. c. 38. l. 4. c. 22.—*Virg. Æn.* 6. v. 773. l. 7. v. 712.—*Servius locis.*

NO'MIA, an Arcadian nymph represented in a picture by Polygnotus, with Callisto, daughter of Lycaon, whose feet she supported on her knees. The picture was preserved at Delhi, where it was still to be seen in the age of Pausanias. *Paus.* 10. c. 31.——A nymph who was so incensed against the shepherd Daphnis because he made no return to her love, that she tore out his eyes. *Servius ad Virg. Ec.* 8. v. 68.

NO'MII, mountains of Arcadia. *Paus.* 8.

NOMISTE'RIUM, a city of Germany. *Ptol.* Its modern name is not known.

NO'MIUS, a surname given to Apollo, because, when banished from heaven, he fed (νέμω, *pasco*) the flocks of king Admetus in Thessaly. *Cic. de Nat. D.* 3. c. 23.—*Servius ad Virg. Ec.* 5. v. 35. —The same name was also applied to Mercury, who was sometimes also considered as the god of shepherds, or because he had established the laws (νόμος) of eloquence.

NO'MUS, a small lake of Attica. *Soph. in Œdip.*— *Paus.* 1.—*Strab.*

NO'NA, one of the Parcæ. *Gellius,* 3. c. 16. The Latins call the Parcæ by the names of Nona, Decima, and Morta.

NON'ACRIS or NONA'CRIS, a town of Arcadia, which received its name from a wife of Lycaon. There was a mountain of the same name in the neighbourhood, from which flowed a stream called the Styx, because its waters were considered as impregnated with poison, and consequently fatal to such as drank them. Alexander is mentioned as one of those who fell a sacrifice to their destructive property. The same improbable report adds, that Antipater was persuaded to poison his master by the advice of Aristotle. Evander is sometimes called *Monacrius heros,* as being an Arcadian by birth, and Atalanta *Nonacria,* as being a native of the place. The town was in ruins in the age of Pausanias. *Curt.* 10. c. 10.—*Ovid. Fast.* 5. v. 97. *Met.* 1. v. 690. l. 2. v. 409. l. 8. v. 426. *De. A.A.* 2. v. 185.—*Paus.* 8. c. 17 & 18.—*Vitruv.* 8. c. 3.—*Tertullian. adv. Val.* 15. *De Anim.* 50.— *Plut. in Alex.*—*Flacc.* 4. v. 141.

NONDI'NA, a goddess who presided over the lustrations made for children before they received their name, which was generally nine days after their birth for boys, or eight for girls. The ceremony of lustration was performed by carrying the child round the fire which blazed on the altar of the divinity, and then sprinkling it with water. *Macrob. Sat.* 1. c. 16.—*Plut. Quæst. R.* 102.— *Tertull. de Idol.* 6.—*Rosin. A.R.* 2. c. 19.

NONIA'NUS C. CONSID., a Roman to whom the province of Gaul was transferred from Cæsar. He was of the Nonian family, and adopted by the Considii. *Cic. Fam.* 16. ep. 12.

NO'NIUS, a Roman soldier imprisoned for paying respect to Galba's statues, &c. *Tacit. Hist.* 1. c. 56.——A Roman who exhorted his countrymen still to oppose J. Cæsar, after the fatal battle of Pharsalia, and the flight of Pompey, by observing that eight standards (*aquilæ*) still remained in the camp, to which Cicero answered, *recte, si nobis cum graculis bellum esset.*——A pro-prætor of Crete, &c. *Cic. Att.* 6. ep. 1.

NO'NIUS ACTIA'NUS, an informer under Nero. *Tac. Hist.* 4. c. 41.

NO'NIUS MARCEL'LUS, a grammarian in the age of Constantine, or, according to Saxius, at the end of the second century. He wrote a book *de proprietate sermonum,* very valuable on account of the many fragments of ancient authors which it has preserved. It was first edited in 1471, and lastly by Mercer, 8vo, Paris, 1614. *Harles. Not. Lit. Rom.* 1. p. 574.—*Sax. Onom.* 1. p. 331.—*G. J. Voss. de Philol.* c. 5.

NON'NUS, a Greek writer of the fifth century, who wrote an account of the embassy which he undertook to Æthiopia, among the Saracens, and other Eastern nations. He is also known by his *Dionysiaca,* a poem in forty-eight books, comprehending a most wonderful collection of heathen mythology and erudition, edited 4to, Antwerp, 1569. His Paraphrase on John was edited by Heinsius, 8vo, L. Bat. 1627. *Sax. Onom.* 2. p. 10. —*Fabr. B. Gr.* 5. c. 12.

NONYM'NA, a city of Sicily. *Steph.*

NO'PIA or CNO'PIA, a town of Bœotia, where Amphiaraus had a temple. *Strab.*

NO'RA, now Nour, a well fortified place of Phrygia, to which Eumenes retired for some time. *C Nepos.* ——A city of Sardinia. *Vid.* Norax.

NOR'ACUS, a city of Pæonia. *Steph.*

NO'RAX, a son of Mercury and Eurythæa, who led a colony of Iberians into Sardinia, where he founded a town, to which he gave the name of Nora. *Paus.* 10. c. 17.—*Solin.* c. 10.

NOR'BA, a town of the Volsci, conquered by Posthumius. *Plin.* 3. c. 5.—*Liv.* 2. c. 34. l. 7. c. 42. l. 8. c. 19.

NOR'BA CÆSARE'A, a town of Spain on the Tagus. *Ptol.* It is now Alcantara.

NORBA'NUS C., a young and ambitious Roman who opposed Sylla, and joined his interest to that of young Marius. In his consulship he marched against Sylla, by whom he was defeated, &c. *Plut.*—*Paterc.* 2. c. 25.——A friend and general of Augustus employed in Macedonia against the republicans. He was defeated by Brutus, &c. ——A prætor of Sicily. *Cic. Verr.* 3. c. 49.

NOREN'SES, a people of Sardinia. *Plin.* 3. c. 7.

NOR'ICUM, a country of ancient Illyricum, which now forms a part of modern Bavaria and Austria. It extended between the Danube, and part of the Alps and Vindelicia. Its savage inhabitants, who were once governed by kings, made many incursions upon the Romans, and were at last conquered under Tiberius, and the country became a Roman province. In the reign of Diocletian, Noricum was divided into two parts, Ripense and Mediterraneum. The iron that was drawn from Noricum was esteemed excellent, and thence *Noricus ensis* was used to express the superior goodness of a sword. *Dionys. Perieg.*—*Strab.* 4. —*Plin.* 34. c. 14.—*Tacit. Hist.* 3. c. 5.—*Horat.* 1. od. 16. v. 9.—*Ovid. Met.* 14. v. 712.—*Ptol.* 2. c. 14.—*Claudian. de Bell. G.* 365.

NOROS'SI, a people of Scythia within Imaus. There was also a mountain there called Norossus. *Ptol.*

NORTHIP'PUS, a Greek tragic poet mentioned as drinking and eating to the greatest excess, from which circumstance he was surnamed *Opsophagus*. *Athen.* 8.—*Gyrald. de P.H.* 7.

NOR'TIA or NUR'TIA, a name given to the goddess of fortune among the Etrurians. *Liv.* 7. c. 3.—*Tertull. in Apol.*—*Juv.* 10. v. 74.—*Mart. Capell* 1.—*Gyrald. H.D.* 6.

NOSCO'PION, a city of Lycia. *Plin.* 5. c. 27.

NOS'ORA, an island of the Red Sea. *Steph.*

NOSTA'NA, a town of Drangiana. *Ptol.*

NO'THUS, a son of Deucalion.——A surname of Darius, king of Persia, from his illegitimacy.

NOS'TIA, a village of Arcadia. *Steph.*

NO'TIUM, a town of Æolia, near the Cayster. It was peopled by the inhabitants of Colophon, who left their ancient habitations because Notium was more conveniently situated in being on the sea-shore. *Liv.* 37. c. 26, 38, 39

NO'TUS, the south wind, called also Auster, and occasionally applied by the poets to all the winds indiscriminately. As it generally produced rain, it is described by Ovid with wet wings, the forehead covered with dark clouds, and the beard heavy and swollen with mists. This personification of the south wind is one of the finest passages in the Metamorphoses. *Hesiod. Th.* 380.—*Homer. Odyss.* 12. v. 289.—*Ovid. Met.* 1. v. 264. *Heroid.* 2. v. 12, &c.—*Flacc.* 1, 2, 5, &c.—*Lucian.* 2, &c.—*Virg. Æn.* 3. v. 268.—*Horat.* 3. od. 7. v. 5.

NO'VÆ (*tabernæ*), the new shops built in the forum at Rome, and adorned with the shields of the Cimbri. *Cic. Orat.* 2. c. 66. The *Veteres tabernæ* were adorned with those of the Samnites. *Liv.* 9. c. 40.

NOVA'NA or CIV'ITAS NO'VA, now Citta Nova, a town of Picenum. *Plin.* 3. c. 13.

NOVA'NUS, a river of Umbria. *Id.* 2. c. 103.

NOVA'RIA, a town of Cisalpine Gaul, now Novara in Milan. *Tacit. Hist.* 1. c. 70.—*Plin.* 3. c. 17.

NOVA'TUS, a man who severely attacked the character of Augustus, under a fictitious name. The emperor discovered him, and only fined him a small sum of money.

NOVAUGUS'TA or NO'VA AUGUS'TA, a town of Spain. *Ptol.*—*Plin.* 3. c. 3. It is now Atienza.

NOVEL'LIUS, a native of Mediolanum, in the time of Tiberius, noted as a great drinker, and thence surnamed *Tricongius*. *Plin.* 14. c. 22

NOVEL'LUS ANTO'NIUS, a general of Otho, who was entrusted with the command of an expedition against Gallia Narbonensis. *Tac. Hist.* 1. c. 87.

NOVENDI'ALE SA'CRUM or NOVEN'DIUM, a funeral sacrifice or oblation made to the dead, nine days after their decease. *Horat.* od. 17. Epod. v. 37.——A sacrifice observed for nine days when the republic was threatened with any calamity. It was then considered as a time of mourning and public sorrow. *Festus de V. Sig.*—*Servius in Æn.* 5. v. 64.—*Tacit. An.* 6.—*Plin.* 2. c. 11.—*Liv.* 1.—*Cæl. Rhod.* 17. c. 19 & 20.

NOVEN'SILES, a name applied to those divinities whose worship was introduced into Rome from foreign countries. Some suppose them to have been those deities whose names were unknown before the foundation of Rome, while others imagine that they were the nine gods to whom alone Jupiter had granted the privilege of hurling his lightnings. According to Servius and the more generally received opinion, the Novensiles were those heroes whom their high descent or their glorious actions raised to the rank and consequence of gods. *Liv.* 8.—*Varro de L. L.* 4. c. 10.—*Servius ad Æn.* 8. v. 187.—*Arnob. adv. Gent.* 3.—*Gyrald. H.D.* 1.—*Mart. Capell. in Nupt. Phil.*

NOVE'SIUM, a town of the Ubii, on the west of the Rhine, now called Nuys, near Cologne. *Tacit. Hist.* 4. c. 26, &c.

NOVIODU'NUM, a town of the Ædui in Gaul, taken by J. Cæsar. It is pleasantly situated on the Ligeris, and now called Noyon, or, as others suppose, Nevers. *Cæs. Bell. G.* 2. c. 12.

NOVIOM'AGUS or NEOM'AGUS, a town of Gaul, now Nizeux in Normandy.——A town of Germany called also Nemetes, now Spire.——A town in Batavia, now Nimeguen, on the south side of the Waal.

NO'VIUM, a town of Spain, now Noya.

NO'VIUS PRIS'CUS, a man banished from Rome by Nero, on suspicion that he was accessory to Piso's conspiracy. *Tacit. An.* 15. c. 71.——A Roman knight who attempted to assassinate the emperor Claudius.

NO'VII, the name of two brothers obscurely born, distinguished in the age of Horace for their officiousness in the exercise of some magisterial employments. *Horat.* 1. sat. 6.

NO'VIUS QUIN'TUS, a comic poet in the age of Africanus, whose plays are mentioned with credit and respect by ancient historians, as full of genuine wit and broad humour. The few fragments that remain of them are often confounded with those of the poet Nævius, and therefore generally collected together.

NOVOCO'MUM or NO'VUM CO'MUM, a town of Insubria on the lake Larinus, of which the inhabitants were called *Novocomensis*. *Cic. ad Div.* 13. c. 35.

NOX, one of the most ancient deities among the heathens, daughter of Chaos. From her union with her brother Erebus, sprang the Day and the Light. She was also the mother of the Parcæ, Hesperides, Dreams, Discord, Death, Momus, Fraud, &c. She is called by some of the poets the mother of all things, of gods as well as of men, and therefore she was worshipped with great solemnity by the ancients. She had a famous statue in Diana's temple at Ephesus. It was usual to offer her a black sheep, as she was the mother of the furies. The cock was also offered to her, as that bird proclaims the approach of day. She is represented as mounted on a chariot and covered with a veil bespangled with stars. The constellations generally went before her as her constant messengers. Sometimes she is seen holding two children under her arms, one of which is black, representing death or rather night, and the other white, representing sleep or day. Some of the moderns have described her as a woman veiled in mourning, and crowned with poppies, and carried on a chariot drawn by owls and bats. *Virg. Æn.* 6. v. 950.—*Ovid. Fast.* 1. v. 455.—*Paus.* 10. c. 38.—*Hesiod. Theog.* 125 & 212.—*Orph. Hym.* 2.—*Cicero de Nat. D.* 3. c. 17.

NUBÆ'I, a people of Arabia Deserta. *Plin.* 6. c. 28.

NUCE'RIA, a town of Campania taken by Annibal. It became a Roman colony under Augustus, and was called Nuceria, Constantia, or Alfaterna. It now bears the name of Nucera, and contains about 30,000 inhabitants. *Lucan.* 2. v. 472.—*Liv.* 9. c. 41. l. 27. c. 3.—*Ital.* 8. v. 531.—*Tacit. Ann.* 13 & 14.—*Flor.* 3. c. 18.—*Polyb.* 3.—*Plin.* 2. c. 5.——A town of Umbria, at the foot of the Apennines. *Strab.*—*Plin.*

NU'CULA, a Roman, intimate with Antony. *Cic. Phil.* 6. c. 5, &c.

NUDIPEDA'LIA, sacrifices at Lacedæmon, offered to the gods in time of public calamity, when the suppliants appeared with naked feet in humiliation, whence the name. The ceremony was probably borrowed from the Jews. *Tertull. in Apol.*—*Gyrald. Var. Crit.*—*Egesippus. apud Ambros.*

NUDITA'NUM, a city of Bastitania, in Spain. *Plin.* 3. c. 1.

NUITH'ONES or NUITHO'NES, a people of Germany, possessing the country now called Mecklenburg and Pomerania. *Tacit. G.* 40.

NU'MA MAR'CIUS, a man made governor of Rome, by Tullus Hostilius. He was son-in-law of Numa Pompilius, and father to Ancus Martius. *Tac. Ann.* 6. c. 11.—*Liv.* 1. c. 20.

NU'MA POMPIL'IUS, a celebrated philosopher born at Cures, a village of the Sabines, on the day that Romulus laid the foundation of Rome. He married Tatia, the daughter of Tatius the king of the Sabines, and, at her death, retired into the country, to devote himself more freely to literary pursuits. At the death of Romulus, the Romans fixed upon him to be their new king, and two senators were sent to acquaint him with the decisions of the senate and of the people. Numa refused their offers, and it was only upon the repeated solicitations of his friends, that he was prevailed upon to accept the honors of royalty. The beginning of his reign was popular, and he dismissed the 300 body guards which his predecessor had kept around his person, observing, that he did not distrust a people who had compelled him to reign over them. He was not, like Romulus, fond of war and military expeditions, but applied himself to tame the ferocity of his subjects, to instil into their minds a reverence for the deity, and to quell their dissensions by dividing all the citizens into different classes. He established different orders of priests, and taught the Romans not to worship the deity by images; and, from his example, no graven or painted statue appeared in the temples or sanctuaries of Rome for upwards of 160 years. He encouraged the report which was spread, of his paying regular visits to the nymph Egeria, and made use of her name to give sanction to the laws and institutions which he had introduced. He established the college of the vestals, and told the Romans that the safety of the empire depended upon the preservation of the sacred *ancyle* or *shield*, which, as was generally believed, had dropped down from heaven. He dedicated a temple to Janus, which, during his whole reign, remained shut, as a mark of peace and tranquillity at Rome. Numa died, after a reign of 43 years, in which he had given every possible encouragement to the useful arts, and in which he had cultivated peace, B.C. 672. Not only the Romans, but also the neighbouring nations, were eager to pay their last offices to a monarch whom they revered for his abilities, moderation, and humanity. He forbade his body to be burnt, according to the custom of the Romans, but ordered it to be buried near mount Janiculum, with many of the books which he had written. These books were accidentally found by one of the Romans, about 400 years after his death, and, as they contain nothing new or interesting, but merely the reasons why he had made innovations in the form of worship and in the religion of the Romans, they were burnt by order of the senate. He left behind him one daughter, called Pompilia, who married Numa Marcius, and became the mother of Ancus Marcius, the fourth king of Rome. Some say that he had also four sons, but this opinion is ill-founded. *Plut. in Vitâ.—Varro.—Liv.* 1. c. 18.—*Plin.* 13 & 14, &c.—*Flor.* 1. c. 2.—*Virg. Æn.* 6. v. 819. l. 9. v. 562.—*Cic. de Nat. D.* 3. c. 2 & 17.—*Val. Max.* 1. c. 2.—*Dionys. Hal.* 2. c. 59. —*Ovid. Fast.* 3. v. 262 & 300. l. 4. v. 652. l. 6. v. 264. *Met.* 15. v. 481. *Trist.* 3. el. 1. v. 30. *Amor.* 2. el. 17. v. 18.—*Lucan.* 7. v. 396. l. 9. v. 478, &c. *Macrob. Sat.* 1. c. 13 & 16.—*Lactant.* 1. c. 22.—*Aug. de Civ. Dei.* 2. c. 16. l. 3. c. 9. l. 11. c. 15. l. 17. c. 35. l. 18. c. 24.—*Solin.* 2.—*Servius ad Æn.* 6. v. 809. l. 7. v. 188, &c.—*Victor. de Viris*, 3. [There is a fine head of Numa Pompilius in the Villa Albani, near Rome.]

NU'MA, one of the Rutulian chiefs, killed in the night by Nisus and Euryalus. *Virg. Æn.* 9. v. 454 & 10. v. 562.

NUMA'NA, a town of Picenum in Italy, of which the people were called *Numanates*. *Mela*, 2. c. 4. —*Plin.* 3. c. 13.—*Sil.* 8. v. 432.

NUMAN'TIA, a town of Spain, near the sources of the river Durius, celebrated for the war of 14 years, which, though unprotected by walls or towers, it bravely maintained against the Romans. The inhabitants obtained some advantages over the Roman forces, till Scipio Africanus was empowered to finish the war, and to see the destruction of Numantia. He began the siege with an army of 60,000 men, and was bravely opposed by the besieged, who consisted of no more than 4,000 men able to bear arms. Both armies behaved with uncommon valor, and the courage of the Numantines was soon changed into despair and fury. Their provisions began to fail, and they fed upon the flesh of their horses, and afterwards of that of their dead companions, and at last were necessitated to draw lots to kill and devour one another. The melancholy situation of their affairs obliged some to surrender to the Roman general. Scipio summoned them to deliver themselves up on the morrow; they refused, and when a longer time had been granted to their petitions, retired and set fire to their houses, and all destroyed themselves, B.C. 133, so that not even one remained to adorn the triumph of the conqueror. Some historians, however, deny this fact, and assert that a number of Numantines delivered themselves into Scipio's hands, and that 50 of them graced the conqueror's triumph at Rome, and the rest were sold as slaves. The fall of Numantia was more glorious than that of Carthage or Corinth, though inferior to them. The conqueror obtained the surname of *Numantinus*. *Flor.* 2. c. 18.—*Appian. Iber.*—*Paterc.* 2. c. 3.—*Cic.* 1. *Off.*—*Strab.* 3.—*Mela*, 2. c. 6.—*Plut.*—*Horat.* 2. od. 12. v. 1.—*Orosius.* 5. c. 6.—*Frontin.* 4. c. 1.—*Eutrop.* 4. c. 3.—*Vegetius.* 3. c. 10.

NUMANTI'NA, the wife of T. Plautius Sylvanus, accused, under Tiberius, of making her husband insane by enchantments, &c. *Tacit. Ann.* 4. c. 22.

NUMA'NUS REM'ULUS, a Rutulian, who accused the Trojans of effeminacy. He had married the younger sister of Turnus, and was killed by Ascanius during the Rutulian war. *Virg. Æn.* 9. v. 592, &c.

NUME'JUS, a Helvetian, sent as ambassador to *Cæsar*. *Comment.* 1. c. 7.

NUME'NIA or NEOME'NIA, a festival observed by the Greeks at the beginning of every lunar month, in honor of all the gods, but especially of Apollo, or the sun, who was justly deemed the author of light, and of the stated divisions of time, namely, months, seasons, days, and nights. It was observed with games and public entertainments, which were provided at the expense of the rich citizens, and which were always frequented by the poor. Solemn prayers were offered at Athens during the solemnity for the prosperity of the republic. The demigods, as well as the heroes of the ancients, were honored and invoked in the festival. *Homer. Schol. Od.* ύ.—*Eustath. Od.* ύ & Φ'.—*Herod.* 1. 8. —*Hesych.*—*Plutarch. de Gr. Quæst.*

NUME'NIUS, a Pythagorean and Platonic philosopher of Apamea, in Syria. He was a writer of eminence, and left several works. *Eusæb. Præp. Evang.* l. 11.—*Origen. contra Cels.* l. 1.——A philosopher and disciple of Pyrrho. *Diog. Laert.* 9. ——A rhetorician who flourished under Adrian. *Suidas.*

NUMENTA'NA VI'A, a road at Rome which led to mount Sacer through the gate Viminalis. It was also called Figulnensis. *Liv.* 3. c. 52.

NUME'RIA, a goddess at Rome, who presided over numbers. *Aug. de Civ. D.* 4. c. 11.

NUMERIA'NUS M. AURE'LIUS, a son of the emperor Carus. He accompanied his father into the East with the title of Cæsar, and at his death succeeded him with his brother Carinus, A.D. 282. His reign was short. Eight months after his father's death, he was murdered in his litter by his father-in-law, Arrius Aper, who accompanied him in an expedition. The murderer, who hoped to ascend the vacant throne, continued to follow the litter as if the emperor was still alive, till he found a proper opportunity of declaring his sentiments. The stench of the body, however, soon discovered his perfidy, and he was sacrificed to the fury of the soldiers. Numerianus has been admired for his learning as well as his moderation. He was naturally an eloquent speaker, and in poetry he was inferior to no writer of his age. *Vopisc. in Numerian.*—*Aur. Vict.*—*Eutrop.* &c.

NUMERIA'NUS, a friend of the emperor Severus, collected a large army in Gaul. *Ælian. Spartian. in vit. Sever.* c. 12.

NUME'RIUS, a man who favored the escape of Marius to Africa, &c.——A friend of Pompey taken by J. Cæsar's adherents, &c. *Plin.*

NUMIC'IA VI'A, one of the great Roman roads which led from the capital to the town of Brundusium.

NUMICIUS C., a tribune of the people mentioned by *Cicero*, 3. *Off.* 30.

NUMI'CUS, now Rivo di Nemi, a small river of Latium falling into the Tyrrhene Sea, near Lavinium, where the dead body of Æneas was found, and where Anna, Dido's sister, drowned herself. Its waters were used in some sacrifices of Vesta, which were discontinued, because, as Servius relates, the river diminished after the death of Æneas, so much that it became merely a little stream, and at last dried up. *Virg. Æn.* 7. v. 150, &c.—*Sil.* 1. v. 359. —*Ovid. Met.* 14. v. 358. &c. *Fast.* 8. v. 643.—*Servius. ad Æn.* 1. v. 263. l. 4. v. 619. l. 6. v. 82. 332. l. 7. v. 798.——A friend of *Horace*, to whom he addressed 1. ep. 6.

NU'MIDA, a surname given by Horace, 1. od. 36. to one of the generals of Augustus, from his conquests in Numidia. Some suppose that he alludes to Pomponius, others to Plotius.

NUMID'IA, an inland country of Africa, which now forms the kingdom of Algiers and Bildulgerid. It was bounded on the north by the Mediterranean Sea, south by Gætulia, west by Mauritania, and east by that part of Libya which was called Africa Propria. The inhabitants were called *Nomades*, and afterwards *Numidæ*. It was the kingdom of Masinissa, who was the occasion of the third Punic war, on account of the offence which he had received from the Carthaginians. Jugurtha reigned there, as also Juba, the father and son. It was conquered, and became a Roman province of which Sallust was the first governor. The Numidians were excellent warriors, and in their expeditions always endeavoured to engage with the enemy in the night time. They rode without saddles or bridles, whence they have been called *infrœni*. They had their wives in common as the rest of the barbarian nations of antiquity. The chief towns of Numidia were Tabraca, Hippo Regius, Rusicada, Zama, Sicca, Cirta, Vaga, Thala and Capsa. *Sallust. in Jug.—Flor.* 2. c. 15.—*Strab.* 2 & 17.—*Mela*, 1. c. 4, &c.—*Ovid. Met.* 15. v. 754.—*Festus. de V. Sig.—Virg. Æn.* 4. v. 41.—*Servius ad Æn.* 4. v. 535.

NUMID'IUS QUADRA'TUS, a governor of Syria under Claudius. *Tac. Ann.* 12 c. 45.

NUMIS'IUS, an officer in the Latin army. *Liv.* 8. c. 11.

Numis'ius Lu'pus, a lieutenant of the eighth legion in Mœsia, who, after being honorably distinguished by Otho, passed over to Vespasian, and was afterwards slain by Tullius Valentinus. *Tac. Hist.* 1. c. 79. 3. c. 10. 4. c. 59 & 70.

Numis'ius Ru'fus, a lieutenant of the German army under Hordeonius Flaccus. *Id. Hist.* 4. c. 22.

NUMIS'TRO, a town of the Brutii, in Italy. *Liv.* 45. c. 17.

NU'MITOR, a son of Procas, king of Alba, who inherited his father's kingdom with his brother Amulius, and began to reign conjointly with him. Amulius was too avaricious to bear a colleague on his throne; he expelled his brother, and, that he might more safely secure himself, put to death his son Lausus, and consecrated his daughter Ilia to the service of the goddess Vesta, an office which demanded perpetual celibacy. These precautions were rendered abortive. Ilia became pregnant, and though the two children which she brought forth were exposed in the river by order of the tyrant, their life was preserved, and Numitor was restored to his throne by his grandsons, and the tyrannical usurper was put to death. *Dionys. Hal. Liv. Plut. in Romul.—Ovid. Fast.* 4. v. 55, &c. —*Virg. Æn.* 6. v. 768.——A son of Phorcus, who fought with Turnus against Æneas. *Virg. Æn.* 10. v. 342.——A rich and dissolute Roman in the age of *Juvenal.* 7. v. 74.

NUMITO'RIA, a woman born at Fregellæ. She married Antonius, the father of M. Antony. *Cic. Phil.* 3. c. 6.

NUMITO'RIUS, a Roman who defended his niece Virginia, to whom Appius wished to offer violence. He was made military tribune. *Liv.* 3. c. 45 & 54.

Numito'rius Q. Pul'lus, a general of Fregellæ, who discovered a conspiracy formed against the Romans by his countrymen. *Cic. de Inv.* 2. c. 34. *Fin.* 5. c. 22.

NUMO'NIUS. *Vid.* Vala.

NUMUTIZIN'THES, a king of Thrace, son of Diogiris, who cruelly sawed men in two, and made fathers feed on the flesh of their slaughtered children and relations. *Val Max.* 9. c. 2.

NUNCO'REUS, a son of Sesostris, king of Ægypt, who made an obelisk, brought some ages after to Rome, and placed in the Vatican. *Plin.* 36. c. 11. He is called Pheron by *Herodotus.*

NUN'DINA, a goddess invoked the ninth day after birth, whence the name *nona dies. Vid.* Nondina. *Macrob. Sat.* 1. c. 16.

NUN'DINÆ. *Vid.* Feriæ

NUP'SIA, a town of Ægypt on the Nile, in the country of the Syenitæ. *Plin.* 6. c. 29.

NUP'SIS, a town near the Nomades of Arabia. *Id.* 6. c. 20.

NUR'SÆ, a town of the Æquicoli, in Italy. *Virg. Æn.* 7. v. 744.

NUR'SICA, a goddess who patronized the Etrurians. *Juv.* 10. v. 74.—*Liv.* 7. c. 3.

NUR'SIA, now Norza, a town of Picenum, the inhabitants of which are called Nursini. Its situation was exposed, and the air considered as unwholesome. *Sil. It.* 8. v. 416.—*Virg. Æn.* 7. v. 716.—*Martial*, 13. epigr. 20.—*Liv.* 28. c. 45.—*Servius ad Virg.* loco.

NU'RUM, a town of Africa Propria. *Ptol.*

NUS, a river of Cilicia, near Cescus. *Ptol.*

NUSAR'IPA, a city of India Citerior. *Id.*

NU'TRIA, a town af Illyricum. *Polyb.* 2. c. 11.

NYCBENI'TÆ or **NYGBENI'TÆ**, a people of Upper Æthiopia. *Ptol.*

NYCDO'SA or **NYGDO'SA**, a city of India within the Ganges. *Id.*

NYC'PII, a people of Africa Propria. *Id.*

NYCTE'IS, a daughter of Nycteus, who was mother of Labdacus. *Apollod.*——A pantronymic of Antiope, the daughter of Nycteus, mother of Amphion and Zethus by Jupiter, who had assumed the shape of a satyr to enjoy her company. *Ovid. Met.* 6. v. 110.

NYCTE'LIA, festivals in honor of Bacchus (*vid.* Nyctelius) observed on mount Cithron. *Plut. in Symp.* 4. c. 5.—*Servius ad Virg. G.* 4. v. 303.

NYCTE'LIUS, a surname of Bacchus, because his orgies were celebrated in the night (νὺξ *nox* τελέω *perficio.*) The words *latex Nyctelius* thence signify wine. *Seneca. in. Œdip.—Paus.* 1. c. 40.—*Ovid. Met.* 4. v. 15.—*Oppian.* 1. *Cyn.—Hesychius.*

NYC'TEUS, a son of Hyrieus and Clonia. *Apollod.* ——A son of Neptune by Celene, daughter of Atlas, king of Lesbus, or of Thebes, according to the more received opinion, He married a nymph of Crete called Polyxo or Amalthæa, by whom he had two daughters, Nyctimene and Antiope. The first of these disgraced herself by her criminal amours with her father, into whose bed she introduced herself by means of her nurse. When the father knew the incest he had committed, he attempted to stab his daughter, who was immediately changed by Minerva into an owl. Nycteus made war against Epopeus, who had carried away Antiope, and died of a wound which he had received in an engagement, leaving his kingdom to his brother Lycus, whom he entreated to continue the war, and punish Antiope for her conduct. *Vid.* Antiope. *Paus.* 2. c. 6.—*Hygin.* fab. 157 & 204.—*Ovid. Met.* 2. v. 590, &c. l. 6. v. 110, &c.—*Propert.* 3. el. 13. v. 12.—*Sch. Apollon.* 4. v. 1090.

NYCTIM'ENE, a daughter of Nycteus. *Vid.* Nycteus.

NYC'TIMUS, a son of Lycaon, king of Arcadia. He died without issue, and left his kingdom to his nephew Arcas, the son of Callisto. *Paus.* 8. c. 4. —*Apollod.* 3.

NYMBÆ'UM, a lake of Laconia, in Peloponnesus. *Paus.* 3. c. 23.

NYM'PHÆ, certain female deities among the ancients. They were generally divided into two classes, nymphs of the land and nymphs of the sea. Of the nymphs of the earth, some presided over woods, and were called Dryades and Hamadryades, others presided over mountains, and were called Oreades, some presided over hills and dales, and were called Napææ, &c. Of the sea nymphs, some were called Oceanides. Nereides, Naiades, Potamides, Limnades, &c. These presided not only over the sea, but also over rivers, fountains, streams, and lakes. The nymphs fixed their residence not only in the sea, but also on mountains, rocks, in woods or caverns, and their grottoes were beautified by evergreens and delightful and romantic scenes. The nymphs were immortal, according to the opinion of some mythologists; others supposed that like men they were subject to mortality, though their life was of long duration. They lived for several thousand years according to Hesiod, or as Plutarch seems obscurely to intimate, they lived about 9720 years. The number of the nymphs is not precisely known. There were above 3000, according to Hesiod, and their power was extended over the different places of the earth, and the various functions and occupations of mankind. They were worshipped by the ancients, though not with so much solemnity as the superior deities. They had no temples raised to their honor, and the only offerings they received were milk, honey, oil, and sometimes the sacrifice of a goat. They were generally represented as young and beautiful virgins, veiled up to the middle, and sometimes they held a vase, from which they seemed to pour water. Sometimes they had grass, leaves, and shells instead of vases. It was deemed unfortunate to see them naked, and such a sight was generally attended by a delirium, to which Propertius seems to allude in this verse, wherein he speaks of the innocence and simplicity of the primitive ages of the world,

Nec feurat nudas pœna videre Deas.

The nymphs were generally distinguished by an epithet which denoted the place of their residence; thus the nymphs of Sicily were called Sicelides; those of Corycus, Corycides, &c. *Ovid. Met.* 1. v. 320. l. 5. v. 412. l. 9. v. 651, &c. *Fast.* 3. v. 769.—*Paus.* 10. c. 3.—*Plut. de Orac. Def.*—*Orpheus, Arg*—*Hesiod. Theog.*—*Propert.* 3. el. 12.—*Homer. Odyss.* 14.—*Servius ad Virg. Æn.* 10. v. 9. 62. *G.* 1. v. 270. l. 4. v. 380. *Æn.* 1. v. 504.—*Schol. Apollon.* 2. v. 481. [The representations of the various nymphs are very numerous, and are noticed under their particular heads.]

NYMPHÆ'A, an island near the Adriatic, where Calypso dwelt. *Steph.*——An island near the Ionian Samus. *Plin.* 5. c. 31.

NYMPHÆ'I CRA'TER, a place in the country of the Apolloniates, in Illyricum. *Id.* 2. c. 106. & 107.

NYMPHÆ'UM, a port of Macedonia.——*Cæs. Bell. Civ.* 3. c. 26.——A harbour of Sardinia. *Ptol.*——A promontory of Epirus on the Ionian Sea. *Lucan.* 5. v. 720.——A promontory of Macedonia, at the foot of mount Athos, now Capo de monte Santo.——A place near the walls of Appollonia, sacred to the nymphs, where also Apollo had an oracle. This oracle was consulted on every occasion except concerning marriage and death, and the suppliant was informed of the will of the divinity, and of the success of his enquiry according to the appearance of the incense which he placed on the altar. If it blazed and was easily consumed, the petition was granted, but if it flew in sparks, or seemed not to yield to the power of the fire, then the answer of the god was unfavorable. The place was also celebrated for the continual flame of fire which seemed to rise at a distance from the plains. It was there that a sleeping satyr was once caught and brought to Sylla as he returned from the Mithridatic war. This monster had the same features as the poets ascribe to the satyr. He was interrogated by Sylla, and by his interpreters, but his articulations were unintelligible, and the Roman spurned from him a creature which seemed to partake of the nature of a beast more than that of a man. *Plut. in Sylla.*—*Dio* 41.—*Plin.* 5. c. 29.—*Strab.* 7.—*Liv.* 42. c. 36 & 49.——A city of Taurica Chersonesus, near Theodosia. It is now Ciprico, according to *Niger.*——A building at Rome where the nymphs were worshipped. It was adorned with their statues and with fountains and waterfalls, which afforded an agreeable and refreshing coolness.

NYMPHÆ'US, a man who went into Caria, at the head of a colony of Melians, &c. *Polyæn.* 8. c. 64.

NYMPHÆ'US, a river of Latium, near Circæi. *Plin.* 3. c. 1. It is now Storace.——A river of Mesopotamia, flowing into the Tigris. *Ammian.*——A mountain of Phthiotis. *Plin.* 4. c. 8.

NYMPHA'IS, an island of the Pamphylian Sea. *Plin.* 5. c. 31.

NYMPHID'IUS, a favorite of Nero, who said that he was descended from Caligula. He was raised to the consular dignity, and soon after disputed the empire with Galba, but was slain by the soldiers. *Tacit. Ann.* 15. 72 & 73. *Hist.* 1. c. 5.

NYM'PHIS, son of Xenagoras, a native of Heraclea, who wrote a history of Alexander's life and actions, divided into 24 books, also of Heraclea in 13 books, down to the time of the expulsion of the tyrants. *Suidas. Athen.* 12 & 13.—*Voss. H. Gr.* 1. c. 16.—*Ælian.* 7. *De Anim.*

NYM'PHIUS, a native of Palæpolis, who made the Romans masters of his country. *Liv.* 8. c. 25. & 26.

NYM'PHO, a native of Colophon, mentioned by *Cicero, ad. Q. Fr.* 1. ep. 2.——A native of Centirypa. *Cic. Verr.* 3. c. 21.

NYMPHODO'RUS, a writer of Amphipolis, published a work on the laws and rites of the Asiatics. *Clem. Alex. Strom.* 1.——A Syracusan who wrote a history of Sicily. *Athen.* 6, 7 & 13.—*Voss. H, Gr.* 1. 3. p. 393.

NYMPHOLEPTES, (from νύμφη *nympha* and ληπτὸς *captus*,) or NYMPHOMA'NES, *possessed by the nymphs*, a name given to the inhabitants of mount Cithæron, who believed that they were inspired by the nymphs. *Plut. in Arist.*

NYM'PHON. *Vid.* Nympho.

NYPHA'TES, a mountain of Armenia Minor. *Ptol.*

NYP'SIUS, a general of Dionysius the tyrant, who took Syracuse, and put all the inhabitants to the sword. *Diod.* 16.

NY'RAX, a city of Gallia Celtica. *Steph.*

NY'SA or NYS'SA, a town of Æthiopia, at the south of Ægypt, or, according to others, of Arabia. This city, with another of the same name in India, was sacred to the god Bacchus, who was educated there by the nymphs of the place, and received the name of Dionysius, which seems to be compounded of Διὸς & Νύσα, the name of his father, and that of the place of his education. The god made this place the seat of his empire and the capital of the conquered nations of the East. *Diodorus* in his 3rd and 4th books has given a prolix account of the birth of the god at Nysa, and of his education and heroic actions. *Mela*, 3. c. 7.—*Ovid. Met.* 4. v. 13, &c.—*Ital.* 7. v. 198.—*Curt.* 8. c. 10.—*Virg. Æn.* 6. v. 805. According to some authors, among whom are *Stephanus* and the *Scholiast* on Homer, there were no less than ten places of the name of Nysa. One of these was on the coast of Eubœa, famous for its vines, which grew in such an uncommon manner that if a twig was planted in the ground in the morning, it immediately produced grapes, which were full ripe in the evening.

NY'SA, a city of Thrace. *Steph.*—*Homer. Il.* ζ. v. 132.

NY'SA, a city seated on the top of mount Parnassus, and sacred to Bacchus. *Juv.* 7. v. 63.

NY'SA, a person killed by Bacchus. *Cic. N. D.* 3. c. 23.

NYSÆ'US, a surname of Bacchus, because he was worshipped at Nysa. *Propert.* 3. el. 17. v. 22.—*Ovid. Met.* 4. v. 13.—*Sil. Ital.* 7. v. 198.——A son of Dionysius of Syracuse. *C. Nep. in Diod.*

NY'SES or NY'SAS, a river of Africa, rising in the mountains of Æthiopia. *Aristot.*

NYSI'ADES, a name given to the nymphs of Nisa, to whose care Jupiter intrusted the education of his son Bacchus. *Ovid. Met.* 3. v. 314, &c. *Fast.* 3. v. 769.—*Meleag. Anthol.* 1. c. 19.

NYS'IÆ POR'TÆ, a small island of Africa.

NYSI'RUS. *Vid.* Nisyrus.

NYS'IUS, a surname of Bacchus as the protecting god of Nysa. *Cic. Flacc.* 25.

NYS'SA, a sister of Mithridates the Great. *Plut.*

O.

O'A, a village of the tribe Pandionis in Attica. *Steph. in* Ὄα.

OÆ'NEUM, or, according to *Ptolemy*, Onæum, a maritime town of Dalmatia.

O'ANI, a people of Taprobane. *Ptol.*

O'ANUS, a city of Lydia. *Steph.*——A river of Sicily. *Pindar.* It is now Frascolari. *Bochart. Geogr. Sacr.* p. 605.

OARAC'TA, OROAC'TA, or OURACH'THA, an island of the Persian Gulph. *Arrian. in Indic.*—*Plin.* 6. c. 23.—*Salmas. ad Solin.* p. 1180.

OAR'SES, the original name of Artaxerxes Mnemon.

O'ARUS, a river of Sarmatia, falling into the Palus Mœotis. *Herodot.* 4.

OA'SIS or O'ASIS, a town about the middle of Libya, at the distance of seven days' journey from Thebes in Ægypt, where the Persian army sent by Cambyses to plunder Jupiter Ammon's temple was lost in the sands. There were two other cities of that name very little known. Oasis became a place of banishment under the lower empire. *Strab.* 17.—*Zosim.* 5. c. 97.—*Herodot.* 3. c. 26.

OAX'ES, a river of Crete, which received its name from Oaxus the son of Apollo. *Virg. Ecl.* 1. v. 66.—*Servius ad Virg. loco.*—*Apollon*, 1 *Arg.*—*Stephan. Byzant.*

OAX'US or OAX'ES, a town of Crete, where Etearchus reigned, who founded Cyrene. *Herodot.* 4.—*Varro.*

OAX'US, a son of Apollo and the nymph Anchiale.

OB'ADA, a small region of the Nabatæi, where king Obodes was buried. *Steph.*

OB'ANA, a town of Assyria. *Ptol.*

OBLOGE'NES, a people of Cyprus, who sent Exagonus to Rome. *Plin.* 28. c. 3. Some read Ophiogenes. *Vid.* Exagonus.

OBOTRI'TÆ or OBOTRII, a people of Germany, inhabiting that part of the country now Mecklenburg.

OB'RAPA, a city of Arabia Felix. *Ptol.*

OB'RIMAS, one of the three rivers near Apamea in Asia. *Plin.* 5. c. 29.

OB'RIMO, a surname of Proserpine. *Cæl. Rhod.* 26. c. 20.

OBRIN'GA, now Ahr, a river of Germany falling into the Rhine above Rimmagen. *Ptol.*

O'BRIS or ORO'BUS, a river of Gallia Narbonensis. *Strab.—Mela,* 2. c. 5, &c. It is now l'Orobe.

OBRO'ATIS, a city of Persia. *Ptol.—Ammian.* It is now Omara.

OB'SEQUENS JUL., a Latin writer, about the time of whose existence the learned differ. *Saxius, Onom.* 1. p. 289, makes him contemporary with Plutarch, A.D. 107. He wrote a work called "de prodigiis," to which Conrad Lycosthenes made additions. The whole was edited by Schesser, Amstel. 1679. The best edition, after Oudendorp's, Lug. Bat. 1720, is that of Kappe, 1772. *Harles. Not. Lit. Rom.* 1. p. 601.

OBUL'CO, a city of Hispania Bætica. *Ptol. Pliny.* 3. c. 1, calls it Pontificense.

OBULTRO'NIUS SABI'NUS, a quæstor put to death by Galba's orders, &c. *Tacit. Ann.* 13. c. 28.—*Hist.* 1. c. 37.

OCA'LEA, OCALE'IA or OCALI'A, a town of Bœotia, to which Rhadamanthus fled after his marriage with Alcmena. *Apollod.* 2.—*Homer. Il.* 2.

OCA'LEA, a daughter of Mantineus, who married Abas, son of Lynceus and Hypermnestra, by whom she had Acrisius and Prœtus. *Apollod.* 2. c. 2.—*Hygin. P. A.* 2. c. 18.—*Lactant. ad Theb.* 1. v. 670. l. 3. v. 458.

OC'CARA, a town of Chalcidica, in Syria. *Antonin.* According to *Simler,* it is the Coara of *Ptolemy.*

OC'CIA, a woman who presided over the sacred rites of Vesta for 57 years, with the greatest sanctity. She died in the reign of Tiberius, and the daughter of Domitius succeeded her. *Tacit. Ann.* 2. c. 86.

OCEAN'IDES and OCEANIT'IDES, sea nymphs, daughters of Oceanus from whom they received their name, and of the goddess Tethys. They were 3000 in number, according to Apollodorus, who mentions the names of seven of them; Asia, Styx, Electra, Doris, Eurynome, Amphitrite, and Metis. Hesiod speaks of the eldest of them and reckons 41, Pitho Admete, Prynno, Ianthe, Rhodia, Hippo, Callirhoe, Urania, Clymene, Idya, Pasithoe, Clythia, Zeuxo, Galuxaure, Plexaure, Perseis, Pluto, Thoe, Polydora. Melobosis, Dione, Cerceis, Xanthe, Acasta, Ianira, Telestho, Europa, Menestho, Petrea, Eudora, Calypso, Tycho, Ocyroe, Crisia, Amphiro, with those mentioned by Apollodorus, except Amphitrite. *Hyginus* mentions 16 whose names are almost all different from those of Apollodorus and Hesiod, which difference proceeds from the mutilation of the original text. The Oceanides, as the rest of the inferior deities, were honored with libations and sacrifices. Prayers were offered to them, and they were entreated to protect sailors from storms and dangerous tempests. The Argonauts, before they proceeded on their expedition, made an offering of flour, honey, and oil, on the sea shore, to all the deities of the sea, and sacrificed bulls to them, and entreated their protection. When the sacrifice was made on the sea shore the blood of the victim was received in a vessel, but when it was in the open sea, the blood was permitted to run down into the waters. When the sea was calm, the sailors generally offered a lamb or a young pig, but if it was agitated by the winds and rough, a black bull was deemed the most acceptable victim. *Homer. Odyss.* 3.—*Horat.*—*Apollon. Arg.*—*Virg. G.* 4. v. 341.—*Hesiod. Theog.* 349.—*Apollod.* 1.

OCE'ANUS, a powerful deity of the sea, son of Cœlus and Terra. He married Tethys, by whom he became father of the gods of the principal rivers, such as the Alpheus, Peneus, Strymon, &c. and a number of daughters who are called from him Oceanides. *Vid.* Oceanides. According to Homer, Oceanus was the father of all the gods, and on that account he received frequent visits from the rest of the deities. He is generally represented as an old man with a long flowing beard, sitting upon the waves of the sea. He often holds a pike in his hand, while ships under sail appear at a distance, or a sea monster stands near him. Oceanus presided over every part of the sea, and even the rivers were subjected to his power. The ancients were superstitious in the worship of this god, and revered with great solemnity a deity to whose care they entrusted themselves when going on any voyage. *Hesiod. Theog.* 135 & 337.—*Ovid. Fast.* 5. v. 81, &c.—*Apollod.* 1.—*Cic. de Nat. D.* 3. c. 20.—*Homer. Il.* [There is a fine recumbent figure representing Oceanus, in the Museum of the Capitol at Rome.]

OCELEN'SES, a people of Lusitania, called Lancienses by *Pliny,* 4. c. 22.

OCE'LIS. *Vid.* Acila.

OCEL'LA SERV., a Roman, intimate with Cicero. He supported Pompey in the civil wars. He was discovered in an intrigue to which *Cicero* alludes, 2 *Fam.* 15. l. 8. ep. 7. *Attic.* 10. ep. 13 & 17.

OCEL'LUS, an ancient philosopher of Lucania. *Vid.* Lucanus.

OC'ELUM, a town of Gaul. *Cæs. Bell. G.* 1. c. 10. ——A town of Hispania Tarraconensis, called Ocelis by *Appian,* and Ocellum Durii by *Antoninus.* It is now Fermosello, according to *Baudrand.*

O'CHA, a mountain of Eubœa, and the name of Eubœa itself. *Plin.* 4. c. 12.—*Casaubon. in Strab.* 10.

O'CHA, a sister of Ochus, buried alive by his orders.

OCHE'SIUS, a general of Ætolia in the Trojan war. *Homer. Il.* 5. v. 843.

O'CHUS, a surname given to Artaxerxes the Third, king of Persia. *Vid.* Artaxerxes.——A man of Cyzicus, who was killed by the Argonauts. *Flacc.* 3. v. 148.——A prince of Persia, who refused to visit his native country for fear of giving all the women each a piece of gold. *Plut.*

O'CHUS, a river of India, or of Bactriana. *Plin.* 6. c. 16. l. 31. c. 7,

O'CHUS, a king of Persia. He exchanged this name for that of Darius. *Vid.* Darius Nothus.

OCILA or OCI'LA. *Vid.* Acila.

OCIN'ARUS, a river of the Brutii. *Lycoph.*

OC'NUS, a son of the Tiber and of Manto, who assisted Æneas against Turnus. He built a town which he called Mantua after his mother's name. Some suppose that he is the same as Bianor. *Virg. Ecl.* 9. *Æn.* 10. v. 198.—*Servius in loco.*——A man remarkable for his industry. He had a wife as remakable for her profusion, who always consumed and lavished away whatever the labors of her husband had earned. Hs is represented as twisting a cord, which an ass standing by eats up as soon as he makes it, whence the proverb of *Ocnus funem torquet* or *contorquet piger funiculum,* often applied to labor which meets no return, and which is totally lost. This fable was represented at Delphi by the pencil of Polygnotus, and it likewise engaged the labors of the painter Socrates according to Pliny. *Propert.* 4. el. 3. v. 21.—*Plin.* 35. c. 11.—*Paus.* 10. c. 29.

O'CRA, the lowest part of the Alps, near the Carni. *Ptol.—Strab.*——A city of the Veneti. *Plin.* 3. c. 19.

OCRIC'ULUM, now Otricoli, a town of Umbria, near Rome. *Cic. pro Mil.—Liv.* 19. c. 41.

OCRID'ION, a king of Rhodes, who was reckoned in the number of the gods after death. He had a temple at Rhodes which heralds were not suffered to enter, because by the treachery of a herald he lost Cydippe, daughter of Ochimus, whom he was going to marry. *Plut. in Græc. Quæst.* 27.

OCRI'NUM, a promontory of Britain. *Ptol.* It is now the Land's End, according to *Camden.*

OCRIS'IA, a woman of Corniculum, who was one of the attendants of Tanaquil, the wife of Tarquinius Priscus. She was mother of Servius Tullius, of the manner of whose conception Pliny and Ovid give an extraordinary account. *Plut. de Fort. Rom.—Plin.* 36. c. 27.—*Ovid. Fast.* 6. v. 627.

OCTACIL'IUS L., a slave who was manumitted, and who afterwards taught rhetoric at Rome. He had Pompey the Great in the number of his pupils and was the author of some historical works. *Voss. H. Lat.* l. c. 9.—*Sueton. in Rhet.*—*Martial.* 10. epigr. 79.

OCTAPITU'RUM, a promontory of Britain. *Ptol.* It is now St. David's head, according to *Camden.*

OCTAP'OLIS, a city of Lycia. *Ptol.*

OCTA'VIA, a Roman lady, sister to the emperor Augustus, and celebrated for her beauty and virtues. She married Claudius Marcellus, and, after his death, M. Antony. Her marriage with Antony was a political step to reconcile her brother and her husband. Antony proved for some time attentive to her, but he soon after abandoned her for Cleopatra, and when she attempted to withdraw him from this unlawful attachment, by going to meet him at Athens, she was secretly rebuked, and rejected with contumelious language. This affront was highly resented by Augustus, and though Octavia endeavoured to pacify him by palliating her husband's behaviour, he resolved to revenge her cause by arms. After the battle of Actium and the death of Antony Octavia, forgetful of the injuries which she had received, took into her house all the children of her husband, and treated them with maternal tenderness. Marcellus, her son by her former husband, was married to a niece of Augustus, and publicly intended as successor to his uncle. His sudden death plunged all his family into the greatest grief. Virgil, whom Augustus patronised, took upon himself to pay a melancholy tribute to the memory of a young man whom Rome regarded as her future father and patron. He was desired to repeat his composition in the presence of Augustus and of his sister. Octavia burst into tears as soon as the poet began; but when he recited the passage beginning with *Tu Marcellus eris*, she swooned away. This tender and pathetic encomium upon the merit and the virtues of young Marcellus was liberally rewarded by Octavia, and Virgil received 10,000 sesterces for every one of the verses. Octavia had two daughters by Antony, Antonia Major and Antonia Minor. The elder married L. Domitius Ahenobarbus, by whom she had Cn. Domitius the father of the emperor Nero by Agrippina, the daughter of Germanicus. Antonia Minor, who was as virtuous and beautiful as her mother, married Drusus the son of Tiberius, by whom she had Germanicus and Claudius, who reigned before Nero. The death of Marcellus continually preyed upon the mind of Octavia, who died of melancholy in her fifty-fourth year, about ten-years B.C. Her brother paid great regard to her memory by pronouncing himself her funeral oration. The Roman people also showed their respect for her virtues by their wish to pay her divine honors. *Suet. in Aug.* 61.—*Plut. in Anton. &c.*—*Dio.* 48, &c.——A daughter of the emperor Claudius by Messalina. She was betrothed to Silanus, but by the intrigues of Agrippina she was married to the emperor Nero in the 16th year of her age. She was soon after divorced on pretence of barrenness, and the emperor married Poppæa, who procured the banishment of Octavia to Campania. She was afterwards recalled at the instance of the people, and Poppæa, who was resolved on her ruin, caused her again to be banished to the island Pandataria, where she was ordered to kill herself by opening her veins. Her head was cut off and carried to Poppæa. *Suet. in Claud.* 27. *In. Ner.* 7, 35 & 57.—*Tacit. Ann.* 14. c. 63.

OCTAVIA'NUS or OCTA'VIUS CÆ'SAR, the nephew of Cæsar the dictator. *Vid.* Augustus.

OCTA'VII, the family of which Augustus became so great an ornament, were originally from Velitræ, and were admitted into the Roman senate by the elder Tarquin, and made patricians by his successor. *Suet. in Aug.*

OCTA'VIUS CN., a Roman, governor of Sardinia, successfully employed in the first Punic war, and afterwards engaged in honorable embassies. *Liv.* 28, &c.

OCTA'VIUS CNE'US, a Roman, who commanded the fleet against Perseus. The king surrendered to him in Samothrace, and Cneus after conducting the royal captive and the Macedonian treasures to Rome, obtained a naval triumph. He was assassinated by Leptines, at Loadicea, when ambassador in Asia, and a statue was erected to his honor in the Roman forum. *Cic. Phil.* 9. c. 2.—*Plin.* 34. c. 6.—*Liv.* 45. c. 5.——His son, was consul with T. Annius, A.U. 625.——His grandson, was consul 667, with Cinna, whom he expelled from the city. Cinna revenged the insult, and at the head of an army, and supported by the influence of Marius, returned to Rome, and after putting his antagonist to death, ignominiously fixed his head on the rostra of the forum. Cneus was admired for his eloquence as well as his integrity. *Cic. Pr.* 3. c. 3. *Br.* 47. *Planc.* 21. *Har.* 25. *Cat.* 3. c. 10. —*Flor.* 3. c. 21.—*Appian. B. Civ.*——The father of Augustus, was respected for his great virtues and superior abilities. As governor of Macedonia he conducted himself with spirit, bravery, and moderation, and after destroying the remains of Spartacus' and Catiline's conspiracy at Thurii, and defeating the Thracians and Bessi, he received the horable appellation of *imperator*, from the gratitude and affection of his troops. He died suddenly on his return from Macedonia to Rome, whilst he meditated to offer himself a candidate for the consulship. He left two daughters, besides Augustus, who was then only four years old. *Suet. in Aug.*—*Paterc.* 2. c. 59.—*Cic. Q. Fr.* 1. ep. 1.

OCTA'VIUS, a man who opposed Metellus in the reduction of Crete, by means of Pompey. He was obliged to retire from the island.——A Roman who boasted of being in the number of Cæsar's murderers. His assertions were false, yet he was punished as if he had been accessory to the conspiracy.——A lieutenant of Crassus in Parthia. He accompanied his general to the tent of the Parthian conqueror, and was killed by the enemy as he attempted to hinder them from carrying away Crassus.——A governor of Cilicia. He died in his province, and Lucullus made applications to succeed him, &c.——A tribune of the people at Rome, whom Tib. Gracchus, his colleague, deposed.——A commander of the forces of Antony against Augustus.——An officer who killed himself, &c.——A poet in the Augustan age, intimate with Horace. He also distinguished himself as an historian. *Horat.* 1. sat. 10. v. 82.—*Vos. H. Lat.* p. 714. *Poet. Lat.* c. 2. p. 34.

OCTA'VIUS SAGIT'TA, a tribune of the people, who debauched a woman of Pontus, and took her away from her husband. She proved unfaithful to him, upon which he murdered her. He was condemned under Nero. *Tacit. Ann.* 13. c. 44.

OCTODU'RUM, a city of Hispania Tarraconensis, on the Durius. *Ptol.* It is now Toro, or, according to some, Sarabris.

OCTODU'RUS, a vilage in the modern country of Switzerland, now called Martigny. *Cæs. B. G.* 3. c. 1.

OCTOGE'SA, a town of Hispania Tarraconensis, a little above the mouth of the Iberus. It is called Etovisa by *Pliny*, 3. c. 3, and Etovissa by *Livy*, and is now Mequinenza. *Cæs. B. G.* 1. c. 61.

OCTOL'OPHUM, a place of Greece. *Liv.* 31. c. 36. & 44. c. 3.

OCY'ALUS, one of the Phæacians with Alcinous. *Homer. Odyss.* 7.

OCYP'ETE, OCYP'ODE or OCYTH'OE, one of the Harpies, who infected whatever she touched. *Hesiod. Theog.* 265.—*Apollod.* 1. c. 9.

OCYP'ETE, a daughter of Thaumas. *Apollod.*——A daughter of Danaus, by Pieria, was the wife of Lampus. *Id.*

OCYP'ODES, a nation of India, of monstrous size. *Salmas. ad Solin.* p. 1006.

OCYR'OE, a daughter of Chiron by Chariclo, who had the gift of prophecy. She was changed into a hare. *Vid.* Menalippe. *Ovid. Met.* 2. v. 638, &c.——A woman, daughter of Chesias, carried away by Appollo, as she was going to a festival at Miletus.

ODAG'ANA, a town of Arabia Deserta. *Ptol.*

OD'ATIS, a daughter of Hormates king of part of Asia Minor, so beautiful in person that she was considered as the daughter of Venus and Adonis. She had frequently heard the praises of Zariadres, a prince who reigned on the borders of the Tanais, and became enamoured of his character, but her father refused to marry her to so distant a suitor. Zariadres, apprised of her partiality for him, visited the Asiatic court, and appeared at a banquet where the princess was ordered by her father to present a cup of wine to the person whom she would honor with her hand. Odatis turned with tears and disdain from the guests of her father, but the appearance of Zariadres reminded her of the favorite of her imagination, she knew him to be the same whom she had seen in a dream, and she gave him the cup and her hand, against the wishes of her father and of the nobles of his court. *Chares, Myth.* 10.—*Athen.* 13.

ODENA'TUS, a celebrated prince of Palmyra. He early inured himself to bear fatigue, and by hunting leopards and wild beasts, accustomed himself to the labors of a military life. He was faithful to the Romans, and when Aurelian had been taken prisoner by Sapor king of Persia, Odenatus warmly interested himself in his cause, and solicited his release by writing a letter to the conqueror and sending him presents. The king of Persia was offended at the liberty of Odenatus, he tore the letter, and ordered the presents which were offered to be thrown into a river. To punish Odenatus who had the impudence, as he observed, to pay homage to so great a monarch as himself, he ordered him to appear before him, on pain of being devoted to instant destruction, with all his family, if he dared to refuse. Odenatus disdained the summons of Sapor, and opposed force to force. He obtained some advantages over the troops of the Persian monarch, and took his wife prisoner with a great and rich booty. These services were seen with gratitude by the Romans; and Gallienus, the then reigning emperor, named Odenatus as his colleague on the throne, and gave the title of Augustus to his children, and to his wife, the celebrated Zenobia. Odenatus, invested with new power, resolved to signalize himself more conspicuously by conquering the northern barbarians, but his exaltation was of short duration, and he perished by the dagger of one of his relations, whom he had slightly offended in a domestic entertainment. He died at Emessa, about 267 A.D. Zenobia succeeded to all his titles and honors. *Trebell. Pollio. de* 30. *Tyr. in vit. Valer. & Galien. c.* 15. Also written Odena'thus.

ODES'SUS, a sea-port town at the west of the Euxine Sea in Lower Mœsia, below the mouths of the Danube. *Ovid.* 1. *Trist.* 9. v. 37.

ODE'UM, a musical theatre at Athens. *Vitruv.* 5. c. 9.

ODI'NUS, a celebrated hero of antiquity, who flourished about 70 years B.C. in the northern parts of ancient Germany, or the modern kingdom of Denmark. He was at once a priest, a soldier, a poet, a monarch, and a conqueror. He imposed upon the credulity of his superstitious countrymen, and made them believe that he could raise the dead to life, and that he was acquainted with futurity. When he had extended his power, and increased his fame by conquest, and by persuasion, he resolved to die in a different manner from other men. He assembled his friends, and with the sharp point of a lance made on his body nine different wounds in the form of a circle, and as he expired declared that he was going into Scythia, where he should become one of the immortal gods. He further added, that he would prepare bliss and felicity for such of his countrymen as lived a virtuous life, who fought with intrepidity, and who died like heroes in the field of battle. These injunctions had the desired effect, his countrymen superstitiously believed him, and always recommended themselves to his protection, whenever they engaged in battle, and entreated him to receive the souls of such as had fallen in war.

ODI'TES, a son of Ixion, killed by Mopsus at the nuptials of Pirithous. *Ovid. Met.* 12. v. 457.——A prince killed at the nuptials of Andromeda. *Id. Ib.* 5. v. 97.

ODO'ACER or ODOA'CER, a king of the Heruli, who destroyed the western empire of Rome, and called himself king of Italy, A.D. 476. *Procop. de Bell. Goth.* 1. 1. *Jornand. de reb. Goth.*—*Cassiodor. in Chron.* &c.

ODOMAN'TI, a people of Thrace, on the eastern banks of the Strymon. *Liv.* 45. c. 4.

ODOMAS'TES, a general or satrap of Sapor, king of Persia. *Salmas.*—*Treb. Poll. de* 30. *Tyr.*

OD'ONES, a people of Thrace. *Dionys. Bassaric.* 1. 14.—*Steph.*

ODRUS'SA, one of the auxiliaries of Æetes against Perses. *Val. Flacc.* 5. v. 594.

OD'RYSÆ, a people of ancient Thrace, between Abdera and the river Ister. The epithet of Odrysius is often applied to a Thracian. *Ovid. Met.* 6. v. 490. 1. 13. v. 554. *Amor.* 3. el. 12. v. 32. *A.A.* 2. 2. v. 134.—*Stat. Ach.* 1. v. 184.—*Liv.* 39. c. 53.

ODYSSE'A, one of Homer's epic poems, in twenty-four books, the adventures of Ulysses on his return from the Trojan war, with other material circumstances. The whole of the action comprehends no more than fifty-five days. Though not so esteemed as the Iliad for boldness of genius and fire of description, yet the Odyssey claims an equal share of approbation for the dignity of its characters. Instead of carnage and blood, we here admire the social virtues, we accompany the hero into domestic scenes, share with him the sweets of private life, admire the steadiness of friendship tried by time and by calamity, and bless the hand of ancient hospitality which was open indiscriminately to those who labored under distress or indigence. The Iliad possesses the powers of the meridian sun, according to the beautiful expression of Longinus, and the Odyssey still preserves the majesty and the serenity of the setting sun. *Vid.* Homerus. *Ovid. Trist.* 2. v. 375.—*Cic. Br.* 18.

ODYSSE'IA, called Edissa by *Cicero, Verr.* 5. c. 34, and *Ulyssis portus* by *Pliny*, 3. c. 8., a harbour and promontory of Sicily, near Pachynus. The promontory is now Capo Marzo, according to *Fazellus*, and the harbor Porto di Palo, according to *Baudrand.*

Œ'A, a city of Africa, now Tripoli. It is called Eoa by *Ptolemy*, Æa by *Silius*, Ææa by *Apuleius. &c. Bochart. Geogr.* p. 526.—*Plin.* 5. c. 4.—*Sil. Ital.* 3. v. 257.——A place in Ægina. *Herodot.* 5. c. 83.

ŒA'GRUS, Œ'AGRUS or Œ'AGER, the father of Orpheus by Calliope. He was king of Thrace, and from him mount Hæmus and also the Hebrus, one of the rivers of the country, received the appellation of Æagrius, though Servius in his commentaries, disputes the explanation of Diodorus, by asserting that the Œagrius is a river of Thrace, the waters of which supply the streams of the Hebrus. *Ovid. in Ib.* 484.—*Apollon.* 1. *Arg.* 23.—*Virg. G.* 4. v. 524.—*Servius, loco.*—*Ital.* 5. v. 463.—*Diod.*—*Apollod.* 1. c. 3.—*Conon. Narr.* 45.—*Propert.* 2. el. 23.—*Flacc.* 4. v. 348.—*Hygin.* fab. 14.—*Manil.* 5. v. 322.

Œ'AGRUS, a tragedian much esteemed at Athens. *Aristoph. Vesp. & Schol.*

ŒAN'THE or ŒANTHI'A, a town of Phocis, where Venus had a temple. *Paus.* 10. c. 38.—*Mela*, 2. c. 3.

Œ'ASO or ŒAS'SO, a promontory of the Vascones in Hispania Tarraconensis. It is called Eason by *Mela*, 1. c. 6. Olarso by *Pliny*, 4. c. 20., Orsona by *Appian*, and Idanusa by *Strabo*. It is now probably le Figuier.

Œ'AX, a son of Nauplius and Clymene. He was brother to Palamedes, whom he accompanied to the Trojan war, and whose death he highly resented on his return to Greece, by raising disturbances in the family of some of the Grecian princes. *Dictys. Cret.*—*Apollod.* 2.—*Sch. Eurip. Orest.* 432.—*Gyrald. de P. H.* 2.—*Hygin.* fab. 117.

ŒBA'LIA, the ancient name of Laconia, which it received from king Œbalus, and thence *Æbalides puer* is applied to Hyacinthus as a native of the country, and *Œbalius Sanguis* is used to denominate his blood. *Paus.* 3. c. 1.—*Stat.* 1. *Ach.* 20. 1. 1. *Sylv.* 2. v. 150. 1. 3. *Sylv.* 2. v. 10. *Theb.* 9. v. 690.—*Apollod.* 3. c. 10.——A name given to Tarentum, because built by a Lacedæmonian colony, whose ancestors were governed by Œbalus. *Virg. G.* 4. v. 125.—*Sil.* 12. v. 451.

ŒBAL'IDES, a patronymic applied to Castor and Pollux the grandson of Œbalus, and also to Hyacinthus. *Ovid. Fast.* 5. v. 705. *Met.* 10. v. 196.

ŒB'ALUS, a son of Argalus or Cynortas, who was king of Laconia. He married Gorgophone the daughter of Perseus, by whom he had Hippocoon, Tyndarus, &c. *Paus.* 3. c. 1.—*Hygin.* fab. 78.—*Apollod.* 3. c. 10.——A son of Telon and the nymph Sebethis, who reigned at Capreæ in the neighbourhood of Neapolis, in Italy. *Virg. Æn.* 7. v. 734.

ŒB'ARES, a satrap of Cyrus employed against the Medes. He fled from the field of battle, and led off his troops with him. *Polyæn.* 7, c. 45.——A groom of Darius, son of Hystaspes. He was the cause that his master obtained the kingdom of Persia, by his artifice in making his horse neigh first. *Vid.* Darius the First. *Herodot.* 3. c. 85.—*Justin.* 1. c, 10.

ŒB'ASUS, one of the auxiliaries of Æetes. *Val. Flacc.* 6. v. 245.

ŒCHA'LIA, a country of Laconia in Peloponnesus, with a small town of the same name. This town was destroyed by Hercules, while Eurytus was king over it, from which circumstance it is often called Eurytopolis.——A small town of Eubœa, where, according to some, Eurytus reigned, and not in Peloponnesus. *Strab.* 8, 9 & 10.—*Virg. Æn.* 8. v. 291.—*Ovid. Heroid.* 9. *Met.* 9. v. 136.—*Sophocl. in Trach.* 74 & *Sch. ibid.*—*Plut. de Orac. Def.*—*Hygin.* fab. 35.—*Apollon.* 1. v. 87.

ŒCHOR'DAS or ŒCHAR'DUS, a river of Serica. *Ptol.* The people in the neighbourhood were called Œchardæ, or Chardi, according to *Ammianus.*

Œ'CHUS, a city of Caria. *Steph.*

ŒCLI'DES, a patronymic of Amphiaraus son of Œcleus. *Ovid. Met.* 8. fab. 7.

Œ'CLEUS. *Vid.* Oicleus.

Œ'CLUS or OE'CLUS, a Centaur. *Ovid. Met.* 12. v. 450.

ŒCUME'NIUS, a Greek writer who wrote in the middle of the tenth century a paraphrase of some of the books of the New Testament in Greek, edited in 2 vols. fol. Paris, 1631.

ŒDAN'TIUM, a city of Illyria. *Steph.*

ŒDIP'ODES or ŒDIPODIONI'DES, a patronymic applied to the sons of Œdipus. *Stat. Theb.* 1. v. 313. l. 2. v. 465.

ŒDIPO'DIA, a fountain of Thebes in Bœotia. *Plut. in Opusc.*

ŒD'IPUS, a son of Laius king of Thebes, and Jocasta. Being descended from Venus by his father's side, Œdipus was born to be exposed to all the calamities and persecutions which Juno could inflict upon the posterity of the goddess of beauty. Laius, the father of Œdipus, was informed by the oracle, as soon as he married Jocasta that he must perish by the hands of his son. Such dreadful intelligence awakened his fears, and to prevent the fulfilment of the oracle, he resolved never to approach Jocasta; but his solemn resolutions were violated in a fit of intoxication. The queen became pregnant, and Laius, still desirous of averting the evil, ordered his wife to destroy the child as soon as it came into the world. The mother had not the courage to obey, yet she gave the child as soon as born to one of her domestics, with orders to expose him on the mountains. The servant was moved with pity, but to obey the command of Jocasta, he bored the feet of the child, and suspended him with a twig by the heels to a tree on mount Cithæron, where he was soon found by one of the shepherds of Polybus, king of Corinth. The shepherd carried him home, and Peribœa, the wife of Polybus, who had no children, educated him as her own child, with maternal tenderness. The accomplishments of the infant, who was named Œdipus on account of the swelling of his feet (οἰδέω *tumeo*, ποῦς *pes*), soon became the admiration of the age. His companions envied his strength and his address, and one of them to mortify his rising ambition, told him that he was an illegitimate child. This raised his doubts; he asked Peribœa who, out of tenderness, told him that his suspicions were ill founded. Not satisfied with this, he went te consult the oracle of Delphi, and was there told not to return home, for if he did, he must necessarily be the murderer of his father, and the husband of his mother. This answer of the oracle terrified him; he knew no home but the house of Polybus, therefore he resolved not to return to Corinth where such calamities apparently attended him. He travelled towards Phocis, and in his journey, met in a narrow road Laius, with his arm-bearer, in a chariot. Laius haughtily ordered Œdipus to make way for him. Œdipus refused, and a contest ensued, in which Laius and his arm-bearer were both killed. As Œdipus was ignorant of the quality and of the rank of the men whom he had just killed, he continued his journey, and was attracted to Thebes by the fame of the Sphynx. This terrible monster which Juno had sent to lay waste the country (*vid.* Sphynx), resorted to the neighbourhood of Thebes, and devoured all those who attempted to explain without success the ænigmas which he proposed. The calamity was now become an object of public concern, and as the successful explanation of an ænigma would end in the death of the Sphynx, Creon, who, at the death of Laius, had ascended the throne of Thebes, promised his crown and Jocasta to him who succeeded in the attempt. The ænigma proposed was this: What animal in the morning walks upon four feet, at noon upon two, and in the evening upon three? This was left for Œdipus to explain; he came to the monster and said, that man, in the morning of life, walks upon his hands and his feet; when he has attained the years of manhood, he walks upon his two legs; and in the evening, he supports his old age with the assistance of a staff. The monster, mortified at the true explanation, dashed his head against a rock, and perished. Œdipus ascended the throne of Thebes, and married Jocasta, by whom he had two sons, Polynices and Eteocles, and two daughters, Ismene and Antigone. Some years after, the Theban territories were visited with a plague; and the oracle declared that it should not cease till the murderer of king Laius was banished from Bœotia. As the death of Laius had never been examined into, and the circumstances that attended it were never known, this answer of the oracle was of the greatest concern to the Thebans; but Œdipus, the friend of the people, resolved to overcome every difficulty by the most exact inquiries. His researches were successful, and he was soon proved to be the murderer of his father. The melancholy discovery was rendered the more alarming, when Œdipus considered, that he had not only murdered his father, but that he had committed incest with his mother. In the excess of his grief he put out his eyes, as unworthy to see the light, and banished himself from Thebes, or as some say, was banished by his own sons. He retired towards Attica, led by his daughter Antigone, and came to Colonos, where there was a grove sacred to the Furies. He remembered that he was doomed by the oracle to die in such a place, and to become the source of prosperity to the country in which his bones were buried. A messenger upon this was sent to Theseus, king of the country, to inform him of the resolution of Œdipus. When Theseus arrived, Œdipus acquainted him, with a prophetic voice, that the gods had called him to die in the place where he stood; and to shew the truth of this he walked, himself, without the assistance of a guide, to the spot where he was to expire. Immediately the earth opened, and Œdipus disappeared. Some suppose that Œdipus had no children by Jocasta, and that the mother murdered herself as soon as she knew the incest which had been committed. His tomb was near the Areopagus, in the age of Pausanias. Some of the ancient poets represent him in hell, as suffering the punishment which crimes like his seemed to deserve. According to some his four children were borne to him by Euriganea, the daughter of Periphas, whom he married after the death of Jocasta. *Apollod.* 3. c. 5.—*Hygin.* fab. 66, &c.—*Eurip. in Phœniss.* &c.—*Sophocl. Œdip. Tyr. & Col. Antig.* &c.—*Hesiod. Theog.* 1.—*Homer. Odyss.* 11. v. 270.—*Paus.* 9. c. 5, &c.—*Stat. Theb.* 8 v. 642.—*Senec. in Œdip.*—*Pindar. Olymp.* 2.—*Diod.* 4.—*Lactant. in Argum. Œdip, Senec.*—*Sch. Eurip. Phœn.* 10, 50, 54 & 1591.—*Sch. Pindar. in Olpmp.* 2. v. 65.—*Sch. Aristoph. in Ran.* 1320.—*Tzetzes in Lycop.* 7, 437 & 1465.—*Servius ad Virg. Æn.* 4. v. 470.—*Athen.* 6 & 10.

Œ'ME, a daughter of Danaus, by Crino. *Apollod.*

Œ'NA, a river of Assyria. *Ammian.*

ŒNAN'THES, a favorite of young Ptolemy, king of Ægypt.

Œ'NE, a small town of Argolis. The people are called Œneadæ. *Steph.*

ŒNE'IS, one of the twelve tribes of Athens, so called from Œneus. *Paus. in Attic.*

Œ'NEUS, a king of Calydon in Ætolia, son of Parthaon or Portheus, and Euryte. He married Althæa, the daughter of Thestius, by whom he had Clymenus, Meleager, Gorge, and Dejanira. After Althæa's death, he married Peribœa, the daughter of Hipponous, by whom he had Tydeus. In a general sacrifice, which Œneus made to all the gods upon reaping the rich produce of his fields, he forgot Diana, and the goddess, to punish this unpardonable neglect, incited his neighbours to take up arms against him, and sent, moreover, a wild boar to lay waste the country of Calydonia. The animal was at last killed by Meleager and the neighbouring princes of Greece, in a celebrated chase known by the name of the chase of the Calydonian boar. Some time after, Meleager died, and Œneus was driven from his kingdom by the sons of his brother Agrius. Diomedes, his grandson, however, soon restored him to his throne; but the continual misfortunes to which he was exposed, rendered him melancholy. He exiled himself from Calydon, and left his crown to his son-in-law Andremon. He died as he was going to Argolis. His body was buried, by the care of Diomedes, in a town of Argolis, which from him received the name Œnoe. It is reported that Œneus received a visit from Bacchus, and that he suffered the god to enjoy the favours of Althæa, and to become the father of Dejanira, for which Bacchus permitted that the wine of which he was the patron, should be called among the Greeks by the name of Œneus (οἶνος) *Hygin.* fab. 129, 171, 174.—*Apollod.* 1. c. 8.—*Homer. Il.* 9. v. 539.—*Diod.* 4.—*Paus.* 2. c. 25.—*Ovid. Met.* 8. v. 510. *Fast.* 4. v. 76.—*Tzetzes. in Lycop.* 493.—*Sch. Apollon.* 3. v. 996.—*Servius. ad Virg. G.* 1. v. 8. l. 2. v. 98.

ŒNEUS or ŒNUS, a river of Liburnia, flowing into the Adriatic. *Ptol.* It is now Fiume di Carnero.

ŒNI'ADÆ, a town of Acarnania, near the Achelous. *Liv.* 26. c. 24. l. 38. c. 11.——A city of Thessaly, near mount Œta. *Steph.*

ŒNI'DES, a patronymic of Meleager, son of Œneus. *Ovid. Met.* 8. fab. 10.

ŒNISTE'RIA, a sacrifice offered by youths at Athens before they shaved their beards. *Hesych.*—*Jul. Pollux.*

Œ'NO, one of the daughters of Anius. *Vid.* Anius.

ŒNOAN'DA, a city of Carbalia, in Lycia, at the foot of mount Taurus. *Steph.*

ŒNOCHE'NUS, a river of Thessaly. *Herodot.* 7.

ŒN'OE, a nymph who married Sicinus, the son of Thoas, king of Lemnus. From her the island of Sicinus has been called Œnoe. *Paus.* 1. c. 33. l. 8. c. 47.—*Sch. Apollon.* 1.

ŒN'OE, the name of two villages of Attica, *Herodot.* 5. c. 74.—*Plin.* 4. c. 7.——A city of Argolis to which Œneus fled when driven from Calydon. *Apollod.* 2.—*Paus.* 2. c. 25.——A town of Elis, in the Peloponnesus. *Strab.*—*Apollod.* 1. c. 8.—*Paus.* 1, &c.

ŒNOM'AUS, a son of Mars by Sterope, the daughter of Atlas. He was king of Pisa, in Elis, and father of Hippodamia by Everete, daughter of Acrisius, or Eurythoa, the daughter of Danaus. He was informed by the oracle that he should perish by the hand of his son-in-law, therefore as he could skilfully drive a chariot, he determined to marry his daughter to him only who could outrun him, on condition that all who entered the lists should agree to lay down their life if conquered. Many had already perished, when Pelops, son of Tantalus, proposed himself. He previously bribed Myrtilus, the charioteer of Œnomaus, by promising him the enjoyment of the favors of Hippodamia, if he proved victorious. Myrtilus gave his master an old chariot, the axle-tree of which broke on the course, which was from Pisa to the Corinthian isthmus, and Ænomaus was killed. Pelops married Hippodamia, and became king of Pisa. As he expired, Œnomaus entreated Pelops to revenge the perfidy of Myrtilus, which was executed. Those who had been defeated when Pelops entered the lists, were Marmax, Alcathous, Euryalus, Eurymachus, Capetus, Lasius, Acrias, Chalcodon, Lycurgus, Tricolonus, Prias, Aristomachus, Æolius, Eurythrus, and Chronius. *Apollod.* 2. c. 4.—*Diod.* 4.—*Paus.* 5. c. 17. l. 6. c. 11, &c.—*Apollon. Rhod.* 1.—*Propert.* 1. el. 2. v. 20.—*Ovid. in Ib.* 367. *Art. Am.* 2. v. 8. *Heroid.* 8. v. 70. *Trist.* 2. v. 386.—*Lucan.* 2. v. 165.—*Tzetzes. in Lyc.* 156.—*Lactant. ad Theb.* 2. v. 166. l. 6. v. 283.—*Servius. in Æn.* 8. v. 130.—*Sch. Pind. Olymp.* 13.—*Hygin.* fab. 84. 253.—*Lucian. in Carid.*—*Philostr. Icon.* 1. c. 17.—*Palœph de Inc,* 30.

Œ'NON, a port of Locris on the bay of Corinth. *Thucyd.* 1. 3.

ŒNO'NA, an ancient name of the island Ægina. It is also called Œnopia. *Herodot.* 8. c. 46.—*Eustath. ad Dionys. Per.* 511.—*Plin.* 4. c. 17.——A town of Troas, the birth-place of the nymph Œnone. *Strab.* 13.

ŒNO'NE, a nymph of mount Ida, daughter of the river Cebrenus in Phrygia. As she had received the gift of prophecy, she foretold to Paris, whom she married before he was discovered to be the son of Priam, that his voyage into Greece would be attended with the most serious consequences, and the total ruin of his country, and that he should have recourse to her medicinal knowledge at the hour of his death. All these predictions were fulfilled; and Paris, when he had received the fatal wound, ordered his body to be carried to Œnone, in hopes of being cured by her assistance. He expired as he came into her presence, and Œnone was so struck at the sight of his dead body, that, after bathing it with her tears, she stabbed herself to the heart. She was mother of Corythus by Paris, and his son perished by the hand of his father, when he attempted, at the instigation of Ænone, to persuade him to withdraw his affections from Helen. *Dictys Cret.*—*Ovid. de Rem. Amor.* v. 457. *Heroid.* 5.—*Propert.* 2. el. 31.—*Apollod.* 3.—*Parthenius.* 4.—*Lucan.* 9.

ŒNOPH'YTA, a city of Bœotia. *Thucyd.*

ŒNO'PIA, one of the ancient names of the island of Ægina. *Ovid. Met.* 7. v. 473.

ŒNOP'IDES, a mathematician of Chius, who studied in Ægypt. *Diod.* 1.—*Euseb. Prœp. Ev.* 10. c. 2.

ŒNO'PION, a son of Ariadne by Theseus, or, according to others, by Bacchus. He married Helice, by whom he had a daughter called Hero, or Merope, of whom the giant Orion became enamoured. The father, unwilling to give his daughter to such a lover, and afraid of provoking him by an open refusal, evaded his applications, and at last put out his eyes when he was intoxicated. Some suppose that this violence was offered to Orion after he had dishonored Merope. Œnopion received the island of Chius from Rhadamanthus, who had conquered most of the islands of the Ægæan Sea, and his tomb was still seen there in the age of Pausanias. Some suppose, and with more probability, that he reigned not at Chius. but at Ægina, which was callen Œnopia from him. *Plut. in Thes.*—*Apollod.* 1. c. 4.—*Diod.*—*Paus.* 7. c. 4.—*Apollon. Rhod.* 3.—*Parthen. Erot.* 20.—*Sch. Apollon.* 3. v. 996.—*Ovid. Met.* 7. v. 472 & 490.

ŒNO'TRI, the inhabitants of Œnotria.

ŒNO'TRIA, a part of Italy which was afterwards called Lucania. It received this name from Œnotrus the son of Lycaon, who settled there with a colony of Arcadians The Œnotrians afterwards spread themselves into Umbria and as far as Latium, and the country of the Sabines, according to some writers. The name of Œnotria is sometimes applied to Italy. That part of Italy where Œnotrus settled, was before inhabited by the Ausones. *Dionys. Hal.* 1. c. 11.—*Paus.* 1. c. 3.—*Virg. Æn.* 1. v. 536. l. 7. v. 85.—*Ital.* 8. v. 220. l. 12 v. 587.—*Flacc.* 1. v. 589.

ŒNOT'RIDES, two small islands on the coast of Lucania, to which some of the Romans were banished by the emperors. They were called Iscia, now Ischia, and Pontia, now Ponza. *Plin.* 3. c. 7.—*Dio.* 59.

ŒNO'TRUS, a son of Lycaon of Arcadia. He passed into Magna Græcia with a colony, and gave the name of Œnotria to that part of the country in which he settled. *Dionys. Hal.* 1. c. 11.—*Paus.* 1. c. 3.

Œ'NUS, a town of Laconia. *Steph.*——A river of Laconia flowing near Sparta. *Polyb.*

ŒNUS'SA, an ancient name of Carthage. *Steph.*——The name of two islands in the Ægæan Sea; one between Tenedus and Samus, the other near Chius. They are called Œnusæ by *Stephanus.*

ŒNUS'SÆ or ŒNU'SÆ, three small islands on the coast of the Peloponnesus, near Messenia. *Mela,* 2. c. 17.—*Plin.* 4. c. 12.

ŒNU'CHUS, an infamous character mentioned by the *Scholiast. Aristoph. on Equit.*

ŒON, a village in the tribe Leontis. *Steph.*

ŒO'NUS, a son of Licymnius, killed at Sparta, to which city he had accompanied Hercules. As the hero had promised Licymnius to bring back his son, he burnt his body and presented the ashes to the afflicted father. From this circumstance arose the custom of burning the dead among the Greeks. *Sch. Hom. Il.* 1.—*Eustath. ibid.*

ŒO'NUS, a small river of Laconia. *Liv.* 34. c. 28.

Œ'OS, a town of Tegea. *Steph.*

ŒR'OE, an island of Bœotia, formed by the Asopus. *Herodot.* 9. c. 50. It is called Ærya by *Pausanias*, l. 9.

ŒS'PORIS, an inland town of Africa. *Ptol.* It is now Sibaca.

ŒS'TRUS, a river of Pamphylia. *Ptol. Mela*, 1. c. 14.

ŒTA, now Banina, a celebrated mountain between Thessaly and Macedonia, upon which Hercules burnt himself. Its height has given occasion to the poets to feign, that the sun, moon and stars rose behind it. Mount Æta, properly speaking, is a long chain of mountains which run from the straits of Thermopylæ and the Gulph of Malia, in a western direction, to mount Pindus, and thence to the bay of Ambracia. The straits or passes of mount Œta are called the straits of Thermopylæ from the hot baths and mineral waters which are in the neighbourhood. These passes are not more than twenty-five feet in breadth. *Mela*, 2. c. 3. —*Catull.* 66. v. 54.—*Apollod.* 2. c. 7.—*Paus.* 7. c. 15. 10. l. c. 20, &c.—*Ovid. Heroid.* 9. *Met.* 2. v. 216. l. 9. v. 204, &c.—*Virg. Ecl.* 8. v. 30.—*Plin.* 25. c. 5.—*Seneca in Med.*—*Lucan.* 3. v. 178. l. 6. v. 389. l. 7. v. 449, &c.—*Servius ad Virg. loco. cit.* & *Æn.* 3. v. 402. l. 8. v. 300.—*Sophoc. in Phil.* 725. —*Aug. de Civ. D.* 18. c. 4.—*Turneb. Adv.* 35. c. 25. ——A small town at the foot of mount Œta near Thermopylæ.

ŒTEN'SII, a people of Lower Mysia. *Ptol.*

Œ'TUS or O'TUS, a giant. *Vid.* Otus.

ŒT'YLUS or ŒT'YLUM, a town of Laconia, which received its name from Œtylus, one of the heroes of Argos. Serapis had a temple there. *Paus.* 3. c. 25.

ŒZE'NIS, a city of Pontus, called also Trapezus. *Steph.*

OFEL'LUS, a man whom, though unpolished, Horace represents as exemplary for wisdom, economy, and moderation. *Horat.* 2. sat. 2. v. 2.

OFIL'IUS, a person mentioned by *Cicero*, *Fam.* 16. ep. 24.——A lawyer. *Cic. Fam.* 7. ep. 21. *Attic.* 13. ep. 37.

O'FI, a nation of ancient Germany. *Tacit. de Germ.* 28.

OGDOL'APIS, a navigable river flowing from the Alps. *Strab.* 6.

OGDO'MI, a people of Marmarica. *Ptol.*

OGDO'US, a king of Ægypt, surnamed Nogæus. *Diod. Sic.* 1, 2.

OGLA'MUS, a mountain of Marmarica. *Ptol.*

OGLA'SA, an island in the Tyrrhene Sea, east of Corsica, famous for wine, and now called Monte Christo. *Plin.* 3. c. 6.

OG'MIUS, a name of Hercules among the Gauls. He was considered by this nation as the god of eloquence and of persuasion, and thence, as reason and the oratorical powers more particularly belong to age, he was represented under the form of an old man, bald and wrinkled, from whose mouth hung suspended a gold chain, which communicated by a thousand others to the ears of an innumerable crowd, who followed without reluctance whatever direction they received. The god wore a lion's skin and a quiver, whilst he held a bow in one hand and his club in the other. *Lucian. in Herc. Gall.*—*Cœl. Rhod.* 6. c. 7.

OGO'AS, a deity of Mylassa in Caria, under whose temple, as it was supposed, the sea passed. *Paus.* 8. c. 10.

OGUL'NIA LEX was introduced by Q. and Cn. Ogulnius, tribunes of the people, A.U.C. 453. It increased the number of pontifices and augurs from four to nine. The addition was made to both orders from plebeian families.

OGUL'NIA, a Roman lady as poor as she was lascivious. *Juv.* 6. v. 351.

OG'YGES, a celebrated monarch, the most ancient of those that reigned in Greece. He was son of Terra, or, as some suppose, of Neptune, and married Thebe the daughter of Jupiter. He reigned in Bœotia, which, from him, is sometimes called Ogygia, and his power was also extended over Attica. It is supposed he was of Ægyptian or Phœnician extraction; but his origin, as well as the age in which he lived, and the duration of his reign are so obscure and unknown, that the epithet of Ogygian is often applied to everything of remote antiquity. In the reign of Ogyges there was a deluge, which so inundated the territories of Attica, that they remained waste for nearly 200 years. This, though it is very uncertain, is supposed to have happened about 1764 years B.C., previous to the deluge of Deucalion. According to some-writers, it was owing to the overflowing of one of the rivers of the country. The reign of Ogyges was also marked by an uncommon appearance in the heavens, and, as it is reported, the planet Venus changed her color, diameter, figure, and course. *Varro. de. R.R.* 3. c. 1.—*Paus.* 9. c. 5. —*Aug. de Civ. D.* 18. c. 8. & *Varro. apud Aug.* 21. c. 8.—*Censorin. de Die Nat.*—*Festus de V. Sig.*—*Strab.* 9.—*Servius. ad Virg. Ec.* 6. v. 41.—*Suidas.* —*Hesychius.*

OGYG'IA, a name of one of the gates of Thebes in Bœotia. *Lucan.* 1. v. 675.——An ancient name of Bœotia, from Ogyges, who reigned there.——The island of Calypso, opposite the promontory of Lacinium in Magna Græcia, where Ulysses was shipwrecked. The situation, and even the existence of Calypso's island, is disputed by some writers. *Plin.* 3. c. 10.—*Homer. Odyss.* 1. v. 52 & 85. l. 5. v. 254. *Callim. in Jov.* 14. *In Del.* 160.—*Mela*, 2. c. 7.—*Philostr. Her.* 10.

OGYG'IA, one of the daughters of Niobe, and Amphion, changed into stones. *Apollod.*—*Paus.*

OGYG'IUS, a surname of Bacchus as worshipped in Thebes, called Ogygia. *Ovid Heroid.* 10. v. 48.

OG'YLUS, an island between Peloponnesus and Crete. *Steph.*

OG'YRIS, an island in the Indian Ocean, opposite Arabia Felix. *Dionys. Perieg.* v. 607. It is now Gerun.

OIC'LEUS or O'ICLEUS, a son of Antiphates and Zeuxippe, who married Hypermnestra, daughter of Thestius, by whom he had Iphianira, Polybœa, and Amphiraus. He was killed by Laomedon when defending the ships which had brought Hercules to Asia, when he made war against Troy. *Homer. Odyss.* 15. v. 243.—*Diod.* 4.—*Apollod.* 1. c. 8. l. 3. c. 6.—*Paus.* 6. c. 17.

OIL'EUS or OI'LEUS, a king of the Locrians. His father's name was Odoedocus, and his mother's Agrianome. He married Eriope, by whom he had Ajax, called Oileus, from his father, to discriminate him from Ajax the son of Telamon. He had also another son called Medon, by a courtezan called Rhene. Oileus was one of the Argonauts. *Virg.* 1. v. 45.—*Apollon.* 1.—*Hygin.* fab. 14 & 18. —*Homer. Il.* 13. v. 697. l. 15. v. 536.—*Apollod.* 3. c. 10.—*Flacc.* 1. v. 372.

O'JUM, a fortified place of Bœotia, near Opus. *Strab.*

OL'ABI, a people of Upper Æthiopia. *Plin.* 6. c. 30.

OLA'CHAS, a river of Bithynia, the waters of which were said to discover perjured people. *Plin.* 31. c. 2.

OL'ANE, one of the mouths of the Po. It is called Olone by *Polybius*, and is now Volana.——A city of Armenia Major. *Strab.*

OLA'NUS, a town of Lesbus.

OLA'PIA, a city of Arabia Felix. *Ptol.*

OLAS'TRÆ, a people of India. *Lucan.* 3. v. 249.—*Plin.* 6. c. 20.

OL'BA, a town of Cilicia. *Strab.*

OL'BASA or OL'BUS, a city of Cilicia. *Strab.*

OLBE'LUS, a city of Macedonia. *Steph.*

OL'BI, a city of Ægypt, near Libya. *Steph.*

OL'BIA, a town of Sarmatia at the confluence of the Hypanis and the Borysthenes, about fifteen miles from the sea, according to Pliny. It was afterwards called Borysthenes, and Miletopolis, because peopled by a Milesian colony, and is now supposed to be Oczakow. *Strab.* 7.—*Plin.* 4. c. 12.——A town of Bithynia on the Propontis, near Nicæa and Apamea. *Mela*, 1. c. 19.——A town of Gallia Narbonensis. *Mela*, 2. c. 5.—*Ptol.* 5. c. 5.—*Strab.* 4. It is now Hyeres.——The capital of Sardinia, on the eastern coast, the residence of the governor. Q. Cicero resided there in that capacity. *Cic. ad Q. Frat.* 2. ep. 3, 6, 8.—*Claudian. de Bell. Gild.* 519.

OLBISIN'II or **OLBIS'II**, a people near the columns of Hercules. *Steph.*

OL'BIUS, a river of Arcadia. *Paus.* 8. c. 14.

OL'BUS, one of the auxiliaries of Æetes, slain by Colaxes. *Val. Fl.* 6. v. 638.

OLCACHI'TES, a bay of Zeugitana. *Ptol.*

OL'CADES, a people of Spain within the Iberus. *Stephanus* calls their city Althæa.

OLCHIN'IUM or **OLCIN'IUM**, now Dulcigno, a town of Dalmatia, at the north of Dyrrachium, on the Adriatic. *Liv.* 45. c. 26.

OL'CION, a city of the Tyrrhenians. *Steph.*

OLE'ADES, a people of Spain. *Liv.* 21. c. 5.

OLE'AROS or **OLI'AROS**, one of the Cyclades, about sixteen miles in circumference, separated from Parus by a strait of seven miles. *Virg. Æn.* 3. v. 126.—*Ovid. Met.* 7. v. 469.—*Strab.* 10.—*Plin.* 4. c. 12.—*Mela*, 2. c. 7.—*Stat. Ach.* 2. v. 3.

OLEAS'TRUM, a town of Spain, near the Sinus Gaditanus. *Ptol.*——A city of the Turdetani, in Hispania Bætica.——A promontory of Mauritania Tingitana, now Capo di Gebba.

OLE'ATRUM, a town of Spain near Saguntum. *Strab.*

O'LEN, a Greek poet of Lycia, who flourished some time before the age of Orpheus, and composed many hymns, some of which were regularly sung at Delphi on solemn occasions. Some suppose that he was the first who established the oracle of Apollo at Delphi, where he first delivered oracles. *Herodot.* 4. 35.—*Paus.* 1. c. 18. 1. 9. c. 27.—*Callim. in Del.* 304.

OLE'NIUS, a Lemnian, killed by his wife. *Val. Fl.* 2. v. 164.

OLEN'NIUS, an officer who incited the Frisii to rebellion. *Tac. Ann.* 4. c. 72.

OL'ENUS, a son of Vulcan, who married Lethæa, a beautiful woman, who preferred herself to the goddesses. She and her husband were changed into stones by the offended deities. *Ovid. Met.* 10. v. 68.——A famous soothsayer of Etruria. *Plin.* 28. c. 2.

Ol'enus, a town of Ætolia, between Calydon and Chalcis on the Evenus. It is now Oleno.——A city of Galatia. *Ptol.*

Ol'enus or **Ol'enum**, a town of Peloponnesus between Patræ and Cyllene. The goat Amalthæa, which was made a constellation by Jupiter, is called Olenia, from its residence there. Hercules was hospitably entertained there by Dexamenes, one of the kings of the country, for which he liberally rewarded his friend. *Plin.* 4. c. 5.—*Ovid. Fast.* 5. v. 113.—*Stat. Theb.* 3. v. 25.—*Senec. in Med.* 313.—*Paus.* 7. c. 22.—*Strab.* 8.—*Apollod.* 1 c. 8.

OLE'ORUS or **OLI'ARUS**, one of the Cyclades, now Anti Paro.

OL'ERUS, a city of Crete, whence Minerva was called Oleria, and a festival in honor of her, Olerium. *Steph.*

OL'GASYS, a mountain of Galatia, called by *Ptolemy* Olyssa, from which the Halys and Parthenius flow. *Strab.*

O'LIA, a city of Mesopotamia, *Ptol.*

OL'IBA, a city of Hispania Tarraconensis. *Ptol.* It is now Oliva. *Ferrar.*

OLIC'ANA, a city of Britain. *Ptol.* It is now Ilkely according to *Camden*, Halifax according to others.

OLIGYR'TUS, a town of Peloponnesus, *Polyb.* By others it is called Ologuntum.

OLI'NA, a river of Gallia Lugdunensis. *Ptol.* It is now Orne.

OLIN'THUS or **OLYN'THUS**, a town of Macedonia. *Vid.* Olynthus.

OLISI'PO, now Lisbon, a town of ancient Spain, on the Tagus, surnamed Felicitas Julia, (*Plin.* 4. c. 22.) and called by some Ulyssippo, and said to have been founded by Ulysses. *Mela*, 3. c. 1.—*Solinus*, 23.

OLITIN'GI, a town of Lusitania. *Mela*, 3. c. 1.

OLI'ZON, a town of Magnesia in Thessaly. *Homer. Il.* 2. v. 717.

OLLICULA'NI, a people of Italy. *Plin.* 3. c. 5.

OL'LINA, a city near the Caspian Sea. *Steph.*

OL'LIUS T., the father of Poppæa, destroyed on account of his intimacy with Sejanus, &c. *Tacit. Ann.* 13. c. 45. *Lipsius* reads Ellius, and *Muretus* T. Ælius.

Ol'lius, a river rising in the Alps, and falling into the Po, now called the Oglio. *Plin.* 2. c. 103.

OLLOV'ICO, a prince of Gaul, called the friend of the republic by the Roman senate. *Cæs. B. Gall.* 7. c. 31.

OLME'JUS, a river flowing from mount Helicon, sacred to the Muses. *Barth. ad Stat. Theb.* 7. v. 284.—*Boccat. de Flum.*

OL'MIA or **HOL'MIA**, a city of Cilicia, afterwards called Seleucia. *Plin.* 5. c. 27.—*Salmas. ad Solin.* p. 619.

OL'MIÆ, a promontory near Megara, on the Sinus Saronicus. *Strab.*

OL'MIUS. *Vid.* Olmejus.

OLMO'NES, a city of Bœotia. *Steph.*

OLOARI'TUS, a centurion of the fleet at Misenum. *Tacit. Ann.* 14. c. 8.

OLOB'AGRA, a city of Macedonia. *Steph.*

OLOCH'ARA, a city of India within the Ganges. *Ptol.*

OLOES'SA, an island near Rhodes. *Plin.* 5. c. 31.

OLON'DÆ, a people of Asiatic Sarmatia. *Ptol.*

OLOOS'SON, now Alessone, a town of Magnesia. *Hom. ap Steph.* We should probably read Oloesson.

OLOPHYX'US, a town of Macedonia on mount Athos. *Herodot.* 7. c. 22.

OL'PÆ, a fortified place of Epirus, now Forte Castri, or Soporto according to *Niger*.

OLU'LIS, a city of Crete. *Ptol.*——A city of Sicily. *Id.* It is now Olulo.

OLU'RUS, a town of Achaia, not far from Pallene. *Steph.*

O'LUS, (*-untis*). a town at the west of Crete. *Steph.*

OL'YCA, a city of Macedonia. *Steph. in Theopompo.*

OLYMPE'NE, a city of Mysia, near Olympus. *Plin.* 5. c. 32.

OLYM'PEUM, a place in Delus. *Steph.*——Another in Syracuse. *Thucyd.* 6 & 7.—*Diod. Sic.* 16.

OLYM'PIA (*-orum*), celebrated games which received their name either from Olympia where they were observed, or from Jupiter Olympius, to whom they were dedicated. They were, according to some, instituted by Jupiter after his victory over the Titans, and first observed by the Idæi Dactyli, B.C. 1453. Some attribute the institution to Pelops, after he had obtained the victory over Œnomaus and married Hippodamia; but the more probable, and indeed the more received opinion is, that they were first established by Hercules in honor of Jupiter Olympius, after a victory obtained over Augias, B.C. 1222. Strabo objects to this opinion by observing, that if they had been established in the age of Homer, the poet would have undoubtedly spoken of them, as he is in every particular careful to mention the amusements and diversions of the ancient Greeks. But they were neglected after their first institution by Hercules, and no notice was taken of them, according to many writers, till Iphitus, in the age of the lawgiver of Sparta, renewed them, and revived the celebration with greater solemnity. This re-institution, which happened B.C. 884, forms a celebrated epoch in Grecian history, and is the beginning of the Olympiads. *Vid.* Olympias. They, however, were neglected for some time after the age of Iphitus, till Corœbus, who obtained a victory B.C. 776, re-instituted them to be regularly and constantly celebrated. The care and superintendence of the games were entrusted to the people of Elis, till they were excluded by the Pisæans, B.C. 364, after the destruction of Pisa. They obtained great privileges from this appointment; they were in danger neither of violence nor war, but were permitted to enjoy their possessions without molestation, as the games were celebrated within their territories. Only one person superintended till the 50th Olympiad, when two were appointed. In the 103rd Olympiad, the number was increased to twelve, according to the number of the tribes of Elis. But in the following Olympiad, they were reduced to eight, and afterwards increased to ten, which number continued till the reign of Adrian. The presidents were obliged solemnly to swear that they would act impartially, and not take any bribes, or discover why they rejected some of the combatants. They generally sat naked, and held before them the crown which was prepared for the conqueror. There were also certain officers to keep good order and regularity called ἄλυται, much the same as the Roman lictors; of whom the chief was called ἀλυτάρχης. No women were permitted to appear at the celebration of the Olympian games, and whoever dared to trespass this law was immediately thrown down from a rock. This, however, was sometimes neglected, for we find not only women present at the celebration, but some also among the combatants, and rewarded with the crown. The preparations for these festivals were great. No person was permitted to enter the lists if he had not regularly exercised himself ten months before the celebration at the public gymnasium of Elis. No unfair dealings were allowed, and whoever attempted to bribe his adversary, was subjected to a severe fine. No criminals, or such as were connected with impious and guilty persons, were suffered to present themselves as candidates; and even the father and relations were obliged to swear that they would have recourse to no artifice which might decide the victory in favor of their friends. The wrestlers were appointed by lot. Some little balls superscribed with a letter, were thrown into a silver urn, and such as drew the same letter were obliged to contend one with the other. He who had an odd letter remained the last, and he often had the advantage, as he was to encounter the last who had obtained the superiority over his adversary. He was called ἔφεδρος. In these games were exhibited running, leaping, wrestling, boxing, and the throwing of the quoit, which was called altogether πένταθλον, or *quinquertium.* Besides these, there were horse and chariot races, and also contentions in poetry, eloquence, and the fine arts. The only reward that the conqueror obtained, was a crown of olive; which, as some suppose, was in memory of the labors of Hercules, which were accomplished for the universal good of mankind, and for which the hero claimed no other reward but the consciousness of having been the friend of humanity. So small and trifling a reward stimulated courage and virtue, and excited more emulation than the most unbounded treasures. The statues of the conquerors, called Olympionicæ, were erected at Olympia, in the sacred wood of Jupiter. Their return home was that of a warlike conqueror; they were drawn in a chariot by four horses, and every where received with the greatest acclamations. Their entrance into their native city was not through the gates, but, to make it more grand and solemn, a breach was made in the walls. Painters and poets were employed in celebrating their names; and indeed the victories severally obtained at Olympia are the subjects of the most beautiful odes of Pindar. The combatants were naked; a scarf was originally tied round their waist, but when it had entangled one of the adversaries, and been the cause that he lost the victory, it was laid aside, and no regard was paid to decency. The Olympic games were observed every fifth year, or, to speak with greater exactness, after a revolution of four years, and in the first month of the fifth year, and they continued for five successive days. As they were the most ancient and the most solemn of all the festivals of the Greeks, it will not appear wonderful that they drew so many people together, not only inhabitants of Greece, but of the neighbouring islands and countries. *Pind. Olym.—Strab.* 8.—*Paus.* 5. c. 67, &c.—*Diod.* 1, &c.—*Plut. in Thes. Lyc.* &c.—*Ælian. V. H.* 10. v. 1.—*Cic. Tusc.* 1. c. 46.—*Lucian. de Gym*—*Tzetz. in Lycophr.*—*Aristotel.*—*Stat. Theb.* 6.—*C. Nep. in Præf.*—*Virg. G.* 3. v. 49.—*Cœl. Rhod.* 12, c. 19.—*Xenoph. de Laced.*—*Aristoph. in Plut.* 586.—*Vitruv. in Præf.* 9. *de Arch.*

Olym'pia, a town of Elis in Peloponnesus, where Jupiter had a temple with a celebrated statue 50 cubits high, reckoned one of the seven wonders of the world. The Olympic games were celebrated in the neighbourhood. *Strab.* 8.—*Paus.* 3. c. 8.

OLYM'PIAS, a certain space of time which elapsed between the celebration of the Olympic games. The Olympic games were celebrated after the expiration of four complete years, whence some have said that they were observed every fifth year. This period of time was called an Olympiad, and became a celebrated era among the Greeks, who computed their time by it. The custom of reckoning time by the celebration of the Olympic games was not introduced at the first institution of these festivals, but, to speak accurately, only in the year in which Corœbus obtained the prize. This Olympiad, which has always been reckoned the first, was, according to the accurate and learned computations of some of the moderns, exactly 776 years B.C., in the year of the Julian period 3938, and 23 years before the building of Rome. The games were exhibited at the time of the full moon after the summer solstice; therefore the Olympiads were of unequal lengths, because the time of the full moon differs 11 days every year, and for that reason they sometimes began the next day after the solstice, and at other times four weeks after. The computations by Olympiads ceased, as some suppose, after the 34th, in the year 440 A.D. It was universally adopted, not only by the Greeks, but by many of the neighbouring countries, though the Pythian games served as an epoch to the people of Delphi and to the Bœotians, the Nemean games to the Argives and Arcadians, and the Isthmian to the Corinthians, and the inhabitants of the Peloponnesian isthmus. To the Olympiads history is much indebted. They have served to fix the time of many momentous events, and indeed before this method of computing time was observed, every page of history is mostly fabulous, and filled with obscurity and contradiction, and no true chronological acconnt can be properly established and maintained with certainty. The mode of computation, which was used after the suppression of the Olympiads and of the consular fasti of Rome, was more useful as it was more universal; but while the era of the creation of the world prevailed in the East, the western nations in the 6th century began to adopt with more propriety the Christian epoch, which was used in historical writings in the 8th century, and in the 10th became legal and popular.

Olym'pias, a celebrated woman who was daughter of a king of Epirus, and who married Philip king of Macedonia, by whom she had Alexander the Great. Her haughtiness, and more probably, her infidelity, obliged Philip to repudiate her, and to marry Cleopatra, the niece of king Attalus. Olympias was sensible of this injury, and Alexander showed his disapprobation of his father's measures by retiring from the court to his mother. The murder of Philip which soon followed this disgrace, and which some have attributed to the intrigues of Olympias, was productive of the greatest extravagancies. The queen paid the highest honor to her husband's murderer. She gathered his mangled limbs, placed a crown of gold on his head, and laid his ashes near those of Philip. When Alexander was dead, Olympias seized the government of Macedonia, and to establish her usurpation, cruelly put to death Aridæus, with his wife Eurydice, as also Nicanor, the brother of Cassander, with 100 leading men of Macedon, who were inimical to her interest. Such barbarities did not long remain unpunished; Cassander besieged her in Pydna, whither she had retired with the remains of her family, and she was obliged to surrender after an obstinate siege. The conqueror ordered her to be accused, and to be put to death. A body of 200 soldiers were directed to put the bloody commands into execution, but the splendor and majesty of the queen disarmed their courage, and she was at last massacred by those whom she had cruelly deprived of their children, about 316 years B.C. *Justin.* 7. c. 6. l. 9. c. 7. l. 14. c. 6.—*Plut. in Alex.*—*Curt.*—*Cic. Div.* 1. c. 23.—*Paus.*—*Aul. Gell.* 13. c. 4.

Olym'pias, a fountain of Arcadia, which flowed for one year and the next was dry. *Paus.* 8. c. 29.

OLYMPIODO'RUS, a musician, who taught Epaminondas music. *C. Nep.*—*Athen.* 4.——A native of Thebes in Ægypt, who flourished under Theodosius the Second, and wrote 22 books of history, in Greek, beginning with the seventh consulship of Honorius, and the second of Theodosius, and continued to the period at which Valentinian was made emperor. He wrote also an account of an embassy to some of the barbarian nations of the north, besides the life of Plato, &c. His style is censured by some as low, and unworthy of an historian. The commentaries of Olympiodorus on the Meteora of Aristotle, were edited apud Ald. 1550, in fol. *Voss. H. Gr.* 2. c. 20.—*Fabr. B. Gr.* 5. c. 5, &c.—*Sax. Onom.* 1. p. 491.——An Athenian officer, present at the battle of Platæa, where he behaved with great valor. *Plut.*——A physician. *Plin.* 1. c. 12 ——A peripatetic philosopher of Alexandria, preceptor of Proclus, who wrote some commentaries on the works of Aristotle and Plato, A.D. 480. *Laert. in Plato.*

OLYM'PIUS, a surname of Jupiter at Olympia, where the god had a celebrated temple and statue, which passed for one of the seven wonders of the world. It was the work of Phidias, and made of gold and ivory, and of the height of 60 feet. *Homer. Odyss.* 4. v. 74 & 173.—*Paus.* 7. c. 2. [The finest statue of Jupiter now extant, that in the Vatican, removed from the Verospi Palace, also the colossal bust in the same Museum, are supposed to be copied from this celebrated statue of Phidias.]——A native of Carthage, called also Nemesianus. *Vid.* Nemesianus.——A favorite at the court of Honorius, who was the cause of Stilicho's death.

OLYM'PUS, a physician of Cleopatra, queen of Ægypt, who wrote some historical treatises. *Plut. in Anton.*——A poet and musician of Mysia, son of Mæon and disciple of Marsyas. He lived before the Trojan war, and distinguished himself by his amatory elegies, his hymns, and particularly by the beautiful airs which he composed, which were still preserved in the age of Aristophanes. *Plato in Min. De Ione. De Leg.* 3.—*Aristot. Pol.* 8. c. 5. —*Philostrat. Icon.* 1. c. 21.—*Aristophan. in Equit* 9. *& Schol. loco.*—*Ovid. Met.* 6. v. 393. *De Ponto*, 3. el. 3.—*Hygin.* fab. 165.—*Plut. de Mus.*——A musician of Phrygia, who lived in the age of Midas. He is frequently confounded with the preceding. *Pollux.* 4. c. 10.—*Gyrald. de P. H.* 2.—*Fabric B. Gr.*——A son of Hercules and Eubœa. *Apollod.*

OLYM'PUS, a mountain of Macedonia and Thessaly, now Lacha. The ancients supposed that it touched the heavens with its top; and, from that circumstance, they have placed the residence of the gods there, and have made it the court of Jupiter. It is about one mile and a half in perpendicular height, and is covered with pleasant woods, caves, and grottoes. On the top of the mountain, according to the notions of the poets, there was neither wind nor rain, nor clouds, but an eternal spring. *Homer. Il.* 1. v. 44. 1. 5. v. 753. l. 8. v. 3 & 349, &c. —*Claudian. de Mal. Theod. Cons.* 206.—*Stat. Theb.* 2. v. 35.—*Val. Flacc.* 1. v. 199. l. 5. v. 1, &c. —*Virg. Æn.* 2. v. 779. l. 6, v. 586. l. 10. v. 1.—*Ovid. Met.*—*Lucan.* 5. v. 620.—*Mela*, 2. c. 3.— —*Strab.* 8.——A mountain of Mysia, called the Mysian Olympus.——A mountain of Elis.——A mountain of Arcadia.——A mountain of the island of Cyprus, now Santa Croce. Some suppose the Olympus of Mysia and of Cilicia to be the same. The *Scholiast* on *Apollonius* enumerates six mountains of this name, others only four.——A town on the coast of Lycia. *Strab.*—*Plin.* 5. c. 27.—*Salmas. ad Solin.* p. 102.

OLYMPU'SA, a daughter of Thespius. *Apollod.*

OLYN'THUS, a celebrated town and republic of Macedonia, on the isthmus of the peninsula of Pallene. It was famous for its advantageous situation, and for its frequent disputes with the Athenians, the Lacedæmonians, and king Philip, who destroyed it, and sold the inhabitants for slaves. *Cic. in Verr.* 3. c. 21.—*Plut. de Ir. Coh. &c.*—*Mela*, 2. c. 2.—*Herodot.* 1. c. 127.—*Curt.* 8. c. 9.

OLY'RAS, a river near Thermopylæ, which, as the mythologists report, attempted to extinguish the funeral pile on which Hercules was consumed. *Strab.* 9.

OLYS'SE, a city of Crete. *Strab.*

OLY'ZON. *Vid.* Olizon.

OMA'LIS, a river of India, emptying itself into the Ganges. *Arrian. in Ind.*

OMA'NA, a city of Arabia Felix. *Steph. Ptolemy* calls it Omanum, and the people Omanitæ, but *Pliny*, 6. c. 28., calls them Omani. It is now Omanagda.

OMA'RIUM, a city of Thessaly, in which Jupiter and Pallas were worshipped. *Steph.*

OMA'RIUS, a Lacedæmonian sent ambassador to Darius, and taken by Parmenio at Damascus. *Curt.* 3. c. 13. Some read Monimus.

OM'BI and TENTY'RA, two neighbouring cities of Ægypt, the inhabitants of which were always in discord one with another. *Juv.* 15. v. 35.

OMBRE'A, a city of Mesopotamia. *Ptol.*

OM'BRI. *Vid.* Umbri.

OM'BRIOS, one of the Fortunate Islands. *Plin.* 6. c. 32. It is called Porto Santo by *Niger*, who thinks it to be the Aprositos of *Ptolemy*.

OMBRO'NES, a people of European Sarmatia. *Plin.* 4. c. 12.

OM'BRUS, a river of Italy. *Steph.*

OMENOG'ARA, a city of India within the Ganges. *Ptol.*

OMI'ZA, a town of Gedrosia. *Id.*

OM'NÆ, a town of the Amani, in Arabia Felix. *Plin.* 6. c. 28.

OMOE'NUS, an island of Arabia Felix, in the Persian Gulph. *Id.* 6. c. 28.

OM'OLE or HOM'OLE, a mountain of Thessaly. *Virg. Æn.* 7. v. 675.

OMOLO'IA or HOMOLO'IA, a festival at Thebes, in honor of Jupiter Homoloius, or Ceres Homoloia, who were so called from Homole in Bœotia, or the prophetess Homoloia, or from Ὁμολος, which in the Æolian dialect signifies *peaceable*. *Theocr. Schol. Idyl.* 8.

OMOPHA'GIA, a festival in honor of Bacchus. The word signifies, *esus crudarum carnium*, the eating of raw flesh. *Clem. Protrept.*—*Arnob.* 1. 5. *Vid.* Dionysia.

OM'PHACE, a city of Sicily. *Steph.*

OM'PHALE or OMPHA'LE, *Propert*, a queen of Lydia, daughter of Jardanus. She married Tmolus, who, at his death, left her mistress of his kingdom. Omphale had been informed of the great exploits of Hercules, and wished to see so illustrious a hero. Her wish was soon gratified. After the murder of Eurytus, Hercules fell sick, and was ordered to be sold as a slave, that he might recover his health and the right use of his senses. Mercury was commissioned to sell him, and Omphale bought him, and restored him to liberty. The hero became enamoured of his mistress, and the queen favored his passion, and had a son by him, whom some call Agelaus, and others Lamon. From this son were descended Gyges and Crœsus; but this opinion is at variance with the account which makes these Lydian monarchs spring from Alcæus, a son of Hercules, by Malis, one of the female servants of Omphale. Hercules is represented by the poets as so desperately enamoured of the queen that, to conciliate her esteem, he spins by her side among her women, while she covers herself with the lion's skin, and arms herself with the club of the hero, and often strikes him with her sandals for the uncouth manner in which he holds the distaff, &c. Their fondness for each other was mutual. As they once travelled together, they came to a grotto on mount Tmolus, where the queen dressed herself in the habit of her lover, and obliged him to appear in a female garment. After they had supped, they both retired to rest in different rooms, as a sacrifice on the morrow to Bacchus required. In the night, Faunus, or according to others, Pan, who was enamoured of Omphale, introduced himself into the cave. He went to the bed of the queen, but the lion's skin persuaded him that it was the dress of Hercules, and therefore he repaired to the bed of Hercules, in hopes to find there the object of his affection. The female dress of Hercules deceived him, and he laid himself down by his side. The hero awaking, kicked the intruder into the middle of the cave. The noise awoke Omphale, and Faunus was discovered lying on the ground greatly disappointed and ashamed. *Ovid. Fast.* 2. v. 305, &c.—*Apollod.* 1. c. 9. l. 2. c. 7.—*Diod.* 4.—*Propert.* 3. el. 11. v. 17.—*Servius in Æn.* 8. v. 300.—*Hygin.* fab. 32. *P. A.* 2. c. 14.—*Seneca in Hipp.* 317. *In Herc. Fur.* 465.—*Palæph.* 45.—*Schol. Hom. Odyss.* 21. v. 23.—*Lucian. de Mod. Scrib. Hist.*—*Terent. in Eun.* 5. sc. 8. [There is a head of Omphale in the Musée Royale at Paris]

OM'PHALOS, a place of Crete, sacred to Jupiter, on the borders of the river Triton. It received its name from the unbilical cord (ὀμφαλός) of Jupiter which fell there soon after his birth. *Diod.* 5.

OM'PHIS, a king of India, who delivered himself up to Alexander the Great. *Curt.* 8. c. 12. *Diodorus Siculus*, l. 17. calls him Mophis.

ON'ABA, a city of Spain. *Ptol.*

ONÆ'UM or OÆ'NEUM, a promontory and town of Dalmatia on the Adriatic. *Liv.* 43. c. 19. The modern name is Cabo Cumano, or Cabo Lovischa, according to some.

ON'ARUS or ONA'RUS, a priest of Bacchus, who is supposed to have married Ariadne, after she had been abandoned by Theseus. *Plut. in Thes.*

ONAS'IMUS, a sophist of Cyprus or of Sparta, who flourished in the reign of Constantine, and wrote several works on the art of oratory. *Suidas.*——An historian. *Vid.* Onesimus.

ONA'TAS, a famous statuary of Ægina, son of Micon. He made a statue of Ceres for the people of Phigalia, and also a brazen chariot drawn by two horses, which was consecrated by Dinamenes, according to the wishes of Hiero his father, to Jupiter Olympius, and which long continued to be the admiration of travellers. He also made equestrian statues for the Tarentines, which were placed in the temple of Delphi. *Plin.* 34. c. 8.—*Paus.* 8. c. 42.

ON'CA, the name of Minerva among the Phœnicians. *Nonn. Dion.* l. 44.—*Selden. de Dis Syr. Syntag.* 2. c. 4, &c.

ON'CÆ, a city of Arcadia. *Isac. in Lycophr.*

ONCÆ'UM, a small region of Arcadia. *Steph.*

ONCHEMI'TES, a wind which blows from Onchesmus, a harbour of Epirus, towards Italy. The word is sometimes spelt Anchesites and Anchemites. *Cic. ad Attic.* 7. ep. 2.—*Ptolemæus.*

ONCHES'TIA, a Bœotian festival in honor of Neptune, surnamed Onchestius from the town of Onchestus. *Paus. Bœot.*

ONCHES'TUS, a town of Bœotia, founded by Onchestus, a son of Neptune. It was in ruins in the age of Pausanias, though the temple and statue of Neptune still remained, and the sacred grove which *Homer* has mentioned, *Il.* 2. v. 506. *Strab.* 9.—*Paus.* 9. c. 26.——A lake near Thebes. *Ælian.* 12. c. 57.——A river near Mycalessus. *Polyb.* 17. c. 16.—*Stat. Theb.* 7. v. 272.

ONCHOB'RICE, an island of Arabia Felix. *Plin.* 6.

ON'CHOE, a city of Phocis. *Steph.*

ON'CIUM, a small region of Arcadia. *Paus.* 8. c. 25.

ONEABA'TES, a city of Ægypt. *Steph.*

ONEN'SES, a people of Hispania Citerior. *Plin.* 3. c. 3.

ONESIC'RITUS, a cynic philosopher of Ægina, who went with Alexander into Asia, and was sent to the Indian Gymnosophists. He wrote a history of the king's life, which has been censured for the romantic, exaggerated, and improbable narrative it gives. It is asserted, that Alexander, upon reading it, said, that he should be glad to come to life again for some time, to see what reception the historian's work met with. *Plut. in Alex.*—*Curt.* 9. c. 10.—*Strab.* 15.—*Ælian. An.* l. 16, *&c.*——A preceptor of the emperor Commodus. *Æl Lamprid.* c. 1.

ONES'IMUS, a Macedonian nobleman, treated with great kindness by the Roman emperors. He wrote an account of the life of the emperor Probus and of Carus with great precision and elegance. *Vopisc. in Bonos.* c. 14. *in Procul.* c. 13. *in Caro*, c. 7. ——A Macedonian noble, disgraced by king Perseus for dissuading him to go to war with the Romans. Onesimus upon this fled to the Romans, by whom he was well received. His father's name was Python. *Liv.* 44. c. 16.

ONESIP'PUS, a son of Hercules. *Apollod.*

ONE'SIUS, a king of Salamis, who revolted from the Persians.

ONETOR'IDES, an Athenian officer, who attempted to murder the garrison which Demetrius had stationed at Athens, &c. *Polyæn.* 5. c. 17.

ONEV'ATHA, a city of Phœnicia. *Lib. Notit.*

ONIABA'THES, a city of Ægypt. *Steph.*

ONI'UM, a place of Peloponnesus, near Corinth. *Polyæn.* 2. c. 3.—*Thucyd.* 2. c. 52.—*Xenoph. Gr.* l. 6 & 7.

ON'NA, a town of Arabia Felix. *Steph.*

ON'OBA, a town near the columns of Hercules. *Mela*, 3. c. 1.—*Plin.* 3. c. 1.

ONOBRISA'TES, a people of Gallia Aquitanica. *Plin.* 4. c. 19.

ONOCHO'NUS, a river of Thessaly, falling into the Peneus. It was dried up by the army of Xerxes. *Herodot.* 7. c. 196.—*Plin.* 4. c. 8.

ONOMAC'RITUS, a soothsayer of Athens. It is generally believed, that the Greek poem, on the Argonautic expedition, attributed to Orpheus, was written by Onomacritus. The elegant poems of Musæus are also, by some, supposed to be the production of his pen. He flourished about 516 years B.C. and was expelled from Athens by Hipparchus, one of the sons of Pisistratus. *Herodot.* 7. c. 6.—*Suidas.*—*Voss. poet. Gr.* p. 23 & 29.——A Locrian, who wrote concerning laws. *Arist.* 2. *Pol. fin.*

ONOMAR'CHUS, a Phocian, son of Euthycrates, and brother of Philomelus, whom he succeeded, as general of his countrymen, in the sacred war. After various exploits of valor and perseverance, he was defeated and slain in Thessaly by Philip of Macedon, who ordered his body to be ignominiously hung up, for the sacrilege offered to the temple of Delphi. He died 353 B.C. *Arist. Pol.* 5. c. 4.—*Diod.* 16.——A man to whose care Antigonus entrusted the keeping of Eumenes. *C. Nep. in Eum.*

ONOMASTOR'IDES, a Lacedæmonian ambassador who was sent to Darius, and fell into the hands of Parmenio at Damascus. *Curt.* 3. c. 13.

ONOMAS'TUS, a freedman of the emperor Otho. *Tacit. Hist.* 1. c. 25.

ON'OPHAS, one of the seven Persians who conspired against the usurper Smerdis. *Ctesias.*——An officer in the expedition of Xerxes against Greece.

ONOSAN'DER, a Platonic philosopher, in the reign of Claudius, wrote a celebrated book, in Greek, *De Imperatoris Institutione*, which he dedicated to Q. Veranius. This work was first published in Latin, by Nicol. Sagundinus, Rome, 1493: in Greek, by Rigaltius, Paris, 1599; and lastly by Schwebel, with the French translation of Zur-Lauben, fol. Norimb. 1762. *Fabr. B. Gr.* 3. c. 28. —*Sax. Onom.* 1. p. 248.

ONU'PHIS, a celebrated city of Ægypt. *Steph.*

ONYCH'ION, a place of Crete, to which the Amyclæans sent a colony. *Steph.*

ONY'THES, a friend of Æneas, killed by Turnus. *Virg. Æn.* 12. v. 514.

ONYTH'RION, a city of Thessaly, near Arne. *Steph.*

OPA'LIA, festivals celebrated by the Romans, in honor of Ops, on the fourteenth of the calends of January. *Mocrob. Sat.* 1. c. 10.—*Varro, L. L.* 5. c. 3.—*Festus de V. Sig.*—*Auson. de Fer. R.* 25.

OPA'NE or OPO'NE, a city of Upper Æthiopia. *Ptol.*

OPHARI'TÆ, a people of Asiatic Sarmatia, near the river Opharus. *Plin.* 6. c. 7.

OPH'ELAS, a general of Cyrene, defeated by Agathocles. *Polyæn.* 5. c. 3.

OPHE'LIAS, a general of the first Ptolemy sent against Thimbro, whom he took prisoner. *Diod.* 18.

OPHEL'TES, a son of Lycurgus, king of Thrace. He is the same as Archemorus. *Vid.* Archemorus. *Apollod.* 1 *&* 3.—*Paus.* 2. c. 15.—*Hygin.* fab. 74.—*Ælian. V. H.* 4. c. 5.—*Lactant. ad Theb.* 4. v. 74. l. 5. v. 630. —The father of Euryalus, whose friendship with Nisus is proverbial. *Virg. Æn.* 9. v. 201.——One of the companions of Acœtes, changed into a dolphin by Bacchus for offering violence to the person of the god. *Hygin.* 134.—*Ovid. Met*· 3. fab. 8.——A native of Cyzicus slain by Telamon in a nocturnal conflict. *Val. Flacc.* 3. v, 198.

OPHEN'SIS, (*civitas*), a town of Africa. *Tacit. Hist.* 4. c. 50. *Lipsius* and *Cujacius* conjecture that we should read Opensis.

O'PHIAS, a patronymic given to Combe, as daughter of Ophius, an unknown person. *Ovid. Met.* 7. v. 382.

OPH'ICI or OP'ICI. *Vid.* Opici.

OPHIO'DES, an island on the coast of Arabia, so called from the great number of serpents found there. It belonged to the Ægyptian kings, and was considered valuable on account of the topaz which it produced, and which was discovered among the rocks during the night only, as the light of the sun made its dazzling beauty disappear. The island was so vigilantly guarded on account of its treasures, that strangers were put to death if they presumed to approach it. *Diod.* 3. *Strab.* 16.

OPHIOG'ENES, a people of Asia on the Hellespont. *Plin.* 28. c. 3.

OPHI'ON, one of the giants killed by Hercules. *Apollod. Rhod.* 1. v. 503.—*Tzetzes ad Lyc.* 1192.—*Schol. Hom. Il.* 8. v. 497.—*Schol. Apol. R.* 2. v. 40.——The father of Amycus. *Ovid. Met.* 12. v. 545.

OPHIO'NEUS or OPHI'ONEUS, an ancient soothsayer in the age of Aristodemus. He was born blind.

OPHIOPH'AGI, a people of Æthiopia. *Plin.* 6. c. 29.—*Solin.* c. 36.

O'PHIS, a small river of Arcadia which falls into the Alpheus.——A river of Cappadocia, flowing into the Euxine. *Arrian.*

OPHIU'CHUS (*Anguitenens*), a constellation in the heavens. *Cic. N. D.* 2. c. 42.—*Ovid. Met.* 8. v. 182.—*Manil.* 1. v. 331.

OPHIU'SA, the ancient name of Rhodes. *Strab.* 14.——A small island near Crete. *Plin.* 4. c. 12.——A town of Sarmatia.——An island near the Baleares, so called from the number of serpents (ὄφις *serpens*) which it produced. It is now called Formentera. *Ptol.*

OPH'LONES, a people of European Sarmatia. *Ptol.*

OPH'RADUS, a river near the Indus. *Plin.* 6. c. 23.

OPHRYNE'UM or OPHRYN'IUM, a town of Troas on the Hellespont. Hector had a grove there. *Strab.* 13.

OPHTHALMI'TIS, a surname of Minerva, given her by Lycurgus, because she cured his eye, which Alcandor had injured. *Paus.* 2. c. 24. l. 3. c. 18.—*Plut. in Lyc.*

OPH'THIS, a city of Libya, near Ægypt. *Steph.*

O'PIÆ, a people near the river Indus. *Id.*

OP'ICI, the ancient inhabitants of Campania, from whose mean occupations the word *Opicus* has been used to express disgrace. *Juv.* 3. v. 207.—*Servius Æn.* 7. v. 730.

OPICONSI'VA, a festival in honor of Vesta, celebrated at Rome on the eighth of the calends of September. No person, except the vestals and the priest, was permitted to enter into the temple of the goddess during the celebration. *Varro de L. L.* 5.—*Voss. de Idolol.* 2. c. 58.

OPIG'ENA, a surname under which Juno was implored by pregnant women for assistance. *Festus de V. Sig.*—*Martian. Capell.*

OPIL'IUS, a grammarian, who flourished about 94 B.C. He wrote a book called *Libri Musarum.*

OPIM'IUS L., a Roman who obtained the consulship, in opposition to the interest and efforts of the Gracchi. He shewed himself a most inveterate enemy to C. Gracchus and his adherents, and behaved himself, whilst in office, with the greatest severity against the popular party. When sent to Africa at the head of an embassy to settle the disputes in the family of Masinissa, he suffered himself to be bribed by the gold of Jugurtha, and made an unfair division of the provinces referred to his arbitration. He was accused and condemned for this criminal conduct, under the Mamilian law, and retired in disgrace and banishment to Dyrrachium, where he died in extreme poverty. Cicero speaks in commendation of Opimius, but the orator's partiality might arise from the bias which he entertained for patrician greatness and unlimited power over the plebeians. The year in which Opimius was consul was remarkable for a superabundant vintage, hence *Opimianum vinum* was used to denote wine of superior quality. Some of this wine was still preserved in Pliny's age, two centuries after Opimius' death. *Cic. pro Sext. Planc. & in Pis.*—*Plut.*—*Sallust. Jug.* 16.—*Plin.* 14. c. 4, &c.—*Martial.* 9. epigr. 89.—*Paterc.* 2. c. 7.——A Roman, who killed one of the Cimbri in single combat.——A rich usurer at Rome in the age of *Horace.* 2. sat. 3. v. 142.

OPI'NUM, a town of Corsica. *Ptol.* It is now Pino.

O'PIS, a town on the Tigris, afterwards called Antiochia. *Xenoph. Anab.* 2.

O'pis, a nymph who was among Diana's attendants, and who avenged the death of her favorite Camilla, by shooting Aruns, by whose weapons the queen had fallen. The goddess herself is likewise called Opis by the Greek poets, and that name is likewise applied to one of the three Hyperborean nymphs, who introduced the worship of the goddess into Delus. The other two were Loxo and Hecaerge. *Virg. Æn.* 11. v. 532 & 867.—*Palæph. de Inc.* 32.—*Cic. de Nat. D.* 3. c. 23.—*Callim. in Dian.* 204. *In Del.* 292.—*Macrob.* 5. *Sat.* 22.—*Servius in Virg. loco cit.*—*Paus.* 5. c. 7.—*Gyrald. de H. Deor.* 12.——One of Cyrene's attendants. *Virg. G.* 4. v. 343.

OPISI'NA, an inland city of Thrace. *Ptol.* It is probably the Opizum of *Antoninus.*

OP'ITER VIRGIN'IUS TRICOS'TUS, a Roman consul who took Cameria, A. U. C. 253.

OPITERGI'NI, a people near Aquileia, on the Adriatic. Their chief city was called Opitergum, now Oderzo. *Lucan.* 4. v. 462.—*Tac. Hist.* 3. c. 6.

OPI'TES, a native of Argos, killed by Hector in the Trojan war. *Homer. Il.* λ. v. 301.

OPIT'ULUS, a surname of Jupiter, because he extended his assistance to mankind. *Festus de V. Sig.*

OPOTU'RA, a city of India within the Ganges. *Ptol.*

OP'PIA, a vestal virgin, buried alive for her incontinence. *Liv.* 2. c. 42.

Op'pia Lex, enacted by C. Oppius, the tribune, A.U.C. 540. It required that no woman should wear above half an ounce of gold for ornament, have party-colored garments, or be carried in any city or town, or to any place within a mile's distance, unless during the celebration of some sacred festivals or public solemnities. This famous law, which was made while Annibal was in Italy, and while Rome was in distressed circumstances, soon created discontent, and 18 years after, the Roman ladies petitioned the assembly of the people that it might be repealed. Cato opposed it strongly, and made many satirical reflections upon the women for their appearing in public to solicit votes. The tribune Valerius, who had presented their petition to the assembly, answered the objections of Cato, and his eloquence had such an influence on the minds of the people, that the law was instantly abrogated with the unanimous consent of all the *comitia*, Cato alone excepted. *Liv.* 33 & 34.—*Cic. de Orat.* 3.—*Tac. Ann.* 3. c. 34.

OPPIAN'ICUS, a surname of Statius Albius. *Cic. Clu.* 4.

OPPIA'NUS, a Greek poet of Anazarbus, in Cilicia, in the second century. His father's name was Agesilaus, and his mother's Zenodota. He wrote some poems, celebrated for their elegance and sublimity. Two of his poems are now extant, consisting of five books on fishing, called *halieuticon*, and four on hunting called *cynegeticon*. The emperor Caracalla was so pleased with his poetry that he gave him a piece of gold for every verse of his cynegeticon; from which circumstance the poem received the name of the golden verses of Oppian. The poet died of the plague in the 30th year of his age. His countrymen raised statues to his honor, and engraved an inscription on his tomb, to the effect that the gods had hastened to call back Oppian in the flower of youth, only because he had already excelled all mankind. The best editions of his works are that of Schneider, 8vo, Argent. 1776; that of De Ballu, Argentor. 1786; and that of Rittershusius, Lug. Bat. 1597. Among the translations are, in French, that of Christianus, Paris, 1575; in German, that of Lierberkühn, Lips. 1755; in Italian, that of Salvini, Florent. 1728; in English, that of Somerville, London, 1788. *Fabr. B. Gr.* 4. c. 24.—*Sax. Onom.* 1. p. 344.

OPPID'IUS, a rich old man, introduced by *Horace*, 2. sat. 3. v. 168, as wisely dividing his possessions among his two sons, and warning them against the follies and extravagance which he believed he saw rising in them.

OP'PIUS C., a friend of Julius Cæsar, celebrated for his life of Scipio Africanus, and of Pompey the Great. In the latter, he paid not much regard to historical facts, and took every opportunity of defaming Pompey, in order that he might extol the character of his patron Cæsar. In the age of Suetonius, he was deemed the author of the Alexandrian, African, and Spanish wars, which some attribute to Cæsar, and others to A. Hirtius. *Harles. Not. Lit. Rom.* 1. p. 174.—*Plut. in Pomp.*

—*Cic. Att.* 5. ep. 1.—*Tacit. Ann.* 12.—*Suet. in Cæs.* 53, &c.——An officer sent by the Romans against Mithridates. He met with ill success, and was sent in chains to the king.——A Roman who saved his aged father from the dagger of the triumvirate.——The name of bankers from Velia, mentioned by *Cicero, Att.* 7. ep. 13. l. 8. ep. 7, &c.

OP'PIUS MAR'CUS, a leader of the plebeians at Rome, when they retired to mount Aventine from the Decemviri. *Liv.* 3. c. 51.

OP'PIUS COR'NICEN, one of the Decemvirs, who shared the crimes of Appius, and, on being put in prison, destroyed himself. *Liv.* 3. c. 35, &c.

OP'PIUS CA'IUS, the author of the Oppian law. *Vid.* Oppia Lex.

OP'PIUS CHA'RES, a grammarian, who taught in Gaul. *Suet. de Illustr. Gramm.* c. 3.—*Voss. de Hist. Lat.* 1. c. 13.

OPS (*opis*), a daughter of Cœlus and Terra, the same as the Rhea of the Greeks, who married Saturn, and became mother of Jupiter. She was known among the ancients by the different names of Cybele, Bona Dea, Magna Mater, Thya, Tellus, Proserpina, and even of Juno, and Minerva; and the worship which was paid to these apparently several deities was offered merely to one and the same person, mother of the gods. The word *Ops* seems to be derived from the word *Opus;* because the goddess, who is the same as the earth, gives nothing without *labor*. Tatius built her a temple at Rome. She was generally represented as a matron, with her right hand opened, as if offering assistance to the helpless, and holding a loaf in her left hand. Her festivals were called Opalia. *Varro de L. L.* 4.—*Dionys. Hal.* 2, &c.—*Tibull.* el. 4. v. 68.—*Tzetzes ad Lyc.* 710.—*Lactant. ad Theb.* 4. v. 457. *De Fals. R.* 1. c. 13 & 14.—*Servius. ad G.* 2. v. 326. *Ad Æn.* 8. v. 84. l. 10. v. 83.—*Varro. apud Aug. de Civ. D.* 7. c. 24.—*Auson. de Fer. R.* 15.—*Plin.* 19. c. 6.

OPSICEL'LA, a town of Cantabria, in Spain. *Strab.*

OP'SIUS M., a prætor, desirous of being made consul, &c. *Tac. Ann.* 4. c. 68.

OPTA'TUS, a freedman of Cæsar, præfect of the fleet under Claudius. *Plin.* 9. c. 17.——One of the fathers, whose works were edited by Du Pin, fol. Paris, 1700. *Hieron. de Script. Eccles.* c. 110.—*Augustin. de doctr. Christ.* 2. c. 40.

OPTILE'TIS, a surname of Minerva, the same as Ophthalmitis. *Vid.* Ophthalmitis.

OP'TIMUS MAX'IMUS, an epithet given to Jupiter to denote his greatness, omnipotence, and supreme goodness. *Cic. de N. D.* 2. c. 25.

O'PUS, (-*untis*), a city of Locris, on the Asopus, destroyed by an earthquake. It was the native place of Abderus, the favorite of Hercules, and it was there that Patroclus accidentally killed Elysonimus. *Apollod.* 2 & 3.—*Ovid. ex Pont.* 1. el. 3. v. 73.—*Strab.* 9.—*Mela*, 2. c. 3.—*Liv.* 28. c. 7.

O'RA, a town of India, taken by Alexander. *Arrian. Curtius*, 8. c. 11. calls it Nora.——A town of Carmania. *Ptol.*

O'RA, one of Jupiter's mistresses.

OR'ABA, a city of Osrhoene. *Lib. Notit.*

ORABAN'TIUS, a poet of Trœzene, anterior to Homer. *Diod. Sic.* l. 3.—*Fabr. B. Gr.* l. c. 17.

ORACULUM, an answer of the gods to the questions of men, or the place where those answers are given. Nothing is more famous than the ancient oracles of Ægypt, Greece, Rome, &c. They were supposed to be the will of the gods themselves, and they were consulted, not only upon very important matter, but even in the common affairs of private life. To make peace or war, to introduce a change of government, to plant a colony, to enact laws, to raise an edifice, to marry, were sufficient reasons for consulting the will of the gods. Mankind, in consulting them, showed that they wished to pay implicit obedience to the command of the divinity, and, when they had been favored with an answer, they acted with more spirit and with more vigor, conscious that the undertaking had met with the sanction and approbation of heaven. In this, therefore, it will not appear wonderful that so many places were sacred to oracular purposes. The small province of Bœotia could once boast of her 25 oracles, and Peloponnesus of the same number. Not only the chief of the gods gave oracles but in process of time heroes were admitted to enjoy the same privileges; and the oracles of Trophonius and Antinous were soon able to rival the fame of Apollo and Jupiter. The most celebrated oracles of antiquity were those of Dodona, Delphi, Jupiter Ammon, &c. *Vid.* Dodona, Delphi, Ammon. The temple of Delphi seemed to claim a superiority over the other temples; its fame was once more extended, and its riches were so great, that not only private persons, but even kings and numerous armies made it an object of plunder and of rapine. The manner of delivering oracles was different. A priestess at Delphi (*vid.* Pythia) was permitted to pronounce the oracles of the god, and her delivery of the answers was always attended with acts of apparent madness and desperate fury. Not only women, but even doves, were the ministers of the temple of Dodona, and the suppliant votary was often startled to hear his questions readily answered by the decayed trunk, or the spreading branches of a neighbouring oak. Ammon conveyed his answer in a plain and open manner, but Amphiaraus required many ablutions and preparatory ceremonies, and generally communicated his oracles to his suppliants in dreams and visions. Sometimes the first words that were heard, after issuing from the temple, were deemed the answers of the oracle, and sometimes the nodding or shaking of the head of the statue, the motions of a fish in a neighbouring lake, or their reluctance in accepting the food which was offered to them, were as strong and valid as the most express and the minutest explanations. The answers were also sometimes given in verse, or written on tablets, but their meaning was always obscure, and often the cause of disaster to such as consulted them. Crœsus, when he consulted the oracle of Delphi, was told, that if he crossed the Halys, he should destroy a great empire: he supposed that that empire was the empire of his enemy, but unfortunately it was his own. The words, *Credo te, Æacida, Romanos vincere posse*, which Pyrrhus received for answer when he wished to assist the Tarentines against the Romans, being interpreted in his own favour proved his ruin. Nero was ordered by the oracle of Delphi, to beware of 73 years, but the pleasing idea that he should live to that age rendered him careless, and he was soon convinced of his mistake, when Galba, in his 73rd year had the presumption to dethrone him. It is a question among the learned, whether the oracles were given by the inspiration of evil spirits, or whether they proceeded from the imposture of the priests. Imposture, however, and forgery, cannot long flourish, and falsehood becomes its own destroyer; and, on the contrary, it is well known how much confidence the credulous and the superstitious place in dreams and romantic stories. Some believe, that all the oracles of the earth ceased at the birth of Christ, but the supposition is false. It was, indeed, the beginning of their decline, but they remained in repute, and were consulted, though perhaps not so frequently, till the fourth century, when Christianity began to triumph over paganism. The oracles often suffered themthemselves to be bribed. Alexander did it, but it is well known that Lysander failed in the attempt. Herodotus, who first mentioned the corruption which often prevailed in the oracular temples of Greece and Ægypt, has been severely treated for his remarks by the historian Plutarch. Demosthenes was also a witness of this corruption, and observed that the oracles of Greece were servilely subservient to the will and pleasure of Philip, king of Macedonia, as he beautifully expresses it by the word φιλιππίζειν. If some of the Greeks, and of the inhabitants of other European and Asiatic countries paid so much attention to oracles, and were so fully persuaded of their veracity, and even divinity, many of their leading men and philosophers were apprized of the deceit, and paid no regard to the command of priests whom money could corrupt, and interposition silence. The Ægyptians showed themselves the most superstitious of mankind, by their blind acquiescence in the imposition of the priests, who persuaded them that the safety and happiness of their life depended upon the mere motions of an ox, or the tameness of a crocodile. *Homer. Il. Odyss.* 10.—*Herodot.* 1 & 2.—*Xenoph. Memor.*—*Strab.* 5, 7, &c.—*Paus.* 1,

&c.—*Plut. de Defec. Orac. de Ages. & de Her. Malign.—Cic. de Div.* 1. c. 19.—*Justin.* 24. c. 6.—*Liv.* 37.—*Ælian. V. H.* 6.—*C.Nep. in Lys.—Aristoph. in Equit. & Plut.—Demosth. Phil.—Ovid. Met.* 1.

ORÆ'A, a small country of Peloponnesus. *Paus.* 2. c. 30.

ORÆ'A, certain solemn sacrifices of fruits offered in the four seasons of the year, to obtain mild and temperate weather. They were offered to the goddess who presided over the seasons, who attended upon the sun, and who received divine worship at Athens. *Athen.* l. 14.

ORA'NI, a people of Asiatic Sarmatia. *Plin.* 6. c. 7.

OR'ASUS, a man who killed Ptolemy, the son of Pyrrhus.

ORA'TES, a river of European Scythia. *Ovid. ex Pont.* 4. el. 10. v. 47. As this river is not now known, *Vossius* reads Crete, a river which is found in Scythia. *Thucyd.* 4.—*Val. Flacc.* 4. v. 719.—*Eustath. ad Dionys. Per.*

ORA'THA, a city of Mesopotamia. *Steph.*

ORAX'US, a fountain of Campania, between Neapolis and Puteoli. *Plin.* 18. c. 11. It is now Astruno, according to *Ortelius.*

ORBANAS'SA, a city of Pamphylia. *Ptol.*

ORBE'LIA, a region of Macedonia, so called from mount Orbelus.

ORBE'LUS or OR'BELUS, a mountain of Macedonia, which it divides from Mœsia. *Plin.* 4, c. 10. It is now M. Caropnitze.

ORBESIO'NA, a region of Armenia Minor. *Ptol.*

ORBIL'IUS PUPIL'LUS, a grammarian of Beneventum, who was the first instructor of the poet Horace. After serving for some time in the Roman armies, he, in his 50th year, came to Rome in the consulship of Cicero, and there, as a public teacher, acquired more fame than money. He was naturally of a severe disposition, of which his pupils often felt the effects. He lived almost to his 100th year, and lost his memory some time before his death. His countrymen raised a marble statue to his honor at Beneventum. *Suet. de Illustr. Gr.* 9.—*Horat.* 2. ep. 1. v. 71.—*Vossius, Inst. Orat.* 6.

ORBI'TÆ, a people of India. *Steph.*

ORBITA'NIUM, a town of the Samnites. *Liv.* 24. c. 20.

OR'BIUS P., a lawyer, who was for some time prætor in Asia. *Cic. Flacc.* 31. *Br.* 48.

ORBO'NA, a goddess at Rome, who was supplicated not to deprive children of their parents. She was the protectress of orphans. Her altar at Rome was near the gods Lares. *Cic. de Nat. D.* 3. c. 25. *Plin.* 2. c. 7.—*Arnob.* 4.

OR'CADES, islands on the northern coasts of Britain, now called the Orkneys. They were unknown till Britain was discovered to be an island by Agricola, who presided there as governor. *Tacit. in Agric.—Juv.* 2. v. 161.—*Plin.* 4. c. 16.

OR'CELIS, a city of the Bastitani, in Hispania Tarraconensis. *Ptol.* It is now Horiguela or Orihuella.

OR'CHÆ, a city of the Babylonians. *Ptol.* It is called Urchao by others, and was the Ur of the Chaldæans in Scripture.

ORCHA'LIS, an eminence of Bœotia, near Haliartus, called also Alopecos. *Plut. in Lys.*

OR'CHAMUS, a king of Assyria, father of Leucothoe, by Eurynome. He buried his daughter alive for her amours with Apollo, and the god changed her into the tree which bears the frankincense. *Ovid. Met.* 4. v. 212.

ORCHE'NI, a people of Arabia Deserta. *Ptol.*

OR'CHIA LEX, by Orchius. the tribune, A.U.C. 566. It was enacted to limit the number of guests that were to be admitted at an entertainment; and it also enforced, that during supper, which was the chief meal among the Romans, the doors of every house should be left open. *Macrob. Sat.* 3. c. 18.

OR'CHIMUS, the father of Cydippe, according to *Stephanus.*

ORCHIV'IUS C., a man who was colleague to Cicero in the prætorship. *Cic. Clu.* 34 & 53.

ORCHOM'ENUS or ORCHOM'ENUM, a town of Bœotia, at the west of the lake Copais, and on the delightful borders of the Cephisus. It was anciently called Minyeia, and, from that circumstance, the inhabitants were often called Minyans of Orchomenus. There was at Orchomenus a celebrated temple built by Eteocles, son of Cephisus, sacred to the Graces, who were from thence called the Orchomenian goddesses. The inhabitants founded Teos in conjunction with the Ionians, under the sons of Codrus. *Plin.* 4. c. 8.—*Herodot.* 1. c. 146.—*Paus.* 9. c. 37.—*Strab.* 9.—*Sch. Apollon.* 1. *Arg.* v. 230. l. 4. v. 264.—*Sch. Aristoph. in Nub.* 397.—*Pindar. Olymp.* 14.—*Plut. in Quæst, Gr.* 38.——A town of Arcadia, at the north of Mantinea.——A town of Thessaly, with a river of the same name. *Strab.—Homer. Il.* 2. v. 511.

ORCHOM'ENUS, a son of Lycaon, king of Arcadia, who gave his name to a city of Arcadia, &c. *Homer. Il.* 2. en. v. 112.—*Apollod.* 3.—*Paus.* 8. c. 3.——A son of Minyas, king of Bœotia, who gave the name of Orchomenians to his subjects, and repressed, by wise and severe laws, the crime of adultery. He died without issue, and the crown devolved upon Clymenus, the son of Presbon, &c. *Paus.* 9. c. 36 & 37.—*Apollod.* 2.—*Tzetzes. in Lyc.* 871.

OR'CUS, one of the names of the god of hell, the same as Pluto, though confounded by some with Charon. He had a temple at Rome under the name of Orcus Quietalis. Those slaves who were made free by the will of a master were called Orcini liberti, to be distinguished from those to whom a master in his lifetime had granted their liberty. The word Orcus is generally used to signify the infernal regions. *Horat.* 1. od. 29, &c. —*Virg. Æn.* 4. v. 502, &c.—*Ovid. Met.* 14. v. 116, &c,—*Varro de L. L.* 4.—*Cic. Verr.* 4. c. 50.—*Petron.* 162.

ORCYN'IA, a place of Cappadocia, where Eumenes was defeated by Antigonus. *Plut.*

ORCYN'IUM, a mountain of Lesbus. *Theophrast. Hist.* 3. c. ult. *Pliny,* 5. c. 31, calls it Ordymnus.

ORDÆ'A, a city of Macedonia. *Steph.*

ORDES'SUS, a river of Scythia, which falls into the Ister. There is a town of that name at the west of the mouths of the Borysthenes, on the Euxine. *Herodot.*

ORDOVI'CES, the people of North Wales in Britain, mentioned by *Tacitus, Ann.* 12. c. 53.

ORE'ADES, nymphs of the mountains, (ὄρος *mons,*) daughters of Phoroneus and Hecate. Some call them Orestiades, and give them Jupiter for father. They generally attended upon Diana, and accompanied her in hunting. It was by their influence and example, according to *Mnaseas,* that mankind exchanged human flesh for the fruits of trees and the roots of the earth. *Virg. Æn.* 1. v. 504.—*Homer. Il.* 6.—*Strab.* 10.—*Ovid. Met.* 8. v. 787.—*Nat. Com.* 5. c. 11.—*Servius ad Virg. Ec.* 10. v. 9 & 62.

O'REAS or ORE'AS, a son of Hercules and Chrissey. *Apollod.* 2.

OREB'ATIS, an inland city of Persia. *Ptol.*

OR'EGES, a hill forming part of mount Imaus. *Plin.* 5. c. 27.

ORE'I or OROE'I, a people of Arabia. *Id.* 6. c. 9. See also *Salmas. ad Solin.* p. 625.

OREI'NE, an island in the Arabian Gulph. *Arrian. in Peripl.* It is now. probably, Maczua.

ORE'IUS and A'GRIUS, were twin sons of the nymph Polyphonte and a bear, according to mythologists, who represent the mother as thus punished in this unnatural connection, by Venus, whose rites and mysteries she had despised. These two sons were of a ferocious temper, and not only insulted, but devoured travellers, so that Jupiter, incensed against them, ordered Mercury to destroy them. The god obeyed, but Mars interfered, and because their mother was daughter of Thrassa, his own child, he obtained of Jupiter that they might be changed into birds of prey *Anton. Lib.* 21.

OREOPHAN'TA, a city of India within the Ganges. *Ptol.*

O'REOS, a city of Eubœa. *Steph.*

ORESIT'ROPHUS, one of Actæon's dogs. *Ovid. Met.* 3. v. 233.

ORES'TÆ, a people of Epirus. They received their name from Orestes, who fled to Epirus when cured of his insanity; but, according to others, it was the hero's son of the same name who seized the country, and removed the obscurity in which his father had concealed his birth by making himself master of part of Epirus, and giving it his name. *Lucan.* 3. v. 249 —*Steph. Byzant.—Solin.* 15.——A people of Macedonia. *Liv.* 33. c. 34.

ORES'TE, a city of Eubœa, according to *Hesychius.*

ORES'TES, a son of Agamemnon and Clytæmnestra. When his father was cruelly murdered by Clytæmnestra and Ægisthus, young Orestes was saved from his mother's dagger by means of his sister Electra, called Laodicea by Homer, and was privately conveyed to the house of Strophius, who was king of Phocis, and who had married a sister of Agamemnon. He was tenderly treated by Strophius, who educated him with his son Pylades. The two young princes soon became acquainted, and, from their familiarity, arose the most inviolable attachment and the most sincere friendship. When Orestes was arrived at years of manhood, he visited Mycenæ, and avenged his father's death by assassinating his mother Clytæmnestra and the adulterer Ægisthus. The manner in which he committed this murder is variously reported. According to Æschylus, he was commissioned by Apollo to avenge his father, and, therefore, he introduced himself, with his friend Pylades, at the court of Mycenæ, pretending to bring the news of the death of Orestes from king Strophius. He was at first received with coldness, and, when he came into the presence of Ægisthus, who wished to inform himself of the particulars, he murdered him, and Clytæmnestra soon after shared the adulterer's fate. Euripides and Sophocles relate the same circumstances. Ægisthus was assassinated after Clytæmnestra, according to Sophocles; and, in Euripides, Orestes is represented as murdering the adulterer, while he offers a sacrifice to the nymphs. This murder, as the poet relates, irritated the guards, who were present, but Orestes appeased their fury by telling them who he was, and he was immediately acknowledged king of the country. Afterwards he stabs his mother, at the instigation of his sister Electra, after he has upbraided her for her infidelity and cruelty to her husband. Such meditated murders received the punishment which, among the ancients, was always supposed to attend parricide. Orestes is tormented by the Furies, and exiles himself to Argos, where he is still pursued by the avengeful goddesses. Apollo himself purifies him, and he is acquitted by the unanimous opinion of the Areopagites, which assembly Minerva herself instituted on this occasion, according to the narrative of the poet Æschylus, who flatters the Athenians in his tragical story, by representing them as passing judgment even upon the gods themselves. According to Pausanias, Orestes was purified of the murder, not at Delphi, but at Trœzene, where was still seen a large stone at the entrance of Diana's temple, upon which the ceremonies of purification had been performed by nine of the principal citizens of the place. There was, also, at Megalopolis in Arcadia, a temple dedicated to the Furies, near which Orestes cut off one of his fingers with his teeth in a fit of insanity. These different traditions are confuted by Euripides, who says, that Orestes, after the murder of his mother, consulted the oracle of Apollo at Delphi, where he was informed that nothing could deliver him from the persecutions of the Furies, if he did not bring into Greece Diana's statue, which was in the Taurica Chersonesus, and which, as it is reported by some, had fallen down from heaven. This was an arduous enterprize. The king of the Chersonesus always sacrificed on the altars of the goddess all such strangers as entered on the borders of his country. Orestes and his friend were both carried before Thoas, the king of the place, and were doomed to be sacrificed. Iphigenia was then priestess of Diana's temple, and it was her office to immolate these strangers. The intelligence that they were Grecians delayed the preparations, and Iphigenia was anxious to learn something about a country which had given her birth. *Vid.* Iphigenia. She even interested herself in their misfortunes, and offered to spare the life of one of them, provided he would convey letters to Greece from her hand. This was a difficult trial; never was friendship more truly displayed, according to the words of Ovid, *Ex Pont.* 3. el. 2.

Ire jubet Pylades carum moriturus Orestem,
Hic negat; inque vicem pugnat uterque mori.

At last Pylades gave way to the pressing entreaties of his friend, and consented to carry the letters of Iphigenia to Greece. These were addressed to Orestes himself, and, therefore, these circumstances soon led to a discovery of the connections of the priestess with the man whom she was going to immolate. Iphigenia was convinced that he was her brother Orestes, and, when the causes of their journey had been explained, she resolved, with the two friends, to flee from Chersonesus, and to carry away the statue of Diana. Their flight was discovered, and Thoas prepared to pursue them, but Minerva interfered, and told him, that all had been done by the will and approbation of the gods. Some suppose that Orestes came to Cappadocia from Chersonesus, and that he left there the statue of Diana, at Comana. Others contradict this tradition, and, according to Pausanias, the statue of Diana Orthia was the same as that which had been carried away from the Chersonesus. Some also suppose that Orestes brought it to Aricia, in Italy, where Diana's worship was established. After these celebrated adventures, Orestes ascended the throne of Argos, where he reigned in perfect security, and married Hermione, the daughter of Menelaus, and gave his sister to his friend Pylades. The marriage of Orestes with Hermione is a matter of dispute among the ancients. All are agreed that she had been promised to the son of Agamemnon, but Menelaus had married her to Neoptolemus, the son of Achilles, who had shown himself so truly interested in his cause during the Trojan war. The marriage of Hermione with Neoptolemus displeased Orestes, he remembered that she had been early promised to him, and therefore he resolved to recover her by force or artifice. This he effected by causing Neoptolemus to be assassinated, or assassinating him himself. According to Ovid's epistle of Hermione to Orestes, Hermione had always been faithful to her first lover, and it was even by her persuasions that Orestes removed her from the house of Neoptolemus. Hermione was dissatisfied with the partiality of Neoptolemus for Andromache, and her attachment for Orestes was increased. Euripides, however, and others, speak differently of Hermione's attachment to Neoptolemus: she loved him so tenderly that she resolved to murder Andromache, who seemed to share, in a small degree, the affections of her husband. She was ready to perpetrate the horrid deed when Orestes came into Epirus, and she was easily persuaded by the foreign prince to withdraw herself, in her husband's absence, from a country which seemed to contribute so much to her sorrows. Orestes, the better to secure the affections of Hermione, assassinated Neoptolemus (*vid.* Neoptolemus,) and retired to his kingdom of Argos. His old age was crowned with peace and security, and he died in the 90th year of his age, leaving his throne to Tisamenes, his son by Hermione. Three years after, the Heraclidæ recovered the Peloponnesus, and banished the descendants of Menelaus from the throne of Argos. Orestes died in Arcadia, as some suppose, by the bite of a serpent; and the Lacedæmonians, who had become his subjects at the death of Menelaus, were directed by an oracle to bring his bones to Sparta. They were, some time after, discovered at Tegea, and his statue appeared to have been seven cubits, according to the traditions mentioned by Herodotus and others. The friendship of Orestes and of Pylades became proverbial, and the two friends received divine honors among the Scythians, and had temples erected to them. *Paus.* 1, 2, 4, &c.—*Paterc.* l. c. 1 & 3.—*Apollod.* 1, &c.—*Strab.* 9 & 13.—*Ovid. Heroid.* 8. *Ex Pont.* 3. el. 2. *Met.* 15. *In Ib.*—*Euripid. in Orest. Andr. &c. Iphig.*—*Sophocl. in Electr. &c.*—*Æschyl. in Eum. Agam. &c.*—*Herodot.* l. c. 69.—*Hygin.* fab. 120 & 261.—*Plut. in Lyc.*—*Dictys.* 6, &c.—*Pindar. Pyth.* 2.—*Plin.* 33.—*Virg. Æn.* 3, &c.—*Homer. Odyss.* 3. v. 304. l. 4. v. 530. l. 11. v. 404.—*Ptol. Heph.*—*Servius ad Virg. Æn.* 2. v. 116. l. 3. v. 331. l. 4. v. 471. l. 6. v. 136.—*Hesych. Etym.*—*Lactant. ad Theb.* 8. v. 437.—*Eustath. in Odyss.* 4.—*Sch. Eurip. in Orest. &c.*—*Solin.* 5.—*Tzetz. ad Lycophr.* 1374.——A son of Achelous. *Apollod.*——A man sent as ambassador by Attila, king of the Huns, to the emperor Theodosius. He was highly honored at the Roman court, and his son Augustulus was the last emperor of the western empire. *Cassiodor. in Chron.—Jornand.—Procopius.*——A governor of Ægypt under the Roman emperors.——A robber of Athens who pretended madness, &c. *Aristoph. Ach.* 4. 7.——A general of Alexander. *Curt.* 4. c. 13.

ORES'TES CN AU'REL, a tribune and consul at Rome, &c. *Cic. Dom.* 13. *Off.* 2. c. 17.

ORES'TES LU'CIUS, another consul, A.U.C. 627. *Cic. Br.* 28.

ORESTEUM, a town of Arcadia, about eighteen miles from Sparta. It was founded by Orestheus, a son of Lycaon, and originally called Oresthesium, and afterwards Oresteum, from Orestes, the son of Agamemnon, who resided there for some time after the murder of Clytæmnestra. *Paus.* 8 c. 8.—*Euripid. in Orest.*—*Tzetzes. in Lyc.* 1374.—*Steph.*

ORES'TIA, a city of Orestis, in Macedonia, where Ptolemy, son of Lagus, first king of Ægypt, was born.——A city of Arcadia. *Steph.*

ORESTI'DÆ, the descendants or subjects of Orestes. the son of Agamemnon. They were driven from the Peloponnesus by the Heraclidæ, and came to settle in a country which, from them, was called Orestis, at the south-west of Macedonia. Some suppose that that part of Greece originally received its name from Orestes, who fled to this place, and built there a city, which gave its founder's name to the whole province. *Thucyd.* 2.—*Liv.* 31.

ORESTIL'LA AUREL., a mistress of Catiline. *Sallust. Cat.* 15.—*Cic. ad. Div.* 7. c. 7.

ORESTIS or ORES'TIAS, a part of Macedonia, on the west, extending between the towns of Apollonia and Oricum. *Cic. de Harusp.* 16.

ORES'TIS POR'TUS, a harbour of Calabria. *Plin.* 3. c. 5. It is now Porto Ravaglioso.

OR'ETÆ, a people of Asiatic Sarmatia, on the Euxine Sea. *Dionys.* This is, however, a corrupt reading for Toretæ, a people placed here by *Pliny*, 6. c. 5., *Ptolemy*, *Stephanus*, and others.

ORETA'NI, a people of Spain, whose capital was Oretum, now Oreto *Liv.* 21. c. 11. l. 35. c. 7. Their country is now La Mancha.

ORETIL'IA, a woman who married Caligula, by whom she was soon after banished.

ORE'UM, one of the principal towns of Eubœa. *Liv.* 28. c. 6.—*Plin.* 4. c. 12. *Ptoleny* calls it Horæus, *Pausanias* Istiæa, *Thucydides* Hostiæa, and *Stephanus* Histiæa. It is now l'Oreo.

OR'GA or OR'GAS, a river of Phrygia, falling into the Mæander. *Strab.*—*Plin.* 5. c. 29.

ORGALE'MA, a city near the Ister. *Steph.*

OR'GANA, an epithet of Minerva. *Hesych.*

OR'GANA, an island adjacent to Arabia Felix. *Ptol.*

OR'GASI, a people of Scythia within Imaus. *Ptol.*

OR'GE, a river of Gallia Narbonensis, called Sulga by *Strabo*, and Sorge by *Pliny*, 18. c. 22. It is now La Sorgue.

ORGE'LIUM or OR'GIA, a city of Hispània Citerior. *Ptol.* It is now Urgel.

ORGES'SUM, a town of Macedonia. *Liv.* 31. c. 27

ORGET'ORIX, one of the chief men of the Helvetii while Cæsar was in Gaul. He formed a conspiracy against the Romans, and, when accused, destroyed himself. *Cæs.*

OR'GIA, festivals in honor of Bacchus. They were the same as the *Bacchanalia*, *Dionysia*, *&c.* which were celebrated by the ancients to commemorate the triumph of Bacchus in India. *Vid.* Dionysia.

ORGOME'NÆ, a city of Illyria. *Steph.*

OR'GON, an island near Etruria. *Id.*

ORIBA'SIUS, a celebrated physician greatly esteemed by the emperor Julian, in whose reign he flourished. He abridged the works of Galenus, and of all the most respectable writers on physic, at the request of the emperor. He accompanied Julian into the east, but his skill proved ineffectual in attempting to cure the fatal wound which his benefactor had received. After Julian's death, he fell into the hands of the barbarians. The best edition of his works is that of Dundas, 4to, L. Bat. 1745. *Sax. Onom.* 1. p. 416.—*Fabr. B. Gr.* 5. c. 38, &c.—*Voss. de Philos.* c. 12. sec. 28.

ORIB'ASUS, one of Actæon's dogs, *ab ὄρος, mons*, and *βαίνω, scando. Ovid. Met.* 3. v. 210.

OR'ICUM or OR'ICUS, a town of Epirus, on the Ionian Sea, founded by a colony from Colchis, according to Pliny. It was called Dardania because Helenus and Andromache, natives of Troy or Dardania, reigned over the country after the Trojan war. It had a celebrated harbour, and was greatly esteemed by the Romans on account of its situation, but it was not well defended. The tree which produces the turpentine grew there in abundance. *Virg. Æn.* 10. v. 136.—*Liv.* 24. c. 40.—*Plin.* 2. c. 89.—*Cæs. Bell. Civ.* 3. c. 1, &c.—*Lucan.* 3. v. 187. It is now Orco.

O'RIENS, in ancient geography, is taken for all the most eastern parts of the world, such as Parthia, India, Assyria, &c.

ORIG'ENES, a Greek writer, as much celebrated for the easiness of his manners, his humility, and modesty, as for his learning and genius. He was surnamed *Adamantius*, from his assiduity, and became so rigid a Christian, that he made himself a eunuch, by following the literal sense of a passage in the Greek testament, which speaks of the voluntary eunuchs of Christ. He suffered martyrdom in his 69th year, A.C. 254. His works were excellent and numerous, and contained a number of homilies, commentaries on the holy Scriptures, and different treatises, besides the *Hexapla*, so called from its being divided into six columns, the first of which contained the Hebrew text, the second the same text in Greek characters, the third the Greek version of the Septuagint, the fourth that of Aquila, the fifth that of Symmachus, and the sixth Theodotion's Greek version. This famous work first gave the hint for the compilation of our Polyglot Bibles. The works of Origen have been learnedly edited by the Benedictine monks, though the whole is not yet completed, in four vols. fol. Paris, 1733. 1740, and 1759. The Hexapla was published in 8vo, at Lips. 1769, by Car. Frid. Bahrdt. *Fabr. B. Gr.* 3. c. 13.—*Sax. Onom.* 1. p. 358.

ORIG'ENI or ORIGEVIO'NES, according to *Mela*, 3. c. 1., a people of Hispania Tarraconensis, whose chief town was Flaviobriga.

ORI'GO, a courtezan in the age of Horace. *Horat.* 1. sat. 2. v. 55.

ORILOCHI'A, a surname of Iphigenia, given her by Diana, after the goddess had removed her from Taurica to Leuce, where she married Achilles according to Nicander, quoted by *Antonius Liberalis*, 27.

ORI'NUS, a river of Sicily. *Ptol.* It is called Erineus by *Thucydides.*

ORIOB'ATES, a general of Darius, at the battle of Arbela. *Curt.* 4.

ORI'ON, a celebrated giant sprung from the urine of Jupiter, Neptune, and Mercury. These three gods, as they travelled over Bœotia, met with great hospitality from Hyrieus, a peasant of the country, who was ignorant of their character and dignity. They were entertained with whatever the cottage afforded, and, when Hyrieus had discovered that they were gods, because Neptune told him to fill up Jupiter's cup with wine, after he had served it before the rest, the old man welcomed them by the voluntary sacrifice of an ox. Pleased with his piety, the gods promised to grant him whatever he required, and the old man, who had lately lost his wife, whom he had promised never to marry again, desired them that, as he was childless, they would give him a son without another marriage. The gods consented, and ordered him to bury in the ground the skin of the victim. Hyrieus did as they commanded, and, when nine months after, he dug for the skin, he found in it a beautiful child, whom he called *Urion, ab urinâ.* The name was changed into Orion by the corruption of one letter, as Ovid says, *Perdidit antiquum litera prima sonum.* Orion soon rendered himself celebrated, and Diana took him among her attendants, and even became deeply enamoured of him. His gigantic stature, however, displeased Œnopion, king of Chius, whose daughter, Hero or Merope, he demanded in marriage. The king, not to deny him openly, promised to make him his son-in-law as soon as he delivered his island from wild beasts. This task, which Œnopion deemed impracticable, was soon performed by Orion, who eagerly demanded his reward. Œnopion, on pretence of complying, intoxicated his illustrious guest. and put out his eyes on the sea shore, where he had laid himself down to sleep. Orion, finding himself blind when he awoke, was conducted by the sound to a neighbouring forge, where he placed one of the workmen on his back, and by his directions, went to a place where the rising sun was seen with the greatest advantage. Here he turned his face towards the luminary, and, as it is reported, immediately recovered his eye-sight, and hastened to punish the perfidious cruelty of Œnopion. It is said that Orion was an excellent workman in iron, and that he fabricated a subterraneous palace for Vulcan. Aurora, whom Venus had inspired with love, carried him away into the island of Delus, to enjoy his company with greater security; but Diana, who was jealous of this, destroyed Orion with her arrows. Some say, that Orion had provoked Diana's resentment, by offering violence to Opis, one of her female attendants, or, according to others, because he had attempted the virtue of the goddess herself. According to Ovid, Orion died of the bite of a scorpion, which the earth produced, to punish his vanity in boasting that there was not on earth any animal which he could not conquer. Some say that Orion was son of Neptune and Euryale, and that he had received from his father the privilege and power of walking over the sea without wetting his feet. Others make him son of Terra, like the rest of the giants. He had married a nymph called Sida, before his connection with the family of Œnopion; but Sida was the cause of her own death, by boasting herself fairer than Juno. According to Diodorus, Orion was a celebrated hunter, superior to the rest of mankind in strength and uncommon stature. He built the port of Zancle, and fortified the coast of Sicily against the frequent inundations of the sea, by heaping up a mound of earth, called Pelorum, on which he built a temple to the gods of the sea. After death, Orion was placed in heaven, where one of the constellations still bears his name. The constellation of Orion, placed near the feet of the bull, was composed of 17 stars in the form of a man holding a sword, which has given occasion to the poets often to speak of Orion's sword. As the constellation of Orion, which rises about the 9th day of March, and sets about the 21st of June, is generally supposed to be accompanied, at its rising, with great rains and storms, it has acquired the epithet of *aquosus*, given it by Virgil. Orion was buried in the island of Delus, and the monument which the people of Tanagra in Bœotia, showed, as containing the remains of this celebrated hero, was nothing but a cenotaph. The daughters of Orion distinguished themselves as much as their father, and, when the oracle had declared that Bœotia should not be delivered from a dreadful pestilence before two of Jupiter's children were immolated on the altars, they joyfully accepted the offer, and voluntarily sacrificed themselves for the good of their country. Their names were Menippe and Metioche. They had been carefully educated by Diana, and Venus and Minerva had made them very rich and valuable presents. The deities of hell were struck at the patriotism of the two females, and immediately two stars were seen to arise from the earth, which still smoked with the blood, and they were placed in the heavens in the form of a crown. According to Ovid, their bodies were burned by the Thebans, and, from their ashes arose two persons whom the gods soon after changed into constellations. *Diod.* 4.—*Homer. Odyss.* 5. v. 121. l. 11. v. 309.—*Virg. Æn.* 3. v. 517.—*Apollod.* 1. c. 4.—*Ovid. Met.* 8. v. 207. l. 13. v. 294 & 693. *Fast.* 5. v. 495 & 535.—*Val. Fl.* 1. v. 647. l. 2 & 4.—*Hygin.* fab. 125. 195. & *P.A.* 2. c. 44, &c.—*Propert.* 2. el. 13.—*Horat.* 2. od. 13. l. 3 od. 4 & 27. *Epod.* 10, &c.—*Lucan.* 1, &c.—*Catull. de Beren.*—*Palæphat.* 1.—*Parthen. Erotic.* 20.—*Tzetzes. in Lyc.* 328.—*Servius in Æn.* 539.—*Lactant. ad Theb.* 3. v. 27. l. 7. v. 237.—*Sch. Homer. Il.* 18. v. 488.—*Eustath. ad Il.* 17. v. 200.—*Sch. Eurip. in Hec.* 1088.—*Nicand.* 4.—*Ant. Lib.* 25.

ORIS'IA, a city of Iberia. *Steph.*

ORIS'SUS, a prince of Spain, who put Hamilcar to flight.

ORISUL'LA LIV'IA, a Roman matron, taken away from Piso.

ORISTI'DES, two islands in the Arabian Gulph. *Ptol.*

ORI'TÆ, a people of India, who submitted to Alexander. *Strab.* 15.

ORITA'NUM, a city of Eubœa. *Plin.* 4. c. 12.

ORITHY'IA, a daughter of Erechtheus, king of Athens, by Praxithea. She was courted and carried away by Boreas, king of Thrace, as she crossed the Ilissus, and became mother of Cleopatra, Chione, Zetes, and Calais. *Apollon.* 1. v. 211.—*Apollod.* 3. c. 15.—*Orpheus*, 220.—*Val. Fl.* 1. v. 469.—*Stat. Theb.* 12. v. 640.—*Ovid. Met.* 6. v. 706. *Fast.* 5. v. 204.—*Paus.* 1. c. 19. l. 5. c. 19.——One of the Nereides. *Hygin.*——A daughter of Cecrops, who bore Europus to Macedon. *Sch. Apollon.* 1. v. 211.——One of the Amazons, famous for her warlike and intrepid spirit. *Justin.* 2. c. 4.

ORIT'IAS, one of the hunters of the Calydonian boar. *Ovid. Met.* 8. fab. .

ORIUN'DUS, a river of Illyricum. *Liv.* 44. c. 31.

ORI'ZA, a city of Palmyrene. *Ptol.*

ORMA'NUS, a river of Arabia Felix, flowing into the Red Sea. *Ptol.*

ORME'NIUM, a town of Thessaly, on the Sinus Pagasæus. *Strab.*

OR'MENUS, a king of Thessaly, son of Cercaphus. He built a town which was called Ormenium from him. He was a father of Amyntor. *Homer. Il.* 9. 448. *Ovid. Heroid.* 9. v. 50.—*Strab.* 9.——A man who settled at Rhodes. *Strab.* 14.—*Gyrald. H. D.* 1.——The father of Astydamia, killed by Hercules. *Diod.* 4.——A son of Eurypylus.

ORMISDA'TIS, a name under which the Persians worshipped the god, whom they considered as the author of all good. The god whom they dreaded as the source of all evil, was called Arimanes, and they believed that these two divinities were perpetually at war together, and that therefore it was necessary to sacrifice to one for his protection, and to the other to escape his resentment. *Agathias*, 2 *Hist.*—*Gyrald. H. D.* 7.—*Plut. de Is. & Os.*

OR'NEA, a town of Argolis, famous for a battle fought here between the Lacedæmonians and Argives. *Diod. Sic.*

ORNEA'TES, a surname of Priapus among the people of Ornea. His festivals were called Ornea, and were also celebrated by young maidens at Colophon in Ionia. *Strab.* 8.—*Gyrald. H.D.* 8.

ORNE'US, a Centaur, son of Ixion and the Cloud. *Ovid. Met.* 12. v. 302.

OR'NEUS, a son of Erechtheus, king of Athens, who built Ornea, in Peloponnesus. He was father of Peteus. *Paus.* 2. c. 25.

ORNITH'IÆ, a wind blowing from the north in the spring, and so called from the appearance of birds ὀρνιθες, *aves*) *Colum.* 11. c. 2.—*Plin.* 2. c. 47.

ORNI'THON, a town of Phœnicia, between Tyre and Sidon. *Strab.*—*Plin.* 5. c. 19.

OR'NITUS or OR'PHITUS, a friend of Æneas, killed by Camilla in the Rutulian war. *Virg. Æn.* 11. v. 677.

ORNOS'PADES, a Parthian, driven from his country by Artabanus. He assisted Tiberius, and was made governor of Macedonia. *Tacit. Ann.* 6. c. 37.

ORNYT'ION, a son of Sisyphus, king of Corinth, father of Phocus. *Paus.* 9. c. 17.

OR'NYTUS, a man of Cyzicus, killed by the Argonauts. *Val. Fl.* 3. v. 173.

OROAN'DA, a town of Pisidia, now Haviran. *Liv.* 38. c. 18.—*Plin.* 5. c. 27.

OROAN'DES, a mountain of Asia, part of Taurus. *Plin. ibid.*

OROA'TES, a large river of Susiana. *Strabo.* It is called Oroatis by *Ptolemy. Pliny*, 6. c. 25, erroneously calls it Oratis.

OR'OBA, an inland city of Assyria. *Ptol.*

OROB'ATIS, an inland city of Persia. *Id.*

ORO'BIA, a town of Eubœa.

ORO'BII, a people of Italy, near Milan.

OR'OBIS, a river of Gallia Narbonensis. *Ptol.* It is called Orbis by *Mela*, 2. c. 5, and is now l'Orbe.

OROC'ANA, a city of Media. *Ptol.*

ORO'DES the First, a prince of Parthia, who murdered his brother Mithridates, and ascended his throne. He, either in person, according to Paterculus, or by Surena, his general, as several authors assert, defeated Crassus, the Roman triumvir, and poured melted gold down the throat of his fallen enemy, to reproach him for his avarice and ambition. He followed the interest of Cassius and Brutus at Philippi. It is said, that, when Orodes became old and infirm, his 30 children applied to him, and disputed, in his presence, their right to the succession. Phraates, the eldest of them, obtained the crown from his father, and, to hasten him out of the world, attempted to poison him. The poison had no effect, and Phraates, still determined on his father's death, strangled him with his own hands, about 37 years B.C. Orodes had then reigned about fifty years. *Justin.* 42. c. 4.—*Paterc.* 2. c. 30.—*Servius in Æn.* 11. v. 19.—*Dio.* 40. c. 27. l. 49. c. 23.—*Liv.* 106.—*Flor.* 3. c. 11.—*Cic. Fam.* 15. ep. 1.

ORO'DES the Second, king of Parthia, was murdered for his cruelty. *Josephus.* 18. *Jud.*

ORO'DES, a son of Artabanus, king of Armenia. *Tacit. Ann.* 6. c. 33.——One of the friends of Æneas in Italy, killed by Mezentius. *Virg. Æn.* 10. v. 732, &c.

ORŒ'TES, a Persian governor of Sardis, under Darius, famous for his cruel murder of Polycrates. He died B.C. 521. *Herodot.* 3. c. 128.—*Cic. Fin.* 5. c. 30.

OROLAU'NUM, a town of Gallia Belgica. *Antonin.* It is now Arlun.

OROMAN'DRUS, a city of Armenia Minor.

OROMAS'DES. *Vid.* Ormisdatis.

OROM'EDON, a lofty mountain in the island of Cos. *Theocrit.* 7.

OROM'EDON, a giant who made war against Jupiter. *Propert.* 3. el. 7. v. 48. The mountain was probably so called from his being buried under it.

ORON'DICI, a people of Galatia. *Ptol.*

ORON'TAS, a relation of Artaxerxes, sent to Cyprus, where he made peace with Evagoras. He was afterwards put to death at Columnia. *Polyæn.* 7. c. 13.—*Diod. Sic.* 15.

ORON'TES, a satrap of Mysia, B.C. 385, who rebelled from Artaxerxes, and afterwards betrayed his companions to him, *Diod. Sic.* 15.——A governor of Armenia, one of the Epigoni of Alexander the Great. *Polyæn.* 4. *com.* 3. *in Eumen.*——A king of the Lycians during the Trojan war, who followed Æneas, and perished in a shipwreck. *Virg. Æn.* 1. v. 117. 16. v. 34.

ORON'TES, a river of Syria, rising in Cœlesyria, and falling, after a rapid and troubled course, into the Mediterranean, below Antioch. According to Strabo, who mentions some fabulous accounts concerning it, the Orontes disappeared under ground for the space of five miles. The course of the river was altered by one of the Roman emperors to improve the navigation, and in the dried bed there was found, as Pausanias relates, a brick tomb, containing a body eleven cubits long, which the oracle of Apollo at Clarus declared to be the remains of an Indian hero called Orontes. The word Oronteus is often used for Syrius. *Dionys. Perieg.*—*Ovid. Met.* 2. v. 248.—*Strab.* 16.—*Paus.* 8. c. 20.—*Plin.* 2. c. 103. l. 5. c. 22.—*Propert.* 2. el. 18. v, 77.—*Lucan.* 3. v. 214. l. 6. v. 51.——A mountain of Media, near Ecbatana. *Ptol.*

OROPHER'NES, a man who seized the kingdom of Cappadocia. He died B.C. 154.

ORO'PUS, a town of Bœotia on the borders of Attica, near the Euripus, which received its name from Oropus, a son of Macedon. It was the frequent cause of quarrels between the Bœotians and the Athenians, whence some have called it one of the cities of Attica, and was at last confirmed in the possession of the Athenians by Philip, king of Macedon. Amphiaraus had a temple there. *Plin.* 4. c. 7.—*Paus.* 1. c. 34.—*Strab.* 9.——A small town of Eubœa, called Græa by *Aristotle.*——A city of Syria, called also Telmissa. *Steph.*

OR'OSA, an inland city of Media, called also Alinza. *Ptol.*

OROS'COPA, a city of Africa, concerning which there was a quarrel between Masinissa and the Carthaginians. *Appian. in Pun.*

OROSI'NES, a river of Thrace. *Plin.* 4. c. 11.

ORO'SIUS PAU'LUS, a Spanish writer, A.D. 416, who published a universal history in seven books, from the creation to his own time, in which, though learned, diligent, and pious, he betrayed a great ignorance of the knowledge of historical facts, and of chronology. The best edition is that of Havercamp, 4to. L. Bat. 1767. He wrote also a work called *Apologeticus contra Pelagium de arbitrii libertate*, edited by Coster, Louan 1558., and Fran. Fabricius, Mogunt. 1615. *Harles. Not. Lit. Rom.* 1. p. 673.—*Sax. Onom.* 1. p. 482.

OROS'PEDA, a mountain of Hispania Tarraconensis. *Strab.* 3. It is called Ortospeda by *Ptolemy.* It extends through a great portion of the country, and is called in different parts, Sierra de Segura, Sierra d'Alcaraz, and Montes de los Alpujaras.

OR'PHE, a daughter of Dion, king of Laconia, by Iphitea, daughter of Prognaus, changed into a rock with her sister Lyco by Bacchus. These two, together with a younger sister, Carya, received the gift of prophecy from Apollo, as a reward for the hospitality which their father had shown to the god, but on condition never to use this mark of divine favor, and never to inquire after secrets of which it became women to remain ignorant. Their promise was disregarded when Bacchus visited Laconia, and convinced Carya of his love. The two sisters, jealous of the intrigue, watched the god so attentively when he returned a second time, that he was not permitted to have an interview with Carya, so that in his resentment he carried them to mount Taygeta, where they were changed into stones. Carya was also changed into a tree, so called in Greek, the *nux* (walnut) of the Latins, the fruit of which was considered by the ancients, in consequence of these intrigues, to promote the powers of love. *Servius ad Virg. Ec.* 8. v. 30.—*Salmas. ad Solin.* p. 603.

OR'PHEUS, a son of Œager by the muse Calliope. Some suppose him to have been the son of Apollo, to render his birth more illustrious. He received a lyre from Apollo, or, according to some, from Mercury, upon which he played with such a masterly hand that even the most rapid rivers ceased to flow, the savage beasts of the forest forgot their wildness, and the mountains moved to listen to his song. All nature seemed charmed and animated, and the nymphs were his constant companions. Eurydice was the only one who made a deep and lasting impression upon the melodious musician, and their nuptials were celebrated. Their happiness, however, was short; Aristæus became enamoured of Eurydice, and, as she fled from her pursuer, a serpent, that was lurking in the grass, bit her foot, and she died of the poisoned wound. Her loss was severely felt by Orpheus, and he resolved to recover her or perish in the attempt. With his lyre in his hand he entered the infernal regions, and gained an easy admission to the palace of Pluto. The king of hell was charmed with the melody of his strains, and, according to the beautiful expression of the poets, the wheel of Ixion stopped, the stone of Sisyphus stood still, Tantalus forgot his perpetual thirst, and even the Furies relented. Pluto and Proserpine were moved with his sorrow, and consented to restore to him Eurydice, provided he forbore looking behind till he had come to the extremest borders of hell. The conditions were gladly accepted, and Orpheus was already in sight of the upper regions of the air when he forgot his promise, and turned back to look at his long lost Eurydice. He saw her, but she instantly vanished from his eyes. He attempted to follow her, but he was refused admission, and the only comfort he could find was to soothe his grief by the sound of his musical instrument in grottos or on the mountains. He totally separated himself from the society of mankind; and the Thracian women, whom he had offended by his coldness to their amorous passions, or, according to others, by his unnatural gratifications und impure indulgences, attacked him while they celebrated the orgies of Bacchus, and after they had torn his body to pieces, they threw into the Hebrus his head, which still articulated the words Eurydice! Eurydice! as it was carried down the stream into the Ægean Sea. Orpheus was one of the Argonauts, of which celebrated expedition he wrote a poetical account, still extant. This is doubted by Aristotle, who says, according to Cicero, that there never existed an Orpheus, but that the poems which pass under his name, are the compositions of a Pythagorean philosopher named Cecrops. According to some of the moderns the

Argonautica, the *Hymns*, the fragments *de lapidibus*, and the *Votum ad Musæum*, all attributed to Orpheus, are the production of the pen of Onomacritus, a poet who lived in the age of Pisistratus, tyrant of Athens. Pausanias, however, and Diodorus Siculus, speak of Orpheus as a great poet and musician, who rendered himself equally celebrated by his knowledge of the art of war, by the extent of his understanding, and by the laws which he enacted. Some maintain that he was killed by a thunderbolt. He was buried at Pieria in Macedonia, according to Apollodorus. The inhabitants of Dion boasted that his tomb was in their city, and the people of mount Libethrus, in Thrace, claimed the same honor, and farther observed, that the nightingales, which built their nests near his tomb, sang with greater melody than all other birds. Orpheus, as some report, after death received divine honors, the muses gave an honorable burial to his remains, and his lyre became one of the constellations in the heavens. The best edition of Orpheus is that of Gesner 8vo. Lips. 1764. *Diod.* 1, &c.—*Paus.* 1, &c.—*Apollod.* 1. c. 9, &c.—*Cic. de Nat. D.* 1. c. 38.—*Apollon.* 1.—*Virg. Æn.* 6. v. 645. *G.* 4. v. 457, &c.—*Hygin.* fab. 14, &c.—*Ovid. Met.* 10. fab. 1, &c. l. 11. fab. 1.—*Plato. Polit.* 10.—*Horat.* 1. od. 13 & 35.—*Orpheus.—Tzetzes ad Lyc.* 175 & 831.—*Servius ad G.* 4. v. 52. *Æn.* 6. v. 645.—*Propert.* 2. el. 23. v. 31.—*Philostr. Her.* 5.—*Val. Flacc.* 1. v. 187. 470. l. 2. v. 426. l. 4. v. 328.—*Aristoph. in Ran.* 1064.—*Euripid. in Alc.* 968.—*Pindar. Pyth.* 4.—*Conon. Narr.* 45.—*Fabr B. Gr.* 1. c. 18 & 19.—*Sax. Onom.* 1. p. 7.

OR'PHICA, a name by which the orgies of Bacchus were called, because they had been introduced into Europe from Ægypt by Orpheus. *Servius in* 6 *Æn.* v. 645.—*Diod.* 4.

ORPHID'IUS BENIG'NUS, a lieutenant of the first legion, slain in an engagement between that legion and the twenty-first. *Tacit.* 2. *Hist.* 43. 45.

ORPH'NE, a nymph of the infernal regions, mother of Ascalaphus by Acheron. The word signifies obscurity. *Ovid Met.* 5. v. 549.

ORPHNÆ'US, one of Pluto's horses. *Claudian. de Rap. Pr.* 1. v. 283.

OR'SA, a town of India within the Ganges. *Ptol.*

OR'SARA, a city of Armenia Minor. *Id. Simler* supposes it to be the Tonasa of *Antoninus.*

ORSED'ICE, a daughter of Cinyras and Metharme. *Apollod.*

ORSE'IS, a nymph who married Hellen. *Apollod.*

OR'SES, a Trojan killed in Italy. *Virg. Æn.* 10. v. 748.

ORSIL'LUS, a Persian who fled to Alexander, when Bessus murdered Darius. *Curt.* 5. c. 13.

ORSIL'OCHE, a surname of Diana Taurica, ironically expressive of hospitality, because all strangers were inhumanly offered on her altars. *Am. Marcel.* 22. c. 8.

ORSIL'OCHUS, a son of Idomeneus, killed by Ulysses in the Trojan war, &c. *Homer. Odyss.* 13. v. 260.——A son of the river Alpheus, father of Diocles, a rich citizen of Phoræ in Messenia, who was father of Orsilochus, killed by Æneas during the Trojan war. *Homer. Il.* 5. v. 546.—*Paus.* 4. c. 30.——A Trojan killed by Camilla in the Rutulian wars. *Virg. Æn.* 11. v. 636 & 690.

OR'SIMA, a town of Upper Æthiopia. *Plin.* 6. c. 29.

OR'SINES, one of the officers of Darius at the battle of Arbela. He was slain by order of Alexander, when Bagoas had calumniously accused him of profaning the sepulchre of Cyrus. *Curt.* 10. c. 1.

ORSIP'PUS a man of Megara, who was prevented from obtaining a prize at the Olympic games, because his clothes were entangled as he ran. This circumstance was the cause that, for the future, all the combatants were obliged to appear naked. *Paus.* 1. c. 44.

ORSOLOGI'ACUM, a city of Galatia, between Ancyra and Nysa. *Antonin.* It is probably the Orsologia of *Ptolemy.*

ORSO'NA or UR'SO, a town of Hispania Bætica. *Strab.—Plin.* 3. c. 1.

OR'TALUS M., a grandson of Hortensius, who was induced to marry by a present from Augustus, who wished that ancient family not to be extinguished. *Tacit. Ann.* 2. c. 37.—*Val. Max.* 3. c. 5.—*Suet. in Tiber.*

ORTHAG'ORAS, a man who wrote a treatise on India. *Ælian. de Anim.* 16. c. 35 & 17. c. 6.——A musician in the age of Epaminondas, whose instructor he was. *Athen.* l. 4.——A tyrant of Sicyon, who mingled severity with justice in his government. The sovereign authority remained upwards of 100 years in his family. *Aristot. Polit.* 5. c. 12.—*Plut. de Virt. & Vit.*

ORTHÆ'A, a daughter of Hyacinthus, immolated by the Athenians.—*Apollod.*

OR'THE, a town of Magnesia. *Plin.* 4. c. 9. According to *Strabo*, it was in Perrhæbia.

ORTHE'AGA, a city of Mesopotamia. *Ptol.*

ORTHE'SIA, an epithet of Diana among the Thracians, ἀπὸ τοῦ ὀρθοῦν, because she was supposed to *lift up* the afflicted, especially the women in labor. *Herod. Melpom.*

OR'THIA, a surname of Diana at Sparta. In her sacrifices it was usual for boys to be whipped. *Vid.* Diamastigosis. *Plut. in Thes. &c.—Paus.* 3. c. 16.—*Servius ad Virg. Æn.* 2. v. 116.

ORTHIUM'AGUS, a place on the sea coast of Phœnicia. *Polyæn.* 4. c. 6. *com.* 9.

ORTHOCORYBAN'TII, a people of Asiatic Scythia. *Herodot.* l. 3.

ORTHO'SIA, a town of Caria, on the confines of Pisidia. *Liv.* 45. c. 25.——A city of Phœnicia, formerly called Anataradus. *Plin.* 5. c. 20.

OR'THUS, a dog which belonged to Geryon, from whom and the Chimæra sprang the Sphinx, and the Nemean lion. He had two heads, and was sprung from the union of Echidna and Typhon. He was destroyed by Hercules. *Hesiod. Theog.* 310.—*Apollod.* 2. c. 5.—*Sil. Ital.* 13. v. 843.

ORTO'NA *Vid.* Artona.

ORTOP'ULA or ORTOP'LA, a town of Liburnia. *Ptol.*

ORTOSPANA, a city of Paropanisus. *Ptol.* It is now Candahor.

ORTOS'PANUM, a city of India. *Plin.* 6. c. 17.

ORTYG'IA, a grove near Ephesus. *Tacit. Ann.* 3. c. 61.——A small island of Sicily, within the bay of Syracuse, which once formed one of the four quarters of that great city. It was in this island that the celebrated fountain Arethusa arose. Ortygia is now the only part remaining of the once famed Syracuse, about two miles in circumference, and inhabited by 18,000 souls. It has suffered, like the towns on the eastern coast, by the eruptions of Ætna. *Virg. Æn.* 3. v. 694.—*Homer. Odyss.* 15. v. 403. *In Hymn. in Apoll.* 16.—*Pindar. Nem.* 1. v. 4.—*Paus.* 8. c. 54.——An ancient name of the island of Delus. Some suppose that it received this name from Latona, who fled thither when changed into a quail (ὄρτυξ), by Jupiter, to avoid the pursuit of Juno. Diana was called Ortygia, as being born there; as also Apollo. *Ovid. Met.* 1. v. 651. *Fast.* 5. v. 692.—*Virg. Æn.* 3. v. 124.—*Schol. Apollon.* 1. v. 308 & 419.

ORTYG'IUS, a Rutulian killed by Æneas. *Virg. Æn.* 9. v. 573.

OR'VIUM, a promontory of Hispania Tarraconensis. *Ptol.*

ORU'ROS, a place of Mesopotamia. *Plin.* 6. c. 26.

O'RUS or HO'RUS, one of the gods of the Ægyptians, son of Osiris and of Isis. He assisted his mother in avenging his father, who had been murdered by Typhon. Orus was skilled in medicine, acquainted with futurity, and made the good and the happiness of his subjects the sole object of his government. He was the emblem of the sun among the Ægyptians, and was generally represented as an infant, swathed in variegated clothes. In one hand he held a staff, which terminated in the head of a hawk, in the other a whip with three thongs. *Herodot.* 2.—*Plut. de Isid. & Os.—Diod.* 1. ——The first king of Trœzene. *Paus.* 2. c. 30.——A grammarian mentioned by *Eustathius in Il.* λ.—*Selden. de Dis. Syr. Synt.* 2. c. 16.——An historian or geographer mentioned by *Stephanus in* Νικίου κώμη.

ORYAN'DER, a satrap of Persia, set over Ægypt, but his cruelty was so great that the Ægyptians rebelled against him. *Polyæn.* 7. c. 11.

O'RYX, a place of Arcadia on the Ladon. *Paus.* 8. c. 25.

OS'ACES, a Parthian general, who received a mortal wound from Cassius. *Cic. ad Att.* 5. ep. 20.—*Dio.* 40. c. 28.

OSÆ'A, a town of Sardinia. *Ptol. Simler* conjectures it to be the Othoca of *Antoninus*, and it is now probably l'Oseo.

OS'CA, a town of Spain, now Huesca in Arragon. *Liv*. 34. c. 10. Sertorius founded an academy here, and here also he was slain. *Plut. in Sertor.—Vell*, 2. c. 30.

OSCA'NA, a city of Gedrosia. *Ptol*.

OSCEL'LA, a town of Insubria on the confines of the Lepontii. *Ptol*. It is now Domo d'Oscela.

OS'CI, a people between Campania and the country of the Volsci, who assisted Turnus against Æneas. Some suppose them to have been the same as the Opici, the word Osci being a diminutive or abbreviation of the other. The language, plays, and ludicrous expressions of this nation, are often mentioned by the ancients, and from their indecent tendency some suppose the word *obscœnum* (*quasi oscenum*) is derived. *Tacit. Ann*. 4. c. 14.—*Cic Fam*. 7. ep. 1.—*Liv*. 10. c. 20.—*Strab*. 5.—*Plin*. 3. c. 5.—*Horat*. 1. sat. 5. v. 54.—*Virg. Æn*. 7. v. 730.

OS'CIUS, a mountain with a river of the same name, in Thrace. *Thucyd*.

OSCHOPHO'RIA, a festival observed by the Athenians. It receives its name ἀπό τοῦ φέρειν τὰς ὄσχας *from carrying boughs* called ὄσχας, hung with grapes. The following is Plutarch's account of its institution. Theseus, at his return from Crete, forgot to hang out the white sail, by which his father was to be apprized of his success. This neglect was fatal to Ægeus, who threw himself into the sea and perished. Theseus no sooner reached the land, than he sent a herald to inform his father of his safe return, and in the meantime, began to make the sacrifices which he vowed when he first set sail from Crete. The herald, on his entrance into the city, found the people in great agitation. Some lamented the king's death, while others, elated at the sudden news of the victory of Theseus, crowned the herald with garlands in demonstration of their joy. The herald carried back the garlands on his staff to the sea shore, and after he had waited till Theseus had finished his sacrifice, he related the melancholy story of the king's death. Upon this the people ran in crowds to the city, showing their grief by cries and lamentations. From that circumstance therefore, at the feast of Oschophoria, not the herald but his staff was crowned with garlands, and all the people that were present always exclaimed ἐλελεῦ, ἰοὺ ἰοὺ, words expressive of grief or of consternation or depression of spirits. The historian further mentions, that Theseus when he went to Crete, did not take with him the usual number of virgins, but that instead of two of them, he filled up the number with two youths of his acquaintance, whom he made pass for women, by disguising their dress, and by using them to the ointments and perfumes of women, as well as by a long and succesful imitation of their voice. The imposition succeeded, their sex was not discovered in Crete, and when Theseus had triumphed over the Minotaur, he with these two youths, led a procession with branches in their hands, in the same habit which is still used at the celebration of the Oschophoria. The branches which were carried were in honor of Bacchus or Ariadne, or because they returned in autumn, when the grapes were ripe. Besides this procession, there was also a race exhibited, in which only young men, whose parents were both alive, were permitted to engage. It was usual for them to run from the temple of Bacchus to that of Minerva, which was on the sea shore. The place where they stopped was called ὀσχοφόριον, because the *boughs* which they carried in their hands were deposited there. The reward of the conqueror was a cup called Πενταπλόα or Πενταπλῆ, *five-fold*, because it contained a mixture of five different things, wine, honey, cheese, meal and oil. *Plut. in Thes.—Hesych.—Harpocrat.—Paus. Att.—Athen*. 1. 11.

OS'CUS, a freedman of Otho, præfect of the fleet sent against Gallia Narbonensis. *Tacit. Hist*. 1. c. 87.

OS'DARA, a city of Armenia Minor. *Antonin*. It is probably the same as Asdara.

OSERIC'TA, a small island. *Plin*. 37. c. 5. According to *Cluverius*, it is now Oesel, an island in the Baltic.

O'SI, a people of Germany. *Tacit. G*. 28 & 43.

OSIA'NA, a city of Cappadocia. *Antonin*.

OS'IBA, a city of Albania. *Ptol*.

OSICER'DA or **OS'SERA**, a town of Hispania Tarraconensis. *Ptol*. *Pliny*, 3. c. 3, calls it Osigerdense.

O'SII or **OS'ILI**, a people of European Sarmatia. *Ptol*.

OSIN'CUM, a town of Corsica. *Id*. It is thought to be now Omiso.

OSIN'TIGI, a city of Hispania Bætica. *Plin*. 3. c. 1.

OSIN'IUS, a king of Clusium, who assisted Æneas against Turnus. *Virg. Æn*. 10. v. 655.

OSI'RIS, a great deity of the Ægyptians, son of Jupiter and Niobe. The ancients greatly differ in their opinions concerning this celebrated god, but they all agree that, as king of Ægypt, he took particular care to civilize his subjects, to polish their morals, to give them good and salutary laws, and to teach them agriculture. After he had accomplished a reform at home, Osiris resolved to go and spread civilization in the other parts of the earth. He left his kingdom to the care of his wife Isis, and of her faithful minister Hermes or Mercury. The command of his troops at home was left to the trust of Hercules, a warlike officer. In his expedition Osiris was accompanied by his brother Apollo, and by Anubis, Macedo, and Pan. His march was through Æthiopia, where his army was increased by the addition of the Satyrs, a hairy race of monsters, who made dancing and playing on musical instruments their chief study. He afterwards passed through Arabia, and visited the greatest part of the kingdoms of Asia and of Europe, where he enlightened the minds of men by introducing among them the worship of the gods, and a reverence for the wisdom of a supreme being. At his return home Osiris found the minds of his subjects roused and agitated. His brother Typhon had raised seditions, and endeavoured to make himself popular. Osiris, whose sentiments were always of the most pacific nature, endeavoured to convince his brother of his ill conduct, but fell a sacrifice to the attempt. Typhon murdered him in a secret apartment, and cut his body to pieces, which were divided among the associates of his guilt. Typhon, according to Plutarch, shut up his brother in a coffer, and threw him into the Nile. The inquiries of Isis discovered the body of her husband on the coasts of Phœnicia, where it had been conveyed by the waves, but Typhon stole it as it was being carried to Memphis, and divided it among his companions, as was before observed. This cruelty incensed Isis; she revenged her husband's death, and, with her son Orus, defeated Typhon and the partisans of his conspiracy. She recovered the mangled pieces of her husband's body, a small part excepted, which the murderer had thrown into the sea, and to render him all the honor which his humanity deserved, she made as many statues of wax as there were mangled pieces of his body. Each statue contained a piece of the flesh of the dead monarch; and Isis, after she had summoned into her presence one by one, the priests of all the different deities in her dominions, gave them each a statue, intimating, that in doing that she had preferred them to all the other communities of Ægypt, and she bound them by a solemn oath that they would keep secret that mark of her favor, and endeavour to show their sense of it by establishing a form of worship, and paying divine honors to their prince. They were further directed to choose whatever animals they pleased to represent the person and the divinity of Osiris, and were enjoined to pay the greatest reverence to that representative of his divinity, and to bury it when dead with the greatest solemnity. To render their establishment more popular, each sacerdotal body had a certain portion of land allotted to them to maintain them, and to defray the expenses which necessarily attended the sacrifices and ceremonial rites. That part of the body of Osiris which had not been recovered, was treated with more particular attention by Isis, and she ordered that it should receive honors more solemn and at the same time more mysterious than the other members. *Vid*. Phallica. As Osiris had particularly instructed his subjects in cultivating the ground, the priests chose the ox to represent him, and paid the most superstitious veneration to that animal. *Vid.* Apis. Osiris, according to the opinion of some mythologists, is the same as the sun, and the adoration which is paid by different nations to an Anubis, a Bacchus, a Dionysius, a Jupiter, a Pan, &c. is the same as that which Osiris received in the Ægyptian temples. Isis also after death received divine honors as well as her husband, and as the ox was the symbol of the sun, or Osiris, so the cow was the emblem of the moon, or of Isis. Nothing can give a clearer idea of the power and greatness of Osiris than this inscription which has been found on some ancient monuments: "Saturn, the youngest of all the gods, was my father: I am Osiris, who conducted a large and numerous army as far the deserts of India, and travelled over the greatest part of the world, and visited the streams of the Ister, and the remotest shores of the ocean, diffusing benevolence to all the inhabitants of the earth." Osiris was generally represented with a cap on his head like a mitre, with two horns; he held a stick in his left hand, and in his right a whip with three thongs. Sometimes he appears with the head of a hawk, as that bird, by its quick and piercing eyes, is a proper emblem of the sun. *Plut. in Isid. & Os.—Herodot.* 2. c. 144.—*Diod.* 1.—*Homer. Odyss.* 12. v. 323.—*Ælian. de Anim.* 3.—*Lucian. de Deâ. Syr.—Tibull.* 2. el. 1.—*Porphyr. de Abst.—Servius. ad Virg. G.* 1. v. 166. *Æn.* 4. v. 154 & 609.—*Gyrald. H.D.* 8.—*Plin.* 8.——A Persian general, who lived 450 B.C.——A friend of Turnus, killed in the Rutulian war. *Virg. Æn.* 12. v. 458.

OSIS'MII, a people of Gaul in Britany. *Mela*, 3. c. 2.—*Cæs. B. G.* 2. c. 34.—*Plin.* 4. c. 18.

OS'PHAGUS, a river of Macedonia. *Liv.* 31. c. 39.

OS'PHRYON, one of those who mutilated the Hermæ or statues of Mercury, at Athens. *Schol. in Aristoph. Aves.*

OSQUIDA'TES, a people Gallia Aquitanica. *Plin.* 4. c. 19.

OSRHOE'NE, a country of Syria on the confines of Mesopotamia. It received this name from one of its kings called Osrhoes, and is now probably Tsisire in the province of Diarbeck. *Procop.—Paus.—Dion.—Steph.* &c.

OS'RHOES, a king of Parthia, subdued by Trajan. *Dionis. Fragm. e. Theodis.* 1. 68.

OS'SA, a lofty mountain of Thessaly, once the residence of the Centaurs. It was formerly joined to mount Olympus, but Hercules, as some report, separated them, and made between them the celebrated valley of Tempe. This separation of the two mountains was more probably effected by an earthquake, which happened, as fabulous accounts represent, about 1885 years B.C. Ossa was one of those mountains which the giants, in their wars against the gods, heaped up one on the other to scale the heavens with more facility. It is now Monte Cassovo, or Olira, according to others. *Mela*, 2. c. 3.—*Ovid. Met.* 1. v. 155. 1. 2. v. 225. 1. 7. v. 224. *Fast.* 1. v. 307. 1. 3. v. 441.—*Strab.* 9.—*Lucan.* 1. v. 389. 1. 6. v. 334 & 412.—*Virg. G.* 1. v. 281.—*Seneca. in Herc. Fur.* 285.——A town of Macedonia. *Ptol.*——A mountain of Peloponnesus. *Strab.*——A river of Etruria. *Ptol.* It is now Fiore.

OSSERIA'TES, a people of Upper Pannonia. *Plin.* 3. c. 25.—*Ptol.*

OSSIGITA'NIA, a city of Hispania Bætica. *Plin.* 3. c. 1.

OSSON'OBA, a city of Lusitania, called Lusturia by *Pliny*, 3. c. 1., Onoba by *Mela*, 3. c. 1., and Sonoba by *Strabo*. It is now Estombar.

OSTAMA, a city of Arabia Felia. *Ptol.*

OSTEO'DES, islands near the Lipari isles. *Plin.* 3. c. 8. They were so called from the bones of some Carthaginians who perished there by famine, according to *Diodorus Siculus*, and are now called Li Pozzeli.

OS'THA, a city of India Citerior. *Ptol.*

OS'TIA, a town built at the mouth of the river Tiber by Ancus Martius, king of Rome, about sixteen miles distant from Rome. It had a celebrated harbour, and was so pleasantly situated that the Romans generally spent a part of the year there. There was a small tower in the port like the Pharos of Alexandria, built upon the wreck of a large ship which had been sunk there, and which contained the obelisks of Ægypt, with which the Roman emperors intended to adorn the capital of Italy. In the age of Strabo the sand and mud deposited by the Tiber had choked the harbour, and added much to the size of the small islands, which sheltered the ships at the entrance of the river. Ostia and her harbour called Portus, became gradually separated, and are now at a considerable distance from the sea. *Flor.* 1. c. 4. 1. 3. c. 21.—*Liv.* 1. c. 33.—*Mela*, 2. c. 4.—*Sueton.—Plin.—Servius ad Virg. Æn.* 7. v. 31.

OSTIP'PO, a city of Hispania Bætica. *Plin.* 3. c. 1. It is now Estepona.

OSTOB'ARA, a city of Bactriana. *Ptol.*

OSTO'RIUS SCAP'ULA, a man made governor of Britain by Claudius. He defeated and took prisoner the famous Caractacus, and died A.D. 55. *Tacit. Ann.* 12. c. 31, &c.——A Roman who put himself to death when accused before Nero of having allowed verses reflecting upon the emperor to be recited in his house. *Id.* 14. c. 48.

OSTO'RIUS SABI'NUS, a man who accused Soranus, in Nero's reign. *Id.* 16. c. 33.

OS'TRA, a town of Umbria. *Ptol. Pliny.* 3. c. 14, calls the people Ostrani.

OSTRACI'NA, a town of Ægypt on the confines of Palestine. *Plin.* 5. c. 12.

OSYMAN'DYS, an ancient king of Ægypt. He erected, in a splendid style, an enormous statue of himself, the feet of which were of the length of seven cubits. *Joh. Marsham. Can. Chron.* sec. 15. p. 426, &c.

OT'ACES, one of the auxiliaries of Perses against Æetes. *Val. Flacc.* 6. v. 121. Some MSS. read Sotaces.

MAR'CIA OTACIL'IA SEVE'RA, wife of Philippus the elder, was a Christian, and for her sake the emperor treated the Christians with lenity. There are many medals extant which bear her effigy. *Casaubon. Not. ad Hist. Aug. Script.—Euseb.* 6. c. 31.—*Spon. Itiner.* part. 3. p. 180 & 193. [There is a bust of Otacilia in the Vatican.]

OTACIL'IUS, a Roman consul sent against the Carthaginians.

OTADI'NI or OTADE'NI, a people of Albion. *Ptol.* According to *Camden*, they inhabited the country now Northumberland.

OTA'NES, a noble Persian, one of the seven who conspired against the usurper Smerdis. It was through him that the usurpation was first discovered. He was afterwards appointed by Darius over the sea coast of Asia Minor, and took Byzantium. *Herodot.* 3. c. 70, &c.

OTAX'ES, an auxiliary of Perses, who assumed the habit of Pan, and terrified the Colchians. He was slain by Aron. *Val. Flacc.* 6. v. 529.

OTESI'NI, a people of Italy in Gallia Togata. *Plin.* 3. c. 15.

O'THO M. SYL'VIUS, a Roman emperor descended from the ancient kings of Etruria. He was one of Nero's favorites, and as such he was raised to the highest offices of the state, and made governor of Pannonia by the interest of Seneca, who wished to remove him from Rome, lest Nero's love for Poppæa should prove his ruin. After Nero's death Otho conciliated the favor of Galba, the new emperor; but when he did not gain his point, and when Galba had refused to adopt him as his successor, he resolved to make himself absolute without any regard to the age or dignity of his friend. The great debts which he had contracted encouraged his avarice, he caused Galba to be assassinated, and made himself emperor. He was acknowledged by the senate and the Roman people, but the sudden revolt of Vitellius in Germany rendered his situation precarious, and it was mutually resolved that their respective right to the empire should be decided by arms. Otho obtained three victories over his enemies, but in a general engagement near Brixellum, his forces were defeated, and he stabbed himself, when all hopes of success were vanished, after a reign of about three months, on the 20th of April, A.D. 69. It has been justly observed that the last moments of Otho's life were those of a philosopher. He comforted his soldiers who lamented his fortune, and expressed his concern for their safety, when they earnestly solicited to pay him the last friendly offices before he stabbed himself, and he observed, that it was better that one man should die, than that a whole empire should be involved in ruin for his obstinacy. His nephew was pale and distressed, fearing the anger and haughtiness of the conqueror; but Otho comforted him, and observed that Vitellius would be kind and affectionate to the friends and relations of Otho, since Otho was not ashamed to say, that in the time of their greatest enmity the mother of Vitellius had received every friendly treatment from his hands. He also burnt the letters which, by falling into the hands of Vitellius, might provoke his resentment against those who had favored the cause of an unfortunate general. These noble and humane sentiments in a man who was the associate of Nero's shameful pleasures, and who stained his hand in the blood of his master, have appeared to some wonderful, and passed for the features of policy, and not of a naturally virtuous and benevolent heart. *Plut. in Vitâ.—Suet. in Oth.—Tacit.* 2. *Hist.* c. 50, &c.—*Martial.* 6. epigr. 32.—*Juv.* 2. v. 90, &c. [A bust of Otho will be found in the Capitol at Rome.]

O'THO JU'NIUS, a tribune of the people, banished for interceding for Acutia. *Tac. Ann.* 6. c. 47.

O'THO ROS'CIUS, a tribune of the people, who, in Cicero's consulship, made a regulation to permit the Roman knights at public spectacles to have the fourteen first rows after the seats of the senators. This was opposed with virulence by some, but Cicero ably defended it. *Horat.* ep. 4. v. 10. —*Juv.* 3. v. 159. sat. 14. v. 324.

O'THO, the father of the Roman emperor Otho, a favorite of Claudius.

OTH'OCA, a city of Sardinia. *Antonin.*

OTHRIO'NEI, a people of Macedonia, between the Amantii and Lyncestæ. *Plin.* 4. c. 10.

OTHRONIEN'SES, a people near Mæonia. *Plin.* 5. c. 29.

OTHRO'NUS, a city or an island near Sicily. *Steph.*

OTHRY'ADES, one of the 300 Spartans who fought against 300 Argives, when those two nations disputed their respective right to Thyrea. Two Argives, Alcinor and Cronius, and Othryades, survived the battle. The Argives went home to carry the news of their victory, but Othryades, who had been reckoned among the number of the slain, on account of his wounds, recovered himself and carried some of the spoils of which he had stripped the Argives into the camp of his countrymen; and after he had raised a trophy, and had written with his own blood, the word *Vici* on his shield, he killed himself, unwilling to survive the death of his countrymen. *Val. Max.* 3. c. 2—*Plut. Parall.—Suidas.—Herodot.* 1. c. 82.——A patronymic given to Pantheus the Trojan priest of Apollo, from his father Othrys. *Virg. Æn.* 2. v. 319.——A person wounded in the thigh by the Calydonian boar. *Ovid. Met.* 8. v. 371.

OTHRY'ONEUS, a Thracian who came to the Trojan war in hopes of marrying Cassandra. He was killed by Idomeneus. *Homer. Il.* 13. v. 375.

O'THRYS, a mountain, or rather a chain of mountains in Thessaly, the residence of the Centaurs. Though covered by almost perpetual snows it abounded with forests of pine. *Stat. Ach.* 1. v. 238.—*Lucan.* 6. v. 338.—*Strab.* 9.—*Herodot.* 7. c. 129.—*Virg. Æn.* 7. v. 675.—*Solin.* 13.——A Trojan, father of Pantheus. *Virg. Æn.* 2.

O'TREUS, a king of Phrygia, son of Cisseus, and brother to Hecuba. *Hesych.*——A chief of the Maryandini, and suitor of Hesione, was slain by Amycus. *Val. Flacc.* 4. v. 162.——A son of Dascylus and Anthemoïsa, slain by Ambenus in the war between Perses and Æetes.

OTROE'A, a town on the borders of Bithynia. *Strab.*

OT'RYE, a town of Phrygia Major, on the confines of Lydia. *Plin.* 5. c. 29.

OTTOROC'ORÆ, a people of Serica, whose city was Ottorocora. *Ptolemy* mentions also a mountain of this name, which *Appian*, l. 3, calls Opurocarra. *Plin.* 6. c. 17.

O'TUS and EPHIAL'TES, sons of Neptune. *Vid.* Aloides.

O'TYS, a prince of Paphlagonia, who revolted from the Persians to Agesilaus. *Xenoph.* l. 4.

O'VIA, a Roman lady, wife of C. Lollius. *Cic. Att.* 21, &c.

P. OVID'IUS NA'SO, a celebrated Roman poet, born at Sulmo, on the 20th March, about 43 years B.C. As he was intended for the bar, his father sent him early to Rome, and removed him to Athens in the 16th year of his age. The progress of Ovid in the study of eloquence was great, but the father's expectations were frustrated; his son was born a poet, and nothing could deter him from pursuing his natural inclination, though he was often reminded that Homer lived and died in the greatest poverty. Everything he wrote was expressed in poetical numbers, as he himself says, *et quod tentabam scribere, versus erat.* A lively genius and a fertile imagination soon gained him admirers; the learned became his friends: Virgil, Propertius, Tibullus, and Horace, honored him with their correspondence, and Augustus patronised him with the most unbounded liberality. These favors, however, were of short duration, and the poet was soon after banished, in his 50th year, to Tomus, on the Euxine Sea, by the emperor. The true cause of this sudden exile is unknown. Some attribute it to a shameful amour with Livia, the wife of Augustus, while others maintain that it arose from the knowledge which Ovid had of the unpardonable incest of the emperor with his daughter Julia. These reasons are indeed merely conjectural, the cause was of a very private and secret nature, of which Ovid himself is afraid to speak, as it arose from error and not from criminality. It was, however, something improper in the family or court of Augustus which he had seen, as these lines seem to indicate:

Cur aliquid vidi? Cur noxia lumina feci?
Cur imprudenti cognita culpa mihi est?
Inscius Actæon vidit sine veste Dianam.
Præda fuit canibus non minus ille suis.

Again,

Inscia quod crimen viderunt lumina plector,
Peccatumque oculos est habuisse meum.

And in another place,

Perdiderunt cum me duo crimina, carmen et error,
Alterius facti culpa silenda mihi est.

In his banishment, Ovid betrayed his pusillanimity, and however afflicted and distressed his situation was, yet the flattery and impatience which he showed in his writings are a disgrace to his pen, and expose him more to ridicule than pity. Though he prostituted his pen and his time to adulation, yet the emperor proved deaf to all entreaties, and refused to listen to his most ardent friends at Rome, who wished for the return of the poet. Ovid, who undoubtedly wished for a Brutus to deliver Rome of her tyrannical Augustus, continued his flattery even to meanness; and, when the emperor died, he was so mercenary as to consecrate a small temple to the departed tyrant, on the shore of the Euxine, where he regularly offered frankincense every morning. Tiberius proved as regardless as his predecessor, to the entreaties which were made for Ovid, and the poet died in the 7th or 8th year of his banishment, in the 59th year of his age, A.D. 17, and was buried at Tomus. In the year 1508 A.D., the following epitaph was found at Stain, in the modern kingdom of Austria:

Hic situs est vates quem Divi Cæsaris ira.
Augusti patriâ cedere jussit humo.
Sæpe miser voluit patriis occumbere terris,
Sed frustra! Hunc illi fata dedêre locum.

This, however, is an imposition, to render celebrated an obscure corner of the world, which never contained the bones of Ovid. The greatest part of Ovid's poems are remaining. His *Metamorphoses* in 15 books are extremely curious on account of the different mythological facts and traditions which they relate, but they can have no claim to the name of an epic poem. In composing this, the poet was more indebted to the then existing traditions, and to the theogony of the ancients, than to the powers of his own imagination. His *Fasti* were divided into 12 books, the same number as the constellations in the zodiac; but of these six have perished, and the learned world have reason to lament the loss of a poem, which must have thrown so much light upon the religious rites and ceremonies, festivals and sacrifices of the ancient Romans as we may judge from the six that have survived the ravages of time and barbarity. His *Tristia*, which are divided into five books, contain much elegance and softness of expression, as also his *Elegies* on different subjects. The *Heroides* are nervous, spirited, and diffuse, the poetry is excellent, the language varied, but the expressions are often too wanton and indelicate, a fault which is common in his compositions. His three books of *Amorum*, and the same number *de Arte Amandi*, with the other *de Remedio Amoris*, are written with great elegance, and contain many flowery descriptions; but the doctrine which they hold forth is dangerous, and, as the composition of an experienced libertine and refined sensualist, they are to be read with caution, as they seem to be calculated to corrupt the heart, and sap the foundations of virtue and morality. His *Ibis*, which is written in imitation of a poem of Callimachus of the same name, is a satirical performance. Besides these, there are extant some fragments of other poems, and among these, some of a tragedy called *Medea*. The talents of Ovid as a dramatic writer have been disputed, and some have observed, that he who is so often void of sentiment, was not born to shine as a tragedian. Ovid has attempted, perhaps, too many sorts of poetry at once. On whatever he has written, he has totally exhausted the subject, and left nothing unsaid. He every where paints nature with a masterly hand, and gives strength to the most common expressions. It has been judiciously observed, that his poetry, after his banishment from Rome, was destitute of that spirit and vivacity which we admire in his other compositions. His *Fasti* are, perhaps, the best written of all his poems, and, after them, we may fairly rank his love verses, his *Heroides*, and, after all, his *Metamorphoses*, which were not totally finished when Augustus sent him into banishment. His *Epistles from Pontus* are the language of an abject and pusillanimous flatterer. However critics may censure the indelicacy and the inaccuracies of Ovid, it is to be acknowledged that his poetry contains great sweetness and elegance, and, like that of Tibullus, charms the ear and captivates the mind. Ovid married three wives, but of the last alone he speaks with fondness and affection. He had only one daughter, but by which of his wives is unknown: and she herself became mother of two children, by two husbands. The best editions of Ovid's works, are those of Burman, 4 vols. 4to. Amst. 1727; of L. Bat. 1670, in 8vo, and of Utrecht, in 12mo, 4 vols, 1713. *Ovid. Trist.* 1. el. 2. v. 77. l. 2. v. 97, 108 & 207. l. 3. el. 5. v. 49. el. 7. v. 12. el. 12. v. 37. l. 4. v. 81, 625 & 673. *Fast.* 3. v. 7 & 809. l. 4. v. 81, 625 & 673. *Am.* 1. el. 3. v. 7. l. 2. v. 110. l. 3. el. 15. v. 5.—*Quintil.*—*Paterc.* 2.—*Martial.* 3 & 8.—*Harles. Not. Lit. Rom.* 1. p. 276.—*Sax. Onom.* 1. p. 190.

OVID'IUS, a man who accompanied his friend Cæsonius when banished from Rome by Nero. *Martial.* 7. epigr. 43.

OVIN'IA LEX, was enacted to permit the censors to elect and admit among the number of the senators the best and worthiest of the people. *Joh. Rosin. Ant. Rom.* 8. c. 5.

OVIN'IUS, a freedman of Vatinius, the friend of Cicero. *Quintil.* 3. c. 4.

OVIN'IUS QUIN'TUS, a Roman senator, punished by Augustus for disgracing his rank in the court of Cleopatra. *Eutrop.* 1.—*Orosius*, 6. c. 49.

O'VIUS, a man who gave information to Cicero of the state of his son at Athens. *Cic.* 16. *Att.* 1.

OX'AMA or UX'AMA, a city of Hispania Tarraconensis. *Ptol.* The city has perished, but a neighbouriug town, Borgo d'Osma, has sprung from its ruins.

OX'ATHRES, a brother of Darius, greatly honored by Alexander, and made one of his generals. *Curt.* 7. c. 5.——A Persian, who favored the cause of Alexander. *Curt.*

OX'EAS, a son of Hercules by Megara. *Boccat.*

OX'EI, a people of Epirus, between Nicopolis and Naupactum. *Antonin.*

OXI'Æ, a name of the Echinades. *Steph. in Dulich.*

OXIA'NE, a lake of Sogdiana, formed by the Oxus. *Niger* says that it is now Chorasmuni, and *Ptolemy* calls the people in the neighbourhood Oxiani.

OXI'ONES, a people of European Sarmatia, whom superstitious traditions represented as having the countenance human, and the rest of the body like that of beasts. *Tacit. de Germ.* 46.

OXIO'PIUM, a city of Asiatic Mysia. *Plin.* 5. c. 30.

OX'US, a large river of Sogdiana, flowing through Margiana, and falling into the east of the Caspian Sea. Its modern name is Geichon, according to some, but there are a variety of opinions upon the subject. *Dionys.* v. 746.—*Strab.* 11.

OXYAR'TES, a king of Bactriana, who surrendered to Alexander. *Curt.* 8. c. 2.—*Diod. Cic.* l. 18.

OXYB'II, a people of Liguria. *Strab.*—*Steph.*

OXYCA'NUS, an Indian prince in the age of Alexander. *Curt.* 9. c. 8.

OXYDA'TES or OXID'ATES, a Persian whom Darius condemned to death. Alexander took him prisoner, and some time after made him governor of Media. He became oppressive, and was removed. *Curt.* 8. c. 3. l. 9. c. 8.

OXYDER'CE, a surname of Minerva, from the sharpness and penetrating power of her eyes. She was worshipped under that name in a temple erected at Argos by Diomedes, whom, in the Trojan war, she had relieved from the darkness with which he was surrounded in battle. Thence also arose her names of Opiletes and Ophthalmitis. *Paus.* 2. c. 24. l. 3. c. 18.—*Plut. in Lyc.*—*Gyrald. Hist. D.* 11.

OXYD'RACÆ, a nation of India. *Curt.* 9. c. 4.

OX'YLUS, a king of Elis, son of Andremon, or according to others, of Hæmon, son of Thoas. An accidental murder obliged him to flee from his country, after he had lost one eye in battle. He was met on horseback by the Heraclidæ, who meditated the conquest of Peloponnesus, and whom the oracle had directed to take three eyes for their guide, and his appearance confirmed the supposition, that in him the will of the gods was fulfilled. He was therefore appointed leader by Cresphontes, who was then at the head of the Heraclidæ, and in that character he advised them not to make their attack on the country by land, but by sea. The attempt was made, and succeeded; Peloponnesus was conquered, and Oxylus demanded and obtained as his reward Elis, which had given him birth, and where he established his kingdom, and rendered himself popular by hospitably inviting all strangers to his court. He adorned his capital, and established festivals, not only in honor of Jupiter, but of the greatest heroes whose life had been distinguished in the service of mankind. He had by his wife Pieris two sons, the eldest of whom died in his infancy, and the younger called Laias succeeded him on the throne, and received by order of the oracle, as a regal partner, a descendant of Pelops, Agorius, son of Damosius. *Aristot. Pol.* 6. c. 4.—*Strab.* 10.—*Apollod.* 2.—*Euseb. Præp. Ev.* 5.—*Paus.* 5. c. 4.——A son of Mars and Protogenia.—*Apollod.* 1. c. 7.

OXYM'AGIS, a river of India, falling into the Ganges. *Arrian. in Ind.*

OXYNI'A, a city of Greece, on the river Ion, which joins the Peneus. *Strab.*

OXYN'THES, a king of Athens, B.C. 1149. He reigned twelve years. *Joh. Marsham, Can. Chron.* Sec. 12.

OXYP'ORUS, a son of Cinyras and Metharme. *Apollod.* 3. c. 14.

OXYRYN'CHUS, a town of Ægypt, on the Nile. *Strab.*

OX'YTHRES, a brother of Artabazus. *Polyæn.* 7. c. 33.

OZE'NE, a city of India Citerior. *Ptol.*

OZI'NES, a Persian imprisoned by Craterus, because he attempted to revolt from Alexander. *Curt.* 9. c. 10.

OZOGARDA'NA, a town mentioned by *Ammianus Marcellinus*. It was probably in Mesopotamia.

OZ'OLÆ or OZ'OLI, a people who inhabited the eastern parts of Ætolia, which were called Ozolea. This tract of territory lay at the north of the bay of Corinth, and extended about twelve miles northward. They received their name from the *bad stench* (ὄζη) of their bodies and of their clothing, which consisted of the raw hides of wild beasts, or from the offensive smell of the body of Nessus the Centaur, which after death was left to putrify in the country, without the honors of a burial. Some derive it with more probability from the stench of the stagnated water in the neighbouring lakes and marshes. According to a fabulous tradition, they received their name from a very different circumstance: during the reign of a son of Deucalion, a bitch brought into the world a stick instead of whelps. The stick was planted in the ground by the king, and grew up to be a large vine and produced grapes, from which the inhabitants of the country were called *Ozolæ*, not from ὄζειν, *to smell badly*, but from ὄζος, *a branch or sprout*. The name of Ozolæ, on account of its indelicate signification, highly displeased the inhabitants, and they soon exchanged it for that of Ætolians. *Paus.* 10. c. 38.—*Herodot.* 8. c. 32.—*Servius in Æn.* 3. v. 399.

OZ'ZALA, a city of Galatia. *Antonin.*

P.

PACATIA'NUS TI'TUS JU'LIUS, a general of the Roman armies, who proclaimed himself emperor in Gaul, about the latter part of Philip's reign. He was soon after defeated, A.D. 249, and put to death.

LATI'NUS PACA'TUS DREPA'NIUS, a poet in the fourth century, whom Ausonius compares with Virgil, and prefers to Catullus. His panegyric on Theodosius is the only one of his works which is extant. The best editions are that of Scheffer, Holmiæ, 1651, and that of Arnzenius, Amstel. 1753. *Harles. Not. Lit. Rom.* 1. p. 626.

PACA'VIUS T., a Roman knight mentioned by *Cicero, Mil.* 27.

PAC'CIUS, an insignificant poet in the age of Domitian. *Juv.* 7. v. 12.——A friend of Atticus. *Cic.* 4. *Att.* 16.

PA'CHES, an Athenian, who took Mitylene. *Arist. Polit.* 5. c. 4.

PA'CHIA, a promontory of Sardinia. *Ptol.*

PACHI'NUS or PACHY'NUS, now Passaro, a promontory of Sicily, projecting about two miles into the sea, in the form of a peninsula, at the south-east corner of the island, with a small harbour of the same name *Strab.* 6.—*Mela*, 2. c. 7.—*Virg. Æn.* 3. v. 699.—*Paus.* 5. c. 25.—*Ovid. Met.* 13. v. 725. *Fast.* 4. v. 479.—*Lucan.* 7. v. 871.—*Servius ad Æn.* 1. v. 200 1. c. 3. v. 687 & 699.

PACIDIA'NUS, a gladiator. *Cic. Tusc.* 4. c. 21.

PACIL'IUS, a Roman whose house Cicero's brother wished to purchase. *Cic.* 1. *Att.* 14.

PACO'NIA, an island between Lilybæum and Africa. *Ptol.*

PACO'NIUS M., a Roman, proconsul of Asia, under Silanus, put to death by Tiberius. *Suet. in Tib.* 61.—*Tacit. An.* 3. c. 66.

PACO'NIUS AGRIPPI'NUS, a stoic philosopher, son of the preceding. He was banished from Italy by Nero, and retired from Rome with the greatest composure and indifference. *Arrian.* 1. c. 1.

PACO'RIA, a city of Mesopotamia. *Ptol.*

PAC'ORUS the First, the eldest of the thirty sons of Orodes, king of Parthia, sent against Crassus, whose army he defeated, and whom he took prisoner. He took Syria from the Romans, and supported the republican party of Pompey, and of the murderers of Julius Cæsar. He was killed in a battle by Ventidius Bassus, B.C. 39, on the same day (9th of June) that Crassus had been defeated. *Flor.* 4. c. 9.—*Horat.* 3. od. 6. v. 9.—*Paterc.* 2. c. 78.—*Justin.* 42. c. 46. 1. 16. c. 17.—*Martial*, 9, epigr. 36.

PAC'ORUS the Second, a king of Parthia, who succeeded Artabanus the Third, and made a treaty of Alliance with the Romans in Trojan's reign. *Plin.* 10. ep. 16. The name was common to the Parthian sovereigns.

PAC'TIA, one of the Cyclades. *Steph.* It is now Pazzi.

PAC'TIUS AFRICA'NUS, an informer under Nero. *Tac. Hist.* 4. c. 41.

PAC'TIUS ORPHI'TUS, an officer who fought with the Parthians, against the orders of Corbulo. *Tac. Ann.* 13. c. 36. *Muretus*, however, reads P. Attius.

PAC'TIUS, a river of Apulia Peucetia. *Plin.* 3. c. 11.

PACTO'LUS, a celebrated river of Lydia, rising in mount Tmolus, and falling into the Hermus after it has watered the city of Sardes. It was in this river that Midas washed himself when he turned into gold whatever he touched, and from that circumstance it ever after rolled golden sands in its stream, and received the name of Chrysorrhoas. It is called Tmolus by Pliny. Strabo observes, that it had no golden sands in his age; but, according to Pliny, its waters possessed great medicinal properties, and proved very conducive to the cure of the various diseases of those who bathed there. *Apollon.* 4. Arg. v. 1300.—*Lycoph.* 273.—*Propert.* 1. el. 6. v. 32. el. 14. v. 11. 1. 3. 1. 16. v. 28.—*Virg. Æn.* 10. v. 142.—*Strab.* 18.—*Ovid. Met.* 11. v. 86.—*Herodot.* 3. c. 110.—*Plin.* 33. c. 8.—*Varro apud Nonium.*—*Hygin.* fab. 191.—*Nonn. Bassar.* 13, 21 & 41.—*Eustath. ad Dionys. Per.* 830.—*Max. Tyr.* 34. *Diss.*—*Sil. Ital.* 1. v. 234.—*Juv.* 14. v. 298.

PAC'TYAS, a Lydian entrusted with the care of the treasures of Crœsus at Sardes. The immense riches which he could command corrupted him, and to make himself independent, he gathered a large army. He laid siege to the citadel of Sardes, but the arrival of one of the Persian generals soon put him to flight. He retired to Cumæ, and afterwards to Lesbus, where he was delivered into the hands of Cyrus. *Herodot.* 1. c. 154, &c.—*Paus.* 2. c. 35.

PAC'TYE, a town of the Thracian Chersonesus. *Plin.* 5. c. 31.

PAC'TYES, a mountain of Ionia, near Ephesus. *Strab.* 14. It is now Monte de Figena.

PACU'RA, a city of Mæsolia, in India Citerior. *Ptol.*

PACU'VIUS M., a native of Brundusium, son of the sister of the poet Ennius, who distinguished himself by his skill in painting, and by his poetical talents. He wrote satires and tragedies which were represented at Rome, and of some of which the names are preserved, as Peribœa, Hermione, Atalanta, Ilione, Teucer, Antiope, Medea, Chryse, Niptris, Paulus, Orestes, and Armorum Judicium. Orestes was considered as the best finished performance; the style, however, though rough and without either purity or elegance, deserved the commendation of Cicero and Quintilian, who perceived strong rays of genius and perfection frequently beaming through the clouds of the barbarity and ignorance of the times. The poet in his old age retired to Tarentum, where he died in his 90th year, about 131 years B.C. Of all his compositions about 437 scattered lines are preserved in the collections of Latin poets. *Cic. de Orat.* 2. *Ad. Heren.* 2. c. 27.—*Horat.* 2. ep. 1. v. 56.—*Martial.* 11. epigrs. 91. v. 5.—*Perseus*, 1. v. 77.—*Plin.* 35. c. 4.—*Quintil.* 10. c. 1.—*A. Gell.* 13. c. 8.—*Harles. Not. Lit. Rom.* 1. p. 97.—*Sax Onom.* 1. p. 131.

PACU'VIUS CALA'VIUS, a native of Capua who induced his countrymen to revolt from Rome and join Annibal. His son threatened to murder the Carthaginian general, which was prevented by the interference of the father. *Liv.* 23. c. 2, 3, 5 & 9.

PACU'VIUS, a lieutenant of Cn. Sentius, in Syria. *Senec. Ep.* 12.

S. PACU'VIUS TAU'RUS, a friend of Augustus, who, when tribune of the people, introduced a law that the month Sextilis should, for the future, be called Augustus. *Macrob. Sat.* 1. c. 12.—*Dio.* 53.

PAC'YRIS, or rather HYPAC'YRIS, a river of European Scythia. *Plin.* 4. c. 12.

PADÆ'I, an Indian nation who are said to have devoured their sick when at the point of death. *Herodot.* 3. c. 99.

PADA'GRUS, a river of Persia. *Arrian. Pliny*, 6. c. 23, calls it Phirstimus.

PADA'SIA, a city of Galatia. *Cedren.*

PADI'NUM, now Bondeno, a town on the Po, at the point where it begins to branch into different channels. *Plin.* 3. c. 15.

PAD'UA, a town called also Patavium, in the country of the Venetians, at the north of the Athesis, founded by Antenor, immediately after the Trojan war. It was the native place of the historian Livy. The inhabitants were once so powerful that they could levy an army of 20,000 men. *Strab.* 5.—*Mela*, 2. c. 4.—*Virg. Æn.* 1. v. 251.

PA'DUS, now the Po, a river in Italy. known also by the name of Eridanus, which forms the northern boundary of the territories of Italy. It rises in mount Vesulus, one of the highest mountains of the Alps, and after it has collected in its course the waters of above 30 rivers, discharges itself in an eastern direction into the Adriatic Sea by seven mouths, two of which only, the Plana or Volana, and the Padusa, were formed by nature. It was formerly said it rolled gold dust in its sands, which was carefully searched for by the inhabitants. The consuls C. Flaminius Nepos, and P. Furius Philus, were the first Roman generals who crossed it. The Po is famous for the death of Phaethon, who, as the poets mention, was hurled into it by the thunderbolts of Jupiter. *Ovid. Met.* 2. v. 258, &c. *Fast.* 4. v. 170. *Am.* 2. el. 17. v. 32.—*Mela,* 2. c. 4.—*Lucan.* 2, &c.—*Virg. Æn.* 9. v. 680.—*Strab.* 5. —*Plin.* 37. c. 2.

PADU'SA, the most southern mouth of the Po, considered by some writers as the Po itself. *Vid.* Padus. It was said to abound in swans, and from it there was a cut to the town of Ravenna. *Virg. Æn.* 11. v. 457.

PÆ'AN, a surname of Apollo, derived from the word *pœan,* a hymn which was sung in his honor, because he had killed the serpent Python, which had given cause to the people to exclaim Io Pæan! The exclamation of Io Pæan! was made use of in invoking the other gods, and was also often a demonstration of joy. *Juv.* 6. v. 171.—*Ovid. Met.* 1. v. 538. l. 14. v. 720.—*Lucan.* 1, &c.—*Strab.* 18.

PÆ'AN, or rather PŒAN, the father of Philoctetes. *Vid.* Pœan.

PÆA'NIUM, a town of Acarnania. *Polyb.*

PÆDAR'ITUS, a Spartan, who, not being elected in the number of the 300 sent on an expedition, declared, that instead of being mortified, he rejoiced that 300 better men than himself could be found in Sparta. *Plut. in Lyc.*

PÆ'DIUS Q., a lieute nant of J. Cæsar, in Spain, who proposed a law to punish with death all such as were concerned in the murder of his patron. *Vell. Paterc.* 2. c. 69.—*Joh. Rosin. Antiq. Rom.* l. 8. c. 27.

PÆDOP'ILES or PÆDOP'ULES, a river mentioned by *Pliny,* 6. c. 1. See also *Salmas. ad Solin.* p. 888.

PÆMA'NI, a people of Belgic Gaul, supposed to have dwelt in the country situate at the west of Luxemburg. *Cæs. G.* 2. c. 4.

PÆNA, an island of the Atlantic Sea. *Ptol.*

PÆ'ON, a Greek historian who wrote an account of his native city Amathus. *Hesychius.*—*Plut. in Thes.*——A celebrated physician who cured the wounds which the gods received during the Trojan war. From him physicians are sometimes called *Pæonii,* and herbs serviceable in medicinal processes *Pæoniæ herbæ.* *Virg. Æn.* 7. v. 769.—*Ovid. Met.* 15. v. 535.—*Homer. Il.* 5. *in ex.*—*Isidor.* 17. c. 9.—*Plin.* 25. c. 4.——One of the three sons of Endymion, king of Elis, who, being dissatisfied with the loss of the succession to the kingdom which his father had promised to superiority of running, left his native home, and settled on the borders of the Axius. *Paus.* 5. c. 1.

PÆ'ONES, a people of Macedonia, who inhabited a small part of the country called Pæonia. Some believe that they were descended from a Trojan colony. *Paus.* 5. c. 1.—*Herodot.* 5. c. 13, &c.

PÆO'NIA, a country of Macedonia, at the west of the Strymon, watered by the Axius, the Erigon, and the Chidorus. It abounded with buffaloes in the age of Pausanias. It received its name from Pæon, a son of Endymion, who settled there. *Paus.* 5. c. 1. l. 10. c. 13.—*Dio.* 49.—*Plin.* 4. c. 10.—*Justin.* 7. c. 1.—*Stat. Ach.* 417.—*Ovid. ex Ponto,* 2. ep. 2. v. 77. *Met.* 5. v. 313.—*Liv.* 42. c. 51. l. 45. c. 29.——A small town of Attica.

PÆON'IDES, a name given to the daughters of Pierus, who were defeated by the Muses, because their mother was a native of Pæonia. *Ovid. Met.* 5. *ult. fab.*

PÆONIUS, a rhetorician, in the number of whose pupils were the son and nephew of Cicero. *Cic. ad Fr.* 3. ep. 3

PÆ'OS, a small town of Arcadia.

PÆ'PIA, a town of Mauritania Cæsariensis. *Ptol.*

PÆSAMAR'CI, a people of Hispania Tarraconensis. *Salmas. ad Solin.* p. 276.

PÆSAR'CÆ, a people under Caucasus. *Steph.*

PÆSTUM, a town of Lucania, called also Neptunia and Posidonia by the Greeks, where the soil produced roses which blossomed twice a year. The ancient walls of the town, about three miles in extent, are still standing, and likewise venerable remains of temples and porticoes. The Sinus Pæstanus on which it stood is now called the Gulph of Salerno. *Virg. G.* 4. v. 119.—*Ovid. Met.* 15. v. 708.—*Pont.* 2. el. 4. v. 28.

PÆSU'RI or PÆSU'RES, a people of Lusitania, near the Tagus. *Plin.* 4. c. 20. Their country is now La Comarca de Covilhan.

PÆ'SUS, a town of the Hellespont, called also Apæsus, situated at the north of Lampsacus. When it was destroyed the inhabitants migrated to Lampsacus, where they settled. They were of Milesian origin. *Strab.* 13.—*Homer. Il.* 2.

PÆTA'LIA, a part of Thrace. *Steph.*

PÆ'TI, a people of Thrace, between the Hebrus and Mela, whose country is called Pætica by *Arrian.*

PÆTO'VIUM, a town of Upper Pannonia, on the Dravus. *Ptol.*—*Tacitus, Hist.* 3. c. 1, calls it Pætovio, and others Pætonia; it is now Betta.

PÆ'TUS, a governor of Armenia under Nero.——A man who made Cicero a present of his library. *Cic.* 2. *Att.* 1.——A Greek, to whom Cæsar presented the honors of Roman citizenship. *Cic.* 13. *Phil.* 15.——A Roman who conspired with Catiline against his country.——A man drowned as he was going to collect money. *Propert.* 3. el. 7. v. 5.——A person who accused Pallas and Burrhus of wishing to seat Cornelius Sulla, a relation of Claudius, upon the throne. *Tacit. Ann.* 13. c. 23. —The name of Pætus was common to the Ælian and Papirian families.

PÆ'TUS CÆCIN'NA, the husband of Arria. *Vid.* Arria.

PA'GÆ, a town of Megaris, subdued by Philip, son of Amyntas, Olymp. 106. an. 3. It is now Pago. *Pliny,* 4. c. 7. calls the inhabitants Pagæi.

PAGANA'LIA, festivals among the Romans yearly, celebrated in the month of January, in honor of Ceres, in the villages and in the country, when processions were made, and waters of lustration sprinkled on the corn as if to purify it. Dionysius attributes the institution to king Tullius. *Ovid. Fast.* 1. v. 689.—*Varro de L. L.* 5.—*Dionys. Hal.* 5.

PAG'ASÆ or PAG'ASA, a town of Magnesia, in Macedonia, with a harbour and promontory of the same name. The ship Argo was built there, as some suppose, and, according to Propertius, the Argonauts set sail from that harbour. From that circumstance not only the ship Argo, but also the Argonauts themselves were ever after distinguished by the epithet of *Pegasœus.* Pliny confounds Pagasæ with Demetrias, but they are different, and the latter was peopled by the inhabitants of the former, who preferred the situation of Demetrias for its convenience. *Ovid. Met.* 7. v. 1. l. 8. v. 349. *Fast.* 1. v. 491. l. 5. v. 401. *Heroides,* 16. v. 45 & 345. ep. 19. v. 175.—*Flacc.* 1. v. 422. l. 8. v. 451.—*Lucan.* 2. v. 715. l. 6. v. 400.—*Mela,* 2. c. 3 & 7.—*Strab.* 9.—*Propert.* 1. el. 20. v. 17.—*Plin.* 4. c. 8.—*Apollon. Rhod.* 1. v. 238, &c.

PAG'ASUS, a Trojan killed by Camilla. *Virg. Æn.* 11. v. 670.——One of the Hyperborean gods, who is said to have been the first who erected a temple to Apollo at Delphi. *Paus.* 10. c. 5.

PAGOAR'GAS, a town on the Red Sea. *Plin.* 6. c. 29.

PA'GRÆ, a town of Syria on the borders of Cilicia. *Strab.* 16. It is called Pacræ by *Antoninus,* and is now Begras.

PAG'RASA, a city of India without the Ganges. *Ptol.*

PA'GUS, a mountain of Æolia, on the river Meles. *Paus.* 7. c. 5.

PAG'YDA or BE'LUS, a river of Phœnicia. *Plin.* 5. c. 19.

PALA'CIUM or PALA'TIUM, a town of the Thracian Chersonesus. *Strab.*

PALA'CIUM, a small village on the Palatine hill, where Rome was afterwards built.

PA'LÆ, a town at the south of Corsica, now St. Bonifacio.

PALÆ'A, a town of Cyprus, now Pelandre. *Strab.*——A town of Cephallenia. *Polyb.*—*Steph.*

PALÆALAZ'ICA STA'TIO, a station on the Euxine Sea, in Asiatic Sarmatia. *Arrian. Peripl.*

PALÆBEU'DOS, a town of Phrygia Major. *Ptol.* It is called Beudos by Pliny.

PALÆB'YBLUS. *Vid.* Byblus.

PALÆ'MON, a sea deity, son of Athamas and Ino. His original name was Melicerta, and he assumed that of Palæmon, after he had been changed into a sea deity by Neptune. *Vid.* Melicerta.——A son of Neptune, or, according to others, of Ætolus or Vulcan, who was amongst the Argonauts.

Apollod.——A son of Hercules and Autonoe. *Id.* ——A son of Priam. *Apollod.* 1 & 2.—*Hygin.* fab. 14.—*Orph. Arg.* 208.—*Apollon. Arg.* 1. v. 202. ——A shepherd mentioned in *Virgil. Ecl.* 5. v. 50.

PALÆ'MON RHEM'NIUS FAU'NIUS, a noted grammarian at Rome, in the age of Tiberius, who made himself ridiculous by his arrogance and luxury. He wrote on grammar, besides a poem on weights and measures, though some ascribe the latter to Favinus, others to Priscianus. His work on grammar may be found in the "Grammat. Illustres, 12." Paris, 1516, and was also published by Petrus, Basil, 1527. The poem was published with Priscianus, Venet. 1496.—*Harles. Not. Lit. Rom.* 1. p. 353.—*Sax. Onom.* 1. p. 244.—*Juv.* 6. v. 451. —*Martial.* 2. epigr. 86.

PALÆOP'OLIS, a small island on the coast of Spain. *Strab.*

PALÆP'APHOS, the ancient town of Paphus in Cyprus, adjoining to the new. *Strab.* 14.

PALÆPAT'MA, a town of India Citerior. *Arrian. in Peripl.*

PALÆPHARSA'LUS, the ancient town of Pharsalus in Thessaly. *Cæs. B. G.* 48.

PALÆPH'ATUS, an ancient Greek philosopher, whose age is unknown, though it can be ascertained that he flourished between the times of Aristotle and Augustus. He wrote five books *De incredibilibus*, of which only the first remains, and in it he endeavours to explain fabulous and mythological traditions, by historical facts. The best edition of Palæphatus is that of J. Frid. Fischer, in 8vo. Lips. 1773.—*Suidas.*—*Virg. in Cir.* 88.—*Eustath. in Homer. Il.* 1 & *Odyss.* 14.—*Orosius*, 1. c. 13.—*Tzetzes. Chil.* 1. *Hist.* 20. c. 2. *Hist.* 47. c. 7. *Hist.* 99.——An heroic poet of Athens, who wrote a poem on the creation of the world, another on the birth of Apollo and Diana, and a third on the dispute of Minerva and Neptune, about giving a name to Athens. *Suidas.*—*Gyrald. de P.H.* 2.—*Voss. de H. Gr.* 1. c. 9.——A disciple of Aristotle, born at Abydus.——An historian of Ægypt.

PALÆP'OLIS, a town of Campania, built by a Greek colony, where Naples was afterwards erected. *Liv.* 8. c. 22.

PALÆSCAMAN'DRUS, a river of Phrygia, or Mysia. *Plin.* 5. c. 30.

PALÆS'TE, a village of Epirus, near Oricus, where Cæsar first landed from his fleet. *Lucan.* 5. v. 460.

PALÆSTI'NA, a province of Syria, which afterwards was called Judæa, though Judæa, properly so named, formed only a part of the ancient Palestine. *Strab.* 16.—*Mela*, 1. c. 11.—*Tacit. Hist.* 1. —*Plin.* 5. c. 12.—*Lucan.* 5. v. 460.—*Ovid. Met.* 4. v. 46. *Fast.* 2. v. 464. 1. 4. v. 236. *De A.A.* 1. v. 416.—*Herodot.* 1. c. 105.—*Sil. It.* 3. v. 606.

PALÆSTI'NUS, an ancient name of the river Strymon. *Plut.*

PALÆS'TRIUM, a town of Macedonia. *Plin.* 4. c. 10.

PALÆT'YRUS, the ancient town of Tyre on the continent. *Strab.* 16.

PALAME'DES, a Grecian chief, son of Nauplius, king of Eubœa, by Clymene. He was sent by the Greek princes who were going to the Trojan war to bring Ulysses to the camp, who, to withdraw himself from the expedition, pretended insanity; and the better to impose upon his friends, used to harness different animals to a plough, and sow salt instead of barley. The deceit was soon perceived by Palamedes, he knew that his unwillingness to part from his wife Penelope, whom he had lately married, was the only reason of the pretended insanity of Ulysses; and to demonstrate this, Palamedes took Telemachus, whom Penelope had lately brought into the world, and put him before the plough of his father. Ulysses showed that he was not insane, by turning the plough a different way not to hurt his child. This having been discovered, Ulysses was obliged to attend the Grecian princes to the war, but an implacable enmity arose between Ulysses and Palamedes. The king of Ithaca resolved to take every opportunity to distress him, and, when all his expectations were frustrated, he had the meanness to bribe one of his servants, and to make him dig a hole in his master's tent, and there conceal a large sum of money. After this, Ulysses forged a letter in Phrygian characters, which king Priam was supposed to have sent to Palamedes. In the letter the Trojan king seemed to entreat Palamedes to deliver into his hands the Grecian army, according to the conditions which had been previously agreed upon when he received the money. This forged letter was carried, by means of Ulysses, before the princes of the Grecian army. Palamedes was summoned, and made the most solemn protestations of innocence, but all was in vain, the money that was discovered in his tent served to corroborate the accusation. He was found guilty by all the army, and stoned to death. Homer is silent about the miserable fate of Palamedes, and Pausanias mentions that it had been reported by some, that Ulysses and Diomedes had drowned him in the sea, as he was fishing on the coast. Philostratus, who mentions the tragical story above related, adds, that Achilles and Ajax buried his body with great pomp on the sea shore, and that they raised upon it a small temple, in which sacrifices were regularly offered by the inhabitants of Troas. Palamedes was a learned man as well as a soldier, and, according to some, completed the alphabet of Cadmus, by the addition of the four letters θ, ξ, χ, φ, during the Trojan war. To him, also, is attributed the invention of dice and back-gammon; and, it is said, that he was the first who regularly ranged an army in a line of battle, and who placed sentinels round a camp, and excited their vigilance and attention by giving them a watchword. *Hygin.* fab. 95, 105, &c.—*Apollod.* 2, &c.—*Dictys. Cret.* 2. c. 15. —*Ovid. Met.* 13. v. 56 & 308.—*Paus.* 1. c. 31.—*Manil.* 4. v. 205.—*Philostrat. Her.* 10.—*Euripid. in Phœniss.*—*Martial*, 13. epigr. 75.—*Plin.* 7. c. 56.—*Servius. in Æn.* 2. v. 81.—*Lactant. in Ach.* 1. v. 92. *Ad Theb.* 2. v. 432. 1. 6. v. 288.—*Tzetzes in Lyc.* 384 & 1097.—*Sch. Eurip. in Orest.* 54.—*Photius*, ep. 142.—*Polyd. Virg.* 1. c. 6.——A grammarian of Elea, who wrote a work called *Onomasticon* on the words used by tragic and comic writers, and on the properties of the Attic and Doric dialects. *Suidas.*—*Voss. H. Gr.* p. 396. ——A Theban, preceptor of Corinnus, both of whom wrote before the Trojan war, according to *Suidas in* Παλαμ & Κόρ.

PALAME'DIUM, a town of Troas. *Plin.* 5. c. 30.

PALAN'TA, a town of Corsica. *Ptol.*

PALAN'TIA, a town of Spain, in the country of the Cantabri, at the north of the Durius. *Mela*, 2. c. 6. It is now Palencia.

PALAN'TIUM, a town of Arcadia. *Steph.*

PALATI'NUS MONS, a celebrated hill, the largest of the seven hills on which Rome was built. It was upon it that Romulus laid the first foundation of the capital of Italy, in a quadrangular form, and there also he kept his court, as well as Tullus Hostilius, and Augustus, and all the succeeding emperors, from which circumstance the word *Palatium* has ever since been applied to the residence of a monarch or prince. The Palatine hill received its name from the goddess *Pales*, or from the *Palatini*, who originally inhabited the place, or from the *balare* or *palare*, the bleatings of sheep, which were frequent there, or perhaps from the word *palantes*, *wandering*, because Evander, when he came to settle in Italy, gathered all the inhabitants, and made them one society. Some games celebrated in honor of Augustus, were called Palatine, because kept on the hill. *Dio. Cass.* 53.—*Ital.* 12. v. 709.—*Liv.* 1. c. 7 & 33.—*Ovid. Met.* 14. v. 822.—*Juv.* 9. v. 23.—*Virg. G.* 1. v. 499.—*Sueton. in Aug.* 56.—*Martial*, 1. epigr. 71.—*Varro. de. L.L.* 4. c. 3.—*Cic. in Catil.* 1.—*Servius ad G.* 3. v. 1. *Æn.* 8. v. 51.—*Cœl. Rh. Ant. Lec.* 8. c. 1. —*Arnob.* 3 & 5.

PALATI'NUS APOL'LO, was worshipped on the Palatine hill. His temple there had been built or rather repaired, by Augustus, who had enriched it with a library, valuable for the various collections of Greek and Latin manuscripts which it contained, as also for the Sibylline books deposited there. *Horat.* 1. ep. 3. v. 17.

PA'LEIS or PALÆ'A, a town in the island of Cephallenia. *Paus.* 6. c. 15.—*Strab.* 10. It is now Palichi.

PA'LES, the goddess of sheepfolds and of pastures among the Romans. She was worshipped with great solemnity at Rome, and her festivals, called Palilia, were celebrated on the 21st of April, the very day on which it is said that Romulus began to lay the foundation of the city of Rome. Servius considers her the same as Vesta, but *Varro* calls this deity a god, and not a goddess. *Virg. G.* 3. v. 1 & 294. *Ecl.* 5. v. 25. *Cul.* 28 & 76 & *Servius in locis. cit.—Ovid. Fast.* 4. v. 722, &c.—*Paterc.* 1. c 8.—*Tibul.* 1. el. 1. v. 15.

PALESIMUN'DUS, a city and river of Taprobane. *Plin.* 6. c. 22.

PALFU'RIUS SU'RA, a writer, removed from the senate by Domitian, who suspected him of attachment to Vitellius. *Juv.* 4. v. 53.—*Martial*, 6. ep. 64. v. 13.—*Suet. Domit.* 13.

PALIA'NA, a city of the Seræ. *Ptol.*

PALIBO'THRA, or **PALIB'OTHRA**, a city of India on the river Ganges. *Strab.* 15. Its modern name is much disputed.

PALI'CI or **PALIS'CI**, two deities, sons of Jupiter by Thalia, whom Æschylus calls Ætna, in a tragedy which is now lost, according to the words of Macrobius. The nymph Ætna when pregnant entreated her lover to remove her from the pursuit of Juno. The god concealed her in the bowels of the earth, and when the time of her delivery was come, the earth opened and brought into the world two children, who received the name of Palici, ἀπὸ τοῦ παλιν ἱκέσθαι, *because they came again into the world from the bowels of the earth.* These deities were worshipped with great ceremonies by the Sicilians, and near their temple were two small lakes of sulphureous water, which were supposed to have sprung out of the earth, at the same time that they were born. Near these pools it was usual for those who wished to decide controversies and quarrels, to take the most solemn oaths. If any of the persons who took the oaths perjured themselves, they were immediately punished in a supernatural manner; and those whose oath, by the deities of the place, was sincere, departed unhurt. The Palici had also an oracle which was consulted upon great emergencies, and which gave the truest and most unequivocal answers. In a superstitious age the altars of the Palici were stained with the blood of human sacrifices, but this barbarous custom was soon abolished, and the deities were satisfied with their usual offerings. *Virg. Æn.* 9. v. 585.—*Ovid. Met.* 5. v. 506.—*Diod.* 2.—*Macrob. Saturn.* 5. c. 10.—*Ital.* 14. v. 219.—*Servius ad Virg. loc.*

PALICO'RUM. *Vid.* Paliscorum.

PALIL'IA, a festival celebrated by the Romans, in honor of Pales. The ceremony consists in burning heaps of straw, and in leaping over them. No sacrifices were offered but the purifications were made with the smoke of horses' blood, and with the ashes of a calf that had been taken from the belly of its mother, after it had been sacrificed, and with the ashes of beans. The purification of the flocks was also made with the smoke of sulphur, of the olive, the pine, the laurel, and rosemary. Offerings of mild cheese, boiled wine, and cakes of millet, were afterwards made. This festival was observed on the 21st of April, and it was during this celebration that Romulus first began to build his city. Some call this festival Parilia *quasi a pariendo*, because the sacrifices were offered to the divinity for the fecundity of the flocks. *Ovid. Met.* 14. v. 774. *Fast.* 4. v. 721, &c. 1. 6. v. 257.—*Propert.* 4. el. 19. v. 1.—*Varro L. L.* 5. c. 3. *R. R.* 2. c. 1, 9.—*Cic. Div.* 2. c. 74.—*Vell.* 1. c. 8.—*Tibull.* 2. el. 5. v. 87.—*Servius in Virg. G.* 3. v. 1 & 294.

PALIMBO'THRA, a city of India. *Steph.*

PALIN'DROMOS, a promontory of Arabia Felix. It is the Acila of *Pliny*, 6. c. 28, according to *Villanovanus.*

PALINU'RUS, son of Jasus, was the skilful pilot of the ship of Æneas. He fell into the sea in his sleep, and was three days exposed to the tempests and the waves of the sea, and at last came safe to the sea shore near Velia, where the inhabitants of the place inhumanly murdered him to obtain his clothes. His body was left unburied on the sea shore, and as, according to the religion of the ancient Romans, no person was suffered to cross the Stygian lake before 100 years were elapsed, if his remains had not been decently buried, we find Æneas, when he visited the infernal regions, speaking to Palinurus, and assuring him, that though his bones were deprived of a funeral, yet the place where his body was exposed should soon be adorned with a monument, and bear his name, and accordingly a promontory was called Palinurus after him. It is now Palinura. *Virg. Æn.* 3. v. 513. 1. 5. v. 840, &c. 1. 6. v. 341.—*Ovid. de Rem.* 577. *Trist.* 5. el. 6. v. 7. *Ibis.* 596.—*Martial.* 3. epigr. 78—*Mela*, 2. c. 4.—*Strab.* 6.—*Horat.* 3. od. 4. v. 28.

PALISCO'RUM or **PALICO'RUM STAG'NUM**, a sulphureous pool in Sicily, at the west of Syracuse. *Vid.* Palici. *Ovid. Pont.* 2. el. 10.

PALIU'RA, a city of Macedonia. *Suidas.*

PALIU'RUS, now Nahil, a river of Africa, with a town of the same name at its mouth, at the west of Ægypt, on the Mediterranean. *Strab.* 17.

PAL'LA or **PAL'LÆ**, a city of Corsica. *Ptol.* It is now Pola, or as others assert Bonifacio,

PAL'LADES, certain virgins of illustrious parents who were consecrated to Jupiter by the Thebans of Ægypt. It was required that they should prostitute themselves, an infamous custom which was considered as a purification, during which they were publicly mourned as dead, and afterwards were permitted to marry. *Strab.* 17.—*Eustath.* 1 *Il. & Od.* 13.

PALLA'DIUM, a celebrated statue of Pallas. It was about three cubits high, and represented the goddess as sitting and holding a pike in her right hand, and in her left a distaff and a spindle. It fell down from heaven near the tent of Ilus, as that prince was building the citadel of Ilium. Some nevertheless suppose that it fell at Pessinus in Phrygia, or, according to others, Dardanus received it as a present from his mother Electra. There are some authors who maintain that the Palladium was made with the bones of Pelops by Abaris; but Apollodorus seems to say, that it was no more than a piece of clock-work which moved of itself. However discordant the opinions of ancient authors are about this famous statue, it is universally agreed that on its preservation depended the safety of Troy. This fatality was well known to the Greeks during the Trojan war, and therefore Ulysses and Diomedes were commissioned to steal it away. They effected their purpose, and if we rely upon the authority of some authors, they were directed how to carry it away by Helenus the son of Priam, who proved in this unfaithful to his country, because his brother Deiphobus, at the death of Paris, had married Helen, of whom he was enamoured. Minerva was displeased with the violence which was offered to her statue, and, according to Virgil, the Palladium itself appeared to have received life and motion, and by the flashes which started from its eyes, and its sudden springs from the earth, seemed to shew the resentment of the goddess. The true Palladium, as some authors observe, was not carried away from Troy by the Greeks, but only one of the statues of similar size and shape, which were placed near it, to deceive whatever sacrilegious persons attempted to steal it. The Palladium, therefore, as they say, was conveyed safe from Troy to Italy by Æneas, and was afterwards preserved by the Romans with the greatest secrecy and veneration, in the temple of Vesta, a circumstance which none but the vestal virgins knew. *Herodian.* 1. c. 14, &c.—*Ovid. Fast.* 6. v. 422, &c. *Met.* 13. v. 336.—*Dictys. Cret.* 1. c. 5.—*Lucan.* 9. v. 994.—*Plin.* 7. c. 44.—*Apollod.* 3. c. 12.—*Dionys. Hal.* 1, &c.—*Homer. Il.* 10.—*Virg. Æn.* 2. v 166. 1. 9. v. 151.—*Plut. de Reb. Rom,—Dares Phryg.—Juv.* 3. v. 139.—*Eustath. in* 6 *Il.—Clem. Alex.* 6 *Str.—Herodian.* 1. c. 14 & 35.—*Tzetzes in Lycop.* 353.—*Conon. Narr.* 14 & 34.

PALLA'DIUS, a Greek physician whose treatise on fevers was edited 8vo, L. Bat. 1745.

PALLA'DIUS RUTIL'IUS TAU'RUS ÆMILIA'NUS, a learned Roman, who flourished under Adrian, though the age in which he lived is disputed by some writers. He wrote *de re rusticâ* in 13 books, usually edited with Cato, and other writers *de R. R.* The work was also published separately at Paris, 1536, and Heidelberg, 1598. *Harles. Not. Lit. Rom* 1. p. 367.—*Sax. Onom.* 1. p. 458.

PALLANTE'UM, a town of Italy, or perhaps more properly a citadel built by Evander on mount Palatine, from whence its name originates. Virgil says, it was called after Pallas, the grandfather of Evander; but Dionysius derives its name from Palantium, a town of Arcadia. *Dionys.* 1. c. 31.—*Virg. Æn.* 8. v. 54 & 341.

PALLAN'TIA or PALAN'TIA. *Vid.* Palantia.

PALLAN'TIAS, a patronymic of Aurora, as being related to the giant Pallas. *Ovid. Met.* 9. fab. 12.

PALLAN'TIDES, the 50 sons of Pallas, the son of Pandion, and the brother of Ægeus. They were all killed by Theseus, the son of Ægeus, whom they opposed when he came to take possession of his father's kingdom. This opposition they showed in hopes of succeeding to the throne, as Ægeus left no children, except Theseus, whose legitimacy was disputed, as he was born at Trœzene. *Plut. in Thes.—Paus.* 1. c. 22.

PAL'LAS, (*-adis*), a daughter of Jupiter, the same as Minerva. The goddess received this name either because she killed the giant Pallas, or perhaps from the spear which she seems to *brandish* (παλλειν) in her hands. For the functions, power, and character of the goddess, *vid.* Minerva.

PAL'LAS, (*-antis,*) a son of king Evander, sent with some troops to assist Æneas. He was killed by Turnus, the king of the Rutuli, after he had made a great slaughter of the enemy. *Virg. Æn.* 8. v. 104, &c.——One of the giants, son of Tartarus and Terra. He was killed by Minerva, who covered herself with his skin, whence, as some suppose, she is called Pallas. *Tzetzes in Lycop.* 355.—*Hygin. Præf. Fab.—Apollod.* 3. c. 12.——A son of Crius and Eurybia, who married the nymph Styx, by whom he had Victory, Valor, &c. *Hesiod. Theog.* 385.——A son of Lycaon. *Apollon.*——A son of Pandion, father of Clytus and Butes. *Ovid. Met.* 7. fab. 17.—*Apollod.*——A writer who composed a history of the mysteries of Mithras, the chief deity of the Persians. *Porphyrus. —Voss. Hist. Gr.* 1. 3. p. 397.——A freedman of Claudius, famous for the power and the riches which he obtained. He advised the emperor, his master, to marry Agrippina, and to adopt her son Nero for his successor. It was by his means, and those of Agrippina, that the death of Claudius was hastened, and that Nero was raised to the throne. Nero forgot to whom he was indebted for the crown. He discarded Pallas, and some time after caused him to be put to death, A.D. 61, that he might make himself master of his great riches, which, it is said, amounted to nearly two millions and a half of English money. *Tacit. Ann.* 11 c. 29. l. 12. c. 2. 13, &c.—*Plin.* 7. ep. 29. l. 8. ep. 6.—The father of one of the Minervas mentioned by Cicero. He was put to death by his daughter. *Cic. N. D.* 3. c. 23.

PALLE'NE, a small peninsula of Macedonia, formerly called Phlegra, situate above the bay of Thermæ on the Ægæan Sea, and containing five cities, the principal of which is called Pallene. It was in this place, according to some of the ancients, that an engagement happened between the gods and the giants. *Diod.* 4.—*Stat.* 4. *Syl.* 2.—*Seneca in Herc. Fur.* 978.—*Liv.* 31. c. 45. l. 45. c. 30.—*Virg. G.* 4. v. 391.—*Ovid. Met.* 15. v. 357.——A village of Attica, where Minerva had a temple, and where the Pallantides chiefly resided. *Herodot.* 1. c. 161.—*Plut. in Thes.*

PALLE'NE, a daughter of Sithon Hodomanthus, king of Thrace. Her beauty gained her many admirers, though her father required her suitors to contend with him in a chariot race, and to forfeit their life if conquered. Many had already been defeated by his superior dexterity, when Dryas and Clytus presented themselves, but the monarch who felt his strength daily decrease, instead ef entering the list, permitted the rivals to contend together, and promised his daughter to the conqueror. Pallene favored the cause of Clytus. One of her servants bribed the charioteer of Dryas, who was furnished with a disabled chariot, the wheels of which flew off on the course, so that Clytus obtained with an easy conquest the hand of his mistress, and destroyed his rival. *Hegesippus apud Parthen.* 6.

PALLE'NE, a town of Peloponnesus, better known as Pellene. *Vid.* Pellene.

PALLEN'SES, a people of Cephallenia, whose chief town was called Pala or Palæa. *Liv.* 38. c. 18.—*Polyb.* 5. c. 3.

PAL'LON, a town of Arabia Felix. *Plin.* 6. c. 28.

PAL'LOR, the goddess of Paleness, daughter of Mars and Venus, who was one of the attendants of Fear. As the word is masculine, among the Latins she was considered as a god to whom Tullus Hostilius devoted and erected a temple, when he saw his troops thrown into flight in a battle. The sacrifices offered were a dog or sheep. *Hesiod. Theog.* 934.—*Plut. in Cleom.—Aug. de Civ. D.* 4. c. 2, 15 & 23. l. 6, c. 10.—*Lactant.* 1. c. 20.—*Liv.* 1. c. 27.

PALLU'RA, a city of India Citerior. *Ptol.*

PALMA'RIA, a small island opposite Tarracina in Latium. *Plin.* 3. c. 6. It is now Palmarola, according to *Niger*.

PALMY'RA, the capital of Palmyrene, a country on the eastern boundaries of Syria. It is famous for having been the residence of the celebrated Zenobia and of Odenatus, in the reign of the emperor Aurelian. It is now in ruins, and the splendid and magnificent remains of its porticos, temples, and palaces, are visited with astonishment and rapture by the curious and the learned. *Plin.* 6. v. 26 & 30.

PALMYRE'NE. *Vid.* Palmyra.

PALPHU'RIUS, one of the flatterers of Domitian. *Juv.* 4. v. 53.

PALSIC'IUM, a town of Istria. *Plin.* 3. c. 11.

PAL'SUS, a river of Mauritania. *Id.* 5. c. 1.

PAL'TUS, now Boldo, a city of Phœnicia. *Strab.—Mela,* 1. c. 12.

PALUMBI'NUM, a town of Samnium. *Liv.* 10. c. 45.

PAMBŒO'TIA, a festival celebrated by *all* the *Bœotians,* who assembled near Coronea, at the temple of Minerva Itonia. *Strab.* 9.—*Paus. Bœot.*

PAMI'SUS, a river of Thessaly, falling into the Peneus. *Herodot.* 7. c. 129.—*Plin.* 4. c. 8.——A river of Messenia in Peloponnesus.

PAM'MENES, an Athenian general, sent to assist Megalopolis against the Mantineans, in Olymp. 104. an. 3. *Polyæn.* 5. c. 16.——An astrologer in the time of Nero.——A learned Grecian, who was preceptor to Brutus. *Cic. Brut.* 97. *Orat.* 29.

PAMMIL'IA, sacrifices among the Greeks. *Lil, Gyrald.*

PAM'MON, a son of Priam and Hecuba. *Apollod.*

PAM'PA, a village near Tentyra in Thrace. *Juv.* 15. v. 76.

PAM'PANIS, an inland town of Ægypt. *Ptol.*

PAM'PHAGUS (*qui omnia edit*), one of the surnames of Hercules, and also the name of one of Actæon's dogs. *Ovid. Met.* 3. v. 210.

PAM'PHILA, a writer in the age of Nero, a daughter of Soteris by Socratides. She wrote a miscellaneous history, and other works. *A. Gell.* 15. c. 17.—*Diog. Laert.—Phot. Cod.* 175. —*Suidas.—Voss. Hist. Gr.* 2. c. 7.

PAM'PHILA or PAM'PHILE, a woman of Cos, who first invented the weaving of silk dresses. *Plin.* 11. c. 22.

PAM'PHILUS, a celebrated painter of Macedonia, in the age of Philip, distinguished above his rivals by a superior knowledge of literature, and the cultivation of those studies which taught him how to infuse more successfully grace and dignity into his pieces. He was founder of the school for painting at Sicyon, and he made a law which was observed not only in Sicyon, but all over Greece, that none but the children of noble and dignified persons should be permitted to learn painting. Apelles was one of his pupils. *Diog.—Plin.* 35. c. 10.—*Voss. de Scient. Matth.* c. 2. sec. 13.——A son of Neoclides, among the pupils of Plato. *Diog. Laert.—Cic. N. D.* 2. c. 26.——A philosopher of Amphipolis, or of Sicyon, or of Nicopolis, was the preceptor of Aristotle, and wrote a history of illustrious painters. Some suppose that he was the same person as the last. *Suidas.—Voss. Hist. Gr.* 1. c. 8.—*Athen.* 13.—The name of Pamphilus is frequently used by the ancient comedians. *Ter.*

PAM'PHOS, a Greek poet, supposed to have lived before Hesiod's age. He was a native of Athens, and wrote hymns and a poem on the Graces. Some of his verses are quoted by ancient authors. *Paus.* 1. c. 38.—*Philostr. Her.* 2.—*Gyrald. de P. Hist.* 2.

PAMPHYL'IA, a province of Asia Minor, anciently called Mopsopia, and bounded on the south by a part of the Mediterranean, called the Pamphylian Sea, on the west by Lycia, on the north by Pisidia, and on the east by Cilicia. It abounded with pastures, vines, and olives, and was peopled by a Grecian colony. *Strab.* 14.—*Mela,* 1. c. 2, 13 & 14. *Stat.* 1. *Sylv.* 4. v. 77.—*Paus.* 7. c. 3.—*Plin.* 5. c.

26.—*Liv.* 37. c. 23 & 40.——A city of Media. *Steph.*

PAMPRE'TIUS, a poet of Panopolis, pupil of the great Proclus.—*Suidas.*—*Voss. Hist. Gr.* c. 21.

PAMYL'IA, festivals observed in Ægypt, in honor of Pamyle, the nurse of Osiris, who lived at Thebes. During the celebration the statue of Osiris and the Phalli were carried in procession. *Diod.* 1.—*Plut. de Isid. & Os.*—*Ggrald. H.D.* 8.

PAN was the god of shepherds, of huntsmen, and of all the inhabitants of the country. He was the son of Mercury, by Dryope, according to Homer. Some give him Jupiter and Callisto for parents, others Jupiter and Ybis or Oneis. Lucian, Hyginus, &c. assert that he was the son of Mercury and Penelope, the daughter of Icarius, and the god gained the affections of the princess under the form of a goat, as she tended her father's flocks on mount Taygetus, before her marriage with the king of Ithaca. Some authors maintain that Penelope became mother of Pan during the absence of Ulysses in the Trojan war, and that he was the offspring of all the suitors that frequented the palace of Penelope, whence he received the name of *Pan*, which signifies *all* or *everything*. Pan was a monster in appearance, he had two small horns on his head, his complexion was ruddy, his nose flat, and his legs, thighs, tail, and feet were those of a goat. The education of Pan was entrusted to a nymph of Arcadia, called Sinoe; but the nurse, according to Homer, terrified at the sight of such a monster, fled away and left him. He was wrapped up in the skin of beasts by his father, and carried to heaven, where Jupiter and the gods long entertained themselves with the oddity of his appearance. Bacchus was greatly pleased with him, and gave him the name of Pan. The god of shepherds chiefly resided in Arcadia, where the woods and the most rugged mountains were his habitation He invented the flute with seven reeds, which he called Syrinx, in honor of a beautiful nymph of the same name, to whom he attempted to offer violence, and who was changed into a reed. He was continually employed in deceiving the neighbouring nymphs, and often with success. Though deformed in his shape and features, yet he had the good fortune to captivate Diana, and to gain her favors by transforming himself into a beautiful white goat. He was also enamoured of a nymph of the mountains called Echo, by whom he had a son called Lynx. He also paid his addresses to Omphale, queen of Lydia, and it is well known in what manner he was received. *Vid.* Omphale. The worship of Pan was well established, particularly in Arcadia, where he gave oracles on mount Lycæus. His festivals, called by the Greeks *Lycæa*, were brought to Italy by Evander, and were well known at Rome by the name of the Lupercalia. *Vid.* Lupercalia. The worship and different functions of Pan were derived from the mythology of the ancient Ægyptians. This god was one of the eight great gods of the Ægyptians, who ranked before the other twelve gods, whom the Romans called *Consentes.* He was worshipped with the greatest solemnity all over Ægypt. His statues represented him as a goat, not because he really was such, but this was done for mysterious reasons. He was the emblem of fecundity, and they looked upon him as the principle of all things. His horns, as some observe, represented the rays of the sun, and the brightness of the heavens was expressed by the vivacity and the ruddiness of his complexion. The star which he wore on his breast was the symbol of the firmament, and his hairy legs and feet denoted the inferior parts of the earth, such as the woods and plants. Some suppose that he appeared as a goat, because when the gods fled into Ægypt, in their war against the giants, Pan transformed himself into a goat, an example which was immediately followed by all the deities. Pan, according to some, is the same as Faunus, and he is the chief of all the Satyrs. *Plutarch* mentions, that in the reign of Tiberius, an extraordinary voice was heard near the Echinades in the Ionian Sea, which exclaimed that the great Pan was dead. This was readily believed by the emperor, and the astrologers were consulted, but they were unable to explain the meaning of so supernatural a voice, which probably proceeded from the imposition of one of the courtiers who attempted to terrify Tiberius. In Ægypt, in the town of Mendes, which word also signifies a *goat*, there was a sacred goat kept with the most ceremonious sanctity. The death of this animal was always attended with the greatest solemnities, and like that of another Apis, became the cause of a universal mourning. As Pan usually terrified the inhabitants of the neighbouring country, that kind of fear which often seizes men, and which is only ideal and imaginary, has received from him the name of *panic fear.* The kind of terror has been exemplified not only in individuals, but in numerous armies, such as that of Brennus, which was thrown into the greatest consternation at Rome, without any cause or plausible reason. *Ovid. Fast.* 1. v. 396. l. 2. v. 277. *Met.* 1. v. 689.—*Virg. G.* 1. v. 17. *Æn.* 8. v. 343 *G.* 3. v. 392.—*Juv.* 2. v. 142.—*Paus* 8. c. 30.—*Ital.* 13. v. 327.—*Varro de L.L.* 5. c. 3.—*Liv.* 1. c. 5.—*Dionys. Hal.* 1.—*Herodot.* 2. c. 46 & 145, &c.—*Diod.* 1. *Orpheus Hymn.* 10.—*Homer Hymn. in Pan.*—*Lucian. Dial. Merc. & Pan.*—*Apollod.* 1. c. 4.—*Euripid in Iphi. Taur.* 1126.—*Epimen. apud Sch. Theocr.* 1. v. 123. *Id.* 4. v. 62. *Id.* 7. v. 109.—*Servius ad Virg. Ecl.* 2. v. 34. *G.* 1. v. 14 & 16. *Æn* 2. v. 43.—*Tzetzes. Lyc.* 772.—*Cic.* 16. *Fam.* 23.—*Val. Flacc.* 3. v. 46. There was an anniversary festival in honor of Pan at Athens, where he had a temple near the Acropolis. *Herodot.* 6. c. 106. Pan had likewise a festival in Arcadia, at which they used to beat his statue with Σκίλλαι, *sea onions. Theocrit. Schol. Idyll.* 7. [There is a fine group of Pan and a youth, in the gardens of the Villa Ludovisi, near Rome.]

PANACE'A, a goddess, daughter of Æsculapius, who presided over health. The word was afterwards applied to salt, because it was considered as able to remove pain. It was also applied to medicinal preparations extracted from various herbs, which were supposed to possess the power of healing. *Plin.* 35. c. 11. l. 25. c. 4. l. 26. c. 8.—*Lucret.* 4. v. 112.—*Celsus,* 5. c. 4 & 27.—*Servius ad Æn.* 12. v. 419.—*Lucan.* 9. v. 918.—*Voss. de Idolol.* 4. c. 58. A festival called Panacea was celebrated in her honor. *Theodor.* 7. *Therap.*

PAN'ACRA, mountains of Crete. *Callimach.*

PANAC'TOS, a place of Attica. *Steph. Harpocration* says that it is a town between Attica and Bœotia. *Salmas. ad Solin.* p. 1278.

PANÆ'TIUS, a stoic philosopher of Rhodes, disciple to Antipater of Tarsus, 138 B.C. He studied at Athens for some time, of which he refused to become a citizen, observing, that a good and modest man ought to be satisfied with one country. He came to Rome, where he reckoned among his pupils Lælius and Scipio the second Africanus. To the latter he was attached by the closest ties of friendship and familiarity, he attended him in his expeditions, and partook of all his pleasures and amusements. To the interest of their countrymen at Rome the Rhodians were greatly indebted for their prosperity, and the immunities which they for some time enjoyed. Besides the works on providence, on the bearing of pain, on the duties of magistrates, Panætius wrote a treatise on the duties of man, the merit of which can be ascertained from the encomiums which Cicero bestows upon it. *Fabr. B. Gr.* 3. c. 10. *de Stoicis.*—*Sax. Onom.* 1. p. 132.—*Cic. in Offic. Finib.* 4. c. 9. *De Div.* 1. *Leg.* 3. c. 6. *In Acad.* 2. c. 2. *De Orat.* 1. *De N.D.* 2. c. 46.—*Horat.* 1. od. 3. v. 14.—*Suidas.*—*Athen.* 13. *Sch. Aristophan in Ran.* 1539.——A tyrant of Leontini in Sicily, B.C. 613. *Polyæn.* 5. c. *ult.*—*Aristot. Polit.* 5. c. 10 & 12.—*Euseb. Chron.*

PANÆTO'LIUM, a general assembly of the Ætolians. *Liv.* 31. c. 29. l. 35. c. 32. *Plin.* 4. c. 2.

PANÆU'RA, a city near the Indus. *Steph.*

PANÆ'US. *Vid.* Paneus.

PANAGÆ'A, a surname of Diana, from the frequent changes of her residence in the woods, in the heavens, and in the infernal regions. *Erasmus. Adag. Chil.* 2. *Cent.* 9. c. 47.

PAN'AGRA, a city of the interior of Libya. *Ptol.*

PAN'ARES, a general of Crete, defeated by Metellus.

PANARIS'TE, one of the waiting women of Berenice the wife of king Antiochus. *Polyæn.* 8. c. 50.

PANAS'SA, a town of India within the Ganges. *Ptol.*

PANATHENÆ'A, festivals in honor of Minerva the patroness of Athens. They were first instituted by Erichthonius or Orpheus, and called Athenæa, but Theseus afterwards renewed them and caused them to be celebrated and observed by all the tribes of Athens, which he had united into one, for which reason the festivals were called Panathenæa. Some suppose that they are the same as the Roman Quinquatria, as they are often called by that name among the Latins. In the first years of the institution, they were observed only during one day, but afterwards the time was prolonged, and the celebration was attended with greater pomp and solemnity. The festivals were two: *the Great* (μεγαλα) *Panathenæa*, which were observed every fifth year, beginning on the 22nd of the month called Hecatombœon, or 7th of July, and the *Lesser* (μικρα) *Panathenæa*, which were kept every third year, or rather annually, beginning on the 21st or 20th of the month called Thargelion, corresponding to the 5th or sixth day of the month of May. In the lesser festivals there were three games conducted by ten presidents chosen from the ten tribes of Athens, who continued four years in office. On the evening of the first day there was a race with torches, in which men on foot, and afterwards on horseback, contended. The same was also exhibited in the greater festivals. The second combat exhibited a trial of strength and bodily dexterity. The last was a musical contention, first instituted by Pericles. In the songs they celebrated the generous undertaking of Harmodius and Aristogiton, who opposed the Pisistratidæ, and of Thrasybulus, who delivered Athens from its thirty tyrants. Phrynis of Mitylene was the first who obtained the victory by playing upon the harp. There were besides other musical instruments, on which they played in concert, such as flutes, &c. The poets contended in four plays, called from their number τετραλογια. The last of these was a satire. There was also at Sunium an imitation of a naval fight. Whoever obtained the victory in any of these games was rewarded with a vessel of oil, which he was permitted to dispose of in whatever manner he pleased, and it was unlawful for any other person to transport that commodity. The conqueror also received a crown of the olives which grew in the groves of Academus, and were sacred to Minerva, and called μοϱίαι, from μοϱός, *death*, in remembrance of the tragical end of Hallirrhotius the son of Neptune, who cut his own legs when he attempted to cut down the olive which had given the victory to Minerva in preference to his father, when these two deities contended about giving a name to Athens. Some suppose that the word is derived from μέϱος, *a part*, because these olives were given by contribution by all such as attended at the festivals There was also a dance called Pyrrhichia, performed by young boys in armour, in imitation of Minerva, who thus expressed her triumph over the vanquished Titans. Gladiators were also introduced when Athens became tributary to the Romans. During the celebration no person was permitted to appear in dyed garments, and if any one transgressed he was punished according to the discretion of the president of the games. After these things, a sumptuous sacrifice was offered, towards which every one of the Athenian boroughs contributed an ox, and the whole was concluded by an entertainment for all the company with the flesh that remained from the sacrifice. In the greater festivals the same rites and ceremonies were usually observed but with more solemnity and magnificence. Others were also added, particularly the procession, in which Minerva's sacred πέπλος, or *garment* was carried. This garment was woven by a select number of virgins, called ἐϱγαςἶναι, from ἔϱγον, *work*. They were superintended by two of the ἀῤῥηφόϱοι, or young virgins. not above seventeen years of age, nor under eleven, whose garments were white and set off with ornaments of gold. Minerva's *peplus* was of a white color, without sleeves, and embroidered with gold. Upon it were described the achievements of the goddess, particularly her victories over the giants. The exploits of Jupiter and the other gods were also represented there, and from that circumstance men of courage and bravery were said to be αξιοι πέπλου, worthy to be pourtrayed on Minerva's sacred garment. In the procession of the *peplus*, the following ceremonies were observed. In the Ceramicus, without the city, there was an engine built in the form of a ship, upon which Minerva's garment was hung as a sail, and the whole was conducted, not by beasts, as some have supposed, but by subterraneous machines, to the temple of Ceres Eleusinia, and thence to the citadel, where the *peplus* was placed upon Minerva's statue, which was laid upon a bed woven or strewed with flowers, which was called πλακίς. Persons of all ages, of every sex and quality, attended the procession, which was led by old men and women carrying olive branches in their hands, from which reason they were called θαλλοφόϱοι, *bearers of green boughs*. Next followed men of full age with shields and spears. They were attended by the μέτοικοι, or *foreigners*, who carried small boats as a token of their foreign origin, and from that account they were called σκαφηφόϱοι, *boat bearers*. After them came the women attended by the wives of the foreigners called ὑδϱιαφόϱοι, because they carried *water-pots*. Next to these came young men crowned with millet and singing hymns to the goddess, and after them followed select virgins of the noblest families, called κανηφόϱοι, *basket bearers*, because they carried baskets, in which were certain things necessary for the celebration, with whatever utensils were also requisite. These several necessaries were generally in possession of the chief manager of the festival called αϱχιθέωϱος, who distributed them when occasion offered. The virgins were attended by the daughters of the foreigners, who carried umbrellas and little seats, from which they were named διφϱηφόϱοι, *seat carriers*. The boys, called πανδαμικοί, led the rear clothed in coats generally worn at processions. The necessaries for this and every other festival were prepared in a public hall erected for that purpose, between the Piræan gate and the temple of Ceres. The management and the care of the whole was entrusted to the νομοφύλακες, or people employed in seeing the rites and ceremonies properly observed. It was also usual to set all prisoners at liberty, and to present golden crowns to such as had deserved well of their country. Some persons were also chosen to sing some of Homer's poems, a custom which was first introduced by Hipparchus, the son of Pisistratus. It was also customary in this festival and every other quinquennial festival to pray for the prosperity of the Platæans, whose services had been so conspicuous at the battle of Marathon. *Plut. in Thes.—Paus. Arc.* 2.—*Ælian. V.H.* 8. c. 2.—*Apollod.* 3. c. 14.—*Virg. in Cir.* 29.—*Plin.* 35. c. 11.—*Hygin. P.A.* 2. c. 13.—*Servius. ad Virg. G.* v. 113.—*Thucyd.* 6. c. 56.—*Pollux.* 8. c. 9.—*Plato in Euthy.—Schol. Pind. Nem.* 10. v. 65.—*Sch. Aristoph. in Nub.* 1001.—*Plant. in Mercat.* 1. sc. 1. v. 67.—*Meurs. in Thes.* 17.

PAN'CALE, a name of Amorgus, one of the Cyclades. *Steph.*

PANCHÆ'A, PANCHE'A or **PANCHA'IA**, a part of Arabia Felix, celebrated for the myrrh, frankincense, and perfumes which it produced. Diodorus considered it as an island on which he enumerates four principal towns, Penara, Hyracia, Dalis, and Oceanis, the first of which contained a temple of Jupiter Triphylius, celebrated for its beauty, the magnificence of its ornaments, and its great riches. *Virg. G.* 2. v. 139. l. 4. v. 379. *Culex*, 87.—*Ovid. Met.* 1. v. 309, &c.—*Diod.* 5.—*Lucret.* 2 v. 417.—*Servius ad Virg. G.* 2. v. 115, 117, & 139, &c.—*Gyrald. H. D.* 2.—*Salmas. ad Solin.* p. 549.

PANCLA'DIA, a festival so called απὸ παντων κλαδων, from *all* sorts of *boughs*. It was celebrated by the Rhodians when they pruned their vines. *Hesych.*

PAN'CRATES, a poet of Alexandria, a flatterer of the emperor Adrian. *Salmas. ad Solin.* p. 976.

PAN'CRATO, a daughter of Haloteus and Iphimede, of Thessaly, who was carried away with her mother by Thracian pirates, and who boldly determined to destroy herself rather than to yield to the dishonorable solicitations of her ravishers. *Andrisc. apud Parthen.* 19.

PAN'DA, two deities at Rome, who presided one over the openings of roads, and the other over the openings of towns. The former of these was first worshipped by Tatius, who invoked her assistance to open to him and to his troops the way to the Capitol, and she afterwards presided also over travellers. Some imagine that Panda was the same as Ceres, but they are distinguished as different deities by most ancient authors. *Aul. Gellius*, 13. c. 22.—*Arnob.* 4 *Adv. Turneb. Adv.* 19. c. 11.—*Varro de P. R.* 1.

PAN'DA, a town not far from Alexandria. *Plin.* 6. c. 16.

PAN'DAMA, a girl of India adopted by Hercules. *Polyœn.* 1. c. 3. n. 4.

PANDA'RIA or PANDATA'RIA, a small island of the Tyrrhene Sea. *Vid.* Pandataria.

PAN'DARUS, a son of Lycaon, who assisted the Trojans in their war against the Greeks. He went to the war without a chariot, and he therefore generally fought on foot. He broke the truce which had been agreed upon between the Greeks and Trojans, and wounded Menelaus and Diomedes and shewed himself very courageous. He was at last killed by Diomedes; and Æneas, who then carried him in his chariot, by attempting to revenge his death, nearly perished by the hand of the enraged enemy. *Dictys. Cret.* 2. c. 35.—*Homer. Il.* 2. *en.* 331. l. 5. v. 795.—*Philostr. Ner.* 14, —*Hygin.* fab. 112.—*Virg. Æn.* 5. v. 495. *& Servius loco.*—*Strab.* 14.——A son of Alcanor, killed with his brother Bitias by Turnus. *Virg. Æn.* 9. v. 735.——A native of Crete, punished with death for being accessary to the theft of Tantalus. What this theft was is unknown. Some, however, suppose that Tantalus stole the ambrosia and the nectar from the tables of the gods to which he had been admitted, or that he carried away a dog which watched Jupiter's temple in Crete, in which crime Pandarus was concerned and for which he suffered. Pandarus had two daughters, Camiro and Clytia, who were also deprived of their mother by a sudden death, and left without friends or protectors. Venus had compassion upon them, and fed them with milk, honey, and wine. The goddesses were all equally interested in their welfare. Juno gave them wisdom and beauty, Diana a handsome figure and regular features, and Minerva instructed them in domestic accomplishments. Venus wished still to make their happiness more complete, and when they were come to nubile years, the goddess prayed Jupiter to grant them kind and tender husbands. But in her absence the Harpies carried away the virgins and delivered them to the Eumenides to share the punishment which their father suffered. *Paus.* 10. c. 30. —*Homer. Odyss.* 20. v. 66.—*Hygin.* fab. 82.—*Tzetzes ad Lyc.* 152.—*Lactant. ad Theb.* 1. v. 246. l. 7 v. 51.—*Sch. Pind. Ol.* 1. v. 97.

PAN'DARUS or PAN'DAREUS, a man whom some suppose to be the same as Pandion, king of Athens, from the fate of his daughters. According to Nicander, he was a native of Ephesus, and highly favored by Ceres. He had two daughters, Aido and Chelidona, the former of whom married Polytechnus, an artisan of Colophon, by whom she had a son called Itys. The happiness of these two lovers was disturbed when they imprudently boasted that their union was more cordial than that of Jupiter and Juno. The offended goddess sent Discord, who raised dissensions among them. As the husband was going to finish a chair, and the wife a piece of tapestry, it was agreed as a trial of dexterity, that whoever had finished first should claim a slave from the other. Aido won, and Polytechnus irritated, went to Pandareus, and on pretence of being sent by his wife, he easily obtained Chelidona, to whom, on his return, he offered violence. This insult, however, was concealed on pain of death, and Chelidona, with her head shorn and in a squalid dress was presented to her sister as a slave. Aido was severe in her exactions, and she soon was led by the melancholy of the stranger, to inquire into and discover the causes of her sorrow. Chelidona revealed the scources of her grief, and the two sisters to avenge the insult, murdered Itys, and presented his flesh as food before his ignorant father. After this they fled, and were pursued by Polytechnus to the house of Pandareus, who seized the unfortunate husband, and carried him loaded with chains, naked, and besmeared with honey, for the derision of his country. Aido was moved with compassion for his misfortunes, and drove away the swarms of flies which tormented him, for which she was doomed to death by her incensed family, but the gods changed her into a nightingale, Chelidona into a swallow, Pandareus into a sea bird, and Polytechnus into a pelican. *Nicander. apud Anton. Lib.—Stat.*

PANDATA'RIA, an island in the Tyrrhene Sea, on the coast of Lucania, now called Santa Maria. Julia, the licentious daughter of Augustus, and her virtuous daughter Agrippina, were sent here into perpetual exile.

PANDA'TES, a friend of Datames at the court of Artaxerxes. *C. Nep. in Dat.* 5.

PANDELE'TUS, a malicious and litigious character at Athens, ridiculed by the comic poets. *Schol. Aristoph. Nub.*

PANDE'MIA, a surname of Venus expressive of great power over the affections of mankind.

PANDE'MON, a festival, the same as the Athenæa and Chalcea so called from the great concourse of people that met at the solemnity. *Suidas.*

PANDE'MUS or PANDE'MOS, one of the surnames of the god of love among the Ægyptians and the Greeks. *Plut. in Erot.*

PANDI'A, a festival at Athens established by Pandion, from whom it received its name, or because it was observed in honor of Jupiter who can τα παντα δινεύειν, *move and turn all things* as he pleases. Some suppose that it concerned the moon, because it does παντοτε ίέναι, *move incessantly*, by showing itself day and night, rather than the sun which never appears but in the day time. It was celebrated after the Dionysia, because Bacchus is sometimes taken for the sun, or Apollo, and therefore the brother, or as some will have it, the son of the moon. *Etymol. Auctor.—Suidas.*

PANDICULA'RES, a name applied by the Romans to those days on which sacrifices were offered to all the gods in common. *Festus. de V. Sig.—Gyrald. de An. & Mens.*

PANDI'ON, a son of Phineus and Cleopatra, deprived of his eye-sight by his father. *Apollod.* 3. c. 5.——A son of Ægyptus and Hephæstina, married Callidice. *Id.*——A king of the Indies in the age of Augustus. *Strab.* 15.——A king of Nelcynda, in the time of *Pliny*.

PANDI'ON, the First, a king of Athens, son of Erichthonius and Pasithea, who succeeded his father, B.C. 1437. He became father of Procne and Philomela, Erechtheus and Butes. During his reign there was such an abundance of corn, wine, and oil, that it was publicly reported that Bacchus and Minerva had personally visited Attica. He waged a successful war against Labdacus king of Bœotia, and gave his daughter Procne in marriage to Tereus king of Thrace, who had assisted him. The treatment which Philomela received from her brother-in-law Tereus (*vid.* Philomela) was the source of infinite grief to Pandion, and he died through excess of sorrow after a reign of forty years. *Euseb. in Chron.—Ovid. Met.* 6. v. 675.—*Meurs. de reg. Att.* l. 2.

PANDI'ON, the Second, son of Cecrops the Second by Metiadusa, succeeded his father, B.C. 1307. He was driven from his paternal dominions, and fled to Pylas, king of Megara, who gave him his daughter Pelia in marriage, and resigned his crown to him. Pandion became father of four children, called from him Pandionidæ, Ægeus, Pallas, Nisus, and Lycus. The eldest of these children recovered his father's kingdom. Some authors have confounded the two Pandions together in such an indiscriminate manner, that they seem to have been only one and the same person. Many believe that Philomela and Procne were the daughters, not of Pandion the First, but of Pandion the Second. *Lucan. ad Pis.* 675.—*Apollod.* 3. c. 15.—*Paus.* 1. c. 5.—*Hygin.* fab. 48.—*Meursius de Reg. A.* 1. c. 6, 7 & 8. *In Cecrop.* 13.

PANDI'ONIS, one of the twelve tribes of Athens, so called from Pandion. *Rossæus, Archæolog. Att.* l. c. 6.

PANDO'RA, a celebrated woman, the first mortal female that ever lived, according to the opinion of the poet Hesiod. She was made with clay by Vulcan, at the request of Jupiter, who wished to punish the impiety and artifice of Prometheus, by giving him a wife. When this woman of clay had been made by the artist, and received life, all the gods vied in making her presents. Venus gave her beauty and the art of pleasing; the Graces gave her the power of captivating; Apollo taught her how to sing; Mercury instructed her in eloquence, and Minerva gave her the most rich and splendid ornaments. From all these valuable presents, which she had received from the gods, the woman was called *Pandora*, which intimates that she had received *every* necessary *gift*, πᾶν δῶρον. Jupiter after this gave her a beautiful box, which she was ordered to present to the man who married her, and by the commission of the god, Mercury conducted her to Prometheus. The artful mortal was sensible of the deceit, and as he had always distrusted Jupiter, as well as the rest of the gods, since he had stolen fire away from the sun to animate his man of clay, he sent away Pandora without suffering himself to be captivated by her charms. His brother Epimetheus was not possessed of the same prudence and sagacity. He married Pandora, and when he opened the box which she presented to him, there issued from it a multitude of evils and distempers, which dispersed themselves all over the world, and which, from that fatal moment, have never ceased to afflict the human race. Hope was the only one who remained at the bottom of the box, and it is she alone who has the wonderful power of easing the labors of man, and of rendering his troubles and sorrows less painful in life. *Hesiod. Theog.* 570, *& Dies.* 60.—*Apollod.* 1. c. 7.—*Paus.* 1. c. 24.—*Hygin.* 142. ——A daughter of Erechtheus king of Athens. She was sister to Protogenia, who sacrificed herself for her country at the beginning of the Bœotian war.

PANDO'RUS, a son of Erechtheus, king of Athens.

PANDO'SIA, a town in the country of the Brutii, situate on a mountain south of Sybaris. Alexander, king of the Molossi, died there. *Strab.* 6. —*Liv.* 8.——A town of Epirus on the river Acheron. *Plin.* 4. c. 1.

PAN'DROSUS, a daughter of Cecrops, king of Athens, sister of Aglaurus and Herse. She was the only one of the sisters who had not the fatal curiosity to open a basket which Minerva had entrusted to their care, *(vid.* Erichthonius,) for which sincerity a temple was raised to her, near that of Minerva, and a festival instituted to her honor, called *Pandrosia. Ovid. Met.* 2. v. 738.—*Apollod.* 3.—*Paus.* 1. c. 2 & 27.—*Athenag. in Apolog.*—*Hesych.*

PANDYS'IA, public rejoicings, when unusually stormy seasons forced the mariner to stay at home. *Æneas. Tactic.*—*Proclus in Hesiod.* Εργ β'.

PANELLE'NIA, a public festival celebrated by an assembly of people from all parts of Greece. *Eustath. Il.* 2.

PAN'ELUS, a city near Pontus, so called from an inhabitant of Heraclea, a descendant of Peneleus. *Steph.*

PAN'ENUS or PANÆ'US, a celebrated painter, who was for some time engaged in painting the battle of Marathon, which was still seen and admired in the Pœcile in the age of Pausanias. His pieces were among those which adorned the temple of Jupiter Olympus. *Paus.* 5. c. 11.—*Plin.* 35. c. 8. l. 36. c. 23.

PANEPH'YSIS, a town of Ægypt. *Ptol.*

PANEU'RA, a city of India within the Ganges, near the Indus. *Steph.*

PANGÆ'US, a mountain of Thrace, anciently called *Mons Caraminus*, and joined to mount Rhodope, near the sources of the river Nestus. It was inhabited by four different nations. It was on this mountain that Lycurgus, the Thracian king, was torn to pieces, and that Orpheus called the attention of the wild beasts, and of the mountains and woods to listen to his song. It abounded in gold and silver mines. *Herodot.* 5. c. 16. &c. l. 7. c. 113.—*Virg. G.* 4. v. 462 —*Ovid. Fast.* 3. v. 739.—*Thucyd.* 2.—*Lucan.* 1. v. 679. l. 7. v. 482.—*Hygin. P.A.* 2. c. 7.—*Pindar. Pyth.* 4. v. 120.—*Euripid. in Bacc.* 560.

PA'NIA, an ancient name of Arcadia. *Steph.*

PANIAR'DIS, a city of Asiatic Sarmatia. *Ptol.*

PANI'ASIS. *Vid.* Panyasis.

PANIG'ENA, a city of India Citerior. *Ptol.*

PANIO'NIUM, a place at the foot of mount Mycale, near the town of Ephesus in Asia Minor, sacred to Neptune of Helice. It was in this place that all the states of Ionia assembled, either to consult for their own safety and prosperity, or to celebrate festivals, or to offer a sacrifice for the good of all the nation, whence the name Πανιώνιον *all Ionia.* The deputies of the twelve Ionian cities which assembled were those of Miletus, Myus, Priene, Ephesus, Lebedus, Colophon, Clazomenæ, Phocæa, Teos, Chius, Samus, and Erythræ. If the bull offered in sacrifice bellowed, it was accounted an omen of the highest favor, as the sound was particularly acceptable to the god of the sea, as in some manner it resembled the roaring of the waves of the ocean. *Herodot.* 1. c. 148, &c.—*Strab.* 14. —*Mela*, 1. c. 17.—*Eustath. Il.* ό.

PA'NIS or PAN'IDES, a king of Chalcis, who preferred Hesiod to Homer, which foolish opinion gave rise to the proverb *Paniäis suffragium. Philostr. in Euphorb.*

PA'NIS, an island in the Arabic Gulph. *Ptol.* It is probably the Orine of *Arrian. in Peripl.*

PANIS'CI (*quasi Panes parvi*), inferior divinities who presided over woods, fields, &c. *Cic. Div.* 2. c. 21. *N. D.* 3. c. 17.—*Plin.* 35. c. 11.

PANIS'SA, a river of Thrace not far from Apollonia. *Plin.* 4. c. 11.

PA'NIUS, a place of Cœlesyria, where Antiochus defeated Scopas, B.C. 198.

PANNO'NIA, a large country of Europe, bounded on the east by Upper Mœsia, on the south by Dalmatia, on the west by Noricum, and on the north by the Danube. It was divided by the ancients into Lower and Upper Pannonia. The inhabitants were of Celtic origin, and were first invaded by J. Cæsar, and conquered in the reign of Tiberius. Philip and his son Alexander, some ages before, had successively conquered it. Sirmium was the ancient capital of all Pannonia, which contains the modern provinces of Croatia, Carniola, Sclavonia, Bosnia, Windisch, March, with part of Servia, and of the kingdoms of Hungary and Austria. *Lucan.* 3. v. 95. l. 6. v. 220.—*Tibull.* 4. el. 1. v. 109.—*Plin.* 3.—*Dion. Cas.* 49.—*Strab.* 4 & 7.—*Jornand.*—*Paterc.* 2. c. 9. — *Suet. Aug.* 20.—*Ovid. Trist.* 2. v. 225.

PANOL'BIUS, a Greek poet mentioned by *Suidas* and *Gyraldus, de P. H.* 3.

PANOMPHÆ'US, a surname of Jupiter derived from πᾶς *omnis* and ὀμφὴ *vox*, either because he was worshipped by every nation on earth, or because he heard the prayers and the supplications which were addressed to him, or because the rest of the gods derived from him their knowledge of futurity. *Ovid. Met.* 11. v. 198.—*Homer. Il.* 8. v. 251. & *Eustath. loco.*

PAN'OPE or PANOPE'A, one of the Nereides, whom sailors generally invoked in storms. *Hesiod. Theog.* 251.—*Virg. Æn.* 5. v. 825. *G.* 1. v. 437.—*Ovid. ad Liv.* 435. *Fast.* 6. v. 499. *Flacc.* 1. v. 134. l. 2. v. 590.

PAN'OPE, one of the daughters of Thespius, mother of Threpsippa by Hercules. *Apollod.* 2. c. 7.

PAN'OPE, a town of Phocis, called Panopeus. *Ovid. Met.* 3. v. 19.—*Liv.* 32. c. 18.—*Paus.* 10. c. 4.—*Stat. Theb.* 7. v. 344.—*Homer. Il.* 2. v. 27. *Odyss.* 11. v. 580.

PAN'OPES, a famous huntsman among the attendants of Acestes, king of Sicily. He was one of those that engaged in the games exhibited by Æneas in Sicily. *Virg. Æn.* 5. v. 300.

PAN'OPEUS, a son of Phocus and Asterodia, who accompanied Amphitryon when he made war against the Teleboans. He was father to Epeus, who made the celebrated wooden horse at the siege of Troy. *Paus.* 2. c. 29.—*Apollod.* 2. c. 4.—*Ovid. Met.* 8. v. 313.—*Servius ad Æn.* 2. v. 263.—*Tzetzes ad Lyc.* 939.

PAN'OPEUS, a town of Phocis. *Vid.* Panope.

PANO'PION, a Roman saved from death by the uncommon fidelity of his servant. When the assassins came to murder him as being proscribed, the servant exchanged clothes with his master, and let him escape by a back door. He afterwards went into his master's bed, and suffered himself to be killed in his stead. *Val. Max.*

PANOP'OLIS, *the city of Pan*, a town of Ægypt,

called also Chemmis. Pan had there a temple, where he was worshipped with great solemnity. Perseus and Danae had also a temple there. The poet Nonnus, the author of the Dionysiaca and Gigantomachia, was born there. *Herodot.* 2.—*Diod.* 5.—*Strab.* 17.—*Gyrald. de P.H.* 5.

PANOP'TES, a name of Argus, from the power of his eyes. *Apollod.* 2.

PANOR'MUS, a Messenian, who insulted the religion of the Lacedæmonians. *Vid.* Gonippus.

PANOR'MUS, now Palermo, the capital of Sicily, built by the Phœnicians, on the north-west part of the island. It had a good and capacious harbour, and was the strongest hold of the Carthaginians in Sicily, and was at last taken with difficulty by the Romans. When captured by the Saracens, A.D. 821, it became the capital of the island, and under the Normans, in 1071, it was made the metropolis of their empire. *Diod.* 22.—*Mela*, 2. c. 7.—*Ital.* 14. v. 262.——A town of the Thracian Chersonesus. *Plin.* 4. c. 11.——A town of Ionia, ner Ephesus. ——A town in Crete. *Ptol.*—*Plin.* 4. c. 12. It is now Mirabello, according to *Niger*.——A town of Macedonia, on the shore near mount Athos. *Ptol.* ——A town of Achaia. *Polyb.* 3.—*Plin.* 4. c. 5.—*Paus.* 7.—*Thucyd.*——A town of Samus. *Liv.* 24. c. 36. It is now Macri. It was the name also of many harbours.

PANO'TII, a people of Scythia, said to have very large ears. *Plin.* 4. c. 13.—*Salmas. ad Solin.* p. 219.

PAN'SA C. VIB'IUS, a Roman consul, who, with A. Hirtius made war against the murderers of J. Cæsar, and was killed in a battle near Mutina. On his death-bed he advised young Octavius to unite his interest with that of Antony, if he wished to revenge the death of Julius Cæsar, and from this friendly advice soon after rose the celebrated second triumvirate. Some suppose that Pansa was put to death by Octavius himself, or at his suggestion by the physician Glicon, who poured poison into the wounds of his patient. Pansa and Hirtius were the two last consuls who enjoyed the dignity of chief magistrate of Rome, with full power. The authority of the consuls afterwards dwindled into a shadow. *Cic. Phil.* 5. c. 19. *Fam.* 10. ep. 33. *Brut.* 6.—*Paterc.* 2. c. 6.—*Dio.* 46.—*Ovid. Trist.* 3. el. 5. v. 6.—*Plut. & Appian.*

PANTÆ'NUS or PANTE'NUS, a stoic philosopher of Sicily, who taught in the Alexandrian school, in the reign of Commodus, A.D. 181. By his discourses as well as by his writings he greatly promoted the cause of Christianity. *Euseb. Hist. Eccles.* 2. c. 32 & 36. l. 5. c. 10.

PANTA'GIAS or PANTA'GIES, a small river on the eastern coast of Sicily, which falls into the sea, after running for a short distance in rough cascades over rugged stones and precipices. Ceres, whose most favored residence was in Sicily, is said to have commanded the river, whose noisy current disturbed her repose, to flow more quietly, and the obedient stream from that time, as the mythologists relate, was scarcely ever heard in its way to the sea. *Ovid. Fast.* 4. v. 471.—*Claudian de Rapt. P.* 2. v. 58.—*Virg. Æn.* 3. v. 689. *Servius loco.*—*Ital.* 14. v. 232.

PANTAGNOS'TUS, a brother of Polycrates, tyrant of Samus. *Pylyæn.* 1. c. 23.

PANTA'LEON, a king of Pisa, who presided at the Olympic games, B.C. 664, after excluding the Eleans, who on that account expunged the Olympiad from the Fasti, and called it the second Anolympiad. They had called for the same reason the eighth the first Anolympiad, because the Piseans presided. ——An Ætolian chief. *Liv.* 42. c. 15.

PANTA'LIA, a city of Thrace. *Procop.*

PANTA'NUS LA'CUS, the lake of Lesina, is situated in Apulia, at the mouth of the Frento. *Plin.* 3. c. 12.

PANTAU'CHUS, a man appointed over Ætolia by Demetrius. *Plut.*

PAN'TEUS, a friend of Cleomenes, king of Sparta. *Plut.*

PAN'THIDES, a man who married Italia the daughter of Themistocles.

PANTHE'A, the wife of Abradates, celebrated for her beauty and conjugal affection. She was taken prisoner by Cyrus, who refused to visit her, that he might not be ensnared by the power of her personal charms. She killed herself on the body of her husband, who had been slain in battle. *Vid.* Abradates. *Xenoph. Cyrop.* 7.—*Suidas.*—*Cœl. Rhod.* 13. c. 33.——The mother of Eumæus, the faithful servant of Ulysses. *Euphorion apud Eustath.* 15. *Odyss.*

PANTHE'JUM, a place of Attica, sixty stadia from the Ilissus, where the victors at the Olympic games were crowned. *Suidas.*

PAN'THEON or PANTHE'ON, a celebrated temple at Rome built by Agrippa, in the reign of Augustus, and dedicated to all the gods, whence the name πᾶς θεός. It was struck with lightning some time after, and partly destroyed, but Adrian repaired it, and it still exists, having been converted into a Christian temple by Pope Boniface the fourth, and dedicated to the virgin and all the martyrs, and is still the admiration of the curious. *Plin.* 36. c. 15.—*Marcell.* 16 c. 10.—*Lips. Adm. Rom.* 3. c. 6.

PAN'THEUS or PAN'THUS, a son of Othryas of Phocis who was carried away from his country by Antenor, whom king Priam had sent to inquire of the oracle of Delphi, whether he might be permitted to rebuild the walls of Troy which Hercules had destroyed. This insult offered to his person was alleviated by the kindness of the monarch, who loaded him with presents and made him priest of Apollo. When Troy was laid in ruins Pantheus escaped through the flames, carrying the secret utensils in one hand, and leading in the other his grandson, that he might follow the fortune of Æneas. *Virg. Æn.* 2. v. 429. *& Servius loco.*

PANTHO'IDES, a patronymic of Euphorbus, the son of Panthous. Pythagoras is sometimes called by that name, as he asserted that he was Euphorbus during the Trojan war. *Horat.* 1. od. 28. v. 10.—*Ovid. Met.* 15. v. 161.——A Spartan general, killed by Pericles at the battle of Tanagra.

PAN'THOUS, the father of Euphorbus.

PANTICAPÆ'UM, now Kertch, a town of Taurica Chersonesus, built by the Milesians, and governed for some time by its own laws, and afterwards subdued by the kings of Bosporus. It was, according to Strabo, the capitol of the European Bosporus. Mithridates the Great died there. *Plin.* 4. c. 12.—*Strab.*

PANTIC'APES, a river of European Scythia, which falls into the Borysthenes, supposed to be the Samara of the moderns. *Herodot.* 4. c. 54.

PANTICH'IUM, a place of Bithynia, near Chalcedon. *Antonin.*

PANTIL'IUS, a buffoon ridiculed by *Horace*, 1. sat. 10. v. 78.

PANTIP'OLIS, a city of India within the Ganges. *Ptol.*

PANTOMA'TRIUM, a maritime town of Crete. *Plin.* 4. c. 12.

PANY'ASIS, an ancient Greek, uncle to the historian Herodotus. He celebrated Hercules in one of his poems in fourteen books, and the Ionians in another. Some authors make him a native of Samus and not of Halicarnassus, whilst others assert that he rendered himself odious to Lygdamis by attempting to prophecy future events, and that he was put to death by him. He was restored to life by Æsculapius, according to Apollodorus. Some of his verses, to the number of twenty-three, are preserved in the collection of Greek poets, and they are in praise of wine, and of drinking. *Athen.* 2.—*Apollod.* 3.—*Quintil.* 10. c. 1.—*Gyrald. de P.H.* 3.—*Salmas ad Solin.* p. 856.

PANY'ASUS, a river of Illyricum, falling into the Adriatic, near Dyrrachium. *Ptol.*

PAPÆ'US, a name of Jupiter, among the Scythians. *Herodot.* 4.

PAPHA'GES, a king of Ambracia, killed by a lioness deprived of her whelphs. *Ovid. in Ib.* v. 502.

PAPH'ARA, a city of Cyrrhestica, in Syria. *Ptol.*

PA'PHIA, a surname of the goddess Venus, because she was worshipped at Paphus. *Vid.* Paphus.——An ancient name of the island of Cyprus.

PAPHLAGO'NIA, now Penderachia, a country of Asia Minor, situate at the west of the river Halys, by which it was separated from Cappadocia. It was divided on the west from Bithynia, by the river Parthenius. *Herodot.* 1. c. 72.—*Strab.* 4.—*Mela.*—*Plin.*—*Curt.* 6. c. 11.—*Cic. Rull.* 2. c. 2. & 19.

PA'PHUS, now Basso, a famous city of the island of

Cyprus, founded, as some suppose, about 1184 years B.C., by Agapenor, at the head of a colony from Arcadia. The goddess of beauty was particularly worshipped there in a celebrated temple which attracted the attention of travellers, and which was visited and admired, among others, by the emperor Titus. It had been built, according to some, by Ærias, king of the country, or rather by Cinyras, on the very spot where the goddess landed when she rose from the waters of the sea. Thamiras of Cilicia introduced there the science of augury, and for his great services the office of high priest remained in his family even beyond the age of Pliny, though it was for some time usurped by the descendants of Cinyras. In this sacred temple all male animals, and particularly goats, were immolated to the goddess, and her altars, though 100 in number, daily smoked with the profusion of Arabian frankincense. Some, however, suppose, that no victims were offered, as it was unlawful to shed blood on the altars of the goddess, to whom fire and prayers were said to be the only acceptable oblations. The altar, though exposed to the open air, was said never to be wetted by the rain. The inhabitants of Paphus were very effeminate and lascivious, and the young virgins were permitted by the laws of the place to obtain a dowry by prostitution. *Strab.* 8. &c.—*Plin.* 2. c. 96.—*Mela*, 2.c. 7.—*Homer. Odyss.* 8.—*Virg. Æn.* 1. v. 419, &c. l. 10. v. 51, &c.—*Horat.* 1. od. 39. v. 1.—*Tacit. Ann.* 3. c. 62. *H.* 2.c. 2.—*Arnob.—Servius ad Æn.* 1. v. 339. c. 2. v. 380.—*Lactant.—Clemens. Alex. Strom.*

Paph'us, a son of Pygmalion, by a statue which had been changed into a woman by Venus. *Vid.* Pygmalion. *Ovid. Met.* 10. v. 297.—*Hygin.* fab. 242, 270 & 275.

Pa'pia Lex, *de peregrinis*, introduced by Papius, the tribune, A.U.C. 688, required that all strangers should be expelled from Rome. It was afterwards confirmed and extended by the Junian law.—Another called *Papia Poppæa*, because it was enacted by the tribunes, M. Papius Mutilus, and Q. Poppæus Secundus, who had received consular power from the consuls for six months. It was called the Julian law, after it had been published by order of Augustus, who was himself of the Julian family. *Vid.* Julia lex, *de maritandis ordinibus. Dio.* 56. c. 3 & 4.—Another, to empower the high priest to choose 20 virgins for the service of the goddess Vesta.—Another in the age of Augustus. It gave the patron a certain right to the property of his client, if he had left a specified sum of money, or if he had not three children.

Papia'nus, a man who proclaimed himself emperor some time after the Gordians. He was put to death.

Pa'pias, an early Christian writer, bishop of Hierapolis in Asia Minor. He first propagated the doctrine of the Millennium. There are remaining some historical fragments of his. *Euseb. Eccles. Hist.* 3. c. 33, &c.—*Hieron de script. Eccles.*

Papinia'nus, a writer, A.D. 212. When ordered to write an oration to excuse or palliate the murder of Geta by his brother Caracalla, he with noble indignation refused, and for this virtuous support of principle he was brutally put to death by the tyrant. He was then only in his 37th year, but so great was the progress of his improvement and the extent of his erudition as a lawyer, that he was unanimously called "the honor of jurisprudence, and the treasure of the laws." *Harles, Not. Lit. Rom.* 1. p. 514.—*Sax. Onom.* 1. p. 337. *Vid.* Æmylius Papinianus.

Papin'ius, a tribune who conspired against Caligula.

Papin'ius Sex'tus, a man who destroyed himself when brought into difficulties by his luxurious living. *Tacit. Ann.* 6. c. 49.

Papir'ia, the wife of Paulus Æmylius. She was divorced. *Plut.*

Papir'ia lex, was introduced by Papirius Carbo, A.U.C. 621. It required that in passing or rejecting laws in the *comitia*, the votes should be given on tablets.—Another, by the tribune Papirius, which enacted that no person should consecrate any edifice, place, or thing, without the consent and permission of the people. *Cic. pro Domo*, 50.—Another, A.U.C. 563, to diminish the weight, and increase the value of the Roman *as*.—Another, A.U.C. 421, to give the freedom of the city to the citizens of Acerræ.—Another, A.U.C. 623. It was proposed, but not passed. It recommended the right of choosing a man tribune of the people as often as he wished.

Papir'ius, a centurion engaged to murder Piso, the proconsul of Africa. *Tacit. Hist.* 4. c. 49. ——A patrician, chosen *rex sacrorum*, after the expulsion of the Tarquins from Rome. *Liv.* l. 2. ——A Roman who ill-treated one of his slaves called Publilius. This called for the interference of justice, and a decree was made, which forbad any person to be detained in fetters, but only for a crime that deserved such a treatment, and only till the criminal had suffered the punishment which the laws directed. Creditors also had a right to seize upon the goods, but not the person of their debtors. *Liv.* 8. c. 28.

Papir'ius Car'bo, a Roman consul who undertook the defence of Opimius, who was accused of condemning and putting to death a number of citizens on mount Aventinus without the formalities of a trial. His client was acquitted.——A friend of Cinna and Marius. He raised cabals against Sylla and Pompey, and was at last put to death by order of Pompey, after he had rendered himself odious by a tyrannical consulship, and after he had been proscribed by Sylla.

Papir'ius Cur'sor, a man who first erected a sun-dial in the temple of Quirinus at Rome. B.C. 293; from which time the days began to be divided into hours.

Papir'ius L. Cur'sor, a dictator who ordered his master of the horse to be put to death, because he had fought and conquered the enemies of the republic without his consent. The people interfered, and the dictator pardoned him. Cursor made war upon the Sabines and conquered them, and also triumphed over the Samnites. His great severity displeased the people so much that *Papiria sævitia* became proverbial. He flourished about 320 years B.C. *Liv.* 8. c. 29. l. 9. c. 14. l. 10. c. 3.

Papir'ius, a Roman surnamed *Prætextatus*, from an action of his whilst he wore the prætexta, a certain gown for young men. His father, of the same name, carried him to the senate-house, where affairs of the greatest importance were then in debate before the senators. The mother of young Papirius wished to know what had passed in the senate; but Papirius, unwilling to betray the secrets of that august assembly, amused his mother by telling her, that it had been considered whether it would be more advantageous to the republic to give two wives to one husband, than two husbands to one wife. The mother of Papirius was alarmed, and communicated the secret to the other Roman matrons, and on the morrow they assembled in the senate, petitioning that one woman might have two husbands, rather than one husband two wives. The senators were astonished at the petition, but young Papirius unravelled the whole mystery, and from that time it was made a law among the senators, that no young man should for the future be introduced into the senate house, except Papirius. This law was carefully observed till the age of Augustus, who permitted children of all ages to hear the debates of the senators. *Macrob. Sat.* 1. c. 6.——A consul defeated by the armies of the Cimbri.——A consul murdered by the Gauls.——A son of Papirius Cursor, who defeated the Samnites and dedicated a temple to Romulus Quirinus.

Papir'ius Cras'sus, a dictator who triumphed over the Samnites. *Cic. Fam.* 9. c. 21.

Papir'ius L. Fregella'nus, a Roman famed for his eloquence. *Cic. Br.* 46.

Papir'ius Mar'cus, a Roman knight assassinated by Clodius on the Appian way. *Cic. Mil.* 7. *Dom.* 19.

Papir'ius L. Pæ'tus, a man intimate with Cicero. He possessed wit, learning, and political influence. *Cic. Fam.* 9. *Att.* 1. ep. 20.

Papir'ius Ma'so, a consul who conquered Sardinia and Corsica, and reduced them into the form of a province. At his return to Rome he was refused a triumph, upon which he introduced a triumphal procession, and walked with his victorious army to the Capitol, wearing a crown of myrtle on his head. His example was afterwards followed by such generals as were refused a triumph by the Roman senate. *Val. Max.* 3. c. 6.—The family of the Papirii, anciently called Papisii, was patrician, and long distinguished for its services to the state. It bore the different surnames of Crassus, Cursor, Mugillanus, Maso, Prætextatus, and Pætus, of which the three first branches became the most illustrious.

PAPIT'IUM, a city of Paphlagonia. *Steph.*

PA'PIUS C., a tribune, author of the Papian law, much condemned by Cicero. *Cic. Arch.* 5. *Balb.* 23. *Att.* 4. ep. 14. *Off.* 3. c. 11.

PAP'PA, a city of the Orondici, in Galatia. *Ptol.*

PAP'PIA LEX was enacted to settle the rights of husbands and wives if they had no children.—Another by which a person less than 50 years old could not marry another of 60.

PAP'PUS, a philosopher and mathematician of Alexandria of very great eminence, in the reign of Theodosius the Great. Many of his works have been lost, the best edition of those which have been preserved is that of Bologna, in fol. 1660, by Carol. Manolessius. *Fabr. B. Gr.* 5. c. 17.—*Sax. Onom.* 1. p. 452.

PAPRE'MIS, a city of Ægypt. *Steph.* Here was formerly an oracle of Mars. *Joh. Marsham. Can. Chron.* sec. 4.

PAPYRIUS. *Vid.* Papirius.

PARABYS'TON, a tribunal at Athens, where causes of inferior consequence were tried by 11 judges. It received this name because it was held in a remote and obscure place. *Pollux.* 8.—*Paus.* 1. c. 40.—*Meurs. Attic. Lect.* 2. c. 9.—*Maussae. ad Harpocrat.*

PARACHELOI'TÆ, a people of Thessaly, near Malia. *Strab.*

PARADI'SUS, a town of Syria or Phœnicia. *Plin.* 5. c. 23.—*Strab.* 16.—*Ptol.*——A small town of Sicily. *Steph.*

PARADI'SUS BAL'SAMI, a place in the plains of Jericho, where was a large palace with a garden beautifully planted with trees.

PARÆTACE'NI, a people between Media and Persia, in whose country Antigonus was defeated by Eumenes. *C. Nep. in Eum.* 8.—*Strab.* 11 & 16. —*Plin.* 6. c 26.

PARÆTO'NIUM, a town of Ægypt at the west of Alexandria, where Isis was worshipped. The word *Parætonius* is used to signify Ægyptian, and is sometimes applied to Alexandria, which was situate in the neighbourhood. *Strab.* 17.—*Flor.* 4. c. 11.—*Lucan.* 3. v. 295. l. 10. v. 9.—*Ovid, Met.* 9. v. 712. *A.* 2. el. 13. v. 7.

PARAGONTI'CUS SI'NUS, a bay of Carmania. *Ptol.* It is now Golfo de Gugerath, according to *Niger.*

PARALA'IS, a town of Lycaonia, in Cappadocia. *Ptol.*

PAR'ALI, a division of the inhabitants of Attica. They received this name from their being near the *sea coast*, παρὰ and ἅλς. *Plut. Solon.*

PAR'ALUS, a friend of Dion, by whose assistance he expelled Dionysius. *Diod. Sic.* 16.——An Athenian who is said to have first built a three-oared galley. *Cic. Verr.* 4. c. 60.—*Plin.* 7. c. 56.——A son of Pericles. His premature death was greatly lamented by his father. *Plut.*——The founder of Clazomenæ. *Strab.* 13.—*Plin.* 5. c. 30.

PARAM'MON, one of the surnames of Mercury at Elis, because the son of Jupiter Ammon. *Paus.* 5. c. 15.

PARAPA'SIUS, one of the kings of Parthia, called also Arsaces. *Alex. ab. Alex.* 1. c. 2.

PARAPIA'NI, a people of India. *Plin.* 6. c. 23.

PARAPOTA'MIA, a town of Phocis, on the Cephisus. *Strab.*——A region near the Tigris. *Plin.* 6. c. 27.

PARA'SIA, a country at the east of Media. *Strab.* —*Polyb.*

PARASI'NUM, a town of Taurica Chersonesus. *Plin.* 2. c. 96.

PARA'SIUS, a son of Philonomia by a shepherd. He was exposed on Erymanthus by his mother, with his twin brother Lycastus. Their lives were preserved. *Plut.*

PARATIA'NÆ, a city of Mauritania Cæsariensis. *Antonin.*

PARAVÆ'I, a people of Thesprotia, in Epirus. *Steph.*

PAR'CA, a city of the Jazyges Metanastæ. *Ptol.*

PAR'CÆ, powerful goddesses who presided over the birth and the life of mankind. They were three in number, Clotho, Lachesis, and Atropos, daughters of Nox and Erebus, according to Hesiod, or of Jupiter and Themis, according to the same poet in another poem. Some make them daughters of the sea. Clotho, the youngest of the sisters, presided over the moment in which men were born, and held a distaff in her hand; Lachesis spun out all the events and actions of human life; and Atropos, the eldest of the three, cut the thread of life with a pair of scissors. Their different functions are well expressed in this ancient verse:

Clotho colum retinet, Lachesis net, & Atropos occat.

The name of the Parcæ, according to Varro is described *a partu* or *parturiendo*, because they presided over the birth of men, and by corruption the word *parca* is formed from *parta* or *partus;* but, according to Servius, they are so called by antiphrasis *quod nemini parcant.* The power of the Parcæ was great and extensive. Some suppose that they were subjected to none of the gods but Jupiter, while others assert that even Jupiter himself was obedient to their commands, and indeed the father of the gods is represented in Homer's Iliad as unwilling to see Patroclus perish, yet obliged by the superior power of the Fates to abandon him to his destiny. According to the more received opinions, they were the arbiters of the life and death of mankind, and whatever good or evil befel men in the world proceeded immediately from the Fates or Parcæ. Some make them ministers of the king of hell, and represent them as sitting at the foot of his throne; others represent them as placed on radiant thrones, amidst the celestial spheres, clothed in robes spangled with stars, and wearing crowns on their heads. According to Pausanias, the names of the Parcæ were different from those already mentioned. The most ancient of all, as the geographer observes, was Venus Urania, who presided over the birth of men. the second was Fortune, the third Ilithyia. To these some add a fourth, Proserpina, who often disputed with Atropos the right of cutting the thread of human life. The worship of the Parcæ was established in some cities of Greece, and though mankind were well convinced that they were inexorable, and that it was impossible to mitigate them, yet they were eager to show a proper respect to their divinity, by raising them temples and statues. They received the same worship as the Furies, and their votaries yearly sacrificed to them black sheep, during which solemnity the priests were obliged to wear garlands of flowers. The Parcæ were generally represented as three old women with chaplets made of wool, and interwoven with the flowers of the Narcissus. They were covered with a white robe, and fillet of the same color, bound with chaplets. One of them held a distaff, another a spindle, and the third was armed with scissors, with which she cut the thread which her sisters had spun. Their dress is differently represented by some authors. Clotho sometimes appears in a variegated robe, and on her head is a crown of seven stars. She holds a distaff in her hand reaching from heaven to earth. The robe which Lachesis wore, was variegated with a great number of stars, and near her were placed a variety of spindles. Atropos was clothed in black, she held scissors in her hand, with clues of thread of different sizes, according to the length or shortness of the lives of the persons whose destiny they seemed to contain. Hyginus attributes to them the invention of these Greek letters α, β, η, τ, υ, and others call them the secretaries of heaven, and the keepers of the archives of eternity. The Greeks call the Parcæ by the different names of μοῖρα, αἶσα, κὴρ, εἱμαρμένη, which are expressive of their power and of their inexorable decrees. *Hesiod. Theog.* 219 & 903. *In Scuto,* 250.—*Paus.* 1. c. 40. l. 3. c. 11. l. 5. c. 15.—*Homer. Il.* 20. *Odyss.* 7.—*Theocrit.* 1.—*Callimach. in Dian.*—*Ælian Anim.* 10.—*Pind. Olymp.* 10. *Nem.* 7.—*Eurip. in Iphig.*—*Plut. de Facie in Orbe Lunæ.*—*Hygin.* in præf. fab. & fab. 277.—*Varro.*—*Orph. Hymn.* 58.—*Apollon.* 1, &c. —*Claudian de Rapt. Pros.*—*Lycophr. & Tzetz.* 144. —*Horat,* 2. od. 6, &c.—*Ovid. Met.* 5. v. 532.—*Lu-*

can. 3. v. 19. l. 6. v. 703 & 777.—*Stat. Theb.* 6. v. 642. l. 8. v. 775.—*Virg. Ecl.* 4. *Æn.* 3, &c.—*Senec. in Herc. Fur.*—*Aul. Gell.* 3. c. 16.—*Tertull. apud Turneb.* 18. c. 34.—*Servius ad Ecl. Virg.* 4. v. 46. *Æn.* l. v. 26.—*Martial.* 4. epigr. 54.—*Phurnut. de N.D.* 13.—*Sch. Soph. in Œd. Col.* 42.—*Albric. de D. Imag.* 10.—*Apul. Met.* 11.

PAREM'PHIS, a city of Ægypt. *Steph.*

PARENTA'LIA, a festival observed annually at Rome in honor of the dead. The friends and relations of the deceased assembled on the occasion, when sacrifices were offered and banquets provided. Æneas first established it. *Ovid. Fast.* 2. v. 544. *Virg. Æn.* 3. v. 66. l. 5. v. 77 & 94. l. 9. v. 215. l. 10. v. 519.—*Tac. Hist.* 2. c. 95.—*Suet. Cal.* 3. 15.

PAREN'TIUM, a port and town of Istria, on the Adriatic. *Plin.* 3. c. 19. It is now Parenzo.

PARICA'NE, a city of Persia. *Steph.*

PAR'IS, the son of Priam, king of Troy, by Hecuba, called also Alexander. He was destined, even before his birth, to become the ruin of his country, and when his mother, in the first month of her pregnancy, had dreamed that she should bring forth a torch which would set fire to her palace, the soothsayers foretold the calamities which might be expected from the imprudence of her future son, and which would end in the destruction of Troy. Priam, to prevent so great and so alarming an evil, ordered his slave Archelaus to destroy the child as soon as born. The slave, either touched with humanity or influenced by Hecuba, did not destroy him, but was satisfied to expose him on mount Ida, where the shepherds of the place found him, and educated him as their own son. Some attribute the preservation of his life, before he was found by the shepherds, to the motherly tenderness of a she-bear which suckled him. Young Paris, though educated among shepherds and peasants, gave early proofs of courage and intrepidity, and from his care in protecting the flocks of mount Ida against the rapacity of the wild beast, he obtained the name of Alexander (*helper* or *defender*). He gained the esteem of all the shepherds, and his graceful countenance and manly deportment recommended him to the favour of Œnone, a nymph of mount Ida, whom he married, and with whom he lived in the most perfect harmony. Their conjugal peace was soon disturbed. At the marriage of Pelius and Thetis, the goddess of discord, who had not been invited to partake of the entertainment, showed her displeasure, by throwing into the assembly of the gods who were at the celebration of the nuptials, a golden apple, on which were written the words, *Detur pulchriori.* All the goddesses claimed this gift as their own, and the contention at first became general, but at last only three, Juno, Venus, and Minerva, wished to dispute their respective right to preeminence in beauty. The gods, unwilling to become arbiters in an affair of so tender and delicate a nature, appointed Paris to adjudge the prize of beauty to the fairest of the goddesses, and, indeed, the shepherd seemed properly qualified to decide so difficult a contest, as his wisdom was so well established, and his prudence and sagacity so well known. The goddesses appeared before their judge without any covering, and devoid of ornament, and each tried by promises and entreaties to gain the attention of Paris, and to influence his judgment. Juno promised him a kingdom; Minerva, military glory; and Venus, the fairest woman in the world for his wife, as Ovid expresses it, *Heroid.* 17. v. 111.

Unaque cum regnum; belli daret altera laudem;
Tyndaridis conjux, Tertia dixit, eris.

After he had heard their several claims and promises, Paris adjudged the prize to Venus, and gave her the golden apple, to which, indeed, she seemed entitled, as the goddess of beauty. This decision of Paris in favour of Venus, drew upon the judge and his family the resentment of the two other goddesses. Soon after, Priam proposed a contest among his sons and other princes, and promised to reward the conqueror with one of the finest bulls of mount Ida. His emissaries were sent to procure the animal, and it was found in the possession of Paris, who reluctantly yielded it up. The shepherd was desirous of obtaining again this favorite animal, and went to Troy and entered the list of combatants. The display of his strength and agility was received with the greatest applause, and he obtained the victory over his rivals, Nestor, the son of Neleus; Cycnus, son of Neptune; Polites, Helenus, and Deiphobus, sons of Priam. He also obtained a superiority over Hector himself; and the prince, enraged to see himself conquered by an unknown stranger, pursued him with such violent resentment that Paris must have fallen a victim to his brother's vengeance had he not fled to the altar of Jupiter. This sacred retreat preserved his life, and Cassandra, the daughter of Priam, struck with the similarity of the features of Paris to those of her brothers, enquired his birth and his age. Being made acquainted with these circumstances, she soon discovered that he was her brother, and as such, she introduced him to her father and to his children. Priam acknowledged Paris as his son, forgetful of the alarming dreams which had influenced him to meditate his death, and all jealousy ceased among the brothers. Paris, however, did not long suffer himself to remain inactive; he equipped a fleet, as if willing to redeem Hesione, his father's sister, whom Hercules had carried away, and obliged to marry Telamon the son of Æacus. This was the pretended motive of his voyage, but the causes were far different. Paris recollected that he was to be the husband of the fairest of women, and, if he had been led to form these expectations while he was an obscure shepherd of Ida, he now expected to see them realized, since he was acknowledged son of the king of Troy. Helen was the fairest woman of the age, and Venus had promised her to him. On these grounds, therefore, he visited Sparta, the residence of Helen, who had married Menelaus. He was received at the court of Sparta with every mark of respect, but he abused the hospitality of Menelaus, and, while the husband was absent in Crete, Paris persuaded Helen to elope with him, and to flee to Asia. Helen consented, and Priam received her into his palace without difficulty, as his sister was then detained in a foreign country, and as he wished to show himself as hostile as possible to the Greeks. This affair was soon productive of serious consequences. When Menelaus had married Helen, all her suitors had bound themselves by a solemn oath to protect her person, and to defend her against all violence, (*vid.* Helena,) and, therefore, the injured husband reminded them of their engagements, and called upon them to recover Helen. Upon this, all Greece took up arms in the cause of Menelaus; Agamemnon was chosen general of the combined forces, and a regular war was begun. *Vid.* Troja. Paris, meanwhile, who, had refused Helen to the petitions and embassies of the Greeks, armed himself with his brothers and subjects, to oppose the invaders; but the success of the war was neither hindered nor accelerated by his means. He fought with little courage, and, at the very sight of Menelaus, whom he had so recently injured, all his resolution vanished, and he retired, with the greatest timidity, from the front of the army, where he had walked before like a conqueror. In a combat with Menelaus, which he undertook at the persuasion of his brother Hector, Paris must have perished had not Venus interfered and conveyed him away from the resentment of his adversary. He nevertheless wounded in another battle, Machaon, Eurypylus, and Diomedes, and, according to some opinions, he killed with one of his arrows the great Achilles. *Vid.* Achilles. The death of Paris is differently related; some suppose that he was mortally wounded by one of the arrows of Philoctetes, which had been in the possession of Hercules, and that when he found himself languid on account of his wounds, he ordered himself to be carried to the residence of Œnone, whom he had basely abandoned, and who, in the years of his obscurity, had foretold him that he would solicit her assistance in his dying moments. He expired before he came into the presence of Œnone, and the nymph, still mindful of their former love, threw herself upon his body, and stabbed herself to the heart, after she had plentifully bathed it with her tears. According to some authors, Paris did not immediately go to Troy after he had left the Peloponnesus, but he was driven by a storm upon the coasts of

Ægypt, where Proteus, the king of the country detained him, and when he heard of the violence which had been offered to the king of Sparta, kept Helen at his court, but permitted Paris to return to his country. *Vid.* Helena. *Dictys. Cret.* 1, 3 & 4.—*Apollod.* 3. c. 12.—*Homer. Il.*—*Ovid. Heroid.* 5, 16 & 17. *De A.A.* 2. v. 5, 6 & 360.—*Quint. Calab.* 10. v. 290.—*Horat.* od. 3.—*Eurip. in Iphig.* 1036.—*Hygin.* fab. 92. & 273.—*Virg. Æn.* 1, &c.—*Ælian. V.H.* 12. c. 42.—*Paus.* 10. c. 27.—*Cic. de Div.*—*Lycoph.* 138.—*Coluthus. de Rap. Hel.*—*Ital.* 7. v. 465.—*Servius ad Æn.* 1. v. 31. & 48. l. 2. v. 13. l. 3. v. 402. l. 5. v. 370. l. 7. v. 320. —*Lactant. ad Ach.* 1. v. 21.—*Conon. Narr.* 23.—*Ptol. Hæph. apud Photium.* 4 & 5.—*Tzetz. in Lyc.* 57. [The finest statue of Paris is now in the Vatican, having been removed from the Altempo Palace, at Rome.]——A name satirically applied to Mummius, because he seduced the wives of Pompey and Lucullus. *Cic. N.D.* 3. c. 38. *Att.* 1. ep. 18. *Orat.* 49.——A celebrated player at Rome, who, for a while, enjoyed the favor of the emperor Nero; he was afterwards put to death by Domitian. *Tacit. Ann.* 13. c. 19, &c.—*Suet. Ner.* 54.—*Dio.* 63. c. 18.

PARIS'ADES, a king of Pontus, in the age of Alexander the Great. *Polyæn.* 7. c. 37.——A king of Bosporus.

PARIS'II, a people and city of Celtic Gaul, on the Sequana, now called Paris, the capital of the kingdom of France. *Cæs. Bell. G.* 6. c. 3. *Vid.* Lutetia.

PAR'ISUS, a river of Pannonia, falling into the Danube. *Strab.*

PA'RIUM, now Pario or Parisio, a town of Asia Minor, on the Propontis, where Archilochus was born, as some say. *Strab.* 10.—*Plin.* 7. c. 2. l. 36. c. 5.

PA'RIUS, a son of Iasion, founded Parium. *Steph.*

PAR'MA, a town of Italy, near Cremona, celebrated for its wool, and now for its cheese. The poet Cassius, and the critic Macrobius were born there. It was made a Roman colony, A.U.C. 569. The inhabitants are called Parmenenses and Parmeni. *Liv.* 39. c. 55.—*Strab.* 5.—*Horat.* 1. ep. 4. v. 3. —*Cic. Phil.* 14. c. 3.—*Varro, L. L.* 7. c. 31.—*Martial.* 2. epigr. 43. v. 4. l. 5. epigr. 13. v. 8 & 14. v. 155.

PARMEN'IDES, a Greek philosopher of Elis, who flourished about 430 years B.C. He was son of Pyres of Elis, and pupil of Xenophanes, or of Anaximander, according to some. He maintained, that there were only two elements, fire and the earth; and he taught that the first generation of men was produced from the sun. He first discovered that the earth was round, and habitable only in the two temperate zones, and asserted that it was suspended in the centre of the universe, in a fluid lighter than air, so that all bodies left to themselves fell to its surface. There were, as he supposed, only two sorts of philosophy; one founded on reason, and the other on opinion. He digested this unpopular system into verses, of which a few fragments remain, and may be found in Henry Stephens, *de Poesi Philosoph.* *Fabr. B. Gr.* 2. c. 26.—*Sax. Onom.* 1. p. 43.—*Diog.* 9.—*Plut. in Erot.*—*Cic. de Nat. D.* 1. c. 11. *In Quæst. Ac.* 4. c. 5 & 23.—*Gyrald. de P. H.* 3.

PARME'NIO or PARME'NION, a celebrated general in the armies of Alexander, who enjoyed the king's confidence, and was more attached to his person as a man than as a monarch. When Darius, king of Persia, offered Alexander all the country which lies at the west of the Euphrates, with his daughter Statira in marriage, and 16,000 talents of gold, Parmenio took occasion to observe, that he would, without hesitation, accept of these conditions if he were Alexander, "So would I, were I Parmenio," replied the conqueror. This friendship, so true and inviolable, was meanly sacrificed to a moment of resentment and suspicion; and Alexander, who had too eagerly listened to a light, and, perhaps, a false accusation, ordered Parmenio and his son to be put to death, as if guilty of treason against his person, B.C. 330. Parmenio was in the 70th year of his age. He died in possession of the greatest popularity, and it has been judiciously observed, that Parmenio obtained many victories without Alexander, but Alexander not one without Parmenio. *Curt.* 3. c. 6. l. 7. c. 1.—*Plut. in Alex.*

PARMENIS'CUS, a grammarian and astrologer, who wrote on autumn and the vintage. He wrote also a commentary on Aratus, and a history of the stars, praised by *Hyginus, P. A.* c. 2 & 13.—*Plin.* 18. c. 31.—*Varro L. L.* l. 9.—*Voss. Hist. Gr.* p. 397. *De Scient. Mathem.* c. 33. sec. 21.

PARNAS'SUS, a mountain of Phocis, anciently called Larnassus, from the *boat* of Deucalion (λάρναξ), which was carried thither in the universal deluge. It received the name of Parnassus from Parnassus the son of Neptune, by Cleobula, and was sacred to the Muses, and to Apollo and Bacchus. The soil was barren, but the valleys and the green woods that covered its sides rendered it agreeable, and fit for solitude and meditation. Parnassus is one of the highest mountains of Europe, and is easily seen from the citadel of Corinth, though at the distance of about 80 miles. According to the computation of the ancients, it is one day's journey round. At the north of Parnassus, there is a large plain about eight miles in circumference. The mountain, according to the poets, had only two tops, called Hyampea and Tithorea, on one of which the city of Delphi was situated, and thence it was called Biceps. *Strab.* 8, 9.—*Ovid. Met.* 1. v. 317. l. 2. v. 221. l. 5. v. 278.—*Lucan.* 5. v. 71. l. 3. v. 173.—*Liv.* 42. c. 16.—*Sil. It.* 15. v. 311.—*Mela,* 2. c. 3.—*Paus.* 10. c. 6.—*Propert.* 2. el. 23. v. 13. l. 3. el. 11. v. 54.—*Persius,* c.—*Catull. de Nupt. Pel.* 386.—*Stat. Th.* 1. v. 628.

PARNAS'SUS, a son of Neptune, who gave his name to a mountain of Phocis.

PAR'NES (*-etis*), a mountain of Attica, abounding in vines. *Stat.* 12. *Theb.* v. 620.

PARNES'SUS, a mountain of Asia, near Bactriana. *Dionys. Per.* 737.

PAR'NI, a tribe of the Scythians, who, under Arsaces, invaded Parthia, and conquered it. *Strab.* 11.

PARNO'PIUS, a surname of Apollo in Bœotia, given him because he drove away the locusts (πάρνοπες). *Paus.* 1. 1.

PARODA'NA, a city of Persia. *Ptol.*

PARŒCOP'OLIS, a city of Macedonia. *Id.*

PARŒTE'A, a region near the Red Sea. *Steph.*

PA'RON and HERACLI'DES, two youths who killed a man who had insulted their father. *Plut. Apopth.*

PAROPAMIS'ADÆ or PAROPAMIS'II, a people of Asia, whose territories were bounded by Bactriana on the west, India on the east, Arachosia on the south, and Caucasus on the north. Their soil was barren, and the inhabitants barbarous. *Curt.* 7. c. 3, 4, 5.—*Strab.* 11.—*Plin.* 6. c. 20, 23, &c.

PAROPAM'ISUS or PAROPAMI'SUS, a ridge of mountains at the north of India, forming part of mount Taurus. It is called Parapanisus by *Ptolemy*, Parnasus by *Aristotle*, and Parnessus by *Dionysius*. The river Bactrus rises here, and also the Indus, according to *Pliny*, 5. c. 27., and *Arrian*, 5 *de Exped. Alex.*—*Strab.* 15.

PARO'PUS, now Colisano, a town at the north of Sicily, on the shores of the Tyrrhene Sea. *Polyb.* 1. c. 24.—*Plin.* 3. c. 8.

PARORÆ'A, a city of Arcadia. *Steph.*——A city of Macedonia. *Id.*

PARORE'IA, a town of Thrace, near mount Hæmus. *Liv.* 39. c. 27.——A town of Peloponnesus. ——A district of Phrygia Magna. *Strab.* 12.

PAROS'PUS, a river of India. *Plin.* 6. c. 23.

PAROS'TA, a city of Taurica Chersonesus. *Ptol.*

PAR'PHORUS, a native of Colophon, who, at the head of a colony, built a town at the foot of Ida, which was abandoned for a situation nearer his native city. *Strab.* 14.—*Paus.* 7. c. 3.

PARRHA'SIA, a town of Arcadia, founded by Parrhasius, the son of Jupiter. The Arcadians are sometimes called Parrhasians, and Arcus Parrhasis, and Carmenta, Evander's mother, Parrhasiadea. *Lucan.* 2. v. 237.—*Virg. Æn.* 8. v. 334.—*Ovid. Met.* 8. v. 315. *Fast.* 1. v. 618. l. 2. v. 276. l. 4. v. 577. *Trist.* 1. el. 3. v. 47. l. 2. v. 190.—*Paus.* 8. c. 27.—*Servius ad Virg. loc. cit.*

PARRHASI'NI, a people of Asia, near Sogdiana. *Plin.* 6. c. 16.

PARRHA'SIUS, a famous painter, son of Evenor

of Ephesus, in the age of Zeuxis, about 415 years B.C. He was a great master of his profession, and particularly excelled in strongly expressing the violent passions. He was blessed with a great genius and much invention, and was peculiarly happy in his designs. He acquired great reputation by his pieces, but by none more than that in which he allegorically represented the people of Athens, with all the injustice, the clemency, the fickleness, the timidity, the arrogance, and the inconsistency which so eminently characterized that celebrated nation. He once entered the lists against Zeuxis, and when they had produced their respective pieces, the birds came to pick with the greatest avidity the grapes which Zeuxis had painted. Parrhasius immediately exhibited his piece, and Zeuxis said, "Remove your curtain, that we may see the painting." The curtain was the painting, and Zeuxis acknowledged himself conquered by exclaiming, "Zeuxis has deceived birds, but Parrhasius has deceived Zeuxis himself." Parrhasius grew so vain of his art, that he clothed himself in purple, and wore a crown of gold, calling himself the king of painters. He was lavish in his own praises, and by his vanity too often exposed himself to the ridicule of his enemies. However great and admired as an artist, the licentiousness of his pencil deserves the severest reprehension. The powers of genius should be directed to the improvement and the morality of mankind; but the painter is little entitled to the applauses of posterity, who, like Parrhasius, devotes his talents, by the representation of libidinous scenes and wanton attitudes, to corrupt, not to purify the heart, to inflame, not to correct the passions. *Plut. in Thes. de Poet. Aud.*—*Paus.* 1. c. 28 & 43. l. 6. c. 25.—*Plin.* 35. c. 10.—*Athen.* 12.—*Cic. Tusc.* 1. c. 2.—*Propert.* 3. el. 7. v. 12.—*Suet. Tib.* 44.—*Horat.* 4. od. 8. v. 6.——A son of Jupiter, or, according to some, of Mars, by a nymph called Philonomia.

PAR'RHAX, a Parthian, who treacherously delivered Meherdates to Gotarzes. *Tacit. Ann.* 12. c. 14.

PAR'SIA and PARSIA'NA, cities of Paropanisus. *Ptol.*

PAR'TA, a city of Persia. *Id.*

PARTHAMAS'PATES, a king placed over Parthia by Trajan, after the defeat of Osroes. *Xiphilin.* l. 68.

PARTHAMASI'RIS or PARTHAMOSIR'IUS, a king of Armenia. *Æl. Spartian. in Hadrian.* c. 5.

PARTHA'NUM, a city of Vindelicia. *Antonin.*

PARTHA'ON, a son of Agenor and Epicaste, who married Euryte, daughter of Hippodamus, by whom he had many children, among whom were Œneus, and Sterope. Parthaon was brother to Demonice, the mother of Evenus by Mars, and also to Molus, Pylus, and Thestius. He is called Portheus by *Homer, Il.* 14.—*Apollod.* 1. c. 7.—*Hygin.* fab. 129 & 239.—*Sch. Apollon.* 1. *Arg.*—*Ovid. Met.* 8. v. 54.—*Stat. Theb.* 1. v. 670.——A son of Peripetus and father of Aristas. *Paus.* 8. c. 24.

PARTHE'NIA, a surname of Minerva from her perpetual celibacy.——An ancient name of Samus. *Steph.*—*Schol. in Nicandr.*—*Plin.* 5. c. 31.

PARTHE'NIÆ or PARTHE'NII, a certain number of desperate citizens of Sparta. During the Messenian war the Spartans were absent from their city for the space of ten years, and it was unlawful for them to return, as they had bound themselves by a solemn oath not to revisit Sparta before they had totally subdued Messenia. This long absence alarmed the Lacedæmonian women, as well as the magistrates. The Spartans were reminded by their wives that if they continued in their resolution, the state must at last decay for want of citizens; and when they had duly considered this embasy, they empowered all the young men in the army who had come to the war while yet under age, and who therefore were not bound by the oath, to return to Sparta, and by a familiar and promiscuous intercourse with all the unmarried women of the state, to raise a future generation. It was carried into execution, and the children that sprang from this union were called Partheniæ, or *sons of virgins* (παρθένος). The war with Messenia was some time after ended, and the Spartans returned victorious; but the cold indifference with which they looked upon the Partheniæ was attended with serious consequences. The Partheniæ knew they had no legitimate fathers, and no inheritance, and that therefore their life depended upon their own exertions. This drove them almost to despair. They joined with the Helots, whose situation was as unpleasant as their own, and it was mutually agreed to murder all the citizens of Sparta, and to seize their possessions. This massacre was to be done at a general assembly, and the signal was to be the throwing of a cap into the air. The whole, however, was discovered through the diffidence and apprehensions of the Helots, and when the people had assembled, the Partheniæ discovered that all was known, by the voice of a crier, who proclaimed that no man should throw up his cap. The Partheniæ, though apprehensive of punishment, were not visibly treated with greater severity; their calamitous condition was attentively examined, and the Spartans, afraid of another conspiracy, and awed by their numbers, permitted them to sail for Italy, with Phalantus their ringleader at their head. They settled in Magna Græcia, and built Tarentum, about 707 years B.C. *Justin.* 3. c. 5.—*Strab.* 6.—*Paus. in Lacon. &c.*—*Plut. in Apoph.*

PARTHE'NIAS, a river of Peloponnesus, flowing by Elis. *Paus.* 6. c. 21.

PARTHE'NION, a mountain of Peloponnesus at the north of Tegea. *Paus.*

PARTHE'NIUS, a river which, after separating Bithynia from Paphlagonia, falls into the Euxine Sea, near Sesamum. It received its name either because the *virgin* Diana (παρθένος) bathed there, or from the purity and mildness of its waters. *Herodot.* 2. c. 104.—*Plin.* 6. c. 2.——A mountain of Arcadia, which was said to abound in tortoises. Here Telephus had a temple. Atalanta was exposed on its top, and brought up there. *Paus.* 8. c. 54.—*Ælian. V. H.* 13.—*Apollod.* 2. c. 7.—*Seneca. in Her. Œt.* 1885.——A river of European Sarmatia. *Ovid. ex Pont.* 4. el. 10. v. 49.

PARTHE'NIUS, a favorite of the emperor Domitian. He conspired against his imperial master, and assisted to murder him. *Dio. Cass.* l. 67. *in Domitian.*——A friend of Æneas killed in Italy. *Virg. Æn.* 10. v. 748.——A friend of *Martial.* 8. epigr. 28. l. 9. epigr. 50.——A poet of Nicæa, in Liguria, in the age of Augustus. He wrote a book in prose, *de Amatoriis Affectionibus*, which he dedicated to Cornelius Gallus. It was first edited by Cornarius, Basil, 1531, and afterwards by Galeus, Paris, 1675. *Fabr. B. Gr.* 3. c. 27.—*Sax. Onom.* 1. p. 182.

PAR'THENON, a temple of Athens, sacred to Minerva. It was destroyed by the Persians, and afterwards rebuilt by Pericles in a more magnificent manner. All the circumstances which related to the birth of Minerva were beautifully and minutely represented in bas-relief, on the front of the entrance. The statue of the goddess, 26 cubits high, and made of gold and ivory, passed for one of the master pieces of Phidias. The name of Hecatompedon has been applied to the temple, because its nave measured 100 feet in length. This beautiful monument of antiquity has been greatly mutilated by the rapacity of modern travellers, and many of the splendid specimens of sculpture which it contained, have been transferred to this country. *Plut. in Per.*—*Paus.* 1. c. 24.—*Plin.* 34. c. 8.

PARTHENOPÆ'US, a son of Meleager and Atalanta, or, according to some, of Milanion and another Atalanta, celebrated among the ancients for the beauty of his person and the elegance of his manners. He was one of the seven chiefs who accompanied Adrastus, the king of Argos, in his expedition against Thebes. He was killed by Amphidicus. *Apollod.* 3. c. 9.—*Paus.* 3. c. 12. l. 9. c. 19.—*Hygin.* fab. 70 & 99.—*Lactant. ad Theb.* 4. v. 309.—*Æschyl. Sept. contra. Theb.*—*Martial.* 9. epigr. 57. v. 8.——A son of Talaus. *Apollod.*

PARTHEN'OPE, one of the Sirens, who threw herself into the sea, when she saw that Ulysses had escaped from her snares.——A daughter of Stymphalus. *Apollod.*

PARTHEN'OPE, a city of Campania, afterwards called Neapolis, *or the new city*, when it had been beautified and enlarged by a colony from Eubœa and Pithecusa. It is now called Naples. It received the name of Parthenope from one of the Sirens, whose body was found on the sea-shore there. *Virg. G.* 4. v. 564.—*Strab.* 1 & 5.—*Paterc.* 1. c. 4.—*Homer. Odyss.* 12. v. 167.—*Ital.* 12. v. 33.—*Servius. ad Virg. loco.*—*Hygin.* 141.—*Plin.* 3. c. 5.—*Ovid.* 14. *Met.* 101.

PARTHIA, a celebrated country of Asia, bounded on the west by Media, on the south by Carmania, on the north by Hyrcania, and on the east by Aria, containing, according to Ptolemy, 25 large cities, the most capital of which was called Hecatompylos, from its *hundred gates.* Some suppose that the present capital of the country is built on the ruins of Hecatompylos. According to some authors, the Parthians were Scythians by origin, who made an invasion into the more southern provinces of Asia, and at last fixed their residence near Hyrcania. They long remained unknown and unnoticed, and became successively tributary to the empires of the Assyrians, Medes, and Persians. When Alexander invaded Asia, the Parthians submitted, like the other dependent provinces of Persia, and were for some time under the power of Eumenes, Antigonus, Seleucus Nicanor, and Antiochus, till the rapacity and oppression of Agathocles, a lieutenant of the latter, roused their spirit, and fomented rebellion. Arsaces, a man of obscure origin, but endowed with great military powers, placed himself at the head of his countrymen, and laid the foundation of the Parthian empire, about 250 years B.C. The Macedonians attempted in vain to recover it; a race of active and vigilant princes, who assumed the surname of *Arsacides*, from the founder of their kingdom, increased its power, and rendered it so formidable, that, while it possessed 18 kingdoms betweeen the Caspian and Arabian Seas, it even disputed the empire of the world with the Romans, and could never be subdued by that nation, which had seen no people on earth unconquered by their arms. It remained a kingdom till the reign of Artabanus, who was killed about A.D. 229, and from that time it became a province of the newly re-established kingdom of Persia, under Artaxerxes. The Parthians were naturally strong and warlike, and were esteemed the most expert horsemen and archers in the world. Their peculiar custom of discharging their arrows while they were retiring at full speed, has been greatly celebrated by the ancients, particularly by the poets, who all observe that their flight was more formidable than their attacks. This manner of fighting, and the wonderful address and dexterity with which it was performed, gained them many victories. They were much addicted to drinking, and to every manner of lewdness, and their laws permitted them to raise children even by their mothers and sisters. *Strab.* 2, 6, &c.—*Curt.* 6. c. 11.—*Flor.* 3. c. 5.—*Virg. G.* 3. v. 31, &c. *Æn.* 7. v. 606.—*Ovid. Art. Am.* 1, &c. *Fast.* 5. v. 580.—*Dio. Cass.* 40.—*Ptol.* 6. c. 5.—*Mela,* 1. c. 2. l. 3. c. 4.—*Propert.* 2, el. 8. v. 18. l. 11. v. 23. l. 3. el. 10. v. 3. l. 4. el. 5. v. 26. el. 6. v. 79.—*Plin.* 6. c. 25. —*Polyb.* 5, &c.—*Marcellin.*—*Herodian.* 3, &c.—*Lucan.* 1. v. 230. l. 6. v. 50. l. 10. v. 53.—*Justin.* 41. c. 1.—*Horat.* 1. od. 19. v. 11. l. 2. od. 13. v. 17.

PARTHI'NI, a people of Illyricum. *Liv.* 29. c. 12. l. 33. c. 34. l. 44. c. 30.—*Suet. Aug.* 19.—*Cic. in Pis.* 40.

PARTHUS, a city of Illyricum. *Steph.*

PARTHYE'NE, a province of Parthia, according to *Ptolemy,* though some authors maintain that it was the name of Parthia itself.

PARTIS'CUM, a city of the Jazyges Metanastæ. *Ptol.*

PARTUN'DA, a deity among the Romans, who presided over child-birth, and was therefore invoked by women in labour. *Gyrald. H. D.* 1.—*Rosin.* 2. c. 19.

PA'RUS or PA'ROS, a celebrated island among the Cyclades, about seven miles and a half distant from Naxus, and 28 from Delus. According to Pliny, it is half as large as Naxus, that is, about 36 or 37 miles in circumference, a measure which some of the moderns have extended to 50 and even 80 miles. It has borne the different names of Pactya, Minoa, Hyria, Demetrias, Zacynthus, Caharnis, and Hyleessa. It received the name of Parus, which it still bears, from Parus, a son of Jason, or as some maintain, of Parrhasius. The island of Parus was rich and powerful, and well known for its famous marble, which was always used by the best statuaries. The best quarries were those of Marpesus, a mountain in which caverns, of the most extraordinary depth, are still seen by modern travellers, and admired as the sources whence the labyrinth of Ægypt and the porticoes of Greece received their splendour. According to Pliny, the quarries were so uncommonly deep, that in the clearest weather the workmen were obliged to use lamps, from which circumstance the Greeks have called the marble *Lychnites,* worked by the light of lamps. Parus is also famous for the fine cattle which it produces, and for its partridges and wild pigeons. The capital city was called Parus. It was first peopled by the Phœnicians, and afterwards a colony of Cretans settled in it. The Athenians made war against it, because it had assisted the Persians in the invasion of Greece, and took it, and it became a Roman province in the age of Pompey. Archilochus was born there. The Parian marbles, better known, perhaps, by the appellation of Arundelian, were engraved in this island in capital letters, B.C. 264, and as a valuable chronicle, preserved the most celebrated epochas of Greece from the year 1582 B.C. These valuable pieces of antiquity were procured originally by M. de Peirisc, a Frenchman, and afterwards purchased by the earl of Arundel, by whom they were given to the university of Oxford, where they are still to be seen. Though in some places defaced and mutilated, yet the incriptions have been rendered intelligible by the learned labors of Selden, Lydiat, and Prideaux, the last of whom published his account in 1676. *Mela.* 2. c. 7.—*Strab.* 5.—*C. Nep. in Milt.* 7. *& Alc.*—*Virg. Æn.* 1. v. 593. *G.* 3. v. 34.—*Ovid. Met.* 3. v. 419. l. 7. v. 466.—*Plin.* 3. c. 14. l. 36. c. 17. *Diod.* 5. *& Thucyd.* 1.—*Herodot.* 5, &c.—*Horat.* 1. od. 19. v. 6. l. 1. ep. 19. v. 23.

PARY'ADRIS, a mountain of Armenia Major. *Ptol.*

PARYS'ADES, a king of Pontus, B.C. 310. He was the son of Leucon, and reigned 30 years. *Diod. Sic.* 16.——A king of the Cimmerian Bosporus, who flourished 284 B.C.

PARYS'ATIS or PARYSA'TIS, a Persian princess, wife of Darius Ochus, by whom she had Artaxerxes Mnemon, and Cyrus the younger. She was so extremely partial to her younger son, that she committed the greatest cruelties to encourage his ambition, and she supported him with all her interest in his rebellion against his brother Mnemon. The death of Cyrus at the battle of Cunaxa was revenged with the grossest barbarity, and Parysatis sacrificed to her resentment all such as she found concerned in his fall. She also poisoned Statira, the wife of her son Artaxerxes, and ordered one of the eunuchs of the court to be flayed alive, and his skin to be stretched on two poles before her eyes, because he had, by order of the king, cut off the hand and the head of Cyrus. These cruelties offended Artaxerxes, and he ordered his mother to be confined in Babylon, but they were soon after reconciled, and Parysatis regained all her power and influence, which she maintained till the time of her death. *Plut. in Art.*—*Ctes.*

PASAR'GADA or PASAR'GADÆ, a town of Persia, near Carmania, founded by Cyrus on the very spot where he had conquered Astyages. The kings of Persia were always crowned there in the temple of Minerva, and as part of the ceremony, they put on the garments which had been worn by Cyrus, and which were there religiously preserved, and they afterwards chewed the leaves of the turpentine tree, ate a dry fig, and drank a mixture of vinegar and milk. The Pasargadæ were the noblest families of Persia, in the number of which were the Achæmenides. *Strab.* 15.—*Plin.* 8. c. 26.—*Herodot.* 1 c. 125.—*Plut. in Artax.*—*Mela,* 3. c. 8.

PASAR'NA, a city of Armenia Minor. *Ptol.*

PA'SEAS, a man of Sicyon, in Peloponnesus, father of Abantidas, who seized the sovereign power of his country. When Abantidas was killed by Aratus, Paseas seated himself in his son's place, and was soon after assassinated by Nicocles, his successor. *Paus.* 2. c. 8.—*Plut. in Arat.*

PASIC'ANA, a city of India Citerior. *Ptol.*

PAS'ICLES, a grammarian of Tarentum. *Suet. de illustr. Gramm.*

PASIC'RATES, a king of part of the island of Cyprus. *Plut.*

PASIPE'DA, a city of India within the Ganges. *Ptol.*

PASIPH'AE, a daughter of the Sun and of Perseis, who married Minos, king of Crete. She disgraced herself by her unnatural passion for a bull, which, according to some authors, she was enabled to gratify by means of the artist Dædalus. This celebrated bull had been given to Minos by Neptune, to be offered on his altars. But as the monarch refused to sacrifice the animal on account of his beauty, the god revenged his disobedience by inspiring Pasiphae with an unnatural love for it. This fabulous tradition which is universally believed by the poets, who observed that the Minotaur was the fruit of this infamous commerce, is refuted by some writers, who suppose that the infidelity of Pasiphae to her husband was betrayed in her affection for an officer called Taurus; and that Dædalus, by permitting his house to be the asylum of the two lovers, was looked upon as accessary to Pasiphae's crime. From this amour with Taurus, as it is further remarked, the queen became the mother of twins, and the name of *Minotaurus* arose from the resemblance of the children to the husband and the lover of Pasiphae. Minos had four sons by Pasiphae, Castreus, Deucalion, Glaucus, and Androgeus, and three daughters, Hecate, Ariadne, and Phædra. *Vid.* Minotaurus. *Plato de Min.—Plut. in Thes.—Apollod.* 2. c. 1.—*Virg. Æn.* 6. v. 24.—*Hygin.* fab. 40.—*Diod.* 4.—*Propert.* 2. el. 21 & 34. l. 3. el. 19. l. 4. el. 7.—*Ital.* 8. v. 472.—*Auson. Id.* 6. v. 30.—*Palæph. de Pasiph.* 2.—*Servius in Æn.* 5. v. 588. l. 6. v. 46, 64, & 447.—*Ovid. Heroid.* 4. v. 57 & 165.—*Cic. N.D.* 3. c. 18.

PASI'RA, the metropolis of Gedrosia. *Ptol.* The country around was called Pasirena. *Salmas ad Solin.* p. 1176.

PAS'IRIS, a city of European Sarmatia. *Ptol.*

PASIT'ELES, a famous Grecian sculptor, presented with the freedom of Rome. *Plin.* 35. c. 12.

PASITH'EA, one of the Graces, also called Aglaia, or Euphrosyne, and made by *Homer* the wife of Somnus. *Il.* 14. v. 267.—*Stat. Theb.* 2. v. 286.—*Catull.* 61.—*Paus.* 9. c. 35.——One of the Nereides. *Hesiod. Th.* 246.——A daughter of Atlas. ——A nymph who married Erisichthon, king of Athens. *Apollod.* 3.——One of the names applied to Cybele or Terra, as mother of all the gods.

PASIT'IGRIS, a name given to the river Tigris. *Strab.* 15.—*Plin.* 6. c. 20.

PAS'SA, a city of Thrace. *Steph.*

PAS'SALON, a city of Ægypt. *Ptol.* According to *Villanovanus*, it is the Pesta of *Antoninus.*

PASSAN'DA, a small region or place near the city of Adramyttium. *Steph.*

PAS'SARON, a town of Epirus at the east of Dodona, where, after sacrificing to Jupiter, the kings swore to govern according to law, and the people to obey and to defend the country. *Plut. in Pyrr.—Liv.* 45. c. 26 & 33.

PASSIE'NUS, a Roman who reduced Numidia. *Tacit. Ann.*

PASSIE'NUS PAU'LUS, a Roman knight, nephew to the poet Propertius, whose elegiac compositions he imitated. He likewise attempted lyric poetry, and with success, and chose for his model the writings of Horace. *Plin.* ep. 6 & 9.

PASSIE'NUS CRIS'PUS, a man distinguished as an orator, but more as the husband of Domitia, and afterwards of Agrippina, Nero's mother. *Tac. Ann.* 6. c. 20.—*Quintil.* 6. c. 2.

PAS'TERIS, a city of Ægypt. *Steph.*

PASTO'NA, a city on the Euphrates. *Plin.* 5. c. 24.

PAS'TOS, a town on the Ægæan Sea, not far from Neapolis in Thrace. *Plin.* 4. c. 11.

PA'SUS, a Thessalian in Alexander's army. *Curt.* 10. c. 8.

PAT'AGA, a city of Arabia. *Plin.* 6. c. 29.

PAT'AGE, one of the Cyclades, called also Platage and Amorgus. *Plin.* 4. c. 12.

PAT'ALA, a harbour at the mouth of the Indus, in an island called Patale. The river here begins to form a Delta like the Nile. Pliny places this island within the torrid zone. *Plin.* 2. c. 73.—*Curt.* 9. c. 7.—*Strab.* 15.—*Arrian.* 6. c. 17.——A city of Italy. *Steph.*

PATELLA'NA or PATEL'LA, a goddess invoked by the Romans to protect their corn, because she presided over the ears of corn when they first made their appearance. *Varro. apud. Aug.Civ. D.* 4. c.8.

PAT'ALUS, an island near Caria. *Steph.*

PAT'ARA (*-orum*), now Patera, a town of Lycia, situate on the eastern side of the mouth of the river Xanthus, with a capacious harbour, a temple, and an oracle of Apollo, surnamed *Patareus*, in which was preserved and shown in the age of Pausanias a brazen cup, which had been made by the hands of Vulcan, and presented by the god Telephus. The god was supposed by some to reside for the six winter months at Patara, and the rest of the year at Delphi. The city was greatly embellished by Ptolemy Philadelphus, who attempted in vain to change its original name into that of his wife Arsinoe. *Liv.* 37. c. 15.—*Strab.* 14.—*Paus.* 9. c. 41.—*Horat.* 3. od. 14. v. 64.—*Ovid. Met.* 1. v. 516.—*Servius. ad Æn.* 4. v. 143. l. 6. v. 37.—*Lactant. ad Theb.* 1. v. 696.—*Mela*, 1. c. 15.

PATA'VIUM, a city of Italy, at the north of the Po, on the shores of the Adriatic, now called Padua, and said to have been once capable of sending 20,000 men into the field. *Vid.* Padua. It was the birth-place of Livy, from which reason some writers have denominated *Patavinity* those peculiar expressions and provincial dialect, which they seem to discover in the historian's style, and which are not strictly agreeable to the purity and refined language of the Roman authors who flourished in or near the Augustan age. *Martial.* 11. epigr. 17. v. 8.—*Quintil.* 1. c. 5. 56. l. 8. c. 13.—*Liv.* 10. c. 2. l. 41. c. 27.—*Strab.* 5.—*Mela*, 2. c. 4.—*Servius ad Virg. Æn.* 1. v. 246, 251. l. 4. v. 377.

PATER'CULUS, a Roman whose daughter, Sulpitia, was pronounced the chastest matron at Rome. *Plin.* 7. c. 35.

PATER'CULUS VELLE'IUS, an historian. *Vid.* Velleius.

PATE'RIA, an island not far from Lemnus. *Plin.* 4. c. 12.

PATERNIA'NA, a city of Hispania Tarraconensis. *Ptol.*

PATIS'CUS, a Cilician intimate with Cicero when pro-consul. He was commander of the fleet after Cæsar's death. *Cic. Fam.* 2. ep. 8, 9, 11. l. 12. ep. 15.

PATIS'TAMA, a city of India within the Ganges. *Ptol.*

PATIZI'THES, one of the Persian Magi, who raised his brother to the throne because he resembled Smerdis, the brother of Cambyses. *Herodot.* 3. c. 61.

PAT'MUS or PATMOS, one of the Cyclades, with a small town of the same name, situate at the south of Icaria, and measuring thirty miles in circumference, according to Pliny, or only eighteen according to modern travellers. It has a large harbour, near which are some broken columns, the most ancient in that part of Greece. The Romans generally banished their culprits there, and it was to this island that St. John was banished by Domitian, and where he composed the Apocalypse. It is now called Palmosa. *Strab.—Plin.* 4. c. 12.

PA'TRÆ, an ancient town at the north-west of Peloponesus, anciently called Aroe. Diana had there a temple, and a famous statue of gold and ivory, which was considered in the age of Pausanias as a masterpiece. *Strab.* 10.—*Plin.* 4. c. 4.—*Ital.* 15. v. 310.—*Paus.* 7. c. 6.—*Ovid. Met.* 6. v. 417.—*Liv.* 27. c. 29.—*Mela*, 2. c. 3.

PAT'RASIS, a city of Pontus. *Steph.*

PATRIAG'ADÆ, a place in Persia. *Id.*

PATRIAM'PHES, a Persian charioteer of Xerxes. *Herodot.* 1. 7.

PA'TRIUS, a surname of Apollo, from the temple erected to his honor at Patræ, where he had a celebrated statue raised by Æsculapius, or, according to others, by Icadius. *Servius ad Æn.* 3. v. 332.——A name applied also to Mars. *Stat. Theb.* 4. v. 111.

PA'TRO, a daughter of Thestius, mother of Archemachus by Hercules. *Apollod.*——An Epicurean philosopher intimate with Cicero. *Cic. Fam.* 13. c. 1.

PATRO'BIUS, a freedman of Nero, who caused sand to be fetched from the Nile, for the purpose of wrestling upon it. He was put to death by Galba. *Plin.* 35. c. 13.—*Tac. Hist.* 1. c. 49.

PAT'ROCLES or **PATRO'CLES**, an officer in the fleet of Seleucus and Antiochus. He discovered several countries, and it is said wrote a history of the world. *Strab.*—*Plin.* 6. c. 17.—*Voss. Hist. Gr.* 3. p. 39.

PATRO'CLI IN'SULA, a small island on the coast of Attica. *Paus.* 4. c. 5.

PATRO'CLUS, one of the Grecian chiefs during the Trojan war, son of Menœtius, by Sthenele, whom some call Philomela, or Polymela. The accidental murder of Cleonymus, or, according to others, of Æas, the son of Amphidamas, in the time of his youth, obliged him to fly from Opus, where his father reigned. He retired to the court of Peleus king of Phthia, where he was kindly received, and where he contracted the most intimate friendship with Achilles the monarch's son. When the Greeks went to the Trojan war, Patroclus also accompanied them at the express command of his father, who visited the court of Peleus, and he embarked with ten ships from Phthia. He was the constant companion of Achilles, lodged in the same tent, and when his friend refused to appear in the field of battle, because he had been offended by Agamemnon, Patroclus imitated his example, and by his absence was the cause of the overthrow of the Greeks; but at last Nestor prevailed upon him to return to the war, and Achilles permitted him to appear in armour. The valor of Patroclus, together with the terror which the sight of the arms of Achilles inspired, soon routed the before victorious Trojans, and obliged them to flee within their walls for safety. He would have broken down the walls of the city, but Apollo, who interested himself for the Trojans, placed himself to oppose him, and Hector, at the instigation of the god, dismounted from his chariot to attack him, as he attempted to strip one of the Trojans whom he had slain. The engagement was obstinate, but at last Patroclus was overpowered by the valor of Hector, and the interposition of Apollo. His arms became the property of the conqueror, and Hector would have severed his head from his body had not Ajax and Menelaus interfered. His body was at last recovered and carried to the Grecian camp, where Achilles received it with the bitterest lamentations. His funeral was observed with the greatest solemnity. Achilles sacrificed twelve young Trojans, near the burning pile, besides four of his horses and two of his dogs, and the whole was concluded by the exhibition of funeral games, in which the conquerors were liberally rewarded by Achilles. The death of Patroclus, as it is described by Homer, gave rise to new events; Achilles forgot his resentment to Agamemnon, and entered the field to avenge the fall of his friend, and his anger was only appeased by the slaughter of Hector, who had more powerfully kindled his wrath by appearing at the head of the Trojan armies in the armour which had been taken from the body of Patroclus. The patronymic of Actorides is often applied to Patroclus, because Actor was father of Menœtius. *Dictys. Cret.* 1, &c.—*Homer. Il.* 9. v. 201. l. 11, 15, 16, 17, 18, & 23.—*Philostr. Her.* 19.—*Eustath. ad Il.* 1. v. 337.—*Schol. Pind. Olymp.* 9. v. 104.—*Apollod.* 3. c. 13.—*Hygin.* fab. 97 & 275.—*Ovid. Met.* 13. v. 273. *A.A.* 1. v. 743. *Ex Pont.* 2. ep. 4. v. 42. *Fast.* 2. v. 39. *Trist.* 1. el. 8. v. 29.—*Flacc.* 1. v. 407. [There is a group of Menelaus protecting the dead body of Patroclus, in the possession of the Grand Duke of Tuscany at Florence; of which mention has already been made under the article Menelaus.——A son of Hercules by Pyrippe. *Apollod.* ——An officer of Ptolemy Philadelphus.——A rich but avaricious person who would not allow himself the use of the bath through parsimony. From this circumstance arose the proverb of *Patroclo sordidior*. *Aristoph. in Plut.*—*Erasm. in Adag.* ——A person raised from the lowest rank to the consulship, in the time of Nero. *Mart.* 1. 12. epigr. 78. v. 9.

PA'TRON, an Arcadian present at the games exhibited by Æneas in Sicily. *Virg. Æn.* 5. v. 298.

PATRO'US, a surname of Jupiter among the Greeks, represented by his statue, especially in Minerva's temple at Argos, as having three eyes, which some suppose to signify that he reigned in three different places, in heaven, on earth, and in hell. *Paus.* 2. c. 24.—*Homer. Il.* 9. v. 457.

PATUL'CIUS, a surname of Janus, which he received *a pateo*, because the doors of his temple were always *open* in the time of war. Some suppose that he received it because he presided over gates, or because the year began by the celebration of his festivals. *Ovid. Fast.* 1. v. 129.—*Servius, Æn.* 7. v. 610.—*Rosin. R. A.* 2. c. 3.——A man who owed money to Cicero. *Cicc. Att.* 14. ep. 18.

PATU'MUS, a city of Arabia. *Steph.*

PAT'YCUS, an inland city of the Œnotri. *Steph.*

PAU'LA, the first wife of the emperor Heliogabalus. She was daughter of the præfect of the Prætorian guards. The emperor divorced her, and Paula retired to solitude and obscurity with composure.

PAULI'NA, a Roman lady who married Saturninus, a governor of Syria, in the reign of the emperor Tiberius. Her conjugal peace was disturbed, and violence was offered to her virtue by a young man called Mundus, who was enamoured of her, and who had caused her to come to the temple of Isis by means of the priests of the goddess, who declared that Anubis wished to communicate to her something of moment. Saturninus complained to the emperor of the violence which had been offered to his wife, and the temple of Isis was overturned and Mundus banished. *Joseph. A.* 18. c. 4.——The wife of the philosopher Seneca, who attempted to kill herself when Nero had ordered her husband to die. The emperor, however, prevented her, and she lived some few years after in the greatest melancholy. *Tacit. Ann.* 15. c. 60, 63, 64. ——A sister of the emperor Adrian, married to Julius Servianus. *Æl. Spart. Hadrian.* c. 1. ——The wife of the emperor Maximinus.

PAULI'NUS POMPE'IUS, an officer in Nero's reign, who had the command of the German armies, and finished the works on the banks of the Rhine, which Drusus had begun 63 years before. *Tacit. Ann.* 13. c. 53.

PAULI'NUS SUETO'NIUS, a Roman general, the first who crossed mount Atlas with an army. He wrote a history of this expedition in Africa, which is lost. Paulinus also distinguished himself in Britain, &c. He followed the arms of Otho against Vitellius. *Plin.* 5. c. 1.—*Salmas ad Solin.* p. 295.

PAULI'NUS VALE'RIUS, a friend of Vespasian.

PAULI'NUS JU'LIUS, a Batavian nobleman, put to death by Fonteius Capito, on pretence of rebellion. *Tacit. H.* 4. c. 13.

PAULI'NUS MERO'PIUS PON'TIUS ANIC'IUS, a Latin Christian poet, who flourished in the age of the emperor Gratian, and is by some supposed to have been allied to Ausonius. He was made bishop of Nola, where he invented bells. He wrote several pieces in hexameter verse, with singular felicity of expression, and with great marks of genius. Fifty-one of his epistles are extant, besides poems. They were edited by Le Brun, Paris, 1685; reprinted at Verona, 1736; and by Muratorius, with the addition of four newly discovered poems, Mediolan, 1697. His style is elegant, but his verses, though correct, are destitute of poetic genius. *Harles. Not. Lit. Rom.* 1. p. 741.

PAU'LUS ÆMYL'IUS, a Roman, son of the Æmylius who fell at Cannæ, was celebrated for his victories, and received the surname of *Macedonicus*, from his conquest of Macedonia. In the early part of life he distinguished himself by his uncommon application, and by his fondness for military discipline. His first appearance in the field was attended with great success, and the barbarians who had revolted in Spain were reduced with unusual rapidity under the power of the Romans. In his first consulship his arms were directed against the Ligurians, whom he totally subdued. His application for a second consulship proved abortive; but when Perseus the king of Macedonia had declared war against Rome, the abilities of Paulus were remembered, and he was honored with the office of consul about the 60th year of his age. After this appointment he behaved with well-known activity, and a general engagement was soon fought near Pydna. The Romans obtained the victory, and Perseus, unsuccessful in the field, found himself deserted by his subjects. In two days the conqueror made himself master of all Macedonia, and soon after the fugitive monarch was brought into his presence. Paulus did not exult over his fallen enemy, but when he had gently rebuked him for his temerity in attacking the Romans, he addressed himself in a pathetic speech to the officers of his army who surrounded him, and feelingly enlarged on the instability of fortune, and the vicissitude of all human affairs. When he had finally settled the government of Macedonia with ten commissioners from Rome, and after he had sacked 70 cities of Epirus, and divided the booty among his soldiers, Paulus returned to Italy. He was received at Rome with acclamations, and though some of the seditious soldiers attempted to prevent his triumphal entry into the Capitol, yet three days were appointed to exhibit the magnificent fruits of his victories. Perseus with his wretched family adorned the triumph of the conqueror, and as they were dragged through the streets before the chariot of Paulus, they drew tears of compassion even from the assembled people. The riches which the Romans derived from this conquest were immense, and the people were freed from all taxes till the consulship of Hirtius and Pansa; but while every one of the citizens received some benefit from the victories of Paulus, the conqueror himself was poor, and appropriated to his own use nothing of the Macedonian treasure except the library of Perseus. In his office of censor, to which he was afterwards elected, Paulus behaved with the greatest moderation, and at his death, which happened about 168 years B.C.. not only the Romans, but tributary nations and the very enemies of the republic confessed, by their lamentations, the loss which they had sustained. He had married Papiria, by whom he had two sons, one of which was adopted by the family of Maximus, and the other by that of Scipio Africanus. He had also two daughters, one of whom married a son of Cato, and the other Ælius Tubero. He afterwards divorced Papiria, and when his friends wished to reprobate his conduct in thus disgracing the wife of his youth, by observing that she was young and handsome, and that she had made him the father of a fine family, Paulus replied, that the shoe which he then wore was new and well made, but that he was obliged to leave it off, though no one but himself, as he said, knew where it pinched him. He married a second wife, by whom he had two sons, whose sudden death exhibited to the Romans, in the most engaging view, their father's philosophy and stoicism. The elder of these sons died five days before Paulus triumphed over Perseus, and the other three days after the public procession. This domestic calamity did not shake the firmness of the conqueror; yet, before he retired to a private station, he harangued the people, and in mentioning the severity of fortune towards his family, expressed his wish that every evil might be averted from the republic by the domestic prosperity of an individual. *Plut. in Vitâ.—Liv.* 43, 44, &c.—*Cic. Ver.* 1. c. 21. *Off.* 2. c. 22. *Mur.* 14.—*Justin.* 33. c. 1, &c.

PAU'LUS MAX'IMUS. *Vid.* Maximus Fabius.

PAU'LUS ÆGINE'TA. *Vid.* Ægineta.

PAU'LUS L. ÆMY'LIUS, a consul, who, when opposed to Annibal in Italy, checked the rashness of his colleague Varro, and recommended an imitation of the conduct of the great Fabius, by harassing and not facing the enemy in the field. His advice was rejected, and the battle of Cannæ, so glorious to Annibal, and so fatal to Rome, soon followed. Paulus was wounded, but when he might have escaped from the slaughter, by accepting a horse generously offered him by one of his officers, he disdained to flee, and perished by the darts of the enemy. *Horat.* od. 12. v. 38.—*Liv.* 22. c. 39.—*Cic. Div.* 2. c. 33. *Or.* 2. c. 87.

PAU'LUS JU'LIUS, a Latin poet in the age of Adrian and Antoninus. He wrote some poetical pieces recommended by *A. Gellius.*

PAU'LUS CY'RUS FLO'RUS, an historian, in the age of Justinian, whose actions he recorded in verse. *Suidas.—Voss. de Poet. Gr.* c. 9, &c. *Hist. Gr.* 4. c. 20. *Hist. Lat.* 2. c. 19.

PAU'LUS. *Vid.* Æmylius.

PAUPER'TAS, a divinity among the ancients called daughter of Luxury, and represented as pale and emaciated. The inhabitants of Gadara in Palestine worshipped her as the mother of Industry and of talents. *Plaut. in Stich.* 1. sc. 3. v. 24, *Horat.* 2. ep. 2. v. 51.—*Petron.* 84.—*Arrian. apud Gyrald. H. D.* 1.

PAUSA'NIAS, a Spartan general, son of Cleombrotus, who greatly signalized himself at the battle of Platæa, against the Persians. The Greeks, sensible of his services, rewarded his meritorious exertions, with a tenth of the spoils taken from the enemy. He was afterwards placed at the head of the Spartan armies, and extended his conquests in Asia; but the haughtiness of his behaviour created him many enemies, and the Athenians, in consequence, soon obtained a superiority in the affairs of Greece. Pausanias gradually became dissatisfied with the jealousy which his countrymen displayed toward their public magistrates, and offered to betray Greece to the Persians, if he received in marriage, as the reward of his perfidy, the daughter of their monarch. His intrigues were discovered by means of a youth, who was intrusted with his letters to Persia, and who refused to go, on the recollection that such as had been employed in that office before had never returned. The letters were delivered to the Ephori of Sparta, and the perfidy of Pausanias laid open. He fled for safety to a temple of Minerva, and, as the sanctity of the place screened him from the violence of his pursuers, the sacred building was surrounded with heaps of stones, the first of which was said to have been carried there by the indignant mother of the unhappy man. He was starved to death in the temple, and died about 471 years B.C. There was a festival, with solemn games, instituted in his honor, in which only free-born Spartans contended. There was also an oration spoken in his praise, in which his actions were celebrated, particularly the battle of Platæa, and the defeat of Mardonius. *C. Nep. in Vitâ.—Plut. in Arist. & Them.—Herodot.* 9.—*Pausan. Lacon.* ——A favorite of Philip king of Macedonia. He accompanied the prince in an expedition against the Illyrians, in which he was killed.——A youth at the court of king Philip, very intimate with the preceding. He was grossly and unnaturally abused by Attalus, one of the friends of Philip, and, when he complained of the injuries which he had received, the king, in some measure, disregarded his remonstrances, and wished them to be forgotten. This seeming denial of justice incensed Pausanias; he resolved to revenge himself, and, when he had heard from his master, Hermocrates the sophist, that the most effectual way to render himself illustrious, was to murder a person who had signalized himself by uncommon actions, he stabbed Philip, as he entered a public theatre. After this bloody action, he attempted to make his escape to his chariot, which waited for him at the gates of the city, but he was stopped accidentally by the twig of a vine, and fell down. Attalus, Perdiccas, and other friends of Philip, who pursued him, immediately fell upon him, and put him to death. Some say that Pausanias committed this murder at the instigation of Olympias, the wife of Philip, and of her son Alexander. *Diod.* 16.—*Justin.* 9. c. 6.—*Plut. in Apoph.*——A king of Macedonia, in the 96th Olympiad, deposed by Amyntas, after a year's reign. *Diod.*——A person who attempted to seize upon the kingdom of Macedonia, which he was prevented from doing by Iphicrates the Athenian.——A friend of Alexander the Great, made governor of Sardis.——A physician, in the age of Alexander, *Plut.*——A learned orator and historian, born at Cæsarea in Cappadocia, and instructed by the celebrated Herodes Atticus. He settled at Rome A.D. 170. where he died at a very advanced age. He wrote a history of Greec, in ten books, in the Ionic dialect, in which he gives, with great precision and geographical accuracy, an account of the situation of its different cities, their antiquities, and the several curiosities which they contained. He has also interwoven mythology in his historical account, and introduced many of the fabulous traditions and superstitious stories which were prevalent in his age. In each book the author treats of a separate country, such as Attica, Arcadia, Messenia, Elis, &c. Some suppose that he gave a similar description of Phœnicia and Syria. Among the editions of Pausanias, are that of Khunius, fol. Lips. 1696; and that of Facius, Lips. 1794, &c. which is the most critical and the best. *Fabr. B. Gr.* 4. c. 17. *Sax. Onom.* 1. p. 321.——A Lacedæmonian, who wrote a partial account of his country.——A statuary of Apollonia, whose abilities were displayed in adorning Apollo's temple at Delphi. *Paus.* 10. c. 9.——A king of Sparta, of the family of the Eurysthenidæ, who died 397 B.C. after a reign of 14 years.

PAU'SIAS, a painter of Sicyon, pupil of Pamphilus and Erigmus. He distinguished himself by the delicate manner in which he adorned the palaces and public buildings of Greece, by emblematical paintings and historical representations, especially on their ceilings, and he is mentioned as the first who understood how to apply colors to wood or ivory, by means of fire. He made a beautiful painting of his mistress Glycera, whom he represented as sitting on the ground, and making garlands with flowers, and, from this circumstance, the picture, which was bought afterwards by Lucullus for two talents, received the name of *Stephanoplocon.* Some time after the death of Pausias, the Sicyonians were obligod to part with the pictures which adorned their public edifices, to deliver themselves from an enormous debt, and M. Scaurus, the Roman, bought them all, in which were those of Pausias, to decorate the theatre, which had been built during his ædileship. Pausias lived about 350 years B.C. *Plin.* 35. c. 11.—*Horat.* 2. sat. 7. v. 95.

PAUSILY'PUS, a mountain near Naples, which received its name from the beauty of its situation, (τῆς παύσεως τῆς λύπης,) *a mœroris cessatione*). The natives shew there the tomb of Virgil, and regard it with the highest veneration. There were near it some fish ponds belonging to the emperor. The mountain is now famous for a subterraneous passage nearly half a mile in length, and 22 feet in breadth, which affords a safe and convenient passage to travellers. *Stat.* 4. *Sylv.* 4. v. 52.—*Plin.* 9. c. 53.—*Strab.* 5.—*Senec.* ep. 5 & 57.

PAUSIM'ACHUS, a Samian, who wrote a history of the earth, according to *Festus Avienus.*

PAUSI'NUS, a river of Liburnia. *Plin.* 3. c. 21. It is now Buzanich, according to *Ortelius.*

PAU'SON, a painter, ridiculed for his poverty by *Aristophanes in Pluto.*

PAU'SUS, (ἀπὸ τοῦ παύειν), a deity averse to war. *Arnob.* 1. 1.—*Turneb. Advers.* 15. c. 21.

PAUTA'LIA, an inland town of Thrace, according to *Ptolemy.*

PAVEN'TIA, a goddess at Rome, who was invoked to protect her votaries from the effects of terror. *Aug. de Civ. D.* 4. c. 11.

PA'VOR, an emotion of the mind, which received divine honors among the Romans, and was considered as possessed of a most tremendous power, as the ancients swore by her name in the most solemn manner. Tullus Hostilius, the third king of Rome, was the first who built her temples, and raised altars to her honor, as also to Pallor, the goddess of Paleness. Her divinity was also honored with a sacrifice by Theseus before he fought the Amazons, and by Alexander the Great before the battle of Arbela, and she was intreated to remove all fear and perturbation from her votaries. She was also worshipped at Corinth, where a statue was erected to her in consequence of the murder of Pheres and Mermerus, sons of Medea. *Liv.* 1. c. 27.—*Lactant. de Fals. R.* 1. c. 20.—*Aug. de Civ. D.* 4. c. 2, 15, 23. 1. 6. c. 10.—*Paus.* 2. c. 3.—*Hesiod. Th.* 934.—*Plut. in Thes.*—*Cic. de Nat. D.* 3. c. 17.—*Gyrald. H. D.* 1.

PAX, an allegorical divinity among the ancients. The Athenians raised her a statue, which represented her as holding the infant Plutus, god of wealth, in her lap, to intimate that peace gives rise to prosperity and to opulence, and they were the first who erected an altar to her honor after the victories obtained by Timotheus over the Lacedæmonian power, though Plutarch asserts it had been done after the conquests of Cimon over the Persians. She was represented among the Romans with the horn of plenty, and also carrying an olive branch in her hand. The emperor Vespasian built her a celebrated temple at Rome, which was consumed by fire in the reign of Commodus. It was customary for men of learning to assemble in that temple, and even to deposit their writings there, as in a place of the greatest security. Therefore, when it was burnt, not only books, but also many valuable things, jewels, and immense treasures were lost in the conflagration. *C. Nep. in. Timoth.* 2.—*Plut. in Cim.*—*Paus.* 9. c. 16.—*Gyrald. H. D.* 1.—*Mercurial. V. Lect.* 1. c. 13.

PAX AUGUS'TA, a city of Lusitania, now Badajoz. It is called by *Pliny,* 3. c. 4., Pax and Colonia Pacensis.

PAX'US, a small island, or rather rock, without inhabitants, between Ithaca and the Echinades in the Ionian Sea. *Plut.*

PE'AS, a shepherd, who, according to some, set on fire the pile on which Hercules was burnt. The hero gave him his bow and arrows. Philoctetes, however, according to the more general opinion, was the person employed in this melancholy office. *Apollod.* 2.

PEDA'CIA, a woman of whom *Horace*, 1. sat. 8. v. 39., speaks as a contemptible character.

PEDÆ'US, an illegitimate son of Antenor. *Homer. Il.* 7.

PEDA'LIUM or **PEDA'SIUM**, a promontory of Cyprus. *Ptol. Mercator* calls it Cabo de Griego.

PEDA'NI. *Vid.* Pedum.

PEDA'NIUS COS'TA, a Roman, who, not being nominated to the consulship by Vitellius, proved ungrateful to him. *Tac. Hist.* 2. c. 71.

PEDA'NIUS SECUN'DUS, a præfect of Rome, killed by one of his slaves, for having denied him his liberty. This violence was avenged by the laws, in the slaughter of the 400 slaves who were in the family, for not protecting the person of their master. *Tacit.* 14. *Ann.* c. 42.

PED'ASA (*-orum*), a town of Caria, near Halicarnassus. *Liv.* 33. c. 30.

PED'ASUS, a son of Bucolion, the son of Laomedon. His mother was one of the Naiades. He was killed in the Trojan war by Euryalus. *Homer. Il.* 6. v. 21.——One of the four horses of Achilles. As it was not immortal like the three others, it was killed by Sarpedon. *Id.* 16. v. 152 & 468.

PED'ASUS, a town near Pylus in the Peloponnesus. *Id. Il.* 9.——An inland town of Caria, given by Cyrus to Pytharchius. *Athen.*

PEDI'ADIS, a part of Bactriana, through which the Oxus flows. *Polyb.*

PEDIA'NUS ASCO'NIUS. *Vid.* Asconius.

PEDIAR'CHUS, a leader of Gelo's archers. *Polyæn.* 1. c. 27. n. 2.

PE'DIAS, the wife of Cranaus. *Apollod.*——A tribe of Attica. *Steph.*

PEDIC'ULI, a people of Italy, bordering upon Apulia and the Salentini. *Plin.* 3. c. 5.

PED'ILI, a people inhabiting the Alps. *Plin.*

PE'DIUS BLÆ'SUS, a Roman, accused by the people of Cyrene of plundering the temple of Æsculapius. He was condemned under Nero, and banished from the senate, but restored to his privileges by Otho. *Tacit. Ann.* 14. c. 18. *Hist.* 1. c. 77.

PE'DIUS QUIN'TUS, a nephew of Julius Cæsar, who commanded one of his legions in Gaul, and was afterwards one of his heirs. He was consul with Augustus after Pansa's death, and was author of the *Lex Pedia* against Cæsar's murderers. *Suet. Cæs.* 83. *Ner.* 3.—*Dio.* 46. c. 46.—*Cic. Planc.* 7. *Att.* 9. ep. 14.

PE'DIUS POPLIC'OLA, son of Quintus, was a lawyer in the age of Horace.

PE'DIUS QUIN'TUS, the grandson of Quintus, distinguished himself at Rome as a painter. He was born dumb, but his superior abilities compensated for all the defects of nature. *Plin.* 35. c. 4.

PED'NA, a small island of the Ægean Sea, near Lesbus. *Plin.* 5. c. 31.

PE'DO, a lawyer patronized by Domitian. His ambition of appearing rich ruined his affairs. *Juv.* 7. v. 129.

PE'DO ALBINOVA'NUS. *Vid.* Albinovanus.

PEDUCÆ'A LEX, a law enacted concerning incest. *Cic. N. D.* 1. 3.

PEDUCÆ'US C., the lieutenant of Pansa, killed at the battle of Mutina. *Cic.* 10. *Fam.* 33.

PEDUCÆ'US SEXT., a prætor in Sicily, distinguished for his great integrity. *Cic. Fin.* 2. c. 18. *Verr.* 2. c. 56.

PE'DUM, a town of Latium, about 10 miles from Rome, conquered by Camillus. The inhabitants were called Pedani. *Liv.* 2. c. 39. l. 8. c. 13 & 14. —*Horat.* 1. ep. 4. v. 2.

PE'GÆ, a fountain at the foot of mount Arganthus in Bithynia into which Hylas fell. *Propert.* 1. el. 20. v. 33.——A town of the Megarensians, 20 miles from Megara. *Pliny*, 4. c. 3, calls it Pagæ. *Steph.* It is now Livadosta.

PEG'ASA, a city of Caria. *Steph.*

PEGASE'UM STAG'NUM, a lake near Ephesus, which arose from the earth when Pegasus struck it with his foot. *Plin.* 5. c. 29.

PEGAS'IDES, a name given to the Muses from the horse Pegasus, or from the fountain which Pegasus had raised from the ground, by striking it with his foot. *Ovid. Heroid.* 15. v. 27.—*Avienus. Orat.* 495.

PEG'ASIS, a name given to Œnone by *Ovid. Her.* 5., because she was daughter of the *river* (πηγή), Cebrenus.

PEG'ASUS, a winged horse sprung from the blood of Medusa, when Perseus had cut off her head. He received his name from his being born, according to Hesiod, near the *source* (πηγή) of the ocean. As soon as born he left the earth, and flew up into heaven, or, rather, according to Ovid, he fixed his residence on mount Helicon, where, by striking the ground with his foot, he instantly raised a fountain, which has been called Hippocrene. He became the favorite of the Muses, and being afterwards tamed by Neptune, or Minerva, he was given to Bellerophon, to conquer the Chimæra. No sooner was this fiery monster destroyed, than Pegasus threw down his rider, because he was a mortal, or, rather, according to the more received opinion, because he attempted to fly to heaven. This act of temerity in Bellerophon was punished by Jupiter, who set an insect to torment Pegasus, which occasioned the melancholy fall of his rider. Pegasus continued his flight up to heaven, and was placed among the constellations by Jupiter. Perseus, according to Ovid, was mounted on the horse Pegasus, when he destroyed the sea monster which was going to devour Andromeda. *Hesiod. Theog.* 282.—*Horat.* 4. od. 11. v. 26.—*Homer. Il.* 6. v. 179.—*Apollod.* 2. c. 3 & 4.—*Lycophr.* v. 17.—*Paus.* 12. c. 3 & 4. —*Ovid. Met.* 4. v. 785. *Ex. Pont.* 4. ep. 7. v. 52. *Trist.* 3. el. 7. v. 15. *Ibin.* 257.—*Tzetzes. ad Lyc.* 17 & 843.—*Servius ad Virg. G.* 1. v. 12. *Æn.* 2. v. 616. l. 5. v. 118. l. 10. v. 163.—*Sch. Pind. Isth.* 7. v. 66.—*Eustath. ad Dionys. Per.* 867.—*Fulgent. Myth.* 3. c. 1.—*Hygin.* fab. 57.

PEG'ASUS, a Trojan who was slain by Camilla. *Virg. Æn.* 11. v. 670.——A lawyer, governor of Rome under the emperors. *Juv.* 4. v. 77.

PEGUN'TIUM, or PEGUN'TIÆ, according to *Pliny* an inland city of Illyricum. *Ptol.*

PE'JUM, a fortified place of Galatia. *Strabo.*

PELA'GO, a eunuch, one of Nero's favorites, employed with a centurion and sixty soldiers, to murder Rubellius Plautus. *Tac. Ann.* 14. c. 59.

PEL'AGON, a man killed by a wild boar. *Ovid. Met.* 8. v. 360.——A son of Asopus and Metope. *Apollod.*——A Phocian, one of whose men conducted Cadmus, and showed him where, according to the oracle, he was to build a city. *Id.*

PELAGO'NIA, one of the divisions of Macedonia at the north. *Liv.* 26. c. 25. l. 31. c. 28.—*Plin.* 4. c. 10. According to *Stephanus*, it was a region of Sicily.

PELAR'GE, a daughter of Potneus, who re-established the worship of Ceres in Bœotia, which had been interrupted by the war of the Epigoni. By the command of the oracle of Dodona she received divine honors after death, and her altars received for sacrifices only female victims, and those in a pregnant state. *Paus.* 9. c 25.

PELAS'GI, a people of Greece, supposed to be one of the most ancient in the world. They first inhabited Argolis in Peloponnesus, which from them received the name of Pelasgia, and about 1883 years B.C. they passed into Æmonia, and were afterwards dispersed in several parts of Greece. Some of them fixed their habitation in Epirus, others in Crete, others in Italy, and others in Lesbus. From these different changes of situation in the Pelasgians, all the Greeks are indiscriminately called Pelasgians, and their country Pelasgia, though, more properly speaking, it should be confined to Thessaly, Epirus, and Peloponnesus, in Greece. Some of the Pelasgians, that had been driven from Attica, settled in Lemnus, whither, some time after, they carried some Athenian women, whom they had seized in an expedition on the coast of Attica. They raised some children by these captive females, but afterwards destroyed them with their mothers, through jealousy, because they differed in manners as well as language from them. This horrid murder was attended by a dreadful pestilence, and they were ordered, to expiate their crime, to do whatever the Athenians commanded them. This was to deliver their possessions into their hands. The Pelasgians seem to have received their name from Pelasgus, the first king and founder of their nation. *Paus.* 8. c. 1.—*Strab.* 5.—*Herodot.* 1.—*Plut. in Rom.*—*Seneca in Med. & Agam.*—*Plin.* 4. c. 6.—*Virg. Æn.* 1. v. 624. l. 2. v. 83, 106 & 152. l. 8. v. 600. l. 9. v. 154.—*Flacc.* 2. v. 658. l. 3. v. 45, 126, &c. l. 4 & 5.—*Ovid. Met.* 7. v. 49. l. 12. v. 7, 19 & 612. l. 13. v. 13, 268, &c. l. 14. v. 562. l. 15. v. 452.—*Seneca in Med.* 240 & 528. *In Aga.* 632.

PELAS'GIA or PELASGIO'TIS, a country of Greece, the inhabitants of which were called Pelasgi or Pelasgiotæ. Every country of Greece, and all Greece in general, is indiscriminately called Pelasgia, though the name should be more particularly confined to a part of Thessaly, situate between the Peneus, the Aliacmon, and the Sperchius. The maritime borders of this part of Thessaly were afterwards called Magnesia, though the sea or its shore still retained the name of Pelasgicus Sinus, now the Gulph of Volo. Pelasgia was also one of the ancient names of Epirus, as also of Peloponnesus. *Vid.* Pelasgi.

PELAS'GUS, a son of Terra, or, according to others, of Jupiter and Niobe, who reigned in Sicyon. He gave his name to the ancient inhabitants of Peloponnesus, and by establishing laws, and teaching them to clothe themselves, and how to make the fruits of the cultivated earth subservient to their wants, he gained the respect and the veneration of his country. He was the father of Lycaon, and also of fifty other children, whose names are mentioned by Apollodorus. *Hesiod. & Acusilas apud Apollod.* 3.—*Servius ad Æn.* 2. v. 83.—*Paus.* 8. c. 1.—*Flacc.* 5. v. 683.——A son of Triopas, who raised a temple to Ceres at Argos. *Paus.* 2. c. 22.——A son of Jupiter and Larissa. *Servius ad Æn.* 1. v. 628.

PE'LE, the name of two cities in Thessaly, one of which was subject to Eurypylus, the other to Achilles *Steph.*

PELE'CES, a city of Libya. *Id.*

PELENA'RIA, a city on the Sinus Traglodyticus. *Plin.* 6. c. 29.

PELEN'DONES, a people of Hispania Tarraconensis. *Id.* 3. c. 3.

PELETHRO'NII, an epithet given to the Lapithæ, because they inhabited the town of Pelethronium, at the foot of mount Pelion in Thessaly; or because one of their number bore the name of Pelethronius. It is to them that mankind are indebted for the invention of the bit with which they tamed their horses with so much dexterity. *Virg. G.* 3. v. 115.—*Ovid. Met.* 12. v. 452.—*Lucan.* 6. v. 387.

PE'LEUS, a king of Thessaly, son of Æacus and Endeis, the daughter of Chiron. He married Thetis, one of the Nereids, and was the only one among mortals who married an immortal. He was accessary to the death of his brother Phocus, and on that account was obliged to leave his father's dominions. He retired to the court of Eurytus, the son of Actor, who reigned at Phthia, or according to the less received opinion of Ovid, he fled to Ceyx, king of Trachinia. He was purified of his murder by Eurytus, with the usual ceremonies, and the monarch gave him his daughter Antigone in marriage. Some time after this Peleus and Eurytus went to the chase of the Calydonian boar, where the father-in-law was accidentally killed by an arrow which his son-in-law had aimed at the beast. This unfortunate event obliged him to banish himself from the court of Phthia, and he retired to Iolcus, where he was purified of the murder of Eurytus by Acastus the king of the country. His residence at Iolcus was short; Astydamia, the wife of Acastus, became enamoured of him, and when she found him insensible to her passionate declaration, she accused him of attempts upon her virtue. The monarch partially believed the accusation of his wife, but not to violate the laws of hospitality, by putting him instantly to death, he ordered his officers to conduct him to mount Pelion, on pretence of hunting, and there to tie him to a tree, that he might become the prey of the wild beasts of the place. The orders of Acastus were faithfully obeyed, but Jupiter, who knew the innocence of his grandson Peleus, ordered Vulcan to set him at liberty. As soon as he had been delivered from danger, Peleus assembled his friends to punish the ill treatment which he had received from Acastus. He forcibly took Iolcus, drove the king from his possessions, and put to death the wicked Astydamia. After the death of Antigone, Pelius courted Thetis, of whose superior charms Jupiter himself had been enamoured. His pretensions, however, were rejected, and as he was a mortal, the goddess fled from him with the greatest abhorrence; and the more effectually to evade his inquiries, she generally assumed the shape of a bird, or of a tree, or of a tigress. Peleus became more animated from her refusal, he offered a sacrifice to the gods, and Proteus informed him that to obtain Thetis he must surprise her while she was asleep in her grotto, near the shores of Thessaly. This advice was immediately followed, and Thetis, unable to escape from the grasp of Peleus, at last consented to marry him. Their nuptials were celebrated with the greatest solemnity, and all the gods attended, and made them each the most valuable presents. The goddess of discord was the only one of the deities who was not present, and she punished this seeming neglect by throwing an apple into the midst of the assembly of the gods with the inscription of *detur pulchriori*. *Vid.* Discordia. From the marriage of Peleus and Thetis was born Achilles, whose education was early entrusted to the Centaur Chiron, and afterwards to Phœnix, the son of Amyntor. Achilles went to the Trojan war, at the head of his father's troops, and Peleus gloried in having a son who was superior to all the Greeks in valor and intrepidity. The death of Achilles was the source of grief to Peleus; and Thetis, to comfort her husband, promised him immortality, and ordered him to retire into the grottos of the island of Leuce, where he would see and converse with the manes of his son. Peleus had a daughter called Polydora, by Antigone. *Homer. Il.* 9. v. 432.—*Eurip. in Androm.*—*Catull. de Nupt. Pel. & Thet.*—*Ovid. Heroid.* 5. *Fast.* 2. *Met.* 11. fab. 7 & 8.—*Apollod.* 3. c. 12.—*Paus.* 2. c. 29.—*Diod.* 4.—*Hygin.* fab. 54.—*Sch. Apollon.* 4. v. 613.—*Sch. Hom. Il.* 16.—*Schol. Pind. Nem.* 6. *& Pyth.* 4. v. 182.—*Tzetzes in Lycop.* 175.—*Sch. Aristoph. Nub.* 1059.—*Coluthus de Raptu. Hel.*—*Servius in Æn.* 1. v. 31.—*Euripid. in Andr.*—*Eustath. in Il.* 9.

PELIA, a river of Etruria. *Cato. in Origin.* It is now Paglia, according to *Leander*.

PELI'ADES, the daughters of Pelias. *Vid.* Pelias.

PELI'ALA, a city of Mesopotamia. *Ptol.*

PELIAS, the twin brother of Neleus, was the son of Neptune by Tyro, the daughter of Salmoneus. His birth was concealed from the world by his mother, who wished her father to be ignorant of her incontinence. He was exposed in the woods, but his life was preserved by shepherds, and he received the name of Pelias from a spot of the colour of *lead* in his face. Some time after this adventure, Tyro married Cretheus, son of Æolus, king of Iolcus, and became mother of three children, of whom Æson was the eldest. Meantime Pelias visited his mother, and was received into her family, and after the death of Cretheus, he unjustly seized the kingdom which belonged to the children of Tyro, by the deceased monarch. To strengthen himself in his usurpation, Pelias consulted the oracle, and when he was told to beware of one of the descendants of Æolus, who should come to his court with one foot shod, and the other bare, he privately removed the son of Æson, after he had publicly declared that he was dead. These precautions proved abortive. Jason the son of Æson, who had been educated by Chiron, returned to Iolcus, when arrived at years of maturity, and as he had lost one of his shoes in crossing the river Anaurus, or the Evenus, Pelias immediately perceived that this was the person against whom he had been warned. His unpopularity prevented him from acting with violence against a stranger, whose uncommon dress and commanding aspect, had raised admiration in his subjects. But his astonishment was excited when he saw Jason arrive at his palace, with his friends and relations, and boldly demand the kingdom which he had usurped. Pelias was conscious that his complaints were well founded, and, therefore, to divert his attention, told him that he would voluntarily resign the crown to him, if he went to Colchis to avenge the death of Phryxus, the son of Athamas, whom Æetes had cruelly murdered. He further observed that the expedition would be attended with the greatest glory, and that nothing but the infirmities of old age had prevented him from vindicating the honor of his country, and the injuries of his family by punishing the assassin. This expedition, so warmly recommended, was as warmly accepted by the young hero, and made known all over Greece. *Vid.* Jason. During the absence of Jason, in the Argonautic expedition, Pelias murdered Æson and all his family; but, according to the more received opinion of Ovid, Æson was still living when the Argonauts returned, and was restored to the vigor of youth by the magic of Medea. This sudden change in the vigor and constitution of Æson, astonished all the inhabitants of Iolcus, and the daughters of Pelias, who had received the patronymic of Peliades, expressed their desire to see their father's infirmities vanish, by the same powerful arts. Medea, who wished to avenge the injuries which her husband Jason had received from Pelias, raised the desire of the Peliades by cutting an old ram to pieces, and boiling the flesh in a cauldron, and afterwards turning it into a fine young lamb. After they had seen this successful experiment, the Peliades cut their father's body to pieces, after they had drawn all the blood from his veins, on the assurance that Medea would replenish them by her incantations. The limbs were immediately put into a cauldron of boiling water, but Medea suffered the flesh to be totally consumed, and refused to give the Peliades the promised assistance, and the bones of Pelias did not even receive a burial. The Peliades were four in number, Alceste, Pisidice, Pelopea, and Hippothoe, to whom Hyginus adds Medusa. Their mother's name was Anaxibia, the daughter of Bias, or Philomache, the daughter of Amphion. After this parricide, the Peliades fled to the court of Admetus, where Acastus, the son-in-law of Pelias, pursued them, and took their protector prisoner. The Peliades died and were buried in Arcadia. *Hygin.* fab. 12, 13 & 14.—*Ovid. Met.* 7. fab. 3 & 4. *Heroid.* 12. v. 129.—*Cic. Orat.* 3. c. 5.—*Paus.* 8. c. 11.—*Apollod.* 1. c. 9.—*Seneca in Med.*—*Apollon. Arg.* 1.—*Pindar. Pyth.* 4.—*Diod.* 4.—*Sch. Pind. ad Pyth.* 4.—*Tzetzes. in Lyc.* 175.—*Servius ad Virg. Ecl.* 4. v. 34.——A Trojan chief wounded by Ulysses during the Trojan war. He survived the ruin of his country, and followed the fortune of Æneas. *Virg. Æn.* 2. v. 435.

PE'LIAS AR'BOR, a name of the ship Argo, because it was built from the trees of mount Pelion.

PE'LIAS (*adis*), the spear of Achilles. *Vid.* Pelion.

PELI'DES, a patronymic of Achilles, and of Pyrrhus as being descended from Peleus. *Virg. Æn.* 2. v. 264.

PELIG'NI, a people of Italy who dwelt near the Sabines and Marsi, and had Corfinium and Sulmo for their chief towns. The most expert magicians were among the Peligni, according to Horace. *Liv.* 8. c. 6 & 29. l. 9. c. 41.—*Ovid. ex Pont.* 1. el. 8. v. 42. l. 4. ep. 14. v. 49. *Am.* 2. el. 16. v. 5 & 37. l. 3. el. 15. v. 3 & 8. *Fast.* 4. v. 685.—*Strab.* 5.—*Horat*, 3. od. 19. v. 8.

PELIG'NUS JU'LIUS, a friend of the emperor Claudius, made governor of Cappadocia. *Tacit. Ann.* 12. c. 49.

PELINÆ'US, a mountain of Chius. *Strab.* 4.—*Ælian. An.* 16. c. 39.

PELINÆ'UM or PELIN'NA, a town of Macedonia, taken from king Philip by M. Acilius. *Strab.* 14 —*Liv.* 36. c. 10 & 14.

PE'LION or PE'LIOS, a celebrated mountain of Thessaly, the top of which was covered with pine trees. It is situate in Magnesia, at the south of the Sinus Thermaicus. In their wars against the gods, the giants, as the poets assert, placed mount Ossa upon Pelion, to scale the heavens with greater facility. The celebrated huge spear of Achilles, which none but the hero could wield, had been cut down on this mountain, and was thence called Pelias. It was a present from his preceptor Chiron, who, like the other Centaurs, had fixed his residence here. *Ovid, Met.* 1. v. 155. l. 13. v. 199. —*Mela*, 2. c. 3.—*Strab.* 9.—*Virg. G.* 1. v. 281. l. 3. v. 94.—*Senec. in Herc. & Med.*—*Lucan.* 6. v. 335. l. 7. v. 481.—*Flacc.* 2. v. 6. l. 3. v. 353. l. 8. v. 417 & 451.—*Servius in Georg.* 3. v. 93.

PE'LIUM, a town of Macedonia, near the source of the river Aliacmon. *Liv.* 31. c. 40.

PEL'LA, a celebrated town of Macedonia, on the Ludias, not far from the Sinus Thermaicus, which became the capital of the country after the ruin of Edessa. Philip, king of Macedonia, was educated there, and Alexander the Great was born there, whence he is often called *Pellæus juvenis.* The tomb of the poet Euripides was in the neighbourhood. The epithet Pelleus is often applied to Ægypt or Alexandria, because the Ptolemies, kings of the country, were of Macedonian origin. *Martial.* 13. epigr. 85.—*Lucan.* 5. v. 60. l. 8. v. 475 & 607. l. 9. v. 1016 & 1073. l. 10. v. 55.—*Mela*, 2. c. 3.—*Strab.* 7.—*Liv.* 42. c. 41.—*Juv.* 10. v. 168. ——A town of Thessaly.——A town of Achaia. *Steph.*

PELLACON'TA, a river of Media, which flows near Bura. *Plin.* 6. c. 26.

PELLA'NA, a town of Laconia, with a fountain, the waters of which were said to have a subterraneous communication with the waters of another fountain. *Paus.* 3. c. 21.—*Strab.* 8.

PELLA'ON, a town on the Adriatic Sea. *Plin.* 3. c. 19.

PELLE'NE, a town of Achaia, in the Peloponnesus, at the west of Sicyon, famous for its wool. It was built by the giant Pallas, or, according to others, by Pellen of Argos, son of Phorbas, and was the country of Proteus, the sea god. *Strab.* 8.—*Paus.* 7. c. 26.—*Liv.* 33. c. 14.—*Tzetzes. ad Lyc.* 911.

PELLI'DI, a people of Sardinia. *Liv.*

PELLO'NIA, (*a pellere*), a goddess at Rome, whose power was exerted in repelling the attacks of enemies. *Arnob.* 4.—*Aug. de Civ. D.* 4. c. 21.—*Gyrald. H. D.* 1.

PEL'OPE, a small town of Lydia, near Phrygia. *Steph.*

PELOPE'A, a daughter of Thyestes, the brother of Atreus. She had a son by her father, who had offered her violence in a wood, without knowing that she was his own daughter. Some suppose that Thyestes purposely committed this incest, as the oracle had informed him that his wrongs would be avenged, and his brother destroyed by a son who should be born from him and his daughter. This proved too true. Pelopea afterwards married her uncle Atreus, who kindly received into his house his wife's illegitimate child, called Ægisthus, because preserved by goats, (αἶγες) when exposed on the mountains. Ægisthus became his uncle's murderer. *Vid.* Ægisthus. *Hygin.* fab. 87, &c.—*Ælian. V.H.* 12.—*Ovid. in Ib.* v. 359.—*Seneca in Agam.* v. 7 & 165.—*Lactant. in Theb.* 1. v. 684. l. 4. v. 306.—*Servius ad Æn.* 11. v. 262.—*Juv.* 7. v. 92.——A daughter of Pelias. *Apollod.* 1. c. 9.

PELOPE'A, a festival observed by the people of Elis in honor of Pelops. It was kept in imitation of Hercules, who sacrificed to Pelops in a trench, as it was usual, when the manes and the infernal gods were the objects of worship. *Pausan. Eliac. Vid.* Pelops.

PELOPE'A MŒ'NIA, is applied to the cities of Greece, but more particularly to Mycenæ and Argos, where the descendants of Pelops reigned. *Virg. Æn.* 2. v. 193.

PELOPI'A a daughter of Niobe. *Apollod.* 3. c. 5. ——The mother of Cycnus by Mars. *Id.*

PELOPI'A, a city of Ephesus, washed by the river Lycus. *Plin.* 5. c. 19.

PELOP'IDAS, a celebrated general of Thebes, son of Hippoclus. He was descended from an illustrious family, and was remarkable for his great possessions, which he bestowed with unusual liberality on the poor and necessitous. Many were the objects of his generosity, but when Epaminondas had refused to accept his presents, Pelopidas disregarded all his wealth, and preferred before it the enjoyment of his friend's conversation and of his poverty. From the friendship and intercourse of these two illustrious citizens the Thebans derived the most important advantages. No sooner had the interest of Sparta prevailed at Thebes, and the friends of liberty and national independence been banished from the city, than Pelopidas, who was in the number of the exiles, resolved to free his country from foreign slavery. His plan was bold and animated, and his deliberations were slow but maturely weighed. Meanwhile Epaminondas, who had been left by the tyrants at Thebes, as being in appearance a worthless and insignificant philosopher, animated the youths of the city, and at last Pelopidas, with eleven of his associates, boldly entered Thebes, and easily put to death the supporters of the tyranny, and freed the country from the usurpation of foreigners. After this successful enterprise, Pelopidas was unanimously placed at the head of the government, and so confident were the Thebans of his abilities, as a general and a magistrate, that they re-elected him thirteen times successively to fill the honorable office of governor of Bœotia. Epaminondas shared with him the sovereign power, and it was to their valor and prudence that the Thebans were indebted for the superior discipline of their armies, and for the celebrated victory of Leuctra. In a war which Thebes carried on against Alexander, tyrant of Pheræ, Pelopidas was appointed commander, but his imprudence in trusting himself unarmed into the enemy's camp nearly proved fatal to him. He was taken prisoner, but Epaminondas restored him to liberty. The perfidy of Alexander so iritated him, that he made war against him, and was killed bravely fighting in a celebrated battle in which his troops obtained the victory, B.C. 364 years. His remains received an honorable burial, the Thebans showed their sense of his merit by their lamentations, sent a powerful army to revenge his death, by the destruction of the tyrant of Pheræ and his relations, and his children were presented, out of respect to the virtues of their father, with large donations by the city of Thessaly. Pelopidas was admired for his valor, as he never engaged an enemy without obtaining the advantage. The impoverished state of Thebes before his birth and after his fall, plainly demonstrated the superiority of his genius and of his abilities, and it has been justly observed as the highest eulogy on their characters and services, that with Pelopidas and Epaminondas the glory and the independence of the Thebans rose and set. *Plut. & C. Nep. in Vitâ.*—*Xenoph. Hist. G.*—*Diod.* 15.—*Polyb.*——An ambassador from Mithridates to the Roman generals in Asia. *Appian. Mith. Bell.*

PELOPONNESI'ACUM BEL'LUM, a celebrated war which continued for 27 years between the Athenians and the inhabitants of Peloponnesus with their respective allies. It was the most famous and most interesting of all the wars which happened between the inhabitants of Greece; and for the minute and circumstantial description which we have of the events and revolutions which mutual animosity produced, we are indebted more particularly to the writings of Thucydides and Xenophon. The circumstances which gave birth to this memorable war were these. The power of Athens, under the prudent and vigorous administration of Pericles, was already extended over Greece, and had procured itself many admirers and more enemies, when the Corcyreans, who had been planted by a Corinthian colony, refused to pay to their founders those marks of respect and reverence which among the Greeks every colony was obliged to show to its mother country. The

Corinthians wished to punish that infidelity; and when the people of Epidamnus, a considerable town on the Adriatic, had been invaded by some of the barbarians of Illyricum, the people of Corinth gladly granted to the Epidamnians that assistance which had in vain been solicited from the Corcyreans, their founders and patrons. The Corcyreans were offended at the interference of Corinth in the affairs of their colony; they manned a fleet, and obtained a victory over the Corinthian vessels which had assisted the Epidamnians. The subsequent conduct of the Corcyreans, and their insolence to some of the Ælians, who had furnished a few ships to the Corinthians, provoked the Peloponnesians, and the discontent became general. Ambassadors were sent by both parties to Athens to claim its protection and alliance, and to justify these violent proceedings. The greatest part of the Athenians heard their various reasons with moderation and with compassion, but the enterprizing ambition of Pericles prevailed, and when the Corcyreans had reminded the people of Athens, that in all states of Peloponnesus they had to dread the most malevolent enemies, and the most insidious of rivals, they were listened to with attention and were promised support. This step was no sooner taken than the Corinthians appealed to the other Grecian states and particularly to the Lacedæmonians. Their complaints were accompanied by those of the people of Megara and of Ægina, who bitterly inveighed against the cruelty, injustice, and insolence of the Athenians. This had due weight with the Lacedæmonians, who had long beheld with concern and with jealousy the ambitious power of the Athenians, and they determined to support the cause of the Corinthians. However, before they proceeded to hostilities, an embassy was sent to Athens to represent the danger of entering into a war with the most powerful and flourishing of all the Grecian states. This alarmed the Athenians; but when Pericles had eloquently spoken of the resources and the actual strength of the republic and of the weakness of the allies, the clamours of his enemies were silenced, and the answer which was returned to the Spartans was a declaration of war. The Spartans were supported by all the republics of the Peloponnesus except Argos and part of Achaia, besides the people of Megara, Bœotia, Phocis, Locris, Leucas, Ambracia, and Anactorium. The Platæans, Lesbians, Carians, Chians, Messenians, Acarnanians, Zacynthians, Corcyreans, Dorians, and Thracians, were the friends of the Athenians, with all the Cyclades except Eubœa, Samus, Melus, and Thera. The first blow had already been struck, May 7, B.C. 431, by an attempt of the Bœotians to surprize Platæa, and therefore Archidamus king of Sparta, who had in vain recommended moderation to the allies, entered Attica at the head of an army of 60,000 men, and laid waste the country by fire and sword. Pericles, who was at the head of the government, did not attempt to oppose them in the field, but a fleet of 150 ships set sail without delay to ravage the coasts of the Peloponnesus. Megara was also depopulated by an army of 20,000 men, and the campaign of the first year of the war was concluded in celebrating with the most solemn pomp the funerals of such as had nobly fallen in battle. The following year was remarkable for a pestilence which raged in Athens, and which destroyed the greatest part of the inhabitants. The public calamity was still heightened by the approach of the Peloponnesian army on the borders of Attica, and by the unsuccessful expedition of the Athenians against Epidaurus and in Thrace. The pestilence which had carried off so many of the Athenians proved also fatal to Pericles, and he died about two years and six months after the commencement of the war. The following years did not give rise to decisive events; but the revolt of Lesbus from the alliance of the Athenians tended more powerfully to embitter the inveterate enmity of the rival states. Mitylene, the capital of the island, was recovered, and the inhabitants treated with the greatest cruelty. The island of Corcyra became also the seat of new seditions, and those citizens who had been carried away prisoners by the Corinthians, and for political reasons treated with lenity, and taught to despise the alliance of Athens, were no sooner returned home than they raised commotions, and endeavoured to persuade their countrymen to join the Peloponnesian confederates. This was strongly opposed, but both parties obtained by turns the superiority, and massacred, with the greatest barbarity, all those who obstructed their views. Some time after Demosthenes the Athenian general invaded Ætolia, where his arms were attended with the greatest success. He also fortified Pylus in the Peloponnesus, and gained so many advantages over the confederates that they sued for peace, which the insolence of Athens refused. The fortune of the war soon after changed, and the Lacedæmonians, under the prudent conduct of Brasidas, made themselves masters of many valuable places in Thrace. But this victorious progress was soon stopped by the death of their general, and of Cleon the Athenian commander, and the pacific disposition of Nicias, who was now at the head of Athens, induced him to make overtures for peace and universal tranquillity. Plistoanax, the king of the Spartans, wished them to be accepted, but the intrigues of the Corinthians prevented the discontinuation of the war, and therefore hostilities began anew. But while the war was carried on with various success in different parts of Greece, the Athenians engaged in a new expedition; they yielded to the persuasive eloquence of Gorgias of Leontium, and the ambitious views of Alcibiades, and sent a fleet of twenty ships to assist the Sicilian states against the tyrannical power of Syracuse, B.C. 416. This was warmly opposed by Nicias, but the eloquence of Alcibiades prevailed, and a powerful fleet was sent against the capital of Sicily. These vigorous, though impolitic measures of the Athenians, were not viewed with indifference by the confederates. Syracuse, in her distress, implored the assistance of Corinth, and Gylippus was sent to direct her operations, and to defend her against the power of her enemies. The events of battles were dubious, and though the Athenian army was animated by the cool prudence and intrepid valor of Nicias, and the more impetuous courage of Demosthenes, yet the good fortune of Syracuse prevailed, and after a campaign of two years of bloodshed, the fleets of Athens were totally ruined, and the few soldiers that survived the destructive siege made prisoners of war. So fatal a blow threw the people of Athens into consternation and despair, and while they sought for resources at home, they severely felt themselves deprived of support abroad, their allies were alienated by the intrigues of the enemy, and rebellion was fomented in their dependent states and colonies on the Asiatic coast. The threatened ruin, however, was timely averted; and Alcibiades, who had been treated with cruelty by his countrymen, and who had for some time resided in Sparta, and directed her military operations, now exerted himself to defeat the designs of the confederates, by inducing the Persians to espouse the cause of his country. But a short time after the internal tranquillity of Athens was disturbed, and Alcibiades, by wishing to abolish the democracy, called away the attention of his fellow-citizens, from the prosecution of a war which had already cost them so much blood. This, however, was but momentary; the Athenians soon after obtained a naval victory, and the Peloponnesian fleet was defeated by Alcibiades. The Athenians beheld with rapture the success of their arms; but when their fleet, in the absence of Alcibiades, had been defeated and destroyed near Andrus, by Lysander, the Lacedæmonian admiral, they showed their discontent and mortification by eagerly listening to the accusations which were brought against their naval leader, to whom they had gratefully acknowledged themselves indebted for their former victories. In the violence of popular frenzy Alcibiades was disgraced in the public assembly, and ten commanders were appointed to succeed him in the management of the republic. This change of admirals, and the appointment of Callicratidas to succeed Lysander, whose office had expired with the revolving year, produced new operations. The Athenians fitted out a fleet, and the two nations decided their superiority near Arginusæ, in a naval battle. Callicratidas was killed, and the Lacedæmonians conquered; but the rejoicings which the intelligence of this victory occasioned, were soon stopped, when it was known that the wrecks of some of the disabled ships of the Athenians, and the bodies of the slain had not been saved from the sea. The admirals were accused in the tumultuous assembly, and immediately condemned. Their successors in office were not so prudent, but they were more unfortunate in their operations. Lysander was again placed at the head of the Peloponnesian forces, instead of Eteonicus, who had succeeded to the command on the death of Callicratidas. The age and the expeaience of this general seemed to promise something decisive, and indeed an opportunity was not long wanting for the display of his military character. The superiority of the Athenians, over that of the Peloponnesians, rendered the former insolent, proud, and negligent; and when they had imprudently forsaken their ships to indulge their indolence, or pursue their amusements on the sea shore at Ægospotamos, Lysander attacked their fleet, and his victory was complete. Of one hundred and eighty sail, only nine escaped, eight of which fled under the command of Conon, to the island of Cyprus, and the other carried to Athens the melancholy news of the defeat. The Athenian prisoners were all massacred, and when the Peloponnesian conquerors had extended their dominion over the states and communities of Europe and Asia, which formerly acknowledged the power of Athens, they returned home to finish the war by the reduction of the capital of Attica. The siege was carried on with vigor, and supported with firmness, and the first Athenian who mentioned capitulation to his countrymen, was instantly sacrificed to the fury and the indignation of the populace, and all the citizens unanimously declared, that the same moment would terminate their independence and their lives. This animated language, however, was not long continued; the spirit of faction was not yet extinguished at Athens, and it proved perhaps more destructive to the public liberty than the operations and assaults of the Peloponnesian besiegers. During four months, negociations were carried on with the Spartans, by the aristocratical part of the Athenians, and at last it was agreed, that to establish the peace, the fortifications of the Athenian harbours must be demolished, together with the long walls which joined them to the city; all their ships, except twelve, were to be surrendered to the enemy: they were to resign every pretension to their ancient dominions abroad; to recall from banishment all the members of the late aristocracy; to follow the Spartans in war, and, in time of peace, to frame their constitution according to the will and the directions of their Peloponnesian conquerors. The humiliating terms were accepted, and the enemy entered the harbour, and took possession of the city, that very day on which the Athenians had been accustomed to celebrate the anniversary of the immortal victory which their ancestors had obtained over the Persians about seventy-six years before, near the island of Salamis. The walls and fortifications were instantly levelled with the ground, and the conquerors observed, that from the demolition of Athens, succeeding ages would date the commencement of Grecian freedom. The day was concluded with a festival, and the recitation of one of the tragedies of Euripides, in which the misfortunes of the daughter of Agamemnon, who was reduced to misery, and banished from her father's kingdom, excited a kindred sympathy in the bosom of the audience, who melted into tears at the recollection that one moment had likewise reduced to misery and servitude the capital of Attica, which in happier times was deservedly called the common patroness of Greece, and the scourge of Persia. This memmorable event happened 404 years B.C. and thirty tyrants were appointed by Lysander to govern the city. *Xen. Græc. Hist.—Plut. in Lys. Per. Alcib. Nic. & Ages.—Diod.* 11, &c.—*Aristophan.—Thucyd.—Plato.—Arist.—Lysias.—Isocrates.—C. Nep. in Lys. Alcib.* &c.—*Cic. in Off.* l. 24.

PELOPONNE'SUS, a celebrated peninsula, which comprehends the most southern parts of Greece. It received this name from Pelops, who settled there, as the name indicates (Πέλοπος νῆσος, *the island of Pelops.*) It had been called before Argia, Pelasgia, and Argolis, and its form, as it has been observed by the moderns, resembles the leaf of the plane tree. Its present name is Morea, which seems to be derived either from the Greek word *μορέα*, or the Latin *morus*, which signifies a *mulberry tree*, which is found there in great abundance. The ancient Peloponnesus was divided into six different provinces, Messenia, Laconia, Elis, Arcadia, Achaia Propria, and Argolis, to which some add Sicyon. These provinces all bordered on the sea shore, except Arcadia. The Peloponnesus was conquered, some time after the Trojan war, by the Heraclidæ or descendants of Hercules, who had been forcibly expelled from it. The inhabitants of this peninsula rendered themselves illustrious like the rest of the Greeks by their genius, their fondness for the fine arts, the cultivation of learning, and the profession of arms, but in nothing more than by a celebrated war which they carried on against Athens and her allies for twenty-seven years, and which from them received the name of the Peloponnesian war. *Vid.* Peloponnesiacum Bellum. The Peloponnesus scarcely extends 200 miles in length, and 140 in breadth, and is about 563 miles in circumference. It was separated from Greece by the narrow isthmus of Corinth, which, as being only five miles broad, Demetrius, Cæsar, Nero, and some others, attempted in vain to cut through, to make a communication between the bay of Corinth and the Saronicus Sinus. *Strab.* 8.—*Thucyd.*—*Diod.* 12, &c.—*Paus.* 3. c. 21. l. 8. c. 1.—*Mela*, 2. c. 3.—*Plin.* 4. c. 86.—*Herodot.* 8. c. 40.—*Tzetzes. ad Lyc.* 178.—*Eustath. ad Dionys. Per.* 414.

PE'LOPS, a celebrated prince, son of Tantalus, king of Phrygia. His mother's name was Euryanassa, or according to others, Euprytone, or Eurystemista, or Dione. He was murdered by his father, who wished to try the divinity of the gods who had visited Phrygia, by placing on their table the limbs of his son. The gods perceived his perfidious cruelty, and all, except Ceres, whom the recent loss of her daughter had rendered melancholy and inattentive, refused to touch the meat which was set before them. She ate one of the shoulders of Pelops, and therefore when Jupiter had had compassion on his fate, and restored him to life, he substituted a shoulder of ivory instead of that which Ceres had devoured. This shoulder, according to mythologists, had an uncommon power, and could heal, by its very touch, every complaint, and remove every disorder. Some time after, the kingdom of Tantalus was invaded by Tros, king of Troy, on pretence that he had carried away his son Ganymedes. This rape had been committed by Jupiter himself; the war, nevertheless, was carried on, and Tantalus defeated and ruined, was obliged to flee with his son Pelops, and seek shelter in Greece. This tradition is confuted by some who maintain that Tantalus did not flee into Greece, as he had been some time before confined by Jupiter in the infernal regions, for his impiety, and therefore Pelops was the only one whom the enmity of Tros persecuted. Pelops came to Pisa, where he became one of the suitors of Hippodamia, the daughter of king Œnomaus, and entered the lists against the father, who promised his daughter to him only who could out-run him in a chariot race. Pelops was not terrified at the fate of the thirteen lovers, who, before him, had entered the course against Œnomaus, and had, according to the conditions, been put to death when conquered. To insure himself the victory, he previously bribed Myrtillus, the charioteer of Œnomaus. He then married Hippodamia, and threw headlong into the sea Myrtillus, when he claimed the favours of the bride as a reward of his perfidy. According to some authors, Pelops had received some winged horses from Neptune, with which he was enabled to out-run Œnomaus. When he had established himself on the throne of Pisa, Hippodamia's possession, he extended his conquests over the neighbouring countries, and from him the peninsula, of which he was the most powerful monarch, received the name of Peloponnesus. Pelops, after death, received divine honors, and was as much revered above all the other heroes of Greece, as Jupiter was above the rest of the gods. He had a temple at Olympia, near that of Jupiter, where Hercules consecrated to him a small portion of land, and offered to him a sacrifice. The place where this sacrifice had been offered was religiously observed, and the magistrates of the country yearly, on coming into office, made there an offering of a black ram. During the sacrifice the soothsayer was not allowed, as at other times, to have a share of the victim, but he alone who furnished the wood, was permitted to take the neck. The wood for sacrifices was always furnished by some of the priests, to such as offered victims, and they received a price equivalent to what they gave. The white poplar was generally used in the sacrifices made to Jupiter and to Pelops. The children of Pelops by Hippodamia were Pittheus, Trœzen, Atreus, Thyestes, &c. besides some by concubines. The time of his death is unknown, though it is universally agreed that he survived Hippodamia for some time. Some suppose that the Palladium of the Trojans was made with the bones of Pelops. His descendants were called Pelopidæ. Pindar, who in his first Olympic speaks of Pelops, confutes the tradition of his ivory shoulder, and says, that Neptune took him up to heaven to be the cupbearer to the gods, from which office he was expelled when the impiety of Tantalus wished to make mankind partake of the nectar and the entertainments of the gods. Some suppose that Pelops first instituted the Olympic games in honor of Jupiter, and to commemorate the victory which he had obtained over Œnomaus. *Paus.* 5. c. 1, &c. *Apollod.* 2. c. 5.—*Eurip. in Iphig.*—*Diod.* 3.—*Strab.* 8.—*Mela*, 1. c. 18.—*Pindar. Ol.* 1.—*Virg. G.* 3. v. 7.—*Ovid. Met.* 6. v. 404, &c.—*Hygin.* fab. 9, 82 & 83.—*Tibull.* 1. el. 4. v. 58.—*Plut. in Par.* 33.—*Tzetzes in Lyc.* 152. *Chil.* 5. *Hist.* 10. —*Schol. Eurip. in Orest.* 11.—*Servius ad Virg. G.* 1. v. 205. l. 3. v. 7. *Æn.* 6. v. 603. l. 8. v. 130.—*Palæph. de Inc.* 30.—*Philost. Icon.* 9.—*Lactant. ad Theb.* 4. v. 306.—*Arnob.* 4.—*Alex.* 6. *Strom.*

PE'LOR, one of the men who sprang from the teeth of the dragon killed by Cadmus. *Paus.* 9. c. 5.—*Apollod.* 3.

PELO'RIA, a festival observed by the Thessalians in commemoration of the news which they received by one Pelorus, that the mountains of Tempe had been separated by an earthquake, and that the waters of the lake which lay there stagnated, had found a passage into the Alpheus, and left behind a vast, fertile, pleasant, and most delightful plain. *Athen.* l. 14.

PELO'RUS, PELO'RUM, or PELO'RIS, now Cape Faro, one of the three great promontories of Sicily, on the top of which was erected a tower to direct the sailor on his voyage. It lies near the coast of Italy, and received its name from Pelorus, the pilot of the ship which carried Annibal away from Italy. This celebrated general, as it is reported, was carried by the tides into the straits of Charybdis, and, as he was ignorant of the coast, he asked the pilot of his ship the name of the promontory which appeared at a distance. The pilot told him that it was one of the capes of Sicily, but Annibal gave no credit to his information, and murdered him on the spot, apprehending that he would betray him into the hands of the Romans. He was, however, soon convinced of his error, and found that the pilot had spoken with great fidelity, and therefore, to pay honour to his memory, and to atone for his cruelty, he gave him a magnificent funeral, and ordered that the promontory should bear his name, and from that time it was called Pelorum. Some authors assert that this account is an invention of the moderns, and observe, that it bore that name before the age of Annibal. *Val. Max.* 9. c. 8.—*Mela*, 2. c. 7.—*Strab.* 5.—*Virg. Æn.* 3. v. 411 & 687.—*Ovid. Met.* 5. v. 350. l. 13. v. 727. l. 15. v. 706.—*Arrian. Descrip. Orb.* 636 —*Servius. in Æn.* 1. v. 200. l. 3. v. 411 & 687.—*Flacc.* 1. v. 579.—*Seneca in Her. Œt.* 80. & *in Med.* 350.

PEL'TÆ, a town of Phrygia Major. *Strab.* It is now Pelti or Felti.

PELTE'NI, a people of Lycaonia. *Plin.* 5. c. 27.

PE'LUS, an island near Chius. *Steph.*——A mountain of Etruria. *Cato.*

PELU'SIUM, now Tineh, a town of Ægypt situate at the entrance of the most eastern mouth of the Nile, called from it Pelusian. It is about twenty stadia from the sea, and has received the name of Pelusium from the lakes and marshes (πηλός. *lutum*,) which are found in its neighbourhood. Pelusium was the key of Ægypt on the side of Phœnicia, as it was impossible to enter the Ægyptian territories without passing by it, and therefore on that account it was always well fortified and garrisoned, as it was of such importance for the security of the country. It produced lentils, and was celebrated for the linen stuffs made there. It is now in ruins. *Mela*, 2. c. 9.—*Colum.* 5. c. 10.—*Sil. It.* 3. v. 25.—*Lucan.* 8. v. 466. l. 9. v. 83. l. 10. v. 53.—*Liv.* 44. c. 19. l. 45. c. 11.—*Strab.* 17.—*Virg. G.* 1. v. 228.—*Servius. loco.*—*Plin.* 15. c. 28.—*Martial.* 13. epigr. 9.

PEL'VA, a town of Pannonia. *Antonin.*

PEM'MA, a town of Arabia. *Plin.* 6. c. 29.

PEMP'TE, a city of Ægypt. *Steph.* The region was called Pemptitis.

PEMP'TUS, a name by which Achilles was known in Crete. *Servius ad Æn.* 1. v. 34.

PENA'TES, certain inferior deities among the Romans, who presided over houses and the domestic affairs of families. They were called Penates, because their images were generally placed in the innermost and most secret parts of the house, *in penitissimâ ædium parte, quod* as Cicero says, *penitus insident.* The place where they stood was afterwards called *Penetralia*, and they themselves received the name of Penetrales. It was in the option of every master of a family to choose his Penates, and therefore Jupiter, as well as some of the superior gods, are often invoked as patrons of domestic affairs. According to some, the gods Penates were divided into four classes; the first comprehended all the celestial gods, the second, the sea gods, the third the gods of hell, and the last all such heroes as had received divine honors after death. The Penates were originally the manes of the dead, but when superstition had taught mankind to pay more than common reverence to the memory and to the images of their deceased friends, their attention was soon exchanged for regular worship, and they were admitted by their votaries to share immortality and power over the world with a Jupiter or a Minerva. The statues of the Penates were generally made of wax, ivory, silver, or earth, according to the taste or affluence of the worshipper, and the only offerings which they received were wine, incense, fruits, and sometimes the sacrifice of lambs, sheep, goats, &c. In the early ages of Rome, human sacrifices were offered to them, but Brutus, who expelled the Tarquins, abolished this unnatural custom. When offerings were made to them, their statues were crowned with garlands, poppies, or garlick, and besides the monthly day that was set apart for their worship, their festivals were celebrated during the Saturnalia. Some have confounded the Lares and the Penates, but they were different. *Cic. de Nat. D.* 2. c. 27. *Ver.* 2.—*Dionys.* 1.—*Servius. in Æn.* 2. v. 296. l. 3. v. 12 & 148. l. 8. v. 679.—*Lamprid. V. Alex.* 29.—*Festus de V. Sig.*

PENDA'LIUM, a promontory of Cyprus.

PENE'IA or PENE'IS, an epithet applied to Daphne, as daughter of the Peneus. *Ovid. Met.* 1. v. 452.

PENE'LEUS or PENE'LEOS, one of the Greeks killed in the Trojan war. *Homer, Il.* 2. v. 494.—*Schol. Euripid. Orest.* 5.——A son of Hippalmus, who was among the Argonauts. *Apollod.* 1 & 3.

PENEL'OPE, a celebrated princess of Greece, daughter of Icarius, and wife of Ulysses, king of Ithaca. Her marriage with Ulysses was celebrated about the same time that Menelaus married Helen, and she retired with her husband to Ithaca, against the inclination of her father, who wished to detain her at Sparta, her native country. She soon after became mother of Telemachus, and was obliged, with great reluctance, to part from her husband, whom the Greeks obliged to go to the Trojan war. *Vid.* Palamedes. The continuation of hostilities for ten years, rendered her sad and melancholy; but when Ulysses did not return like the other princes of Greece at the conclusion of the war, her fears and anxiety for his safety were increased. As she received no intelligence of his situation, she was soon beset by a number of importuning suitors, who wished her to believe that her husband was shipwrecked, and that therefore she ought no longer to expect his return, but forget his loss, and fix her choice and affections on one of her numerous admirers. She received their addresses with coolness and disdain; but as she was destitute of power, and a prisoner as it were in their hands, she yet flattered them with hopes and promises, and declared that she would make a choice of one of them, as soon as she had finished a piece of tapestry on which she was employed. The work was continued in a dilatory manner, and she baffled their eager expectations, by undoing in the night what she had worked in the day-time. This artifice of Penelope has given rise to the proverb of *Penelope's web*, which is applied to whatever labor can never be ended. The return of Ulysfes, after an absence of twenty years, however, delivered her from her fears and dangerous suitors. Penelope is described by Homer as a model of female virtue and chastity, but some more modern writers dispute her claims to the character of modesty and continence, and represent her as the most debauched and voluptuous of her sex. According to their opinions, therefore, she liberally gratified the desires of her suitors, in the absence of her husband, and had a son, whom she called Pan, as if to show that he was the offspring of all her admirers. Some, however, suppose that Pan was born of Penelope by Mercury, and that he was born before his mother's marriage with Ulysses. The god, as it is said, deceived Penelope, under the form of a beautiful goat, as she was teuding her father's flocks on one of the mountains of Arcadia. After the return of Ulysses, Penelope had a daughter, who was called Ptoliporthe, but if we believe the traditions that were long preserved at Mantinea, Ulysses repudiated his wife for her incontinence during his absence, and she fled to Sparta, and afterwards to Mantinea, where she died and was buried. After the death of Ulysses, according to Hyginus, she married Telegonus, her husband's son by Circe, by order of the goddess Minerva. Some say that her original name was Arnea or Amirace, and that she was called Penelope, when some river birds called Penelopes had saved her from the waves of the sea, upon which her father had exposed her. Icarius had attempted to destroy her, because the oracles had told him that his daughter by Periboea would be the most dissolute of her sex, and a disgrace to his family. *Cic. N.D.* 3. c. 22.—*Apollod.* 3. c. 10.—*Paus.* 3. c. 12. —*Homer. Il. & Odyss.*—*Ovid. Heroid.* 1. *Met.*—*Aristot. Hist. Anim.* 8.—*Hygin.* fab. 127 & 256.—*Aristoph. in Avib.*—*Plin.* 37. c. 2.—*Eustath. Odyss.* 1, &c.—*Sch. Pind.* 9. *Ol.*—*Tzetzes. ad Lyc.* 792.—*Lucian. in Dial. Pan. & Merc.*—*Sch. Theocr. Id.* 7.—*Servius. in G.* 1. v. 16.—*Æn.* 2. v. 43.

PENES'TÆ, a people of Thessaly. *Steph.*

PENES'TIA, a people of Illyria. *Liv.* 43. c. 21.

PENE'US, a river of Thessaly, rising in mount Pindus, falling into the Thermæan Gulph, after a wandering course between mounts Ossa and Olympus, through the plains of Tempe. It received its name from Peneus, a son of Oceanus and Tethys. The Peneus anciently inundated the plains of Thessaly, till an earthquake separated the mountains Ossa and Olympus, and formed the beautiful vale of Tempe, where the waters were formerly stagnant. From this circumstance, therefore, it obtained the name of Araxes, *ab ἀράσσω, scindo.* Daphne, the daughter of the Peneus, according to the fables of the mythologists, was changed into a laurel on the banks of this river. This tradition arises from the quantity of laurels which grow on the banks of the Peneus. *Ovid. Met.* 1. v. 452, &c.—*Strab.* 9.—*Mela*, 2. c. 3.—*Virg. G.* 4. v. 317.—*Diod.* 4.——A small river of Elis in Peloponnesus, better known under the name of Araxes. *Apollod.* 2.—*Strab.* 8 & 11.—*Paus.* 6. c. 24.

PEN'IDAS, one of Alexander's friends, who went to examine Scythia, under pretence of being sent on an embassy. *Curt.* 6. c. 6.

PENNI'NÆ AL'PES, a certain part of the Alps, between the sources of the Rhone on the north and the Verbanus Lacus on the south. *Liv.* 21. c. 38.

PEN'NUS M., a tribune at Rome, who opposed the violent measures of C. Gracchus. *Cic. Off.* 3. c. 11.

PEN'NUS, a divinity worshipped by the Gauls, as the greatest of the gods. His temple was on one of the Alps, now called Mount St. Bernard, and his statues represented him as a young man, naked, and with only one eye in the middle of the forehead. Some suppose that the sun was worshipped under that name. *Liv.* 21. c. 38.

PENTEDAC'TYLUS or PENTEDAC'TYLON, a mountain of Ægypt, on the Arabian Gulph. *Ptol.*

PENTAGRAM'MA, a city of India within the Ganges. *Id.*

PENTAP'OLIS, a part of Africa, near Cyrene. It received this name on account of the *five cities* which it contained: Cyrene, Arsinoe, Berenice, Ptolemais or Barce, and Apollonia. *Plin.* 5. c. 5. —*Servius in Æn.* 4. v. 42.——Part of Palestine, containing the five cities of Gaza, Gath, Ascalon, Azotus, and Ekron.

PENTAP'YLON, a temple of Jupiter Arbitrator at Rome, so called from its *five doors.* *Rosin. R. Ant.* 2. c. 5.

PENTE'LEUM, a city of Peloponnesus. *Plut.*

PENTE'LIA, a mountain of Arcadia, from which the Ladon flows. *Hesych.*

PENTEL'ICUS, a mountain of Attica, where were found quarries of beautiful marble, with which the chief of the Athenian artists formed some of their most celebrated statues. *Cic. ad Att.* 1. ep. 8.—*Paus.* 1. c. 32.—*Strab.* 9. It is now Pentely.

PENTHESILE'A, a queen of the Amazons, daughter of Mars, is said, by *Justin*, 2. c. 4, to have succeeded Ottera or Orithyra in the kingdom. She came to assist Priam in the last years of the Trojan war, and fought against Achilles, by whom she was slain. The hero was so struck with the beauty of Penthesilea, when he stripped her of her arms, that he even shed tears for having too violently sacrificed her to his fury. Thersites laughed at the partiality of the hero, for which ridicule he was instantly killed. Lycophron says, that Achilles slew Thersites because he had put out the eyes of Penthesilea when she was yet alive. The scholiast of Lycophron differs from that opinion, and declares, that it was commonly believed, that Achilles offered violence to the body of Penthesilea when she was dead, and that Thersites was killed because he had reproached the hero for this infamous action, in the presence of all the Greeks. The death of Thersites so offended Diomedes that he dragged the body of Penthesilea out of the camp, and threw it into the Scamander. It is generally supposed, that Achilles was enamoured of the Amazon before he fought with her, and that she had by him a son called Cayster. According to Helen and Ptolemæus, Penthesilea conquered and killed Achilles, whom Thetis restored to life again for a few moments, that he might revenge his fall by the death of the victorious Amazon. *Dictys. Cret.* 3 & 4.—*Paus.* 10. c. 31.—*Q. Calab.* 1.—*Virg. Æn.* 1. v. 495. l. 11. v. 662.—*Dares. Phryg.*—*Lycophr. in Cass.* 995, &c. —*Hygin.* fab. 112.—*Tzetzes. ad Lyc. loco. cit.*—*Eustath. Il.* 2, *& Hellen apud Eustath. ad Homer. Odyss.* 11.—*Ptolemæus Heph.* 6.—*Seneca in Troad.* 243.—*Servius in Æn. loco. cit.*—*Justin.* 2. c. 4.

PEN'THEUS, son of Echion and Agave, was king of Thebes in Bœotia. His refusal to acknowledge the divinity of Bacchus was attended with the most fatal consequences. He forbad his subjects to pay adoration to the new god; and when the Theban women had gone out of the city to celebrate the orgies of Bacchus, Pentheus, apprized of the debauchery which attended the solemnity, ordered the god himself, who conducted the religious multitude, to be seized. His orders were obeyed with reluctance, but when the doors of the prison in which Bacchus had been confined, opened of their own accord, Pentheus became more irritated, and commanded his soldiers to destroy the whole band of the bacchanals. This, however, was not executed, for Bacchus inspired the monarch with the ardent desire of seeing the celebration of the orgies. Accordingly he hid himself in a wood on mount Cithæron, whence he could see all the ceremonies unperceived. But his curiosity soon proved fatal to him, he was descried by the bacchanals, and they all rushed upon him. His mother was the first who attacked him, and her example was instantly followed by her two sisters, Ino and Autonoe, and his body was torn to pieces. Euripides introduces Bacchus among his priestesses, when Pentheus was put to death; but Ovid, who relates the whole in the same manner, differs from the Greek poet only in saying, that not Bacchus himself, but one of his priests, was present. The tree on which the bacchanals found Pentheus, was cut down by the Corinthians, by order of the oracle, and with it two statues of the god of wine were made, and placed in the forum. *Hygin.* fab. 184.—*Theocrit.* 26 v. 26.—*Ovid. Met.* 3. fab. 7, 8 & 9.—*Virg. Æn.* 4. v. 469.—*Servius in loco.*—*Lactant. ad Theb.* l. v. 11, 69 & 230. l. 2. v. 80. l. 4. v. 566 & 570.—*Paus.* 2. c. 5.—*Apollod.* 3. c. 5.—*Euripid. in Bacch.*—*Senec. in Phœnis. & Hipp.*

PEN'THILE, a city of Lesbus. *Steph.*

PENTHILUS, a son of Orestes by Erigone, the daughter of Ægisthus, who reigned conjointly with his brother Tisamenus at Argos. He was driven some time after from his throne by the Heraclidæ, and retired to Achaia, and thence to Lesbus, where he planted a colony. *Paus.* 5. c. 4.—*Strab.* 13.—*Paterc.* l. c. 1.—*Tzetzes. ad Lyc.* 1369.

PEN'THYLUS, a prince of Paphus, who assisted Xerxes with twelve ships. He was seized by the Greeks, to whom he communicated many important things concerning the situation of the Persians. *Herodot.* 7. c. 195.

PEN'TRI, a people of Samnium, whose city was called Bovianum. *Liv.* 9. c. 31.

PEPARETHUS, a small part of the Ægean Sea, on the coast of Macedonia, at the entrance of the Sinus Thermaicus, about twenty miles in circumference. It abounded in olives, and its wines have always been reckoned excellent. They were not, however, palatable before they were seven years old. *Plin.* 4. c. 12.—*Ovid. Met.* 7. v. 470.—*Liv.* 28. c. 5. l. 31. c. 28.—*Senec. in. Troad.* 842.

PEPERI'NA or PEPERI'NE, an island of India within he Ganges. *Ptol.*

PEPH'NUS, a town of Laconia, near a small island of the same name, where, according to some, Castor and Pollux were born, and where they had two small statues which remained immoveable though continually beaten by the waves, a circumstance regarded as supernatural by the inhabitants. The little island, which was scarcely more than a rock, abounded with white ants. *Paus.* 3. c. 26.

PEPHRE'DO, a sea nymph, daughter of Phorcys and Ceto. She was born with white hair, and thence surnamed Graia. She had a sister called Enyo. *Hesiod. Th.* 270.—*Sch. Apollon.* 4. v. 1515.—*Apollod.* 2.

PE'RA, a city of Pisidia.——A city of Thessaly. *Steph.*

PERÆ'A or BERÆ'A, a part of Judæa, near Ægypt. *Plin.* 5. c. 14.——A part of Caria, opposite Rhodes. *Liv.* 32. c. 33.——A colony of the Mityleneans, in Æolia. *Liv.* 57. c. 21.

PERÆ'BE or PERÆ'BUS, a town of Thessaly. *Steph.*

PERAN'TIA, a city of Ætolia. *Steph.*

PERASIP'PUS, an ambassador sent to Darius by the Lacedæmonians. *Curt.* 3. c. 13.

PER'CE, an ancient name of Thrace. *Steph.*

PERCEIA'NA, a city of Spain, near Emerita. *Antonin.*

PER'CES, a name given to the river Bætis by the inhabitants of the neighbouring country. *Steph.*

PERCO'PE or PERCO'TE, a city near Pontus, the inhabitants of which assisted Priam during the Trojan war. *Vid.* Percote.

PERCO'SIUS, a man acquainted with futurity. He attempted in vain to dissuade his two sons, Adrastus and Amphius, from going to the Trojan war, by telling them that they should perish there.

PERCO'TE, a town on the Hellespont, between Abydus and Lampsacus, near the sea shore. Artaxerxes gave it to Themistocles to supply his wardrobe. It is sometimes called Percope. *Herodot.* 1. c. 117.—*Hom.*

PERDIC'CAS the First, king of Macedonia, B.C. 729, was descended from Temenus. He increased his dominions by conquest, and in the latter part of his life, he showed his son Argæus where he wished to be buried, and told him that as long as the bones of his descendants and successors on the throne of Macedonia were laid in the same grave, so long would the crown remain in their family. These injunctions were observed till the time of Alexander, who was buried out of Macedonia. *Herodot.* 7 & 8. *Justin.* 7. c. 2.

PERDIC'CAS the Second, a king of Macedonia, son of Alexander. He reigned during the Peloponnesian war, and assisted the Lacedæmonians against Athens. He behaved with great courage at the head of his armies, and died B.C. 413, after a long and successful reign, during which he had subdued some of his barbarian neighbours. *Thucyd.* l. 3, 4, 6, &c. *Diod.* l. 12, &c.

PERDIC'CAS the Third, the third son of Amyntas, was king of Macedonia after his brothers Alexander and Ptolemy. He was supported on his throne by Iphicrates the Athenian, against the intrusions of Pausanias. He was killed in a war against the Illyrians, B.C. 360, after a reign of six years. *Justin.* 7, &c.

PERDIC'CAS, son of Orontes, was one of the friends and favourites of Alexander the Great. At the king's death he wished to make himself absolute, and the ring which he had received from the hand of the dying Alexander, seemed in some measure to favor his pretensions to be his successor. The better to support his claims to the throne, he married Cleopatra, the sister of Alexander, and strengthened himself by making a league with Eumenes. His ambitious views were early discovered by Antigonus, and the rest of the generals of Alexander, who all wished, like Perdiccas, to succeed to the kingdom and honors of the deceased monarch. Antipater, Craterus, and Ptolemy leagued with Antigonus against him, and, after much bloodshed on both sides, Perdiccas was totally ruined, and at last assassinated in his tent in Ægypt, by his own officers, about 321 years B.C. Perdiccas possessed not the prudence and address necessary to conciliate the esteem and gain the attachment of his fellow-soldiers, and this impropriety of his conduct alienated the heart of his friends, and at last proved his destruction. *Plut. in Alex.*—*Diod.* 17 & 18.—*Curt.* 10.—*C. Nep. in Eum.*—*Ælian. V. H.* 12.—*Justin.* 13. c. 8.

PERDIC'IA, a region and harbour of Lycia. *Steph.*

PER'DIX, a young Athenian, son of the sister of Dædalus. He invented the saw, and seemed to promise to become a greater artist than had ever been known. His uncle was jealous of his rising fame, and, as it is said, threw him down from the top of a tower, and put him to death. Perdix was changed into a bird which bears his name. *Hygin.* fab. 39 & 274.—*Apollod.* 3. c. 15.—*Ovid. Met.*—8. v. 220, &c.—*Servius ad Virg. G.* l. v. 143. *Æn.* 6. v. 14.

PEREI'A, a region of Thessaly. *Steph.*

PEREN'NA. *Vid.* Anna.

PEREN'NIS, a favorite of the emperor Commodus. He is described by some as a virtuous and impartial magistrate, while others represent him as a cruel, violent, and oppressive tyrant, who committed the greatest barbarities to enrich himself. He was put to death for aspiring to the empire. *Herodian.*—*Lamprid. in Comment.* c. 5.

PE'REUS, a son of Elatus and Laodice, grandson of Arcas. He left only one daughter called Neæra, who was mother of Auge, and of Cepheus and Lycurgus. *Apollod.* 3.—*Paus.* 8. c. 4.

PER'GA, a town of Pamphylia. *Vid.* Perge. *Liv.* 38. c. 57.

PER'GAMUS, a place of Crete, where was the sepulchre of Lycurgus. *Plut. Pliny,* 9, 12. c. 4, calls it Pergamum.

PER'GAMUS, PER'GAMA, *(plur.)* the citadel of the city of Troy. It was situated in the most elevated part of the town, on the banks of the river Scamander. Xerxes mounted to the top of this citadel when he reviewed his troops as he marched to the invasion of Greece. *Herodot.* 7. c. 43.—*Virg. Æn.* 1. v. 466, &c.—*Ovid Met.* 12. v. 445, &c.—*Flacc.* 2. v. 489, 570. l. 3. v. 513.—*Propert.* 2. el. 1. v. 21, &c.—*Horat.* 1. od. 16. v. 36, &c.

PER'GAMUS, now Pergamo, a town of Mysia, on the banks of the Caycus. It was the capital of a celebrated empire called the kingdom of Pergamus, which was founded by Philæterus, a eunuch, whom Lysimachus, after the battle of Ipsus, had entrusted with the treasures he had obtained in the war. Philæterus made himself master of the treasures and of Pergamus, in which they were deposited, B.C. 283, and laid the foundations of an empire, over which he himself presided for 20 years. His successors began to reign in the following order: His nephew Eumenes ascended the throne 263 B.C.; Attalus, 241; Eumenes the Second, 197; Attalus Philadelphus, 159; Attalus Philomator, 138; who, B.C. 133, left the Roman people heirs to his kingdom, as he had no children. The right of the Romans, however, was disputed by a usurper, who claimed the empire as his own, and Aquilius, the Roman general, was obliged to conquer the different cities one by one, and to gain their submission by poisoning the waters which were conveyed to their houses, till the whole was reduced into the form of a dependent province. The capital of the kingdom of Pergamus was famous for a library of 200,000 volumes, which had been collected by the different monarchs who had reigned there. This noble collection was afterwards transported to Ægypt by Cleopatra, with the permission of Antony, and it adorned and enriched the Alexandrian library, till it was destroyed by the Saracens, A.D. 642. Parchment was first invented and made use of at Pergamus, to transcribe books, as Ptolemy, king of Ægypt, had forbidden the exportation of Papyrus from his kingdom, in order to prevent Eumenes from making a library as valuable and as choice as that of Alexandria. From this circumstance parchment has been called *charta Pergamena*. Galenus the physician, and Apollodorus, the mythologist, were born there. Æsculapius was the chief deity of the country. *Plin.* 5. c. 30. 10. c. 21. l. 13. c. 11.—*Isid.* 6. c. 11.—*Strab.* 13.—*Liv.* 29. c. 11. l. 31. c. 46.

PER'GAMUS, a son of Neoptolemus and Andromache, who, as some suppose, retired from Epirus when his brother Molossus ascended the throne, and went into Asia, where he founded Pergamus. *Paus.* 1. c. 11.

PERGAN'TIUM, a city of Liguria. *Steph.* It is now Berganeon.

PER'GASE, a village of the tribe Erechtheis. *Steph.*

PER'GE or PER'GA, a town of Pamphylia, where Diana had a magnificent temple, whence her surname of Pergæa. Apollonius, the geometrician, was born there. *Mela*, 1. c. 14.—*Strab.* 14. It is now Pirgi.

PER'GUS, a lake of Sicily, near Enna, where Proserpine was carried away by Pluto. *Ovid. Met.* 5. v. 386.—*Claudian. de Rap. Pros.* 2. v. 112.

PERI'ADA, a city of Eubœa. *Steph.*

PERIAN'DER, a tyrant of Corinth, son of Cypselus. The first years of his government were mild and popular, but he soon learnt to become oppressive, when he had consulted the tyrant of Sicily about the surest way of reigning. Of the method to be pursued, he might judge from the Sicilian tyrant's having, in the presence of his messenger, plucked, in a field, all the ears of corn which seemed to tower above the rest. Periander understood the meaning of this answer. He immediately surrounded himself with a numerous guard, and put to death the richest and most powerful citizens of Corinth. He was not only cruel to his subjects, but his family also were objects of his vengeance. He committed incest with his mother, and put to death his wife Melissa, upon a false accusation. He also banished his son Lycophron to the island of Corcyra, because the youth pitied and wept at the miserable end of his mother, and detested the barbarities of his father. Periander died about 585 years B.C., in his 80th year, and, by the meanness of his flatterers, he was reckoned one of the seven wise men of Greece. Though he was tyrannical, yet he patronised the fine arts; he was fond of peace, and showed himself the friend and protector of genius and learning. He used to say, that a man ought solemnly to keep his word, but not to hesitate to break it if ever it clashed with his interest. He said also, that not only crimes ought to be punished, but also every wicked and corrupt thought. *Diog in Vitâ.*—*Aristot.* 5. *Polit.*—*Paus.* 2. c. 28.—*Auson.* ep. *de* 7. *Sap.* [There is a bust of Periander in the Museum of the Vatican, at Rome.]——A tyrant of Ambracia, whom some rank as one of the seven wise men of Greece, and not the tyrant of Corinth. *Aristot. Polit.* 5. c. 19.——A man distinguished as a physician, but contemptible as a poet. *Plut.*—*Lucan.*

PERI'APIS, a daughter of Pheres, mother of Patroclus by Menœtius. *Apollod.* 3.

PERIAR'CHUS, a naval commander of Sparta conquered by Conon. *Diod. Sic.* 14.

PERIBŒ'A, the second wife of Œneus, king of Calydon, was daughter of Hipponous. She became mother of Tydeus. Some suppose that Œneus debauched her, and afterwards married her. *Hygin.* fab. 69.—*Apollod.* 1.—*Hesiod. apud. Apoll.*—*Diod.* 4.—*Lact. ad Theb.* 1. v. 41.——A daughter of Alcathous, sold by her father on suspicion that she was courted by Telamon, son of Æacus, king of Ægina. She was carried to Cyprus, where Telamon the founder of Salamis married her, and she became mother of Ajax. She accompanied Theseus, according to some, into Crete, and returned with him to Athens, after she had escaped the arts of Minos, who is said to have attempted her virtue. She is also called Eribœa. *Sophoc. in Aj.* 570.—*Pind. Isth.* 6. v. 65.—*Apollod.* 3 —*Diod.* 4.—*Plut. in Thes. & Par.*—*Schol. Homer. Il.* 16. v. 14.—*Paus.* 1. c. 17 & 42.—*Hygin.* 97. ——The wife of Polybus, king of Corinth, who educated Œdipus as her own child. *Apollod.* 3. c. 8.—*Hygin.* fab. 66.—*Soph. in Œd. Tyr.* 785. The name of the wife of Polybus, according to Seneca and others, was Merope and not Peribœa. *Senec. in Œdip.* 272.—*Pisander. apud Sch. Eurip. Phœniss.* 1050. ——A daughter of Eurymedon, celebrated for her beauty. She became mother of Nausithous by Neptune. *Homer. Odyss.* 7. v. 57.——A Naiad, wife of Icarius, and the mother of Penelope, according to some authors. *Apollod.*

PERIBO'MIUS, a noted debauchee, mentioned by *Juvenal* 2. v. 16.

PERI'CLES, an Athenian of a noble family, son of Xanthippus and Agariste. He was naturally endowed with great powers, which he improved by attending the lectures of Damon, of Zeno, and of Anaxagoras. Under these celebrated masters he became a commander, a statesman, and an orator, and gained the affections of the people by his uncommon address and well-directed liberality. When he took a share in the administration of public affairs, he rendered himself popular by opposing Cimon, who was the favourite of the nobility, and to remove every obstacle which stood in the way of his ambition, he lessened the dignity and the power of the court of the Areopagus, which the people had been taught for ages to look up to with confidence and veneration. He also attacked Cimon, and caused him to be banished by the ostracism. Thucydides also, who had succeeded Cimon on his banishment, shared the same fate, and Pericles remained for 15 years the sole minister, and as it may be said the absolute sovereign of a republic which always showed itself so jealous of its liberties, and which distrusted so much the honesty of her magistrates. In his ministerial capacity Pericles did not enrich himself, but the prosperity of Athens was the sole object of his administration. He made war against the Lacedæmonians, and restored the temple of Delphi to the care of the Phocians, who had been illegally deprived of that honorable trust. He obtained a victory over the Sicyonians near Nemea, and waged a successful war against the inhabitants af Samus, at the request of his favorite mistress Aspasia. The Peloponnesian war was fomented by his ambitious views (*vid.* Peloponnesiacum bellum), and when he had warmly represented the flourishing state, the opulence and actual power of his country, the Athenians did not hesitate to undertake a war against the most powerful republics of Greece, a war which continued for 27 years, and which ended in the destruction of their empire, and the demolition of their walls. The arms of the Athenians were for some time crowned with success, but an unfortunate expedition raised clamors against Pericles, and the enraged populace attributed all their losses to him, and to make atonement for their ill success, they condemned him to pay 50 talents. The loss of popular favor by republican caprice, did not so much affect Pericles as the recent death of all his children, and when the tide of unpopularity was passed by, he condescended to come into the public assembly, and to view with secret pride the contrition of his fellow-citizens, who universally begged his forgiveness for the violence which they had offered to his ministerial character. He was again restored to all his honors, and, if possible, invested with more power and more authority than before, but the dreadful pestilence which had diminished the number of his family, proved fatal to him, and about 429 years B.C. in his 70th year, he fell a sacrifice to that terrible malady which robbed Athens of so many of her citizens. Pericles was for 40 years at the head of the administration, 25 years with others, and 15 years alone, and the flourishing state of the empire during his government gave occasion to the Athenians publicly to lament his loss and venerate his memory. As he was expiring, and seemingly senseless, his friends expatiated with warmth on the most glorious actions of his life, and the victories which he had won, when he suddenly interrupted their tears and conversation, by saying that in mentioning the exploits that he had achieved, and which were common to him with all generals, they had forgotten to mention a circumstance which reflected far greater glory upon him as a minister, a general, and above all, as a man. It is, says he, that not a citizen in Athens has been obliged to put on mourning on my account. The Athenians were so captivated with his eloquence that they compared it to thunder and lightning, and, as to another father of the gods, they gave him the surname of Olympian. The poets, his flatterers, said that the goddess of persuasion, with all her charms and her attractions, dwelt upon his tongue. When he marched at the head of the Athenian armies, Pericles observed that he had the command of a free nation that were Greeks, and citizens of Athens. He also declared that not only the hand of a magistrate, but also his eyes and his tongue should be pure and undefiled. Yet great and venerable as his character may appear, we must not forget the follies of Pericles. His vicious partiality for the celebrated courtezan Aspasia subjected him to the ridicule and the censure of his fellow-citizens; but if he triumphed over satire and malevolent remarks, the Athenians had occasion to execrate the memory of a man who by his example corrupted the purity and innocence of their morals, and who made licentiousness respectable, and the indulgence of every impure desire the qualification of the soldier as well as the senator. Pericles lost all his legitimate children by the pestilence, and to call a natural son by his own name he was obliged to repeal a law which he had made against spurious children, and which he had enforced with great severity. This son, called Pericles, became one of the ten generals who succeeded Alcibiades in the administration of affairs, and like his colleagues, he was condemned to death by the Athenians after the unfortunate battle of Arginusæ. *Paus.* 1. c. 25.—*Plut. in Vitâ.*—*Qnintil.* 12. c. 9.—*Cic. de Orat.* 3.—*Ælian. V.H.* 4. c. 10. — *Xenoph. Hist. G.* — *Thucyd.* [There are many fine busts of Pericles, some perhaps by the hand of Phidias himself. One of the best will be found in the British Museum.]

PERICLIDAS, one of the ambassadors sent by the Lacedæmonians to Athens in the 8th year of the Peloponnesian war. *Schol. Aristoph. Equit.*

PERICLYM'ENUS, one of the twelve sons of Neleus, brother to Nestor, killed by Hercules. He was one of the Argonauts, and had received from Neptune his grandfather the power of changing himself into whatever shape he pleased, and therefore before he perished by the blows of the hero, he attempted in vain to conceal himself in the form of a fly, a bee, a serpent, an ant, and an eagle. Under this last transformation, he wounded Hercules with his talons, but was at length shot by an arrow. *Orpheus. Arg.* 153.—*Apollon. Rh.* 1. v. 156.—*Ovid. Met.* 12. v. 556.—*Hygin.* fab. 10 & 14.—*Tzetzes. Chil.* 2. *H.* 45.—*Sch. Pindar.* 4. v. 309.—*Apollod.* 1.——A son of Neptune, who, in the Theban war against Adrastus, killed Amphidicus and Parthenopæus, and wounded Amphiaraus. *Apollod.* 3.—*Paus.* 9. c. 18.

PERIDI'A, a Theban woman, whose son was killed by Turnus in the Rutulian war. *Virg. Æn.* 12. v. 515.

PERIEGE'TES DIONYS'IUS, a poet. *Vid.* Dionysius.

PERIER'BIDI, a people of Asiatic Sarmatia. *Ptol.*

PERIE'RES, a son of Æolus, or, according to others, of Cynortas by Enaretta. He married Gorgophone, daughter of Perseus, by whom he had Aphareus, Leucippus, Icarius, and Tyndarus. He reigned in Messenia. *Pausanias,* 3. c. 1. l. 4. c. 2., says that Gorgophone was mother of Tyndarus, by Œbalus son of Cynortes, whom she married after the death of Perieres. *Apollod.* 1 & 3.——The charioteer of Menœceus. *Apollod.*

PERIG'ENES, an officer of Ptolemy.

PERIG'ONE, a woman who had a son called Melanippus, by Theseus. She was daughter of Synnis the famous robber, whom Theseus killed, and she was so terrified, that she concealed herself among wild reeds not to share his fate, till she was recalled and promised protection by the conqueror. She married Deioneus the son of Eurytus, by consent of Theseus, and as during the concealment she had sworn never to burn or injure reeds, her promise was solemnly observed by the descendants of her son Joxus. *Plut. inThes.*—*Paus.* 10. c. 25.

PERILAM'PES, a friend of Pericles, who kept peacocks. *Aristoph. Vesp.*—*Plut. in Pericl.*

PERILA'US, an officer in the army of Alexander the Great, sent by Aridæus to Perdiccas and Leonatus, to put an end to the dissensions between the infantry and cavalry. *Curt.* 10. c. 8.——A tyrant of Argos, who destroyed the brazen tower which Acrisius had erected for the protection of Danae. *Paus.* 2. c. 23.——A son of Icarius and Peribœa. *Apollod.*

PERIL'LA, a daughter of Ovid the poet. She was extremely fond of poetry and literature. *Ovid. Fast.* 3. el. 7. v. 1.

PERIL'LUS, an ingenious artist at Athens, who made a brazen bull for Phalaris, tyrant of Agrigentum. This machine was fabricated to put criminals to death by burning them alive, and was so constructed that their cries were like the roaring of a bull. When Perillus gave it Phalaris, the tyrant made the first experiment upon the donor, and cruelly put him to death by lighting a slow fire under the belly of the bull. *Plin.* 34. c. 8.—*Propert.* 2. el. 19. v. 52.—*Juv.* 8. v. 81.—*Pers.* 3. v. 39.—*Ovid. Trist.* 5. el. 1. v. 53. *In Art. Am.* 1. v. 653. *in Ib.* 439.——A lawyer and usurer in the age of Horace. *Horat.* 2. sat. 3. v. 75.

PERIME'DE, a daughter of Æolus, who married Achelous. *Apollod.*——The wife of Lycimnius, sister of Amphitryon. *Id.*——A daughter of Eurystheus, immolated by the Athenians. *Id.*——A daughter of Œneus of Calydon, who according to some, married Phœnix, and became mother of Astypalea and Europa. *Asius apud Paus.* 7. c. 4.——A woman skilled in the knowledge of herbs and of enchantments. *Theocrit.* 2.

PERIME'DES one of the companions of Ulysses who prepared the victims, which, by the advice of Circe, the hero offered to the manes before his descent to the infernal regions. Those victims, though not mentioned by Homer, were supposed to be black rams, according to a picture of Polygnotus. *Homer. Odyss.* 11. v. 23.—*Paus.* 10. c. 29.

PERIME'LA or PERIME'LE, a daughter of Hippodamus, thrown into the sea for receiving the addresses of Achelous. She was changed into an island in the Ionian Sea, and became one of the Echinades. *Ovid. Met.* 8. v. 690.

PERIME'LES, a son of Admetus and Alceste. *Sch. Eurip. in Alc.* 264 & 405.

PERIMEL'IDES, a name given to the nymphs who presided over the sheep-folds in the country. *Servius ad Virg. Ec.* 10. v. 62.

PERINCA'RI, a city of India Citerior. *Ptol.*

PERIN'THUS, a town of Thrace on the Propontis, anciently called Mygdonia. It was afterwards called Heraclea, in honor of Hercules, and is now Erekli. It was first peopled by a Samian colony. *Plut. in Qu. Gr.* 57.—*Mela,* 2.c. 2.—*Paus.* 1. c. 29.—*Plin.* 4. c. 11.—*Liv.* 33. c. 30.

PERIPATET'ICI, a sect of philosophers at Athens, disciples of Aristotle. They received this name from the place in the Lyceum, where they were taught, which was called *Peripaton*, or because they received the philosopher's lectures as they *walked* (περιπατοῦντες). The Peripatetics acknowledged the dignity of human nature, and placed their *summum bonum*, not in the pleasures of sense, but in the due exercise of the moral and intellectual faculties. The habit of this exercise, when guided by reason, constituted the highest excellence of man. The philosopher contended that our own happiness chiefly depends upon ourselves, and though he did not require in his followers that self-command to which others pretended, yet he allowed a moderate degree of perturbation, as becoming human nature, and he considered a certain sensibility of passion necessary, as by resentment we are able to repel injuries, and the smart which past calamities have inflicted renders us careful to avoid their repetition. *Cic. Acad.* 2, &c. For an account of Peripatetic philosophers, *vide Fabr. B. Gr.* 3. c. 8.

PER'IPHAS, a man who attempted, with Pyrrhus, Priam's palace. He was a native of Scyrus, and had accompanied the young hero to the war. *Virg. Æn.* 2. v. 476.——A son of Ægyptus who married Actæa. *Apollod.* 2. c. 1.——One of the Lapithæ. *Ovid. Met.* 12. v. 449.——One of the first kings of Attica, before the age of Cecrops, according to some authors. It is said that his subjects paid him divine honors, for which Jupiter determined to destroy him with his thunder, but at the prayer of Apollo, changed him only into an eagle, which he made his favorite bird, and guardian of his thunderbolts. The wife of Periphas, unable to survive her husband, entreated the gods to remove her from life, and she was changed into a moor-hen. *Autonin. Lib.* 6.—*Ovid. Met.* 7. v. 400.

PERIPHE'MUS, an ancient hero of Greece, to whom Solon sacrificed at Salamis, by order of the oracle.

PERIPHE'TES, a robber of Attica, son of Vulcan, destroyed by Theseus. He is also called Corynetes, because he was generally armed with a club, (κορύνη,) with which he killed those whom he plundered. Some call him son of Neptune. *Hygin.* fab. 38.—*Apollod.* 3. cap. ult.—*Diod.* 5.—*Plut. in Thes.*—*Paus.* 2. c. 1.—*Ovid. Met.* 7. v. 438.——A king of Mygdonia, killed by Æthon, son of Neptune, king of the Thracian Chersonesus. *Conon. Narr.* 10.——A son of Nyctimus of Arcadia, father of Parthaon. *Paus.* 8. c. 24.

PERIPHO'SIUS, a harbour of Lower Libya. *Ptol.*

PERIP'OLIS, a town of the Bruti on the river Halex. *Plin.* It is called Peripolium by *Thucydides.*

PERIRRHEU'SA, a small town near Ephesus. *Plin.* 3. c. 31.

PERIS'ADES, a people of Illyricum. *Strab.* 7.

PERIS'TERE, a city of the Phœnicians. *Steph.*

PERISTER'IDES, some small islands of the Ægæan Sea, near Ionia. *Plin.* 5. c. 31.

PERIS'THENES, a son of Ægyptus, who married Electra, by whom he was murdered. *Apollod.* 2.

PER'ITA, a favorite dog of Alexander the Great, in whose honor the monarch built a city. *Plut.* c. 107.—*Jul. Poll.* 5. c. 5.

PERIT'ANUS, an Arcadian who enjoyed the company of Helen after her elopement with Paris. The offended lover punished the crime with mutilation, whence mutilated persons were called Peritani in Arcadia. *Ptol. Heph.* 1. *in Init.*

PERITHOE'DA, a village in the tribe Œneis. *Steph.*

PERITO'NIUM, a town of Ægypt on the western shores of the Nile, esteemed of great importance, as being one of the keys of the country. Antony was defeated there by C. Gallus, the lieutenant of Augustus.

PERMES'SUS, a river of Bœotia, rising in mount Helicon, and flowing all round it. It received its name from Permessus the father of a nymph called Aganippe, who also gave her name to one of the fountains of Helicon. The river Permessus, as well as the fountain Aganippe, were sacred to the Muses. *Strab.* 8.—*Propert.* 2. el. 8. v. 30.—*Martial.* 1. epigr. 77.—*Paus.* 9. c. 29.—*Servius ad Virg. Ec.* 6. v. 64.

PER'NE, a city of Thrace. *Steph.*

PE'RO, a daughter of Neleus, king of Pylus, by Chloris. Her beauty drew many admirers, but she married Bias son of Amythaon, because he had by the assistance of his brother Melampus, (*vid.* Melampus,) and according to her father's desire, recovered some oxen which Hercules had stolen away, and she became mother of Talaus. *Homer. Odyss.* 1. v. 284.—*Propert.* 2. el. 2. v. 17. *Paus.* 4. c. 36.——A daughter of Cimon, remarkable for her filial affection. When her father had been sent to prison, where his judges had condemned him to starve, she supported his life by giving him the milk of her breasts, as to her own child. *Val. Max.* 5. c. 4.——The mother af Asopus by Neptune. *Apollod.*

PER'OE, a fountain of Bœotia, called after Pero. *Paus.* 9. c. 4.

PER'OLA, a Roman who meditated the death of Annibal in Italy. His father Pacuvius dissuaded him from assassinating the Carthaginian general.

PERON'TICUM, a city of Thrace. *Ptol.*

PEROR'SI, a people of Æthiopia, on the borders of Mauritania. *Plin.* 6. c. 30. They are called Petorsi by *Stephanus.*

PERPER'NA or **PERPEN'NA M.**, a Roman who conquered Aristonicus in Asia, and took him prisoner. He died B.C. 130. *Liv.* 59.—*Vell. Paterc.* 2. c. 30.—*Strab.* 13.——A Roman who joined the rebellion of Sertorius, and opposed Pompey. He was defeated by Metellus, and some time after he had the meanness to assassinate Sertorius, whom he had invited to his house. He fell into the hands of Pompey, who ordered him to be put to death. *Plut. in Sert.*—*Paterc.* 2. c. 30.——A Greek who obtained the consulship at Rome. *Val. Max.* 3. c. 4.

PERPEN'NA HOSTIL'IUS LICINIA'NUS, a person proclaimed emperor, in the age of Decius. He died of the plague soon after.

PERPERE'NA, a place of Phrygia, where, as some suppose, Paris adjudged the prize of beauty to Venus. *Strab.* 5.

PERRAN'THES, a hill of Epirus, near Ambracia. *Liv.* 38. c. 4. It is now monte di Larta.

PERRHÆ'BIA, a part of Thessaly, situate on the borders of the Peneus, extending between the town of Artax and the vale of Tempe. The inhabitants were driven from their possessions by the Lapithæ, and retired into Ætolia, where part of the country received the name of Perrhæbia. *Propert.* 2. el. 5. v. 33.—*Strab.* 9.—*Liv.* 33. c. 34. 1. 36. c. 34.

PERRHI'DÆ, a village in the tribe Antiochus. *Steph.*

PER'SA or **PERSE'IS**, one of the Oceanides, mother of Æetes, Circe, and Pasiphae, by Apollo. *Hesiod. Theog.* 355 & 955.—*Hygin.* fab. 40.—*Apollod.* 3.

PERSA'CRA, a city of India within the Ganges. *Ptol.*

PER'SÆ, the inhabitants of Persia. *Vid.* Persia.

PERSÆP'OLIS, a celebrated city, the capital of the Persian empire, situated on the river Araxes. It was laid in ruins by Alexander after the conquest of Darius. The reason of this is unknown. Diodorus says that the sight of about 800 Greeks, whom the Persians had shamefully mutilated, so irritated Alexander that he resolved to punish the barbarity of the inhabitants of Persæpolis, and of the neighbouring country, by permitting his soldiers to plunder their capital. Others suppose that Alexander set it on fire at the instigation of Thais, one of his courtezans, when he had passed the day in drinking, and in riot and debauchery. The ruins of Persæpolis, now Chehil Menara, i.e. forty columns, still astonish the modern traveller by their grandeur and magnificence. *Curt.* 5. c. 7.—*Diod.* 17, *&c.*—*Arrian.*—*Plut. in Alex.*—*Justin.* 11. c. 14.

PERSÆ'US, a philosopher intimate with Antigonus, by whom he was appointed over the Acrocorinthus. He flourished B.C. 274. *Diog. Laert. in Zenon.*

PERSE'A or **PERSE'E**, a fountain near Mycenæ, in Peloponnesus. *Paus.* 2. c. 16.

PERSE'IS. *Vid.* Persa.——A patronymic of Hecate as daughter of Perses. *Ovid. Met.* 7. v. 69.

PERSEPH'ONE, a daughter of Jupiter and Ceres, called also Proserpine. *Vid.* Proserpina. It was not lawful for any except the initiated to pronounce the word at the Eleusinian mysteries. Ceres herself received the same appellation. *Homer. Odyss.* 10. v. 491, 494, & 509.—*Paus.* 8. c. 37.—*Ovid. Heroid.* 21. v. 46. *Met.* 5. v. 470. l. 10. v. 15 & 730. *Fast.* 4. v. 452, &.——The mother of Amphion by Jasus.

PER'SES, a son of Perseus and Andromeda. From him the Persians, who were originally called Cephenes, received their name. *Herodot.* 7. c. 61. ——A son of Crius and Eurybia, who married Asteria, by whom he had Hecate. *Hesiod. Th.* 134 & 409.——A brother of Hesiod, to whom the poet addressed his Opera and Dies. The two brothers, according to the beginning of the poem, had been at enmity in consequence of the division of their property.——A king of Macedonia. *Vid.* Perseus.

PER'SEUS, a son of Jupiter and Danae, the daughter of Acrisius. As Acrisius had confined his daughter in a brazen tower to prevent her becoming a mother, because he was to perish, according to the words of an oracle, by the hands of his daughter's son, Perseus was no sooner born, (*vid.* Danae,) than he was thrown into the sea with his mother Danae. The hopes of Acrisius were frustrated; the slender boat which carried Danae and her son was driven by the winds upon the coasts of the island of Seriphus, one of the Cyclades, where they were found by a fisherman called Dictys, and carried to Polydectes, the king of the place. They were treated with great humanity, and Perseus was entrusted to the care of the priests of Minerva's temple. His rising genius and manly courage, however, soon displeased Polydectes, and the monarch, who wished to offer violence to Danae, feared the resentment of her son. Yet Polydectes resolved to remove every obstacle. He invited all his friends to a sumptuous entertainment, and it was requisite that all who accepted the invitation should present the monarch with a beautiful horse. Perseus was in the number of the invited, and the more particularly so, as Polydectes knew that he could not receive from him the present which he expected from all the rest. Nevertheless, Perseus, who wished not to appear inferior to the others in magnificence, told the king that as he could not give him a horse he would bring him the head of Medusa, the only one of the Gorgons who was subject to mortality. The offer was doubly agreeable to Polydectes, as it would remove Perseus from Seriphus, and on account of its seeming impossibility, the attempt might perhaps end in his ruin. But the innocence of Perseus was patronised by the gods. Pluto lent him his helmet, which had the wonderful power of making its bearer invisible; Minerva gave him her buckler, which was as resplendent as glass; and he received from Mercury wings and the talaria, with a short dagger made of diamonds, and called herpe. According to some it was from Vulcan and not from Mercury, that he received the herpe, which was in form like a scythe. With these arms Perseus began his expedition, and traversed the air, conducted by the goddess Minerva. He went to the Graiæ, the sisters of the Gorgons, who, according to the poets, had wings like the Gorgons, but only one eye and one tooth between them all, of which they made use, each in her turn. They were three in number, according to Æschylus and Apollodorus, or only two, according to Ovid and Hesiod. With Pluto's helmet, which rendered him invisible, Perseus was enabled to steal their eye and their tooth while they were asleep, and he returned them only when they had informed him where their sisters the Gorgons resided. When he had received the necessary information, Perseus flew to the habitation of the Gorgons, which was situate beyond the western ocean, according to Hesiod and Apollodorus; or in Libya according to Ovid and Lucan; or in the deserts of Asiatic Scythia, according to Æschylus. He found these monsters asleep, and as he knew that if he fixed his eyes upon them, he should be instantly changed into a stone, he continually looked on his shield, which reflected all objects as clearly as the best of glasses. He approached them, and with a courage which the goddess Minerva supported, he cut off Medusa's head with one blow. The noise awoke the two immortal sisters, but Pluto's helmet rendered Perseus invisible, and the attempt of the Gorgon's to revenge Medusa's death proved fruitless; the conqueror made his way through the air, and from the blood which dropped from Medusa's head sprang those innumerable serpents which have ever since infested the sandy deserts of Libya. Chrysaor also, with his golden sword, sprang from these drops of blood, as well as the horse Pegasus, which immediately flew through the air and stopped on mount Helicon, where he became the favorite of the Muses. Meantime Perseus continued his journey across the deserts of Libya, but the approach of night obliged him to alight in the territories of Atlas, king of Mauritania. He went to the monarch's palace, where he hoped to meet with a kind reception by announcing himself as the son of Jupiter, but in this he was disappointed. Atlas recollected that, according to an ancient oracle, his gardens were to be robbed of their fruit by one of the sons of Jupiter, and therefore he not only refused Perseus the hospitality he demanded, but even offered violence to his person. Perseus finding himself inferior to his powerful enemy, showed him Medusa's head, and Atlas was instantly changed into a large mountain which bore the same name in the deserts of Africa. On the morrow Perseus continued his flight, and as he passed across the deserts of Libya, he discovered, on the coasts of Æthiopia, the naked Andromeda, exposed to a sea monster. He was struck at the sight, and offered her father Cepheus to deliver her from instant death if he obtained her in marriage as the reward of his labors. Cepheus consented, and Perseus, raising himself in the air, flew towards the monster, which was advancing to devour Andromeda, and plunging his dagger into his right shoulder, destroyed it. This happy event was attended with the greatest rejoicings. Perseus raised three altars to Mercury, Jupiter, and Pallas, and after he had offered the sacrifice of a calf, a bullock, and a heifer, the nuptials were celebrated with the greatest festivity. The universal joy, however, was soon disturbed. Phineus, Andromeda's uncle, entered the palace with a number of armed men, and attempted to carry away the bride, whom he had courted and admired long before the arrival of Perseus. The father and mother of Andromeda interfered, but in vain; a bloody battle ensued, and Perseus must have fallen a victim to the rage of Phineus, had not he defended himself at last with the same arms which proved fatal to Atlas. He showed the Gorgon's head to his adversaries, and they were instantly turned to stone, each in the posture and attitude in which he then stood. The friends of Cepheus, and such as supported Perseus, shared not the fate of Phineus, as the hero had previously warned them of the power of Medusa's head, and of the service which he received from it. Soon after this memorable adventure, Perseus returned to Seriphus, at the very moment that his mother, Danae, had fled to the altar of Minerva, to avoid the pursuit of Polydectes, who attempted to offer her violence. Dictys, who had saved her from the sea, and who, as some say, was the brother of Polydectes, defended her against her enemies, and therefore, Perseus, sensible of his merit and of his humanity, placed him on the throne of Seriphus, after he had, with Medusæ's head, turned into stones the wicked Polydectes, and the officers who were the associates of his guilt. He afterwards restored to Mercury his talaria and his wings, to Pluto his helmet, to Vulcan his sword, and to Minerva her shield; but as he was more particularly indebted to the goddess of wisdom for her assistance and protection, he placed the Gorgon's head on her shield, or, rather, according to the more received opinion, on her ægis. After he had finished these celebrated exploits, Perseus expressed a wish to return to his native country, and he accordingly embarked for the Peloponnesus, with his mother and Andromeda. When he reached the Peloponnesian coasts, he was informed that Teutamias, king of Larissa, was then celebrating funeral games in honor of his father. This intelligence drew him to Larissa, to signalize himself in throwing the quoit, of which, according to some, he was the inventor. But here he was attended by an evil fate, and had the misfortune to kill a man with a quoit which he had thrown in the air. This was no other than his grandfather Acrisius, who on the first intelligence that his grandson had reached the Peloponnesus, fled from his kingdom of Argos to the court of his friend and ally Teutamias, to prevent the fulfilling of the oracle, which had obliged him to treat his daughter with so much barbarity. Some suppose with Pausanias, that Acrisius had gone to Larissa to be reconciled to his grandson, whose fame had been spread in every city in Greece; and Ovid asserts, that the grandfather was under the strongest obligations to his son-in-law, as, through him he had received his kingdom, from which he had been forcibly driven by the sons of his brother Prœtus. This unfortunate murder greatly depressed the spirits of Perseus: by the death of Acrisius he was entitled to the throne of Argos, but he refused to reign there; and to remove himself from a place which reminded him of the parricide he had unfortunately committed, he exchanged his kingdom for that of Tirynthus, and the maritime coast of Argolis, where Megapenthes, the son of Prœtus then reigned. When he had finally settled in this part of the Peloponnesus, he determined to lay the foundations of a new city, which he made the capital of his dominions, and which he called *Mycenæ*, because the pommel of his sword, called by the Greeks μύκης, had fallen there. The time of his death is unknown, yet it is universally agreed, that he received divine honors, like the rest of the ancient heroes. He had statues at Mycenæ, and in the island of Seriphus, and the Athenians raised him a temple, in which they consecrated an altar in honor of Dictys, who had treated Danae and her infant son with so much paternal tenderness. The Ægyptians also paid particular honor to his memory, and asserted that he often appeared among them wearing shoes two cubits long, which was always interpreted as a sign of fertility. Perseus had by Andromeda, Alceus, Sthenelus, Nestor, Electryon, and Gorgophone, and, after death, according to some mythologists, he became a constellation in the heavens. *Herodot.* 2. c. 91.—*Apollod.* 2. c. 4, &c.—*Paus.* 2. c. 16 & 18. l. 3. c. 17, &c.—*Apollon. Arg.* 4. v. 1509.—*Ovid. Met.* 4. fab. 16. l. 5. fab. 1, &c. *Am.* 2. el. 19. v. 27. *De A.A.* 3. v. 415.—*Lucan.* 9. v. 668.—*Hygin.* fab. 64.—*Hesiod. Theog.* 270. *In Scut.* 217.—*Ital.* 9. v. 442.—*Pind. Pyth.* 7. & *Olymp.* 3.—*Propert.* 2. el. 16. v. 10. el. 21. v. 115. *Lactant. ad Theb.* 6. v. 286.—*Athen.* 13.—*Homer. Il.* 14. v. 319.—*Servius in Æn.* 4. v. 246. l. 6. v. 289. l. 7. v. 372. l. 8. v. 435.—*Sch. Apollon.* 4.—*Eustath. ad Dionys. Per.* 225 & 910.—*Arat. phæn.* [There is a statue of Perseus in the Museum of the Vatican, at Rome.]——A governor of Troy, when Paris returned from Greece with Helen. *Hegus. apud. Parth. erot.* 18.—*Tzetzes. in Lycoph.*——A son of Nestor and Anaxibia. *Apollod.* 1. c. 9. ——A writer who published a treatise on the republic of Sparta. *Athen.* 4.——A philosopher, disciple to Zeno. *Vid.* Persæus.

PER'SEUS or PER'SES, a son of Philip king of Macedonia. He distinguished himself, like his father, by his enmity to the Romans, and when he had made sufficient preparations, he declared war against them. His operations, however, were slow and injudicious, he wanted courage and resolution, and though he at first obtained some advantage over the Roman armies, yet his avarice and his timidity proved destructive to his cause. When Paulus was appointed to the command of the Roman armies in Macedonia, Perseus showed his inferiority by his imprudent encampments, and when he had at last yielded to the advice of his officers, who recommended a general engagement, and drawn up his forces near the walls of Pydna, B C. 168, he was the first who ruined his own cause, and, by fleeing as soon as the battle was begun, he left the enemy masters of the field. From Pydna, Perseus fled to Samothrace, but he was soon discovered in his obscure retreat, and brought into the presence of the Roman conqueror, where the meanness of his behaviour exposed him to ridicule, and not to mercy. He was carried to Rome, and dragged along the streets of the city to adorn the triumph of the conqueror. His family were also exposed to the sight of the Roman populace, who shed tears on viewing in their streets, dragged like a slave, a monarch who had once defeated their armies, and spread alarm all over Italy, by the greatness of his military preparations, and by his bold undertakings. Perseus died in prison, or according to some, he was put to a shameful death the first year of his captivity. He had two sons, Philip and Alexander, and one daughter, whose name is not known. Alexander, the younger of these, was apprenticed to a Roman carpenter, and led the greatest part of his life in obscurity, till his ingenuity raised him to notice. He was afterwards made secretary to the senate. *Liv.* 40, &c. —*Justin.* 33. c. 1, &c.—*Plut. in Paulo.*—*Flor.* 2. c. 12.—*Propert.*—4. el. 12. v. 39.—*Cic. Tusc.* 5. c. 40.

PER'SIA, a celebrated kingdom of Asia, which, in its ancient state, extended from the Hellespont to the Indus, above 2800 miles, and from Pontus to the shores of Arabia, above 2000 miles. As a province, Persia was but small, and, according to the description of *Ptolemy*, it was bounded on the north by Media, on the west by Susiana, on the south by the Persian Gulph, and on the east by Carmania. The empire of Persia, or the Persian monarchy, was first founded by Cyrus the Great, about 559 years B.C, and under the succeeding monarchs, it became one of the most considerable and powerful kingdoms of the earth. The kings of Persia began to reign in the following order: Cyrus, B.C. 559; Cambyses, 529; and, after the usurpation of Smerdis for seven months, Darius, 521; Xerxes the Great, 485; Artabanus, seven months, and Artaxerxes Longimanus, 464; Xerxes the Second, 425; Sogdianus seven months, 424; Darius the Second, or Nothus, 423; Artaxerxes the Second, or Mnemon, 404; Artaxerxes the Third, or Ochus, 358; Arses or Arogus, 337; and Darius the Third, or Codomanus, 335, who was conquered by Alexander the Great, 331. The destruction of the Persian monarchy by the Macedonians was easily effected, and, from that time, Persia became tributary to the Greeks. After the death of Alexander, when the Macedonian empire was divided among the officers of the deceased conqueror, Seleucus Nicanor made himself master of the Persian provinces, till the revolt of the Parthians introduced new revolutions in the east. Persia was partly reconquered from the Greeks, and remained tributary to the Parthians for nearly 500 years. After this, the sovereignty was again placed in the hands of the Persians, by the revolt of a common soldier, A.D. 229, who became the founder of the second Persian monarchy, which proved so inimical to the power of the Roman emperors. In their national character the Persians were warlike, they were early taught to ride and to handle the bow, and, by the manly exercise of hunting, they were inured to bear the toils and fatigues of a military life. Their national valor, however, soon degenerated, and their want of employment at home soon rendered them unfit for war. In the reign of Xerxes, when the empire of Persia was in its most flourishing state, a small number of Greeks was enabled repeatedly to repel, for three successive days, an almost innumerable army. This celebrated action, which happened at Thermopylæ, shows in a strong light the superiority of the Grecian soldiers over the Persians, and the battles that before, and a short time after, were fought between the two nations at Marathon, Salamis, Platæa and Mycale, are an incontestible proof that these Asiatics had more reliance upon their numbers and upon the splendor and richness of their arms, than upon the valor and discipline of their troops. Their custom, too prevalent among eastern nations, of introducing luxury into the camp, proved also, in some measure, destructive to their military reputation, and the view which the ancients give us of the army of Xerxes, of his cooks, stage-dancers, concubines, musicians, and perfumers, is no very favourable sign of the sagacity of a monarch, who, by his nod, could command millions of men to flock to his standard. In their religion the Persians were very superstitious, they paid the greatest veneration to the sun, the moon, and the stars, and they offered sacrifices to fire, but the supreme deity was never represented by stars among them. They permitted Polygamy, and it was no incest among them to marry a sister or a mother. In their punishments they were extremely severe, even to barbarity. The monarch always appeared with the greatest pomp and dignity; his person was attended by a guard of 15,000 men, and he had, besides, a body of 10,000 chosen horsemen, called immortal. He styled himself, like the rest of the eastern monarchs, the King of Kings, as expressive of his greatness and his power. The Persians were formerly called Cephenes, Achæmenians, and Artæi, and they are often confounded with the Parthians by the ancient poets. They received the name of Persians from Perses, the son of Perseus and Andromeda, who is supposed to have settled among them. Persepolis was the capital of the country. *Curt.* 4. c. 14. l. 5. c. 3.—*Plut. in Artax. Alex. &c.*—*Mela*, 1. c. 2. l. 2. c. 2. l. 3. c. 8.—*Ovid. Fast.* 1. v. 385.—*Lucan.* 8. v. 400.—*Catull.* 91.—*Seneca*, ep. 32.—*Heliodor.* 6 & 9 *Æth.*—*Strab.* 2, 15.—*Xenoph. Cyrop.*—*Herodot.* 1. c. 125, &c.—*Apollod.* 2.—*Marcell.* 23.—*Eustath.* 1 *Il.*

PER'SICUM MA'RE or PER'SICUS SI'NUS, a part of the Indian Ocean on the coast of Persia and Arabia, now called the Gulph of Bassora. *Mela*, 3. c. 8.

PER'SIS, a province of Persia bounded by Media, Carmania, Susiana, and the Persian Gulph. It is often taken for Persia itself.

AU'LUS PER'SIUS FLAC'CUS, a Latin poet, born at Volaterræ in Etruria. He was of an equestrian family, and made himself known by his intimacy with the most illustrious Romans of the age. The early part of his life was spent in his native town, and, at the age of sixteen, he was removed to Rome, where he studied philosophy under Cornutus the celebrated Stoic. He also received the instruction of Palemon the grammarian, and Virginius the rhetorician. Naturally of a mild disposition, his character was unimpeached, his modesty remarkable, and his benevolence universally admired. As a writer he early distinguished himself by his satirical humor, and made the faults of the orators and poets of his age the subjects of his poems. He did not even spare Nero, and, the more effectually to expose the emperor to ridicule, he introduced into his satires some of his verses. The *torva mimalloneis implerunt cornua bombis*, with the three following verses, are Nero's, according to some. But, though he was so severe upon the vicious and ignorant, and attacked the debaucheries of his countrymen with the bold and licentious freedom of vulgar indignation, rather than with the judicious delicacy of a virtuous moralist, he did not forget the homage due to private merit and sincere friendship. The fame and the virtues of Cornutus were celebrated in the pages of the poet, and the character of the preceptor is viewed with additional lustre in lines dictated by the gratitude and respect of the pupil. It was by the advice of this worthy man that he corrected one of his poems, in which he had compared Nero to Midas, and, at his representation, he altered the words *Auriculas asini Mida rex habet*, into *Auriculas asini quis non habet?* Persius died in the 30th year of his age, A D. 62, and left all his books, which consisted of 700 volumes, and a large sum of money, to his venerated preceptor, but Cornutus accepted only the books, and, with commendable generosity, returned the money to the sisters and relations of the deceased. The satires of Persius are six in number, containing 664 verses, blamed by some for obscurity of style and language. But, though they may appear almost unintelligible to some, it ought to be remembered that they were read with pleasure and avidity by his contemporaries, and that the only difficulties which now appear to the moderns, arise from their not knowing the various characters which they describe, the vices which they lash, and the errors which they censure. The satires of Persius are generally printed with those of Juvenal, the best of which will be found to be that of Hennin, 4to, L. Bat. 1695; of Hawkey, 12mo. Dublin, 1746; of Is. Casaubon, Paris, 1605, edited again by Meric Casaubon, London, 1647. Among the English translations are those of Dryden, Owen, and Brewster. *Harles. Not. Lit. Rom.* 1. p. 442.—*Sax. Onom.* 1. p. 252.—*Martial.* 4. epigr. 29. v. 7.—*Euseb. Chron.*—*Quintil.* 10, c. 1.—*Augustin de Magist.* 9.—*Lactant.*—*Crinitus*, 3. *de P. Lat.* [There is a bust of Persius in the Museum of the Vatican, at Rome.]——A man whose quarrel with Rupilius is mentioned in a ridiculous manner by *Horace*, sat. 7. He is called Hybrida, as being the son of a Greek by a Roman woman.

PER'SIUS CA'IUS, an orator in the age of the Gracchi. *Cic. Fin.* 1. c. 3. *Or.* 2. c. 6. *Br* 26.

PER'TA, a town of Galatia. *Ptol.*

PER'TINAX PUB'LIUS HEL'VIUS, a Roman, made emperor after the death of Commodus. He was descended from an obscure family, and, like his father, who was either a slave or the son of a manumitted slave, he for some time followed the mean employment of drying wood and making charcoal. His indigence, however, did not prevent him from receiving a liberal education, and, indeed, he was for some time employed in teaching a number of pupils the Greek and Roman languages in Etruria. He left this laborious profession for a military life, and, by his valor and intrepidity, gradually rose to offices of the highest trust in the army, and was made consul by M. Aurelius for his eminent services. He was afterwards entrusted with the government of Mœsia, and, at last, presided over the city of Rome as governor. When Commodus was murdered, Pertinax was selected by the general voice to succeed to the imperial throne, and his refusal, and the plea of old age and increasing infirmities, did not prevent his being saluted emperor and Augustus. He acquiesced with reluctance, but his mildness, economy, and the popularity of his administration, convinced the senate and the people of the prudence and the justice of their choice. Pertinax forbade his name to be inscribed on such places or estates as were part of the imperial domain, and exclaimed that they belonged not to him but to the public. He melted all the silver statues which had been raised to his vicious predecessor, and exposed to public sale all his concubines, horses, arms, and all the instruments of his pleasure and extravagance. With the money raised from these he enriched the empire, and was enabled to abolish all the taxes which Commodus had laid on the rivers, ports, and highways through the empire. This patriotic administration gained him the affection of the worthiest and most discerning of his subjects, but the extravagant and luxurious raised their clamors against him, and, when Pertinax attempted to introduce among the prætorian guards that discipline which was so necessary to preserve the peace and tranquillity of Rome, the flames of rebellion were kindled, and the affection of the soldiers gradually alienated. Pertinax was apprised of this mutiny, but refused to flee in the hour of danger. He scorned the advice of his friends who wished him to withdraw from the impending storm, and unexpectedly appeared before the seditious prætorians, and without fear or concern, boldly asked them whether they, who were bound to defend their prince and emperor, were come to betray him and to shed his blood. His undaunted assurance and intrepidity would have had the desired effect, and the soldiers had already begun to retire with submission and repentance, when one of the most seditious advanced and darted his javelin at the emperor's breast, exclaiming, "The soldiers send you this." The rest immediately followed the example, and Pertinax muffling up his head, and calling upon Jupiter to avenge his death, remained unmoved, and was instantly despatched. His head was cut off, and carried upon the point of a spear, as in triumph, to the camp. This happened on the 28th March, A.D. 193. Pertinax reigned only 87 days, and his death was the more universally lamented, as it proceeded from the violence of a sudden tumult, and robbed the Roman empire of a wise, virtuous, and benevolent emperor. *Dio.*—*Herodian.*—*Capitol.* c. 12. [A bust of Pertinax will be found in the Vatican, at Rome.]

PERTUN'DA, a goddess among the Romans, who presided over the consummation of marriage. Her statue was generally placed in the bridal chamber. *Varro, apud. Aug. Civ. D.* 6. c. 9.—*Gyrald. H.D.* 1.—*Rosin. R.A.* 5. c. 37.

PERU'SIA, now Perugia, an ancient town of Etruria, on the Tiber, built by Ocnus. L. Antonius was besieged there by Augustus, and obliged to surrender. *Strab.* 5.—*Lucan.* 1. v. 41.—*Paterc.* 2. c. 74.—*Liv.* 9. c. 37. l. 10. c. 30 & 37.—*Propert.* 1. el. 21. v. 1.—*Servius ad Virg. Æn.* 6. v. 133. l. 12. v. 198.

PESCEN'NIUS. *Vid.* Niger.

Pescen'nius, a man intimate with Cicero. *Cic.* 14. *Fam.* 4.

PESENDIÆ, a people of Upper Æthiopia. *Ptol.*

PES'ICI, a people of Hispania Tarraconensis. They are called Pæsici by *Ptolemy*. Their town is now S. Ander.

PES'SINUS or PESSI'NUS (*-untis*), a town of Phrygia Magna, near the Sangaris, where Atys, as some suppose, was buried. It was particularly famous for a temple and statue of the goddess Cybele, who was thence called Pessinuntia. *Strab.* 12.—*Paus.* 7. c. 17.—*Liv.* 29. c. 10 & 11. It is now Possene.

PES'SIUM, a city of the Jazyges Metanastæ. *Ptol.*

PESU'RI, a people of Lusitania. *Plin.* 4. c. 21. The country inhabited by them is now la Comarca di Covilhan.

PE'TA, a goddess who presided over the petitions which were to be offered to the gods, and who, therefore, was consulted to know whether they would prove acceptable. *Arnob. contra Gent.* 3. —*Gyrald. H D.* 1.

PETA'LIA, a town of Eubœa. *Strab.*

PETA'LIÆ, four islands in the Euripus, near the city of Chalcis. *Plin.* 4. c. 12.

PETE'LIA or PETEL'LIA. *Vid.* Petilia.

PETELI'NUS LU'CUS, a grove near one of the gates of Rome. *Liv.* 6. c. 20.

PETEL'LIDES, an historian of Gnossus. *Hygin. P.A.*

PETENI'SUS, a town of Galatia. *Ptol.*

PE'TEON, a town of Bœotia. *Stat. Theb.* 7. v. 333. —*Strab.* 9.

PETESU'CUS, a king of Ægypt, who first built the Labyrinth. *Plin.* 36. c. 13.

PE'TEUS or PE'TEOS, a son of Orneus, and grandson of Erechtheus. He reigned in Attica, and became father of Mnestheus, who went with the Greeks to the Trojan war. He is represented by some of the ancients as a monster, half a man and half a beast. *Apollod.* 3. c. 10.—*Paus.* 10. c. 35.—*Diod.* 1.

PETIL'IA, now Strongoli, a town of Magna Græcia, the capital of Lucania, built, or perhaps, only repaired, by Philoctetes, who, after his return from the Trojan war, left his country, Melibœa, because his subjects had revolted. *Mela*, 2. c. 4.—*Liv.* 23. c. 20.—*Virg. Æn.* 3. v. 402.—*Strab.* 6.—*Plut. in Ann.*—*Servius. ad Virg. loco.*

Petil'ia Lex was enacted by Q. Petilius, the tribune in the consulship of Æmilius Lepidus, and C. Flaminius Nepos, to inquire how much money had been obtained from the conquests over king Antiochus. *Joh. Rosin. Antiq. Rom.* 8. c. 28.

PETIL'II, two tribunes who accused Scipio Africanus of extortion, in his expedition against Antiochus. After Scipio's death, the charge was repeated against his brother Lucius and others, who were condemned. *Liv.* 38. c. 50, 54 & 55.

PETIL'IUS, a prætor who persuaded the people of Rome to burn the books which had been found in Numa's tomb, about 400 years after his death. His advice was followed. *Plut. in Num.*—*Liv.* 40. c. 29.——A plebeian decemvir.——A governor of the Capitol who stole away a golden crown from Jupiter's statue. He was accused, but, though guilty, he was acquitted as being the friend of Augustus. *Horat.* 1. sat. 4. v. 94. & 10. v. 26.——A Roman knight of Syracuse. *Cic. Ver.* 2. c. 29.

Petil'ius Ceria'lis, a lieutenant of the ninth legion in Britain. He afterwards superintended the German war, under Vespasian. *Tacit. Hist.* 3. c. 59.

Petil'ius Quin'tus, one of the judges at the trial of Milo. *Cic. Mil.* 16.

Petil'ius Ru'fus, a prætorian who sought to be nominated consul by the interest of Sejanus. *Tac. Ann.* 4. c. 68.

PETIR'GALA, a city of India within the Ganges. *Ptol.*

PETIS'SIUS, a native of Urbinum whom extravagance and consequent poverty attached to the party of Antony. *Cic. Ph.* 3. c. 8. l. 13. c. 2.

PETOR'SI, a great and populous nation of Libya. *Steph.*

PETOSI'RIS, a celebrated mathematician and astrologer of Ægypt. *Juv.* 6. v. 580.—*Plin.* 7. c. 49.

PETO'VIO, a colony and city of Upper Pannonia. It is called Petavium by *Ptolemy*, Petobio by *Ammianus*, Pœtovio by *Appian* and *Antoninus*, and is now Pettaw.

PE'TRA, the capital town of Arabia Petræa. *Plin.* 8. c. 28.—*Strab.* 16.——A town of Sicily, near Hybla, the inhabitants of which were called Petrini and Petrenses. *Ital.* 14. v. 249.—*Solin.* 11. —*Cic. Verr.* 1. c. 39.——A town of Thrace. *Liv.* 40. c. 22.——A town of Pieria in Macedonia. *Liv.* 39. c. 26.—*Cic. in Verr.* 1. c. 39.——An elevated place near Dyrrachium. *Lucan.* 6. v. 16 & 70.—*Cæs. Civ.* 3. c. 42.

Pe'tra, the name of two Roman knights put to death under Claudius for some superstitious dream. *Tacit. Ann.* 11. c. 4.

PETRA'CHUS, a mountain hanging over Chæronea, in Bœotia. *Plutarch* calls it Petrochous.

PETRÆ'A, one of the Oceanides. *Hesiod. Th.* v. 357.

Petræ'a, a part of Arabia which has Syria on the east, Ægypt on the west, Palestine on the north, and Arabia Felix on the south. This part of Arabia was rocky, whence it received its name. It was for the most part also covered with barren sands, though occasionally interspersed with some fruitful spots. Its capital was called Petra. *Salmas ad Solin.* p. 482.

PETRE'IUS ATI'NAS, a Roman soldier who killed his tribune during the Cimbrian wars, because he hesitated to attack the enemy. He was rewarded for his valour with a crown of grass. *Plin.* 22. c. 6.

Petre'ius, a lieutenant of C. Antonius, the consul, who attacked and defeated the troops of Catiline. He took the part of Pompey against Julius Cæsar, by whom he was defeated in Spain. When Cæsar had been victorious in every part of the world, Petreius, who had retired into Africa, attempted to destroy himself by fighting with his friend king Juba in single combat. Juba was killed first, and Petrius obliged one of his slaves to run him through. *Sallust. Catil.*—*Appian. Cæs.* 1, 2, 3. *Civ.*—*Lucan.* 4. v. 5.—*Cic. ad Fam.* 16. ep. 12. *Att.* 8. ep. 2.—*Sext.* 5. *Vell.* 2. c. 50.—*Hirt. Afr.* 94.——A nobleman of Thessaly, who favored the party of *Cæsar. Bell. Civ.* 3. c. 35.

Petre'ius Mar'cus, a centurion in Cæsar's army in Gaul, slain whilst attempting to break down the gates of Gergovia. *Cæs. Comm.* 7. c. 50. Some read Petronius.

PETRI'NUM, a town of Campania. *Horat.* 1. ep. 5. v. 5. It is now Rocha M di Dragone.

PETROCO'RII, the inhabitants of the modern town of Perigord, in France. *Cæs.* 7. *B. G.* c. 75.

PETROD'AVA, a town of Dacia. *Ptol.*

PETRO'NIA, the wife of Vitellius, whilst a private person. She afterwards married Dolabella. *Tac. Hist.* 2. c. 64.

PETRO'NIUS MAX'IMUS, a Roman emperor. *Vid.* Maximus.

Petro'nius, a Roman appointed governor of Ægypt after Cornelius Gallus. He behaved with great humanity to the Jews, and made war against Candace, queen of Æthiopia. *Strab.* 17.——A favourite of Nero, put to death by Galba.——A tribune killed in Parthia with Crassus. *Polyæn.* 7. c. 41. ——A man banished by Nero to the Cyclades, when Piso's conspiracy was discovered. *Tacit. Ann.* 15. c. 71.——A governor of Britain in Nero's reign. He was put to death by Galba's orders. ——A person raised by means of Ælius to the equestrian order. When Ælius fell on his sword at Placentia, Petronius followed his example. *Val. Max.* 4. c. 7. *de Amicit. ex.* 5.——A præfect of Syria, whom Caligula ordered to place his statue in the temple at Jerusalem. *Joseph. A.J.* 18. c. 11.——A præfect of Noricum, faithful to Otho. *Tac. Hist.* 1. c. 70.

Petro'nius Ar'biter, a native of Massilia, was a favourite of the emperor Nero, and one of the ministers and associates of all his pleasures and debauchery. He was naturally fond of pleasure, and effeminate, and passed his nights in revels, and his days in sleep. He indulged himself in all the delights and gaieties of life, but though he was the most voluptuous of the age, yet he affected moderation in his pleasures and wished to appear curious and refined in luxury and extravagance. Whatever he did seemed to be performed with an air of unconcern and negligence, he was affable in his behaviour, and his witticisms and satirical remarks appeared artless and natural. He was appointed proconsul of Bithynia, and was afterwards rewarded with the consulship, in both of which honorable employments he behaved with all the dignity which became one of the successors of a Brutus or a Scipio. With his offices he laid down his artificial gravity, and again gave himself up to the pursuit of pleasure, the emperor became more attached to him, and seemed fonder of his company, but he did not long enjoy the imperial favour. Tigellinus, likewise one of Nero's favourites, jealous of his fame, accused him of conspiring against the emperor's life. The accusation was credited, and Petronius immediately resolved to withdraw himself from Nero's vengeance by a voluntary death. This was performed in a manner altogether unprecedented, A.D. 66. Petronius ordered his veins to be opened, but to show that he was not eager to hasten the termination of his agonies, he directed them to be closed at intervals. Some time after they were re-opened, and as if he wished to die in the same careless and unconcerned manner as he had lived, he passed his time in discoursing with his friends upon trifles, and listened with the greatest avidity to love verses, amusing stories, or laughable epigrams. Sometimes he manumitted his slaves or punished them with stripes. In this ludicrous manner he spent his last moments till nature was exhausted, and before he expired he wrote an epistle to the emperor, in which he described with a masterly and unsparing hand, his nocturnal extravagances, and the gross impurities of his actions. This letter was carefully sealed, and after he had conveyed it privately to the emperor, Petronius broke his signet, that it might not after his death become a snare to the innocent. Petronius was distinguished by his writings as well as by his luxury and voluptuousness. He is the author of many elegant but obscene compositions still extant, among which is a poem on the civil wars of Pompey and Cæsar, superior in some respects to the Pharsalia of Lucan. Some, however, attribute this to another person, whom they assert to have lived in the age of the Antonines. There is also the feast of the Trimalchion, in which he paints with too much licentiousness, the pleasures and the debaucheries of a corrupt court and of an extravagant monarch; reflections on the instability of human life; a poem on the vanity of dreams; another on the education of the Roman youth; two treatises, &c. The best editions of Petronius are those of Burmann, 4to, Ut. 1709, edited again by his son Caspar Burmann, Lug. Bat. 1743, and that of Antonius, Lips. 1781. *Harles. Not. Lit. Rom.* 1. p. 374.—*Tacit. Ann.* 16, 18, 19.

PETRO'NIUS DIODO'RUS, a physician, who wrote a work called Antilegomena. *Plin,* 20. c. 8.

PETRO'NIUS GRA'NIUS, a centurion of the eighth legion, under Cæsar in Gaul. He fell into the hands of Scipio, as he was sailing to Africa, in the capacity of quæstor, and slew himself. *Plut. in Cæs.*

M. PETRO'NIUS PAS'SER, a Roman, who, when Cato was ordered to prison by Cæsar, followed him. Being reproved for this by the consul, he answered *Malo esse cum Catone in carcere, quam hîc tecum. Varro, de R. R.* 1. 3.

PETROS'ACA, a small region of Arcadia. *Steph.*

PETROSID'IUS LU'CIUS, a standard bearer, who being pressed by the troops of Ambiorix, threw the eagle over the rampart, and fell bravely fighting before the camp. *Cæs. Com.* 5. c. 36.

PETROS'SA, an island of Cilicia. *Steph.*

PET'TALUS, a friend of Phineus, who assisted him in his attempts to disturb the marriage of Perseus and Andromeda. He was killed by Lycormas. *Ovid. Met.* 5. v. 115.

PET'TIUS a friend of *Horace,* to whom the poet addressed his eleventh epode.

PETUA'RIA, a town of the Parisii, in Britain. *Ptol.* It is now Beverley.

PE'TUS, an architect. *Vid.* Satyrus.

PEU'CE, a small island at the mouth of the Danube. The inhabitants were called Peucæ, and Peucini. *Strab.* 7.—*Mela,* 2. c. 7.—*Flacc.* 8. v. 217, 256, &c. —*Lucan.* 3. v. 202.—*Plin.* 4. c. 12.

PEUCELAI'TÆ, a people at the mouth of the Indus. *Dionys.*

PEUCELAO'TIS, a region of India. *Arrian. in Indic. Pliny,* 6. c. 23, calls a city near the Indus Peucolais.

PEUCES'TES or PEUCES'TAS, a Macedonian set over Ægypt by Alexander. He received Persia at the general division of the Macedonian empire at the king's death, but behaved with great cowardice after he had joined himself to Eumenes. *C. Nep. in Eum.—Plut.—Curt.* 4. c. 8.

PEUCES'TES, an island which was visited by the Argonauts on their return from Colchis.

PEUCE'TIA, a part of Magna Græcia at the north of the bay of Tarentum, between the Apennines and Lucania, called also Mesapia and Calabria. It received its name from Peucetus the son of Lycaon of Arcadia. *Strab.* 6.—*Plin.* 3. c. 11.—*Ovid. Met.* 14. v. 513.—*Apollod.* 3.—*Paus.* 10. c. 13.—*Curt.* 1. c. 11.—*Servius in Æn,* 8. v. 9. It is now Terra di Bari.

PEUCI'NI, a nation of Germany, called also Basternæ. *Tacit. de Germ.* 46.

PEUCOLA'US, an officer who conspired with Dymnus against Alexander's life. *Curt.* 6. c. 9.——An officer set over Sogdiana, with 3000 infantry. *Id.* 7. c. 10.

PEU'CRON, a son of the god of the Palus Mæotis, was one of the auxiliaries of Perses, and was slain in the Colchian war. *Val. Flacc.* 6. v. 564.

PEXODO'RUS, a governor of Caria, who offered to give his daughter in marriage to Aridæus the illegitimate son of Philip. *Plut.* Some read Pizodorus.

PHA'CE, a sister of Ulysses, called by others Callisto. *Athen.* 4. c. 15.

PHA'CIUM, a town of Thessaly on the Peneus. *Liv.* 32. c. 13. l. 36. c. 13.—*Thucyd.* 4.

PHACU'SA, a town of Ægypt, on the eastern mouth of the Nile.

PHADIZ'ANA, a fortified place of Cappadocia. *Arrian.*

PHÆ'A, a celebrated sow which infested the neighbourhood of Crommyon. It was destroyed by Theseus as he was travelling from Trœzene to Athens to make himself known to his father. Some supposed that the boar of Calydon sprang from this sow. Phæa, according to some authors, was no other than a woman who prostituted herself to strangers, whom she murdered, and afterwards plundered. *Plut. in Thes.—Strab.* 8.

PHÆA'CIA, an island of the Ionian Sea, near the coast of Epirus, anciently called Scheria, afterwards Corcyra, and now Corfu. The inhabitants, called Phæaces, were a luxurious and dissolute people, for which reason a glutton was generally stigmatized by the epithet of *Phœax.* When Ulysses was shipwrecked on the coast of Phæacia, Alcinous, whose gardens have been greatly celebrated, was then king of the island. *Horat.* 1. ep. 15. v. 24.—*Ovid. Met.* 13. v. 719.—*Strab.* 6 & 7.—*Propert.* 3. el. 2. v. 13.—*Homer. Odyss.* 6. v. 3. l. 7. v. 80. l. 8. v. 6 & 335.—*Virg. Æn.* 3. v. 291.—*Ptol.* 3. c. 14.—*Mela,* 2. c. 7.—*Tibull.* 4. el. 1. v. 78.—*Lucan.* 5. v. 420.

PHÆ'AX, an inhabitant of the island of Phæacia. *Vid.* Phæacia.——A man who sailed with Theseus to Crete.——An Athenian who opposed Alcibiades in his administration.

PHÆCA'SIA, one of the Sporades in the Ægæan Sea. *Plin.* 4. c. 12.

PHÆC'OMES, a Centaur killed by Nestor. *Ovid. Met.* 12. v. 431.

PHÆD'IMUS, one of Niobe's children. *Ovid. Met.* 6. v. 239.—*Apollod.* 3. c. 5.——A Macedonian general who betrayed Eumenes to Antigonus.——A celebrated courier of Greece. *Stat.* 6. v. 558.

PHÆ'DON, an Athenian put to death by the thirty tyrants. His daughters, to escape their oppressors and preserve their chastity, threw themselves together into a well.——A disciple of Socrates. He had been seized by pirates in his younger days, and the philosopher, who seemed to discover something uncommon and promising in his countenance, procured his liberty for a sum of money, and ever after esteemed him. Phædon, after the death of Socrates, returned to Elis his native country, where he founded a sect of philosophers called Elean. The name of Phædon is affixed to one of the dialogues of Plato. *Macrob. Sat.* 1. c. 11.—*Diog.*—*Cic. de N. D.* 1. c. 33.—*Aul. Gell.* 2. c. 18.——An archon at Athens, when the Athenians were directed by the oracle to remove the bones of Theseus to Attica. *Plut. in Thes.*

PHÆ'DRA, a daughter of Minos and Pasiphae, who married Theseus, by whom she became mother of Acamas and Demophoon. They had already lived for some time in conjugal felicity, when Venus, who hated all the descendants of Apollo, because that god had discovered her amour with Mars, inspired Phædra with an unconquerable passion for Hippolytus, the son of Theseus by the amazon Hippolyte. This shameful passion Phædra long attempted to stifle, but in vain, and therefore, in the absence of Theseus, she addressed Hippolytus with all the impatience of a desponding lover. Hippolytus rejected her with horror and disdain; but Phædra, incensed on account of the reception which she met with, resolved to punish him for his refusal. At the return of Theseus she accused Hippolytus of attempts upon her virtue. The credulous father listened to the accusation, and without hearing the defence of Hippolytus, banished him from his kingdom, and implored Neptune, who had promised to grant three of his requests, to punish him in some exemplary manner. As Hippolytus fled from Athens, his horses were suddenly terrified by a huge sea-monster, which Neptune, in compliance with the request of Theseus, had sent on the shore. He was dragged through precipices and over rocks, trampled under the feet of his horses, and crushed to death under the wheels of his chariot. When the tragical end of Hyppolytus was known at Athens, Phædra confessed her crime, and hanged herself in despair, unable to survive one whose death her wickedness and guilt had occasioned. The death of Hippolytus, and the infamous passion of Phædra, form the subject of one of the tragedies of Euripides, and also of Seneca. Phædra was buried at Trœzene, where her tomb was still seen in the age of the geographer Pausanias, near the temple of Venus, which she had built to render the goddess favourable to her incestuous passion. There was near her tomb a myrtle, the leaves of which were all full of small holes, and it was reported that Phædra had done this with a hair pin, when the vehemence of her passion had rendered her melancholy and almost desperate. She was represented in a painting in Apollo's temple at Delphi, as suspended by a cord and balancing herself in the air, while her sister Ariadne stood near to her, and fixed her eyes upon her; a delicate idea, by which the genius of the artist intimated her melancholy end. *Plut. in Thes. & Par.* 47.—*Paus.* 1. c. 22. l. 2. c. 32. l. 10. c. 29.—*Diod.* 4.—*Hygin.* fab. 47, &c. 243.—*Eurip. & Senec. in Hippol.*—*Virg. Æn.* 6. v. 445.—*Ovid. Heroid.* 4.—*Servius.in Æn.* 6. v. 14, 47 & 445. l. 7, v. 61.

PHÆ'DRIA, a village of Arcadia. *Paus.* 8. c. 35.

PHÆ'DRUS, one of the disciples of Socrates, intimate with Plato, who has given his name to one of his treatises. *Cic. de Nat. D.* 1. c. 33.——An Epicurean philosopher. *Cic. ad Att.* 13. ep. 30.

PHÆ'DRUS or PHÆ'DER, a Thracian, who became one of the freedmen of the emperor Augustus. He translated into iambic verses the fables of Æsop, in the reign of the emperor Tiberius. They are divided into five books, valuable for their precision, purity, elegance, and simplicity. They remained long buried in oblivion, till they were discovered in the library of St. Remi, at Rheims, and published by Peter Pithou, a Frenchman, at the end of the sixteenth century. It is remarkable that none of the ancients made mention of the name of the poet, whose literary fame would have remained buried in obscurity, had not the indefatigable zeal of the moderns been directed to the discovery of the long lost monuments of Roman literature and genuine poetry. Phædrus was for some time persecuted by Sejanus, because this corrupt minister believed that he was satirised and abused in the encomiums which the poet everywhere pays to virtue. The best editions of Phædrus are those of Burmann, 4to. Leyd. 1727; Hoogstraten, 4to, Amst. 1701; Barbou, 12mo, Paris, 1754; and Bentley, Cantab. & London, 1726, Amstel. 1727. *Harles. Not. Lit. Rom.* 1. p. 437.

PHÆDY'MA, a daughter of Otanes, who first discovered that Smerdis, who had ascended the throne of Persia at the death of Cambyses was an impostor. *Herodot.* 3. c. 69.

PHÆMON'OE, the first priestess of Apollo at Delphi, who is said to have invented heroic verse. *Plin.* 10. c. 3.—*Strab.* 9.—*Lucan.* 5. v. 126.

PHÆNAR'ETE, the mother of the philosopher Socrates. She was a midwife by profession.

PHÆNIA'NA, a city of Rhætia. *Ptol.* It was called also *Rhæbiana Castra.*

PHÆ'NIAS, a peripatetic philosopher, disciple of Aristotle. He wrote a history of tyrants. *Diog. Laert.*—*Athen.*—*Plut.*—*Suid.*—*Voss. Hist. Gr.* 1. c. 9.

PHÆN'NA, one of the two Graces worshipped at Sparta, together with her sister Clita. Lacedæmon first paid them particular honor. *Paus.* 9. c. 35.

PHÆN'NIS, a famous prophetess in the age of Antiochus. She was daughter of a Chaonian prince, and foretold the irruption of the Gauls from Europe into Asia, nearly 30 years before the event took place. *Paus.* 10. c. 15.

PHÆNODE'MUS, an ancient historian. *Schol. in Aristoph. Crabr.*

PHÆS'ANA, a town of Arcadia on the Alpheus, near Olympia. *Pindar. Olymp.* od. 6.

PHÆS'TUM, a town of Crete. *Homer. Odyss.* 3. v. 296.—*Eustath. ad Dionys. Per.* 88.—*Philostr. de Apol. Thyan.* 6. c. 10.——A town in the middle of Thessaly, at the north of the Peneus. *Liv.* 36. c. 13.

PHÆS'TUS, son of Borus, assisted Priam against the Greeks, and was killed by Idomeneus. *Homer. Il.* 5. v. 43.

PHA'ETHON, a son of Cephalus and Aurora, according to Hesiod and Pausanias, or of Tithonus and Aurora, according to Apollodorus. He is, however, according to the more generally received opinion of Ovid, Hyginus, Lucian, and others, supposed to have been the son of Phœbus and Clymene, one of the Oceanides. Phaethon was naturally of a lively disposition, and possessed of a handsome figure. Venus became enamoured of him, and entrusted him with the care of one of her temples. This distinguishing favor of the goddess, rendered him vain and aspiring, and when Epaphus, the son of Io, had told him to check his pride, that he was not the son of Phœbus, Phaethon resolved to know his true origin, and at the instigation of his mother visited the palace of the sun. He begged Phœbus, that if he really were his father, he would give him incontestible proofs of his paternal tenderness, and convince the world of his legitimacy. Phœbus swore by the Styx, that he would grant him whatever he required, and no sooner was the oath uttered, than Phaethon demanded of him to drive his chariot for one day. Phœbus represented the impropriety of such a request, and the dangers to which it would expose him, but in vain; and as the oath was inviolable, and Phaethon unmoved, his father instructed his son how he was to proceed in his way through the regions of the air. His explicit directions were forgotten, or little attended to; and no sooner had Phaethon received the reins from his father, than he betrayed his ignorance and incapacity to guide the chariot. The flying horses became sensible of the confusion of their driver, and immediately departed from the usual track. Phaethon repented too late of his rashness, and already heaven and earth were threatened with a universal conflagration, when Jupiter, who had perceived the disorder of the horses of the sun, struck the rider with one of his thunderbolts, and hurled him headlong from heaven into the river Po. His body, consumed with fire, was found by the nymphs of the place, and honored with a decent burial. His sisters mourned his unhappy end, and were changed into poplars by Jupiter. *Vid.* Phaethontiades. According to the poets, while Phaethon was unskilfully driving the chariot of his father, the blood of the Æthiopians was dried up, and their skin became black, a color which is still preserved among the greatest part of the inhabitants of the torrid zone. The territories of Libya were also parched up, according to the same tradition, on account of their too great vicinity to the sun; and Africa ever since, unable to recover her original verdure and fruitfulness, has exhibited a sandy country and uncultivated waste. According to those who explain this poetical fable, Phaethon was a Ligurian prince, who studied astronomy, and in whose age the neighbourhood of the Po was visited with uncommon heats. The horses of the sun are called *Phaethontis equi*, either because they were guided by Phaethon, or from the Greek word Φαέθων, which expresses the splendor and lustre of that luminary. *Virg. Æn.* 5. v. 105.—*Hesiod. Theog.* 985.—*Ovid. Met.* 1. fab. 17. l. 2. fab. 1, &c.—*Apollon.* 4. *Arg.*—*Horat.* 4. od. 11.—*Senec. in Medea.*—*Apollod.*—*Hygin.* fab. 156.—*Paus. Att.* 3.—*Lucian. Dial. de Jov. & Ph.*—*Servius ad Æn.* 6. v. 659. l. 10. v. 189.—*Palæph de Inc.* 22.—*Lucret.* 5. v. 397.—*Cic. Off.* 3. c. 25.—*Stat. Theb.* 1. v. 219 —*Tzetzes. ad Lyc.* 704. *Chil.* 4. *Hist.* 134.——A slave mentioned by *Cicero, ad Att.* 3. ep. 8.

PHAETHONTI'ADES or PHAETHON'TIDES, the sisters of Phaethon, who were changed into poplars by Jupiter. *Ovid. Met.* 2. v. 346. *Vid.* Heliades.

PHAETHU'SA, one of the Heliades changed into poplars, after the death of their brother Phaethon. *Ovid. Met.* 2. v. 346.——A daughter of Sol and Neæra. She is represented as keeping her father's herds in Sicily. *Homer. Odyss.* 12. v. 132.

PHÆ'US, a town of Peloponnesus. *Diod. Sic.* 15.

PHAGE'SIA, a festival among the Greeks, observed during the celebration of the Dionysia. It received its name from the good *eating* φαγεῖν and living that then universally prevailed. *Athen.* 1. 7.

PHAG'ITA, a freedman of Sylla, to whom his patron gave the name of Cornelius. *Sueton. Cæs.* c. 74. *Plut. Crass.*

PHA'GO, a remarkable glutton, mentioned by ancient authors. *Varr. apud Non.* 1. 237.

PHA'GRES, a city of Thrace on the Strymon. *Steph. ex Thucyd.* 1. 2.

PHA'INIS, one of the priestesses of Juno at Argos. *Joh. Marsham. Can. Chron.* sec. 9.

PHA'INUS, a native of Elis, an illustrious astronomer, and the preceptor of Meton. *Vitruv.* 9. c. 7.—*Salmas. ad Solin.* p. 737.——The name of a grammarian, often praised by the *Scholiast* on *Aristophanes*.

PHALACH'THIA, a city of Thessaly. *Ptol.*

PHALAC'REUS, a town of Libya.

PHALAC'REUS, a son of Æolus. *Homer. Od.* 10.

PHALACRI'NE, a village of the Sabines, where Vespasian was born. *Suet. Vesp.* 2. It is now Falacrino.

PHALAC'RIUM, a promontory of Sicily. It is now Capo Rascocolmo.

PHAL'ACRON, a promontory of Corcyra. *Steph.*

PHA'LÆ, wooden towers at Rome erected in the circus. *Juv.* 6. v. 589.

PHALÆ'CUS, a general of Phocis, against the Bœotians, killed at the battle of Cheronæa. *Diod.* 16.

PHALÆ'SIA, a town of Arcadia. *Paus.* 8. c. 35.

PHALAN'GES, a people of Æthiopia, on the Sinus Barbaricus. *Plin.* 6. c. 30.

PHALAN'NA, a town of Perrhæbia, at the south of Thessaly. *Liv.* 42. c. 54.

PHALAN'THUS, a Lacedæmonian, who, at the head of the Partheniæ, founded Tarentum, in Italy. His father's name was Aracus. As he went to Italy he was shipwrecked on the coast, and carried to shore by a dolphin, and for that reason, there was a dolphin placed near his statue in the temple of Apollo at Delphi. *Vid.* Partheniæ. He received divine honors after death. *Justin* 3. c. 4.—*Paus.* 10. c. 10.—*Horat.* 2. od. 6. v. 11.—*Sil. It.* 11. v. 16.—*Servius. Virg. Ec.* 10. v. 37.

PHALAN'THUS, a town and mountain of Arcadia. *Paus.* 8. c. 35.

PHALA'RA or PHAL'ARA, a city of Bœotia. *Plin.* 4. c. 7.——A city of Thessaly, near Lamia. *Steph.*

PHAL'ARIS, a tyrant of Agrigentum, who made use of the most excruciating torments to punish his subjects on the smallest suspicion. Perillus made him a brazen bull, and when he had presented it to Phalaris, the tyrant ordered the inventor to be seized, and the first experiment to be made on his body. These cruelties did not long remain unrevenged, the people of Agrigentum revolted in the tenth year of his reign, and put him to death in the same manner as he had tortured Perillus, and many of his subjects after him, B.C. 552. The brazen bull of Phalaris was carried by Amilcar to Carthage; when that city was taken by Scipio, it was delivered again to the inhabitants of Agrigentum by the Romans. There are now some letters extant written by a certain Abaris to Phalaris with their respective answers, but they are supposed by some to be spurious, and their authenticity was the subject of the famous controversy between Boyle and Bentley. The best editions are that of the learned Boyle, Oxon, 1718, and that of Lennep, finished after his death by Valcknaer, Groning. 1777. *Fabr. B. Gr.* 2. c. 10.—*Sax. Onom.* 1. p. 21.—*Cic. in Verr.* 4. *ad Attic.* 7. ep. 12. *de Offic.* 2.—*Ovid. de Art. Am.* 1. v. 663.—*Juv.* 8. v. 81.—*Plin.* 34. c. 8.—*Diod.*——A Trojan killed by Turnus. *Virg. Æn.* 9. v. 762.——A city of Etruria. *Cato.* It is called Phalerium by *Strabo* and *Dionysius.* It is now Falare, according to *Leander*.

PHALA'RIUM, a citadel of Syracuse, where Phalaris' bull was placed.

PHALA'RUS, a river of Bœotia, falling into the lake Cephisus. *Paus.* 9. c 34.

PHALASAR'NA, a city of Crete. *Steph.* It is now Contarini.

PHALA'SIA, a promontory of Eubœa. *Ptol.*

PHAL'CES, an auxiliary of Perses against Æetes, slain by Argus, son of Phryxus. *Val. Flacc.* 6. v. 88.

PHAL'CIDON, a town of Thessaly. *Polyæn.* 4. c. 2.

PHA'LEAS or PHAL'LEAS, a philosopher and legislator, who established an equality of property. *Aristot. Polit.* 11. c. 7.

PHALE'REUS, a man who being given over by his physican, sought death in the field of battle, but being wounded, was cured. *Plin.* 7. c. 50.

PHALE'REUS DEME'TRIUS. *Vid.* Demetrius.

PHALE'RIA, a town of Thessaly at the mouth of the Peneus. *Liv.* 32. c. 15.

PHAL'ERIS, a Corinthian who led a colony to Epidamnus from Corcyra.

PHALE'RON, a city of Thessaly, near Œta. *Steph.*—*Liv.* 27. c. 30, &c.

PHALE'RUM PHALE'RA, (*orum*), or PHALE'REUS POR'TUS, an ancient harbour of Athens, about 25 stadia from the city, which, from its situation and small size, was not very fit for the reception of many ships.

PHALE'RUS, a son of Alcon, one of the Argonauts, who is said to have built a town afterwards called Naples, in Italy, and another in Thessaly, and to have given his name to the port of Athens. *Flacc.* 1. v. 398.—*Paus.* 2. c. 1.—*Tzetzes. in Lyc.* 717.—*Apollòn.* 1. *Arg.* 96.—*Orpheus*, v. 142.

PHA'LIAS, a son of Hercules and Heliconis, daughter of Thestius. *Apollod.* 2.

PHAL'IUS, a Corinthian, son of Eratoclides, who led a Corcyrean colony to Epidamnum. *Thucyd.* 1. 1.

PHAL'LICA, festivals observed by the Ægyptians in honor of Osiris. The institution originated in this: after the murder of Osiris, Isis was unable to recover, among the other limbs, the privities of her husband, and therefore as she paid particular honor to every part of his body, she distinguished that which was lost with more honor, and paid it more attention. Its representation, called *phallus*, was made with wood, and carried during the sacred festivals which were instituted in honor of Osiris. The people held it in the greatest veneration, it was looked upon as an emblem of fecundity, and the mention of it among the ancients never conveyed any impure thought or lascivious reflection. The festivals of the *phallus* were imitated by the Greeks, and introduced into Europe by the Athenians, who made the procession of the *phallus* part of the celebration of the Dionysia of the god of wine. Those that carried the *phallus* at the end of a long pole, were called *phalliphori*. They generally appeared among the Greeks besmeared with the dregs of wine, covered with skins of lambs, and wearing on their heads a crown of ivy. Some of the Greeks suppose that the ceremonies of the *phallus* were not derived from Ægypt, but they assert that Pegasus of Eleusis first taught the Athenians how to worship Bacchus, and that he introduced the use of the *phallus* in the orgies. He was banished, according to their opinion, by the Athenians, who were, for that insult to his person, visited with a terrible distemper in the member which the *phallus* represented, and that they, to appease the god, and in gratitude for the relief which he extended to them, established the procession of the *phallus*. *Lucian. de Deâ Syr.—Plut. de Isid. & Osir.—Natal. Com.* 5. c. 13.—*Paus.* 1. c. 2.—*Herodot.* 2.—*Athen.* 14.—*Gyrald. H. D.* 8.—*Clem. Alex. in Cohort. ad Gent.*

PHALO'RA or **PHALO'RIA**, a city of Thessaly. *Steph.*

PHALO'RIAS, a city of Locris. *Id.*

PHALYS'IUS, a citizen of Naupactum, who recovered his sight by reading a letter sent him by Æsculapius. The letter was carried to him by Anyte, a woman of a poetical genius, and he no sooner recovered his powers of vision than he presented her with 2000 pieces of gold, agreeably to the contents of the letter which he had received, and afterwards erected a temple in honor of the god at Naupactum. *Paus.* 10. *cap. ult.*

PHANÆ'US, a promontory of the island of Chius. famous for its wines. It was called after a king of the same name, who reigned there. *Liv.* 36. c. 43.—*Virg. G.* 2. v. 98, *& Servius loco.*—Apollo received the surname of Phanæus from a temple raised to his honor on the promontory. *Plut.*

PHANAGO'RIA, a city of Asiatic Sarmatia, on the Bosphorus, opposite Theodosia, in Taurica. *Dionys.* v. 552.

PHANARŒ'A, a town of Cappadocia, near the sources of the Thermoden. *Plin.* 6. c. 3.—*Strab.*

PHA'NAS, a famous Messenian, who died B.C. 682.

PHANAS'ORA, a daughter of Pæon, the second wife of Minyas, king of Bœotia, and by him mother of three sons, the eldest of whom was Orchomenus.

PHANDA'NA, a city of Armenia Major. *Ptol.*

PHANDO'RÆ or **PANDO'RÆ**, a people of India. *Plin.* 7. c. 2.

PHA'NEAS, a noble Carthaginian, who revolted to the Romans in the third Punic war. *Liv. Epit.* l. 50.

PHA'NES, a man of Halicarnassus, who fled from Amasis, king of Ægypt, to the court of Cambyses, king of Persia, whom he advised, when he invaded Ægypt, to pass through Arabia. *Herodot.* 3. c. 4.

PHANE'TA, a town of Epirus. *Liv.* 32. c. 28.

PHA'NIA, a man who pretended to be rich, whence the proverb *Phaniæ janua* was applied to such as magnified their possessions. *Eustath. in Od.* 24.—*Cœl. Rh. Art. Lect.* 6. c. 18.

PHA'NIAS, a freedman of Appius Pulcher. *Cic. Fam.* 2. ep. 13.

PHA'NIUM, a character in Terence's Phormio.

PHAN'OCLES, an elegiac poet of Greece, who wrote a poem upon that unnatural sin of which Socrates is accused by some. He maintained that Orpheus was the first who disgraced himself by that filthy indulgence. Some of his fragments are remaining. *Euseb. Chr.—Orosius.* 1. c. 12.—*Stobœus,* 62.—*Clem. Alex. Strom.* 6.—*Gyrald. de P. Hist.* 3.—*Voss. Hist. Gr.* 1. c. 9.

PHANODE'MUS, an historian who wrote on the antiquities of Attica. *Dion. Hal.* l. 1.—*Voss. Hist. Gr.* 1. p. 399.

PHANOD'ICUS, a writer, author of a work called Deliaca, quoted by the *Scholiast* on *Apollonius,* l. 1.—*Laert. in Thal. & Biant.*—*Voss. Hist. Gr.* 1. p. 400.

PHANOS'TRATUS, an archon at Athens, Olymp. 99. an. 2.

PHAN'OTEUS, a city of Phocis. *Steph.*

PHANTA'SIA, a daughter of Nicarchus of Memphis, in Ægypt. Some have supposed that she wrote a poem on the Trojan war, and another on the return of Ulysses to Ithaca, from which compositions Homer copied the greatest part of his Iliad and Odyssey, when he visited Memphis, where they were deposited. *Ptol. Heph.* 5.

PHAN'TASUS, one of the dreams, son of Somnus, and brother of Morpheus and Phobetor. He generally changed himself into rocks, rivers, towns, and mountains, and all inanimate bodies, whilst Morpheus assumes the shape of human beings, and Phobetor that of animals. *Ovid. Met.* 11. v. 642.

PHAN'TES, a son of Ægyptus by Caliande, married Theano. *Apollod.*

PHAN'TIA, a city of Troas. *Steph.*

PHA'NUS, a son of Bacchus, who was among the Argonauts. *Apollod.* 1.

PHA'ON, a boatman of Mitylene in Lesbus. He received a small box of ointment from Venus, who had presented herself to him in the form of an old woman, to be carried over into Asia, and as soon as he had rubbed himself with what the box contained, he became one of the most beautiful men of his age. Many were captivated with the charms of Phaon, and among others, Sappho, the celebrated poetess. Phaon gave himself up to the pleasures of Sappho's company, but, however, he soon conceived a disdain for her, and Sappho, mortified at his coldness, threw herself into the sea. Some say that Phaon was beloved by the goddess of beauty, who concealed him for some time among lettuces. Ælian says, that Phaon was killed by a man whose bed he was defiling. *Ælian. V. H.* 12.—*Ovid. Heroid.* 21. v. 44.—*Palæphat. de In.* c. 49.—*Athen.* 2.—*Lucian. in Sim. & Polistr.*—*Martial.* 10. epigr. 35. v. 17.—*Plin.* 22. c. 8.—*Servius Æn.* 3. v. 279.

PHA'RA, a town of Africa Propria, burnt by Scipio's soldiers. *Strab.*

PHARAC'IDAS, a general of the Lacedæmonian fleet, who assisted Dionysius the tyrant of Sicily against the Carthaginians. *Polyæn.* 2. c. 11.

PHA'RÆ or **PHE'RÆ**, a town of Crete. *Plin.* 4. c. 2.——A town in Messenia. *Paus.* 4. c. 30. *Vid.* Pheræ.

PHARAM'BARA, a town of Media. *Ptol.*

PHA'RAN or **PA'RAN**, a city of Arabia Petræa, and a mountain on the Arabian Gulph. *Ptol.*

PHARAS'MANES, a king of Iberia, reconciled by Tiberius to his brother Mithridates. *Tacit. Ann.* 6. c. 33. There were three kings of this name in the reign of Adrian. See *Casaubon. ad Spartian.* c. 6. *in Hadr.*

PHARAS'TIA, a city of Media. *Ptol.*

PHA'RAX, a Lacedæmonian officer, who attempted to make himself absolute in Sicily. *Diod. Sic.* 14.——A Thessalian, whose son, called Cyanippus, married a beautiful woman called Leucone, who was torn to pieces by his dogs. *Parth. Erot.* 10.

PHARBÆ'THUS, a city of Ægypt. *Steph.*

PHARBE'LUS, a city of the Eretrians. *Id.*

PHARCE'DON, a city of Thessaly. *Id.*

PHAREN'SES, a people of Ionia on the river Melas. *Strab.* 8.

PHA'RIA, an island on the coast of Illyricum with a town and harbour of the same name, called also Pharus, and originally Parus, because peopled by a Parian colony. *Plin.* 3. c. 26.—*Strab.* 7.

PHA'RIO, a river of Armenia flowing into the Tigris. *Plin.* 6. c. 27.

PHA'RIS, a town of Laconia, the inhabitants of which are called Pharitæ. *Paus.* 3. c. 30.——A son of Mercury and Philodamea, who built Pharæ in Messenia. He had only one daughter called Telegone. *Strab.* 8.—*Homer. Il.* 5. v. 544.—*Paus* 4. c. 30.

PHARMACOT'ROPHI, a people of Asia, near Margiana and Susiana. *Plin.* 6. c. 16.

PHARMACU'SA, an island of the Ægean Sea, where Julius Cæsar was seized by some pirates. *Suet. Cæs.* 4.——Another, where Circe's tomb was shewn. *Strab.*

PHARMATE'NUS, a river of Cappadocia. *Arrian. Peripl.*

PHAR'MICAS, a city of Bithynia. *Plin.* 5. c. 32.

PHARNABA'ZUS, a satrap of Persia, son of a person of the same name, B.C. 409. He assisted the Lacedæmonians against the Athenians, and gained their esteem by his friendly behaviour and support. His conduct, however, towards Alcibiades, was of the most perfidious nature, and he did not scruple to betray to his mortal enemies the man whom he had long honored with his friendship. *C. Nep. in Alc.*—*Plut.*——An officer under Eumenes.——A king of Iberia.——A Persian, substituted by the last Darius in the place of Memnon. *Curt.* 3. c. 8. l. 4. c. 5.

PHAR'NACE, a town of Pontus. *Plin.* 6. c. 4.

PHAR'NACE, the mother of Cinyras king of Pontus. *Suidas.*——A daughter of Megessaris, wife of Sandacus. *Apollod.*

PHARNA'CIA, a region and city of Pontus between Cerasus and Trapezus. *Steph.* It is now Farnace.

PHAR'NACES, a son of Mithridates, king of Pontus, who favored the Romans against his father. He revolted against Mithridates, and even caused him to be put to death, according to some accounts. In the civil wars of Julius Cæsar and Pompey, he interested himself for neither of the contending parties, but hoped from their dissensions to raise the fallen power of Pontus, and regain the extensive dominions lost by his father. Cæsar was aware of his ambitious views, and therefore, after the conquest of Ægypt, marched against the unsuspecting monarch, and easily defeated him. It was to express the celerity of his operations in conquering Pharnaces, that the victorious Roman made use of these words *Veni, vidi, vici*. *Flor.* 3.—*Suet. in. Cæs.* 37.—*Paterc.* 2. c. 55.—*Plut. in Cæs.*—*Servius in Æn.* 1. v. 292. —*Hirtius de Alex.*—*Appian. Mithr.* 250.—*Dio.* 42. p. 134.——A king of Pontus, who made war with Eumenes, B.C. 181.——A king of Cappadocia.——A librarian of Atticus. *Cic. ad Att.* ep. 44. l. 13.——A son of Pharnabazus. *Aristoph. Av.*——A noble Persian, brother of the last Darius, slain at the battle of the Granicus.

PHARNA'CIUM, a city of Phrygia. *Steph.*

PHARNAPA'TES, a general of Orodes, king of Parthia, killed in a battle by the Romans.

PHARNAS'PES, the father of Cassandra the mother of Cambyses.

PHAR'NUS, a king of Media, conquered by Ninus king of Assyria.

PHARNU'TIS, a river of Bithynia, near Nicæa. *Suidas.*

PHARODE'NI or PHARODI'NI, a people of Germany. *Ptol.* According to some authors, they were the Suardones of *Tacitus, Germ.* c. 40.

PHARPAR'IDES, part of mount Taurus. *Plin.* 5. c. 27. Read Paryadres.

PHARSA'LUS, now Farsa, a town of Thessaly, near the Enipeus, at the south of Larissa, in the neighbourhood of which is a large plain called Pharsalia, famous for a battle which was fought there between Julius Cæsar and Pompey, in which the former obtained the victory. In that battle, which was fought on the 12th of May, B.C. 48, Cæsar lost about 200 men, or according to others 1200. Pompey's loss was 15,000, or 25,000, according to others, and 24,000 of his army were made prisoners of war by the conqueror. *Lucan.* 1, &c.—*Plut. in Pomp. & Cæs.*—*Appian. Civ.*—*Cæsar. Civ.*—*Sueton. in Cæs.*—*Strab.* 8.—*Catull.* 65. v. 37.—*Cic. Ph.* 14. c. 8.—*Servius in Æn.* 4. v. 696.—*Dio. Cass.*—The poem of Lucan, in which he gives an acconnt of the civil wars of Cæsar and Pompey, bears the name of Pharsalia. *Vid.* Lucanus.

PHAR'TE, a daughter of Danaus, wife of Eurydamas. *Apollod.*

PHA'RUS, a Rutulian killed by Æneas. *Virg. Æn.* 10. v. 322.

PHA'RUS or PHA'ROS, a small island in the bay of Alexandria, about seven furlongs distant from the continent. It was joined to the Ægyptian shore with a causeway by Dexiphanes, B.C. 284, and upon it was built a celebrated tower, in the reign of Ptolemy Soter, and Philadelphus, by Sostratus, the son of Dexiphanes. This tower, which was called the tower of Pharus, and which passed for one of the seven wonders of the world, was built with white marble, and could be seen at the distance of 100 miles. On the top, fires were constantly kept to direct sailors in the bay, which was dangerous and difficult of access. The building of this tower cost the Ægyptian monarch 800 talents, which are equivalent to above 165,000*l.* English, if Attic; or if Alexandrian, double that sum. There was this inscription upon it, "King Ptolemy to the gods the saviours, for the benefit of sailors;" but Sostratus the architect, wishing to claim all the glory, engraved his own name upon the stones, and afterwards filled the hollow with mortar, and wrote the above-mentioned inscription. When the mortar had decayed by time, Ptolemy's name disappeared, and the following inscription then became visible: "Sostratus the Cnidian, son of Dexiphanes, to the gods the saviours, for the benefit of sailors." The word Pharius is often used for Ægyptian. *Lucan.* 2. v. 636. l. 3. v. 260. l. 6. v. 308. l. 9. v. 1005, &c.—*Ovid. A. A.* 3. v. 635.—*Plin.* 4. c. 31 & 85. c. 11. l. 38. c. 12. 13. l. 36. c. 13.—*Strab.* 17.—*Mela,* 2. c. 7.—*Servius Æn.* 11. v. 262.—*Flacc.* 2. v. 318.—*Homer. Odyss.* 4. v. 355.—*Stat.* 3. *Sylv.* 5. v. 102.——A watch-tower near Capreæ.——An island on the coast of Illyricum, now called Lesina. *Mela,* 2. c. 7.—The emperor Claudius ordered a tower to be built at the entrance of the port of Ostia, for the benefit of sailors, and it likewise bore the name of Pharus, an appellation afterwards given to every other edifice which was raised to direct the course of sailors, either with lights, or by signals. *Juv.* 11. v. 76.—*Suet.*——A river of Cilicia. *Suid.*

PHARU'SII or PHAURU'SII, a people of Africa, beyond Mauritania. It was said that they came originally from Asia when Hercules went in quest of the apples of the Hesperides. They lived partly in caves under the earth, and had no covering but the skins of serpents and fishes. *Strab.* 17.—*Plin.* 5. c. 8.—*Sallust, Jug.*—*Mela,* 1. c. 4

PHAR'YBUS, a river of Macedonia, falling into the Ægæan Sea. It is called Helicon by *Pausanias,* l. 9., Bephyrus by *Lycophron,* Baphyrus, by *Livy,* 44. c. 6., and is now Faribo.

PHARYC'ADON, a town of Macedonia on the Peneus. *Strab.* 9.

PHAR'YGÆ, a town of Locris. *Homer. Il.* 2. v. 533. calls it Tarphe.

PHARYG'IUM, a promontory of Phocis. *Strab.*

PHARYN'GÆ, a town of Phocis. *Plut. in Phoc.* Some read Pharygæ.

PHASA'NIA, a town of Africa above the Syrtis Minor. *Plin.* 5. c. 5.

PHAS'CA, a city of Armenia Major. *Ptol.*

PHASE'LIS, a town of Pamphylia, at the foot of Taurus, which was long the residence of pirates. The inhabitants were censured for their impiety towards the gods, to whom they contemptuously offered only small fishes in sacrifice, hence *Phaselitarum Sacrificium* became proverbial. *Mela.* 1. c. 14.—*Virg. G.* 4. v. 289.—*Zenob. Cent.* 6. c. 36.—*Strab.* 14.—*Lucan.* 8. v. 251.—*Cic. Agra.* 2. c. 19.

PHASELUS'SÆ, two islands of Libya, near the river Siris. *Steph.*

PHASIA'NA, a country of Asia, near the river Phasis. The inhabitants, called Phasiani, were of Ægyptian origin. *Diod. Sic.* 14.—*Strab.*—*Plin.* 10. c. 48.

PHA'SIAS, a patronymic given to Medea, as being born near the Phasis. *Ovid Met.* 7.

PHA'SIS, a son of Phœbus and Ocyroe. He slew his mother upon finding her in the arms of an adulterer, for which crime he was so persecuted by the furies, that he drowned himself in the river Arcturus, which afterwards bore his name. Some say that he was father of Colchus. *Plut. de Flum.* —*Eustath. ad Dionys Per.* 692.

PHA'SIS, a river of Colchis rising in the mountains of Armenia, now called Faoz, and falling into the east of the Euxine. It is famous for the expedition of the Argonauts, who entered it, after a long and perilous voyage, from which reason all dangerous voyages have been proverbially intimated by the words of *sailing to the Phasis.* There were on the banks of the Phasis a great number of large birds, of which, according to some of the ancients, the Argonauts brought some to Greece, and which were called on that account *pheasants.* The Phasis was reckoned by the ancients one of the largest rivers of Asia. The ancients often denoted the country of Colchis by the epithet of Phasiacus. *Virg. G.* 4. v. 367.—*Propert.* 1. el. 20. v. 18. l. 3. el. 21. v. 11.—*Val. Flacc.* 1. v. 2. l. 5. v. 422, &c. —*Lucan.* 2. v. 585 & 715. l. 3 & 4.—*Sidon.* 9. v. 63. —*Seneca in Her. Œt.* 948.—*Plin.* 10. c. 48.—*Martial.* 13. epigr. 62.—*Strab.* 11.—*Mela,* 1. c. 19.—*Apollod.* 1, &c.—*Paus.* 4. c. 44.—*Orpheus.*——A river of Taprobane.

PHAS'SUS, a son of Lycaon. *Apollod.*

PHATERUNE'SOS, a desert island near the Thracian Chersonesus. *Plin.* 4. c. 11.

PHATNIT'ICUM, one of the mouths of the Nile.

PHAU'DA, a town of Pontus. *Strab.* 12.

PHAU'RA, a small island of Attica. *Strab.*

PHAUS'GA, a city of Armenia Major. *Ptol.*

PHAVORI'NUS, a writer, the best edition of whose Greek Lexicon is that in fol. Venet. 1712.

PHAYL'LUS, a tyrant of Ambracia, who seduced the wife of Aristo the governor of Œta by his munificent presents. He not only gave her a celebrated collar which was in Minerva's temple, and which was said to be that which once belonged to Eryphile, but also robbed the sacred shrine of all its treasures to gratify her avarice. Like all those who had possessed the fatal collar, the wife of Aristo met a terrible death; her son in a fit of madness set fire to her house, and, with his mother, perished in the flames. Phayllus was likewise punished for his crimes, and as he was hunting, Diana sent a young lion to meet him. This he would have easily vanquished, when the mother rushed to his assistance, and tore the pursuer to pieces. The people of Ambracia were so elated at their sudden deliverance that they erected a statue to Diana, at the foot of which was represented a lioness; and it is even said that they paid adoration to the animal. *Parthen Erot.* 25.—*Antonin Lib.* 4.—*Ælian. H. A.* 12. c. 40.—*Ovid. in Ibin.* 504.——A native of Crotona who built the ship which went from his country to assist the Grecian states in their war against Persia. He had obtained some victories at the Pythian games, and was honored with a statue at Delphi. *Paus.* 10. c. 9.—*Eustath. ad Dionys. Per.* 569.——The brother of Onomarchus, engaged in the Phocian war. *Vid.* Phocis. *Paus.* 10. c. 2.—*Diod.* 5.

PHE'A or PHE'IA, a town of Elis. *Homer. Il.* 7. v. 135.

PHECA'DUM, an inland town of Macedonia. *Liv.* 31. c. 41.

PHE'DIUS, a person who was esteemed by the oracle of Delphi as the wisest and happiest of men. *Plin.* 7. c. 46.

PHE'GIA, a city of Azania in Arcadia, founded by Pheges brother of Phoroneus. It was at first called Erymanthus, and afterwards Psophis. *Steph.* It is now Dimizana, according to *Niger.*——A village of the tribe Ægeis. *Steph.*

PHEGÆ'E, a village of the tribe Pandionis. *Id.*

PHE'GEUS or PHLE'GEUS, a companion of Æneas, killed by Turnus. *Virg. Æn.* 9. v. 765.

PHE'GEUS, another likewise killed by Turnus. *Id.* 12. v. 371, &c.——A son of Alpheus, king of a small town in Arcadia, which afterwards bore his name. He had two sons Temenus and Axion, and a daughter called Arsinoe by *Apollodorus*, and Alphesibœa by *Pausanias*. When Alcmæon, after the murder of his mother, fled to him, he hospitably received him, and, when he had purified himself of the foul crime, gave him his daughter in marriage. He was afterwards put to death by the children of Alcmæon by Callirhoe, because he had ordered Alcmæon to be killed when he attempted to recover a collar which he had given to his daughter. *Vid.* Alcmæon. *Ovid. Met.* 9. v. 412.——A Trojan prince, son of Darces, killed by Diomedes after many acts of valor in defence of his country. *Homer. Il.* 5. v. 11.——A Trojan slave who followed the fortune of Æneas. *Virg. Æn.* 5. v. 263.——A son of Inachus and Melia, brother to Phoroneus, often confounded with the son of Alpheus. *Sch. Eurip. Orest.* 1248.——A priest of Bacchus, who accompanied the god in his Indian expedition. *Stat. Theb.* 2. v. 609. l. 7. v. 603.—*Sch. ad Theb.* 2. v. 303.

PHE'GUS, a village in the tribe Erechtheis. *Steph.*

PHELE-SÆ'I, a people in Japygia. *Id.*

PHEL'LEUS, a mountain of Attica. *Steph.—Schol. in Acharn.*

PHEL'LIA, a river of Laconia. *Paus.* 3. c. 20.

PHEL'LOE, a town of Achaia near Ægira, where Bacchus and Diana had each a temple. *Paus.* 7. c. 26.

PHEL'LUS, a place of Attica.——A town of Elis, near Olympia. *Strab.*

PHEL'LUS, a festival of Bacchus, preparatory to the Dionysia. *Suidas.—Aristoph. Schol. Nub.*

PHE'MIÆ, a city of Arne, so called from Phemius, son of Ampyx. *Steph.*

PHEMIUS, a man introduced by Homer as a musician among Penelope's suitors. Some say that he taught Homer, for which the grateful poet immortalized his name. *Homer. Odyss.* 1 & 22.—*Plut. de Mus.—Gyrald. P. H.* 2.——A man who, according to some, wrote an account of the return of the Greeks from the Trojan war. The word is applied by *Ovid. Am.* 3. v. 7, indiscriminately to any person who excels in music.

PHEMON'OE, a priestess of Apollo, who is supposed to have invented heroic verses, as she was the first who delivered the oracles of the gods in poetry. *Paus.* 10. c. 6.——The name of the Sibyl whom Æneas consulted in Italy, according to *Servius in Æn.* 3. v. 445.——The Pythia, whom Appius consulted. *Lucan.* 5. v. 126.—*Gyrald. de P. H.* 2.

PHE'NEUM, a town of Arcadia, near a small lake of the same name, which was said to emit very dangerous vapours in the night. The inhabitants called Pheneatæ, pretended that Hercules had for some time resided among them in the house of Laonome the mother of Amphitryon. Minerva Tritonia had there a temple, as also Diana, and Neptune Hippeus a statue, which had been raised by Ulysses, who found there his horses, which he had searched for all over Peloponnesus. The chief deity of the place, however, was Mercury, in whose honor games called Hermæa were regularly celebrated. The tomb of Myrtillus, the son of Mercury, was shown there behind his temple, and it was said that the herb called *moly*, a powerful antidote to poison, grew there in great abundance. *Pause.* 8. c. 14.—*Ovid. Met.* 15. v. 332.—*Servius in Æn.* 3. v. 167. l. 8. v. 165.—*Plin.* 4. c. 4.—*Cic. de Nat. D.* 3.

PHE'NEUS, a town with a lake of the same name in Arcadia, the waters of which were very unwholesome in the night, and wholesome in the day time. *Cic. de N. D.* 3. c. 22.—*Virg. Æn.* 8. v. 165.—*Ovid. Met.* 15. v. 332.

PHE'NEUS, a son of Melas, killed by Tydeus. *Apollod.*

PHENOD'AMAS, a Trojan under Laomedon, father of three daughters whom he tenderly loved. He prevailed on his countrymen to decree that the lot should decide which of the Trojan women should be devoured by the sea monster which Neptune had sent to ravage the country, and when Hesione, Laomedon's daughter, was doomed to death, the monarch showed his resentment against Phenodamas, by ordering his three daughters to be exposed to wild beasts. The command was executed by some Sicilian sailors, but Venus preserved their lives, and one of them called Ægesta, became mother of Acestus by Crinisus. *Tzetzes. in Lycoph.* 472 & 952.—*Servius in Æn.* 5. v. 554.

PHE'RÆ, a town of Thessaly, at the west of the Pegasæus Sinus, where the tyrant Alexander reigned, whence he was called Pheræus. *Strab.* 8.—*Cic.* 2. *De Offic.—Ovid in Ib.* 321.—*Val. Max.* 9. c. 13.——A town of Achaia, near Patræ, at the west of the Peloponnesus. There was in the middle of the market-place a beautiful statue of Mercury Agoreus, with a long beard, placed there by Simylus of Messenia, and there also oracles were delivered. Such as wished to consult the god, first offered their prayers to Vesta, whose statue, surrounded with lamps, stood before that of Mercury, and after they had filled the lamps with oil and lighted them, they were permitted to approach the god, and in placing a piece of money in his right hand, to whisper into his ear their petition. They then reverently retired from the altar stopping their ears, and the first words that were heard from those that passed by, were considered as the answer of the divinity. *Paus.* 7. c. 22.—*Strab.* 8.——A town of Laconia in Peloponnesus. *Liv.* 35. c. 30.

PHERÆ'US, a surname of Jason, as being a native of Pheræ, and also of Admetus, whence the epithet is given to his herds. *Ovid de A. A.* 2. v. 239.——A name applied to Alexander the tyrant of Pheræ. *Vid.* Alexander.

PHERAU'LES, a Persian whom Cyrus raised from poverty to affluence. He afterwards gave up all his possessions to enjoy tranquililty and retirement. *Xenoph. Cyr.* 1. 8.

PHER'ECLUS, a Trojan, son of Harmonus, who built the fatal ships in which Paris brought back Helen to his country. He was killed in the Trojan war. *Homer. Il.* 5.—*Ovid. Her.* 15. v. 22.——A pilot of the ship of Theseus when he went to Crete. *Plut. in Thes.*

PHEREC'RATES, a comic poet of Athens, in the age of Plato and Aristophanes. He is supposed to have written twenty-one comedies, of which only few verses remain. He introduced living characters on the stage, but never abused the liberty he had taken either by satire or defamation. He invented a sort of verse which from him has been called Pherecratian. It consisted of the three last feet of an hexameter verse, of which the first was always a spondee, as for instance, the third verse of *Horace's* 1. od. 5. *Grato Pyrrha sub antro. Suidas.—Jul. Pollux.—Fabr. B. Gr.* 2. c. 22. ——An intimate friend of Plato. *Athen.* 3. c. 13. ——A poet descended from Deucalion. His μυρμηκάνθρωπος is praised by the *Scholiast* on *Aristoph. Vesp.—Cic. Tus.*

PHERECY'DES, a philosopher of Scyrus, disciple of Pittacus, one of the first who delivered his thoughts in prose. He was acquainted with the periods of the moon, and foretold eclipses with the greatest accuracy. The doctrine of the immortality of the soul was first supported by him, as also that of the metempsychosis. Pythagoras was one of his disciples, and was remarkable for his esteem and attachment to his learned master. When Pherecydes lay dangerously ill in the island of Delus, Pythagoras hastened to give him every assistance in his power, and when all his efforts had proved ineffectual, he buried him, and after he had paid him the last offices, retired to Italy. Some, however, suppose, that Pherecydes threw himself down from a precipice as he was going to Delphi, or, according to others, he fell a sacrifice to the lousy disease, B.C. 515, in the eighty-fifth year of his age. *Diog.—Lactant.—Paus.* 1. c. 20.—*Cic. Tusc.* 1. c. 16. *Div.* 1. c. 50.—*Servius in Æn.* 3. v. 76.—*Tzetzes. Chil.* 2. *Hist.* 55.—*Vossius. H. Gr.* 4. c. 4.——An historian of Lerus, surnamed the Athenian. He wrote a history of Attica, now lost, and lived in the age of Darius Hystaspes. *Germanic. in Arat.—Laert.* 1.—*Voss. Hist. Gr.* p. 445.——Another historian, supposed to be more ancient than Herodotus. *Cic. Or.* 2. c. 13.—*Salmas. ad Solin.* p. 842.——A tragic poet.

PHERENDATES, a Persian set over Ægypt by Artaxerxes. Olymp. 137. an. 3.

PHEREN'DIS, a town of Armenia Major. *Ptol.*

PHERENI'CUS, an historian of Heraclea, who wrote in heroic verse. *Athen.* 1. 3.—*Tzetz. Chil.* 7. *Hist.* 144.

PHEREPHAT'TA, a surname of Proserpine from the production of corn.

PHEREPHAT'TIA, a festival celebrated at Cyzicus, in which a black heifer was sacrificed to Proserpine. *Plut. in Lucull.—Appian in Mithridatic.*

PHEREP'OLUS, a surname of the goddess of fortune, because she was represented at Smyrna, as bearing the globe on her head with a cornucopia under her arm. *Pindar, &c.—Schol.* 2. *Pyth.—Paus.* 4. c. 30.

PHE'RES, a son of Cretheus and Tyro, who built Pheræ in Thessaly, where he reigned. He married Clymene, by whom he had Admetus and Lycurgus. *Apollod.* 1. c. 9.——A son of Medea, stoned to death by the Corinthians on account of the poisonous clothes which he had given to Glauce, Creon's daughter. Some are of opinion that he perished through the cruelty of his mother. *Vid.* Medea. *Hygin.* fab. 239.—*Apollod.* 2.—*Paus.* 2. c, 3.——A friend of Æneas, killed by Halesus. *Virg. Æn.* 10. v. 413.

PHERE'TIAS, a patronymic of Admetus, son of Pheres. *Ovid. Met.* 8. v. 291

PHERETI'MA, the wife of Battus, king of Cyrene, and mother of Arcesilaus. After her son's death, she recovered the kingdom by means of Amasis king of Ægypt, and to avenge the murder of Arcesilaus she caused all his assassins to be crucified round the walls of Cyrene, and cut off the breasts of their wives, and hung them up near the bodies of their husbands. It is said that she was devoured alive by worms, a punishment which, according to some of the ancients, was inflicted by Providence for her unparalleled cruelties. *Polyæn.* 8. c. 47.—*Herodot.* 4. c. 204, &c.

PHERI'CLES, the eighth perpetual archon at Athens.

PHER'INUM, a town of Thessaly. *Liv.*

PHE'RON, a king of Ægypt, who succeeded Sesostris. He was blind, and recovered his sight by washing his eyes, according to the directions of the oracle, in the urine of a woman who had never had any unlawful connections. He tried his wife first, but she appeared to have been faithless to his bed, and was burnt with all those whose urine could not restore sight to the king. He married the woman whose urine proved beneficial. *Herodot.* 2. c. 111.

PHERO'NIA, a town of Sardinia. *Ptol.*

PHERU'SA, one of the Nereides. *Apollod.* 1.—*Hygin. Præf. Fab.*

PHES'TI, a place of Latium, five miles from the city, where the Ambarvalia were celebrated. *Strab.*

PHES'TUM, a town of Thessaly. *Liv.* It is called Phestos by *Ptolemy.*

PHEUGA'RUM, a city of the Cherusci in Germany. *Ptol.* It is now Halberstad.

PHI'ALE, one of Diana's nymphs. *Ovid. Met.* 3. v. 172.——A celebrated courtezan. *Juv.* 10. v. 238.

PHIA'LIA or PHIGA'LIA, a town of Arcadia. It was destroyed by the Lacedæmonians, Olymp. 30. an. 2. *Paus.* 8. c. 3.

PHI'ALUS, a king of Arcadia. *Id. ib.*

PHI'ARA, a city of Sagarausena, in Cappadocia *Ptol.*

PHICE'ON or PHIC'IUM, a mountain of Bœotia. *Steph.* It was the resort of the Sphinx. *Plut.*

PHIC'ORES, a people near the Palus Mæotis. *Mela*, 1. c. 19.

PHID'IAS, a celebrated statuary of Athens, son of Charmidas, and pupil to Eladas of Argos, who died B.C. 432. He made a statue of Minerva at the request of Pericles, which was placed in the Parthenon. It was made of ivory and gold, and measured thirty-nine feet in height. It was universally admired, not only for its majestic appearance, but for the mythological representations with which it was judiciously adorned, such as the battles of the Centaurs, the Amazons, the birth of Pandora, and of twenty of the gods, in which the workman had shown, not only his taste, but his learning and superior judgment. The serpent and the sphinx, on which the lance in the hand of the goddess was supported, was particularly entitled to approbation, as Pliny mentions in his circumstantial description of it; but as most of these historical events were represented on the shield of the statue, which was ten feet in diameter, their effect was in a great degree lost, as the image placed on a pedestal rendered a distant examination very difficult and indistinct. So celebrated a statue, while it displayed the merit of the artist, did not, however, diminish satirical reflections and malevolent insinuations; and Phidias, charged with arrogance and presumption, was no sooner accused of having carved his own image and that of Pericles on the shield of the goddess, than he was banished from Athens by the clamorous populace. He retired to Elis, where he determined to revenge the ill treatment he had received from his countrymen, by making a statue which would eclipse the fame of that of Minerva. He was successful in the attempt, and the statue which he made of Jupiter Olympius, likewise in gold and ivory, sixty feet high, was always reckoned the best of all his pieces, and passed for one of the wonders of the world. The people of Elis were so sensible of his merit, and of the honour he had done to their city, that they appointed his descendants to the honorable office of keeping clean that magnificent statue, and of preserving it from injury. *Paus.* 9. c. 4. *Cic. de Orat.—Plin.* 36. c. 5. & 8.—*Strab.* 8.—*Quintil.* 12. c. 10.—*Plut. in Per.*

PHID'ILE. *Vid.* Phidyle.

PHIDIP'PIDES, a celebrated courier, who ran from Athens to Lacedæmon, about 152 English miles in two days, to ask of the Lacedæmonians assistance against the Persians. The Athenians raised a temple to his memory. *Herodot.* 6. c. 105.—*C. Nep in Milt.—Solin.* 6.—*Suidas.*

PHIDIT'IA, a public entertainment at Sparta, where much frugality was observed, as the word (Φειδίτια from φειδομαι, *parco*,) denotes. Persons of all ages were admitted; the younger frequented it as a school of temperance and sobriety, where they were trained to good manners and useful knowledge, by the example and the discourse of the elders. *Cic. Tusc.* 5. c. 34.—*Plut. in. Lyc.—Paus.* 3. c. 10.

PHIDO'LAS, an athlete of Corinth, who, after he had fallen from his horse at the Olympic games, had the pleasure to see the faithful animal continue the course, and arrive victorious at the goal. *Paus.* 6. c. 13.

PHI'DON, a man who enjoyed the sovereign power at Argos, and is supposed to have invented scales and measures, and coined silver at Ægina. He died B.C. 854. *Aris. Pol.* 5. c. 10.—*Strab.* 8.—*Paus.* 11.—*Plin.* 7. c. 56.—*Herodot.* 6. c. 127. ——An ancient legislator at Corinth. *Aristot. Polit.* l. 2.

PHID'YLE, a female servant on *Horace's* farm, to whom he addressed 3. od 23.

PHIGA'LEI, a people of Peloponnesus, near Messenia. They were naturally fond of drinking, and negligent of domestic affairs. *Paus.* 8. c. 39.

PHIGA'LIA, a town of Arcadia called after Phigalus, son of Lycaon. Bacchus and Diana had each a temple there, and the public place was adorned with statues of illustrious natives. *Paus.* 8. c. 40.—*Lycoph.* 212.

PHIG'AMUS, a river of Cappadocia. *Arrian. in Peripl.*

PHIG'IA, a city of Arabia Felix. *Ptol.*

PHI'LA, the eldest daughter of Antipater, who married Craterus. She afterwards married Demetrius, and when her husband had lost the kingdom of Macedonia, she poisoned herself. *Plut.*

PHI'LA, a town of Macedonia, founded by Demetrius son of Antigonus Gonatas, near the Peneus. It is now Fello. *Liv.* 42. c. 67. l. 44. c. 2 & 34.——An island of Gallia Narbonensis. *Plin.* 3. c. 5.

PHIL'ACE, a lover of Stratocles. *Plut.*

PHILADEL'PHI'A, now Alah-sher, a town of Lydia. *Plin.* 5. c. 29.——A town of Cilicia. *Plin.* 5. c 18. *Strab.*——A town of Arabia.——A town of Cœlesyria.

PHILADEL'PHUS, a king of Paphlagonia, who followed the interest of M. Antony.——The surname of one of the Ptolemies, king of Ægypt, by antiphrasis, because he destroyed all his brothers. *Vid.* Ptolemæus the Second.

PHI'LÆ, a town and island of Ægypt, above the smaller cataract, but placed opposite Syene by *Pliny*, 5. c. 9. Isis was worshipped there. *Servius Æn.* 6. v. 154.—*Lucan.* 10. v. 313.—*Senec.* 2. *Nat.* 4. c. 2.——One of the Sporades. *Plin.* 4. c. 12.——Four small islands in the Nile. *Plin.* 5. c 9.

PHILÆ'NI, two brothers of Carthage. When a contest arose between the Cyreneans and Carthaginians, about the extent of their territories, it was mutually agreed, that, at a stated hour, two men should depart from each city, and that wherever they met, there they should fix the boundaries of their country. The Philæni accordingly departed from Carthage, and met the Cyreneans, when they had advanced far into their territories. This produced a quarrel, and the Cyreneans asserted that the Philæni had left Carthage before the appointment, and that therefore they must retire, or be buried in the sand. The Philæni refused, upon which they were overpowered by the Cyreneans, and accordingly buried in the sand. The Carthaginians, to commemorate the patriotic deed of the Philæni, who had sacrificed their lives that the extent of their country might not be diminished, raised two altars on the place where their bodies had been buried, which they called *Philænorum aræ*. These altars were the boundaries of the Carthaginian dominions, which on the other side extended as far as the columns of Hercules, which is about 2000 miles, or, according to the accurate observations of the moderns, only 1420 geographical miles. *Sallust. de Bell. Jug.* 19 & 79.—*Sil. It.* 15. v. 704.

PHILÆ'NIS or PHILE'NIS, a courtezan. *Vid.* Philenis.

PHILÆ'US, a son of Ajax by Lyside, the daughter of Coronus, one of the Lapithæ. Miltiades, as some suppose, was descended from him. *Apollon.* 1. v. 57.—*Apollod.* 1.—*Marcell. in Thucyd.*—*Herodot.* 6. c. 35.——A son of Augeas, who upbraided his father for not granting what Hercules justly claimed for clearing his stables. *Vid.* Augeas. He was placed upon his father's throne by Hercules. *Apollod.* 2.

PHILAM'MON, a celebrated musician, son of Apollo by Chione, or, according to others, by Philonis. He was loved by a nymph called Agryope, whom he forsook, and by whom he had Thamyris. He is mentioned as the first who introduced the choral songs in the sacrifices of Apollo Delphius. *Paus.* 4. c. 33.—*Conon. Narr.* 7.—*Hygin.* fab. 200.—*Ovid. Met.* 11. v. 317.—*Apollod.* 1.—*Schol. Homer. Odyss.* 19. v. 432.—*Schol. Apollon.* 1. *Arg.* v. 24.——A man who murdered Arsinoe, and who was slain by her female attendants.

PHILAN'THUS, a son of Prolaus of Elis, killed at the Olympic games. *Paus.* 5. c. 2.

PHILAR'CHI, a people of Arabia Felix. *Strab.*

PHILAR'CHUS, a hero who gave assistance to the Phocians when the Persians invaded Greece. *Paus.* 10.—*Plin.* 35. c. 11.——An historian, mentioned by *Plutarch, in vit. Arat. & l. de Isid. & Osir.*—*Ælian. Hist. An.* 6. c. 29.

PHI'LE or PHI'LES, a Greek writer, under whose name there is extant a miscellaneous collection of verses on birds and animals, in ninety-three different portions, to which fifteen more subjects have been added by Joach. Camerarius.

PHILE'AS, a geographer, who published a work on Asia. *Macrob. Sat.* l. 5. c. 20.

PHILE'MON, a Greek comic poet, contemporary with Menander, son of Damon of Syracuse, or according to *Strabo*, of Pompeiopolis in Cilicia. He wrote ninety plays, and obtained some poetical prizes over Menander, not so much by the merit of his composition as by the intrigues of his friends. Plautus imitated some of his comedies. He lived to his 97th, or, according to some, to his 101st year, and died, as it is reported, of laughing on seeing an ass eat figs, B.C. 274. Some fragments of his plays remain, and have been collected by Hertelius and Grotius. *Fabr. B. Gr.* 2. c. 22.—*Sax. Onom.* 1. p. 86.——His son, wrote fifty-four comedies, of which some few fragments remain, which do not seem to entitle him to a high rank among the Greek comic writers. *Val. Max.* 9. c. 12.—*Quintil.* 10. c. 1.—*Suidas.*—*Lucian. de Macr.*—*Plut. de Irâ. Coh.*—*Strab.* 14.——A poor man of Phrygia. *Vid.* Baucis.——An illegitimate son of Priam. *Apollod.* 3.

PHILE'NE, a town of Attica, between Athens and Tanagra. *Stat. Theb.* 4. v. 102.

PHILE'NIS, an immodest woman, whom Philocrates the poet lampooned. She had written a poem upon lascivious attitudes. *Martial.* 7. epigr. 67 & 70. Read Philænis.

PHIL'EROS, a town of Macedonia. *Plin.* 4. c. 10.

PHILE'SIUS, a leader of the 10,000 Greeks after the battle of Cunaxa.——A surname of Apollo. *Plin.* 34. c. 8 —*Boccat.* I. 3.

PHILETÆ'RUS, a eunuch made governor of Pergamus by Lysimachus. He quarrelled with Lysimachus, and made himself master of Pergamus, where he laid the foundations of a kingdom called the kingdom of Pergamus, B.C. 283. He reigned there for twenty years, and at his death he appointed his nephew Eumenes his successor. *Strab.* 13.—*Paus.* 1. c. 8.—*Justin.* 27. c 3.——A Cretan general; who revolted from Seleucus, and was conquered. *Polyæn.* 4. c. 17.——A comic poet, son of Aristophanes, wrote twenty-one comedies. *Fabr. B. Gr.* 2. c. 22.—*Sax. Onom.* 1. p. 66.

PHILE'TAS, a grammarian and poet of Cos, in the reign of king Philip, and of his son Alexander the Great. He was made preceptor to Ptolemy Philadelphus. The elegies and epigrams which he wrote have been greatly commended by the ancients, and so highly esteemed was his poetry, that he is placed next to Callimachus among elegiac writers. Some fragments of his poetry are still preserved in Athenæus. The poet was so small and slender, according to the improbable accounts of Ælian, that he always carried pieces of lead in his pockets, to prevent being blown away by the wind. *Ælian. V. H.* 9. c. 14.—*Ovid. Fast.* 1. el. 5. *A. A.* 3. v. 330. *Rem.* 760.—*Athen.* 12.—*Propert.* 3. el. 1. v. 1. el. 3. v. 52. l. 4. el. 6. v. 3.—*Suidas.*—*Hesychius.*—*Senec.* ep. 51.—*Quintil.* 10. c. 1.——An historian, who wrote a book called Attica, cited by *Athenæus*, 1. 11, and other books. Some suppose him to be the same as the last. *Voss. H. Gr.* 3. p. 401. *Poet. Gr.* c. 7.

PHILE'TIUS, a faithful steward of Ulysses, who, with Eumæus, assisted him in destroying the suitors, who not only had insulted the queen, but wasted the property of the absent monarch. *Homer. Odyss.* 20, 21 & 22.

PHIL'IA, a promontory of Thrace, at the mouth of the Euxine Sea. *Ptol.*

PHIL'IDAS, a friend of Pelopidas, who favored the conspiracy formed to expel the Spartans from

Thebes. He received the conspirators into his own house.

PHIL'IDES, a dealer in horses in the age of Themistocles. *Plut. in Them.*

PHILIN'NA, a courtezan, mother of Aridæus, by Philip, the father of Alexander.

PHILI'NUS, a native of Agrigentum, who fought with Annibal against the Romans. He wrote a partial history of the Punic wars. *C. Nep. in Annib.—Polyb.* 1.—*Diod. Sic. in Eclog.* l. 23 & 24. ——An archon at Athens in the third year of Heliogabalus.

PHILIPPE'I or **PHILIP'PI**, certain pieces of money coined in the reign of Philip of Macedonia, and with his image. *Horat.* 2. ep. 1. v. 284.—*Liv.* 34. c. 52. l. 37. c. 59. l. 39. c. 5 & 7.

PHILIP'PI, a town of Macedonia, anciently called Datos, and situate at the east of the Strymon on a rising ground, which abounds with springs and water. It was called Philippi, after Philip, king of Macedonia, who fortified it against the incursions of the barbarians of Thrace, and became celebrated for two battles which were fought there in October, B.C. 42, at the interval of about 20 days, between Augustus and Antony, and the republican forces of Brutus and Cassins, in which the former obtained the victory. *Ovid. Met.* 15. v. 824.—*Plin.* 7. c. 45.—*Flor.* 4. c. 7.—*Paterc.* 2. c. 7, &c.—*Appian.* 2. *Civ. Bell.*—*Plut. in Anton.*—*Virg. G.* 1. v. 490.—*Suet. Aug.* 3.—*Mela*, 2. c. 2.—*Val. Max.* 1. c. 5.

PHILIP'PIDES, a Greek comic poet, son of Morsius, or Philocles, according to some. His verses were admired for their elegance and precision, and, from the fragments quoted by Plutarch and Athenæus, and collected by Hertelius and Grotius, appear to have deserved the encomiums bestowed upon them. Philippides was patronized by Lysimachus, whose favors and friendship he largely enjoyed, and he died through excess of joy, on finding unexpectedly one of his compositions rewarded with the poetical prize above one of his rivals. *Plut. in Dem.—Aul. Gell.* 3. c. 15.—*Gyrald. de P. Gr.* 6.—*Fabr. B. Gr.* 2. c. 2.——A courier. *Vid.* Philippides.

PHILIPPOP'OLIS, now Philippopoli, a town of Thrace, near the Hebrus, built by Philip, the father of Alexander. *Liv.* 39. c. 53.——A town of Thessaly, called also Philippi.

PHILIP'PUS the First, son of Argeus, succeeded his father on the throne of Macedonia, and reigned 35 years B.C. 40. *Petav. part.* 2. *rat. temp.* 2. c. 14, &c.

PHILIP'PUS the Second, was the fourth son of Amyntas, king of Macedonia. He was sent to Thebes as a hostage by his father, where he learnt the art of war under Epaminondas, and studied with the greatest care the manners and the pursuits of the Greeks. He was recalled to Macedonia, and, after the death of his brother Perdiccas, ascended the throne as guardian and protector of his youthful nephew. His ambition, however, soon discovered itself, and he made himself independent. The valor of a prudent general, and the policy of an experienced statesman seemed requisite to ensure his power. The neighbouring nations, ridiculing the youth and inexperience of the new king of Macedonia, appeared in arms, but Philip soon convinced them of their error. Unable to meet them as yet in the field of battle, he suspended their fury by presents, and soon turned his arms against Amphipolis, a colony tributary to the Athenians. Amphipolis was conquered, and added to the kingdom of Macedonia, and Philip meditated no less than the destruction of a republic which had rendered itself so formidable to the rest of Greece, and had even claimed submission from the princes of Macedonia. His designs, however, were as yet immature, and before he could make Athens an object of conquest, the Thracians and Illyrians demanded his attention. He made himself master of a Thracian colony, to which he gave the name of Philippi, and from which he received the greatest advantages, on account of the gold mines in the neighbourhood. In the midst of his political prosperity, Philip did not neglect the honour of his family. He married Olympias, the daughter of Neoptolemus, king of the Molossi, and when, some time after, he became father of Alexander, the monarch, conscious of the inestimable advantages which arise from the lessons, the example, and the conversation of a learned and virtuous preceptor, wrote a letter with his own hand to the philosopher Aristotle, and begged him to retire from his usual pursuits, and to dedicate his whole time to the instruction of the young prince. Everything seemed to contribute to his aggrandizement, and historians observed that Philip received in one day the intelligence of three things which could gratify the most unbounded ambition, and flatter the hopes of the most aspiring monarch; the birth of a son, an honorable crown at the Olympic games; and a victory over the barbarians at Illyricum. But all these increased rather than satiated his ambition, he manifested his hostility to the power of Athens and the independence of Greece by laying siege to Olynthus, a place, which, on account of its situation and consequence, would prove most injurious to the interests of the Athenians, and most advantageous to the intrigues and military operations of every Macedonian prince. The Athenians, roused by the eloquence of Demosthenes, sent 17 vessels and 2000 men to the assistance of Olynthus, but the money of Philip prevailed over all their efforts. The greatest part of the citizens suffered themselves to be bribed by the Macedonian gold, and Olynthus surrendered to the enemy, and was instantly reduced to ruins. His successes were as great in every part of Greece, he was declared head of the Amphictyonic council, and was entrusted with the care of the sacred temple of Apollo at Delphi. If he was recalled to Macedonia, it was only to add fresh laurels to his crown, by victories over his enemies in Illyricum and Thessaly. By assuming the character of a moderator and peacemaker he gained the confidence of his too weak and credulous neighbours, and in attempting to protect the Peloponnesians against the encroaching power of Sparta, he rendered his cause popular, and by ridiculing the insults that were offered to his person as he passed through Corinth, he displayed to the world his moderation and philosophic virtues. In his attempts to make himself master of Eubœa, Philip was unsuccessful; and Phocion, who despised his gold as well as his meanness, obliged him to evacuate an island, the inhabitants of which were as insensible to the charms of money as they were unmoved at the horrors of war, and the bold efforts of a vigilant enemy. From Eubœa he turned his arms against the Scythians, but the advantages which he obtained over this indigent nation were inconsiderable, and he again made Greece an object of plunder and rapine. He advanced far into Bœotia, and a general engagment was fought at Chæronea. The fight was long and bloody, but Philip obtained the victory. His behaviour after the battle reflects great disgrace upon him as a man, and as a monarch. In the hour of festivity, during the entertainment which he had given to celebrate the trophies which he had won, Philip sallied from his camp, and with the inhumanity of a brute, insulted the bodies of the slain, and gloried in the calamities of the prisoners of war. His insolence, however, was checked when Demades, one of the Athenian captives, reminded him of the brutal indecency of his conduct, by exclaiming, "Why do you, O king! act the part of a Thersites, when you can represent with so much dignity the elevated character of an Agamemnon?" The reproof was felt, Demades received his liberty, and Philip learned how to gain popularity even among his fallen enemies, by relieving their wants and easing their distresses. At the battle of Chæronea the independence of Greece was extinguished; and Philip, unable to find new enemies in Europe, formed new enterprises and meditated new conquests. He was by the influence of his conquests, and the flattery of his slaves, nominated general of the Greeks against the Persians, and was called upon, as well from inclination as duty, to revenge those injuries which Greece had suffered from the invasions of Darius and Xerxes. But he was stopped in the midst of his warlike preparations, he was stabbed by Pausanias as he entered the theatre at the celebration of the nuptials of his daughter Cleopatra. This murder has given rise to various reflections upon the causes which produced it, and many who consider the recent repudiation of Olympias, and the resentment of Alexander, are apt to trace the causes of his death into the bosom of his family. The ridiculous honours which Olympias paid to her husband's murderer strengthened the suspicion, yet Alexander declared that he invaded the kingdom of Persia to revenge his father's death upon the Persian satraps and princes, by whose immediate intrigues the assassination had been committed. The character of Philip was that of a sagacious, artful, prudent, and intriguing monarch, he was brave in the field of battle, eloquent and dissimulating at home, and possessed the wonderful art of changing his conduct according to the disposition and caprice of mankind, without ever altering his purpose, or losing sight of his ambitious aims. He possessed much perseverance, and in the execution of his plans he was always vigorous. The hand of an assassin prevented him from achieving the boldest and the most extensive of his undertakings, and he might have acquired as many laurels, and conquered as many nations as his son Alexander did in the succeeding reign, and the kingdom of Persia might have been added to the Macedonian empire, perhaps with greater moderation, with more glory, and with more lasting advantages. The private character of Philip lies open to censure, and raises indignation. The admirer of his virtues is disgusted to find him among the most abandoned prostitutes, and disgracing himself by the most unnatural crimes and lascivious indulgences which can make even the most debauched and the most profligate blush. He was murdered in the 47th year of his age, and the 24th of his reign, about 336 years B.C. His reign is become uncommonly interesting, and his administra ion a matter of instruction. He is not only the first monarch whose life and actions are described with peculiar accuracy and historical faithfulness, but the sagacious prince who elevated Macedonia to an eminent rank among nations, and laid the foundations of those victorious armies which a few years after changed the face of the world, by the destruction of an ancient monarchy, and the introduction of the arts, the language, the manners, and intrigues of Greece into Asia. Philip was the father of Alexander the Great and of Cleopatra, by Olympias; he had also by Audaca, an Illyrian, Cyna, who married Amyntas, the son of Perdiccas, Philip's elder brother; by Nicasipolis, a Thessalian, Nicæa, who married Cassander; by Philinna, a Larissæan dancer, Aridæus, who reigned some time after Alexander's death; by Cleopatra, the niece of Attalus, Caranus, and Europa, who were both murdered by Olympias; and Ptolemy, the first king of Ægypt, by Arsinoe, who in the first month of her pregnancy was married to Lagus. *Demosth. in Phil. & Olynth.—Justin.* 7, &c.—*Diod.* 16.—*Plut. in Alex. Dem. & Apoph.—Isocrat. ad. Phil.—Curt.* 1, &c.—*Æschines.—Paus. Bœotic.* &c.—*Juv.* 10. v. 125. [There is a bust of Philip in the Palace of the Conservators at Rome.]

PHILIP'PUS the Third, was brother of Alexander the Great. *Vid.* Aridæus.

PHILIP'PUS the Fourth, succeeded his father Cassander, A.U.C. 456, and reigned one year. *Justin.* 1. 15 & 16.—*Diod. Sic.—Euseb.*

PHILIP'PUS the Fifth, the last king of Macedonia, of that name, was son of Demetrius. His infancy, after the death of his father, was protected by Antigonus Doson, one of his friends, who ascended the throne, and reigned for twelve years. When Antigonus died, Philip recovered his father's throne, though only 15 years of age, and early distinguished himself by his boldness and ambitious views. His cruelty, however, to Aratus, soon displayed his character in its true light. Not satisfied with the kingdom of Macedonia, Philip aspired to become the friend of Annibal, and wished to share with him in the spoils which the distresses and long continued defeats of the Romans seemed soon to promise. But his expectations were frustrated, the Romans discovered his intrigues, and though weakened by the valor and artifice of the Carthaginians, yet they were soon enabled to meet him in the field of battle. The consul Lævinus entered without delay his territories in Macedonia, and, after he had obtained a victory over him near Apollonia, and reduced his fleet to ashes, he compelled him to sue for peace. This peace was not permanent; and, when the Romans discovered that he had assisted their immortal enemy, Annibal, with men and money, they appointed T. Q. Flaminius to punish his perfidy, and the violation of the treaty. The Roman consul with his usual expedition, invaded Macedonia, and, in a general engagement, which was fought near Cynocephale, the hostile army was totally defeated, and the monarch saved his life with difficulty by fleeing from the field of battle. Destitute of resources, without friends either at home or abroad, Philip was obliged to submit to the mercy of the conqueror, and to demand peace by his ambassadors. It was granted with difficulty, the terms were humiliating, but the poverty of Philip obliged him to accept the conditions, however disadvantageous and degrading to his dignity. In the midst of these public calamities, the peace of his family was disturbed; and Perses, the eldest of his sons by a concubine, raised seditions against his brother Demetrius, whose condescension and humanity had gained popularity among the Macedonians, and who, from his residence at Rome, as a hostage, had procured the good graces of the senate, and by the modesty and innocence of his manners, had obtained forgiveness from that venerable body for the hostilities of his father. Philip listened with too much avidity to the false accusation of Perses; and when he heard it asserted that Demetrius wished to rob him of his crown, he no longer hesitated to punish with death so unworthy and so ungrateful a son. No sooner was Demetrius sacrificed to credulity, than Philip became convinced of his cruelty and rashness, and, to punish the perfidy of Perses, attempted to make Antigonus, another son, his successor on the Macedonian throne. But he was prevented from executing his purpose by death, in the 42nd year of his reign, 179 years B.C. The assassin of Demetrius succeeded his father, and, with the same ambition, with the same rashness and oppression, renewed the war against the Romans, till his empire was destroyed, and Macedonia became a Roman province. Philip has been compared with his great ancestor of the same name, but, though they possessed the same virtues, the same ambition, and were tainted with the same vices, yet the father of Alexander was more sagacious and more intriguing, and the son of Demetrius was more suspicious, more cruel, and more implacable, and, according to the pretended prophecy of one of the Sibyls, Macedonia was indebted to one Philip for her rise and consequence among nations, and under another Philip she lamented the loss of her power, her empire, and her dignity. *Polyb.* 16, &c.—*Justin,* 29, &c.—*Plut. in Flam.—Paus.* 7. c. 8.—*Liv.* 31, &c.—*Val. Max.* 4. c. 8.—*Orosius,* 4. c. 20.—*Eutrop.* 4. c. 1.—*Ital.* 15. v. 286.

PHILIP'PUS M. JU'LIUS, a Roman emperor, of an obscure family in Arabia, from whence he was surnamed Arabian. From the lowest rank in the army he gradually rose to the highest offices, and, when he was made general of the prætorian guards, he assassinated Gordian to make himself emperor. To establish himself with more certainty on the imperial throne, he left Mesopotamia a prey to the continual invasions of the Persians, and hurried to Rome, where his election was universally approved by the senate and the Roman people. Philip rendered his cause popular by his liberality and profusion, and it added much to his splendour and dignity that the Romans during his reign commemorated the foundation of their city, a solemnity which was observed but once every hundredth year, and which was celebrated with more pomp and more magnificence than under the preceding reigns. The people were entertained with games and spectacles, the theatre of Pompey was successively crowded during three days and three nights, and 2000 gladiators bled in the circus at once, for the amusement and pleasure of a gazing populace. His usurpation, however, was short, Philip was defeated by Decius, who had proclaimed himself emperor in Pannonia, and he was assassinated by his own soldiers near Verona, in the 45th year of his age, and the fifth of his reign A.D. 249. His son who bore the same name, and who had shared with him the imperial dignity, was also massacred in the arms of his mother. *Aurel. Victor.—Zosim.—Jul. Capitol. in vit. Gordian.*

PHILIP'PUS, a son of Antiochus Gryphus, king of part of Syria. *Joseph.* 13. c. 21.——A native of Acarnania, physician to Alexander the Great. When the monarch had been suddenly taken ill, after bathing in the Cydnus, Philip undertook to remove the complaint, when the rest of the physicians believed that all medical assistance would be ineffectual. But as he was preparing his medicine, Alexander received a letter from Parmenio, in which he was advised to beware of his physician Philip, as he had conspired against his life. The monarch was alarmed, and, when Philip presented him his medicine, he gave him Parmenio's letter to peruse, and began to drink the potion. The serenity and composure of Philip's countenance, as he read the letter, removed every suspicion from Alexander's breast. He pursued the directions of his physician, and in a few days recovered. *Plut. in Alex.—Curt.* 9. c. 5.—*Arrian.* 2.——A son of Alexander the Great, murdered by Olympias.——A leader of the Thessalians in the army of Alexander the Great, slain in India, where Alexander had left him with the command. *Curt.* 10. c. 1.——A governor of Sparta.——A son of Cassander.——A man who pretended to be the son of Perses, that he might lay claim to the kingdom of Macedonia. He was called *Pseudophilippus.*——A general of Cassander, in Ætolia.——A Phrygian, made governor of Jerusalem by Antiochus.——A son of Herod the Great, in the reign of Augustus, was governor of Gaulonitis, Ituræa, and Trachonitis. He died without issue, and Tiberius added these provinces to Syria. *Luc.* c. 3. v. 1.—*Joseph. J.A.* 17. c. 1, &c.——A freedman of Pompey the Great. He found his master's body on the seashore, in Ægypt, and gave it a decent burial with the assistance of an old Roman soldier, who had fought under Pompey.——The father-in-law of the emperor Augustus.——A Lacedæmonian who wished to make himself absolute in Thebes.——An officer, made master of Parthia, after the death of Alexander the Great.——A son of Antipater, in the army of Alexander. *Curt.* 6. c. 10.——A brother of Lysimachus, who died suddenly after hard walking and labour. *Curt.* 8. c. 2.——An historian of Amphipolis. *Suidas.*——A man who wrote a history of Caria. *Strab.* l. 14.—*Athen.* l. 6.——A native of Megara, mentioned by *Diogenes Laertius in Stilpon.*——A native of Sida in Pamphylia, under Theodosius, who wrote a diffuse history from the creation down to his own time. It was not much valued. *Socr. Hist.* 7. c. 27.—*Niceph. Calist.* 14. c. 29.—*Phot. Cod.* 35.—*Voss. Hist. Gr.* 2. c. 20. The Marcian family at Rome took the name of Philippi, of whom L. Marcius, an orator of some eminence, and a man of great integrity, was consul, A.U. 663. *Cic. Off.* 2. c. 17. His son Lucius was consul, A.U. 698, and was step-father to Octavius. *Cic. Phil.* 3. c. 10. *Fam.* 1. ep. 9. [There are busts of Lucius Marcus and his son in the Museum of the Capitol, at Rome.]

PHILIS'CUM, a town of Parthia on the Euphrates. *Plin.* 5. c. 26.

PHILIS'CUS, a famous sculptor, whose statues of Latona, Venus, Diana, the Muses, and a naked Apollo, were preserved in the portico belonging to Octavia.——A Greek comic poet. Some of his plays are mentioned by *Suidas. Fabr. B. Gr.* 2. c. 22. *Plin.* 11. c. 9.

PHILIS'CUS or PHIL'ICUS, a native of Corcyra, one of the poets called Pleiades. He wrote 42 tragedies. *Fabr. ibid.* 2. c. 19.——A tragic poet of Ægina. He was author of the epigram upon Lycias, which *Plutarch* has preserved in his lives of the ten orators. *Fabr. ibid.*——An Athenian who received Cicero when he fled to Macedonia. *Dion. Epit. in Pomp.*——An officer of Artaxerxes, appointed to make peace with the Greeks. *Diod. Sic.* 15.

PHILISTI'DES, an historian or geographer mentioned by *Pliny*, 4. c. 12. *Salmas ad Solin.* p. 169.

PHILISTI'NÆ FOS'SÆ, one of the mouths of the Po, called by some Tartarus. *Plin.* 3. c. 16. *Tacitus, Hist.* 3. c. 9, mentions a river called Tartarus.

PHILIS'TION, a comic poet of Nicæa, in the age of Socrates, who is said to have died from excessive laughter. Rigaltius edited a work under the title of "Σύγκρισις *sententiarum Philistionis,*" Paris, 1613: but he supposes, and so does Burmann, that these verses are the production of Philemon. This work was re-edited with a translation by Rutgersius, and notes by Heinsius, L. Bat. 1618. Amstel. 1654. *Fabr. B. Gr.* 2. c. 22.—*Suidas—Cassiodor.* 4. *Var.—Gyrald. de P. H.* 8.—*Martial.* 2 epigr. 41.——A physician of Locris. *A. Gell.* 7. c. 12.

PHILIS'TUS, a musician of Miletus.——A Syracusian, who, during his banishment from his native country, wrote a history of Sicily in 12. books, which was commended by some, though censured for inaccuracy by *Pausanias.* He was afterwards sent against the Syracusans by Dionysius the younger, and killed himself when overcome by the enemy, 356 B.C. *Plut. in Dion.—Diod.* 5 & 13.—*Dionys. Hal.* 1.—*Cic. Div.* 1. c. 20, &c.—*Voss. H. Gr.* 1 c. 6.

PHIL'LO, an Arcadian maid, by whom Hercules had a son. The father, named Alcmedon, exposed his daughter, but she was saved by means of her lover, who was directed to the place by the chirping of a magpie, which imitated the plaintive cries of a child. *Paus.* 8. c. 12.

PHI'LO, a Jewish writer of Alexandria, A.D. 40, sent as ambassador from his nation to Caligula. He was unsuccessful in his embassy, of which he wrote an entertaining account; and the emperor, who wished to be worshipped as a god, expressed his dissatisfaction with the Jews, because they refused to places his statues in their temples. He was so happy in his expressions, and elegant in his variety, that he was called the Jewish Plato, and the Greeks in admiration of his great talent, used the common saying of "Either Plato Philonizes or Philo Platonizes;" and the book which he wrote on the sufferings of the Jews in the reign of Caius, met with such unbounded applause in the Roman senate, where he read it publicly, that he was permitted to consecrate it in the public libraries. His works were divided into three parts, of which the first related to the creation of the world, the second spoke of sacred history, and in the third the author made mention of the laws and customs of the Jewish nation. The best editions of Philo are that of Mangey, 2 vols. fol. London, 1742, and that of Pfeiffer, Erlang. 1785. *Fabr. B. Gr.* 4. c. 6.—*Sax. Onom.* 1. p. 240.——A man who fell in love with his daughter called Proserpine, as she was bathing. He had by her a son, Mercurius Trismegistus.——A man who wrote an account of a journey to Æthiopia. *Strab.* 2.——A philosopher who followed the doctrines of Carneades, B.C. 100.——A philosopher of Athens, who left his country in the Mithridatic war, and came to Rome where he taught rhetoric, and was preceptor to Cicero. *Cic. in Acad.* 4. c. 6. *In Bruto,* 89. *Tusc.* 2. c. 3. *Fam.* 13. ep. 1.——A Theban, at whose house Philip lodged when sent as a hostage to Bœotia. *Plut. de Scite Dict.*——A grammarian in the first century.——An architect of Byzantium, who flourished about three centuries before the Christian era. He built a dock at Athens, into which ships were drawn in safety and protected from the storm. *Plut. in Syll.—Cic. in Orat.* 1. c. 14.——A Greek Christian writer, whose work was edited at Rome, 4to, 1772.——A dialectic philosopher, 260 B.C.——A freedman of Pompey. *Cic. Att.* 16, ep. 3. *Jonsius,* 1. 3, *de script. hist. Philos. & Fabricius, B. Gr.* 4. c. 6, have enumerated many more persons of this name.

PHILO'BIA, the wife of Perseus the governor of Troy in the reign of Priam.

PHILOBŒO'TUS, a mountain of Bœotia. *Plut.*

PHILOCALI'A or PHILOCALE'A, a fortified place of Themiscyra, not far from the river Tripolis. *Plin.* 6. c. 4.

PHILOCAN'DRUS, one of the Cyclades. *Ptol.*

PHILOCH'ARES, a painter, one of whose pieces was placed in the senate-house by Augustus. *Plin.* 35. c. 4.

PHILOCH'ORUS, a man who wrote a history of Athens in 17 books, besides a catalogue of the archons, two books of Olympiads, an account of Salamis, a treatise on sacrifices, &c. He died B.C.

222. *Vossius, H. Gr.* 1. c. 18.—*Fabr. B. Gr.* 2. c. 22.

PHIL'OCLES, one of the admirals of the Athenian fleet, during the Peloponnesian war. He recommended to his countrymen to cut off the right hand of such of the enemies as were taken, that they might be rendered unfit for future service. His plan was adopted by all the ten admirals except one, but their expectations were frustrated, and instead of being conquerers, they were totally defeated at Ægospotamus by Lysander, and Philocles with 3000 of his countrymen were put to death, and refused the honors of sepulture. *Paus.* 9. c. 32.—*Plut. in Lys.*——A general of Ptolemy, king of Ægypt. *Polyæn.* 3. *in. fin.* c. 16. Some MSS. read Diocles.——A tragic poet of Athens, nephew to Æschylus. He was ugly in his person and morose in his temper. He gained the prize, though Sophocles was one of his competitors and recited the Œdipus, a circumstance mentioned with indignation by Aristides. *Fabr. B. Gr.* 2. c. 19.—*Suidas.*—*Gyrald. P. H.* 7.——A tragic poet, son of Astydamas. *Aristoph. Schol. ad aves.* 282.—*Fabr. Ibid.*

PHILOCRATES, an Athenian accused of betraying his country to Philip, and of disgracing himself by his effeminate morals and intemperance. *Lucian. Dial. Paras.*—*Demosth. Ph.* 2.—*Plut. in Symp.* 4, *& de Fort.*——A writer who published a history of Thessaly. *Athen.* l. 6.——A servant of C. Gracchus.——A Greek orator.

PHILOCTE'MON, a luxurious Athenian. *Aristoph. in Crabr. & Scholiast.*

PHILOCTETES, son of Pœan and Demonassa, was one of the Argonauts, according to Flaccus and Hyginus, and the arm-bearer and particular friend of Hercules. He was present at the death of Hercules, and because he had erected the burning pile on which the hero was consumed, he received from him the arrows which had been dipped in the gall of the hydra, after he had bound himself by a solemn oath not to betray the place where his ashes were deposited. He had no sooner paid the last offices to Hercules, than he returned to Melibœa, where his father reigned. He next visited Sparta, where he became one of the numerous suitors of Helen, and soon after, like the rest of those princes who had courted the daughter of Tyndarus, and who had bound themselves to protect her from injury, he was called upon by Menelaus to accompany the Greeks to the Trojan war, and immediately set sail from Melibœa with seven ships, and repaired to Aulis, the general rendezvous of the combined fleet. He was here prevented from joining his countrymen, and the offensive smell which arose from a wound in his foot, obliged the Greeks, at the instigation of Ulysses, to remove him from the camp, and he was accordingly carried to the island of Lemnus, or, as others say, to Chryse, where Phimachus, the son of Dolophion, was ordered to wait upon him. In this solitary retreat he was suffered to remain for some time, till the Greeks, in the tenth year of the Trojan war, were informed by the oracle that Troy could not be taken without the arrows of Hercules, which were then in the possession of Philoctetes. Upon this Ulysses, accompanied by Diomedes, or according to others by Pyrrhus, was commissioned by the rest of the Grecian army to go to Lemnus, and to prevail upon Philoctetes to come and finish the tedious siege. Philoctetes recollected the ill-treatment he had received from the Greeks, and particularly from Ulysses, and therefore he not only refused to go to Troy, but even persuaded Pyrrhus to conduct him to Melibœa. As he embarked, the manes of Hercules forbade him to proceed, but immediately to repair to the Grecian camp, where he should be cured of his wounds, and put an end to the war. Philoctetes obeyed; and after he had been restored to his former health by Æsculapius, or, according to some, by Machaon, or Podalirius, he destroyed a greta number of the Trojans, among whom was Paris, the son of Priam, with the arrows of Hercules. When by his valor Troy had been ruined, he set sail from Asia, but as he was unwilling to visit his native country, he came to Italy, where, by the assistance of his Thessalian followers, he was enabled to build a town in Calabria, which he called Petilia. Authors disagree about the causes of the wound which Philoctetes received on the foot. The most ancient mythologists support, that it was the bite of the serpent which Juno had sent to torment him, because he had attended Hercules in his last moments, and had buried his ashes. According to another opinion, the princes of the Grecian army obliged him to discover where the ashes of Hercules were deposited, and as he had made an oath not to mention the place, he only with his foot struck the ground where they lay, and by this means concluded he had not violated his solemn engagement. For this, however, he was soon after punished, and the fall of one of the poisoned arrows from his quiver upon the foot which had struck the ground, occasioned so offensive a wound that the Greeks were obliged to remove him from their camp. The sufferings and adventures of Philoctetes are the subject of one of the best tragedies of Sophocles. *Homer. Il.* 2. *Enum.* 225, &c.—*Virg. Æn.* 3. v. 46.—*Pindar. Pyth.* 1.—*Dictys. Cret.* 1. c. 14.—*Senec in. Herc.*—*Sophocl. Phil.*—*Quint. Calab.* 9 & 10.—*Hygin.* fab. 26, 97 & 102.—*Diod.* 2 & 4.—*Ovid. Met.* 13. v. 329. l. 9. 5. 234. *Trist.* 5. el. 2.—*Cic. Tusc.* 2. 7.—*Ptolem. Hæph.* 6.—*Philostr.* ic. 17, & her. 5.—*Lactant. de Fals. R.* 9.—*Servius. Æn.* 3. v. 402. l. 8. v. 300.—*Eustath. in Hom.*—*Tzetzes ad Lyc.* 911.—*Propert.* 2. el. 1. v. 61.—*Flacc.* 2. v. 571.—*Schol. ad Hom. Il.* 2, &c.—*Conon. Narr.* 23.

PHILOCY'PRUS, a prince of Cyprus in the age of Solon, by whose advice he changed the situation of a city, which in gratitude he called Soli. *Plut. in Sol.*

PHILODAME'A or PHILODAMI'A, one of the Danaides, mother of Phares by Mercury. *Paus.* 7. c. 22.

PHILODA'MUS, a man of Lampsacus, to whose daughter Verres attempted to offer violence. His disappointment was revenged by the murder of the innocent woman and of her father. *Cic. Ver.* 1 c. 25, &c.

PHILODE'MUS, a poet of Gadara, in the age of Cicero, who rendered himself known by his lascivious and indelicate verses. *Cic. de Finib.* 2. c 35.—*Anthol.* 1.—*Gassend. Vita Epicur.* 2. c. 6.—*Horat.* 1. sat. 2. v. 121.——A comic poet, ridiculed by *Aristophanes. Athenæus.*

PHILOD'ICE, a daughter of Inachus, who married Leucippus. *Apollod.*

PHILOD'OCUS, a Lacedæmonian sent to Rhodes, to put down a faction, Olymp. 97. an. 2.

PHILODO'RUS, a native of Tralles in Lydia, mentioned by *Cicero, Flacc.* 22.

PHILOG'ENES, a slave in the family of Atticus. *Cic. Att.* 5. ep. 13.

PHILOLA'US, a son of Minos, by the nymph Paria, from whom the island of Parus received its name. Hercules put him to death, because he had killed two of his companions. *Apollod.* 3. c. 1.——A Pythagorean philosopher of Crotona, B.C. 374, who first maintained the diurnal motion of the earth round its axis, and its annual motion round the sun. Cicero, *in Arcad.* 4. c. 39, has ascribed this opinion to the Syracusan philosopher Nicetas, and likewise to Plato; and from this passage some suppose that Copernicus derived the idea of the system which he afterwards established. Philolaus is considered by some as the author of the famous verses better known by the name of the golden verses of Pythagoras. *Cic. de Orat.* 3. c. 34.—*Diog.* 8.—*Plat. de Opin. Phil.* 3. c. 13.—*Fabr. B. Gr.* 2. c. 13.——A lawgiver of Thebes. He was a native of Corinth; and of the family of the Bacchiades. *Aristot.* 2.—*Polit. cap. ult.*——A mechanic of Tarentum. *Vitruv.* 9. c. 9.—*Salmas. ad Solin.* p. 636.——A surname of Æsculapius, who had a temple in Laconia, near the Asopus. *Paus.* 3. c. 22.

PHILOL'OGUS, a freedman of Cicero. He betrayed his master to Antony, for which he was cruelly tortured by Pomponia, the wife of Cicero's brother. *Plut. in Cic.* &c.

PHILOM'ACHE, the wife of Pelias, king of Iolcus. According to some writers, she was daughter of Amphion, king of Thebes, though she is more generally called Anaxibia, daughter of Bias. *Apollod.* 1.

PHILOM'BROTUS, an archon at Athens, Olymp.

46, in whose age the state was intrusted to Solon, when torn by factions. *Plut. in Sol.*

PHILOME'DUS, a man who made himself absolute in Phocis, by promising to assist the inhabitants. *Polyæn.* 5. c. 45. We should probably read Philomelus.

PHILOME'LA, a daughter of Pandion, king of Athens, and sister of Procne, who had married Tereus, king of Thrace. Procne, separated from Philomela, to whom she was particularly attached, spent her time in great melancholy till she prevailed upon her husband to go to Athens, and bring her sister to Thrace. Tereus obeyed his wife's injunctions, but had no sooner obtained Pandion's permission to conduct Philomela to Thrace, than he became enamoured of her, and resolved to gratify his passion. He dismissed the guards, whom the suspicions of Pandion had appointed to watch his conduct, offered violence to Philomela, and afterwards cut out her tongue, that she might not be able to discover his barbarity, and the indignities which she had suffered. He confined her also in a lonely castle, and after he had taken every precaution to prevent a discovery, he returned to Thrace, and told Procne that Philomela had died by the way, and that he had paid the last offices to her remains. Procne, at this sad intelligence, put on mourning for the loss of Philomela; but a year had scarcely elapsed before she was secretly informed that her sister was not dead. Philomela, during her captivity, described, on a piece of tapestry, her misfortunes, and the brutality of Tereus, and privately conveyed it to Procne. She was going to celebrate the orgies of Bacchus when she received it, but she disguised her resentment, and as, during the festivals of the god of wine, she was permitted to rove about the country, she hastened to deliver her sister Philomela from her confinement, and concerted with her on the best measures of punishing the cruelty of Tereus. She murdered her son Itylus, who was in the sixth year of his age, and served him up as food before her husband during the festival. Tereus, in the midst of his repast, called for Itylus, but Procne immediately informed him, that he was then feasting on his flesh, and that instant Philomela, by throwing on the table the head of Itylus, convinced the monarch of the cruelty of the scene. He drew his sword to punish Procne and Philomela, but as he was going to stab them to the heart, he was changed into a hoopoe, Philomela into a nightingale, Procne into a swallow, and Itylus into a pheasant. This tragical scene happened at Daulis, in Phocis; but Pausanias and Strabo, who mention the whole of the story, are silent about the transformation; and the former observes, that Tereus, after this bloody repast, fled to Megara, where he destroyed himself. The inhabitants of the place raised a monument to his memory, where they offered yearly sacrifices, and placed small pebbles instead of barley. It was on this monument that the birds called hoopoes were first seen; whence the fable of his metamorphosis. Procne and Philomela died through excess of grief and melancholy, and as the notes of the nightingale and of the swallow are peculiarly plaintive and mournful, the poets have embellished the fable, by supposing that the two unfortunate sisters were changed into birds. *Apollod.* 3. c. 14.—*Paus.* 1. c. 42. l. 10. c. 4.—*Hygin.* fab. 45.—*Strab.* 9.—*Ovid. Met.* 6. fab. 9 & 10.—*Virg. G.* 4. v. 15 & 511.—*Heraclit. de Inc.* 35.—*Lactant. in Arg.* 6.—*Catull.* 66.—*Plut. in Symp.* 8. quæst. 7.—*Conon. Narr.* 31.—*Sch. Sophoc. in Elec.* 107.—*Servius. in Ecl.* 6. v. 78. *in G.* 3. v. 89.——A daughter of Actor, king of the Myrmidons.

PHILOME'LIUM or PHILOME'LUM, a town of Phrygia. *Cic. ad Attic.* 5. ep. 20. *in Verr.* 3. c. 83.—*Strab.* 12.

PHILOME'LUS, a general of Phocis, who plundered the temple of Delphi. He threw himself headlong from a rock, and was killed B.C. 354. *Justin.* 8. c. 1.—*Paus. in Phoc.*—*Diod. Sic.* 16, &c. *Vid.* Phocis.——A rich musician. *Mart.* 4. epigr. 5. v. *ult.*

PHILOM'ENES, a king of Paphlagonia. *Alex. ab Alex.* 1. c. 1.

PHI'LON, a general of some Greeks, who settled in Asia. *Diod.* 18.——A celebrated physician who discovered some valuable remedies. *Cœl. Rhod.* 28. c. 11.——An inhabitant of Phocis, punished with death for squandering away money dedicated to sacred purposes, Olymp. 108. an. 2.——A son of Phricodemus. *Polyæn.* 8. c. 46.

PHILON'IDES, a courier of Alexander, who ran from Sicyon to Elis, 160 miles, in nine hours, and returned the same journey in 15 hours. *Plin.* 2. c. 71.—*Salmas. ad Solin.* c. 1. p. 45.——A Greek comic poet of Athens, before the age of Aristophanes. He was tall in stature, but unpolished in mind, whence the proverb of *Philonide indoctior*. *Suidas.*—*Erasm. Ch.* 2. *Cent.* 6. c. 30.—*Gyrald. de. H. P.* 6.—*Fabr. B. Gr.* 2. c. 22.

PHILO'NIS, a name of Chione, daughter of Dædalion, made immortal by Diana. *Vid.* Chione.

PHILO'NIUS, a harbour of Corsica. *Ptol.* It is now Porto Vecchio, according to *Leander* and *Niger.*

PHILON'OE, a daughter of Tyndarus, king of Sparta, by Leda, daughter of Thestius. *Apollod.*——A daughter of Iobates, king of Lycia, who married Bellerophon. *Id.* 2.—*Tzetzes ad Lyc.* 17.

PHILON'OME, a daughter of Nyctimus, king of Arcadia, who threw into the Erymanthus two children, whom she had borne to Mars. The children were preserved, and afterwards ascended their grandfather's throne. *Plut. in Par.*—*Zopyr. in Byzant.*——The second wife of Cycnus, the son of Neptune. She become enamoured of Tennus, her husband's son by his first wife Proclea, the daughter of Clytius, and, when he refused to gratify her passion, she accused him of attempts upon her virtue. Cycnus believed the accusation, and ordered Tennus to be thrown into the sea. The father of Philonome was Crausagus. *Paus.* 10. c. 14.

PHILON'OMUS, a son of Electryon, king of Mycenæ, by Anaxo. *Apollod.* 2.

PHILON'OMUS and CAL'LIAS, two brothers of Catana, who, during an irruption of Ætna, carried away their parents on their shoulders. *Stobæus ex Ælian.*

PHILO'NUS, a village of Ægypt, between the Nile and the Arabian Gulph. *Strab.*——A village of the Pentapolis in Africa. *Ptol.*

PHILOP'ATOR, a surname of one of the Ptolemies, king of Ægypt. *Vid.* Ptolemæus.——A king of Cilicia, A.C. 17, who succeeded Polemon. *Tac. Ann.* 2. c. 42.

PHIL'OPHRON, a general, who, with 5000 soldiers, defended Pelusium against the Persians, who invaded Ægypt. *Diod.* 16.

PHILOPŒ'MEN, a celebrated general of the Achæan league, born at Megalopolis. His father's name was Grangis. His education was begun and finished under Cassander, Ecdemus, and Diophantus, and he early distinguished himself in the field of battle, though he appeared more fond of agriculture and a country life. He proposed to himself Epaminondas for a model, and he was not unsuccessful in imitating the prudence and the simplicity, the disinterestedness and the activity of this famous Theban. When Megalopolis was attacked by the Spartans, Pilopœmen, then in the 30th year of his age, gave the most decisive proofs of his valor and intrepidity. He afterwards assisted Antigonus and was present in the famous battle in which the Ætolians were defeated. Raised to the rank of chief commander, he showed his ability by the faithful discharge of that important trust, and his personal valor by killing with his own hand Mechanidas, the tyrant of Sparta; and if he was defeated in a naval battle by Nabis, he soon after repaired his losses by taking the capital of Laconia, B.C. 188, and by abolishing the laws of Lycurgus which had flourished there for such a length of time. Sparta, after its conquest, became tributary to the Achæans, and Philopœmen enjoyed the triumph of having reduced to ruins one of the greatest and the most powerful of the cities of Greece. Some time after, the Messenians revolted from the Achæan league, and Philopœmen, who headed the Achæans, unfortunately fell from his horse, and was dragged to the enemy's camp. Dinocrates, the general of the Messenians, treated him with great severity; he was thrown into a dungeon, and obliged to drink a dose of poison.

When he received the cup from the hand of the executioner, Philopœmen asked him how his countrymen had behaved in the field of battle: and when he heard that they had obtained the victory, he drank the whole with pleasure, exclaiming, that this was comfortable news. The death of Philopœmen, which happened about 183 years B.C. in his 70th year, was universally lamented, and the Achæans, to revenge his death, immediately marched to Messenia, where Dinocrates, to avoid their resentment, killed himself. The rest of his murderers were dragged to his tomb, where they were sacrificed; and the people of Megalopolis, to show farther their great sense of the merits of their brave countryman, ordered a bull to be yearly offered on his tomb, and hymns to be sung in his praise, and his actions to be celebrated in a panegyrical oration. He had also statues raised to his memory, which some of the Romans attempted to violate, and to destroy, to no purpose, when Mummius took Corinth. Philopœmen has been called by his countrymen, and with some justice, the last of the Greeks. *Plut. in Vitâ.—Justin.* 32. c. 4.—*Polyb.—Liv.* 35. c. 25. l. 39. c. 49.——A native of Pergamus, who died B.C, 138.

PHI'LOS, an island opposite Persia, not far from Cassandra. *Plin.* 6. c. 25. *Salmasius, ad Solin*, p. 1181, wishes to read Ilas, a place mentioned by *Arrian.*

PHILOS'OE, the wife of Tlepolemus. king of Rhodes. She honored the memory of her husband, who had been slain before Troy, by raising him a superb monument, and instituting games, in which the conqueror received a prize and a poplar crown. The wife of Tlepolemus is called Polyxo by *Pausanias. Tzetzes in Lyc.* 911.—*Sch. Pind.* 7. *Olymp.*

PHILOSTEPH'ANUS, an historian of Cyrene, intimate with Callimachus, He flourished under Ptolemy Philadelphus, and wrote *de fluviis, rebus Epyroticis, Cypriis, &c. Athen.* 7 & 8.—*Plut. in Lyc.—Clem. Strom.* l. 1.—*Voss. H. Gr.* 1. c. 15.

PHILOS'TRATUS FLA'VIUS, a famous sophist, born at Lemnus, or, according to some, at Athens. He came to Rome, where he lived under the patronage of Julia, the wife of the emperor Severus. and was entrusted by the empress with all the papers which contained some account, or anecdotes of Apollonius Tyanensis, and he was ordered to review them, and with them to compile a history. The life of Apollonius is written with elegance, but the improbable accounts, fabulous stories, and exaggerated details which it gives, render it disgusting. He wrote also "Heroica," "Icones," two books on the lives of the sophists, letters, epigrams, &c. He died A.D. 244. The best edition of his writings is that of Olearius, fol. Lips. 1709. *Fabr. B. Gr.* 4. c. 22.

PHILOS'TRATUS, a nephew of the preceding, wrote one book of "Icones" and some epistles, besides several other works which are lost. *Suidas.—Fabr. Ibid.* There were several other persons of this name, for an account of whom see *Meursius*' diatribe in the edition of *Philostratus* published Lug. Bat. 1616, *Vossius.* 2. *H. Gr.* 15. *Jonsius*, 3. c. 14. and *Fabricius* in the chapter above quoted.

PHILO'TAS, a son of Parmenio, distinguished for bravery in the battles of Alexander, and at last accused of conspiring against his life. He was in consequence tortured, and stoned to death, or, according to some, struck through with darts by the soldiers, B.C. 330. *Curt.* 2. c. 3 & 10. l. 4. c. 5 & 13. l. 6. c. 11.—*Plut in Alex.—Arrian.*——An Officer in the army of Alexander. *Curt.* 5. c. 2. This is probably the præfect of Cadmea and Phrygia mentioned by *Diodorus*, l. 17.—— One of the companions of Alexander, who was made master of Cilicia after his death. *Curt.* 18. c. 10.——A physician in the age of Antony. He ridiculed the expenses and the extravagance of this celebrated Roman. *Plut.*

PHILOT'ERA, the mother of Milo, put to death by her son. *Polyæn.* 8. c. 52.

PHILOT'ERA, a city near the Troglodytæ founded by Satyrus. *Apollod.*——A city of Cœlesyria. *Steph.*

PHILOTI'MUS, a freedman of Cicero. *Cic. ad Div.* 3. c. 9.——A physician at Athens. *Plut. de Aud.*——A statuary of Ægina. *Paus.* 6. c. 14.

PHILO'TIS, a servant maid at Rome, who saved her countrymen from destruction. After the siege of Rome by the Gauls, the Fidenates assembled an army under the command of Lucius Posthumius, and marched against the capital, demanding all the wives and daughters in the city, as the conditions of peace. This extraordinary demand astonished the senators, and when they refused to comply, Philotis advised them to send all their female slaves disguised in matrons' clothes, and offered herself to march at their head. Her advice was followed, and when the Fidenates had feasted to a late hour, and were quite intoxicated and fallen asleep, Philotis lighted a torch as a signal for her countrymen to attack the enemy. The plot was successful, the Fidenates were conquered, and the senate, to reward the fidelity of the female slaves, permitted them to appear in the dress of the Roman matrons. An annual festival was also appointed to commemorate the happy event, on the 7th of July, hence called *Caprotidæ nonæ*, because, from a fig-tree, *caprificus*, Philotis gave the signal to her countrymen. *Plut. in Rom.—Varro de L. L.* 5.—*Ovid. de Art. Am.* 2.—*Macrob.* 1. *Sat.* 11.

PHILOX'ENUS, an officer of Alexander the Great, who received Cilicia, at the general division of the provinces. *Polyæn.* 7. c. 49.——A son of Ptolemy, who was delivered to Pelopidas as a hostage.——A dithyrambic poet of Cythera, who enjoyed the favour of Dionysius, tyrant of Sicily, for some time, till he offended him by seducing one of his female singers. During his confinement, Philoxenus composed an allegorical poem, called Cyclops, in which he had delineated the character of the tyrant under the name of Polyphemus, and represented his mistress under the name of Galatæa, and himself under that of Ulysses. The tyrant, who was fond of writing poetry, and of being applauded, removed Philoxenus from his dungeon, but the poet refused to purchase his liberty, by saying things unworthy of himself, and applauding the wretched verses of Dionysius, and therefore he was sent to the quarries. When he was asked his opinion at a feast about some verses which Dionysius had just repeated, and which the courtiers had received with the greatest applause, Philoxenus gave no answer, but ordered the guards that surrounded the tyrant's table, to take him back to the quarries. Dionysius was pleased with his pleasantry and with his firmness, and immediately forgave him. Philoxenus died at Ephesus about 380 years B.C. *Cic.* 4. *Att.* 6.—*Plut. de Virt. Alex.—Diod.—Fabr. B. Gr.* 2. c. 19.——A celebrated musician of Ionia. *Polyæn.* 6. c. 10.——A painter of Eretria, who made for Cassander an excellent representation of the battle of Alexander with Darius. He was pupil to Nicomachus. *Plin.* 35. c. 10.——A philosopher, who wished to have the neck of a crane, that he might enjoy the taste of his aliments longer, and with more pleasure. *Arist. eth.* 3. c. 9.——A grammarian of Alexandria who wrote *de monosyllabis verbis, de Hellenismo, de genere linguarum, &c. Suidas.*——An Athenian debauchee of effeminate manners. *Aristoph. Schol. in Vesp.*

PHILYL'LIUS, a comic poet. *Athen.* 3, 4, 9.—*Fabr. B. Gr.* 2. c. 22.——A poet of the old comedy. *Athen.* 14.—*Pollux.* 7.

PHI'LUS, the surname of the Fulvii at Rome. *Cic.* 4 *Att.* 16. *Amic.* 4, 7, 19.

PHIL'YRA, one of the Oceanides who was met by Saturn in Thrace. The god, to escape from the vigilance of Rhea, changed himself into a horse to enjoy the company of Philyra, by whom he had a son, half a man and half a horse called Chiron. Philyra was so ashamed at giving birth to such a monster, that she entreated the gods to change her nature. She was metamorphosed into the linden tree, called by her name among the Greeks. *Servius*, 3. *Virg. G.* 3. v. 91.—*Sch. Apollon.* 1.—*Arg.* v. 544. l. 2. v. 1235.—*Apollod.* 1.—*Tzetzes. ad Lyc.* 1200.—*Sch. Pind. Pyth.* 4. v. 180.—*Hygin.* fab. 138.——The wife of Nauplius. *Apollod.*

PHIL'YRES, a people near Pontus. *Dionys.* v. 766.

PHILYR'IDES, a patronymic of Chiron, the son of Philyra. *Ovid. Art. Am. Fast.* 6.—*Propert.* 2. el. 1.—*Hesiod. Th. & Scuto.—Virg. G.* 3. v. 550.

PHI'NA, a town of Macedonia. *Plin.* 4. c. 10.

PHINE'UM, a town of Pontus founded by Phineus. *Steph.*

PHI'NEUS, a son of Agenor, king of Phœnicia, or, according to some, of Neptune, who became king of Thrace, or. as the greater part of the mythologists assert, of Bithynia. He married Cleopatra the daughter of Boreas, whom some call Cleobula, by whom he had Plexippus and Pandion. After the death of Cleopatra, he married Idæa, the daughter of Dardanus. Idæa, jealous of Cleopatra's children, accused them of attempts upon their father's life and crown, or, according to some, of attempts upon her virtue, and they were immediately condemned by Phineus to be deprived of their eyes. This cruelty was soon after punished by the gods, Phineus suddenly became blind, and the Harpyes were sent by Jupiter to keep him under continual alarm, and to spoil the meats that were placed on his table. He was some time after delivered from these dangerous monsters by his brothers-in-law, Zethes and Calais, who pursued them as far as the Strophades. He also recovered his sight by means of the Argonauts, whom he had received with great hospitality, and instructed in the easiest and speediest way by which they might reach Colchis. The causes of the blindness of Phineus are a matter of dispute among the ancients, some supposing that this was inflicted by Boreas, for his cruelty to his grandson, whilst others attribute it to the anger of Neptune, because he had directed the sons of Phryxus how to escape from Colchis to Greece. Many, however, think that it proceeded from his having rashly attempted to develope futurity, while others assert that Zethes and Calais put out his eyes on account of his cruelty to their nephews. The second wife of Phineus is called by some Dia, Eurytia, Danae, and Idothea. Phineus was killed by Hercules. *Arg.* 2.—*Apollod.* 1. c. 9. 1. 3. c. 15.—*Diod.* 4.—*Hygin.* fab. 19.—*Orpheus* —*Flacc.* 4. v. —*Sch. Eurip. in Phœn.* 225.—*Sch. Sophoc. in Trachin.* 980.—*Tzetzes. in Lyc.* 1286.—*Sch. Hom. in Odyss.* 12. v. 76.—*Servius in Virg. Æn.* 3. v. 209. l. 8. v. 334.—*Lactant. ad Theb.* 8. v. 254.—*Lucian. in Tim.*——The brother of Cepheus, king of Æthiopia. He was going to marry his niece Andromeda, when her father Cepheus was obliged to give her up to be devoured by a sea monster, to appease the resentment of Neptune. She was, however, delivered from her perilous situation by Perseus. who married her with the consent of her parents, for having destroyed the sea monster. This marriage displeased Phineus; he interrupted the ceremony, and with a number of attendants attacked Perseus and his friends. Perseus defended himself, and turned into stone Phineus, and his companions, by showing them the Gorgon's head. *Apollod.* 2. c. 1 & 4.—*Ovid. Met.* 5. fab. 1. & 2.—*Tzetzes. ad Lyc.* 838.—*Hygin.* fab. 64.——A son of Melas.——A son of Lycaon, king of Arcadia.—*Apollod.*——An Athenian remarkable for his justice.—*Ovid. Met.* 7. v. 399.

PHINOP'OLIS, a city of Pontus, founded by Phineus. *Steph.*—*Plin.* 4. c. 11. It is now Phinopoli.

PHIN'TA, a king of Messenia, who succeeded Sybotas, and was succeded by Antiochus. *Paus.* 4. c. 4.

PHIN'THIA, a fountain in which it was said nothing could sink. *Plin.* 31. c. 2.

PHIN'TIAS, a town of Sicily, at the mouth of the Himera. *Cic. in Verr.* 3. c. 83.

PHIN'TIAS, called also Pithias, Pinthias and Phytias, a man famous for his unparalleled friendship for Damon. *Vid.* Damon.—*Cic. de Off.* 3. c. 10. *Tusc.* 5. c. 22.—*Diod.* 6, &c.—*Val. Max.* 4. c. 7.—*Hygin.* fab. 254.——A tyrant of Agrigentum, B.C. 282.

PHINTO'NIS or PHIN'TON, a small island between Sardinia and Corsica, now called Figo. *Plin.* 3. c. 6.—*Ptol.*

PHIRÆ'SI, a people of the island of Scandia. *Ptol.*

PHIR'STIMUS, a river of Persia flowing into the Persian Gulph. *Plin.* 6. c. 23.

PHISER'SA, a town of Corsica, at the west of the island. *Ptol.*

PHLA, a small island in the lake Tritonis, in Africa. *Herodot.* 4. c. 178.

PHLAN'ATES, a people of Illyricum. *Plin.* 3. c. 19.

PHLA'NON, a city and harbour near the island Absyrtus. *Steph.*

PHLEG'ELAS, an Indian king beyond the Hydaspes, who surrendered to Alexander. *Curt.* 9. c. 1.

PHLEG'ETHON, one of the rivers of hell, the waters of which were *burning*, as the word φλεγέθω, from which the name is derived, seems to indicate. *Virg. Æn.* 6. v. 550.—*Lucan.* 6. v. 704.—*Ovid. Met.* 15. v. 532.—*Senec. in Hip.*—*Sil.* 13. v. 564 & 836.—*Flacc.* 1. v. 735.

PHLE'GIA, a city of Bœotia, on the Cephisus. *Steph.*

PHLE'GIAS, a man of Cyzicus, when the Argonauts visited it. *Flacc.* 3. v. 125.

PHLE'GON, a native of Tralles in Lydia, one of the emperor Adrian's freedmen. He wrote different treatises on the long-lived, on wonderful things, besides an historical account of Sicily, sixteen books on the Olympiads, an account of the principal places in Rome, three books of Fasti, &c. Of these some fragments remain. His style was not elegant, and he is said to have written without judgment or precision. His name is particularly noticed by the moderns, as he made mention of the darkness which prevailed during the crucifixion of our Saviour. The passage is now lost, though the substance is preserved by Eusebius. The works of Phlegon had been edited by Meursius, 4to, L. Bat. 1620, and by Franzius, Halæ, 1775. *Fabr. B. Gr* 4. c. 15.—*Sax. Onom.* 1. p. 305.——One of the horses of the sun. The word signifies *burning*. *Ovid. Met.* 2. v. 154.

PHLE'GRA or PHLEGRÆ'US CAM'PUS, a place of Macedonia, afterwards called Pallene, where the giants attacked the gods and were defeated by Hercules. The combat was afterwards renewed in Italy, in a place of the same name near Cumæ, afterwards called Vesuvius. *Sil* 8. v. 538. l. 9. v. 305.—*Strab.* 5.—*Diod.* 4 & 5.—*Ovid. Met.* 10. v. 151. l. 12. v. 378. l. 15. v. 532.—*Stat.* 5. *Sylv.* 3. v. 196.—*Plin.* 3. c. 5.—*Servius ad Æn.* 3. v. 578.—*Propert.* 2. el. 1. v. 39. l. 3. el. 7. v. 48.

PHLE'GYÆ, a people of Thessaly. Some authors place them in Bœotia. They received their name from Phlegyas the son of Mars, with whom they plundered and burned the temple of Apollo at Delphi. Some few of them escaped to Phocis, where they settled. *Paus.* 9. c. 36.—*Homer. Il.* 13. v. 301.—*Strab.* 9.

PHLE'GYAS, a son of Mars, king of the Lapithæ, in Thessaly, by Chryse, daughter of Halmus. He was father of Ixion and Coronis, to whom Apollo offered violence. When the father heard that his daughter had been so wantonly abused, he marched an army against Delphi, and reduced the temple of the god to ashes. This was highly resented, Apollo killed Phlegyas and placed him in hell, where a huge stone was suspended over his head, and kept him in continual alarms by its threatening appearance. *Paus.* 9. c. 36.—*Apollod.* 3. c. 5.—*Pind. Pyth.* 3.—*Ovid. Met.* 5. v. 87.—*Servius ad Virg. Æn.* 6. v. 618.—*Stat. Theb.* 1. v. 703.

PHLI'AS, one of the Argonauts, son of Bacchus and Ariadne. He married Chthonophyle, by whom he had Androdamas. *Orph.* 192.—*Apollon. Arg.* 1. v. 115.—*Flacc.* 1. v. 412. l. 3. v. 148.—*Paus.* 2. c. 12.

PHLIA'SIA, a country of Peloponnesus, near Sicyon, of which Phlius was the capital. It bore the names of Arantia from Aras, and Arethyrea, from a daughter of Aras, and Phliasia from Phlias son of Bacchus. Hebe was particularly worshipped there, but, though she had no statues, her temple was venerated as an asylum for the unfortunate, and her name was honored by annual festivals. Ceres had also a temple there. The country was peopled by an Argive colony. *Homer. Il.* 2. v. 572 & 604.—*Paus.* 2. c. 12 & 13.

PHLI'US, (*-untis*,) a town in Peloponnesus, now Staphlica, in the territory of Sicyon. *Pausan.* 1. 2.——A town in Elis. *Plin.* 4. c. 5.——A town in Argolis, now Drepano.

PHLŒ'A, a name of Proserpine. *Hesychius.*

PHLŒ'US, a surname of Bacchus, expressive of his youth and vigor. *Plut. in Symp.* 5. qu. 8.

PHLO'GIUS and DEI'LON, sons of Deimachus, joined the Argonauts at Sinope. *Apollod.* 2.—*Flacc.* 5. v. 115.

PHLORY'JA, a town of Mauritania Cæsariensis. *Ptol.*

PHLYGA'DIA, a mountain of Illyricum. *Strab.*

PHLYGO'NIUM, a city of Phocis. *Steph.*

PHLY'A, a municipal town of Attica. *Hesych.*

PHOBE'TOR, one of the sons of Somnus, and his principal minister. His office was to assume the shape of serpents and wild beasts, to inspire terror in the minds of men, as his name intimates. (φοβέω). The other two ministers of Somnus were Phantasia and Morpheus. *Ovid. Met.* 11. v. 640.

PHO'BOS or PHO'BUS, son of Mars, and god of terror among the ancients, was represented with a lion's head, and sacrifices were offered him to deprecate his appearance in battles. *Plut. in Erot.*

PHO'CÆ, small islands off Crete, near the promontory of Sommonium. *Plin.* 4. c. 12.

PHOCÆ'A, now Fochia, a maritime town in Ionia. in Asia Minor, with two harbours, between Cumæ and Smyrna, founded by an Athenian colony. It received its name from Phocus, the leader of the colony, or from (*phocæ*) *sea calves*, which are found in great abundance in the neighbourhood. The inhabitants called Phocæi and Phocæenses were expert mariners, and founded many cities in different parts of Europe. They left Ionia, when Cyrus attempted to reduce them under his power, and came, after many adventures, to Gaul, where they founded Massilia, now called Marseilles. The town of Marseilles is often distinguished by the epithet of Phocaica, and its inhabitants called Phocæenses. Phocæa was declared independent by Pompey, and under the first emperors of Rome it became one of the most flourishing cities of Asia Minor. *Liv.* 5. c. 34. l. 37. c. 31. l. 38. c. 39.—*Mela*, 1. c. 17.—*Paus.* 7. c. 3.—*Herodot.* 1. v. 165. *Strab.* 14.—*Horat.* epod. 16.—*Ovid Met.* 6. v. 9.—*Plin.* 3. c. 4.—*Solin.* 8.—*Eustath. ad Dionys. Per.* 437.

PHOCA'RIA, an island of the Ægæan Sea, opposite Attica. *Plin.* 4. c. 12.

PHOCÆ'A, a town of Sicily. *Thucyd.*

PHOCEN'SES and PHO'CICI, the inhabitants of Phocis in Greece.

PHO'CEUS, son of Olenus, slain at Cyzicus by Telamon. *Val. Flacc.* 3. v. 204.

PHO'CION, an Athenian, celebrated for his virtues, private as well as public. He was educated in the school of Plato and of Xenocrates, and as soon as he appeared among the statesmen of Athens, he distinguished himself by his prudence and moderation, his zeal for the public good, and his military abilities. He often checked the violent and inconsiderate measures of Demosthenes, and when the Athenians seemed eager to make war against Philip, king of Macedonia, Phocion observed that war should never be undertaken without the strongest and most certain expectations of victory and success. When Philip endeavoured to make himself master of Eubœa, Phocion stopped his progress, and soon obliged him to relinquish his enterprize. During the time of his administration he was always inclined to peace, though he never suffered his countrymen to become indolent, or to forget the jealousy and rivalship of their neighbours. He was forty-five times appointed governor of Athens, and no greater encomium can be passed upon his talents as a minister and statesman, than that he never solicited that high though dangerous office. In his rural retreat, or at the head of the Athenian armies, he always appeared barefooted, and without a cloak, whence one of his soldiers had occasion to observe, when he saw him dressed more warmly than usual during a severe winter, that since Phocion wore his cloak, it was a sign of the most inclement weather. If he was a friend of temperance and discipline, he was not a less brilliant example of true heroism. Philip, as well as his son Alexander, attempted to bribe him, but to no purpose; and Phocion boasted in being one of the poorest of the Athenians, and in deserving the appellation of *the Good*. It was through him that Greece was saved from an impending war, and he advised Alexander rather to turn his arms against Persia, than to shed the blood of the Greeks, who were either his allies or his subjects. Alexander was so sensible of his merit and of his integrity, that he sent him 100 talents from the spoils which he had obtained from the Persians, but Phocion was too great to suffer himself to be bribed; and when the conqueror had attempted a second time to oblige him, and to conciliate his favor, by offering him the government and possession of five cities, the Athenian rejected the presents with the same indifference, and with the same independent mind. But not totally to despise the favors of the monarch, he begged Alexander to restore to their liberty four slaves that were confined in the citadel of Sardis. Antipater, who succeeded to the government of Macedonia after the death of Alexander, also attempted to corrupt the virtuous Athenian, but with the same success as his royal predecessor; and when a friend had observed to Phocion, that if he could so refuse the generous offers of his patrons, yet he should consider the good of his children, and accept them for their sake, Phocion calmly replied, that if his children were like him they could maintain themselves as well as their father had done, but if they behaved otherwise, he declared that he was unwilling to leave them any thing which might either supply their extravagancies, or encourage their debaucheries. But virtues like these could not long stand against the insolence and fickleness of an Athenian assembly. When the Piræus was taken, Phocion was accused of treason, and, therefore, to avoid the public indignation, he fled for safety to Polyperchon. Polyperchon sent him back to Athens, where he was immediately condemned to drink the fatal poison. He received the indignities of the people with unparalleled composure; and when one of his friends lamented his fate, Phocion exclaimed, "This is no more than what I expected, this treatment the most illustrious citizens of Athens have received before me." He took the cup with the greatest serenity of mind; and, as he drank the fatal draught, he prayed for the prosperity of Athens, and bade his friends to tell his son Phocus not to remember the ignominious treatment which his father had received from the Athenians. He died about 318 years B.C. His body was deprived of a funeral by order of the ungrateful Athenians, and if it was at last interred, it was by stealth, under a hearth, by the hand of a woman, who placed this inscription over his bones: "Keep inviolate, O sacred hearth, the precious remains of a good man, till a better day restores them to the monument of his forefathers, when Athens shall be delivered of her frenzy, and shall be more wise." It has been observed of Phocion, that he never appeared elated in prosperity, or dejected in adversity, and never betrayed pusillanimity by a tear, or joy by a smile. His countenance was stern and unpleasant, but he never behaved with severity, his expressions were mild, and his rebukes gentle. At the age of eighty he appeared at the head of the Athenian armies like the most active officer; and to his prudence and cool valor. in every period of life, his fellow-citizens acknowledged themselves much indebted. His merits were not long buried in oblivion; the Athenians repented of their ingratitude, and honored his memory by raising him statues, and putting to a cruel death his guilty accusers. *Plut.* & *C. Nep in vitâ.*—*Diod.* 16. [There is a remarkably fine statue in the Musée Royale, at Paris, which is designated Phocion.]——A Spanish peripatetic philosopher, who wrote a work called Cornucopia. *A. Gell.* 1. c. 8.

PHO'CIS, a country of Greece, bounded on the east by Bœotia, and on the west by Locris. It originally extended from the bay of Corinth to the sea of Eubœa, and reached on the north as far as Thermopylæ, but its boundaries were afterwards more contracted. Phocis received its name from Phocus, a son of Ornytion, who settled there. The inhabitants were called Phocenses, and thence also the epithet of Phocicus was formed. Parnassus was the most celebrated of the mountains of Phocis, and Delphi was the greatest of its towns. Phocis is rendered famous for a war which it maintained against some of the Grecian republics, and which has received the name of the Phocian war. This celebrated war originated in the following circumstances: When Philip king of Macedonia had, by his intrigues and well-concerted policy, fomented divisions in Greece, and disturbed the peace of every republic, the Greeks universally became discontented in their situation, fickle in their resolutions, and jealous of the prosperity of the neighbouring states. The Amphictyons, who were the supreme rulers of Greece, and who at that time were subservient to the views of the Thebans, the inveterate enemies of the Phocians, showed the same spirit of fickleness, and, like the rest of their countrymen, were actuated by the same fears, the same jealousy and ambition. As the supporters of religion, they accused the Phocians of impiety for ploughing a small portion of land which belonged to the god of Delphi. They immediately commanded that the sacred field should be laid waste, and that the Phocians, to expiate their crime, should pay a heavy fine to the community. The inability of the Phocians to pay the fine, and that of the Amphictyons to enforce their commands by violence, gave rise to new events. The people of Phocis were roused by the eloquence and the popularity of Philomelus, one of their countrymen, and when this ambitious ringleader liberally contributed the great riches which he possessed to the public service, and for the support of national honor, they resolved to oppose the Amphictyonic council by force of arms. He seized the rich temple of Delphi, and employed the treasures which it contained to raise and equip a mercenary army. During two years, hostilities were carried on between the Phocians and their enemies, the Thebans and the people of Locris, but no decisive battles were fought; and it can only be observed, that the Phocian prisoners were always put to an ignominious death, as guilty of the most abominable sacrilege and impiety, a treatment which was liberally retaliated on such of the army of the Amphictyons as became the captives of the enemy. The defeat, however, and death of Philomelus, for a while checked the successes of his countrymen, but the deceased general was soon succeeded in the command by his brother called Onomarchus, his equal in boldness and ambition, and his superior in activity and enterprize. Onomarchus rendered his cause popular, the Thessalians joined his army, and the neighbouring states observed at least a strict neutrality, if they neither opposed nor favored his arms. Philip of Macedonia, who had assisted the Thebans, was obliged to retire from the field with dishonor; but a more successful battle was fought near Magnesia, and the monarch, by crowning the head of his soldiers with laurel, and telling them that they fought in the cause of Delphi and heaven, obtained a complete victory. Onomarchus was slain, and his body exposed on a gibbet, 6000 of his fellow-soldiers shared his fate, and their bodies were thrown into the sea, as unworthy of funeral honors, and 3000 were taken alive. This fatal defeat, however, did not ruin the Phocians; Phayllus, the only surviving brother of Philomelus, took the command of their armies, and doubling the pay of his soldiers, increased his forces by the addition of 9000 men from Athens, Lacedæmon, and Achaia. But all this numerous force at last proved ineffectual; the treasures of the temple of Delphi, which had long defrayed the expenses of the war, began to fail; dissensions arose among the ringleaders of Phocis; and when Philip had crossed the straits of Thermopylæ, the Phocians, relying on his generosity, claimed his protection, and implored him to plead their cause before the Amphictyonic council. His dissimulated intercession was not attended with success, and the Thebans, the Locrians, and the Thessalians, who then composed the Amphictyonic council, unanimously decreed, that the Phocians should be deprived of the privilege of sending members among the Amphictyons. Their arms and their horses were to be sold, for the benefit of Apollo; they were to pay the annual sum of 60.000 talents, till the temple of Delphi had been restored to its ancient splendor and opulence; their cities were to be dismantled, and reduced to distinct villages, which were to contain no more than sixty houses each, at the distance of a furlong from one another; and all the privileges and the immunities of which they were stripped, were to be conferred on Philip, king of Macedonia, for his eminent services in the prosecution of the Phocian war. The Macedonians were ordered to put these cruel commands into execution. The Phocians were unable to make resistance, and ten years after they had undertaken the sacred war, they saw their country laid desolate, their walls demolished, and their cities in ruins, by the wanton jealousy of their enemies, and the inflexible cruelty of the Macedonian soldiers, B.C. 348. They were not, however, long under this disgraceful sentence; their well known valor and courage recommended them to favor, and they gradually regained their influence and consequence, by the protection of the Athenians and the favor of Philip. *Liv.* 32. c. 18.—*Ovid.* 2. *Am.* 6. v. 15. *Met.* 5. v. 276.—*Demosth.*—*Justin.* 8, &c.—*Diod.* 16, &c.—*Plut. in Dem. Lys. Per. &c.*—*Strab.* 5.—*Paus.* 4. c. 5. l. 10. c. 1.—*Mela*, 2. c. 3.—*Lucan* 1. v. 144.

PHO'CLIS, a city of Arachosia. *Ptol.*

PHO'CRA, a mountain of Mauritania Tingitana. *Ptol.*

PHO'CUS, son of Phocion, was dissolute in his manners, and unworthy of the virtues of his great father. He was sent to Lacedæmon to imbibe there the principles of sobriety, of temperance, and of frugality. He cruelly revenged the death of his father, whom the Athenians had put to death. *Plut. in Phoc. & Apoph.* —— A son of Æacus by Psamathe, killed by Telamon and Peleus, his eldest brothers, by Endeis. Pausanias mentions, but upon no authority, that he reigned in Phocis. *Anton. Lib.* 38.—*Hygin.* fab. 14.—*Paus.* 10. c. 1.—*Diod.* 4.—*Apollod* 3. c. 12.—— A son of Ornytion, who led a colony of Corinthians into Phocis. He cured Antiope, a daughter of Nycteus, of insanity, and married her, and by her became father of Panopeus and Crisus. *Paus.* 2. c. 4 & 29. l. 9. c. 17.—*Sch. Eurip. in Orest.* 1096. —*Tzetzes. ad Lyc.* 1073.—*Eustath. ad Dionys. Per.* 437.

PHOCU'SA, one of the Sporades. *Plin.* 4. c. 12.

PHOCU'SÆ, two islands in the Ægyptian Sea. *Ptol.*

PHOCYL'IDES, a Greek poet and philosopher of Miletus, about 540 years B.C. The poetical piece now extant, called νουθετικόν, comprehending about 217 lines and attributed to him, is supposed not to have been his composition, but that of another poet of the same name, who lived in the reign of Adrian. It was edited by Schier, Lips. 1751. *Gyrald. de P.H.* 3.—*Scal. ad Eus. Chron.*—*Fabr. B. Gr.* 2. c. 11.—*Sax. Onom.* 1. p. 24.

PHO'DA, a town of Arabia Felix. *Plin.* 6. c. 28.

PHŒ'BAS, (-*adis*), a name applied to a prophetess, as Cassandra, but more particularly to the priestess of Apollo's temple at Delphi. *Servius in Æn.* 6. v. 78 & 662.—*Lucan.* 5. v. 128, &c.—*Propert.* 3. el. 11. v. 62.—*Ovid. Am.* 2. el. 8. v. 12.—*Ital.* 15. v. 282.

PHŒBA'TIS, a city of Macedonia. *Polyb.*

PHŒ'BE, a name given to Diana or the moon, on account of the brightness of that luminary. She was considered as daughter of Cœlus and Terra, and by Ceus she became, according to Apollodorus, mother of Asteria and Latona. *Vid.* Diana. *Hesiod. Theog.* 136 & 407.—*Apollod.* 1.—— A daughter of Leucippus and Philodice, carried away, with her sister Hilaira, by Castor and Pollux, as she was going to marry one of the sons of Aphareus. *Vid.* Leucippides. *Apollod.* 2. c. 10. —*Paus.* 2. c. 22.—*Ovid. Fast.* 5. v. 701. *A.A.* 1. v. 681.

PHŒ'BE, a small island of the Propontis. *Plin.* 5. c. *ult.*

PHŒBE'UM, a place near Sparta.

PHŒ'BI, a promontory of Mauritania Tingitana. *Ptol.* It is now Cabo de Gomera.

PHŒ'BIA, a town of the Sicyonians. *Steph.*

PHŒB'IDAS, a Lacedæmonian general, sent by the Ephori to the assistance of the Macedonians against the Thracians. He seized the citadel of Thebes; but, though he was disgraced and banished from the Lacedæmonian army for this perfidious measure, yet his countrymen kept possession of the town. He died B.C. 377. *C. Nep. in Pelop.*—*Diod.* 14, &c.

PHŒBIG'ENA, a surname of Æsculapius, as being descended from Phœbus. *Virg. Æn.* 7. v. 773.

PHŒ'BUS, a name given to Apollo or the sun. The word (φοῖβος) expresses the brightness and splendor of that luminary. *Vid.* Apollo.

PHŒDI'NUS, a person slain by Nicocreon, on account of the beauty of his wife Aretaphile. *Plut.*

PHŒ'MOS, a lake of Arcadia. *Ovid. Met.* 15.

PHŒNICÆ'UM, a mountain of Peloponnesus, near Corinth. *Steph.*

PHŒNI'CE or PHŒNIC'IA, a country of Asia, at the east of the Mediterranean, the boundaries of which have been different in different ages. Some suppose that the names of Phœnicia, Syria, and Palestine, are indiscriminately used for one and the same country. Phœnicia, according to *Ptolemy*, extended on the north as far as the Eleutherus, a small river which falls into the Mediterranean Sea, a little below the island of Aradus, and it had Pelusium or the territories of Ægypt as its more southern boundary, and Syria on the east. Sidon and Tyre were the most capital towns of the country. The inhabitants were naturally industrious, the invention of letters is attributed to them, and commerce and navigation were among them in the most flourishing state. They planted colonies on the shores of the Mediterranean, parcularly Carthage, Hippo, Marseilles, and Utica, and their manufactures acquired such a superiority over those of other nations, that among the ancients, whatever was elegant, great, or pleasing either in apparel or domestic utensils, received, as expressive of its value the epithet of Sidonian. The Phœnicians were originally governed by kings. They were subdued by the Persians and afterwards by Alexander, and remained tributary to his successors and the Romans. They were called Phœnicians from Phœnix, son of Agenor, who was one of their kings, or, according to others, from the great number of *palm trees* (φοίνικες) which grew in the neighbourhood. *Herodot.* 4. c. 42. l. 5. c. 58, *Homer, Odyss.* 15 v. 415.—*Mela*, 1. c. 11. l. 2. c. 7. —*Strab.* 16.—*Apollod.* 3. c 1.—*Lucret.* 2. v. 829. —*Plin.* 2. c. 47. l. 5. c. 12 —*Curt.* 4. c. 2.—*Virg. Æn.* 1, &c.—*Ovid. Met.* 12. v. 104. l. 14. v. 345. l. 15. v. 288.—*Propert.* 2. el. 1. v 62. el. 20. v. 61.—*Ital.* 1. v. 89. l. 17. v. 147 & 636.

PHŒNI'CE, a town of Epirus. *Liv.* 29. c. 12.

PHŒNIC'IA. *Vid.* Phœnice.

PHŒNIC'IUS MONS, a mountain of Bœotia, near Thebes. *Strab.*——A mountain in Lycia, called also Olympus.

PHŒNI'CUS, a town of Lycia. *Liv.* 36. c. 45 ——A city of Crete with a harbour, now Fenichia.

PHŒNICU'SA, now Fenicusa, one of the Æolian islands, at the north of Sicily. *Ptol.*

PHŒNICUS'SÆ, a city of the Phœnicians, in Syria. *Steph.*

PHŒNIS'SA, a patronymic given to Dido as a native of Phœnicia. *Virg. Æn.* 4. v. 529.

PHŒ'NIX, son of Amyntor king of Argos, by Cleobule or Hippodamia, was preceptor to Achilles. When his father proved faithless to his wife, on account of his fondness for a concubine, called Clytia, Cleobule, jealous of her husband, persuaded her son Phœnix to ingratiate himself into the favours of his father's mistress. Phœnix easily succeeded, but when Amyntor discovered his intrigues, he drew a curse upon him, and the son, soon after, was deprived of his sight by divine vengeance. According to some, Amyntor himself put out the eyes of his son, which so cruelly provoked him, that he meditated the death of his father. Reason and piety, however, prevailed over passion, and Phœnix, not to become a parricide, fled from Argos to the court of Peleus, king of Phthia. Here he was treated with tenderness, Peleus carried him to Chiron, who restored to him his eye-sight, and he was soon after made preceptor to Achilles, his benefactor's son. He was also presented with the government of many cities, and made king of the Dolopes. He accompanied his pupil to the Trojan war, and Achilles was ever grateful for the instructions and precepts he had received from Phœnix. After the death of Achilles, Phœnix, with others, was commissioned by the Greeks to return into Greece, to bring to the war young Pyrrhus. This commission he performed with success, and, after the fall of Troy, he returned with Pyrrhus and died in Thrace. He was buried at Æon, or according to Strabo, near Trachinia, where a small river in the neighbourhood, which, after joining the Asopus fell into the sea near Thermopylæ, received the name of Phœnix. *Strab.* 9.—*Homer. Il.* 9, &c.—*Ovid. in Ib.* v. 259.—*Apollod.* 2. c. 7.—*Virg. Æn.* 2. v. 762.—*Eustath. in Il.* 2.—*Lycop.* 422.—*Tzetzes. in Lycoph.* 421.—*Propert.* 2. el. 1. v. 99.—*Servius ad Virg. loco.*—*Vives ad Aug. Civ. D.* 1. c. 4.——A son of Agenor, by a nymph who was called Telephassa, according to Apollodorus and Moschus, or, according to Epimedusa, Perimeda, or Agriope. He was, like his brothers Cadmus and Cilix, sent by his father in pursuit of his sister Europa, whom Jupiter had carried away under the form of a bull, and, when his enquiries proved unsuccessful, he settled in a country, which, according to some, was from him called Phœnicia. From him, as some suppose, the Carthaginians were called Pœni. *Apollod.* 3.—*Hygin.* fab. 178.—*Mosch. Id.*—*Sch. Eurip. in Ph.*—*Lactant. ad Theb.* 2.—*Paus.* 7. c. 4.—*Nonnus. in Dionys.* 3.—*Tzetzes. in Chil.* 7. *Hist.* 117.—*Servius in Æn.* 3. v. 88.——The father of Adonis, according to *Hesiod.*——A Theban, delivered to Alexander, &c. ——A native of Tenedus, who was an officer in the service of Eumenes.

PHŒ'NIX, a city of Crete. *Ptol.* It is now S. Niqueta, according to *Niger.*——A mountain of Caria, opposite Rhodes. *Plin.* 4. c. 8.—*Strab.*—*Ptol.*

PHŒ'TIÆ or PHŒ'TIUM, a city of Acarnania, founded by Phoetius, son of Alcmæon. *Polyb.* 4. —*Steph.*

PHOLEGAN'DRUS, one of the Sporades. *Ptol.*—*Hesych.*—*Strab.* 10.

PHOL'OE, one of the horses of Admetus. *Stat. Theb.* 6. v. 461.

PHOL'OE, now Xiria, a mountain of Arcadia, near Pisa. It received its name from Pholus, the friend of Hercules, who was buried there. It is often confounded with another of the same name in Thessaly, near mount Othrys. *Plin.* 4. c. 6.—*Lucan.* 3. v. 198. l. 6. v. 388. l. 7. v. 449.—*Ovid.* 2. *Fast.* 2. v. 273.

PHOL'OE, a female servant, of Cretan origin, given to Sergestus with her two sons, by Æneas. *Virg. Æn.* 5. v. 285.——A courtezan in the age of Horace.—*Horat.* 1. od. 33 v. 7. l. 2. od. 5. v. 17. l. 3. od. 15. v. 7.—*Tibull.* 1. el. 8. v. 69 & 77.

PHO'LON, a town of Arcadia, so called from the Centaur Pholus. *Steph.*

PHO'LUS, one of the Centaurs, son of Silenus and Melia, or, according to others, of Ixion and the cloud. He kindly entertained Hercules when he was going against the boar of Erymanthus, but he refused to give him wine, as that which he had belonged to the rest of the Centaurs. Hercules, upon this, without ceremony, broke the cask and drank the wine. The smell of the liquor drew the Centaurs from the neighbourhood to the house of Pholus, but Hercules stopped them when they forcibly entered the habitation of his friend, and killed the greatest part of them. Pholus gave the dead a decent funeral, but mortally wounded himself with one of the arrows which were poisoned with the venom of the hydra, and which he attempted to extract from one of the bodies of the Centaurs. Hercules, unable to cure him, buried him when dead, and called the mountain where his remains were deposited, by the name of Pholoe.—*Apollod.* 1.—*Paus.* 3. c. 18 —*Virg. G.* 2. v. 456. *Æn.* 8. v. 294.—*Diod.* 4.—*Ital.* 1. v. 438.—*Stat. Theb.* 2. v. 564.—*Lucan.* 3. v. 198, 388. l. 6. v. 391. l. 7. v. 449 & 827.—*Servius ad Virg. loco.* ——One of the friends of Æneas, killed by Turnus. *Virg. Æn.* 12. v. 341.

PHO'RA, a city of Armenia Major. *Ptol.*

PHOR'AGA, a city of Aria. *Id.*

PHOR'BÆ, a city of the Achæans, in Thessaly. *Steph.*

PHORBAN'TIA, the most northerly island of the Ægates, near Sicily. *Vid.* Ægates.

PHORBAN'TIUM, a mountain of Trœzene, *Steph.*

PHOR'BAS, a son of Priam and Epithesia, killed during the Trojan war by Menelaus. The god Somnus borrowed his features when he deceived Palinurus, and threw him into the sea near the coast of Italy. *Virg. Æn.* 5. v. 842. *& Servius in Æn.* 1. v. 525.——A son of Lapithes, who married Hyrmine, the daughter of Epeus, by whom he had Actor. Pelops, according to Diodorus, shared his kingdom with Phorbas, who also, says the same historian, established himself at Rhodes, at the head of a colony from Elis and Thessaly, by the order of the oracle, which promised by his means only, deliverance from the numerous serpents which infested the island. *Diod.* 2 & 4 — *Paus.* 5. c. 1.—*Schol. Apollon.* 1. v. 171.—*Hygin. P. A.* 2. c. 14.——A shepherd of Polybus, king of Corinth.——A man who profaned Apollo's temple, &c. *Ovid. Met.* 11. v. 414.——A king of Argos, A.M. 2466. *Euseb. in Chron.*——An Archon at Athens, who presided 31 years, and was succeeded by Megacles.——A native of Syene, son of Methion, killed by Perseus. *Ovid. Met.* 5. fab. 3.

PHOR'CUS or PHOR'CYS, a sea deity, son of Pontus and Terra, who married his sister Ceto, by whom he had the Gorgons, the dragon that kept the apples of the Hesperides, and other monsters. *Hesiod. Theogn*, v. 270 & 352.—*Apollon.* 4.—*Schol. Æschyl. ad Prom.* 792.—*Apollod.*——A son of Phenops, one of the auxiliaries of Priam, killed by Ajax, during the Trojan war. *Homer. Il.* 17.——A man whose seven sons assisted Turnus against Æneas. *Virg. Æn.* 10. v. 328.——A sculptor and painter. *Plin.* 36. c. 5.

PHORIA'MI, a place of Elis. *Steph.*

PHOR'ICA, a city of Arcadia. *Id.*

PHOR'MIO or PHOR'MION, an Athenian general, whose father's name was Asopicus. He impoverished himself to maintain and support the dignity of his army. His debts were some time after paid by the Athenians, who wished to make him their general, an office which he refused, while he had so many debts, observing, that it was unbecoming an officer to be at the head of an army, when he knew that he was poorer than the meanest of his soldiers. *Paus.* 1. c. 23.—*Thucyd.* 2.—*Aul. Gell.* 17. c. 21.——A general of Crotona, who conquered the Lacedæmonians in a naval battle.——A Peripatetic philosopher of Ephesus, who once gave a lecture upon the duties of an officer, and of the military profession. The philosopher was himself ignorant of the subject upon which he treated, upon which Annibal the Great, who was one of his auditors, exclaimed that he had seen many doting old men, but never one worse than Phormio. From this circumstance the name of Phormiones has been applied to such persons as attempt to teach what they do not comprehend. *Cic. de Orat.* 2. c. 18.——An Athenian archon. Olymp. 96. an. 1.——A disciple of Plato, chosen by the people of Elis, to make a reformation in their government, and their jurisprudence. *Plut. de Rep. Ger.*

PHOR'MIO or PHOR'MION, one of *Terence's* plays, so called from one of the principal characters in it.

PHOR'MIS, an Arcadian who acquired great riches at the court of Gelon and Hiero in Sicily. He dedicated the brazen statue of a mare to Jupiter Olympius in Peloponnesus, which so much resembled nature, that horses came near it, as if it had been alive. *Paus.* 5. c. 27.—*Servius ad Virg. G.* 3. v. 280.

PHORMIS'IUS, a person ridiculed by *Aristophanes. Schol. in ran.*

PHOR'MUS or PHOR'MIS, a tragic poet of Syracuse. *Fabr. B. Gr.* 2. c. 19.—*Voss. poet. Gr.* c. 5.

PHORNA'CIS, a city of the Turdetani in Hispania Bætica. *Ptol.* It is now Alhama.

PHOROBRENTA'RIUM, a city of Libya. *Steph.*

PHORO'NEUS, the god of a river of Peloponnesus of the same name. He was son of the river Inachus, by Melissa, and was the second king of Argos. He married a nymph called Cerdo, or Laodice, by whom he had Apis, from whom Argolis was called Apia, and Niobe, the first woman of whom Jupiter became enamoured. Phoroneus taught his subjects the utility of laws, and the advantages of a social life, and of friendly intercourse, whence the inhabitants of Argolis are often called Phoronæi. Pausanias relates, that Phoroneus, with the Cephisus, Asterion, and Inachus, were appointed umpires in a quarrel between Neptune and Juno, concerning their right of patronizing Argolis. Juno gained the preference, upon which Neptune, in a fit of resentment, dried up all the four rivers, whose decision he deemed partial, but afterwards restored them to their dignity and consequence. Phonoreus was the first who raised a temple to Juno. He received divine honors after death, and his temple still existed at Argos in the age of Antoninus the Roman emperor. *Paus.* 2. c. 15, &c.—*Apollod.* 2. c. 1.—*Stat. Theb.* 4. v. 589. l. 3. *Sylv.* 2. v. 101.—*Lactant. ad Theb.* 1. v. 252.—*Plin.* 7. c. 56.—*Schol. Eurip. in Orest.* 933. — *Sch. Æschyl. ad Prom.* 921. — *Hygin.* fab. 143.

PHORO'NIS, a pantronymic of Io as sister of Phoroneus. *Ovid. Met.* 1. v. 625.

PHORO'NIUM, a town of Argolis, built by Phoroneus.

PHORON'TIS, a town on the borders of Caria in Asia Minor. *Plin.* 5. c. 29.

PHO'RUM, a harbour of Attica. *Strab.*

PHORUN'NA, a city of Thrace. *Steph. ex Strab.*

PHOS'PHORUS, the name of Venus, or the morning, signifying its ushering forth the light, (φῶς φέρω, *lucem fero*). *Martial.* 8. epigr. 21.—*Cic. N.D.* 2. c. 20.

PHOTINÆ'ON, a city of Thessaly. *Steph.*

PHOTI'NUS, a eunuch that was prime minister to Ptolemy, king of Ægypt. When Pompey fled to the court of Ptolemy, after the battle of Pharsalia, Photinus advised his master not to receive the illustrious fugitive, but to put him to death. His advice was strictly followed. Julius Cæsar some time after visited Ægypt, and Photinus raised a sedition against him, for which he was put to death. When Cæsar triumphed over Ægypt and Alexandria, the pictures of Photinus and of some of the Ægyptians, were carried in the procession at Rome. *Plut.*——A native of Ancyra in Galatia, in the fourth century, famous as the head of a sect called Photinians, which for a while disturbed the peace of the Church. He died A.D. 375, in Galatia. *Epiphan. Hær.* 73.—*Theodoret. Hær.* fab. 1. 2.

PHO'TIUS, a son of Antonin, who betrayed to Belisarius his wife's debaucheries.——A patrician in Justinian's reign.——A patriarch of Constantinople in the 9th century, known by his Bibliotheca, edited by Schottus, August. Vindel. 1606. *Fabr. B. Gr.* 5. c. 35.—*Sax. Onom.* 2. p 121.

PHOVIBAGI'NA, a town of Galatia. *Ptol.*

PHOX'US, a general of the Phocæans, who built Lampsacus. *Polyæn.* 8. c. 37.——A tyrant of Chalcis, banished by his subjects. *Aristot. Pol.* 5. c. 4.

PHRAA'TA, a city of Media. *Steph.*

PHRAA'TES the First, a king of Parthia, called also Phriapatius, succeeded Arsaces the Third. He made war against Antiochus, king of Syria, and was defeated in three successive battles. He left several children behind him, but as they were all too young, and unable to support the dignity of the throne, he appointed his brother Mithridates, of whose abilities and military prudence he had often been a spectator. *Justin.* 41. c. 6.

PHRAA'TES the Second, succeeded his father Mithridates as king of Parthia; and made war against the Scythians, whom he called to his assistance against Antiochus, king of Syria, and whom he refused to pay, on the pretence that they came too late. He was murdered by some Greek mercenaries who had been once his captives, and who had afterwards enlisted into his army, B.C. 129. *Justin.* 42. c. 1.—*Plut. in Pomp.*

PHRAA'TES the Third, succeeded his brother Pacorus on the throne of Parthia, and gave one of his daughters in marriage to Tigranes, the son of Tigranes king of Armenia. Soon after, he invaded the kingdom of Armenia, to place his son-in-law on the throne of his father, but this unnatural expedition was attended with ill success. He renewed a treaty of alliance which his father had made with the Romans, and at his return into Parthia was assassinated by his sons Orodes and Mithridates. *Justin.*

PHRAA'TES the Fourth, was nominated king of Parthia by his father Orodes, whom he soon after murdered, as also 30 of his own brothers, that he might the more securely possess the supreme power. He made war against M. Antony with success, and obliged him to retire after he had received some severe defeats. Some time after, he was dethroned by the Parthian nobility, but by the assistance of the Scythians, he soon regained his power, and drove away the usurper, called Tiridates. The usurper claimed the protection of Augustus the Roman emperor, and Phraates sent ambassadors to Rome to plead his cause, and gain the favor of his powerful judge. He was successful in his embassy, made a treaty of peace and alliance with the Roman emperor, restored the ensigns and standards which the Parthians had taken from Crassus and Antony, and gave up his four sons with their wives as hostages, till his engagements were performed. Some suppose that Phraates delivered his children into the hands of Augustus to be confined at Rome, that he might reign with greater security, as he knew that his subjects would revolt as soon as they found any one of his family inclined to countenance their rebellion, though at the same time they scorned to support the interest of any usurper who was not of the royal house of the Arsacidæ. He was however at last murdered by one of his concubines, who placed her son called Phraataces on the throne. *Val. Max.* 7. c. 6.—*Justin.* 42. c. 5.—*Dio. Cas.* 51, &c.—*Plut. in Anton. &c.*—*Horat.* 2. od. 2. v. 17.—*Tacit. Ann.* 6. c. 32.

PHRAA'TES or PHRAHA'TES, a prince of Parthia in the reign of Tiberius. *Tac. Ann.* 6. c. 31.——A satrap of Parthia. *Tacit. Ann.* 6. c. 42.

PHRAAT'ACES, a son of Phraates the Fourth. He with his mother murdered his father, and took possession of the vacant throne. His reign was short, he was deposed by his subjects, whom he had offended by his cruelty, avarice, and oppression.

PHRA'DA, a city of Drangiana, which Alexander the Great afterwards called Prophthasia. *Steph.*

PHRADA'TES, an officer in the army of Darius at the battle of Arbela.

PHRAGAN'DÆ, a people of Thrace. *Liv.* 26. c. 25.

PHRAHA'TES, the same as Phraates. *Vid.* Phraates.

PHRANIC'ATES, a general of the Parthian armies, who fought with Ventidius at Trapezus. *Strab.* 16.

PHRAOR'TES, succeeded his father Deioces on the throne of Media. He made war against the neighbouring nations, and conquered the greatest part of Asia. He was defeated and killed in a battle by the Assyrians, after a reign of 22 years, B.C. 625. His son Cyaraxes succeeded him. It is supposed that the Arphaxad mentioned in Judith is Phraortes. *Paus.* 4. c. 24.—*Herodot.* 1. c. 102.——A king of India remarkable for his frugality. *Philostr. in vit. Apollon.*

PHRAS'ICLES, a nephew of Themistocles, whose daughter Nicomacha he married. *Plut. in Them.*

PHRASICLI'DES, an archon at Athens, Olymp. 102. an. 2.

PHRAS'IMUS, a Grecian hero, father of Praxithea, the wife of Erechtheus. *Apollod.* 3. c. 29.

PHRA'SIUS, a Cyprian soothsayer, sacrificed on an altar by Busiris king of Ægypt. *Id.*

PHRATAPHER'NES, a general of the Massagetæ, who surrendered to Alexander. *Curt.* 8. c. 1.——A satrap, who, after the death of Darius, fled to Hyrcania, and surrendered himself to Alexander. *Id.* 6. c. 4.

PHRA'ZI, a city of Bactriana. *Ptol.*

PHREAR'RHI, a village in the tribe Leontis *Steph.*

PHREA'TA, a town of Garsauria in Cappadocia. *Ptol.*

PHRE'TES, a people of Libya. *Steph.*

PHRIAPA'TIUS, a king of Parthia who flourished B.C. 195. *Vid.* Phraates.

PHRIC'IUM, a town near Thermopylæ. *Liv.* 36. c. 13.

PHRICODE'MUS, a tyrant of the Œantii. *Polyæn.* 8. c. 46.

PHRIX'A, a town of Triphylia, afterwards Phæstus. *Steph.*

PHRIX'US, a river of Argolis. *Pausan.* 1. 2.——A small town of Elis, built by the Minyæ. *Herodot.* 4. c. 148.——A harbour of Asiatic Sarmatia, at the mouth of the Cimmerian Bösporus. *Steph.*

PHRON'IMA, a daughter of Etearchus, king of Crete. She was delivered to a servant to be thrown into the sea, by order of her father, at the instigation of his second wife. The servant was unwilling to murder the child, but as he was bound by an oath to throw her into the sea, he accordingly let her down into the water by a rope, and took her out again unhurt. Phronima was afterwards in the number of the concubines of Polymnestus, by whom she became mother of Battus, the founder of Cyrene. *Herodot.* 4. c. 154.

PHRON'TIS, son of Onetor, pilot of the ship of Menelaus, after the Trojan war, was killed by Apollo just as the ship reached Sunium. *Homer. Odyss.* 3. v. 282.—*Paus.* 10. c. 25.——One of the Argonauts, son of Phryxus and Chalciope. *Hygin.* 3 & 14.—*Sch. Apollon.* 2. v. 390 & 1125.—*Apollon.* 1. v. 1159.—*Apollod.* 1.

PHRUDAR'CIDAS, one of the three Lacedæmonians who offered violence to the daughters of Scedasus. *Vid.* Scedasus.

PHRU'DIS, a river of Gallia Belgica. *Ptol.*

PHRUGUNDI'ONES, a people of European Sarmatia. *Ptol.*

PHRU'RI, a Scythian nation. *Dionys.*

PHRU'RIUM, a city of India within the Ganges. *Ptol.*

PHRY'GES, a river of Asia Minor, dividing Phrygia from Caria, and falling into the Hermus. *Paus.* 2.

PHRYG'IA, a country of Asia Minor, generally divided into Phrygia Major and Minor. Its boundaries are not properly or accurately defined by ancient authors, though it appears that it was situate between Bithynia, Lydia, Cappadocia, and Caria. It received its name from the Bryges, a nation of Thrace, or Macedonia, who came to settle there, and from their name, by corruption, arose the word Phrygia. Cybele was the chief deity of the country, and her festivals were observed with the greatest solemnity. The most remarkable towns besides Troy, were Laodice, Hierapolis, and Synnada. The invention of the pipe of reeds, and of all sorts of needlework, is attributed to the inhabitants, who are represented by some authors as stubborn, but yielding to correction (hence *Phryx verberatus melior*), as imprudent, effeminate, servile, and voluptuous; and to this *Virgil* seems to allude, *Æn.* 9. v. 617. The Phrygians, like all other nations, were called Barbarians by the Greeks; their music (*Phrygii cantus*) was of a grave and solemn nature when opposed to the brisker and more cheerful Lydian airs. *Mela.* 1. c. 19.—*Strab.* 2, &c.—*Ovid. Met.* 13. v. 429, &c.—*Cic.* 7. *ad Fam.* ep. 16.—*Flacc.* 27.—*Dio.* 1. c. 50.—*Plin.* 8. c. 48.—*Horat.* 2. od. 9. v. 16.—*Paus.* 5. c. 25.—*Herodot.* 7. c. 73.—*Servius in Æn.* 1. v. 276 & 472. l. 2. v. 504. l. 4. v. 215.——A city of Thrace.

PHRY'NE, a celebrated courtezan who flourished at Athens about 328 years B.C. She was mistress to Praxiteles, who exhibited all the powers of his art in a statue which he made of her. *Vid.* Praxiteles. This was one of his best pieces, and it was placed in the temple of Apollo at Delphi. It is said that Apelles painted his Venus Anadyomene after he had seen Phryne on the sea shore naked, and with dishevelled hair. Phryne became so rich by the liberality of her lovers, that she offered, at her own expense, to rebuild Thebes, which Alexander had destroyed, provided this inscription was placed on the walls: *Alexander diruit, sed meretrix Phryne refecit.* This offer was indignantly refused by the Thebans. *Plin.* 34. c. 8. l. 36. c. 5.—*Athen.* 13.—*Clem. Alex. ad Gentes.*—*Arnob. adv. Gent.*—*Paus.* 1. c. 20. l. 9. c. 27.—*Cic. Verr.* 4.—*Tibull.* 2. el. 5. v. 6. el. 7.——Another courtezan, who was accused of impiety, though some consider her to be the same person as the mistress of Praxiteles. When she saw that in spite of the eloquence of her defender Hyperides she was going to be condemned, she unveiled her bosom, and by this sudden display of her charms so influenced her judges, that she was immediately acquitted. *Quintil.* 2. c. 15.

PHRYN'ICHUS, a general of Samus, who endeavoured to betray his country to the Athenians. *Polyæn.* 3. c. 6.——A tragic poet of Athens, disciple to Thespis. He was the first who introduced a female character on the stage. His plays are lost, though some of the titles are preserved, such as Pleuronia, Alcestes, Actæon, the Ægyptians, Antheus, the Danaides, the taking of Miletus, &c. This last was so unpopular at Athens that the poet was fined a thousand drachmas, because he had interested, in too forcible a manner, the citizens in favour of a city which the Athenians regarded with jealousy and hatred. The name of his father was Polyphradmon, or, according to others, Minyrus, or Choroclis. *Herodot.* 6.—*Plut.*

in Præc. Polit. & Symph. 1.—*Fabr. B. Gr.* 2. c. 19.——Another tragic poet of Athens, son of Melanthes. Among his compositions are mentioned the tragedies of Erigone and Andromeda, &c. *Gyrald. de P. H.* 6.—*Strab.* 14.—*Fabr. ibid.*——A comic poet in the 76th Olympiad. He wrote ten comedies. Some fragments of his works have been collected by Hertelius and Grotius. *Fabr. B. Gr.* 2. c. 22.——An Archon at Athens, Olymp. 110. an. 5.——A writer in the reign of Commodus, who made a collection, in 36 books, of phrases and sentences from the best Greek authors, &c. *Phot. Bib. Cod.* 158.—*Suidas.*

PHRY'NIS, a musician of Mitylene, the first who obtained a musical prize at the Panathenæa at Athens. He added two strings to the lyre, which had always been used with seven by all his predecessors B.C. 438. It is said that he was originally a cook at the house of Hiero, king of Sicily, who observed his musical genius, and recommended him to the care of Aristoclitus.—*Pollux*, 4. c. 9.—*Suidas.*—*Plut. de Laud.*—*Schol. Aristoph. ad Nub.* 961.—*Gyrald. de P. H.* 7.

PHRY'NON, *(-ontis)*, a celebrated general of Athens, who died B.C. 590. *Polyæn.* 1. c. 25.

PHRYX'US or **PHRIX'US**, a son of Athamas, king of Thebes, by Nephele. After the repudiation of his mother, he was persecuted with the most inveterate hatred by his step-mother Ino, because he was to sit on the throne of Athamas, in preference to the children of a second wife. He was apprized of Ino's intention upon his life, by his mother Nephele, or, according to others, by his preceptor; and the better to make his escape, he secured part of his father's treasure, and privately left Bœotia with his sister Helle, to go to their friend and relation Æetes, king of Colchis. The two fugitives embarked on board a ship, or, according to the fabulous accounts of the poets and mythologists, they mounted on the back of a ram, the fleece of which was of gold, and proceeded on their journey through the air. The height to which they were carried made Helle giddy, and she fell into the sea. Phryxus gave her a decent burial on the sea shore, and after he had called the place Hellespont, from her name, he continued his flight, and arrived safe in the kingdom of Æetes, where he offered the ram on the altar of Mars. The monarch received him with great hospitality, and gave him his daughter Chalciope in marriage. She had by him Phrontis, Melias, Argos, Cylindrus, whom some call Cytorus, Catis, Lorus, and Hellen. Some time after Phryxus was murdered by his father-in-law, who envied him the possession of the golden fleece; and Chalciope, to prevent her children from sharing their father's fate, sent them privately from Colchis to Bœotia, as nothing was to be dreaded there from the jealousy or resentment of Ino, who was then dead. The fable of the flight of Phryxus to Colchis on a ram, has been explained by some, who observe, that the ship on which he embarked was either called by that name, or carried on her prow the figure of that animal. The fleece of gold is explained by recollecting that Phryxus carried away immense treasures from Thebes. Phryxus was placed among the constellations of heaven, after death. The ram which carried him to Asia, is said to have been the fruit of Neptune's amour with Theophane. This ram had been given to Athamas by the gods, to reward his piety and religious conduct, and Nephele procured it for her children, just as they were going to be sacrificed to the jealousy of Ino. The murder of Phryxus was some time after amply revenged by the Greeks. It gave rise to a celebrated expedition which was achieved under Jason, at the head of the most illustrious princes of Greece, and which had for its object the recovery of the golden fleece, and the punishment of the king of Colchis, for his cruelty to the son of Athamas. *Diod.* 4.—*Herodot.* 7. c. 197.—*Apollon. Arg.*—*Orpheus.*—*Flaccus.*—*Strab.*—*Apollod.* 1. c. 9.—*Pindar. Pyth* 4.—*Hygin.* fab. 14, 188, &c.—*Ovid. Heroid.* 18. *Met.* 4. fab. 13.—*Lactant. ad Achill.* 1. v. 65.—*Manil.* 4.—*Tzetzes. in Lyc.* 22.—*Sch. Pind.* 4. *Pyth.*—*Palæph. de Inc.* 31.—*Heraclit. Pont.* 24.

PHRYX'US, a small river of Argolis

PHTHI'A, a town of Phthiotis, at the east of mount Othrys in Thessaly, where Achilles was born, from which circumstance he is often called *Phthius heros*. *Horat.* 4. od. 6. v. 4.—*Ovid. Met* 13. v. 156.—*Strab.* 9.—*Virg. Æn.* 1. v. 288.—*Servius in Æn.* 2. v. 97.—*Seneca in Troad.* 817.—*Mela*, 2. c. 3.—*Propert.* 2. el. 14. v. 38.—*Cic. Tusc.* 1. c. 10.

PHTHI'A, a nymph of Achaia beloved by Jupiter, who, to seduce her, disguised himself under the shape of a pigeon. *Ælian. V.H.* 1. c. 15.—*Athen.* 9.——A daughter of Menon, of Thessaly, who married Æacides, king of Epirus, one of the descendants of Achilles, and had by him two daughters, and a son called Pyrrhus. *Plut. in Pyrr.*——The wife of Admetus, king of the Molossi. *Plut. in Them.*——A daughter of Amphion and Niobe, killed by Diana. *Apollod.*

PHTHIO'TIS, a small province of Thessaly, between the Pelasgicus Sinus and the Maliacus Sinus, Magnesia, and mount Œta. It was also anciently called Achaia. *Paus.* 10. c. 8.

PHTHI'RA, a mountain of Caria. *Steph.*

PHTHIROPH'AGI, a people of Asiatic Sarmatia, on the Euxine Sea. *Strab.*

PHTHON'TIS, a small town of Ægypt. *Ptol.*

PHTHU'RIS, a town of Ægypt, taken by C. Petronius, when set over Ægypt by Augustus. *Plin.* 6. c. 29.

PHUCA'RI or **PHYCA'RI**, a people inhabiting Caucasus. *Plin.* 37. c. 8.

PHU'PHENA, a city of Armenia Minor. *Ptol.* It is the Euspœna of *Antoninus*, according to *Simler.*

PHURNI'TA, a city of Libya. *Steph.*

PHUS'CA or **PHYS'CUS**, a maritime city of Caria. *Diod.*—*Strab.* It is now Fiesco.

PHY'A a tall and beautiful woman of Attica, whom Pisistratus, when he wished to re-establish himself a third time as absolute sovereign of Athens, dressed like the goddess Minerva, and led to the city on a chariot, making the populace believe that the goddess herself was come to restore him to power. The artifice succeeded. *Herodot.* 1. c. 59.—*Polyæn.* 1. c. 40.—*Val. Max.* 1 c. 2.

PHY'CUS *(-untis)*, a promontory near Cyrene, now called Ras-al-sem. *Lucan.* 9. v. 40.

PHYCUS'SÆ, islands of Libya. *Steph.*

PHYG'ELA, a town of Pannonia founded by some fugitives. *Pin.* 5. c. 29.

PHYL'ACE, a town of Thessaly, built by Phylacus. Protesilaus reigned there, whence he is often called Phylacides. *Lucan.* 6. v. 252.—*Ovid. de A.A.* 2. v. 356.—*Propert.* 1. el. 19. v. 7.——A town of Arcadia. *Paus.* 8. c. 54.——A town of Epirus. *Liv.* 45. c. 26.

PHYLACEN'SII, a people of Bithynia. *Ptol.*

PHYL'ACIS and **PHYLAN'DER**, sons of Apollo and Acacallis, were born in Crete, where a goat brought them up. To commemorate this event, the inhabitants of that part of the country sent as a present to Delphi, the brazen image of a goat suckling two infants. *Paus.* 10. c. 16.

PHYL'ACUS, a son of Deion, king of Phocis. He married Clymene, the daughter of Mynias, by whom he had Iphiclus, Pœas, and Alcimede. He was the founder of Phylace, in Phthiotis of Thessaly. *Flacc.* 1. v. 295.—*Eustath. ad Il.* 2. v. 697.—*Apollon.* 1. v. 47.—*Apollod.* 1.——A native of Delphi who distinguished himself in the Persian wars. *Paus.* 10. c. 8 & 13.

PHY'LÆ or **PHI'LÆ**, a small island of Ægypt. *Strab.*—*Salmas ad Solin.* p. 437.

PHYLAN'DER, a son of Apollo. *Vid.* Phylacis.

PHYLAR'CHUS, a Greek biographer, who flourished, B.C. 221. He is accused of partiality by *Plutarch in Arat.*

PHY'LAS, a king of Ephyre, son of Antiochus, and grandson of Hercules. *Apollod.* 2.—*Paus.* 2. c. 4.—*Diod.* 4.

PHY'LE, a well fortified village of Attica, at a little distance from Athens. *C. Nep. in Thras.*

PHYLE'IS, a daughter of Thespius. *Apollod.* 1.

PHY'LEUS, one of the Greek captains during the Trojan war.——A son of Augeas. He blamed his father for refusing to pay Hercules what he had promised him for cleaning his stables, and for this honorable conduct he was placed on the throne by Hercules. *Apollod.* 2.—*Paus.* 5. c. 2 & 3.

PHYL'IRA. *Vid.* Philyra.

PHYLIT'Æ, a people of India within the Ganges. *Ptol.*

PHYL'LA, the wife of Demetrius Poliorcetes, and mother of Stratonice, the wife of Seleucus.

PHYLLA'LIA, a part of Arcadia called also Phylos. *Stat. Theb.* 4. v. 45. *Stephanus* and *Strabo*, l. 9. give this name to a place in Thessaly. *Vid. Barthii animadvers. ad loc. cit.*

PHYLLE'IUS, a mountain, country, and town of Macedonia. *Apollon. Arg.* 1.

PHYL'LIS, a daughter of Sithon, or, according to others of Lycurgus, king of Thrace, who hospitably received Demophoon, the son of Theseus, who, at his return from the Trojan war had stopped on her coasts. She became enamoured of him, and did not find him insensible to her passion. After some months of mutual tenderness and affection, Demophoon set sail for Athens, where his domestic affairs recalled him. He promised faithfully to return as soon as a month was expired; but either his dislike for Phyllis, or the irreparable situation of his affairs, obliged him to violate his engagement, and the queen, grown desperate on account of his absence, hanged herself, or, according to others, threw herself down a precipice into the sea and perished. Her friends raised a tomb over her body, where there grew up certain trees, the leaves of which, at a particular season of the year, suddenly became wet, as if shedding tears for the death of Phyllis. According to an old tradition, mentioned by Servius, Virgil's commentator, Phyllis was changed by the gods into an almond-tree, which is called Phylla by the Greeks. Some days after this metamorphosis, Demophoon re-visited Thrace, and when he heard of the fate of Phyllis, he ran and clasped the tree, which, though at that time stripped of its leaves, suddenly shot forth and blossomed as if still sensible of tenderness and love. The absence of Demophoon from the house of Phyllis has given rise to a beautiful epistle of Ovid, supposed to have been written by the Thracian queen about the fourth month after her lover's departure. *Ovid. Heroid.* 2. *De Art. Am.* 2. v. 353. *Trist.* 2. v. 437.—*Aul. Sabin.* 2.—*Hygin.* fab. 59.—*Servius. ad Virg. Ec.* 5. v. 10.—*Tzetzes. Chil.* 1. c. 4. & *Lyc.* 495. This last author calls the lover of Phyllis, Acamas, the brother of Demophoon, and not Demophoon himself.——A country woman introduced into *Virgil's* eclogues ——The nurse of the emperor Domitian, who buried him when murdered. *Suet. in Dom.* 17.——A musician mentioned by the *Scholiast* on *Aristoph. Ran.*

PHYL'LIS, a country of Thrace, near mount Pangæus. *Herodot.* 7. c. 113.——A river of Bithynia. *Strab.—Steph.*

PHYL'LIUS, a young Bœotian, uncommonly fond of Cygnus, the son of Hyria, a woman of Bœotia. Cygnus slighted his passion, and told him that to obtain a return of affection, he must previously destroy an enormous lion, take alive two large vultures, and sacrifice on Jupiter's altar a wild bull that infested the country. This he easily effected by means of artifice, and by the advice of Hercules he forgot his partiality for the son of Hyria, who became so desperate at his coldness, that he threw himself into the lake Canopus, and was changed into a swan. His mother, unable to survive his death, threw herself down a precipice, and from the tears which she had shed there arose a stream which bore her name in Bœotia. Ovid speaks of this metamorphosis in a different manner. *Homer. Il.* 2. v. 496.—*Hesiod. apud Sch. Pind.* 4. *Pyth.* v. 36.—*Antonin. Lib.* 3. c 12. —*Ovid. Met.* 7. v. 372.——A Spartan remarkable for the courage with which he fought against Pyrrhus, king of Epirus.

PHYLLOD'OCE, one of Cyrene's attendant nymphs. *Hygin. in Præf. Fab.—Virg. G.* 4. v. 336.

PHYLLO'NE, daughter of Alcimedon, became mother of Æchmacoras by Hercules. *Pausan.* 8. c. 12.

PHYL'LOS, a country of Arcadia. *Vid.* Phyllalia.

PHYL'LUS, a general of Phocis during the Phocian or sacred war against the Thebans. He assumed the command after the death of his brothers Philomelus and Onomarchus. He is called by some Phayllus. *Vid.* Phocis.

PHY'LO, one of the female attendants of Helen. *Hom. Odyss.* 4. v. 133.

PHYS'CA, a city of Mygdonis in Macedonia. *Ptol.*

PHYS'CE, a town of Lower Mœsia. *Id.* It is now Chosabet, according to *Niger.*

PHYSCEL'LA, a town of Macedonia. *Mela*, 2. c. 3.—*Plin.* 4. c. 10.

PHYS'CIA, a city of Lycia, on a lofty mountain. *Steph.*

PHYS'CION or PHIC'IUM, a famous rock of Bœotia, which was the residence of the Sphinx, and against which the monster destroyed himself when his enigmas were explained by Œdipus. *Plut.*

PHYS'CIUS, a son of Amphictyon, father of Locrus. *Plut. in Qu. Gr.* 15.

PHYS'COA, a woman of Elis, mother of Narcæus, by Bacchus. *Vid.* Narcæus. *Paus.* 5. c. 16.

PHYS'CON, a surname of one of the Ptolemies kings of Ægypt, from the great prominence of his belly (φύσκη, *venter*). *Vid.* Ptolemæus. *Athen.* 2. c. 23.—*Galen.* 2. *Ad. Epid.—Vitruv.* 7. *in* præf.

PHYS'COS, a town of Caria, opposite Rhodes. *Strab.* 14.——A mountain of Magna Græcia, near Crotona. *Theocr.*——A town of Locris, founded by Physcus the Ætolian. *Steph.*

PHYS'CUS, a river of Asia, falling into the Tigris. The ten thousand Greeks crossed it on their return from Cunaxa.

PHYS'IUS, a son of Lycaon of Arcadia. *Apollod.* 3.

PHYTE'UM, a city of Ætolia. *Steph.*

PHYTAL'IDES, the patronymic of the descendants of Phytalus.

PHYTAL'MIUS, a surname of Neptune, expressive of his presiding over and nourishing plants. *Plut. Symp.* 8. *Qu.* 8.

PHYT'ALUS, a man who hospitably received and entertained Ceres, when she visited Attica, for which, besides the gift of the fig-tree, the care of the mysteries of the goddess was entrusted to his family, and confirmed by Theseus. Phytalus died at Cephisus, near Athens, where a monument was raised to honor his memory. *Paus. in Att.* c. 37. —*Plut. in Thes.*

PHYTE'UM, a city of Elis. *Steph.*

PHY'TO, the name of the Samian Sibyl, called also Phemenoe by Isidorus. *Clem. Alex. Strom.* 1.—*Isidor.* 8. c. 8.—*Gyrald. de P. H.* 2.

PHY'TON, a general of the people of Rhegium against Dionysius, the tyrant of Sicily. He was taken by the enemy, and tortured, B.C. 387, and his son was thrown into the sea. *Diod.* 14.

PHYTO'NIA, an island of the Tyrrhene Sea. *Mela*, 2. c. 7.

PHYX'IUM, a town of Elis. *Polyb.*

PHYZA'NIA, a region of Africa. *Ptol.*

PI'ACUS, a city of Sicily. *Steph.*

PI'ADA, a city of Serica. *Ptol.*

PI'ALA, a city of Cappadocia, in the Galatian Pontus. *Ptol.*

PI'ALÆ, a people of Scythia. *Plin.* 6. c. 17.

PIA'LIA, festivals instituted in honor of Adrian, by the emperor Antoninus. They were celebrated at Puteoli, in the second year of the Olympiads. ——A city of Thessaly. *Steph.*

PIAREN'SII, a people of Lower Mysia. *Ptol.*

PIAS'TÆ, a people near Pontus. *Steph.*

PI'ASUS, a general of the Pelasgi. *Strab.* 13.

PICEN'DACA, a city of India within the Ganges. *Ptol.*

PICE'NI, the inhabitants of Picenum, called also Picentes. They received their name from *picus*, a bird by whose auspices they had settled in that part of Italy. *Ital.* 8. v. 425.—*Strab.* 5.—*Mela*, 2. c. 4.

PICEN'TIA, the capital of the Picentini. *Strab.* 5.

PICENTI'NI, a people of Italy, between Lucania and Campania on the Tuscan Sea. They are different from the Piceni or Picentes, who inhabited Picenum. *Sil. It.* 8. v. 580.—*Tacit. H.* 4. c. 62.

PICE'NUM or PICE'NUS A'GER, a country of Italy near the Umbrians and Sabines, on the borders of the Adriatic, now called the March of Ancona. The inhabitants were called Piceni or Picentes. *Liv.* 21 c. 6. l. 22. c. 9. l. 27. c. 43.—*Sil.* 10. v. 313.—*Horat.* 2. sat. 3. v. 272.—*Mart.* 1. epigr. 44.—*Strab.* 5 & 6.—*Mela.* 2. c. 4.—*Servius in Æn.* 7. v. 175.—*Festus de V. Sig.*

PICNE'SII, a people of Upper Mysia. *Ptol.*

PI'CRA, a lake of Africa, which Alexander crossed when he went to consult the oracle of Ammon. *Diod.*

PIC'TÆ or PIC'TI, a people of Scythia, called also Agathyrsæ. They received this name from their painting their bodies different colors, to appear more terrible in the eyes of their enemies. A colony of these, according to Servius, Virgil's commentator, emigrated to the northern parts of Britain, where they still preserved their name and savage manners, but they are mentioned only by later writers. *Marcell.* 27. c. 18.—*Claudian. de Hon. Cons.* v. 54.—*Plin.* 4. c. 12.—*Herodot.* 4. c. 10.—*Servius in Æn* 4. v. 146.—*Mela*, 2. c. 1.

PICTA'VI or PIC'TONES, a people of Gaul, in the modern country of Poictou. *Cæs.* 7. *Bell. G.* c. 4.

PICTA'VIUM, a town of Gaul.

PIC'TOR FA'BIUS, a consul under whom silver was first coined at Rome, A U. C. 485.

Q. FA'BIUS PIC'TOR. *Vid.* Fabius.

PICUEN'TUM, an inland city of Istria. *Ptol.* It is now Pinguento, according to *Leander*.

PICUM'NUS and PILUM'NUS, two deities at Rome, who presided over the auspices that were required before the celebration of nuptials. Pilumnus was supposed to patronize children, as his name seems in some manner to indicate, *quod pellat mala infantiæ.* The manuring of lands was first discovered by Picumnus, from which reason he is called Sterquilinius. Pilumnus was also invoked as the god of bakers and millers, as he is said to have first discovered how to grind corn. Turnus boasted of being one of his lineal descendants. *Virg. Æn.* 9. v. 4.—*Varro de Vit. P. R.* 2. *Apud. Nonn.*—*Servius in Æn.* 9. v. 4. l. 10. v. 76.—*Gyrald. de H. D.* 1.

PI'CUS, a king of Latium, son of Saturn, who married Venilia, who is also called Canens, by whom he had Faunus. He was tenderly loved by the goddess Pomona, and loved her with mutual affection. As he was one day hunting in the woods, he was met by Circe, who became deeply enamoured of him, and who, upon finding her addresses treated with contempt, struck him with her wand, and changed him into a woodpecker, called by the name of *picus* among the Latins. His wife Venilia was so disconsolate when she was informed of his death, that she pined away. Some suppose that Picus was the son of Pilumnus, and that he gave prophecies to his subjects, by means of a favorite woodpecker, from which circumstance originated the fable of his being metamorphosed into a bird. *Virg. Æn.* 7. v. 48. 171, &c.—*Ovid. Met.* 14. v. 320, &c.—*Festus de V. Sig.*—*Servius in Æn.* 7. v. 190. l. 10. v. 76.

PI'DA, a city of the Galatian Pontus in Cappadocia. *Ptol.*

PI'DE, a town of Æthiopia on the Red Sea. *Plin.* 6. c. 29.

PIDIBO'TAS, a town of Upper Æthiopia. *Plin. Ibid.*

PIDO'RUS, a town near mount Athos. *Herodot.* 7. c. 122.

PIDO'SUS, a small island of Caria, near Helicarnassus. *Plin.* 5. c. 31. It is now probably Isola di S. Pietro.

PIDY'TES, a man killed by Ulysses during the Trojan war. *Hom. Il.* 7.

PI'ELUS, a son of Neoptolemus, king of Epirus, after his father. *Justin.* 17. c. 3.—*Hygin.* fab. 123.—*Paus.* 1. c. 11.

PIEPH'IGI, a people of Dacia. *Ptol.*

PI'ERA, a fountain of Peloponnesus, between Elis and Olympia. It was necessary that persons who presided over the Olympic games should be purified with the waters of this fountain, and offer a pig before they entered on the exercise of their functions. *Paus.* 5. c. 16.

PI'ERES, a people of Macedonia, near the Dardani. *Plin.* 4. c. 10.

PIE'RIA, a small tract of country in Thessaly or Macedonia, from which the epithet of *Pierian* was applied to the Muses and to poetical compositions. *Mela*, 2. c. 3.—*Apollod.* 1 & 3.—*Martial.* 9. epigr. 88. v. 3.—*Horat.* 4. od. 8. v. 20.

PIE'RIA, a place between Cilicia and Syria.

PIE'RIA, one of the wives of Danaus, mother of six daughters, called Actea, Podarce, Dioxippe, Adyte, Ocypete, and Pilarge. *Apollod.* 2.——The wife of Oxylus, the son of Hæmon, and mother of Ætolas and Laias. *Paus.* 5. c. 3 & 4.——The daughter of Pythas, a Milesian. *Polyæn.* 8. c. 35.

PIER'IDES, a name given to the Muses, either because they were born in Pieria, in Thessaly, or resided on mount Pierus, or because they were supposed by some to be the daughters of Pierus, a king of Macedonia, who settled in Bœotia. *Hesiod. Th.* 54.—*Propert.* 2. el. 8. v. 16.—*Virg. Ecl* 3. v. 85. 6. v. 13. & 8. v. 63, &c.—*Horat.* 4. od. 8 v. 20.—*Cic. de N. D.* 3. c. 21.—*Festus de V. Sig.* ——The daughters of Pierus, who challenged the Muses to a trial in music, in which they were conquered, and changed into magpies. It may perhaps be supposed, that the victorious Muses assumed the name of the conquered daughters of Pierus, and ordered themselves to be called Pierides, in the same manner as Minerva was called Pallas because she had killed the giant Pallas. *Ovid. Met.* 5. v. 300.—*Nicander ad Anton. Liber.* 9.

PI'ERIS, a mountain, the same as Pierus. *Paus.* 9. c. 29.

PI'ERUS, a mountain of Thessaly, at the west of Olympus, sacred to the Muses, who were from thence, as some imagine, called Pierides. *Horat.* 3. od. 4. v. 40.—*Lucret.* 1. v. 945.—*Ovid. ex Pont.* 1. ep. 5. v. 58. ep. 9. v. 62. *Am.* 3. ep. 9. v. 26.—*Propert.* 2. el. 10. v. 5.

PI'ERUS, a son of Apollo, who is said to have raised a temple to the Muses. *Servius Æn.* 7. v. 21.——A rich man of Thessaly, father of nine daughters by Evippe. These daughters, called Pierides from their father, relying on their musical powers, had the presumption to challenge the Muses, and were changed into magpies, when conquered. Pierus is called by some the son of Linus, or, according to Apollodorus, of Magnes, who says that he had a son called Hyacinthus by Clio. *Apollod.* 1.—*Plut. de Music.*—*Tzetzes Chil.* 6. v. 90.—*Fabr. B. Gr.* 1. c. 26.—*Gyrald. P. H.* 2.—*Paus.* 9. c. 29.

PI'ERUS, a river of Achaia, in Peloponnesus.——A town of Thessaly. *Plin.* 4. c. 8.——A mountain, with a lake of the same name, in Macedonia. *Paus.* 7. c. 22.

PI'ETAS, a virtue which denotes veneration for the deity, and love and tenderness to our friends. It received divine honors among the Romans, and was made one of their gods. Acilius Glabrio first erected a temple to this new divinity, on the spot where a woman had fed with her own milk her aged father, or, according to others, her mother, who had been imprisoned by the order of the senate, and deprived of all aliments. *Cic. de Div.* 1. c. 43.—*Val. Max.* 5. c. 4.—*Lactant.* 1. c. 20. —*Plin.* 7. c. 36.—*Festus de V. Sig.*

PI'GRES and MAT'TYAS, two brothers, &c. *Herodot.* 5. c. 12.

PI'GRES, a brother of Artemisia, wife of Mausolus. *Suidas.*

PI'GRES, the name of three rivers according to *Herodotus.* *Vid. Salmas. ad Solin.* p. 694.

PI'GRUM MA'RE, a name applied to the Northern Sea, from its being frozen. The word Pigra is applied to the Palus Mæotis. *Ovid.* 4. *Pont.* 10. v. 61.—*Plin.* 4. c. 13.—*Tacit. G.* 45.

PILUM'NUS, the god of bakers at Rome. *Vid.* Picumnus.

PIMOLI'SA, a fortified place of Pontus, within the Halys. The country was called Pimolisena, and was probably the Pimolitis of *Strabo. Steph.*

PIM'PLA or PIMPLE'A, a mountain of Macedonia, with a fountain of the same name on the confines of Thessaly, near Olympus, sacred to the Muses, who on that account are often called Pimpleæ and Pimpleades. *Horat.* 1. od. 26. v. 9.—*Strab.* 10.—*Martial.* 12. epigr. 11. v. 3.—*Stat.* 1. *Sylv.* 4. v. 26. *Sylv.* 2. v. 36.—*Catull.* 10. v. 1.—*Festus de V. Sig.*—*Gyrald. H. D.* 7.

PIMPRA'NA or PIMPRA'MA, a town on the Indus. *Arrian. in Indic.*

PIN'AMUS, a city of Ægypt. *Steph.*

PIN'ARA, an island of the Ægæan Sea. *Plin.* 4. c. 12.——A town of Syria, at the south of mount Amanus. *Plin.* 5. c. 25.—— A town of Lycia. *Strab.* 14.

PINA'RIUS and POTIT'TIUS, two old men of Arcadia, who came with Evander to Italy. They were instructed by Hercules, who visited the court of Evander, how they were to offer sacrifices to his divinity, in the morning, and in the evening at sun-set. The morning sacrifices they punctually performed, but in the evening Potitius was obliged to offer the sacrifice alone, as Pinarius neglected to come until after the appointed time

This negligence offended Hercules, and he ordered that for the future, Pinarius and his descendants should preside over the sacrifices, but that Potitius, with his posterity, should wait upon the priests as servants, when the sacrifices were offered to him on mount Aventine. This was religiously observed till the age of Appius Claudius, who persuaded the Potitii, by a large bribe, to discontinue their sacred office, and to have the ceremony performed by slaves. For this negligence, as the Latin authors observe, the Potitii were deprived of sight, and the family became a little time after, totally extinct. *Liv* 1. c. 7.—*Virg. Æn.* 8. v. 269, &c.—*Victor. de Orig.* c. 8.—*Macrob. Sat.* 1. c. 12. l. 3. c. 6.—*Servius ad Virg. loco cit.*

M. PINA'RIUS POS'CA, a prætor, who conquered Sardinia and defeated the Corsicans. *Civ. de Orat.* 2.

PINA'RIUS TI'TUS, a Roman, intimate with Cicero. *Cic.* 12. *Fam.* 24. *Att.* 6. ep. 1. l. 8. ep. 15.

PIN'ARUS, now Delifou, a river falling into the sea near Issus, after flowing between Cilicia and Syria. *Dionys. Per.*

PIN'CUM, a town of Mœsia Superior, now Gradisca.

PIN'DARUS, a celebrated lyric poet of Thebes. He was carefully trained from his earliest years to the study of music and poetry, and was taught by Myrtis and Corinna how to compose verses with elegance and simplicity. When he was young, it is said that a swarm of bees settled on his lips, and there left some honey-combs as he reposed on the grass. This was universally explained as a prognostic of his future greatness and celebrity, and indeed he seemed entitled to notice when he had conquered Myrtis in a musical contest. He was not, however, so successful against Corinna, who obtained five times, while he was competitor, a poetical prize, which, according to some, was adjudged rather to the charms of her person, than to the brilliancy of her genius, or the superiority of her composition. In the public assemblies of Greece, where females were not permitted to contend, Pindar was rewarded with the prize, in preference to every other competitor; and as the conquerors at Olympia were the subjects of his compositions, the poet was courted by statesmen and princes. His hymns and pæans were repeated before the most crowded assemblies in the temples of Greece; and the priestess of Delphi declared that it was the will of Apollo that Pindar should receive the half of all the first-fruit offering that were annually heaped upon his altars. This was not the only public honor which he received; after his death, he was honored with every mark of respect, even to adoration. His statue was erected at Thebes in the public places where the games were exhibited, and six centuries after it was viewed with pleasure and admiration by the geographer Pausanias. The honors which had been paid to him while alive, were also shared by his posterity; and at the celebration of one of the festivals of the Greeks, a portion of the victim which had been offered in sacrifice, was reserved for the descendants of the poet. Even the most inveterate enemies of the Thebans showed regard for his memory, and the Spartans spared the house which the prince of Lyrics had inhabited when they destroyed the buildings and the walls of Thebes. The same respect was also paid him by Alexander the Great, when Thebes was reduced to ashes. It is said that Pindar died at the advanced age of 86, B.C. 435. The greatest part of his works has perished. He had written some hymns to the gods, poems in honour of Apollo, dithyrambics to Bacchus, and odes on several victories obtained at the four greatest festivals of the Greeks, the Olympic, Isthmian, Pythian, and Nemean games. Of all these, the odes are the only compositions extant, and they are admired for sublimity of sentiment, grandeur of expression, energy and magnificence of style, boldness of metaphor, harmony of numbers, and elegance of diction. In these odes which were repeated with the aid of musical instruments, and accompanied by the various inflections of the voice, with suitable attitudes and proper motions of the body, the poet has not merely celebrated the place where the victory was won, but has introduced beautiful episodes, and by unfolding the greatness of his heroes, the dignity of their characters, and the glory of the several republics where they flourished, has rendered the whole truly beautiful, and in the highest degree interesting. Horace has not hesitated to call Pindar inimitable, and this panegyric will not perhaps appear too extravagant, when we recollect that succeeding critics have agreed in extolling his beauties and his excellence, and the fire, animation, and enthusiasm of his genius. He has been censured for his affectation in composing an ode from which the letter S was excluded. The best editions of Pindar are those of Heyne, 4to, Gottingen, 1773; of Glasgow, 12mo, 1774; and of Schmidius, 4to, Witteberg. 1616. *Athen.*—*Quintil.* 10. c. 1.—*Horat.* 4. od. 2.—*Ælian. V.H.* 3. c. 26. l. 12. c. 45. l. 13. c. 7 & 25.—*Paus.* 1. c. 8. l. 9. c. 23.—*Val. Max.* 9. c. 12.—*Plut. in Alex.*—*Curt.* 1. c. 13.—*Fabr. B. Gr.* 2. c. 15.—*Sax. Onom.* 1. p. 33. [A fine bust of Pindar, inscribed with his name, will be found in the Capitoline Museum at Rome. There are several repetitions of it in other collections.]——A tyrant of Ephesus, who retired to Peloponnesus, leaving Pasis guardian of his son. *Ælian. V. H.* 3. c. 16.——A Theban, who wrote a poem on the Trojan war. *Voss. Hist. Lat.* 3. c. 11.

PIN'DASUS, a mountain of Troas. *Plin.* 5. c. 30.

PINDENIS'SUS, a town of Cilicia on the borders of Syria. Cicero, when pro-consul in Asia, besieged it for twenty-five days and took it. *Cic. ad M. Cœlium. Ad Fam.* 2. ep. 10.

PIN'DUS, a mountain, or rather a chain of mountains, between Thessaly, Macedonia, and Epirus. It was greatly celebrated as being sacred to the Muses and to Apollo. *Ovid. Met.* 1. v. 570.—*Strab.* 7 & 8.—*Plin.* 4.—*In Prœm.*—*Horat.* 1. od. 13. v. 6.—*Virg. Ecl.* 10. v. 11.—*Lucan.* 1. v. 674. l. 6. v. 339.—*Mela*, 2. c. 3.——A town of Doris in Greece, called also Cyphas. It was watered by a small river of the same name which falls into the Cephisus, near Lilæa. *Herodot.* 1. c. 56.

PINE'TUS, a town of Hispania Tarraconensis. *Antonin.* It is now Peneda.

PIN'GUS, a river of Mysia, falling into the Danube. *Plin.* 3. c. 26.

PIN'NA, a town of Italy, at the mouth of the Matrinus, south of Picenum. *Sil.* 8. v. 518.

PIN'NIUS, a Roman, who showed his respect to Cicero, by appointing him his second heir. *Cic.* 13. *Fam.* 61.

PI'NON, a town of Dacia. *Ptol.*.

PINTHIAS. *Vid.* Phinthias.

PIN'TIA, a town of Spain, now supposed to be Valladolid.

PIN'ZON, a town of Thrace. *Procopius.*

PI'ONIS, one of the descendants of Hercules, who built Pionia, near the Caycus in Mysia. It is said that smoke issued from his tomb as often as sacrifices were offered to him. *Paus.* 9. c. 18.

PI'ONE, one of the Nereides. *Apollod.* 1.

PIO'NIA, a town of Mysia, near the Caycus. *Plin.* 5. c. 30.—*Paus.* 9.

PIPLE'A, the mistress of Daphnis, a Grecian shepherd. She was carried away by pirates, and sold to Lytiersas of Lydia, a cruel prince, who obliged all strangers to cut down his ripe corn, and who put them to death if they worked too slowly. Daphnis came in quest of Piplea, and was about to fall a sacrifice to the barbarity of Lytiersas, when Hercules arrived, and not only delivered him by putting the tyrant to death, but gave him the treasures of his palace. *Servius in Ecl.* 8. v. 68.

PIRÆ'A, an ancient name of Amisus. *Strab.* 12.

PIRÆ'US or PIRÆ'EUS, a celebrated harbour at Athens, at the mouth of the Cephisus, about three miles distant from the city. It was joined to the town by two walls, in circumference seven miles and a half, and sixty feet high, which Themistocles wished to raise in a double proportion. One of these was built by Pericles, and the other by Themistocles. The towers which were raised on the walls to serve as a defence, were turned into dwelling-houses, as the population of Athens gradually increased. It was the most capacious of all the harbours of the Athenians, and was naturally divided into three large basins called Cantharon, Aphrodisium, and Zea, improved by the labours of Themistocles, and made sufficiently commodious for the reception of a fleet of 400 ships in the greatest security. The walls which joined it to Athens, with all its fortifications, were totally demolished when Lysander put an end to the Peloponnesian war by the reduction of Attica. *Paus.* 1. c. 1.—*Strab.* 9.—*C. Nep. in Them.*—*Flor.* 3. c. 5.—*Justin.* 5. c. 8.—*Ovid. Met.* 6. v. 446. *Fast.* 4. v. 563.—*Vitruv.* 7. *In Pr.* & l. 8. c. 3.—*Propert.* 3. el. 21. v. 23.—*Catull.* 65. v. 74.

PIRAN'THUS, a son of Argus and Evadne, brother of Iasus, Epidaurus, and Perasus. *Paus.* 2. c. 16. & 17.—*Apollod.* 2.

PI'RAS, the husband of Styx, by whom he had the Lernæan hydra. *Epimenid. apud Paus.* 8. c. 18.

PI'REN, a son of Glaucus, killed by his brother Bellerophon. He is more frequently called Alcimenus or Beller. *Apollod.* 2.

PIRE'NE, a daughter of Danaus, wife of Agaptolemus. *Apollod.*——A daughter of Œbalus, or, according to others, of the Achelous. She had by Neptune two sons called Leches and Cenchrius, who gave their name to two of the harbours of Corinth. Pirene was so disconsolate at the death of her son Cenchrius, who had been killed by Diana, that she pined away, and was dissolved by her continual weeping into a fountain of the same name, which was still seen at Corinth in the age of Pausanias. The fountain Pirene was sacred to the Muses, and, according to some, the horse Pegasus was drinking some of its waters, when Bellerophon took it to go and conquer the Chimæra. *Paus* 2. c. 3.—*Ovid. Met.* 2. v. 240. *Ex Pont.* 1. ep. 3. v. 75.—*Plin.* 4. c. 4.—*Pers. Prol.*—*Stat.* 1. *Sylv.* 4. v. 27.

PIRE'SIA, a city of Thessaly, formerly called Asterion. *Orpheus in Argon.*

PIR'IDES, islands in the Ægæan Sea. *Antonin.*

PIRI'NA, a town of Sicily. *Id.*

PIRITH'OUS, a son of Ixion and the cloud, or, according to others, of Dia, the daughter of Deioneus. Some make him son of Dia, by Jupiter, who assumed the shape of a horse whenever he paid his addresses to his mistress. He was king of the Lapithæ, and, as an ambitious prince, he wished to become acquainted with Theseus, king of Athens, of whose fame and exploits he had heard so many reports. To see him, and at the same time to be a witness of his valour, he resolved to invade his territories with an army. Theseus immediately met him on the borders of Attica, yet at the sight of one another the two enemies did not begin the engagement, but, struck with the appearance of each other, stepped between the hostile armies. Their meeting was like that of the most cordial friends, and Pirithous, by giving Theseus his hand as a pledge of his sincerity, promised to repair all the damages which his hostilities in Attica might have occasioned. From that time, therefore, the two monarchs became the most intimate and the most attached of friends, so much, that their friendship, like that of Orestes and Pylades, is become proverbial. Pirithous some time after married Hippodamia, and invited not only the heroes of his age, but also the gods themselves, and his neighbours the Centaurs, to celebrate his nuptials. Mars was the only one of the gods who was not invited, and to punish this neglect, the god of war was determined to raise a quarrel among the guests and to disturb the festivity of the entertainment. Eurythion, captivated with the beauty of Hippodamia, and intoxicated with wine, attempted to offer violence to the bride, but he was prevented by Theseus and immediately killed. This irritated the rest of the Centaurs, the contest became general, but the valour of Theseus, Pirithous, Hercules, and the rest of the Lapithæ, triumphed over their enemies. Many of the Centaurs were slain, and the rest saved their lives by flight. *Vid.* Lapithes. The death of Hippodamia left Pirithous very disconsolate, and he resolved, with his friend Theseus, who had likewise lost his wife, never to marry again, except he was united to a goddess, or one of the daughters of the gods. This determination occasioned the rape of Helen by the two friends; the lot was drawn, and it fell to the share of Theseus to have the beautiful prize. Pirithous upon this undertook with his friend to carry away Proserpine and to marry her. They descended into the infernal regions, but Pluto, who was apprized of their machinations to disturb his conjugal peace, stopped the two friends, and confined them there. Pirithous was tied to his father's wheel, or, according to Hyginus, was delivered to the furies to be continually tormented. His punishment, however, was short, and when Hercules visited the kingdom of Pluto, he obtained from Proserpine the pardon of Pirithous, and brought him back to his kingdom safe and unhurt. Some, however, assert that Theseus only was liberated by the intercession of Hercules, and that the punishment of Pirithous became more severe, while others suppose that he was torn to pieces by the dog Cerberus. *Vid.* Theseus. *Ovid. Met.* 12. fab. 4 & 5.—*Hesiod. in Scut. Her.* 176.—*Homer. Il.* 2. v. 247. *Enum. Od.* 21. 293.—*Paus.* 5. c. 10.—*Apollod.* 1. c. 8. l. 2. c. 5.—*Hygin.* fab. 14, 79, 155.—*Diod.* 4.—*Plut. in Thes.*—*Horat.* 4. od. 7.—*Virg. Æn.* 7. v. 304.—*Mart.* 7. epigr.—*Sch. ad Hom. Il.* 1. v. 168.—*Sch. Apollon.* 3. *Arg.* v. 62 *Eustath. in Odyss.* 21.—*Servius in Æn.* 6. v. 121 & 601. l. 7. v. 304

PIROBORIDA'VA, a town of Lower Mysia. *Ptol.*

PI'RUM, a city of Dacia. *Id.*

PI'RUS, a captain of the Thracians during the Trojan war, killed by Thoas, king of Ætolia. *Homer. Il.* 4.

PIRUS'TÆ, a people of Illyricum. *Liv.* 45. c. 26.

PI'SA, a town of Elis, on the Alpheus at the west of the Peloponnesus, founded by Pisus the son of Perieres and grandson of Æolus. Its inhabitants accompanied Nestor to the Trojan war, and they long enjoyed the privilege of presiding at the Olympic games, which were celebrated near their city. This honorable appointment was envied by the people of Elis, who made war against the Piseans, and after many bloody battles took their city, and totally demolished it. It was at Pisa that Œnomaus murdered the suitors of his daughter, and that he himself was conquered by Pelops. The inhabitants were called Pisæi. Some have doubted the existence of such a place as Pisa, but this doubt originates from Pisa's having been destroyed in so remote an age. The horses of Pisa were famous. The year in which the Olympic games were celebrated was often called *Pisæus annus*, and the victory which was obtained there was called *Pisææ ramus olivæ*. *Vid.* Olympia. *Strab.* 8.—*Ovid. Trist.* 2. v. 386. l. 4. el. 10. v. 95.—*Mela*, 2. c. 3.—*Virg. G.* 3. v. 180.—*Stat. Theb.* 7. v. 416.—*Paus.* 6. c. 22.—*Plin.* 4. c. 5.—*Lucan.* 2. v. 165. l. 3. v. 175.—*Juv.* 13. v. 99.

PI'SÆ, a town of Etruria, at the mouth of the river Arnus, built by a colony from Pisa in the Peloponnesus. The inhabitants were called Pisani. *Dionysius* of *Halicarnassus* affirms that it existed before the Trojan war, but others assert that it was built by a colony of Piseans who were shipwrecked on the coast of Etruria, at their return from the Trojan war. Pisæ was once a very powerful and flourishing city, which conquered the Baleares, together with Sardinia and Corsica. The sea on the neighbouring coast was called the bay of Pisæ. *Virg. Æn.* 10. v. 179.—*Strab.* 5.—*Lucan.* 2. v. 401.—*Liv.* 39. c. 2. l. 45. c. 13.—*Mela*, 2. c. 4.—*Plin.* 2. c. 103.—*Servius in Æn.* 10. v. 179.

PISÆ'US, a surname of Jupiter at Pisa. The god by an oracle forbade Hercules to injure the inhabitants of the place, as he particularly patronized them. *Paus.* 5. c. 3.

PISAN'DER, a son of Bellerophon, killed by the Solymi. *Homer. Il.* 9.——A Trojan chief killed by Menelaus. *Homer. Il.* 13. v. 601.——One of Penelope's suitors, son of Polyctor. *Ovid. Heroid.* 1. v. 91.—*Homer. Od.* 18. v. 298. l. 22. v. 243.——A son of Antimachus, killed by Agamemnon during the Trojan war. He had had recourse to entreaties and promises, but in vain, as the Grecian wished to resent the advice of Antimachus, who opposed the restoration of Helen. *Homer. Il.* 11. v. 123.——An Athenian prætor. *C. Nep.* 7. c. 5.——An admiral of the Spartan fleet during the Peloponnesian war. He abolished the democracy at Athens, and established the aristocratical government of the four hundred tyrants. He was killed in a naval battle by Conon, the Athenian general, near Cnidus, in which the Spartans lost fifty gallies, B.C. 394. *C. Nep.* 9. c. 2.—*Diod.*——A poet of Rhodes, who composed a poem called *Heraclea*, in which he gave an account of all the labors and all the exploits of Hercules. He was the first who ever represented his hero armed with a club. The time in which he flourished is not precisely known, though some place him in the 33d Olympiad. In one of his poems he gave an account of the principal events of history and fable, from which some have imagined that Virgil copied almost word for word the particulars about the wooden horse and the treachery of Sinon. *Eratosth. Catast.* 12.—*Athen.* 11.—*Paus.* 2. c. 37. l. 8. c. 22.—*Macrob. Sat.* 5. c. 2.—*Gyrald. de P. H.* 3.

PISA'TES or PISÆ'I, the inhabitants of Pisa in the Peloponnesus.

PISAU'RUS, now Foglia, a river of Picenum, falling into the Adriatic, with a town called Pisaurum, now Pesaro, which became a Roman colony in the consulship of Claudius Pulcher. The town was destroyed by an earthquake in the beginning of the reign of Augustus. *Mela*, 2. c. 4.—*Catull.* 82. v. 3.—*Plin.* 3. c. 4.—*Liv.* 39. c. 44. l. 41. c. 27.—*Servius Æn.* 6. v. 826.

PIS'CA, a city of India within the Ganges. *Ptol.*

PISCE'NÆ, a town of Gallia Narbonensis. *Ptol.*

PISCIO'TA, a town of Lucania. *Plin.* 3. c. 5.

PISCU'RI, a people of Asia. *Strab.*

PISE'NOR, a son of Ixion and the cloud. *Ovid. Met.* 12. v. 303.——One of the ancestors of the nurse of Ulysses. *Homer. Od.* 1. v. 429. l. 19. v. 401.

PIS'EUS, a king of Etruria, about 260 years before the foundation of Rome. *Plin.* 7. c. 26.

PIS'IAS, a general of the Argives in the age of Epaminondas. *Xenoph.*——A statuary at Athens, celebrated for his pieces. *Paus.* 1. c. 3.

PIS'IDA GEOR'GIUS, one of the Greek fathers, who wrote a poem on the six days' labor, or creation of the world. There is also remaining, besides a few other fragments, an unfinished poem, comprehending 261 verses, on the vanity of human life.

PISID'IA, an inland country of Asia Minor, between Phrygia, Pamphylia, Galatia, and Isauria. It was rich and fertile. The inhabitants, called Pisidæ, were industrious and warlike. *Cic. de Div.* 1. c. 1.—*Mela*, 1. c. 2.—*Strab.* 12.—*Liv.* 37. c. 54 & 56.—*Claudian. in Eutr.* 2. v. 241 & 465.

PISID'ICE, a daughter of Æolus, who married Myrmidon, and became mother of Antiphus and Actor. *Apollod.* 1.——A daughter of Nestor. *Id.*——A daughter of Pelias. *Id.*——The daughter of a king of Methymna in Lesbus. She became enamoured of Achilles when he invaded her father's kingdom, and promised to deliver the city into his hands if he would marry her. Achilles agreed to the proposal, but when he became master of Methymna, he ordered Pisidice to be stoned to death for her perfidy. *Parthen. erot.* 21.

PISID'IUM, a maritime town of Asia Minor, not far from Seleucia. *Diod. Holstenius* reads Positium.

PISI'DON, a harbour of Africa Propria. *Ptol.*

PIS'ILIS, a town of Caria, between Caunus and the river Calbis. *Strab.*

PISINA'TES, a people of Umbria. *Plin.* 3. c. 14.

PISIN'DA, a city of Africa Propria. *Ptol.*——A city of Pamphylia. *Id.*

PISIN'GARA, a town of Armenia Minor. *Ptol.*

PI'SIS, a native of Thespis, who gained uncommon influence among the Thebans, and behaved with great courage in the defence of their liberties. He was taken prisoner by Demetrius, who made him governor of Thespiæ.

PI'SIS, a city and mountain of Armenia or Susiana. *Steph.*

PISISTRAT'IDÆ, the descendants of Pisistratus. *Vid.* Pisistratus.

PISISTRATIDES, a man sent by the Spartans as ambassador to the satraps of the king of Persia.

PISIS'TRATUS, an Athenian, son of Hippocrates, who early distinguished himself by his valor in the field, and by his address and eloquence at home. After he had rendered himself the favorite of the populace by his liberality and by the intrepidity with which he had fought their battles, particularly near Salamis, he resolved to make himself master of his country. Every thing seemed favorable to his ambitious views; but Solon alone, who was then at the head of affairs, and who had lately instituted his celebrated laws, opposed him, and discovered his duplicity and artful behaviour before the public assembly. Pisistratus was not disheartened by the measures of his relation Solon, but had recourse to artifice. In returning from his country house, he cut himself in various places, and after he had exposed his mangled body to the eyes of the populace, deplored his misfortunes, and accused his enemies of attempts upon his life, because he was the friend of the people, the guardian of the poor, and the reliever of the oppressed; he claimed a chosen body of 50 men from the populace to defend his person in future from the malevolence and cruelty of his enemies. The unsuspecting people unanimously granted his request, though Solon opposed it with all his influence; and Pisistratus had no sooner received an armed band, on the fidelity and attachment of which he could rely, than he seized the citadel of Athens, and made himself absolute. The people perceived their credulity too late; yet, though the tyrant was popular, two of the citizens, Megacles and Lycurgus, conspired together against him, and by their means he was forcibly ejected from the city. His house and all his effects were exposed to sale, but there was found in Athens only one man who would buy them. The private dissensions of the friends of liberty proved favorable to the expelled tyrant; and Megacles, who was jealous of Lycurgus, secretly promised to restore Pisistratus to all his rights and privileges in Athens, if he would marry his daughter. Pisistratus consented, and by the assistance of his father-in-law, he was soon enabled to expel Lycurgus, and to re-establish himself. By means of a woman called Phya, whose shape was tall, and whose figure was noble and commanding, he imposed upon the people, and created himself adherents even among his enemies. Phya was conducted through the streets of the city, and showing herself subservient to the artifice of Pisistratus, she was announced as Minerva, the goddess of wisdom, and the patroness of Athens, who was come down from heaven to re-establish her favorite Pisistratus, in a power which was sanctioned by the approbation of the gods, and favored by the affection of the people. In the midst of his triumph, however, Pisistratus found himself unsupported, and some time after, when he repudiated the daughter of Megacles, he found that not only the citizens, but even his very troops were alienated from him by the influence, the intrigues, and the bribery of his father-in-law. He fled from Athens where he could no longer maintain his power, and retired to Eubœa. Eleven years after he was drawn from his obscure retreat, by means of his son Hippias, and was a third time received by the people of Athens as their master and sovereign. Upon this he sacrificed to his resentment the friends of Megacles, but did not lose sight of the public good; and while he sought the aggrandizement of his family, did not neglect the dignity and the honor of the Athenian name. He died about 527 years B.C., after he had enjoyed the sovereign power at Athens for thirty-three years, including the years of his banishment, and was succeeded by his son Hipparchus. Pisistratus, though a usurper and a tyrant, claims our admiration for his justice, his liberality, and his moderation. If he was dreaded and detested as a master, the Athenians loved and respected his private virtues and his patriotism, as a fellow-citizen, and the opprobrium which generally fell on his head may be attributed not to the severity of his administration, but to the republican principles of the Athenians, who hated and exclaimed against the moderation and equity of the mildest sovereign, while they flattered the pride and gratified the guilty desires of the most tyrannical of their fellow subjects. Pisistratus often refused to punish the insolence of his enemies, and when he had one day been virulently accused of murder, rather than inflict immediate punishment upon the man who had criminated him, he went to the Areopagus, and there convinced the Athenians that the accusations of his enemies were groundless, and that his life was irreproachable. It is to his labors that we are indebted for the preservation of the poems of Homer, and he was the first, according to Cicero, who introduced them at Athens, in the order in which they now appear. He also established a public library at Athens, and the valuable books which he had diligently collected were carried into Persia when Xerxes made himself master of the capital of Attica. Hipparchus and Hippias, the sons of Pisistratus, who have received the name of Pisistratidæ, rendered themselves as illustrious as their father, but the flames of liberty were too powerful to be extinguished. The Pisistratidæ governed with great moderation, yet the name of a master, whether softened by mildness of manners or rendered odious by oppression, was insupportable to the Athenians. Two of the most respectable of the citizens, called Harmodius and Aristogiton, conspired against them, and Hipparchus was dispatched in a public assembly. This murder was not, however, attended with any advantages, and though the two leaders of the conspiracy, who have been celebrated through every age for their patriotism, were supported by the people, yet Hippias quelled the tumult by his uncommon firmness and prudence, and for a while preserved that peace in Athens, which his father had often been unable to command. This was not long to continue. Hippias was at last expelled by the united efforts of the Athenians and of their allies of Peloponnesus, and he left Attica, when he found himself unable to maintain his power and preserve his independence. The rest of the family of Pisistratus followed him in his banishment, and after they had refused to accept the liberal offers of the princes of Thessaly, and of the king of Macedonia, who wished them to settle in their respective territories, the Pisistratidæ retired to Sigæum, which their father had in the summit of his power conquered and bequeathed to his posterity. After the banishment of the Pisistratidæ, the Athenians became more than commonly jealous of their liberty, and often sacrificed the most powerful of their citizens, apprehensive of the influence which popularity, and a well-directed liberality, might gain among a fickle and unsettled populace. The Pisistratidæ were banished from Athens about eighteen years after the death of Pisistratus, B.C. 510. *Ælian. V. H.* 13. c. 14.—*Justin.* 2. c. 8.—*Gell.* 17. c. 21.—*Paus.* 7. c 26.—*Herodot.* 1. c. 59. l. 6. c. 103.—*Cic. de Orat.* 3. c. 33 & 34.—*Val. Max.* 1. c. 2.——A son of Nestor. *Apollod.*——A king of Orchomenus, who rendered himself odious by his cruelty towards the nobles. He was put to death by them, and they carried away his body from the public assembly, by hiding each a piece of his flesh under their garments, to prevent a discovery by the people, with whom he was a great favorite. *Plut. in Par.*——A Theban attached to the Roman interest, while the consul Flaminius was in Greece. He assassinated the prætor of Bœotia, for which he was put to death, &c.——An historian of Larissa. *Suidas.*——A son of Nestor and Eurydice. *Homer. Odyss.* 3.

PI'SO, a celebrated family at Rome, which was a branch of the Calpurnians, descended from Calpus, the son of Numa. They received the name of Piso either from the cultivation of *pease* by one of the family, or from the invention of the *pestle* of a mortar. Before the death of Augustus, eleven of this family had obtained the consulship, and many had been honored with triumphs, on account of their victories, in the different provinces of the Roman empire. *Lucan. ad Pis.* 15.—*Plin.* 18. c. 3.—*Festus.*——One of the 30 tyrants appointed over Athens by Lysander.

PI'SO LU'CIUS CALPUR'NIUS, was tribune of the people, about 149 years B.C., and afterwards consul. His frugality procured him the name of *Frugi*, and he gained the greatest honors as an orator, a lawyer, a statesman, and an historian. He made a successful campaign in Sicily, and rewarded his son, who had behaved with great valour during the war, with a crown of gold, which weighed 20 pounds. He composed some annals and harangues, which were lost in the age of Cicero. His style was obscure and inelegant. *Cic. Br.* l. 2.—*A. Gell.* 11. c. 14.—*Voss. Hist. Lat.* 1. c. 6.

PI'SO CA'IUS, a Roman consul, A.U.C. 687, who supported the consular dignity against the tumults of the tribunes, and the clamours of the people. He made a law to restrain the cabals which generally prevailed at the election of the chief magistrates.——A Roman who was at the head of a celebrated conspiracy against the emperor Nero. He had rendered himself a favorite of the people by his private as well as public virtues, by the generosity of his behaviour, his fondness for pleasure with the voluptuous, and his austerity with the grave and the reserved. He had been marked by some as a proper person to succeed the emperor; but the discovery of the plot by a freedman, who was among the conspirators, soon cut him off, with all his partizans. He refused to court the affections of the people, and the army, when the whole had been made public, and, instead of taking proper measures for his preservation, either by proclaiming himself emperor, as his friends advised, or by seeking a retreat in the distant provinces of the empire, he retired to his own house, where he opened the veins of both his arms and bled to death. *Tac. Ann.* 15. c. 48.——A son-in-law of Cicero, remarkable for his abilities, as well as for the mildness of his disposition and the goodness of his heart. He died before Cicero's return from banishment. *Cic. Br.* 78. *Ad Fam.* 14. ep. 1. *Ad. Quir.* 3. *Pis.* 1.

PI'SO CNE'IUS, another consul under Augustus. He was one of the favorites of Tiberius, by whom he was appointed governor of Syria, where he rendered himself odious by his cruelty. He was accused of having poisoned Germanicus, and when he saw, on his return to Rome, that he was shunned and despised by his friends, and brought to a trial, in which his crimes and his ingratitude were laid open to public view, he destroyed himself, A.D. 20. *Tacit. Ann.* 3. c. 10, &c.—*Suet. Tib.* 52.——A factious and turbulent youth, who conspired against his country with Catiline. He was among the friends of Julius Cæsar.

PI'SO LU'CIUS, a governor of Spain, who was assassinated by a peasant, as he was travelling through the country. The murderer was seized and tortured, but refused to confess the cause of the murder. *Tac. Ann.* 4. c. 45.——A private man, accused of having uttered seditious words against the emperor Tiberius. He was condemned, but a natural death saved him from the hands of the executioner.——A governor of Rome for twenty years, an office which he discharged with the greatest justice and credit. He was greatly honoured by the friendship of Augustus, as well as of his successor, a distinction he deserved, both as a faithful citizen and a man of learning. Some, however, say, that Tiberius made him governor of Rome, because he had continued drinking with him a night and two days, or two days and two nights, according to Pliny. *Horace* dedicated his poem *de Arte Poeticâ* to his two sons, whose partiality for literature had distinguished them among the rest of the Romans, and who were fond of cultivating poetry in their leisure hours. *Plut. in Cæs.*—*Plin.* 18. c. 3.——A senator, who followed the emperor Valerian into Persia. He proclaimed himself emperor after the death of Valerian, but was defeated and put to death a few weeks after, A.D. 261, by Valens, &c.

PI'SO LICINIA'NUS, a senator adopted by the emperor Galba. He was put to death by Otho's orders, though his many virtues deserved a better fate. *Tacit. Hist.* 1. c. 14. &c.—*Suet. Galb.* 17.

PI'SO LU'CIUS CÆSONIA'NUS, a patrician, whose daughter married Julius Cæsar. He supported Clodius in procuring the banishment of Cicero, and disgraced himself in an embassy to Antony, who was engaged at the siege of Mutina. *Cic.* 4. *Fam.* 4. *Phil.* 8. c. 9 & 10. c. 5. *de Offic. &c.*—*Horat*—*Tacit. Ann. & Hist.* — *Val. Max.* — *Liv.* — *Sueton.*—*Plut. in Cæs.*, &c.

PISO'NIS VIL'LA, a place near Baiæ in Campania, which the emperor Nero often frequented. *Tacit. Ann.* 1. It is now Truglio.

PISO'NOS, a city of Armenia Minor. *Antonin.*

PISSANTI'NI, a people of Macedonia. *Polyb.*

PIS'SIRUS, a town of Thrace, near the river Nestus. *Herod.* 7. c. 109.

PIS'TOR, a surname signifying *baker*, given to Jupiter by the Romans, because when the city was taken by the Gauls, the gods persuaded them to throw down loaves from the Tarpeian hill where they were besieged, that the enemy might, from that circumstance, suppose that they were not in want of provisions, though in reality they were near surrendering through famine. This deceived the Gauls, and they soon after raised the siege. *Ovid. Fast.* 6. v. 350, 394, &c.

PISTO'RIA, now Pistoja, a town of Etruria, at the foot of the Apennines, near Florence, where Catiline was defeated. *Sallust. Cat.* 57. —*Plin.* 3. c. 4.

PI'SUS, a son of Aphareus, or, according to others, of Perieres. *Apollod.* 3.—*Paus.* 5. c. 17.

PISUTH'NES, a Persian Satrap of Lydia, who revolted from Darius Nothus. His father's name was Hystaspes. *Plut in Art.*

PIT'ANE, a town of Æolia in Asia Minor, at the mouth of the Caycus. It was the native place of the philosopher Archesilaus. The inhabitants made bricks which were said to swim on the surface of the water. *Lucan.* 3. v. 305.—*Strab.* 13. —*Vitruv.* 2. c. 3.—*Mela*, 1. c. 18.—*Ovid. Met.* 7. v. 357.——A town of Laconia. *Pindar. Ol.* 6. v. 46.

PITA'NUS, a river of Corsica. *Ptol.*

PITA'ON, a city of Caria, so called from Pitaus, a friend of Midas. *Steph.*

PIT'ARA, a town of Upper Æthiopia. *Plin.*

PITARA'TUS, an Athenian archon, during whose magistracy Epicurus died. *Cic. Fat.* 9.

PITHE'CON COL'POS, i.e. *Simiarum sinus*, a harbour of Libya, near Carthage. *Steph.*

PITHECU'SA, a small island on the coast of Etruria, anciently called Ænaria and Inarime, and now Ischia, with a town of the same name, on the top of a mountain. The frequent earthquakes to which it was subject, obliged the inhabitants to leave it. There was a volcano in the middle of the island, called St. Julian, which gave occasion to the ancients to say, that the giant Typhon was buried there. Some suppose that it received its name from πίθηκοι *monkeys*, into which the inhabitants were changed by Jupiter. *Ovid. Met.* 14. v. 90.—*Plin.* 3. c. 6.—*Pindar. Pyth.* 1.—*Strab.* 1.

PITHECUS'SÆ, three islands off Africa, where monkeys were worshipped. *Diod. Sic.*

PITH'EUS. *Vid.* Pittheus.

PITHNIS'SA or PITNIS'SA, a city of Lycaonia. *Steph.*

PI'THO, called also Suada, the goddess of persuasion among the Greeks and Romans, supposed to be the daughter of Mercury and Venus. She was represented with a diadem on her head, to intimate her influence over the hearts of men. One of her arms appears raised, as in the attitude of an orator haranguing a public assembly, and with the other she holds a thunderbolt and fetters, made with flowers, to signify the powers of reasoning, and the attractions of eloquence. A *caduceus* as a symbol of persuasion, appears at her feet, with the writings of Demosthenes and Cicero, the two most celebrated orators among the ancients, who understood how to command the attention of their audience, and to rouse and animate their various passions. *Paus.* 1. c. 22. l. 9. c. 35.—*Cic. de Clar. Orat.* 15.——A Roman courtezan. She received this name on account of the allurements which her charms possessed, and of her winning expressions. *Ovid. Am.* 3. el. 7. v. 23.

PITHODE'MUS, a famous wrestler mentioned by *Pliny*, 34. c. 8.

PITHOLA'US and LYCO'PHRON, seized upon the sovereign power of Pheræ, by killing Alexander. They were ejected by Philip of Macedonia. *Diod.* 16.

PITHO'LEON, an insignificant poet of Rhodes, who mingled Greek and Latin in his compositions. He wrote some epigrams against J. Cæsar, and drew upon himself the ridicule of Horace, on account of the inelegance of his style. *Macrob. Sat.* 2. c. 2.—*Suet. de cl. Rhet.*—*Horat.* 1. sat. 10. v. 21.

PI'THON, one of the body guards of Alexander, put to death by Antiochus.

PITH'ONIS, a place of Asia. *Plin.* 10. c. 23.

PITHONOBAS'TÆ, a city of India without the Ganges. *Ptol.*

PI'THOS, a village of the tribe Cecropis, so called ἀπὸ τῶν πίθων, *the vessels*, made there. *Steph.*

PI'THYS, a nymph beloved by Pan. Boreas was also fond of her, but she slighted his addresses, upon which he dashed her against a rock, and she was changed into a pine-tree, which ever after became sacred to the god of the shepherds. *Propert.* 1. el. 18. v. 20.

PITI'NUM, an inland town of Umbria. *Ptol.*

PIT'TACUS, a native of Mitylene in Lesbus, was one of the seven wise men of Greece. His father, whose name was Caicus, or Cyrrhadius, was a native of Thrace, and his mother was a citizen of Lesbus. With the assistance of the brothers of Alcæus, he delivered his country from the oppression of the tyrant Melanchrus, and in the war which the Athenians waged against Lesbus, he appeared at the head of his countrymen, and challenged to single combat, Phrynon, the enemy's general. As the event of the war seemed to depend on this combat, Pittacus had recourse to artifice, and, when he engaged, he entangled his adversary in a net, which he had concealed under his shield, and easily dispatched him. He was amply rewarded for this victory, and his countrymen, sensible of his merit, unanimously appointed him governor of their city with unlimited authority. In this capacity, Pittacus behaved with great moderation and prudence, and, after he had governed his fellow-citizens with the strictest justice, and had established and enforced the most salutary laws, voluntarily resigned the sovereign power, after he had enjoyed it for ten years, observing, that the virtues and innocence of private life were incompatible with the power and influence of a sovereign. His disinterestedness gained him many admirers, and, when the Mityleneans wished to reward his public services by presenting him with an immense tract of territory, he refused to accept more land than what should be contained within the distance to which he could throw a javelin. He died in the 82d year of his age, about 570 years B.C., after he had spent the last ten years of his life in literary ease and peaceful retirement. He had married the sister of Draco, the son of Penthilus, a woman so proud of the consequence of her family, that she despised the inferior birth of her husband, and often added insults and violence to the virulence of her language. He had an only son called Tyrrheus, whose sudden death he bore with the resignation which became the character of his philosophy. One of his favorite maxims was to know and to take advantage of opportunity; that man ought to provide against misfortunes, to avoid them; but, that if they ever happened, he ought to support them with patience and resignation. In prosperity friends were to be acquired, and in the hour of adversity their faithfulness was to be tried. He also observed, that in our actions it was imprudent to make others acquainted with our designs, for, if we failed, we exposed ourselves to censure and to ridicule. Many of his maxims were inscribed on the walls of Apollo's temple at Delphi, to show to the world how great an opinion the Mityleneans entertained of his abilities as a philosopher, a moralist, and a man. By one of his laws, every fault committed by a man when intoxicated, deserved double punishment. The titles of some of his writings are preserved by Laertius, among which are mentioned elegiac verses, some laws in prose, addressed to his countrymen, epistles and moral precepts called *Adomena*. *Diog. in Vit.*—*Aristot. Polit.*—*Plut. in Symp.*—*Paus.* 10. c. 24 —*Ælian. V. H.* 2. c. 29. l. 3. c. 17. l. 7. c. 15.—*Auson. ep. Sept. Sap.*—*Val. Max.* 6. c. 5.—*Athenæus*, 10.—*Stobæus*, 3.—*Lucian. longæv.*—*Sax. Onom.* 1. p. 17. ——A grandson of Porus king of India. *Polyæn.* 4. c. 3.——A lawgiver, surnamed the Less. He is mentioned by *Phavorinus* and *Demetrius. Laert.* 1. c. 79.

PIT'TALUS, an Athenian physician. *Schol. Aristoph. Acarn. & Crabr.*

PIT'THEA, a town near Trœzene. Hence the epithet of Pittheus in *Ovid. Met.* 15. v. 296.

PIT'THEUS, a king of Trœzene in Argolis, son of Pelops and Hippodamia. He was universally admired for his learning, wisdom, and application; he publicly taught in a school at Trœzene, and even composed a book, which was seen by Pausanias the geographer. He gave his daughter

Æthra in marriage to Ægeus, king of Athens, and he himself took particular care of the youth and education of his grandson Theseus. He was buried at Trœzene, which he had founded, and on his tomb were seen, for many ages, three seats of white marble, on which he sat, with two other judges, whenever he gave laws to his subjects, or settled their disputes. *Paus.* 1. c. 22 & 27. l. 2. c. 30 & 31.—*Plut. in Thes.—Ovid. Heroid.* 10.—*Strab.* 8.—*Eurip. in Hipp. & Med.*

PITUA'NIUS LU'CIUS, a mathematician in the age of Tiberius, thrown down from the Tarpeian rock. *Tacit. Ann.* 2. c. 32.

PITULA'NI, a people of Umbria in Italy. Their chief town was called Pitulum. *Plin.* 3. c. 5 & 14.

PITYE'A, a town of Asia Minor. *Apollon.*

PITYAS'SUS, a town of Pisidia. *Strab.*

PITYN'DA or PYTIN'DRA, the metropolis of India within the Ganges. *Ptol.* It is now probably Narsingapatan.

PITYONE'SUS, a small island on the coast of Peloponnesus, near Epidaurus. *Plin.* 4. c. 12.

PIT'YUS, (*-untis*), now Pitchinda, a town of Colchis. *Plin.* 6. c. 5.

PITYU'SA, a small island on the coast of Argolis. *Plin.* 4. c. 12.——A name of Chius.——A name of Lampsacus.

PITYU'SÆ, two small islands in the Mediterranean, near the coast of Spain, of which the larger was called Ebusus, and the smaller Ophiusa. They received their name from the quantity of pines (πίτυς) which grew there. *Mela*, 2. c. 7.—*Strab.* 13.—*Plin.* 3. c. 5. l. 4. c. 12. l. 5. c. 31.

PI'US, a surname given to the emperor Antoninus, on account of his piety and virtue.——A surname given to Metellus, because he interested himself so warmly to have his father recalled from banishment.

PIX'IUS, one of Jupiter's surnames among the Latins, which signified the name as the Sanctus or Sangus of the Sabines. *Dionys. Hal.* 4.

PLA'CAS or PLACU'SIUS, a mountain of Cilicia. *Hesych.*

PLA'CE, a city of the Hellespont. *Steph.*

PLACEN'TIA, now called Piacenza, an ancient town and colony of Italy, at the confluence of the Trebia and Po. *Liv.* 21. c. 25 & 56. l. 37. c. 10. ——A city of Hispania Tarraconensis. It is now La Vera de Placentia.

PLA'CIA, a town of Mysia, near Cyzicum. *Plin.* 5. c. *ult.*

PLACI'ADÆ, a municipal town of Attica. *Suidas.*

PLACIDEIA'NUS, a gladiator in the age of *Horace.* 2. sat. 7.

PLACID'IA GAL'LA, a daughter of Theodosius the Great, sister of Honorius and Arcadius. She married Adolphus king of the Goths, and afterwards Constantius, by whom she had Valentinian the Third. She died A.D. 449. *Isodor. in. Chron.* —*Olympiod. apud Phot.*——A daughter of Valentinian the Third, was led away by Genseric into Africa, but afterwards sent back to Constantinople, where she married the senator Olybrius.

PLAC'IDUS JU'LIUS, a tribune of a cohort, who imprisoned the emperor Vitellius. *Tacit. H.* 3. c. 85.

PLACIL'LA, the wife of Theodosius the Great, remarkable for her piety. *Theodor. Eccl. Hist.* 9. c. 31.——A daughter of the emperor Arcadius.

PLÆTO'RIUS M., a curule ædile at Rome, prætor with Cicero. He became the accuser of M. Fonteius. *Cic. Clu.* 45, &c. *Att.* 5. ep. 20.

PLAGE'REUM, a place of Sicily between Agrigentum and Syracuse. *Antonin.*

PLA'GIA, a harbour of Liguria. *Id.*

PLAGIA'RIA, a city of Spain. *Id.* It is now Neustra Sennora de Betove.

PLAGULEIUS C. ATEI., a friend of Clodius. *Cic. Att.* 10. ep. 8.—*Dion.* 33.

PLA'MUS, a city of Caria. *Steph.*

PLANA'SIA, a small island of the Tyrrhene Sea. ——An island on the coast of Gaul, where Tiberius ordered Agrippa, the grandson of Augustus, to be put to death. *Tacit. Ann.* 1. c. 3.——A town on the Rhone. *Strab.* It is now Pont S. Esprit.

PLANCI'NA, a woman celebrated for her intrigues and her crimes, who married Piso, and was accused with him of having murdered Germanicus, in the reign of Tiberius. She was acquitted either by means of the empress Livia, or on account of the partiality of the emperor for her person. She had long supported the spirits of her husband during his confinement, but when she saw herself freed from the accusation, she totally abandoned him to his fate. Subservient in every thing to the will of Livia, she, at her instigation, became guilty of the greatest crimes, to injure the character of Agrippinia. After the death of Agrippina, Plancina was accused of the most atrocious villanies, and, as she knew that she could not elude justice, put herself to death, A.D. 33. *Tacit. Ann.* 6. c. 26, &c.

PLAN'CUS LU'CIUS MUNA'TIUS, a Roman, who rendered himself ridiculous by his follies and his extravagance. He had been consul, and had presided over a province in the capacity of governor, but he forgot all his dignity, and became one of the most servile flatterers of Cleopatra and Antony. At the court of the Ægyptian queen in Alexandria, he appeared in the character of the meanest stage dancer, and, in comedy, personated Glaucus, and painted his body of a green color, dancing on a public stage quite naked, with only a crown of green reeds on his head, while he had tied behind his back the tail of a large sea fish. This exposed him to the public derision, and, when Antony had joined the rest of his friends in censuring him for his unbecoming behaviour, he deserted to Octavius, who received him with great marks of friendship and attention. It was he who proposed, in the Roman senate, that the title of Augustus should be conferred on his friend Octavius, as expressive of the dignity and the reverence which the greatness of his exploits seemed to claim. Horace has dedicated 1. od. 7. to him; and he certainly deserved the honor, from the elegance of his letters, which are still extant, written to Cicero. It appears that Plancus did not fully enjoy the confidence of Augustus, since he wished to retire in disgust from Italy, and pass the remainder of his life at Rhodes, a determination which the friendship of Horace combated with wit and success. Plancus, by the direction of the Roman senate, founded a city in Gaul at the confluence of the Rhone and Arar, which he called Lugdunum, now modern Lyons. *Dio.* 46. c. 40, &c.—*Plut. in Anton.—Horat.* 1. od. 7. l. 3. od. 14.—*Cic. Fam.* 4. ep. 7. l. 7. ep. 3. l. 10. ep. 4.

PLAN'CUS T. BUR'SA, his brother, burnt the senate-house, after the death of Clodius, for which he was accused and banished by means of Cicero, against whom he afterwards manifested the most violent enmity. He favored the party of Antony after Cæsar's death. *Cic. Phil.* 6. c. 4. l. 1. c. 6. l. 12. c. 18. l. 13. c. 11. *Fam.* 7. ep. 2.

PLAN'CUS M. HÆ'RES, a Roman knight who espoused Pompey's side. He was the friend of Cicero. *Cic.* 9. *Fam.* 13.

PLAN'CUS CNE'US, a knight of Atinum, who showed great civility to Cicero during his banishment at Dyrrachium. He was defended by Cicero when accused, and joined Pompey in the civil wars, and after the battle of Pharsalia retired into exile to Corcyra. *Cic.* 4. *Fam.* 14 & 15.—*Plin.* 31. *post redit.*

PLAN'CUS, a patrician, proscribed by the second triumvirate. His servants wished to save him from death, but he refused it, rather than expose their persons to danger. The Planci were so called from one of the family who was born with the soles of his feet unusually plain. *Festus.*—*Plin.* 11. c. 45.

PLANGEN'SES, a people of Umbria. *Plin.* 3. c. 14.

PLAN'GON, a famous courtezan of Miletus, who tried the fidelity of a young Colophonian by demanding a necklace which belonged to Bacchis her rival. The necklace was obtained, and Bacchis and Plangon were reconciled. *Athen.* 13.

PLARÆ'I, a people of Epirus. *Steph.*

PLARAS'SA, a city of Caria. *Id.*

PLATÆ'A, a daughter of Asopus, king of Bœotia. When Juno was dissatisfied with Jupiter, the god, to obtain a reconciliation, pretended that he was going to marry Platæa, and by the advice of Cithæron, a wooden image was dressed in the habits of a new bride, and drawn in a chariot through the streets. The artifice succeeded, Juno was easily reconciled, and to commemorate the event, the Platæans yearly celebrated a festival called Dædala. Plutarch wrote a treatise on the subject, which is quoted by Eusebius. *Paus.* 9. c. 1, &c. —*Euseb. præf. ev.* 3.

PLATÆ'A, an island on the coast of Africa, in the Mediterranean. It belonged to the Cyreneans. *Herodot.* 4. c. 157.——One of the Sporades, in the Ægæan Sea. It is now Placeda.

PLATÆ'A or PLATÆ'Æ, (*arum*), a town of Bœotia, near mount Cithæron, on the confines of Megaris and Attica, celebrated for a battle fought there between Mardonius, the commander of Xerxes king of Persia, and Pausanias the Lacedæmonian, and the Athenians. The Persian army consisted of 300,000 men, of which scarcely 3000 escaped with their lives. The Grecian army, which was greatly inferior, lost but few men, and among these ninety-one Spartans, fifty-two Athenians, and sixteen Tegeans, were the only soldiers found in the number of the slain. The plunder which the Greeks obtained in the Persian camp was immense. Pausanias received the tenth of all the spoils, on account of his uncommon valor during the engagement, and the rest were rewarded each according to their respective merit. This battle was fought on the 22d of September, the same day as the battle of Mycale, 479 B.C., and by it Greece was delivered for ever from the continual alarms to which she was exposed on account of Persian invasions, and from that time none of the princes of Persia dared to advance with a hostile force beyond the Hellespont. The Platæans were naturally attached to the interest of the Athenians, and furnished them with a thousand soldiers when Greece was attacked by Datis, the general of Darius. Platæa was taken by the Thebans after a famous siege, in the beginning of the Peloponnesian war, and destroyed by the Spartans, B.C. 427. Alexander rebuilt it, and passed great enconiums upon the inhabitants, on account of their ancestors, who had so bravely fought against the Persians at the battle of Marathon and under Pausanias. *Herodot.* 8. c. 50. —*Paus.* 9. c. 1.—*Plut. in Alex. &c.*—*C. Nep. &c.* —*Cic. de Offic.* 1. c. 18.—*Strab.*—*Justin.*

PLATAMO'DES, a place of Peloponnesus, 120 stadia distant from Coryphasium. *Strab.*

PLATANÆ'US, a river of Bithynia. *Plin.* 5. c. 32.

PLATANIS'TON, a promontory on the coast of Laconia in Peloponnesus. *Paus.* 3. c. 23.——A river of Arcadia, flowing through Lycosura. *Paus.* 8. c. 39.

PLATANIS'TUS, a promontory of Æolis. *Plin.* ——A maritime place of Pamphylia or Cilicia. *Strab.*

PLATA'NIUS, a river of Bœotia. *Paus.* 9. c. 24.

PLAT'ANUS, a city of Phœnicia, between Antiochia Magna and Laodicea. *Steph.*—*Antonin.*

PLATE'A or PLAT'EA, an island of Lybia. *Steph.*

PLATIÆ, small islands off Crete. *Plin.* 4. c. 12. They are now, probably, Dielassa and Cardes.

PLA'TO, a celebrated philosopher of Athens, son of Ariston and Parectonia. His original name was Aristocles, and he received that of Plato from the largeness of his shoulders. As one of the descendants of Codrus, and as the offspring of a noble, illustrious, and opulent family, Plato was educated with care, his body was formed and invigorated with gymnastic exercises, and his mind was cultivated and enlightened by the study of poetry and of geometry, from which he derived that acuteness of judgment, and warmth of imagination, which have stamped his character as the most subtle and flowery writer of antiquity. He first began his literary career by writing poems and tragedies; but he was soon disgusted with his own productions, when, at the age of twenty, he was introduced into the presence of Socrates, and when he was enabled to compare and examine, with critical accuracy, the merit of his compositions with those of his poetical predecessors. He, therefore, committed to the flames those productions of his early years, which could not command the attention or gain the applause of a maturer age. During eight years he continued to be one of the pupils of Socrates; and, if he was prevented by momentary indisposition from attending the philosopher's last moments, yet he collected, from the conversation of those that were present, the minutest and most circumstantial accounts, which exhibit, in their truest colors, the concern and sensibility of the pupil, and the firmness, virtues, and moral sentiments of the dying philosopher. After the death of Socrates, Plato retired from Athens; and, to acquire that information which the accurate observer can derive in foreign countries, began to travel over Greece. He visited Megara, Thebes, and Elis, where he met with the kindest reception from his fellow disciples, whom the violent death of their master had likewise removed from Attica. He afterwards visited Magna Græcia, attracted by the fame of the Pythagorean philosophy, and by the learning, abilities, and reputation of its professors, Philolaus, Archytas, and Eurytus. He afterwards passed into Sicily, and examined the eruptions and fires of the volcano of that island. He also visited Ægypt, where the mathematician Theodorus then flourished. When he finished his travels, Plato retired to the groves of Academus, in the neighbourhood of Athens, where his lectures were soon attended by a crowd of learned, noble, and illustrious pupils; and the philosopher, by refusing to have a share in the administration of affairs, rendered his name more famous, and his school more frequented. During forty years he presided at the head of the academy, and there he devoted his time to the instruction of his pupils, and composed those dialogues which have been the admiration of every age and country. His studies, however, were interrupted for a while, whilst he obeyed the pressing calls and invitations of Dionysius, and whilst he persuaded the tyrant to become the father of his people, and the friend of liberty. *Vid.* Dionysius the Second. In his dress the philosopher was not ostentatious, his manners were elegant, but modest, simple, without affectation, and the great honors which his learning deserved were not paid to his appearance. When he came to the Olympian games, Plato resided, during the celebration, in a family who were entire strangers to him. He ate and drank with them, he partook of their innocent pleasures and amusements; but though he told them his name was Plato, yet he never spake of the employment he pursued at Athens, and never introduced the name of that philosopher whose doctrines he followed, and whose death and virtues were favorite topics of conversation in every part of Greece. When he returned home, he was attended by the family which had so kindly entertained him; and, as being a native of Athens, he was desired to show them the great philosopher whose name he bore; their surprise was great when he told them that he himself was the Plato whom they wished to behold. In his diet he was moderate, and, indeed, to sobriety and temperance in the use of food, and to the want of those pleasures which enfeeble the body and enervate the mind, some have attributed his preservation during the tremendous pestilence which raged at Athens with so much fury at the beginning of the Peloponnesian war. Plato was never subject to any long or lingering indisposition; and though change of climate had enfeebled a constitution naturlly strong and healthy, the philosopher lived to an advanced age, and was often heard to say, when his physicians advised him to leave his residence at Athens, where the air was impregnated with the pestilence, that he would not advance one single step to gain the top of mount Athos, where he certain of attaining the great longevity which the inhabitants of that mountain were said to enjoy above the rest of mankind. Plato died on his birthday, in the 81st year of his age, about 348 years B.C. His last moments were easy and without pain; and, according to some, he expired in the midst of an entertainment, or, according to Cicero, as he was writing. The works of Plato are numerous; they are all written in the form of a dialogue, except twelve letters, and each of them have three names for title, the first proper, the second expressive of the subject, and the third an epithet denoting its nature. He speaks always by the mouth of others, and the philosoqher has no where made mention of himself except once in his dialogue entitled

Phædon, and, another time, in his apology for Socrates. His writings were so celebrated, and his opinion so respected, that he was called divine; and for the elegance, melody, and sweetness of his expressions, he was distinguished by the appellation of the Athenian bee. Cicero had such an esteem for him, that, in the warmth of panegyric, he exclaimed *Errare mehercule malo cum Platone quam cum istis vera sentire;* and Quintilian said, that when he read Plato, he seemed to hear not a man, but a divinity speaking. His style, however, though admired and commended by the best and most refined of critics among the ancients, has not escaped the censure of some of the moderns; and the philosopher has been blamed for asserting that fire is a pyramid tied to the earth by numbers, that the world is a figure consisting of twelve pentagons, and who, to prove the metempsychosis and the immortality of the soul, asserts, that the dead are born from the living, and the living from the dead. The speculative mind of Plato was employed in examining things divine and human, and he attempted to fix and ascertain, not only the practical doctrines of morals and politics, but the more subtle and abstruse theory of mystical theogony. His philosophy was universally received and adopted, and it has not only governed the speculative part of mankind, but it continues still to influence the reasoning, and to divide the sentiments of the moderns. In his system of philosophy he followed the physics of Heraclitus, the metaphysical opinions of Pythagoras, and the morals of Socrates. He maintained the existence of two beings, one self-existent, and the other formed by the hand of a pre-existent creature, God and man. The world was created by that self-existent cause, from the rude indigested mass of matter which had existed from all eternity, and which had ever been animated by an irregular principle of motion. The origin of evil could not be traced under the government of a deity, without admitting a stubborn intractability and wildness congenial to matter, and from these, consequently, could be demonstrated the deviations from the laws of nature, and from hence the extravagant passions and appetites of men. From materials like these were formed the four elements, and the beautiful structure of the heavens and the earth, and into the active, but irrational principle of matter, the divinity infused a rational soul. The souls of men were formed from the remainder of the rational soul of the world, which had previously given existence to the invisible gods and demons. The philosopher, therefore, supported the doctrine of ideal forms, and the pre-existence of the human mind, which he considered as emanations from the Deity, which can never remain satisfied with objects or things unworthy of their divine original. Men could perceive, with their corporeal senses, the types of immutable things, and the fluctuating objects of the material world; but the sudden changes to which these are continually obnoxious, create innumerable disorders, and hence arise deception, and, in short, all the errors and miseries of human life. Yet, in whatever situation man may be, he is still an object of divine concern; and, to recommend himself to the favor of the pre-existent cause, he must comply with the purposes of his creation, and, by proper care and diligence, he can recover these immaculate powers with which he was naturally endowed. All science the philosopher made to consist in reminiscence, and in recalling the nature, forms, and proportions of those perfect and immutable essences with which the human mind had been conversant. From observations like these, the summit of felicity might be attained by removing from the material and approaching nearer to the intellectual world, by curbing and governing the passions, which were ever agitated and inflamed by real or imaginary objects. The passions were divided into two classes; the first consisted of the irascible passions, which originated in pride or resentment, and were seated in the breast; the other, founded on the love of pleasure, was the concupiscible part of the soul, seated in the belly, and inferior parts of the body. These different orders induced the philosopher to compare the soul to a small republic, of which the reasoning and judging powers were stationed in the head, as in a firm citadel, and of which the senses were its guards and servants. By the irascible part of the soul men asserted their dignity, repelled injuries, and scorned dangers; and the concupiscible part provided for the support and the necessities of the body, and, when governed with propriety, gave rise to temperance. Justice was produced by the regular dominion of reason, and by the submission of the passions; and prudence arose from the strength, acuteness, and perfection of the soul, without which all other virtues could not exist. But, amidst all this, wisdom was not easily attained; at their creation all minds were not endowed with the same excellence, the bodies which they animated were not always in harmony with the divine emanation; some might be too weak, others too strong, and on the first years of a man's life depended his future consequence; as an effeminate and licentious education seemed calculated to destroy the purposes of the divinity, while the contrary produced different effects, and tended to cultivate and improve the reasoning and judging faculty, and to produce wisdom and virtue. Plato was the first who maintained the immortality of the soul upon arguments solid and permanent, deduced from truth and experience. He did not imagine that the diseases, and the death of the body, could injure the principle of life and destroy the soul, which, of itself, was of divine origin, and of an incorruptible and immutable essence, which, though inherent for a while in matter, could not lose that power which emanated from God. From doctrines like these, the great founder of Platonism concluded, that there might exist in the world a community of men, whose passions could be governed with moderation, and who, from knowing the evils and miseries which arise from ill conduct, might aspire to excellence, and attain that perfection which can be derived from the proper exercise of the rational and moral powers. To illustrate this more fully, the philosopher wrote a book, well known by the name of the republic of Plato, in which he explains with acuteness, judgment, and elegance, the rise and revolutions of civil society; and so respected was his opinion as a legislator, that his scholars were employed in regulating the republics of Arcadia, Elis, and Cnidus, at the desire of those states, and Xenocrates gave political rules for good and impartial government to the conqueror of the east. The best editions of Plato are those of Francof. fol. 1602; and Bipont. 12 vols. 8vo. 1788. Some of the dialogues have been edited separately by Fischer, Lips. 1770, 1774, &c., but for an account of the various editions of Plato's works, the reader is referred to the third chapter of the third book of *Fabricius, B. Gr.—Sax. Onom.* 1. p. 36.—*Plato, Dial.* &c.—*Cic. de Offic.* 1. *De Div.* 1. c. 36. *De Nat. D.* 2. c. 12. *Tusc.* 1. c. 17.—*Plut. in Sol.* &c.—*Seneca*, ep. 58.—*Quintil.* 10. c. 1, &c.—*Ælian. V.H.* 2. c. 9. l. 4. c. 9.—*Paus.* 1. c. 30.—*Diog.* 7 & 8.—*Apuleius de Phil. Nat.* [The finest bust of Plato is in the collection at Florence.]——A son of Lycaon, king of Arcadia.——A Greek poet, called the prince of the middle comedy, who flourished B.C. 445. Some fragments remain of his pieces. *Suidas.—Pollux.—Athen.*——An Athenian who led a reinforcement to Alexander, into Media. *Curt.* 5. c. 7.

PLA'TOR, a man of Dyrrachium, put to death by Piso. *Cic. Pis.* 34.——A general of Macedonia. *Liv.* 28. c. 6.

PLAUTIA LEX, was enacted by M. Plautius, the tribune, A.U.C. 664. It required every tribe annually to chose fifteen persons of their body, to serve as judges, making the honor common to all the three orders, according to the majority of votes in every tribe. Another, called also Plotia, A.U.C. 675. It punished with the *interdictio ignis & aquæ*, all persons who were found guilty of attempts upon the state, or the senators, or magistrates, or such as appeared in public armed, with an evil design, or such as forcibly expelled any person from his legal possessions.

PLAUTIA'NUS FUL'VIUS, an African of mean birth, who was banished for his seditious behaviour in the years of his obscurity. In his banishment,

Plautianus formed an acquaintance with Severus, who, some years after, ascended the imperial throne. This was the beginning of his prosperity; Severus paid the greatest attention to him, and, if we believe some authors, their familiarity and intercourse were carried beyond the bounds of modesty and propriety. Plautianus shared the favors of Severus on the throne as well as in obscurity. He was invested with as much power as his patron at Rome, and in the provinces, and, indeed, he wanted but the name of emperor to be his equal. His table was served with more delicate meats than that of the emperor; when he walked in the public streets he received the most distinguishing honors, and a number of criers ordered the most noble of citizens, as well as the meanest beggars to make way for the favorite of the emperor, and not to fix their eyes upon him. He was concerned in all the rapine and destruction that was committed through the empire, and enriched himself with the possessions of those who had been sacrificed to the emperor's cruelty or avarice. To complete his triumph, and to make himself still greater, Plautianus married his favorite daughter Plautilla to Caracalla, the son of the emperor; and so eager was the emperor to indulge his inclination in this, and in every other respect, that he declared he loved Plautianus so much, that he would even wish to die before him. The marriage of Caracalla with Plautilla was attended with serious consequences. The son of Severus had complied with great reluctance; and though Plautilla was amiable in her manners, commanding in aspect, and of a beautiful countenance, yet the young prince often threatened to punish her haughty and imperious behaviour as soon as he succeeded to the throne. Plautilla reported the whole to her father, and to save his daughter from the vengeance of Caracalla, Plautianus conspired against the emperor and his son. The conspiracy was discovered, and Severus forgot his attachment to Plautianus, and the favors he had heaped upon him, when he heard of his perfidy. The wicked minister was immediately put to death, and Plautilla banished to the island of Lipara, with her brother Plautius, where, seven years after, she was put to death by order of Caracalla, A.D. 211. Plautilla had two children, a son, who died in his childhood, and a daughter, whom Caracalla murdered in the arms of her mother. *Dion. Cass.—Herodian.* 3. c. 10, 11, 12, &c.

PLAUTIL'LA, a daughter of Plautianus, the favorite minister of Severus. *Vid.* Plautianus.——The mother of the emperor Nerva, descended from a noble family.

PLAU'TIUS, a Roman, who became so disconsolate at the death of his wife, that he threw himself upon her burning pile. *Val. Max.* 4. c. 6.——One of Otho's friends. He dissuaded him from killing himself.——A Roman, who presided as prætor over Bithynia and Pontus. *Cic.* 13. *Fam.* 29. ——A man put to death by order of Caracalla.

Plau'tius Ca'ius, a consul sent against the Privernates, &c.——Another general defeated in Lusitania.

Plau'tius Au'lus, a governor of Britain, who obtained an ovation for the conquests he had gained there over the Barbarians. *Tac. Agric.* c. 14. ——A general who defeated the Umbrians and the Etrurians.

Plau'tius Latera'nus, an adulterer of Messalina, who conspired against Nero, and was capitally condemned. *Tac. Ann.* 33. c. 11 & 15. c. 49.

Plau'tius T. Sylva'nus, a tribune who made a law to prevent seditions in the public assemblies. *Tac. Ann.* 4. c. 22.

Plau'tius Rubel'lius, a man accused before Nero, and sent to Asia, where he was assassinated.

PLAUTUS M. AC'CIUS, a comic poet, born at Darsinna, in Umbria. Fortune proved unkind to him, and, from competence, he was reduced to abject poverty. To maintain himself he entered into the family of a baker as a common servant, and while he was employed in grinding corn, he sometimes dedicated a few moments to the comic muse. Some, however, reject this account as false, and assert that Plautus was never obliged to have recourse to the laborious employments of a bakehouse for his maintenance. He wrote 130 comedies, of which only 20 are extant; the Amphitryon, Aulularia, Asinaria, Captivi, Curculio, Casina, Cistellaria, Epidicus, Bacchides, Mostellaria, Menæchmi, Miles gloriosus, Mercator, Pseudolus, Pœnulus, Persa, Rudens, Stichus, Trinummus, and Truculentus. He died about 184 years B.C., and Varro, his learned countryman, wrote this stanza, which deserved to be engraved on his tomb:

> *Postquam morte captus est Plautus,*
> *Comœdia luget, scena est deserta;*
> *Deinde risus, ludus, jocusque, & numeri*
> *Innumevi simul omnes collacrymârunt.*

The plays of Plautus were universally esteemed at Rome, and the purity, the energy, and the elegance of his language, were, by other writers considered as objects of imitation; and Varro, whose judgment is great, and generally decisive, declares, that if the Muses were willing to speak Latin, they would speak in the language of Plautus. In the Augustan age, however, when the Roman language became more pure and refined, the comedies of Plautus did not appear free from inaccuracy. The poet, when his style was compared with the more elegant language of Terence, was censured for his negligence in versification, his low wit, execrable puns, and disgusting obscenities. Yet, however censured as to language or sentiments, Plautus continued to be a favorite on the stage. If his expressions were not choice or delicate, it was universally admitted that he was more happy than other comic writers in his pictures, the incidents of his plays were more varied, the acts more interesting, the characters more truly displayed, and the catastrophe more natural. In the reign of the emperor Diocletian, his comedies were still acted on the public theatres; and no greater compliment can be paid to his abilities as a comic writer, and no greater censure can be passed upon his successors in dramatic composition, than to observe, that for 500 years, with all the disadvantage of obsolete language and diction, in spite of the change of manners, and the revolutions of government, he commanded and received that applause which no other theatrical author dared to dispute with him. The best editions of Plautius are that of Gronovius, 8vo. L. Bat. 1684; that of Barbou, 12mo, in 3 vols. Paris, 1759; that of Esnesti, 2 vols. 8vo, Lips. 1760; and that of Glasgow, 3 vols. 12mo, 1763. *Harles. Not. Lit. Rom.* 1. p. 89.—*Sax. Onom.* 1. p. 122.—*Varro apud Quintil.* 10. c. 1.—*Cic. de Offic.* 1. c. 29. *De Orat.* 3. c. 12. *Ad. Br* 2.—*Aul. Gell.* 1. c. 24.—*Festus.* l. 3. c. 3.—*Horat.* 2. ep. 1. v. 58, 170. *De Art. Poet.* 54 & 270.

Plau'tus Ælia'nus, a high priest, who consecrated the Capitol in the reign of Vespasian. *Tacit. Hist.* 4. c. 53.

PLA'VIS, a river of Venetia, in Italy, now la Piave.

PLEGE'RIUM, a town of India on the Choaspes. *Strab.*

PLE'GRA, a city of Galatia. *Ptol.* 5. c. 6.

PLEI'ADES or **PLE'IADES**, a name given to seven of the daughters of Atlas by Pleione or Æthra, one of the Oceanides. They were placed in the heavens after death, where they formed a constellation called Pleiades, near the back of the bull in the Zodiac. Their names were Alcyone, Merope, Maia, Electra, Taygeta, Sterope, and Celæno. They all, except Merope, who married Sisyphus, king of Corinth, had some of the gods for their suitors. On that account, therefore, Merope's star is dim and obscure among the rest of her sisters, Electra's star alone was dim ever after the fall of Troy, of which her son Dardanus was the king and founder. The name of the Pleiades is derived from the Greek word πλέειν, *to sail*, because that constellation shows the time most favourable to navigators, which is in the spring. The name of Vergiliæ they derive from *ver, the spring*. They are sometimes called Atlantides, from their father, or Hesperides, from the gardens of that name which belonged to Atlas. *Hygin.* fab. 192. *P. A.* 2. c. 21. —*Ovid. Met.* 13. v. 293 *Fast.* 5. v. 106 & 170.— *Hesiod. Oper. & Dies*, v. 615.—*Homer. Odyss.* 5. v. 272.—*Horat.* 4. od. 14.—*Virg. G.* 1. v. 138. l. 4. v. 233. *Æn.* 1. v. 744. l. 3. v. 316.—*Lucan.* 2. v. 722. l. 5. v. 4. l. 8. v. 852.—*Stat. Theb.* 4. v. 119.

l. 9. v. 460.—*Flacc.* 5. v. 46, &c.—*Servius ad Virg. G.* 4. v. 100 & 232.

PLEI'ADES or PLE'IADES, seven poets, who have received their name from their number. They flourished in the age of Philadelphus Ptolemy, king of Ægypt. Their names were Lycophron, Theocritus, Aratus, Nicander, Apollonius, Philicus, and Homerus the Younger. *Sax. Onom.* 1. p. 95.—*Fabr. B. Gr.* 2. c. 19.—*Leisner. de Pleiad. Trag. Gr.*

PLEI'ONE, one of the Oceanides, who married Atlas, king of Mauritania, by whom she had twelve daughters, and a son called Hyas. Seven of the daughters were changed into a constellation called Pleiades, and the rest into another called Hyades. *Ovid. Fast.* 5. v. 84.

PLEMMYR'IUM, now Massa Olivieri, a promontory with a small castle of that name, in the bay of Syracuse. *Virg. Æn.* 3. v. 693.

PLEM'NEUS, a king of Sicyon, son of Peratus. His children always died as soon as born, till Ceres, pitying his misfortune, offered herself as a nurse to his wife, as she was going to be brought to bed. The child, called Chrysorte, lived by the care and protection of the goddess, and Plemneus was no sooner acquainted with the dignity of his nurse, than he raised her a temple. *Paus.* 2. c. 5 & 11.

PLERÆ'I, a people near Dalmatia. *Strab.*

PLESIM'ACHUS, an author who wrote on the return (νόστον) of the Greeks. *Plut. de Flum.*

PLESTIN'IA, a town of the Marsi in Italy. *Plin.*

PLES'TORUS, a god of the Thracians. *Herod.* l. 9.

PLETAU'RI, a people of Lusitania. *Strab.*

PLEUMOX'II, a people of Belgium, the inhabitants of modern Tournay. *Cæs. G.* 5. c. 38.

PLEURA'TUS, a king of Illyricum. *Liv.* 26. c. 24.

PLEU'RON, a son of Ætolus, who married Xantippe, the daughter of Dorus, by whom he had Agenor. He founded a city in Ætolia on the Evenus, which bore his name. *Apollod.* 1. c. 7.—*Plin.* 4. c. 2.—*Sil.* 15. v. 310.—*Paus.* 7. c. 13.—*Ovid. Met.* 7. v. 382.—*Tzetzes. in Lyc.* 143.—*Sch. Hom. Il.* 1. v. 525.—*Sch. Soph. in Trach.* 7.

PLEU'RON, a town of Ætolia. *Vid.* Pleuron.

PLEXAU'RE, one of the Oceanides. *Hesiod. Theog.* v. 39.

PLEXIP'PUS, a son of Thestius, brother of Althæa, the wife of Œneus. He was killed by his nephew Meleager, in hunting the Calydonian boar. His brother Toxeus shared his fate. *Apollod. Vid.* Althea & Meleager.——A son of Phineus and Cleopatra, brother of Pandion, king of Athens. *Apollod.* 3.

C. PLIN'IUS SECUN'DUS, surnamed *Major*, was born at Verona, or, according to some, at Novicomum, and was of a noble family. He distinguished himself in the field, and after he had been made one of the augurs at Rome, was appointed governor of Spain. In his public character he did not neglect the pleasures of literature; the day was employed in the administration of the affairs of his province, and the night was dedicated to study. Every moment of time was precious to him; at his meals one of his servants read to him books valuable for their information, and from them he immediately made copious extracts in a memorandum book. Even while he dressed himself after bathing, his attention was called away from surrounding objects, and he was either employed in listening to another, or in dictating himself. To a mind so earnestly devoted to learning, nothing appeared too laborious, no undertaking too troublesome. He deemed every moment lost which was not dedicated to study, and from these reasons, he never appeared at Rome but in a chariot, and wherever he went, he was always accompanied by his amanuensis. He even censured his nephew, Pliny the Younger, because he had indulged himself with a walk, and sternly observed, that he might have employed those moments to better advantage. But, if his literary pursuits made him forget public affairs, his prudence, his abilities, and the purity and innocence of his character, made him known and respected. He was courted and admired by the emperors Titus and Vespasian, and received from them all the favors which a virtuous prince could offer, and an honest subject receive. As he was at Misenum, where he commanded the fleet, which was then stationed there, Pliny was surprised at the sudden appearance of a cloud of dust and ashes. He was then ignorant of the cause which produced it, and immediately set sail in a small vessel for Mount Vesuvius, which he at last discovered to have made a dreadful eruption. The sight of a number of boats that fled from the coast to avoid the danger, might have deterred another, but the curiosity of Pliny excited him to advance with more boldness; and, though his vessel was often covered with stones and ashes, that were continually thrown up by the mountain, yet he landed on the coast. The place was deserted by the inhabitants, but Pliny remained there during the night, the better to observe the mountain, which, during the obscurity, appeared to be one continual blaze. He was soon disturbed by a terrible earthquake, and the contrary wind on the morrow prevented him from returning to Misenum. The eruptions of the volcano increased, and at last, the fire approached the place where the philosopher made his observations. Pliny endeavoured to flee before it, but though he was supported by two of his servants, he was unable to escape. He soon fell down, suffocated by the thick vapours that surrounded him, and the insupportable stench of sulphureous matter. His body was found three days after, and decently buried by his nephew, who was then at Misenum with the fleet. This memorable event happened in the 79th year of the Christian era; and the philosopher who perished by the eruptions of the volcano, has been called by some the martyr of nature. He was then in the 56th year of his age. Of the works which he composed none are extant but his natural history in thirty-seven books. It is a work, as Pliny the Younger says, full of erudition, and as varied as nature herself. It treats of the stars, the heavens, wind, rain, hail, minerals, trees, flowers, and plants, besides an account of all living animals, birds, fishes, and beasts; a geographical description of every place on the globe, and a history of every art and science, of commerce and navigation, with their rise, progress, and several improvements. He is happy in his descriptions as a naturalist, he writes with force and energy, and though many of his ideas and conjectures are sometimes ill-founded, yet he possesses that fecundity of imagination, and vivacity of expression, which are requisite to treat a subject with propriety, and to render a history of nature pleasing, interesting, and, above all, instructive. His style possesses not the graces of the Augustan age, it has neither its purity, elegance, or its simplicity, but is rather cramped and obscure, and sometimes unintelligible. Yet, for all this, it has ever been admired and esteemed, and it may be called a compilation of every thing which had been written before his age on the various subjects of which it treats, and a judicious collection from the most excellent treatises which had been composed on the various productions of nature. Pliny was not ashamed to mention the authors whom he quoted, he speaks of them with admiration, and while he pays the greatest compliment to their abilities, his encomiums show, in the strongest light, the goodness, the sensibility, and the ingenuousness of his own mind. He had written 160 volumes of remarks and annotations on the various authers which he had read, and so great was the opinion entertained by his contemporaries of his erudition and abilities, that a man called Lartius Lutinius offered to buy his notes and observations for the enormous sum of about 3242*l*. English money. The philosopher, who was himself rich and independent, rejected the offer, and his compilations, after his death, came into the hands of his nephew Pliny. The best editions of Pliny are that of Harduin, 3 vols. fol. Paris, 1723; that of Franzius, 10 vols, 8vo, Lips. 1778; that of Brotier, 6 vols. 12mo. Paris, 1779; and the Variorum, 8vo, in 8 vols. Lips 1778 to 1789. *Tacit. Ann.* 1. c. 69. l. 13. c. 20. l. 15. c. 53.—*Harles. Not. Lit. Rom.* 1. p. 376.—*Sax. Onom.* 1. p. 265.—*Plin. Ep.* &c.

C. PLIN'IUS CÆCIL'IUS SECUN'DUS, surnamed *Junior*, was son of L. Cæcilius by the sister of Pliny the elder. He was adopted by his uncle, whose name he assumed, and whose estates and effects he inherited. He received the greatest part of his education under Quintilian, and at the age of nineteen appeared at the bar, where he distinguished himself so much by his eloquence, that he and Tacitus were reckoned the two greatest orators of their age. He did not make his profession an object of gain like the rest of the Roman orators, but refused fees from the richest as well as from the poorest of his clients, and declared that he cheerfully employed himself for the protection of innocence, the relief of the indigent, and the detection of vice. He published many of his harangues and orations, which have been lost. When Trajan was invested with the imperial purple, Pliny was created consul by the emperor. This honor the consul acknowledged in a celebrated panegyric, which, at the request of the Roman senate, and in the name of the whole empire, he pronounced on Trajan. Some time after he presided over Pontus and Bithynia, in the capacity and with the power of pro-consul, and by his humanity and philanthropy the subject was freed from the burden of partial taxes, and the persecution which had been begun against the Christians of his province was stopped when Pliny solemnly declared to the emperor that the followers of Christ were a meek and inoffensive sect of men, that their morals were pure and innocent, that they were free from all crimes, and that they voluntarily bound themselves by the most solemn oaths to abstain from vice, and to relinquish every sinful pursuit. If he rendered himself popular in his province, he was not less respected at Rome. He was there the friend of the poor, the patron of learning, great without arrogance, affable in his behaviour, and an example of good breeding, sobriety, temperance, and modesty. As a father and a husband, his character was amiable; as a subject, he was faithful to his prince; and as a magistrate, he was candid, open, and compassionate. His native country shared, among the rest, his unbounded benevolence; and Comum, a small town of Insubria, which gave him birth, boasted of his liberality in the valuable and choice library of books which he collected there. He also contributed towards the expenses which attended the education of his countrymen, and liberally spent part of his estate for the advancement of literature, and for the instruction of those whom poverty otherwise deprived of the advantages of a public education. He made his preceptor Quintilian, and the poet Martial, objects of his benevolence, and when the daughter of the former was married, Pliny wrote to the father with the greatest civility; and while he observed that he was rich in the possession of learning, though poor in the goods of fortune, he begged of him to accept, as a dowry for his beloved daughter, 50,000 sesterces, about 300*l.* "I would not," continued he, "be so moderate, were I not assured from your modesty and disinterestedness, that the smallness of the present will render it acceptable." He died in the 52d year of his age, A.D. 113. He had written a history of his own times, which is lost. It is said, that Tacitus did not begin his history till he had found it impossible to persuade Pliny to undertake that laborious task; and, indeed, what could not have been expected from the panegyrist of Trajan, if Tacitus acknowledged himself inferior to him in delineating the character of the times? Some suppose, but falsely, that Pliny wrote the lives of illustrious men, universally ascribed to Cornelius Nepos. He also wrote poetry, but his verses have all perished, and nothing of his learned works remains but his panegyric on the emperor Trajan, and ten books of letters, which he himself collected and prepared for the public, from a numerous and respectable correspondence. These letters contain many curious and interesting facts, and abound with many anecdotes of the generosity and humane sentiments of the writer. They are written with elegance and great purity, and the reader every where discovers that affability, that condescension and philanthropy which so egregiously marked the advocate of the Christians. These letters are esteemed by some equal to the voluminous epistles of Cicero. In his panegyric, Pliny's style is florid and brilliant; he has used, to the greatest advantage, the liberties of the panegyrist, and the eloquence of the courtier. His ideas are new and refined, but his diction is distinguished by that affectation and pomposity which marked the reign of Trajan. The best editions of Pliny, are those of Gesner, 8vo, Lips. 1770, and of Lallemand, 12mo, Paris apud Barbou, and of the panegyric separate, that of Schwartz, 4to. 1746, and of the epistles, the Variorum L. Bat. 1669, 8vo. *Harles. Not. Lit. Rom.* 1. p. 407.—*Sax. Onom.* 1. p. 283.—*Plin. Ep.*—*Vossius.*—*Sidonius.*

PLIN'THINE or PLINTHI'NE, a town of Ægypt on the Mediterranean. *Steph.* It is now Torre de gl'Arabi.

PLISTAR'CHIA, a town of Caria, called also Heracleum. *Steph.*

PLISTAR'CHUS, son of Leonidas, of the family of the Eurysthenidæ, succeeded to the Spartan throne at the death of Cleombrotus. *Herodot.* 9. c. 10.——A brother of Cassander.

PLIS'THANUS, a philosopher of Elis who succeeded in the school of Phædon. *Diog. Laert. in Phæd.* l. 1.

PLIS'THENES, a son of Atreus king of Argos, father of Menelaus and Agamemnon, according to Hesiod and others. Homer, however, calls Menelaus and Agamemnon sons of Atreus, though they were, in reality, the children of Plisthenes. The father died very young, and the two children were left in the house of their grandfather, who took care of them and instructed them. From his attention to them, therefore, it seems probable that Atreus was universally acknowledged as their protector and father, and thence their surname of *Atridæ. Ovid. Rem. Am.* v. 778.—*Dictys. Cret.* 1.—*Homer. Il.*—*Hesiod. apud Eustath. Il.* 1.—*Servius in Æn.* 1. v. 462.—*Lactant. in* 1. *Ach.*—*Schol. Homer. Il.* 1, &c.——A son of Thyestes, presented at an entertainment as meat to his father by Atreus. *Senec. Thyest.* 724.

PLISTI'NUS, a brother of Faustulus the shepherd, who saved the life of Romulus and Remus. He was killed in a scuffle which happened between the two brothers.

PLISTO'ANAX or PLISTO'NAX, son of Pausanias, was general of the Lacedæmonian armies in the Peloponnesian war. He was banished from his kingdom of Sparta for 19 years, and was afterwards recalled by order of the oracle of Delphi. He reigned 68 years. He had succeeded Plistarchus. *Thucyd.*

PLISTONI'CUS or PLISTONI'CES, an author mentioned by *Athenæus.*

PLIS'TUS, a river of Phocis falling into the bay of Corinth. *Strab.* 9.

PLITA'NIÆ, islands near Troas. *Plin.* 5. c. 31.

PLO'TÆ, the name of the two islands in the Ionian Sea, called afterwards Strophades. *Apollon.* 2. v. 297.—*Servius in Æn.* 3. v. 209.—*Plin.* 4. c. 12.—*Eustath. ad Dionys. Per* 461.

PLOTHE'A, a village in the tribe Ægeis. *Steph.*

PLOTI'NA POMPE'IA, a Roman lady who married Trajan while he was yet a private man. She entered Rome in the procession with her husband when he was saluted emperor, and distinguished herself by the affability of her behaviour, and by her humanity and liberal offices to the poor and friendless. She accompanied Trajan into the east, and at his death brought back his ashes to Rome, and still enjoyed all the honors and titles of a Roman empress under Adrian, who, by her means had succeeded to the vacant throne. At her death, A.D. 122, she was ranked among the gods, and received divine honors, which, according to the superstition of the times, she seemed to deserve, from her regard for the good and the prosperity of the Roman empire, and for her private virtues. *Dion. & Spartian. in Adrian.* [The finest bust of Plotina will be found in the Museum of the Capitol, at Rome.]

PLOTINOP'OLIS, a town of Thrace, built by the emperor Trajan, and called after Plotina, the founder's wife. *Ptol.* It is now Ploudin, according to *Niger.*——A town in Dacia.

PLOTI'NUS, a Platonic philosopher of Lycopolis in Ægypt. He was for eleven years a pupil of Ammonius the philosopher, and, after he had profited by the instruction of his learned preceptor, he determined to improve his knowledge, and to visit the territories of India and Persia to acquire information. He accompanied Gordian in his expedition into the east, but the day which proved fatal to the emperor, nearly terminated the life of the philosopher. He saved himself by flight, and the following year retired to Rome, where he publicly taught philosophy. His school was frequented by people of every sex, age, and quality; by senators, as well as by plebeians; and, so great was the opinion entertained by the public of his honesty and candor, that many, on their death-bed, left all their possessions to his care, and entrusted their children to him, as to a superior being. He was the favorite of all the Romans, and, while he charmed the populace by the force of his eloquence, and the senate by his doctrines, the emperor Gallienus courted his friendship and admired and valued the extent of his learning. It is even said, that the emperor and the empress Salonina intended to rebuild a decayed city of Campania, and to appoint the philosopher over it, that there he might experimentally know, while he presided over a colony of philosophers, the validity and the use of the ideal laws of the republic of Plato. This plan was not executed, through the envy and malice of the enemies of Plotinus. The philosopher, at last became helpless and infirm, returned to Campania, where the liberality of his friends for awhile maintained him. He died A.D. 270, in the 66th year of his age, and as he expired, he declared that he made his last and most violent efforts to give up what there was most divine in him to that Divine Being which fills the whole universe. Amidst the great qualities of the philosopher, we discover some ridiculous singularities. Plotinus never permitted his picture to be taken, and he observed, that to see a painting of himself in the following age, was beneath the notice of an enlightened mind. These reasons also induced him to conceal the day, the hour, and the place of his birth. He never made use of medicines, and though his body was often debilitated by abstinence or too much study, he disdained to have recourse to a physician, and thought that it would degrade the gravity of a philosopher. His writings have been collected by his pupil Porphyry. They consist of 54 different treatises divided into six equal parts, written with great spirit and vivacity; but his reasoning is abstruse, and the subjects metaphysical. The best edition is that of Ficinus, fol. Basil, 1580. *Fabr. B. Gr.* 4. c. 29.—*Sax. Onom.* 1. p. 367.

PLO'TIUS CRISPI'NUS, a stoic philosopher and poet, whose verses were inelegant, and whose disposition was morose, for which he has been ridiculed by Horace, and surnamed *Aretalogus*. *Horat.* 1. sat. 1. v. 4. sat. 3. v. 139. sat. 4. v. 14. l. 2. sat. 7. v. 45.—*Gyrald. de P. H.* 4.

PLO'TIUS FIR'MUS, a commander set over the guards, after the murder of Galba. *Tacit. Hist.* 1. c. 46.

PLO'TIUS GAL'LUS, a native of Lugdunum, who taught grammar at Rome, and had Cicero among his pupils. *Cic. de Orat.* 1.—*Quintil.* 2. c. 4.

PLO'TIUS GRI'PHUS, a man made senator by Vespasian. *Tacit. Hist.* 3. c. 52.

PLO'TIUS LU'CIUS, a poet in the age of the great Marius, whose exploits he celebrated in his verses. *Gyrald. de. H. P.* 4.

PLO'TIUS MAR'CUS, a centurion in Cæsar's army. *Cœs. B. C.* 3. c. 19.

PLO'TIUS A. SYLVA'NUS, a prætor at Rome, in the consulship of Marcellus and Sulpicius. *Cic.* 13. *Fam.* 29.

PLO'TIUS TUC'CA, a friend of Horace and of Virgil, who made him his heir. He was selected by Augustus, with Varius, to review the Æneid of Virgil. *Horat.* 1. sat. 5. v. 40. sat. 10. v. 81.—*Gyrald. de H. P.* 4.—*Harles. Not. Lit. Rom.* 1. p. 305.

PLU'BIUM, a town of Sardinia. *Ptol.* It is now Sossari, according to *Niger*.

PLU'SIUS, a surname of Jupiter at Sparta, expressive of his power to grant riches. *Paus.* 3. c. 19.

PLUTAR'CHUS, a native of Chæronea, descended from a respectable family. His father, whose name is unknown, was distinguished for his learning and virtues, and his grandfather, called Lamprias, was also as conspicuous for his eloquence and the fecundity of his genius. Under Ammonius, a reputable teacher at Delphi, Plutarch was made acquainted with philosophy and mathematics, and his character was so well established, that he was appointed by his countrymen, while yet very young, to go to the Roman proconsul, in their name, upon an affair of the most important nature. This commission he executed with honor to himself, and with advantage to his country. He afterwards travelled in quest of knowledge; and, after he had visited, like a philosopher and historian, the territories of Ægypt and Greece, retired to Rome, where he opened a school. His reputation made his school frequented. The emperor Trajan admired his abilities, and honored him with the office of consul, and appointed him governor of Illyricum. After the death of his imperial benefactor, Plutarch removed from Rome to Chæronea, where he lived in the greatest tranquillity, respected by his fellow-citizens, and raised to all the honors which his native town could bestow. In this peaceful and solitary retreat, Plutarch closely applied himself to study, and wrote the greatest part of his works; and particularly his lives. He died in an advanced old age at Chæronea, about 140 A.D. Plutarch had five children, four sons and one daughter, by his wife, called Timoxena. Two of the sons and the daughter died when young, and those that survived were called Plutarch and Lamprias, and the latter did honor to his father's memory, by giving to the world an accurate catalogue of his writings. In his private and public character, the historian of Chæronea was the friend of discipline. He boldly asserted the natural right of mankind, liberty; but he recommended obedience and submissive deference to magistrates, as necessary to preserve the peace and security of the community. He maintained, that the most violent and dangerous public factions arose too often from private disputes and from misunderstanding. To render himself more intelligent, he always carried a common-place book with him, and preserved with the greatest care whatever judicious observations occurred in the course of conversation. The most esteemed of his works are his lives of illustrious men, of whom he examines and delineates the different characters with wonderful skill and impartiality. He neither misrepresents the virtues, nor hides the foibles of his heroes. He writes with precision and fidelity, and though his diction is neither pure nor elegant, yet there is energy and animation in it, and in many descriptions he is inferior to no historian. In some of his narrations, however, he is often too circumstantial, and his remarks are often injudicious; and when he compares the heroes of Greece with those of Rome, the candid reader can easily remember which side of the Adriatic gave the historian birth. Some have accused him of not knowing the genealogy of his heroes, and have censured him for his superstition; yet, for all this, he is the most entertaining, the most instructive, and the most interesting of all the writers of ancient history; and were a man of true taste and judgment asked what book he wished to save from destruction, of all the profane compositions of antiquity, he would perhaps without hesitation, reply with Theodore Gaza, the lives of Plutarch. In his moral treatises, Plutarch appears in a different character, and his misguided philosophy, and erroneous doctrines, render some of these inferior compositions puerile and disgusting. They, however, contain many useful lessons and curious facts, and though they are composed without connexion, compiled without judgment, and often abound with improbable stories and false reasonings, yet they contain much information, and many useful reflections. The best editions of Plutarch are that of Frankfort, 2 vols. fol. 1599; that of Stephens, 6 vols. 8vo, 1572; the Lives by Reiske, 12 vols. 8vo, Lips. 1775; and the Moralia, &c. by Wyttenbach. Among the translations are that of Dacier in French, and of Langhorne in English, besides several others. *Fabr. B. Gr.* 4. c. 13.—*Sax. Onom.* 1. p. 286.——A native of Eretria, during the Peloponnesian war. He was defeated by the Macedonians. *Plut. in Phoc.* Several other persons of this name are mentioned by *Fabricius*, and *Jonsius, de Script. Hist. Phil.* 3. c. 6.

PLU'TIA, a town of Sicily. *Cic. in Verr.*

PLU'TIUM, a city of the Tyrrhenes. *Steph.*

PLU'TO, a daughter of Himas of Phrygia, mother

of Tantalus by Jupiter. Some call her one of the Oceanides. *Paus.* 2. c. 22.—*Hygin.* fab. 155.—*Schol. Pind.* 3. *Olymp.*—*Sch. Hesiod. in Th.* 355.

PLU'TO, a son of Saturn and Ops, inherited his father's kingdom with his brothers Jupiter and Neptune. He received as his lot the kingdom of hell, and whatever lies under the earth, and as such he became the god of the infernal regions, of death, and of funerals. From his functions, and the place he inhabited, he received different names. He was called Dis, Hades, or Ades, Clytopolon, Agelastus, Orcus, Eubulus, Isidotes, Leptinis, Clymenon, Anapompus, &c. As the place of his residence was obscure and gloomy, all the goddesses refused to marry him; but he determined to obtain by force what was denied to his solicitations. As he once visited the island of Sicily, after a violent earthquake, he saw Proserpine, the daughter of Ceres, gathering flowers in the plains of Enna, with a crowd of female attendants. He became enamoured of her, and immediately carried her away upon his chariot drawn by four horses. To make his retreat more unknown, he opened himself a passage through the earth, by striking it with his sceptre in the lake of Cyane, in Sicily, or, according to others, on the borders of the Cephisus in Attica. Proserpine called upon her attendants for help, but in vain, and she became the wife of her ravisher, and the queen of hell. Pluto is generally represented as holding a sceptre with two teeth, he has also keys in his hand, to intimate that whoever enters his kingdom can never return. He was regarded as a hard-hearted and inexorable god, with a grim and dismal countenance, and for that reason no temples were raised to his honor as to the rest of the superior gods. Black victims, and particularly a bull, were the only sacrifices that were offered to him, and their blood was not sprinkled on the altars, or received in vessels, as at other sacrifices, but was permitted to run down into the earth, as if it were to penetrate as far as the realms of the god. The Syracusans yearly sacrificed to him black bulls, near the fountain of Cyane, where, according to the received traditions, he had disappeared with Proserpine. Among plants, the cypress, the narcissus, and the maiden-hair were sacred to him, as also everything which was deemed inauspicious, particularly the number Two. According to some of the ancients, Pluto sat on a throne of sulphur, from which issued the rivers Lethe, Cocytus, Phlegethon, and Acheron. The dog Cerberus watched at his feet, the Harpies hovered around him, Proserpine sat on his left hand, and near the goddess stood the Eumenides, with their heads covered with snakes. The Parcæ occupied the right, each of whom held in her hand the symbol of her office, the distaff, the spindle, and the scissors. Pluto is called by some the father of the Eumenides. During the war of the Gods and the Titans, the Cyclopes made a helmet, which rendered the bearer invisible, and gave it to Pluto. Perseus was armed with it when he conquered the Gorgons. *Hesiod. Theog.* 185 & 455.—*Apollod.* 1, &c.—*Hygin.* fab. 155. *P.A.* 2.—*Stat. Theb.* 8. v. 37.—*Diod* 5.—*Hom. Il.* 5. v. 395. l. 13. v. 389. l. 15. v. 187.—*Claudian. de Raptu. Pr.*—*Ovid. Met.* 5. fab. 6. *Fast.* 4. v. 439.—*Palæph. de Inc.*—*Paus.* 2. c. 36.—*Orpheus, Hymn.* 17, &c.—*Cic. de Nat. D.* 2. c. 26.—*Plato de Rep.*—*Eurip. in Med. Hippol.*—*Æschyl. in Pers. Prom.*—*Varro. L.L.* 4.—*Catull.* ep. 3.—*Virg. G.* 4. v. 502. *Æn.* 6. v. 273. l. 8. v. 296.—*Lucan.* 6. v. 715.—*Horat.* 2. od. 3 & 18.—*Senec. in Herc. Fur.*—*Servius in Æn.* 1. v. 133. l. 5. v. 134. l. 8. v. 276.—*Tzetzes. ad Lyc.* 838.—*Aug. de Civ. D.* 7. c. 28.—*Gyrald. H.D.* 6.—*Suidas.*—*Phurn. de Nat. D.* 5.—*Hesychius.*—*Isid.* 8. c. 11.—*Albricius de D. Imag.* 10. [There is a small statue of Pluto in the Vatican, where will also be found a very fine colossal head of this deity.]

PLUTO'NIUM, a temple of Pluto in Lydia. *Cic. de Div.* l. c. 36.—*Strab.*

PLU'TUS, son of Jasion or Jasius, by Ceres, the goddess of corn, has been confounded by many of the mythologists with Pluto, though plainly distinguished from him as being the god of riches. He was born at Tripolis in Crete, where his mother was employed in bestowing cultivation on the earth, and was brought up by the goddess of peace, and, on that account, Pax was represented at Athens, as holding the god of wealth in her lap. The Greeks spoke of him as of a fickle divinity. They represented him as blind, because he distributed riches indiscriminately; he was lame, because he came slow and gradually; but had wings, to intimate that he flew away with more velocity than he approached mankind. *Lucian. in Tim.*—*Paus.* 9. c. 16 & 26.—*Hygin P.A.*—*Aristoph. in Plut.*—*Diod.* 5.—*Hesiod. Th.* 970.—*Theog. apud Stobæum.*—*Dionys. Hal.* 1. c. 53.

PLU'VIUS, a surname of Jupiter as the god of *rain*. His worship was established at Athens, where, on mount Hymettus, an altar and a statue were erected to him, and sacrifices regularly offered in the time of drought. He was also invoked by that name amongst the Romans, whenever the earth was parched up by continual heat, and was in want of refreshing showers. He had an altar in the temple on the Capitol, and the Romans had reason to be grateful to a divinity who sent a plentiful shower of rain to the prayers of the thirsty army of Trajan. In consequence of this event a bas-relief of the god was placed on Trajan's column, representing him as an old man with a long beard, and extended arms, while at his feet the soldiers spread their shields to receive the showers which dropped from his beard and hands. *Tibull.* 1. el. 7. v. 26.—*Sueton. in Traj.*—*Paus.* 2. c. 19.—*Phurnut. de N.D.* 9.—*Spanh. ad. Aristoph. in Nub.* 370.

PLYN'EÆ, an island of the Nile. *Steph.*

PLYNTE'RIA, a festival among the Greeks, in honor of Aglaurus, or rather of Minerva, who received from the daughter of Cecrops the name of Aglaurus. The word seems to be derived from πλύνειν, *lavare*, because during the solemnity, they undressed the statue of the goddess and *washed* it. The day on which it was observed, was universally looked upon as unfortunate and inauspicious, and, on that account, no person was permitted to appear in the temples, as they were purposely surrounded with ropes. The arrival of Alcibiades in Athens that day, was deemed very unfortunate; but, however, the success that ever after attended him, proved it to be otherwise. It was customary at this festival to bear in procession a cluster of figs, which was called Ηγητορία or Ηγήτρια, from ἡγέομαι, because figs were ἡγεμόνες τοῦ καθαροῦ βιοῦ, i.e. *leaders of humanity*, and intimated the progress of civilization among the first inhabitants of the earth, as they served them for food after they had conceived a dislike for acorns. *Pollux.* 8. c. 12.—*Hesych.*—*Plut. Alcib.*—*Athen.* l. 3.—*Xenoph. Hell.* 1.—*Gyrald. de Sacr.*

PLY'NUS, a city of Libya, near mount Atlas. *Herodot.*

PLYSE'NUM, a town of Thrace. *Procopius.*

PNEB'EBIS, a city of Ægypt. *Steph.*

PNEVEN'TIA, a town of Picenum. *Strab.*

PNI'GEUS, a village of Ægypt, near Phœnicia. *Strab.* 16.

PNUPS, a small town of Æthiopia, near the Nile. *Ptol.*

PNYX, a place of Athens, set apart by Solon for holding assemblies. The windows, because they opened towards the sea, were closed by the 30 tyrants, and others opened towards the land, as it was considered that the dominion of the sea was favorable to democracy, but that the cultivation of the land was productive of greater tranquillity under an oligarchical government. *Plut. in Thes. & Themis.*—*C. Nep. Att.* 3.

POBLICIUS MAR'CUS, a lieutenant of Pompey in Spain.

PODALI'A or PODALE'A, a city of Lydia. *Steph.*

PODALIR'IUS, a son of Æsculapius and Epione. He was one of the pupils of the Centaur Chiron, and made himself under him, such a master of medicine, that during the Trojan war, the Greeks invited him to their camp, to stop a pestilence which had baffled the skill of all their physicians. Some however suppose, that he went to the Trojan war, not in the capacity of a physician in the Grecian army, but as a warrior, attended by his brother Machaon, in 30 ships, with soldiers from Œchalia, Ithome, and Trica. At his return from the Trojan war, Podalirius was shipwrecked on the coast of Caria, where he cured of the falling sickness and married, a daughter of Damœtas, the king of the place. He fixed his habitation there, and built two towns, one of which he called Syrna, after the name of his wife. The Carians, after his death, built him a temple, and paid him divine honors. *Homer. Il.* 2. *enum.* v. 236.—*Dictys. Cret.*—*Q. Smyrn.* 6. v. 464. l. 9. v. 460.—*Ovid. de Art. Am.* 2. 735.—*Trist.* el. 6.—*Paus.* 3.——A Rutulian, engaged in the wars of Æneas and Turnus. *Virg. Æn.* 12. v. 394.

PODAR'CE, a daughter of Danaus. *Apollod.*

PODAR'CES, a son of Iphiclus of Thessaly, who went to the Trojan war, with his brother Protesilaus, at the head of forty ships. He succeeded to the command of the army after his brother's death. *Homer. Il.* 2. *En.* v. 211.—*Apollod.* 1.—*Dictys. Cret.* 1.——The first name of Priam. When Troy was taken by Hercules, he was carried away in the number of the captives, but his sister Hesione, to whom the hero had given the power of choosing any one she pleased, redeemed him from slavery by giving the golden ornaments of her head to the conqueror, and from that circumstance he received the name of Priam. *Vid.* Priamus. *Apollod.* 2 & 3.

PODA'RES, a general of Mantinea, in the age of Epaminondas. He was killed in a battle against the Thebans, and his countrymen rewarded his valor by erecting him a statue in the public forum. *Paus.* 8. c. 9.

PODAR'GE, one of the Harpies, mother of two of the horses of Achilles, by Zephyrus. The word intimates the *swiftness* of her *feet. Homer. Il.* 16.

PODAR'GI, a people of Thrace. *Steph.*

PODAR'GUS, a charioteer of Hector. *Homer.* Ψ. v. 295.

PODO'CA, a city of India within the Ganges. *Ptol. Niger* calls it Pedephetan.

PODU'CE, a city of Taprobane. *Ptol.*

PŒ'AN, the father of Philoctetes. The son is often called *Pœantia proles*, on account of his father. *Ovid. Met.* 13. v. 45.

PŒ'AS, son of Thaumacus, was among the Argonauts. *Apollod.*

PŒC'ILA PE'TRA, a maritime town of Cilicia. *Strab. Mercator* calls it Paxoli.

PŒCILA'SIUM or PŒCILAS'SUS, a city of Crete. *Ptol.* It is now Pentalo.

PŒCILE, a celebrated portico at Athens, which received its name from the variety (ποικίλος) of paintings which it contained. It was there that Zeno kept his school, and the Stoics also received their lessons there, whence their name (ἁ ςοά, *a porch*). The pœcile was adorned with pictures of gods and benefactors, and among many others were those of the siege and sacking of Troy, the battle of Theseus with the Amazons, the fight between the Lacedæmonians and Athenians at Œnoe in Argolis, and of Atticus, the great friend of Athens. The only reward which Miltiades obtained after the battle of Marathon, was to have his picture drawn in the fore-ground, and more conspicuous than the rest of the officers that fought with him, in the representation which was made of the engagement, which was hung up in the pœcile, in commemoration of that celebrated victory. *C. Nep. in Milt. & in Attic.* 3.—*Paus.* 1. c. 15 & 16.—*Meursius. Att. Lect.* 6. c. 18.—*Plin.* 35. c. 9.

PŒDIC'ULI, a people of Italy, *Strab.*—*Appian.*—*Val. Max.* 1. 7.

PŒD'ICUM, a town of Carinthia. *Ptol.* It is now Peckfelde.

PŒEES'SA, a city of Ceus. *Steph.*

PŒMA'NIUM, a small region of Cyzicum. *Steph.* Some read Pœmœnion.

PŒ'MEN, a mountain of Pontus, from which the Parthenius flows.

PŒME'NIUM, a mountain of Macedonia. *Steph.*

PŒ'NA, a monster sent by Apollo to Argos, to punish the inhabitants, because they had not prevented the death of the son he had by Psamathe. This monster, which Hesychius places among the furies, tore with savage barbarity children from their mothers' breasts, and devoured them. It was at last killed by Corœbus. *Paus.* 1. c. 43.—*Stat. Theb.* 1. v. 570 *& seq.*—*Hesychius.*

PŒ'NI, a name given to the Carthaginians. It seems to be a corruption of the word Phœni or Phœnices, as the Carthaginians were of Phœnician origin. *Serv. ad Virg.* 1. v. 302.

PŒNI'NA, a divinity worshipped by the inhabitants of the Pœninæ Alpes, now St. Bernard. *Servius* 10. *Æn.* v. 13.

PŒ'NIUS, an architect, who assisted Demetrius in finishing the temple of Diana at Ephesus. *Vitruv.* l. 7. *in Proœm.*

PŒ'NIUS POS'TUMUS, a præfect of the camp in Britain. *Tac. Ann.* 14. c. 37.

PŒ'ON. *Vid.* Pæon.

PŒO'NIA, a part of Macedonia, at the north of the Thermaicus Sinus. *Vid.* Pæonia.

PŒ'US, a part of mount Pindus, from which the Peneus flows. *Strab.*

PO'GLA, a city of Pamphylia. *Ptol.*

POGOAR'GAS, a town of Upper Æthiopia. *Plin.*

PO'GON, a harbour of the Trœzenians, on the coast of the Peloponnesus. It received this name on account of its appearing to come forward before the town of Trœzene, as the *beard* (πώγων) does from the chin. *Strab.* 8.—*Mela*, 2.

PO'LA, a city of Istria, founded by the Colchians who followed Medea when she fled with Jason. The gulph in the neighbourhood was called Polaticus or Polarius Sinus. The town was afterwards made a Roman colony, and called Pietas Julia. *Plin.* 3. c. 9.—*Mela*, 2. c. 3.—*Strab.* 1 & 5.—*Hygin.* 23.

POLEMAR'CHUS. *Vid.* Archon.——The assassin of Polydorus, king of Sparta, *Paus.* 3. c. 3.——An elder brother of Lysias the orator.

POLEMOC'RATES, son of Machaon, was placed among the gods after death. His temple in Attica was greatly frequented, as it was said that he cured all his diseased suppliants. *Paus.* 2. c. *ult.*

POLEMOCRA'TIA, a queen of Thrace, who fled to Brutus after the murder of Cæsar. She retired from her kingdom because her subjects had lately murdered her husband.

POL'EMON, a youth of Athens, son of Philostratus. He was much given to debauchery and extravagance, and spent the greatest part of his life in riot and drunkenness. He once, when intoxicated, entered the school of Xenocrates, and with an air of insolence derided the remarks and stifled indignation of the spectators. Xenocrates did not notice the conduct of his former pupil with pointed severity, but, changing the discourse in which he was engaged, mildly enlarged on the virtues of modesty and the horrors of intemperance. The rebuke was felt, and Polemon was so struck with the eloquence of the academician, and the force of his arguments, that from that moment he renounced the dissipated life he had led, and applied himself totally to the study of philosophy. He was then in the 30th year of his age, and from that time he never drank any other liquor than water; and, after the death of Zenocrates, succeeded to the superintendence of the school where his reformation had been effected. He died about 270 years B.C., in an extreme old age. *Diog. in Vitâ.*—*Horat.* 2. sat. 3. v. 254.—*Val. Max.* 6. c. 9.——A son of Zeno the rhetorician, made king of Pontus by Antony. He attended his patron in his expedition against Parthia. After the battle of Actium he was received into favor by Augustus, though he had fought in the cause of Antony. He was killed some time after by the barbarians near the Palus Mæotis, against whom he had made war. *Strab.*—*Dion.*——His son, was confirmed on his father's throne by the Roman emperors, and the province of Cilicia was also added to his kingdom by Claudius.——An officer in the army of Alexander, intimate with Philotas. *Curt.* 7. c. 1, &c.——A rhetorician at Rome, who wrote a poem on weights and measures, still extant. He was master of Persius the celebrated satirist, and died in the age of Nero.

POL'EMON ANTO'NIUS, a sophist of Laodicea in Asia Minor, in the reign of Adrian. He was often sent to the emperor with an embassy by his countrymen, which he executed with great success. He was greatly favored by Adrian, from whom he exacted much money. In the 56th year of his age he buried himself alive, as he was much afflicted with the gout. He wrote declamations in Greek. *Gyrald. de P.H.* 5.

POLEMO'NIUM, now Vatiza, a town of Pontus, at the east of the mouth of the Thermodon. *Ptol.*

POLEN'DOS, an island of the Ægæan Sea. *Plin.* 4. c. 12.

POLE'NOR, one of the Centaurs, wounded by the poisoned darts of Hercules. The river Anigrus, where he washed himself, was remarkable from that time for its offensive and dangerous exhalations. *Paus.* 5. c. 5.

POLETES, an ambassador sent by the Epidaurians to the Illyrians. *Alex. ab Alex.* 4. c. 10.

POLE'UR, a city of India within the Ganges. *Ptol.*

POLLIA'NUS, a mountain of Macedonia near Epirus. *Steph.*

PO'LIAS, a surname of Minerva as protectress of cities. She was particularly worshipped under that name at Trœzene, where her statue of gold and ivory was one of the best pieces of Phidias. She was also worshipped at Tegea in Arcadia, where her temple, served by one priest, was entered only once a-year. The locks of Medusa's head were said to be preserved there, which had the power of rendering those who possessed them more than a match for their enemies. *Apollod.* 2. —*Strab.* 9.—*Steph. Byz.*—*Paus.* 2. c. 30. l. 3. c. 17. l. 8. c. 47.

POLICH'NA, a town of Troas on mount Idas. *Herodot.* 6. c. 28.——A town of Crete. *Thucyd.* 2. c. 85.

POL'ICHUS, a statuary of Ægina, son of Synnoon, and pupil of Aristocles of Sicyon. *Paus.* 6. c. 9.

POLIE'A, a festival at Thebes in honor of Apollo, who was represented there with *grey hair* (πολιός), contrary to the practice of all other places. The victim was a bull, but when it happened once that no bull could be found, an ox was taken from the cart and sacrificed. From that time the sacrifice of labouring oxen was deemed lawful, though before it was looked upon as a capital crime. *Paus. Bœot.*

POLIE'UM, a city of Italy, before called Siris. *Steph.*

PO'LIEUS, a surname of Jupiter at Athens, derived from πόλις and Ζεύς, as the god who protected cities. His temple and statue were erected by Leochares. At the time of sacrifice, a mixture of wheat and barley was placed on the altar, which the ox was permitted to taste, and no sooner was he immolated than the priest fled. The people who stood by, as if unconscious of the act, cited the bloody hatchet as a criminal, to answer in judgment, because the killing of oxen in ancient times was considered as unlawful. *Phurnut. de D.N.* 20.—*Paus.* 1. c. 24.—*Hesychius.*—*Steph. Byz. de Urb.* —*Gyrald. H.D.* 2.

POLIME'LA, a daughter of Æolus, seduced by Ulysses during his residence at the Æolian islands. The intrigue was only known to the father after the departure of Ulysses, and he was so irritated that he would have put his daughter to death, had not her brother Diores declared that he would not survive her, as he had placed all his affections upon her. This confession appeased Æolus, who gave Diores permission to marry his sister. *Philetas apud Parthen. Erot.* 2.

POLIME'LUS, an illegitimate son of Peleus, who was father of Patroclus. *Philoc. apud Apollod.* 3.

POLIORCE'TES (*destroyer of cities*), a surname given to Demetrius, son of Antigonus. *Plut. in Demet.*

POLIS'MA a town of Troas, on the Simois. *Strab.* 13.

POLIS'TRATUS, an Epicurean philosopher, born the same day as Hippoclides, with whom he always lived in the greatest intimacy. They both died at the same hour. *Diog.* 10.—*Val. Max.* 1. c. *ult.*

POLI'TES, a son of Priam and Hecuba, remarkable for his swiftness, and therefore frequently engaged to watch the motions of the Grecian army. Iris once assumed his form to inform the Trojans of the unexpected approach of the Grecian forces. Polites was killed by Pyrrhus, in his father's presence, on the night of the sacking of the city. *Virg. Æn.* 2. v. 526, &c.—*Homer. Il.* 2. v. 298. l. 13. v. 533. l. 24. v. 250.—*Apollod.* 3.—*Hygin.* fab. 90.—*Dictys.* 2. c. 43.——Son of the preceding, followed Æneas into Italy, and was one of the friends of young Ascanius. *Virg. Æn.* 5. v. 564.

POLIT'IA, a city of Achaia. *Steph.*

POLITICEOR'GAS, a region of Asia Propria, called afterwards Amphrodisias. *Plin.* 5. c. 30.

POLITO'RIUM, a city of the Latins destroyed by the Romans, 639 B.C. *Liv.* 1. c. 33.

POL'LA ARGENTA'RIA, the wife of the poet Lucan. She assisted her husband in correcting the three first books of his Pharsalia. *Stat. Sylv.* 1 & 2.

POLLEN'TIA, now Polenza, a town of Liguria in Italy, famous for wool. There was a celebrated battle fought here between the Romans and Alaric, king of the Huns, about the 403rd year of the Christian era, in which the former, according to some, obtained the victory. *Mela,* 2. c. 7.—*Plin.* 8. c. 48.—*Suet. Tib.* 37.—*Sil.* 8. v. 598.—*Cic.* 11. *Fam.* 13.——A town of Majorca. *Plin. & Mela.* ——A town of Picenum. *Liv.* 39. c. 44. l. 41. c. 27.

POL'LES, a Greek poet whose writings were so obscure and unintelligible that his name became proverbial. *Suidas.*—*Gyrald. de P.H.* 2.

POL'LIA, one of the thirty-five tribes of the city of Rome. *Liv.* 8. c. 37.—*Val. Max.* 9. c. 10.

POLLIN'EA, a prostitute, &c. *Juv.* 2. v. 68.

POL'LIO C. ASIN'IUS, a Roman consul, under the reign of Augustus, who distinguished himself as much by his eloquence and writings as by his exploits in the field. He defeated the Dalmatians, and favoured the cause of Antony against Augustus. He patronized, with great liberality, the poets Virgil and Horace, who have immortalized his name in their writings. He was the first who collected a public library at Rome, and indeed his example was afterwards followed by many of the emperors. In his library were placed the statues of all the learned men of every age, and Varro was the only person who was honored there during his life-time. He was with J. Cæsar when he crossed the Rubicon. He was greatly esteemed by Augustus, whose cause he espoused upon the disgraceful alliance of Antony with Cleopatra, and did not offend him by refusing to share his dangers at the battle of Actium. Pollio wrote some tragedies, orations, and a history of the civil wars of Pompey and Cæsar, which was divided into seventeen books. All these compositions are lost, and nothing remains of his writings except a few letters to Cicero. He died in the 80th year of his age, A.D. 4. He is the person to whom Virgil has inscribed his fourth eclogue, called *Pollio*, as a reconciliation was effected between Augustus and Antony during his consulship. The poet, as is supposed by some, makes mention of a son of the consul born about this time, and is lavish in his excursions into futurity, and his predictions of approaching prosperity. *Horat.* 2. od. 1. sat. 10. l. 1.—*Appian. de B. Civ.* 5.—*Vell. Pat.* 2. c. 44 & 86.—*Suidas.*—*Virg. Ecl.* 3. v. 8. & 4. v. 12.—*Val. Max.* 8. c. 13.—*Quint.* 10. c. 1.

POL'LIO AN'NIUS, a man accused of sedition before Tiberius, and acquitted. He afterwards conspired against Nero. *Tacit.* 6. c. 9. l. 15. c. 56.

POL'LIO VE'DIUS, one of the friends of Augustus, who used to feed his fishes with human flesh. This cruelty was discovered when one of his servants broke a glass in the presence of Augustus, who had been invited to a feast. The master ordered the servant to be seized: but he threw himself at the feet of the emperor, and begged him to interfere, and not to suffer him to be devoured by fishes. Upon this the causes of his apprehension were examined, and Augustus, astonished at the barbarity of his favorite, caused the servant to be dismissed, all the fish-ponds to be filled up, and the crystal glasses of Pollio to be broken to pieces.

POL'LIO, a man who poisoned Britannicus at the instigation of Nero.——An historian in the age of Constantine the Great.——A sophist in the age of Pompey the Great.——A friend of the emperor Vespasian.

POL'LIS, a commander of the Lacedæmonian fleet, defeated at Naxus, B.C. 377. *Diod. Sic.* 15.—*Polyæn.* 3. c. 11.

POL'LIUS FE'LIX, a friend of the poet Statius, to whom he dedicated his second Sylva.

POLLUP'ICE, a city of Liguria. It is now Finale, according to *Simler.*

POLLUS'CA or POLUS'CA, a town of Latium, formerly the capital of the Volsci. The inhabitants were called Pollustini. *Liv.* 2. c. 39.—*Plin.* 3. c. 5.

POLLUSTI'NI. *Vid.* Polusca.

POLLU'TIA, a daughter of L. Vetus, put to death after her husband Rubellius Plautus, by order of Nero. *Tacit.* 16. *Ann.* c. 10 & 11.

POL'LUX, a son of Jupiter, by Leda the wife of Tyndarus. He was brother of Castor. *Vid.* Castor.

Pol'lux Ju'lius, a Greek writer, who flourished A.D. 186, in the reign of Commodus, and died in the 58th year of his age. He was born at Naucratis, and taught rhetoric at Athens, and wrote a useful work called Onomasticon, of which the best edition is that of Hemsterhusius, 2 vols fol. Amst. 1706 *Fabr B. Gr.* 4. c. 35.—*Sax. Onom.* 1. p. 328.

POLO'SUS, a place in Bœotia, where it was said that Atlas made his observations on the heavens. *Paus.* 9. c. 20.

POL'TIS, a king of Thrace, in the time of the Trojan war. He was solicited by both parties to espouse their quarrels, but wisely rejected their offers, and observed to the Greeks, that as one woman was the cause of their warfare, he would give them two instead, and at the same time advised the Trojans to restore Helen to her lawful husband. *Plut. Apoph.*—*Apollod* 2.

POLTYM'BRIA, a city of Thrace. *Steph.*

PO'LUS, a celebrated Grecian actor.——A sophist of Agrigentum.

POLYÆ'NUS, a native of Macedonia, who wrote in Greek eight books of stratagems, which he dedicated to the emperors Antoninus and Verus, while they were making war against the Parthians. He wrote also other books which have been lost, among which was a history, with a description of the city of Thebes. The best editions of his stratagems are those of Maasvicius, 8vo, L. Bat. 1690, and of Mursinna, 12mo, Berlin, 1756. *Fabr. B. Gr.* 4. c. 17.—*Sax. Onom.* 1. p. 316.——A friend of Philopœmen.——An Orator in the age of Julius Cæsar. He wrote, in three books, an account of Antony's expedition into Parthia, and likewise published orations.——A mathematician, who afterwards followed the tenets of Epicurus, and disregarded geometry as a false and useless study. *Cic. in Acad. Quæst.* 4. c. 33.

POLYÆ'GUS, one of the Sporades. *Plin.* 4. c. 12.

POLYAN'DUS, a city of Cataonia, in Armenia Minor. *Ptol.*

POLYAN'THUS, a native of Cyrene, who wrote *de ortu Asclepiadarum.* *Sext. Emp.* 1. 3. *adv. Mathem.* c. 12.

POLYA'NUS, a mountain of Macedonia, near Pindus. *Strab.*

POLY'ARA, a city of Caria. *Steph.*

POLYAR'CHUS, the brother of a queen of Cyrene. *Polyæn*, 8. c. 41.

POLYB'IDAS, a general after the death of Agesipolis the Lacedæmonian. He reduced Olynthus.

POLYB'IUS or **POL'YBUS**, a king of Corinth, who married Peribœa, whom some have called Merope. He was son of Mercury by Chthonophyle, the daughter of Sicyon, king of Sicyon. He permitted his wife, who had no children, to adopt and educate as her own son, Œdipus who had been found by his shepherds exposed in the woods. He had a daughter called Lysianassa, whom he gave in marriage to Talaus, son of Bias king of Argos. As he had no male child, he left his kingdom to Adrastus, who had been banished from his throne, and who had fled to Corinth for protection. *Hygin.* fab. 66.—*Seneca. in Œdip.* 812.—*Sch. Sophoc. in Tyr.* 785.—*Sch. Eurip. in Phœn.* 1050 & 1591.—*Stat. Theb.* 1. v. 64.—*Martial.* 7. epigr. 71.—*Paus.* 2. c. 6.—*Apollod.* 3. c. 5.

Polyb'ius, a native of Megalopolis in Peloponnesus, son of Lycortas. He was early initiated into the duties, and made acquainted with the qualifications of a statesman, by his father, who was a strong supporter of the Achæan league, and under him Philopœmen was taught the art of war. In Macedonia he distinguished himself by his valor against the Romans, and when Perseus had been conquered, he was carried to the capital of Italy as a prisoner of war. But he was not long buried in the obscurity of a dungeon. Scipio and Fabius were acquainted with his uncommon abilities as a warrior and as a man of learning, and made him their friend by their kindness and attention. Polybius was not insensible to their merit; he accompanied Scipio in his expeditions, and was present at the taking of Carthage and Numantia. In the midst of his prosperity, however, he felt the distresses of his country, which had been reduced into a Roman province, and, like a true patriot, he relieved its wants, and eased its servitude by making use of the influence which he had acquired by his acquaintance with the most powerful Romans. After the death of his friend and benefactor Scipio, he retired from Rome, and passed the rest of his days at Megalopolis, where he enjoyed comforts and honors which every good man can receive from the gratitude of his fellow citizens, and from the self-satisfaction which attends a humane and benevolent heart. He died in the 82nd year of his age, about 124 years B.C. of a wound which he had received by a fall from his horse. He wrote a universal history in Greek, divided into 40 books, which began with the wars of Rome with the Carthaginians, and finished with the conquest of Macedonia by Paulus. The greatest part of this valuable history is lost; the five first books are extant, and of the twelve following the fragments are numerous. The history of Polybius is admired for its authenticity, and he is, perhaps, the only historian among the Greeks, who was experimentally acquainted with the military operations, and the political measures of which he makes mention. He has been recommended in every age and country as the best master in the art of war, and nothing can more effectually prove the esteem in which he was held among the Romans, than to mention, that Brutus, the murderer of Cæsar, perused his history with the greatest attention, epitomized it, and often retired from the field where he had drawn his sword against Octavius and Antony, to read the instructive pages which described the great actions of his ancestors. Polybius, however great and entertaining, is sometimes censured for his unnecessary digressions, for his uncouth and ill-digested narrations, for his negligence, and the inaccurate arrangement of his words. But every where there is instruction to be found, information to be collected, and curious facts to be obtained; and it reflects not much honor upon Livy to have called the historian, from whom he has copied whole books almost word for word, without gratitude or acknowledgment, *haudquaquam spernendus auctor.* Dionysius of Halicarnassus also, is one of his most violeat accusers; but the historian has rather exposed his ignorance of true criticism, than discovered inaccuracy or inelegance. The best editions of Polybius are those of Gronovius, 3 vols. 8vo. Amst. 1670; of Ernesti, 3 vols. 8vo, 1764; and of Schweighäuser, 7 vols. 8vo, Lips. 1789—1793.—*Fabr. B. Gr.* 3. c. 28.—*Sax. Onom.* 1. p. 133.—*Plut. in Phil. in præc.*—*Liv.* 30. c. 45.—*Paus.* 8. c. 9, 30, 44, &c.—*Cic. Att.* 13. ep 30. 5. *Fam.* 12. *Off.* 3. c. 32.—*Vossius. de H. Gr.* 1. c. 19.—*Lucian. Macr.*——A freedman of Augustus, employed with Hilarion to write his will. *Suet. Aug.* c. 101.——A physician, disciple and successor of Hippocrates. *Justus in Chron.*—*Vander Linden de script. med.*——A soothsayer of Corinth, who foretold to his son the fate that attended them in the Trojan war.

POLYBŒ'A, a daughter of Amyclas and Diomede, sister of Hyacinthus. She died young, and probably on that account was represented on a monument between Sparta and Amyclæ, as carried up to heaven, with her brother, by Venus, Minerva, and Diana. *Paus.* 3. c. 19.——The first wife of Actor, son of Myrmidon. *Eustath. in Il.* 2.

POLYBŒ'TES. *Vid.* Polypœtes.

POLYBO'TES, one of the giants who made war against Jupiter. He was killed by Neptune, who crushed him under a part of the island of Cos, as he was walking across the Ægæan, and with the mangled body formed, as the mythologists relate, the island of Nisyrus. *Apollod.* 1.—*Paus.* 1. c. 2.—*Hygin. in præf. fab.*

POL'YBUS, a king of Thebes in Ægypt in the time of the Trojan war. He kindly received Menelaus and Helen on their return to Greece from Troy, and loaded them with rich presents. *Hom. Odyss.* 4. v. 126.——A son of Mercury and Eubœa, father of Glaucus. *Athen.* 7.——One of Penelope's suitors. *Ovid. Heroid.* 1.—*Hom. Od.* 22. v. 284.——A king of Sicyon.——A king of Corinth. *Vid.* Polybius.

POLYCA'ON, a son of Lelex, who succeeded his brother Myles in the government of Laconia. He, with his wife Messene, received divine honors at Lacedæmonia after death. *Paus.* 4. c. 1, &c.——A son of Butes, who married Erechme, daughter of Hyllus. *Paus. ib.*

POLYCAR'PUS, a famous Greek writer, born at Smyrna, and educated at the expense of a rich but pious lady. Some suppose that he was St. John's disciple. He became bishop of Smyrna, A.D. 167. His epistle to the Philippians is simple and modest, yet replete with useful precepts and rules for the conduct of life. The best edition of Polycarp's epistle is that of Smith, Oxon. 8vo. 1708, being annexed to the works of Ignatius. *Fabr. B. Gr.* 5. c. 1.—*Sax. Onom.* 1. p. 318.

POLCYAS'TE, the youngest of the daughters of Nestor. According to some authors she married Telemachus, when he visited her father's court in quest of Ulysses, and had by him a son called Perseptolis. *Hom. Od.* 3. v. 464.—*Hesiod. apud Eustath.* in 26. *Od.*

POLYCH'ARES, a rich Messenian, the cause of the first Messenian war. He fed his herds, it is said, in the fields of a Spartan called Enephnus, on condition that he should give him half of the produce, but his confidence was betrayed. Enephnus sold the herds and their keepers, and then complained that they had been carried away by pirates, a falsehood which was quickly discovered by the appearance of one of the slaves who revealed his perfidy. The crime was, however, forgiven by Polychares, who was persuaded by his pretended friend to send his son to Sparta, to receive the money which the sale of the herds had produced. The son was basely murdered, and when Polychares repaired to Sparta, to complain of the violation of all laws divine and human, and to demand the punishment due to the crimes of Enephnus, his applications were slighted, and therefore, grown disconsolate, melancholy, and frantic by disappointment, he attacked and slaughtered every Spartan whom he met on his return to Messenia. The Lacedæmonians demanded vengeance, and when the Messenians refused all reparation, war was formally declared. *Paus.* 4. c. 4.

POLYCHAR'MUS, a prætor at Athens, in the age of Cicero. *Cicero.* 5. *Att.* 11.——A celebrated artist who sculptured a statue of Venus bathing. *Plin.* 36. c. 5.

POL'YCHUS, one of Lycaon's fifty sons. *Apollod.* 3.

POLYCLE'A, the mother of Thessalus. *Plut.*—*Polyæn.* 8. c. 44.

POL'YCLES, an Athenian, one of the conspirators who strove to expel Heraclides, the præfect of Demetrius. *Polyæn.* 5, c. 17.——A Naxian appointed governor of his country.——A statuary of Athens, son of Timarchides, and pupil of Stadicus. *Plin.* 34. c. 8. l. 36. c. 5.—*Paus.* 4. c. 4.——A famous athlete, often crowned at the four solemn games of the Greeks. He had a statue in Jupiter's grove at Olympia, which represented him as holding a ribbon in his right hand, and two infants in his left, one of which had a top, whilst the other raised his arm to seize the ribbon. *Paus.* 6. c. 1.

POLYCLE'TUS or POLYCLI'TUS, a celebrated statuary of Sicyon, who flourished about 232 years B.C. He was universally reckoned the most skilful artist of his profession among the ancients, and the second rank was given to Phidias. One of his pieces, in which he had represented one of the body guards of the king of Persia, was so happily executed, and so nice and exact in all its proportions, that it was looked upon as a perfect model, and accordingly called the Rule. He was also acquainted with architecture, and was therefore employed to finish the beautiful temple and elegant theatre of Æsculapius, at Epidaurus. *Paus.* 2. c. 17 & 27. l. 6. c. 6.—*Plut. in Per.*—*Stat.* 4. *Sylv.* 6. v. 28.—*Juv.* 3. v. 217.—*Martial.* 8. epigr. 51. l. 10. epigr. 89.—*Quintil.* 12. c. 10.——Another artist who lived about thirty years after the former.

POLYCLE'TUS, a favorite of the emperor Nero, put to death by Galba. *Tac. Ann.* 14. c. 39.

POLYCLI'TUS, an historian of Larissa. *Athen.* 12.—*Ælian.* 16. c. 41.—*Voss. H. Gr.* 3. p. 405.

POLYC'RATES, a tyrant of Samus, son of Ajax, well known for the continual flow of good fortune that attended him. He became very powerful, and made himself master, not only of the neighbouring islands, but also of some cities on the coast of Asia. He had a fleet of one hundred ships of war, and was so universally respected, that Amasis, the king of Ægypt, made a treaty of alliance with him. The Ægyptian monarch, however, terrified by his continued prosperity, advised him to chequer his enjoyments, by relinquishing some of his most favorite objects. Polycrates complied, and threw into the sea a beautiful seal, the most valuable of his jewels. The voluntary loss of so precious a seal afflicted him for some time, but a few days after, he received as a present a large fish, in the belly of which the jewel was found. Amasis no sooner heard this, than he declined all further alliance with the tyrant of Samus, observing, that sooner or later his good fortune would vanish. Some time after Polycrates visited Magnesia on the Mæander, whither he had been invited by Orontes, the governor. He was shamefully put to death, 522 years B.C., merely because the governor wished to terminate the prosperity of Polycrates. The daughter of Polycrates had dissuaded her father from going to the house of Orontes, on account of some extraordinary dreams which she had had, but her advice was disregarded. *Paus.* 8. c. 14.—*Strab.* 14.—*Cic.* 5. *Fin.* 30.—*Herodot.* 3. c. 39, &c.—*Plut. de Phil.*—*Plin.* 33. c. 1. l. 37. c. 1.—*Lucian. in Char.*——A sophist of Athens, who, to engage the public attention, wrote a panegyric on Busiris and Clytæmnestra. *Quintil.* 2. c. 17.——An ancient statuary. *Plin.* 34. c. 8.

POLYCRE'TA or POLYCRI'TA, a young woman of Maxus, who, when her country, according to Polyænus and Plutarch, was besieged by the Milesians, assisted by Diognetus the Erythrean, and herself a prisoner in the hand of the enemy, meditated and ensured the deliverance of her fellow-citizens. As she had gained the affections of Diognetus, she easily obtained permission to send to her brother Philocles within the besieged town a cake containing a writing which informed him that the Milesians were going to celebrate a festival, the riot and debauchery of which would render any attack upon them successful. As the cake was one of those prepared for the feast, Philocles was desired to eat it the very day he received it, and therefore, the contents were no sooner known than the enemy was attacked and all put to the sword, except Diognetus, whom Polycreta hoped to honor with her hand. Her exhortations were in vain, the congratulations of her countrymen were too powerful, and she expired through excess of joy; and a monument was all that the gratitude of her country was permitted to pay to her memory. Aristotle and others differ in the relation of this history, by mentioning that Polycreta was not a prisoner, but that she persuaded Diognetus, as the price of her favors, to betray his trust, and to invite Philocles to the destruction of the Milesians. Diognetus was killed in the engagement that followed, according to the same historians. *Plut. de Virt. Mul.*—*Aristot. apud eund.*—*Theophr. apud Parth. Erot.* 9.—*Andrisc. apud eund.*

POLYC'RITUS, a man who wrote the life of Dionysius, the tyrant of Sicily. *Diog.* 2. c. 63.

POLYC'TOR, the husband of Stygna, one of the Danaides. *Apollod.* 2. c. 1.——The father of Pisander, one of Penelope's suitors. He was killed by Philætius. *Hom. Odyss.* 22. v. 243 & 268.——An athlete of Elis. It is said that he obtained a victory at Olympia by bribing his adversary Sosander, who was superior to him in strength and courage. This intrigue, it is reported, was discovered, and both were fined by the judges a sum of money, which was employed in making two statues to Jupiter, which were placed in the sacred grove of Olympia. *Paus.* 5. c. 21. l. 6. c. 23.

POLYDÆ'MON, an Assyrian prince killed by Perseus. *Ovid. Met.* 5. fab. 3.

POLYD'AMAS, a Trojan, son of Antenor, by Theano the sister of Hecuba. He married Lycaste, a natural daughter of Priam. He is accused by some of having betrayed his country to the Greeks. *Dares Phry.*—*Quint. Smyr.* 2. v. 41. l. 10. v. 10.—*Servius Æn.* 1. v. 246.——A son of Panthous, born the same night as Hector. He was inferior in valor to none of the Trojans except Hector; and his prudence, the wisdom of his counsels, and the firmness of his mind claimed equal admiration, and proved most salutary to his unfortunate and often misguided countrymen. He was at last killed by Ajax, after he had slaughtered a great number of the enemy. *Dictys. Cret.* 1, &c.—*Homer. Il.* 12. v. 60. l. 13. v. 725. l. 14. v. 425 & 449. l. 18. v. 285.——A celebrated athlete, son of Nicias, who imitated Hercules in whatever he did. He killed a lion with his fist, and it is said he could stop a chariot with his hand in its most rapid course. He was one day with some of his friends in a cave, when, on a sudden, a large piece of rock came tumbling down, and while all fled away, he attempted to receive the falling fragment in his arms. His prodigious strength, however, was insufficient, and he was instantly crushed to pieces under the rock. *Paus.* 6. c. 5.—*Plin.* 7. c. 49.—*Val. Max.* 9. c. 12.——One of Alexander's officers, intimate with Parmenio. *Curt.* 4. c. 15.

POLYDAM'NA, the wife of Thonis, king of Ægypt. It is said that she gave Helen a certain powder, which had the wonderful power of driving away the most poignant cares and the most rooted melancholy. *Homer. Odyss.* 4. v. 228.

POLYDEC'TES, a king of Sparta, of the family of the Proclidæ. He was son of Eunomus. *Paus.* 3. c. 7.—*Plut. in Lyc.*——A son of Magnes and Nais, king of the island of Seriphus. He received with great kindness Danae and her son Perseus, who had been exposed on the sea by Acrisius. *Vid.* Perseus. He took particular care of the education of Perseus; but when he became enamoured of Danae, he removed him from his kingdom, apprehensive of his resentment. Some time after he paid his addresses to Danae, and, when she rejected him, prepared to offer her violence. Danae fled to the altar of Minerva for protection, and Dictys, the brother of Polydectes, who had himself saved her from the sea, opposed her ravisher, and armed himself in her defence. At this critical moment, Perseus arrived, and with Medusa's head turned into stones Polydectes and the associates of his guilt. The crown of Seriphus was given by the victor to Dictys, who had shown himself so active in the cause of innocence. *Ovid. Met.* 5. v. 242.—*Hygin.* fab. 63, &c. —*Paus.* 1. c. 22.—*Apollod.* 1 & 2.—*Servius ad Æn.* 6. v. 289.—*Tzetzes. ad Lyc.* 838.—*Sch. Hom. Il.* 14. v. 319.——A sculptor of Greece. *Plin.* 36. c. 5.

POLYDEUCE'A, a fountain of Laconia, near Therapne. *Strab.* 9.

POLYD'ICE, a woman who betrayed her father Pterelas, king of Thebes, to Creon. *Servius.*

POLYDO'RA, a daughter of Peleus king of Thessaly, by Antigone, the daughter of Eurytion. She married the river Sperchius, by whom she had Mnestheus. *Hom. Il.* 16. v. 175.—*Apollod.* 3.——One of the Oceanides. *Hesiod.*——A daughter of Meleager king of Calydon, who married Protesilaus. She killed herself when she heard that her husband was dead. The wife of Protesilaus is more commonly called Laodamia. *Vid.* Protesilaus. *Paus.* 4. c. 2.——A daughter of Perieres.

POLYDO'RA, an island of the Propontis, near Cyzicus. *Steph.*—*Plin.* 5. c. *ult.*

POLYDO'RUS, a son of Alcamenes, king of Sparta. He put an end to the war which had been carried on during 20 years, between Messenia and his subjects, and during his reign the Lacedæmonians planted two colonies, one at Crotona, and the other at Locri. He was universally respected. He was assassinated by a nobleman, called Polemarchus, but his memory was honored by the gratitude and the tears of his countrymen. His son Eurycrates succeeded him 724 years B.C. *Paus.* 3.—*Herodot.* 7. c. 204.——A celebrated carver at Rhodes, who with one stone made the famous statue of Laocoon and his children. *Plin.* 34. c. 8.——A son of Hippomedon, who went with the Epigoni to the second Theban war. *Paus.* 2. c. 20.——A son of Cadmus and Hermione, who married Nycteis, by whom he had Labdacus, the father of Laius. He had succeeded to the throne of Thebes, when his father had gone to Illyricum. *Apollod.* 3.——A brother of Jason of Pheræ, who killed his brother, and seized upon his possessions. *Diod.* 15.——A son of Priam by Hecuba, or according to others by Laothoe, the daughter of Altes, king of Pedasus. As he was young and inexperienced when Troy was first besieged by the Greeks, his father forbad him to appear in the field, but his valor and swiftness made him disregard the parental admonition, and he was, according to Homer, killed by Achilles. Succeeding poets and historians have given a different account, and mentioned, that instead of appearing in the war, Polydorus was sent by his father to the court of Polymnestor, king of Thrace, and that with him also were entrusted to the care of the monarch a large sum of money, and the greatest part of the treasures of Troy, till the country was freed from foreign invasion. No sooner was the death of Priam known in Thrace, than Polymnestor made himself master of the riches that were in his possession, and to ensure them the better, assassinated young Polydorus, and threw his body into the sea, where it was found by Hecuba. *Vid.* Hecuba. According to Virgil, the body of Polydorus was buried near the shore by his assassin, and there grew on his grave a myrtle, the boughs of which dropped blood, when Æneas, going to Italy, attempted to tear them from the tree. *Vid.* Polymnestor. *Virg. Æn.* 3. v. 21, &c.—*Apollod.* 3. c. 12.—*Ovid. Met.* 13. v. 432.—*Homer. Il.* 20. v. 407. l. 21. v. 85.—*Dictys. Cret.* 2. c. 18.—*Euripid. in Hec.* 1.—*Hygin.* fab. 90 & 109.—*Servius ad Virg. loco. cit.*

POLYG'IUS, a surname of Mercury. *Paus.* 1. 2.

POLYGNO'TUS, a celebrated painter of Thasus, about 422 years B.C. His father's name was Aglaophon. He adorned the public porticoes of Greece with his paintings, but those which claimed the highest admiration were the two which were preserved at Delphi, the one of which represented the most striking events of the Trojan war, and the other the descent of Ulysses to the infernal regions. The subjects of these pieces are interwoven with the history and mythology of the ancient times, and it has fortunately happened, that a very minute description of them is preserved and embellished by Pausanias in a manner which, in showing his taste and judgment, presents to our view the actions and characters of the heroic ages. Polygnotus was said particularly to excel in giving grace, liveliness, and expression to his pieces. He rose superior to his predecessors, and instead of employing, like them, the various shades of black and white only, improved his art by the introduction of new materials, and applied to his pieces with delicacy and taste the different powers of four colours. The Athenians were so pleased with him, that they offered to reward his labours with whatever he chose to accept. He declined this generous offer, and the Amphictyonic council, which was composed of the representatives of the principal cities of the country of all Greece, ordered that Polygnotus should be honored with the thanks of Greece, and that for his services and his merits he should be maintained at the public expense wherever he went. *Quintil.* 12. c. 10.—*Plin.* 33. c. 13. l. 34. c. 8. l. 35. c. 6, 9 & 11.—*Plut. in Cim.*—*Paus.* 10. c. 25, &c.——A celebrated statuary. *Plin.* 34. c. 11.

POLYG'ONUS and TELEG'ONUS, sons of Proteus and Coronis, were famous for their dexterity in wrestling. They not only challenged all strangers to a trial of skill, but cruelly put them to death when defeated. They were at last both conquered and killed, by Hercules, in their favorite exercise. *Apollod.* 2.—*Servius. Georg.* 4. v. 387.

POLYHIS'TOR, a name given to Corn. Alexander, as expressive of his great knowledge of history. *Suet. de Il. Gr.* 20. Apion is also so called by *Gellius*, 5. c. 14.

POLYHYMN'IA or POLYM'NIA, one of the Muses, daughter of Jupiter and Mnemosyne. She presided over singing and rhetoric, and was deemed the inventress of harmony and of theatrical gestures. She was represented veiled in white, holding a sceptre in her left hand, and with her right raised up, as if ready to harangue. She had a crown of jewels on her head. *Hesiod. Theog.* 75 & 915.—*Plut. in Symp.* 9 & 53.—*Horat.* 1. od. 1. v. 33.—*Ovid. Fast.* 5. v. 9. [The finest representation of this Muse will be found in the Vatican at Rome.]

POLYI'DUS, a physician who brought back to life Glaucus, the son of Minos, by applying to his body a certain herb, with which he had seen a serpent restore life to another which was dead. *Vid.* Glaucus. *Apollod.* 3. c. 3.——A son of Hercules by one of the daughters of Thestius. *Apollod.*——A Corinthian soothsayer, called also Polybius.——A dithyrambic poet, painter, and musician.——A son of Eurydamas, skilful in the interpretation of dreams. He was killed by the Greeks during the Trojan war. *Homer. Il.* 5. v. 150.——An engineer who wrote *de arte machinali. Vitruv. præf.* 7.

POLYLA'US, son of Hercules and Crathe, daughter of Thespius. *Apollod.* 2.

POLYME'DE, a daughter of Autolycus, who married Æson, by whom she had Jason. She survived her husband only a few days. *Apollod.* 1. c. 13.

POLYME'DIA, a town of Troas, near the Hellespont. *Plin.* 5. c. 30.

POLYM'EDON, one of Priam's illegitimate children. *Apollod.* 3.

POLYME'LA, one of Diana's companions. She was daughter of Phylas, and had by Mercury a son called Eudorus, who signalized himself during the Trojan war. She afterwards married Echeleus, whose origin is not known, but whose riches are celebrated. *Homer. Il.* 16. v. 176.——A daughter of Æolus. *Vid.* Polimela.——A daughter of Actor. She was the first wife of Peleus, the father of Achilles. *Tzetzes ad Lyc.* 175.—*Eustath.* 2. *Il.*—*Sch. Liban. in* 2 *Plut.*

POLYME'LUS, a Trojan killed before Troy by Patroclus. *Homer. Il.* 16. v. 417.

POLYM'ENES, an officer appointed to take care of Ægypt after it had been conquered by Alexander. *Curt.* 4. c. 8.

POLYMNES'TES, a Greek poet of Colophon, son of Meles or Miletus. He used a particular sort of metre, which from him was called Polymnestian. Some of his compositions were still extant in the age of Pausanias. *Plut. de Mus.*—*Suidas.*—*Gyrald. de P.H.* 2 & 3.—*Vossius. de P. Gr. Pag.* 94.—*Paus.* 1. c. 14.——A native of Thera, father of Battus or Aristocles, by Phronima, the daughter of Etearchus. *Herodot.* 4. c. 150.—*Strab.* 17.—*Pind. Pyth.* 4. v. 104.

POLYMNES'TOR, a king of the Thracian Chersonesus, who married Ilione, the eldest of Priam's daughters. When the Greeks besieged Troy, Priam sent the greatest part of his treasures, together with Polydorus, the youngest of his sons, to Thrace, where they were entrusted to the care of Polymnestor. The Thracian monarch paid every attention to his brother-in-law; but when he was informed that Priam was dead, he murdered him to become master of the riches that were in his possession. At that time, the Greeks were returning victorious from Troy, followed by all the captives, among whom was Hecuba, the mother of Polydorus. The fleet stopped on the coast of Thrace, where one of the female captives discovered on the shore the body of Polydorus, which Polymnestor had thrown into the sea. The dreadful intelligence was immediately communicated to the mother, and Hecuba, who recollected the frightful dream which she had had on the preceding night, concluded that Polymnestor was the cruel assassin. She resolved to revenge her son's death, and immediately called out Polymnestor as if wishing to impart to him a matter of the most important nature. The tyrant was drawn into the snare, and was no sooner introduced into the apartments of the Trojan princess, than the female captives rushed upon him, and put out his eyes with their pins, while Hecuba murdered his two children who had accompanied him. According to Euripides, the Greeks condemned Polymnestor to be banished into a distant island for his perfidy. Hyginus, however, relates the whole differently, and observes, that when Polydorus was sent to Thrace, Ilione, his sister, apprehensive of her husband's cruelty, took him instead of her son Deiphilus, who was of the same age. The monarch was unacquainted with the imposition, he looked upon Polydorus as his own son, and treated Deiphilus as the brother of Ilione. After the destruction of Troy, the conquerors, who wished the house and family of Priam to be totally extirpated, offered Electra, the daughter of Agamemnon, to Polymnestor, if he would destroy Ilione and Polydorus. The monarch accepted the offer, and immediately despatched his own son Deiphilus, whom he had been taught to regard as Polydorus. Polydorus, who passed for the son of Polymnestor, consulted the oracle after the murder of Deiphilus, and when he was informed that his father was dead, his mother a captive in the hands of the Greeks, and his country in ruins, he communicated the answer of the god to Ilione, whom he had always regarded as his mother. Ilione told him the measure she had pursued to save his life, and upon this he avenged the perfidy of Polymnestor, by putting out his eyes. *Eurip. in Hecub.*—*Hygin.* fab. 109.—*Virg. Æn.* 3. v. 45, &c.—*Ovid. Met.* 13. v. 430, &c.—*Propert.* 3. el. 11. v. 55.—*Auson. Epitap. Polyd.*—*Servius in Æn.* 1. v. 658. 1. 3. v. 15 & 49.——A king of Arcadia, succeeded on the throne by Ecmis. *Paus.* 8.——A young Milesian, who took a hare in running, and afterwards obtained a prize at the Olympic games. *Solin.* 6.

POLYNI'CES, a son of Œdipus, king of Thebes, by Jocasta. He inherited his father's throne with his brother Eteocles, and it was mutually agreed between the two brothers, that they should reign, each a year, alternately. Eteocles first ascended the throne by right of seniority; but when the year was expired refused to resign the crown to his brother. Polynices, upon this, fled to Argos, to implore the assistance of the Argives, and there married Argia, the daughter of Adrastus, king of the country, and levied a large army, at the head of which he marched against Thebes. The command of this army was divided among seven celebrated chiefs, who were to attack the seven gates of the city of Thebes. The battle was decided by a single combat between the two brothers, who both killed one another. *Vid.* Eteocles. *Æschyl. sept. contra Theb.*—*Eurip. Phœniss.*—*Senec. in Theb.*—*Diod.* 4.—*Hygin.* fab. 68, 69, 71, 72, & 254.—*Paus.* 2. c. 20. 1. 9. c. 5.—*Apollod.* 3. c. 5.

POLYN'OE, one of the Nereides. *Apollod.* 1. c. 2.

POLYPE'MON, a famous thief, called also Procrustes, who plundered all the travellers about the Cephisus, and near Eleus in Attica. He was killed by Theseus. Ovid calls him father of Procrustes, and Apollodorus of Sinis. *Vid.* Procrustes.—*Paus.* 1. c. 38.—*Ovid. in Ib.* 409.—*Diod.* 4.—*Plut. in Thes.*

POLYPER'CHON or POLYSPER'CHON, one of the officers of Alexander the Great. Antipater, at his death, appointed him governor of the kingdom of Macedonia, in preference to his own son Cassander. Polyperchon, though old, and a man of experience, showed great ignorance in the administration of the government. He became cruel not only to the Greeks, or such as opposed his ambitious views, but even to the helpless and innocent children and friends of Alexander, to whom he was indebted for his rise and military reputation. He was killed in a battle 309 B.C. *Curt.*—*Diod.* 17, &c.—*Justin.* 13.

POLYPHE'MUS, king of all the Cyclopes in Sicily, was son of Neptune and Thoosa, the daughter of Phorcys. He is represented to have been a monster of strength, of tall stature, and with one eye only, in the middle of the forehead. He fed upon human flesh, and kept his flocks on the coasts of Sicily, when Ulysses, at his return from the Trojan war, was driven there. The Grecian prince, with twelve of his companions, visited the coast, and were seized by Polyphemus, who confined them in his cave, and daily devoured two of them. Ulysses would have shared the fate of his companions, had he not intoxicated the Cyclops, and put out his eye with a fire-brand while he was asleep. Polyphemus was awakened by the sudden pain, and stopped the entrance of his cave, but Ulysses made his escape by creeping between the legs of the rams of the Cyclops, as they were led out to feed on the mountains. Polyphemus became enamoured of Galatæa, but his addresses were disregarded, and the nymph shunned his presence. Her refusal only made the Cyclops more earnest in his addresses, and when he saw Galatæa surrender herself to the pleasures of Acis, he crushed his rival with a piece of a broken rock. *Theocrit.* 1.—*Ovid. Met.* 13. v. 772.—*Hom. Odyss.* 1. v. 71. l. 9. v. 188.—*Eurip. in Cyclop.*—*Hygin.* fab. 125.—*Virg. Æn.* 3. v. 619, &c.—*Tzetzes. in Lyc.* 659.——One of the Argonauts, son of Elatus and Hippea. He married Laonome, sister of Hercules, and assisted the hero in his enquiries after Hylas. He was killed by the Chalybes in Mysia. *Apollod.* 1.—*Orph. Arg.* 167.—*Flacc.* 1. v. 457. l. 4. v. 107.—*Schol. Apollon.* 1. v. 41 & 1240.—*Hygin.* 14.——One of the Lapithæ. *Homer. Il.* 1. v. 264.

POLYPH'IDUS, a king of Sicyon. *Vid.* Ægisthus.

POLYPH'ITUS, a Lacedæmonian, who with his father Calliteles, distinguished himself at the Olympic games. They both obtained the victory, the father in wrestling and the son in a horse race. *Paus.* 6. c. 16.

POLYPHON'TA, one of Diana's nymphs, daughter of Hipponus and Thraosa. She devoted herself to celibacy, and to a retired life with such constancy, that Venus, irritated at the contempt she showed her divinity, inspired her with an unnatural passion for a bear, which the unfortunate nymph is said to have gratified. This was no sooner known, than she was detested by Diana, and pursued by all the wild beasts of the forest, but she escaped to her father's house, where she brought forth twins, to whom she gave the name of Oreius and Agrius. These children, inheriting all the barbarity of the beast from which they derived their origin, employed themselves in killing passengers and feeding upon their flesh, till Jupiter, incensed against them, sent Mercury to destroy them. The god would have executed his office, but reflecting that they were sprung from him, he changed them into birds of prey, Oreius into a crow, and Agrius into a vulture, whilst the unfortunate Polyphonta became a bird of monstrous appearance called Styx, which was generally considered as the harbinger of war and of all evils. *Boeus in Ornith.* 2. *apud Anton. Lib.* 21.

POLYPHON'TES, one of the Heraclidæ, who killed Cresphontes, king of Messenia, and not only usurped his crown, but killed two of his children, and forced Merope, the widowed queen, to his bed. This unnatural treatment was resented; a third son called Ægyptus or Telephontes, who was absent from Messenia, was recalled by the unhappy mother, and succeeded in destroying the tyrant and recovering the crown. *Apollod.* 2.—*Hygin* fab. 137 & 184.——One of the Theban generals under Eteocles. *Æschyl. Sept. contra Theb.*

POLYPHRAD'MON, a tragic poet, son of Phrynichus, also a poet. *Schol. in Aves Aristoph.*—*Suidas.*

POL'YPHRON, a prince killed by his nephew Alexander, the tyrant of Pheræ.

POLYPODU'SA, an island near Cnidus. *Steph.*

POLYPŒ'TES, a son of Pirithous and Hippodamia, who went to the Trojan war at the head of the inhabitants of Argissa, Helone, Oloosson, &c. in twenty ships, or forty according to Dictys. He behaved there with all the valor which characterized his father, and distinguished himself particularly at the funeral games of Patroclus. *Homer. Il.* 2. *Enu.* v. 247. l. 6. v. 29. l. 12. v. 182. l. 23. v. 844.—*Dictys.*—*Apollod.* 3.—*Hygin.* fab. 97.—*Qu. Calab.* 4. v. 501.—*Paus.* 10. v. 26.——A son of Apollo by Pythia, killed by Ætolus son of Endymion. *Apollod.* 1.——One of the Trojans whom Æneas saw when he visited the infernal regions. *Virg. Æn.* 6. v. 484.

POLYRRHE'NIA, a city of Crete. *Steph.*

POLYSPER'CHON. *Vid.* Polyperchon.

POLYSTEPH'ANUS, an historian praised by the *Scholiast* on *Apollonius* 1. and by *Gellius*, 9. c. 4.——An ancient name of Tibur, in Italy. *Steph.*

POLYS'TRATUS, a Macedonian soldier, who found Darius after he had been stabbed by Bessus, and who gave him water to drink, and carried the last injunctions of the dying monarch to Alexander. *Curt.* 5. c. 13.——An Epicurean philosopher who flourished B.C. 238.

POLYTECH'NUS, an artist of Colophon, who married Ædone, th daughter of Pandarus, by whom he had a son called Itys, changed into a bird. *Vid.* Pandarus.

POLYTIME'TUS, a river of Scythia within Imaus. *Ptol.* According to *Q. Curtius*, 6. c. 4. & 7. c. 10, it was a river of Sogdiana. *Niger* calls it Amo.

POLYT'ION, a friend of Alcibiades, with whom he profaned the mysteries of Ceres. *Paus.* 1. c. 2.—*Plut. in Alc.*

POLYT'ROPUS, a man sent by the Lacedæmonians with an army against the Arcadians. He was killed at Orchomenus. *Diod.* 15.

POLYX'ELUS, a Greek comic poet, whose plays are enumerated by *Suidas.*

POLYX'ENA, a daughter of Priam and Hecuba, celebrated for her beauty and accomplishments. Achilles became enamoured of her, and solicited her hand, and their marriage would have been consummated, had not Hector her brother opposed it. Polyxena, according to some authors, accompanied her father when he went to the tent of Achilles to redeem the body of his son Hector. Some time after, the Grecian hero came into the temple of Apollo to obtain a sight of the Trojan princess, but he was murdered there by Paris; and Polyxena, who had returned his affection, was so afflicted at his death, that she went and sacrificed herself on his tomb. Some, however, suppose that this sacrifice was not voluntary, but that the manes of Achilles appeared to the Greeks, as they were going to embark, and demanded of them the sacrifice of Polyxena. The princess, who was in the number of the captives, was upon this dragged to her lover's tomb, and there immolated by Neoptolemus, the son of Achilles. *Ovid. Met.* 13. fab. 5, &c.—*Dictys. Cret.* 3 & 5.—*Virg. Æn.* 3. v. 321.—*Catul.* ep. 65. v. 368.—*Hygin.* fab. 90 & 100.—*Philostr. Her.* 19. *In Ap. Th.* 4. c. 16.—*Servius in Æn.* 3. v. 322.—*Lactant. ad Achill.* 1. v. 134.—*Euripid. in Hec.*—*Paus.* 1. c. 22.—*Propert.* 2. el. 10. v. 38.—*Q. Catab.* 14. v. 212 & 266.

POLYXEN'IDAS, a Syrian general who flourished B.C. 192.

POLYX'ENUS, one of the Greek princes who went to the Trojan war at the head of the Ætolians in ten, or, according to Hyginus, in forty ships. His father's name was Agasthenes. *Homer. Il.* 2. *en.* 130.—*Paus.* 5. c. 3.—*Hygin.* fab. 97.——A son of Medea by Jason. *Hellanic. apud. Paus* 2. c. 3.——A young Athenian who became blind, &c. *Plut. in Par.*——A general of Dionysius, from whom he revolted.

POLYX'O, a priestess of Apollo's temple in Lemnus. She was also nurse to queen Hipsipyle. It was by her advice that the Lemnian women murdered their husbands. *Apollon.* 1. v. 664.—*Flacc.* 2. v. 316—*Stat. Theb.* 5. v. 90 & 327.—*Hygin.* fab. 15.——One of the Atlantides.——A native of Argos, who married Tlepolemus, son of Hercules. She followed him to Rhodes, after the murder of her uncle Licymnius, and when he went to the Trojan war with the rest of the Greek princes, she became the sole mistress of the kingdom. After the Trojan war, Helen fled from Peloponnesus to Rhodes, where Polyxo reigned. Polyxo detained her, and to punish her as being the cause of a war, in which Tlepolemus had perished, ordered her to be hanged on a tree by her female servants disguised in the habit of Furies. *Vid.* Helena. *Paus.* 5. c. 19.——The wife of Nycteus.——One of the wives of Danaus.

POLYZE'LUS, a Greek poet of Rhodes. He had written a poem on the origin and birth of Bacchus, Venus, the Muses, &c. Some of his verses are quoted by *Athenæus*, 1 & 8.—*Hygin. P. A.* 2. c. 14.—*Gyrald. de P. H.* 7.——An Athenian Archon. Ol. 103. an. 2.——A Messenian historian in Olymp. 50, father of the poet Ibycus. *Suidas in* Ἴβυκος.

POMAXÆ'THRES, a Parthian soldier who killed Crassus, according to some. *Plut.*

POME'TIA, POME'TII, or POME'TIA SUES'SA, a town of the Volsci in Latium, totally destroyed by the Romans, because it had revolted. *Virg. Æn.* 6. v. 775.—*Liv.* 2. c. 17.

POMETI'NA, one of the thirty-five tribes of the people, at Rome.

POMO'NA, a nymph at Rome who was supposed to preside over gardens, and all sorts of fruit-trees. She had a temple at Rome, and a regular priest called *Flamen Pomonalis,* who offered sacrifices to her divinity, for the preservation of fruit. She was generally represented as sitting on a basket full of flowers and fruit, and holding a bough in one hand, and apples in the other. Pomona was particularly delighted with the cultivation of the earth, she disdained the toils of the field, and the fatigues of hunting. Many of the gods of the country endeavoured to gain her affections, but she received their addresses with coldness. Vertumnus was the only one, who, by assuming different shapes, and introducing himself into her company, under the form of an old woman, prevailed upon her to break her vow of celibacy, and to marry him. This deity was unknown among the Greeks. *Ovid. Met.* 14. v. 628, &c.—*Festus de V. Sig.—Servius in Æn.* 7. v. 190. [There is a statue of this deity in the collection at Florence.]

POMPE'IA, a daughter of Sextus Pompeius, by Scribonia. She was promised to Marcellus, as a means of procuring a reconciliation between her father and the triumvirs, but she married Scribonius Libo.——A daughter of Pompey the Great, Julius Cæsar's third wife. She was accused of incontinence, because Clodius had introduced himself in women's clothes into the room where she was celebrating the mysteries of Cybele. Cæsar repudiated her upon this accusation. *Suet. & Plut. in Julio.*——The wife of Annæus Seneca, was the daughter of Pompeius Paullinus.

POMPE'IA MACRI'NA, wife of Argolicus, was sent into banishment by Tiberius. *Tac. Ann.* 6. c. 18.

POMPE'IA, a portico at Rome, much frequented by all orders of people. *Ovid. Art. Am.* v. 67.—*Mart.* 11. epigr. 48.

POMPE'IA LEX, was enacted by Pompey the Great, *de ambitu,* A.U.C. 701. It ordained that whatever person had been convicted of the crime of *ambitus,* should be pardoned, provided he could impeach two others of the same crime, and occasion the condemnation of one of them. Another by the same, A.U.C. 701, which forbad the use of *laudatores* in trials, or persons who gave a good character of the prisoner then impeached. *Plut. in vitâ.—Val. Max.* 6. c. 2.—Another by the same, A.U.C. 683. It restored to the tribunes their original power and authority, of which they had been deprived by the Cornelian law.—Another by the same, A.U.C. 701. It shortened the forms of trials, enacted that the three first days of a trial should be employed in examining witnesses, and allowing only one day to the parties to make their accusation and defence. The plaintiff was confined to two hours, and the defendant to three. This law had for its object the riots, which happened from the quarrels of Clodius and Milo.—Another by the same, A.U.C. 698. It required, that the judges should be the richest of every century, contrary to the usual form. It was however requisite that they should be such as the Aurelian law prescribed. *Cicer. in Pison.*—Another of the same, A.U.C. 701. Pompey was by this empowered to continue in the government of Spain five years longer. *Dio.* 38.—*Plut. in vit.*

POMPEIA'NUS JU'PITER, a large statue of Jupiter, near Pompey's theatre, whence it received its name. *Plin.* 34. c. 7.

POMPEIA'NUS, a Roman knight of Antioch, raised to offices of the greatest trust, under the emperor Aurelius, whose daughter Lucilla he married. He lived in great popularity at Rome, and retired from the court when Commodus succeeded to the imperial crown. He ought, according to Julian's opinion, to have been chosen and adopted as successor to M. Aurelius.——A general of Maxentius, killed by Constantine.——A Roman put to death by Carcalla.

POMPE'II or POMPE'IUM, a town of Campania, built, as some suppose, by Hercules, and so called because the hero there exhibited the long procession (*Pompa,*) of the herd of Geryon, which he had obtained by conquest. It was partly demolished by an earthquake, A.D. 63, and afterwards rebuilt. Sixteen years after it was swallowed up by another earthquake, which accompanied one of the eruptions of mount Vesuvius Herculaneum in its neighbourhood, shared the same fate. The people of the town were then assembled in the theatre, where public spectacles were exhibited. *Vid.* Herculaneum. Some interesting discoveries have lately been made among the ruins of these two cities, which have thrown considerable light on the customs of the ancients. *Liv.* 9. c. 38.—*Strab.* 6.—*Mela,* 2. c. 4.—*Dionys.* 1.—*Seneca Quæst.* 4.—*Solin.* 8.—*Servius in Æn.* 7. v. 662.

POMPEIOP'OLIS, a town of Cilicia, formerly called Soli. *Mela,* 1. c. 13. *Strab.* 12.—*Solin.* 51. It is now Polesoli.——A town in Paphlagonia, originally called Eupatoria, which name was exchanged when Pompey conquered Mithridates. *Plin.* 5. c. 27.—*Ptol.—Solin.* c. 46.

POMPE'IUS Q., a consul who carried on war against the Numantines and made a shameful treaty. He is the first of that noble family, of whom mention is made. *Flor.* 2. c. 18.

POMPE'IUS CNE'US, a Roman general, who made war against the Marsi, and triumphed over the Piceni. He declared himself against Cinna and Marius, and supported the interest of the republic. He was surnamed *Strabo,* because he squinted. While he was marching against Marius, a plague broke out in his army and raged with such violence, that it carried off 11,000 men in a few days. He was killed by a flash of lightning, and, as he had behaved with cruelty while in power, the people dragged his body through the streets of Rome with an iron hook, and threw it into the Tiber. *Paterc.* 2. c. 21.—*Plut. in Pomp.*

POMPE'IUS RU'FUS, a Roman, consul with Sylla. He was sent to finish the Marsian war, but the army mutinied at the instigation of Pompeius Strabo, whom he was to succeed in the command, and he was assassinated by some of the soldiers. *Appian. Civ.* 1.

POMPE'IUS, a general who succeeded Metellus in Spain, and was the occasion of a war with Numantia.——A general taken prisoner by Mithridates.——A tribune of the soldiers in Nero's reign, deprived of his office when Piso's conspiracy was discovered. *Tacit. Ann.* 15. c. 71.——A consul praised for his learning and abilities. *Ovid. ex Pont.* 4. ep. 1.——A tribune of a prætorian cohort under Galba. *Tac. Hist.* 1. c. 31.——A Roman knight put to death by the emperor Claudius for his adultery with Messalina. *Tacit.* 11. *Ann.*

POMPE'IUS SEX'TUS, a governor of Spain, who cured himself of the gout by placing himself in corn above the knee. *Plin.* 22. c. 25.

Q. POMPE'IUS RU'FUS, a grandson of Sylla, tribune of the people with T. Numantius Plancus, was a great enemy of Milo.

M. POMPE'IUS, a son of Theophanes of Mitylene, famous for his intimacy with Pompey the Great, and for his writings. *Tacit. Ann.* 6. c. 14.

POMPE'IUS CNE'US, surnamed Magnus, from the greatness of his exploits, was the son of Pompeius Strabo and Lucilia. He early distinguished himself in the field of battle, and fought with success and bravery under his father, whose courage and military prudence he imitated. He began his career with great popularity; the beauty and elegance of his person gained him admirers, and by pleading at the bar he displayed his eloquence, and received the most unbounded applause. In the disturbances which agitated Rome, and which were caused by the ambition and avarice of Marius and Sylla, Pompey followed the interest of the latter, and, by levying three legions for his service, gained his friendship and protection. In the 26th year of his age he conquered Sicily, which was in the power of Marius and his adherents, and in forty days regained all the territories of Africa, which had forsaken the interest of Sylla. This rapid success astonished the Romans, and Sylla, who admired and dreaded the rising power of Pompey, recalled him to Rome. Pompey immediately obeyed, and the dictator, by saluting him with the title of Great, showed to the world what expectations he formed from the maturer age of his victorious lieutenant. This sounding title was not sufficient to gratify the ambition of Pompey; he demanded a triumph, and when Sylla refused to grant it, he emphatically exclaimed, that the sun shone with more ardour at his rising than at his setting. His assurance gained what petitions and entreaties could not obtain, and he was the first Roman knight who, without an office under the appointment of the senate, marched in triumphal procession through the streets of Rome. He now appeared, not as a dependent, but as a rival of the dictator, and his opposition to his measures totally excluded him from his will. After the death of Sylla, Pompey supported himself against the remains of the Marian faction, which were headed by Lepidus. He defeated them, put an end to the war which the revolt of Sertorius in Spain had occasioned, and obtained a second triumph, though still a private citizen, about 73 years B.C. He was soon after made consul, and in that office he restored the tribunitial power to its original dignity, and in forty days removed the pirates from the Mediterranean, where they had reigned for many years, and, by their continual plunder and audacity, almost destroyed the whole naval power of Rome. While he was prosecuting the piratical war, and extirpating these maritime robbers in their obscure retreats in Cilicia, Pompey was called to greater undertakings, and by the influence of his friends at Rome, and of the tribune Manilius, he was empowered to finish the war against two of the most powerful monarchs of Asia, Mithridates, king of Pontus, and Tigranes, king of Armenia. In this expedition, Pompey showed himself by no means inferior to Lucullus, who was then at the head of the Roman armies, and who resigned with reluctance an office which would have made him the conqueror of Mithridates, and the master of all Asia. His operations against the king of Pontus were bold and vigorous, and in a general engagement, the Romans so totally defeated the enemy, that the Asiatic monarch escaped with difficulty from the field of battle. *Vid.* Mithridaticum Bellum. Pompey did not lose sight of the advantages which despatch would ensure; he entered Armenia, received the submission of the king Tigranes, and after he had conquered the Albanians and Iberians, visited countries which were scarcely known to the Romans, and, like a master of the world, disposed of kingdoms and provinces, and received homage from twelve crowned heads at once; he entered Syria, and pushed his conquests as far as the Red Sea. Part of Arabia was subdued, Judæa became a Roman province, and when he had now nothing to fear from Mithridates, who had voluntarily destroyed himself, Pompey returned to Italy with all the pomp and majesty of an eastern conqueror. The Romans dreaded his approach; they knew his power and his influence among his troops, and feared the return of another tyrannical Sylla. Pompey, however, banished their fears; he disbanded his army at Brundusium, and the conqueror of Asia entered Rome like a private citizen. This modest and prudent behaviour gained him more friends and adherents than the most unbounded power, aided with profusion and liberality, could have done. He was honored with a triumph, and the Romans, for three successive days, gazed with astonishment on the riches and the spoils which their conquests had acquired in the east, and expressed their raptures at the sight of the different nations, habits, and treasures which preceded the conqueror's chariot. But it was not this alone which gratified the ambition, and flattered the pride of the Romans; the advantages of their conquests were more lasting than an empty spectacle, and when 20,000 talents were brought into the public treasury, and the revenues of the republic raised from fifty to eighty-five millions of drachmæ, Pompey became more powerful, more flattered, and more envied. To strengthen himself, and to triumph over his enemies, Pompey soon after united his interest with that of Cæsar and Crassus, and formed the first triumvirate, by solemnly swearing, that their attachment should be mutual, their cause common, and their union permanent. The agreement was completed by the marriage of Pompey with Julia, the daughter of Cæsar, and the provinces of the republic were arbitrarily divided among the triumvirs. Africa and the two Spains were allotted to Pompey, while Crassus repaired to Syria, to add Parthia to the empire of Rome, and Cæsar remained satisfied with the rest, and the continuation of his power as governor of Gaul for five additional years. But this powerful confederacy was soon broken; the sudden death of Julia, and the total defeat of Crassus in Syria, shattered the political bands which united the jarring interests of Cæsar and Pompey. Pompey dreaded his father-in-law, and yet affected to despise him; and by suffering anarchy to prevail in Rome, he convinced his fellow-citizens of the necessity of investing him with dictatorial power. But while the conqueror of Mithridates was as a sovereign at Rome, the adherents of Cæsar were not silent. They demanded either that the consulship should be given to him, or that he should be continued in the government of Gaul. This just demand would perhaps have been granted, but Cato opposed it; and when Pompey sent for the two legions which he had lent to Cæsar, the breach became more wide, and a civil war became inevitable. Cæsar was privately preparing to meet his enemies, while Pompey remained indolent, and gratified his pride in seeing all Italy celebrate his recovery from an indisposition by public rejoicings. But he was soon roused from his inactivity, and it was now time to find his friends, if anything could be obtained from the caprice and the fickleness of the people which he had once delighted and amused, by the exhibition of games and spectacles in a theatre which could contain 20,000 spectators. Cæsar was now near Rome, he had crossed the Rubicon, which was a declaration of hostilities, and Pompey, who had once boasted that he could summon legions to his assistance by stamping on the ground with his foot, fled from the city with precipitation, and retired to Brundusium with the consuls, and part of the senators. His cause indeed was popular; he had been invested with discretionary power, the senate had entreated him to protect the republic against the usurpation and tyranny of Cæsar, and Cato, by embracing his cause, and appearing in his camp, seemed to indicate, that he was the friend of the republic, and the assertor of Roman liberty and independence. But Cæsar was now master of Rome, and in sixty days all Italy acknowledged his power, and the conqueror hastened to Spain, there to defeat the interests of Pompey, and to alienate the hearts of his soldiers. He was too successful: and when he had gained to his cause the western parts of the Roman empire, Cæsar crossed into Greece, to which country Pompey had retired, supported by all the power of the east, the wishes of the republican Romans, and by a numerous and well-disciplined army. Though superior in numbers, he refused to give the enemy battle, while Cæsar continually harassed him, and even attacked his camp. Pompey repelled him with great success, and he might have decided the war if he had continued to pursue the enemy, while their confusion was great, and their defeat almost inevitable. Want of provisions obliged Cæsar to advance towards Thessaly; Pompey pursued him, and in the plains of Pharsalia the two armies engaged. The whole was conducted against the advice and approbation of Pompey; and by suffering his troops to wait for the approach of the enemy, he deprived his soldiers of that advantage which the army of Cæsar obtained by running to the charge with spirit, vigor, and animation. The cavalry of Pompey soon gave way, and the general retired to his camp overwhelmed with grief and shame. But here there was no safety; the conqueror pushed on his forces on every side, and Pompey disguised himself, and fled to the sea-coast, whence he passed to Ægypt, where he hoped to find a safe asylum, till better and more favourable moments returned, in the court of Ptolemy, a prince whom he had once protected and ensured on his throne. When Ptolemy was told that Pompey claimed his protection, he consulted his ministers, and by their advice he had the baseness to betray and deceive him. A boat was sent to fetch him on shore, and the Roman general left his galley, after an affectionate and tender parting with his wife Cornelia. The Ægyptian sailors sat in sullen silence in the boat, and before Pompey disembarked, Achillas, an Ægyptian, and Septimus, a Roman, who had served under the banners of this unhappy exile, assassinated him. His wife, who had followed him with her eyes to the shore, was a spectator of the bloody scene, and she hastened away from the bay of Alexandria, not to share his miserable fate. Pompey died B.C. 48, in the 58th or 59th year of his age, the day after his birth-day. His ade was cut off, and, after being embalmed, was sent to Cæsar, who turned away from it with horror, and shed a flood of tears. The body was left for some time naked on the sea-shore, till the humanity of Philip, one of his freedmen, and an old soldier, who had often followed his standard to victory, raised a burning pile, and deposited his ashes under a mound of earth. Cæsar erected a monument over his remains, and the emperor Adrian, two centuries after, when he visited Ægypt, ordered it to be repaired at his own expense, and paid particular honor to the memory of a great and good man. The character of Pompey is that of an intriguing and artful general, and the *oris probi*, and *animo inverecundo* of Sallust, short and laconic as it may appear, is the best and most descriptive picture of his character. He wished it to be thought that he obtained all his honors and dignity by merit alone, and as the free and unprejudiced favors of the Romans, while he secretly claimed them by faction and intrigue; and he who wished to appear the patron, and an example of true discipline and ancient simplicity, was not ashamed publicly to bribe the populace to gain an election, or to support his favorites. His great misfortunes interest, indeed, the heart, and his character, compared to that of his successful rival, who at last overthrew the liberties of Rome, appears with more splendid lustre, and more strongly claims our respect, but had Pompey obtained the victory, he might have become a more tyrannical master than Cæsar. The same thirst after power, the same ambition, and the same overbearing consequence, prevailed in the characters of the two rivals, and it was not unknown to the friends of Pompey, of those who shared his retirement, his pleasures, and his confidence, that he meditated subjection for his country, and had frequently threatened to forge for the Romans those chains of slavery, which, with more dissimulation and dexterity, Cæsar gradually imposed. Yet, amidst all these proofs of public ambition and private intrigue, which were perhaps but too congenial to the age, we perceive many other striking features; Pompey was kind and clement to the conquered, and generous to his captives, and he buried at his own expense Mithridates, with all the pomp and solemnity, which the greatness of his power and the extent of his dominions seemed to claim. He was an enemy to flattery, and, when his character was impeached by the malevolence of party, he condescended, though consul, to appear before the censorial tribunal, and to show that his actions and measures were not subversive either of the public peace or the independence of the people. In his private character he was as remarkable; he lived with great temperance and moderation, and his house was small, and not ostentatiously furnished. He destroyed with great prudence the papers which were found in the camp of Sertorius, lest mischievous curiosity should find cause to accuse the innocent, or jealousy meditate their destruction. With great disinterestedness he refused the presents which princes and monarchs offered to him, and he ordered them to be added to the public revenue. He might have seen a better fate, and terminated his days with more glory, if he had not acted with such imprudence when the flames of civil war were first kindled; and he reflected with remorse, after the battle of Pharsalia, upon the absence of his usual sagacity and military prudence, in fighting at such a distance from the sea, and in leaving the fortified places of Dyrrhachium, to meet in the open plain an enemy, without provisions, without friends, and without resources. The misfortunes which attended him after the conquest of Mithridates, are attributed by Christian writers, to his impiety in profaning the temple of the Jews, and in entering, with the insolence of a conqueror, the Holy of Holies, where even the sacred person of the high priest of the nation was not admitted but upon the most solemn occasions. His duplicity of behaviour in regard to Cicero is deservedly censured, and he should not have violently sacrificed to party and sedition, a Roman, whom he had ever found his firmest friend and adherent. In his meeting with Lucullus he cannot but be taxed with pride, and he might have paid more deference and more honor to a general, who was as able and more entitled than himself to finish the Mithridatic war. Pompey was married four times. His first matrimonial connection was with Antistia, the daughter of the prætor Antistius, whom he divorced with great reluctance to marry Æmylia, the daughter-in-law of Sylla. Æmylia died in child-bed; and Pompey's marriage with Julia, the daughter of Cæsar, was a step more of policy than affection. Yet Julia loved Pompey with great tenderness, and her death in child-bed was the signal of war between her husband and her father. He afterwards married Cornelia, the daughter of Metellus Scipio, a woman commended for her virtues, beauty, and accomplishments. *Plut in vitâ.—Flor.* 4.—*Paterc.* 2. c. 29.—*Dio. Cass.—Lucan.—Appian.—Cic. ad Att.* 7. ep. 25. *Ad. Fam.* 13. ep. 19. *Pro. lege Manil. & de cl. Orat.* 68.—*Cæs. Bell. Civ.—Eutrop.* [There is a very fine statue of Pompey at the Palazzo Spada, at Rome.]

POMPE'IUS CNE'US, son of the preceding, was slain at the battle of Munda.

POMPE'IUS SEX'TUS, likewise a son of Pompey the Great, after the battle which proved fatal to his brother fled to Sicily, where he for some time supported himself; but the murder of Cæsar gave rise to new events, and if Pompey had been as prudent and sagacious as his father, he might have become perhaps as great and as formidable. He treated with the triumvirs as an equal, and when Augustus and Antony had the imprudence to trust themselves without arms and without attendants, in his ship, Pompey, by following the advice of his friend Menas, who wished him to cut off the illustrious persons who were masters of the world, and now in his power, might have made himself as absolute as Cæsar; but he refused, and observed it was unbecoming the son of Pompey to act with such duplicity. This friendly meeting of Pompey with two of the triumvirs was not productive of lasting advantages to him; he wished to have no superior, and hostilities soon after began. Pompey was at the head of 350 ships, and appeared so formidable to his enemies, and so confident of success in himself, that he called himself the son of Neptune, and the lord of the sea. He was, however, soon defeated in a naval engagement by Octavius and Lepidus, and of all his numerous fleet only 17 sail accompanied his flight to Asia. Here for a while he raised seditions, but Antony ordered him to be seized, and he was put to death by Titius at Miletus, about 35 years B.C., in his 46th year. *Plut. in Anton. &c.—Paterc.* 2. c. 55, &c.—*Flor.* 4. c. 2, &c.—*Strab.—Appian.*

POMPE'IUS TRO'GUS. *Vid.* Trogus.

SEX'TUS POMPE'IUS FES'TUS, a Latin grammarian, of whose treatise *de verborum significatione*, the best edition is in 4to, Amst. 1699. *Harles. Not. Lit. Rom.* 1. p. 576.

POM'PELON, a town of Spain, now Pampeluna, the capital of Navarre. *Plin.* 3. c. 3.

POMPIL'IA, a daughter of Numa Pompilius. She married Numa Martius, by whom she had Ancus Martius, the fourth king of Rome. The family of the Pompilii once flourished among the Sabines, and was rendered illustrious by the elevation of Numa to the Roman throne.

POMPIL'IUS NU'MA, the second king of Rome. *Vid.* Numa. The descendents of the monarch were called *Pompilius Sanguis*, an expression applied by *Horace* to the Pisones. *Art. Poet.* v. 292.

POMPIL'IUS ANDRONI'CUS, a grammarian of Syria, who opened a school at Rome, and had Cicero and Cæsar among his pupils. *Sueton. in illustr. gramm.* c. 8.

POMPIL'IUS, a person intimate with Catiline. *Cic. Pet. Cons.*——A slave of Theophrastus the peripatetic, who afterwards became a philosopher. *Gell.* 2. c. 18.

POMPI'LUS, a fisherman of Ionia. He carried into Miletus, Ocyroe, the daughter of Chesias, of whom Apollo was enamoured, but before he had reached the shore, the god changed the boat into a rock, Pompilus into a fish of the same name, and carried away Ocyroe. *Ovid. Halieut.* 101.—*Plin.* 6. c. 29. l. 9. c. 15. l. 32. c. 11.—*Apollon. Rh. apud Athen.*

POMPIS'CUS, an Arcadian general. *Polyæn.* 5. c. 33.

POMPO'NIA, the wife of Q. Cicero, sister of Pomponius Atticus. She punished with the greatest cruelty, Philologus, the slave who had betrayed her husband to Antony, and ordered him to cut off his flesh by piecemeal, and afterwards to boil it and eat it in her presence. *Cic.* 1. *Att.* 5.——A matron banished from Rome by Domitian, and recalled by Nerva.——The mother of Africanus. *Sil.* 13. v. 615.——A daughter of Atticus, who married Agrippa, by whom she was divorced, that he might marry Julia, the daughter of Augustus. She was mother of Vipsania Aggrippina who married Tiberius, and afterwards Asinius Gallus.

POMPO'NIA GRÆCI'NA, a daughter of Pomponius Græcinus, in the age of Augustus, was wife of Plautius, and suspected of being a Christian. *Tac. Ann.* 13. c. 32.—*Ovid.* 1. 4. *de Ponto.*

POMPONIA'NA, an island of Gallia Narbonensts, near Massilia. *Plin.* 3. c. 5.

POMPO'NIUS, the father of Numa, advised his son to accept the regal dignity, which the Roman ambassadors offered to him.——A celebrated Roman, intimate with Cicero. He was surnamed *Atticus*, from his long residence at Athens, and by this name he is best known. *Vid.* Atticus.——A tribune of the people, in the time of Servilius Ahala the consul.——A Roman tribune who accused Manlius the dictator of cruelty, but did not prosecute his purpose through the threats of the son of the accused. He triumphed over Sardinia, of which he was made governor. He escaped from Rome, and the tyranny of the triumvirs, by assuming the habit of a prætor, and by travelling with his servants disguised in the dress of lictors with their fasces. *Liv.* 7. c. 4 & 5.——A friend of C. Gracchus. He was killed in attempting to defend him. *Plut. in Gracc.*——An officer taken prisoner by Mithridates.——A dissolute youth, &c. *Horat.* 1. sat. 4. v. 52.

POMPO'NIUS FLAC'CUS, a man appointed governor of Mœsia and Syria by Tiberius, because he had continued eating and drinking with him for two days without intermission. *Suet. in Tib.* 42.

POMPO'NIUS LA'BEO, a governor of Mœsia, accused of mismanagement in his province. He destroyed himself by opening his veins. *Tacit. Ann.* 6. c. 29.

POMPO'NIUS LU'CIUS, a native of Bologna on the Po, who flourished at Rome about the age of Cicero, and excelled as a writer of comedies. His delineation of the human character was happy, his characters striking, and his humour sprightly and elegant. Above 30 of his plays are mentioned by ancient authors and grammarians, such as his Aleones, Nuptiæ, Privignus, Piscatores, Rusticus, Asinaria, Buccho, Verres, &c., of all of which only 138 lines are preserved in the collection of Latin poets. *Cic.—Seneca.—Quintil.—Aul. Gell.*

POMPO'NIUS ME'LA, a Spaniard who wrote a book on geography. *Vid.* Mela.

POMPO'NIUS SILVA'NUS, a proconsul of Africa, accused by the inhabitants of his province and acquitted. *Tac. Ann.* 13. c. 52.

POMPO'NIUS SECUN'DUS, an officer in Germany in the age of Nero. He was honored with a triumph for a victory over the barbarians of Germany. He wrote some poems, and especially tragedies so highly celebrated by the ancients for their beauty, elegance, and sublimity, that he has been called the tragic Pindar of Rome. As he was in affluent circumstances, he was intimate with the great men of his age, among whom is particularly mentioned Cæsar Germanicus. His character was so illustrious, that Pliny wrote an account of his life in two books, and proved that the virtues and the merit he possessed were deserving of immortality. Only five of his verses are preserved. *Quintil.* 10. c. 1.—*Plin.* 3. ep. 5—*Gyrald.*

POMPO'NIUS SEX'TUS, a lawyer, disciple to Papinian. The fragments of his works which are extant, were published by Ruperti, Jena, 1661. *Harles. Not. Lit. Rom.* 1. p. 507.—*Sax. Onom.* 1. p. 302.

POMPOSIA'NUS, a Roman put to death by Domitian. He had been before made consul by Vespasian.

POMPTI'NA. *Vid.* Pontina.

POMPTI'NUS C., a Roman officer, who conquered the Allobroges after the death of Catiline. *Cic. Att.* 4. ep. 16. 1. 6. ep. 3. *Fam.* 2. ep. 15. 1. 2. c. 2. 1. 15. ep. 4.

POM'PUS, a king of Arcadia, son and successor of Simus. He encouraged commerce among his subjects, and rendered his country flourishing by introducing the commodities in which the people of Ægina traded. *Paus.* 8. c. 5.

PONEROP'OLIS, a city of Thrace, under mount Rhodope. It was first called Philippopolis, from its founder, and lastly Trimontium, from its situation. *Plin.* 4. c. 11.

PONS Æ'LIUS was built by the emperor Adrian at Rome. It was the second bridge of Rome in following the current of the Tiber. It is still to be seen, and is the largest and most beautiful in Rome. It is now called Ponte di S. Angelo.

PONS ÆMYL'IUS, an ancient bridge at Rome, originally called Sublicius, because built with wood *(sublicæ)*. It was raised by Ancus Martius, and dedicated with great pomp and solemnity by the Roman priests. It was rebuilt of stone by Æmylius Lepidus, whose name it assumed. It was much injured by the overflowing of the river, and the emperor Antoninus repaired it with white marble. It was the last of all the bridges of Rome, in following the course of the river, and some vestiges of it may still be seen. It is now Marmorato.

PONS ANIEN'SIS was built across the river Anio, about three miles from Rome. It was rebuilt by the eunuch Narses, when it had been destroyed by the Goths, and was called after his name.

PONS ARMONIEN'SIS was built by Augustus, to join the Flaminian to the Æmylian road.

PONS AURELIA'NUS was built with marble by the emperor Antoninus.

PONS BAJA'NUS was built at Baiæ in the sea by Caligula. It was supported by boats, and measured about six miles in length.

PONS CES'TIUS was built in the reign of Tiberius by a Roman called Cestius Gallus, from whom it received its name, and carried back from an island of the Tiber, to which the Fabricius conducted. It is now Ponte de S. Bartholomeo.

PONS FABRIC'IUS was built by Fabricius, and carried to an island of the Tiber. It is now Ponte de quattro capi.

PONS GAR'DIUS was built by Agrippa.

PONS JANICULA'RIS received its name from its vicinity to mount Janiculum. It is still standing.

PONS MIL'VIUS was about one mile from Rome. It was built by the censor Æmylius Scaurus. It was near it that Constantine defeated Maxentius. It is now Ponte Molle.

PONS NARNIEN'SIS, built by Augustus, joined two mountains near Narnia. It was of stupendous height, and was sixty miles from Rome; one arch of it remains, about 100 feet high.

PONS PALATI'NUS, near mount Palatine, was also called Senatorius, because the senators walked over it in procession when they went to consult the Sibylline books. It was begun by M. Fulvius, and finished in the censorship of L. Mummius, and some remains of it are still visible. It is now called Ponte S. Maria, or Ponte rotto.

PONS SUFFRAGIO'RUM was built in the Campus Martius, and received its name, because the populace were obliged to pass over it whenever they delivered their suffrages at the elections of magistrates and officers of the state.

PONS TRAJA'NI was built by Trajan across the Danube, and was celebrated for its size and magnificence. The emperor built it to assist more expeditiously the provinces against the barbarians, but his successor destroyed it, as he supposed that it would be rather an inducement for the barbarians to invade the empire. It was raised on 20 piers of hewn stone, 150 feet from the foundation, sixty feet broad, and 170 feet distant one from the other, extending in length above a mile. Some of the pillars are still standing.——A bridge built by Trajan over the Tagus, part of which still remains.

PONS TIREN'SIS, a bridge of Latium, between Arpinum and Minturnæ.

PONS TRIUMPHA'LIS was on the way to the Capitol, and passed over by those who triumphed.

PONS VETE'RIS BRIVA'TIS, the largest single arched bridge known, over the river Elaver in France. The pillars stand on two rocks, at the distance of

195 feet. The arch is 84 feet high above the water. Of temporary bridges, that of Cæsar over the Rhine was the most famous.

PON'TIA, a Roman matron who committed adultery with Sagitta, and was slain by him. *Tacit. Ann.* 13. c. 44.——A mother infamous for her cruelty. *Martial.* 1. epigr. 34.——A surname of Venus at Hermione, on the isthmus of Corinth, because she was considered as a sea deity, from her emerging from the waves. Her statue of white marble was considered an elegant piece of sculpture. *Paus.* 2. c. 34.——A woman condemned by Nero as guilty of a conspiracy. She killed herself by opening her veins. She was daughter of Petronius, and wife of Bolanus. *Juv.* 6. v. 637.——An island in the Tyrrhene Sea, where Pilate, surnamed Pontius is supposed to have lived. *Ptol.* 3. c. 1.—*Plin.* 3. c. 6. *Vid.* Œnotrides.

PON'TICUM MA'RE, the sea of Pontus, generally called the Euxine. *Macrob. Sat.* 7. c. 12.

PON'TICUS, a poet of Rome, contemporary with Propertius, by whom he is compared to Homer. He wrote an account of the Theban war in heroic verse. *Propert.* 1. el. 7.—*Ovid. Trist.* 4. 1. 10. v. 47.——A man in Juvenal's age, fond of boasting of the antiquity and great actions of his family, yet without possessing himself one single virtue.

PONTID'IUS, a native of Arpinum, distinguished as an orator. *Cic Br.* 70. *Orat.* 2. c. 67.

PONTI'NA or POMPTI'NA PA'LUS, a lake in the country of the Volsci, through which the great Appian road passed. Travellers were sometimes conveyed in a boat, drawn by a mule, in the canal that ran along the road from Forum Appii to Tarracina. This lake is now become so dangerous, from the exhalations of its stagnant waters, that travellers avoid passing near it. *Horat.* 1. sat. 5. v. 9 —*Lucan.* 3. v. 85.

PONTI'NUS, a friend of *Cicero. De Provinc. Consul.*

PONTI'NUS AQ'UILA, a tribune of the people, who refused to rise up when Cæsar passed in triumphal procession. He was one of Cæsar's murderers, and was killed at the battle of Mutina. *Sueton. in Cæsar.* 78.—*Cic.* 10. *ad. Fam.*

PONTI'NUS, a mountain of Argolis, with a river of the same name. Minerva Saitis was worshipped in a temple built there. *Paus.* 2. c. 73.

PONTIUS AUFIDIA'NUS, a Roman citizen, who, upon hearing that violence had been offered to his daughter by Fannius Saturninus, her preceptor, punished her and her ravisher with death. *Val. Max.* 6. c. 1.

PON'TIUS HEREN'NIUS, a general of the Samnites, who surrounded the army under the consuls T. Veturius and P. Posthumius. As there was no possibility of the Romans escaping, Pontius consulted his father what he could do with an army that were prisoners in his hands. The old man advised him either to let them go untouched, or put them all to the sword. Pontius rejected his father's advice, and spared the lives of the enemy, after he had obliged them to pass under the yoke with the greatest ignominy. He was afterwards conquered, and obliged in his turn to pass under the yoke. Fabius Maximus defeated him, when he appeared at the head of another army, and he was afterwards shamefully put to death by the Romans, after he had adorned the triumph of the conqueror. *Liv.* 9. c. 1, &c.—*Cic. Off.* 2. c. 21.

PON'TIUS COMIN'IUS, a Roman who gave information to his countrymen who were besieged in the Capitol, that Camillus had obtained a victory over the Gauls. *Plut.*

PON'TIUS PILA'TUS, the Roman governor of Judæa, under whom our Saviour was crucified. *Tacit.* 15. *Ann.* 44.

PON'TIUS, a Roman slave, who told Sylla in a prophetic strain, that he brought him success from Bellona.

PON'TIUS FREGELLA'NUS, one of the favorites of Albucilla. He was degraded from the rank of senator. *Tacit. Ann.* 6. c. 48.

PON'TIUS TI'TUS, a Roman centurion, whom *Cicero, de Senect.* mentions as possessed of uncommon strength.

PON'TIUS PAULI'NUS, a writer. *Vid.* Paulinus.

PONTON'OUS, one of the heralds who attended at the court of Antinous when Ulysses was wrecked on the island of Phæacia. *Homer. Od.* 7. v. 180.

PONTOPORI'A, one of the Nereides. *Hesiod. Th.* 256.

PON'TUS, a kingdom of Asia Minor, bounded on the east by Colchis, on the west by the Halys, on the north by the Euxine Sea, and on the south by part of Armenia. It was divided into three parts according to Ptolemy; Pontus *Galaticus*, of which Amasia was the capital, Pontus *Polemoniacus*, from its chief town Polemonium, and Pontus *Cappadocius*, of which Trapezus was the capital. It was governed by kings, the first of whom was Artabazes, either one of the seven Persian noblemen, who murdered the usurper Smerdis, or one of their descendants. The kingdom of Pontus was in its most flourishing state under Mithridates the Great. When J. Cæsar had conquered it, it became a Roman province, though it was often governed by monarchs who were tributary to the power of Rome. Under the emperors a regular governor was always appointed over it. Pontus produced castors, the oil of which was highly valued among the ancients for its salutary medicinal qualities. *Virg. G.* 1. v. 58.—*Mela*, 1. c. 1 & 19. 1. 2. c. 1, 2 & 7.—*Servius ad Virg. Ecl.* 8. v. 95. *Æn.* 3. v. 312. 1. 9. v. 582.—*Strab.* 12.—*Cic. pro Lege Manil.* 9.—*Appian.*—*Ptol.* 5. c. 6.——A part of Mysia in Europe, on the borders of the Euxine Sea, to which Ovid was banished, and where he wrote his four books of epistles *de Ponto*, and his six books *de Tristibus*, *Ovid. de Pont.*

PONTUS, an ancient deity, son of Thya, and father of Phorcys, Thaumas, Nereus, Eurybia, Ceto, and according to some, the Harpies, by Terra. He is the same as Oceanus. *Apollod.* 1. c. 2.—*Hesiod. Th.* 131 & 233.—*Servius in Æn.* 3. v. 241.

PON'TUS EUXI'NUS, a celebrated sea, situate at the west of Colchis, between Asia and Europe, at the north of Asia Minor. It is called the Black Sea by the moderns. *Vid.* Euxinus.

POPA'NIUM, a city of the Tyrrhenes. *Aristot. in Mirabil.*

POPIL'IA, a plebeian family at Rome, many of the members of which were distinguished for their public services. *Cic.* 2. *Leg.* 22.——The mother of Q. Catulus. Her virtues were celebrated in an oration, by her son, at her funeral, and this is the first person of whom such public mention is made. *Cic.* 2. *Or.* 2.

POPIL'IUS M., a consul who was informed, as he was offering a sacrifice, that a sedition was raised in the city against the senate. Upon this he immediately went to the populace in his sacerdotal robes, and quieted the multitude with a speech, from which circumstance he was surnamed *Lænas*. He lived about 404 A.U.C. *Liv.* 9. c. 21.—*Val. Max.* 7. c. 8.—*Cic. Br.* 14.

POPIL'IUS CA'IUS, a consul, who, when besieged by the Gauls, abandoned his baggage to save his army. *Cic. ad Heren.* 1. c. 15.

POPIL'IUS LÆ'NAS, a Roman ambassador to Antiochus, king of Syria. He was commissioned to order the monarch to abstain from hostilities against Ptolemy, king of Ægypt, who was an ally of Rome. Antiochus wished to evade him by his answers, but Popilius, with a stick which he had in his hand, made a circle round him on the sand, and bade him, in the name of the Roman senate and people, not to go beyond it before he spake decisively. This boldness intimidated Antiochus; he withdrew his garrisons from Ægypt, and no longer meditated a war against Ptolemy. *Cic. Ph.* 8. c. 8.—*Val. Max.* 6. c. 4.—*Justin.* 34. c. 3. —*Plin.* 34. c. 6.—*Plut. in Apoph.*—*Liv.* 45. c. 12. —*Paterc.* 1. c. 10.

POPIL'IUS, a tribune of the people, born at Picenum. He was accused of parricide, but saved from disgrace and death by the eloquence of Cicero. These services were forgotten, and when the orator was proscribed, Popilius offered himself to destroy him, and when Herennius, the centurion, had cut off his head, he desired that the hands which had written the Philippics might also be severed from the body, as a pleasing offering to Antony. *Plut. in Cic.*—*Appian. Civ. B.* 4.—*Val. Max.* 5. c. 3. ——A prætor who banished the friends of Tiberius Gracchus from Italy.——A Roman consul, who made war against the people of Numantia, on pretence that the peace had not been firmly established. He was defeated by them.——A senator who alarmed the conspirators against Cæsar, by telling them that the whole plot was discovered.——A Roman emperor. *Vid.* Nepotianus.

POPLIC'OLA, one of the first consuls. *Vid.* Publicola.

POPPÆ'A SABI'NA, a celebrated Roman matron, daughter of Titus Ollius. She married a Roman knight called Rufus Crispinus, by whom she had a son. Her personal charms, and the elegance of her figure, captivated Otho, who was then one of Nero's favorites. He carried her away and married her; but Nero, who had seen her, and had often heard her accomplishments extolled, soon deprived him of her company, and sent him out of Italy, on pretence of presiding over one of the Roman provinces. After he had taken this step, Nero repudiated his wife Octavia, on pretence of barrenness, and married Poppæa. The cruelty and avarice of the emperor did not long permit Poppæa to share the imperial dignity, and though she had already made him father of a son, he began to despise her, and even to use her with barbarity. She died of a blow which she received from his foot when many months advanced in her pregnancy, about the 65th year of the Christian era. Her funeral was performed with great pomp and solemnity, and statues raised to her memory. It is said that she was so anxious to preserve her beauty and the elegance of her person, that 500 asses were kept on purpose to afford her milk in which she used daily to bathe. Even in her banishment she was attended by 50 of these animals for the same purpose, and from their milk she invented a kind of ointment, or pomatum, to preserve beauty, called *Poppæanum* from her. *Plin.* 11. c. 41.—*Dio.* 62.—*Juv.* 6. v. 461.—*Sueton. in Ner. & Oth.*—*Tacit.* 13 & 14. [The finest bust of Poppæa will be found in the Capitol, at Rome.]

POPPÆ'A, a beautiful woman at the court of Nero. She was mother of the preceding. *Tacit. Ann.* 11. c. 1, &c.

POPPÆ'US SABI'NUS, a Roman of obscure origin, who was made governor of some of the Roman provinces. He destroyed himself. *Tacit.* 6. *Ann.* 39.

POPPÆ'US SYLVA'NUS, a man of consular dignity, who brought to Vespasian a body of 600 Dalmatians. *Tac. Hist.* 3. c. 50. & 4. c. 47.

POPPÆ'US VOPIS'CUS, a favourite of Otho. *Tac. Hist.* 1. c. 77.

POPULIFU'GIA, a festival celebrated at Rome in June, to commemorate the retreat of the Roman populace, who were irritated against the senators, whom they suspected of killing Romulus. Some believe that it was instituted rather to commemorate the flight of the Romans when the city was taken by the Gauls. *Macrob. Sat.* 3. c. 2.—*Ovid. Fast.* 2. v. 496.—*Varro de L.L.* 5. c. 3.—*Dionys. Hal.* 2.

POPULO'NIA, a surname of Juno worshipped at Rome, because she was considered as the patroness of marriage, which contributes to the increase and population of a state. *Macrob.* 3. c. 11.—*Mart. Cap. de Nupt.* 2.—*Arnob.* 3.—*Aug. de Civ. D.* 6. c. 10.

POPULO'NIA or POPULO'NIUM, a maritime town of Etruria, near Pisæ, supposed to have been founded by a Corsican colony. It was destroyed in the civil wars of Sylla. *Strab.* 5.—*Virg. Æn.* 10. v. 172. *& Servius loco.*—*Mela*, 2. c. 5.—*Plin.* 3. c. 5.

POR'ATA, a river of Dacia, now the Pruth, falling into the Danube a little below Axiopoli.

POR'CE, the name of one of the serpents which killed Laocoon. *Servius. Æn.* 2. v. 211.

POR'CIA, a sister of Cato of Utica, greatly commended by Cicero. She married Domitius Ahenobarbus, and her great virtues received a funeral encomium from Cicero. *Cic. Att.* 13. ep. 37 & 48. l. 15. ep. 11.——A daughter of Cato of Utica, who married Bibulus, and, after his death, Brutus, after he had previously divorced Claudia. She was remarkable for her prudence, philosophy, courage, and conjugal tenderness. She gave herself a heavy wound in the thigh, to see with what fortitude she could bear pain; and when her husband asked her the reason of it, she said that she wished to try whether she had courage enough to share not only his bed, but to partake of his most hidden secrets. Brutus was astonished at her constancy, and no longer detained from her knowledge the conspiracy which he and many other illustrious Romans had formed against J. Cæsar. Porcia wished them success, and though she betrayed fear, and fell into a swoon the day that her husband was gone to assassinate the dictator, yet she was faithful to her promise, and dropped nothing which might affect the conspirators. When Brutus was dead, she refused to survive him, and attempted to end her life in a manner worthy of a daughter of Cato. Her friends attempted to terrify her; but when she saw that every weapon was removed from her reach, she swallowed burning coals, and died about 42 years B.C. Valerius Maximus says, that she was acquainted with her husband's conspiracy against Cæsar when she gave herself the wound. *Val. Max.* 3. c. 2. l. 4. c. 6.—*Plut. in Brut. &c.*—*Dio.* 47 & 63.—*Appian. de B. Civ.* 4.—*Cic. ad Att.* 13. ep. 37 & 48.—*Martial.* 1. epigr. 42.—The Porcian family was plebeian, and came originally from the town of Tusculum. *Tacit. Ann.* 11. c. 24.—*Plut. iu Cat. Cens.*

POR'CIA LEX, *de civitate*, was enacted by M. Porcius the tribune, A.U.C. 453. It ordained that no magistrate should punish with death, or scourge with rods, a Roman citizen when condemned, but only permit him to go into exile. *Sallust. in Cat.*—*Liv.* 10.—*Cic. pro Rab.*

PORCIF'ERA, a river of Liguria, flowing from the Apennines. *Plin.* 3. c. 5. According to *Leander*, it is now Porcevera.

PORCI'NA, a surname of the orator M. Æ. Lepidus, who lived a little time before Cicero's age, and was distinguished for his abilities. *Cic. ad Her.* 4. c. 5.

M. POR'CIUS LA'TRO, a celebrated orator who killed himself when laboring under a quartan ague, A.U.C. 750. *Senec. in præf. Contr.*—*Voss. de Rhet. Nat.* 1. l. c. 15.

POR'CIUS LICIN'IUS, a Latin poet during the time of the third Punic war, commended for the elegance, gracefulness, and happy wit of his epigrams. He is described as a man of dissolute morals and of Epicurean principles. Only six of his verses are preserved. *Catull.* 48.—*Horat.* 2. sat. 8. v. 22.—*Aul. Gell.* 17. c. 21. l. 19. c. 9.——A consul. *Liv.* 39. c. 32.

POR'CIUS LÆ'CA, a Roman senator who joined the conspiracy of Catiline. *Sal. Cat.* 27.—*Cic. Cat.* 1. c. 4.

POR'CIUS, a son of Cato of Utica, much given to drinking.

POR'CIUS NAS'ICA, an orator. *Cic. Or.* 2. c. 64.

POR'CIUS SEPTIM'INUS, a præfect of Rhætia, very faithful to Vitellius. *Tacit. Hist.* 3. c. 5.

PORDOSOLE'NE, an island near Lesbus, with a city of the same name. Some call it Poroselene. *Steph.*—*Strab.* 13.—*Plin.* 5. c. 31.—*Paus.* 3. c. 25.

PORED'ORAX, one of the forty Gauls whom Mithridates ordered to be put to death, and to remain unburied, for conspiring against him. His mistress at Pergamus buried him against the orders of the monarch. *Plut. de Virt. Mul.* c. 23.

PORI'NA, a river of Peloponnesus, near Cyllene. *Paus.* 8. c. 15.

POROLIS'SUM, a river of European Sarmatia. *Ptol.*

POROSELE'NE. *Vid.* Pordoselene.

PORPHYR'ION, a son of Cœlus and Terra, one of the giants who made war against Jupiter. He was so formidable, that Jupiter, to conquer him, inspired him with love for Juno, and while the giant endeavored to obtain his wishes, he, with the assistance of Hercules, overpowered him. *Horat.* 3. od. 4. v. 54.—*Apollod.* 1. c. 6.——A charioteer who wore a green livery, &c. *Martial.* 13. epigr. 78.——A city of Phœnicia, at the foot of mount Carmel. *Steph*

PORPHYRIO'NE, an island of the Propontis, opposite Cyzicus. *Plin.* 5. c. *ult.* It is now Isola di Chizico.

POR'PHYRIS, a name of the island Cythera.

PORPHYRI'TE, a town of Arabia, near Ægypt. *Steph.* According to *Eusebius*, it was in the Thebais.

PORPHYR'IUS, a Platonic philosopher of Tyre, whose original name was Malchus He studied eloquence at Athens under Longinus, and afterwards retired to Rome, where he perfected himself under Plotinus. Porphyry was a man of universal information, and, according to the testimony of the ancients, excelled his contemporaries in the knowledge of history, mathematics, music, and philosophy. He expressed his sentiments with elegance and dignity, and while other philosophers studied obscurity in their language, his style was remarkable for its simplicity and grace. He applied himself to the study of magic, which he called a theourgic or divine operation. The books that he wrote were numerous, and some of his smaller treatises are still extant. His most celebrated work, which is now lost, was against the religion of Christ; and in this theological contest he appeared so formidable, that most of the fathers of the church have been employed in confuting his arguments, and developing the falsehood of his assertions. He has been universally called the greatest enemy which the Christian religion had, and indeed his doctrines were so pernicious, that a copy of his book was publicly burnt by order of Theodosius, A.D. 388. Porphyry resided for some time in Sicily, and died at the advanced age of seventy-one, A.D. 304. The best edition of his life of Pythagoras is that of Kuster, 4to, Amst. 1707; of his treatise *De Abstinentia*, that of De Rhoer. Traj. ad Rhen. 8vo, 1767; and of *De Antro Nympharum*, that of Van Goens, in 8vo, Traj. ad Rhen. 1765. *Fabr. B. Gr.* 4. c. 30.—*Sax. Onom.* 1. p. 375.

PORPHYR'IUS PUB'LIUS OPTATIA'NUS, a Latin poet in the reign of Constantine the Great. He was banished from his country, but recalled on condition that he should write a poem in praise of the emperor. This panegyric is extant, and may be found among the "Epigrammata & poemata vetera" of Pithoeus, Paris, 1590; and in the works of Velser, Noriberg, 1682, edited by Arnold. *Harles. Not. Lit. Rom.* 1. p. 712.—*Sax. Onom.* 1. p. 396.

POR'RIMA, one of the attendants of Carmente when she came from Arcadia. *Ovid.* 1. *Fast.* v. 633.—*Servius Æn.* 8. v. 336.—*Gell.* 16. c. 16.

PORSEN'NA, POR'SENA, or PORSE'NA, a king of Etruria, who declared war against the Romans, because they refused to restore Tarquin to his throne and royal priviliges. He was at first successful, the Romans were defeated, and Porsenna would have entered the gates of Rome, had not Cocles stood at the head of a bridge, and resisted the fury of the whole Etrurian army, while his companions behind were cutting off the communication with the opposite shore. This act of bravery astonished Porsenna; but when he had seen Mutius Scævola enter his camp with an intention to murder him, and burn his hand without emotion, to convince him of his fortitude and intrepidity, he no longer dared to make head against a people so brave and so generous. He concluded a peace with the Romans, and for ever after abandoned the cause of Tarquin. The generosity of Porsenna's behaviour to the captives was admired by the Romans, and to reward his humanity they raised a brazen statue to his honor. *Liv.* 2. c. 9, &c.—*Plut. in Public.*—*Flor.* 1. c. 10.—*Horat. Ep.* 16. v. 4.—*Virg. Æn.* 8. v. 646.—*Aur. Vict.* 12.—*Martial.* 1. epigr. 22. l. 14. epigr. 98.

POR'SICA, or PER'SA according to *Stephanus*, a town of Mesopotamia on the Euphrates.

POR'TA ASINA'RIA, called also Cœliomontana, and now S. Giovanni, led to mount Cœlius. It received its name from the family of the Asinii.

POR'TA AURE'LIA, a gate at Rome, which received its name from Aurelius, a consul who made a road which led to Pisa, all along the coast of Etruria.

POR'TA CAPE'NA, a gate at Rome, which led to the Appian road. It is now Porte di S. Sebastiano. *Ovid. Fast.* 6. v. 192.

PORTA CARMENTA'LIS was at the foot of the Capitol, built by Romulus. It was afterwards called Scelerata, because the 300 Fabii marched through it when they went to fight an enemy, and were killed near the river Cremera. *Virg. Æn.* 8. v. 338.

POR'TA CATULA'RIA was near the Carmentalis Porta, at the foot of mount Viminalis.

POR'TA COLLATI'NA received its name from its leading to Collatia.

POR'TA COLLI'NA, called also Quirinalis Agonensis and Salaria, was near Quirinalis Mons. Annibal rode up to this gate and threw a spear into the city.

POR'TA ESQUILI'NA was also called Metia, Taurica, or Libitinensis, and all criminals who were going to be executed generally passed through it, as also dead bodies which were carried to be burnt on mount Esquilinus.

POR'TA FLAMIN'IA, called also Flumentana, was situate between the Capitol and mount Quirinalis, and through it the Flaminian road passed.

POR'TA FONTINA'LIS led to the Campus Martius. It received its name from the great number of fountains that were near it.

POR'TA JANUA'LIS was near the temple of Janus.

POR'TA NAVA'LIS was situate near the place where the ships came from Ostia.

POR'TA TRIGEM'INA, called also Ostiensis, led to the town of Ostia.

POR'TA VIMINA'LIS was near mount Viminalis.—It is to be observed, that at the death of Romulus there were only three or four gates at Rome, but the number was increased, and in the time of *Pliny* there were thirty-seven, when the circumference of the walls was thirteen miles and 290 paces.

PORTACRA, a city of Taurica Chersonesus. *Ptol.*

PORTHA'ON or PARTHA'ON, a son of Agenor. *Vid.* Parthaon.

PORTHA'ON, a son of Lycaon, king of Arcadia. *Apollod.* 3.

POR'TIA and POR'TIUS. *Vid.* Porcia & Porcius.

PORTH'MIA, a village at the mouth of the Palus Mæotis. *Steph.*

PORTH'MOS, a town of Eubœa, now Portimo or Portmo. *Demosth. Poil.* 1.—*Plin.* 3. c. 5. l. 4. c. 12.

PORTICA'NUS, a king of the Præsti, a people of India. He was slain by Alexander the Great. *Curt.* 9. c. 8.

PORTOS'PANA, a city of Carmania. *Ptol.* It is called Ortospana by *Ammianus*.

PORTUMNA'LIA, festivals of Portumnus at Rome, celebrated on the 17th of August, on the borders of the Tiber, in a very solemn and lugubrious manner. *Varro de L. L.* 5. c. 3.—*Ovid. Fast.* 6. v. 547.—*Rosin. A. R.* 4. c. 12.

PORTU'NUS or PORTUM'NUS, a sea deity. *Vid.* Melicerta.

PORTUNA'TA, an island of Illyricum or Liburnia. *Plin.* 3. c. 21.

POR'TUS AUGUS'TI, a city of Etruria, at the mouth of the Tiber. *Antonin.*—*Procop.*—*Cassiod.* It is now Porto.

POR'TUS HER'CULIS, a harbour of Liguria. *Val. Max.* It is now Monacho.——A harbour of Etruria, near mount Argentarius. *Strab.*—*Antonin.* It is now Porto Ercole.——A harbour of the Brutii. *Plin.* 3. c. 5. It is now le Formicole.

POR'TUS LU'NÆ, a harbour of Liguria. *Strabo.*—*Ennius ap Pers.* sat. 6. v. 9. It is now Golfo della Spezzia.

POR'TUS MAG'NUS, a harbour of Hispania Bætica. It is now Almeria. *Ptol.*—*Plin.* 5. c. 2.

POR'TUS MENES'THEI, a town of Hispania Bætica. *Strab.*—*Ptol.* Is is now Porto di S. Maria.

POR'TUS NAVO'NIUS. a harbour of Corsica. *Antonin.* It is now Porto Navon.

POR'TUS ORES'TIS, a harbour of the Brutii, now Porto Ravaglioso. *Plin.* 3. c. 5.

POR'TUS ROMATI'NUS, a town of the Carni, on the river Romatius. *Plin.* 3. c. 18. It is now Porto Gruaro.

POR'TUS SANTO'NUM, a city of Aquitania. *Ptol.* It is now la Rochelle.

POR'TUS VELI'NUS, a harbour of Lucania. *Virg.* 6. v. 366. It is now Porto di Castellamare.

POR'TUS VENE'RIS, a town of Liguria, opposite the island of Palmaria. *Antonin.*—*Ptol.* It is now Porto Venere.

POR'TUS ULYS'SIS, a harbour of Sicily. *Plin.* 3. c. 8. It is now Lognina, and is choked up with stones discharged from mount Ætna.

PO'RUS, the god of plenty at Rome, was son of Metis or Prudence. At a feast given by the gods in honor of Venus he is said to have become, by Penia or Poverty, the father of Cupid, who, however, always passed as the son of the goddess of beauty. *Plato in Symp.*——A king of India when Alexander invaded Asia. The conqueror of Darius ordered him to come and pay homage to him, as a dependent prince. Porus scorned his commands, and declared he would go and meet him on the frontiers of his kingdom sword in hand,

and immediately marched a large army to the banks of the Hydaspes. The stream of the river was rapid; but Alexander crossed it in the obscurity of the night, and defeated one of the sons of the Indian monarch. Porus himself renewed the battle; but the valor of the Macedonians prevailed, and the Indian prince retired covered with wounds, on the back of one of his elephants. Alexander sent one of the kings of India to demand him to surrender, but Porus killed the messenger, exclaiming, "Is not this the voice of the wretch who has abandoned his country?" And when he at last was prevailed upon to come before the conqueror, he approached him as an equal. Alexander demanded of him how he wished to be treated; "Like a king," replied the Indian monarch. This magnanimous answer so pleased the Macedonian conqueror, that he not only restored him his dominions, but increased his kingdom by the addition of new provinces; and Porus, in acknowledgment of such generosity and benevolence, became one of the most faithful and attached friends of Alexander, and never violated the assurances of peace which he had given him. Porus is represented as having been a man of uncommon stature, great strength, and proportionable dignity. *Plut. in. Alex.—Philostr.* 2. c. 10.—*Curt.* 8. c. 8, &c.—*Claud. Cons. Honor.* 4. v. 375.—*Sidon. Carm.* 2. v. 446. ——A king of Babylon.

POSI'DES, a eunuch and freedman of the emperor Claudius, who rose to honors by the favor of his master. *Juv.* 14. v. 94.

POSIDE'UM or POSID'IUM, a promontory and town of Ionia, where Neptune had a temple. *Strab.* 14. ——A town of Syria near Libanus. *Plin.* 5. c. 20 & 29.——A town near the Strymon, on the borders of Macedonia. *Plin.* 4. c. 10.

POSIDIP'PUS, a comic poet, who flourished three years after the death of Menander. *Suidas* enumerates 30 of his plays. *Lil. Girald.—Voss. H. Gr.* 3. p. 407. [There are many statues of Posidippus, and among them one very fine in the Museum at Naples.]——A writer who composed a book on Cnidus. He is mentioned by *Clemens, Tzetzes Chil.* 7. *Hist.* 144, and *Arnobius.* Some of his epigrams are preserved in the Anthologia *Athen.—Stobæus,* &c.

POSI'DON, a name of Neptune among the Greeks, about the derivation of which the moderns are greatly divided. Some form it from ποὺς, σείω and γῆ, because the divinity shook the earth; others from πολλὰ εἰδων, because the God sees many things; and others from πόσις, because Neptune is the god of water. But it is with greater probability derived from the Punic word *Pesitan,* which signifies *latus* or *expansus,* and is with great propriety applied to the ocean. *Gyrald, H. D.* 4.—*Phurnut. de N. D.* 3.—*Fulgent. Myth,* 1. c. 3.—*Heraclid. Pont. Alleg.—Bochart. Phaleg.* 1. c. 1.—*Herodot. in Euterpe.*

POSIDO'NIA, a town of Lucania, better known by the name of Pæstum. *Vid* Pæstum.

POSIDO'NIUM or POSID'IUM, a town or temple of Neptune, near Cænis in Italy, where the straits of Sicily are narrowest, and scarcely a mile distant from the opposite shore.

POSIDO'NIUS, a philosopher of Apamea. He lived at Rhodes for some time, and afterwards came to Rome, where, after cultivating the friendship of Pompey and Cicero, he died in his 84th year. He wrote a treatise on the nature of the gods, and also attempted to measure the circumference of the earth; he accounted for the tides from the motion of the moon, and calulated the height of the atmosphere at 400 stadia. *Cic. Tusc.* 2. c. 25. l. 5. c. 37. *De N. D.* 1. c. *ult. Att.* 2. c. 1. *Off.* 3. c. 2.—*Lactant.* 2. c. 34.—*Plut. in Pomp.—Strab.* 14, [The most authentic bust of Posidonius is in the Farnese collection at Naples. There is also a statue which goes by his name, in the Borghese collection, now at Paris.]——A philosopher, born at Alexandria in Ægypt.——An Ephesian sculptor, mentioned by *Pliny,* 33. c. 12.

POS'SIS, a native of Magnesia, who wrote a history of the Amazons. *Athen.* l. 7 & 12.

POSTHU'MIA, a vestal virgin, accused of adultery and acquitted. *Volaterr. ex Plut.*——The wife of Servius Sulpicius. *Cic.* ep. 4.——A daughter of Sylla.

POSTHU'MIUS ALBI'NUS, a man who suffered himself to be bribed by Jugurtha, against whom he had been sent with an army. *Sallust. Jug.* 36.

POSTHU'MIUS, a writer at Rome, whom Cato ridiculed for composing a history in Greek, and afterwards offering apologies for the inaccuracy and inelegance of his expressions.——A general who defeated the Sabines, and who was the first who obtained an ovation.——A man poisoned by his wife.——A soothsayer in the age of Sylla. *Plut. in Syll.*——A man who married Lælia Galla, whom he left, to accompany Tiberius in his expedition into Armenia. *Propertius* had dedicated the 11th elegy of his third book to him. ——A Roman to whom *Horace* inscribed the 14th ode of his third book.

POSTHU'MIUS TU'BERO, a master of the horse to the dictator Æmilius Mamercus. He was himself made dictator in the war which the Romans waged against the Volsci, and punished his son with death for fighting against his orders, A.U.C. 312. *Liv.* 4. c. 23, &c.

POSTHU'MIUS SPU'RIUS, a consul sent against the Samnites. He was taken in an ambush by Pontus the enemy's general, and obliged to pass under the yoke with all his army. He saved his life by a shameful treaty, and, when he returned to Rome, persuaded the Romans not to reckon as valid the engagements he had made with the enemy, as it was without their advice. He was given up to the enemy because he could not perform his engagements; but he was released by Pontius for his generous and patriotic behaviour. ——An enemy of Tib. Gracchus.

POSTHU'MIUS AU'LUS, a dictator who defeated the Latins and the Volsci. *Liv.* 2. c. 19 & 20.

POSTHU'MIUS TUBER'TUS, another dictator who defeated the Æqui and the Volsci. *Cœl. Rhod. ex Liv.* 2. c. 19.

POSTHU'MIUS LU'CIUS, a consul sent against the Samnites.——A Roman consul, who was defeated by the Boii. He was left among the slain. and his head was cut off from his body, and carried in triumph by the barbarians into their temple, where they made with the skull a sacred vessel to offer libations to their gods. *Liv.* l. 22.

POSTHU'MIUS REGILLEN'SIS, a general who conquered the Æqui, and was stoned to death by the army, because he refused to divide the promised spoils. *Liv.* 4. c. 49 & 50.—*Flor.* 22.

POSTHU'MIUS MAR'CUS CAS'SIUS LATIE'NUS, an officer proclaimed emperor in Gaul, A.D 260. He reigned with great popularity, and gained the affection of his subjects by his humanity and moderation. He took his son of the same name as a colleague on the throne. They were both assassinated by their soldiers, after a reign of six years. *Trebell. Pollio in Gallien.* c. 4.

POSTHU'MIUS MEGIL'THUS, a consul sent against the Samnites and Tarentines.

POSTHU'MIUS QUIN'TUS, a man put to death by Antony.

POSTHU'MIUS AL'BUS, a Roman Decemvir, sent to Athens to collect the most salutary laws of Solon, &c. *Liv.* 3. c. 31.

POST'HUMUS RA'BIR, a Roman knight who assisted Gabinius in reseating Pompey on the Ægyptian throne. He was, when accused, ably defended by Cicero.

POST'HUMUS SYL'VIUS, a son of Æneas and Sylvia.

POSTU'MIA VI'A, a Roman road about the town of Hostilia. *Tac. Hist.* 3. c. 21.

POSTU'MIUS. *Vid.* Posthumius.

POSTVER'TA, a goddess at Rome, who presided over the painful travails of women. Some suppose her to have been one of Carmente's attendants, who was acquainted with futurity, but others imagine that it is only a surname of Juno, who was invoked to grant an easy, quick, and safe birth to children. *Ovid. Fast.* 1. v. 633.—*Aul. Gell.* 16. c. 16.—*Servius in Æn.* 8. v. 336.—*Macrob.* 1. c. 7.

POTAM'IDES, nymphs who presided over rivers and fountains, as their name (πόταμὸς, *fluvius*) implies.

POT'AMON, a philosopher of Alexandria, in the age of Augustus. He wrote several treatises, and confined himself to the doctrines of no particular sect of philosophers. *Diog. Laert. in Præf. Phil.*

cit.—Suidas.—Voss. de Sect. Phil. c. 21.——A rhetorician of Lesbus or Mitylene, son of Lesbonax. He flourished in the age of Tiberius, and left several works. *Strab.* 13.—*Hesych.—Voss. H. Gr.* 2. c. 7.—*Gesner in Biblioth.*

POTAMOS'ACUM, a river and island of Æolis. *Stephanus* calls it Sacon.

POT'AMUS, a town of Attica, near Sunium. *Strab.* 9.—*Plin.* 4. c. 7.

POTEN'TIA, a town of Picenum on the shores of the Adriatic. *Liv.* 39. c. 44. It is now S. Maria di Loretto.——An inland town of Lucania. *Ptol.* It is now Potenza.

POTHE'REUS, a river of Crete, flowing between Gnossus and Gortyna. *Vitruv.*

POTHI'NUS, a eunuch, tutor to Ptolemy, king of Ægypt. He advised the monarch to murder Pompey, when he claimed his protection after the battle of Pharsalia. He stirred up commotions in Alexandria, when Cæsar came there, upon which the conqueror ordered him to be put to death. *Lucan.* 8. v. 483. l. 10. v. 95.

PO'THOS, one of the deities of the Samothracians. He had a statue made by Cephissodorus, son of Praxiteles. *Plin.* 36. c. 5.

POTIC'ARA, a city of Persia. *Ptol.*

POTIDÆ'A, a town of Macedonia, situate in the peninsula of Pallene. It was founded by a Corinthian colony, and became tributary to the Athenians, from whom Philip of Macedonia took it. The conqueror gave it to the Olynthians, to render them more attached to his interest. Cassander repaired and enlarged the town and called it Cassandria, a name which it still preserves, and which has given occasion to Livy to say, that Cassander was the original founder of that city. *Liv.* 44. c. 11.—*Demosth. Olymp.—Strab.* 7.—*Paus.* 5. c. 23.—*Mela,* 2. c. 2.

POTIDA'NIA, a town of Ætolia. *Liv.* 28. c. 8.

POTI'NA or POT'UA, a goddess at Rome, who presided over children's potions. *Varro apud Nonium.* 2. No. 310.—*Aug. de Civ. D.* 4. c. 8.—*Arnob.* 3.

POTIT'IUS. *Vid.* Pinarius.

POT'NIÆ, a town of Bœotia, where Bacchus had a temple. The Potnians, having once murdered the priest of the god, were ordered by the oracle, to appease his resentment, yearly to offer on his altars a young man. This unnatural sacrifice was continued for some years, till Bacchus himself substituted a goat, from which circumstance he received the appellations of *Ægobolus* and *Ægophagus.* There was here a fountain the waters of which were said to make horses run mad as soon as they were touched. There were also here certain goddesses called Potniades, on whose altars, in a grove, sacred to Ceres and Proserpine, victims were sacrificed. It was also usual, at a certain season of the year, to conduct into the grove young pigs, which were found the following year in the groves of Dodona. The mares of Potnia destroyed their master Glaucus, son of Sisyphus. *Vid.* Glaucus. *Paus.* 9. c. 8.—*Virg. G.* 3. v. 267. *& Servius, ib.—Ælian. V. H.* 15. c. 25.——A town of Magnesia, the pastures of which caused madness in asses, according to *Pliny,* 25. c. 8.

POTULATEN'SII, a people of Dacia. *Ptol.*

PRAC'NUS, a city of Illyria. *Steph.*

PRAC'TIUM, a town and small river of Asia Minor, on the Hellespont. *Hom. Il.* 2. v. 835.

PRÆ'CIA, a courtezan at Rome, who influenced Cethegus, and procured Asia as a consular province for Lucullus. *Plut. in Luc.*

PRÆNES'TE, a town of Latium, about 21 miles north-east from Rome, built by Telegonus, son of Ulysses and Circe, or according to others by Cæculus the son of Vulcan. There was a celerbated temple ofFortune there, with two famous images, as also an oracle, which was long in great repute. The answers were given by lots, which were said to have been discovered in a rock by Numerius Suffucius, a native of the town, whom repeated dreams had directed to the inquiry and to the spot. These lots were small pieces of wood, on which the predictions were written in ancient characters, and were preserved in an olive chest, whence, when the oracle was consulted, one of them was drawn out and considered the answer. *Cic. de Div.* 2. c. 41.—*Virg. Æn.* 7. v. 680. *& Servius loco.—Horat.* 3. od. 4.—*Stat.* 1. *Sylv.* 3. v. 80.

PRÆ'SOS, a small town of Crete, destroyed in a civil war by one of the neighbouring cities.

PRÆS'TI, a nation of India. *Curt.* 9. c. 8.

PRÆ'TOR, one of the chief magistrates at Rome. The office of Prætor was first instituted A.U.C. 388, by the senators, who wished by some new honor to compensate for the loss of the consulship, of which the plebeians had claimed a share. The prætor received his name *a præeundo.* Only one was originally elected, and another A.U.C. 501. One of them was totally employed in administering justice among the citizens, whence he was called Prætor *urbanus,* and the other appointed judges in all causes which related to foreigners. In the year of Rome 520, two more prætors were created to assist the consul in the government of the provinces of Sicily and Sardinia, which had been lately conquered, and two more when Spain was reduced into the form of a Roman province, A.U.C. 551. Sylla the dictator added two more, and Julius Cæsar increased the number to 10, and afterwards to 16, and the second triumvirate to 64. After this their numbers fluctuated, being sometimes 18, 16, or 12, till, in the decline of the empire, their dignity decreased, and their number was reduced to three. The prætor administered justice, protected the rights of widows and orphans, presided at the celebration of public festivals, and, in the absence of the consul, assembled or prorogued the senate as he pleased. He also exhibited shows to the people, and in the festivals of the Bona Dea, where no males were permitted to appear, his wife presided over the rest of the Roman matrons. Feasts were announced and proclaimed by him, and he had the power to make and repeal laws, if it met with the approbation of the senate and people. The quæstors were subject to him, and in the absence of the consuls, he appeared at the head of the armies, and in the city he kept a register of all the freedmen of Rome, with the reasons for which they had received their freedom. In the provinces the prætors appeared with great pomp, six lictors with the fasces walked before them, and when the empire was increased by conquest, they divided like the consuls their government, and provinces were given them by lot. When the year of their prætorship was elapsed, they were called proprætors, if they still continued at the head of their province. At Rome, the prætors appeared also with much pomp, two lictors preceded them, they wore the *prætexta,* or the white robe with purple borders, they sat in curule chairs, and their tribunal was distinguished by a sword and a spear, while they administered justice. The tribunal was called *prætorium.* When they rode, they appeared on white horses as a mark of distinction. The prætor who appointed judges to try foreign causes, was called *prætor peregrinus.* The *prætores Cereales,* appointed by Julius Cæsar, were employed in providing corn and provisions for the city. They were on that account often called *frumentarii.*

PRÆTO'RIA, a town of Dacia at the north of the Danube, now Cronstadt.——A town, now Aoust. in Piedmont.

PRÆTO'RIUS, a name ironically applied to As. Sempronius Rufus, because he was disappointed in his solicitations for the prætorship, as being too dissolute and luxurious in his manners. He was the first who had a stork brought to his table. *Horat.* 2. sat. 2. v. 50.

PRÆTU'TIUM, a town of Picenum. The inhabitants were called Prætutiani, and occupied the country between the two small rivers called Helvia and Vomanus which fall into the Adriatic. *Ital.* 15. v. 568.—*Liv.* 22. c. 9. l. 27. c. 43.

PRAS, a city of Perrhæbia. *Steph.*

PRAS'IÆ or BRAS'IÆ, a village of Athens, in the tribe Pandionis. *Steph.*

PRASIA'NE, now Verdant, a large island at the mouth of the Indus. *Plin.* 6. c. 20.

PRA'SIAS, a lake between Macedonia and Thrace, where were silver mines. *Herodot.* 5. c. 17.

PRA'SII, a nation of India in Alexander's age. *Curt.* 9. c. 2.

PRA'SON, a promontory near the Red Sea. *Steph. Salmas. ad Solin.* p. 244.

PRASSÆ'BI, a nation of Thesprotia. *Steph.*

PRASTIL'LUS, a city of Macedonia, otherwise Crastillus. *Id.*

PRATEL'LIA LEX, was enacted by Pratellius the tribune, A.U.C. 398, to curb and check the ambitious views of men who were lately advanced in the state. *Liv.* 7. c. 15.—*Rosin. Antiq. Rom.* 8. c. 29.

PRAT'INAS, a Greek poet of Phlius, son of Pyrrhonides, called by some Encomius, and contemporary with Æschylus. He was the first among the Greeks who composed satires, which were represented as farces. Of these 32 were acted, as also 18 of his tragedies, only one of which obtained the poetical prize. Some of his verses are quoted by Athenæus. His son Aristias also excelled in the composition of satire. *Paus.* 2. c. 13.—*Suidas.*—*Athen.* 1. c. 19. l. 9. c. 11. l. 14. c. 2.—*Gyrald. P. H.* 6.—*Fabr. B. Gr.* 1. c. 17.

PRATI'TÆ, a people near the Caspiæ Portæ; they were also called Paredoni. *Plin.* 6. c. 15.

PRAU'SI, a people of Gaul, of whom Brennus was general. *Strab.*

PRAXAG'ORAS, an Athenian writer, who published a history of the kings of his own country. He was then only 19 years old, and three years after, he wrote the life of Constantine the Great. He had also written the life of Alexander. His works have all perished. *Phot. Cod.* 62.—*Voss. H. Gr.* 2. c. 17.

PRAXAS'PES. *Vid.* Prexaspes.

PRAX'IAS, a celebrated statuary of Athens, who was employed by the Delphians to adorn their temple. He made for them the beautiful statues which were seen on the pediment of the temple, representing Diana, Latona, the Muses, Apollo, Bacchus, and the Thyades. *Paus.* 10. c. 18.

PRAXIBU'LUS, an archon at Athens, Olymp. 116. an. 2. *Plin.* 33. c. 7.

PRAXID'AMAS, a famous athlete of Ægina, the first honored with a statue at Olympia. *Paus.* 6. c. 18.

PRAXID'ICE, a goddess among the Greeks, who presided over the execution of enterprizes, and who punished all evil actions. Her attributes and festivals employed the pen of Orpheus, and Menelaus raised her a statue at Sparta after the Trojan war. She was generally represented by a human head separated from the rest of the body. *Orpheus, Arg.* 31 & *Hym.* 28. v. 5.—*Suidas.*—*Hesychius*—*Paus.* 9. c. 33.

PRAX'ILA, a lyric poetess of Sicyon, who flourished about 492 years B.C. She invented a kind of metre which received her name, and which is used by Pindar in his Isthmian odes. From a song which she wrote, the words, *Stolidior Praxilæ Adonide*, became proverbial, because Adonis is there said, on his entrance into the infernal regions, to have been asked what he had left most beautiful on earth, to which he answered, the sun, the moon, cucumbers, and apples, a connection of ideas in itself totally ridiculous. *Athen.* 15. c. 15.—*Eustath. Il.* 2.—*Euseb. Chron.*—*Sch. Aristoph. in Vesp.* 1231.—*Gyrald. P. H.* 3.—*Paus.* 3. c. 13.

PRAX'ILUS, a city of Macedonia. *Steph.*

PRAXI'ON, a person who wrote a history of Megara. *Suidas.*—*Aristoph. Schol.*

PRAXIPH'ANES, a Rhodian, who wrote a learned commentary on the obscure passages of Sophocles. ——An historian. *Diog. in Plat.*

PRAX'IS, a surname of Venus at Megara, where, in a temple near that of Bacchus, she had a beautiful statue of ivory. *Paus.* 1. c. 43.—*Gyrald. H. D.* 13.

PRAXIT'ELES, a famous sculptor of Magna Græcia, who flourished about 324 years B.C. He chiefly worked on Parian marble, on account of its beautiful whiteness. He carried his art to the greatest perfection, and was so happy in copying nature, that his statues seemed to be animated. The most famous of his pieces was a Cupid which he gave to Phryne. This celebrated courtezan, who wished to have the best of all the statues of Praxiteles, and who could not depend upon her own judgment in the choice, alarmed the sculptor, by telling him that his house was on fire. Praxiteles upon this showed his eagerness to save his Cupid from the flames, above all his other pieces; but Phryne restrained his fears, and by discovering her artifice, obtained the favorite statue. The sculptor employed his chisel in making a statue of this beautiful courtezan, which was dedicated in the temple of Delphi, and placed between the statues of Archidamus, king of Sparta, and Philip, king of Macedon. He also made a statue of Venus, at the request of the people of Cos, and gave them their choice of the goddess, either naked or veiled. The former was superior to the other in beauty and perfection, but the inhabitants of Cos preferred the latter. The Cnidians, who did not wish to patronize modesty and decorum with the same eagerness as the people of Cos, bought the naked Venus, and it was so universally esteemed, that it was visited as an object of admiration by travellers from distant countries, and Nicomedes, king of Bithynia, offered the Cnidians to pay an enormous debt under which they labored, if they would give him their favorite statue. This offer was not accepted. The famous Cupid was bought of the Thespians by Caius Cæsar, and carried to Rome, but Claudius restored it to them, and Nero afterwards obtained possession of it. *Paus.* 1. c. 40. l. 8. c. 9.—*Plin.* 7. c. 34 & 36.—*Propert.* 3. el. 7. v. 16.—*Papin.* 4. *Sylv.* 6.

PRAXITH'EA, a daughter of Phrasimus and Diogenea. She married Erechtheus, king of Athens, by whom she had Cecrops, Pandarus, and Metion, and four daughters Procris, Creusa, Chthonia, and Orithyia. *Apollod.* 3. c. 15.—*Servius ad Virg. G.* 4. v. 463.—*Schol. Apoll. Rhod.* 1. v. 212. ——A daughter of Thestius, mother of some children by Hercules. *Apollod.* 2. c. 7.——A daughter of Erechtheus, sacrificed by order of the oracle. *Plut. in Par.*

PRECIA'NUS, a Roman lawyer, intimate with Cicero and Cæsar. *Cic.* 7. *Fam.* 8.

PRE'CIUS or PRE'LIUS, a lake in Tuscany, now Castiglione. *Cic. Mil.* 27.—*Plin.* 3. c. 5.—*Cluv. Ital. Ant.* p. 474.

PRE'MA, a goddess at Rome, supposed to preside over the consummation of marriage. *Aug. de Civ. D.* 6. c. 9.

PRES'BON, a son of Phryxus, father of Clymenus. ——A son of Minyas and Clytodora. *Paus.* 9. c. 34 & 37.—*Sch. Apollon.* 1. v. 185 & 230.

PREU'GENES, a son of Agenor, son of Areus. He was directed by a dream to convey away the statue of Diana Limnatis, from Sparta, when the Dorians became masters of that city, and he carried it to Mesoa. He had a statue erected to him, and received the honors of a hero, with his son Patreus, in the town which Patreus had built in Achaia, and called Patra. *Paus.* 3. c. 2. l. 7. c. 18 & 20.

PREXAS'PES, a Persian, who by order of king Cambyses put Smerdis to death. *Herodot.* 3. c. 30.

PRIÆ'SUS, a city of Crete. *Steph.*

PRIAM'IDES, a patronymic applied to Paris as being son of Priam. It is also given to Hector, Deiphobus, and all the other children of the Trojan monarch. *Ovid. Heroid.*—*Virg. Æn.* 3. v. 295.

PRI'AMUS, the last king of Troy, was son of Laomedon, by Strymo, called Placia by some. When Hercules took the city of Troy, (*vid.* Laomedon), Priam was in the number of his prisoners, but his sister Hesione redeemed him from captivity, and he exchanged his original name of Podarces for that of Priam, which signifies *bought* or *ransomed*. *Vid.* Podarces. He was also placed on his father's throne by Hercules, and employed himself with well directed diligence in repairing, fortifying, and embellishing the city of Troy. He had married, by his father's orders, Arisba, whom he now divorced for Hecuba, the daughter of Dimas, or Cisseus, a neighbouring prince. He had by Hecuba 17 children, according to Cicero, or, according to Homer, 19; the most celebrated of whom were Hector, Paris, Deiphobus, Helenus, Pammon, Polites, Antiphus, Hipponous, Troilus, Creusa, Laodice, Polyxena, and Cassandra. Besides these he had many others by concubines. Their names, according to *Apollodorus*, were Melanippus, Gorgythion, Philæmon, Glaucus, Agathon, Evagoras, Hippothous, Chersidamas, Hippodamas, Mestor, Atas, Doryclus, Dryops, Lycaon, Astygonus, Bias, Evander, Chromius, Telestas, Melius, Cebrion, Laodocus, Idomeneus, Archemachus, Echephron, Hyperion, Ascanius, Arrhetus, Democoon, Dejoptes, Echemon, Clonius, Ægioneus, Hypirochus, Lysithous, Polymedon, Medusa, Lysimache, Medesicaste, and Aristodeme. After he had reigned for some time in the greatest prosperity, Priam expressed a desire to recover his sister Hesione, whom Hercules had carried into Greece, and married to Telamon his friend. To carry this plan into execution, Priam manned a fleet, of which he gave the command to his son Paris, with orders to bring back Hesione. Paris, to whom the goddess of beauty had promised the fairest woman in the world, (*vid.* Paris.) neglected in some measure his father's injunctions, and, as if to make reprisals upon the Greeks, carried away Helen, the wife of Menelaus, king of Sparta, during the absence of her husband. Priam beheld this with satisfaction, and countenanced his son by receiving into his palace the wife of the king of Sparta. This rape kindled the flames of war; all the suitors of Helen, at the request of Menelaus, (*vid.* Menelaus), assembled to revenge the violence offered to his bed, and a fleet, according to some, of 140 ships, under the command of the 69 chiefs who furnished them, set sail for Troy. Priam might have averted the impending blow by the restoration of Helen; but this he refused to do, when the ambassadors of the Greeks came to him, and he immediately raised an army to defend himself. Troy was soon besieged, frequent skirmishes took place, in which the success was various, and the advantages on both sides inconsiderable. The siege was continued for ten successive years, and Priam had the misfortune to see the greatest part of his children massacred by the enemy. Hector, the eldest of these, was the only one to whom the Trojans now looked for protection and support; but he at last fell a sacrifice to his own courage, and was killed by Achilles. Priam severely felt his loss, and, as he loved him with the greatest tenderness, wished to ransom his body which was in the enemy's camp. The gods, according to Homer, interested themselves in favor of the aged Priam. Achilles was prevailed upon by his mother, the goddess Thetis, to restore Hector to Priam, and the king of Troy passed through the Grecian camp conducted by Mercury the messenger of the gods, who with his rod had made him invisible. The meeting of Priam and Achilles was solemn and affecting, the conqueror paid to the Trojan monarch that attention and reverence which were due to his dignity, his years, and his misfortunes, and Priam in a suppliant manner addressed the prince whose favors he claimed, and kissed the hands that had robbed him of the greatest and the best of his children. Achilles was moved by the sorrows of a venerable old man, whose grey hairs presented to his agitated mind the recollection of his own respected sire in his native land, he restored Hector, and consented to a truce of twelve days for the funeral of the fallen hero. Some time after Troy was betrayed into the hands of the Greeks by Antenor and Æneas, and Priam upon this resolved to die in the defence of his country He put on his armour, and advanced to meet the Greeks, but Hecuba by her tears and entreaties detained him near an altar of Jupiter, to which she had fled for protection. While Priam yielded to the prayers of his wife, Polites, one of his sons, fled also to the altar before Neoptolemus, who pursued him with fury. Polites. wounded and overcome, fell dead at the feet of his parents, and the aged father, fired with indignation, vented the most bitter invectives against the Greek who paid no regard to the sanctity of altars and temples, and raising his spear darted it upon him. The spear, hurled by the feeble hand of Priam, touched the buckler of Neoptolemus, and fell to the ground. This irritated the son of Achilles, he seized the grey hair of Priam, and, without compunction or reverence for the sanctity of the place, plunged his dagger into his breast. His head was cut off, and the mutilated body was left among the heaps of slain. *Dictys. Cret.* 1, &c.—*Dares. Phryg.*—*Herodot.* 2. c. 120.—*Paus.* 10. c. 27.—*Homer. Il.* 22, &c.—*Eurip. in Troad.* 135.—*Cic. Tusc.* 1. c. 35.—*Q. Smyrn.* 1. v. 104.—*Virg. Æn.* 2. v. 507, &c.—*Horat.* od. 10. v. 14.—*Hygin.* fab. 110.—*Q. Calaber.* 15. v. 226.—*Tzetzes ad Lyc.* 12 & 32.—*Sch. Theocr.* 15. v. 139.—*Servius ad Virg. Æn.* 2. v. 506.

PRIAN'TES, a people of Thrace. *Plin.* 4. c. 11.—*Solin.* c. 10. *Herodotus* calls them Briantes.

PRIAPA'TIUS, the third king of Parthia, succeeded Arsaces the Second, and reigned fifteen years, leaving two sons Mithridates and Phraates. *Justin.* 41. c. 5. But see the note of *Vossius* on this passage of *Justin*.

PRIAPONNE'SUS, an island in the Sinus Ceramicus. *Plin.* 5. c. 31.

PRIA'PUS, a deity among the ancients, who presided over gardens. He was son of Venus by Mercury or Adonis; or, according to the more received opinion, by Bacchus. The goddess of beauty, who was enamoured of Bacchus, went to meet him as he returned victorious from his Indian expedition, and by him she had Priapus, who was born at Lampsacus. Priapus was so deformed in all his limbs, by means of Juno, who had assisted at the delivery of Venus, that the mother, ashamed to have given birth to such a monster, ordered him to be exposed on the mountains. His life, however, was preserved by shepherds, and he received the name of Priapus. He soon became a favorite of the people of Lampsacus, but he was expelled by the inhabitants on account of the freedom which he took with their wives. This violence was punished by the son of Venus. and, when the Lampsacenians had been afflicted with a disease, Priapus was recalled, and temples erected to his honor. Festivals were also celebrated, and the people, naturally idle and indolent, gave themselves up to every lasciviousness and impurity during the celebration. His worship was also introduced at Rome; but the Romans revered him more as the god of orchards and gardens, than as the patron of licentiousness. A crown painted with different colors was offered to him in the spring, and in the summer a garland of ears of corn. An ass was generally sacrificed to him, because that animal, by its braying, awoke the nymph Lotis, to whom Priapus was going to offer violence. He is generally represented with a human face and the ears of a goat; he holds a stick in his hand, with which he terrifies birds, as also a club to drive away thieves, and a scythe to prune the trees and cut down the corn. He was crowned with the leaves of the vine, and sometimes with laurel or rocket. The last of these plants was sacred to him, and it is said to raise the passions and excite love Priapus is often distinguished by the epithets of *phallus*, *fascinus*, *Ithyphallus*, or *ruber*, or *rubicundus*, which are all expressive of his deformity. *Catull.* ep. 19 & 20.—*Colum.* 2. *De Cult. hort.*—*Horat.* 1. sat. 1.—*Tibull.* 1. el. 1. v. 18.—*Ovid. Fast.* 1. v. 415. l. 6. v. 319.—*Virg. Ecl.* 7. v. 33. *G.* 4. v. 111. *& Servius locis*—*Paus.* 9. c. 31.—*Hygin.* fab. 160.—*Diod.* 1.—*Tzetzes in Lyc.* 830.—*Lactant. de Fals. R.* 21.—*Aug. de Civ. D.* 2. c. 14.—*Plin.* 5. c. 32. l. 19. c. 8.—*Suidas.*—*Sch. Apollon.* 1. v. 932.—*Cœl. Rh.* 7. c. 16. [There is a terminus, a representation of Priapus, in the Villa Albani, near Rome.]

PRIA'PUS, a town of Asia Minor, near Lampsacus, now Caraboa. Priapus was the chief deity of the place, and from him the town received its name, because he had taken refuge there when banished from Lampsacus. *Strab.* 12.—*Plin.* 5. c. 32.—*Mela*, 1. c. 19.——An island near Ephesus. *Plin.* 5, c. 31.

PRIE'NE, a maritime town of Asia Minor at the foot of mount Mycale. one of the twelve independent cities of Ionia. It gave birth to Bias, one of the seven wise men of Greece. It had been built by an Athenian colony. *Paus.* 9. c. 2. l. 8. c. 24.—*Strab.* 12.—*Solin.* 43.—*Auson. de* 7. *Sap.* v. 8.

PRI'MA, a daughter of Romulus and Hersilia.

PRI'MIS or PRIM'MIS, a city of Upper Æthiopia. *Ptol.*—*Plin.* 6. c. 29. It is called Premnis by *Strabo*.

PRINAS'SUS, a city of Caria. *Steph.*

PRINOES'SA, a small island of Epirus, opposite Leucadia. *Plin.* 4. c. 12. It is now Isola di S. Maura.

PRI'ON, a place at Carthage. *Polyb.*——A place of Ephesus. *Strab.*—*Salmas. ad Solin.* p. 808.——A river of Arabia Felix, flowing into the Red Sea. *Ptol.* It is now Prim.——A mountain of the island of Cous. *Plin.* 5. c. 31.

PRI'ON, a prince of the Getæ, an auxiliary of Perses against Æetes. He was slain by Jason. *Val. Flacc.* l. 6. *Argon.* v. 19.

PRISCIA'NUS, a celebrated grammarian at Athens, in the age of the emperor Justinian. He wrote a work *de arte grammaticâ*, addressed to Julian the Consul. He also wrote a book *de naturalibus quæstionibus* addressed to Chosroes, king of Persia, and translated the Periegesis of Dionysius into Latin, besides other works. The first edition of his works was published at Venice 1470; and they may be also found in the "Grammatici Veteres" of Putschius. *Harles. Not. Lit. Rom.* 1. p. 759.—*Sax. Onom.* 2, p. 19.

PRISCIL'LA, a woman praised for her conjugal affection by *Statius*, 5. *Sylv.* 1.

PRIS'CUS SERVIL'IUS, a dictator at Rome who defeated the Veientes and the Fidenates.

Pris'cus, a surname of the elder Tarquin, king of Rome. *Vid.* Tarquinius.——A governor of Syria, brother to the emperor Philip. He proclaimed himself emperor in Macedonia, when he was informed of his brother's death, A.C. 249, but was soon after conquered and put to death by Decius, Philip's murderer. *Aurel. Vict. de Cæs.*——A friend of the emperor Severus.——A friend of the emperor Julian, almost murdered by the populace. ——One of the emperor Adrian's friends.——A friend of Domitian.——An orator, whose dissipated and luxurious manners *Horace* ridicules, 1, sat. 7. v. 9.

Pris'cus Helvid'ius, a quæstor in Achaia during the reign of Nero, remarkable for his independent spirit. *Tacit. Hist.* 4. c. 6.—*Juvenal.*

Pris'cus Ju'lius, an officer under Vitellius. *Tac. Hist.* 3. c. 55.

PRIS'TIS, the name of one of the ships that engaged in the naval combat which was exhibited by Æneas at the anniversary of his father's death. She was commanded by Mnestheus. *Virg. Æn.* 1. v. 116.

PRIVER'NUS, a Rutulian killed by Capys in the wars between Æneas and Turnus. *Virg. Æn.* 9. v. 576.

PRIVER'NUM, now Piperno Vecchio, a town of the Volsci in Italy, the inhabitants of which were called Privernates. Metabus, father of Camilla, was king there, when Æneas came into Italy. It became a Roman colony. *Liv.* 8. c. 10.—*Virg. Æn.* 11. v. 540.—*Val. Max.* 6. c. 2.—*Servius. ad Virg. Æn.* 7. v. 803. l. 11. v. 567.—*Cic.* 1. *Div.* 43.

PROA'NA, a city of Thessaly. *Steph.*

PRO'BA, the wife of the emperor Probus.——A woman who opened the gates of Rome to the Goths. *Vid.* Falconia.

PRO'BUS M. AURE'LIUS VALE'RIUS, a native of Sirmium, in Pannonia. His father was originally a gardener, who by entering the army rose to the rank of a military tribune. His son obtained the same office in the 22d year of his age, and distinguished himself so much by his probity, valor, intrepidity, moderation, and clemency, that, at the death of the emperor Tacitus, he was invested with the imperial purple by the voluntary and uninfluenced choice of his soldiers. His election was universally approved by the Roman senate and the people; and Probus, strengthened on his throne by the affection and attachment of his subjects, marched against the enemies of Rome, in Gaul and Germany. Several battles were fought, and after he had left 400,000 barbarians dead in the field, Probus turned his arms against the Sarmatians. The same success attended him, and after he had quelled and terrified to peace the numerous barbarians of the north, he marched through Syria against the Blemmyes in the neighbourhood of Ægypt. The Blemmyes were defeated with great slaughter, and the military character of the emperor was so well established, that the king of Persia sued for peace by his ambassadors, and attempted to buy the conqueror's favors with the most splendid presents. Probus was feasting upon the most common food when the ambassadors were introduced; but without even casting his eyes upon them, he said, that if their master did not give proper satisfaction to the Romans, he would lay his territories desolate, and as naked as the crown of his head. As he spoke, the emperor took off his cap, and showed the baldness of his head to the ambassadors. His conditions were gladly accepted by the Persian monarch, and Probus returned to Rome to convince his subjects of the greatness of his conquests, and to claim from them the applause which their ancestors had given to the conqueror of Macedonia or the destroyer of Carthage, as he passed along the streets of Rome. His triumph lasted several days, and the Roman populace were long entertained with shows and combats. But the Roman empire, delivered from its foreign enemies, was torn by civil discord, and peace was not re-established till three usurpers had been severally defeated. While his subjects enjoyed tranquillity, Probus encouraged the liberal arts, he permitted the inhabitants of Gaul and Illyricum to plant vines in their territories, and himself repaired 70 cities in different parts of the empire which had been reduced to ruins. He also attempted to drain the stagnant waters in the neighbourhood of Sirmium, by conveying them to the sea by artificial canals. His armies were employed in this laborious undertaking; but as they were unaccustomed to such toils, they soon mutinied, and fell upon the emperor as he was passing into one of the towns of Illyricum. He fled into an iron tower which he himself had built to observe the marshes, but as he was alone and without arms, he was soon overpowered, and murdered in the 50th year of his age, after a reign of six years and four months, on the second of November, B.C. 282. The news of his death was received with the greatest consternation; not only his friends, but his very enemies deplored his fate; and even the army, which had been concerned in his fall, erected a monument over his body, and placed upon it this inscription: *Hic Probus, imperator vere probus, situs est, victor omnium gentium barbararum, victor etiam tyrannorum.* He was then preparing, in a few days, to march against the Persians that had revolted, and his victories there might have been as great as those he obtained in the two other quarters of the globe He was succeeded by Carus, and his family, who had shared his greatness, immediately retired from Rome, not to become objects either of private or public malice. *Zos.*—*Prob.*—*Saturn.*

Pro'bus Æmil'ius, a grammarian in the age of Theodosius. The lives of excellent commanders, written by Cornelius Nepos, have been falsely attributed to him by some authors.

Pro'bus, an oppressive præfect of the prætorian guards, in the reign of Valentinian.

PRO'CAS, a king of Alba, after his father Aventinus. He was father of Amulius and Numitor. *Liv.* 1, c. 3.—*Ovid. Met.* 14. v. 622. *Fast.* 4. v. 52. l. 6. v. 143.—*Aurel. Vict.* 1.—*Virg. Æn.* 6. v. 767.—*Servius in Æn.* 4. v. 276. l. 7. v. 657.

PROCERAS'TIS, a town of Bithynia on the Thracian Bosporus, better known by the name of Chalcedon. *Plin.* 5. c. *ult.*

PROCHARISTE'RIA, a festival annually observed by the Athenian magistrates, in honor of Minerva, when the spring first appeared. *Suidas.*

PROCH'YTA. an island of Campania, in the bay of Puteoli, now Procida. It was situated near Inarima, from which it was said that it had been separated by an earthquake. It received its name, according to Dionysius, from the nurse of Æneas. *Virg. Æn.* 9. v. 715.—*Strab.* 1, 2, 5 & 6.—*Mela*, 2. c. 7.—*Ovid. Met.* 14. v. 89.—*Dionys. Hal.* 1.

PROCIL'LIUS, a Latin historian in the age of Pompey the Great. *Varro L. L.* 4.—*Cic. Att.* 2. c. 2. —*Plin.* 8. c. 2.

PROCIL'LA JU'LIA, a woman of uncommon virtue, killed by the soldiers of Otho. *Tacit. Agric.* 4.

PROCIL'LUS C. VALE'RIUS, a prince of Gaul, intimate with *Cæsar. Com.* 1. c. 19.

Procil'lus, a freedman of Augustus, condemned to death for his incontinence. *Suet. Aug.* 37.—*Plin.* 7. c. 46.

PROCLA'IS, a city of India within the Ganges. *Ptol.*—*Salmas. ad Solin.* p. 992.

PRO'CLE, a city of Lydia. *Steph.*

PROCLE'A, a daughter of Clytius, who married Cycnus, a son of Neptune, by whom she had Tenes and Hemithea. After her death her husband married Philonome, who entertained an illicit passion for Tenes. *Homer. Il.* 15. v. 419. —*Paus.* 10. c. 14.

PRO'CLES, a son of Aristodemus and Argia, born at the same birth as Eurysthenes. There were continual dissensions among the two brothers, who both sat on the Spartan throne. *Vid.* Eurysthenes & Lacedæmon.——A native of Andrus, in the Ægean Sea, son of Lycastidas. He was crowned at the Olympic games. *Dionys. Hal.* 1.—*Paus.* 6. c. 14.——A man descended from Ion, son of Xuthus, who headed the Ionians when they took Samus. *Paus.* 7. c. 4.——A Carthaginian writer, son of Eucrates. He wrote some historical treatises, of which Pausanias has preserved some fragments. *Paus.* 2. c. 2. l. 4. c. 35.——A tyrant of Epidaurus, put to death and thrown into the sea.—*Plut. de Orac.*——A general of the Naxians, in Sicily, who betrayed his country to Dionysius the tyrant, for a sum of money.

PROCLI'DÆ, the descendants of Procles, who sat on the throne of Sparta together with the Eurysthenidæ. *Vid.* Lacedæmon & Eurysthenes.

PRO'CLUS, a patriarch at Constantinople, who wrote homilies, &c., and flourished A.D. 446. *Fabr. B. Gr.* 5. c. 23.——A Platonic philosopher surnamed Diadochus. He left several works, chiefly commentaries on Plato, &c. Some of his verses are preserved in the collection of Greek poets. They consist of hymns on the Sun, the Muses, and Venus. He died at Athens 485, in his 75th year. *Voss. de Sect. Phil.* c. 16.—*Jonsius Script. Hist. Phil.* 3. c. 10.—*Fabr. B. Gr.* 5. c. 21.

PROC'NE. *Vid.* Progne.

PROCONNE'SUS, now Marmora, an island of the Propontis, at the north of the Cyzicus; also called Elaphonnesus and Neuris. It was famous for its fine marble. *Plin.* 5. c. 32.—*Strab.* 13.—*Flacc.* 3. v. 34.—*Vitruv.* 2. c. 8.—*Mela*, 2. c. 7.

PROCO'PIUS, a celebrated officer of a noble family in Cilicia, related to the emperor Julian, with whom he lived in great intimacy. He was universally admired for his integrity, but he was not destitute of ambition or pride. After he had signalized himself under Julian and his successor, he retired from the Roman provinces among the barbarians in the Thracian Chersonesus, and, some time after, suddenly made his appearance at Constantinople, when the emperor Valens had marched into the east, and he there proclaimed himself master of the eastern empire. His usurpation was universally acknowledged, and his victories were so rapid, that Valens would have resigned the imperial purple had not his friends interposed. But now fortune changed, Procopius was defeated in Phrygia, and deserted by his army. His head was cut off, and carried to Valentinian in Gaul, A.D. 366. Procopius was slain in the 42nd year of his age, after he had enjoyed the title of emperor for about eight months. *Ammian. Marcell.* 25 & 26.——A Greek historian of Cæsarea, in Palestine, secretary to the celebrated Belisarius, A.D. 534. He wrote the history of Justinian, and greatly celebrated the hero whose favors and patronage he enjoyed. This history is divided into eight books, two of which gave an account of the Persian war, two of the Vandals, and four of the Goths, to the year 553, which was afterwards continued in five books by Agathias till 559. Of this performance the character is great, though perhaps the historian is often too severe on the emperor. The history of the Gothic war was first published in the fifteenth century, in a Latin translation by Leonard Aretin, who imposed them upon the world as his own original composition. The discovery of other manuscripts unveiled the fraud, and exposed the impostor to merited ignominy. The whole was edited in two volumes, folio, Paris, 1662. *Fabr. B. Gr.* 5. c. 1.—*Sax. Onom.* 2. p. 23.——A rhetorician and sophist of Gaza, who wrote a work called "Catena Patrum," on the first eight books of Scripture, &c. *Fabr. B. Gr.*

PRO'CRIS, a daughter of Erechtheus, king of Athens. She married Cephalus. *Vid.* Cephalus. *Virg. Æn.* 6. v. 445.——A daughter of Thestius. *Apollod.*

PROCRUS'TES, a famous robber of Attica, killed by Theseus, near the Cephisus. He tied travellers on a bed, and, if their length exceeded that of the bed, cut off part of their limbs to make their length equal to that of the bed; but if they were shorter he stretched their bodies till they were of the same length. He is called by some Damastes and Polypemon. *Ovid. Heroid.* 2. v. 69. *Met.* 7. v. 43.—*Plut. in Thes.*

PROC'ULA, a prostitute in *Juvenal's* age.——The wife of Codrus, represented as short. *Juv.* 3. v. 203.

PROCULE'IUS, a Roman knight, very intimate with Augustus, and brother of Terentia, the wife of Mecænas. He is celebrated for his humanity and fraternal kindness to his brothers Muræna and Scipio, with whom he divided his possessions, after they had forfeited their estates, and incurred the displeasure of Augustus for siding with young Pompey. He was sent by Augustus to Cleopatra, to endeavour to bring her alive into his presence, but to no purpose. He destroyed himself when laboring under a heavy disease. His son showed himself very undutiful to him. *Quintil.* 9. c. 3.—*Horat.* 2. od. 2.—*Plut. in Anton.*—*Juv.* 7. v. 95. *Plin.* 36. c. 24.——A debauchee in Nero's reign. *Juv.* 1. v. 40.

PROC'ULUS JU'LIUS, a Roman who, after the death of Romulus, declared that he had seen him in appearance more than human, and that he had ordered him to bid the Romans to offer him sacrificer under the name of Quirinus, and to assure them that Rome was destined by the gods to become the capital of the world. *Plut. in Rom.*—*Liv.* 1. c. 16.—*Cic.* 1 *Leg.* 1.—*Ovid. Fast.*

PROC'ULUS GEGA'NIUS, a Roman consul, A.U.C. 315.

PROC'ULUS PLACIT'IUS, a Roman who conquered the Hernici.

PROC'ULUS, a Greek poet, one of the most learned of the Platonic philosophers of his age. He studied under Plutarch of Athens, and wrote several works, some of which are preserved, and generally placed with the poems af Orpheus, and among the commentaries on Hesiod and Plato. *Suidas.*—*Gyrald. de P.H.* 3.——A friend of Vitellius.——A consul under Nerva.——A man accused of extortion.——An African in the age of Aurelius. He published a book entitled *de regionibus* or *religionibus*, on foreign countries, &c.——An officer who proclaimed himself emperor in Gaul, in the reign of Probus. He was soon after defeated and exposed on a gibbet. He was very debauched and licentious in his manners, and had acquired riches by piratical excursions. *Vopisc. in Proculo.* c. 12 & 13.

PROCU'RI, a city of Taprobane. *Ptol.*

PRO'CYON, a star near Sirius, or the dog Star, before which it generally rises in July. Cicero calls it *Anticanis*, which is of the same signification (πρὸ κυνῶν.) *Horat.* 3. od. 29. v. 18.—*Plin.* 18. c. 28.—*Cic. de Nat. D.* 2. c. 44.

PROD'ICUS, a sophist and rhetorician of Cos, who flourished about 396. B.C. He was sent by his countrymen as ambassador to Athens, where he publicly taught, and had among his pupils Euripides, Socrates, Theramenes, and Isocrates. He travelled from town to town in Greece, to procure admirers and get money. He made his auditors pay to hear him harangue, which has given occasion to some of the ancients to speak of the orations of Prodicus, for fifty drachmas. In his writings, which were numerous, he composed a beautiful episode, in which virtue and pleasure were introduced, as attempting to make Hercules one of their votaries. The hero at last yielded to the charms of virtue, and rejected pleasure. This has been imitated by Lucian. Prodicus was at last put to death by the Athenians, on pretence that he corrupted the morals of their youth. *Cic. N.D.* 1. c. 42, *Off.* 1. c. 32.—*Orat.* 3. c. 22.—*Laert.* 9. c. 50.—*Xenoph. Memor.*——A physician, pupil of Æsculapius. *Plin.* 29. c. 1.——An epic poet of Phocis. *Paus. in Phoc.*—*Suid.*

PROER'NA, a town of Phthiotis, near the Sinus Maliacus. *Liv.* 63. c. 14.—*Strab.* 9.

PROERO'SIA or PRERO'SIA, a surname of Ceres. Her festivals, celebrated at Athens and Eleusis before the sowing of the corn, bore the same name. *Meurs. de Myst. El.*—*Hesych.*—*Suid.*—*Aristoph. Schol. Equit.*

PRŒT'IDES, the daughters of Prœtus, king of Argolis, were three in number, Lysippe, Iphinoe, and Iphianassa. They became insane for neglecting the worship of Bacchus, or, according to others, for preferring themselves to Juno, and they ran about the fields believing themselves to be cows, and fearful lest they should be harnessed to the plough or to the chariot. Prœtus applied to Melampus to cure his daughters of their insanity, but he refused to employ him when he demanded a third part of his kingdom as a reward. This neglect of Prœtus was punished, the insanity became contagious, and the monarch at last promised Melampus two parts of his kingdom and one of his daughters, if he would restore them and the Argian women to their senses. Melampus consented, and, after he had wrought the cure, married the most beautiful of the Prœtides. Some have called them Lysippe, Ipponoe, and Cyrianassa. *Apollod.* 2. c. 2.—*Virg. Ecl.* 6. v. 48.—*Servius. loco. & G.* 3. v. 550.—*Ovid. Met.* 15.—*Lactant. ad Stat. Theb.* 1. v. 670. l. 3. v. 453.

PRŒ'TUS, a king of Argos, son of Abas and Ocalea. He was twin brother to Acrisius, with whom he quarrelled even before their birth. This dissension between the brothers increased with their years. After their father's death, they both tried to obtain the kingdom of Argos; but the claims of Acrisius prevailed, and Prœtus left Peloponnesus, and retired to the court of Jobates, king of of Lycia, where he married Stenobœa, called by some Antea or Antiope. He afterwards returned to Argolis, and, by means of his father-in-law, made himself master of Tyrinthus. Stenobœa had accompanied her husband to Greece, and became by him mother of the Prœtides, and of a son called Megapenthes, who, after his father's death, succeeded to the throne of Tiryntbus. *Vid.* Stenobœa. *Homer. Il.* 6. v. 160.—*Lactant. ad Theb.* 1. v. 670.—*Servius. Ecl. Virg.* 6. v. 48.—*Apollod.* 2. c. 2.

PROGA'SIA, a town of Lydia. *Steph.*

PROG'NE, a daughter of Pandion, king of Athens, by Zeuxippe. She married Tereus, king of Thrace, by whom she had a son called Itylus, or Itys. *Vid.* Philomela.

PROG'NE, a small island of Asia, near Rhodes. *Plin.* 5. c. 31.

PROLA'US, a native of Elis, father of Philanthus and Lampus, by Lysippe. These two youths went to Corinth to enter the lists of wrestling at the Isthmian games, but were strangled by their antagonists before they appeared on the arena, upon which their mother uttered a dreadful curse against such of her fellow-citizens as attended the celebration. The dread of being exposed to the curse prevented the people of Elis from afterwards appearing at the Isthmian games. *Paus.* 5. c. 2.

PROLO'GIA, a festival celebrated by the people of Laconia, before they gathered their fruits. *Hesychius.*

PROMA'CHIA, a festival in which the Lacedæmonians crowned themselves with reeds. *Athen.* l. 15.

PROM'ACHUS, one of the Epigoni, son of Parthenopæus. He was honored with a statue, which was still to be seen at Argos in the age of Pausanias. He had also another at Delphi. *Lactant. ad Theb.* 4. v. 309.—*Apollod.* 1 & 3.—*Paus.* 2. c. 20. l. 10. c. 10.——A son of Psophis, daughter of Eryx, king of Sicily. *Paus.* 8. c. 34.——An athlete of Pallene, son of Dyon. He was honored in his lifetime with several statues for obtaining the prize in the pancratiastic exercise three times at the Isthmian games, twice at the Nemean, and once at Olympia. *Paus.* 6. c. 8. l. 7. c. *ult.*——A son of Æson, killed by Pelias. *Apollod.*

PROMATH'IDES, an historian of Heraclea. *Athen.* 7.—*Voss. H. Gr.* p. 408.

PROMA'THION, a man who wrote a history of Italy. *Plut. in Rom.*—*Voss. ibid.*

PROM'EDON, a native of the island of Naxus, who went to Miletus to see his friend Hypsicreon, whose bed he defiled by yielding to the strong and repeated solicita ions of his wife Neæra during her husband's absence. *Theophr. apud Parthen. erot.* 18.

PROMENE'A, one of the priestesses of the temple of Dodona. It was from her that Herodotus received the tradition that two doves had flown from Thebes in Ægypt, one to Dodona, and the other to the temple of Jupiter Ammon, where they gave oracles. *Herodot.* 2. c. 55.

PROMETHE'A, a festival celebrated at Athens, in honor of Prometheus. *Aristoph. Schol. Ran.*

PROMETHEI JU'GUM or AN'TRUM, a place on the top of mount Caucasus, in Albania. *Propert.* l. el. 12. v. 10.

PROMETHEUS, a son of Iapetus by Clymene, one of the Oceanides. He was brother to Atlas, Menœtius, and Epimetheus, and surpassed all mankind in cunning and fraud. He ridiculed the gods, and deceived Jupiter himself. He sacrificed two bulls, and filled their skins, one with the flesh and the other with the bones, and asked the father of the gods which he preferred as an offering. Jupiter became the dupe of his artifice, and chose the bones, and from that time the priests of the temple were ever after ordered to burn the whole victims on the altars, the flesh and the bones altogether. To punish Prometheus and the rest of mankind, Jupiter took fire away from the earth, but the son of Iapetus outwitted the father of the gods. He climbed the heavens by the assistance of Minerva, and stole fire from the chariot of the sun, which he brought down at the end of a ferula. This provoked Jupiter the more; he ordered Vulcan to make a woman of clay, and after he had given her life, sent her to Prometheus, with a box of the richest and most valuable presents which she had received from the gods. *Vid.* Pandora. Prometheus, who suspected Jupiter, took no notice of Pandora or her box, but made his brother Epimetheus marry her; and the god, now more irritated, ordered Mercury, or Vulcan, according to Æschylus, to carry this artful mortal to mount Caucasus, and there tie him to a rock, where for 30,000 years a vulture was to feed upon his liver, which was never diminished though continually devoured. He was delivered from this painful confinement about 30 years afterwards by Hercules, who killed the bird of prey. The vulture, or according to others, the eagle which devoured the liver of Prometheus, was born from Typhon and Echidna. According to Apollodorus, Prometheus made the first man and woman that ever were upon the earth, with clay, which he animated by means of the fire which he had stolen from heaven. On this account therefore the Athenians raised him an altar in the groves of Academus, where they yearly celebrated games in his honor. During these games there was a race, and he who carried a burning torch in his hand without extinguishing it, obtained the prize. Prometheus, as it is universally credited, had received the gift of prophecy, and all the gods, and even Jupiter himself, consulted him as a most infallible oracle. To him mankind are indebted for the invention of many of the useful arts; he taught them the use of plants, with their medicinal powers, and from him they received the knowledge of taming horses and different animals, either to cultivate the ground, or for the purpose of luxury. He is generally represented tied to the rock, and at the moment that Hercules killed the bird that preyed on his vitals. *Propert,* 3. el. 3. v. 29.—*Hesiod. Theog.* 510 & 550.—*Apollod.* 1 & 2.—*Paus.* 1, c. 30. l. 5. c. 11.—*Hygin.* fab. 144.—*Æschyl. in Prom.*—*Virg. Ecl.* 6. v. 42..—*Ovid. Met,* 1. v. 82.—*Horat.* 1.od. 3.—*Seneca in Med.* v. 823.—*Sch. Æsch. in Prom.* 1021.—*Sch. Apollon. Rh.* 1253.—*Tertull. Apol.* 18.

PROMETHIS or PROMETHI'DES, a patronymic applied to the children of Prometheus, as to Deucalion, &c. *Ovid. Met.* 10. v. 390.

PROME'THUS and DAMASICH'THON, two sons of Codrus, who conducted colonies into Asia Minor. Here a misunderstanding arose, and Prometheus killed Damasichthon, and fled to Naxus, where he died. His body was brought back to Ionia, where the son of Damasichthon honored it with a funeral and a monument. *Paus.* 1. c. 3.

PROM'ONA, a city of Liburnia. *Appian.* There is a mountain now called Promina, on which the town stood, and on which there are still some remains of the ancient city.

PROM'ULUS, a Trojan killed by Turnus. *Virg. Æn.* 9. v. 574.

PRONAP'IDES, an ancient Greek poet of Athens, who was, according to some, preceptor to Homer. It is said, that he first taught the Greeks how to write from the left to the right, contrary to the custom of writing from the right to the left, which is still observed by some of the eastern nations.

Diod. 3.—*Joh. Marsham. Can. Chron. Sec.* 15. *de Hesiodo.*

PRONAS'TÆ, an ancient people of Bœotia. *Steph.*

PRO'NAX, a brother of Adrastus king of Argos, son of Talaus and Lysimache. He was father of Lycurgus, one of the Epigoni. *Apollod.* 1.—*Paus.* 3. c. 18.—*Tzetzes ad Lyc.* 439.

PRON'OE, a daughter of Phorbus, mother of Pleuron and Calydon, by Ætolus. *Apollod.* 1.

PRON'OMUS, a Theban who played so skilfully on the flute, that the invention of that musical instrument is attributed to him. Before his time separate flutes were requisite to play the three musical airs then most admired, the Dorian, Phrygian, and Lydian, but that which he invented could be accommodated with the greatest facility to all. A statue was raised to his honor by the Thebans, and his merits were considered so great that it was placed by the side of that of Epaminondas. *Paus.* 9. c. 12.—*Athen.* 14. c. 7.

PRON'OUS, a son of Phlegeas, killed by the sons of Alcmæon. *Apollod.* 3.

PRON'UBA, a surname of Juno, because she presided over marriages. *Virg. Æn.* 4. v. 166.

PROP'ALÆ, a city of Sicily. *Steph.*

PROPER'TIUS SEX'TUS AURE'LIUS, a Latin poet, was born in Umbria; and though Mevania is more generally supposed to have been the place of his birth, yet four other cities of Umbria have disputed the honor of it; Hespillus, Ameria, Perusia, and Assisium. His father was a Roman knight, whom Augustus proscribed, because he had followed the interest of Antony. He came to Rome, where his genius and poetical talents soon recommended him to the notice of the great and powerful. Mecænas, Gallus, and Virgil became his friends, and Augustus his patron. Mecænas wished him to attempt an epic poem; of which he proposed the emperor for hero; but Propertius refused, observing that his abilities were unequal to the task. He died about 19 years B.C. in the 40th year of his age. His works consist of four books of elegies, which are written with so much spirit, vivacity, and energy, that many authors call him the prince of the elegiac poets among the Latins. He may justly be considered as inferior to Tibullus in tenderness, and to Ovid in variety of imagination and facility of expression, yet he may claim the palm of greater correctness, of more art, and of superior learning. His poetry, though elegant, is not, however, free from faults, and the many lascivious expressions which he uses, deservedly expose him to censure. Cynthia, who is the heroine of all his elegies, was a Roman lady, whose real name was Hostia, or Hostilia, of whom the poet was deeply enamoured. The best editions are that of Santenius, 4to, Traj ad Rh. 1780, and that of Barthius, Leips. 1777; and when published together with Catullus and Tibullus, those of Grævius, 8vo. Utr, 1680, of Vulpius, 4 vols, Patavii, 1737, 1749, 1755, and the edition of Barbou, 12mo, Paris, 1754. *Harles. Not. Lit. Rom.* 1. p. 227.—*Sax. Onom.* 1. p. 184.—*Ovid. Trist.* 2. v. 465. 1. 4. el. 10. v. 53. *de Art. Am.* 3. v. 333.—*Martial.* 8. epigr. 73. 1. 14. epipr. 189.—*Quintil.* 10 c. 1.—*Plin.* 6. ep. 1. 9. ep. 22.—*Stat.* 1. *Sylv.* 2. v. 247.—*Lactant. de Div. Ins.* 2, c. 6.—*Gyrald. de P. H.* 4.—*Turneb. Adv.* 8. c. 2. 1. 11. c. 15.

PROPER'TIUS CE'LER, a prætorian under Tiberius. *Tac. Ann.* 1. c. 75.

PROPHTHA'SIA, a city of Drangiana. *Steph.*—*Plin.* 6. c. 17.

PROPH'YTUS, a tyrant of Pygela in Ionia. *Polyæn.* 7. c. 23. Some, however, read Phytus.

PROPŒT'IDES, some women of Cyprus, severely punished by Venus, whose divinity they had despised. They sent their daughters to the sea shore, where they prostituted themselves to strangers. The poets have feigned, that they were changed into stones, on account of their insensibility to every virtuous sentiment. *Justin.* 18. c. 5.—*Ovid. Met.* 10. v. 238. *& Lactant. Ib.*

PROPON'TIS, a sea between Europe and Asia, which has a communication with the Euxine, by the Thracian Bosporus, and with the Ægæan by the Hellespont. It is now called the Sea of Marmora, and is about 175 miles long and 62 broad. It received its name from its vicinity to Pontus. *Mela*, 1. c 19.—*Strab.* 2.—*Ovid.* 1. *Trist.* 9. v. 29. *Lucan.* 9. v. 960.—*Val. Flacc.* 2. v. 646.—*Apollod.* 1.—*Propert.* 3. el. 22.

PROPYLE'A, a surname of Diana. She had a temple at Eleusis in Attica. *Paus.* 1. c. 38.

PRO'SA or PROR'SA, a deity at Rome invoked by pregnant women, that she might grant an easy position to the child, and a safe delivery. *Aul. Gel.* 16. c. 16.—*Servius ad Æn.* 8. v. 326.—*Gyrald. H. D.* 1.

PROSAC'TIUM, a river flowing from the Idæan mountains, and falling into the sea between the Hellespont and the Euxine. *Arrian.* 1. 1.

PROSCHÆRETE'RIA, a day of rejoicing when a new married wife went to the house of her husband. *Suidas.*—*Harpocration.*

PROS'CHIUM, a town of Ætolia. *Strab.*

PROSCLYS'TIUS, a surname of Neptune, among the Greeks, because he was prevailed upon by the entreaties of Juno not to oblige the rivers of Argolis to inundate the country, as he threatened to do, in consequence of the superiority over the province which they had adjudged to the goddess in opposition to himself. A temple was raised to the god on the spot where the waters had retired to their bed, by the name of Prosclystius, expressive of the subsiding of the streams. *Paus.* 2. c. 22.

PROSELE'NE, a city of Phrygia Minor. *Ptol.* It is now S. Anania.

PROSER'PINA, a daughter of Ceres by Jupiter, called by the Greeks *Persephone.* She was so beautiful, that the father of the gods himself became enamoured of her, and deceived her by changing himself into a serpent, and folding her in his wreaths. Proserpine made Sicily the place of her residence, and delighted herself with the beautiful views, flowery meadows, and limpid streams, which surrounded the plains of Enna. In this solitary retreat, as she amused herself with her female attendants in gathering flowers, Pluto carried her away into the infernal regions, of which she became the queen. *Vid.* Pluto. Ceres was so disconsolate at the loss of her daughter, that she travelled all over the world, but her inquiries were in vain, and she never would have discovered whither she had been carried, had she not found the girdle of Proserpine on the surface of the waters of the fountain Cyane, near which the ravisher, by striking the earth with his trident, had opened to himself a passage to his kingdom. Ceres soon learned from the nymph Arethusa that her daughter had been carried away by Pluto; she immediately repaired to Jupiter, and demanded of him to punish the ravisher. Jupiter in vain attempted to persuade the mother that Pluto was not unworthy of her daughter, and when he saw that she was inflexible, he said that she might return on earth, if she had not taken any aliments in the infernal regions. Her return, however, was impossible; Proserpine, as she walked in the Elysian fields, had gathered a pomegranate from a tree and eaten it, and Ascalaphus, who was the only one who saw it, was, for discovering the circumstance, instantly turned into an owl. Jupiter, to appease the resentment of Ceres, and soothe her grief, consented that Proserpine should remain six months with Pluto in the infernal regions, and should spend the rest of the year with her mother on earth. As queen of hell, and wife of Pluto, Proserpine presided over the death of mankind, and, acccording to the opinion of the ancients, no one could die, if the goddess herself, or Atropos her minister, did not cut off one of the hairs from the head. From this superstitious belief, it was usual to cut off some of the hair of the deceased, and to strew it at the door of the house, as an offering to Proserpine. The Sicilians were very particular in their worship of Proserpine, and, as they believed that the fountain Cyane had risen from the earth at the very place where Pluto had opened himself a passage, they annually sacrificed there a bull, the blood of which they suffered to run into the water. Proserpine was universally worshipped by the ancients, and was known by the different names of *Core, Theogamia, Libitina, Hecate, Juno inferna, Anthesphoria, Azesia, Chthonia, Cotyto, Deois, Libera, &c. Plut. in Luc.*—*Paus.* 8. c. 27. 1. 9 c. 31.—*Ovid. Met.* 5. fab. 6. *Fast.* 4. v. 417.—*Virg. Æn.* 4. v. 698. 1. 6. v. 138.—*Strab.* 7.—*Diod.*

5.—*Cic. in Verr.* 4.—*Hygin.* fab. 146.—*Hesiod. Theog.* 911.—*Apollod.* 1. c. 3.—*Orpheus, Hymn.* 28.—*Claudian. de Rapt. Pros.*—*Eurip. in Alc.*—*Arnob.* 5.—*Sch. Soph. ad Col.* 674.—*Lactant. in Theb.* 5. v, 357.—*Servius ad Virg. loc. cit.* [There is a statue of Proserpine in the Villa Albani, near Rome.]

PROSODI'TÆ, a people of Marmarica. *Ptol.*

PROSOPI'TIS, an island in one of the mouths of the Nile. *Herodot.* 2. c. 4.

PROSO'PUM, an island of Africa, opposite Carthage. *Steph.*

PROSPALE'A, a village of the tribe Acmantis. *Steph.*

PROS'PER, one of the fathers who died A.D. 466. His works have been edited by Mangeant, fol. Paris, 1711.

PROSTROPÆ'A, a city of Sicily. *Steph.*

PROSYM'NA, a part of Argolis, where Juno was worshipped. It received its name from a nymph of the same name, daughter of Atserion, who nursed Juno. *Paus.* 2. c. 7.

PRO'TA, an island of the Thracian Bosporus. *Steph.*

PROTAG'ORAS, a Greek philosopher of Abdera in Thrace, who was originally a porter. He became one of the disciples of Democritus, when that philosopher had seen him carrying faggots on his head, poised in a proper equilibrium. He soon rendered himself ridiculous by his doctrines, and in a book which he published, he denied the existence of a Supreme Being. This doctrine he supported by observing, that his doubts arose from the uncertainty of the existence of a Supreme Power, and from the shortness of human life. This book was publicly burnt at Athens, and the philosopher banished from the city, as a worthless and contemptible being. Protagoras visited, from Athens, different islands in the Mediterranean, and died in Sicily in a very advanced age, about 400 years. B.C. He generally reasoned by dilemmas, and always left the mind in suspense about all the questions which he proposed. Some suppose that he was drowned. *Diog.* 9.—*Plato in Protag.*—*Aul. Gell.* 5. c. 10.—*Cic. N. D.* 1. c. 1 & 23. *Orat.* 3. c. 32. *Br.* 12.——A king of Cyprus, tributary to the court of Persia.

PROTAGOR'IDES, an historian of Cyzicus, who wrote a treatise on the games of Daphne, celebrated at Antioch. *Athen.* 1. 3 & 4.

PROTAR'CHUS, an historian of Tralles, praised by *Macrobius,* 1. 1. *Sat.* c. 7.

PROTE, a small island of the Ionian Sea. *Plin.* 3. c. 5.

PRO'TEAS, a Macedonian, a noted drinker. *Leon.* 3. c. 89.

PROTEI COLUM'NÆ, a place in the remotest parts of Ægypt. *Virg. Æn.* 11. v. 262.

PROTESILAE'A, a festival celebrated by the Chersonesians and Thessalians, in memory of Protesilaus, who was the first Grecian slain by Hector. *Pind. Schol. Isthm.* od. 11.—*Lucian. Deor. Con.*

PROTESILA'I TUR'RIS, the monument of Protesilaus, on the Hellespont. *Plin.* 4. c. 11.—*Mela,* 2. c. 2.

PROTESILA'US, a king of part of Thessaly, son of Iphiclus, originally called Iolaus, grandson of Phylacus, and brother of Alcimede, the mother of Jason. He married Laodamia, the daughter of Acastus, and, some time after, departed with the rest of the Greeks for the Trojan war with 40 sail. He was the first of the Greeks who set foot on the Trojan shore, and, as such, he was doomed by the oracle to perish; he was killed therefore as soon as he had leaped from his ship, by Æneas or by Hector. Homer has not mentioned the person who killed him. His wife Laodamia destroyed herself, when she heard of his death. *Vid.* Laodamia. Protesilaus has received the patronymic of, Phylacides, either because he descended from Phylacus, or because he was a native of Phylace. He was buried on the Trojan shore, and, according to *Pliny,* there were near his tomb certain trees which grew to an extraordinary height, and which, as soon as they could be discovered and seen from Troy, immediately withered and decayed, and afterwards grew up again to their former height, and suffered the same vicissitude. *Homer. Il.* 2. v. 205.—*Philostr. Her.* 2.—*Ovid. Met.* 12. fab. 1. *Heroid.* 13. v. 17.—*Propert.* 1. el. 19.—*Hygin.* fab. 103, &c.

PRO'TEUS, a sea deity, son of Oceanus and Tethys, or, according to some, of Neptune and Phœnice. He had received the gift of prophecy from Neptune, because he had tended the monsters of the sea, and from his knowledge of futurity mankind received the greatest services. He usually resided in the Carpathian Sea, and, like the rest of the gods, he reposed himself on the sea shore, where such as wished to consult him generally resorted. He was difficult of access, and when consulted refused to give answers, by assuming different shapes, and, if not properly secured in fetters, eluding the grasp of his enquirers in the form of a tiger or a lion, or disappearing in a flame of fire, a whirlwind, or a rushing stream. Aristæus and Menelaus were in the number of those who consulted him, as also Hercules. Some suppose that he was originally a king of Ægypt, known among his subjects by the name of Cetes, and they assert that he had two sons, Telegonus and Polygonus, who were both killed by Hercules. He had also some daughters, among whom were Cabira, Eidothea, and Rhetia. *Homer. Odyss.* 4. v. 360.—*Ovid. Met.* 8. fab. 10. *Am.* el. 12. v. 36.—*Hesiod. Theog.* 243.—*Virg. G.* 4. v. 387.—*Hygin.* fab. 188.—*Herodot.* 2. c. 112.—*Diod.* 1.—*Servius ad Virg. loco cit.*—*Lactant. ad Achill.* 1. v. 136.—*Philostr. Ic.* 17.—*Tzetzes Chil.* 2. *H.* 44.—*Eustath. ad Od.* 4.

PROTHE'NOR or PROTHOE'NOR, a Bœotian, who went to the Trojan war, at the head of the Thespians, in eight ships. He was brother of Arcesilaus son of Lycus. *Hygin.* fab. 97.

PRO'THEUS, a Greek at the Trojan war.——A Spartan who endeavoured to prevent a war with the Thebans.

PROTHIN'GI, a people of Scythia, beyond the Ister. *Zosim.* 1. 4.

PRO'THIS, a person of Cyzicus, slain by Pollux. *Val. Flacc.* 3. v. 158.

PROTH'OUS, a son of Lycaon of Arcadia. *Apollod.* 3.——A son of Agrius, who united with his brothers Celeutor, Melanippus, and Lycopeus, in driving Œneus from the throne of Calydon, and in placing Agrius in his room. *Apollod.* 1.——A son of Teuthredon who went to the Trojan war with forty ships, at the head of the inhabitants of that part of Thessaly which borders on the Peneus and near Pelion. *Homer. Il.* 2. v. 756.—*Dict. Cret.* 1.—*Dar. Phryg.* 14.

PROTOG'ENES, a painter of Rhodes, who flourished about 328 years B.C. He was originally so poor that he painted ships to maintain himself. His countrymen were ignorant of his ingenuity before Apelles came to Rhodes, who, in the rapture of his admiration, offered to buy all the pieces of the neglected artist, and to submit them to the public taste as the labours of his own hand. This disinterested and highly flattering compliment opened the eyes of the Rhodians, they became sensible of the merit of their countryman, and liberally rewarded him. Protogenes was employed for seven years in finishing a picture of Jalysus, a celebrated huntsman, supposed to have been the son of Apollo, and the founder of Rhodes. During the whole of this time the painter lived only upon lupines and water, thinking that such aliments would leave him greater flights of fancy; but this diet did not seem to make him more successful in the perfection of his picture. He was to represent in the piece a dog panting, and with froth at his mouth, but this he never could do with satisfaction to himself; and when all his labours seemed to be without success, he threw his sponge upon the piece in a fit of anger. Chance alone brought to perfection what the labours of art could not do, the fall of the sponge represented the froth at the mouth of the dog in the most expressive and natural manner, and the piece was universally admired. Protogenes was very exact in his representations, and copied nature with the greatest nicety, and this was blamed as a fault by his friend Apelles. When Demetrius besieged Rhodes, he refused to set fire to a part of the city which might have made him master of the whole, because he knew that Protogenes was then working in that quarter. When the town was taken, the painter was found closely employed in a garden in finishing a picture; and when the conqueror asked him why he showed not more concern at the general calamity? he replied, that Demetrius made war against the Rhodians, and not against the fine arts. *Paus.* 1. c. 3.—*Plin.* 35. c. 10.—*Ælian. V.H.* 12.—*Juv.* 3. v. 120. *Plut. in Dem.*——One of Caligula's favorites, infamous for his cruelty and extravagance.——A reader to M. Marius. *Cic.* 7. *Fam.* 1.

PROTOGENI'A or PROTOGENE'A, a daughter of Calydon by Æolia the daughter of Amythaon. She had a son called Oxillus, by Mars. *Apollod.* 1.——A daughter of Deucalion and Pyrrha. She was beloved by Jupiter, by whom she had Æthlius, the father of Endymion. *Apollod.* 1. c.7.—*Paus.* 5. c. 1.—*Hygin.* fab. 155.

PROTOM'ACRA, a town of Bithynia. *Ptol.*

PROTOMEDU'SA, one of the Nereides, called Protomelia by Hesiod. *Hesiod. Th.* 245.—*Apollod.* 1.

PROTRO'PI, a people of Apulia, not far from Beneventum. They were called Abellinates. *Plin.* 3. c. 11.

PROTRYGE'A, a festival in honor of Neptune, and Bacchus, surnamed Προτρύγης or Προτρυγαῖος, ἀπὸ τῆς τρυγὸς, *new wine. Hesychius.*

PROTUS, a Phocian, who, according to *Plutarch in Solon.* founded Massilia.

PROXENUP'OLIS, a city near Naucratia. *Steph.*

PROX'ENUS, a Bœotian of great authority at Thebes, in the age of Xenophon. *Polyæn.* 7. c. 18.——A writer who published historical accounts of Sparta. *Athen.* 1. 6.

AURE'LIUS, PRUDEN'TIUS CLE'MENS, a Latin poet who flourished A.D. 392, and was successively a soldier, an advocate, and a judge. His poems are numerous, and all theological, devoid of the elegance and purity of the Augustan age, and yet greatly valued for the zeal which he manifests in the cause of Christianity, and for the learning and good sense which he everywhere displays. He lived to a great age, and his piety was rewarded with the highest offices of the church. The best editions of his works are the Delphin, 4to, Paris, 1687; that of Cellarius, 12mo, Halæ, 1703; that of Parma, 2 vols. 4to, 1788; and that of Areval, Rome. *Harles. Not. Lit. Rom.* 1. p. 731.—*Sax. Onom.* 1. p. 475.

PRUM'NIDES, a king of Corinth.

PRU'SA, a town of Bithynia, built by king Prusias, from whom it received its name, and also celebrated for the asylum which it afforded to the persecuted Annibal. *Strab.* 12.—*Cic. de Div.* 2. c. 24.—*Liv.* 45. c. *ult.*—*Ital.* 13. v. 888.—*Paus.* 8. c. 12.—*Nepos.* 23. c. 12.—*Plin.* 10. ep. 16.

PRUSÆ'US DI'ON, flourished A.D. 105.

PRU'SIAS, a king of Bithynia, who flourished 221 B.C.——A king of Bithynia, surnamed *Venator*, who made an alliance with the Romans when they waged war with Antiochus, king of Syria. He gave a kind reception to Annibal, and, by his advice, made war against Eumenes, king of Pergamus, and defeated him. Eumenes, who was an ally of Rome as well as Prusias, complained before the Romans of the hostilities of the king of Bithynia. Q. Flaminius was sent from Rome to settle the disputes of the two monarchs, and he was no sooner arrived in Bithynia, than Prusias, to gain his favour, prepared to deliver to him, at his request, the celebrated Carthaginian, to whom he was indebted for all the advantages which he had obtained over Eumenes; but Annibal prevented it by a voluntary death. Prusias was obliged by the Roman ambassador to make restitution of the provinces which he had conquered, and by his meanness he continued to enjoy the favour of the Romans. When he some time after visited the capital of Italy, he appeared in the habit of a manumitted slave, calling himself a freedman of the Romans; and when he was introduced into the senate house, he saluted the senators by the name of visible deities, of saviours and deliverers. Such abject behaviour rendered him contemptible not only in the eyes of the Romans, but of his subjects, and when he returned home the Bithynians revolted, and placed his son Nicomedes on the throne. The banished monarch fled to Nicomedia, where he was assassinated near the altar of Jupiter, about 149 years B.C. Some say that his son was his murderer. Prusias, according to Polybius, was the meanest of monarchs, without honesty, morals, virtue, or principle; he was cruel and cowardly, intemperate and voluptuous, and an enemy to all learning. He was naturally deformed, and often appeared in public in the habit of a woman, to render his deformities more visible. He married the sister of Perseus, king of Macedonia. *Polyb.*—*Liv.* 39. c. 46. 51. l. 45. c. 44. l. 50.—*Justin.* 31, &c.—*C. Nep. in Annib.*—*Plut in Flam, &c.*

PRYMNE'SIA, a city of Mæonia, on the borders of Lydia. It was founded by Mimæthus. *Steph.*

PRYM'NO, one of the Oceanides. *Hesiod. Theog.* v. 350.

PRYT'ANES, certain magistrates at Athens who presided over the senate, and had the privilege of assembling it when they pleased, festivals excepted. They generally met in a large hall called *prytaneum*, where they gave audiences, offered sacrifices, and feasted together with all those who had rendered signal service to their country. The Prytanes were elected from the senators, who were in number 500, fifty of which were chosen from each tribe. When they were elected, the names of the ten tribes of Athens were thrown into one vessel, and in another were placed nine black beans and a white one. The tribe the name of which was drawn with the white bean presided the first, and the rest in the order in which they were drawn. They presided each for 35 days, as the year was divided into ten parts; but it is unknown what tribe presided on the supernumerary days. When the number of tribes was increased to twelve, each of the Prytanes presided one full month. *Paus.* 1. c. 18.—*Meurs. in Areop.* 11. Some of the principal magistrates of Corinth were also called Prytanes.

PRYT'ANIS, a king of Sparta, of the family of the Proclidæ. *Paus.* 2. c. 36.——One of the friends of Æneas, killed by Turnus. *Virg. Æn.* 9. v. 767.——A son of Europus, father of Lycurgus, the legislator of Sparta. *Salmas. ad Solin.* p. 16.

PRYT'ANIS, a river of Pontus. *Arrian.*

PSA'CUM, a promontory of Crete. *Ptol.* It is called Capo Spada, by *Niger.*

PSALACHAN'TA, a nymph of Icaria who endeavoured in vain to gain the affections of Bacchus, and in revenge attempted to destroy her rival Ariadne, for which the irritated god changed her into a plant that bore her name. This plant, unknown to botanists, was placed upon Ariadne's crown, and was said to have the singular power of conferring happiness on such as were crowned with it. *Ptol. Heph.* 5.

PSAM'ATHE, one of the Nereides, mother of Phocus by Æacus, king of Ægina. *Apollod.* 3. c. 12. *Ovid. Met.* 11. v. 398.—*Flacc.* 1. v. 364.——A daughter of Crotopus, king of Argos. She became mother of Linus by Apollo, and, to conceal her shame from her father, exposed her child, which was found by dogs and torn to pieces. *Stat. Theb.* 1. v. 570.—*Paus.* 1. c. 43.

PSAM'ATHE, a fountain and town of Thebes. *Flacc.* 1. v. 364.

PSAM'ATHOS a town and port of Laconia, near the city of Tænarus. *Plin.* 4. c. 5.—*Paus.* 3. c. 25.

PSAMMENI'TUS, succeeded his father Amasis on the throne of Ægypt. Cambyses made war against him, and as he knew that the Ægyptians paid the greatest veneration to cats, the Persian monarch placed some of these at the head of his army, and the enemy, unable to defend themselves, and unwilling to kill those objects of their adoration, were easily conquered. Psammenitus was twice beaten, at Pelusium and in Memphis, and became one of the prisoners of Cambyses, who treated him with great humanity. Psammenitus, however, raised seditions against the Persian monarch, and attempted to make the Ægyptians rebel, for which he was put to death by drinking bull's blood. He had reigned about six months. He flourished about 525 years B.C. *Herodot.* 3. c. 10, &c.

PSAMMET'ICHUS, a king of Ægypt. He was one of the twelve princes who shared the kingdom among themselves; but as he was more popular than the rest, he was banished from his dominions, and retired into the marshes near the sea-shore. A descent of some of the Greeks upon Ægypt proved favorable to his cause; he joined the enemy, and defeated the eleven princes who had expelled him from the country. He rewarded the Greeks, by whose valor he had recovered Ægypt, allotted them some territory on the sea coast, patronized the liberal arts, and encouraged commerce among his subjects. He made useless inquiries after the sources of the Nile, and stopped, by bribes and money, a large army of Scythians that were marching against him. He died 617 years B.C., and was buried in Minerva's temple at Sais. During his reign there was a contention among some of the neighbouring nations about the antiquity of their language. Psammetichus took part in the contest, and confining two young children, fed them with milk; the shepherd to whose care they were entrusted, was ordered never to speak to them, but to watch diligently their articulations. After some time the shepherd observed, that whenever he entered their place of confinement they repeatedly exclaimed *Beccos*, and he gave information of this to the monarch. Psammetichus made inquiries, and found that the word *Beccos* signified bread in the Phœnician language, and from that circumstance, therefore, it was universally concluded that the language of Phœnicia was of the greatest antiquity. *Herodot.* 2. c. 28, &c.—*Polyæn.* 8.—*Strab.* 16.——A son of Gordius, brother to Periander, who held the tyranny at Corinth for three years, B.C. 584. *Aristot. Polit.* 5. c. 12.

PSAM'MIS or PSAM'MITES, a king of Ægypt, B.C 376.

PSAM'MUS, the sixteenth of the shepherd kings of Ægypt, contemporary with Gideon judge of Israel. *Joh. Marsham. Can. Chron. ex Manethone.*

PSA'PHIS, a town on the confines of Attica and Bœotia. There was an oracle of Amphiaraus, who, according to *Sophocles*, was swallowed up here in his chariot by the earth. *Strab.* 9.

PSA'PHO, a Libyan who taught a number of birds which he kept to say, "Psapho is a god," and afterwards gave them their liberty. The birds did not forget the words which they had been taught, and the Africans paid divine honors to Psapho. The same story is related of Hanno of Carthage by Ælian. *Alex. ab. Alex.* 6. c. 14.—*Ælian. V. H.* 14. c. 39.

PSA'PIS, a river of Asiatic Sarmatia. *Ptol.* Some read Psatis.

PSAU'MIS, son of Acron, rebuilt the town of Camarina, in Sicily. *Pindar. Ol.* 5. v. 18.

PSEBO'A or PSE'BO, a region of Æthiopia. *Artemidorus* calls it a lake. *Steph.—Salmas. ad Solin.* p. 111.

PSE'CAS, one of Diana's attendant nymphs. *Ovid. Met.* 3

PSENE'RUS, a small town of Ægypt. *Steph.*

PSEN'TRIS, a village of Ægypt. *Id.*

PSES'SII or PSES'SI, a people of Taurinia. *Id.*

PSEUDAR'TACE, a hill of Scythia. *Id.*

PSEU'DO, a word prefixed to the name of persons whose character was falsely assumed for the purpose of political intrigue or insurrection. Thus Pseudo-Philippus is applied to Andriscus, an obscure individual who pretended to be the son of king Perseus, that he might free Macedonia from the Roman yoke. Amatius is called Pseudo-Marius, because he called himself the son of C. Marius, and attempted to revenge the murder of J. Cæsar.

PSEUDOCE'LIS, a city of Arabia Felix. *Ptol.*

PSEUDOPE'NIAS, a promontory of Cyrenaica, on which was the city of Berenice. *Strab.* It is now Capo Bernich.

PSEUDOS'TOMUM, one of the mouths of the Ister. *Plin* 4. c. 12.—*Ptol.*

PSI'LAS, a name of Bacchus at Amyclæ. *Paus.* l. 3. c. 19.

PSI'LE, an island near Ephesus. *Plin.* 5. c. 31.

PSI'LIS, a river of Bithynia, flowing into the Euxine Sea. *Arrian.—Salmas. ad Solin.* p. 880.

PSI'LUM, a small mouth of the Danube. *Arrian.* It is called Stenostoma by *Solinus*, c. 19., Spireostoma by *Pliny*, 4. c. 12., and Thiagola by *Ptolemy*.

PSIM'ADA, a small region of Isauria. *Steph.*

PSIN'APHOS, a town of Ægypt. *Ptol.*

PSINEC'TABIS, a village of Ægypt. *Steph.*

PSIT'TACE, a city near the Tigris. *Id.*

PSITTACHEM'MIS, a small town of Ægypt. *Id.*

PSITUL'CIS or SCILLUS'TIS, an island of India. *Plut. in vit. Alex. Mag.* *Arrian* calls it Cilluta, but it is not mentioned by *Curtius*.

PSOCHEM'MIS, a small town of Ægypt. *Steph.*

PSO'PHIS, a town of Arcadia, near the river Erymanthus, the name of which it originally bore, and afterwards that of Phegia. It is now Dimizana. *Stat. Theb.* 4. v. 290.—*Paus.* 8. c. 24.—*Ovid. Met.* 5. v. 607.——A river and town of Elis.——A town of Acarnania.——A town of Libya.

PSO'PHIS, a daughter of Eryx.

PSY'CHE, a nymph whom Cupid married and conveyed to a place of bliss where he long enjoyed her company. Venus put her to death because she had robbed the world of her son; but Jupiter, at the request of Cupid, granted immortality to Psyche. The word signifies *the soul*, and this personification of Psyche, first mentioned by Apuleius, is consequently posterior to the Augustan age, though it is connected with ancient mythology. Psyche is generally represented with the wings of a butterfly, to imitate the lightness of the soul, of which the butterfly is the symbol, and on that account, among the ancients, when a man had just expired, a butterfly was said to appear fluttering above, as if rising from the mouth of the deceased. Psyche was daughter of the nymph Endelechia, or of a certain Grecian king whose name is not mentioned. *Apul. Met.* 4, 5, 6.—*Fulgent. Myth.* 3. c. 6.—*Cœl. Rh. H. L.* 24. c. 9.—*Martian. Cap.* [The most beautiful representation of Psyche is in a group with Cupid, to be found in the Capitol, at Rome.]

PSYCH'IA, a name of Amorgus, one of the Cyclades. *Steph.*

PSYCH'RUS, a river of Thrace. When sheep drank of its waters they were said to bring forth black lambs. *Aristot.*

PSYL'LA or PSYL'LIUM, a city of Bithynia, not far from Heraclea. *Steph.* It is now Picello.

PSYL'LI, a people of Libya near the Syrtes, very expert in curing the bite of venomous serpents. *Strab.* 17.—*Dio.* 51. c. 14.—*Lucan.* 2. v. 894.—937.—*Herodot.* 4. c. 173.—*Paus.* 9. c. 28.—*Aul. Gell.* 16. c. 11.—*Plin.* 7. c. 2. l. 8. c. 25. l. 25. c. 10. l. 28. c. 3.

PSY'RA, an island of the Ægean Sea, near Chius. *Steph.*

PSYTTALI'A, a small island of the Sinus Saronicus, between Salamis and the Piræus. *Strab.*—*Steph.*

PTE'LEA, a name of Ephesus. *Steph.—Salmas. ad Solin.* p. 110.——A village in the tribe Œneis. *Steph.*

PTE'LEON, a youth who is said to have seduced the affections of Procris by the offer of a crown of gold. Procris, upon the discovery of her amour by her husband, fled to Crete. *Apollod.* 3.

PTE'LEUM, now Fitleo, a town of Thessaly between the Pagasæus Sinus and the island of Eubœa. *Lucan.* 6. v. 852.—*Liv.* 35. c. 43.

PTE'RAS, an architect of Delphi who was employed in beautifying the temple of Apollo. *Paus.* 10. c. 5.

PTERELA'US, a son of Taphius, presented with immortality by Neptune, provided he kept on his head a yellow lock. When Taphus, over which he reigned, was besieged by Amphitryon and the Teleboans, his daughter Cometho became enamoured of the general of the enemy, and cut off the fatal hair, on which depended her father's life and the prosperity and independence of her country. Her perfidy, however, was punished; she was put to death by order of Amphitryon. *Tzetzes ad Lyc.* 934.—*Apollod.* 2. c. 4.

PTE'RIA, a well fortified town of Cappadocia. It was in its neighbourhood, according to some, that Crœsus was defeated by Cyrus. *Herodot.* 1. c. 76.

PTEROPH'OROS, a region of Scythia, near the Hyperborean mountains. *Plin.* 4. c. 12.

PTE'ROS, an island of Arabia Felix, in the Indian Sea. *Id.* 6. c. 28.

PTE'RUM, a promontory of Lower Mysia. *Ptol.*

PTISCIA'NA, an inland city of Mauritania Tingitana. *Ptol.* It is now Dar al Hamara.

PTOLEDER'MA, a town of Arcadia. *Paus.* 8. c. 27.

PTOLEMÆUM, a certain place at Athens dedicated to exercise and study. *Cic.* 5. *de fin.*

PTOLEMÆUS the First, surnamed *Lagus*, a king of Ægypt, son of Arsinoe, who, when pregnant by Philip of Macedonia, married Lagus, a man of mean extraction. *Vid.* Lagus. Ptolemy was educated in the court of the king of Macedonia, he became one of the friends and confidential attendants of Alexander, and when that monarch invaded Asia, the son of Arsinoe attended him as one of his generals. During the expedition, he behaved with uncommou valor; he killed one of the Indian monarchs in single combat, and it was to his prudence and courage that Alexander was indebted for the reduction of the rock Aornus. After the conqueror's death, in the general division of the Macedonian empire, Ptolemy obtained, as his share, the government of Ægypt, with Libya, and part of the neighbouring territories of Arabia. In this appointment the governor soon gained the esteem of the people by the wisdom of his administration, and by his benevolence and clemency, and though he did not assume the title of independent monarch till nineteen years after, yet he established himself so firmly that the attempts of Perdiccas to expel him from his possessions proved abortive; and Ptolemy, after the murder of his rival by Grecian soldiers, might have added the kingdom of Macedonia to his Ægyptian territories. He made himself master of Cœlesyria, Phœnicia, and the neighbouring coast of Syria; and when he had reduced Jerusalem, he carried above 100,000 prisoners to Ægypt to people the extensive city of Alexandria, which then became the capital of his dominions. After he had rendered these prisoners the most attached and faithful of his subjects by his liberality and the grant of various privileges, Ptolemy assumed the title of king of Ægypt, and soon after reduced Cyprus under his power. He made war with success against Demetrius and Antigonus, who disputed his right to the provinces of Syria; and from the assistance which he gave to the people of Rhodes against their common enemies, he received the honorable appellation of Soter. While he extended his dominions, Ptolemy was not negligent of the advantages of his people, nor of the local improvement of his provinces. As the bay of Alexandria was dangerous of access, he built a tower upon which he placed a light for the guidance of sailors in the obscurity of the night, (*vid.* Pharus,) and that his subjects might imbibe a taste for literature, he laid the foundation of a public library, which, under succeeding reigns, became the most celebrated in the world. He also established in the capital of his dominions a society called Museum, of which the members, maintained at the public expense, were employed in philosophical researches, and in the advancement of science and the liberal arts. Ptolemy died in the 84th year of his age, after a reign of thirty-nine years, about 284 B.C. He was succeeded by his son Ptolemy Philadelphus, who had been his partner on the throne for the last ten years of his reign. Ptolemy Lagus has been commended for his abilities, not only as a sovereign but as a writer; and among the many valuable compositions which have been lost, we have to lament a history of Alexander the Great, by the king of Ægypt, greatly admired and valued for the elegance of its style and the correctness of its information. All his successors were called Ptolemies from him. *Paus.* 10. c. 7.—*Justin.* 13, &c.—*Polyb.* 2.—*Arrian.*—*Curt.*—*Plut. in Alex.*—*Tacit.* 4. *Hist.* 83. [There is a fine bronze bust of Ptolemy Lagus. in the Portici Museum; and a statue of him will be found in the Capitol, at Rome.]

PTOLEMÆUS the Second, son of Ptolemy the First, succeeded his father on the Ægyptian throne, and was called *Philadelphus* by antiphrasis, because he killed two of his brothers. He showed himself worthy in every respect to succeed his illustrious father, and, conscious of the advantages which arise from an alliance with powerful nations, he sent ambassadors to Italy to solicit the friendship of the Romans, whose name and military reputation had become universally known for the victories which they had just obtained over Pyrrhus and the Tarentines. His ambassadors were received with marks of the greatest attention; and immediately after four Roman senators came to Alexandria, where they gained the admiration of the monarch and of his subjects, and, by refusing the crowns of gold and rich presents which were offered to them, convinced the world of the virtue and of the disinterestedness of their nation. But while Ptolemy strengthened himself by alliances with foreign powers, the internal peace of his kingdom was disturbed by the revolt of Magas, his brother, the dependent king of Cyrene. The sedition however was stopped, though encouraged and supported by Antiochus king of Syria, and the death of the rebellious prince re-established peace for some time in the family of Philadelphus. Antiochus, the Syrian king, married Berenice the daughter of Ptolemy, and the father, to render the union more sincere and lasting, though old and infirm, conducted his daughter to her husband's kingdom, and assisted at the nuptials. Philadelphus died in the 64th year of his age, 246 B.C. He left two sons and a daughter, by Arsinoe, the daughter of Lysimachus. He had afterwards married his sister Arsinoe, whom he loved with uncommon tenderness, and to whose memory he began to erect a celebrated monument. *Vid.* Dinocrates. During the whole of his reign Philadelphus was employed in exciting industry, and in encouraging the liberal arts and useful knowledge among his subjects. The inhabitants of the adjacent countries were allured by promises, presents, and immunities to increase the number of the Ægyptian subjects, and Ptolemy could boast of reigning over 33,339 well peopled and flourishing cities. He gave every possible encouragement to commerce, and, by keeping two powerful fleets, one in the Mediterranean and the other in the Red Sea, he made Ægypt the centre of mercantile intercourse with foreign nations, and Alexandria, his capital, the repository of the most valuable productions of the earth. His army consisted of 200,000 foot, 40,000 horse, besides 300 elephants, and 2000 armed chariots. With justice therefore has he been called the richest of all the monarchs of his age, and indeed the remark was fully justified when it is observed, that at his death he left in his treasury 750,000 Ægyptian talents, a sum equivalent to two hundred millions sterling. His palace was the asylum of learned men, whom he admired and patronized. He paid particular attention to Euclid, Theocritus, Callimachus, and Lycophron, and by increasing the library, which his father had founded, he showed his taste for learning, and his wish to encourage genius. This celebrated library at his death contained 200,000 volumes of the best and choicest books, and it was afterwards increased to 700,000 volumes. Part of it was burnt by the flames of Cæsar's fleet when he set it on fire to save himself, a circumstance however not mentioned by the Roman general, and the whole was again magnificently repaired by Cleopatra, who added to the Alexandrian library the valuable collection made by the kings of Pergamus. It is said that the Old Testament was translated into Greek by his direction, which translation has been called the Septuagint, because executed by the labors of seventy different persons. *Eutrop.*—*Justin.* 17. c. 2, &c.—*Liv.*—*Plut.*—*Theocrit.*—*Athen.* 12.—*Plin.* 13. c. 12.—*Dio*, 42.—*Gellius*, 6. c. 17.

PTOLEMÆUS the Third, succeeded his father Philadelphus on the Ægyptian throne. He early engaged in a war against Antiochus Theus, for his unkindness to Berenice the Ægyptian king's sister, whom he had married with the consent of Philadelphus. With the most rapid success he conquered Syria and Cilicia, and advanced as far as the Tigris, but a sedition at home stopped the progress of his victorious arms, and he returned to Ægypt loaded with the spoils of conquered nations. Among the immense riches which he brought, he recovered above 2500 statues of the Ægyptian gods, which Cambyses had carried away into Persia when he conquered Ægypt. These were restored to the temples, and the Ægyptians called their sovereign *Evergetes*, in acknowledgment of his attention, beneficence, and religious zeal for the gods of his country. The last years of Ptolemy's reign were passed in peace, if we except the refusal of the Jews to continue to pay the tribute of twenty silver talents which their ancestors had always paid to the Ægyptian monarchs. He also interested himself in the affairs of Greece, and assisted Cleomenes the Spartan king against the leaders of the Achæan league; but he had the mortification to see his ally defeated, and even a fugitive in Ægypt. Evergetes died 221 B.C. after a reign of twenty-five years, and, like his two ilustrious predecessors, he deserved the gratitude of his country as a munificent patron of learning, but unfortunately, as if the fates envied the Ægyptians the succession of a race of virtuous and patriotic sovereigns, he was the last of the Lagides who gained popularity among his subjects by the clemency, moderation, and humanity of his government, and who commanded respect, even from his enemies, by his valor, prudence, and reputation. It is said that he deposited fifteen talents in the hands of the Athenians to be permitted to transcribe the original manuscripts of Æschylus, Euripides, and Sophocles. *Plut. in. Cleom. &c.—Polyb.* 2.—*Justin.* 27, 29, &c.—*Tacit. Hist.* 4. c. 84.—*Am.* 6. c. 28.

Ptolemæ'us the Fourth, succeeded his father Evergetes on the throne of Ægypt, and received the surname of *Philopater* by antiphrasis, because, according to some historians, he destroyed his father by poison. He began his reign with acts of the greatest cruelty, and successively sacrificed to his avarice his mother, his wife, his sister, and his brother. Regardless of the exemplary conduct which alone can entitle a monarch to the approbation of his subjects, he disgraced himself by his licentious amours with the courtezan Agathoclea, who, for a while, assisted by her brother Agathocles, converted the influence which she posssessed over a sceptered profligate to the purposes of public oppression and national venality. His vices however were branded with infamy by the general voice of the people, and he received the name of *Tiphon*, from his extravagance and debauchery, and that of *Gallus*, because he appeared in the streets of Alexandria like one of the bacchanals, and with all the gestures of the priests of Cybele. In the midst of his pleasures Philopater was called to support a war against Antiochus king of Syria, and at the head of a powerful army he soon invaded his enemy's territories, and might have added the kingdom of Syria to Ægypt, if he had made a prudent use of the victory which attended his arms at the battle of Raphia. In his return he visited Jerusalem, but the Jews forcibly prevented him from entering their temple, for which indignity the monarch determined to extirpate the whole nation. He ordered a great number of Jews to be exposed in a plain, and trodden under the feet of elephants, but by a supernatural instinct the generous animals turned their fury not on those that had been devoted to death, but upon the Ægyptian spectators. This circumstance so terrified Philopater, that, as if struck with remorse, he behaved with more than common kindness to a nation which he had so lately devoted to destruction. In the latter part of his reign the Romans, whom a dangerous war with Carthage had weakened, but at the same time roused to superior activity, renewed, for political reasons, the treaty of alliance which had been made with the Ægyptian monarchs. Philopater at last, enervated by intemperance and continual debauchery, died in the 37th year of his age, after a reign of 17 years, 204 B.C. His death was immediately followed by the murder of the companions of his voluptuousness and extravagance, and their carcases were dragged by the populace, with the greatest ignominy, through the streets of Alexandria. *Polyb.*—*Justin.* 30, &c.—*Plut. in Cleom.*

Ptolemæ'us the Fifth, succeeded his father Philopater as king of Ægypt, though only in the fourth year of his age. During the years of his minority he was under the able protection of Sosicius and of Aristomenes of Acarnania, by whose prudent administration Antiochus was dispossessed of the provinces of Cœlesyria and Palestine, which he had conquered. The Romans also renewed their alliance with the young king after their victories over Annibal, and the conclusion of the second Punic war. This flattering embassy induced Aristomenes to offer the care of the patronage of the young monarch to the Romans, but the regent was confirmed in his honorable office, and by making a treaty of alliance with the people of of Achaia, he convinced the Ægyptians that he was qualified to wield the sceptre and to govern the nation. When Ptolemy reached his fourteenth year, according to the laws and customs of Ægypt, his minority expired. He received the surname of *Epiphanes*, or illustrious, and was crowned at Alexandria with the greatest solemnity, on which occasion the faithful Aristomenes resigned into his hands an empire which he had governed with honor to himself and with credit to his sovereign. Young Ptolemy was no sooner delivered from the shackles of a superior, than he betrayed the same vices which had characterized his father; the counsels of Aristomenes were despised, and the minister who for ten years had governed the conntry with equity and moderation, was sacrificed to the capricious cruelty of the sovereign, who abhorred him for the salutary advice which his own vicious inclinations did not permit him to follow. His repeated cruelties at last raised seditions among his subjects, but these were twice quelled by the prudence and moderation of Polycrates, the most meritorious and faithful of his corrupt ministers. In the midst of his extravagance Epiphanes did not forget his alliance with the Romans; above all others he showed himself eager to cultivate friendship with a nation from which he could derive so many advantages, and during their war against Antiochus he offered to assist them with money against a monarch, whose daughter Cleopatra he had married, but whom he secretly hated on account of the seditions which he had raised in the very heart of Ægypt. After a reign of twenty-four years, Ptolemy was poisoned 180 B.C., by his ministers, whom he had threatened to rob of their possessions to carry on a war against Seleucus, king of Syria. *Liv.* 35. c. 13, &c.—*Justin.* &c.

Ptolemæ'us the Sixth, succeeded his father Epiphanes on the Ægyptian throne, and received the surname of *Philometor*, on account of his hatred against his mother Cleopatra. He was in the sixth year of his age when he ascended the throne, and during his minority the kingdom was governed by his mother, and, at her death, by a eunuch who had obtained a strong ascendancy over him, and was one of his principal favorites. He made war against Antiochus Epiphanes, king of Syria, to recover the provinces of Palestine and Cœlesyria, which had formed for several years part of the Ægyptian dominions, and after some successes he fell into the hands of his enemy, who detained him in confinement. During the captivity of Philometor, the Ægyptians raised to the throne his younger brother Ptolemy Evergetes, or Physcon, also son of Epiphanes, but he was no sooner established in his power than Antiochus turned his arms against Ægypt, expelled the usurper, and restored Philometor to all his rights and privileges as king of Ægypt. This artful behaviour of Antiochus was soon comprehended by Philometor, and when he saw that the valuable town of Pelusium, the key of Ægypt, had remained in the hands of his Syrian ally, he recalled his brother Physcon, and made him his partner on the throne, and concerted with him how to repel their common enemy. This union of interest in the two royal brothers incensed Antiochus; he entered Ægypt with a large army, but the Romans generously interfered, checked his progress, and obliged him to retire. No sooner were they delivered from the impending war than Philometor and Physcon, whom the fear of danger had united, began with mutual jealousy to oppose each other's views. Physcon was at last banished by the superior influence of his brother, and as he could find no support in Ægypt, he immediately repaired to Rome. To excite more effectually the compassion of the Romans, and to gain their assistance, he appeared in the meanest dress, and took up his residence in the most obscure corner of the city. He was admitted to an audience by the senate, and the Romans settled the dispute between the two royal brothers, by making them independent of one another, and by giving the government of Libya and Cyrene to Physcon, and confirming Philometor in the possession of Ægypt, and the island of Cyprus. These terms of accommodation were gladly accepted, but Physcon soon claimed the dominion of Cyprus, and in this he was secretly supported by the Romans, who wished to aggrandize themselves by the diminution of the Ægyptian power. Philometor refused to deliver up the island of Cyprus, and, to call away his brother's attention, he fomented the seeds of rebellion in Cyrene. But the death of Philometor 145 B.C., left Physcon master of Ægypt, and all the dependent provinces. Philometor has been commended by some historians for the clemency and moderation of his government. *Justin.* 34. c. 2 & 3. l. 38. c. 8.—*Liv.* 44. c. 19. l. 45. c. 11 & 12. l. 46.—*Polyb. Leg.* 113.—*Val. Max.* 5. c. 1.—*Diod.*

PTOLEMÆ'US the Seventh, surnamed *Physcon*, on account of the prominence of his belly, ascended the throne of Ægypt after the death of his brother Philometor, and as he had reigned for some time conjointly with him, (*vid* Ptolemæus the Sixth), his succession was approved, though the wife and the son of the deceased monarch laid claims to the crown. Cleopatra was supported in her claims by the Jews, but to avoid the dangers attendant upon a disputed succession, it was at last agreed that Physcon should marry the queen, and that her son should be heir to the throne at his death. The nuptials were accordingly celebrated, but on that very day the tyrant murdered Cleopatra's son in her arms. He ordered himself to be called *Evergetes*, but the Alexandrians refused, and stigmatized him with the appellation of *Kakergetes*, or evil doer, a surname which he deserved by his tyranny and oppression. A series of barbarities rendered him odious; but as no one attempted to rid Ægypt of her tyrant, the Alexandrians abandoned their habitations, and fled from a place which continually streamed with the blood of their massacred fellow-citizens. If their migration proved fatal to the commerce and prosperity of the long-flourishing city of Alexandria, it was of the most essential service to the countries whither they retired; and the numbers of Ægyptians who sought a safer asylum in Greece and Asia, introduced among the inhabitants of those countries the different arts and professions that were practised with success in the capital of Ægypt. Physcon endeavoured to re-people the city which his cruelty had laid desolate; but the fear of sharing the fate of its former inhabitants, prevailed more than the promise of riches, civil rights, and commercial immunities. The king, at last, disgusted with Cleopatra, repudiated her, and married her daughter by Philometor, called also Cleopatra. Though he still continued to exercise the greatest cruelty upon his subjects, the prudence and vigilance of his ministers kept the people in tranquillity, till all Ægypt revolted when the king had basely murdered all the young men of Alexandria. Without friends or support in Ægypt, the tyrant fled to Cyprus, and Cleopatra, the divorced queen. ascended the throne. In his banishment Physcon dreaded lest the Alexandrians should also place the crown on the head of his son, by his sister Cleopatra, who was then governor of Cyrene, and under these apprehensions he sent for the young prince, called Memphitis, to Cyprus, and murdered him as soon as he reached the shore. To make the barbarity more complete, he sent the limbs of Memphitis to Cleopatra, and they were received as the queen was going to celebrate her birth-day. Soon after this he invaded Ægypt with an army, and obtained a victory over the forces of Cleopatra, who being left without friends or assistance, fled to her eldest daughter Cleopatra, who had married Demetrius, king of Syria. This decisive blow restored Physcon to his throne, where he continued to reign for some time, hated by his subjects and feared by his enemies. He died at Alexandria in the 67th year of his age, after a reign of 29 years, about 116 B.C. Some authors have extolled Physcon for his fondness for literature; they have observed that from his extensive knowledge he was called the philologist, and that he wrote a commentary upon Homer, besides a history in twenty-four books, admired for its elegance, and often quoted by succeeding authors whose pen was employed on the same subject. *Diod.*—*Justin.* 38, &c. *Athen.* 2.—*Porphyr.*

PTOLEMÆ'US the Eighth, surnamed *Lathyrus*, from an excrescence on the nose like a pea, succeeded his father Physcon as king of Ægypt. He had no sooner ascended the throne than his mother Cleopatra, who reigned conjointly with him, banished him to Cyprus, and placed the crown on the head of Ptolemy Alexander, her favourite son. Lathyrus, banished from Ægypt became king of Cyprus; and soon after appeared at the head of a large army to make war against Alexander Jannæus, king of Judæa, through whose assistance and intrigue he had been expelled by Cleopatra. The Jewish monarch was conquered, and 50,000 of his men were left on the field of battle. Lathyrus, after he had exercised the greatest cruelty upon the Jews, and made vain attempts to recover the kingdom of Ægypt, retired to Cyprus till the death of his brother restored him to his dominions. Some of the cities of Ægypt refused to acknowledge him as their sovereign; and Thebes, for its obstinacy, was closely besieged for three successive years, and from a powerful and populous city was reduced to ruins. In the latter part of his reign Lathyrus was called upon to assist the Romans with a navy for the conquest of Athens, but Lucullus, who had been sent to obtain the required aid, though received with kingly honors, was dismissed with evasive and unsatisfactory answers, and the monarch refused to part with troops which he deemed necessary to preserve the peace of his kingdom. Lathyrus died 81 B.C., after a reign of thirty-five years, eleven of which he had passed with his mother Cleopatra on the Ægyptian throne, eighteen in Cyprus, and seven after his mother's death. He was succeeded by his only daughter Cleopatra, whom Alexander the son of Ptolemy Alexander, upon the recommendation of the dictator Sylla, soon after married and murdered. *Joseph. Hist.*—*Justin.* 39. c. 4.—*Plut. in Luc.*—*Appian. in Mithrid. & B. Civ.*

PTOLEMÆ'US, the Ninth. *Vid.* Alexander Ptolemy the First.

PTOLEMÆ'US the Tenth. *Vid.* Alexander Ptolemy the Second.

PTOLEMÆ'US the Eleventh. *Vid.* Alexander Ptolemy the Third.

PTOLEMÆ'US the Twelfth, the illegitimate son of Lathyrus, ascended the throne at the death of Alexander the Third. He received the surname of *Auletes*, because he played skilfully on the flute. The means by which he raised himself to the throne showed great marks of prudence and circumspection, and as his predecessor by his will had left the kingdom of Ægypt to the Romans, Auletes knew that he could not be firmly established in his power, without the approbation of the Roman senate. He was successful in his applications, and Cæsar, who was then Consul, and in want of money, confirmed his succession, and granted him the alliance of the Romans after he had received the enormous sum of about £1,162,500 sterling. But these measures, the effects of timidity rather than of wisdom, rendered him unpopular at home, and when he had suffered the Romans quietly to take possession of Cyprus, the Ægyptians revolted, and Auletes was obliged to flee from his kingdom, and seek protection among his powerful allies. His complaints were heard at Rome at first with indifference, and the murder of 100 noblemen of Alexandria, whom the Ægyptians had sent to justify their proceedings before the Roman senate, rendered him deservedly unpopular and suspected. Pompey, however, supported his cause, and the senators decreed to re-establish Auletes on his throne; but as they proceeded slowly in their plans, the monarch retired from Rome to Ephesus, where he lay concealed for some time in the temple of Diana. During his absence from Alexandria, his daughter Berenice had made herself absolute, and established herself on the throne by a marriage with Archelaus, a priest at Comana, but she was soon driven from Ægypt when Gabinius, at the head of a Roman army, approached to replace Auletes on his throne. Auletes was no sooner restored to power than he sacrificed to his ambition his daughter Berenice, and behaved with the greatest ingratitude and perfidy to Rabirius, a Roman who had supplied him with money when expelled from his kingdom. Auletes died four years after his restoration, about 51 B.C. He left two sons and two daughters, and by his will ordered the eldest of his sons to marry the eldest of his sisters, and to ascend with her the vacant throne. As these children were young, the dying monarch recommended them to the protection and paternal care of the Romans, and accordingly Pompey the Great was appointed by the senate to be their patron and guardian. Their reign was as turbulent as that of their predecessors, and it is remarkable for no uncommon events, only we may observe that the young queen was the Cleopatra who soon after became so celebrated as being the mistress of J. Cæsar, the wife of M. Antony, and the last of the Ægyptian monarchs of the family of Lagus. *Cic. pro. Rabir.* 1. *Fam.* 7, &c.—*Strab.* 17.—*Dion.* 39.—*Appian. de Civ.*—*Lucan.* 8. v. 824.—*Plut. in Ant.*

PTOLEMÆ'US the Thirteenth, surnamed *Dionysius* or *Bacchus*, ascended the throne of Ægypt conjointly with his sister Cleopatra, whom he had married, according to the directions of the will of his father Auletes. He was under the care and protection of Pompey the Great, (*vid.* Ptolemæus the Twelfth), but the avarice of his ministers soon obliged him to reign independent. He was then in the 13th year of his age, when his guardian, after the battle of Pharsalia, came to the shores of Ægypt, and claimed his protection. He refused to grant the required assistance, and by the advice of his ministers basely murdered Pompey, after he had invited him to the shore under the mask of friendship and cordiality. To curry favour with the conqueror of Pharsalia, Ptolemy cut off the head of Pompey, but Cæsar turned with becoming indignation from such perfidy, and when he arrived at Alexandria he found the king of Ægypt as faithless to his cause as to that of his fallen enemy. Assuming the character of umpire as master of the Roman world, Cæsar sat as judge to hear the various claims of the brother and sister to the throne; and to satisfy the people, he ordered the will of Auletes to be read, and confirmed Ptolemy and Cleopatra in the possession of Ægypt, and appointed the two younger children masters of the island of Cyprus. This fair and candid decision might have left no room for dissatisfaction, but Ptolemy was governed by cruel and avaricious ministers, and therefore he refused to acknowledge Cæsar either as a judge or as a mediator. The Roman enforced his authority by arms, and three victories were obtained over the Ægyptian forces. Ptolemy, who had been for some time a prisoner in the hands of Cæsar, found means to escape, and place himself at the head of his armies, but a defeat was fatal, and as he attempted to save his life by flight, he was drowned in the Nile, about 46 B C., and three years and eight months after the death of Auletes. Cleopatra, at the death of her brother, became sole mistress of Ægypt; but as the Ægyptians were no friends to female government, Cæsar obliged her to marry her younger brother Ptolemy, who was then in the eleventh year of his age. *Appian. Civ.*—*Cœsar. in Alex.*—*Strab.* 17.—*Joseph. Ant.* 15. c. 4.—*Dio*, 42, 44.—*Plut. in Ant*, *&c.*—*Sueton. in Cœs.*

PTOLEMÆ'US A'PION, king of Cyrene, was the illegitimate son of Ptolemy Physcon. After a reign of 20 years he died; and as he had no children, made the Romans heirs of his dominions. The Romans presented his subjects with their independence, but, afterwards, in consequence of the turbulence of party and insurrection among the people, the country was reduced into the shape of a Roman province. *Plut. in Lyc.*—*Eutrop.* 6. —*Liv.* 70.—*Justin.* 39.

PTOLEMÆ'US CERAU'NUS, a son of Ptolemy Soter by Eurydice the daughter of Antipater. Unable to ascend the throne of Ægypt, either by force or by intrigues, Ceraunus fled to the court of Seleucus, where he was received with friendly marks of attention. Seleucus was then king of Macedonia, an empire which he had lately acquired by the death of Lysimachus, in a battle in Phrygia, but his reign was short, and Ceraunus perfidiously murdered him and ascended his throne, 280 B.C. The murderer, however, could not be firmly established in Macedonia, as long as Arsinoe the widow and the children of Lysimachus were alive, and entitled to claim the kingdom as the lawful possession of their father. To remove these obstacles Ceraunus insidiously made offers of marriage to Arsinoe, who was his own sister. The queen at first refused, but the protestations and solemn promises of the usurper at last prevailed upon her to consent. The nuptials, however, were no sooner celebrated than Ceraunus murdered the two young princes, and confirmed his usurpation by rapine and cruelty. But now three powerful princes claimed the kingdom of Macedonia as their own; Antiochus, the son of Seleucus; Antigonus, the son of Demetrius; and Pyrrhus, the king of Epirus. These enemies, however, were soon removed by the arts and intrigues of Ceraunus, who conquered Antigonus in the field of battle, and stopped the hostilities of his other rivals by promises and money. He was not however permitted to remain long inactive; a barbarian army of Gauls claimed tribute from him, and the monarch immediately marched to meet them in the field. The battle was long and bloody, but the Macedonians might have obtained the victory if Ceraunus had shown more prudence. He was thrown from his elephant, and taken prisoner by the enemy, who immediately tore his body to pieces, and fixed his head on a lance in triumphant exultation. Ptolemy had been king of Macedonia only 18 months. *Justin.* 24. c. 1, &c.—*Paus.* 10. c. 10.—*Polyb.* l. 5.

PTOLEMÆ'US, an illegitimate son of Ptolemy Lathyrus, king of Cyprus, of which he was tyranically dispossessed by the Romans at the instance of the tribune Clodius, whom the king's avarice and great penuriousness had offended and excited to future revenge. Cato was at the head of the forces which were sent against Ptolemy by the senate, and in obedience to his instructions he proposed to the monarch to retire from the throne, and to pass the rest of his days in the obscure office of high priest in the temple of Venus at Paphus. This offer was rejected with the contempt which it merited, and the monarch, unable to make effectual resistance, poisoned himself at the approach of the enemy. The treasures found in the island amounted to the enormous sum of £1,356,250 sterling, which were carried to Rome by the couquerors. *Plut. in Caton. min.*—*Flor.* 3.—*Strab.* 4.—*Cic. Dom.* 8. 20. 25. *Sext.* 26, *&c.*—*Paterc.* 2. *c.* 45. —*Lucan.* 3. v. 164.—*Val. Max.* 9. c. 4.—*Appian. Civ. B.* 2.——A man who attempted to make himself king of Macedonia in opposition to Perdiccas. He was expelled by Pelopidas the Theban.——A son of Pyrrhus king of Epirus, by Antigone, the daughter of Berenice. He was left governor of Epirus when Pyrrhus went to Italy to assist the Tarentines against the Romans, where he presided with great prudence and moderation. He was killed bravely fighting in the expedition which Pyrrhus, after his return from Italy, undertook against Sparta and Argos.——A eunuch, by whose friendly assistance Mithridates the Great saved his life, after a battle with Lucullus.——A king of Epirus, who died very young as he was marching an army against the Ætolians, who had seized part of his dominions. *Justin.* 28.——A king of Chalcidica in Syria, about 30 B.C.——He opposed Pompey when he invaded Syria, but was defeated, and the conqueror spared his life upon receiving 1000 talents. *Joseph. Ant.* 13.——A nephew of Antigonus, who commanded an army in the Peloponnesus. He revolted from his uncle to Cassander, and some time after attempted to bribe the soldiers of Ptolemy Lagus, king of Ægypt, who had invited him to his camp. He was seized and imprisoned for this treachery, and the Ægyptian monarch at last ordered him to be put to death, by causing him to drink the juice of hemlock.——A son of Seleucus, killed in the celebrated battle at Issus, between Darius and Alexander the Great.——A son of Juba, made king of Mauritania. He was son of Cleopatra Selene, the daughter of M. Antony, and the celebrated Cleopatra. He was put to death by Caius Caligula. *Dio.—Tacit. Ann.* 11.——A friend of the emperor Otho.——A favourite of Antiochus, king of Syria. He was surnamed *Macron.*——A Jew, famous for his cruelty and avarice. He was for some time governor of Jericho, about 135 B.C.——A powerful Jew, during the troubles which disturbed the peace of Judæa, in the reign of Augustus.——A son of Antony, by Cleopatra, surnamed *Philadelphus* by his father, and made master of Phœnicia, Syria, and all the territories of Asia Minor which were situated between the Ægean and the Euphrates. *Plut. in Anton.*——A general of Herod, king of Judæa.——A son of Chrysermus, who visited Cleomenes, king of Sparta, when imprisoned in Ægypt.——A governor of Alexandria, put to death by Cleomenes.

PTOLEMÆ'US CLAU'DIUS, a celebrated geographer and astrologer in the reign of the emperors Adrian and Antoninus. He was a native of Alexandria, or, according to others, of Pelusium or Ptolemais, and on account of his great learning received the name of most wise, and most divine, among the Greeks. In his well known system of the world called the Ptolemaic system, he places the earth in the centre of the universe, and accounts for the motion of the heavenly bodies by the ingenious, but almost unintelligible application of cycles and epicycles, a doctrine universally believed and adopted by the learned of all nations till the 16th century, when it was confuted and rejected by Copernicus. His geography is valued for its learning, and the very useful information which it communicates. Besides his system and geography, Ptolemy wrote other books, in one of which he preserves a very valuable account of the fixed stars, of 1022 of which he gives the certain and definite longitude and latitude. The best edition of Ptolemy's geography in seven books, is that of Bertius, fol. Amst. 1618, and that of his treatise, *de Judiciis Astrologicis* by Camerar. 4to, 1535, and of the *Harmonica*, 4to, Wallis, Oxon. 1683. *Fabr. B. Gr.* 4. c. 16.—*Sax. Onom.* 1. p. 314.

PTOLEMA'IS, a large town of Thebais in Ægypt, called after the Ptolemies, who beautified it.——A city in the territories of Cyrene. It was situate on the coast, and according to some, it was the same as Barce. *Vid.* Barce.——A city of Palestine, called also Acon, and now better known by the name of Acre. *Mela*, 1. c. 8. l. 3. c. 8.—*Plin.* 2. c. 73.—*Strab.* 14, &c.——A city of Upper Æthiopia on the Arabian Gulph, called Theron by *Ptolemy*, and Epithera by *Pliny*, 6. c. 29. It is now Suachen.

PTOL'ICHUS, a statuary of Corcyra, pupil to Critias the Athenian. *Paus.* 6. c. 3.

PTO'US, a son of Athamas and Themisto, who gave his name to a mountain in Bœotia, upon which he built a temple to Apollo, surnamed Ptous. The god had also a celebrated oracle on mount Ptous. *Plut. de orac. def.—Paus.* 9. c. 23.—*Apollod.* 1. c. 9. Tzetzes derives the surname of Ptous, applied to Apollo, from the fear (πτόα) which Latona felt at the sight of a large boar which she saw after the birth of Apollo and Diana. *Tzetzes. Lyc.* 265 & 352.

PTU'A, a city of Armenia Minor. *Ptol.*

PTYCH'IA, an island near Corcyra. *Steph.*

PU'AN, a city of Arabia Felix. *Ptol.*

PUBLICI'A LEX forbad any person to play with bad or fraudulent designs. *Joh. Rosin. Antiq.* 8. c. 31.

PUBLIC'IUS, a Roman freedman, so much like Pompey the Great, that they were often confounded together. *Val. Max.* 9. c. 14.

PUBLIC'OLA, a name given to Publius Valerius on account of his great popularity. *Vid.* Valerius. *Plut. in Pub.—Liv.* 2. c. 8.—*Plin.* 30. c. 15.

PUBLIL'IA, the wife of Cicero, after the divorce of Terentia. *Cic.* 12. *Att.* 32.——A tribe at Rome. *Liv.* 7. c. 15.

PUBLIL'IA LEX was introduced by Publius Philo the dictator, A.U.C. 445. It permitted one of the censors to be elected from the Plebeians, since one of the consuls was chosen from that body. *Liv.* 8. c. 12—Another, by which it was ordained, that all laws should be previously approved by the senators, before they were proposed by the people.

Q PUBLIL'IUS PHI'LO, a consul and dictator who conquered the Latins. *Liv.* 8. c. 12.

PUB'LIUS SY'RUS, a Syrian mimic poet, who flourished about 44 B.C. He was originally a slave sold to a Roman patrician, called Domitius, who brought him up with great attention, and gave him his freedom when of age. He gained the esteem of the most powerful at Rome, and reckoned J. Cæsar among his patrons. He soon eclipsed the poet Laberius, whose burlesque compositions were in general esteem. There remains of Publius, a collection of moral sentences about 400 in number, written in iambics and placed in alphabetical order, the newest of which is that of Patav. Comin. 1740. They are also to be found at the end of some editions of Phædrus. *Harles. Not. Lit. Rom.* 1. p. 294.—*Cic.* 12. *Fam.* 18. *Att.* 14. ep. 2.—*Macrob.* 2. *Sat.* 7.—*Plin.* 8. c. 21. l. 35. v. 17. —*Seneca Contr.* 3. c. 18.—*Aul. Gell.* 17. c. 14.—*Gyrald. P. H.* 8.

PUB'LIUS, a prænomen, common among the Romans.——A prætor, who conquered Palæopolis. He was only a plebeian, and though neither consul nor dictator, obtained a triumph in spite of the opposition of the senators. He was the first who was honored with a triumph during a prætorship.——A Roman consul who defeated the Latins, and was made dictator.——A Roman flatterer in the court of Tiberius.——A tribune who accused Manlius, &c.

PUB'LIUS CA'IUS, a man who conspired with Brutus against J. Cæsar.

PUCIA'LIA, a city of the Bastitani, in Spain. *Ptol.*

PUCI'NUM, a town in the interior of Istria. *Ptol.* 3. c. 1. It is now Prosecho. Its wines *(Pucina)* are much praised by *Pliny*, 14. c. 6, and are now called *Beinfal* by the Germans.

PUCLA'TA or PUDA'TA, a city of Macedonia, between Larissa and Thessalonica. *Antonin.* It is probably the Pudna of other writers, and the Pautalia of *Ptolemy.*

PUDI'CA, a surname applied by the moderns to the statue of Venus of Cnidus, on account of its modest attitude.

PUDICIT'IA, a goddess, who, as her name implies, presided over chastity. She had two temples at Rome: the one erected by Æmilius for the patricians; and the other, for the plebeians, was raised by Virginia the wife of Volumnius, and none but women, and those of known virtue and exemplary modesty, and such as had espoused only one husband, were permitted to approach her sacred threshold. Among those females whose virtues history has recorded, the names of Penelope queen of Ithaca, of Evadne wife of Capaneus, of Laodamia wife of Protesilaus, of Alceste queen of Thessaly, of Hecuba wife of Priam, of Lucretia, of Virginia, &c. may be mentioned as deserving the honors which the goddess of chastity was supposed to bestow in a peculiar degree on her deserving votaries. *Gyrald. H. D. Synt.* 1.—*Rosin. A. Rom.* 2. c. 18.—*Festus de V. Sig.*—*Liv.* 10. c. 7. —*Val. Max.* 2. c. 1. [The finest statue of Pudicitia is in the Vatican, at Rome.]

PUD'NI or PU'DIN, a town of Arabia Felix. *Ptol.* It is now Ziden.

PUG'ELA, a city of Ionia, near Ephesus. *Mela.*

PULCHEL'LUS, a name opprobriously applied to Clodius. *Cic. Att.* 2. ep. 1.

PUL'CHER, the surname of some of the Appian family. *Liv.* 33. c. 44, &c.

PULCHE'RIA, a daughter of the emperor Theodosius the Great, famous for her piety, moderation, and virtue.——A daughter of Arcadius, who held the government of the Roman empire for many years. She was mother of Valentinian. Her piety, and private as well as public virtues have been universally admired. She died A.D. 452, and was interred at Ravenna, where her tomb is still to be seen. *Niceph. hist. Eccles—Theodoret. —Baron. in Annal.*

PUL'CHRUM, a promontory near Carthage, now Rasafran. *Liv.* 29. c. 27.

PULIP'ULA, a city of India within the Ganges. *Ptol.*

PUL'LUS, a surname of Numitorius.

PUMENTUM, an inland town of Lucania. *Strab.* 6. *Xylander* reads Grumentum.

PUNICUM BELLUM, the first Punic war was undertaken by the Romans against Carthage, B.C. 264. The ambition of Rome was the origin of this war. For upwards of 240 years the two nations had beheld each other's power with secret jealousy, but had totally eradicated every cause of contention, by settling in three different treaties, the boundaries of their respective territories, the number of their allies, and how far one nation might sail in the Mediterranean without giving offence to the other. Sicily, an island of the highest consequence to the Carthaginians as a commercial nation, was the seat of the first dissensions. The Mamertini, a body of Italian mercenaries, were appointed by the king of Syracuse, to guard the town of Messana, but this tumultuous tribe, instead of protecting the citizens, basely massacred them, and seized their possessions. This act of cruelty raised the indignation of all the Sicilians, and Hiero, king of Syracuse, who had employed them, prepared to punish their perfidy; and the Mamertini, besieged in Messana and without friends or resources, resolved to throw themselves for protection under the hands of the first power that could relieve them. They were, however, divided in their sentiments, and while some implored the assistance of Carthage, others called upon the Romans for protection. Without hesitation or delay the Carthaginians entered Messana, and the Romans also hastened to give to the Mamertini that aid which had been claimed from them with as much eagerness as from the Carthaginians. At the approach of the Roman troops, the Mamertini, who had implored their assistance, took up arms and forced the Carthaginians to evacuate Messana. Fresh forces were poured in on every side, and though Carthage seemed superior in arms and in resources, yet the valor and intrepidity of the Romans daily appeared more formidable, and Hiero, the Syracusan king, who had hitherto embraced the interest of the Carthaginians, became the most faithful ally of the republic. From a private quarrel the war became general. The Romans obtained a victory in Sicily, but as their enemies were masters at sea, the advantages they gained were small and inconsiderable. To make themselves equal to their adversaries they aspired to the dominion of the sea, and in sixty days timber was cut down and a fleet of 120 gallies completely manned and provisioned. The successes they met by sea were trivial, and little advantage could be gained over an enemy whose sailors had become formidable by actual practice and long experience. Duilius at last obtained a victory, and he was the first Roman who ever received a triumph after a naval battle. The losses they had already sustained induced the Carthaginians to sue for peace, and the Romans, whom an unsuccessful attempt upon Africa, under Regulus (*vid.* Regulus), had rendered diffident, listened to the proposal, and the first Punic war was concluded B.C. 241, on the following terms: The Carthaginians pledged themselves to pay to the Romans, within twenty years the sum of 3000 Euboic talents; they promised to release all the Roman captives without ransom; to evacuate Sicily, and the other islands in the Mediterranean; and not to molest Hiero, king of Syracuse, or his allies. After this treaty the Carthaginians, who had lost the dominion of Sardinia and Sicily, made new conquests in Spain, and soon began to repair their losses by industry and labor. They planted colonies, confirmed their connections with foreign states, and secretly prepared to revenge themselves upon their powerful rivals. The Romans were not insensible of their successes in Spain, and, to stop their progress towards Italy, made a stipulation with the Carthaginians, by which they were not permitted to cross the Iberus, or to molest the cities of their allies the Saguntines. This was for some time observed, but when Annibal succeeded to the command of the Carthaginian armies in Spain, he spurned the boundaries which the jealousy of Rome had set to his arms, and immediately formed the siege of Saguntum. The Romans were apprised of the hostilities which had been begun against their allies, but Saguntum was in the hands of the active enemy before they had taken any steps to oppose him. Complaints were carried to Carthage, but war was determined upon by the influence of Annibal in the Carthaginian senate. Without delay or diffidence B.C. 218, Annibal marched a numerous army of 90,000 foot and 12,000 horse towards Italy, resolved to carry on the war to the gates of Rome. He crossed the Rhone, the Alps, and the Apennines, with uncommon celerity, and the Roman consuls who were stationed to stop his progress were severally defeated. The battle of Trebia, and that of the lake Thrasymenus, threw Rome into the greatest apprehensions, but the prudence and the dilatory measure of the dictator Fabius soon taught them to hope for better times. Yet the conduct of Fabius was universally censured as cowardice, and the two consuls who succeeded him in the command, by pursuing a different plan of operations, soon brought on a decisive action at Cannæ, in which 45,000 Romans were left on the field of battle. This bloody victory caused so much consternation at Rome, that some authors have declared, that if Annibal had immediately marched from the plains of Cannæ to the city, he would have met with no resistance, but would have terminated a long and dangerous war with glory to himself, and the most inestimable advantages to his country. This celebrated victory at Cannæ left the conqueror master of two camps, and of an immense booty; and the cities which had hitherto observed a neutrality, no sooner saw the defeat of the Romans, than they eagerly embraced the interest of Carthage. The news of this victory was carried to Carthage by Mago, and the Carthaginians refused to believe it till three bushels of golden rings, which had been taken from the Roman knights in the field of battle, were spread before them. After this Annibal called his brother Asdrubal from Spain with a large reinforcement: but the march of Asdrubal was intercepted by the Romans, his army was defeated, and himself slain. Affairs had now taken a different turn, and Marcellus, who had the command of the Roman legions in Italy, soon taught his countrymen that Annibal was not invincible in the field. In different parts of the world the Romans were making very rapid conquests, and if the sudden arrival of a Carthaginian army in Italy at first raised fears and apprehensions, they were soon enabled to dispute with their enemies for the sovereignty of Spain, and the dominion of the sea. Annibal no longer appeared formidable in Italy; if he conquered towns in Campania or Magna Græcia, he remained master of them only while his army hovered in the neighbourhood, and if he marched towards Rome the alarm he occasioned was but momentary; the Romans were prepared to oppose him, and his retreat was therefore the more dishonorable. The conquests of young Scipio in Spain had now raised the expectations of the Romans, and he had no sooner returned to Rome than he proposed to remove Annibal from the capital of Italy by carrying the war to the gates of Carthage. This was a bold and hazardous enterprize, but though Fabius opposed it, it was universally approved by the Roman senate, and Scipio was empowered to sail to Africa. The conquests of the young Roman were as rapid in Africa as in Spain, and the Carthaginians, apprehensive for the fate of their capital, recalled Annibal from Italy, and preferred their safety at home to the maintaining a long and expensive war in another quarter of the globe. Annibal received their orders with indignation, and with tears in his eyes left Italy, where for sixteen years he had known no superior in the field of battle. At his arrival in Africa, the Carthaginian general soon collected a large army, and met his insulting adversary in the plains of Zama. The battle was long and bloody, and though one nation fought for glory and the other for liberty, the Romans obtained the victory; and Annibal, who had sworn eternal enmity to the gods of Rome, fled from Carthage, after he had advised his countrymen to accept the terms of the conqueror. This battle of Zama was decisive; the Carthaginians sued for peace, which the haughty conquerors granted with difficulty. The conditions were these: Carthage was permitted to hold all the possessions she had in Africa before the war, and to be governed by her own laws and institutions. She was ordered to make restitution of all the ships and other effects which had been taken in violation of a truce that had been agreed upon by both nations. She was to surrender the whole of her fleet, except ten gallies; she was to release and deliver up all her captives, deserters, or fugitives taken or received during the war; to indemnify Masinissa for all the losses which he had sustained; to deliver up all her elephants, and for the future never to tame or break any more of these animals. She was not to make war upon any nation whatever, without the consent of the Romans; and she was to reimburse the Romans, to pay the sum of 10,000 talents, at the rate of 200 talents a year for fifty years, and she was to give up hostages from the noblest families for the performance of these several articles; and till the ratification of the treaty, to supply the Roman forces with money and provisions. These humiliating conditions were accepted 201 B.C., and immediately 4000 Roman captives were released, 500 gallies were delivered and burnt on the spot, but the immediate exaction of 200 talents was more severely felt, and many of the Carthaginian senators burst into tears at the melancholy humiliation of their country. During the 50 years which followed the conclusion of the second Punic war, the Carthaginians were employed in repairing their losses by unwearied application and industry; but they found still in the Roman power a jealous rival and a haughty conqueror, and in Masinissa, the ally of Rome, an intriguing and ambitious monarch. The king of Numidia made himself master of one of their provinces; but as they were unable to make war without the consent of Rome, the Carthaginians sought relief by embassies, and made continual complaints in the Roman senate, of the oppression and encroachments of Masinissa. Commissioners were appointed to examine the cause of their complaints; but as Masinissa was the ally of Rome, the interest of the Carthaginians was neglected, and whatever seemed to depress their republic was agreeable to the Romans. Cato, who was in the number of the commissioners, examined the capital of Africa with a jealous eye; he saw it with concern, rising as it were from its ruins; and when he returned to Rome, declared in full senate, that the peace of Italy would never be established while Carthage was in being. The senators, however, were not guided by his opinion, and the *delenda est Carthago* of Cato did not prevent the Romans from acting with moderation. But while the senate were debating about the existence of Carthage, and while they considered it a dependent power, and not as an ally, the wrongs of Africa were without redress, and Masinissa continued his depredations. Upon this the Carthaginians resolved to do to their cause that justice which the Romans had denied them; they entered the field against the Numidians, but were defeated in a bloody battle by Masinissa, who was then 90 years old. By this bold measure they had broken the peace; and as their late defeat had rendered them desperate, they hastened with all possible speed to the capital of Italy, to justify their proceedings, and to implore the forgiveness of the Roman senate. The news of Masinissa's victory had already reached Italy, and some forces were immediately sent to Sicily, and thence ordered to pass into Africa. The ambassadors of Carthage received evasive and unsatisfactory answers from the senate; and when they saw the Romans landed at Utica, they resolved to purchase peace by the most submissive terms which even the most abject slaves could offer. The Romans acted with the deepest policy, no declaration of war had been made, though hostilities appeared inevitable; and in answer to the most submissive offers of Carthage the consuls replied that to prevent every cause of quarrel, the Carthaginians must deliver into their hands 300 hostages, all children of senators, and the most respectable families. The demand was great and alarming, but it was no sooner granted, than the Romans made another demand, and the Carthaginians were told that peace could not continue, if they refused to deliver up all their ships, their engines of war, with all their naval and military stores. The Carthaginians complied, and immediately 40,000 suits of armour, 20,000 large engines of war, with a plentiful store of ammunition and missile weapons were surrendered. After this duplicity had succeeded, the Romans laid open the final resolution of the senate, and the Carthaginians were then told that to avoid hostilities, they must leave their ancient habitations, and retire into the inland parts of Africa, and found another city, at the distance of not less than ten miles from the sea. This was heard with horror and indignation; the Romans were fixed and inexorable, and Carthage was filled with tears and lamentations. But the spirit of liberty and independence was not yet extinguished in the capital of Africa, and the Carthaginians determined to sacrifice their lives for the protection of their gods, the tombs of their forefathers, and the place which had given them birth. Before the Roman army approached the city preparations to support a siege were made, and the ramparts of Carthage were covered with stones, to compensate for the weapons and instruments of war, which they had ignorantly betrayed to the duplicity of their enemies. Asdrubal, whom the despair of his countrymen had banishsd on account of his unsuccesful expedition against Masinissa, was immediately recalled; and, in the moment of danger, Carthage seemed to have possessed more spirit and more vigor, than when Annibal was victorious at the gates of Rome. The town was blocked up by the Romans, and a regular siege was begun. Two years were spent in useless operations, and Carthage seemed still able to rise from its ruins, to dispute for the empire of the world; when Scipio, the descendant of the great Scipio, who finished the second Punic war, was sent to conduct the siege. The vigour of his operations soon baffled the efforts and the bold resistance of the besieged; the communications which they had with the land were cut off, and the city, which was twenty miles in circumference, was completely surrounded on all sides by the enemy. Despair and famine now raged in the city, and Scipio gained access to the city walls, where the battlements were low and unguarded. His entrance into the streets was disputed with uncommon fury, the houses as he advanced were set on fire to stop his progress; but when a body of 50,000 persons of either sex, had claimed quarter, the rest of the inhabitants were disheartened, and such as disdained to be prisoners of war, perished in the flames, which gradually destroyed their habitations, 147 B.C., after a continuation of hostilities for three years. During 17 days Carthage was in flames; and the soldiers were permitted to redeem from the fire whatever possessions they could. But while others profited from the destruction of Carthage, the philosophic general, struck by the melancholy aspect of the scene, repeated two lines from Homer, which contained a prophecy concerning the fall of Troy. He was asked by the historian Polybius, to what he then applied his prediction? "To my country," replied Scipio, "for her too I dread the vicissitude of human affairs, and in her turn she may exhibit another flaming Carthage." This remarkable event happened about the year of Rome 606. The news of this victory caused the greatest rejoicings at Rome; and commissioners were immediately appointed by the Roman senate, not only to raze the walls of Carthage, but even to demolish and burn the very materials of which they were made; and in a few days, that city, which had been once the seat of commerce, the model of magnificence, the common store of the wealth of nations, and one of the most powerful states of the world, left behind no traces of its splendor, of its powers, or even of its existence. *Polyb.—Orosius.—Appian. de Punic*, &c.—*Flor.—Plut. in Cat.* &c.—*Strab.—Liv. epit.—Diod.*

PU'NICUM, an inland town of Istria. *Ptol.* 3. c. 1. *Plin.* 14. c. 6.

PU'PIA LEX, *de senatu*, required that the senate should not be assembled from the 18th of the calends of February to the calends of the same month, and that before the embassies were either accepted or rejected, the senate should be held on no account.

PUPIE'NUS MAR'CUS CLAU'DIUS MAX'IMUS, a man who, though the son of a blacksmith, raised himself by his merit to the highest offices of the Roman armies, and gradually became a prætor, consul, præfect of Rome, and a governor of the provinces. After the death of the Gordians, Pupienus was elected with Balbinus to the imperial throne, and to rid the world of the usurpation and tyranny of the Maximini, he immediately marched against these tyrants; but he was informed that they had been sacrificed to the fury and resentment of their own soldiers; and therefore he retired to Rome, to enjoy the tranquillity which his merit claimed. He soon after prepared to make war against the Persians, who insulted the majesty of Rome, but in this he was prevented, and was massacred A.D. 236, by the prætorian guards. Balbinus, his imperial colleague, shared his fate. Pupienus is sometimes called Maximus. In his private character he always appeared grave and serious, he was the firm and constant friend of justice, moderation, and clemency, and no greater encomium can be passed upon his virtues than to say that he was invested with the purple without soliciting it, and that the Roman senate said that they had selected him from thousands, because they knew no person more worthy or better qualified to support the dignity of an emperor. *Jul. Capitol in Gordianis.* c. 10. & *Maximin.* c. 20. 24.—*Herodian.* 1. 7.—*Aur. Victor. de Cæs.* [There is a fine statue of Pupienus in the Villa Albani, near Rome: and a bust in the Capitol.]

PU'PIUS, a centurion of Pompey's army, seized by Cæsar's soldiers. *Cæs. B. C.* 1. c. 13.——A prætor mentioned by *Livy*, 39. c. 45.——A plebeian quæstor. *Liv.* 4. c. 54.——An ædile. *Liv.* 39. c. 39.——A poet. *Vid.* Puppius.

PUP'PIUS, a tragic poet in the age of J. Cæsar. His tragedies were so pathetic, that when they were represented on the Roman stage, the audience melted into tears, from which circumstance Horace calls them *lachrymosa.* He was himself sensible of his own merits, as the words of his epitaph seem to indicate: *Flebunt amici & bene noti mortem meam, nam populus omnis, me vivo, lacrymatus est.* *Horat.* 1. ep. 1. v. 67.—*Gyrald. de P. H.* 8.

PURPURA'RIÆ, two islands of the Atlantic on the African coast, now Lancarota and Fortuventura. *Plin.* 6. c. 31. l. 35. c. 6.

PU'TA, a divinity at Rome, who presided over the pruning of trees. *Arnob.* 4.—*Gyrald. H. D.* 7.

PUTE'OLI, a maritime town of Campania, between Baiæ and Naples, founded by a colony from Cumæ. It was originally called Dicæarchia, and afterwards Puteoli, from the great number of *wells* that were in the neighbourhood. It was much frequented by the Romans, on account of its mineral waters and hot baths, and near it Cicero had a villa called Puteolanum. It is now called Puzzoli, and contains, instead of its ancient magnificence, not more than 10.000 inhabitants. *Sil.* 13. v. 385.—*Strab.* 5.—*Varro L. L.* 4. c. 5.—*Cic. Phil.* 8. c. 3. *fam.* 5. ep. 15.—*Mela,* 2. c. 4.—*Paus.* 8. c. 7.

PUTIC'ULÆ, a place of the Esquiline gate, where the meanest of the Roman populace were buried. Part of it was converted into a garden by Mecænas, who received it as a present from Augustus. *Horat.* 1. sat. 8. v. 8.—*Varro L. L.* 4. c. 5.

PYANEP'SIA, sometimes called Pœanopsia or Panopsia, an Athenian festival, celebrated in honor of Theseus and his companions, who, after their return from Crete, were entertained with all manner of fruits, and particularly pulse. From this circumstance the Pyanepsia was ever after commemorated by the *boiling of pulse,* ἀπὸ τοῦ ἕψειν πύανα. Some however suppose that it was observed in commemoration of the Heraclidæ, who were entertained with pulse by the Athenians. *Plut. in Thes.*—*Pollux,* 8. c. 8.—*Hesychius.* —*Meursius, Gr. Fer.*

PYC'NUS, a river of Crete. *Ptol.*

PY'DES, a city and river of Pisidia. *Steph.*

PYD'NA, a town of Macedonia, originally called Citron, situate between the mouth of the rivers Aliacmon and Lydius. It was in this city that Cassander massacred Olympias the mother of Alexander the Great, his wife Roxana, and his son Alexander. Pydna is famous for a battle which was fought there, on the 22d of June, B.C. 168, between the Romans under Paulus, and king Perseus, in which the latter was conquered, and Macedonia soon after reduced into the form of a Roman province. *Justin.* 14. c. 6.—*Flor.*—*Plut. in Paul.*—*Liv.* 44. c. 10.—*Paterc.* 1. c. 9.

PYE'NIS, a city of the Colchi. *Steph.*

PYG'ELA, a sea-port town of Ionia. *Liv.* 37. c. 11.

PYGMÆ'I, a nation of dwarfs, in the extremest parts of India, or, according to others, in Æthiopia. Some authors affirm, that they were no more than one foot high, and that they built their houses with egg-shells. Aristotle says that they lived in holes under the earth, and that they came out in the harvest time with hatchets to cut down the corn as if to fell a forest. They went on goats and lambs of proportionable stature to themselves, to make war against certain birds called cranes, which came there yearly from Scythia to plunder them. They were originally governed by Gerana a princess, who was changed into a crane, for boasting herself fairer than Juno. *Ovid. Met.* 6. v. 90.—*Homer. Il.* 3. v. 6. —*Strab.* 7.—*Arist. Anim.* 8. c. 12.—*Juv.* 13. v. 186.—*Mela,* 3. c. 8.—*Suet. in Aug.* 83.—*Athen.* 9. —*Plin.* 4. c. 11. l. 5. c. 29. l. 6. c. 19 & 30. l. 7. c. 2.—*Marcell.*—*Aul. Gell.* 9. c. 4.—*Nonnus in Dionys.* 4.—*Stat.* 1.—*Sylv.* 6. v. 63.—*Anton.* lib. 16. *Philostratus, icon.* 2. c. 22, mentions that Hercules once fell asleep in the deserts of Africa, after he had conquered Antæus, and that he was suddenly awakened by an attack which had been made upon his body by an army of these Lilliputians, who discharged their arrows with great fury upon his arms and legs. The hero, pleased with their courage, wrapped a great number of them in the skin of the Nemean lion, and carried them to Eurystheus.

PYGMÆ'ON, a surname of Adonis in Cyprus. *Hesychius.*

PYGMA'LION, a king of Tyre, son of Belus, and brother to the celebrated Dido, who founded Carthage. At the death of his father he ascended the vacant throne, and soon became odious to his subjects by his cruelty and avarice. He sacrificed every thing to the gratification of his predominant passions, and did not even spare the life of Sichæus, Dido's husband, because he was the most powerful and opulent of all the Phœnicians. This murder he committed in a temple, of which Sichæus was the priest; but instead of obtaining the riches which he desired, Pygmalion was still more abhorred by his subjects, and Dido, to avoid further acts of cruelty, fled away with her husband's treasure, and a large colony, to the coast of Africa, where she founded a city. Pygmalion died in the 56th year of his age, and in the 47th of his reign. *Virg. Æn.* 1. v. 347, &c.—*Justin.* 18. c. 5.—*Apollod.* 3.—*Eustath. in Dionys. Per.*— *Servius Æn.* 1. v. 646.—*Ital.* 1. v. 21.

PYGMA'LION, a celebrated statuary of the island of Cyprus. The debauchery of the females of Amathus, to which he was a witness, created in him such an aversion for the fair sex, that he resolved never to marry. The affection which he denied to the other sex, he liberally bestowed upon the works of his own hands. He became enamoured of a beautiful statue ef marble which he had made, and at his earnest request and prayers, according to the mythologists, the goddess of beauty changed this favorite statue into a woman, whom the artist married, and by whom he had a son called Paphus, who founded the city of that name in Cyprus. *Ovid. Met.* 10. fab. 9.

PYLACE'UM, a city of Phrygia. *Ptol.*

PYL'ADES, a son of Strophius, king of Phocis, by one of the sisters of Agamemnon. He was educated, together with his cousin Orestes, with whom he formed the most inviolable friendship, and whom he assisted to revenge the murder of Agamemnon, by assassinating Clytæmnestra and Ægisthus. He also accompanied him to Taurica Chersonesus, and for his services Orestes rewarded him, by giving him his sister Electra in marriage.

Pylades had by her two sons, Medon and Strophius. The friendship of Orestes and Pylades became proverbial. *Vid.* Orestes. *Eurip. in Iphig.—Æschyl. in Ag.* &c.—*Paus.* 1. c. 28.—*Hygin.* fab. 119 & 120.—*Sch. Pind.* 11. *Pyth.* v. 53.——A celebrated Greek musician, in the age of Philopœmen. *Plut. in. Phil.*——A mimic in the reign of Augustus, banished, and afterwards recalled. *Sueton. in Aug.*

PY'LÆ, a town of Asia, between Cappadocia and Cilicia. *Cic.* 5. *ad Att.*——An island of the Arabian Gulf, called also Pseudopylæ. *Plin.* 6. c 29. The word *Pylœ*, which signifies *gates*, was often applied by the Greeks to any straits or passages which opened a communication between one country and another, such as the straits of Thermopylæ, of Persia, Hyrcania, &c.

PYLÆ'A, a town of Trachinia, near mount Œta. *Strabo*, 1. 9.——A festival at Pylæ, called also Thermopylæ, in honor of Ceres. *Id. ibid.*

PYLÆM'ENES, a Paphlagonian, son of Melius, who came to the Trojan war, and was killed by Menelaus. His son, called Harpalion, was killed by Meriones. *Dictys. Cret.* 2. c. 34.—*Homer. Il.* 2. v. 358. 1. 5. v. 575. 1. 13. v. 644.——A king of Mæonia, who sent his sons, Mestes and Antiphus, to the Trojan war. *Homer. Il.* 2. *en.* 371.—*Dict.* 2. c. 35.——A son of Nicomedes, banished from Paphlagonia by Mithridates, and restored by Pompey. *Eutrop.* 5 & 6.

PYLÆ'US, a mountain of Lesbus. *Strab.*

PYLAG'ORÆ, a name given to the Amphictyonic council, because they always assembled at Pylæ, near the temple of Delphi. *Justin.* 8. c. 1.

PYLA'ON, a son of Neleus and Chloris, killed by Hercules with his brothers. *Apollod.* 1. c. 9.

PYLAR'GE, a daughter of Danaus. *Apollod.*

PYLARTES, a Trojan killed by Patroclus. *Homer. Il.* 16. v. 695.

PY'LAS, a king of Megara. He had the misfortune accidentally to kill his uncle Bias, for which he fled away, leaving his kingdom to Pandion, his son-in-law, who had been driven from Athens. *Apollod.* 3. c. 15.—*Paus.* 1. c. 39.—*Strab.* 9.—*Suidas.*

PYLENE, a town of Ætolia. *Homer. Il.* 2.

PYLER'DUS, a son of Hercules by Astybia, daughter of Thestius. *Apollod.* 2.

PYLE'TIS or PYLÆ'TIS, a surname of Minerva, because her statue was placed at the entrance of the Grecian temples. *Gyrald. H. D.* 11.

PYL'EUS, a Trojan chief, killed by Achilles. *Dictys*, 3. c. 14.—*Dares*, 21.——A son of Clymenus, king of Orchomenus. *Paus.* 9. c. 37.

PYL'LEON, a town of Thessaly. *Liv.* 42. c. 40.

PY'LO, a daughter of Thespius, mother of Hippotas. *Apollod.*

PYLO'RA, an island of Persia. *Arrian.*

PYLO'RUS, a city in the interior of Crete. *Plin.* 4. c. 12.

PY'LUM, a city of Macedonia, near the borders of Illyria. *Strab.*

PY'LUS, now Navarino, a town of Messenia, situate on the western coast of the Peloponnesus, opposite the island Sphacteria in the Ionian Sea. It was also called Coryphasion, from the promontory on which it was erected. It was built by Pylus, at the head of a colony from Megara. The founder was dispossessed of it by Neleus, and fled into Elis, where he dwelt in a small town, which he also called Pylus.——A town of Elis, at the mouth of the river Alpheus, between the Peneus and the Selleis. It is now Pilos.——Another town of Elis, called Triphyliacha, from Triphylia, a province of Elis, where it was situate. These three cities, which bore the name of Pylus, disputed their respective right to the honor of having given birth to the celebrated Nestor, son of Neleus. The Pylus which was situate near the Alpheus seems to win the palm, as it had in its neighbourhood a small village called Geranus, and a river called Geron, of which Homer makes mention. Pindar, however, calls Nestor king of Messenia, and gives the preference to the first-mentioned of these three cities. *Apollod.* 1. c. 19. 1. 3. c. 15.—*Paus.* 1. c. 39.—*Strab.* 9.—*Homer. Il.* 2. *Od.* 3.—*Schol. Hom. Il.* 2.—*Sch. Pind.* 6. *Pyth.*——An island near Peloponnesus, seized by Laches during the Peloponnesian war. It was taken by the Lacedæmonians, and afterwards retaken by Cleon. *Schol. Equit. Aristoph.* p. 291.

PY'LUS, a son of Mars by Demonice, the daughter of Agenor. He was present at the chase of the Calydonian boar. *Apollod.* 1.

PYN'DIS, a town of Upper Æthiopia. *Plin.* 6. c. 29.

PY'RA, a part of mount Œta, on which the body of Hercules was burnt. *Liv.* 36. c. 30.

PYRAC'MON, one of Vulcan's workmen in the forges of mount Ætna. The name is derived from πῦρ, and ἄκμων, which signify *fire* and *an anvil*. *Virg. Æn.* 8. v. 475.

PYRAC'MOS, a man killed by Cæneus. *Ovid, Met.* 12. v. 460.

PY'RÆ, a town of Latium, near Minturnæ. *Plin.* 3. c. 5. It is now in ruins.

PYRÆ'A, part of Thessaly. *Steph.*

PYRÆCH'MES, a king of Eubœa, who was conquered by the Bœotians, headed by Hercules, and torn to pieces between two horses. *Plut. in Par.* 7.——A king of Pæonia during the Trojan war. He assisted Priam, and was killed by Diomedes, or, according to Homer, by Patroclus. *Dictys*, 2 & 3.—*Homer. Il.* 16. v. 286.——A celebrated slinger. *Paus.* 5. c. 3.

PYRÆ'I, a people of Dalmatia. *Plin.* 3. c. 22.

PYR'AMUS, a youth of Babylon, who became enamoured of Thisbe, a beautiful virgin, who dwelt in the neighbourhood. The flame was mutual, and the two lovers, whom their parents forbade to marry, regularly received each other's addresses, through the chink of a wall, which separated their houses. After the most solemn vows of sincerity, they both agreed to elude the vigilance of their friends, and to meet one another at the tomb of Ninus, under a white mulberry tree, without the walls of Babylon. Thisbe came first to the appointed place, but the sudden arrival of a lioness frightened her away; and as she fled into a neighbouring cave she dropped her veil, which the lioness found and besmeared with blood. Pyramus soon arrived, he found Thisbe's veil all bloody, and concluding that she had been torn to pieces by the wild beasts of the place, stabbed himself with his sword. Thisbe, when her fears were vanished, returned from the cave, and at the sight of the dying Pyramis, fell upon the sword which still reeked with his blood. This tragical scene happened under a mulberry tree, which, as the poets mention, was stained with the blood of the lovers, and ever after bore fruit of the color of blood. *Ovid. Met.* 4. v. 55, &c.—*Hygin.* fab. 243.

PYR'AMUS, a river of Cilicia, rising in mount Taurus, and falling into the Pamphylian Sea. *Cic.* 3. *Fam.* 11.—*Dionys. Perieg.*—*Curt.* 3. c. 4. 1. 7. c. 5.—*Apollod.* 3. It is now Malmistra, according to *Niger*.

PYRAN'DER, a quæstor at Athens, slain by the populace for the parsimonious manner in which he distributed the corn. *Plut.*——An historian, who wrote on the Peloponnesian war. *Plut. in Par.* c. 37.

PYRAN'THUS, a small city of Crete, near Gortynia. *Steph.* It is now in ruins.

PYR'ASUS, a Trojan slain by Ajax. *Homer.*

PYR'ASUS, a city of Phthia. *Steph.*

PYRE'ICUS, a celebrated painter. *Plin.* 35. c. 10.

PYRENÆ'A, a city of Locris. *Steph.*

PYRENÆ'A VE'NUS, a town of Gallia Narbonensis. It is called *Portus Venerus* by *Mela*, 2. c. 5, and *Templum Veneris* by others. It is now Capo de Creuz, or Port *Vendres*, according to *Baudrand*.

PYRENÆ'I, a mountain, or a long ridge of high mountains, which separate Gaul from Spain, and extend from the Atlantic to the Mediterranean Sea. They receive the name from Pyrene the daughter of Bebrycius, (*vid.* Pyrene,) or from the fire (πῦρ) which once raged there for several days. This fire was originally kindled by shepherds, and so intense was the heat which it occasioned, that all the silver mines of the mountains were melted, and ran down in large rivulets. This account is deservedly deemed fabulous by Strabo and others. *Diod.* 6.—*Strab.* 8.—*Mela*, 2. c. 6.—*Ital.* 3. v. 415.—*Liv.* 21. c. 60.—*Plin.* 4. c. 20.—*Eustath. ad Dionys. Per.* 288.—*Tibul.* 1. el. 8. v. 9.—*Auson.* 24. v. 69,

PYRENÆ'US, a king of Thrace, who during a shower of rain, gave shelter in his house to the nine muses, and attempted to offer them violence. The goddesses, upon this, took to their wings and flew away. Pyrenæus, who attempted to follow them as if he had wings, threw himself down from the top of a tower and was killed. *Ovid. Met.* 5. v. 274.

PYRE'NE, a daughter of Bebrycius, king of the southern parts of Spain. Hercules offered violence to her before he went to attack Geryon, and she brought into the world a serpent, which so terrified her, that she fled into the woods, where she was torn to pieces by wild beasts. *Sil. Ital.* 3 v. 420.——A nymph, mother of Cycnus by Mars. *Apollod.* 2.

PYRE'NE, a fountain near Corinth. *Plin.* 4. c. 4.—*Ovid. Met.* 1. 2.——A small village in Celtic Gaul, near which, according to some, the river Ister took its rise.

PYR'ETHI, certain Magi in Cappadocia. *Strab.* l. 15.

PYRGA'NUM, a maritime place of Etruria. *Antonin.*

PYRGEN'SES, a people of Achaia. *Plin.* 4. c. 6.

PYR'GI, an ancient town of Etruria, on the sea coast, between Antium and Graviscæ. *Martial.* 12. epigr. 2.—*Virg. Æn.* 10. v. 184.—*Servius loco.*—*Mela*, 2. c. 5.—*Liv.* 36. c. 3.

PYR'GION, an historian who wrote on the laws of Crete. *Athen.* l. 4.

PYR'GO, the nurse of Priam's children who followed Æneas in his flight from Troy. *Virg. Æn.* 5. v. 645.

PYRGOT'ELES, a celebrated engraver on gems, in the age of Alexander the Great. He had the exclusive privilege of engraving the conqueror, as Lysippus was the only sculptor who was permitted to make statues of him. *Plin.* 37. c. 1.

PYR'GUS, a fortified place of Elis in the Peloponnesus. *Liv.* l. 7. dec. 3.——A city of Marmarica, now Barda.

PYR'GUS EUPHRAN'TA, a town of Africa, near the Syrtis Major. *Ptol.*

PYRILAM'PES, an athlete of Ephesus, who obtained a prize at the Olympic games. His statue at Olympia was made by an artist of the same name, a native of Messenia. *Paus.* 6. c. 4. & 15.

PYRIN'DUS and PYR'NUS, cities of Caria. *Steph.*

PYRIPHLEG'ETHON, a river of Thesprotia, more generally called Phlegethon. *Hom. Odyss.* 10. v 513.—*Lycoph.* 669. & *Tzetzes loco.*

PYRIP'PE, a daughter of Thespius. *Apollod.*

PYRIS'OUS, the first name of Achilles, because his father saved him from the flames when his mother Thetis had placed him on coals to try whether he was, like herself, immortal, or, according to others, to destroy all the mortal parts he had. *Apollod.* 3.—*Ptol. Hephæst.* 7.

PY'RO, one of the Oceanides. *Hesiod. Theog.*

PYRO'DES, a son of Cilix, said to be the first who discovered and applied to human purposes the fire concealed in flints. *Plin.* 7. c. 56.

PYR'OIS, (*-entos,*) one of the horses of the sun. *Ovid. Met.* 2. v. 153.—*Val. Flacc.* 5. v. 432.

PYR'OIS, a name given to the planet Mars from its redness or fiery appearance. *Colum.* 10. v. 290.—*Hygin. P. A.* 2. c. 42.—*Sch. Apollon.* 3. v. 1376.

PYRONÆ'A, a city of Locris. *Steph.* Some read Vyrenæa.

PYRO'NIA, a surname of Diana, from her temple on mount Cratis in the country of the Brutii in Italy, whence the Argians from Peloponnesus came to fetch fire for their festivals at Lerna. *Paus.* 8. c. 16.

PYR'RHA, a daughter of Epimetheus and Pandora, who married Deucalion, the son of Prometheus, who reigned in Thessaly. In her age all mankind were destroyed by a deluge, and she and her husband alone escaped from the general destruction, by saving themselves in a boat which Deucalion had made by his father's advice. When the waters had retired from the surface of the earth, Pyrrha, with her husband, went to the oracle of Themis, where they were directed to repair the loss of mankind, by throwing stones behind their backs. They obeyed, and the stones which Pyrrha threw were changed into women, and those of Deucalion into men. *Vid.* Deucalion. Pyrrha became mother of Amphictyon, Hellen, and Protegenea, by Deucalion. *Ovid. Met.* 1. v. 350, &c.—*Hygin.* fab. 153.—*Apollon. Rhod.* 3. v. 1085.—*Schol. Theocrit.* 15. v. 141.—*Sch. Hom. Il.* 1. v. 10.——A daughter of Creon, king of Thebes. *Paus.* 9. c. 10.——The name which Achilles bore when he disguised himself in women's clothes, at the court of Lycomedes. *Hygin.* fab. 96.—*Servius ad Virg. Æn.* 1. v. 34.—*Tertull. de Pall.* 4.

PYR'RHA, a town of Eubœa. *Plin.* 4. c. 12.—*Mela*, 2. c. 7.——A promontory of Phthiotis, on the bay of Malia. *Strab.*——A town of Lesbus.——A city of Caria. *Plin.* 2. c. 92.——A city of Ionia, at the mouth of the Mæander. *Ptol.* It is now Demonage.

PYR'RHA, a beautiful courtezan at Rome, of whom Horace was long an admirer. *Horat.* 1. od. 5.

PYRRHÆ'I, a people of Æthiopia, in the interior of Libya. *Ptol.*

PYRRHE'UM, a place in the city of Ambracia. *Liv.* 38. c. 5.—*Plin.* 4. c. 1.

PYR'RHI CAS'TRA, a place of Lucania. *Liv.* 35. c. 27.

PYR'RHIAS, a boatman of Ithaca, remarkable for his humanity. He delivered from slavery an old man who had been taken by pirates, and robbed of some pots full of pitch. The old man was so grateful for this kindness, that he gave the pots to his deliverer, after he had told him that they contained gold under the pitch. Pyrrhias, upon this, offered the sacrifice of a bull to the old man, and retained him in his house with every act of kindness and attention till the time of his death. *Plut. in quæst. G.*——A general of the Ætolians, defeated by Philip, king of Macedonia.

PYR'RHICHA, (*saltatio*), a kind of dance said to have been invented and introduced into Greece by Pyrrhus, the son of Achilles, or by the Corybantes or Dactyli. The dancers were generally armed, and exhibited at the sound of the flute all the evolutions of military discipline. *Xenoph. Cyr.* 6.—*Dionys. Hal.* 2.—*Suet. in Cæs.* 39. *Ner.* 12.—*Plin.* 7. c. 56.—*Athen.* 14.—*Alex. ab Alex.* 6. c. 19.—*Solin.* 16.

PYR'RHICUS, a free town of Laconia. *Paus.* 3. c. 21.

PYR'RHIDÆ, a patronymic given to the successors of Neoptolemus in Epirus. *Alex. ab. Alex.* 1. c. 2.

PYR'RHION, an archon at Athens, Olymp. 98. an. 1. *Diod. Sic.* l. 14.

PYR'RHO, a philosopher of Elis, disciple to Anaxarchus, and originally a painter. His father's name was Plistarchus or Pistocrates. He was in continual suspense, doubted of every thing, never made any conclusions, and when he had carefully examined a subject, and investigated all its parts, he concluded by still doubting of its evidence. This manner of doubting in the philosopher has been called *Pyrrhonism*, and his disciples have received the appellation of sceptics, inquisitors, examiners, &c. He pretended to have acquired an uncommon dominion over opinion and passions. The former of these virtues he called *ataraxia*, and the latter *metriopathia*, and so far did he carry his want of common feeling and sympathy, that he passed with unconcern near a ditch into which his master Anaxarchus had fallen, and where he had nearly perished. He was once in a storm, and when destruction appeared almost certain, the philosopher remained unconcerned; and while the rest of the crew were lost in lamentations, he desired them to look at a pig which was then feeding himself on board the vessel, exclaiming, "This is a true model for the wise man." As he shewed so much indifference in every thing, and declared that life and death were the same thing, some of his disciples asked him why he did not hurry himself out of the world; "because," said he, "there is no difference between life and death." When he walked in the streets he never looked behind, or moved from the road for a chariot, even in its most rapid course; and indeed, as some authors remark, this indifference for his safety, often exposed him to the greatest and most imminent dangers, from which he was saved by the interference of his friends who followed him. He flourished B.C. 304 and died at the advanced age of 90. He left no writings behind him. His countrymen were so partial to him, that they raised statues to his memory, and exempted all the philosophers of Elis from taxes. *Diog.* 9.—*Cic. de Orat.* 3. c. 17.

—*Paus.* 6. c. 24.—*Aul. Gell.* 11. c. 5.—*Gyrald. P. H.* 3.—*Voss. de sect. Phil.* c. 20.

PYR'RHUS, a son of Achilles and Deidamia, the daughter of king Lycomedes, received this name from the *yellowness* of his hair. He was also called Neoptolemus, or *new warrior*, because he came to the Trojan war in the last years of the celebrated siege of the capital of Troas. *Vid.* Neoptolemus.——A king of Epirus, descended from Achilles, by the side of his mother, and from Hercules by that of his father, and son of Æacides and Phthia. He was saved when an infant, by the fidelity of his servants, from the pursuit of the enemies of his father, who had been banished from his kingdom, and he was carried to the court of Glautius, king of Illyricum, who educated him with great tenderness. Cassander, king of Macedonia, wished to despatch him, as he had so much to dread from him; but Glautius not only refused to deliver him up into the hands of his enemy, but even went with an army, and placed him on the throne of Epirus, though only twelve years of age. About five years after, the absence of Pyrrhus, to attend the nuptials of one of the daughters of Glautias, raised new commotions. The monarch was expelled from his throne by Neoptolemus, who had usurped it after the death of Æacides; and being still without resources, he applied to his brother-in-law Demetrius for assistance. He accompanied Demetrius at the battle of Ipsus, and fought there with all the prudence and intrepidity of an experienced general. He afterwards passed into Ægypt, where by his marriage with Antigone, the daughter of Berenice, he soon obtained a sufficient force to attempt the recovery of his throne. He was successful in the undertaking; but to remove all causes of quarrel, he took the usurper to share with him the sovereignty, and some time after put him to death, under pretence that he had attempted to poison him. In the subsequent years of his reign Pyrrhus engaged in the quarrels which disturbed the peace of the Macedonian monarchy, he marched against Demetrius, and gave the Macedonian soldiers fresh proofs of his valor and activity. By dissimulation he ingratiated himself into the minds of his enemy's subjects, and when Demetrius laboured under a momentary illness, Pyrrhus made an attempt upon the crown of Macedonia, which, if not then successful, soon after rendered him master of the kingdom. This he shared with Lysimachus for seven months, till the jealousy of the Macedonians, and the ambition of his colleague obliged him to retire. Pyrrhus was meditating new conquests when the Tarentines invited him to Italy to assist them against the encroaching power of Rome. He gladly accepted the invitation, but his passage across the Adriatic nearly proved fatal; and he reached the shores of Italy after the loss of the greater part of his troops in a storm. At his entrance into Tarentum B.C. 280, he began to reform the manners of the inhabitants, and by introducing the strictest discipline among their troops, to accustom them to bear fatigue and to despise dangers. In the first battle which he fought with the Romans, he obtained the victory; but for this he was more particularly indebted to his elephants, the bulk and uncommon appearance of which astonished the Romans, and terrified their cavalry. The number of the slain was equal on both sides, and the conqueror said that such another victory would totally ruin him. He also sent Cineas, his chief minister, to Rome, and though victorious, sued for peace. These offers of peace were refused; and when Pyrrhus questioned Cineas about the manners and the character of the Romans, the sagacious minister replied, that their senate was a venerable assembly of kings, and that to fight against them was to attack another Hydra. A second battle was soon after fought near Asculum, but the slaughter was so great, and the valor so conspicuous on both sides, that the Romans and their enemies reciprocally claimed the victory as their own. Pyrrhus still continued the war in favour of the Tarentines, when he was invited into Sicily by the inhabitants, who labored under the yoke of Carthage, and the cruelty of their own petty tyrants. His fondness for novelty soon determined him to quit Italy; he left a garrison at Tarentum, and crossed over to Sicily, where he obtained two victories over the Carthaginians and took many of their towns. He was for a while successful, and formed the project of invading Africa; but his popularity soon vanished, his troops became insolent, and he behaved with haughtiness, and shewed himself oppressive, so that his return to Italy was deemed a fortunate event for all Sicily. He had no sooner arrived at Tarentum, than he renewed hostilities with the Romans with great acrimony, but when his army of 80,000 men had been defeated by 20,000 of the enemy under Curius, he left Italy with precipitation, B.C. 274, ashamed of the enterprize, and mortified by the victories which had been obtained over one of the descendants of Achilles. In Epirus, he began to repair his military character, by attacking Antigonus, who was then on the Macedonian throne. He gained some advantages over his enemy, and was at last restored to the throne of Macedonia. He afterwards marched against Sparta, at the request of Cleonymus; but when all his vigorous operations were insufficient to take the capital of Laconia he retired to Argos, whither the treachery of Aristeus invited him. The Argives desired him to retire, and not to interfere in the affairs of their republic, which were confounded by the ambition of two of their nobles. He apparently complied with their wishes, but in the night he marched his forces into the town, and might have made himself master of the place, had he not retarded his progress by entering it with his elephants. The combat that ensued was obstinate and bloody; and the monarch, to fight with more boldness, and to encounter dangers with more facility, exchanged his dress. He was attacked by one of the enemy, but as he was going to run him through in his own defence, the mother of the Argive, who saw her son's danger from the top of a house, threw down a tile, and brought Pyrrhus to the ground. His head was cut off, and carried to Antigonus, who gave his remains a magnificent funeral, and presented his ashes to his son Helenus, 272 B.C. Pyrrhus has been deservedly commended for his talents as a general; and not only his friends, but also his enemies, have been warm in extolling him; and Annibal declared, that for experience and sagacity the king of Epirus was the first of commanders. He had chosen Alexander the Great for a model, and in every thing he wished not only to imitate, but to surpass him. In the art of war none were superior to him; he made it not only his study as a general, but even wrote many books on encampments, and the different ways of training up an army, and whatever he did was by principle and rule. His uncommon understanding, and his penetration have been also admired; but the general is severely censured, who has no sooner conquered a country, than he looks for other victories, without regarding or securing what he has already obtained, by measures and regulations honorable to himself, and advantageous to his subjects. The Romans passed great encomiums upon him, and Pyrrhus was no less struck with their magnanimity and valor; so much indeed, that he exclaimed that if he had soldiers like the Romans, or if the Romans had him for a general, he would leave no corner of the earth unseen, and no nation unconquered. Pyrrhus married many wives, and all for political reasons; besides Antigone he had Lanassa the daughter of Agathocles, as also a daughter of Autoleon king of Pæonia. His children, as his biographer observes, derived a warlike spirit from their father, and when he was asked by one to which of them he should leave the kingdom of Epirus, he replied to him who has the sharpest sword. *Ælian. Hist. An.* 10.—*Plut, in Vitâ.*—*Justin.* 17, *&c.*—*Liv.* 13 & 14.—*Horat.* 3. od. 6. [There is a fine statue, called Pyrrhus of Epirus, in the Museum of the Capitol, at Rome.]——A king of Epirus son of Ptolemy, murdered by the people of Ambracia. His daughter, called Laudamia, or Deidamia, succeeded him. *Paus.*——A son of Dædalus.

PYR'RUM, a town of Upper Pannonia, *Antonin.*

PY'RUS, a town of Caria. *Steph.*

PYS'TE, the wife of Seleucus, taken prisoner by the Gauls. *Polyæn.* 8. c. 61.

PYSTIL'LUS, a person who founded Agrigentum with a colony from Gela, 579 B.C. *Thucyd.* 4.

PYSTI'RA, an island opposite Smyrna. *Plin.* 5. c. 31.

PYTHÆN'ETUS, a writer on Ægina. The *Scholiast* on *Apollonius*, 1. 4, quotes his first book. *Athen.* l. 13.

PYTHAG'ORAS, a celebrated philosopher born at Samus. His father Mnesarchus was a person of distinction, and therefore the son received that education which was most calculated to enlighten his mind and invigorate his body. Like his contemporaries, he was early made acquainted with poetry and music; eloquence and astronomy became his private studies, and, in gymnastic exercises, he often bore away the palm for strength and dexterity. He first made himself known in Greece, at the Olympic games, where he obtained in the 18th year of his age, the prize for wrestling; and, after he had been admired for the elegance and dignity of his person, and the brilliancy of his understanding, he retired into the east. In Ægypt and Chaldæa he gained the confidence of the priests, and learned from them the artful policy, and the symbolic writings, by which they governed the princes as well as the people, and, after he had spent many years in gathering all the information which could be collected from antique tradition concerning the nature of the gods and the immortality of the soul, Pythagoras revisited his native island. The tyranny of Polycrates at Samus disgusted the philosopher, who was a great advocate for national independence, and, though he was the favorite of the tyrant, he retired from the island, and a second time assisted at the Olympic games. His fame was too well known to escape notice; he was saluted in the public ascembly by the name of *Sophist*, or wise man; but he refused the appellation, and was satisfied with that of philosopher, or, *the friend of wisdom*. "At the Olympic games," said he, in explanation of this new appellation, which he wished to assume, "some are attracted with the desire of obtaining crowns and honors, others come to expose their different commodities to sale, while curiosity draws a third class, and the desire of contemplating whatever deserves notice in that celebrated assembly; thus, on the more extensive theatre of the world, while many struggle for the glory of a name, and many pant for the advantages of fortune, a few, and indeed but a few, who are neither desirous of money, nor ambitious of fame, are sufficiently gratified to be spectators of the wonder, the hurry, and the magnificence of the scene." From Olympia the philosopher visited the republics of Elis and Sparta, and retired to Magna Græcia, where he fixed his habitation in the town of Crotona, about the 40th year of his age. Here he founded a sect which has received the name of the Italian, and soon saw himself surrounded by a great number of pupils, which the recommendation of his mental, as well as his personal accomplishments, had procured. His skill in music and medicine, and his knowledge of mathematics, and natural philosophy, gained him friends and admirers; and amidst the voluptuousness that prevailed among the inhabitants of Crotona, the Samian sage found his instructions respected, and his approbation courted; the most debauched and effeminate were pleased with the eloquence and the graceful delivery of the philosopher, who boldly upbraided them for their vices, and called them to more virtuous and manly pursuits. These animated harangues were attended with rapid success, and a reformation soon took place in the morals and the lives of the people of Crotona. The females were exhorted to become modest, and they left off their gaudy ornaments; the youths were called away from the pursuit of pleasure, and they instantly forgot their intemperance, and paid to their parents that submissive attention and deference which the precepts of Pythagoras required. As to the old, they were directed no longer to spend their time in amassing money, but to improve their understanding, and to seek that peace and those comforts of mind which frugality, benevolence, and philanthropy alone can produce. The sober and religious behaviour of the philosopher strongly recommended the necessity and importance of these precepts. Pythagoras was admired for his venerable aspect, his voice was harmonious, his eloquence persuasive, and the reputation he had acquired by his distant travels, and by being crowned at the Olympic games, was great and important. He regularly frequented the temples of the gods, and paid his devotion to the divinity at an early hour; he lived upon the purest and most innocent food; he clothed himself like the priests of the Ægyptian gods, and by his continual purifications and regular offerings, seemed to be superior to the rest of mankind in sanctity. These artful measures united to render him an object not only of reverence, but of imitation. To set himself at a greater distance from his pupils, a number of years was required to try their various dispositions; the most talkative were not permitted to speak in the presence of their master before they had been his auditors for five years, and those who possessed a natural taciturnity were always allowed to speak after a probation of two years. When they were capable of receiving the secret instructions of the philosopher, they were taught the use of cyphers and hieroglyphic writings, and Pythagoras might boast that his pupils could correspond together, though in the most distant regions, in unknown characters; and by the signs and words which they had received, they could discover, though strangers and barbarians, those who had been educated in the Pythagorean school. So great was his authority among his pupils, that to dispute his word was deemed a crime, and the most stubborn were drawn to coincide with the opinions of their opponents when they helped their arguments by the words of *the master said so*, an expression which becamo proverbial in *jurare in verba magistri*. The great influence which the philosopher possessed in his school was transferred to the world; the pupils divided the applause and the approbation of the people with their venerated master, and, in a short time, the rulers and the legislators of all the principal towns of Greece, Sicily, and Italy, gloried in being the disciples of Pythagoras. The Samian philosopher was the first who supported the doctrine of metempsychosis, or the transmigration of the soul into different bodies, and those notions he seemed to have imbibed among the priests of Ægypt, or in the solitary retreat of the Brachmans. More strenuously to support this chimerical system, he declared that he recollected the different bodies which his soul had animated before that of the son of Mnesarchus. He remembered to have been Æthalides, the son of Mercury, to have assisted the Greeks during the Trojan war in the character of Euphorbus, *(vid.* Euphorbus,) to have been Hermotimus, afterwards a fisherman, and last of all Pythagoras. He forbad his disciples to eat flesh, as also beans, because he supposed them to have been produced from the same putrified matter from which, at the creation of the world man was formed. In his theological system Pythagoras maintained that the universe was created from a shapeless heap of passive matter, by the hands of a powerful being, who himself was the mover and soul of the world, and of whose substance the souls of mankind were a portion. He considered numbers as the principles of everything, and perceived in the universe regularity, correspondence, beauty, proportion, and harmony, as intentionally produced by the creator. In his doctrines of morality he perceived in the human mind propensities common to us with the brute creation; but, besides these, and the passion of avarice and ambition, he discovered the nobler seeds of virtue, and declared that the most ample and perfect gratification was to be found in the enjoyment of moral and intellectual pleasures. The thoughts of the past he considered as always present to us, and he believed that no enjoyment could be had where the mind was disturbed by consciousness of guilt or fears about futurity. This opinion induced the philosopher to recommend to his followers a particular mode of education. The tender years of the Pythagoreans were employed in continual labour, in study, in exercise, and repose; and the philosopher maintained this well known and important maxim, that many things, especially love, are best learnt late. In a more advanced stage, the adult was desired to behave with caution, and patriotism, and to remember, that the community and civil society demanded his exertions, and that the good of the public, and not his own private enjoyments, were the ends of his creation. From lessons like these, the Pythagoreans were strictly enjoined to call to mind, and carefully to review, the actions, not only of the present, but of the preceding days. In their acts of devotion, they early repaired to the most solitary places of the mountains, and after they had examined their private and public conduct, and conversed with themselves, they joined in the company of their friends, and refreshed their body with light and frugal aliments. Their conversation was of the most innocent nature; political or philosophic subjects were discussed with propriety, but without warmth, and, after the conduct of the following day was regulated, the evening was spent with the same religious ceremony as the morning, in a strict and impartial self-examination. From such regularity, nothing but the most salutary consequences could arise, and it will not appear wonderful that the disciples of Pythagoras were so much respected and admired as legislators, and imitated for their constancy, friendship, and humanity. The authors that lived in and after the age of Alexander have rather tarnished than brightened the glory of the founder of the Pythagorean school, and have obscured his fame by attributing to him actions which were at variance with his character as a man and a moralist. To give more weight to his exhortation, as some writers mention, Pythagoras retired into a subterraneous cave, where his mother sent him intelligence of everything which happened during his absence. After a certain number of months he again re-appeared on the earth with a grim and ghastly countenance, and declared, in the assembly of the people, that he was returned from hell. From similar exaggerations, it has been asserted that he appeared at the Olympic games with a golden thigh, and that he could write in letters of blood whatever he pleased on a looking-glass, and that, by setting it opposite to the moon when full, all the characters which were on the glass became legible on the moon's disc. They also assert, that by some magical words, he tamed a bear, stopped the flight of an eagle, and appeared on the same day and at the same instant in the cities of Crotona and Metapontum, &c. The time and the place of the death of this great philosopher are unknown; yet many suppose that he died at Metapontum about 497 B.C.; and so great was the veneration of the people of Magna Græcia for him, that he received the same honors as were paid to the immortal gods, and his house became a sacred temple. Succeeding ages likewise acknowledged his merits, and when the Romans A.U.C. 411, were commanded by the oracle of Delphi to erect a statue to the bravest and wisest of the Greeks, the distinguished honor was conferred on Alcibiades and Pythagoras. Pythagoras had a daughter called Damo. There is now extant a poetical composition, comprehended in seventy-one lines, ascribed to the philosopher, and called the *golden verses of Pythagoras*, which contain the greater part of his doctrines and moral precepts; but many conceive that it is a supposititious composition, and that the true name of the writer was Lysis. Pythagoras distinguished himself also by his discoveries in geometry, astronomy, and mathematice, and it is to him that the world is indebted for the demonstration of the 47th proposition of the first book of Euclid's elements, about the square of the hypothenuse. It is said that he was so elated after making the discovery, that he made an offering of a hecatomb to the gods; but the sacrifice was undoubtedly of small oxen, made with wax, as the philosopher was ever an enemy to shedding the blood of all animals. His system of the universe, in which he placed the sun in the centre, and all the planets moving in elliptical orbits round it, was deemed chimerical and improbable, till the deep enquiries and philosophy of the 16th century proved it, by the most accurate calculations to be true and incontestible. Diogenes, Porphyry, Iamblichus, and others, have written an account of his life, but with more erudition than veracity. *Fabr. B. Gr.* l. 2. c. 12.—*Sax. Onom.* 1. p. 27.—*Cic. de Nat. D.* 1. c. 5. *Tusc.* 4. c. 1.—*Diog. &c.* 8.—*Hygin.* fab. 112.—*Ovid. Met.* 15. v. 60, &c.—*Plato.*—*Plin.* 34. c. 6.—*Gell.* 9. v. 11.—*Iamblic.*—*Porphyr.*—*Plut.* [A bust of Pythagoras will be found in the Vatican at Rome.]——A soothsayer at Babylon, who foretold the death of Alexander and of Hephæstion, by consulting the entrails of victims.——A tyrant of Ephesus.——One of Nero's wicked favorites.

PYTHANG'ELI, a place of Ægypt. *Strab.*

PYTHANG'ELUS, a Greek tragic poet of inferior merit. *Gyrald. P. H.* 7.

PYTHAU'LES, a celebrated flute player at Delphi, in honor of whose skill all other players were called by his name. *Varr. apud Non.* 2. n. 743.—*Hygin.* fab. 273.

PYTH'EAS, an archon at Athens, Olymp. 100. an. 1.——A native of Massilia, famous for his knowledge of astronomy, mathematics, philosophy, and geography. He also distinguished himself by his travels, and, with a mind that wished to seek information in every corner of the earth, he advanced far into the northern seas, and discovered the island of Thule, and entered that then unknown sea which is now called the Baltic. His discoveries in astronomy and geography were ingenious, and, indeed, modern navigators have found it expedient to justify and accede to his conclusions. He was the first who established a distinction of climate by the length of days and nights. He wrote different treatises in Greek, which have been lost, though some of them were extant in the fifth century. Pytheas lived, according to some, in the age of Aristotle. *Plut. de Opin. Phil.* 3. c. 17.—*Strab.* 2, &c.—*Plin.* 37.—*Voss. H. Gr.* 1. c. 17. & 4. c. 11. *de Phil.* c. 11. sec. 6. *de scient. Math.* c. 43. sec. 1.——An Athenian rhetorician, in the age of Demosthenes, who distinguished himself by his intrigues, rapacity, and opposition to the measures of Demosthenes, of whom he observed, that his orations smelt of the lamp. Pytheas joined Antipater after the death of Alexander the Great. His orations were devoid of elegance, harsh, unconnected, and diffuse, and from this circumstance he has not been ranked among the orators of Athens. *Ælian. V. H.* 7. c. 7.—*Plut. in Dem. & Polit. Pr.*——A celebrated turner. *Plin.* 33. c. 12.—*Salmas. ad Solin.* p. 1048.

PYTHER'MUS, an historian of Ephesus. *Athen.* l. 7.——A Phocian sent as ambassador to Sparta, to persuade the Lacedæmonians to assist the Ionians. *Herodot.* l. 2.

PY'THES, a native of Abdera, in Thrace, son of Andromachus, who obtained a crown at the Olympian games. His statue at Olympia was the work of Lysippus. *Plin.* 34. c. 7.—*Paus.* 6. c. 14.

PYTH'EUS, a Lydian in the age of Xerxes, famous for his riches. He kindly entertained the monarch and all his army, when he was marching on his expedition against Greece, and offered him to defray the expenses of the whole war. Xerxes thanked him with much gratitude, and promised to give him whatever he should require. Pytheus asked him to dismiss his son from the expedition; upon which the monarch ordered the young man to be cut into two, and one half of the body to be placed on the right hand of the way, and the other on the left, that his army might march between them. *Plut. de mul. virt.*—*Herodot.*

PYTH'IA, the priestess of Apollo at Delphi. She delivered the answers of the god to such as came to consult the oracle, and was supposed to be suddenly inspired by the sulphureous vapours which issued from the hole of a subterraneous cavity within the temple, over which she sat bare on a three-legged stool, called a tripod. In the stool was a small aperture, through which the vapor was inhaled by the priestess, and, at this divine inspiration, her eyes suddenly sparkled, her hair stood on end, and a shivering ran over all her body. In this convulsive state she spoke the oracles of the god, often with loud howlings and cries, and her articulations were taken down by the priest, and set in order. Sometimes the spirit of inspiration was more gentle, and not always violent; yet Plutarch mentions one of the priestesses who was thrown into such an excessive fury, that not only those who consulted the oracle, but also the priests that conducted her to the sacred tripod, and attended her during the inspiration, were terrified, and forsook the temple; and so violent was the fit, that she continued for some days in the most agonizing tortures, and at last died. The Pythia, before she placed herself on the tripod, used to wash her whole body, and particularly her hair, in the waters of the fountain Castalis, at the foot of mount Parnassus. She also shook a laurel tree that grew near the place, and sometimes ate the leaves with which she crowned herself. The priestess was originally a virgin, but the institution was changed when Echecrates, a Thessalian, had offered violence to one of them, and none but women who were above the age of fifty were permitted to enter upon that sacred office. They always appear dressed in the garments of virgins, to intimate their purity and modesty, and were solemnly bound to observe the strictest laws of temperance and chastity, that neither fantastical dresses nor lascivious behaviour might bring the office, the religion, or the sanctity of the place into contempt. There was originally but one Pythia, besides subordinate priests, yet afterwards two were chosen, and sometimes more. The most celebrated of all these was Phemonoe, who is supposed by some to have been the first who gave oracles at Delphi. The oracles were always delivered in hexameter verse, a custom which was some time after discontinued. The Pythia was consulted only one month in the year, about the spring. It was always required that those who consulted the oracle should make large presents to Apollo, and thence arose the opulence, the splendor, and the magnificence of that celebrated temple of Delphi. Sacrifices were also offered to the divinity, and if the omen proved unfavourable the priestess refused to give an answer. There were generally five priests who were engaged at the offering of the sacrifices, and there was also another who attended the Pythia, and assisted her in receiving the oracle. *Vid.* Delphi & Oraculum. *Paus.* 10. c. 5.—*Diod.* 16.—*Strab.* 6 & 9.—*Justin.* 24. c. 5.—*Plut. de Orac. Def.*—*Eurip. in Ion.*—*Chrysost. Hom.* 20. *In Cor.* 22.—*Origen. contra Cels.* 3 & 7.—*Sch. Aristoph. ad Plut.* 39.—*Lucan.* 5. v. 80.

PYTH'IA, games celebrated in honor of Apollo, near the temple of Delphi. They were first instituted, according to the more received opinion, by Apollo himself, in commemoration of the victory which he obtained over the serpent Python, from which they received their name; though others maintain that they were first established by Agamemnon, or Diomedes, or by Amphictyon, or, lastly, by the council of the Amphictyons, B.C. 1263. They were originally celebrated once in nine years. but afterwards every fifth year, in the second year of every Olympiad, according to the number of the Parnassian nymphs who congratulated Apollo after his victory. The gods themselves were originally among the number of the combatants, and, according to some authors, the first prizes were won by Pollux, in boxing; Castor, in horse-races; Hercules, in the pancratium; Zetes, in fighting with the armour; Calais, in running; Telamon, in wrestling; and Peleus, in throwing the quoit. These illustrious conquerors were rewarded by Apollo himself, who was present, with crowns and laurel. Some however observe, that at first it was nothing but a musical contention, in which he who sang best the praises of Apollo obtained the prize, consisting of presents of gold or silver, which were afterwards exchanged for a garland of the palm-tree, or of beech leaves. It is said that Hesiod was refused admittance to these games, because he was not able to play upon the harp, which was required of all such as entered the lists. The songs which were sung were called πυθικόι νόμοι, *the Pythian modes*, divided into five parts, which contained a representation of the fight and victory of Apollo over Python: ἀνακρόυσις, *the preparation for the fight;* ἔμπειρα, *the first attempt;* κατακελευσμὸς. *taking breath and collecting courage;* ἴαμβοι καὶ δάκτυλοι, *the insultiug sarcasms of the god over his vanquished enemy;* σύριγγες, *an imitation of the hissing of the serpent*, just as he expired under the blows of Apollo. A dance was also introduced; and in the 48th Olympiad, the Amphictyons, who presided over the games, increased the number of musical instruments by the addition of a flute, but, as it was more peculiarly used in funeral songs and lamentations, it was soon rejected, as unfit for merriment, and the festivals which represented the triumph of Apollo over the conquered serpent. The Romans, according to some, introduced them into their city, and called them *Apollinares ludi.* *Paus.* 10. c. 13 & 37.—*Strab.* 9.—*Ovid. Met.* 1. v. 447.—*Plin.* 7.—*Liv.* 25.

PYTH'IAS, a Pythagorean philosopher, called also Phintias, intimate with Damon. *Vid.* Phintias.

PYTH'IAS, a road which led from Thessaly to Tempe. *Ælian.* 3. c. 1.

PYTH'ION, an Athenian, killed, with 420 soldiers. when he attempted to drive the garrison of Demetrius from Athens *Polyæn.* 5. c. 17.

PY'THIS, a sculptor and painter, mentioned by *Pliny*, 35. c. 9. l. 36. c. 5.

PY'THIS, a promontory of Marmarica, on the coast of the Mediterranean. *Ptol.*

PYTH'IUM, a town of Thessaly. *Liv.* 42. c. 53. l. 44. c. 2.——A place near Gortyna in Crete. *Steph.*

PYTH'IUS, a Syracusan, who defrauded Canius, a Roman knight, to whom he had sold his gardens. *Cic. de Off.* 3. c. 14.——A surname of Apollo, which he received from having conquered the serpent Python, or because he was worshipped at Delphi, called also Pytho. *Macrob.* 1. *Sat.* 17.—*Propert.* 2. el. 23. v. 16.

PY'THO, the ancient name of the town of Delphi, which it received ἀπό τȣ πύθεσθαι, because the serpent which Apollo killed *rotted there.* It was also called Parnassia Nape. *Vid.* Delphi. *Paus.* 10. c. 6.

PYTHOCH'ARIS, a musician who assuaged the fury of some wolves by playing on a musical instrument. *Ælian. H. Anim.* l. 11.

PYTH'OCLES, an Athenian descended from Aratus. It is said, that on his account, and for his instruction, Plutarch wrote the life of Aratus. ——A man put to death with Phocion.——A man who wrote on Italy. *Plut. Par. Min.* c. 14.—*Clem. Strom.* l. 1.—*Voss. H. Gr.* 3. p. 410.

PYTHODO'RIS, wife of Polemon king of Pontus, was celebrated for her prudence and many virtues. She governed the kingdom after her husband's death.

PYTHODO'RUS, an Athenion archon, Olym. 109. an. 2. He was probably the person who succeeded Laches in Sicily. *Thucyd.* l. 3. & 4.——A native of Tralles in Lydia, mentioned by *Cicero, Flacc.* 22.——A carver. *Plin.* 36. c. 5.——An Athenian victor at the games in Olymp. 103. [A bust in the Capitol is inscribed with ths name of Pythodorus.

PYTHOLA'US, the brother of Theba, the wife of Alexander tyrant of Pheræ. He assisted his sister in despatching her husband. *Plut.*

PY'THON, a native of Byzantium, in the age of Philip of Macedonia. He was a great favorite of the monarch, who sent him to Thebes, when that city, at the instigation of Demosthenes, was going to take up arms against Philip. *Plut. in Dem.*—*Diod.* l. 16.——One of the friends of Alexander, put to death by Ptolemy Lagus.——A man who killed Cotys king of Thrace, at the instigation of the Athenians.

PY'THON, a celebrated serpent sprung from the mud and stagnant waters which remained on the surface of the earth after the deluge of Deucalion. Some, however, suppose that it was produced from the earth by Juno, and sent by the goddess to persecute Latona, who was then pregnant by Jupiter. Latona escaped his fury by means of her lover, who changed her into a quail during the remaining months of her pregnancy, and afterwards restored her to her original shape in the island of Delus, where she gave birth to Apollo and Diana. Apollo, as soon as he was born, attacked the monster, and killed him with arrows, and, in commemoration of the victory which he had obtained, instituted the celebrated Pythian games. *Strab.* 8.—*Paus.* 2. c. 7. l. 10. c. 6.—*Hygin.* præf.—*Ovid. Met.* 1. v. 438, &c.—*Lucan.* 5. v. 134.—*Orpheus.* 991.—*Tibull.* 2. el. 3. v. 27.

PYTHONI'CE, an Athenian prostitute greatly honored by Harpalus, whom Alexander some time before had entrusted with the treasures of Babylon. He married her; and, according to some, she died the very moment that the nuptials were going to be celebrated. He raised her a splendid monument, which cost him 30 talents, on the road which led from Athens to Eleusis. *Plut. in Phoc.*—*Curt.* 10. c. 1.—*Justin.* 13. c. 5.—*Diod.* 17.—*Paus.* 1. c. 37.—*Athen.* 13, &c.

PYTHONIS'SA, a name given to the priestess of Apollo's temple at Delphi. She is more generally called Pythia. *Vid.* Pythia. The word Pythonissa was commonly applied to women who attempted to explain futurity.

PYTHOP'OLIS, a city of Mysia.——A city of Caria, called also Nysa. *Steph.*

PYTIO'NIA, a small island of the Ionian Sea, near Corcyra.

PYT'NA, a part of mount Ida, in Crete. *Strab.* 10.

PYT'TALUS, a celebrated athlete, son of Lampis of Elis, who obtained a prize at the Olympic games. *Paus.* 9. c. 16.

PYX'A, a town of Cos. *Theocr.* It is not now in existence.

PYXIRA'TES, a name of the Euphrates, near its source. *Plin.* 5. c. 24.—*Salmas. ad Solin.* p. 627.

PYX'IS, an inland city of the Œnotri. *Steph.*

PYXI'TES, a river of Themiscyrena, near Trapezus. *Plin.* 6. c. 4.

PYXODO'RUS, a person worshipped by the Ephesians, as the discoverer of marble. *Vitruv.* 1. 10. c. 7.—*Voss. de Idolol.* 1. c. 21.

PYX'US (*-untis*), a city of Sicily founded by Mianthus. *Steph.*

Q.

QUACER'NI or QUERQUER'NI, a people of Hispania Tarraconensis, whose town was called Forum Quacernorum. *Plin.* 3. c. 3.—*Antonin.*—*Ptol.*

QUA'DI, an ancient nation of Germany, near the country of the Marcommanni, on the borders of the Danube, in modern Moravia. They rendered themselves celebrated by their opposition to the Romans, by whom they were often defeated, though not totally subdued. *Tacit. in Germ.* 42 & 43. *An.* 2. c. 63.

QUADRA'TA, a town of Germany. *Antonin.* According to *Cluverius* it was in Pannonia, and is now Wiselburg.

QUADRA'TUS, a surname given to Mercury, because some of his statues were square. The num-4, according to Plutarch, was sacred to Mercury, because he was born on the fourth day of the month. *Plut. in Symp.* 9. *Qu.* 2 & 3.

QUADRA'TUS T. UMMID'IUS, a governor of Syria in the age of Nero. *Tacit. Ann.* 12. c. 45 & 54.

QUAD'RIFRONS or QUAD'RICEPS, a surname of Janus, because he was represented with four heads. He had a temple on the Tarpeian rock, raised by L. Catulus, with four equal fronts, and one door and three windows in each, with the intention that three windows should represent the three months of each season of the year. *Aug. de Civ. D.* 7. c. 2 & 4.—*Macrob.* 1. c. 9.—*Servius ad Æn.* 7. v. 607.—*Gyrald. H. D.* 4.

QUADRIGA'RIUS, Q. CL., an ancient Roman historian, contemporary with Sisenna and Valerius Antias. *Voss. Hist. Lat.* 1. c. 10.

QUÆSTO'RES, two officers at Rome, first created A.U.C. 269. They received their name *a quærendo*, because they collected the revenues of the state, and had the management of the public treasury. The quæstorship was the first office which could be had in the state. It was requisite that the candidate should be 24 or 25 years of age, or, according to some, 27. In the year 332 A.U.C., two more were added to the others, to attend the consuls, to take care of the pay of the armies abroad, and to sell the plunder and booty which had been acquired by conquest. These were called *Peregrini*, whilst the others, whose employment was in the city, received the name of *Urbani*. When the Romans were masters of all Italy, four more were created, A.U.C. 439, to attend the proconsuls and proprætors in their provinces, and to collect all the taxes and customs which each particular district owed to the republic. They were called *Provinciales*. Sylla, the dictator, created 20 quæstors, and J. Cæsar 40, to fill up the vacant seats in the senate; whence it is evident the quæstors ranked as senators. The quæstors were always appointed by the senate, and if any person was appointed to the quæstorship without their permission, he was only *Proquæstor*. The *Quæstores urbani* were apparently of more consequence than the rest, the treasury was entrusted to their care, they kept an account of all receipts and disbursements, and the Roman eagles or ensigns were always in their possession when the armies were not on an expedition. They required every general before he triumphed to tell them, upon his oath, that he had given a just account of the number of slain on both sides, and that he had been saluted *imperator* by the soldiers, a title which every commander generally received from his army after he had obtained a victory, and which was afterwards confirmed and approved by the senate. The quæstors had also the care of the ambassadors; they lodged and received them, and some time after, when Augustus was declared emperor, they kept the decrees of the senate, which had been before entrusted to the keeping of the ædiles and tribunes. This gave rise to two new offices of trust and honor, One of which was *quæstor palatii*, and the other *quæstor principis* or *augusti*, sometimes called *candidatus principis*. The tent of the quæstor in the camp was called *quæstorium*. It stood near that of the general. *Varro. de L.L.* 4.—*Liv.* 4. c. 43.—*Dionys. Hal.* 5. c. 34.—*Plut. in Publ.*—*Dio.* 43.—*Val. Max.* 2. c. 8.—*Aul. Gell.* 13. c. 13.—*Servius. Æn.* 6. v. 432.—*Voss. in Quæstor.*

QUA'RI, a people of Gallia Narbonensis, between the Salii and Vocontii. *Strab.* 1. 4.

QUARIA'TES or CAV'ARÆ, a people of Gallia Narbonensis. *Plin.* 3. c. 4.

QUA'RIS, a city of Bactriana, on the Oxus. *Ptol.*

QUA'RIUS, a river of Bœotia, near Coronea. It is called Coralius by Alcæus. *Strab.*——A river of Thessaly. *Id.*

QUARQUE'NI, a people of Transpadane Italy. *Plin.* 3. c. 19.

QUER'CENS, a Rutulian who fought against the Trojans. *Virg. Æn.* 9. v. 684.

QUERQUETULA'NUS, a name given to mount Cœlius at Rome, from the oaks which grew there. *Tacit. An.* 4. c. 65.

QUIE'TUS FA'NUM, a temple without the walls of the city of Rome, near the Colline gate. Quies was the goddess of rest, whom the Romans refused to receive within their city, probably because the glory of their empire rested on activity. Some suppose that Quies means death, or Proserpine. *Liv.* 4. c. 41.—*Aug. de Civ. D.* 4. c. 16.—*Alex. ab Alex.* 2. c. 4. l. 4. c. 16.

QUIE'TUS L., an officer under the emperor Trajan, who behaved with great valor in the expeditions which were undertaken by the army which he commanded. He was put to death by Adrian.

QUI'NA, a colony and town of Africa Propria. *Ptol.*

QUINC'TIA PRA'TA. *Vid.* Quintia.

QUINCTIA'NUS a man who conspired against Nero, for which he was put to death.

QUINCTIL'IA, a comedian, who refused to betray a conspiracy which had been formed against Caligula.

QUINC'TIUS AT'TICUS, a friend of Vespasian, put into chains by the followers of Vitelliua, &c. *Tac. Hist.* 3. c. 73 & 75.

QUINC'TIUS CER'TUS, a Roman knight, slain by order of Decimus Pacarius, because he would not aid Vitellius against Otho. *Tac. Hist.* 2. c. 16.

QUINC'TIUS T., a Roman consul who gained some victories over the Æqui and the Volsci, and obtained a triumph for subduing Præneste.

QUINC'TIUS CÆ'SO, a man accused before the Roman people, and vindicated by his father Cincinnatus.

QUINC'TIUS, a Roman celebrated for his frugality. *Vid.* Cincinnatus.——A master of horse.——A Roman consul when Annibal invaded Italy.——A brother of Flaminius, banished from the senate by Cato, for killing a Gaul.——An officer killed by the Carthaginians.——An officer under Dolabella.——Another who defeated the Latins.——A consul who obtained a victory over the Volsci.

QUINC'TIUS HIRPI'NUS. *Vid.* Hirpinus.

QUIN'DA, a town of Cilicia. *Plut.—Arat.*

QUINDECIM'VIRI, an order of priests whom Tarquin the Proud appointed to take care of the Sibylline books. They were originally two, but afterwards the number was increased to ten, and Sylla added five more, whence their name. *Vid.* Decemviri & Duumviri. *Liv.* 1. c. 26. l. 7. c. 28. l. 9. c. 30.—*Tacit. An.* 3. c. 64. l. 6. c. 12.—*Lactant.* 1. c. 6.—*Suet. in Cæs.* 79.—*Servius ad Æn.* 3. v. 332. l. 6. v. 73.

QUINQUA'TRIA, a festival in honor of Minerva at Rome, which continued during five days. The beginning of the celebration was the 18th of March. The first day sacrifices and oblations were presented, but, however, without the effusion of blood. On the second, third, and fourth days, shows of gladiators were exhibited, and on the fifth day there was a solemn procession through the streets of the city. On the days of the celebration scholars obtained holidays, and it was usual for them to offer prayers to Minerva for learning and wisdom, which the goddess patronized; and, on their return to school, they presented their master with a gift, which has received the name of *Minerval.* They were much the same at the Panathenæa of the Greeks. Plays were also acted, and disputations were held on subjects of literature. They received their name from the *five* days which were occupied in their celebration. *Ovid. Fast.* 3. v. 809. l. 6. v. 651 & 693. *Am.* 1. el. 8. v. 65.—*Macrob.* 1. c. 12.—*Varro de de L. L.* 5. *De R. R.* 3. c. 2.—*Horat.* 2. ep. 2. v. 197.—*Festus de V. Sig.—Alex. ab Alex.* 2. c. 22.

QUIN'QUE-COL'LES, a place of Laconia, near Lacedæmon. *Athen.* It is now Monti di Misitra.

QUIN'QUE-DIG'ITUS, a mountain of Upper Æthiopia. *Ptol.* It is now Montagne di Ceser.

QUINQUENNA'LES LU'DI, games celebrated by the Chians every fifth year in honor of Homer. There were also some games among the Romans which bore this name. They are the same as the Actian games. *Vid.* Actia.

QUIN'TIA PRA'TA, a place on the borders of the Tiber, near Rome, which had been cultivated by the great Quintius Cincinnatus. *Liv.* 3. c. 26.

QUINTIA'NUS, a noble youth who attempted to assassinate Commodus. *Herodian.* 1. c. 8.

QUINTILIA'NUS MAR'CUS FA'BIUS, a celebrated rhetorician born in Spain. He opened a school of rhetoric at Rome, and was the first who obtained a salary from the state as being a public teacher. After he had remained twenty years in this laborious employment. and obtained the merited applause of the most illustrious Romans, not only as a preceptor, but as a pleader at the bar, Quintilian, by the permission of the emperor Domitian, retired to enjoy the fruits of his labors and industry. In his retirement he assiduously dedicated his time to the study of literature, and wrote a treatise on the causes of the corruption of eloquence. Some time after, at the pressing solicitations of his friends, he wrote his *institutiones oratoriæ*, the most perfect and complete system of oratory extant. It is divided into twelve books, in which the author explains, from observation as well as from experience, what is required to constitute a good and perfect orator, and in this he not only mentions the pursuits and the employments of the rhetorician, but also speaks of his education, and begins with the attention which ought to be shown him even in his cradle. He was appointed preceptor to the two young princes whom Domitian destined for his successors on the throne, but the pleasure which the rhetorician received from the favors and the attention of the emperor, and from the success with which his writings met in the world, was embittered by the loss of his wife, and of his two sons. It is said that Quintilian was poor in his retirement, and that his indigence was relieved by the liberality of his pupil Pliny the younger. The innocence of his manners and the integrity of his heart deservedly claim the highest praise, but out of respect to his good sense and virtuous character we must attribute the fulsome adulation which he bestowed on the execrable Domitian to personal fear and extorted gratitude, rather than to sober truth and real feeling. Quintilian died A.D. 95, in a good old age. His institutes were discovered A.D. 1415 in an old tower of a monastery at St. Gall, by Poggio Bracciolini, a native of Florence. The best editions of Quintilian are those of Gesner, 4to, Gotting. 1738; of L. Bat. 8vo, *cum notis variorum*, 1655; of Gibson, 4to, Oxon. 1693; and that of Rollin, republished in 8vo, London, 1792. *Harles. Not. Lit. Rom.* 1. p. 387.

QUINTIL'IUS VA'RUS, a Roman governor of Syria. *Vid.* Varus.

QUINTIL'IUS, a friend of the emperor Alexander. ——A man put to death by the emperor Severus.

QUINTIL'IUS SEX'TUS, a consul who died of the plague. *Liv.* 3. c. 32.

QUINTIL'IUS CN., a man created dictator A.U.C. 423, to drive a nail in the Capitol. *Liv.* 8. c. 18.

QUINTIL'IUS LU'CIUS, a prætor in the second Punic war who defeated Mago in Insubria. *Liv.* 30. c. 18.

QUINTIL'LA, a courtesan at Rome, &c. *Juv.* 7. v. 75.

QUINTIL'LUS M. AURE'LIUS, a brother of Claudius, who proclaimed himself emperor, and destroyed himself seventeen days after by opening his veins in a bath, when he heard that Aurelian was marching against him, about the 270th year of the Christian era. *Trebell. Poll. in Claud.* c. 12. —*Vopisc. in Aurelian.* c. 16.—*Euseb. in Chron.*

QUIN'TIUS or QUINC'TIUS, one of the names of Cincinnatus. *Pers.* 1. v. 73.

QUIN'TIUS PE'DIUS, a painter. *Vid.* Pedius.

QUIN'TIUS CÆ'SO, the son of Cincinnatus, was banished for opposing the tribunes. He was the first who gave bail for his appearance, and, by forfeiting it, his father was almost reduced to ruin, and obliged to sell his property, and live in obscure retirement. *Liv.* 3. c. 11, &c.

QUIN'TIUS BARBA'TUS, a man six times consul.

QUIN'TIUS PUB'LIUS, a plebeian defended by Cicero.

QUIN'TIUS TI'TUS FLAMIN'IUS, the famous conqueror of Philip of Macedonia. *Vid.* Flaminius.—The family of the Quintii came originally from Alba. *Liv.* 1. c. 30. l. 3. c. 12.

QUIN'TUS CUR'TIUS RU'FUS, a Latin historian, who flourished, as some suppose, in the reign of Vespasian or Trajan. He has rendered himself known by his history of the reign of Alexander the Great. This history was divided into ten books, of which the two first, the end of the fifth, and the beginning of the sixth are lost. This work is admired for the elegance, purity, and floridness of its style. It is however blamed for great anachronisms, and glaring mistakes in geography, as well as history. Freinshemius has written a supplement to Curtius, in which he seems to have made some very satisfactory amends for the loss which the history has suffered, by a learned collection of facts and circumstances from all the different authors who have employed their pen in writing an account of Alexander, and of his Asiatic conquests. Some suppose that the historian is the same with that of Curtius Rufus who lived in the age of Claudius, under whom he was made consul. This Rufus was born of an obscure family, and attended a Roman quæstor into Africa, when he was met at Andrumetum by a woman of more than human shape, as he was walking under the porticos in the middle of the day. This extraordinary character addressed the indigent Roman, and told him that the day should come in which he should govern Africa with consular power. This strange prophecy animated Rufus; he repaired to Rome, where he gained the favor of the emperor, obtained consular honors, and at last retired as pro-consul to Africa, where he died. The best editions of Curtius are those of Elzevir, 8vo, Amst. 1673; of Snakenburg, 4to. L. Bat. 1724; and of Barbou, 12mo, Paris, 1757. *Tacit. Ann.* 11. c. 23, &c.—*Harles. Not. Lit. Rom.* 1. p. 356.

QUIN'TUS VERA'NIUS, a governor of Cappadocia.

QUIN'TUS CIC'ERO, the brother of Cicero.

QUIN'TUS CAT'ULUS, a Roman consul.

QUIN'TUS, a friend of Cæsar.

QUIRI'NA a tribe at Rome. *Cic. pro Quinct.—Rosin. Antiq. Rom.* 6. c. 25.

QUIRINA'LIA, festivals in honor of Romulus surnamed *Quirinus*, celebrated on the 13th of the calends of March. *Cic. ad Q. fr.* 2. ep. 3.—*Ovid. Fast.* 2. v. 513.—*Festus. de V. Sig.*

QUIRINA'LIS, a hill at Rome, originally called Agonius, and afterwards Collinus. It obtained the name of Quirinalis from the inhabitants of Cures, who settled there under their king Tatius. It was also called Caballinus, from two marble statues, one of which was the work of Phidias, and the other of Praxiteles. *Liv.* 1. c. 44.—*Ovid. Fast.* 375. *Met.* 14. 845.——One of the gates of Rome, near Quirinalis.

QUIRI'NUS, a surname of Mars among the Romans. This name was also given to Romulus when he had been made a god by his superstitious subjects. *Liv.* 1. c. 13, &c.—*Lactant.* 1. c. 15.—*Ovid. Fast.* 2. v. 475.——A surname of the god Janus. *Macrob.* 1. c. 9.

QUIRI'NUS PUB'LIUS SULPIT'IUS, a Roman consul born at Lanuvium, and called Cyrenius in Scripture. Though descended from an obscure family, he was raised to the greatest honours by Augustus. He was appointed governor of Syria, and afterwards made preceptor of Caius, the grandson of the emperor. He married Æmilia Lepida, the grand-daughter of Sylla and Pompey, but some time after he shamefully repudiated her. He died A.D. 22. *Tacit. Ann.* 3, &c.

QUIRI'TES, a name given to the citizens of Rome, because they admitted into their city the Sabines, who inhabited the town of Cures, and who on that account were called Quirites. After this union, the two nations were indiscriminately and promiscuously called by that name. It is, however, to be observed that the word was confined to Rome, and not used in the armies, as we find some of the generals applying it only to such of their soldiers as they dismissed or disgraced. Some of the emperors even appeased a sedition, by calling their rebellious soldiers by the degrading appellation of Quirites. *Sueton. Cæs.* 70.—*Lamprid.* 53.—*Lucan.* 5. v. 558.—*Horat.* 4. od. 14. v. 1.—*Varro de L.L.* 4.—*Liv.* 1. c. 13.—*Ovid. Fast.* 2. v. 479.—*Servius. ad Virg. Æn.* 7. v. 710.

QUI'ZA or BUI'ZA, a maritime city of Mauritania Cæsariensis. *Ptol.*

R.

RA'BA, a city on the Ionian Gulph. *Steph.*

RABBATAM'MANA, a city of Arabia Petræa. *Steph.*

RABIR'IUS C. POS'THUMUS, a Roman knight, who lent a large sum of money to Ptolemy Auletes, king of Ægypt. The monarch afterwards not only meanly refused to repay him, but even confined him, and endangered his life. Rabirius escaped from Ægypt with difficulty, but at his return to Rome was accused of having lent money to an African prince, for unlawful purposes. He was ably defended by Cicero, and acquitted with difficulty. *Cic. pro Rab.*

RABIR'IUS CA'IUS, a senator accused by Labienus, at the solicitation of Cæsar, of killing the tribune Saturninus thirty years before. He appealed from the sentence of death pronounced against him by Cæsar, and was acquitted by the assembly of the people. Hortensius and Cicero were his defenders. *Cic. Rab.*—*Dio.* 37. c. 26, &c.—*Sueton. Cæs.* 12.

RABIR'IUS, a Latin poet in the age of Augustus, who wrote, besides satires and epigrams, a poem on the victory which the emperor had gained over Antony at Actium. Seneca has compared him to Virgil for elegance and majesty, but Quintilian does not give so favorable a character to his poetry. *Ovid. ex Pont.* 4. el. 16. v. 5.—*Senec. de Ben.* 6. c. 6.—*Quintil.* 10. c. 1.—*Voss. H. Lat.* 1. c. 21.—*Fulgent. expos. sermon. antiq.*——An architect in the reign of Domitian, who built a celebrated palace for the emperor, of which the ruins are still seen at Rome.

RA'BIUS L., a friend of Marius, who fled to Mithridates, whom he afterwards betrayed. *Cic. Verr.* 1. c. 34.

RABOCEN'TUS, a leader among the Bessi, put to death by Piso. *Cic. Pis.* 34.

RABO'NIUS L., a man who had the care of Castor's temple at Rome. *Cic. Verr.* 1. c. 50.

RACIL'IA, the wife of Cincinnatus. *Liv.* 3. c. 26.

RACIL'IUS L., a tribune who complained in the senate of the faction of Clodius. *Cic. in Verr.* 2. c. 12. *Ad. Q. fr.* 2. c. 1.

RAD'ALUS, an auxiliary of Perses against Æetes. *Val. Flacc. Argon.* 6. v. 70.

RÆSA'CES, an officer of Artaxerxes. He revolted from his master, and fled to Athens.

RÆTIA'RIA, a town of Upper Mysia. *Ptol.* It is now Nicopoli, according to *Niger*.

RAGE'JA, a town of Media, founded by Nicanor. *Strab.*—*Bochart. Geogr.* p. 106.

RAGUNDO'NA, a town of Upper Pannonia. *Antonin.* It is now Robisch.

RAI'THI, a region of Arabia Petræa. The people were called Ratheni.

RAM'ELOS, an auxiliary of Perses against Æetes. *Val. Flacc. Argon.* 6. v. 530.

RAMES'SES, a name common to some kings of Ægypt. *Vid. Joh. Marsham. Can. Chron. ex Syncello.*

RAMI'SES, a king of Ægypt. *Vid.* Rhamses.

RAM'NES or RHAMNEN'SIS, one of the three centuries instituted by Romulus. After the Roman people had been divided into three tribes, the monarch selected out of each, 100 young men of the best and noblest families, with whom he formed three companies of horse. One of them was called Rhamnensis, either from the tribe of which it was chosen, or from Romulus. Another was called Tatiensis from Tatius, and the third Luceres from Lucumon. *Varr. de L.L.* 4. c. 9.—*Liv.* 1. c. 13.—*Horat. de Art. Poet.* 340.—*Plut. in Rom.*—*Propert.* 4. el. 1. v. 31.—*Servius ad Æn.* 5. v. 560.

RAN'DA, a village of Persia, where 3000 rebellious Persians were slain by Chiles. *Polyæn.* 7. c. 39.

RA'NI, a people of Scythia, dwelling near Caucasus. *Plin.* 6. c. 7.

RA'NIUS, a freedman of Brutus. *Cic. Att.* 12. ep. 21.

RAPHA'NE, a city of Media, on the confines of Parthia. *Plin.* 6. c. 26.

RAPHI'A, a town of Palestine, near the sea-coast, at the south of Gaza. It was near it that Antiochus, king of Syria, was defeated by the forces of Ptolemy the fourth king of Ægypt, under the conduct of Nicolaus, the Ætolian general. *Polyb.* 5. c. 82.—*Ptol.*—*Steph.*

RAP'SA, a town in the Pentapolis or Cyrenaica. *Plin.* 5. c. 5.

RA'PO, a Rutulian chief, &c. *Virg. Æn.* 10. v. 748.

RAP'TUM, a promontory of Upper Æthiopia. *Ptol.*—*Steph.*

RARAS'SA, a city of India within the Ganges. *Ptol.* The Greek MS. has Cragausa.

RAREN'TUS, a city of Italy. *Steph.*

RARUN'GÆ, a people of India. *Plin.* 6. c. 22.

RASCIP'OLIS, a Macedonian sent to the assistance of Pompey. *Cæs. Bell. Civ.* 3. c. 4.

RATA'NEUM, a town of Illyricum. *Plin.* 3. c. 23.

RATOSTATHYB'IUS, a river of Albion. *Ptol.*

RAU'RACI or RAURA'CI, a people of Gaul, whose chief town is now Augst on the Rhine. *Cæs. G.* 1. c. 5.

RAUSIM'ODUS, a king of Sarmatia, conquered and slain by Constantine the Great, A.D. 321. *Eutrop.* 1. 10, &c.

RAVEN'NA, a town of Italy on the Adriatic, which became celebrated under the Roman emperors. Augustus embellished it by building a new and capacious harbour able to contain 250 ships, and communicating with the sea by means of a canal three miles in length. The place was some time the seat of the western empire, especially under Valentinian, and under Theodoric, king of the Goths, who there defeated Odoacer, king of the Heruli, A.D. 493. It was difficult of access by land, as it stood on a small peninsula; and was so ill supplied with water, that it sold at a higher price than wine, according to Martial. The emperors kept one of their fleets there, and the other at Misenum, on the other side of Italy. Ravenna was founded by a colony of Thessalians, according to Strabo, or, according to Pliny, of Sabines. It is now fallen from its former grandeur, and is a wretched town, the capital of Romagnia, situate at the distance of about four miles from the sea, and surrounded with swamps and marshes. *Strab.* 5.—*Suet. in Aug.* 49.—*Plin.* 36. c. 12.—*Mela*, 2. c. 4.—*Sil. Ital.* 8. v. 604.—*Servius. ad Virg. G.* 1. v. 262.—*Martial.* c. epigr. 93. v. 8, &c.

RAV'OLA, a celebrated debauchee, &c. *Juv.* 9.

RAX, an island of Lycia. *Steph.*

REA'TE, now Rieti, a pleasant town of Umbria, built, as Dionysius supposes, before the Trojan war, about fifteen miles from Fanum Vacunæ, near the lake Velinus. Cybele, called also Rhea, was the chief deity of the place. It was famous for its asses, which were said by Varro and Pliny to be superior to those of Arcadia. *Strab.* 5.—*Dionys. Hal.* 1.—*Varro de R.R.* 1.—*Liv.* 25. c. 7. l. 26. c. 11. l. 28. c. 45.—*Cic. Cat.* 3. c. 2. *N.D.* 2. c. 2.—*Ital*, 8. v. 519.—*Servius ad Æn.* 7. v. 712.

REB'ILUS T. CANIN., a lieutenant in Cæsar's army, elected consul for a few hours. *Cic. Fam.* 7. ep. 30. *Att.* 12. ep. 37.

REDÆS'TUM, a city of Thrace on the Propontis. It is called Bisanthe by *Ptolemy*, and is now Rodosto.

REDIC'ULUS, a deity whose name is derived from the word *redire* (to return.) The Romans raised a temple to this imaginary deity on the spot whence Annibal had retired, as if struck by a sudden panic, when he approached Rome as if to besiege it. *Festus de V. Sig.*—*Gyrald. H. D.* 1.

REDINTUI'NUM, a city of Germany. *Ptol.* It is now Tein, in Bohemia.

RED'ONES, a nation among the Armorici, now the people of Rennes, and St. Maloes, in Brittany. *Cæs. B.G.* 2. c. 41.

RE'GIA, a temple at Rome sacred to Mars, in which on the 13th of December, the sacrifice of a horse was yearly offered, for the head of which it was usual for the young people of the neighbourhood to dispute in two opposite bands. *Plut. in Rom.* & *Qu. R.* 97.

REGIFU'GIUM or **FUGA'LIA**, a festival at Rome, to celebrate the flight of the Tarquins. On that occasion, after sacrifices were offered to the goddess of liberty, the chief or king of the priests was obliged to flee from the temple, and to take refuge in the country for a few days. *Ovid. Fast.* 2. v. 685. l. 5. v. 728.—*Festus de V. Sig.*—*Auson. ecl. de fer R.* 13.

REGIL'LÆ or **REGIL'LUM**, a town in the country of the Sabines in Italy, about twenty miles from Rome, celebrated for a battle which was fought there, A.U.C. 258, between 24,000 Romans and 40,000 Etrurians, who were headed by the Tarquins. The Romans obtained the victory, and scarcely 10,000 of the enemy escaped from the field of battle. Castor and Pollux, according to some accounts, were seen mounted on white horses, and fighting at the head of the Roman army. *Liv.* 2. c. 16.—*Dionys. Hal.* 5.—*Plut. in Cor.*—*Val. Max.* 1.—*Flor.* 1.—*Suet. Tib.* 1.—*Eutrop.* 1. c. 11.—*Oros.* 2. c. 13.—*Lactant.* 2. c. 8.

REGILLIA'NUS Q. NO'NIUS, a Dacian who entered the Roman armies, and was raised to the greatest honors under Valerian. He was elected emperor by the populace, who were dissatisfied with Gallienus, and was soon after murdered by his soldiers, A.D. 262. *Trebell. Poll. de 30 tyran.* c. 10.

REGIL'LUS, a small lake of Latium, the waters of which fall into the Anio, at the east of Rome. The dictator Posthumius defeated the Latin army near it. *Liv.* 2. c. 19.—*Cluver. Ital. Antiq.* 3. c. 5. It is now Lago di Castiglione.

REGI'NA, a surname of Juno at Rome. Her temple was on mount Aventine, and was adorned with a huge statue brought from Veii, after the destruction of that city. Rhea, wife of Saturn, was also known by that name among the Greeks. *Diod. Sic.* 4.—*Ovid. Fast.* 6. v. 37.—*Festus de V. Sig.*

Regi'na, a town of the Turdetani, in Spain. *Ptol.*

REGI'NUM, a town of Germany, now supposed to be Ratisbon or Regensburg.

REGI'NUS, an officer who was entrusted by Pompey with the command of the Etrurian Sea. *Cic.* 10. *Att.* 12.

RE'GIUM LEP'IDUM, a town of Modena, now Regio, at the south of the Po. *Plin.* 3. c. 15.—*Cic.* 12. *Fam.* 5. l. 13. ep. 7.

REG'NI, a people of Britain. *Ptol.* Their town, Regnum, is now Ringwood.

REG'ULUS M. ATTIL'IUS, a consul during the first Punic war. He reduced Brundusium, and in his second consulship he took sixty-four and sunk thirty gallies of the Carthaginian fleet, on the coast of Sicily. He afterwards landed in Africa, and so rapid was his success, that in a short time he defeated three generals, and made himself master of about 200 places of consequence on the coast. The Carthaginians, terrified at his approach, sued for peace, but the conqueror refused to grant it, and was soon after defeated in a battle by Xanthippus, and 30,000 of his men were left on the field of battle, and 15,000 taken prisoners. Regulus fell into the hands of the enemy, and was carried in triumph to Carthage. He was afterwards sent by the enemy to Rome, to propose an accommodation, and an exchange of prisoners; and if his commission was unsuccessful. he was bound by the most solemn oaths to return to Carthage, without delay. When he came to Rome, Regulus dissuaded his countrymen from accepting the terms which the enemy proposed; and when his opinion had had due influence on the senate, he rctired to Carthage agreeably to his engagements. The Carthaginians were no sooner informed that their offers of peace had been rejected at Rome by the means of Regulus, than they prepared to punish him with the greatest severity. His eyebrows were cut off, and he was exposed for some days to the excessive heat of the meridian sun, and afterwards confined in a barrel, the sides of which were everywhere filled with large iron spikes, till he died in the greatest agonies. His sufferings were reported at Rome, and the senate permitted his widow to inflict whatever punishment she pleased on some of the most illustrious captives of Carthage, who were in their hands. She confined them in presses filled with sharp iron points, and was so exquisite in her cruelty, that the senate at last interfered, and stopped the barbarity of her punishments. Regulus died about 251 B.C. *Sil.* 6. v. 319.—*Flor.* 2. c. 3.—*Horat.* 3 od. 5.—*Cic. de Off.* 1. c. 13.—*Val. Max.* 1. c. 1. l. 9. c. 2.—*Liv.* ep. 16.—*Aurel. Vict.* 37 & 40.—*Eutrop.* 2. c. 3. —*Aul. G.* c. 3 & 4.—*Ovid. in Ib.* 283.—*Aug. de Civ. D.* 1. c. 14 & 15.

Reg'ulus Mem'mius, a Roman made governor of Greece by Caligula. While Regulus was in his province, the emperor wished to bring to Rome the celebrated statue of Jupiter Olympius, by Phidias; but this, according to the credulous historians, was supernaturally prevented; the ship which was to convey it was destroyed by lightning, and the workmen who attempted to remove the statue, were terrified away by sudden noises. *Dio. Cass.*

Reg'ulus, a man who condemned Sejanus.

Reg'ulus Ros'cius, a man who held the consulship for one day only, in the reign of Vitellius.

Reg'ulus L. Livin, a Roman very intimate with *Cicero. Fam.* 13. ep. 60.

RE'MI, a nation of Gaul, whose principal town was Durocortorum, now Rheims, in the north of Champagne. *Plin.* 4. c. 17.—*Cæs. B. G.* 2. c. 5.

REM'MIA LEX, *de judiciis*, was enacted to punish all calumniators. The letter K was marked on their foreheads. This law was repealed by Constantine the Great. *Cic. pro Ros.*—*Rosin. Antiq. Rom.* 8. c. 22.

REM'ULUS, a chief of Tibur, whose arms were seized by the Rutulians, and afterwards became part of the plunder which Euryalus obtained. *Virg. Æn.* 9. v. 360.——A friend of Turnus, trampled to death by his horse, which Orsilochus had wounded. *Id.* 11. v. 636, &c.

Rem'ulus Syl'vius, a king of Alba, descended from Tiberinus, destroyed by lightning on account of his impiety. *Ovid. Trist.* 4. v. 50.

REMU'RIA, festivals established at Rome by Romulus, to appease the manes of his brother Remus. They were afterwards called Lemuria, and celebrated yearly in the month of May. *Vid.* Lemures.

RE'MUS, the brother of Romulus, was exposed together with him, by the cruelty of his grandfather. In the contest which happened between the two brothers about building a city, Romulus obtained the preference, and Remus, for ridiculing the mean appearance of the rising walls, was put to death by his brother's orders, or, according to some authors, by Romulus himself. *Vid.* Romulus. The Romans were visited with a plague after the murder, upon which the oracle was consulted, and the manes of Remus appeased by the institution of festivals called from him Remuria. *Ovid. Fast.* 4. v. 837. l. 5. v. 469.—*Dionys.* 1. c. 87.—*Cic. Div. ex. Enn.* 1. c. 48. ——One of the auxiliaries of Turnus against Æneas. *Virg. Æn.* 9. v. 330.

RESÆ'NA or RHÆS'ENA, a town of Mesopotamia, famous for the defeat of Sapor by Gordian. *Aurel. Victor.*

RE'SUS, a small river of Asia Minor, falling into the Mæander. *Strab.* 12.

RETI'NA, a village near Misenum. *Plin.* 5. c. 5.

REUDIG'NI, a nation of Germany. *Tacit. de Germ.* 40.

REX, a surname of the family of the Marcii. *Suet. Cæs.* 6.

RHA, a large river, now the Volga, which rises on the borders of Lithuania in Russia, in the north of Europe, and falls into the Caspian Sea, after a course of upwards of 1,200 miles. A medicinal root which grew on its bank was called *Rha barbarum*, Rhubarb. *Mela*, 3. c. 5.

RHACE'LUS, a city of Macedonia. *Steph.*

RHA'CIA, a promontory in the Mediterranean Sea, projecting from the Pyrenean mountains. *Polyb.* It appears to be called Aphrodisium by *Ptolemy.*

RHA'CIUS, a Cretan prince, the first of that nation who entered Ionia with a colony. He seized Clarus, of which he became the sovereign. He married Manto, the daughter of Tiresias, who had been seized on his coasts, after she had been driven with some of her countrymen from Thebes, when Thersander, son of Polynices, had obtained a victory over his enemies. *Paus.* 7. c. 3.

RHACO'TES or RHACO'TIS, an ancient name of Alexandria, the capitol of Ægypt. *Strab.*—*Paus.* 5. c. 21.

RHADAMAN'THUS, a son of Jupiter and Europa. He was born in Crete, which he abandoned about the 30th year of his age. He passed into some of the Cyclades, where his government was marked by so much justice and impartiality, that the ancients have said he became one of the judges of hell, and that he was employed in the infernal regions in obliging the dead to confess their crimes, and in punishing them for their offences. Rhadamanthus reigned not only over some of the Cyclades, but over many of the Greek cities of Asia. *Paus.* 8. c. 53.—*Ovid. Met.* 9. v. 435.—*Diod.* 5.—*Plato in Min. & Axioch.*—*Homer. Il.* 4. v. 564.—*Virg. Æn.* 6. v. 66.—*Servius loco.*

RHADAMIS'TUS, a son of Pharnasmanes king of Iberia. He married Zenobia, the daughter of his uncle Mithridates, king of Armenia, and some time after put him to death. He was put to death by his father for his cruelties about the year 52 of the Christian era. *Tacit. Ann.* 13. c. 37.

RHADANU'SIAS or RHODANU'SIA, a name of the city of Massilia. *Steph.* It was probably so called from its vicinity to the Rhodanus.

RHADA'TA, a town of the Syenitæ in Æthiopia. *Plin.* 6. c. 29.

RHAD'INE and LEONTI'CHUS had a tomb at Samus, on which unfortunate lovers offered vows. *Paus.* 7. c. 5.

RHA'DIUS, a son of Neleus. *Apollod.*

RHÆ'A, a city between Scythia and Hyrcania. *Steph.*

RHÆS'ENA. *Vid.* Resæna.

RHÆTE'UM, a city of Phrygia.

RHÆ'TI or RÆ'TI, an ancient and warlike nation of Etruria. They were driven from their native country by the Gauls, and went to settle on the other side of the Alps. *Vid.* Rhætia. *Plin.* 3. c. 20.—*Justin.* 20. c. 5.

RHÆ'TIA, a country at the north of Italy, between the Alps and the Danube, which now forms the territories of the Grisons, of Tyrol, and part of Italy. It was divided into two parts, *Rhætia prima* and *Rhætia secunda.* The first extended from the sources of the Rhine to those of the Licus or Lek, a small river which falls into the Danube. The other, called also Vindelicia, extended from the Licus to another small river called Œnus or Inn, towards the east. The principal towns of Rhætia were Curia, Tridentum, Belunum, and Feltria. The Rhætians rendered themselves formidable by their frequent invasions of the Roman empire, and were at last conquered by Drusus, the brother of Tiberius, and other generals of the Roman emperors. *Virg. G.* 2. v. 96.—*Strab.* 4.—*Plin.* 3. c. 20. l. 14. c. 2, &c.—*Horat.* 4. od. 4 & 14.—*Servius ad Æn.* 1. v. 247.—*Claudian. de Bell. G.* 330.

RHAGÆ'A, a city of Parthia. *Ptol.*

RHA'GE or RA'GE, a town of Britain. *Ptol.* It is supposed to be now Nottingham.

RHA'GES, a town of Thessaly, on the Peneus. *Liv.* l. 2. dec. 4.

RHAMNÆ'I, a people of Arabia Felix, *Plin.* 6. c. 28.

RHAM'NES, a king and augur, who assisted Turnus against Æneas. He was killed in the night by Nisus. *Virg. Æn.* 9. v. 325.

RHAM'NUS, a town of Attica, famous for a temple of Amphiaraus, and a statue of the goddess Nemesis, who was thence called Rhamnusia. This statue was made by Phidias, out of a block of Parian marble which the Persians intended as a pillar to be erected to commemorate their expected victory over Greece. The goddess was represented with a crown of victory on her head, and holding in her left hand the bough of an apple tree, and in her right a cup. *Ovid. Trist.* 5. el. 9. v. 9.—*Claudian. de Bell. G.* 601.—*Paus.* 1. c. 33.—*Plin.* 36. c. 5 ——A town and harbour of Crete. *Ptol.*

RHAMNU'SIA, a name of Nemesis. *Vid.* Rhamuns.

RHAMPSINI'TUS or RHAMPSIN'ITUS, an opulent king of Ægypt who succeeded Proteus. He built a large stone tower at Memphis, where his riches were deposited, and of which he was robbed by the artifice of the architect, who had left a stone in the wall easily moveable, so as to admit a plunderer. *Herodot.* 2. c. 121, &c.—*Plut. Cons. ad Apollon.*—*Paus.* 9. c. 37.

RHAM'SES or RAMI'SES, a powerful king of Ægypt, who, with an army of 700,000 men, conquered Æthiopia, Libya, Persia, and other eastern nations. In his reign, according to Pliny, Troy was taken. Some authors consider him to be the same as Sesostris. *Tacit. Ann.* 2. c. 60.—*Plin.* 36. c. 8.

RHA'NIS, one of Diana's attendant nymphs. *Ovid. Met.* 3. v. 171.

RHAP'PHA, a city of India without the Ganges. *Ptol.*

RHA'RIAS, a surname of Ceres from Rharus. *Steph.*

RHA'RUS or RHA'RIUM, a plain of Attica where corn was first sown by Triptolemus. It received its name from the sower's father, who was called Rharus. *Paus.* 1. c. 14 & 38.

RHASCU'PORIS, a king of Thrace, who invaded the possessions of Cotys, and was put to death by order of Tiberius, &c. *Tacit. Ann.* 2. c. 64. He is called Thrascypolis by *Suetonius in Tiber.* c. 37.

RHAU'RARIS. *Vid.* Araurius.

RHAZUN'DA, a town of Media. *Ptol.*

RHE'A, a daughter of Cœlus and Terra, who married Saturn, by whom she had Vesta, Ceres, Juno, Pluto, Neptune, &c. Her husband, however, devoured all his children as soon as born, as he had succeeded to the throne with the solemn promise that he would raise no male offspring, or, according to others, because he had been informed by an oracle, that one of his sons would dethrone him. To stop the cruelty of her husband, Rhea consulted her parents, and was advised to impose upon him, or perhaps to flee into Crete. Accordingly, when she brought forth, the child was immediately concealed, and Saturn devoured a stone wrapped up in linen, which his wife had given him as her own child. The fears of Saturn were soon proved to be well founded. A year after, the child, whose name was Jupiter, became so strong and powerful, that he drove his father from his throne. Rhea has been confounded by the mythologists with some of the other goddesses, and many have supposed that she was the same divinity that received adoratoin under the various names of Bona Dea, Cybele, Dindymene, Magna mater, Ceres, Vesta, Titæa and Terra, Tellus, and Ops. *Vid.* Cybele, Ceres, Vesta, &c. Rhea, after the expulsion of her husband from his throne, followed him to Italy, where he established a kingdom. His benevolence in this part of Europe was so great, that the golden age of Saturn is often called the age of Rhea. *Hesiod. Theog.* 460.—*Orpheus in Hymn.*—*Homer. ib.*—*Æschyl. Prom.*—*Euripid. Bacc. & Elect.*—*Ovid. Fast.* 1. v. 197.—*Apollod.* 1. c. 1, &c.

RHE'A SYL'VIA, daughter of Numitor king of Alba, was mother of Romulus and Remus. She is also called Ilia. *Vid.* Ilia.

RHE'A, a nymph of Italy, who is said to have borne to Hercules a son called Aventinus. *Virg. Æn.* 7. v. 659.

RHE'BAS or RHE'BUS, a river of Bithynia, flowing from mount Olympus into the Euxine Sea. *Flacc.* 7. v. 698.

RHE'CAS, a leader of the Lacedæmonians. *Strab.* 11.

RHED'ONES. *Vid.* Redones.

RHEGIA'NUM, a town of Lower Mysia. *Ptol.* It is now Rosi, according to *Niger.*

RHE'GIUM, now Rheggio, a town of Italy, in the country of the Brutii, opposite Messana in Sicily, where a colony of Messenians under Alcidamidas settled, B.C. 723. It was originally called Rhegium, and afterwards Rhegium Julium, to distinguish it from Rhegium Lepidi, a town of Cisalpine Gaul. Some suppose that it received its name from the Greek word ῥήγνυμι, *to break*, because it is situate on the straits of Charybdis, which were formed when the island of Sicily, as it were, was broken and separated from the continent of Italy. This town has always been subject to great earthquakes, by which it has often been destroyed. The neighbourhood is remarkable for its great fertility, and for its delightful views. *Sil.* 13. v. 94.—*Cic. pro Arch.* 3.—*Ovid. Met.* 14. v. 5 & 48.—*Justin.* 4. c. 1.—*Mela*, 2. c. 4.—*Strab.* 6.—*Macrob.* 2. c. 11.—*Tzetzes in Lyc.* 45.

RHEG'MA, a city of Cilicia.——A bay near the Persian Gulph. *Steph.*——A lake near Anchiale. *Strab.*

RHEGUS'CI, a people of the Alps. *Plin.* 3. c. 20.

RHE'MI. *Vid.* Remi.

RHE'NE, a small island of the Ægæan, about 200 yards from Delus, 18 miles in circumference. The inhabitants of Delus always buried their dead there, and their women also retired thither during their labor, as in their own island, which was consecrated to Apollo. Latona had brought forth, and no dead bodies were allowed to be buried there. Strabo says, that it was uninhabited, though it was once as populous and flourishing as the rest of the Cyclades. Polycrates conquered it, and consecrated it to Apollo, after he had tied it to Delus by means of a long chain. Rhene was sometimes called the small Delus, and the island of Delus, the great Delus. *Thucyd.* 3.—*Strab.* 10.—*Mela*, 2. c. 7.—*Steph.*—*Plin.* 4. c. 12.

RHE'NI, a people on the borders of the Rhine. *Pers. Sat.* 6. v. 47.

RHE'NUS, one of the largest rivers of Europe, which divides Germany from Gaul. It rises in the Rhætian Alps, and falls into the German Ocean. Virgil has called it *bicornis*, because it divides itself into two streams. The river Rhine was a long time a barrier between the Romans and the Germans, and on that account its banks were covered with strong castles. J. Cæsar was the first Roman who crossed it to invade Germany. The waters of that river were held in great veneration, and were supposed by the ancient Germans to have some peculiar virtue, as they threw their children into it, either to try the fidelity of the mothers, or to brace and invigorate their limbs. If the child swam on the surface, the mother was acquitted of suspicion, but if it sank to the bottom, it was deemed illegitimate. In modern geography the Rhine is known as dividing itself into four large branches, the Waal, Lech, Issel, and Rhine. That branch which still retains the name of Rhine, loses itself in the sands above modern Leyden, and is afterwards no longer known by its ancient appellation, since the year 860, A.D., when the inundations of the sea destroyed the regularity of its mouth. *Ovid. Met.* 2. v. 258. *Fast.* 1. v. 286. l. 4. v. 571. *Trist.* 2. v. 42. *Ex Pont.* 3. el. 4. v. 88 & 108.—*Horat. de A. P.* 18.—*Ital.* 8. v. 601.—*Strab.* 4.—*Mela.* 2. c. 5. l. 3. c. 2.—*Cæsar. de Bell. G.* 4. c. 10.—*Tacit. Ann.* 2. c. 6.—*Virg. Æn.* 8. v. 727.——A small river of Italy, falling into the Po on the south, now Reno. It was in a small island formed by this river that Augustus, Antony, and Lepidus met after the battle of Mutina, and arbitrarily divided among them the provinces of the Roman empire. *Sil.* 8. v. 600.—*Plin.* 3. c. 16. l. 16. c. 36.

RHEOMI'TRES, a Persian who revolted from Artaxerxes, &c. *Diod.* 15.——A Persian officer killed at the battle of Issus. *Curt.* 2. c. 5.

RHES'ALA, a city of Umbria. *Steph.*

RHE'SUS, a king of Thrace, son of the Strymon and Terpsichore, or, according to others, of Eioneus by Euterpe. After many warlike exploits and conquests in Europe, he marched to the assistance of Priam, king of Troy, against the Greeks. He was expected with great impatience, as an ancient oracle had declared, that Troy should never be taken, if the horses of Rhesus drank the waters of the Xanthus, and fed upon the grass of the Trojan plains. This oracle was well known to the Greeks, and therefore two of their best generals, Diomedes and Ulysses, were commissioned by the rest to intercept the Thracian prince. The Greeks entered his camp in the night, slew him, and carried away his horses in triumph to their camp. Rhesus had married a little before his arrival in Asia, a beautiful woman of Cios, called Arganthone. *Homer. Il.* 10.—*Dictys. Cret.* 2.—*Apollod.* 1. c. 3.—*Virg. Æn.* 1. v. 473.—*Ovid. Met.* 13. v. 98. & *Heroid.* 1. v. 39. *Am.* 1. el, 9. v. 23.—*Eustath. ad Hom.* 10. *Il.*—*Servius ad Virg. loco*, & l. 12. v. 347.—*Parthen.* 36.—*Schol. Euripid. in Rhes.*—*Catul.* 56. v. 26.

RHETE'NOR, one of the friends of Diomedes, changed by Venus into a bird. *Ovid. Met.* 14. v. 504.

RHET'ICO, a mountain of Rhætia. *Mela*, 2. c. 3.

RHETOG'ENES, a prince of Spain, who surrendered to the Romans, and was treated with great humanity.

RHEU'NUS, a place in Arcadia. *Paus.* 8. c. 23.

RHEXE'NOR, a son of Nausithous, king of Phæacia. *Homer. Odys.* 7. v. 63.——The father of Chalciope, wife of Ægeus, king of Athens. *Apollod.* 3.——A musician who accompanied Antony in Asia. *Plut. in Ant.*

RHEXIB'IUS, an athlete of Opus, who obtained a prize at the Olympic games, in the 61st Olympiad, and had a statue in the grove of Jupiter. *Paus.* 6. c. 18.

RHI'A, a festival annually celebrated by the people of Locris, on mount Rhion. *Plut. in Conv.*

RHIA'NUS, a Greek poet of Thrace, originally a slave. He wrote an account of the war between Sparta and Messenia, which continued for twenty years, as also a history of the principal revolutions and events which had taken place in Thessaly. Of this poetical composition nothing but twenty-one verses are extant. He flourished about 200 years B.C. *Paus.* 4. c. 6.—*Suidas.*—*Stephan. Byz.*—*Gyrald. de P. H.* 3.—*Salmas. ad Solin.* p. 856.

RHID'AGO, a river of Hyrcania, falling in a northern direction into the Caspian Sea. *Curt.* 6. c. 4.

RHIGI'NA or RHIGIN'IA, a river of Macedonia. *Strab.*

RHIMOT'ACLES, a king of Thrace, who revolted from Antony to Augustus. He boasted of his attachment to the emperor's person at an entertainment, upon which Augustus said, *proditionem amo, proditores vero odi. Plut.*

RHINOCOLU'RA, a town on the borders of Palestine and Ægypt. *Liv.* 45. c. 11.—*Plin.* 5. c. 13.—It is now Faramida, according to *Niger.*

RHINOCOLUS'TES, a surname of Hercules, derived from his having ordered the ears and nose of the Orchomenian heralds to be cut off, because they claimed the tribute of 100 oxen which Erginus had imposed upon the Thebans whom he had conquered. *Paus.* 9. c. 25.—*Apollod.* 2.

RHIN'THON, a Greek poet of Tarentum, in the age of Alexander. He first composed tragi-comic plays which bore his name, but of the thirty-eight pieces which he wrote not one has escaped the ravages of time. *Fabr. B. Gr.* 2. c. 19.—

Cic. ad Att. 1. ep. 20.—*Suidas.*—*Antholog.* 3. —*Athen.* 3.—*Gyrald. P. H.* 7.—*Varro, R. R.* 3. c. 3.

RHIOCH'ARUS, a river of Colchis, flowing into the Euxine Sea. *Strab.*

RHI'ON, a promontory of Achaia, opposite to Antirrhium in Ætolia, at the mouth of the Corinthian Gulf, called also the Dardanelles of Lepanto. The strait between Naupactum and Patræ bore also the same name. The tomb of Hesiod was at the top of the promontory, and a festival called Rhia was annually celebrated there. *Liv.* 27. c. 30. l. 38. c. 7.—*Plin.* 4. c. 2.—*Paus.* 7. c. 22.—*Plut. in conv.*

RHI'PHA or RHI'PHE, a town of Arcadia. *Stat.* 4. *Theb.* v. 286.

RHIPHÆ'I, large mountains at the north of Scythia, where, as some suppose, the Gorgons had fixed their residence. The name of Rhiphæan was applied to any cold mountain in a northern country, and indeed these mountains seem to have existed only in the imagination of the poets, though some make the Tanais rise there. *Plin.* 4. c. 12.—*Lucan.* 3. v. 272. l. 3. v. 382. l. 4. v. 418.—*Virg. G.* 1. v. 240. l. 4. v. 518.—*Strab.* 7.—*Servius ad Virg. G.* 3. v. 382.

RHIPHÆOR'MA, a town of Arabia. *Plin.* 6. c. 28.

RHI'PHEUS, one of the Centaurs, killed by Theseus. *Ovid. Met.*——A Trojan praised for his justice. *Virg. Æn.* 2. v. 426. *Vid.* Ripheus.

RHIS'PIA, a town of Upper Pannonia. *Ptol.*

RHIT'TIUM, a town of Lower Pannonia, on the Danube. *Ptol.*

RHITYM'NA or RHITHYM'NA, a city of Crete. *Ptol.*—*Steph.*—It is now Retimo.

RHI'UM. *Vid.* Rhion.

RHIUSIA'VA, a city of Germany. *Ptol.*

RHIZE'NIA, a city of Crete. *Steph.*

RHI'ZIS, a promontery of the Troglodytæ. *Steph.*

RHIZ'IUS or RHI'ZUS, a harbour near the Euxine Sea. *Ptol.*

RHIZONI'TÆ, a people of Illyricum, whose chief town was called Rhizinium. *Liv.* 45. c. 26.—*Plin.* 3. c. 22.

RHIZOPH'AGI, a people of Æthiopia. They are called Elii by *Strabo.*

RHI'ZUS, a city of Magnesia, near Melibœa. *Plin.* 4. c. 9.

RHO'AS, a river of Colchis, flowing from mount Caucasus into the Euxine Sea. *Plin.* 6. c. 4.

RHO'DA, now Reses, a sea-port town of Spain, at the extremity of the Pyrenean mountains, in the Mediterranean. *Liv.* 34. c. 8.——A town of the Rhone, from which the river received its name. It was ruined in Pliny's age. *Plin.* 3. c. 4.

RHOD'ANUS, a river of Gallia Narbonensis, rising in the Rhætian Alps, and falling by several mouths into the Mediterranean Sea, near Marseilles. It is one of the largest and most rapid rivers of Europe, and is now known by the name of the Rhone. *Mela,* 2. c. 5. l. 3. c. 3.—*Ovid. Met.* 2. v. 258.—*Sil.* 3. v. 447.—*Marcel.* 15. c. 28. —*Cæsar. Bell. G.* 1. c. 1.—*Plin.* 3. c. 4.—*Strab.* 4.—*Lucan.* 1. v. 433. l. 6. v. 475.—*Tibull.* 1. el. 8. v. 11.—*Claudian. in Ruf.* 2. v. 111.

RHO'DE, a daughter of Neptune. *Apollod.*——A daughter of Danaus. *Id.*

RHODI'A, one of the Oceanides. *Hesiod. Theog.* v. 351.——A daughter of Danaus. *Apollod.*

RHO'DIA, a city of Lycia, called also Rhodiopolis and Rhodiorum Colonia. *Steph.*—*Plin.* 5. c. 27. —*Salmas. ad Solin.* p. 785. It is now Machri.

RHO'DO, a Roman intimate with Thermus. *Cic.* 2. *Fam.* 18.

RHOD'OE, a city of India. *Steph.*

RHODOGY'NE, a daughter of Phraates, king of Parthia, who married Demetrius, when he was in banishment at her father's court. *Polyæn.* 8. c. 27.

RHOD'OPE or RHODO'PIS, a celebrated courtezan of Greece, who was fellow-servant with Æsop, at the court of a king of Samus. She was carried to Ægypt by Xanthus, and her liberty was at last bought by Charaxes of Mitylene, the brother of Sappho, who was enamoured of her, and who married her. She sold her favors at Naucratis, where she collected so much money, that, to render her name immortal, she consecrated a number of spits in the temple of Apollo at Delphi, or, according to others, erected one of the pyramids of Ægypt. Ælian says, that, as Rhodope was one day bathing, an eagle carried away one of her sandals, and dropped it near Psammetichus, king of Ægypt, at Memphis. The monarth was struck with the beauty of the sandal, strict inquiry was made to find the owner, and Rhodope, when discovered, married Psammetichus. *Herodot.* 2. c. 134, &c.—*Strab.* 17.—*Athen.* 13. c. 7.—*Plin.* 36. c. 12.—*Plut. de Pyth.*—*Ovid. Heroid.* 15. v. 63.—*Ælian. V. H.* 13. c. 33. *Perizonius* supposes there were two persons of that name. *Ælian in loco.*

RHOD'OPE, a high mountain of Thrace, extending across the country as far as the Euxine Sea, nearly in an eastern direction. Rhodope, according to the poets, was the wife of Hæmus king of Thrace, who was changed into this mountain, because she considered herself more beautiful than Juno. The festivals of Bacchus were celebrated by the Mænades on this mountain. *Ovid. Met.* 6. v. 87, &c.—*Virg. Ecl. G.* 3. v. 351.—*Mela,* 2. c. 2.—*Strab.* 7.—*Ital.* 2. v. 73.—*Seneca in Herc. Œt.* 1538.—*Lactant. ad Theb.* 2. v. 81 & l. 5. v. 188.—*Eustath. ad Dionys. Per.* 298.——A city of Ionia. *Steph.*

RHODOPE'IUS, is used in the same signification as Thracian, because Rhodope was a mountain of that country. *Ovid. A. A.* 3. v. 321. *Heroid.* 2. —*Virg. G.* 4. v. 461.

RHODU'NIA, the top of mount Œta. *Liv.* 36. c. 16.

RHO'DUS, a celebrated island in the Carpathian Sea, 120 miles in circumference, at the south of Caria, from which it is distant about twenty miles. Its principal cities were Rhodes, founded about 408 B.C., Lindus, Camirus, and Jalysus. Rhodes was famous for the siege which it supported against Demetrius, and for a celebrated statue of Apollo. *Vid.* Colossus. The Rhodians were originally governed by kings, and were independent, but this government was at last exchanged for a democracy and an aristocracy. They were naturally given to commerce, and, during many ages, were the most powerful nation by sea. Their authority was respected, and their laws were so universally approved, that every country made use of them to decide disputes concerning maritime affairs, and they were at last adopted by other commercial nations, and introduced into the Roman code, whence they have been extracted to form the basis of the maritime regulations of modern Europe. When Alexander made himself master of Asia, the Rhodians lost their independence, but they soon after asserted their natural privileges under his cruel successors, and continued to hold that influence among nations to which their maritime power and consequence entitled them. They assisted Pompey against Cæsar, and were defeated by Cassius, and became dependent upon the Romans. The island of Rhodes has been known under the several names of Ophiusa, Stadia, Telchinis, Corymbia, Trinacria, Æthræa, Asteria, Peressa, Athabyria, Colossa, Macaria, and Pelagia. It received the name of Rhodes, either on account of Rhode, a beautiful nymph who dwelt there, and who was one of the favorites of Apollo, or because *roses* (ῥόδον) grew in great abundance in the island. As the Rhodians were the first who offered sacrifices to Minerva, Jupiter, to reward their piety towards his daughter, overshadowed the island with a golden cloud, from which showers of treasures and plenty descended upon the inhabitants. *Strab.* 14.—*Homer. Il.* 2. *Æn.* 163.—*Mela,* 2. c. 7.—*Diod.* 5.—*Plin.* 2. c. 62 & 87. l. 5. c. 31.—*Flor.* 2. c. 7.—*Pindar. Olymp.* 7.—*Lucan.* 8. v. 248.—*Cic. pro Man. leg. in Brut.* 13.—*Liv.* 27. c. 30 l. 31. c. 2.—*Marcell.* 17.—*Catull.* 4.—*Ptol.* 5. c. 2.—*Vitruv.* 7.—*Isidor. Orig.* 14. c. 6.—*Philostr. Icon.* 2. c. 27.—*Claudian. de Stil.* 3. v. 226. —*Lactant. de Fals. R.* 21.—*Aul. G.* 7. c. 3.

RHODUS'SA, an island of the Argives. *Steph.* ——The name of two islands in the Thracian Bosporus. *Plin.* 5. c. 32.

RHŒ'BUS, a horse of Mezentius, which his master addressed with the determination to die or conquer, when he saw his son Lausus brought lifeless from the battle. This beautiful address is copied from Homer, who has likewise represented Achilles as addressing his horses. *Virg. Æn.* 10. v. 861.

RHŒ'CUS, one of the Centaurs, who attempted to offer violence to Atalanta. He was killed by Bacchus at the nuptials of Pirithous. *Ælian. V. H.* 13. c. 1.—*Flacc.* 1. v. 140.—*Ovid. Met.* 12. v. 301. *Virg. G.* 2. v 455.——One of the giants killed by Bacchus, under the form of a lion, in the war which these sons of the earth waged against Jupiter and the gods. *Horat.* 2. od. 19. v. 23.——A Samian, said to have been the inventor of the plastic art. *Plin.* 35. c. 12.

RHŒ'DIAS, a river of Macedonia flowing into the Axius. *Plin.* 4. c. 10.

RHŒ'O, a nymph beloved by Apollo, and mother of Anius by him. It is said that she was thrown by her father, Staphylus, in a coffer, into the sea, and that she was cast on the shore of Delus, where her son was found in the coffer with her, and placed by her on Apollo's altar, who brought him up, and convinced him of his legitimacy. *Diod.* 5.—*Tzetzes. in Lyc.* 570.

RHŒT'ACES, a river of Armenia. *Strab.*

RHŒTE'UM or RHŒ'TUS, a promontory of Troas, on the Hellespont, near which the body of Ajax was buried. *Ovid. Met.* 11. v. 197. 4. *Fast.* v. 279. —*Virg. Æn.* 6. v. 505. l. 12. v, 456.

RHŒ'TIA, a daughter of Sithon, son of Mars, who gave her name to the Rhœtean promontory near Troy. *Tzetz. ad Lyc.* 582 & 1160.—*Serv. Æn.* 2. 506. 3. 108. & 6. 505.

RHŒ'TIA, a city of the Bactri. *Steph.*

RHŒ'TIUS, a mountain of Corsica. *Ptol.* It is now Monte di Mezzo.

RHŒ'TUS, a king of the Marubii, who married a woman called Casperia, to whom Anchemolus, his son by a former wife, offered violence. After this incestuous attempt, Anchemolus fled to Turnus king of the Rutuli. *Virg. Æn.* 10. v. 388.—*Servius in loco.*—*Lucan.* 6. v. 390.——A Rutulian killed by Euryalus in the night. *Virg.* 9. v. 344. ——An Æthiopian killed by Perseus. *Ovid. Met.* 5. v. 38.

RHŒX'US, a naval station of Cilicia. *Steph.*

RHOGA'NE, a city of India. *Id.*

RHO'GE, an island near Lycia. *Id.*

RHOMBI'TES, a river of Asiatic Sarmatia. *Ptol.* It is now Kuban.

RHON, a city of Scythia. The gentile name was Rhonius or Rhonites. *Steph.*

RHONDÆ'I, a people of Thrace. *Id.*

RHOSA'CES, a Persian killed by Clitus as he was going to stab Alexander at the battle of Granicus. *Curt.* 8. c. 1.

RHOSPODU'SA, an island in the Sinus Carcinitis. *Plin.* 4. c. 13.

RHO'SUS, a town of Syria, on the Gulph of Issus, celebrated for its earthenware. *Cic.* 6. *Att.* 1.—*Strab.* 16.—*Plin.* 5. c. 22.—*Mela*, 1. c. 12.

RHOTA'NA, a city of India. *Steph.*

RHOTA'NUS, a river of Corsica. *Ptol.* It is now Tavignani.

RHO'TUS, a man engaged as architect at the erection of the Lemnian labyrinth. *Plin.* 36. c. 13.

RHOXOLA'NI, a people at the north of the Palus Mæotis. *Tacit. Hist.* 1. c. 79.—*Plin.* 4. c. 12.

RHOXA'NA or ROXA'NA, a mistress of Alexander. *Vid.* Roxana.

RHOXA'NI, a nation against whom Mithridates made war, &c.

RHUCAN'THII, a people of Rhætia. *Strab.*

RHUSPI'NA, a city of Africa Propria. *Ptol.* It is now Souse.

RHUSUCCO'RÆ, a city of Mauritania Cæsariensis. *Ptol.* It is probably the Ruscurium of *Pliny*, 5. c. 2., and is now Alger.

RHUTE'NI or RUTHE'NI, a people of Germano-Sarmatia.

RHUTE'NI, a people of Gallia Aquitanica. *Cæs. B. G.* l. 1. c. 45. Their country is now Rovergue, and their city Rodez.

RHYB'DUS, a fortified place of Sicily. *Steph.*

RHYN'CHE, a small region of Eubœa. *Steph.*

RHYN'DACUS, a large river of Mysia in Asia Minor. *Plin.* 5. c. 32.

RHYN'THON. *Vid.* Rhinthon.

RHY'PÆ, a town of Achaia, at the west of Helice. *Steph.*

RHYP'ARA, a small island of the Ægæan Sea, near Samus. *Plin.* 5. c. 31.

RHYSA'DIUS, a mountain in the interior of Libya. *Ptol.*

RHYT'IUM, a city of Crete. *Hom. Il.* 2.

RIGODU'LUM, a village of Germany, now Rigol, near Cologne. *Tacit. H.* 4. c. 71.

RIG'MUS, son of Pires of Thrace, assisted Priam against the Greeks, and was killed by Achilles. *Homer. Il.* 20. v. 484.

RIPHÆ'I. *Vid.* Rhipæi.

RIPHEAR'MA, a city of Arabia Felix. *Plin.* 6. c. 28.

RI'PHEUS, a Trojan who joined Æneas the night that Troy was reduced to ashes, and was at last killed after making a great carnage among the Greeks. He is commended for his love of justice and equity. *Virg. Æn.* 2. v. 339 & 426.——One of the Centaurs killed by Theseus at the nuptials of Pirithous. *Ovid. Met.* 12. v. 352.

RI'RA, a river of Thrace. *Plin.* 4. c. 11.

RISAM'ORI, a people of the Celtiberi, in Hispania Tarraconensis. *Martial.* l. 4. epigr. 55. v. 16.

RISAR'DIS, a harbour of Mauritania. *Plin.* 5. c. 1.

RIZONI'TÆ. *Vid.* Rhizonitæ.

ROBI'GO or RUBI'GO, a goddess at Rome, particularly worshipped by husbandmen, as she presided over corn. Her festivals, called *Robigalia*, were celebrated on the 25th of April, and incense was offered to her, as also the entrails of a sheep, and of a dog. She was entreated to preserve the corn from blights. *Ovid. Fast.* 4. v. 911.—*Virg. G.* 1. v. 151.—*Horat.* 3. od. 23. v. 6.—*Tertul. de Spect.* 5.—*Varro. de L.L.* 5. *de R.R.* 1. c. 1.

RODUM'NA, now Roanne, a town of the Ædui, on the Loire.

RO'MA, a city of Italy, the capital of the Roman empire, situate on the banks of the river Tiber, at the distance of about sixteen miles from the sea. The name of its founder, and the manner of its foundation, are not precisely known. Romulus, however, is universally supposed to have laid the foundations of that celebrated city, on the 20th of April, according to Varro, in the year 3961 of the Julian period, 3251 years after the creation of the world, 753 before the birth of Christ, 431 years after the Trojan war, and in the fourth year of the sixth Olympiad. In its original state, Rome was but a small castle on the summit of mount Palatine; and the founder, to give his followers the appearance of a nation, or a barbarian horde, was obliged to erect a standard as a common asylum for every criminal, debtor, or murderer, who fled from his native country to avoid the punishment which attended him. From such an assemblage a numerous body was soon collected; and before the death of the founder, the Romans had covered with their habitations, the Palatine, Capitoline, Aventine, and Esquiline hills, with mounts Cœlius and Quirinalis. After many successful wars against the neighbouring states, the views of Romulus were directed to regulate a nation naturally fierce, warlike, and uncivilized. The people were divided into classes, the interests of the whole were linked in a common chain, and the labors of the subject, as well as those of his patron, tended to the same end, the aggrandizement of the state. Under the successors of Romulus, the power of Rome was increased, and the boundaries of her dominions extended; while one was employed in regulating the forms of worship, and in inculcating in the minds of his subjects a reverence for the deity, the other was engaged in enforcing discipline among the army, and raising the consequence of the soldiers in the government of the state, and a third made the object of his administration consist in adorning his capital, in beautifying its edifices, and fortifying it with towers and walls. During 244 years, the Romans were governed by kings, but the tyranny, the oppression, and the violence of the last of these monarchs and of his family, became so atrocious, that a revolution was effected in the state, and the democratical government was established. The monarchical government existed under seven princes, who began to reign in the following order: Romulus, B.C. 753; and after one year's interregnum, Numa, 715; Tullus Hostilius, 672; Ancus Martius, 640; Tarquinius Priscus, 616; Servius Tullius, 578; and Tarquinius Superbus, 534, expelled twenty-five years after, B.C. 509; and this regal administration has been properly denominated the infancy of the Roman empire. After the expulsion of the Tarquins from the throne, the Romans became more sensible of their consequence: with their liberty they acquired a spirit of faction, and became so jealous of their independence, that the first of their consuls, who had been the most zealous and animated in the assertion of their freedom, was banished from the city, because he bore the name, and was of the family, of the tyrants; and another, to stop their suspicions, was obliged to pull down his house, the stateliness and magnificence of which seemed incompatible with the duties and the rank of a private citizen. They knew more effectually their power when they had fought with success against Porsenna, the king of Etruria, and some of the neighbouring states, who supported the claims of the tyrant, and attempted to replace him on his throne by force of arms. A government which is entrusted into the hands of two of the most distinguished of its members, for the limited space of one year, cannot but give rise to great men, glorious exploits, and tremendous seditions. The general who is placed at the head of an army during a campaign, must be active and diligent, when he knows that his power is terminated with the year, and if he has a becoming ambition, he will distinguish his consulship by some uncommon act of valor, before he descends from the dignity of an absolute magistrate to the inconsequence of a common citizen. Yet these attempts for the attainment of glory often fail of success; and though the Romans could once boast that every individual in their armies could discharge with fidelity and honour the superior offices of magistrates and consul, there are to be found in their annals many years marked by overthrows, or disgraced by the ill conduct, the oppression, and the wantonness of their generals. *Vid.* Consul. To the fame which their conquests and daily successes had gained abroad, the Romans were not a little indebted for their gradual rise to superiority; and to this may be added the policy of the census, which every year told them their actual strength, and how many citizens were able to bear arms. And indeed it was no small satisfaction to a people who were continually making war, to see, that in spite of all the losses which they might sustain in the field, the increase of the inhabitants of the city was prodigious, and almost incredible; and had Romulus lived after the battle of Actium, he would have been persuaded with difficulty that above four millions of inhabitants were contained within the walls of a city, which in the most flourishing period of his reign could scarcely muster an army of 3000 infantry and 300 horse. But when Rome had flourished under the consular government for about 120 years, and beheld with pleasure the conquests of her citizens over the neighbouring states and cities, which, according to a Roman historian, she was ashamed to recollect in the summit of her power, an irruption of the barbarians of Gaul rendered her very existence precarious, and her name was nearly extinguished. The valor of an injured individual (*vid.* Camillus) saved it from destruction, yet not before its buildings and temples were reduced to ashes. This celebrated event, which gave the appellation of another founder of Rome to Camillus, has been looked upon as a glorious era to the Romans. The huts and cottages which Romulus had erected, and his successors repaired, were totally consumed, and when the city rose again from its ruins, the streets were enlarged, convenience as well as order was observed, taste and regularity were consulted, and the poverty, ignorance and rusticity of the Romans seemed to be extinguished with their old habitations. But no sooner were they freed from the fears of their barbarian invaders, than they turned their arms against those states which refused to acknowledge their superiority, or yield their independence. Their wars with Pyrrhus and the Tarentines displayed their character in a different view; if they had before fought for freedom and independence, they now drew their sword for glory; and here we may see them conquered in the field, and yet refusing to grant that peace for which their conqueror himself had sued. The advantages they gained from their battles with Pyrrhus were many. The Roman name became known in Greece, Sicily and Africa; and in losing or gaining a victory, the Romans were enabled to examine the manœuvres, observe the discipline, and contemplate the order and encampments of those soldiers whose friends and ancestors had accompanied Alexander the Great in the conquest of Asia. Italy became subject to the Romans at the end of the war with the Tarentines, and that period of time has been called the second age, or the adolescence of the Roman empire. After this memorable era they tried their strength not only with distant nations, but upon a new element; and in the long wars which they waged against Carthage, they acquired territory, and obtained the sovereignty of the sea; and though Annibal for sixteen years kept them in continual alarm, hovered round their gates, and destroyed their armies almost before their walls, yet they were doomed to conquer, (*vid.* Punicum Bellum.) and soon to add the kingdom of Macedonia, (*vid.* Macedonicum Bellum), and the provinces of Asia, (*vid.* Mithridaticum Bellum), to their empire. But while we consider the Romans as a nation subduing their neighbours by war, their manners, their counsels, and their pursuits at home are not to be forgotten. To be warriors was their profession; their assemblies in the Campus Martius were a meeting of armed men, and very properly denominated an army. Yet, while their conquests were so extensive abroad, we find them torn by factions at home; and so far was the resentment of the poorer citizens carried, that we see the enemy at the gates of the city, while all are unwilling to take up arms, and to unite in the defence of their common liberty. The senators and nobles were ambitious of power, and endeavoured to retain in their hands that influence which had been exercised with so much success, and such cruelty by their monarchs. This was the continual occasion of tumults and sedition. The people were jealous of their liberty. The oppression of the nobles irritated them, and the stripes to which they were too often exposed without mercy, was often productive of revolutions. The plebeians, though originally the poorest and most contemptible citizens of an indigent nation, whose food in the first ages of the empire was only bread and salt, and whose drink was water, soon gained rights and privileges by their opposition. Though really slaves, they became powerful in the state; one concession from the patricians produced another, and, when their independence was boldly asserted by the tribunes, they were admitted to share in the highest offices of the state, and the laws which forbad the intermarriage of plebeian and patrician families were repealed, and the meanest peasant could by valor and fortitude be raised to the dignity of dictator and consul. It was not till these privileges were obtained by the people from the senate, that Rome began to enjoy internal peace and tranquillity; her battles were then fought with more vigor, her soldiers were more animated, and her sovereignty was more universally established. But supreme power lodged in the hands of a factious and ambitious citizen, becomes too often dangerous. The greatest oppression and tyranny took the place of subordination and obedience, and from those causes proceeded the unparalleled slaughter and effusion of blood under Sylla and Marius. It has been justly observed, that the first Romans conquered their enemies by valor, temperance, and fortitude; their moderation also and their justice are well known among their neighbours, and not only private possessions, but even mighty kingdoms and empires, were left in their power, to be distributed among a family, or to be ensured in the hands of a successor. They were also chosen umpires, to decide quarrels, but in this honorable office they consulted their own interest; they artfully supported the weaker side, that the more powerful might be reduced, and gradually become their prey. Under J. Cæsar and Pompey the rage of civil war was carried to unprecedented excess; it was not merely to avenge a private injury, but it was a contest for the sovereignty, and though each of the adversaries wore the mask of pretended sincerity, and professed himself to be the supporter of the republic, not less than the abolition of freedom and public liberty was the aim. What Julius began, his adopted son achieved; the ancient spirit of national independence was extinguished at Rome; and after the battle of Actium, the Romans seemed unable to govern themselves without the assistance of a chief, who, under the title of *imperator*, an appellation given to every commander by his army after some signal victory, reigned with as much power and as much sovereignty as another Tarquin. Under their emperors the Romans lived a luxurious and indolent life; they had long forgotten to appear in the field, and their wars were left to be waged by mercenary troops, who fought without spirit or patriotism, and who were ever ready to yield to him who bought their allegiance and fidelity with the greatest sum of money. Their leaders themselves were not the most prudent or the most humane; the power which they had acquired by bribery was indeed precarious, and among a people, where not only the highest offices of the state, but even the imperial purple itself, are exposed to sale, there cannot be expected much happiness or tranquillity in the palace of the emperor. The reigns of the successors of Augustus were distinguished by variety; one was the most abandoned and profligate of men, whom his own vices and extravagance hurried out of the world, while his successor, perhaps the most clement, just, and popular of princes, was sacrificed in the midst of his guards and attendants by the dagger of some offended favorite or disappointed eunuch. Few indeed were the emperors of Rome whose days were not shortened by poison or the sword of an assassin. If one for some time had the imprudence to trust himself in the midst of a multitude, to perish at last by his own credulity, the other consulted his safety, but with no better success, in the innumerable chambers of his palace, and changed every day, to elude discovery, the place of his retirement. After they had been governed by a race of princes, remarkable for the variety of their characters, the Roman possessions were divided into two distinct empires by the emperor Constantine, A.D. 328. Constantinople became the seat of the eastern empire, and Rome remained in the possession of the western emperors, and continued the capital of their dominions. In the year 800 of the Christian era, Rome with Italy was delivered by Charlemagne, the then emperor of the west, into the hands of the Pope, who still continues to hold the sovereignty, and to maintain his independence under the name of the Ecclesiastical States. The original poverty of the Romans has often been disguised by their poets and historians, who wished it to appear, that a nation who were masters of the world, had had a better beginning than to be a race of shepherds and robbers. Yet it was to this simplicity they were indebted for their successes. Their houses were originally destitute of every ornament, they were made with unequal boards and covered with mud, and these served them rather as a shelter against the inclemency of the seasons than for relaxation and ease. Till the age of Pyrrhus they despised riches, and many salutary laws were enacted to restrain luxury and punish indolence. They observed great temperance in their meals: young men were not permitted to drink wine till they had attained their 30th year, and it was totally forbidden to women. Their national spirit was supported by policy; the triumphal procession of a conqueror along the streets amidst the applause of thousands, was well calculated to promote emulation, and the numbers of gladiators which were regularly introduced, not only in public games and spectacles, but also at private meetings, served to cherish their fondness for war, whilst it steeled their hearts against the calls of compassion; and when they could gaze with pleasure upon wretches whom they forcibly obliged to murder one another, they were not inactive in the destruction of those whom they considered as inveterate foes or formidable rivals in the field. In their punishments, civil as well as military, the Romans were strict and rigorous; a deserter was severely whipped and sold as a slave, and the degradation from the rank of a soldier and dignity of a citizen, was the most ignominious stigma which could be fixed upon a seditious mutineer. The transmarine victories of the Romans proved at last the ruin of their innocence and bravery. They grew fond of the luxury of the Asiatics; and, conquered by the vices and indolence of those nations whom they had subdued, they became as effeminate and dissolute as their captives. Marcellus was the first who introduced a taste for the fine arts among his countrymen. The spoils and treasures that were obtained in the plunder of Syracuse and Corinth, rendered the Romans partial to elegant refinement and ornamental splendor. Though Cato had despised philosophy (*vid.* Carneades), and declared that war was the only profession of his countrymen, the Romans, by their intercourse with the Greeks, soon became fond of literature; and, though they had once banished the sophists of Athens from their city, yet they beheld with rapture their settlement amongst them, in the principal towns of Italy, after the conquest of Achaia. They soon after began to imitate their polished captives, and to cultivate poetry with success. From the valour of their heroes and conquerors, indeed, the sublimest subjects were offered to the genius of their poets; but of the little that remains to celebrate the early victories of Rome, nothing can be compared to the nobler effusions of the Augustan age. Virgil has done so much for the Latin name that the splendour and the triumphs of his country are forgotten for a while, when we are transported in admiration at the majesty of his numbers, the elegance and delicacy of his expressions, and the fire of his muse; and the applause given to the lyric powers of Horace, the softness of Tibullus, the vivacity of Ovid, and to the superior compositions of other respectable poets, shall be unceasing as long as the name of Rome excites our reverence and our praises, and so long as genius, virtue, and abilities are honored amongst mankind. Though they originally rejected with horror a law which proposed the building of a public theatre, and the exhibition of plays, like the Greeks, yet the Romans soon proved favourable to the compositions of their countrymen. Livius was the first dramatic writer of consequence at Rome, whose plays began to be exhibited A.U.C. 514. After him Nævius and Ennius wrote for the stage; and in a more polished period Plautus, Terence, Cæcilius, and Afranius claimed the public attention, and gained the most unbounded applause. Satire did not make its appearance at Rome till 100 years after the introduction of comedy, and so celebrated was Lucillus in this kind of writing, that he was called the inventor of it. In historical writing the progress of the Romans was slow and inconsiderable, and for many years they employed the pen of foreigners, to compile their annals, till the superior abilities of Livy were made known. In their worship and sacrifices the Romans were uncommonly superstitious; the will of the gods was consulted on every occasion, and no general marched on an expedition without previous assurance from the augurs, that the omens were propitious, and his success almost indubitable. Their sanctuaries were numerous; they raised altars not only to the gods, who, as they supposed, presided over their city, but also to the deities of the conquered nations, as well as to the different passions and virtues. There were no less than 420 temples at Rome, crowded with statues, the priests were as numerous, and each divinity had a particular college of sacerdotal servants. Their wars were declared in the most awful and solemn manner, and prayers were always offered in the temples for the prosperity of Rome, when a defeat had been sustained or a victory won. The power of fathers over their children was very extensive, and indeed unlimited; they could sell them or put them to death at pleasure, without the forms of trial or interference of the civil magistrates. Many of their ancient families were celebrated for the great men which they had produced, but the vigorous and interested part they took in the management of the republic exposed them often to danger, and some have observed that the Romans sank into indolence and luxury when the Cornelii, the Fabii, the Æmylii, the Marcelli, &c. who had so often supported their spirit, and led them to victory, had been extinguished in the bloody wars of the two triumvirates. When Rome was become powerful, she was distinguished from other cities by the flattery of her neighbours and citizens; adoration was paid to her as a deity, and temples were raised in her honor not only in the city but in the provinces. The goddess Roma was represented like Minerva, completely armed, and sitting on a rock, holding a pike in her hand, with her head covered with a helmet, and a trophy at her feet. *Liv.* 1, &c.—*Cato de R.R.*—*Virg. Æn. G. & Ecl.*—*Horat.* 2. sat. 6, &c.—*Flor.* 1. c. 1, &c. —*Paterc.*—*Tacit. Ann. & Hist.*—*Tibull.* 4.—*Lucan*—*Plut. in Rom. Num. &c.*—*Cic. de Nat. D.* 1, &c.—*Plin.* 7. &c.—*Justin.* 43.—*Varro de LL.* 5.—*Val. Max.* 1, &c.—*Martial.* 12. epigr. 8. [There is a fine colossal statue of Rome in the gardens of the Villa Medicis, near Rome, and a good head in the Vatican.]

RO'MA, a daughter of Evander.——A Trojan woman who came to Italy with Æneas.——A daughter of Italus and Luceria. It was after one of these females, according to some authors, that the capital of Italy was called Roma. *Servius ad Æn.* 1. v. 277.—*Festus de V. Sig.*

ROMA'NI, the inhabitants of Rome. *Vid.* Roma.

ROMA'NUS, an officer under Theodosius.——An officer poisoned by Nero.——A son of Constans, &c.

ROMATI'NUS, a river of the Carni. *Plin.* 3. c. 18. It is now Limino, according to *Leander*.

ROME'CHIUM, a place of Magna Græcia, between Locri and Caulon. *Ovid Met.* 15. v. 705.

ROMIL'IUS MARCEL'LUS, a Roman centurion in Galba's reign. *Tacit.* 1. *Hist.* c. 56 & 59.

ROM'ULA, a name given to the fig-tree under which Romulus and Remus were found. *Ovid.* 2. *Fast.* v. 412.——A village of Liburnia. *Antonin.* It is now Radstchach.

ROMU'LEA, a town of the Samnites. *Liv.* 10. c. 17.

ROMU'LIDÆ, a patronymic given to the Roman people from Romulus their first king, and the founder of the city. *Virg. Æn.* 8. v. 638.

ROMU'LIUS POL'LIO, a Roman who lived to a very advanced age. *Plin.* 22. c. 24.

ROM'ULUS, a son of Mars and Ilia, grandson of Numitor, king of Alba, was born at the same birth with Remus. These two children were thrown into the Tiber by order of Amulius, who usurped the crown of his brother Numitor; but they were preserved, and, according to Florus, the river stopped its course, and a she-wolf came and fed them with her milk till they were found by Faustulus, one of the king's shepherds, who educated them as his own children. When they knew their real origin, the twins, called Romulus and Remus, put Amulius to death, and restored the crown to their grandfather Numitor. They afterwards undertook to build a city; and, to determine which of the brothers should have the management of it, they had recourse to omens and the flight of birds. Remus went to mount Aventine, and Romulus to mount Palatine. Remus saw first a flight of six vultures, and soon after, Romulus, twelve; and therefore, as his number was greater, he began to lay the foundations of the city, hopeful that it would become a warlike and powerful nation, as the birds from which he had received the omen were fond of prey and slaughter. Romulus marked with a furrow the place where he wished to erect the walls; but their slenderness was ridiculed by Remus, who leaped over them with the greatest contempt. This irritated Romulus, and Remus was immediately put to death, either by the hands of his brother or one of the workmen. When the walls were built, the city was without inhabitants; but Romulus, by making an asylum of a sacred grove, soon collected a multitude of fugitives, foreigners and criminals, whom he received as his lawful subjects. Yet, however numerous these might be, they were despised by the neighbouring inhabitants, and none were willing to form matrimonial connections with them. But Romulus obtained by force what was denied to his petitions. The Romans celebrated games in honor of the god Consus, and forcibly carried away all the females who had assembled there to be spectators of these unusual exhibitions. These violent measures offended the neighbouring nations; they made war against the ravishers with various success, till at last they entered Rome, which had been betrayed to them by one of the stolen virgins. A violent engagement was begun in the middle of the Roman forum; but the Sabines were conquered, or, according to Ovid, the two enemies laid down their arms when the women had rushed between the two armies, and by their tears and entreaties raised compassion in the bosoms of their parents and husbands. The Sabines left their original possessions and came to live in Rome, where Tatius, their king, shared the sovereign power with Romulus. The introduction of the Sabines into the city of Rome was attended with the most salutary consequences, and the Romans, by pursuing this plan, and admitting the conquered nations among their citizens, rendered themselves more powerful and more formidable. Afterwards Romulus divided the lands which he had obtained by conquest; one part was reserved for religious uses, to maintain the priests, to erect temples, and to consecrate altars; the other was appropriated for the expenses of the state; and the third part was equally distributed among his subjects, who were divided into three classes or tribes. The most aged or experienced, to the number of 100, were also chosen, whom the monarch might consult in matters of the highest importance, and from their age they were called *senators*, and from authority *patres*. The whole body of the people was also distinguished by the name of patricians and plebeians, patron and client, who by mutual interest were induced to preserve the peace of the state, and to promote the public good. Some time after, Romulus disappeared as he was giving instructions to the *senators*, and the eclipse of the sun, which happened at that time, was favorable to the rumour which asserted that the king had been taken up to heaven, 714 B.C., after a reign of 39 years. This was further confirmed by J. Proculus, one of the senators, who solemnly declared, that as he returned from Alba, he had seen Romulus in a form above human, and that he had directed him to tell the Romans to pay him divine honors under the name of Quirinus, and to assure them that their city was doomed one day to become the capital of the world. This report was immediately credited, and the more so as the senators dreaded the resentment of the people who suspected them of having offered him violence. A temple was raised to him, and a regular priest, called *Flamen Quirinalis*, was appointed to offer him sacrifices. Romulus was ranked by the Romans among the 12 great gods, and it is not to be wondered at that he received such distinguished honors, when the Romans considered him as the founder of their city and empire, and the son of the god of war. He is generally represented like his father, so much that it is difficult to distinguish them. The fable of the two children of Rhea Sylvia being nourished by a she-wolf, arose from Lupa, Faustulus's wife having brought them up. *Vid.* Acca. *Dionys. Hal.* 1 & 2.—*Liv.* 1. c. 4, &c.—*Justin.* 43. c. 1. & 2.—*Flor.* 1. c. 1.—*Plut. in Romul.*—*Val. Max.* 3. c. 2. l. 5. c. 3.—*Plin.* 15. c. 18, &c.—*Virg. Æn.* 8. v. 342. 635.—*Ovid. Met.* 14. v. 616 & 845. *Fast.* 4, &c.—*Horat.* 3. od. 3.—*Juv.* 18. v. 272.—*Eutrop.* 1. c. 4.—*Aug. de Civ. D.* 2. c. 17. l. 3. c. 6. l. 13. c. 15.—*Lactant.* 1. c. 20. l. 2. c. 7.—*Servius ad Virg. Æn.* 1. v. 280 & 296. l. 2. v. 261. l. 6. v. 778. l. 7. v. 678.

ROM'ULUS SYL'VIUS, or ALLA'DIUS, a king of Alba. He succeeded Agrippa, and reigned 19 years. *Dion. Hal.*

ROM'ULUS MOMYL'LUS AUGUS'TULUS, the last of the emperors of the western empire of Rome. His country was conquered A.D. 476, by the Heruli, under Odoacer, who assumed the name of king of Italy.

RO'MUS, a son of Æneas, by Lavinia. Some suppose that he was the founder of Rome. *Apollod.*

in Euxen.——A son of Æmathion sent by Diomedes to Italy, and also supposed by some to be the founder of Rome.——A son of Ulysses and Circe. *Steph.*

ROPI'CUM, a town of Corsica. *Ptol.* It is now Rogela.

ROS'CIA LEX, *de theatris*, was introduced by L. Roscius Otho the tribune, A.U.C. 685. It required that none should sit in the first 14 seats of the theatre, if they were not in possession of 400 sestertia, which was the fortune required to be a Roman knight.

ROSCIA'NUM, the port of Thurii now Rosano.

ROS'CIUS Q., a Roman actor, born at Lanuvium, so celebrated on the stage, that every person of superior excellence and merit in every employment of life may be honorably called the *Roscius* of his profession. His eyes were naturally distorted, and he always appeared on the stage in a mask, but the Romans obliged him to act his characters without, and overlooked the deformities of his face, that they might the better hear his elegant pronunciation, and be delighted with the sweetness of his voice. In his private character Roscius was so respectable that he was raised to the rank of senator. When falsely accused on suspicion of dishonorable practices, Cicero, who had been one of his pupils, undertook his defence, and cleared him of the malevolent aspersions of his enemies, in an elegant oration, still extant. Roscius wrote a treatise now lost, in which he compared, with great success and much learning, the profession of the orator with that of the comedian. He died about 60 years B.C. The daily stipend of Roscius for acting was 1000 denarii, or about £32 6s. English money, though Cicero makes his yearly income amount to about £48,434 10s. *Horat.* 2. ep. 1. v. 82.—*Quintil.* 11. c. 3.—*Cic. pro. Ros. de Orat.* 3. c. 56, 57, & 223. *De Div.* 1. c. 133. l. 2. c. 101. *Tusc.* 3. c. 75. *Arch.* 8.—*Athen.* 14.—*Macrob.* 3. c. 14.—*Plut. in Cic.*

Ros'cius Sex'tus, a rich citizen of Ameria, murdered in the dictatorship of Sylla. His son, of the same name, was accused of the murder, and eloquently defended by Cicero, in an oration still extant, A.U.C. 673. The murder of this unfortunate man had been perpetrated by means of two Roscii, Capito and Magnus, who obtained possession of his estate during the troubled times of Sylla, and, to avoid the restitution, caused his innocent son to be accused by C. Erucius. *Cic. pro S. Roscio Amer. Brut.* 90. *Off.* 2. c. 14.

Ros'cius Lu'cius, a lieutenant of Cæsar's army in Gaul. *Cæs. Com.* 5. c. 24.

Ros'cius O'tho, a tribune, who made a law to discriminate the knights from the common people at a public spectacle. *Vid.* Roscia Lex. *Cic. Mur.* 19.—*Vell.* 2. c. 32.—*Hor.* 1. ep. 1. v. 62.—*Juv.* 3. v. 159.

Ros'cius Cœ'lius, a lieutenant of the 20th legion, in Britain. *Tac. Hist.* 1. c. 60.

L. Ros'cius Faba'tus, a prætor mentioned by *Cæsar, B. C.* 1. c. 3.

ROSE'Æ CAM'PUS or RO'SIA, a beautiful plain in the country of the Sabines, near the lake Velinus. *Varro. R. R.* 1. c. 7.—*Virg. Æn.* 7. v. 712.—*Cic.* 4. *Att.* 15.

ROSELLA'NUS, A'GER, a territory in Etruria. *Liv.* 10. c. 37.

RO'SIUS POR'TUS, a harbour of Cilicia. *Polyæn.* 4. c. 6. It should be written Rhosius.

Ro'sius, a man made consul for one day only under Vitellius, &c. *Tacit. Hist.* 3. c. 37.

ROS'CIUS REG'ULUS, a man made consul, &c.

ROS'TRUM NEMA'VIÆ, a town of Rhætia. *Ptol.* It is now, probably, Mindelheim.

ROS'ULUM, a town of Etruria, now Monte Rosi.

ROTOM'AGUS, a town of Gaul, now Rouen, at the mouth of the Seine.

ROVE'SIUM, a town of the Velauni, in Gallia Aquitanica. *Ptol.* It is now S. Flour.

ROXA'NA, a Persian woman, taken prisoner by Alexander the Great. The conqueror became enamoured of her, and married her. She behaved with great cruelty to Statira after Alexander's death, and was at last put to death, together with her infant son, by order of Cassander. She was daughter of Darius, or, according to others, of Oxyartes, one of his satraps. *Plut. in. Alex.*—*Paus.* 1. c. 6. l. 9. c. 7.—*Strab.* 11.—*Justin.* 13. c. 4. l. 14. c. 2.—*Curt.* 8. c. 4. l. 10. c. 6.—*Diod.* 18.——A wife of Mithridates the Great, who poisoned herself.

ROXA'NI, a people near the Tigris. *Plut. de flum.*

ROXOLA'NI, a people of European Sarmatia, who proved very active and rebellious in the reign of the Roman emperors. *Tac. Germ.* c. 46.

RUBE'Æ, the north cape at the north of Scandinavia. *Plin.* 4. c. 13.

RUBEL'LIUS BLAN'DUS, a man who married Julia, the daughter of Drusus. *Tac. Ann.* 3. c. 23, &c.

Rubel'lius Plau'tus, an illustrious Roman, one of the descendants of Augustus, who disgraced himself by his arrogance and ambitious views. He was put to death by Nero. *Juv.* 8. v. 39.—*Tac. Ann.* 13. c. 19.

RU'BI, now Ruvo, a town of Apulia, from which the epithet Rubeus is derived, applied to osiers and bramble bushes, which grew there in great abundance. The inhabitants were called Rubitini. *Horat.* 1. sat. 5. v. 94.—*Virg. G.* 1. v. 266, *& Servius loco.*

RU'BICON, now Rugon, a small river of Italy, which it separates from Cisalpine Gaul. It rises in the Apennine mountains, and falls into the Adriatic Sea. By crossing it, and thus advancing beyond the boundaries of his province, and transgressing the decrees of the senate, J. Cæsar declared war against Pompey and his adherents, and began the civil wars. *Lucan.* 1. v. 185 & 213.—*Strab.* 5.—*Suet. in Cæs.* 32.—*Plin.* 3. c. 15.

RUBIE'NUS LAP'PA, a tragic poet in the age of Juvenal, conspicuous as much for his great genius as for his extreme poverty. *Juv.* 7. v. 72.

RUBI'GO, a goddess. *Vid.* Robigo.

RU'BO, the Dwina, which falls into the Baltic at Riga. *Ptol.*

RU'BRA, a town of Corsica. *Ptol.* It is now Solensara.

Ru'bra Sax'a, a place of Etruria, near Veii, at the distance of about eight miles from Rome. *Mart.* 4. epigr. 64. v. 15.—*Liv.* 2. c. 49.

RU'BRIA LEX was enacted after the taking of Carthage, to make an equal division of the lands in Africa. *Rosin. Antiq.* l. 8. c. 8.

RUBRICA'TUS, a river of Hispania Tarraconensis. *Ptol.*—*Mela*, 2. c. 6.——A river of Africa, called Armua by *Pliny.* 5. c. 3.

RU'BRIUS, a Roman knight accused of treason under Tiberius. *Tacit. Ann.* 1. c. 73.

Ru'brius Faba'tus, a man who fled to Parthia, on suspicion that the Roman affairs were ruined. *Tac. Ann.* 6. c. 14.

Ru'brius Gal'lus, a friend of Vitellius. *Tac. Hist.* 2. c. 51.

Ru'brius, an obscure Gaul in great favour with Domitian. *Juv.* 4. v. 105.——A worthless character employed by Verres. *Cic. Verr.* 1. c. 25 & 26.

Ru'brius L., an officer in Cæsar's army. *Cæs. B. C.* c. 23.

RU'BRUM MA'RE, (*the Red Sea,*) is situate between Arabia, Ægypt, and Æthiopia, and is often called Erythræum Mare, and confounded with the Arabicus Sinus, and the Indian Sea. *Plin.* 6. c. 23 & 24.—*Liv.* 36. c. 17. l. 42. c. 52. l. 45. c. 9.—*Virg. Æn.* 8. v. 686.—*Lucan.* 8. v. 853.

RUCCO'NIUM, a city of Dacia. *Ptol.* It is now Ragen.

RU'DIÆ, a town of Calabria, near Brundusium, built by a Greek colony, and famous for giving birth to the poet Ennius. *Cic. pro Arch.* 10.—*Ital* 12. v. 396.—*Mela*, 2. c. 4.

RU'FÆ. *Vid.* Rufræ.

RUFFI'NUS, a general of Gaul in the reign of Vitellius. *Tacit. H.* 2. c. 94.——A Latin writer, some of whose verses on the composition and metres of orators are preserved to the number of seventy-four in the Corpus Poetarum.——A consul in the wars against Pyrrhus. Sylla was said to be descended from him.

RU'FIUS CRISPI'NUS, an officer of the prætorian guards under Claudius. He was banished by Agrippina for his attachment to Britannicus and Octavius, the sons of Messalina, and put himself to death. His wife Poppæa Sabina, by whom he had a son called Ruffinus Crispinus, afterwards married Nero. *Tacit.* 12. *Hist.* c. 42. l. 16. c. 17.

RU'FUS HEL'VIUS, a soldier presented with a civic crown for preserving the life of a Roman citizen. *Tac. Ann.* 3. c. 21.

RUFINIA'NA, a town of Gaul, now Rufash in Alsace.

RUFIL'LUS, a Roman ridiculed by *Horace*, sat. 2. v. 27. for his great effeminacy.

RUFINIA'NUS JUL., a rhetorician in the age of Constantine. He wrote a small treatise on figures of speech, &c., which has been edited by Ruhnken with Rutilius Lupus. *Harles. Not. Lit. Rom.* 1. p. 634.

RUFI'NUS, a general of the emperor Theodosius. He was left by him guardian of Arcadius and Honorius. He excited the Goths to besiege Constantinople, and was at length slain by the soldiers. *Zosim.* l. 5.—*Niceph.* l. 15.

RU'FRÆ, a town of Campania, of which the inhabitants were called Rufreni. *Cic.* 10. *Fam.* 71.—*Sil.* 8. v. 568.—*Virg. Æn.* 7. v. 739.

RU'FRIUM, a town of Samnium, now Ruvo. *Liv.* 8. c. 25.

RU'FUS, a Latin historian. *Vid.* Quintus.——A centurion under Scipio Africanus, of whose actions he wrote an account. *Appian.*——A Greek who wrote a history of the drama and of music. *Phot.* 161.——A friend of Commodus, famous for his avarice and ambition.——One of the ancestors of Sylla, degraded from the rank of a senator because ten pounds weight of gold was found in his house.——A governor of Judæa.——A man who conspired against Domitian.——A poet of Ephesus in the reign of Trajan. He wrote six books on simples, now lost.——A Latin poet.

RU'FUS SEX'TUS, a man of consular dignity, who wrote a work called Breviarium, on the victories and provinces of the Romans, which he dedicated to Valens. The best edition is that of Verheyk, Lug. Bat. 1762. *Harles. Not. Lit. Rom.* 1. p. 589.

RU'FUS MUNA'TIUS, a Latin historian, praised by *Valerius Maximus*, 4. c. 3.

RU'FUS GEMIN'IUS, an illustrious Roman, who nobly refused to pay honor to the worthless Sejanus, for which he was accused before the senate, and when condemned by that assembly, fell upon his sword.

RU'FUS SEMPRO'NIUS. *Vid.* Prætorius.

RU'GIA, now Rugen, an island of the Baltic.

RU'GII, a nation of Germany. *Tacit. de Germ.* 43.

RUL'LUS P. SERVIL'IUS, a tribune, who, in Cicero's consulship, proposed an agrarian law, which the eloquence of Cicero alone prevented from being adopted. Cicero's three orations on this subject are extant.

RU'MIA or RUMI'NA, a goddess at Rome, who presided over the female breasts and infants whilst still at the breast. The oblations made by women in her temple consisted of milk only, and no wine. Some consider the words as signifying the breast or milk, whence the fig tree under which Romulus and Remus were found bore the name of Ruminal. *Plin.* 5. c. 18.—*Varro de R. R.* 2. c. 11.—*Festus de V. Sig.*—*Plut. in Qu. & in Rom.*—*Aug. de Civ. D.* 4. c. 2. l. 6. c. 1.—*Servius ad Virg. Æn.* 8. v. 90.

RU'MINAL, RU'MINUS or RUMI'NUS, a surname of Jupiter, as presiding over the nourishment of mankind. *Aug. de Civ. D.* 7. c. 11.

RUNCI'NA, a goddess at Rome, invoked when the corn was cut down. The name is derived *a runcare*, to cut, hence the god Averuncus who removed evil from mankind. *Varro de L. L.* 5. c. 10. l. 6. c. 5.—*Aug. de Civ. D.* 4. c. 8.

RUPIL'IUS, a officer surnamed *Rex*, for his authoritative manners. He was proscribed by Augustus, and fled to Brutus. *Horat.* 1. sat. 7. v. 1.

RUPIL'IUS PUB'LIUS, a consul A U.C. 621. He was severe against the faction of the Gracchi, and put an end to the servile war in Sicily, and introduced wholesome regulations in the government of that island. *Flor.* 3. c. 19.—*Liv.* 59.—*Oros.* 5. c. 9.—*Paterc.* 2. c. 17.—*Cic. Verr.* 4. c. 50. *Am.* 11. *Cæcil.* 5. & *Ascon. Ibi.*

RUSA'ZUS or RUZA'SUS, a maritime town and colony of Mauritania Cæsariensis. *Plin.* 5. c. 2. —*Ptol.*

RUS'CA M. PINA'RIUS, a tribune who proposed a law to settle the age at which the offices of the state should be solicited. *Cic. Or.* 2. c. 65.

RUS'CIA, a city of Magna Græcia. *Procop.*

RUS'CINO, a town of Gaul at the foot of the Pyrenees. *Liv.* 21. c. 24.—*Plin.* 3. c. 5.—*Strab.* &c.—It is now Rousillon.——A river of Gallia Narbonensis. *Strab.*—*Ptol.* It is now La Tet.——A sea-port town of Africa. *Liv.* 30. c. 10. It is called Rustænium by *Ptolemy*, and Rungoniæ by *Antoninus*.

RUS'CIUS, a town of Gaul.

RUSCO'NIA, a town of Mauritania. *Liv.* 21. c. 24. *Vid.* Ruscino.

RUSEL'LÆ, an inland town of Etruria, destroyed by the Romans. *Liv.* 28. c. 45. It is now Rosella.

RU'SIBIS or RU'SUBIS, a harbour and town of Mauritania Tingitana. *Pliny*, 5. c. 1., calls it Rutubis.

RUSI'NA or RURI'NA, a goddess at Rome who presided over the country. *Aug. de Civ. D.* 4. c. 8.

RU'SIUM, a city of Thrace, near Rhodope. *Cedrenus* It is called Topirus by *Ptolemy*, Doberus by *Thucydides*, and Toprus by *Procopius*, and is now Rusio.

RUS'PÆ, a maritime city of Africa Propria. *Ptol.* It is now, probably, Alfaques.

RUS'PINA or RUSPI'NUM, a town of Africa near Adrumetum. *Sil. It.* 3. v. 260.—*Hirt. Af.* 6 & 10.

RUSSA'DIUM, a promontory of Africa. *Salmas. ad Solin.* p. 305.

RUSTICIA'NA, a town of the Vettones, near Placentia. *Antonin.* According to some it is now Cuidad Rodrigo.

RUS'TICUS L. JUN ARULE'NUS, a tribune of the people who offered to intercede with Nero for Thrasea, against whom a decree of the senate had been passed. He was put to death by Domitian. *Tac. Ann.* 16. c. 26, &c.—*Plin.* ep. 14. l. 1.—*Plut. de Curios.*—*Suet. in Dom.* c. 9. [There is a fine bust of Junius Rusticus in the Capitol, at Rome.

RUSUCUR'RIUM, a town of Mauritania, believed to be modern Algiers.

RUTE'NI, a people of Gaul, now Roüerge, in Guienne. *Cæs. B. G.* 7. c. 7.

RUTILA, a deformed old woman, who lived nearly 100 years, &c. *Plin.* 7. c. 48.—*Juv.* 10. v. 294.

RUTIL'IA, the sister of Rutulius, was wife of M. Aurel. Cotta. Her many virtues, and the magnanimity with which she bore the banishment of her brother and the death of her favorite son, are proposed as examples of imitation by Seneca to his mother, during his own disgrace and exile. *Seneca.*

P. RUTIL'IUS RU'FUS, a Roman consul in the age of Sylla, celebrated for his virtues and writings. He refused to comply with the requests of his friends because they were unjust. When Sylla had banished him from Rome he retired to Smyrna amidst the acclamations and praises of the people; and when some of his friends wished him to be recalled by means of a civil war, he severely reprimanded them, and said, that he wished rather to see his country blush at his exile, than to plunge it into distress by his return. He was the first who taught the Roman soldiers the principles of fencing, and by thus mixing dexterity with valor, rendered their attacks more certain and irresistible. During his banishment he employed his time in study, and wrote a history of Rome in Greek, and an account of his own life in Latin, besides many other works. *Ovid. Fast.* 6. v. 563. *Ex Pont.* 1. el. 3. v. 63.—*Seneca de Benefic.* 6. c. 37.—*Cic. in Brut. de Orat.* 1. c. 53.—*Val. Max.* 2. c. 3. l. 6. c. 4.—*Paterc.* 2. c. 9.

RUTIL'IUS, a Roman proconsul, who is supposed to have encouraged Mithridates to murder all the Romans who were in his provinces.——A man who went against Jugurtha.——A friend of Nero.

RUTIL'IUS LU'PUS, a prætor who fled away with three cohorts from Tarracina. *Cæs. B. C.* 1. c. 24.——A rhetorician. *Quintil.* 3. c. 1. He wrote two books on figures of speech, which have been edited by Dav. Ruhnken. *Harles. Not. Lit. Rom.* 1. p. 210.

RUTIL'IUS CLAU'DIUS NUMATIA'NUS, a poet of Gaul, in the reign of Honorius. According to some he wrote a poem on mount Ætna. He wrote also an itinerary in long and short verses, addressed to Venerius Rufius, elegant in style, but severe against the Christians and Jews whom he affects to despise and ridicule. This work, which is incomplete, was published by Burmann in the Poetæ Latini Minores, L. Bat. 4to, 1731. There is also an edition by Wernsdorf, Altorf. 1741, and another by Kappe, Erlang. 1788. *Harles. Not. Lit. Rom.* 1. p. 740.—*Sax. Onom.* 1. p. 484.—*Vossius de P. Latin.*

RUTILUS, a rich man reduced to beggary by his extravagance. *Juv.* 11. v. 2.——The first plebeian dictator. *Vid.* C. Marcius.

RU'TUBA, a small river of Liguria, falling from the Apennines into the Mediterranean. *Lucan.* 2. v. 422.—*Plin.* 3. c. 5.

RU'TUBUS, a gladiator, &c. *Horat.* 2. sat. 7. v. 96.

RU'TULI, a people of Latium, anciently known as well as the Latins, by the name of Aborigines. When Æneas came into Italy, Turnus was their king, and they supported him in the war which he waged against this foreign prince. The capital of their dominions was called Ardea. *Ovid. Fast.* 4. v. 883. *Met.* 14. v. 455, &c.—*Virg. Æn.* 7, &c.—*Plin.* 3. c. 5.—*Servius ad Virg. Æn.* 4. v. 615.

RU'TUPÆ, a sea-port town on the southern coasts of Britain, abounding in excellent oysters, whence the epithet of Rutupinus. Some suppose that it is the modern town of Dover, but others Richborough or Sandwich. *Lucan.* 6. v. 67.—*Juv.* 4. v. 141.

RYPHÆ'I MON'TES. *Vid.* Rhipæi.

RYSSADI'RUM, a city of Mauritania Tingitana. *Ptol.*

RYSSA'DIUM, a promontory of Libya. *Id.* It is now Capo de Riogrande.

S.

SA'BA, a town of Arabia, famous for frankincense, myrrh, and aromatic plants, and thence probably its name arose (*a σάζειν, adorare.*) The inhabitants were called *Sabœi. Strab.* 16.—*Diod.* 3.—*Virg. G.* 1. v. 57. *Æn.* 1. v. 420.—*Mela,* 3. c. 8.—*Plin.* 12. c. 14.—*Horat.* 1. od. 29. v. 3.—*Flacc.* 6. v. 138.—*Lucan.* 9. v. 821.—*Servius ad Virg. loco cit.*—*Sch. Dionys. Per.* 958.——A country of Æthiopia, of which Candace, the guest of king Solomon, was queen. *Joseph. A. J.* 1. c. 6.

SAB'ACUS or SAB'ACON, a king of Æthiopia, who invaded Ægypt, and reigned there after the expulsion of king Amasis. After a reign of 59 years he was terrified by a dream, and retired into his own kingdom. *Herodot.* 2. c. 137, &c.

SABADI'BÆ, three islands in the Indian Sea. *Ptol.*

SABÆ'I, a people of Arabia. *Vid.* Saba.

SABAGE'NA, a city of Armenia Minor. *Ptol.*

SABAITICU'MOS, a place of Æthiopia, on the Arabian Gulph. *Strabo.*

SABALAS'SA, one of the mouths of the river Indus. *Ptol.*

SAB'ANA, a city of the Golden Chersonesus. *Id. Mercator* calls it Saendebar, and places it in the island of Japan.

SABAR'CÆ, a people of India, whose government was democratical. *Curt.* 9. c. 8.

SABA'RIA, a town of Noricum, a colony of Claudius. *Plin.* 3. c. 24. *Amm. Marcell.* 19. c. 5, &c.

SABA'TA, a town of Liguria, with a safe and beautiful harbour, supposed to be the modern Vadi. It was also called *Vada Sabatorum. Sil.* 8. v. 461.—*Strab.* 4.—*Mela,* 2. c. 4.—*Liv.* 28.——A town of Assyria.

SABA'THA, a town of Arabia, now Sanaa. *Plin.* 6. c. 27.

SABA'THRA, a town of Syria. *Sil.* 3. v. 256.——A city of Arabia Felix. *Plin.* 6. c. 28. It is now, probably, Saada.——A maritime town of Africa.

SABATI'NI, a people of Samnium, living on the banks of the Sabatus, a river which falls into the Vulturnus. *Liv.* 26. c. 33.

SABA'ZIA, nocturnal mysteries in honor of Jupiter Sabazius, or of Bacchus, surnamed Sabazius, from the Sabæ, a people of Thrace. *Clemens, Protrept.*—*Diod. Sic.* 1. 4.—*Aristoph. Schol. Vesp.*—*Harpocrat.*—*Cic. N. D.* 3. c. 23. *Vid.* Sabazius.

SABA'ZIUS, a surname of Bacchus in Thrace, where his orgies called Sabazia were observed only in the night, on account of the disorder and debauchery of their secret mysteries. Bacchus Sabazius is called by Diodorus son of Jupiter and Proserpine, and is said to be far more ancient than the son of Semele. Cicero calls him son of Caprius, and king of Asia. *Plut. in Symp.* 4.—*Apul. Met.* 8.—*Cic. de N.D.* 3. c. 23.—*Arnob.* 4.—*Diod.* 4.——A surname of Jupiter, whose worship was introduced at Rome under the emperors, though in vain attempted during the times of the republic, by Cornel. Hispallus. *Val. Max.* 1. c. 3.

SAB'BAS, a king of India.

SABBA'TIA, a village of Gallia Celtica. *Steph.*

SABEL'LA, the nurse of the poet *Horace.* 1. sat. 9. v. 29.

SABEL'LI, a people of Italy, descended from the Sabines, or, according to some, the Samnites. They inhabited that part of the country which lies between the Sabines and the Marsi. Hence the epithet of *Sabellicus. Horat.* 3. od. 6. v. 38. l. 5. od. 17. v. 28. l. 2. sat. 1. v. 36.—*Sil. It.* 4. v. 221.—*Virg. G.* 3. v. 255.—*Servius ad Virg. G.* 2. v. 167.

SABEL'LIUS, a consul mentioned by *Cicero. in Br.* 34.

SABEL'LUS, a Latin poet in the reigns of Domitian and Nerva. *Martial.* 12 epigr. 43.

SA'BI, a people of Phrygia. *Steph.*

SABID'IUS, a Roman family. *Cic. Pet. Cons.* 2. *Martial.* 3. epigr. 17, mentions one of the family who was a terrible glutton.

SABI'NA JU'LIA, a Roman matron, who married Adrian by means of Plotina, the wife of Trajan. She was celebrated for her private as well as public virtues. Adrian treated her with the greatest asperity, though he had received from her the imperial purple; and the empress was so sensible of his unkindness, that she boasted in his presence that she had disdained to make him a father, lest his children should become more odious or more tyrannical than he himself was. The behaviour of Sabina at last so exasperated Adrian, that he poisoned her, or, according to some, obliged her to destroy herself. The emperor at that time, labored under a mortal disease, and he was therefore the more encouraged to sacrifice Sabina to his resentment, that she might not survive him. Divine honors were paid to her memory. She died A.D. 138, after she had been married 31 years to Adrian. *Sext. Aurel.*—*Æl. Spartian.* c. 23. [There is a statue of Sabina in the character of Venus, in the Museum of the Vatican, where also will be found the finest of numerous busts of her.]

SABI'NI, an ancient people of Italy, reckoned among the aborigines, or those inhabitants whose origin was not known. Some suppose that they were originally a Lacedæmonian colony, which settled in that part of the country. The possessions of the Sabines were situated in the neighbourhood of Rome, between the rivers Nar and Anio, and bounded on the north by the Apennines and the Umbria, on the south by Latium, on the east by the Æqui, and by Ætruria on the west. The greatest part of the contiguous nations were descended from them, such as the Umbrians, the Campanians, the Sabelli, the Osci. Samnites, Hernici, Æqui. Marsi, Brutii, &c. The Sabines are celebrated in ancient history as having been the first who took up arms against the Romans, to avenge the rape of their females at a spectacle to which they had been invited. After some engagements, the greatest part of the Sabines left their ancient possessions, and migrated to Rome, where they settled with their new allies. Those who still continued in their ancient possessions were at last totally subdued, about the year of Rome 373, and ranked as Roman citizens. Their chief cities were Cures, Fidenæ, Reate, Crustumerium, Corniculum, Nomentum, Collatia, &c. The character of the nation for chastity, for purity of morals, and for the knowledge of herbs and incantations, was very great. *Horat. Epod.* 17. v. 28.—*Cic. Vat.* 15.—*Plin.* 3. c. 12.—*Liv.* 1. c. 9 & 18.—*Dionys.* 2. c. 51.—*Strab.* 5.—*Flor.* 1. c. 1. l. 3. c. 18.—*Ital.* 8. v. 424.—*Ovid. Met.* 14. v. 775 & 797.—*Am.* 1. v 101. l. 3. 8. v. 61.—*Juv.* 10. v. 197.—*Aur. Vict.* 2. 63 & 73.—*Festus de V. Sig.*—*Martial.* 1. epigr. 67.—*Servius ad Virg. Æn.* 6. v. 809. l. 7. v. 710. l. 8. v. 638. l. 11. v. 785.

SABINIA'NUS, a general who revolted in Africa, in the reign of Gordian, and was defeated soon after, A.D. 240. *Zosimus.—Jul. Capitol in Gordian.* c. 23.

SABI'NUS AU'LUS, a Latin poet intimate with Ovid. He wrote some epistles and elegies, in the number of which were mentioned, an epistle from Æneas to Dido, from Hippolytus to Phædra, and from Jason to Hipsipyle, from Demophoon to Phylis, from Paris to Œnone, from Ulysses to Penelope; the three last of which, though said to be his composition, are spurious. *Ovid. Am.* 2. el. 18. v. 27. *Ex Pont.* 4. el. 16. v. 16.

SABI'NUS, a man from whom the Sabines received their name. He received divine honors after death, and was one of those deities whom Æneas invoked when he entered Italy. He was supposed to be of Lacedæmonian origin. *Virg. Æn.* 7. v. 178.——An officer of Cæsar's army defeated by the Gauls.——A friend of Domitian.——A Roman who attempted to plunder the temple of the Jews. *Joseph. B. J.* 6. c. 1.——A friend of the emperor Alexander.——A lawyer in the reign of Heliogabalus, called the Cato of his age. *Æl. Lamprid. in Vit. Heliogab.* c. 16.——A sophist under Adrian, author of several works. *Suidas.*

SABI'NUS JU'LIUS, an officer among the Lingones in Gaul, who, by pretending to be descended from Julius Cæsar, gained popularity, and proclaimed himself emperor in the beginning of Vespasian's reign. He was soon after defeated in a battle, and, to escape from the conqueror, hid himself in a subterraneous cave, with two faithful domestics, where he continued unseen for nine successive years. His wife Empona found out his retreat, and spent her time with him, till her frequent visits to the cave discovered the place of his concealment. He was dragged before Vespasian, and, by his orders, put to a cruel death, though his friends interested themselves in his cause, and his wife endeavoured to raise the emperor's pity, by showing him the twins which she had brought forth in their subterraneous retreat. *Plut. in Erot.—Tacit. H.* 4. c. 55.

SABI'NUS SABIN'IUS, a friend of Claudius, born at Reate. *Cit. Sext.* 37.

SABI'NUS CORNE'LIUS, a man who conspired against Caligula, and afterwards destroyed himself.

SABI'NUS TIT'IUS, a Roman senator, shamefully accused and condemned by Sejanus. His body, after execution, was dragged through the streets of Rome, and treated with the greatest indignities. His dog constantly followed the body, and, when it was thrown into the Tiber, the faithful animal plunged in after it, and was drowned. *Plin.* 8. c. 40.—*Tac. Ann.* 4. c. 68.

SABI'NUS POPPÆ'US, a Roman consul, who presided above 24 years over Mœsia, and obtained a triumph for his victories over the barbarians. He was a great favorite of Augustus and of Tiberius. He died in Achaia, of which he was governor. *Tacit. Ann.* 1. c. 80. l. 4. c. 96. l. 6. c. 39.

SABI'NUS FLA'VIUS, a brother of Vespasian, killed by the populace. He was well known for his fidelity to Vitellius. He commanded in the Roman armies for 35 years, and was governor of Rome for 12. *Tacit. Hist.* 1. c. 46. l. 2. c. 63. l. 3. c. 74.

SABI'NUS ASID'IUS, a declaimer of great genius. *Senec. Suasor.* 2.

SABI'NUS CALVIS'IUS, a person accused of treason under Tiberius. *Tac. Ann.* 6. c. 9.

SABI'NUS PUB'LIUS, the præfect of a cohort, afterwards set over the prætorian guards by Vitellius. *Tac. Hist.* 11. c. 92. l. 3. c. 36.

SABI'NUS TY'RO, an author who wrote *De Hortensibus*. *Plin.* 19. c. 10.

SA'BIS, now *Sambre*, a river of Belgic Gaul, falling into the Maese at Namur. *Cæsar*, 2. c. 16 & 18.——A river of Carmania flowing into the Persian Gulph. *Plin.* 6. c. 23.

SABO'THA, the same as Sabatha.

SAB'RACÆ, a powerful nation of India. *Curt.* 9. c. 8.

SAB'RATA, a maritime town of Africa, near the Syrtes. It was a Roman colony, about 70 miles from the modern Tripoli. *Ital.* 3. v. 256. *& Drakenb. in loc.—Plin.* 5. c. 4.

SABRI'NA, a river of Britain. It is now the Severn. *Tac. Ann.* 12. c. 31.

SAB'URA, a general of Juba, king of Numidia, defeated and killed in battle. *Lucan.* 4. v. 722.

SABURA'NUS, an officer of the prætorian guards. When he was appointed to this office by the emperor Trajan, the prince presented him with a sword, saying, "Use this weapon in my service as long as my commands are just, but turn it against my own breast whenever I become cruel or malevolent." *Aurel. Victor.*

SA'BUS, one of the ancient kings of the Sabines, son of Sangus, the same, according to Virgil, as Sabinus. He is said to have been wrecked with a Lacedæmonian colony on the shores of Italy, where he fixed his residence. *Vid.* Sabinus.

SAC'ADAS, a musician and poet of Argos, who obtained three several times the prize on the flute at the Pythian games. His statue was placed in the grove sacred to the muses at the top of Helicon, and his tomb was still to be seen at Argos in the age of Pausanias. *Plut. de Mus.—Paus.* 6. c. 14. l. 9. c. 30.—*Gyrald. de P.H.* 3.

SA'CÆ, a people of Scythia, who inhabited the country that lies at the east of Bactriana and Sogdiana, and towards the north of mount Imaus. The name of Sacæ was given in general to all the Scythians, by the Persians. They had no towns, according to some writers, but lived in tents. Their descendants on the borders of Europe were afterwards called Dacæ. *Ptol.* 6. c. 13.—*Herodot.* 3. c. 93. l. 7. c. 63.—*Plin.* 6. c. 17.—*Solin.* 62.

SACA'RUM FES'TA or **SACÆ'A**, festivals observed for five days by the Persians and Syrians in honor of the goddess Anaitis. Slaves on those occasions were waited upon by their masters as at the Saturnalia of the Romans. *Athen.* 14.—*Cœl. Rhod.* 18. c. 29.

SAC'ALA, a place of India, near the mouth of the Indus. *Arrian.*

SACAPE'NA, a region of Armenia Major. *Ptol.—Salmas ad Solin.* p. 621.

SACARAU'ZÆ or **SAGARAU'CÆ**, a people of Scythia. *Ptol.—Oros.*

SACCHE'NI, a people of Arabia. *Steph.*

SACER'DOS C. LICIN., a Roman prætor, who was governor of Sicily before Verres, and served also under Metellus in Crete. *Cic. Planc.* 11. *Verr.* 1. c. 10.

SA'CER MONS, a mountain near Rome. *Vid.* Mons. Sacer.

SA'CER LU'CUS, a wood of Campania, on the Liris *Strab.* It is now Selva di Hami.

SA'CER PORTUS or **SA'CRI POR'TUS**, a town of Italy, near Præneste, famous for a battle that was fought there between Sylla and Marius, in which the former obtained the victory. *Paterc.* 2. c. 26. —*Lucan.* 2. v. 134.—*Appian. de B. Civ.* 1.—*Flor.* 3. c. 21 —*Liv.* 84.—*Aurel. Vict.* 86.

SACES'PHARES, a king of the Sacæ. *Polyæn.* 7. *in Dario.*

SACHALI'TÆ, a people of India. *Steph.* There was a bay in their country called Sinus Sachalites, now Golfo di Sachalat.

SACRA'NI, a people of Latium, who assisted Turnus against Æneas. They were descended from the Pelasgians, or from a priest of Cybele. *Virg. Æn.* 7. v. 796.

SACRA'TOR, one of the friends of Turnus. *Virg. Æn.* 10. v. 747.

SAC'RA SO'LIS, a promontory of Arabia Felix. *Ptol.*

SA'CRA VI'A, a celebrated street of Rome, where a treaty of peace and alliance was made between Romulus and Tatius. It led from the amphitheatre to the Capitol, by the temple of the goddess of Peace, and the temple of Cæsar. The triumphal processions passed through it to go to the Capitol. *Horat.* 4. od. 2. l. 1. sat. 9.—*Liv.* 2. c. 15.—*Cic. Planc.* 7. *Att.* 4. ep. 3.——The road which led to Eleusis from Athens. *Athen.* l. 12.

SACRA'TA LEX *militaris*, introduced A.U.C 411., by the dictator Valerius Corvus, as some suppose, enacted that the name of no soldier which had been entered on the muster-roll should be struck out but by his consent, and that no person who had been a military tribune should execute the office of *ductor ordinum*. *Liv.* 7. c. 41, &c.

SACRAT'IVIR, a friend of Cæsar, killed at Dyrrachium. *Cæs. Bell. G.* 3. c. 71.

SA'CRI POR'TUS. *Vid.* Sacer Portus.

SA'CRUM BEL'LUM, a name given to the wars carried on concerning the temple of Delphi. The first began B.C. 448., and in it the Athenians and Lacedæmonians were auxiliaries on opposite sides. The second war began 357 B.C., and was finished nine years after by Philip of Macedonia, who destroyed all the cities of the Phocians. *Vid.* Phocis.

SA'CRUM PROMONTO'RIUM, a promontory of Spain, now Cape St. Vincent, called by *Strabo* the most westerly part of the earth.——A promontory of Corsica. *Ptol.* It is now Cabo Corso, according to *Leander.*——A promontory of Lycia. *Ptol.* It is now Capo Chelidoni.

SAD'ALES, a son of Cotys, king of Thrace, who assisted Pompey with a body of 500 horsemen. *Cæs. Bell. C.* 3. c. 4.—*Cic. Verr.* 1.

SADA'LIS, a city of Ægypt. *Steph.*

SADU'CA, a river of Hispania Bætica. *Ptol.*

SA'DUS, a river of India.

SADYATTES, one of the Mermnadæ, who reigned in Lydia 12 years after his father Gyges. He made war against the Milesians for six years. *Herodot.* 1. c. 16, &c.

SÆDE'NE, a mountain near Cumæ in Æolia. *Steph.*

SÆ'NA, an inland town of Etruria. *Ptol.* It is now Siena.

SÆ'NOS, a river of the Sinæ. *Ptol.*

SÆPI'NUM, a city of the Samnites. *Ptol.*

SÆP'ONE, a city of Hispania Bætica. *Ptol.* 3. c. 1.

SÆ'PRUS, a river of Sardinia. *Ptol.*

SÆT'ABIS, a town of Spain near the Lucro, on a rising hill, famous for its fine linen. *Sil.* 3. v. 373.

SAFIN'IUS, a citizen of Atella, mentioned by *Cicero, Clu.* 25.

SAGALAS'SUS, a town of Pisidia, on the borders of Phrygia, now *Sadjaklu. Liv.* 38. c. 15.

SAG'ANA, a woman acquainted with magic and enchantments, and known as the friend of Pisidia. She is ridiculed by *Horace*, epod. 5. v. 25. l. 1. sat. 8. v. 41 & 48.

SAG'ANAS, a river of Carmania. *Ptol. Pliny* calls it Siccanas. *Vid. Salmas ad Solin.* p. 1181. It is now Basiri.

SAG'ARIS or SAN'GARIS, a river of Asia, rising from mount Dindymus in Phrygia, and falling into the Euxine. *Vid.* Sangaris. *Ovid. ex Pont.* 4. ep. 10. v. 47.——One of the companions of Æneas, killed by Turnus. *Virg. Æn.* 5. v. 263. l. 9. v. 575.

SAGAR'TIA, a peninsula near the Caspian Sea. *Steph.*

SA'GES, a native of Cyzicus, slain by Hylas. *Val. Flacc. Argon.* l. 3. v. 182.

SAGIT'TA C., an officer who encouraged Piso to rebel against the emperor Nero. *Tacit. Hist.* 4. c. 49.

SAGON'TIA, a town of Spain, between Cæsar Augustus and Bilbilis. *Appian.* It is called Secontia by *Antoninus*, and is now Epila.

SA'GRA, a small river of Italy in the country of the Brutii, where 130,000 Crotoniatæ were routed by 10,000 Locrians and Rhegians. *Cic. Nat. D.* 2. c. 2.—*Strab.* 6. It is now the Sagriano, or Suchriano.

SA'GRUS, a river of Cilicia according to *Strabo*, of Caramania and Armenia Minor according to *Pliny*, 3. c. 10. It is now Sangro, or Sanguino according to *Niger.*

SAGUN'TUM or SAGUN'TUS, a town of Hispania Tarraconensis, at the west of the Iberus, about one mile from the sea shore, now called Morvedro. It had been founded by a colony of Zacynthians, and by some of the Rutuli of Ardea. Saguntum was celebrated for the clay in its neighbourhood, with which cups, *pocula Saguntina*, were made, but it was more particularly famous as having been the cause of the second Punic war, and for the attachment of its inhabitants to the interest of Rome. Hannibal took it after a siege of about eight months; and the inhabitants, not to fall into the enemy's hands, destroyed themselves in the conflagration of their houses, and of all their effects. The conqueror afterwards rebuilt it, and placed a garrison there, with all the noblemen whom he detained as hostages from the several neighbouring nations of Spain. Some suppose that he called it *Spartagene. Flor.* 2. c. 6.—*Liv.* 21. c. 2, 7, 9.—*Sil.* 1. v. 271.—*Lucan.* 3. v. 350.—*Strab.* 3.—*Mela*, 2. c. 6.

SA'I, a people of Thrace, opposite the island of Samothrace. *Eustath.*——A town of Upper Æthiopia. *Plin.* 6. c. 30.

SA'IS, now *Sa*, a town in the Delta of Ægypt, situate between the Canopic and Sebennytican mouths of the Nile, and anciently the capital of Lower Ægypt. There was there a celebrated temple dedicated to Minerva, with a room cut out of one stone, which had been conveyed by water from Elephantis by the labours of 2000 men in three years. The stone measured on the outside 21 cubits long, 14 broad, and 8 high. Osiris was also buried near the town of Sais. The inhabitants were called *Saitæ*. One of the mouths of the Nile, which is adjoining to the town, has received the name of *Saiticum. Strab.* 17.—*Herodot.* 2. c. 17, &c.—*Mela*, 1. c. 9.—*Cic. de N. D.* 3. c. 23.—*Tzetzes. in Lyc.* 111.—*Gyrald. H. D.* 11.

SAIX'Æ, a people near the Ister. *Steph.*

SA'LA, a town of Thrace, near the mouths of the Hebrus. *Herodot.*——A town of Mauritania. *Ptol.*——A town of Phrygia.——A river of Germany falling into the Elbe, near which are saltpits. *Tacit. Ann.* 13. c. 57.——A river falling into the Rhine, now the *Issel.*

SALABAS'TRÆ, a people near the Indus. *Plin.* 6. c. 20.

SALA'BRIA or SARABRÆ'A, a city of Cappadocia. *Ptol.*

SALA'CIA, the Latin name of Amphitrite (*ab aquâ salsâ*). *Festus de V. Sig.*—*Servius ad Virg. G.* 1. v. 31. *Æn.* 1. v. 148.—*Gell.* 13. c. 22.——A city of the Turdetani in Lusitania. *Ptol.* It is now Alcazor do Sal.

SAL'ACON, a poor man who pretended to be uncommonly rich, and therefore behaved insolently, whence the name is proverbial to express impudence. *Cic. Fam. Ep.* 7. c. 24.

SA'LÆ, a nation of Colchis, called by the ancients Phthirographi. *Plin.* 6. c. 4.

SALAMBO'RIA, an inland town of Cappadocia. *Ptol.* It is called Harberic by the Turks.

SALAMI'NÆ, small islands of Cyprus, near Salamis. *Plin.* 5. c. 31.

SALAMIN'IA, a name given to a ship at Athens, which was employed by the republic in conveying the officers of state to their different administrations abroad, &c.——A name given to the island of Cyprus, on account of Salamis, one of its capital cities.

SALAMINIA'DA, a city of Cœlosyria. *Antonin.*

SALAMI'NUS, one of the Idæi Dactyli. *Lil. Gyrald.* l. 6. *Hist. Deor.*

SAL'AMIS, a daughter of the river Asopus, by Methone. Neptune became enamoured of her, and carried her to an island of the Ægæan, which afterwards bore her name, and where she gave birth to a son called Cenchreus. *Diod.* 4.

SAL'AMIS, SAL'AMIN, or SALAMI'NA, now Coluri, an island in the Saronicus Sinus, on the southern coast of Attica, opposite Eleusis, at the distance of about a league, with a town and harbour of the same name. It is about fifty miles in circumference. It was originally peopled by a colony of Ionians, and afterwards by some of the Greeks from the adjacent islands and countries. It is celebrated for a battle which was fought there between the fleet of the Greeks and that of the Persians, when Xerxes invaded Attica. The enemy's ships amounted to above 2,000, and those of the Peloponnesians to 380 sail. In this engagement, which was fought on the 20th of October, B.C. 480, the Greeks lost 40 ships, and the Persians about 200, besides an immense number which were taken, with all the ammunition they contained. The island of Salamis was anciently called Sciras, Cychria, or Cenchria, and its bay the Gulf of Engia. It is said that Xerxes attempted to join it to the continent. Teucer and Ajax, sons of Telamon, who joined the rest of the Greeks in the Trojan war, were natives of Salamis. *Strab.* 2.—*Herodot.* 8. c. 56, &c.—*Plut. & C. Nep. in Them.* &c.—*Diod.* 4.—*Val Max.* 5. c. 3.—*Paus.* 1. c. 35, &c.—*Mela*, 2. c. 7.—*Lucan.* 5. v. 109.—*Sil.* 14. v. 283.—*Pindar. Nem.* 2.—*Anton. lib.* 38.—*Servius ad Virg, Æn.* 3. v. 80. l. 8. v. 157.—*Æschyl. in Pers* 34.

SALAMIS, or SALAMI'NA, a town at the east of the island of Cyprus. It was built by Teucer, son of Telamon, who gave it the name of the island Salamis, from which he had been banished, about 1270 years B.C.; and from this circumstance the epithets of *ambigua* and of *altera* were applied to it, as the mother country was also called *vera*, for the sake of distinction. His descendants continued masters of the town for above 800 years. It was destroyed by an earthquake, but rebuilt in the 4th century, and called Constantia. *Strab.* 9.—*Herodot.* 8. c. 94, &c.—*Horat.* 1 od. 7. v. 21.—*Paterc.* 1. c. 1.—*Lucan.* 3. v. 183.—*Servius in Æn.* 1. v. 625.

SALAMP'SII, a people of Mauritania Cæsariensis. *Ptol.*

SALAN'GUS, a nation of Italy.——A nation of India. *Steph.*

SALANIA'NA, a town of Lusitania, between Ebora and Pax Julia. *Antonin.*

SALAPÆ'I, a people of Thrace. *Appian.*

SALAPE'NI, a nation of Arabia Felix. *Ptol.*

SALAPHITA'NUM, a town of Africa Propria. *Plin.* 5. c. 4.

SALA'PIA, or SALA'PIÆ, now Salpe, a town of Apulia, to which Annibal retired after the battle of Cannæ, and where he devoted himself to licentious pleasures, forgetful of his fame, and of the interests of his country. It was taken from the Carthaginian general by Marcellus. Some remains of this place may be traced near a lake called *Salapina Palus*, now called Lago di Andoria, and used for making salt, which, from the situation near the sea, is easily conveyed by small boats to ships of superior burden. *Lucan.* 5. v. 377.—*Val. Max.* 3. c. 8.—*Plin.* 3. c. 11.—*Ptol.* 3. c. 1.—*Appian de Bell. Civ.* 1.—*Liv.* 24. c. 2 & 20.

SAL'ARA, a town of Africa Propria, taken by Scipio. *Liv.* 29. c. 34, &c.

SALA'RIA, a street and gate at Rome which led towards the country of the Sabines. It received the name of Salaria, because salt (*sal*) was generally conveyed to Rome that way. *Mart.* 4. epigr. 64.——A city of Hispania Tarraconensis. It is called in ancient inscriptions Colonia Julia Salariensis, and is now Cazorla.

SALA'RIUS PONS, a bridge built four miles from Rome, through the Salarian gate on the river Anio.

SA'LARS, an island of Libya. *Steph.*

SA'LAS, a river of Germany. *Strab.* It is now Saal.

SAL'ASI, SALAS'SI, or SALAS'SII, a people of Cisalpine Gaul, who were continually engaged in war with the Romans. They cut off 10,000 Romans under Appius Claudius, A.U.C. 610, and were soon after defeated, and at last totally subdued and sold as slaves by Augustus. Their country, now called Val d'Osta, after a colony settled there, and called Augusta Prætoria, is situated in a valley between the Alpes Graiæ and Penninæ, or Great and Little St. Bernard. *Liv.* 21. c. 38.—*Plin.* 3. c. 17.—*Strab.* 4.

SALAS'SUS Q., a Roman, brother to P. Curtius. and mentioned by *Cicero*. *Fam.* 6. ep. 18.

SAL'DÆ, a colony and city of Mauritania Cæsariensis *Ptol.* It is now Tadelis, according to *Mercator*.

SA'LE, a city of Hyrcania. *Ptol.*

SALE'IUS BAS'SUS, a poet of great merit in the age of Domitian, yet pinched by poverty, though born of illustrious parents, and distinguished by purity of manners and integrity of mind. *Juv.* 7. v. 80.—*Quint.* 10. c. 1.—*Harles. Not. Lit. Rom.* 1. p. 456.

SALE'NÆ, an inland town of Albion. *Ptol.* It is now Salndy in Bedfordshire, according to *Camden*.

SALE'NI, a people of Spain. *Mela*, 3. c. 1.

SALENTI'NI, a people of Italy, near Apulia, on the southern coast of Calabria. They originally came from Crete and Illyricum, and received their name from their voyage across the sea (*a salo.*) Their chief towns were Brundusium, Tarentum, and Hydruntum. *Ital.* 8. v. 579.—*Virg. Æn.* 3. v. 400.—*Varro de R.R.* 1. c. 24.—*Strab.* 6.—*Mela*, 2. c. 4.—*Festus. de V. Sig.*—*Cato de R.R.* 6.—*Ovid. Met.* 15. v. 51.—*Servius. ad Virg. loco.*

SAL'ERA, a town of Africa Propria, seized by Cato. *Liv.* 29. c. 34.

SALER'NUM, now Salerno, a town of the Picentini, on the shores of the Tyrrhene Sea, south of Campania, and famous for a medical school in the lower ages. *Plin.* 13. c. 3.—*Liv.* 34. c. 45.—*Lucan.* 2. v. 425.—*Paterc.* 1. c. 15.—*Horat.* 1. ep. 15.

SALE'SII, a people of Pœonia. *Steph.*

SALE'TAS, a daughter of Jupiter, the Minerva of the Ægyptians, said to be sprung from the Nile. *Alex. ab. Alex.* 6. c. 4.

SAL'GANEUS, or SALGA'NEA, a town of Bœotia, on the Euripus. *Liv.* 35. c. 37, &c.

SA'LIA, a town and river of Spain, where Prudentius was born. *Mela.* It is now Rio de Sella.

SAL'ICA, a town of the Oretani in Spain. *Ptol.*

SALIE'NUS CLE'MENS, a senator in the time of Nero. *Tac. Hist.* 5. c. 73.

SA'LII, a college of priests at Rome, instituted in honor of Mars, and appointed by Numa, to take care of the sacred shields called Ancylia, B.C. 709, *Vid.* Ancyle. They were twelve in number, the three elders among them had the superintendence of all the rest; the first was called *præsul*, the second *vates*, and the third *magister*. Their number was afterwards doubled by Tullius Hostilius, after he had obtained a victory over the Fidenates, in consequence of a vow which he made to Mars. The Salii were all of patrician families, and the office was very honorable. The first of March was the day on which the Salii observed their festivals in honor of Mars. They were generally dressed in a short scarlet tunic, of which only the edges were seen; they wore a large purple-coloured belt about the waist, which was fastened with brass buckles. They had on their heads round bonnets with two corners standing up, and carried in their right hands a small rod, and in their left a small buckler. In the observation of their solemnities they first offered sacrifices, and afterwards went through the streets dancing in measured motions, sometimes altogether, or at other times separately, while musical instruments were playing before them. They placed their bodies in different attitudes, and struck with the rods the shields they held in their hands. They also sang hymns in honor of the gods, particularly of Mars, Juno, Venus, and Minerva, and were accompanied in the chorus by a certain number of virgins, habited like themselves, and called *Saliæ*. The Salii instituted by Numa were called *Palatini*, in contradistinction to the others, because they lived on mount Palatine, and offered their sacrifices there. Those that were added by Tullus were called *Collini*, *Agonales*, or *Quirinales*, from a mountain of the same name, on which they had fixed their residence. Their name seems to have been derived *a saliendo* or *saltando*, because, during their festivals it was particularly requisite that they should leap and dance. Their feasts and entertainments were uncommonly rich and sumptuous, whence *dapes saliaries* is proverbially applied to such repasts as are most splendid and costly. It was usual among the Romans when they declared war, for the Salii to shake their shields with great violence, as if to call upon the god Mars to come to their assistance. *Liv.* 1. c. 20.—*Varro de L.L.* 4. c. 15.—*Ovid. Fast.* 3. v. 387.—*Dionys.* 3.—*Flor.* 1. c. 2, &c.—*Virg. Æn.* 8. v. 285.—*Festus. de V. Sig.*—*Servius ad Virg.* 2. v. 166, & 325, &c. *loco cit.*——A nation of Germany who invaded Gaul, and were conquered by the emperor Julian. *Amm. Mar.* 17.

SALINA'TOR, a surname common to the family of the Livii, and others, because one of them when censor imposed a tax upon salt. *Cic. Sen.* 3. *Orat.* 2. c. 67. *Brut.* 18 —*Liv.* 29. c. 37.

SALI'NUM, a town of Lower Pannonia, on the Danube. *Ptol.*

SALIS'SO, a town between the Treviri and Argentoratum. *Antonin.*

SALISUB'SULUS, a surname given to Mars either from the dances of his priest the Salii, or from the levity of his character in espousing different parties in the time of war. During their military expeditions the Spartans tied the statue of the god that he might not pass over to their enemies. *Catull.* 17. v. 6.—*Pacuvius apud Non. Marcel.* & *Scaliger in loco.*

SALIUN'CA, a city of the Autrigones in Hispania

Tarraconensis. *Ptol.* It is now probably, Orduna.

SA'LIUS, an Acarnanian present at the games exhibited by Æneas in Sicily, and killed in the wars with Turnus. It is said by some that he taught the Latins those ceremonies accompanied with dancing, which afterwards bore his name in the apellation of the Salii. *Virg. Æn.* 5. v. 298. l. 10. v. 753.—*Servius ad Virg. loco—Festus. de V. Sig.*——A Pelignian who distinguished himself against the Macedonians in the Roman army under Paulus. *Plut in Paul. Æm.*

SALLUN'TUM, a city of Dalmatia. *Antonin.*

SALLUS'TIUS CRIS'PUS, a Latin historian, born at Amiternum, in the country of the Sabines. He received his education at Rome, and made himself known as a public magistrate in the office of quæstor and consul. His licentiousness and the depravity of his manners, however, did not escape the censure of the age, and Sallust was degraded from the dignity of a senator, B.C. 50, by the censor Claudius Pulcher. His amour with Fausta, the daughter of Sylla, was a strong proof of his debauchery; and Milo, the husband, who discovered the adulterer in his house, revenged the violence offered to his bed by beating him with stripes, and selling him his liberty at a high price. A continuation of extravagance could not long be supported by the income of Sallust, but he extricated himself from all difficulties by embracing the cause of Cæsar. He was restored to the rank of senator, and made governor of Numidia. In the administration of his province, Sallust behaved with unusual tyranny; he enriched himself by plundering the Africans, and at his return to Rome, built himself a magnificent house, and bought gardens, which from their delightful and pleasant situation, still preserve the name of the gardens of Sallust. He married Terentia the divorced wife of Cicero: and from this circumstance, according to some, arose an immortal hatred between the historian and the orator. Sallust died in the 51st year of his age, 35 years B.C. As a writer he is peculiarly distinguished. He had composed a history of Rome, which some of the ancients declared superior to Livy's, but this valuable work has perished, excepting a few fragments. His only compositions extant are his history of Catiline's conspiracy, and of the wars of Jugurtha king of Numidia. In these celebrated works the author is greatly commended for his elegance, and the vigor and animation of his sentences; he everywhere displays a wonderful knowledge of the human heart, and paints with a masterly hand the causes of the great events which he relates. No one was better acquainted with the vices that prevailed in the capital of Italy, and no one seems to have been more severe against the follies of the age, and the failings of which he himself was guilty in the eyes of the world. His descriptions are elegantly correct, and his harangues are nervous and animated, and well suiting the character and the different pursuits of the great men in whose mouths they were placed. The historian, however, is blamed for tedious and insipid exordiums, which often disgust the reader without improving him; his affectation of old and obsolete words and phrases is also censured, and particularly his unwarrantable partiality in some of his narrations. Though faithful in every other respect, he has not painted the character of Cicero with all the fidelity and accuracy which the reader claims from the historian; and in passing in silence over many actions which reflect the greatest honor on the first husband of Terentia, the rival of Cicero has disgraced himself, and rendered his compositions less worthy of credit. There are two orations or epistles to Cæsar, concerning the regulations of the state, attributed to him, as also an oration against Cicero, the authenticity of which some of the moderns have disputed. Quintilian, who well knew the merit of the two historians of Rome, compares Sallust to Thucydides, and Livy to Herodotus. The best editions of Sallust, are those of Haverkamp, 2 vols. 4to. Amst. 1742; and of Edinburgh, 12mo. 1755. *Quintil.* 2, 3, &c.—*Suet. de Gram. in Cæs.—Martial*, 14 epigr. 191.—*Macrob.* 5. c. 1.—*Aul. Gell.* 3 c. 1. l. 17. c. 18.—*Lactant*, 2. c. 12.—*Servius. in Æn.* 2. v. 468.—*Seneca contr.* 3. c. 22.—*Euseb. Chron.* 1931.—*Dio.* 42.—*Harles. Not. Lit. Rom.* 1. p. 182.—*Sax. Onom.* 1. p. 165.——A grand-nephew of the historian, by whom he was adopted. He imitated the moderation of Mæcenas, and remained satisfied with the dignity of a Roman knight, when he could have made himself powerful by the favors of Augustus and Tiberius. He was very effeminate and luxurious. *Horace* dedicated od. 2. lib. 2 to him. *Tacit. Ann.* 1. c. 6. l. 2. c. 40. l. 3. c. 30. *Hist.* 3. c. 82.—*Plin.* 34.

SALLUS'TIUS CNE'US, a friend of Cicero. His brother Publius is also mentioned by the orator. *Att.* 11. ep. 11 & 20. *Div.* 1. c. 28. *Fam.* 14. ep. 4 & 11.

SALLUS'TIUS SECUN'DUS PROMO'TUS, a native of Gaul, very intimate with the emperor Julian. He was remarkable for his integrity and the soundness of his counsels. Julian made him prefect of Gaul.

SALLUS'TIUS SECUN'DUS, a person whom some have improperly confounded with Promotus. Secundus was also one of Julian's favorites, and was made by him prefect of the east. He conciliated the good graces of the Romans by the purity of his morals, his fondness for discipline, and his religious principles. After the death of the emperor Jovian, he was universally named by the officers of the Roman empire to succeed to the imperial throne; but he refused this great though dangerous honor, and pleaded infirmities of body and old age. The Romans wished upon this to invest his son with the imperial purple, but Secundus opposed it, and observed that he was too young to support the dignity.

SALLUS'TIUS, a prefect of Rome in the reign of Valentinian.——An officer in Britain.

SAL'LYES or SA'LYI, a people of Gallia Narbonensis, whose metropolis was Aquæ Sextiæ. *Plin.* 3. c. 4.—*Strabo.—Liv.* 21. c. 26.

SAL'MA, the name of three towns in Arabia. *Ptol.*

SAL'MACIS, a fountain of Caria, near Halicarnassus, which rendered effeminate all those who drank of its waters. It was there that Hermaphroditus changed his sex, though he still retained the characteristics of his own. *Ovid. Met.* 4. v. 285. l. 15. v. 319.—*Hygin.* fab. 271.—*Vitruv.* 2. c. 8.—*Strab.* 14.—*Auson.* ep. 69 & 101.—*Festus de V. Sig.*

SALMAN'TICA, a town of Spain, now Salamanca. It is called Salmatis by *Polyænus*, 7. c. 48.

SALMO'NE, a town of Elis in Peloponnesus, with a fountain, from which the Enipeus takes its source, and falls into the Alpheus, about 40 stadia from Olympia, which on account of that is called Salmonis. *Ovid. Amor.* 3. el. 6. v. 43.——A promontory at the east of Crete. *Dionys.* 5.—*Act. Apost.* 27. v. 7.

SALMO'NEUS, a king of Elis, son of Æolus and Enarette, who married Alcidice, by whom he had Tyro. He wished to be called a god, and to receive divine honors from his subjects; therefore to imitate the thunder, he used to drive his chariot over a brazen bridge, and darted burning torches on every side, as if to imitate the lightning. This impiety provoked Jupiter. Salmoneus was struck with a thunderbolt, and placed in the infernal regions near his brother Sisyphus. *Homer. Odyss.* 11. v. 235.—*Apollod.* 1. c. 9.—*Hygin.* fab. 60.—*Diod.* 4.—*Virg. Æn.* 6. v. 585.—*Tzetzes ad Lyc.* 980.—*Servius ad Virg. Æn.* 4. v. 696. l. 6. v. 585.

SALMO'NIS, a name given to Olympia. *Vid.* Salmone.——The patronymic of Tyro, daughter of Salmoneus. *Ovid. Am.* 3. el. 6. v. 43.

SAL'MOS, a town of Bœotia. *Steph.*

SAL'MUS, (*-untis*), a town of Asia near the Red Sea, where Alexander saw a theatrical representation. *Diod.* 17.

SAL'MYCA, a city near the columns of Hercules. *Steph.*

SALMYDES'SUS or HALMYDES'SUS, a bay on the Euxine Sea, with a town of the same name on the east of Thrace. *Steph.—Strab.* 7. It is now Stagnara.

SA'LO, now Xalon, a river in Spain, falling into the Iberus. *Mart.* 10. epigr. 20.

SALOBRI'ASÆ, a people near India. *Plin.* 6. c. 20.

SALODU'RUM, now Soleure, a town of the Helvetii.

SALOM'ACUM, a town of Aquitania. *Antonin.*

SALO'ME, a queen of Judæa. This name was common to some of the princesses of the family of Herod, &c.

SA'LON, a country of Bithynia. *Strab.* 12.

SALO'NA or SALO'NÆ, a town of Dalmatia, about 10 miles distant from the coast of the Adriatic, conquered by Pollio, who, on that account, called his son Salonius, in honor of the victory. It was the native place of the emperor Diocletian, and he retired there to enjoy peace and tranquillity, after he had abdicated the imperial purple, and built a stately palace, the ruins of which were still seen in the 16th century. A small village of the same name preserves the traces of its fallen grandeur. Near it is Spalatro. *Lucan.* 4. v. 404.—*Cæs. Bell. Civ.* 9.—*Mela*, 2. c. 3.—*Strab.* 7.—*Ptol.* 2. c. 17.—*Servius ad Virg. Ecl.* 4. v. 1 & 11. *Ecl.* 8. v. 12.

SALONIA'NA, an inland city of Dalmatia. *Ptol.* It is now Czernicz.

SALONI'NA, a celebrated matron who married the emperor Gallienus, and distinguished herself by her private as well as public virtues. She was the patroness of all the fine arts, and to her clemency, mildness, and benevolence, Rome was indebted some time for her peace and prosperity. She accompanied her husband in some of his expeditions, and often called him away from the pursuits of pleasure to make war against the enemies of Rome. She was put to death by the hands of the conspirators, who also assassinated her husband and family, about A.D. 268. *Trebell. Pollio in Gallien.* c. 3. [There is a bust of Salonina in the Museum of the Capitol.]——A wife of Alienus Cæcina, a general of Vitellius. *Tac. Hist.* 2. c. 20.

SALONI'NUS, a son of Asinius Pollio. He received his name from the conquest of Salonæ by his father. Some suppose that he is the hero of Virgil's fourth eclogue, in which the return of the golden age is so warmly and beautifully anticipated.

SALONI'NUS P. LICIN'IUS CORNE'LIUS, a son of Gallienus, by Salonina, sent into Gaul, there to be taught the art of war. He remained there some time, till the usurper Posthumius arose, and proclaimed himself emperor. Salonius was upon this delivered up to his enemy, and put to death in the 10th year of his age. *Trebell. Pollio in Galllien.*—*Aur. Vict.*—*Oros. &c.* [There is a bust of Saloninus in the Museum of the Capitol.

SALO'NIUS, a friend of Cato the censor. His daughter became the second wife of Cato, in his 80th year, and bore him a son, who was the father of Cato of Utica. *Plin.* 7. c. 14.—*Gell.* 13. c. 18.——A tribune and centurion of the Roman army, hated by the populace for his strictness.

SAL'PIS, a colony of Etruria, the inhabitants of which were called *Salpinates*. *Liv.* 5. c. 31.

SAL'SUM, a river of Hispania Bætica. *Hirt. Bell. Hisp* c. 9.

SAL'TIGA, a town of Hispania Tarraconensis. *Ptol.* It is now Suorniglia.

SAL'TIUS SEX., one of the magistrates of Capua. *Cic. Rull.* 2. c. 34.

SAL'VA, a town of Lower Pannonia. *Ptol.* It is now Scalmar.

SA'LUC, a town in the interior of Libya. *Ptol.*

SAL'VIA, the mother of Apuleius.

SAL'VIA, a town of the Triacenses, in Italy. *Ptol.*

SALVIA'NUS, one of the fathers of the 5th century, of whose works the best edition is the 12mo. Paris, 1684. *Harles. Not. Lit. Rom.* 1. p. 688.—*Sax. Onom.* 1. p. 506.

SALVIA'NUS CALPUR'NIUS, a person banished under Tiberius for accusing S. Marius. *Tac. Ann.* 4. c. 36.

SALVIDIE'NUS, an officer in the army of Augustus. He was betrayed by Antony, and put to death.——A Latin writer in the age of the emperor Probus. *Vopisc. in Saturnin.* c. 10.

SAL'VIUS, a flute-player saluted king by the rebellious slaves of Sicily in the age of Marius, he maintained war for some time against the Romans.——A friend of Pompey.——A freedman of Atticus. *Cic. ad Fam.* 9. c. 11.——A freedman of the son of Hortensius. *Cic. ad Fam.* 10. ep. 18.

SAL'VIUS COCCEIA'NUS, a nephew of the emperor Otho. He was slain by Domitian. *Tac. Hist.* 2. c. 48.—*Sueton. in Domit.* c. 10.

SA'LUR, a town of India within the Ganges. *Ptol.*

SA'LUS, the goddess of health at Rome, worshipped by the Greeks under the name of Hygiea. Her first temple at Rome was erected by C. Junius Babulcus the censor, and from it one of the gates was called Salutaris. *Liv.* 9 & 10.—*Paus.* 7. c. 24.—*Cic. de Div.* 1. c. 47.—*Plaut. in Captiv.* 3. sc. 3. v. 14.—*Suet. in Aug.* 31.—*Tacit. Ann.* 12. c. 23.—*Macrob.* 1. c. 16.—*Festus de V. Sig.*

SA'LYES, or SA'LII, a people of Gaul on the Rhone. *Liv.* 5. c. 34 & 35. l. 21. c. 26. *Vid.* Sallyes.

SAMAMYC'II, a people near the Syrtis Major. *Ptol.*

SAM'ARA, a river of Gaul, now called the Somme, which falls into the British Channel near Abbeville.

SAMARA'BRIÆ, nations in the neighbourhood of India. *Plin.* 6. c. 20.

SAMARI'A, a city and country of Palestine, famous in sacred history. The inhabitants, called Samaritans, were composed of heathen and rebellious Jews, and on having a temple built there after the form of that of Jerusalem, a lasting enmity arose between the people of Judæa and of Samaria, so that no intercourse took place between the two countries, and the name of Samaritan became a word of reproach, as if it were a curse. The English form is Sama'ria.

SAMAROBRI'VA, a town of Gaul, now Amiens in Picardy. *Cæs. B. G.* l. 5. c. 53.

SAMBA'NA, a place of Asia. *Diod. Sic.* 17.

SAM'BETHA, the most ancient of the Sibyls who was supposed to reside in Ægypt or Babylon. The time in which she lived, and even her very existence are doubted by ancient and modern writers. *Paus.* 10. c. 12.—*Nicanor apud Lactant.* l. c. 6.—*Varro apud eundem.*—*Tatian. Orat. adv. Gr.*—*Aug. de Civ. D.* 18. c. 25.

SAM'BOS, a city of Arabia, the inhabitants were called Sambi or Sambitæ. *Steph.*

SAM'BRI, a town of Upper Æthiopia. *Plin.* 6. c. 30.

SAM'BROCA, a river of Hispania Tarraconensis. *Ptol.* It is now the Ter.

SAMBRUCE'NI, a people near Judæa. *Plin.* 6. c. 20.

SAMBU'LOS, a mountain near Mesopotamia, where Hercules was worshipped. *Tacit. A.* 12. c. 13.

SAM'BUS, an Indian king defeated by Alexander. *Diod.* 17.

SAM'BUS, a river of India flowing into the Ganges. *Arrian. Ind.*——A town of Arabia. *Steph.*

SA'ME, SA'MOS or SA'MUS, a small island in the Ionian Sea near Ithaca, called also Cephallenia. *Virg. Æn.* 3. v. 271.

SAME'NI, a people of the Nomades. *Steph.*

SA'MIA, a daughter of the river Mæander, who married Ancæus, son of Neptune, by whom she had four sons, Pericas, Alithersus, Enudus, Samus, and a daughter Parthenope. *Paus.* 7 c. 4.——A surname of Juno, because she was worshipped at Samus.

SAM'ICUM, a city of Triphylia. *Steph.*

SAMI'NA, a city of Media, on the Caspian. *Ptol.*

SA'MIUS, an illustrious Roman knight, who slew himself. *Tac. Ann.* 11. c. 5.

SAMMON'ICUS Q. SERE'NUS, a poet in the age of young Gordian, whose preceptor he was. He was in the number of those who shared the favors and the severity of his imperial patron, as it is generally believed that he was stifled in a bath. There are remaining under his name some small poems on medical subjects, the latest and best edition is that of Ackermann, Lips. 1784. 8vo. *Harles. Not. Lit. Rom.* 1. p. 706.—*Sax. Onom.* 1. p. 349.

SAMMO'NIUM, a promontory of Crete. *Strab.* It is now Capo Salamon.

SAM'NIS. *Vid.* Samnites.

SAMNIT'Æ or AMNIT'Æ, a people of Gaul. *Strab.*—*Ptol.*

SAMNITES, a people of Italy, who inhabited the country situate between Picenum, Campania, Apulia, and ancient Latium. They distinguished themselves for their implacable hatred against the Romans, in the first ages of that empire, till after various bloody contests, they were at last totally extirpated, B.C. 272, after a war of 71 years. Their chief town was called Samnium or Samnis. *Liv.* 7, &c.—*Flor.* 1. c. 16, &c. 1. 3. c.

18.—*Strab.* 5.—*Lucan.* 2. v. 201 & 236.—*Ital.* 1. v. 666. l. 4. v. 560 —*Servius ad Virg. Æn.* 6. v. 825 & 845. l. 7. v. 715. l. 10. v. 145.—*Orosius.* 3. c. 20.—*Eutrop.* 2. The English form is Sam'nites.

SAM'NIUM, a town and country of Italy inhabited by the Samnites. *Vid.* Samnites.

SAMOCHONI'TIS, a small lake of Palestine.

SAMOS'ATA, a town of Syria, near the Euphrates, below mount Taurus, where Lucian was born.

SAMOTHRA'CE or SAMOTHRA'CIA, an island in the Ægæan Sea, opposite the mouth of the Hebrus, on the coast of Thrace, from which it is distant about 32 miles. It was known by the ancient names of Leucosia, Melitis, Electria, Leucania, and Dardania. It was afterwards called Samus, and distinguished from the Samus which lies on the coast of Ionia, by the epithet of Thracian, or by the name of Samothrace. It is about 38 miles in circumference, according to Pliny, or only 20, according to modern travellers. The origin of the first inhabitants of Samothrace is unknown. Some, however, suppose that they were Thracians, and that the place was afterwards peopled by the colonies of the Pelasgians, Samians, and Phœnicians. Samothrace is famous for a deluge which inundated the country, and reached the very top of the highest mountains. This inundation, which happened before the age of the Argonauts, was owing to the sudden overflow of the waters of the Euxine, which the ancients considered merely as a lake. The Samothracians were very religious; and as all mysteries were supposed to have taken their origin there, the island received the name of *sacred*, and was considered a safe and inviolable asylum for all fugitives and criminals. The island was originally governed by kings, but afterwards the government became democratical. It enjoyed all its rights and immunities under the Romans till the reign of the emperor Vespasian, who reduced it, with the rest of the islands in the Ægæan, into the form of a province.. *Strab.* 10.—*Herodot.* 7. c. 108, &c.—*Virg. Æn.* 7. v. 208.—*Mela,* 2. c. 7.—*Paus.* 7. c. 4.—*Flor.* 2. c. 12.—*Plin.* 23. c. 1.—*Servius Æn.* 1. v. 382. l. 3. v. 264. l. 7. v. 207.

SAM'PHE, a city of Phœnicia. *Steph.*

SAMSICERA'MUS, a prince of the Arabians. His son Jamblichus cultivated the alliance of the Romans. *Strab.* l. 10.—*Cic. Att.* 2. ep. 14, &c.

SAMPSI'RA, a city of Ægypt. *Steph.*

SAM'ULA, a woman who lived 110 years. *Plin.* 7. c. 48.

SAMU'NIS, a city of Albania. *Ptol.* It is called Samacha by *Niger.*

SA'MUS, an island in the Ægæan Sea, on the coast of Asia Minor, from which it is divided by a narrow strait, with a capital of the same name, built B.C. 986. It is about 87 miles in circumference, and is famous not only for the birth of Pythagoras, and Duris, but for the industry, the commerce, and the arts of the inhabitants, especially pottery, and for the fertility of the soil, where the fig-tree, the vine, and the apple-tree plentifully rewarded twice a year the labors of the cultivator. It was anciently called Parthenia, Anthemusa, Stephane, Melamphylus, Cyparissia, and Dryusa. It was first in the possession of the Leleges, and afterwards of the Ionians. The people of Samus were at first governed by kings, and afterwards the form of their government became democratical and oligarchical. Samus was in its most flourishing situation under Polycrates, who had made himself absolute there. The Samians assisted the Greeks against the Persians when Xerxes invaded Europe, and were reduced under the power of Athens, after a revolt by Pericles, B.C. 441. They were afterwards subdued by Eumenes, king of Pergamus, and were restored to their ancient liberty by Augustus. Under Vespasian, Samus became a Roman province. Juno was held in the greatest veneration there, her temple was uncommonly magnificent, and it was even said that the goddess had been born there under a willow tree, on the banks of the Imbrasus. *Mela,* 2. c. 7.—*Paus.* 7. c. 2 & 4.—*Plut. in Per.*—*Plin.* 5. c. 31.—*Virg. Æn.* 1. v. 20.—*Thucyd.*—*Strab.* 10 & 14.—*Cic. ad Fratr.* ep. 1.—*Ovid. Met.* 8. v. 220. *Fast.* 3. v. 153.—*Servius ad Æn.* 3. v. 271. l. 7. v. 207.—*Lucan.* 8. v. 246.——The islands of Samothrace and Cephallenia were also known by that name.

SA'MUS, a son of Ancæus and Samia, grandson of Neptune. *Paus.* 7. c. 4.

SAMYD'ACE, a city of Carmania. *Steph.*

SAMYL'IA, a city of Caria. *Steph.*

SA'NA or SA'NE, a town of Macedonia, near mount Athos. It was here that Xerxes began to make a channel to convey the sea round the mountain.

SANAGEN'SES, a people of Gallia Narbonensis. *Plin.* 3. c. 4.

SAN'AIS, a city of Media. *Ptol.* It is now Sena.

SAN'AOS, a town of Phrygia. *Strab.*

SAN'ARI, a people of Asiatic Sarmatia. *Ptol.*

SANCHONI'ATHON, a Phœnician historian born at Berytus, or, according to others, at Tyre. He flourished a few years before the Trojan war, and wrote, in the language of his country, a history in nine books, in which he amply treated of the theology and antiquities of Phœnicia, and the neighbouring places. It was compiled from the various records found in cities, and the annals which were usually kept by the ancients in the temples of the gods. This history was translated into Greek by Philo, a native of Byblus, who lived in the reign of the emperor Adrian. Some few fragments of this Greek translation are extant. Some, however, suppose them to be spurious, while others contend that they are genuine. *Fabr. B. Gr.* l. c. 28.—*Sax. Onom.* 1. p. 7.

SAN'CUS, SAN'GUS, or SANC'TUS, a deity of the Sabines, introduced among the gods of Rome under the name of Dius Fidius. Some authors consider Sanctus to be the same as Hercules, though the word is applied to all those gods whose aid is solicited by mortals. According to Dionysius and others, Sancus was father of Sabus, or Sabinus, the first king of the Sabines. *Ital.* 8. v. 421.—*Varro. de L.L.* 4. c. 10.—*Ovid. Fast.* 6. v. 213 —*Festus de V. Sig.*—*Dionys. Ital.* 2. c. 51. l. 4.—*Aug. de Civ. D.* 18. c. 19.—*Lactant. de Fals. R.* l. c. 15.—*Liv.* 8. c. 20.

SANDAB'ALA, a river of India. *Ptol.*

SANDA'CE, a sister Xerxes.

SANDA'LION, a small region of Pisidia. *Steph.*—*Strab.*

SANDALIO'TIS, a name given to Sardinia from its resemblance to a sandal. *Plin.* 3. c. 7.

SANDA'LIUM, a small island of the Ægæan, near Lesbus.

SAN'DANIS, a Lydian, who advised Crœsus not to make war against the Persians. *Herodot.* l. 1.

SAN'DANUS, a river of Thrace, near Pallene. *Plut.*

SANDAR'ACA, a harbour of Bithynia, on the Euxine Sea. *Strab.*

SANDARACUR'GIUM, a mountain of Paphlagonia, near Pompeiopolis. *Strab.*

SANDA'RIO, a general of Aurelian, slain by the people of Palmyra. *Vopisc. in Vit. Aurel.*

SANDA'VA, a city of Dacia. *Ptol.*

SAN'DO, the father of the Stoic philosopher Athenodorus. *Cic. Fam.* 3. ep. 7.

SAN'DACUS, grandson of Phaethon, married Thanace, by whom he had Cinyras the founder of Paphus. *Apollod.* 3. c. 7.

SANDROCOT'TUS, an Indian of mean origin. His impertinence to Alexander was the beginning of his greatness; the conqueror ordered him to be seized, but Sandrocottus fled away, and at last threw himself down overwhelmed with fatigue. As he slept on the ground a lion came to him and gently licked the sweat from his face. This uncommon action of the animal appeared supernatural to Sandrocottus, and raised his ambition. He aspired to the monarchy, and after the death of Alexander made himself master of a part of the country which was in the hands of Seleucus. *Justin.* 15. c. 4.

SA'NE, a town of Macedonia. *Vid.* Sana.

SANE'A, a city of India. *Steph.*

SAN'GA C. FAB., a senator who patronised the Allobroges. It was to him that the discovery of Catiline's conspiracy was first made. *Cic. Pis.* 31.—*Sallust. Cat.* 41.

SAN'GA, a river of the Cantabri in Spain. *Plin.* 4. c. 20.

SAN'GALA, a town of India destroyed by Alexander. *Arrian.* 5. *Ptolemy* calls it Sagala.

SANGAMAR'TA, a city of India within the Ganges. *Ptol.*

SANGA'RIUS or **SAN'GARIS**, a river of Phrygia, rising in mount Dindymus and falling into the Euxine. The daughter of the Sangarius became pregnant of Altes merely from gathering the boughs of an almond tree on the banks of the river. Hecuba, according to some, was daughter of this river. Some of the poets call it Sagaris. *Ovid. ex Pont.* 4. el. 10.—*Homer. Il.* 3. v. 187.—*Virg. Æn.* 5. v. 263. l. 9. v. 575.—*Strab.* 12 & 14. *Ptol.* 5. c. 1.—*Liv.* 38. c. 18.—*Dionys. Per.* 811.—*Eustath. ad D. Per.* 793 & 809.—*Servius ad Æn.* 6. v. 785.—*Claudian in Eutrop.* 2.—*Paus.* 7. c. 17.

SANGUIN'IUS, a man condemned for ill language, &c. *Tacit. Ann.* 6. c. 7.

SAN'GUS. *Vid.* Sancus.

SANI'GÆ, a people of Scythia, near the Abasci. *Arrian.—Plin.* 6. c. 4.

SANI'NA, a city on the Red Sea. *Steph.*

SAN'NIO, a slave.——A low character in *Terence's Adelphi*, Act 2. sc. 2. v. 13.

SANNYR'ION, a tragic poet of Athens. He composed many dramatical pieces, one of which was called Io, and another Danae. *Athen.* 9 & 11.—*Suidas.—Gyrald. P. H.* 6.

SANQUIN'IUS, the accuser of L. Arruntius. *Tac. Ann.* 6. c. 7.

SAN'TONES or **SAN'TONI**, now Saintonge, a people with a town of the same name in Gaul. *Lucan.* 1. v. 422.—*Martial.* 3. epigr. 96.

SAN'UA, a city of Albania. *Ptol.*

SA'O, one of the Nereides. *Apollod.* 1. c. 6.

SA'ON, an historian. *Dion. Hal.* Some suspect that he is the same person as Sæus mentioned by *Athenæus*, l. 4.——A man who first discovered the oracle of Trophonius. *Paus.* 9. c. 40.

SAPÆ'I or **SAPHÆ'I**, a people of Thrace called also Sintii. *Ovid. Fast.* 1. v. 389.—*Strab.* 10.—*Plin.* 4. c. 11. l. 6. c. 7.

SAP'ALA, a man intimate with Catiline. *Cic. Pet. Cons.* 3.

SAP'PHAR, a royal city of the Arabians. *Plin.* 6. c. 20.

SAPIRI'NE, an island of the Arabic Gulph. *Plin.* 6. c. 29.

SAPI'RES, a people near Pontus. *Orpheus in Argon. Stephanus* calls them Sabires, and *Agathias* Sabiri.

SA'PIS, now Savio, a river of Gallia Cispadana, falling into the Adriatic. *Lucan.* 2. v. 406.

SA'POR the First, a king of Persia, who succeeded his father Artaxerxes about the year 238 A.D. Naturally fierce and ambitious, Sapor wished to increase his paternal dominions by conquest: and as the indolence of the emperors of Rome seemed favourable to his views, he laid waste the provinces of Mesopotamia, Syria, and Cilicia; and he might have become master of all Asia, if Odenatus had not stopped his progress. If Gordian attempted to repel him, his efforts were weak and unavailing, and Philip, who succeeded him on the imperial throne, bribed Sapor into a cessation of hostilities. Valerian, who was afterwards invested with the purple, marched against the Persian monarch, but was defeated and taken prisoner. Odenatus no sooner heard that the Roman emperor was a captive in the hands of Sapor, than he attempted to release him by force of arms. The forces of Persia were cut to pieces, the wives and the treasures of the monarch fell into the hands of the conqueror, and Odenatus penetrated, with little opposition, into the very heart of the kingdom. Sapor, soon after his defeat, was assassinated by his subjects, A.D. 273, after a reign of 32 years. He was succeeded by his son called Hormisdas. *Pollio de 30 Tyrann.*—*Agathias.—Eusebius, &c.*

SA'POR the Second, succeeded his father Hormisdas on the throne of Persia. He was as great as his ancestor of the same name: and by undertaking a war against the Romans, he attempted to enlarge his dominions, and to add the provinces on the west of the Euphrates to his empire. His victories alarmed the Roman emperors, and Julian would have perhaps seized him in the capital of his dominions, if he had not received a mortal wound. Jovian, who succeeded Julian, made peace with Sapor; but the monarch, always restless and indefatigable, renewed hostilities, invaded Armenia, and defeated the emperor Valens. Sapor died A.D. 380, after a reign of 70 years, in which he had often been the sport of fortune. He was succeeded by Artaxerxes. *Sozomen.* 1. 2.—*Socr.—Agath.—Ammian.—Euseb.* &c.

SA'POR the Third, a prince who died after a reign of five years, A D. 389, in the age of Theodosius the Great. *Marcellin, &c.*

SAPPIRE'NE, an island in the Arabian Gulph. *Steph.*

SAP'PHO, or **SA'PHO**, celebrated for her beauty, her poetical talents, and her amorous disposition, was born in the island of Lesbus, about 600 years B.C. Her father's name, according to Herodotus, was Scamandronymus, or, according to others, Symon, or Semus, or Etarchus, or Ecritus, and her mother's name was Cleis. She married Cercolas, a man of opulence and consequence, and by him she had a daughter called Cleis. Her tender passions were so violent, that some have represented her attachment with three of her female companions, Telesippe, Atthis, and Megara, as criminal, and, on that account have given her the surname of Tribas. She conceived such a passion for Phaon, a youth of Mitylene, that upon his refusal to gratify her desires, she threw herself into the sea from mount Leucas. She had composed nine books in lyric verses, besides epigrams, elegies, &c. Of all these compositions, nothing now remains but two fragments, the uncommon sweetness and elegance of which show how meritoriously the praise of the ancients have been bestowed upon a poetess, who, for the sublimity of her genius, was called the tenth Muse. Her compositions were all extant in the age of Horace. The Lesbians were so sensible of the merit of Sappho, that after her death they paid her divine honors, and raised her temples and altars, and stamped their money with her image. The poetess has been censured for writing with a licentiousness and freedom which disgraced her character as a woman. The Sapphic verse has been called after her name. *Ovid. Heroid. Od.* 15 & 21. *Trist.* 2. v. 365.—*Horat.* 2. od. 13.—*Herodot.* 2. c. 135.—*Stat.* 5. *Sylv.* 3. v. 155.—*Ælian. V. H.* 12. c. 18 & 29.—*Plin.* 22. c. 8.—*Auson. Idyl.* 6. v. 25 ep. 31.—*Athen.* 13. c. 7.—*Suidas.—Gyrald de P. H.* 9.—*Turneb. adv.* 10. c. 2.—*Antipater, in 2 Anthol.—Fab. B. Gr.* 2. c. 15.—*Sax. Onom.* l. p. 18. [There is a statue of Sappho in the Museum of the Vatican; and the most esteemed bust is to be found in the Capitol, at Rome.

SAPTINE, a daughter of Darius, the last king of Persia, offered in marriage to Alexander. *Curt.* 4. c. 5.

SAPU'RI, mountains of Scythia, within Imaus. *Ptol.*

SA'RA, a city of the Chersonesus Aurea.——A city of Cappadocia. *Antonin.*

SAR'ABUS, a river of India within the Ganges. *Ptol.*

SAR'ACA, an inland town of Media. *Id.*

SAR'ACE, a city of Colchis. *Id.*

SARACE'NE, part of Arabia Petræa, the country of the Saracens who embraced the religion of Mahomet.

SAR'ACES, a prætor of Ægypt, slain at the battle of Issus. *Curt.* 3. c. 11. Read *Sataces.*

SARACO'RI, a people who went to war mounted on asses. *Ælian. V. H.* 12.

SAR'AGA, a city of the Sinæ. *Ptol.*

SAR'ALUS, a town of Galatia. *Id.*

SARAMAN'NE, a city of Hyrcania. *Id.*

SARAME'NA, a region of Asia Minor, near Amisus. *Strab.*

SARAN'GÆ, a people near Caucasus. *Plin.* 6. c. 16.

SARAN'GES, a river of India, falling into the Hydraotes, and thence into the Indus. *Polyæn.* 1. c. 1.

SARAPA'NI, a people of Colchis. *Strab.* 10.

SARAPA'RÆ, a people near Caucasus, not far from Hyrcania. *Plin.* 6. c. 16.

SARA'PIS, an island in the Indian Gulph. *Steph.*

SAR'APUS, a surname of Pittacus, one of the seven wise men of Greece. *Diog Laert.* 1. c. 81.

SAR'ASA, a fortified place of Mesopotamia, on the Tigris. *Strab.*

SARAS'PADES, a son of Phraates, king of Parthia, sent as a hostage to Augustus, &c. *Strab.*

SARAVUS, now the Soar, a river of Belgium, falling into the Moselle.

SARBANIS'SA, a city of Cappadocia. *Ptol.*

SAR'BATHA, a city of Assyria. *Id.*

SARBE'NA, a city of Assyria. *Id.*

SARDAB'ALA, a river of Mauritania Tingitana. *Plin.* 5. c. 2.

SARDA'NA, a city of India within the Ganges. *Ptol.*

SARDANAPA'LUS, the 40th and last king of Assyria, celebrated for his luxury and voluptuousness. The greatest part of his time was spent in the company of his eunuchs, and the monarch generally appeared in the midst of his concubines disguised in the habit of a female, and spinning wool for his amusement. This effeminacy irritated his officers, and two of them, Belesis and Arsaces, conspired against him and collected a numerous force to dethrone him. Sardanapalus quitted his voluptuousness for a while, and appeared at the head of his armies. The rebels were defeated in three successive battles; but he was at last beaten and besieged in the city of Ninus for two years. When he despaired of success, he burned himself in his palace, with his eunuchs, concubines, and all his treasures, and the empire of Assyria was divided among the conspirators. This remarkable event happened B.C. 820, according to Eusebius, though Justin and others, with less probability, place it 80 years earlier. Sardanapulus was made a god after death. His tomb was seen at Anchiale, a town which he built in Cilicia, or more properly at Ninus, where an inscription commemorated his effeminacy, and informed the reader, that during life he had luxuriously enjoyed himself in drinking and in eating, and in every sort of voluptuousness; an epitaph, as Aristotle observes, more becoming a brute than a king. *Herodot.* 2. c. 150.—*Diod* 2.—*Strab.* 14.—*Cic. Tus.* 5. c. 35.—*Athen.* 12. c. 7.—*Arrian de ex Al.* 2. c. 5.—*Suidas.*—*Schol. Aristoph. in Av.* 1. v. 22.—*Aug. de Civ. D.* 2. c. 20.—*Sueton.* 1. c. 3.

SARDEMI'SOS, a promontory of mount Taurus, between Lycia and Pamphylia. *Plin.* 5. c. 27.

SARDE'NE, a mountain on the river Hermus. *Herodot.*

SAR'DES. *Vid.* Sardis.

SARDES'SUS, a city of Lycia, near Lyrnessus, where Jupiter Sardessius was worshipped. *Steph.*

SARDEU'NA, a town of Armenia Minor. *Ptol.*

SAR'DI, the inhabitants of Sardinia. *Vid.* Sardinia.

SARDIÆ'I. *Vid.* Ardiæi.

SARDIÆ'ON, a mountain of Bœotia, near the Asopus. *Steph.*

SAR'DICA, an inland city of Thrace. *Ptol.* It is now Sophia.

SARDIN'IA, the largest island in the Mediterranean, after Sicily, is situate between Italy and Africa, at the south of Corsica. It was originally called Sandaliotis or Ichmusa, from its resembling the human foot (ἴχνος) and received the name of Sardinia from Sardus, a son of Hercules, who settled there a colony which he had brought with him from Libya. Other colonies of Greeks under Aristæus, of Iberians under Norax, and of Thespians and Athenians under Iolas, also settled there. The Carthaginians were long masters of it, and were dispossessed by the Romans in the Punic wars, B.C. 231. Some call it, with Sicily, one of the granaries of Rome. The air was very unwholesome, though the soil was fertile in corn, in wine, and oil. Neither wolves nor serpents are found in Sardinia, nor any poisonous herb, except one, which, when eaten, contracts the nerves, and is attended with a paroxysm of laughter, the forerunner of death; hence *risus Sardonicus*, or *Sardous*. *Cic. Fam.* 7. c. 25.—*Servius ad Virg.* 7. ecl. 41.—*Tacit. Ann.* 2. c. 85.—*Mela*, 3. c. 7.—*Strab.* 2 & 5.—*Cic. pro Manil. ad Q. Frat.* 2. ep. 3.—*Plin.* 3. c. 7.—*Paus.* 10. c. 17.—*Varro de R. R.*—*Tzetzes. ad Lyc.* 796.—*Solin.* 4 & 10.—*Val. Max.* 7. c. 6.—*Martial.* 4. epigr. 60.—*Liv.* 30. c. 37.

SAR'DIS or SAR'DES, now Sart, a town of Asia Minor, the capital of the kingdom of Lydia, situate at the foot of mount Tmolus, on the banks of the Pactolus. It is celebrated for the many sieges which it sustained against the Cimmerians, Persians, Medes, Macedonians, Ionians, Athenians, and for the battle in which, B.C. 262, Antiochus Soter, was defeated by Eumenes, king of Pergamus. It was destroyed by an earthquake in the reign of Tiberius, who ordered it to be rebuilt. It fell into the hands of Cyrus, B.C. 548, and was burnt by the Athenians, B.C. 504, which became the cause of the invasion of Attica by Darius. *Plut. in Alex.*—*Ovid. Met.* 11. v. 137. 152, &c.—*Strab.* 13.—*Herodot.* 1. c. 7, &c.—*Horat.* 1. ep. 2 v. 2.—*C. Nep.* 1. c. 4.—*Eustath. ad Dionys. Per.* 830.—*Servius ad Virg. G.* 1. v. 56.

SAR'DONES, the people of Roussilon in France, at the foot of the Pyrenees. *Plin.* 3. c. 4.

SARDO'NIÆ, a city of India within the Ganges. *Ptol.*

SAR'DUS, a son of Macerio, the Hercules of the Ægyptians, who led a colony to Sardinia, and gave it his name.

SAR'DUS, an inland town of Dalmatia. *Strab.*

SAREP'TA, a town of Phœnicia, between Tyre and Sidon, now Sarafendi.

SARGAN'THA, a city of Iberia. *Steph.*

SARGAN'TIS, a city of Ægypt. *Id.*

SARIAS'TER, a son of Tigranes, king of Armenia, who conspired against his father, &c. *Val. Max.* 9. c. 11.

SAR'ICHA, a city of Cappadocia. *Steph.*

SARIOLE'NUS VOC'ULA, an informer under Nero and Vitellius, condemned under Vespasian. *Tac. Hist.* 4. c. 41.

SAR'IPHI, mountains at the east of the Caspian.

SARIS'ABIS, a city of India within the Ganges. *Ptol.*

SARI'TÆ, a people of Arabia Felix. *Id.*

SAR'MATÆ or SAUROM'ATÆ, the inhabitants of Sarmatia. *Vid.* Sarmatia.

SARMA'TIA, an extensive country at the north of Europe and Asia, divided into European and Asiatic. The European was bounded by the ocean on the north, by Germany and the Vistula on the west, by the Jazygæ on the south, and by the Tanais on the east. The Asiatic was bounded by Hyrcania, the Tanais, and the Euxine Sea. The former contained the modern kingdoms of Russia, Poland, Lithuania, and Little Tartary; and the latter, Great Tartary, Circassia, and the neighbouring country. The Sarmatians were a savage uncivilized nation, often confounded with the Scythians, naturally warlike, and famous for painting their bodies to appear more terrible in the field of battle. They were well known for their lewdness, and passed among the Greeks and Latins by the name of barbarians. In the time of the emperors they became very powerful, and disturbed the peace of Rome by their frequent incursions; till at last, increased by the savage hordes of Scythia, under the barbarous names of Huns, Vandals, Goths, Alans, &c. they successfully invaded and ruined the empire in the 3d and 4th centuries of the Christian era. They generally lived on the mountains without any habitation except their chariots, whence they have been called *Hamazobii*. They lived upon plunder, and fed upon milk mixed with the blood of horses. *Strab.* 7, &c.—*Mela*, 2. c. 4.—*Diod.* 2.—*Flor.* 4. c. 12.—*Lucan.* 1, &c.—*Juv.* 2. v. i. sat. 3. v. 79. sat. 15. v. 125.—*Ovid. Trist.* 3, &c.—*Herodot.* 4. c. 99.—*Ptol.* 3. c. 5. 1. 5. c. 5.—*Tacit. Hist.* 1. c. 79.—*Dionys. Per.* 14.—*Plin.* 6. c. 7.—*Martial.* 8. epigr. 11.

SARMAT'ICA, an island of Lower Mysia, opposite the mouth of the Danube called Calostoma. *Plin.* 4. c. 12.

SARMAT'ICUM MA'RE, a name given to the Euxine Sea, because on the coast of Sarmatia. *Ovid.* 4. *ex Pont* ep. 10. v. 38.

SARMEN'TUS, a scurrilous person, whose ludicrous dispute with Messius Cicerrus is particularly mentioned by *Horace*, 1. sat. 5. v. 56.

SARMYDES'SUS, a place of Thrace. *Suidas.*

SAR'NACA, a city of Troas or Mysia. *Plin.* 5. c. 30.

SAR'NADA, a town of Pannonia. *Antonin.*

SAR'NIUS, a river of Asia, near Hyrcania. *Strab.*

SAR'NUS, a river of Picenum, dividing it from Campania, and anciently falling through Pompeii into the Tuscan Sea. *Stat.* 1. *Sylv.* 2. v. 256.—*Virg. Æn.* 7. v. 738.—*Strab.* 5.—*Orosius*, 4. c. 15.—*Servius ad Virg. loco. cit.*

SA'RON, a king of Trœzene, after Althepus son of Mercury, unusually fond of hunting. He was drowned in the sea, into which he had swam for some miles in pursuit of a stag. He was made a sea-god by Neptune, and divine honors were paid to him by the Trœzenians. It was customary for sailors to offer him sacrifices before they embarked. That part of the sea where he was drowned was called *Saronicus Sinus*, and is situate on the coast of Achaia, near the Isthmus of Corinth. Saron built a temple to Diana at Trœzene, and instituted festivals in her honor, called from himself Saronia. *Paus.* 2. c. 30.—*Mela*, 2. c. 3.—*Strab.* 8.—*Aristid. in Them.*—*Gyrald. H. D.* 5.

SARO'NIA, a festival. *Paus. Corinth. Vid.* Saron.

SARON'ICUS SI'NUS, now the Gulph of Engia, a bay of the Ægæan Sea, lying at the south of Attica, and on the north of the Peloponnesus. The entrance into it is between the promontory of Sunium and that of Scyllæum. Some suppose that this part of the sea received its name from Saron, who was drowned there, or from a small harbour of the same name. The Saronic bay is about 62 miles in circumference, 23 miles in its broadest, and 25 in its longest part, according to modern calculation.

SAROPH'AGES, a people of India on the Indus. *Plin.* 6. c. 20.

SARPE'DON, a son of Jupiter, by Europa, the daughter of Agenor. He banished himself from Crete, after he had in vain attempted to make himself king, in preference to his elder brother Minos, and retired to Caria, where he built the town of Miletus. He went to the Trojan war to assist Priam against the Greeks, where he was attended by his friend and companion Glaucus. He was at last killed by Patroclus, after he had made a great slaughter of the enemy, and his body, by order of Jupiter, was conveyed to Lycia by Apollo, where his friends and relations paid him funeral honors, and raised a monument to perpetuate his valor. According to some mythologists, the brother of king Minos, and the prince who assisted Priam, were two different persons. This last was king of Lycia, and son of Jupiter, by Laodamia, the daughter of Bellerophon, and lived about a hundred years after the age of the son of Europa. His succession to the kingdom of Lycia is variously related. Isander and Hippolochus, sons of Bellerophon and brothers to Laodamia, disputed their respective right to the crown, and at last determined to settle it upon him who could dart an arrow from a distance through a ring, placed on the body of a person reclining on the ground, and without wounding him. When none seemed desirous to support the ring in the manner required, Laodamia offered her only son; and this noble generosity which tended to reconcile her family, drew upon her the applause of the whole nation, and upon her brothers universal hatred, so that the crown was immediately conferred upon Sarpedon in gratitude to his mother. More probably, however, as Eustathius observes, Isander died without children, and Glaucus and Sarpedon the sons of Hippolochus and Laodamia, shared the sovereignty which was due to their friendship and their virtues. *Apollod.* 3. c. 1.—*Herodot.* 1. c. 173.—*Strab.* 12.—*Homer. Il.* 16.—*Servius in Æn.* 1. v. 104.—*Eustath. ad Il.* 6.—*Tertull. Apol.* 14.——A son of Neptune, killed by Hercules for his barbarous treatment of strangers.——A preceptor of Cato of Utica, famous for his learning and the excellent qualities of his mind. *Plut. in Cat.*—*Val. Max.* 3. c. 1.——A Syrian general who flourished B.C. 143.

SARPE'DON, a town of Cilicia famous for a temple sacred to Apollo and Diana.——A promontory of Cilicia, beyond which Antiochus was not permitted to sail by a treaty of peace which he had made with the Romans. *Liv.* 38. c. 38.—*Mela*, 1. c. 13.——A promontory of Thrace.

SAR'RA, a town of Phœnicia, the same as Tyre. It received this name from a small shell-fish of the same name, which was found in the neighbourhood, and with the blood of which garments were dyed. Hence arose the epithet of *Sarranus*, so often applied to Tyrian colors, as well as to the inhabitants of the colonies of the Tyrians, particularly Carthage. *Sil.* 6. v. 662. l. 15. v. 205.—*Virg. G.* 2. v. 506.—*Servius ad Virg. loco.*—*Festus de V. Sig.*

SARRANA'TES, a people of Umbria. *Plin.* 3. c. 14.

SARRAS'TES, a people originally from Peloponnesus, who settled in Campania and built Nuceria on the Sarnus, and assisted Turnus against Æneas. *Virg. Æn.* 7. v. 738.—*Servius loco.*

SAR'RITOR, SAR'TOR, or SA'TOR, a divinity who presided over weeding and agriculture among the Romans. *Servius in Virg. Georg.* 1. v. 21.—*Varro R. R.* 1. c. 29.

SAR'RON, a king of the Celtæ, so famous for his learning, that from him philosophers were called *Sarronidæ*. *Diod.* 6. c. 9.

SARS, a town of Spain, near Cape Finisterre. *Mela*, 3. c. 1.

SAR'SAGA, a city of Armenia Minor. *Antonin.*

SAR'SINA, an ancient town of Umbria, where the poet Plautus was born. The inhabitants are called Sarsinates. *Martial.* 9. epigr. 59.—*Plin.* 3. c. 14.—*Ital.* 8. v. 462. & *Drakenb. in loco.*

SAR'TE, a city near Athos. *Steph.*

SA'RUM, a town of Arabia Felix. *Ptol.*

SARUNE'TES, a people of Helvetii. *Plin.* 3. c. 20.

SA'RUS, a river of Cappadocia, which, after crossing mount Taurus, falls into the Mediterranean at the north of Cyprus. *Liv.* 33. c. 41.

SASAN'DA, a town of Caria. *Diod.* 14.

SASER'NA, a writer on husbandry.——Another writer also mentioned by *Varro, R.* 1. c. 2. 22.—*Colum.* 1. l. 4.—*Plin.* 17. c. 23.——A person intimate with Antony. *Cic. Phil.* 13. c. 13. *Att.* 15. ep. 7.

SA'SON, an island at the entrance of the Adriatic Sea, lying between Brundusium and Aulon, on the coast of Thrace. It was barren and inhospitable. *Strab.* 6.—*Lucan.* 2. v. 627. & 5. v. 650.—*Sil. It.* 7. v. 480.

SA'SON, a river falling into the Adriatic.

SAS'ONES, a people of Scythia, near mount Imaus, *Ptol.*

SAS'SIA, a Roman matron, mother of Cluentius. *Cic. Clu.* 5.

SASU'RI, a people of India. *Plin.* 6. c. 19.

SAT'ALA, a city of Armenia. *Steph.*

SATAR'CHÆ, a people near the Palus Mæotis. *Mela*, 2. c. 1.—*Flacc.* 6. v. 144.

SAT'AROS, a city of Lycia, called also Patara. *Plin.* 5. c. 27.

SATAS'PES, a Persian crucified by order of Xerxes, for offering violence to the daughter of Megabyzus. His father's name was Theaspes. *Herodot.* 4.

SATER'NEI, a people near the Mæotis. *Plin.* 6. c. 7.

SATIBARZA'NES, a Persian made satrap of the Arians by Alexander, from whom he afterwards revolted. *Curt.* 6 & 7.

SATIC'ULA or SATIC'ULUS, a town near Capua. *Virg. Æn*, 7. v. 729.—*Liv.* 9. c. 21. l. 23. c. 39.—*Servius ad Virg. loco.*

SA'TIO, a town of Macedonia, near the Lake Lychnis. *Polyb.* 1. 5.

SAT'NIUS, one of the auxiliaries of Priam against the Greeks, killed by Ajax Oileus. He was son of Enops, and a sea nymph. *Homer. Il.* 14. v. 441.

SA'TRA, a city of Crete, afterwards Eleutherina. *Steph.*

SAT'RACHUS, a city and river of Cyprus. *Lyc.*

SA'TRÆ, a people of Thrace. *Herodot.* 7. c. 111.

SATRA'IDÆ, a people of Ariana. *Dionys.* v. 1098.

SATRAPE'NI, a people of Media, under Tigranes. *Plut.*

SA'TRIA, a city of Italy. *Steph.*

SATRIC'ULA, a town of the Samnites taken by the Romans, A.U.C. 439.

SAT'RICUM or SATRI'CUM, a town of Italy taken by Camillus. *Liv.* 6. c. 8.

SA'TRIUS, M., the nephew and heir of M. Minuc. Basilus. *Cic. Off.* 3. c. 18.——A lieutenant of Trebonius. *Cic. ad Br.* 6.

SA'TRIUS SECUN'DUS, a vile informer, who was entrusted with the intrigues of Sejanus to make himself absolute, and betrayed them to Tiberius. *Tacit. Ann.* 6. 47.

SATROCEN'TÆ, a people of Thrace. *Steph.*

SATROP'ACES, an officer in the army of Darius, &c. *Curt.* 4. c. 9.

SATTAGY'LÆ, a people of Asia. *Herodot.*

SAT'TALA, a city of Phrygia. *Ptol.*

SAT'ULA, a city of Arabia Felix. *Id.*

SAT'URA, a lake of Latium, forming part of the Pontine lakes. *Sil.* 8. v. 382.—*Virg. Æn.* 7. v. 801.—*Horat.* 1. sat. 6. v. 59.—*Servius ad Virg. loco.*

SATURE'IUM or **SATU'RIUM**, a town of Calabria, near Tarentum, with famous pastures and horses, whence the epithet of *Satureianus* in *Horace*, 1. sat. 6. v. 59.

SATURE'IUS, one of Domitian's murderers.

SATU'RIUS, a lawyer at Rome, employed by Chærea against Roscius, &c. *Cic. Q. Rosc.* 1.

SATURNA'LIA, festivals in honor of Saturn, celebrated on the 16th or 17th, or, according to others, the 18th of December. They were instituted long before the foundation of Rome, in commemoration of the freedom and equality which prevailed on earth in the golden reign of Saturn. Some, however, suppose that the Saturnalia were first observed at Rome in the reign of Tullius Hostilius, after a victory obtained over the Sabines; while othesr assert, that Janus first instituted them in gratitude to Saturn, from whom he had learnt agriculture. Others maintain, that they were first celebrated A.U.C. 257, after a victory obtained over the Latins by the dictator Posthumius. The Saturnalia were originally celebrated for only one day, but afterwards the solemnity continued for three, four, five, and at last for seven days. The celebration was remarkable for the liberty which universally prevailed. The slaves were permitted to ridicule their masters, and to speak with freedom upon every subject. It was usual for friends to make presents one to another, all animosity ceased, no criminals were executed, schools were shut, war was never declared, all was mirth, riot, and debauchery. In the sacrifices the priests made their offerings with their heads uncovered, a custom which was never observed at other festivals. *Senec.* ep. 18.—*Cato de R.R.* 57.—*Sueton. in Vesp.* 19.—*Cic. ad Attic.* 5. ep. 20.—*Macrob.* 1. c. 7 & 10.—*Tertull. de Idol.* 10.—*Solin.* 3.

SATUR'NIA, a name given to Italy, because Saturn had reigned there during the golden age. *Virg. G.* 2. v. 173.——A name given to Juno, as being the daughter of Saturn. *Virg. G.* 2. v. 173. *Æn.* 3. v. 380.

Satur'nia, an ancient town of Italy, supposed to have been built by Saturn on the Tarpeian rock. *Virg. Æn.* 8. v. 358.——A colony of Etruria. *Liv.* 39. c. 55.—*Plin.* 3. c. 5.

SATURNI'NUS P. SEMPRO'NIUS, a general of Valerian, proclaimed emperor in Ægypt by his troops after he had rendered himself celebrated by his victories over the barbarians. His integrity, complaisance, and affability, had gained him the affection of the people, but his fondness for ancient discipline provoked his soldiers, who wantonly murdered him in the 43rd year of his age, A.D. 262. *Treb. Poll. in* 30 *Tyrann.* c. 23.

Saturni'nus Sex'tus Ju'lius, a Gaul, intimate with Aurelian. The emperor esteemed him greatly, not only for his private virtues, but for his abilities as a general, and for the victories which he had obtained in different parts of the empire. He was saluted emperor at Alexandria, and compelled by the clamorous army to accept of the purple, which he rejected with disdain and horror. Probus, who was then emperor, marched his forces against him, and besieged him in Apamea, where he destroyed himself when unable to make head against his powerful adversary. *Vospisc. in Prob.* c. 18.

Saturni'nus Lu'cius Appule'ius, a tribune of the people who raised a sedition at Rome, intimidated the senate, and tyrannized for three years. Meeting at last with opposition, he seized the Capitol, but being induced by the hopes of a reconciliation to trust himself among the people, he was suddenly torn to pieces. His sedition has received the name of *Appuleiana* in the Roman annals. *Flor.* 3. c. 16.—*Plut. in Mar.*—*Cic. Cat.* 1. *Rabir. Phil.* 8. c. 5.

Saturni'nus, an officer in the court of Theodosius, murdered for obeying the emperor's orders, &c.

Saturni'nus Pompe'ius, a writer in the reign of Trajan. He was greatly esteemed by Pliny, who speaks of him with great warmth and approbation as an historian, a poet, and an orator. Pliny always consulted the opinion of Saturninus before he published his compositions.

Saturni'nus Sen'tius, a friend of Augustus and Tiberius. He succeeded Agrippa in the government of the provinces of Syria and Phœnicia.

Saturni'nus, Vitel'lius, an officer among the friends of the emperor Otho.

Saturni'nus Cne'us, a son of Saturninus of Atinum. As his father was honored with a curule office at Rome, he was acquainted with some of the leading men of the city. *Cic. Plan.* 8. *Fam.* 8. ep. 14.

SATUR'NIUS, a name given to Jupiter, Pluto, and Neptune. as being the sons of Saturn.

SATUR'NUS, a son of Cœlus, or Uranus, by Terra, called also Titea, Thea, or Titheia. He was naturally artful, and by means of his mother, revenged himself on his father, whose cruelty to his children had provoked the anger of Thea. The mother armed her son with a scythe, which was fabricated with the metals drawn from her bowels, and as Cœlus was going to unite himself to Thea, Saturn mutilated him, and for ever prevented him from increasing his children, whom he treated with unkindness, and confined in the infernal regions. After this the sons of Cœlus were restored to liberty, and Saturn obtained his father's kingdom by the consent of his brothers, provided he did not bring up any male children. Pursuant to this agreement, Saturn always devoured his sons as soon as born, because, as some observe, he dreaded from them a retaliation of his unkindness to his father, till his wife Rhea, unwilling to see her children perish, concealed from her husband the birth of Jupiter, Neptune, and Pluto, and, instead of the children, presented to him large stones, which he immediately swallowed without perceiving the deceit. Titan was some time after informed that Saturn had concealed his male children, therefore he made war against him, and dethroned, and imprisoned him, together with Rhea; and Jupiter, who was secretly educated in Crete, was no sooner grown up, than he hastened to deliver his father, and to replace him on his throne. Saturn, unmindful of his son's kindness, conspired against him when he heard that he raised cabals against him, but Jupiter banished him from his throne, and the father fled for safety into Italy, where the country preserved the name of *Latium*, as being the place of his *concealment* (*lateo*) Janus, who was then king of Italy, received Saturn with every mark of attention, and made him his partner on the throne; and the king of heaven employed himself in civilizing the barbarous manners of the people of Italy, and in teaching them agriculture and the useful and liberal arts. His reign there was so mild and popular, so beneficent and virtuous, that mankind have called it the *golden age*, to intimate the happiness and tranquillity which the earth then enjoyed. Saturn was father of Chiron the centaur by Philyra, whom he had changed into a mare, to avoid the importunities of Rhea. The worship of Saturn was not so solemn or so universal as that of Jupiter. It was usual to offer human victims on his altars, but this barbarous custom was abolished by Hercules, who substituted small images of clay. In the sacrifices of Saturn, the priest always performed the ceremony with his head uncovered, which was unusual at other solemnities. The god is generally represented as an old man bent double through age and infirmity. He holds a scythe in his right hand, with a serpent biting its own tail, which is an emblem of time and the revolution of the year. In his left hand he holds a child, which he raises up as if to devour it. Tatius, king of the Sabines, first built a temple to Saturn on the Capitoline hill, a second was afterwards added by Tullus Hostilius, and a third by the first consuls. On his statues were generally hung fetters in commemoration of the chains which he had worn when imprisoned by Jupiter. From this circumstance, all slaves who obtained their liberty, generally dedicated their fetters to him. During the celebration of the Saturnalia, the chains were taken from the statues to intimate the freedom and the independence which mankind enjoyed during the golden age. One of the temples of Saturn at Rome was appropriated for the preservation of public treasures, and it was there also that the names of foreign ambassadors were enrolled. *Hesiod. Theog.* v. 138. 209 & 460.—*Cic. de Nat. D.* 2. c. 24.—*Apollod.* 1. c. 1.—*Virg. Æn.* 8. v. 319. —*Paus.* 8. c. 8.—*Tibull.* el. 3. v. 35.—*Homer. Il.*—*Ovid. Fast.* 4. v. 197. *Met.* 1. v. 123.—*Macrob.* 1. c. 8.—*Servius ad Virg. Æn.* 3. v. 104. l. 8. v. 322. l. 9. v. 83. [There is a fine head, veiled and of colossal size, representing Saturn, in the Museum of the Vatican.

SAT'URUM, a town of Calabria, where stuffs of all kinds were dyed in different colors with great success. *Virg. G.* 2. v. 197. l. 4. v. 335 *& Servius loco.*

SAT'YRI, demigods of the country, whose origin is unknown. They are represented like men, but with the feet and legs of goats, short horns on the head, and the whole body covered with thick hair. They chiefly attended upon Bacchus, and rendered themselves known in his orgies by their riotous demeanour and lasciviousness. The first fruits of everything were offered to them. The Romans called them indifferently Fauni, Panes, or Sylvani. It is said that a Satyr was brought to Sylla as that general returned from Thessaly. The monster had been surprised asleep in a cave; but his voice was inarticulate when brought into the presence of the Roman general, and Sylla was so disgusted with it, that he ordered it to be instantly removed. This monster answered in every degree the description which the poets and painters have given of the Satyrs. *Paus.* 1. c. 28. —*Plut. in Syll.*—*Virg. Ec.* 5. v. 13.—*Ovid. Heroid.* 4. v. 171.—*Horat.* 1. od. 1. v. 31.—*Nonnius.* 4, 14, 15, 18 & 21—*Servius ad Virg. Ecl.* 6. v. 13.—*Hieronym. in vita Paul, Erem.* [There are many representations of Satyrs in sculpture, the finest of which are generally considered statues of Pan. But there is also an exceedingly beautiful group of a Nymph and Satyr, in the Vatican.]

SAT'YRUS, a king of Bosporus, who reigned 14 years, &c. His father's name was Spartacus. *Diod.* 14.——An Athenian who attempted to eject the garrison of Demetrius from the citadel, &c. *Polyæn.* 5. c. 17.——A Greek actor who instructed Demosthenes, and taught him how to acquire a good and strong delivery. *Plut.*—*Diod. Sic.* 16. —*Voss. H. Gr.* 3. p. 411.——A man who assisted in murdering Timophanes, by order of his brother Timoleon.——A Rhodian sent by his countrymen to Rome, when Eumenes had accused some of the allies of intentions to favour the interests of Macedonia against the republic.——A peripatetic philosopher and historian who flourished B.C. 148. *Athen.* 6.—*Voss. H. G.* p. 411.——A tyrant of Heraclea, 346 B.C.——An architect, who, together with Petus, is said to have planned and built the celebrated tomb which Artemisia erected to the memory of Mausolus, and which became one of the wonders of the world. The honor of erecting it is, however, ascribed to others.

SAUBAA'NA, a city of Armenia Major. *Id.*

SAU'BATHA, the metropolis of Arabia Felix. *Id.* It is the Sabbatha of *Arrian*, and probably the Sabora of *Pliny.*

SAUCI'VA, a city of Pannonia. *Antonin.*

SAUFE'IUS TRO'GUS, one of Messalina's favorites, punished by Claudius, &c. *Tacit. Ann.* 11. c. 35.

Saufe'ius Ap'pius, a Roman, who died on his return from the bath upon taking mead, &c. *Plin.* 7. c. 53.

Saufe'ius, a friend of Saturninus who supported him in his seditious views. *Cic. Att.* 1. ep. 3, &c.

SAU'NIS, a city of Arabia. *Steph.*

SAU'NIUS, a fountain near Bulis in Phocis. *Paus.* 1. 10.

SAU'RA, a city of the Samnites. *Steph.*——A city of Susiana. *Ptol.*

SAU'RIUM, a river of Hispania Tarraconensis. *Mela*, 3. c. 1.

SAUROM'ATÆ, a people in the northern parts of Europe and Asia. They are called Sarmatæ by the Latins. *Vid.* Sarmatia.

SAU'RUS, a famous robber of Elis, killed by Hercules. *Paus.* 6. c. 21.——A statuary of Lacedæmon, who with Batrachus was employed in adorning the temples of Rome. Though their labours were voluntary and gratuitous, they were not permitted to inscribe their names on their works, in consequence of which, Saurus introduced with taste and delicacy the figures of lizards (σαῦρα) on the bases and chapiters of the columns, and Batrachus those of frogs (βάτραχος) and thus perpetuated their memory. *Plin.* 36, c. 6.

SA'VA, a town of Arabia Felix. *Steph.*——A town of Arabia Deserta. *Ptol.*

SAV'ARA, a town of Assyria. *Id.*

SAVARABA'TIS, a region of India within the Ganges. *Id.*

SAV'ARI, a people of European Sarmatia. *Id.*

SAVE'RA, a village of Lycaonia. *Strab.* 12.

SA'VIA, a town of the Pelendones in Spain. *Ptol.*

SA'VO or **SAVO'NA**, a town with a small river of the same name in Campania. *Stat.* 4.—*Plin.* 3. c. 5.——A town of Liguria.

SA'VUS, a river of Pannonia, rising in Noricum, at the north of Aquileia, and falling into the Danube, after flowing through Pannonia in an eastern direction. *Claudius de Stil.* 2. v. 191.——A small river of Numidia, falling into the Mediterranean.

SAX'A, a Celtiberian made tribune by J. Cæsar. He espoused Antony's party against Augustus. *Cic. Phil.* 11. c. 5. &c.

SAX'I, a people near Pontus. *Steph.*

SAXI'NÆ, a nation of the Troglodytæ in Æthiopia. *Plin.* 6. c. 29.

SAX'ONES, a people of Germany, near the Chersonesus Cimbrica. Their descendants invaded England. *Ptol.* 3. 11.—*Claud.* 1. *Eutr.* v. 392.

SAXON'TIUM, a town of India within the Ganges. *Ptol.*

SAZARA'NA, a city of Thrace. *Antonin.*

SAZ'ICHES, an ancient Ægyptian, said to have been the second legislator of the country. He lived prior to the age of Sesostris, and not only introduced a purer and more perfect worship of the gods, but invented geometry, and improved the means of astronomical observation. *Diod.* 2.

SCÆ'A, one of the gates of Troy, where the tomb of Laomedon was seen. The name is derived by some from σκαιὸς (*sinister*), because it was through this avenue that the wooden horse was introduced. *Homer. Il.*—*Sil.* 13. v. 73.—*Virg. Æn.* 2. v. 612. —*Eustath. in Il.* 2.—*Servius in Æn.* 2. v. 234 & 612.

Scæ'a, one of the Danaides. Her husband's name was Dayphron. *Apollod.* 2.

SCÆ'VA, a soldier in Cæsar's army, who behaved with great courage at Dyrrachium. *Lucan.* 6. v. 144.——A man who poisoned his own mother. *Horat.* 2, sat. 1. v. 53.——A friend of *Horace*, to whom the poet addressed ep. 17. lib. 1. He was a Roman knight.——A slave belonging to Q. Croto, who killed the seditious Saturninus, for which he was manumitted. *Cic. Rab. Perd.* 11.

Scæ'va Me'mor, a Latin poet in the reign of Titus and Domitian. *Mart.* 11. epigr. 11.

SCÆV'OLA. *Vid.* Mutius.

SCAL'ABIS, now Santaren, a town of ancient Spain. *Plin.* 4. c. 22.

SCAL'DIS or **SCAL'DIUM**, a river of Belgium, now called the Scheldt, and dividing the modern country of the Netherlands from Holland. *Cæs. B. G.* 6. v. 33.

Scal'dis Pons, a town on the same river, now called Conde. *Cæs.*

SCAMAN'DER or **SCAMAN'DROS**, a celebrated river of Troas, rising at the east of mount Ida, and falling into the sea below Sigæum. It receives the Simois in its course, and towards its mouth it is very muddy, and flows through marshes. This river, according to Homer, was called Xanthus by the gods, and Scamander by men. The waters of the Scamander had the singular property of giving a beautiful colour to the hair or wool of such animals as bathed in them; and from this circumstances the three goddesses, Minerva, Juno, and Venus, bathed there before they appeared before Paris, to obtain the golden apple. It was usual among all the virgins of Troas to bathe in the Scamander, when they were arrived at nubile years. The god of the Scamander had a regular priest, and sacrifices offered to him. Some suppose that the river received its name from Scamander, the son of Corybas, but others give it a different origin. Hercules, as they say in his war against Troy, when laboring under great thirst, implored Jupiter for relief, and immediately, from a hole which he opened in the earth, issued forth a river, called from that circumstance Scamander (σκάμμα ἀνδρὸς, *hominis fossio.*) *Ælian. Anim.* 1. c. 21.—*Strab.* 1 & 13.—*Plin.* 5. c. 30.—*Mela*, 1. c. 18.—*Homer. Il.* 5. v. 77.—*Arist.* 3. *Hist. An.* c. 12.—*Sch. Hom. in Il.* 21.—*Plut. de Flum.*—*Eustath. in Hom. Il.* 20.—*Æschin.* ep. 10.

SCAMAN'DER or SCAMAN'DRUS, a son of Corybas and Demodice, who led a colony from Crete into Phrygia, and settled at the foot of mount Ida, where he introduced the festivals of Cybele, and the dances of the Corybantes. He some time after lost the use of his senses, and threw himself into the river Xanthus, which ever after bore his name. His son-in-law, Teucer succeeded him in the government of his colony. He had two daughters, Thymo and Callirhoe. *Apollod.* 3. c. 12.—*Diod.* 4.—*Servius in Virg. Æn.* 3. v. 108 & 167.——The son of Hector and Andromache, called also Astyanax. *Homer. Il.* 21. v. 223.

SCAMAN'DER, a freed-man mentioned by *Cicero. Clu.* 16.

SCAMAN'DRIA, a town on the banks of the Scamander. *Plin.* 4. c. 30.

SCAMAN'DRIUS, one of the generals of Priam, son of Strophius. He was killed by Menelaus, *Homer. Il.* 5. v. 49.

SCAMBE'NA, a town of Media. *Ptol.*

SCAMBON'IDÆ, a village of Attica, in the tribe Leontis. *Schol. in Vesp.*

SCA'MON, a Mitylenean, who wrote a book *De rerum inventione. Clem. Strom.* 1.—*Athen.* l. 4.

SCANDA'RIA, a promontory in the island of Cos. *Strab.* 14.

SCAN'DIA, a town and dock-yard of Cythera. *Steph. ex Paus.* l. 3.

SCANDIL'IUS P., a Roman knight of Syracuse. *Cic. Ver.* 3. c. 58.

SCANDINA'VIA, a name given by the ancients to that tract of territory which contains the modern kingdoms of Norway, Sweden, Denmark, Lapland, Finland, &c., supposed by them to be an island. *Plin.* 4. c. 13.

SCANTA'TE, a town of the Zimareni, a people near the Nabatæi. *Plin.* 6. c. 28.

SCAN'TIA, a woman of whom *Cicero* makes mention. *Mil.* 27.

SCAN'TIA SYL'VA, a wood of Campania, the property of the Roman people. *Cic.*—*Plin.* 2. c. 107.

SCANTIL'LA, the wife of Didius Julianus. It was by her advice that her husband bought the empire which was exposed to sale at the death of Pertinax. [There is a bust of this empress in the Museum of the Vatican, at Rome.]

SCANTIN'IA LEX. *Vid.* Scatinia.

SCAN'TIUS, a Roman who devoted himself to gardening, and the cultivation of apples, &c. *Plin.* 15. c. 14.—*Cato.* 7. c. 2.

SCA'PHE, a city of Mesopotamia. *Ptol.*

SCA'POS, an island of the Mediterranean Sea. *Plin.* 4. c. 12.

SCAPTES'YLE, a town of Thrace, near Abdera, abounding in silver and gold mines, belonging to Thucydides, who is supposed there to have written his history of the Peloponnesian war. *Lucret.* 6. v. 810.—*Plut. in Cim.*

SCAP'TIA, a town of Latium. *Sil.* 8. v. 396.—*Plin.* 3. c. 5.—*Liv.* 8. c. 7.

SCAP'TIUS, a merchant appointed by the influence of Brutus, prefect at Cyprus. In his office, Scaptius vexed the Cyprians, and especially the people of Salamis, that he might recover some money which his patron Brutus had lent to the people of the island, at an extravagant interest. The settling of this affair proved troublesome to Cicero in his pro-consulship in Asia. *Cic. ad Att.* 5. *ult.* 6. 1. 2.

SCAP'TIUS MAR'CUS, the brother of the preceding, was raised to the office of prefect by Cicero. *Cic. ad Att.* 5. *ult.* 6. ep. 1.

SCAP'TIUS PUB'LIUS, a plebeian, by whose testimony the Romans unlawfully seized as their own, some land, for the settlement of which they were appointed umpires by the people of Aricia and Ardea. *Liv.* 3. c. 71, 72.

SCAP'ULA, a native of Corduba, who defended that town against Cæsar, after the battle of Munda. When he saw that all his efforts against the Roman general were useless, he destroyed himself. *Cæs. Bell. H.* 33.—*Cic. Fam.* 9. ep. 13.——A usurer. *Cic. ad Att.* 12. ep. 37.——The surname of the family of the Quintii. *Plin.* 7. c. 53.

SCARABAN'TIA JU'LIA, a town of the Boii in Noricum. *Plin.* 3. c. 24.

SCAR'DII, a ridge of mountains of Macedonia, which separated it from Illyricum. *Liv.* 43. c. 20.

SCARDO'NA, a town on the confines of Dalmatia. *Ptol.*—*Plin.* 3. c. 21. It is now Scardo.

SCA'RI, a city of Lycia. *Steph.*

SCARNIUN'GA, a river of Pannonia.

SCARPHI'A, SCARPHE'A or SCAR'PHE, a town near Thermopylæ, on the confines of Phthiotis. Its inhabitants went with Ajax to the Trojan war. *Senec. in Tr.*

SCAR'THON, a river of Asia. *Strab.* 13.

SCATIN'IA LEX *de pudicitia*, by C. Scatinius Aricinus, the tribune, was enacted against those who kept catamites, and such as prostituted themselves to any vile or unnatural service. The penalty was originally a fine, but it was afterwards made a capital crime under Augustus. It is sometimes called *Scantinia* from a certain *Scantinius* upon whom it was first carried into effect. *Juv.* 2. v. 44.—*Cic. Phil.* 3. c. 6. *Fam.* 8. ep. 13.—*Suet. Dom.* 8.—*Val. Max.* 6. c. 1 & 7.

SCAURI'NUS, a celebrated grammarian in the age of Adrian.——Son of the preceding, was also a grammarian, and preceptor of Alexander Severus. *Jul. Capitol. in Ver.* c. 2. & *Salmas. in loco.*

SCAU'RUS M. ÆMIL'IUS, a Roman consul, who distinguished himself by his eloquence at the bar, and by his successes in Spain. He was sent against Jugurtha, but his exertions as commander and ambassador were checked by the bribes of the Numidian prince, and the Romans seemed more anxious to obtain the gold of Jugurtha, than to avenge the wrongs of Masinissa's murdered family. Every accusation against Scaurus for corruption or dereliction of duty was silenced by his superior influence, and he was invested with new offices. In an ensuing campaign he conquered the Ligurians, and in his censorship he built the Milvian bridge at Rome, and began to pave the road, which from him was called the Æmilian. He was originally very poor. He wrote some books, and among these a history of his own life, compared by Cicero for its great elegance and usefulness to the Cyrus of Xenophon. All his works have unfortunately perished. *Cic. Mur.* 7. *Orat.* 2. c. 64. *Br.* 29, 30, &c. *Font.* 7. *Sex.* 47.—*Sallust. Jug.* 15, &c.—*Quintil.* 5. c. 12, &c.—*Tacit. Agr.* 1.—*Plin.* 33. c. 1.——Son of the preceding, made himself known by the large theatre which he built during his ædileship. This theatre, which could contain 30,000 spectators, was supported by 360 columns of marble, was 38 feet in height, and was adorned with 3,000 brazen statues. This celebrated edifice, according to Pliny, proved more fatal to the manners and simplicity of the Romans, than the proscriptions and wars of Sylla had done to the inhabitants of the city. Scaurus afterwards endeavoured to recruit his shattered fortune, and as governor of Sardinia showed himself oppressive and vexatious, but, though accused of extortion, he was acquitted by the eloquence of Cicero. Scaurus in his attempts to obtain the consulship had recourse to bribery, for which, even in these corrupted times, he was banished. He was engaged in the Mithridatic wars under Pompey, and by him appointed governor of Judæa. He married Mucia when divorced by Pompey. *Plut. in Syll.*—*Joseph. B. J.* 1. c. 7.—*Cic. Off.* 2. c. 16. *Sext.* 5. c. 4. *Att.* 4. ep. 16. *Fr.* 3. ep. 1.—*Ascon. in Scaur.*—*Val. Max.* 7. c. 1.—*Plin.* 36. c. 15. These two characters, father and son, are ranked by Horace among the most illustrious sons of Rome, though they possessed few of the virtues of their ancestors, and gained distinction by dissimulation, and by an artful subserviency to the public opinion, and the caprices of the people. *Horat.* 1. od. 12. v. 37.—*Juv.* 2. v. 35. 6. v. 603. 11. v. 91.

SCAU'RUS, a Roman of consular dignity. When the Cimbri invaded Italy, the son of Scaurus behaved with great cowardice, upon which the father sternly ordered him never to appear again in the field of battle. The severity of this command rendered young Scaurus melancholy, and he plunged a sword into his own heart to free himself from further ignominy.

SCAU'RUS AURE'LIUS, a Roman consul taken prisoner by the Gauls. He was put to a cruel death because he told the king of the enemy not to cross the Alps to invade Italy, which was universally deemed unconquerable. *Liv.* 1. 67.

SCAU'RUS MAMER'CUS, a man in the reign of Tiberius, accused of adultery with Livia, and put to death. He was an eloquent orator, but very lascivious and debauched in his morals. *Tac. Ann.* 6. c. 29.—*Senec.* l. 4. *de Benef.* c. 31.

SCAU'RUS MAX'IMUS, a man who conspired against Nero.

SCAU'RUS TEREN'TIUS, a Latin grammarian. He had been preceptor to the emperor Adrian. *A. Gellius.* 11. c. 15. The surname of Scaurus, which was applied to the Aurelian and Æmilian families, was probably derived from the weak or distorted ancles of some of them. *Horat.* 1. sat. 3. v. 48 *& Acron. ib.*—*Plin.* 11. c. 45

SCED'ASUS, a native of Leuctra in Bœotia. His two daughters, Miletia and Molpia, whom some call Theano, or Hippo, were ravished by some Spartans, in the reign of Cleombrotus, and killed themselves, unable to survive the loss of their honor. The father became so disconsolate, that when he was unable to obtain redress from his country, he killed himself on their tomb. *Paus.* 9. c. 13.—*Plut. in Amat.* 3.

SCELAT'ICI, a people of Mauritania *Plin.* 5. c. 1.

SCELERA'TA POR'TA, one of the gates of Rome, so called because the 300 Fabii, who were killed at the river Cremera, had passed through it when they went to attack the enemy. It was before named Carmentalis.

SCELERA'TUS CAM'PUS, a plain at Rome near the Colline gate, where the vestal Minucia was buried alive, when convicted of adultery. *Liv.* 8. c. 15.

SCELERA'TUS VI'CUS, a street at Rome formerly called Cyprius, which received this name because it was in this street that Tullia ordered her postilion to drive her chariot over the body of her father, king Servius. *Liv.* 1. c. 48.—*Ovid. Ib.* 365.

SCEM'PSA, a city of Thrace. *Steph.*

SCE'NA, a town on the confines of Babylon. *Strab.* 16.——A river of Ireland, now the Shannon. *Orosius,* 1. c. 2.

SCENI'TÆ, Arabians who live in tents, whence their name. *Plin.* 5. c. 11.—*Solin.* 23.—*Ammian.* 22. c. 15. l. 23. c. 6.

SCEP'SIS, a town of Troas, where the works of Theophrastus and Aristotle were long concealed under ground, and damaged by the wet, &c. *Strab.* 10.

SCEPTRU'CHI, a people of the Sarmatians. *Tac.* 6. c. 33.

SCHE'DIA, a small village of Ægypt with a dockyard between the western mouths of the Nile and Alexandria. *Strab.*—*Salmas. ad Solin.* p. 476.

SCHEDIUS, son of Iphitus, king of Phocis, was one of Helen's suitors, and accompanied Menelaus to the Trojan war at the head of the inhabitants of Crissa, Panopea, Daulis, and other neighbouring cities, in 40 ships. He was slain by Hector. Some make him son of Epistrophus, who is called by others his brother. *Homer. Il* 2. v. 24. l. 17. v. 865.—*Paus.* 10. c. 4 & 30.—*Apollod.* 3.

SCHE'RA, an inland city of Sicily. *Ptol.*

SCHE'RIA, an ancient name of Corcyra. *Paus.* 2. c. 5.—*Plin.* 4. c. 12.

SCHINUS'SA, a small island of the Ægæan Sea. *Plin.* 4. c 12.

SCHŒNE'IS, a patronymic of Atalanta, as daughter of Schœneus, king of Arcadia. *Ovid. Am.* 1. el. 7. v. 13. ep. 16. v. 263.

SCHŒ'NEUS, a son of Athamas and Themisto, father of Atalanta. *Paus.* 8, c. 35.—*Apollod.* 1 & 3.

SCHŒ'NUS, now SCHE'NO, a port of Peloponnesus on the Sinus Saronicus.

SCHŒ'NUS, a village near Thebes, with a river of the same name.——A river of Arcadia.——A river near Athens.

SCI'A, a town of Eubœa. *Steph.*

SCIAS'TES, a surname of Apollo at Lacedæmon, from the village Scias, where he was particularly worshipped. *Lycoph.* 562. *& Tzetzes. loco.*

SCI'ATHIS, a mountain of Arcadia. *Paus.* 8 c. 14.——A city of Ægypt, near mount Scetis. *Ptol.*

SCI'ATHUS or SCI'ATHOS, an island in the Ægæan Sea, opposite mount Pelion, on the coast of Thessaly. *Val. Flacc.* 2. v. 8.

SCI'DRUS, a town of Magna Græcia. *Steph.*

SCIE'RIA, a festival observed annually at Alea in Arcadia, in honor of Bacchus. During its celebration it was customary to whip women before the altar of the god, which was in a shady spot ὑπὸ τῇ σκιᾷ, whence the name. *Paus. Arcad.* —*Pollux,* 8. c. 33.

SCIL'LUS (*-untis*), a town of Peloponnesus, near Olympia, where Xenophon wrote his history. *Plut.*

SCILU'RUS, a king of Scythia, who had 80 sons. *Vid.* Scylurus.

SCINGOM'AGUS, a town beyond the Alps. *Strabo,* 4. It is now Sesans.

SCI'NIS, a cruel robber, who tied men to the boughs of trees which he had forcibly brought together, and which he afterwards unloosened, so that their limbs were torn in an instant from their body. He was son of Polypemon, or, according to others, of Neptune, and generally fixed his residence on the Isthmus of Corinth. It was here that Theseus, going from Trœzene to Athens, met him, and inflicted on him the same punishment which he cruelly practised on innocent travellers. His daughter was spared by the conqueror, by whom she had a son, after which she married Deioneus son of Eurytus, king of Œchalia. *Apollod.* 3.—*Diod.* 4.—*Hygin.* fab 38. —*Plut. in Thes.*—*Propert.* 3. el. 21. v. 37.—*Ovid. Met.* 7. v. 440.

SCIN'THI, a people of Germany, near the Cheruscia. *Claudian. de bell. Get.* v. 420.

SCIO'NE, a town of Thrace, in the possession of the Athenians, which revolted from them to the Lacedæmonians, during the Peloponnesian war. It was built by a Grecian colony on their return from the Trojan war. *Thucyd.* 4.—*Mela,* 2. c. 2. —*Plin.* 4. c. 10.

SCIPI'ADÆ, a name applied to the two Scipios, who obtained the surname of Africanus, from the conquest of Carthage. *Virg. Æn.* 6. v. 843.

SCIP'IO, a celebrated family at Rome, the members of which obtained the greatest honors in the republic. The name seems to be derived from Scipio, which signifies a stick, because one of the family had conducted his blind father, and had been to him as a staff. The Scipios were a branch of the Cornelian family. *Macrob.* 2. sat. 6.——A Roman dictator.——A consul A.U.C. 495.

SCIP'IO P. CORN., a man made master of the horse by Camillus, &c. *Liv.* 5. c. 13, &c.

SCIP'IO L. CORNEL, a consul A.U. C. 456, who defeated the Etrurians near Volaterra. *Liv.* 10.

SCIP'IO CN, surnamed Asina, was consul A.U.C. 494 & 500. He was conquered in his first consulship in a naval battle, and lost 17 ships. The following year he took Aleria, in Corsica, and defeated Hanno, the Carthaginian general, in Sardinia. He also took 200 of the enemy's ships, and the city of Panormum, in Sicily. He was father of Publius and Cneus Scipio. *Liv.* 17.— *Val. Max.* 5. c. 1.—*Zonar. in Annal &c.*

SCIP'IO PUB'LIUS was sent in the beginning of the second Punic war, with an army to Spain to oppose Annibal; but when he heard that his enemy had passed over into Italy, he attempted by his quick marches and secret evolutions to stop his progress. He was vanquished by Annibal near the Ticinus, and would have lost his life, had not his son, who was afterwards surnamed Africanus, courageously defended him. He again passed into Spain, where he obtained some memorable victories over the Carthaginians, and the inhabitants of the country. His brother Cneus shared the supreme command with him, but their great confidence proved their ruin. They separated their armies, and soon after Publius was furiously attacked by the two Asdrubals and Mago, who commanded the Carthaginian armies. The forces of Publius were too few to resist with success the three Carthaginian generals. The Romans were

cut to pieces, and their commander was left on the field of battle. No sooner had the enemy obtained this victory, than they marched to meet Cneus Scipio, whom the revolt of 30,000 Celtiberians had weakened and alarmed. The general, who was already apprized of his brother's death, secured an eminence, where he was soon surrounded on all sides. After desperate acts of valor he was left among the slain, or, according to some, he fled into a tower, where he was burnt with some of his friends by the victorious enemy, 28 days after the fall of his brother. *Cic. Off.* 1. c. 18. *Planc.* 25. *Balb.* 15.—*Liv.* 21, &c.—*Polyb.* 4.—*Flor.* 2, c. 6. &c.—*Eutrop.* 3. c. 8, &c.

SCIP'IO CNE'US. *Vid.* Scipio Publius.

SCIP'IO PUB'LIUS CORNE'LIUS, surnamed *Africanus*, was son by Pomponia, of Publius Scipio, who was killed in Spain. He first distinguished himself at the battle of Ticinus, where he saved his father's life by deeds of unexampled valor. The battle of Cannæ, which proved so fatal to the Roman arms, instead of disheartening Scipio, raised his expectations, and he no sooner heard that some of his desperate countrymen wished to abandon Italy, and to flee from the insolence of the conqueror, than with his sword in his hand, and by his firmness of example, he obliged them to swear eternal fidelity to Rome, and that they would put to immediate death the first man who attempted to retire from his country. In his 21st year Scipio was made œdile, an honorable office which was never given but to such as had reached their 27th year. Some time after, the Romans were alarmed by the intelligence that the commanders of their forces in Spain, Publius and Cneus Scipio, had been slaughtered, and immediately young Scipio was appointed to avenge the death of his father, and of his uncle, and to vindicate the military honor of the republic. It was soon known how able he was to be at the head of an army; the various nations of Spain were conquered, and in four years the Carthaginians being banished from that part of the continent, the whole province became tributary to Rome; New Carthage submitted in one day, and in a battle 54,000 of the enemy were left dead on the field. After these signal victories, Scipio was recalled to Rome, which still trembled at the continual alarms of Annibal, who was at her gates. The conqueror of the Carthaginians in Spain was looked upon as a proper general to encounter Annibal in Italy; but Scipio opposed the measure which his countrymen wished to pursue, and declared in the senate, that if Annibal was to be conquered, he must be conquered in Africa. These bold measures were immediately adopted, though opposed by the eloquence, age and experience of the great Fabius, and Scipio was empowered to conduct the war on the coasts of Africa. Being invested with the dignity of consul he embarked for Carthage. Success attended his arms, his conquests here were as rapid as in Spain; the Carthaginian armies were routed, the camp of the crafty Asdrubal was set on fire during the night, and his troops totally defeated in a bloody battle. These repeated losses alarmed Carthage; Annibal, who was victorious at the gates of Rome, was instantly recalled to defend the walls of his country, and the two greatest generals of the age met each other in the field. Terms of accommodation were proposed; but in the parley which the two commanders had together, nothing satisfactory was offered, and while the one enlarged on the vicissitude of human affairs, the other wished to dictate like a conqueror, and recommended the decision of the controversy to the sword. This celebrated battle was fought near Zana, and both generals displayed their military knowledge in drawing up their armies and in choosing their ground. Their courage and intrepidity were not less conspicuous in charging the enemy; a thousand acts of valor were performed on both sides, and though the Carthaginians fought in their own defence, and the Romans for fame and glory, yet the conqueror of Italy was vanquished. About 20,000 Carthaginians were slain, and the same number made prisoners of war, B.C. 202. Only 2,000 of the Romans were killed. This battle was decisive; the Carthaginians sued for peace, which Scipio at last granted on the most severe and humiliating terms. The conqueror after this returned to Rome, where he was received with the most unbounded applause, honored with a triumph, and dignified with the appellation af Africanus. Here he enjoyed for some time the tranquillity and the honors which his exploits merited, but to him, as to other great men, fortune showed herself inconstant. Scipio offended the populace in wishing to distinguish the senators from the rest of the people at the public exhibitions, and when he canvassed for the consulship for two of his friends, he had the mortification to see his applicatien slighted, and the honors which he claimed, bestowed on a man of no character, and recommended neither by abilities nor meritorious actions. He retired from Rome that he might no longer be a spectator of the ingratitude of his countrymen. and, in the capacity of lieutenant, accompanied his brother against Antiochus, king of Syria. In this expedition his arms were attended with the usual success, and the Asiatic monarch submitted to the conditions which the conquerors dictated. At his return to Rome, Africanus found the malevolence of his enemies still unabated. Cato, his inveterate rival, raised seditions against him, and the Petilii, two tribunes of the people, accused the conqueror of Annibal of extortion in the provinces of Asia, and of living in an indolent and luxurious manner. Scipio condescended to answer the accusation of his calumniators; the first day was spent in hearing the different charges, but when he again appeared on the second day of his trial, the accused interrupted his indges, and exclaimed, "Tribunes and fellow citizens, on this day, this very day, did I conquer Annibal and the Carthaginians, come therefore with me, Romaus; let us go to the Capitol, and there return our thanks to the immortal gods for the victories which have attended our arms." These words had the desired effect, the tribes and all the assembly followed Scipio, the court was deserted, and the tribunes were left alone on the seat of judgment. Yet when this memorable day was past and forgotten, Africanus was a third time summoned to appear; but he had fled before the impending storm, and retired to his country house at Liternum. The accusation was therefore stopped, and the accusers silenced, when one of the tribunes, formerly distinguished for his malevolence against Scipio, rose to defend him, and declared in the assembly, that it reflected the highest disgrace on the Roman people, that the conqueror of Annibal should become the sport of the populace, and be exposed to the malice and envy of disappointed ambition. Some time after Scipio died in the place of his retreat, about 184 years B.C., in the 48th year of his age; and so great an aversion did he express, as he expired, for the depravity of the Romans, and the ingratitude of their senators, that he ordered his bones not to be conveyed to Rome. They were accordingly inhumated at Liternum, where his wife Æmilia, the daughter of Paulus Æmilius, who fell at the battle of Cannæ, raised a mausoleum on his tomb, and placed upon it his statue, with that of the poet Ennius, who had been the companion of his peace and of his retirement. If Scipio was robbed, during his life-time, of the honors which belonged to him as conqueror of Africa, he was not forgotten when dead. The Romans viewed his character with reverence; they read his warlike actions with rapture, and Africanus was regarded in the following ages as a pattern of virtue, innocence, courage, and liberality. The fame and the greatness of his conquests sufficiently stamp his character as a general, and indeed we hear that Annibal declared himself inferior to no general that ever lived except Alexander the Great, and Pyrrhus king of Epirus; when Scipio asked him what rank he would claim if he had conquered him, the Carthaginian general answered, "If I had conquered you, Scipio, I should have called myself greater than the conqueror of Darius, and the ally of the Tarentines." As an instance of Scipio's continence, ancient authors have recorded that the conqueror of Spain refused to see a beautiful princess that had fallen into his hands after the taking of New Carthage, and that he not only restored her inviolate to her parents, but also added immense presents for the person to whom she was betrothed. It was to the artful complaisance of Africanus, that the Romans owed their alliance to Massinissa, king of Numidia, and also that with king Syphax. The friendship of Scipio and Lælius is well known. *Polyb.* 6.—*Liv.* 21, &c.—*Plut.*—*Flor.* 2. c. 6.—*Cic. in Brut. &c.*—*Eutrop.* [There are two fine busts of Scipio Africanus, one in the Capitol at Rome, and the other in the Museum at Herculaneum.]

Scip'io Lu'cius Corne'lius, surnamed *Asiaticus*, accompanied his brother Africanus in his expeditions in Spain and Africa. He was rewarded with the consulship, A.U.C. 560, for his services to the state, and was empowered to attack Antiochus, king of Syria, who had declared war against the Romans. Lucius was accompanied in this campaign by his brother Africanus; and by his own valor, and the advice of the conqueror of Annibal, he soon routed the enemy, and in a battle near the city of Sardes, killed 50,000 foot, and 4,000 horse. Peace was soon after settled by the submission of Antiochus, and the conqueror, at his return home, obtained a triumph, and the surname of Asiaticus. He did not, however, long enjoy his prosperity; Cato, after the death of Africanus, turned his fury against Asiaticus, and the two Petilii, his devoted favorites, presented a petition to the people, in which they prayed that an enquiry might be instituted to discover what money had been received from Antiochus and his allies. The petition was instantly received, and Asiaticus, charged with having suffered himself to be corrupted by Antiochus, was summoned to appear before the tribunal of Terentius Culeo, who was on this occasion created prætor. The judge, who was an inveterate enemy of the family of the Scipios, soon found Asiaticus, with his two lieutenants and his quæstor, guilty of having received, the first 6,000 pounds' weight of gold, and 480 pounds' weight of silver, and the others nearly an equal sum, from the monarch against whom, in the name of the Roman people, they were enjoined to make war. They were condemned to pay large fines; but while the others gave security, Scipio declared that he had accounted to the public for all the money which he had brought from Asia, and that he was therefore innocent. For this obstinacy Scipio was dragged to prison, but his cousin Nasica pleaded his cause before the people, and the prætor instantly ordered the goods of the prisoner to be seized and confiscated. The sentence was executed, but the effects of Scipio were insufficient to pay the fine, and it was the greatest justification of his innocence, that whatever was found in his house had never been in the possession of Antiochus or his subjects. This, however, did not totally liberate him; he was reduced to poverty, and refused to accept the offers of his friends and of his clients. Some time after he was appointed to settle the disputes between Eumenes and Seleucus, and at his return, the Romans, ashamed of their severity towards him, rewarded his merit with such uncommon liberality, that Asiaticus was enabled to celebrate games in honor of his victory over Antiochus, for ten successive days, at his own expense. *Liv.* 37. c. 59. l. 38. c. 55.—*Cic. Mur.* 14.—*Plin.* 35. c. 11, &c.—*Eutrop.* 4.

Scip'io Nas'ica was son of Cneus Scipio, and cousin of Scipio Africanus. He was refused the consulship, though supported by the interest and fame of the conqueror of Annibal; but he afterwards obtained it, and in that honorable office conquered the Boii, and gained a triumph. He was also successful in an expedition which he undertook in Spain. When the statue of Cybele was brought to Rome from Phrygia, the Roman senate determined to delegate one of their body who was the most remarkable for the purity of his manners and the innocence of his life, to go and meet the goddess in the harbour of Ostia. Nasica was the object of their choice, and as such he was enjoined to bring the statue of the goddess to Rome with the greatest pomp and solemnity. Nasica also distinguished himself by the active part he took in confuting the accusations laid against the two Scipios, Africanus and Asiaticus. *Cic. Mur. Res.* 13. *Orat.* 3. c. 33.—*Liv.* 29. c. 14. l. 35, c. 10, &c.—*Plin.* 7. c. 34.——The son of Nasica, was for his wisdom surnamed Corculum. He was raised to the consulship and censorship, and distinguished himself by the opposition which he made to the violent measures of Cato, who recommended the total destruction of Carthage. *Cic. N. D.* 2. c. 4. *Div.* 2. c. 35. *Br.* 29 & 58.—*Plut. Cat. Mag.* ——The son of the preceding, was known by the surname of Serapion, which he received through derision, because he resembled either a slave or a dealer in swine of that name. Nasica was consul with D. Brutus, and, in those turbulent times, felt the virulence of the tribunes, who imprisoned him for his opposition to their decrees. He was afterwards Pontifex Maximus, and distinguished himself chiefly by killing, with his own hand, the seditious Tib. Gracchus, and thus conciliating the favor and the applause of the senate, while he exposed himself to the persecution of the popular party. He retired from the tumultuous cabals of Rome to Pergamus, where he died in honorable retirement. *Val. Max.* 5. c. 3.—*Cic. Flacc.* 31. *Amic.* 12. *Dom.* 34. *Plan.* 36. *Offic.* 22. *Att.* 6. ep. 1.—*Plin.* 21. c. 3.—*Liv.* 55.

Scip'io Q. Metel'lus Cæcil. Pius, the great grandson of Serapion, was one of the advocates of Verres against Cicero. Pompey married his daughter Cornelia, and took him as his colleague in the consulship, an honor which he had solicited in vain. As the friend of Pompey, he opposed the measures of Cæsar, and, rather than fall into the enemy's hands, destroyed himself, when he found that his ship could not reach the Spanish coast unpursued. Scipio had been adopted by Metellus. *Hirt. B.A.* 96.—*Lucan.* 7. v. 221.—*Cæs. B. G.* 3. c. 88.—*Dio.* 41.—*Appian. B. C.* 2.—*Cic. Att.* 6. ep. 1. *Verr.* 4. c. 35. *Fam.* 8. ep. 8.

Scip'io Publ. Æmilia'nus, son of Palus the conqueror of Perseus, was adopted by the son of Scipio Africanus. He received the same surname as his grandfather, and was called *Africanus the younger*, on account of his victories over Carthage. Æmilianus first appeared in the Roman armies under his father, and afterwards distinguished himself as a legionary tribune in the Spanish provinces, where he killed a Spaniard of gigantic stature, and obtained a mural crown at the siege of Intercatia. He passed into Africa to demand a reinforcement from king Masinissa, the ally of Rome, and was the spectator of a long and bloody battle which was fought between the monarch and the Carthaginians, and which soon produced the third Punic war. Some time after Æmilianus was made ædile, and next appointed consul, though under the age required for that important office. The surname which he had received from his grandfather, he was doomed lawfully to claim as his own. He was empowered to finish the war with Carthage, and as he was permitted by the senate to choose his colleague, he took with him his friend Lælius, whose father of the same name had formerly enjoyed the confidence and shared the victories of the first Africanus. The siege of Carthage was already begun, but the operations of the Romans were not continued with vigor. Scipio had no sooner appeared before the walls of the enemy than every communication with the land was cut off, and that they might not have the command of the sea, a stupendous mole was thrown across the harbour with immense labor and expense. This, which might have disheartened the most active enemy, rendered the Carthaginians more eager in the cause of freedom and independence; all the inhabitants, without distinction of rank, age, or sex, employed themselves without cessation in digging another harbour, and building and equipping another fleet. In a short time, in spite of the vigilance and activity of Æmilianus, the Romans were astonished to see another harbour formed, and 50 gallies suddenly issuing under sail, ready for the engagement. This unexpected fleet, by immediately attacking the Roman ships, might have gained the victory, but the delay of the Carthaginians proved fatal to their cause, and the enemy had sufficient time to prepare themselves. Scipio soon got possession of a small eminence in the harbour, and by the success of his subsequent operations, broke open one of the gates of the city and entered the streets, where he made his way by fire and sword. The surrender of about 50,000 men was followed by the reduction of the citadel, B.C. 147. The city was set on fire, and though Scipio was obliged to demolish its very walls to obey the orders of the Romans, yet he wept bitterly over the melancholy and tragical scene; and in bewailing the miseries of Carthage, expressed his fears, lest Rome in her turn, in some future age, should exhibit such a dreadful conflagration. The return of Æmilianus to Rome was that of another conqueror of Annibal, and, like him, he was honored with a magnificent triumph, and received the name of Africanus. He was not long left in the enjoyment of his glory before he was called to obtain fresh honors. He was chosen consul a second time, and appointed to finish the war which the Romans had hitherto carried on without success or vigorous exertion against Numantia. The fall of Numantia was more noble than that of the capital of Africa, and the conqueror of Carthage obtained the victory only when the garrison had been consumed by famine, or by self-destruction, B.C. 133. From his conquests in Spain, Æmilianus was honored with a second triumph, and with the surname of *Numantinus*. Yet his popularity was short, and by telling the people that the murder of their favorite, his brother-in-law, Gracchus, was lawful, since he was turbulent, and inimical to the peace of the republic, Scipio incurred the displeasure of the tribunes, and was received with hisses. His authority for a moment, quelled their sedition, when he reproached them for their cowardice, and exclaimed, "Factious wretches, do you think that your clamours can intimidate me; me, whom the fury of your enemies never daunted? Is this the gratitude that you owe to my father Paulus, who conquered Macedonia, and to me? Without my family you were slaves. Is this the respect you owe to your deliverer? Is this your affection?" This firmness silenced the murmurs of the assembly, and some time after Scipio retired from the clamours of Rome to Caieta, where, with his friend Lælius, he passed the rest of his time in innocent pleasures and amusement, in diversions which had pleased them when children; and the two greatest men that had ruled the state were often seen on the sea-shore picking up light pebbles, and throwing them on the smooth surface of the waters. Though fond of retirement and literary ease, yet Scipio often interested himself in the affairs of the state. His enemies accused him of aspiring to the dictatorship, and the public displeasure was at the highest, when he had opposed the Sempronian law, and declared himself the patron of the inhabitants of the provinces of Italy. This active part of Scipio was seen with pleasure by the friends of the republic, and not only the senate, but also the citizens, the Latins and neighbouring states, conducted their illustrious friend and patron to his house. It seemed almost the universal wish that the troubles might be quieted by the election of Scipio to the dictatorship; and many presumed that that honor would be on the morrow conferred upon him. In this, however, the expectations of Rome were frustrated; Scipio was found dead in his bed to the astonishment of the world; and those who enquired for the causes of this sudden death, perceived violent marks on his neck, and concluded that he had been strangled, B.C. 128, in the 56th year of his age. This assassination, as it was then generally believed, was committed by the triumvirs, Papirius Carbo, C. Gracchus, and Fulvius Flaccus, who supported the Sempronian law, and by his wife Sempronia, who is charged with introducing the murderers into his room. No enquiries were made after the authors of his death: Gracchus was the favorite of the mob, and the only atonement which the populace made for the death of Scipio, was to attend his funeral, and to show their concern by their cries and loud lamentations. The second Africanns has often been compared to the first of that name; they seemed to be equally great and equally meritorious, and the Romans were unable to decide which of the two was entitled to a greater share of their regard and admiration. Æmilianus, like his grandfather, was fond of literature, and saved from the flames of Carthage many valuable compositions, written by Phœnician and Punic authors. In the midst of his greatness he died poor, and his nephew Q. Fabius Maximus, who inherited his estates, found in his house 32 pounds' weight of silver, and two and a half of gold. His liberality to his brother and sisters deserve the greatest commendations, and indeed no higher encomium can be passed upon his character, private as well as public, than the words of his rival Metellus, who told his sons at the death of Scipio, to go and attend the funeral of the greatest man that ever lived or should live in Rome. *Liv.* 44, &c.—*Cic. de Senec. Orat. in Brut. &c.*—*—Polyb.—Appian. B. C.* 1.—*Paterc.* 1. c. 12, &c. *—Flor.—Plut. in Gr.—Quintil.* 8. c. 6.—*Val. Max.* 4. c. 1. [A bust of Scipio Æmilianus is to be found in the collection at the Villa Albani, near Rome.]

SCIP'IO, a son of the first Africanus, taken captive by Antiochus, king of Syria, and restored to his father without a ransom. He adopted as his son young Æmilianus, the son of Paulus Æmilius, who was afterwards surnamed Africanus. Like his father Scipio, he distinguished himself by his fondness for literature, and his valor in the Roman armies. *Cic. Sen.* 9 & 11.—*Liv.* 40. c. 42. ——The commander of a cohort in Mauritania, in the reign of Vitellius. *Tac. Hist.* 2. c. 59.

SCIP'IO SALU'TIO, a mean person in Cæsar's army in Africa. The general appointed him his chief commander either to ridicule him, or because there was an ancient oracle that declared that the Scipios would ever be victorious in Africa. *Plut. in Cæs.*

SCIP'IO L. CORNE'LIUS, a consul who opposed Sylla. He was at last deserted by his army and proscribed.

SCI'RA or SCIROPHO'RIA, an annual solemnity observed at Athens in honour of Minerva, or, according to others, of Ceres and Proserpine. It received its name either from Sciras, a small town of Attica, or from a native of Dodona called Scirus, who was killed in a battle between the Eleusinians and Erechtheus king of Athens. He was buried by the people of Eleusis in a neighbouring village, which, to commemorate his memory assumed his name. The festival was celebrated in the month of June, called *Scirophorion* from that circumstance. During its continuance there was a race called ὀσχοφόρια, because they carried vine branches full of grapes in their hands. *Paus.* 1. c. 36.—*Strab.* 9.—*Gyrald. H. D.* 11.—*Aristoph. Schol.—Suidas.—Harpocration.*

SCIRA'DIUM, a promontory of Attica on the Sinus Saronicus. *Plut. in Solon.*

SCI'RAS, an ancient name of Ægina. Minerva was also called Sciras. *Strab.* 9. *Vid.* Scira.

SCIRA'TÆ, a people of India, in whose country were immense serpents. *Ælian, de Anim.* l. 26.

SCIRES'SA, a mountain of Arcadia. *Plin.* 4. c. 5.

SCI'RI or SCIR'RI, a people of Galatia.——A people of Pæonia. *Steph.*

SCIRI'TIS, a region of Caria, containing twelve cities. *Steph.*

SCI'RON, a celebrated thief in Attica, who plundered the inhabitants of the country, and threw them down from the highest rocks into the sea, after he had obliged them to wait upon him and to wash his feet Theseus attacked him, and treated him as he treated travellers. According to Ovid, the earth as well as the sea, refused to receive the bones of Sciron, which remained for some time suspended in the air, till they were changed into large rocks called *Scironia Saxa*, situate between Megara and Corinth. There was a road near them, which bore the name of Sciron; it was naturally small and narrow, but was afterwards enlarged by the emperor Adrian. Some suppose that Ino threw herself into the sea from one of these rocks. Sciron had married the daughter of Cychreus, a king of Salamis. He was brother-in-law to Telamon the son of Æacus. *Ovid. Met.* 7. v. 444, *Heroid.* 2. v. 69.—*Strab.* 9. *—Mela*, 2. c. 13.—*Plin.* 2. c. 47.—*Diod.* 4.—*Hygin.* fab. 38.—*Propert.* 3. el. 14. v. 12.—*Paus.* 1. c. 44.—*Plut. in Thes.—Tzetzes, Chil.* 5. *Hist.* 10. *—Seneca. N. Q.* 5. c. 17.

SCIRTH'ARI, a people of Dalmatia. *Plin.* 3. c. 22.
SCIRTO'NIUM, a city of Arcadia. *Steph. ex Paus.*1.8.
SCIR'TUS a river of Syria, flowing through Edessa into the Euphrates.
SCI'RUS, a village of Arcadia, of which the inhabitants were called Sciritæ. *Steph.*——A plain and river of Attica near Megara. *Paus.* 1. c. 36.
SCIS'SIS, a town of Spain. *Liv.* 21. c. 60.
SCI'THÆ, a town of Thrace, or Macedonia, near Potidæa. *Steph.*
SCO'DRA, a town of Illyricum, where Gentius resided. *Liv.* 43. c. 20.
SCOE'NUS a river of Thrace near Maronea. *Mela*, 1. c. 16.
SCO'LUS, a mountain of Bœotia.——A town of Macedonia near Olynthus. *Strab.*
SCOM'BRUS or SCO'MIUS, a mountain of Thrace, near Rhodope. *Aristot.*
SCOP'ADÆ, a people of Thessaly. *Schol. Theocr.*
SCO'PAS, an architect and sculptor of Ephesus, for some time employed in making the mausoleum which Artemisia raised to her husband, and which was reckoned one of the seven wonders of the world. One of his statues of Venus was among the antiquities with which Rome was adorned. Scopas lived about 430 years B.C. *Paus.* 1. c. 43. 1 2. c. 10. l. 6. c. 25.—*Plin.* 34. c. 8. l. 36. c. 5.—*Cic. Div.* 1. c. 13.—*Horat.* 4. od. 8. v. 6.—*Vitr.* 9. c. 9.——An Ætolian who raised some forces to assist Ptolemy Epiphanes, king of Ægypt, against his enemies Antiochus and his allies. He afterwards conspired against the Ægyptian monarch, and was put to death, B.C. 196. *Liv.* 26. c. 24.——An ambassador to the court of the emperor Domitian.——A Thessalian who refused to pay Simonides the whole of the reward which he had promised him for a poem in his praise, desiring him to recover the rest from Castor and Pollux, whose names he had introduced into his composition. Some time after, Simonides was called away from a banquet by two young men who were supposed to be the two despised gods, and immediately the roof of the house in which he was fell and crushed to death Scopas and the rest of his guests. *Cic. Orat.* 2. c. 86.—*Phædr. Fab.*
SCO'PE, an island in the Rhodian Sea. *Plin.* 5. c. 31.——A small town of Libya. *Ptol.*
SCO'PIA, *plur.*, a city of Upper Mysia. It is called Scupa by *Ptolemy.*
SCO'PIA EXTRE'MA, a promontory of Doris. *Ptol. Strabo* seems to call it Termerium.
SCO'PIUM, a town of Thessaly. *Polyb.* 1. 5.—*Cedren.*
SCO'PIUS, a mountain of Macedonia. *Plin.* 4. c. 10.——A mountain of Thrace.——A river of Bithynia.
SCORDIS'CI or SCORDIS'CÆ, a people of Pannonia and Thrace, well known during the reign of the Roman emperors for their barbarity and uncivilized manners. They were fond of drinking human blood, and generally sacrificed their captives to their gods. *Liv.* 41. c. 19.—*Strab.* 7.—*Flor.* 3. c. 4.—*Ammian.* 27. c. 4.—*Justin.* 23. c. 3.—*Herodot.* 4.
SCORDIS'CUS, a mountain of Cappadocia. *Ptol.*
SCOR'PIO, one of the signs of the zodiac. Anciently the place of Scorpio was the sixth part of the zodiac, but the sign of Libra was afterwards introduced where it extended its claws (*Brachia*, or *Chelæ*). The Scorpion was placed among the constellations by Jupiter, because the vanity of Orion had been punished by its bite. *Vid.* Orion. *Lactant. ad Stat. Theb.* 7. v. 237.—*Virg. G.* 1. v. 35.—*Plin.* 17. c. 24.—*Colum.* 11. c. 1.—*Horat.* 2. od. 17. v. 17.—*Ovid. Met.* 2. v. 195.
SCOR'PUS, a person who often won the prize in the chariot race, in the Ludi Circenses, under Domitian. *Mart.* l. 4. epigr. 67. & l. 10. epigr. 50.
SCOTA'NA, a small town in Arcadia. *Paus. in Arcad.*
SCO'TI, the ancient inhabitants of Scotland, mentioned as different from the Picts. *Claudian. de Hon.* 3. *cons.* v. 54.
SCOTI'NUS, a surname of Heraclitus. *Strab.* 15.
SCOTUS'SA, a town of Thessaly, at the north of Larissa, and of the Peneus. It was perfidiously destroyed by Alexander of Pheræ, and the inhabitants all slaughtered. *Liv.* 28. c. 5 & 7. l. 36. c. 14.—*Strab.* 7 & 9.—*Paus.* 6. c. 5.—*Polyb.* 8. c. 39.——A town in Macedonia. *Plin.* 4. c. 10.
SCRIBO'NIA, a daughter of Scribonius, who married Augustus after he divorced Claudia. He had by her a daughter, the celebrated Julia. Scribonia was some time after repudiated, that Augustus might marry Livia. She had been married twice before she became the wife of the emperor. *Sueton. in Aug.* 62.—*Paterc.* 2. c. 100.—*Tacit. Ann.* 2. c. 7.——A woman who married Crassus.——The wife of Sext. Pompeius. *Cæs. B. C.* 1. c. 26.
SCRIBONIA'NUS CRAS'SUS, a man in the age of Nero. Some of his friends wished him to be competitor for the imperial purple against Vespasian, which he declined. *Tacit. H.* 4. c. 39.
SCRIBONIA'NUS, the name of two brothers who did nothing without each other's consent. *Tacit. H.* 4. c. 41.
SCRIBO'NIUS, a man who made himself master of the kingdom of Bosporus.——A physician in the age of Augustus and Tiberius. He wrote a book *De medicamentorum compositione. Castellan. de Ill. Med.* p. 119.
SCRIBO'NIUS LI'BO, a man who wrote annals, A.D. 22. The best edition of Scribonius is that of Patav. 4to. 1655. *Cic. in Br.* l. 2. *de Orat.* 12, &c. —*Val. Max.* 8. c. 1.——A friend of Pompey, &c.——A tribune who accused Serv. Galba of misconduct in the province of Spain. *Cic. Orat.* 1. c. 53. l. 2. c. 65.
SCRIBO'NIUS LI'BO DRU'SUS, a prætor put to death under Tiberius, upon the information of Firmius Catus. *Tac. Ann.* 2. c. 27.
SCROB'ILUS, a promontory of Africa, on the Arabian Gulf. *Ptol.*
SCRO'PHA, a surname of the Tremellii, one of whom wrote on husbandry, &c. *Plin.* 17. c. 27. —*Varro, R. R.* 2. c 4.—*Macrob.* 1. c. 6.—*Cic. Att.* 5. ep. 4. l. 6. ep. 1.
SCULTEN'NA, a river of Gallia Cispadana, falling into the Po, now called Panaro. *Liv.* 41. c. 12 & 18.—*Plin.* 3. c. 16.
SCY'BIS, a marble sculptor of Crete. *Plin.* 36. c. 4.
SCY'BROS, a small region of Macedonia. *Steph.*
SCYDIS'SA, a mountain near Colchis. *Strab.* 12.
SCY'DRA, a city of Macedonia. *Steph.*
SCYLACE'UM, SCYLA'CIUM or SCYLLE'TIUM, a town of the Brutii, built by Mnestheus at the head of an Athenian colony. As Virgil has applied the epithet *Navifragum* to Scylaceum, some suppose that either the poet was mistaken in his knowledge of the place, because there are no apparent dangers to navigation there, or that he confounds this place with a promontory of the same name on the Tuscan Sea. Servius explains this passage by supposing that the houses of the place were originally built with the shipwrecked vessels of Ulysses' fleet, a most puerile explanation! *Virg. Æn.* 3. v. 553. —*Strab.* 6.—*Mela*, 2. c. 4.—*Flacc.* 3. v. 36.—*Servius ad Virg. loco. cit.*—*Turneb. Adv.* 19. c. 21. 20. c. 30.—*Plin.* 3. c. 10.
SCY'LAX, a geographer and mathematician of Caria, in the age of Darius, son of Hystaspes, about 550 years B.C. He was commissioned by Darius to make discoveries in the east, and, after a journey of 30 months, visited Ægypt. Some suppose that he was the first who invented geographical tables. The latest edition of the *Periplus* of Scylax is that of Gronovius, 4to. L. Bat. 1697. *Herodot.* 4. c. 44.—*Strab.*—*Fabr. B. Gr.* 4. c. 2.—*Sax. Onom.* 1. p. 29.—*Is. Voss. ad Scylac. Caryand. Peripl.*
SCY'LAX, a river of Cappadocia. *Strab.*
SCYL'LA, a daughter of Nisus, king of Megara, who became enamoured of Minos, as that monarch besieged her father's capital. To make him sensible of her passion, she informed him that she would deliver Megara into his hands, if he promised to marry her. Minos consented; and as the prosperity of Megara depended on the golden hair which was on the head of Nisus, Scylla cut it off as her father was asleep, and from that moment the sallies of the Megareans were unsuccessful, and the enemy easily became master of the place. Scylla was disappointed in her expectations, and Minos treated her with such contempt

and ridicule, that she threw herself from a tower into the sea, or, according to other accounts, she was changed into a lark by the gods, and her father into a hawk. *Ovid. Trist.* 2. v. 393. *Met.* 8. fab. 1.—*Paus.* 2. c. 34.—*Propert.* 3. el. 19. v. 21.—*Hygin.* fab. 198.—*Virg. G.* 1. v. 405, &c.—*Servius ad Virg. G.* 1. v. 404. *Æn.* 3. v. 420. l. 6. v. 286.—*Lactant. ad Theb.* 1. v. 332.—*Tzetzes ad Lyc.* 934.——A daughter of Typhon, or, as some say, of Phorcys, who was greatly loved by Glaucus, one of the deities of the sea. Scylla scorned the addresses of Glaucus, and the god, to render her more propitious, applied to Circe, whose knowledge of herbs and incantations were universally admitted. Circe no sooner saw him than she became enamoured of him, and, instead of giving him the required assistance, attempted to make him forget Scylla, but in vain. To punish her rival, Circe poured the juice of some poison ous herbs into the waters of the fountain where Scylla bathed; and no sooner had the nymph touched the place, than she found every part of her body below the waist changed into frightful monsters like dogs, which never ceased barking. The rest of her body assumed an equally hideous form. She found herself supported by twelve feet, and had six different heads, each with three rows of teeth. This sudden metamorphosis so terrified her, that she threw herself into that part of the sea which separates the coast of Italy from Sicily, where she was changed into rocks, which continued to bear her name, and which were universally deemed by the ancients as dangerous to sailors as the whirlpool of Charybdis on the coast of Sicily. The waves are described by modern navigators as roaring dreadfully, when driven into the rough and uneven cavities of the rock during a storm. *Homer. Odys.* 12. v, 85.—*Ovid. Met.* 14. v. 66, &c.—*Paus.* 2. c. 34.—*Hygin.* fab. 199.—Some authors, as *Propertius*, 4. el. 4. v. 39., and *Virgil*, ecl. 6. v. 74., with *Ovid, Fast.* 4. v. 500., have confounded the daughter of Typhon wlth the daughter of Nisus. *Virg. Æn.* 3. v. 424, &c.—*Servius ad Æn.* 3. v. 420.

SCYL'LA, the name of a ship in the fleet of Æneas, commanded by Cloanthus, &c. *Virg. Æn.* 5. v. 122.

SCYLLÆ'UM, a promontory of Peloponnesus, on the coast of Argolis. It is called Scillium by *Ptolemy*, and is now Cape Scigli. *Steph.*——A promontory of the Brutii in Italy, supposed to be the same as Scylaceum, near which was the famous whirlpool Scylla, from which the name is derived. It is now Capo di Volpe.

SCYLLETIUM, a city of the Brutii, founded by a colony of Athenians under Mnestheus. *Cassiod.* —*Strab.* 6.—*Joh. Marsh. Can. Chron.* sec. 17. It is now Squillaci. *Vid.* Scylaceum.

SCYL'LIAS, a celebrated swimmer of Scione, who enriched himself by diving after the goods which had been lost in the Persian ships near Pelium. Is is said that he could dive 80 stadia under the water. *Herodot.* 8. c. 8.—*Paus.* 10. c. 19.—*Plin.* 35. c. 11.

SCYL'LIS and DIPŒ'NUS, statuaries of Crete, before the age of Cyrus, king of Persia. They were said to be sons and pupils of Dædalus, and established a school at Sicyon, where they taught successfully the principles of their art. *Paus.* 2. c. 15.—*Plin.* 36. c. 4.

SCYL'LUS (*-untis*), a town of Achaia, given to Xenophon by the Lacedæmonians. *Strab.*

SCYLU'RUS, a monarch of Tartary who left 80 sons. He called them to his bedside as he was on the point of expiring, and by enjoining them to break a bundle of sticks tied together, and afierwards separately, convinced them, that, when firmly united, their power would be insuperable; but that, if they were ever disunited, they would fall an easy prey to their enemies. *Plut. de Garr.*——A king of Chersonesus, who built many fortified places. *Strab.* 7.

SCYMNI'ADÆ, a people dwelling with the Getæ. *Steph.* They were probably the Scymnitæ of *Ptolemy*, whom he places in European Sarmatia.

SCYM'NUS, a geographer of Chius. *Steph. in* Πάρας.

SCYPH'IA, a town of the Clazomenians. *Id.*

SCYP'PIUM, a town in the neighbourhood of Colophon. *Paus.* 7. c. 3.

SCY'RAS, a river of Laconia. *Paus.* 3. c. 25.

SCY'RI, a people of Arabia. *Plin.* 6. c. 23.

SCYR'IAS, a name applied to Deidamia as a native of Scyrus. *Ovid. A.* 1. v. 682.

SCYRI'TÆ, a people of the Nomades. *Id.* 6. c. 28.

SCYR'MUS, a city near Cyzicus. *Steph.*

SCY'RON, a follower of Epicurus. *Cic.* 4. *Acad.* 33.

SCY'ROS or SCY'RUS, a rocky and barren island in the Ægæan, at the distance of about 28 miles north-east from Eubœa, sixty miles in circumference. It was originally in the possession of the Pelasgians and Carians. Achilles retired to this island, that he might not go to the Trojan war, and became father of Neoptolemus by Deidamia, the daughter of king Lycomedes. Scyrus was conquered by the Athenians under Cimon. *Homer. Odys.* 10. v. 508.—*Ovid. Met.* 7. v. 464. l. 13. v. 156.—*Paus.* l. c. 7.—*Strab.* 9.—*Mela*, 2. c. 7.—*Plin.* 4. c. 12. l. 36. c. 17.—*Servius in Æn.* 2. v. 477.—*Tzetzes ad Lyc.* 184.

SCY'THÆ, the inhabitants of Scythia. *Vid.* Scythia.

SCY'THES or SCY'THA, a son of Jupiter by a daughter of Tellus. Half his body was that of a man, and the rest that of a serpent. He became king of a country which he called Scythia. *Diod.* 2.——A son of Hercules and Echidna.

SCYTHE'NI, a people near the Macrones. *Steph. ex Xenoph. Anab.* 1. 4.

SCYTH'IA, a large country situate in the most northern parts of Europe and Asia, from which circumstance it is generally denominated European and Asiatic. The most northern parts of Scythia were uninhabited on account of the extreme coldness of the climate. The more southern parts in Asia which were inhabited were distinguished by the name of Scythia *intra et extra Imaum*, &c. The boundaries of Scythia were unknown to the ancients, as no traveller had penetrated beyond tho vast tracts of land which lay at the north, east, and west. Scythia comprehended the modern kingdoms of Tartary, Russia in Asia, Siberia, Muscovy, the Crimea, Poland, part of Hungary, Lithuania, the northern parts of Germany, Sweden, Norway, &c. The Scythians were divided into several nations or tribes; they had no cities, but continually changed their habitations. They inured themselves to bear labor and fatigue; they despised money, lived upon milk, and covered themselves with the skins of their cattle. The virtues seemed to flourish among them, and that philosophy and moderation which other nations wished to acquire by study, seemed natural to them. Some authors, however, represent them as a savage and barbarous people, who fed upon human flesh, drank the blood of their enemies, and used the skulls of travellers as vessels in their sacrifices to their gods. The Scythians made several irruptions upon the more southern provinces of Asia, especially B.C. 624, when they remained in possession of Asia Minor for 28 years; and we find them at different periods extending their conquests in Europe, and penetrating as far as Ægypt. Their government was monarchical, and the deference which they paid to their sovereigns was unparalleled. When the king died, his body was carried through every province, where it was received iu solemn procession, and afterwards buried. In the first centuries after Christ, they invaded the Roman empire with the Sarmatians. *Vid.* Sarmatia. *Herodot.* 1. c. 4, &c.—*Strab.* 7. —*Diod.* 2.—*Val. Max.* 5. c. 4.—*Justin.* 2. c. 1, &c.—*Ovid. Met.* 1. v. 64. l. 2. v. 224.—*Paus.* 8. c. 43.—*Servius ad Virg. Ecl.* 2. v. 11. *G.* 3. v. 349. *Æn.* 4, &c.

SCYTHI'NUS, a Greek poet of Teos in Ionia, who wrote Iambics. *Diog. in Herac.*—*Athen.* 11.—*Plut. cur Pyth.*—*Gyrald. H. P.* 3.

SCY'THON, a man said to have had the power of changing himself into a woman whenever he pleased. *Ovid. Met.* 4. v. 280.

SCYTHOP'OLIS, a town of Syria, anciently called Nysa, from the nurse of Bacchus, who was said to have been its founder. *Strab.* 16.—*Plin.* 5. c. 18.—*Marcell.* 19. c. 29.——A city of Libya. *Steph.*

SCYTHOTAU'RI, a people of Chersonesus Taurica, who barbarously offered, on the altars of their goddess Diana, all strangers who were unhappily thrown on their shores. *Plin.* 4. c. 12.—*Solin.* 25.

SCYTHRA'NIUS, a town of Marmarica. *Ptol.*

SEBAS'TA or SEBAS'TE, a town of Judæa, so called in honor of Augustus by Herod, who had embellished it. Its ancient name was Samaria. *Strab.* 16.—*Joseph. Ant. Jud.* 15. c. 11.

Sebas'ta, a town of Cilicia. It is now Sevesta. ——A town of the Damnonii in Britain. It is now Liskeard. The name was common to several cities, being given to them in compliment to Augustus.

SEBASTI'A or SEBAS'TIA, a city of Armenia. *Antonin.*

SEBA'TUM, a town of Noricum. *Id.*

SEB'EDA, a harbour of Lycia. *Steph.*

SEBENDU'NUM, a city of the Castellani in Spain. *Ptol.*

SEBEN'ICUM or SI'CUM, a city of Dalmatia. *Id.* It is now Sebenico.

SEBENNY'TUS, a town of the Delta in Ægypt. That branch of the Nile which flows near it is called *Sebennytic.* *Plin.* 5. c. 10.

SEBE'THUS, now Fiume della Maddalena, a small river of Campania, falling into the bay of Naples, whence the epithet *Sebethis*, given to one of the nymphs who frequented its borders, and became mother of Œbalus by Telon. *Virg. Æn.* 7. v. 734.—*Stat.* 1. *Sylv.* 2. v. 263.—*Servius ad Virg. loco.*

SEBO'SUS, a friend of Catulus. *Cic. Att.* 11. ep. 14, &c.

SEBRI'APA, a city of Asiatic Sarmatia. *Ptol.*

SEBUSIA'NI or SEGUSIA'NI, a people of Celtic Gaul.

SECAN'DE, a town of Upper Æthiopia. *Plin.* 6. c. 30.

SEC'ELA, a city of Palestine. *Steph. ex Josepho.*

SECHNU'PHIS, an Ægyptian priest, preceptor of Plato. *Clem. Strom.* l. 1.

SECON'TIA or SEGUN'TIA, now Siguenza, a city of Hispania Tarraconensis. *Liv.* 34. c. 18.

SE'COR, a harbour of Gallia Aquitanica. *Ptol.*

SECTA'NUS, an infamous debauchee in the age of *Horace.* 1. sat. 4. v. 112.

SECUNDA'NI, a people of Gaul. *Plin.* 3. c. 4.

SECUN'DUS JU'LIUS, a man who published some harangues and orations in the age of the emperor Titus.

Secun'dus, a favorite of Nero.——One of the associates of Sejanus.

Secun'dus Pompo'nius, a poet. *Vid.* Pomponius.

SECUS'SES, a people of the Alps. *Plin.* 3. c. 20.

SEDETA'NI or SEDENTA'NI. *Vid.* Hedetani.

SEDIBONIA'TES, a people of Gallia Aquitanica. *Plin.* 4. c. 19.

SEDIG'ITUS VOLCA'TIUS, a Latin poet who made a comparison of the merits of the ancient Roman poets, in Iambic verse, in which he showed himself a critic of learning, genius, and discernment. Some suppose that he was called Sedigitus because he had six fingers on each hand. Only thirteen of his verses are preserved. *Plin.*

SEDITA'NI or SEDENTA'NI, a people of Spain. *Ital.* 3. v. 372.

SEDOCHE'ZI, a people of Pontus, one of whose kings is mentioned by *Tacitus. Hist.* 3. c. 48. Some consider it a corrupt reading.

SEDU'LIUS, a man of mean occupation employed by Clodius. *Cic. pro Dom.* 30.

Sedu'lius Cœ'lius, a native of Ireland, who, after travelling for information, settled at Rome, where he distinguished himself as a Christian writer and poet, in the reign of Theodosius the younger. His poems possess elegance and spirit, and prove him to have been a man of genius and learning. They are all on scriptural subjects, the largest of which is divided into five books, containing 1739 heroic verses, besides shorter pieces to the number of 262 lines. The best editions are that of Eisenberg, Lips. 1499, and that of Gruner, Lips. 1747. *Harles. Not. Lit. Rom.* 1. p. 743.—*Sax. Onom* 1. p. 494.

SEDU'NI, an ancient nation of Belgic Gaul. *Cæs. B. G.* 3. c. 7. *Plin.* 3. c. 20.

SEDU'SII, a people of Germany, near the Suevi. *Cæs. B. G.* 1. c. 51.

SEGALLAU'NI or SEGOVELLAU'NI, a people of Gallia Narbonensis, on the Rhone. *Plin.* 3. c. 4.

SEG'EDA or SEG'IDA, a town of Hispania Tarraconensis. *Strab.*—*Steph.* It is now Seges.

Seg'eda a town of Hispania Bætica, called also Julia Contributa. *Plin.* 3. c. 1.

SEGEL'OCUM, a town of Britain. *Antonin.* It is now Littleborough in Nottinghamshire, according to Camden.

SEGER'RA, a town of Hispania Tarraconensis. *Ptol.* It is now Cigura.

SEGES'TA, a town of Sicily, founded by Æneas, or, according to some, by Crinisus. *Vid.* Ægesta.

SEGES'TES, a German friendly to the Roman interest in the time of Germanicus. His daughter married Arminius. *Tacit. Ann.* 1. c. 55.

SEGE'TIA or SEGES'TA, a divinity at Rome, invoked by the husbandmen that their harvests might be plentiful. *Aug. de Civ. D.* 4. c. 8.—*Macrob.* 1. c. 16.—*Plin.* 18. c. 2.

SEGET'ICA, a city of Mœsia, taken by M. Crassus. *Dio.*

SEGIME'RUS, a brother of Segestes, was general of the Cherusci. *Tac. Ann.* 1. c. 71.—*Strab.* 7.

SEGIMUN'DUS, a son of Segestes, sent as ambassador to Germanicus. *Tac. Ann.* 1. c. 57.—*Strab.* 6. c. 7.

SEGI'SA, a town of the Bastitani in Spain. *Ptol.*

SEGIS'AMA JU'LIA or SEGES'AMA, a town on the borders of the Varduli in Hispania Tarraconensis. *Strab.*—*Steph.* It is now Veyzama.

SEGISAMUN'CLUM, or SEGISMON'CULUM, a town of Hispania Tarraconensis. *Ptol.*

SEG'NI, a people with a town of the same name in Belgic Gaul. *Cæs. B. G.* 6. c. 31.

SEGOBRI'GA, a town of Spain, near Saguntum. *Plin.* 3. c. 3.

SEGODU'NUM, a city of Germany. *Ptol.*

SEG'ONAX, a prince in the southern parts of Britain, who opposed Cæsar by order of Cassivelaunus, &c. *Cæs. Bell. G.* 5. c. 22.

SEGON'TIA or SEGUN'TIA, a town on the north of Hispania Tarraconensis. *Liv.* 34. c. 10.——A town a little at the north of Calpe.

SEGONTI'ACI, a people of Belgic Gaul, who submitted to J. Cæsar. *B. G.* 5. c. 21.

SEGO'VIA, a town of Spain, of great power in the age of the Cæsars. *Ptol.* There was also another of the same name in Lusitania. Both were founded by the Celtiberi.

SEGU'LIUS, a man of worthless character who irritated Augustus against Cicero. *Cic. Fam.* 11. ep. 20 & 21.

SEGUN'TIUM, a town of Britain, supposed to be Carnarvon in Wales. *Cæs. G.* 5. c. 21.

SEGUSIA'NI, a people of Gaul on the Loire. *Cæs. G.* 1. c. 10.—*Plin.* 4. c. 18.

SEGU'SIO, a town of Piedmont on the Durius. *Plin.* 3. c. 17.

SE'IA, a rural divinity at Rome, who presided over corn, before it sprang up above the earth, after sowing. The growth of corn was under the particular protection of different deities, especially among a nation devoted to agricultural improvement; hence the worship paid to Seia, to Occator, the god of harrowing, to Sarritor, the god of weeding, to Nodotus, the god who watched over the blade when it became knotty, to Robigus, &c. *Plin.* 18. c. 2.—*Servius ad Virg. G.* 1. v. 21.—*Aug. de Civ. D.* 4. c. 8.—*Gyrald. H. D.* 1.—*Arnob.* 4.

SEJA'NUS Æ'LIUS, a native of Vulsinum, in Tuscany, who distinguished himself in the court of Tiberius. His father's name was Seius Strabo, a Roman knight, commander of the prætorian guards. His mother was descended from the Junian family. Sejanus first gained the favor of Caius Cœsar, the grandson of Augustus, but afterwards attached himself to the views and interest of Tiberius, who then sat on the imperial throne. The emperor, who was naturally of a suspicious temper, was free and open with Sejanus, and, while he distrusted others, communicated his greatest secrets to this fawning favorite. Sejanus improved this confidence, and when he had found that he possessed the esteem of Tiberius, next endeavoured to become the favorite of the soldiers and the darling of the senate. As commander of the prætorian guards he was the second man in Rome, and in that important office he made use of insinuations and every mean artifice to make himself beloved and revered. His affability and condescension gained him the hearts of the common soldiers, and by appointing his own favourrites and adherents to places of trust and honor, all the officers and centurions of the army became devoted to his interest. The views of Sejanus in this were well known; yet to advance with more success, he attempted to gain the affections of the senators. In this he met with no opposition. A man who has the disposal of places of honor and dignity, and who has the command of the public money, cannot but be the favorite of those who need his assistance. It is even said, that Sejanus gained to his views all the wives of the senators, by a private and most secret promise of marriage to each of them, whenever he had made himself independent and sovereign of Rome. Yet however successful with the best and noblest families in the empire, Sejanus had to combat numbers in the house of the emperor; but these seeming obstacles were soon removed. All the children and grand-children of Tiberius were sacrificed to the ambition of the favorite under various pretences; and Drusus, the son of the emperor, by striking Sejanus, made his destruction sure and inevitable. Livia, the wife of Drusus, was gained by Sejanus, and though the mother of many children, she was prevailed upon to assist her adulterer in the murder of her husband, and consented to marry him when Drusus was dead. No sooner was Drusus poisoned, than Sejanus openly declared his wish to marry Livia. This was at first strongly opposed by Tiberius, but the emperor by recommending the son of Germanicus to the senators for his successor, rendered Sejanus bold and determined. He was more urgent in his demands; and when he could not gain the consent of the emperor, persuaded him to retire to solitude from the noise of Rome, and the troubles of government. Tiberius, naturally fond of ease and luxury, yielded to his representations, and retired to Campania, leaving Sejanus at the head of the empire. This was highly gratifying to the favorite, who was now without a master. Prudence and moderation might have made him what he wished to be, but Sejanus offended the whole empire when he declared that he was emperor of Rome, and Tiberius only the dependent prince of the island of Capræa, to which he had retired. Tiberius was upon this fully convinced of the designs of Sejanus, and when he had been informed that his favorite had had the meanness and audacity to ridicule him by introducing him upon the stage, the emperor ordered him to be accused before the senate. Sejanus was deserted by all his pretended friends, as soon as by fortune; and the man who aspired to the empire, and who called himself the favorite of the people, the darling of the prætorian guards, and the companion of Tiberius, was seized without resistance, and the same day strangled in prison, A.D. 31. His remains were exposed to the fury and insolence of the populace, and afterwards thrown into the Tiber. His children and all his relations were involved in his ruin, and Tiberius sacrificed to his resentment and suspicions, all those who were even connected with Sejanus, or had shared his favors or enjoyed his confidence. *Tacit. Ann.* 3, &c.—*Dio.* 58.—*Suet. in Tib.*—*Juv.* 10. v. 74.

SE'IUS CN., a Roman who had a famous horse of large size, and uncommon beauty, supposed to have been of the same breed as the horses of Diomedes, which were slain by Hercules. Seius was put to death by Antony, and as Dolabella, the next owner of the horse, was slain in battle against Cassius, and Cassius himself, and Antony, the next possessors of the animal, fell by their own hand, it was observed that whoever obtained possession of this horse became unfortunate, and lost all his property, with every member of his family. Hence arose the proverb, *ille homo habet Sejanum equum*, applied to such as were oppressed with misfortunes. *Aul. Gellius*, 3. c. 9.—*Erasm. Chil.* 1. *Cent.* 10. c. 97.

SE'IUS STRA'BO, the father of Sejanus, was a Roman knight and commander of the prætorian guards.

SE'IUS, a freedman of Atticus. *Cic.* 5. *Att.* 18.

SE'IUS CNE'US, a senator, mentioned by *Cicero. Cluent.* 38.

SE'IUS MAR'CUS, a Roman who sold corn during a famine at so cheap a rate, that though reduced to poverty, he procured his election against Piso, a man of elevated rank and great fortune. *Cic. Planc.* 5.

SE'IUS Q. POST'HUMUS, a Roman knight, poisoned by means of Clodius, because he refused to sell him his house. *Cic. Har.* 14. *Dom.* 44.

SELAMBI'NA, a city of Hispania Bætica. *Ptol.*

SELAMPU'RA or LAMPU'RA, a city of India without the Ganges. *Ptol.*

SELA'SIA. *Vid.* Sellasia.

SELEM'NUS, a river of Achaia. *Paus.* 7. c. 23. *Vid.* Selimnus.

SELE'NE, the wife of Antiochus king of Syria, put to death by Tigranes, king of Armenia. She was daughter of Physcon, king of Ægypt, and had first married her brother Lathurus, according to the custom of her country, and afterwards, by desire of her mother, her other brother Gryphus. At the death of Gryphus she had married Antiochus Cyzicenus, by whom she had two sons Antiochus Asiaticus, and Seleucus Cybiosactes. According to Appian, she first married the father, and after his death, his son Eusebes. *Cic. Verr.* 4. c. 27.—*Joseph. Ant.* 13. c. 29.—*Appian. Syr.* &c. The word signifies in Greek the moon, whence it is taken in the same sense in Greek writers as Diana, or Luna, among the Latins. *Hesiod. Th.* 136 & 137.—*Diod.* 3.

SELE'NE, a city of Tyrrhenia. *Steph.*

SELENU'SIA PA'LUS, a lake of Ionia, near Colophon. *Strab.* It is now Lago di Altobosco.

SELEUCE'NA or SELEU'CIS, a country of Syria, in Asia. *Vid.* Seleucis.

SELEUCI'A, a town of Syria, on the sea shore, generally called Pieria, to distinguish it from others of the same name. There were no less than 13 cities which were called Seleucia, and which had all received their name from Seleucus Nicanor. They were situate in the kingdom of Syria, in Cilicia, and near the Tigris and Euphrates. *Flor.* 3. c. 11.—*Plut. in Dem.*—*Mela*, 1. c. 12.—*Strab.* 11 & 15.—*Plin.* 6. c. 26.——The residence of the Parthian kings. *Cic.* 8. *Fam.* 14. The English form is Seleu'cia.

SELEU'CIDÆ, a surname given to those monarchs who sat on the throne of Syria, which was founded by Seleucus, the son of Antiochus. The era of the Seleucidæ begins with the taking of Babylon by Seleucus, B.C. 312, and ends at the conquest of Syria by Pompey, B.C. 65. The order in which these monarchs reigned is shown in the account of Syria. *Vid.* Syria.

SELEU'CIS, a division of Syria which received its name from Seleucus, the founder of the Syrian empire after the death of Alexander the Great. It was also called Tetrapolis from the four cities it contained, called also sister cities; Seleucia called after Seleucus, Antioch called after his father, Laodicea after his mother, and Apamea after his wife. *Strab.* 16.

SELEU'CUS the First, one of the captains of Alexander the Great, surnamed *Nicanor* or *Victorious*, was son of Antiochus. After the king's death he received Babylon as his province; but his ambitious views, as he passed through his territories, rendered him so unpopular that he fled for safety to the court of his friend Ptolemy king of Ægypt. He was soon after enabled to recover Babylon, which Antigonus had seized in his absence, and increased his dominions by the immediate conquest of Media, and some of the neighbouring provinces. When he had strengthened himself in his empire, Seleucus imitated the rest of the generals of Alexander, and assumed the title of independent monarch. He afterwards made war against Antigonus, with the united forces of Ptolemy, Cassander, and Lysimachus; and after that monarch had been conquered and slain, his territories were divided among his victorious enemies. When Seleucus became master of Syria, he built a city there, which he called Antioch, in honor of his father, and made the capital of his dominions. He also made war against Demetrius and Lysimachus, though he had originally married Stratonice, the daughter of the former, and had lived in the closest friendship with the latter. Seleucus was at last murdered by one of his servants called Ptolemy Ceraunus, a man on whom he had bestowed the greatest favours, and whom he had distinguished by acts of the most unbounded confidence. According to Arrian, Seleucus was the greatest and most powerful of the princes who inherited portions of the Macedonian empire after the death of Alexander. His benevolence has been commended: and it has been observed, that he conquered, not to enslave nations, but to make them more happy. He founded no less than 59 cities in different parts of his empire, which he peopled with Greek colonies, whose national industry, learning, religion, and spirit were communicated to the indolent and luxurious inhabitants of Asia. Seleucus was a great benefactor to the Greeks; he restored to the Athenians the library and statues which Xerxes had carried away from their city when he invaded Greece, and among them were Harmodius and Aristogiton. Seleucus was murdered 280 years B.C. in the 32nd year of his reign, and the 78th, or, according to others, the 73rd year of his age, as he was going to conquer Macedonia, where he intended to finish his days in peace and tranquillity in that province where he was born. He was succeeded by Antiochus Soter. He is sometimes represented in statues and medals, with horns on his head, because at a sacrifice he seized with his own hands the bull that was escaping from the priest, and brought it back by the horns to the altar. *Justin.* 13. c. 4. l. 15. c. 4. l. 16. c. 3, &c.—*Plut. in Dem.*—*Plin.* 6. c. 17. l. 29. c. 1.—*Paus.* 8. c. 51.—*Joseph. Ant.* 12. c. 3.—*Appian. in Syr.*—*Val. Max.* 2. c. 10.—*Suidas.*

SELEU'CUS the Second, surnamed *Callinicus*, succeeded his father Antiochus Theus on the throne of Syria. He attempted to make war against Ptolemy, king of Ægypt, but his fleet was shipwrecked in a violent storm, and his armies soon after defeated by his enemy. He was at last taken prisoner by Arsaces, an officer who had made himself powerful by the dissensions which reigned in the house of Seleucidæ, between the two brothers, Seleucus and Antiochus; and after he had been a prisoner for some time in Parthia, he died of a fall from his horse, B.C. 226, after a reign of 20 years. Seleucus had received the surname of *Pogon*, from his long beard; that of *Callinicus* was ironical, to express his very unfortunate reign. He had married Laodice, the sister of one of his generals, by whom he had two sons, Seleucus and Antiochus, and a daughter whom he gave in marriage to Mithridates, king of Pontus. *Strab.* 16.—*Justin.* 27.—*Appian. de Syr.*

SELEU'CUS, the Third, succeeded his father Seleucus the Second on the throne of Syria, and received the surname of *Ceraunus*, by antiphrasis, as he was a very weak, timid, and irresolute monarch. He was murdered by two of his officers, after a reign of three years, B.C. 223, and his brother Antiochus, though only 15 years old, ascended the throne and rendered himself so celebrated, that he acquired the name of the Great. *Appian.*—*Euseb. in Chron.*

SELEU'CUS the Fourth succeeded his father Antiochus the Great on the throne of Syria. He was surnamed *Philopator*, or, according to Josephus, *Soter*. His empire had been weakened by the Romans when he became monarch, and the yearly tribute of a thousand talents to these victorious enemies contributed to lessen his power and consequence among nations. Seleucus was poisoned after a reign of 12 years, B.C. 175. His son Demetrius had been sent to Rome, there to receive his education, and he became a prince of great abilities. *Strab.* 16.—*Justin.* 32.—*Appian.*

SELEU'CUS the Fifth succeeded his father Demetrius Nicanor on the throne of Syria, in the 20th year of his age. He was put to death in the first year of his reign, by Cleopatra his mother, who had also sacrificed her husband to her ambition. He is not reckoned by many historians in the number of the Syrian monarchs. *Appian. in Syriac*,—*Justin.* l. 39.—*Euseb. in Chron.*

SELEU'CUS the Sixth, son of Antiochus Gryphus, killed his uncle Antiochus Cyzicenus, who wished to obtain the crown of Syria. He was some time after banished from his kingdom by Antiochus Pius son of Cyzicenus, and fled to Cilicia, where he was burnt in a palace by the inhabitants, B.C. 93. *Appian.*—*Joseph.*

SELEU'CUS, a prince of Syria, to whom the Ægyptians offered the crown of which they had robbed Auletes. Seleucus accepted it, but he soon disgusted his subjects, and received the surname of *Cybiosactes*, or *Scullion*, from his meanness and avarice. He was at last murdered by Berenice, whom he had married.——A servant of Cleopatra, the last queen of Ægypt, who accused his mistress before Octavianus, of having secreted part of her jewels and treasures.——A mathematician, intimate with Vespasian the Roman emperor. *Tacit.* 2. *Hist.* 78.——A Roman consul, A.U.C. 573.——A celebrated singer. *Juv.* 10. v. 211.——A king of the Bosporus, who died B.C. 429.——A slave. *Cic.* 6. *Att.* 18.——A grammarian of Emessa, who wrote two books on the affairs of the Parthians. *Suidas.*——A grammarian of Alexandria, surnamed *Homericus*, who wrote commentaries on nearly all the poets. *Suidas.*—*Strab.* 1.—*Porphyr.* 2.—*Voss. H. Gr.* 3. p. 412.

SELEU'CUS, a part of the Alps.

SEL'GE, a town of Pamphylia, made a colony by the Lacedæmonians. *Liv.* 35. c. 13.—*Strabo.* It is now Philadelphia, according to *Niger*.

SEL'GIA, a city of Armenia Major. *Ptol.*

SELIC'IA, a woman mentioned by Cicero, and proprobably the daughter of Selicius. *Cic.* 15. *Att.* 12.

SELIC'IUS Q., a friend of Lent. Spinther, mentioned asa usurer. *Cic. Fam.* 1. ep. 5. *Att.* 1. ep. 12.

SELIM'NUS, a shepherd of Achaia, who for some time enjoyed the favors of the nymph Argyra without interruption. Argyra was at last disgusted with her lover, and the shepherd died through melancholy, and was changed into a river of the same name. Argyra was also changed into a fountain, and was fond of mingling her waters with those of the Selimnus. He forgot, however, afterwards, his affection for the ungrateful nymph, by the permission of Venus, and thence those who bathed in the Selimnus were said to become regardless of former attachments. *Paus.* 7. c. 23.

SELI'NUNS or SELI'NUS (*-untis*), a town in the southern parts of Sicily, founded A.U.C. 127 by a colony from Megara. It received its name from σέλινον, *parsley*, which grew there in abundance. The marks of its ancient consequence are visible in the venerable ruins now found in its neighbourhood. *Virg. Æn.* 3. v. 705.—*Paus.* 6. c. 19.—*Strab.* 6.—*Plut. cur. Pyth.*

SELI'NUS, a river of Elis in Peloponnesus, which watered the town of Scillus. *Paus.* 5. c. 6.——A river of Achaia.——A river of Sicily, near the town of the same name. *Strab.* 6.——A river and town of Cilica, where Trajan died. *Liv.* 33. c. 20.—*Strab.* 14.——The name of two small rivers near Diana's temple at Ephesus. *Plin.* 5. c. 29.——A lake at the entrance of the Cayster. *Strab* 14.

SE'LIUS, an orator of mean capacity. *Cic.* 7. *Fam.*32.

SE'LIUS CNE'US and PUB'LIUS, two men of great literary fame, intimate with the great Lucullus. *Cic.* 4. *Acad.* 4.

SEL'LÆ. a people of Epirus. *Lucan.* 3. v. 180.

SELLA'SIA, a town of Laconia, where Cleomenes was defeated by the Achæans, B.C. 222. Scarcely 200, out of a body of 5000 Lacedæmonians, survived the battle. *Plut.*

SELLE'IS, a river of Peloponnesus falling into the Ionian Sea. *Hom. Il.* o. v. 531.

SELLE'NES, a river of Thesprotia. *Hesych.*

SELLE'TÆ, a people of Thrace, near Mount Hæmus. *Liv.* 38. c. 40.

SEL'LI, an ancient nation of Epirus, near Dodona. *Lucan.* 3. v. 180.—*Strab.* 7.

SEL'LUS, the name of the father of Æschines. *Aristoph. Vesp.*

SELOCHU'SA, a small island of Peloponnesus. *Plin.* 4. c. 12.

SE'LUR, a city of India Citerior. *Ptol.*

SELYMB'RIA, a town of Thrace, on the Propontis. *Liv.* 39. c. 39.

SEMBRACE'NA, a city of the Sabæi, near the Arabian Gulf. *Ptol.*

SEM'ELE, a daughter of Cadmus by Hermione, the daughter of Mars and Venus. She was tenderly loved by Jupiter; but Juno, who was always jealous of her husband's amours, and who hated the house of Cadmus, because they were related to the goddess of beauty, determined to punish her successful rival. She borrowed tho girdle of Ate, which made its wearer an adept in wickedness, deceit, and perfidy, and, in the form of Beroe, Semele's nurse, visited the house of Jupiter's mistress. Semele listened with attention to the artful address of the false Beroe, and was at last persuaded to entreat her lover to visit her with the same majesty as he approached Juno. This rash request was heard with horror by Jupiter; but as he had sworn by the Styx to grant Semele whatever she required, he came to her attended by the clouds, the lightning, and the thunderbolts. The mortal nature of Semele could not endure the presence of such majesty, and she was instantly consumed with fire. The child, however, of which she was pregnant, was saved from the flames by Mercury, or, according to others, by Dirce, one of the nymphs of the Achelous, and Jupiter placed him in his thigh till the completion of the time during which he ought to have remained in his mother's womb. This child was called Bacchus, or Dionysius. Semele immediately after death was honored with immortality under the name of Thyone. Some, however, suppose that she remained in the infernal regions till Bacchus her son was permitted to bring her back. There were in the temple of Diana, at Trœzene, two altars raised to the infernal gods, one of which was over an aperture, through which, as Pausanias reports, Bacchus returned from hell with his mother. Semele was particularly worshipped at Brasiæ in Laconia, whither, according to a certain tradition, she had been driven by the winds with her son, after Cadmus had exposed her on the sea, on account of her amour with Jupiter. The mother of Bacchus, though she received divine honours, had no temples; she had a statue in a temple of Ceres, at Thebes, in Bœotia. *Paus.* 3. c. 24. l. 9. c. 5 & 16.—*Hesiod. Theog.* 940 & 975.—*Homer. Il.* 14. v. 323.—*Orpheus, Hymn.*—*Eurip. in. Bacch.*—*Apollod.* 3. c. 4.—*Ovid. Met.* 3. v. 254. *Fast.* 3. v. 715.—*Diod.* 3 & 4.—*Servius in Æn.* 5. v. 241.

SEMENTI'NÆ, festivals observed at Rome at the time of sowing the corn on a day appointed at the option of the high priest or chief magistrate. *Varro de L. L.* 5. *R. R.* 1. c. 2.—*Festus de V. Sig.*—*Ovid. Fast.* 1. v. 661.—*Macrob.* 1. c. 16.

SEMIGERMA'NI, a name given to the Helvetii, a people of Germany. *Liv.* 24. c. 38.

SEMIGUN'TUS, a general of the Cherusci, taken prisoner by Germanicus, &c. *Strab.* 7.

SEMIR'AMIS, a celebrated queen of Assyria, daughter of the goddess Derceto, by a young Assyrian. She was exposed in a desert, but her life was preserved by doves for one whole year, till Simmas, one of the shepherds of Ninas, found her and brought her up as his own child. Semiramis, when grown up, married Menones, the governor of Nineveh, and accompanied him to the siege of Bactra, where, by her advice and prudent directions, she hastened the king's operations and took the city. These eminent services, but chiefly her uncommon beauty, endeared her to Ninus. The monarch asked her of her husband, and offered him instead, his daughter Sosana; but Menones, who tenderly loved Semiramis, refused, and when Ninus had added threats to entreaties, he hanged himself. No sooner was Menones dead than Semiramis, who was of an aspiring soul, married Ninus, by whom she had a son called Ninyas. Ninus was so fond of Semiramis, that at her request he resigned the crown to her, and commanded her to be proclaimed queen and sole empress of Assyria. Of this, however, he had cause to repent; Semiramis put him to death, the better to establish herself on the throne, and when she had no enemies to fear at home, she began to embellish the capital of her empire, and by her means Babylon became the most magnificent city in the world, She visited every part of her dominions, and left every where immortal monuments of her greatness and benevolence. To render the roads passable, and communication easy, she hollowed mountains and filled up valleys, and water was conveyed at a great expense, by large and convenient aqueducts, to barren deserts and unfruitful plains. She was not less distinguished as a warrior, since many of the neighbouring nations were conquered; and when Semiramis was once told, as she was dressing her hair, that Babylon had revolted, she left her toilette with precipitation, and though only half dressed, refused to have the rest of her head adorned before the sedition was quelled, and tranquillity re-established. Semiramis has been accused of licentiousness, and some authors have observed, that she regularly called the strongest and stoutest men in her army to her arms, and afterwards put them to death that they might not be living witnesses of her incontinence. Her passion for her son was also unnatural, and it was this criminal propensity which induced Ninyas to destroy his mother with his own hands. Some say that Semiramis was changed into a dove after death, and received immortal honors in Assyria. It is supposed that she lived 1965 years before the Christian era, and that she died in the 62d year of her age, and the 25th of her reign. Many fabulous reports have been propagated about Semiramis, and some have declared that for some time she disguised herself and passed for her son Ninyas. *Val. Max.* 9. c. 3.—*Herodot.* 1. c. 184.—*Diod.* 2.—*Mela*, 1. c. 3.—*Strab.* 5.—*Paterc.* 1. c. 6.—*Justin.* 1. c. 1, &c.—*Propert.* 3. el. 11. v. 21.—*Plut. de Fort. &c.*—*Ovid. Amor.* 1. el. 5. v. 11. *Met.* 4. v. 58.—*Marcell.* 14. c. 6.—*Juv.* 2. v. 108.—*Claudian. de Cons. Prob.* 162.

SEMI'RUS, now Simari, a river of Magna Græcia. *Plin.* 3. c. 10.

SEM'NONES or SEN'ONES, a people of Italy, on the borders of Umbria. *Ptol.*

SEM'NONES, a people of Germany, on the Elbe and Oder. *Ptol.*

SEMO'NES, inferior deities of Rome, who were not in the number of the 12 great gods. Among these were Faunus, the Satyrs, Priapus, Vertumnus, Janus, Pan, Silenus, and all such illustrious heroes as had received divine honors after death. The word seems to be the same as *semi homines*, because they were inferior to the supreme gods, and superior to men. *Ovid. Fast.* 6. v. 213.

SEMOSANC'TUS, one of the gods of the Romans among the Indigetes, or such as were born and educated in their country. *Ovid. Fast.* 6. v. 213.

SEMPRO'NIA CORNEL, a Roman matron, daughter of Scipio Africanus, and mother of the two Gracchi, celebrated for her learning, and her private as well as public virtues.

SEMPRO'NIA, a sister of the Gracchi, who is accused of having assisted the triumvirs Carbo, Gracchus, and Flaccus, to murder her husband, Scipio Africanus the younger. The name of Sempronia was common to the female descendants of the family of the Sempronii, Gracchi, and Scipiones.

SEMPRO'NIA LEX *de magistratibus*, was introduced by C. Sempronius Gracchus, the tribune, A.U.C. 630; it ordained that no person who had been legally deprived of an office of magistracy for misdemeanours should be capable of bearing an office again. This law was afterwards repealed by the author.—Another, *de civitate*, by the same, A.U.C. 630. It ordained that no capital judgment should be passed on a Roman, without the concurrence and authority of the senate. There were also some other regulations included in this law.—Another, *de comitiis*, by the same, A.U.C. 635. It ordained that in giving their votes, the centuries should be chosen by lot, and not give it according to the order of their classes.—Another, *de comitiis*, by the same, the same year, which granted to the Latin allies of Rome, the privilege of giving their votes at elections, as if they were Roman citizens.—Another, *de provinciis*, by the same, A.U.C. 630. It enacted that the senators should be permitted before the assembly of the consular *comitia*, to determine as they pleased the particular provinces which should be proposed to the consuls, to be divided by lot, and that the tribunes should be deprived of the power of interposing against a decree of the senate.—Another, called *agraria prima*, by T. Sempronius Gracchus the tribune, A.U.C. 620. It confirmed the *lex agraria Licinia*, and enacted that all such as were in possession of more lands than that law allowed, should immediately resign them, to be divided among the poorer citizens.

Three commissioners were appointed to put this law into execution, and its consequences were so violent, as it was directly made against the nobles and senators, that it cost the author his life.—Another, called *agraria altera*, by the same. It required that all the ready money which was found in the treasury of Attalus king of Pergamus, who had left the Romans his heirs, should be divided among the poorer citizens of Rome, to supply them with all the various instruments requisite in husbandry, and that the lands of that monarch should be farmed by the Roman censors, and the money drawn from thence divided among the people.—Another called *frumentaria*, by C. Sempronius Gracchus. It required that a certain quantity of corn should be distributed among the people, so much to every individual, for which it was required that they should only pay the trifling sum of a *semissis* and a *triens*.—Another, *de usurâ*, by M. Sempronius, the tribune, A.U.C. 560. It ordained that in lending money to the Latins and the allies of Rome, the Roman laws should be observed as well as among the citizens.—Another, *de judicibus*, by the tribune C. Sempronius, A.U.C. 630. It required that the right of judging, which had been assigned to the senatorial order by Romulus, should be transferred from them to the Roman knights.—Another, *militaris*, by the same, A.U.C. 630. It enacted that the soldiers should be clothed at the public expense, without any diminution of their usual pay. It also ordered that no person should be obliged to serve in the army before the age of seventeen. *Rosin. Antiq. Rom. passim.*

SEMPRO'NIUS A. ATRATI'NUS, a senator who opposed the agrarian law, which was proposed by the consul Cassius, soon after the election of the tribunes.——A military tribune, A.U.C. 310. He was one of the first censors with his colleague in the consulship, Papirius.

SEMPRO'NIUS CA'IUS, a consul summoned before an assembly of the people, because he had fought with ill success against the Volsci.

SEMPRO'NIUS BLÆ'SUS, a consul who obtained a triumph for some victories gained in Sicily.

SEMPRO'NIUS SO'PHUS, a consul sent against the Æqui. He also fought against the Picentes, and during the engagement there was a dreadful earthquake. The soldiers were terrified, but Sophus encouraged them, and observed that the earth trembled only for fear of changing its old masters.

SEMPRO'NIUS, a man who proposed a law that no person should dedicate a temple or altar, without the previous approbation of the magistrates, A.U.C. 449. He repudiated his wife because she had gone to see a spectacle without his permission or knowledge.——A legionary tribune, who led away from Cannæ the remaining part of the soldiers who had not been killed by the Carthaginians. He was afterwards consul, and fought in the field against Annibal with great success. He was killed in Spain.——A eunuch, made governor of Rome by Caracalla.——The father of the Gracchi. *Vid.* Gracchus.——A censor, who was also sent as ambassador to the court of Ægypt. ——A tribune of the people, &c. *Tacit.—Flor.—Liv.—Plut.—Cæs.—Appian.*——An emperor. *Vid.* Saturninus.

SEMPRO'NIUS RU'FUS, a senator banished from the senate because he had killed a crane to serve him as food. *Salmas. ad Tertull. de pall. c. ult.*

SEMPRO'NIUS TUDITA'NUS, a man sent against Sardinia by the Romans.

SEMPRO'NIUS TIBE'RIUS LON'GUS, a Roman consul defeated by the Carthaginians in an engagement which he had begun contrary to the advice of his colleague C. Scipio. He afterwards obtained victories over Hanno and the Gauls.

SEMPRO'NIUS TIBE'RIUS GRAC'CHUS, a consul who defeated the Carthaginians and the Campanians. He was afterwards betrayed by Fulvius, a Lucanian, into the hands of the Carthaginians. and was killed, after he had made a long and bloody resistance against the enemy. Hannibal showed great honor to his remains; a funeral pile was raised at the head of the camp, and the enemy's cavalry walked round it in solemn procession.

SEMPRO'NIUS GRAC'CHUS, a man who debauched Julia. *Vid.* Gracchus.

SEMPRO'NIUS DEN'SUS, a centurion of a prætorian cohort, who defended the person of Galba against the assassins. He was killed in the attempt. *Tac. Hist.* 1. c. 43.

SEMU'RIUM, a place near Rome, where Apollo had a temple. *Cic. Phil.* 6. 6.—*Macrob.* 1. 1. sat. 10.

SE'NA or SENOGAL'LIA, a town of Umbria in Italy, on the Adriatic, built by the Senones, after they had made an irruption into Italy, A.U.C. 396; and on that account called Gallicia. There was also a small river in the neighbourhood which bore the name of Sena. It was near it that Asdrubal was defeated by Cl. Nero. *C. Nep. in Catone.*—*Sil.* 8. v. 454.—*Liv.* 27. c. 46.—*Cic. Brut.* 18.

SENA'TUS, the chief council of the state among the Romans. The members of this body, called *senators* on account of their age, and *patres* on account of their authority, were of the greatest weight and consequence in the republic. The senate was first instituted by Romulus to govern the city, and to preside over the affairs of the state during his absence. This body was continued by his successors; but Tarquin the Second disdained to consult them, and by having his own council chosen from his favorites, and from men totally devoted to his interest, he diminished the authority and consequence of the senators, and slighted the concurrence of the people. The senators whom Romulus created were a hundred, to whom he afterwards added the same number when the Sabines were incorporated among the citizens of Rome. Tarquinius Priscus made the senate consist of 300, and this number remained fixed for a long time. After the expulsion of the last Tarquin, whose tyranny had thinned the patricians, as well as the plebeians, 164 new senators were chosen to complete the 300; and as they were called *conscripts*, the senate ever afterwards consisted of members who were denominated *patres* and *conscripti*. The number continued to fluctuate during the times of the republic, but gradually increased to 700, and afterwards to 900 under Julius Cæsar, who, to reward the services of his adherents, filled the senate with men of every rank and order. Under Augustus the senators amounted to 1000, but this number was reduced to 300, which being the cause of complaints, induced the emperor to limit the number to 600. The place of a senator was always bestowed upon merit; the monarchs had the privilege of choosing the members, and after the expulsion of the Tarquins it was one of the rights of the consuls, till the election of the censors, who from their office seemed most capable of making choice of men whose character was irreproachable, whose morals were pure, and relations honorable. Sometimes the assembly of the people elected senators, but it was only upon some extraordinary occasions; there was also a dictator chosen to fill up the number of the senate, after the battle of Cannæ. Only particular families were admitted into the senate; and when the plebeians were permitted to share the honors of the state, it was then required that they should be born of free citizens. It was also required that the candidates should be knights before their admission into the venerable assembly. They were to be above the age of 25, and to have previously passed through the inferior offices of quæstor, tribune of the people, ædile, prætor, and consul. Some, however, suppose that the senators whom Romulus chose were all old men; yet his successors neglected this, and often men who were below the age of 25 were admitted by courtesy into the senate. The dignity of a senator could not be supported without the possession of 80,000 sesterces, or about £7000 English money, and therefore such as squandered away their money, and whose fortune was reduced below this sum, were generally struck out of the list of senators. This regulation was not made in the first ages of the republic, when the Romans boasted of their poverty as of a national virtue. The senators were not permitted to be of any trade or profession. They were distinguished from the rest of the people by their dress; they wore the laticlave, half boots of a black color, with a crescent or silver buckle in the form of a C; but this last honor was confined only to the descendants of those hundred senators who had been elected by Romulus, as the letter C (*Centum*) seems to imply. They had the sole right of feasting publicly in the Capitol in ceremonial habits; they sat in curule chairs, and at the representation of plays and public spectacles, were honored with particular seats. Whenever they travelled abroad, even on their own business, they were maintained at the public expense, and always found provisions for themselves and their attendants ready prepared on the road; a privilege that was generally termed *free legation*. On public festivals they wore the *prætexta*, or long white robes with purple borders. The right of convoking the senate belonged only to the monarchs; and after the expulsion of the Tarquins, to the consuls, the dictator, master of the horse, governor of Rome, and tribunes of the people; but no magistrate could exercise this privilege except in the absence of a superior officer, the tribunes excepted. The time of meeting was generally three times a month, on the calends, nones, and ides. Under Augustus they were not assembled on the nones, and it was requisite that the place where they assembled should have been previously consecrated by the augurs. This was generally in the temple of Concord, of Jupiter Capitolinus, Apollo, Castor and Pollux, &c. or in the Curiæ called Hostilia, Julia Pompeia, &c. When audience was given to foreign ambassadors, the senators assembled without the walls of the city, either in the temples of Bellona or of Apollo; and the same ceremony as to their meeting was also observed when they transacted business with their generals, as the ambassadors of foreign nations, and the commanders of armies, while in commission, were not permitted to appear within the walls of the city. To render their decrees valid, a certain number of members was requisite, and such as were absent without some proper cause, were always fined. In the reign of Augustus, 400 senators were requisite to make a senate. Nothing was transacted before sunrise, or after sunset. In their office the senators were the guardians of religion, they disposed of the provinces as they pleased, prorogued the assemblies of the people, appointed thanksgivings, nominated ambassadors, distributed the public money, and, in short, had the management of every thing political or civil in the republic, except the creating of magistrates, the enacting of laws, and the declarations of war or peace, which were confined to the assemblies of the people. Rank was always regarded in their meetings: the chief magistrates of the state, such as the consuls, the prætors, and the censors sat first; after these the inferior magistrates, such as the ædiles and quæstors, and last of all, those that then exercised no office in the state. Their opinions were originally collected, each according to his age; but when the office of censor was instituted, the opinion of the *princeps senatus*, or person whose name stood first on the censor's list, was first consulted, and afterwards those who were of consular dignity, each in their respective order. In the age of Cicero, the consuls elect were first consulted; and in the age of Cæsar, he was permitted to speak first till the end of the year, on whom the consul had originally conferred that honor. Under the emperors the same rules were observed, but the consuls were generally consulted before all others. When any public matter was introduced into the senate, which was always called *referre ad senatum*, any senator whose opinion was asked, was permitted to speak upon it as long as he pleased, and on that account it was often usual for the senators to protract their speeches till it was too late to determine. When the question was put, they passed to the side of that speaker, whose opinion they approved, and a majority of votes was easily collected, without the trouble of counting the numbers. This mode of proceeding was called *pedibus in alicujus sententiam ire*, and, therefore, on that account, the senators who had not the privilege of speaking, but only the right of giving a silent vote, such as bore some curule honors, and on that account were permitted to sit in the senate, but not to deliberate, were denominated *pedarii senatores*. After the majority had been known, the matter was determined, and a *senatus consultum* was immediately written by the clerks of the house, at the feet of the chief magistrates, and it was signed by all the principal members of the house. When there was not a sufficient number of members to make a senate, the decision was called *senatus autoritas*, but it was of no consequence if it did not afterwards pass into a *senatus consultum*. The tribunes of the people by the word *veto*, could stop the debates, and the decrees of the assembled senate, as also any one who was of equal authority with him who had proposed the matter. The *senatus consulta* were left in the custody of the consuls, who could suppress or preserve them; but about the year of Rome 304, they were always deposited in the temple of Ceres, and afterwards in the treasury, by the ædiles of the people. The degradation of the senators was made by the censor, by omitting their names when he called over the list of the senate. This was called *præterire*. A senator could be again introduced into the senate if he could repair his character or fortune, which had been the causes why the censor had lawfully called him unqualified, and had challenged his opposition. The meeting of the senate was often sudden, except the particular times already mentioned, upon any emergency. After the death of J. Cæsar, they were not permitted to meet on the ides of March, which were called *parricidium*, because on that day the dictator had been assassinated. The sons of senators, after they had put on the *tòga virilis*, were permitted to come into the senate, but this privilege was afterwards limited. *Vid.* Papirius. The rank and authority of the senators, which were so conspicuous in the first ages of the republic, and which caused the minister of Pyrrhus to declare, that the Roman senate was a venerable assembly of kings, dwindled into nothing under the emperors. Men of the lowest character were admitted into the senate; the emperors took pleasure in robbing this illustrious body of their privileges and authority, and the senators themselves, by their meanness and servility, contributed as much as the tyranny of their sovereign to diminish their own consequence; and by applauding the follies of a Nero, and the cruelties of a Domitian, they convinced the world that they no longer possessed sufficient importance or dignity to entitle them to be consulted on matters of weight and public interest. In the election of successors to the imperial purple after Augustus, the approbation of the senate was consulted, but it was only a matter of courtesy, and the concurrence of a body of men who were without power, and under the control of a mercenary army, was little regarded. The title of *Clarissimus* was given to the senators, under the emperors, and indeed this was the only distinction they had in compensation for the loss of their former independence. The senate was abolished by Justinian, thirteen centuries after its first institution by Romulus.

SEN'ECA M. ANNÆ'US, a native of Corduba in Spain, who married Helvia, a woman of Spain, by whom he had three sons, Seneca the philosopher, Annæus Novatus, and Annæus Mela, the father of the poet Lucan. Seneca made himself known by some declamations of which he had made a collection from the most celebrated orators of the age, and from that circumstance, and for the sake of distinction, he obtained the appellation of *declamator*. He left Corduba, and went to Rome, where he became a Roman knight. His works are usually edited with those of his son. His *Controversiæ* were first published at Venice 1490. and again in 1503, to which the *Suasoriæ* were added in 1492. The latest edition is the Bipontine 1783. *Harles. Not. Lit. Rom.* 1. p. 319.—*Sax. Onom.* 1. p. 213.

SEN'ECA L. ANNÆ'US, son of the preceding, was born about six years before Christ, and was early distinguished by his extraordinary talents. He was taught eloquence by his father, and received lessons in philosophy from the best and most celebrated Stoics of the age. As one of the followers of the Pythagorean doctrines, Seneca observed the most reserved abstinence, and never ate the flesh of animals; but this custom he abandoned at the representation of his father, when Tiberius threatened to punish some Jews and Ægyptians who abstained from certain meats. In the character of a pleader, Seneca appeared with great advantage, but the fear of Caligula, who aspired to the name of an eloquent speaker, and who was consequently jealous of his fame, deterred him from pursuing his favorite study, and he sought a safer employment in canvassing for the honors and offices of the state. He was made quæstor, but the aspersions which were thrown upon him on account of a shameful amour with Julia Livilla, the daughter of Germanicus, removed him from Rome, and the emperor banished him for some time into Corsica. During his banishment the philosopher wrote some spirited epistles to his mother, remarkable for elegance of language and sublimity; but he soon forgot the dignity of philosophy, and disgraced himself by his flatteries to the emperor, and in wishing to be restored to favor, even at the expense of his innocence and character. The disgrace of Messalina, and the marriage of Agrippina with Claudius, proved favorable to Seneca, and after he had remained five years in Corsica, he was recalled by the empress to take care of the education of her son Nero, who was destined to succeed to the empire. In the honorable duty of preceptor, Seneca gained applause, and as long as Nero followed his advice, Rome enjoyed tranquillity, and believed herself safe and happy under the administration of the son of Agrippina. Some, however, are clamorous against the philosopher, and observe that Seneca initiated his pupil into those unnatural vices, and abominable indulgences, which afterwards disgraced him as a monarch and as a man. This may be the language of malevolence, or the insinuation of jealousy. In the corrupted age of Nero, the preceptor had to withstand the clamors of wicked and profligate ministers, and if he had recommended himself to the favor of the emperor, by sharing his pleasures, his debaucheries, and his extravagance, Nero would not perhaps have been so anxious to destroy a man whose example, from vicious inclinations, he could not follow, and whose salutary precepts his licentious associates forbad him to obey. Seneca was too well acquainted with the disposition of Nero, to think himself secure; he had been accused of having amassed the most ample riches, and of having built sumptuous houses, and adorned beautiful gardens, during the four years in which he had attended Nero as a preceptor, and therefore he desired his imperial pupil to accept of the riches, and the possessions which his attendance on his person had procured, and to permit him to retire to solitude and study. Nero refused with artful duplicity, and Seneca, to avoid further suspicions, kept himself at home, as if labouring under disease. In the conspiracy of Piso, which happened some time after, and in which some of the most noble of the Roman senators were concerned, Seneca's name was mentioned either designedly or by accident by Natalis, and Nero, who was glad of an opportunity of sacrificing him to his secret jealousy, ordered him to destroy himself. Seneca very probably was not accessary to the conspiracy, though it is said that the conspirators wished to elevate him to the imperial throne on account of his great virtues, and the only thing which could be produced against him as a crimination, was trivial and unsatisfactory. Piso, as Natalis declared, had complained that he never saw Seneca, and the philosopher had observed in answer, that it was not proper or conducive to their common interest, to see one another often. He further pleaded indisposition, and said that his own life depended upon the safety of Piso's person. Seneca was at table with his wife Paulina and two of his friends, when the messenger from Nero arrived. He heard the words which commanded him to destroy himself, with philosophical firmness, and even with joy, and observed, that such a mandate might have long been expected from a man who had murdered his own mother, and assassinated all his friends. He wished to dispose of his possessions as he pleased, but this was refused, and when he heard this, he turned to his friends who were weeping at his melancholy fate, and told them, that since he could not leave them what he believed to be his own, he would leave them at least his own life for an example which they might imitate, and by which they might acquire immortal fame. Against their tears and wailings he exclaimed with gentleness but firmness, and asked them whether they had not learnt better to withstand the attacks of fortune, and the violence of tyranny. As for his wife, he attempted to calm her emotions, and when she seemed resolved to die with him, he said he was glad to find his example followed with so much fortitude. Their veins were opened at the same moment, but the life of Paulina was preserved, and Nero, who was partial to her, ordered the blood to be stopped, and from that moment, according to some authors, the philosopher's wife seemed to rejoice that she could still enjoy the comforts of life. Seneca's veins bled but slowly, and it has been observed that the sensible and animated conversation of his dying moments was happily collected by his friends, and preserved among his works. To hasten his death he drank a dose of poison, but it had no effect, and he therefore ordered himself to be carried into a hot bath, to accelerate the operation of the draught, and to make the blood flow more freely. This was attended with no better success, and, as the soldiers were clamorous and impatient, he was carried into a stove, and suffocated by the steam, on the 12th of April, in the 65th year of the Christian era, and in his 53rd year. His body was burnt without pomp or funeral ceremony, according to his will which he had made when he enjoyed the most unbounded favours of Nero. The compositions of Seneca are numerous, and chiefly on moral subjects. He is so much admired for his refined sentiments and virtuous precepts, his morality, his constancy, and his innocence of manners, that St. Jerome has not hesitated to rank him among Christian writers. His style is nervous, abounds with ornament, and seems well suited to the tastes of the age in which he lived, but the desire of recommending himself and his writings to the world obliged him too often to depreciate the merits of the ancients. His treatises are "de irâ, de consolatione, de Providentiâ, de tranquillitate animi, de clementiâ, de sapientis constantiâ, de otio sapientis, de brevitate vitæ, de beneficiis, de vitâ beatâ," besides his "naturales quæstiones, ludus in Claudium, moral letters, &c." There are also some tragedies ascribed to Seneca, in imitation of the sublime works of Æschylus, and Euripides, but they are more probably the composition of some writer of his name or of his family. Quintilian supposes that the "Medea" is his composition; and, according to others, the "Troas" and the "Hippolytus" were also written by him; and the "Agamemnon, Hercules furens, Œdipus, Thebais, Octavia, Thyestes, and Hercules in Œta," by his father, Seneca the declaimer. The best editions of Seneca are those of Antwerp, fol. 1615, and of Gronovius, 3 vols. Amst. 1672; and those of his tragedies are that of Schroeder, 4to. Delph. 1728, and the 8vo. of Gronovius, L. Bat. 1682. *Tac. Ann.* 12. c. 8. l. 14. c. 52 & 53. l. 15. c. 60.—*Dio.*—*Juv.* 5. v. 108. sat. 8. v. 211. sat. 10. v. 16.—*Plin.* 14. c. 4.—*Schol. in Juv.*—*Martial.* 1. epigr. 62. l. 12. epigr. 36 —*Quintil.* 9. c. 2. l. 10. c. l. 125, &c.—*Sueton. in Ner. &c.*—*Harles. Not. Lit. Rom.* 1. p. 320.—*Sax. Onom.* 1. p. 250. [The finest bust of Seneca is to be found in the Museum at Herculaneum; it is of bronze. There is also a double terminus of Seneca and Sotion his preceptor, in the Vatican at Rome.]

SENE'CIO CLAU'DIUS, one of Nero's favorites, and the associate of his pleasure and debauchery.

SENE'CIO TUL'LUS, a man who conspired against Nero, and was put to death, though he turned informer against the rest of the conspirators.

SENE'CIO, a man put to death by Domitian, for writing an account of the life of Helvidius, one of the emperor's enemies.——One of Constantine's enemies.——A man who from his restless and aspiring disposition acquired the name of Grandio. *Seneca, Suas.* 1.

SE'NIA, a town of Liburnia, now Segna. *Plin.* 3. c. 21.

SE'NIUS RU'FUS. *Vid.* Fenius.

SEN'NA or SE'NA, a river of Umbria. *Vid.* Sena. *Lucan.* 2. v. 407.

SENO'NES or SEN'ONES, an uncivilized nation of Gaul between the rivers Sequana and Icauna, who left their native possessions, and under the conduct of Brennus, invaded Italy, and pillaged Rome. They afterwards united with the Umbri, Latins, and Etrurians, to make war against the Romans till they were totally destroyed by Dolabella. The chief of their towns in that part of Italy where they settled near Umbria, and which from them was called Senogallia, were Fanum Fortunæ, Sena, Pisaurum, and Ariminum. *Vid.* Cimbri. *Lucan.* 1. v. 254.—*Sil.* 8. v. 454.—*Liv.* 5. c. 35, &c.—*Flor.* ——A people of Germany near the Suevi. *Paterc.* 2. c. 106.——A people of the Salentini, on the shores of the bay of Tarentum. Their city was Galliopolis. *Plin.* 4. c. 18.

SEN'TA FAU'NA. *Vid.* Fauna.

SEN'TIA LEX *de senatu*, introduced by C. Sentius the consul, A.U.C. 734, enacted the choosing of proper persons to fill up the number of senators. *Tac. Ann.* 11. c. 25.

SEN'TICE, a city of the Vaccæi in Hispania Tarraconensis.

SENTI'NUM, a town of Umbria. *Liv.* 10. c. 27 & 30.

SENTI'NUS, a god among the Romans whose power was exerted in opening and maturing the sense and feelings of children newly born. *Aug. de Civ. D.* 7. c. 2.

SENTI'NUS AU'GUR. *Vid.* Sentius.

SEN'TIUS CN., a governor of Syria under the emperors.

SEN'TIUS, a governor of Macedonia, A.U.C. 671. *Cic. Verr.* 3. c. 93. *Pis.* 34.——A Roman emperor. *Vid.* Severus.——A writer in the reign of the emperor Alexander, of whose life he wrote an account in Latin, or, according to others, in Greek.

SEN'TIUS SEPTIM'IUS, one of the soldiers of Pompey, who assisted the Ægyptians in murdering him.

SEN'TIUS AU'GUR, a poet at Rome, who distinguished himself as a writer of epigrams, in which he displayed a correct judgment, great genius, and an untainted heart. He imitated his predecessors Catullus and Calvus, though he occasionally forgot his general character in the severity of his satire. He was intimate with Spurina and Antoninus. Only eight of his verses are said to be extant. *Plin. in Epist.*—*Pet. Crinitus in vitâ.*

SE'NUS, a city of Ægypt. *Steph.*

SEPEL'ACUS, a place of Spain, near Saguntum. *Antonin.*

SE'PIAS, a cape of Magnesia in Thessaly, at the north of Eubœa, above the Pegasæus Sinus, now St. George.

SEPI'NUM or SÆPI'NUM, a colony and town of Samnium. *Ptol.* It is now Supino.

SEPIUS'SA, an island of Doris in the Sinus Ceranicus. *Plin.* 5. c. 31.

SEPLA'SIA, a place of Capua, where ointments were sold, whence came the epithet *Seplasiarius* for an effeminate person. *Cic. Pis.* 7 & 11.

SEPON'TIA PARAMI'CA, a city of the Vaccæi in Spain. It is now Penedo.

SEP'TEM A'QUÆ, a portion of the lake near Reate. *Cic.* 4. *Att.* 15.

SEP'TEM FRA'TRES, seven mountains of Mauritania, now Gebel-Mousa. *Strab.* 17.

SEP'TEM MARI'A, the entrance of the seven mouths of the Po. *Herodian.* 8. c. 7. It is now Lagune di Venetia.

SEPTEM'PEDA, a town of Picenum. *Ptol.* It is now S. Severino.

SEPTE'RION, a festival observed once in nine years at Delphi, in honor of Apollo. It was a representation of the pursuit of Python by Apollo, and of the victory obtained by the god. *Plut. Gr. Qu.* 12.

SEPTIMAN'CÆ, a city of the Vaccæi in Hispania Tarraconensis. *Antonin.* It is now Simanca.

SEPTIM'IUS TIT., a Roman knight distinguished by his poetical compositions both lyric and tragic. He was intimate with Augustus as well as Horace, who has addressed the sixth of his second book of Odes to him. *Harles Not. Lit. Rom.* 1. p. 305.

SEPTIM'IUS CA'IUS, a prætor mentioned by *Cicero, pro Red.* 9.

SEPTIM'IUS LU'CIUS, a Roman at the court of Ptolemy, who slew Pompey.

SEPTIM'IUS a centurion put to death by his seditious soldiers. *Tacit. Ann.* 1. c. 32.——A native of Africa, who distinguished himself at Rome as a poet. He wrote among other things a hymn in praise of Janus. Only eleven of his verses are preserved. *M. Terent.*—*Crinitus in vitâ.*——The author of the history of Alexander Severus. *Lamprid. in vit. huj.* c. 17.——A translator of the history of the Trojan war by Dictys of Crete, *Voss. H. Lat.* 3. p. 719.

SEPTIMON'TIUM, a festival at Rome yearly observed in December, and first celebrated when the seventh hill was inclosed within the walls of the city. The sacrifices on the occasion were offered in seven different places. *Varro de L. L.* 5. —*Festus de V. Sig.*

SEPTIMULE'IUS L., a native of Anagnia intimate with C. Gracchus. He suffered himself to be bribed by Opimius, and had the meanness to carry his friend's head fixed on a pole through the streets of Rome. *Cic.* 2. *Or.* 67.

SEPTIT'IUS Q., a Roman knight mentioned by *Cicero, Verr.* 3. c. 4.

SEP'YRA, a town of Cilicia, taken by Cicero, when he presided over that province. *Cic. ad Fam.* 15. c. 4.

SEQ'UANA, a river of Gaul, which separates the territories of the Belgæ and the Celtæ, and is now called the Seine. After passing through Paris and receiving the waters of the Marne, the Allier, and other streams, it falls into the British Channel. *Plin.* 4. c. 17.—*Ptol.* 2. c. 8.—*Martial.* 4. epigr. 19.—*Strab.* 4.—*Mela,* 3. c. 2.—*Lucan.* 1. v. 425.

SEQ'UANI, a people of Gaul, near the territories of the Ædui, between the Soane and mount Jura, famous for their wars against Rome. *Vid.* Ædui. The country which they inhabited is now called Franche Comptè, or Upper Burgundy. *Cæsar. Bell. G.*

SEQUIN'TIUS, a native of Alba, who married one of his daughters to Curiatius of Alba, and the other to Horatius, a citizen of Rome. The two daughters were brought to bed on the same day, each of three male children.

SE'RA, the metropolis of the Seres. *Ptol.* It is now Cambalech according to *Niger*; Sindinfu according to *Mercator.*

SERA'PIO, a surname given to one of the Scipios, because he resembled a swineherd of that name. ——A Greek poet and physician, who flourished in the reign of Trajan. He was intimate with Plutarch. *Plut. de orac. Delph.*—*Castellan. in vit. med.*——An Ægyptian put to death by Achilles, when he came at the head of an embassy from Ptolemy, who was a prisoner in the hands of J. Cæsar.——A painter. *Plin.* 35. c. 10.——A geographer of Antioch. *Cic.* 2. *Att.* 4 & 6.—*Plin. in elench. script.* l. 5.

SERA'PIO ÆLIA'NUS, an orator of Alexandria, who wrote many works. *Suidas.*

SERA'PIS, one of the Ægyptian deities, supposed to be the same as Osiris. He had a magnificent temple at Memphis, another at Alexandria, remarkable for its opulence, and a third at Canopus. The worship of Serapis was introduced at Rome, by the emperor Antoninus Pius, A.D. 146, and the mysteries celebrated on the 6th of May, but with so much licentiousness that the senate were soon after obliged to abolish them. Herodotus, who speaks in a very circumstantial manner of the deities, and of the religion of the Ægyptians, makes no mention of the god Serapis. Apollodorus says he was the same as the bull Apis. Some writers suppose that Æsculapius or Pluto was worshipped under this name. *Plut. in Isid.*—*Bochart. Hieroz.* part. 1. l. 2. c. 34.—*Salmas ad Vopisc. in Saturnin.* c. 8.—*Paus.* 1. c. 18. l. 2. c. 34.—*Tacit. Hist.* 4. c. 83.—*Strab.* 17.—*Martial.* 9. epigr. 30.—*Varro apud. Aug. Civ. D.* 18. c. 5. —*Macrob.* 1. c. 7 & 20.—*Tertull. de Spect.* 8 *et in Apol.* 18. [There is a fine colossal bust of Jupiter Serapis in the Vatican, where will also be found a small statue of this deity.]

SER'BES (*-etis*), a river of Mauritania Cæsariensis. *Ptol.* It was the Sardabala of *Pliny,* 5. c. 2.

SER'BI, a people near the Mæotis. *Plin.* 6. c. 7.

SER'BIA or SER'VIA, a city of Macedonia, near Berrhœa. *Zonar. Ann.* l. 3.

SERBI'NUM, a town of Lower Pannonia. *Ptol.*

SERBO'NIS, a lake near the Mediterranean, between Ægypt and Palestine.

SE'REN, a city of the Arabians, not far from the Troglodytæ. *Plin.* 6. c. 29.

SERE'NA, a daughter of Theodosius, who married Stilicho. She was put to death, &c. *Claudian.*

SERENIA'NUS, a favorite of Gallus, the brother of Julian. He was put to death.

SERE'NUS. *Vid.* Sammonicus.

SERE'NUS AU'LUS SEPTIM'IUS, a Latin poet who excelled as a lyric writer, and deserved to be ranked with the first Roman authors for his genius and learning. His poems were highly elegant, and he was particularly happy in his love descriptions, and in the humorous sallies of his muse. Only 16 of his verses are preserved. *Martin. Capell.—Non. Marcell.—Harles Not. Lit. Rom.* 1, p. 254.

SERE'NUS VIB'IUS, a governor of Spain, accused of cruelty in the government of his province, and put to death by order of Tiberius.

SERE'NUS CA'IUS, a consul with Cæpio. *Cic. Planc.* 5.

SERE'NUS ANNÆ'US, a præfect of Nero's guards, very intimate with Seneca. *Plin.* 22. c. 3.—*Senec.* ep. 64.—*Lips. ad Tac. Ann.* l. 3.

SE'RES, a nation of Asia, according to Ptolemy, between the Ganges and the Eastern Ocean, now the modern Thibet. They were naturally of a meek disposition. Silk, of which the fabrication was unknown to the ancients, who imagined that the materials were collected from the leaves of trees, was brought to Rome from their country, and on that account it received the name of *sericum*, and thence a garment or dress of silk is called *serica vestis*. Heliogabalus the Roman emperor was the first who wore a silk dress, which at that time was sold for its weight in gold. It afterwards became very cheap, and consequently was the common dress among the Romans. Some suppose that the Seres are the same as the Chinese. *Ptol.* 6. c. 16.—*Horat.* 1. od. 29. v. 9.—*Lucan.* 1. v. 19. l. 10. v. 142 & 292.—*Ovid. Am.* 1. el. 14. v. 6.—*Virg. G.* 2. v. 121.—*Oros.* 3. c. 24.—*Plin.* 21. c. 3.—*Lamprid. Heliog.* 29.—*Solin.* 63.—*Sidon. Carm.* 5. v. 43.

SERES'TUS, a Trojan who followed the fortunes of Æneas.—*Virg. Æn.* 2. v. 171.

SERGES'TUS, a sailor in the fleet of Æneas, from whom the family of the Sergi at Rome were descended. *Virg. Æn.* 5. v. 121.

SER'GIA, a Roman matron. She conspired with others to poison their husbands. The plot was discovered, and Sergia, with some of her accomplices, drank poison and died.

SER'GIUS, one of the names of Catiline.——A military tribune at the siege of Veii. *Liv.* 6. c. 5. ——A military tribune. *Id.* 5. c. 16.

SER'GIUS CNE'US, a prætor. *Id.* 31. c. 4.

SER'GIUS L. FIDE'NAS, a consul. *Id.* 4. c. 17.

SER'GIUS MAR'CUS SI'LUS, a lieutenant under the consul Æmilius. *Id.* 44. c. 40. The family of the Sergii was patrician, and branched out into the several families of the Fidenates, Sili, Catilinæ, Nattæ, Ocellæ, and Planci.

SER'GIUS or SERGI'OLUS, a deformed youth, greatly admired by the Roman ladies in Juvenal's age. *Juv.* 6. v. 105. *et seq.*

SERI'PHUS, an island among the Sporades, in the Ægæan Sea, about 36 miles in circumference, according to Pliny only 12, very barren, rocky, and uncultivated. The Romans generally sent their criminals into banishment there; and it was there that Cassius Severus the orator was exiled, and where he died. According to Ælian, the frogs of this island never croaked; but when they were removed from the island to another place, they were more noisy and clamorous than others; hence the proverb *Seriphia rana*, applied to a man who neither speaks nor sings. This, however, is found by modern travellers to be erroneous. It was on the coast of Seriphus that the chest was discovered in which Acrisius had exposed his daughter Danae, and her son Perseus. *Strab.* 10.—*Ælian. Anim.* 3. c. 37.—*Mela.* 2. c. 7. —*Apollod.* 1. c. 9.—*Tacit. Ann.* 4. c. 21.—*Ovid. Met.* 5. v. 242, l. 7. v. 65.—*Plin.* 27. c. 7. l. 32. c. 9. —*Juv.* 6. v. 564. sat. 10. v. 170.—*Stat. Ach.* 1. v. 205.

SER'MYLA, a town of Sithonia, in Macedonia. *Herodot.* 7. c. 122.

SERMYL'IUS, a city near Athos. *Steph.*

SERNIC'IUM, a place in Italy between Sulmo and Venusium. *Antonin.*

SE'RON, a general of Antiochus Epiphanes.

SERPENTA'RIUS, one of the constellations of the northern hemisphere, called also Anguitenens and Ophiuchus. Some authors suppose that this constellation represented Æsculapius, others Triopas king of Thessaly, who was punished for profaning the temple of Ceres. *Hygin. P.A.* 2. c. 14.—*Diod.* 4.—*Eratosth.* 6.

SERRA'NUS, a surname given to Cincinnatus, *a serendo*, because he was found sowing his fields when he was told that he had been elected dictator. Some, however, suppose that Serranus was a different person from Cincinnatus. *Plin.* 18. c. 3.—*Liv.* 3. c. 26.—*Virg. Æn.* 6. v. 844. l. 9. v. 335 & 455.—*Ital.* 6. v. 62.—*Servius ad Virg. Æn.* 6. v. 844.——One of the auxiliaries of Turnus killed in the night by Nisus. *Virg. Æn.* 9. v. 335.——A poet of some merit in Domitian's reign. *Juv.* 7. v. 80.

SERRA'NUS SEX'TUS GAVIN'IUS, a tribune inimical to Cicero's fame. *Cic. Att.* 4. ep. 2. *Sext.* 33.

SERRA'NUS DOMES'TICUS, a Roman who delivered a funeral oration over his son, in the composition of which he was assisted by Cicero. *Cic. Fr.* 3. ep. 8.

SERREP'OLIS, a city of Cilicia. *Ptol.* It is called Cassipolis by *Pliny*, 5. c. 27.

SERRE'TES, a people of Pannonia, on the river Dravus. *Plin.* 3. c. 25.

SERRHE'UM or SERRHI'UM, a fortified place of Thrace. *Liv.* 31. c. 16.

SER'RI, a people near the Colchi. *Plin.* 6. c. 5.

SERTO'RIUS QUIN'TUS, a Roman general, son of Quintus and Rhea, born at Nursia. His first campaign was under the great Marius, against the Teutones and Cimbri. He visited the enemy's camp as a spy, and had the misfortune to lose one eye in the first battle which he fought. When Marius and Cinna entered Rome, and indiscriminately slaughtered all their opponents, Sertorius accompanied them; but he expressed his sorrow and concern at the melancholy death of so many of his countrymen. He afterwards fled for safety into Spain, when Sylla had proscribed him; and in this distant province he behaved himself with so much address and valor, that he was looked upon as the sovereign of the country. The Lusitanians universally revered and loved him; and the Roman general, in gratitude for the public support which he received, showed himself particularly attentive to their interest, by establishing schools, and educating the children of the country in the polite arts, and the literature of Greece and Rome. He selected also a council under the name of a senate, over which he presided with consular authority, and the Romans who followed his standard paid equal reverence to his person. They were experimentally convinced of his valor and magnanimity as a general; and the artful manner in which he imposed upon the credulity of his adherents in the garb of religion, did not diminish his reputation. He pretended to hold commerce with heaven by means of a white hind which he had tamed with great success, and which followed him everywhere, even into the field of battle. The success of Sertorius in Spain, and his popularity among the natives alarmed the Romans. They sent some troops to oppose him, but with little effect. Four armies were found insufficient to crush, or even to injure the power of Sertorius; and Pompey and Metellus, who never engaged an enemy without obtaning the victory, were driven with dishonor from the field. But the favorite of the Lusitanians was exposed to the dangers which usually attend greatness. Perpenna, one of his generals, who was jealous of his fame, and tired of a superior, conspired against him, and gained over some of the other officers to his party. At a banquet, the conspirators began to open their intentions by speaking with freedom and licentiousness in the presence of Sertorius, whose age and character had hitherto claimed deference from others. Perpenna overturned a glass of wine as a signal to the the rest of the conspirators, and immediately Antonius, one of his officers, stabbed Sertorius, and the example was followed by all the rest, 73 years B.C. Sertorius has been commended for his love of justice and moderation. The flattering description which he heard of the Fortunate Islands, when he passed into the west of Africa, almost tempted him to bid adieu to the world; and perhaps he would have retired from the noise of war, and the clamors of envy, to end his days in the bosom of a peaceful and solitary island, had not the stronger calls of ambition and the thirst for fame prevailed. It has been observed that Sertorius in his latter days became indolent, and fond of luxury and wanton cruelty; yet we must confess that in affability, complaisance, generosity, and military valor, he surpassed not only his contemporaries, but the rest of the Romans. *Plut. in Vitâ.—Paterc.* 2. c. 30, &c.—*Appian. de Civ.* 1.—*Flor.* 3. c. 21, &c.—*Val. Max.* 1. c. 2. l. 7. c. 3.—*Eutrop.* 6.—*Auctor. de Vir. Illust.* 63 & 67.—*Frontin.* 1. c. 2, &c.—*Orosius*, 5. c. 22. *Plin.* 8. c. 32.—*Aul. Gell.* 15. c. 22.

SERVÆ'US QUIN'TUS, a man accused by Tiberius of being privy to the conspiracy of Sejanus. *Tacit. A.* 6. c. 7.

SERVIA'NUS, a consul in the reign of Adrian. He was a great favorite of the emperor Trajan. *Spartian. in Adrian.* c. 15.—*Vopisc. in Saturnin.* c. 8.

SERVIL'IA, a sister of Cato of Utica, greatly enamoured of Julius Cæsar, though her brother was one of the most inveterate enemies of her lover. To convince Cæsar of her affection, she sent him a letter filled with the most tender expressions of regard for his person. The letter was delivered to Cæsar in the senate-house, where they were debating about punishing the associates of Catiline's conspiracy; and when Cato saw it, he exclaimed that it was a letter from the conspirators, and insisted on its being made public. Upon this Cæsar gave it to Cato, and the stern senator had no sooner read its contents, than he threw it back with the words of "Take it, drunkard." From the intimacy which existed between Servilia and Cæsar, some have supposed that the dictator was the father of M. Brutus. *Plut. in Cæs. & Cat. Brut.—Suet. in Cæs.—C. Nep. in Attic.*——Another sister of Cato, who married Silanus.——A daughter of Bareas Soranus, put to death with her father, by order of Nero. Her crime was only the consulting of magicians to know what would happen in her family. *Tac. Ann.* 16. c. 30.

SERVIL'IA LEX *de pecuniis repetundis*, was introduced by C. Servilius the prætor, A.U.C. 653. It punished severely such as were guilty of peculation and extortion in the provinces. Its particulars are not precisely known.—Another, *de judicibus*, by Q. Servilius Cæpio the consul, A.U.C. 648. It divided the right of judging between the senators and the equites; a privilege which, though originally belonging to the senators, had been taken from them and given to the equites.—Another, *de civitate*, by C. Servilius ordained, that, if a Latin accused a Roman senator, so that he was condemned, the accuser should be honored with the name and the privileges of a Roman citizen —Another, *agraria*, by P. Servilius Rullus the tribune, A.U.C. 690. It required the immediate sale of certain houses and lands which belonged to the people for the purchase of others in a different part of Italy. It required that ten commissioners should be appointed to see it carried into execution, but Cicero prevented its passing into a law by the three orations which he pronounced against it.

SERVILIA'NUS, a Roman consul defeated by Viriathus in Spain, &c.

SERVIL'IUS QUIN'TUS, a Roman who, in his dictatorship, defeated the Æqui.

SERVIL'IUS PUB'LIUS, a consul who supported the cause of the people against the nobles, and obtained a triumph in spite of the opposition of the senate, after defeating the Volsci. He afterwards changed his opinions, and very violently opposed the people, because they had illiberally treated him.

SERVIL'IUS, a pro-consul killed at the battle of Cannæ by Annibal.——An augur prosecuted by Lucullus for his inattention in his office. He was acquitted.——A prætor ordered by the senate to forbid Sylla to approach Rome. He was ridiculed and insulted by the conqueror's soldiers.——A man appointed by Pompey to guard the sea-coast of Pontus.——A Roman general who defeated an army of Etrurians.——An informer in the court of Tiberius.——A favourite of Augustus.

SERVIL'IUS AHA'LA, a master of the horse to the dictator Cincinnatus. When Mælius refused to appear before the dictator, to answer the accusations which were brought against him on suspicion of his aspiring to tyranny, Ahala slew him in the midst of the people, whose protection he claimed. Ahala was accused for this murder, and banished, but this sentence was afterwards repealed. He was raised to the dictatorship.

SERVIL'IUS MAR'CUS, a man who pleaded in favour of Paulus Æmilius, &c.

SERVIL'IUS PUB'LIUS, a pro-consul of Asia during the age of Mithridates. He conquered Isauria, for which service he was surnamed *Isauricus*, and rewarded with a triumph.

SERVIL'IUS GEM'INUS, a Roman consul who opposed Annibal with success.

SERVIL'IUS NONIA'NUS, a Latin historian who wrote a history of Rome in the reign of Nero. There were more than one writer of this name, as *Pliny* speaks of a Servilius remarkable for his eloquence and learning; and *Quintilian* mentions another equally illustrious for his genius and literary merit.

SERVIL'IUS CAS'CA, one of Cæsar's murderers. The family of the Servilii was of patrician rank, and came to settle at Rome after the destruction of Alba, where they were promoted to the highest offices of the state. To the several branches of this family were attached the different surnames of Ahala, Axilla, Priscus, Cæpio, Structus, Geminus, Pulex, Vatia, Casca, Fidenas, Longus, and Tucca.

SERVIL'IUS LA'CUS, a lake near Rome. *Cic. S. Ros.* 32.

SER'VIUS TUL'LIUS, the sixth king of Rome, was son of Ocrisia, a slave of Corniculum, by Tulleus, a man slain in the defence of his country against the Romans. Ocrisia was given by Tarquin to Tanaquil his wife, and she brought up her son in the king's family, and added the name of Servius to that which he had inherited from his father, to denote his slavery. Young Servius was educated in the palace of the monarch with great care, and though originally a slave, raised himself to so much consequence, by his good conduct and valor, that Tarquin gave him his daughter in marriage. His own private merit and virtues recommended him to public notice not less than the royal favor, and Servius, become the favorite of the people and the darling of the soldiers, by his liberality and complaisance, was easily raised to the throne on the death of his father-in-law. Rome had no reason to repent of her choice. Servius endeared himself to the people still more as a warrior and a legislator. He defeated the Veientes and the Tuscans, and by a proper act of policy established the census, which told him that the population of Rome amounted to about 84 thousand inhabitants. He increased the number of the tribes, beautified and adorned the city, and enlarged its boundaries by taking within its walls the hills Quirinalis, Viminalis, and Esquilinus. He also divided the Roman people into tribes, and, that he might not seem to neglect the worship of the gods, he built several temples to the goddess of fortune, to whom he deemed himself particularly indebted for obtaining the kingdom. He also built a temple to Diana on mount Aventine, and raised himself a palace on the hill Esquilinus. Servius married his two daughters to the grandsons of his father-in-law; the elder to Tarquin, and the younger to Aruns. This union, it might have been supposed, would have tended to ensure the peace of his family; but if such were his expectations, he was unhappily deceived. The wife of Aruns, naturally fierce and impetuous in her disposition, murdered her own husband to unite herself to Tarquin, who had likewise assassinated his wife. These bloody measures were no sooner effected, than Servius himself was murdered by his own son-in-law, and his daughter Tullia showed herself so inimical to filial gratitude and piety, that she ordered her chariot to be driven over the mangled remains of her father, B.C. 534. The death of Servius was universally lamented, and the slaves annually celebrated a festival in his honor, in the temple of Diana, on mount Aventine, on the day that he was murdered. Tarquinia his wife buried his remains privately, and died of excess of grief on the following day. *Liv.* 1. c. 41.—*Dionys. Hal.* 4.—*Flor.* 1. c. 6.—*Cic. de Div.* 1. c. 53.—*Val. Max.* 1. c. 6.—*Ovid. Fast.* 6. v. 601.—*Juv.* 9. v. 259.—*Plin.* 2. c. 100. l. 36. c. 27.—*Servius ad Æn.* 2. v. 682.

SER'VIUS GAL'BA, a seditious person who wished to refuse a triumph to Paulus Æmilius after the conquest of Macedonia.

SER'VIUS CLAU'DIUS, a grammarian. *Suet. de cl. Gr.*

SER'VIUS, a friend of Sylla, who applied for the consulship to no purpose.——A despicable informer in the Augustan age. *Horat.* 2. sat. 1. v. 47.

SER'VIUS CORNE'LIUS, a consul in the first ages of the republic, &c.

SER'VIUS SULPIT'IUS, an orator in the age of Cicero and Hortensius. He was sent as ambassador to M. Antony, and died before his return. Cicero obtained a statue for him from the senate and the Roman people, which was raised in the Campus Martius. Besides orations, he wrote verses which were highly censured for their indelicacy. His works are lost. *Cic. in Brut. Phil.* 9, &c.—*Plin.* 5. ep. 3.

SER'VIUS MAU'RUS or MA'RIUS SER'VIUS HONORA'TUS, a learned grammarian in the age of Honorius and Theodosius. He wrote Latin commentaries upon Virgil, still extant. The first edition of these was published at Rome, 1471, by Udalricus Gallus; and afterwards at Venice, 1471. His *centimetrum* was edited by Santenius, Lug. Bat. 1788. He wrote also other works, some of which are not yet edited. *Harles. Not. Lit. Rom.* 1. p. 603.

SES'AMUM, a city of Paphlagonia. *Steph.*

SESA'NIUM, a town between Ægypt and Æthiopia. *Plin.* 6. c. 29.

SES'ARA, a daughter of Celeus king of Eleusis, and Metanira, was sister of Triptolemus. *Paus.* 1. c. 38. l. 7. c. 18.

SESARE'THUS, a city of the Taulantii. *Steph.*

SESA'TÆ, a people of the Sinæ. *Arrian. in Peripl.*

SESIN'DIUM, a city of India. *Steph.*

SESITH'ACUS, a son of Ægemerus leader of the Cherusci. *Strab.* l. 7.

SESOS'TRIS, a celebrated king of Ægypt some ages before the Trojan war. His father ordered all the children in his dominions who were born on the same day with him to be publicly educated, and to pass their youth in the company of his son. This scheme succeeded in the highest degree, and Sesostris had the pleasure to find himself surrounded by a number of faithful ministers and active warriors, whose education and intimacy with their prince rendered them inseparably devoted to his interest. When Sesostris had succeeded to his father's throne, he became ambitious of military fame, and after he had divided his kingdom into 36 different districts, he marched at the head of a numerous army to make the conquest of the world. Libya, Æthiopia, Arabia, with all the islands of the Red Sea, were conquered, and the victorious monarch marched through Asia and penetrated farther into the east than the conqueror of Darius. He also invaded Europe and subdued the Thracians; and that the fame of his conquests might long survive him, he placed columns in the several provinces which he subdued; and many ages after, this pompous inscription was read in many parts of Asia: "Sesostris, the king of kings, has conquered this territory by his arms." At his return home the monarch employed his time in encouraging the fine arts, and improving the revenues of his kingdom. He erected 100 temples to the gods for the victories he had obtained, and mounds of earth were heaped up in several parts of Ægypt, where cities were built for the reception of the inhabitants during the inundations of the Nile. Some canals were also dug near Memphis to facilitate navigation and the communication of one province with another. In his old age Sesostris, grown infirm and blind, destroyed himself, after a reign of 44 years, according to some. His mildness towards the conquered has been admired, while some have upbraided him for his cruelty and insolence in causing his chariot to be drawn by some of the monarchs whom he had vanquished. The age of Sesostris is so remote from every authentic record, that many suppose that the actions and conquests ascribed to this monarch are fabulous. *Herodot.* 2. c. 102, &c.—*Diod.* 1.—*Val. Flacc.* 5. v. 419.—*Plin.* 33. c. 3.—*Lucan.* 10. v. 276.—*Strab.* 16.

SESSI'TES, now Sessia, a river of Cisalpine Gaul, falling into the Po. *Plin.* 3. c. 16.

SESTIA'RIA EXTRE'MA, a promontory of Mauritania Tingitana, on the shores of the Mediterranean. *Ptol.* It is now Gebba, in the Kingdom of Fez.

SES'TIAS, a name applied to Hero, as born at Sestus. *Stat. Theb.* 6. 547.

SESTINA'TES, a people of Umbria. *Plin.* 3 c. 14.

SESTI'NUM, an inland city of the Œnotri. *Steph.*

SES'TIUS, a friend of Brutus with whom he fought at the battle of Philippi. Augustus resigned the consulship in his favor, though he still continued to reverence the memory of Brutus.——A governor of Syria.——A decemvir. *Liv.* 3. c. 33.——A physician mentioned by *Pliny*, 20. c. 21.

SES'TUS, a town of Thrace on the shores of the Hellespont, exactly opposite Abydus on the Asiatic side. It is celebrated for the bridge which Xerxes built there across the Hellespont, as also for being the seat of the amours of Hero and Leander. It is now Sesto. *Mela*, 1, c. 19. l. 2. c. 2.—*Strab.* 13.—*Musæus de L. & H.*—*Virg. G.* 3. v. 258.—*Ovid. Heroid.* 18. v. 2. *Trist.* 3. el. 10. v. 41.—*Lucan.* 9. v. 995.

SESU'VII, a people of Celtic Gaul. *Cæsar. Bell. G.*

SE'TA, a sister of Rhesus, mother of Bithys by Mars. *Steph.*

SET'ABIS, a town of Spain between New Carthage and Saguntum, famous for the manufacture of linen. There was also a small river of the same name in the neighbourhood. *Sil.* 16. v. 474.—*Strab.* 2.—*Mela*, 2. c. 6.—*Plin.* 3. c. 3. l. 19. c. 1.—*Catull.* 12. v. 14. ep. 25 v. 7.

SE'TÆ, a people of India, very rich in silver. *Plin.* 6. c. 19.

SETÆ'UM, a small region of Magna Græcia, between Sybaris and Thurii. *Steph.*

SETEL'SIS, a city of the Jaccetani in Hispania Tarraconensis. *Ptol.*

SE'THON, a priest of Vulcan, who made himself king of Ægypt after the death of Anysis. He was attacked by the Assyrians and delivered from this powerful enemy by an immense number of rats, which in one night gnawed their bowstrings and thongs, so that on the morrow their arms were found to be useless. From this wonderful circumstance Sethon had a statue which represented him with a rat in his hand, with the inscription of, "Whoever fixes his eyes upon me, let him be pious." *Herodot.* 2. c. 141.—*Joh. Marsham. Can. Chron. Sec.* 17.

SETHREI'TES or SETHROI'TES, a city and district of Ægypt within the Delta. *Ptol.*

SE'THRON, a city of Ægypt. *Joh. Marsham. Can. Chron. Sec.* 8.

SE'TIA, a town of Latium, above the Pontine Marshes, celebrated for its wines, which Augustus is said to have preferred to all others. *Plin.* 3. c. 5. l. 14. c. 6.—*Juv.* 5. v. 34. sat. 10. v. 27.—*Martial.* 13. epigr. 112.—*Strab.* 5.—*Stat.* 2. *Sylv.* 6. v. 90.——A city of Hispania Citerior. *Ptol.* It is now Sesse.

SETIDA'VA, a city of Germany. *Ptol.* It is now Posen.

SETIEN'SIS, a city of Africa Propria. *Id.*

SETO'VIA, a city of Dalmatia. *Appian.*

SETU'BIA, a city of Hispania Tarraconensis. *Ptol.* It is now Sepulveda.

SETU'IA, a city of Germany. *Id.* It is now Zittaw.

SETUN'DUM, a city of Upper Æthiopia. *Plin.*

SEV'ACES, a people of Noricum. *Ptol.*

SEVE'RA JU'LIA AQUIL'IA, a Roman lady, whom the emperor Heliogabalus married. She was soon after repudiated, though possessed of all the charms of mind and body which could captivate the most virtuous.

SEVE'RA VALE'RIA, the wife of Valentinian, and the mother of Gratian, was well known for her avarice and ambition. The emperor, her husband, repudiated her, and afterwards took her again. Her prudent advice at last ensured her son Gratian on the imperial throne.

SEVE'RA, the wife of Philip the Roman emperor.

SEVERIA'NUS, a governor of Macedonia, father-in-law to the emperor Philip.——A general of the Roman armies in the reign of Valentinian, defeated by the Germans.——A son of the emperor Severus.

SEVERIS'SIMUS, a centurion, slain by his seditious soldiers. *Tac. Hist.* 1. c. 80.

SEVE'RUS LU'CIUS SEPTIM'IUS, a Roman emperor born at Leptis in Africa, of a noble family. He gradually exercised all the offices of the state, and recommended himself to the notice of the world by an ambitious mind, and a restless activity, that could, for the gratification of avarice, endure the most complicated hardship. After the murder of Pertinax, Severus resolved to remove Didius Julianus, who had bought the imperial purple when exposed to sale by the licentiousness of the prætorians, and therefore proclaimed himself emperor on the borders of Illyricum, where he was stationed against the barbarians. To support himself in this bold measure, he took as his partner in the empire, Albinus, who was at the head of the Roman forces in Britain, and immediately marched towards Rome, to crush Didius and his partizans. He was received as he advanced through the country with universal acclamations, and Julianus was soon deserted by his favorites, and assassinated by his own soldiers. The reception of Severus at Rome was sufficient to gratify his pride; the streets were strewed with flowers, and the submissive senate was ever ready to grant whatever honors or titles the emperor claimed. In professing that he had assumed the purple only to avenge the death of the virtuous Pertinax, Severus gained many adherents, and was enabled not only to disarm, but to banish the prætorians, whose insolence and avarice were becoming alarming not only to the citizens, but to the emperor. But while he was victorious at Rome, Severus did not forget that there was another competitor for the imperial purple. Pescennius Niger was in the east at the head of a powerful army, and with the name and ensigns of Augustus. Many obstinate battles were fought between the troops and officers of the imperial rivals, till on the plains of Issus, which had been above five centuries before covered with the blood of the Persian soldiers of Darius, Niger was totally ruined by the loss of 20,000 men. The head of Niger was cut off, and sent to the conqueror, who punished in a most cruel manner all the partizans of his unfortunate rival. Severus afterwards pillaged Byzantium, which had shut her gates against him; and after he had conquered several nations in the east, returned to Rome, resolved to destroy Albinus, with whom he had hitherto reluctantly shared the imperial power. He attempted to assassinate him by his emissaries; but when this had failed of success, Severus had recourse to arms, and the fate of the empire was again decided on the plains of Gaul. Albinus was defeated, and the conqueror was so elated with the recollection that he had now no longer a competitor for the purple, that he insulted the dead body of his rival, and ordered it to be thrown into the Rhone, after he had suffered it to putrify before the door of his tent, and to be torn to pieces by his dogs. The family and the adherents of Albinus shared his fate; and the return of Severus to the capital exhibited a repetition of the bloody triumphs of Marius and Sylla. The richest of the citizens were sacrificed, and their money became the property of the emperor. The wicked Commodus received divine honors, and his murderers were punished in the most wanton manner. Tired of the inactive life he led in Rome, Severus marched into the east, with his two sons, Caracalla and Geta, and with uncommon success made himself master of Seleucia, Babylon, and Ctesiphon, and advanced without opposition, far into the Parthian territories. From Parthia the emperor marched towards the more southern provinces of Asia; after he had visited the tomb of Pompey the Great, he entered Alexandria; and after he had granted a senate to that celebrated city, he viewed with the most criticising and inquisitive curiosity the several monuments and ruins which that ancient kingdom contains. The revolt of Britain recalled him from the east. After he had reduced it under his power, he built a wall across the northern parts of the island, to defend it against the frequent invasions of the Caledonians. Hitherto successful against his enemies, Severus now found the peace of his family disturbed. Caracalla attempted to murder his father, as he was concluding a treaty of peace with the Britons; and the emperor was so shocked at the undutifulness of his son, that on his return home he called him into his presence, and after he had upbraided him for his ingratitude and perfidy, he offered him a drawn sword, adding, "If you are so ambitious of reigning alone, now imbrue your hands in the blood of your father, and let not the eyes of the world be witnesses of your want of filial tenderness." If these words checked Caracalla, yet he did not show himself concerned, and Severus, worn out with infirmities which the gout and the uneasiness of his mind increased, soon after died, exclaiming that he had been everything man could wish, but that he was then nothing. Some say that he wished to poison himself, but that when this was denied, he ate to great excess, and soon after expired at York on the 4th of February, in the 211th year of the Christian era, in the 66th of his age, after a reign of 17 years, 8 months, and three days. Severus has been so much admired for his military talents, that some have called him the most warlike of the Roman emperors. As a monarch he was cruel, and it has been observed that he never did an act of humanity, or forgave a fault. In his diet he was temperate, and always showed himself an open enemy to pomp and splendor. He loved the appellation of a man of letters, and even composed a history of his own reign, which some have praised for its correctness and veracity. However cruel Severus may appear in his punishments and in his revenge, many have endeavoured to exculpate him, and observed that there was need of severity in an empire the morals of which were so corrupted, and where no less than 3,000 persons were accused of adultery during the space of 17 years. Of him, as of Augustus, some were found to say, that it would have been better for the world, if he had never been born, or had never died. *Dio.—Herodian.—Victor, &c.—Spartian. in vita.—Eutropius.—Orosius.* [The busts of this emperor are very numerous; that in the Vatican is the best; there is a statue in the Villa Albani, near Rome.]

SEVE'RUS ALEXAN'DER MAR'CUS AURE'LIUS, a native of Phœnicia, adopted by Heliogabalus. His father's name was Genesius Marcianus, and his mother's Julia Mammæa, and he received the surname of Alexander the Great. He was carefully educated, and his mother, by paying particular attention to his morals, and the character of his preceptors, preserved him from those infirmities, and that licentiousness which old age too often attributes to the depravity of youth. At the death of Heliogabalus, who had been jealous of his virtues, Alexander, though only in the 14th year of his age, was proclaimed emperor, and his nomination was approved by the universal shouts of the army, and the congratulations of the senate. He had not long been on the throne before the peace of the empire was disturbed by the incursions of the Persians. Alexander marched into the east without delay, and soon obtained a decisive victory over the barbarians. At his return to Rome he was honored with a triumph, but the revolt of the Germans soon after called him away from the indolence of the capital. His expedition into Germany was attended with some success, but the virtues and amiable qualities of Alexander were forgotten in the stern and sullen strictness of the disciplinarian. His soldiers, fond of repose, murmured against his severity; their clamours were fomented by the artifice of Maximinus, and Alexander was murdered in his tent, in the midst of his camp, after a reign of 13 years and 9 days, on the 18th of March, A.D. 235. His mother Mammæa shared his fate, with all his friends; but this was no sooner known than the soldiers punished with immediate death all such as had been concerned in the murder, except Maximinus. Alexander has been admired for his many virtues, and every historian, except Herodian, is bold to assert, that if he had lived, the Roman empire might soon have been freed from those tumults and abuses which continually disturbed her peace, and kept the lives of her emperors and senators in perpetual alarms. His severity in punishing offences was great, and such as had robbed the public, were they even the most intimate friends of the emperor, were indiscriminately sacrificed to the tranquillity of the state which they had violated. The great offices of the state, which had before his reign been exposed to sale, and occupied by favorites, were now bestowed upon merit, and Alexander could boast that all his officers were men of trust and abilities. He was a patron of literature, and dedicated the hours of relaxation to the study of the best Greek and Latin historians, orators, and poets; and in the public schools, which his liberality and the desire of encouraging learning had founded, he often heard with pleasure and satisfaction the eloquent speeches and declamations of his subjects. The provinces were well supplied with provisions, and Rome was embellished with many stately buildings and magnificent porticos by him. *Alex. vit.—Herodian.—Zosim.—Victor. Æl. Lamprid. in vitâ.* [A bust of Alexander Severus will be found in the Vatican; where also is a statue of Sallustia Barbia his wife, in the character of Venus, with a Cupid.]

Seve'rus Fla'vius Vale'rius, a native of Illyricum, nominated Cæsar by Galerius. He was put to death by Maximianus, A.D. 307. *Zosim.* l. 12.—*Eutrop.* l. 9, *&c.*

Seve'rus Ju'lius, a governor of Britain, under Adrian.

Seve'rus, a general of Valens.——An officer under the emperor Julian.——An officer of Valentinian, &c.——A prefect of Rome, &c.——A celebrated architect employed in building Nero's golden palace at Rome, after the burning of that city. *Tac. Ann.* 15. c 42.

Seve'rus, a mountain of the Sabines in Italy, near the Fabaris. *Virg. Æn.* 7. v. 713.—*Servius loco.*

Seve'rus Aquil'ius, a native of Spain, who wrote an account of his own life, in the reign of the emperor Valens.

Seve'rus Lib'ius, a man proclaimed emperor of the west, at Ravenna, after the death of Majorianus. He was soon after poisoned, A.D. 465. *Marcellin. & Cassiodor. in Chron.*

Seve'rus Lu'cius Corne'lius, a Latin poet in the age of Augustus, for some time employed in the judicial proceedings of the forum. He wrote a pathetic elegy on the death of Cicero, and attempted an heroic poem on the wars of Sicily, which remained imperfect on account of his untimely death. Some of the ancients have commended his genius and abilities, but Quintilian considered him rather as a correct writer than a sublime poet. Besides his Ætna only 33 of his verses are preserved. The remains of his works may be found in the "Fragmenta Veterum Poetarum" of Rob. et Hen. Stephens, Paris, 1564. They were edited also by Le Clerc, with the notes of Jos Scaliger and Lindenbroch, Amstel. 1703 & 1715. *Harles. Not. Lit. Rom.* p. 293.—*Seneca.—Quintil.*

Seve'rus Cas'sius, an orator banished to the island of Crete, by Augustus, for his illiberal language. He remained an exile for 17 years, and died in Seriphus. He is commended as an able orator, yet declaiming with more warmth than prudence. His writings were destroyed by order of the senate. *Suet. in Oct.—Quint.*

Seve'rus Sulpit'ius, an ecclesiastical historian who died A.D. 420. The best of his works is his "Historia Sacra," from the creation of the world to the consulship of Stilicho, of which the style is elegant, and superior to that of the age in which he lived. The best edition is in 2 vols. 4to Patavii, 1741.

SEVI'NUS PROMPTI'NUS, a person restored to the dignity of senator by Otho. *Tac. Hist.* 1. c. 77.

SEU'MARA, a city of Iberia in Asia. *Strab.* l. 11.

SE'VO, a ridge of mountains between Norway and Sweden, now called Dofrefield. *Plin.* 4. c. 15.

SEU'RI, a people of Hispania Tarraconensis. *Ptol.* They are called Seurbi by *Pliny*, 4. c. 20.

SEU'THES, a man who dethroned his monarch, &c. *Aristot.* l. 5. *Polit.* c. 10.——A friend of Perdiccas, one of Alexander's generals.——A Thracian king, who encoureged his countrymen to revolt, &c. This name is common to several of the Thracian princes, one of whom engaged in service the 10,000 Greeks, on their return from Cunaxa, and kept them two or three months in his pay. *C. Nep.*

SEX'ANA, a city of Sicily. *Phavorinus.*

SEXIGNA'NI or **SEXAGNA'NI**, a people of Gallia Aquitanica. *Plin.*

SEXOLI'TÆ, a people near the Euxine Sea. *Pompon.*

SEXTA'NI, a people of Gaul. *Id.*

SEXTA'TIO or **SEXTAN'TIO**, a city of Gallia Narbonensis. *Antonin.* It is now Soustancion.

SEX'TIA, a woman celebrated for her virtue and her constancy, put to death by Nero. *Tacit. Ann.* 16 c.10.

Sex'tia Licin'ia Lex, *de magistratibus*, was introduced by C. Licinius and L. Sextius the tribunes, A.U.C 386. It ordained that one of the consuls should be elected from among the Plebeians.—Another, *de religione*, by the same, A.U.C. 385. It enacted that a decemvirate should be chosen from the patricians and plebeians instead of the *decemviri sacris faciundis.*

Sex'tiæ A'quæ, now Aix, a place in Cisalpine Gaul, where the Cimbri were defeated by Marius. It was built by C. Sextius, and is famous for its cold and hot springs. *Liv.* 61.—*Vell. Pater.* 1. c. 15.

SEXTIL'IA, the wife of Vitellius. She became mother of two children. *Suet. in Vit.—Tacit H.* 2. c. 64.

SEXTIL'IUS, a governor of Africa, who ordered Marius when he landed there to depart immediately from his province. Marius heard this with some concern, and said to the messenger, "Go and tell your master that you have seen the exiled Marius sitting on the ruins of Carthage." *Plut. in Mar.*——A Roman preceptor, who was seized and carried away by pirates, &c.——One of the officers of Lucullus.——A friend of Milo. *Cic. Fr.* 2. ep. 1.

Sextil'ius Hæ'na, a poet. *Vid.* Hæna.

Sextil'ius Fe'lix, an officer sent to Germany, &c. *Tacit. H.* 3. c 7.

SEX'TIUS TI'TUS, a lieutenant of Cæsar in Gaul. *Cæs. Comm.* 6. c. 1 & 7. c. 49.

Sex'tius Pub'lius, a tribune, who favored the interests of Cicero, and was earnest for his recal from banishment. When accused of sedition and of the murder of those who had fallen in the tumult occasioned by Clodius, he was ably defended by Cicero and Hortensius, and acquitted. *Cic. pro Sext. Fr.* 2. ep. 4,

Sex'tius, a seditious tribune in the first ages of the republic.——A dictator.——One of the sons of Tarquin. *Vid.* Tarquinius.

Sex'tius Lu'cius, was remarkable for his friendship with Brutus; he gained the confidence of Augustus, and was afterwards consul. *Horace*, who was in the number of his friends, dedicated od. 4. lib. 1. to him.——The first plebeian consul. *Plut.—Fast. Capitolin.*

SEX'TUS, a prænomen given to the sixth son of a family.——A son of Pompey the Great. *Vid.* Pompeius.——A stoic philosopher, born at Cheronæa in Bœotia. Some suppose that he was Plutarch's nephew. He was preceptor to M. Aurelius and L. Verus. *Jul. Capitol. in vit. M. Antonin.* c. 3. [There is a statue of this philosopher in the Vatican.]——A governor of Syria.——A philosopher in the age of Antoninus. He was one of the followers of the doctrine of Pyrrho. Some of his works are still extant. The best edition of the treatise of Sextus Pompeius Festus "De Verborum Significatione" is that of Amst. 4to. 1699. *Sax. Onom.* 1. p. 332, &c.

SI'Æ, a city of Armenia Major. *Ptol.*

SI'AGUL, a maritime city of Africa Propria. *Id.*

SI'ALA, a city of Tyanitis in Cappadocia. *Id.*

SIAN'TICUM, a city of Noricum, on the confines of Pannonia. *Id.* It is now Sanneck.

SI'ARA, a city of Armenia Minor. *Antonin.*

SIATUTAN'DA, a town of Germany. *Ptol.*

SIAVA'NA, a city of Armenia Major. *Id.*

SI'BÆ, a people of India. *Strabo.—Dionys.* v. 1141.

SIBA'RÆ, a people of India. *Plin.* 6. c. 20.

SIB'ARIS. *Vid.* Sybaris.

SIB'DA, a city of Caria. *Steph.*

SIBI'NI, a people near the Suevi. *Strab.* 7.

SIB'ORA, a city of Cappadocia. *Antonin.*

SIB'OTES, an auxiliary in the war between Perses and Æetes, slain by Ambenus. *Val. Flacc.* 6. v. 249.

SIB'RIUM, a city of India within the Ganges. *Ptol.*

SI'BRUS, a river of Lycia. *Steph.*

SIBUR'TIUS, a satrap of Arachosia, in the age of Alexander, &c. *Plut. in Eumen.—Polyæn.* 4.—*Diod.* l. 19.

SIBUTZA'TES, a people of Gallia Aquitanica, near the Garumni. *Ptol.* Their town is now Sobusse.

SI'BY, a town of Arabia Felix, or of the Elamitæ, called by the Greeks Apate. *Plin.* 6. c. 28.

SIBYL'LÆ, certain women said to have been inspired by heaven with the knowledge of futurity. They flourished in different parts of the world, but their exact number is unknown. Plato speaks of one, Capella of two, Pliny of three, Pausanias and Ælian of four, and Varro of ten, an opinion which is universally adopted by the learned. These ten Sibyls generally resided in the following places, Persia, Libya, Delphi, Cumæ in Italy, Erythræa, Samus, Cumæ in Æolia, Marpessa on the Hellespont, Ancyra in Phrygia, and Tiburtis. The most celebrated of the Sybils is that of Cumæ in Italy, whom some have called by the different names of Amalthæa, Demophile, Herophile, Daphne, Manto, Phemonoe, and Deiphobe. It is said that Apollo became enamoured of her, and that to make her sensible of his passion he offered to give her whatever she should ask. The Sibyl requested that she might live as many years as she had grains of sand in her hand, but unfortunately forgot to ask for the enjoyment of health, vigor, and bloom, of which she was then in possesion. The god granted her request, but she refused to gratify the passion of her lover, though he offered her perpetual youth and beauty. Some time after she became old and decrepid, her form decayed; melancholy, paleness, and haggard looks succeeded to bloom, and cheerfulness. She had already lived about 700 years when Æneas came to Italy, and some have imagined that she had three centuries more to live before her years were as numerous as the grains of sand which she had in her hand. She gave Æneas instructions how to find his father in the infernal regions, and even conducted him to the entrance of hell. It was usual in the Sybil to write her prophecies on leaves which she placed at the entrance of her cave, and it required particular care in such as consulted her to take up these leaves before they were dispersed by the wind, as their meaning then became incomprehensible. According to the most correct historians of the Roman republic, one of the Sibyls came to the palace of Tarquin the elder, some say the second, with nine volumes, which she offered to sell for a very high price. The monarch disregarded her, and she immediately disappeared, and soon after returned, when she had burned three of the volumes. She asked the same price for the remaining six books; and when Tarquin refused to buy them she burned three more, and still persisted in demanding the same sum of money for the three that were left. This extraordinary behaviour astonished Tarquin; he bought the books, and the Sibyl instantly vanished, and never after appeared to the world. These books were preserved with great care by the monarch, and called the "Sibylline verses." A college of priests called *Decemviri*, and afterwards *Quindecemviri*, from their number, was appointed to have the care of them; and such reverence did the Romans entertain for these prophetic books, that they were consulted with the greatest solemnity, and only when the state seemed to be in the most imminent danger. When the Capitol was burnt in the troubles of Sylla, the Sibylline verses, which were deposited there, perished in the conflagration; and to repair the loss which the republic seemed to have sustained, commissioners were immediately sent to different parts of Greece, to collect whatever verses could be found of the inspired writings of the Sibyls. The fate of these Sibylline verses, which were collected after the conflagration of the Capitol, is unknown. There are now eight books of Sibylline verses extant, but they are universally reckoned spurious. They speak so plainly of our Saviour, of his sufferings, and of his death, as even to surpass the sublime predictions of Isaiah in minuteness of description, and therefore, from this very circumstance, it is evident that they were composed in the second century, by some of the followers of Christianity, who wished to convince the heathens of their error, by assisting the cause of truth with the arms of pious artifice. The word Sibyl seemed to be derived from Σιοῦ, Æolice for Διὸς, *Jovis*, and βουλὴ *consilium*. *Plut. in Phæd.—Ælian. V. H.* 12. c. 35.—*Paus.* 10. c. 12, &c.—*Diod.* 4.—*Ovid. Met.* 14. v. 109 & 140.—*Virg. Æn.* 3. v 445. l. 6. v. 36.—*Servius. locis.*—*Lucan.* 1. v. 564.—*Plin.* 13. c. 13.—*Flor.* 4. c. 1.—*Sallust.*—*Cic. Catil.* 3. c. 4.—*Val. Max.* 1. c. 1. l. 8. c. 15. &c.—*Propert.* 2. el. 2. v. 68. el. 19. v. 19.—*Aul. Gell.* 1. c. 19.—*Solin.* 8.—*Lactant.* 1. c. 6.—*Isidor. Orig.* 8. c. 8.—*Tacit. Ann.* 6. c. 12.—*Suidas.*

SIBYR'TUS, a city of Crete. *Steph.*

SI'CA, a man who showed much attention to Cicero in his banishment. Some suppose that he is the same as the Vibius Siculus mentioned by *Plutarch in Cic.—Cic. ad Attic.* 3. ep. 2. l. 8. ep. 12. *Ad. div.* 14. c. 4, 15.

SICAM'BRI, SYCAM'BRI, SYGAM'BRI, SUGAM'BRI or SUCAM'BRI, a people of Germany, near the Lippe, the Weser, and the Rhine, conquered by the Romans after an obstinate resistance. They revolted under Augustus, who marched against them, but did not totally reduce them. Drusus conquered them, and they were carried away from their native country to inhabit some of the more westerly provinces of Gaul, between the Rhine and the Meuse. These provinces now form the duchies of Gueldres and Cleves. *Dio.* 54.—*Strab.* 4.—*Horat.* 4. od. 2. v. 36. od. 14. v. 51.—*Tacit.* 2. *Ann.* 26.—*Propert.* 4. el. 6. v. 77.—*Martial. de Spect.* 3.—*Claudian. in Eutr.* 1. v. 383.

SICAM'BRIA, the country of the Sicambri, formed the modern province of Guelderland. *Claud. in Eutrop.* 1. v. 383.

SICA'NE, a city of Iberia. *Steph*

SICA'NI, a people of Spain, who left their native country and passed into Italy, and afterwards into Sicily, which they called Sicania. They inhabited the neighbourhood of mount Ætna, where they built some cities and villages. Some reckoned them the next inhabitants of the island after the Cyclopes. They were afterwards driven from their ancient possessions by the Siculi, and retired into the western parts of the island. *Dionys. Hal.* 1.—*Ovid. Met.* 5 & 13.—*Virg. Ecl.* 10. *Æn.* 7. v. 795.—*Servius ad Æn.* 1. v. 587. l. 8. v. 328. l. 10. v. 4. l. 11. v. 317.—*Lucan.* 2. v. 548. l. 3. v. 59 & 176. l. 6. v. 66.—*Ital.* 14. v. 40.—*Diod.* 5.—*Horat Ep.* 17. v. 32.

SICA'NIA or SICANI'A, an ancient name of Italy, which it received from the Sicani, or from Sicanus, their king, or from Sicanus, a small river in Spain, in the territory where they lived, as some suppose. The name was more generally given to Sicily. *Vid.* Sicani.

SIC'APHA, a town of Africa Propria. *Ptol.*

SICAS'SA, an island of the Ægean Sea, opposite Ephesus. *Plin.* 31. c. 5.

SIC'CA, or SIC'CA VENE'RIA, a town of Numidia, at the west of Carthage. *Sall. in Jug.* 56.

SICEL'IA CÆSARE'A, a city of Mauritania, the native place of Macrinus. *Xiphilinus.*

SIC'ELIS (*Sicelides*, plur.), an epithet applied to the inhabitants of Sicily. The Muses are called *Sicelides* by Virgil, because Theocritus, whom the Latin poet, as a writer of Bucolic poetry professed to imitate, was a native of Sicily. *Virg. Ecl.* 4.

SICE'MUS, a city of Arabia. *Steph.*

SICEN'DUS, a lake of Thessaly, the frogs of which were mute. *Plin.* 8. c. 58.

SICE'NUS, an island near Crete, formerly called Œnoe. *Steph.*

SICHÆ'US, called also Sicarbus and Acerbas, was a priest of the temple of Hercules in Phœnicia. His father's name was Plisthenes. He married Elisa, the daughter of Belus, and sister of king Pygmalion, better known by the name of Dido. He was so extremely rich that his brother-in-law murdered him to obtain his possessions. This murder Pygmalion concealed from his sister Dido; and amused her by telling her that her husband was gone upon an affair of importance, and that he would soon return. This would perhaps have succeeded had not the shade of Sichæus appeared to Dido, and related to her the cruelty of Pygmalion, and advised her to flee from Tyre, after she had previously secured some treasures, which, as he mentioned, were concealed in an obscure and unknown place. According to Justin, Acerbas was the uncle of Dido. *Virg. Æn.* 1. v. 347, &c. *Servius loco.—Paterc.* 1. c. 6.—*Justin.* 18. c. 4.

SICIL'IA, the largest and most celebrated island in the Mediterranean Sea, at the bottom of Italy. It was anciently called Sicania, Trinacria, and Triquetra. It is of a triangular form, and has three celebrated promontories: one looking towards Africa, called Lilybæum; Pachynum looking towards Greece; and Pelorum towards Italy. Sicily is about 600 miles in circumference, and so much celebrated for its fertility, that it was called one of the granaries of Rome, and Pliny says that it rewards the husbandman a hundred fold. Its most famous cities were Syracuse, Messana, Leontini, Lilybæum, Agrigentum, Gela, Drepanum, Eryx, Catana, Hybla, Cuma, and Naxus. The highest and most celebrated mountain in the island is Ætna, the frequent eruptions of which are dangerous, and often fatal, to the country and its inhabitants, from which circumstance the ancients supposed that the forges of Vullcan and the Cyclopes were placed there. The poets feign that the Cyclopes were the original inhabitants of this island, and that after them it came into the possession of the Sicani, a people of Spain, and at last of the Siculi, a nation of Italy. *Vid.* Siculi. The plains of Enna are well known for their excellent honey, and, according to Diodorus, the hounds lost their scent in hunting on account of the many odoriferous plants that profusely perfumed the air. Ceres and Proserpine were the chief deities of the place, and it was from the plains of Enna according to poetical tradition, that the latter was carried away by Pluto. The Phœnicians and Greeks settled some colonies there, and at last the Carthaginians became masters of the whole island, till they were dispossessed of it by the Romans in the Punic wars. Some authors suppose that Sicily was originally joined to the continent, and that it was separated from Italy by an earthquake, and that the straits of the Charybdis were thus formed. The inhabitants of Sicily were so fond of luxury, that *Siculæ mensæ* became proverbial. The rights of citizens of Rome were extended to them by M. Antony. *Cic.* 14. *Att* 12. *Verr.* 2. c. 13.—*Homer. Odyss* 9. v. 109.—*Strab.* 1.—*Mela*, 2. c. 7 1. 3. c. 6.—*Ptol.* 3. c. 4.—*Ovid. Met.* 5. v. 385. *Fast.* 4. v. 417.—*Claudian. de Rapt. Pr.* 1. v. 140, &c.—*Justin.* 4. c. 1, &c.—*Virg. Æn.* 3. v. 414, &c. *Servius ad Ecl.* 10. v. 4. *Æn.* 3. v. 384 & 687.—*Seneca, Cons. ad Mar.* 17.—*Ital.* 14. v. 11, &c.—*Plin.* 3. c. 8. 1. 18. c. 10.—*Apul. Met.* 11.

SICIL'IA MI'NOR, a name given to the island of Naxus, in the Ægean, on account of its fruitfulness.

SICILIB'BA or SICILIB'RA, a city of Africa Propria. *Antonin.*

L. SICIN'IUS DENTA'TUS, a Roman tribune, celebrated for his valor and the honors which he obtained in the field of battle, during the period of 40 years, in which he was engaged in the Roman armies. He was present in 121 battles; obtained 14 civic crowns; 3 mural crowns; 8 crowns of gold; 183 golden collars; 160 bracelets; 18 lances; 23 horses, with all their ornaments, and all as the reward of his uncommon services. He could show the scars of 45 wounds, all of which he had received in the breast, particularly in opposing the Sabines when they took the Capitol. The popularity of Sicinius became odious to Appius Claudius, who wished to make himself absolute at Rome, and therefore to remove him from the capital, he sent him to the army, by which, soon after his arrival, he was attacked and murdered. Of 100 men who were ordered to fall upon him, Sicinius killed 15, and wounded 30; and according to Dionysius, the surviving number had recourse to artifice to overpower him, by killing him with a shower of stones and darts thrown at a distance, about 405 years B.C. For this uncommon courage Sicinius has been called the Roman Achilles. *Val. Max.* 3. c. 2.—*Dionys.* 8.—*Plin.* 7. c. 27.—*Aul. Gell.* 11. c. 11.—*Festus de V. Sig.*

SICIN'IUS CA'IUS, a man by whose influence the Roman populace retired from the city to mount Sacer. He was one of the first tribunes made. *Liv.* 2. c. 33 & 58. 1. 3. c. 54.

SICIN'IUS VELLU'TUS, one of the first tribunes in Rome. He raised cabals against Coriolanus, and was one of his accusers. *Plut. in Cor.*

SICIN'IUS SUBI'NUS, a Roman general who defeated the Volsci.

SIC'INUS or SICIN'NUS, a man privately sent by Themistocles to deceive Xerxes, and to advise him to attack the combined forces of the Greeks. He had been preceptor to Themistocles. *Plut.*

SIC'INUS or SIC'INOS, an island of the Ægæan Sea. *Ptol.—Strab.—Plin.* 4. c. 12.

SICOBASILIS'CES, a city of Armenia. *Antonin*

SICOBO'TES, a people of European Sarmatia. *Jul. Capitol. in vit M. Antonin.* c. 22.

SIC'ORIS, now Segre, a river of Hispania Tarraconensis, rising in the Pyrenean mountains, and falling into the Iberus a little above its mouth. It was near this river that J. Cæsar conquered Afranius and Petreius, the partizans of Pompey. *Lucan.* 4. v. 14. 133, &c. *Plin.* 3. c. 3.—*Auson.* 25. v. 58.—*Servius ad Æn.* 8. v. 328.

SIC'ULI, a people of Italy, driven from their possessions by the Opici. They fled into Sicania or Sicily, where they settled in the territories which the Sicani inhabited. They soon extended their borders, and after they had conquered their neighbours the Sicani, they gave their name to the island. This, as some suppose, happened about 300 years before Greek colonists settled in the island, or about 1059 years B.C. *Diod.* 5.—*Dionys. Hal.—Strab.* 6.—*Thucyd.* 6.—*Servius ad Virg. Æn.* 8. c. 328.

SIC'ULUM FRETUM or MA'RE, the sea which separated Sicily from Italy, is 15 miles long, but in some places so narrow that the barking of dogs can be heard from shore to shore. The strait is supposed to have been formed by an earthquake, which separated the island from the continent. *Plin.* 3. c. 8.

SIC'ULUS, a son of Neptune, king of Sicily after Sicanus. *Solin.* c. 5.

SIC'YON, now Basilico, a town of Peloponnesus, the capital of Sicyonia. It was celebrated as being the most ancient kingdom of Greece, having begun B.C. 2089, and ended B.C. 1088, under a succession of monarchs of whom little is known, except the names. Ægialeus was the first king. Some ages after, Agamemnon made himself master of the place, and it afterwards fell into the hands of the Heraclidæ. It became very powerful in the time of the Achæan league, which it joined B.C. 251, at the persuasion of Aratus. It was destroyed by Demetrius, son of Antigonus, who rebuilt it, and endeavoured to impose upon it the name of Demetrias, which was soon exchanged for its more respectable and ancient appellation The inhabitants of Sycion are characterised by some authors as dissolute, and fond of luxury, hence the Sicyonian shoes, which were once very celebrated, were deemed marks of effeminacy among the Romans. *Apollod.* 3. c. 5.—*Lucret.* 1. v. 118.—*Liv.* 32. c. 19 1. 33. c. 15.—*Strab.* 8.—*Mela*, 2. c. 3.—*Plut. in Dem.—Paus.* 2. c. 1, &c.—*Cic. de Orat.* 1. c. 54.—*Virg. G.* 2. v. 519.—*Plin.* 36. c. 4.—*Festus V. Sig.—Servius ad Virg. loco. cit. & Æn.* 6. v. 480.——A place of Africa. where the Crathis falls into the ocean. *Plin.* 19. c. 8. ——A city of Thessaly. *Niceph.* 1. 5.

SICYO'NIA, a province of Peloponnesus, on the bay of Corinth, of which Sicyon was the capital. It is the most eminent kingdom of Greece, and in it flourishing situation not only its dependens states, but also the whole Peloponnesus were called Sicyonia. The territory is said to abound with corn, wine, and olives, and also with iron mines. It produced many celebrated men, particularly painters and statuaries. *Vid.* Sicyon.

SID'ACE, a city of Lycia, so called from Sidace, daughter of Amisodorus.

SID'ALA, a city of Armenia Major. *Ptol.*

SI'DE, the wife of Orion, thrown into hell by Juno for boasting herself fairer than the goddess. *Apollod.* 1. c. 4.——A daughter of Belus.——A daughter of Danaus. *Paus.* 3. c. 22.

SI'DE, a town of Pamphylia. *Liv.* 37. c. 23.—*Cic.* 3. *Fam.* 6.

SIDE'LE, a city of Ionia. *Steph.*

SI'DEN or SYD'ERIS, a lake in India. *Plin.* 6. c. 16 It is called Silia by *Strabo*, Silla by *Diodorus*, and Sila by *Arrian*.

SIDE'NA or SIDE'NE, a city of Mysia Minor on the Granicus. *Strab.*

SIDE'NE, a region of Cappadocia. *Plin.* 6. c. 4.

SIDE'RO, wife of Salmoneus, was harsh in her treatment of her daughter-in-law Tyro, for which she was put to death by Pelias.

SIDETA'NI, a people of Africa, near Carthage. *Strab.* 3.

SIDICI'NUM, a town of Campania, at the east of the Liris, called also Teanum. *Vid.* Teanum. *Virg. Æn.* 7. v. 727. *& Servius ad Virg. loc.*—*Ital.* 5. v. 551. l. 12. v. 521.—*Plin.*—*Strab.* 5.

SI'DO, a king of the Suevi. *Tac. Ann.* 12. c. 29.

SI'DON, an ancient city of Phœnicia, the capital of the country, with a famous harbour, now called Saide. It is situate on the shores of the Mediterranean, at the distance of about 50 miles from Damascus, and 24 from Tyre. The people of Sidon were well known for their industry, their skill in arithmetic, in astronomy, in commercial affairs, and in sea voyages. They, however, had the character of being very dishonest. Their women were peculiarly happy in working embroidery. The invention of glass, of linen, and beautiful purple dye, is attributed to them. The city of Sidon was taken by Ochus, king of Persia, after the inhabitants had burnt themselves and the city B.C. 351; but it was afterwards rebuilt by its inhabitants. *Lucan.* 3. v. 217. l. 10. v. 141.—*Diod.* 16.—*Justin.* 11. c. 10.—*Plin.* 36. c. 26.—*Homer. Odyss.* 15. v. 411.—*Mela*, 1. c. 12.—*Strab.* 1.—*Virg. Æn.* 1. v. 613. l. 4. v. 75.—*Ovid, in Ib.* 448. *Met.* 3. v. 129. l. 4. v. 574.—*Propert.* 2. el. 13 v. 55. el. 22. v. 15.

SIDO'NA, a region of Cappadocia Pontus. *Ptol.*

SIDO'NES, a people of Thrace, near the Hebrus. *Plin.*

SIDO'NIA, a city of Troas. *Steph.*

SIDONIO'RUM IN'SULÆ, islands in the Persian Gulf. *Strab.* 16.

SID'ONIS or SIDO'NIS, the country of which Sidon is the capital, is situate at the west of Syria, on the coast of the Mediterranean. *Ovid. Met.* 2. fab. 19. Dido, as a native of the country, is often called Sidonis. *Ovid. Met.* 14. v. 80.

SIDO'NIUS CAIUS SOL'LIUS APOLLINA'RIS MODES'TUS, a Christian writer, born A.D. 430. He was for 15 years bishop of Clermont in France, a town which he vigorously defended against the Goths, and distinguished himself for his learning, his subtle and penetrating wit, and by the elegance and graces of his diction, both as a writer of prose and poetry. He died in the 52d year of his age. There are remaining of his compositions, some letters and different poems, consisting chiefly of panegyrics on the great men of his time, written in heroic verse, and occasionally in other metre, of which the best edition is that of Sirmondus, 1614, a second edition of which was afterwards published by Labbeus, Paris, 4to. 1652. *Harles. Not. Lit. Rom.* 1. p. 746.—*Sax. Onom.* 1. p. 513 —*Fabr. B. Lat.* 2. p. 634. & 3. p. 174.

SIDO'NIUS, an epithet applied not only to the natives of Sidon, but used to express the excellence of any thing, especially embroidery or dyed garments. Carthage is called *Sidonia urbs*, because built by Sidonians. *Virg. Æn.* 1. v. 682.

SID'ONES, a people of Germany. *Ptol.*

SI'DUS, a small town near Corinth.——A village near Clazomenæ.——A place of Pamphylia. *Steph.*

SIDUS'SA, a city of Ionia. *Id.*

SID'YMA, a city of Lycia. *Id.*

SIE'NA JU'LIA, a town of Etruria. *Cic. Brut.* 18.—*Tacit.* 4. *Hist.* 45.

SI'GA, a town of Numidia, famous as the residence of Syphax. *Plin.* 5. c. 11.

SIGÆ'UM or SIGE'UM, now Cape Ineihisari, a town of Troas, on a promontory of the same name, where the Scamander falls into the sea, extending six miles along the shore. It was near Sigæum that the greatest part of the battles between the Greeks and Trojans were fought, and that Achilles was buried. *Virg. Æn.* 2. v. 312. l. 7. v. 294. *& Servius locis.*—*Ovid. Met.* 12. v. 71.—*Lucan.* 9. v. 962.—*Mela*, 1. c. 18.—*Strab.* 13.—*Dictys. Cret.* 5. c. 12.

SIG'ALA, a city of India within the Ganges. *Ptol.*

SIGA'LION, the name of the god of silence, honored by the Ægyptians under the appellation of Harpocrates. His statue was placed at the entrance of the temples of Isis and Serapis, to intimate that the mysteries of religion were to be kept secret, and he was represented with the fore-finger of the right hand pressing his lips. *Varro de L. L.* 3 & 4.—*Auson.* ep. 25. v. 27.—*Aug. de Civ. D.* l. 8. c. 5.

SIG'ANAS or SAG'ANAS, a river of Carmania. *Plin.* 6. c. 25.—*Salmas ad Solin*, p. 1181.

SIGA'NIA, a river of Colchis. *Plin.* 6. c. 4.

SIG'ATHA, a city of Libya. *Steph. ex Strab.* 17.

SIGILLA'RIA, a festival observed at Rome at the conclusion of the Saturnalia, for two days. Small human figures of paste, wood, or wax were offered to Pluto, and presented to friends. Hercules was supposed to be the first who introduced this ceremony, as a substitute for human victims, which before were sacrificed to Pluto and Saturn. *Macrob.* 1. c. 10 & 11.

SIGINDU'NUM, a town of Upper Mysia. *Ptol.* *Niger* calls it Simedro.

SIG'NIA, an ancient town of Latium, the inhabitants of which were called Signini. The wine of Signia was used by the ancients as an astringent in medicinal preparations. *Liv.* 1. c. 56.—*Plin.* 3. c. 5. l. 14. c. 6.—*Strab.* 5.—*Martial.* 13. epigr. 116.——A mountain of Phrygia near Apamea. *Plin.* 5. c. 29.

SIGOVE'SUS, a prince among the Celtæ, in the reign of Tarquin. *Liv.* 5. c. 34.

SIG'UA, a city of Armenia Major. *Ptol.*

SIGY'NI, SIGU'NÆ, SIGYN'NÆ or SIGYN'NES, a nation of European Scythia, beyond the Danube. *Herodot.* 5. c. 9.

SI'LA or SY'LA, a large wood in the country of the Brutii near the Apennines, abounding with much pitch, and famous for its wines. *Cassiodor.* 12. c. 4.—*Strab.* 6.—*Virg. Æn.* 12. v. 715.

SILÆ'UM, a town of Arabia Felix. *Ptol.*

SILA'NA JU'NIA, a woman at the court of Nero, remarkable for her licentiousness and impurities. She had married C. Julius, by whom she was divorced.

SILA'NION, a statuary at Athens in high estimation. *Cic. in Verr.* 9.—*Plin.* 34. c. 8.—*Diog.* 3. *in Plat.*—*Paus.* 6. c. 4.—*Plut.*

SILA'NUS D., a son of T. Manlius Torquatus, accused of extortion in the management of the province of Macedonia. The father himself desired to hear the complaints laid against his son, and, after he had spent two days in examining the charges of the Macedonians, on the third day pronounced his son guilty of extortion, and unworthy to be called a citizen of Rome. He also banished him from his presence, and the son was so struck at the severity of his father, that he hanged himself on the following night. *Liv.* 54. —*Cic. de Finib.* 1.—*Val. Max.* 5. c. 8.

SILA'NUS C. JU'NIUS, a consul under Tiberius, accused of extortion, and banished to the island of Cythera. *Tacit. Ann.* 3. c. 69.

SILA'NUS MAR'CUS, a lieutenant of Cæsar's armies in Gaul. *Cæs. Comm.* 1. 6.

SILA'NUS, the father-in-law of Caligula. *Suet. Cal.* 22.——A proprætor in Spain, who routed the Carthaginian forces there, while Annibal was in Italy.——An augur in the army of the 10,000 Greeks, at their return from Cunaxa.

SILA'NUS TURPIL'IUS, a lieutenant of Metellus sent against Jugurtha. He was accused by Marius, though totally innocent, and condemned by the malice of his judges.

SILA'NUS TORQUA'TUS, a man put to death by Nero.

SILA'NUS LU'CIUS, a man betrothed to Octavia, the daughter of Claudius. Nero took Octavia away from him, and on the day of her nuptials, Silanus killed himself. *Tacit. Ann.* 12. c. 3 & 8.

SILA'NUS DEC'IMUS JU'NIUS, a consul with Muræna, who voted for the death of Cataline's associates. *Sallust. Cat.* 50.—*Cic. Cat.* 4. c 4.

SIL'ARUS, a river of Picenum, rising in the Apennine mountains, and falling into the Tyrrhene Sea. Its waters, as it is reported, petrified all leaves that fell into it, a property which they do not now possess. *Dionys. Per.* 361. *& Eustath. loco.*—*Sil. It.* 8. v. 582.—*Strab.* 5.—*Mela*, 2. c. 4.—*Virg. G.* 3. v. 146.—*Plin.* 2. c. 103.

SIL'BIUM, a city of Phrygia, between Apamea and Philomelium. *Ptol.*

SIL'DA, a colony and city of Mauritania Tingitana. *Id.* It is called Gilda by *Antoninus.*

SI'LE, a town of Lower Ægypt. *Antonin.*

SILE'NI, a people on the banks of the Indus. *Plin.* 2. c. 20.

SILE'NUS, a demi-god, who became the nurse, the preceptor, and the attendant of the god Bacchus. He was, as some suppose, the son of Pan, or, according to others, of Mercury, or of Terra. Malea in Lesbus was the place of his birth. After death he received divine honors, and had a temple in Elis. Silenus is generally represented as a fat jolly old man, riding on an ass, crowned with flowers, and always intoxicated. He was once found by some peasants in Phrygia, after he had lost his way and could not follow Bacchus, and was carried to king Midas, who received him with great attention. He detained him for ten days, and afterwards restored him to Bacchus, for which he was rewarded with the power of turning into gold whatever he touched. Some authors assert, that Silenus was a philosopher, who accompanied Bacchus in his Indian expedition, and assisted him by the soundness of his counsels. From this circumstance, therefore, he is often introduced, speaking with all the gravity of a philosopher concerning the formation of the world, and the nature of things. The Fauns in general, and the Satyrs are often called Sileni. *Paus.* 3. c. 25. l. 6. c. 24.—*Philost.* 23.—*Ovid. Met.* 4.—*Hygin.* fab. 191.—*Diod.* 3, &c.—*Cic. Tusc.* 1. c. 48.—*Ælian. V. H.* 3. c. 18.—*Virg. Ecl.* 6. v. 13.—*Conon. apud. Phot.* 1.—*Lactant. Arg.* 11. *Met.* fab. 3.—*Servius ad Virg. loco.* [The statues of Silenus are very numerous; by far the best is that with the infant Bacchus in his arms, formerly in the Villa Borghese, now at Paris, in the Musée Royale.] ——A Carthaginian historian who wrote an account of the affairs of his country in the Greek language. ——An historian who wrote an account of Sicily. *Liv.* 26. c. 49.—*Cic. Div.* 1. c. 24.—*Voss. H. Gr.* p. 414.

SIL'IA, the wife of a senator, sent into exile, &c. *Tac. Ann.* 16. c. 20.

SILICEN'SE (*flumen*), a river of Hispania Bætica. *Hirt. B. Alex.* c. 57. It is now Las Agalmidas.

SILICER'NIUM, the name of a festival celebrated among the Romans after the burial of a friend. *Varro apud Non.* 1. 234.—*Festus de V. Sig.*—*Donat. ad Terent. Adelph.* 4. 2. v. 48.

SIL'ICE, a people of Assyria, *Plin.* 6. c. 26.

SIL'ICI MONS, a town near Padua.

SILIN'DIUM, a small town near Ida. *Steph.*

SI'LIS, a small river of Venetia in Italy, falling into the Adriatic. *Plin.* 3. c. 18.

C. SIL'IUS ITAL'ICUS, a Latin poet, who was originally at the bar, where he for some time distinguished himself, till he retired from Rome, in order to devote his time exclusively to study. He was consul the year that Nero was murdered. Pliny has observed, that when Trajan was invested with the imperial purple, Silius refused to come to Rome, and congratulate him like the rest of his fellow-citizens; a neglect which was never resented by the emperor, or insolently mentioned by the poet. Silius was in possession of a house where Cicero had lived, and another in which was the tomb of Virgil; and it has been justly remarked, that he looked upon no temple with greater reverence than upon the sepulchre of the immortal poet, whose steps he followed, but whose fame he could not equal. The birth-day of Virgil was yearly celebrated with unusual pomp and solemnity by Silius; and for his partiality, not only to the memory, but to the compositions of the Mantuan poet, he has been called the ape of Virgil. Silius starved himself, when labouring under an imposthume which his physicians were unable to remove, in the beginning of Trajan's reign, about the 75th year of his age. There remains a poem of Italicus on the second Punic war, divided into 17 books, greatly commended by Martial. The moderns have not been so favorable in their opinions concerning its merits. The poetry is weak and inelegant, yet the author deserves to be commended for his purity, the authenticity of his narrations, and his interesting descriptions. He has everywhere imitated Virgil, but with little success. Silius was a great collector of antiquities. His son was honored with the consulship during his father's life-time The best editions of Italicus will be found to be Drakenborch's in 4to. Utr. 1717, and that of Cellarius, 8vo, Lips. 1695. *Mart.* 11. epigr. 49, &c.—*Plin. Jun.* ep. & paneg. 58.—*Harles. Not. Lit. Rom.* 1. p. 477.—*Sax. Onom.* 1. p. 256.

SIL'IUS CA'IUS, a man of consular dignity, greatly loved by Messalina for his comely appearance and elegant address. Messalina obliged him to divorce his wife, that she might enjoy his company without intermission. Silius was forced to comply, though with great reluctance, and was at last put to death for the adulteries which the empress obliged him to commit. *Tacit.* 11. *Ann.* c. 5, &c.—*Suet.*—*Dio.*—*Juv.* 10. v. 330 ——A commander in Germany, put to death by Sejanus, who was jealous of his virtue, and of his attachment to the family of Germanicus. *Tacit. Ann.* 3 & 4.

SIL'IUS TI'TUS, a tribune in Cæsar's legions in Gaul. *Cæs. Comm.* 3. c. 8.

SIL'LYOS, a city of Ionia, near Smyrna. *Steph.*

SIL'PHII, a people of Libya. *Herodot.* l. 4.

SIL'PIA, a town of Spain. *Liv.* 28. c. 12.

SIL'PIUS, a mountain of Syria, on which Antiochia Magna was built by Seleucus. *Suidas.*

SIL'URES, the people of South Wales, in Britain. *Ptol.*

SILVA'NUS, a rural deity, son of Crathis, an Italian shepherd, by a goat, according to Ælian and Probus. From this circumstance he is generally represented as half a man and half a goat. According to Virgil, he was son of Picus, or, as others report, of Mars, or, according to Plutarch, of Valeria Tusculanaria, a young woman who introduced herself into her father's bed, and became pregnant by him. The worship of Silvanus was established only in Italy, where, as some authors have imagined, he reigned in the age of Evander. This deity was sometimes represented holding a cypress in his hand, because he became enamoured of a beautiful youth called Cyparissus, who was changed into a tree of the same name. Silvanus presided over gardens and limits, and he is often confounded with the Fauns, Satyrs, and Silenus. *Plut. in Parall.*—*Virg. Ecl.* 10. *G.* 1. v. 20. l. 2. v. 493.—*Servius locis, & Æn.* 6. v. 776. l. 8. v. 601.—*Probus ad Virg. Georg.* 1.—*Aug. de Civ. D.* 6. c. 9. l. 15. 23.—*Ælian. Anim.* 6. c. 42.—*Ovid. Met.* 10.—*Horat.* ep. 2.—*Dionys. Hal.* 1.——A man who murdered his wife Apronia, by throwing her down from one of the windows of his chamber.——One of those who conspired against Nero.——An officer of Constantius, who revolted and made himself emperor. He was assassinated by his soldiers.

SILVA'NUS PLO'TIUS, a tribune, author of the Plotian or Plautian law, to regulate the granting of citizenship. *Cic. Arch.* 4.

SIL'VIUM, a town of Apulia Peucetia, now Gorgolione. *Plin.* 3. c. 11.——A town of Istria.

SI'LYS, a river of European Scythia. *Plin.* 6. c. 7 & 16

SIMÆ'THEUS or SYMÆ'THUS, a town and river at the east of Sicily, which served as a boundary between the territories of the people of Catana and the Leontini. In its neighbourhood the gods Palici were born and particularly worshipped. *Virg. Æn.* 9. v. 584.—*Strab.* 6.—*Ital.* 14. v. 232.

—*Ovid. Met.* 13. v. 750 & 879.—*Fast.* 4. v. 472.—*Servius ad Virg. loco.*

SIMA'NA, a city of Bithynia, between two rivers. *Steph.*

SIMBRIVI'US or SIMBRU'VIUS, a lake of Latium, formed by the Anio. *Tacit.* 14. *Ann.* 22.

SIME'NA, a town of Lycia, near Chimæra. *Plin.* 5. c. 27.—*Steph.*

SIM'ENI, a people of Britain. *Ptol.* Where they dwelt is a matter of dispute, some stating it to be in Hampshire, and others in Norfolk and Suffolk.

SIME'NUS, an engraver of silver. *Plin.* 34. c. 8.

SIM'ILÆ, a grove at Rome, in which the orgies of Bacchus were celebrated. *Liv.* 39. c. 12.

SIM'ILIS, one of the courtiers of Trajan, who retired from Rome into the country to enjoy peace and solitary retirement. *Dio. Cass. in Adrian.*

SIM'MIAS, a philosopher of Thebes who wrote 25 dialogues. *Diog. Laert.* 1. 2. *Vit. Phil.*——A grammarian of Rhodes. *Strab.* 4.——A poet of Rhodes, who wrote two poems called Ovum and Πέλεκυς, which *Salmasius* has illustrated with notes. He seems also to have published a book on the antiquities of Samus. *Suidas. in Lex.*—*Tzetz. Chil.* 7. *H.* 144.—*Voss. de Poet. Gr.* p. 59.——A Macedonian suspected of conspiracy against Alexander, on account of his intimacy with Philotas. *Curt.* 7. c. 1.

SI'MO, a comic character in Terence, &c.

SIM'OIS (-*entis*), a river in Troas, which rises in mount Ida, and falls into the Xanthus. It is celebrated by Homer and most of the ancient poets, as in its neighbourhood were fought many battles during the Trojan war. It is found to be but a small rivulet by modern travellers, and some have even disputed its existence. *Homer. Il.* 6. v. 4. l. 12. v. 22.—*Propert.* 2. l. 7. v. 50. l. 3. el. 1. v. 27.—*Lucan.* 9. v. 262.—*Virg. Æn.* 1. v. 104. l. 3. v. 302, &c.—*Ovid. Met.* 13. v. 324.—*Mela*, 1. c. 18.

SIMO'IS, a son of Oceanus and Tethys. He was the god of the river Simois.

SIMOISIUS, a Trojan prince, son of Anthemion, killed by Ajax. He was so called because he was born on the banks of the Simois. *Homer. Il.* 4. v. 473.

SI'MON, a currier at Athens, whom Socrates often visited on account of his great sagacity and genius. He collected all the information which he could receive from the conversation of the philosopher, and afterwards published it, with his own observations, in 33 dialogues. He was the first of the disciples of Socrates who attempted to give an account of the opinions of his master concerning virtue, justice, poetry, music, honor, &c. These dialogues were extant in the age of the biographer Diogenes, who has preserved their title. Pericles honored Simon with his friendship, and wished him to exchange his situation; but he nobly answered, that he chose rather to live a currier with independence, than a great man, however subservient, in the house of another. *Diog.* 2. c. 14.——An author who wrote on rhetoric. *Id.*——A sculptor.——A name common among the Jews.

SIMON'IDES, a celebrated poet of Cos, who flourished about 529 B.C. His father's name was Leoprepis, or Theoprepis. He wrote elegies in so tender and pathetic a style, that they are called by Catullus the tears of Simonides. He wrote also epigrams and dramatical pieces, esteemed for their elegance and sweetness, and epic poems, one on Cambyses, king of Persia, another on the battle of Salamis, &c. Simonides was universally courted by the princes of Greece and Sicily, and, according to the fables of Phædrus, he was such a favorite of the gods, that his life was miraculously preserved at an entertainment, when the roof of the house fell upon all those who were seated at the table. He obtained a poetical prize in the 80th year of his age, and lived to his 90th or 96th year. The people of Syracuse, who had hospitably honored him when alive, erected a magnificent monument to his memory. Simonides, according to some, added the four letters, η, ω, ξ, ψ, to the alphabet of the Greeks. Some fragments of his poetry are extant, chiefly preserved in Stobæus, among which is his celebrated satire upon the different temper and character of women, most of which have been elegantly translated into Latin verse by Buchanan. According to some, the grandson of the elegiac poet of Cos was also called Simonides, and flourished a few years before the Peloponnesian war. He was the author of some books of inventions, genealogies, &c. *Quintil.* 10. c. 1.—*Phædr.* 4. fab. 21 & 24.—*Horat.* 2. od. 1. v. 38.—*Herodot.* 5. c. 102.—*Cic. de Orat. &c.*—*Pindar. Isth.* 2.—*Catull.* 1. ep. 39.—*Lucian. de Macrob.*—*Ælian. V. H.* 8. c. 2.—*Plato. in Protag.*—*Arist. Rh.* 3. c. 2.—*Val. Max.* 1. c. 8.—*Plut. in cons. ad Ap. &c.*—*Suidas.*—*Stobæus.*—*Athen.* 4. 11, *&c.*—*Philostr. in Apoll.* 1.—*Fabr. B. Gr.* 2. c. 15.—*Sax. Onom.* 1. p. 24.

SIMPLIC'IUS, a Greek commentator in the sixth century, born in Cilicia, and strongly attached to the tenets of the heathen philosophy. He wrote some valuable commentaries on Aristotle and Epictetus, which are esteemed by the learned on account of the interesting fragments of antiquity which they preserve. Andr. Dacier published a translation of his commentary on Epictetus in 1715, and Dr. Stanhope in 1704. The latest edition of this commentary is that of Schweighäuser, in the 4th and 5th volumes of his "*Epicteteæ Philosophiæ Monumenta*," Lips. 1800. For other editions, see *Fabricii B. Gr.* 5. c. 24.—*Sax. Onom.* 2. p. 46.

SIMPSIM'IDA, a town of Parthia. *Ptol.*

SIM'ULUS or SIM'YLUS, an ancient poet who wrote some verses on the Tarpeian rock. *Plut. in Rom.*

SI'MUS, a king of Arcadia after Phialus. *Paus.* 8. c. 5 ——A painter mentioned by *Pliny*, 35. c. 11.

SIMYL'LA, a city of India Citerior. *Ptol.*

SIM'YRA, a town of Phœnicia. *Mela*, 1. c. 12.

SIM'YRUS, a city of the Syrians. *Steph.*

SI'NA, a city of Margiana. *Ptol.*

SIN'ACA, a city of Hyrcania. *Id.*

SI'NÆ, a people of India, called by *Ptolemy* the most eastern nation of the world.

SINAPATIN'GA, a city of India within the Ganges. *Ptol.*

SIN'ARUS, a river of India which falls into the Hydaspes. *Arrian. in Indic.*

SIN'CAR, a city of Media. *Ptol.*

SIN'CIUM, a town of Pannonia. *Antonin.*

SIN'DA, a city of Pisidia. *Steph.*——A maritime city of India without the Ganges. *Ptol.*

SIN'DÆ, islands in the Indian Ocean, supposed to be the Nicabar islands.

SINDES'SUS, a city of Caria. *Steph.*

SIN'DI, a people of European Scythia, on the Palus Mæotis. *Flacc.* 6. v. 86.

SIN'DIA, a city of Lycia. *Steph.*

SINDOCAN'DA, a city of Taprobane. *Ptol.*

SINDO'GA, a town of Parthia. *Id.*

SINDONÆ'I, a people of Thrace. *Steph.*

SINE'RA, a city of Phœnicia. *Id.*

SINER'VAS, a city of Armenia Minor. *Antonin.*

SIN'GA, a name of Pallas, in Phœnicia. *Paus.* 1. 9.

SIN'GA, a town of Comagene. *Ptol.*

SIN'GÆ, a people of India. *Plin.* 6. c. 20.

SINGÆ'I, a people on the confines of Macedonia and Thrace. *Thucyd.* 1. 5. They were probably the inhabitants of Singus. *Vid.* Singus.

SIN'GAMES, a river of Colchis, probably the Sigania of *Pliny*, 6. c. 4.—*Arrian.*

SIN'GARA, a city at the north of Mesopotamia, now Sinjar. *Ptol.*——A city of Arabia, near Edessa. *Steph.*

SINGIDA'VA, a city of Dacia. *Ptol.*

SIN'GULIS, a river of Spain falling into the Guadalquiver. *Plin.* 3. c. 1.

SIN'GUS, a town of Macedonia, on the eastern coast. The bay near it is called Singiticus Sinus.

SIN'GYA, a city of Pamphylia. *Steph.*

SI'NIS, a famous robber. *Vid.* Scinis.

SI'NIS, a colony and city of Armenia Minor, on the Euphrates. *Ptol.*

SIN'NA, a city near Libanus. *Ptolemy* places two cities of this name in Mesopotamia.

SIN'NACES, a Parthian of an illustrious family, who conspired against his prince, &c. *Tacit.* 6. *Ann.* c. 31.

SIN'NACHA, a town of Mesopotamia, where Crassus was put to death by Surena. *Plut.*

SIN'NAUS, a lake in Asia. *Plin.* 2. c. 103.

SIN'OE, a nymph of Arcadia who educated Pan. *Paus.* 8. c. 30.

SIN'OE, a city of Sicily. *Steph.*

SI'NON, a son of Sisyphus, who accompanied the Greeks to the Trojan war, and there distinguished himself by his cunning and fraud, and his intimacy with Ulysses. When the Greeks had fabricated the famous wooden horse, Sinon went to Troy with his hands bound behind his back, and by the most solemn protestations assured Priam that the Greeks were gone from Asia, and that they had been ordered to sacrifice one of their soldiers, to render the wind favourable to their return; and that, because the lot, at the instigation of Ulysses, had fallen upon him, he had fled away from their camp, not to be cruelly immolated. These false assertions were immediately credited by the Trojans, and Sinon advised Priam to bring into his city the wooden horse which the Greeks had left behind them, and to consecrate it to Minerva. His advice was followed, and Sinon in the night, to complete his perfidy, opened the side of the horse, from which issued a number of armed Greeks, who surprised the Trojans and pillaged their city. *Dares, Phryg.*—*Homer. Odyss.* 8. v. 492. l. 11. v. 521.—*Virg. Æn.* 2. v. 79, &c.—*Paus.* 10. c. 27.—*Q. Smyrn.* 12. v. 239, 355, 367. l. 13. v. 24.—*Hygin.* fab. 208.

SINO'PE, a daughter of the Asopus by Methone. She was beloved by Apollo, who carried her away to the borders of the Euxine Sea, in Asia Minor, where she gave birth to a son called Syrus. *Diod.* 4.—*Steph.*—*Byz.*——The original name of Sinuessa in Italy.

SINO'PE, now Sinopi, a town of Pontus in Asia Minor, with a seaport on the shores of the Euxine, founded or rebuilt by a colony of Milesians. It was long an independent state, till Pharnaces, king of Pontus, seized it. It was the capital of Pontus, under Mithridates, and was the birthplace of Diogenes, the cynic philosopher. It received its name from Sinope, whom Apollo carried thither. *Ovid. Pont.* 1. el. 3. v. 67.—*Strab.* 2 & 12.—*Diod.* 4.—*Mela*, 1. c. 19.—*Flacc.* 5. v. 109.—*Plin.* 33. c. 7. l. 35. c. 6.

SIN'ORIX, a governor of Gaul, &c. *Polyæn.* 8. c. 39.

SINO'TIUM, the names of two towns in Dalmatia, distinguished by the appellations of *Novum* and *Vetus*. *Strab.*

SIN'SII, a people of Dacia. *Ptol.*

SIN'THIA, an inland town of Macedonia. *Thucyd.* —*Liv.* 26. c. 9.

SIN'TI or SINTIES, a nation of Thracians, who inhabited Lemnus, when Vulcan fell there from heaven. *Homer. Il.* 1. v. 594. *Od.* 8. v. 294.—*Servius ad Virg. Ec.* 4. v. 62. *Æn.* 8. v. 414.

SINTOE'UM, a fortified place of Armenia, founded by the Galatians. *Steph.*

SINUES'SA, a maritime town of Campania, originally called Sinope. It was celebrated for its hot-baths and mineral waters, which were said to cure people of insanity, and render women prolific. *Ovid. Met.* 15. v. 715.—*Mela*, 2. c. 4.—*Strab.* 5.—*Liv.* 10. c. 21. l. 22. c. 13.—*Mart.* 6. epigr. 42. l. 11. epigr, 8.—*Tacit. Ann.* 12. c. 66.—*Plin.* 31. c. 2. —*Ital.* 8. v. 529.

SINU'NIA, a city of Parthia. *Ptol.*

SINZI'TA, a city of Armenia Minor. *Id.*

SI'ODA, a town of Albania.

SI'ON, one of the hills on which the city of Jerusalem was built.

SIO'NIA, a city of Pontus. *Steph.*

SIPARUN'TUM, an inland town of Dalmatia on the borders of Upper Mysia. *Ptol.*

SIPH'ARA, a city of Aria. *Ptol.*

SIPH'NOS or SIPH'NUS, now Sifano, one of the Cyclades, situate at the west of Parus, twenty miles in circumference, according to Pliny, or, according to modern travellers, forty. Siphnus had many excellent harbours, and produced great plenty of delicious fruits. The inhabitants were so depraved that their licentiousness became proverbial. They however behaved with spirit in the Persian wars, and refused to give earth and water to the emissaries of Xerxes in token of submission. There were some gold mines in Siphnus, of which Apollo demanded the tenth part. When the inhabitants refused to continue to offer part of the gold to the god of Delphi, the island was inundated and the mines disappeared. The air is so wholesome, that many of the natives are said to live to their 120th year. *Paus.* 10. c. 11.—*Herodot.* 8. c. 46.—*Mela*, 1. c. 7.—*Strab.* 10.—*Steph. Byz.*

SIPON'TUM, SIPUN'TUM, SI'PUS or SE'PIUS, a maritime town of Apulia in Italy, near the mouth of the river Cerbalus on the Adriatic, founded by Diomedes, after his return from the Trojan war. *Strab.* 6.—*Lucan.* 5. v. 377.—*Mela*, 2. c. 4.—*Liv.* 8.—*Ital.* 8. v. 332.—*Plin.* 3. c. 11.—*Servius ad Virg. Æn.* 11. v. 247.

SIP'PARA, a city of India within the Ganges. *Ptol.*

SIP'PAS or SIS'PAS, a prætor set over Macedonia by Antipater. *Diod.* l. 18.

SIP'PHARA, a city of Mesopotamia. *Ptol.*

SIP'TE, a city of Thrace. *Paus. in Eliac.*

SIP'YLUM or SIP'YLUS, a town of Lydia with a mountain of the same name near the Meander, formerly called Ceraunius. The town was destroyed by an earthquake, with 12 others in the neighbourhood, in the reign of Tiberius. Cybele was said to preside over the place. *Strab.* 1 & 12. —*Paus.* 1. c. 20.—*Apollod.* 3. c. 5.—*Homer. Il.* 24. v. 615.—*Hygin.* fab. 9.—*Plin.* 2. c. 91.—*Propert.* 2. el. 20. v. 7.—*Tacit. Ann.* 2. c. 47.

SIP'YLUS, one of Niobe's children, killed by Apollo. *Ovid. Met.* 6. fab. 6.

SIRAM'NÆ, a people of India within the Ganges. *Ptol.*

SIRAN'GÆ, an inland people of Libya. *Id.*

SIR'BI, a people of Asiatic Sarmatia. *Ptol.*

SIRBO'NIS LA'CUS, a lake between Ægypt and Palestine, now Sebaket Bardoil. *Plin.* 4. c. 13.

SIRE'NES, sea nymphs who charmed so much with their melodious voice, that all forgot their employments to listen with more attention, and at last died for want of food. They were daughters of the Achelous, by the muse Calliope, or, according to others, by Melpomene or Terpsichore. They were three in number, called Parthenope, Ligea, and Leucosia, or, according to others, Molpe, Aglaophonos, and Thelxiope, or Thelxione, and they usually lived in a small island near Cape Pelorus in Sicily. Some authors suppose that they were monsters, who had the form of a woman above the waist, and the rest of the body like that of a bird; or rather that the whole body was covered with feathers, and had the shape of a bird, except the head, which was that of a beautiful female. This monstrous form they had received from Ceres, who wished to punish them, because they had not assisted her daughter when carried away by Pluto. But according to Ovid, they were so disconsolate at the rape of Proserpine, that they prayed the gods to give them wings that they might seek her in the sea as well as by land. The Sirens were informed by the oracle, that as soon as any persons passed by them without suffering themselves to be charmed by their songs, they should perish, and their melody had prevailed in calling the attention of all passengers, till Ulysses, informed of the power of their voice by Circe, stopped the ears of his companions with wax, and ordered himself to be tied to the mast of his ship, and no attention to be paid to his commands, should he wish to stay and listen to the song. This was a salutary precaution. Ulysses made signs for his companions to stop, but they were disregarded, and the fatal coast was passed with safety. Upon this artifice of Ulysses, the Sirens were so disappointed, that they threw themselves into the sea and perished. Some authors say, that the Sirens challenged the Muses to a trial of skill in singing, and that the latter proved victorious, and plucked the feathers from the wings of their adversaries, with which thay made themselves crowns. The place where the Sirens destroyed themselves, was afterwards called Sirenis, on the coast of Sicily. Virgil, however, *Æn.* 5. v. 864, places the *Sirenum Scopuli* on the coast of Italy, near the island of Caprea. Some suppose that the Sirens were a number of lascivious women in Sicily, who prostituted themselves to strangers, and made them forget their pursuits while drowned in unlawful pleasures. The Sirens are often represented holding, one a lyre, a second a flute, and the third singing. *Paus.* 9. c. 34. l. 10. c. 6.—*Homer. Odyss.* 12. v. 167.—*Strab.* 6.—*Ammian.* 29. c. 2. —*Hygin.* fab. 141.—*Apollod.* 2. c. 4.—*Ovid. Met.* 5. v. 555. *de Art Am.* 3. v. 311.—*Ital.* 12. v. 33.—

—*Martial.* 3. epigr. 64.—*Auson. Id* 11. v. 20.—*Tzetzes ad Lyc.* v. 653 & 712.—*Servius ad Æn.* 5. v. 864.—*Aul. Gell.* 16. c. 8.

SIRENU'SÆ, three small rocky islands near the coast of Campania, where the Sirens were supposed to reside. *Mela*, 2. c. 4.—*Solin.* c. 8.

SI'RES, a people of Thrace, above Byzantium. *Steph.*

SIR'ICIS, a city of Armenia Minor. *Antonin.*

SIR'ION, a city of Gallia Aquitanica. *Antonin.*

SI'RIS, SI'RÆ or **SER'HÆ**, a town of Magna Græcia, founded by a Grecian colony after the Trojan war, at the mouth of a river of the same name. There was a battle fought near it between Pyrrhus and the Romans. *Dionys. Perieg.* v. 221.—*Plin.* 5. c. 9.—*Strab.* 6.

SI'RIS, a name given by the Æthiopians to the Nile before its divided streams united into one current. *Plin.* 5. c. 9.——A town of Pæonia in Thrace.

SIR'IUS or **CANIC'ULA**, the dog star, the appearance of which, as the ancients supposed, always caused great heat on the earth. *Virg. Æn.* 3. v. 141.—*Lucan.* 10. v. 211.

SIR'MIO, now Sermione, a peninsula in the lake Benacus, where Catullus had a villa. *Carm.* 29.

SIR'MIUM, the capital of Pannonia at the confluence of the Savus and Bacuntius, very celebrated during the reign of the Roman emperors. *Ptol.*—*Jornand.*—*Evagr. &c.*

SI'RON, an Epicurean philosopher, preceptor to Varro and Virgil. *Servius Virg. Ecl.* 6. v. 13.

SI'ROS, a river of Bythynia. *Plin.* 5. c. 32.

SIR'PICUS, a centurion of a legion in Pannonia, who was the cause of a sedition among the troops. *Tac. Ann.* 1. c. 23.

SIR'RHA, a city of Thrace. *Steph.*

SIR'RHAS, the king of a nation bordering upon Macedonia, against whom Archelaus waged war. *Aristot.* 5. *Polit.* c. 10.

SIS'ALO, a city of Spain between Emerita and Cæsar-augusta. *Antonin.*

SISAM'NES, a judge flayed for his partiality, by order of Cambyses. His skin was nailed on the bench of the other judges to incite them to act with candour and impartiality. *Herodot.* 5. c. 25.

SIS'APHO, a Corinthian who murdered his brother, because he had put his children to death. *Ovid. in Ib.*

SIS'APO, a town of Spain, famous for its vermilion mines, the situation of which is not well ascertained. *Plin* 33. c. 7.—*Cic. Phil.* 2. c. 19.

SI'SAR, a river of Mauritania Cæsariensis. *Ptol. Pliny*, 5. c. 2., calls it Usar.

SIS'ARA, a lake in Africa Propria. *Ptol.*——A place near Nisibis. *Amm. Marcell.*

SISAR'ACA, a city of the Murbogi in Hispania Tarraconensis. *Ptol.*

SISAURA'NUM, a small city of Persia. *Procop. Persic.* l. 2.

SIS'CIA, SEGES'TA or **SEGES'TICA**, a town of Pannonia, now Sisseg. *Ptol.*

SIS'ENES, a Persian deserter who conspired against Alexander, &c. *Curt.* 3. c. 7.

SISEN'NA L., a Roman historian, 91 B.C. He wrote an account of the civil wars between Marius and Sylla, of which Cicero speaks with great warmth, and also translated from the Greek the Milesian fables of Aristides. Some fragments of his compositions are quoted by different authors. *Ovid. Trist.* 2. v. 443.—*Cic. in. Brut.* 64 & 67.—*Paterc.* 2. c. 9.—*Sallust. Jug.* 95.—*Voss. H. Gr.* l. 3. p. 331. *& H. Lat.* 1. c. 10.

SISEN'NA CORN., a Roman, who on being reprimanded in the senate for the ill conduct and depraved manners of his wife, publicly accused Augustus of unlawful commerce with her. *Dio.* 54. The family of the Cornelii and Apronii received the surname of Sisenna. They are accused of intemperate loquacity in the Augustan age, by *Horace*, 1. sat. 7. v. 8.

SISIGAM'BIS or **SISYGAM'BIS**, the mother of Darius the last king of Persia. She was taken prisoner by Alexander the Great, at the battle of Issus, with the rest of the royal family. The conqueror treated her with uncommon tenderness and attention; saluted her as his own mother, and what he had sternly denied to the petitions of his favorites and ministers, he often granted to the intercession of Sisygambis. The regard of the queen for Alexander was uncommon, and indeed she no sooner heard that he was dead than she killed herself, unwilling to survive the loss of so generous an enemy; though she had seen with less concern, the fall of her son's kingdom, the ruin of his subjects, and himself murdered by his servants. She had also lost in one day her husband and 80 of her brothers, whom Ochus had assassinated to make himself master of the kingdom of Persia. *Curt.* 4. c. 9. l. 10. c. 5.

SISIG'YLIS, a large city near Gallia Celtica. *Steph.*

SISIMITH'RÆ, a fortified place of Bactriana, 15 stadia high, 80 in circumference, and plain at the top. Alexander married Roxana there, *Strab.* 11.

SISOCOS'TUS, one of the friends of Alexander, entrusted with the care of the rock Aornus. *Curt* 8. c. 11.

SISOLEN'SES, a people of Italy. *Plin.* 3. c. 5.

SISO'PA, a town of Upper Pannonia. *Ptol.*

SISYPHAM'IDAS, a son of Aristodemus, one of the ambassadors sent by the Lacedæmonians to Athens in the 8th year of the Peloponnesian war. *Schol. Aristoph. Equit.*

SISYPH'IUM, a place of Asia. *Strab.* 8.

SIS'YPHUS, a brother of Athamas and Salmoneus, son of Æolus and Enaretta, the most crafty prince of the heroic ages. He married Merope the daughter of Atlas, or, according to others, of Pandareus, by whom he had several children. He built Ephyre, called afterwards Corinth, and debauched Tyro the daughter of Salmoneus, because he had been told by an oracle that his children by his brother's daughter would avenge the injnries which he had suffered from the malevolence of Salmoneus. Tyro, however, as Hyginus says, destroyed the two sons, whom she had by her uncle. It is reported that Sisyphus mistrusting Autolycus, who stole the neighbouring flocks, marked his bulls under the feet, and when they had been carried away by the dishonesty of his friend, he confounded and astonished the thief by selecting from his numerous flocks those bulls, which by the mark he knew to be his own. The artifice of Sisyphus was so pleasing to Autolycus, who had now found one more cunning than himself, that he permitted him to enjoy the company of his daughter Anticlea, whom a few days after he gave in marriage to Laertes of Ithaca. After his death, Sisyphus was condemned in hell, to roll to the top of the hill a large stone, which had no sooner reached the summit than it fell back into the plain with impetuosity, and rendered his punishment eternal. The causes of this rigorous sentence are variously reported. Some attribute it to his continual depredations in the neighbouring country, and his cruelty in laying heaps of stones on those whom he had plundered, and suffering them to expire in the most agonizing torments. Others, to the insult offered to Pluto, in chaining Death in his palace and detaining her till Mars, at the request of the king of hell, went to deliver her from confinement. Others suppose that Jupiter inflicted this punishment upon him because he told Asopus whither his daughter Ægina had been carried by her ravisher. The more received opinion, however, is, that Sisyphus, on his deathbed, entreated his wife to leave his body unburied, and when he came into Pluto's kingdom, he received permission to return upon earth to punish this seeming negligence of his wife, but, however, on promise of immediately returning. But he was no sooner out of the infernal regions, than he violated his engagements, and when he was at last brought back to hell by Mars, Pluto, to punish his want of fidelity and honor, condemned him to roll a huge stone to the top of a mountain. The institution of the Pythian games is attributed by some to Sisyphus. To be of the blood of Sisyphus was deemed disgraceful among the ancients. *Homer. Odyss.* 11. v. 592.—*Virg. Æn.* 6. v. 616.—*Ovid. Met.* 4. v. 459. l. 13. v. 32. *Fast.* 4. v. 175. *in Ibin.* 191.—*Paus.* 2. c. 1 & 3.—*Hygin.* fab. 60.—*Horat.* 2. od. 14. v. 20.—*Apollod.* 3. c. 4.—*Lucret.* 3 v. 1009.—*Propert.* 2. el. 20. v. 32. l. 4. el. 11. v. 23.—*Servius ad Virg. G.* 1. v. 137. *Æn.* 6. v. 529.—*Tzetzes ad Lyc.*—107, 175, 343 & 380.—*Schol. Apollon. Rh.* 3. v. 1093 & 1239.—*Sch. Aris-*

toph. in Ach. 390.—*Eustath. ad Il.* 6. & *Od.* 11.—*Seneca, in Herc. Fur.* 751.——A son of M. Antony, who was born deformed, and received the surname of Sisyphus, because he was endowed with genius and an excellent understanding. *Horat.* 1. sat. 3. v. 47.——A native of Cos, the scribe of Teucer, who wrote on the Trojan war before Homer. *Tzetz. Chil.* v. 29, 30.

SISYR'BA, a part of Ephesus, so called from an Amazon of this name. *Steph.*

SIT'ACE, a city of Assyria. The region around it was called Sitacene. *Xenoph.*—*Plin. de Ladano*, l. 12. c. 15, &c.

SITAL'CES, one of Alexander's generals, imprisoned for his cruelty and avarice in the government of his province. *Curt.* 10. c. 1.——A king of Thrace, B.C. 436, who led an army against Perdiccas.

SITA'NA, a city of Hispania Tarraconensis. *Sext. Avien.*

SITHE'NI, a people near the Red Sea. *Steph.*

SITH'NIDES, certain nymphs of a fountain in Megara. The daughter of one of the sea nymphs became mother of Megarus, by Jupiter. *Paus.* 1. c. 40.

SI'THON, a king of Thrace.

SI'THON, an island in the Ægæan. *Ovid.*

SITHO'NIA, a country of Thrace, between mount Hæmus and the Danube. Sithonia is often applied to all Thrace, and thence the epithet Sithonis, so often used by the poets. It received its name from king Sithon. *Horat.* 1. od. 18. v. 9.—*Ovid. Met.* 6. v. 588. l. 7. v. 466. l. 13. v. 571.—*Herodot.* 7. c. 122.—*Steph. Byz.*—*Lucan.* 3. v. 280.—*Virg. Ec.* 10. v. 66.

SIT'IA, a town of Hispania Bætica. *Plin.* 3. c. 1.

SITICUM, a town of Italy. *Steph.*

SITIOEN'TA, a town of Lower Mysia. *Ptol.* It is now Tulza according to *Niger*.

SITIOG'AGUS, a river flowing through Carmania. *Plin.* 6. c. 23.

SIT'IPHA, a colony of Mauritania Cæsariensis. *Ptol.*

SIT'IPHIS, the metropolis of Mauritania Tingitana. *Procop.*

SIT'IUS P., a native of Nuceria, who favored the views of Catiline, and passed over into Africa with a number of brave and devoted adherents. By espousing, as an independent prince, the cause of different parties, he enriched himself, and was at last rewarded by Cæsar with a large portion of land in Africa, and ably supported his benefactor in his war against Scipio and Juba. He was slain by Arabio the son of Manasses. *Cic. Att.* 15. ep. 17.—*Appian. B.C.* 4.—*Dio.* 43.—*Flor.* 3. c. 18.—*Sallust. Jug.* 21.—*Hirt. Afr.* 95 & 96.

SITOM'AGUS, a city of Anglia. *Antonin.* *Camden* calls it Thetford.

SI'TON or I'TON, a city of Thessaly. *Steph.*

SIT'ONE, a city near mount Athos. *Plin.* 4. c. 10.

SIT'ONES, a nation of Germany, or modern Norway, according to some. *Tacit. de Germ.* 45.

SIT'TACE. *Vid.* Sitace.

SITTA'PHIUS, a plain in Africa Propria. *Ptol.*

SITTEBE'RIS, a city of India within the Ganges. *Ptol.*

SITTOCA'TES, a river of India flowing into the Ganges. *Arrian.*

SIT'UA, a city of Paphlagonia. *Ptol.*

SI'UR, a city of Africa Propria. *Id.*

SI'VA, a city of Cilicia. *Id.*

SIVA'TA, a city of Galatia. *Id.*

SIX'US, a city of the Mastienii. *Steph.*

SIZA'TA, a city of Syria, otherwise called Larissa. *Steph.*

SIZ'YGES, a nation of the Seres. *Ptol.*

SMARAG'DUS, a town of Ægypt on the Arabian Gulph, where emeralds (*smaragdi*) were dug. *Strab.* 16.

SME'NUS, a river in Laconia rising in mount Taygetus, and falling into the sea near Hypsos. Its waters were remarkable for their sweetness and excellence. *Paus.* 3. c. 24.

SMER'DIS, a son of Cyrus, put to death by order of his brother Cambyses. As his execution was not public, and as it was only known to one of the officers of the monarch, one of the Magi of Persia, who was himself called Smerdis, and who greatly resembled the deceased prince, declared himself king, upon the death of Cambyses. This usurpation would not perhaps have been known, had not he taken too many precautions to conceal it. After he had reigned six months with universal approbation, seven noblemen of Persia conspired to dethrone him, and when this had been executed with success, they chose one of their number to reign in the usurper's place, B.C. 521. This was Darius, the son of Hystaspes. *Herodot.* 3. c 30.—*Justin.* 1. c. 9.

SMIC'YTHUS or MIC'YTHUS, a servant of Anaxilaus. *Vid.* Micythus.

SMI'LA, a city of Thrace. *Steph.*

SMI'LAX or MI'LAX, a beautiful shepherdess who became enamoured of Crocus. She was changed into a flower, as was also her lover. *Ovid. Met.* 4. v. 283. *Fast.* 5. v. 227.—*Plin.* 16. c. 35.—*Servius ad Virg. G.* 4. v. 182.—*Nonnus in Dionys.* 32.

SMI'LIS, a statuary of Ægina, in the age of Dædalus, son of Euclides. *Paus.* 7. c. 4.—*Euseb. Præp. Ev.* 3. c. 8.—*Clem. Alex. in Protrep.*

SMINDYR'IDES, a native of Sybaris, noted for his luxury. *Ælian. V. H.* 9. c. 24. & 12. c. 24.

SMIN'THE, a city of Troas. *Steph.*

SMIN'THEUS, one of the surnames of Apollo in Phrygia, where the inhabitants raised him a temple, because he had destroyed a number of rats that had infested the country. These rats were called σμίνθαι, in the language of Phrygia, whence the surname. According to Strabo and others, a Cretan colony accompanied Teucer in search of a settlement, and they were told by Apollo to settle where the natives of the place came to make war against them. They came into Phrygia, where their girdles and bucklers were one night gnawed to pieces by a number of rats, which they considered as the completion of the oracle, and they accordingly built a city there, and erected in gratitude a temple to Apollo Smintheus. One of the scholiasts of Homer says, that Apollo was so surnamed by his priest Crines at Chrysa, whose gardens and whose fruits were preserved by the god from the devastation of rats. *Homer. Il.* 1. v. 39.—*Strab.* 13.—*Ovid. Met.* 12. v. 585.—*Servius Æn.* 3. v. 108.—*Tzetzes in Lyc.* 1301.—*Arnob. adv. Gent.* 3.—*Plin.* 5. c. 30.

SMYR'NA, a celebrated sea-port town of Ionia in Asia Minor, built, as some suppose, by Tantalus, or, according to others, by the Æolians. It has been subject to many revolutions, and been severally in the possession of the Æolians, Ionians, Lydians, and Macedonians. Alexander, in compliance with the direction of a vision which he saw near the temple of the Eumenides, or, according to Strabo, Lysimachus, rebuilt it 400 years after it had been destroyed by the Lydians. It was one of the richest and most powerful cities of Asia, and became one of the twelve cities of the Ionian confederacy. The inhabitants were much given to luxury and indolence, but were universally esteemed for their valor and intrepidity, when called into action. Marcus Aurelius repaired it after having been destroyed by an earthquake, about the 180th year of the Christian era. Smyrna, once so famous for its stately buildings, its magnificent temples, and marble porticos, still continues to be a very flourishing and commercial place, though some imagine that the modern town is at the distance of more than three miles from the site of the ancient city. The river Meles flows near its walls. The inhabitants of Smyrna believed that Homer was born among them, and, to confirm this opinion, they not only paid him divine honors, but showed a place which bore the poet's name, and also had a brass coin in circulation which was called *Homerium*. Some suppose that it was called Smyrna from an Amazon of the same name, who took possession of it. Cinna the Roman poet was a native of the place. *Herodot.* 1. c. 16, &c.—*Strab.* 12 & 14.—*Ital.* 8. v. 565.—*Paus.* 4. c. 21. l 5. c. 8. l. 7. c. 5.—*Mela*, 1. c. 17.—*Lucan.* 9. v. 984.—*Catull.* 66.

SMYR'NA, a daughter of Thias, mother of Adonis.——An Amazon.

SMYR'NA, the name of a poem which Cinna, a Latin poet, composed in nine years, and which was worthy of admiration, according to Catullus, 94.

SMYRNÆ'US Q., a Greek poet of the 3d century, called also Calaber. *Vid.* Calaber.

SO'ACA, a town of Arabia Felix. *Ptol.*

SOÆ'MUS, a king of Ituræa, in the time of Claudius. *Tac. Ann.* 12. c. 23.——Another monarch to whom Nero delivered Sophene. He went over to the party of Vespasian. *Tac. Hist.* 13. c. 7. 2. c. 81.

SO'AMUS, a river of India. *Arrian. in Indic.*

SOA'NA, a river of Asiatic Sarmatia. *Ptol. Niger* calls it Terchin.

SOAN'DA, a town of Armenia Minor. *Strab.* 12.

SOA'NES, a people of Colchis, near Caucasus, in whose territories the rivers abound with golden sands, which the inhabitants gather in wool skins, whence perhaps arose the fable of the golden fleece. *Strab.* 11.—*Plin.* 33. c. 3.—*Eustath. Dionys. Per.*

SOB'ALA, a city of Caria. *Steph.*

SOBA'NUS, a river of India without the Ganges. *Ptol.*

SOB'IDAS, a region of Parthia. *Id.*

SOBOT'ALE, a city of the Sabæi on the Red Sea. It had sixty temples within its walls. *Plin.* 6. c. 28.

SO'CHIS, a king of Ægypt, who dedicated four obelisks to the sun, at Heliopolis. *Plin.* 36. c. 8.

SOC'RATES, the most celebrated philosopher of all antiquity, was a native of Athens. His father Sophroniscus, was a statuary, and his mother Phenarete was by profession a midwife. For some time he followed the occupation of his father, and some have mentioned the statues of the Graces in the citadel of Athens, admired for their simplicity and elegance, as the work of his hands. He was called from this meaner employment, of which, however, he was never ashamed, by Crito, who admired his genius and courted his friendship. Philosophy soon became the study of Socrates, and under Archelaus and Anaxagoras he laid the foundation of that great and exemplary virtue which succeeding ages have ever loved and venerated. He appeared like the rest of his countrymen in the field of battle; he fought with boldness and intrepidity, and to his courage two of his friends and disciples, Xenophon at the battle of Delium, and Alcibiades at the battle of Potidæa, owed the preservation of their lives. But the character of Socrates appears more conspicuous as a philosopher and moralist than as a warrior. He was fond of labour; he inured himself to suffer hardships, and acquired that serenity of mind, and firmness of countenance which the most alarming dangers could never destroy, or the most sudden calamities alter. If he was poor, it was from choice, and not the effects of vanity or the wish of appearing singular. He bore injuries with patience, and the insults of malice or resentment he not only treated with contempt, but even received with a mind that expressed some concern, and felt compassion for the depravity of human nature. So singular and so venerable a character was admired by the most enlightened of the Athenians. Socrates was attended by a number of illustrious pupils, whom he instructed by his exemplary life, as well as by his doctrines. He had no particular place where to deliver his lectures; but as the good of his countrymen, and the reformation of their corrupted morals, and not the aggregation of riches, was the object of his study, he was present everywhere, and drew the attention of his auditors either in the groves of Academus, the Lyceum, or on the banks of the Ilyssus. He spoke with freedom on every subject, religious as well as civil, and had the courage to condemn the violence of his countrymen, and to withstand the torrent of resentment, by which the Athenian generals were capitally punished for not burying the dead at the battle of Arginusæ. This independence of spirit, and visible superiority of mind and genius over the rest of his countrymen, created many enemies to Socrates; but as his character was irreproachable, and his doctrines pure, and void of all obscurity, the voice of malevolence was silent. Yet Aristophanes soon undertook, at the instigation of Melitus, in his comedy of the Clouds, to ridicule the venerable character of Socrates on the stage; and when once the way was open to calumny and defamation, the fickle and licentious populace paid no reverence to the philosopher whom they had before regarded as a being of a superior order. When this had succeeded, Melitus stood forth to criminate him, together with Anytus and Lycon, and the philosopher was summoned before the tribunal of the five hundred. He was accused of corrupting the Athenian youth, of making innovations in the religion of the Greeks, and of ridiculing the many gods which the Athenians worshipped; yet, false as this might appear, the accusers relied for the success of their cause upon the perjury of false witnesses, and the envy of the judges, whose ignorance would readily yield to misrepresentation, and be guided by eloquence and artifice. In this their expectations were not frustrated; and while the judges expected submission from Socrates, and that meanness of behaviour and servility of defence which characterised criminals, the philosopher perhaps accelerated his own fall by the firmness of his mind, and his uncomplying integrity. Lysias, one of the most celebrated orators of the age, composed an oration in a laboured and pathetic style, which he offered to his friend to be pronounced as his defence in the presence of his judges. Socrates read it, but, after he had praised the eloquence and the animation of the whole, he rejected it, as neither manly nor expressive of fortitude, and, comparing it to Sicyonian shoes, which, though fitting, were proofs of effeminacy, he observed, that a philosopher ought to be conspicuous for magnanimity and for firmness of soul. In his apology he spoke with great animation, and confessed that while others boasted that they were acquainted with everything, he himself knew nothing. The whole discourse was full of simplicity and noble grandeur, the energetic language of offended innocence. He modestly said, that what he possessed was applied for the service of the Athenians; it was his wish to make his fellow-citizens happy, and it was a duty which he performed by the special command of the gods, "whose authority," said he emphatically, to his judges, "I regard more than yours." Such language from a man who was accused of a capital crime, astonished and irritated the judges. Socrates was condemned, but only by a majority of three voices; and when he was desired, according to the spirit of the Athenian laws, to pass sentence of death upon himself, and to mention the death he preferred, the philosopher said, "For my attempts to teach the Athenian youth justice and moderation, and to render the rest of my countrymen more happy, let me be maintained at the public expense the remaining years of my life in the Prytaneum, an honor, O Athenians, which I deserve more than the victors of the Olympic games. They make their countrymen happy in appearance, but I have made you so in reality." This exasperated the judges in the highest degree, and he was condemned to drink hemlock. Upon this he addressed the court, and more particularly the judges who had decided in his favor, in a pathetic speech. He told them that to die was a pleasure, since he was going to hold converse with the greatest heroes of antiquity; he recommended to their paternal care his defenceless children, and as he returned to the prison he exclaimed: "I go to die, you to live; but which is the best the divinity alone can know." The solemn celebration of the Delian festivals (*Vid.* Delia), prevented his execution for thirty days, and during that time he was confined in the prison and loaded with irons. His friends, and particularly his disciples, were his constant attendants; he discoursed with them upon different subjects with all his usual cheerfulness and serenity. He reproved them for their sorrow; and when one of them was uncommonly grieved because he was to suffer, though innocent, the philosopher replied, "would you then have me die guilty?" With this composure he spent his last days, he continued to be a preceptor till the moment of his death, and instructed his pupils on questions of the greatest importance; he told them his opinions in support of the immortality of the soul, and reprobated with acrimony the prevalent custom of suicide. He disregarded the intercession of his friends, and when it was in his power to make his escape out of prison he refused it, and asked with his usual pleasantry, where he could escape death? "Whither," says he to Crito, who had bribed the gaoler, and made his escape certain, "whither shall I flee to avoid this irrevocable doom passed on all mankind?" When the hour to drink the poison was come, the executioner presented him the cup with tears in his eyes. Socrates received it with composure, and after he had made a libation to the gods, drank it with an unaltered countenance, and a few moments after expired. Such was the end of a man whom the uninfluenced answer of the oracle of Delphi had pronounced the wisest of mankind. Socrates died about 400 years B.C. in the 70th year of his age. He was no sooner buried than the Athenians repented of their cruelty, his accusers were universally despised and shunned, one suffered death, some were banished, and others, with their own hands, put an end to the life, which their severity to the best of the Athenians had rendered insupportable. The actions, sayings, and opinions of Socrates have been faithfully recorded by two of the most celebrated of his pupils, Xenophon and Plato, and everything which relates to the life and circumstances of this great philosopher is now minutely known. To his poverty, his innocence, his example, the Greeks were particularly indebted for their greatness and splendor; and the learning which was universally disseminated by his pupils, gave the whole nation a consciousness of their superiority over the rest of the world, not only in the polite arts, but in the more laborious exercises, which their writings celebrated. The philosophy of Socrates forms a celebrated epoch in the human mind. The son of Sophroniscus derided the more abstruse enquiries and metaphysical researches of his predecessors, and by first introducing moral philosophy, induced mankind to consider themselves, their passions, their opinions, their duties, actions, and faculties. From this it was said, that the founder of the Socratic school drew philosophy down from heaven upon the earth. In his attendance upon religious worship, Socrates was himself an example; he believed the divine origin of dreams and omens, and publicly declared that he was accompanied by a dæmon or invisible conductor. (*Vid.* Dæmon), whose frequent interposition stopped him from the commission of evil, and the guilt of misconduct. This familiar spirit, however, according to some, was nothing more than a sound judgment assisted by prudence and long experience, which warned him at the approach of danger, and from a general speculation of mankind could foresee what success would attend an enterprize, or what calamities would follow an ill-managed administration. As a supporter of the immortality of the soul, he allowed the perfection of a supreme knowledge, from which he deduced the government of the universe. From the resources of experience as well as nature and observation, he perceived the indiscriminate dispensation of good and evil to mankind by the hand of heaven, and was convinced that nothing but the most inconsiderate would incur the displeasure of their creator to avoid poverty or sickness, or gratify a sensual appetite, which must in the end harass their soul with remorse and the consciousness of guilt. From this natural view of things, he perceived the relation of one nation with another, and how much the tranquillity of civil society depended upon the proper discharge of their respective duties. The actions of men furnished materials also for his discourses; to instruct them was his aim, and to render them happy was the ultimate object of his daily lessons. From principles like these, which were enforced in Socrates, by the unparalleled example of an affectionate husband, a tender parent, a warlike soldier, and a patriotic citizen, the celebrated sects of the Platonics, the Peripatetics, the Academics, Cyrenaics, Stoics, &c. soon after arose. Socrates never wrote for the public eye, yet many assert that the tragedies of his pupil Euripides, were partly composed by him. He was naturally of a licentious disposition, and a physiognomist observed, in looking into the face of the philosopher, that his heart was the most depraved, immodest, and corrupted that ever was in the human breast. This nearly cost the satirist his life, but Socrates upbraided his disciples, who wished to punish the physiognomist, and declared that his assertions were true, but that all his vicious propensities had been duly corrected and curbed by means of reason. Socrates made a poetical version of Æsop's fables, while in prison. The most celebrated of his pupils, besides Xenophon and Plato, were Antisthenes, Alcibiades, Simon, Æschines, Phædon, and Aristippus. He married two wives, Myrtone daughter of the great Aristides, by whom he had Sophroniscus and Menexenus, and Xantippe, remarkable for her violent and morose temper, by whom he had Lamprocles. *Aristot. apud Laert.—Xenoph.—Plato.—Diog Laert.—Paus.* 1. c. 22.—*Plut. de op. Phil. &c.—Cic. de Orat.* 1. c. 54. *Tusc.* 1. c. 41, &c.—*Val. Max.* 3. c. 4. [The most authentic bust of Socrates is in the Neapolitan Museum.]——A leader of the Achæans at the battle of Cunaxa. He was seized and put to death by order of Artaxerxes. *Polyæn.* 7. c. 18.——A governor of Cilicia under Alexander. *Curt.* 4. c. 5.——A painter. *Plin.* 35. c. 11.——A Rhodian in the age of Augustus. He wrote an account of the civil wars. *Athen.* l. 4.——A scholiast born A.D. 380, at Constantinople. He wrote an ecclesiastical history from the year 309, at which period the history of Eusebius ends, down to 440, with great exactness and judgment, of which the best edition is that of Reading, fol. Cantab. 1720. *Sax. Onom.* 1. p. 509.—*Fabr. B. Gr.* 5. c. 4.

SOC'RATIS IN'SULA, an island on the coast of Arabia. *Ptol.*

SOCUN'DA, a town of Arcadia. *Id.* It is called Socaana by *Ammianus*.

SO'DII, a people of Iberia. *Plin.* 6. c. 10.

SO'DRÆ, a people on the banks of the Indus. *Diodor.*

SODUCE'NA, a region of Armenia Minor. *Ptol.*

SŒ'MIAS JU'LIA, mother of the emperor Heliogabalus, was made president of a senate of women, which she had elected to decide the quarrels and the affairs of the Roman matrons. She at last provoked the people by her debaucheries, extravagance, and cruelties, and was murdered with her son and family. She was a native of Apamea; her father's name was Julius Avitus, and her mother's Masa. Her sister Julia Mammæa married the emperor Septimus Severus. [The statues and busts of Julia Sœmias are very numerous. The finest of each will be found in the Vatican at Rome.]

SOE'TA, a city of Scythia without Imaus. *Ptol.*

SOGDIA'NA, a country of Asia, bounded on the north by Scythia, on the east by the Sacæ, on the south by Bactriana, and on the west by Margiana, and now known by the name of Zagatay, or Usbek. The people are called Sogdiani. The capital was Marcanda. *Herodot* 3. c. 93.—*Curt.* 7. c. 10.

SOGDIA'NUS, a son of Artaxerxes Longimanus, who murdered his elder brother, king Xerxes, to make himself master of the Persian throne. He was but seven months in possession of the crown. His brother Ochus, who reigned under the name of Darius Nothus, conspired against him, and suffocated him in a tower full of warm ashes. *Euseb. in Chron.*

SOGDON'ACUS, father of Pasines, king of Arabia, rebuilt Charace. *Plin.* 6. c. 27.

SOGIUN'TII, a people of the Alps. *Plin.* 3. c. 20.

SOGOC'ARA, a city of Armenia Major. *Ptol.*

SOI'TA, a city of Armenia Major. *Id.*

SOL (*the sun*) was an object of veneration among the ancients. It was particularly worshipped by the Persians, under the name of Mithras, and was the Baal or Bel of the Chaldæans, the Belphegor of the Moabites, the Moloch of the Canaanites, the Osiris of the Ægyptians, and the Adonis of the Syrians. The Massagetæ sacrificed horses to the sun on account of their swiftness. According to some of the ancient poets Sol and Apollo are two different persons. Apollo, however, and Phœbus and Sol, are universally supposed to be the same deity. *Macrob.* c. 17.—*Strab.* 21.—*Herodot.* 2.—*Paus.* 2. c. 43. l. 4. c. 31.—*Homer. Odyss.* 8.

SOLA'NA, a city of the Seres. *Ptol.*

SOLAN'IDÆ, islands of Arabia Felix. *Plin.* 6. c. 28.

SOLA'NUS, a friend of Ovid. *Pont.* l. 2.

SOL'ENUS, a river of India within the Ganges. *Ptol.*

SOLE'TUM, a city of Calabria. *Plin.* 3. c. 11. It is now Soleto according to *Leander*.

SOLICIN'IUM, a town of Germany, now Sultz, on the Neckar. *Antonin.—Cluver.*

SOLIM'NA, a city of India. *Steph.*

SOLIM'NIA, an island of the Ægean Sea. *Plin.* 4. c. 12.

SOLINA'TES, a people of Umbria. *Id.* 3. c. 14.

SOLI'NUS C. JU'LIUS, a grammarian who flourished at the end of the first century, or, according to others, in the middle of the third century. He wrote a book called "Polyhistor," which is a collection of historical remarks and geographical annotations on the most celebrated places of every country. He has been called Pliny's ape, because he imitated that well known naturalist. Of the Polyhistor there have been several editions; the best, however, is that of Salmasius, first published at Paris in 1629. The last impression is that of Noriberg. 1777, edited by Goezius. *Harles. Not. Lit. Rom.* 1. p. 534.—*Sax. Onom.* 1. p. 351.

SO'LIS COLUM'NA, some rocks in the highest part of the Alps, whence the Rhodanus flows. *Sex. Avien.*

So'lis Fons, a celebrated fountain in Libya. *Vid.* Ammon.

So'lis Por'tus, a harbour in the island of Taprobane.

SOLITAURA'LIA, sacrifices at Rome, at which were offered a ram, a bull, and a pig. *Rosin. Antiq. Rom.* 4. c. 17.

SOL'LIUM, or **SO'LIUM**, a town of Corinth. *Steph.*

SOLMIS'SUS, a mountain of Ionia, near Ephesus. *Strab.*

SOL'OE or **SO'LI**, a town of Cyprus, built on the borders of the Clarius by an Athenian colony. It was originally called Æpeia, till Solon visited Cyprus, and advised Philocyprus, one of the princes of the island, to change the situation of his capital. His advice was followed, a new town was raised in a beautiful plain, and called after the name of the Athenian philosopher. *Strab.* 14.—*Plut. in Sol.*

Sol'oe, a town of Cilicia on the sea coast, built by the Greeks and Rhodians. It was afterwards called Pompeiopolis, from Pompey, who settled a colony of pirates there. *Plin.* 5. c. 27. l 6. c. 34. —*Dionys.*—*Mela*, 1. c. 13.—*Aul. Gell.* 1. c. 7. l. 5. c. 20. l. 7. c. 2. Some suppose that the Greeks, who settled in either of these two towns, forgot the purity of their native language, and thence arose the term Solecismus, applied to an inelegant or improper expression. Crantor, Aratus, Chrysippus, and Philemon were natives of Soli.

SOL'OEIS, a city of Sicily. *Thucyd.* 1, 6.—*Cic. Verr.* 3. c. 43. It is called Solanto by *Leander.*

SOLOEN'TIA, a promontory of Libya at the extremity of mount Atlas, now cape Cantin. *Ptol.*—*Mela*, 1. c. 13.

SOLOMA'TIS, a river flowing into the Ganges. *Arrian. in Indic.*

SO'LON, one of the seven wise men of Greece, was born at Salamis and educated at Athens. His father's name was Euphorion, or Execestides, one of the descendants of king Codrus, and by his mother's side he reckoned among his relations the celebrated Pisistratus. After he had been for some time employed in commercial pursuits, and thus acquired a sufficient independence, he devoted himself to philosophical and political studies, and then travelled over the greater part of Greece. At his return he was distressed at the dissensions which were kindled among his countrymen, and, as in the public offices which he had discharged, he had displayed the greatest integrity and the most consummate wisdom, all fixed their eyes upon him as a deliverer, and he was unanimously elected archon and sovereign legislator. He might have become absolute, but he refused the dangerous office of king of Athens, and in the more honourable capacity of lawgiver, began to make a reform in every department The complaints of the poorer citizens found redress, all debts were remitted, and no one was permitted to seize the person of his debtor if unable to make a restoration of his money. After he had made the most salutary regulations in the state, and bound the Athenians by a solemn oath, that they would faithfully observe his laws for 100 years, Solon resigned the office of legislator, and removed himself from Athens. He visited Ægypt, and in the court of Crœsus, king of Lydia, convinced the monarch of the instability of fortune, and told him, when he wished to know whether he was not the happiest of mortals, that Tellus, an Athenian, who had always seen his country in a flourishing state, who had seen his children lead a virtuous life, and who had himself fallen in defence of his country, was more entitled to happiness than the possessor of riches and the master of empires. After ten years' absence Solon returned to Athens, but he had the mortification to see the greater part of his regulations disregarded by the factious spirit of his countrymen, and the usurpation of Pisistratus. Not to be longer a spectator of the divisions that reigned in his country, he retired to Cyprus, where he died at the court of king Philocyprus, in the 80th year of his age, 558 years B.C. The salutary consequences of the laws of Solon can be discovered in the length of time they were in force in the republic of Athens. For above 400 years they flourished in full vigor, and Cicero, who was himself a witness of their benign influence, passes the highest encomiums upon the legislator, whose superior wisdom framed such a code of regulations. It was the intention of Solon to protect the poorer citizens, and by dividing the whole body of the Athenians into four classes, three of which were permitted to discharge the most important offices and magistracies in the state, and the last to give their opinion in the assemblies, but not have a share in the distinctions and honors of their superiors, the legislator gave the populace a privilege which, though at first small and inconsiderable, soon rendered them masters of the republic, and of all the affairs of government. He made a reformation in the Areopagus, increased the authority of the members, and permitted them yearly to inquire how every citizen maintained himself, and to punish such as lived in idleness, and were not employed in some honorable and lucrative profession. He also regulated the Prytaneum, and fixed the number of its judges at 400. The sanguinary laws of Draco were all cancelled, except that against murder, and the punishment denounced against every offender was proportioned to his crime; but Solon made no law against parricide or sacrilege. The former of these crimes, he said, was too horrible to human nature for a man to be guilty of it, and the latter could never be committed, because the history of Athens had never furnished a single instance. Such as had died in the service of their country, were buried with great pomp, and their family was maintained at the public expense; but such as had squandered away their estates, such as refused to bear arms in defence of their country, or paid no attention to the infirmities and distress of their parents, were branded with infamy. The laws of marriage were newly regulated; it became a union of affection and tenderness, and no longer a mercenary contract. To defame the dead or the living, was made a crime, and the legislator wished that the character of his fellow-citizens should be freed from the aspersions of malevolence and envy. A person that had no children, was permitted to dispose of his estate as he pleased; and the females were not allowed to be extravagant in their dress or expenses. To be guilty of adultery was a capital crime, and the friend and associate of lewdness and debauchery was never permitted to speak in public; for, as the philosopher observed, a man who has no shame is not capable of being intrusted with the government of the people. These celebrated laws were engraved on several tables, and that they might be the better known, more familiar to, and more deeply impressed upon the minds of the Athenians, they were written in verse. The indignation which Solon expressed on seeing the tragical representations of Thespis, is well known; and he sternly observed, that if falsehood and fiction were tolerated on the stage, they would soon find their way among the common occupations of men. According to Plutarch he was reconciled to Pisistratus, but this seems to be false, as the legislator refused to live in a country where the privileges of his fellow-citizens were trampled upon by the usurpation of a tyrant. *Vid.* Lycurgus. About 154 verses are preserved in the collection of the

Greek poets under the name of Solon's elegies, and they contain precepts for the regulation of human life and observations on the power of Providence, &c. *Plut. in Sol.—Herodot.* 1. c. 29.—*Diog.* 1.—*Paus.* 1. c. 49.—*Cic. in Sen.—Auson. de Sept. Sap.—Persius.* 3. v. 79.—*Juv.* 10. v. 174.—*Sax. Onom.* 1. p. 20.—*Fabr. B. Gr.* 2. c. 14. [The most authentic bust of Solon is to be found in the Vatican at Rome.]

SO'LON or SOLO'NIUM, a city of the Allobroges. *Dio.—Epitome. Liv.* 103. It is now probably la Sone.

SOLO'NIUM, a town of Latium on the borders of Etruria. *Plut. in Mar.—Cic. de Div.* 1.—*Festus. de V. Sig.*

SOLO'RIUS, a mountain of Spain, separating Tarraconensis from Bætica and Lusitania. *Plin.* 3. c. 1.——A harbour of Hispania Tarraconensis. *Dion. Hal.—Sex. Ruf.* It is now Porto Salo.

SOLUEN'TII, a nation of Lower Libya. *Ptol.*

SO'LUS (*-untis*) or SOLUN'TUM, a maritime town of Sicily. *Vid.* Soloeis. *Strab.* 14.—*Plin.* 3. c. 7.—*Hesych.*

SOLUSA'PRA, a town of Sicily. *Antonin.*

SOL'VA, a town of Noricum. *Plin.* 3. c. 24. It is now Solveld.

SOL'YMA or SOL'YMÆ, a town of Lycia. The inhabitants, called Solymi, were anciently called Milyades, and afterwards Termili, and Lycians. Sarpedon settled among them. *Strab.* 14.—*Homer. Il.* 6. v. 184.—*Apollon.* 2. v. 724.—*Plin.* 5. c. 27 & 29.

SOL'YMA, an ancient name of Jerusalem. *Vid.* Hierosolyma. *Juv.* 6, v. 543.—*Tacit. H.* 5. c. 8.—*Joseph. Ant.* 7. c. 3.

SOM'NUS, son of Erebus and Nox, was one of the infernal deities, and presided over sleep. His palace, according to some mythologists, was a dark cave, where the sun never penetrated. At the entrance were a number of poppies and somniferous herbs. The god himself is represented as asleep on a bed of feathers with black curtains. The dreams stand by him, and Morpheus as his principal minister, watches to prevent the noise from awakening him. The Lacedæmonians always placed the image of Somnus near that of death. *Hesiod, Theog.* 212.—*Homer. Il.* 14. v. 230.—*Virg. Æn.* 6. v. 893.—*Ovid. Met.* 11. fab. 10.—*Stat. Th.* 10. v. 89.—*Paus.* 2. c. 31. l. 5. c. 18. [The finest statue of Somnus was in the Museum of the Vatican at Rome.]

SONCHE'DES, an Ægyptian prophet, the preceptor of Pythagoras. *Clem. Strom.* l. 11.

SON'CHIS, an Ægyptian priest in the age of Solon. It was he who told that celebrated philosopher a number of traditions, particularly about the Atlantic isles, which he represented as more extensive than the continent of Asia and Africa. These islands disappeared, and as it is said, in one day and one night. *Plut. in Isid. & in Solon.*

SON'DRÆ, a people of India. *Plin.* 6. c. 20.

SONTIA'TES or SOTIA'TES, a people in Gaul. *Cæs. B. G.* 3. c. 20 & 21.

SO'NUS, a river flowing into the Ganges. *Plin.* 6. c. 18.—*Arrian in Indic.*

SOPAR'MA, a market town of India within the Ganges. *Arrian in Peripl.*

SOP'ATER, a philosopher of Apamea, in the age of the emperor Constantine. He was one of the disciples of Iamblichus, and after his death he was at the head of the Platonic philosophers. *Suidas.—Sozom.* 1. c. 5.—*Phot. Cod.* 141.——An officer of Macedonia, whom king Philip sent with 4000 men to assist the Carthaginians against Rome. *Liv.* 30. c. 26 & 42.——A general of king Perseus. *Liv.* 42. c. 62.——A magistrate at Syracuse. *Liv.* 24. c. 23.——A native of Halycia in Sicily. *Cic. Verr.* 2. c. 38.

SO'PHAX, a son of Hercules and Tinga the widow of Antæus, who founded the kingdom of Tingis, in Mauritania, and from whom were descended Diodorus and Juba, king of Mauritania. *Strab.* 3.—*Plut. in Sertor.*

SOPHÆN'ETUS, an historian who wrote an account of the expedition of Cyrus. *Steph. in Carduch.*

SOPHE'NE, a country of Armenia, on the borders of Mesopotamia. *Lucan.* 2. v. 593.

SOPH'ILUS, a writer of the middle comedy, in the time of Ptolemy Lagus. *Athen.—Diog. Laert.—Lil. Girald.—Voss. de Poet. Gr.* c. 8.

SOPH'OCLES, a celebrated tragic poet of Athens, educated in the school of Æschylus. He distinguished himself not only as a poet, but also as a statesman. He commanded the Athenian armies, and in several battles shared the supreme command with Pericles, and exercised the office of archon with credit and honor. The first appearance of Sophocles as a poet reflects great honor on his abilities. The Athenians had taken the island of Scyrus, and to celebrate that memorable event, an annual contest for a prize for the best tragedy was instituted. Sophocles on this occasion obtained the prize over many competitors, in the number of whom was Æschylus, his friend and master. This success contributed to encourage the poet, he wrote for the stage with applause, and obtained the poetical prize, and was publicly crowned 20 different times. Sophocles was the rival of Euripides for public praise; they divided the applause of the populace, and while the former surpassed in the sublime and majestic, the other was not inferior in the tender and pathetic. The Athenians were pleased with their contention, and as the theatre was at that time an object of importance and magnitude, and deemed an essential and most magnificent part of the religious worship, each had his admirers and adherents: but the two poets, captivated at last by popular applause, gave way to jealousy and rivalship. Of 120 tragedies which Sophocles composed, only seven are extant; Ajax, Electra, Œdipus Tyrannus, Antigone, the Trachiniæ, Philoctetes, and Œdipus Coloneus. The ingratitude of the children of Sophocles is well known. They wished to become immediate masters of their father's possessions, and therefore, tired of his long life, accused him before the Areopagus of insanity. The only defence the poet made was to read his tragedy of Œdipus at Colonus, which he had lately finished, and then he asked his judges, whether the author of such a performance could be taxed with insanity? The father upon this was acquitted, and the children returned home covered with shame and confusion. Sophocles died in the 91st year of his age, 406 years B.C., through excess of joy, as some authors report, at having obtained a poetical prize at the Olympic games; though Lucian asserts that he was choked with a grape stone, in his 95th year. Athenæus has accused Sophocles of licentiousness and debauchery, particularly when he commanded the armies of Athens. When he was in his cradle it is reported that bees settled upon his lips, as if to prognosticate the great sweetness of his compositions, on that account he was called the Athenian bee, and a swarm of bees was sculptured on his tomb. The best editions of Sophocles are those of Capperonnier, 2 vols. 4to. Paris, 1780; of Glasgow, 2 vols. 12mo. 1745; of Geneva, 4to. 1603; and that by Brunck, 4 vols. 8vo. 1789. The best English translation is that of Potter. *Sax. Onom.* 1. p. 41.—*Fabr. B. Gr.* 2. c. 17.—*Cic. in Cat. de Div.* 1. c. 25.—*Plut. in Cim. & Pompil. &c.—Quintil.* 1. c. 10. l. 10. c. 1.—*Val. Max.* 8. c. 7. l. 9. c. 12.—*Plin.* 7. c. 53.—*Athen.* 10, &c. [There is a fine bust of Sophocles in the Museum of the Vatican, at Rome.]——A native of Agrigentum, mentioned by Cicero as learned and eloquent. *Verr.* 3. c. 88.

SOPHO'NIA, a small island of the Ægean Sea. *Plin.* 2. c. 89.

SOPHONIS'BA, a daughter of Asdrubal the Carthaginian, celebrated for her beauty. She married Syphax, a prince of Numidia; and when her husband was conquered by the Romans and Masinissa, she fell into the hands of the enemy. Masinissa became enamoured of her, and married her. This behaviour displeased the Romans, and Scipio, who at that time had the command of the armies of the republic in Africa, rebuked the monarch severely, and desired him to part with Sophonisba. This was an arduous task for Masinissa, yet he dreaded the Romans. He entered Sophonisba's tent with tears in his eyes, and told her, that as he could not deliver her from captivity and the jealousy of the Romans, he recommended her, as the strongest pledge of his love and affection for her person, to die like the daughter of Asdrubal. Sophonisba obeyed, and drank, with unusual composure and serenity, the cup of poison which Masinissa sent to her, about 203 years. B.C. *Lic.* 30. c. 12, &c.—*Sallust de Jug.*—*Justin.* 33. c. 1.

SO'PHRON, a comic poet of Syracuse, son of Agathocles and Damasyllis. His compositions were so universally esteemed, that Plato is said to have read them with rapture. A few of his verses are extant. *Val. Max.* 8, c. 7.—*Quintil.* 1. c. 10.—*Athen.* 13 & 14.—*Plut. de Cic.*—*Gyrald. P. H.* 7.—*Fabr. B. Gr.* 2. c. 22.

SOPHRO'NIA, a Roman lady whom Maxentius took by force from her husband's house, and married. Sophronia killed herself when she saw that her affections were abused by the tyrant.

SOPHRONIS'CUS, the father of Socrates.

SOPHROS'YNE, a daughter of Dionysius by Dion's sister.

SOPH'THA, an island of the Persian Gulf. *Ptol.* It is supposed to be the Phara of *Marcellinus.*

SOPIA'NÆ, a city of Lower Pannonia.

SOP'OLIS, the father of Hermolaus. *Curt.* 8. c. 7.——A painter in Cicero's age. *Att.* 4. ep. 16.

SO'RA, a town of the Volsci, of which the inhabitants were called Sorani. *Ital.* 8. v. 395.—*Cic. pro Pl.*—*Liv.* 6 & 7.—*Juv.* 3. v. 223.—*Strab.* 5.—*Servius ad Æn.* 9. v. 590.——A city of India Citerior. *Ptol.*

SORACTES or **SORAC'TE**, a mountain of Etruria, near the Tiber, seen from Rome, though at the distance of 26 miles. It was sacred to Apollo, who is thence surnamed Soractis; and it is said that the priests of the god, called Hirpi, could walk over burning coals without hurting themselves. There was, as some report, a fountain on mount Soracte, the waters of which boiled at sun-rise, and instantly killed all such birds as drank of them. The modern name of Soracte is Monte S. Oreste or S. Œdisti. *Strab.* 5.—*Plin.* 2. c. 93. l. 7. c. 2,—*Horat.* 1. od. 9.—*Virg. Æn.* 11. v. 785.—*Ital.* 5. v. 175.—*Solin.* 8.—*Servius ad Æn.* 7. v. 696. l. 11. v. 762 & 785.

SORAC'TIA, a city of the Omani, in Arabia Felix. *Plin.* 6. c. 28.

SORA'DEUS, a dæmon worshipped by the Indians. *Athen.* l. 1.

SORA'NUS, a man put to death by Nero. *Vid.* Valerius.——The father of Atilia, the first wife of Cato.——A physician of Ephesus, in the age of Trajan and Adrian. *Suidas*——A surname of Pluto. *Plin.* 2. c. 93.——An Ephesian physician, who wrote *De Morbis Mulierum.* A fragment of this work was edited by Turnebus. *Harles. Not. Lit. Rom.* 1. p. 513.

SORBO'TÆ, a people of Æthiopia. *Plin.*

SO'REX, a favorite of Sylla, and the companion of his debaucheries. *Plut.*

SOR'GE, a daughter of Œneus, king of Calydon, by Æthea, daughter of Thestius. She married Andremon, and was mother of Oxilus. She is sometimes called Horge. *Apollod.* 1 & 2.

SORIT'IA, a city of Hispania Bætica. *Hirt, B. Hisp* c. 27.

SOR'OGA, a city of Upper Pannonia. *Ptol.*

SO'RON, a city of Paphlagonia. *Paus.* l. 8.

SORO'NA, a wood of Arcadia. *Id. ibid.*

SORO'RES, a name given to the cities of Antiochia Magna, Seleucia Pieria, Apamea, and Laodicea, founded at the same time by Seleucus Nicanor. *Strab.*

SORTHIDA, a city of Babylonia. *Ptol.*

SOSAN'DER, an athlete of Smyrna, bribed at the Olympic games. *Vid.* Polyctor.

SOSAN'DRA, an island near Crete. *Steph.*

SO'SIA GAL'LA, a woman at the court of Tiberius, banished, &c. *Tacit. Ann.* 4. c. 19.——The name of a slave in Terence.

SOSIA'NUS, a surname of Apollo, who had a cedar statue at Rome, brought from Seleucia. *Plin.* 13. c. 5.

SOSIB'IUS, a grammarian of Laconia, B.C. 255. He was a great favorite of Ptolemy Philopator, and advised him to murder his brother, and the queen his wife, called Arsinoe. He lived to a great age, and was on that account called Polychronos. He was afterwards permitted to retire from the court, and spend the rest of his days in peace and tranquillity, after he had disgraced the name of minister by the most abominable crimes, and the murder of many of the royal family. His son of the same name was preceptor to king Ptolemy Epiphanes. *Suidas.*—*Athen.*——The preceptor of Britannicus, the son of Claudius. *Tacit. Ann.* 11. c. 1.

SOS'ICLES, a Greek who behaved with great valor when Xerxes invaded Greece ——An archon at Athens, Olymp. 113. an. 4.——A poet of Syracuse, one of the Pleiades. He wrote 73 plays, and gained seven prizes. *Suidas.*

SOSIC'RATES, a noble senator among the Achæans, put to death because he wished his countrymen to make peace with the Romans.——A writer *De Rebus Cretensibus. Athen.* l. 6.—*Voss. H. Gr.* 3. p. 415.——A comic poet. *Fabr. B. Gr.* 2. c. 22.

SOSIC'URÆ, a town of India within the Ganges. *Ptol.*

SOSIG'ENES, an Ægyptian mathematician of superior merit, who assisted Julius Cæsar in regulating the Roman calendar. *Suet.*—*Dio.*—*Plin.* 18. c. 25.——A commander of the fleet of Eumenes. *Polyæn.* 4. c. 6.——A friend of Demetrius Poliorcetes. —— A man who introduced the mysteries of Ceres of Eleusis at Megalopolis. He was honored with a statue. *Paus.* 8. c. 31.

SO'SII, celebrated booksellers at Rome, in the age of *Horace*, 1. ep. 20. v. 2. & *Art. P.* 345.

SOS'ILUS, a Lacedæmonian in the age of Annibal. He lived in great intimacy with the Carthaginian, taught him Greek, and wrote the history of his life. *C. Nep. in Annib.*

SOS'IMUS, an author who wrote Περὶ χρόνων. *Athen.* l. 14.

SOSIP'ATER, a grammarian in the reign of Honorius. He published five books of observations on grammar.——A Syracusian magistrate.——A general of Philip, king of Macedonia.——A comic poet. *Fabr. B. Gr.* 2. c. 22.

SOSIP'OLIS, a divinity worshipped at Elis. A female was the minister of his temple, and a cake made with honey formed the chief part of the oblations she presented. In an eruption of the Arcadians into Elis, a woman with a child at her breast appeared in the army of the Eleans, who were going to meet the enemy, and told them that the child would fight for them. The child was placed naked at the head of the army, and as the battle began, assumed the shape of a serpent, which so terrified the Arcadians, that they fled, and were easily conquered. In gratitude for this signal service, the child, as a deliverer, was honored with a temple and statue near the temple of Lucina, and to swear by his divinity became one of the most solemn oaths observed in Elis. *Paus.* 6. c. 20.——A surname of Jupiter.

SOSIP'PUS, a harbour of Arabia Felix. *Ptol. Niger* thinks that it is the Becare of *Pliny*, 6. c. 23.

SOSIRA'TE, a city of Susiana. *Plin.* 6. c. 27.

SO'SIS, a seditious Syracusan, who raised tumults against Dion. When accused before the people, he saved himself by flight, and thus escaped capital punishment.

SOSIS'TRATUS, a tyrant of Syracuse, in the age of Agathocles. He invited Pyrrhus into Sicily, and afterwards revolted from him. He was at last removed by Hermocrates. *Polyæn.* 1. c. 43. ——Another tyrant mentioned by the same author, 5. c. 37.

SOSITH'EUS, a poet of Syracuse, one of the Pleiades. *Suidas.*—*Lil. Girald. Dial. in Poet.*—*Fabr. B. Gr.* l. 2. c. 22.

SO'SIUS, a consul who followed the interest of Mark Antony.——A Roman of consular dignity, to whom Plutarch dedicated his Lives.——A prætor. *Cic. Att.* 8. p. 6.

So'sius Ca'ius, a governor of Syria, A.M. 3925.

So'sius Quin'tus, a Roman knight who camd from Picenum. *Cic. N. D.* 3. c. 30.

SOS'PITA, a surname of Juno in Latium. Her most famous temple was at Lanuvium. She had also two at Rome, and her statue was covered with a goat's skin, and armed with a buckler, &c. *Liv.* 3. 6. 8. 26.—*Festus de V. Sig.*—*Cic. de Div.* 1. c. 2. *De Nat. D.* 1. c. 129.—*Ovid. Fast.* 2. v. 56.—*Ital.* 13. v. 363. [There is a colossal statue of Juno in this character, in the Vatican, at Rome.

SOSSINA'TI, a people of Sardinia. *Strab.*

SOS'SIUS, a small river of Sicily. *Ptol.* It is now Pulici, according to *Leander.*

SOSTHENES, a general of Macedonia, who flourished B.C. 281. He defeated the Gauls under Brennus, and was killed in the battle. *Justin.* 24. c. 5.——A native of Cnidus, who wrote a history of Iberia. *Plut. in Nilo, &c.*

SOS'THENIS, a city of the Thessalians in Macedonia. *Ptol.*

SOS'TRATA, a female character in Terence.

SOSTRA'TE, a town of Elymais. *Plin.* 6. c. 17.—*Salmas ad Solin.* p. 368.

SOS'TRATUS, a friend of Hermolaus, put to death for conspiring against Alexander. *Curt.* 8. c. 6. ——A grammarian in the age of Augustus. He was Strabo's preceptor. *Strab.* 14.——A statuary. *Plin.* 34. c. 8.—*Paus.* 6. c. 9.——An architect of Cnidus, son of Dexiphanes, B.C. 284, who built the white tower of Pharus, in the bay of Alexandria. He inscribed his name upon it. *Strab.* 17. —*Plin.* 30. c. 12. *Vid.* Pharus.——A priest of Venus at Paphus, among the favorites of Vespasian. *Tacit. H.* 2. c. 4.——A favorite of Hercules, in honor of whom the hero erected a monument at Dymæ in Achaia, and also cut off his own hair as a funeral offering on his tomb. *Paus.* 7. c. 17. ——A Greek historian who wrote an account of Etruria. *Plut. in Par.*——A poet who wrote a poem on the expedition of Xerxes into Greece. *Juv.* 10. v 178.——An athlete of Sicyon, who obtained 12 times the prize in the great games of Greece, and was honoured with a statue at Olympia. The strength of his hand was so great, that by squeezing he crushed the fingers of his antagonists, and obliged them to yield the victory. *Paus.* 6. c. 4.

SOSX'ETRA, a city of Gedrosia. *Ptol.*

SOT'ADES, an athlete of Crete, who obtained a prize at the Olympic games. His reputation was so great, that the Ephesians prevailed upon him, by a large bribe, to call himself a native of their city, for which perfidy he was banished by his irritated countrymen. *Paus Eliac.* 18.——A Greek poet of Thrace, or, according to some. Maronea in Crete. He wrote verses against Philadelphus Ptolemy, for which he was thrown into the sea in a cage of lead. He was called *Cinædus*, not only because he was addicted to the abominable crime which the surname indicates, but because he wrote a poem in commendation of it. Some suppose that instead of the word *Socraticos* in the 2nd satire, verse 10th of Juvenal, the word *Sotadicos* should be inserted, as the poet Sotades, and not the philosopher Socrates, deserved the appellation of Cinædus. Obscene verses were generally called *Sotadea carmina* from him. They could be turned and read different ways without losing their measure or sense, such as the following, which can be read backwards .—

Roma tibi subito motibus ibit amor.
Si bene te tua laus taxat, sua laute tenebis.
Sole medere pede, ede, perede melos.

Quint. 1. c. 8. l. 9. c. 4.—*Auson.* ep. 17. v. 29.—*Plin.* 5. ep. 3.—*Scaliger. P.* 2. c. 30.—*Fabr. B. Gr.* 2. c. 22.

SO'TER, surname of the first Ptolemy. It was also common, not only to other monarchs, but to the gods themselves, as the saviours of mankind.

SOTE'RIA, days appointed for thanksgivings and the offering of sacrifices for deliverance from danger. One of these was observed at Sicyon, to commemorate the deliverance of that city from the hands of the Macedonians. *Stat.* 1. *Sylv.* 4.—*Martial.* 12. epigr. 56.—*Plut. Arat.*—*Polyb.* 1. 2.—*Cic. de Off.* 1 3.

SOTER'ICHUS, a poet and historian in the age of Diocletian. He wrote a panegyric on that emperor, as also a life of Apollonius Thyanæus. His works, greatly esteemed, are now lost, except some few fragments preserved by the scholiast of Lycophron.—*Suidas.*—*Voss. H. Gr.* 2. c. 16.—*Lil. Girald. de H. Poet.* dial. 4.——A freed man mentioned by *Cicero, Balb.* 25.——A musician of Alexandria. *Plut. de Music.*—*Voss. H. Gr.* 2. c. 16. *& Poet Gr.* c. 9.

SOTER'IDAS, an Epidaurian who wrote on music. *Dionys.*—*Fabr. B. Gr.* 2. c. 22.

SOT'ERUS, a harbour of the Arabian Gulph. *Diod. Sic.*

SO'THIS, an Ægyptian name of the constellation called Sirius, which received divine honors in that country. *Plut. de Isid. et. Osir.*—*Voss. de Idolol.* 2. c. 36.

SOTIA'TES or SONTIA'TES, a people of Gaul conquered by Cæsar. *Cæs. B. G.* 3. c. 20 & 21.

SOTIG'ENA, a surname of Juno, the same as Opigena, from her affording assistance to the distressed. *Festus de V. Sig.*

SO'TION, a grammarian of Alexandria, preceptor to Seneca. *Senec.* ep. 49 & 58. [There is a head of Sotion combined with another of Seneca, forming a double terminus, in the Vatican.]——A writer on the succession of the philosophers. *Diog. Laert.* 1. c. 1.—*Voss. H. Gr.* 2. c. 7.——A writer on rivers, fountains, and lakes. *Phot. Cod.* 189.

SOTI'RA, a midwife of eminence. *Plin.* 28. c. 7. ——A surname of Juno.

SOTI'RA, a city of the Arieni, founded by Antiochus, son of Seleucus. *Steph.*

SO'TIUS, a philosopher in the reign of Tiberius.

SOVENOCHALE'I, a people of Asiatic Sarmatia. *Ptol.*

SO'US, a king of Sparta, who made himself known by his valor. *Paus. Lacon.*

SOX'OLÆ, a nation of Carmania. *Ptol.*

SOZO'A, a city of Media. *Id.*

SOZOM'ENUS HER'MIAS, an ecclesiastical historian of Bethelia in Palestine, who died 450 A.D. His history extends from the year 324 to 439, and is dedicated to Theodosius the younger. It is written in a style of inelegance and mediocrity. The best edition is that of Reading, fol. Cantab. 1720. *Cassiodor. de divin. Lect.* c. 17.—*Phot. Cod.* 30.

SPA'CO, the nurse of Cyrus. The word signifies a bitch in the Persian language. *Justin.* 1. c. 4.—*Herodot.*

SPACO'RUM, a town of Spain, between Bracara and Asturica. *Antonin.*

SPALÆ'I a people near the Palus Mæotis. *Plin.* 6. c. 7.

SPALA'I, a people of Asiatic Sarmatia. *Id.* 4. c. 12.

SPAL'ETHRA, a city of Thessaly. *Steph.*—*Plin*, 4. c. 9. calls *Spalathra* a city of Magnesia.

SPARGAPI'SES, a son of queen Tomyris, killed by Cyrus in battle. *Herodot.* 1. 1.

SPAR'TA, a celebrated city of Peloponnesus, the capital of Laconia, situate on the Eurotas, at the distance of about 30 miles from its mouth. It received its name from Sparta, the daughter of Eurotas, who married Lacedæmon. *Vid.* Lacædemon.

SPAR'TACUS, a king of Pontus. *Diod. Sic.* 1. 16. ——A king of Bosporus, who died B.C. 433. His son and successor of the same name died B.C. 407. ——Another, who died 284. B.C *Diod.* 12.—— A Thracian shepherd celebrated for his abilities and the victories which he obtained over the Romans. Being one of the gladiators who were kept at Capua in the house of Lentulus, he escaped from the place of his confinement with 70, or, according to some, 74 or 78 of his companions, and took up arms against the Romans. He soon found himself at the head of 10,000 men, equally resolute with himself, and though at first obliged to hide himself in the woods and solitary retreats of Campania, he quickly laid waste the country; and when his followers were increased by additional numbers, better disciplined, and more completely armed, he attacked the Roman generals in the field of battle. Clodius Glaber was defeated on mount Vesuvius, Lentulus on the Apennines, and Cassius met with the same disgrace near Modena; and Spartacus, superior in counsel and abilities, appeared more terrible, though often deserted by his fickle attendants. Crassus was at last sent against him, but this celebrated general at first despaired of success. A bloody battle was fought, in which, at last, the gladiators were defeated. Spartacus behaved with great valor; when wounded in the leg, he fought on his knees, covering himself with his buckler in one hand, and using his sword with the other; and when at last he fell, he fell upon a heap of Romans, whom he had sacrificed to his fury, B.C. 71. In this battle no less than 40,000 of the rebels were slain, and the war was totally finished. *Flor.* 3. c. 20.—*Liv.* 95.—*Eutrop.* 6. c. 2.—*Plut. in Crass.*—*Paterc.* 2. c. 30.—*Appian. de*

B. Civ. 1.—*Horat.* 3. od. 14. v. 19. epod. 16. v. 5. —*Cic. Phil.* 4. c. 6.—*Orosius*, 5. c. 25.—*Aug. de. Civ. D.* 3. c. 26.

SPAR'TACUS, a city of Thrace. *Steph.*

SPAR'TÆ or SPAR'TI, a name given to those men who sprang from the dragon's teeth, which Cadmus sowed. They all destroyed one another, except five, who assisted Cadmus in building Thebes. *Ovid. Met.* 3. v. 125.—*Apollod.* 3.—*Lactant.* 3. c. 4.—*Paus.* 9. c. 5.—*Sch. Soph. in Antig.* 128—*Sch. Apollon. Rhod.* 3. v. 1178 & 1185.—*Sch. Eurip. in Phœn.* 675, 825 & 1069.

SPARTA'NI or SPARTIATÆ, the inhabitants of Sparta. *Vid.* Sparta Lacedæmon.

SPARTIA'NUS DE'LIUS, a Latin historian, who wrote the lives of all the Roman emperors, from J. Cæsar to Diocletian. He dedicated them to Diocletian, to whom, according to some, he was related. Of these compositions only the life of Adrian, Verus, Didius Julianus, Septimus Severus, Pescennius Niger, Caracalla, and Geta, are extant, published among the Scriptores Historiæ Augustæ, 1787. Spartianus is not highly esteemed as an historian or biographer. *Harles. Not. Lit. Rom.* 1. p. 547.

SPARTO'LUS, a city of Macedonia. *Steph.*

SPAR'TON, a brother of Phoroneus. *Id.*

SPAS'INES, a king of Arabia. *Plin.* 6. c. 27.—*Salmas ad Solin.* p. 489.

SPAT'ANA, a harbour of Taprobane. *Ptol.*

SPE'CHIA, an ancient name of the island of Cyprus.

SPEN'DIUS, a Campanian deserter, who rebelled against the Romans, and raised tumults, and made war against Amilcar, the Carthaginian general.

SPEN'DON, a poet of Lacedæmon.

SPERCHI'A, a town of Thessaly on the banks of the Sperchius. *Ptol.*

SPERCHI'US, a river of Thessaly, rising in mount Œta, and falling into the sea in the bay of Malia, near Anticyra. The name is supposed to be derived from its rapidity (σπέρχειν, *festinare*), though Apollodorus says that it was called after Sperchius, son of Perieres. Peleus vowed to the god of this river the hair of his son Achilles, if ever he returned safe from the Trojan war. *Herodot.* 7. c. 198.—*Strab.* 9.—*Homer. Il.* 23. v. 144.—*Apollod.* 3. c. 13.—*Mela*, 2. c. 3.—*Ovid. Met.* 1. v. 557. l. 2. v. 250. l. 7. v. 230.—*Plin.* 4. c. 7.—*Servius ad Virg. G.* 2. v. 487.—*Statius. Theb.* 4. v. 838. *Ach.* 1. v. 98 & 237.—*Paus.* 1. c. 37.

SPERMATOPH'AGI, a people who lived in the extremest parts of Ægypt. They fed upon the fruits that fell from the trees. *Strabo*, l. 16.

SPEUSIP'PUS, an Athenian philosopher, nephew, and also successor of Plato. His father's name was Eurymedon, and his mother's, Potone, Plato's sister. He presided in Plato's school for 8 years, and disgraced himself by his extravagance and debauchery. Plato, who had received him when banished from his father's house for ill conduct, and who had formed and polished his mind by the light of science, attempted to check him, but to no purpose. He died of the lousy sickness, or killed himself according to some accounts, B.C. 339. *Plut. in Lys. & Syll.*—*Diog.* 4.—*Val. Max.* 4. c. 1.—*Aul. Gell.* 3. c. 17.—*Aug. de Civ. D.* 8. c. 12.

SPHACTE'RIÆ, three small islands opposite Pylus, on the coast of Messenia. They are also called Sphagiæ.

SPHÆ'RIA, an island belonging to the Trœzenians in the Sinus Argolicus. *Paus.* 2.

SPHÆ'RUS, an arm-bearer of Pelops, son of Tantalus. He was buried in a small island near the isthmus of Corinth, which from him was called Spheria. *Paus.* 5. c. 10.——A Greek philosopher, disciple to Zeno of Cyprus, 243 B.C. He came to Sparta in the age of Cleomenes, and opened a school there. The titles of the books which he wrote are preserved by Diogenes. *Diog. Laert.* 7. —*Voss. H. Gr.* 1. c. 16.—*Jonsius. de Script. Hist. Phil.* 2. c. 6.

SPHAGI'TES, a promontory of Scythia. *Steph.*

SPHEN'DALE, a village of the tribe Hippothoontis. *Id.*

SPHET'TUS, a village of the tribe Acamantis. *Id.*

SPHINX, a monster which had the head and breasts of a woman, the body of a dog, the tail of a serpent, the wings of a bird, the paws of a lion, and a human voice. It sprang from the union of Orthos with the Chimæra, or Typhon with Echidna. The Sphinx had been sent into the neighbourhood of Thebes, by Juno, who wished to punish the family of Cadmus, which she persecuted with immortal hatred, and it laid this part of Bœotia under continual alarms by proposing enigmas, and devouring the inhabitants if unable to explain them. In the midst of their consternation the Thebans were told by the oracle, that the Sphinx would destroy herself as soon as one of the enigmas she proposed was explained. In this enigma she wished to know what animal walked on four legs in the morning, two at noon, and three in the evening. Upon this Creon, king of Thebes, promised his crown and his sister Jocasta in marriage to him who could deliver his country from the monster by a successful explanation of the enigma. It was at last happily explained by Œdipus, who observed that man walked on his hands and feet when young, or in the morning of life, at the noon of life he walked erect, and in the evening of his days he supported his infirmities upon a stick. *Vid.* Œdipus. The Sphinx no sooner heard this explanation than she dashed her head against a rock, and immediately expired. Some mythologists wish to unriddle the fabulous traditions about the Sphinx, by the supposition that one of the daughters of Cadmus, or Laius, infested the country of Thebes by her continual depredations, because she had been refused a part of her father's possessions. The lion's paw expressed, as they observe, her cruelty, the body of the dog her lasciviousness, her enigmas the snares she laid for strangers and travellers, and her wings the dispatch which she used in her expedition. *Hesiod. Theog.* v. 326.—*Hygin* fab. 68.—*Apollod.* 3. c. 5.—*Diod.* 4.—*Ovid. in Ib.* 378.—*Strab.* 9.—*Sophocl. in Œdip. Tyr.*—*Athen.* 6. & 10.—*Plut. in Gryll.*—*Stat. Theb.* 2.—*Sch. Soph. in Tyr. & Eurip. in Phœn.* 813 & 1026.—*Palæphat. de Sphin.*—*Paus.* 9. c. 26.—*Nat. Comes.* 9. c. 18.

SPHO'DRIAS, a Spartan, who, at the instigation of Cleombrotus, attempted to seize the Piræus. *Diod.* 15.

SPHRAGID'IUM, a retired cave on mount Cithæron in Bœotia. The nymphs of the place, called Sphragitides, were yearly honored with a sacrifice by the Athenians, by order of the oracle of Delphi, because they had lost few men at the battle of Platæa. *Plin.* 35. c. 6.—*Celsus*, 5. c. 20.—*Paus.* 9. c. 3.—*Plut. in Arist.*

SPICIL'LUS, a favorite of Nero. He refused to assassinate his master, for which he was put to death in a cruel manner.

SPI'NA, now Primaro, a town on the most southern mouth of the Po. *Plin.* 3. c. 16.

SPINEN'SIS or SPINIEN'SIS, a god among the Romans, whose power was invoked to clear the fields from thorns and briars, whence the name. *Gyrald. H. D.* 1.—*August. de Civ. D.* 4. c. 21.

SPI'NO, a deity among the Romans. *Cic. N. D.* 3. c. 20.

SPIN'THARUS, a Corinthian architect, who built Apollo's temple at Delphi. *Paus.* 10. c. 5.——A freedman of Cicero. *Ad. Att.* 13. ep. 25.

SPIN'THER LEN'TUL., a Roman consul. He was one of Pompey's friends, and accompanied him at the battle of Pharsalia, where he betrayed his meanness by being too confident of victory, and contending for the possession of Cæsar's offices and gardens before the action. *Plut.*—*Plin.* 19. c. 1.

SPI'O or SPEI'O, one of the Nereides. *Virg. Æn.* 5. v. 826.—*Hesiod. Th.* 245.

SPIRÆ'UM, a promontory of Peloponnesus. *Ptol*

SPITAM'ENES, one of the officers of king Darius, who conspired against the murderer Bessus, and delivered him to Alexander. *Curt.* 7. c. 5.

SPITHOB'ATES, a satrap of Ionia, son-in-law of Darius. He was killed at the battle of the Granicus. *Diod.* 17.

SPITHRIDA'TES, a Persian killed by Clitus, as he was going to strike Alexander dead.——A Persian satrap in the age of Lysander.

SPOLE'TIUM, now Spoletro, a town of Umbria, which bravely withstood Annibal while he was in Italy. The people were called Spoletani. Water is conveyed to this town from the neighbouring mountain called St. Francis, by an aqueduct of such a great height, that in one place the top is raised above the foundation 230 yards. An inscription over the gates still commemorates the defeat of Annibal. *Mart.* 13. epigr. 120.—*Liv.* 22. c. 9.

SPON'GIA, a nickname applied to one of the judges on Clodius' trial. *Cic.* 1. *Att.* 16.

SPOR'ADES, a number of islands in the Ægean Sea. They received their name a σπείρω, *spargo*, because they are scattered in the sea, at some distance from Delus, and in the neighbourhood of Crete. Those islands that are contiguous to Delus, and that encircle it, are called Cyclades. *Mela*, 2. c. 7.—*Strab.* 2.—*Plin.* 4. c. 12.—*Servius ad Æn.* 3. v. 126.

SPO'RUS, one of Nero's favorites. *Suet. Ner.* 28.

SPURI'NA, a mathematician and astrologer, who told J. Cæsar to beware of the ides of March. As he went to the senate-house on the morning of the ides, Cæsar said to Spurina, "The ides are at last come." "Yes," replied Spurina, "but not yet past." Cæsar was murdered a few moments after. *Suet. in Cæs.* 81.—*Dio.* 44. c. 18.—*Appian. B. C.* 2. p. 522 & 525.—*Val. Max.* 1. c. 6. l. 8. c. 11.——A young Etrurian, whose personal accomplishments were so attractive that many women forgot their character to court his acquaintance. Sensible of his powers to please, Spurina voluntarily disfigured his countenance, that he might preserve his virtue and deserve the applauses of his country. *Val. Max.* 4. c. 5.

SPU'RIUS, a prænomen common to many of the Romans.

SPU'RIUS, one of Cæsar's murderers.——A friend of Otho, &c.

SPU'RIUS LAR'TIUS, a Roman who defended the bridge over the Tiber against Porsenna's army.

STABE'RIUS L., a friend of Pompey set over Apollonia, which he was obliged to yield to Cæsar, because the inhabitants favored his cause. *Cæsar. B.C.*

STABE'RIUS, an avaricious fellow, who wished it to be known that he was uncommonly rich. *Horat.* 2. sat. 3. v. 89.

STA'BIÆ, a maritime town of Campania on the bay of Puteoli, destroyed by Sylla, and converted into a villa, whither Pliny endeavoured to escape from the eruption of Vesuvius, in which he perished. *Plin.* 3. c. 5. ep. 6. c. 16.

STAB'ULUM, a place in the Pyrenees, where a communication was open from Gaul into Spain.

STA'CHIR, a river in the interior of Libya. *Ptol.*

STAD'ISIS, a town of Upper Æthiopia, where the Nile flows between the mountains with such noise, as to deprive the inhabitants of the power of hearing. *Plin.* 6. c. 29.

STAGI'RA or STAGI'RUS, a town on the borders of Macedonia, near the bay into which the Strymon discharges itself, at the south of Amphipolis; founded 665 years B.C. Aristotle was born there, from which circumstance he is called Stagirites. A law of the country, *quod non deposuisti, ne tollas*, was on account of its excellence and great morality adopted by Solon, in the laws which he introduced at Athens. *Thucyd.* 4.—*Paus.* 6. c. 4.—*Laert. in Sol.*—*Ælian. V. H.* 3. c. 46.

STA'IUS, an unprincipled wretch in Nero's age, who murdered all his relations. *Pers.* 2. v. 19.

STALE'NUS C. or STAIE'NUS, a senator condemned for his attempts to bribe a jury. He sat as judge on the trial of Cluentius. *Cic. Clu.* 7 & 24. & *Br.* 68.

STALIOCA'NUS, a harbour of Gallia Narbonensis. *Ptol.*

STAM'ENE, a city of the Chalybes. *Steph.*

STAN'ACUM, a city of Noricum. *Antonin.*

STAPH'YLUS, one of the Argonauts, son of Theseus, or according to others, of Bacchus and Ariadne. He had according to some, two daughters, Hemithea and Rhoio, when Lyrcus, son of Phoroneus, visited him, on his return from consulting the oracle with respect to his raising children. Staphylus, informed of the answer of the oracle, intoxicated his guest, and introduced Hemithea into his bed, who thus became mother of Basilus, who afterwards inherited the possessions of his father. The other daughter of Staphylus married Æson, and was, as some report, mother of Jason. *Nicenœt. & Apoll. apud Parthen.* 1.—*Tzetzes in Chil.* 7. c. 96.—*Flacc.* 1. v. 295.—*Hygin.* fab. 3 & 14.—*Ovid. Heroid.* 6. v. 105.—*Apollod.* 1. c. 9.——A son of Sithenus, who first mixed wine and water, according to *Pliny*, 7. c. 56.——A native of Naucratis, who wrote on the affairs of the Thessalians, &c. *Schol. in Apollon.* l. 4.—*Harpocrat.*

STASA'NOR, an officer of Alexander, who succeeded Arsames as præfect of Caria. *Curt.* 8. c. 3.

STA'SEAS, a peripatetic philosopher, engaged to instruct young M. Piso in philosophy. *Cic. in Orat.* 1. c. 22.

STASIC'RATES, a famous statuary of Alexandria, who offered to Alexander to form a statue of the monarch on mount Athos, and to represent him as holding in his left a town peopled by 10,000 inhabitants, and in his right pouring a large river; an extravagant proposal which the good sense of the conqueror rejected. *Plut. in Alex. & in Com.*

STASIL'EUS, an Athenian killed at the battle of Marathon. He was one of the ten prætors.

STATA'NUS or STATILI'NUS, (*a stare*,) a god invoked at Rome to assist infants, and to give them the power of standing upright and walking. *Varro apud Nonium.* 12.—*Aug. de Civ. D.* 4. c. 21.—*Rosin.* 2. c. 19.

STATEL'LI or STATIL'LI, a people of Liguria, between the Tænarus and the Apennines. *Liv.* 42. c. 7. *Cic.* 11. *Fam.* 11.

STATIL'IA, a woman who lived to a great age, as mentioned by *Seneca*, ep. 77. *Vid.* Messalina.

STATIL'IUS, a young Roman celebrated for his courage and constancy. He was an inveterate enemy to Cæsar, and when Cato murdered himself, he attempted to follow his example, but was prevented by his friends. The conspirators against Cæsar wished him to be in their number, but the answer which he gave displeased Brutus. He was at last killed by the army of the triumvirs. *Plut.*——A young general in the war which the Latins undertook against the Romans. He was killed with 25,000 of his troops.——A general who fought with Augustus against Antony. *Cic. Att.* 12. ep. 13, &c.—*Paterc.* 2. c. 127.

STATIL'IUS LU'CIUS, one of the friends of Catiline. He joined in his conspiracy, and was put to death. *Cic. Cat.* 3. c. 3 & 6.—*Sallust. Cat.* 17, 44, &c.

STATIL'IUS TAU'RUS, a pro-consul of Africa. He was accused of consulting magicians, upon which he put himself to death. *Tacit. Ann.* 12. c. 59.

STAT'INÆ, islands on the coast of Campania, raised from the sea by an earthquake. *Plin.* 2. c. 88.

STATI'RA, a daughter of Darius, who married Alexander. The conqueror had formerly refused her, but when she had fallen into his hands at Issus, the nuptials were celebrated with uncommon splendour. No less than 9000 persons attended, to each of whom Alexander gave a golden cup, to be offered to the gods. Statira had no children by Alexander. She was cruelly put to death by Roxana, after the conqueror's death. *Justin.* 12. c. 12.—*Curt.* 4. c. 4.—*Plut. in Alex.*——A sister of Darius the last king of Persia. She also became his wife, according to the manners of the Persians. She died after an abortion, in Alexander's camp, where she was detained as prisoner. She was buried with great pomp by the conqueror. *Plut. in Alex.*——A wife of Artaxerxes Mnemon, poisoned by her mother-in-law, queen Parysatis. *Plut. in Art.*——A sister of Mithridates the Great. *Plut.*

STA'TIUS CÆCIL'IUS, a comic poet in the age of Ennius. He was a native of Gaul, and originally a slave. His Latinity was bad, yet he acquired great reputation by his comedies. He died a little after Ennius, and was buried at the foot of mount Janiculum. *Cic. de Sen.* 7. *Orat.* 2. c. 64.—*Aul. Gell.* 4. c. 20.—*Gyrald. de H.P.* 8.

STA'TIUS ANNÆ'US, a physician, the friend of the philosopher Seneca. *Tacit. Ann.* 15. c. 64.

STA'TIUS P. PAPIN'IUS, a poet born at Naples, in the reign of the emperor Domitian. His father's name was Statius of Epirus, and his mother's Angelina. Statius has made himself known by two epic poems, the "Thebais" in 12 books, and the "Achilleis" in two books, which remained unfinished on account of his premature death. There are besides other pieces composed on several subjects, which are extant, and well known under the name of "Sylvæ," divided into four books. The two epic poems of Statius are dedicated to Domitian, whom the poet ranks among the gods. They were universally admired in his age at Rome, but the taste of the times was corrupted, though some of the moderns have called them inferior to no Latin composition except Virgil's. The style of Statius is bombastic and affected, he often forgets the poet to become the declaimer and the historian. In his "Sylvæ," which were for the most part composed *ex tempore*, are many beautiful expressions and strokes of genius. Statius, as some suppose, was poor, and was obliged to maintain himself by writing for the stage. None of his dramatic pieces are extant, but Juvenal insinuates that poverty compelled him to sell to Paris the imperial favorite, his play of Agave. Though he was contemporary with Martial, yet it is remarkable that his name is not mentioned in any of his epigrams, a circumstance ascribed by some writers to envy and a mean spirit of emulation. What Juvenal had written in his praise, some have interpreted as an illiberal reflection upon him. Statius died about the 100th year of the Christian era, probably a natural death, though some imagine that he was mortally stabbed by Domitian with a sharp stylus, a report not well supported, and which, if the favors of tyrants were not capricious and uncertain, the great and repeated kindness of the emperor to the poet would render highly improbable. The best editions of his works are that of Barthius, 2 vols 4to. Cygneæ, 1664, and that of the Variorum, 8vo. L. Bat. 1671; and of the Thebais, separate, that of Warrington, 2 vols. 12mo. 1778. *Juv.* 7. v. 82.—*Gyrald.*—*Vossius de P. Lat.* 3. p. 45.—*Harles. Not. Lit. Rom.* 1. p. 465. —*Sax. Onom.* 1. p. 273.

STA'TIUS L. MUR'CUS, a Roman general, who, on the day that the battle of Philippi was fought, defeated, in a naval engagement, Domitius Calvinus, who came with reinforcements to Antony and Augustus. He afterwards joined S. Pompey, who cruelly caused him to be put to death, though his services and merits deserved every proof of kindness and gratitude. *Appian. B.C.* 656.—*Vell.* 2. c.72.—*Cic. Ph.* 11.c.12.—*Dio*.48.c.19.

STA'TIUS DOMIT'IUS a tribune in the age of Nero, deprived of his office when Piso's conspiracy was discovered. *Tacit. Ann.* 15. c. 17.

STA'TIUS, a general of the Samnites.——An officer of the prætorian guards who conspired against Nero. *Tacit, Ann.* 15. c. 50.

STA'TOR, a surname of Jupiter, given him by Romulus because he *stopped* the flight of the Romans in a battle against the Sabines. The conqueror erected him a temple under that name, part of which is still in existence. *Ovid. Fast.* 6. v. 793.—*Flor.* 1. c. 1.—*Seneca de Benef.* 4. c. 7.

STATO'RIUS, a Roman, sent by Scipio as ambassador to Syphax. *Liv.* 24. c. 48. l. 30. c. 28.

STAU'RI, a people near the Caspian sea. *Plin.* 6. c. 16.

STAVA'NI, a nation of European Sarmatia. *Ptol.*

STAVE'NI, a people of Aria. *Ptol.*

STE'LÆ, a city of Crete, near Paræsus, and Rhythimna. *Steph.*

STEL'LA ARUN'TIUS, a poet of great opulence in the age of Statius and Martial, whose friendship he deserved and enjoyed. All his works are lost. *Martial.* 1. 5. epigr. 11.

STELLA'TIS CAM'PUS, a field in Campania, remarkable for its fertility. *Cic. Ag.* 1. c. 70.—*Sueton. Cæs.* 10.

STEL'LIO, a youth turned into an elf by Ceres, because he derided the goddess, who drank with avidity when tired and afflicted in her vain pursuits after her daughter Proserpine. *Ovid. Met.* 5. v. 445.—*Anton. Liber.* 24.—*Nicander in Alex.* 128. *& Ther.* 484.—*Sch. Euripid. in Orest.* 962.

STE'NA, a narrow passage on the mountains near Antigonia, in Chaonia. *Liv.* 32. c. 5.

STE'NE-DEI'RE, an island of the Arabian Gulph. *Plin.* 6. c. 29.

STE'NIAS, a surname of Minerva among the people of Trœzene expressive of her power. She had disputed with Neptune the honor of presiding over that part of the Peloponnesus, and obtained it. *Paus.* 2. c. 30.—*Gyrald. H. D.* 11.

STENOBŒ'A. *Vid.* Sthenobœa.

STENOC'RATES, an Athenian who conspired to murder the commander of the garrison which Demetrius had placed in the citadel, &c. *Polyæn.* 5.

STEN'TOR, one of the Greeks who went to the Trojan war. His voice was said to be so powerful that it equalled in loudness that of 50 men together. Juno assumed his form to animate the Greeks whose power was exhausted in a war against the Trojans. *Homer. Il.* 5. v. 784.—*Juv.* 13. v. 112.

STEN'TORIS LA'CUS, a lake near Enus in Thrace. *Herodot.* 7. c. 58.—*Plin.* 4. c. 11.

STEPH'ANE or STEPH'ANIS, a maritime town of Paphlagonia. *Steph.*

STEPHA'NIO, a pantomimic writer or actor, who lived to a great age. *Plin.* 7. c. 48.

STEPH'ANUS, a musician of Media, upon whose body Alexander made an experiment in burning a certain sort of bitumen called naphtha. *Strab.* 16.—*Plin.* 2. c. 105. l. 35. c. 15.—*Hygin.* fab. 25. —*Seneca in Medea*, 573.—*Schol. Eurip. in Med.* 1387.—*Plut. in Alex.*——A Greek writer of Byzantium in the 5th or 6th century, known for his dictionary, giving an account of the towns and places of the ancient world, a valuable performance which has descended to us in the injudicious abridgment of the grammarian Hermolaus. The best edition is that of Gronovius, 2 vols. fol. L. Bat. 1694.—*Fabr. B. Gr.* 4 c. 2.—*Sax. Onom*, 1. p. 520. —*Voss. H. Gr.* 2. c. 22.——The name of the god, who, according to Parmenides, surrounded the heavens with a luminous circle like a crown. *Cic. de N. D.* 1. c. 11.

STE'PHON, a place near Tanagra in Bœotia. *Plut. Q. Gr.*

STER'CES, one of the kings of the Aborigines of Italy, whom, according to some, Virgil calls Dercennus. *Servius ad Virg. Æn.* 11. v. 850.

STERCU'LIUS, STERCU'TIUS, STERQUILI'NUS or STERCULI'NUS, a god at Rome who presided over the manuring of land, and other offices of agriculture. He is said by some authors to be son of Faunus; while others call Saturn by this name or that of Stercutius. *Servius ad Virg. G.* 1. v. 21. *Æn.* 9. v. 4. l. 10. v. 70.—*Aug. de Civ. D.* 18. c. 15.—*Lactant.* 1. c. 20.—*Macrob.* 1. c. 1.—*Plin.* 16. c. 9.

STERE'A, a village of the tribe Pandionis. *Steph.*

STEREON'TIUM, a city of Germany. *Ptol.* It is now Cassel.

STE'RIS, an inland town of Phocis. *Paus.* 1. 10.

STER'OPE, one of the Pleiades, daughters of Atlas. She married Œnomaus, king of Pisa, by whom she had Hippodamia. According to some, however, she was not the wife of Œnomaus, but his mother by the god Mars. *Apollod.* 3.—*Paus.* 5. c. 10.—*Hygin.* fab. 84 & 159. *P.A.* 2. c. 21.—*Servius ad Virg. Æn.* 8. v. 130.—*Tzetzes. ad Lyc* 156.—*Ovid Fast.* 4. v. 172.——A daughter of Parthaon, supposed by some to be the mother of the Sirens.——A daughter of Cepheus, son of Aleus, to whom Hercules gave as a present, part of the Gorgon's hair. *Apollod.* 2.——A daughter of Pleuron.——A daughter of Acastus.——A daughter of Danaus. ——A daughter of Cebrion, who married Æsacus, son of Priam. *Apollod.* 3.—*Tzetzes. ad Lyc.* 224.

STER'OPES, one of the Cyclopes. *Virg. Æn.* 8, v. 425.—*Hesiod. Th.* 142.—*Stat.* 1. *Sylv.* 1. v. 4.

STERTIN'IUS, a stoic philosopher, ridiculed by *Horace*. 2. sat. 3. He wrote in Latin verse 220 books on the philosophy of the Stoics.

STERTIN'IUS LU'CIUS, a proconsul of Spain. *Liv.* 31. c. 20.

STESAG'ORAS, a brother of Miltiades. *Vid.* Miltiades.

STESICH'ORUS, a Greek Lyric poet of Himera, in Sicily, highly esteemed by the ancients, and said by Dionysius to be superior to Pindar and Simonides. Some say that he was son of Hesiod and Clymene, and others call his father Euphorbus or Euclides. He was originally called Tisias, and obtained the name of Stersichorus, from the alterations which he made in music and dancing, or, in the words of Suidas, ὅτι πρῶτος κιθαρῳδίᾳ χορὸν ἔστησεν, His compositions were written in the Doric dialect, and comprised in 26 books, all now lost except a few fragments preserved in Athenæus, and other writers. Some say he lost his eyesight for writing invectives against Helen, and that he received it only upon making a recantation of what he had said. He was the first inventor of that fable of the horse and the stag, which Horace and some other poets have imitated, and this he wrote to prevent his countrymen from making an alliance with Phalaris, to avenge themselves more effectually against their enemies. According to some, he was the first who wrote an epithalamium. He flourished 556 B.C. and died at Catana, in the 85th year of his age. His countrymen honored him in his old age with a statue, and Cicero, who saw and admired this homage paid to genius, says it was a highly finished piece of sculpture, which represented the poet in a leaning posture, and holding a book in his hand. Some fragments of his poetry have been collected by Neander, H. Stephens, and Fulvius Ursinus. They have been also published and illustrated by Suchfort, Gotting. 1771. *Fabr. B. Gr.* 2. c. 15.—*Sax. Onom.* 1. p. 22.—*Isocrat. in Hel.*—*Arist. Rhet.* 2. c. 21.—*Strab.* 3.—*Lucian. in Macr.*—*Cic. in Verr.* 2. c. 35.—*Plut de Mus.*—*Quintil.* 10. c. 1.—*Paus.* 3. c. 19. l. 10 c. 26.—*Plato. in Phœd*—*Athen.* 4.—*Pollux.* 9. c. 7.—*Suidas.*—*Gyrald. P. H.* 9.

STESICLI'DES, an Athenian praised by *Laertius in Xenophonte.*

STESILE'A, a beautiful woman of Athens, loved by Themistocles and Aristides, and the cause of jealousy and dissension between these celebrated men. *Plut in Them.*

STESIM'BROTUS, an historian very inconsistent in his narrations. He wrote an account of Cimon's exploits.—*Plut. in Cim.*—*Voss. H. Gr.* 4. c. 7. ——A son of Epaminondas, put to death by his father, because he had fought contrary to his orders, and obtained a victory over the Lacedæmonian forces. *Ctesiph. apud Plut. in Par.* 12.——A musician of Thasus, *Corn. Nep. in Epamin.*

STEU'NOS, a cave of Phrygia. *Paus. in Achaic.*

STHEN'ELE, a daughter of Acastus, wife of Menœtius, and mother of Patroclus. *Apollod.* 3. c. 13. ——A daughter of Danaus by Memphis. *Id.* 2. c. 1.

STHEN'ELUS, a king of Mycenæ, son of Perseus and Andromeda. He married Nicippe, the daughter of Pelops, by whom he had two daughters, and a son called Eurystheus, who was born, by Juno's influence, two months before the natural time, that he might obtain a superiority over Hercules, as being older. Sthenelus made war against Amphitryon, who had killed Electryon and seized his kingdom. He fought with success and transmitted to Eurystheus an undisputed crown and an extended kingdom. *Homer. Il.* 19. v. 91.—*Apollod.* 2. c. 4.—*Hygin.* fab. 30 & 32.—— One of the sons of Ægyptus by Tyria.——A son of Capaneus He was one of the Epigoni, and of the suitors of Helen. He went to the Trojan war, and was one of those who were shut up in the wooden horse, according to Virgil. His tomb was to be seen at Argos in the age of Pausanias. *Homer. Il.* 4 v. 367. l. 5. v. 835.—*Hygin.* fab. 175 & 257.—*Virg. Æn.* 2. v. 261. l. 10. v. 388. l. 12. v. 341. *& Servius locis*, & l. 11. v. 269.—*Paus.* 2. c. 18.——A son of Androgeus the son of Minos. Hercules made him king of Thrace. *Apollod.* 2. c. 5.——A king of Argos, who succeeded his father Crotopus. *Paus.* 2. c. 16.——A son of Actor, who accompanied Hercules in his expedition against the Amazons. He was killed by one of these females.——A son of Melas, killed by Tydeus. *Apollod.* 1. c. 8.

STHENIP'PUS, a Lacedæmonian, who being fined by the Ephori fled to Tegea. *Polyœn.* 2. c. 26.

STHE'NIS, a statuary of Olynthus, some of whose statues were seen in the grove of Jupiter at Olympia, and in the Capitol at Rome. *Paus.* 6. c. 16. —*Plin.* 34. c. 8.—*Plut. in Lyc.*——An orator of Himera, in Sicily, during the civil wars of Pompey. He saved himself and his countrymen from the severity of punishment which Pompey prepared against them for adhering to his enemies, and by boldly taking the whole blame upon himself, gained the pardon which his magnanimity deserved. *Plut. in Pomp.*

STHE'NIUS, a native of Thermæ in Sicily, greatly insulted by Verres. *Cic. in Verr.* 2. c. 34, &c.

STHE'NO or STHEN'YO, one of the three Gorgons, was immortal. *Vid.* Gorgones.

STHENOBŒ'A, a daughter of Jobates, king of Lycia, who married Prœtus, king of Argos. She became enamoured of Bellerophon who had taken refuge at her husband's court, after the murder of his brother, and when he refused to gratify her criminal passion, she accused him before Prœtus of attempts upon her virtue. According to some, she killed herself after his departure. *Homer. Il.* 6. v. 162.—*Hygin.* fab. 57 & 243.—*Juv.* 10. v. 327. —*Tzetzes ad Lyc.* c. 17.—*Apollod.* 2.—*Zenob.* 11. c. 87.—*Statian. ad Stat. Theb.* 4. c. 586. Many mythologists call her Antæa.

STHENOC'RATES, an Athenian, one of the conspirators who attempted to slay Heraclides. *Polyœn.* 5. c. 17.

STIL'BE or STIL'BIA, a daughter of Peneus by Creusa, who became mother of Centaurus and Lapithes, by Apollo. *Diod.* 4.

STIL'BO, a name given to the planet Mercury by the ancients, from its shining appearance. *Cic. de Nat. D.* 2. c. 20.—*Martian. Cap* 8.

STIL'ICHO, a general of the emperor Theodosius the Great. He behaved with much courage, but under the emperor Honorius showed himself turbulent and disaffected. Being of barbarian extraction, he wished to see the Roman provinces laid desolate by his countrymen, but in this he was disappointed. Honorius discovered his intrigues, and ordered him to be beheaded, about the year of Christ 408. His family were involved in his ruin. *Claudian* has been loud in his praises, and *Zosimus. Hist.* 5., denies the truth of the charges laid against him.

STIL'IO, a philosopher, one of the preceptors of Alexander Severus. *Lamprid.* c. 3.

STIL'PÆ, a city of Sicily. *Steph.*

STIL'PO, a celebrated philosopher of Megara, who flourished 336 years B.C., and was greatly esteemed by Ptolemy Soter. He was naturally addicted to riot and debauchery, but reformed his manners when he opened a school at Megara. He was universally respected, his school was frequented, and Demetrius, when he plundered Megara, ordered the house of the philosopher to be left safe and unmolested. It is said that he intoxicated himself when ready to die, to alleviate the terrors of death. He was one of the chiefs of the stoics, and had among his disciples Crates and Zeno. *Plut. in Dem. Diog.* 2.—*Seneca de Const. Sap.* 5. & ep. 9.—*Cic. de Fato.*

STIM'ICON, a shepherd's name in *Virgil's* 5th *eclogue.*

STIM'ULA, a goddess at Rome who roused and animated the indolent, though, according to some, she presided over excess of all kinds, and patronised debauchery. *Aug. de Civ. D.* 4. c. 11. —*Sch. Juv.* 2.

STIPHA'NA, a lake near Amasia in Pontus. *Strabo*, 12.

STIPH'ILUS, one of the Lapithæ, killed in the house of Pirithous. *Ovid. Met.* 12. v. 459.

STI'RIS, a town of Phocis. The inhabitants were a colony from Stirium, a village of Attica. *Paus* 1.10.

STIRI'TIS, a surname of Ceres from the temple at Stiris in Phocis, where her statue of marble represented her as holding a torch in each hand. *Paus.* 10. c. 35.

STOBÆ'US, a Greek writer who flourished A.D. 405. His work, though mutilated, is valuable for the precious relics of ancient literature which he has preserved. Among the editions are that of Gesner, Tigur. 1549, and of Wechelius, Francofurt, 1581. *Fabr. B. Gr.* 5. c. 25.—*Phot. Cod.* 167.—*Gesn. in Proleg. Collect. sent. Stobæi, & in. Biblioth.*

STO'BI, a town of Pœonia in Macedonia. *Liv.* 33. c. 19. l. 40. c. 21.

STOBOR'RUM, a promontory of Africa Propria. *Ptol.*

STŒCH'ADES, five small islands in the Mediterranean, on the coast of Gaul, now the Hieres, near Marseilles. They were called Ligustides by some, but Pliny speaks of them as only three in number. *Steph. Byzant.*—*Lucan.* 3. v. 516.—*Strab.* 4.—*Mela*, 2. c. 7.—*Plin.* 3. c. 5.

STŒ'NI, a people living among the Alps. *Liv.* ep. 62.

STO'ICI, a celebrated sect of philosophers founded by Zeno of Citium. They received their name from the *portico* (στοὰ), where the philosopher delivered his lectures. They preferred virtue to every thing else, and whatever was opposite to it, they looked upon as the greatest of evils. They reqnired, as well as the disciples of Epicurus, an absolute command over the passions, and they maintained that man alone, in the present state of his existence, could attain perfection and felicity. They encouraged suicide, and believed that the doctrine of future punishments and rewards was unnecessary to excite or intimidate their followers. *Vid.* Zeno.

STO'LA SEXT., a Roman judge in the trial of Flaccus. *Cic. Flacc.* 20.

STO'LO, a surname common to some Roman families. *Varr. R. R.* 1. c. 2.—*Plin.* 17 & 27.

STO'LUS, a city of Thrace. *Steph.*

STO'MA, a lake of Troas near the mouth of the Scamander. *Strab.*

STO'NIA, a city of Cappadocia. *Ptol.*

STOR'NA, a city of India without the Ganges. *Id.*

STOVI'NUS, a town of Liguria. *Steph.*

STRABELLI'NI, a town of Apulia. *Plin.* 3. c. 11.

STRA'BO, a name among the Romans, given to those whose eyes were naturally deformed or distorted. Pompey's father was distinguished by that name.

STRA'BO, a native of Amasia, on the borders of Cappadocia, who flourished in tho age of Augustus and Tiberius. He first studied under Xenarchus, the peripatetic, and afterwards warmly embraced the tenets of the stoics. Of all his compositions nothing remains but his geography, divided into 17 books, a work justly celebrated for its elegance and purity, and the erudition and universal knowledge of the author. It contains an account, in Greek, of the most celebrated places of the world, the origin, religion, prejudices, and government of nations; the foundation of cities, and the accurate history of each separate province. Strabo travelled over great part of the world in quest of information, and to examine with the most critical enquiry, not only the situation of the places, but also the manners of the inhabitants, whose history he meant to write. In the two first books the author wishes to show the necessity of geography; in the third he gives a description of Spain; in the fourth of Gaul and the British isles. The fifth and sixth contain an account of Italy and the neighbouring islands; the seventh, which is mutilated at the end, gives a full description of Germany, and the country of the Getæ, Illyricum, Taurica Chersonesus, and Epirus. The affairs of Greece and the adjacent islands are separately treated of in the 8th, 9th, and 10th; and in the four next, Asia within mount Taurus; and in the 15th and 16th, Asia without Taurus, India, Persia, Syria, and Arabia; the last book gives an account of Ægypt, Æthiopia, Carthage, and other places of Africa. Among the books of Strabo which have been lost, were historical commentaries; the sixth of which he quotes in the 11th book of his geography. This celebrated geographer died A.D. 25. The best editions of his geography are those of Casaubon, fol. Paris, 1620; and of Amst. 2. vols. fol. 1707. *Fabr. B. Gr.* 4. c. 1.—*Sax. Onom.* 1. p. 209.—*Plut. in Pomp.*—*Strab.* 2. 10 & 12.—*Suidas.*—*Vossius de Hist. Gr.* 2. c. 6.——A Sicilian, so clear-sighted, that it is said he could distinguish objects at the distance of 130 miles with the same ease as if they had been near.

STRAG'ONA, a city of Germany. *Ptol.*

STRAM'BÆ, a city of Thrace. *Steph.*

STRATAR'CHAS, the grandfather of the geographer Strabo. His father's name was Dorylaus. *Strab.* 10.

STRATH'OCLES, an Athenian magistrate in the age of Demetrius Poliorcetes, represented by Plutarch as vile and insinuating. *Plut. de Am. de Civil. Inst. et Dem.*

STRA'TIA, a city of Arcadia, so called from the daughter of Phanæus. *Steph.*

STRAT'ICHUS, a son of Nestor of Pylus and Anaxibia. *Apollod.* 1. c. 25.

STRATIP'PUS, a son of Nicias the Athenian general.

STRA'TIS, a tragic poet. *Schol. in Aristoph. Ran.*

STRA'TIUM, a city of Acarnania. *Steph.*

STRA'TIUS, a surname of Jupiter among the Carians. *Herod.* 1. 5.

STRA'TO or STRA'TON, a king of the island Aradus, received into alliance by Alexander. *Curt.* 4. c. 1.

STRA'TO, a king of Sidon, dependant upon Darius. Alexander deposed him because he refused to surrender. *Curt. ibid.*——A philosopher of Lampsacus, disciple and successor in the school of Theophrastus, about 289 years B.C. He applied himself with uncommon industry to the study of nature, and was surnamed *Physicus*; and after the most mature investigation, he asserted that nature was inanimate, and that there was no god but nature. He was appointed preceptor to Ptolemy Philadelphus, who not only revered his abilities and learning, bnt also rewarded his labors with unbounded liberality. He wrote different treatises, all now lost, the titles of which, however, are preserved by Diogenes, as also the philosopher's will, which proves that he died immensely rich. *Diog.* 5.—*Cic. de Nat. D.* 1. c. 13. *Acad.* 1. c. 9. 1. 4. c. 38. *De Finib.* 5. c. 5.—*Plut. de Exil. &c.*—*Seneca apud Aug. de Civ. D.* 6. c. 10.——A physician, pupil of Erasistratus.——A peripatetic philosopher.——A native of Epirus, very intimate with Brutus, the murderer of Cæsar. He killed his friend at his own request. *Plut. in Brut.*——A rich Orchomenian who destroyed himself because he could not obtain in marriage a young woman of Haliartus. *Plut. in Amat.* 1.——A Greek historian who wrote the lives of the Macedonian kings. *Diog. Laert.* 5.——A statuary, whose statue of Æsculapius in white marble was admired as the most perfect model in all Argos. *Paus.* 1. c. 23.——An athlete of Achaia, crowned twice in one day at the Olympic games. *Paus.* 7. c. 23.——*Voss. H. Gr.* 1. c. 20.

STRAT'OCLES, an Athenian general at the battle of Cheronæa, &c. *Polyæn.*——A stage player in Domitian's reign. *Juv.* 3. v. 99.——An orator of Greece, said to have first invented the story that Themistocles destroyed himself by drinking bull's blood. *Cic. Br.* 11.

STRA'TON. *Vid.* Strato.

STRATONI'CE, a daughter of Thespius. *Apollod.*——A daughter of Pleuron. *Id.*——A daughter of Ariarathes, king of Cappadocia, who married Eumenes, king of Pergamus, and became mother of Attalus. *Strab.* 13.——A daughter of Demetrius Poliorcetes, who married Seleucus, king of Syria. Antiochus, her husband's son by a former wife, became enamoured of her, and married her by his father's consent, when the physician had told him, that if he did not comply, his son's health would be impaired. *Plut. in Dem.*—*Val. Max.* 5. c. 7.——A concubine of Mithridates, king of Pontus, whom she betrayed. *Plut. in. Pomp.*——The wife of Antigonus, mother of Demetrius Poliorcetes. Her father's name was Corræus. *Plut. in Demet.*

STRATONI'CE, a town of Caria, made a Macedonian colony, and afterwards adorned and beautified by the Syrian monarchs. *Plut.* 5. c. 21.—*Strab.* 14.—*Liv.* 33. c. 18 & 33.——A city of Mesopotamia.——A city near mount Taurus.

STRATONI'CUS, an opulent person in the reign of Philip, and of his son Alexander, whose riches became proverbial. *Diod.* 13.—*Plut. in Lyc*——A musician of Athens in the age of Demosthenes. He was treated with kindness by Ptolemy, king of Ægypt, and gained both reputation and money by the number of his pupils. He was at last put to death by order of Nicocles, king of Cyprus, against whose sons he had spoken with great disrespect. *Ælian. V. H.* 14. c. 14, & *Perizon. in loco.*—*Athen.* 6. c. 6. 1. 8. c. 12.——A native of Alabanda, mentioned as remarkable for his wit and humour. *Cic. N. D.* 3. c. 19.

STRATO'NIS IN'SULA, an island in the Arabian Gulf. *Plin.* 6. c. 29.—*Strab.*

STRATO'NIS TUR'RIS, a city of Judæa, afterwards called Cæsarea by Herod, in honor of Augustus.

STRATO'RIUS a lieutenant of Africa, under Cornificius. *Cic.* 12. *Fam.* 23.

STRA'TOS, a city of Æolia. *Liv.* 36. c. 11. l. 38. c. 4.——A city of Acarnania. *Strab.*
STRAT'TIS, a Greek historian of Olynthus, a companion of Alexander the Great. *Suidas.*
STRE'NA, a city of Crete. *Steph.*
STRE'NIA, a goddess at Rome, who presided over the presents which relations and friends made to each other on the return of the new year. *Varro. de L.L.* 4. c. 8.—*Festus de V. Sig.*
STRENU'A, a goddess at Rome who gave vigor and energy to the weak and indolent. *Aug. de Civ. D.* 4. c. 11 & 16.—*Gyrald. H. D.* 1.—*Symmach.* 10. ep. 35.
STREP'SA, a city of Macedonia. *Steph.*
STREVIN'TA, a town of Germany. *Ptol.*
STRO'BUS, a city of Macedonia, built by the Romans. *Steph.*
STRO'E, a city of Libya. *Id.*
STROGO'LA, a city of Lydia. *Id.*
STRON'GYLE, or STRON'GYLOS, now Strombolo, one of the islands called Æolides in the Tyrrhene Sea, near the coast of Sicily. It has a volcano, ten miles in circumference, which throws up flames continually, and of which the crater is on the side of the mountain. *Mela*, 2. c. 7.—*Strab.* 6.—*Paus.* 10. c. 11.—*Servius in Æn.* 1. v. 56.
STROPH'ADES, now Strivali, two islands in the Ionian Sea, on the western coasts of the Peloponnesus. They were anciently called *Plotæ*, and received the name of Strophades from *στρέφω, verto*, because Zethes and Calais, the sons of Boreas, returned thence by order of Jupiter, after they had driven the Harpyies from the tables of Phineus. The fleet of Æneas stopped near the Strophades. The largest of these two islands is not above five miles in circumference. *Hygin.* fab. 19.—*Mela*, 2. c. 7.—*Ovid. Met.* 13. v. 709.—*Virg. Æn.* 3. v. 210.—*Strab.* 8.—*Apollod.* 1.—*Flacc.* 4. v. 513.—*Eustath. ad Dionys. Per.* 461.—*Apollon. R.H.* 2. v. 297.
STRO'PHIUS, a son of Crisus, king of Phocis. He married a sister of Agamemnon, called Anaxibia, or Astyochia, or, according to others, to Cyndragora, by whom he had Pylades, celebrated for his friendship with Orestes. After the murder of Agamemnon by Clytæmnestra and Ægisthus, the king of Phocis, educated at his own house, with the greatest care, his own nephew whom Electra had secretly removed from the dagger of his mother and her adulterer. Orestes was enabled by means of Strophius to revenge the death of his father. *Paus.* 2. c. 29. l. 10. c. 30.—*Eustath. in Od.* 3.—*Tzetzes ad Lyc.* 1374.—*Schol. Eurip. in Orest.* 764 & 1235.—*Hygin.* fab. 1. 17.——A son of Pylades by Electra the sister of Orestes. *Paus. Cor.* 16.
STRU'THAS, a general of Artaxerxes, employed against the Lacedæmonians, Olymp. 97. an. 3.
STRUTHI'A, a city of Phrygia, on the borders of Lycaonia. *Steph.*
STRUTHOPH'AGI, a people of Æthiopia, who feed on sparrows, as their name signifies. *Strab.*—*Ptol.*
STRUTHUN'TUM, a promontory of Argolis. *Paus.* 1. 2.
STRYB'IA, one of the Sporades. *Steph.*
STRY'MA, a town of Thrace, founded by a Thasian colony, on the sea shore at the mouth of the Lissus. *Herodot.* 7. c. 109.——An island of the Ægæan Sea, near Thasus.
STRYM'NO, a daughter of the Scamander, who married Laomedon, and became mother of Tithon, Clytus, Lampon, Podarces, Hesione, &c. *Apollod.* 3. c. 12.
STRYMODO'RUS, an Athenian citizen. *Aristoph. Acharn & Vesp.*
STRY'MON, a river which separates Thrace from Macedonia, and falls into a part of the Ægæan Sea, which has been called *Strymonicus sinus*. A number of cranes, as the poets say, resorted to its banks in the summer time. Its eels were excellent. *Mela*, 2. c. 2.—*Apollod.* 2. c. 5.—*Virg. G.* 1. v. 120. l. 4. v. 508. *Æn.* 10. v. 265.—*Propert.* 4. el. 5. v. 70.—*Lucan.* 3. v. 199. l. 5. v. 711.—*Seneca Agam.* 843. & *Œdip.* 604.—*Ovid. Met.* 2. v. 251.—*Athen.* 7. c. 13.
STU'BERA, a town of Macedonia, between the Axius and Erigon. *Liv.* 31. c. 39.
STUI'NUS, a city of Liguria. *Steph.*
STULPI'NI, a people of Liburnia. *Plin.* 3. c. 21.
STU'RA, a river of Cisalpine Gaul falling into the Po.
STU'RÆ, some islands in the Gallic Ocean. *Plin.* 3. c. 16.
STUR'NI, a people of European Sarmatia. *Ptol.*
STURNI'NI, a people of Calabria. *Plin.* 3. c. 11.
STYEL'LA, a fortified place of Megara, in Sicily. *Steph.*
STYLLAN'GIUM, a city of Triphylia. *Id.*
STYM'BARA, a city of Greece. *Strab.* l. 7. It was probably the Stubera of *Livy*. *Vid.* Stubera.
STYM'PHA, a mountain of Epirus, from which the Arachthus flows. *Strab.*
STYMPHA'LIA or STYMPHA'LIS, a part of Macedonia. *Liv.* 45. c. 30.
STYMPHA'LIA, a surname of Diana, the vault of whose temple at Stymphalus was adorned with the figure of the birds called Stymphalides. There were also statues of white marble which represented young women, with the lower part of the body like birds. *Paus.* 8. c. 22.
STYMPHA'LUS, a king of Arcadia, son of Elatus and Laodice. He made war against Pelops, and was killed in a truce. *Apollod.* 3. c. 9.—*Paus.* 8. c. 4.—*Stat. Th.* 4. v. 298.
STYMPHA'LUS, a town, river, lake, and fountain of Arcadia, which receives its name from king Stymphalus. The neighbourhood of the lake Stymphalus was infested by a number of voracious birds like cranes or storks, which fed upon human flesh, and which were called *Stymphalides*. They were at last destroyed by Hercules with the assistance of Minerva. Some have confounded them with the Harpyies, while others pretend that they never existed but in the imagination of the poets. Pausanias, however, asserts that there were carnivorous birds like the Stymphalides, which he describes as hostile to the travellers of the desert, as lions and tigers. Diana was particularly worshipped at Stymphalus, as also Juno, to whom the inhabitants pretended that Temenus, the son of Pelasgus, had erected three temples, relating to three different periods of her history, to her infancy, her marriage with Jupiter, and her banishment from his company, during which time she fixed her residence in that part of Arcadia. *Apollod.* 2.—*Strab.* 8.—*Plin.* 11. c. 37.—*Lucret.* 5. v. 31.—*Apollon. Rh.* 2. v. 384.—*Ovid. Fast.* 2. v. 273.—*Plaut. in Pers.* sc. 1. v. 4.—*Servius in Æn.* 8. v. 300.—*Catull.* 69. v. 112.—*Auson. Id.* 19. v. 5.—*Paus.* 8. c. 4.—*Stat. Theb.* 4. v. 298.——A lofty mountain of Arcadia in Peloponnesus.
STYG'NE, a daughter of Danaus. *Stat. Syl.* 4. 6.—*Apollod.*
STY'RA, a town of Eubœa, near Carystus. *Steph.*
STYRA'CIUM, a mountain of Crete, whence Apollo was called Styracites. *Id.*
STYRE'I, a people of Greece. *Herod.* 6 & 8.
STY'RUS, a king of Albania, to whom Æetes promised his daughter Medea in marriage, to obtain his assistance against the Argonauts. *Flacc.* 3. v. 497. l. 8. v. 358.
STYX, a daughter of Oceanus and Tethys. She married Pallas, by whom she had three daughters, Victory, Strength and Valor, and a fourth, by some called Emulation; and all these became the companion of Jupiter after he had gained by their assistance, his victory over the Titans. *Hesiod. Theog.* 363 & 384.—*Apollod.* 1. c. 2.—*Lactant. ad Ach.* 3. v. 84.—*Servius ad Æn.* 6. v. 134 & 324.
STYX, a celebrated river of hell, round which it flows nine times. According to some writers, the Styx was a small river flowing from mount Nonacris, in Arcadia, the waters of which were so cold and venomous, that they proved fatal to such as tasted them. Among others, Alexander the Great is mentioned as having fallen a victim to their fatal power, in consequence of drinking them. They even consumed iron, and broke all vessels, and, according to Pausanias and Plutarch, could be preserved only in horns made from horses' hoofs. The wonderful properties of this water suggested the idea that it was a river of hell, especially when it disappeared in the earth a little below its fountain head. The gods held the waters of the Styx in such veneration, that they always swore by them, an oath which was inviolable. If any of the gods had perjured themselves, Jupiter obliged them to drink the waters of the Styx, which lulled them for one whole year into a senseless stupidity; for the nine following years they were deprived of the

ambrosia and the nectar of the gods; and after the expiration of the years of their punishment, they were restored to the assembly of the deities, and to all their original privileges. It is said that this veneration was shown to the Styx, because it received its name from the nymph Styx, who, with her three daughters, assisted Jupiter in his war against the Titans. *Hesiod. Theog.* v. 384, 775. *Homer. Odyss.* 10. v. 513.—*Herodot.* 6. c. 74. —*Virg. Æn.* 6. v. 323, 439, &c.—*Apollod.* 1. c. 3. —*Ital.* 13. v. 553 & 570.—*Plut. in Alex.*—*Vitruv.* 8. c. 3.—*Tertull. adv. Valent.* 15. *De Anim.* 58.—*Servius ad Æn.* 6. v. 134, 154, &c.—*Ovid. Met.* 3. v. 29, &c.—*Lucan.* 6. v. 378, &c.—*Paus.* 8. c. 17 & 18.—*Curt.* 10. c. 10.——A fountain of Arabia Felix. *Ptol.* 6. c. 7.——A lake of Ægypt. *Servius Æn.* 6. v. 154.

SUA'DA or SUADE'LA, the goddess of Persuasion, called Pitho, by the Greeks. Theseus was the first person who paid adoration to her, and established her worship. She had a statue in the temple of Venus Praxis at Megara. *Cic. de Cl. Orat.* 15, *Brut.* 15.—*Paus.* 1. c. 22 & 43. l. 9. c. 35.—*Horat.* 1. ep. 6. v. 38.

SUAG'ELA, a city of Caria, which was the burial place of the Carian kings. *Steph.*

SUA'NA, a town of Etruria. *Ptol.* It is now Soana.

SUANAGU'RA, a city of India without the Ganges. *Id.* It is now, probably, Patua.

SUANE'TES, a people of Rhætia, called Suanitæ by *Ptolemy.*

SUA'NI, a people of Colchis, whose country abounded with gold. *Plin.* 33. c. 3.

SUARDO'NES, a people of Germany. *Tacit. G.* 40.

SUAR'NI, a people who habited the Gordiæan mountains. *Plin.* 6. c. 11.

SU'ASA, a town of Umbria. *Ptol.*——A town of Upper Æthiopia. *Id.* 6. c. 29.

SUBA'TRII, a people of Germany, over whom Drusus triumphed. *Strab.* 7.

SU'BI, a small river of Hispania Citerior. *Plin.* 3. c. 3. It is now the Beles.

SUB'LACUM, a town of the Æqui, in Latium. It is called Sublaqueum by *Tacitus, Ann.* 14. c. 22. & *Pliny*, 3. c. 12. It is now Sollago according to *Leander.*

SUBLA'VIO, a city of Noricum. *Antonin.*

SUBLIC'IUS, the first bridge erected over the Tiber at Rome. *Vid.* Pons.

SUBMONTO'RIUM, a town of Vindelicia, now Augsburg.

SUBOCRI'NI, a people of Istria. *Plin.* 3. c. 20.

SU'BOTA, small islands at the east of Athos. *Liv.* 44. c. 28.

SUBRI'TA, a city of Crete. *Ptol.*

SU'BRIUS DEX'TER, a tribune of the prætorian cohort under Galba. *Tac. Hist.* 1. c. 31.

Su'brius Fla'vius, a tribune of the prætorian cohort, who conspired against Nero. *Id. Ann.* 15. c. 49.

SUBROM'ULA, a city of Italy between Hydruntum and Equotuticum. *Antonin.*

SUBSICI'NUM, a city of Calabria, near the river Medana. *Id.*

SUBSOLA'NUS, the name of the east wind, or Eurus, amongst the Romans, who had a particular dislike to it. *Aul. Gell.* 2. c. 22.—*Plin.* 2. c. 47. —*Seneca, Qu. Nat.* 5. c. 16.

SU'BUR, a river of Mauritania Tingitana, falling into the Atlantic Ocean. *Ptol.*—*Plin.* 5. c. 1.——A town of Hispania Citerior. It is now Siges or Ciges, or, according to others, Cubilles.

SUBUR'GIA, now Burgi, an inland town of Mauritania Cæsariensis. *Ptol.*

SUBUR'RA, a street in Rome, where all the licentious, dissolute, and lascivious Romans and courtezans resorted. It was situate between mounts Viminalis and Quirinalis, and was remarkable as having been the residence of the obscurer years of J. Cæsar. *Horat. Epod.* 5. v. 58.—*Suet. in Cæs.*—*Varro de L. L.* 4. c. 8.—*Martial.* 6. epigr. 66.—*Juv.* 3. v. 5.

SUBUI'TUM, a city of India Citerior. *Ptol.*

SUCCAS'SES, a people of Gallia Aquitanica. *Plin.* 4. c. 19.

SUC'CI, a town of Upper Mysia. *Ammian.*

SUC'CABAR, a colony of Tingitana, among the Mauri. *Plin.* 5. c. 2.

SU'CHE, a town of Æthiopia, near the Sinus Adulitanus. *Id.* 6. c. 29.

SUCIDA'VA, a town of Lower Mysia, on the Danube. *Antonin.*

SU'CRO, now Xucar, a river of Hispania Tarraconensis, celebrated for a battle fought there between Sertorius and Pompey, in which the former obtained the victory. *Plut.*

Su'cro, a Rutulian killed by Æneas. *Virg. Æn.* 12. v. 505.

SUC'ULÆ, a name improperly given to the Hyades, daughters of Atlas, as mentioned by *Cicero, de Nat. D.* 2. *Plin.* 18. c. 26.

SUDE'NI, a people of European Sarmatia. *Ptol.*

SUDER'TUM, an inland city of Etruria. *Id.* It is now Muderno according to *Leander.*

SUDERTA'NI, a people of Etruria. *Liv.* 26. c. 23. Their town is now Souretto.

SUDE'TI or SUDI'TI, mountains of Germany. *Ptol.*

SUDIDE'NIS, a city of Africa Propria. *Id.*

SUE'BI, mountains of Scythia within Imaus. *Id.*

SUECO'NII, a people of Belgium. *Plin.* 4. c. 17.

SUE'DIUS CLE'MENS, a commander to whom Otho entrusted the conduct of the war in Gallia Narbonensis. *Tac. Hist.* 1. c. 87

SU'EL, a town of Hispania Bætica. Ptolemy calls it Σοῦλ. *Mela*, 2. c. 6.—*Plin.* 3. c. 1.

SUES'SA, a town of Campania, called also Aurunca, to distinguish it from Suessa Pometia. The poet Lucilius was born there. *Ital.* 8. v. 400.—*Strab.* 5.—*Plin.* 3. c. 5.—*Dionys. Hal.* 4.—*Liv.* 1 & 2.—*Virg. Æn.* 6. v. 775.—*Cic. Phil.* 3. c. 4. l. 4. c. 2.—*Auson.* 15. v. 9.

Sues'sa Pome'tia, a city of the Volsci. *Strab.* 5.—*Dionys.*—*Liv.* 2.

SUESSITA'NI, a people of Spain. *Liv.* 25. c. 34.

SUESSO'NES, or SUESSI'ONES, a powerful nation of Belgic Gaul reduced by J. Cæsar. *Cæs. Bell. G.* 2.

SUES'SULA, a town of Campania. *Liv.* 7. c. 37. l. 23. c. 14.—*Plin.* 3. c. 5.

SUE'TES, an auxiliary of Perses against Æetes. *Val. Flacc.* 6. v. 550.

SUETO'NIUS C. PAULI'NUS, the first Roman general who crossed mount Atlas with an army, of which expedition he wrote an account. He presided over Britain as governor for about 20 years, where he conquered Boadicea, and he was afterwards made consul. He forsook the interest of Otho, and attached himself to Vitellius. He wrote a history. *Tacit. Ann.* 14. c. 29.—*Voss. H. Lat.* 1. c. 26.

Sueto'nius C. Tranquil'lus, a Latin historian, son of a Roman knight of the same name. He was favored by Adrian, and became his secretary, but he was afterwards banished from the court for want of attention and respect to the empress Sabina. In his retirement Suetonius enjoyed the friendship and correspondence of Pliny the younger, and dedicated his time to study. He wrote a history of the Roman kings, divided into three books; a catalogue of all the illustrious men of Rome, a book on the games and spectacles of the Greeks, &c. which are all now lost. The only one of his compositions extant is the lives of the twelve first Cæsars, and some fragments of his catalogue of celebrated grammarians. Suetonius, in his lives, is praised for his impartiality and correctness. His expressions, however, are often too indelicate, and it has been justly observed, that while he exposed the deformities of the Cæsars, he wrote with all the licentiousness and extravagance with which they lived. The best editions of Suetonius are that of Pitiscus, 4to. 2 vols. Leovard. 1714; that of Oudendorp, 2 vols. 8vo. L. Bat. 1751; and that of Ernesti, 8vo. Lips. 1755. *Plin.* 1. ep. 18. l. 5. ep. 11, &c.—*Harles. Not. Lit. Rom.* 1. p. 147.—*Sax. Onom.* 1. p. 285.—*Suet. Oth.* 10.

SUE'TRI, a people of Gaul near the Alps.

SUE'VI, a people of Germany, between the Elbe and the Vistula, who made frequent incursions into the territories of Rome under the emperors. *Lucan.* 2. v. 51.

SUE'VIUS, a Latin poet in the age of Ennius, some of whose elegant verses Virgil is said to have adopted in his own poems. A few verses to the number of ten are preserved. An idyllium called "Moretum," ascribed by some to him, is preserved in the Corpus Poetarum. *Macrob.* 6. c. 1 & 5. —*Gyrald. P. H.* 4.

SUFFE'NUS, a Latin poet in the age of Catullus.

He was but of moderate abilities, but puffed up with a high idea of his own excellence, and therefore deservedly exposed to the ridicule of his contemporaries. *Catull.* 22.

SUFFE'TIUS or SUFE'TIUS. *Vid.* Metius.

SUFFET'ULA or SUFET'ULA, an inland town of Mauritania. *Antonin.*

SUFFU'CIUS NUME'RIUS, a man of Præneste, who, it is said, by the direction of a dream discovered the *sortes* or oracles of Præneste. *Cic. Div.* 2. c. 41.

SU'IDAS, a Greek writer who flourished about the 11th century. He was the author of an excellent Lexicon, which, though mutilated in some parts, abounds with a most valuable collection of anecdotes and historical materials from ancient authors. The best edition is that of Kuster 3 vols. fol. Cantab. 1705. For further particulars respecting this writsr, see the 40th chapter of the 5th book of *Fabricius' Bibl. Gr.*

SUIL'LIUS PUB., an informer in the court of Claudius, banished under Nero, by means of Seneca, and sent to the Baleares. *Tacit. A.* 14. c. 42, &c.

SUIL'LIUS CÆSONI'NUS, a guilty favorite of Messalina. *Id. ib.* 11. c. 36.

SUI'ONES, a nation of Germany, supposed to be the modern Swedes. *Tacit. de Germ.* c. 44.

SUL'CHI or SUL'CI, a town at the south of Sardinia, built by the Carthaginians, and considered as the second city of the island. The air was unwholesome from the great heat and southerly winds which prevailed there. *Paus.* 10. c. 17.—*Mela*, 2. c. 7.—*Claudian. de Gild.* 518.—*Strab.* 5.

SUL'CIUS, an informer whom Horace describes as hoarse with the number of informations which he daily gave *Horat.* 1. sat. 4. v. 65.

SUL'GA, now Sorgue, a small river of Gaul falling into the Rhone. *Strab.* 4.

SUL'LA or SYL'LA. *Vid.* Sylla.

SUL'LA, a son-in-law of Claudius, banished to Massilia, where he was murdered by order of Nero. *Tac. Ann.* 13. c. 23. l. 14. c. 57.

SUL'LUCUM, a city of Numidia. *Antonin.*

SUL'MO, now Sulmona, an ancient town of the Peligni, at the distance of about 90 miles from Rome, founded by Solymus, or one of the followers of Æneas. Ovid was born there. *Ovid. passim.*—*Ital.* 8. v. 511. l. 9. v. 70,—*Strab.* 5.—*Cæs. B. Civ.* 1.—*Plin.* 3. c. 5 & 12.—*Flor.* 3. c. 21.

SUL'MO, a Latian chief killed in the night by Nisus, as he was going with his companions to destroy Euryalus. *Virg. Æn.* 9. v. 412.

SULPIT'IA, a daughter of Paterculus, who married Fulvius Flaccus. She was so famous for her chastity, that she consecrated a temple to Venus Verticordia, a goddess who was implored to turn the hearts of the Roman women to virtue. *Plin.* 7. c. 35.——A poetess in the age of Domitian, against whom she wrote a poem, because he had banished the philosophers from Rome. This composition is still extant, consisting of 70 well-written verses. She had also written a poem on conjugal affection, commended by *Martial.* 10. epigr. 35. now lost. It was first published with Ausonius by Ugoletus, Venet. 1499, and afterwards by Schwarzius, Altorf. 1721. *Harles. Not. Lit. Rom.* 1. p. 490.——A daughter of Serv. Sulpitius mentioned in the book of elegies falsely attributed to Tibullus.

SULPIT'IA LEX, *militaris*, by C. Sulpitius, the tribune, A.U.C. 665, invested Marius with the direction of the war against Mithridates, of which Sylla was to be deprived.——Another, *de senatu*, by Servius Sulpitius the tribune, A.U.C. 665. It required that no senator should owe more than 2,000 drachmæ.——Another, *de civitate*, by P. Sulpitius the tribune, A.U.C. 665. It ordered that the new citizens who composed the eight tribes lately created, should be divided among the 35 old tribes as a greater honor.——Another, called also Sempronia, *de religione*, by P. Sulpitius Saverrio and P. Sempronius Sophus, consuls, A.U.C. 449. It forbad any person to consecrate a temple or altar without the permission of the senate and the majority of the tribunes.——Another to empower the Romans to make war against Philip of Macedonia.

SULPIT'IUS or SULPIC'IUS, an illustrious family at Rome.

SULPIT'IUS PET'ICUS, a man chosen dictator against the Gauls. His troops mutinied when first he took the field, but he soon after engaged the enemy, and totally defeated them. *Liv.* 7.

SULPIT'IUS SEVER'RIO, a consul who gained a victory over the Æqui. *Id.* 9. c. 45.

SULPIT'IUS C. PATER'CULUS, a consul sent against the Carthaginians. He conquered Sardinia and Corsica, and obtained a complete victory over the enemy's fleet. He was honored with a triumph at his return to Rome. *Id.* 17.

SULPIT'IUS SPU'RIUS, one of the three commissioners whom the Romans sent to collect the best laws which could be found in the different cities and republics of Greece. *Liv.* 3. c. 10, &c.

SULPIT'IUS, one of the first consuls who received intelligence that a conspiracy was formed in Rome to restore the Tarquins to power, &c.——A priest who died of the plague in the first ages of the republic at Rome.——A Roman consul who fought against Pyrrhus and defeated him.——One of Messalina's favorites, put to death by Claudius.

SULPIT'IUS P. GAL'BA, a Roman consul who signalized himself greatly during the war which his countrymen waged against the Achæans and the Macedonians.

SULPIT'IUS SEVE'RUS, a writer. *Vid.* Severus.

SULPIT'IUS PUB'LIUS, one of the associates of Marius, well known for his intrigues and cruelty. He made some laws in favour of the allies of Rome, and kept about 3,000 young men in continual pay, whom he called his anti-senatorial band, and with these he had often the impertinence to attack the consuls in the popular assemblies. He became at last so seditious, that he was proscribed by Sylla's adherents, and immediately murdered. His head was fixed on a pole in the rostrum, where he had often made many seditious speeches in the capacity of tribune. *Liv.* 77.—*Cic. Har.* 19. *Br.* 63.—*Plut. in Syll.*.

SULPIT'IUS C. LON'GUS, a Roman consul, who defeated the Samnites, and killed 30,000 of their men. He obtained a triumph for this celebrated victory. He was afterwards made dictator to conduct a war against the Etrurians.

SULPIT'IUS RU'FUS, a lieutenant of Cæsar in Gaul.

SULPIT'IUS SERV. RU'FUS, a competitor for the consulship with Murena. When pro-consul of Achaia, he wrote an elegant consolatory letter to his friend Cicero on the death of his daughter Tullia. He died on his way to Mutina, where he was going at the head of an embassy to Antony. *Cic. Mur.* 3. *Fam.* 4. ep. 3. l. 8. ep. 6.—*Plut.* 9. c. 1.

SULPIT'IUS P. QUIRI'NUS, a consul in the age of Augustus.

SULPIT'IUS CAMERI'NUS, a pro-consul of Africa, under Nero, accused of cruelty, &c. *Tacit. An.* 13. c. 52.

SULPIT'IUS GAL'LUS, a celebrated astrologer in the age of Paulus. He accompanied the consul in his expedition against Perseus, and told the Roman army that the night before the day on which they were to give the enemy battle there would be an eclipse of the moon, this explanation encouraged the soldiers, whereas such an event would have intimidated them, if not previously acquainted with the causes of it. Sulpitius was universally regarded, and he was honoured a few years after with the consulship. *Liv.* 44. c. 37. l. 45. c. 44.—*Plin.* 2. c. 12.—*Cic. Off.* 1. c. 6. *Sen.* 16.

SULPIT'IUS APPOLINA'RIS, a grammarian in the age of the emperor M. Aurelius. He left some letters and a few grammatical observations now lost. *Civ —Liv.—Plut.—Polyb.—Flor.—Eutrop.*

SUMMA'NUS, a surname of Pluto, as prince of the dead, *summus manium*. He had a temple at Rome, erected during the wars with Pyrrhus; and the Romans believed that the thunder-bolts of Jupiter were in his power during the night. *Cic. de Div.* 1. c. 10 —*Ovid. Fast.* 6. v. 731.—*Plin.* 2. c. 52.—*Aug. de Civ. D.* 4. c. 23.—*Turneb. Adv.* 11. c. 7.

SUMMA'RUM, a town of Upper Æthiopia, on the banks of the Nile. *Ptol.*

SU'NICI, a people of Germany on the shores of the Rhine. *Tacit. H.* 4. c. 66.

SU'NIDES, a soothsayer in the army of Eumenes. *Polyæn.* 4. c. 19.

SU'NIUM, a promontory of Africa, about 45 miles

distant from the Piræus. There was there a small harbour, as also a town. Minerva had there a beautiful temple, whence she was called Sunias. There are still in being, according to *Spon*, nineteen columns among the venerable ruins of this temple, from which circumstance it is called Capo delle Colonne. *Plin.* 4. c. 7.—*Strab.* 9.—*Paus.* 1. c. 1.—*Cic. ad Attic.* 7. ep. 3. l. 13. ep. 10.—*Ovid. Fast.* 4. v. 561.

SU'NIUS, a writer on Arabian affairs. *Steph. in* Ἐδουμαῖοι.

SUNONEN'SIS LA'CUS, a lake near Nicomedia in Bithynia. *Ammian.* It is called by *Pliny*, 5. c. *ult. Nicomediensis*, and is now Lago di Comidia.

SUOD'ANA, a city of Arabia Felix. *Ptol.*

SUOVETAURIL'IA, a sacrifice among the Romans, which consisted of the immolation of a sow (*sus*), a sheep (*ovis*), a bull (*taurus*), whence the name. It was generally observed every fifth year. *Varro, de R. R.* 2. c. 1.—*Cato, de R. R.* 141.—*Liv.* 1. c. 44. l. 8. c. 10.—*Tacit. An.* 16. c. 37. *Hist.* 4. c. 53.—*Festus de V. Sig.*

SUP'PARA, a city of India within the Ganges. *Ptol.* It appears to have been the Uppara of *Arrian.*

SU'PERUM MA'RE, a name of the Adriatic Sea, because it was situate above Italy. The name of *Mare Infernum* was applied, for the opposite reasons, to the sea below Italy. *Cic. pro Cluent.* c. 8. & *pro Flacc.* c. 13.

SUP'TU, a city of Mauritania Cæsariensis. *Ptol.*

SU'RA ÆMYL'IUS, a Latin writer, *de annis P. R. V. Pat.* 1. c. 6.

SU'RA LEN'TULUS, one of the accomplices in Catiline's conspiracy. *Plut. in Cic.*

SU'RA L LICIN'IUS, a favorite of Trajan honored with the consulship.

SU'RA, a freedman mentioned by *Cicero*. 5. *Fam.* 10. ——A writer in the age of the emperor Gallienus. He wrote a history of the reign of the emperor.

SU'RA, a city on the Euphrates.——A city in Iberia. ——A river of Germany, the waters of which fall into the Moselle. *Aus. in Mos.*

SURDA'ONES, a people of Hispania Tarraconensis. *Plin* 3. c. 3.

SURE'NA, a powerful officer in the armies of Orodes king of Parthia. His family had the privilege of crowning the kings of Parthia. He was appointed to conduct the war against the Romans, and to protect the kingdom of Parthia against Crassus, who wished to conquer it. He defeated the Roman triumvir, and after he had drawn him perfidiously to a conference, he ordered his head to be cut off. He afterwards returned to Parthia, mimicking the triumphs of the Romans. Orodes ordered him to be put to death, B.C. 52. Surena has been admired for his valour, his sagacity as a general, and his prudence and firmness in the execution of his plans; but his perfidy, his effeminate manners, and his lasciviousness, have been deservedly censured. *Polyæn.* 7.—*Plut. in Crass.*

SURI'GA, a town of Mauritania Tingitana. *Ptol.*

SU'RIUM, a town at the south of Colchis.

SU'RIUS, a river of Colchis, flowing into the Phasis. *Plin.* 2. c. 103.

SURREN'TUM, a town of Campania, on the bay of Naples, famous for the wine which was made in the neighbourhood. *Mela*, 2. c. 4.—*Strab.* 5.—*Horat.* 1. ep. 17. v. 52.—*Ovid. Met.* 15. v. 710.—*Mart.* 13. epigr. 110. l. 14. epigr. 102.—*Plin.* 3. c. 5. l. 23. c. 1.—*Tacit. Ann.* 6. c. 1.

SUR'TA, a city of Armenia Major. *Ptol.*

SUR'UBA, a city of Asiatic Sarmatia. *Id.*

SU'RUS, one of the Ædui, who made war against Cæsar. *Cæs. G.* 8. c. 45.

SUS, the name of a small brook near Libethra in Thrace. *Strab.* 10.—*Paus.* 9. c. 30.

SU'SA (-*orum*), now Souster, a celebrated city of Asia, the chief town of Susiana, and the capital of the Persian empire, built by Tithonus the father of Memnon. Cyrus took it. The walls of Susa were about 120 stadia in circumference. The treasures of the kings of Persia were generally kept there, and the royal palace was built with white marble, and its pillars were covered with gold and precious stones. It was usual with the kings of Persia to spend the summer at Ecbatana, and the winter at Susa, because the climate was more warm there than at any other royal residence. It has been called Memnonia, or the palace of Memnon, because that prince reigned there. *Plin.* 6. c. 26, &c.—*Lucan.* 2. v. 49.—*Strab.* 15.—*Xenophon, Cyr.*—*Propert.* 2. el. 13.—*Claudian. de Gild.* 33.

SU'SANA, a town of Hispania Tarraconensis. *Sil.* 3. v. 384.

SUSA'RION, a Greek poet of Megara, who is supposed, with Dolon, to have been the inventor of comedy, and to have first introduced it at Athens on a moveable stage. B C. 562. His father's name was Philinus. A few of his verses are extant. *Gyrald. P. H.* 6.—*Fabr. B. Gr.* 2. c. 22.—*Sax. Onom.* 1. p. 22.

SUSIA'NA or SU'SIS, a country of Asia, of which the capital was called Susa, situate at the east of Assyria. Lilies grow in great abundance in Susiana, and it is from that plant that the province received its name. according to some, as Susan is the name of a lily in Hebrew.

SU'SIDÆ PY'LÆ, narrow passes over mountains from Susiana into Persia. *Curt.* 3. c. 5.

SUSUDA'TA, a city of Germany. *Ptol.*

SU'THUL, a town of Numidia, where the king's treasures were kept. *Sall. Jug.* 37.

SU'TRIUM, now Sutri, a town of Etruria, about 24 miles north-west of Rome. Some suppose that the phrase *Ire Sutrium*, to act with despatch, arises from the celerity with which Camillus recovered the place, but Festus explains it differently. *Plaut. Cas.* 3, 1. v. 10.—*Liv.* 26. c. 34.—*Paterc.* 1. c. 13.—*Strab.* 5.—*Ital.* 8. v. 492.

SY'AGRA, a region of Cilicia. *Steph.*

SY'AGRUS or SYA'GRUS, an ancient poet, the first who wrote on the Trojan war. He is called Sagaris by *Diogenes Laertius*, who adds that he lived in Homer's age, of whom he was the rival. *Ælian. V. H.* 14. c. 21.—*Gyrald. P. H.* 2.—*Fabric. B. Or.* 34.

SY'ALIS, a city of the Mastieni. *Steph.*

SYB'ARIS, a river of Lucania in Italy, the waters of which were said to render men more strong and robust. *Strab.* 6.—*Pliny.* 3. c. 11. l. 31. c. 2.—*Eustath. ad Dion. Per.* 373.—*Schol. Theocr. Idyl.* 5. v. 15.—*Tzetzes ad Lycoph.* 1021.——A town on the river of the same name, on the bay af Tarentum, which had been founded by a colony of Achæans. Sybaris became very powerful, and in its most flourishing situation it had the command of four neighbouring nations, of 25 towns, and could send an army of 300,000 men into the field. The walls of the city were said to extend six miles and a half in circumference, and the suburbs covered the banks of the Crathis for the space of seven miles. It made a long and vigorous resistance against the neighbouring town of Crotona, till it was at last totally reduced by the disciples of Pythagoras, B.C. 508. Sybaris was destroyed no less than five times, and always repaired. In a more recent age the inhabitants became so effeminate, that the word Sybarite became proverbial to intimate a man devoted to pleasure. Every excess, either in luxury or voluptuousness, could be found there, and the indolence of the inhabitants was so great, that they never saw the sun rise or set. That their slumbers might not be disturbed, all professions which were attended with noise, were carefully forbidden in the city, and even cocks were destroyed. The greatest encouragement on the other hand was liberally lavished on such as invented new pleasures, and golden crowns were the reward of those who had given the most sumptuous entertainments. So great was their dissipation, that guests were generally invited one year before the day of conviviality, that suitable preparations might be made, and while every one was sunk in sloth and effeminacy, the noble arts of peace and industry were forgotten, insomuch that, Sybaris in the period of a long prosperity cannot boast of one citizen whose name may claim immortality, either by deeds of heroism, or the practice of the milder virtues of a domestic life. After several revolutions there was a small town built in the neighbourhood about 444 years before the Christian era, and called Thurium, from a small fountain called Thuria, where it was built. *Diod.* 12.—*Strab.* 6.—*Ælian. V.H.* 9. c. 24—*Martial.* 12. epigr. 96.—*Plut. in Pelop.* &c.—*Plin.* 3. c. 10. l. 13. c. 2.—*Eustath. ad*

Dionys. Per. 353.—*Tzetzes. ad Lyc.* 1021.—*Athen.* 12.—*Mela*, 2. c. 4.—*Suidas.*

SYB'ARIS, a friend of Æneas killed by Turnus. *Virg. Æn.* 12. v. 363.——A youth enamoured of Lydia, &c. *Horat.* 1. od. 8. v. 2.

SYBARI'TA, an inhabitant of Sybaris. *Vid.* Sybaris.

SYBENNIT'ICA, a maritime province of Ægypt. *Steph.*

SYB'EROS, a city of Illyria. *Id.*

SYB'OTA, two or three small islands with a harbour of the same name, between Thesprotia in Epirus, and the south-east of Corcyra, opposite the promontory of Leucinna in that island. *Thucyd.* 1. c. 52.—*Strab.* 7.—*Cic.* 5. *Att.* 9.

SYB'OTAS, a king of the Messenians in the age of Lycurgus, the Spartan legislator. *Paus.* 4. c. 4.

SY'BRA, a fortified place of Phrygia. *Steph.*

SYB'RIDÆ, a village in the tribe Erechtheis.

SYBUR'PORES, a people of Libya. *Ptol.*

SYCAM'INON, a city of the Phœnicians. *Steph.*

SY'CE, a small island of Ionia. *Steph.*—*Plin.* 5. c. 31.

SY'CEUS, one of the Titans.

SYCIN'NUS, a slave of Themistocles, sent by his master to engage Xerxes to fight against the fleet of the Peloponnesians. *Polyæn.* 1. c. 30.

SYCI'TES, a surname of Bacchus ἀπὸ τῶν συκῶν. *Hesychius*, however, calls him Syceates.

SYC'TA, a city of Persia. *Ptol.*

SYCU'RIUM, a town of Thessaly at the foot of Ossa. *Liv.* 42. c. 54.

SYCUS'SA, a small island opposite Ephesus. *Plin.* 8. c. 31.

SYD'ERIS, a river of Parthia or Media, flowing into the Caspian Sea. *Id.* 6. c. 16.

SYD'IMA, a city in the mountainous parts of Lycia. *Id.* 5. c. 27.

SY'DRUS, a city of India Citerior. *Ptol.*

SY'EDRA, a town of Cilicia Trachea. *Steph. Strabo* calls it Sydre. *Lucan.* 8. v. 258.

SYE'NE, now Asna, a town of Thebais, on the extremities of Ægypt, nearly under the tropic of Cancer. Juvenal the poet was banished thither on pretence of commanding a prætorian cohort stationed in the neighbourhood. It was famous for its quarries of marble. *Strab.* 1 & 2.—*Mela*, 1. c. 9.—*Plin.* 36. c. 8.—*Ovid. ex Pont.* 1. el. 5. v. 79. *Met.* 5. v. 74.—*Lucan.* 2. v. 587. 1. 8. v. 851. 1. 10. v. 234.—*Stat. Theb.* 4. v. 739. 1. 2. *Sylv.* 2. v. 86.

SYENE'SIUS, a Cicilian who, with Labinetus of Babylon, concluded a peace between Alyattes, king of Lydia, and Cyaxares, king of Media, while both armies were terrified by a sudden eclipse of the sun, B.C. 585. *Herodot.* 1. c. 74.

SYEN'NESIS, a satrap of Cilicia, when Cyrus made war against his brother Artaxerxes. He wished to favor both the brothers by sending one of his sons into the army of Cyrus, and another to Artaxerxes.

SYES'SA, a city of the Tyrrhenians. *Steph.*

SYG'ARUS, an island in the Arabic Gulf. *Plin.* 6. c. 28.

SYI'A, a small city of Crete. *Steph.*

SYL'EA, a daughter of Corinthus.

SYLE'UM, a town of Pamphylia.

SY'LEUS, a king of Aulis.

SYLI'ONES, a people of Chaonia. *Steph.*

SYL'LA L. CORNE'LIUS, a celebrated Roman of a noble family. The poverty of his early years was relieved by the liberality of the courtezan Nicopolis, who left him heir to a large fortune; and with the addition of the immense wealth of his mother-in-law, he soon appeared one of the most opulent of the Romans. He first entered the army under the great Marius, whom he accompanied in Numidia, in the capacity of quæstor. He rendered himself conspicuous in military affairs; and Bocchus, one of the princes of Numidia, delivered Jugurtha into his hands for the Roman consul. The rising fame of Sylla gave umbrage to Marius, who was always jealous of an equal, as well as of a superior; but the ill language which he used, rather inflamed than extinguished the ambition of Sylla. He left the conqueror of Jugurtha, and carried arms under Catullus. Some time after, he obtained the prætorship, and was appointed by the Roman senate to place Ariobarzanes on the throne of Cappadocia, against the views and interests of Mithridates, king of Pontus. This he easily effected; one battle left him victorious, and before he quitted the plains of Asia, the Roman prætor had the satisfaction to receive in his camp the ambassador of the king of Parthia, who wished to make a treaty of alliance with the Romans. Sylla received them with haughtiness and behaved with such arrogance, that Orabazus, one of them, exclaimed, "Surely this man is master of the world, or doomed to be such!" At his return to Rome, he was commissioned to finish the war with the Marsi, and when this was successfully ended, he was rewarded with the consulship, in the 50th year of his age. In this capacity he wished to have the administration of the Mithridatic war; but he found an obstinate adversary in Marius, and he attained the summit of his wishes only when he entered Rome sword in hand. After he had slaughtered all his enemies, set a price upon the head of Marius, and put to death the tribune Sulpitius, who had continually opposed his views, he marched towards Asia, and disregarded the flames of discord which he left behind him unextinguished. Mithridates was already master of the greatest part of Greece; and Sylla, when he reached the coast of Peloponnesus, was delayed by the siege of Athens, and of the Piræus. His operations were carried on with vigor, and when he found his money fail, he made no scruple to take the riches of the temples of the gods to bribe his soldiers. and render them devoted to his service. His boldness succeeded, the Piræus surrendered; and the conqueror, as if struck with reverence at the beautiful porticos where the philosophic followers of Socrates and Plato had often disputed, spared the city of Athens, which he had devoted to destruction, and forgave the living for the sake of the dead. Two celebrated battles at Cheronæa and Orchomenus, rendered him master of Greece. He crossed the Hellespont, and attacked Mithridates in the very heart of his kingdom. The artful monarch, who well knew the valor and perseverance of his adversary, made proposals of peace; and Sylla, whose interest at Rome was then decreasing, did not hesitate to put an end to a war which had rendered him master of so much territory, and which enabled him to return to Rome like a conqueror, and to dispute with his rival the sovereignty of the republic with a victorious army. Muræna was left at the head of the Roman forces in Asia, and Sylla hastened to Italy. In the plains of Campania he was met by a few of his adherents, whom the success of his rivals had banished from the capital, and he was soon informed that if he wished to contend with Marius, he must encounter 15 generals followed by 25 well disciplined legions. In these critical circumstances he had recourse to artifice, and while he proposed terms of accommodation to his adversaries, he secretly strengthened himself, and saw with pleasure his armies daily increase, by the revolt of soldiers whom his bribes or promises had corrupted. Pompey, who afterwards merited the surname of Great, embraced his cause, and marched to his camp with three legions. Soon after, he appeared in the field with advantage; the confidence of Marius decayed with his power, and Sylla entered Rome like a tyrant and a conqueror. The streets were daily filled with dead bodies, and 7000 citizens, to whom the conqueror had promised pardon, were suddenly massacred in the circus. The senate, at that time assembled in the temple of Bellona, heard the shrieks of their dying countrymen; and when they inquired into the cause of it, Sylla coolly replied, "They are only a few rebels whom I have ordered to be chastised." If this had been the last and most dismal scene, Rome might have been called happy; but it was only the beginning of her misfortunes, each succeeding day exhibited a greater number of slaughtered bodies, and when one of the senators had had the boldness to ask the tyrant when he meant to stop his cruelties, Sylla, with an air of unconcern, answered, that he had not yet determined, but that he would take it into his consideration. The slaughter was continued, and a list of such as were proscribed was daily stuck in the public streets. The slave was rewarded to bring his master's head, and the son was not ashamed to imbrue his hands in the blood of his father for money. No less than 4700 of the most powerful and opulent were slain, and Sylla wished the Romans to forget his cruelties in aspiring to the title of perpetual dictator. In this capacity he made new laws, abrogated such as were inimical to his views, and changed every regulation by which his ambition was obstructed. After he had finished whatever the most absolute sovereign may do, from his own will and authority, Sylla abdicated the dictatorial power, and retired to a solitary retreat at Puteoli, where he spent the rest of his days, if not in literary ease and tranquillity, yet far from the noise of arms, in the midst of riot and debauchery. The companions of his retirement were the most base and licentious of the populace, and Sylla took pleasure still to wallow in voluptuousness, though on the verge of life, and covered with infirmities. His intemperance hastened his end, his blood was corrupted, and an imposthume was bred in his bowels. He at last died in the greatest torments of the lousy disease, about 78 years B.C., in the 60th year of his age: and it has been observed, that like Marius, on his death-bed, he wished to drown the stings of conscience and remorse by continual intoxication. His funeral was very magnificent; his body was attended by the senate and the vestal virgins, and hymns were sung to celebrate his exploits and to honor his memory. A monument was erected in the field of Mars, on which appeared an inscription written by himself, in which he said, that the good services he had received from his friends, and the injuries of his enemies, had been returned with unexampled usury. The character of Sylla was that of an ambitious, dissimulating, credulous, tyrannical, debauched and resolute commander. He was revengeful in the highest degree, and the surname of *Felix* or *the fortunate*, which he assumed, showed that he was more indebted to fortune than to valor for the great fame he had acquired. But in the midst of all this, who cannot admire the moderation and philosophy of a man, who when absolute master of a republic, which he has procured by his cruelty and avarice, silently abdicates the sovereign power, challenges a critical examination of his administration, and retires to live securely in the midst of thousands whom he has injured and offended? The Romans were pleased and astonished at his abdication; and when the insolence of a young man had been vented against the dictator, he calmly answered, "This usage may perhaps deter another from following my example in resigning his power, if ever he becomes absolute." Sylla has been commended for the patronage he gave to the arts and sciences. He brought from Asia the extensive library of Apellicon, the Peripatetic philosopher, in which were the works of Aristotle and Theophrastus, and he himself composed 22 books of memoirs concerning himself. *Cic in Verr.* 1. *Pro lege Man.—C. Nep. in Attic.—Paterc.* 2. c. 17, &c.—*Liv.* 75, &c.—*Paus.* 1. c. 20.—*F or.* 3. c. 5, &c. l. 4. c. 2, &c.—*Val. Max.* 1. c. 5. l. 2. c. 3. l. 4. c. 6. l. 6. c. 8 & 9, &c.—*Plin.* 2. c. 97. l. 7. c. 24. l. 25. c. 2, &c.—*Orosius*, 5. c. 19.—*Aug. de Civ. D.* 3. c. 22. 27 & 28.—*Polyb.* 5.—*Justin.* 37 & 38. —*Eutrop.* 5. c. 2.—*Plut. in Vitâ.* [A statue of Sylla, a sitting figure, will be found at Florence.]

SYL'LA FAUS'TUS CORN., son of the dictator, honored his father's memory by the exhibition of a show of gladiators and a public entertainment. He espoused the side of Pompey in the civil wars, and was put to death after the battle of Thapsus. *Plin.* 19. c. 1.—*Liv.* 114.—*Cic. Vat.* 13.

SYL'LA PUB'LIUS, a relation of the dictator, who lost the consulship on account of his bribery. He was accused of having a share iu Catiline's conspiracy, of which, however, he was acquitted by the eloquence of Hortensius and Cicero. In the battle of Pharsalia he commanded Cæsar's right wing, and he was afterwards engaged in disposing of the effects of those who had been proscribed by his friend. *Sallust. Cat.* 18.—*Cæs. B. C.* 3. c. 89. —*Cic.* 9. *Fam.* 9. ep. 10. l. 15. ep. 17.

SYL'LA SER'VIUS, the brother of the preceding, was in the number of Catiline's conspirators. *Cic. Syll.* 1.

SYL'LA, a man put to death by Nero at Marseilles, to which place he had been banished.——A friend of Cato, defeated and killed by one of Cæsar's lieutenants.——A senator banished from the senate, for his prodigality, by Tiberius. *Tac. Ann.* 2. c. 48.

SYL'LIS, a nymph, who became, by Apollo, mother of Zeuxippus, king of Sicyon after Phæstus, son of Hercules. *Paus.* 2. c. 6.

SYL'LUS, a Pythagorean philosopher. *Cic. N.D.* 1. c. 34.——A general of the Cretan forces. *Liv.* 42. c. 51.

SYL'OES, a promontory of Africa. *Herodot.*

SYL'OSON, a man who gave a splendid garment to Darius, son of Hystaspes, when a private man Darius, when raised to the throne of Persia, remembered the gift of Solyson with gratitude. *Strab.* 14.

SYLVA'NUS, a god of the woods. *Vid.* Silvanus.

SYL'VIA or IL'IA, the mother of Romulus. *Vid.* Rhea.

SYL'VIA, a daughter of Tyrrhenus, whose favourite stag was wounded by Ascanius. *Virg. Æn.* 7. c. 503.

SYL'VIUS, a son of Æneas by Lavinia, from whom afterwards all the kings of Alba were called Sylvii. *Virg. Æn.* 6. v. 763.

SY'MA or SY'ME, a town of Asia. *Homer. Il.* 2.

SY'MA, a nymph, mother of Chthonius, by Neptune. *Diod.* 5.—*Strab.* 14.

SYMÆ'THA, a city of Thessaly. *Steph.*

SYMÆ'THUS. *Vid.* Simethus.

SYM'BOLUM, a place of Macedonia, near Philippi, the confines of Thrace. *Plut.*

SY'ME, an island between Rhodes and Cnidus. *Plin.* 5. c. 38. It was so called from Syme, daughter of Jalysus, having been before known by the name of Metapontis and Ægle.

SYM'ITHA, a town of Mauritania Cæsariensis. *Ptol.*

SYM'MACHUS, an officer in the army of Agesilaus. *Polyæn.* 2. c. 1.——A writer in the second century. He translated the Bible into Greek, of which but few fragments remain. *Euseb. Hist. Ecl.* 6. c. 14.——A noble Macedonian youth, remarkable for his rashness. *Curt.* 8. c. 13.——A wretched grammarian, ridiculed by *Scholiast* on *Aristophanes.*——The author of a history of the Medes and Assyrians. *Agath.* 1. 2.

SYM'MACHUS Q. AURE'LIUS, a celebrated orator in the age of Theodosius the Great. His father was præfect of Rome. He wrote with great virulence against the Christians, and ten books of his letters are extant, which have been refuted by Ambrose and Prudentius. The best editions of Symmachus are that of Genev. 8vo. 1598, and that of Paris, 4to. 1604. *Harles. Not. Lit. Rom.* 1. p. 629.—*Macrob.* sat. 5. c. 5.

SYM'NI, a people of Æthiopia. *Curt.* 4. c. 7.

SYMPLEG'ADES or CYAN'EÆ, two islands or rocks at the entrance of the Euxine Sea. *Vid.* Cyaneæ.

SYMPO'SIUS CŒLIUS, a Latin poet under the emperors. He has left enigmas which are not only well written, but abound with genuine wit, and are not unworthy of the more refined tastes of modern times. They are 100 in number, and must be considered as curious, if considered as probably the first and oldest collection of this lighter sort of poetry.

SY'MUS, a mountain of Armenia, from which the Araxes flows. *Orph. in Argon.*

SYNAN'GUS, a city of Phœnicia. *Steph.*

SYN'AUS, a city of Phrygia Magna, near the Sangarius. *Ptol.*

SYNCEL'LUS, one of the Byzantine historians, whose works were edited in fol. Paris, 1652. *Fabr. B. Gr.* 5. c. 5.

SYNE'SIUS, a bishop of Cyrene in the age of Theodosius the younger, as conspicuous for his learning as his piety. He wrote 155 epistles besides other treatises in Greek, in a style pure and elegant, and bordering much upon the poetic. He has also left ten sacred hymns, containing altogether 1537 verses. Among the editions are that of Turnebus, Paris, 1553, and that of Petavius, fol. Paris 1612 & 1633. *Fabr. B. Gr.* 5. c. 17.

——The author of a book *de febribus*. Some consider him the same person as the preceding. The best edition is that of Barnard, Amst. 1749. *Fabr. ibid.*

SYN'NADA. *Vid.* Synnas.

SYNNALAX'IS, a nymph of Ionia, who had a temple at Heraclea in Elis. *Paus.* 6. c. 22.

SYN'NAS, (*-adis*), or SYN'NADA (*plur.*), a town of Phrygia, famous for its marble quarries. *Strab.* 12.—*Claudian. in Eutr.* 2.—*Martial.* 9. epigr. 77. —*Stat.* 1. *Sylv* 5. v. 41.—*Cic.* 5. *Ad. Att.* ep. 16.

SYN'NIS, a famous robber. *Vid.* Scinis.

SYNO'PE, a town on the borders of the Euxine. *Vid.* Sinope.

SYO'PII, a people near Liburnia. *Steph.*

SYPALET'TUS, a village in the tribe Cecropis. *Steph.*

SY'PHAX, a king of the Massyli in Libya, who married Sophonisba, the daughter of Asdrubal, and forsook the alliance of the Romans to join himself to the interests of his father-in-law, and of Carthage. He was conquered in a battle by Masinissa, the ally of Rome, and given to Scipio the Roman general. The conqueror carried him to Rome, where he adorned his triumph. Syphax starved himself to death in prison, 201 B.C., and his possessions were given to Masinissa. According to some, the descendants of Syphax reigned for some time over a part of Numidia, and continued to make opposition to the Romans. *Liv.* 24, &c.—*Plut. in Scip.*—*Flor.* 2. c. 6.—*Polyb.*—*Propert.* 3. el. 9. v 61.—*Ital.* 16. v. 171 & 188.—*Ovid. Fast.* 6. v. 769.

SYPHÆ'UM, a town of the Brutii in Italy. *Liv.* 30. c. 19. It is now Castrovillare.

SYR'ACES, one of the Sacæ who mutilated himself, and, by pretending to be a deserter, brought Darius, who made war against his country, into many difficulties. *Polyæn.* 7.

SYRACO'SIA, festivals at Syracuse, celebrated during ten days, in which women were busily employed in offering sacrifices.—Another yearly observed near the lake of Syracuse, where, as they supposed, Pluto had disappeared with Proserpine.

SYRACU'SÆ, a celebrated city of Sicily, founded about 732 years B.C. by Archias, a Corinthian, and one of the Heraclidæ. In its flourishing state it extended 22½ English miles in circumference, and was divided into four districts, Ortygia, Acradina, Tyche, and Neapolis, to which some add a fifth division, Epipolæ, a district little inhabited. These were of themselves separate cities, and were fortified with three citadels, and three-folded walls. Syracuse had two capacious harbours, separated from one another by the island of Ortygia. The greatest harbour was above 5000 paces in circumference, and its entrance 500 paces wide. The people of Syracuse were very opulent and powerful, and, though subject to tyrants, were masters of vast possessions and dependent states. The city of Syracuse was well built, its houses were stately and magnificent: and it has been said that it produced the best and most excellent of men when they were virtuous, but the most wicked and depraved when addicted to vicious pursuits. The women of Syracuse were not permitted to adorn themselves with gold, or wear costly garments, except such as prostituted themselves. Syracuse gave birth to Theocritus and Archimedes. It was under different governments: and after being freed from the tyranny of Thrasybulus, B.C. 446, it enjoyed security for 61 years, till the usurpation of the Dionysii, who were expelled by Timoleon, B.C. 343. In the age of the elder Dionysius, an army of 100,000 foot and 10,000 horse, and 400 ships, were kept in constant pay. It fell into the hands of the Romans, under the consul Marcellus, after a siege of three years, B.C. 212. The city of Syracuse is now confined to the small islands of Ortygia, and contains about 18,000 inhabitants. *Cic. in Verr.* 4. c. 52 & 53.—*Strab.* 1 & 8.—*C. Nep.* 20. c. 3.—*Mela*, 2. c. 7 —*Liv.* 23, &c.—*Plut. in Marcell.* &c.—*Flor.* 2. c. 6 —*Ital.* 14. v. 278 & 343.

SYRACU'SIUS, an Athenian lawyer, ridiculed by the comic writers for his garrulity. *Schol. in Aristoph. Aves.*

SYRASTRE'NE, a region of India Citerior, near the mouth of the Indus. *Ptol.*

SYRAS'TRA, a small town of India within the Ganges. *Id.*

SYRBA'NE, an island in the Euphrates. *Steph.*

SYREN'TION or SYRCEN'TIUM, a town of Etruria. *Id.* It is mentioned, however, by no other writer.

SYR'IA, a large country of Asia, the boundaries of which were not accurately ascertained by the ancients. Syria, generally speaking, was bounded on the east by the Euphrates, on the north by mount Taurus, on the west by the Mediterranean, and on the south by Arabia. It was divided into several districts and provinces, among which were Phœnicia, Seleucis, Judæa or Palestine, Mesopotamia, Babylon, and Assyria. It was also called Assyria; and the words Syria and Assyria, though distinguished and defined by some authors, were often used indifferently. Syria was subjected to the monarchs of Persia; but after the death of Alexander the Great, Seleucus, surnamed Nicanor, who had received this province as his lot in the division of the Macedonian dominions, raised it into an empire, known in history by the name of the kingdom of Syria or Babylon, B.C. 312. Seleucus died after a reign of 32 years, and his successors, surnamed the *Seleucidæ*, ascended the throne in the following order:—Antiochus, surnamed Soter, 280 B.C.; Antiochus Theos, 261; Seleucus Callinicus, 246; Seleucus Ceraunus, 226; Antiochus the Great, 223; Seleucus Philopator, 187; Antiochus Epiphanes, 175; Antiochus Eupator, 164; Demetrius Soter, 162; Alexander Balas, 150; Demetrius Nicanor, 146; Antiochus the Sixth, 144; Diodotus Tryphon, 143; Antiochus Sidetes, 139; Demetrius Nicanor restored, 130; Alexander Zebina, 127, who was dethroned by Antiochus Gryphus, 123; Antiochus Cyzicenus, 112, who takes part of Syria, which he calls Cœlesyria; Philip and Demetrius Eucerus, 93, and in Cœlesyria, Antiochus Pius; Aretas was king of Cœlesyria, 85; Tigranes, king of Armenia, 83; and Antiochus Asiaticus, 69, who was dethroned by Pompey, B.C. 65; in consequence of which Syria became a Roman province. The deity most particularly worshipped by the Syrians was Astarte, supposed to be Diana or the moon, or, according to others, Venus; and her magnificent temple at Hierapolis was attended by 300 priests. Adonis received there also distinguished homage. *Herodot.* 2, 3, & 7.—*Apollon.* 1. *Arg.*—*Strab.* 12 & 16.—*C. Nep. in Dat.*—*Mela*, 1. c. 2.—*Ptol.* 5, c. 6.—*Curt.* 6. c. 4.—*Dionys. Perieg.* 784. —*Sueton. in Ner.* 56.—*Voss. de Idol.* 1. c. 23. l. 2. c. 55.

SYRI'ACUM MA'RE, that part of the Mediterranean Sea which is on the coast of Phœnicia and Syria. *Tacit. Hist.* 5. c. 7.

SYRIMAL'AGA, a city of India within the Ganges. *Ptol.*

SYRIN'GES, a place of Ægypt, near Thebes. *Paus.* 1.—*Amm. Marcell.* l. 22.

SY'RINX, a nymph of Arcadia, daughter of the river Ladon. Pan became enamoured of her, and attempted to offer her violence; but Syrinx escaped, and at her own request was changed by the gods into a reed called Syrinx by the Greeks. The god made himself a pipe with the reed into which his favorite nymph had been changed. *Ovid. Met.* 1. v. 691.—*Martial*, 9. epigr. 63 —*Servius ad Virg. Ecl.* 2 v. 31. *Ecl.* 10. v. 26.

SYRMÆ'UM, a plain between the Nomades and the Nabatæi. *Steph.*

SYR'MATÆ, a people the same as the Sauromatæ. *Steph.*

SYR'MUS, a king of the Triballi. *Arrian.* l. 1.

SYR'NA, a city of Caria, founded by Podalirius. *Steph.*

SYROCIL'ICES, a people on the confines of Syria, near mount Amanus. *Mela*, 1. c. 2.

SYROPHŒ'NIX, the name of an inhabitant of the maritime coast of Syria. *Juv.* 8. v. 158.

SYR'TES, two large sand-banks in the Mediterranean, on the coast of Africa, distinguished by the appellation of *Major* and *Minor*, one of which was near Leptis, and the other near Carthage. As they often changed places, and were sometimes very high or very low under the water, they were deemed most dangerous in navigation, and proved fatal to whatever ships touched upon them. From this circumstance, therefore, the word has been used to denote any part of the sea of which the navigation was attended with danger, either from whirlpools or hidden rocks. *Mela*, l. c. 7. l. 2. c. 7.—*Virg. Æn.* 4. v. 41.—*Lucan.* 9. v. 303.—*Sallust. in J.* c. 78.—*Ital.* 17. v. 629.—*Solin.* 40.—*Plin.* 5. c. 4.—*Servius ad Æn.* 1. v. 579. l. 5. v. 192. l. 10. v. 678.

SY'RUS, or SY'ROS, one of the Cyclades in the Ægæan Sea, at the east of Delus, about 29 miles in circumference, very fruitful in wine and corn of all sorts. The inhabitants lived to a great old age, because the air was wholesome. *Homer. Odyss.* 15. v. 504.—*Strab.* 10,—*Mela*, 2 c. 7.——A town of Caria. *Paus.* 3. c. 26.—*Steph. Byz.*

SY'RUS, a son of Apollo by Sinope, the daughter of the Asopus, who gave his name to Syria. *Plut. in Luc.*——A writer. *Vid.* Publius.——The name of a slave in Terence. Many slaves were brought into Italy from Syria, whence the expression of *Syri venales.* *Cic. Orat.* 2. c. 66. *Att.* 12. ep. 22.

SYSIGAM'BIS, the mother of Darius. *Vid.* Sisygambis.

SYSIM'ETHRES, a Persian satrap, who had two children by his mother, an incestuous commerce tolerated by the laws of Persia. He opposed Alexander with 2,000 men, but soon surrendered. He was greatly honored by the conqueror. *Curt.* 8. c. 4.

SYS'INAS, the elder son of Datames, who revolted from his father to Artaxerxes. *Nep.* 14. c. 7.

SY'THAS, a river of Peloponnesus, flowing through Sicyonia into the bay of Corinth. *Paus.* 2. c. 7.

SYVE'RUS, a river of Attica. *Plin.* 37. c. 8.

T.

TAAU'TES, a Phœnician deity, the same as the Saturn of the Latins, and probably the Thoth, or Thaut, the Mercury of the Ægyptians. *Cic. de N.D.* 3. c. 22.—*Servius ad Virg. Æn.* 4. v. 577.—*Euseb. Præp. Ev.* 1. c. 10.—*Varro de L.L.* 4. c. 9.—*Voss. de Idolol.* 1. c. 22.

TA'BÆ, a town of Pisidia. *Liv.* 38. c. 13.——A promontory in the Arabian Gulph.—*Auct. Peripl.*—*Salmas. ad Solin.* p. 996.

TAB'ANA, a town of Chersonesus Taurica. *Ptol.*

TA'BAS, a town in Parætacene. *Curt.* 5. c. 13.

TABELLA'RIÆ LE'GES, laws made by suffrages delivered upon tablets (*tabellæ*) and not *vivâ voce.* There were four of these laws; the *Gabinia lex*, A.U.C. 614, by Gabinius; the *Cassia*, by Cassius, A.U.C. 616; the *Papiria*, by Carbo, A.U.C. 621; and the *Cælia*, by Cælius, A.U.C. 635. *Cic. de Leg.* 3. c. 16.

TABE'NI, a people dwelling near the desert of Carmania. *Steph.*

TABER'NÆ NO'VÆ, a street in Rome where shops were built. *Liv.* 3. c. 48.

TABER'NÆ RHENA'NÆ, a town of Germany on the confluence of the Felbach and the Rhine, now Rhin-Zabern.

TABER'NÆ RIG'UÆ, now Bern-Castel, on the Moselle.

TABER'NÆ TRIBOC'CORUM, a town of Alsace in France, now Saverne.

TABIA'NA or TIBIA'NA, an island of the Persian Gulph. *Ptol.*

TABI'NUM, a promontory of Scythia. *Plin.* 5. c. 5.

TA'BIS, a city of Arabia. *Steph.*——A promontory of Scythia. *Mela*, 3. c. 7.—*Salmas. ad Solin.* p. 995.

TA'BOR, a mountain of Palestine.

TAB'RACA, a maritime town of Africa, near Hippo, made a Roman colony. The neighbouring forests abounded with monkeys. *Juv.* 10. v. 194.—*Plin.* 5. c. 3.—*Mela*, 1. c. 7.—*Ital.* 3. v. 256.

TABU'DA, a river of Germany, now the Scheldt. *Ptol.*

TABUR'NUS, a mountain of Campania, which abounded with olives. *Virg. G.* 2. v. 38. *Æn.* 12. v. 715. & *Servius locis.*

TAC'APE, a town of Africa, near the Syrtis Minor. *Ptol.*

TACAT'UA, a maritime town of Numidia. *Plin.* 5. c. 3.—*Ptol.*

TACFARI'NAS, a Numidian who commanded an army against the Romans in the reign of Tiberius. He had formerly served in the Roman legions; but in the character of an enemy, he displayed the most inveterate hatred against his benefactor. After he had severally defeated the officers of Tiberius, he was at last routed, and killed in the field of battle, fighting with uncommon fury, by Dolabella. *Tacit. Ann.* 2. c. 52. l. 4. c. 23.

TACHAS'ARA, a city of Media. *Ptol.*

TACHOMP'SO, an island in the Nile, near Thebais. The Ægyptians held one half of this island, and the rest was in the hands of the Æthiopians. *Herodot.* 2.

TA'CHUS, or TA'CHOS, a king of Ægypt, in the reign of Artaxerxes Ochus, against whom he sustained a long war. He was assisted by the Greeks, but his confidence in Agesilaus, king of Lacedæmon proved fatal to him. Chabrias the Athenian had been entrusted with the fleet of the Ægyptian monarch, and Agesilaus was left with the command of the mercenary army. The Lacedæmonian disregarded his engagements, and by joining with Nectanebus, who had revolted from Tachus, he ruined the affairs of the monarch, and obliged him to save his life by flight. Some observe, that Agesilaus acted with that duplicity to avenge himself upon Tachus, who had insolently ridiculed his short and deformed stature. The expectations of Tachus had been raised by the fame of Agesilaus; but when he saw the lame monarch, he repeated on the occasion the fable of the mountain which brought forth a mouse, upon which he replied with asperity, that though he called him a mouse, yet he soon should find him to be a lion. *C. Nep. & Plut. in Ages.*

TACI'NA, a river of Magna Græcia. *Antonin.* It is probably the Targines of *Pliny.*

TAC'ITA, a goddess who presided over silence. Numa, as some say, paid very particular veneration to this divinity.

TAC'ITUS M. CLAU'DIUS, a Roman, elected emperor by the senate after the death of Aurelian. He would have refused this important and dangerous office, but the pressing solicitations of the senate prevailed, and in the 70th year of his age, he complied with the wishes of his countrymen, and accepted the purple. The time of his administration was very popular, the good of his people was his care, and as a pattern of moderation, economy, temperance, regularity, and impartiality, Tacitus found no equal. He abolished the several brothels which under the preceding reigns had filled Rome with licentiousness and obscenity; and by ordering all public baths to be shut at sunset, he prevented the commission of many irregularities, which the darkness of the night had hitherto sanctioned. The senators under Tacitus seemed to have recovered their ancient dignity, and long-lost privileges. They were not only the counsellors of the emperor, but they even seemed to be his masters; and when Florianus, the brother-in-law of Tacitus, was refused the consulship, the emperor said, that the senate, no doubt, could fix upon a more deserving object. As a warrior, Tacitus was inferior to few of the Romans, and during a short reign of about six months, he not only repelled the barbarians who had invaded the territories of Rome in Asia, but he prepared to make war against the Persians and Scythians. He died in Cilicia as he was on his expedition, of a violent distemper, or, according to some, he was destroyed by the secret dagger of an assassin, on the 13th of April in the 276th year of the Christian era. Tacitus has been commended for his love of learning, and it has been observed, that he never passed a day without consecrating some part of his time to reading or writing. He has been accused of superstition, and authors have recorded, that he never studied on the second day of each month, a day which he deemed inauspicious and unlucky. *Tacit. Vita.*—*Zosim.*—*Vopisc. in Tacit.*—*& Florian.*

TAC'ITUS C. CORNE'LIUS, a celebrated Latin historian, born in the reign of Nero. His father was a Roman knight, who had been appointed governor of Belgic Gaul. The native genius and rising talents of Tacitus, were beheld with rapture by the emperor Vespasian, and as he wished to protect and patronise merit, he raised the young historian to places of trust and honor. The succeeding emperors were not less partial to Tacitus, and Domitian seemed to forget his cruelties, when virtue and innocence claimed his patronage. Tacitus was honored with the consulship, and he gave proofs of his eloquence at the bar, by supporting the cause of the injured Africans against the proconsul Marius Priscus, and in causing him to be condemned for his avarice and extortion. The friendly intercourse of Pliny and Tacitus has often been admired, and many have observed, that the familiarity of these two great men, arose from similar principles, and a perfect conformity of manners and opinions. Yet Tacitus was as much the friend of a republican government, as Pliny was an admirer of the imperial power, and of the short-lived virtue of his patron Trajan. Pliny gained the hearts of his adherents by affability, and all the elegant graces which became the courtier and the favorite, while Tacitus conciliated the esteem of the world by his virtuous conduct, which prudence and love of honor ever guided. The friendship of Tacitus and of Pliny almost became proverbial, and one was scarce mentioned without the other, as the following instance may indicate. At the exhibition of the spectacles in the circus, Tacitus held a long conversation on different subjects with a Roman knight, with whom he was unacquainted; and when the knight asked him whether he was a native of Italy, the historian told him that he was not unknown to him, and that for their distant acquaintance he was indebted to literature. "Then you are," replied the knight, "either Tacitus or Pliny." The time of Tacitus was not employed in trivial pursuits, the orator might have been now forgotten if the historian had not flourished. Tacitus wrote a treatise on the manners of the Germans, a composition admired for the beauty and exactness with which it is executed, though some have declared that the historian delineated manners and customs with which he was not acquainted, and which never existed. His life of Cn. Julius Agricola, whose daughter he had married, is celebrated for its purity, elegance, and the many excellent instructions and important truths which it relates. His history of the Roman emperors is imperfect; of the 28 years of which it treated, that is from the 69th to the 96th year of the Christian era, nothing remains but the 69th year and part of the 70th. His annals were the most extensive and complete of his works. The history of the reign of Tiberius, Caius, Claudius, and Nero, was treated with accuracy and attention, yet we are to lament the loss of the reign of Caius, and the beginning of that of Claudius. Tacitus had reserved for his old age, the history of the reign of Nerva and Trajan, and he also proposed to give the world an account of the interesting administration of Augustus; but these important subjects never employed the pen of the historian, and as some of the ancients observe, the only compositions of Tacitus were contained in 30 books, of which we have now only left 16 of his annals, and five of his history. The style of Tacitus has always been admired for peculiar beauties; the thoughts are great; there is sublimity, force, weight, and energy; every thing is treated with precision and dignity, yet many have called him obscure, because he was fond of expressing his ideas in few words. This was the fruit and experience of judgment; the history appears copious and diffuse, while the annals which were written in his old age, are less flowing as to style, more concise, and more heavily laboured. His Latin is remarkable for being pure and classical, and though a writer in the decline of the Roman empire, he has not used obsolete words, antiquated phrases, or barbarous expressions, but with him everything is sanctioned by the writers of the Augustan age. In his biographical sketches he displays an uncommon knowledge of human nature; he paints every scene with a masterly hand, and gives each object its proper size and becoming colors. Affairs of importance are treated with dignity, the secret causes of events and revolutions are investigated, from their primeval source, and the historian every where shows his reader that he was a friend of public liberty and national independence, a lover of truth, and the general good and welfare of mankind, and an inveterate enemy to oppression and to a tyrannical government. The history of the reign of Tiberius is his master-piece, the deep policy, the dissimulation and various intrigues of this celebrated prince, are painted with all the fidelity of the historian, and Tacitus boasted in saying, that he neither would flatter the follies, nor maliciously or partially represent the extravagance of the several characters he delineated. Candour and impartiality were his standard, and his claim to these essential qualifications as an historian has never been disputed. It is said that the emperor Tacitus, who boasted in being one of the descendants of the historian, ordered the works of his ancestor to be placed in all public libraries, and directed that ten copies, well ascertained for accuracy and exactness, should be yearly written, that so great and valuable a work might not be lost. Some ecclesiastical writers have exclaimed against Tacitus for the partial manner in which he speaks of the Jews and Christians; but it should be remembered, that he spoke the language of the Romans, and that the peculiarities of the Christians could not but draw upon them the odium and ridicule of the Pagans, and the imputation of superstition. Among the many excellent editions of Tacitus these may pass for the best; that of Rome, fol. 1515; that in 8vo. 2 vols. L. Bat. 1673; that in usum Delphini, 4 vols. 4to. Paris, 1682; that of Lips. 2 vols 8vo. 1714; of Gronovius, 2 vols. 4to. 1721; that of Brotier, 7 vols. 12mo. Paris, 1776; that of Ernesti, 2 vols. 8vo. Lips. 1777; and Barbou's 3 vols. 12mo. Paris, 1760. *Plin.* ep. 1, &c. *Tacit. Agr.* 9. *Hist.* 1. c. 1.—*Harles. Not. Lit. Rom.* 1. p. 396.—*Sax. Onom.* 1. p. 277.

TACO'LA, a city of India without the Ganges. *Ptol.*

TACOMP'SUS, or TACHOMP'SO, a town on the borders of Ægypt and Æthiopia. *Steph.*

TACU'BIS, a town of Lusitania. *Ptol.*—*Antonin.*

TA'DER, a river of Spain near New Carthage. It is now Rigo Seguro.

TA'DIUS P., a lieutenant of Verres in Sicily, originally a trader at Athens. *Cic. Verr.* 1. c. 39. l. 5. c. 25.

TA'DIUS QUIN'TUS, a relation of Verres who appeared against him at his trial. *Cic. Verr.* 1. c, 49.

TÆ'DIA, a prostitute at Rome, &c. *Juv.* 2. v. 49.

TÆDIF'ERA, a surname of Diana. She had a temple at Ægium in Achaias where she was represented in a statue covered from head to foot with a veil, with one hand extended, and with a torch in the other. *Paus.* 1. c. 31. The name is also applied to Ceres, either because she lighted torches in Ætna, when in pursuit of Proserpine, or because a torch was borne by her priests at the Eleusinian mysteries. *Ovid. Heroid.* 2. v. 42.

TÆN'ARUS, or TÆN'ARUM, now Matapan, a promontory of Laconia, the most southern part of Europe, where Neptune had a temple in the form of a grotto, with a statue. There was there a large and deep cavern, whence issued a black and unwholesome vapour, from which circumstance the poets have imagined that it was one of the entrances of hell, through which Hercules dragged Cerberus from the infernal regions. This fabulous tradition arose, according to Pausanias, from the continual resort of a large serpent near the cavern of Tænarus, whose bite was mortal. This serpent, as the geographer observes, was at last killed by Hercules, and carried to Eurystheus. The town of Tænarus was at the distance of about forty stadia from the promontory, and was famous for marble of a beautiful green colour, and for the excellent wool of its sheep. The town, as well as the promontory, received its name from Tænarius, a son of Neptune. There were some festivals celebrated there called Tænaria, in honour of Neptune, surnamed Tænarius. *Homer. Hymn. in Apoll.* 413.—*Paus.* 3. c. 14 & 25.—*Lucan.* 6. v. 648.—*Ovid. Met.* 2. v. 247. l. 10. v. 13 & 83.—*Apollod.* 2. c. 5.—*Mela*, 2. c. 3.—*Strab.* 8.—*Sch. Aristoph. in Ach.* 509.—*Seneca. in Herc. Fur.* 586, 663, &c. *in Œt.* 1061, &c.

TÆ'NIAS, a part of the lake Mareotis. *Strab.*

TÆNIOLON'GA, a town of Mauritania Tingitana. *Ptol.*

TAGABES'SA, a city of India within the Ganges. *Ptol.*

TA'GÆ, a people of Asia, on the Oxus. *Solin.* c. 52.——A city of Parthia. *Polyb.* 10. c. 26.

TAGAS'TE, a town of Numidia. It was the birthplace of St. Augustin. *Plin.* 5. c. 4.

TA'GES, a son of Genius, grandson of Jupiter, was the first who taught the 12 nations of the Etrurians the science of augury and divination. It is said that he was found by a Tuscan ploughman in the form of a clod, and that he assumed a human shape to instruct this nation, which became so celebrated for their knowledge of omens and incantations. *Cic. de Div.* 2. c. 23.—*Ovid. Met.* 15. v. 558.—*Lucan.* 1. v. 673.—*Stat.* 5. *Sylv.* 2. v. 1. —*Gyrald. H. D* 1.—*Arnob. adv. Gent.* 2.—*Marcellin.* 17 & 21.—*Columell. de Cult.* 345.

TAGO'NIUS, a river of Hispania Tarraconensis. *Plutarch.* It is now Rio de Henares.

TA'GUS, a river of Spain, which falls into the Atlantic after it has crossed Lusitania, or Portugal, and now bears the name of Tajo. The sands of the Tagus, according to the poets, were covered with gold. *Mela,* 3. c. 1.—*Ovid. Met.* 2. v. 251.—*Sil.* 4. v. 234.—*Lucan.* 7. v. 755.—*Martial,* 4. epigr. 55, &c.—*Strab.* 3.—*Juv.* 3. v. 55, sat. 14. v. 299.

TA'GUS, a Latin chief killed by Nisus. *Virg. Æn.* 9. v. 418.——A Trojan, killed by Turnus. *Id.* 12. v. 513.

TAI'RA, a female attendant of Cleopatra. *Plut. in Anton.*

TAIZ'ALUM or TEXA'LIUM, a promontory of Albion, in the east of Scotland. *Ptol.*

TALABRI'CA or TALABRI'GA, a city of Lusitania. *Ptol.*

TALAB'ROCA, a town of Hyrcania. *Steph.*

TALALA'TUM, a city of Africa Propria. *Antonin.*

TALAMI'NA, a town of Hispania Tarraconensis. *Ptol.* It is now La Vega.

TAL'ARA, a city of India within the Ganges. *Ptol.*

TALA'RIA, a city of the Syracusans. *Steph.*

TALA'SIUS, TALAS'SIUS, or TALAS'SIS. *Vid.* Thalasius.

TAL'AUS, a son of Bias and Pero, brother to Laodocus and Areius. He was father of Adrastus and of Eriphyle, by Lysimache, daughter of Abas. According to Hyginus, the name of his wife was Eurynome, daughter of Iphitus, or, according to Pausanias, Lysianassa, daughter of Polybus. He was one of the Argonauts. *Orph. Arg.* 142.—*Apollon.* 1. v. 118.—*Hygin.* fab. 69 & 71.—*Paus.* 2. c. 6 & 21.—*Flacc.* 1. v. 358.—*Apollod.* 1. c. 9. 1. 3. c. 6.

TALA'YRA, the sister of Phœbe. She is also called Hilaira. *Vid.* Phœbe.

TALBEN'DA, a city of Pamphylia. *Ptol.*

TAL'CA or TAL'GA, a fertile island of the Caspian Sea. *Ptol.*—*Mela,* 3. l. 6. It is called Tazata by *Pliny,* 6. c. 17., and is now Alea.

TALCI'NUM, now Talsini, an inland town of Corsica. *Ptol.*

TAL'ETUM, a temple sacred to the sun on mount Taygetus in Laconia. Horses were generally offered there for sacrifice. *Paus.* 3.

TALI'A, a city of Upper Mœsia. *Antonin.*

TA'LIUS GEM'INUS, the accuser of Fabricius Veiento. *Tac. Ann.* 14. c. 50. *Muretus* reads T. Allius.

TAL'NA, the name of one of the judges at the trial of Clodius, for violating the solemnities of Bona Dea. *Cic. Att.* 1. ep. 6.——A philologist rejected in his offers of marriage to Cornificia, on account of his small fortune. *Cic.* 13. *Att.* 29.

TAL'NUS, a Rutulian killed by Æneas. *Virg. Æn.* 12. v. 513.

TA'LOS, a youth, son of the sister of Dædalus, who invented the saw, compasses, and other mechanical instruments. His uncle became jealous of his growing fame, and murdered him privately; or, according to others, he threw him down from the citadel of Athens. Talus was changed into a partridge by the gods. He is also called Calus, Acalus, Perdix, and Taliris. *Apollod.* 3. c. 1.—*Paus.* 1. c. 21.—*Ovid. Met.* 8. v. 237.—*Hygin.* fab. 39 & 244.—*Servius ad Virg. Æn.* 6. v. 14. *G.* 1. v. 143.—*Tzetzes, Chil.* l. c. 1. 9 & 11. c. 394.—*Suidas.*—*Schol. Euripid. ad Orest.* 1650.——A son of Œnopion. *Paus.* 7. c. 4.——A son of Cres, the founder of the Cretan nation. *Id.* 8. c. 53.——A friend of Æneas killed by Turnus. *Virg. Æn.* 12. v. 513.

TALTHYB'IUS, a herald in the Grecian camp during the Trojan war, the particular minister and friend of Agamemnon. He brought away Briseis from the tent of Achilles by order of his master. Talthybius died at Ægium in Achaia, where his monument was still to be seen in the age of Pausanias, though the people of Sparta boasted that his remains had been buried in their territory. The inhabitants of both these cities annually paid him funeral honors. *Homer. Il.* 1. v. 320, &c.—*Paus.* 7. c. 23.—*Ovid. Heroid.* 3. v. 9.

TA'LY, a river of Ægypt, flowing into the sea through the Bolbitic mouth of the Nile. *Ptol.*—*Salmas. ad Solin.*.

TAM'ALE, a city, with a harbour and promontory of India without the Ganges. *Salmas. ad Solin.* p. 997.—*Voss. in Melam.*

TAM'ARE, a town of the Damnonii in Albion. *Ptol.* According to *Camden* it was Tamerton.

TAM'ARIS or TAM'ARA, a river of the Callaici in Spain. *Ptol.* It is now the Tamar.

TAM'ARUS, a mountain of Epirus, called also Tmarus and Tomarus. *Strab.*

TAMA'SEA a beautiful plain of Cyprus, sacred to the goddess of beauty. It was in this place that Venus gathered the golden apples with which Hippomanes was enabled to overtake Atalanta. *Ovid. Met.* 10. v. 644.—*Plin.* 5. c. 31.—*Strab.* 14. —*Steph. Byz.*

TAMASIDA'VA, a city of Lower Mœsia. *Ptol.*

TAM'ASIS, a city of India within the Ganges. *Id.*

TAM'ESA, or TAM'ESIS, a river of Britain, now the Thames. *Cæs. G.* 5. c. 11.

TAMIA'THIS, a city of Ægypt. *Steph.* It is now Damietta.

TAM'NA, a city of Arabia. *Steph.*

TAM'NUM, a town of Aquitania, on the Garumna. *Antonin.* It is now Talmont.

TA'MOS, a native of Memphis, made governor of Ionia, by young Cyrus. After the death of Cyrus. Tamos fled into Ægypt, where he was murdered on account of his immense treasures. *Diod.* 14. —*Thucyd.* 8.

TA'MOS, a promontory of India near the Ganges. *Mela,* 3. c. 7. & *Voss. in loc.*

TAM'PIUS, a Roman historian. *Suet in Vitâ Julii.* c. 77. Some read T. Ampius. *Casaubon in loc.*

TAM'UDA, a town of Mauritania Tingitana, with a river of the same name. *Mela,* 1. c. 5.

TAMU'SIDA, an inland city of Mauritania Tingitana. *Ptol.*

TAM'YNÆ, a city of Eretria. *Strab.* Jupiter was surnamed Tamynæus from this place. *Steph.*

TAMYR'ACA, a town of European Sarmatia. *Strab.*

TAM'YRAS, a river of Phœnicia, between Tyre and Sidon. It is called Damyras by *Polybius,* 5. c. 68., Nagoras or Magoras by *Pliny,* 5. c. 20., and is now Damor.

TAM'YRIS. *Vid.* Thomyris.

TAN'AGRA, or TANA'GRA, a town of Bœotia, near the Euripus, between the Asopus and Thermodon, famous for fighting cocks. It was founded by Pœmandros, a son of Chæresilaus, the son of Jasius, who married Tanagra. Corinna was a native of Tanagra. *Strab.* 9.—*Paus.* 9. c. 20 & 22.—*Ælian. V.H.* 13. v. 25.—*Plin.* 4. c. 7.—*Stat. Theb.* 7. v. 254. l. 9. v. 745.

TAN'AGRA, or TANA'GRA, a nymph, daughter of Æolus, or according to others of Asopus. She married Pœmandros, who gave her name to a city which he founded in Bœotia. Tanagra lived to a great old age, when she received the name of Graia, by which also the town was for some time known. *Homer. Il.* 2. en. v. 5.—*Paus.* 9. c. 20.

TAN'AGRUS or TAN'AGER, now Negro, a river of Lucania in Italy, remarkable for its cascades and the beautiful meanders of its streams, through a fine picturesque country. *Virg. G.* 3. v. 151. & *Servius loco.*

TAN'AIS, a Rutulian, killed by Æneas. *Virg. Æn.* 12. v. 513.——A eunuch, freed-man to Mæcenas. *Horat.* 1. sat. 1. v. 105.

TAN'AIS, a river of Scythia, now the Don, which divides Europe from Asia, and falls into the Palus Mæotis after a rapid course, and after it has received the additional streams of many small rivulets. A town at its mouth bore the same name. *Mela,* 1. c. 19.—*Strab.* 11 & 16.—*Curt.* 6. c. 2.—*Lucan.* 3. v. 273. l. 8. v. 319. l. 9. v. 414 & 751.—*Propert.* 2. el. 23. v. 54.—*Macrob. in Som. Scip.* 2. c. 7.

TAN'AIS, a deity among the Persians and Armenians, who patronised slaves, and is supposed to have been the same as Venus. The daughters of the noblest Persians and Armenians prostituted themselves in honor of this deity, and were received with greater regard and affection by their suitors. Artaxerxes, the son of Darius, was the first who raised statues to Tanais, in the different provinces of his empire, and taught his subjects to pay her divine honors. *Strab.* 11.—*Curt.* 5. c. 1.—*Clem. Alex. in Adm. ad Gent.*

TAN'AQUIL, called also Caia Cæcilia, was the wife of Tarquin the 5th king of Rome. She was a native of Tarquinia, where she married Lucumon, better known by the name of Tarquin, which he assumed after he had come to Rome at the request of his wife, whose knowledge of augury promised him something uncommon. Her expectations were not frustrated: her husband was raised to the throne, and she shared with him the honors of royalty. After the murder of Tarquin, Tanaquil raised her son-in-law Servius Tullius to the throne, and ensured him the succession. She distinguished herself by her liberality; and the Romans in succeeding ages had such a veneration for her character, that the embroidery which she had made, her girdle, as also the robe of her son-in-law, which she had worked with her own hands, were preserved with the greatest sanctity. Juvenal bestows the appellation of Tanaquil on all such women as were imperious, and had the command of their husbands. *Liv.* 1. c. 34, &c.—*Dionys. Hal.* 3. c. 59.—*Flor.* 1. c. 5 & 8.—*Ital.* 13. v. 818.—*Eutrop.* 1. c. 7.—*Plin.* 33. c. 1 & 3. l. 35. c. 12.—*Aug. de Civ. D.* 3. c. 15.—*Juv.* 6. v. 566. —*Auson.* ep. 23, 31.

TAN'ARUS, a river of Italy. It is now Tanaro according to *Leander.*

TA'NAS, a river of Numidia. *Sallust. J.* 90.

TAN'ATIS, a town of Upper Mœsia on the Danube. *Ptol.* It is called Terriana by *Niger.*

TANE'TUM, or TANNE'TUM, a town of Italy, now Tonedo, in the duchy of Modena. *Anton.*—*Ptol.*

TANE'TUS, a small island of Albion. *Ptolemy* calls it Tolianis. It is now Thanet.

TANFA'NÆ LU'CUS, a sacred grove in Germany, in the country of the Marsi, between the Ems and Lippe. *Tacit. Ann.* 1. c. 51.

TA'NIS, a city of Ægypt, on one of the eastern mouths of the Nile. *Plin.* 5. c. 9.

TA'NOS, or TA'NUS, a city of Crete. *Steph.*

TANTAL'IDES, a patronymic applied to the descendants of Tantalus, such as Niobe, Hermione, &c.—Agamemnon and Menelaus, as grandsons of Tantalus, are called *Tantalidæ fratres. Ovid. Heroid.* 8. v. 45 & 122.

TAN'TALUS, a king of Lydia, son of Jupiter, by a nymph called Pluto. He was father of Niobe, Pelops, &c. by Dione, one of the Atlantides, called by some Euryanassa. Tantalus is represented by the poets as punished in hell, with an insatiable thirst, and placed up to the chin in the midst of a pool of water, which, however, flowed away as soon as he attempted to taste it. There hung also above his head, a bough, richly loaded with delicious fruit; which, as soon as he attempted to seize it, was carried away from his reach by a sudden blast of wind. According to some mythologists, his punishment was to sit under a huge stone hung at some distance over his head, and as it seemed every moment ready to fall, he was kept under continual alarms and never-ceasing fears. The causes of this eternal punishment are variously explained. Some declare that it was inflicted upon him because he stole a favorite dog, which Jupiter had entrusted to his care to keep his temple in Crete. Others say that he stole away the nectar and ambrosia from the tables of the gods when he was admitted into the assemblies of heaven, and that he gave it to mortals on earth. Others maintain, this proceeded from his cruelty and impiety in killing his son Pelops, and in serving up his limbs as food before the gods, whose divinity and power he wished to try, when they had stopped at his house as they passed over Phrygia. There are also others who impute it to his lasciviousness in carrying away Ganymedes to gratify the most unnatural of passions. *Pindar. Olymp.* 1.—*Homer. Odyss.* 11. v. 581.—*Cic. Tusc.* l. c. 5. l. 4. c. 16.—*Eurip. in Iphig. Taur.* 386. *& in Orest.*—*Paus.* 2. c. 22.—*Plut. in Par.*—*Ovid. Am.* 2. el. 2. v. 43. *Met.* 6. v. 404.—*Propert.* 2. el. 1. v. 66.—*Horat.* 1. sat. 1. v. 68.—*Tzetzes. in Chil.* 4. c. 141. *Ch.* 5. c. 10.—*Phanocles apud Oros.* 1. c. 12.—*Hygin.* fab. 82 & 83.—*Seneca in Herc. Fur.* 752 *In Thy.* 76 & 144.—*Claudian. de Rap. Pr.* 2, v. 336.—*Lactant. ad Theb.* 1. v. 230. l. 7. v. 51.——A son of Thyestes, the first husband of Clytæmnestra. *Paus.* 2. c. 18 & 22.—*Hygin.* fab. 88.—*Eurip. in Iphig. Aul.* 5. sc. 3.——One of Niobe's children. *Ovid. Met.* 6. fab. 6.

TAN'TALUS, a mountain of Lesbus. *Steph.*

TA'NUS, a river of Peloponnesus flowing through Argolis. *Paus.* 3. *Euripides* calls it Tanaus.

TANU'SIUS GEM'INUS, a Latin historian intimate with Cicero. *Suet. Cæs.* 9,—*Seneca.* ep. 93.

TA'OCE, a city of Persia. *Ptol.*—*Dionys.* v. 1060.

TAPANI'TÆ, a people of Lower Libya. *Ptol.*—*Salmas. ad Solin.* p. 1019.

TA'PE, a royal city of Hyrcania, on the shores of the Caspian Sea. *Strab.*

TA'PHIÆ, islands in the Ionian Sea, between Achaia and Leucadia. They were also called Teleboides. They received these names from Taphius and Telebous, the sons of Neptune who reigned there. The Taphians made war against Electryon king of Mycenæ, and killed all his sons, upon which the monarch promised his kingdom and his daughter in marriage to whoever could avenge the death of his children upon the Taphians. This was effected by Amphitryon with the assistance of his friend Cephalus, the husband of Procris, whom he seated on the throne of the conquered nation, and obtained the promised reward. The Taphians were expert sailors, but too fond of plunder and piratical excursions. *Homer. Odyss.* l. v. 181 & 419. l. 15. v. 426.—*Apollod.* 2. c. 4.—*Plin.* 4. c. 12.—*Strab.* 10.—*Tzetzes ad Lyc.* 932.

TA'PHIUS, a son of Neptune by Hippothoë the daughter of Nestor. He was king of the Taphiæ, to which he gave his name, and he became father of Pterelaus by a nymph. *Strab.* 10.—*Apollod.* 2. c. 4.—*Tzetz. ad Lyc.* 932.

TA'PHIUS or TAPHIAS'SUS, a mountain of Locris on the confines of Ætolia. *Strab.*—*Plin.* 4. c. 2.

TAPHIU'SA, a place near Leucas where a stone is found called Taphiusius. *Plin.* 36. c. 21.

TAPHIUS'SA, a city of Cephallenia, formerly called Taphos. *Steph.*

TA'PHRA, a city of Africa Minor. It is called Taphrura by *Ptolemy.*

TA'PHRÆ, a town on the isthmus of the Taurica Chersonesus, now Precop. *Mela,* 2. c. 1.—*Plin.* 4. c. 12.

TA'PHRON, a city of Arabia Felix. *Marcellinus.*

TA'PHROS or TA'PHRÆ, the strait between Corsica and Sardinia, now Bonifacio.

TAPOSI'RIS or TAPHOSI'RIS, a town of Ægypt. *Plut.*

TAPROB'ANE, an island of the Indian Ocean, now called Ceylon. Its inhabitants were very rich and lived to a great age. Their country was visited by two summers and two winters. Hercules was their chief divinity, and as the sovereignty was elective and only from among unmarried men, the monarch was immediately deposed if he became a father. *Ptol.* 6.—*Strab.* 2.—*Ovid. ex Pont.* 8. el. 5. v. 80.—*Servius ad Virg. G.* 1. v. 48.—*Solin.* 66.—*Tzetzes. Chil.* 8. c. 213.—*Dionys. Per.* 777.

TAP'SACUM, a town of Cyrenaica. *Plin.* 5. c. 5.

TAP'SUS, a maritime town of Africa. *Sil. It.* 3. ——A small and lowly situated peninsula on the eastern coast of Sicily. *Virg. Æn.* 3. v. 689.

TAP'SUS, a man of Cyzicus, killed by Pollux. *V. Flacc.* 2. v. 191.

TAP'YRI or TAPU'RI, a people near Hyrcania. *Dio. Perieg.*

TARACH'IE, a small island near Corcyra. *Plin.* 4. c. 12.

TARAN'DRUS, a region of Phrygia. *Steph.*

TAR'ANIS, a name of Jupiter among the Gauls, to whom human sacrifices were offered. *Lucan.* 1, v. 446.

TARAN'TUS, a city of Bithynia, whence Jupiter was surnamed Taranteus. *Steph.*

TARA'RIUM, a town of Bithynia, on the shores of the Propontis. *Ptol.*

TA'RAS, a son of Neptune or Hercules according some, who built Tarentum, as some suppose. He had a statue at Delphi, erected there by the Tarentines. *Paus.* 10. c. 10 & 13.

TA'RAS, a river of Italy near Tarentum. *Steph.*—*Appian.*—*Paus. in Phoc.*

TARAS'CO, a town of Gaul, now Tarascon in Provence.

TARAXIP'PUS, a deity, son of Neptune, worshipped at Elis. His statue was placed near the race-ground, and his protection was implored, that no harm might happen to the horses during the games. *Paus.* 6. c. 20. l. 10. c. 37.—*Dionys. Hal.* 2.—*Gyrald. H. D.* 1.

TARBEL'LI, a people of Gaul, at the foot of the Pyrenees, which from thence are sometimes called Tarbellæ. *Tibul.* 1. el. 7. v. 13.—*Lucan.* 4. v. 121.—*Cæs. G.* 3. c. 27.

TARCHE'TIUS, an impious king of Alba. *Plut. in Rom.*

TAR'CHIA, a city of Sicily. *Steph.*

TAR'CHON, an Etrurian chief, who assisted Æneas against the Rutuli. Some suppose that he founded Mantua. *Virg. Æn.* 8. v. 603. l. 10. v. 153 & 290. l. 11. v. 184 & 729.—*Servius ad Virg. loc.* ——A prince of Cilicia. *Lucan.* 9. v. 219.

TARCHONDIM'OTUS, a prince of Cilicia in the age of Cicero, who visited him. *Cic. Fam.* 15. ep. 1. —*Lucan.* 11. v. 219.

TARCHO'NIUM, a city of Tyrrhenia, founded by Telephus, son of Tarchon. *Steph.*

TARELE'I, a people of Æthiopia, near the source of the Niger. *Plin.* 5. c. 8.

TAREN'TUM, TAREN'TUS, or **TA'RAS**, a town of Calabria, situate on a bay of the same name, near the mouth of the river Galesus. It was founded, or rather repaired, by a Lacedæmonian colony, about 707 years before Christ, under the conduct of Phalanthus. Long independent, it maintained its superiority over 13 tributary cities; and could once arm 100,000 foot, and 3000 horse. The people of Tarentum were very indolent, and as they were easily supplied with all necessaries as well as luxuries from Greece, they gave themselves up to voluptuousness, so that "the delights of Tarentum" became proverbial. The war which they supported against the Romans, with the assistance of Pyrrhus, king of Epirus, and which has been called the Tarentine war, is greatly celebrated in history. This war, which had been undertaken by the Romans, B.C. 281, to avenge the insults the Tarentines had offered to their ships when near their harbours, was terminated after ten years; 30,000 prisoners were taken, and Tarentum became subject to Rome. The government of Tarentum was democratical; there were, however, some monarchs who reigned there. It was for some time the residence of Pythagoras, who inspired the citizens with the love of virtue, and rendered them superior to their neighbours in the cabinet as well as in the field of battle. The large, beautiful and capacious harbour of Tarentum is greatly commended by ancient historians. Tarentum, now called Tarento, is inhabited by about 18,000 souls, who still maintain the character of their forefathers for idleness and effeminacy, and live chiefly by fishing. *Flor.* 1. c. 18.—*Val. Max.* 2. c. 2.—*Plut. in Pyr.*—*Plin.* 8. c. 6. l. 15. c. 10. l. 34. c. 7.—*Liv.* 12. c. 13, &c.—*Mela*, 2. c. 4.—*Strab.* 6.—*Horat.* 1. ep. 7. v. 45.—*Ælian. V.H.* 5. c. 20.—*Auct. de Vir. Ill.* 35.—*Macrob.* 2. c. 14. —*Aug. de Civ. D.* 3. c. 17.—*Oros.* 4. c. 1.—*Servius. ad Virg. G.* 4. v. 126. *Æn.* 3. v. 551. l. 6. v. 773.—*Lucan.* 5. v. 376.—*Stat.* 1. *Sylv.* 1. v. 105.

TARGA'RUM, a town of Africa Propria. *Ptol.*

TARICHE'A, TARICH'EÆ, or **TARICHÆ'Æ**, a fortified town of Judæa. *Cic. ad Div.* 12. c. 11. Several towns on the coast of Ægypt bore this name from their *pickling* fish. *Herodot.* 2. c. 15, &c.

TARIO'NA, a fortified place of Liburnia. It is called Tuina by *Niger. Pliny*, 3. c. calls the inhabitants Tariotæ.

TAR'NA, TAR'NE, or **TAR'NÆ**, a town mentioned by *Homer. Il.* 5.——A fountain of Lydia, near Tmolus. *Strab.*——A river of Aquitania. *Plin.* 4. c. 19. It is now le Tarn.

TARODU'NUM, a town of the Alemanni. *Ptol.* It is now Fribourg.

TAR'PA SPU'RIUS MÆTIUS, a critic at Rome in the age of Augustus. He was appointed with four others in the temple of Apollo, to examine the merit of every poetical composition, which was to be deposited in the temple of the Muses. In this office he acted with great impartiality, though many taxed him with want of candor. All the pieces that were represented on the Roman stage had previously received his approbation. *Horat.* 1. sat. 10. v. 38. *A.P.* 387 *& Scholiast.*

TARPE'IA, the daughter of Tarpeius, the governor of the citadel of Rome, promised to open the gates of the city to the Sabines, provided they gave her their golden bracelets, or, as she expressed it, what they carried on their left hands. Tatius, the king of the Sabines consented, and as he entered the gates, to punish her perfidy, he threw not only his bracelet, but his shield upon Tarpeia. His followers imitated his example, and Tarpeia was crushed under the weight of the bracelets and shields of the Sabine army. She was buried in the Capitol, which from her was called the Tarpeian rock, and there afterwards many of the Roman malefactors were thrown down a deep precipice. *Plut. in Rom.*—*Ovid. Fast.* 1. v. 261. *Amor.* 1. el. 10. v. 50 —*Liv.* 1. c. 11.—*Propert.* 4. el. 4.——A vestal virgin in the reign of Numa. ——One of the warlike female attendants of Camilla in the Rutulian war. *Virg. Æn.* 11. v. 656.

TARPE'IA LEX was enacted A.U.C. 269, by Sp. Tarpeius, to empower all the magistrates to lay fines on offenders. This power before belonged to the consuls only. The fine was not to exceed two sheep and thirty oxen.

TARPE'IUS SP., the governor of the citadel of Rome, under Romulus. His descendants were called Montani and Capitolini.

TARPE'IUS MONS, a hill at Rome about eighty feet in perpendicular height, whence the Romans threw down their condemned criminals. It received its name from Tarpeia, who was buried there, and is the same as the Capitoline hill. *Liv.* 6. c. 20.—*Lucan.* 7. v. 758.—*Virg. Æn.* 8. v. 347 & 652.

TAR'PHA, a city of the Locri Epicnemidii. *Steph.* —*Hom. in Catal.*

TAR'PHARA, a city of Arabia. *Steph.*

TARQUIN'IA, a daughter of Tarquinius Priscus, who married Servius Tullius. When her husband was murdered by Tarquinius Superbus, she privately conveyed away his body by night, and buried it. This preyed upon her mind, and the following night she died. Some have attributed her death to excess of grief, or suicide, while others, perhaps more justly, have suspected Tullia, the wife of young Tarquin of the murder.——A vestal virgin, who, as some suppose, gave the Roman people a large piece of land, which was afterwards called the Campus Martius.

TARQUIN'II, now Turchina, a town of Etruria, built by Tarchon, who assisted Æneas against Turnus. Tarquinius Priscus was born and edu-ted there, and he made it a Roman colony when he ascended the throne. *Strab.* 5.—*Plin.* 2. c. 95. —*Liv.* 1. c. 34. l. 27. c. 4.

TARQUIN'IUS the First, surnamed *Priscus*, and the fifth king of Rome, was son of Demaratus, a native of Greece. His first name was Lucumon, but this he changed when by the advice of his his wife Tanaquil he had come to Rome. He called himself Lucius, and assumed the surname of Tarquinius, because born in the town of Tarquinii in Etruria. At Rome he distinguished himself so much by his liberality and engaging manners, that Ancus Martius, the reigning monarch, nominated him at his death, the guardian of his children. This was insufficient to gratify the ambition of Tarquin; the princes were young, and an artful oration delivered to the people immediately transferred the crown of the deceased monarch to the head of Lucumon. The people had every reason to be satisfied with their choice. Tarquin reigned with moderation and popularity. He increased the senate and made himself friends by electing 100 new senators from the plebeians, whom he distinguished by the appellation of *Patres minorum gentium*, from those of the patrician body, who were called *Patres majorum gentium*. The glory of the Roman arms, which was supported with so much dignity by the former monarchs was not neglected in this reign, and Tarquin showed that he possessed valour and military prudence in the victories which he obtained over the united forces of the Latins and Sabines, and in the conquest of the twelve nations of Etruria. He repaired, in the time of peace, the walls of the capital, the public places were adorned with elegant buildings, and useful ornaments, and many centuries after, such as were spectators of the stately mansions and golden palaces of Nero, viewed with more admiration and greater pleasure the more simple though less magnificent edifices of Tarquin. He laid the foundations of the Capitol, and to the industry and the public spirit of this monarch, the Romans were indebted for their aqueducts and subterraneous sewers, which supplied the city with fresh and wholesome water, and removed all the filth and ordure, which in a great capital too often breed pestilence and diseases. Tarquin was the first who introduced among the Romans the custom of canvassing for offices of trust and honor; he distinguished the monarch, the senators, and other inferior magistrates with particular robes and ornaments, with ivory chairs at spectacles, and the hatchets carried before the public magistrates, were by his order surrounded with bundles of sticks, to strike more terror and to be viewed with greater reverence. Tarquin was assassinated by the two sons of his predecessor, in the 80th year of his age, 38 of which he had sat on the throne, 578 years before Christ. *Dionys. Hal.* 3. c. 59.—*Val. Max.* 1. c. 4. l. 3. c. 2.—*Flor.* 1. c. 5, &c.—*Liv.* 1. c. 31.—*Virg. Æn.* 6. v. 817.—*Eutrop.* 1. c. 7.—*Auct. de Vir.* 6.—*Lactant.* 2. c. 1 & 7.

TARQUIN'IUS the Second, surnamed *Superbus*, from his pride and insolence, was grandson of Tarquinius Priscus. He ascended the throne of Rome after his father-in-law Servius Tullius, and was the seventh and last king of Rome. He married Tullia the daughter of Tullius, and it was at her instigation that he murdered his father-in-law, and seized the kingdom. The crown which he had obtained with violence, he endeavoured to keep by a continuation of tyranny. Unlike his royal predecessors, he paid no regard to the decisions of the senate, or the approbation of the public assemblies, and by wishing to disregard both, he incurred the jealousy of the one and the odium of the other. The public treasury was soon exhausted by the continual extravagance of Tarquin, and to silence the murmurs of his subjects, he resolved to call their attention to war. He was successful in his military operations, as the neighbouring cities submitted; but while the siege of Ardea was continued, the wantonness of the son of Tarquin at Rome, for ever stopped the progress of his arms; and the Romans, whom a series of barbarity and oppression had hitherto not provoked, no sooner saw the virtuous Lucretia stab herself, not to survive the loss of her honor, (*Vid.* Lucretia,) than the whole city and camp arose with indignation against the monarch. The gates of Rome were shut against him, and Tarquin was for ever banished from his throne in the year of Rome 244. Unable to find support from even one of his subjects, Tarquin retired among the Etrurians, who attempted in vain to replace him on his throne. The republican government was established at Rome, and all Italy refused any longer to support the cause of an exiled monarch against a nation, who heard the name of Tarquin, of king, and of tyrant, mentioned with equal horror and indignation. Tarquin died in the 90th year of his age, about fourteen years after his expulsion from Rome. He had reigned about 25 years. Though Tarquin appeared so odious among the Romans, his reign was not without its share of glory. His conquests were numerous; to beautify the buildings and porticos of Rome was his wish, and with great magnificence and care he finished the Capitol, which his predecessor of the same name had begun. He also bought the Sybilline books which the Romans consulted with such religious solemnity. *Vid.* Sibyllæ. *Cic. pro Rab. & Tusc.* 3. c. 27.—*Liv.* 1. c. 46, &c.—*Dionys. Hal.* 4. c. 48, &c.—*Flor.* 1. c. 7 & 8.—*Plin.* 8. c. 41.—*Plut.*—*Val. Max.* 9. c. 11.—*Ovid. Fast.* 2. v. 687.—*Virg. Æn.* 6. v. 817.—*Eutrop.*

TARQUIN'IUS COLLATI'NUS, one of the relations of Tarquin the proud, who married Lucretia. *Vid.* Collatinus.

TARQUIN'IUS SEX'TUS, the eldest of the sons of Tarquin the Proud, rendered himself well known by a variety of adventures. When his father besieged Gabii, young Tarquin publicly declared that he was at variance with the monarch, and the report was the more easily believed when he came before Gabii with his body all mangled and bloody with stripes. This was an agreement between the father and the son, and Tarquin had no sooner declared that this proceeded from the tyranny and oppression of his father, than the people of Gabii entrusted him with the command of their armies, fully convinced that Rome could never have a more inveterate enemy. When he had thus succeeded, he dispatched a private messenger to his father, but the monarch gave no answer to be returned to his son. Sextus enquired more particularly about his father, and when he heard from the messenger that when the message was delivered, Tarquin cut off with a stick the tallest poppies in his garden, the son followed the example by putting to death the most noble and powerful citizens of Gabii. The town soon fell into the hands of the Romans. The violence which some time after Tarquinius offered to Lucretia, was the cause of his father's exile, and the total expulsion of his family from Rome. *Vid.* Lucretia. Sextus was at last killed, bravely fighting in a battle during the war which the Latins sustained against Rome in attempting to re-establish the Tarquins on their throne. *Ovid. Fast.*—*Liv.*

TARQUIN'IUS, a Roman senator who was accessary to Catilline's conspiracy, but perhaps the word should be more properly Tarquitius, as the very name of Tarquin was proscribed at Rome. *Sall. Cat.* 48. The English form is Tarquin.

TARQUIT'IUS CRES'CENS, a centurion under Cæsennius Pætus. *Tac. Ann.* 15. c. 11.

TARQUIT'IUS PRIS'CUS, an officer in Africa, who accused the pro-consul Statilius Taurus. *Id.* 12. c. 59. l. 14. c. 46.

TARQUIT'IUS LU'CIUS, a master of the horse at Rome. *Liv.* 3. c. 27.

TARQUIT'IUS, a writer on the augury of the Etrurian nation. *Plin. in Cat. Auct.*

TAR'QUITUS, a son of Faunus and Dryope, who assisted Turnus against Æneas. He was killed by Æneas. *Virg. Æn.* 10. v. 550.

TARRABE'NI, a people of Corsica. *Ptol.* According to *Leander* their town is now Bastilica, but it is more probably Carabeni.

TARRACI'NA, a town of the Volsci, in Latium, between Rome and Neapolis. It was also called Anxur, because Jupiter the infant was worshipped there under that name, which signifies beardless. *Liv.* 4. c. 29.—*Strab.* 5.—*Mela*, 2 c. 4.—*Festus de V. Sig.*—*Virg. Æn.* 7. v. 699. l. 10. v. 545.—*Servius ad Æn.* 8. v. 564.

TAR'RACO, now Tarragona, a city of Spain, situate on the shores of the Mediterranean, founded by the two Scipios, who planted a Roman colony there. The province of which it was the capital was called Tarraconensis, and was famous for its wines. Hispania Tarraconensis, which was also called by the Romans Hispania Citerior, was bounded on the east by the Mediterranean, by the ocean on the west, by the Pyrenean mountains and the sea of the Cantabri on the north, and by Lusitania and Bætica on the south. *Martial.* 10. epigr. 104. l. 13. epigr. 118.—*Mela*, 2. c. 6.—*Sil.* 3. v. 369. l. 15. v. 177.

TAR'RAGA, a colony and town of Hispania Citerior. *Plin.* 3. c. 3.

TAR'RAS, a city of Sardinia. It is called Tharros by *Antoninus*.

TAR'RHA, a city of Lydia, whence Apollo was surnamed Tarrhæus. *Steph.*——A city near Caucasus. a colony of the Cretans. *Steph.*

TARRU'BIUS LU'CIUS, a mathematician. *Plut. Rom.*—*Solin.* c. 2.

TARRU'TIUS. *Vid.* Acca Laurentia.

TAR'SA, a Thracian who rebelled under Tiberius, &c. *Tacit. Ann.* 4. c. 50.

TARSAT'ICA or TARSAT'ICUM, a town of Liburnia. *Antonin*

TARSE'A, a city of Bithynia, called also Tarsus. *Steph.*

TARSEI'ON, a town of Spain near the columns of Hercules. It is called Carteia by other authors.

TAR'SIUM, a town of Lower Pannonia. *Ptol.*

TAR'SIUS, a river of Troas. *Strab.*

TARSU'RAS, a river of Colchis. *Arrian.*

TAR'SUS, now Terassa, a town of Cilicia, on the Cydnus, founded by Triptolemus and a colony of Argives, or, as others say, by Sardanapalus, or by Perseus. Tarsus was celebrated for the great men it produced, particularly for the birth of Antipater, Archidamus, the Athenodori, and St. Paul. It was once the rival of Alexandria and Athens in literature and the study of the polite arts. The people of Tarsus wished to ingratiate themselves into the favor of J. Cæsar by giving the name of Juliopolis to their city, but it was soon lost. *Lucan.* 3. v. 225.—*Mela*, 1. c. 13.—*Strab.* 14.

TAR'TARUS (pl. *a*, -*orum*), one of the regions of hell, where, according to the ancients, the most impious and guilty among mankind were punished. It was surrounded with a brazen wall, and its entrance was continually hidden from the sight by a cloud of darkness, which is represented three times more gloomy than the obscurest night. According to Hesiod it was a separate prison, at a greater distance from the earth than the earth is from the heavens. Virgil says it was surrounded by three impenetrable walls, and by the impetuous and burning streams of the river Phlegethon. The entrance was by a large and lofty tower, the gates of which were supported by columns of adamant, which neither gods nor men could open. In Tartarus, according to Virgil, were punished such as had been disobedient to their parents, traitors, adulterers, faithless ministers, and such as had undertaken unjust and cruel wars, or had betrayed their friends for the sake of money. It was also the place where Ixion, Tityus, the Danaides, Tantalus, Sisyphus, &c. were punished, according to Ovid. *Hesiod. Theog.* v. 720.—*Sil.* 13. v. 591.—*Virg. Æn.* 6.—*Homer. Odyss.* 11.—*Ovid. Met.* 4. fab. 13.

TAR'TARUS, a small river of Italy, near Verona. *Tacit. H.* 3. c. 9.

TARTES'SUS, a town in Spain near the columns of Hercules, on the Mediterranean. Some suppose that it was afterwards called Carteia, and it was better known by the name of Gades, when Hercules had set up his columns on the extremities of Spain and Africa. There was also a town called Tartessus, in a small island formed by a river of the same name, near Gades in Iberia. Tartessus has been called the most distant town in the extremities of Spain, by the Romans, as also the place where the poets imagined the Sun unharnessed his tired horses. *Sil.* 3. v. 399 & 411. l. 10. v. 538.—*Mela*, 2. c. 6.—*Paus.* 6. c. 19.—*Ovid. Met.* 14. v. 416.—*Strab.* 3.—*Martial.* 3 ep. 28. l. 8. epigr. 27. l. 9. epigr. 62.

TARUA'NA, a town of Gaul now Terrouen, in Artois.

TAR'UDA, a city of Mauritania Cæsariensis *Ptol.*

TARUN'TIUS, L., a mathematician who flourished 61 years B.C., and was well skilled in divination. *Cic. ad Div.* 2. c. 47.—*Plut. Rom.*

TA'RUS, a river of Gaul, falling into the Po. *Plin.* 3. c. 16. It is called Taro by *Leander.*

TARUSA'TES, a people of Gaul, now Tursan. *Cæs. G.* 3. c. 23 & 27.

TARUS'CUM, a town of Gaul. *Ptol.*

TARVIS'IUM, a town of Italy, now Treviso, in the Venetian States.

TASACO'RA, a city of Mauritania Cæsariensis. *Antonin.*

TASAR'TA, a town of Africa Propria. *Id.*

TASCODUNITA'RI, a people of Occitania. *Plin.* 3. c. 4.

TASCUTI'NI, a people of Pontus, near Colchis. *Diod. Sic.* l. 14.

TASGE'TIUS CARNU'TUS, a prince of Gaul, assassinated in the age of Cæsar. *Cæs. B. G.* 5. c. 25.

TAS'TACHE, a city of Parthia. *Ptol.*

TATIA'NUS, one of the Greek fathers, A.D. 172. Of all his works the only one which remains is his "Oratio adversus Græcos;" of this there have been several editions, but the best is that of Worth, Oxon. 1700. *Fabr. B. Gr.* 5. c. 1.—*Sax. Onom.* 1. p. 320. The English form is Tatian.

TATIEN'SES, a name given to one of the tribes of the Roman people by Romulus, in honor of Tatius, king of the Sabines. The Tatienses, who were partly the ancient subjects of the king of the Sabines, lived on mounts Capitolinus and Quirinalis.

TA'TIUS TI'TUS, king of Cures among the Sabines, made war against the Romans after the rape of the Sabines. The gates of the city were betrayed into his hands by Tarpeia, and the army of the Sabines advanced as far as the Roman forum, where a bloody battle was fought. The cries of the Sabine virgins at last stopped the fury of the combatants, and an agreement was made between the two nations. Tatius consented to leave his ancient possessions, and, with his subjects of Cures, to come and live in Rome, which, as stipulated, was permitted still to bear the name of its founder, whilst the inhabitants adopted the name of Quirites in compliment to the new citizens. After he had for six years shared the royal authority with Romulus, in the greatest union, he was murdered at Lanuvium, B.C. 742, for an act of cruelty to the ambassadors of the Laurentes. This was done by order of his royal colleague, according to some authors. *Liv.* 1. c. 10, &c.—*Plut. in Rom.*—*Cic. pro Balb.* 13.—*Ovid. Met.* 14. v. 804. *Fast.* 3. v. 131.—*Flor.* 1. c. 1.

TA'TIUS ACHIL'LES, an ancient Greek writer of Alexandria. *Vid.* Achilles.

TA'TIUS GRATIA'NUS, a prætor executed for treason under Tiberius. *Tac. Ann.* 6. c. 38.

TAT'TA, a large lake of Phrygia on the confines of Pisidia. *Strab.*—*Plin.* 5. c. 27.

TAUCHI'RA, or **TEUCHI'RA**, a city of Libya, afterwards called Arsinoe. *Steph.*

TAU'A, a town of the Delta in Ægypt.

TAULAN'TII, a people of Illyricum on the Adriatic. *Liv.* 45. c. 26.—*Lucan.* 6. v. 16.

TAU'NUS, a mountain in Germany, now Hayrich or Hoherucke, opposite Mentz. *Tacit.* 1. *Ann.* c. 56.

TAURA'NIA, a town of Italy in the country of the Brutii.—*Mela*, 2. c. 7.—*Plin.* 3. c. 5.

TAURAN'TES, a people of Armenia, between Artaxata and Tigranocerta. *Tacit. Ann.* 14. c. 24.

TAU'REA JUBEL'LIUS, a chief of Capua, famous for his valor, and skill in horsemanship. He revolted from the Romans to Annibal, and at last stabbed himself. *Liv.* 23. c. 8 & 46. l. 26. c. 15.

TAUREN'TA, a city of Gallia Narbonensis. *Cæs. B. C.* 2. c. 4.

TAU'RI, a people of European Sarmatia, who inhabited Taurica Chersonesus, and sacrificed all strangers to Diana. The statue of this goddess, which they believed to have fallen from heaven, was carried away to Sparta, and not to Athens, as asserted by Euripides, by Iphigenia, and Orestes.—*Strab.* 12.—*Herodot.* 4. c. 99, &c.—*Mela*, 2. c. 1.—*Paus.* 3. c. 16.—*Eurip. Iphig.*—*Ovid. ex Pont.* 1. el. 2. v. 80.—*Sil.* 14. v. 260.—*Juv.* 15. v. 116.—*Aug. de Civ. D.* 7. c. 21 & 26.

TAURIA'NUS SCOP'ULUS, a place in the country of the Brutii, on the sea coast. *Ptol.* It is called Terinæus by *Pliny*, 3. c. 5.

TAU'RICA CHERSONE'SUS, a large peninsula of Europe, at the south-west of the Palus Mæotis, now called the Crimea. It is joined by an isthmus to Scythia, and is bounded by the Cimmerian Bosporus, the Euxine Sea, and the Palus Mæotis. The inhabitants, called Tauri, were a savage and uncivilized nation. *Strab.* 4.—*Plin.* 4. c. 12. *Vid.* Tauri.

TAU'RICA, a surname of Diana, because she was worshipped by the inhabitants of Taurica Chersonesus.

TAURI'NI, the inhabitants of Taurinum, a town of Cisalpine Gaul, now called Turin in Piedmont. *Sil.* 3. v. 646.—*Plin.* 3. c. 17.—*Liv.* 5. c. 34.

TAURI'NUS, a person proclaimed emperor in the time of Alexander Severus, at whose approach he was so terrified that he drowned himself in the Euphrates. *Lamprid. in Alex. Sever.* c. 36.

TAURIS'CI, a people of Mysia. *Strab.* 7.——A people of Noricum, among the Alps. *Id.* 4.

TAURIS'CUS, a sculptor. *Vid.* Appollonius.——A player mentioned by *Cicero, Or.* 3. c. 59.

TAU'RIUM, a town of Peloponnesus, taken by Antigonus in the time of the Peloponnesian war. *Polyb.*

TAUROMIN'IUS. *Vid.* Tauromininium.

TAUROMIN'IUM, a town of Sicily, between Messana and Catana, built by the Zancleans, Sicilians, and Hybleans, in the age of Dionysius, the tyrant of Syracuse. The hills in the neighbourhood were famous for the fine grapes which they produced, and they surpassed almost the whole world for the extent and beauty of their prospects. There was a small river near it called Tauromnius. *Diod.* 16.

TAU'RON, a leader of the Agriani in the army of Alexandria. *Curt.* 8, c. 15.

TAUROSTHENES, an athlete of Ægina, who obtained a crown at the Olympic games. It is said that his victories were proclaimed to his countrymen by a phantom which assumed his form. *Paus.* 6. c. 9.

TAU'RUS, the largest mountain of Asia, as to extent. One of its extremities is in Caria, and it extends not only as far as the most eastern extremities of Asia, but it also branches into several parts, and runs far into the north. Mount Taurus was known by several names, particularly in different countries. In Cilicia, where it reaches as far as the Euphrates, it was called Taurus. It was known by the name of Amanus, from the bay of Issus as far as the Euphrates; of Antitaurus from the western boundaries of Cilicia up to Armenia; of Montes Matieni in the country of the Leucosyrians; of Mons Moschicus at the south of the river Phasis; of Caucasus between the Hyrcanian and Euxine Seas; of Hyrcanii Montes near Hyrcania; of Imaus in the more eastern parts of Asia. The word Taurus was more properly confined to the mountains that separate Phrygia and Pamphylia from Cilicia. The several passes which were opened in the mountain were called Pylæ, and hence frequent mention is made in ancient authors of the Armenian Pylæ, Cilician Pylæ, &c. *Mela*, 1. c. 15. l. 3. c. 7 & 8.—*Plin.* 5. c. 27.—*Strab.* 14.—*Ptol.* 5 & 6.——A mountain in Germany. *Tacit. Ann.* 6. c. 41.——A promontory of Sicily. It is now Capo di St. Croce.

TAU'RUS, a proconsul of Africa accused by Agrippina, who wished him to be condemned, that she might become mistress of his gardens. *Tacit. Ann.* 12. c. 59.——An officer of Minos, king of Crete. He had an amour with Pasiphäe, whence arose the fable of the Minotaur, from the son, who was born some time after. *Vid.* Minotaurus. Taurus was vanquished by Theseus, in the games which Minos exhibited in Crete. *Plut. in Thes.*——A Platonic philosopher in the age of Antoninus Pius. He wrote on the difference between the Platonic and Aristotelic philosophies. *Suidas.*—*Gesner. in Biblioth.*

TAU'RUS STATIL'IUS, a consul distinguished by his intimacy with Augustus, as well as by a theatre which he built, and the triumph he obtained after a prosperous campaign in Africa. He was made præfect of Italy by his imperial friend. *Tac. Ann.* 6. c. 11.

TAU'TICE, a city of Media. *Ptol.*

TA'VA, a city of Ægypt. *Steph.*

TAV'ACA, a city of Sicily. *Id.*

TA'VIUM, a city of Galatia. *Ptol.*—*Plin.* 5. c. 32.

TAV'OLA, a river of Corsica.

TAX'ES, an auxiliary engaged in the war between Perses and Æetes. *Val. Flacc. Argon.* 6. v. 252.

TAX'ILA (*plur.*) a large country in India, between the Indus and the Hydaspes. *Strab.* 15.

TAX'ILUS or TAX'ILES, a king of Taxila, in the age of Alexander, called also Omphis. He submitted to the conqueror, who rewarded him with great liberality. *Diod.* 17.—*Plut. in Alex.*—*Ælian. V.H.* 5. c. 6.—*Curt.* 8. c. 14.

TAX'ILUS, a general of Mithridates, who assisted Archelaus against the Romans in Greece. He was afterwards conquered by Muræna, the lieutenant of Sylla. *Plut. in Syll.*

TAXIMAG'ULUS, a king in the southern parts of Britain when Cæsar invaded it. *Cæs.* 5. *G.* c. 22.

TAX'US, a river of Thrace. *Suidas.*

TAY'GETE or TAY'GETA, a daughter of Atlas and Pleione, mother of Lacedæmon by Jupiter. She became one of the Pleiades, after death. *Hygin.* fab. 155 & 192.—*Apollod.* 3.—*Paus. in Lac.* 1 & 18.—*Virg. G.* 4. v. 232.

TAY'GETUS or TAY'GETA (*-orum,*) a mountain of Laconia, in Peloponnesus, at the west of the river Eurotas. It hung over the city of Lacedæmon, and it is said that once a part of it fell down by an earthquake, and destroyed the suburbs. It was on this mountain that the Lacedæmonian women celebrated the orgies of Bacchus. *Mela*, 2. c. 5.—*Paus.* 3. c. 1 & 20.—*Strab.* 8.—*Lucan.* 5. v. 52.—*Virg. G.* 2. v. 488.—*Propert.* 3. el. 12. v. 13.—*Plin.* 2. c. 79.—*Servius ad G.* 2. v. 488. l. 3. v. 44.

TAZ'ATA, an island in the Scythian Ocean. It is called Talga by *Mela*, 3. c. 6., and Chalca by *Ptolemy*.

TA'ZUS, an inland town of the Taurica Chersonesus. *Ptol.* It is now Theodoro according to *Niger.*——A town of Asiatic Sarmatia. *Ptol. Mercator* calls it Susaco.

TEA'NUM, a town of Campania, on the Appian road, at the east of the Liris, called also Sidicinum, to distinguish it from another town called Apulum at the west of Apulia, at a small distance from the coast of the Adriatic. The rights of citizenship were extended to it under Augustus. *Cic. Clu.* 9 & 69. *Phil.* 12. c. 11.—*Horat.* 1. ep. 1.—*Plin.* 31. c. 2.—*Sil. Ital.* 8. v. 513.—*Liv.* 22. c. 27.—*Mela*, 2. c. 4.

TE'ARI, a people of Hispania Citerior, called also Julienses. *Plin.* 3. c. 3.

TE'ARUS, a river of Thrace, rising in the same rock from 38 different sources, some of which are hot and others cold. Darius raised a column there when he marched against the Scythians, to denote the sweetness and salubrity of the waters of that river. *Herodot.* 4. c. 90, &c.—*Plin.* 4. c. 11.

TEA'TE, or TEGEA'TE, a town of Latium. *Sil. It.* 8. v. 522. l. 17. v. 457.

TEBEN'DA, a city of the Galatian Pontus. *Ptol.*

TEBES'CA or TEVES'TA, an inland city of Africa. *Ptol.*—*Antonin.*

TECE'LIA, a town of Germany. *Ptol.* It is now Tekelenborch according to *Ortelius.*

TECHE'DIA, a small island of the Ægæan Sea. *Plin.* 4. c. 12.

TE'CHES, a mountain of Pontus, from which the 10,000 Greeks first had a view of the sea. *Xenoph. Anab.* 4.

TECMES'SA, the daughter of a Phrygian prince, called by some Teuthras, and by others Teleutas. When her father was killed in war by Ajax, son of Telamon, the young princess became the property of the conqueror, and by him she had a son called Eurysaces. Sophocles, in one of his tragedies, represents Tecmessa as moving her husband to pity by her tears and entreaties, when he wished to stab himself. *Horat.* 2. od. 1. v. 6.—*Dictys. Cret.*—*Sophocl. in Ajac.*—*Q. Calab.* 5. v. 355 & 525.—*Servius ad Æn.* 1. v. 623.—*Ovid. A.A.* 3. v. 517 & 523.

TEC'MON, a town of Epirus. *Liv.* 45. c. 26.

TEC'NATIS, a king of Ægypt. *Plut. de Isid.*

TEC'TAMUS, son of Dorus, grandson of Hellen, the son of Deucalion, went to Crete with the Ætolians and Pelasgians, and there reigned. He had a son called Asterius, by the daughter of Cretheus.

TECTOS'AGES, TECTOS'AGÆ, or TECTOS'AGI, a people of Gallia Narbonensis, whose capital was the modern Toulouse. They received the name of Tectosagæ, *quod sagis tegerentur.* Some of them passed into Germany, where they settled near the Hercynian forest, and another colony passed into Asia, where they conquered Phrygia, Paphlagonia, and Cappadocia. The Tectosagæ were among those Gauls who pillaged Rome under Brennus, and who attempted some time after to plunder the temple of Apollo at Delphi. On their return from Greece they were visited by a pestilence, and ordered, to stop it, to throw into the river all the riches and plunder which they had obtained in their distant excursions. Nearly 200 years afterwards they became the objects of the pillage which they had before barbarously exercised, and Cæpio carried, to enrich Rome, the gold and the silver of their submissive capital. *Cæs. Bell. G.* 6. c. 23.—*Strab.* 4.—*Cic. de Nat. D.* 3. c. 30.—*Liv.* 38. c. 16.—*Flor.* 2. c. 11 —*Justin.* 32. c. 3.—*Oros.* 5. c. 15. *Auson. Ordo Nob. Urb.*

TE'CUM, a river of Gaul falling from the Pyrenees into the Mediterranean.

TEDA'NIUS, a river of Liburnia. *Plin.* 3. c. 21.

TEDIAS'TUM, an inland city of Liburnia. *Ptol.* It is now Smodrusch.

TEGANU'SA or THIGANU'SA, an island on the coast of Peloponnesus.

TE'GEA or TEGÆ'A, now Moklia, a town of Arcadia in the Peloponnesus, founded by Tegeates, a son of Lycaon, or, according to others, by Aleus. The gigantic bones of Orestes were found buried there, and removed to Sparta. Apollo and Pan were worshipped there, and there also Ceres, Proserpine, and Venus had each a temple. The inhabitants were called Tegeates: and the epithet Tegæa is given to Atalanta, as a native of the place. It is said that a war with the people of Pheneæ was concluded by referring the decision to a combat between the three twin sons of Demostratus of Pheneæ against the three twins of Reximachus of Tegea, in which Critolaus, one of the Tergeates, obtained the victory, after he had slain his antagonists and seen his two brothers fall. His sister Demodice, who was betrothed to one of his opponents, reviled him, and was in the moment of victory sacrificed to his resentment, for which crime he was accused, and through his popularity acquitted. The story of the Horatii and Curiatii of Rome is probably copied from this. *Ovid. Met.* 8. fab. 7. *Fast.* 6. v. 531.—*Virg. Æn.* 5. v. 299.—*Strab.* 8.—*Paus.* 8. c. 45, &c.—*Stobœus.* p. 228.—*Liv.* 8. c. 40.

TEGEÆ'US, a surname of Pan from the worship he received at Tegea. *Propert.* 3. el. 2. v. 30.—*Virg. G.* 1. v. 18. *Æn.* 8. v. 459.—*Ital.* 13. v. 329.

TEGES'SUS, a city of Cyprus. *Steph.*—*Hesych.*

TEGES'TRA, a city of Illyria. *Id.*

TEG'ULA P. LICIN., a comic poet who flourished B.C. 198.

TEG'YRA, a town of Bœotia where Apollo Tegyræus was worshipped. There was a battle fought there between the Thebans and Peloponnesians.

TE'IOS. *Vid.* Teos.

TE'IUM, a town of Paphlagonia on the Euxine Sea.

TE'LA, a town of Spain. *Antonin.*

TEL'AMON, a king of the island of Salamis, son of Æacus and Endeis. He was brother to Peleus and father to Teucer and Ajax, who on that account is often called *Telamonius heros.* He fled from Megara, his native country, after he had accidentally killed his brother Phocis in playing with the quoit, and he sailed to the island of Salamis, where he soon after married Glauce, the daughter of Cychreus, the king of the place. At the death of the father-in-law, who had no male issue, Telamon became king of Salamis. He accompanied Jason in his expedition to Colchis, and was armour-bearer to Hercules, when that hero took Laomedon prisoner, and destroyed Troy. Telamon was rewarded by Hercules for his services with the hand of Hesione, whom the conqueror had obtained among the spoils of Troy, and with her he returned to Greece. He also married Peribœa, whom some call Eribœa. *Ovid. Met.* 13. v. 151.—*Sophocl. in Aj.* 570.—*Pindar. Isthm.* 6.—*Stat. Theb.* 5. v. 378.—*Apollod.* 1, 2, &c.—*Hygin.* fab. 97, &c.—*Anton. Liber.* 38.—*Paus.* 2. c. 29.—*Tzetzes. in Lyc.* 452 & 469.—*Flacc.* 1. v. 351.

TEL'AMON, a seaport town of Etruria. *Mela*, 2. c. 4.—*Plin.* 3. c. 5.

TELAMONI'ADES, a patronymic given to the descendants of Telamon.

TELAN'DRUS, TELAN'DRUM, or TELAN'DRIA, a city of Caria. *Steph.*

TELA'NE, a very ancient city of Syria. *Id.*

TELAU'GES, a philosopher, son of Pythagoras, was preceptor of Empedocles of Agrigentum, in the 65th Olympiad. *Suidas.*—*Diog. Laert.*

TELCHI'NES, a people of Rhodes, said to have been originally from Crete. They were the inventors of many useful arts, and according to Diodorus, passed for the sons of the sea. They were the first who raised statues to the gods. They had the power of changing themselves into whatever shape they pleased, and according to Ovid, they could poison and fascinate all objects with their eyes, and cause rain and hail to fall at pleasure. The Telchinians insulted Venus, for which the goddess inspired them with a sudden fury, so that they committed the grossest crimes, and offered violence even to their own mothers. Jupiter destroyed them all by a deluge. Epimenides of Crete was said to have written a history of this fabulous race of men. *Strab.* 10 & 14.—*Diod.* 5.—*Ovid. Met.* 7. v. 365, &c.—*Euseb. Chron.*—*Tzetzes, Ch.* 7. c. 113. *Ch.* 12. c. 447.

TELCHIN'IA, a surname of Minerva at Teumessa in Bœotia, where she had a temple. *Paus.* 9. c. 19.——A surname of Juno in Rhodes, where she had a statue at Ialysus raised by the Telchinians, who settled there. *Diod.* 5.——An ancient name of Crete, as the place from which the Telchines of Rhodes were descended. *Stat.* 4. *Sylv.* 6. v. 47.

TELCHIN'IUS, a surname of Apollo among the Rhodians, *Diod.* 5.—*Gyrald. H D.* 11.

TEL'CHIR, a city of India within the Ganges. *Ptol.*

TEL'CHIS, a son of Europs, the son of Ægialeus. He was one of the first kings of the Peloponnesus. *Æschyl. in Supp.*—*Paus.* 2. c. 5.

TEL'CHIS, a city of Æthiopia. *Steph.*

TEL'CHIUS, a charioteer in the service of Castor and Pollux. *Plin.* 6. c. 5.

TELE'A, or TELI'A, a surname of Juno in Bœotia.

TEL'EBA, a town of Albania. *Ptol.*

TELEB'OÆ or TELEB'OES, a people of Ætolia, called also Taphians; some of whom left their native country, and settled in the island of Capreæ. According to Apollodorus, the name of Teleboans was given by Taphius to those natives of Achaia, Ætolia, and Greece, who assisted him in seizing the islands of the Ionian Sea, as expressive of the distance from their country. *Apollod.* 2.—*Ital.* 7. v. 418.—*Tacit. Ann.* 4. c. 67.—*Virg. Æn.* 7. v. 735 *Vid.* Taphiæ.

TELEB'OAS, a son of Ixion and the cloud. *Ovid. Met.* 11.——A son of Lycaon. *Apollod.*

TELEBO'IDES, islands opposite Leucadia. *Plin.* 4. c. 12.

TELEB'OIS, a region of Acarnania. *Steph.*

TEL'ECLES or TEL'ECLUS, a Lacedæmonian king, son of Archelaus, of the family of the Ægidæ, who reigned 40 years B.C. 813, and was killed in a sedition. *Plut. Apoph.*—*Herodot.* 7. c. 205.—*Paus.* 3. c. 2.

TEL'ECLES, a philosopher, disciple of Lacidas. B.C. 214. *Diog. Laert.* 4. c. 60.——A Milesian lawgiver. *Aristot. Polit.* 4. c. 14

TELECLI'DES, an Athenian comic poet in the age of Pericles, one of whose plays, called the Amphictyons is mentioned by ancient authors. *Plut. in Nicia.*—*Athen.* 8.

TELEC'OON, a native of Cyzicus, slain by Ancæus. *Val. Flacc.* 3. v. 140.

TELEG'ONUS, a son of Ulysses and Circe, born in the island of Ææa, where he was educated. When arrived at years of manhood, he went to Ithaca to make himself known to his father; but he was shipwrecked on the coast, and, being destitute of provisions, he plundered some of the inhabitants of the island. Ulysses and Telemachus came to defend the property of their subjects against this unknown invader; a quarrel arose, and Telegonus killed his father without knowing who he was. He afterwards returned to his native country, and, according to Hyginus, he carried thither his father's body, where it was buried. Telemachus and Penelope also accompanied him in his return, and soon after, the nuptials of Telegonus with Penelope were celebrated by order of Minerva. Penelope had by Telegonus a son called Italus, who gave his name to Italy. Telegonus founded Tusculum and Tibur or Præneste in Italy, and, according to some, he left one daughter called Mamilia, from whom the patrician family of the Mamilii at Rome were descended. *Horat.* 3. od. 29. v. 8.—*Ovid. Fast.* 3 & 4.—*Trist.* 1. el. 1.—*Plut. in Par.*—*Hygin.* fab. 127.—*Diod.* 7.—*Ital.* 7. v. 692.—*Servius. ad Æn.* 2. v. 43.—*Festus de V. Sig.*——A son of Proteus killed by Hercules. *Apollod.*——A king of Ægypt who married Io after she had been restored to her usual form by Jupiter. *Id.*

TELEM'ACHUS, a son of Ulysses and Penelope. He was still in the cradle when his father went with the rest of the Greeks to the Trojan war. At the end of this celebrated expedition, Telemachus, anxious to see his father, went to seek him; and as the place of his residence and the cause of his long absence were then unknown, he visited the court of Menelaus and Nestor to obtain information. He afterwards returned to Ithaca, where the suitors of his mother Penelope had conspired to murder him; but he avoided their snares, and, by means of Minerva, he discovered his father, who had arrived in the island two days before him, and was then in the house of Eumæus. With this faithful servant and Ulysses, Telemasuch concerted how to deliver his mother from the importunities of her suitors, and it was effected with success. After the death of his father, Telemachus went to the island of Ææa, where he married Circe, or, according to others, Cassiphone, the daughter of Circe, by whom he had a son called Latinus. He some time after had the misfortune to kill his mother-in-law, Circe, and fled to Italy, where he founded Clusium. Telemachus was accompanied in his visit to Nestor and Menelaus by the goddess of wisdom, under the form of Mentor. It is said, that, when a child, Telemachus fell into the sea, and that a dolphin brought him safe to shore, after he had remained some time under water. From this circumstance Ulysses had the figure of a dolphin engraved on the seal which he wore on his ring. *Hygin.* fab. 95 & 125.—*Ovid. Heroid.* 1. v. 98.—*Horat.* 1. ep. 7. v. 41.—*Homer. Odyss.* 2, &c.—*Lycoph. in Cass. & Tzetzes.* v. 658 & 805 —*Plut. Terr. an Aquit.*—*Sabin.* 1. v. 115.—*Servius ad Virg. Æn.* 10. v. 167.

TEL'EMUS, a Cyclops, son of Eurymus, who was acquainted with futurity. He foretold Polyphemus all the evils which he some time after suffered from Ulysses. *Ovid. Met.* 13. v. 771. & *in Ib.* 720.—*Homer. Odyss.* 9. v. 509.—*Theocr. Id.* 6. v. 23.—*Hygin.* fab. 128.

TELEPH'AE, the wife of Cadmus, whom he married before Hermione. *Steph. in Dardan.*

TELEPHAS'SA, the mother of Cadmus, Phœnix, and Cilix, by Agenor. She died in Thrace, as she was seeking her daughter Europa, whom Jupiter had carried away. *Apollod.* 3. c. 1 & 4.

TEL'EPHUS, a king of Mysia, son of Hercules and Auge, the daughter of Aleus. He was exposed as soon as born on mount Parthenius; but his life was preserved by a goat and some shepherds. According to Apollodorus, he was exposed, not on a mountain, but in a temple of Minerva, at Tegea, or, according to a tradition mentioned by Pausanias, he was left to the mercy of the waves with his mother, by the cruelty of Aleus, and carried by the winds to the mouth of the Caycus, where he was found by Teuthras, king of the country, who married, or rather adopted as his daughter, Auge, and educated her son. Some, however, suppose that Auge fled to Teuthras to avoid the anger of her father, on account of her amour with Hercules. Yet others declare that Aleus gave her to Nauplius to be severely punished for her incontinence, and that Nauplius, unwilling to injure her, sent her to Teuthras, king of Bithynia, by whom she was adopted. Telephus, according to the more received opinion, was ignorant of his origin; and he was ordered by the oracle, if he wished to know his parents, to go to Mysia. Obedient to this injunction, he came to Mysia, where Teuthras offered him his crown, and his adopted daughter in marriage, if he would deliver his country from the hostilities of Idas, the son of Aphareus. Telephus readily complied, and at the head of the Mysians he soon routed the enemy, and received the promised reward. As he was going to unite himself to Auge, the sudden appearance of an enormous serpent separated the two lovers. Auge implored the assistance of Hercules, and was soon informed that Telephus was her own son. When this was known, the nuptials were not celebrated, and Telephus some time after married one of the daughters of king Priam. As one of the sons of the Trojan monarch, Telephus prepared to assist Priam against the Greeks, and he attacked them with heroic valour when they had landed on his coasts. The carnage was great, and Telephus would have been victorious had not Bacchus, who protected the Greeks, suddenly raised a vine from the earth, which entangled the feet of the monarch, and laid him flat on the ground. Achilles immediately rushed upon him, and wounded him so severely, that he was carried away from the battle. The wound was mortal, and Telephus was informed by the oracle, that he alone who inflicted it could totally cure it. Upon this, applications were made to Achilles, but in vain; the hero observed that he was no physician; till Ulysses, who knew that Troy could not be taken without the assistance of one of the sons of Hercules, and who wished to make Telephus the friend of the Greeks, persuaded Achilles to obey the directions of the oracle. Achilles consented; and as the weapon which had given the wound could alone cure it, the hero scraped the rust from the point of his spear, and by applying it to the sore gave it immediate relief. It is said that Telephus showed himself so grateful to the Greeks, that he accompanied them to the Trojan war, and fought with them against his father-in-law. *Hygin.* fab. 101.—*Paus.* 8. c. 48.—*Apollod.* 2. c. 7, &c.—*Ælian. V.H.* 12. c. 42.—*Diod.* 4.—*Ovid. Fast.* 1. el. 1, &c.—*Philostr. Her.* 2.—*Plin.* 25. c. 5. l. 34. c. 15.—*Tzetzes ad Lyc.* 206 & 212. *Propert.* 2. el. 1. v. 65.—*Eustath. ad Il.* 1.——A friend of Horace, remarkable for his beauty and the elegance of his person. He was the favorite of Lydia, the mistress of Horace, &c. *Horat.* 1. od. 12. l. 4. od. 11. v. 21.——A slave who conspired against Augustus. *Sueton. in Aug.*

TEL'EPHUS L. VE'RUS, wrote a book on the rhetoric of Homer, as also a comparison of that poet with Plato, and other treatises, all lost. *Voss. H. Gr.* 4. c. 16.

TELESE'TES or TELES'TES, a comic poet in the 95th Olympiad. *Suidas.*

TELE'SIA, or TELES'SIA, a town of Campania, taken by Annibal. *Liv.* 21. c. 13. l. 24. c. 20.

TELES'ICLES, a Parian, father to the poet Archilochus, by a slave called Enippo. *Ælian. V.H.* 10. c. 13.

TELESIL'LA, a lyric poetess of Argos, who bravely defended her country against Cleomenes and the Lacedæmonians, and obliged them to raise the siege. A statue was raised to her honor in the temple of Venus, which represented her with some volumes of poetry at her feet, and with a helmet in her hands, which she appeared to raise towards her head. *Herodot.* 6.—*Plut. de Mul. Virt.*—*Apollod.* 3.—*Paus.* 2. c. 20.

TELESINI'CUS, a Corinthian auxiliary at Syracuse, &c. *Polyæn.* 5. c. 28.

TELESI'NUS PON'TIUS, a general of the Samnites, who joined the interest of Marius, and fought against the generals of Sylla. He marched towards Rome, and defeated Sylla with great loss. He was afterwards routed in a bloody battle, and left in the number of the slain, after he had given repeated proofs of valor and courage. *Pat.* 2. c. 27.—*Plut. in Mar, &c.*

TELESI'NUS, a poet of considerable merit in Domitian's reign. *Juv.* 7. v. 25.

TELESIP'PUS, a poor man of Pheræ, father to the tyrant Dinias. *Polyæn.* 2. c. 34.

TELES'PHORUS, a divinity who presided over medicine, and the recovery of diseased persons. He was called Acesius at Epidaurus, and Evemerion at Titana. On some of Adrian's medals he is represented as a young man. *Paus.* 2. c. 11.—*Gyrald. H. D* 1. [A small statue of Telesphorus, by the side of a fine figure of Æsculapius, was lately in the Massimi palace at Rome; but we have every reason to think that it is now in the Vatican.]

TELESTAG'ORAS, a man of Naxus whose daughters were ravished by some of the nobles of the island, in consequence of which they were expelled by the direction of Lygdamis. *Athen.* 8.

TELES'TAS, a son of Priam. *Apollod.* 3. c. 12.——An athlete of Messenia, who obtained a prize, and was honored with a statue at Olympia, the work of Silanion. *Paus.* 6. c. 14.——A king of Corinth, who died 779 B.C.

TELES'TES, a dithyrambic poet, who flourished B.C. 402. A few of his verses are preserved in *Athenæus.*

TELES'TO, one of the Oceanides. *Hes. Theog.*

TELETHRION or TELEPHRIUS MONS, a mountain of Œchalia in Eubœa. *Steph.*

TELETHU'SA, the wife of Lygdus or Lyctus, a native of Crete. She became mother of a daughter, who was afterwards changed into a boy. *Vid.* Iphis. *Ovid. Met.* 9. v. 681.

TELEU'TIAS, a prince of Macedonia, &c. *Xenophon.*

TE'LEUS, a surname of Jupiter at Tegea, as expressive of his full growth, because he had as an infant a statue there. *Paus.* 8. c. 48.——An Argive, son of Clymenus, criminally fond of his own daughter. *Parthen.* 13.

TELEU'TE, a surname of Venus among the Ægyptians. *Plut. de Is. & Os.*

TELEU'TIA, a Lacedæmonian matron, who, on hearing that her son Pædaretus disgraced himself at Chius, where he was governor, wrote to him to bid him alter his conduct, or to renounce his country, as his return would be attended not only with disgrace, but death. *Plut. in Apop. Lac.*

TELEU'TIAS, the brother of Agesilaus who was killed by the Olynthians, &c.

TELLE'NÆ, a town of Latium now destroyed. *Liv.* 1. c 33.

TEL'LES, a king of Achaia, son of Tisamenes. *Paus.* 7. c. 6.

TEL'LIAS, a famous soothsayer of Elis, in the age of Xerxes. He was greatly honored in Phocis, where he had settled, and the inhabitants raised him a statue in the temple of Apollo at Delphi. *Paus.* 10. c. 1.—*Herodot.* 8. c. 27.

TEL'LIS, or TEL'LEN, a Greek lyric poet, the father of Brasidas. He made great improvements in music. *Zenob. Cent.* 1. p. 45. *Cent.* 2. p. 15.—*Gyrald. de P,H.* 9.

TEL'LUS, a divinity the same as the earth, the most ancient of all the gods after Chaos. She was mother, by Cœlus, of Oceanus, Hyperion, Ceus, Rhea, Japetus, Themis, Saturn, Phœbe, Tethys, &c. Tellus is the same as the divinty who is honored under the several names of Cybele, Rhea, Vesta, Ceres, Tithea, Bona Dea, Proserpine, &c. She was generally represented in the character of Tellus, as a woman with many breasts, distended with milk to express the fecundity of the earth. She also appeared crowned with turrets, holding a sceptre in one hand, and a key in the other, expressive of her sovereignty, and of the treasures which she contains, while at her feet was lying a tame lion without chains, as if to intimate that every part of the earth can be made fruitful by means of cultivation. *Hesiod. Theog.* v. 130.—*Virg. Æn.* 7. v. 137.—*Apollod.* 1. c. 1.—*Varro apud Aug. Civ.* 7. c. 24. [The representations of Tellus have been mentioned under the head of Cybele, another name of the same deity.]——A poor man, whom Solon called happier than Crœsus, the rich and ambitious king of Lydia. Tellus had the happiness to see a strong and healthy family of children, and at last honorably to fall in the defence of his country. *Herodot.* 1. c. 30. ——An Italian who is said to have had commerce with his mares, and to have had a daughter called Hippone, who became the goddess of horses. *Agesilaus apud Plut. Par.* 29.

TEL'MERA, a city of Caria. *Steph.*

TELMES'SUS, or TELMIS'SUS, a town of Caria, the inhabitants of which were skilled in augury and the interpretation of dreams. *Cic. de Div.* 1. —*Strab.* 14.—*Liv.* 37. c. 16.

TELMES'SUS, a city of Lycia.——A city of Pisidia.

TELMI'SUS or TELMES'SUS, a river of Bœotia. *Orph.*

TE'LO MAR'TIUS, a town at the south of Gaul, now Toulon. *Antonin.*

TEL'OBIS, a town of the Jaccetani in Hispania Tarraconensis. *Ptol.*

TE'LON, a skilful pilot of Massilia, killed during the siege of that city by Cæsar. *Lucan.* 3. v. 592. ——A king of the Teleboæ, who married Sebethis, by whom he had Œbalus. *Virg. Æn.* 7. v. 734. l. 12. v. 513. & *Servius Æn.* 7. v. 734.

TE'LOS, a small island near Rhodes. *Plin.* 4. c. 12. & 13. c. 1.

TELPHU'SA or TELPHUS'SA, a nymph of Arcadia, daughter of the Ladon, who gave her name to a town and fountain of that place. The waters of the fountain Telphussa were so cold, that Tiresias died by drinking them. *Diod.* 4.—*Strab.* 9.—*Lycophron.* 1040.—*Athen.* 2.—*Paus.* 8. c. 25.

TELUM'NUM, a city of Aquitania. *Antonin.*

TELXI'OPE, one of the muses according to *Cicero de N.D.* 3. c. 21.

TE'LYS, a tyrant of Sybaris. *Herodot.* 1. 5.

TEM'ALA, a city and river of India without the Ganges. *Ptol.*

TEMA'THIA, a mountain of Messenia. *Paus.* 4. c. 34. It is now Monte di Coron.

TEM'BASA, a town of Lycaonia on mount Taurus. *Plin.* 5. c. 27.

TEM'BRIUM, a city of Phrygia. *Steph.*

TEM'BRIUS, a river near Pontus. *Orph. in Argon.*

TEMBRO'GIUS, a river of Phrygia flowing into the Sangarius. *Plin.* 6. c. 1.

TEM'BROS, a city of Cyprus, in which Apollo, surnamed Helates, was worshipped. *Steph.*

TEMENI'A, a city of Phrygia. *Id.*

TEMENI'TES, a surname of Apollo, which he received from Temenus, a small place near Syracuse, where he was worshipped. *Cic. in Verr.* 4. c. 53. —*Turneb. Adv.* 8. c. 12.

TEME'NIUM, a place in Messene, where Temenus was buried. *Strab.*

TEM'ENUS, a place of Syracuse, where Apollo, called Temenites had a statue. *Cic. Verr.* 4. c. 53.—*Suet. Tib.* 74.

TEME'NUS, the son of Aristomachus, was the first of the Heraclidæ, who returned to Peloponnesus with his brother Cresphontes, in the reign of Tisamenes, king of Argos. Temenus made himself master of the throne of Argos, from which he expelled the reigning sovereign. After death he was succeeded by his son-in-law, Deiphon, who had married his daughter Hyrneto, and this succession was in preference to his own son. *Apollod.* 2. c. 7.—*Paus.* 2. c. 18 & 19.—*Hygin.* fab. 219.—*Paterc.* 1. c. 1.——A son of Pelasgus, who was entrusted with the care of Juno's infancy. *Paus.* 8. c. 22.

TEMERIN'DA, the name of the Palus Mæotis among the inhabitants of the neighbourhood. *Plin.* 6. c. 7.

TEM'ESA or TAM'ASUS, a town of Cyprus. *Steph.*

TEM'ESA or TEMP'SA, a town in Calabria, in Italy, famous for its mines of copper, which were exhausted in the age of Strabo. *Cic. Verr.* 5. c. 15.—*Liv.* 34. c. 35.—*Homer. Odys.* 1. l. 184.—*Ovid. Fast.* 5. v. 441. *Met.* 7. v. 207. *De Rem. A.* 41.—*Stat. Ach.* 1. v. 413.—*Mela,* 2. c. 4.—*Strab.* 6.

TEM'NES, a king of Sidon. *Diod. Sic.*—*Oros.* 3. c. 7.

TEM'NOS, a town of Æolia, at the mouth of the Hermus. *Herodot.* 1. c. 49.—*Cic. Flacc.* 18.—*Plin.* 5. c. 30.

TEM'PE, (*plur.*) a valley in Thessaly, between mount Olympus at the north, and Ossa at the south, through which the river Peneus flows into the Ægæan. The poets have described it as the most delightful spot on the earth, with continually cool shades, and verdant walks, which the warbling of birds rendered more pleasant and romantic, and which the gods often honored with their presence. Tempe extended about five miles in length, but varied in the dimensions of its breadth so as to be in some places scarce one acre and a a half wide. All valleys that are pleasant, either for their situation or the mildness of their climate, are called Tempe by the poets. *Strab.* 9.—*Mela,* 2. c. 3.—*Diod.* 4.—*Dionys. Perieg.* 219.—*Ælian. V.H.* 3. c. 1.—*Plut. de Mus.*—*Virg. G.* 2. v. 469. —*Ovid. Met.* 1. v. 569. *Am.* 1. el. 1. v. 15.—*Horat.* 3. od. 1. v. 24.

TEM'PLUM, a part of Liguria. *Tac. Agric.* c. 7. ——A place of Africa Propria. *Antonin.*

TEMP'SIS, the top of mount Tmolus. *Plin.* 7. c. 48.

TEN'AGUS, a place of Susiana on the Persian Gulph. *Ptol.*

TENC'TERI, TENCH'TERI, or TENCHTE'RI, a nation of Germany, who frequently changed the place of their habitation. *Tacit. Ann.* 13. c. 56. *H.* 4. c. 21. They are called Tanchari by *Appian*, Tenterides by *Plutarch*, and Tenchateri by *Livy*.

TEN'DEBA, a town of Caria. *Liv.* 33. c. 18.

TE'NEA, or TENÆ'A, according to *Suidas* a part of Corinth. *Mela,* 2. c. 3.

TENE'DIA SECU'RIS. *Vid.* Tenes.

TEN'EDUS, or TEN'EDOS, a small and fertile island of the Ægæan Sea, opposite Troy, at the distance of about 12 miles from Sigeum, and 56 miles north from Lesbus. It was anciently called Leucophrys, till Tenes, the son of Cycnus, settled there and built a town, which he called Tenedus, from which the whole island received its name. It became famous during the Trojan war, as it was there that the Greeks concealed themselves the more effectually to make the Trojans believe that they were returned home without finishing the siege. Apollo was particularly worshipped there. The earthen vessels made there were in high estimation among the ancients. *Homer. Odys.* 3. v. 59.—*Diod.* 5.

Strab. 13.—*Virg. Æn.* 2. v. 21.—*Ovid. Met.* 1. v. 540. l. 12. v. 109.—*Mela*, 2. c. 7.—*Plin.* 5. c. 13. —*Servius ad Virg. loco.*—*Eustath. ad Il.* 2. p. 233. *Schol. Hom. ad* 13 *Il.* v. 33.

TENER'ICUS CAM'PUS, a plain near the lake Copais. *Strab.*

TEN'ERUS, son af Apollo and Melia, received from his father the knowledge of futurity, *Paus.* 9. c. 10.—*Sch. Pindar. Pyth.* 11.

TE'NES, or TEN'NES, a son of Cycnus and Proclea. He was exposed on the sea, on the coast of Troas, by his father, who credulously believed his wife Philonome, who had fallen in love with him, and accused him of attempts upon her virtue, when he refused to gratify her passion. Tenes arrived safe in Leucophrys, which he called Tenedus, and of which he became the sovereign. Some time after Cycnus discovered the guilt of his wife Philonome, and as he wished to be reconciled to his son whom he had so grossly injured, he went to Tenedus. But when he had tied his ship to the shore, Tenes cut off the cable with a hatchet, and suffered his father's ship to be tossed about in the sea. From this circumstance the "hatchet of Tenes" is become proverbial to intimate a resentment that cannot be pacified. Some, however, suppose that the proverb arose from the severity of a law made by a king of Tenedus against adultery, by which the guilty were both put to death with a hatchet. The hatchet of Tenes was carefully preserved at Tenedus, and afterwards deposited by Periclytus, son of Eutymachus, in the temple of Delphi, where it was still to be seen in the age of Pausanias. Tenes, as some suppose, was killed by Achilles, as he defended his country against the Greeks, and received divine honors after death. His statue at Tenedus was carried away by Verres. *Strab.* 13.—*Paus.* 10. c. 14.—*Cic. N.D.* 3. c. 15. *in Verr.* 1. c. 19.—*Diod.* 5.—*Eustath. in Il.* 1.—*Conon. Nar.* 29.——A general of 3000 Greek mercenaries, sent by the Ægyptians to assist the Phœnicians. *Diod.* 16.

TEN'ESIS, a part of Æthiopia. *Strab.*

TE'NION, a city of Achaia. *Steph.*

TENIS'SA, a town of Mauritania Cæsariensis. *Ptol. Niger* calls it Tremissen.

TENNAGO'RA, a city of India within the Ganges. *Ptol.*

TEN'NES, a king of Sidon, who when his country was besieged by the Persians, burnt himself and the city together, B.C. 351.

TEN'NUM, a town of Æolia. *Strab.* 14.

TE'NOS, a city of Laconia. *Steph.*

TEN'TYRA, (*plur.*) and TEN'TYRIS, a small town of Ægypt, on the Nile, the inhabitants of which were at enmity with the crocodiles, and made war against those who paid them adoration. *Seneca, N.Q.* 4. c. 2.—*Strab.* 17.—*Juv.* 15.—*Plin.* 25. c. 8.

TENTY'RA, (*melius* Tempy'ra), a place of Thrace, opposite Samothrace. *Ovid. Trist.* 1. el. 9. v. 21.

TENUP'SIS, a town of the Nubæi in Upper Æthiopia. *Plin.* 6. c. 30.

TE'NUS, a small island in the Ægæan, near Andrus, called Ophiussa, and also Hydrussa, from the number of its fountains. It is very mountainous, but it produces excellent wines, which were universally esteemed by the ancients. Tenus was abont 15 miles in extent. The capital was also called Tenus. It is now Teno. *Strab.* 10.—*Mela*, 2. c. 7.—*Ovid. Met.* 7. v. 469. *Heroid.* 21. v. 81. *Trist.* 3. el. 13. v. 8.—*Apollod.* 3.—*Arist. apud Plin.* 12. c. 4.—*Athen.* 1.

TE'OS (Τέως,) or TE'IOS, now Sigagik, a maritime town on the coast of Ionia in Asia Minor, opposite Samus. It was one of the 12 cities of the Ionian confederacy, and gave birth to Anacreon and Hecatæus, who is by some deemed a native of Miletus. According to Pliny, Teos was an island. Augustus repaired Teos, whence he is often called the founder of it on ancient medals. *Strab.* 14.—*Mela*, 1. c. 17.—*Paus.* 7. c. 3.—*Ælian. V.H.* 8. c. 5—*Horat.* 1. od. 17. v. 18.—*Plin.* 5. c. 31.—*Ovid. de A.A.* 3. v. 330. *de Rem. Am.* 762.—*Propert.* 4. el. 8. v. 13 & 58.

TEPHE'NE, a small province (*toparchia*) of Palestine. *Plin.* 5. c. 14.

TERACA'TRIÆ, plains of Germany near the Danube. *Ptol.*

TERAM'BUS, a shepherd, son of Euseirus, and grandson of Neptune, who settled in Thessaly, at the foot of mount Othrys, whither he invited, by the power of his songs, the neighbouring nymphs, to assist him in the tending of his numerous flocks. Pan, jealous of his popularity among the nymphs, laid snares for him, and at last deprived him of his mental powers, in consequence of which he insulted the nymphs, by whom he was changed into an insect nearly resembling the beetle, and called by the ancients Cerambix, or *Bos Lignivorus.* Some suppose him, and with great propriety, to be the same with Cerambus, who, as Ovid mentions, was changed into a bird. *Nicander. in Heter. apud Ant. Liber.* 22.—*Ovid. Met.* 7. v. 353.

TERAP'SA, a small island near Carthage. *Steph.*

TERBE'TIA, a city of Sicily. *Id.*

TERE'DON, a town on the Arabian Gulph. *Dionys. Per.* 982.

TEREN'TIA, the wife of Cicero. She became mother of M. Cicero, and of a daughter called Tulliola. Cicero repudiated her, because she had been faithless to his bed, when he was banished into Asia. Terentia married Sallust, Cicero's enemy, and afterwards Messala Corvinus. She lived to her 103rd year, or, according to Pliny, to her 117th year. *Plut. in Cic.*—*Val. Max.* 8. c. 13.—*Plin.* 7. c. 48.—*Cic. ad Attic.* 11. ep. 16, &c.——The wife of Scipio Africanus.——The wife of Mecænas, with whom it was said that Augustus carried on an intrigue. *Dio.* 54. c. 19. — *Sueton. Aug.* 66 & 69.

TEREN'TIA LEX, called also Cassia *frumentaria*, was introduced by M. Terentius Varro Lucullus, and C. Cassius, A.U.C. 680. It ordered that the same price should be given for all corn bought in the provinces, to hinder the exactions of the quæstors. ——Another by Terentius the Tribune, A.U.C. 291, to elect five persons to define the power of the consuls, lest they should abuse the public confidence by violence or rapine. *Liv.* 3. c. 9 & 11.

TERENTIA'NUS, a Roman, to whom Longinus dedicated his treatise on the sublime.

TERENTIA'NUS MAU'RUS, a native of Carthage who flourished about 240 A.D. and wrote a useful treatise on the rules of versification, which had been observed by the poets of the Augustan age, and by succeeding authors. This work, called *Tractatus de Literis, Syllabis, Pedibus & Metris*, which is written in varied metre, is valuable for the curious information which it contains upon ancient poetry. There have been several editions; it was first published with Ausonius, Mediolan, 1497; and again with Marius Victorinus, Genev. 1684. It is also among the "Grammaticæ Latinæ Auctores," of Putsch, Hanov. 1605. *Harles. Not. Lit. Rom.* 1. p. 482.—*Sax. Onom.* 1. p. 272.—*Martial*, 1. epigr. 70.

TEREN'TIUS PUB'LIUS, a native of Carthage in Africa, celebrated for the comedies which he wrote. He was sold as a slave to Terentius Lucanus, a Roman senator, who educated him with great care, and manumitted him for the brilliancy of his genius. He bore the name of his master and benefactor, being called Terentius. He applied himself to the study of the Greek comedy with uncommon assiduity, and merited the friendship of the learned and powerful. Scipio, the elder Africanus, and his friend Lælius, have been suspected, on account of their intimacy, of assisting the poet in the composition of his comedies; and the fine language, the pure expressions, and delicate sentiments with which the plays of Terence abound, seem perhaps to favor the supposition. Terence was in the 25th year of his age, when his first play appeared on the Roman stage. All his compositions were received with great applause; but when the words

Homo sum, humani nil a me alienum puto,

were repeated, the plaudits were reiterated, and the audience, though composed of foreigners, conquered nations, allies, and citizens of Rome, were unanimous in applauding the poet, who spoke with such elegance and simplicity the language of nature, and supported the native independence of man. The talents of Terence were employed rather in translations than in the effusions of originality. It is said, that he translated 108 of the comedies of the poet Menander, six of which only are extant, his Andria, Eunuch, Heautontimorumenos, Adelphi, Phormio and Hecyra. Terence is admired for the purity of his language, and the artless elegance and simplicity of his diction, and for a continued delicacy of sentiment. There is more originality in Plautus, more vivacity in the intrigues and more surprise in the catastrophes of his plays; but Terence will ever be admired for his taste, his expressions, and his faithful pictures of nature and manners, and the becoming dignity of his several characters. Quintilian, who candidly acknowledges the deficiencies of the Roman comedy, declares that Terence was the most elegant and refined of all the comedians whose writings appeared on the stage. The time and manner of his death are unknown. He left Rome in the 35th year of his age, and never after appeared there. Some suppose that he was drowned in a storm as he returned from Greece, about 159 years before Christ, though others imagine that he died in Arcadia or Leucadia, and that his death was accelerated by the loss of his property, and particularly of his plays, which perished in a shipwreck. The best editions of Terence are those of Westerhovius, 2 vols. 4to. Amst. 1726; of Edinb. 12mo. 1758; of Bentley, Cambridge, 4to. 1726; of Hawkey, 12mo. Dublin, 1745; and that of Zeunius, 8vo. Lips. 1774. *Cic. ad Attic.* 7. ep. 3.—*Paterc.* 1. c. 17.—*Quintil.* 10. c. 1.—*Horat.* 2. ep. 1. v. 59.—*Cæsar. apud Sueton.*—*Liv.* 30.—*Cor. Nep. apud Donatum in vita Ter.*—*Aul. Gell.* 7. c. 14. l. 17. c. 21. [The finest bust of Terence is to be found in the Vatican.]

TEREN'TIUS Q. CU'LEO, a tribune intimate with Cicero. He consulted with Atticus about the recal of his friend from banishment. *Cic. Att.* 3. ep. 15. *Har.* 7.——A Roman senator, taken by the Carthaginians, and redeemed by Africanus. When Africanus triumphed, Culeo followed his chariot with a pileus on his head. He was some time after appointed judge between his deliverer and the people of Asia, and had the meanness to condemn him and his brother Asiaticus, though both innocent. *Liv.* 30. c. 45.

TEREN'TIUS, a tribune who wished the number of the citizens of Reme to be increased.——A consul with Æmilius Paulus at the battle of Cannæ. He was the son of a butcher, and had followed for some time the profession of his father. He placed himself totally in the power of Hannibal, by making an improper disposition of his army. After he had been defeated, and his colleague slain, he retired to Canusium, with the remains of his slaughtered countrymen, and sent word to the Roman senate of his defeat. He received the thanks of this venerable body, because he had engaged the enemy however improperly, and not despaired of the affairs of the republic. He was offered the dictatorship, which he declined. *Plut.*—*Liv.* 22. &c.——An ambassador sent to Philip king of Macedonia.

TEREN'TIUS EVOCA'TUS, a man, who, as it was supposed, murdered Galba. *Tacit. Hist.* 1. c. 41.

TEREN'TIUS LENTI'NUS, a Roman knight condemned for perjury. *Tac. Ann.* 14. c. 41.

TEREN'TIUS VAR'RO, a writer. *Vid.* Varro.

TEREN'TIUS MASSALIO'TA, an ædile of the people, &c.

TEREN'TIUS MAR'CUS, a friend of Sejanus, accused before the senate for his intimacy with that discarded favorite. He made a noble defence, and was acquitted. *Tacit. Ann* 6. c. 8.

TEREN'TUS, a place in the Campus Martius near the Capitol, where Pluto and Proserpine had an altar. Those festivals which were celebrated every 100th year were called Ludi Terentini. *Festus. de V. Sig.*—*Stat.* 1. *Sylv.* 4. v. 18. l. 4. *Syl.* 1. v. 38.—*Auson. Id.* 4. v. 34.—*Ovid. Fast.* 1. v. 504.

TERENU'THIS, a city of Ægypt. *Steph.*

TE'RES, a son of Sitalces king of Thrace, presented with the rights of citizenship at Athens. *Aristoph. Acharn.*

TE'REUS, a king of Thrace, son of Mars and Bistonis, who married Progne, the daughter of Pandion king of Athens, whom he had assisted in a war against Megara. He afterwards offered violence to his sister-in-law Philomela, whom he conducted to Thrace by desire of Progne. *Vid.* Philomela and Progne.——A friend of Æneas, killed by Camilla. *Virg. Æn.* 11. v. 675.

TER'GEDUM, a town of Upper Æthiopia. *Plin.* 6. c. 29.

TERGEM'INUS or TRICOR'POR, a name applied to Cerberus, and also to Geryon, from having three bodies or three heads. Diana is also called Tergemina, because called Diana on earth, Luna in heaven, and Hecate in hell. *Virg. Æn.* 4. v. 511. l. 8. v. 202.

TERGES'TE or TERGES'TUM, now Trieste, a town of Italy on the Adriatic Sea, made a Roman colony. The adjacent gulf bears its name. *Mela*, 2. c. 3, &c.—*Dionys. Perieg.* v. 380.—*Paterc.* 2. c. 110.—*Plin.* 3. c. 18.—*Steph. Byz.*

TERGILA'NI, a people of Lucania. *Plin.* 3. c. 11.

TER'GIS, a city of Libya, near Æthiopia. *Steph.*

TE'RIAS, a river of Sicily near Catana. It is called Tyrias by *Diodorus.*

TERIBA'ZUS, a nobleman of Persia, sent with a fleet against Evagoras king of Cyprus. He was accused of treason and removed from office. *Polyæn.* 7. c. 13.

TERID'AE, a concubine of Menelaus.

TERIDA'TA, a city of Mesopotamia. *Ptol.*

TERIDA'TES, a favorite eunuch at the court of Artaxerxes. At his death the monarch was in tears for three days, and was consoled at last only by the arts, and the persuasion of Aspasia, one of his favorites. *Ælian. V.H.* 12. c. 1.

TER'IGUM, a town of Macedonia.

TERI'NA, a town of the Brutii.

TERI'OLA or TERI'OLIS, now Tirol, a town at the north of Italy, in the country of the Grisons.

TERIOL'TES, a præfect of Parapamisas, slain by Alexander for his avarice and oppression. *Curt.* 9. c. 8.

TERI'RES, a victor at the Olympic games, Olymp. 97. Ann. 1. *Diod.* l. 14.

TE'RIUM, a city of Pieria in Macedonia. *Polyb.* l. 4.

TERMAN'TIA or TER'MES, a town of Hispania Tarraconensis. *Ptol.* It is now Neustra Senora de Tiermes. The people are called Termestini by *Tacitus, Ann.* 4. c. 45.

TER'MERA, a town of Lycia. *Steph.*

TER'MERUS, a robber of Peloponnesus, who killed people by crushing their heads against his own. He was slain by Hercules in the same manner. *Plut. in Thes.*

TER'MES, a mountain of Asia Minor. *Plin.* 5. c. 29.

TERMES'SUS, a river of Arcadia. *Paus.* 9. *Strabo* and others call it Permessus. *Barth. ad Stat. Theb.* 7. v. 283.

TERMI'EUS, a surname of Jupiter, because he is the origin and principle of every thing. *Lycop.* 706. & *Tzetzes. in loco.*

TER'MILÆ, a name given to the Lycians.

TERMINA'LIA, annnal festivals at Rome, observed in honor of the god Terminus, in the month of February. It was then usual for the peasants to assemble near the principal land-marks which separated their fields, and after they had crowned them with garlands and flowers, to make libations of milk and wine, and to sacrifice a lamb or a young pig. They were originally established by Numa, and though at first it was forbidden to shed the blood of victims, yet in process of time land-marks were plentifully sprinkled with it. *Ovid. Fast.* 2. v. 641.—*Cic. Phil.* 12. c. 10. *Att.* 1. c. 6. ep. 1.—*Macrob.* 1. c. 13.—*Varro. L.L.* 5. c. 3.—*Alex. ab Alex.* 2. c. 22.

TERMINA'LIS, a surname of Jupiter, because he presided over the boundaries and lands of individuals before the worship of the god Terminus was introduced. Some, and particularly Dionysius, suppose that Jupiter and Terminus are the same divinity. *Dionysius. Hal.* 2.

TER'MINUS, a divinity at Rome who was supposed to preside over bounds and limits, and to punish all unlawful usurpation of land. His worship was first introduced at Rome by Numa, who persuaded his subjects that the limits of their lands and estates were under the immediate inspection of heaven. His temple was on the Tarpeian rock, and he was represented at first by a large square stone, but afterwards by a human head without feet or arms, to intimate that he never moved wherever he was placed. The people of the country assembled once a year, with their families, and crowned with garlands and flowers the stones which separated their different possessions, and sprinkled them in a solemn manner with the blood of the victim which was offered to the god who presided over the boundaries, or sometimes with pure oil. It is said that when Tarquin the Proud wished to build a temple on the Tarpeian rock to Jupiter, the god Terminus refused to give way, though the other gods resigned their seats with cheerfulness: whence Ovid has said,

Restitit, et magno cum Jove templa tenet.

Dionys. Hal. 2.—*Ovid. Fast.* 2. v. 641.—*Plut. in Num.*—*Liv.* 5.—*Virg. Æn.* 9. v. 449.—*Servius. ad Virg. loco.*—*Aug. de Civ. D.* 7. c. 7.—*Lactant.* 1. c. 20.—*Arnob. Adv. Gent.* 1.—*Aul. Gell.* 12 c. 6. [The representations of this deity are very numerous, but none of them are of superior workmanship. The best will be found in the collection at the Villa Albani near Rome. The name has been extended to all busts and half figures which terminate in a square block of stone, similar to the representations of the god Terminus.]

TER'MISUS or TERMES'SUS, a town of Pisidia. *Strab*—*Ptol.*—*Liv.* 38. c. 15.

TER'MUS, a river of Sardinia. *Ptol.*

TERPAN'DER, a lyric poet and musician of Antissa in Lesbus, 675 B.C. It is said that he appeased a tumult at Sparta by the melody and sweetness of his notes. He added three strings to the lyre, which before his time had only four. He was four times crowned at the Pythian games, and was the first who obtained a prize at the Carnea. According to the Parian marbles his father's name was Dardeneus. *Fabr. B. Gr.* 1. c. 34.—*Ælian. V.H.* 12. c. 50.—*Plut. de Mus.*—*Strab.* 13.—*Suidas.*—*Steph. Byzant.*—*Zenob. Cent.* 5. *Prov.* 9.—*Athen.* 14. c. 9.—*Euseb. in Chron. & in Strom.* 1.

TERPO'LIUS, a tribune at Rome. *Cic. Corn.* 2.

TERPSICH'ORE, or TERPSICH'ORA, one of the Muses, daughter of Jupiter and Mnemosyne. She presided over dancing, of which she was reckoned the inventress, as her name intimates, and with which she delighted her sisters. She is represented like a young virgin crowned with laurel, and holding in her hand a musical instrument. She was, according to some, mother of the Sirens, and, as others assert, she became mother of Rhesus by the Strymon, and of Biston by Mars. *Juv.* 7. v. 35.—*Apollod.* 1.—*Aus.* ep. 138.—*Eustath. in Il.* 10.—*Sch. Euripid. in Arg. Rh.*—*Tzetzes. Chil.* 13. *H.* 496. *& ad Lyc.* 653. [The finest statue of this Muse is in the Vatican, at Rome.]

TERPSIC'RATE, a daughter of Thespius. *Apollod.* 2. c. 7.

TER'RA, one of the most ancient deities in mythology, wife of Uranus, and mother of Oceanus, the Titans, Cyclopes, Giants, Thea, Rhea, Themis, Phœbe, Thetys, and Mnemosyne. By the Air she had Grief, Mourning, Oblivion, Vengeance, &c. According to Hyginus, she is the same as Tellus. *Vid.* Tellus. Her worship was very universally established, and there was scarcely a country where she had not temples, priests, altars, and statues. She gave her oracle at Delphi to Themis, and Themis afterwards to Apollo. *Hesiod. The.* 134 & 160.—*Apollod.* 1.—*Hygin.* præf. fab.—*Ovid. Met.* 1. v. 321.—*Lucan.* 5. v. 81.—*Marcell.* 21.—*Orph. Hymn.* 78.—*Sidon.* 9. [Terra as well as Tellus is undistinguishable from Cybele. *Vid.* Cybele.]

TERRACI'NA. *Vid.* Tarracina.

TERRASID'IUS, a Roman knight in Cæsar's army in Gaul. *Cæs. B. C.* 3. c. 7 & 8.

TER'ROR, an emotion of the mind which the ancients made a deity, and one of the attendants of the god Mars, and of Bellona.

TER'TA, a town of Thrace, between Sardica and Philippopolis. *Ptol.*

TER'TIA, a sister of Clodius the tribune, &c.——A daughter of Paulus, the conqueror of Perseus, called also Æmilia. *Cic. ad Div.* 1. c. 46. l. 2. c. 40.——A daughter of Isidorus. *Cic. in Verr.* 3. c. 34.——A sister of Brutus who married Cassius. She was also called Tertulla and Junia. *Tacit. Ann.* 3. c. 76.—*Suet. Cæs.* 50.—*Cic. ad B.* 5 & 6. *ad Att.* 15. ep. 11. l. 16. ep. 20.

TER'TIUS JULIA'NUS, a lieutenant in Cæsar's legions. Read Titius.

TERTULLIA'NUS SEPTIM'IUS FLO'RENS, a celebrated Christian writer of Carthage, who flourished A.D. 196. He was originally a Pagan, but afterwards embraced Christianity, of which he became an able advocate by his writings, which showed that he was possessed of a lively imagination, impetuous eloquence, elevated style, and strength of reasoning. The most famous and esteemed of his numerous works, are his Apology for the Christians, and his Prescriptions. He also attempted poetry, but his five books against Marcion, consisting of 1301 verses, and his book De Judicio Domini, in 398 verses, though they show his zeal, are not much in favour of his poetical abilities. The best edition of Tertullian is that of Semler, 4 vols. 8vo. Hal. 1770; and of his Apology, that of Havercamp, 8vo. L. Bat. 1718. Rigaltius' edition, Paris, 1675, is considered the best. *Harles. Not. Lit. Rom.* 1. p. 516.—*Sax. Onom.* 1. p. 339.

TER'VA, a city of Armenia. *Ptol.*

TE'SA, a city of Carmania. *Id.*

TES'TA, a name applied to Trebatius the lawyer. *Cic.* 7. *Fam.* 22.

TES'TIUS PENA'RIUS, an orator, whose distortions in speaking are mentioned by *Cicero*, 2. *Or.* 66.

TE'THYS, the greatest of the sea deities, was wife of Oceanus, and daughter of Uranus and Terra. She was mother of the chief rivers of the universe, such as the Nile, the Alpheus, the Mæander, Simois, Peneus, Evenus, Scamander, &c. and about 3000 daughters called Oceanides. Tethys is confounded by some mythologists with her granddaughter Thetis, the wife of Peleus, and the mother of Achilles. The word Tethys is poetically used to express the sea. *Apollod.* 1. c. 1, &c.—*Virg. G.* 1. v. 31.—*Ovid. Met.* 2. v. 509. l. 9. v. 498. *Fast.* 2. v. 191.—*Hesiod. Theog.* v. 336.—*Homer. Il.* 14. v. 302.—*Seneca in Troad.* 879.

TE'TOS or TE'TUS, a small river of Gaul flowing from the Pyrenees. *Mela.* 2. c. 5.

TETRAGO'NIS, a town of Arachosia, under Caucasus. *Plin.* 6. c. 23. It was before called Cartana.

TETRAP'OLIS, a name given to the city of Antioch, the capital of Syria, because it was divided into four separate districts, each of which resembled a city. Some apply the word to Seleucis, which contained the four large cities of Antioch near Daphne, Laodicea, Apamea, and Seleucia in Pieria.——A division of Attica containing four towns. *Strab.* 8.

TET'RICUS, a mountain of the Sabines near the river Fabaris. It was very rugged, and difficult of access, whence the epithet Tetricus was applied to persons of a morose and melancholy disposition. *Virg. Æn.* 7. v. 713.—*Varro apud Nonium.* 2. no. 865.—*Liv.* 1. c. 18.—*Ital.* 8. v. 419.—*Martial.* 3. epigr. 10.—*Servius ad Virg. loco.*—*Ovid. Amor.* 3. el. 8. v. 61. *De A.A.* 1. v. 721. *Fast.* 2. v. 397.

TET'RICUS, a Roman senator, saluted emperor in the age of Aurelian. He was led in triumph by his successful adversary, who afterwards heaped the most unbounded honors upon him and his son of the same name. *Trebell. Poll. de 30 tyrann.* c. 23.—*Vopisc. in Aurel.* c. 39.

TET'TIX, a Cretan prince who is said to have founded the town of Tænarus on the promontory of the same name in Laconia. *Plut. de his qui serò pun.*

TEU'CER, a king of Phrygia, son of the Scamander by Ida. According to some authors, he was the first who introduced among his subjects the worship of Cybele, and the dances of the Corybantes. This report, however, though supported by Virgil, is confuted by his commentators, and by others who mention Scamander as the prince by whose exertions the ceremonies of the goddess were established in Phrygia. The country where he reigned was from him called Teucria, and his subjects Teucri. His daughter Batea married Dardanus, a Samothracian prince, who succeeded him in the government of Teucria. *Apollod.* 3. c. 12. —*Virg. Æn.* 3. v. 108.—*Dionys. Hal.* 1.—*Trogus apud Servium Æn.* 3. v. 108.—*Servius Æn.* 1. v. 42 & 239. l. 3. v. 94, 95, 104 & 108.——A son of Telamon, king of Salamis, by Hesione, the daughter of Laomedon. He was one of Helen's suitors, and accordingly accompanied the Greeks to the Trojan war, where he signalized himself by his valor and intrepidity. It is said that his father refused to receive him into his kingdom, because he had left the death of his brother Ajax unrevenged. This severity of the father did not dishearten the son; he left Salamis, and retired to Cyprus, where, with the assistance of Belus king of Sidon he built a town, which he called Salamis, after his native country. He attempted to recover the island of Salamis after his father's death, but his efforts were successfully opposed by Eurysacus the son of Ajax, and he retired to Cyprus, where his posterity remained seated on the throne till the time of Evagoras. He afterwards built a temple to Jupiter in Cyprus, in which a man was annually sacrificed till the reign of the Antonines. Some suppose that Teucer did not return to Cyprus, but that, according to a less received opinion, he went to settle in Spain, where New Carthage was afterwards built, and thence into Galatia. *Homer. Il.* 8. v. 281.—*Virg. Æn.* 1. v. 623. —*Apollod.* 3. c. 12.—*Paus.* 2. c. 29.—*Justin.* 44. c. 3.—*Paterc.* 1. c. 1.—*Dictys. Cret.* 1, &c.—*Horat.* 1. od. 7. v. 7.—*Ovid. Heroid.* 7. v. 130.—*Hygin.* fab. 39.—*Lactant. de Fals. R.* 21.——One of the servants of Phalaris of Agrigentum. *Tzetzes. Ch.* 5. c. 31.

TEU'CRI, a name given to the Trojans, from Teucer, their king. *Virg. Æn.* 1. v. 42 & 239.

TEU'CRIA, a name given to Troy, from Teucer, one of its kings. *Virg. Æn.* 2. v. 26.

TEUC'TERI, a people of Germany at the east of the Rhine. *Tacit. de Germ.* c. 22.

TEUMES'SUS, a mountain of Bœotia with a village of the same name, where Hercules, when young, killed an enormous lion. Europa was kept concealed on this mountain by Jupiter, according to some. Minerva Telchinia had a temple there but no statue. The place was celebrated in the verses of Antimachus. *Strab.* 9 —*Paus.* 9. c. 19. —*Stat. Theb.* 1. v. 331. l. 9. v. 462.

TEUO'CHIS, a city and lake of Ægypt. *Steph.*

TEURIOCHÆ'MÆ, a people of Germany. *Ptol.*

TEU'TA or TEU'THA, a queen of Illyricum, B.C. 231, who ordered the Roman ambassadors, P. Junius and L. Coruncanius, to be put to death. This unprecedented murder was the cause of a war, which ended in her defeat and disgrace. *Flor.* 2. c. 5.—*Liv.* 20.—*Plin.* 34. c. 6.

TEUTAG'ONUS, a general of the Bastarnæ, an auxiliary of Perses against Æetes. *Flacc. Argon.* 6. v. 97.

TEUTA'MIAS or TEU'TAMIS, a king of Larissa. He instituted games in honor of his father, where Perseus killed his grandfather Acrisius with a quoit. *Apollod.* 2.—*Tzetzes. ad Lyc.* 838.

TEU'TAMUS, a king of Assyria, the same as Tithonus, the father of Memnon. *Diod.* 5.

TEUTA'NA, a place of Sicyon, before called Titana. *Steph.*—*Plin.* 3. c. 5.

TEU'TAS or TEUTA'TES, a name of Mercury among the Gauls, probably the same as the Thoth of the Ægyptians. The people offered human victims to this deity. *Lucan.* 1. v. 445.—*Cæsar. Bell. G.* 6—*Liv.* 26.—*Lactant de Fals. R.* 21.

TEUTHAD'AMAS, the father of Pelasgus. *Hom. Il.* 2.

TEU'THIS, a city of Arcadia. *Steph.*

TEUTHRA'NIA, a part of Mysia where the Caycus rises. *Ovid. Trist.* 2. v. 19.

TEU'THRAS, a king of Mysia on the borders of the Caycus. He adopted as his daughter, or, according to others, married, Auge, the daughter of Aleus, when she fled away into Asia from her father, who wished to punish her for her amours with Hercules. Some time after, his kingdom was invaded by Idas, the son of Aphareus, and to remove this enemy, he promised Auge and his crown to any one who could restore tranquillity to his subjects. This was executed by Telephus, who afterwards proved to be the son of Auge, who was promised in marriage to him by right of his successful expedition. Some authors call Teuthras the father of Thespius, and thence the 50 Thespiades, who became mothers by Hercules, are called *Teuthrantia turba*. *Apollod.* 2. c. 7, &c.—*Paus.* 3. c. 25.—*Ovid. Trist.* 2. v. 19. *Heroid.* 9. v. 51.—*Hygin.* fab. 99 & 100.——One of the companions of Æneas in Italy. *Virg. Æn.* 10. v. 402.

TEU'THRAS, the name of a river. *Propert.* 1. 2. el. 11. v. 11.

TEUTHRO'NE, a city of Laconia. *Ptol.* It is called Scopia by *Niger.*

TEUTOBODI'ACI, a people of Gaul. *Plin.* 5. c. 32 —*Salmas. ad Solin.* p. 876.

TEUTOBERGIEN'SIS SAL'TUS, a forest of Germany between the Ems and Lippe, where Varus and his legions were cut to pieces. *Tacit. Ann.* 1. c. 60.

TEUTOM'ATUS, a prince of Gaul among the allies of Rome. *Cæs. Comm.* 7. c. 31.

TEU'TONI or TEU'TONES, a people of Germany, who with the Cimbri made incursions upon Gaul, and cut to pieces two Roman armies. They were at last defeated by the consul Marius, and an infinite number made prisoners. *Vid.* Cimbri. *Cic. pro Manil.*—*Flor.* 3. c. 3.—*Plut. in Mar.*—*Martial.* 14. epigr. 26.—*Plin.* 4. c. 14.—*Propert.* 3. el. 3. v. 44.—*Claudian. in Eutr.* 1. v. 406.

TEU'TUS, a prince of Vessa or Inessa, subdued by Phalaris. *Polyæn.* 5. c. 1.

THABEN'NA, an inland town of Africa. *Hirt. Afric.* 77. It is called Thabba by *Ptolemy.*

THA'BIS, a mountain of Scythia. *Mela*, 3. c. 7.

THABU'SIUM, a fortified place of Phrygia. *Liv.* 38. c. 14.

THÆ'MA, an inland city of Arabia Felix. *Ptol.*

THA'IS, a famous courtezan of Athens, who accompanied Alexander in his Asiatic conquests, and gained such an ascendancy over him, that she made him burn the royal palace of Persæpolis. After Alexander's death, she married Ptolemy king of Ægypt. Menander celebrated her charms, both mental and personal, which were of a superior nature, and on this account she is called Menandrea, by *Propertius* 2. el. 6. v. 3. l. 4. el. 5. v. 43. —*Ovid. de Art. Am.* 3. v. 604. *de Rem. Am.* v. 384. —*Plut. in Alex.*—*Juv.* 3. v. 93.—*Athen.* 13. c. 13.

THA'LA, a town of Africa. *Tacit. Ann.* 3. c. 21. According to *Ptolemy* it was a mountain in the interior of Libya, where also he places a people called Thalæ.

THAL'AMÆ, a town of Messenia, famous for a temple and oracle of Pasiphäe. *Plut. in Agid.*

THALAMANÆ'I, a people under the dominion of the Persians. *Steph.*

THALAMI'A, a city of Thessaly, called also Thameia. *Steph.*

THALAS'SIUS, TALAS'SIUS or TALAS'SIO,* a beautiful young Roman in the reign of Romulus. At the rape of the Sabines, one of these virgins appeared remarkable for her beauty and elegance, and her ravisher, afraid of many competitors, exclaimed as he carried her away, that it was for Thalassius. The name of Thalassius was no sooner mentioned, than all were eager to preserve so beautiful a prize for him. Their union was attended with so much happiness, that it was ever after usual at Rome to make use of the word Thalassius at nuptials, and to wish those that were married the felicity of Thalassius. He is supposed by some to be the same as Hymen, as he was made a deity. *Plut. in Rom.*—*Martial.* 1. epigr. 36. l. 3. epigr. 92. l. 12. epigr. 42.—*Liv.* 1. c. 9.—*Servius ad Virg. Ecl.* 6. v. 31.

THA'LES, one of the seven wise men of Greece, born at Miletus in Ionia. He was descended from Cadmus: his father's name was Examius, and his mother's Cleobula. Like the rest of the ancients, he travelled in quest of knowledge, and for some time resided in Crete, Phœnicia, and Ægypt. Under the priests of Memphis he was taught geometry, astronomy, and philosophy, and enabled to measure with exactness the vast height and extent of a pyramid merely by its shadow. His discoveries in astronomy were great and ingenious; he was the first who calculated with accuracy a solar eclipse, and he is said particularly to have foretold that which so remarkably put an end to the hostilities of the armies of the Medes and Lydians. He discovered the solstices and equinoxes, he divided the heavens into five zones, and recommended the division of the year into 365 days, which was universally adopted by the Ægyptian philosophers. Like Homer, he looked upon water as the principle of everything. He was the founder of the Ionic sect, which distinguished itself for its deep and abstruse speculations under the successors and pupils of the Milesian philosopher, Anaximander, Anaximenes, Anaxagoras, and Archelaus the master of Socrates. Thales was never married; and when his mother pressed him to choose a wife, he said he was too young. The same exhortations were afterwards repeated, but the philosopher eluded them by observing, that he was then too old to enter the matrimonial state. He died in the 96th year of his age, about 548 years before the Christian era. His compositions on philosophical subjects are lost. *Fabr. B. Gr.* 1. c. 35.—*Herodot.*

l. c. 7.—*Plato in Ph. & in Tim.*—*Strab.* 14.—*Clem. Alex. Strom.* 2.—*Euseb. Præp. Ev.* 4. c. 14.—*Auson. de Sept.* ep.—*Diog.* 1.—*Cic. de Nat. D.* 1. c. 10. [The finest bust of Thales is in the Vatican, at Rome.]——An orator of Calantes, considered as an affected and turgid imitator.——A painter of Sicyon, whose pieces were finished with spirit and boldness.——A person mentioned by Duris. *Laert.* 1. c. 38.——A writer mentioned by *Dionysius, in Critic.*

THALES'TRIA or THALES'TRIS, a queen of the Amazons, who, accompanied by 300 women, came 35 days' journey to meet Alexander in his Asiatic conquests, to raise children by a man whose fame was so great and courage so uncommon. She is called Minithya or Minithœa by Justin. *Curt.* 6 c. 5.—*Strab.* 11.—*Justin.* 2. c. 4. l. 12. c. 3.

THALE'TAS, a Greek poet of Crete, 900 B.C. He was visited by the lawgiver Lycurgus, whom he accompanied back to Sparta; and his poetry and musical powers proved highly instrumental in paving the way for the introduction of his friend's famous laws, by softening the manners of the Spartans, and inculcating the necessary duties of amity, submission, and concord. It is said that he put an end to a pestilence that raged in Laconia, and thus commanded the reverence and gratitude of his newly adopted countrymen. He is often called Thales, and consequently confounded with the philosopher of that name. *Strab.* 10.—*Plut. de Mus. & in Lyc. &c.*—*Suidas.*—*Fabric. B. Gr.* 1. c. 35.—*Gyrald. de P.H* 3.

THA'LI or THAL'LI, a people near the Sauromatæ.

THALI'A, one of the Muses, who presided over festivals, and over pastoral and comic poetry. She is represented leaning on a column, holding a mask in her right hand, by which she is distinguished from her sisters, as also by a shepherd's crook. Her dress appears shorter, and not so much ornamented as that of the other Muses. The name is derived by some from θάλλω (*floreo*), and therefore the goddess is considered as presiding over botany; while others deduce it from θάλεια (*convivium*), on which account Varro recommends frequent and moderate feasting among poets and musicians, where the conviviality is preserved by the introduction of no more guests than are equal in number to the nine Muses and the three Graces. *Horat.* 4. od. 6. v. 25.—*Mart.* 9. epigr. 75.—*Plut. in Symp. &c.*—*Virg. Ecl.* 6. v. 2.—*Phurnut de N.D.* 14. [The finest representation of this Muse is to be found in the Vatican.] ——One of the Nereides. *Hesiod. Theog.* 245.—*Virg. Æn.* 5. v. 286.

THALI'A, an island in the Tyrrhene Sea. *Aristot. in Mirabil.*

THALIAR'CHUS, a word used by Horace to denote the person who presided at a convivial meeting. *Horat.* 1. od. 9.

THAL'LO, one of the Horæ or Seasons, who presided over the Spring. *Paus.* 9. c. 35.

THALLUME'TUS, a slave of T. Pomp. Atticus. *Cic. ad Att.* 5. ep. 12.

THAL'LUS, a native of Greece, distinguished as the author of a history of Syria, of great worth and authenticity. *Euseb. Præp. Ev.* 10. c. 3.

THAL'PIUS, a son of Eurytus, one of Helen's suitors. He consequently attended Menelaus to the Trojan war at the head of 20 ships, of which he shared the command with his brother Amphimachus. *Homer. Il.* 2. en. 127.—*Paus.* 5. c. 3.—*Apollod.* 3. c. 10.

THALUC'TÆ, a people of India. *Plin.* 6. c. 19.

THAL'UDA, a river of Mauritania Tingitana. *Ptol.*

THALYS'IA, Greek festivals celebrated by the people of the country in honor of Ceres, to whom the first fruits were regularly offered. *Schol. Theocrit.* 5.—*Cœl. Rh. Lect.* 12. c. 19.

THAM'ARA, a city of Arabia Felix. *Plin.* 6. c. 28.

THAMARI'TA, a town of Mauritania Cæsariensis. *Ptol.*

THAM'ARUS, a river of Samnium flowing from the Apennines. *Antonin.*

THAM'IRAS, a Cilician who first introduced the art of augury into Cyprus, where it was religiously preserved in his family for many years. *Tacit.* 2. *Hist.* c. 3.

THAMIS'SA, a city of Africa, near Utica. *Ptol.* We should probably read Thinissa.

THAM'NA, a city of Palestine. *Steph.*

THAM'UDA, a part of Arabia Felix. *Il.*

THAM'YRAS or THAM'YRIS, a celebrated musician of Thrace. His father's name was Philammon, and his mother's Argiope. He became enamoured of the Muses, and challenged them to a trial of skill near Dorion. His challenge was accepted, and it was mutually agreed that the conquered should be totally at the disposal of his victorious adversary. He was conquered, and the Muses deprived him of his eye-sight and his melodious voice, and broke his lyre. Some accuse him of having first introduced into the world the unnatural vice of which Sotades is accused. Among his poems the ancients have mentioned a theogony in 3000 verses, a cosmogony in 5,000, and hymns, the excellency of which has induced Plato to compare him to Orpheus, and to say that the soul of Orpheus transmigrated into the swan, and that of Thamyras into the nightingale. *Homer. Il.* 2. v. 594. l. 5. v. 599.—*Apollod.* 1. c. 3.—*Ovid. Amor.* 3. el. 7. v. 62. *Art. Am.* 3. v. 399.—*Lucan.* 6. v. 352.—*Paus.* 4. c. 33.—*Plato de Leg.* 8 *de Rep.* 10.—*Suidas.*—*Tzetzes. Chil.* 7. c. 108.

THAM'YRIS, one of the petty princes of the Sacæ, in the age of Darius. *Polyæn.* 7. c. 10.——A queen of the Massagetæ. *Vid.* Thomyris.——A Trojan killed by Turnus. *Virg. Æn.* 12. v. 341.

THAN'ACE, wife of Astynous, son of Tithon, was mother of Cinyras, king of Cyprus. *Apollod.* 3.

THAP'SACUS, a city on the Euphrates. *Steph.* It was before called Europus, and afterwards Amphipolis. *Plin* 5. c. 24.

THAPSIP'OLIS, a city near Chalcedon. *Steph.*

THAP'SUS, a town of Africa Propria, where Scipio and Juba were defeated by Cæsar. *Sil.* 3. v. 261.—*Liv.* 29. c. 30. l. 33. c. 48.——A town at the north of Syracuse in Sicily. *Virg. Æn.* 3. v. 698.

THARGE'LIA, festivals in Greece, celebrated in May in honor of Apollo and Diana. They lasted two days, and the youngest of both sexes carried olive branches, on which were suspended cakes and fruits. *Athen.* 12.—*Suidas. Schol.*—*Aristoph. in Equit.*

THARGEL'LA, a noble female, fond of philosophy. *Plut. in Pericl.*

THARI'ADES, one of the generals of Antiochus, &c. *Strab.* l. 11.

THA'RO, an island in the Persian Gulph. *Ptol.* It is called Dora by *Stephanus.*

THA'ROPS, the father of Œager, to whom Bacchus gave the kingdom of Thrace, after the death of Lycurgus. *Diod.* 3.

THA'SIUS or THRA'SIUS, a famous soothsayer of Cyprus, who told Busiris, king of Ægypt, that to stop a dreadful plague which afflicted his country, he must offer a foreigner to Jupiter. Upon this the tyrant ordered him to be seized and sacrificed to the god, as he was not a native of Ægypt. *Ovid. de Art. Am.* 1. v. 649.—*Apollod.* 2.

THA'SIUS, a surname of Hercules, who was worshipped at Thasus. *Paus.* 5. c. 25.

THA'SUS or THA'SOS, a small island in the Ægæan Sea, on the coast of Thrace, opposite the mouth of the Nestus, anciently known by the names of Æria, Odonis, Æthria, Acte, Ogygia, Chryse, and Ceresis. It received that of Thasus, from Thasus the son of Agenor, who settled there when he despaired of finding his sister Europa. It was about 40 miles in circumference, and so uncommonly fruitful, that the fertility of Thasus became proverbial. Its wine was universally esteemed, and its marble quarries were also in great repute, as well as its mines of gold and silver. The capital of the island was also called Thasus, and it was famous for the birth of Theagenes the athlete, and Polygnotus the painter. *Liv.* 33. c. 30 & 35.—*Herodot.* 2. c. 44.—*Mela,* 2. c. 7.—*Paus.* 5. c. 25.—*Ælian. V.H.* 4, &c.—*Virg. G.* 2. v. 91.—*C. Nep. Cim.* 2.—*Plut. de Exil.*—*Plin.* 14. c. 3. l. 14 & 18. l. 15. c. 22.

THA'SUS, a son of Neptune, who went with Cadmus to seek Europa. He built the town of Thasus in Thrace. Some make him brother of Cadmus. *Apollod.* 3. c. 1.—*Con. Nar.* 37.—*Paus.* 5. c. 25.—*Eustath. ad D. Per.* 522.——A son of Anius, a priest of Apollo at Delus. He was devoured by his own dogs. *Hygin.* fab. 247.—*Ovid. in Ib.* 480.

THAUMA'CIA, a town of Thessaly on the Maliac Gulph. *Liv.* 32. c. 4.

THAUMAN'TIAS or THAUMAN'TIS, a name given to Iris, the messenger of Juno, because she was the daughter of Thaumas, the son of Oceanus and Terra, by one of the Oceanides. *Hesiod. Th.* —*Virg. Æn.* 9. v. 5.—*Ovid. Met.* 4. v. 479. l. 14. v. 845.—*Stat. Theb.* 10. v. 123. l. 3. *Sylv.* 3. v. 80. —*Aristot. Meteor.* 3. c. 3.—*Plut. de Plac. Phil.*

THAU'MAS, a son of Neptune and Terra, who married Electra, one of the Oceanides, by whom he had Iris and the Harpyies, &c. *Apollod.* 1. c. 2. —*Hesiod. Th.* 265.—*Hygin præf.* fab.—*Ptol. Heph.*—*Servius in Æn.* 3. v. 241.

THAUMA'SIUS, a mountain of Arcadia, on the top of which, according to some accounts, Jupiter was born. In the age of Pausanias, a grotto was still shown there, called the grotto of Rhea, which no females were permitted to enter, except the women who celebrated the mysteries of the goddess. The rivers Mylaon and Malœtas flowed at the bottom of the mountain. *Paus.* 8. c. 36.

THE'A, a daughter of Uranus and Terra. She married her brother Hyperion, by whom she had the sun, the moon, Aurora, &c. She is called Thia, Titæa, Rhea, Tethys, &c. *Hesiod. Th.* 136 & 371.—*Apollod.* 1

THE'A, one of the Sporades.——A city of Laconia. *Steph.*

THEÆTE'TUS, a mathematician in the 80th Olympiad. He wrote some geometrical treatises. *Procl. Diadoch.* 2. *Comm. in Eucl.*

THEAG'ENES, a man who made himself master of Megara, &c. *Aristot. Polit.* 5. c. 5.——An athlete of Thasus, famous for his strength. His father's name was Timosthenes, a friend of Hercules, though some say that the god himself was his father, and that he had introduced himself to his mother in the features of her husband. He was of superior strength to the rest of his fellow-citizens, and therefore in the public games of Greece he universally distinguished himself, and was crowned not less than 1200 times, according to Plutarch. Statues were raised in different places to honor and commemorate his great actions, and after death he was ranked among the gods. *Plut. in Præc. Pol.*—*Dio. Chrys.* 41.—*Heliodor. Æth.* 16.—*Plin.* 7. c. 47.—*Herodot.* 5. c. 47.—*Paus.* 6. c. 6 & 11.——A Theban officer who distinguished himself at the battle of Cheronæa. *Plut. de Virt. Mul.*——A writer of Athens, who published commentaries on Homer's works. *Tatian.*—*Euseb. Præp. Evan.* l. 10.——An Athenian surnamed καπνος (*fumus*), because he promised much and performed nothing. *Schol. in Aristoph. Aves.* ——A person highly esteemed on account of his riches. *Suidas.* There were several other persons of this name, but of little note. *Voss. H. Gr.* 1. c. 1, &c.

THE'AGES or THEA'GES, a Greek philosopher, disciple of Socrates, who was indebted to a long illness for the zeal and the application which he afterwards showed in the pursuit of science. *Plato Polit. & in Dial. Theog.*—*Ælian. V.H.* 4. c. 15. l. 8, c. 1.

THEAN'GELA, a town of Caria. *Steph.*

THEA'NO, the wife of Metapontus, son of Sisyphus, presented some twins to her husband, when he wished to repudiate her for her barrenness. The children were educated with the greatest care, and some time afterwards, Theano herself became mother of twins. When they were grown up she encouraged them to murder the supposititious children who were to succeed to their father's throne in preference to them. They were both killed in the attempt, and the father, displeased with the conduct of Theano, repudiated her to marry the mother of the children whom he had long considered as his own. *Eustath. ad Dionys. Per.* 368.—*Hygin.* fab. 186.——A daughter of Cisseus, sister to Hecuba, who married Antenor, and was supposed to have betrayed the Palladium to the Greeks, as she was priestess of Minerva. *Homer. Il.* 6. v. 298.—*Paus.* 10. c. 27.—*Dictys. Cret.* 5. c. 8.—*Servius in Virg. Æn.* 1. v. 246 & 484. ——One of the Danaides. Her husband's name was Phantes. *Apollod.* 2. c. 1.——A poetess of Locris. *Voss. de Poet. Gr.* c. 4 —*Jamblich. de Vit. Pythagor.* c. 17, &c.——The wife of the philosopher Pythagoras, daughter of Pythonax of Crete, or, according to others, of Brontinus of Crotona. *Plut. de Præc. Matr. & in Narr. Am.* 3.—*Gyrald. de P.H.* 9.—*Diog.* 8. c. 42.——A priestess of Athens, daughter of Menon, who refused to pronounce a curse upon Alcibiades, when he was accused of having mutilated all the statues of Mercury. *Plut.*——The mother of Pausanias. She was the first, as it is reported, who brought a stone to the entrance of Minerva's temple to shut up her son, when she heard of his crimes and perfidy to his country. *Polyæn.* 8. c. 31.—*Corn. Nep. in Paus.* c. 5.——A daughter of Scedasus, to whom some of the Lacedæmonians offered violence at Leuctra.——A Trojan matron, who became mother of Mimas by Amycus, the same night that Paris was born. *Virg. Æn.* 10. v. 703.

THEA'NUM, a town of Italy. *Vid.* Teanum.

THEAR'IDAS, a brother of Dionysius the elder. He was made admiral of his fleet. *Diod.* 14.

THEA'RIUS, a surname of Apollo at Trœzene. The temple raised to this god was considered as the most ancient of Greece, and had been repaired by Pittheus the son of Pelops. *Hesychius.*—*Schol. Pind. Nem.* 3. v. 122.—*Paus.* 2, c. 31.

THEATE'TES or THEÆTE'TUS, a Greek epigrammatist, some of whose verses are still extant. ——A philosopher, disciple of Socrates, who established himself at Heraclea in Pontus. *Diog.* 4.—*Gyrald. P.H.* 10. —*Plato in The.*

THEA'VA, a town of Hispania Tarraconensis. *Ptol.*

THE'BA or THE'BE, a town of Cilicia. *Vid.* Thebæ.

THE'BÆ (*-arum*), a celebrated city, the capital of Bœotia, situate on the banks of the river Ismenus. The manner of its foundation is not precisely known. Cadmus is supposed to have first begun to found it by building the citadel Cadmea. It was afterwards finished by Amphion and Zethus, but, according to Varro, it owed its origin to Ogyges. The government of Thebes was monarchical, and the sovereigns reigned in the following order after Cadmus: Pentheus son of Echion, Polydorus son of Cadmus, Nycteus son of Neptune, Lycus brother of Nycteus, Labdacus son of Polydorus, Amphion and Zethus sons of Jupiter, Laius son of Labdacus, Œdipus son of Laius, and Eteocles son of Œdipus, whose misfortunes are celebrated and immortalized in the writings of Æschylus, Euripides, and Sophocles. The war which Eteocles and the Thebans supported against the Argives headed by Polynices is famous, as well as that of the Epigoni. The Thebans were looked upon as an indolent and sluggish nation, and the words of Theban pig, became proverbial to express a man remarkable for stupidity and inattention. This, however, was not literally true; under Epaminondas, the Thebans, though before dependent, became masters of Greece, and every thing was done according to their will and pleasure. When Alexander invaded Greece, he ordered Thebes to be totally demolished, because it had revolted against him, except the house where the poet Pindar had been born and educated. In this dreadful period 6,000 of its inhabitants were slain, and 30,000 sold for slaves. Thebes was afterwards repaired by Cassander, the son of Antipater, but it never rose to its original consequence, and Strabo, in his age, mentions it merely as an inconsiderable village. The monarchical government was abolished there at the death of Xanthus, about 1190 years before Christ, and Thebes became a republic. It received its name from Thebe, the daughter of Asopus, to whom the founder Amphion was nearly related. *Apollod.* 2. c. 4, &c.—*Mela,* 2. c. 3.—*Paus.* 2. c. 6. l. 9. c. 5.—*Strab.* 9.—*Plut. in Pel. Flam. & Alex.*—*C. Nep. in Pel. Epam. &c.*—*Horat. Art. Poet.* 394. *Ovid. Met.* 3. v. 561. 14. v. 416, &c.—*Strab.* 9.—*Quintil.* 5. c. 10.—*Servius. ad Virg. Æn.* 2. v. 601. l. 3. v. 466. l. 4. v. 469. l. 6. v. 445. l. 12. v. 514.—*Macrob. in Somn. Scip.*—*Stat. Theb.*——A town at the south of Troas, built by Hercules, and also called Placia and Hypoplacia. It fell into the hands of the Cilicians, who occupied it during the Trojan war. *Curt.* 3. c. 4.—*Liv.* 37. c. 19.—*Strab.* 11.——An ancient celebrated city of Thebais in Ægypt, called also Hecatompylos, on account of its hundred gates, and Diospolis, as being sacred to Jupiter. In the time of its splendour, it extended above 23 miles, and upon any emergency could send into the field 700,000 men according to Tacitus, but agreeable to the more credible opinion of Homer, it could pour through each of its hundred gates 200 armed men with their chariots and horses, or about 40,000 men, allowing two men to each chariot. Thebes was ruined by Cambyses king of Persia, and though its walls were 24 feet in thickness, and its buildings the most solid and magnificent, yet in the times of Strabo and of Juvenal, only mutilated columns, broken obelisks, and temples levelled with the dust. remained to mark its situation, and inform the traveller of the desolation which time or the more cruel hand of tyranny can spread over the proudest monument of human art. *Plin.* 5. c. 9. l. 36. c. 3.—*Juv.* 15. v. 16.—*Tacit. Ann.* 2. c. 60.—*Herodot.* 2 & 3.—*Diod.* 2.—*Homer, Il.* 9. v. 381.—*Propert.* 2. el. 8. v. 9—*Schol. Apollon. Rhod.* 5. v. 262.—*Strab.* 17.—*Mela,* 1. c. 9.——A town of Africa built by Bacchus.——A town in Thessaly. *Liv.* 28. c. 7.——A town in Phthiotis. *Steph. Byz.*—*Eustath. ad Dionys. Per.* 248.—*Schol. Apollon. Rh.* 4. v. 262. The English form is Thebes.

THEB'AIS, a country in the southern parts of Ægypt, of which Thebes was the capital. There were some poems which bore the name of Thebais, but of these the only one extant is the Thebais of Statius. It gives an account of the war of the Thebans against the Argives, in consequence of the dissension of Eteocles with his brother Polynices. The poet was twelve years in composing it, and though the style is often inelegant, yet the poem is highly valuable for the information which it contains respecting the mythology and the more unknown particulars of ancient times.

THEB'AIS, a river of Lydia.

THEB'AIS, a name given to a native of Thebes.

THE'BE or THE'BA, a daughter of the Asopus, who married Zethus. *Apollod.* 3. c. 5.—*Paus.* 2. c. 5.——The wife of Alexander, tyrant of Pheræ. She abhorred so much the cruelties which were daily practised before her, and she lamented so feelingly the death of Pelopidas, that she conspired against her husband, and with the assistance of her three brothers, murdered him. *Plut. in Pelop.*—*Cic. Inv.* 2. c. 49. *Conon. Narr.* 50.

THEBE'TA, a fortified place in Mesopotamia. *Steph.*

THEG'ILIS, an epithet of Minerva. *Steph. in Pamphyl.*

THEGO'NIUM, a city of Thessaly. *Steph.*

THE'IA, a goddess. *Vid.* Thea.

THE'IAS, a son of Belus, who had an incestuous intercourse with his daughter Smyrna.

THELAI'RA, a daughter of Leucippus, better known by the name of Hilaira. *Vid.* Hilaira.

THELAMU'SA, a fortified place of Arabia near the Euphrates. *Steph.*

THELBENCA'NE, a city of Babylon, near the river Euphrates. *Ptol.* It is now Maraga.

THEL'DA, a town of Mesopotamia. *Id.*

THELEPHAS'SA, the second wife of Agenor, called also Telephassa.

THELMINIS'SUS, a town of Syria on the river Orontes. *Ptol.*

THELPU'SA, a nymph of Arcadia. *Vid.* Telpusa.

THELSE'A, a town of Cœlesyria, on the confines of Phœnicia. *Antonin.*

THELXI'ON, a son of Apis, who conspired against his father, who was king of Peloponnesus. *Apollod.* 2. c. 1.—*Paus.* 2. c. 5.

THELXI'OPE, one of the muses, according to some writers. *Cic. de Fin.* 3. c. 21.

THEM'ACI, a village in the tribe Erechtheis. *Steph.*

THEMBRI'MUS, a city of Caria. *Steph.*

THEM'ENUS, one of the Heraclidæ, son of Aristomachus, better known by the name of Temenus. *Vid.* Temenus.

THEME'SION, a tyrant of Eretria. *Diod.* 15.

THEMIL'LAS, a Trojan, &c. *Virg. Æn.* 9. v. 576.

THE'MIS, a daughter of Cœlus and Terra, who married Jupiter against her own inclination. She became mother of Dice, Irene, Eunomia, the Parcæ and Horæ, and was the first to whom the inhabitants of the earth raised temples. Her oracle was famous in Attica in the age of Deucalion, who consulted it with great solemnity, and was instructed how to repair the loss of mankind. She was generally attended by the seasons, and was considered as the first of the gods who established the laws of religion, of sacrifices, of divination, and whatever tends to the harmony and peace of society. She was supposed to preside over the petitions which were presented to the gods, and as she was vigilant that nothing improper or unreasonable was asked from the divinity, so she regarded the due execution and fulfilling of all agreements among mankind. Her image was carried into the tribune at Rome, whenever an orator was permitted to address the people, that he might remember that everything he uttered must be conformable to truth, to equity, and to religion. Among the moderns she is represented as holding a sword in one hand, and a pair of scales in the other. *Ovid. Met.* 1. v. 321.—*Hesiod. Th.* 902.—*Amm. Marc.* 21. c. 1.—*Apollod.* 1. c. 1, &c.—*Paus.* 1. c. 22. l. 5. c. 17.—*Servius in Æn.* 3. v. 104. l. 4. v. 246.—*Festus de V. Sig.*——A daughter of Ilus who married Capys, and became mother of Anchises. *Apollod.* 8 c. 12.

THE'MIS, a town of Africa Propria. *Ptol.*

THEMIS'CYRA or THEMISCY'RA, a town of Cappadocia, at the mouth of the Thermodon, belonging to the kingdom of the Amazons. The territories round it bore the same name. *Strab.* 2.—*Barth. ad Stat. Theb.* 12. v. 635.

THEM'ISON, a famous physician of Laodicea, disciple to Asclepiades. He was founder of a sect called methodists, because he wished to introduce methods to facilitate the learning and the practice of physic. He flourished in the Augustan age. *Cels. Præf.*—*Plin.* 29. c. 1.—*Dioscorid.* 7. c. 2.—*Seneca,* ep. 95.——A physician in the age of Juvenal of established reputation, but too often unsuccessful in his care of his patients. *Juv.* 10. v. 221.——One of the generals and ministers of Antiochus the Great. He was born at Cyprus. *Ælian. V.H.* 2. c. 41.—*Athen.* 7.

THEMIS'SUA, a town of Africa Propria. *Ptol.*

THEMIS'SUS, a city of Caria. *Steph.* It was so called from Themissus, son of Dadus, the founder. *Steph.*

THEMIS'TA or THEMIS'TIS, a goddess, the same as Themis, but more probably a learned woman of Lampsacus, disciple to Epicurus. *Diog.* 10. c. 5.—*Cic. de Fin.* 2. c. 21. *Pis.* 26.

THEMIS'TIUS, a celebrated philosopher of Paphlagonia in the age of Constantius, greatly esteemed by the Roman emperors, and called Euphrades, the fine speaker, from his eloquent and commanding delivery. He was made a Roman senator, and was always distinguished for his liberality and munificence. His school was greatly frequented. He wrote, when young, some commentaries on Aristotle, fragments of which are still extant, and 33 of his orations. He professed himself to be an enemy to flattery, and though he often deviates from this general rule in his addresses to the emperors, yet he strongly recommends humanity, wisdom, and clemency. The best edition of Themistius is Harduin, fol. Paris, 1684. *Fabr. B. Gr.* 5. c. 18.—*Sax. Onom.* 1. p. 415.

THEMIS'TO, daughter of Hypseus, was the third wife of Athamas, king of Thebes, by whom she had four sons, called Ptous, Leucon, Schœneus, and Erythroes, or only two, according to Hyginus, who mentions Orchomenus as one of them. She endeavoured to kill the children of Ino, her husband's second wife, but she killed her own by means of Ino, who lived in her house in the disguise of a servant maid, and to whom she entrusted her bloody intentions, upon which she destroyed herself. *Hygin.* fab. 4, 157 & 239.—*Paus.* 9. c. 23.—*Apollod.* 1. c. 9.—*Tzetzes ad Lyc.* 22.——The mother of the poet Homer, according to a tradition mentioned by *Pausanias,* 10 c 24.——A woman mentioned by *Polynæus,* 8. c. 46.

THEMIS'TOCLES, a celebrated general born at Athens. His father's name was Neocles, and his mother's Euterpe, or Abrotonum a native of Halicarnassus, or of Thrace, or Acarnania. The beginning of his youth was marked by vices so flagrant, and an inclination so incorrigible, that his father disinherited him. This, which might have disheartened others, roused the ambition of Themistocles, and the protection which he was denied at home he sought in courting the favours of the populace, and in sharing the administration of public affairs. When Xerxes invaded Greece, Themistocles was at the head of the Athenian republic, and in this capacity the fleet was entrusted to his care. While the Lacedæmonians, under Leonidas, were opposing the Persians at Thermopylæ, the naval operations of Themistocles, and the combined fleet of the Peloponnesians, were directed to destroy the armament of Xerxes, and to ruin his maritime power. The obstinate wish of the generals to command the Grecian fleet, might have proved fatal to the interests of the allies, had not Themistocles freely relinquished his pretensions, and by nominating his rival Eurybiades master of the expedition, shown the world that his ambition could stoop when his country demanded his assistance. The Persian fleet was distressed at Artemisium by a violent storm, and the feeble attack of the Greeks; but a decisive battle had never been fought, if Themistocles had not used threats and entreaties, and even called religion to his aid, and the favorable answers of the oracle to second his measures. The Greeks, actuated by different views, were unwilling to make head by sea against an enemy whom they saw victorious by land, plundering their cities, and destroying all by fire and sword; but before they were dispersed, Themistocles sent intelligence of their intentions to the Persian monarch. Xerxes, by immediately blocking them up with his fleet in the bay of Salamis, prevented their escape, and while he wished to crush them all at one blow, he obliged them to fight for their safety, as well as for the honour of their country. This battle, which was fought near the island of Salamis, B.C. 480, was decisive, the Greeks obtained the victory, and Themistocles the honour of having destroyed the formidable navy of Xerxes. Further to ensure the peace of his country, Themistocles informed the Asiatic monarch, that the Greeks had conspired to cut the bridge which he had built across the Hellespont, and to prevent his retreat into Asia. This met with equal success: Xerxes hastened away from Greece, and while he believed, on the words of Themistocles, that his return would be disputed, he left his forces without a general, and his fleets an easy conquest to the victorious Greeks. These signal services to his country, endeared Themistocles to the Athenians, and he was universally called the most warlike and most courageous of all the Greeks who fought against the Persians. He was received with the most distinguished honours, and, by his prudent administration, Athens was soon fortified with strong walls, her Piræus was rebuilt, and her harbours were filled with a numerous and powerful navy, which rendered her the mistress of Greece. Yet in the midst of that glory, the conqueror of Xerxes incurred the displeasure of his countrymen, which had proved so fatal to many of his illustrious predecessors. He was banished from the city, and after he had sought in vain a safe retreat among the republics of Greece, and the barbarians of Thrace, he threw himself into the arms of a monarch, whose fleets he had defeated, and whose father he had ruined. Artaxerxes, the successor of Xerxes, received the illustrious Athenian with kindness; and though he had formerly set a price upon his head, yet he made him one of his greatest favorites, and bestowed three rich cities upon him, to provide him with bread, wine and meat. Such kindness from a monarch, from whom he perhaps expected the most hostile treatment, did not alter the sentiments of Themistocles. He still remembered that Athens gave him birth, and according to some writers, the wish of not injuring his country, and therefore his inability of carrying on war against Greece, at the request of Artaxerxes, obliged him to destroy himself by drinking bull's blood. The manner of his death, however, is uncertain, and while some affirm that he poisoned himself, others declare that he fell a prey to a violent distemper in the city of Magnesia, where he had fixed his residence, while in the dominions of the Persian monarch. His bones were conveyed to Attica, and honored with a magnificent tomb by the Athenians, who began to repent too late of their cruelty to the saviour of his country. Themistocles died in the 65th year of his age, about 449 years before the Christian era. He has been admired as a man naturally courageous of a disposition fond of activity, ambitious of glory and enterprize. Blessed with a provident and discerning mind, he seemed to rise superior to misfortunes, and, in the midst of adversity, was possessed of resources which could enable him to regain his splendour, and even command fortune. *Plut. & C. Nep. in Vitâ.—Paus.* 1. c. 1. l. 8. c. 52.—*Ælian. V.H.* 2. c. 12. l. 9. c. 18. l. 13. c. 40. —*Ovid. ex Pont.* 1. el. 3. v. 69. [The finest and most authentic bust of Themistocles will be found in the Museum of the Vatican, at Rome.]——A writer, some of whose letters are extant.——An Archon at Athens, Olymp. 108. an. 2.

THEMISTOG'ENES, an historian of Syracuse in the age of Artaxerxes Mnemon. He wrote on the wars of Cyrus the younger, a subject ably treated afterwards by Xenophon. *Xenoph. H. Gr.* 3. c. 1.

THEM'MA, a town of Arabia Deserta. *Ptol.*

THEN'NA or THE'NÆ, a city of Africa Propria. *Antonin.*

THEOBRICU'LA, a city of Spain, near Auria. *Id.*

THE'OCLES, an opulent citizen of Corinth, who liberally divided his riches among the poor. Thrasonides, a man equally rich with himself, followed the example. *Ælian. V. H.* 14. c. 24. ——A Greek statuary. *Paus.* 6. c. 19.

THEOCLI'A, a sister of Alexander Severus. *Capitol. in Maximin.* c. 3.

THE'OCLUS, a Messenian poet and soothsayer, who died B.C. 671. *Paus.* 4. c. 15, &c.—*Gyrald. de P.H.* 3.

THEOCLYM'ENUS, a soothsayer of Argolis, descended from Melampus. His father's name was Thestor. An accidental murder obliged him to flee from Argos, and he reached Pylus just as Telemachus was going to return to Ithaca, and he easily obtained permission to accompany him. Here, at the sight of some birds, he foretold to his patron and to Penelope the speedy return of Ulysses, and the prophecy was soon after fulfilled. *Homer. Odyss.* 15. v. 225, &c.—*Hygin.* fab. 128.

THEOCRES'TOS or THEOCHRES'TUS, a writer on Libyan affairs. *Apollod. Schol.* l. 4.

THEOC'RITUS, a Greek poet who flourished at Syracuse in Sicily, 282 B.C. His father's name was Praxagoras or Simichus, and his mother's Philina. He lived in the age of Ptolemy Philadelphus, whose praises he sang, and whose favours he enjoyed. Theocritus distinguished himself by his poetical compositions, of which 30 idyllia and some epigrams are extant, written in the Doric dialect, and admired for their beauty, elegance, and simplicity. Virgil, in his eclogues, has imitated and often copied him. Theocritus has been blamed for many indelicate and obscene expressions which he uses; and while he introduces shepherds and peasants with all the rusticity and ignorance of nature, he often disguises their character by making them speak on high and exalted subjects. It is said that he wrote some invectives against Hiero king of Syracuse, who ordered him to be strangled. He also wrote a ludicrous poem called Syrinx, and placed his verses in such order that they represented the pipe of the god Pan. The best editions of Theocritus are Warton's, 2 vols. 4to. Oxon. 1770; that of Heinsius, 8vo. Oxon. 1699; that of Valkenaer, 8vo. L. Bat. 1779; and that of Reiske, 2 vols. 4to. Lips. 1765. *Fabr. B. Gr.* 3. c. 16.—*Sax. Onom.* 1. p. 96—*Quintil.* 10. c. 1.—*Laert.* 5.—*Suidas.*—*Servius ad Virg. Ecl.* 5. v. 55.—*Zarotus ad Ovid. in Ib.*—A Greek historian of Chius, who wrote an account of Libya. *Plut. in Symp.*—*Suidas.*—*Fulgent. Myth.* 1. c. 26.

THEOD'AMAS or THIOD'AMAS, a king of Mysia, in Asia Minor, father of Hylas by Menodice or Mecionice. He was killed by Hercules, because he refused to treat him and his son Hyllus with hospitality, and the hero carried away Hylas, on whom he bestowed his tenderest regards. *Ovid. in Ib.* v. 438.—*Apollod.* 2. c. 7.—*Hygin.* fab. 271. —*Tzetzes, Chil.* 2. c. 43.—*Propert.* 1. el. 20. v. 6. —*Schol. Apollon. Rh.* 1. v. 131.

THEOD'ATUS, an archon at Athens Olymp. 98. an. 2.

THEODEC'TES, a Greek orator and poet of Phaselis, in Pamphylia, son of Aristander, and disciple of Isocrates. He wrote 50 tragedies besides other works now lost, and he was the first who gave rules for acquiring perfection in oratory, which were written in verse. He had such a happy memory that he could repeat with ease whatever verses were spoken in his presence. When Alexander passed through Phaselis, he crowned with garlands the statue which had been erected to the memory of the deceased poet. Aristotle, it is said, rewarded his friendship by presenting him with his books on oratory. *Fabr. B. Gr.* 2. c. 19.—*Sax. Onom.* 1. p. 68.—*Cic. Tusc.* 1. c. 24. *In. Orat.* 51, &c.—*Plut. in Isoc. & Alex.*—*Val. Max.* 8. c. 14.—*Diog.* 5. c. 24.—*Quintil.* 11. c. 2.—*Gyrald. de P. H.* 7.——An orator, son of the preceding, wrote a panegyric on Alexander king of Epirus, and six books on Rhetoric. *Suidas.*—*Voss. de Poet. & H. Gr.*

THEODO'NIS, a town of Germany, now Thionville, on the Moselle,

THEODO'RA, a daughter-in-law of the emperor Maximian, who married Constantius.

THEODO'RA, a woman who from being a prostitute became empress to Justinian, and distinguished herself by her intrigues and enterprises. *Procop. de bell. Goth.*—*Evagr. Hist.* 7. The name of Theodora was common to the empresses of the East in a later period.

THEODORE'TUS or THEODORI'TUS, one of the Greek fathers, who flourished A.D. 425. His works have been edited by Sirmond, 5 vols. fol. Paris 1642, and 5 vols. Halæ, 1769 to 1774. His historical works have been best edited by Reading, fol. Cantab. 1720. *Fabr. B. Gr.* 5. c. 7.—*Sax. Onom.* 1. p. 489. The English form is Theodoret.

THEODO'RUS, a Syracusan of great authority among his countrymen, who severely inveighed against the tyranny of Dionysius.——A philosopher, disciple to Aristippus. He was banished from Cyrene his native town, and fled to Athens, where the friendship of Demetrius Phalereus saved him from the accusations which were carried to the Areopagus against him. Some suppose that he was at last condemned to death for his impiety, and that he drank poison. *Cic. N.D.* 1. c. 1. *Tusc.* 1. c. 43.—*Laert.* 2. c. 86, 101.——A preceptor to one of the sons of Antony, whom he betrayed to Augustus. He was probably the philosopher at Rhodes, who had for some time Tiberius in the number of his pupils. *Quintil.* 2. c. 15. l. 3. c. 1, 17, 18.——A consul in the reign of Honorius. Claudian wrote a poem upon him, in which he praises him with great liberality.——A secretary of Valens. He conspired against the emperor, and was beheaded.——A man who compiled a history of Rome. Of this nothing but his history of the reigns of Constantine and Constantius is extant.——A comic actor.——A player on the flute in the age of Demetrius Poliorcetes, who contemptuously rejected the favors of Lamia, the mistress of the monarch.——A Greek poet of Colophon, whose compositions are lost.——A sophist of Byzantinm called Lagodaidalos by Plato. *Cic. Br.* 12. *Orat.* 12.—*Quintil.* 3. c. 1.——A Greek poet in the age of Cleopatra. He wrote a book of metamorphoses, which Ovid imitated, as some suppose.——An artist of Samus about 700 years B.C. He was the first who found out the art of melting iron, with which he made statues, and to his ingenious experiments it is said that mankind are indebted for the invention of locks, of the rule, the level, and the turning lathe. *Plin.* 7, c. 55.——A priest, father of Isocrates.——A Greek writer, called also Podromus. The time in which he lived is unknown. There is a romance of his composition extant, called the Amours of Rhodanthe and Dosicles, the only edition of which was by Gaulminus, 8vo. Paris, 1625. *Plut. in Isocr. In Symp.* 9. c. 1. *De Opin. Phil.* 1. c. 7. *In Par.* 22, &c.—*Ælian. V.H.* 12. c. 17. l. 14. c. 40.—*Diog.* 2. *In Arist.*—*Paus.* 1. c. 37. l. 3. c 12.

THEODO'SIA, now Caffa, a town in the Cimmerian Bosporus. *Mela*, 2. c. 1.

THEODOSIOP'OLIS, a town of Armenia, built by Theodosius, &c.

THEODO'SIUS FLA'VIUS, a Roman emperor surnamed *Magnus* from the greatness of his exploits. He was invested with the imperial purple by Gratian, and appointed over Thrace and the eastern provinces, which had been in the possession of Valentinian. The first years of his reign were marked with different conquests over the barbarians. The Goths were defeated in Thrace, and 4000 of their chariots, with an immense number of prisoners of both sexes were the reward of this victory. This glorious campaign intimidated the inveterate enemies of Rome; they sued for peace, and treaties of alliance were made with distant nations, who wished to gain the favours and the friendship of a prince whose military virtues were so conspicuous. Some conspiracies were formed against the emperor, but Theodosius totally disregarded them; and while he punished his competitors for the imperial purple, he thought himself sufficiently secure in the love and affection of his subjects. His reception at Rome was that of a conqueror; he triumphed over the barbarians, and restored peace in every part of the empire. He died of a dropsy at Milan, in the 60th year of his age, after a reign of 16 years, the 17th of January, A.D. 395. His body was conveyed to Constantinople, and buried by his son Arcadius in the tomb of Constantine. Theodosius was the last of the emperors who was the sole master of the whole Roman empire. He left three children, Arcadius and Honorius, who succeeded him, and Pulcheria. Theodosius has been commended by ancient writers as a prince blessed with every virtue, and debased by no vicious propensity. Though master of the world he was a stranger to that pride and arrogance which too often disgrace the monarch; he was affable in his behaviour, benevolent and compassionate, and it was his wish to treat his subjects as himself was treated when a private man, and a dependant. Men of merit were promoted to places of trust and honor, and the emperor was fond of patronizing the cause of virtue and learning. His zeal as a follower of Christianity has been applauded by all the ecclesiastical writers, and it was the wish of Theodosius to support the revealed religion, as much by his example, meekness, and Christian charity, as by his edicts and ecclesiastical institutions. His want of clemency, however, in one instance, was too openly betrayed, and when the people of Thessalonica had unmeaningly, perhaps, killed one of his officers, the emperor ordered his soldiers to put all the inhabitants to the sword, and no less than 6000 persons, without distinction of rank, age, or sex, were cruelly butchered in that town in the space of three hours. This violence irritated the ecclesiastics, and Theodosius was compelled by St. Ambrose to do open penance in the church, and publicly to make atonement for an act of barbarity which had excluded him from the bosom of the church and the communion of the faithful. In his private character Theodosius was an example of soberness and temperance, his palace displayed becoming grandeur, but still with moderation. He never indulged luxuries or countenanced superfluities. He was fond of bodily exercise, and never gave himself up to pleasure and enervating enjoyments. The laws and regulations which he introduced in the Roman empire, were of the most salutary nature. *Socrat.* 5, &c.—*Zosim.* 4, &c.—*Ambros.*—*Augustin.*—*Claudian, &c.*

THEODO'SIUS the Second, succeeded his father Arcadius as emperor of the western Roman empire, though only in the 8th year of his age. He was governed by his sister Pulcheria, and by his ministers and eunuchs, in whose hands was the disposal of the offices of the state, and all places of trust and honor. He married Eudoxia, the daughter of a philosopher called Leontius, a woman remarkable for her virtues and piety. The territories of Theodosius were invaded by the Persians, but the emperor soon appeared at the head of a numerous force, and the two hostile armies met on the frontier of the empire. The consternation was universal on both sides; without even a battle, the Persians fled, and no less than 100,000 were lost in the waters of the Euphrates. Theodosius raised the siege of Nisibis, where his operations failed of success, and he averted the fury of the Huns and Vandals by bribes and promises. He died on the 29th of July, in the

49th year of his age, A.D. 450, leaving only one daughter Licinia Eudoxia, whom he had married to the emperor Valentinian the Third. The carelessness and inattention of Theodosius to public affairs are well known. He signed all the papers that were brought to him without even opening them or reading them, till his sister apprized him of his negligence, and rendered him more careful and diligent, by making him sign a paper, in which he delivered into her hands Eudoxia his wife as a slave and menial servant. The laws and regulations which were promulgated under him, and selected from the most useful and salutary institutions of his imperial predecessors, have been called the Theodosian code. Theodosius was a warm advocated for the Christian religion, but he has been blamed for his partial attachment to those who opposed the orthodox faith. *Sozom.—Socrates, &c.*

THEODO'SIUS, a lover of Antonina the wife of Belisarius.——A mathematician of Tripoli, who flourished 75 B.C. His treatise called Sphærica, is best edited by Hunt, 8vo. Oxon. 1707. *Sax. Onom.* 1. p. 281.—*Fabr. B. Gr.* 3. c. 5.——A Roman general, father of Theodosius the Great; he died A.D. 376.——A native of Chius who came to Rome as ambassador from his nation, and was assassinated by means of Clodius. *Cic. Resp. Har.* 16.

THEOD'OTA or THEOD'OTE, a beautiful courtezan of Elis, whose company was frequented by Socrates. *Xenoph. de Socrat. Fact. &c.—Ælian. V. H.* 13. c. 32.

THEOD'OTA, a Roman empress, &c.

THEODO'TION, an interpreter, in the reign of Commodus.

THEOD'OTUS, an admiral of the Rhodians, sent by his countrymen to make a treaty with the Romans.——A native of Chius, who, as preceptor and counseller of Ptolemy, advised the feeble monarch to murder Pompey. He carried the head of the unfortunate Roman to Cæsar, but the resentment of the conqueror was such that the mean assassin fled, and, after a wandering and miserable life in the cities of Asia, he was at last put to death by Brutus. *Plut. in Brut. & Pomp.*——A Syracusan, accused of a conspiracy against Hieronymus the tyrant of Syracuse.——A governor of Bactriana in the age of Antiochus, who revolted and made himself king, B C. 250. *Justin.* 41. c. 4.——A friend of the emperor Julian.——A Greek who wrote a history of Phœnicia. *Suidas.*——One of the generals of Alexander.

THEOGAMI'A, festivals celebrated by the Greeks, in honor of Proserpine and Pluto. *Gyrald. de Sacrif.* 17.

THEOGNE'TE, the name of Jason's mother, according to the *scholiast* of *Apollonius* of *Rhodes*, l. 3.

THEOGNE'TES or THEOGNE'TUS, a Greek tragic poet, whose plays, called Philargyrus, Philodespotus, and Centaurus, are mentioned by ancient authors. *Athen.*

THEOG'NIS, a Greek poet of Megara, who flourished about 549 years before Christ, and wrote several poems. His sentences, which are intended as precepts for the conduct and the regulation of human life, are often quoted by Plato, and other Greek historians and philosophers. They are collected together, and comprehended in 1220 verses, in which the poet very frequently addresses himself to Cyrnus, a person at present unknown, but who probably was his friend and patron. The morals of the poet have been censured as neither decorous nor chaste. The best edition of Theognis is that of Blackwall, 12mo. London, 1706. *Plut. cur Pyth. &c.—Fabr. B. Gr.* 2. c. 11.—*Sax. Onom.* 1. p. 23.——A tragic poet, whose compositions were so lifeless and inanimated, that they procured him the name of *Chion* or *snow*. *Plut. de Comm. Not.—Gyrald. de P. H.* 7.

THEOI'NOS, a surname of Bacchus, expressive of his presiding over wine.

THEOM'BROTUS, a philosopher, disciple of Metrocles, who had among his pupils Demetrius of Alexandria. *Plin.* 7. c. 37.—*Diog.* 6.

THEOMNAS'TUS or THEORAC'TUS, a native of Syracuse intimate with Verres. *Cic. Verr.* 2. c. 21. l. 4. c. 66.

THEOMNES'TUS, a rival of Nicias in the administration of public affairs at Athens. *Strab.* 14.——A statuary of Sardinia. *Paus.* 6. c. 15.—*Plin.* 34. c. 10.——An Athenian philosopher among the followers of Plato's doctrines. He had Brutus, Cæsar's murderer, among his pupils. *Plut. in Brut.*——A painter. *Plin.* 35. c. 10.

THE'ON, a philosopher, who used frequently to walk in his sleep. *Diog.*——An astronomer of Smyrna, in the reign of Adrian.——A painter of Samus. *Ælian. V. H.* 2. c. 44.—*Plut.*——A philosopher. *Diog.*——An infamous reviler, hence *Dente Theonino circumrodi* became proverbial. *Horat.* 1. ep. 18. v. 82, *& Scholiast.—Auson.* 4. v. 102.——An Alexandrian philosopher and mathematician who flourished under Theodosius the Great. He wrote commentaries on Ptolemy. *Socr. H.* 7. c 15.—*Voss. Scient. Math.* c. 16. sec. 9, &c. For other persons of this name, and their works, see *Sax. Onom.* 1. p. 293, 394, & 452. *& Fabr. B. Gr.* 3. c. 5. 4. c. 31. & 5. c. 22.

THEON'OE, a daughter of Thestor, sister of Calchas. She was carried away by pirates, and sold to Icarus, king of Caria. Her father pursued the ravishers and was wrecked on the coast of Caria, where he was seized by the natives and imprisoned. Leucippe, another sister of Theonoe, anxious for her father's and her sister's fate, consulted the oracle, and was directed to disguise herself, and to travel in the dress and character of a priest of Apollo. In this assumed habit she visited Caria, and was introduced to Theonoe, who became enamoured of her, and ordered her to be assassinated when she refused to yield to her intreaties. Thestor was employed as the assassin of this unknown stranger, but he discovered in the prison that this pretended priest was his own daughter Leucippe, and when he espoused her quarrel, and united to destroy their common murderer, he found her to be Theonoe, to whom he was reconciled. Icarus was informed of this strange adventure, and he loaded this unhappy family with presents, and permitted them to return home. *Hygin.* fab. 190.——A daughter of Proteus and a Nereid, who became enamoured of Canobus, the pilot of a Trojan vessel. *Euripid. in Hel.* 325.—*Conon, Narr.* 8.

THE'OPE, one of the daughters of Leos.

THEOPH'ANE, a daughter of Bisaltus, whom Neptune changed into a sheep, to remove her from her numerous suitors, and conveyed to the island Crumissa. The god afterwards assumed the shape of a ram, and under this transformation he had by the nymph a ram with a golden fleece, which carried Phryxus to Colchis. *Ovid. Met.* 6. v. 177. *Hygin.* fab. 188.

THEOPH'ANES, a Greek historian, born at Mitylene. He was very intimate with Pompey, of whose actions he wrote the history, and from his friendship with the Roman general, his countrymen derived many advantages. After the battle of Pharsalia, he advised Pompey to retire to the court of Ægypt. *Cic. pro Arch. &c.—Paterc.* 2. c. 18.—*Plut. in Cic. & Pomp.*

THEOPH'ANES M. POMPE'IUS, son of the preceding, was made governor of Asia, and enjoyed the intimacy of Tiberius.

THEOPH'ANES, an historian of Byzantium, who flourished under Justin the Second. His works were published at Paris, fol. 1649. *Voss. H. Gr.* 2. c. 24.

THEOPHA'NIA or THEOPHANI'A, festivals celebrated at Delphi in honor of Apollo.

THEOPH'ILA, a city of India within the Ganges. *Ptol.*

THEOPH'ILUS, a comic poet of Athens.——A freedman of Marcellus. *Cic. Fam.* 9. ep. 10.——A governor of Syria in the age of Julian.——A friend of Piso. *Tac. Ann.* 2. c. 55.——A physician, whose treatise *de Urinis* is best edited by Guidotius, L. Bat. 1728, and another by Morell, 8vo. Paris, 1556.——One of the Greek fathers, whose work *ad Autolycum* is best edited in 12mo. by Wolf, Hamb. 1724. The name of Theophilus was common among the primitive Christians.

THEOPHRAS'TUS, a native of Eresus, in Lesbus, son of a fuller. He studied under Plato, and afterwards under Aristotle, whose friendship he gained, and whose warmest commendations he deserved. His original name was Tyrtamus, but this the philosopher made him exchange for that of Euphrastus, to intimate his excellence in speaking, and afterwards for that of Theophrastus, which he deemed still more expressive of his eloquence, the brilliancy of his genius, and the elegance of his language. After the death of Socrates, when the malevolence of the Athenians drove all the philosopher's friends from the city, Theophrastus succeeded Aristotle in the Lyceum, and rendered himself so conspicuous that in a short time the number of his auditors was increased to two thousand. Not only his countrymen courted his applause, but kings and princes were desirous of his friendship; and Cassander and Ptolemy, two of the most powerful of the successors of Alexander, regarded him with more than usual partiality. Theophrastus composed many books, and Diogenes has enumerated the titles of about 200 treatises, which he wrote with great elegance and copiousness. About 20 of these are extant, among which are his history of stones, his treatise on plants, on the winds, on the signs of fair weather, &c. and his Characters, an excellent moral treatise, which was begun in the 99th year of his age. He died loaded with years and infirmities in the 107th year of his age, B C. 288, lamenting the shortness of life, and complaining of the partiality of nature in granting longevity to the crow and to the stag, but not to man. To his care we are indebted for the works of Aristotle, which the dying philosopher entrusted to him. The best edition of Theophrastus is that of Heinsius, fol. L Bat. 1613; and of his Characters, that of Needham, 8vo. Cantab. 1712, and that of Fischer, 8vo. Coburg, 1763. *Fabr. B. Gr.* 3. c. 9.—*Sax. Onom.* 1. p. 83.—*Cic. Tusc.* 3. c. 28. *in Brut.* c. 31. *in Orat.* 19, &c.—*Strab.* 13.—*Diog. in Vitâ.*—*Ælian. V. H.* 2. c. 8. l. 34. c. 20. l. 8. c. 12.—*Quintil.* 10. c. 1.—*Plut. adv. Colot.*—*Hieronym. ep. ad Nep.* [A bust of Theophrastus will be found in the Museum of the Capitol, at Rome.]——An officer entrusted with the care of the citadel of Corinth by Antigonus. *Polyæn.* ——An archon at Athens, Olymp. 110. an. 1.

THEOPOL'EMUS, a man who, with his brother Hiero, plundered Apollo's temple at Delphi, and fled away for fear of being punished. *Cic. in Verr.* 5.

THEOP'OLIS, a name given to Antioch because the Christians first received their name there.

THEOPOM'PUS, a king of Sparta, of the family of the Proclidæ, who succeeded his father Nicander, and distinguished himself by the many new regulations which he introduced. He created the Ephori, and died, after a long and peaceful reign, B.C. 723. While he sat on the throne the Spartans made war against Messenia. *Plut. in Lyc.*—*Paus.* 3. c. 7.——A famous Greek historian of Chius, disciple of Isocrates, who flourished B.C. 354. All his compositions are lost, except a few fragments quoted by ancient writers. He is compared to Thucydides and Herodotus, as an historian, yet he is severely censured for his satirical remarks and illiberal reflections. He obtained a prize in which his master was a competitor, and he was liberally rewarded for composing the best funeral oration in honor of Mausolus. His father's name was Damasistratus. *Fabr. B. Gr.* 5. c. 38.—*Sax. Onom.* 1. p. 73.—*Dionys. Hal.* 1.—*Plut. in Lys.*—*C. Nep.* 7. c. 11.—*Paus.* 6. c. 18.—*Quintil.* 2. c. 8. l. 10. c. 1.—*Cic. de Att.* 2. ep. 6. *Leg.* 1. c. 1. *Br.* 56.—*Diod.* 14.——An Athenian, who attempted to deliver his country from the tyranny of Demetrius. *Polyæn.* 5.——A comic poet in the age of Menander. He wrote 24 plays, all lost. *Suidas.*—*Plut. in Lys.*—*Athen.*—*Gyrald. de P. H.* 7.—*Fabr. B. Gr.* 2. c. 22.—*Sax. Onom.* 1. p. 67.——A son of Demaratus, who obtained several crowns at the Olympic games, and was rewarded with his son of the same name, and his father, with statues in the grove of Jupiter at Olympia. *Paus.* 1. c. 10.——An orator and historian of Cnidus, very intimate with J. Cæsar. *Strab.* 14.—*Cic.* 13. *Att.* 7.——A Spartan general, killed at the battle of Tegyra.——A philosopher of Cheronæa, in the reign of the emperor Philip. *Eutrop.* l. 10.

THEOPHYLACTUS SIMOCAT'TUS, a Byzantine historian, whose works were edited fol. Paris, 1647. *Phot. Cod.* 65.—*Suidas in Lex.*—*Voss. H. Gr.* 2. c. 23.

THEOPHYLAC'TUS, one of the Greek fathers, who flourished A.D. 1070. His works were edited at Venice, 4 vols. 1754 to 1763.

THEO'RIA, a festival at Athens in honor of Apollo, which was yearly observed, according to the vow which Theseus had made when going on his Cretan expedition, to send the ship in which he sailed to Delus with offerings and sacrifices for the god. The ship was called Theoris, and the persons sent Theores, or Deliastæ. *Suidas.*—*Plato in Phæd.*—*Gyrald de Navig.*

THEO'RIUS, a surname of Apollo at Trœzene, where he had a very ancient temple. The word signifies clear-sighted. *Paus.* 2. c. 31.—*Plut. de ei Inscrip.*

THEO'RUS, a comic poet of infamous character. *Aristoph. Schol. Equit.*

THEOTI'MUS, a wrestler of Elis, son of Moschion, in the age of Alexander. *Paus.* 6. c. 17.——A Greek who wrote a history of Italy.—*Plut. in Par.*

THEOXE'NA, a noble lady of Thessaly, who destroyed herself, her husband, and children, when unable to escape from the soldiers of king Philip, who pursued her. *Liv.* 40. c. 4.

THEOXE'NIA, a festival celebrated in honor of all the gods in every city of Greece, but especially at Athens. Games were then observed, and the conqueror who obtained the prize received a large sum of money, or, according to others, a net beautifully ornamented. The Dioscuri established a festival of the same name, in honor of the gods who had visited them at one of their entertainments. *Strab.* 8.—*Paus.* 7. c. 27.—*Hesych.*—*Schol. Pindar. Olymp.* 3.

THEOXE'NIUS, a surname of Apollo. *Salmas ad Solin.* p. 149.

THEOX'ENUS, a general of the Achæan league. *Liv.* 33. c. 18.

THE'RA, a daughter of Amphion and Niobe, called also Ethodea, or Neæra. *Apollod.* 3.—*Schol. Stat. ad Theb.* 3. v. 191.—*Hygin.* fab. 69.

THE'RA, one of the Sporades in the Ægæan Sea, anciently called Calista, now Santorin. It was first inhabited by the Phœnicians, who were left there under Membliares by Cadmus, when he went in quest of his sister Europa. It was called Thera by Theras, the son of Autesion, who settled there with a colony from Lacedæmon. *Paus.* 3. c. 1.—*Herodot.* 4.—*Strab.* 8.—*Plin.* 2. c. 89.—*Tzetzes ad Lyc.* 885.——A town of Caria. *Steph.*

THERAM'BOS or THERAM'BUS, a town near Pallene. *Herodot.* 7. c. 123.

THERAM'ENES, an Athenian philosopher and general in the age of Alcibiades. His father's name was Agnon. He was one of the 30 tyrants at Athens, but he had no share in the cruelties and oppression which disgraced their administration. He was accused by Critias, one of his colleagues, because he opposed their views, and he was condemned to drink hemlock, though defended by his own innocence, and the friendly intercession of the philosopher Socrates. He drank the poison with great composure, and poured some of it on the ground, with the sarcastical exclamation of, "This is to the health of Critias." This happened about 404 years before the Christian era. Theramenes, on account of the fickleness of his disposition, has been called *Cothurnus*, a part of the dress used by both men and women. *Cic. de Orat.* 3. c. 16.—*Plut. in Alcib., &c.*—*C. Nep.*—*Tzetzes. Chil.* 12. v. 416.

THERAP'NE or TERAP'NE, a town of Laconia, at the west of the Eurotas, where Apollo had a temple called Phœbeum. It was at a very short distance from Lacedæmon, and indeed some authors have confounded it with the capital of Laconia. It received its name from Terapne, a daughter of Lelex. Castor and Pollux were born there, and on that account they were sometimes called *Therapnæi fratres.* Menelaus had a temple there, where his tomb was also shown. *Orph. Arg.* 204. *Paus.* 3. c. 14.—*Ovid. Fast.* 5. v. 223.—*Sil.* 6. v. 303. l. 8. v. 414. l. 13. v. 43.—*Liv.* 2. c. 16.—*Dionys. Hal.* 2. c. 49.—*Stat.* 7. *Theb.* v. 793.—*Tzetzes ad Lyc.* 149 & 590.

THE'RAS, a son of Autesion of Lacedæmon, who conducted a colony to Callista, to which he gave the name of Thera. He received divine honors after death. *Paus.* 3. c. 1 & 15.

THER'GUBIS, a city of Mesopotamia. *Ptol.*

THER'ICLES, a potter of eminence at Corinth in the age of Aristophanes. *Cic. Verr.* 4. c. 18.—*Lucian. Lexic.* 7.—*Athen.* 8.——A sculptor. *Plin.* 16. c. 40.

THERIM'ACHUS, a son of Hercules by Megara. *Apollod.* 2. c. 4 & 7.

THERIONAR'CE, a small island of Doris, near Cnidus. *Plin.* 5. c. 31.

THERIP'PIDAS, a Lacedæmonian, &c. *Diod.* 15.

THERI'TAS or THER'ITAS, a surname of Mars in Laconia, from a statue which he had at Therapne. This statue was said to receive the name from Thero, a supposed nurse of the god, or from the place whence it was brought, though some believed it to have been placed there by Castor and Pollux from Colchis. *Paus.* 3. c. 19.

THER'MA, a town of Africa. *Strabo.*——A town of Macedonia, afterwards called Thessalonica, in honor of the wife of Cassander, and now Salonichi. The bay in the neighbourhood of Thema is called Thermæus, or Thermaicus Sinus, and advances far into the country, so much that *Pliny* has named it Macedonicus Sinus, by way of eminence, to intimate its extent. *Strab.*—*Tacit. Ann.* 5. c. 10.—*Herodot.*

THER'MÆ (*baths*), a town of Sicily, where were the baths of Selinus, now Sciacca.——A town near Panormus, now Thermini. *Sil.* 14. v. 23.—*Cic. Ver.* 2. c. 35.

THER'MIDA, a city of the Carpetani. *Ptol.*

THERMIDA'VA, a town of Dalmatia. *Id.*

THERMO'DON, now Termeh, a famous river of Cappadocia, in the ancient country of the Amazons, falling into the Euxine Sea, near Themiscyra. There was also a small river of the same name in Bœotia, near Tanagra, which was afterwards called Hæmon. *Strab.* 11.—*Herodot.* 9. c. 27.—*Mela,* 1. c. 19.—*Paus.* 1. c. 1. l. 9. c. 19.—*Plut. in Dem.*—*Virg. Æn.* 11. v. 659.—*Plin.* 37. c. 8.—*Propert.* 3. el. 12. v. 16. l. 4. el. 4. v. 69.—*Ital.* 2. v. 80.—*Ovid. Met.* 2. v. 249, &c.

THERMOP'YLÆ, a small pass leading from Thessaly into Locris and Phocis. It has a large ridge of mountains on the west, and the sea on the east, with deep and dangerous marshes, being in the narrowest part only 25 feet in breadth. Thermopylæ receives its name from the hot baths which are in the neighbourhood. It is celebrated for a battle which was fought there, B.C. 480, on the 7th of August, between Xerxes and the Greeks, when 300 Spartans resisted for three successive days the repeated attacks of the most brave and courageous of the Persian army, which, according to some historians, amounted to five millions. There was also another battle fought there between the Romans and Antiochus, king of Syria. *Herodot.* 7. c. 176, &c.—*Strab.* 9.—*Liv.* 36. c. 15.—*Mela,* 2. c. 3.—*Plut. in Cat. & in Cleom.*—*Paus.* 7. c. 15.

THER'MUM or THER'MUS, a town of Ætolia, on the Evenus, at one time the chief town of the country. *Polyb.* 5.

THER'MUS, a man accused in the reign of Tiberius, &c.——A man put to death by Nero.

THER'MUS, a town of Ætolia. *Vid.* Thermum.

THER'MUS A. MINUC., a man defended twice by Cicero. *Cic. Flacc.* 39.

THER'MUS QUIN'TIUS, a prætor of Asia intimate with Cicero. *Cic.* 2. *Fam.* 18. l. 13. ep. 59.

THER'MYDRA, the harbour of a city in Rhodes. *Steph.*

THER'NE, a city of Thrace. *Id.*

THEROD'AMAS, a king of Scythia, who as some report, fed lions with human blood, that they might be more cruel. *Ovid. Ib.* 383. *Pont.* 1. el. 2. v. 121.

THE'RON, a tyrant of Agrigentum, who died 472 B.C. He was a native of Bœotia, son of Ænesidamus, and he married Demarete, the daughter of Gelon of Sicily. *Herodot.* 7.—*Pind. Olymp.* 2.——A Rutulian who attempted to kill Æneas. He perished in the attempt. *Virg. Æn.* 10. v. 312.——A priest in the temple of Hercules at Saguntum, when the town was besieged by Annibal. *Sil.* 2. v. 149.——A Theban descended from the Spartæ, killed in the Argive war by Hippomedon. *Stat. Theb.* 2. v. 572.——A daughter of Phylas beloved by Apollo, by whom she had a son called Cheron. *Paus.* 9. c. 40.

THE'RON, one of Actæon's dogs. *Ovid. Met.* 2. v. 211.

THEROTH'OÆ, a nation of the Troglodytæ. *Plin.* 6. c. 29.

THERPAN'DER. *Vid.* Terpander.

THER'SALUS, a native of Lampsacus, a great enemy to Verres. *Cic. Verr.* 1. c. 33.

THERSAN'DER, a son of Polynices and Argia. He accompanied the Greeks to the Trojan war, but was killed in Mysia by Telephus, before the confederate army reached the enemy's country. Homer makes no mention of him. He, as some suppose, gave Eryphile the famous necklace of Harmonia. He was succeeded by his son Tisamenes on the throne of Thebes. *Paus.* 7. c. 3. l. 9. c. 6.—*Stat. Theb.* 3. v. 683.—*Virg. Æn.* 2. v. 261.—*Apollod.* 3. c. 7.—*Sch. Homer. Il.* 1. v. 405.——A son of Sisyphus, king of Corinth, and also of Agamedidas, king of Cleonæ in Peloponnesus. *Paus.* 2. c. 4. l. 3. c. 16.——A musician of Ionia.

THER'SARA, a city of Assyria. *Ptol.*

THER'SES, a native of Thebes, the friend of Anius. *Ovid. Met.* 13. v. 682.

THERSIL'OCHUS, son of Antenor, and leader of the Pæonians in the Trojan war, was killed by Achilles. *Virg. Æn.* 6. v. 483.——A friend of Æneas killed by Turnus. *Id.* 12. v. 363.——An athlete of Corcyra, crowned at the Olympic game. *Paus.* 6. c. 13.

THERSIP'PUS, a son of Agrius, who drove Œneus from the throne of Calydon.——A man who carried a letter from Alexander to Darius. *Curt.*——An Athenian author who died 954 B.C.

THERSI'TÆ, a nation of Iberia. *Steph.*

THERSI'TES, an officer the most deformed and illiberal of the Greeks during the Trojan war. He was fond of ridiculing his fellow-soldiers, particularly Agamemnon, Achilles and Ulysses. Achilles killed him with one blow of his fist, because he laughed at his mourning the death of Penthesilea. The name is used as most expressive of a deformed person and cowardly character. *Ovid. ex Pont.* 4. el. 13. v. 15: *Am.* 2. el. 6. v. 41. *de R.A.* 482.—*Juv.* 8. v. 269. sat. 11. v. 31.—*Apollod.* 1. c. 8.—*Homer. Il.* 2. v. 212, &c.—*Tzetzes ad Lyc.* 995.—*Quint. Smyr.* 1. v. 720, 756, &c.

THESE'IDÆ, a patronymic given to the Athenians from Theseus, one of their kings. *Virg. G.* 2. v. 383.

THESE'IS, a poem written by Codrus, containing an account of the life and actions of Theseus, and now lost. *Juv.* 1. v. 2.

THE'SEUS, king of Athens, and son of Ægeus, by Æthra, the daughter of Pittheus, was one of the most celebrated heroes of antiquity. He was educated at Trœzene, in the house of Pittheus; and as he was not publicly acknowledged to be the son of the king of Athens, he passed for the son of Neptune. When he came to years of maturity, he was sent by his mother to his father, and a sword was given him, by which he might make himself known to Ægeus in a private manner. *Vid.* Ægeus. His journey to Athens was not across the sea, as it was usual with travellers, but Theseus determined to signalize himself by going by land, and encountering difficulties. The road which led from Trœzene to Athens was infested with robbers and wild beasts, and rendered impassable; but these obstacles were easily removed by the courageous son of Ægeus. He destroyed Corynetes, Synnis, Sciron, Cercyon, Procrustes, and the celebrated Phæa. At Athens, however, his reception was not cordial. Medea lived there with Ægeus, and as she knew that her influence would fall to the ground if Theseus was received into his father's house, she attempted to destroy him before his arrival was made public. Ægeus was himself to give the cup of poison to this unknown stranger at a feast; but the sight of his sword on the side of Theseus reminded him of his amours with Æthra. He knew him to be his son, and the people of Athens were glad to find that this illustrious stranger who had cleared Attica from robbers and pirates was the son of their monarch. The Pallantides, who expected to succeed their uncle Ægeus on the throne, as he apparently had no children, attempted to assassinate Theseus; but they fell a prey to their own barbarity, and were all put to death by the young prince. The bull of Marathon next engaged the attention of

Theseus. The labor seemed arduous, but he caught the animal alive; and after he had led it through the streets of Athens, he sacrificed it to Minerva, or the god of Delphi. After this, Theseus went to Crete among the seven chosen youths whom the Athenians yearly sent to be devoured by the Minotaur. The wish to deliver his country from so dreadful a tribute engaged him to undertake this expedition. He was successful, by means of Ariadne, the daughter of Minos, who was enamoured of him; and after he had escaped from the labyrinth with a clue of thread, and killed the Minotaur, (*Vid.* Minotaurus), he sailed from Crete with six boys and seven maidens, whom his victory had equally redeemed from death. In the island of Naxus, whither he was driven by the winds, he had the meanness to abandon Ariadne, to whom he was indebted for his safety. The rejoicings which his return might have occasioned at Athens were interrupted by the death of Ægeus, who threw himself into the sea when he saw his son's ship return with black sails, which was the signal of ill success. *Vid.* Ægeus. His ascension on his father's throne was universally applauded, B.C. 1235. The Athenians were governed with mildness, and Theseus made new regulations, and enacted new laws. The number of the inhabitants of Athens was increased by the liberality of the monarch; a court was instituted which had the care of all civil affairs; and Theseus made the government democratical, while he reserved for himself only the command of the armies. The fame which he had gained by his victories and policy made his alliance courted; but Pirithous, king of the Lapithæ, alone wished to gain his friendship by meeting him in the field of battle. He invaded the territories of Attica, and when Theseus had marched out to meet him, the two enemies, struck at the sight of each other, rushed between their two armies to embrace one another in the most cordial and affectionate manner, and from that time began the most sincere and admired friendship, which has become proverbial. Theseus was present at the nuptials of his friend, and he was the most eager and courageous of the Lapithæ in the defence of Hippodamia and her female attendants, against the brutal attempts of the Centaurs. When Pirithous had lost Hippodamia, he agreed with Theseus, whose wife Phædra was also dead, to carry away some of the daughters of the gods. Their first attempt was upon Helen, the daughter of Leda; and after they had obtained this beautiful prize, they cast lots, and she became the property of Theseus. The Athenian monarch entrusted her to the care of his mother Æthra, at Aphidnæ, till she was of nubile years; but the resentment of Castor and Pollux soon obliged him to restore her safe into their hands. Helen, before she reached Sparta, became mother of a daughter by Theseus; but this tradition, confirmed by some ancient mythologists, is confuted by others, who affirm that she was but nine years old when carried away by the two royal friends; and Ovid introduces her in one of his epistles, saying, *Excepto redii passa timore nihil.* Some time after, Theseus assisted his friend in procuring a wife, and they both descended into the infernal regions to carry away Proserpine. Pluto, apprized of their intentions, stopped them. Pirithous was placed on his father's wheel, and Theseus was tied to a huge stone, on which he had sat to rest himself. Virgil represents him in this eternal state of punishment, repeating to the shades in Tartarus the words of *Discite justitiam moniti, et non temnere divos.* Apollodorus, however, and others declare, that he was not long detained in hell. When Hercules came to steal the dog Cerberus, he tore him away from the stone, but with such violence that his skin was left behind him. The same assistance was given to Pirithous, and the two friends returned upon the earth by the favor of Hercules and the consent of the infernal deities, not, however, without suffering the most excruciating torments. During the captivity of Theseus in the kingdom of Pluto, one of the descendants of Erechtheus ingratiated himself into the favors of the people of Athens, and obtained the crown in preference to the children of the absent monarch. At his return, Theseus attempted to eject the usurper, but to no purpose. The Athenians had forgotten his many services, and he retired with great mortification to the court of Lycomedes, king of the island of Scyrus. After paying him much attention, Lycomedes, either jealous of his fame, or bribed by the presents of Mnestheus, carried him to a high rock, on pretence of showing him the extent of his dominions, and threw him down a deep precipice. Some suppose that Theseus inadvertently fell down this precipice, and that he was crushed to death without receiving any violence from Lycomedes. The children of Theseus, after the death of Mnestheus, recovered the Athenian throne, and that the memory of their father might not be without the honors due to a hero, they brought his remains from Scyrus, and gave them a magnificent burial. They also raised statues and a temple, and festivals and games were publicly instituted to commemorate the actions of a hero who had rendered such services to the people of Athens. These festivals were celebrated with original solemnity in the age of Pausanias and Plutarch, about 1200 yeas after the death of Theseus. The historians disagree with the poets in their accounts of this hero, and they all suppose, that, instead of attempting to carry away the wife of Pluto, the two friends wished to seduce a daughter of Aidoneus, king of the Molossi. This daughter, as they say, bore the name of Proserpine, and the dog which kept the gates of the palace was called Cerberus, and hence, perhaps, arises the fiction of the poets. Pirithous was torn to pieces by the dog, but Theseus was confined in prison, whence he made his escape some time after by the assistance of Hercules. Some authors place Theseus and his friend in the number of the Argonauts, but they were both detained, either in the infernal regions, or in the country of the Molossi, at the time of Jason's expedition to Colchis. *Plut. in Vitâ.—Apollod.* 3.—*Hygin.* fab. 14, 33, 38, & 79.—*Paus.* 1. c. 2, &c.—*Ovid. Met.* 7. v. 433. l. 12. v. 227. *Ib.* 412. *Fast* 3. v. 473 & 491. *Heroid.* 10.—*Diod.* 1 & 4.—*Lucan.* 2. v. 612.—*Homer Odyss.* 21. v. 293.—*Hesiod. in Scut. Herc.* v. 176.—*Ælian. V.H.* 4. c. 5.—*Stat. Theb.* 5. v. 432. *& Ach.* 1. v. 156.—*Propert.* 3.—*Lactant. ad Theb. Stat.* 5. v. 430.—*Philost. Icon.* 1.—*Flacc.* 2. v. 193.—*Apollon.* 1. v. 103.—*Virg. Æn.* 6. v. 617.—*Seneca in Hippol.* 951.—*Catul. de Nup. Pel. & Th.* 52.—*Tzetzes Ch.* 5. c. 10. *Ad Lycoph.* 143.—*Sch. Euripid. in Hippol.* 980.—*Servius ad Virg. Æn.* 3. v. 74 & 123. l. 6. v. 14 & 21. [The splendid figure brought from the Parthenon by Lord Elgin, and placed in the British Museum, is generally known by the name of Theseus, but is in reality a Hercules. There is a fine group called Theseus and Æthra in the Villa Ludovisi, near Rome.]

THESI'DE or THESEI'DÆ, a name given to the people of Athens because they were governed by Theseus. *Virg. G.* 2. v. 383. *Servius loco.*

THESI'DES, a patronymic applied to the children of Theseus, especially Hippolytus. *Ovid. Her.* 4. v. 65.

THESMOPH'ORA, a surname of Ceres, as lawgiver, in whose honor festivals were instituted, called *Thesmophoria.* The Thesmophoria were instituted by Triptolemus, or, according to some, by Orpheus, or the daughters of Danaus. The greatest part of the Grecian cities, especially Athens, observed them with great solemnity. The worshippers were free-born women, whose husbands were obliged to defray the expenses of the festival. They were assisted by a priest called στεφανόφορος, because he carried a *crown* on his head. There were also certain virgins who officiated, and were maintained at the public expense. The free-born women were dressed in white robes to intimate their spotless innocence; they were charged to observe the strictest chastity during three or five days before the celebration, and during the four days of the solemnity, and on that account it was usual for them to strew their bed with *agnus castus, fleabane,* and all such herbs as were supposed to have the power of expelling all libidinous propensities. They were also charged not to eat pomegranates, or to wear garlands on their heads, as the whole was to be observed with the greatest signs of seriousness and gravity, without any display of wantonness or levity. It was however usual to jest at one another, as the goddess Ceres had been made to smile by a merry expression when she was sad and melancholy for the recent loss of her daughter Proserpine. Three days were required for the preparation, and upon the 11th of the month called Pyanepsion, the women went to Eleusis, carrying books on their heads, in which the laws which the goddess had introduced were contained. On the 14th of the same month the festival began, on the 16th day a fast was observed, and the women sat on the ground in token of humiliation. It was usual during the festival to offer prayers to Ceres, Proserpine, Pluto, and Calligenia, whom some suppose to have been the nurse or favorite maid of the goddess of corn, or perhaps one of her surnames. There were some sacrifices of a mysterious nature, and all persons whose offence was small were released from confinement. Such as were initiated at the festivals of Eleusis assisted at the Thesmophoria. The place of high priest was hereditary in the family of Eumolpus. *Ovid. Met.* 10. v. 431. *Fast.* 4. v. 619.—*Apollod.* 1. c. 4.—*Virg. Æn.* 4. v. 58.—*Sophocl. in Œdip. Col.*—*Clem. Alex. Strom.* 4. *& in Protr.*—*Callimach. in Cerer.*—*Parthen. Erot.* 8.—*Sch. Theocr.* 4. v. 25.—*Plin.* 24. c. 9.—*Paus.* 10. c. 33.—*Hygin.* fab. 47, 274, & 277.—*Phurnut. de N.D.* 28.

THESMOTH'ETÆ, a name given to the last six Archons among the Athenians, because they took particular care to enforce the laws, and to see justice impartially administered. They were at that time nine in number. *Plut. in Antiph.*

THESPE'A or THESPI'A, now Neocorio, a town of Bœotia, at the foot of mount Helicon, which received its name from Thespia, the daughter of Asopus, or from Thespius. *Plin.* 4. c. 7.—*Paus.* 9. c. 26.—*Strab.* 9.

THESPI'A, a city of Thessaly. *Val. Flacc.* 1. v. 92.

THESPI'ADÆ, the sons of the Thespiades. *Vid.* Thespius.

THESPI'ADES, a name given to the 50 daughters of Thespius. *Vid.* Thespius. *Diod.* 4.—*Seneca in Her. Œt.* 369.——A surname of the nine muses, because they were held in great veneration at Thespia. *Flacc.* 2. v. 368.—*Ovid. Met.* 5. v. 310.

THESPI'EUS, the 10th perpetual archon of Athens, who reigned 27 years.

THES'PIS, a Greek poet of Attica, supposed by some to have been the inventor of tragedy, 536 years before Christ. His representations were very rustic and imperfect. He went from town to town upon a cart, on which were erected a temporary stage, where two actors, whose faces were daubed with the lees of wine, entertained the audience with choral songs, &c. Solon was a great enemy to his dramatic representations. *Horat. Art. P.* 276.—*Diog.* 5. *in Heracl. Pont.*—*Suidas.*—*Plut. in Sol.*—*Gyrald. de P.H.* 6.

THES'PIUS, a king of Thespia, in Bœotia, son of Erechtheus, according to some authors. He was desirous that his 50 daughters should have children by Hercules, and therefore when that hero was at his court he permitted him to enjoy their company. All the daughters of Thespius brought male children into the world, and some of them twins, particularly Procris the eldest, and the youngest. Some suppose that one of the Thespiades refused to admit Hercules to her arms, for which the hero condemned her to pass all her life in continued celibacy, and to become the priestess of a temple he had at Thespia. The children of the Thespiades, called Thespiadæ, went to Sardinia, where they made a settlement with Iolaus, the friend of their father. Thespius is often confounded by ancient authors with Thestius, though the latter lived in a different place, and, as king of Pleuron, sent his sons to the hunting of the Calydonian boar. *Apollod.* 2. c. 4.—*Paus.* 9. c. 26 & 27.—*Plut. de Fluv.*—*Diod.* 4.—*Sch. Apollon.* 1. v. 146.—*Athen.* 13. c. 2.—*Suidas.*—*Arnob. adv. Gent.* 2.

THESPRO'TIA, a country of Epirus, at the west of Ambracia, bounded on the south by the sea. It is watered by the rivers Acheron and Cocytus, which the poets, after Homer, have called the streams of hell. The oracle of Dodona was in Thesprotia. *Homer. Odyss.* 14. v. 315.—*Strab.* 7, &c.—*Paus.* 1. c. 17.—*Lucan.* 3. v. 179.—*Sil. It.* 15. v. 297.—*Plin. in. Pr.* 4.

THESPRO'TUS, a son of Lycaon, king of Arcadia. *Apollod.* 3. c. 8.

THESSA'LIA, a country of Greece, the boundaries of which have been different at different periods. Properly speaking, Thessaly was bounded on the south by the southern parts of Greece, or Græcia propria; on the east by the Ægæan; on the north by Macedonia and Mygdonia; and on the west by Illyricum and Epirus. It was generally divided into four separate provinces, Thessaliotis, Pelasgiotis, Istiæotis, and Phthiotis, to which some add Magnesia. It has been severally called Æmonia, Pelasgicum Argos, Hellas, Argeia, Dryopis, Pelasgia, Pyrrhæa, Æmathia, &c. The name of Thessalia is derived from Thessalus, one of its monarchs. Thessaly is famous for a deluge which happened there in the age of Deucalion. Its mountains and cities are also celebrated, such as Olympus, Pelion, Ossa, Larissa, &c. The Argonauts were partly natives of Thessaly. The inhabitants of the country passed for a treacherous nation, so that false money was called Thessalian coin; and a perfidious action, a Thessalian deceit. Thessaly was governed by kings, till it became subject to the Macedonian monarchs. The cavalry were universally esteemed, and the people were superstitious, and addicted to the study of magic and incantations. Thessaly is now called Janna. *Lucan.* 6 v. 438, &c.—*Dionys.* 210.—*Curt.* 3. c. 2.—*Ælian. V. H.* 3. c. 1.—*Paus.* 4. c. 36. l. 10. c. 1.—*Mela,* 2. c. 3.—*Justin.* 7. c. 6.—*Diod.* 4.—*Strab.* 8.—*Paterc.* 1. c. 3.—*Liv.* 32. c. 13.—*Tibull.* 2. el. 4, 56.—*Propert.* 1. el. 5. v. 6. el. 19. v. 10.—*Ovid. Am.* 3. el. 7. v. 27.

THESSA'LION, a servant of Mentor, of Sidon, in the age of Artaxerxes Ochus, &c. *Diod.* 16.

THESSALIO'TIS, a part of Thessaly at the south of the river Peneus.

THESSALONI'CA, an ancient town of Macedonia, first called Therma, and afterwards Thessalonica after the wife of Cassander. According to ancient writers it was once very powerful. It still continues to be a place of note, and is called Salonichi. *Strab.* 7.—*Dionys.*—*Cic. in Pis.* c. 17—*Liv.* 29. c. 17. l. 40. c. 4. l. 44. c. 10 & 45.—*Tzetzes in Chil.* 13. c. 486.—*Mela,* 2. c. 3.

THESSALONI'CE, a daughter of Philip, king of Macedonia, by Nicasipolis, and sister to Alexander the Great. She married Cassander, by whom she had a son called Antipater who put her to death. *Paus.* 8. c. 7.

THES'SALUS, a son of Æmon the son of Lycaon. *Step. Byz.*——A son of Hercules and Calliope, daughter of Euryphilus. Thessaly received its name from one of these. *Apollod.* 2.—*Dictys. Cr.* 2.—*Schol. Apollon.* 3. v. 1089.—*Sch. Pind.* 4. *Nem.* v. 40.——A physician who invited Alexander to a feast at Babylon to give him poison. *Curt.* 10. c. 41.——A physician of Lydia, in the age of Nero. He gained the favour of the great and opulent at Rome, by the meanness and servility of his behaviour. He treated all physicians with contempt, and thought himself superior to all his predecessors. *Plin.* 29. c. 1.—*Galen.* 1. *Meth.* c. 2.—*Castellan. in illustr. Med.*——A son of Cimon, who accused Alcibiades because he imitated the mysteries of Ceres.——A son of Pisistratus.——A player in the age of Alexander.——An archon at Athens, Olymp. 107. an. 2.

THES'SYRIS, a river of European Sarmatia. *Ptol.*

THES'TALUS, a son of Hercules and Epicaste. *Apollod.* 2. c. 7.

THES'TE, a sister of Dionysius the elder, tyrant of Syracuse. She married Philoxenus, and was greatly esteemed by the Sicilians.

THES'TIA, a town of Ætolia, between the Evenus and Achelous. *Polyb.* 5. c. 7.

THESTI'ADÆ amd THESTI'ADES. *Vid.* Thespiadæ and Thespiades.

THESTI'ADÆ, the sons of Thestius, Toxeus and Plexippus. *Ovid. Met.* 8. v. 286.

THES'TIAS, a patronymic of Althæa, daughter of Thestius. *Ovid. Met.* 8. v. 452.

THES'TIS, a fountain in the country of Cyrene. *Herodot.*——A city of Arabia.—A city of Libya. *Steph.*

THES'TIUS, king of Pleuron, and son of Parthaon, was father to Toxeus, Plexippus, and Althæa. The sons of Thestius, called Thestiadæ, were killed by Meleager at the chase of the Calydonian boar. *Apollod.* 2. c. 7.—*Ovid. Met.* 8. v. 304, 434, 452. *Trist.* 1. el. 6. v. 18.——A king of Thespia. *Vid.* Thespius.

THES'TOR, a son of Idmon and Laothoe, father of Calchas and Theonoe. From him Calchas is often called Thestorides. *Ovid. Met.* 12. v. 19.—*Stat.* 1. *Ach.* v. 497.—*Apollon.* 1. v. 239.—*Homer. Il.* 1. v. 69.

THESTOR'IDES, a schoolmaster, who published as his own the lesser Iliad, which had been given him by Homer. *Herodot. in vit. Hom.*—*Salmas. ad Solin.* p. 853.

THES'TORUS, a city of Thrace. *Steph.*

THES'TYLIS, a countrywoman mentioned by Theocritus and Virgil.

THETID'IUM, a city of Thessaly. *Steph.*

THE'TIS, one of the sea deities, daughter of Nereus and Doris, often confounded with Tethys her grandmother. She was courted by Neptune and Jupiter; but when the gods were informed that the son she should bring forth must become greater than his father, their addresses were stopped, and Peleus, the son of Æacus, was permitted to solicit her hand. Thetis refused him, but the lover had the artifice to catch her when asleep, and by binding her strongly, he prevented her from escaping from his grasp, in assuming different forms. When Thetis found that she could not elude the vigilance of her lover, she consented to marry him, though much against her inclination. Their nuptials were celebrated on mount Pelion, with great pomp; all the deities attended except the goddess of discord, who punished the negligence of Peleus, by throwing into the midst of the assembly a golden apple, to be given to the fairest of all the goddesses. *Vid.* Discordia. Thetis became mother of several children by Peleus, but all these she destroyed by fire in attempting to see whether they were immortal. Achilles must have shared the same fate, if Peleus had not snatched him from her hand as she was going to repeat the cruel operation. She afterwards rendered him invulnerable by plunging him into the waters of the Styx, except that part of the heel by which she held him. As Thetis well knew the fate of her son, she attempted to remove him from the Trojan war by concealing him in the court of Lycomedes. This was useless, he went with the rest of the Greeks. The mother, still anxious for his preservation, prevailed upon Vulcan to make him a suit of armour; but when it was done, she refused the god the favors which she had promised him. When Achilles was killed by Paris, Thetis issued out of the sea with the Nereides to mourn his death, and after she had collected his ashes in a golden urn, she raised a monument to his memory, and instituted festivals in his honor. *Hesiod. Theog.* v. 244, &c.—*Apollod.* 1. c. 2 & 9. l. 3. c. 13.—*Hygin.* fab. 34, 107 & 110.—*Homer. Il.* 1. v. 496. l. 18. v. 52, &c. *Od.* 24. v. 55.—*Paus.* 5. c. 18, &c.—*Ovid. Met.* 11. fab. 7. l. 12. fab. 1, &c.—*Catull. de Nupt. P. & Th.*—*Lactant.* 1. c. 11.—*Tzetzes ad Lyc.* 175.—*Sch. Pind. Pyth.* 3. v. 160 & 168. *Nem.* 4. v. 101.—*Ptol. Heph.* 6.—*Lact. ad Stat. Ach.* 1. v. 134. [There is a beautiful statue of Thetis in the Villa Albani, near Rome.]

THEU'DALE, a city of Africa Propria. *Ptol.*

THEUPROSO'PON or THEOUPROSO'PON, a promontory of Phœnicia. *Id.*

THEU'TIS or TEU'THIS, a prince of a town of the same name in Arcadia, who went to the Trojan war. He quarrelled with Agamemnon at Aulis, and when Minerva, under the form of Melas son of Ops, attempted to pacify him, he struck the goddess and returned home. Some say that the goddess afterwards appeared to him and showed him the wound which he had given her in the thigh, and that he died soon after. As the country which gave him birth was visited by a pestilence, the inhabitants, to appease the gods, erected a statue to Minerva, representing her with a wounded thigh. *Paus.* 8. c. 28.

THI'A, the mother of the sun, moon, and Aurora, by Hyperion. *Vid* Thea. *Hesiod. Theog.* 1. v. 37.

THI'A, one of the Sporades that rose out of the sea in the age of Pliny. *Plin.* 2. c. 87.

THIAG'OLA, a lake of Lower Mysia, at the mouths of the Ister. *Ptol.*

THI'AS, a king of Assyria.

THIB'II, a people of Pontus. *Plin.* 7. c. 2.—*Salmas ad Solin.* p. 46 & 47.

THI'BRUS, the name of a city mentioned by Lycophron. *Steph.*

THI'CHIS, a river of Hispania Tarraconensis. *Mela*, 2. c. 5.

THIM'BRON or THI'BRON, a Lacedæmonian, chosen general to conduct a war against Persia. He was recalled, and afterwards re-appointed. The 10,000 after their return from Cunaxa, joined his army, and assisted him against Tisaphernes. He died, B.C. 391. *Diod.* 17.—*Xenoph. Anab.*

THIM'BRON, a friend of Harpalus. *Diod. Sic.* 17 & 18.

THI'NÆ, the metropolis of the Sinæ. *Ptol.*

THIN'GE, a city of Libya. *Steph.*

THIN'IAS, a promontory of Thrace on the Euxine Sea. *Ptol.*

THINIS'SA, a city of Zeugitana. *Ptol.* It is now Tunis.

THIOD'AMAS, the father of Hylas. *Vid.* Theodamas.

THIR'MIDA, a town of Numidia, where Hiempsal was slain. *Sall. Jug.* 2.

THIRSIP'PUS, the fourth perpetual archon at Athens, who reigned forty-one years. *Joh. Marsham. Can. Chron. Sec.* 13.

THIS, a city of Ægypt near Abydus. *Steph.*

THIS'BE, a beautiful woman of Babylon. *Vid.* Pyramus.

THIS'BE, a town of Bœotia between two mountains. *Paus.* 9. c. 32. *Hom. Il.* 2. v. 502.

THIS'IAS, a Sicilian writer. *Quintil.* 3. c. 6.

THIS'ICA, a city of Africa Propria. *Ptol.*

THIS'OA, one of the three nymphs who fed Jupiter in Arcadia. The two others were Neda and Hagno or Agno. She built a town in Arcadia which bore her name. *Paus.* 8. c. 38.—*Gyrald. H. D.* 5.

THISSAMIS'SA, a harbour of Caria. *Mela.* 1. c. 16.

THIS'TIE, a town of Bœotia. *Plin.* 4. c. 7.

THMU'IS, a city of Ægypt. *Steph.*

THNO'CIA or THOC'NIA, a city of Arcadia. *Pausan. in Arcad.*

THOA'NA, a town of Arabia Petræa. *Ptol.*

THOA'NES, a people above Colchis, near the Phthirophagi. *Strab.*

THOAN'TIUM, a place on the coast of Rhodes. *Strab.*—*Stat. Theb.* l. 5.

THO'ARIS or THOA'RIUS, a river of Cappadocia. *Arrian.*

THO'AS, a king of Taurica Chersonesus, in the age of Orestes and Pylades. He would have immolated these two celebrated strangers on Diana's altars, according to the barbarous custom of the country, had they not been delivered by Iphigenia. *Vid.* Iphigenia. According to some, Thoas was the son of Borysthenes. *Eurip. in Iphig. Taur.*—*Anton. Liber.* 27.—*Hygin.* fab. 120.—*Servius ad Æn.* 2. v. 116. l. 6. v. 136.—*Ovid. Pont.* 3. el. 2.——A king of Lemnus, son of Bacchus and Ariadne, the daughter of Minos, and husband to Myrine. He had been made king of Lemnus by Rhadamanthus. He was still alive when the Lemnian women conspired to kill all the males in the island, but his life was spared by his only daughter Hypsipyle, in whose favour he had resigned the crown. Hypsipyle obliged her father to depart secretly from Lemnus, to escape from the fury of the women, and he arrived safe in a neighbouring island, which some call Chius, though many suppose that Thoas was assassinated by the enraged females before he had left Lemnus. Some mythologists confound the king of Lemnus with that of Chersonesus, and suppose they were one and the same man. According to their opinion, Thoas was very young when he retired from Lemnus, and after that he went to Taurica Chersonesus, where he settled. *Flac.* 8. v. 208.—*Hygin.* fab. 74, 120.—*Ovid. in Ib.* 384. *Heroid.* 6. v. 114.—*Stat. Theb.* 5. v. 262 & 486.—*Apollon. Rhod.* 1. v. 209 & 615—*Apollod.* 1. c. 9. l. 3. c. 6.—*Eurip. in Iphig.*——A son of Andremon and Gorge, the daughter of Œneus. He went to the Trojan war with 15 or rather 40 ships, where he behaved with so much valour that Neptune borrowed his features to animate the Greeks to battle. *Homer. Il*, en. 2. v. 145. l. 4. v. 527. l. 13. v. 215. l. 15. v. 281.—*Paus*. 5. c. 3. l. 10. c 38.—*Dictys. Cret*. 1. *Hygin*. fab. 97.——A famous huntsman, who promised to consecrate to Diana the head and feet of all animals which he might kill. He however, one day, offered to the goddess only the head of a large boar which he had caught in hunting, and suspended it on a tree, whence it fell upon him when asleep, and killed him. *Schol. Aristoph. in Plut.*—*Ovid. in Ib*. 507.—*Diod*. 4.——A son of Icarius. *Apollod*. 3. c. 10. ——A son of Jason and Hypsipyle queen of Lemnus. *Stat. Theb*. 6. v. 342.——A son of Ornytion, grandson of Sisyphus. *Paus*. 2. c. 4.——A king of Assyria, father of Adonis and Myrrha, according to *Apollodorus*, 3. c. 14.——A man who made himself master of Miletus.——An officer of Ætolia, who strongly opposed the views of the Romans, and favoured the interest of Antiochus, B C. 193. *Liv*. 35. c. 12.——One of the friends of Æneas, killed in Italy by Halesus. *Virg. Æn*. 10. v. 415.

THO'E, one of the Nereides. *Hesiod. Th*. 245.—*Homer. Il*. 18. v. 40.——One of the Amazons, &c. *Val. Fl*. 6. v. 376.

THO'E one of the horses of Admetus. *Stat. Theb*. 6. v. 461.

THOLUBA'NA, a city of India within the Ganges. *Ptol*.

THO'MUM, a city of Ægypt, near Chenoboscia. *Antonin*.

THOM'YRIS, called also Tamyris, Tameris, Thamyris, and Tomeris, was queen of the Massagetæ. After her husband's death she marched against Cyrus, who wished to invade her territories, cut his army to pieces, and killed him on the spot. The barbarous queen ordered the head of the fallen monarch to be cut off and thrown into a vessel full of human blood, with the insulting words of *Satia te sanguine quem sitisti*. Her son had been conquered by Cyrus before she marched herself at the head of her armies. *Herodot*. 1. c. 205.—*Justin*. 1. c. 8.—*Lucian. in Char.*—*Tibul*. 4. el. 1. v. 143.

THON, an Ægyptian physician, &c. *Hom. Od*. 4.

THON, a city of Africa Propria. *Appian*.

THO'NIS, a courtezan of Ægypt. *Plut. in Dem.*—*Ælian. V.H*. 12. c. 63.—*Athen*. 13.

THONI'TES, a lake of Armenia Major, on the confines of Mesopotamia. *Eustath. Dionys*. v. 987.

THONI'TIS, a lake and river of Ægypt, near Canopus. *Strab*.

THO'ON, a Trojan chief killed by Ulysses. *Homer. Il*. 11. v. 422.—*Ovid. Met*. 13. v. 259.——One of the giants who made war against Jupiter. *Apollod*. 1. c. 6.

THOO'SA, a sea nymph, daughter of Phorcys, and mother of Polyphemus, by Neptune. *Hesiod. Th*. v. 236.—*Homer. Odyss*. 1. v. 71.

THOO'TES, one of the Grecian heralds. *Homer. Il*. 12.

THO'RA, a town of Campania. *Florus*. 3. c. 20.

THO'RÆ, a village in the tribe Antiochus. *Steph*.

THORA'NIUS or TORA'NIUS, a general of Metellus, killed by Sertorius. *Plut*.

THORA'TES, a surname of Apollo in Laconia. *Hesych*.

THO'RAX, a mountain near Magnesia, in Ionia, where the grammarian Daphitas was suspended on a cross for his abusive language against kings and absolute princes, whence the proverb *Cave a Thorace*. *Strab*. 14.

THO'RAX, a Lacedæmonian officer who served under Lysander, and was put to death by the Ephori. *Plut. in Lys*.——A man of Larissa who paid much attention to the dead body of Antigonus, &c.

THO'RIA LEX, *agraria*, by Sp. Thorius the tribune. It ordained that no person should pay any rent for the land which he possessed. It also made some regulations about grazing and pastures. *Cic. in Brut*.

THOR'ICUS, a small town of Ægypt, near Canopus. *Steph*.

THO'RIUS L. BAL'BUS, a native of Lanuvium, represented as a great voluptuary. *Cic. Fin*. 2. c. 20 & 22.

THO'RIUS SPU'RIUS, a popular orator and tribune at Rome, author of the *Thoria lex*, A.U.C. 646. *Cic. Brut*. 31. *Orat*. 2. c. 70.—*Appian. B.C*. 1. c. 367.

THOR'NAX, a mountain of Argolis. It received its name from Thornax, a nymph who became mother of Buphagus, by Japetus. The mountain was afterwards called Coccygia, because Jupiter there changed himself into a cuckoo. *Paus*. 8. c. 27.

THOR'SUS, a river of Sardinia. *Paus*. 10. c. 17. It is called Thyrsus by *Ptolemy*.

THORUN'UBA, a city of Africa Propria. *Ptol*.

THORYC'ION, an Athenian, who aided the Peloponnesians in their attack upon this country. *Aristoph. Ran*.

THORYC'IUM, a city of Italy near Croton and Crimissa. *Isac. in Lycophr*.

THOS'PIA, a city of Armenia Major. *Ptol*.

THOSPI'TIS, a region and city of Armenia Major. *Id*.

THOTH, an Ægyptian deity, the same as Mercury. It was also the name of the first month of the Ægyptian year. *Cic. de N.D*. 3. c. 22.—*Lactant*. 1. c. 6.—*Servius ad Æn*. 4. v. 577.

THO'US, a Trojan chief, &c. *Homer*.

THO'US, one of Actæon's dogs. *Ovid. Met*. 3. v. 221.

THRABUNAC'TUM, a city of Africa Propria. *Antonin*.

THRA'CE, a daughter of Titan.

THRA'CE, a name of Thrace. *Vid*. Thracia.

THRA'CES, the inhabitants of Thrace. *Vid*. Thracia.

THRA'CIA, a large country of Europe, at the south of Scythia, bounded by mount Hæmus. It had the Ægæan Sea on the south, on the west Macedonia and the river Strymon, and on the east the Euxine Sea, the Propontis, and the Hellespont. Its northern boundaries extended as far as the Ister, according to Pliny and others. The Thracians were looked upon as a cruel and barbarous nation; they were naturally brave and warlike, addicted to drinking and venereal pleasures, and they sacrificed without the smallest humanity their enemies on the altars of their gods. Their government was originally monarchical, and divided among a number of independent princes. Thrace is barren as to its soil. It received its name from Thrax, the son of Mars, the chief deity of that country. The first inhabitants lived upon plunder, and on the milk and flesh of sheep. It now forms the province of Romania. *Herodot*. 4. c. 99. l. 5. c. 3.—*Strab*. 1 & 7.—*Virg. Æn*. 3, &c.—*Mela*, 2. c. 2, &c.—*Paus*. 9. c 29, &c.—*Ovid. Met*. 11. v. 92. l. 13. v. 565, &c.—*C. Nep. in Alc*. 11.—*Flor*. 3. c. 4.—*Veget. de R.R*. 1. c. 28.—*Claudian. de* 4 *Cons. Hon*. 179 & 474.

THRAC'IDÆ, an illustrious family at Delphi, destroyed by Philomelus, because they opposed his views. *Diod*. 16.

THRA'CIS, a town of Phocis. *Paus*. 10. c. 3.

THRA'CON, a village near Antiochia. *Steph*.

THRAM'BUS, a promontory of Macedonia. *Steph*.

THRA'SEAS or THRA'SIUS, a soothsayer. *Vid*. Thasius.

THRA'SEA PÆ'TUS, a stoic philosopher of Patavium, in the age of Nero, famous for his independence and generous sentiments. He was put to death by Nero, A.D. 66. *Juv*. 5. v. 36.—*Mart*. 1. epigr. 19.—*Tacit. A*. 15. c. 16. l. 16. c. 21.

THRASID'EUS succeeded his father Theron as tyrant of Agrigentum. He was conquered by Hiero, and soon after put to death. *Diod*. 11.

THRASIME'NUS. *Vid*. Thrasymenus.

THRA'SIUS, a general of some Phocian mercenaries in Sicily, who raised a sedition against Timoleon. *Diod*. 16.——A spendthrift at Rome, &c. *Horat*. 2. *Sat*. 2. v. 99.——A soothsayer of Cyprus. *Vid*. Thasius.

THRA'SO, a painter. *Strab*. 14.——A favorite of Hieronymus, who espoused the interest of the Romans. He was put to death by the tyrant. ——The character of a boasting captain in *Terence*. ——A statuary. *Plin*. 34. c. 8.——A native of Tyndaris, a town of Sicily, mentioned by *Cicero. Verr*. 4. c. 22.

THRASYBU'LUS, a famons general of Athens who began the expulsion of the 30 tyrants of his country, though he was only assisted by 30 of his friends. His efforts were attended with success,

B.C. 401, and the only reward which he received for this patriotic action was a crown made with two twigs of an olive branch; a proof of his own disinterestedness and of the virtue of his countrymen. The Athenians employed a man whose abilities and humanity were so conspicuous, and Thrasybulus was sent with a powerful fleet to recover their lost power in the Ægæan, and on the coast of Asia. After he had gained many advantages, this great man was killed in his camp by the inhabitants of Aspendus, whom his soldiers had plundered without his knowledge, B.C. 391. *Diod.* 14.—*C. Nep. in vitâ.*—*Cic. Phil.*—*Val. Max.* 4. c. 1.—*Xenoph. H. Gr.* 2.—*Paus.* 1. c. 29.——A tyrant of Miletus, B. C. 634. He made war against Alyattes, king of Lydia. *Polyæn.* 6. c. 47.—*Frontin.* 3. c. 9 & 15.——A soothsayer descended from Imaus the son of Apollo by Evadne. He had a statue in the wood sacred to Jupiter at Olympia, in which he was represented with a lizard on his right shoulder, and at his feet was a dog whose body was open that the entrails might be examined by the augurs. *Pind. Olymp.* 6.—*Plin.* 18. c. 3.—*Paus.* 6. c. 2.——A son of Gelon banished from Syracuse, of which he was the tyrant, B.C. 466. *Aristot. Polit.* 5. c 10.—*Diod. Sic.* 11.——An Athenian in the army of the Persians, who supported the siege of Halicarnassus. *Diod. Sic.* 17.

THRASYDÆ'US, a king of Thessaly, &c.

THRASYL'LUM or THRASYL'LUS, a mountain of Mysia, near the Caicus. It was afterwards called Theutras, according to *Plutarch, de flum.*

THRASYL'LUS, a man of Attica, so disordered in his mind, that he believed all the ships which entered the Piræus to be his own. He was cured by means of his brother, whom he liberally reproached for depriving him of that happy illusion of mind. *Ælian. V.H.* 4. c. 25.—*Athen.* 12.——A general of the Athenians in the age of Alcibiades, with whom he obtained a victory over the Persians. *Thucyd.* 8.——A Thessalian slain by Eurydamus, who himself immediately perished by the hand of Simo, the brother of Thrasyllus. *Ovid. Ib.* 3. 334.—*Schol. in Homer. Il.* 22. v. 398.——A Greek Pythagorean philosopher and mathematician, who enjoyed the favor and the friendship of Augustus and Tiberius. *Suet. in Tib.* 14.—*Tacit. An.* 6. c. 21.—*Plut. de Music.*—*Diog.* 9. c. 38.

THRASYM'ACHUS, a native of Carthage who became the pupil of Isocrates and Plato. Though he was a public teacher at Athens, he was starving for want of bread, and at last hanged himself. He was the first who wrote on the harmonious arrangement of words. *Cic. Orat.* 3, 12, 16.—*Juv.* 7. v. 204.——A man who abolished democracy at Cumæ. *Arist. Pol.* 5. c. 5.

THRASYME'DES, a son of Nestor, king of Pylus, by Anaxibia, the daughter of Bias. He was one of the Grecian chiefs during the Trojan war. *Hygin.* fab. 57.—*Paus.* 2. c. 26. l. 4, c. 31 & 36.——A sculptor of Parus, son of Arignotus. He made a statue of Æsculapius in gold and ivory, for the temple of the god at Epidaurus. *Paus.* 2. c. 27.——A son of Philomelus, who carried away a daughter of Pisistratus, whom he married. *Polyæn.* 5. c. 14.

THRASYME'NUS, a lake of Italy near Perusium, celebrated for a battle fought there between Annibal and the Romans, under Flaminius, B.C. 217. No less than 15,000 Romans were left dead on the field of battle, and 10,000 taken prisoners, or, according to Livy, 6,000, or Polybius, 15,000. The loss of Annibal was about 1500 men. About 10,000 Romans made their escape covered with wounds. This lake is now called the lake of Perugia. *Strab.* 5.—*Ovid. Fast.* 6. v. 765.—*Plut.*—*Sidon.* 9. v. 248. *Ital.* 4. v. 66 & 698.

THREIC'IUS, of Thrace. Orpheus is called by way of eminence *Threicius Sacerdos. Virg. Æn.* 6, 645.

THREIS'SA, an epithet applied to Harpalyce, a native of Thrace. *Virg. Æn.* 1. v. 320.

THREPSIP'PAS, a son of Hercules and Panope. *Apollod.*

THRI'A, a village in the tribe Æneis. *Steph.*

THRIAM'BUS, one of the surnames of Bacchus.

THRIA'SIUS, a village of Attica, with a river of the same name between Athens and Eleusis. *Hesiod.*—*Plin.* 4. c. 7.

THRIN'CE, a city near the columns of Hercules. *Steph.*

THRISTIS'IMA, a city of Mauritania Cæsariensis. *Ptol.*

THROA'NA, a city of the pirates in India without the Ganges. *Id.*

THRO'NIUM, a town of Phocis, where the Boagrius falls into the sea, in the Sinus Maliacus. *Liv.* 36. c. 20.—*Strab.* 9.—*Plin.* 4. c. 7.——A city of Thesprotia.

THRYAN'DA, a city of Lycia. *Steph.*

THRY'ON, a town of Messenia, near the Alpheus. *Strab.* 8.—*Homer. Il.* 2.

THRY'US, a town of Peloponnesus near Elis. *Strab.*—*Stat. Theb.* 4. v. 180.

THUBUR'SICA, a city of Africa Propria. *Ptol.*

THUCYD'IDES, a celebrated Greek historian, born at Athens. His father's name was Olorus, and among his ancestors he reckoned the great Miltiades. His youth was distinguished by an eager desire to excel in the vigorous exercises and gymnastic amusements, which called the attention of his contemporaries, and when he had reached the years of manhood, he appeared in the Athenian armies. During the Peloponnesian war he was commissioned by his countrymen to relieve Amphipolis; but the quick march of Brasidas, the Lacedæmonian general, defeated his operations, and Thucydides, unsuccessful in his expedition, was banished from Athens. This happened in the eighth year of this celebrated war, and in the place of his banishment the general began to write an impartial history of the important events which had happened during his administration, and which still continued to agitate the several states of Greece. This famous history is continued only to the 21st year of the war, and the remaining part of the time till the demolition of the wall of Athens was described by the pens of Theopompus and Xenophon. Thucydides wrote in the Attic dialect, as possessed of more vigor, purity, elegance, and energy. He spared neither time nor money to procure authentic materials; and the Athenians, as well as their enemies, furnished him with many valuable communications, which contributed to throw great light on the different transactions of the war. His history has been divided into eight books, the last of which is imperfect, and supposed to have been written by his daughter. The character of this interesting history is well known, and the noble emulation of the writer will ever be admired, who shed tears when he heard Herodotus repeat his history of the Persian wars at the public festivals of Greece. The historian of Halicarnassus, has often been compared with the son of Olorus, but each has his peculiar excellence. Sweetness of style, grace, and elegance of expression, may be called the characteristics of the former, while Thucydides stands unequalled for the fire of his descriptions, the conciseness, and at the same time, the strong and energetic manner of his narratives. His relations are authentic, as he himself was interested in the events which he mentions; his impartiality is indubitable, as he no where betrays the least resentment against his countrymen, and the factious partizans of Cleon, who had banished him from Athens. Many have blamed the historian for the injudicious distribution of his subject, and while, for the sake of accuracy, the whole is divided into summers and winters, the thread of the history is interrupted, the scene continually shifted, and the reader, unable to pursue events to the end, is transported from Asia to Peloponnesus, or from the walls of Syracuse to the coast of Corcyra. The animated harangues of Thucydides have been universally admired: he found a model in Herodotus, but he greatly surpassed the original: and succeeding historians have adopted with success, a peculiar mode of writing, which introduces a general addressing himself to the passions and feelings of his armies. The history of Thucydides was so much admired, that Demosthenes, to perfect himself as an orator, transcribed it eight different times, and read it with such attention, that he could almost repeat it by heart. Thucydides died at Athens, where he had been recalled from his exile, in his 80th year, 391 years before Christ. The best editions of Thucydides are those of Duker, fol. Amst. 1731; of Glasgow, 12mo, 8 vols. 1759; of Hudson, fol. Oxon. 1696, and the 8vo. of Bipont. 1788. *Fabr. B. Gr.* 2. c. 25.—*Sax. Onom.* 1. p. 50.—*Cic. de Orat.* 2. c. 13, &c.—*Diod.* 12.—*Dionys. Hal. de Thuc.* — *Ælian V.H.* 12. c. 50.—*Quintil.*—*Aul. Gell.* 15. c. 23.—*Marcell. in Thucyd.*—*Suidas.*—*Photius. Tm.* 60. [There is a fine bust of Thucydides in the Capitol, at Rome.]——A son of Milesias, in the age of Pericles. He was banished for his opposition to the measures of Pericles. *Plut. in Per.*—*Marcell. in Thuc.*

THUIS'TO, one of the deities of the Germans. *Tacit. Germ.* c. 2.

THU'LE, an island in the most northern parts of the German Ocean, to which, on account of its great distance from the continent, the ancients gave the epithet of *ultima*. Its situation was never accurately ascertained, hence its present name is unknown by modern historians. Some suppose that it is the island now called Iceland, or part of Greenland, whilst others imagine it to be the Shetland Isles. *Stat.* 3. *Sylv.* 5 v. 20.—*Strab.* 1.—*Mela,* 3. c. 6.—*Tacit. Agric.* 10.—*Plin.* 2. c. 75. l. 4. c. 16.—*Virg. G.* 1. v. 30.—*Juv.* 15. v. 112.—*Solin.* 20.—*Servius ad Virg. loco. cit.*

THU'RAS or THUR'RAS, the name of Mars among the Assyrians. *Suidas. in voce.*

THU'RI, a people near the Athacori. *Plin.* 6. c. 17.

THU'RIA, a town of Messenia, on the borders of Laconia. *Strab.* It is called Thurium by *Ptolemy,* & Thyrea by *Pliny,* 4. c. 5.

THU'RIÆ, THU'RII or THU'RIUM, a town of Lucania, in Italy, built by a colony of Athenians, near the ruins of Sybaris, B.C. 444. In the number of this Athenian colony were Lysias and Herodotus. *Strab.* 6.—*Mela,* 2. c. 4.—*Plin.* 12. c. 4.—*Plut. de Exil.*

THURI'NUS or THU'RINUS, a name given to Augustus when he was young, either because some of is progenitors were natives of Thurium, or because they had distinguished themselves there. *Sueton. Aug.* 7.

THUS'CIA, a country of Italy, the same as Etruria. *Vid.* Etruria.

THY'A or THY'IA, a daughter of the Cephisus; the first, according to some authors, who was instructed in the orgies of Bacchus. *Herodot.* 7. c. 178.

THY'A, a place near Delphi.

THY'ADES (*sing.* THY'AS), a name of the Bacchanals. They received their name from Thyas, daughter of Castalius, and mother of Delphus by Apollo. She was the first woman who was priestess of the god Bacchus. *Virg. Æn.* 4. v. 302.—*Paus.* 10. c. 4.—*Horat.* 2. od. 9. v. 19. l. 3. od. 15. v. 10.—*Flacc.* 6. v. 757.

THY'AMIS, a river of Epirus falling into the Ionian Sea. *Paus.* 1. c. 11.—*Cic.* 7. *Att.* 2.—*Plin.* 4.

THY'ANA, a town of Cappadocia. *Strab.*—*Plin.* 6. c. 3.—*Ptol. &c.*

THYATI'RA, a town of Lydia, now Ak-hissar. *Liv.* 37. c. 8 & 44.

THYATI'RA, one of the Echinades. *Plin.* 4. c. 12.

THYBAR'NI, a people near Sardes. *Diod.* 17.

THYES'SUS, a city of Lydia.——A city of Pisidia. *Steph.*

THYES'TA, a sister of Dionysius, the tyrant of Syracuse.

THYES'TES, a son of Pelops and Hippodamia, and grandson of Tantalus, debauched Ærope, the wife of his brother Atreus, because he refused to take him as his colleague on the throne of Argos. This was no sooner known, than Atreus divorced Ærope, and banished Thyestes from his kingdom; but soon after, the more effectually to punish his infidelity, he expressed a wish to be reconciled to him, and recalled him to Argos. Thyestes was received by his brother at an elegant entertainment, but he was soon informed that he had been feeding upon the flesh of one of his own children. This Atreus took care to communicate to him by showing him the remains of his son's body. This action appeared so barbarous, that, according to the ancient mythologists, the sun changed his usual course, not to be a spectator of so bloody a scene. Thyestes escaped from his brother, and fled to Epirus. Some time after he met his daughter Pelopea in a grove sacred to Minerva, and offered her violence without knowing who she was. This incest, however, according to some, was intentionally committed by the father, as he had been told by an oracle, that the injuries he had received from Atreus would be avenged by a son born from himself and Pelopea. The daughter, pregnant by her father, was seen by her uncle Atreus and married, and some time after she brought into the world a son, whom she exposed in the woods. The life of the child was preserved by goats; he was called Ægisthus, and presented to his mother, and educated in the family of Atreus. When grown to years of maturity, the mother gave her son Ægisthus a sword, which she had taken from her unknown ravisher in the grove of Minerva, with hopes of discovering who he was. Meantime Atreus, intent to punish his brother, sent Agamemnon and Menelaus to pursue him, and when at last they found him, he was dragged to Argos, and thrown into a close prison. Ægisthus was sent to murder Thyestes, but the father recollected the sword, which was raised to stab him, and a few questions convinced him that his assassin was his own son. Pelopea was present at this discovery, and when she found that she had committed incest with her father, she asked Ægisthus to let her examine the sword, and immediately plunged it into her own breast. Ægisthus rushed from the prison to Atreus, with the bloody weapon, and murdered him near an altar, as he wished to offer thanks to the gods for the supposed death of Thyestes. At the death of Atreus, Thyestes was placed on his brother's throne by Ægisthus, from which he was soon after driven by Agamemnon and Menelaus. He retired from Argos, and was banished into the island of Cythera by Agamemnon, where he died. *Apollod.* 2. c. 4.—*Sophocl. in Ajac.* 1311.—*Ovid. in Ib.* 359. *A. A.* 1. v. 327. *Ex. Pont.* 4. el. 16. v. 47.—*Hygin.* fab. 86, &c.—*Lucan.* 1. v. 544, l. 7. v 451.—*Senec. in Thyest.*—*Tzetzes. Ch.* 1. c. 18.—*Sch. Euripid. ad Orest.* 5—*Lactant. ad Theb.* 4. v. 306. —*Servius ad Æn.* 1. v. 572. l. 6. v. 623. l. 11. v. 262.

THY'IA. *Vid.* Thya.

THY'IA, a nymph intimate with Chloris, daughter of Amphion, and loved by Neptune. She had a statue in the temple of Delphi. *Paus. Phoc.* 29.

THY'IA, a festival celebrated annually in honor of Bacchus by the people of Elis. *Paus.* 6. c. 26.

THYMAR'ADÆ, a village in the tribe Hippothoontis.

THYM'BRA, a small town of Lydia, near Sardes, celebrated for a battle which was fought there between Cyrus and Crœsus, in which the latter was defeated. The troops of Cyrus amounted to 196,000 men, besides chariots, and those of Crœsus were twice as numerous.——A plain in Troas through which a small river, called Thymbrius,, flows in its course to the Scamander. Apollo had there a temple, and thence he is called Thymbræus. Achilles was killed there by Paris, according to some. *Strab.* 13.—*Stat.* 4. *Sylv.* 7. v. 22.—*Dictys. Cret.* 2. c. 52. l. 3. c. l.—*Tzetzes ad Lyc.* 269.—*Sch. Hom. Il.* 10. v. 430.

THYMBRÆ'US, a surname of Apollo from Thymbra. *Virg. G.* 5. v. 323. *Æn.* 3. v. 85.—*Strab.* 13. *Vid.* Thymbra.

THYM'BRIA, a village of Caria, near Myus, on the Mæander. *Strab.*

THYM'BRIS, a concubine of Jupiter, said to have been mother of Pan. *Apollod.*

THYM'BRIS, a fountain and river of Sicily. *Theoc.* 1. v. 100.——A river of Bithynia, which rises in Galatia, and flows into the Sangarius. *Liv.* 38. c. 18. It is called Thymbrius by *Strabo,* and Tembrogius by *Pliny,* 6. c. 1.

THYM'BRON. *Vid.* Thimbron.

THYM'ELE, a celebrated female dancer, favoured by Domitian. She was the wife of Latinus, a well-known mimic of those times. *Mart.* 1. epigr. 5. v. 5.—*Juv.* 1. v. 36. sat. 6. v. 36.

THYMIATE'RION, a city of Libya. *Steph.*

THYMI'ATHIS, a river of Epirus. *Strab.* 7.

THYMI'TUS or THYMŒ'TES, a Greek poet in the age of Orpheus. He travelled through several countries, and was initiated at Nysa in Africa into the mysteries of Bacchus, and afterwards wrote some dithyrambic poems, one of which was called Phrygia. He is said by some to have been son of Laomedon. *Diod.* 3.—*Gyrald. de P.H.* 2.

THYM'NIAS, a bay of Doris, with a promontory, between Gnidus and Larumna. *Plin.* 5. c. 28.—*Mela*, 1. c. 16.

THYMOCH'ARES or THYMOCH'ARIS, an Athenian defeated in a battle by the Lacedæmonians.

THYMON'DAS, son of Mentor, general of Darius. *Curt.* 3. c. 8.

THYMŒ'TES, a king of Athens, son of Oxynthes, the last of the descendants of Theseus, who reigned at Athens. He was deposed because he refused to accept a challenge sent by Xanthus, king of Bœotia, and was succeeded by a Messenian, B.C. 1128, who repaired the honor of Athens by fighting the Bœotian king. *Paus.* 2. c. 18.——A Trojan prince, whose wife and son were put to death by order of Priam. It was to revenge the king's cruelty that he persuaded his countrymen to bring the wooden horse within their city. He was son of Laomedon, according to some. *Virg. Æn.* 2. v. 32.—*Servius loco.*—*Dictys. Cret.* 4. c. 4.——A son of Hicetaon, who accompanied Æneas into Italy, and was killed by Turnus. *Virg. Æn.* 10. v. 123. l. 12. v. 364.

THY'NE, a city of Libya. *Steph.*

THY'NI or BITHY'NI, a people of Bithynia, hence the word *Thyna merx* applied to their commodities. *Horat.* 3. od. 7. v. 3.—*Plin.* 4. c. 11.

THYN'IAS or THYN'NIAS, an island in the Euxine Sea, on the coast of Pontus, opposite Bithynia. *Plin.* 5. *c. ult.*—*Mela*, 2. c. 7.

THY'NOS or TY'NOS, a town of Cilicia. *Plin.* 5. c. 27

THYOD'AMAS. *Vid.* Theodamas.

THYO'NE, a name given to Semele after she had been presented with immortality by her son. *Diod.* 4.—*Apollod.* 3. c. 5.

THYO'NEUS or THYONIA'NUS, a surname of Bacchus from his mother Semele, who was called Thyone. *Apollod.* 3. c. 5.—*Horat.* 1. od. 17. v. 23. —*Ovid. Met.* 4. v. 13.—*Stat. Theb.* 5. v. 262.—*Catull.* 27. v. 7.

THYO'TES or THY'OTES, a priest of the Cabiri, in Samothrace. *Flacc.* 2. v. 438.

THY'RE, a town of the Messenians, famous for a battle fought there between the Argives and Lacedæmonians. *Herodot.* 1. c. 82.—*Stat. Theb.* 4. c. 48.

THYR'EA or THYREA'TIS, an island on the coast of Peloponnesus, near Hermione. *Herodot.* 6. c. 76.

THYR'EUM or THYR'IUM, a town of Acarnania, the inhabitants of which are called Thyrienses. *Liv.* 36. c. 11. l. 38. v. 9.

THYR'EUS, a son of Lycaon, king of Arcadia. *Paus.* 8. c. 3.——A son of Œneus, king of Calydon. *Apollod.* 1. c. 8.

THYR'IDES, three small islands of the Ionian Sea, on the coast of Messenia. *Plin.* 4. c. 12. ——The top of mount Tænarus, or a promontory on the coast of Laconia. *Paus.* 3.

THYRSAG'ETÆ or THYSSAG'ETÆ, a people of Sarmatia who lived upon hunting. *Plin.* 4. c. 12.

THYR'SUS or TYR'SUS, a river of Sardinia, now Oristagni.

THYS'DRUS or TIS'DRUS, a colony and city in the interior of Africa. *Hirt. B. Afr.* c. 36.—*Plin.* 5. c. 4.

THYS'SOS, a town near mount Athos. *Herodot.* —*Strab.*

THYS'TRUS, a city of Libya. *Herodian.* 1. 6.

THY'US or THYS, a satrap of Paphlagonia, who revolted from Artaxerxes, and was defeated and taken prisoner by Datames. *C. Nep. in Dat.*

THYXE'US, a surname of Apollo at Cyanea, in Lycia. In a fountain there consecrated to the god, was represented every thing which those who consulted his oracle wished to know. *Paus.* 7. c. 21.

TIA'RA JU'LIA, a city of Hispania Tarraconensis. *Ptol.*

TI'ASA or TIA'SA, a daughter of the Eurotas, who gave her name to a river in Laconia. *Paus.* 3. c. 18.

TIBARE'NI, a people of Cappadocia, on the borders of the Thermodon. *Dionys.* v. 776.——A people of Pontus. *Mela*, 1. c. 20.

TIBERIA'NUS, a governor of Syria in the age of Trajan. *Plin. Epist.* 10.—*Oros.* 7. c. 8.—*Euseb.* 3. c. 30.——A prefect of the prætorian cohort under Constantine the Great. He was also a poet.—*Hieron. in Chron.*—*Lil. Gyrald. H. Poet.* —*Voss. H. Lat.* 2.

TIBE'RIAS, a town of Galilee built by Herod, near the lake of the same name, and called after Tiberius. *Plin.* 5. c. 16.—*Joseph. A.* 18. c. 3.

TIBERI'NUS SYL'VIUS, son of Capetus, and king of Alba, was drowned in the river Albula, which on that account assumed the name of Tiberis, and of which he became the protecting god. *Liv.* 1. c. 3.—*Cic. de Nat.* 2. c. 20.—*Varro. de L.L.* 4. c. 5, &c.—*Ovid. Fast.* 2. v. 389. l. 4. v. 47.—*Minuc. Felix.* 25.

TIB'ERIS, TYB'ERIS, TI'BER, TI'BRIS, TY'BRIS or THY'BRIS, a river of Italy, on the banks of which the city of Rome was built. It was originally called Albula, from the whiteness of its waters, and afterwards Tiberis, when Tiberinus, king of Alba had been drowned there. It was also named Tyrrhenus, because it watered Etruria, and Lydius, because the inhabitants in the neighbourhood were supposed to be of Lydian origin. The Tiber rises in the Apennines, and falls into the Tyrrhene Sea, 16 miles below Rome, after dividing Latium from Etruria. *Ovid. Fast.* 4. v. 47, 329, &c. l. 5. v. 641. *In Ib.* 514.—*Lucan.* 1. v. 381, &c.—*Varro de L.L.* 4. c. 5.—*Virg. Æn.* 7. v. 30.—*Horat.* 1. od. 2. v. 13.—*Mela*, 2. c. 4.—*Liv.* 1. c. 3.—*Strab.* 5.—*Paus.* 8. c. 43. [There is a very fine statue of the Tiber, in the Vatican at Rome.]

TIBE'RIUS CLAU'DIUS DRU'SUS NE'RO, a Roman emperor after the death of Augustus, descended from the family of the Claudii. In his early years he commanded popularity by entertaining the populace with magnificent shows and fights of gladiators; and he gained some applause in the funeral oration which he pronounced over his father, though only nine years old. His first appearance in the Roman armies was under Augustus, in the war against the Cantabri; and afterwards in the capacity of general, he obtained victories in different parts of the empire, and was rewarded with a triumph. Yet in the midst of his glory, Tiberius fell under the displeasure of Augustus, and retired to Rhodes, where he continued for seven years as an exile, till, by the influence of his mother Livia with the emperor, he was recalled. His return to Rome was the more glorious; he had the command of the Roman armies in Illyricum, Pannonia, and Dalmatia, and seemed to divide the sovereign power with Augustus. At the death of this celebrated emperor, Tiberius, who had been adopted, assumed the reins of government; and while with dissimulation and affected modesty he wished to decline the dangerous office, he found time to try the fidelity of his friends, and to make the greatest part of the Romans believe that he was invested with the purple, not from his own choice, but from the recommendation of Augustus, and the urgent entreaties of the Roman senate. The beginning of his reign seemed to promise tranquillity to the world: Tiberius was a watchful guardian of the public peace; he was the friend of justice, and never assumed the sounding titles which most disgust a free nation; but he was satisfied to say of himself that he was the master of his slaves, the general of his soldiers, and the father of the citizens of Rome. This seeming moderation, however, which was but the fruit of the deepest policy, soon disappeared, and Tiberius was viewed in his real character. His ingratitude to his mother Livia, to whose intrigues he was indebted for the purple, his cruelty to his wife Julia, and his tyrannical oppression and murder of many noble senators, rendered him odious to the people, and suspected even by his most intimate favorites. The armies mutinied in Pannonia and Germany; but the tumults were silenced by the prudence of the generals and the fidelity of the officers, and the factious demagogues were abandoned to condign punishment. This acted as a check upon Tiberius in Rome; he perceived, as his successors experienced, that his power was precarious, and his very existence in perpetual danger. He continued as he had begun, to pay the greatest deference to the senate; all libels against him he disregarded, and observed, that in a free city, the thoughts and the tongue of every man should be free. The taxes were gradually lessened, and luxury restrained by the salutary regulations, as well as by the prevailing example and frugality of the emperor. While Rome exhibited a scene of peace and public tranquillity, the barbarians were severally defeated on the borders of the empire, and Tiberius gained new honors by the activity and valor of Germanicus and his other faithful lieutenants. Yet the triumphs of Germanicus were beheld with jealousy. Tiberius dreaded his power; he was envious of his popularity, and the death of that celebrated general in Antioch was, as some suppose, accelerated by poison, and the secret resentment of the emperor. Not only his relations and friends, but the great and opulent, were sacrificed to his ambition, cruelty, and avarice; and there was scarcely one single family in Rome that did not reproach Tiberius for the loss of a brother, a father, or a husband. He at last retired to the island of Capræa, on the coast of Campania, where he buried himself in unlawful pleasures. The care of the empire was entrusted to favorites, among whom for a while Sejanus shone with uncommon splendour. In his solitary retreat the emperor proposed rewards to such as invented new pleasures, or could produce fresh luxuries. He forgot his age as well as his dignity, and disgraced himself by the most unnatural vices and enormous indulgences, which can draw a blush even upon the countenance of the most debauched and abandoned. While the emperor was lost to himself and the world, the provinces were harassed on every side by the barbarians, and Tiberius found himself insulted by those enemies whom hitherto he had seen fall prostrate at his feet with every mark of submissive adulation. At last, grown weak and helpless through infirmities, he thought of his approaching dissolution; and as he well knew that Rome could not exist without a head, he nominated as his successor Caius Caligula. Many might inquire, why a youth naturally so vicious and abandoned as Caius was chosen to be the master of an extensive empire; but Tiberius wished his own cruelties to be forgotten in the barbarities which might be displayed in the reign of his successor, whose natural propensities he had well defined, in saying of Caligula, that he bred a serpent for the Roman people, and a Phaethon for the rest of the empire. Tiberius died at Misenum the 16th of March, A.D. 37, in the 78th year of his age, after a reign of 22 years, six months, and 26 days. Caligula was accused of having hastened his end by suffocating him. The joy was universal when his death was known; and the people of Rome, in the midst of sorrow, had a moment to rejoice, heedless of the calamities which awaited them in the succeeding reigns. The body of Tiberius was conveyed to Rome, and burnt with great solemnity. A funeral oration was pronounced by Caligula, who seemed to forget his benefactor while he expatiated on the praises of Augustus, Germanicus, and himself. The character of Tiberius has been examined with particular attention by historians, and his reign is the subject of the most perfect and elegant of all the compositions of Tacitus. When a private man, Tiberius was universally esteemed; when he had no superior, he was proud, arrogant, jealous, and revengeful. If he found his military operations conducted by a warlike general, he affected moderation and virtue; but when he got rid of the powerful influence of a favorite, he was tyrannical and dissolute. If, as some observe, he had lived in the times of the Roman republic, he might have been as conspicuous as his great ancestors; but the sovereign power lodged in his hands, rendered him vicious and oppressive. Yet, though he encouraged informers and favored flattery, he blushed at the mean servilities of the senate, and derided the adulation of his courtiers, who approached him, he said, as if they approached a savage elephant. He was a patron of learning; he was an eloquent and ready speaker, and dedicated some part of his time to study. He wrote a lyric poem, entitled, "A Complaint on the death of Lucius Cæsar," as also some Greek pieces in imitation of some of his favorite authors. He avoided all improper expressions, and all foreign words he wished totally to banish from the Latin tongue. As instances of his humanity, it has been recorded that he was uncommonly liberal to the people of Asia Minor, whose habitations had been destroyed by a violent earthquake, A.D. 17. One of his officers wished him to increase the taxes, "No," said Tiberius, "a good shepherd must shear not flay his sheep." The senators wished to call the month of November, in which he was born, by his name, in imitation of J. Cæsar and Augustus, in the months of July and August; but this he refused, saying, "What will you do, conscript fathers, if you have thirteen Cæsars?" Like the rest of the emperors, he received divine honors after death, and even during his life. It was wittily observed by Seneca, that he never was intoxicated but once all his life, for he continued in a perpetual state of intoxication from the time he gave himself to drinking to the last moment of his existence. *Sueton. in Vitâ, &c.—Tacit. Ann.* 6, &c.—*Dion. Cass.* [The finest bust of Tiberius is in the Capitol at Rome.]

TIBE'RIUS, a friend of Julius Cæsar, whom he accompanied in the war of Alexandria. Tiberius forgot the favours he had received from his friend; and when he was assassinated, he wished all his murderers to be publicly rewarded.——One of the Gracchi. *Vid.* Gracchus.——A son of Brutus, put to death by his father, because he had conspired with other young noblemen to restore Tarquin to his throne.——A Thracian, made emperor of Rome in the latter ages of the empire. *Niceph.* 18. c. 6.—*Evagr.* 6.

TIBE'RIUS SEMPRO'NIUS, a son of Drusus and Livia, the sister of Germanicus, put to death by Caligula.

TIBE'SIS, a river of Scythia, flowing from mount Hæmus into the Ister. *Herodot.* 4. c. 49.

TIBIS'CA, a town of Lower Mœsia. *Ptol.*

TIBIS'CUS, now Teisse, a river of Dacia, with a town of the same name, now Temeswar. It falls into the Danube.

TI'BRIS. *Vid.* Tiberis.

TIB'ULA, a town of Sardinia, now Lango Sardo.

TIBUL'LUS AL'BIUS, a Roman knight, celebrated for his poetical compositions. He followed Messala Corvinus into the island of Corcyra, but he was soon dissatisfied with the toils of war, and retired to Rome, where he gave himself up to literary ease, and to all the effeminate indolence of an Italian climate. His first composition was to celebrate the virtues of his friend Messala, but his more favorite study was writing love verses, in praise of his mistresses Delia and Plautia, of Nemesis and Neæra, and in these elegant effusions he showed himself the most correct of the Roman poets. As he had espoused the cause of Brutus he lost his possessions when the soldiers of the triumvirate were rewarded with lands; but he might have recovered them, if he had condescended, like Virgil, to make his court to Augustus. This, however, he nobly refused to do; and while he lamented his poverty, and attributed his misfortunes to the violence of the times, he did not disgrace his muse by calumny, but passed in silent contempt over the virtues and vices which he might have discovered in the character of his imperial oppressor. Four books of elegies are the only remaining pieces of his composition. They are uncommonly elegant and beautiful, and possessed of so much grace and purity of sentiment, that the writer is deservedly ranked as the prince of elegiac poets. Tibulus was intimate with the literary men of the age, and he for some time had a poetical contest with Horace, in gaining the favors of an admired courtezan. Ovid has written a beautiful elegy on the death of his friend. The poems of Tibullus are generally published with those of Propertius Catullus, of which the best editions are, that of Vulpius, Patavii, 1737, 1749, 1755; that of Barbou, 12mo. Paris, 1754; and that by Heyne, 8vo. Lips. 1776: this last is considered the best edition. *Harles Not. Lit. Rom.* 1. p. 224.—*Sax. Onom.* 1. p. 183.—*Ovid.* 3. *Am.* el. 9. v. 15 & 39. *Trist.* 2. v. 447 & 463. l. 4. el. 10. v. 51. l. 5. el. 1. v. 8. *de A.A.* 1. v. 764. l. 3. v. 334. *de Rem.* 763.—*Gyrald de P.H.* 4.—*Horat.* 1. ep. 4. l. 1. od. 33. v. 1.—*Quintil.* 10. c. 1.

TI'BUR, an ancient town of the Sabines, about 20 miles north of Rome, built, as some say, by Tibur the son of Amphiarus. It was watered by the Anio, and Hercules was the chief deity of the place, from which circumstance it has been called *Herculei Muri*. In the neighbourhood, the Romans, on account of the salubrity of the air, had their several villas to which they retired; and there also Horace had his favorite country seat, though some place it nine miles higher. *Strab.* 5.—*Cic.* 2. *Orat.* 65.—*Suet. Cal.* 21.—*Virg. Æn.* 7. v. 630.—*Horat.* 3. od. 4, &c.—*Ovid. Fast.* 6. v. 61, &c.—*Sil. It.* 4. v. 225.—*Propert.* 2. el. 23. v. 43. l. 3. el. 14. v. 2. el. 21. v. 23.—*Servius ad Æn.* 7. v. 670.

TIBUR'TIUS L., a centurion in Cæsar's army, wounded by Pompey's soldiers. *Cæs. B. Civ.* 3. c. 19.

TIBUR'TUS, the founder of Tibur, often called *Tiburtia Mœnia*. He was assisted in the building by his brothers Coras and Catillus, sons of Amphiarus. *Virg. Æn.* 7. v. 670. & *Servius loco.*

TICA'RIUS or FICA'RIUS, a river of Corsica. *Ptol.* It is called Grosso by *Leander*.

TICH'ASA, a city of Africa Propria. *Ptol.*

TICHI'CES, a fortified place near Trachinia. *Steph*

TI'CHIS, now Tec, a river of Spain, falling into the Mediterranean. *Mela*, 2. c. 5.

TICH'IUM, a town of Ætolia. *Thucyd.*

TICH'IUS, a name given to the top of Mount Œta. *Liv.* 36. c. 16.

TI'CHOS or TEI'CHOS, a fortified place of Achaia. *Steph.*

TIC'IDA CA'IUS, a poet of Rome, who flourished a few years before the age of Cicero. He wrote epigrams in an easy and elegant style, and praised his mistress Metella under the fictitious name of Perilla, and chiefly excelled in amorous poetry. Only eight of his verses are preserved. *Ovid Trist.* 2. v. 433.—*Priscian.*

TICI'NUS, now Tesino, a river near Ticinum, a small town of Italy, where the Romans were defeated by Annibal. The town of Ticinum was also called Pavia. The Ticinus falls into the Po. *Strab.* 5.—*Ital.* 4. v. 81.—*Plin.* 2. c. 103.—*Claudian de Cons. Hon.* 6. v. 195.

TID'IUS, a man who joined Pompey, &c.

TIES'SA, a river of Laconia, falling into the Eurotas. *Paus.* 3. c. 18.

TIFA'TA or TIF'ATA, a mountain of Campania, near Capua. It is now Monte di Capoa and di Caserta. *Stat. Sylv.* 4. v. 85.

TIFER'NUM, a name common to three towns of Italy. One of them, for distinction's sake, was called *Metaurense*, near the Metaurus in Umbria; the other *Tiburnium*, on the Tiber; and the third *Samniticum*, in the country of the Sabines. *Liv.* 10. c. 14.—*Plin.* 3. c. 14.—*Plin.* sec. 4. ep. 1.

TIFER'NUS, a mountain and river in the country of the Samnites. *Plin.* 3. c. 11.—*Liv.* 10. c. 30.—*Mela*, 2. c. 4.

TIG'ASIS, a son of Hercules.

TIGA'VA, an inland city of Mauritania Cæsariensis. *Ptol.* It is called Tigavia by *Antoninus*.

TIGELLI'NUS SOPHO'NIUS, a Roman celebrated for his intrigues and perfidy in the court of Nero. He was appointed judge at the trial of the conspirators who had leagued against Nero, for which he was liberally rewarded with triumphal honors. He afterwards betrayed the emperor, and, on the accession of Galba, was ordered to destroy himself, 68 A.D. *Tacit.* 1. *H.* c. 72.—*Plut.*—*Juv.* 1. v. 155.

M. TIGEL'LIUS HERMOG'ENES, a native of Sardinia, who became the favorite of J. Cæsar, of Cleopatra, and of Augustus, by his mimicry and facetiousness. He was celebrated for the melody of his voice, yet he was of a mean and ungenerous disposition, and of unpleasing manners, as *Horace*, 1. sat. 2. v. 3. *et seq.* insinuates. *Cic.* 7. *Fam.* 24. *Att.* 13. ep. 49 & 51.

TI'GIS, a town of Mauritania Cæsariensis. *Ptol.*

TI'GRA, a city of Lower Mœsia. *Antonin.*

TIGRA'NES, a king of Armenia, who made himself master of Assyria and Cappadocia. He married Cleopatra, the daughter of Mithridates, and, by the advice of his father-in-law, declared war against the Romans. He despised these distant enemies, and even ordered the head of the messenger to be cut off who first told him that the Roman general was boldly advancing towards his capital. His pride, however, was soon abated; and though he ordered the Roman consul Lucullus, to be brought alive into his presence, he fled with precipitation from his capital, and was soon after defeated near mount Taurus. This totally disheartened him; he refused to receive Mithridates into his palace, and even set a price upon his head. His mean submission to Pompey, the successor of Lucullus in Asia, and a bribe of 60,000 talents, insured him on his throne, and he received a garrison in his capital, and continued at peace with the Romans. His second son of the same name revolted against him, and attempted to dethrone him with the assistance of the king of Parthia, whose daughter he had married. This did not succeed, and the son had recourse to the Romans, by whom he was put in possession of Sophene, while the father remained quiet on the throne of Armenia. The son was afterwards sent in chains to Rome for his insolence to Pompey. *Cic. pro Man. Sext.* 27.—*Val. Max.* 5. c. 1. l. 8. c. 15. l. 9. c. 11.—*Dio.* 38, 30.—*Lucan.* 2. v. 637.—*Paterc.* 2. c. 33 & 37.—*Justin.* 40. c. 1 & 2.—*Plut. in Luc. Pomp. &c.*——A king of Armenia in the reign of Tiberius. He was put to death. *Tacit.* 6. *Ann.* c. 40.——One of the royal family of the Cappadocians, chosen by Tiberius to ascend the throne of Armenia.——A general of the Medes. *Herodot.* l. 7.——A man appointed king of Armenia by Nero. *Tacit. Ann.* 14. c. 26.——A prince of Armenia, in the age of Theodosius.

TIGRANOCER'TA, now Sered, the capital of Armenia, built by Tigranes, during the Mithridatic war, on a hill between the springs of the Tigris and mount Taurus. Lucullus, during the Mithridatic war, took it with difficulty, and found in it immense riches, and no less than 8000 talents in ready money. *Tacit. Ann.* 15. c. 4.—*Plin.* 6. c. 9.

TI'GRES, a river of Peloponnesus, called also Harpys, from one of the Harpies who was drowned in it. *Apollod.* 1. c. 9.

TI'GRIS, now Basilensa, a river of Asia, rising on mount Niphate in Armenia, and falling into the Persian Gulf. It is the eastern boundary of Mesopotamia. The Tigris now falls into the Euphrates, though in the age of Pliny the two separate channels of these rivers could be easily traced. *Plin.* 6. c. 27.—*Justin.* 42. c. 3.—*Lucan.* 3. v. 256.—*Ptol.* 5. c. 13.—*Mela*, 1. c. 11. l. 3. c. 8.—*Virg. Ecl.* 1. v. 63.

TI'GRIS, one of Actæon's dogs. *Ovid. Met.* 3. v. 217.

TIGURI'NI, a warlike people among the Helvetii, now forming the modern cantons of Switz, Zurich, Scaffhausen, and St. Gall. Their capital was Tigunum. *Cæs. Bell. G.*

TILATÆ'I, a people of Thrace. *Thucyd.* 2.

TILAVEMP'TUS, a river of Italy falling into the Adriatic, at the west of Aquileia. *Ptol.*—*Plin.* 3. c. 18.

TILABA'RUM, a city of Africa Propria. *Antonin.*

TIL'LIUM, a town of Sardinia, now Argentera.

TIL'LIUS CIM'BER. *Vid.* Tullius.

TILOGRAM'MUM, a city of India within the Ganges. *Ptol.*—*Plin.* 12. c. 3.

TI'LOX, a promontory of Corsica, near Calvia. *Ptol.*

TILPHOS'SA or TILPHU'SIA, a fountain of Bœotia, near which was the tomb of Tiresias. *Apollod.*—*Paus. Bœot.* 32.—*Bochart. Chan.* 1. c. 16.

TILPHOS'SÆUM or TILPHOS'SIUM, a small region of Thessaly. *Steph.*

TIM'ACUS, a river of Mœsia falling into the Danube. The neighbouring people were called Timachi. *Plin.* 3. c. 26.

TIMÆ'A, the wife of Agis, king of Sparta, was debauched by Alcibiades, by whom she had a son. This child was rejected in the succession to the throne, though Agis, on his death-bed, declared him to be legitimate. *Plut. in Ag.*

TIMÆ'A, a city of Bithynia. *Ptol.*

TIMÆ'I, a people of Sicily. *Steph. in* Ευκαρπια.

TIMÆ'US, a friend of Alexander, who came to his assistance when he was alone, surrounded by the Oxydracæ. He was killed in the encounter. *Curt.* 9. c. 5.——An historian of Tauromenium in Sicily, who flourished about 262 B.C., and died in the 96th year of his age. His father's name was

Andromachus. He was banished from Sicily by Agathocles. His general history of Sicily, and that of the wars of Pyrrhus, were in general esteem, and his authority was great, except when he treated of Agathocles. Polybius, however, and others, accuse him of want of veracity, and mention his satirical propensities with respect to characters as most severe and illiberal. All his compositions are lost. *Plut. in Nic.—Cic. de Orat.* 2.—*Longinus*, 3.—*Polyb.* 12. c. 3 & 6.—*Lucian. de Macrob.—Diod.* 5.—*C. Nep.* 7. c. 11. ——A writer who published some treatises concerning ancient philosophers. *Diog. in. Emp.* ——A Pythagorean philosopher, born at Locris, in the age of Plato. He followed the doctrines of the founder of the metempsychosis; but in some parts of his system of the world he differed from him. He wrote a treatise in the Doric dialect, on the nature and the soul of the world, still extant. *Plato in Tim.—Plut. de Opin. Phil.* 3. c. 17.—*Cic. Fin.* 5. c. 29.—*Voss. H. Gr.* 1. c. 12. *Jons. de Script. Phil.* p. 32.——An Athenian in the age of Alcibiades. *Plut.*——A sophist who wrote a book called *Lexicon vocum Platonicarum. Phot. Ecl.* 151.

TIMAG'ENES, a Greek historian of Alexandria, 54 B.C., brought to Rome by Gabinius, and sold as a slave to Faustus, the son of Sylla. His great abilities procured him his liberty, and gained the favour of the great, and of Augustus. The emperor discarded him for his impertinence; and Timagenes, to revenge himself on his patron, burnt the interesting history which he had composed of his reign. He afterwards lived universally respected in the family of Asinius Pollio. *Seneca de Ira*, 3. c. 23. *Contr.* 34.—*Plut.—Horat.* 1. ep. 19. v. 15.—*Quintil.* 1. c. 10.—*Amm. Marcell.* 15. c. 9.—*Suidas.*——An historian and rhetorician of Miletus. *Voss. H. Gr.* 1. c. 24. ——A man who wrote an account of the life of Alexander. *Curt.* 9. c. 5.——A general killed at Cheronæa.

TIMAG'ORAS, an Athenian capitally punished by his countrymen for paying homage to Darius, according to the Persian manner of kneeling on the ground, when he was sent to Persia as ambassador. *Val. Max.* 6. c. 3.—*Suidas.*—— *Vid.* Meles.

TIMAN'DRA, a daughter of Leda, sister to Helen She married Echemus of Arcadia. *Paus.* 8 c. 5. ——A mistress of Alcibiades.——A widow on the borders of Thessaly, who, with her son Neophron and her lover Ægypius, and his mother Bulis, were changed into birds, as mentioned by *Antoninus Liberalis, Met.* 5.

TIMAN'DRIDES, a Spartan celebrated for his virtues. *Ælian. V. H.* 14. c. 32.

TIMAN'THES, a painter of Sicyon, in the reign of Philip, father of Alexander the Great. In his celebrated painting of Iphigenia going to be immolated, he represented all the attendants overwhelmed with grief; but his superior genius, by covering the face of Agamemnon, left to the conception of the imagination the deep sorrows of the father. He obtained a prize for which the celebrated Parrhasius was a competitor. This was in painting an Ajax with all the fury which his disappointment could occasion, when deprived of the arms of Achilles. *Cic. de Orat.* 22.—*Val. Max.* 8. c. 11.—*Ælian. V. H.* 9. c. 11.—*Quintil.* 2. c. 13.—*Plin.* 35. c. 10.—*Plut. in Arato.*——An athlete of Cleone, who burnt himself when he perceived that his strength began to fail. *Paus.* 6. c. 8.

TIMAR'CHIDES, a worthless freedman of Verres in Sicily. *Cic. Verr.* 2. c. 28.——A celebrated sculptor. *Plin.* 36. c. 5.

TIMAR'CHUS, a philosopher of Alexander, intimate with Lamprocles, the disciple of Socrates. *Diog.* 6.—*Plut. de Socr.*——A rhetorician who hanged himself when accused of licentiousness by Æschines. *Plut. in Æsch.—Tzetzes Ch.* 6. c. 36. ——A Cretan, accused before Nero of oppression. *Tacit. Ann.* 15. c. 20.——An officer in Ætolia, who burnt his ships to prevent the flight of his companions, and to ensure himself the victory. *Polyæn.* 5. c. 25.——An Athenian accused of treason by Æschines. He fled to Epidaurus, where he was murdered by Procles the tyrant of the place, who wished to obtain possession of the large sum of money he had brought with him. *Plut. cur Pyth., &c.*——A statuary. *Plin.* 34. c. 8.——A king of Salamis.——A tyrant of Miletus, in the age of Antiochus, &c.

TIMAR'ETA, TIMAR'ETE, TIMARE'TA, or TIMARE'TE, a priestess of the oracle of Dodona. *Herodot.* 2. c. 94.——A daughter of the painter Mycon, who likewise excelled in her father's profession. *Plin.* 35. c. 9.

TI'MAS, a native of Mariandynum put to death by Amycus. *Val. Flacc.* 4. v. 187.

TIMA'SION, one of the leaders of the 10,000 Greeks, &c.

TIMASITH'EUS, a prince of Lipara, who obliged a number of pirates to spare some Romans who were going to make an offering of the spoils of Veii to the god of Delphi. The Roman senate rewarded him very liberally, and 137 years after, when the Carthaginians were dispossessed of Lipara, the same generosity was nobly extended to his descendants in the island. *Diod.* 14.—*Plut. in Cam.*——A famous athlete of Crotona, superior to Milo in strength. *Paus.* 6. c. 14.

TIMA'VUS, now Timavo, a broad river in Italy, rising from a mountain, and, after running a short space, falling by seven mouths, or, according to some, by one only, into the Adriatic Sea. There are at the mouth of the Timavus small islands with hot springs of water. *Mela,* 2. c. 4. —*Virg. Ecl.* 8. v. 6. *Æn.* 1. v 44 & 248.—*Stat.* 4. —*Sylv. ult.—Strab* 5.—*Plin.* 2. c. 103.

TIME'SIUS or TIME'SIAS, a native of Clazomenæ, who began to build Abdera. He was prevented by the Thracians, but honored as a hero at Abdera. *Herodot.* 1. c. 168.—*Ælian V.H.* 12. c. 9. —*Plut. in Præc. Pol.—Salmas. ad Solin.* p. 161.

TIM'ICA, an inland city of Mauritania Cæsariensis. *Ptol.*

TIMOCH'ARES, the physician of Pyrrhus, who offered to Fabricius the Roman general to poison his master: a proposal which was indignantly rejected. *Gell.* 3. c. 8.

TIMOCH'ARIS, an astronomer of Alexandria, 294 B.C. *Vid.* Aristillus.

TIMOCLE'A a Theban lady, sister to Theogenes, who was killed at Cheronæa. One of Alexander's soldiers offered her violence, after which she led her ravisher to a well, and while he believed that immense treasures were concealed there, Timoclea threw him into it. Alexander commended her virtue, and forbad his soldiers to hurt the Theban females. *Plut. in Alex. & de Virt. Mul.*

TIM'OCLES, the name of two Greek poets of Athens who wrote some theatrical pieces, the one six and the other eleven, some verses of which are extant. *Athen.* 6.—*Stobæus.*——A statuary of Athens. *Paus.* 10. c. 34.—*Plin.* 34. c. 8.——A dancer who accompanied L. Piso into Macedonia. *Cic. Pis.* 36.

TIMOC'RATES, a Greek philosopher of uncommon austerity. He was one of the heirs of Epicurus, though he differed in opinions from him, and drew down upon himself his severest censures. *Cic. N. D.* 1. c. 33 & 40. *Fin.* 2. c. 31.—*Diog.* 10, 16.——A Syracusan who married Arete when Dion had been banished into Greece by Dionysius. He commanded the forces of the tyrant.——An archon at Athens. Olymp. 104. an. 1.

TIMO'CREON, a comic poet of Rhodes, who obtained poetical as well as gymnastic prizes at Olympia. He lived about 476 years B.C., and was distinguished for his voracity, and resentment against Simonides and Themistocles. The following epitaph was written on his grave:

Multa bibens, et multa vorans, mala denique dicens
Multis, hic jaceo Timocreon Rhodius.

TIMODE'MUS, the father of Timoleon.

TIMOGIT'TIA, a town of Lower Mysia, on the shores of the Euxine Sea. *Antonin.*

TIMOLA'US, a Spartan, intimate with Philopœmen, &c.——A son of the celebrated Zenobia. *Trebell. in eo.* c. 28.——A general of Alexander, put to death by the Thebans.——A native of Larissa, pupil of Anaximenes. He wrote a poem on the Trojan war.—*Suidas.*

TIMO'LEON, a celebrated Corinthian, son of Timodemus and Demariste. He was such an enemy to tyranny, that he did not hesitate to murder his own brother Timophanes, when he attempted, against his representations, to make himself absolute in Corinth. This was viewed with pleasure by the friends of liberty; but the mother of Timoleon conceived the most inveterate aversion for her son, and for ever banished him from her sight. This proved painful to Timoleon; a settled melancholy dwelt upon his mind, and he refused to accept any offices in the state. When the Syracusans, oppressed with the tyranny of Dionysius the younger, and of the Carthaginians, had solicited the assistance of the Corinthians, all looked upon Timoleon as a proper deliverer; but all applications would have been disregarded, if one of the magistrates had not awakened in him the sense of natural liberty. "Timoleon," says he, "if you accept of the command of this expedition, we will believe that you have killed a tyrant; but if not, we cannot but call you your brother's murderer." This had due effect, and Timoleon sailed for Syracuse with ten ships, accompanied by about 1000 men. The Carthaginians attempted to oppose him, but Timoleon eluded their vigilance. Icetas, who had possession of the city, was defeated, and Dionysius, who despaired of success, gave himself up into the hands of the Corinthian general. This success gained Timoleon adherents in Sicily; many cities which had hitherto looked upon him as an impostor, claimed his protection; and when he became at last master of Syracuse by the total overthrow of Icetas and of the Carthaginians, he razed the citadel which had been the seat of tyranny, and erected on the spot a common hall. Syracuse was almost destitute of inhabitants, and at the solicitation of Timoleon, a Corinthian colony was sent to Sicily; the lands were equally divided among the citizens, and the houses were sold for a thousand talents, which were appropriated to the use of the state, and deposited in the treasury. When Syracuse was thus delivered from tyranny, the conqueror extended his benevolence to the other states of Sicily, and all the petty tyrants were reduced and banished from the island. A code of salutary laws was framed for the Syracusans; and the armies of Carthage, which had attempted again to raise commotions, were defeated, and peace was at last re-established. The gratitude of the Sicilians was shown everywhere to their deliverer. Timoleon was received with repeated applause in the public assemblies, and, though a private man, unconnected with the government, he continued to enjoy his former influence at Syracuse; he was consulted on matters of importance, and his authority respected. He ridiculed the accusations of malevolence; and when some informers had charged him with oppression, he rebuked the Syracusans, who were going to put the accusers to immediate death. A remarkable instance of his providential escape from the dagger of an assassin has been recorded by one of his biographers. As he was going to offer a sacrifice to the gods after a victory, two assassins sent by the enemies, approached his person in disguise. The arm of one of the assassins was already lifted up, when he was suddenly stabbed by an unknown person, who made his escape from the camp. The other assassin, struck at the fall of his companion, fell before Timoleon, and confessed, in the presence of the army, the conspiracy that had been formed against his life. The unknown assassin was in the meantime pursued, and when he was found, he declared that he had committed no crime in avenging the death of a beloved father, whom the man he had stabbed had murdered in the town of Leontini. Enquiries were made, and his confessions were found to be true. Timoleon died at Syracuse about 337 B.C. His body received an honorable burial in a place called from him *Timoleonteum*; but the tears of a grateful nation were more convincing proofs of the public regret than the institution of festivals, and games yearly to be observed on the day of his death. *C. Nep. & Plut. in Vitâ.—Polyæn.* 5. c. 3.—*Diod.* 16.

TIMO'LUS. *Vid.* Tmolus.

TIMOM'ACHUS, a painter of Byzantium, in the age of Sylla and Marius. His paintings of Medea murdering her children, and his Ajax, were purchased for 80 talents by J. Cæsar, and deposited in the temple of Venus at Rome *Plin.* 35. c. 11. —*Athen.* 14.—*Plut. quomodo Adol. Poet.*——A general of Athens, sent to assist the Thebans. *Xenoph.*

TI'MON, a native of Athens, son of Echecratides, called Misanthrope, for his unconquerable aversion to mankind and all society. He was fond of Apemantus, another Athenian whose character was similar to his own, and he said he had some partiality for Alcibiades, because he was one day to be his country's ruin. He once went into the public assembly, and told his countrymen, that he had a fig-tree on which many had ended their lives with a halter, and that he was going to cut it down to raise a building on the spot, he advised all such as were inclined to destroy themselves, to hasten and go and hang themselves in his garden. *Plut. in Alc. &c.—Lucian. in Tim.—Paus.* 6. c. 12.—*Tzetzes Chil.* 7. c. 129.——Son of Timarchus, a Greek poet of Phlius in Peloponnesus, in the age of Ptolemy Philadelphus. He wrote several dramatic pieces all now lost, and died in the 90th year of his age. *Diog.* 9.—*Aul. Gell.* 3. c. 17.—*Athen.* 6 & 13.—*Suidas.*——An athlete of Elis. *Paus.* 6. c. 12.

TIMO'NIUM or TIMO'LÆUM, a fortified place of Paphlagonia. *Steph. Strabo* and *Ptolemy* call the country around it Timonites, and *Pliny*, 5. c. 32. calls the people Timoniacenses.

TIMOPH'ANES, a Corinthian, brother to Timoleon. He attempted to make himself tyrant of his country, by means of the mercenary soldiers with whom he had fought against the Argives and Cleomenes. Timoleon wished to convince him of the impropriety of his measures, and when he found him unmoved, he caused him to be assassinated. *Plut. & C. Nep. in Tim.*——A man of Mitylene, celebrated for his riches, &c. *Aristot. Polit.* 5. c. 4.

TI'MOR, *fear*, a divinity among the Romans, worshipped by the Greeks under the name of Phobos.

TIMO'THEUS, a poet and musician of Miletus, son of Thersander or Philopolis. He is said to have used eleven strings to his lyre, and not seven, according to the custom of his predecessors, a circumstance which was offensive to the Lacedæmonians, so that they reduced the strings to their original number. He was received with hisses the first time he exhibited as musician in the assembly of the people, and further application would have totally been abandoned, had not Euripides discovered his abilities, and encouraged him to follow a profession in which he afterwards gained so much applause. He received the immense sum of 1000 pieces of gold from the Ephesians, because he had composed a poem in honor of Diana. He died about the 90th year of his age, two years before the birth of Alexander the Great, and left behind him 21 hymns, 19 sacred nomi or songs, three tragedies, and other poems now lost. ——A musician of Bœotia, in the age of Alexander, often confounded with the musician of Miletus. He was a great favorite of the conqueror of Darius. *Cic. de Leg.* 2. c. 15.—*Paus.* 3. c. 12.—*Plut. de music. de fort, &c.—Suidas.—Macrob.* sat. 5. c. 22.—*Steph. Byz —Athen.* 12.—*Lucian. in Harmon.—Quintil.* 2. c. 3.——An Athenian general, son of Conon. He signalized himself by his valor and magnanimity, and showed that he was not inferior to his great father in military prudence. He seized Corcyra, and obtained several victories over the Thebans, but ill success in one of his expeditions disgusted the Athenians, and Timotheus, like the rest of his noble predecessors, was fined a large sum of money. He retired to Chalcis, where he died. He was so disinterested, that he never appropriated any of the plunder to his own use, but after one of his expeditions he filled the treasury of Athens with 1200 talents. Some of the ancients, to intimate his continual successes, have represented him sleeping by the side of Fortune, while the goddess drove cities into his net. He was intimate with Plato, at whose table he learned temperance and moderation. *Athen.* 10. c. 3.—*Cic. Tusc.* 5. c. 35. *Off.* 1. c. 32.—*Paus.* 1. c. 29.—*Plut. in Syl. &c.—Ælian. V.H.* 2. c. 10 & 18. l. 3. c. 16 l. 12. c. 43. —*C. Nep.*——A Greek statuary, engaged in the mausoleum erected by Artemisia. *Paus.* 2. c. 32.

Plin. 34. c. 10.——A tyrant of Heraclea, who murdered his father. *Diod.* 16.——A king of the Sapæi.

TIMO'TIUS, a dithyrambic poet, who flourished in the 95th Olympiad.

TIMOX'ENUS, a governor of Sicyon, who betrayed his trust, &c. *Polyæn.* 7. c. 33.——A general of the Achæans.

TIMPI'RUM, a city of Thrace. *Antonin. Simler* reads Tomporis.

TIMY'RA, a city near Isauria.——*A* river of India. *Steph.*

TI'NA, a river of Albion. *Ptol.* It is now Tyne according to *Camden.*

TIN'CA T., a citizen of Placentia, mentioned by Cicero, as distinguished for wit and genuine humour. *Cic. Br.* 46.—*Quintil.* 1. c. 5.

TIN'DA, an inland town of Thrace. *Plin.* 4. c. 11. is called *Stabulum Diomedis* by *Antoninus. Salmas. ad Solin.* p 160.

TIN'DE, a city of Thrace. *Steph.*

TIN'DIUM, a city of Libya. *Id.*

TIN'GIS, now Tangier, a maritime town of Africa, in Mauritania, built by the giant Antæus, or according to others, by Sophax son of Hercules, by Tinga the wife of Antæus. Sertorius took it, and as the tomb of the founder was near the place, he caused it to be opened, and found in it a skeleton sixty cubits long. This increased the veneration of the people for their founder. *Plut. in Sert.*—*Mela,* 1. c. 5.—*Plin.* 5. c. 1.—*Sil.* 3. v. 258.—*Strab.* 3 & 17.

TIN'IA, a river of Umbria, now Topino, falling into the Clitumnus. *Strab.* 5.—*Sil.* 8. v. 454.—*Plin.* 3. c. 5.

TINIS'SA, a city of Armenia Major. *Ptol.*

TIO'RA, a town of the Sabines, on the lake Velinus. It was also called Matiena. *Dion. Hal.*

TIPANIL'LÆ, a people near Caucasus. *Steph.*

TIPARE'NUS, an island of the Peloponnesus, in the Argolic Gulph. *Plin.* 4. c. 12.

TIP'ASA, a city and colony of Mauritania Cæsariensis. *Ptol.*

TI'PHA, a town of Bœotia, where Hercules had a temple. It was the native place of the pilot Tiphys. *Ovid.* ep. 6. v. 48.—*Paus.* 9. c. 32.

TI'PHYS, the pilot of the ship of the Argonauts, was son of Hagnius, or, according to some, of Phorbas and Hymane. He died before the Argonauts reached Colchis, at the court of Lycus in the Propontis, where his tomb was to be seen many ages after, and Eriginus was chosen in his place. *Orph.* 120.—*Apollod.* 1. c. 9.—*Apollon.* 1. v. 105. l. 2. v. 856.—*Val. Flacc.* v. 481. l. 5. v. 65. l. 8. v. 177.—*Seneca in Med.* 617.—*Amm. Marcel.* 22. c. 8.—*Paus.* 9. c. 32.—*Hygin.* fab. 14 & 18.

TIPH'YSA, a daughter of Thestius. *Apollod.* 2. c. 7.

TIQUA'DRA, an island of the Balearic Sea. *Plin.* 3. c. 5.

TIRACIEN'SES, a people of Sicily. *Plin.* 3. c. 8.

TIRE'SIAS, a celebrated prophet of Thebes, son of Everus and Chariclo. He lived to a great age, which some authors have called as long as seven generations of men, others six, and others nine, during the time that Polydorus, Labdacus, Laius, Œdipus, and his sons sat on the throne of Thebes. It is said that in his youth he found two serpents on the top of mount Cyllene, and that when he had struck them with a stick to separate them, he found himself suddenly changed into a girl. Seven years after he again found some serpents together in the same manner, and he recovered his original sex, by striking them a second time with his wand. When he was a woman, Tiresias had married, and it was from these reasons, according to some of the ancients, that Jupiter and Juno referred to his decision, a dispute in which the deities wished to know, which of the sexes received greater pleasures from the connubial state. Tiresias decided in favour of Jupiter. Juno, upon this, punished Tiresias by depriving him of his eye-sight. But this dreadful loss was in some measure repaired by the humanity of Jupiter, who bestowed upon him the gift of prophecy, and permitted him to live seven times more than the rest of men. This account of the origin of the blindness of Tiresias, which is supported by the authority of Ovid, Hyginus, and others, is contradicted by Appollodorus, Callimachus, Propertius, &c, who declare that this misfortune was inflicted upon him as a punishment, because he had seen Minerva bathing in the fountain Hippocrene, on mount Helicon. Chariclo, who accompanied Minerva, complained of the severity with which her son was treated; but the goddess, who well knew that this was the irrevocable punishment inflicted by Saturn on such mortals as fixed their eyes upon a goddess without her consent, alleviated the misfortunes of Tiresias, by making him acquainted with futurity, and giving him a staff which could conduct his steps with as much safety as if he had the use of his eye-sight. During his life-time, Tiresias was an infallible oracle to all Greece. The generals, during the Theban war, consulted him, and found his predictions verified. He drew his prophecies sometimes from the flight or the language of birds, in which he was assisted by his daughter Manto, and sometimes he drew the Manes from the infernal regions with mystical ceremonies. He at last died, after drinking the waters of a cold fountain, which froze his blood. He was buried with great pomp by the Thebans on mount Tilphussus, and honored as a god. His oracle at Orchomenus was in universal esteem. Homer represents Ulysses as going to the infernal regions to consult Tiresias concerning his return to Ithaca. *Apollod.* 3. c. 6.—*Theocrit. Id.* 24. v. 70.—*Stat. Theb.* 2. v. 96.—*Hygin.* fab. 69 & 75.—*Æschyl. sep. contra. Theb,*—*Sophocl. in Œdip. tyr.*—*Pindar. Nem.* 1.—*Diod.* 4.—*Homer. Odyss.* 11. v. 1.—*Plut. in Symp. &c.*—*Paus.* 9. c. 33.—*Callim. Hym. in Pall. lav.* 81 & 128.—*Tzetzes. in Lyc.* 682.—*Lactant. ad Theb.* 2. v. 95. l. 4. v. 407, 626.—*Lucian. in Macrob. Ptolem. Heph.* 1.—*Propert.* 4. el. 9. v. 57.—*Nonnus. in Dionys.* 20.—*Anton. Lib.* 17.—*Heraclit. de Iner.* 7.—*Porphyr.* 3.—*Philostr. in Apoll.* 1. c. 14.—*Athen.* 2 c. 4.

TIRGATA'O, the wife of Hecates, king of the Sindi. She was repudiated by him. *Polyæn.* 8. c. 55.

TIRIBA'ZUS, TERIBA'ZUS, TIRIBA'SES or TERIBA'SES, an officer of Artaxerxes, killed by the guards for conspiring against the king's life, B.C. 394. *Plut. in Art.*

TIR'IDA, a town of Thrace where Diomedes lived. *Plin.* 4. c. 11.

TIRIDA'TES, or TERIDA'TES, a king of Parthia, after the expulsion of Phraates by his subjects. He was soon after deposed by his antagonist, assisted by the Scythians, and he fled to Augustus in Spain for protection. *Justin.* 4. c. 5.—*Plin.* 30. c. 2.—*Suet. in Ner.* 13.—*Horat.* 1. od. 26.——A man made king of Parthia by Tiberius, after the death of Phraates, in opposition to Artabanus. *Tacit. Am.* 6, &c.——A keeper of the royal treasures at Persæpolis, who offered to surrender to Alexander the Great. *Curt.* 5. c. 5, &c.——A king of Armenia, in the reign of Nero.——A son of Phraates, &c.

TI'RIS, a general of the Thracians, who opposed Antiochus. *Polyæn.* 4. c. 16.

TIRIS'SA, a city of Æmathia, in Macedonia. *Ptol.*

TIRIS'TA, a city of Lower Mysia. *Id.* It is now Drista.

TIRIS'TRIA, a promontory of Lower Mysia, on the shores of the Euxine Sea. *Id.* It is now Capo Lemano.

TIRI'ZA, a town of Paphlagonia. *Steph.*

TI'RO TUL'LIUS, the slave, and afterwards the freedman of Cicero, greatly esteemed by his master for learning and good qualities. It is said that he invented short-hand writing among the Romans. He wrote the life of Cicero and other treatises now lost. *Harles. Not. Lit. Rom.* 1. p. 165.—*Cic. ad Att.* 16. ep. 4. *Ad. Fam.* 16. ep. 1, 2, 3, &c.—*Cor. Nep. in Att.*

TIR'SE, a city of Mygdonia. *Steph.*

TIRYN'THIA, a name given to Alcmena, because she lived at Tirynthus. *Ovid. Met.* 6.

TIRYN'THUS, a town of Argolis in the Peloponnesus, founded by Tirynx, son of Argus, with very large stones and without cement. Hercules generally resided there, whence he is called *Tirynthius heros,* an appellation given also to Fab. Maximus from his great exploits. Tirynthus was destroyed by the Argives, who carried the inhabitants to repeople their own city. *Paus.* 2. c. 16 & 25.—*Plin.* 4. c. 5.—*Ælian. V. H.* 3. c. 15 & 49.

—*Virg. Æn.* 7. v. 662.—*Servius loco,* & l. 8. v 228.—*Sil.* 8. v. 217.

TISÆ'UM or **TISÆ'US**, a mountain of Thessaly. *Polyb.*

TISAG'ORAS, a brother of Miltiades, called also Stesagoras. *C. Nep. in Milt.*

TISAM'ENES or **TISAM'ENUS**, a son of Orestes and Hermione, the daughter of Menelaus, who succeeded his father on the throne of Lacedæmon. The Heraclidæ entered his kingdom in the third year of his reign, and he was obliged to retire with his family into Achaia. He was some time after killed in a battle against the Ionians, near Helice, and his remains, which had been entombed in the town, were, by order of the oracle, removed to Sparta. *Apollod.* 2. c. 7.—*Paus.* 3. c. 1. l. 7. c. 1.—*Tzetzes. ad Lyc.* 1374.

TISAM'ENES, a king of Thebes, son of Thersander, and grandson of Polynices The Furies, who continually persecuted the house of Œdipus, permitted him to live in tranquillity, but they tormented his son and successor Autesion, and obliged him to retire to Doris. *Paus.* 3. c. 5. l. 9. c 6.——A native of Elis, crowned twice at the Olympic games, and regarded for the services which he rendered to the Spartans. *Paus.* 3. c. 11.

TISAN'DRUS, one of the Greeks concealed with Ulysses in the wooden horse. Some suppose him to be the same as Thersander, the son of Polynices. *Virg. Æn.* 2. v. 261.

TIS'ARA, a harbour and town of Latium. *Steph.*

TISARAN'THUS, a river of Scythia. *Herodot.* l. 4. Read Tiarantus.

TISAR'CHUS, a friend of Agathocles, by whom he was murdered. *Polyæn.* 5. c. 3.

TIS'DRA, a town of Africa. *Cæs. Afr.* 76.

TIS'IA, a city of Italy. *Steph.*

TISI'ARUS, a town of Africa.

TI'SIAS, an ancient philosopher of Sicily, considered by Cicero as the inventor of rhetoric, &c. *Cic. de Inv.* 2. c. 2. *Orat.* 1. c. 48.—*Quintil.* 2. c. 17.

TISIA'US, a city of Africa Propria, destroyed by Scipio. *Strab.*

TISIPH'ONE, one of the Furies. daughter of Nox and Acheron, who was the minister of divine vengeance upon mankind, who visited them with plagues and diseases, and punished the wicked in Tartarus. She was represented with a whip in her hand: serpents hung from her head, and were hung round her arms instead of bracelets. By Juno's direction she attempted to prevent the landing of Io in Ægypt, but the god of the Nile repelled her, and obliged her to retire to hell. *Stat. Theb.* 1. v. 59.—*Virg. G.* 3. v. 552. *Æn.* 6. v. 555.—*Horat.* 1. sat. 8. v. 34.——A daughter of Alcmæon and Manto.

TISIPH'ONUS, a man who conspired against Alexander, tyrant of Pheræ, and seized the sovereign power. *Diod.* 16.

TI'SIS, a city of Ægypt. *Steph.*

TIS'SA, now Randazo, a town of Sicily. *Sil.* 14. v. 268.—*Cic. Verr.* 3. c. 38.

TISSAM'ENUS. *Vid.* Tisamenus.

TISSAPHER'NES, an officer of Darius.——A satrap of Persia, commander of the forces of Artaxerxes, at the battle of Cunaxa. It was by his valor and intrepidity that the king's forces gained the victory, and for this he obtained the daughter of Artaxerxes in marriage, and all the provinces of which Cyrus was governor. His popularity did not long continue, and the king ordered him to be put to death when he had been conquered by Agesilaus, 395 B.C. *C. Nep.*——An officer in the army of Cyrus, killed by Artaxerxes at the battle of Cunaxa. *Plut.*

TISU'RUS, a town of Africa Propria. *Ptol.*

TITAC'IDÆ, a village in the tribe Antiochis. *Steph.*

TITÆ'A, the mother of the Titans. She is supposed to have been the sama as Thea, Rhea, Terra, &c.

TI'TAN or **TITA'NUS**, a son of Cœlus and Terra, brother to Saturn and Hyperion. He was the eldest of the children of Cœlus; but he gave his brother Saturn the kingdom of the world, provided he raised no male children. When the birth of Jupiter was concealed, Titan made war against Saturn, and with the assistance of his brothers the Titans, imprisoned him till he was replaced on his throne by his son Jupiter. This tradition is recorded by Lactantius, a Christian writer, who took it from the dramatic compositions of Ennius, now lost. None of the ancient mythologists, such as Apollodorus, Hyginus, &c. have made mention of Titan. Titan is a name applied to Saturn by Orpheus and Lucian; to the sun by Virgil and Ovid; and to Prometheus by Juvenal. *Ovid. Met.* l. v. 10.—*Juv.* 14. v. 35.—*Diod.* 5.—*Paus,* 2. c. 11. —*Orpheus. Hymn.* 13.—*Virg. Æn.* 4. v. 119.—*Lactant. de Fals. R.* 14. [There is a fine head in the British Museum, which has been considered a representation of Titan.]

TIT'ANA or **TIT'ANE**, a town of Sicyonia in Peloponnesus, where Titanus, a man skilled in astronomy, was said to live. *Paus.* 2. c. 11.

TITA'NES, a name given to the sons of Cœlus and Terra. They were 45 in number, according to the Ægyptians. Apollodorus mentions 13, Hyginus 6, and Hesiod 23, among whom are the Titanides. The most known of the Titans are Saturn, Hyperion, Oceanus, Japetus, Cottus, and Briareus, to whom Horace adds, Tiphoeus, Mimas, Porphyrion, Rhœtus, and Enceladus, who are by other mythologists reckoned among the giants. They were all of a gigantic stature and proportionate strength. They were treated with great cruelty by Cœlus, and confined in the bowels of the earth, till their mother pitied their misfortunes, and armed them against their father. Saturn with a scythe wounded his father, as he was going to unite himself to Terra, and from the mutilated parts which he threw into the sea, and the froth, sprang a new deity called Venus; as also Alecto, Tisiphone, and Megæra, according to Apollodorus. When Saturn succeeded his father, he married Rhea; but he devoured all his male children, as he had been informed by an oracle, that he should be dethroned by them as a punishment for his cruelty to his father. The war of the Titans against the gods is very celebrated in mythology. It is often confounded with that of the giants; but it is to be observed that the war of the Titans was against Saturn, and that of the giants against Jupiter. *Hesiod. Theog.* 135, &c. —*Apollod.* 1. c. 1.—*Æschyl. in Prom.*—*Callim, in Del.*17 —*Diod.* 1.—*Hygin. Præf.* fab. The English form is Titans.

TITA'NIA, a patronymic applied to Pyrrha as grand-daughter of Titan, and likewise to Diana. *Ovid. Met.* 1. v. 395. l. 2, &c.

TITAN'IDES, the daughters of Cœlus and Terra: reduced in number to six, according to Hesiod, or to seven according to Orpheus The most celebrated were Tethys, Themis, Dione, Thea, Mnemosyne, Ops, Cybele, Vesta, Phœbe, and Rhea. *Hesiod. Theog.* 135, &c.—*Apollod.* 1. c. 1.—*Æschyl. in Pr.* 205 & 873.—*Callimac. in Del.* 17.

TIT'ANUS, a river in Peloponnesus, with a town and mountain of the same name.

TITARE'SIUS, a river of Thessaly, called also Eurotas, flowing into the Peneus, but without mixing its thick and turbid waters with the transparent stream. From the unwholesomeness of its water, it was considered as deriving its source from the Styx. *Lucan.* 6. v. 376.—*Homer. Il.* 2. en. 258.—*Strab.* 8.—*Paus.* 8. c. 18.

TIT'ARON, a city of Thessaly. *Steph.*—*Lycophr.*

TITE'NUS or **TIT'ENUS**, a river of Colchis, falling into the Euxine Sea. *Apollon.* 4.

TITHENID'IA, a festival of Sparta, in which nurses, τιθῆναι, conveyed male infants entrusted to their charge, to the temple of Diana, where they sacrificed young pigs. During the time of the solemnity, they generally danced and exposed themselves in ridiculous postures; there were also some entertainments given near the temple, where tents were erected. Each had a separate portion allotted him, together with a small loaf, a piece of new cheese, part of the entrails of the victim, and figs, beans, and green vetches, instead of sweetmeats.

TITHO'NUS, a son of Laomedon, king of Troy, by Strymo, the daughter of the Scamander. He was so beautiful that Aurora became enamoured of him, and carried him away. He had by her Memnon and Æmathion. He begged of Aurora to be made immortal, and the goddess granted it; but as he had forgotten to ask the vigor, youth, and beauty which he then enjoyed, he soon grew old, infirm, and decrepid; and as his life became insupportable to him, he prayed Aurora to remove him from the world. As he could not die, the goddess changed him into a cicada or grasshopper. *Apol. lod.* 3. c. 5.—*Virg. G.* 1. v. 447. *Æn.* 4. v. 585. l. 8. v. 384.—*Hesiod. Theog.* 984.—*Diod.* 1.—*Ovid. Fast.* 1. c. 461. l. 9. v. 403.—*Horat.* 1. od. 28. l. 2. od. 16.—*Athen.* 12. c. 12.—*Tzetzes ad Lyc.* 15, 18. —*Quint. Cal.* 2. v. 114.—*Servius ad Æn.* 1. v. 493. l. 4. v. 585. *Ad. G.* 1. v. 447. l. 3. v. 328.—*Eustath. ad Hom.* 23. *Il. & Od.* 1 & 5.—*Flacc.* 1. v. 311. l. 3. v. 1.

TITHO'REA, one of the tops of Parnassus. *Herodot.* 8. c. 32.

TI'THRAS, a village in the tribe Ægeis. *Steph.*

TITH'RASUS, a river and town in the interior of Libya. *Suidas.*

TITHRAUS'TES, a Persian satrap, B.C. 395, ordered by Artaxerxes to murder Tisaphernes. He succeeded to the offices which the slaughtered favorite enjoyed. He was defeated by the Athenians under Cimon.——An officer in the Persian court, &c. The name was common to some of the superior officers of state in the court of Artaxerxes. *Plut.—C. Nep. in Dat. & Conon.*

TITHRONI'UM, a city of Phocis. *Steph.*

TIT'IA, a deity among the Milesians. *Apollon. Argon.* 1. 1.

TIT'IA LEX, *de magistratibus*, by P. Titius, the tribune, A.U.C 710. It ordained that a triumvirate of magistrates should be invested with consular power to preside over the republic for five years The persons chosen were Octavius, Antony, and Lepidus.—Another, *de provinciis*, which required that the provincial quæstors, like the consuls and prætors should receive their provinces by lot.

TITIA'NA FLA'VIA, the wife of the emperor Pertinax, disgraced herself by her debaucheries and incontinence. After the murder of her husband she was reduced to poverty, and spent the rest of her life in obscurity.

TITIA'NUS ATIL'IUS, a noble Roman, put to death A.D. 156, by the senate, for aspiring to the purple He was the only one proscribed during the reign of Antoninus Pius.

TITIA'NUS, a brother of Otho.

TIT'II, priests of Apollo at Rome, who observed the flight of doves, and drew omens from it. *Varro de L.L.* 4.—*Lucan.* 1. v. 602.

TITIN'IA, the wife of Cotta, mentioned by *Cicero, Br.* 60.

TITIN'IUS, a tribune of the people in the first ages of the republic.——The name of some persons put to death by Catilline, &c. *Cic. Pet. Cons.* 2.——A friend of Cassius, who killed himself.——One of the slaves who revolted at Capua. He betrayed his trust to the Roman generals.——A poet at Rome, of whose plays some few fragments, to the number of 111 verses are preserved in the Corpus Poetarum.

TITIN'IUS QUIN'TUS, a brother of C. Fannius by the same mother. He was intimate with Cicero. *Cic. Att.* 5. ep. 21. *Verr.* 1. c. 49.

TITIN'IUS CNE'US, a Roman knight. *Cic. Clu.* 56.

TIT'IUS, a friend of Claudius. *Cic. Dom.* 29.——A man who foretold a victory.——One of Pompey's murderers.——One of Antony's officers.

TIT'IUS PROC'ULUS, a Roman knight, appointed to watch Messalina. *Tacit.* 11. *Ann.* c. 35.

TIT'IUS SEX'TUS, a tribune of the people who enacted the Titian law. He was so effeminate in his manners that a dance was called by his name. *Cic. Br.* 62. *Leg.* 2. c. 6 & 12.—*Quintil.* 11. c. 3.

TIT'IUS C. RU'FUS, a city prætor when Paulus went to Macedonia. He was lieutenant to Dolabella in Asia. *Cic. Fam.* 13. ep. 57.

TIT'IUS CA'IUS, an orator and a writer of tragedies, of a very dissolute character. *Cic. Br.* 45.

TIT'IUS SEPTIM'INUS, a poet in the Augustan age, who distinguished himself by his lyric and tragic compositions, now lost. *Horat.* 1. ep. 3. v. 9.

TITOR'MUS, a shepherd of Ætolia, called another Hercules, on account of his strength. He was stronger than his contemporary, Milo of Crotona, as he could lift on his shoulders a stone which the Crotonian moved but with difficulty. *Ælian. V.H.* 12. c. 22.—*Herodot.* 6. c. 127.—*Athen.* 10.—*Eustath. Od.* 5.

TITUA'CIA, a city of the Carpetani in Hispania Tarraconensis. *Ptol.*

TITUL'CIA, a place of Spain, between Emerits and Cæsaraugusta. *Antonin.*

TITU'RIUS, a friend of Junius Silana, who informed against Agrippa, &c. *Tacit. Ann.* 13.

TITU'RIUS SABI'NUS, a lieutenant of Cæsar in Gaul, killed by Ambiorix. *Cæs. Bell. G.* 5. c. 29, &c.

TITUR'NIUS M. RU'FUS, a man mentioned by *Cicero, Fam.* 13. ep. 39.

TI'TUS VESPASIA'NUS, son of Vespasian and Flavia Domitilla, became known by his valor in the Roman armies, particularly at the siege of Jerusalem. In the 79th year of the Christian era, he was invested with the imperial purple, and the Roman people had every reason to expect in him the barbarities of a Tiberius, and the debaucheries of a Nero. While in the house of Vespasian, Titus had been distinguished for his incontinence and extravagance; his attendants were the most abandoned and dissolute, and it seemed that he wished to be superior to the rest of the world in the gratification of every impure desire, and in every unnatural vice. From such a private character, which still might be curbed by the authority and example of a father, what could be expected but tyranny and oppression? Yet Titus became a model of virtue, and in an age and office in which others wish to gratify all appetites, the emperor abandoned his usual profligacy, forgot his debaucheries, and Berenice, whom he had loved with such uncommon ardour, as even to render himself despised by the Roman people, was dismissed from his presence. When raised to the throne, he thought himself bound to be the father of his people, the guardian of virtue, and the patron of liberty; and Titus is perhaps the only monarch who, when invested with uncontrollable power, bade adieu to those vices, those luxuries and indulgences, which as a private man he never ceased to gratify. He was moderate in his entertainments, and though he often refused the donations which were due to sovereignty, no emperor was ever more generous or more magnificent than Titus. All informers were banished from his presence, and even severely punished. A reform was made in the judicial proceedings, and trials were no longer permitted to be postponed for years. The public edifices were repaired, and baths were erected for the convenience of the people. Spectacles were exhibited, and the Roman populace were gratified with the sight of a naval combat in the ancient naumachia, and the sudden appearance of 5000 wild beasts brought into the circus for their amusement. To do good to his subjects was the ambition of Titus, and it was on the recollection that he had done no service, and granted no favor one day, that he made use of the memorable words of "My friends, I have lost a day!" A continual wish to be benevolent and kind, made him popular; and it will not occasion surprise, that he who could say that he had rather die himself, than be the cause of the destruction of one of his subjects, was called the love and delight of mankind. Two of the senators conspired against his life, but the emperor disregarded their attempts, he made them his friends by kindness, and like another Nerva, presented them with a sword to destroy him. During his reign, Rome was three days on fire, the towns of Campania were destroyed by an eruption of Vesuvius, and the empire was visited by a pestilence which carried away an infinite number of inhabitants. In this time of public calamity, the emperor's benevolence and philanthropy were conspicuous. Titus comforted the afflicted as a father, he alleviated their distresses by his liberal bounties, and as if they were but one family, he exerted himself for the good and preservation of the whole. The Romans, however, had not long to enjoy the favors of a magnificent prince; Titus was taken ill, and as he retired into the country of the Sabines to his father's house, his indisposition was increased by a burning fever. He lifted his eyes to heaven, and with modest submission complained of the severity of fate which removed him from the world when young, where he had been employed in making a grateful people happy. He died on the 13th of September A.D. 81, in the 41st year of his age, after a reign of two years, two months, and

20 days. The news of his death was received with lamentations; Rome was filled with tears, and all looked upon themselves as deprived of the most benevolent of fathers. After him Domitian ascended the throne, not without incurring the suspicion of having hastened his brother's end, by ordering him to be placed, during his agony, in a tub full of snow, where he expired. Domitian has also been accused of raising commotions, and of making attempts to dethrone his brother; but Titus disregarded them and forgave the offender. Some authors have reflected with severity upon the cruelties which Titus exercised against the Jews, but though his treatment of them disgraces his character, we must consider him as an instrument in the hands of Providence, raised up for the punishment of a wicked and infatuated people. *Joseph. B. J.* 7. c. 16, &c.—*Suetonius.*—*Dio, &c.* [There is a bust of Titus in the Museum of the Capitol, at Rome.]

TI'TUS TA'TIUS, a king of the Sabines. *Vid.* Tatius.

TI'TUS LIV'IUS, a celebrated historian. *Vid.* Livius.

TI'TUS, a son of Junius Brutus, put to death by order of his father, for conspiring to restore the Tarquins.——A friend of Coriolanus.——A native of Crotona, engaged in Catiline's conspiracy.

TIT'YRUS, a shepherd introduced in Virgil's eclogues, and in Theocritus. The ancients often gave the name of Tityri to the Satyrs and Sileni, who were the companions of Pan and Bacchus. *Ælian V.H.* 3. c. 40.

TIT'YRUS, a large mountain of Crete.

TIT'YUS, a celebrated giant, son of Terra; or, according to others, of Jupiter, by Elara, the daughter of Orchomenus. He was of such a prodigious size, that his mother died in travail after Jupiter had drawn her from the bowels of the earth, where she had been concealed during her pregnancy to avoid the anger of Juno. His portentous appearance rendered him powerful, and Juno, who was jealous of Jupiter's amours with Latona, employed the strength of Tityus to bring her rival into her presence, but the attempt was resented by the god, who hurled the ravisher into Tartarus. According, however, to the more received opinion, Tityus became enamoured of Latona, and attempted to offer her violence, but the goddess delivered herself from his importunities, by calling to her assistance her children, who killed the giant with their arrows. He was placed in hell, where a serpent continually devoured his liver; or, according to others, where vultures perpetually fed upon his entrails, which grew again as soon as devoured. It is said that Tityus covered nine acres when stretched on the ground. He had a small temple with an altar in the island of Eubœa. *Apollod.* 1. c. 4.—*Pind. Pyth.* 4.—*Homer. Odyss.* 7. v. 325. l. 11. v. 575.—*Apollon. Rh.* 1. v 182, &c.—*Virg. Æn.* 6. v. 595.—*Horat.* 3. od. 4. v. 77.—*Hygin.* fab. 55.—*Ovid. Met.* 4. v. 457.—*Tibull.* 1. el. 3. v. 75.—*Callimac. in Dian.* 110.—*Lucill. in Anthol.* 2.—*Lucret.* 3. v. 999.—*Seneca in Thyest.* 10. *In Herc. Œt.* 1070.—*Strab.* 6.—*Paus,* 10. c. 4.——A loquacious orator. *Cicer. Br.* c. 62.

TI'US, TI'UM, or TI'ON, a maritime town of Paphlagonia, built by the Milesians. *Mela,* 1. c. 19.

TLEPOL'EMUS, a son of Hercules, by Astyochia, or, according to Pindar, by Astydamia, was born at Argos. He left his native country after the accidental murder of Licymnius, and retired to Rhodes, by order of the oracle, where he was chosen king, as being one of the sons of Hercules. He left his kingdom to the care of Butes, and went to the Trojan war with nine ships, and was killed by Sarpedon. There were some festivals established at Rhodes in his honor, called Tlepolemia in which men and boys contended. The victors were rewarded with poplar crowns. *Homer. Il.* 2, en. 161. l. 5. v. 655.—*Apollod.* 2. c. 7.—*Diod.* 5.—*Hygin.* fab. 97 & 113.—*Tzetzes. ad Lyc.* 911.—*Meursius de Rhod.* 1. c. 5.——One of Alexander's generals, who obtained Carmania at the general division of the Macedonian empire. *Diod.* 18.——An Ægyptian general who flourished B.C. 207.——A painter of Cibyra, patronised by Verres. *Cic. Verr.* 3. c. 28. l. 4. c. 13 & 21.

TLE'TES, a people of Iberia. *Steph.*

TMA'RUS, a Rutulian engaged in the wars of Æneas. *Virg. Æn.* 9. v. 685.

TMA'RUS, a mountain of Thesprotia, called Tomarus by *Pliny.*

TMO'LUS, a king of Lydia, who married Omphale, and was son of Sipylus and Chthonia. He offered violence to a young nymph called Arriphe, at the foot of Diana's altar, for which impiety he was afterwards killed by a bull. The mountain on which he was buried bore his name. Tmolus is called by some the father of Tantalus. He, according to Ovid and Hyginus, sat as umpire between Pan and Apollo, and adjudgèd to the latter the prize of superior singing. *Apollod.* 2. c. 6.—*Ovid. Met* 11. fab. 4.—*Hygin.* fab. 191.—*Tzetzes Chil.* 5. *H.* 10.—*Schol. Euripid. in Bacc.* 154.—*Eustath. Il.* 2.—*Sch. Hom. ad Od.* 21. v. 23.

TMO'LUS, a town of Asia Minor destroyed by an earthquake.——A mountain of Lydia, now Bouzdag, in which the river Pactolus rises. The air was so wholesome near Tmolus, that the inhabitants generally lived to their 150th year. The neighbouring country was very fertile, and produced plenty of vines, saffron, and odoriferous flowers. *Strab.* 13, &c.—*Herodot.* 1. c. 84, &c.—*Ovid. Met.* 2, &c.—*Sil.* 7. v. 210.—*Virg. G.* 1. v. 56. l. 2. v. 98.—*Plin.* 5. c. 29. l. 7. c. 49.—*Solin.* 53.—*Tzetzes ad Lyc.* 272.—*Schol. Soph. ad Phil.* 392.—*Dionys. Per.* 831.—*Stat. Theb.* 7. v. 686.—*Seneca in Thy.* 602. *In Her. Œt.* 371.——A river of Lydia. *Plin.* 33. c. 8.—*Salmas ad Solin.* p. 1103.

TNYS'SUS, a city of Caria. *Steph.*

TOA'NI, a people of Arabia Felix. *Plin.* 6. c. 28.

TO'BRUS, a city of Africa Propria. *Ptol. Simler* supposes it to be the same as the Tuburbis of *Antoninus.*

TOCH'ARI, a people of India. *Ptol.*—*Dionys.*—*Plin.* 6. c. 17.

TOCHA'TA, a city of Cappadocia, on the river Lycus. It is now Tocato.

TOCOLOS'IDA, a town of Mauritania Tingitana. *Ptol.*

TOGA'TA, an epithet applied to a certain part of Gaul, where the inhabitants were distinguished by the peculiarity of their dress. *Vid.* Gallia.

TOGIS'ONUS, a river of the Veneti. *Plin.* 3. c. 16. It is called Sciocco by *Leander.*

TOGO'NIUS GAL'LUS, a senator of ignoble birth, devoted to the interests of Tiberius, whom he flattered. *Tacit. Ann.* 6. c. 2.

TOLBI'ACUM. a town of Gallia Belgica, south of Juliers. *Tac. Hist.* 4. c. 79.

TO'LEN, a town of Upper Æthiopia. *Plin.* 6. c. 30.

TOLENTI'NUM, or TOLLENTI'NUM, a city of Picenum. The inhabitants are called Tolentinates by *Pliny,* 3. c. 13.

TOLE'NUS, a river of Latium, now Salto, falling into the Velinus. *Ovid. Fast.* 6. v. 561.

TOLE'RIUM, a city of ancient Latium. *Steph. Pliny,* 3. c. 5., calls the inhabitants Tolerienses.

TOLE'TUM, now Toledo, a town of Spain on the river Tagus.

TOLISTO'BII, TOLISTOBO'GII, TOLISTOBO'GI, or TOLISTOBO'II, a people of Galatia in Asia. *Plin.* 5. c. 32.—*Liv.* 58. c. 15 & 16.

TOL'MIDES, an Athenian officer, defeated and killed in a battle in Bœotia, 447 B.C. *Polyæn.* 7.

TOLMIDES'SA, a city of Chalcidica in Syria. *Ptol.*

TOL'OPHON, a city of the Locri Ozoli. *Steph.*

TOLO'SA or THOLO'SA, now Toulouse, the capital of Languedoc, a town of Gallia Narbonensis. which became a Roman colony under Augustus, and was afterwards celebrated for the cultivation of the sciences. Minerva had there a rich temple, which Cæpio the consul plundered, and as he was never after fortunate, the words *aurum Tolosanum* became proverbial. *Cæs. Bell. G.*—*Mela,* 2. c. 5.—*Cic. de Nat. D.* 3. c. 20.—*Strab.* 4.—*Justin.* 32. c. 3.—*Aul. G.* 3. c. 9.—*Sidon.* 7. v. 436.—*Martial.* 9. epigr. 101.—*Auson. de Urb.* 11. *& in Parent.* 3.

TOLUM'NIUS, an augur in the army of Turnus against Æneas. *Virg. Æn.* 11. v. 429. l. 12. v. 258.——A king of Veii, killed by Cor. Cossus after he had ordered the ambassadors of Rome to be assassinated. *Liv.* 4. c. 19.—*Propert.* 4. el. 11. v. 25.—*Virg. Æn.* 6. v. 842 *& Servius loco.*

TO'LUS, a man whose head was found in digging

for the foundation of the Capitol, in the reign of Tarquin, whence the Romans concluded that their city should become the head or mistress of the world. *Dionys.* 4. c. 59.

TOMADÆ'ORUM (*insulæ*,) two islands in the Arabic Gulf. *Plin.* 4. c. 8.

TOMÆ'UM, a mountain of Peloponnesus. *Thucyd.*

TOM'ARUS or TOMA'RUS. *Vid.* Tmarus.

TOME'RUS, a river of India. *Plin.* 6. c. 23.—*Arrian. in Indic.*—*Salmas ad Solin.* p. 1176.

TO'MEUS, a city near Odessus. *Steph.*

TOM'ISA, a country between Cappadocia and Taurus. *Strabo.*

TO'MOS or TO'MIS, a town situate on the western shores of the Euxine Sea, about 36 mils from the mouth of the Danube. The word is derived from τέμνω, *seco*, because Medea, as it is said, cut to pieces the body of her brother Absyrtus there. It is celebrated as being the place where Ovid was banished by Augustus. Tomos was the capital of Lower Mœsia, founded by a Milesian colony, B.C. 633. *Strab.* 7.—*Apollod.* 1. c. 9.—*Mela*, 2. c. 2. —*Ovid. ex Pont.* 4. el. 14. v. 59. *Trist.* 3. el. 9. v. 33, &c.—*Stat.* 1. *Sylv.* 2. v. 255.

TOM'YRIS. *Vid.* Thomyris.

TONE'A, a solemnity observed at Samus. It was usual to carry Juno's statue to the sea shore, and to offer cakes before it, and afterwards to replace it again in the temple. This was in commemoration of the theft of the Tyrrhenians, who attempted to carry away the statue of the goddess, but were detained in the harbour by an invisible force.

TONGIL'LIUS, an avaricious lawyer, &c. *Juv.* 7. v. 130.

TONGIL'LUS, a friend of Catiline. *Cic. Cat.* 2. c. 2.

TONI'CE, a city of Upper Æthiopia. *Ptol.*

TON'SUS or TON'ZUS, an inland city of Thrace. *Id.*—*Salmas ad Solin.* p. 214.

TOPA'ZUS, an island in the Arabian Gulf, anciently called Ophiodes from the quantity of serpents that were there. These reptiles were gradually destroyed, and none were to be seen there in the age of Diodorus. The valuable stone called topaze is found there. *Plin.* 6. c. 20. l. 37. c. 8. —*Diod.* 3.

TOP'ICI, a name given to those deities who were worshipped only in certain countries, such as Astarte in Syria, Isis and Osiris in Ægypt, and Quirinus at Rome. *Servius ad Æn.* 7. v. 47.—*Gyrald. H. D.* 1.

TOP'IRIS, TOPI'RIS, TOPI'RUS or TO'PRUS, a town of Thrace. *Ptol.* It is called Topirium by *Antoninus*, and Doperus by *Thucydides.*

TORA'NIUS, a friend of Pompey, who, after sharing his fortunes, was betrayed byhis own son, and put to death by the proscription of Augustus and Antony. *Val. Max.* 9. c. 11.

TORE'TÆ or TOREA'TÆ, a people of Pontus. *Steph.*

TOR'INI, a people of Scythia. *Val. Flacc.* 6. v. 145.

TORNA'TES, a people of Aquitania. *Plin.* 4. c. 19. Their country is now Tournay.

TORO'NE, a town of Macedonia. *Liv.* 31. c. 45. A bay in the neighbourhood was called Toroniacus Sinus.——A city of Epirus. It is now Parga according to *Niger.*

TORPI'DI, a people of Thrace, on the confines of Macedonia. *Appian.*

TORQUA'TA, one of the vestal virgins, daughter of C. Silanus. She was a vestal for 64 years. *Tacit. An.* c. 69.

TORQUA'TUS, a surname of Titus Manlius. *Vid.* Manlius.——A governor of Oricum, in the interest of Pompey. He surrendered to J. Cæsar, and was killed in Africa. *Hirt. Afric.* 96.——An officer in Sylla's army.——A Roman, sent ambassador to the court of Ptolemy Philometor of Ægypt.

TORQUA'TUS SILA'NUS, an officer put to death by Nero. *Tac. Ann.* 15. c. 35.

TOR'RHEBUS, a city of Lydia. *Steph.*

TORTOMI'ON, a city between Syria and Armenia. *Id.*

TORTO'NA, a city of Sicily *Id.*

TOR'TOR, a surname of Apollo. He had a statue at Rome under that name. *Suet. in Aug.* c. 70.—*Rosin. Ant. Rom.* 2. c. 7.

TORTYRA, a town of Asia, one of the seven cities given by Cyrus to Pytharchus. *Athen.*

TO'RUS, a mountain of Sicily, near Agrigentum. *Polyb.*

TORY'NE, a small town near Actium. The word in the language of the country signifies a ladle, which gave Cleopatra occasion to make a pun when it fell into the hands of Augustus. *Plut. in Ant.*

TOTTA'IUM, TOTTÆ'UM, or TUTA'IUM, a city of Bithynia between Nicæa and Dablis. *Antonin.*

TOXAN'DRI, a people of Gallia Belgica. *Plin.* 4. c. 17.

TOX'ARIS, a Scythian hero contemporary with Solon and Anacharsis, in whose honor games were instituted. *Voss. de Idolol.* 1. c. 13.

TOX'EUS, a son of Œneus, killed by his father. *Apollod.* 1. c. 8.

TOXIC'RATE, a daughter of Thespius.

TRAB'ALA, a city of Lycia. *Steph.*

TRA'BEA Q., a comic poet at Rome, in the age of Regulus, highly esteemed and ranked in merit next to Terence and Turpilius. Only eight lines remain of his poetry collected in the Corpus Poetarum. *Cic. in Tusc.* 4. c. 31. *Fin.* 2. c. 4. *Fam.* 9. ep. 21.

TRACH'ALUS M. GALE'RIUS, a consul in the reign of Nero, celebrated for his eloquence as an orator, and for a majestic and commanding aspect. *Quintil.* 10. c. 1.—*Tacit.*

TRACH'ALUS, one of the friends and ministers of Otho.

TRA'CHAS, a town of Latium. *Ovid. Met.* 15. v. 717.

TRACHE'A or TRACHI'A, a name given to Isauria by *Strabo. Steph.*

TRACHIN'IA, TRA'CHIS, or TRA'CHIN, a small country of Phthiotis, on the bay of Malea near mount Œta. The capital was called Trachis, or Trachina, and it was thither that Hercules retired after he had killed Eunomus, son of Architeles. The hero was received with kindness and hospitality by Ceyx, who was their king, and on that account the town was called Heraclea Trachinia. *Thucyd.* 2.—*Plin.* 12. c. 25.—*Lucan.* 3. v. 178. l. 6. v. 353.—*Seneca in Herc. Œt.* 194. *In Troad.* 818 —*Strab.* 9. —*Apollod.* 2. c. 7.—*Ovid. Met.* 11. v. 269.

TRACHONI'TIS, a part of Judea on the other side of the Jordan. *Plin.* 5. c. 18.

TRÆMENOTHYRI'TÆ, a people of Troas; they are called Grimenothyritæ by *Tzetzes.*

TRAG'ASÆ, a region of Epirus. *Steph.*

TRA'GIA, TRA'GIAS, or TRAGÆ'A, a small island of the Ægean Sea near Samus. *Steph.*——A town of Naxus, where Apollo was worshipped. *Id.*

TRAG'ILOS or TRAG'ILUS, a city of Thrace, near the Macedonian Chersonesus. *Id.*

TRAGU'RIUM, a small island on the coast of Dalmatia, joined to the continent by a bridge. *Plin.* 4. c. 21.

TRA'GUS, a river of Arcadia, falling into the Alpheus. *Paus.* 8. c. 33.

TRAJA'NA LE'GIO, a town of Upper Germany, on the Rhine. *Ptol.*

TRAJANOP'OLIS, a town of Thrace.——A name given to Selinus in Cilicia, where Trajan died.

TRAJA'NUS M. UL'PIUS CRINI'TUS, a Roman emperor, born at Italica, in Spain. His great virtues, and his private as well as public character, and his services to the empire, both as an officer, a governor, and a consul, recommended him to the notice of Nerva, who adopted him as his son, invested him during his lifetime with the imperial purple, and gave him the name of Cæsar and of Germanicus. A little time after, Nerva died, and the election of Trajan to the vacant throne was confirmed by the unanimous rejoicings of the people, and the free concurrence of the armies on the confines of Germany, and the banks of the Danube. The noble and independent behaviour of Trajan evinced the propriety and goodness of Nerva's choice, and the attachment of the legions; and the new emperor seemed calculated to ensure peace and domestic tranquillity to the extensive empire of Rome. All the actions of Trajan showed a good and benevolent prince, whose virtues truly merited the encomiums which the pen of an elegant and courteous panegyrist has paid. The barbarians continued quiet, and the hostilities which they generally displayed at the election of a new emperor whose military abilities they distrusted, were not few,

Trajan, however, could not behold with satisfaction and unconcern, the insolence of the Dacians, who claimed from the Roman people a tribute which the cowardice of Domitian had offered. The sudden appearance of the emperor on the frontiers awed the barbarians to peace; but Decebalus, their warlike monarch, soon began hostilities by violating the treaty. The conqueror entered the enemy's country, by throwing a bridge across the rapid streams of the Danube, and a battle was fought in which the slaughter was so great, that in the Roman camp linen was wanted to dress the wounds of the soldiers. Trajan obtained the victory, and Decebalus despairing of success, destroyed himself, and Dacia became a province of Rome. That the ardour of the Roman soldiers in defeating their enemies might not cool, an expedition was undertaken into the east, and Parthia threatened with immediate war. Trajan passed through the submissive kingdom of Armenia, and by his well directed operations, made himself master of the provinces of Assyria and Mesopotamia. He extended his conquests in the east, he obtained victories over unknown nations, and when on the extremities of India, he lamented that he possessed not the vigour and youth of an Alexander, that he might add unexplored provinces and kingdoms to the Roman empire. These successes in different parts of the world gained applause, and the senators were profuse in the honors which they decreed to the conqueror. This, however, was but the blaze of transient glory. Trajan had no sooner signified his intentions of returning to Italy, than the conquered barbarians appeared again in arms, and the Roman empire did not acquire one single acre of territory from the conquests of her sovereign in the east. The return of the emperor towards Rome was hastened by indisposition, he stopped in Cilicia, and in the town of Selinus, which afterwards was called Trajanopolis, he was seized with a flux, and a few days after expired, in the beginning of August, A.D 117, after a reign of 19 years, 6 months, and 15 days, in the 64th year of his age. He was succeeded on the throne by Adrian, whom the empress Plotina introduced to the Roman armies, as the adopted son of her husband. The ashes of Trajan were carried to Rome, and deposited under the stately column which he had erected a few years before. Under this emperor the Romans enjoyed tranquillity, and for a moment supposed that their prosperity was complete under a good and virtuous sovereign. Trajan was fond of popularity, and he merited it. The sounding titles of Optimus, and the father of his country, was not unworthily bestowed upon a prince who was equal to the greatest generals of antiquity, and who, to indicate his affability, and his wish to listen to the just complaints of his subjects, distinguished his palace by the inscription of the public palace. Like other emperors he did not receive with an air of unconcern the homage of his friends, but rose from his seat and went cordially to salute them. He refused the statues which the flattery of favorites wished to erect to him, and he ridiculed the follies of an enlightened nation, that could pay adoration to cold inanimate pieces of marble. His public entry into Rome gained him the hearts of his people; he appeared on foot, and showed himself an enemy to parade, and an ostentatious equipage. When in his camp, he exposed himself to the fatigues of war like the meanest soldier, and crossed the most barren deserts and extensive plains on foot, and in his dress and food displayed all the simplicity which once gained the approbation of the Romans in their countryman Fabricius. He knew all the oldest soldiers by name, he conversed with them with great familiarity, and never retired to his tent before he had visited the camp, and by a personal attendance convinced himself of the vigilance and security of his army. As a friend he was not less distinguished than as a general. He had a select number of intimates, whom he visited with freedom and openness, and at whose tables he partook many a moderate repast without form or ceremony. His confidence, however, in the good intentions of others, was perhaps carried to excess. His favorite Sura had once been accused of attempts upon his life, but Trajan disregarded the informer, and as he was that same day invited to the house of the supposed conspirator, he went thither early. To try farther the sincerity of Sura, he ordered himself to be shaved by his barber, directed a medicinal application to be made to his eyes by the hand of his surgeon, and bathed together with him. The public works of Trajan are also celebrated, he opened free and easy communications between the cities of his provinces, he planted many colonies, and furnished Rome with all the corn and provisions which could prevent a famine in the time of calamity. It was by his directions, that the architect Apollodorus built that celebrated column which is still to be seen at Rome, under the name of Trajan's column. The area on which it stands was made by the labours of men, and the height of the pillar proves that a large hill 144 feet high was removed at a great expense. A.D. 114, to commemorate the victories of the reigning prince. His persecutions of the Christians were stopped by the interference of the humane Pliny, but he was uncommonly severe upon the Jews, who had barbarously murdered 200,000 of his subjects, and even fed upon the flesh of the dead. His vices have been obscurely seen, through a reign of continued splendour and popularity, yet he is accused of incontinence and many unnatural indulgences. He was too much addicted to drinking, and his wish to be styled lord has been censured by those who admired the dissimulated moderation, and the modest claims of Augustus. *Plin. Paneg. &c.—Dio. Cass.—Eutrop.—Ammian.—Spartian.—Joseph. Bell. J.—Victor.* [The statues and busts of this emperor are very numerous, and very fine; the best of the former will be met with in the Vatican and Capitoline Museums, at Rome, and one of the best of the latter in the British Museum.]

TRAJA'NUS, the father of the emperor, was honored with the consulship, and a triumph, and the rank of a patrician, by the emperor Vespasian.——A general of the emperor Valens. *Theodoret.* 4. c. 31.——A son of the emperor Decius.——A patrician under Justinian, who wrote a work called *Temporum Epitome. Suidas.*

TRAJA'NUS, a river of Ægypt. *Ptol.*

TRAJEC'TUM AD MO'SAM, a city of Lower Germany, now Maestricht.

TRAJEC'TUM AD RHE'NUM, a large city of the Batavi in Lower Germany. It is now Utrecht.

TRAL'LES or TRAL'LIS, a town of Lydia, now Sultanhisar. *Juv.* 3. v. 70.—*Liv* 37. c. 45.

TRAL'LI or TRAL'LII, a people of Illyria.

TRALLIA'NUS ALEX., a native of Tralles, who flourished A.D. 550, and distinguished himself as a physician. His works are divided into twelve books, which show him to have been a man of great erudition, accurate judgment, and indefatigable industry, though in the difficult paths of medical knowledge occasionally superstitious. *Fabr. B. Gr.* 6. c. 7.—*Sax. Onom.* 2. p. 42.

TRAM'PE, a city of Ionia. *Steph.*

TRAM'PYA, a city of Epirus. *Id.*

TRANSDUC'TA or TRADUC'TA, a city of Bœtica. *Ptol.—Plin.* 5 c. 1.

TRANSTIBERI'NA, a part of the city of Rome on the side of the Tiber. Mount Vatican was in that part of the city. *Mart.* 1. epigr. 109.

TRAPEZOP'OLIS, a city of Caria on the Mæander. *Ptol.*

TRAPE'ZUM, a hill of Syria hanging over Antiochia. *Strab.*

TRAPE'ZUS, a city of Pontus, built by the people of Sinope, now called Trebizond. It had a celebrated harbour on the Euxine Sea, and was the first friendly spot where the 10,000 Greeks reached after their arduous retreat from Cunaxa. Trapezus became famous under the emperors of the eastern empire, of which it was for some time the magnificent capital. *Tacit. H.* 3. c 47. *Plin.* 6. c. 4.—*Xenoph Anab.*——A town of Arcadia, near the Alpheus. It received its name from a son of Lycaon. *Apollod.* 3. c. 8.

TRASIME'NUS. *Vid.* Thrasymenus.

TRASUL'LUS, a man who taught Tiberius astrology at Rhodes. He wrote also on medicine, and his works are repeatedly praised by *Pliny. Tac. Ann.* 6. c 20.

TRAUCHE'NII, a people near Pontus. *Steph.*

TRAU'LUS MONTA'NUS, a Roman knight, one of Messalina's favorites, put to death by Claudius. *Tacit. Ann.* 11. c. 36.

TRE'BA or TRE'BIA, a town of the Æqui. *Plin.* 3. c. 12.

C. TREBA'TIUS TES'TAS, a man banished by Julius Cæsar for following the interests of Pompey, and recalled by the eloquence of Cicero. He was afterwards reconciled to Cæsar, and enjoyed the favor and patronage of his successor Augustus. He wrote nine books on religious ceremonies, and treatises on civil law; and the verses that he wrote proved him a poet of no inferior consequence. *Horat.* 2. sat. 1. v. 4.—*Cic. Ep. ad Fam.* 1. 7.

TREBELLIA'NUS C. AN'NIUS, a pirate who proclaimed himself emperor of Rome, A.D. 264. He was defeated and slain in Isauria by the lieutenants of Gallienus. *Trebell. Pollio de* 30 *Tyr.* c. 26.

TREBELLIE'NUS RU'FUS, a prætor appointed governor of the children of Cotys, by Tiberius. *Tac. Ann.* 6. c. 39.

TREBELLIE'NUS, a tribune who opposed the Gabinian law.——A Roman who murdered the inhabitants of Gaul. He was made governor of Britain.

TREBEL'LIUS POL'LIO, a Latin historian, who wrote an account of the lives of the emperors. The beginning of this history is lost; part of the reign of Valerian, and the lives of the two Gallieni and of Claudius, with the 30 tyrants, are the only fragments remaining. He flourished A.D. 305. His works are edited with those of Spartian. *Harles. Not. Lit. Rom.* 1. p. 557.—*Sax. Onom.* 1. p. 380.

TREBEL'LIUS LU'CIUS, an opponent of Antony's measures, but afterwards his devoted friend. *Cic. Phil.* 6. c. 4. l. 13. c. 12.

TREBEL'LIUS, a governor of Britain, odious for his extortions. He was succeeded by Bolanus, and rejected by Vitellius. *Tacit. H.* 1. c. 60, &c.

TRE'BIA, a river of Cisalpine Gaul, rising in the Apennines, and falling into the Po, at the west of Placentia. It is celebrated for the victory which Annibal obtained there over the forces of L. Sempronius the Roman consul. *Sil.* 4. v. 486.—*Strab.* 5.—*Plin.* 15. c. 18.—*Lucan.* 2. v. 46.—*Liv.* 21. c. 54 & 56.——A town of Latium. *Liv.* 2. c. 39. ——A town of Campania. *Id.* 28. c. 14.——A town of Umbria. *Plin.* 3. c. 14.

M. TRE'BIUS GAL'LUS, an officer in Cæsar's army in Gaul. *Cæs. Com.* 2. c. 7 & 8. Some MSS. have Trebonius Gallus.

TRE'BIUS, a parasite in Domitian's reign. *Juv.* 5. v. 19, 135, &c.

TREBO'NIA LEX, *de provinciis*, by L. Trebonius the tribune, A.U.C. 698. It gave Cæsar the chief command in Gaul for five years longer than was enacted by the Vatinian law, and in this manner prevented the senators from recalling or superseding him.—Another by the same, in the same year conferred the command of the provinces of Syria and Spain on Cassius and Pompey for five years. *Dio. Cass.* 39.—Another by L. Trebonius, the tribune, A.U.C. 305, which confirmed the election of tribunes in the hands of the Roman people. *Liv.* 3 & 5.

VIB'IUS TREBONIA'NUS GAL'LUS, a præfect of Mœsia who rebelled against Decius, A.C. 254. *Journand. de Reb. Goth.*—*Zonar.* tom. 2. *Vid.* Gallus, a Roman who assassinated Decius. [There is a fine head of Trebonianus in the Vatican, and another in the Capitol at Rome.]

TREBO'NIUS, a soldier remarkable for his continence. *Plut.*——One of the adherents of Marius. ——A man caught in adultery, and severely punished, in the age of *Horace.*

TREBO'NIUS CA'IUS, one of Cæsar's friends, made through his interest prætor and consul. Though thus raised to the honors of office by Cæsar, he yet preferred the safety of the republic to gratitude, and joined in the conspiracy against his benefactor. On the fatal day, while the bloody deed was done, he detained Antony at the door in conversation, and thus preserved his life. After the dictator's death, Trebonius obtained Asia as his province, where he was treacherously killed by Dolabella at Smyrna. *Cæs. Bell.* 5. c. 17.—*Cic. in Phil.* 11. c. 2.—*Paterc.* 56 & 69.—*Liv.* 119.—*Dio.* 47. c. 29.—*Appian. B.C.* 3. p. 542.—*Horat.* 1. sat. 4. v. 114. [A bust of Trebonius is to be found in the Vatican.]

TREBO'NIUS GARUCIA'NUS, a governor of Africa, who put to death the proconsul Clodius Macer, by Galba's orders. *Tacit. H.* 1. c. 7.

TREBO'NIUS LU'CIUS, a tribune who proposed a law at Rome, and imprisoned Cato because he opposed it. *Plut. in Pomp. & Caton. Utic.*

TREB'ULA, a town of the Sabines celebrated for cheese. The inhabitants were called Trebulani. *Cic. in Agr.* 2. c. 25.—*Liv.* 23.—*Plin.* 3. c. 5 & 12. —*Martial.* 5. epigr. 72. l. 13. epigr. 33.——A city in Campania. *Liv.* 23. c. 39.

TRE'CHUS, an Ætolian, slain by Mars. *Homer. Il.* 5.

TREMEL'LIUS SCRO'PHA, a writer on husbandry. *Plin.* 17. c. 27.—*Varr. R.R.* 2. c. 4.—*Macrob.* 1. c. 6.

TREM'ILE, an ancient name of Lycia. *Steph.*

TREMI'THUS or TREM'ETHUS, a small town of Cyprus. *Ptol.*

TRE'RUS, a river of Latium, falling into the Liris. *Strab.* It is now Trere.

TRES TABER'NÆ, a place on the Appian road, where travellers took refreshment. *Cic. A.* 1. ep. 13. l. 2. ep. 10 & 11. It is now Zabern.

TRE'TUM or TRI'TUM, a promontory of Africa Propria. *Strab.*

TREVEN'TUM or TEREVEN'TUM, a city of Samnium. *Plin.* 3. c. 12.

TREV'ERI or TREV'IRI, a town and people of Belgium, now called Triers or Treves. *Mela*, 3. c. 2.

TRIAM'BUS or THRIAM'BUS, a surname of Bacchus, given to him on his return from India, because he was the first conqueror honored with a triumph. *Diod* 4.

TRIAR'CHIA, a city of Armenia Minor. *Antonin.*

TRIA'RIA, a woman well known for her cruelty. She was the wife of L. Vitellius. *Tacit. H.* 1 & 3.

TRIA'RIUS C., an orator commended by Cicero, and made the guardian of his children. *Cic. Att.* 12. ep. 28. *Fin.* 1. c. 5.

TRIA'RIUS CA'IUS, a friend of Pompey. He had for some time the care of the war in Asia against Mithridates, whom he defeated, and by whom he was afterwards beaten. He was killed in the civil wars of Pompey and Cæsar. *Cæs. Bell. Civ.* 3. c. 5.

TRIBAL'LI, a people of Thrace, or according to some, of Lower Mœsia. They were conquered by Philip, the father of Alexander; and some ages after, they maintained a long war against the Roman emperors. *Plin.*

TRIBAN'TA, a city of Phrygia Major. *Ptol.*

TRIB'OCI, a people of Alsace in Gaul. *Tacit. in Germ.* 28.—*Plin.* 4. c. 17.

TRIBU'LIUM, a town of Dalmatia.

TRIBU'NI PLE'BIS, magistrates at Rome, created in the year U.C. 261, when the people, after a quarrel with the senators, had retired to Mons. Sacer. The two first were C. Licinius and L. Albinus, but their number was soon after raised to five, and 37 years after to ten, which remained fixed. Their office was annual; and as the first had been created on the 4th of the ides of December, that day was ever after chosen for the election. Their power, though at first small, and granted by the patricians to appease the momentary seditions of the populace, soon became formidable, and the senators repented too late of having consented to elect magistrates who not only preserved the rights of the people, but could summon assemblies, propose laws, stop the consultations of the senate, and even abolish their decrees by the word *Veto.* Their approbation was also necessary to confirm the *senatûs consulta*, and this was done by affixing the letter T under it. If any irregularity happened in the state, their power was almost absolute; they criticised the conduct of all the public magistrates, and even dragged a consul to prison, if the measures he pursued were hostile to the peace of Rome. The dictator alone was their superior; but when that magistrate was elected, the office of tribune was not, like that of all other inferior magistrates, abolished while he continued at the head of the state. The people paid them so much deference, that their person was held sacred, and thence they were always *Sacrosancti.* To strike them was a capital crime, and to interrupt them while they spoke in the assemblies called for the immediate interference of power. The marks by which they were distinguished from other magistrates were not very conspicuous. They wore no particular dress, only a beadle called *victor* marched before them. They never sat in the senate, though some time after, their office, entitled them to the rank of senators. Yet great as their power might appear, it was rendered almost useless by their number; and as their consultations and resolutions were of no effect if they were not unanimous, the senate often took advantage of their avarice, and by gaining one of them by bribes, they, as it were, suspended the authority of the rest. The office of tribune of the people, though at first deemed mean and servile, was afterwards one of the first steps that led to more honorable employments; and as no patrician was permitted to canvass for the tribuneship, we find many that descended among the plebeians to exercise that important office. From the power with which they were at last invested by the activity, the intrigues, and continual applications of those who were in office, they became almost absolute in the state; and it has been properly observed, that they caused far greater troubles than those which they were at first created to silence. Sylla, when raised to the dictatorship, gave a fatal blow to the authority of the tribunes; and by one of his decrees they were no longer permitted to harangue and inflame the people; they could make no laws; no appeal lay to their tribunal; and such as had been tribunes were not permitted to solicit for other offices of the state. This disgrace, however, was but momentary. At the death of the tyrant, the tribunes recovered their privileges by means of Cotta and Pompey the Great. The office of tribune remained in full force till the age of Augustus, who, to make himself more absolute, and his person sacred, conferred the office on himself, whence he was called *tribunitiâ potestate donatus*. His successors on the throne imitated his example; and as the emperor was the real and official tribune, such as were appointed to the office were merely nominal, without power or privilege. Under Constantine the tribuneship was totally abolished. The tribunes were never permitted to sleep out of the city, except at the *Feriæ Latinæ*, when they went with other magistrates to offer sacrifices upon a mountain near Alba. Their houses were always open, and they received every complaint, and were ever ready to redress the wrongs of their constituents. Their authority was not extended beyond the walls of the city. There were also other officers who bore the name of tribunes, such as the *tribuni militum*, or *militares*, who commanded a division of the legions. They were empowered to decide all quarrels that might arise in the army, they took care of the camp, and gave the watch-word. There were only three at first chosen by Romulus, but the number was at last increased to six in every legion. After the expulsion of the Tarquins, they were chosen by the consuls, but afterwards the right of electing them was divided between the people and the consul. They were generally of senatorian and equestrian families, and the former were called *laticlavii*, and the latter *augusticlavii*, from their peculiar dress. Those that were chosen by the consuls were called *Rutuli*, because the right of the consuls to elect them was confirmed by Rutulus, and those elected by the people were called *Comitiati*, because chosen in the comitia. They wore a golden ring, and were in office no longer than six months. When the consuls were elected, it was usual to choose 14 tribunes from the knights, who had served five years in the army, and who were called *juniores*, and ten from the people who had been in ten campaigns, who were called *seniores*. There were also some officers called *tribuni militum consulari potestate*, elected instead of consuls, A.U.C. 310. There were only three originally, but the number was afterwards increased to six, or more according to the will and pleasure of the people, and the emergencies of the state. Part of them were plebeians, and the rest of patrician families. When they had subsisted for about 70 years, not without some interruption, the office was totally abolished, as the plebeians were admitted to share the commonwealth. The *tribuni cohortium prætorianarum* were entrusted with the person of the emperor, which they guarded and protected. The *tribuni ærarii* were officers chosen from among the people, who kept the money which was to be applied to defray the expenses of the army. The richest persons were always chosen, as much money was requisite for the pay of the soldiers. They were greatly distinguished in the state, and they shared with the senators and Roman knights the privileges of judging. They were abolished by Julius Cæsar, but Augustus re-established them, and created 200 more, to decide causes of smaller importance. The *tribuni celerum* had the command of the guard which Romulus chose for the safety of his person. They were 100 in number, distinguished for their probity, their opulence, and their nobility. The *tribuni voluptatum* were commissioned to take care of the amusements which were prepared for the people, and that nothing might be wanting in the exhibitions. This office was also honorable.

TRICAD'IBA, a city of India within the Ganges. *Ptol.*

TRIC'ALA or TRIOC'ALA, a fortified place at the south of Sicily, between Selinus and Agrigentum. *Sil.* 14. v. 271.

TRICARA'NUM, a town of Philasia. *Steph.*

TRICAS'SES, a people of modern Champagne in Gaul, between the Matrona and Sequana. *Plin.* 4 c. 18.

TRICASTI'NI, a people of Gallia Narbonensis. *Sil.* 3. v. 466.—*Liv.* 21. c. 31. Their country is now Troyes.

TRICAT'ANA, a fortified place of Phliasia. *Steph.*

TRIC'CA, a town of Thessaly, where Æsculapius had a temple. The inhabitants went to the Trojan war. *Liv.* 32. c. 13.—*Homer. Il.* 2. en. 240.—*Apollon. Rh.* 2. v. 957.—*Seneca in Troad.* 821.—*Steph. Byz.*—*Avienus in Arat.* 206.—*Plin.* 4. c. 8.

TRICHO'NIUM, a town of Ætolia. *Steph.*

TRICIPITI'NUS, a surname of the Lucretii. *Vid.* Lucretius.

TRICLA'RIA, a festival celebrated yearly by the inhabitants of three cities in Ionia, to appease the anger of Diana *Triclaria*, whose temple had been defiled by the adulterous commerce of Menalippus and Cometho. It was usual to sacrifice a boy and a girl, but this barbarous custom was abolished by Eurypylus. The three cities were Aroe, Mesatis, and Anthea, the united labors of which had erected the temple of the goddess. *Paus.* 7. c. 19.

TRICOLO'NUS, a son of Lycaon, who gave his name to a town of Arcadia. He left a son called Zæteus, who also gave his name to an Arcadian city. *Paus.* 6. c. 21. l. 8. c. 35.

TRICOLLO'RII, a people of Gallia Narbonensis. *Plin.* 3. c. 4.

TRICO'RII, a people of Gaul, now Dauphiny, at the east of the Rhone. *Liv.* 31. c. 31.

TRICORNEN'SII, a people of Upper Mysia. *Ptol.*

TRICOR'NIUM, a town of Upper Mysia. *Id.*

TRICORY'THUS. *Vid.* Trycorythus.

TRICO'SUS, a surname of Hercules, from the hairy appearance of his body.

TRICRE'NA, a place of Arcadia, where, according to some, Mercury was born. *Paus.* 8. c. 16.

TRIDEN'TUM or TRIDEN'TE, a town of Cisalpine Gaul, now called Trent, famous in history for the ecclesiastical council, which sat there 18 years to regulate the affairs of the church, A.D. 1545.

TRIE'RES or TRIE'RIS, a city of Syria.

TRIE'RUM or TRIE'RON, a promontory of Africa. *Ptol.*

TRIETER'ICA, festivals in honor of Bacchus celebrated every three years, because his expedition in the Indies had continued for that time. *Virg. Æn.* 4. v. 302. *Servius loco.*—*Gyrald. de Sacrific.*

TRIFA'NUM, a place of Latium near Sinuessa. *Liv.* 8. c. 11.

TRIFOLI'NUS, a mountain of Campania, famous for its wine. *Mart.* 13. epigr. 104.—*Plin.* 14. c. 7.

TRIFOR'MIS, a surname of Diana from her three names of Luna, Hecate, and Diana.

TRIGA'RIUS, a place near the Campus Martius. *Plin.* 37. c. 13.

TRIGEM'INA, one of the Roman gates, so called because the three Horatii went through it against the Curiatii. *Liv.* 4. c. 16. l. 35. c. 41. l. 40. c. 51.

TRIG'LYPHON, a city of India without the Ganges. *Ptol.*

TRIMAM'MIUM, a town of Lower Mysia. *Antonin.*

TRINA'CRIA or TRIN'ACRIS, one of the ancient names of Sicily, from its triangular form. *Virg. Æn.* 3. v. 384, &c. l. 5. v. 450 & 555.—*Homer. Odyss.* 12. v. 127.—*Ovid. Met.* 5. v. 347 & 476. *Fast.* 4. v. 287 & 420.—*Servius ad Virg. Æn.* 1. v. 200. l. 3. v. 687.—*Tzetzes. ad Lyc.* 740.

TRINEME'IS or TRINEMI'A, a village in the tribe Cecropis. *Steph.*

TRINE'MII, a people of Hellas, near the spot where the Cephisus rises. *Strab.*

TRINE'SIA, an island of India within the Ganges. *Ptol.*

TRINES'SA, a place of Phrygia. *Steph.*

TRIN'IUS, a river of Italy falling into the Adriatic.

TRINOBAN'TES, a people of Britain in modern Essex and Middlesex. *Tacit. Ann.* 14. c. 31.—*Cæs. G.* 5. c. 20.

TRIOC'ALA, or TRI'OCLA, a town in the southern parts of Sicily. *Vid.* Tricala. *Sil.* 14. v, 271.

TRIOC'ULUS, a surname of Jupiter, because in a temple of Minerva at Argos, he had a statue which represented him with a third eye in the middle of the forehead. *Paus.* 2. c. 24.

TRI'OPAS or TRI'OPS, a son of Neptune by Canace, the daughter of Æolus. He was father of Iphimedia and of Erisichthon, who is called on that account Triopeius, and his daughter Triopeis. *Callimac. in Cerer.* 24 & 97.—*Ovid. Met.* 8. v. 754.—*Apollod.* 1. c. 7.

TRI'OPAS, a son of Phorbas, father to Agenor, Jasus, and Messene. *Homer. Hymn. in Ap.* 211.—*Diod.* 4.—*Paus.* 2. c. 16. l. 4. c. 1.——A son of Piranthus, supposed to be the same as the son of Phorbas. *Hygin.* fab. 145.

TRIO'PIUM, TRIO'PION or TRIO'PIA, a city and promontory of Caria. *Steph* It is now Capo Chio.

TRIORE'NA, a place of Arcadia, where there were three fountains, and Mercury was born. *Paus. in Arcad.*

TRIPHYL'IA, one of the ancient names of Elis. *Liv.* 28. c. 8.——A mountain in the island Panchaia, where Jupiter had a temple, whence he is called Triphylius. This report, though supported and enlarged upon by Diodorus, is refuted by Plutarch, and by the moderns, who assert that there is no such place or island. *Diod.* 5.—*Plut. de Isid. & Os.*—*Gyrald. H.D.* 2.—*Salmas. ad Solin.* p. 549.

TRIPHY'LUS, one of the ancient heroes born at Tegea in Arcadia. He was son of Laodamia, daughter of Amyclas, and not of Erato, and he had a statue in the temple of Apollo at Delphi *Paus.* 10. c. 9.

TRIO'PIUM, a town of Caria.

TRIPO'LIS, an ancient town of Phœnicia, built by the united efforts of the inhabitants of Tyre, Sidon, and Aradus, whence the name. *Dionys.* v. 914. ——A town of Pontus.——A district of Arcadia. ——A district of Laconia. *Liv.* 35. c. 27.——A district of Thessaly. *Liv.* 42. c. 53.——A town of Lydia or Caria.——A district of Africa between the Syrtes.

TRIPOLYS'SI, a people of Thesprotia. *Steph.*

TRIPTOL'EMUS, a son of Oceanus and Terra, or according to some, of Trochilus, a priest of Argos. According to the more received opinion he was son of Celeus, king of Attica, by Neæra, whom some have called Metanira, Cothonea, Hyona, Melania or Polymnia. He was born at Eleusis in Attica, and was cured in his youth of a severe illness by the care of Ceres, who had been invited into the house of Celeus by the monarch's children, as she travelled over the country in quest of her daughter. To repay the kindness of Celeus, the goddess took particular notice of his son. She fed him with her own milk, and placed him on burning coals during the night, to destroy whatever particles of mortality he had received from his parents. The mother was astonished at the uncommon growth of her son, and had the curiosity to watch Ceres. She disturbed the goddess by a sudden cry, when Triptolemus was laid on the burning ashes, and as Ceres was therefore unable to make him immortal, she taught him agriculture, and rendered him serviceable to mankind, by instructing him how to sow corn, and make bread. She also gave him her chariot, which was drawn by two dragons, and in this celestial vehicle he travelled over all the earth, and distributed corn to all the inhabitants of the world. In Scythia the favorite of Ceres nearly lost his life; but Lyncus, who had conspired to murder him, was changed into a lynx. At his return to Eleusis, Triptolemus restored Ceres her chariot, and established the Eleusinian festivals and mysteries in honor of the deity. He reigned for some time, and after death received divine honors, and was ranked by some authors, among the judges of the infernal regions. Some suppose that he accompanied Bacchus in his Indian expedition. *Cic. Tusc.* 1. c. 4.—*Diod.*—*Hygin.* fab. 147.—*Paus.* 2. c. 14. l 8. c. 4.—*Justin.* 2. c. 6.—*Apollod.* 1. c. 5.—*Callim. in Cer.* 22.—*Ovid. Met.* 5. v. 646. *Fast.* 4. v. 501. *Trist.* 3. el. 8. v. 1.—*Lactant. ad Theb.* 2. v. 382. l. 12. v. 628.—*Schol. Apollon.* 3. v. 242.—*Aug. de Civ. D.* 18. c. 13.—*Servius ad Æn.* 1. v. 327. *G.* 1. v. 163.

TRIQ'UETRA, a name given to Sicily by the Latins, from its triangular form. *Lucret.* 1. v. 78. —*Horat.* 2. sat. 6. v. 55.—*Servius ad Æn.* 1. v. 200.

TRIS'IDIS, an inland town of Mauritania Tingitana. *Ptol.*

TRISMEGIS'TUS, a famous Egyptian. *Vid.* Mercurius.

TRIS'PLÆ, a people of Thrace. *Steph.*

TRIS'SUM, a city of the Jazyges Metanastæ. *Ptol.*

TRIS'TOLUS, an inland town of Macedonia. *Ptol.*

TRITÆ'A, a city of Achaia. *Steph.*

TRITAN'NUS, a Roman centurion, mentioned by Cicero, as remarkable for his strength. *Cic. Fin.* 1. c. 3.—*Plin.* 7. c. 20.

TRI'TE, a city near the columns of Hercules. *Steph.*

TRIT'IA, TRIT'TIA or TRITÆ'A, a daughter of the river Triton, mother of Menalippus, by Mars. A town in Achaia, built by her son, bore her name. *Paus.* 7. c. 22.

TRIT'IUM, a town of Hispania Tarraconensis. It is called Tuboricum by *Ptolemy*, and Tobolicum by *Mela*, 3. c. 1.

TRITOGENI'A or TRI'TO, a surname of Pallas, because she was born on the 3d of the month, or because she was born on the borders of the lake Tritonis, &c. *Diod.* 1.—*Festus de V. Sig.*

TRI'TON, a sea deity, son of Neptune, by Amphitrite; or, according to some, by Celeno, or Salacia. He was very powerful among the sea deities, and could calm the ocean and abate storms at pleasure. He is generally represented as blowing a shell, his body above the waist, is like that of a man, and below, a dolphin. Some represent him with the fore feet of a horse. Many of the sea deities are called Tritons, but the name is generally applied to those only who are half men and half fishes. Pausanias has given a particular description of them, and he, as well as Pliny, believed that there exists in the sea a species of monsters half human and half fishes. *Apollod.* 1. c. 4.—*Hesiod. Theog.* v. 930.—*Ovid. Met.* 1. v. 333.—*Cic. de Nat. D.* 1 c. 28.—*Virg. Æn.* 1. v. 148. l. 6. v. 173.—*Paus.* 9. c. 20.—*Tzetzes ad Lyc.* 35 & 887.—*Servius ad Æn.* 1. v. 148 —*Plin.* 9. c. 5. l. 32. c. 11.—*Stat. Theb.* 5. v. 707. [There is an exceedingly fine half figure in the Vatican, representing Triton.]

TRI'TON, a river of Africa, falling into the lake Tritonis. *Claud. de laud. Stil.* 1. v. 251.——One of the names of the Nile.——A small river of Bœotia or Thessaly.

TRITO'NIA, a surname of Minerva. *Vid.* Tritonis.

TRITO'NIS, a lake and river of Africa, near which Minerva had a temple, whence she is surnamed Tritonis, or Tritonia. The Bœotians gave the name of Tritonis to a small river of their country, that they might claim the privilege of saying that Minerva was born within their territory. *Hesiod. Op. & Di.* 76.—*Ovid. Met.* 3. v. 127. l. 5. v. 270. l. 6. v. 1. *Fast.* 6. v. 655.—*Lucan.* 9. v. 354 & 682.—*Eustath. ad Dionys. Per.* 267.—*Herodot.* 4. c. 178. l. 5. c. 704. l. 11. c. 483.—*Lactant. ad Theb.* 2. v. 722.—*Schol. Apollon.* 4. v. 1311.—*Paus.* 9. c. 33.—*Virg. Æn.* 2. v. 171.—*Mela,* 1. c. 7.——A name given to Athens, because dedicated to Minerva. *Ovid. Met.* 5.

TRIT'ONON, a town of Doris. *Liv.* 28. c. 7.

TRITO'NUS, a town of Macedonia. *Steph.*

TRIVEN'TUM, a town of the Samnites.

TRIV'IA, a surname given to Diana, because she presided over all places where three roads meet, where her image was placed with three faces, one looking towards each way. At the new moon the Athenians offered her sacrifices, and a sumptuous entertainment, which was generally distributed among the poor. *Virg. Æn.* 6. v. 13. l. 7. v. 774. l. 10. v. 537. l. 11. v. 566. *Catull.* ep. 35. v. 15. *De Beren.* 67. v. 5.—*Propert.* 2. el. 23. v. 40.—*Ovid. Met.* 2. v. 416. *Fast.* 1. v. 141 & 389.

TRIV'IÆ AN'TRUM, a place in the valley of Aricia, where the nymph Egeria resided. *Mart.* 6. epigr. 47.

TRIV'IÆ LU'CUS, a place of Campania, in the bay of Cumæ. *Virg. Æn.* 6. v. 13.

TRIVI'CUM, a town in the country of the Hirpini in Italy. *Horat.* 1. sat. 5. v. 79.

TRIUM'VIRI *republicæ constituendæ* were three magistrates appointed equally to govern the Roman state with absolute power. These officers gave a fatal blow to the expiring independence of the Roman people, and became celebrated for their different pursuits, their ambition, and their various fortunes. The first triumvirate, B.C. 60, was in the hands of J. Cæsar, Pompey, and Crassus, who, at the expiration of their office, kindled a civil war. The second and last triumvirate, B.C. 43, was under Augustus, M. Antony, and Lepidus, and through them the Romans totally lost their liberty. Augustus disagreed with his colleagues, and after he had defeated them, he made himself absolute in Rome. The triumvirate was in full force at Rome for the space of about 12 years.—There were also other officers who were called *triumviri capitales*, created A.U.C. 464. They took cognizance of murders and robberies, and every thing in which slaves were concerned. Criminals under sentence of death were entrusted to their care, and they had them executed according to the commands of the prætors.—The *triumviri nocturni* watched over the safety of Rome in the night-time, and in case of fire were ever ready to give orders, and to take the most effectual measures to extinguish it.—The *triumviri agrarii* had the care of colonies that were sent to settle in different parts of the empire. They made a fair division of the lands among the citizens, and exercised over the new colony all the power which was placed in the hands of the consuls at Rome.—The *triumviri monetales* were masters of the mint, and had the care of the coin, hence their office was generally intimated with the following letters often seen on ancient coins and medals; IIIVIR. A. A. A. F. F. i. e. *Triumviri auro, argento, ære, flando, feriendo.* Some suppose that they were created only in the age of Cicero, as those who were employed before them, were called *Denariorum flandorum curatores.*—The *triumviri valetudinis* were chosen when Rome was visited by a plague or some pestiferous distemper, and they took particular care of the temples of health and virtue.—The *triumviri senatus legendi* were appointed to name those that were most worthy to be made senators from among the plebeians. They were first chosen in the age of Augustus, as before this privilege belonged to the kings, and afterwards devolved upon the consuls and the censors, A.U.C. 310.—The *triumviri mensarii* were chosen in the second Punic war, to take care of the coin and prices of exchange.

TRIUMVIRO'RUM IN'SULA, a place on the Italian Rhine, which rising from the Apennines, after a short course, falls into the Po, where the triumvirs Antony, Lepidus, and Augustus, met to divide the Roman empire after the battle of Mutina. *Dio.* 46. c. 55.—*Appian. Civ.* 4.

TRI'ZI, a people near the Ister. *Steph.*

TRO'ADES, the inhabitants of Troas.

TRO'AS, a country of Phrygia in Asia Minor, of which Troy was the capital. When Troas is taken for the whole kingdom of Priam, it may be said to contain Mysia and Phrygia Minor; but if only applied to that part of the country where Troy was situated, its extent is confined within very narrow limits. Troas was anciently called Dardania. *Vid.* Troja.

TROCH'OIS or TROCHŒIDES, a lake in the island of Delus, near which Apollo and Diana were born.

TROC'MI, a people of Galatia. *Liv.* 38. c. 16.

TROC'TES, a Phœnician mentioned by *Homer, Odys.* 11.

TRŒ'ZON, son of Pelops and Hippodamia reigned for some time in the isthmus of Corinth, and was succeeded by his brother Pittheus, who for some time had been partner with him on the throne. *Paus.* 2. c. 30.—*Plut. in Thes.*

TRŒZE'NE, a town of Argolis, in Peloponnesus, near the Saronicus Sinus. Two towns Hyperea and Anthia had been founded on the isthmus of Corinth by Hyperetes and Anthas, sons of Neptune and Alcyone, and they were afterwards united and called Trœzene by Pittheus, in honor of his brother Trœzen, whom he succeeded. Trœzene is often called Theseis, because Theseus was born there; and Posidonia, because Neptune was worshipped there. *Stat. Theb.* 4. v. 81.—*Paus.* 2. c. 50.—*Plut. in Thes.*—*Ovid. Met.* 8. v. 566. l. 15. v. 296. *Fast.* 6. v. 739. *Heroid.* 4. v. 107. *Ex. Pont.* 4. el. 16. v. 15.—*Apollod.* 2.—*Tzetzes ad Lyc.* 449. —— A town at the south of the Peloponnesus. *Plin.* 31. c. 2.

TROGIL'IÆ, three small islands near Samus.

TROGIL'IUM, a part of mount Mycale, projecting into the sea. *Strab.* 14.

TROG'ILUS, a harbour of Sicily. *Sil.* 14. v. 259.

TROGLODY'TÆ, a people of Æthiopia, who dwelt in caves (τρώγλη *specus*, δῦμι *subeo*). They were all shepherds, and thence called Nomades, and they all, except the king, had their wives in common. *Strab.* 1.—*Mela*, 1. c. 4 & 8.—*Diod.* 3. —*Plin.* 5. c. 8. l. 37. c. 10.—*Tzetzes ad Lyc.* 827.

TRO'GUS POMPE'IUS, a Latin historian, B.C. 41, born in Gaul. His father was one of the friends and adherents of J. Cæsar, and his ancestors had obtained privileges and honors from the most illustrious of the Romans. Trogus wrote a universal history of all the most important events that had happened from the beginning of the world to the age of Augustus, divided into 44 books. This history, which was greatly admired for its purity and elegance, was epitomized by Justin, and is still extant. Some suppose that the epitome is the cause that the original of Trogus is lost. *Justin.* 47. c. 5.—*Aug. de Civ D.* 4. c. 6.—*Harles. Not. Lit. Rom.* 1. p. 211.—*Voss. H. Lat.* 1. c. 19.

TRO'JA, a city, the capital of Troas, or according to others, a country of which Ilium was the capital. It was built on a small eminence near mount Ida, and the promontory of Sigæum, at the distance of about four miles from the sea shore. Dardanus the first king of the country built it, and called it Dardania, and from Tros one of his successors it was called Troja, and from Ilus, Ilion. Neptune is also said to have built, or more properly repaired, its walls, in the age of king Laomedon. This city has been celebrated by the poems of Homer and Virgil, and of all the wars which have been carried on among the ancients, that of Troy is the most famous. The Trojan war was undertaken by the Greeks, to recover Helen, whom Paris the son of Priam king of Troy had carried away from the house of Menelaus. All Greece united to avenge the cause of Menelaus, and every prince furnished a certain number of ships and soldiers. According to Euripides, Virgil, and Lycophron, the armament of the Greeks amounted to 1000 ships. Homer mentions them as being 1186, and Thucydides supposes that they were 1200 in number. The number of men which these ships carried is unknown; yet as the largest contained about 120 men each, and the smallest 50, it may be supposed that no less than 100,000 were engaged in this celebrated expedition. Agamemnon was chosen general of all these forces; but the princes and kings of Greece were admitted among his counsellors, and by them all the operations of the war were directed. The most celebrated of the Grecian princes that distinguished themselves in this war, were Achilles, Ajax, Menelaus, Ulysses, Diomedes, Protesilaus, Patroclus, Agamemnon, Nestor, Neoptolemus, &c. The Grecian army was opposed by a more numerous force. The king of Troy received assistance from the neighbouring princes in Asia Minor, and reckoned among his most active generals, Rhesus king of Thrace, and Memnon, who entered the field with 20,000 Assyrians and Æthiopians. Many of the adjacent cities were reduced and plundered before the Greeks approached the walls; but when the siege was begun, the enemies on both sides gave proofs of valor and intrepidity. The army of the Greeks, however, was visited by a plague, and their operations were not less retarded by the quarrel of Agamemnon and Achilles. The loss was great on both sides; the most valiant of the Trojans, and particularly the sons of Priam, were slain in the field; and indeed, so great was the slaughter, that the rivers of the country are represented as filled with dead bodies and suits of armour. After the siege had been carried on for ten years, some of the Trojans, among whom were Æneas and Antenor, betrayed the city into the hands of the enemy, and Troy was reduced to ashes. The poets, however, assert that the Greeks made themselves masters of the place by artifice. They secretly filled a large wooden horse with armed men, and led away their army from the plains, as if to return home. The Trojans brought the wooden horse into their city, and in the night the Greeks that were confined within the sides of the animal, rushed out and opened the gates to their companions, who had returned from the place of their concealment. The greatest part of the inhabitants were put to the sword, and the others carried away by the conquerors. This happened, according to the Arundelian marbles, about 1184 years before the Christian era, in the 3530th year of the Julian period, on the night between the 11th and 12th of June, 408 years before the first Olympiad. Some time after, a new city was raised, about 30 stadia from the ruins of the old Troy; but though it bore the ancient name, and received ample donations from Alexander the Great, when he visited it in his Asiatic expedition, yet it continued to be small, and in the age of Strabo it was nearly in ruins. It is said that J. Cæsar, who wished to pass for one of the descendants of Æneas, and consequently to be related to the Trojans, intended to make it the capital of the Roman empire, and to transport thither the senate and the Roman people. The same apprehensions were entertained in the reign of Augustus, and according to some, an ode of Horace, *Justum et tenacem propositi virum* was written purposely to dissuade the emperor from putting into execution so wild a project. *Vid.* Paris, Æneas, Antenor, Agamemnon, Ilium, Laomedon, Menelaus, &c. *Virg. Æn.—Homer.—Ovid.—Diod, &c.*

TROJA'NI and TROJU'GENÆ, the inhabitants of Troy.

TROJA'NI LU'DI, games instituted by Æneas or his son Ascanius, to commemorate the death of Anchises, and celebrated in the circus at Rome. Boys of the best families, dressed in a neat manner, and accoutred with suitable arms and weapons, were permitted to enter the list. After Ascanius had taught them to the people of Alba, they were adopted by the Romans, and Sylla exhibited them in his dictatorship, and under Augustus they were observed with unusual pomp and solemnity. A mock fight on horseback, or sometimes on foot, was exhibited. The leader was called *princeps juventutis*, and was generally the son of a senator, or the heir apparent to the empire. *Virg. Æn.* 5. v. 602.—*Sueton. in Cæs. & in Aug.—Plut. in Syll.—Servius ad Virg. loc.*

TROI'LUS, a son of Priam and Hecuba, during whose life the fates had decreed that Troy should not fall. This important oracle did not deter him from attacking Achilles, by which he lost his life, and his country her independence. Some have said that Achilles was immoderately fond of this Trojan prince, and that he actually killed him by the excess of his embraces. *Apollod.* 3. c. 11.—*Horat.* 2. od. 9. v. 16.—*Virg. Æn.* 1. v. 474.—*Dictys. Cret.* 4.—*Dares. Phryg.* 4 & 34.—*Servius ad Æn.* 1. v. 478.—*Tzetzes ad Lyc.* 307.

TROMENTI'NA, one of the Roman tribes. *Liv.* 6. c. 5.

TROPÆ'A, a town of the Brutii. *Steph.*

TROPÆ'A, a stone monument on the Pyrenees, erected by Pompey.

TROPÆ'A AUGUS'TA, a maritime town of Liguria. *Ptol.* It is now Torbia.

TROPÆ'A DRU'SI, a town of Germany where Drusus died, and Tiberius was saluted emperor by the army. *Tac.* l. 2.

TROPHO'NIUS, a celebrated architect, son of Erginus, king of Orchomenus in Bœotia. He built Apollo's temple at Delphi, with the assistance of his brother Agamedes; and when he demanded of the god a reward for his trouble, he was told by the priestess to wait eight days, and to live during that time with all cheerfulness and pleasure. When the days were past, Trophonius and his brother were found dead in their bed. According to Pausanias, however, he was swallowed up alive by the earth; and when the country was afterwards visited by a great drought, the Bœotians were directed to apply to Trophonius for relief, and to seek him at Lebadea, where he gave oracles in a cave. They discovered this cave by means of a swarm of bees, and Trophonius told them how to ease their misfortunes. From that time Trophonius was honored as a god; he passed for the son of Apollo, a temple and a statue were erected to him, and sacrifices were offered to his divinity, when consulted to give oracles. The cave of Trophonius became one of the most celebrated oracles of Greece. Many ceremonies were required, and the suppliant was obliged to make particular sacrifices, to annoint his body with oil, and bathe in the waters of certain rivers. He was to be clothed in a linen robe, and, with a cake of honey in his hand, he was directed to descend into the cave by a narrow entrance, whence he returned backwards after he had received an answer. He was always pale and dejected at his return, and thence it became proverbial to say of a melancholy man, that he had consulted the oracle of Trophonius. There were games annually exhibited in honor of Trophonius at Lebadea. Some authors consider Trophonius as a surname of Mercury, and they make him son of Valens and Phoronis. *Cic. N.D.* 3. c. 22. *Div.* 1. c. 34 *Tusc.* 1. c. 47.—*Paus.* 9. c. 37, &c.—*Plut. in Orac. Cons. ad Apoll.*—*Philostr. in Apoll.* 8. c. 19.—*Plin.* 34. c. 7.—*Ælian V. H.* 3. c. 45.—*Schol. Aristoph. in Nub.* 508.

TROS, a son of Erichthonius, king of Troy, who married Callirhoe, the daughter of the Scamander, by whom he had Ilus, Assaracus and Ganymedes. He made war against Tantalus, king of Phrygia, whom he accused of having stolen the youngest of his sons. The capital of Phrygia was called Troja from him, and the country itself Troas. *Virg. G.* 3. v. 36.—*Homer. Il.* 20. v. 219.—*Apollod.* 3. c. 12.—*Servius ad Virg. G.* 3. v. 36. *Æn.* 3. v. 108. l. 5. v. 252.—*Dictys. Cret.* 1. c. 9.——A Trojan warrior, son of Alastor, who fought against the Greeks, and was killed by Achilles. *Homer. Il.* 20. v. 463.

TRO'SIUS A'PER, a Latin grammarian. *Jul. Capit. in vit. Marc.*

TROS'OBOR, a leader of the Clitæ who rebelled under Claudius. *Tac, Ann.* 12. c. 55.

TROS'SULUM, a town of Etruria, which gave the name of Trossuli to the Roman knights who had taken it without the assistance of foot-soldiers. *Plin.* 32. c. 2.—*Senec.* ep. 86 & 87.—*Pers.* 1 v. 82.

TROT'ILUM, a town of Sicily. *Thucyd.* 6.

TRUCULEN'TUS (*the churl*), the name of one of Plautus's plays. *Cic. Sen.* 14.

TRUEN'TUS or TRUENTI'NUS, now Tronto, a river of Picenum, falling into the Adriatic. There is also a town of the same name in the neighbourhood. *Sil.* 8. v. 434.—*Mela,* 2. c. 4.—*Plin.* 3. c. 13.

TRY'CHÆ, a city of Eubœa. *Steph.*

TRYCOR'YTHUS, a town of Attica.

TRY'GO, a nymph of Arcadia, nurse to Æsculapius. Her tomb was to be seen in the town of Telpusa. *Paus.* 8. c. 25.

TRYPH'ERUS, a celebrated cook, &c. *Juv.* 11.

TRYPHIODO'RUS, a Greek poet and grammarian of Ægypt in the 6th century, who wrote a poem on the destruction of Troy, comprehended in 677 verses, which have been elegantly translated by Merrick It is generally published with the works of Coluthus. He wrote an Odyssey in 24 books, called after the 24 letters of the alphabet, from each of which he excluded the corresponding letter, that is, α from the first book, β from the second, γ from the third, &c. *Fabr. B. Gr.* 2. c. 7.—*Sax. Onom.* 2. p. 21.—*Suidas.*

TRY'PHON, a tyrant of Apamea in Syria, put to death by Antiochus. *Strab.* 16.—*Joseph. A.J.* 13. c. 12.—*Justin.* 36. c. 1.——A surname of one of the Ptolemies. *Ælian. V.H.* 14. c. 31.——A grammarian of Alexandria, in the age of Augustus, who wrote, among other works, a treatise on orthography, and another on style. *Suidas.*——A slave. *Cic.* 3. *Att.* 8. *Fam.* 13. ep. 61.

TUÆ'SIS, a river of Albion. *Ptol.* It is now the Tweed, according to *Camden.*

TUBAN'TES or TUBAN'TII, a people of Germany. *Tacit.* 1. c. 51.

TU'BERO Q. Æ'LIUS, a Roman consul, son-in-law of Paulus the conqueror of Perseus. He is celebrated for his poverty, in which he seemed to glory, as well as the rest of the family. Sixteen of the Tuberones, with their wives and children, lived in a small house, and maintained themselves with the produce of a little field, which they cultivated with their own hands. The first piece of silver plate that entered the house of Tubero was a small cup, which his father-in-law presented to him after he had conquered the king of Macedonia. *Val. Max.* 4. c. 4, 9,—*Plin.* 33. c. 11.

Tu'bero Quin'tus, son of the preceding, was known for his integrity and great worth. He was a rigid stoic in principle and in practice, which he displayed so much at the funeral games of his uncle Africanus, that the Romans refused him the prætorship. *Cic. Br.* 31. *Mur.* 36.—*Tacit. Ann.* 16. c. 22.

Tu'bero Pub'lius, brother of the preceding, spoke the funeral oration on his uncle Africanus, which Lælius had written. *Cic. Or.* 2. c. 84.

Tu'bero Lu'cius, an intimate friend of Cicero, who supported Pompey during the civil wars, and was afterwards reconciled to Cæsar with his son Quintus, who became the accuser of Ligarius. Tubero was a man of great learning, and composed a history which is mentioned with approbation by the ancients. *Cic. Lig. Leg.* 7 & 8. *Planc.* 41.—*Dionys.* 1.—*Liv.* 4. c. 23.

Tu'bero, a governor of Africa.——A Roman general who marched against the Germans under the emperors. He was accused of treason and acquitted.

TUBER'TUS PUB'LIUS, a consul with Poplicola and Menenius in the first ages of the consulship. He was buried within the city, a privilege retained by his posterity. *Cic. Leg.* 2. c. 23.

Tuber'tus A. Posthu'mius, a dictator who obtained a victory over the Æqui and Volsci. *Liv.* 4. c. 26. 29.

TUBILUS'TRIA, a festival at Rome when a purification was made of the sacred trumpets, and the sacrifice of a sheep made to Vulcan. *Varro de L.L.* 5. c. 3.—*Festus de V. Sig.*—*Ovid. Fast.* 5. c. 725.

TUBUC'CI or TACU'BIS, according to *Antoninus*, a town of Lusitania on the Tagus.

TU'BULUS C. HOSTIL., a prætor who opposed Annibal with success. *Liv.* 27. c. 6, &c.

Tu'bulus Lu'cius, a prætor who suffered himself to be bribed in his magisterial capacity. He retired, when accused, into voluntary banishment. *Cic. Fin* 2. c. 16, &c. *N.D.* 3. c. 20.

TUBUR'BIS or TUBUR'BO, the name of two towns of Africa, called Major and Minor, both near the river Bagrada. *Antonin.*

TUBURNI'CA, an inland colony and city of Africa. *Ptol.*

TUBUSUP'TUS, a city of Mauritania Cæsariensis. *Ptol.*—*Antonin.* It is now probably Couco.

TUC'CA PLAU'TIUS, a friend of Horace and Virgil. He was, with Varius, ordered by Augustus, as some report, to revise the Æneid of Virgil, which remained uncorrected on account of the premature death of the poet, with a particular injunction to add nothing to the poem. *Horat.* 1. sat. 5. v 40. sat. 10. v. 84.—*Servius ad Virg. Æn.* 2. v. 566. l. 5. v. 871. l. 7. v. 464.—*Donat. in Virg. Vitâ.*

Tuc'ca, a town of Mauritania on the river Bagrada, at the south of Carthage. *Antonin.*

TUC'CI, a city of the Turduli in Hispania Bætica. *Ptol.* It is called Tuccis by *Strabo*, and Augusta Gemella by *Pliny*, 3. c. 1.

TUC'CIA, an immodest woman in Juvenal's age. *Juv.* 6. v. 64.——A vestal virgin accused of incontinence, A.U.C. 609, of which she cleared herself, and proved her innocence by drawing water out of the Tiber with a sieve. *Val. Max.* 8. c. 1.—*Plin.* 28. c. 2.—*Aug. de Civ. D.* 10. c. 16.—*Dionys. Hal.* 2. c. 69.

TUC'CIUS, an ædile and prætor, commander in Apulia and Brutii. *Liv.* 35. c. 41 l. 36. c. 45, &c.——A man who accused C. Sempronius Rufus, by whom also he himself was accused. *Cic.* 8. *Fam.* 8.

TU'CIA, a river near Rome. *Sil.* 13. v. 5.

TU'CRIS, a city of Spain. *Ptol.* It is now Trudela.

TU'DER or TUDER'TIA, an ancient town of Umbria. The inhabitants were called Tudertes. *Sil.* 4. v. 222.

TUDITA'NUS, a surname of the Sempronian family, because one of them had a head like a mallet (*tuditi caput simile*). *Festus.*——An insane person who was grandfather to Fulvia, the wife of the triumvir. *Cic. Phil.* 3. c. 6.—*Val. Max.* 7. c. 8.

Tudita'nus Mar'cus was consul when Livius Andronicus exhibited his first play at Rome. *Cic. Br.* 18. *Tusc.* 1. c. 1.

Tudita'nus Pub'lius, a colleague of Cethegus in the consulship, A.U.C. 549, and of the censorship. *Cic. Br.* 15.

TU'DRI, a people of Germany. *Tacit. de Germ.* 42.

TU'GIA, now Toia, a town of Spain. *Plin.* 3. c. 1.

TUGI'NI, TUGE'NI or TU'GENI, a people of ancient Helvetia, whose chief town was called Tugium, now Zug. *Strab.* 4 & 7.

TUG'MA, a city of India without the Ganges. *Ptol.*

TUGURI'NUS JU'LIUS, a Roman knight who conspired against Nero, &c. *Tacit. A.* 15. c. 50.

TUIS'CO, a deity of the Germans, son of Terra, and the founder of the nation. He left a son called Mannus, and Mannus had three children, the eldest of whom gave his name to the Ingevones, who dwelt near the ocean; the second to the Hermiones in the middle of Germany; and the third to the Istevones, who completed the rest of the nation. *Tacit. de Germ.* 2.—*Voss. de Idolol.* 1. c. 31.

TUL'CIS, a river of Spain falling into the Mediterranean, now Francolin. *Mela*, 2. c. 6.

TULIN'GI, a people of Germany between the Rhine and the Danube. *Cæs. B. G.* 1. c. 25.

TULIPHUR'DUM, a city of Germany. *Ptol.*

TULISUR'GIUM, a city of Germany. *Ptol.* It is now Brunswick. A more correct reading is Tubisurgium.

TUL'LA, one of Camilla's attendants in the Rutulian war. *Virg. Æn.* 11. v. 656.

TUL'LIA, a daughter of Servius Tullius, king of Rome. She married Tarquin the Proud, after she had murdered her first husband Aruns, and consented to see Tullius assassinated, that Tarquin might be raised to the throne. It is said that she ordered her chariot to be driven over the body of her aged father, which had been thrown mangled and bloody into one of the streets of Rome. She was afterwards banished from Rome with her husband. *Ovid. in Ib.* 363. [There is a head in the Villa Pamfili near Rome, which bears the name of Tullia.]——Another daughter of Servius Tullius, who married Tarquin the Proud. She was murdered by her husband, that he might marry her ambitious sister of the same name.——A daughter of Cicero. *Vid.* Tulliola.——A debauched woman. *Juv.* 6. v. 306.

Tul'lia Lex, *de senatu*, by M. Tullius Cicero, A.U.C. 690, enacted that those who had a *libera legatio* granted them by the senate, should hold it no more than one year. Such senators as had a *libera legatio* travelled through the provinces of the empire without any expense, as if they were employed in the affairs of the state. Another, *de ambitu*, by the same, the same year. It forbade any person, two years before he canvassed for an office, to exhibit a show of gladiators, unless that case had devolved upon him by will. Senators guilty of the crime of *ambitu*, were punished with the *aquæ et ignis interdictio*, for ten years, and the penalty inflicted on the commons was more severe than that of the Calpurnian law. *Rosin. Antiq. Rom.* 8. c. 4.

TULLIA'NUM, a subterraneous prison in Rome, built by Servius Tullius, and added to the other called Robur, where criminals were confined. *Sallust, in B. Catil.*—*Rosin. Antiq. Rom.* 9. c. 31.

TULLI'OLA or TUL'LIA, a daughter of Cicero by Terentia. She married Caius Piso, and afterwards Furius Crassipes, and lastly P. Corn. Dolabella. With this last husband she had every reason to be dissatisfied. Dolabella was turbulent, and consequently the cause of much grief to Tullia and her father. Tullia died in childbed, about 44 years B.C. Cicero was so inconsolable on this occasion, that some have accused him of an unnatural partiality for his daughter. According to a ridiculous story which some of the moderns report, in the age of pope Paul the Third a monument was discovered on the Appian road, with the inscription of *Tulliolæ filiæ meæ*. The body of a woman was found there, which was reduced to ashes as soon as touched; there was also a lamp burning, which was extinguished as soon as the air gained admission, and which was supposed to have been lighted above 1500 years. *Cic.—Plut. in Cic.*

TUL'LIUS CIM'BER, the son of a freedman, who rose to great honors, and followed the interest of Pompey. He was reconciled to Julius Cæsar, whom he murdered with Brutus. He was afterwards governor of Bithynia, where he had a powerful fleet, which he entrusted to the quæstor Turulius, whilst he passed over to Syria to assist Cassius. *Dio.* 47. c. 31.—*Cic. Fam.* 12. ep. 13. *Phil.* 2. c. 11.—*Plut. in Brut.—Sueton. in Cæs.*

TUL'LIUS LAU'REA, a poet. *Vid.* Laurea.

TUL'LIUS CIC'ERO, a celebrated orator. *Vid.* Cicero.

TUL'LIUS, the son of the orator Cicero. *Vid.* Cicero ——A leading man among the collectors of the public revenue at Rome. *Cic. Verr.* 3 c. 71.——A friend of Otho.——One of the kings of Rome. *Vid.* Servius.

TUL'LIUS LU'CIUS, a relation of Cicero, his lieutenant in Cilicia. *Cic. Att.* 5. epp. 21.—*Verr.* 4. c. 11.

TUL'LIUS L. MONTA'NUS, a Roman who accompanied Cicero's son to Athans. *Cic.* 12. *Att.* 52.

TUL'LIUS MA'NIUS, a consul with Sulpitius 10 years after the expulsion of the Tarquins. *Cic. Br.* 16. —*Liv.* 2. c. 19.

TUL'LIUS SER'VIUS, a king of Rome. *Vid.* Servius.

TUL'LIUS SENE'CIO, a man accused of conspiracy against Nero with Piso. *Tac. Ann.* 15. c. 50.

TUL'LUS HOSTIL'IUS, the third king after the death of Numa. He was of a warlike and active disposition, and signalized himself by his expedition against the people of Alba, whom he conquered, and whose city he destroyed after the famous battle of the Horatii and Curiatii. He afterwards carried his arms against the Latins and the neighbouring states with success, and enforced reverence for majesty among his subjects. He died with all his family about 640 years B.C, after a reign of 32 years. The manner of his death is not precisely known. Some suppose that he was killed by lightning while he was performing some magical ceremonies in his own house; or, according to the more probable account of others, he was murdered by Ancus Martius, who set fire to the palace, to make it believed that the impiety of Tullus had been punished by heaven. *Flor.* 1. c. 3.—*Dionys. Hal.* 3. c. 1.—*Eutrop.* 1. c. 6.—*Plut.* —*Plin.* 2. c. 35. l. 28. c. 2.—*Val. Max.* 3. c. 4. l. 7. c. 4. l. 9. c. 12.—*Servius ad Æn.* 1. v. 11 & 276. l. 2. v. 315. l. 8. v 642.—*Aug. de Civ. D.* 3. c. 15.— *Juv.* 5. v. 57.—*Virg. Æn.* 6. v. 814.—*Liv.* 1. c. 22.

TUL'LUS, a consul, A.U.C. 686. *Horat.* 3. od. 8. v. 12.——The patron of the poet Propertius. *Prop.* 1. el. 1. v. 9.

TUL'LUS CLU'VIUS, a Roman ambassador put to death by Lars Tolumnius. *Cic. Ph.* 9. c. 3.

TUL'LUS L. VOLCA'TIUS, a consul, A.U.C. 688. *Cic. Cat.* 1. c. 6. *Att.* 8. ep. 15.

TUL'LUS HOSTIL'IUS, a friend and strong partisan of Antony. *Cic. Phil.* 13. c. 12.

TUL'LUS AT'TIUS, a chief of the Volsci who hospitably received Coriolanus. *Liv.* 2. c. 55.

TULO'NIUM or TULLO'NIUM, a town of the Vandali in Spain. *Ptol.—Antonin.*

TUN'DIS, a maritime town of India. *Salmas ad Solin.* p. 1185.

TU'NES or TU'NIS, a town of Africa on the Mediterranean, at the east of Carthage, near which Regulus was defeated and taken by Xanthippus. *Liv.* 30. c. 9.

TUN'GRI, a name given to some of the Germans, supposed to live on the banks of the Maese, whose chief city, called Aduatuca, is now Tongeren. *Amm. Marcel.* l. 26 & 27. The river of the country is now the Spaw. *Tacit. de Germ.* 2.

TUNICA'TES, a people of Vindelicia. *Ptol.*

TU'OLA, a river of Corsica. *Ptol.*

TURA'NIUS C., a Latin tragic poet in the age of Augustus. *Ovid. ex Pont.* 4. el. 16. v. 29.

TUR'BA, a town of Spain. *Liv.* l. 35.

TUR'BO, a gladiator mentioned by *Horace*, 2. sat. 3. v. 310. He was of small stature, but uncommonly courageous.——A governor of Pannonia under the emperors.

TURDETA'NI, or TUR'DULI, a people of Spain, inhabiting both sides of the Bætis. *Liv.* 21. c. 6. l. 28. c. 39. l. 34. c. 17.

TUR'DUS, a tribune. *Liv.* 41. c. 6. The Turdi were a branch of the family of the Papirii. *Cic.* 9. *Fam.* 21.

TURE'SIS, a Thracian who revolted from Tiberius. *Tac. Ann.* 4. c. 50.

TUR'GAN, an island of Arabia Felix. *Ammian.* l. 23. *Ortelius* supposes it to be the same as the Serapis of *Ptolemy*.

TU'RIA, TU'RIAS, or TU'RIUM, a river of Spain falling into the Mediterranean, now Guadalaviar. *Plin.* 3. c. 3.

TURIA'SO, a city of Hispania Tarraconensis. *Ptol.* —*Plin.* 3. c. 3. It is now Tarracona.

TU'RICUM, a town of Gaul, now Zurich, in Switzerland.

TU'RIUS, a corrupt judge in the Augustan age. *Horat.* 2. sat. 1. v. 49.——A freedman of the preceding.

TU'RIUS Q. a trader in Africa. *Cic.* 12. *Fam.* 26.

TU'RIUS LU'CIUS, an orator of no great merit. *Cic. Br.* 67.

TURME'DA, a city of Syria, called also Amphipolis. *Steph.*

TURMOD'IGI, a people or town of Hispania Tarraconensis. *Plin.* 3. c. 3.

TUR'MULI, a place in Lusitania. *Antonin.* It is now Roccha Fredda.

TUR'NI, an inland town of Calabria. *Ptol.* Some MSS. have Sturni.

TUR'NUS, a king of the Rutuli, son of Daunus and Venilia. He made war against Æneas, and attempted to drive him from Italy, that he might not marry the daughter of Latinus, who had been previously engaged to him. His efforts were attended with no success, though supported with great courage and a numerous army. He was conquered, and at last killed in single combat by Æneas. He is represented as a man of uncommon strength. *Virg. Æn.* 7. v. 56, &c.—*Tibul.* 2. el. 5. v. 49.—*Ovid. Fast.* 4. v. 879. *Met.* 14. v. 451.—*Servius ad Æn.* 6. v 90. l. 7. v. 366. l. 9. v. 737. l. 10. v. 76. l. 12. v. 29.

TUROBRI'CA, a town of Hispania Bætica. *Plin.* 3. c. 1. It is now Alcantara.

TU'RONES, TU'RONI or TURO'NII, a people of Gaul, whose capital, Cæsarodunum, is the modern Tours. *Cæs. Com. B. G.* 3. c. 35.—*Tac. Ann.* 3. c. 41.

TURPIL'IUS SEXT., a comic poet of merit at Rome His plays were esteemed by the learned, and deserved to be placed near those of Terence in the public opinion. Some critics have assigned him the seventh place among the Roman comic poets, and in their comparisons of literary merit, have ranked his poetry before that of Luscius, Ennius, and Trabea. He wrote 15 comedies, some of which are mentioned, as the Philopater, Demetrius, Bethones, Lemnii, Pedius, Epiclerus, Thrasyleo, Canephorus, Hecyra, Demiurgos, Leucadia, Paraterusa, Lyndia, &c.; but of all these only about 148 scattered verses have escaped the ravages of time. The poet lived to a great old age, and died at Sinuessa some years before the time of Cicero. *Suidas.—Fabric. B. Latin.*

TUR'PIO, an actor of eminence in Terence's plays. *Vid.* Ambivius.——A shoemaker at Rome, mentioned by *Cicero*. 6. *Att.* 1.

TURRA'NIUS M. or TURA'NIUS, a Roman of great integrity, refused to accept a province offered to him by Antony, of whose conduct he disapproved. *Cic. Ph* 3. c. 10.

TURRA'NIUS DE'CIUS, a man known for his extensive learning. He was very intimate with Cicero and with his brother, and generally lived with them. *Cic.* 1. *Att.* 6. l. 6. ep. 9. l. 7. ep. 1.—*Plin.* 3. c. 1.

TUR'RES, a town of Apulia Peucetia. *Antonin.* It is now Turi.——A town of Etruria. *Id.* It is now S. Severa.——A town of the Brutii. *Id.* It is now S. Biaso.——A town of Liburnia. *Id.* It is now Thurn.

TUR'RIS LIBYS'SONIS, a city of Sardinia. *Plin.* 3. c. 7. It is called Turris Bissonis by *Ptolemy*, and is now Torre.

TUR'RUS, a river of Italy falling into the Adriatic. *Plin.* 3. c. 18. It is now Torre or Turre.

TURSE'LIUS L., a Roman whose property was seized by Antony by means of a forged will. *Cic. Phil.* 2. c. 16.

TURU'LIS, a river of Spain, with a city of the same name. *Ptol.* The river is now Rio de Morvedre.

TURUL'LIUS, a quæstor to Cimber in Bithynia. *Cic.* 12. *Fam.* 13. His name is mentioned in the number of Cæsar's murderers. *Suet. in J. Cæs.* c. 80.

TURUL'LIUS CERIA'LIS, an officer who deserted to Vitellius. *Tac. Hist.* 2. c. 22.

TUR'ULUM, a city of Thrace. *Suidas.* It is called Tzurulum by *Cedrenus*, and is now Zorlich.

TURUN'TUS, a river of Sarmatia, supposed to be the Dwina or Duna. *Ptol.*

TURUPTIA'NA, a city of Hispania Tarraconensis. *Ptol.* It is now Tui.

TUR'ZO, a city of Africa Propria. *Ptol.*

TUS'CA, a river of Africa. *Plin.* 5. c. 3.

TUSCA'NIA or TUS'CIA, a large country at the west of Rome, the same as Etruria. *Vid.* Etruria.

TUSCE'NIUS, a man of obscure rank, who complained of Q. Cicero's conduct. *Cic. Fr.* 1. ep. 1, &c.

TUS'CI or THUS'CI, the inhabitants of Etruria. *Plin.* 3. c. 5.—*Liv.* 2. c. 51.

TUS'CI, the villa of Pliny the younger, near the sources of the Tiber. *Plin.* ep. 5 & 6

TUSCULA'NUM, a country-house of Cicero, near Tusculum, where, among other books, the orator composed his Quæstiones, concerning the contempt of death, &c. in five books. *Cic. Tusc.* 1. c. 4. *Att.* 15. ep. 2. *Div.* 2. c. 1. *Pro Leg. Agr.* 3. c. 2.

TUS'CULUM, a town of Latium, on the declivity of a hill, about twelve miles from Rome, founded by Telegonus, the son of Ulysses and Circe. It is now called Frescati, and is famous for the magnificent villas in its neighbourhood. *Cic. ad Attic.*—*Strab.* 5.—*Horat.* 3. od. 23. v. 8, &c.—*Propert.* 2. el. 23. v. 42.—*Ital.* 7. v. 693.—*Martial.* 9. epigr. 61. l. 13. epigr. 30.—*Tibull.* 1. el. 8. v. 57.

TUS'CUM MA'RE, a part of the Mediterranean, on the coast of Etruria. *Vid.* Tyrrhenum.

TUS'CUS, belonging to Etruria. The Tiber is called *Tuscus amnis* from its situation. *Virg. Æn.* 10. v. 199.

TUS'CUS VI'CUS, a small village near Rome. It received this name from the Etrurians of Porsenna's army, that settled there. *Liv.* 2. c. 14.

TU'TA, a queen of Illyricum, &c. *Vid.* Teuta.

TUTELI'NA or TUTULI'NA, a Roman goddess invoked to protect the harvest. *Varro apud Nonium*, 1. No. 243.—*Aug. de Civ. D.* 4. c. 8.—*Macrob.* 1. c. 16.—*Gyrald. H. D.* 1.—*Voss. Idolol.* 2. c. 61.

TUTIA, a vestal virgin accused of incontinence. She proved herself to be innocent by carrying water from the Tiber to the temple of Vesta in a sieve, after a solemn invocation to the goddess. *Liv.* 20.

TU'TIA, a small river six miles from Rome, where Annibal pitched his camp when he retreated from the city. *Liv.* 26. c. 11.

TU'TICUM, a town of the Hirpini. *Horat.* 1. sat. 5. v. 87. It is now Ariano.

TUTI'NUS or TUTU'NUS, a deity at Rome, who presided over the conjugal duties, and whose statue persons lately married touched, to remove sterility. Women made their offering, the head covered with a veil. *Aug. de Civ. D.* 4. c. 11. l. 6. c. 9.—*Festus de V. Sig. voce Mutini.*—*Lactant.* 1. c. 20.—*Arnob. Adv. Gent.* 4.

TU'TOR, a ridiculous comedy mentioned by *Cicero, Orat.* 2. c. 64.

TU'TOR JU'LIUS, a præfect of the Treviri. *Tac. Hist.* 4. c. 55.

TY'ANA, a town at the foot of mount Taurus in Cappadocia, where Apollonius was born, whence he is called Tyaneus. *Ovid. Met.* 8. v. 719.—*Strab.* 12.—*Plin.* 5. c. 29. l. 6. c. 3.

TYANI'TIS, a province of Asia Minor, near Cappadocia. *Strab.*

TYB'II, a people between the Getæ and the Thracians. *Plin.* 7. c. 2.

TY'BRIS. *Vid.* Tiberis.

TY'BRIS, a Trojan who fought in Italy with Æneas against Turnus. *Virg. Æn.* 10. v. 124.

TY'BUR, a town of Latium on the Anio. *Vid.* Tibur.

TY'CHE, one of the Oceanides. *Paus.* 4. c. 30.—*Hesiod. Theog.* v. 360.

TY'CHE, a part of the town of Syracuse. *Cic. in Verr.* 4. c. 53.

TY'CHE, a name applied to fortune since the days of Homer and Hesiod. *Pindar Olymp.* 12. v. 2.

TYCH'IUS, a celebrated artist of Hyle in Bœotia, who made Hector's shield, which was covered with the hides of seven oxen. *Ovid. Fast.* 3. v. 823.—*Strab.* 9.—*Homer. Il.* 7. v. 220.

TY'CUS, a general of Maximinus, proclaimed emperor by his soldiers. He was slain after a reign of six months. *Jul. Capitol. in Maxim.* c. 11.—*Herodian.* 7. c. 1.—*Treb. Poll. in* 30. *Tyr.* c. 32.

TY'DE, a town of Hispania Tarraconensis. *Ital.* 3. v. 367.

TY'DEUS, a son of Œneus king of Calydon, by Peribœa. He fled from his country after the accidental murder of one of his friends, and found a safe asylum in the court of Adrastus, king of Argos, whose daughter Deiphile he married. When Adrastus wished to replace his son-in-law on the throne of Thebes, Tydeus undertook to go and declare war against Eteocles, who had usurped the crown. The reception he met with provoked his resentment; he challenged Eteocles and his officers to single combat, and defeated them. On his return to Argos he slew 50 of the Thebans who had conspired against his life, and lain in ambush to surprise him; and only Meon, one of the number, was permitted to return to Thebes, to bear the tidings of the fate of his companions. He was one of the seven chiefs of the army of Adrastus, and during the Theban war he behaved with great courage. Many of the enemy expired under his blows, till he was at last wounded by Melanippus. Though the blow was fatal, Tydeus had the strength to dart at his enemy, and to bring him to the ground, before he was carried away from the field by his companions. At his own request, the dead body of Melanippus was brought to him, and after he had ordered the head to be cut off, he began to tear out the brains with his teeth. The savage barbarity of Tydeus displeased Minerva, who was coming to bring him relief, and to make him immortal; and the goddess left him to his fate, and suffered him to die. He was buried at Argos, where his monument was still to be seen in the age of Pausanias. He was father to Diomedes. Some suppose that the cause of his flight to Argos, was the murder of the son of Melus, or, according to others, of Alcathous his father's brother, or perhaps of his own brother Olenius. *Homer. Il.* 4. v. 365, 387.—*Apollod.* 1. c. 8. l. 3. c. 6.—*Æschyl. Sept. contra Theb.*—*Paus.* 9. c. 18. l. 10. c. 10.—*Diod.* 2.—*Eurip. in Sup.*—*Virg. Æn.* 6. v. 479.—*Ovid. in Ib.* 350, &c.—*Stat. Theb.* 1. v. 401 & 451. l. 2. v. 113 & 488. l. 8. v. 458, &c.—*Servius ad Æn* 1. v. 101. l. 11. v. 239.—*Tzetzes ad Lyc.* 1066.—*Hygin.* fab. 69.

TYDI'DES, a patronymic of Diomedes, as son of Tydeus. *Homer. Il.* 5. v. 163. l. 9. v. 53. l. 10, &c.—*Virg. Æn.* 1. v. 101.—*Horat.* 1. od. 15. v. 28.

TY'DRUS, a son of Caucasus, an auxiliary of Æetes, slain by Colaxes. *Val. Flacc. Argon.* 6. v. 640.

TYEL'LA, a town of Sicily. *Diod. Sic.*

TYE'NIS, a mountain of the Colchi. *Steph.*

TYLAN'GIUM, a city of Triphylia. *Polyb.*

TY'LIS, a city of Thrace near Hæmus. *Steph.*

TY'LUS, a town of Peloponnesus near Tænarus. *Strab.*——An island in the Persian Gulf. *Plin.* 6. c. 28.—*Arrian.* l. 7.

TYM'BER, a son of Daunus, who assisted Turnus.

His head was cut off in an engagement by Pallas. *Virg. Æn.* 10. v. 391, &c.

TYM'BRIA, a town of Caria, on the Mæander. *Strab.*

TYMBRIA'NI, a people between Pisidia and Lycaonia. *Plin.* 5. c. 27.

TYMENÆ'ON, a city near Phrygia. *Steph.*

TYMEN'NA, a village of Lycia. *Id.*

TY'MES (-*etis*), a city of Libya. *Id.*

TYMNIS'SUS, a city of Caria. *Id.*

TYM'NUS, a city of Caria. *Id.*

TYMO'LUS, a mountain. *Ovid. Met.* 6. v. 15. *Vid.* Tmolus.

TYMPA'NIA, an inland town of Elis. *Plin.* 4. c. 6.—*Ptol.*—*Polyb.*

TYMPHÆ'I, a people between Epirus and Thessaly. *Strab.* 7.—*Plin.* 4. c. 2.

TYM'PHE, a mountain of Thesprotia. *Steph.*

TYNDAR'IDÆ, a patronymic of the children of Tyndarus, as Castor, Pollux, and Helen, &c. *Ovid. Met.* 8. v. 301. *Fast.* 5. 700. *Trist.* 1. el. 10. c. 45.—*Cic. de N.D.* 3. c. 5 & 15.

TYNDAR'IDÆ, a people of Asiatic Sarmatia. *Dionys. Af.*

TYN'DARIS, a patronymic of Helen, daughter of Tyndarus. *Virg. Æn.* 2. v. 569.——A name given by *Horace* to one of his mistresses, as best expressive of all female accomplishments. 1. od. 17. v. 10.——A name given to Cassandra. *Ovid. A. A.* 2. v. 408.

TYN'DARIS, a town of Sicily near Pelorus, founded by a Messenian colony. *Strab.* 6.—*Plin.* 2. c. 91.—*Sil.* 14. v. 209.——A town of Colchis on the Phasis. *Plin.*

TYN'DARUS, a son of Œbalus and Gorgophone, or, according to some, of Perieres. He was king of Lacedæmon, and married the celebrated Leda, who bore him Timandra, Philonoe, &c. and also became mother of Pollux and Helen by Jupiter. *Vid.* Leda, Castor, Pollux, Clytæmnestra, &c.

TYN'DIS, a town of Limyrice in India. *Plin.* 6. c. 25.—*Salmas. ad Solin.* p. 1187.

TY'NES (-*etis*), a city of Sicily. *Steph.*

TYN'NA, a city of Catalonia in Armenia Minor. *Ptol.*

TYN'NICHUS, a general of Heraclea. *Polyæn.* 5. c. 23.

TYPÆ'ON, a mountain of Elis. *Steph.*

TYPHO'EUS or TY'PHON, a famous giant, son of Tartarus and Terra, who had a hundred heads like those of a serpent or a dragon. Flames of devouring fire were darted from his mouth and eyes, and he uttered horrid yells, like the dissonant shrieks of different animals. He was no sooner born, than, to avenge the death of his brothers the giants, he made war against heaven, and so frightened the gods, that they fled away and assumed different shapes. Jupiter became a ram, Mercury an ibis, Apollo a crow, Juno a cow, Bacchus a goat, Diana a cat, Venus a fish, &c. The father of the gods at last resumed courage, and put Typhœus to flight with his thunderbolts, and crushed him under mount Ætna, in the island of Sicily, or according to some, under the island Inarime. Typhœus became father of Geryon, Cerberus, and Orthos, by his union with Echidna. *Hygin.* fab. 152 & 196.—*Ovid. Met.* 5. v. 325.—*Æschyl. Sept. contra Theb.*—*Hesiod. Theog.* 306 & 820.—*Homer. Hym.*—*Herodot.* 2. c. 156.—*Virg. Æn.* 9. v. 716.—*Anton. Lib.* 28.—*Servius ad G.* 1. v. 279.—*Philostr.* 2. *Ic.* 17. *& in Apoll.* 5. c. 13.—*Manil. Astr.* 2 & 4.—*Tzetzes in Lyc.* 177 & 1194. *& Chil.* 8. *H.* 171.—*Schol. Pindar. Olym.* 4. v. 11.—*Schol. Apollon.* 2 v. 1214, &c.

TY'PHON, a giant whom Juno produced by striking the earth. Some of the poets make him the same as the famous Typhœus. *Vid.* Typhœus.——A brother of Osiris, who married Nepthys. He laid snares for his brother during his expedition, and murdered him at his return. The death of Osiris was avenged by his son Orus, and Typhon was put to death. *Vid.* Osiris. He was reckoned among the Ægyptians to be the cause of every evil, and on that account generally represented as a wolf and a crocodile. *Plut. in Is. & Os.*—*Diod.* 1.

TY'RA. *Vid* Tyras.

TYRACI'NÆ or TYRACI'NA, a city of Sicily. *Steph.*

TYRAM'BE or TYRAM'BIS, a city of Asiatic Sarmatia. *Ptol.*

TYRAN'NION, a grammarian of Amisa in Pontus, intimate with Cicero. His original name was Theophrastus, and he received that of Tyrannion, from his austerity to his pupils. He was taken by Lucullus, and restored to his liberty by Muræna. He opened a school in the house of his friend Cicero, and enjoyed his friendship. He was extremely fond of books, and collected a library of about 30,000 volumes. To his care and industry the world is indebted for the preservation of Aristotle's works. *Cic. ad Q. Frat.* 2. ep. 4. l. 3. ep. 4 & 5.—*Hesychius.*—*Suidas* ——One of the disciples of the preceding, called Diocles. He was a native of Phœnicia, and was made prisoner in the war of Augustus and Antony. He was bought by Dymas, one of the emperor's favorites, and afterwards by Terentia, who gave him his liberty. He wrote 67 different volumes, in one of which he proved that the Latin tongue was derived from the Greek; and another in which Homer's poems were corrected, &c. *Suidas.*

TYRANNOS'BOAS or TYRANNOB'OAS, a town of India within the Ganges. *Arrian. in Peripl.*

TYRAN'NUS, a son of Pterelaus.——A sophist who wrote 10 books, *de divisione orationis. Suidas.*

TY'RAS or TY'RA, a river of European Sarmatia, falling into the Euxine Sea, between the Danube and the Borysthenes, now called the Niester. *Ovid. Pont.* 4. el. 10 v. 50.——A city of Lower Mysia. *Ptol.*

TYREDI'ZA or TYRODI'ZA, a city of Thrace *Steph.*

TY'RES, one of the companions of Æneas in his wars against Turnus. He was brother of Teuthras. *Virg. Æn.* 10. v. 403.

TY'RES, a river of Scythia. *Herodot.* 4. c. 11.

TYRIDA'TES, a rich man in the age of Alexander, &c. *Curt.* 8. c. 6.

TYR'II or TY'RUS, a town of Magna Græcia. *Plut.*

TYRI'OTES, a eunuch of Darius, who fled from Alexander's camp, to inform his master of the queen's death. *Curt.* 4. c. 10.

TYRIS'SA, a town of Æmathia. *Plin.* 4. c. 10.

TYRIS'TASIS, a town of the Thracian Chersonesus. *Id.* 4. c. 11.—*Demosthen.*

TYRITACI'TE, a city of Pontus. *Steph.*

TYRI'TÆ, a people of European Sarmatia, near the mouth of the Tyras. They are called Tyrangitæ by *Ptolemy*, Tyrigetæ by *Strabo*, and Tyragetæ by *Pliny*, 3. c. 1.

TYR'IUS, a surname of Hercules, from the worship which he received at Tyre. *Herodot.* 2.

TYRME'NII, a people of Scythia *Steph.*

TYR'MIDÆ, a village in the tribe Œneis. *Steph.*

TY'RO, a beautiful nymph, daughter of Salmoneus, king of Elis, and Alcidice. She was treated with great severity by her mother-in-law, Sidero, and was at last removed from her father's house by her uncle Cretheus. She became enamoured of the Enipeus; and as she often walked on the banks of the river, Neptune assumed the shape of her favoured lover, and gained her affections. She had two sons, Pelias and Neleus, by Neptune, whom she exposed, to conceal her incontinence from the world. The children were preserved by shepherds, and when they had arrived at years of maturity, they avenged their mother's injuries by assassinating the cruel Sidero. Some time after her amour with Neptune, Tyro married her uncle Cretheus, by whom she had Amythaon, Pheres, and Æson. Tyro is often called Salmonis from her father. *Homer. Od.* 11. v. 234.—*Pindar. Pyth.* 4.—*Apollod.* 1. c. 9.—*Diod.* 4.—*Propert.* 1. el. 13. v. 20. l. 2. el. 30. v. 51. l. 3. el 19. v. 13.—*Ovid. Am.* 3. el. 6. v 43.—*Ælian. V. H.* 12. c. 42.——The mother of Venus the goddess of the Syrians *Cic. N. D.* 3. c. 23.

TYRON'IDAS, a native of Tegea in Arcadia, who made laws for his countrymen, and for his services was rewarded with a statue in the forum. *Paus.* 8. c. 48.

TY'ROS, an island of Arabia. *Strab.* 16.——A city of Phœnicia. *Vid.* Tyrus.

TYRRHE'IDÆ, a patronymic given to the sons of Tyrrheus, who kept the flocks of Latinus. *Virg. Æn.* 7. v. 484.

TYRRHE'NI, the inhabitants of Etruria, distinguished themselves by their knowledge of augury and their religious ceremonies. They were supposed to be acquainted with navigation, and supported the dignity ef their magistrates and public officers by assigning them particular seats, and appropriating to them a distinguishing dress. They invented brazen trumpets, and were the first who placed porticos before their houses. *Vid.* Hetruria. *Diod.* 5.—*Mela*, 1. c. 13.—*Strab.* 5.—*Plut. in Qu. R.* 53.—*Athen.* 4. c. 6.—*Servius ad Æn.* 1. v. 71. l. 7. v. 426. l. 8. v. 479.—*Plin.* 5. c. 5.—*Hygin.* fab. 134.—*Paus.* 2. c. 21.—*Pollux.* 4. c. 11.—*Ital.* 5. v. 11.

TYRRHE'NUM MA'RE, that part of the Mediterranean which lies on the coast of Etruria. It is also called *Inferum*, as being at the bottom or south of Italy. It is now Il Mare di Toscana.

TYRRHE'NUS, a son of Atys king of Lydia, brother to Lydus. In the time of a great scarcity the lot decided which of the two brothers should leave his native country, and Tyrrhenus, obliged to yield, came to Italy, where part of the country was called after him. He was, according to Servius, brother of Tarchon who founded Mantua, and father of Clusius who built Clusium. *Strab.* 5.—*Tacit. Ann.* 4. c. 55.—*Paterc.* 1. c. 1.—*Servius ad Æn.* 2. v. 781. l. 10. v. 164. 167 & 198. ——A friend of Æneas. *Virg. Æn.* 11. v. 612.

TYR'RHEUS, a shepherd of king Latinus, whose stag being killed by the companions of Ascanius, was the cause of war between Æneas and the inhabitants of Latium. Lavinia afterwards took refuge in his house, and there gave birth to Sylvius, who became king of Alba. Hence the word Tyrrheides. *Virg.* 6. v. 760. l. 7. v. 485.—*Servius in loco, & Æn.* 1. v. 274 ——An Ægyptian general, B.C. 91.——A son of the philosopher Pittacus, who was accidentally killed by a brazier with the blow of a hatchet, in a barber's shop at Carmel, which he had frequented to learn the news. The offender was seized and sent to the father, who, however, forgave the cause of his affliction, saying, with the serenity of a philosopher, that pardon was more becoming than penitence. *Diog. Laert.* 1. c. 76.

TYR'SIS, a place in the Balearides, supposed to be the palace of Saturn. *Homer.*—*Pindar.*

TYRTÆ'US, son of Archimbrotus, a Greek elegiac poet, born in Attica. In the second Messenian war, the Lacedæmonians were directed by the oracle to apply to the Athenians for a general, if they wished to finish their expedition with success, and they were contemptuously presented with Tyrtæus. The poet, though ridiculed for his many deformities, and his ignorance of military affairs, animated the Lacedæmonians with martial songs, just as they wished to raise the siege of Ithome, and inspired them with so much courage, that they defeated the Messenians. For his services, he was made a citizen of Lacedæmon, and treated with great attention. Of the compositions of Tyrtæus, nothing is extant but the fragments of four or five elegies, comprehending 136 verses full of strong and powerful exhortations to deeds of valour and heroism, and such as were calculated to lead a martial people to battle and to victory. He flourished 684 B.C. The fragments of his works have been edited by Woldenberg, Rostoch. 1658; by Fulvius Ursinus, Antwerp, 1568; by Klotzius, Bremæ, 1764. His elegies have been translated into English by Polwhele, London, 1787. *Fabr. B. Gr.* 2. c. 11.—*Sax. Onom.* 1. p. 15.—*Justin.* 2. c. 5.—*Strab.* 8.—*Aristot. Polit.* 5. c. 7.—*Horat. de Art. P.* 402.—*Ælian. V. H.* 12. c. 50.—*Paus.* 4. c. 6, &c.—*Plato de Leg.* 1.—*Plut. in Apoph.*—*Pollux.* 4. c. 15.

TY'RUS, a very ancient city of Phœnicia, built by the Sidonians, on a small island at the south of Sidon, about 200 stadia from the shore, and now called Sur. There were, properly speaking, two places of that name, the old Tyrus, called Palætyrus, on the sea shore, and the other in the island. It was about 19 miles in circumference, including Palætyrus, but without it, about four miles. Tyre was destroyed by the princes of Assyria, and afterwards rebuilt. It maintained its independence till the age of Alexander, who took it with much difficulty, and only after he had joined the island to the continent by a mole, after a siege of seven months, on the 20th of August, B.C. 332. The Tyrians were naturally industrious; their city was the emporium of commerce, and they were deemed the inventors of scarlet and purple colors. They founded many cities in different parts of the world, such as Carthage, Gades, Leptis, Utica, &c. which on that account are often distinguished by the epithet of *Tyria.* The buildings of Tyre were very splendid and magnificent; the walls were 150 feet high, and of a proportionable breadth. Hercules was the chief deity of the place, and he was worshipped in a stately temple decorated with the most sumptuous ornaments, particularly with a pillar of gold, and another of emeralds of unusual brightness. Tyre had two large and capacious harbours, and a powerful fleet; and was built, according to some writers, about 2760 years before the Christian era. *Strab.* 16.—*Herodot.* 2. c. 44. —*Mela*, 1. c. 12. l. 3. c. 6.—*Curt.* 4. c. 4.—*Virg. Æn.* 1. v. 6, 339, &c.—*Ovid. Fast.* 1, &c. *Met.* 5 & 10.—*Lucan.* 3. v. 217. l. 5. v. 108. l. 10. v. 122. —*Martial.* 1. epigr. 54. l. 8. epigr. 9. l. 9. epigr. 23. l. 10. epigr. 16.—*Stat. Theb.* 1. v. 161. l. 10. v. 3.—*Flac.* 1. v. 17. l. 2. v. 342.

TY'RUS, a nymph, mother of Venus. *Vid.* Tyro.

TYS'CA, a small region of Africa, the cause of a contest between the Carthaginians and Masinissa. *Appian. Alex.*

TYS'IAS, a man celebrated by Cicero. *Vid.* Tisias.

U.

U'BII, a people of Germany, near the Rhine, transported across the river by Agrippa, who gave them the name of Agripinenses, from his daughter Agrippina, who had been born in the country. Their chief towns, *Ubiorum oppidum*, is now Cologne. *Tacit. G.* 28. *Ann.* 12. c. 27.—*Plin.* 4. c. 17.—*Cæs.* 4. c. 30.

UCAL'EGON, a Trojan chief, remarkable for his great age, and praised for the soundness of his principles and good intentions, though accused by some of betraying his country to the enemy. His house was first set on fire by the Greeks. *Virg. Æn.* 2. v. 312.—*Homer. Il.* 3. v. 148.—*Servius ad Virg. loco.*—*Dares.* 38.

UCE'TIA, a town of Gallia Narbonensis. It is now Uzez.

UCHO'REUS, a king of Ægypt, the eighth descendant of Osymandes, who built Memphis. *Diod.* 2. —*Joh. Marsham. Can. Chron. sec.* 3.

U'CUBIS, now Lucubi, a town of Hispania Bætica. *Hirt. B. Hisp.* c. 7, 8, 20, 24 & 27.

UCULTINI'ACUM, a city of Hispania Bætica. *Plin.* 3. c. 1.

U'DEUS, one of the Spartæ who sprang from the dragon's teeth. He was the father or the grandfather of Tiresias. *Paus.* 9. c. 5.—*Apollod.* 3.

UDI'NA or VEDI'NUM, now Udino, a town of Italy.

UDI'NI, a people of Albania, in Asia, near the Caspian. *Plin.* 6. c. 13.

U'FENS, a river of Italy near Tarracina. *Virg. Æn.* 7. v. 892.—*Plin.* 3. c. 5.——A river of Picenum. *Liv.* 5. c. 35.

U'FENS, a prince who assisted Turnus against Æneas. The Trojan monarch made a vow to sacrifice his four sons to appease the manes of his friend Pallas, in the same manner as Achilles is represented as killing some Trojan youths on the tomb of Patroclus. *Virg. Æn.* 7. v. 745. l. 10. v. 518. He was afterwards killed by Gyas. *Id.* 12. v. 460.

UFENTI'NA, a Roman tribe first created, A.U.C. 435. with the tribe Falerina, in consequence of the great increase of population at Rome. *Liv.* 9. c. 20.—*Festus.*

UF'FUGUM, a city of the Brutii. *Liv.*

UGGA'DE, a town of the Aulerci, on the Sequana, in Gallia Lugdunensis. *Antonin.* According to some it is now Elbeuf.

U'LÆ, a people of Asiatic Sarmatia. *Ptol.*

UL'CI, a city of Lucania. *Ptol.*

U'LIA, a city of the Turduli in Hispania Bætica. *Id.*

ULIBILIA'NI, a people of Mauritania Tingitana. *Id.*

ULIZIBI'RA, a city of Africa Propria. *Id. Pliny*, 5. c. 4., calls it *Ulusubritanum oppidum.*

UL'MI, a town of Lower Pannonia. *Antonin.* It is now Iltz according to *Simler.*

UL'PIA TRAJA'NA, a Roman colony planted in Sarmatia by Trajan.

ULPIA'NUS DOMI'TIUS, a native of Tyre, a lawver in the reign of Alexander Severus, of whom he became the secretary, and principal minister. He raised a persecution against the Christians, and was at last murdered by the prætorian guards, of which he had command, A.D. 226. There are some fragments of his compositions on civil law still extant. They have been edited by Cannegieter, Traject. ad Rhen. 1768, and by Hugo, Gotting. 1788. The Greek commentaries of Ulpian on Demosthenes were printed in fol. 1527, *apud Aldum*. *Harles. Not. Lit. Rom.* 1. p. 526.

ULPIA'NUS MARCEL'LUS, an officer in the age of Commodus.

ULPIA'NUS JULIA'NUS, a man sent to oppose Heliogabalus, &c.

U'LUBRÆ, a small town of Latium, on the river Astura, east of Ardea, where Augustus was educated *Juv.* 10. v. 102.—*Horat.* 1. ep. 11.

ULYS'SES, a king of the islands of Ithaca, and Dulichium, son of Anticlea and Laertes, or according to some, of Sisyphus. *Vid.* Sisyphus and Anticlea. He became, like the other princes of Greece, one of the suitors of Helen, but as he despaired of success in his applications, on account of the great number of his competitors, he solicited the hand of Penelope, the daughter of Icarius. Tyndarus, the father of Helen, favored the addresses of Ulysses, as by him he was directed to choose one of his daughter's suitors without offending the others, and to bind them all by a solemn oath, that they would unite together in protecting Helen if any violence was ever offered to her person. Ulysses had no sooner obtained the hand of Penelope, than he returned to Ithaca, where his father resigned him the crown, and retired to peace and rural solitude. The rape of Helen, however, by Paris, did not long permit him to remain in his kingdom, and as he was bound to defend her against every intruder, he was summoned to the war with the other princes of Greece. Pretending to be insane, not to leave his beloved Penelope, he yoked a horse and a bull together, and ploughed the sea-shore, where he sowed salt instead of corn. This dissimulation was soon discovered, and Palamedes, by placing before the plough of Ulysses, his infant son Telemachus, convinced the world, that the father was not mad, as he had sense enough to turn away the plough from the furrow, not to hurt his child. Ulysses was therefore obliged to go to the war, but he did not forget him who had discovered his pretended insanity. *Vid.* Palamedes. During the Trojan war, the king of Ithaca was courted for his superior prudence and sagacity. By his means Achilles was discovered among the daughters of Lycomedes, king of Scyrus, (*Vid.* Achilles), and Philoctetes was induced to abandon Lemnus, and to fight the Trojans with the arrows of Hercules. *Vid.* Philoctetes. He was not less distinguished for his activity and valour. With the assistance of Diomedes, he murdered Rhesus, and slaughtered the sleeping Thracians in the midst of their camp, (*Vid.* Rhesus & Dolon,) and he introduced himself into the city of Priam, and carried away the Palladium of the Trojans. *Vid.* Palladium. For these eminent services he was universally applauded by the Greeks, and was rewarded with the arms of Achilles, for which Ajax had contended with him. After the Trojan war Ulysses embarked on board his ships to return to Greece, but he was exposed to a number of misfortunes before he reached his native country. He was thrown by the winds upon the coasts of Africa, and visited the country of the Lotophagi, and of the Cyclopes in Sicily. Polyphemus, who was king of the Cyclopes, seized Ulysses with his companions, five of whom he devoured, (*Vid.* Polyphemus,) but the prince of Ithaca intoxicated him and put out his eye, and at last escaped from the dangerous cave where he was confined, by tying himself under the belly of the sheep of the Cyclops when led to pasture. In Æolia he met with a friendly reception, and Æolus gave him, confined in bags, all the winds which could obstruct his return to Ithaca, but the curiosity of his companions to know what the bags contained, proved nearly fatal. The winds rushed out with impetuosity, and all the fleet was destroyed except the ship which carried Ulysses. Thence he was thrown upon the coasts of the Læstrygones, and of the island Æea, where the magician Circe changed all his companions into pigs for their voluptuousness. He escaped their fate by means of an herb which he had received from Mercury, and after he had obliged the musician by force of arms to restore his companions to their original shape, he yielded to her charms, and made her mother of Telegonus. He visited the infernal regions, and consulted Tiresias how to regain his country in safety; and after he had received every necessary information, he returned on earth. He passed along the coasts of the Sirens unhurt, by the directions of Circe, (*Vid.* Sirenes,) and escaped the whirlpools and shoals of Scylla, and Charybdis. On the coasts of Sicily his companions stole and killed some oxen that were sacred to Apollo, for which the god destroyed the ships, and all were drowned, except Ulysses, who saved himself on a plank, and swam to the island of Calypso, in Ogygia. There, for seven years, he forgot Ithaca, in the arms of the goddess, by whom he had two children. The gods at last interfered, and Calypso, by order of Mercury, suffered him to depart after she had furnished him a ship, and everything requisite for the voyage. He had almost reached the island of Corcyra, when Neptune, still mindful that his son Polyphemus had been robbed of his sight by the perfidy of Ulysses, raised a storm and sank his ship. Ulysses swam with difficulty to the island of the Phæacians, where the kindness of Nausicaa, and the humanity of her father, king Alcinous, entertained him for a while. He related the series of his misfortunes to the monarch, and, at last, by his benevolence, he was conducted in a ship to Ithaca. The Phæacians laid him on the sea-shore as he was asleep, and Ulysses found himself safely restored to his country, after a long absence of 20 years. He was well informed that his palace was besieged by a number of suitors, who continually disturbed the peace of Penelope, and therefore he assumed the habit of a beggar, by the advice of Minerva, and made himself known to his son, and his faithful shepherd Eumæus. With them he took measures to re-establish himself on his throne; he went to the palace, and was personally convinced of the virtues and the fidelity of Penelope. Before his arrival was publicly known, all the importuning suitors were put to death, and Ulysses restored to the peace and bosom of his family. *Vid.* Laertes, Penelope, Telemachus, Eumæus. He lived about 16 years after his return, and was at last killed by his son Telegonus, who had landed in Ithaca, with the hopes of making himself known to his father. This unfortunate event had been foretold to him by Tiresias, who assured him that he should die by the violence of something that was to issue from the bosom of the sea. *Vid.* Telegonus. According to some authors, Ulysses went to consult the oracle of Apollo after his return to Ithaca, and he had the meanness to seduce Erippe, the daughter of a king of Epirus, who had treated him with great kindness. Erippe had a son by him whom she called Euryalus. When come to years of puberty, Euryalus was sent to Ithaca by his mother, but Penelope no sooner knew who he was, than she resolved to destroy him. When, therefore, Ulysses returned, he put to immediate death his unknown son, on the crimination of Penelope his wife, who accused him of attempts upon her virtue. The adventures of Ulysses in his return to Ithaca from the Trojan war are the subject of Homer's Odyssey. *Homer. Il. & Odyss.*—*Virg. Æn.* 2, 3, &c.—*Dictys. Cret.* 1, &c.—*Ovid. Met* 13. *Heroid.* 1.—*Hygin.* fab. 125, 126, 201, &c.—*Apollod.* 3. c. 10.—*Paus.* 1. c. 17 & 22. l. 3. c. 12. l. 6. c. 6. l. 7. c. 4. l. 8. c. 3. l. 10. c. 28.—*Ælian. V.H.* 13. c. 12. —*Horat.* 3. od. 29. v. 8.—*Parthen. Erot.* 3.—*Plut. in qu Gr.* 43. *Propert.* 1. el. 11.—*Ptol. Heph.* 3. *apud Phot.*—*Apul. de Deo.*—*Socr.*—*Lactant. ad Ach.* 1. v. 5. l. 3. v. 76.—*Schol. Sophoc. in Aj.* 190, *& in Phil.* 417.—*Servius. ad Æn.* 2. v. 81. l. 6. v. 529, &c.—*Schol. Hom. Il.* 2. v. 339.—*Sch. Thucyd.* 1. c. 9.—*Qu. Smyr.* 3, 5, &c.—*Plin.* 35. c. 11.—*Tzetzes. ad Lyc.* 344, 384, & 1031, &c.

ULYSSE'UM, a promontory of Sicily west of Pachinus.

UM'BER, a lake of Umbria near the Tiber. *Propert.* 4. el 1. v. 124.

UM'BRA POMPE'IA, a portico of Pompey at Rome. *Mart.* 5 epigr. 10.

UMBRE'NUS P., a freedman who joined in Catiline's conspiracy. *Cic. Cat.* 3. c. 6.—*Sallust. Cat.* 40.

UM'BRIA, a country of Italy, separated from Etruria by the Tiber, bounded on the north by the Adriatic Sea, on the east by Picenum, and the country of the Sabines, and on the south by the river Nar. Some derive the word Umbria *ab imbribus.*, the frequent showers that were supposed to fall there, or from the shadow (*umbra*) of the Apennines which hung over it. Umbria had many cities of note. The Umbrians opposed the Romans in the infancy of their empire, but afterwards became their allies abour the year U.C. 434. *Catull.* 40, v. 11.—*Strab.* 5.—*Plin.* 3. c. 12. l. 8. c. 49.—*Dionys. Hal.*—*Aul. Gell.* 3. c. 2.

UMBRIC'IUS, a soothsayer, who foretold approaching calamities to Galba. *Juv.* 3. v. 21.—*Tacit. H.* 1. c. 27.

UM'BRO, a navigable river of Italy. *Plin.* 3. c. 5. It is now l'Ombrone.

UM'BRO, a general who assisted Turnus against Æneas, and was killed during the war. He could assuage the fury of serpents by his songs, and counteract the poisonous effects of their bites. *Virg. Æn.* 7. v. 752. l. 10. v. 544.

U'NA, a river of Mauritania Tingitana, flowing into the Atlantic Ocean. *Ptol.*

UN'CA, a surname of Minerva among the Phœnicians and the Thebans. The goddess was first known in Ægypt by that name, and Æschylus is the first Greek writer who gives her that appellation, which probably had been introduced into Bœotia by Cadmus. *Æsch. Sep, cont. Th.*—*Euphoris apud Steph. Byz.*—*Schol. Æschy. loco.*—*Hesychius.*—*Gyrald. H.D.* 11.

UN'CHÆ, a town of Mesopotamia, or of Assyria. *Curt.* 4.

UNDECEM'VIRI, magistrates at Athens to whom such as were publicly condemned were delivered to be executed. *C. Nep. in. Phoc.*

UNEL'LI, a people of Cotantin of Normandy in Gaul, conquered by Cæsar. *Cæs. Bell. G.* 2. c. 34.

UNIG'ENA, a surname of Minerva, as sprung from Jupiter alone.

UNX'IA, a surname of Juno, derived from *ungere*, to anoint, because it was usual among the Romans for the bride to anoint the threshhold of her husband, and from this necessary ceremony wives were called Unxores, and afterwards Uxores, from Unxia, who presided over them. *Arnob.* 3.—*Servius in Æn.* 4. v. 458.—*Mart. Capell.* 2.

U'PIS, the father of one of the Dianas mentioned by the ancients, from which circumstance Diana herself is called Upis. *Cic. de Nat. D.* 3. c. 23.—*Callim. in Dian.*—*Palœphat.* c. 32.

U'RA, a place on the Euphrates. *Plin.* 5. c. 24.

URA'NIA, one of the Muses, daughter of Jupiter and Mnemosyne, who presided over astronomy. She is generally called mother of Linus by Apollo, and of the god Hymenæus by Bacchus. She was represented as a young virgin dressed in an azure coloured robe, crowned with stars, and holding a globe in her hands, and having many mathematical instruments placed round. *Hesiod. Theog.* 77.—*Apollod.* 1. c. 2—*Hygin.* fab. 161.—*Catull.* 62. v. 2. [The finest representatien of this Muse will be found in the Vatican at Rome.]——A surname of Venus, the same as Celestial. She was supposed in that character, to preside over beauty and generation, and was called daughter of Uranus or Cœlus by the Light. Her temples in Asia, Africa, Greece, and Italy were numerous. *Plato in Symp.*—*Cic. de Nat. D.* 3. c. 23.—*Paus.* 1. c. 14. l. 3. c. 23. l. 6. c. 25. l. 7. c. 26. l. 9. c. 16.—*Phurnut. de N.D.* 14.—*Voss. Idolol.* 2. c. 21.

URA'NIA, a town of Cyprus.

URA'NII or U'RII, a people of Helvetia.

URANOP'OLIS, a town at the foot of mount Athos, founded by Alexander, brother of Cassander. *Plin.* 4. c. 10.——A city of Pamphylia. *Ptol.*

U'RANUS, a deity the same as Cœlus, the most ancient of all the gods. He married Tithea, or the earth, by whom he had Ceus, Creus, Hyperion, Mnemosyne, Cottus, Phœbe, Briareus, Thetis, Saturn, Giges, called from their mother Titans. His children conspired against him, because he confined them in the bosom of the earth, and his son Saturn mutilated him and drove him from his throne. *Hesiod. Th.* 134.—*Apollod.* 1.—*Lactant.* l. c 11 & 12.

URATHI'NÆ, a city of India without the Ganges. *Ptol.*

UR'BA, now Orbe, a town of the Helvetii, on a river of the same name, at the north of the Lemannus Lacus, now the lake of Geneva.

UR'BARA, a town of Mauritania Cæsariensis. *Ptol.*

URBA'TA, a city of Pannonia. *Antonin.*

UR'BI, a people of India. *Plin.* 6. c. 23.

URBIC'UA, a town of Hispania Tarraconensis. *Liv.* 41. c. 16. It is now Arbecha.

UR'BICUS, an actor at Rome in Domitian's reign. *Juv.* 6.

URBI'NUM, now Urbino, a town of Umbria. *Plin.* 3. c. 14.

URBUB'UMA, a town of Upper Æthiopia. *Plin.* 6. c. 29.

UR'CE, a city of Hispania Tarraconensis. *Ptol.* It is now Aquile.

URCE'SA, a city of the Celtiberi in Hispania Tarraconensis. *Ptol.*

URCIN'IUM, a town of Corsica. *Id.*

U'REMA, a city of Syria. *Id.*

UR'GENUM, a town of Gallia Narbonensis. *Strab.* It is called Enargium by *Antoninus*, and Ernagium by *Ptolemy*.

UR'GI, a people of Sarmatia, between the Ister and the Borysthenes. *Strab.*

UR'GO. now Gorgona, an island in the bay of Pisa, 25 miles west of Leghorn, famous for anchovies. *Plin.* 3. c. 6.

URGULA'NIA, a friend of Livia, in the reign of Tiberius. *Tac. Ann.* 2. c. 34.

U'RI, a people near the Euxine Sea. *Orpheus*—*Plin.* 6. c. 20.

U'RIA, a town of Calabria, built by a Cretan colony. It was also called Hyria, and now bears the name of Oria. *Herodot.* 7. c. 170.—*Plin.* 3. c. 11.—*Strab.* 6.——A town of Apulia.

U'RITES or URI'TES, a people of Italy. *Liv.* 42. c. 48.

URPA'NUS, a river of Pannonia. *Plin.* 3. c. 25. It is now Sarvvicze.

URSEN'TUM, a town of the Brutii, now Orso. *Plin.* 3. c. 11. The people were called Ursentini.

URSE'OLA or URSO'LIS, a city of Gallia Narbonensis. *Antonin.*

URSID'IUS, an adulterer mentioned by *Juvenal*, 6. v. 38.

URTICI'NI, a people of Picenum. *Plin.* Their town is now Ortezzana.

USA'DIUM, a promontory of Mauritania Tingitana. *Ptol.*

USCA'NA, a town of Macedonia. *Liv.* 43. c. 18.

US'CENUM, a town of the Jazyges. *Ptol.*

USCE'TA, a town of Africa Propria. *Hirt. Af.* 89.

USCUD'AMA, a town of Thrace, afterwards called Adrianopolis. *Amm. Marcell.*

USEL'LIS, a city of Sardinia. *Ptol.*

USIL'LA, a city of Byzacene. *Id.*

USIP'ETES or USIP'II, a people of Germany at the east of the Rhine. *Cæs. Bell. G.* 4. c. 1, &c.

US'PEN, a city of the Siraci. *Tacit. Ann.* 12. c. 16.

USTI'CA, a town in an island on the coast of Sicily, near Panormum. *Horat.* 1. od. 17. v. 11.

U'TENS, a river of Gallia Cispadana, now Montone, falling into the Adriatic by Ravenna. *Liv.* 5 c. 35.

U'TICA, now Biserta or Beusert, a celebrated city of Africa, on the coast of the Mediterranean, on the same bay as Carthage, founded by a Syrian colony about 287 years before Carthage. It had a large and commodious harbour, and became the metropolis of Africa, after the destruction of Carthage, in the third Punic war, and the Romans granted it all the lands situate between Hippo and Carthage. It is celebrated for the death of Cato, who from that event is called *Uticensis*, or of Utica. *Strab.* 17.—*Lucan.* 6. v. 306—*Justin.* 18. c. 4.—*Plin.* 16. c. 40.—*Liv.* 25. c. 31.—*Sil.* 3. v. 242.—*Horat.* 1. ep. 20. v. 13.

UTIDA'VA, a town of Dacia. *Ptol.*

UX'AMA, a town of Spain on the Iberus. *Sil.* 3. v. 384.—*Plin.* 3. c. 3.

UXAN'TIS, now Ushant, an island on the coast of Britany.

UXELLODU'NUM, a town of Gallia Aquitanica, on the Oldus, one of the branches of the Garonne, defended by steep rocks now Puech d'Issoudun. *Cæs B. G.* 8. c. 38.

UXEN'TUM, a town of Calabria, now Ugento.

UXEN'TUS, a mountain of India Citerior. *Ptol.*

UX'II, mountains of Armenia, with a nation of the same name, conquered by Alexandria. The Tigris rises in their country.—*Strab.*—*Diod.*

UXIS'AMA, an island in the western ocean. *Strab.* It was probably one of the Azores.

UZE'CIA, a city of Africa Propria. *Ptol.*

U'ZITA or **UZI'TA**, an inland town of Africa, destroyed by Cæsar. *Hirt. de Afric.* 41, &c.

V.

VA'BAR, a town of Mauritania Cæsariensis. *Ptol.*

VACA'RIA or **AVACA'RIA**, a place in Africa Propria. *Antonin.*

VACATIO'NE (*lex de*), was enacted concerning the exemption from military service, and contained this very remarkable clause, *nisi bellum Gallicum exoriatur*, in which case the priests themselves were not exempted from service. This intimates how apprehensive the Romans were of the Gauls, by whom their city had once been taken.

VAC'CA, a town of Numidia. *Sallust. Jug.* c. 66. ——A river of Spain. It is called Vacua by *Strabo* and Vacus by *Ptolemy*, and is now Vouga.

VACCÆ'I, a people of Hispania Tarraconensis, through whose country the Durius flows. Their country is now Regno di Leon. *Liv.* 21. c. 5. l. 35. c. 7. l. 46. c. 47.

VAC'CUS M. VITRUV., a general of the Fundani and Privernates against Rome. His house at Rome was pulled down, and the land (*Vacci prata*) appropriated to the public. *Cic. Dom.* 38.—*Liv.* 8. c. 19.

VACER'RA, a lawyer in the age of Cicero. *Cic.* 7. *Fam.* 8.

VACOM'AGI, a people of Albion. *Ptol.*

VACON'TIUM, a town of Lower Pannonia. *Id.*

VACO'RIUM, a city of Noricum. *Id.*

VACU'NA, a goddess at Rome, who presided over repose and leisure, as the word (*vacare*) indicates. Her festivals were observed in the month of December. Her temple and grove at Reate in the country of the Sabines were famous. *Plin.* 3. c. 12.—*Ovid. Fast.* 6. v. 307.—*Horat.* 1. ep. 10. v. 49.

VADA'TA, a city of Cappadocia. *Ptol.*

VADDA'SI, a people of Media, *Id.*

VADE'NI, a people of Arabia Felix. *Id.*

VADICAS'SII, a people of Gallia Lugdunensis. *Plin.* 4. c. 18.

VADIMO'NIS LA'CUS, now Bassanella, a lake of Etruria, the waters of which were sulphureous. The Etrurians were defeated there by the Romans; and the Gauls by Dolabella. *Plin.* 2. c. 96.—*Liv.* 9. c. 39.—*Flor.* 1. c. 13.—*Plin.* 8. ep. 20.

VAD'NIA, a city of the Cantabri. *Ptol.*

VÆRI'ACA, a city of Phœnicia. *Lib. Notit.*

VÆS'APA, a city of Armenia Minor. *Ptol.*

VA'GA or **VAGEN'SE** (*oppidum*), a town of Africa. *Sil.* 3. v. 259.—*Plin.* 5. c. 4.

VA'GAL, a town of Mauritania Cæsariensis. *Antonin.*

VAGEDRU'SA, a river of Sicily between the towns of Camarina and Gela. *Sil.* 14. v. 229.

VAGEL'LIUS, an obscene lawyer of Mutina. *Juv.* 16. v. 23.

VAGE'NI or **VAGIEN'NI**, a people of Liguria, at the sources of the Po, whose capital was called *Augusta Vagiennorum*. *Sil.* 8. v. 606.—*Plin.* 3. c. 5. They are called Bagienni by *Varro*, Batieni by *Ptolemy*, and Bacienni by *Paterculus*.

VAGITA'NUS, a god at Rome who presided over the cries of children. He was represented under the form of a weeping genius. *Aug. de Civ. D.* 4. c. 8.—*Gyrald. H. D.* 1.

VAGNI'ACUM or **VAGNI'ACÆ**, a town of Albion. *Antonin.* It is now Maidstone according to *Camden*; or Wrotham according to *Talbot*.

VA'HALIS, a river of the Batavi, or rather a part of the Rhine. It is now called the Waal. *Tacit. Ann.* 2. c. 6.

VA'LA, a city of Thrace. *Ptol.*——A city of Mauritania Tingitana. *Id.*

VA'LA C. NUMO'NIUS, a friend of *Horace*, to whom the poet addressed 1. ep. 15.

VAL'CUM, a town of Lower Pannonia. *Antonin.* It is now Veltz according to *Simler*, or Valcowar according to others.

VALDA'NUS, a river of Lower Pannonia. *Plin.* 3. c. 25. It is now Valpo.

VAL'ENA, a town of Upper Pannonia. *Ptol.* It is now Valbach.

VA'LENS FLA'VIUS, a son of Gratian, born in Pannonia. His brother Valentinian took him as his colleague on the throne, and appointed him over the eastern parts of the Roman empire. The bold measures and threats of the rebel Procopius frightened the new emperor; and if his friends had not intervened, he would have willingly resigned all his pretensions to the empire, which his brother had entrusted to his care. By perseverance, however, Valens was enabled to destroy his rival, and to distinguish himself in his wars against the northern barbarians. But his lenity to these savage intruders proved fatal to the Roman power; and by permitting some of the Goths to settle in the provinces of Thrace, and to have free access to every part of the country, Valens encouraged them to make depredations on his subjects, and to disturb their tranquillity. His eyes were opened too late; he attempted to repel them, but he failed in the attempt. A bloody battle was fought, in which the barbarians obtained some advantage, and Valens was hurried away by the obscurity of the night, and the affection of his soldiers for his person, into a lonely house, which the Goths set on fire. Valens, unable to make his escape, was burnt alive in the 50th year of his age, after a reign of 15 years, A.D. 378. He has been blamed for his superstition and cruelty, in putting to death all such of his subjects whose name began with *Theod.*, because he had been informed by his favorite astrologers, that his crown would devolve upon the head of an officer whose name began with these letters. Valens did not possess many of the high qualities which distinguish a great and powerful monarch. He was illiterate, and of a disposition naturally indolent and inactive. Yet though timorous in the highest degree, he was warlike; and though fond of ease, he was acquainted with the character of his officers, and preferred none but such as possessed merit. He was a great friend of discipline, a pattern of chastity and temperance, and showed himself always ready to listen to the just complaints of his subjects, though he gave an attentive ear to flattery and malevolent informations. *Ammian. Marcell. Hist.* l. 31.—*Ruffin.*—*Socrat.*—*Theodoret.*—*Oros.* &c.——A general of the emperor Honorius.——The name of the father of the second Mercury mentioned by *Cicero de Nat. D.* 3. c. 22. This appellation may be considered as more properly belonging to Jupiter.

VA'LENS PUB'LIUS VALE'RIUS, a proconsul of Achaia, who proclaimed himself emperor of Rome, when Macrian, who had been invested with the purple in the east, attempted to assassinate him. He reigned only six months, and was murdered by his soldiers, A.D. 261. *Poll. de* 30. *Tyran.* c. 19.

VA'LENS FA'BIUS, a friend of Vitellius, whom he saluted emperor, in opposition to Otho. He was greatly honored by Vitellius, &c.

VALEN'TIA, one of the ancient names of Rome. *Servius ad Æn.* 1. v. 277.—*Solin.* 2.

VALEN'TIA, a goddess worshipped at Ocriculum in Italy. *Tertull. Apol.* 24.—*Gyrald. H. D.* 1.

VALEN'TIA, a town of Spain, a little below Saguntum, founded by J. Brutus, and for some time known by the name of Julia Colonia. *Plin.* 3. c. 3 & 4.——A town of Italy.——A town of Sardinia. ——A colony and city of Gallia Narbonensis. *Ptol.*

VALENTI'NI, a people of Sardinia. *Ptol.*—*Plin.* 3. c. 7.——A people of Calabria. *Plin.* 3. c. 11.

VALENTINIA'NUS the First, son of Gratian, raised to the imperial throne by his merit and valor. He kept the western part of the empire for himself, and appointed his brother Valens over the east. He gave the most convincing proof of his military valor in the victories which he obtained over the barbarians in the provinces of Gaul, the deserts of Africa, and on the banks of the Rhine and the Danube. The insolence of the Quadi he punished with great severity; and when these desperate and indigent barbarians entreated the conqueror for mercy, Valentinian treated them with contempt, and upbraided them with every mark of resentment. While he spoke with much warmth, he broke a blood vessel, and fell lifeless on the ground. He was conveyed into his palace by his attendants, and soon after died, after suffering the greatest agonies, violent fits, and contortions of his limbs, on the 17th of November, A.D. 375. He was then in the 55th year of his age, and had reigned 12 years. He has been represented by some, as cruel and covetous in the highest degree. He was naturally of an irascible disposition, and he gratified his pride in expressing a contempt for those who were his equals in military abilities, or who shone for gracefulness or elegance of address. *Ammian. Marcell.* l. 30.—*Prosper. & Cassiodor. in Chron.* &c.

Valentinia'nus the Second, second son of the preceding, was proclaimed emperor a few days after his father's death, though only 10 years old. He succeeded his brother Gratian, as sole emperor, A.D. 383, but his youth seemed to favor dissension, and the attempts and the usurpations of rebels. He was robbed of his throne by Maximus, four years after the death of Gratian; and in this helpless situation he had recourse to Theodosius, who was then emperor of the east. He was successful in his applications; Maximus was conquered by Theodosius, and Valentinian entered Rome in triumph, accompanied by his benefactor. He was some time after strangled by one of his officers, a native of Gaul, called Arbogastus, in whom he had placed too much confidence, and from whom he expected more deference than the ambition of a barbarian could pay. This happened on the 15th of May, A.D. 392, at Vienne, one of the modern towns of France. Valentinian reigned nine years. He has been commended for his many virtues, and the applause which the populace bestowed upon him was bestowed upon real merit. He abolished the greater part of the taxes; and because his subjects complained that he was too fond of the amusements of the circus, he ordered all such festivals to be abolished, and all the wild beasts that were kept for the entertainment of the people to be slain. He was remarkable for his benevolence and clemency, not only to his friends, but even to such as had conspired against his life; and he used to say, that tyrants alone are suspicious. He was fond of imitating the virtues and exemplary life of his friend and patron Theodosius, and if he had lived longer, the Romans might have enjoyed peace and security. *Marcell. in Chron.*—*Ambros. in Valent.*—*Socrat.*—*Sozom.*—*Ruffin.*, &c.

Valentinia'nus the Third, was son of Constantius and Placidia, the daughter of Theodosius the Great, and therefore, as related to the imperial family, he was saluted emperor in his youth, and publicly acknowledged as such at Rome, the 3rd of October, A.D. 423, about the 6th year of his age. He was at first governed by his mother, and the intrigues of his generals and courtiers; and when he came to years of discretion, he disgraced himself by violence, oppression, and incontinence. He was murdered in the midst of Rome, A.D. 454, in the 36th year of his age, and the 31st of his reign, by Petronius Maximus, to whose wife he had offered violence. The vices of Valentinian the Third were conspicuous; he wished to gratify every passion at the expense of his honor, his health, and his character; and as he lived without one single act of benevolence or kindness, he died lamented by none, though pitied for his imprudence and vicious propensities. He was the last of the family of Theodosius. *Cassiodor. & Marcellin. in Chron.*—*Evagr.* l. 2.—*Procop*, &c.

Valentinia'nus, a son of the emperor Gratian, who died when very young.

VALEN'TIUS A., an interpreter in the service of Verres in Sicily. *Cic. Verr.* 3. c. 37.

VALEPON'GA, a city of Spain between Liminium and Cæsaraugusta. *Antonin.*

VALE'RIA, a sister of Poplicola, who advised the Roman matrons to go and deprecate the resentment of Coriolanus. *Plut. in Cor.*——A daughter of Poplicola, given as a hostage to Porsenna by the Romans. She fled from the enemy's country with Clœlia, and swam across the Tiber. *Plut. de Virt. Mul.*——A woman of Tusculum, who committed incest with her father, and became mother of Sylvanus. *Plut. in Par.* 22.——A daughter of Messala, sister to Hortensius, who married Sylla. ——The wife of the emperor Valentinian.——The wife of the emperor Galerius.

Vale'ria, a town of Spain. *Plin* 3. c. 3.

Vale'ria Vi'a, a road in Sicily, which led from Messana to Lilybæum. *Strab.*

Vale'ria Lex, *de provocatione*, by P. Valerius Poplicola, the sole consul, A.U.C. 243. It permitted an appeal from a magistrate to the people, and forbade the magistrate to punish the citizen for making an appeal. It further made it a capital crime for a citizen to aspire to the sovereignty of Rome, or to exercise any office without the choice and approbation of the people. *Val. Max.* 4. c. 1.—*Liv.* 2. c. 8.—*Dion Hal.* 4.—Another, *de debitoribus*, by Valerius Flaccus. It required that all creditors should discharge their debtors, on receiving a fourth part of the whole sum.—Another by M. Valerius Corvinus, A.U.C. 453, which confirmed the first Valerian law, enacted by Poplicola.—Another, called also *Horatia*, by L. Valerius and M. Horatius the consuls, A.U.C. 304. It revived the first Valerian law, which, under the triumvirate had lost its force.—Another, *de magistratibus*, by P. Valerius Poplicola, sole consul, A.U.C. 243. It created two quæstors to take care of the public treasure, which was for the future to be kept in the temple of Saturn. *Plut. in Pop.*—*Liv.* 2.

VALERIA'NUS PUB'LIUS LICIN'IUS, a Roman, proclaimed emperor by the armies in Rhætia, A.D. 254. The virtues which shone in him when a private man, were lost when he ascended the throne. Formerly distinguished for his temperance, moderation, and many virtues, which fixed the uninfluenced choice of all Rome upon him, Valerian, when invested with the purple, displayed inability and meanness. He was cowardly in his operations, and, though acquainted with war, and the patron of science, he seldom acted with prudence, or favored men of true genius and merit. He took his son Gallienus as his colleague in the empire, and showed the malevolence of his heart by persecuting the Christians whom he had for a while tolerated. He also made war against the Goths and Scythians; but in an expedition which he undertook against Sapor, king of Persia, his arms were attended with ill success. He was conquered in Mesopotamia, and when he wished to have a private conference with Sapor, the conqueror seized his person, and carried him in triumph to his capital, where, and in all the cities of his empire, he exposed him to the ridicule and insolence of his subjects. When the Persian monarch mounted on horseback, Valerian served as a footstool, and the many other insults which he suffered, excited indignation even among the courtiers of Sapor. The monarch at last ordered him to be flayed alive, and salt to be thrown over his mangled body, so that he died in the greatest torments. His skin was tanned and painted red; and, that the ignominy of the Roman empire might be lasting, it was nailed up in one of the temples of Persia. Valerian died in the 71st year of his age, A.D. 260, after a reign of seven years. *Aurel. Victor. de Cæs. Eutrop.*—*Euseb.*—*Oros.* &c. [A bust larger than life of this emperor will be found in the Vatican at Rome.]

Valeria'nus P. Licin'ius Saloni'nus, a grandson of Valerian, the emperor. He was put to death, when his father, the emperor Gallienus, was killed. *Trebell. Poll. in Gallien.* c 14.

Valeria'nus, one of the generals of the usurper Niger.——A worthy senator, put to death by Heliogabalus.

Valeria'nus Asiat'icus a governor of Gallia Belgica, in the age of Vitellius. *Tac. Hist.* 1. c. 59.

VALE'RII, a patrician family at Rome, anciently called Valesii. The Valerian family branched into the Lævini, Flacci, Messalæ, Maximi, &c., and distinguished itself for patriotism, military valor, and an ardent love of liberty. *Liv.* 2. c. 8, &c.—*Dionys.* 5. c. 19.—*Quintil.* 1. c. 4.

VALE'RIUS AN'TIAS, an excellent Roman historian in the age of Marius and Sylla, often quoted, and particularly by Livy. *Plin.* 2. c. 107.—*Plut.* —*Priscian.* l. 9.—*A. Gell.* 7. c. 9.—*Voss. H. Lat.* 1. c. 10.

VALE'RIUS ASIAT'ICUS, a celebrated Roman, accused of having murdered one of the relations of the emperor Claudius. He was condemned by the intrigues of Messalina though innocent, and he opened his veins and bled to death. *Tacit. Ann.* 11. c. 3.—*Senec. de Tranquill. Animi.* 2. c. 18.

VALE'RIUS CAP'ITO, a prætor disgraced by Agrippina, but restored by Nero after her death. *Tacit. Ann.* 14. c. 12.

VALE'RIUS CORVI'NUS, a tribune of the soldiers under Camillus. When the Roman army was challenged by one of the Senones, remarkable for his strength and stature, Valerius undertook to engage him, and obtained an easy victory, by means of a crow that assisted him, and attacked the face of the Gaul, whence his surname of Corvinus. Valerius triumphed over the Etrurians, and the neighbouring states that made war against Rome, and was six times honored with the consulship. He died in the 100th year of his age, admired and regretted for many private and public virtues. *Val. Max.* 8. c. 13.—*Liv.* 7. c. 27, &c.—*Plut. in Mar.* —*Cic. in Cat.*

VALE'RIUS MAR'CUS CORVI'NUS MESSA'LA, a Roman, made consul with Augustus. He distinguished himself by his learning as well as military virtues. He lost his memory about two years before his death, and, according to some, he was even ignorant of his own name. *Sueton. in Aug.*—*Cic. in Brut.*

VALE'RIUS FABIA'NUS, a youth condemned under Nero, for counterfeiting the will of one of his friends. *Tacit. Ann.* 14. c. 48.

VALE'RIUS FLAC'CUS, a Roman intimate with Cato the censor. He was consul with him, and cut off an army of 10,000 Gauls in one battle. He was also chosen censor, and prince of the senate. *Liv.* 34. c. 1, 2, 3.

VALE'RIUS CA'IUS FLAC'CUS SETI'NUS, a Latin poet born at Padua, or, according to others, at Setia, a town of Campania, in the age of Vespasian. He wrote a poem in eight books on the Argonautic expedition, containing 5605 verses, but it remained unfinished on account of his premature death. The Argonauts were there left on the sea in their return home. Some critics have been lavish in their praises upon Flaccus, and have called him the second poet of Rome, after Virgil. His poetry, however, is deemed by some, frigid and languishing, his style uncouth and inelegant, and many of his lines are translated from the Argonautica of Apollonius of Rhodes. The best editions of Flaccus are those of Burman. L. Bat. 1724, and 12mo. Utr. 1702, and the Bipont, 1786, 8vo. *Harles. Not. Lit. Rom.* 1. p. 463.—*Sax. Onom.* 1. p. 264.—*Martial.* 1. epigr. 62, 77, &c.—*Quintil.* 10. c. 1. 90.

VALE'RIUS LÆVI'NUS, a consul who fought against Pyrrhus during the Tarentine war. *Vid.* Lævinus.

VALE'RIUS MAR'CUS, a brother of Poplicola, who defeated the army of the Sabines in two battles. He was honored with a triumph, and the Romans, to show their sense of his great merit built him a house on mount Palatine, at the public expense.

VALE'RIUS MAX'IMUS, a Latin historian who carried arms under the sons of Pompey. He dedicated his time to study, and wrote an account of all the most celebrated sayings and actions of the Romans, and other illustrious persons, which is still extant, and divided into nine books. It is dedicated to Tiberius. Some have supposed that he lived after the age of Tiberius, from the want of purity and elegance, which so conspicuously appear in his writings, unworthy of the correctness of the golden age of the Roman literature. The best editions of Valerius are that of Torrenius, 4to. L. Bat. 1726, of Vorstius, 8vo. Berolin. 1672. of Knappe, Lips. 1782, and the Bipont of 1783. *Harles. Not. Lit. Rom.* 1. p. 344.—*Sax. Onom.* 1. p. 235.—*Voss. de H. L.* p. 122.——A brother of Poplicola.

Q. VALE'RIUS OR'CA, a lieutenant of Cæsar, sent by him into Sicily. *Cæsar. B. C.* l. 1. c. 29.

VALE'RIUS PAULI'NUS, a friend of the emperor Vespasian. *Tac. Hist.* 3. c. 42.

VALE'RIUS POTI'TUS, a general who stirred up the people and army against the decemvirs, and Appius Claudius in particular. He was chosen consul, and conquered the Volsci and Æqui. *Plut.*

VALE'RIUS PRÆCONI'NUS, a lieutenant of Cæsar's army in Gaul, slain in a skirmish. *Cæs. Com.* 3. c. 20.

VALE'RIUS PRO'BUS, a grammarian under Adrian. *Servius in Æn.*

M. VALE'RIUS PRO'BUS, another grammarian who wrote commentaries on the Bucolics and Georgics of Virgil. His "Instituta Artium" were published, Mediolan. 1504, and in the "Grammatici Veteres" of Putsch. His book "De Interpretandis Romanorum Literis" was edited by Ernstius, Soræ, 1647. *Harles. Not. Lit. Rom.* 1. p. 355.—*Sax. Onom.* 1. p. 249.

VALE'RIUS, a friend of Vitellius.

VALE'RIUS PUB'LIUS, a celebrated Roman, surnamed *Poplicola*, for his popularity. He was very active in assisting Brutus to expel the Tarquins, and he was the first who took an oath to support the liberty and independence of his country. Though he had been refused the consulship, and had retired with great dissatisfaction from the direction of affairs, yet he regarded the public opinion, and when the jealousy of the Romans inveighed against the towering appearance of his house, he acknowledged the reproof, and in making it lower, he showed his wish to be on a level with his fellow-citizens, and not to erect what might be considered as a citadel for the oppression of his country. He was afterwards honored with the consulship, on the expulsion of Collatinus, and triumphed over the Etrurians, after he had gained a victory in the battle in which Brutus and the sons of Tarquin had fallen. Valerius died after he had been four times consul, and enjoyed the popularity, and received the thanks and the gratitude, which a people redeemed from slavery and oppression usually pay to their patrons and deliverers. He was so poor, that his body was buried at the public expense. The Roman matrons mourned his death a whole year. *Plut. in Vitâ.* —*Flor.* 1. c. 9.—*Liv.* 1. c. 58, &c.

VALE'RIUS SORA'NUS, a Latin poet, in the age of Julius Cæsar, put to death for betraying a secret. He acknowledged no god, but the soul of the universe.

VAL'ERUS, a friend of Turnus against Æneas. *Virg. Æn.* 10. v. 752.

VAL'GIUS TI'TUS RU'FUS, a Roman poet in the Augustan age, celebrated for the elegance and happy turn of his poetry. He was intimate with Horace, Tibullus, and other great men, and the wits of the age, and was considered as highly capable of celebrating the wars, the heroic actions, and superior eloquence of his friend Messala Corvinus. He has, however, been accused of ignorance, in saying that Ætna was the only volcano in the world. Only five verses remain of his poetry. *Tibull.* 3. el. 1. v. 180.—*Horat.* 1. sat. 10. v 82.—*Harles. Not. Lit. Rom.* 1. p. 305.

VAL'GIUS C. HIPPIA'NUS, a friend of Cicero, adopted into the family of the Valgii. *Cic.* 13. *Fam.* 76.

VAL'GIUS CA'IUS, a botanist who presented an unfinished work on herbs to Augustus. *Plin.* 25. c. 2.

VAL'GIUS, a rhetorician, disciple to Apollodorus. *Quintil.* 3. c. 1, &c.——A son-in-law of Sylla. *Cic. Rull.* 3. c. 1.

VA'LI, a people of Asia, on the Palus Mæotis. *Plin.* 6. c. 7.

VA'LII, a people of Æthiopia. *Plin.* 6. c. 30.

VAL'LÆ, a city of Pieria in Macedonia. *Ptol.* *Pliny*, 4. c. 10, calls the inhabitants Vallæi.

VAL'LI, a people of Asia near the *Portæ Caucasiæ*. *Plin.* 6. c. 11.

VALLI'NA or VALLO'NIA, a goddess at Rome, who presided over valleys. *Aug. de Civ. D.* 4. c. 8.—*Gyrald. H. D.* 1.—*Voss. Idolol.* 2. c. 62.

VAL'LIS AL'BA, a place of Phœnicia. *Lib. Not.*

VAL'LIS CARMIA'NA or CARINIA'NA, a city of Pannonia. *Antonin.*

VAL'LIS DOMITIA'NI, a place of Lower Mysia, near the mouth of the Danube. *Id.*

VAL'LIUS, a celebrated declaimer mentioned by *Seneca.*

VA'LON, a river of Mauritania Tingitana. *Ptol.*

VA'MA, a river emptying itself into the Ganges. *Plin.* 6. c. 18.——A city of the Celtici, in Spain. It is Οὔαμα in Greek, some read Οὔλμα.

VAMAC'URES, a people of Africa Propria. *Plin.* 5. c. 4.

VAMICE'LA, a town of Mauritania Cæsariensis. *Ptol.*

VANACI'NI, a people of Corsica, near the promontory now called Capo Corso. *Id.*

VANDABAN'DA, a region of Sogdiana. *Id.*

VAN'DALI, VANDA'LII, VIN'DILI or VAN'-DULI, a people of Germany. *Tacit. de Germ.* c. 3.

VANGA'LIA, an island near Taprobane. *Id.*

VAN'GIO, the nephew of Vannius, king of the Suevi. He attempted to depose his uncle. *Tac. Ann.* 12. c. 29.

VANGI'ONES, a people of Germany. Their capital, Borbetomagus, is now called Worms. *Lucan.* 1. v. 431.—*Cæs. G.* 1. c. 51.

VA'NIUS, a city of Lower Libya. *Ptol.*

VAN'NIA, a town of Italy, north of the Po, now called Civeda. *Id.*

VAN'NIUS, a king of the Suevi, banished under Claudius, &c. *Tacit. Ann.* 12. c. 29.

VAPIN'CUM, a town of Gallia Narbonensis. *Antonin.*

VAR'ADA, a city of the Carpetani, in Spain. *Ptol.*

VAR'AMUS, a river of Venetia. *Plin.* 3. c. 18. It is now Varamo.

VARA'NES, a name common to some of the Persian monarchs, in the age of the Roman emperors.

VAR'BARA, a city of Mauritania Cæsariensis. *Ptol.*

VAR'CIA, a city of Gallia Belgica. *Antonin.*

VARDÆ'I, a people of Dalmatia. *Cic. Fam.* 5. ep. 9.—*Plin.* 3. c. 22.

VAR'DULI, a people of Hispania Tarraconensis. *Plin.* 4. c. 22.—*Mela*, 3. c. 1.—*Ptol.* Their country is now Guipuscoa.

VARENTA'NUM, now Valentano, an inland town of Etruria. *Antonin.*

VARE'NUS L., a man accused of murder and defended by Cicero. The oration spoken on the occasion is lost. *Quintil.* 4. c. 2, &c.

VARETA'TÆ, a people of India. *Plin.* 6. c. 20.

VARE'TUM, a river of Cappadocia. *Id.* 6. c. 2.

VARGID'IUS M., a Roman knight, mentioned by *Cicero*, 10. *Fam.* 7.

VAR'GULA, a man mentioned as witty and loquacious by *Cicero*, *Orat.* 2 c. 60.

VARGUNTE'IUS, a Roman senator, engaged in Catiline's conspiracy. His part was the murder of Cicero in his bed. *Sall. Cat.* 28.—*Cic. Sull.* 2.

VARGUNTE'IUS Q., a Roman who repeated the annals of Ennius, after the manner of the Greek rhapsodists. *Suet. de Gramm.* c. 2.—*A. Gell.* 18. c. 5.

VA'RIA, a town of Hispania Tarraconensis. *Strab.*—*Plin.* 3. c. 3.—*Ptol.*

VA'RIA LEX, *de majestate*, by the tribune L. Varius. A.U.C. 662. It ordained that all such as had assisted the confederates in their war against Rome, should be publicly tried.—Another *de civitate*, by Q. Varius Hybrida of Sucro. It punished all such as were suspected of having assisted or supported the people of Italy in their petition to become free citizens of Rome. *Cic. pro Mil.* 36. *in Brut.* 56, 88, &c.

VARIA'NA, a town of Upper Pannonia. *Antonin.*——A town of Lower Mysia, on the Danube. *Id.*

VARI'NI, a people of Germany. *Tacit. de Ger.* 40.

VARI'NUS P., a governor of Asia, mentioned by *Cicero*, *Flacc.* 19.

VARIS'TI, a people of Germany. *Tac. Germ.* c. 42.

VA'RIUS or VA'RUS LU'CIUS, a tragic poet, intimate with Horace and Virgil. He was one of those whom Augustus appointed to revise Virgil's Æneid. Besides tragedies, he wrote a panegyric on the emperor, and indeed so highly were his abilities esteemed, that Horace, not less in the language of truth than of partiality, declares, that he was the only poet capable of celebrating the heroic achievements and illustrious character of M. Agrippa. Among his tragedies his Thyestes has been particularly mentioned by Quintilian as a most happy effusion, as possessing all the elegance, pathos, and sublimity which we admire on the Grecian stage. Only 13 verses of all his compositions have survived the ravages of time, and they seem little inferior to the finished lines of his friend and favorite Virgil. *Harles. Not. Lit. Rom.* 1. p. 305.—*Virg. Ecl.* 6. v. 10. *Ecl.* 9. v. 26.—*Quintil.* 10.—*Horat.* 1. sat. 5. v. 40.—*Martial.* 8. epigr. 17. l. 12. epigr. 4.—*Servius ad Virg. Ecl.* 3. v. 20. *Ecl.* 6. v. 12. *Ecl.* 9. v. 35.

VA'RIUS, a native of Sucro in Spain, who, though of a disagreeable appearance, raised his reputation by the power of his oratory. He was the author of the Varia lex, which at last proved fatal to himself. *Cic. de Orat.* 1. c. 25. *Br.* 89 *N. D* 3. c. 33.—*Val. Max.* 3. c. 7.——One of the friends of Antony, surnamed Cotylon. *Cic. Ph.* 8. c. 10. l. 13. c. 12.——A man in the reign of Otho, punished for his adulteries, &c. *Tac. Ann.* 4. c. 42.

VARONIA'NUM, a town of Lower Pannonia. *Antonin.*

VARP'NA, a city of Aria. *Ptol.*

VAR'RO M. TERENTIUS, a Roman consul defeated at Cannæ, by Annibal. *Vid.* Terentius.——A Latin writer, celebrated for his great learning. He wrote no less than fifty different volumes, which are all lost, except some fragments of six books of a treatise *de linguâ Latinâ*, written in his eightieth year, and dedicated to the orator Cicero, and three books *de re rusticâ*. He was Pompey's lieutenant in his piratical wars, and obtained a naval crown. In the civil wars he was taken by Cæsar, and proscribed, but escaped. He has been greatly commended by Cicero for his erudition, and St. Augustin says, that it cannot but be wondered how Varro, who read such a number of books, could find time to compose so many volumes; and how he who composed so many volumes, could be at leisure to peruse such a variety of books, and gain so much literary information. He died B.C. 28, in the 88th year of his age. The best editions of Varro are that of Durdrecht, 8vo, 1619, of Amstel. 1623, and Bipont. 1788. *Harles. Not. Lit. Rom.* 1. p. 119. *Cic. in Acad.* 1. *ad Fam.* 11. ep. 10.—*Quintil.* 10. c. 1.—*Lactant. de fals. Rel.* 6.—*Aul. Gell.* 4. c. 9.—*Servius ad Æn.* 10. v. 175. l. 11. v. 787.—*Arnob.* 5.

VAR'RO P. TERENT., surnamed *Atacinus*, because born near the Atax or Aude, a river of Gaul, flourished in the age of J. Cæsar. He translated into Latin verse the Argonautica of Apollonius Rhodius, with great correctness and elegance. He also wrote a poem entitled *De bello Sequanico*, besides many epigrams and an elegiac poem in which he celebrated the beauty and accomplishments of his favorite Leucadia. Some fragments of his verses are still extant to the number of only 12 verses. He failed in his attempts to write satire. *Harles. Not. Lit. Rom.* 1. p. 124.—*Ruhnken. Epist. crit.* 2. p. 199.—*Horat.* 1. sat. 10. v. 46.—*Ovid. Am* 1. el. 15.—*Quint.* 10. c. 1.—*Propert.* 2. el. 25. v. 85.—*Gyrald. H. P.* 4.

VARRO'NIS VIL'LA, now Vicovaro, was situate on the Anio, in the country of the Sabines. *Cic. Phil.* 2. ep. 41.

.S. VA'RUS QUINTIL'IUS, a Roman proconsul, descended from an illustrious family. He was appointed governor of Syria, and afterwards made commander of the armies in Germany. He was surprised by the enemy, under Arminius, a crafty and dissimulating chief, and his army was cut to pieces. When he saw that every thing was lost, he killed himself, A.D. 10, and his example was followed by some of his officers. His head was afterwards sent to Augustus at Rome, by one of the barbarian chiefs, as also his body; and so great was the influence of this defeat upon the emperor, that he continued for whole months to show all the marks of dejection and deep sorrow, often exclaiming, "O Varus, restore me my legions." The bodies of the slain were left on the field of battle, where they were found six years after by Germanicus, and buried with great pomp. Varus has been taxed with insolence and cowardice, and some have intimated, that if he had not trusted too much to the insinuations of the barbarian chiefs, he might have not only escaped ruin, but have awed the Germans into their duty. His avarice was also conspicuous; he went poor to Syria, whence he returned loaded with riches. *Horat.* 1. od. 24.—*Paterc.* 2. c. 117.—*Flor.* 4. c. 12.—*Virg. Ecl.* 6.

Va'rus Quintil'ius, a son of Varus, who married a daughter of Germanicus.—*Tacit. Ann.* 4. c. 6. ——A friend of Horace, and other great men in the Augustan age. He was a good judge of poetry, and a great critic, as *Horace, Art. P.* 438, seems to insinuate. The poet has addressed the 18th ode of his first book to him, and in the 24th he mourns pathetically his death. Some suppose this Varus to be the person killed in Germany, while others believe him to be a man who devoted his time more to the muses than to war. *Vid.* Varius.

Va'rus, the name of the father and grandfather of the Varus who was killed in Germany They slew themselves with their own swords, the one after the battle of Philippi, and the other in the plains of Pharsalia. *Paterc.* 2. c. 71.

Va'rus Lu'cius, an Epicurean philosopher intimate with Julius Cæsar. Some suppose that it was to him that Virgil inscribed his sixth eclogue. He is commended by *Quintilian*, 6. c. 3. 78.

Va'rus Alfe'nus, a Roman, who though originally a shoemaker, became consul, and distinguished himself by his abilities as an orator. He was buried at the public expense, an honor granted to few, and only to persons of merit. *Horat.* 1. sat. 3.

Va'rus Ac'cius, one of the friends of Cato in Africa, &c.

Va'rus, a river which falls into the Mediterranean, at the west of Nice, after separating Liguria from Gallia Narbonensis. *Lucan.* 1. v. 404.

VAS'ACES, a leader of the Parthian cavalry under Vologeses. *Tac. Ann*, 15. c. 14.

VASA'TES or **VASA'TÆ**, a people of Gallia Aquitanica. They are called Vassei by *Pliny*, 4. c. 19.

VASCO'NES or **VAS'CONES**, a people of Spain, on the Pyrenees. They were reduced to such a state of famine by Metellus, that they fed on human flesh. *Plin.* 3. c. 3.—*Auson.* 2 v. 100.—*Juv.* 15. v. 93.

VA'SIO, a town of Gaul in modern Provence. *Cic. Fam.* 10. ep. 34.—*Mela*, 2. c. 5.

VATICA'NUS, a hill at Rome, near the Tiber and the Janiculum, which produced wine of no great esteem. It was disregarded by the Romans on account of the unwholesomeness of the air, and the continual stench of the filth that was there, and of stagnated waters. Heliogabalus was the first who cleared it of all disagreeable nuisances. There was there a temple sacred to a god of the same name, who presided over the cries of infants, and the first words which they articulate. His name is derived by A. Gellius from the oracles (*a vaticiniis*) which he gave. The Vatican is now admired for ancient monuments and pillars, for a celebrated public library, and for the palace of the pope. *Horat.* 1. od. 20.—*Aug. de Civ. D.* 4. c. 8 & 11.—*Aul. Gell.* 16. c. 17.—*Gyrald. H.D.* 1.

VATIE'NUS P., a peasant, who, as historians relate, was informed by Castor and Pollux, of the victory of Paulus over the Macedonian king, before the regular intelligence could reach Rome. *Cic. N.D.* 2. c. 2. l. 3. c. 5.

VATIN'IA LEX, *de provinciis*, by the tribune P. Vatinius, A.U.C. 694. It appointed Cæsar governor of Gallia Cisalpina and Illyricum, for five years, without a decree of the senate. His army was to be paid out of the public treasury, and he was empowered to plant a Roman colony in the town of Novocomum in Gaul.—Another by P. Vatinius the tribune, A.U.C. 694, *de repetundis*, for the better management of the trials of those who were accused of extortion.

VATIN'IUS, an intimate friend of Cicero, once distinguished for his enmity to the orator. He hated the people of Rome for their great vices and corruption, whence excessive hatred became proverbial in the words *Vatinianum odium*. *Catull.* 14. v. 3.——A shoemaker, ridiculed for his great deformities, and the oddity of his character. He was one of Nero's favorites, and surpassed the rest of the courtiers in flattery, and in the commission of every impious deed. Large cups, of no value, are called Vatiniana from him, because he used one which was both ill-shaped and uncouth. *Tacit. Ann.* 13. c. 34.—*Juv.*—*Mart* 14. epigr. 96.

Vatin'ius Pub'lius, a tribune, author of the Lex Vatinia, in favor of Cæsar, whose friend and determined partisan he was. When accused of bribery by Calvus, he was, at the request of Cæsar and Pompey, defended by Cicero, against whom he had shown himself malignantly violent. After Cæsar's death Vatinius resigned to Brutus the command of his legions in Illyricum, where he was grown unpopular from the baseness of his disposition and the deformity of his person. *Cic.* 2. *Att.* 9. *Phil.* 10. c. 6. *Fam.* 1. ep. 9.—*Vell.* 2. c. 69.—*Liv.* 118.—*Dio.* 47.—*Plut. in Cat.*—*Val. Max.* 7. c. 5.

VATRE'NUS, now Saterno, a river rising in the Apennines and falling into the Po. *Martial.* 3. epigr. 67.—*Plin.* 3. c. 16.

VEAS'CIUM, a town of Italy destroyed by the Gauls when they abandoned Rome. *Diod. Sic.* l. 14.

VE'CA, a town of Hispania Tarraconensis. *Plin.* 4. c. 20.

VECTIE'NUS or **VETTIE'NUS**, a Roman intimate, with Cicero. He is called Monetalis, because probably he was engaged in money matters. *Cic.* 10. *Att.* 5 & 11, &c.

VEC'TA or **VEC'TIS**, the isle of Wight, south of Britain. *Suet. Cl.* 4. The modern name appears to be derived from the Vitæ, a people of Germany who settled there. *Spelman. in Glossar. Archæol.*

VEC'TIUS, a rhetorician, &c. *Juv.* 7. v. 150.——A senator. *Cic. Flacc.* 34.

Vec'tius Bola'nus, an officer sent to succeed Trebellius Maximus in Britain. *Tac. Hist.* 2. c. 65.

VECTO'NES. *Vid.* Vettones.

VEDELI'ACUS, one of the Ædui. *Cæs. B. Gall.* 7. c. 32.

VEDIAN'TII, a people of Gallia Narbonensis, between the *Alpes maritimæ*, and the river Varus. *Plin.* 3. c. 5.

VE'DIUS POL'LIO, a friend of Augustus, very cruel to his servants, &c. *Vid.* Pollio.

Ve'dius Aq'uila, an officer at the battle of Bebriacum, &c. *Tacit. H.* 2. c. 44.

VEGES'ELA, a city of Numidia. *Antonin.*

VEGETIUS FLA'VIUS RENA'TUS, a Latin writer, who flourished A.D. 386. The best editions of his treatise, *de re militari* are that of Paris, 4to, 1607, and that of Schwebelius, Norimberg. 1767. *Harles. Not. Lit. Rom.* 1. p. 613.—*Sax. Onom.* 1. p. 422.

Vege'tius, a writer *de mulomedicina* or *de arte veterinaria*. Some suppose him to be the same as the preceding. This treatise was edited at Basil, 1574, and also by Gesner in his writers *de R.R.* p. 1033. *Harles. & Sax. ibid.*—*Fabr. B. Lat.* 3. p. 173.

VE'GIA or **VE'GIUM**, an island on the coast of Dalmatia.

VEHIL'IUS P., a Roman, who refused to accept a province, offered him by Antony. *Cic. Phil.* 3. c. 10.

VE'IA, a sorceress in the age of *Horace.* Ep. 5. v. 29.

VEIA'NIUS, a gladiator in the age of *Horace.* 1. ep. 1. v. 4.

VEIEN'TES, the inhabitants of Veii. They were carried to Rome, where the tribe they composed was called Veientina. *Vid.* Veii.

VEIEN'TO FABR., a Roman, as arrogant as he was satirical. Nero banished him for his libellous writings. *Juv.* 3. v. 185.

Veien'to, a governor of Syria, after Bibulus. *Cic.* 7. *Att.* 3.

VE'II, a powerful city of Etruria, at the distance of about 12 miles from Rome. It sustained many long wars against the Romans, and was at last taken and destroyed by Camillus, after a siege of ten years. At the time of its destruction Veii was larger and far more magnificent than the city of Rome. Its situation was so eligible, that the Romans, after the burning of their city by the Gauls, were long inclined to migrate thither, and abandon their native home, and this would have been carried into execution if it had not been opposed by the authority and eloquence of Camillus. *Ovid.* 2. *Fast.* v. 195.—*Cic. de Div.* 1. c. 44.—*Horat.* 2. sat. 3. v. 143.—*Liv.* 5. c. 21, &c.—*Sueton. in Ner.* 39.—*Dionys. Hal.* 2. c. 55.

VEJ'OVIS or **VEDI'US**, a deity of ill omen at Rome. He had a temple at Rome on the Capitoline hill, built by Romulus. Some suppose that he was the same as Jupiter the infant, or in the cradle, because he was represented without thunder, or a sceptre, and had only by his side the goat Amalthæa, and the Cretan nymph who fed him when young.—*Ovid. Fast.* 3. v. 430.—*Aul. Gell.* 5. c. 12.

VELA'BRUM, a marshy piece of ground on the side of the Tiber, between the Aventine, Palatine, and Capitoline hills, which Augustus drained, and where he built houses. The place was frequented as a market, where oil, cheese, and other commodities were exposed to sale. *Horat.* 2. sat. 3. v. 229.—*Ovid. Fast.* 6. v. 401.—*Tibull.* 2. el. 5. v. 33. —*Plaut.* 3. c. 1. v. 29.

VELA'NIUS Q., One of Cæsar's officer's in Gaul, &c. *Cæs. Com.* l. 3. c. 7.

VELATODU'RUM, a town of the Sequani iu Gallia Lugdunensis. *Antonin.*

VELAU'NI, a people at the south of Gaul, on the west of the Rhone. *Plin.* 3. c. 20.

VEL'CERA, a town of Liburnia. *Ptol.*

VELDIDE'NA, a town of Rhætia Propria, on the borders of Vindelicia. *Antonin.*

VEL'EDA, a prophetess honored by the Germans as a goddess. *Tac. Hist.* 4. c. 66.

VELE'IA, a city of Hispania Tarraconensis. *Antonin.*—*Plin.* 3. c. 3.

VE'LIA, a maritime town of Lucania, founded by a colony of Phoceans, about 600 years after the coming of Æneas into Italy. Virgil, in making Palinurus, in the infernal regions, exhort Æneas to sail to Velia, is inadvertently guilty of a gross error, by giving existence to a place which was founded so many centuries afterwards. The port in its neighbourhood was called *Velinus portus. Strab.* 6.—*Mela,* 2. c. 4.—*Cic. Phil.* 10. c. 4.—*Virg. Æn.* 6. v. 366.—*Hygin. apud A. Gell.* 10. c. 16.——An eminence near the Roman forum, where Poplicola built himself a house. *Liv.* 2. c. 6.—*Cic.* 7. *Att.* 15.

VEL'ICA or VEL'LICA, a town of the Cantabri in Spain. *Ptol.*

VELIEN'SES, a people of Latium. *Plin.* 3. c. 5.

VELI'NA, a part of the city of Rome, adjoining mount Palatine. It was also one of the Roman tribes. *Horat.* 1. ep. 6. v. 52.—*Cic.* 4. *ad Attic.* ep. 15.

VELI'NUS, a lake in the country of the Sabines, formed by the stagnant waters of the Velinus, between some hills near Reate. The river Velinus rises in the Apennines, and after it has formed the lake, it falls into the Nar, near Spoletium. As the Velinus rolls down a precipice 300 feet high three miles from Interamna, dashing with such impetuosity against the opposing rocks, that the neighbouring country is perpetually covered with a thick misty cloud from the watery vapors, Addison has imagined, and with classical judgment, that Virgil probably alludes to this majestic cascade when he describes the descent of Alecto to the infernal regions through a passage in the middle of Italy. The lake Amsactus has been considered by the ancients as the spot where this scene was laid. *Virg. Æn.* 7. v. 517.—*Plin.* 2. c. 93.—*Cic. Div.* 1. c. 36.

VELIOCAS'SI, a people of Gaul, the same as the Velocasses. *Vid.* Velocasses.

VELIS'CUM, a city of Mauritania Cæsarensis. *Antonin.*

VELITER'NA, VEL'ITRÆ or VELI'TRÆ, an ancient town of Latium on the Appian road, 26 miles at the east of Rome. The inhabitants were called Veliterni. It became a Roman colony under the dictator Posthumius. *Liv.* 8. c. 12, &c.—*Sueton. in Aug.*—*Ital.* 8. v. 378. l. 13. v. 229.—*Strab.* 5.—*Plin.* 3. c. 5. l. 16. c. 45.

VEL'LANIS, a city of Upper Mysia. *Ptol.*

VELLA'TES, a people of Gallia Aquitanica. *Plin.* 4. c. 19.

VEL'LAVI, a people of Gaul. *Cæs. Comm.* 7. c. 25.

VELLAUNODU'NUM, a town of the Senones, now Beaune. *Cæs.* 7. c. 11

VEL'LEDA. *Vid.* Veleda.

VELLEJA'CIUM, a town in Italy, near Placentia. *Plin.* 7. c. 49.

C. VELLE'IUS PATER'CULUS, a Roman historian descended from an equestrian family of Campania. He was at first a military tribune in the Roman armies, and for nine years served under Tiberius in the various expeditions which he undertook in Gaul and Germany. Velleius wrote an epitome of the history of Greece, and of Rome, and of other nations of the most remote antiquity, but of this composition there remain only fragments of the history of Greece and Rome from the conquest of Perseus, by Paulus, to the 17th year of the reign of Tiberius, in two books. It is a judicious account of celebrated men, and illustrious cities; the historian is happy in his descriptions, and accurate in his dates, his pictures are true, and his narrations lively and interesting. The whole is candid and impartial, but only till the reign of the Cæsars, when the writer began to be influenced by the presence of the emperor or the power of his favorites. Paterculus is deservedly censured for his invectives against Cicero and Pompey and his encomiums on the cruel Tiberius, and the unfortunate Sejanus. Some suppose that he was involved in the ruin of this disappointed courtier, whom he had extolled as a pattern of virtue and morality. The best editions of Paterculus are those of Ruhnken, 8vo. 2 vols. L. Bat. 1779; of Barbou, Paris, 12mo. 1777; and of Burman, L. Bat. 1719. *Hen. Dodwell. Annal. Velleian, Oxon.* 1678.—*Harles. Not. Lit. Rom.* 1. p. 313.—*Sax. Onom.* 1. p. 212.—*Liv.* 1. c. 13, 41, 52, 56, 58.—*Vossius. de H. Lat.*—*Lipsius Cent.* 3. *Misc* ep. 61.

VELLE'IUS CA'IUS, the grandfather of the historian of that name, was one of the friends of Livia. He killed himself when old and unable to accompany Livia in her flight. *Vell.* 2. c. 76.——A tribune, A.U.C. 663, who strongly attached himself to the opinions and philosophy of Epicurus. *Cic. N. D.* 1. c. 6. *Orat.* 3. c. 21.

VEL'LICA. *Vid.* Velica.

VELLOCA'TUS, an arm-bearer of Venutius, whom Cartismandua, queen of the Brigantes, married. *Tac. Hist.* 3. c. 45.

VELOCAS'SES or VELLOCAS'SI, the people of Vexin, in Normandy, on the eastern banks of the Seine. *Cæs. G.* 2. c. 4.—*Plin.* 4. c. 18.

VELU'CA, a city of Hispania Tarraconensis. *Antonin.*

VENA'FRUM, a town of Campania, near Arpinum, abounding in olive trees. It became a Roman colony. It had been founded by Diomedes. *Horat.* 2. od. 6. v. 16. l. 2. sat. 6. v. 69. sat. 8. v. 45. —*Martial.* 13. epigr. 98.—*Juv.* 5. v. 86.—*Strab.* 5. —*Plin.* 3. c. 5.—*Servius ad Æn.* 10. v. 246.

VENAN'TIUS HONO'RIUS CLEMENTIA'NUS FORTUNA'TUS, a Latin writer of the western empire, who distinguished himself so much by his zeal and piety that he was appointed bishop of Poictiers. His poems are various, but all upon evangelical subjects, or in praise of the first martyrs and proselytes to Christianity, and they are divided into ten books, consisting of several thousand lines. His works have been edited by the Jesuit Brouverius. *Harles. Not. Lit. Rom.* 1. p. 769.—*Sax. Onom.* 2. p. 55.

VENA'RIA, a small island in the Sinus Formianus. *Mela.* According to *Pliny,* 3. c. 6., it was in the Tyrrhene Sea.

VEN'EDI or VENE'DÆ, a people of Germany, near the mouth of the Vistula, or gulph of Dantzic. *Tacit. de Germ.* 46.—*Plin.* 4. c. 13.

VEN'ELI, a people of Gaul on the coast of modern Normandy, near Cape La Hogue. *Cæs. Bell. G.* 3. c. 34.

VENE'RIA, a name given to Sicca in Africa.——A name of Nebrissa in Hispania Bætica. *Plin.* 3. c. 1.

VENERIA'NUS, a general of Gallienus, who conquered the Goths in a naval battle. *Treb. Poll. in Gallien.* c. 13.

VEN'ERIS POR'TUS, a town on the coast of Liguria. *Antonin.*

VEN'ERIS URBS, a city of Ægypt. *Plin.* 5. c. 9. It is called Aphrodites and Aphroditopolis by *Ptolemy.*

VEN'ETI, a people of Italy in Cisalpine Gaul, near the mouth of the Po. They were descended from a nation of Paphlagonia, who settled there under Antenor, some time after the Trojan war The Venetians, who have been long a powerful and commercial nation, were originally very poor, whence a writer in the age of the Roman emperor said, that they had no other fence against the waves of the sea than hurdles, no food but fish, no wealth besides their fishing-boats, and no merchandise but salt. *Strab.* 4, &c.—*Liv.* 1. c. 1.—*Mela,* 1. c. 2. l. 2. c. 4.—*Cæs. Bell. G.* 3. c. 8.—*Lucan.* 4. v. 134.—*Ital.* 8. v. 605.—*Plin.* 3. c. 19.—*Curt.* 3. c.

1.—*Propert.* 1. el. 12. v. 4.—*Servius ad Æn.* 1. v. 247 & 605.——A nation of Gaul, at the south of Armorica, on the western coast, powerful by sea. Their chief city is now called Vannes. *Cæs.* 3. *G.* 8.

VENE'TIA (Venice.) a part of Gallia Transpadana, at the north of the mouths of the Po. *Vid.* Veneti.

VEN'ETUS PAU'LUS, a centurion who conspired against Nero with Piso, &c. *Tacit.* 15. *Ann.* c. 50.

VEN'ETUS LA'CUS, a lake through which the Rhine passes, now Bodensee, or Constance. *Mela*, 3. c. 2.

VENIL'IA, a nymph, sister to Amata, and mother of Turnus, by Daunus. Amphitrite the sea goddess is also called Venilia. *Virg. Æn.* 10. v. 76. —*Ovid. Met.* 14. v. 334.—*Varro de L. L.* 4. c. 10. *Aug. de Civ. D.* 4. c. 11 l. 7. c. 22.—*Servius ad Æn.* 6 v. 90. l. 7. v. 366. l. 10. v. 76. l. 12. v. 29.

VEN'NONES or VENNO'NES, a people of the Rhætian Alps. *Plin.* 3. c. 20.

VENO'NIUS or VENNO'NIUS, a Latin historian. mentioned by *Cicero ad Attic.* 12. ep. 3, &c. *Voss. H. Lat.* p. 726.

VEN'TA BELGA'RUM, a town of Britain, near Winchester.

VEN'TA ICENO'RUM. a town of Britain, now Norwich.

VEN'TA SILU'RUM, a town of Britain, now Caerwent, in Monmouthshire.

VENTI. The ancients, and especially the Athenians, paid particular attention to the winds, and offered them sacrifices as deities intent upon the destruction of mankind, by continually causing storms, tempests, and earthquakes. The winds were represented in different attitudes and forms. The four principal winds were *Eurus*, the south-east; who is represented a young man flying with great impetuosity, and often appearing in a playful and wanton humour. *Auster*, the south wind, appeared generally as an old man with gray hair, a gloomy countenance, a head covered with clouds, a sable vesture, and dusky wings. He is the dispenser of rain, and of all heavy showers. *Zephyrus* is represented as the mildest of all the winds. He is young and gentle, and his lap is filled with vernal flowers. He married the goddess Flora, with whom he enjoyed the most perfect felicity. *Boreas*, or the north wind, appears always rough and shivering. He is the father of rain, snow, hail, and tempests, and is always represented surrounded with impenetrable clouds. Those of inferior note were *Solanus*, whose name is seldom mentioned; he appeared as a young man holding fruit in his lap, such as peaches, oranges, &c. *Africus*, or south-west, represented with black wings, and a melancholy countenance. *Corus*, or the north-west, drives clouds of snow before him; and *Aquilo*, the north-east, is equally dreadful in appearance. The winds, according to some mythologists, were confined in a large cave, of which Æolus had the management; and without this necessary precaution they would have overturned the earth, and reduced everything to its original chaos. *Virg. Æn.* 1. v. 57, &c.—*Homer. Il.* 23. v. 194. *Od.* 10. v. 1.—*Hesiod. Th.* 870.—*Herodot.* 1 & 7.—*Xenoph. in Cyr.* 1.—*Ovid. Met.* 6. v. 683. l. 14. v. 233. *Fast.* 2. v. 456.—*Ælian. V. H.* 12. c. 61.—*Strab.* 15.—*Seneca in Q. Nat.* 5. c. 17.—*Hygin.* præf. fab.

VENTID'IUS BAS'SUS, a native of Asculum in Picenum, born of an obscure family When Asculum was taken, he was carried before the triumphal chariot of Pompeius Strabo, hanging on his mother's breast. A bold, aspiring soul, aided by the patronage of the family of Cæsar, raised him from the mean occupation of a chairman and muleteer to dignity in the state. He displayed valor in the Roman armies, and gradually rose to the offices of tribune, prætor, high priest, and consul. He made war against the Parthians, and conquered them in three great battles, B.C. 39. He was the first Roman ever honoured with a triumph over Parthia. He died greatly lamented by all the Roman people, and was buried at the public expense. *Plut. in Anton.*—*Juv.* 7. v. 199.—*Val. Max.* 6. c. 9.—*Gell.* 15. c. 4.—*Cic.* 10. ep. 18. —*Dio.* 43.

VENTID'IUS CUMA'NUS, a governor of Palestine, &c. *Tacit. A.* 13. c. 54.

VENTID'IUS, the name of two brothers in the age of Pompey, who favored Carbo's interest, &c. *Plut.*

Q. VENULETIUS SATURNI'NUS, a writer in the age of the emperor Alexander. Fragments of his four books *De Officio Proconsulis* have been edited by Hermann Oosterdyk, Trajac. ad Rhenum. 1755. *Harles. Not. Lit. Rom.* 1. p. 533.

VENULE'IUS, a friend of Verres. *Cic. Verr.* 3. c. 42.

VEN'ULUS, one of the Latin elders sent into Magna Græcia to demand the assistance of Diomedes, &c. *Virg. Æn.* 8. v. 9.

VE'NUS, one of the most celebrated deities of the ancients. She was the goddess of beauty, the mother of love, the queen of laughter, the mistress of the graces and of pleasure, and the patroness of courtezans. Some mythologists speak of more than one Venus. Plato mentions two, Venus Urania, the daughter of Uranus, and Venus Popularia, the daughter of Jupiter and Dione. Cicero speaks of four, a daughter of Cœlus and Light, one sprung from the froth of the sea, a third, daughter of Jupiter and the Nereid Dione, and a fourth born at Tyre, and the same as the Astarte of the Syrians. Of these, however, the Venus sprung from the froth of the sea, after the mutilated part of the body of Uranus had been thrown there by Saturn, is the most known, and of her in particular ancient mythologists, as well as painters, make mention. She arose from the sea near the island of Cyprus, or, according to Hesiod, of Cythera, whither she was wafted by the zephyrs, and received on the sea shore by the seasons, daughters of Jupiter and Themis. She was soon after carried to heaven, where all the gods admired her beauty, and all the goddesses became jealous of her personal charms. Jupiter attempted to gain her affections, and even wished to offer her violence; but Venus refused, and the god, to punish her obstinacy, gave her in marriage to his ugly and deformed son Vulcan. This marriage did not prevent the goddess of love from gratifying her favorite passions, and she defiled her husband's beds by her amours with the gods. Her intrigue with Mars is the most celebrated. She was caught in her lover's arms, and exposed to the ridicule and laughter of all the gods. *Vid.* Alectryon. Venus became mother of Hermione, Cupid, and Anteros, by Mars; by Mercury, she had Hermaphroditus; by Bacchus, Priapus; and by Neptune, Eryx. Her great partiality for Adonis made her abandon the seats of Olympus (*Vid.* Adonis), and her regard for Anchises obliged her often to visit the woods and solitary retreats of mount Ida. *Vid.* Anchises & Æneas. The power of Venus over the heart was supported and assisted by a celebrated girdle, called *zone* by the Greeks, and *cestus* by the Latins. This mysterious girdle gave beauty, grace and elegance, when worn even by the most deformed; it excited love, and rekindled extinguished flames. Juno herself was indebted to this powerful ornament to gain the favors of Jupiter, and Venus, though herself possessed of every charm, no sooner put on her cestus, than Vulcan, unable to resist the influence of love, forgot all the intrigues and infidelities of his wife, and fabricated arms even for her illegitimate children. The contest of Venus for the golden apple of Discord is well known. She gained the prize over Pallas and Juno (*Vid.* Paris & Discordia), and rewarded her impartial judge with the hand of the fairest woman in the world. The worship of Venus was universally established; statues and temples were erected to her in every kingdom, and the ancients were fond of paying homage to a divinity who presided over generation, and by whose influence alone mankind existed. In her sacrifices and in the festivals celebrated in her honor, very great licentiousness prevailed, and public prostitution was often part of the ceremony. Victims were seldom offered to her, or her altars stained with blood, though we find Aspasia making repeated sacrifices. No pigs, however, or male animals, were deemed acceptable. The rose, the myrtle, and the apple, were sacred to Venus; and among birds, the dove, the swan, and the sparrow, were her favorites; and among fishes, those called the aphya and the lycostomus. The goddess of beauty was represented among the ancients in different forms. At Elis she appeared seated on a goat, with one foot resting on a tortoise. At Sparta and Cythera she was represented armed like Minerva, and sometimes wearing chains on her feet. In the temple of Jupiter Olympius she was represented by Phidias as rising from the sea, received by love, and crowned by the goddess of persuasion. At Cnidus her statue made by Praxiteles (*Vid.* Cnidus) represented her naked. Her statue at Elephantis was the same, with only a naked Cupid by her side. In Sicyon she held a poppy in one hand, and in the other an apple, while on her head she had a crown, which terminated in a point, to intimate the pole. She is generally represented with her son Cupid, on a chariot drawn by doves, or at other times by swans or sparrows. The surnames of the goddess are numerous, and only serve to show how well established her worship was all over the earth. She was called Cypria, because particularly worshipped in the island of Cyprus, and in that character she was often represented with a beard, with a sceptre in her hand, and the body and dress of a female, whence she is called *duplex Amathusia* by Catullus. She received the name of Paphia, because worshipped at Paphus, where she had a temple with an altar, on which rain never fell, though exposed in the open air. Some of the ancients called her Apistrophia or Epistrophia, as also Venus Urania, and Venus Pandemos. The first of these she received as presiding over wantonness and incestuous enjoyments; the second because she patronized pure love, and chaste and moderate gratifications; and the third because she favored the propensities of the vulgar, and was fond of sensual pleasures. The Cnidians raised her temples under the name of Venus Acræa, of Doris, and of Euploea. In her temple under the name of Euploea at Cnidus, was the most celebrated of her statues, being the most perfect piece of Praxiteles. It was made with white marble, and appeared so engaging and so much like life, that, according to some historians, a youth of that place became enamoured of it. Venus was also surnamed Cytheræa, because she was the chief deity of Cythera; Exopolis, because her statue was without the city at Athens; Philomeda, from her affection for the phallus; Philommeis, because the queen of laughter; Telessigama, because she presided over marriage; Coliada, Colotis, or Colias, because worshipped on a promontory of the same name in Attica; Area, because armed like Mars; Verticordia, because she could turn the hearts of women to cultivate chastity; Apaturia, because she deceived; Calva, because she was represented bald; Ericyna, because worshipped at Eryx; Etaria, because the patroness of courtezans; Acidalia, because of a fountain of Orchomenus; Basilea, because the queen of love; Myrtea, because the myrtle was sacred to her; Libertina, from her licentious inclinations; Mechanitis, in allusion to the many artifices practised in love, &c., &c. As goddess of the sea, because born in the bosom of the waters, Venus was called Pontia, Marina, Limnesia, Epipontia, Pelagia, Saligenia, Pontogenia, Aligena, Thalassia, &c., and as rising from the sea, the name of Anadyomene is applied to her, and rendered immortal by the celebrated painting of Apelles, which represented her as issuing from the bosom of the waves, and wringing her tresses on her shoulder. *Vid.* Anadyomene. *Cic. de Nat. D.* 2. c. 27. l. 3. c, 23.—*Orpheus Hymn.* 54.—*Hesiod. Theog.*—*Sappho.*—*Homer. Hymn. in Ven., &c.*—*Virg. Æn.* 5. v. 800. &c.—*Ovid. Heroid.* 15, 16, 19, &c. *Met.* 4. fab. 5, &c.—*Diod.* 1 & 3.—*Hygin.* fab. 94, 271.—*Paus.* 2. c. 1. l. 4. c. 30. l. 5. c. 18.—*Martial.* 6. epigr. 13.—*Eurip. in Hel. in Iphig. In Troad.*—*Plut. in Erotic.*—*Ælian. V. H.* 12. c. 1. —*Athen*, 12, &c.—*Catullus.*—*Calaber*, 11.—*Lucian dial. &c.*—*Strab.* 14.—*Tacit. Ann.* 3, &c.—*Val. Max.* 8. c. 11.—*Plin.* 36.—*Horat.* 3. od. 26. l. 4. od. 11, &c.—*Lactant. de Fals. R. Ad. Theb.* 4. v. 226.—*Fulgent. Myth.* 2. c. 4.—*Servius ad Virg. passim.*—*Tzetzes ad Lyc.* 403. 449 & 832.—*Gyrald. H. D. Synt.* 13.—*Steph. Byzant.*—*Macrob.* l. c. 21.—*Suidas.*—*Hesychius.*—*Aug. de Civ. D.* 4. c. 8 & 16, &c.—*Tertullian. de Spect.*—*Festus de V. Sig.*—*Coluth. de Rapt. Hel.* 80, &c.—*Priap. Carm.* 36.—*Sappho in Vener.*—*Eustath. ad Il.* [The statues of this deity are very numerous, and many of them are very fine. The most celebrated are the Venus de Medici, in the Museum, at Florence; the Venus of the Capitol, at Rome; and the Townley Venus, in the British Museum. There is an exquisite fragment, the hands and feet being lost, which is supposed to be a copy from the famous Venus of Praxiteles, in the Braschi Palace, at Rome.]

VE'NUS, a planet, called by the Greeks Phosphorus, and by the Latins Lucifer, when it rises before the sun, but when it follows it, Hesperus or Vesper. *Cic. de Nat. D.* 2. c. 20. *In somn. Scip* 4.

VE'NUS PYRENÆ'A, a town of Spain, near the borders of Gaul. *Plin.* 3. c. 3.

VENU'SIA or VENU'SIUM, a town of Apulia, where Horace was born. Part of the Roman army fled thither after the defeat at Cannæ. The town, though in ruins, contains still many pieces of antiquity, especially a marble bust preserved in the great square, and falsely said to be an original representation of Horace. Venusia was on the confines of Lucania, whence the poet said *Lucanus an Apulus anceps*, and it was founded by Diomedes, who called it Venusia or Aphrodisia, after Venus, whose divinity he wished to appease. *Strab.* 5 & 6.—*Horat.* 2. sat. 1. v. 35.—*Liv.* 22. c. 54.—*Plin.* 3. c. 11.—*Juv.* 1. v. 51.—*Servius ad Æn.* 11. v. 246.

VENU'TIUS, a king of the Brigantes, for a long time faithful to the Romans. *Tac. Ann.* 12. c. 40.

VERAGRA'NI or VEREGRA'NI, a people of Picenum. *Plin.* 3. c. 20.

VER'AGRI or VERA'GRI, a people between the Alps and the Allobroges. *Liv.* 21. c. 38.—*Cæs. G.* 3. c. 1.

VERA'NIA, the wife of Piso Licinianus, whom Galba adopted. *Tac. Hist.* 1. c. 47.

VERA'NIUS, a governor of Britain under Nero. He succeeded Didius Gallus. *Tacit.* 14. *Ann.* c. 29.

VERBA'NUS LA'CUS, now Lago Maggiore, a lake of Italy, from which the Ticinus flows. It is in the Milanese, and extends 50 miles in length from south to north, and five or six in breadth. *Strab.* 4.

VERBIG'ENUS, a village in the country of the Celtæ. *Cæs. Comm.* 1. c. 27.

VERBI'NUM, a town at the north of Gaul on the Isara, which falls into the Seine. *Antonin.* It is now Vervins.

VERCEL'LÆ, a town on the borders of Insubria, at the north of the Po, where Marius defeated the Cimbri. *Plin.* 3. c. 17.—*Cic. Fam.* 11 ep. 19.—*Sil.* 8. v. 598.

VERCINGET'ORIX, a celebrated chief of the Gauls, in the time of Cæsar. By his powerful influence the nations of Gaul united to shake off the Roman yoke, but the superior valor and fortune of Cæsar prevailed, and Vercingetorix, after severe losses, surrendered himself up at Alesia to the conqueror, who, after dragging him in chains to adorn his triumph, ordered him, with a cruelty unworthy of his fame, to be put to death. *Flor.* 3. c. 10.—*Dio*, 40, 41, & 43, 19.—*Cæs Bell. G.* 7. c. 4.

VER'ESIS, a small river of Latium falling into the Anio.

VER'GÆ, a town of the Brutii. *Liv.* 30. c. 19.

VERGASILLAU'NUS, one of the generals and friends of Vercingetorix. *Cæsar. Bell. G.* 7. c. 88.

VERGEL'LUS, a small river near Cannæ, falling into the Aufidus, over which Annibal made a bridge with the slaughered bodies of the Romans. *Flor.* 2. c. 6,—*Val. Max.* 9. c. 11. It is now Fiume di Canne.

VERGEN'TUM, a town of Spain. *Plin.* 3. c. 1.

VERGIL'IA, the wife of Coriolanus, &c.

VERGIL'IA, a town of Spain, supposed to be Murcia.

VERGIL'IÆ, seven stars, called also *Pleiades.* When they set, the ancients began to sow their corn. They received their name from the spring, *quia vere oriantur.* *Propert.* 1. el. 8. v. 18.—*Cic. de Nat. D.* 2. c. 44.—*Plin.* 18. c. 25.—*Aul. Gell.* 13. c. 9.—*Servius ad Virg. G.* 1. v. 137 & 219. *Æn.* 1. v. 748.

VERGIN'IUS, one of the officers of the Roman troops in Germany, who refused the absolute power which his soldiers offered to him. *Tacit.* 1. *Hist.* c. 8.——A rhetorician in the age of Nero, banished on account of his great fame. He was the preceptor of Persius, and wrote *de materia Rhetoricorum.* *Id. An.* 15. c. 71.

VER'GIUM, a town of Hispania Bætica. *Liv.* 43. c. 1. It is called Bergidum by *Ptolemy.*

VERGOB'RETUS, the name of the supreme magistrate among the Ædui, who was created annually, and had the power of life and death. *Cæs. B. G.* 1. c. 16.

VER'ITAS (*truth*) was not only personified by the ancients, but also made a deity, and called the daughter of Saturn and the mother of Virtue. She was represented like a young virgin, dressed in white apparel, with all the marks of youthful diffidence and modesty. Democritus used to say, that she hid herself at the bottom of a well, to intimate the difficulty with which she is found, and Apelles in his celebrated picture of Calumny, represented her dressed in a modest manner, and standing at a distance. *Pindar. Olymp.* 10. v. 5.—*Hippocrat. in Ep ad Philop.*—*Plut. in Qu. R.* 12.—*Philostrat. Ic.* 1. c. 28.—*Lucian. de Calumniâ.*

VERJUGODUM'NUS, a deity worshipped by the Gauls. *Car. du Fresne, de infer. ævi Numism. num.* 54.

VE'RO, a river of Celtiberia. *Martial.* epigr. 50. v. 5.

VERODOC'TIUS, one of the Helvetii. *Cæs. G.* 1. c. 7.

VEROMAN'DUI, a people of Gaul, the modern Vermandois. The capital is now St. Quintin. *Cæs. G. B.* 2.—*Plin.* 4. c. 17.

VERO'NA, a town of Venetia, on the Athesis, in Italy, founded, as some suppose, by Brennus, the leader of the Gauls. C. Nepos, Catullus, and Pliny the elder, were born there. It was adorned, by the Roman emperors, with a circus and an amphitheatre, which still exist, and it still preserves its ancient name. *Plin.* 9. c. 22.—*Strab.* 5.—*Ovid. Am.* 3. el. 15. v. 7.—*Catull.* 68. v. 34.—*Martial.* 14. epigr. 152.

VERO'NES, a people of Hispania Tarraconensis. *Sil.* 3. v. 378.

VERREGI'NUM, a town in the country of the Volsci. *Liv.* 4. c. 1, &c.—*Val. Max.* 6. c. 5.

VER'RES C., a Roman who governed the province of Sicily as prætor. The oppression and rapine of which he was guilty while in office, so offended the Sicilians, that they brought an accusation against him before the Roman senate. Cicero, who was connected with the unfortunate Sicilians by a former quæstorship, undertook their cause, and pronounced those celebrated orations which are still extant. Verres was defended by Hortensius, but as he despaired of the success of his defence, he left Rome without waiting for his sentence, and lived in great affluence in one of the provinces. He was at last killed by the soldiers of Antony the triumvir, about 26 years after his voluntary exile from the capital. *Cic. in Ver.*—*Plin.* 34. c. 2.—*Lactant.* 2. c. 4.

VER'RES QUIN'TUS, a relation of Verres. *Cic.* 1. *in Verr.*

VER'RITUS, a general of the Frisii in the age of Nero, &c. *Tacit. Ann.* 13. c. 54.

M. VER'RIUS FLAC'CUS, a freedman and grammarian famous for his powers in instructing. He was appointed over the grand-children of Augustus, and also distinguished himself by his writings. The chief of these were, a book entitled "Saturnus;" "De obscuris Catonis;" "De Verborum Significatione," and "Fasti." They have been edited by Fogginius, Rome, 1779, and others. *Vid.* Festus Pompeius. *Harles. Not. Lit. Rom.* 1. p. 209 & 577.—*Gell.* 4. c. 5.—*Suet. de Gram.*

VER'RIUS, a friend of Cicero and of Pætus. *Cic. Fam.* 9. ep. 20, 26.

VERRU'GO, a town in the country of the Volsci. *Liv.* 4. c. 1.

VERRU'TIUS C., a name which Verres assumed the better to conceal himself. *Cic. Verr.* 5. c. 76.

VER'TICO, one of the Nervii who deserted to Cæsar's army, &c. *Cæs. B. G.* 5. c. 45.

VERTICOR'DIA, one of the surnames of Venus, the same as the Apostrophia of the Greeks. This name was given her because her asssistance was implored to turn the hearts of the Roman matrons, and teach them to follow virtue and modesty. *Ovid.* 4. *Fast.* v. 157., thus describes the origin of the name:

Roma pudicitiâ proavorum tempore lapsa est,
Cumæam, Veteres, consuluistis anum:
Templa jubet Veneri fieri: quibus ordine factis
Inde Venus verso *nomine* corda *tenet.*

Val. Max. 8. c. 15.—*Plin.* 7. c. 35.

VERTI'NÆ, a town of Calabria. *Strab.* It is now Verzine.

VERTIS'CUS, one of the Rhemi, who commanded a troop of horse in Cæsar's army. *Cæs. B. G.* 8. c. 12.

VERTOBRI'GA, a town of Hispania Bætica. *Plin.* 3. c. 1.

VERTUMNA'LIA, festivals in honor of the god Vertumnus, celebrated by the Romans in October. *Varro, L. L.* 5. c. 3.

VERTUM'NUS or VORTUM'NUS, a deity among the Romans, who presided over spring and over orchards. He endeavoured to gain the affections of the goddess Pomona; and to effect this, he assumed the shape and dress of a fisherman, of a soldier, a peasant, a reaper, &c., but all to no purpose, till under the form of an old woman, he prevailed upon his mistress and married her. He is generally represented as a young man crowned with flowers, covered up to the waist, and holding in his right hand fruit, and a crown of plenty in his left. *Ovid. Met.* 14. v. 642, &c.—*Propert.* 4. el. 2. v. 2.—*Horat.* 2. sat. 7. v. 14

VER'ULÆ or VER'ULUM, a town of the Hernici *Liv.* 9. c. 42.—*Plin.* 3. c. 5. It is now Veroli.

VERULA'NUS SEVE'RUS, a lieutenant under Corbulo, who drove away Tiridates from Media, &c. *Tacit. Ann.* 14. c. 26.

VE'RUS LU'CIUS CEIO'NIUS COM'MODUS, a Roman emperor, son of Ælius and Domitia Lucilla. He was adopted in the 7th year of his age by M. Aurelian, at the request of Adrian, and married Lucilla the daughter of his adopted father, who also took him as his colleague on the throne. He was sent by M. Aurelius to oppose the barbarians in the east. His arms were attended with success, and he obtained a victory over the Parthians. He was honored with a triumph on his return home, and soon after marched with his imperial colleague against the Marcomanni in Germany. He died in this expedition of an apoplexy, in the 39th year of his age, after a reign of eight years, and some months. His body was brought back to Rome, and buried by M. Aurelius with great pomp and solemnity. Verus has been greatly censured for his debaucheries, which appeared more enormous and more disgusting, when compared to the temperance, meekness, and popularity of Aurelius. The example of his father did not influence him, and he often retired from the frugal and moderate repast of Aurelius, to the profuse banquets of his own palace, where the night was spent in riot and debauchery, with the meanest of the populace, with stage dancers, buffoons, and lascivious courtezans. At one entertainment, where there were no more than twelve guests, the emperor spent no less than six millions of sesterces, or about 32,200*l.* sterling. But it is to be observed, that whatever was most scarce and costly was there; the guests never drank twice out of the same cup; and whatever vessels they had touched, they received as a present from the emperor when they left the palace. In his Parthian expedition, Verus did not check his vicious propensities; for four years he left the care of the war to his officers, while he retired to the voluptuous retreats of Daphne, and the luxurious banquets of Antioch. His fondness for a horse has been faithfully recorded. The animal had a statue of gold; he was fed with almonds and raisins by the hand of the emperor; he was clad in purple, and kept in the most splendid of the halls of the palace, and when dead, the emperor, to express his sorrow, raised him a magnificent monument on mount Vatican. Some have suspected M. Aurelius of dispatching Verus to rid the world of his debaucheries, and guilty actions, but this seems to be the report of malevolence. *Jul. Capitol.* c. 5. [The statues and busts of this emperor are very numerous; the finest of the former will be found in the Vatican, at Rome, and the most esteemed bust is in the Borghese collection, at Paris.]

VE'RUS L. ANNÆ'US, a son of the emperor Aurelius, who died in Palestine. [A bust of Annæus Verus will be found in the Museum of the Capitol, at Rome.]

VE'RUS, the father of the emperor Verus. He was adopted by the emperor Adrian, but like his son he disgraced himself by his debaucheries and extravagance. He died before Adrian.

VES'BIUS or VESU'BIUS. *Vid.* Vesuvius.

VES'CI or VES'CIS, called also Faventia, a city of Hispania Bætica. *Ptol.*

VES'CIA, a town of Campania. *Liv.* 8. c. 11.

VESCIA'NUM, a country house of Cicero in Campania, between Capua and Nola. *Cic.* 15. *Ad Attic.* 2.

VESCULA'RIUS FLAC'CUS, a Roman knight intimate with Tiberius, &c. *Tacit. Ann.* 2. c. 28, &c.

VESEN'TIUM, a town of Tuscany.

VES'ERIS, a place or river near mount Vesuvius. *Liv.* 8 c. 8.—*Cic. Off.* 3. c. 31.

VESE'VIUS or VESE'VUS. *Vid.* Vesuvius.

VESID'IA, a river of Tuscany.

VESON'NA, a town of Gaul, now *Perigueux.*

VESON'TIO, a town of Gaul, now Besançon. *Cæs.* 1. *G.* 38.

VESPA'SIÆ, a small village of Umbria near Nursia. *Suet. Vesp.* 1.

VESPASIA'NUS TI'TUS FLA'VIUS, a Roman emperor descended from an obscure family at Reate. He was honored with the consulship, not so much by the influence of the imperial conrtiers, as by his own private merit and his public services. He accompanied Nero into Greece, but he offended the prince by falling asleep while he repeated one of his poetical compositions. This momentary resentment of the emperor did not prevent Vespasian from being sent to carry on a war against the Jews. His operations were crowned with success; many of the cities of Palestine surrendered, and Vespasian began the siege of Jerusalem. This was, however, achieved by the hands of his son Titus, and the death of Vitellius and the affection of his soldiers, hastened his rise, and he was proclaimed emperor at Alexandria. The choice of the army was approved by every province of the empire; but Vespasian did not betray any signs of pride at so sudden and so unexpected an exaltation, and though once employed in the mean office of a horse-doctor, he behaved, when invested with the imperial purple, with all the dignity and greatness which became a successor of Augustus. In the beginning of his reign Vespasian attempted to reform the manners of the Romans, and he took away an appointment which he had a few days before granted to a young nobleman who approached him to return him thanks, smelling of perfumes and covered with ointment, adding, "I had rather you had smelt of garlick." He repaired the public buildings, embellished the city, and made the great roads more spacious and convenient. After he had reigned with great popularity for 10 years, Vespasian died of a pain in his bowels, A.D. 79, in the 70th year of his age. He was the first Roman emperor that died a natural death, and he was also the first who was succeeded by his own son on the throne. Vespasian has been admired for his great virtues. He was clement, he gave no ear to flattery, and for a long time refused the title of father of his country, which was often bestowed upon the most worthless and tyrannical of the emperors. He despised informers, and rather than punish conspirators, he rewarded them with great liberality. When the king of Parthia addressed him with the superscription of "Arsaces king of kings to Flavius Vespasianus," the emperor was no way dissatisfied with the pride and insolence of the monarch, and answered him again in his own words; "Flavius Vespasianus to Arsaces king of kings." To men of learning and merit, Vespasian was very liberal: one hundred thousand sesterces were annually paid from the public treasury to the different professors that were appointed to encourage and promote the arts and sciences. Yet in spite of this apparent generosity some authors have taxed Vespasian with avarice. According to their accounts he loaded the provinces with new taxes, he bought commodities, that he might sell them to a greater advantage, and even laid an impost upon urine, which gave occasion to Titus to ridicule the meanness of his father. Vespasian, regardless of his son's observation, was satisfied to show him the money that was raised from so productive a tax, asking him at the same time whether it smelt offensive. His ministers were the most avaricious of his subjects, and the emperor used very properly to remark that he treated them as sponges, by wetting them when dry, and squeezing them when they were wet. He has been accused of selling criminals their lives, and of condemning the most opulent to make himself master of their possessions. If, however, he was guilty of these meaner practices, they were all under the name of one of his concubines, who wished to enrich herself by the avarice and credulity of the emperor. *Sueton. in Vitâ.—Tacit. Hist.* 4.—*Aurel. Victor. de Cæsar.* —*Joseph. de B. J.—Euseb.* 3. c. 3. [A bust of Vespasian will be found in the Capitol, and another in the Vatican, at Rome.]

VES'PER or HES'PERUS, a name applied to the planet Venus, when it is the evening star. *Virg. G.* 1. v. 251.—*Horat.* 3. od. 19. v. 26.

VES'SA, a town of Sicily, conquered by Phalaris. *Polyæn.* 5. c. 1.

VES'TA, a goddess, daughter of Rhea and Saturn, sister to Ceres and Juno. She is often confounded by the mythologists with Rhea, Ceres, Cybele, Proserpine, Hecate, and Tellus. When considered as the mother of the gods, she is the mother of Rhea and Saturn; and when considered as the patroness of the vestal virgins and the goddess of fire, she is called the daughter of Saturn and Rhea. Under this last name she was worshipped by the Romans. Æneas was the first who introduced her mysteries into Italy, and Numa built her a temple which no males were permitted to enter. The Palladium of Troy was supposed to be preserved within her sanctuary, and a fire was constantly kept lighted by a certain number of virgins, who had dedicated themselves to the service of the goddess. *Vid.* Vestales. If the fire of Vesta was ever extinguished, it was supposed to threaten the republic with some sudden calamity. The virgin by whose negligence it had been extinguished was severely punished, and it was kindled again by the rays of the sun. The temple of Vesta was of a round form, and the goddess was represented in a long flowing robe with a veil on her head, holding in one hand a lamp, or a two-eared vessel, and in the other a javelin, or sometimes a Palladium. On some medals she appears holding a drum in one hand, and a small figure of victory in the other. *Hesiod. Theog.* v. 454.—*Cic. de Leg.* 2. c. 12.—*Apollod.* 1. c. 1.—*Virg. Æn.* 2. v. 296. 1. 5. v. 744.—*Ovid. Fast.* 6. v. 265 & 450. *Trist.* 3. v. 29.—*Val. Max.* 1. c. 1.—*Plut. in Num.—Paus.* 5. c. 14.—*Lucan.* 9. v. 996. *Propert.* 4. el. 4.—*Festus de V. Sig.—Albric. de D. Imag.*

VESTA'LES, priestesses among the Romans, consecrated to the service of Vesta, as their name indicates. This office was very ancient, as the mother of Romulus was one of the vestals. Æneas is supposed to have first chosen the vestals. Numa first appointed four, to which Tarquin added two. They were always chosen by the monarchs, but after the expulsion of the Tarquins, the high priest was entrusted with the care of them. As they were to be virgins, they were chosen young, from the age of six to ten; and if there was not a sufficient number presented themselves as candidates for the office, twenty virgins were selected, and they upon whom the lot fell were obliged to be priestesses. Plebeians as well as patricians were permitted to propose themselves, but it was required that they should be born of a good family, and be without blemish or deformity in any part of their body. For thirty years they were to remain in the greatest continence; the ten first years were spent in learning the duties of the order, the ten following were employed in discharging them with fidelity and sanctity, and the last ten in instructing such as had entered the noviciate. When the thirty years were elapsed they were permitted to marry, or if they still preferred celibacy, they waited upon the rest of the vestals. As soon as a vestal was initiated, her head was shaved to intimate the liberty of her person, as she was then free from the shackles of parental authority, and was permitted to dispose of her possessions as she pleased. The employment of the vestals was to take care that the sacred fire of Vesta was not extinguished, for if it ever happened, it was deemed the prognostic of great calamities to the state; the offender was punished for her negligence, and severely scourged by the high priest. In such a case all was consternation at Rome, and the fire was again kindled by glasses with the rays of the sun. Another equally particular charge of the vestals was to keep a sacred pledge, on which depended the very existence of Rome, which, according to some, was the Palladium of Troy, or some of the mysteries of the gods of Samothrace. The privileges of the vestals were great; they had the most honorable seats at public games and festivals; a lictor with the fasces always preceded them when they walked in public; they were carried in chariots when they pleased, and they had the power of pardoning criminals when led to execution, if they declared that their meeting was accidental. Their declarations in trials were received without the formality of an oath; they were chosen as arbiters in cases of moment, and in the execution of wills, and so great was the deference paid them by the magistrates, as well as by the people, that the consuls themselves made way for them, and bowed their fasces when they passed before them. To insult them was a capital crime, and whoever attempted to violate their chastity was beaten to death with scourges. If any of them died while in office, their body was buried within the walls of the city, an honor granted to few. Such of the vestals as proved incontinent were punished in the most rigorous manner. Numa ordered them to be stoned, but Tarquin the elder dug a large hole under the earth, where a bed was placed with a little bread, wine, water, and oil, and a lighted lamp, and the guilty vestal was stripped of the habit of her order, and compelled to descend into the subterraneous cavity, which was immediately shut, and she was left to die through hunger. Few of the vestals were guilty of incontinence, and for the space of one thousand years, during which the order continued established, from the reign of Numo, only 18 were punished for the violation of their vow. The vestals were abolished by Theodosius the Great, and the fire of Vesta extinguished. The dress of the Vestals was peculiar; they wore a white vest with purple borders, a white linen surplice called *lintcum supernum*, above which was a great purple mantle which flowed to the ground, and which was tucked up when they offered sacrifices. They had a close covering on their heads, called *infula*, from which hung ribands, or *vittæ*. Their manner of living was sumptuous, as they were maintained at the public expense, and though originally satisfied with the simple diet of the Romans, their tables soon after displayed the luxuries and the superfluities of the great and opulent. *Liv.* 2 & 8 c. 15.—*Plut. in Num. &c.*—*Val. Max.* 1. c. 1.—*Cic. de. Nat. D.* 3. c. 30.—*Flor.* 1.—*Propert.* 4. el. 11.—*Tacit. An.* 4. c. 16.—*Festus de V. Sig.*

VESTA'LIA, festivals in honor of Vesta, observed at Rome on the 9th of June. Banquets were then prepared before the houses, and meat was sent to the vestals to be offered to the gods, millstones were decked with garlands, and the asses that turned them were led round the city covered with garlands. The ladies walked in the procession, bare-footed, to the temple of the goddess, and an altar was erected to Jupiter surnamed Pistor. *Ovid. Fast* 6. v. 305.

VESTA'LIUM MATER, a title given by the senate to Livia the mother of Tiberius, with the permission to sit among the vestal virgins at plays. *Tacit.* 4. *Ann.* c. 16.

VES'TIA OP'PIA, a common prostitute of Capua. *Liv.* 6. c. 2.

VESTIL'IUS SEX'TUS, a prætorian, disgraced by Tiberius, because he was esteemed by Drusus. He killed himself. *Tacit. Ann.* 4. c. 16.

VESTIL'LA, a matron of a patrician family, who declared publicly before the magistrates that she was a common prostitute. She was banished to the island of Seriphus for her immodesty.

VESTI'NI, a people of Italy near the Sabines, famous for the making of cheese. Their cities were Amiternum, Aternum, and Pinna. *Plin.* 3. c. 5.—*Strab.* 5.—*Ital.* 8. v. 516.—*Lucan.* 2. v. 425.—*Martial.* 13. epigr. 31.

VESTI'NUS L., a Roman knight appointed by Vespasian to repair the Capitol, &c. *Tacit. H.* 4. c. 53. *Liv.* 8. c. 29.

VESTI'NUS, a consul put to death at the time of Piso's conspiracy.

VESTO'RIUS C., a banker in the town of Puteoli, mentioned by *Cicero*, 8. *Fam.* 8. *Att.* 4. ep. 6.

VESTRIC'IUS SPURIN'NA, an officer sent by Otho to the borders of the Po, &c. *Tacit. Hist.* 2. c. 11.

VES'VIUS. *Vid.* Vesuvius.

VES'ULUS, now Viso, a large mountain of Liguria near the Alps, where the Po takes its rise. *Virg. Æn.* 10. v. 708.—*Plin.* 3. c. 19.—*Servius ad Virg. loco cit.*

VESU'VIUS, a mountain of Campania, about six miles at the east of Naples, celebrated for its volcano, and now called Mount Soma. The ancients, and particularly the writers of the Augustan age, spoke of Vesuvius as a place covered with orchards and vineyards, of which the middle was dry and barren. The first eruption of this volcano was in the 79th year of the Christian era, under Titus. It was accompanied by an earthquake, which overturned several cities of Campania, particularly Pompeii and Herculaneum, and the burning ashes which it threw up, were carried not only over the neighbouring country, but as far as the shores of Ægypt, Libya, and Syria. This eruption proved fatal to Pliny the naturalist. From that time the eruptions have been frequent, and there now exists an account of twenty-nine of these. Vesuvius continually throws up a smoke, and sometimes ashes and flames. The perpendicular height of this mountain is 3780 feet. *Dio. Cass.* 46.—*Varro de R.* 1. c. 6.—*Liv.* 23. c. 39.—*Strab.* 5.—*Tacit. Hist.* 1. c. 2.—*Mela*, 2. c. 4.—*Plin.* 6. ep. 16.—*Ital.* 12. v. 152. l. 17. v. 598.—*Virg. G.* 2. v. 224.—*Mart.* 4. epigr. 43 & 44.—*Columell.* 3. c. 2.—*Stat.* 4. *Sylv.* 4. v. 79.—*Flacc.* 3. v. 208. l. 4. v. 587.

VET'ERA CASTRA, a Roman encampment in Germany, which became a town, now Santen, near Cleves. *Tacit. H.* 4. c. 18. *Ann.* 1. c. 45.

VETERA'NIUS or VETRA'NIO, an illiterate general proclaimed emperor in Pannonia, A.D. 350. Constantius compelled him to return to a private station, A.D. 351. *Amm. Marcell.*—*Socr. &c.*

VET'TIUS BOLA'NUS, the tribune of a legion under Corbulo. He was consul with C. Calphurnius Piso. *Stat. Sylv.* 1. 5.

VET'TIUS CHI'LO, a person slain in Gaul by order of Galba, on suspicion of treasonable practices. *Tac. Hist.* 1. c. 37.

VET'TIUS CA'TO, one of the officers of the allies in the Marsian war. He defeated the Romans, and was at last betrayed and murdered. *Cic. Ph.* 12. c. 11.

VET'TIUS SP., a Roman senator who was made interrex at the death of Romulus, till the election of another king. He nominated Numa, and resigned his office. *Plut. in Num.*

L. VET'TIUS JU'DEX, a man who accused Cæsar of being concerned in Catiline's conspiracy. He afterwards devoted himself to the cause of Cæsar, as an informer, and was strangled in prison, it is said, by Cæsar's orders. *Cic.* 2. *Fam.* 24. *Vat.* 10 & 11.—*Dio.* 37.—*Appian. B. C.* 2. 434.—*Suet. Cæs.* 20.

VET'TIUS, a quæstor to Verres in Sicily. *Cic. Verr.* 5. c. 44.——A Roman knight who became enamoured of a young female at Capua, and raised a tumult amongst the slaves, who proclaimed him king. He was betrayed by one of his adherents, upon which he laid violent hands upon himself.

VETTO'NA, a town of Umbria. *Plin.* 3. c. 14.

VETTO'NES, VETO'NES, or VECTO'NES, an ancient nation of Spain, between the Durius and Tagus. *Sil.* 3. v. 378.—*Plin.* 25. c. 8.

VETULO'NIA or VETULO'NIUM, one of the chief cities of Etruria, whose waters were famous. The Romans were said to derive the badges of their magisterial officers thence. *Plin.* 2. c. 103. l. 3. c. 5.—*Ital.* 8. v. 484.—*Dionys. Hal.* 3.

VETU'RIA, one of the Roman tribes, divided into

the two branches of the Junii and Senii. It received its name of the Veturian family, which was originally called Vetusian. *Liv.* 36.

VETU'RIA, the mother of Coriolanus. She was solicited by the Roman matrons to go to her son with her daughter-in-law, and entreat him not to make war against his country. She went and prevailed over Coriolanus, and for her services to the state, the Roman senate offered to reward her as she pleased. She only asked to raise a temple to the goddess of female fortune, which was done on the very spot where she had pacified her son. *Liv.* 2. c. 40. *Dionys. Hal.* 7, &c.

VETU'RIUS, a Roman artist, who made shields for Numa. *Vid.* Mamurius.——A Roman who conspired against Galba. *Tacit. Hist.* 1. c. 25.——A consul appointed one of the Decemvirs.——A consul defeated by the Samnites, and obliged to pass under the yoke with great ignominy.——A tribune of the people, &c.

VETU'RIUS CA'IUS, a Roman consul, accused before the people, and fined because he had acted with imprudence while in office.

VE'TUS L., a Roman who proposed to open a communication between the Mediterranean and the German oceans, by means of a canal. He was put to death by order of Nero.

VE'TUS, a man accused of adultery, &c.

VI'A a city of Mauritania Cæsariensis. *Ptol.*——A river of Hispania Tarraconensis. *Id.*

VI'A ÆMYL'IA, a celebrated road, made by the consul M. Æmylius Lepidus, A.U.C. 567. It led with the Flaminian road to Aquileia. There was also another of the same name in Etruria, which led from Pisæ to Dertona.

VI'A AP'PIA was made by the censer Appius, and led from Rome to Capua, and from Capua to Brundusium, a distance of 350 miles, which the Romans called a five days' journey. It passed successively through the towns and stages of Aricia, Forum Appii, Tarracina, Fundi, Minturnæ, Sinuessa, Capua, Claudium, Beneventum, Equotuticum, Herdonia, Canusium, Barium, and Egnatia to Brundusium. It was called by way of eminence *regina viarum*, and was made so strong, and the stones so well cemented together, that it remained entire for many hundred years. Some parts of it are still to be seen in the neighbourhood of Naples. Appius carried it only 130 miles, as far as Capua, A U.C. 442, and it was finished as far as Brundusium by Augustus.

VI'A MINU'CIA or NUMIC'IA, a road which led to Brundusium, but by what places is now uncertain.

VI'A FLAMIN'IA was made by the censor Flaminius, A.U.C. 533. It led from the Campus Martius, to the modern town of Rimini, on the Adriatic, through the country of the Osci and Etrurians, at the distance of about 360 miles.

VI'A LA'TA, one of the ancient streets of Rome.

VI'A VALE'RIA led from Rome to the country of the Marsi, through the territories of the Sabines. There were besides many streets and roads of inferior note, such as the Aurelia, Cassia, Campana, Ardeatina, Lavicana, Domitiana, Ostiensis, Prænestina, &c., all of which were made and constantly kept in repair at the public expense. For an account of these and other roads, see *Hoffman's Lexicon Universale.*

VIACIEN'SES, a people of Spain. *Plin.* 3. c. 3.

VI'ADUS VI'ADRUS or VIA'DRUS, the classical name of the Oder, which rises in Moravia, and falls by three mouths into the Baltic. *Ptol.*

VIA'LIS, a surname of Mercury, because he presided over public roads. The Lares were also called Viales. *Voss. de Idolol.* 1. c. 11.

VIB'ERI, a people dwelling near the source of the Rhone. *Plin.* 3. c. 20.

VIBID'IA, one of the Vestal virgins in the favour of Messalina, &c. *Tacit. Ann.* 11. c. 32.

VIBID'IUS, a friend of Mæcenas. *Hor.* 2. sat. 8. v. 22.

VIBID'IUS VAR'RO, a prodigal and needy senator degraded by Tiberius. *Tac. Ann.* 2. c. 48.

VIBIE'NUS, a senator who died in consequence of the wounds he received from the partisans of Clodius in a tumult. *Cic. Mil.* 14.

VIB'IUS, a Roman who refused to pay any attention to Cicero when banished, though he had received from him the most unbounded favors.

VIB'IUS SIC'ULUS. *Vid.* Sica.

VIB'IUS SECUN'DUS, a Roman knight, accused of extortion in Africa, and banished. *Tac Ann.* 14. c. 28.

VIB'IUS AVI'TUS, a præfect of Gaul and Germany, under Nero. *Plin.* 34. c. 7.

VIB'IUS FRON'TO, a præfect of horse. *Tac. Ann.* 2. c. 68.

VIB'IUS MAR'SUS, a person accused by Satrius Secundus of adultery with Albucilla. *Tacit. Ann.* 6 c. 47.

VIB'IUS SERE'NUS, a proconsul of Hispania Citerior, banished for his atrocities to Amorgus, under Tiberius. *Tac. Ann.* 4. c. 13.——An accuser of Fonteius Capito, under Tiberius. *Id. ibid.* 4. c. 36.

VIB'IUS TREBONIA'NUS GAL'LUS, a præfect of Mæsia, proclaimed emperor by one legion. He took for his colleague his son Volusianus, but was slain when Æmilianus was proclaimed emperor, A.D. 255. *Aur. Victor. Jornand de reb. Goth.*—*Zonar.* tom. 2.

VIB'IUS VIR'IUS, a man at Capua who advised his countrymen to revolt to Annibal. When Capua was retaken by the Romans, he poisoned himself not to fall into the hands of the conspirators. *Liv.* 26. c. 13 & 14.

VIB'IUS SEQUES'TER, a Latin writer, whose treatise *De Flaminibus*, &c. is best edited by Oberlin, 8vo. Argent. 1778. *Harles. Not. Lit. Rom.* 1. p. 625. —*Sax. Onom.* 1. p. 450.

VI'BO, a town of Lucania, anciently called Hipponium and Hippo. *Cic. ad Att.* 3. c. 3.—*Plin.* 3. c. 5.——A town of Spain.——A town of the Brutii.

VIBULE'NUS AGRIP'PA, a Roman knight accused of treason. He attempted to poison himself, and was strangled in prison, though almost dead. *Tacit.* 6. *An.* c. 40.

VIBULE'NUS, a mutinous soldier in the army of Germanicus, &c. *Id. ibid.* 1. c 22, &c.

VIBUL'LIUS RU'FUS, a friend of Pompey, taken by Cæsar, &c. *Cic. ad Att.* 8. ep. 1, 2.—*Cæs. B. C.* 3. c. 10.

VIBUL'LIUS, a prætor in Nero's reign. *Tac. Ann.* 13. c. 28.

VICAP'OTA or VI'CA PO'TA, a goddess at Rome, who presided over victory (à *vincere* et *potiri*) *Liv.* 2. c. 7.—*Cic.* 2 *de Leg.* c. 11.—*Seneca.*

VICEL'LIUS, a friend of Galba, who brought him news of Nero's death.

VICEN'TIA or VICE'TIA, a town of Cisalpine Gaul, at the north-west of the Adriatic. *Tacit. Hist.* 3. c. 8.—*Plin.* 3. c. 19. It is now Vicenza.

VIC'TOR SEXT. AURE'LIUS, a writer in the age of Constantius. He gave the world a concise history of the Roman emperors, from the age of Augustus to his own time, or A.D. 360. He also wrote an abridgment of the Roman history before the age of Julius Cæsar, which is now extant, and ascribed by different authors to C. Nepos, to Tacitus, Suetonius, Pliny, &c. Victor was greatly esteemed by the emperors, and honored with the consulship. The best edition of Victor is that of Pitiscus, 8vo. Utr. 1696; and that of Arntzenius, 4to. Amst. 1733. *Vid.* Aurelius.

VIC'TOR a surname of Hercules among the Romans. He had two temples, one near the ox market, and other near the Tergemina Porta. *Servius ad Æn.* 8. v. 361.——A surname of Jupiter, under which he had two temples at Rome. *Rosinus. A. R.* 2. c. 5.

VIC'TOR CLAU'DIUS MA'RIUS, a Christian Latin writer of Marseilles under the emperor Zeno, who composed a poem in three books on Genesis, in 1850 heroic lines, addressed to his son Æthereus, and also an epistle on the degenerate manners of the age in 105 verses, in which he displays his learning more than his genius, or the effusions of a brilliant mind. *Harles. Not. Lit. Rom.* 1. p. 751.

VIC'TOR CLAU'DIUS, a general sent against Vocula. *Tac. Hist.* 4. c. 33.

VICTO'RIA, one of the deities of the Romans, called by the Greeks Nice, supposed to be daughter of the giant Pallas, or of Titan and Styx. The goddess of Victory was sister to Strength and Valor, and was one of the attendants of Jupiter. She was greatly honored by the Greeks, particularly at Athens. Sylla raised her a temple at Rome, and instituted festivals in her honor. She was represented with wings, crowned with laurel, and holding the branch of a palm-tree in her hand. A golden statue of this goddess, weighing 320 pounds, was presented to the Romans by Hiero, king of Syracuse, and deposited in the temple of Jupiter, on the Capitoline hill. The Ægyptians, who worshipped Victory under the appellation of Naphte, represented her under the form of an eagle, as that bird is strong and always victorious against all other birds. *Liv.* 22.—*Varr. de L.L.* 4. c. 10.—*Hesiod. Theog.* 384.—*Hygin.* fab.—*Aul. Gell.* 6. c. 6.—*Paus.* 1. c. 22. l. 3. c. 15.—*Dio. Cass.* 51.—*Apul. Met.* 2.—*Turneb. adv.* 27. c. 5.—*Sueton. in Aug.* 100.—*Tac. Ann.* 14. c. 32.—*Servius ad Virg. Æn.* 6. v. 134.—*Aug. de Civ. D.* 4. c. 14 & 15.—*Ovid. Met* 1. v. 13.—*Auson.* ep. 1. v. 2.—*Claudian. de Stil.* 3. v. 203. & *de* 6. *Cons. H.* 597. [A statue of Victory will be found in the collection at Florence.]

VICTO'RIA, an inland city of Mauritania Cæsariensis. *Ptol.* It is now Moascar according to *Sanson.*

VICTO'RIÆ MONS, a place of Spain at the mouth of the Iberus. *Liv.* 24. c. 41. It is now Monzia.

VICTORI'NA or VICTO'RIA, a celebrated matron who placed herself at the head of the Roman armies, and made war against the emperor Gallienus. Her son Victorinus, and her grandson of the same name, were declared emperors, but when they were assassinated, Victorina invested with the imperial purple one of her favorites called Tetricus. She was some time after poisoned, A.D. 269, and, according to some, by Tetricus himself. *Trebell. Poll. de* 30. *Tyran.* c. 5, &c.

VICTORI'NUS MAR'CUS PIAVVO'NIUS, a colleague of Posthumus in the empire. He was put to death by a person whose wife he had debauched. *Id ibid.* c. 5 & 6.

VICTORI'NUS JU'NIOR, son of the preceding, was proclaimed Cæsar by his father, and slain soon after by the soldiers. *Id. ibid* c. 7.

VICTORI'NUS FA'BIUS LAUREN'TIUS MA'RIUS, a Christian writer in the age of Constantius, who composed an inelegant epic poem in 338 verses on the death of the seven children mentioned in the Maccabees, and several other theological and critical works, and distinguished himself by the active part which he took in his writings against the Arians. His commentary on the "Rhetorica" of Cicero was published, Mediolan. 1474 & 1509, and is in the "Rhetores Antiqui" of Pithoeus, Paris, 1599, and of Caperoner. Argentor. 1756. His treatise "De Enunciatione Literarum, &c.," is among the "Rei Grammaticæ Auctores," published at Basil, 1527, and of Putschius, p. 2450, &c. *Vid. Harles. Not. Lit. Rom.* 1. p. 582 & 663.—*Sax. Onom.* 1. p. 407.—*Vossius de P. Lat.*

VICTO'RIUS, a man of Aquitain, who, A.D. 463, invented the paschal cycle of 532 years. *Harles. Not. Lit. Rom.* 1. p. 685.—*Sax. Onom.* 1. p. 514.

VICTO'RIUS MARCEL'LUS, a Roman of eminence, to whom Quintilian inscribed his system of rhetoric. *Quintil,*

VICTUM'VIÆ, a small town of Insubria near Placentia. *Liv.* 21. c. 45.

VI'CUS LON'GUS, a street at Rome, where an altar was raised by Virginia to the goddess Pudicitia, or the modesty of the Plebeians. *Liv.* 10. c. 23.

VI'CUS CYP'RIUS, a place on the Esquiline hill, where the Sabines dwelt.

VIDUCAS'SES, a people of Normandy. *Plin.* 4. c. 18.

VIEN'NA, a town of Gallia Narbonensis, on the Rhone below Lyons. *Strab.* 1.—*Cæs. Bell. G.* 7. c. 9.

VIGEL'LIUS M., a disciple and friend of Panætius. *Cic. Orat.* 3. c. 21.

VIL'LIA LEX, *annalis* or *annaria*, by L. Villius, the tribune, A.U.C. 574, defined the proper age required for exercising the office of a magistrate, 25 years for the quæstorship, 27 or 28 for the ædileship or tribuneship, for the office of prætor 30, and for that of consul 43. *Liv.* 11. c. 44.

VIL'LIUS L., a tribune of the people, author of the Villian law, and thence called Annalis, a surname borne by his family. *Liv.* 11. c. 44.—*Cic. Rull.* 2. c. 2.

VIL'LIUS PUB'LIUS, a Roman ambassador sent to Antiochus. He held a conference with Annibal, who was at the monarch's court.

VIL'LIUS, a man who disgraced himself by his criminal amours with the daughter of Sylla. *Horat.* 1. sat. 2. v. 64.

VILUM'BRI, a people in the east of Umbria. *Ptol.* Their chief town was Spoletium.

VIMINA'LIS, one of the seven hills on which Rome was built, so called from the number of osiers (*vimines*) which grew there. Servius Tullius first made it part of the city. Jupiter had a temple there, whence he was called Viminalis. *Liv.* 1. c. 44.—*Varro. de L.L.* 4. c. 8.—*Festus de V. Sig.* —*Rosinus, A. R.* 2. c. 4.

VINA'LIA, festivals at Rome in honor of Jupiter and Venus. In the ceremonies observed in honor of Venus, and thence called Veneralia, and celebrated in April, wine was liberally distributed to the people in the temple of the goddess, and her sanctuary, as surnamed Erycina, was frequented by the courtezans of Rome, who, in offering her roses, myrtle, and incense, implored her protection, the gifts of beauty and personal attraction, and the favor of the public. In the Vinalia of Jupiter observed in August, the priest of the god made on the altar the first oblation of wine, and before this festival it was not lawful to drink the new made wine. *Varro. de L.L.* 5.—*Festus. de V. Sig.*—*Ovid. Fast.* 4. v. 861.—*Plin.* 18. c. 29.—*Rosin. A.R.* 4. c. 8 & 12.

VINCEN'TIUS, surnamed Lirinensis or Lerenensis from the place of his birth, one of the Christian fathers, A.D. 434, whose works are best edited by Baluzius, Paris, 1669. *Harles. Not. Lit. Rom.* 1. p. 689.—*Fabr. B. Lat.* 6. p. 300.—*Sax. Onom.* 1. p. 409.

VIN'CIUS RUFI'NUS, a Roman knight condemned under Nero. *Tacit. Ann.* 14. c. 40.

VIN'CIUS, an officer in Germany.

VINDA'LIUS, a writer in the reign of Constantius, who wrote ten books on agriculture.

VINDEL'ICI, an ancient people of Germany, between the heads of the Rhine and the Danube. Their country, which was called Vindelicia, now forms part of Swabia and Bavaria, and their chief town, Augusta Vindelicorum, is now Ausburgh. *Horat.* 4 od. 4. v. 18.

VIN'DELIS, an island of the Durotriges on the coast of Britain. *Antonin.* It is now Portland. *Camden.*

VINDEMIA'TOR, a constellation that rose about the nones of March. *Ovid. Fast.* 3. v. 407.—*Plin.* 18. c. 31.

VIN'DEX JU'LIUS, a governor of Gaul, who revolted against Nero, and determined to deliver the Roman empire from his tyranny. He was followed by a numerous army, but at last defeated by one of the emperor's generals. When he perceived that all was lost, he laid violent hands upon himself, A.D. 68. *Sueton. in Galb.*—*Ner.* 41.—*Tacit. H.* 1. c. 51.—*Plin.* 9. ep. 19.

VINDIC'IUS, a slave who discovered the conspiracy which some of the most noble of the Roman citizens had formed to restore Tarquin to his throne. He was amply rewarded, and made a citizen of Rome. *Liv.* 2. c. 5.—*Plut. in Popl.*

VIN'DILI or VAN'DALI, a nation of Germany. *Plin.* 4. c. 14.

VIN'DIUS, a mountain of Hispania Tarraconensis. *Ptol.* 2. c. 6. It is now Monte de las Asturias.

VINDOM'AGUS, a city of Gallia Narbonensis. *Ptol.*

VINDONIS'SA, now Windisch, a town of the Helvetii on the Aar, in the territory of Berne. *Tacit.* 4. *Hist.* 61 & 70.

VINIC'IUS or VINU'CIUS, a Roman consul poisoned by Messalina, &c.

VINIC'IUS, a man who conspired against Nero, &c. ——A young man intimate with Augustus. *Suet. Aug.* 46, 71.

VINID'IUS, a miser mentioned by *Horace*, 1. sat. 1. v. 95. Some manuscripts read Numidius and Umidius.

VIN'IUS T., a commander in the prætorian guards, intimate with Galba, of whom he became the first minister. He was honored with the consulship, and some time after, in consequence of his profligacy and many crimes, he was murdered. *Tacit. H.* 1. c. 11, 42 & 48.—*Plut.*

VIN'IUS, a man who revolted from Nero.

VIN'IUS, a river of Samnium, flowing into the Liris. *Varro.* It is now Fiume di S. Germano.

VIN'NIUS ASEL'LA, a servant of Horace, to whom *Ep.* 13. is addressed to instruct him how to deliver to Augustus some poems from his master.

VIPSA'NIA, a daughter of M. Agrippa, mother of Drusus She was the only one of Agrippa's daughters who died a natural death. She was married to Tiberius when a private man, and when she had been repudiated, she married Asinius Gallus. *Tacit. A.* 1. c 12. l. 3. c. 19.

VIPSA'NIUS LE'NAS, a proconsul condemned for his avaricious conduct in Sardinia. *Tac. Ann.* 13. c. 30.

VIPSA'NIUS MESSA'LA, a tribune of the army in Mæsia. *Tac. Hist.* 3. c. 9.

VIRA'GO, a name applied to Minerva and Diana, as expressive of the boldness, the fortitude, and manly exertions of their character. *Ovid. Met.* 2. v. 765. l. 6. v. 130.—*Seneca in Hippol.* 54.—*Stat.* 4. *Sylv.* 5. v. 33.——A name applied to Medusa and to Jupiter. *Stat. Theb.* 11. v. 414.—*Virg. Æn.* 12. v. 468.

VIR'BIUS, (qui inter *viros bis* fuit,) a name given to Hippolytus, after he had been brought back to life by Æsculapius, at the instance of Diana, who pitied his unfortunate end. Some suppose that Æsculapius was destroyed by Jupiter for raising him to life, and that he was concealed in a forest in Italy by Diana, under the name of Virbius. Here he married Aricia, and had a son called also Virbius, who supported Turnus against Æneas. *Virg. Æn.* 7. v. 762.—*Ovid. Met.* 15. v. 544.—*Hygin.* fab. 251.—*Servius ad Æn.* 5. v. 95. l. 7. v. 761.—*Lactant. ad Ovid. Met.* 15.

VIR'CAO, a town of Hispania Bætica, between Corduba and Iliturgis. *Antonin.*

VIR'DIUS GEM'INUS, a general of Vespasian. *Tac. Hist.* 3. c. 48.

PUBL. VIRGIL'IUS or VERGIL'IUS MA'RO, called the prince of the Latin poets, was born at Andes, a village near Mantua, about 70 years before Christ, on the 15th of October. His first years were spent at Cremona, where his taste was formed, and his rising talents first exercised. The distribution of the lands of Cremona to the soldiers of Augustus, after the battle of Philippi, nearly proved fatal to the poet, and when he attempted to dispute the possession of his fields with a soldier, Virgil was obliged to save his life from the resentment of the lawless veteran, by swimming across a river. This was the beginning of his greatness, he with his father repaired to Rome, where he soon formed an acquaintance with Mæcenas, and recommended himself to the favor of Augustus. The emperor restored his lands to the poet, whose modest muse knew so well how to pay the tribute of gratitude, and his first bucolic was written to thank the patron, as well as to tell the world that his favors were not unworthily bestowed. The ten bucolics were written in about three years. The poet showed his countrymen that he could write with grateful simplicity, with elegance, delicacy of sentiment, and with purity of language. Some time after Virgil undertook the Georgics, a poem the most perfect and finished of all Latin compositions. The Æneid (*Vid.* Æneis) was begun, as some suppose, at the particular request of Augustus, and the poet, while he attempted to prove that the Julian family was lineally descended from the founder of Lavinium, visibly described in the pious and benevolent character of his hero, the amiable qualities of his imperial patron. The great merit of this poem is well known, and it will ever remain undecided, which of the two poets, Homer or Virgil, is more entitled to our praise, our applause, and our admiration. The writer of the Iliad stood as a pattern to the favorite of Augustus. The voyage of Æneas is copied from the Odyssey, and for his battles, Virgil found a model in the wars of Troy, and the animated descriptions of the Iliad. The poet died before he had revised this immortal work, which had already engaged his time for eleven successive years. He had attempted to attend his patron in the east, but he was detained at Naples on account of his ill health. He however went to Athens, where he met Augustus on his return, but he soon after fell sick at Megara, and ordered himself to be removed to Italy. He landed at Brundusium, where he expired a few days after, on the 22nd of September, in the 51st year of his age, B.C. 19. He left the greatest part of his immense possessions to his friends, particularly to Mæcenas, Tucca, and Augustus, and he ordered as his last will his unfinished poem to be burnt. These last injunctions were disobeyed, and according to the words of an ancient poet, Augustus saved his favorite Troy from a second and more dismal conflagration. The poem was delivered by the emperor to three of his literary friends. They were ordered to revise and to expunge whatever they deemed improper, but they were strictly enjoined not to make any additions, and this, as some suppose, is the cause that so many lines of the Æneid are unfinished, particularly in the last books. The body of the poet, according to his own directions, was conveyed to Naples, and interred with much solemnity in a monument erected on the road that leads from Naples to Puteoli. The following modest distich was engraved on the tomb, written by the poet some few moments before he expired:

Mantua me genuit; Calabri rapuere; tenet nunc
Parthenope: cecini pascua, rura duces.

The Romans were not insensible to the merit of their poet. Virgil received much applause in the capital, and when he entered the theatre he was astonished and delighted to see the crowded audience rise up to him, as an emperor, and welcome his approach by repeated plaudits. He was naturally modest and of a timorous disposition. When people crowded to gaze upon him, or pointed at him with the finger with raptures, the poet blushed and stole away from them, and often hid himself in shops to be removed from the curiosity and the admiration of the public. The most liberal and gratifying marks of approbation which he received were from the emperor and from Octavia. He attempted in Æneid to paint the virtues, and to lament the premature death of the son of Octavia, and he was desired by the emperor to repeat the lines in the presence of the afflicted mother. He had no sooner begun *O nate*, &c. than Octavia burst into tears; he continued, but he had artfully suppressed the name of her son, and when he repeated in the 16th line the well-known words *Tu Marcellus eris*, the princess swooned away, and the poet withdrew, but not without being liberally rewarded. Octavia presented him ten sesterces for every one of his verses in praise of her son, the whole of which was equivalent to £2000 English money. As an instance of his modesty, the following circumstance has been recorded. Virgil wrote this distich, in which he compared his patron to Jupiter,

Nocte pluit totâ, redeunt, spectacula mane
Divisum imperium cum Jove Cæsar habet,

and placed it in the night on the gates of the palace of Augustus. Enquiries were made for the author by order of Augustus, and when Virgil had the diffidence not to declare himself, Bathyllus, a contemptible poet of the age, claimed the verses as his own, and was liberally rewarded. This displeased Virgil; he again wrote the verses near the palace, and under them

Hos ego versiculos feci, tulit alter honores;

with the beginning of another line in these words

Sic vos non vobis,

four times repeated. Augustus wished the lines to be finished, Bathyllus seemed unable, and Virgil at last, by completing the stanzas in the following order—

Sic vos non vobis nidificatis aves;
Sic vos non vobis vellera fertis oves;
Sic vos non vobis mellificatis apes;
Sic vos non vobis fertis aratra boves,

proved himself to be the author of the distich, and the poetical usurper became the sport and ridicule of Rome. In the works of Virgil we can find a more perfect and satisfactory account of the religious ceremonies and customs of the Romans, than in all the other Latin poets, Ovid excepted. Everything he mentions is founded upon historical truth; and though he borrowed much from his predecessors, and even whole lines from Ennius, yet he has the happiness to make it all his own. He was uncommonly severe in revising his own poetry, and he used often to compare himself to a bear that licks her cubs into shape. In his connecetions, Virgil was remarkable; his friends enjoyed his unbounded confidence, and his library and possessions seemed to be the property of the public. Like other great men, he was not without his enemies and detractors in his life-time, but from their aspersions he received additional lustre. Among the very numerous and excellent editions of Virgil, these few may be collected as the best: that of Masvicius, 2 vols 4to. Leovardiæ, 1717; of Baskerville, 4to. Birmingham, 1757; Of the Variorum, L. Bat. 1661; of Heyne, 4 vols. 8vo. Lips. 1767; of Edinburgh, 2 vols. 12mo. 1755; and of Glasgow, 12mo. 1758. Some deny that Virgil was the author of the poems Culex, Ciris, Moretum, Copa, &c. usually ascribed to him. *Harles. Not. Lit. Rom.* 1. p. 232. & 2. p. 276.—*Paterc.* 2. c. 36.—*Horat.* sat. 5. v, 40.—*Propert.* 2. el. 34. v. 61.—*Ovid. Trist.* 4. el. 10. v. 51. *Am.* 1. el. 15. v. 27. *De. A.A.* 3. v. 337.—*Stat. Theb.* 12. v. 827.—*Mart.* 8. ep. 56.—*Juv.* 11. v. 178.—*Quintil.* 10 c. 1.—*Plin* 3. ep. 21.—*Lamprid. in vit. Sever.* [Both a statue and a bust of Virgil will be found in the Capitol at Rome.]

VIRGIL'IUS CA'IUS, a prætor of Sicily, who, when Cicero was banished, refused to receive the exiled orator, though his friend, for fear of the resentment of Clodius. *Cic. ad Q. Fratr.* 1. ep. 2. *Planc.* 40. *Att.* 12. ep. 51. l. 13. ep. 26.

VIRGIL'IUS MAR'CUS, a tribune who opposed the going of Sylla to the Mithridatic war. *Cic. Br.* 48.—*Plut. in Syll.*

VIRGIL'IUS, a comic poet at Rome in the age of Trajan. commended by *Pliny*, 6. ep. 21. *ad Canin.*

VIRGINEN'SIS, a deity at Rome, to whom women on their marriage consecrated their girdle. Her statue was placed in the bridal chamber late on the evening of the nuptials. She was honored at Athens under the name of Lysizone. *Aug. de Civ. D.* 6. c. 9.

VIRGIN'IA, a daughter of the centurion L. Virginius. Appius Claudius, the decemvir, became enamoured of her, and attempted to remove her from the place where she resided. She was claimed by one of his favorites as the daughter of a slave, and Appius, in the capacity and with the authority of judge, had pronounced the sentence, and delivered her into the hands of his friend, when Virginius, informed of his violent proceedings, arrived from the camp. The father demanded to see his daughter; and when this request was granted, he snatched up a knife and plunged it into Virginia's breast, exclaiming, "This is all, my dearest daughter, I can give thee, to preserve thy chastity from the lust and violence of a tyrant." No sooner was the blow given than Virginius ran to the camp with the bloody knife in his hand. The soldiers were astonished and incensed, not against the murderer, but the tyrant who was the cause of Virginia's death, and they immediately marched to Rome Appius was seized, but he destroyed himself in prison, and prevented the execution of the law. Spurius Oppius, another of the decemvirs, who had not opposed the tyrant's views, killed himself also, and Marcus Claudius, the favorite of Appius, was put to death, and the decemviral power abolished, about 449 years B.C. *Liv.* 3. c, 44, &c.—*Juv.* 10. v. 294. ——A daughter of A. Virginius, the patrician. She married the plebeian consul Volumnius, and admission to the celebration of the festival in honor of patrician chastity being refused her by the patrician matrons, she erected a temple to plebeian chastity. *Liv.* 10. c. 23.

VIRGIN'IUS, the father of Virginia, made tribune of the people. *Vid.* Virginia.——A tribune of the people who accused Q. Cæso, the son of Cincinnatus. He increased the number of the tribunes to ten, and distinguished himself by his seditions against the patricians.——A tribune in the age of Camillus, fined for opposition to a law which proposed the going to Veii.——An augur who died of the plague.——A tribune who encouraged Cinna to criminate Sylla.——One of the generals of Nero in Germany. He made war against Vindex, and conquered him. He was treated with great coldness by Galba, whose interest he had supported with so much success. He refused all dangerous situations, and, though twice offered the imperial purple, he rejected it with disdain. *Plut.*——A Roman orator and rhetorician in the age of Quintilian. *Quintil.* 3. c. 1, &c

VIRGIN'IUS CA'IUS, a prætor of Sicily, who opposed the entrance of Cicero into his province, though under many obligations to the orator. Some read Virgilius.

VIRIA'THUS, a mean shepherd of Lusitania, who gradually rose to power, and, by first leading a gang of robbers, saw himself followed by a numerous army. He made war against the Romans with uncommon success, and for 14 years enjoyed the envied title of protector of public liberty in the provinces of Spain. Many generals were defeated, and Pompey himself was ashamed to find himself beaten. Cæpio was at last sent against him, but his despair of conquering him by force of arms obliged him to have recourse to artifice, and he had the meanness to bribe the servants of Viriathus to murder their master, B.C. 40.—*Flor.* 2. c. 17.—*Val, Max.* 6. c. 4.—*Liv.* 52 & 54.—*Auct. de Vir. Ill.* 71.—*Eutrop.* 4. c. 15.—*Sil. It.* 3. v. 354.—*Orosius*, 5. c. 4.——A Spanish general in the second Punic war, slain by Paulus Æmylius. *Ital.* 3. v. 354. l. 10. v. 233.

VIRIDOM'ARUS, a young man of great power among the Ædui. Cæsar greatly honored him, but he fought at last against the Romans, and was killed in single combat by Marcellus.—*Plut. in Marc.*—*Cæs. Bell. G.* 7. c. 39, &c.

VIRID'OVIX, a general of the Unelli. *Cæs. B. G.* 3. c. 17.

VIRIPLA'CA or VIRIP'LACA, a goddess among the Romans who presided over the peace of families, whence her name (*virum placare*). If any quarrel happened between a man and his wife, they generally repaired to the temple of the goddess, which was erected on the Palatine mount, and came back reconciled. *Val. Max.* 2. c. 1.—*Pub. Victor.*

VIROVES'CA or BURVES'CA, a town of Hispania Tarraconensis. *Ptol.* It is now Breviesca.

VIR'RO, a fictitious name introduced into *Juvenal's* 5th sat. v. 49, &c.

VIR'TUS, a deity worshipped at Rome. Marcellus erected two temples, one to Virtue, and the other to Honor. They were built in such a manner, that, to see the temple of Honor, it was necessary to pass through that of Virtue; a happy allegory among a nation free and independent. The principal virtues were distinguished each by their attire. Prudence was known by her rule, and her pointing to a globe at her feet; Temperance had a bridle; Justice had an equal balance, and Fortitude leant against her sword: Honesty was clad in a transparent vest; Modesty appeared veiled; Clemency wore an olive branch, and Devotion threw incense upon an altar; Tranquillity was seen to lean on a column; Health was known by her serpent, Liberty by her cap, and Gaiety by her myrtle. *Cic, de Nat. D.* 2. c. 23.—*Plaut. in Amph. Prol.*—*Liv.* 29. c. 11.—*Val, Max.* 1. c. 1.—*Aug de Civ. D.* 4. c. 20.

VIRU'NUM, a town of Noricum. *Ptol.* Geographers are not agreed as to its modern name.

VIS'BIUS, an author who flourished under Domitian. He wrote the life of Dionysius the Areopagite. *Voss. H. Lat.* 1. c 29.

VISBUR'GII, a people of Germany. *Ptol.*

VISCEL'LÆ, now Weltz, a town of Noricum, between the Ens and Mure. *Cic. Am.* 11.

VISCELLI'NUS, a surname of Sp. Cassius, who was thrown down from the Tarpeian rock for aspiring to sovereignty. *Cic. Am.* 11.

VISE'IUS, a man of mean occupation at Pisaurum, made tribune by Antony. *Cic. Ph.* 13. c. 12.

VISEL'LIA LEX was made by Visellius Varro the consul, A.U.C. 776, to restrain the introduction of improper persons into the offices of the state. *Dempster. Antiq. Rom.* 8. c. 15.

L. VISEL'LIUS VAR'RO, a lieutenant in Germany under Tiberius. *Tac. Ann.* 3. c. 41. l. 4. c. 17.

CA'IUS VISEL'LIUS VAR'RO, a relation of Cicero. *Cic. Br.* 76.

VISEL'LUS, a man whose father-in-law the commentators of Horace believe to have been afflicted with a hernia, from their observations on this verse, 1. sat. 1. v. 105 *Est inter Tanaim quiddam, socerumque Viselli.*

VISID'IUS L., a Roman knight who defended Cicero when threatened during Catiline's conspiracy. He afterwards opposed Antony's party with great spirit. *Cic. Phil.* 7. c. 9.

VIS'IO, a town of Gallia Narbonensis. *Antonin.*

VIS'TULA or VISTIL'LUS, a river falling into the Baltic, the eastern boundary of ancient Germany.

VISUR'GIS, a river of Germany, now called the Weser, and falling into the German Ocean. Varus and his legions were cut to pieces near it by the Germans. *Vell.* 2. c. 105.—*Tacit. An.* 1. c. 70. l. 2. c. 9.

VIT'ACA, a town of Mauritania Cæsariensis. *Ptol.*

VITEL'LIA, a Roman colony on the borders of the Æqui. *Liv.* 5. c. 29.

VITEL'LIUS AU'LUS, a Roman raised by his vices to the throne. He was descended from one of the most illustrious families of Rome, and as such he gained an easy admission into the palace of the emperors. The greatest part of his youth was spent at Capreæ, where his willingness to gratify the most vicious propensities of Tiberius raised his father to the dignity of consul, and governor of Syria. The applause which he gained in this school of debauchery was too great and flattering to induce Vitellius to alter his conduct, and no longer to be one of the votaries of vice. Caligula was pleased with his skill in driving a chariot; Clodius loved him because he was a great gamester; and he recommended him to the favors of Nero by wishing him to sing publicly in the crowded theatre. With such an insinuating disposition, it is not to be wondered that Vitellius became so great. He did not fall with his patrons, like the other favorites, but the death of an emperor seemed to raise him to greater honors, and to procure him fresh applause. He passed through all the offices of the state, and gained the soldiery by donations and liberal promises. He was at the head of the Roman legions in Germany when Otho was proclaimed emperor; and the exaltation of his rival was no sooner heard in the camp, than he was likewise invested with the purple by his soldiers. He accepted with pleasure the dangerous office, and instantly marched against Otho. Three battles were fought, and in all Vitellius was conquered. A fourth, however, between the plains of Mantua and Cremona, left him master of the field and of the Roman empire. He feasted his eyes in viewing the bodies of the slain, and the ground covered with blood; and, regardless of the insalubrity of the air, proceeding from so many carcasses, he told his attendants that the smell of a dead enemy was always sweet. His first care was not like that of a true conqueror, to alleviate the distresses of the conquered, or patronise the friends of the dead, but it was to insult their misfortunes, and to intoxicate himself, with the companions of his debauchery, in the field of battle. Each successive day exhibited a scene of greater extravagance. Vitellius feasted four or five times a day, and such was his excess, that he often made himself vomit to begin his repast afresh, and to gratify his palate with more luxury. His food was of the most rare and exquisite nature: the deserts of Libya, the shores of Spain, and the waters of the Carpathian sea, were diligently searched to supply the table of the emperor. The most celebrated of his feasts was that with which he was treated by his brother Lucius. The table, among other meats, was covered with two thousand different dishes of fish, and seven thousand of fowls; and so expensive was he in every thing, that above seven millions sterling were spent in maintaining his table in the space of four months; and Josephus has properly observed, that if Vitellius had reigned long, the great opulence of all the Roman empire would have been found insufficient to defray the expenses of his banquets. This extravagance, which delighted the favorites soon raised the indignation of the people. Vespasian was proclaimed emperor by the army, and his minister Primus was sent to destroy the imperial glutton. Vitellius concealed himself under the bed of the porter of his palace; but this obscure retreat betrayed him, he was dragged naked through the streets, his hands were tied behind his back, and a drawn sword was placed under his chin to make him lift up his head. After suffering the greatest insults from the populace, he was at last carried to the place of execution, and put to death with repeated blows. His head was cut off and fixed to a pole, and his mutilated body dragged with a hook, and thrown into the Tiber, A.D. 69, after a reign of one year except twelve days. *Suet.*—*Tac. Hist.* 2.—*Eutrop.*—*Dio.*—*Plut.* [The finest bust of Vitellius will be found in the Museum of the Capitol at Rome.]

Vitel'lius Lu'cius, the father of the emperor, obtained great honors by his flattery to the emperors. He was made governor of Syria, and in this distant province he obliged the Parthians to sue for peace. His adulation to Messalina is well known, and he obtained as a particular favor the honorable office of pulling off the shoes of the empress, &c. *Suet, &c.*

Vitel'lius, a brother of the emperor, who enjoyed his favors by encouraging his gluttony, &c. ——One of the flatterers of Tiberius.——A son of the emperor Vitellius, put to death by one of his father's friends.—Some of the family of the Vitellii conspired with the Aquilii and other illustrious Romans to restore Tarquin to his throne. Their conspiracy was discovered by the consuls, and they were severely punished. *Plut. &c.*

Vitel'lius Pub'lius, an uncle of the emperor of that name. He was accused under Nero of attempts to bribe the people against the emperor, with money from the treasury. He killed himself before his trial.

Vitel'lius Saturni'nus, an officer of the prætorians under Otho. *Tacit. H.* 1. c. 82.

VITER'BUM, a town of Tuscany, where Fanum Volumnæ stood. It is not mentioned by classical writers. *Liv.* 4. c. 23 & 61. l. 5. c. 17.

VIT'IA, the mother of Fusius Geminus, put to death by Tiberius, for weeping at the death of her son, &c. *Tacit. Ann.* 6. c. 10.

VITIS'ATOR, a surname of Saturn and Bacchus, they presided over the cultivation of the vine. *Ennius, apud Macrob.* 6. c. 5.—*Virg. Æn.* 7. v. 199.—*Arnob. Adv.* 3.

VIT'RICUS, a surname of Mars. *Ovid.*

M. VITRU'VIUS POL'LIO, a celebrated architect, born at Formiæ, in the age of Augustus. He is known only by his writings, and nothing is recorded in history of his life or private character. He wrote a treatise on his profession, in 10 books, which he dedicated to Augustus, and it is the only book on architecture now extant, written by the ancients. In this work he plainly shows that he was master of his profession, and that he possessed both genius and abilities. The best edition of Vitruvius is that of De Laet, Amst. 1649. *Harles. Not. Lit. Rom.* 1. p. 207.—*Sax. Onom.* 1. 177.

VIT'ULA, a deity among the Romans who presided over festivals and rejoicings. *Macrob.* 3. c. 2.

VITULA'RIA VI'A, a road in the country of Arpinum. *Cic. Q. Fr.* 3. ep. 1.

VITUM'NUS, a deity at Rome, who was invoked by women after conception, that he might preserve the fœtus and bring it to maturity. *Aug. de Civ. D.* 7. c. 3.

VI'VA, a city of Africa Propria. *Antonin.*

VIVENTA'NI, a people of Umbria. *Ptol.*

VIVIA'NUS AN'NIUS, a son-in-law of Corbulo, lieutenant of the 5th legion, in the Armenian war. *Tac Ann.* 15. c. 28.

VOBER'CA or **VOBER'TA**, a town of Hispania Tarraconensis. *Martial.* 4. epigr. 50. v. 14.

VO'BRIX, a town of Mauritania Tingitana. *Ptol.*

VO'CA, a city of the Callaici in Spain. *Id.*

VOCE'TUS or **VOCE'TIUS**, part of mount Jura. *Tacit. H.* 1. c. 68.

VOCO'NIA LEX, *de testamentis*, by Q. Voconius Saxa, the tribune, A.U.C. 524, enacted, that no woman should be left heiress to an estate, and that no rich person should leave by his will more than the fourth part of his fortune to a woman. This step was taken to prevent the decay of the noblest and most illustrious of the families of Rome. This law was abrogated by Augustus. *Dempster. Antiq. Rom.* 8. c. 18.

VOCO'NII FO'RUM, a town of Gaul, between Antibes and Marseilles. *Cic.* 10. *Fam.* 17.

VOCO'NIUS VIC'TOR, a Latin poet, &c. *Martial.* 7. epigr. 28.—*Plin.* 2. ep 13.

Voco'nius Sax'a, a tribune who made the Voconian law.

Voco'nius, an officer of Lucullus in Asia. The family of the Voconii were originally from Africa. *Cic. Ph.* 3. c. 6.

VOCON'TIA, VOCUN'TIA or **VOCON'TII**, a people of Gallia Narbonensis. *Silius*, 3. v. 467. Their country is now Val de Viso.

VOC'ULA DIL'LIUS, a Roman general under Vespasian, defeated and slain by the Gauls, after a successful campaign. *Tacit. Hist.* 2. c. 24, &c.

VODOM'ARUS, a king of part of Gaul. The emperor Constantius urged him to make war against Julian the Apostate; but his letters were intercepted, and he was sent prisoner to Spain, *Amm. Marcell.* l. 21.

VOG'ESUS, now Vauge, a mountain of Belgic Gaul, which separates the Sequani from the Lingones. *Lucan.* 1. v. 397.—*Cæs. G.* 4. c. 10.

VO'GIA, a town of the Turduli in Hispania Bætica. *Ptol.*

VOL, a city of Africa Propria. *Id.*

VO'LÆ, a city of the Æqui. *Liv.* 4. c. 49.

VOLAGIN'IUS, a soldier who assassinated Scribonianus. *Tacit. H.* 2. c. 75.

VOLA'NA, a town of the Samnites, taken by Carvilius. *Liv.* 10. c. 44.

VOLAN'DUM, a fortified place of Armenia. *Tac. Ann.* 13. c. 39.

VOLATER'RÆ, an ancient town of Etruria, famous for hot baths. Persius the satirist was born there. *Liv.* 10. c. 12.—*Strab.* 5.—*Cic.* 13. *Fam.* 4.—*Plin.* 3. c. 5. It is now Volterra.

VOL'CÆ or VOL'GÆ, a people of Gaul between the Garonne and the Rhone. They were divided into the Arecomici and the Tectosages, and their country is now Languedoc. *Liv.* 21. c. 26.—*Mela*, 2. c. 5.

VOLCA'TIUS, a friend of Verres. *Cic. Verr.* 2. c. 19, &c.

VOLCA'TIUS SEDIG'ITUS, a poet. *Vid.* Sidigitus.

VOLCA'TIUS CA'IUS, a man improperly treated by Dolabella. He died a sudden death. *Plin.* 7. c. 53.—*Cic. Corn.* 1. *Frag.*

VOLCA'TIUS LU'CIUS, a prætor, &c. *Cic. Fam.* 13. ep. 14.

VOLCA'TIUS LU'CIUS TUL'LUS, a Roman who was consul with Lepidus, A.U.C. 687. He distinguished himself for his patriotism and good conduct. *Cic.* 4. *Fam.* 4.—*Sallust. Cat.* 18.

VOLCA'TIUS EPID'IUS, a grammarian who wrote an account of the actions of Pompey the Great. He had M. Antony and Augustus among his pupils. *Corn. Nep. in Fragm.* c. 6.

VOLCA'TIUS GALLICA'NUS, an author who was five times consul, and wrote the lives of the emperors to Diocletian. The life of Avidius Cassius is the only one of his compositions which is extant. *Voss. H. Lat.* 2. c. 5.

VOLCA'TIUS TERENTIA'NUS, an author who wrote a history of his own times. He lived in the age of the Gordians. *Jul. Capitol. in Gordian.* c. 21.

VOLCENTA'NI, a people of Lucania. *Plin.* 3. c. 11.

VOL'CI, an inland town of Lucania, now Lauria. *Liv.* 27. c. 15.——A town of Etruria. *Plin.* 3. c. 3.

VOLCIA'NI, a people of Hispania Tarraconensis. *Liv.* Their town is now Villa Dolce.

VOLE'RIUS, a river of Corsica. *Ptol.*

VOL'ERO PUBLIL., a plebeian, made a tribune, and author of the Publilian law. *Liv.* 2. c. 55, &c.

VOL'ESUS, a Sabine who accompanied king Tatius to Rome. *Ovid. Pont.* 3. el. 2. v. 105.

VOL'ESUS MESSA'LA, a brutal proconsul of Asia under Augustus. *Sen. Ir.* 1 c. 5.

VOLGE'SIA, a city of Babylonia. *Ptol.* It is called Vologesocerta by *Pliny*, 6. c. 26., and Vologessia by *Ammianus*, l. 23.

VOL'IBA, a harbour of Albion. *Ptol.* It is now Falmouth according to *Camden.*

VOLOG'ESES, a name common to many of the kings of Parthia, who made war against the Roman emperors. *Tacit.* 12. *Ann.* 14, 50, &c.

VOLS'CÆ or VUL'CI, a city of Etruria. *Ptol.*

VOL'SCENS, a Latin chief who discovered Nisus and Euryalus as they returned from the Rutulian camp loaded with spoils. He killed Euryalus, and was himself immediately stabbed by Nisus. *Virg. Æn.* 9. v. 370 & 442.

VOL'SCI or VOL'CI, a people of Latinum, whose territories are bounded on the south by the Tyrrhene Sea, on the north by the country of the Hernici and Marsi, on the west by the Latins and Rutulians, and on the east by Campania. Their chief cities were Antium, Circea, Anxur, Corioli, Fregellæ, Arpinum, &c. Ancus king of Rome made war against them, and in the time of the republic they became formidable enemies, till they were at last conquered with the rest of the Latins. *Liv.* 3 & 4.—*Virg. G.* 2. v. 168. *Æn.* 9. v. 505. l. 11. v. 546, &c.—*Strab.* 5.—*Mela*, 2. c. 4 & 5.—*Plin.* 3. c. 5.—*Servius ad Æn.* 7. v. 803. & *G.* 2. v. 168.

VOLSIN'IUM, now Bolsena, a town of Etruria in Italy, destroyed, according to *Pliny*, 2. c. 53, by fire from heaven. The inhabitants numbered the years by fixing nails in the temple of Nortia, a Tuscan goddess. A lake in the neighbourhood called Volsiniensis Lacus, is now Lago di Bolsena. *Liv.* 5. c. 31. l. 7. c. 3. l. 10. c. 37.—*Juv.* 3. v. 191.—*Tacit. Ann.* 4.—*Ptol*, 3. c. 1.—*Plin.* 2. c. 54 & 55.—*Columell.* l. 12.

VOLTIN'IA, one of the Roman tribes. *Cic. pro. Planco.*

VOLTUM'NA or VULTUR'NA, a goddess at Rome, who presided over kindness and good will. She had a temple near mount Ciminus in Etruria. She is the same as Volumna. *Vid.* Volumnus. *Liv.* 4. c. 23 & 61. l. 5. c. 17.—*Gyrald. H.D.* 1.

VOLU'BILIS, a town of Africa, supposed to be now Fez, the capital of Morocco. *Plin.* 5. c. 1.

VOL'UCE, a city of Spain between Cæsaraugusta and Asturica. *Antonin.*

VOLUM'NÆ FA'NUM, a temple in Etruria, sacred to the goddess Volumna, who presided over the will and over complaisance, where the states of the country used to assemble. Viterbo now stands on the spot. *Liv.* 4. c. 23. l. 5. c. 17. l. 6. c. 2.

VOLUM'NIA, the wife of Coriolanus. *Liv.* 2. c. 40. ——The freedwoman of Volumnius Eutrapelus, mistress to Antony. *Cic. Phil.* 2. c. 24.

VOLUM'NIUS T., a Roman famous for his friendship towards M. Lucullus, whom M. Antony had put to death. His great lamentations were the cause that he was dragged to the triumvir, of whom he demanded to be conducted to the body of his friend, and there to be put to death. His request was readily granted. *Liv.* l. 24. c. 29

VOLUM'NIUS, a mimic whom Brutus put to death. ——An Etrurian who wrote tragedies in his own native language.——A consul who defeated the Samnites and the Etrurians, &c. *Liv.* 9.——A friend of M. Brutus. He was present when that great republican killed himself, and he wrote an account of his death and of his actions, from which Plutarch selected some remarks. *Voss. H. Lat.* 1. c. 17.——A præfect of Syria, B.C. 11.——A Roman knight, put to death by Catiline.

VOLUM'NIUS EUTRAP'ELUS, a friend of Antony. *Cic. Ph.* 13. c. 2.

VOLUM'NIUS LU'CIUS, a friend of Cicero. *Cic. Fam.* 7. ep. 32.—*Varro, R.R.* 2, 4, 12.

VOLUM'NUS and VOLUM'NA, so called *a Volendo*, two deities who presided over the will. They were chiefly invoked at marriages, to preserve concord between the husband and wife. They were particularly worshipped by the Etrurians. *Liv.* 4. c. 61. l. 5. c. 17.—*Rosin. A.R.* 2. c. 19.—*Gyrald. H.D.* 1.

VOLUN'TII, a people of Hibernia. *Ptol.*

VOLUP'TAS or VOLU'PIA, the goddess of sensual pleasures, worshipped at Rome, where she had a temple. She was represented as a young and beautiful woman, well dressed, and elegantly adorned, seated on a throne, and having Virtue under her feet. *Cic, de N. D.* 2. c. 23.—*Macrob.* 1. c. 10.—*Aug. de Civ. D.* 4. c. 8.

VOLUSE'NUS C. QUADRA'TUS, a military tribune in Cæsar's army, &c. *Cæs. Bell. G.* 3. c. 5.—*Hirt.* 8. c. 23.

VOLUSIA'NUS, a Roman taken as colleague on the imperial throne, by his father Gallus. He was killed by his soldiers. *Vid.* Gallus. [A bust of Volusianus will be found in the Capitol, at Rome.]——A soothsayer with Verres. *Cic. Verr.* 3. c. 21.

VOLU'SIUS, a poet of Patavia, who wrote, like Ennius, the annals of Rome in verse, a work by no means respectable. *Seneca.* ep. 93.—*Catull.* 96. v. 7.——A friend of Cicero, who was in his retinue in Cilicia. *Cic.* 5. *Att.* 11. *Fam.* 5. ep. 10.

VOLU'SIUS SATURNI'NUS, a governor of Rome, who died in the 93rd year of his age, beloved and respected, under Nero. *Tacit. Ann.* 13. c. 30.

VOLU'SIUS CA'IUS, a soldier at the siege of Cremona, &c. *Tacit. Hist.* 3. c. 29.

VOLU'SIUS PROC'ULUS, one of Nero's officers. *Tacit. Ann.* 13. c. 51.

VOL'USUS, a friend of Turnus. *Virg. Æn.* 11. v. 463.

VOLUTRI'NA, a goddess invoked by countrymen to prosper their crops, and not leave the ears of corn exposed, but to surround them with a protecting integument. *Aug. de Civ. D.* 4. c. 8.—*Voss. Idolol.* 2. c. 61.

VO'LUX, a son of Bocchus, whom the Romans defeated. Sylla suspected his fidelity, &c. *Sallust. Jug.* 105, &c.

VOMA'NUS, a river of Picenum in Italy, falling into the Adriatic. *Plin.* 3. c. 13.—*Sil. It.* 8. v. 4c8. It is now Vomano.

VONO'NES, a king of Parthia, expelled by his subjects, and afterwards placed on the throne of Armenia. *Tacit. Ann.* 12. c. 10.——Another king of Armenia.——A man made king of Parthia by Augustus. *Justin.* 42. c. 5.

VOPIS'CUS FLA'VIUS, a native of Syracuse, 303, A D. who wrote the life of Aurelian, Tacitus, Florianus, Probus, Firmus, Saturninus, Proculus, Bonosus, Carus, Numerianus, and Carinus. He is one of the six authors who are called *Historiæ Augustæ scriptores*, bnt he excels all the others in the elegance of his style, and the manner in which he relates the various actions of the emperors. He is not, however, without his faults, and we look in vain for the purity or perspicuity of the writers of the Augustan age. *Harles. Not. Lit. Rom.* 1. p. 559.—*Sax. Onom.* 1. p. 381.—*Voss. H. Lat.* 2. c. 7.

VOPIS'CUS J. CÆ'SAR, a man to whom J. Cæsar gave the freedom of Rome. He was a warm partisan of Antony. *Cic. Ph. H.* 11. c. 5. Pliny supposes that Vopiscus was a name originally given to one of two twins who was born safe, after the abortion or death of the other. *Plin.* 7. c. 10.

VORA'NUS, a freedman of Q. Luctatius Catulus, famous for his robberies as well as his cunning, &c. *Horat.* 1. sat. 8. v. 39.—*Cœl. Rhod.* 19. c. 2.

VORA'TES, a prince of the Jazyges, father of Gesander *Val. Flacc.* 6. v. 288.

VOR'EDA, a city of Anglia. *Antonin.* It is now Old Carlisle, according to *Camden.*

VOTIE'NUS MONTA'NUS, a man of learning banished to one of the Baleares for his malevolent reflections upon Tiberius. Ovid has celebrated him as an excellent poet. *Tacit. Ann.* 4. c. 42.

VOTU'RI, a people who formerly inhabited Galatia. *Plin.* 5. c. 32.—*Solin.* c. 43.

VULCANA'LIA, festivals in honor of Vulcan, first celebrated at Præneste, whence they were brought to Rome, and observed in the month of August. The streets were illuminated, fires kindled every where, and animals thrown into the flames as a sacrifice to the deity. The victims offered were a boar pig and a calf. *Varro de L.L.* 5.—*Dionys. Hal.* 1.—*Columell.* 11. c. 3.—*Plin.* 18. c. 13.—*Plin. Jun.* 3. ep. 5.

VULCA'NIÆ IN SULÆ or VULCA'NIA, a name given to the islands between Sicily and Italy, now called Lipari. *Virg. Æn.* 1. v. 52. 1. v. 791. 1. 8. 422.—*Diod.* 5.—*Strab.* 1 & 8.—*Mela*, 2. c. 7. They received it because there were there subterraneous fires, supposed to be excited by Vulcan, the god of fire.

VULCA'NIUS TERENTIA'NUS. *Vid.* Volcanius.

VULCA'NUS, a god of the ancients who presided over fire, and was the patron of all who worked in iron and metals. He was son of Juno alone. who in this wished to imitate Jupiter, who had produced Minerva from his brains. According to Homer, he was son of Jupiter and Juno, and the mother was so disgusted with the deformities of her son, that she threw him into the sea as soon as born, where he remained nine years. According to the more received opinion, Vulcan was educated in heaven with the rest of the gods, but his father kicked him down from Olympus, when he attempted to deliver his mother, who had been fastened by a golden chain for her insolence. He was nine days in coming from heaven to earth, and fell in the island of Lemnus, where, according to Lucian, the inhabitants seeing him in the air, caught him in their arms. He however broke his leg by the fall, and ever after remained lame of one foot. He fixed his residence in Lemnus, where he built himself a palace, and raised forges to work metals. The inhabitants of the island became sensible of his industry, and were taught all the useful arts which could civilize their rude manners, and render them serviceable to the good of society. The first work of Vulcan was, according to some, a throne of gold with secret springs, which he presented to his mother to avenge himself for her want of affection towards him. Juno no sooner was seated on the throne than she found herself unable to move. The gods attempted to move her by breaking the chains which held her, but to no purpose, and Vulcan alone had the power of setting her at liberty. Bacchus intoxicated him, and prevailed upon him to come to Olympus, where he was reconciled to his parents. Vulcan has been celebrated by the ancient poets for the ingenious works and anatomical figures which he made, and many speak of two golden statues, which not only seemed animated, but which walked by his side, and even assisted him in the working of metals. It is said, that at the request of Jupiter, he made the first woman that ever appeared upon earth, well known under the name of Pandora. *Vid.* Pandora. The Cyclopes of Sicily were his ministers and attendants, and with him they fabricated, not only the thunderbolts of Jupiter, but also arms for the gods and the most celebrated heroes. His forges were supposed to be under mount Ætna, in the island of Sicily, as well as in every part of the earth where there were volcanos. The most known of the works of Vulcan which were presented to mortals are, the arms of Achilles, those of Æneas, the shield of Hercules, described by Hesiod, a collar given to Hermione, the wife of Cadmus, and a sceptre, which was in the possession of Agamemnon king of Argos and Mycenæ. The collar proved fatal to all those who wore it, but the sceptre, after the death of Agamemnon, was carefully preserved at Cheronæa, and regarded as a divinity. The amours of Vulcan are not numerous. He demanded Minerva from Jupiter, who had promised him in marriage whatever goddess he should choose, and when she refused his addresses, he attempted to offer her violence. Minerva, however, resisted with success. *Vid.* Erisichthonius. This disappointment in his love was repaired by Jupiter, who gave him one of the Graces. Venus is universally acknowledged to have been the wife of Vulcan; her infidelity is well known, as well as her amours with Mars, which were discovered by Phœbus, and exposed to the gods by her own husband. *Vid.* Alectryon. The worship of Vulcan was well established, particularly in Ægypt, at Athens, and at Rome. It was usual, in the sacrifices that were offered to him, to burn the whole victim, and not reserve part of it as in the immolations to the rest of the gods. A calf and a boar pig were the principal victims offered. Vulcan was represented as covered with sweat, blowing with his nervous arm the fire of his forges. His breast was hairy, and his forehead was blackened with smoke. Some represent him lame and deformed, holding a hammer raised in the air, ready to strike; while with the other hand he turns, with pincers, a thunderbolt on his anvil, for which an eagle waits by his side, to carry it to Jupiter. He appears on some monuments with a long beard, dishevelled hair, half naked, and a small round cap on his head, while he holds a hammer and pincers in his hand. The Ægyptians represented him under the figure of a monkey. Vulcan has received the names of Mulciber, Pamphanes, Clytotechnes, Pandamator, Cyllus, Amphigyëis, Lemnius, Cyllopodion, Chalæpus, Tardipes, &c., all expressive of his lameness and his profession. He was father of Cupid by Venus; and of Cæculus, Cecrops, Cacus, Periphetes, Cercyon, Ocrisia, &c. Cicero speaks of more than one deity of the name of Vulcan. One he calls son of Cœlus, and father of Apollo, by Minerva; the second he mentions is son of the Nile, and called Phtas by the Ægyptians; the third was son of Jupiter and Juno, and fixed his residence in Lemnus; and the fourth who built his forges in the Lipari islands was son of Menalius. Vulcan seems to have been admitted into heaven more for ridicule than any other purpose. He seems to be the great cuckold of Olympus, and even his wife is represented as laughing at his deformities, and mimicking his lameness to gain the smiles of her lovers. *Hesiod. Theog.* 570, 927, *& in Scut. Herc.* 140 & 320.—*Apollod.* 1. c. 3, &c.—*Homer. Il.* 1. 578, 593, &c. l. 11. v. 397. l. 15. v. 18. l. 18. v. 373, &c. —*Diod.* 5.—*Paus.* 1. c. 20. l. 3. 17. l. 8. c. 24. l. 9. c. 40.—*Catull.* 37. c. 7.—*Aul. Gell.* 15. c. 21.—*Herodot.* 2. c. 99 & 191. l. 3. c. 37.—*Cic. de Nat. D.* 3. c. 22.—*Varro de L.L.*—*Ovid. Fast.* 5. v. 251.—*Met.* 4. v. 173. l. 5, &c.—*Lucian. de Sacrif.* —*Plato de Rep.* 2.—*Aristot. Polit.* 1.—*Lactant. ad Theb.* 2. v. 272. *De Fals. R.* 1. c. 17.—*Aug. de Civ. D.* 18. c. 2.—*Hygin.* fab. 38, 158, & 166, *& P.H.* 2. c. 13.—*Philostrat. in Apoll.* 7. c. 24.—*Servius ad Virg. G.* 3. v. 113.—*Fulgent. Myth.* 2. c. 14.—*Arnob. ad Gent.* 5.—*Meurs. Athen. Att.* 1. &. c. 4. l. 2. c. 12.—*Albricius de D. Imag.* 15.—*Vossius. de Idol.* 2. c. 66.—*Virg. Æn.* 7, &c. There is a head of Vulcan in the Vatican, at Rome.]

VULCA'TIUS ARARI'CUS, a Roman knight, who conspired with Piso against Nero, &c. *Tacit. Ann.* 15. c. 58.

VULCA'TIUS, an historian. *Vid.* Volcatius Gallicanus.

VULCATIUS MOS'CHUS, an exile who left his property to the people of Masillia. *Tac. Ann.* 4. c. 43.

VULSI'NUM, a town of Etruria, where Sejanus was born. *Vid.* Volsinium.

VUL'SO, a Roman consul who invaded Africa with Regulus.——A consul who had the provinces of Asia while in office, and triumphed over the Galatians.

VULTE'IUS or VOLTE'IUS, a man in the retinue of Metellus in Sicily. *Verr.* 3. c. 66.

VULTE'IUS ME'NA, a common crier mentioned by *Horace*, 1. ep. 7. v. 55 & 65.

VUL'TURA or VULTURA'RIA, a city of the Hirpini on the borders of Apulia. *Horat.* 3. od. 4. v. 9.—*Lucan.* 9. v. 183.

VULTUR'CIUS or VOLTUR'CIUS, a man of Crotona, who conspired against his country with Catiline. *Cic. Cat.* 3. c. 2.—*Sallust. Cat.* 44, &c.

VULTUR'NIUS, a surname of Apollo. *Vid.* Vulturnus.

VULTUR'NUM, a town of Campania, near the mouth of the Vulturnus. *Liv.* 25. c. 20.—*Plin.* 3. c. 5. It is now Castel del Volturno.——An ancient name of Capua. *Liv.* 4. c. 37.

VULTUR'NUS, a river of Campania, rising in the Appennines, and falling into the Tyrrhene Sea, after passing by the town of Capua. *Lucret.* 5. v. 664.—*Virg. Æn.* 7. v. 729.—*Liv.* 4. c. 37. l. 8. c. 11. l. 22. c. 46 & 47.—*Aul. Gell.* 2. c. 22.——A wind which received the name of Vulturnus when it blew from the side of the Vulturnus: it highly incommoded the Romans at the battle of Cannæ. *Liv.* 22. c. 43 & 46.

VULTUR'NUS, a name of the god of the Tiber. *Varro de L. L.* 4. c. 5.——A surname of Apollo on mount Lissus in Ionia, near Ephesus. The god received this name from a shepherd who raised him a temple, after he had been drawn out of a subterraneous cavern by vultures. *Conon. Narr.* 35.

X.

XAN'THE, one of the Oceanides. *Hesiod. Theog.* v. 356.

XAN'THI, a people of Thrace. *Steph.* Their city was called Xanthia.——The inhabitants of Xanthus in Asia. *Vid.* Xanthus.

XAN'THIAS PHO'CEUS, a Roman whom *Horace* addressed in the fourth ode of his second book, and of whom he speaks as enamoured of a servant maid.

XAN'THICA, a festival observed by the Macedonians in the month called Xanthicus, the same as April. It was then usual to make a lustration of the army with great solemnity. A bitch was cut into two parts, and one half of the body placed on one side, and the other part on the other side; after which the soldiers marched between, and imitated a real battle by a sham engagement.

XANTHIP'PE, a daughter of Dorus. *Vid.* Xantippe.

XANTHIP'PUS, a son of Melas, killed by Tydeus, *Vid.* Xantippe.

XAN'THO, one of Cyrene's attendant nymphs. *Hesiod. Th.* 355.—*Hygin.* præf. fab.—*Virg. G.* 4. v. 336.

XAN'THUS, a river of Troas in Asia Minor. It is the same as the Scamander, but, according to Homer, it was called Xanthus by the gods, and Scamander by men. *Vid.* Scamander. The word signifies yellow or auburn (*flavus*), and the ancients supposed that the waters of the river had the property of changing into that beautiful color the fleeces of sheep that drank there, or the hair of such as bathed in the stream. *Homer. Il.* 12. v. 19. l. 20. v. 74.—*Strab.* 1 & 13.—*Virg. Æn.* 3. 50 & 497. l. 5. v. 807. l. 10. v. 69.—*Aristot. H. Anim.* 3. c. 15.—*Ælian. H. A.* 8. c. 21.—*Dionys. Per.* 819.—*Plin.* 2. c. 103. l. 5. c. 30.—*Servius Æn.* 1. v. 473. l. 3. v. 108.—*Eustath. ad Dionys. P.* 847.—*Schol. Homer. Il.* 2. v. 4 & 465. l. 20. v. 74.——A river of Lycia, anciently called Sirbes. It was sacred to Apollo, and fell into the sea near Patara. *Homer. Il.* 6. v. 172.—*Virg. Æn.* 4. v. 143.—*Mela*, 1. c. 15.—*Strab.* 14.—*Ptol.* 5. c. 3.—*Stat. Theb.* 4. v. 837.—*Plin.* 5. c. 27.——A town of Lycia on the river of the same name, at the distance of about 15 miles from the sea-shore. The inhabitants were celebrated for their love of liberty and national independence. Brutus laid siege to their city; and when at last they were unable longer to support themselves against the enemy, they set fire to their houses and destroyed themselves. The conqueror wished to spare them; but though he offered rewards to his soldiers if they brought any of the Xanthians alive into his presence, only 150 were saved, much against their will. *Appian.* 4.—*Plut. in Brut.*

XAN'THUS, one of the horses of Achilles, who spoke to his master when chid with severity, and told him that he must soon be killed. *Homer. Il.* 19. *Claudian. de* 4. *Hon.* 566.—*Servius ad Æn.* 11. v. 90.——One of the horses given to Juno by Neptune, and afterwards to the sons of Leda. *Servius ad G.* 3. v. 89.

XAN'THUS, an historian of Sardes in the reign of Darius.——A Greek historian of Lydia, who wrote an account of his country, of which some fragments remain. *Dionys. Hal.* l. 1.—*Athen.* l. 12.—*Voss. H. Gr.* 4. p. 451.——A king of Lesbus.——A king of Bœotia, who made war against the Athenians. He was killed by the artifice of Melanthus. *Vid.* Apaturia.——A Greek poet. *Ælian. V. H.* 4. c. 26.—*Suidas.*——A philosopher of Samus, in whose house Æsop lived some time as servant. *Planud. in Æs. Vitâ.*

XAN'TICLES, one of the leaders of the 10,000 Greeks, after the battle of Cunaxa.

XANTIP'PE, a daughter of Dorus who married Pleuron, by whom she had Agenor, &c. *Apollod.* 1. c. 7.——The wife of Socrates, remarkable for her ill humour and peevish disposition, which are become proverbial. Some suppose that the philosopher was acquainted with her moroseness and insolence before he married her, and that he took her for his wife to try his patience, and inure himself to the malevolent reflections of mankind. She continually tormented him with her impertinence; and one day, not satisfied with using the most bitter invectives, she emptied a vessel of dirty water on his head, upon which the philosopher coolly observed, "After thunder there generally falls rain." *Cic. Tusc.* 3. c. 15. —*Ælian. V. H.* 7. c. 10. l. 9. c. 7. l. 11. c. 12.—*Diog. in Socrat.*—*Aul. Gell.* 1. c. 17.

XANTIP'PUS, a Lacedæmonian general who assisted the Carthaginians in the first Punic war. He defeated the Romans, 256 B C., and took the celebrated Regulus prisoner. Such signal service deserved to be rewarded; but the Carthaginians looked with envious jealousy upon Xantippus, and he retired to Corinth after he had saved them from destruction. Some authors assert, that the Carthaginians ordered him to be assassinated, and his body to be thrown into the sea as he was returning home; while others say that they had prepared a leaky ship to convey him to Corinth, which he artfully avoided. *Liv.* 18 & 28 c. 43.—*Appian. de Pun.*—*Cic. Off.* 3. c. 26.—*Frontin. Strat.* 2. c. 2 & 14.—*Sil.* 6. v. 680.——An Athenian general, who, with Leotychides, defeated the Persian fleet at Mycale. A statue was erected to his honor in the citadel of Athens. He made some conquests in Thrace, and increased the power of Athens. He was father to the celebrated Pericles by Agariste the niece of Clisthenes, who expelled the Pisistratidæ from Athens. *Paus.* 1. c. 25. l. 3. c. 7. l. 8. c. 52.——A son of Pericles, who disgraced his father by his disobedience, his ingratitude, and his extravagance. He died of the plague in the Peloponnesian war. *Plut.*

XA'RAX or ZA'RAX, a town of Laconia. *Paus.* l. 3.

XARXI'ARE, a city of Drangiana. *Ptol.*

XA'THRI, a free people of India near the Indus. *Arrian* l. 6.

XAU'RUS, a place of Macedonia. *Steph.*

XE'NA, a place of Crete where Lycurgus was buried, according to *Plutarch.*

XENAG'ORAS, an historian. *Dionys. Hal.* l. 1.—*Macrob.* 5. c. 19.—*Voss. H. Gr.* 3. p. 422, &c. ——A philosopher who measured the height of mount Olympus.

XENAR'CHUS, a comic poet, whose plays are mentioned by *Athenæus, Aristotle, & Suidas.* ——A Peripatetic philosopher of Selucia, who taught at Alexandria and at Rome, and was intimate with Augustus. *Strab.* 14.——A prætor of the Achæan league who wished to favor the interest of Perseus, king of Macedonia, against the Romans.

XEN'ARES, an intimate friend of Cleomenes, king of Sparta.

XEN'ETUS, a rich Locrian, whose daughter Doris married Dionysius of Sicily, &c. *Arist. Pol.* 5. c. 7.

XE'NEUS, a Chian writer who composed a history of his country. *Athen.* l. 14.

XENI'ADES, a Corinthian who went to buy Diogenes the Cynic, when sold as a slave. He asked him what he could do; upon which the Cynic answered, "Command freemen." This noble answer so pleased Xeniades, that he gave the Cynic his liberty, and entrusted him with the care and education of his children. *Diog.—Gell.* 2. c. 18.—*Macrob.* 4. c. 11.

XE'NION, an author who wrote a work on Crete, and also on Italy. *Steph.—Macrob.* l. c. 9.

XENIP'PA, a region on the confines of Scythia. *Q. Curt.* 8. c. 2.

XE'NIUS, a surname given to Jupiter as the god of hospitality. His statue was placed in the rooms where the Lacedæmonians publicly ate. *Plato* 5. *de Leg.—Paus* 3. c. 11.

XENOCLE'A, a priestess of Apollo's temple at Delphi, from whom Hercules extorted an oracle by force, when she refused to answer him, because he was not purified of the blood and death of Iphitus. *Paus.* 10. c. 13.—*Gyrald. P. H.* 2.

XEN'OCLES, a tragic writer who obtained four times a poetical prize in a contention in which Euripides was his competitor, either through the ignorance or by the bribery of his judges. The names of his tragedes which obtained the victory were Œdipus, Lycaon, Bacchæ, Athamas Satyricus, against the Alexander, Palamedes, Trojani, and Sisyphus Satyricus, of Euripides. His grandson bore also the name of Xenocles, and excelled in tragical compositions. *Ælian. V. H.* 2. c. 8.—*Aristoph. Ran.* 1. sc. 2. *Schol. Arist. loco.*——A Spartan officer in the expedition which Agesilaus undertook against the Persians. *Diod.* l. 14.——An architect of Eleusis.——A friend of Aratus. ——A celebrated rhetorician of Adrymittium, who accompanied Cicero into Asia. *Cic. Br.* 91. —*Strab.* 13.

XENOCLI'DES, a Greek poet in the 105th Olympiad. *Demosth.*

XENOC'RATES, an ancient philosopher born at Calchedonia, and educatedin the school of Plato, whose friendship he gained, and whose approbation he merited. Though of a dull and sluggish disposition, he supplied the defects of nature by unwearied attention and industry, and was at last found capable of succeeding to the school of Plato after Speusippus, about 339 years before Christ. He was remarkable as a disciplinarian, and he required that his pupils should be acquainted with mathematics before they came under his care, and he even rejected some who had not the necessary qualification, saying that they had not yet found the key to philosophy. He not only recommended himself to his pupils by precepts, but more powerfully by example, and after the wonderful change he had made upon the conduct of one of his auditors, (*Vid.* Polemon,) his company was as much shunned by the dissolute and extravagant, as it was courted by the virtuous and the benevolent. Philip of Macedon attempted to gain his confidence with money, but with no success. Alexander in this imitated his father, and sent some of his friends with 50 talents for the philosopher. They were introduced, and supped with Xenocrates. The repast was small, frugal, and elegant, without ostentation. On the morrow, the officers of Alexander wished to pay down the 50 talents, but the philosopher asked them whether they had not perceived from the entertainment of the preceding day, that he was not in want of money: "Tell your master," said he, "to keep his money, he has more people to maintain than I have." Yet not to offend the monarch, he accepted a small sum, about the 200th part of one talent. His character was not less conspicuous in every other particular, and he has been cited as an instance of virtue from the following circumstance. The courtezan Lais had pledged herself to forfeit an immense sum of money, if she did not triumph over the virtue of Xenocrates. She tried every art, assumed the most captivating looks, and used the most tempting attitudes to gain the philosopher, but in vain; and she declared at last, that she had not lost her money, as she had pledged herself to conquer a human being, not a lifeless stone. Though so respected and admired, yet Xenocrates was poor, and he was dragged to prison, because he was unable to pay a small tribute to the state. He was delivered from confinement by one of his friends. His integrity was so well known, that when he appeared in the public courts as a witness, the judges dispensed with his oath. He died B.C. 314, in his 82d year, after he had presided in the academy for above 25 years. It is said, that he fell in the night with his head into a basin of water, and was suffocated. He had written above 60 treatises on different subjects, all now lost. He acknowledged no other deity but heaven, and the seven planets. *Voss. H. Gr.* 3. p. 423.—*Diog.—Cic. ad Attic.* 10. ep. 1, &c.—*Tusc.* 5. c. 32.—*Val. Max.* 2. c. 10.—*Lucian. de Macr.—Macrob. in Som. Scip.* 1. c. 14.——A physician in the age of Nero, not in great esteem. His Greek treatise, *De Alimento ex Aquatilibus*, is best edited by Franzius, Lips. 8vo. 1774. *Sax. Onom.* 1. p. 239.—*Fabr. B. Gr.* 3. c. 3. l. 5. c. 38. &c.——An excellent painter. *Plin.* 34. c. 8.

XENODA'MUS, an illegitimate son of Menelaus, by Gnossia. *Apollod.* 3. c. 11.——An athlete of Anticyra, who obtained a prize at the Olympic games. *Paus.* 10. c. 36.

XENOD'ICE, a daughter of Syleus, killed by Hercules. *Apollod.* 2. c. 6.——A daughter of Minos and Pasiphae. *Id.* 3. c. 1.

XENOD'OCHUS, a Messenian crowned at the Olpmpic games. *Paus.* 4. c. 5.——A native of Cardia, &c.

XENODO'RUS, a celebrated statuary. *Plin.* 34. c. 8.

XENOM'ENES, a man who hospitably received Cicero at Thyreum. *Cic.* 16. *Fam.* 5.

XENOPH'ANES, a Greek philosopher of Colophon, disciple of Archelaus, B.C. 535. He wrote several poems and treatises, and founded a sect, which was called the Eleatic, in Sicily. Wild in his opinions about astronomy, he supposed that the stars were extinguished every morning, and rekindled at night: that eclipses were occasioned by the temporary extinction of the sun; that the moon was inhabited, and eighteen times bigger than the earth; and that there were several suns and moons for the convenience of the different climates of the earth. He maintained the uncertainty of human knowledge, and imagined that God and the world were the same. He also credited the eternity of the universe, but his incoherent opinions about the divinity, raised the indignation of his countrymen, and he was banished. He died very poor when about 100 years old. *Cic. Quæst.* 4. c. 37. *de Div.* 1. c. 3. *de Nat. D.* 1. c. 11.—*Lactant. Div. Inst.* 3. c. 23.—*Apollod. apud Clem. Alex. Strom.* 1.—*Sext. Empir*

p. 15.——A governor of Olbus, in the age of M. Antony. *Strab.* 14.——One of the ministers of Philip, who went to Annibal's camp, and made a treaty of alliance between Macedonia and Carthage.——An Iambic poet of Lesbus. *Suid.*—*Diod* l. 5.

XENOPH'ILUS, a Pythagorean philosopher of Chalcis, who lived to his 170th year, and enjoyed all his faculties to the last. He wrote upon music, and was thence called the musician. *Lucian. de Macr.*—*Plin.* 7. c. 50.—*Val. Max.* 8. c. 13.——One of Alexander's generals. *Curt.* 5. c. 2.——A robber of whom Aratus hired some troops.

XEN'OPHON, an Athenian, son of Gryllus, celebrated as a general, an historian, and a philosopher. In the school of Socrates he received those instructions and precepts which afterwards so eminently distinguished him at the head of an army, in literary solitude, and as the prudent father of a family. He was invited by Proxenus, one of his intimate friends, to accompany Cyrus the younger in an expedition against his brother Artaxerxes, king of Persia; but he refused to comply without consulting his venerable master, and enquiring into the propriety of such a measure. Socrates strongly opposed it, and observed that it might raise the resentment of his countrymen, as Sparta had made an alliance with the Persian monarch; but, however, before he proceeded further, he advised him to consult the oracle of Apollo. Xenophon paid due deference to the injunctions of Socrates, but as he was ambitious of glory, and eager to engage in a distant expedition, he hastened with precipitation to Sardis, where he was introduced to the young prince, and treated with great attention. In the army of Cyrus, Xenophon showed that he was a true disciple of Socrates, and that he had been educated in the warlike city of Athens. After the decisive battle in the plains of Cunaxa, and the fall of young Cyrus, the prudence and vigor of his mind were called into action. The ten thousand Greeks who had followed the standard of an ambitious prince, were now at the distance of above 600 leagues from their native home, in a country surrounded by a victorious enemy, without money, without provisions, and without a leader. Xenophon was selected from among the officers, to superintend the retreat of his countrymen, and though he was often opposed by malevolence and envy, yet his persuasive eloquence and activity convinced the Greeks that no general could extricate them from every difficulty, better than the disciple of Socrates. He rose superior to danger, and though under continual alarms from the sudden attacks of the Persians, he was enabled to cross rapid rivers, penetrate through vast deserts, gain the tops of mountains, till he could rest secure for a while, and refresh his tired companions. This celebrated retreat was at last happily effected; the Greeks returned home after a march of 1155 parasangs, or leagues, which was performed in 215 days, after an absence of fifteen months. The whole perhaps might now be forgotten, or at least but obscurely known, if the great philosopher who planned it, had not employed his pen in describing the dangers which he escaped, and the difficulties which he surmounted. He was no sooner returned from Cunaxa, than he sought new honors in following the fortune of Agesilaus, in Asia. He enjoyed his confidence, he fought under his standard, and conquered with him in the Asiatic provinces, as well as at the battle of Coronæa. His fame, however, did not escape the aspersions of jealousy, he was publicly banished from Athens for accompanying Cyrus against his brother, and being now without a home, he retired to Scillus, a small town of the Lacedæmonians, in the neighbourhood of Olympia. In this solitary retreat he dedicated his time to literary pursuits, and as he had acquired riches in his Asiatic expeditions, he began to adorn and variegate by the hand of art, for his pleasure and enjoyment, the country which surrounded Scillus. He built a magnificent temple to Diana, in imitation of that at Ephesus, and spent part of his time in rural employments, or in hunting in the woods and mountains. His peaceful occupations, however, were soon disturbed, when a war arose between the Lacedæmonians and Elis. The sanctity of Diana's temple, and the venerable age of the philosopher, who lived in the delightful retreats of Scillus, were disregarded, and Xenophon, driven by the Elians from his favorite spot, where he had composed and written for the information of posterity, and honor of his country, retired to the city of Corinth. In this place he died in the 90th year of his age, 359 years before the Christian era. The works of Xenophon are numerous; he wrote an account of the expedition of Cyrus, called *the Anabasis*, and as he had no inconsiderable share in the enterprise, his description must be authentic, having been himself an eye-witness. Many, however, have accused him of partiality. He appeared often too fond of extolling the virtues of his favorite Cyrus, and while he describes with contempt the operations of the Persians, he does not neglect to show that he was a native of Greece. His *Cyropœdia*, divided into eight books, has given rise to much criticism, and while some warmly maintain that it is a faithful account of the life and the actions of Cyrus the Great, and declare that it is supported by the authority of Scripture; others as vehemently deny its authenticity. According to the opinions of Plato and of Cicero, the Cyropædia of Xenophon was a moral romance, and they assert, that the historian did not so much write what Cyrus had been, as what every true, good, and virtuous monarch ought to be. His *Hellenica* were written as a continuation of the history of Thucydides; and in his *Memorabilia* of Socrates, and in his *Apology*, he has shown himself as Valerius Maximus observes, a perfect master of the philosophy of that great man, and has explained his doctrines and moral precepts with all the success of persuasive eloquence and conscious integrity. These are the most famous of his compositions, besides which there are other small tracts, his eulogium given on Agesilaus, his œconomics, on the duties of domestic life, the dialogue intituled Hiero, in which he happily describes and compares the misery which attended the tyrant, with the felicity of a virtuous prince; a treatise on hunting, the symposium of the philosophers, on the government of Athens and Sparta, a treatise on the revenues of Attica, &c. The simplicity and elegance of Xenophon's diction have procured him the name of the Athenian muse, and the bee of Greece, and have induced Quintilian to say, that the graces dictated his language, and that the goddess of Persuasion dwelt upon his lips. He received however a more noble appellation, the surname of Benefactor, when with arms in his hands, and with all the eagerness of humanity and valor, he forced his victorious troops to abandon the plunder of Byzantium, and to spare a prostrate enemy. His sentiments, as to the Divinity and religion, were the same as those of the venerable Socrates: he asserted the immortality of the soul, and exhorted his friends to cultivate those virtues which ensure the happiness of mankind. He has been quoted as an instance of tenderness and of resignation to the will of providence. As he was offering a sacrifice, he was informed that Gryllus, his eldest son, had been killed at the battle of Mantinea. Upon this he tore the garland from his head, but when he was told that his son had died like a Greek, and given a mortal wound to Epaminondas, the enemy's general, he replaced the flowers upon his head, and continued the sacrifice, exclaiming that the pleasure he derived from the valor of his son, was greater than the grief which his unfortunate death occasioned. The best editions of Xenophon are those of Leunclavius, fol. Francof. 1596, of Ernesti, 4 vols. 8vo. Lips. 1763, and the Glasgow edition 12mo. of the Cyropædia 1767, the expedition of Cyrus, 1764, the Memorabilia, 1761, and the history of Greece, 1762, and likewise the edition of Zeunius, published at Leipsic, in 8vo. in six vols. between the years 1778 & 1791. *Sax. Onom.* 1. p. 56.—*Fabr. B. Gr.* 3. c. 4.—*Cic. in Orat.* 19. *Val. Max.* 5. c. 10.—*Quintil.* 10. c. 2.—*Ælian. V.H.* 3. c. 13. l. 4. c. 5.—*Diog. in Xenoph.*—*Seneca ad Marc.* 12.—*Stobæus.* 106. [There is a bust of Xenophon in the collection of the Villa Albani, near Rome.]——A writer of Ephesus, in the beginning of the fourth century, known by his entertaining Greek romance in five books, *De Amoribus Anthiæ et Abrocomæ*, published in 8vo. and 4to. Cocceius, Lond. 1726.——A physician of the emperor Claudius, born in the island of Cos, and said to be descended from the Asclepiades. He enjoyed the emperor's favor, and through him the people of Cos were exempt from all taxes. He had the meanness to poison his benefactor at the instigation of Agrippina. *Tacit.* 12 *Ann.* c. 61 & 67.——An officer under Adrian, &c.

XE'RA, a town of Spain, now Xerez, where the Moors gained a battle over Roderic king of the Goths, and became masters of the country.

XEROLIB'YA, a part of Africa between Ægypt and Cyrene. *Virg. Æn.* 4. v. 42.

XERXE'NE, a part of Armenia. *Strab.* 11.

XER'XES the First succeeded his Father Darius on the throne of Persia, and, though but the second son of the monarch, was preferred to his elder brother Artabazanes. The causes alleged for this preference were, that Artabazanes was son of Darius when a private man, and that Xerxes was born, after his father had been raised to the Persian throne, of Atossa, the daughter of Cyrus. Xerxes continued the warlike preparations of his father, and added the revolted kingdom of Ægypt to his extensive possessions. He afterwards invaded Europe, and entered Greece with an army which together with the numerous retinue of servants, eunuchs, and women that attended it, amounted to no less than 5,283,220 souls. This multitude, which the fidelity of historians has not exaggerated, was stopped at Thermopylæ, by the valor of 300 Spartans under king Leonidas. Xerxes, astonished that such a handful of men should dare to oppose his progress, ordered some of his soldiers to bring them alive into his presence, but for three successive days the most valiant of the Persian troops were repeatedly defeated in attempting to execute the monarch's injunctions, and the courage of the Spartans might perhaps have triumphed longer, if a Trachinian had not led a detachment to the top of the mountain, which suddenly fell upon the devoted Leonidas. The king himself nearly perished on this occasion, and it has been reported, that in the night, the desperate Spartans sought, for a while, the royal tent, which they found deserted, and wandered through the Persian army, slaughtering thousands before them. The battle of Thermopylæ was the beginning of the disgrace of Xerxes; he advanced only to experience new disappointments, his fleet was defeated at Artemisium and Salamis, and though he burnt the deserted city of Athens, and trusted to the artful insinuations of Themistocles, yet he found his millions unable to conquer a nation that was superior to him in the knowledge of war and maritime affairs. Mortified with the ill success of his expedition, and apprehensive of imminent danger in an enemy's country, Xerxes hastened to Persia, and in 30 days marched over all that territory which before he had passed with much pomp and parade in the space of six months. Mardonius, the best of his generals was left behind with an army of 300,000 men, and the rest that had survived the ravages of war, of famine, and of pestilence, followed their timid monarch into Thrace, where his steps were marked by the numerous birds of prey that hovered round him, and fed upon the dead carcasses of the Persians. When he reached the Hellespont, Xerxes found the bridge of boats which he had erected there, totally destroyed by the storms, and he crossed the straits in a small fishing vessel. Restored to his kingdom and safety, he forgot his dangers, his losses, and his defeats, and gave himself up to riot and debauchery. His indolence and luxurious voluptuousness offended his subjects, and Artabanus, the captain of his guards, conspired against him, and murdered him in his bed, in the 21st year of his reign, about 464 years before the Christian era. The personal accomplishments of Xerxes have been commended by ancient authors, and Herodotus observes that there was not one man among the millions of his armies, that was equal to the monarch in comeliness or stature, or that was as worthy to preside over a great and extensive empire. The picture is finished, and the character of Xerxes completely known, when we hear Justin exclaim that the vast armament which invaded Greece, was without a head. Xerxes has been cited as an instance of humanity. When he reviewed his millions from a stately throne in Asia, he suddenly shed a torrent of tears on the recollection that the multitude of men which he saw before his eyes, in one hundred years, should be no more. His pride and insolence have been deservedly censured; he ordered chains to be thrown into the sea, and the waves to be whipped because the first bridge he had laid across the Hellespont had been destroyed by a storm. He cut a channel through mount Athos, and saw his fleet sail in a place which before was dry ground. The very rivers were dried up by his army as he advanced towards Grece, and the cities which he entered reduced to want and poverty. *Herodot.* 1. c. 183. l. 7. c. 2, &c.—*Diod.* 11.—*Strab.* 9.—*Ælian.* 3. *V.H.* 25.—*Justin.* 2. c. 10, &c.—*Paus.* 3. c. 4. l. 8. c. 46.—*Lucan.* 2. v. 672. l. 3. v. 285.—*Plut. in Them. &c.*—*Val. Max.*—*Isocrat. in Panath.*—*Seneca. de Const. Sap.* 4.—*Propert.* 2. el. 1. v. 22.—*Juv.* 10. v. 174.—*Tzetzes. ad Lyc.* 1283.

XER'XES the Second succeeded his father Artaxerxes Longimanus on the throne of Persia, 425 B.C., and was assassinated in the first year of his reign by his brother Sogdianus.

XER'XES, a painter of Heraclea, who made a beautiful representation of Venus. *Ælian.*

XEUX'ES, an officer of Antiochus the Great, king of Syria.

XIL'IA, a city of Libya. *Steph.*

XILI'NE, a town of the Cappadocian Pontus. *Ptol.* It is now Sentina.

XIPHO'NIA, a promontory of Sicily, at the north of Syracuse, now Cruce. *Strab.* 6.——A town near it, now Agousta.

XOA'NA, a town of India within the Ganges. *Ptol.*

XOD'RACA, a city of India within the Ganges. *Id.*

XO'ES or XO'IS, an island formed by the mouths of the Nile. *Strab.* 17.

XOL'LA, a city of Africa. *Appian. in Punic.*

XU'CHES, a city of Libya. *Steph.*

XU'THIA, the ancient names of the plains of Leontium in Sicily. *Diod.* 5.

XU'THUS, a son of Hellen, grandson of Deucalion. He was banished from Thessaly by his brothers, and came to Athens, where he married Creusa, the daughter of king Erechtheus, by whom he had Achæus and Ion. He retired, after the death of his father-in-law, into Achaia, where he died. According to some, he had no children, but adopted Ion, the son whom Creusa, before her marriage, had bore to Apollo. *Apollod.* 1. c. 7.—*Paus.* 7. c. 1.—*Euripid. in Ion.* 1. sc. 1.

XY'CHUS, a Macedonian who told Philip of his cruelty, when he had put his son Demetrius to death, at the instigation of Perseus.

XYLENOP'OLIS, a town at the mouth of the Indus, built by Alexander, supposed to be Laberi. *Plin.* 6 c. 23.

XYLICEN'SES, a people of the interior of Libya. *Ptol.*

XYLI'NE, a town of Pamphylia. *Liv.* 38. c. 15.

XYLOP'OLIS, a town of Macedonia. *Plin.* 4. c. 10.

XY'LOS, a town of Caria. *Steph.*—*Hecatæus.*

XYME'THUS, a city of Marmarica. *Ptol.*

XYN'IA, a city of Thessaly. *Steph.*

XYN'IAS, a lake of Thessaly, or, according to some, of Bœotia. *Liv.* 32. c. 13. l. 33. c 3.

XYNŒ'CIA, an anniversary day observed at Athens, in honor of Minerva, and in commemoration of the time in which the people of Attica left their country seats, and by advice of Theseus, all united into one body. *Thucyd.* 1. 2.

XYP'ETE, a village in the tribe Cecropis. *Steph.* ——A village of Attica, formerly called Troja. *Id.*

XYS'TIS, a city of Caria. *Pliny*, 5. c. 29., calls the people Xystiani.

Z.

ZA'ARAM or ZA'BRAM, a region of Arabia Felix. *Ptol.*

ZA'BA, a city of India without the Ganges. *Id.* ——An island near Taprobane. *Id.*

ZAB'ATUS, a river of Media, falling into the Tigris, near which the ten thousand Greeks stopped on their return. *Xenophon.*

ZABDICE'NE, a province of Persia. *Amm. Marcell.*

ZA'BI, a place of Mauritania Cæsariensis. *Antonin.*

ZABI'DA, a village in the interior of Arabia Felix. *Steph.*

ZA'BII, a people of India who fought against Bacchus. *Id.*

ZABIR'NA, a town of Libya, where Bacchus destroyed a large beast that infested the country. *Diod.* 3.

ZA'BUS, a river of Assyria, falling into the Tigris.

ZACAN'THA, a town of Iberia taken by Annibal. *Steph.—Polyb.*

ZACA'TÆ, a people of Asiatic Sarmatia, near the sources of the Tanais. *Ptol.*

ZAC'ORUS, an auxiliary of Perses, slain by Argus, son of Phryxus. *Val. Flacc.* 6. v. 554.

ZACYN'THUS, a native of Bœotia, who accompanied Hercules when he went into Spain to destroy Geryon. At the end of the expedition, he was entrusted by the hero, with the care of Geryon's flocks, and ordered to conduct them to Thebes. As he went on his journey, he was bitten by a serpent, and some time after died. His companions carried his body away, and buried it in an island of the Ionian Sea, which from that time was called Zacynthus. The island of Zacynthus, now called Zante, is situate at the south of Cephalenia, and at the west of the Peloponnesus. It is about 60 miles in circumference. *Liv.* 26. c. 24.—*Plin.* 4. c. 12.—*Strab.* 2 & 8.—*Mela*, 2. c. 7.—*Homer. Odyss.* 1. v. 246. l. 9. v. 24.—*Ovid. de Art. Am.* 2. v. 432. *Heroid.* 1. v. 87.—*Paus.* 4. c. 23.—*Virg. Æn.* 3. v. 270.——A son of Dardanus. *Paus.* 8. c. 24.

ZADA'DRUS, a river of India. *Ptol.*

ZADRACARTA, a city of Hyrcania. *Arrian.* l. 3.

ZADRA'ME, a region of Arabia Felix. *Steph.*

ZA'DRIS, a town of Colchis, on the borders of Albania. *Ptol.*

ZÆ'A or ZE'A, a very ancient city of Bæotia. *Steph.*

ZAGACUP'ODA, a city of Africa Propria. *Ptol.*

ZAG'ATIS, a river of Pontus. *Arrian. in Peripl.*

ZAG'ERÆ, a people of the Troglodytæ in Æthiopia. *Plin.* 6. c. 29.

ZAGILLOVI'TIS, a region of Asia Minor. *Strab. Casaubon* reads Galvatis.

ZAGI'RA, a town of Paphlagonia, between the rivers Parthenius and Halys.

ZAGMA'IS, a city of Arabia Deserta. *Ptol.*

ZAGO'RA, ZAGO'RUM or ZAGO'RUS, a maritime place of Galatia. *Arrian. in Peripl.*

ZAGRÆ'US, a son of Jupiter and Proserpine, the same as the first Bacchus, of whom Cicero speaks. Some say that Jupiter obtained Proserpine's favors, in the form of a serpent in one of the caves of Sicily, where her mother had concealed her from his pursuits, and that from this union Zagræus was born. The child was carried to Olympus, where Juno, through jealousy, incited the Titans to destroy him. His ashes, according to an ancient mythologist, were collected by the offended god, and formed into a philtre, which he gave to Semele, who became mother of Bacchus. *Diod.* 1 & 3.—*Arrian. de Gest. Alex. & apud Eustath. ad Dionys. Per.* 1153.—*Hygin.* fab. 155 & 167.—*Clem. Alex. in Protrept.—Arnob. adv. Gent.—Cor. Nep. in Dion.* 9.—*Nonnus Dionys.* 5 & 6.—*Tzetzes. ad Lyc.* 212 & 355.—*Etymolog. Mag. voce* Ζαγρευς.—*Sch. Aristoph. ad Ranas*, 326 & 346. —*Ampelius.* 9.

ZA'GRUS, a mountain on the confines of Media and Babylonia. *Strab.* 11.

ZAG'YLIS, a maritime town of Marmorica. *Ptol.*

ZAGYS'TIS, a small region of Libya. *Steph.*

ZAI'RA, a town of Mesopotamia, on the eastern bank of the Euphrates.

ZAL'ACA, a city of Media. *Ptol.*

ZAL'ACUS, a mountain of Mauritania.

ZAL'APA, a city of Africa Propria. *Ptol.*

ZAL'ATES, an effeminate youth brought to Rome from Armenia, as a hostage, &c. *Juv.* 2. v. 164.

ZALE'NI, a people near Persia. *Zosim.* l. 3.

ZALEU'CUS, a lawgiver of the Locrians in Italy, and one of the disciples of Pythagoras, 550 B.C. He was very humane, and at the same time very austere, and attempted to enforce his laws more by inspiring shame than dread. He had decreed that a person guilty of adultery should lose both his eyes. His philosophy was called to a trial when he was informed that his son was an adulterer. He ordered the law to be executed; the people interfered, but Zaleucus resisted, and rather than violate his own institutions, he commanded one of his own eyes, and one of those of his son, to be put out, This made such an impression upon the people, that while Zaleucus presided over the Locrians, no person was again found guilty of adultery. *Val. Max.* 1. c. 2. l. 6. c. 5.—*Cic. de Leg.* 2. c. 6. *Ad. Attic.* 6. ep. 1.—*Ælian. V. H.* 2. c. 37. l. 3. c. 17. l. 13. c. 24.—*Strab.* 6.—*Diod.* 12.—*Symmach.* 10. ep. 18.—*Clem. Alex. Strom.* 1.—*Zenob. Cent.* 4. *Prov.* 10.

ZALIS'CUS or ZAL'ICUS, a river of Galatia, flowing through Paphlagonia into the Euxine Sea. *Ptol.*

ZALIS'SA, a royal city of Iberia. *Id.*

ZA'MA, a town of Numidia, 300 miles from Carthage, celebrated for the victory which Scipio obtained there over the great Annibal, B.C 202. Metellus besieged it, and was obliged to retire with great loss. After Juba's death it was destroyed by the Romans. *Hirt. Af* 91.—*C. Nep. in Annib.* —*Liv.* 30. c. 29.—*Sallust. de Jug.*—*Flor.* 3. c. 1.—*Ital.* 3 v. 261.—*Strab.* 17.—*Vitruv.* 8. c. 4.—*Dio.* 48.——A town of Cappadocia.——A town of Mesopotamia,

ZA'ME, a fountain of Africa, which rendered shrill the voices of those who drank its waters. *Plin.* 31. c. 2.

ZAMA'ZI, a nation in the interior of Libya. *Ptol.*

ZA'MEIS, a debauched king of Assyria, son of Semiramis and Ninus, as some report. He reigned thirty-eight years. *Diod.* l. 3.—*Justin.* l. 1. c. 1. *Euseb. Chron.—Beros.* l. 5.

ZAME'TES, a mountain of Arabia Felix. *Ptol.*

ZAM'NES, a city of Upper Æthiopia. *Plin.* 6. c. 29.

ZAMOL'XIS or ZALMOX'IS, a slave and disciple of Pythagoras. He accompanied his master into Ægypt, and afterwards retired into the country of the Getæ, which had given him birth. He began to civilize his countrymen; and the more easily to gain reputation, he concealed himself for three years in a subterraneous cave, and afterwards made them believe that he was just raised from the dead. Some place him before the age of Pythagoras. After death he received divine honors. *Diog.* 8. c. 1.—*Herodot.* 4. c. 19, &c.—*Lucian. in Scyth.—Voss. de Sect. Philos.* c. 3. sec. 1.

ZANA'ATHA, a city of Arabia Petræa. *Ptol.*

ZAN'CLE, a town of Sicily, on the straits which separate that island from Italy. It received its name from appearing like a scythe, which was called ζαγκλον in the language of the country, or, as others say, because the scythe with which Saturn mutilated his father fell there, or because, as Diodorus reports, a person named Zanclus had either built it or had been its sovereign. Zancle fell into the hands of the Samians 497 years B.C., and three years after it was recovered by Anaxilaus, the Messenian tyrant of Rhegium, who gave it the name of his native country, and called it Messana. It was founded, as most chronologists suppose, about 1058 years B.C., by the pirates of Cumæ in Italy, and peopled by Samians, Ionians, and Chalcidians. *Vid.* Messana. *Ptol.* 3. c. 4.—*Mela*, 2. c. 7.—*Strab.* 6.—*Diod.* 4.—*Ital.* l. v. 662.—*Ovid. Fast.* 4. v. 499, *Met.* 14. v. 6. l. 15. v. 290. *Trist.* 5. el. 2. v. 73.—*Paus.* 4. c. 23.——A town of Achaia. *Plin* 4. c. 5.

ZAN'CLES, a native of Samothrace, who had a fresh set of teeth when 104 years old. *Plin.* 11. c. 37.

ZA'NES, the name of six statues of Jupiter which had been erected in the sacred grove of Olympia, in the 98th Olympiad, from the fines paid by wrestlers for using fraud or corruption during the combat. Of these statues, two were made by Cleon of Sycyon. The word is the plural of Ζευς, corrupted by the Olympians into Ζαν. *Paus.* 5. c.21.

ZAN'JA, a city of Media. *Ptol.*

ZAPAVORTE'NE, a region near the Caspian. *Trogus*, 41. c. 5.

ZA'RA, a city near Armenia Minor. *Antonin.*

ZARAGAR'DIA, a city of Mesopotamia on the Euphrates. *Zosim.* l. 3.

ZAR'AI, a city of Mauritania Cæsariensis. *Antonin.*

ZA'RAM, a region of Arabia Felix. *Ptol.*

ZAR'AMA, a city of Media. *Id.*

ZARANGÆ'I or ZARAN'GI, a people of Asia. *Arrian.* l. 2 & 6.

ZAR'ANIS, a city of Media. *Ptol.*

ZARAS'PÆ, a people of Asia. Their chief city was Prophthasia. *Plin.* 6. c. 13.

ZAR'ATHA, a city of Mauritania Cæsariensis. *Ptol.*

ZA'RAX, a town of Peloponnesus on the sea shore of Laconia, as also a mountain of Eubœa near Bœotia, called after Zarax, son of Carycus or Caristus, the grandson of Chiron. *Lycophr.* 373.—*Tzetzes loco, & v.* 580.—*Paus.* 1. c. 38.—*Philaris. in Epist.*

ZARBIE'NUS, a petty monarch of Asia, who was gained over to the interest of the Romans by one of the officers of Lucullus. Tigranes put him to death for his desertion, and his funeral was celebrated with great magnificence by the Roman general. *Plut. in Luc.*

ZARGIDA'VA, a town of Lower Mœsia. *Ptol.*

ZARIAS'PA, a city of Bactriana. *Strab.*

ZARIAS'PES, a Persian who attempted to revolt from Alexander, &c. *Curt.* 9. c. 10.

ZARIAS'PES. a river, now Dehash, on which Bactra, the capital of Bactriana, was built. It is called Bactrus by *Curtius*, 7. c. 4.—*Plin.* 6. c. 15 & 16.—*Salmas. ad Solin.* p. 985.

ZARMIZEGETHU'SA, a city of Dacia, called also Ulpia Trajana. *Ptol.*

ZARVA'NA, a city of Armenia Minor.—*Ptol.*—*Salmas. ad Solin.* p. 698.

ZA'THES, a river of Armenia. *Xenoph. Cyrop.* l. 3.

ZA'THUA, a town of Armenia Major. *Ptol.*

ZAUE'CES or ZAVE'CES, a people of Libya. *Herodot.* 4. c 193.

ZEBI'NA ALEXAN'DER, an impostor who usurped the throne of Syria at the instigation of Ptolemy Physcon.

ZEBYT'TIS a city of Libya. *Steph.*

ZEERI'TÆ, a people of Arabia Felix. *Ptol.*

ZEGREN'SII, a people of Mauritania Tingitana. *Id.*

ZEIRIN'IA, a town of Thrace. *Steph. ex Theopompo.*

ZE'LA, a town of Pontus near the river Lycus, where Cæsar defeated Pharnaces, son of Mithridates. In expressing this victory, the general used the words *Veni, vidi, vici. Suet. Cæs.* 37.—*Hirt. Alex.* 72.

ZELA'SIUM, a promontory of Thessaly. *Liv.* 31. c. 46.

ZE'LES, a native of Cyzicus, beaten and left half dead by Pollux. *Val. Flacc.* 3. v. 152.

ZE'LES, a town of Spain. *Strab.* It is now Arzila.

ZELI'A, a town of Troas at the foot of Ida. *Steph.* ——A town of Lycia.

ZE'LIAS or ZE'ILAS, son of Nicomedes, who seized Cresta, a city of Paphlagonia. *Steph.*

ZEL'LA, a city of Africa, destroyed in the war between Cæsar and Scipio. *Strab.*

ZE'LUS, a daughter of Pallas.

ZE'LUS, a city of Æthiopia. *Steph.*

ZENGI'ZA, a promontory of Africa. *Ptol.* 1. c. 17.

ZENICE'TUS, a noted robber. *Strab.*—*Salmas. ad Solin.* p. 802.

ZE'NIS, the chief of the Dardan cities. *Polyæn.* 8. c. 54.

ZE'NO, a philosopher of Elea or Velia in Italy, the disciple, or, according to some, the adopted son of Parmeniades, and the supposed inventor of dialectics. His opinions about the universe, the unity, incomprehensibility, and immutability of all things, were the same as those of Xenophanes and the rest of the Eleatic philosophers. It is said that he attempted to deliver his country from the tyranny of Nearchus. His plot was discovered, and he was exposed to the most excruciating torments to reveal the names of his accomplices; but this he bore with unparalleled fortitude; and not to be at last conquered by tortures, he cut off his tongue with his teeth, and spat it in the face of the tyrant. Some say that he was pounded alive in a mortar, and that in the midst of his torments he called to Nearchus as if to reveal something of importance; the tyrant approached him, and Zeno, as if willing to whisper to him, caught his ear with his teeth. and bit it off. *Cic. Tusc.* 2. c. 22. *de Nat. D.* 3. c. 33.—*Diod. in Frag.*—*Val. Max.* 3. c. 3.—*Diog.* 9.—*Clem. Alex. Strom.* 4.—*Tertull. Apolog.*—*Valesias. ad Ammian.* 14. c. 9. [The finest bust of Zeno will be found in the Museum at Naples.]

ZE'NO, the founder of the sect of the Stoics, born at Citium, in the island of Cyprus. The first part of his life was spent in commercial pursuits, but he was soon called to more elevated employments. As he was returning from Phœnicia, a storm drove his ship on the coast of Attica, and he was shipwrecked near the Piræus. This moment of calamity he regarded as the beginning of his fame. He entered the house of a bookseller, and, to dissipate his melancholy reflections, he began to read. The book was written by Xenophon, and the merchant was so pleased and captivated by the eloquence and beauties of the philosopher, that from that time he renounced the pursuits of a busy life, and applied himself to the study of philosophy. Ten years were spent in frequenting the school of Crates, and the same number under Stilpo, Xenocrates, and Polemon. Perfect in every branch of knowledge, and improved from experience as well as observation, Zeno opened a school at Athens, and soon saw himself attended by the great, the learned, and the powerful. His followers were called *Stoics*, because they received the instructions of the philosopher in the portico called στοά. He was so much respected during his life-time that the Athenians publicly decreed him a brazen statue and a crown of gold, and engraved their decree, to give it more publicity, on two columns in the academy, and in the Lyceum. His life was an example of soberness and moderation, his manners were austere, and to his temperance and regularity he was indebted for the continual flow of health which he always enjoyed. After he had taught publicly for 48 years, he died in the 98th year of his age, B.C. 264, a stranger to disease. He was buried in that part of the city called Ceramicus, where the Athenians raised him a monument. The founder of the Stoic philosophy shone before his followers as a pure example worthy of imitation. Virtue was the great object of his search. He wished to live in the world as if nothing was properly his own; he loved others, and his affections were extended even to his enemies. He felt a pleasure in being kind, benevolent, and attentive, and he found that these sentiments of pleasure were reciprocal. He saw a connection and dependence in the system of the universe, and perceived that thence arose the harmony of civil society, the tenderness of parents, and filial gratitude. In the attainment of virtue, the goods of the mind were to be preferred to those of the body; and when that point was once gained, nothing could equal our happiness and perfection, and the Stoic could view with indifference health or sickness, riches or poverty, pain and pleasure, which could neither move nor influence the serenity of his mind. Zeno recommended resignation; he knew that the laws of the universe cannot be changed by man, and he therefore wished that his disciples should not by prayer deprecate impending calamities, but rather beseech Providence to grant them fortitude to bear the severest trials with pleasure and due resignation to the will of Heaven. An arbitrary command over the passions was one of the rules of Stoicism; to assist our friends in the hour of calamity was our duty, but to give way to childish sensations was unbecoming our nature. Pity, therefore, and anger, were to be banished from the heart, propriety and decorum were to be the guides in everything, and the external actions of men were the best indications of their inward feelings, their secret inclinations, and their character. It was the duty of the Stoic to study himself; in the evening he was enjoined to review, with critical accuracy, the events of the day, and to regulate his future conduct with more care, and always to find an impartial witness within his own breast. Such were the leading characters of the Stoic philosophy, the followers of which were so illustrious, so perfect, and so numerous, and the effects of which were productive of such exemplary virtues in the annals of the human mind. Zeno in his maxims used to say, that with virtue men could live happy under the most pressing calamities. He said that nature had given us two ears and only one mouth, to tell us that we ought to listen more than speak. He compared those whose actions were dissonant with their professions to the coin of Alexandria, which appeared beautiful to the eye, though made of the basest metals. He acknowledged only one God, the soul of the universe, which he conceived to be the body, and therefore he believed that those two together united, the soul and the body, formed one perfect animal which was the god of Stoics. Amongst the most illustrious followers of his doctrine, and as the most respectable writers, may be mentioned Epictetus, Seneca, the emperor Antoninus, &c. *Cic. Acad.* 1. c. 12. *De Nat. D.* 1. c. 14. l. 2. c. 8 & 24. l. 3. c. 24. *pro. Mur. de Orat.* 32, &c. *Finib.—Seneca.—Epictetus.—Arrian.—Ælian. V. H.* 9. c. 26.—*Diog.—Suidas.—Hesychius.* [The finest bust of this Zeno will be found in the Museum of the Vatican.]——An Epicurean philosopher of Sidon, who numbered among his pupils Cicero, Pomponius Atticus, Cotta, Pompey, &c. *Cic. de Finib.* 1. c. 5. *De Nat. D.* 1. c. 21 & 34. [The finest bust of this Zeno is in the Vatican.]——A rhetorician, father to Polemon, who was made king of Pontus.——The son of Polemon, was king of Armenia. *Strab.* 12.—*Tacit. Ann.* 2. c. 56.——A native of Lepreos, son of Calliteles, crowned at the Olympic games, and honored with a statue in the grove of Jupiter at Olympia. *Paus.* 6. c. 15.——A general of Antiochus. ——A philosopher of Tarsus, B.C. 207. The name of Zeno was common to some of the Roman emperors on the throne of Constantinople, in the 5th and 6th centuries. *Voss. H. Gr.* 1. c. 16. *& De Sect. Philos.* 1. sec. 30. c. 19, &c.

ZENOBIA, a queen of Iberia, wife to Rhadamistus. She accompanied her husband when he was banished from his kingdom by the Armenians, but as she was unable to follow him on account of her pregnancy, she entreated him to murder her. Rhadamistus long hesitated, but fearful of her falling into the hands of his enemy, he obeyed and threw her body into the Araxes. Her clothes kept her up on the surface of the water, where she was found by some shepherds, and as the wound was not mortal, her life was preserved, and she was carried to Tiridates, who acknowledged her as queen. *Tacit. Ann.* 12. c. 51.

ZENO'BIA, a town of Syria, on the Euphrates.

ZENO'BIA SEPTIM'IA, a celebrated princess of Palmyra, who married Odenatus, whom Gallienus acknowledged as his partner on the Roman throne. After the death of her husband, which, according to some authors, she is said to have hastened, Zenobia reigned in the east as regent of her infant children, who were honored with the title of Cæsars. She assumed the name of Augusta, appeared in imperial robes, and ordered herself to be styled the queen of the east. The troubles which at that time agitated the western parts of the empire, prevented the emperor from checking the insolence and ambition of this princess, who boasted to be sprung from the Ptolemies of Ægypt. Aurelian was no sooner invested with the imperial purple than he marched into the east, determined to punish the pride of Zenobia. He well knew her valor, and he was not ignorant that in her wars against the Persians, she had distinguished herself no less than Odenatus. She was the mistress of the east; Ægypt acknowledged her power, and all the provinces of Asia Minor were subject to her command. When Aurelian approached the plains of Syria, the Palmyrean queen appeared at the head of 700,000 men. She bore the labors of the field like the meanest of her soldiers, and walked on foot fearless of danger. Two battles were fought; the courage of the queen gained the superiority, but an imprudent evolution of the Palmyrean cavalry ruined her cause; and while they pursued with spirit the retreating enemy, the Roman infantry suddenly fell upon the main body of Zenobia's army, and the defeat was inevitable. The queen fled to Palmyra, determined to support a siege. Aurelian followed her, and after he had almost exhausted his stores, he proposed terms of accommodation, which were rejected with disdain by the warlike princess. Her hopes of victory, however, soon vanished, and though she harassed the Romans night and day by continual sallies from her walls, and the working of her military engines, she despaired of success when she heard that the armies which were marching to her relief from Armenia, Persia, and the east, had partly been defeated and partly bribed from their allegiance. She fled from Palmyra in the night, but Aurelian, who was apprised of her escape, pursued her, and she was caught as she was crossing the river Euphrates. She was brought into the presence of Aurelian, and though the soldiers were clamorous for her death, she was reserved to adorn the triumph of the conqueror. She was treated with great humanity, and Aurelian gave her large possessions near Tibur, where she was permitted to live the rest of her days in peace, with all the grandeur and majesty which became a queen of the east, and a warlike princess. Her children were patronised by the emperor, and married to persons of the first distinction at Rome. Zenobia has been admired, not only for her military abilities, but also for her literary talents. She was acquainted with every branch of useful learning, and spoke with fluency the language of the Ægyptians, the Greeks, and the Latins. She composed an abridgment of the history of the oriental nations, and of Ægypt, which was greatly commended by the ancients. She received no less honor from the patronage she afforded to the celebrated Longinus, who was one of her favorites, and who taught her the Greek tongue. She has also been praised for her great chastity, and her constancy, though she betrayed too often her propensities to cruelty and intoxication, when in the midst of her officers. She fell into the hands of Aurelian about the 273rd year of the Christian era. *Aur. Vict.—Zos. &c.*

ZENO'BII IN'SULÆ, small islands at the mouth of the Arabian Gulph. *Ptol.*

ZENODO'RUS, a sculptor in the age of Nero. He made a statue of Mercury, as also a colossus for the emperor, which was 110 or 120 feet high, and which was consecrated to the Sun. The head of this colossus was some time after broken off by Vespasian, who placed there the head of Apollo surrounded with seven beams, each of which was seven feet and a half long. From this famous colossus the modern Coliseum, the ruins of which are now so much admired at Rome, took its name. *Plin.* 34. c. 7.

ZENODO'TIA, a town of Mesopotamia, near Nicephorium. *Plut. in Crass.*

ZENOD'OTUS, a native of Trœzene, who wrote a history of Umbria. *Dion. Hal.* 2.——A grammarian of Alexandria in the age of Ptolemy Soter, by whom he was appointed to take care of the celebrated library of Alexandria, and to preside over the education of his children. He wrote on Homer, and died B.C. 245. *Suidas.*——A sophist, also of Alexandria, who wrote on Hesiod, Homer, and against the doctrines of Plato, and also revised the works of Aristarchus. *Suidas.—Vossius. H. Gr.* 1. c. 11.

ZENOTH'EMIS, a Greek author who wrote *de rebus monstrosis. Plin.* 37. c 2.—*Tzetz. Chil.* 7. *Hist.* 44. —*Voss. H. Gr.* 3. p. 425.—*Ælian. V.H.* 17. c. 30.

ZEPH'YRE, a small island of Crete. *Plin.* 4. c. 12.

ZEPHYR'IUM, a promontory of Magna Græcia towards the Ionian Sea, whence, according to some, the Locrians are called *Epizephyrii.—Ovid. Met.* 15. v. 705.——A town of Cilicia. *Liv.* 33. c. 20. ——A cape of Crete, now San Zuane.——A promontory in the island of Cyprus, where Venus had a temple built by Ptolemy Philadelphus, whence she was called Zephyria. It was in his temple that Berenice made an offering of her hair to the goddess of beauty. *Eratosth.* 12.—*Catull.* 67.—*Hygin. P.A.* 2. c. 24.—*Justin.* 26. c. 3.

ZEPH'YRUS, one of the winds, son of Astreus and Aurora, the same as the Favonius of the Latins. He married a nymph called Chloris, or Flora, by whom he had a son called Carpos. Zephyr was said to produce flowers and fruits by the sweetness of his breath. He had a temple at Athens, where he was represented as a young man of delicate form, with two wings on his shoulders, and with his head covered with all sorts of flowers. He was supposed to be the same as the west wind. *Hesiod. Theog.* 377.—*Virg. Æn.* 1. v. 135. l. 2. v. 417. l. 4. v. 233, &c.—*Ovid. Met.* 1. v. 64. l. 15. v. 700.—*Propert.* 1. el. 16. v. 34 el. 18. v. 2.—*Lucret.* 5. v. 738.—*Catull.* 75. v. 270 & 282.—*Paus.* 1. c. 36.—*Plin.* 2. c. 47. l. 18. c. 34.—*Aul. Gell*

2. c. 22 & 25.—*Apul. de Mund.* 2. c. 4.—*Servius ad Virg. Ecl.* 4. v. 48.

ZERA'NIA, a region of Thrace. *Steph.*

ZER'BIS, a river of Mesopotamia, falling into the Tigris. *Plin.* 6. c. 26.

ZERMIZIR'GA, a city of Dacia. *Ptol.*

ZER'NA, a city of Thrace. *Antonin.*

ZERYN'THUS, a town of Samothrace, with a cave sacred to Hecate. The epithet of Zerynthius is applied to Apollo. *Ovid. Trist.* 1. el. 9. v. 19.—*Liv.* 38. c. 41.

ZE'TEON, a town of Arcadia. *Paus.* 1. 8.

ZE'THA, a promontory of Africa near the Syrtis Minor. *Ptol.*

ZE'THES, ZE'TES or ZETUS, a son of Boreas, king of Thrace, and Orythia, who, with his brother Calais, accompanied the Argonauts to Colchis. In Bithynia, the two brothers, who are represented with wings, delivered Phineus from the continual persecution of the Harpies, and drove these monsters as far as the islands called Strophades, where at last they were stopped by Iris, who promised them that Phineus should no longer be tormented by them. They were both killed, as some say, by Hercules during the Argonautic expedition, and were changed into those winds which generally blow eight or ten days before the dog-star appears, and are called Prodromi by the Greeks. Their sister Cleopatra married Phineus king of Bithynia. *Orpheus. Arg.* 220.—*Apollod.* 1. c. 9. l. 3. c. 15.—*Hygin.* fab. 14, 157 & 273.—*Ovid. Met.* 8. v. 716.—*Paus.* 3. c. 18.—*Val. Flacc.* 1. v. 469. l. 4. v. 465.—*Apollon.* 1. v. 211.—*Oppian.* 2. *Cyn.* 621.—*Servius ad Æn.* 3. v. 209.—*Fulgent. Myth.* 3. c. 11.—*Seneca. in Med.* 634.—*Palæph. de Inc.* 23.

ZETHIS, a town of Carmania. *Plin.* 6. c. 23. *Hermolaus*, however, reads Cethis.

ZE'THUS, a freeman mentioned by *Cicero*, 9. *Fam.* 15.

ZET'TA, a town of Africa Propria, at the west of Thapsus, now Zerbi. *Strab.* 14.—*Hirt. Afr.* 68.

ZE'TUS or ZE'THUS, a son of Jupiter and Antiope, brother to Amphion. The two brothers were born on mount Cithæron, whither Antiope had fled to avoid the resentment of her father Nycteus. When they had attained the years of manhood, they collected a number of their friends to avenge the injuries which their mother had received from Lycus, the successor of Nycteus on the throne of Thebes, and his wife Dirce. Lycus was put to death, and his wife tied to the tail of a wild bull, that dragged her over rocks and precipices till she died. The crown of Thebes was seized by the two brothers, not only as the reward of this victory, but as their inheritance, and Zethus surrounded the capital of his dominions with a strong wall, while his brother amused himself with playing on his lyre. Music and verses were disagreeable to Zethus, and, according to some, he prevailed upon his brother to pursue so unproductive a study no longer. Zethus married Thebe, and Amphion Niobe daughter of Tantalus. *Hygin.* fab. 7.—*Paus.* 2. c. 6. l. 9. c. 5 & 17.—*Tzetzes. ad Lyc.* 436 & 602.—*Apollod.* 3. c. 5 & 10.—*Horat.* 1. ep. 18. v. 41. [Zethus is a principal figure in the celebrated "Toro Farnese," at Naples.]

ZEU'GIS or ZEUGITA'NA, a portion of Africa, in which Carthage is situated. The other division more to the south was called Byzacium. *Isidor.* 14, 5.—*Plin.* 5. c. 4.

ZEUG'MA, a town of Mesopotamia, on the western banks of the Euphrates, where was a well known passage across the river. It was the eastern boundary of the Roman empire, and in Pliny's age, a chain of iron was said to extend across it. *Plin.* 5. c. 24.—*Strab.* 16.—*Curt* 3. c. 7.—*Tacit. Ann.* 12. c. 12.——A town of Dacia. *Ptol.*

ZE'US, a name of Jupiter among the Greeks, expressive of his being the father of mankind, by whom all things live. *Diod.* 5.

ZEUXIDA'MUS, a king of Sparta, of the family of the Proclidæ. He was father of Archidamus, and grandson of Theopompus, and was succeeded by his son Archidamus. *Paus.* 3. c. 7.

ZEUX'IDAS, a prætor of the Achæan league, deposed because he had proposed to his countrymen an alliance with the Romans.

ZEUXIPPE, a daughter of Eridanus, mother of Butes, one of the Argonauts. Some make her daughter of Apidamus, and wife of Pandion king of Athens, by whom she had Butes and Erechtheus, and two daughters Procne and Philomela. *Hygin.* fab. 14.—*Meursius de Reg. A.* 2. c. 6 & 18.—*Apollod.* 3. c. 15.——A daughter of Laomedon. She married Sicyon, who after his father-in-law's death became king of that city of Peloponnesus, which from him has been called Sicyon. *Paus.* 2. c. 6.

ZEUX'IS, a celebrated painter, born at Heraclea, which some suppose to be the Heraclea of Sicily. He flourished about 468 years before the Christian era, and was the disciple of Apollodorus, and contemporary with Parrhasius. In the art of painting he not only surpassed all his contemporaries, but also his master, and became so sensible, and at the same time so proud of the value of his pieces, that he refused to sell them, observing that no sum of money, however great, was sufficient to buy them. His most celebrated paintings were his Jupiter sitting on a throne surrounded by the gods; his Hercules strangling the serpents in the presence of his affrighted parents; his modest Penelope; and his Helen, which was afterwards placed in the temple of Juno Lacinia, in Italy. This last piece he had painted at the request of the people of Crotona, and that he might not be without a model, they sent him the most beautiful of their virgins. Zeuxis retained five, from whose graces and elegance united, he conceived in his mind the form of the most perfect woman in the universe, which his pencil at last executed with wonderful success. His contest with Parrhasius is well known (*Vid.* Parrhasius); but though he represented nature in such perfection, and copied all her beauties with such exactness, he often found himself deceived. He painted grapes, and formed an idea of the goodness of his piece from the birds which came to eat the fruit on the canvass. But he soon acknowledged that the whole was an ill executed piece, as the figure of the man who carried the grapes was not done with sufficient expression to terrify the birds. According to some, Zeuxis died from laughing at a comical picture which he had painted of an old woman. *Cic. de Inv.* 2. c. 1.—*Plut. in Par. &c.*—*Quintil.* 12. c. 10.—*Plin.* 35. c. 9 & 10.—*Festus de V. Sig.*——A person suspected of parricide in the province over which Quintus, Cicero's brother, presided. *Cic. Q. Fr.* 1. ep. 2. 2.

ZEUX'O, one of the Oceanides. *Hesiod Theog.* v. 352.

ZIG'ANA, a city of Armenia, or of the Cappadocian Pontus. *Antonin.*

ZIG'ERA, a town of Africa Propria, south of Hippo. *Ptol.*

ZIG'ERE, a city of Thrace, near Lower Mœsia. *Plin.* 4. c. 11.

ZIGI'RA, a city of Assyria.

ZIL'IA or ZE'LIS, a town of Mauritania, at the mouth of the river of the same name, which falls into the Atlantic Sea. *Plin.* 5. c. 1.

ZIM'ARA, a town of Armenia Minor, twelve miles from the sources of the Euphrates. *Plin.* 5. c. 24.

ZIMY'RA, a city of Aria. *Ptol.*

ZIN'CHI, a people of Asiatic Sarmatia, on the Euxine Sea. *Arrian.*

ZIN'GIS, a promontory of Æthiopia, near the entrance of the Red Sea, now Cape Orfui.

ZIOB'ERIS a river of Hyrcania, whose rapid course is described by *Curtius*, 6. c. 4.

ZIPŒ'TES or ZIBŒ'TES, a king of Bithynia, who died in his 70th year, B.C. 279.

ZIRIDA'VA, a city of Dacia. *Ptol.*

ZI'THA, a town of Mesopotamia.——A promontory and town of Africa. *Ptol.*

ZI'ZA, a town of Arabia Petræa. *Ptol.*

ZI'ZERUS, a harbour of India. *Plin.* 6. c. 23.

ZO'ELÆ, a people of Hispania Tarraconensis. *Id.* 3. c. 3.

ZO'ES, a place of Cyrene founded by Battus. *Herodot.* l. 4.

ZOE'TIUM, a city of Armenia. *Steph.*

ZOGOC'ARA, a city of Armenia Major. *Ptol.*

ZO'ILUS, a sophist and grammarian of Amphipolis, B.C. 259. He rendered himself known by his severe criticisms on the works of Isocrates and Plato, and the poems of Homer, for which he received the name of Homeromastix, or the chastiser of Homer. He presented his criticisms to Ptolemy Philadelphus, but they were rejected with indignation, though the author declared that he starved for want of bread. Some say, that Zoilus was cruelly stoned to death, or exposed on a cross, by order of Ptolemy, while others assert, that he was burnt alive at Smyrna. The name of Zoilus is generally applied to austere critics. The works of this unfortunate grammarian are lost. *Ælian. V.H.* 11 c. 10.—*Dionys. Hal. in Ep. ad Cn. Pomp.*—*Vitruv. in Præf.*—*Ovid. de Rem. Am.* 266.——An officer in the army of Alexander. *Curt.* 6. c. 6.

ZOIP'PUS, a son-in-law of Hiero of Sicily.

ZOIT'IUM, a city of Arcadia. *Steph.*

ZOL'CA, a town of the Paphlagonians in Galatia. *Ptol.*

ZOM'BIS, a city of Media. *Steph.*

ZO'NE, a town of Africa. *Dio.* 48.——A town of Thrace on the Ægæan Sea, where the woods are said to have followed the strains of Orpheus. *Mela,* 2. c. 2.—*Herodot.*

ZON'ARAS or ZONA'RAS, one of the Byzantine historians, whose Greek Annals were edited 2 vols fol. Paris, 1686.

ZOPARIS'TUS, a city of Armenia Major. *Ptol.*

ZOPYR'IO, one of Alexander's officers, left in Greece when the conqueror was in Asia, &c. *Curt.* 10. c. 1.

ZOPYR'ION, a governor of Pontus, who made war against Scythia, &c. *Justin.* 2. c. 3.

ZOP'YRUS, a Persian, son of Megabyzus, who, to show his attachment to Darius, the son of Hytaspes, while he besieged Babylon, cut off his ears and nose, and fled to the enemy, telling them that he had received such treatment from his royal master because he had advised him to raise the siege, as the city was impregnable. This was credited by the Babylonians, and Zopyrus was appointed commander of all their forces. When he had totally gained their confidence, he betrayed the city into the hands of Darius, for which he was liberally rewarded. The regard of Darius for Zopyrus could never be more strongly expressed than in what he used often to say, that he had rather have Zopyrus not mutilated than twenty Babylons. *Herodot.* 3. c. 154, &c.—*Plut. in Apoph. Reg.* 3.—*Justin.* 1. c. 10.——An orator of Clazomenæ. *Quintil.* 3. c. 6.——A physician in the age of Mithridates He gave the monarch a description of an antidote which wonld prevail against all sorts of poisons. The experiment was tried upon criminals and succeeded.——A physician in the age of Plutarch.——An officer of Argos, who cut off the head of Pyrrhus. *Plut.*——A man appointed master of Alcibiades, by Pericles. *Plut.*——A physiognomist. *Cic. Tusc.* 4. c. 37. *De Sat.* 5.——A rhetorician of Colophon. *Diog*

ZORI'GA, a city of Armenia Major. *Ptol.*

ZOROAN'DA, a part of Taurus, between Mesopotamia and Armenia, near which the Tigris flows. *Plin.* 6. c. 27.

ZOROAS'TER, a king of Bactria, supposed to have lived in the age of Ninus, king of Assyria, some time before the Trojan war. According to Justin, he first invented magic, or the doctrines of the Magi, and rendered himself known by his deep and acute researches in philosophy, the origin of the world, and the studty of astronomy. He was respected by his subjecrs and contemporaries for his abilities as a monarch, a law-giver, and a philosopher, and though many of his doctrines are puerile and ridiculous, yet his followers are still found in numbers in the wilds of Persia, and the extensive provinces of India. Like Pythagoras, Zoroaster admitted no visible object of devotion, except fire, which he considered as the most proper emblem of the supreme being; which doctrines seem to have been preserved by Numa, in the worship and ceremonies which he instituted in honor of Vesta. According to some of the moderns, the doctrines, laws, and regulations of this celebrated Bactrian are still extant, and they have been lately introduced into Europe in a French translation by M. Anquetil, of the academy of Belles Lettres. The history of Zoroaster is so little known, that many speak of two, three, four, and even six lawgivers of that name. Some authors, who assert that two persons only of this name flourished, describe the first as an astronomer, living in Babylon, 2459 years B.C. whilst the era of the other, who is supposed to have been a native of Persia, and the restorer of the religion of the Magi, is fixed 589, and by some 519 years B.C. *Fabr. B. Gr.* 1. 1. c. 36.—*Sax. Onom.* 1. p. 26.—*Justin.* 1. c. 1.—*August. de Civ.* 21. c. 14.—*Oros.* 1. c. 4.—*Plin.* 7. c. 10. 1. 30. c. 1.—*Fragment. Berosi.*—*Arnob.* 1.—*Gyrald. de P. H.* 2.

ZOROPAS'SUS, a city of Armenia Major. *Ptol.*

ZOR'ZINES, a king of the Siraci, in the time of Claudius. *Tac. Ann.* 12. c. 15.

ZOS'IMUS, an officer in the reign of Theodosius the younger, about the year 410 of the Christian era. He wrote the history of the Roman emperors in Greek, from the age of Augustus to the beginning of the 5th century, of which only the five first books and the beginning of the sixth are extant. In the first of these he is very succinct in his account from the time of Augustus to the reign of Diocletian, but in the succeeding he becomes more diffuse and interesting. His composition is written with elegance, but not much fidelity, and the author showed his malevolence against the Christians in his history of Constantine, and some of his successors. The best editions of Zosimus are that of Cellarius, 8vo. Jenæ, 1728, and that of Reitemier, 8vo. Lips. 1784 *Fabr. B. Gr.* 5. c. 5 & 38.——*Sax. Onom.* 1. p. 498.——A freedman in the house of the younger Pliny. *Plin.* 5. ep. 19.

ZOS'INE, the wife of king Tigranes, led in triumph by Pompey. *Plut.*

ZOSIP'PUS, a man of consequence at Tyndaris in Sicily. *Cic. Verr.* 4. c. 42.

ZOS'TER, a town, harbour, and promontory of Attica. *Cic. ad Att.* 5. ep. 12.

ZOSTE'RIA, a surname of Minerva. She had two statues under that name in the city of Thebes, in Bœotia. The word signifies girt, or armed for battle, expressions synonymous among the ancients. *Paus.* 9. c. 17.—*Hom. Il.* 2. v. 478. 1. 11. v. 15.

ZOT'ALE, a place near Antioch in Margiana, where the Margus was divided into small streams. *Plin.* 6. c. 16.

ZO'TON, a city of Upper Æthiopia. *Plin.*

ZOTUAS'TES or ZATRAS'TES, a lawgiver among the Arimaspi. *Diod. Sic. Antiq.* 2 & 3. c. 5.

ZUCHAB'ARUS or ZUCHAB'BARI, a mountain of Africa Propria. *Ptol.*

ZU'CHIS, a lake to the east of the Syrtis Minor, with a town of the same name, famous for a purple dye, and salt-fish. *Strab.* 17.

ZU'GANA, a city of Arabia Felix. *Ptol.*

ZU'GAR, a city of Africa Propria. *Id.*

ZU'RACHI, a people of Arabia. *Plin.* 6. c. 28.

ZUROB'ARA, a city of Dacia. *Ptol.*

ZURZU'RA, a city of Armenia Major. *Id.*

ZUSIDA'VA, a city of Dacia. *Id.*

ZYDRE'TÆ. a people near the Euxine Sea, according to *Arrian in Peripl.* They are called Sisilissi by *Procopius.*

ZYGAC'TES, a river of Thrace near Philippi, in the passage of which Pluto, when he carried of Proserpine, is said to have *broken* the *yoke* of his chariot, whence the name. *Appian. Civil.* 1. 4.

ZYGAN'TES, a people of Africa. *Herodot.* 1. 4.

ZYG'ENA, an island in the Red Sea. *Steph.*

ZYGEN'SES, a people of Marmarica. *Ptol.*

ZY'GI, a people near the Asiatic Bosporus. The town of Zygopolis, near Trapezus, seems to have belonged to them. *Steph.*

ZYG'IA, a surname of Juno, because she presided over marriage (*a ζεύγνυμι, jungo*). She is the same as the *Pronuba* of the Latins. *Pindar.*—*Pollux.* 3. c. 3.—*Virg. Æn.* 4. v. 59.—*Apul. Met.* 6.

ZYGIA'NA, a region of Bithynia. *Ptol.*

ZYG'II, a savage nation, at the north of Colchis. *Strab.* 11.

ZYGOP'OLIS, a town of Cappadocia, on the borders of Colchis. *Strab.* 12. *Vid.* Zygi.

ZY'GRIS, a town of Marmarica. *Ptol.* The people were called Zygritæ

ZYM'NA, a city of Syria, between Edessa and Cyrrhus. *Antonin.*

ZYPOETES, the father of Nicomedes, who founded Nicomedia. He waged war with Lysimachus, and conquered him in many battles. *Salmas. not. ad Treb. Poll. in Gallien.* c. 4.

ZY'RAS, a river of Thrace which flows by Dionysiopolis.

GRECIAN MEASURES OF LENGTH REDUCED TO

												English paces.	ft.	in.	dec.
											Dactylus or *Digit* (Δακτυλος)	0	0	0	$7554\frac{1}{16}$
4											*Doron* (Δῶρον) or *palm* (Δοχμή)	0	0	3	$0218\frac{3}{4}$
10	$2\frac{1}{2}$										*Lichas* (Λιχας)	0	0	7	$5546\frac{7}{8}$
11	$2\frac{3}{4}$	$1\frac{1}{10}$									*Orthodoron* (Ορθόδωρον)	0	0	8	$3101\frac{9}{16}$
12	3	$1\frac{1}{5}$	$1\frac{1}{11}$								*Spithame* (Σπιθαμή)	0	0	9	$0656\frac{1}{4}$
16	4	$1\frac{3}{5}$	$1\frac{5}{11}$	$1\frac{1}{3}$							*Foot* (Ποῦς.)	0	1	0	0875
18	$4\frac{1}{2}$	$1\frac{4}{5}$	$1\frac{7}{11}$	$1\frac{1}{2}$	$1\frac{1}{8}$						*Cubit* (Πύγμη)	0	1	1	$5984\frac{3}{8}$
20	5	2	$1\frac{9}{11}$	$1\frac{2}{3}$	$1\frac{1}{4}$	$1\frac{1}{9}$					*Pygon* (Πυγών)	0	1	3	$1093\frac{3}{4}$
24	6	$2\frac{2}{5}$	$2\frac{2}{11}$	2	$1\frac{1}{2}$	$1\frac{1}{3}$	$1\frac{1}{5}$				*Larger Cubit* (Πῆχυς)	0	1	6	13125
96	24	$9\frac{3}{5}$	$8\frac{8}{11}$	8	6	$5\frac{1}{3}$	$4\frac{4}{5}$	4			*Pace* (Ὀργυία)	0	6	0	525
9600	2100	960	$872\frac{8}{11}$	800	600	$533\frac{1}{3}$	480	400	100		*Stadium* (Σταδιον)	100	4	4	5
76800	19200	7680	$6981\frac{9}{11}$	6400	4800	$4266\frac{2}{3}$	3840	3200	800	8	*Milion* (Μίλιον, *milliare*)	805	5	0	

To these may be added the Δίαυλος, equal to two stadia; the Δόλιχος, to twelve stadia; and the Κλίμα, to sixty feet.

ROMAN MEASURES OF LENGTH REDUCED TO

										English paces.	ft.	in.	dec.
									Digitus transversus	0	0	0	$725\frac{1}{4}$
$1\frac{1}{3}$									*Uncia*	0	0	0	967
4	3								*Palmus*	0	0	2	901
16	12	4							*Pes*	0	0	11	604
20	15	5	$1\frac{1}{4}$						*Palmipes*	0	1	2	505
24	18	6	$1\frac{1}{2}$	$1\frac{1}{5}$					*Cubitus*	0	1	5	406
40	30	10	$2\frac{1}{2}$	2	$1\frac{2}{3}$				*Gradus*	0	2	5	01
80	60	20	5	4	$3\frac{1}{3}$	2			*Passus*	0	4	10	02
10000	7500	2500	625	500	$416\frac{2}{3}$	250	125		*Stadium*	120	4	4	5
80000	60000	20000	5000	4000	$3333\frac{1}{3}$	2000	1000	8	*Milliare, Lapis,* or *Cippus*	967	0	0	

The Grecian square Measures were the *Plethron* or Acre, containing 1444, as some say, or, as others report, 10000 square feet; the *Aroura*, which was half the *Plethron*. The *Aroura* of the Ægyptians was the square of 100 Cubits,

The Roman square Measure was the *Jugerum*, which, like their *Libra* and their *As*, was divided into twelve Parts called *Unciæ*, as the following Table shows:

		Unciæ	Square feet.	Scruples.	English roods	Square poles.	Square feet.
1	*As* or......	12	28800	288	2	18	250,05
$\frac{11}{12}$	*Deunx* ...	11	26400	264	2	10	183,85
$\frac{5}{6}$	*Dextans*	10	24000	240	2	2	117,64
$\frac{3}{4}$	*Dodrans*	9	21600	216	1	34	51,42
$\frac{2}{3}$	*Bes*	8	19200	192	1	25	257,46
$\frac{7}{12}$	*Septunx*	7	16800	168	1	17	191,25
$\frac{1}{2}$	*Semis* ...	6	14400	144	1	9	125,03
$\frac{5}{12}$	*Quincunx*	5	12000	120	1	1	58,82
$\frac{1}{3}$	*Triens* ...	4	9600	96	0	32	264,85
$\frac{1}{4}$	*Quadrans*	3	7200	72	0	24	198,64
$\frac{1}{6}$	*Sextans*...	2	4800	48	0	16	132,43
$\frac{1}{12}$	*Uncia* ...	1	2400	24	0	8	66,21

N. B. The *Actus Major* was 14400 square feet, equal to a *Semis*. The *Clima* was 3600 square feet, equal to a *sescuncia*, or an *uncia* and a half, and the *actus minimus* was equal to a *sextans*.

The Roman *as*, or *æs*, was called so because it was made of brass.

ATTIC MEASURES OF CAPACITY, FOR THINGS LIQUID, REDUCED TO THE ENGLISH WINE MEASURE.

										gals.	pts.	sol.in.	dec.
Cochlearion										0	1/120	0	0356 5/12
2	*Cheme*									0	1/60	0	0712 5/6
2½	1¼	*Mystron*								0	1/48	0	0891 1/24
5	2½	2	*Conche*							0	1/24	0	1782 1/12
10	5	4	2	*Cyathus* (Κύαθος)						0	1/12	0	3564 1/6
15	7½	6	3	1½	*Oxybaphon* (Ὀξύβαφον)					0	½	0	5346¼
60	30	24	12	6	4	*Cotyle* (Κοτύλη)				0	⅛	2	1385
120	60	48	24	12	8	2	*Xestes* (Ξέστης)			0	1	4	277
720	360	288	144	72	48	12	6	*Chous* (Χοῦς)		0	6	25	662
8640	4320	3456	1728	864	576	144	72	12	*Metretes* (Μετρητής)	10	2	10	632

There is a measure called by Herodotus 'Αρυστήρ, but what it held is unknown.

ROMAN MEASURES OF CAPACITY FOR THINGS LIQUID, REDUCED TO ENGLISH WINE MEASURE.

										gals.	pts.	sol.in.	dec.
Ligula										0	1/48	0	117 6/12
4	*Cyathus* or *Sympulus*									0	1/12	0	469⅔
6	1½	*Acetabulum*								0	⅛	0	704½
12	3	2	*Quartarius*							0	¼	1	409
24	6	4	2	*Hemina* (à Gr. Ἥμισυ)						0	½	2	818
48	12	8	4	2	*Sextarius*					0	1	5	636
288	72	48	24	12	6	*Congius*				0	7	4	942
1152	288	192	96	48	24	4	*Urna*			3	4½	5	33
2304	576	384	192	96	48	8	2	*Amphora* or *Quadrantal*		7	1	10	66
46080	11520	7680	3840	1920	960	160	40	20	*Culeus*	143	3	11	095

N. B. The *cadus*, *congiarius*, and *dolium* denote no certain measure. The Romans divided the *sextarius* like the *libra*, into 12 equal parts, called *cyathi*, and therefore their *calices* were called *sextantes*, *quadrantes*, *trientes*, &c. according to the number of *cyathi* which they contained.

ATTIC MEASURES OF CAPACITY FOR THINGS DRY, REDUCED TO ENGLISH CORN MEASURE.

							pecks.	gals.	pts.	sol.in.	dec.
Cochlearion							0	0	0	0	276 7/20
10	*Cyathus*						0	0	0	2	763½
15	1½	*Oxybaphon*					0	0	0	4	144¾
60	6	4	*Cotyle*				0	0	0	16	579
120	12	8	2	*Xestes*			0	0	0	33	158
180	18	12	3	1½	*Chœnix* (Χοῖνιξ)		0	0	1	15	705¾
8040	864	576	144	72	48	*Medimnus* (Μέδιμνος)	4	0	6	3	501

N. B. Besides this *Medimus*, which is the *Medicus*, there was a *Medimnus Georgicus*, equal to six Roman *Modii*.

ROMAN MEASURES OF CAPACITY FOR THINGS DRY, REDUCED TO ENGLISH CORN MEASURE.

							pecks.	gals.	pts.	sol.in.	dec.
Ligula							0	0	$\frac{1}{48}$	0	01
4	*Cyathus*						0	0	$\frac{1}{12}$	0	04
6	$1\frac{1}{2}$	*Acetabulum*					0	0	$\frac{1}{8}$	0	06
24	6	4	*Hemina*				0	0	$\frac{1}{2}$	0	24
48	12	8	2	*Sextarius*			0	0	1	0	48
384	96	64	16	8	*Semimodius*		0	1	0	3	84
768	192	128	32	16	2	*Modius*	1	0	0	7	68

THE MOST ANCIENT GRECIAN WEIGHTS REDUCED TO ENGLISH TROY WEIGHT.

			lb.	oz.	dwt.	gr.
Drachma (Δραχμή)			0	0	2	$14\frac{22}{49}$
100	*Mina* (Μνᾶ)		1	1	0	$4\frac{44}{49}$
6000	60	*Talentum* (Τάλαντον)	65	0	12	$5\frac{43}{49}$

The *Talentum Majus* weighed 80 *Minæ.*

LESS ANCIENT GRECIAN AND ROMAN WEIGHTS REDUCED TO ENGLISH TROY WEIGHT.

											lb.	oz.	dwt.	gr.
Lentes											0	0	0	$0\frac{85}{112}$
4	*Siliquæ*										0	0	0	$3\frac{1}{28}$
12	3	*Obolus*									0	0	0	$9\frac{3}{28}$
24	6	2	*Scriptulum*								0	0	0	$18\frac{3}{14}$
72	18	6	3	*Drachma*							0	0	2	$6\frac{9}{14}$
96	24	8	4	$1\frac{1}{3}$	*Sextula*						0	0	3	$0\frac{6}{7}$
144	36	12	6	2	$1\frac{1}{2}$	*Sicilicus*					0	0	4	$13\frac{2}{7}$
192	48	16	8	$2\frac{2}{3}$	2	$1\frac{1}{3}$	*Duella*				0	0	6	$1\frac{5}{7}$
576	144	48	24	8	6	4	3	*Uncia*			0	0	18	$5\frac{1}{7}$
6912	1728	576	288	96	72	48	36	12	*Libra*		0	10	18	$13\frac{5}{7}$

N. B. The Roman ounce is the English *avoirdupois* ounce, which was anciently divided into seven *denarii*, and eight *drachmæ*, and as they reckoned their *denarius* equal to an Attic *drachma*, the Attic weights were $\frac{1}{8}$th heavier than the corresponding weights among the Romans.

The Greeks divided their *obolus* into *chalci* and smaller proportions; some into six *chalci*, and every *chalcus* into seven smaller parts, and others divided it into eight *chalci*, and each *chalcus* into eight parts.

THE GREATER WEIGHTS REDUCED TO ENGLISH TROY WEIGHT.

				lb.	oz.	dwt.	gr.
Libra				0	10	18	$13\frac{5}{7}$
$1\frac{1}{24}$	*Mina Attica communis*			0	11	7	$16\frac{2}{7}$
$1\frac{1}{3}$	$1\frac{7}{25}$	*Mina Attica medica*		1	2	11	$10\frac{2}{7}$
$62\frac{1}{2}$	60	$46\frac{7}{8}$	*Talentum Atticum commune*	56	11	0	$17\frac{1}{7}$

N. B. There was also another Attic talent which consisted of 80, or, according to some, of 100 *minæ*. It must however be remembered, that every *mina* contains 100 *drachmæ*, and every *talent* 60 *minæ*. The talents differ according to the standard of their *minæ* and *drachmæ*, as the following table indicates:

		Consists of Attic drachmæ	Equivalent to English troy weight			
The Mina	*Ægyptiaca*	133⅓	1	5	6	22 26/49
	Antiochica	133⅓	1	5	6	22 26/49
	Cleopatræ Ptolemaica	144	1	6	14	16 32/49
	Alexandrina Dioscoridis	160	1	8	16	7 41/49

		Consists of Attic minæ	Equivalent to English troy weight			
The Talentum	*Ægyptiacum*	80	86	8	16	8
	Antiochicum	80	86	8	16	8
	Ptolemaicum Cleop.	86⅔	93	11	11	0
	Alexandriæ	96	104	0	19	14
	Insulanum	120	130	1	4	12
	Antiochiæ	360	390	3	13	11

THE VALUE AND PROPORTION OF THE GRECIAN COINS.

											l.	s.	d.	q.
Lepton											0	0	0	0 31/336
7	*Chalcus*										0	0	0	0 31/48
14	2	*Dichalcus*									0	0	0	1 7/24
28	4	2	*Hemiobolus*								0	0	0	2 7/12
56	8	4	2	*Obolus*							0	0	1	1⅙
112	16	8	4	2	*Diobolus*						0	0	2	2⅓
224	32	16	8	4	2	*Tetrobolus*					0	0	5	0⅔
336	48	24	12	6	3	1½	*Drachma*				0	0	7	3
672	96	48	24	12	6	3	2	*Didrachmon*			0	1	3	2
1344	192	96	48	24	12	6	4	2	*Tetradrachmon Stater*		0	2	7	0
1680	384	120	60	30	15	7½	5	2½	1¼	*Pentadrachmon*	0	3	2	3

N. B. The *drachma*, and the *didrachmon*, were silver, the others generally of brass. The *tridrachmon*, *triobolus*, &c. were sometimes coined. The *drachma* and the *denarius* are here supposed to be equal, though the former often exceeded in weight.

	l.	s.	d.
The gold Coin among the Greeks was the *stater aureus*, which weighed two Attic *drachmæ*, or half the *stater argenteus*, and was worth 25 Attic *drachmæ*, of silver, or in English money	0	16	1¾
Or according to the proportion of gold to silver, at present	1	0	9
The *Stater Cyzicenus* exchanged for 28 Attic *drachmæ*, or	0	18	1
The *Stater Philippi* and *Stater Alexandri* were of the same value			
The *Stater Daricus*, according to Josephus, was worth 50 Attic *drachmæ*, or	1	12	3½
The *Stater Crœsi* was of the same value.			

THE VALUE AND PROPORTION OF THE ROMAN COINS.

						l.	s.	d.	q.
Teruncius						0	0	0	0 775/1000
2	*Sembella*					0	0	0	1 11/20
4	2	*Libella*, or *As*				0	0	0	3 1/10
10	5	2½	*Sestertius*			0	0	1	3¾
20	10	5	2	*Quinarius*, or *Victoriatus*		0	0	3	3½
40	20	10	4	2	*Denarius*	0	0	7	3

N. B. The *denarius, victoriatus, sestertius*, and sometimes the *as*, were of silver, the others were of brass. The *triens, sextans, uncia, sextula*, and *dupondius*, were sometimes coined of brass.

THE COMPUTATION OF MONEY AMONG THE GREEKS, WAS BY DRACHMÆ, AS FOLLOWS:

	l.	s.	d.	q.
1 *Drachma*	0	0	7	3
10 *Drachmæ*	0	6	5	2
100 *Drachmæ* equal to a *Mina*	3	4	7	
10 *Minæ*	32	5	10	

	l.	s.	d.
60 *Minæ* equal to a *Talent*	193	15	0
10 *Talents*	1937	10	0
100 *Talents*	19375	0	0

AMONG THE ROMANS, THE COMPUTATION WAS BY SESTERTII NUMMI, AS

	£.	s.	d.	q.
A *Sestertius*	0	0	1	3¾
10 *Sestertii*	0	1	7	1½
1000 *Sestertii* equal to one *Sestertium* ...	8	1	5	2
10 *Sestertia*	80	14	7	0
100 *Sestertia*	807	5	10	0

	£.	s.	d.	q.
1000 *Sestertia* or *decies sestertiûm* (centies und.) or *decies centena millia nummûm*	8072	18	4	0
Centies vel *centies H. S.* ...	80729	3	4	0
Millies H. S.	807291	13	4	0
Millies centies H. S. ...	888020	16	8	0

	Was worth of Attic *drachmæ.*
The Mina Syra	25
Ptolemaica	33⅓
Antiochica	100
Euboica	100
Babylonica	116
Attica major	133⅓
Tyria	133⅓
Æginæa	166⅔
Rhodia	166⅔

	Was worth of Attic *minæ.*
The Talentum Syrum	15
Ptolemaicum	20
Antiochicum	60
Euboicum	60
Babylonicum	70
Atticum majus	80
Tyrium	80
Æginæum	100
Rhodium	100
Ægyptium	80

The Roman gold coin was the *aureus*, which generally weighed double the *denarius.*	£.	s.	d.	q.
The value of it, according to the first proportion of coinage, mentioned by Pliny, was ...	1	4	3	3
Or according to the proportion of coinage at present	1	0	9	
According to the decuple proportion mentioned by Livy and Julius Pollux	0	12	11	
According to Tacitus, as it was afterwards valued and exchanged for 25 *denarii* ...	0	16	1	3

The Value of Coin underwent many change during the existence of the Roman Republic, and stood, according to Pliny, as follows:

	The *as* weighed of brass.
In the reign of Servius,	1 pound.
A.U.C. 490	2 ounces.
A.U.C. 537	1 ounce.
A.U.C. 586	½ ounce.

	The *denarius* exchanged for
A.U.C. 485	10 *asses.*
A.U.C. 537	16 *asses.*

A.U.C. 547, a scruple of gold was worth 20 *sestertii;* coined afterwards of the pound of gold, 20 *denarii aurei;* and in Nero's reign of the pound of gold, 45 *denarii aurei.*

N.B.—In the above tables of money, it is to be observed that the silver has been reckoned at 5s., and the gold at 4*l.* per ounce.

A talent of gold among the Jews was worth 5475*l.*, and one of silver 342*l.* 3*s.* 9*d.*

The greater talent of the Romans was worth 99*l.* 6*s.* 8*d.*, and the less 60*l.*, or, as some say, 75*l.*, and the great talent 1125*l.*

The value of the Roman *pondo* is not precisely known, though some suppose it to have been equivalent to an Attic *mina*, or 3*l.* 4*s.* 7*d.* It is used indifferently by ancient authors for *æs*, *as*, and *mina*, and was supposed to consist of 100, or 96 *denarii.* It is to be observed, that whenever the word *pondo* is joined to numbers, it signifies the same as *libra;* but when it is used with other words, it bears the same signification as the σάθμη or Ολκή of the Greeks, or the *pondus* of the Latins. The word *nummus*, when mentioned as a sum of money, was supposed to be equivalent to a *sestertius;* and though the words *sestertius* and *nummus* are often joined together, yet their signification is the same, and they intimate no more than either does separately.

We must particularly remark, that in reckoning their *sesterces*, the Romans had an art which can be rendered intelligible by the observation of these rules:—If a numeral noun agreed in case, gender, and number, with the word *sestertius*, it denoted precisely as many *sestertii;* as, for example, *decem sestertii* was ten *sestertii.* If a numeral noun of another case was joined with the genitive plural of *sestertius*, it denoted so many thousand, as *decem sestertiûm* signifies so many thousand *sestertii.* If the adverb numeral was joined, it denoted so many hundred thousand, as *decies sestertiûm* was ten hundred thousand *sestertii.* If the numeral adverb was put by itself, the signification was not altered; therefore *decies*, *vigesies*, &c., in a sentence, imply as many hundred thousand *sestertii*, or hundred *sestertia*, as if the word *sestertium* was expressed.

The *denarius*, which was the chief silver coin used at Rome, received its name because it contained *denos æris*, ten *asses.*

The *as* is often expressed by an L., because it was one pound weight: and the *sestertius*, because it was equivalent to two pounds and a half of brass, is frequently denoted by H. S., or by L. L. S.

The Roman *libra* contained twelve ounces of silver, and was worth about 3*l.* sterling.

The Roman talent was supposed to be equivalent to twenty-four *sestertia*, or nearly 193*l.* sterling.